THE OXFORD
DICTIONARY OF
ENGLISH
PROVERBS

THE OXFORD
DICTIONARY OF
ENGLISH
PROVERBS

THIRD EDITION

REVISED BY F. P. WILSON

WITH AN INTRODUCTION
BY JOANNA WILSON

OXFORD
AT THE CLARENDON PRESS

Oxford University Press, Walton Street, Oxford OX2 6DP

Oxford New York Toronto
Delhi Bombay Calcutta Madras Karachi
Petaling Jaya Singapore Hong Kong Tokyo
Nairobi Dar es Salaam Cape Town
Melbourne Auckland
and associated companies in
Berlin Ibadan

Oxford is a trade mark of Oxford University Press

First edition 1935
Second edition 1948
Third edition 1970
Reprinted 1974, 1975, 1979, 1980, 1982, 1984, 1989

ISBN 0–19–869118–1

Printed in Great Britain by
Courier International
Tiptree, Essex

PREFACE TO THE SECOND EDITION

THE arrangement of a collection of proverbs in such a way that the inquirer may readily find the proverb he is looking for is a matter of some difficulty. The difficulty arises from the fact that many proverbs have not a precise, invariable, and generally known and accepted form. On the contrary, there are frequently variant or uncertain versions, particularly in the opening words and in respect of the use of the definite or indefinite article, the choice between 'He that' and 'He who', the inclusion or exclusion of the first 'as' in proverbs of the type of 'As red as a rose', and similar points of doubt. Who shall say whether it is 'A burnt child' or 'The burnt child' who dreads the fire, or whether, according to the true version, it is 'You' or 'A man' who may lead a horse to the water but cannot make him drink? It follows that no convenient arrangement of proverbs in alphabetical order is possible if the proverbs are set out in their ordinary form.

The proverbs in this collection are arranged in the alphabetical order of some (usually the first) significant word in each, the part (if any) of the proverb preceding the significant word being transferred to the end of the proverb, or, if more convenient, to an intermediate point in it. The transferred part begins with a capital letter, and if placed in the middle of the proverb is terminated by an upright hair-stroke. Thus

> To give a Roland for an Oliver,

becomes

> Roland for an Oliver, To give a;

and

> When you are at Rome, do as Rome does,

becomes

> Rome, When you are at | do as Rome does.

Some proverbs have only one significant word (e.g. 'Blood will have blood'), or a significant word so dominant that, if the inquirer does not know it, he cannot know the proverb at all (e.g. 'Curses like chickens come home to roost'). In these cases nothing further is required. But where, as is more frequent, there are two or more words in a proverb of comparable significance, an inquirer may be uncertain which of these, on the above system, has been chosen as the opening word; or again he may know only the general tenor of the proverb, not its precise wording. Accordingly, under any other word of importance in the proverb a cross-reference has been given showing the opening word under which the proverb appears, together with so much of the rest of it as will indicate its general sense. Thus if the proverb 'He that will play at bowls must expect to meet with rubbers' is looked for under 'Bowls', it will not be found there, but, instead, a cross-reference: 'Bowls, *see* Play at b. must expect rubbers', and the proverb with the relevant quotations will be found under 'Play at bowls'. These cross-references, which are very numerous, should make it possible to trace without difficulty any proverb in the collection.

The cross-references under any word have as a rule been placed immediately after the last proverb beginning with that word. Some slight departures from strict alphabetical order occur here and there, where this appears convenient; but in general the order may be exemplified as follows:

> Dog . . .
> Dog's . . .
> Dogged . . .
> Dogs . . .
> Dogs' . . .
> Dog(s) (cross-references).

It may further be noted that when the alphabetical position of any proverb was being settled, any parenthesis, whether between brackets or between a comma and a vertical stroke, was disregarded. Thus

> Necessity (Need) has no law

is placed before

> Necessity is a hard dart;

and

> Rome, When you are at | do as Rome does

is placed before

> Rome was not built in a day.

A certain number of proverbs (mostly Scottish) which appeared in the original edition of *The Oxford Dictionary of Proverbs* have been omitted from the present work because of their somewhat trivial character, and have been replaced by others of greater interest. For many of the latter the publishers are indebted to Professor F. P. Wilson, whose profound knowledge of sixteenth- and seventeenth-century English literature and extensive collections of proverbs and quotations have furnished a multitude of instances of the appearance of proverbs at earlier dates than had previously been recorded. Professor Wilson has also given invaluable advice and assistance on many bibliographical and other points. A number of proverbs and interesting quotations have also been drawn from a collection made by the late G. G. Loane and from notes by Mr. Vernon Rendall.

In the present edition acknowledgement is also due to G. L. Apperson's *English Proverbs and Proverbial Phrases*, published by Messrs. J. M. Dent & Sons Ltd. in 1929, for some early examples which Mr. Apperson's careful researches first made available. These are indicated by (A) after the reference.

P. H.

INTRODUCTION

'WISE men make proverbs and fools repeat them': so says a proverb, but the proverb telling what a proverb is cannot be discovered and men who have worked for years on the subject have hardly bettered the dictionary definition.[1] To G. L. Apperson, the first editor with a historical approach, a proverb is a crystallized summary of popular wisdom or fancy, whilst M. P. Tilley could find no satisfactory definition, nor could he distinguish between proverbs, proverbial phrases, and proverbial similes; he resorted to reliance on our ancestors' understanding and an acceptance of what they included in their collections.

To turn from the hopeless task of their definition to the age of proverbs: their use is centuries old, dating probably from the time when wisdom and precept were transmitted by story and song. Their acceptance and eventual general rejection is a comment on the history of manners, educational development, and morals. In medieval times and later they were constantly on men's lips as accepted wisdom, in the sixteenth and much of the seventeenth century they were an essential ornament in a fashionable writer's or talker's equipment, until from the end of the seventeenth century onwards they deteriorated into 'vulgar sayings', only fit for ignorant men. Yet every day we still hear proverbs, many of ancient origin, many transmitted in print, many debased to clichés. From time to time new ones are coined, to meet the need of a 'pithy saying' for some development or discovery.

The antiquity of proverbs is recognized by our ancestors. Thus Lyly: 'I haue heard my great grandfather tell how his great grandfather should saie, that it was an olde prouerbe, when his greate grandfather was a childe, that it was a good winde that blew a man to the wine.'[2] Or Nashe speaks of a 'hackney prouerb in mens mouths euer since K. Lud was a little boy'.[3] Their wisdom too is attested. 'Why speaks he Prouerbes?' is asked in *Two Angry Women of Abingdon*[4]—'Because he would speak trueth, And proverbes youle confesse, are ould said sooth.' 'Proverbs bear age, and he who would do well may view himself in them as in a Looking-glass' is a comment by Mapletoft as late as 1707, although by then their down-grading had begun. Eventually they were dismissed by Jane Austen as 'gross and illiberal',[5] or as the 'reckless maxims of our worthy grandsires' by Blackmore.[6]

A justification for the study of proverbs, if any is needed, may be found in its usefulness for philology, psychology, folk-lore, the history of manners, and for literary studies, to help to establish a text or interpret a meaning.[7] Some have

---

[1] *O.E.D.*: 'a short pithy saying in common recognized use.'
[2] *Mother Bombie*, II. v. 4 (1594).   [3] *Have with you to Saffron Walden*, iii. 129 (1596).
[4] *Two Angry Women of Abingdon*, ll. 499–501 (1597).
[5] *Sense and Sensibility*, ch. 9 (1811).   [6] *Perlycross*, ch. 15 (1894).
[7] See F. P. Wilson, 'The Proverbial Wisdom of Shakespeare', his Presidential Address to Modern Humanities Research Association (1961).

changed their form with changing habits. 'Do not spoil the hog for a halfpenny-worth of tar' is recorded in 1600, 'hog' becomes 'sheep' in 1651, and by 1823 the present usage of 'ship' is established. To give another example, the current 'I would not touch him with a barge-pole' was in earlier times 'I would not touch him with a pair of hedging-mittins'. What, we may ask, will be substituted for a barge-pole when it no longer exists? Several proverbs are restricted to one type of society. 'To drive a coach and horses through' is parliamentary, recurring in politicians' speeches. Many are coined by the Services, who have their own dictionaries of proverbs and of slang. Regional examples are numberless and many still keep within their original boundaries.

In England the appearance of proverbs in manuscripts and books naturally varied according to the interest in the subject. Janet Heseltine, in her Introduction to the first edition of the *Oxford Dictionary of English Proverbs*, has pointed out that proverbial sayings, generally of a sententious nature, can be found in religious manuscripts from the first half of the eighth century onwards, with, occasionally, brief collections of proverbs inserted half in the vernacular, the whole in Latin, presumably to facilitate the teaching of Latin to a novice. But more important was the influence of the rhetoricians, who illustrated their dicta by proverbs, a fashion which spread from a narrow trickle to the wide channel of Chaucer, Gower, and Lydgate, in whose works proverbs new and old reflect life in cottage and court, in foreign countries or in the smallest English hamlet, where the saws of husbandry, many still current today, were passed through the years from father to son.

By the beginning of the sixteenth century the channel was becoming a torrent, and eventually a flood which, overreaching itself, nearly brought destruction. The *Adagia* of Erasmus, published in 1500, consisting of strings of proverbs which illustrate the opinions of classical philosophers, was ravenously devoured by men hungry for knowledge and for novelty. Heywood in his *Dialogue of Proverbs* (1545), 'conteinyng the nomber in effect of all the prouerbes in the englishe tongue', clothed his advice from an older man to a younger in narrative form and embroidered it with innumerable 'old said saws' in the accepted and popular manner. But the height of fashion was reached in 1579 by Lyly, whose habit in his *Euphues* of wrapping a phrase in golden tissue added a new word to our language. His influence was enormous, an overgilded style in an overgilded age. Camden, Fergusson, Draxe, Herbert, and other collectors followed, each borrowing from the other according to his interest in rhetoric, morals, or antiquity. Arrangement is as fancy dictates, although a theme such as Seasons, Philosophy, Wisdom is sometimes roughly followed. There were contributions too from abroad, particularly during the latter half of the sixteenth century, by, among others, Sanford, Minsheu, Stepney, Florio, and Howells. These enriched our language, for many proverbs of foreign origin were quickly absorbed into English life and these have a rightful place in an English dictionary.

In the second half of the seventeenth century Torriano provided some kind of index for his *Italian Proverbs and Proverbial Phrases* (1666). Ray (1670 and 1678) is both more scholarly and more original, in that he gives his sources and adds examples that have not appeared before. His method was to read all former collections, and then for ten years listen to talk, and gather contributions from friends in several parts of England. He begins alphabetically and afterwards classes his excerpts under subject matter, with the inevitable result that he repeats himself. He excludes improper proverbs, not wishing to be guilty of 'administring fewel to lust, which I am sensible needs no incentives, burning too eagerly of it self'. He admits, however, that some proverbial phrases using 'dirty words' are most witty and significant, and in these cases he compromises with the initial letter only for the offending word. Probably it is these 'indecent sayings' that Apperson rejected in 1929.

The eighteenth century reflects a varying attitude. Thomas Fuller the physician in 1732 was of the opinion that 'Sentences and Sayings . . . are usual and useful in Conversation and Business', with the warning that they 'are to be accounted only as Sauce to relish Meat with', and that to apply them wrongly is 'abominably foppish, ridiculous, and nauseous'. He is modest about the value of his collection, which he endearingly describes as a 'vast confus'd heap of unsorted Things, Old and new, which you may pick over and make use of, according to your Judgment and Pleasure'. James Kelly's attitude is different. His *Scottish Proverbs* (1721) is prefaced with extraordinary statistics; he tells us how from memory he jotted down 1,200 examples before he even began to think of his volume, thus having a head-start over his fellow-countryman Fergusson who published only 945. Kelly has a high opinion of proverbs, quoting on the title-page Bacon's dictum that the 'Genius, Wit, and Spirit of a Nation, are discovered by their Proverbs'. They are, Kelly says, 'accomodated to the Principal Concerns of Life . . . especially used among the better Sort of the Commonalty'. He is interested to find that many which he thought were genuine Scottish proverbs originated in other countries, and he observes that the mind of man concerning elemental things is much the same the world over.

Polite writers, however, in the eighteenth century despised these 'vulgar sayings', and Swift pilloried them. The tide had turned against them, though in plays and novels they abound, particularly when low life is depicted. By the nineteenth century they were used more self-consciously, in legions by Scott, frequently by Dickens and Trollope, and in search of old times by Hardy. There were further Scots collections, and W. C. Hazlitt in 1869 published his extensive contribution, which was marred as usual by uncertain arrangement and an untrustworthy index. More shapeless still was Lean's monumental work (1902-4), which, like others, may possibly have stemmed from an awareness that with an increase in reading and greater sophistication proverbs were beginning to change or die and should be recorded for posterity.

In 1929 there was a new approach, with the publication of Apperson's dictionary. This is historical and on it the *Oxford Dictionary of English Proverbs* may be said to be based, its purpose being to cite for each entry the earliest literary reference in manuscript or book, with a few examples from later centuries. Medieval proverbs of which there is no literary evidence in a later period are only admitted if they are of special interest in themselves or by reason of the text in which they occur. The first edition of the *Oxford Dictionary of English Proverbs* was published in 1935, compiled by W. G. Smith; a second edition, revised by Sir Paul Harvey, appeared in 1948. The present edition is the result of F. P. Wilson's lifelong interest in proverbs, which began with his early work on Dekker and continued with his wide and deep knowledge of Elizabethan literature. This study was for him a relaxation from more arduous work, and as time went on he likened his course to that of James Kelly, who pursued his way 'without any Regard either to Honour or Profit, but only to give myself a Harmless, Innocent, Scholar-like Divertisement in my declining years'.

In 1950 M. P. Tilley's *Dictionary of the Proverbs in England in the Sixteenth and Seventeenth Centuries* was published. The unrestricted use of this work, which is exemplary for clarity, for references, particularly to Shakespeare, and for paucity of errors, was generously granted by the University of Michigan to the Clarendon Press. Shortly before his death in 1963 F. P. Wilson finished collating Tilley's dictionary with the second edition of the *Oxford Dictionary of English Proverbs*, adding many proverbs to the projected new edition, and many earlier examples of those already there, partly from Tilley, partly from his own extensive reading. The principle of the second edition is largely adhered to, that proverbs should be listed according to the first significant word. It is hoped that a more liberal entry of cross-references to words will facilitate the labour of searching. Let those who look in vain be reminded that this collection is selective, and also, if this brief Introduction may end, as it began, with a proverb, that 'In many words the truth goes by . . . a lye or twayne sone maie escape'.

In 1959, when a third edition of this dictionary was planned, a team of ten contributors agreed to submit examples of proverbs, some new, and some earlier versions of those in the second edition. F. P. Wilson was grateful for the assistance of Professor J. A. W. Bennett, Mr. R. W. Burchfield, the late Professor J. Butt, the late Mr. J. Crow, the late Professor H. J. Davis, Professor Norman Davis, Professor the Revd. James Kinsley, Mr. J. C. Maxwell, Mr. A. G. Rigg, and Professor James Sutherland.

In addition I am grateful for suggestions made by Mrs. Jean Bromley and Miss Gwyneth Lloyd Thomas. I am particularly indebted to Mr. J. C. Maxwell both for his advice on proverbial matters and for his help with proof-reading and the arduous task of preparing this volume for the press.

JOANNA WILSON

BOOKS REFERRED TO BY AUTHOR, COMPILER, OR ABBREVIATED TITLE ONLY AND NOTES OF THE EDITIONS USED

* after a date indicates that later dates are quoted for later works.

c. 1594	BACON	Francis Bacon, *Promus*.
1736	BAILEY	Nathan Bailey, *Dictionarium Britannicum*, 2nd edn., 1736.
1547	BALDWIN	William Baldwin, *A treatise of Morall Phylosophie, contayning the sayinges of the wyse*.
1509*	BARCLAY	Alexander Barclay, *Ship of Fools*, ed. Jamieson (1874). *Eclogues*, E.E.T.S.
1573*	BARET	John Baret, *An Alveary or Triple Dictionary, in Englishe, Latin, and French*.
1754	BERTHELSON	Andreas Berthelson, *An English and Danish Dictionary*.
1702	BLAU	Robert Blau, *The Locutions of the Latin Tongue*.
1629	*Bk. Mer. Rid.*	*The Book of Merry Riddles*.
1694*	BOYER	Abel Boyer, *The Compleat French-Master, for Ladies and Gentlemen*.
1609–18	BRETNOR	Thomas Bretnor, Yearly almanacs. His lists of good and evil days are reprinted by J. Crow in *Elizabethan and Jacobean Studies*, presented to F. P. Wilson (1959).
1616*	BRETON 1 and 2 *Crossing*	Nicholas Breton, *Crossing of Proverbs*, in two Parts.
1626	BRETON 1 and 2 *Soothing*	Nicholas Breton, *Soothing of Proverbs: With only True forsooth*, in two Parts.
1917	BRIDGE	J. C. Bridge, *Cheshire Proverbs*.
1541	BULLINGER	H. Bullinger, *Christian State of Matrimony*, tr. M. Coverdale. Quotations are from the edition of 1543.
1883	BURNE	C. S. Burne, *Shropshire Folk-lore*.
1614*	CAMDEN	William Camden, *Remaines Concerning Britaine*.
a. 1628	CARMICHAELL	*The James Carmichaell Collection of Proverbs in Scots. From the Original Manuscript in the Edinburgh University Library*, ed. M. L. Anderson (1957).
1545	CATO *Precepts*	*Precepts of Cato, with annotacions of D. Erasmus*, tr. R. Burrant.
1882	CHAMBERLAIN	E. L. Chamberlain, *A Glossary of West Worcestershire Words*.
1359*	CHAUCER	Geoffrey Chaucer, *Works*, ed. F. N. Robinson (1957).
1896	CHEVIOT	A. Cheviot, *Proverbs, Proverbial Expressions, and Popular Rhymes of Scotland*.
1639	CLARKE	John Clarke, *Parœmiologia Anglo-Latina*.
1664	CODRINGTON	Robert Codrington, *A Collection of Many Select and Excellent Proverbs out of Severall Languages*.
1565*	COOPER	Thomas Cooper, *Thesaurus linguae Romanae et Britannicae*.
1611	COTGRAVE	Randle Cotgrave, *A Dictionary of the French and English Tongues*.
1578	*Courtly Controv.*	Jacques Yver, *A courtlie controversie of Cupids Cantles*, tr. H. Wotton.

1894	COWAN	F. Cowan, *Dictionary of the Proverbs . . . of the English Language relating to the Sea.*
1611	DAVIES	John Davies of Hereford, *The Scourge of Folly.*
1592	DELAMOTHE	G. Delamothe, *The French Alphabeth . . . Together with the Treasure of the French toung.*
1846	DENHAM	M. A. Denham, *A Collection of Proverbs . . . relating to the Weather.*
c. 1526	*Dicta Sap.*	Erasmus, *Dicta Sapientum. The sayenges of the wyse men of Grece in Latin with the Englysshe folowyng.*
c. 1350	DOUCE MS. 52	*Douce MS. 52* (Förster) in *Festschrift z. XII. deutschen Neuphilologentage.* Erlangen, 1906.
1616	DRAXE	Thomas Draxe, *Bibliotheca Scholastica Instructissima. Or, A Treasurie of ancient Adagies, and sententious Prouerbes, selected out of the English, Greeke, Latine, French, Italian and Spanish.* The English proverbs were reprinted by Max Förster in *Anglia*, xlii (1918).
	DRAYTON	Michael Drayton, *Works*, ed. J. W. Hebel, 5 vols. (1931–41).
1709	DYKES	Oswald Dykes, *English Proverbs with Moral Reflections.* 3rd edn., 1713.
1699	E., B.	*A New Dictionary of the . . . Canting Crew . . . with an Addition of some Proverbs, Phrases, Figurative Speeches, etc.* By B. E. Gent.
1557	EDGEWORTH	Roger Edgeworth, *Sermons very fruitfull, godly, and learned.*
1538*	ELYOT *Dict.*	Sir Thomas Elyot, *The dictionarie.*
1542	ERASM. *Apoph.*	Erasmus, *Apophthegmes, that is to saie, prompte, quicke, wittie and sentencious saiynges . . . First gathered . . . by . . . Erasmus . . . And now translated . . . by Nicolas Udall.* The edition of 1564 is a reprint, ed. Roberts (1877).
1881	EVANS	A. B. Evans, *Leicestershire Words, &c.*
1641	FERGUSSON	David Fergusson, *Fergusson's Scottish Proverbs From the Original Print of 1641 Together with a larger Manuscript Collection of about the same period . . .*, ed. Erskine Beveridge, S.T.S. (1924).
1578	FLORIO	John Florio, *Florio His firste Fruites*, ed. A. del Re, Taihoku (1936).
1591	FLORIO	John Florio, *Florios Second Frutes*, ed. R. C. Simonini, Gainesville (1953).
1830	FORBY	R. Forby, *The Vocabulary of East Anglia.*
1662	FULLER	Thomas Fuller, D.D., *The History of the Worthies of England.*
1732	FULLER	Thomas Fuller, M.D., *Gnomologia: Adagies and Proverbs; Wise Sentences and Witty Sayings, Ancient and Modern, Foreign and British.*
1566*	GASCOIGNE	George Gascoigne, *Works*, ed. Cunliffe, 2 vols. (1907–10).
1654	GAYTON	Edmund Gayton, *Pleasant Notes upon Don Quixote.*
c. 1450–1500	*The Gd. Wife*	*The Good Wife taught her Daughter. The Good Wife would a Pilgrimage. The Thewis of Good Women*, ed. T. F. Mustanoja, *Annales Academiae Scientiarum*, Fennicae B LXI, 2, Helsinki (1948).
1579	GOSSON	Stephen Gosson, *School of Abuse.*
1785*	GROSE	Francis Grose, *A Classical Dictionary of the Vulgar Tongue.*
1787*	GROSE	Francis Grose, *A Provincial Glossary with a Collection of Local Proverbs, and Popular Superstitions.*

1611	GRUTER	Janus Gruterus, *Florilegii Ethico-Politici . . . Pars Altera.*
1581–6	GUAZZO	Stefano Guazzo, *The Civile Conversation . . . Written first in Italian, and nowe translated out of French by George Pettie.* References are to T.T. edition (1925).
1548	HALL	Edward Hall, *Chronicle, The Union of the Two Noble and Illustre Famelies of Lancastre & Yorke.* Quotations are from reprint of 1809.
1596	HARINGTON	Sir John Harington, *A New Discourse of a Stale Subiect, Called the Metamorphosis of Ajax.* Quotations are from the edition by P. Warlock and J. Lindsay (1927).
1609	HARWARD	Simon Harward, An unprinted MS. in the Library of Trinity College, Cambridge.
1869*	HAZLITT	W. C. Hazlitt, *English Proverbs.*
1874–6	HAZL.-DODS.	*A Select Collection of Old English Plays. Originally published by Robert Dodsley in the year 1744,* 4th edn., ed. W. C. Hazlitt, 15 vols.
1832	HENDERSON	Andrew Henderson, *Scottish Proverbs . . .,* with an Introductory Essay, by W. Motherwell.
1640	HERBERT	George Herbert, *Outlandish Proverbs,* in *Works,* ed. F. E. Hutchinson (1941). See also *Jacula Prudentum* 1651.
1546–c. 1549	HEYWOOD	John Heywood, *A dialogue conteinyng the number in effect of all the prouerbes in the englishe tongue, . . . set foorth by John Heywood.* Quotations are from the edition by R. Habernicht (1963).
c. 1594*	T. HEYWOOD	Thomas Heywood, *Dramatic Works,* ed. R. H. Shepherd, 6 vols. (1874).
a. 1530	HILL	Richard Hill, *Songs, Carols . . . from Richard Hill's commonplace book,* ed. R. Dyboski, E.E.T.S. (1907).
1862	HISLOP	A. Hislop, *The Proverbs of Scotland,* 3rd edn.
1576	HOLYBAND	C. Holyband [or Desainliens] *The Frenche Littelton. A most easy . . . way to learne the French tongue.*
1659	HOWELL	James Howell, *ΠΑΡΟΙΜΙΟΓΡΑΦΙΑ. Proverbs . . . in English . . . Italian, French and Spanish . . . British.*
1552	HULOET	Richard Huloet, *Alredarium Anglico Latinum.*
1869*	INWARDS	R. Inwards, *Weather Lore.*
1615	*Janua Linguarum,*	tr. W. Welde.
1598*	JONSON	Ben Jonson, *Works,* ed. Herford and Simpson, 11 vols. (1925–52).
1721	KELLY	James Kelly, *A Complete Collection of Scotish Proverbs Explained and made Intelligible to the English Reader.*
1834*	J. B. KER	John Bellender Ker, *An Essay on the Archaeology of Popular English Phrases and Nursery Rhymes.*
1902–4	LEAN	V. S. Lean, *Collectanea.*
1579*	LYLY	John Lyly, *Works,* ed. R. W. Bond, 3 vols. (1902).
1707	MAPLETOFT	John Mapletoft, *Select Proverbs.*
1590*	MARLOWE	Christopher Marlowe, *Works,* ed. Case (1930–33).
1583	MELBANCKE	Brian Melbancke, *Philotimus. The Warre betwixt Nature and Fortune.*
1525–40	*Merry Dial.*	Erasmus, *A merry Dialogue, declaringe the propertyes of shrowde shrewes, and honest wyues,* ed. H. de Vocht (1928).
1567	*Merry Tales*	*Merry tales, Wittie questions, and quicke answeres.* Reprinted in W. C. Hazlitt's *Shakespeare Jest-Books,* vol. i (1864).

1688   MIÈGE   Guy Miège, *The Great French Dictionary. In two Parts.*

1599   MINSHEU   John Minsheu, *A Dictionarie in Spanish and English.* Part of the same book, but with separate title-pages, are *A Spanish Grammar* and *Pleasant and Delightfull Dialogues.*

1559*   *Mirror for Mag.*   *The Mirror for Magistrates.* References are to the edition by L. B. Campbell (1938).

1603   MONTAIGNE   *Essays of Michael Lord of Montaigne Translated by John Florio.* References are to T.C. edn., 6 vols.

1659   N.R.   N. R., Gent., *Proverbs English, French, Dutch, Italian, and Spanish.*

1589*   NASHE   Thomas Nashe, *Works*, ed. R. B. McKerrow, 5 vols. (1904–10).

1892   NORTHALL   G. F. Northall, *English Folk-Rhymes.*

1894   NORTHALL   G. F. Northall, *Folk Phrases of Four Counties*, E.D.S., Sec. 3, 73.

1566–7   PAINTER   William Painter, *The Palace of Pleasure*, 2 vols. Quotations are from the edition of J. Jacobs, 3 vols. (1890).

1623   PAINTER   William Painter, *Chaucer New Painted.*

1710   PALMER   S. Palmer, *Moral Essays on some of the most curious and significant English, Scotch and Foreign Proverbs.*

1530   PALSGRAVE   John Palsgrave, *L'éclairissement de la langue francoyse*, ed. F. Genin (1852).

1540   PALSGRAVE   John Palsgrave, *Acolastus*, ed. P. L. Carver, E.E.T.S.

1576   PETTIE   George Pettie, *A Petite Pallace of Pettie his Pleasure.* Quotations are from the edition of I. Gollancz, 2 vols. (1908).

1597   *Politeuphuia*   *Politeuphuia Wits Commonwealth.*

1586*   LA PRIMAUDAYE   P. de la Primaudaye, *The French Academie*, tr. by T. B[owes].

c. 1500   *Proverbs at Leconfield* (Wressell) printed from British Museum MS. Bibl. Reg. 18. D. 11, in F. Grose, T. Astle, *et al., Antiquarian Repertory* iv (1809).

1737   RAMSAY   Allan Ramsay, *A Collection of Scots Proverbs.*

1695   RAVENSCROFT   Edward Ravenscroft, *The Canterbury Guests; Or, A Bargain Broken. A Comedy.*

1670*   RAY   John Ray, *A Collection of English Proverbs.*

1681   ROBERTSON   W. Robertson, *Phraseologia Generalis.*

1621   ROBINSON   Bartholomew Robinson, *Adagia in Latine and English.*

1883   ROPER   W. Roper, *Weather Sayings.*

c. 1350   *Rylands Latin MS.*   Latin MS. 394 in the John Rylands Library, Manchester. Proverbs printed by W. A. Pantin in Bulletin IV (Jan. 1930).

1573   SANFORD   James Sanford, *The Garden of Pleasure: Contayinge most pleasante Tales . . . Done out of Italian into English, by Iames Sanforde Gent. Wherein are also set forth diuers Verses and Sentences in Italian, with the Englishe to the same.*

1691   SEWEL   *A New Dictionary English and Dutch.*

1590*   SHAKES.   William Shakespeare, *Works*, ed. Peter Alexander (1951).

1612–20   SHELTON   Miguel de Cervantes, *Don Quixote*, tr. by Thomas
1 and 2 *Quix.*   Shelton. References are to book and chapter and also to the edition in Macmillan's Library of English Classics, first issued in 1900.

1489*   SKELTON   John Skelton, dates as given in W. Nelson's *John Skelton* (New York, 1939).

c. 1640	SMYTH	John Smyth, *Berkeley MSS.*
1663	STAMPOY	'Pappity Stampoy', *A Collection of Scotch Proverbs.* (A plagiarism of one of the editions of Fergusson.)
1591	STEPNEY	William Stepney, *The Spanish Schoole-master.*
1706	STEVENS	J. Stevens, *A New Spanish and English Dictionary.*
1692*	SWIFT	Jonathan Swift, *Works*, ed. H. J. Davis (1939–67).
1738	SWIFT	Jonathan Swift, *A Complete Collection of Genteel and Ingenious Conversation . . . in Three Dialogues*, E.L. edn. (1911).
c. 1532	*Tales*	*Tales and quicke answeres, very merry, and pleasant to rede.*
1539	TAVERNER	*Proverbes or adagies with newe addicions gathered out of the Chiliades of Erasmus by Richard Tauerner. Hereunto be also added Mimi Publiani.*
1642*	TORRIANO	Giovanni Torriano, *Select Italian Proverbs.*
1659	TORRIANO	John Florio, *Vocabolario Italiano & Inglese . . . whereunto is added a Dictionary English & Italian, with severall Proverbs . . . by Gio: Torriano.*
1666	TORRIANO	Giovanni Torriano, *Piazza universale di Proverbi Italiani Or, A Common Place Of Italian Proverbs And Proverbial Phrases.*
1853	TRENCH	R. C. Trench, *On the Lessons in Proverbs* (1894 edn.).
1557*	TUSSER	Thomas Tusser, *A Hundreth good pointes of husbandrie.* Enlarged editions appeared in 1573, 1577, and 1580. The edition of 1580 was called *Fiue hundreth points of good Husbandrie.*
1534	UDALL	Nicholas Udall, *Floures for Latine speakyng selected and gathered out of Terence.*
1773	VIEYRA	A. Vieyra, *A Dictionary of the Portuguese and English Languages,* 2 vols.
1670	WALKER	William Walker, *Idiomatologia.*
1672	WALKER	William Walker, *Paroemiologia Anglo-Latina Or, English and Latin Proverbs, and Proverbial Sentences and Sayings matched together.*
1771*	WESLEY	John Wesley. References are to the editions of the *Works* (1872); of the *Letters*, ed. J. Telford (1931); of the *Journal*, ed. N. Curnock (1909, 1938); and of the *Sermons*, ed. E. H. Sugden (1921, 1935).
c. 1576	WHYTHORNE	Thomas Whythorne, *Autobiography*, ed. Osborn (1961).
1581*	WITHALS	John Withals, *A short dictionary most profitable for young beginners: the thirde time corrected and augmented.* Important additions were made in 1584 by Abraham Fleming, in 1602 by William Clerk, and in 1616.
1623	WODROEPHE	John Wodroephe, *The spared houres of a souldier. Or, the true marrowe of the French tongue.*

ABBREVIATIONS

Arb.	Arber
B.S.	Ballad Society
C.U.P.	Cambridge University Press
E.D.S.	English Dialect Society
E.E.T.S.	Early English Text Society
E.L.	Everyman's Library
E.P.P.	*Early Popular Poetry* (ed. Hazlitt)
F.L.S.	Folk Lore Society
Gros.	Grosart
H.M.C.	Historical Manuscripts Commission
Hunt. Cl.	Hunterian Club
Merm.	Mermaid Series
N. & Q.	*Notes and Queries*
New Sh. S.	New Shakespeare Society
OE	Old English
O.E.P.	*Old English Plays* (ed. Hazlitt)
O.H.S.	Oxford Historical Society
O.U.P.	Oxford University Press
P.S.	Parker Society
Roxb. Cl.	Roxburghe Club
Ser.	Series
Sp. S.	Spenser Society
S.T.S.	Scottish Text Society
s.v.	*sub voce*, under the word
T.C.	Temple Classics
T.L.S.	*Times Literary Supplement*
T.T.	Tudor Translations
W.C.	World's Classics

NOTES ON REFERENCES

The letter and number in brackets immediately following a proverb refers to M. P. Tilley's *Dictionary of the Proverbs in England in the Sixteenth and Seventeenth Centuries*.

When possible the date cited refers to the first edition, with a note when a quotation comes from a later edition. A double date, the first in square brackets, indicates that the work was known to have been composed some years earlier than it was published.

Plays are referred to by act and scene, or by act only. Other works are referred to by page unless otherwise indicated. Volumes are referred to by lower-case numerals, pages by number only, omitting 'p'.

The absence of a quotation following a reference means that in the passage referred to the proverb is given without significant change. This is indicated by omission marks (. . .) where an addition to the quotation follows.

Titles are usually modernized, but not quotations. Contractions are expanded.

A

Ab, *see* Make ab or warp of the business.

Abbey, *see* Bring an a. to a grange; Bury an a.

Abbot, *see* Horner, Popham . . . when the a. went out.

A-bed, All are not | that shall have ill rest. (A 114)

1509 BARCLAY *Ship of Fools* i. 13 All are nat in bed whiche shall haue yll rest. 1546 HEYWOOD II. vii. K1ᵛ But take vp in tyme, or els I protest, All be not abedde, that shall haue yll rest. 1670 RAY 60 All that are in bed, must not have quiet rest.

Abed, *see also* Lies long a.; Name is up (His), he may lie a. till noon.

Aberdeen and twelve miles round, Take away | and where are you?

1896 CHEVIOT 309. 1911 *Brit. Wkly.* 27 Jul. 419 A country that has as good a conceit of itself as Scotland, a city where the best-known proverb is 'Tak' awa' Aberdeen and twal' mile round aboot it, an' far¹ are ye?' [¹ where.]

Abide a bad market, He that cannot | deserves not a good one. (M 673)

1678 RAY 173.

Abide, *see also* Grin and a. it.

Ability, *see* Gentility without a.; Nobility without a.

A-bleeding, *see* All (Love) lies a.

Above, *see* Comes from a. let no man question; Things that are a. us are nothing.

Above-board. (D 128)

a. 1607 T. MIDDLETON *Family of Love* III. i Play fair yet above board. 1616 BEAUM. & FL. *Cust. Country* I. i. 145 Yet if you play not fair Play, and above-board too, I have a foolish gin here. 1617 BRATHWAIT *Solemn Disputation* 45 Faire play above boord. 1788 BURKE *Sp. agst. Hastings*, Wks. xiii. 293 All that is in this trans-action is fair and above-board.

Abra(ha)m, *see* Sham A.

Abraham's bosom, In. (A 8)

[LUKE xvi. 23 He seeth Abraham afar off, and Lazarus in his bosom.] *c.* 1533 J. FRITH *Dispn.*

of Purgatory K8ᵛ Abrahams bosome were nothing els then Abrahams fayth. 1550 *Answer to the Commons* Camden Soc. ed. N. Pocock 1884 173 The souls of them that die in the state of grace . . . sleep in Abraham's lap. 1580 A. FLEMING *Epitaph upon William Lambe* A8 His soule in Abrahams bosome restes, in quietnesse I truste. [1592] 1597 SHAKES. *Rich. III* IV. iii. 38 The sons of Edward sleep in Abraham's bosom. 1599 *Id. Hen. V* II. iii. 10 He's in Arthur's bosom, if ever man went to Arthur's bosom [malapropism]. *a.* 1797 WALPOLE *Letters* Toyn-bee VI. 310 Two or three old ladies, who are languishing to be in Abraham's bosom.

Abroad, *see* All a. and nothing at home; Argus a. and mole at home; Children hear at home, (What) soon flies a.; Saint a., devil at home; Schoolmaster is a.; Turns lie dead and one ill deed report a. does spread, (Ten good).

Absence sharpens (hinders) love, pres-ence strengthens it. (A 10)

1557 TOTTEL *Songs and Sonnets* Rollins i. 224 Absence works wonders. 1572 E. PASQUIER tr. G. FENTON *Monophylo* 29ᵛ Absence reuiueth our affection, enforceth our desire, and redoubleth our hope. 1581 W. AVERELL *Charles and Julia* B7ᵛ Three thinges there be that hinder Loue, that's Absence, Feare, and Shame. 1589 Letter of SIR H. WOTTON [Pearsall Smith i. 232] Nothing able to add more to it [affection] than absence. 1591 ARIOSTO *Orl. Fur.* Harington XXXI. 3 Long absence grieues, yet when they meet againe, That absence doth more sweet and pleasant make it. 1597 *Politeuphuia* 127 Absence in loue, makes true loue more firme and constant. *a.* 1633 G. HERBERT *Priest to Temple* 284 Absence breedes strangeness, but presence love. 1732 FULLER no. 755. 1850 T. HAYNES BAYLY *Isle of Beauty* Absence make the heart grow fonder.

Absence, *see also* Salt water and a. wash away love.

Absent are always in the wrong, The. (P 86)

c. 1440 LYDGATE *Fall of Princes* III, l. 3927 For princis ofte . . . Will cachche a quarel . . . Ageyn folk absent. 1640 HERBERT no. 318 The absent partie is still faultie. 1710 S. PALMER 51 The Absent Party is always to Blame. 1736 FRANK-LIN July The absent are never without fault, nor the present without excuse. [Fr. *Les absents ont toujours tort.*]

Absent without fault, nor present with-out excuse, He is neither. (F 109)

1616 DRAXE no. 488. 1659 HOWELL *Span. Prov.* 6.

Absent, *see also* Dead men and a. no friends left; Lion when he is a., (Who takes a.) fears a mouse present; Long a. soon forgotten; Master a. and house dead.

Abstain from beans. (B 119)

[L. *Abstineto a fabis*, Abstain from beans, i.e. from elections (ERASM., who quotes EMPEDOCLES, κυάμων ἀπο χεῖρας ἔχεσθε).] *c.* 1535 ELYOT *Educ.* F2 Absteyne from Beanes, Busy not they selfe with ouer mani matters. 1539 TAVERNER f. lv There be sondry interpretacions of thys symbole. But Plutarche and Cicero thynke beanes to be forbydden of Pythagoras, because they be wyndye and do engender impure humours and for that cause prouoke bodely lust. 1579 LYLY *Euph.* i. 281 To absteine from beans, that is, not to meddle in ciuill affayres or businesse of the common weale, for in the olde times the election of magistrats was made by the pullinge of beanes. 1662 FULLER Leics. 126 I read a Latine prouerb, A Fabis abstineto, Forbear beans; whereof some make a civil interpretation, meddle not with matters of State; because anciently men cast in a Bean when they gave their Suffrages in publick elections.

Absurdities. *See* quotn.

1619 J. FAVOUR *Antiquity triumphing over Novelty* 535 According to the old saying, *Uno absurdo dato, mille sequuntur*, a man may build a thousand absurdities vpon one.

Abundance, like want, ruins many.

1766 *Goody Two-Shoes* v. iii.

Abundance of law breaks no law.

[L. *Abundantia juris non nocet*.] *a.* 1628 CAR-MICHAELL no. 27. 1721 KELLY 45 . . . Do more than the Law requires, rather than leave any thing undone that it does.

Abundance of money ruins youth, The. (A 11)

1611 COTGRAVE s.v. Argent Th'aboundant, or free vse of money ruines youth. 1670 RAY 18.

Abundance of things engenders disdainfulness. (A 12)

c. 1533 BELLENDEN *Hist. Rome* III, S.T.S. i. 241 Plente generis contemptioun. 1548 E. HALL *Chron.* 1809 ed., 499 The olde prouerbe, that men throughe abundaunce of ryches waxe more insolent, hedstronge and robustius. 1573 SAN-FORD 50ᵛ. 1578 FLORIO *First F.* 32 The plenty of things dooth ingender care. 1594 *King Leir* ed. S. Lee III. ii. 30 Abundance maketh us forget The fountains whence the benefits do spring. 1597 DELONEY I *Gentle Craft* ed. Mann 121. 1659 HOWELL *It. Prov.* 3 Abundance engenders loathing, and scarcity an appetite.

Abuse(d), *see* Best things may be a.; No case, a. attorney.

Accidents will happen in the best-regulated families.

1763 COLMAN *Deuce is in him* I Accidents, accidents will happen—no less than seven brought

into our infirmary yesterday. 1823 SCOTT *Peveril* ch. 49 Nay, my lady, . . . such things will befall in the best regulated families. 1850 DICKENS *Dav. Cop.* ch. 28 'Copperfield,' said Mr. Micawber, 'accidents will occur in the best-regulated families.' 1884 21 Nov. Kipling Letter cited C. Carrington *Life* (1955) 58.

Accipe, see Better is one *a.*

Accord, There is no good | where every man would be a lord. (A 15)

c. 1450 *Salomon's Proverbs* in *Cambridge M. E. Lyrics* ed. Person 1962 l. 1 Salomon seyth ther is none accorde Ther euery man wuld be a lord. 1546 HEYWOOD II. vi. Ii . . . Wherefore my wyfe will be no lorde, but lady. 1573 TUSSER 113 *Author's* l. 21 E.D.S. 210 But when I spide That Lord with Lord could not accord, . . . Then left I all. 1659 N. R. 95.

Accords, *see* Rhyme (It may), but it a. not.

Account for himself and others, Who must | must know both. (A 18)

1640 HERBERT no. 209.

Accounting for tastes, There is no. (D 385)

[L. *De gustibus non est disputandum.* There is no disputing about tastes.] 1599 MINSHEU *Span. Dial* 6ᵛ Against ones liking there is no disputing. 1760 STERNE *T. Shandy* I. viii. init. *De gustibus non est disputandum*: that is there is no disputing against Hobby-horses. 1779–81 JOHNSON *Lives of Poets* (1908) ii. 209 *De gustibus non est disputandum*; men may be convinced, but they cannot be pleased, against their will. 1823 GALT *Entail* ch. 29 (But you know . . .). 1867 TROLLOPE *Last Chron. Bars.* ch. 31 He had not the slightest objection to recognizing in Major Grantly a suitor for his cousin's hand. . . There was . . . no accounting for tastes.

Accounts, *see* Cast up a.; Short reckonings (a.) long friends.

Accusation(s), *see* Conscience fears not . . . false a., (A. clear).

Accuser, *see* Advocate becomes a. (Woe to him whose).

Accuses, *see* Excuses himself (Who) a. himself.

Ace, *see* Bate me an a.

Ache(s), *see* Better eye out than always a.; Head a. (When), all body the worse; Head may never a. till (Wish my); Heart (Every) has own a.; Works after his manner (He that), head a. not.

Achilles, *see* Heel of A.; Spear of A.

Aching teeth, Who has | has ill tenants.

1659 HOWELL *Fr. Prov.* 11 Who hath sore teeth, hath ill neighbours. *Id. New Sayings*, 8a (Who hath sore teeth). 1670 RAY 26. 1706 STEVENS s.v. Diente (has a bad Relation).

Aching tooth at one, To have an.
(T 421)

1667 L'ESTRANGE *Visions* III.'191 You have still'... an aching tooth at those poor varlets. **1678** RAY 274. **1730** BAILEY *Dict.* s.v. Ake To have an Aking tooth at one, to be angry at, to have a mind to rebuke or chastise one.

A-cold than a cuckold, It is better to be.
(C 881)

1678 RAY 69.

Acorns better than corn, To esteem.

1581 P. BOQUINUS *A Defence of Christianitie* 67 Some, that esteeme Achornes better then corne according to the prouerbe.

Acorns were good till bread was found.
(A 21)

c. **1580** SIDNEY *Arcadia* Wks. IV. 200 Ys hee carryed away with the greedy desyer of Ackornes, that hathe had his sences ravished with a garden of moste Delightfull Fruites? *c.* **1594** BACON no. 871 *Satis quercus.* **1597** BACON *Col. Good and Evil* no. 6.

Acorn(s), *see also* Hog never looks up to him who threshes a.; Horse that was foaled of a.; Oak has been an a.

Acquaintance(s), *see* Friends, (Have but few), but many a.; Old a. will be remembered; Short a. brings repentance.

Acquittance, *see* Forbearance is no a.

Acre(s), *see* Half an a. is good land; Performance, (One a. of); Reputation is commonly measured by a.; Sits above that deals a.; Three a. and cow.

Act, *see* Women may blush to hear what they were not ashamed to a.

Act of Parliament, *see* Coach and four; Honest by A. of P. (Cannot make people).

Actions are our security, Our own | not others' judgements.
(A 27)

1640 HERBERT no. 173.

Actions speak louder than words.

1628 PYM *Debate on a Message from Charles I* A word spoken in season is like an apple of silver, and actions are more precious than words. **1856** A. LINCOLN *Fragment on Sectionalism* (1953 Wks. ii. 352) 'Actions speak louder than words' is the maxim. **1889** J. MIDDLEMORE *Proverbs* 36. **1906** F. MCCULLAGH *With Cossacks* 178 The gallant foreigner, who could not tell them how he sympathized with them, but whose actions spoke louder than words.

Action(s), *see also* Innocent a. carry warrant; Mad a. (One); Man punishes a., God intention.

Adam, The old.
(A 29)

[= the fallen nature inherited from Adam. *c.* **456** SIDONIUS APOLLINARIS *Op.* p. 561 Veteremque novus . . . Adam.] **1537** W. TURNER *Old Learn. and New*, A6 Thys doctryne . . . beateth downe the pryde and arrogancye of the olde Adam. **1577** A. GOLDING *Murther of George Sanders* ed. L. T. Golding, *An Eliz. Puritan* 179 Wee be the impres of the olde Adam. **1579** J. CALVIN *Thirteen Sermons* A4ᵛ Mortifying the olde Adam in vs, and . . . quickening the inwarde man. **1599** SHAKES. *Hen. V* I. i. 29 Consideration like an angel came, And whipp'd the offending Adam out of him. **1642** D. ROGERS *Naaman* To Rdr. Corrupt self . . . is (upon point) no other then old Adam; the depravedness and disorder of the appetite before spoken of. **1852** E. FITZGERALD *Polonius* 92 Let him who would know how far he has changed the old Adam, consider his dreams. **1910** G. W. E. RUSSELL *Sketch. & Snap.* 62 As time goes on, we find the old Adam in Manning's nature reasserting itself.

Adam delved and Eve span, When | who was then a (the) gentleman?
(A 30)

c. **1340** HAMPOLE in *Relig. Pieces fr. Thornton MS.* 79 When Adam dalfe and Eve spane . . . Whare was þan þe pride of man? [**1381**] J. R. GREEN *Short Hist.* (1893) ii. 484 A spirit fatal to the whole system of the Middle Ages breathed in the popular rime which condensed the levelling doctrine of John Ball:[1] 'When Adam delved and Eve span, who was then the gentleman?' *c.* **1470** *Harl. MS. 3362*, f. 5a When Adam dalf and Eve span, who was then a gentleman? *c.* **1500** *Songs & Carols* Warton Club 2 Now bething the, Gentilman How Adam dalf and Eve span. **1562** J. PILKINGTON *Aggeus* P.S. 125 When Adam dalve, and Eve span, Who was then a gentleman? Up start the carle, and gathered good, And thereof came the gentle blood. **1605** ROWLANDS *Hell's Broke Loose* 15 For when old Adam delu'd, and Euah span, Where was my silken veluet Gentleman? **1659** HOWELL *Eng. Prov.* 13b. [1 executed 1381.]

Adam's children, We are all.

c. **1497** *Fulgens & Lucres* F7ᵛ Both he and I cam of adam and eue. *c.* **1530** *Of Gentleness & Nobility* A4ᵛ We cam all of adam and eue. *Ibid.* Bl Ye cam of one furst stok and progenye Both of adam and eue ye wyll not denye. **1564** *Cap and Head* 1565 ed., C2ᵛ We come all of Adam which tilled the earth. **1572** CRADOCKE *Ship of Assured Safety* 182 What hath one deserued more . . . than an other . . . Were we not all descended from our father Adam? **1598–9** SHAKES. *M.A.* II. i. 53 Adam's sons are my brethren; and truly I hold it a sin to match in my kindred. **1600** *Weakest to the Wall* E4 I know thy bringing vp though not thy birth, Thou art deriu'd from Adam, form'd of earth: From that first Parent all descended are, Then who begat or bare thee that's not my care.

Adam's children but silk makes the difference, We are all.
(A 31)

1659 HOWELL *Span. Prov.* 13 We are all Adams sons, silk onely distinguisheth us. **1732** FULLER no. 5425. **1706** STEVENS s.v. Hijo (Adam and Eve's children).

Adam, *see also* Died half a year ago dead as A.; Know one from A. (Not to).

Add, *see* Fuel to the fire, (To a. more); Insult to injury.

Adder could hear, and the blind worm could see, If the | neither man nor beast would ever go free.

1856 *N. & Q.* 2nd Ser. I. 331 There is a Kentish proverb about the adder . . . 'If I could hear as well as see, Nor man nor beast should pass by me.' **1869** HAZLITT 228 If I could hear, and thou couldst see, there would none live but you and me, as the adder said to the blindworm. **1879** G. JACKSON *Shropshire Word-Bk.* 135 Shropshire rustics say—'If the *ether* 'ad the blindworm's ear, An' the blindworm 'ad the *ether's* eye, Neither mon nor beäst could safe pass by'. **1883** BURNE 239 I learnt this version when young—'If the adder could hear, and the blindworm could see, Neither man nor beast would ever go free'. Current near London.

Adder, *see also* Deaf as an a.; March comes in with a. heads; March wind kindles the a.; Put your hand in creel and take out either a. or. . . .

Addled egg as an idle bird, As good be an.

1579 LYLY *Euph.* I. 325. **1602** SHAKES. *T.C.* I. ii. 127 If you love an addle egg as well as you love an idle head. **1617** J. SWETNAM *School of Defence* C3 Better an addle Egge then an ill Bird. **1732** FULLER no. 681.

Addle(d), *see* Brains are a.; Egg, (But one), and that a.

Adlant, *see* Turn a narrow a.

Admonish your friends in private, praise them in public.　　　(F 683)

[PUB. SYRUS *Secrete amicos admone, lauda palam.*] *c.* **1526** ERASMUS *Dicta Sapientum* A4 Comende thy frende openly, but whan he erreth correcte hym secretely. **1597** *Politeuphuia* 90 (secretly . . . openly). **1621** BURTON *Anat. Mel.* II. iii. VII (1651) 360.

Ado, *see* Jack-an-apes (More a. with); Make a. and have a.; Mickle a., and little help; Much a. about nothing; Much a. to bring beggars to stocks.

Advantage, *see* Spending (In) lies the a.

Adventures are to the adventurous.

1844 DISRAELI *Coningsby* iii. I. **1914** H. H. MUNRO ('Saki') *Beasts and Super-Beasts* 'The Name-Day' (Adventures, according to the proverb).

Adverbs, *see* God is better pleased with a. than with nouns.

Adversity makes a man wise, not rich.　　　　　　　　　　　　　　　(A 42)

1574 J. BALE *Pageant of Popes* tr. J. Studley 113 This Celestine [IV] vsed this sayinge commonly: It is harder to keepe moderation in prosperity, then in aduersitye. **1579** (1607 ed., E3ᵛ) J. FOXE *Christ Jesus Triumphant* As it was said of the Phrygians in a Greeke Prouerbe, that stripes strike wisdome into them. **1591** SHAKES. *3 Hen. VI* III. i. 24 Let me embrace thee, sour adversity, For wise men say it is the wisest course. **1599** *Id. A.Y.* II. i. 12 Sweet are the uses of adversity, Which, like the toad, ugly and venomous, Wears yet a precious jewel in his head. **1616** DRAXE no. 54. In Aduersitie men finde eies. **1659** N. R. 17 Adversity makes men wise. **1678** RAY 92.

Adversity, *see also* Misery (A.) makes strange bedfellows; Poet in a. can hardly make verses; Prosperity is blessing of O.T., a. of New; Prosperity makes friends, a. tries them.

Advice, We may give | but we cannot give conduct.

1736 FRANKLIN *Way to Wealth* in Wks. I. 451 (Bigelow). **1782** WESLEY *Sermons* ii. 74 The advice is good; but it comes too late! I have made a breach already.

Advice comes too late, When a thing is done.　　　　　　　　　　　　　　(T 159)

1592 DELAMOTHE 45 When a thing is done, all counsell is in vayne. **1659** TORRIANO no. 128 (I am sorry, comes too late). **1664** CODRINGTON 224. **1670** RAY I.

Advice, If you wish good | consult an old man.

c. **1386** CHAUCER *Melibeus* l. 2354 For the book seith that 'in olde men is the sapience, and in longe tyme the prudence'. **1616** G. HAKEWILL *Answer to a Treatise Written by Dr. Carrier* 161 The aduice of an old man is commonly best, but the execution of young. **1813** RAY I. *Lusit.*

Advice, *see also* First a. of a woman (Take); In vain he craves a.; Woman's a. best at a dead lift; Woman's a. is no great thing; Write down a. of him who loves you.

Advise none to marry or go to war.　　　　　　　　　　　　　　　　　(W 39)

1640 HERBERT no. 236.

Advise, *see also* Discreet a.; Old and wise, yet still a.

Advisement, *see* Good a. (Came never ill of).

Advocate becomes his accuser, Woe be to him whose.　　　　　　　　　(W 596)

1678 RAY *Adag. Hebr.* 403 . . . God required propitiatory sacrifices of his people . . . But if they offered the blind or lame, &c. they . . .

increased their guilt: And thus their advocate became their accuser.

Affairs, like salt fish, ought to be a good while a soaking.

1707 MAPLETOFT 15.

Affection blinds reason.   (A 48)

[*c.* 1609] 1616 JONSON *Ev. Man In* I. ii. 110 Affection makes a foole Of any man.   1616 DRAXE no. 57.   1659 J. HOWELL *Letter of Advice.*   1664 CODRINGTON 205 Meer Affection is blind Reason.

Affection, *see also* Heat of a. joined with idleness of brain.

Afflictions are sent to us by God for our good.   (A 53)

1541 H. BULLINGER *Christ. State Matrimony* tr. Coverdale 1543 ed. L6 Affliccion[s] tech to know god.   1579 CALVIN *Sermons* tr. L.T. Table. Affliction is the triall of our faith.   1610 SHAKES. *Cym.* III. vi. 9 Will poor folks lie, That have afflictions on them, knowing 'tis A punishment or trial?   1611 *Id. W.T.* II. i. 121 This action I now go on [imprisonment] Is for my better grace.   1659 N. R. 17.   1707 MAPLETOFT 35 Afflictions draw Men up towards Heaven.

Afraid of far enough.

1670 RAY 161 . . . *Chesh.* Of that which is never likely to happen.

Afraid of him that died last year. (Y 5)

1670 RAY 161.   1732 FULLER no. 810 Are you afraid of him that dy'd last Year?

Afraid of his own shadow.   (S 261)

c. 1513 SIR T. MORE *Rich. III* 1821 ed., 42 Who maye lette her to feare her owne shadowe?   1533 MORE *Debellation* Wks. 1557 ed., 962a The Ordinaries afeard of their own shadow.   1548 HALL 1809 ed., 259 Whether she wer a fraied of her awne shadow.   1567 G. FENTON *Bandello* ii. 285 T.T. He retorned with more fear of his shadow then true reaporte of that he had in charge.   1568 GRAFTON *Chron.* ii. 659 Whether shee were afrayed of her owne shadowe . . . the truth is, that the whole army returned to their shippes.   *c.* 1576 WHYTHORNE 47 Hee that iz Afraid of every shadow had need to keep him self alwaiz in the dark.   [1592] 1597 SHAKES. *Rich. III* V. iii. 215 Be not afraid of shadows.   1593–4 *Id. Luc.* l. 997 At his own shadow let the thief run mad.   1670 RAY 161.

Afraid of the wagging of feathers, He that is | must keep from among wild fowl.   (F 165)

1611 COTGRAVE s.v. Fueille.   1640 HERBERT no. 48.   1670 RAY 55 . . . Timorous persons must keep as far off from danger as they can . . . also . . . causeless fear works men unnecessary disquiet.

Afraid of wounds, He that is | must not come nigh a battle.   (W 932)

1639 CLARKE 310.   1670 RAY 56.

Afraid, *see also* Good thing cheap (He will never have) that is n. to ask price; More a. than hurt.

Africa always brings something new.
(A 56)

[ARISTOTLE *de Animal. Hist.* 8. 28. 7 'Αεὶ Λιβύη φέρει τι καινόν. PLINY (the Elder) *Nat. Hist.* 8. 16 *Semper aliquid novi Africam afferre.* 1500 ERASM. *Adag.* quoting PLINY 3. 7. 10 *Semper Africa noui aliquid apportat.*]   1548 T. ELYOT *Bibliotheca* Africa semper aliquid noui apportat . . . a prouerbe applied to inconstant and wauering persones.   1559 *A Woorke of Ioannes Ferrarius* tr. W. Bavarde 81 It is saied that Affricque bringeth foorthe the alwaies some newe thing.   1598 SIR R. BARCKLEY *Of the Felicitie of Man* 220 Affrica (that according to the old proverbe, is accustomed alwayes to bring forth some new and strange thing).   1601 HOLLAND tr. *Pliny's Nat. Hist.* 8. 16. 200 The Greekes have this common proverbe, That Affricke evermore bringeth forth some new and strange thing or other.   1642 HOWELL *For. Trav.* iii. Arb. 22 *France*, which as *Africk* produceth always something New, for I never knew week passe in *Paris* but it brought forth some new kinds of Authors.   1928 *Daily Mail* 19 Mar. 5/5 'Semper aliquid novi ex Africa'; so runs the old Latin tag, 'Always something new from Africa', but the newest . . . is the great harbour of the Gold Coast.

After a collar comes a halter.   (C 513)

1583 MELBANCKE *Philotimus* 193 Be ware you accord not to wear an hempton cord, For after a collar comes an haulter.   *c.* 1595 SHAKES. *R.J.* I. i. 4. I mean, an we be in choler, we'll draw. — Ay, while you live, draw your neck out of collar.   *a.* 1596 *K. Edw. IV & Tanner of Tam.* in PERCY *Reliques* II. I. XV. 171 (Gilfillan) II. 74 'After a coller commeth a halter, I trow I shall be hang'd to-morrowe'.   1597 SHAKES. *I Hen. IV* II. iv. 315 Choler, my lord, if rightly taken. — No, if rightly taken, halter.   1600 *Look about You* l. 480 I would slip the coller for feare of the halter.   1659 HOWELL *Eng. Prov.* 17a.

After a dream of a wedding comes a corpse. *Cf.* Dream of a funeral. (D 585)

1639 CLARKE 236.

After a famine in the stall, comes a famine in the hall.

1678 RAY 353. *Som.*

After a lank comes a bank.   (L 67)

1678 RAY 343 . . . Said of breeding women.   1727 BOYER *Eng. Fr. Dict.* A lank makes a bank.

After a sort, as Costlet served the King.

1721 KELLY 44 . . . One Captain Costlet boasting much of his Loyalty, was asked how he serv'd the King, when he was a Captain in Cromwell's Army; answered, After a sort.   1818 SCOTT *Rob Roy* ch. 26 He's honest after a sort, as they say . . Captain Costlett . . . said that he served him *after a sort.*

After a storm comes a calm [*or vice versa*]. (C 24; S 908)

c. 1200 *Ancrene Riwle* Morton 376 Louerd, þet makest stille efter storme. *c.* 1377 LANGLAND *Piers Plowm.* B. xviii. 407 After sharpe showres most shene is the sonne. *c.* 1387 T. USK *Test. Love* I. v. 87 After grete stormes the whether is often mery and smothe. 1576 HOLYBAND E1ᵛ After a storme commeth a calme. 1576 PETTIE ii. 91 Calm continueth not long without a storm. 1580 LYLY *Euph. & his Eng.* ii. 220 Feelyng as it were newe stormes to arise after a pleasaunt calme. 1614 CAMDEN 303. 1616 DRAXE no. 253 After a calme commeth a storme. 1655 FULLER *Ch. Hist.* IX. viii 233 . . . Wearied with a former blustering they began now to repose themselves in a sad silence.

After black clouds, clear weather. (C 442)

c. 1400 *Tale of Beryn* l. 3955 After myȝty cloudis þere comyth a cler sonne. *a.* 1547 J. REDFORD *Wit & Sci.* 828 After stormy clowdes cumth wether clere. 1546 HEYWOOD I. xi. D4 Be of good chére. After clouds blacke, we shall haue wether clére. 1639 CLARKE 294.

After cheese comes nothing. (C 267)

1609 HARWARD 76ᵛ After cheese commeth nothinge. After fish nutts. 1623 CAMDEN 266. 1639 CLARKE 136. 1721 KELLY 52 . . . As being always the last Dish.

After Christmas comes Lent. (C 367)

1611 COTGRAVE s.v. Banquet After feasting fasting. 1632 MASSINGER *City Madam* Merm. IV. iv She hath feasted long, And, after a carnival, Lent ever follows. 1678 RAY 113.

After death the doctor. (D 133)

c. 1374 CHAUCER *Troilus* Bk. 5, l. 741 Al to late comth the letuarie [remedy], Whan men the cors unto the grave carie. 1576 HOLYBAND D7ᵛ We saye in french after death, the phisitian: and the english sayeth after dinner mustard. 1613 SHAKES. *Hen. VIII* III. ii. 40 All his tricks founder, and he brings his physic After his patient's death: the King already Hath married the fair lady. 1670 RAY 78 . . . *Après la mort le médecin.* Parallel to . . . Μετὰ πόλεμον ἡ συμμαχία. Post bellum auxilium.

After dinner sit awhile, after supper walk a mile. (D 340)

[L. *Post prandium stabis, post cœnam ambulabis.* Sch. of Health at Salerno.] 1582 WHETSTONE *Hept. Civil Disc.* E3 After dynner, talke a-while, After . . . 1608 BEAUM. & FL. *Philaster* II. iv. I As men Do walk a mile, women should talk an hour After supper: 'Tis their exercise. 1613 WITHER *Abuses* 171 As having sup't 'tis good to walk a mile, So after dinner men must sit awhile. 1876 BLACKMORE *Cripps Carrier* ch. 4 He neighed . . . for he felt quite inclined for a little exercise, . . . 'After supper, trot a mile'.

After Lammas corn ripens as much by night as by day. (L 43)

[Lammas = 1st of Aug., formerly observed as harvest festival.] 1678 RAY 352. 1902–4 LEAN I. 380 . . . from the heavy night dews.

After meat, mustard. (M 809)

1576 HOLYBAND D7ᵛ The english sayeth 'after dinner, mustard'. 1577 STANYHURST in HOLINSHED *Chron. Ireland* (1587 95b) As we saie, Beware of had I wist, or After meat mustard, or You come a daie after the faire, or Better done than said. 1603 MONTAIGNE (Florio) III. x 122 It is even as good as mustard after dinner. 1670 RAY 119 . . . When there is no more use of it. 1822 SCOTT *Nigel* ch. 3 I could have gi'en you avisement . . ., but now its like after meat mustard.

After peascods, *see* Everything is good in its season (quotn. 1591).

After the house is finished, leave it. (H 748)

1640 HERBERT no. 172. 1706 STEVENS s.v. Casa When the House is finish'd, leave it. Because a new House is damp and unwholesome.

After us the deluge.

[Fr. *Après nous le déluge*: said by Mme de Pompadour to Louis XV.] 1876 BURNABY *Ride to Khiva* Introd. Our rulers did not trouble their heads much about the matter. 'India will last my time . . . and after me the Deluge.'

After wit comes ower late. (A 58)

1594 *King Leir* (ed. Lee) I. i. 47 After-wishes ever come too late. 1663 P. STANPOY 18 Efter word comes weard. 1683 MERITON *Yorkshire Ale* (1697) 83–7.

After wit is dear bought. (A 59)

1590 R. GREENE Gros. viii. 125 After wits are bitten with many sorrowes. 1595 R. SOUTHWELL 'Love's Delay'. 1709 DYKES 6.

'After you' is good manners. (A 61)

1569 T. PRESTON *Cambyses* B3ᵛ Manerly before and let vs be gone. 1600–1 SHAKES. *M.W.W.* I. i. 280 Yourself shall go first . . . I pray you, sir . . . I'll rather be unmannerly than troublesome. 1650 R. HEATH *Clarastella*, Epigrams, 33 Oh! after him is manners. 1658 E. PHILLIPS *Mysteries of Love and Eloquence* 158 After me is manners. 1721 KELLY 42 . . . Spoken when our Betters offer to serve us first. 1738 SWIFT *Dial.* II. E.L. 302.

After your fling, watch for the sting.

1917 BRIDGE 7 . . . After pleasure comes pain.

After-claps, *see* Beware of a.

After-love, *see* Scorn at first makes a. more.

Afterwit, *see* Forewit, (One good) worth two a.

Against the grain. (G 404)

1608 SHAKES. *C.* II. iii. 229 Your minds, Preoccupied with what you rather must do Than what you should, made you against the grain To voice him consul. **1650** HUBBERT *Pill Formality* 65 O this goes against the grain, this cannot be indured. **1861** HUGHES *Tom B. at Oxford* ch. 44 I followed your advice at last, though it went against the grain uncommonly.

Against the hair.   (H 18)

[= against the grain, inclination. Fr. *A contre-poil.*] **1387–8** T. USK *Test. Love* II. iv Ayenst the heere it tourneth. **1530** PALSGRAVE 829a Agaynst the heare, frowardly, or arsewardly. **1579–80** NORTH *Plutarch* (1676) 388 All went utterly against the hair with him. *c.* **1595** SHAKES. *R.J.* II. iv. 91 Thou desirest me to stop in my tale against the hair. **1600–1** *Id. M.W.W.* II. iii. 36 If you should fight, you go against the hair of your professions. **1602** *Id. T.C.* I. ii. 26 He is melancholy without cause and merry against the hair. **1668** HOWE *Bless. Righteous* (1825) 170 Something that crosses them, and goes against the hair.

Against the shins.   (S 342)

1678 RAY 81 That goes against the shins; i.e. It's to my prejudice, I do it not willingly.

Agamemnon, *see* Brave men before A.

Age (Winter) and wedlock tames man and beast (brings a man to his night-cap).   (A 63 and 64)

1589 GREENE *Menaphon* Grosart vi. 105 Why how now, Menaphon, hath your newe change driuen you to a night cap? . . . this is the strangest effect of loue that euer I saw, to freeze so quicklye the heart it set on fire so lately. **1594** *Taming o, A Shrew* F1ᵛ For forward wedlocke as the pro-uerbe says, Hath brought him to his nightcap long ago. **1594–8** SHAKES. *T.S.* IV. i. 20 But, thou knowest, winter tames man, woman, and beast. **1616** DRAXE no. 2395 Mariage and want of sleepe tame both man and beast. **1623** PAINTER C8 Wee forward wedlocke may com-pare thereto, For that vnto a night cap bring a man will doe. **1623** CAMDEN 265. **1639** CLARKE 328 Wedding and ill wintering tames both man and beast. **1670** RAY 47 (bring a man to his nightcap). **1908** E. PHILLPOTTS *The Mother* II. v 'Sometimes I feel that desperate that I could run away' . . . 'Time will tame you . . . Winter and wedlock tames maids and beasts.'

Age is jocund, When | it makes sport for death.   (A 76)

1640 HERBERT no. 637.

Age, *see also* Dies for a. (When he) you may quake; Eagle's old a.; Golden a.; Golden life in iron a.; Look in your mouth to know your a.; Old a. comes stealing on; Old a. is sickness of itself; Page of your own a.; Save while you may (For a.); Youth and a. never agree.

Agony, *see* Pile up the a.

Agree, for the law is costly. (*Cf.* Law is a lickpenny.)   (L 97)

a. **1607** MIDDLETON *Family of Love* V. iii. 24. **1616** BRETON *Cross.* B3 The law is costly. **1623**

CAMDEN 265. *a.* **1633** JONSON *Tale Tub* IV. i. 56 Come to a composition with him, Turfe: The Law is costly, and will draw on charge. **1638** J. TAYLOR *Bull Bear & Horse* B6ᵛ The proverbe says truly, The Law is costly. **1738** SWIFT *Dial.* I. E.L. 260. **1773** VIEYRA s.v. Avenca.

Agree like bells; They | they want nothing but hanging.   (B 281)

1556 J. POYNET *Treatise of Politick Power* E3ᵛ My lorde and I agree almost like belles. [*c.* **1592**] **1594** *Knack to Know a Knave* I. iv. 108, C3 We should gree together lyke belles, if thou wert but hanged first. **1614** T. ADAMS *Fatal Banquet* ii. Wks. 192 The great Theeues agree one with another . . . They tune like Bells, and want but hanging. **1670** RAY 161. **1802** WOLCOT (P. Pindar) *Middl. Elect.* iii. Wks. (1816) IV. 196 Iss,¹ iss, leek *bells* they all agree, Want nothing now but hanging. [¹ yes.]

Agree like cats and dogs, To.   (C 184)

1557 ERASMUS *Merry Dial.* B5ᵛ Ye are alwaies one at a nother, agreinge lyke dogges and cattes. **1576** PETTIE ii. 85 (dogs and cats). **1579** GOSSON *Sch. Abuse* Arb. 27 He that compareth our instruments, with those that were vsed in ancient times, shall see them agree like Dogges and Cattes. **1616** DRAXE no. 338. **1692** L'ESTRANGE *Aesop's Fab.* ccccxxviii (1738) 460 In the days of yore, when men and their wives agreed like dog and cat in a house together. **1882** BLACKMORE *Christowell* ch. 27 They live like cats and dogs, for his lordship has a temper, and so has Mr. G.

Agree like pickpockets in a fair, They.

1813 RAY 178.

Agree like the clocks of London, They.   (C 426)

1589 NASHE *Pasquil's Returne* I. 84 The Preachers of England begin to strike and agree like the Clocks of England. **1604** F. HERRING *Modest Defence* A2. **1659** HOWELL *Fr. Prov.* 21 (viz., not at all). **1672** CODRINGTON no. 1206. **1678** RAY 325 . . . I find this among both the *French* and *Italian* Proverbs for an instance of disagree-ment.

Agree like the fiddle and the stick, To.

1592 LYLY *Midas* I. ii. 8.

Agree like two cats in a gutter, They.   (C 185)

1546 HEYWOOD II. i. F4. **1659** HOWELL *Eng. Prov.* 3a.

Agree, *see also* Beauty and chastity seldom a.; Friends a. best at distance; Hearts may a. though heads differ.

Agreement, *see* Ill a. is better than good judge-ment.

Ague in the spring is physic for a king, An.   (A 79)

1650 A. WELLDON *Secret Hist. Jas. I* (1811) i. 479.

1653 A. WILSON *Hist. Gt. Britain* 285 A Tertian Ague . . . is not dangerous in the Spring (if we believe the Proverb). **1659** HOWELL *Eng. Prov.* 20b. **1670** RAY 32 . . . That is if it comes off well. . . . And an Ague-fit is not thought to go off kindly, unless it ends in a sweat. **1706** STEVENS s.v. Calentura.

Agues (Diseases) come on horseback, but go away on foot.   (A 83)

1593 J. ELIOT *Ortho-Epia Gallica* ed. J. Lindsay 88 Sicknesse comes alwaies on horsebacke, and goeth away on foot. **1611** COTGRAVE s.v. Maladie. **1678** RAY 33. **1869** HAZLITT 336.

Ague(s), *see also* Autumnal a. . . . mortal; No man dies of an a.; Quartan a. kill old men.

Aim, To be out of (beyond) one's.   (A 85)

1586 WARNER *Albion's Eng.* III. xix. L1 Yet (if I shoote not past myne aime) a world of tyme from me, Parte of our blood, in highest pompe, shall Englands glorie be. **1639** CLARKE 6 You are out of your ayme. **1671** CLARKE *Phras. Puer.* 187 He means well, but is clean out of his ayme. He's quite beside the cushion.

Aim, *see also* Archer . . . known . . . by his a., (A good).

Air of a window is as the stroke of a cross-bow, The. *Cf.* Cold wind reach you.   (A 87)

1642 TORRIANO 11. **1678** RAY 42 [Ital.] Aria di[1] finestra, colpo di balestra. [[1] *da*; Giusti].

Air, *see also* Beat the a.; Castles in a., (To build); Free as a.; Ill a. slays sooner than sword; Live on a. like chameleon; Northern wind brings weather fair.

Ajax, *see* Mad as A.

Akin as Lenson[1] Hill to Pilsen[2] Pen, As much.   (L 203)

1662 FULLER *Dorset* 278 . . . That is no kin at all . . . It is spoke of such who have vicinity . . . without the least ·. . . consanguinity or affinity betwixt them. For these are two high hills, the first wholy, the other partly in the Parish of Broad Windsor, whereof once I was Minister. **1670** RAY 226 [as 1662]. **1790** GROSE *Prov. Gloss.* C5 . . . These hills are eminent sea-marks. known to the sailors by the name of the Cow and Calf. This is commonly spoken of persons who are near neighbours, but neither relations nor acquaintance. [[1] Lewesdon. [2] Pillesden.]

Akin to the rich man, Every one is.   (M 580a)

1642 TORRIANO 82. **1659** HOWELL *It. Prov.* 9. Rich men can want no kindred. **1813** RAY 129.

Albion, *see* Perfidious A.

Alchemy to saving, No.   (A 97)

1640 HERBERT no. 114. **1710** PALMER 162 No Alchymy like to Thrift. **1773** VIEYRA s.v. Alchimia.

Alderman, *see* Paced like an a.

Ale and history.

a. **1635** R. CORBET *Iter Boreale* in CHALMERS *English Poets* V. 580 Mine host was full of ale and history. **1676** ETHEREGE *Man of Mode* I. i.

Ale (Drink, Wine) is in, When | wit is out.   (W 471)

c. **1386** CHAUCER *Pard. T.* l. 560 In whom that drynke hath dominacioun He kan no conseil kepe. *c.* **1390** GOWER *Conf. Amantis* VI. 555 For wher that wyn doth wit aweie, Wisdom hath loste the rihte weie. **1555** HEYWOOD *Epigr. upon Prov.* no. 163. **1612–15** BP. HALL *Contempl.* (Wks. 1647) 1072 We use to say, that when drink is in, wit is out; but if wit were not out, drink would not be in. **1640** HERBERT no. 187. **1721** KELLY 340 . . . A slender Excuse for what People may say, or do in their drink. **1858** SURTEES *Ask Mamma* ch. 58 It was just the wine being in and the wit being out . . . that led him away.

Ale is meat, drink, and cloth, Good.   (A 103)

1602 CAREW *Surv. of Cornwall* 1769 ed., 70 The liquor [ale] is the Englishman's ancientest and wholesomest drink, and serveth many for meat and cloth too. *c.* **1612** BEAUM. & FL. *Scornf. Lady* IV. ii. 61 In this short sentence, ale, is all included: Meat, drink, and cloth. **1670** DRYDEN *Almanz. & Alma.* Prol. 15 Like them that find meat, drink, and cloth in ale. **1738** SWIFT *Dial.* II. E.L. 310 O my lord, my ale is meat, drink, and cloth.

Ale sellers should not be tale-tellers.

1721 KELLY 32 . . . Publick House-keepers should not blaze abroad what their Guests may say, or do, in their Houses.

Ale will (Enough to) make a cat speak.   (A 99)

1585–1618 *Shirburn Ballads* (1907) 93 Who is it but loues good liquor? 'Twill make a catte speak. **1596** NASHE *Saffron W.* iii. 50 The wrongs that thou hast offred him are so intollerable, as they would make a Cat speake. **1606** BRETON *Pkt. Lett.* Wks. Gros. ii *h* 51 I haue spoken for Ale that will make a Cat speake. **1608–10** BEAUM. & FL. *Coxcomb* II. i There's Ale will make a Cat speak. **1611** SHAKES. *Temp.* II. ii. 78 Here is that which will give language to you, cat. **1639** J. TAYLOR *Drink & Welcome* D1[v] Braggot, that can teach a Cat to speake. **1678** RAY 88 Ale that would make a cat to speak. **1738** SWIFT *Dial.* II. E.L. 310 My ale . . . will make a cat speak, and a wise man dumb. **1839** DICKENS *N. Nickleby* ch. 12 It's enough to make a Tom cat talk French grammar, only to see how she tosses her head.

Ale, *see also* Banbury a.; Brew good a. (You); Fair chieve good a.; Lemster bread and Weabley a.; Mends as sour a. in summer; Must be if we sell a. (This); Sickle . . . love I not to see, but the good a. tankard, happy might it be; Southwark a.; Water stoups hold no a.

Ale-clout, *see* Wash one's face in a.

Ale-drinkers, *see* Cobblers and tinkers.

Ale-house, *see* Penny to spend; St. Peter's in the Poor, where no a.; Settling an island, first building by Englishman an a.

Alike every day makes a clout[1] on Sunday.

1721 KELLY 46 . . . A Reprimand to them who wear their best Suit every Day, which will soon make them improper to be worn on Sunday. 1732 FULLER no. 785. [¹ rag.]

Alike, *see also* Grooms and householders are a. great (Where); disastrous for houses; Lie all a. in our graves.

Alive, *see* Hope keeps man a.;

All abroad and nothing at home.

1673 MARVELL *Rehearsal Transpros'd* pt. 2, 105.

All are not saints that go to church (seem so).   (A 116)

a. 1576 WHYTHORNE III All iz not gowld that seemeth to be so nor eury on A saint that seemeth to be on. 1584 WITHALS K6ᵛ They be not all saints of this be you sure, that go in and out at the Churche dore. 1659 N. R. I All who come into a Church, say not their Prayers.

All came from and will go to others.
                                             (A 123)

1611 COTGRAVE s.v. Autruy. 1640 HERBERT no. 41.

All complain.   (A 126)

1640 HERBERT no. 750.

All covet, all lose.   (A 127)

1297 *R. of Gloucester's Chron.* (1724) 306 Wo so coueyteþ al, al leseþ ywys. *c.* 1400 LYDGATE *Isopes* 8. I An old prouerbe hath he sayde and shal . . . who al coveiteth, oft he lesith all. 1481 CAXTON *Reynard* xxxiii Arb. 95 Who that wold haue all leseth alle Ouer couetous was neuer good. 1546 HEYWOOD II. ix. L2ᵛ Haue ye not herde tell, all couet all leese? 1663 J. WILSON *Cheats* IV. i This is it when men must manage their business by themselves:—All covet and all lose. 1692 L'ESTRANGE *Aesop's Fab.* vi (1738) 6 Out of a greediness to get both, he chops at the shadow, and loses the substance. . . . All covet, all lose.

All faults to mend, Hard [it] is for any man.   (M 200)

1546 HEYWOOD I. xi. D3ᵛ. 1611 DAVIES no. 345.

All feet tread not in one shoe. *Cf.* Shoe fits not every foot (Every); One shoe will not fit all feet.   (F 574)

1587 J. BRIDGES *Def. of Gov.* 86 Diuerse feete haue diuerse lastes. 1591 LAMBARDE *Archeion* (1635, 78) To apply one generall Law to all particular cases, were to make all shooes by one last. 1640 HERBERT no. 497.

All fellows at football.   (F 182)

[*c.* 1587] 1594 MARLOWE & NASHE *Dido* III. iii. 5 All fellows now, dispos'd alike to sport. 1594 *Taming of a Shrew* Ind. 37 All fellows now, and see you take me so. [*c.* 1591] 1599 [GREENE?] *George a Green* F3ᵛ Come, masters, all fellowes. 1600 SIR J. OLDCASTLE F3ᵛ All friends at footeball, fellows all in field, Harry, and Dick, and George. 1630 *Wine Beer Ale & Tobacco* C3ᵛ At Dancing and at Foot-ball, all fellowes. 1670 RAY 174 . . . If gentlemen . . . will mingle themselves with rusticks in their rude sports; they must look for usage suitable to, or rather courser then others. 1733 SWIFT *Reas. Repeal. Sacr. Test* Wks. (1856) ii. 248 The whole Babel of sectaries joined . . . in a match at football; where the proverb expressly tells us, that all are fellows.

All have and nought forego, He would.
                                             (A 194)

1546 HEYWOOD I. xi. E1ᵛ She will all haue and will right nought forgo. 1562 HEYWOOD Y1 *Epig.* no. 278 He woulde all haue and naught forgo. 1616 DRAXE no. 375. 1639 CLARKE 40 (All would have).

All is good, if God say Amen.   (A 137)

1616 WITHALS 570. All good, and God say Amen. 1639 CLARKE 235.

All Hallows'-tide, Allhallontide, *see* Set trees at A.

All in the day's work, It is.

1738 SWIFT Dial. I. E.L. 271 Will you be so kind as to tie this string for me . . .? it will go all in your day's work. 1820 SCOTT *Monast.* ch. 9 That will cost me a farther ride, . . . but it is all in the day's work. 1896 F. E. YOUNGHUSBAND *Heart of Cont.* 28 The mules merely shook themselves and then stared stonily ahead, as if it were all in the day's work.

All is gone, and nothing left, When | what avails the dagger with the dudgeon-heft?   (A 212)

1582 R. STANYHURST *The First Four Books of Virgil* A4ᵛ When al is goane but thee black scabbard, Wel faer thee haft wyth thee duggeon dagger. 1583 MELBANCKE *Philot.* 28. 1602 WITHALS 34 (what helps). 1659 HOWELL *Eng. Prov.* 14a. [Common daggers had a hilt made of *dudgeon* wood, perhaps boxwood.]

All is lost that goes beside one's own mouth.   (A 141)

1618 D. DYKE *Two Treatises (Philemon)* 108 They . . . snatch it all to themselues, grudging another

the least morsell, thinking all is lost that goes
besides their owne lips. **1639** CLARKE 76 All's
lost that falls beside. **1738** SWIFT Dial. III. E.L.
323 I wish they would be quiet, and let me drink
my tea. — What! I warrant you think all is lost
that goes beside your own mouth.

All is over but the shouting.

1842 APPERLEY *Life Sportsman* ch. 16 It's all over
but shouting . . . Antonio's as dead as a hammer.
1869 A. L. GORDON *How we beat the favourite* The
race is all over, bar shouting. **1891** J. L. KIPLING
Beast & Man 226 The Englishman would say
the back of a job was broken, or 'All is over but
the shouting'.

All (Love) lies a-bleeding. (A 159)

1546 HEYWOOD II. v. H2 Aduise ye well, for here
doeth all lye and bleede. *c.* **1565** *Bugbears* IV.
iii. 36 Thou has sene nothinge yet, to that thou
shalt see for yet it lies and bledes. **1594–5**
SHAKES. *R.J.* III. i. 186 My blood for your rude
brawls doth lie a-bleeding. [**1609**] **1620** BEAUM.
& FL. *Philaster or Love Lies a Bleeding* [play
title]. **1610** BRETNOR *Almanac* Sept. Good days.
It lyes a bleeding. **1611** DAVIES no. 194. **1634**
T. HEYWOOD *Maidenhead Well Lost* (1874 ed. iv.
148) All our fortunes lie a bleeding.

All meats to be eaten, and all maids to be wed. (M 850)

1546 HEYWOOD II. ii. F4ᵛ. **1616** DRAXE no. 1390
That that one will not, another will: so shall all
maids bee married, and all meats eaten. **1678**
RAY 64.

All men are mortal. (M 502)

c. **1386** CHAUCER *Melibeus* l. 2803 Deeth is the
ende of every man as in this present lyf. *Id.
Knight's T.* l. 3030 Of man and womman seen
we wel also, . . . He moot ben deed, the king as
shal a page. *c.* **1430** LYDGATE *Minor Poems*
Percy Soc. 77 Bothe highe and loughe shal go
dethis daunce. [*c.* **1537**] *c.* **1560** UDALL *Thersytes*
C4 And seeinge we be mortall all Let not our
wroth be immortall. **1598** SHAKES. *2 Hen. IV*
III. ii. 36 Death, as the Psalmist saith, is certain
to all; all shall die. **1598–9** *Id. M.A.* I. i. 50
Well, we are all mortal. **1600–1** *Id. H.* I. ii. 72
All that lives must die. [**1598**] **1616** HAUGHTON
Englishman for my Money l. 473 All of vs are
mortall men. **1616** DRAXE no. 435.

All men have what belongs to them, When | it cannot be much. (M 595)

1640 HERBERT no. 979.

All men must die. (M 505)

[Ps. lxxxix 48 : What man is he that liveth and shall
not see death?] **1560** T. PALFREYMAN *Mirror*
P2ᵛ We are al planted within the limits of death.
1578 WHETSTONE *2 Promos and Cass.* v. iii. L4
Death, is but death, and all in fyne shall dye.
1591 SHAKES. *3 Hen. VI* V. ii. 28 And, live we
how we can, yet die we must. *c.* **1593** *Id. R.J.*
III. iii. 92 Well, death's the end of all. *Ibid.* III.
iv. 4 Well, we were born to die. **1595** *Id.
Rich. II* III. ii. 103 Death will have his day.
1595 *Locrine* I. i. 247 Euerie man must tread the

way to death. **1598** SHAKES. *2 Hen. IV* III. ii. 36
Death, as the Psalmist saith, is certain to all; all
shall die. **1639** CLARKE 216 Rich and poore,
old and young must die. **1738** SWIFT Dial. II.
E.L. 315 Dead! . . . . I'm heartily sorry; but, my
lord, we must all die.

All men row galley way.

1642 TORRIANO 96. **1813** RAY 16 . . . i.e. Every
one draweth towards himself.

All men say you are an ass, When | it is time to bray. (M 531)

1616 DRAXE no. 104. **1659** HOWELL *Span. Prov.*
I.

All men speak, When | no man hears. (M 596)

c. **1641** FERGUSSON MS. no. 1462. **1721** KELLY
343 . . . Used when many speak at once in a
Business.

All men will please, He that | shall never find ease. (M 526)

[*Cf.* **1509** BARCLAY *Ship of Fools* i. 208.] *a.* **1581**
N. WOODES *Conflict of Conscience* G1 He that
will seeke eche man to content shall proue him-
selfe at last most vnwise. **1601** *Historical
Collections* (1680) 54 He that seeketh to please
All, shall please None. **1639** CLARKE 282.

All men, *see also* True that a. m. say.

All must be as God will. (A 161)

1548 HALL *Chron.* 627 Some Englishe knightes
sayd, syr you haue sayd well, and as God will
all must be. **1616** DRAXE no. 492. **1639** CLARKE
114 What God will, that must be.

All my eye (and Betty Martin).

[= all humbug, nonsense.] **1768** GOLDSMITH
Good-n. Man III (Globe) 625 That's all my eye.
The King only can pardon. **1785** GROSE *Dict.
Vulg. T.* 1788 ed. s.v. Betty Martin, That's my
eye, Betty Martin. **1819** MOORE *Tom Crib's
Mem. Congress* 2 All my eye, Betty. **1823**
PIERCE EGAN s.v. Betty Martin. That's my eye,
Betty Martin; . . . a corruption of 'Mihi beatae
martinis'. **1824** SCOTT *St. Ronan's W.* ch. 31
Sounds of depreciation, forming themselves
indistinctly into something like the words, 'My
eye and Betty Martin'. **1850** KINGSLEY *Alton L.*
ch. 25 Hullo! my eye and Betty Martin! . . . This
is too ridiculous. **1894** BLACKMORE *Perlycross*
ch. 21 Oh, that's all my eye, and Betty Martin!
Nobody believes that, I should hope.

All one (the same) a hundred (thousand) years hence, It will be. (Y 22)

1611 COTGRAVE s.v. Fiers All will be one at the
latter day, say we. **1738** SWIFT Dial. I. E.L.
276 If people will be rude, I have done: my
comfort is, 'twill be all one a thousand years
hence. **1839** DICKENS *N. Nickleby* ch. 9 Mrs.
Squeers . . . frequently remarked when she made
any . . . mistake, it would be all the same a hundred years hence.

All sorts to make a world, It takes.

(s 666)

1620 SHELTON *Quix.* II. vi (1908) II. 224 In the world there must be of all sorts. **1767** JOHNSON 17 Nov. in *Boswell* (1848) xx. 188 Some lady surely might be found . . . in whose fidelity you might repose. *The World*, says Locke, *has people of all sorts.* **1844** JERROLD *Story of Feather* ch. 28 Click can't get off this time ? . . . Well, it takes all sorts to make a world. **1891** A. LANG *Ess. in Little* 180 'It takes all sorts to make a world', in poetry as in life. Sir Walter's sort is a very good sort.

All Stuarts are not sib to the king.

1721 KELLY 14 . . . Spoken when People boast of some great Man of their Name. **1857** DEAN RAMSAY *Remin.* v (1911) 194 Persons may have the name and appearance of greatness without the reality: *A' Stuarts are na sib to the King.*

All that is sharp is short. *Cf.* Nothing that is violent is permanent. (A 168)

1546 HEYWOOD II. ii. G1. **1592** SHAKES. *T.And.* I. i. 409–10 'Tis good, sir: you are very short with us; But, if we live, we'll be as sharp with you. [1604] **1607** DEKKER & WEBSTER *Sir T. Wyatt* II. ii. 66. **1616** DRAXE no. 2248. **1655** FULLER *Church Hist.* IX. v. III. 55 Short but sharp.

All that shakes falls not. (A 169)

1603 MONTAIGNE (Florio), III. ix. 30 All that shaketh doth not fall: the contexture of so vast a frame holds by more then one naile. **1640** HERBERT no. 1022.

All that you get you may put in your eye, and see never the worse. (w 506)

1530 PALSGRAVE 478a Whan I have all caste my penyworthes, I maye put my wynnyng in myn eye. **1545** ASCHAM *Toxoph.* Arb. 151 That shoter whiche . . . shooteth . . . in rough wether and fayre, shall alwayes put his wynninges in his eyes. **1546** HEYWOOD I. xi. E2ᵛ At ende I myght put my wynnyng in myne iye, And sée neuer the wors. **1588** 'MARPRELATE' *Epitome* ed. Pierce 129 I might carry it in my eye, and see never a whit the worse. **1629** T. ADAMS *Serm.* (1861–2) I. 201 Judas . . . sells his Master to the Pharisees, himself to the Devil. Yet when all is done, he might put his gains in his eye.

All the wit in the world, If you had | fools would fell you.

1721 KELLY 185 . . . Spoken disdainfully, to them that think themselves very wise.

All things are good unseyit.[1] (T 162)

a. **1628** CARMICHAELL no. 223 (unprovin). **1641** FERGUSSON no. 144. [¹ untried.]

All things are to be bought at Rome.

(T 164)

1549 LATIMER *5th Serm. bef. Edw. VI* P.S. 185 We have the old proverb, *Omnia venalia Romae,*

'All things are sold for money at Rome'; and Rome is come home to our own doors. **1571** J. BRIDGES *Sermon at Paul's Cross* 137 The·comon prouerbe, *Omnia venalia Romæ*, al things are sale at Rome. **1624** J. HEWES *Perfect Survey* F2 (are saleable at Rome).

All things fit not all persons. (T 167)

c. **1532** *Tales* no. 7 By this tale ye may perceyue that all thynges beseme nat euery body. **1539** TAVERNER 36ᵛ Nether all thynges, nor in all places, nor of al men. Thys prouerbe teacheth vs, that in takynge of rewardes, we shewe oure selues not only shamefast, but also ware and circumspecte. **1639** CLARKE 82 (not all men). *Ibid.* 89 Omnia non decent omnes.

All things in their being are good for something. (T 170)

1602 WARNER *Albion's Eng.* Bk. 13, ch. 78 All Things in themselues be good. **1640** HERBERT no. 520.

All things require skill but an appetite.

(T 173)

1640 HERBERT no. 378.

All things thrive at thrice. *Cf.* Third time's lucky; Luck in odd numbers.

(T 175)

a. **1628** CARMICHAELL no. 214 (bot thryse). **1641** FERGUSSON no. 107 (but thrice). **1721** KELLY 26 . . . An Encouragement . . . to try the third time. They will say the third's a Charm.

All things to all men, To be.

[I CORINTH. ix. 22 I am made all things to all men, that I might by all means save some.] **1545** TAVERNER G2 Some men do by their blandishmentes and sugred tunge accomodate them selues in all thinges to al men. **1763** C. CHURCHILL *Prophecy of Famine* l. 211 If they, directed by Paul's holy pen, Become discreetly all things to all men, That all men may become all things to them, Envy may hate, but Justice can't condemn.

All truths are not to be told. (T 594)

c. **1350** *Douce MS.* 52 no. 57 Alle the Sothe is not to be sayde. *c.* **1460** *Passe Forthe, Pilgrime* in Herrig's *Archiv* 101. 51 Say not all, that wolde the sothe seme. **1640** HERBERT no. 89. **1670** RAY 150 All truth must not be told at all times. **1721** KELLY 37 All the truth should not be told. Because it may be ill-natured, uncharitable, or unseasonable. **1821** SCOTT *Kenilw.* ch. 6 A man may, in some circumstances, disguise the truth . . .; for were it to be always spoken, and upon all occasions, this were no world to live in. [Fr. *Toutes les vérités ne sont pas bonnes à dire.*]

All women are good. (w 680)

1678 RAY 59 viz., either good for something or good for nothing. **1836** DICKENS *Pickwick* ch. 8 All women are angels, they say.

All's out is good for prisoners, but naught for the eyes. (A 219)

1678 RAY 186 . . . It's good for prisoners to be out, but bad for the eyes to be out. This is a droll used by good fellows when one tells them, all the drink is out.

All, All are (not), All is (not), All the, All this, *see also under significant words following.*

Allowance, *see* Grains of a.

Almanac, *see* Buchanan's a., long foul long fair; Court has no a.

Almond for a parrot, An. (A 220)

1521 SKELTON *Sp. Parrot* 50 ii. 4 An almon now for Parrot, dilycatly drest. **1599** BUTTES *Dyets Dry Dinner* E2 Phillis was turned into an Almond-tree, for telling tales out schoole: euer sithence, it hath bene a by-word: an Almond for the Parrat. **1602** SHAKES. *T.C.* V. ii. 191 The parrot will not do more for an almond than he for a commodious drab. *a.* **1637** JONSON *Magn. Lady* v. vii. 42 Almond for Parrat; Parrat's a brave bird.

Almost and very (well) nigh saves many a lie. (A 221)

1639 CLARKE 106. **1670** RAY 56 . . . *Almost* having some latitude, men are apt to stretch it to cover untruths.

Almost was never hanged. (A 222)

1557 EDGEWORTH *Sermons* 4A1 Aristotle saith, Quod fere fit non fit, sed quod vix fit fit. That is almost done or wel nere done, is not done: but that is scarsely done, yt it is done thoughe it be with much a do. **1639** CLARKE 3.

Alms never make poor. (A 223)

1640 HERBERT no. 189. **1659** HOWELL *It. Prov.* 20. **1706** STEVENS s.v. Limosna.

Alms, *see also* Good memory gives few a.; Preaches (He that) gives a.

Almsgiving lessens no man's living, Great. (A 226)

1640 HERBERT no. 190.

Alone, *see* Better be a. than . . . ; Eats his cock a. (Who), must saddle horse a.; Eagles fly a.; Haste comes not a.; Misfortunes never come a.; Welcome evil if comest a.; Wise man is never less a.; Woe to him that is a.

Altar, He that serves at the | ought to live by the altar. (A 230)

1546 *Suppl. Commons* in FISH *Suppl. for Beggars* E.E.T.S. 72 Affirminge that it is but mete that suche as serue the aulter, should haue a liuynge therby. **1583** G. BABINGTON *Exposition of the Commandments* 234 The workman is worthie of his wages. He that serueth the Altar let him liue of the Altar.

Altar(s), *see also* Friend as far as a. permits; Prosperity no a. smoke (In).

Although it rain, throw not away your watering-pot. (W 133)

1640 HERBERT no. 325.

Although the sun shine, leave not your cloak at home. (S 968)

[*c.* **1190** *Li Proverbe au Vilain* (Tobler) 20 no. 44 Et par pluie et par bel tens doit on porter sa chape, ce dit li vilains.] *c.* **1390** CHAUCER *Proverbs* i What shul thise clothes thus manyfold, Lo! this hote somers day? After greet hete cometh cold; no man caste his pilche [cloak] away. **1640** HERBERT no. 336. **1706** STEVENS s.v. Sol.

Alton, *see* Pass of A. poverty might pass (Through).

Altrincham, *see* Mayor of A.

Always say 'No', If you | you'll never be married.

1721 KELLY 298 Say ay No, and you'll never be married. **1728** SWIFT Dial. I. E.L. 264. No, I thank your lordship. . . . — Well; but if you always say no, you'll never be married.

Always (a) something, There is.

1841 MARRYAT *Poacher* ch. 40 There never was anybody . . . who . . . had mixed with the world, who could afterwards say that they were at any time perfectly happy. . . . 'There is always something.' **1883** J. PAYN *Thicker than W.* ch. 2 [The marriage] 'upon the whole is very satisfactory; it is true Jeannie hates her gudeman, but then there's always a something.'

Always taking out of the meal-tub, and never putting in, soon comes to the bottom. (B 552)

1659 HOWELL *Span. Prov.* 10 Where they take out and put nothing in, they quickly go to the bottom. **1706** STEVENS s.v. Hondon. **1758** FRANKLIN *Way to Wealth* (Crowell) 20 They think . . . a little to be spent . . . is not worth minding; but *Always taking out,* &c.

Always verify your references.

1918 *Times Lit. Sup.* 26 Apr. 197 Routh's[1] advice, 'Always verify your references' evidently never reached him, or made no impression on him. [[1] M. J. Routh, 1755-1854, President of Magdalen College, Oxford. See Dean Burgon, *Lives of Twelve Good Men* i. 73.]

Amantium irae, **see** Falling out of lovers.

Ambassador, *see* Welsh a.

Amber, *see* Fly in a.

Ambition loses many a man.   (A 235)

[1589] 1592 LYLY *Midas* III. i. 11 Ambition . . .
climeth so high by other mens heads, that she
breaketh her owne necke. 1605–6 SHAKES. *M.*
I. vii. 25 I have . . . only Vaulting ambition
which o'erleaps itself And falls on th' other.
1616 BRETON *Crossing* B3ᵛ Ambition endangers
life. 1659 N.R. 14.

Amble, *see* Foal a., If horse and mare trot, (How
can?); Mother trot, (If the) how can the
daughter a.?

Ambry, *see* No sooner up but hand in a.

**Amend when they cannot appair (grow
worse), Some do.**   (A 237)

1530 PALSGRAVE 531b I praye God amende hym,
for he can nat well empayre. 1546 HEYWOOD II.
ix. Lɪᵛ Howe ye will amende, whan ye can not
appayre. 1555 HEYWOOD *Three Hund. Epig.* no.
106 He may soone amend, for he cannot apeyre.
1611 DAVIES no. 264. 1616 DRAXE no. 482
(mend). 1659 HOWELL *Eng. Prov.* 5b He may
mend, but not grow worse.

Amends for ladies (all).

1600 *Look about You* l. 2406 (all). 1611 N.
FIELD *Amends for Ladies* [play title]. 1664 W.
CONYERS *Hemerologicum Astronomicum* 14 Dec.
(all).

Amend(s, ed), *see also* Angry without a cause,
. . . pleased without a.; Best may a.; Chastises
one a. many; Every man mend (a.) one (If);
Heaven will make a.; Little said soonest a.;
World is well a.

**Americans, Good | when they die, go to
Paris.**

1858 O. W. HOLMES *Autocrat of Breakfast Table*
ch. 6 To these must certainly be added that
other saying of one of the wittiest of men
[Thomas Appleton, 1812–84]: 'Good Americans, when they die, go to Paris.' 1879 HENRY
JAMES *International Episode*, ii. 1882 JOWETT in
Life II. 208 The Southern climate . . . is, like
Paris, 'the heaven to which good Americans go'.
1893 O. WILDE *Woman of No Import.* Act I They
say, Lady Hunstanton, that when good Americans die they go to Paris.

Amiss, *see* Goodman is last who knows what's a.;
Thinks a. concludes worse.

Amongst good men two men suffice.
                                                   (M 506)

1640 HERBERT no. 885.

Amorous, *see* Moist hand argues a. nature.

Amuck, *see* Run a.

**Anchor of a ship, Like the | that is
always at sea and never learns to swim.**
                                                   (A 240)

1591 FLORIO *Second F.* 134 Thou art like vnto an

anker, which is alwaies in. *c.* 1594 BACON no.
923 Lyke an anchor that is ever in the water and
will never learn to swym. 1894 COWAN 61 . . .
The writer frequently has had this proverb
applied to him, on account of his inability to
resist sea-sickness even after crossing . . . all . . .
the waters of the world.

Anchor(s), *see also* Dutchman's a.; Good riding
at two a.

Ancient, *see* Blood is alike a., (All).

Ancum (Ancolme) pike, *see* Witham eel.

Angel visits, Like.

1687 J. NORRIS *Miscellanies* 'The Parting'; 18
How fading are the Joves[1] we dote upon, . . .
Like *Angels* visits, *short* and *bright.* 1742 BLAIR
Grave 589 Its visits, Like those of angels, Short
and far between. 1799 CAMPBELL *Pleas. of Hope*
II. 377–8 (1807) 77 My wingèd hours of bliss
have been, Like angel-visits, few and far between!
[[1] joys.]

Angels, On the side of the.

1864 DISRAELI *Sp. on 25 Nov.* Is man an ape or
an angel? Now I am on the side of the angels.
1945 'Watchman' in *Brit. Wkly.* 6 Sept. One
might say [of a U.S. magazine] that it was on the
side of the angels, if that be understood as meaning that it was on the side of *man.*

Angel(s), *see also* Fire (By this) that's God's a.;
Men are not a.; Oil of a.; Physician is a. when
employed; Spoke an a.; Talk of an a.; Write
like a.

Anger and haste hinder good counsel.

1562 A. BROOKE *Romeus & Juliet* (Munro) l. 1655
Two foes that counsel hath, That wont to hinder
sound advice, rash hastiness and wrath. 1707
MAPLETOFT 8.

Anger dies quickly with a good man.
                                                   (A 244)

c. 1526 *Dicta Sap.* B3 The angre of yuell men
moost slowlye asswageth, of good men soone.
1539 TAVERNER *Publius* B2ᵛ With a good man
angre sone dyeth. 1664 CODRINGTON 184.
1670 RAY I.

Anger is a short madness.   (A 246)

[HORACE *Ep.* I. 2. 62 *Ira furor brevis est.*] *c.*
1200 *Ancrene Riwle* 120 Wreththe[1] is a wodshipe[2].
1539 TAVERNER *Publius* B8ᵛ Angre (sayeth
Horace) is a shorte frensy. 1539 TAVERNER 2
Garden 44ᵛ He [Cato] sayde an angrye bodye
dothe nothynge dyffer from a mad man but in
the tariaunce of tyme. Signifyeng that wrathe is
(as Horace the poete sayeth) a short frensye.
1578 FLORIO *First F.* 42ᵛ Petrarcha . . . saith . . .
Anger is a furie short. 1605–8 SHAKES. *T.Ath.*
I. ii. 28 They say my lords, *Ira furor brevis est.*
1621 BURTON *Anat. Mel.* I. ii. I. ix (1651) 104
Anger, a perturbation, . . . preparing the body to
melancholy, and madness itself—*ira furor brevis
est.* 1707 SWIFT *Facult. of Mind* Wks. (1904)
416 These orators inflame the people, whose

anger is really but a short fit of madness. [¹ wrath. ² madness.]

Anger punishes itself. (A 247)

1580 LYLY *Euph. & his Eng.* ii. 66 It fell out with him as it doth commonly, with all those that are cholericke, that he hurt no man but himself. **1732** FULLER no. 799.

Anger, *see also* Enter into a house (When you), leave a. at door; Housetop in a., (To be on); Keep yourself from a. of great man; Meat is in, (When) a. is out.

Angle all day and catch a gudgeon at night, To. (D 106)

1618 BRETON *Courtier & Countryman* Roxb. Libr. 190.

Angle (Fish) with a golden (silver) hook, To. (H 591)

[ERASM. *Ad. Aureo piscari hamo.* To fish with a golden hook.] *c.* **1549** ERASM. *Two Dial.* tr. E. Becke f. 19ʳ Were not he a starke fole that wold fishe with a golden bayte. **1560** *Impat. Poverty* E1ᵛ He made is purgacyon vpon a boke Or els redemed wyth the syluer hoke. **1562** A. BROOKE *Romeus & Juliet* (Munro), l. 712 There is no better way to fish than with a golden hook. **1579** T. F. *News from the North* Iiᵛ. **1580** CHURCHYARD *Charge* 28 Collier Although you fishe with golden hookes. **1605** BRETON *Honour of Val.* 5/2 Wks. Gros. I To fish for honour with a silver hooke. **1678** RAY 226 ... The Italians by this phrase mean, to buy fish in the market. Money is the best bait to take all sorts of persons with. **1796** M. EDGEWORTH *Par. Asst.* (1903) 422 The servants we might corrupt; but even the old proverb of 'Angle with a silver hook', won't hold good with him.

Angler eats more than he gets, An.

1706 STEVENS s.v. Pescador. **1732** FULLER no. 579. **1823** COLLINS 259 'The fisherman with a rod, eats more than he earns.' Applied to persons who, to avoid work, seek employments of little advantage.

Anglesea is the mother of Wales. (A 248)

1387 HIGDEN (tr. Trevisa) ii. 39 (Rolls Ser.) A proverbe and an olde sawe ... Mon moder of Wales. **1613–22** DRAYTON *Polyolb.* ix. 390 Mona ... Was call'd (in former times) her Country *Cambria's* mother. **1662** FULLER Anglesea 18 *Mon Mam Cymbry.* That is, Anglesea is the Mother of Wales ... because, ... she ... is said to afford Corn enough to sustain all Wales.

Angling, *see* Fishing (End of) is not a.

Angry as a pismire,¹ As.

c. **1386** CHAUCER *Sum. T.* l. 1825 He is as angry as a pissemyre, Though þat he haue al that he kan desire. [¹ ant.]

Angry as a wasp, As. (W 76)

c. **1350** *Alexander* l. 738 As wrath as waspe.

a. **1529** SKELTON *Elyn. Rumming* l. 330 Angry as a waspy. **1546** HEYWOOD I. xi. D2 Now mery as a cricket, and by and by, Angry as a waspe. **1659** HOWELL *Eng. Prov.* 3a.

Angry as an ass with a squib in his breech, As.

1611 COTGRAVE s.v. Asne.

Angry, When | count a hundred (recite the alphabet).

[1591] **1623** SHAKES. *2 Hen. VI* I. iii. 150 My choler being overblown with walking once about the quadrangle. [1592] **1597** *Id. Rich. III* I. iv. 118 I hope this passionate humour of mine will change; it was wont to hold me but while one tells twenty. **1616** T. ADAMS *Diseases of the Soul* 16 [Athenodorus to Augustus Caesar] An angry man should not vndertake any action or speech, till hee had recited the Greeke Alphabet: as a pause to coole the heate of choler. **1817** T. JEFFERSON Letter to C. Clay When angry count ten before you speak. If very angry a hundred. **1902–4** LEAN IV. 182.

Angry, He that is | is seldom at ease. (E 37)

1530 PALSGRAVE 682b He that can nat refrayne his anger at a tyme muste nedes have moche busynesse. **1611** COTGRAVE s.v. Courroucé Hee's not at ease thats in a chafe. **1616** DRAXE no. 86. **1670** RAY I.

Angry without a cause, He that is | shall (must) be pleased without amends. (C 200)

c. **1510** STANBRIDGE *Vulg.* E.E.T.S. 23 Yf thou be angry with me without a cause thou shall be made at one without a mendes. **1641** FERGUSSON no. 305 He that crabbes¹ without cause, should mease² without mends. **1670** RAY 56. **1721** KELLY 146 ... must mease² without amends. [¹ grows angry. ² settle, grow calm.]

Angry, If you be | you may turn the buckle of your girdle (belt) behind you. (B 698)

1598–9 SHAKES. *M.A.* V. i. 139 I think he be angry indeed. — If he be, he knows how to turn his girdle. **1621** BURTON *Anat. Mel.* Democ. to Rdr. (1651) 77 If any man take exceptions, let him turn the buckle of his girdle; I care not. **1659** HOWELL *Eng. Prov.* 12b. **1738** SWIFT *Dial.* I. E.L. 287 If miss will be angry for nothing, take my counsel, and bid her turn the buckle of her girdle behind her. **1818** SCOTT *Rob Roy* ch. 25 Nay, never look ... grim at me, man—if ye're angry, ye ken how to turn the buckle o' your belt behind you.

Angry, *see also* Hungry (If thou be), I am a.; Hungry man a. man; Never be a. at (Two things a man should); Short folk are soon a.; Two to one in all things against a. man.

Annoy, *see* Joy without a. (No).

Annuity, *see* Give a man an a. . . . live for ever.

Anon(s), *see* Better keep now than seek a.; Two a. and a by-and-by.

Another yet the same.

[HOR. *Carm. Saec.* 10 *Alme Sol . . . qui alius . . . et idem nasceris.*] **1728** POPE *Dunciad* iii. 40. **1789–91** DARWIN *Botanic Garden* I. 4. 380. **1814** WORDSWORTH *Excursion* ix l. 440 A twofold image; on a grassy bank A snow-white ram, and in the crystal flood, Another and the same. **1826** SCOTT *Journ.* 1 Jan. Singular to be at once another and the same.

Another's bread costs dear.   (B 609)

1640 HERBERT no. 324.

Another, *see also* Block in a.'s way, (To lay a); Dig a pit for a.; Fed at a.'s hand (He that is); Knife whets a. (One); One nail (love) drives out a.; One poison drives out a.; One thing brings up a. thing; You are such a.

Another man, *see* Conscience is cumbered (Whose), of a. m.'s deeds the worse will deem; King's word more than a. m.'s oath; Loss is a. m.'s gain, (One man's); Meddle not with a. m.'s matter; Put a. m.'s child in your bosom; Scald not your lips in a. m.'s pottage; Wholesomest meal at a. m.'s cost.

Answer as a man gives, Such | such will he get.   (A 254)

a. **1628** CARMICHAELL no. 1368. **1641** FERGUSSON no. 766.

Answer, To be (do) more than he can.   (M 1160)

1598–9 SHAKES. *M.A.* IV. ii. 56 And this is more, masters, than you can deny. **1600** DEKKER *Shoemakers' Hol.* I. i. 148 I thinke you doe more then you can answere. [**1600**] **1659** J. DAY *Blind Beggar* II. E1 I haue done No more than I can answer, I and will. *a.* **1633** JONSON *Tale Tub* IV. i. 25 This more: and which is more, then he can answer.

Answer (*noun*), *see also* Demand is a jest, (Where the) the fittest a. is a scoff; Get the poor man's a.; Question (Like) like a.; Shortest a. is doing; Soft a. turns away; Truth has no a.; Woman's a. is never to seek; Wrong hears, wrong a. gives.

Answer(s) (*verb*), *see* Money a. all things; Never a. a question until asked; Understands ill (Who), a. ill.

Ant had wings to her hurt, The.   (A 256)

1584 LYLY *Camp.* IV. ii. 13 Antes liue safely, til they haue gotten wings. **1620** SHELTON *Quix.* II. xxxiii (1908) III. 55 The proverb says the ant had wings to do her hurt, and it may be Sancho the squire may sooner go to heaven than Sancho

the governor. **1644** HOWELL *Dodona's Grove* 20 **1706** STEVENS s.v. Dios.

Ant, *see also* Fly has spleen, a. gall.

Antwerp is a pistol pointed at the heart of England.

1903 H. B. GEORGE *Rel. of Geog. & Hist.* 240 'Antwerp', said Napoleon, 'is a pistol pointed at the heart of England'; and he did his best to create a fleet there.

Anvil fears no blows, The.   (A 257)

1609 HARWARD 70 A sound Anvill feareth no hammer. **1666** TORRIANO *It. Prov.* 118 no. 19 A good anvil fears no hammer. **1732** FULLER no. 4395.

Anvil should have a hammer of feathers, An iron.   (A 259)

1611 COTGRAVE s.v. Marteau By patience we quaile, or quell all harsh attempts. **1666** TORRIANO *It. Prov.* 118 no. 16 (a feather hammer). **1710** PALMER 76 A Rough, Stubborn, and Perverse Humour, must be manag'd with the more tender Address.

Anvil, When you are an | hold you still; when you are a hammer, strike your fill.   (A 261)

1591 FLORIO *Second F.* 101. **1640** HERBERT no. 338. **1710** PALMER 165. **1902** *Spectator* 24 May As a rule, they make the best of a bad job, remembering the old proverbial rhyme—'When you are', &c.

Anvil, *see also* Church is an a.; Hammer and a., (Between); Many strike on an a. (When), strike by measure.

Any port in a storm.

c. **1780** J. COBB *First Floor* II. ii (Inchbald's *Farces*) Here is a door open, i' faith—any port in a storm, they say. **1821** SCOTT *Pirate* ch. 4 As the Scottishman's howf[1] lies right under your lee, why, take any port in a storm. **1882** BLACKMORE *Christowell* I It must be more than twenty years since I saw the inside of a church, . . . but any port in a storm, we say. [[1] haunt.]

Any tooth, good barber.   (T 418)

1659 HOWELL *Eng. Prov.* 12a. **1678** RAY 91. **1695** RAVENSCROFT 57.

Anybody, *see* Law, logic, and the Switzers fight for a.

Anything for a quiet life.   (L 244)

[*c.* **1621**] **1662** MIDDLETON [Title]. **1624** HEYWOOD *Captives* l. 1852. **1639** CLARKE 328. **1670** RAY 135. **1738** SWIFT *Dial.* I. E.L. 286. **1836–7** DICKENS *Pickwick* ch. 43 . . . as the man said wen he took the sitivation at the lighthouse. **1837** MARRYAT *Diary on Cont.* ch. 33 A peaceable sort of man, whose very physiognomy said 'anything for a quiet life'.

Anything, *see also* Gain savours sweetly from a.; Money will do a.

Anythingarian, He is an.

a. **1704** T. BROWN *Wks.* (1760) III. 97 Such bifarious anythingarians, that always make their interest the standard of their religion. **1738** SWIFT Dial. I. E.L. 279 What religion is he of? —Why, he is an Anythingarian. **1850** KINGSLEY *Alton Locke* ch. 22 They made puir Robbie Burns an anythingarian with their blethers.

Apace, *see* Salt beef draws down drink a.

Ape can crack a nut, Before an.

1596 HARINGTON *Met. Ajax* ed. Donno 225 He goeth and ere an Ape can cracke a nut (as they say) he brings the names.

Ape drunk, To be.   (A 265)

[Tradition says that when a man begins to drink he is like a lamb, then he becomes successively like the lion, the ape, and the sow. *See* CHAUCER *Wks.* 763b.] *c.* **1386** CHAUCER *Manc. Prol.* l. 44 I trowe that ye dronken han wyn ape, And that is whan men pleyen with a straw. **1509** BARCLAY *Ship of Fools* i. 96 Some are Ape dronke full of lawghter and of toyes.

Ape's an ape, An | a varlet's a varlet, though they be clad in silk or scarlet.
(A 262–3)

c. **1536–7** ERASMUS *Pilgr. Pure Devotion* 44ᵛ As an ape is euer an ape . . . so is a maryner euer a maryner. **1539** TAVERNER C5 An ape is an ape, although she weare badges of golde. **1549** CHALONER tr. *Erasmus' Praise of Folly* C3. **1563** B. GOOGE *Eglogs* iii Arb. 40 A prouerbe olde, hath ofte ben harde and now full true is tryed: An Ape, wyll euer be an Ape, thoughe purple gaiments hyde. **1586** J. CASE *Praise of Music* 25 You may cloath an Ape in golde, and an Infant in Hercules armour: doth an Infant therfore chaunge his age, or an Ape forgoe his nature? **1592** WARNER *Albion's Eng.* VII. 36, V2ᵛ Apes be euer Apes. [1592] **1596** *Edward III* II. i. 444 Decke an Ape In tissue, and the beautie of the robe Adds but the greater scorne vnto the beast. **1601** JONSON *Poetaster* v. iii. 630. **1668** J. WILSON tr. *Moriae Encomium* 24 *Simïa, est simia, etiamsi purpurâ vestiatur* An ape, is an ape, though clad in scarlet. **1732** FULLER no. 6391.

Ape is of his tail, As free as an.   (A 268)

a. **1500** *15c. School-Bk.* ed. W. Nelson 54 Londyners . . . shall make hym as clen from it [money] as an ape fro tailys. **1670** RAY 205.

Ape's paternoster, To say an. *Cf.*
Devil's paternoster.   (A 274)

1578 *Courtly Controv.* O1ᵛ The coniurer . . . mumbling the Diuels paternoster, like an old ape. **1611** COTGRAVE s.v. Barboter To chatter, or didder for cold; to say an Apes Paternoster. **1653** URQUHART *Gargantua* I. xi, T.T. i. 54 He would . . . say the Apes Paternoster.

Ape(s), *see also* Bare as an a. is behind, (As);

Bit and a knock; Devil is God's a.; Higher the a. goes, the more shows tail; Nuts to an a.; Old a. has old eye; Old maids lead a. in hell; Toy to mock an a.

Apollo, *see* Once in the year A. laughs.

Apothecary's mortar spoils the luter's music, The.   (A 281)

1640 HERBERT no. 925.

Apothecary, *see also* Broken a., new doctor; Stomach an a.'s shop, (Make not thy); Talk like an a.

Appair, *see* Amend when they cannot a. (Some).

Apparel makes the man.   (A 283)

a. **1500** *Prov. Wisdom* l. 59 Euer maner and clothyng makyth man. *c.* **1545** *Jacob and Esau*, E4ᵛ Apparell setteth out a man. **1588** w. AVERELL *Marvellous Combat of Contrarieties* C1ᵛ Vestis virum facit, Apparell makes a man. **1591** FLORIO *Second F.* 115 Though manners makes, yet apparell shapes. **1600–1** SHAKES. *H.* I. iii. 72 For the apparel oft proclaims the man.

Apparel, *see also* God makes and a. shapes.

Appeal from Philip drunk to Philip sober, To.   (P 252)

[VAL. MAX. 6. 2 Ext. 1 *Provocarem ad Philippum, inquit, sed sobrium.*] **1531** SIR T. ELYOT *Governour* II. v 52 (1880) A poure woman, agayne whom the same kynge had gyuen iugement; . . . cried, I appele. . . . To whom appelist thou? said the kyng. I appele, said she, from the, nowe beinge dronke, to kynge Philip the sobre. *c.* **1532** *Tales* no. 46. **1564** GUEVARA *Dial of Princes* tr. North Bk. 4 (1582 ed., 439ᵛ). **1882** W. BATES *Maclise Port. Gal.* (1898) 1 Kinnaird . . . retaining the document . . . till he had an opportunity of appealing 'from Philip drunk to Philip sober', succeeded in dissuading the poet from his angry purpose. **1906** ALEX. MACLAREN *Exposn., Deut.–1 Sam.* 49 Our appeal is not to men in the flush of excitement, but to them in their hours of solitary sane reflection. It is from 'Philip drunk to Philip sober'.

Appear, *see* Rainbows a. (If two) . . . presage rain.

Appearances, *see* Judge from a. (Never).

Appetite comes with eating.   (A 286)

[RABELAIS i. 5 *L'appétit vient en mangeant.*] *c.* **1594** BACON no. 1597 En mangeant l'appétit vient. **1600–1** SHAKES. *H.* I. ii. 143 Why, she would hang on him, As if increase of appetite had grown By what it fed on. *a.* **1721** PRIOR *Dialog. of Dead* (1907) 227 But as we say in France, the appetite comes in eating; so in writing you still found more to write. **1906** W. MAXWELL *Yalu to Pt. Arthur* 10 But appetite comes with eating. Having absorbed Port Arthur and begun on Manchuria, Russia saw no reason why she should not have Korea also.

Appetite, *see also* All things require skill but a.;
Leave (off) with a.; New meat, new a.

Apple, an egg, and a nut, you may eat though dressed by a slut, An. (A 296)

1586 L. EVANS *Revised Withals Dict.* A 7 Apples,
egges and nuttes, a man may eate thoughe they
be dressed by a slute. **1670** RAY 33 . . . *Poma,
ova atque nuces, si det tibi sordida, gustes.* **1720**
Lady Pennyman's Misc. (1740) 18 We got some
boiled eggs, and eat more of our Bacon, which
again put me in Mind of our *English* proverb, of
Egg, Apple and Nut. **1732** FULLER no. 6250.

Apple going to bed, Eat an | make the doctor beg his bread.

c. **1630** *The Soddered Citizen* l. 1051 Hee gott A
terrible heartburnynge, (had hee tane An apple
then to beddwards, he had beene cur'd). **1866**
N. & Q. 3rd Ser. IX. 153. **1911** CROSSING *Folk
Rhymes of Devon* 122.

Apple of discord.

[The golden apple contended for by Juno,
Minerva, and Venus: whence any subject of
dissension.] *a.* **1649** DRUMM. OF HAWTH. *Irene*
Wks. (1711) 173 Who throw the apple of dissension amongst your subjects. **1867** FREEMAN
Norm. Conq. I. iv. 195 This great and wealthy
church constantly formed an apple of discord.

Apple to an apple (crab)[1], As like as an.

1579 LYLY *Euph.* i. 258 The sowre crab hath the
shewe of an apple as well as the sweet pyppin.
c. **1605** SHAKES. *K.L.* I. v. 14 She's [Regan] as
like this [Goneril] as a crab's like an apple.
1654 GAYTON 35. **1705** 11 Aug. DEFOE *Review*
As like a brat of their own begetting, that like
two apples, they could not know them asunder.
[1 crab-apple.]

Apple (egg) to an oyster (nut), As like as an. (A 291)

1532 MORE *Wks.* (1557) 724 No more lyke then
an apple to an oyster. **1555** J. PHILPOT *Fifth
Exam.* P.S. 40 It followeth not the primitive
catholic church, neither agreeth with the same,
no more than an apple is like a nut. **1559** COOPER
s.v. *Similis* (is to a nutte, or as wotemeale to
grene chese). *c.* **1580** JOHN CONYBEARE 24 (nut).
1581 G. ELLIOTT *True Report of taking of E.
Campion* Arb. *Eng. Garner* viii. 207 As far
different from truth as darkness from light; and as
contrary to truth as an egg is contrary in likeness
to an oyster. **1594–8** SHAKES. *T.S.* IV. ii. 100
In countenance somewhat doth resemble you.—
As much as an apple doth an oyster. **1655**
Musarum Deliciae James Smith to Sir John
Mennis 12 For now I haue no more minde to't,
Then is an Apple like a Nut. **1668** *Visions of
Quevedo* 3rd ed. 299 (no more like him than).
1732 FULLER no. 707 (lobster).

Apple-cart, To upset the.

1788 GROSE *Dict. Vulg. T.* s.v. Apple-Cart. Down
with his apple-cart; knock or throw him down.
1796–1801 FESSENDEN *Orig. Poems* (1806) 100 He
talketh big words to congress and threateneth to
overturn their apple-cart. **1848** in HODDER *Life
Shaftesbury* If the Prince goes on like this, why
he'll upset our apple-cart. **1896** C. RHODES in
Daily News 24 July 5/5 Old Jameson has upset
my apple-cart.

Apple-pie order.

1813 SCOTT LOCKHART *Life* 1839, iv. 131 The
children's garden is in apple-pie order. **1830**
July 3 B. RODGERS *Georgian Chronicle* 257 Letter
from A. Aikin to C. Aikin Everything in apple
pye order. **1865** DICKENS *Our Mutual Friend*
Bk. 1 ch. 15 'Apple-pie order!' said Mr. Boffin.

Apples swim! See how we | quoth the horse-turd. (A 302)

1616 WITHALS 570. **1642** D. RODGERS *Naaman*
545 Hypocrites are very glad when Gods and
their ends concurre As the dung swimming in the
same streame with the Apples, said, We apples
swimme. **1692** L'ESTRANGE *Aesop's Fab.* cxxxiv
(1738) 150 Upon a . . . fall of rain, the current
carried away a huge heap of apples, together
with a dung-hill that lay in the watercourse. . . .
As they went thus . . . the horse-turds would be
. . . crying out still, 'Alack-a-day! How we apples
swim!'

Apple(s), *see also* Better an a. given; Choice in
rotten a.; Egg to the a. (From the); Good a. on
sour stock (No); Hog (Every) has own a.; Lost
with an a.; Rotten a. (Not worth a); Rotten a.
injures its neighbours; St. Swithin is christening
a.; Sodom a.

Approve, *see* See and a. the better course.

April blows his horn, When | it's good both for hay and corn. (A 311)

1670 RAY 41 . . . That is, when it thunders in
April.

April flood carries away the frog and her brood, An. (F 379)

1639 CLARKE 307. **1670** RAY 41.

April showers bring forth May flowers. (S 411)

c. **1430** LYDGATE *Reason & Sensuality* I. 6310
Holsom as the Aprile showr fallyng on the herbes
newe. *c.* **1560** WRIGHT *Songs, Philip and Mary*
213 Roxb. Cl. When Aprell sylver showers so
sweet Can make May flowers to sprynge. **1573**
TUSSER (1578) 103 Swéete April showers, Doo
spring Maie flowers. **1606–7** SHAKES. *A.C.* III.
ii. 43 The April's in her eyes. It is love's spring,
And these the showers to bring it on. **1648**
HERRICK *Hesper.* Wks. Gros. I. 38 First, April,
she with mellow showers Opens the way for
early flowers; Then after her comes smiling May,
in a more rich and sweet array. **1670** RAY 41
1821 SCOTT *Kenilw.* ch. 32 I believe'. . . if showers
fall in April, that we shall have flowers in May.
1846 DENHAM 36 March winds and April showers
bring forth May flowers.

April weather, rain and sunshine both together.

1607 TOURNEUR *Rev. Trag.* v. ii Alas! I shine in tears, like the sun in April. **1824** SCOTT *Redg.* ch. 17 Smiles and tears mingled on Lilias's cheeks, like showers and sunshine in April weather. **1893** INWARDS 23.

April, *see also* Blow in A. (If they [cherries]); Cold A. barn will fill; Dove's flood is worth (In A.); First of A. hunt the gowk;—you may send a fool whither you will; March borrowed from A.; March the birds begin; March the cuckoo starts; Third of A. comes cuckoo; Windy March and rainy A.

Apron, *see* Cunning wife makes husband her a.

Apron-strings, To be tied to (hold by) (a woman's). (A 312)

1542 ERASM. *Apoph.* tr. Udall (1877 ed., 118) As we say in english, As wise as a gooce, or as wise as her mothers aperen string. **1581** C. THIMEL-THORPE *Short Inventory* G8 Rockinge in Venus lappe, . . . thrumming of apern strings and with many other idle deuises. **1647** N. WARD *Simple Cobbler* 63 Apron-string tenure is very weak, tyed but of a slipping knot, which a childe may undoe, much more a King. **1678** RAY 226 To hold by the Apron-strings, *i.e.* in right of his wife. **1743** FIELDING *Jonathan Wild* II. iii The hero . . . was not of that low snivelling breed of mortals who, as is generally expressed, *tie themselves to a woman's apron strings.* **1819** I Aug. BYRON *Lett.* Prothero iv. 330 If you wish to secure him, tie him to your petticoat-string. **1849** MACAULAY *Hist. Eng.* II. 649 He could not submit to be tied to the apron strings even of the best of wives.

Archdeacon Pratt, *see* Jack Sprat.

Archer is not known by his arrows, but his aim, A good. (A 313)

1580 LYLY *Euph. & his Eng.* ii. 104. **1732** FULLER no. 135.

Archer(s), *see also* English a. . . . twenty-four Scots; Speak good of a.

Architect, *see* Every man is the a. of own fortune.

Arden, *see* Black bear of A.

Are you there with your bears? (B 133)

1594 LYLY *Mother B.* II. iii. 46 I . . . come to make choise of a mistres. — A ha, are you there with your beares? **1600** C. SNUFFE (= R. Arnim) *Quips upon Questions* C3. **1617** BRATH-WAIT *Solemn Disputation* 45. **1668** SHADWELL *Sullen Lov.* V. iii. — Would she had it, for her own sake, and yours too. — Faith! are you there with your bears? Nay, then, I have brought my hog to a fair market. **1742** RICHARDSON *Pamela* III. 335 O ho, Nephew! are you thereabouts with your bears?

Argue(s), *see* Moist hand a. amorous nature.

Argument(s), *see* Soft words hard a.

Argus abroad and a mole at home (or vice versa), An. (A 314)

[Argus, in fable, had 100 eyes.] **1581** GUAZZO i. 160 Doe you not knowe, that (as the Proverbe is) wee see better a farre of, than hard by us, and that at home wee see no more than Moles, but abroade as muche as Argus. **1636** S. WARD *Serm.* (1862) 74 False zeal loves to be gadding, is eagle-eyed abroad, and mole-eyed at home. **1642** TORRIANO 65. **1732** FULLER no. 582.

Argus, *see also* Eyes as A. (As many).

Argyle, Duke of, *see* God bless the D. of A.

Arithmetic, *see* Cipher in a.

Arm(s), *see* Clothe thee in war, a. thee in peace; God strikes with finger, not with a.; Kings have long a.; Open a. (With); Stretch your a. no further than sleeve; Weapons of war will not a. fear; Wide therm had never long a.

Armour is light at table. (A 319)

1640 HERBERT no. 934.

Armour, *see also* Hog in a.; Ship under sail, man in complete a., . . . ; Warm one in his a. (Absurd to).

Army marches on its stomach. An.

1904 *Windsor Magazine* 268 attributes this to Napoleon. **1911** HACKWOOD *Good Cheer* 313 (says the old proverb).

Army of stags led by a lion would be more formidable than one of lions led by a stag, An.

[PLUTARCH *Chabriae Apophth.* 3 Φοβερώτερόν ἐστιν ἐλάφων στρατόπεδον ἡγουμένου λέοντος ἢ λεόντων ἐλάφου. L. *Formidabilior cervorum exercitus, duce leone, quam leonum cervo.*] **1890** W. F. BUTLER *Sir C. Napier* 150 Many . . . had seen . . . the fruits of bad leadership in Cabul, and had learnt to value the truth of the proverb, . . . that 'a herd of deer led by a lion was more formidable to the enemy than a herd of lions led by a deer'. **1898** G. F. R. HENDERSON *Stonewall Jackson* ch. 12 (the old proverb).

Aroint, *see* Rynt.

Arrow shot upright falls on the shooter's head, An. (A 324)

a. **1536** HILL 27, 129. [c. **1591**] **1592** *Arden of Fev.* IV. iv. 40 For curses are like arrowes shot vpright, Which falling down light on the shuters head. **1595** R. TURNER *Garland of a Green Wit* D4ᵛ Thou didst him constraine And causelesse curse, like arrowe shot vpright Returning downe, on thine owne head will light. **1615** R. A. *Val.*

Welsh. IV. v (as in *Arden*). **1709** KINGSTON
Apoph. Cur. 97, 15 Like Arrows shot against
Heaven, fall upon their own Heads.

Arrows, Not to know of what wood to make.   (W 736)

1567 PAINTER (Jacobs) iii. 24 Hys Wyfe . . . iwas
in great care, and could not tell of what Woode
to make hir arrowes.   **1604** R. DALLINGTON *View
of France* G3   As their prouerbe is, . . . He
knewe not . . .   **1659** HOWELL *Fr. Prov.* 16.

Arrow(s), *see also* Archer not known by his a.,
(A good); Bolt (A.) came never out of your bag
(That); Bow and a. and go to bed, (To take
one's); Shoot a second a. to find first; Swift as
an a.; Wood (Like), like a.

Arse, *see* Bare a. than a furred hood, (Better a);
Cast at cart's a.; Dab, quoth Dawkins, when he
hit his wife on the a.; Dirten a. dreads aye;
Doomsday we shall see whose a. is blackest, (At).

Arsie versie, *see* Kim Kam a. v.

Art consists in concealing art.   (A 335)

[L. *Ars est celare artem.*]   **1581–3** SIDNEY
Apology for Poetry (ed. Gregory Smith, 203)
Vsing Art to shew Art, and not to hide Art (as
. . . he should doe).   **1583** MELBANCKE *Philotimus*
G1 It is a chiefe point of art to dissemble art.
1603 BRETON *Packet Mad Lett.* Wks. Gros. ii.
11 I have heard scholars say, that it is art to
conceal art, and that under a face of simplicity,
is hidden much subtlety.   **1707** SWIFT *Facult. of
Mind* Wks. (1856) II. 285 In oratory the greatest
art is to hide art.   **1907** A. C. BENSON *Upton Lett.*
201 Henry James . . . seems to be so afraid of
anything that is obvious . . . that his art conceals
not art but nature.

Art, He who has an | has everywhere a part.   (*cf.* T 406)

1666 TORRIANO *It. Prov.* 14 no. 19 Who hath a
trade, or an art, every where claims a lively-hood.

Art has no enemy but ignorance.
(A 331)

1589 PUTTENHAM *Art. Eng. Poesy* II. ii. (1936 ed.)
140 Certaine grosse ignorants of whom it is
truly spoken scientia non habet inimicum nisi
ignorantem.   **1599** JONSON *Ev. Man Out* I. i. 219
Arte hath an enemy cal'd Ignorance.   **1653**
Shinkin ap Shone Her Prognostn. for 1654 1.

Art improves nature.

1563 R. RAINOLDES *Foundation of Rhetoric* A1.
1584 LYLY *Camp.* III. v. 19 Arte must yeeld to
nature.   **1587** UNDERDOWNE *Heliodorus* iii. 94
T.T. Arte can breake nature.   **1604** MARSTON
Malcontent Epilogue Art above Nature, Judgment above Art.   **1732** FULLER no. 814 Art
helps Nature, and Experience Art.   **1841**
DICKENS *B. Rudge* ch. 39 Art improves natur'—
that's my motto.

Art is long, life is short. *Cf.* Day is short.
(A 322)

[HIPPOCRATES *Aphor.* 1. 1 'Ο βίος βρα ύς, ἡ δὲ
τέχνη μακρή. Life is short, and art is long.   L.
Ars longa, vita brevis.]   *c.* **1380** CHAUCER *Parl.
Foules* l. 1 The lyf so short, the craft so long to
lerne.   **1552** BULLEIN *Govt. Health* f. 4ᵛ And
although our life be short, yet the art of physick is
long.   **1581** GUAZZO i. 43.   **1710** PALMER 380.
1839 LONGFELLOW *Psalm of Life* Art is long, and
Time is fleeting.   **1869** M. ARNOLD *Culture &
Anarchy,* Our Liberal practitioners. 'Art is long',
says the *Times,* 'and life is short'.

Art, In every | it is good to have a master.   (A 334)

1640 HERBERT no. 619.

Art(s), *see also* Belly teaches all a.; Honours
nourish a.; Poverty is mother of a.

Arthur could not tame woman's tongue.
(A 336)

1659 HOWELL *Brit. Prov.* 23.

Arthur was not, but whilst he was.
(A 337)

1659 HOWELL *Brit. Prov.* 35 Arthur himself had
but his time.   **1662** FULLER Cardigan 26 But
Arthur ond tra fu. That is, Arthur was not, but
whilest he was. It is sad to say, Nos fuimus
Trojes, the greatest eminency when not extant is
extinct.

Arthur, *see also* King A.

As bad as, As fit as, As freely as, As good (as),
As like as, As many, As much, As well, *see under
significant words following.*

Ascend, *see* Descend than a., (Easier to).

Asfordby Bridge, *see* Gone over A. B.

Ash (tree), *see* Oak's before the a. (If).

Ashamed to look one in the face, To be.

a. **1536** HILL E.E.T.S. 111 þou daryst not loke a
man in the face.   **1591** ARIOSTO *Orl. Fur.* Harington
XXXVII. 94.   [1604] **1607** DEKKER *Sir T. Wyatt*
ed. Bowers v. ii. 104.

Ashamed, *see also* Never be a. to eat meat;
Women may blush to hear what they were not a.
to act.

Ashes, *see* Divine a. better than earthly meal;
Dog that licks a.; Eat a peck of dirt (a.); Lay on
more wood, a. give money; Pale as a.

Ashford, *see* Naughty A.

Ask a kite for a feather, and she'll say, she has but just enough to fly with.

1732 FULLER no. 816.

Ask and have. *Cf.* Speak and speed.
(A 343)

[MATT. vii 7: Ask, and it shall be given you.] *c.* 1475 *Mankind* l. 856 Aske mercy, and haue. *a.* 1500 *15c. School-Bk.* ed. W. Nelson 72. **1581** GUAZZO i. 84 Hee which wil have, must aske. **1585** MUNDAY *Fedele and Fortunio* l. 1676. **1592** SHAKES. *T.And.* I. i. 201 Titus, thou shalt obtain and ask the empery. **1755** FRANKLIN 29 Ask and have, is sometimes dear buying.

Ask but enough, and you may lower the price as you list.

1639 CLARKE 172 Be sure to aske enough. **1642** TORRIANO 46. **1813** RAY 2.

Ask, He that cannot | cannot live.
(A 344)

1616 DRAXE no. 228. **1639** CLARKE 41.

Ask for bread and be given a stone, To.

[**1611** MATT. vii. 9 Or what man is there of you, whom if his sonne aske bread, will hee giue him a stone?] **1834** MARRYAT *Jacob Faith.* ch. 37 'We will find you bread, and hard enough you will find it . . . it's like a flint'. 'So we ask for bread, and you give us a stone.' *a.* 1880 MARQ. SALISBURY in *Life* (1921) I. 120 When asked to support a Church scheme for . . . purely secular . . . work . . ., he refused, with the brief comment, 'They are asking you for bread and you are offering them stones.'

Ask mine host whether he have good wine.
(H 725)

1642 TORRIANO 45. **1658** *Comes Fac. in Via* 192.

Ask much to have a little.
(M 272)

1539 TAVERNER 33ᵛ Aske that is vnreasonable that thou mayst beare awaye that is reasonable. **1573** GASCOIGNE *Dulce Bellum* i. 174. **1640** HERBERT 322. **1706** STEVENS s.v. Pedir.

Ask my fellow if I be a thief.
(F 177)

1545 TAVERNER 11ᵛ (an . . . English proverbe). **1546** HEYWOOD II. v. H4. **1549** LATIMER *3rd Serm. bef. Edw. VI* P.S. 139 Thieves and thieves' fellows be all of one sort. They were wont to say, 'Ask my fellow if I be a thief'. **1614** CAMDEN 303. **1615** T. ADAMS *Englands Sicknes* 32 The Prouerbe, Aske the sons if the Father be a thiefe. **1641** FERGUSSON no. 759 Speir at Jock thief my marrow [i.e. companion] if I be a leal man. **1659** FULLER *Appeal Inj. Innoc.* in *Hist. of Camb. Univ.* (1840) 366 'Ask my fellow if I be a thief'; ask a poetical fable, if a monkish legend be a liar.

Ask no questions and you will be told no lies.

1773 GOLDSMITH *She Stoops to C.* III. Ask me no questions and I'll tell you no fibs. **1818** SCOTT *Ht. Midl.* ch. 10 If ye'll ask nae questions, I'll tell ye nae lees. **1860** DICKENS *Gt. Expect.* ch. 2 Drat that boy . . . Ask no questions and you'll be told no lies.

Ask of my sire brown bread, I had rather | than borrow of my neighbour white.
(F 271)

1640 HERBERT no. 269.

Ask pardon, *see* Never a. p. before accused.

Ask pears of an elm tree, To.

1612 SHELTON *Quix.* III. ix (1908, i. 182) To demand such a thing of us is as likely as to seek for pears in an elm-tree. **1706** STEVENS s.v. Pedir.

Ask the mother if the child be like the father.
(M 1193)

1562 HEYWOOD *Epig.* 50 208 Who is thy father childe, axt his mothers husband. Axe my mother (quoth he) that to vnderstand. The boy dalieth with you sir: for verily He knowth who is his father as well as I. **1594-5** SHAKES. *L.L.L.* II. i. 201 Pray you, sir, whose daughter?—Her mother's, I have heard. **1594-8** *Id. T.S.* V. i. 27 Art thou his father?—Ay sir. So his mother says, if I may believe her. **1598-9** *Id. M.A.* I. i. 88 I think this is your daughter. — Her mother hath many times told me so. [**1600**] **1659** DAY & CHETTLE *Blind Beg.* E1ᵛ Is not this your Son?—I cannot tell, his Mother tells me so. **1611** SHAKES. *Temp.* I. ii. 55 Sir, are not you my father?—Thy mother was a piece of virtue, and She said thou wast my daughter. **1616** BRETON *Cross.* B2ᵛ Euery child knowes his owne father. —Not, but as his mother tels him. **1732** FULLER no. 818. *Ibid.,* no. 4676 The Mother knows best, whether the Child be like the Father.

Ask your neighbour if you shall live in peace, You must.
(N 113)

1639 CLARKE 203. **1721** KELLY 258 No Man can live longer in Peace than his Neighbour pleases. For an ill Neighbour, with his Scolding, Noise, Complaints, Law-suits, and Indictments, may be very troublesome. **1732** FULLER no. 5961.

Askers, *see* Devil made a.

Asks faintly begs a denial, He that.
(D 201)

[SENECA *Hipp. Qui timide rogat, docet negare.*] *a.* 1591 H. SMITH *Serm.* (1657) 461 It is an old saying, that he which asketh faintly teacheth us to deny him. **1596** SHAKES. *Rich. II* V. iii. 103 He prays but faintly and would be denied. **1633** P. FLETCHER *Pisc. Eclog.* Wks. (1908) II. 202 Cold beggars freeze our gifts: thy faint suit breeds her no. **1732** FULLER no. 2042.

Asking, The better (None the better) for your.

c. 1380 CHAUCER *Troilus* Bk. 3, l. 1562 And ner he [Pandarus] com, and seyde, 'how stant it now This mury morwe, nece, how kan ye fare?' Criseyde answerde, 'neuer the bet for yow'. [**1598**] **1601** JONSON *Every Man In* l. ii. 76. **1599** H. PORTER *Two Angry Women* l. 1299. **1600-1**

SHAKES. *M.W.W.* I. iv. 122 How now, good woman! how dost thou?—The better that it pleases your good worship to ask. **1607** SHARPHAM *Cupid's Whirligig* F1. **1738** SWIFT *Dial.* I. E.L. 259.

Ask(ed, ing, s), *see also* Good thing cheap (He will never have) that is afraid to a. price; Lose nothing for a.; Never a. pardon before accused; Thought to have a. you (I had); Wait till you're a.

Asleep and awake, Between.

1591 ARIOSTO *Orl. Fur.* Harington x. 20. [*c.* **1590**] **1594** GREENE *Orl. Fur.* I. iii. 390 Between halfe sleeping and awake. **1595** SHAKES. *M.N.D.* IV. i. 144 My lord, I shall reply amazedly Half 'sleep, half waking. *c.* **1605** *Id. K.L.* I. ii. 15 Th' creating a whole tribe of fops Got 'tween asleep and wake. **1611** COTGRAVE s.v. Dormeveille.

Aspen leaf, To quake (tremble) like an.
(L 140)

c. **1374** CHAUCER *Troilus* Bk. 3 l. 1200 Right as an aspes leef she gan to quake. *c.* **1386** *Id. Somnour's Prol.* l. 3 That lyk an aspen leef he quook for yre. *?a.* **1483** *Mankind* l. 727 My body trymmelyth as the aspen leffe. **1530** PALSGRAVE 700a. He shaked and it had ben an aspen leafe. **1592** SHAKES. *T.And.* II. iv. 45 O! had the monster seen those lily hands Tremble, like aspen-leaves, upon a lute. **1598** *Id. 2 Hen. IV* II. iv. 100 Feel, masters, how I shake . . . an 'twere an aspen leaf: I cannot abide swaggerers. **1824** D. M. MOIR *Mansie W.* ch. 25 Tommy and Benje trembled from top to toe, like aspen leaves.

Asquint, *see* Love being jealous.

Ass, As dull as an.   (A 348)

[*a.* **1547**] *c.* **1568** COPLAND *Seven Sorrows* Prol., A2 Yet shoulde we were as dulle as any asse. **1597** Burghley to R. Cecil cited C. Read *Ld. Burghley & Q. Elizabeth* 529 Forced daily to feed on an ass's milk and so subject to be as dull as an ass.

Ass climbs a ladder, When an | we may find wisdom in women.   (A 367)

1678 RAY *Adag. Hebr.* 401. **1732** FULLER no. 5546.

Ass endures his burden, but not more than his burden, An.   (A 350)

1599 MINSHEU *Span. Gram.* 83 . . . *El asno sufre la carga, no la sobre carga.* **1620** SHELTON *Quix.* II. lxxi (1908) III. 317 It now sufficeth . . . that the ass endure his charge, but not the sur-charge. **1651** HERBERT no. 1080.

Ass falls, Where-ever an | there will he never fall again.

1642 TORRIANO 48. **1732** FULLER no. 5643.

Ass goes a-travelling, If an | he'll not come home a horse.

1732 FULLER no. 2668. **1852** E. FITZGERALD *Polonius* xlii 'You must swear by Allah, smoke chibouques, and spell Pasha differently from every predecessor, or we shall scarce believe you have been in a hareem!' 'NEVER WENT OUT ASS, AND CAME HOME HORSE.'

Ass in a lion's skin, An.   (A 351)

[The title of one of Æsop's Fables.] **1484** CAXTON *Fab. Avian.* (1899), IV. 219, title: The fourthe fable is of the asse and of the skynne of the Lyon. **1549** CHALONER tr. *Erasmus' Praise of Folly* A3 Walke lyke Asses in Lyons skinnes, K4 Lyke the asse wrapped in a lyons skinne. [**1591**] **1593** PEELE ed. Bullen i. 145 Nor can an ass's hide disguise A lion, if he ramp and rise. **1632** S. MARMION *Holland's Leaguer* I. 2ᵛ As fearefull as an Asse in a Lyons skinne. **1711** ADDISON *Spect.* No. 13, par. 4 The ill-natured world might call him the Ass in the Lion's Skin. **1748** SMOLLETT *Rod. Rand.* ch. 54 He had talked so much of his valour that I had . . . rated him as an ass in a lion's skin.

Ass is known by his ears, An.   (A 355)

1538 BALE *K. Johan* Mal. Soc. l. 697 34 With long eares lyke an asse. **1548** ELYOT s.v. Asinus The asse waggeth his eares. A prouerb applied to theim, whiche although they lacke learnynge, yet will they babble and make a countenaunce, as if they knewe somewhat. **1584** WITHALS C4 By their wordes we know fooles, and asses by their eares. **1589** *Hay any work for Cooper* (*Marprelate Tracts* ed. Pierce 257) They have turned unto me . . . a beast, whom by the length of his ears I guesse to be his brother; that is, an ass of the same kind. [**1598**] **1616** HAUGHTON *Englishmen for my Money* G2ᵛ We know the Asse by his eares. **1666** TORRIANO *It. Prov.* 15, no. 37. *Ibid.* 190, no. 5 (by his ears, and a fool by too much speech).

Ass kicks you, When an | never tell it.

1834 MISS EDGEWORTH *Helen* ch. 24 Lady Cecilia . . . guessed that Lord Davenant had been circumvented by some diplomatist of inferior talents, and she said to Helen, 'When an ass kicks you never tell it, is a maxim which mamma . . . always acts upon'.

Ass knows well in whose face he brays, The.

1853 TRENCH iii (1894) 52 What a grave humour lurks in this: *The ass knows well in whose face he brays.* [Sp.] Bien sabe el asno en cuya cara rebozna.

Ass laden with gold climbs to the top of the castle, An.   (A 356)

[PLUT. *Apoph. Reg.* 178] **1539** TAVERNER I *Garden* C4 Philip kynge of Macedonie, . . . When on a tyme he had purposed to take a stronge castle . . . and his espyes hadde shewed hym that it was very hard for hym to brynge to passe, . . . He asked them whether it were so harde, that an asse laden with golde myght not

come vnto it. Meanynge that there is nothynge
so stronge, but with golde it maye be wonne.
1562 G. LEGH *Accidence of Armoury* A4ᵛ (that
witty saying of Phillip . . . King of Macedonia).
1572 E. PASQUIER tr. Fenton T4ᵛ Phylip king of
Macedonia, whose common saying was, when he
came afore any towne inassaultable by force, that
if an Asse loaden with Golde could enter, he and
his armie woulde not be kept out. [**1602**] **1637**
HEYWOOD *Royal King* vi. 21 [At court] Asses with
gold laden, free may enter. **1612** T. ADAMS
Gallant's Burden 52 The Prouerbe sayth, There is
no earthly Gate, but an Asse laden with Gold
can enter. **1732** FULLER no. 587 (overtakes
everything).

Ass loaded with gold still eats thistles, The. (A 360)

1581 WHITNEY *Choice of Emblems* 18. [**1591**]
1631 MARLOWE *Jew of Malta* V. ii. 40 He ... Lives
like the ass that Æsop speaketh of, That labours
with a load of bread and wine, And leaves it off
to snap on thistle tops. **1599** SHAKES. *J.C.* IV. i.
21 He shall but bear them [honours] as the ass
bears gold, To groan and sweat under the business
. . . Then take we down his load, and turn him
off (Like to the empty ass) to shake his ears And
graze in commons. **1611** COTGRAVE s.v. Ortle
Applicable to a rich, and most wretched penie-
father; one that all the yeare long bestowes not
a bit of good meat on himselfe. **1632** MASSINGER
City Madam II. i. Merm. 423 Or wilt thou . . .
being keeper of the cash, Like an ass that carries
dainties, feed on thistles? *c.* **1645** HOWELL *Lett.*
(1903) III. 76 He makes not nummum his numen,
money his god . . . The first . . . is worse than the
Arcadian ass, who while he carrieth gold on his
back, eats thistles.

Ass must be tied where the master will have him, An. (A 357)

1581 GUAZZO ii. 110 Let the servaunte . . . tye
the Asse (as they say) where his maister will have
him tyed. **1642** TORRIANO 15. **1732** FULLER no.
589.

Ass of, To make an.

1595 SHAKES. *M.N.D.* III. i. 110 This is to make
an ass of me, to fright me, if they could. **1605**
MARSTON *Dutch Courtezan* III. iii And you make
an asse of me, Ile make an Oxe of you.

Ass of Isis, The.

1598 MARSTON *Sat.* I Asse, take off Isis, no
man honours thee. **1599** DANIEL *Musophilus*
And thinke like Isis Asse, all Honours are Given
unto them alone, the which are done Unto the
painted Idoll which they bear. **1612** CHAPMAN
Widow's Tears I. i. 153 And let the beast's dull
apprehension take the honour done to Isis, done
to himself.

Ass play on a harp (lute)? Did you ever hear an. (A 366)

c. **1380** CHAUCER *Boethius* I. Prose iv. l. 2 Artow
lyke an asse to the harpe? *c.* **1390** *Id. Troilus*
Bk. I. l. 731. **1549** CHALONER tr. *Erasmus'
Praise of Folly* Duᵛ As inapte as an asse is to
finger on harpe. *Ibid.* O1 As if an asse were set
to plaie on a gitterne. **1577** R. STANYHURST in

HOLINSHED *Desc. Ireland* (1587, 16a) As for an
asse to twang quipassa on a harpe or gitterne.
1706 STEVENS s.v. Asno.

Ass pricked must needs trot, An. (A 358)

1573 SANFORD 102. **1629** *Bk. Mer. Rid.* Prov.
no. 58.

Ass (a fool) that brays against another ass, He is an. (A 374)

1616 DRAXE no. 754 He is an asse that braieth
against an asse.

Ass that brays most eats least, The. (A 359)

1611 COTGRAVE s.v. Asne. **1654** GAYTON
Pleasant Notes 143 (few Thistles). **1670** RAY 3.
1762 SMOLLETT *Sir Launcelot Greaves* ch. 10
(little grass).

Ass thinks himself worthy to stand with the king's horses, Every. (A 362)

1616 DRAXE no. 291 There is not an asse amongst
them, but hee is worthy to stand amongst the
Kings horses, in the same stable. **1639** CLARKE
254. **1732** FULLER no. 1405.

Ass to be called a lion? What good can it do an.

1732 FULLER no. 5490.

Ass, *see also* All men say you are an a. (When),
time to bray; Angry as an a.; Beat the a. (He
that cannot) beats the saddle; Better ride on an
a.; Braying of an a. does not reach heaven; Devil
is a.; Drives an a. and leads a whore (Who); Go
to a goat (a.) for wool; Hold the a. by the bridle;
Honey is not for a.'s mouth; Law is an a.; Mere
scholar, mere a.; Mule (A.) does scrub another
(One); Plough with ox and a.; Straw to his dog,
bones to a. (Gives); Tell you, you are an a.
(If one); Thistle is salad for a.'s mouth; Washes
an a.'s head (He that); Wife an a. (If you make).
See also Donkey.

Assault, (*noun*), *see* Gentleman, (He that would
be) let him go to a.

Assault(ed), (*verb*), *see* Man a. is half taken.

Astrology is true, but the astrologers cannot find it. (A 389)

1640 HERBERT no. 641. **1659** HOWELL *It. Prov.* I
(but where is the Astrologer?)

At ease, He that is | seeks dainties. (E 38)

1640 HERBERT no. 985.

At hand, quoth Pickpurse. (H 65)

1575 *App. & Virg.* Mal. Soc. l. 531 At hand
(quoth picke purse) here redy am I. **1597**

SHAKES. *1 Hen. IV* II. i. 46 What, ho! chamberlain. —'At hand, quoth pickpurse.' [1600] 1659
DAY & CHETTLE *Blind Beg.* E2ᵛ Where's my
Son?—At hand quoth Pickpurse,—what's the
matter with you trow? 1631 DRUE *Duch.
Suffolk* II. C4 Now where's this Tiler.—At hand
quoth pickepurse.

At hand, All is not | that helps.

(A 145)

1641 FERGUSSON no. 6. 1695 RAVENSCROFT 44
(in hand). 1721 KELLY 21 . . . Assistance and
support may come from whence we cannot
foresee. 1732 FULLER no. 526.

At last, *see* God stays long, but strikes a. l.;
Long looked for comes a. l.; Loses indeed that
loses a. l.; Lost (It is not) that comes a. l.; Never
long that comes a. l.

Athanasius against the world.

1597 HOOKER *Eccles. Polity* v. xlii (1830) II. 139
This was the plain condition of those times; the
whole world against Athanasius, and Athanasius
against it. 1861 DEAN STANLEY *Hist. East. Ch.*
(1862) vii. 234–6 In the Nicene Council[1] . . . he
was almost the only high ecclesiastic who stood
firm against the Arians . . . *Athanasius contra
mundum*; a proverb which . . . sets forth the
claims of individual . . . judgement. [1 325.]

Atheism, *see* Devil divides . . . between a. and
superstition.

Atheist is one point beyond the devil, An.

1629 T. ADAMS *Serm.* (1861–2) II. 341 Atheists
. . . are in some respects worse than the Devil:
he knows and acknowledgeth a Deity; these say,
'There is no God'. 1732 FULLER no. 593 An
Atheist is got one Point beyond the Devil.

Atheist(s), *see also* Physicians (Where three),
there are two a.

Athens, The modern (i.e. Edinburgh).

[*c.* 1815] 1856 H. COCKBURN *Memorials* 288 It
was about this time that the foolish phrase 'The
Modern Athens' began to be applied to the
capital of Scotland, a sarcasm, or a piece of
affected flattery, when used in a moral sense; but
just enough if meant only as a comparison of the
physical features of the two places. 1822 SCOTT
Nigel (*Introd. Epist.*) I think our Modern Athens
much obliged to me for having established such
an extensive manufacture. 1831 PEACOCK
Crotchet Castle ch. 2 [Mr. Mac Quedy loq.]
Morals and metaphysics, politics and political
economy . . . you have all these to learn from us;
in short, all the arts and sciences. We are the
modern Athenians. 1905 J. OXENHAM *White Fire*
ch. 2 Her husband had been a professor in
Edinburgh, and the society he and she had enjoyed in the modern Athens, thirty years before,
was her standard of what society ought to be.
1911 *Spectator* 25 Nov. 903 Some of the
'Modern Athenians' look on their unfinished
temple on Calton Hill . . . as making the archi-
tecture of Edinburgh even more like that of
fallen Athens than it would otherwise have been.

Athens, *see also* Owls to A.

Atlantic, *see* Mrs. Partington.

Attendance, *see* Dance a.

Attorney(s), *see* Kick an a. downstairs; Two a.
can live in a town.

Auger, *see* Wimble will let in a.

August, *see* Born in A.; Dry A. does harvest no
harm; Twenty-fourth of A. be fair (If).

Aunt had been a man, If my | she'd have been my uncle.

1813 RAY 202 . . . Spoken in derision of those
who make ridiculous surmises. 1910 A. C.
BENSON *Silent Isle* ch. 22 A speaker was recommending a measure . . . that . . . would be a very
satisfactory one if only the conditions . . . were
different. 'As much as to say', said Whately . . . ,
'that if my aunt were a man, he would be my
uncle.'

Aunts, She is one of mine | that made mine uncle go a begging.

(A 398)

1604 DEKKER *I Honest Whore* I. ii. 121 To call
you one a my naunts, sister, were as good as call
you arrant whoore. 1666 TORRIANO *Prov. Phr.*
s.v. Quelle, 162. To be one, viz. of those women
that live a merry life . . . wanton Girls; The
English oft-times express the same by, One of
my Cousins, or one of my Aunts, Ladies of
Pleasure. 1678 RAY 227.

Author, Like | like book.

(A 401)

1611 COTGRAVE s.v. Oeuvre Like Author like
worke; such as the writer such his booke. 1664
CODRINGTON 204. 1670 RAY 15.

Autumn fruit without spring blossoms, No.

1732 FULLER no. 3544. 1846 DENHAM 57 No
tree bears fruit in autumn that does not blossom
in the spring.

Autumn, *see also* Fair things (Of) a. is fair.

Autumnal agues are long or mortal.

(A 84)

1640 HERBERT no. 148. 1706 STEVENS s.v.
Calentura An Ague in Autumn is either very
tedious, or mortal.

Avails, *see* Beauty without bounty a. naught;
Dead a. not . . . , (To lament the).

Avarice, *see* Poverty wants many things and
covetousness (a.) all.

Aver, *see* Holds up her head like hundred
pound a.; Inch of a nag worth an a.; Kindly a.
never good horse.

Avernus, *see* Descent to hell (A.) is easy.

Aw, *see* Well worth a.

Awake, *see* Asleep and a., (Between).

Aware, *see* Too late a.; Wise that is ware in time.

Away goes the devil when he finds the
door shut against him. (D 269)

1599 MINSHEU *Span. Dial.* 7 At a locked doore,
the diuell himselfe goeth his way. **1642** TOR-
RIANO 62 The devil when the door is shut upon
him, will turn his back. **1659** HOWELL *It. Prov.*
4 The Devil turns his back at a gate shut.

Away, *see also* Good that are a. (They are aye);
Good wife's a. (When), keys are tint; Hold that
will a. (Who can); Once a way (a.) and aye a.;
Snatch and a., (A); Whiff and a.

Awe makes Dun draw, *see* Well worth aw, it
makes the plough draw.

Awhile, *see* Lend me your ears a.

Awl(s), *see* Cobbler deals with all [a.]; Six a.
make shoemaker.

Awry, *see* Tread one's shoe a.

Axe to grind, To have an.

[= to have private ends to serve. In a story told
by Benjamin Franklin the expression does not
bear this meaning.] **1810** C. MINER *Who'll turn
Grindstone?* When I see a merchant over-polite
to his customers . . . thinks I, that man has an
axe to grind. **1902** W. BESANT *Autobiog.* ch. 7
Sea-captains . . . have no private axe to grind.
1927 *The Times* 28 Nov. 14/2 Both Germany and
Russia have axes to grind in all that concerns the
Lithuanian Republic.

Axe, *see also* Lochaber a.; Open the door with
an a.; Pine wishes herself shrub when a. at her
root; Sandal tree perfumes a. that fells; Tree is
fallen, everyone runs with a.

Axle-tree for an oven, A pretty fellow
to make an. (F 179)

1670 RAY 162 (*Chesh.*). **1732** FULLER no. 362.

Axle-tree, *see also* Fly sat upon a.

B

B, *see* Knows not a B from battledore (*or* bull's
foot); Say B to battledore.

Babbling is not without offence, Much.
(B 3)

c. **1532** *Tales* no. 59 Bablynge (as Plutarchus
sayth) is a greuous disease. **1616** DRAXE no. 108.
1659 N.R. 76.

Babble, *see* Burn does not b. (When).

Babe(s), *see* Bugbears (Bugs) to scare b.; Innocent as new-born b.; Love the b. for her that
bare it.

Baby of Beelzebub's bower, Ye be a.
(B 7)

1362 LANGLAND *P. Pl.* A. II. 100 A bastard i-boren
of Belsabubbes Kunne. **1546** HEYWOOD II. iv.
G4ᵛ.

Baby (-ies), *see also* Empty the b. with the bath;
Look b.

Babylon, The modern (i.e. London).

1835 J. M. WILSON in *Tales of Borders* I. 355, 6
I proceeded to London . . . and . . . found myself
. . . in a wilderness. . . . Months passed away, and
I was still a wanderer upon the streets of the
modern Babylon.

Babylon, *see also* Way to B. will never bring to
Jerusalem.

Bacchants, *see* Thyrsus-bearers.

Bacchus has drowned more men than
Neptune.

1732 FULLER no. 830.

Bacchus, *see also* Ceres and B. (Without) Venus
grows cold.

Bachelors laugh (grin) and show our
teeth, We | but you married men laugh
till your hearts ache. (B 9)

1621 BURTON *Anat. Mel.* Pref. We bachelors cry
hahho for a wife, but when we are married we
make one moan. **1651** HERBERT no. 1175.
1670 RAY 48. **1732** FULLER no. 5433.

Bachelors' fare: bread and cheese, and
kisses.

1738 SWIFT Dial. I. E.L. 278. **1823** PIERCE
EGAN'S *Grose.*

Bachelors' wives and maids' children
are well taught. (B 10)

1546 HEYWOOD II. vi. I. 1. **1614** CAMDEN 304.
1706 STEVENS s.v. Muger We say . . . Maids
Children and Batchelors Wives, are well govern'd.
1738 SWIFT Dial. I. E.L. 289 Ay, ay! bachelors'
wives and maids' children are finely tutored.
1808 E. HAMILTON *Cottagers of Glenburnie* ch. 8
Maiden's bairns are aye weel bred, ye ken. **1834**

MARRYAT *Jacob Faith*. ch. 42 Bachelors' wives are always best managed, they say. **1857** G. ELIOT *Scenes of Clerical Life* 'Amos Barton' ch. 6 Old maids' husbands are al'ys well managed. If you was a wife you'd be as foolish as your betters, belike.

Bachelor(s), *see also* Lewd b. jealous husband; Son of a b.; Town bull as much a b. as he; Two b. drinking to you . . . soon be married.

Back door robs the house, The. (*Cf.* Nice wife and back door; Postern door; Two daughters.) (B 21)

[*c.* 1590] **1592** *Soliman & Perseda* IV. ii. 53 Haue an eye to the back dore. **1609** HARWARD 71ᵛ The Backdore spoyles the howse. **1616** DRAXE no. 2117 The backe doore maketh theeues. **1640** HERBERT no. 474. **1642** TORRIANO 69. **1659** N.R. 100. **1732** FULLER no. 4402.

Back door(s), *see also* Marries a widow and two children . . . has three b. d. to his house; Nice wife and b. d. make rich man poor; Two daughters and b. d. are thieves. *See also* Postern.

Back is broad enough to bear blame (jests), His. (B 13)

a. **1471** MALORY X. 78 I may beare well the blame, for my bak ys brode ynowghe. *a.* **1529** SKELTON *Manerly Margery* l. 12 Dyce i. 28 Go watch a bole, your bak is brode. *c.* **1560** R. WEVER *Lusty Juventus* D3ᵛ My backe is broade inought to bare away that mock. **1639** CLARKE 86. **1670** RAY 163. **1675** C. COTTON *Burlesque upon Burlesque* III Jeer on, my back is broad enough. **1782** J. RITSON *Observns. on Warton's Hist. of Eng. Poetry* 27.

Back(s), *see also* Bear him on my b.; Bear till his b. break; Beast with two b., (To make the); Belly robs the b.; Claw the b. of; Coat is on one's b., (As sure as the); Fall b. fall edge; Fall on his b. and break his nose; God shapes b. for burden; Good for b. bad for head; Got over the devil's b.; Piss down one's b.; Rod for his own b.; Steel to the b.; Water off duck's b.; Wears a whole lordship on his b.

Backare,[1] quoth Mortimer to his sow. (M 1183)

1546 HEYWOOD I. xi. E2. *a.* **1553** UDALL *Roister D.* I. ii. Arb. 16. **1587** J. BRIDGES *Defence* 123 Emperours, Kings . . . for all their supremacie, must backarie, and come after you. **1594–8** SHAKES. *T.S.* II. i. 73 Bacare! you are marvellous forward. **1611** DAVIES no. 23. [1 stand back.]

Backbiters, *see* Beasts, (The most deadly of wild) is a b. (tyrant), of tame ones a flatterer; Hearers (Were there no), no b.

Backward(s), *see* Crab, (To go b. like the); Lies b. and lets out her fore-rooms, (She).

Bacon, *see* Devil is a hog (When), you shall eat b.; Flitch of b. from Dunmow; Loves b. well

that licks; Save one's b.; Sell one's b.; Think there is b. (Where you), there is no chimney.

Bad a Jill, There is not so | but there's as bad a Will (Jack). (J 6)

1591 ARIOSTO *Orl. Fur.* Harington XVI. 15 As fitly met, As knauish iacke could be for whorish gill. *c.* **1641** FERGUSSON MS. no. 1376 There was never such a sillie Jockie but he gat als sillie a Jennie. **1678** RAY 146. **1706** STEVENS s.v. Escoba (Jack . . . Jill). **1732** FULLER no. 6112.

Bad bush is better than the open field, A. (B 735)

Cf. c. **1300** *Provs. of Hending*, no. 19 in *Anglia* 51. 258 Ounder buskes me shal fair weder abide. *Cf. c.* **1500** *Sloane MS.* 747 f. 66a Under the bosshe yt ys gode fayre weder to abyde. **1670** RAY 58 . . . Better to have . . . a bad friend or relation, then to be quite destitute. **1792** BURNS *Wks.* II. 397 Better a wee bush than nae bield. **1820** SCOTT *Monast.* ch. 3 Elspeth . . . will give us houseroom. . . . These evil showers make the low bush better than no bield.

Bad cause that none dare speak in, It is a. (C 201)

1639 CLARKE 199. **1737** RAMSAY III. 187 It's an ill cause that the lawyers think shame o'.

Bad cloth that will take no colour, It is a. (C 431)

1546 HEYWOOD II. ix. K4ᵛ. **1580** LYLY *Euph. & his Eng.* ii. 169 Be your cloath neuer so badde it will take some colour, & your cause neuer so false, it will beare some shew of probabilytie. **1670** RAY 71 . . . Cattiva è quella lana che non si puo tingere. *Ital.*

Bad custom is like a good cake, better broken than kept, A. (C 931)

1600–1 SHAKES. *H.* I. iv. 15 It is a custom More honour'd in the breach than the observance. **1611** COTGRAVE s.v. Gasteau. **1670** RAY 76.

Bad day that has a good night, It is never a. (D 87)

1581 T. LUPTON *Siuqila* 75 As it is commonlye saide, they haue neuer an euill daye that haue a good night. **1608** JOHN DENISON *Three-fold Resolution* (1616) 422 Wee haue an old saying: That is no bad day, that hath a good night. **1609** HARWARD 83ᵛ He hath never ill day that hath a good night. **1641** FERGUSSON no. 855 They had never an ill day that had a good evening. **1670** RAY 6.

Bad dog never sees the wolf, A. (D 442)

[14 . . *Prov. communs* À mauvais chien on ne peut montrer le loup.] **1611** COTGRAVE s.v. Loup. **1640** HERBERT no. 59.

Bad dog, Into the mouth of a | often falls a good bone. (M 1253)

1592 DELAMOTHE 49. **1639** CLARKE 45. **1670** RAY 82 . . . Souvent à mauvais chien tombe un bon os en gueule. *Gall.*

Bad excuse (shift) is better than none at all, A. (E 214)

1551 T. WILSON *Rule of Reason* S 6 This is as thei saie in English, better a badde excuse, then none at all, in Latine it is called, *non causa pro causa posita.* **1553** UDALL *Royster D.* v. ii Arb. 81 Yea Custance, better (they say) a badde scuse than none. **1579** GOSSON *Sch. Abuse* Arb. 42. **1599** PORTER *Two Angry Women* K1 'Tis good to haue a cloake for the raine, a bad shift is better then none at all. **1616** DRAXE no. 626 (sory). **1639** CLARKE 44. **1692** L'ESTRANGE *Aesop's Fab.* no. 119 (1738) 136.

Bad for the better, To change the. (B 26)

1575 G. GASCOIGNE *Glass of Govt.* ii. 43 Shun the bad, and sew the best. **1591** W. STEPNEY 156 It is alwayes good to change for a better. **1594** SHAKES. *T.G.V.* II. vi. 12 And he wants wit that wants resolved will To learn his wit t'exchange the bad for better. **1594-5** *Id. L.L.L.* IV. iii. 68 If by me broke, what fool is not so wise To lose an oath to win a paradise?

Bad is the best. (*Cf.* Best is as good as stark naught.) (B 316)

1564 BULLEIN *Dial. agst. Fever* E.E.T.S. 77 Bad is the best, the world amends like sour ale in summer. **1587** G. WHETSTONE *Censure of a loyal subject* B1ᵛ Little may be the moue, bad was the best. **1591-2** SHAKES. *3 Hen. VI* V. vi. 91 Counting myself but bad till I be best. *a.* **1609** *Id. Son.* 114 Creating every bad a perfect best. **1678** RAY 96 Where bad's the best, naught must be the choice. **1800** EDGEWORTH *The Will* ch. 2 Bad's the best, if that be the best of her characters.

Bad money drives out good.

1902-4 LEAN III. 425 Bad money drives out good (money), i.e. inconvertible paper drives out gold. —Gresham's Law.

Bad penny (shilling) always comes back, A.

1824 SCOTT *Redg.* ch. 2 Bring back Darsie? little doubt of that—the bad shilling is sure enough to come back again. **1872** BESANT & RICE *Ready-m. Mort.* ch. 8 I always said he'd come back like a bad shilling.

Bad sack that will abide no clouting, It is a. (S 6)

1546 HEYWOOD II. iv. G2ᵛ. **1611** DAVIES no. 369. **1670** RAY 23.

Bad shearer never had a good sickle, A. (S 290)

1641 FERGUSSON no. 72 (hooke). **1721** KELLY 12 (Hook). **1846** DENHAM 50.

Bad Spaniard makes a good Portuguese, A.

1846 GRANT *Rom. of War* ch. 9 The Portuguese are not over nice . . . and we have a proverb among us, 'that a bad Spaniard makes a good Portuguese'. **1853** TRENCH iii. 52 The Spaniard's contempt for his peninsular neighbours finds emphatic utterance in: Take from a Spaniard all his good qualities, and there remains a Portuguese.

Bad woman is worse than a bad man, A.

1893 LIDDON *Serm. O. Test.* 159 The current . . . proverb, that 'a bad woman is much worse than a bad man', owes its force to the fact that women . . . fall deeper, because they fall . . . from a higher level.

Bad (Ill) workman quarrels with his tools, A. (W 857 and 858)

1568 G. B. GELLI *The Fearful Fancies of the Florentine* tr. W. Barker B3 All artificers not cunninge, doe impute all the errowrs they do, to the matter they work on. **1586** J. CASE *Praise of Music* 30 Blame not the hatchet for the Carpenters fault. **1611** COTGRAVE s.v. Outil A bungler cannot find (or fit himselfe with) good tooles. **1640** HERBERT no. 67 Never had ill workman good tools. *Ibid.* no. 408 (An ill labourer). **1670** RAY 158. **1738** SWIFT *Dial.* II. E.L. 311 They say, an ill workman never had good tools. **1907** *Japan Times* 26 Feb. General Bildering . . . says it is only a bad workman who quarrels with his tools and repudiates Kuropatkin's criticism of the rank and file.

Bad, *see also* Best go first, b. remains; Collier's sack, b. without . . . (Like a); Four good mothers have four b. daughters; Good riddance to b. rubbish; Learning in breast of b. man; No man ever . . . b. all at once; Nothing so b. but might have been worse;—in which is not some good; Pardoning b. is injuring good; Rome sees a b. man.

Badge, *see* Blue coat without a b.

Baff, *see* Buff nor b., (He can neither say).

Badger, *see* Gip with an ill rubbing, quoth B.; Grey as a b.

Bag (Sack), To give one the. (B 32)

[= to leave without warning; later, to dismiss.] **1576** *Common Conditions* l. 215 This tinkerly trade, wee geue it the bagge. **1577** *Art of Angling* A1ᵛ I would giue them the bag, and bid them adue. **1592** GREENE *Def. Conny Catching* (Gros. xi. 86) If he meane to giue her the bagge, he selleth whatsoeuer he can, and so leueth her. **1613** T. ADAMS *Heaven and Earth Reconcil'd* 6 As Demas, that gaue Religion the Bagge, when the World offered him the Purse. **1637** SHIRLEY *Hyde Park* I. i—If she would affect one of us, for my part I am indifferent.—So say I too, but to give us both the canvas! [*Note.* From the practice of journeymen mechanics carrying their tools with them, when dismissed, they were said to get the canvas or the bag.] **1825** C. M. WESTMACOTT

Eng. Spy I. 178 You munna split on me, or I shall get the zack for telling on ye. **1908** E. M. SNEYD-KYNNERSLEY *H.M.I.* (1910) ch. 2 A new minister . . . preached against the war. They had a meeting in the vestry after service, and gave him the sack before dinner.

Bag to hold, To give (one) the.

[= to leave in the lurch.] **1793** T. JEFFERSON *Writ.* (1859) IV. 7 She will leave Spain the bag to hold. **1823** SCOTT *Peveril* ch. 7 She gave me the bag to hold, and was smuggling in a corner with a rich old Puritan.

Bag(s), *see also* Beggar beat his b. (Would make); Covetousness (Too much) breaks b.; Put him up in a b.; Toom b. rattle; World wags (I wot how), best loved that hath most b.

Bagpipe; He is like a | he never talks till his belly be full.   (B 34)

1577 *Art of Angling* C5ᵛ Good sir let him eat his meate.—My wife counteth me like the instrument of Lincolneshere. **1616** DRAXE no. 816 A baggepipe will not lightly speake, vntill his belly be full. **1618** D. BELCHIER *Hans Beere-pot* E iv Or Baggepype-like not speake before thou art full. **1678** RAY 291. **1906** QUILLER-COUCH *Sir J. Constantine* ch. 20 There's another saying that even a bagpipe won't speak till his belly be full.

Bagpipes, *see also* Lincolnshire.

Bag-pudding, *see* Deceit in a b. (No); Sweetheart and b.

Bailery, *see* Whiles thou, whiles I, so goes b.

Bailiff of Bedford is coming, The.
(B 37)
1655 FULLER *Hist. Univ. Camb.* V (1840) 105 In the next (being a wet and windy) winter, down comes the bailiff of Bedford (so the country-people commonly call the over-flowing of the river Ouse), . . . and breaks down all their paper-banks.

Bailiff of the Marshland, The.   (B 38)
1662 FULLER *Norfolk* 248 He is arrested by the Baily of the Marshland. The aire of Marshland in this County is none of the wholesomest. . . . Hence . . . strangers coming hither are clapt on the back with an ague. **1897** BP. CREIGHTON *Story of Eng. Shires* 379 The Fenmen . . . counted little of the ague which attacked them, and was called 'the Bailiff of the Marshland'.

Bailiff, *see also* Gerard's b. (Here is).

Bairns o' Falkirk, Like the | they'll end ere they mend.

1862 HISLOP 212 . . . 'This is a proverbial saying of ill-doing persons, as expressive of there being no hope of them.'

Bairn(s), *see also* Christen the b.; Death of a b.

is not skailing of house; Fools and b. . . . half-done work; God's b. is eith to lear; Hands off other folks' b.; Sair dung b. that dare not greet; Scant of b. that brought you up; Thrawn faced b. gotten against father's will; Tod's b. ill to tame.

Bait hides the hook, The.   (B 50)

1539 FRONTINUS *Stratagems of War* tr. R. Morysine a5 They shal . . . hereby perceyue, many swete baytes to couer soure hokes. **1562** A. BROOKE *Romeus & Juliet* l. 388 Oft the poisoned hook is hid, wrapt in the pleasant bait. **1566–8** R. WILMOT *et al. Gismond of Salerne* III. Chorus 41 He geues poison so to drink in gold, And hides vnder such pleasant baite his hoke. **1576** GASCOIGNE *Princelye Pleasures at Kenilworth Castle* ii. 108 The Sugred baite oft hides the harmefull hookes. **1579** LYLY *Euph.* i. 222 Beautie . . . was a deceiptfull bayte with a deadly hooke. **1594–5** SHAKES. *R.J.* Prol. to II, l. 8 And they steal love's sweet bait from fearful hooks. **1600** DEKKER *Old Fort.* I. ii. 50 Her most beautious lookes Are poysned baits, hung vpon golden hookes. **1732** FULLER no. 4403.

Bait, *see also* Burford b.; Escaped mouse feels taste of b.; Fish follows b.; Fish will soon be caught that nibbles at every b.; Welsh b.

Bake so shall you brew (eat), As you. (*Cf.* As they brew so let them bake.)
(B 52)
1548 E. HALL *Hen. VII: Chron.* 7ᵛ Suche breade as they bake, suche muste they eate. **1579** GOSSON *Sch. Abuse* 46 But as bake many times, so they brue. **1583** MELBANCKE D4 Such as thou bakest, such shalt thou eat. **1594** GREENE & LODGE *Look. Glass* F2 Nay, euen as you haue baked, so brue, ielousie must be driuen out by extremities.

Bake, *see* Brew (As they), so let them b.

Baker by his bow legs, He should be a.
(B 54)
1607 DEKKER & WEBSTER *Westward Hoe* II. ii. 156 Wil women's tounges, (like Bakers' legs) neuer go straight! **1678** RAY 91.

Baker, Be not a | if your head be of butter.   (B 53)
1640 HERBERT no. 321. **1659** HOWELL *Span. Prov.* 7.

Baker to the pillory, I fear we part not yet, quoth the.   (L 171)
[There were severe penalties for impurity of bread or shortness of weight.] **1546** HEYWOOD II. ii. G1 And so late met, that I feare we parte not yéet, Quoth the baker to the pillory. **1659** HOWELL *Eng. Prov.* 11b Ile take no leave of you, quoth the Baker to the Pillory.

Baker's daughter, *see* Three dear years will raise a b. d.

Baking beside meal, It is good. (B 56)

a. 1628 CARMICHAELL no. 911. 1641 FERGUSSON no. 523. 1721 KELLY 181 . . . That is, People may do well enough, when they have some to uphold, and supply them.

Balaam's ass, *see* Mackerel is in season.

Balance distinguishes not between gold and lead, The. (B 57)

1640 HERBERT no. 629.

Bald as a coot, As. (c 645)

a. 1300 *Gloss. Walter de Biblesworth* in Wright's *Vocab.* 165 *Une blarye*, a balled cote. 1430 LYDGATE *Chron. Troy.* II. xv And yet he was so balde as is a coote. 1545 *Precepts of Cato* H6 (bare). 1546 HEYWOOD I. v. B2ᵛ What though she be toothlesse, and balde as a coote? 1621 BURTON *Anat. Mel.* III. iii. I. ii (1651) 599 I have an old grim sire to my husband, as bald as a coot.

Bald head is soon shaven, A. (H 237)

14 . . *Reliq. Antiquae* i. 75 A bare berd wyl sone be shave. 1678 RAY 96. 1802 WOLCOT (P. Pindar) *Middl. Elect.* ii Bald pates be quickly shav'd.

Bald moon, A | quoth Benny Gask; another pint, quoth Lesley.

1721 KELLY 53 . . . Spoken when People encourage themselves to stay a little longer in the Ale-house, because they have Moonlight. 1818 SCOTT *Rob Roy* ch. 29 Mind the auld saw, man— It's a bauld moon, quoth Benny Gask—another pint, quoth Lesley; we'll no start for another chappin.

Bald, *see also* Believe he's b. till you see his brains (Will not); Mare has a b. face (When the).

Baldwin's dead, My Lord. (L 448)

1670 RAY 163 . . . It is used, when one tells that for news which everybody knows. A *Sussex* proverb. But who this Lord *Baldwin* was, I could not learn there.

Bale (Need) is hext (highest), When | boot (help) is next (nighest). (B 59)

a. 1250 *Owl & Night.* ll. 687–8 Wone þe bale is alre-hecst, þonne is þe bote alre-necst. [When the evil is highest of all, then the remedy is nighest of all.] *a.* 1300 *Cursor M.* 4775 Quen þe bal ys alder hext þen sum time ys bote next. *c.* 1320 *Reliq. Antiquae* (1841) i. 113 When the bale is hest, Thenne is the bote nest. *c.* 1350 *Douce MS.* 52 no. 91. *c.* 1400 *Beryn* E.E.T.S. I. 3956 So 'aftir bale comyth bote' who-so bydë conne. 1546 HEYWOOD I. xii. E4 Comfort your selfe with this old text, . . . That telth vs, when bale is hekst, boote is next. 1616 DRAXE no. 996. 1822 SCOTT *Nigel* ch. 21 Did you never hear, that when the need is highest the help is nighest? 1827 HARE *Guess. at Truth* (1859) ii. 316 Though a great and momentous truth is involved in the saying, that, when need is highest, then aid is

nighest, this comfort belongs only to such as acknowledge that man's waywardness is ever crost and over-ruled by a higher power.

Balk¹ (balks) of good ground, Make not a. (B 60)

[= don't waste a good chance.] *a.* 1628 CARMICHAELL no. 1104 (bakes). 1636 CAMDEN 302. 1640 FULLER *Joseph's Coat* (1867) 35 The rich Corinthians, in not inviting the poor, made balks of good ground. 1641 FERGUSSON no. 642 Make no balkes of good bear land. 1721 KELLY 247 Make no Baulks in good Bearland. Spoken when it is proposed to marry the youngest Daughter, before the eldest. [¹ a ridge or piece left unploughed by accident or carelessness.]

Balk(s), *see also* By-walkers (Many), many b.

Ball at one's foot (*or* before one), To have the. (B 63)

1563 *Mirror for Mag.* ed. Campbell 380 But when the ball was at my foote to guyde, I played to those that fortune did abide. 1568 H. CHARTERIS, Preface to Lindsay's *Warkis* (Hamer, i. 398) Thay had the ball at thair fute. *c.* 1661 *Papers on Alterat. Prayer-bk.* 24 You have the ball before you, and have the . . . power of contending without controll. 1755 BUBB DODINGTON *Diary* 27 May The Duke of Newcastle had the ball at his foot when his brother died. *c.* 1800 LD. AUCKLAND *Corr.* (1862) 416 We have the ball at our feet, and if the Government will allow us . . . the rebellion will be crushed. 1906 A. T. QUILLER-COUCH *Cornish Wind.* 126, 7 Relief . . . came with his election as Fellow of Oriel . . . and the brilliant young scholar had . . . the ball at his feet.

Ball does not stick to the wall, If the | it will at least leave a mark.

1659 HOWELL *Span. Prov.* 19 If this dab doth not stick to the wall, 'twill at least leave a mark. 1706 STEVENS s.v. Pella. 1732 FULLER no. 2701. 1823 COLLINS 346 . . . It alludes to defamation.

Ball, *see also* Round as a b.; Stricken the b. under the line; World is round, (turns as a b.).

Ballast, *see* Sail too big for b. (Make not).

Balm in Gilead.

[1560 BIBLE (Geneva) *Jer.* viii. 22 Is there no balme at Gilead? is there no Physition there?] 1778 FLETCHER OF MADELEY *Wks.* vii. 303. 1849 C. BRONTË *Shirley* ch. 11 There are two guineas to buy a new frock. Come, Cary, never fear: we'll find balm in Gilead.

Balm, *see also* Sow recks not of b.

Banagher, *see* Bangs B.

Banbury ale. (A 100)

1609 T. RAVENSCROFT *Pammelia* E1ᵛ Banbery Ale where where where, at the Black Smithes house, I would I were there. 1658 MENNIS & SMITH *Wit Restored: Facetiae* i. 281 . . . a halfe-yard-pott.

Banbury zeal, cheese, and cakes. (z 1)

1586 T. BRIGHT *Treat. of Mel.* 26 Of a grosse and melancholicke nourishment . . . are bag puddings, or panpuddings made with flour, frittars, pancakes, such as wee call Banberie cakes, and those great ones confected with butter, egges, &c. vsed at weddings. [**1592**] **1594** *Knack to Know a Knave* Hazl.-Dods. vi. 533 We are as near kin together As the cates [Cats Q] of Banbury be to the bells of Lincoln. **1596** HARINGTON *Anat. Metam. Ajax* (1927 ed.) 116 O that I were at Oxenford to eat some Banberie cakes. **1610** CAMDEN *Britannia* tr. Holland 376 The fame of this towne is for zeale, cheese, and cakes. **1662** FULLER Oxford 328 Banbury Zeale, Cheese, and Cakes. I admire to find these joyned together in so learned an author as Mr. Camden . . . But, . . . no such words are extant in the Latine Camden. . . . In the . . . last Edition, Anno 1637, . . . the error is continued out of design to nick the town of Banbury, as reputed then a place of precise people.

Banbury, *see also* Hogs to a B. market; Thin as B. cheese; Tinkers (B.).

Band(s), *see* Busy will have bonds (b.); Old b. is captain's honour.

Bangs (Beats) Banagher! That.

1830–3 CARLETON *Traits & Stories; Three Tasks* (Routledge) 25 'O, by this and by that', says he, 'but that bates Bannagher!' **1885** W. BLACK *White Heather* ch. 40 'Well, that bangs Banagher!' she said with a loud laugh. . . . 'There's a place for twa lovers to foregather!' **1910** P. W. JOYCE *Eng. as We Speak* 192 Banagher is a village in King's Co., on the Shannon. . . . When anything very unusual or unexpected occurs, the people say, 'Well, that bangs Banagher!'

Bank, *see* After a lank a b.; Safe as the b.

Bankrupt, *see* Beggar can never be b.

Banning, *see* Be as be may is no b.; Wooing for woeing, banna for b.

Bannock should burn than you should turn it, I had rather my.

1721 KELLY 192 . . . Spoken to those, whose intermedling with our Business we think not for our Profit.

Bannock, *see also* Grace of gray b. is in baking; Kitty Sleitchock's b.

Banquet, There is no great | but some fare ill.   (B 68)

1568 GUEVERA *Dial of Princes* tr. T. North (1582, 437b) There was neuer made feast or bancket but the diuell was euer lightly a guest, by whose presence always happeneth some mischiefe. **1640** HERBERT no. 668. **1642** TORRIANO 79. **1670** RAY 2.

Bapchild, *see* Live a little while.

Barber learns to shave by shaving fools, A.   (B 69)

1611 COTGRAVE s.v. Fol By shauing a foole one learnes to shaue. **1670** RAY 141 . . . He is a fool that will suffer a young beginner to practise first upon him. **1792** WOLCOT (P. Pindar) *Odes to K. Long* v Accept a proverb out of Wisdom's schools, 'Barbers first learn to shave, by shaving fools'.

Barber, One | shaves another gratis.
                                                           (B 71)

1611 COTGRAVE s.v. Barbier. Un barbier rait l'autre. Prov. One knaue trimmes; excuses, helpes; soothes, or flatters, another. **1654** E. GAYTON *Festivous Notes on Don Quixote* 262 One Barber wipes anothers nose. **1658** E. PHILLIPS *Myst. Love and Eloq.* 159 One barber trims another. **1902–4** LEAN IV. 72 . . . L'ung barbier raist l'autre.—Cord., 1538 The custom survives in medical practice. 'Barber' means of course 'barber surgeon'.

Barber shaves so close but another finds work, No.   (B 70)

1640 HERBERT no. 667. **1732** FULLER no. 3737.

Barber, *see also* Any tooth, good b.; Young b. and old physician.

Barber's chair, *see* Common as a b. c.

Bare arse than a furred hood, Better a.

1541 *Sch. of Women* D2ᵛ (Ye had leuer a).

Bare as an ape is behind, As.

c. **1570** INGELAND *Disobedient Child* F3ᵛ. **1591** GREENE *Disc. of Cozenage* ed. Harrison 20 They leaue him as bare of mony, as an ape of a taile.

Bare as the birch at Yule even, He is as.
                                                           (B 356)

a. **1628** CARMICHAELL no. 672 He is als bair as the birk in Yule evin. **1641** FERGUSSON no. 726 *Of Waisters & Debters.*

Bare moor that he goes over and gets not a cow, It is a.   (M 1133)

1641 FERGUSSON no. 529.

Bare walls make giddy housewives.
                                                           (W 18)

1623 PAINTER C8. **1623** CAMDEN 267. **1639** CLARKE 242. **1655** FULLER *Ch. Hist.* XI. ii (1868) III. 427 If in private houses bare walls make giddy housewifes, in princes' palaces empty coffers make unsteady statesmen. **1723** DEFOE *Col. Jack* x Wks. (1912) I. 399 I had . . . a house . . . ; but, as we say, bare walls make giddy hussies. **1732** FULLER no. 839 Bare Walls make gadding Housewives.

Bare words are (make) no good bargain.
                                                           (W 786)

1597 *Politeuphuia* 166ᵛ (no lawfull bargaines).

1639 CLARKE 85. **1721** KELLY 72 . . . A Preface to the demanding of Earnest.

Bare, *see also* Breeches of a b.-arsed man, (To beg); Hair and hair; More b. than the shoemaker's wife.

Bareback, *see* Saddles lack.

Barefoot must not plant thorns, He that goes. (T 235)

c. **1594** BACON *Promus* no. 433 Chi semina spine non vada discalzo. **1599** MINSHEU To the Reader A3 He that soweth thornes, let him not go barefoot. **1605** S. DANIEL *Philotas* Wks. Gros. III. 109 Men must be shod that goe amongst the thornes. **1611** COTGRAVE s.v. Pied. **1640** HERBERT no. 82. **1664** CODRINGTON 187 Barefooted Men need not tread on thorns. **1678** RAY 404 While thy shoee is on thy foot tread upon the thornes. **1736** FRANKLIN Oct. He that scatters thorns let him not go barefoot.

Barefoot, *see also* Dance b.; Dead men's shoes (He goes along b. that wears); Idleness must thank itself if it goes b.

Bargain is a bargain, A. (B 76)

1553 T. WILSON *Arte of Rhet.* (1585 ed.) 34 A bargaine is a bargaine and must stand without all excepcion. **1592** *Arden Fevers.* II. ii *Shaks. Apoc.* 13 I haue had ten pound to steale a dogge, and we haue no more heere to kill a man; but that a bargane is a bargane, . . . you should do it yourselfe. **1894** BLACKMORE *Perlycross* ch. 11 A bargain is a bargain—as we say here.

Bargain is a pick-purse, A good. (B 77)

1611 COTGRAVE s.v. Argent Good cheape commodities are notable picke-purses. **1640** HERBERT no. 12. **1710** PALMER 29.

Bargains dear bought, Some | good cheap should be sold. (B 81)

1546 HEYWOOD I. viii. C1. **1611** DAVIES no. 395.

Bargain(s), *see also* Bare words no b.; Beloved (To be) is above all b.; Best of a bad b.; Good b. (At a) make a pause; Ill b. where no man wins; More words than one to b.; Robin Hood b.; Second word makes b.; Smithfield b.; Two (words) to make a b.

Bargepole, *see* Touch him with a pair of tongs (b.).

Bark against (at) the moon, To.
(D 449 and M 1143)

1401 *Pol. Poems* (1859) II. 53 Thou, as blynde Bayarde, berkest at the mone. *c.* **1410** *Towneley Plays* E.E.T.S. xiii. 662 Can ye bark at the mone? **1520** WHITTINGTON *Vulg.* E.E.T.S. 72 They playe as the dogge doeth that barketh at the moon all nyght. **1616** DRAXE no. 1337 He barketh at the moone. **1655** HEYWOOD *Fort. by Land.* I. i. Wks. (1874) VI. 370 He hath such

honourable friends to guard him, We should in that but bark against the moon.

Bark and the tree, Put not thy hand between the. (H 88)

1546 HEYWOOD II. ii. G1ᵛ It were a foly for mé, To put my hande betwéene the barke and the tré. **1580** TUSSER C1 Nor put to thy hand betwixt bark and the tree, least through thy owne follie so pinched thou bee. **1641** FERGUSSON no. 495 Put not your hand betwixt the rind and the tree. **1721** KELLY 200 It is ill medling between the Bark and the Rind. It is a troublesome and thankless Office to concern our selves in the Jars, and Out-falls of near Relations, as Man and Wife, Parents and Children. **1813** RAY 118 . . . *i.e.* Meddle not in family affairs.

Bark is worse than his bite, His. *Cf.* Barkers are no biters.

1663 *Lauderdale Papers* (1884) I. 131 It . . . is intended that that letter shall be a great bark if not a byt. **1816** SCOTT *Antiq.* ch. 22 'Monkbarns's bark', . . . 'is muckle waur than his bite'. **1842** DE QUINCEY *Cicero* Wks. VI. 184 The bark of electioneering mobs is worse than their bite. **1900** G. C. BRODRICK *Mem. & Impress.* 253 [Freeman] was . . . an unscrupulous controversialist. . . . Yet his bark was worse than his bite, and he was essentially a kind-hearted man.

Bark ourselves ere we buy dogs so dear, We will.

a. **1628** CARMICHAELL no. 1234. **1721** KELLY 357 . . . Spoken when too dear a Rate is asked for what we are buying.

Bark up the wrong tree, To.

1833 *Sketches & Eccentr. D. Crockett* (1834) 58 I told him . . . that he reminded me of the meanest thing on God's earth, an old coon dog, barking up the wrong tree. **1841** *Congress. Globe* 25 Jan. App. 153 The stock-jobbers were barking up the wrong tree when they wrote those letters.

Bark (of a tree), *see also* Near as b. to tree.

Bark(ing) (of a dog), *see also* Dog (wolf) b. in vain at moon; Dog will b. ere he bite; Dog's b. (At) seem not to awake; Dogs b. as bred; Dogs b. not at him (All); Dogs that b. at distance bite not at hand; Dogs (Like) when one b. all b.; Keep a dog and b. myself; Moon does not heed b. of dogs.

Barkers are no biters, Great. (B 85)

1387 TREVISA tr. Higden iii. 427 Rolls Ser. Hit is þe manere of þe feblest houndes for to berke most. **1584** *Fedele and Fortunio or Two Italian Gentlemen* B2ᵛ Great barkers are none of the greatest biters. *a.* **1599** ? GREENE *George-a-G.* IV. iii *Merm.* 439 That will I try. Barking dogs bite not the sorest. **1614** CAMDEN 306. **1721** KELLY 112 . . . Great Boasters are not always best Performers. **1880** BLACKMORE *Mary Aner.* ch. 47 Thousands of men threaten, and do nothing, according to the proverb. [*See also* quotations under next proverb.]

Barking dogs seldom bite.   (D 528)

c. 1275 *Prov. of Alfred* (Skeat) B 652 The bicche bitiþ ille þauh he berke stille.   1539 TAVERNER 49 Fearfull dogges do barke the sorer.   1595 *Locrine* IV. i *Shaks. Apoc.* 56 A barking dog doth seldom strangers bite.   1655 FULLER *Ch. Hist.* VIII. ii 20 [Tunstall's] passion herein may the rather be pardoned, because politickly presumed to barke the more that he might bite the lesse.   1837 CHAMIER *Saucy Areth.* ch. 35 Our dogs which bark, Abdallah, seldom bite. [*See also* quotations under preceding proverb. Fr. *Chien qui aboie ne mord pas.*]

Barley straw's good fodder when the cow gives water.   (B 89)

1678 RAY 51.

Barley, *see also* Cry 'B.'; Long in coming as Cotswold b.; Prizing of green b.; St. David's day put b. in clay; Sloe tree is white (When), sow b.

Barley-corn is better than a diamond to a cock, A.   (B 88)

1553 T. BECON *Jewel of Joy* P.S. 427 Bellied hypocrites, which, like to Esop's cock, set more by a barley-corn than by all the precious stones in the world.   1571 J. BRIDGES *Sermon at Paul's Cross* 124 Esops donghyll Cocke, who fynding a precious stone, hadde rather haue had a sillye barley corne to cramme his croppe, than all the precious stones in the worlde.   1576 PETTIE ii. 148 To give . . . a precious stone for a barleycorn with Aesop's cock.   1587 R. GREENE *Euph. his Censure* in Wks. Gros. vi. 179 Prefer not a barlie corne before a pretious Jewel, set not a fading content before a perpetuall honor.   1635 QUARLES *Div. Emb.* III. ii We snatch at barly grains, whilst pearls stand by Despis'd; such very fools art thou and I.   1692 L'ESTRANGE *Aesop's Fab.* i (1738) I.   1732 FULLER no. 7.

Barleycorn, *see also* John B.

Barm, *see* Brains will work without b.

Barn's full, When the | you may thresh before the door.   (B 90)

c. 1645 HOWELL *Lett.* II. xxiv When the barn was full anyone might thresh in the haggard.   1721 KELLY 354.

Barn, *see also* Robbing the b.

Barnaby bright: the longest day and the shortest night.   (B 92)

[St. Barnabas' Day, the 11th of June, in Old Style reckoned the longest day.]   1595 SPENSER *Epithal.* l. 266 This day the sunne is in his chiefest hight, With Barnaby the bright.   1659 HOWELL *Eng. Prov.* 20a.   1670 EACHARD *Cont. Clergy* 32 Barnaby-bright would be much too short for him to tell you all that he could say.   1858 *N. & Q.* 2nd Ser. VI 522 In some parts of the country the children call the lady-bird Barnaby Bright, and address it thus:—'Barnaby Bright, Barnaby Bright, The longest day and the shortest night'.

Barnaby, *see also* Dance B.

Barrel the (a) better herring, Never a (Neither).   (B 94)

[= never one better than another: nothing to choose between them.]   1542 ERASM. *Apoph.* tr. Udall (1877 ed. 187) Two feloes being like flagicious, and neither barell better herring, accused either other.   1546 HEYWOOD II. xi. M1 A foule olde riche widowe, whether wed wold ye, Or a yonge fayre mayde, beyng poore as ye be. In neither barrell better hearryng (quoth hee).   *c.* 1550 BALE *K. Johan* 1888 Eng. Lyke lorde, lyke chaplayne; neyther barrell better herynge.   1621 BURTON *Anat. Mel.* (1651) 46 Choose out of the whole pack, . . . you shall find them all alike—*never a barrel better herring.*   1680 BUNYAN *Mr. Badman* ed. Brown, 1905, 137 'Hang them Rogues, there is not a barrel better Herring of all the holy Brotherhood of them.'   1882 E. GOSSE *Gray* 167 *A Satire upon the Heads, or Never a barrel the better Herring,* a comic piece in which Gray attacked the prominent heads of houses.

Barrel, *see also* Herring in b.; Knock on the hoop, another on b.; Wine by the b. (Cannot know).

Barren sow was never good to pigs, A.   (S 683)

a. 1628 CARMICHAELL no. 259 A yeild sw was never gude to grises.   1641 FERGUSSON no. 78. 1721 KELLY 1 A Yell Sow was never good to Grices.

Barrow, *see* Bout as B. was.

Barter, *see* Fond of b. that niffers with Old Nick.

Bashful mind hinders his good intent, His.   (M 970)

1678 RAY 66.

Bashfulness is an enemy to poverty.   (B 98)

[ERASM. *Ad. Verecundia inutilis viro egenti.* Bashfulness is useless to a man in want. HOM. *Od.* 17. 347.]   1539 TAVERNER, f. 26 Cast away bashfulnes where nede constrayneth.   1601 9 Aug. W. ALABASTER to Sir Rob. Cecil Hatfield MSS. vol. 87, f. 80–80ᵛ (*HMC* xi. 329) Bashefulnes doth not suite with misery.   1670 RAY 2.

Bashfulness, *see also* Modesty be virtue (Though), b. is vice.

Basilisk's eye is fatal, The.   (B 99)

c. 1400 MANDEVILLE ch. 28, 285 Thei sleu him anon with the beholdynge, as dothe the Basilisk.   1572 E. PASQUIER *Monophylo* tr. G. Fenton Y4ᵛ The mortal sight of the basilicque, by whom we die but of one death onely.   1590 LODGE *Rosalind* ed. Greg 74 Venus . . . is a basilisk, shut thy eyes and gaze not at her lest thou perish.   1590–1 SHAKES. *2 Hen. VI* III. ii. 52 Come, basilisk, And kill the innocent gazer with thy sight.   1597 M.B. *Trial True Frdship* C2 Pouertie . . . shunned as a Basilike of al men, whose sight presently

killeth. **1610** SHAKES. *Cym.* II. iv. 107 It is a
basilisk unto mine eye, Kills me to look on 't.
1611 *Id. W.T.* I. ii. 388 Make me not sighted
like the basilisk.

Basket, To go to the.
[= to go to prison.] **1632** MASS. & FIELD *Fatal
Dowry* v. i *Pontalier* [to Liladam, who is in
custody for debt], Go to the basket and repent.

Basket, You shall have the.   (B 102)
1678 RAY 344 . . . *Taunton.* Said to the journey-
man that is envied for pleasing his master. **1725**
ERASM. *Familiar Colloquies* tr. N. Bailey (1733
217) He demands what's his Right, let him have
the Basket.

Basket, *see also* Eggs in one b.; Youth in a b.

**Basket-justice will do justice right or
wrong, A.**   (B 103)
['Basket justices' allowed themselves to be
bought by baskets of game.] **1601** in TOWNS-
HEND *Hist. Coll.* (1680) 268 A Justice of Peace . . .
for half a Dozen of Chickens will Dispence with
a whole Dozen of Penal Statutes . . . These be
the Basket-Justices. **1678** RAY 74 A basket
Justice; a Jyll Justice; a good forenoon Justice.
He'll do Justice right or wrong.

Bass, The, *see* Ding doun Tantallon; Tammie
Norie o' the B.

Bastard brood is always proud.
1721 KELLY 68. **1736** BAILEY *Dict.* s.v. Bastard.

Bastard, *see also* Fine as a lord (lord's b.);
Hazelnuts (The more), more b.; Looked on me
as cow on b. calf.

Bastes the fat hog, Every man. *Cf.*
Grease the fat sow.   (H 487)
c. **1300** *Provs. of Hending* (ed. Schleich) in *Anglia*
51. 271 Euer man fedit þe fat swine for þe smere.
1509 BARCLAY *Ship of Fools* I. 100 The fat
pygge is baast, the lene cony is brent. **1546**
HEYWOOD I. xi. E4 Euery man basteth the fat hog
we sée, But the leane shall burne er he basted bé.
1648 HERRICK *Hesper.* 64 Wks. (1893) I. 23 The
fattest hogs we grease the more with lard.

Baste, *see also* Goose that will not b. herself.

Baston, *see* Oil of b.

Bat, *see* Blind as a b.

Bate me an ace, quoth Bolton.   (A 20)
1570 EDWARDS *Damon & Pithias* Hazl.-Dods. iv.
77. *c.* **1590** SIR THOMAS MORE II. i *Shaks. Apoc.*
391. **1659** HOWELL *Eng. Prov.* 14b. **1670** RAY
163 Queen Elisabeth, . . . being presented with
a collection of English Proverbs, and told by the
Authour, that it contained all the English
Proverbs, nay replied she, Bate me an ace, quoth
Bolton; which . . . happened to be wanting in his
collection.

Bath, *see also* Beggars of B.

**Bath of the blackamoor has sworn not
to whiten, The.**   (B 105)
1599 J. MINSHEU *Span. Gram.* 83 . . . i. That
which is bred in the bone will neuer out of the
flesh. **1651** HERBERT no. 1105.

**Bathes in May, He who | will soon be
laid in clay; he who bathes in June,
will sing a merry tune; he who bathes
in July, will dance like a fly.**
1827 HONE *Table-Book* 315. **1846** DENHAM 45.
1893 INWARDS 27.

Bathon, Jon of, *see* Speak, spend, quoth J. of B.

Bats in the belfry, To have.
[= to be crazy or eccentric.] **1907** A. BIERCE
(cited *N. & Q.* 207, 426). **1911** R. D. SAUNDERS
Col. Todhunter ch. 9 It's a case of bats in the
belfry on that one subject. **1927** A. E. W. MASON
No Other Tiger ch. 19. Phyllis Harmer exclaimed
. . . 'Dear man, you've got bats in the belfry'.

Battalions, *see* Providence is always on the side
of.

**Battersea, Go to | to be cut for the
simples.**
1787 GROSE (*Surrey*) I3 . . . In Battersea are . . .
market gardeners who grow medicinal herbs,
termed simples, for . . . apothecaries, who used
to . . . see them cut, which they called going to
Battersea to have their simples cut; whence
foolish people were jocularly advised to go
thither for the same purpose. **1788** GROSE
Class. Dict. of Vulgar Tongue s.v. Simples . . .
Battersea is a place famous for its garden grounds,
some of which were formerly appropriated to the
growing of simples for apothecaries, who at a
certain season used to go down to select their
stock for the ensuing year, at which time the
gardners were said to cut their simples; whence
it became a popular joke to advise young people
to go to Battersea, at that time, to have their
simples cut, or to be cut for the simples.

**Battle lost, Next to a | the greatest
misery is a battle gained.**
[1815] WELLINGTON 1912 *Times Lit. Sup.* 14 June
241 Wellington was the centre of all things . . .
'I hope to God', he said one day, 'that I have
fought my last battle . . . I always say that, next
to a battle lost, the greatest misery is a battle
gained'.

Battle, *see also* Ill b. where devil carries colours;
Race is not to swift nor b. to strong; War, (In)
not permitted to err twice.

Battledore, *see* Knows not a B. from a b.; Say B.
to a b.

Bauble, *see* Dote more than fool on b.; Fool will
not gave b.; Fools had b. (If all).

Bauchle(s), *see* Rice for good luck.

Bavin[1] is but a blaze, The.   (B 107)

1579 LYLY *Euph.* i. 218 Hot loue is soone colde...
the Bauin though it bourne bright, is but a blaze.
1584 GREENE *Anat. of Fortune* in Wks. Gros. iii.
194 I went out of my tente . . . hoping that hot
loue would be soone cold, that the greatest bauin
was but a blaze. **1591** ARIOSTO *Orl. Fur.* Harington x. 7 Beardlesse youths . . . Whose fancies
soone like strawne fire kindled are, And sooner
quencht amid their flaming heate. **1597** *Politeuphuia* 182ᵛ The longest date of his man's yeeres,
is but as a bauens blaze. **1597** SHAKES. *1 Hen. IV*
III. ii. 60 The skipping king, he ambled up and
down With shallow jesters and rash bavin wits,
Soon kindled and soon burnt. **1603** H. CROSSE
Vertues Commonw. (1878) 133 Which like a
bauin giueth goodly blaze . . . but is soone out.
[1 a bundle of brushwood.]

Bawbee(s), *see* Placks and b. grow pounds.

Bawd, *see* Opportunity is whoredom's b.

Bawdry, *see* Whoring and b. end in beggary.

Bawling, *see* Scolds and infants never lin b.

Bawtry, *see* Hanged for leaving liquor like
saddler of B.

Bawty, *see* Bourd not with B.

Bayard of ten toes.   (B 110)

1587 J. BRIDGES *Defence of Govt. of C. of E.* 1281
Trot on bayard a tentoes [i.e. on foot]. **1597**
E. S. *Disc. Knights Post* A3 As I traueiled . . .
upon my well approued hacney, (ould Bayard of
ten toes). **1616** BRETON *Good and Bad* (Wks. ii.
14) His trauell is the walke of the wotul and his
horse Bayard of ten toes. **1695** RAVENSCROFT 31
(on).

Bayard, *see also* Bold as blind B.; Keep B. in
stable.

Be as be may (is no banning).   (B 65)

c. **1386** CHAUCER *Monk's T.* l. 3319 Be as be may,
I wol hire noght accusen. *c.* **1406** HOCCLEVE
Mâle Règle l. 289 Be as be may, no more of this
as now. **1530** PALSGRAVE 444b. **1546** HEYWOOD
II. i. F3 God spéde them, be as be maie is no
bannyng. *c.* **1591** PEELE *O.W.T.* l. 6 It shall be
as it may be, so and so. **1591–2** SHAKES. *3 Hen.
VI* I. i. 194. **1594** LYLY *Mother B.* II. ii. 21 Well,
be as be may is no banning. I think I have
charmed my young master. [*Note*, p. 542.
Evidently a proverb with folk who think affairs
are going well and call for no extraordinary
effort.] **1611** DAVIES no. 20 Be as be may, no
banning is: And yet it is a curse To be as now it
is; because the world was neuer worse. **1721**
KELLY 75 Be it so, is no banning. Spoken when
we unwillingly give our consent to a Thing.

Be it for better, be it for worse, do you
after him that bears the purse.   (P 646)

c. **1350** *Douce MS.* 52 no. 64 Do thow better,
do thow worse, Do after hym, that beryth the

purse. *a.* **1530** *R. Hill's Commonpl. Bk.* E.E.T.S.
130. **1546** HEYWOOD I. v. B2. **1817** SCOTT *Rob
Roy* ch. 27 My puir mither used aye to tell me,
Be it better, be it worse, Be ruled by him that has
the purse.

Be not, *see* Baker, if head of butter; Bold with
your biggers; Hasty to outbid.

Be still, and have thy will.

c. **1450** *Provs. of Wysdom* 100 Suffer and haue
þy will. **1853** TRENCH ii 32 That very beautiful
[proverb] . . . in the writings of Tyndal, *Be still,
and have thy will.*

Be what thou wouldst be called (*or
seem to be*).   (s 214)

c. **1377** LANGLAND *Piers Plowman* B text X l. 253
Suche as thow semest in syghte, be in assay
y-founde. **1539** TAVERNER 49ᵛ Se thou be that
thou arte reported and borne in hande to be.
1547 W. BALDWIN *Treatise of Moral Philosophy*
L2ᵛ Be the selfe same that thou pretendest.
1621 BURTON *Anat. Mel.* II. iii. VII (1651) 360 Out
of humane authors take these few cautions, . . .
Seem not greater than thou art. *a.* **1628** CAR-
MICHAELL no. 268 Be the same thing that thow
wald be called. **1640** HERBERT no. 724. **1641**
FERGUSSON no. 195. **1721** KELLY 68 Be what
you seem, and seem what you are. The best way!
for Hypocrisy is soon discovered.

Be, *see also* Answer, To b.(do) more than he can.

Beacon Hill, *see* Bore a hole through B. H. (As
well).

Beadle, *see* Fear, the b. of the law.

Beads in the hand, The | and the devil
in capuch (or, cape of the cloak).

(B 113)

1599 MINSHEU *Span. Gram.* 84 The beades in the
hand, and the diuell in his capuch or cape of his
cloake, i. God in his mouth and the diuell in his
hart: good words and wicked deeds. **1651**
HERBERT no. 1082 (in Capuch (or cape of the
cloak)). **1659** HOWELL *Span. Prov.* 15 Beads
about his neck, and the Devil in his body.

Beam, *see* Kick the b.; Mote in another's eye.

Bean in a monk's hood, Like a.   (B 117)

1546 HEYWOOD II. vi. I. 2 And she must syt lyke
a beane in a monks hood. Bearyng no more rule,
than a goose turd in tems [Thames]. **1571** J.
BRIDGES *Sermon at Paul's Cross* 77 The cause of
God is cleane swallowed vp like a drop in the
sea, a beane in a Monks hoode, a mouse in a
cheese.

Bean in liberty is better than a comfit
in prison, A.   (B 114)

1640 HERBERT no. 653. **1670** RAY 15. **1732**
FULLER no. 9.

Bean has its black, Every. (B 115)

a. 1624 BP. M. SMITH *Serm.* (1632) 178. 1639 CLARKE 211. 1818 SCOTT *Rob Roy* ch. 38 Ye hae had your ain time o't, Mr. Syddall; but ilka bean has its black, and ilka path has its puddle.

Beans blow before May does go, Be it weal or be it woe. (W 186)

1678 RAY 351. 1742 *An Agreeable Companion* 33.

Beans in the wane of the moon, Set. (B 121)

1557 TUSSER B1ᵛ Set gardeine beanes [garlike and beanes *1573*], after saint Edmonde the king: the Moone in the wane, theron hangeth a thing. 1813 RAY 43 Sow or set beans in Candlemas waddle: i.e. Wane of the moon. Som.

Bean(s), *see also* Abstain from b.; Crooked man should sow b.; Dunder do gally the b.; Find the b. in the cake; Hunger makes hard b. sweet; Knows how many b. make five; Pea for a b. (To give); Pease has its veaze, (Every) and a b. fifteen; St. Valentine's day, cast b. in clay; Shake a Leicestershire man; Sow b. in the mud; Sow b. in the wind; Sow four b. in a row; Sow in b., (As still as a); Sow or set b. in Candlemas waddle; Sow peas and b. in wane of moon; Three blue b. in blue bladder.

Bear a bull that has borne a calf, He may. (B 711)

1539 TAVERNER 10 *Taurum tollet qui uitulum sustulerit.* He that hath borne a calfe, shall also beare a bull, he that accustometh hym selfe to lytle thynges, by lytle & lytle shalbe hable to go away wyth greater thynges. 1615 *Janua Linguarum* 27 He will carry a Bull, that carieth a Calfe. 1909 A. MACLAREN *Ephesians* 243 The wrestler, according to the old Greek parable, who began by carrying a calf on his shoulders, got to carry an ox by and by.

Bear all his kin on his back, A man cannot.

1721 KELLY 42 . . . Spoken when we are upbraided with some bad Kinsman.

Bear and forbear. (B 135)

[Epictetus' golden rule, ἀνέχου καὶ ἀπέχου.] 1573 SANFORD 5. 1570 TUSSER U1ᵛ Both beare and forbeare now and then as ye may. 1580 LYLY *Euph. & his Eng.* ii. 206. 1621 BURTON *Anat. Mel.* II. iii. VII *Sustine et abstine.* 1688 BUNYAN *Bldg. of Ho. of God* x. Wks. (Offor) II. 589 To bear and forbear here, will tend to rest. 1832 HENDERSON 50 Bear and forbear is gude philosophy. 1871 SMILES *Character* 313 The golden rule of married life is, 'Bear and forbear'.

Bear goes to the stake, As willingly as the. (B 127)

[i.e. to be baited.] *c.* 1430 LYDGATE *Churl & Bird* l. 132 To gon at large, but as a bere at stake,

To passe his boundis, but if he leve take. 1546 HEYWOOD I. ix. C2 With as good will as a beare goth to the stake. 1551 CRANMER *Ans. to Gardiner* 354 Euen as gladde you be to come to this, as a beare is to come to the stake. 1573 J. BRIDGES *Supremacy of Christ* H2ᵛ With ripe deliberation, that is to say, as a beare goeth to the stake. 1605 SHAKES. *K.L.* III. vii. 53 I am tied to the stake, and I must stand the course. 1606 *Id. M.* V. vii. 1 They have tied me to a stake . . . bearlike I must fight the course. 1659 HOWELL *Eng. Prov.* 15 He goes as a Bear to the stake.

Bear him on my back, I. (B 14)

1639 CLARKE 303 I bore him all the while on my back. 1670 RAY 164 . . . That is, I remember his injuries done to me with indignation and grief, or with a purpose of revenge.

Bear it away, He will | if it be not too hot or too heavy. (N 322)

c. 1386 CHAUCER *Friar's T.* l. 1435 I spare nat to taken, god it woot, But if it be to hevy or to hoot, What I may gete in conseil prively. 1542 UDALL *Apoph. Cicero* § 50 A taker and a bribing [robbing] feloe, and one for whom nothing was to hotte nor to heauie. 1678 RAY 349 . . . *Spoken of a pilferer.*

Bear (Wolf), If it were a | it would bite you. (B 129)

1599 MINSHEU *Span. Dial.* 8 Do you knowe where the brush is? — See there hanged vpon that naile, that if it were a beare it would now haue bit thee. 1616 DRAXE no. 30. 1639 CLARKE 6. 1721 KELLY 196 If it had been a Wolf, it would have worried you. Spoken when one hath, to no purpose, sought a Thing, that was afterwards found hard by them. 1738 SWIFT Dial. I. E.L. 275 I have been searching my pockets for my snuff-box, and, egad, here it is in my hand. — If it had been a bear, it would have bit you.

Bear one in hand, To. (H 94)

[*c.* 1495] *c.* 1530 MEDWALL I *Nature* A4 But yf Reason tykyll hym in the ere Or bere hym on hand the kow ys wood. [*c.* 1517] 1533 SKELTON *Magn.* B1ᵛ They bare me in hande that I was a spye. 1528 TYNDALE *Obed. Chrn. Man* P.S. 247 Ye bear them in hand what ye will, and have brought them in case like unto them which, when they dance naked in nets, believe they are invisible. 1594–8 SHAKES. *T.S.* IV. ii. 3 I tell you sir, she bears me fair in hand. 1598–9 *Id. M.A.* IV. i. 300 What? bear her in hand until they come to take hands. 1697 W. POPE *Life of Seth* [Ward] ed. Bamborough 109 He spoke after this manner; My Lord, I might bear you in hand, a Western Frase, signifying to delay or keep in expectation, and feed you with promises, or at least hopes.

Bear picks muscles, As handsomely as a. (B 126)

1540 PALSGRAVE *Acolastus* 100 It becommeth hym as wel to do, as . . . a beare to pycke muskles. 1546 HEYWOOD II. v. H1 Eche of his ioyntes agaynst other iustles, As handsomly as a beare picketh muscles. 1549 J. PROCTOUR *Fall of the late Arians* O3ᵛ.

Bear (Take, Suffer) this, bear (take, suffer) all.   (A 172)

[1590] 1598 *Mucedorus* v. i. 175.   1592 *Arden F.*, G4ᵛ Ah, Mosbie, Periurde beast, beare this and all.   1599 H. PORTER *Angry Wom. Abing.* H1 Rascall, take that and take all, do yee heare sir, I doe not meane to pocket vp this wrong.   1599 SHAKES. *A.Y.* IV. iii. 14 Bear this, bear all! She says I am not fair, that I lack manners.   [*a.* 1600] 1639 DELONEY *Gentle Craft* ii (Mann) 173 Put vp this and put vp all.   [1633] 1655 MASSINGER *Guardian* I. ii. 203 Easy injunctions, with a mischief to you! Suffer this and suffer all.

Bear till his back break, A man may.
                                                                  (M 256)

1606 T. HEYWOOD 2 *If You Know Not Me* 328 You will beare with me. — I but M. Gresham, a man may beare till his backe breake.   1616 DRAXE no. 1593.   1618 FIELD *Amends Ladies* I. i I come not to be scoffed. A woman may bear and bear, till her back burst.   1639 CLARKE 15.

Bear to a honey-pot, Like a.   (B 130)

1589 LYLY *Pap w. Hatchet* iii. 399 Swarm'd . . . like beares to a honnie pot.

Bear wants a tail, and cannot be lion, The.   (B 128)

1662 FULLER *Warwick* 118 Robert Dudley Earl of Leicester . . . when he was Governour of the Low Countries, . . . signed all Instruments with the Crest of the Bear and Ragged Staff. He was then suspected . . . [of] an Ambitious design to make himself absolute Commander (as the Lion is King of Beasts) over the Low Countries. Whereupon some . . . wrote under his Crest, . . . *Ursa caret caudâ, non queat esse Leo.* The Bear he never can prevail To Lion it, for lack of Tail. . . . This Proverb is applied to such who . . . aspire to what is above their worth to deserve, or Power to achieve.   1909 *Times Wkly.* 18 June iii It is not easy to take bears seriously. . . . Their persons end towards the rear with a suddenness which precludes any affectation of dignity. The Bear he never can prevail To lion it for lack of tail.

Bear wealth, poverty will bear itself.
                                                                  (W 191)

a. 1628 CARMICHAELL no. 319.   1721 KELLY 64 . . . Wealth is subject to a great many more Tentations than Poverty.

Bear with a sore head, As cross as a.

1788 GROSE *Dict. Vulg. T.* s.v. Grumble He grumbled like a bear with a sore ear.   1870 *N. & Q.* 4th Ser. VI. 321 Thus we say 'As sulky as a bear with a sore head'.

Bear with evil and expect good. (E 195)

1573 SANFORD 109ᵛ Suffer the yl, hoping for the good.   1640 HERBERT no. 511.   1670 RAY 8.

Bear's (hound's) tooth, As white as a.

1606 T. HEYWOOD 2 *If You Know Not Me* 227 As white as Beares teeth.   1923 *Devonsh.*

Assoc. Trans. liv. 137 [Of a clean floor] 'Er's so white's a hound's tooth.

Bear(s) (*noun*), *see also* Are you there with your b.; Black b. of Arden; Call the b. 'uncle'; Carry guts to a b. (Not fit to); Congleton rare sold Bible to pay for b.; Course be fair (If), quoth Bunny to his b.; Fight dog, fight b.; Good goose, (b.), do not bite; Iron nails that scratches b. (Must have); Jack-an-apes (More ado with one); Kings and b. oft worry keepers; One thing thinks the b.; Sell the b.'s skin before; Shares honey with b. (He who); Take the b. by the tooth; Tricks as a dancing b. (As many); Young b. with troubles before him.

'Bear' [on Stock Exchange], *see* Price is too low (No).

Bear (*verb*), *see also* Bell, (To b. the); Boughs that b. most hang lowest; Devil himself must b. cross; Grin and abide (b.) it; Misery best, (He b.) that hides it most; Swinge, (To b. a great); Take no more on you than able to b.; Tree often transplanted b. not much fruit; Worthy to b. his books (Not). *See also* Endure.

Bear-garden, He speaks.   (B 146)

1678 RAY 66 . . . That is, such rude and uncivil, or sordid and dirty language, as the Rabble that frequent those sports, are wont to use.

Bear-pie, *see* Eaten a b. (He that has).

Beard that makes the philosopher, It is not the.

[1654 E. GAYTON *Festivous Notes on Don Quixote* 120 Non barba facit Philosophum.]   1732 FULLER no. 5102.

Beard the lion, To.

[I SAM. xvii. 34, 35 There came a lion, . . . and when he arose against me, I caught him by his beard, and . . . slew him.]   1749 SMOLLETT *Regicide* II. vii (1777) 39 Sooner would'st thou beard The Lion in his rage.   1808 SCOTT *Marmion* VI. xiv And dar'st thou then To beard the lion in his den, The Douglas in his hall?   1894 BLACKMORE *Perlycross* ch. 22 Nothing less would satisfy her than to beard . . . the lion in the den, the arch-accuser, in the very court of judgment.

Beard were all, If the | the goat might preach.   (G 169)

[*Anth. Pal.* 11. 430 Εἰ τὸ τρέφειν πώγωνα δοκεῖ σοφίαν περιποιεῖν, καὶ τράγος εὐπώγων αἶψ' ὅλος ἐστὶ Πλάτων.]   1662 FULLER *Wales* 4 Goats . . . afterwards put on . . . great gravity. . . . If that ornamental excrement which groweth beneath the chin be the standard of wisdome, they carry it from Aristotle himself.   1690 D'URFEY *Collin's Walk* iii. 120 If Providence did Beards devise, To prove the wearers of them wise, A fulsome Goat would then by Nature Excel each other human Creature.

Beard will pay (not pay) for the shaving, The.

1830 FORBY 431 . . . When a person is paid for his labour by taking part, or the whole, of that which he is employed about; as cutting bushes, &c. . . . The work will produce enough to pay for itself. **1917** BRIDGE 111 The beard will not pay for the shaving. When a hedge is trimmed the brushings are called 'beardings'.

Beard(s), *see also* Beild aneath auld man's b.; Brains don't lie in b.; Cat knows whose b. she licks; Hares may pull dead lions by b.; Lick the fat from b.; Long b. heartless . . . England thriftless; Merry in hall when b. wag; Red b. and black head; Ride with b. on shoulder; Spite of one's teeth (b. etc.); Teeth are longer than your b.

Bearing, *see* Good b. begins worship (In).

Beast that goes always never wants blows, The. (B 150)

1640 HERBERT no. 260.

Beast with two backs, To make the.
(B 151)

1591 FLORIO *Giardino di Ricreatione* 105 Far la bestia a due dossi. **1604** SHAKES. *O.* I. i. 116 Your daughter and the Moor are now making the beast with two backs. **1611** COTGRAVE s.v. Dos (also s.v. Beste) *Faire ensemble la beste à deux dos.* To leacher. **1666** TORRIANO *Prov. Phr.* s.v. Bestia 14 To play the beast with two backs, viz. to play the Sodomite.

Beasts, The most deadly of wild | is a backbiter (tyrant), of tame ones a flatterer. (B 158)

1539 TAVERNER I *Garden* E8ᵛ Demaunded, what beast hath the moste venemouse bytyng. If of wyld beastes, quoth he [Diogenes], thy questyon be, a backbyter, yf of tame beastes, a flaterer. For a backbyter outwardly pretendeth hatred, but the flatterer inwardly vnder the personage of a frend, hurteth moche more greuously. **1540** TAVERNER *Flores* A8ᵛ There be two whiche byte most deedly, of wylde beastes, the backbyter, and of tame the flatterer. *c.* **1641** FERGUSSON MS. no. 1125 Off al tame creatures a flatterer is the worst. **1710** Addison *Whig-Examiner* (1811 ed.) v. 468 It was a saying of Thales, the wise Milesian, That of all wild beasts, a tyrant is the worst; and of all tame beasts, a flatterer.

Beast(s), *see also* Dies like a b.; Keep your feet dry . . . and live like b.; Many-headed b.; Nature of the b.; Strange b. that hath neither head nor tail; Wolf knows what ill b. thinks.

Beat a horse till he be sad, You may | and a cow till she be mad. (H 706)

1678 RAY 98.

Beat about the bush, To. (B 742)

[= to approach a subject slowly; shilly-shally.] **1520** WHITTINGTON *Vulg.* E.E.T.S. 35 A longe betynge aboute the busshe and losse of tyme to a yonge begynner. *c.* **1530** TERENCE *Andria* B3 Abowt the bush dost thou go. **1588** GREENE *Pandosto* Prose Wks. (1881–3) iv. 284 Dorastus . . . thought it was vaine so longe to beate about the bush. **1892** STEVENSON & OSB. *Wrecker* ch. 18 I did not know how long he might thus beat about the bush with dreadful hintings.

Beat (any one) black and blue, To.
(B 160)

[Originally *blak and bla, blak and blo: blo* became obsolete after 1550.] *c.* **1425** *Castle of Perseverance* l. 2176 Whanne he was betyn blo and blak. *Ibid.* l. 2220 I am al betyn blak and blo. *c.* **1460** *Towneley Myst.* 206 Bett hym blak and bloo. **1594** LYLY *Mother B.* v. iii. 120 Do you not thinke it would beate my heart blacke and blew? **1600–1** SHAKES. *M.W.W.* IV. v. 103 Mistress Ford, good heart, is beaten black and blue.

Beat one at one's own weapon, To.
(W 204)

1591 R. W. *Martin Mar-Sixtus* E1 Who would not breake out and laugh, to see how hee beateth himselfe with his owne weapon. *c.* **1600** *Tarlton's Jests* Pt. i. ed. Shakes. Soc. 8. **1608** LORDING BARRY *Ram Alley* v. iii (overthrow). **1672** WALKER 14 no. 12 You challenge me at mine own game; weapon.

Beat one like a stockfish, To. (s 867)

[With reference to the beating of the dried fish before cooking.] *c.* **1475** *The Boke of Brome* ed. L. Toulmin-Smith 1886 1b Ther be iiij thyngs take gret betyng: A stockfisch, a milston, a fedirbed, a wooman. **1533** J. HEYWOOD *Johan Johan* l. 114 I harde the say thou woldest one bete. Mary, wyfe, it was stokfysshe in temmes street. **1552** HULOET s.v. Beate Beate often as a stockfyshe is beaten, *retundo.* **1560** BECON *Catech.* P.S. 355 Those parents . . . whiche furiously rage against their children, and . . . beat them as stockfish. **1611** SHAKES. *Temp.* III. ii. 67 I'll turn my mercy out o' doors and make a stockfish of thee.

Beat spice it will smell the sweeter, If you. (s 746)

1576 PETTIE i. 36 As spices the more they are beaten the sweeter sent they send forth. **1579** LYLY *Euph.* i. 191 If you pownde spices they smell the sweeter. **1732** FULLER no. 2741.

Beat the air, To.

1559 T. BECON *Prayers* P.S. 266 Ye do nothing else than beat the air with your breath. **1567** PAINTER (Jacobs) iii. 214 You seeme to kicke against the wynd, and beat Water in a morter. **1676** MARVELL *Dr. Smirke* Gros. 71.

Beat the ass (horse), He that cannot | beats the saddle. (H 656)

1573 SANFORD 103. **1599** MINSHEU *Span. Dial.* 66 This seemes to me, to put the fault of the asse on the packesaddle. **1620** SHELTON *Quix.* II. lxvi (1908) iii. 286 According to the opinion of wise men, the fault of the ass must not be laid upon the pack-saddle. **1640** HERBERT no. 240 The fault of the horse is put on the saddle. **1659** HOWELL *Span. Prov.* 4 They cast the fault of the Ass upon the Panniers. **1666** TORRIANO *It. Prov.* 22 no. 14 Who cannot strike the Ass may strike The Packsaddle. **1706** STEVENS s.v. Asno Since he could not be reveng'd upon the Ass, he falls upon the Packsaddle.

Beat the dog before the lion. (D 443)

[JACOBUS DE VORAGINE: *Quia quando canis flagellatur, leo domesticatur.*] *c.* **1350** *Douce MS.* 52 no. 63 By the litul welpys me chastys þe lyon. *c.* **1386** CHAUCER *Squire's T.* (F1) l. 491 And for to maken othere be war by me, As by the whelp chasted is the leon. *a.* **1547** SURREY ed. Padelford (1938) 22.40 How the lyon chastysed is by beating of the whelpp. **1604** SHAKES. *O.* II. iii. 266 Even so as one would beat his offenceless dog to affright an imperious lion. **1640** HERBERT no. 825.

Beat water in a mortar, To. (W 105)

1567 PAINTER (Jacobs iii. 214) You seeme to kicke against the wind, and beat Water in a morter. **1576** LAMBARDE *Peramb. Kent* 469 The house of Yorke had hitherto but beaten water in a morter, and lost al their former labour. **1666** TORRIANO *Prov. Phr.* s.v. Pietra 148 To labour in vain, To beat water in a morter, the English would say.

Beat your heels against the ground, To no more purpose than to. (H 390 and P 644)

1557 EDGEWORTH *Serm.* 3 Z1ᵛ Leude and folyshe preistes . . . geue them selues to walkinge the stretes, and beatinge the bulkes with theyr heeles. **1602** R. CAREW *Survey Cornwall* (1769 ed. 20ᵛ) Better . . . then to sit idly, knocking his heeles against the wall. **1603** H. CROSSE *Virtue's Commonwealth* R2 Some like Æsops labber, [*sic for* lubber] sit beating their heeles against a stall. **1670** RAY 190 (or wind). **1732** FULLER no. 5209 (than 'twould be to knock one's Heels against the Ground).

Beating proud folks, It is good | for they'll not complain. (B 161)

1551 CRANMER *Answer to Gardiner* 294 The olde englyshe prouerbe is here trewe, that it is good beatyng of a proude man: for when he is all to beaten backe and bone, yet wyll he boast of his victorie, and bragge what a valyant man he is. **1639** CLARKE 31. **1670** RAY 133.

Beats the bush, One | and another catches the birds. (B 740)

c. **1300** *Ipomadon* l. 6021 On the bushe bettes one, A nothere man hathe the bryde. *c.* **1350** *Douce MS.* 52 no. 36 On betyth þe buske anoþer hathe [i.e. hath the] brydde. *c.* **1390** GOWER *Confessio Amantis* ii. l. 2355 His oghne astat thus up he haleth, And takith the bridd to his beyete, Wher othre men the buisshes bete. *c.* **1440** *Generydes* l. 4524 Some bete the bush . . . other men . . . catch the burdes. *c.* **1450** *Cov. Myst.* 119 Many a man doth bete the bow,

Another man hath the brydde. **1526** *Pilgr. Perf.* (W. de W. 1531) 141 Whiche . . . hath . . . betten the busshe that you may catche the byrde. **1546** HEYWOOD i. iii. A4 And whyle I at length debate and beate the bushe, There shall steppe in other men, and catche the burdes. **1614** CAMDEN 311.

Beat(en, s), *see also* Beggar b. his bag (Would make); Better to be b. than in bad company; Friar's b. (When the), then comes James; Hoof, (To b. it on the); Roast meat (Give one) and b. him with spit; Wife (He that has no) b. her oft.

Beauchamp, *see* Bold as B.

Beaulieu Fair, *see* Cuckoo goes to B. F.

Beauty and chastity (honesty) seldom agree. (B 163)

1576 R. EDWARDS *Par. Dainty Dev.*, 59 Twixt comelinesse and chastitie, A deadly strife is thought to be. **1580** LYLY *Euph. & his Eng.* ii. 209 Who knoweth not how rare a thing it is (Ladies) to match virginitie with beautie. **1591** FLORIO *Sec. F.* 193 Beawtie and honesty seldome agree, for of beautie comes temptation, of temptation dishonour. **1599** SHAKES. *A.Y.* I. ii. 34. 'Tis true; for those that she makes fair she scarce makes honest, and those that she makes honest she makes very ill-favouredly. **1600–1** *Id. H.* III. i. 110 Could beauty, my lord, have better commerce than with honesty?—Ay, truly; for the power of beauty will sooner transform honesty from what it is to a bawd than the force of honesty can translate beauty into his likeness. **1666** TORRIANO *It. Prov.* 42 no. 3.

Beauty draws more than oxen. (B 166 and H 20)

[*Anth. Pal.* 5. 230.] **1591** FLORIO *Second F.* 183 Ten teemes of oxen draw much lesse, than doth one haire of Helens tresse. **1640** HERBERT no. 685. **1642** TORRIANO no. 86 One hair of a woman, draweth more then an hundred yoake of oxen. **1659** *Ibid.* no. 85 One hair of benevolence draws more then a hundred pair of oxen. **1693** DRYDEN *Persius* 5. 247 She . . . can draw you to her with a single hair. **1714** POPE *Rape of Lock* II. 28 And beauty draws us with a single hair.

Beauty fades like a flower. (B 165)

1563 RAINOLDE *Found. Rhet.* 26ᵛ Beautie sone fadeth. **1581** W. AVERELL *Charles & Julia* K4ᵛ Flesh at last shall vade, and beauties flowre decay. **1599** SHAKES. *A.Y.* V. iii. 26 How that a life was but a flower, In the spring time. **1601** *Id. T.N.* I. v. 46 As there is no true cuckold but calamity, so beauty's a flower. *c.* **1640** W.S. *Countrym. Commonw.* 27 Beauty's a blossom that fadeth.

Beauty is but a blossom. (B 169)

1592 LYLY *Midas* II. i. 108 Beautie is . . . a blossome. **1601** SHAKES. *T.N.* I. v. 46 As there is no true cuckold but calamity, so beauty's a flower. **1616** DRAXE no. 158. **1732** FULLER no. 947.

Beauty is but skin-deep.   (B 170)

1606 DAVIES OF HEREFORD *Select Sec. Husb.* 6 in
Wks. ii (Gros.) Beauty's but skin-deepe. *c.*
1606 MIDDLETON & DEKKER *Roaring Girl* (1611)
13ᵛ Goodnesse [= beauty] I see is but outside.
a. **1613** OVERBURY *Wife.* i Wks. (1856) 37 All the
carnall beauty of my wife, Is but skin-deep.
1740–1 RICHARDSON *Pamela* (1824) I. xcix. 484
Beauty is but . . . a mere skin-deep perfection.
1829 COBBETT *Adv. to Young Men* iii (1906) 122
The less favoured part of the sex say, that 'beauty
is but skin deep'; . . . but it is very agreeable
though, for all that.

Beauty is no inheritance.   (B 171)

1616 DRAXE no. 160 Beauty is no heritage.
1670 RAY 2.   **1732** FULLER no. 951.

Beauty is potent but money is omni-
potent.   (B 172)

1670 RAY 122.   **1732** FULLER no. 952 (with 'more
potent' for 'omnipotent').

Beauty may have fair leaves, yet bitter
fruit.   (B 173)

1580 LYLY *Euph. & his Eng.* ii. 169 Beautie may
haue faire leaues & foule fruite.   **1732** FULLER
no. 955.

Beauty without bounty avails nought.
                                            (B 174)

1578 *Courtly Controv.* O4 There is so great
enmity betwixt beauty and bounty, as they neuer
remaine togither in one mansion.   **1580** LYLY
Euph. & his Eng. ii. 72 Beautie without riches,
goeth a begging.   **1721** KELLY 68 Beauty but
Bounty availeth nothing.

Beauty, *see also* Fancy passes b.; Poor b. finds
more lovers than husbands; Sweet b. with sour
beggary; Virtue is the b. of the mind.

Because is a woman's reason.   (B 179)

1551 T. WILSON *Rule of Reason* 80 Beyng asked
why they will doe this and that, they aunswere
streight. Marie, because, I will doe it, or because
it pleaseth me beste so to doe . . . Some women
are subiect to this aunswere.   **1594** SHAKES.
T.G.V. I. ii. 23 — Your reason? — I have no
other but a woman's reason: I think him so because I think him so. [*c.* **1589**] **1601** LYLY
Love's Metam. IV. i. 78 Women's reasons; they
would not, because they would not.   **1602**
SHAKES. *T.C.* I. i. 104 Wherefore not afield? —
Because not there. This woman's answer sorts.
1666 TORRIANO *Prov. Phr.* s.v. Raggione 163 To
give a Womans reason, viz. because I will have
it so, so it must be.   **1721** KELLY 68.

Beck¹ is as good as a Dieu-gard, A.
                                            (B 181)

[O.F. *Dieu vous gard* 'God keep (you)!' a polite
salutation.] *c.* **1547** BALE *Three Lawes* iv. E2
As good is a becke, as is a dewe vow garde.
1546 HEYWOOD I. x. D1ᵛ And thus with a becke
as good as a dieu gard, She flang fro me.   **1603**
MONTAIGNE (Florio) III. v. 158 A wink, a cast of
the eye . . . a becke is as good as a Dew guard.
1611 DAVIES no. 315. [¹ bow, nod.]

Becomes it as well as a cow does a cart-
saddle, He. *Cf.* Sow to bear a saddle.
                                            (C 758)

1530 PALSGRAVE 427b Thou art as mete to be a
great mans kerver as a kowe to beare a sadle.
1540 *Id. Acolastus* 100.   **1567** T. STAPLETON
Counterblast i. 78b As well doth a saddle fit a
cowe.   **1639** CLARKE 5.   **1670** RAY 203 (It).

Bed could tell all it knows, If the | it
would put many to the blush.   (B 190)

1614 SIR T. OVERBURY *His Wife* etc. (1622 ed.,
T7ᵛ) If the bed should speake all it knowes, it
would put many to the blush.   **1659** HOWELL
Eng. Prov. 2b.   **1670** RAY 3.

Bed for a dog, It is hard to make a.
                                            (D 523)

1581 GUAZZO ii. 110 This old proverbe . . .   **1588**
J. PRIME *Consolations of David* A2ᵛ So hard a
matter it is (as the prouerbe is) to make a bed for
a dog for he wil alwaies haue it of his own making
and fassion.   **1666** TORRIANO *Prov. Phr.* s.v.
Letto, 89 . . . To undertake a difficult task, and
troublesome; for a dog in his kennel, tumbles,
and stirs the straw, as if it did complain of his
bed-making, as one may say.

Bed with the lamb, Go to | and rise
with the lark.   (B 186)

c. **1555** WRIGHT *Songs &c. Philip and Mary* 38
(Roxb. Cl.) And wythe the larke yche day I
ryes.   *a.* **1558** *Jacob and Esau* A3ᵛ He is vp
day by day before the Crowe is.   **1580** LYLY
Euph. & his Eng. ii. 16.   **1602** WITHALS 21.   **1633**
JONSON *T. Tub.* I. vi. 7 Madam, if he had
couched with the Lambe, He had no doubt beene
stirring with the Larke.   **1833** LAMB *Elia; Newsp.
35 Yrs. Ago* We were compelled to rise, having
been perhaps not above four hours in bed—(for
we were no go-to-beds with the lamb, though we
anticipated the lark oft times in her rising).

Bed straw, *see* Eaten his b. s. (Look as if had).

Bed, *see also* Apple going to b. (Eat an); Bow
and arrows and go to b., (To take one's); Early
to b.; Egg and to b.; Go to b. at noon; Goes to b.
supperless (Who); Heathen went to b. without
candle; Lie in b. and forecast; Lie in b. till meat
falls in mouth; Make your b., so lie on it; Parsley
b.; Procrustes' b.; Put off his clothes before goes
to b. (He will not); Put to b.; Sluggard's guise,
slow to b. *See also* Abed.

Bedfellow(s), *see* Misery (Adversity) makes
strange b.

Bedford, *see* Bailiff of B.

Bedfordshire, To go to.   (B 198)

c. **1591–4** *Thomas of Woodstock* IV. iii. 71 Here's
a note of seven hundred whisperers, most on

'em sleepy knaves, we pulled them out of Bedfordshire. **1608** MIDDLETON *Mad World* II. v. 29 You come rather out of Bedfordshire; we cannot lie quiet in our beds for you. **1657** TORRIANO *Choice It. Dial.* 10. Make me unready, for I will to Bedfordshire. **1664** C. COTTON *Scarron.* IV. (1715 ed. 64) Each one departs to Bedfordshire; And pillows all securely snort on. **1786** 31 Dec. WOODFORDE *Diary Country Parson* Went for Bedfordshire alias to bed.

Bedpost, *see* Between you and me and b.; Twinkling of a b.

Bee in one's bonnet, To have a. *Cf.* Head is full of bees.   (H 255)

[= to have a craze on some point.] **1681** S. COLVIL *Whiggs Sup.* II. 49 A Scripturest thou proves, as he was, In whose fool Bonnetcase a Bee was. **1821** SCOTT *Pirate* ch. 23 As to these Troils . . . there is a bee in their bonnet. **1824** MOIR *Mansie W.* ch. 24 Things were . . . so queer . . . that I . . . began at length to question . . . whether Taffy's master might not have had a bee in his bonnet. **1863** READE *Hard Cash* ch. 40 The doctor had a bee in his own bonnet.

Bee sucks honey out of the bitterest flowers, The.   (B 205)

1567 *Amorous Tales* tr. J. Sanford A5ᵛ The paynful Bee his sauorie Honie takes Of stinking flowre, and Rose which smelleth well. **1578** WHETSTONE *Promos and Cassandra* A2ᵛ. **1589** NASHE *Anat. Absurdity* Wks. i. 30 Euen as the Bee out of the bitterest flowers and sharpest thistles gathers honey.

Bee sucks honey, Where the | the spider sucks poison.   (B 208)

a. **1542** WYATT *Poems* ed. Muir no. 68 Nature, that gave the bee so feet a grace To fynd hony of so wondrous fashion, Hath taught the spider owte of the same place To fetche poyson, by straynge alteration. **1548–9** N. UDALL *Paraphrase* of Erasmus Ded. to Queen Katherine B8ᵛ Out of one and the same flowre the Bee gathereth honey, and the spider sucketh venom. **1571** J. BRIDGES *Sermon at Paul's Cross* 38 Thoughe a Bee sucke Honnie out of a floure, yet all that a Spider sucketh out of the same, be it neuer so wholsome, turneth to venome. **1573** G. HARVEY *Letter-bk.* (Camd. Soc.) 25 As ther is matter of poison to the spider where would be matter of honi to the bee. **1575** G. GASCOIGNE Wks. i. 476 As the venemous spider wil sucke poison out of the most holesome herbe, and the industrious Bee can gather hony out of the most stinking weede. **1579** LYLY *Euph.* i. 186 Ther frequented to his lodging . . . as well the Spider to sucke poyson, of his fine wyt, as the Bee to gather hunny. *a.* **1614** BEAUM & FL. *Four Plays* Wks. (1905) X. 312 Sweet poetry's A flower, where men, like Bees and Spiders, may Bear poison, or else sweets and Wax away. **1616** DRAXE no. 1345. **1853** TRENCH v. 122 . . . Let the student be as the bee looking for honey, and from . . . classical literature he may store of it abundantly in his hive.

Bee(s), *see also* Busy as a b.; Calf, the goose, the b., world is ruled by; Dead b. makes no honey; Head is full of b.; Honey is sweet (Every b.'s); Honey is sweet but b. stings; Humble b.; May b. don't fly this month; Quick as a b.; St. Matthee shut up the b.; Sheep, swine, and b., (He that has) . . . may thrive; Swarm of b. in a churn; Swarm of b. in May; Swine, women, and b. cannot be turned.

Bee-bikes, *see* Scythe cuts (Where), no more b.

Beef, Such | such broth.   (B 215)

1591 T. LODGE *Catharos* (Hunt. Cl.) B4. **1598** MERES *Palladis* f. 218.

Beef to the heels, like a Mullingar heifer.

1837 LOVER *Rory O'More* ch. 2 'The women in Westmeath, they say, is thick in the legs, . . . and so there's a saying again thim, "You're beef to the heels, like a Mullingar heifer".'

Beef, *see also* Buckinghamshire bread and b.; Honour buys no b.; Looks as big as if he had eaten bull b.; No broth . . . no b.; Salt b. draws down drink apace; Weavers' b. of Colchester.

Bees are old, When | they yield no honey.   (B 212)

1616 DRAXE no. 1543. **1670** RAY 19. **1732** FULLER no. 3706 Old bees yield no honey.

Bees are, Where | there is honey.   (B 213)

1616 DRAXE no. 829. **1670** RAY 60 . . . Where there are industrious persons, there is wealth, for the hand of the diligent maketh rich. This we see verified in our neighbours the *Hollanders.*

Bees that have honey in their mouths have stings in their tails.   (B 211)

c. **1440** *Passe forth, pilgrime* (ed. Förster) in *Archiv f. d. Stud. d. neueren Sprachen* 101. 29 Favel farith ryght even as dothe the bee; Honymowthed, full of swetnys is she, But loke behynde and ware ye fro hir stonge. **1576** G. WAPULL *Tide* A3. **1660** W. SECKER *Nonsuch Prof.* i (1891) 22 These bees carry honey in their mouths, but they have a sting in their tails.

Bees, *see also* Bee(s).

Beelzebub, *see* Baby of B.'s bower.

Beer, *see* Heresy and b. came both in a year; New b. . . . make hair grow through hood; Shoulder of mutton and b. make Flemings tarry; Turkeys . . . and b. came into England in one year. *See also* Small beer.

Beer and skittles, *see* Life is not all.

Beetle¹ and the block, Between the.

1589 R. HARVEY *Pl. Perc.*, Thou must come to Knokham faire, and what betweene the block

and the beetle, be thumped like a stock fish.
1613 HAYWARD *Norm. Kings* 274 Earle William
being thus set, as it were, betweene the beetle and
the blocke, was nothing deiected. [¹ mallet.]

**Beetle flies over many a sweet flower,
and lights in a cowshard, The.** (B 221)

1575 GASCOIGNE *Glass of Govt.* ii. 59. Humble
bees . . . tast the flowers, that fairest are to see:
But yet at even, when all thinges go to rest, A
foule cowe sharde, shall then content them best.
1576 PETTIE ii. 124 The humblebee flieth all day
in the pleasant air, and thinketh much to alight
even upon the sweet flowers, but at night taketh
no scorn to lodge in a cow's foul shard. **1606**
SHAKES. *A.C.* III. ii. 20 They are his shards, and
he their beetle. **1640** JONSON *Tale Tub* IV. v. 60
A Squire? And thinke so meanely? fall upon a
Cow-shard?

Beetle, *see also* Blind as a b.; Dull as a b.; Wedge
where b. drives it.

Before one can say Jack Robinson.

1778 BURNEY *Evelina* Lett. 82 Why, then, 'fore
George, I'd do it as soon as say Jack Robinson.
1812 EDGEWORTH *Absentee* ch. 2 I'd get her off
before you could say Jack Robinson. **1837**
SOUTHEY *Doctor* iv. 250 Who was Jack Robinson? . . . the one whose name is in every body's
mouth, because it is so easily and so soon said.
1872 BLACKMORE *Maid of Sker* ch. 10 The ship
must . . . go to pieces . . . , before one could say
'Jack Robinson'.

**Before St. Chad¹ every goose lays, both
good and bad.** (S 39)

1678 RAY 51. **1882** E. L. CHAMBERLAIN 37 By
Valentine's² day every good goose should lay;
But by David³ and Chad both good and bad.
[¹ 2 March. ² 14 Feb. ³ 1 March.]

Before the cat can lick her ear. (C 133)

[**1591**] **1593** PEELE *Ed. I* ii Wks. (Bullen) I. 101
But go and come with gossip's cheer, Ere Gib
our cat can lick her ear. **1665** COTTON *Scarron*.
(1715 ed.) iv. 104 Ere a Cat could lick her Ear.
1670 RAY 168.

**Before you make a friend eat a bushel
of salt with him.** (F 685)

a. **1500** *15c. School-Bk.* ed. W. Nelson 44 As
Cicero saith, men must ete togedre many bushels
of salt before they know their frendes. **1531**
ELYOT *Governour* (Croft ii. 163) As Aristotle
sayeth, in as longe tyme as by them bothe
[friends] beinge to gether conversaunt a hole
busshell of salte moughte be eten. **1539**
TAVERNER 30 *Nemini fidas, nisi cum quo prius
modium salis absumpseris.* Trust no man onles
thou hast fyrst eaten a bushel of salte wyth hym.
1579 LYLY *Euph.* i. 197. **1592** DELAMOTHE 21.
1621 BURTON *Anat. Mel.* III. iii. IV. ii (1651) 627
As Plutarch adviseth, one must eat *modium salis*,
a bushel of salt with him, before he choose his
friend. **1710** PALMER 234 A Man must Eat a
Peck of Salt with Another, before He takes Him
for a Friend. **1844** KINGLAKE *Eothen* ch. 14
They did not offer me the bread and salt (the
pledges of peace amongst wandering tribes).

**Before you marry, be sure of a house
wherein to tarry.** (H 749)

1605 SHAKES. *K.L.* III. ii. 27 The codpiece that
will house Before the head has any, The head and
he shall louse: So beggars marry many. **1642**
TORRIANO 66. **1664** CODRINGTON 187. **1670**
RAY 17. **1706** STEVENS s.v. Casa.

Before, *see also* Ape can crack a nut, (B. an);
Hires the horse (He that) must ride b.; Kingdom
of a cheater (In the) wallet carried b.; Looks not
b. (He that) finds himself behind.

Beforehand with the world, To be.
　　　　　　　　　　　　　　　　　　(W 885)

[*c.* **1640**] **1651** CARTWRIGHT *The Ordinary* V. i.
5 Tis good to be before hand still. **1647** J.
HOWELL *Let.* III. 5, II. 519 He is the happy man
who can square his mind to his means . . . he who
is before-hand with the world. **1666** TORRIANO
Prov. Phr. s.v. Salci 176 To lay up moneys like a
good Husband, and be before-hand with the
World. **1811** J. AUSTEN *Sense and Sensibility*
ch. 6 I shall see how much I am beforehand with
the world . . . and we will plan our improvements
accordingly.

Beg at the wrong door, To. (D 376)

1546 HEYWOOD I ix. C1ᵛ Then of trouth ye beg at
a wrong mans dur. **1616** JONSON *Ev. Man In* II.
i. 79 He has the wrong sow by the eare, ifaith:
and claps his dish at the wrong mans dore.

**Beg from beggars and you'll never be
rich.**

1721 KELLY 62 . . . Spoken when we ask that from
one which they sought from another.

**Beg of him who has been a beggar,
Neither | nor serve him who has been a
servant.**

1706 STEVENS s.v. Servir.

Beg than steal, Better. (B 222)

1586 *Lazarillo* tr. D. Rowland ed. Crofts 45.
a. **1628** CARMICHAELL no. 337 Better thig,¹ nor
steill and be hangit. **1667** R. L'ESTRANGE
Visions (1668 ed.) II. 61 He that asks an alms,
pleads that 'tis Honester to Beg than Steal.
[¹ beg.]

Beg the question, To.

[= to take for granted the matter in dispute.]
1581 W. CLARKE in *Confer.* iv (1584) Ff iij I say
this is still to begge the question. **1680** BURNET
Rochester (1692) 82 This was to assert or beg
the thing in Question. **1788** REID *Aristotle's Log.*
v, § 3. 118 Begging the question is when the thing
to be proved is assumed in the premises.

Beg, *see also* Breeches of a bare-arsed man, (To
b.); Learned timely to steal (b.); Spends before
he thrives, (Who) will b. before he thinks.

Beggar beat his bag, It would make a.
(B 235)

1678 RAY 228.

Beggar can never be bankrupt, A.
(B 226)

1616 WITHALS 572.   1639 CLARKE 243.   1670
RAY 60.   1721 KELLY 36.

Beggar, One | is enough at a door.
(B 236)

1611 COTGRAVE S.V. Huis So many beggers at one
doore, so many suitors for one thing, are not
good, or, are not like to speed.   1621 ROBINSON
19.   1639 CLARKE 187.

Beggar is never out of his way, The.
(B 228)

c. 1553 *Gam. Gurt. Needle.* II. i. 9–10 [Diccon the
Bedlam] Nyght or daye, South, east, north or
west, I am never out of my waye.   1605–6 SHAKES.
K.L. IV. i. 18 I have no way, and therefore want
no eyes.   1616 T. ADAMS Politic Hunting 79
Vagrant Rogues . . . are neuer out of their way.
1616 DRAXE no. 2330.   1659 HOWELL *Eng. Prov.*
15a.   1663 BUTLER *Hud.* I. i. 501 Of vagabonds
we say, That they are ne'er beside their way.

Beggar is woe that another by the door
should go, One.   (B 237)

c. 1350 *Douce MS. 52*, no. 66 On begger is wo
þat anothir in-to þe towne goth.   1520 WHIT-
TINGTON *Vulg.* E.E.T.S. 71 But it is comenly
sayd euery begger is woo that ony other shold by
the dore go.   1545 TAVERNER B1 One begger
byddeth wo that an other by the dore shuld go.
1608 ARMIN *Nest Ninnies* (1842) 47 One foole
cannot indure the sight of another, . . . and one
beggar is woe that another by the doore should
goe.   1641 FERGUSSON no. 39.

Beggar knows his dish (bag), As well as
the.   (B 234)

1546 HEYWOOD I. xi. D4ᵛ (bag).   1579 GOSSON
Sch. Abuse (Arb.) 74 Such as he knew as well as
the Begger his dishe.   1638 T. HEYWOOD *Wise
W. Hogs.* II. i As well as the beggar knows his
dish.   1738 SWIFT Dial. I. E.L. 267.

Beggar may sing before the thief, The.
(B 229)

[JUVENAL *Sat.* 10. 22 *Cantabit vacuus coram
latrone viator.*]   1377 LANGLAND *P. Pl.* B. xiv.
305 And an hardy man of herte amonge an
hepe of theues; *Cantabit pauper coram latrone
viator.*   c. 1386 CHAUCER *W. of Bath's T.* l. 1192
Juvenal seith of poverte, myrily, 'The povre man
whan he goth by the weye, Bifore the theves he
may synge and pleye'.   c. 1440 LYDGATE *Fall of
Princes* III. 582 The poore man affor the theeff
doth synge.   1546 HEYWOOD I. xii. E4ᵛ.   1593
PEELE *Edw. I* Bullen i. 169 A man purse-penni-
less may sing before a thief.   1614 CAMDEN 312.
1875 J. PAYN *Walter's World* ch. 32 'As to my
cheerfulness, there is a proverb that a man with
empty pockets is not cast down by falling among

thieves'.   'That may be so in England, signor,
. . . but with us brigands it is different.'

Beggar on horseback, Set a | and he'll
ride a gallop (*for variants see quotations*).
(B 238)

1576 PETTIE ii. 100 (and he will never alight).
1584 W. AVERELL *A Dyall for Dainty darlings*
C4ᵛ Set a begger on horsebacke and he will
gallop.   1591 SHAKES. *3 Hen. VI* I. iv. 125 It
needs not, . . . proud queen, Unless the adage
must be verified, That beggars mounted run their
horse to death.   1592 NASHE *Pierce Pen.* i. 174.
These whelpes . . . drawne vp to the heauen of
honor from the dunghill of abiect fortune, haue
long been on horsebacke to come riding to your
Diuelship.   [a. 1592] 1599 GREENE *Orpharion* in
Wks. XII 36 (Gros.)   (and they say he will neuer
light).   1611 GRUTER 183 (ride his horse out of
breath).   1616 DRAXE no. 1699 (runne his horse
out of breath).   1621 BURTON *Anat. Mel.* II. iii. II
(651) 319 Nothing so intolerable as a fortunate
fool . . . Asperius nihil est humili, cum surgit in
altum:[1] set a begger on horsebacke and he will ride a
gallop.   1616 T. ADAMS *Sacrifice of Thankfulness*
6 He that serues the *Flesh* serues his fellow; and
a Beggar mounted on the backe of Honour,
rides post to the Diuell.   1809 CORBETT *Pol. Reg.*
XV. xii. 429 Our own old saying: 'Set a beggar
on horse-back, and he'll ride to the devil.'
[1 CLAUDIANUS *In Eutrop.* I. 181.]

Beggar pays a benefit with a louse, A.
(B 230)

1583 MELBANCKE 2D3ᵛ The saying of the pleasaunt Philosopher Mimns [*sic*], Qui cum lasso
familico loquitur rixam quaerit, He that helpes a
begger out of the ditch shalbe stung with his
lyce.   1678 RAY 98.

Beggar, The stoutest | that goes by the
way, can't beg through Long[1] on a
midsummer's day.

1869 HAZLITT 399 *Higson's MSS. Coll.*, 131.
[1 LEAN I. 181 Sharp (*British Gazetteer*, 1852) is
doubtless right in assigning it to Longdon in
Staffordshire, 'a village of some length'.]

Beggar's-bush, This is the way to.
(W 165)

1564 BULLEIN *Dial. agst. Fever* E.E.T.S. 78 In
the ende thei go home . . . by weepyng cross, by
beggers Barne, and by knaues Acre.   1588
MARPRELATE *Epistle* ed. Pierce 51 (go home by
Beggar's Bush).   1592 GREENE *Upst. Courtier*
(1871) 6 Walking home by Beggars Bush for a
penance.   1662 FULLER Hunts. 49. This is the
way to Beggars Bush. It is spoken of such who
use dissolute and improvident courses . . .
Beggars Bush being a tree notoriously known,
on the left hand of London road from Huntington to Caxton. . . . King James . . . having heard
. . . how Sir Francis [Bacon] had prodigiously
rewarded a mean man . . .; Sir Francis (said He)
you will quickly come to beggars bush; and I
may even goe along with you, if both be so
bountifull.   1902–4 LEAN I. 103 This is the way
to BEGGAR'S BUSH. . . . The primary meaning was
a rendezvous for beggars at the bifurcation of
two roads.

Beggar's scrip is never filled, A.

(B 242)

1539 TAVERNER 39. **1615** *Janua Linguarum* tr. W. Welde 83. **1639** CLARKE 38 A beggars purse is bottomless.

Beggars of Bath, The.

(B 250)

1662 FULLER *Som.* 21 The Beggars of Bath. Many in that place, some natives there, others repairing thither from all parts of the Land, the Poor for Alms, the pained for ease.

Beggars breed, and rich men feed.

(B 244)

1639 CLARKE 98. **1670** RAY 60. **1721** KELLY 75 . . . Poor Peoples Children find a Support in the Service of the Rich and Great.

Beggars must (should) be no choosers.

(B 247)

1546 HEYWOOD I. x. D1 Folke saie alwaie, beggers shulde be no choosers. **1579** GOSSON *Sch. Abuse* Arb. 73 Beggars, you know, must bee no choosers. **1594-8** SHAKES. *T.S.* Ind. I. 41. Would not the beggar then forget himself?— Believe me, lord, I thinke he cannot choose. *c.* **1612** BEAUM. & FL. *Scornf. Lady* v. iii. 20. **1863** READE *Hard Cash* ch. 23 So I told him beggars musn't be choosers.

Beggars of Bologna, Like the blind.

(B 251)

1663 J. WILSON *Cheats* II. iv He's like the blind beggars of Bolonia, a man must give 'um a Half-penny to sing, and Two-pence to hold their tongues.

Beggar(s), *see also* Beg from b. and you'll never be rich; Beg from him who has been a b.; Better to be a b.; Better to die a b.; Dainties love (Who) shall b. prove; Drunk as a b.; Every b. descended from a king; Fools nor b. . . . among his kindred, (Who has neither) was born of a stroke of thunder; Great as b.; Lady's heart and b.'s purse; Leeful man is b.'s brother; Louse is b.'s companion; Loves the poor but cannot abide b.; Marry a b. and get a louse; Merry as b.; Misery may be mother where one b. . . . beg of another; Much ado to bring b. to stocks; Old serving-man, young b.; Plain of poverty and die b.; Pride is as loud a b. as want; Proud b. that makes own alms; Proud mind and b.'s purse; Scratch a b. before you die (You will); Simple man is b.'s brother; Slothful man is b.'s brother; Small invitation will serve b.; Sue a b., get a louse; Swear by no b.; Wishes were buttercakes (If), b. might bite; Wishes were horses (If) . . . ; Wishes were thrushes (If) . . . ; Wishes would bide (If) . . . ; Young courtier old b.; Young serving-man, old b.

Beggary, *see* Gentility without ability; Idleness is the key of b.; Sweet beauty with sour b.

Begged for a fool, To be.

(F 496)

1584 D. FENNER *Def. Ministers* (1587) 51 Then would you haue proued vs asses, not begged vs for innocents. *c.* **1592** SHAKES. *C.E.* II. i. 40 But if thou live to see like right bereft, This fool-begg'd patience in thee will be left. **1594** LYLY *Mother B.* I. i. 37 He needs not, sir, Ile beg him for a foole. **1736** HERVEY *Mem.* II. 143 Moyle either deserved to be . . . begged for a fool, or hanged for a knave.

Begging, *see* Sleeps all the morning, (He who) may go a b. all the day after; Year sooner to the b. (It is but a).

Begin a journey on Sunday, I love to.

1738 SWIFT *Dial.* II. E.L. 313 Now I always love to begin a journey on Sunday, because I shall have the prayers of the church to preserve all that travel by land or by water.

Begin well, Good to | better to end well.

(B 253)

1530 PALSGRAVE 656b It is nat they that begyn well, but that persever that shall come to honour. **1664** CODRINGTON 195. **1670** RAY 8.

Beginning is hard, Every.

(B 256)

a. **1500** *15c. Sch.-Bk.* ed. W. Nelson 21 The begynnynge of every thynge is the hardiste. **1530** WHITFORDE *Wk. Householders* B4 (harde and of greate difficulte). **1590** SPENSER *F.Q.* III. iii. 21 Let no whit thee dismay The hard begin, that meets thee in the dore. **1666** TORRIANO *It. Prov.* 219 no. 6 (is difficult).

Beginning, Such | such end.

(B 262)

1546 HEYWOOD II. ix. L1 And suche begyn-nynge suche ende we all daie sée. *c.* **1593** SHAKES. *R.J.* II. vi. 9 These violent delights have violent ends. **1604** *Id. O.* I. iii. 350 It was a violent commencement in her, and thou shalt see an answerable sequestration. **1670** RAY 3. **1611** DAVIES no. 281.

Beginnings come great things, From small.

(B 264)

1609 HARWARD 72ᵛ Of small beginnings do oft come great mischieffs. **1611** Cotgrave s.v. Commencement Of small beginnings are great matters raised. **1659** HOWELL *Fr. Prov.* 7 A small beginning makes a great web.

Begins many things, He who | finishes but few.

(T 217)

1666 TORRIANO *It. Prov.* 48, no. 35.

Begins the song, Let him that | make and end.

(S 634)

1616 DRAXE no. 120.

Begins to build too soon that has not money to finish it, He.

(M 1039)

1616 DRAXE no. 4. **1659** N.R. 46.

Begins to die that quits his desires, He.
(D 214)
1611 COTGRAVE s.v. Abandonner.   **1640** HER-BERT no. 2.

Beginning(s), *see also* Beware b.; Everything must have b.; Good (Hard) b. makes good ending; Ill b. ill ending.

Begin(s), begun, *see also* Better never to b.; End before you b., (Think on the); Sooner b., sooner done; War, (All may begin a), few can end it; Well b. is half done.

Beguile(s, d), *see* Mouth has b. hands; Sorrow be in the house that you're b. in; Think none ill (They that) soonest b.; Wily b. with himself (He has played).

Behind the horseman sits black care.
[HORACE *Odes* 3. 1. 37 *Post equitem sedet atra cura.*] **1603** MONTAIGNE (Florio) I. xxxviii. 89 Care, looking grim and blacke, doth sit Behinde his backe that rides from it. **1857-9** THACKERAY *Virgin.* ch. 85 Does not *Atra Cura* sit behind baronets as well as *equites*?   **1861** G. J. WHYTE-MELVILLE *Market Harbor.* ch. 2 If Care sits behind the horseman on the cantle of his saddle, Ambition may also be detected clinging somewhere about his spurs.

Behind the mountains there are people to be found.
1861 DEAN STANLEY *Hist. East. Ch.* (1862) i. 2 There is a wise German proverb which tells us that it is good . . . to be reminded that 'Behind the mountains there are people to be found'.

Behind, *see also* Bare as an ape is b.; Best is b.; Far b. must follow the faster; Far b. that may not follow (They are); Further we go, further b.; Rides b. another (He who) does not travel when he pleases; Worst is b.

Beild[1] aneath an auld man's beard, There is.
1737 RAMSAY III. 196. [¹ shelter, protection.]

Being, *see* All things in their b. are good for something.

Belfry, *see* Bats in b.; Devil gets up b. by vicar's skirts.

Believe he's bald till you see his brains, You will not.
(B 597)
1580 LYLY *Euph. & his Eng.* ii. 48 As incredulous as those, who thinke none balde, till they see his braynes.   **1601** SHAKES. *T.N.* IV. ii. 112 I'll ne'er believe a madman till I see his brains.   **1639** CLARKE 181.

Believe it (me) if you list. *Cf.* Take it as you will.
1548 HALL *Chron.* (1809, 181) You maie beleue as you list.   **1566** PAINTER ed. Jacobs ii. 140.

1580 LYLY *Euph. & his Eng.* ii. 135 Women will beleeue but what they lyst.   **1586** R. CROWLEY *Father John Francis* O2ᵛ If we wyll beleeue you, we may. But for my parte I can hardly beleeue, that eyther you did then, or doo nowe, knowe the doctrines that Luther and Caluine taught.   **1600** J. LEO *Hist. of Africa* tr. J. Pory 342.   **1600** T. HEYWOOD *et al. 1 Ed. IV* i. 50 My name is Tom Twist.—Belieue, ye that list.   **1617** J. SWETNAM *Sch. of Defence* 197 Beleeue what you list of it, and leaue what you like not.   **1631** P. MASSINGER [Play-title].

Believe it though I saw it myself, I cannot.
(B 267)
1621 ROBINSON 20.   **1639** CLARKE 146.

Believe no tales from an enemy's tongue.
(T 52)
1659 HOWELL *Brit. Prov.* 32.

Believe not all that you see nor half what you hear.
c. **1205** LAYAMON *Brut* (Madden) I. 342 Yif thu ileuest ælcne mon, selde thu sælt wel don. [If thou believest every man, seldom shalt thou do well.]   **1492** *Dialogue of Salomon & Marcolphus* ed. Duff 30 Ye shulde not geue credence to alle thing that ye here.   **1706** STEVENS s.v. Pandero We must not believe all we hear.   **1858** MULOCK *A Woman's Thoughts* 194 'Believe only half of what you see, and nothing that you hear', is a cynical saying, and yet less bitter than at first appears.

Believe well and have well.
(B 265)
1546 HEYWOOD II. ix. K3ᵛ Beleue well, and haue well, men saie.   **1611** DAVIES no. 271.   **1862** HISLOP (1870) 55 Believe a' ye hear, an' ye may eat a' ye see.

Believe what we desire, We soon. *Cf.* Wish is father to the thought.
(B 269)
[CAES. *De Bello G.* 3. 18 *Libenter homines id quod volunt credunt.* Ov. *A.A.* 3. 674 *Prona venit cupidis in sua vota fides.*] c. **1386** CHAUCER *Melibeus* B² l. 2473 'Lo, Lo!' quod dame Prudence, 'how lightly is every man enclyned to his owene desyr and to his owene plesaunce!'   **1576** PETTIE i. 177 I did perceive, if desire to have it so did not deceive me.   **1591** ARIOSTO *Orl. Fur.* (Harington) I. 56 It is a prouerbe vsed long a go, We soone beleeue the thing we would haue so.   **1598** SHAKES. *2 Hen. IV* IV. v. 91 I never thought to hear you speak again. — Thy wish was father, Harry, to that thought.   **1616** DRAXE no. 1985.   We soone beleeue that we would haue. *a.* **1632** DEKKER cited G. E. Bentley *Jac. & Caroline Stage* iii. 245 *Believe It is So and 'Tis So* [play title]. *a.* **1640** J. SMYTH *Lives of the Berkeleys* ii. 286 Facile credimus quod volumus.

Believe(d, s), *see also* Do not all you can, b. not all you hear; Easily done soon b.; Fool b. everything; Husband, don't b. what you see. Liar not b. when speaks truth.

Believers, *see* Quick b. need broad shoulders.

Believes all, misses; He that | he that believes nothing, misses. (A 185)

1631 *Celestina* tr. Mabbe 55 He is unwise, that will beleeve all men; And hee is in an errour, that will beleeve no man. **1640** HERBERT no. 364.

Believing, *see* Seeing is b.

Bell, To bear (*or* carry away) the.
(B 275)

[= to be first.] *c.* **1374** CHAUCER *Troilus* Bk. 3 l. 198 And lat se which of yow shal bere the belle To speke of love aright! *c.* **1460** *Towneley Myst.* 88 Of alle the foles I can telle . . . Ye thre bere the belle. **1594** BARNFIELD *Aff. Sheph.* II. xxxix For pure white the Lilly bears the Bell.— CAREW *Huarte's Exam. Wits* xiii. (1596) 215 Iulius Cæsar . . . bare away the bell (in respect of fortunatenesse) from all other captains of the world. **1596** SPENSER *F.Q.* IV. V. 13. **1621** BURTON *Anat. Mel.* To Rdr. 49 True merchants, they carry away the bell from all other nations. **1817** BYRON *Beppo* x Venice the bell from every city bore.

Bell, book, and candle. (B 276)

[A form of excommunication closed with the words, 'Do to the book, quench the candle, ring the bell!'] *a.* **1300** *Cursor M.* l. 17110 Curced in kirc þan sal þai be wid candil, boke, and bell. *c.***1548** BALE *K. Johan* l. 1033 For as moch as Kyng Johan doth Holy Church so handle, Here I do curse hym wyth crosse, boke, bell and candle. **1596** SHAKES. *K.J.* III. iii. 12 Bell, book, and candle shall not drive me back. **1680** *Spir. Popery* 45 The Field-Preachers damned this Bond with Bell, Book, and Candle. **1896** G. BERNARD SHAW in *The Savoy* Jan. 26 This unseemly wretch should be seized and put out, bell, book, candle and all, until he learns to behave himself.

Bell the cat, To.

[An allusion to the fable of the mice proposing to hang a bell about the cat's neck, to apprise them of her coming.] **1377** LANGLAND *P. Pl.* B. Prol. ll. 168–70 To bugge¹ a belle of brasse . . . And hangen it vp-on the cattes hals. **1482** LD. GRAY IN RAMSAY *Remin.* (1857) v When the nobles of Scotland proposed . . . to take Cochrane, the favourite of James the Third, and hang him, the Lord Gray asked, 'It is well said, but wha will bell the cat?' *a.* **1529** SKELTON *Col. Cloute* 164 Loth to hang the bell aboute the cattes necke. **1642** TORRIANO 10. **1721** KELLY 180 It is well said, but who will bell the Cat? **1881** JESSOPP *Arcady* 149 Their neighbours . . . wink at much which they would gladly see mended; but who is to bell the cat? . . . He would be a very bold man . . . who would have the pluck to lodge a complaint. **1926** *Times* 1 Nov. 13/2 The taxes are illegal. All are prepared to protest, but none is willing to bell the cat. [¹ buy.]

Belle giant, or devil of Mountsorrel, He leaps like the.

1787 GROSE Leics. 1790 E 6. About Mountsorrel, or Mountstrill, says Peck, the country people have a story of a giant or devil, named Bell, who . . . took three prodigious leaps, . . . This story seems calculated to ridicule . . . shooters in the long bow.

Belled wether break the snow, Let aye the.

1832 HENDERSON 129. **1862** HISLOP 135. . . . A 'bell'd wether' is a ram with a bell round its neck; and the proverb means that a difficult or dangerous undertaking should be led by the old and experienced.

Bellerophon, Letters of. (L 214)

[Proetus sent him to Lycia, γράψας ἐν πίνακι πτυκτῷ θυμοφθόρα πολλά, *Il.* vi. 169, having graved in a folded tablet many deadly things. L. *Literae Bellerophontis.*] **1548** SIR T. ELYOT *Bibliotheca* s.v. Bellerophontes, A Prouerbe, whan one bryngeth letters agaynst hym selfe. **1742–6** YOUNG *Night Thoughts* VII He, whose blind thought futurity denies, Unconscious bears, Bellerophon! like thee, His own indictment. **1855** BULFINCH *Age of Fable* xvi Bellerophon being unconsciously the bearer of his own death warrant, the expression 'Bellerophontic letters' arose.

Bellows like a bull, He | but is as weak as a bulrush. (B 709)

[*c.* 1616] **1630** *Pathomachia* II. ii. 18 This Argument may rush like a Bull, but it is as weake as a Bull-rush. **1639** CLARKE 142.

Bellows, *see* Windmill go with b. (Cannot make).

Bells call others, but themselves enter not into the church. (B 278)

1557 NORTH *Diall of Princes* f. 138ᵛ For men yᵗ reade much, and worke litle, are as belles, the which do sound to cal others, and they themselues neuer enter into the church. *a.* **1591** H. SMITH *Serm.* (1866) II. 117 They are like our bells, which can call the people together to the service of God, but cannot perform any service to God. **1640** HERBERT no. 571. **1754** FRANKLIN Feb. The bell calls others to church, but itself never minds the sermon.

Bell(s), *see also* Agree like b., want but hanging; Counsel of fools (To) wooden b.; Cracked b. never sound; Fear not loss of b. more than steeple; Fool thinks (As the), so b. clinks; Fool's b. soon rung; God comes to see without a b.; Hang all my b. on one horse; Hear a toll or knell; Silly flock where ewe bears b.; Sound as a b.; Whip and b.

Bell-wether, *see* Flock follow b.

Belly carries the legs (feet), The.
(B 284)

1599 MINSHEU 33 (feete, and not the feete the bellie). **1620** SHELTON *Quix.* II. xxxiv (1908) III. 63 The belly carries the legs, and not the legs the belly. **1732** FULLER no. 3194 Let the Guts be full, for its they that carry the Legs. **1911** A. COHEN *Anct. Jew. Prov.* 39 The stomach carries the feet . . . Similarly it is said 'The heart carries the feet'.

Belly cries cupboard, His (My). (B 301)

1671 CLARKE *Phras. Puer.* s.v. Hungry 168 Vacuus mihi venter crepitat. **1678** RAY 237.

1738 SWIFT Dial. II. E.L. 296 Dinner's upon the table. — Faith, I'm glad of it; my belly began to cry cupboard.

Belly full of gluttony will never study willingly, A. *Cf.* Fat paunches.   (B 285)

a. **1500** *15c. Sch.-Bk.* ed. W. Nelson 7 It is selde sean that they which ffyll their belys ouermych be disposede to their bookys.   *c.* **1530** BARCLAY *Ecl.* II. 28 A full bely asketh a bed full of rest. **1584** WITHALS H6 A bellie full with gluttonie, will neuer studie willinglie.   **1584** LYLY *Camp.* I. ii. 79 The belly is the heads graue.   **1586** GUAZZO ii. 142 Know that this Proverbe is as true as common, That a fat bellie doth not engender a subtill witte.   **1641** F. QUARLES *Enchiridion* IV. lxxix A full belly makes a dull brain.   **1678** RAY 146 . . . i.e. the old proverbial Verse. Impletvs venter non vult studere libenter.   **1845** LOWELL *Conv. on Old Poets* 55 Impletus venter non vult studere libenter was the old monkish jingle, and let us be grateful . . . to the critics who have made the poets unwillingly illustrate it.

Belly is full, He whose | believes not him who is fasting. *Cf.* Full man and a fasting, etc.   (B 296)

1573 SANFORD 104ᵛ.   **1578** FLORIO *First F.* 29ᵛ He that is fed beleeueth not the fasting.   **1584** WITHALS M1 The man whose bellie filled is, commendeth fasting much Iwis.   **1732** FULLER no. 2399.

Belly is full, When the | the bones would be at rest. *Cf.* Bellyfull, To have a.   (B 303)

[*c.* **1486–1500**] *c.* **1530** MEDWALL *Nature* G1ᵛ And whan I am well fed Than get I me to a soft bed my body to repose. [*c.* **1521**] *c.* **1530** BARCLAY *Ecl.* II. 13 When full is the wombe the bones wolde haue rest.   *a.* **1530** R. *Hill's Commonpl. Bk.* E.E.T.S. 129 Whan the beli is fwll, þe bonis wold hawe rest.   **1530** R. WHITFORD *Werke for Householders* E4ᵛ.   **1546** HEYWOOD II. ii. F4 Husbande (quoth she) I wold we were in our nest. Whan the bely is full, the bones wolde be at rest.   **1580** BURGHLEY to Walsingham cited C. Read *Ld. Burghley & Q. Elizabeth* 215 We . . . mean to survey his [Hatton's] house at Holdenby and we have done to fill our bellies with his meat and sleep also, as the proverb is, our bellies full.   **1641** FERGUSSON no. 722 Quhen the bellie is full, the bones wald have rest.   **1738** SWIFT Dial. II. E.L. 312 I sometimes take a Nap after my Pipe; for . . . .

Belly is full, When the | the mind is among the maids.   (B 304)

1607 H. ESTIENNE *World of Wonders*, tr. R.C., 42 (The *Greeke* verse saith proverbially, that). **1611** COTGRAVE s.v. Pance. When the bellie is full, the breech would be figging.   *c.* **1645** Edw. Brooke MS. *N. & Q.* vol. 154, 27.

Belly is the truest clock, The.
                                        (B 287a and S 872)

[*Cf.* AQUILIUS, Boetia, Rib. 2, 38 (Parasite loq.), cited W. F. H. King *Class. & Foreign Quotations*

no. 2850 Nam unum me puero venter erat solarium, etc.]   **1590** LODGE *Rosalynde* (Greg) 85 Therefore we shepheards say, tis time to goe to dinner: for the Sunne and our stomackes, are Shepheards dialls.   **1592** GREENE *Groatsworth* (G. B. Harrison) 35 Opus and Vsus told him by the chymes in his stomacke it was time to fall vnto meat.   **1592–3** SHAKES. *C.E.* I. ii. 66 Methinks your maw, like mine, should be your clock And strike you home without a messenger. **1599** MINSHEU *Span. Dial.* 27 She [a mule] knowes better then a clocke when it is noone, and foorthwith she lookes for prouender.   **1611** COTGRAVE s.v. Horloge The bellie is the best, or truest Clocke.   **1738** SWIFT Dial. I. E.L. 294 My Stomach serves me instead of a Clock.   **1966** BOWRA *Memories* ch. 1 Chinese amah . . . said . . . 'Baby clock, he inside tummy, he savvy.'

Belly teaches all arts, The.

[**1540** PALSGRAVE *Acolastus* 62 The bely which is the master of wytte.]

Belly, If it were not for the | the back might wear gold. (The belly robs the back).   (B 288)

[*c.* **1553**] **1572** *Gam. Gurt. Needle* II Fyrste a Songe: Backe and syde go bare, go bare, booth foote and hande go colde: But Bellye god sende thee good ale ynoughe, whether it be newe or olde.   **1588** W. AVERELL *Combat of Contrarieties* B1 [The Back to the Belly] Your disorder in feeding, hath made the members weake, and my garments bare.   **1611** COTGRAVE s.v. Estat The bellie is starued by the backe.   **1619** W. HORNBY *Scourge of Drunkennes* 13 That by his paunch his backe should fare the worse.   **1706** STEVENS s.v. Pico (We say, . . .).   **1732** FULLER no. 2690; no. 6043 Your Belly will never let your Back be warm.

Belly thinks the throat is cut, The.
                                        (B 290)

1540 PALSGRAVE *Acolastus* 59 My bealy weneth my throte is cutte.   **1599** BRETON *Anger & Pat.* Wks. Gros. 60 My belly will thinke my throat cut that I feede no faster.   **1623** CAMDEN 279.   **1721** KELLY 379 Your Weime¹ thinks your Wizran² is cutted. Spoken to them who have wanted Meat long.   **1738** SWIFT Dial. II. E.L. 296 Mr. Neverout, you are in great haste; I believe, your belly thinks your throat's cut. [¹ belly, ² throat.]

Belly wants ears, The.   (B 286)

[CATO THE ELDER *Venter famelicus auriculis caret.* A hungry belly hath no ears.]   **1539** TAVERNER 47ᵛ Venter auribus caret. The bely hath no eares. When the belyes mater is in hande, honeste reasons be not admitted, nor herde.   **1562** J. WIGAND *De Neutralibus* M4 The belly wanteth eares.   **1653** WALTON *Angler* 144 It is a hard thing to perswade the belly, because it hath no ears.   *a.* **1673** ABP. LEIGHTON *Theol. Lect.* xxii Wks. (1819) IV. 230 Consider 'that, as Cato said, the belly has no ears', but it has a mouth, into which a bridle must be put.   **1853** TRENCH ii. 27 When we have . . . the English, *Hungry bellies have no ears*, and . . . the Latin, Jejunus venter non audit verba libenter, who can doubt that the first is the proverb, and the second only the versification of the proverb?

Belly (bellies), *see also* Bagpipe (He is like he never talks till b. be full; Better b. burst than drink lost; Better fill a man's b. than his eye; Birth follows b.; Eats the calf in cow's b.; Egg will be in three b. in twenty-four hours; Eye is bigger than b.; Fair words fill not b.; Full b. neither fights; Got over devil's back spent on b.; Hill b. fill b.; Never good that mind b.; Ship under sail . . . woman with a great b.; Yellow b.

Bellyful is a bellyful, whether it be meat or drink, A.   (B 305)

1659 HOWELL *Span. Prov.* 11 A belly full, though it be of hay. **1666** TORRIANO *Prov. Phr.* s.v. Sacco, 175. **1678** RAY 100. **1738** SWIFT Dial. II. E.L. 307 I have made my whole dinner of beef. — . . . A bellyfull's a bellyfull, if it be but of wheat-straw.

Bellyful, To have a. *Cf.* **Belly is full.**   (B 306)

c. **1475** *Mankind* l. 632 Of murder and man-slawter I haue my bely-fyll. [*c.* **1521**] **1533** J. HEYWOOD *Pard. and Friar* B1 Therfore preche hardely thy bely full. **1566** ERASM. *Diversoria* tr. E. H. B2 A manne cannot fill his bellye with pleasaunte talke. **1610** SHAKES. *Cym.* II. i. 19 Every Jackslave hath his bellyfull of fighting. **1670** *Journey into Spain* 9 These inns are sad spectacles, and the sight of them gives one a belly full.

Bellyful, *see also* Feast and a b. (Little difference).

Bellywark, *see* Sick of the . . . b. in the heel.

Belong(s), *see* All men have what b. to them (When), it cannot be much.

Beloved, To be | is above all bargains.   (B 82)

1640 HERBERT no. 631.

Beloved, *see also* Well with him who is b.

Below, *see* Things that are b. us are nothing.

Belt, *see* Angry (If you be), turn buckle of b.; Buckles his b. (Every man); Hit below the b.; Thumb under my b.

Beltanes, *see* Skill of man and beast (You have), born between the B.

Belvoir has a cap, If | yon churls of the Vale look to that.   (B 336)

1662 FULLER *Leics.* 126 If Bever have a capp, Yon churles of the Vale look to that. That is, when the Clouds . . . hang over the Towers of the Castle, it is a prognostick of much rain . . . to . . . that fruitful Vale, lying in the three Counties of Leicester, Lincoln, and Nottingham. **1848** A. B. EVANS *Leics. Words, &c.* (1881) 300 I have heard the proverb . . . always in the form: 'When Belvoir wears his cap, Yon churls of the Vale

look to that'; and . . . when an Albini or a Ros 'wore his cap' in the Manor Court, or rode . . . to the chase . . . there was good cause for the 'churls of the Vale' to look to it.

Bemired, *see* Hog that's b.

Bench(es), *see* Hall b. are slippery; Penniless b.

Bend while it is a twig, Best to.   (T 632)

[*a.* **1465**] **1543** J. HARDYNG *Eng. Chronicle in Metre* fol. xcvii[v] Writh nowe the wand, while it is grene. **1509** A. BARCLAY *Ship of Fools* I. 47 A lytell twygge plyant is by kynde A bygger braunche is harde to bowe or wynde. **1530** PALSGRAVE 448b A man may bende a wande while it is grene, and make it strayght though it be never so croked. **1563** B. GOOGE *Eclog.* vi Arb. 53 The tender twyg, that now doth bend at length refuseth cleane. **1650** BAXTER *Saints Everl. Rest* III. xi They are young . . . and flexible . . . You have a twig to bend, and we an oak. **1670** RAY 61. **1710** PALMER 15.

Bend, *see also* Better b. than break.

Benefice, *see* Gape for a b.

Benefits bind.   (B 310)

1539 TAVERNER *Publius* A7 To take a benefite is to sell thy libertie. He is not his owne man, that vseth another mans benefite. *Ibid.* B3 When thou gyuest a benefite to the worthy thou byndest al. For it is bestowed not vpon the person, but vpon vertue. **1597** *Politeuphuia* 168 He findeth fetters that findeth benefits. **1616** DRAXE no. 918. **1639** CLARKE 283.

Benefits please, like flowers, while they are fresh.   (B 311)

1651 HERBERT no. 40a.

Benson, *see* Hope better, quoth B. . . . cuckold.

Bent of his bow, I have (know) the.   (B 313)

c. **1430** LYDGATE *Minor Poems* E.E.T.S. ii. 680 Hertford 198 We knowe to weel the bent of Iackys bowe. **1530** PALSGRAVE 417a I accustome hym for the bent of my bowe. **1546** HEYWOOD I. xi. D4 Though I, hauyng the bent of your vncles bow, Can no waie bryng your bolt in the butte to stande. **1578** *Courtly Controv.* T1[v] This cruell Pope bending . . . his snares . . . to win and draw to the bent of his bowe. **1670** RAY 164. **1783** AINSWORTH *Lat. Dict.* (Morell) I s.v. Bent I have got the bent of his bow, *ego illius sensum pulchrè calleo.*

Bent, *see also* Bow long b.

Bermudas let you pass, If the | you must beware of Hatteras.

1840 DANA *Two Years* ch. 35 We passed inside of the Bermudas; and notwithstanding the old couplet, . . .—'If the Bermudas let us pass, You

must beware of Hatteras—' we were to the northward of Hatteras, with good weather.

Bernard did not see everything.

[Usually taken as referring to St. Bernard of
Clairvaux, 1091–1153.] *c.* **1385** CHAUCER
L.G.W. Prol. l. 16 Bernard the monk ne saugh
nat al, pardee! **1623** J. BALMFORD *Reply to
Gataker* 47 Bernardus non vidit omnia. **1645**
A. ROSS *Medicus Medicatus* 83 S. *Bernard*, wee
say, saw not all. **1659** FULLER *Appeal Inj.
Innoc.* in *Hist. Camb. Univ.* (1840) 332 *Bernardus
non videt omnia*; I could not come to the know-
ledge of every particular.

Berry, *see* Devil in every b. of grape.

Berry, (*prop. name*) *see* Sheep of B.

Berwick to Dover three hundred miles over, From.   (B 315)

c. **1300** R. BRUNNE tr. LANGTOFT's *Chron.*
(Hearne) 305 Alle Inglond fro Berwick vnto
Kent. **1553** T. WILSON *Arte of Rhet.* (1909) 105
Oftentimes they beginne as much from the matter,
as it is betwixt Douer and Barwike. **1662** FULLER
Northumb. 302 From Berwick to Dover, three
hundred miles over. That is, from one end of the
land to the other. Semnable the Scripture expression, From Dan to Ber-sheba.

Beside the book, To be.   (B 531)

a. **1590** MUNDAY *John a Kent* l. 1096 One of vs
Iohns must play besyde the booke. **1602** N.
BRETON *Old Madcap's Gallimaufry* (*Poems* ed.
Robertson 131) Vpon ynough, it is ynough to
looke, And what is more, is quite beside the
booke. **1605** CHAPMAN *All Fools* II. i. 333 The
poor lawyers . . . Were fair to rail and talk
besides their books Without all order. **1672**
WALKER 32 no. 69.

Beside (Besides) the cushion, To set (*or* put).   (C 929)

[= to depose, or disappoint of an office or dignity.] **1546** HEYWOOD II. ix. L2ᵛ I maie set you
besyde the cushyn yit. And make ye wype your
nose vpon your sléeue. **1589** NASHE *Pasquil's
Return* i. 91. *a.* **1624** BP. M. SMITH *Serm.* 188
Sometimes putting them besides the Cushion,
and placing others in their roome.

Beside, *see also* Think all is lost that goes b. your
mouth.

Besom, *see* Broomstick (B.), (To jump the);
Little for rake after b.; Need of a b. that sweep
with turf (They have).

Best among them, There is never a | as the fellow said by the fox cubs.   (B 327)

1678 RAY 228.

Best bred have the best portion, The.   (E 58)

c. **1630** G. HERBERT *Letters* (Wks. ed. Hutchinson

376) Take this rule and it is an outlandish one,
. . . 'the best bredd child hath the best portion'.
1640 HERBERT no. 953.

Best carpenter makes the fewest chips, The.   (C 93)

1609 HARWARD 79ᵛ He is not the best carpenter
that maketh the most chipps. **1611** CORYATE
Crudities I. 407 (For, according to the old
proverbe, the best carpenters make). [**1632**]
1653 R. BROME *Novella* III. i. 132. **1697** W. POPE
Seth [*Ward*] 158 Every Carpenter makes some
Chips, and he is the best Workman who makes
fewest.

Best cart may overthrow, The.   (C 101)

1550 HEYWOOD I. xi. D3ᵛ Well (quoth his man)
the best cart maie ouerthrowe. **1639** CLARKE
160.

Best cloth may have a moth in it, The.   (C 429)

1492 *Dialogue of Salomon & Marcolphus* ed.
Duff 7 Undre a whyte cloth often are hyd
mothys. **1571** TIGURINUS *Institution of a
Christian Prince* tr. J. Chichester 5 Of the nature
of Moathes, that always follow good clothes.
1576 PETTIE i. 27 The moth which most of all
eateth the best cloth. **1732** FULLER no. 4411.

Best dog leap the stile first, The.   (D 444)

1678 RAY 76 . . . i.e. Let the worthiest person take
place.

Best foot (leg) foremost (foreward), To put (set) one's.   (F 570)

a. **1500** MEDWALL *Nature* C3 Com behynd and
folow me. Set out the better legge I warne the.
1548 HALL *Chron.* (1809, 67) In whiche good and
iust quarel al good persons shal rather set bothe
theyr feete forward, then once to turne theyr one
heale backward. **1562** J. WIGAND *De Neutralibus* A3 Many . . . were wonderous feruente, and
set the better legge afore stoutly. **1590** A.
MUNDAY *The English Roman Life* A3ᵛ Wee
sette the better legge before. **1592** SHAKES.
T.And. II. iii. 192 Come on, my lords, the better
foot before. **1599** NASHE *Lenten Stuff* iii. 205
Thither our Fisherman set the best legge before.
1633 JONSON *T.Tub* II. i. 1 Zonne Clay, cheare up,
the better leg avore. **1678** RAY 245 To set the
best foot forward. **1876** BLACKMORE *Cripps*
ch. 7 Hup! Dobbin there. Best foot foremost
kills the hill.

Best general who makes the fewest mistakes, He is the.

1907 SIR. I. HAMILTON *Staff Off. Scrap-Bk.* II.
347 The highest authority tells us that he is the
best general who makes fewest mistakes.

Best go first, The.

a. **1631** DONNE *Sonnet on Death* And soonest
our best men with thee doe goe. **1645** *Verney*

Memoirs (1892) ii. 75 The best go [= die] first. **1859** C. READE *Love me Little* ch. 21 'She was an angel, . . . sent to bear us company a little while, and now she is a saint in heaven'. 'Ah, ma'am! the best goes first, that is an old saying.'

Best gown that goes up and down the house, That is the. (G 389)

1640 HERBERT no. 742.

Best is as good as stark naught, The. (B 317)

1616 WITHALS 581. **1639** CLARKE 14.

Best is behind, The. (B 318)

c. **1369** CHAUCER *Bk. Duchess* l. 890 The formest was alway behynde. *a.* **1500** *Robin Hood and the Potter* st. 30 Her es more, and affter ys to saye, The best ys beheynde. *a.* **1529** SKELTON *Wks.* (Dyce) I. 17 Take thys in worth, the best is behynde. **1579** LYLY *Euph.* i. 279 But the greatest thinge is yet behinde. **1605–6** SHAKES. *M.* I. iii. 116 Glamis, and Thane of Cawdor: The greatest is behind. **1659** HOWELL *Eng. Prov.* 6b. **1824** MOIR *Mansie W.* ch. 2 In the course of the evening, his lordship whispered to one of the flunkies to bring in some things— they could not hear what. . . . The wise ones thought within themselves that the best aye comes hindmost.

Best is best cheap. (B 319)

1523 FITZHERBERT *Husbandry* (Skeat, 14) Thoughe they be derer at the fyrst, yet at lengthe they be better cheape. **1546** HEYWOOD II. vii. I4. **1605** L. OWEN *Key. Span. Tongue* 124 That which is good, is good cheape. **1616** DRAXE no. 148. **1655–62** GURNALL *Chrn. in Armour* (1865) I. 82 He that sells cheapest shall have most customers, though, at last, best will be best cheap. **1670** RAY 61 . . . For it doth the buyer more credit and more service. **1786** WOLCOT (P. Pindar) *Lousiad* v. Wks. (1816) I. 230 'Best is best cheap'—you very wisely cry.

Best is oftentimes the enemy of the good, The. *Cf.* **Good is the enemy of the best.**

1605–6 SHAKES. *K.L.* I. iv. 347 Striving to better, oft we mar what's well. **1861** TRENCH *Epist. Seven Ch.* Pref. iii. 'The best is oftentimes the enemy of the good'; and . . . many a good book has remained unwritten, . . . because there floated before the mind's eye . . . the ideal of a better or a best. **1925** *Times* 1 Dec. 16/2 This is not the first time in the history of the world when the best has been the enemy of the good; . . . one single step on . . . solid ground may be more profitable than a more ambitious flight. [Fr. *Le mieux est l'ennemi du bien.*]

Best loved furthest off, Men are. (M 539)

a. **1547** SURREY ed. Padelford (1928) 28. 44 The farther of, the more desired. **1639** CLARKE 71.

Best may amend, The. (B 321)

a. **1560** *Cont. betwixt Churchyard and Camell* C3. (be amended, and that is very true). **1563**

J. PILKINGTON *Comfutation* P.S. 611 (be amended). **1584** R. WILSON *Three Ladies of London* Hazl.-Dods. vi. 370 The best of us all may amend. **1587** J. BRIDGES *Defence* 1320 (may be amended). **1616** DRAXE no. 85. **1640** E.B. *Buckler agst. Fear of Death* Ded. (be bettered).

Best men when in the worst health, We are usually the.

1707 MAPLETOFT 79.

Best of a bad bargain (market), Make the. (B 326)

1589 PUTTENHAM *Art Eng. Poesy* Arb. 195 The figure Paradiastole . . . we call the Curry-fauell, as when we make the best of a bad thing. **1663** PEPYS *Diary* 14 Aug. I . . . therefore am resolved to make The best of a bad market. **1664** COTTON *Scarron.* (1715 ed.) i. 18 Let's make the best of a bad Market. **1670** RAY 61. **1712** ARBUTHNOT *John Bull* II. xii Matters have not been carried on with due secrecy; however, we must make the best of a bad bargain. **1721** KELLY 247 *Make the best of a bad Market.* Since you have faln into a troublesome Business, mend it by your Cunning and Industry. **1775** BOSWELL *Johnson* xlviii (1848) 440 A young lady . . . had married . . . her inferior in rank . . . Mrs. Thrale was all for . . . 'making the best of a bad bargain'. **1829** SCOTT *Journ.* 14 July A rainy forenoon . . . I wrote 4½ pages to make the best of a bad bargain. **1876** E. A. FREEMAN *Norm. Conq.* IV. xvii. 7 Men had made up their minds to submit to what they could not help, and to make the best of a bad bargain. **1879** S. COLVIN (*Times Lit. Supp.* 5 June 1959 344) My own object is to get L[ouis] back, if without Mrs. S[tevenson], so much the better; if with her, then as the best of a bad job.

Best of both worlds, To make the.

1855 KINGSLEY *Westward Ho!* ch. 12 Bishop Grandison of Exeter proclaimed . . . 'participation in all spiritual blessings for ever', to all who would promote the bridging of that dangerous ford; and so, consulting alike the interests of their souls and of their bodies, 'make the best of both worlds'. **1871** FROUDE *Calvinism in Short Stud.* II (1900) 57 We have learnt . . . to make the best of both worlds, to take political economy for the rule of our conduct, and to relegate religion into the profession of orthodox doctrines.

Best of men are but men at best, The.

1680 J. AUBREY to Wood (15 June) I remember one saying of Generall Lambert's, 'that the best of men are but men at best'. **1885** HARLEY *Moon Lore* 191.

Best or worst thing to man, for this life, is good or ill choosing his good or ill wife, The. (T 123)

1546 HEYWOOD I. ii. A3. **1721** KELLY 331 The good or ill Hap of a good or ill Life, is the good or ill Choice, of a good or ill Wife. **1732** FULLER no. 6413 (*as* 1721).

Best payment is on the peck bottom, The.

1721 KELLY 95 . . . That is, when you have

measured out your Grain, to receive your Payment on the Peck that measured it.

Best smell, The | is bread, the best savour salt, the best love that of children. (s 555)

1578 FLORIO *First F.* 2A2ᵛ It is an auncient prouerbe, that the odour of odours, is the bread: the sauour of sauours, is the salt, and the loue of loues, is chyldren. 1640 HERBERT no. 741.

Best thing for the inside of a man is the outside of a horse, The.

1603 MONTAIGNE (Florio) I. xlviii. 203 Plato commendeth it [horse-riding] to be availefull for health. And Plinie affirmeth the same to be healthfull for the stomache, and for the joynts. 1906 G. W. E. RUSSELL *Soc. Silhouettes* xxxii. 218 The Squire will wind up . . . with an apocryphal saying which he attributes to Lord Palmerston—'There's nothing so good for the inside of a man as the outside of a horse'.

Best things are worst to come by, The. (T 178)

1556 R. RECORDE *The Castle of Knowledge* (Hebel & F. R. Johnson, 130) The best things are not most easiest to attain. 1635 SWAN *Spec. Mundi* 465 Excellent things are hard to come by. 1639 CLARKE 87.

Best things (Everything) may be abused, The. (N 317)

1530 PALSGRAVE 415b There is nothing so good but it may be abused. *Ibid.*, 639a. 1545 R. ASCHAM *Toxophilus* ed. Wright 22 Shoting (as all other good thinges) may be abused. 1576 PETTIE ii. 138 There is nothing so good, but by ill using may be made naught. 1579 LYLY *Euph.* i. 242 There is nothing but through the mallice of man may be abused. *c.* 1595 SHAKES. *R.J.* II. iii. 19 Nor aught so good but strain'd from that fair use Revolts from true birth, stumbling on abuse. 1624 QUARLES *Job Militant* Med. V And best of things (once abus'd) prove worst of all. 1639 CLARKE 5. 1666 TORRIANO *It. Prov.* I no. 12 (Everything).

Best use of their time, Those that make the | have none to spare.

1732 FULLER no. 5029.

Best wine comes out of an old vessel, The.

1621 BURTON *Anat. Mel.* II. iii. II (1651) 312 *Vilis sæpe cadus nobile nectar habet*: the best wine comes out of an old vessell. How many deformed princes, kings, emperours, could I reckon up, philosophers, orators?

Best wine is that a body drinks of another man's cost, The.

1564 UDALL *Erasm. Apoph.* (1877) 141 To one demanding what wyne he¹ best loued and liked with his good will to drinke, Marie (quoth he) of another mannes purse. [*Margin.* The best wine is that a body drinketh of another mans cost.] [¹ i.e. Diogenes.]

Best, *see also* Bad is the b.; Black b. sets forth white; Every man likes his own thing b.; Good is the enemy of the b.; Grace is b. for the man; Hope for b.; Mean is b.; Misery b., (He bears) that hides it most; Purse is his b. friend; Short follies are b.

Bestill [i.e. *be still*] is worth a groat, A good. (B 329)

c. 1430 LYDGATE *Minor Poems* E.E.T.S. ii. 817 A good be stille is ofte weel wourth a groote. Large language causith repentaunce. 1546 HEYWOOD II. v. H2 A good bestyll is woorth a grote. 1616 DRAXE no. 1977.

Bestows his gifts as broom does honey, He. (G 112)

1584 WITHALS D4ᵛ. 1639 CLARKE 38. 1678 RAY 246 . . . Broom is so far from sweet that it's very bitter.

Bestows, *see also* Plays the whore for apples, then b. them.

Betides, *see* Weel bides, weel b.

Betimes, *see* Rise b. that will cozen devil; Rise b. that would please everybody; Rises b. has something in head (He that).

Better a bare foot than none. (F 561)

1611 COTGRAVE s.v. Nud A bare foot is better then none. 1640 HERBERT no. 78.

Better a castle of bones than of stones. (C 120)

c. 1350 HY. SAVAGE in HOLINSHED *Chron. Ire.* (1577 ed. 72) In this season dwelled in Vlster . . . sir Robert Sauage . . . 'Father (quoth yoong Sauage) I remember the prouerbe "Better a castell of bones than of stones". Where . . . valiant men are . . . neuer will I . . . cumber my selfe with dead walles.' [1571] 1633 E. CAMPION *Hist. Ire.* II. vi. 90 I remember the Proverbe, better a Castle of bones, then of stones, where strength and courage of valiant men are to helpe us.

Better a clout than a hole out. (C 447)

c. 1540 Unpublished Poems in Devonshire MS. (MS. Add. 17492) K. Muir in *Leeds Phil. Soc. Proc. Lit & Hist. Sect.* VI no. 40 The bagars prouerbe ffynd I good: Betar a path [sic for 'patch'] than a hille oute. 1636 CAMDEN 299. 1664 CODRINGTON 188. 1670 RAY 71.

Better a finger off than aye wagging.¹ (F 225)

c. 1200 *Ancrene Riwle* (Morton) 360 Vor betere is finker offe þen he eke euer. *a.* 1628 CARMICHAELL no. 284 (warking¹). 1641 FERGUSSON no. 176 (warkin[1]). **1721** KELLY 56 . . . Better put an end to a troublesome Business, than to be always vex'd with it. **1817** SCOTT *Rob Roy* ch. 18 I hae been thinking o' flitting, . . . and now I am o' the mind to gang in gude earnest . . . better a finger aff as aye wagging. [[1] aching.]

Better a lean jade than an empty halter. (J 28)

1678 RAY 166. **1732** FULLER no. 863.

Better a lean peace than a fat victory. (A 78)

1573 SANFORD 107[v]. **1578** FLORIO *First F.* 32 Better is a leane agreement then a fat sentence. **1605** BRETON *Old Man's Lesson* Wks. (Gros.) ii. 10 The heart of a wise man will bee better pleased with a poore peace, then a Rich Warre. **1732** FULLER no. 864.

Better a little loss than a long sorrow.

1362 LANGLAND *P. Pl.* Prol. 388–9 (Wright) I. 12 For better is a litel los Than a long sorwe.

Better a louse (mouse) in the pot than no flesh at all. (L 468)

1623 CAMDEN 267. **1636** *Ibid.* 293. **1639** CLARKE 241. **1641** FERGUSSON no. 211 (mouse). **1670** RAY 117 . . . The Scotch Proverb saith a mouse. **1732** FULLER no. 867 (mouse).

Better a mischief than an inconvenience. (I 62 and M 995)

c. **1530–60** *The Resurrection of our Lord* l. 462 To suffer a myschiefe, rather then an inconueny-ence. **1572** T. WILSON *Discourse upon Usury* (1925), 237. (As we say) better it is to suffer a mischiefe then an inconvenience. **1611** DEKKER & MIDDLETON *Roaring Girl* F4 Worse, and worse still, you embrace a mischiefe, to preuent an ill. **1639** CLARKE 199 Better once a mischief than ever an inconvenience. **1642** D. ROGERS *Naaman* ix. 255 Redeem a perpetual inconvenience, al-though by a present mischief (as the proverb saith), pulling down a bad chimney with some cost, rather than enduring a perpetual smoky house. **1670** RAY 121 . . . That is, better a present mischief that is soon over, then a constant grief and disturbance.

Better a portion in a wife than with a wife.

1721 KELLY 70 Better a Togher in her than with her. Better marry a . . . vertuous woman, . . . than an idle . . . Drab, with a much greater Portion. **1732** FULLER no. 868. **1886** E. J. HARDY *How to be Happy* ch. 4 Better to have a fortune *in* your wife than with her.

Better a snotty child than his nose wiped off. (C 296)

1611 COTGRAVE s.v. Enfant Better a snottie child then a noselesse. **1640** HERBERT no. 828. **1659** HOWELL *Fr. Prov.* 27.

Better a wee fire to warm us than a mickle fire to burn us. (F 249)

c. **1515** A.BARCLAY *Eclog.* I. l. 1067 Then better is small fire one easyly to warme, Then is a great fire to do one hurt or harme. *a.* **1628** CAR-MICHAELL no. 280. **1641** FERGUSSON no. 194. **1721** KELLY 61 . . . An ordinary Fortune is safest, and exposes us to less Danger. **1824** S. FERRIER *Inheritance* II. xxvii As the old byeword says, 'better a wee ingle to warm ye, than a muckle fire to burn you'.

Better an apple given than eaten. (A 292)

c. **1300** *Provs. of Hending* 13 Betere is appel y-yeue then y-ete. **1641** FERGUSSON no. 154 Better apple given nor eaten. **1721** KELLY 42 . . . (eaten by a time.) A Man may get more Favour by giving a Thing, than using it.

Better an egg to-day than a hen to-morrow. (E 70)

[**1546** RABELAIS III. xlii *Ad præsens ova cras pullis sunt meliora.*] **1642** TORRIANO 49. **1659** HOWELL *It. Prov.* I. **1666** TORRIANO *It. Prov.* 113 no. 24. **1732** FULLER no. 2916 It is better to have a Hen to Morrow than an Egg to Day. **1734** FRANKLIN Sept. An egg to-day is better than a hen to-morrow. **1777** DIBDIN *Quaker* I. ii An egg to-day is better than a chicken to-morrow. **1860** SURTEES *Plain or Ring .?* ch. 13 There is an old adage 'that an egg to-day is worth a hen to-morrow'.

Better an empty house than an ill tenant.

1721 KELLY 67. **1732** FULLER no. 870.

Better an open enemy than a false friend. (F 410)

c. **1200** *Ancrene Riwle* (Morton) 98 Ueond þet þuncheð freond is swike ouer alle swike. [An enemy who seems a friend is of all traitors the most treacherous.] *c.* **1386** CHAUCER *Merch. T.* l. 1784 O famulier foo, that his servyce bedeth! O servant traytour, false hoomly hewe, . . . God shilde us all from youre aqueyntaunce. **1550** R. CROWLEY *One & Thirty Epigrams* E.E.T.S. 30 Of an open enimie a man may be ware: When the flatteryng frend wyl worcke men much care. **1557** EDGEWORTH *Serm.* 3R2 There is none so perilous gyle, as that is hidde vnder the similitude and colour of frendship. **1591–2** SHAKES. *3 Hen. VI* IV. i. 139 I rather wish you foes than hollow friends. **1597** *Id. Rich. III* III. i. 16 God keep me from false friends. **1655–62** GURNALL *Chrn. in Armour* (1865) ii. 27 A false friend is worse than an open enemy in man's judgement; and a hypocritical Judas more ab-horred by God than a bloody Pilate. **1727** GAY *Fables, Shep. Dog & W.* An open foe may prove a curse, But a pretended friend is worse. **1822** SCOTT *Nigel* ch. 9 I thank you for your plainness, . . . an open enemy is better than a hollow friend. **1847** E. BRONTË *Wuthering H.* ch. 10 'You are worse than twenty foes, you poisonous friend!'

Better are meals many than one too merry. (M 788)

1546 HEYWOOD II. vii. I4[v]. *c.* **1594** BACON

Promus no. 594.   **1616** DRAXE no. 2016 Better
meales few, then one too merrie.   *Ibid.* no. 720
(feastes fewe).   **1678** RAY 40.

Better are small fish than an empty dish. (F 303)

1678 RAY 204.   **1862** HISLOP 171 Sma' fish are
better than nane.   **1905** ASHBY-STERRY in
Graphic Christmas No. You will find that the
spider . . . If he only entangles the tiniest flies,
Thinks '*Small fish are better than none!*'

Better be a fool than a knave. (F 446)

1592 DELAMOTHE 21 It is better to show himselfe
without wit, then to enter into the way of vn-
thankfulnesse.   **1595** T. LODGE *A Fig for Momus*
(Hunt. Cl.) B1 'Tis better be a foole then be a
fox.   **1640** HERBERT no. 961.   **1659** HOWELL *Fr.
Prov.* 6 Better be a Cuckold then a Knave.

Better be alone than in bad (ill) company. (C 570)

1477 RIVERS *Dictes and Sayings* (1877) 8 It is
better a man . . . to be a lone than to be acom-
payned with euill people.   **1586** GUAZZO ii. 124
I will withdraw . . . where with this saying I will
remaine. It is better to be alone then in ill companie.   **1609** HARWARD 77ᵛ (ill accompanyed).
1639 CLARKE 291.   **1859** SMILES *Self-Help* 368
Lord Collingwood . . . said, 'Hold it as a maxim
that you had better be alone than in mean company'.

Better be an old man's darling, than a young man's warling.[1] (M 444–5)

1546 HEYWOOD II. vii. I3ᵛ.   **1602** BRETON
Wonders worth Hear. Wks. (Gros.) ii. 12 I see
by my neighbours, it is better being an old mans
darling then a young mans worldling.   **1721**
KELLY 74 . . . than a young Man's Wonderling,
say the Scots, Warling, say the English.   **1738**
SWIFT Dial. I. E.L. 290.   **1886** E. J. HARDY *How
to be Happy* ch. 5 The majority of girls would
rather be a young man's slave than an old man's
darling. [1 one who is despised or disliked.]

Better be envied than pitied. (E 177)

[ERASM. *Ad. Praestat invidiosum esse quam
miserabilem*, quoting Greek authors.]   **1546**
HEYWOOD I. xi. D2ᵛ.   **1557** EDGEWORTH *Sermons*
203ᵛ The old prouerbe, I hadde leauer hee
enuyed me, then bemoned me.   *c.* **1565** W.
WAGER A3 A common saying better is enuy
then rueth.   *c.* **1592** MARLOWE *Jew of Malta* Prol.
27 Let me be envy'd and not pittied.   **1636**
CAMDEN 299 It is better be spited then pittied.
a. **1631** DONNE *Verse Lett.* Wks. (1896) ii. 32
Men say, and truly, that they better be which be
envied than pitied.   **1902** G. W. E. RUSSELL *Coll.
& Recol.* 2 Ser. (1909) ch. 33 Her friend responded sympathetically, 'My dear, I'd much
rather be envied than pitied'.

Better be first in a village than second at Rome. (V 55)

[PLUTARCH, *Caesar* 11. 2.]   **1542** UDALL *Apoph.
of Erasmus* (1877) 297 [Julius Caesar] . . . had
lieffer to bee the firste, or the chief man here,
then the seconde man in Rome.   **1605** BACON
Adv. Learn. II. xxiii. (1900) 240 Caesar, when he
went first into Gaul, made no scruple to profess
*That he had rather be first in a village than second
at Rome.*   **1668** COWLEY *Ess.* vi (1772) 211 I
should be like Caesar . . . and choose rather to be
the first man of the village, than second at Rome.

Better be happy than wise. (H 140)

1546 HEYWOOD II. vi. I1ᵛ.   **1565** W. ALLEY *Poor
Man's Library* (1571 ed., 6) *Est fortunatior quam
prudentior.* It is better to be happy, then wise.
1641 FERGUSSON no. 181.   **1642** TORRIANO 50.

Better be sure than sorry.

1695 RAVENSCROFT 45 It's good to be sure.
1837 LOVER *Rory O'More* ch. 21 'Just countin
them,—is there any harm in that?' said the
tinker; 'it's better be sure than sorry'.

Better be the head of a dog (fox, mouse, lizard) than the tail of a lion. (H 238)

1599 *Master Broughton's Letters* E2 This is a
common prouerb with them [the Rabbinists],
That it is better being the head of a fox, then
the tayle of a lyon; that is, the author of an addle
fancie, then the scholler of a receiued veritie.
1599 MINSHEU *Span. Gram.* 83 (mouse).   **1640**
HERBERT no. 579 (Lyzard).   **1670** RAY 101 (dog).
1791–1823 I. DISRAELI *Curios. Lit.* (Chandos) III.
52 The ancient . . . spirit of Englishmen was once
expressed by our proverb, 'Better be the head of
a dog than the tail of a lion'; i.e. the first of the
yeomanry rather than the last of the gentry.

Better be the head of a pike than the tail of a sturgeon. (H 259)

1659 N.R. 69, 70.   **1670** RAY 101.

Better be the head of an ass than the tail of a horse. (H 239)

1639 CLARKE 105.   *Ibid.* 91 Better be the tayle of
a horse than th' head of an ass.   **1670** RAY 101.
1732 FULLER no. 928.

Better be the head of the yeomanry than the tail of the gentry. (H 240)

1589 L. WRIGHT *Display Duty* 9 It is a true saying,
Better to liue in low degree, then high disdaine.
1609 HARWARD 73 Better it is to be the head of
dames then the tayle of mistresses. Better to be
the head of yeomanry then the tayle of gentry.
1639 CLARKE 22.   **1670** RAY 101.   **1732** FULLER
no. 933 (Yeomen).

Better be unmannerly than trouble-some. (U 15)

1591 FLORIO *Second F.* 15 I am readie, goe before,
and I will folowe you.—I will rather showe myselfe vnmannerlie, than disobedient.   **1599** *Warning for Fair Women* D2 Ile rather be vnmanerly
then ceremonious, Ile leave you sir to recommend my thanks.   **1600–1** SHAKES. *M.W.W.* I.
i. 285.   *a.* **1628** CARMICHAELL no. 947 It is gude
to be courteous bot not over commersome.
1659 HOWELL *Eng. Prov.* 5a.   **1670** RAY 153.

1675 P. FESTEAU *Fr. Gram.* 231 I had rather be vncivil, than troublesom. **1721** KELLY 72 Better my friend think me frame[1] than fashious.[2] He that sees his Friend too seldom, errs on the right side. [[1] strange. [2] troublesome.]

Better beg than steal.   (B 222)

1586 *Lazarillo* tr. D. Rowland ed. Crofts 45. **1639** CLARKE 225.

Better belly burst than good drink (meat) lost.   (B 291)

a. **1628** CARMICHAELL no. 363 (nor gude meit spilt). **1659** HOWELL *Eng. Prov.* 17b. **1678** RAY 100 Better belly burst then good {drink {meat lost.

Better bend (bow) than break.   (B 566)

c. **1374** CHAUCER *Troilus* Bk. I ll. 257–8 The yerde is bet that bowen wole and wynde, Than that that brest. *c.* **1420** *Peter Idle's Instructions to his Son* (Miessner) I. 88 For better is the tree þat bowe þan breste. *c.* **1450** *Provs. of Wysdom* l. 58 Better is to bow þen to brest. **1546** HEYWOOD I. ix. C2 Well (quoth I) better is to boow then breake. **1642** FULLER *H. & P. State* V. xviii (1841) 417 Better, for a time, to bow to our foes, rather than to be broken by them. **1840** DICKENS *Barn. Rudge* ch. 79 I have had . . . sorrows . . . but I have borne them ill. I have broken where I should have bent.

Better blue clothes, He is in his. (C 436)

1678 RAY 66 . . . He thinks himself wondrous fine.

Better bread than is made of wheat, He would have.   (B 622)

1546 HEYWOOD II. vii. I4 Lyke one of fonde fancy so fyne and so neate, That wold haue better bread than is made of wheate. **1568** W. PAINTER (Jacobs iii. 148). **1579** LYLY *Euph.* Ep. Ded. i. 181 English men desire to heare finer speach then the language will allow, to eate finer bread then is made of Wheat. **1706** STEVENS s.v. Trastrigo . . . to be foolishly nice. **1853** TRENCH iv. 87 What warnings do many contain against . . . a looking for perfection is a world of imperfection. . . . We say: *He expects better bread than can be made of wheat.*

Better buy than borrow.   (B 783)

1539 TAVERNER f. 13[v] I had leuer bye than begge. **1616** DRAXE no. 200. **1641** FERGUSSON no. 210 Better buy as borrow. **1721** KELLY 59 . . . True! for he that goes a borrowing goes a sorrowing. **1732** FULLER no. 884.

Better children weep than old (bearded) men.   (C 326)

c. **1350** *Douce MS.* 52 no. 103 Better is a zong chylde wepe than on olde man. **1546** HEYWOOD I. xi. D3[v]. **1641** FERGUSSON no. 186 Better bairnes greit nor bearded men. **1721** KELLY 62 Better Bairns greet as bearded Men. Better you make your Children cry with seasonable Correction, than they make you cry by their after Miscarriage. **1827–30** SCOTT *Tales Grandf.* ch. 32 The king burst into tears. 'Let him weep on', said the Tutor of Glamis[1] fiercely; 'better that bairns (children) weep, than bearded men.' [[1] to King James VI after the Ruthven Raid, 1582.]

Better come at the latter end of a feast than the beginning of a fray.

(C 547 and 548; E 114)

1546 HEYWOOD II. vii. I3[v] It is yll commyng . . . To thend of a shot and begynnyng of a fray. *a.* **1548** R. COPLAND *Jyl of Brentford's Testament* l. 704 He that goeth to a fray at the begynnyng, And to a good meale at the latter endyng. **1597** SHAKES. *1 Hen. IV* IV. ii. 76 To the latter end of a fray and the beginning of a feast Fits a dull fighter and a keen guest. **1636** MASSINGER *Bashful Lover* III. iii They said, Haste to the beginning of a feast, There I am with them; *but to the end of a fray*—That is apocryphal. **1670** RAY 90. **1721** KELLY 73. **1860** PEACOCK *Gryll Grange* ch. 15 Not too late for a feast, though too late for a fray.

Better cut the shoe than pinch the foot.

1580 LYLY *Euph. & his Eng.* ii. 10 Better to cut the shooe, then burne the last. **1732** FULLER no. 887.

Better day (the day), The | the better deed (the deed).   (D 60)

1607 MIDDLETON *Mich. Term.* III. i. **1612** S. ROWLANDS *Knave of Harts* Wks. (1880) II. 46 They say, The better day, the better deede. **1655** FULLER *Ch. Hist.* III. i 34. Upon Christmas-day (the better day the better deed!) he[1]Excommunicated Robert de Broc, because the day before he had cut off one of his horses' tailes. **1721** KELLY 328 The better Day, the better Deed. I never heard this used but when People say that they did such an ill thing on *Sunday*. **1738** SWIFT *Dial.* I. E.L. 284 That won't be proper; you know to-morrow's Sunday.—What then, madam! they say, the better day, the better deed. **1896** J. C. HUTCHESON *Crown & Anchor* ch. 13 'The better the day, the better the deed, . . . it was only the Pharisees who objected to any necessary work being done on the Sabbath'. [[1] Becket.]

Better die with honour than live with shame.   (H 576)

c. **1532** *Tales* no. 56 Better it is with worshyp to dye than with shame to lyue: albe hit that Demosthenes sayde: he that fleeth cometh agayne to batayle. **1591** ARIOSTO *Orl. Fur.* tr. Harington XVIII. 19. **1599** SHAKES. *Hen. V* IV. v. 23 Let life be short; else shame will be too long. **1666** TORRIANO *It. Prov.* 158, no. 23 (with shame and infamy).

Better end of the string, He has the.

1721 KELLY 157 . . . He has the Advantage in this Cause.

Better eye out than always ache.

(E 226)

[*Cf.* Matt. xviii. 9 And if thine eye offend thee, pluck it out, and cast it from thee.] **1546** HEYWOOD I. viii. C1 Continuall penurie, whyche I muste take, Telth me, better eye out than alwaie ake. **1597** BACON *Col. of G. & E.* 10 Arb. 153 Hereof the common fourmes are, Better eye out, then alwayes ake. **1611** DAVIES no. 396 (Eies).

Better eye sore than all blind.

c. **1300** *Provs. of Hending* 8 Betere is eye sor, then al blynd, quoth Hendyng.

Better fed than taught.   (F 174)

a. **1500** *15c. Sch.-Bk.* ed. W. Nelson 13 Ye may say I lake curtesy, and better fedde than taught. **1530** PALSGRAVE 557b He is better fostred than taught. **1546** HEYWOOD I. x. C3ᵛ But ye be better fed then taught farre awaie. **1580** LYLY *Euph. & his Eng.* ii. 179 Better taught then fedde. **1602** SHAKES. *A.W.* II. ii. 3 I will show myself highly fed and lowly taught. **1631** R. BRATHWAIT *Whimzies* (Halliw.) 119 His duck will not swim over with him: which makes him peremptorily conclude she is better fed than taught. **1641** FERGUSSON no. 464 Of drunkards. . . . He is better fed nor nortured. **1820** SCOTT *Monast.* ch. I Those dependents . . . might have been truly said to be better fed than taught.

Better fill a man's belly than his eye. *Cf.* Eye is bigger than the belly.
                                    (E 261 and G 146)

1530 PALSGRAVE 743a It is better to suffyse your bellye than your eye. **1577** *Art of Angling* D2ᵛ It is better to fill my belly than mine eye. **1590** GREENE *Mourning Garm.* Wks. (Huth) ix. 167 Better fill a man's belly than his eye. **1600** J. LANE *Tom Telltroth's Message* New Sh. S. 130. **1636** CAMDEN 293 (gluttons).

Better fleech[1] a fool (the devil) than fight him.

1820 SCOTT *Monast.* ch. 14. **1827** *Id. Highl. Widow* ch. 2 Those in the Lowland line . . . comforted themselves with the old proverb, that it was better to 'fleech the deil than fight him'. [1 flatter.]

Better give a shilling than lend and lose half a crown.   (S 338)

1642 TORRIANO 75 It is better to give a shilling away, then lend twenty. *c.* **1643** *Oxinden and Peyton Letters 1642–1670* ed. D. Gardiner 16 Rather give a little then leese all. **1659** HOWELL *It. Prov.* 14 Better give a peny then lend twenty. **1732** FULLER no. 895.

Better give than take (receive). (G 119)

[ACTS xx. 35] *c.* **1390** GOWER *Conf. Amantis* v. 7725. **1493** H. PARKER *Dives and Pauper* 2ᵛ It is . . . more blysseful to giue than to take. *c.* **1526** *Dicta Sap.* B2 It is better to gyue than to take, for he that takethe a gyfte of another is bonde to quyte it, so that his lyberte is gone. **1546** HEYWOOD I. v. B2. **1555** *Id. Epig. on Prov. no.* XI Better gyue then take, al say, but so thynke none. **1581** MERBURY *Brief Discourse* 43 Honour dependeth more of the giuer, then of the receiuer. **1611** DAVIES no. 123.

Better give the wool than the sheep.
                                    (W 756)

1573 SANFORD 107ᵛ. **1611** DAVIES no. 76 It's better to giue the Fleece then the sheepe. **1659** TORRIANO no. 11 (It is better to part with). **1670** RAY 30.

Better go away longing than loathing.

1732 FULLER no. 942.

Better go by your enemy's grave than his gate.   (E 143)

1621 ROBINSON 30 (doore). **1639** CLARKE 195.

Better go to bed supperless than to rise in debt.   (B 183)

1654 FULLER *Grand Assizes: Serm.* II. 290 The Italians have a Proverb, It is good to goe to Bed without supping, and to rise in the Morning with [out] owing. **1659** HOWELL *Span. Prov.* 6 'Tis wholesomer to go to bed without a supper, then rise in debt. **1670** RAY 7. **1739** FRANKLIN May Rather go to bed supperless than run in debt for a breakfast.

Better go to heaven in rags than to hell in embroidery.

1732 FULLER no. 898.

Better good afar off than evil at hand.
                                    (G 309)

1623 WOD. 503 Better is a Far off Good, then a Neare hand Evill. **1640** HERBERT no. 267.

Better half, My.   (H 49)

1590 SIDNEY *Arcadia* III. xii. 426 Argalus came out of his sowne, and . . . forcing up (the best he could) his feeble voice, My deare, my deare, my better halfe, (said he) I finde I must now leave thee. **1667** MILTON *Parad. Lost* v. 95 Best image of myself, and dearer half. [**1926** FOWLER *Mod. Eng. Usage* s.v. *Hackneyed Phrases* My better half.]

Better hand loose than in an ill tethering.   (H 66)

a. **1628** CARMICHAELL no. 376 Better be louse nor in ane ill teddering. **1641** FERGUSSON no. 160 Better hand louse nor bound to an ill baikine.[1] **1721** KELLY 59 . . . Better at Liberty, than an ill Service. Better a Bachelor, than married to an ill Wife. [1 tethering stake.]

Better is one *Accipe*, than twice to say, *Dabo tibi.*   (A 14)

[*c.* **1190** *Li Proverbe au vilain* (Tobler) 22 Mieuz ain un 'tien' que dous 'tu l'avras'.] **1584** LYLY *Sappho & Phao* I. iv. 25 A dram of 'giue me', is heauier then an ounce of 'heare me'. **1591** STEPNEY L 3ᵛ. **1620** SHELTON *Quix.* II. lxxi (1908) III. 320 One 'Take it' is more worth than two 'Thou shalt have it'. **1651** HERBERT no. 1079.

Better keep now than seek anon. (K 9)

c. **1425** WAKEFIELD PLAYS 'Killing of Abel' 142 It is better hold that I haue then go from doore to doore and craue. **1659** HOWELL *Brit. Prov.* 16. *Id. Span. Prov.* 6 Better keep then ask.

Better keep the devil at the door than turn him out of the house.

1721 KELLY 61 . . . Better to resist the Temptations of the Evil One, than to master them when they are comply'd with.

Better kiss a knave than to be troubled with him, It is.   (K 121)

1611 GRUTER 179. **1614** CAMDEN 308. **1738** SWIFT Dial. I. E.L. 269 Well, I'd rather give a knave a kiss for once than be troubled with him.

Better known than trusted.   (K 187)

c. **1560** HUTH *Anc. Ballads* (1867) 228 They are not so wel trust as knowne. **1648** HERRICK *Hesper.* No. 830 (Saints.) II. 77 Tap (better known then trusted) as we heare. **1818** SCOTT *Rob Roy* ch. 26 (better kenned).

Better late than never.   (L 85)

c. **1200** *Ancrene Riwle* (Morton) 340 Betere is þo þene no, betere is er. *c.* **1350** *Douce MS.* 52 no. 140 Better is late than neuer. *c.* **1386** CHAUCER *Can. Yeom. T.* l. 1410 Lest ye lese al, for bet than nevere is late. *c.* **1450** *Assembly of Gods* (Triggs) l. 1204 Vyce to forsake ys bettyr late then neuer. **1546** HEYWOOD I. x. C4 But better late then neuer to repent this. **1786** WOLCOT (P. Pindar) *Lousiad* ii. Wks. (1816) I. 158 But, says the proverb, 'better late than never'. **1836** MARRYAT *Midsh. Easy* ch. 9 You made your mind up but late to come to sea. However, . . . 'Better late than never'.

Better learn by your neighbour's skaith than by your own.   (N 114)

c. **1374** CHAUCER *Troilus* Bk. 3 l. 329 For wyse ben by foles harm chastysed. *a.* **1628** CARMICHAELL no. 297 Better learne be your neibours hurt, nor be your awin. **1641** FERGUSSON no. 152.

Better leave than lack.   (L 172)

1546 HEYWOOD I. v. B2 Praisyng this bargayne saith, better leaue then lacke. **1642** FULLER *H. & P. State* IV. xiv (1841) 291 His book is a worthy work (wherein the reader may rather leave than lack). **1721** KELLY 66 . . . Better to abound in material Tools, . . . than be in the least deficient.

Better lose a jest than a friend.   (J 40)

[QUINTILIAN 6. 3. 28 *Potius amicum, quam dictum perdere.*] **1581** GUAZZO i. 72 They had rather forgoe a faythfull friende, then a scoffing speeche. **1589** G. HARVEY *Pierce's Supererogation* (1593) in Wks. (Gros.) ii. 125 It is better to loose a new iest, then an old frend. **1601** JONSON *Poetaster* IV. iii. A . . . satyricall rascall, flie him; he . . . wil sooner lose his best friend then his least iest. **1662** FULLER *London* 221 John Heiwood . . . was most familiar with Sir Thomas More, whom he much resembled in quickness of parts, both under valuing their friend to their jest. **1721** KELLY 283 Rather spill[1] your Jest than spite your Friend. **1816** SCOTT *Antiq.* ch. 43 'Aweel, Sir Arthur,' replied the beggar, who

never hesitated an instant between his friend and his jest, 'mony a wise man sits in a fule's seat, and mony a fule in a wise man's.' [[1] spoil.]

Better lost than found.   (L 454)

1546 HEYWOOD I. x. C4ᵛ A geast as good lost as founde. *c.* **1553** UDALL *Roister Doister* IV. iii. 96 A jewell muche better lost then founde. **1576** PETTIE ii. 68 Knowing him better lost than found, being no better unto you. **1576** U. FULWELL *Ars Adulandi* vii. 36 As good such frendes were lost as found that helpeth not at neede. **1580** LYLY *Euph. & his Eng.* ii. 66 Better lost they are with a lyttle grudge, then found with much griefe. **1591** ARIOSTO *Orl. Fur.* Harington xx. 84 A conquest better lost then wonne. **1599** PORTER *Angry Wom. Abingd.* l. 2287 Hee is gone to seeke my young Mistresse; and I thinke she is better lost then found. **1650** BROME *Jov. Crew* IV (1708) 39 A thing that's better lost than found; a woman! **1670** RAY 184 As good lost as found. **1697** W. POPE *Seth* [Ward] 123 An ill Custom . . . is better lost than retaind. **1818** SCOTT *Ht. Midl.* ch. 40 We hae but tint a Scot of her, and that's a thing better lost than found.

Better luck next time.

1834 MARRYAT *Jacob Faith.* ch. 2 'Better luck next time, missus', replied I, wiping my eyes. **1866** BLACKMORE *Cradock N.* ch. 55 Bob . . . thought, 'Better luck next time'.

Better my hog dirty home than no hog at all.   (H 485)

1664 CODRINGTON 187. **1670** RAY 13.

Better ne'er been born as have his nails on a Sunday shorn, A man had. (N 10)

1596 LODGE *Wit's Miserie* Hunt. Cl. 12 He will not . . . paire his nailes while Munday, to be fortunat in his love. **1695** CONGREVE *Love for L.* Merm. III. iv. 253 Thou'rt . . . as melancholic as if thou hadst . . . pared thy nails on a Sunday. **1846** DENHAM 12. **1848** *Athenæum* 5 Feb. Cut your nails on a Sunday, you cut them for evil, For all the next week you'll be ruled by the devil. **1898** HARE *Shropshire* ch. 1 Sabbatarianism is dying out, yet—'A man had better ne'er be born Than on the Sabbath pare his horn' (cut his nails), is still an adage in vogue.

Better never to begin than never to make an end.   (E 115)

1509 BARCLAY *Ship of Fools* I. 176 Than leue a thynge vnendyd better nat begynne. **1616** DRAXE no. 576. *a.* **1628** CARMICHAELL no. 307 Better never begun nor never endit. **1639** CLARKE 247.

Better one house troubled (filled) than two (spilled[1]).   (H 750)

1586 LA PRIMAUDAYE *French Academy* 497 The wicked and reprobate, of whome that common prouerbe is spoken, that it is better one house be troubled with them than twayne. **1587** GREENE *Penelope's Web* in Wks. Gros. v. 162 Where the old prouerb is fulfild, better one house troubled then two. **1594** LYLY *Mother B.* v. iii. 106.

1670 RAY 51 Better one house fill'd then two spill'd. This we use when we hear of a bad Jack who hath married as bad a Jyll. **1721** KELLY 219 It had been a pity to have spoil'd two Houses with them. Spoken when two ill-natur'd People are married. [¹ spoiled.]

Better ride on an ass that carries me than a horse that throws me. (A 361)

c. **1320** HARLEY LYRICS no. 24 l. 12 Þe is bettere on fote gon þen wycked hors to ryde. *c.* **1594** BACON no. 938 Tomar asino que me lleve y no cavallo que me devinque. **1616** DRAXE no. 2322 Better is an asse that carrieth me, then an horse that layeth me on the ground. **1640** HERBERT no. 258 I had rather ride on an asse that carries me, then a horse that throwes me. **1670** RAY 2 Better ride on an Asse that carries me, then an Asse that throws me. **1908** J. A. SPENDER *Com. of Bagshot* xiii. 129 'Better is an ass that carrieth me than a horse that layeth me on the ground.' It is the greatest folly to seek a position to which your abilities are unequal.

Better rue sit than rue flit. (R 199)

a. **1628** CARMICHAELL no. 306 Better rew sit, nor rew flit. **1721** KELLY 59 . . . Spoken to them that long to change Masters, Servants, Hsuses, Farms and the like. **1818** SCOTT *Ht. Midl.* ch. 20 But ye are of my mind, hinny—better sit and rue, than flit and rue.

Better say, 'here it is', than, 'here it was'. (S 109)

a. **1628** CARMICHAELL no. 310. **1641** FERGUSSON no. 179. **1721** KELLY 65 . . . Better be at some Pains to secure a Thing . . . than to lament the Loss of it when it is gone.

Better side the worse, You make the. (S 432)

1678 RAY 355. *Som.*

Better sit still than rise and fall. (S 491)

c. **1410** *Towneley Plays* E.E.T.S. 29. **1546** HEYWOOD II. v. H2 Flée that temptyng of extremitees all. Folke saie, better syt styll than ryse and fall. **1548** W. PATTEN *Expedn. into Scotland* (T.T. 105) The common proverb that saith, 'It is better to sit still than rise up and fall.' **1618** BRETON *Courtier & Countryman* Wks. Gros. ii. 9 I haue heard my father say, that it is better to sit fast, then to rise and fall. **1623** CAMDEN 266 As good sit still, as rise vp and fall. **1808** SCOTT *Marmion* IV. xxix 'Tis better to sit still and rest, Than rise, perchance to fall.

Better some of a pudding than none of a pie. (P 621)

1670 RAY 135.

Better spare at brim than at bottom. (B 674)

[HESIOD *W. & D.* 367 δειλὴ δ' ἐνὶ πυθμένι φειδώ.] **1523** FITZHERBERT *Husbandry* E.D.S. 100 Thou husbande and huswife, that intend to . . . kepe measure, you must spare at the brynke, and not at the bottom. **1546** HEYWOOD II. v. H1. **1573** TUSSER (1878) 23 Some spareth too late, . . . the foole at the bottom, the wise at the brim. **1681** W. ROBERTSON *Phraseol. Gen.* 1153 Better spare at the brim, than at the bottom, *sera est in fundo parsimonia* [SENECA *Ep.* I. 5]. **1721** KELLY 59 (hold) at . . . Better live sparingly while we have something, than spend lavishly, and afterwards want.

Better spare to have of thine own, than ask of other men. (M 508)

1640 HERBERT no. 266.

Better spared than ill spent. (S 711)

1616 DRAXE no. 2040. **1670** RAY 144.

Better speak truth rudely, than lie covertly. (T 563)

1640 HERBERT no. 767. **1659** N.R. 22.

Better suffer ill than do ill. (I 23)

1615 T. ADAMS *England's Sickness* 44 It is far better to suffer, then to offer wrong. **1639** CLARKE 15 Better to suffer wrong than doe wrong. **1640** HERBERT no. 770.

Better than she is bonny, She is. (B 334)

a. **1641** FERGUSSON MS. no. 1203. **1721** KELLY 298 . . . An additional Praise of a Woman who is commended for her Beauty. **1857** DEAN RAMSAY *Remin.* v (1911) 193 This mode of expressing that the worth of a handsome woman outweighs even her beauty has a very Scottish character: *She's better than she's bonny.* **1883** C. READE *Peril. Secret* ch. 13 'She's the loveliest girl in the county, and better than she's bonny.'

Better the devil (harm) you know than the devil (harm) you don't know. (H 166)

1539 TAVERNER 48 Nota res mala, optima. An euyl thynge knowen is best. It is good kepyng of a shrew that a man knoweth. **1576** PETTIE ii. 132 You had rather keep those whom you know, though with some faults, than take those whom you know not, perchance with more faults. **1586** *Lazarillo* tr. Rowland 73 The olde proverbe: Better is the euill knowne, than the good which is yet to knowe. **1600–1** SHAKES. *H.* III. i. 81 The dread of something after death . . . makes us rather bear those ills we have Than fly to others that we know not of. **1857** TROLLOPE *Barch. Tow.* ch. 26 'Better the d— you know than the d— you don't know', is an old saying, . . . but the bishop had not yet realised the truth of it. **1869** HAZLITT 87 Better the harm I know than that I know not. **1905** B. BURLEIGH *Emp. of East* ch. 24 Neither the Koreans nor the Chinese love overmuch the Japanese. . . . The Chinese seem to prefer the old Russian devil they know, to the new devil they don't.

Better the foot slip than the tongue. (F 575)

1573 SANFORD *Anacarsis* . . . was wont to saye, that it was better to slyde with the feete than with the tong. **1581** GUAZZO i. 122 Remembring alwayes that it is better to slip with the foote, then with the tongue. **1640** HERBERT no. 53. **1734** FRANKLIN Jan.

Better the last smile than the first laughter. *Cf.* Laughs best, etc. (s 560)

1546 HEYWOOD II. ix. L1ᵛ. **1664** CODRINGTON 186. **1670** RAY 24.

Better, the worse, The. (B 333)

1542 UDALL *Apoph. of Erasmus* (1877) 121. **1584** LYLY *Camp.* v. i. 5 The better, the worser. **1587** GREENE Gros. iii. 88. **1625** BACON *Apoph.* Wks. Chandos 384 Diogenes said of a young man that danced daintily, and was much commended, 'The better, the worse'.

Better to be a beggar than a fool, It is.

1599 MINSHEU *Span. Gram.* Lett. to Gray's Inn i2ᵛ *Meglio esser mendicante che ignorante,* Better to bee a beggar then barren of good letters. **1642** TORRIANO 49 It is better to be a beggar than an Ignoramus. **1813** RAY 81.

Better to be a martyr than a confessor, It is. (M 703)

1573 SANFORD 107ᵛ (a Confessoure, than a Martir). **1578** FLORIO *First F.* 32 [as 1573]. **1586** GUAZZO ii. 197 If I had not given credence to that Proverbe, That it is better to bee a Martyr than a Confessour. **1616** DRAXE no. 916.

Better to be beaten than be in bad company. (C 562)

1664 CODRINGTON 188. **1670** RAY 2.

Better to be blind than to see ill. (S 200)

1640 HERBERT no. 126.

Better to be half blind than have both his eyes out, A man were. *Cf.* Better to have one eye, etc., *and* One eye (He that has but), etc. (M 303)

1616 WITHALS 576. **1639** CLARKE 86.

Better to die a beggar than live a beggar. (B 231)

1664 CODRINGTON 188. Better die a beggar, than live a beggar. Remember the golden Mean. **1670** RAY 2. **1732** FULLER no. 888.

Better to go about than to fall into the ditch. (D 387)

1659 HOWELL *Span. Prov.* 5. **1670** RAY I. **1706** STEVENS s.v. Rodear (drown in).

Better to have a dog fawn on you than bite (bark at) you. (D 445)

1609 HARWARD 83 As good have a dogg fawne as barck. **1616** DRAXE no. 533 As good to

haue a dogge fawne vpon him, as barke at him. **1639** CLARKE 219. *a.* **1628** CARMICHAELL no. 301 Better the dog faune, nor bark at me. **1641** FERGUSSON no. 155 Better a dog fan nor bark on you. **1678** RAY 128. **1721** KELLY 64 . . . It is good to have the good Will even of the meanest. **1732** FULLER no. 902.

Better to have one eye than be blind altogether. *Cf.* Better to be half blind. (E 227)

1577 N. BRETON *The Works of a Young Wit* (*Poems* ed. J. Robertson, 29) Better one eye, one legge, and but one hand, then be starke blinde, and cannot sturre, nor stand. **1616** DRAXE no. 1258. **1664** CODRINGTON 187. **1670** RAY 8. **1736** BAILEY *Dict.* s.v. Better, Better one eye than quite blind.

Better to have than wish (hear). (H 214)

c. **1530** *Calisto and Melibea* B2ᵛ Better is possession than the desyryng. **1546** HEYWOOD II. iv. G3. **1639** CLARKE 256 Better to have than to heare of a good thing. **1670** RAY 29.

Better to pay and have little than have much and to be in debt. (L 351)

1642 TORRIANO 50. **1659** HOWELL *It. Prov.* 11. **1732** FULLER no. 2918.

Better to rule than be ruled by the rout. (R 193)

1534 MORE *Dial. of Comfort* E.L. 285 As my mother was wonte to saye, God haue mercy on her soule, it is euer more better to rule than to bee ruled. **1546** HEYWOOD I. v. B2. **1611** GRUTER 175. **1614** CAMDEN 304. **1670** RAY 23.

Better to wear out than to rust out. (W 209)

1557 EDGEWORTH *Serm.* Preface Better it is to shine with laboure, then to rouste with idlenes. **1598** SHAKES. *2 Hen. IV* I. ii. 206 I were better to be eaten to death with a rust than to be scoured to nothing with perpetual motion. **1770** G. WHITEFIELD in SOUTHEY, *Wesley* (1858) ii. 170 I had rather wear out than rust out. **1834** EDGEWORTH *Helen* ch. 29 Helen . . . trembled for her health . . . but she repeated her favourite maxim—'Better to wear out than to rust out'. **1859** SMILES *Self-Help* ch. 11 Still we must labour on . . . 'It is better to wear out than to rust out', said Bishop Cumberland.[1] [¹ *ob.* 1718.]

Better two skaiths[1] (seils) than one sorrow. (S 130)

a. **1628** CARMICHAELL no. 311 Better tua seils, nor ane sorrow. **1641** FERGUSSON no. 185. **1721** KELLY 66 . . . Losses may be repaired, but Sorrow will break the Heart, and ruin the Constitution. [¹ harm, injury.]

Better unborn than unbred (untaught). (U 1)

c. **1275** *Prov. of Alfred* (Skeat) A 449 For betere is child vnboren þenne vnbeten. *c.* **1300** *Prov.*

of Hending no. 4 For betere were child ounboren þen ounbeten. *c.* **1300** BRUNNE *Handl. Synne* l. 4855 Better were the chylde unbore than fayle chastysyng and syththen lore. *c.* **1350** *Douce MS. 52,* no. 106 Better is a chylde unborne þen vnlerned. *c.* **1350** *How the Gd. Wife* l. 161 Betere were child unbore þan techingeles forlore. *a.* **1530** *R. Hill's Commonpl. Bk.* E.E.T.S. 129 Better it is to be unborne than untaught. **1546** HEYWOOD I. x. C3ᵛ Better vnborne than vn-tought, I haue herde saie. **1662** FULLER *Shrops.* 11 Unbred! unborn, is better rather.

Better untaught than ill taught.
(U 18)

1678 RAY 345. **1732** FULLER no. 938.

Better wear out shoes than sheets.

1663 P. STAMPOY 12. **1721** KELLY 67 . . . Sick Men wear Sheets and sound Men Shoes, an Excuse of, or for, Boys who wear many Shoes. **1732** FULLER no. 940.

Better wed over the mixen than over the moor.
(M 917)

a. **1628** CARMICHAELL no. 320 Better to wow over middin, nor ouer mure. **1641** FERGUSSON no. 168 (mosse). **1662** FULLER *Chesh.* 174 Better Wed over the Mixon than over the Moor . . . that is, hard by or at home, Mixon being that heap of Compost which lyeth in the yards of good husbands. . . . The gentry in Cheshire find it more profitable to match within their County, then to bring a Bride out of other Shires. **1818** SCOTT *Ht. Midl.* ch. 31 He might hae dune waur than married me . . .—better wed over the mixen as over the moor, as they say in Yorkshire. **1874** HARDY *Far from Mad. Crowd* ch. 22.

Better were within, If | better would come out.

1721 KELLY 217. **1732** FULLER no. 2672.

Better with a rake than a fork, He is.
(R 23 and 25)

1580 LYLY *Euph. & his Eng.* ii. 16 Tedding[1] that with a forke in one yeare, which was not gathered together with a rake, in twentie. **1616** T. ADAMS *Sacrifice of Thankfulness* 96 Most men now-a-dayes (as it is in the Prouerbe) are better at the Rake, then at the Pitch-forke; readier to pull in, then giue out. *c.* **1640** W. S. *Countrym. Commonw.* 9 Two miserable folkes married together, . . . are good with a rake, but naught with a forke. **1678** RAY 266 He is better with a rake then a fork & vice versâ. **1721** KELLY 129 He comes oftener with the Rake than the Sho'el.[2] Spoken of a poor Friend, whose Business is not to give us, but to get from us. [¹ spreading newly cut grass to dry. ² shovel.]

Better, (*adv.*), *see also* Asking, (The b. (none the b.) for your); Bad for the b., (To change the); Bare arse than a furred hood, (B. a); Common a good thing is the b. (The more); Crust is b. than no bread; Do well than to say well, (It is b. to); No b. than she should be; See and approve the b. course; Seldom comes a b.; Severity is b. than

gentleness, (Sometimes); Somewhat is b. than nothing; Sooner the b.; Uses me b. than he is wont (He that).

Betters, (*noun*), *see* Bold with your b.

Betty Martin, *see* All my eye.

Between the cradle and the grave.

1658 W. SANDERSON *A Compleat History of the Life and Raigne of King Charles from his Cradle to his Grave.* [Title]. *c.* **1707** PRIOR (Cambridge) i. 95 Studious the busy moments to deceive That fleet between the cradle and the grave. **1709** STEELE *Tatler* no. 52, ¶ 4 A modest fellow never has a doubt from his cradle to his grave. **1726** DYER *Grongar Hill* A little rule, a little sway, A sunbeam in a winter's day, Is all the proud and mighty have Between the cradle and the grave.

Between two stools one goes (falls) to the ground.
(S 900)

[SENECA *Controversia* 3. 189 *Duabus sellis sedit.* *c.* **1026** EGBERT V. LUTTICH *Fecunda Ratis* (Voigt) l. 175 *Labitur enitens sellis herere duabus. c.* **1190** *Li Proverbe au vilain* (Tobler) 84 no. 202 *Entre dous seles chiet cus a terre.*] *c.* **1390** GOWER *Conf. Amantis* II. 22 Thou farst as he betwen tuo stoles That wolde sitte and goth to grounde. *a.* **1530** *R. Hill's Commonpl. Bk.* E.E.T.S. 129 Betwen two stolis, the ars goth to grwnd. **1546** HEYWOOD I. iii. A4 While betwene two stoles, my taile go to grounde. *c.* **1604** T. HEYWOOD *Wise W. of Hogs.* v. iv Here's even the proverb verified—between two stools, the tail goes to ground. **1730** FIELDING *Tom Thumb* II. x While the two stools her sittingpart confound, Between 'em both fall squat upon the ground. **1857** TROLLOPE *Barch. Tow.* ch. 20 Truly he had fallen between two stools.

Between you and me and the bedpost.

[= in confidence.] **1805** J. DAVIS *The Post-Captain* xxvi (the post). **1839** DICKENS *N. Nickleby* ch. 10 And between you and me and the post, sir, it will be a very nice portrait too. **1875** BROWNING *Inn Album* i. A secret's safe between you and me and the gatepost. **1882** BLACKMORE *Christowell* ch. 13 Between you and me and the bed-post, Short—as the old ladies say—I don't want Jack to have her.

Between, *see also under significant words following.*

Bewails himself has the cure in his hands, He that.
(C 920)

1640 HERBERT no. 441.

Bewail, *see also* Carrion crows b. dead sheep; Death in your house.

Beware beginnings.
(B 263)

1611 COTGRAVE s.v. Pain In the beginning of a cause are faults the soonest made. **1639** CLARKE 259.

Beware (He is happy that can) by other men's harms, It is good to. *Cf.* Learn at other men's costs.　　(M 612 and 615)

[PLAUTUS *Merc.* 893 Feliciter is sapit qui periculo alieno sapit.]　*c.* **1436** *Libell of Engl. Policy* l. 480 Beware . . . of other mennys perylle.　*c.* **1470** *Harl. MS. 3362* f. 1a (Förster) in *Anglia* 42. 200 He ys an happy man, þat ys war be anothyr mannys dedys. Est felix culpa quem castigat aliena.　*c.* **1526** *Dicta Sap.* B 4ᵛ By the errours of other, he that ys wyse, lerneth to take hede and beware.　*a.* **1536** HILL 36, 132 He is wysse, that can beware by an other manys harme. **1539** TAVERNER 3 He is happy, whom other mens perilles maketh ware.　**1546** HEYWOOD I. xi. E2ᵛ. **1567** W. LILY *Short Introd. to Gram.* C5ᵛ Happy is he, whom other mens harms do make to beware. **1578** *Mirr. for Mag.* (Campbell 441) Happie are they whome other mens harmes do make to be ware. **1614** CAMDEN 308. **1706** STEVENS s.v. Varon Happy the Man who takes warning by others, and not by himself.

Beware of a silent dog (man) and still water.　　(M 78)

[L. *Cave tibi a cane muto et aquâ silenti.*] **1585** ROBSON *Choice Change* N 2 A still fellow, for he commonly is subtill and crafty. A still water which is deepe, and therefore dangerous.　**1706** STEVENS s.v. Persona Remove your Dwelling at a distance from a silent Person: They who talk least, generally observe most; and therefore take heed of them. **1750** J. WESLEY *Lett.* iii. 34 I always find there is most hazard in sailing upon smooth water.

Beware of after-claps.　　(A 57)

c. **1400** *Canticum Creat.* l. 471 For drede of after clap.　*c.* **1412** HOCCLEVE *Carpenter* l. 20 I so sore ay dreede an aftir clap.　**1475** *Loud whal.* l. 77 But ȝet be war of after clappys. **1532** SIR T. MORE *To them that trusteth in Fortune* But for all that beware. . . .　**1535** LATIMER *Serm.* P.S. 29 For he can give us an after-clap when we least ween; that is, suddenly return unawares to us, and then he giveth us an after-clap that over-throweth us.　**1548** HALL *Chron.* (1809, 90) The Frenchmen . . . paled their lodgynges for feare of afterclappes. **1550** HEYWOOD *100 Epigrams* no. 6 Touche not to muche, for feare of after claps. **1559** *Mirr. for Mag.* 'Henry VI' (Campbell, 213). **1639** FULLER *Holy War* v. ii (1651) 231 Some therefore in this matter know little, and dare speak less, for fear of after claps.

Beware of breed.　　(B 646)

1670 RAY 65.　**1678** *Id.* 105 Beware of breed, *Chesh.*, i.e. an ill breed.　**1772** FLETCHER OF MADELEY *Wks.* ii. 130 Take care of the breed. **1917** BRIDGE 31 Beware of breed; i.e. *bad* breed. A casual allusion to this proverb helped to lose a Cheshire candidate his seat at the General Election of 1857.

Beware of the man of one book.　　(W 595)

[L. *Cave ab homine unius libri.*]　**1642** TORRIANO 43–4 From one that reads but one book . . . good Lord deliver us.　**1651** HERBERT no. 1146 Wo be to him that reads but one book.　*a.* **1843**

SOUTHEY *Doctor* xlix 113 Upon both subjects he was *homo unius libri*; such a man is proverbially formidable at his own weapon.　**1903** J. MCCARTHY *Port. of Sixties* 152 'I fear the man of one book' is a classic proverb.

Beware, *see also* Buyer b.; Had I wist (B. of); Haldon has a hat, (When) let Kenton b. of a skatt.

Bewitched, *see* Water b.

Beyond, *see* Aim, to be out of (b.) one's; Every man a little b. himself a fool.

Bias again, He turns to his old.
　　　　　　　　　　　　(B 338)

1573 GASCOIGNE *Dan B. of Bath* i. 134 She . . . rangde againe, and to hir byas fell.　**1576** LEMNIUS *Touchstone of Complexions* tr. T. Newton 58 But now againe to fal into my byas, and leauing this digression to retourne to my purpose. **1601** SHAKES. *T.N.* V. i. 252 But nature to her bias drew in that.　**1616** DRAXE no. 687.

Bias, To run against the.　　(B 339)

c. **1580** SIDNEY *Apology* (G. G. Smith *Eliz. Crit. Essays* i. 200) Wee . . . laugh sometimes to finde a matter quite mistaken and goe downe the hill agaynst the bias. **1594–5** SHAKES. *L.L.L.* IV. ii. 104 Study his bias leaves and makes his book thine eyes.　**1594–8** *Id. T.S.* IV. v. 24 Thus the bowl should run, And not unluckily against the bias.　**1596** *Id. Rich. II* III. iv. 5 My fortune runs against the bias.　[**1594–1600**] **1615** T. HEYWOOD *Four Prentices* ii. 181 Fie, fie, you run quite from the byas cleane.　**1600** DEKKER *Shoem. Hol.* II. iii. 84 Al this is from the bias.　**1603** MONTAIGNE (Florio) III. ix. 79. **1639** CLARKE 224.　**1695** RAVENSCROFT 32 These Carrions have put me Quite out of my Byass.

Bible is the religion of Protestants, The.

1637 CHILLINGWORTH *Relig. of Protest.* vi (1846) 463 The BIBLE, I say, the BIBLE only, is the religion of protestants! **1921** *Times Lit. Sup.* 19 Aug. 526 The Bible and the Bible only, . . . is, according to a well-known saying, the religion of Protestants.

Bible, *see also* Congleton rare sold the B.; Peerage is Englishman's B.

Bid(s, den), *see* Breaks his word. (A man that) b. others be false to him; Do as you're b.; Hold up your head, for there is money b. for you; Servant must . . . go when you b. him (A good).

Bides as fast as a cat bound to a saucer, He.　　(C 146)

1641 FERGUSSON no. 410 (bound with).

Bide(s), *see also* Iron shoes, (He should wear) that b. his neighbour's dead; Weel b., weel betides; Worth no weal that can b. no woe.

Big(-ger) *see* God make me great and b., . . .; Looks as b. as if eaten bull beef; Miller's thumb.

(No b. than a); Too b. for one's boots; Two b. will not go in one bag.

Bigger the man, the better the mark, The.

1894 NORTHALL *Folk-phrases* E.D.S. 24 The bigger the man, the better the mark, i.e. to aim, or strike at in combat.

Bilberry, *see* Nineteen bits of a b.

Bill under wing.   (B 348)

[= quiet, hidden, like a bird's bill under its wing.] *c.* **1390** GOWER *Conf. Amantis* v. l. 6526 What he may get of his michinge [i.e. thieving], It is al bile under the winge. *c.* **1425** *Seven Sages* Percy Soc. l. 2196. The byrde . . . bylle undyr wynge layede. *a.* **1548** HALL *Chron., Hen. VI,* 174 After this . . . the duke of Yorke . . . thought it mete neither lenger to dissimule, nor farther to kepe his bill vnder wyng.

Billesdon, *see* In and out, like B.

Billet, *see* Bullet has its b., (Every).

Billingsgate for a box on the ear, You shall have as much favour at.   (F 128)

1576 U. FULWELL *Ars adulandi* ¶4ᵛ A man may buy as much loue at Belinsgate for a box on the eare. **1659** HOWELL *Eng. Prov.* 15b. **1670** RAY 215.

Billingsgate language.   (B 350)

1594 *King Leir* III. v. 77 As bad a tongue . . . as any oyster-wife at Billingsgate. **1654** GAYTON *Pleas. Notes Don Quix.* II. vi. 60 Most bitter Billingsgate Rhetorick. **1676** WYCHERLEY *Pl. Dealer* III. i (1678) 35 With sharp invectives—*Wid.* (Alias Belin'sgate). **1848** THACKERAY *Vanity F.* ch. 13 Mr. Osborne . . . cursed Billingsgate with an emphasis quite worthy of the place.

Bills, *see* Bows and b.

Bind the sack before it be full.   (S 2)

1580 MUNDAY *Zelauto* H2ᵛ Shut vp the sacke when it is but halfe full. **1584** WITHALS G4 Oft haue I founde a sack tied vp that was not ful. **1611** COTGRAVE s.v. Sac A sacke before tis full is well ynough tyed vp; men while they are kept low are easily kept in. **1640** HERBERT no. 842. **1641** FERGUSSON no. 174 Bind the seck or it be full. **1902–4** LEAN III. 433 Bind the sack ere it be full.—Ferg. Do not tax any person or thing to the utmost.

Bind(s), *see also* Benefits b.; Fast (safe, sure) b., fast find; Hold nor to b. (Neither to); Reason b. the man; Willows are weak yet they b.; Words b. men.

Binder, *see* Bread is a b.

Birch, *see* Bare as the b. at Yule even.

Birchen twigs break no ribs.   (T 633)

1583 G. BABINGTON *Exposn. of the Commandments* 223 A small twigge will not kill the tenderest

Prince, Lord or Ladie in the worlde. **1639** CLARKE 75. **1670** RAY 61. **1732** FULLER no. 6380.

Bird caught in lime strives, The more the | the faster he sticks.   (B 380)

1557 EDGEWORTH *Sermons* 3Q1ᵛ Byrdes that bee meshede in a nette, canne not gette out when they woulde wythout helpe, but the more they stryue, the sorer they be holden in the nette. **1572** T. WILSON *Discourse upon Usury* ed. Tawney 227. **1584** WITHALS E6 The more that the little birdes doe striue to rid themselues oute of the lime, the more they intangle themselues therein. **1600–1** SHAKES. *H.* III. iii. 68 O limed soul, that, struggling to be free, Art more engag'd! **1666** TORRIANO *It. Prov.* 296, no. 26 The bird, the more he flutters, the more he intangles himself.

Bird in my bosom, I have saved (kept) the.   (B 386)

1548 HALL 1809 ed. 260 [Of Sir Ralph Percy slain at Hedgeley Moor in 1462] Saiyng, when he was diyng: I haue saued the birde in my bosome: meanyng that he had kept, both his promise and othe. **1662** FULLER Leics. 141 Burdet [in 1477] patiently and chearfully took his Death, affirming he had a Bird in his breast (his own Innocency) that sung comfort unto him. **1820** SCOTT *Abbot* ch. 8 Thou hast kept well . . . the bird in thy bosom. . . . Thou hast kept thy secret and mine own amongst thine enemies. *Note.* An expression used by Sir Ralph Percy, slain in the battle of Hedgely-moor in 1464, to express his having preserved unstained his fidelity to the House of Lancaster. **1902** *Spectator* 24 May Queen Christina may say . . . that she 'has kept the bird in her bosom', an indefeasible loyalty to her task.

Bird in the hand is worth two in the bush, A.   (B 363)

[*c.* **1400** in J. WERNER *Lat. Sprichwörter* . . . *des Mittelalters* (1912) 70 *Plus valet in manibus avis unica fronde duabus.*] *c.* **1450** CAPG. *St. Kath.* 2. 250 It is more sekyr a byrd in your fest, than to haue three in the sky aboue. *c.* **1470** *Harl. MS. 3362,* f. 4a Betyr ys a byrd in þe hond þan tweye in þe wode. *a.* **1530** R. *Hill's Commonpl. Bk.* E.E.T.S. 128 A birde in hond is better than thre in the wode. **1546** HEYWOOD I. xi. D4 Better one byrde in hande than ten in the wood. **1590** LODGE *Rosalynde* (Greg 78) (woorth two in the wood). **1620** SHELTON *Quix.* II. vii (1908) II. 230 A bird in the hand is worth two in the bush. **1678** BUNYAN *Pilgr.* I (1877) 26 That proverb, A bird in the hand is worth two in the bush, is of more authority with them than are all . . . testimonies of the good of the world to come. **1678** RAY *Adag. Hebr.* 404 One bird in the net is better then an hundred flying. **1894** LD. AVEBURY *Use of Life* xv (1904) 92 A bird in the hand is worth two in the bush; but . . . the bird in the bush may never be in the cage, while the future . . . is sure to come.

Bird is known by his note, the man by his words, The.   (B 365)

1579 GOSSON *Sch. Abuse* 51 The Bell is knowen by his sounde, the Byrde by her voyce, the Lyon by his rore, the Tree by the fruite, a man by his woorkes [*sic*]. **1642** TORRIANO 6 The bird is known by his note, and by speech a mans headpiece. **1659** HOWELL *It. Prov.* 10. **1732** FULLER no. 12.

Bird loves her nest, The. (B 385)

c. **1594** BACON no. 1587 A tous oiseaux leurs nids sont beaux. **1611** COTGRAVE s.v. Nid Euerie bird likes his owne neast. **1640** HERBERT no. 75. **1659** HOWELL *Span. Prov.* 9.

Bird loves to hear himself sing, Each. (B 367)

1659 HOWELL *Brit. Prov.* 2 Each bird is well pleased with his own voice.

Bird must flighter[1] that flies with one wing, The.

1721 KELLY 308 . . . Spoken by them who have Interest only in one side of the House. **1824** SUSAN FERRIER *Inheritance* III. xxxii 'The bird maun flichter that flees wi' ae wing'—but ye's haud up your head yet in spite o' them a'. **1914** K. F. PURDON *Folk of Furry F.* ch. 2 He held out a shilling to Hughie. 'A bird never yet flew upon the one wing, Mr. Heffernan!' said Hughie, that was looking to get another shilling. [[1] flutter.]

Bird of the same nest (brood, egg, feather), A. (B 365a and E 81)

1553 N. UDALL *Roister D.* l. 192 (nest). **1559** T. BECON *Displ. of Popish Mass* (*Prayers* P.S. 274) Chickens of the pope's own brood. **1572** *Admonition to Parliament* (Greene and Douglas, *Puritan Manifestoes*, 32) (fether). **1579** S. GOSSON *Sch. of Abuse* Arber 27 (broode). **1579** LOARTE *Exercise of a Christ. Life* tr. Brinkley Ded. (of your owne broode). **1588** E. BULKELEY *An Answer* 49 Master Harpsfield a bird of the same nest. *c.* **1594** BACON no. 765 He came of an egge. **1602** SHAKES. *A.W.* IV. iii. 265 What's he?—E'en a crow o' th' same nest. *a.* **1628** CARMICHAELL no. 91 (foule). **1639** CLARKE 14 A feather of the same wing.

Bird on briar (bough), As merry (light) as. (B 359)

c. **1460** *Wisdom* l. 626, 56 As mery as the byrde on bow. *a.* **1500** *Selection of Carols* ed. R. Greene 63 Man, be merie as bryd on berie. **1554** HILARIE *Resur. Mass* B8 As gladde as byrdes vpon bryers. **1595** SHAKES. *M.N.D.* V. i. 383 As light as bird from brier. **1659** HOWELL *Br. Prov.* 20 As a bird on the bough.

Bird such nest (egg), Such. (B 381)

1584 WITHALS A5[v] The Lapwing being a foule birde maketh her selfe a fowle neast. **1591** STEPNEY 156 Of a good egge comes a good bird. **1601** CHETTLE & MUNDAY *Death of Robert Earl of Huntington* Hazl.-Dods. viii. 263 Look for a good egg, he was a good bird. **1611** COTGRAVE s.v. Nid. **1666** TORRIANO *It. Prov.* 296 no. 35 As the bird, such is the egg.

Bird take back its own feathers, If every | he'll (you'll) be naked. (B 375)

1579–80 LODGE *Def. Poetry* Shaks. Soc. 3 Though men . . . polish their writings with others

sentences, yet the simple truth will . . . bestowing every feather in the body of the right M. turn out the naked dissembler into his own coat. **1605–8** SHAKES. *T.Ath.* II. i. 30 When every feather sticks in his own wing, Lord Timon will be left a naked gull. **1629** T. ADAMS *Serm.* (1861–2) i. 203 Some he steals from the Jew, . . . much from idolatry, . . . If every bird should fetch her own feathers, you should have a naked Pope. **1732** FULLER no. 2675.

Bird to pick out his own eyes, He hath brought up a. (B 372)

1590 LODGE *Rosalynde* Wks. (1883) I. 33 In liking Rosalynde thou hatchest vp a bird to pecke out thine owne eyes. **1662** FULLER Lancs. 111 I know you have hatched up some Chickens that now seek to pick out your eyes. **1732** FULLER no. 1864.

Bird told me, A (little). (B 374)

1546 HEYWOOD II. v. H3 I did lately heere . . . by one byrd that in myne eare was late chauntyng. **1583** MELBANCKE F3[v] I had a litle bird, that brought me newes of it. **1598** SHAKES. *2 Hen. IV* V. v. 108 I heard a bird so sing. **1611** BIBLE *Eccles.* x. 20 A bird of the air shall carry the voice and that which hath wings shall tell the matter. **1822** SCOTT *Nigel* ch. 6 Stone walls have ears, and a bird of the air shall carry the matter. **1833** MARRYAT *Peter Simple* ch. 39 (A little bird).

Birds of a feather flock together. (B 393)

1545 W. TURNER *Rescuing of the Romish Fox* B 8 Byrdes of on kynde and color flok and flye allwayes to gether. **1577** STANYHURST in Hollinshed *Chron. Ireland* (1587, 89a) These foure, as birds of one feather, were supposed to be open enimies to the house of Kildare. **1578** WHETSTONE *Promos and Cass.* C1[v] Byrds of a feather, best flye together. **1591** SHAKES. *3 Hen. VI* II. i. 170 Clifford and the haught Northumberland, And of their feather many more proud birds. *Ibid.* III. iii. 161 Both of you are birds of selfsame feather. **1613** WITHER *Abuses* 72 But as the proverb saith, Birds of a feather Will always use to flock and feed together. **1660** W. SECKER *Nonsuch Prof.* ii (1891) 93 We say, 'That birds of a feather will flock together'. To be too intimate with sinners is to intimate that we are sinners. **1680** BUNYAN *Mr. Badman* iv. Wks. (Offor) III. 615 They were birds of a feather, . . . they were so well met for wickedness. **1828** LYTTON *Pelham* ch. 79 It is literally true in the systematised roguery of London, that 'birds of a feather flock together'.

Birds of this year in last year's nests, There are no. (B 399)

1620 SHELTON *Quix.* II. lxxiv (1908) III. 338 I pray you go not on so fast, since that in the nests of the last year there are no birds of this year. Whilom I was a fool, but now I am wise. **1906** A. T. QUILLER-COUCH *From Cornish W.* 5 With what heart Don Quixote . . . in that saddest of all last chapters, bade his friends look not for this year's birds in last year's nests. **1926** *Times* 19 Jan. 15/6 Things may not be as they were; 'there are no birds in last year's nest', and there may be no fish in the old rivers.

Birds once snared (limed) fear all bushes. *Cf.* Old fox is not easily snared.
(B 394)

c. **1579** MERBURY *Marr. Wit and Wisdom* (Halliwell 1846) viii. 55 The silly bird once caught in net, If she ascape aliue, Will come no more so ny the snare, Her fredome to depriue. **1591** SHAKES. *3 Hen. VI* V. vi. 13 The bird that hath been limed in a bush With trembling wings misdoubteth every bush. [**1592**] **1596** *Edward III* IV. iii. 21 What bird that hath escapt the fowlers gin, Will not beware how shees insnared againe? **1593–4** SHAKES. *Luc.* l. 88 Birds never lim'd no secret bushes fear.

Birds were flown, The.   (B 364)

1546 HEYWOOD I. xii. F1 Er the next daie the byrds were flowne eche one, To séke seruyce. **1575** GASCOIGNE *Posies* i 94 The Byrdes were flowen before I found the nest. **1855** C. KINGSLEY *Westward Ho!* ch. 5 The birds are flown, . . . we can do nothing till we raise the hue and cry tomorrow.

Bird(s), *see also* Addled egg as idle b. (As good be); Beats the bush (One), another catches b.; Bitter b. (Thou art), said raven to starling; Candlemas (As long as b. sings before); Catch b. to-morrow (We shall); Catch old b. with chaff; Child's b. and knave's wife; Crow thinks own b. fairest; Destroy the nests, b. fly away; Early b. catches worm; Feather in hand better than b. in air; Forbear not sowing because of b.; Free as b. in air; Fright a b. not the way to catch; Gape long enough ere b. fall in mouth; God builds nest of blind b.; Good egg nor b. (Neither) Hit the b. in the eye, (To); John Grey's b.; Ill b. that bewrays own n.; Ill b. that pecks out dam's eyes; In for a b.; Kill two b. with one stone; Little b. little nest; Little b. that can sing and won't; March the b. begin; May b. aye cheeping; Rough net not best catcher of b.; St. Valentine . . . all b. in couples; Small b. must have meat. *See also* Ill bird.

Birth follows the belly, The.

1612–15 BP. HALL *Contempl.* x. vi (1825) I. 284 The mother, as she is more tender over her son, . . . can work most upon his inclination. Whence . . . in the history of the Israelitish Kings, the mother's name is commonly noted; and, as civilly, so also morally, the birth follows the belly. **1616** T. ADAMS *The Soldier's Honour* 30 *Partus sequitur ventrem.*

Birth is much, but breeding is more.
(B 402)

1613 J. STEPHENS *Cynthia's Revenge* E1ᵛ Birth may do much, loue makes the low inherit. **1639** CLARKE 103. **1732** FULLER no. 983.

Birth, *see also* Great b. is a poor dish; Pope by voice, king by b.

Birthright, *see* Sell one's b.

Biscuit, *see* Dry as a b.; Weevil in a b.

Bishop has blessed it, The.   (B 405)

1528 TYNDALE *Obed. Chrn. Man* P.S. 304 When a thing speedeth not well, we borrow speech, and say, 'The bishop hath blessed it'; because that nothing speedeth well that they meddle withal.

Bishop has put (set) his foot in it, The.
(B 406)

1528 TYNDALE *Obed. Chrn. Man* P.S. 304 If the porridge be burned too, or the meat over roasted, we say, 'The bishop hath put his foot in the pot', or, 'The bishop hath played the cook'; because the bishops burn whom they lust, and whosoever displeaseth them. **1573** TUSSER 49 E.D.S. 108 Blesse Cisley (good mistris) that Bishop doth ban for burning the milke of hir cheese to the pan. **1641** MILTON *Animad. Rem. Def. Smect.* Prose Wks. (1904) III. 91 I doubt not but they will say, the bishop's foot hath been in your book, for I am sure it is quite spoiled by this just confutation. **1738** SWIFT *Dial.* I. E.L. 262 The cream is burnt too.—Why, madam, the bishop has set his foot in it. **1790** GROSE *Provincial Glossary* s.v. Bishop . . . (set), a saying in the North, used for milk that is burnt-to in boiling. Formerly, in days of superstition whenever a bishop passed through a town or village, all the inhabitants ran out in order to receive his blessing; this frequently caused the milk on the fire to be left till burnt to the vessel, and gave origin to the above allusion. **1917** BRIDGE 112 The Bishop has put his foot in it. Said of burnt milk. '*The milk is bishopped*', is a common phrase in Cheshire.

Bishop, *see also* Devil busy b. in own diocese; No b. no king; Once a b. always a b.; Weel's him . . . that has b. in his kin.

Bit and a knock (bob, buffet), as men feed apes, A.   (B 416 and 420)

1576 GASCOIGNE *Steel Glass* ii. 172 When Fencers fees, are like to apes rewards, A peece of breade, and therwithal a bobbe. **1590** R. HARVEY *Plain Perceval* A 3 As men feed Apes: with a bit and a boxe on the eare. **1623** PAINTER C1 Some are fed like Apes with bits and knockes. **1639** *Clarke* 240 A bit and a knock. **1640** BRAITHWAITE *Art Asleep Husb.* 129 I should bee much better for a bit and a buffet with't. *a.* **1641** FERGUSSON MS. no. 570 He giues him the bit and the buffet with it. **1652** W. LEACH *First, a bitt and a knock for under-sheriffs.* [Title.] **1678** RAY 226. **1706** STEVENS s.v. Pan (as 1639). **1819** SCOTT *Bride Lam.* ch. 21 A fellow, whom he could either laugh with, or laugh at, . . . who would take, according to Scottish phrase, 'the bit and the buffet'.

Bit draws down another, One.   (B 419)

1639 CLARKE 148. **1659** HOWELL *Fr. Prov.* 12 (drawes on).

Bit that one eats no friend makes, The.
(B 415)

1640 HERBERT no. 142. **1706** STEVENS s.v. Bocado.

Bit what the bread is, You may see by
a. *Cf.* Sack is known by the sample.
(B 421)
1616 DRAXE no. 857 (By a little bit, a man may
see). **1639** CLARKE 64.

Bit(s), *see also* Bleating sheep loses her b.;
Nurses put one b. in child's mouth, two in own;
Shoulder of veal . . . good b. (In a); Take the b.
in the teeth; Two b. of a cherry.

Bitch, *see* God loves (Whom), his b. brings forth
pigs; Hasty b. brings forth blind whelps.

Bite and whine. (B 427)
1546 HEYWOOD II. vii. I2 She can and dothe
here, bothe bite and whine. *c.* **1594** BACON no.
668. **1596** WARNER *Albion's Eng.* XII. 76, X 3
Well, bite and whine (quoth he) who trusts a
Woman is saru'd.

Bite, If you cannot | never show your
teeth. (T 425)
1615 20 May J. CHAMBERLAIN Yt were to no
purpose to shew our teeth unles we could bite.
1639 FULLER *Holy War* II. viii (1651) 54 Bernard,
. . . set his title on foot, and then quietly let it
fall to the ground, as counting it no policie to
shew his teeth where he durst not bite. **1670**
RAY 63. **1738** SWIFT *Dial.* III. E.L. 322 I'm sure
you show your teeth when you can't bite. **1906**
SIR I. HAMILTON *Staff Off. Scrap.-Bk.* 77 The
bark-without-preparing-to-bite system of drift-
ing towards war which prevails in England and
America.

Bite one's thumbs, To. (T 273)
[An indication of anger or vexation.] **1573**
GASCOIGNE *Dulce Bellum* i. 173. **1573** *Satir.
Poems Reform.* xlii. 266 The Clerk was like to
byte his thowmis. *c.* **1595** SHAKES. *R.J.* I. i. 43
Do you bite your thumb at us, sir?—I do bite
my thumb, sir. **1608** DEKKER *Dead Term* D4ᵛ
What shouldering, what Justling, what Jeering,
what byting of Thumbs to beget quarrels. **1638**
T. RANDOLPH *Muses' Looking Glass* III. v. 2 Dags
and Pistolls! To bite his thumb at me! **1670**
G. H. *Hist. Cardinals* II. ii. 158 The Spaniards
were nettled, and bit their thumbs . . . in private.

Bite out of your own hip (arm), You
take a.
1721 KELLY 367 . . . What you say reflects upon
your self, or Family. **1732** FULLER no. 5925
You have taken a Bite out of your own Arm.

Bite the hand that feeds you, To.
1711 Ap. 10 ADDISON *Spectator* ed. D. Bond i no.
35 148 He is wonderfully unlucky, insomuch
that he will bite the Hand that feeds him.

Bite upon the bridle (bit), To. (B 670)
[= to be impatient of restraint.] *c.* **1390** GOWER
Conf. Amantis vi. l. 929 As who seith, upon the
bridel I chiewe, so that al is ydel As in effect the
fode I have. [*c.* 1515] **1530** BARCLAY *Eclog.* II.

l. 822 These courtiers . . . Smelling those dishes
they bite vpon the bridle. **1538** J. BALE *Three
Laws* A7ᵛ (gnaw upon the bit). **1549** LATIMER
7th Serm. bef. Edw. VI P.S. 230 His Father gave
him looking on, and suffered him to bite upon
the bridle awhile. **1579** CALVIN *Four Sermons*
tr. J. Field E1 We are heere . . . put in minde,
not to gnawe our bitte, to lament and grudge at
our estate. **1600** ABP. ABBOT *Exp. Johah* 342
Bite upon the bridle, that . . . he may be wiser
afterward. **1612** CHAPMAN *Epicede* 172 The
still-feasted arts, which now on bridles bite.
1709 STEELE *Tatler* No. 25 'Make the rogue bite
upon the bridle', said I; 'pay none of his bills'.

Biter bit, The. (B 429)
1693 D'URFEY *Richmond Heiress* Epil. Once in an
age the biter should be bit. **1710** WARD *Nuptial
Dial.* II. 179 I think she merits equal Praise That
has the Wit to bite the Biter. **1809** MALKIN *Gil
Blas* I. viii I would advise you . . . not to set
your wit a second time against the Church: the
biter may be bit. **1863** C. READE *Hard Cash* ch. 8
He could not sell all the bad paper he had
accumulated for a temporary purpose: the panic
came too swiftly. . . . The biter was bit: the fox
. . . was caught. **1888** MRS. OLIPHANT *Second
Son* ch. 44 They should also hear how the tables
had been turned upon him, how the biter had
been bit.

Biters, *see* Barkers are no b., (Great).

Bites on every weed must needs light
on poison, He that. (W 237)
1597 BODENHAM *Wit's Commonw.* 155. **1639**
CLARKE 211. **1670** RAY 63. **1710** PALMER 24.

Bites the mare by the thumb, This.
(M 654)
1546 HEYWOOD II. vi. I2 This byteth the mare by
the thumbe, as they sey. **1548** J. HALES *Discourse of the Common Weal* ed. Lamond I. ii,
cited C. Read *Mr. Sec. Cecil* 50. This was what
bit the mare by the thumb. **1611** DAVIES no. 82.

Biting and scratching is Scots folk's
wooing. (B 430)
a. **1628** CARMICHAELL no. 381 Byting and scarting is Scots folks wowing. **1641** FERGUSSON no.
204. **1832** HENDERSON 87 (Scarting and nipping).

Bitten by a serpent, He that has been |
is afraid of a rope. (S 227)
1678 RAY *Adag. Hebr.* 407. **1853** TRENCH iii.
71 The Jewish Rabbis had said long before:
One bitten by a serpent, is afraid of a rope's end;
even . . . a resemblance to a serpent . . . shall now
inspire him with terror.

Bitten, Though he be | he's not all
eaten. (B 428)
1639 CLARKE 32.

Bite(s) (noun), *see also* Bark is worse than his b.;
Dog allowed first b., (Every); Two b. of a cherry.

Bite(s), bit (*verb*), *see also* Bear (If it were a), it would b. you; Biter b.; Covers me . . . and b. me with his bill; Cur will b. before bark; Dead men don't b.; Dog to b. him (A man may cause own); Dog will bark ere he b.; Dogs b., (In every country); Dogs that bark at a distance b. not at hand; Drink of the burn when cannot b. of brae; Fish that will not b., (Rare to find); Fools b. one another; Look on the wall and it will not b.; Maggot b.; Mastiff be gentle (Though), b. him not; Never b. unless teeth meet; Once b. twice shy; Trick for trick, . . . when she b. him upon the back and he her upon the buttock.

Biting, *see also* Scratching and b. (By) cats and dogs come together.

Bitter as gall.   (G 11)

c. 1305 *Polit. Songs John to Edw. II* ed. Wright Camden Soc. 193 Ther hi habbeth dronke bittrere then the galle. [*c.* 1525–9] 1561 *Godly Qu. Hester* l. 1174 More bytter than gall. 1560 T. BECON *Catechism* P.S. 343. 1600 DEKKER *Old Fort.* IV. i. 80. 1670 RAY 203.

Bitter bird, Thou art a | said the raven to the starling.   (B 382)

1678 RAY 195.

Bitter in his mouth, Who has | spits not all sweet.   (B 432)

1640 HERBERT no. 422. 1732 FULLER no. 2387 (breast).

Bitter pills may have blessed effects.
                                                   (P 327)

c. 1374 CHAUCER *Troilus* Bk. 3, l. 1212 O! soth is seyd, that heled for to he As of a fevre or other gret syknesse, Men moste drynke, as men may often see, Ful bittre drynke. 1579 LYLY *Euph.* i. 253 The medicine, the more bitter it is, the more better it is in working. 1594 SHAKES. *T.G.V.* II. iv. 145 When I was sick you gave me bitter pills. 1601 JONSON *Poetaster* V. iii. 402 They [the pills] are somewhat bitter . . . but very wholesome. 1604 SHAKES. *M.M.* IV. vi. 8 'Tis a physic That's bitter to sweet end. 1721 KELLY 69 . . . Present Afflictions may tend to our future good. 1732 FULLER no. 985 (wholesome).

Bitter(est), *see* Beauty may have fair leaves yet b. fruit; Bee sucks honey out of the b. flowers; Stomach makes all the meat b., (An ill); Sweet is the nut, but b. the shell. Bitterness, *see* Remembrance of past sorrow.

Blab is a scab, He that is a.   (B 434)

1616 WITHALS 550. 1639 CLARKE 132. 1732 FULLER no. 6296 He that is a Blab, is a meer Scab.

Blab it wist and out it must.   (B 433)

a. 1500 *Harl. MS. 3362* Labbe hyt whyste, and owt yt must. 1546 HEYWOOD I. x. C3 Loke what she knowth, blab it wist, and out it must.

Black and blue, *see* Beat (anyone) b. and b.

Black and white, In (Under).   (B 439)

[= in writing or in print.] *c.* 1374 CHAUCER *Troilus* Bk. 2, l. 1320 And Pandarus gan him the lettre take, And scyde . . . 'Have here a light, and loke on al this blake.' *c.* 1440 LYDGATE *Fall of Princes* E.E.T.S. I Prol. l. 465 Hauyng no colours but onli whit & blak. 1590 *Almond for a Parrot* (Nashe iii. 372) I haue his name in blacke and white. 1598–9 SHAKES. *M.A.* V. i. 290 Which, indeed, is not under white and black. 1601 JONSON *Ev. Man In* IV. iv. 20 He has basted me rarely, sumptuously! but I haue it here in black and white. *a.* 1656 BP. HALL *Rem.* Wks. (1660) 136 We stay not till we have gotten it under black and white. 1712 STEELE *Spect.* No. 286, par. 3 Give us in Black and White your Opinion in the matter. 1866 W. COLLINS *Armadale* IV. xv The whole story of her life, in black and white.

Black as a crow, As.   (C 844)

c. 1320 *Horn Childe* l. 1049 Blac as ani crawe. *c.* 1386 CHAUCER *Knight's T.* l. 2693 Blak he lay as any . . . crowe. 1611 SHAKES. *W.T.* IV. iv. 216 Cypress black as e'er was crow.

Black as a pot-side (pan).

[*c.* 1515] 1530 BARCLAY *Eclog.* I. 238 Blacke as any pan. 1556 J. POYNET *Treatise* C8ᵛ As black as a potte side. 1562 J. WIGAND *De Neutralibus* K 2ᵛ Though thou be neuer so angrye with the Papistes, and cursest them as blacke as a potte syde.

Black as ink.   (I 73)

[*c.* 1515] 1530 BARCLAY *Eclog.* E.E.T.S. IV, l. 96. 1590 SPENSER *F.Q.* I. i. 22. *c.* 1594 SHAKES. *T.G.V.* III. i. 283.

Black as soot (pitch).   (P 357)

c. 1410 *Mirc's Festival* Blake altogether as pitch. 1528 TYNDALE *Obed. Chrn. Man* P.S. 299 They . . . curse thee as black as pitch. 1592 WARNER *Albion's Eng.* VII. 37, X1ᵛ Pathes as darke as pitch. 1591 ARIOSTO *Orl. Fur.* Harington XXXIV. 48. 1678 RAY 281.

Black as the devil.   (D 217)

c. 1390 *Romaunt of the Rose* A 973 Blak as fend in helle. 1509 BARCLAY *Ship of Fools* ii. 269 Defyle theyr faces . . . more fowle than the blacke Deuyll of hell. *c.* 1545 J. REDFORD *Wyt & Sci.* 42 As black as the devyll. *c.* 1600 *Merry Devil of Ed.* IV. ii. 7 As black as Lucifer. 1670 RAY 203.

Black as thunder.

1838 THACKERAY *Yellowplush Papers* ch. 4.

Black bear of Arden, He is the.

1787 GROSE (1790) *Warw.* 14ᵛ . . . Guy Beachamp, Earl of Warwick, was so called, both from his crest . . . a black bear, and from . . . a black and grim countenance, as well as on account of . . . undaunted courage. Arden was a forest [in] . . . this county. . . . The person . . . so denominated, was . . . an object of terror.

Black best sets forth white. (B 435)

c. 1403 LYDGATE *Temple of Glas* st. 104 For white is whitter, if it be set bi blak. 1523 SKELTON *Garl. Laurel* l. 1237 (Dyce i. 411) The whyte apperyth the better for the black. *a.* 1578 T. GARTER *Susanna* l. 835. 1590 SPENSER *F.Q.* III. ix. 2 But never let th'ensample of the bad Offend the good: for good by para- gone Of euill, may more notably be rad, As white seemes fairer, macht with blacke attone. *c.* 1595 SHAKES. *R.J.* I. v. 46 So shows a snowy dove trooping with crows As yonder lady o'er her fellows shows. *Ibid.* III. ii. 19 Whiter than new snow upon a raven's back.

Black book, To be in one's. (B 534)

1592 GREENE *Black Bks. Messenger* Wks. (Gros. xi. 5) Ned Browne's villanies . . . are too many to be described in my Blacke Booke. 1595 SPENSER *Sonnet* X A1 her faults in thy black boke enroll. 1614 JONSON *Barth. Fair.* II. i. 44 This is the speciall day for detection of those foresaid enormities. Here is my blacke booke for the purpose. *a.* 1627 MIDDLETON *Anything for Quiet Life* I. i She hath . . . her Black Book . . . remembers in it . . . all my misdemeanours.

Black dog on one's back, To have the.

[= to be in low spirits, or in the sulks.] 1778 MRS. THRALE in *Piozzi Letters* II. 32 I have lost what made my happiness . . . but the black dog shall not make prey of both my master and my- self. 1816 SCOTT *Antiq.* ch. 6. 1882 STEVENSON *New Arab. Nts.* II. 111 He did not seem to be enjoying his luck. . . . The black dog was on his back, as people say, in terrifying nursery metaphor.

Black hen lays a white egg, A. (H 418)

1611 COTGRAVE s.v. Noir . . . Many a foule woman brings forth a faire child. 1616 DRAXE no. 566 A blacke hen may bring foorth white egges. 1670 RAY 63 . . . This a French Proverb, Noire geline pond blanc œuf. I conceive the meaning of it is, that a black woman may bear a fair child. 1738 SWIFT *Dial.* I. E.L. 275 Oh! the wonderful works of nature, that a black hen should lay a white egg!

Black, Though I am | I am not the devil. (D 297)

1592 GREENE *Upst. Courtier* Wks (1881–3) xi. 259 Marry, quoth hée, that lookte like Lucifer, though I am blacke, I am not the Diuell, but indeed a Colier of Croiden. *a.* 1595 PEELE *O.W.T.* l. 640 Wks. (1888) i. 331 As the old proverb is, though I am black I am not the divel.

Black in the face, *see* Swear till one is b.

Black is any one's eye (eye-brow, nail, etc.), To say. (E 252)

[= to find fault with, to lay anything to his charge.] *c.* 1412 HOCCLEVE *Reg. Princ.* (1860) 102 The riche and myghty man, thoughe he trespace, No man seithe ones that blak is his eye. 1528 RAY & BARLOW *Read me and be not wroth.* ed. Arb. 70. 1675 BROOKS *Gold Key* Wks. (1867) v. 250 He knew that the law could not say black was his eye, and that the judge

upon the bench would pronounce him righteous. 1749 FIELDING *Tom Jones* IX. iv I defy anybody to say black is my eye. 1828 CARR *Craven Dial.* II. 2 'Thou cannot say black's my nail'. 1838 MRS CARLYLE *Let. to Miss H. Welsh* 27 May There is none justified in saying with self- complacency, 'black is the eye' of another.

Black is to white, As like as. (B 438)

1563 J. PILKINGTON *Confutation* P.S. 493 They are as like as black and white. *c.* 1570 *Marr. Wit and Science* V. i E2 They are no more like . . . then blacke to white. 1663 S. BUTLER *Hud.* I. iii. 1372 And contrary as black to white.

Black (white) (is) white (black), To make (say that). (B 440 and 441)

1528 ROY & BARLOW *Read me and be not wroth.* ed. Arb. 51 Makynge as he lyst blacke of whyte. *a.* 1529 SKELTON *Image Hypocrisy* Wks. II. 414 [We] must sey that white is blacke. 1533 SIR T. MORE *Debellation* Wks. 1119b If it tell you blacke is white, and good is badde, . . . yet must ye beleue it. 1551 CRANMER *Ans. to Gardiner* 85 You be wonte to make blacke white, and white blacke: or one thyng yea and nay, blacke and white at your pleasure. 1559 *Mirr. for Mag.* (Campbell, 74) We coulde by very arte haue made the blacke seme white. 1579 J. CALVIN *Thirteen Serm.* 124 Wee turn (as they say) blacke to white, and white into blacke, that wee might iustifie our selues. 1605–8 SHAKES. *T.Ath.* IV. iii. 28 Thus much of this will make blacke white, foul fair. 1613 *Id. Hen. VIII* I. i. 208 That dye is on me Which makes my whit'st part black. 1756 J. WESLEY *Wks.* IX. 220 (prove). 1763 CHURCHILL *The Author* 309–10 Wks. (1855) 196 To make most glaring contraries unite, And prove beyond dispute that black is white.

Black man is a pearl (jewel) in a fair woman's eye, A. (M 79)

1592 SHAKES. *T.And.* V. i. 42 This is the pearl that pleas'd your empress' eye. 1594 *Id. T.G.V.* V. ii. 10 The old saying is, Black men are pearls in beauteous ladies' eyes. 1621 BURTON *Anat. Mel.* III. ii. II. ii (1651) 464 A black man is a pearl in a fair woman's eye, and is as acceptable as lame Vulcan was to Venus. 1670 RAY 51 (jewel).

Black man (men), *see also* God gives b. m. what white forget; God made b. m.; Red man (To a) read thy rede. . . .

Black ox[1] has trod on (his, etc.) foot, The. (O 103)

[The blacke oxe had not trode on his nor hir foote.] [1525–40] 1557 *Merry Dial.* 86 I thinke he passethe not. xxiii. the blacke oxe neuer trode on hys fote. 1546 HEYWOOD I. vii B4. 1575 GASCOIGNE *Glass of Govt.* ii. 81 They never prove stayed untill the blacke oxe hath troden on their toes. 1581 MULCASTER *Positions* xxxvi (1887) 139 Till the blacke oxe, tread vpon his toes, and neede make him trie what mettle he is made of. 1583 H. HOWARD *Defensative* *2 Bos enim lassus fortius figit pedem, for a wearie oxe dooth set downe his foote, and treade somewhat harder. 1621 BURTON *Anat. Mel.* III. ii. vi. iii (1651) 561

Time, care, rivels² her . . . ; after the blacke oxe
hath trodden on her toe, she will . . . wax out of
favour.   **1738** SWIFT *Dial.* I. E.L. 288 I hear
she's grown a mere otomy.³ —. Poor creature!
The black ox has set his foot upon her already.
1850 L. HUNT *Autobiog.* (1928) ch. 4, 128 The
'black ox' trod on the fairy foot of my light-
hearted cousin Fan.   **1859** MEREDITH *R. Feverel*
ch. 27 The Black Ox haven't trod on his foot yet.
[¹ A symbol for misfortune, adversity, old age.
² wrinkles. ³ atomy = skeleton.]

**Black plum (raisin, grape) is as sweet as
a white, A.** (P 439)

1616 DRAXE no. 155 A blacke raisin as good as a
white. (*Ibid.* 16 grape.)   **1670** RAY 63 . . . The
prerogative of beauty proceeds from fancy.

Black puddings, *see* Kill hogs (He who does not)
will not get b. p.

Black sheep, To know one from a.
(S 316)

1609 HARWARD 119ᵛ Whilest I live I will know
him from a black sheepe.   **1616** WITHALS 557
(Hee is knowne from).   **1721** KELLY 203 I'll know
him, by a black Sheep, hereafter. Spoken with
Indignation, of one that has deceived me, and
whom I will not trust again.

**Black sheep in every flock (fold), There
are.**

1816 SCOTT *Old Mort.* ch. 35 The curates . . .
know best the black sheep of the flock.   **1902**
Spectator 1 Nov. There is no great movement
without its black sheep.   **1928** *Times* 17 July 17/5
There is . . . not the slightest intention of impugn-
ing the . . . force as a whole, but there are always
some black sheep in every fold.

Black sheep is a biting beast, A. (S 296)

c. **1550** *Six Ballads* Percy Soc. 4 The blacke
Shepe is a perylous beast.   **1591** LYLY *Endym.*
II. ii. 154 Indeede a blacke sheepe is a perrilous
beast.   **1598** BASTARD *Chrestoleros* IV. xx. 90
Till now I thought the prouerbe did but iest,
which said a blacke sheepe was a biting beast.

Black sheep keep the white, Let the.
(S 305)

1639 CLARKE 69.

Black swan, A. (S 1027)

[JUVENAL *Sat.* 6. 165 *Rara avis in terris, nigroque
simillima cygno.* A bird rarely seen on earth, and
very like a black swan.]   *c.* **1549** ERASM. *Two
Dial.* tr. E. Becke f. 8ᵛ Where shall a man fynde
suche blacke swannes?   **1553** *Respublica* l. 184
Yone the swanne-is-blacke yone.   **1569** C.
AGRIPPA *Vanity of Arts and Sciences* (1575) 104ᵛ
As rare . . . as a black swanne.   **1576** PETTIE
i. 89 As rare as the black swan.   **1580** LYLY
Euph. & his Eng. ii. 16 It is as rare to see a rich
Surety as a black Swan.   **1581** T. W. *A Glass for
Gamesters* C5ᵛ As rare birdes vpon the yearth,
as a blacke Swanne, or a white Rauen.   **1614**
RALEIGH *Hist. of World* Pref. C5 Onely those
few blacke Swannes I must except: who . . .

behold death without dread.   **1843** DICKENS
Christ. Car. Stave 3 A feathered phenomenon
to which a black swan was a matter of course.

**Black, Above | there is no colour, and
above salt no savour.** (G 172)

1573 SANFORD 109ᵛ Aboue God there is no Lorde,
Aboue blacke there is no colour; And Aboue salt
there is found no sauour.   **1659** HOWELL *It.
Prov.* 7.

Black velvet, *see* Little gentleman in b. v.

Black will take no other hue. (B 436)

[PLIN. *H.N.* 8. 193 *Lanarum nigrae nullum
colorem bibunt.*]   *c.* **1540–60** BALE *K. Johan* l.
2347 The crowe wyll not chaunge her hewe.
1546 HEYWOOD II. ix. K4ᵛ Folke haue a saiyng
bothe olde and trew, In that they saie, blacke
will take none other hew.   **1592** SHAKES. *T. And.*
IV. ii. 100 Coal-black is better than another hue,
In that it scorns to bear another hue; For all
the water in the ocean Can never turn the swan's
black legs to white.   **1629** T. ADAMS *Serm.* (1861–
2) II. 363 We were wont to say, that black could
never be coloured into white; yet the devil hath
some painters that undertake it.   **1721** KELLY
66 . . . Intimating the Difficulty of reclaiming
perverse People. Can the Ethiopian change his
Colour.

Black(s, -est) *see also* Bean has its b.
(Every); Beat b. and blue; Books (To be in a
person's b.); Devil is not so b. as painted;
Doomsday we shall see whose arse is b., (At);
Drive b. hogs in the dark; Fair and sluttish, b.
and proud; Keep a man out of mud (Way to),
b. his boots; Necessity is coal b.; Pepper is b.;
Spice is b., but has sweet smack; Two b. do not
make white; Wears b. must hang brush; White
b. (To make); White has its b. (Every).

Blackamoor, *see* Bath of the b.; Wash a b. white.

Blackberries, *see* Devil sets his foot on b. on
Michaelmas; Plentiful as b.

Blackbird, *see* Whistle like a b.

Black-brows, *see* Kettle calls pot b.

Bladders, *see* Swim without b.

**Blade wears out the scabbard (sheath),
The.**

1817 BYRON *We'll go no more a roving.* For the
sword outwears its sheath, And the soul wears
out the breast.   **1823** LOCKHART *Reg. Dalton* III.
vi There is an old Scots saying . . . that 'the
blade wears the scabbard'.

Blade, *see also* Flint (b.) on a feather bed, (To
break a).

Blad'ry, *see* Shame fall the gear and the b.

Blame(d), *see* Back broad enough to bear b.;
Deaf bears injury; Do as you're bidden, never
bear b.; Truth may be b.

Blames his wife for his own unthrift, Many a one.

a. 1628 CARMICHAELL no. 1176 (wytes his wyf of his awin wanthrift). **1721** KELLY 250 . . . I never saw a Scottish Woman who had not this at her Finger's ends.

Blames would buy, He that.   (B 445)

[PROV. xx. 14 It is naught, saith the buyer; but when he is gone his way, then he boasteth.] **1590** H. SMITH *Benefit Contentation* Wks. ii. 279 As Solomon saith of the buyer, while he is in buying, he dispraiseth the things which he buyeth, and saith, It is naught, it is not worth the price which ye ask. *c.* **1604** J. DAY *Law Tricks* l. 723 You will not buy me sure you praise me so. **1640** HERBERT no. 410. **1854** R. SURTEES *Hand. Cross* ch. 60 The stables were thrown open. . . . There was Captain Shortflat admiring Artaxerxes, and abusing Dismal Geordy, that he wanted to buy.

Blanch powder land, *see* Killed the blue spider.

Blanket, *see* Spits on own b.; Wrong side of the b.

Blate[1] cat makes a proud mouse, A.
                                        (C 134)

1568 'King James the Fyft his Pasquil' (Bannertyne MS. I 134 and Melville 23) Quhat maks a wanton mouse But a slow cat. *a.* **1628** CARMICHAELL no. 20 A blait cat maks a proud mowse. **1641** FERGUSSON no. 92. **1721** KELLY 25 . . . When Parents and Masters are too mild and easy, it makes their Children and Servants too saucy and impertinent. [[1] bashful.]

Blaze, *see* Bavin is but a b.; Mare has bald face (When), filly will have b.

Blear-eyed, *see* Blind as b. e., (Not so).

Bleating sheep loses her bit, A.
                                        (S 297)

1599 MINSHEU *Span. Dial.* 20 (a bit). **1623** WODROEPHE 477 The Yewe that doth bleete doth loose the most of her Meate. **1659** TORRIANO no. 41 A bleating sheep loseth her pasture. **1666** TORRIANO *It. Prov.* 28 no. 6 The sheep, for offering to bleat, loseth her bit. **1732** FULLER no. 1471. **1861** HUGHES *Tom B. at Oxford* ch. 23 He said something about a bleating sheep losing a bite; but I should think this young man is not much of a talker.

Bleat(s), *see* Goat must b. where tied.

Bleed your nag on St. Stephen's day, If you | he'll work your work for ever and aye.   (N 2)

1528 MORE *Wks.* (1557) 194 On Saint Stephen's day we must let al our horses bloud with a knife, because saynt Stephen was killed with stones. **1552** LATIMER *Serm. on St. Stephen's Day* P.S. 100 Upon this day we were wont to let our horses blood. **1846** DENHAM 66 If you bleed your nag

on St. Stephen's day, he'll work your wark for ever and ay. Hospinian quotes . . . from Naogeorgus, . . . translated by Barnaby Googe:— Then followeth St. Stephen's day, whereon doth every man, His *horses* jaunt and course abrode, as swiftly as they can, Until they do extremely *sweate,* and then they let them *blood.*

Blessed is he who expects nothing, for he shall never be disappointed.

1727 POPE Letter to Gay, 6 Oct. *Wks.* (1824) x, 184 I have . . . , repeated to you, a ninth beatitude . . . 'Blessed is he who expects nothing, for he shall never be disappointed.' **1739** FRANKLIN May Blessed is he that expects nothing, for he shall never be disappointed. **1911** *Times Lit. Sup.* 6 Oct. 359 Evidently Sir Edwin's hope is not too roseate, and he is among those who are accounted blessed because they expect little.

Blessed is the eye, that is betwixt Severn and Wye.   (E 228)

1659 HOWELL *Eng. Prov.* 14b. **1662** FULLER *Heref.* 35 Blessed is the Eye, That is betwixt Severn and Wye. . . . The Eyes of those Inhabitants are entertained with a pleasant Prospect. **1897** BP. CREIGHTON *Some Eng. Shires* 286 Herefordshire . . . throve, owing to its natural fertility and mild climate, so that the proverb ran—'Blessed is the eye Between Severn and Wye'.

Bless(ed), *see also* Bishop has b. it; Cross to b. himself with; Penny to buy . . . (b. him).

Blessing(s), *see* Child may have too much of mother's b.; God's b. make my pot boil (Will); Godfathers oft give b. in a clout; Means (Use the) and God will give b.; Need of a b. that kneel to a thistle; Sorrow wit you wat where a b. may light.

Blessing of your heart, *see* Brew good ale.

Bletherin' coo soon forgets her calf, A.

1330 *Wright's Polit. Songs* Camd. Soc. 332 Hit nis noht al for the calf that kow louweth. **1553** T. WILSON *Arte of Rhet.* (1909) 77 The Cowe lacking her Caulf, leaueth lowing within three or fower daies at the farthest. **1895** ADDY *Househ. Tales* 142 In the East Riding they say, 'A bletherin' coo soon forgets her calf', meaning that excessive grief does not last long.

Blind as a bat, As.   (O 92)

1588 J. HARVEY *Discursive Problem* 40 As blinde as moules, or bats. **1601** T. WRIGHT *Passions of the Minde* 144 Blinded as battes in their own conceits. **1639** CLARKE 52. **1923** P. G. WODEHOUSE *Leave it to Psmith* ch. 1 Lord Emsworth . . . had mislaid his glasses and without them was as blind, to use his own neat simile, as a bat.

Blind as a beetle.   (B 219)

1529 ERASM. *Exhortation to study of Scripture* B2[v] [Woman] be as men are wonte to saye comonly more blinde then a betle. **1544** T. BECON *Supplication* P.S. 230 More blind than beetles. **1548** UDALL *Erasmus Paraphr. Mark* i.

5 Jerusalem . . . albeit she were in very dede as

67 *Blind | Blind*

5 Jerusalem . . . albeit she were in very dede as blynde as a betell. **1549** ERASM. tr. Chaloner *Praise of Folly* N3ᵛ As poreblinde as a betle. **1881** EVANS 102 'As blind as a beetle' is a very common simile, the cockchafer being the beetle referred to.

Blind as a harper, As. *Cf.* Have among you, blind harpers. (H 175)

1584 LYLY *Sappho & P.* IV. iii. 35 Harping alwaies vpon loue, till you be as blind as a Harpar.

Blind as a mole. (M 1034)

1548 COOPER s.v. Talpa Talpa coecior, blynder then a mole, a prouerbe applied to theim that lacke iudgement in thynges that are plaine. **1557** EDGEWORTH *Sermons* B2ᵛ They be as blinde as the Molle. **1563** *Mirr. Mag., Rivers* Campbell 261 Blynde as molles. *c.* **1580** J. CONYBEARE *Adagia* (F. C. Conybeare 1905) 50 Talpa caecior blinder than a mole. **1713** BENTLEY *Rem. Disc. Freethink.* II. xlix. 269 In the whole compass and last Tendency of Passages he is as blind as a mole.

Blind as an owl. (O 92)

1553 T. BECON *Jewel of Joy* P.S. 427 The blind owls cannot away with the sun-light. **1607** WALKINGTON *Optic Glass* II. 21 Our soule in the body, though it bee not so blinde as a Batt, yet is it like an Owle, or Batt before the rayes of Phoebus, all dimmed and dazled. **1691** *Pepys Bal.* vi. 106 no. 367. Sometimes she wants Rings, with other such things And makes the poor fellow as blind as an Owl.

Blind as I am blear-eyed, I am not so.

1721 KELLY 199 . . . I may think it proper to hold my Tongue, but yet I can very well observe how Things go.

Blind as those who won't see, None so. (S 206)

1546 HEYWOOD II. ix. K4' Who is . . . so blynde, as is hée, That wilfully will nother here nor sée? **1551** CRANMER *Ans. to Gardiner* 58 There is no manne so deafe as hee that will not heare, nor so blynd as he that will not see, nor so dull as he that wyll not vnderstande. **1597** SHAKES. *Rich. III* (Qq.) III. vi. 12 Yet who so blind but sayes he sees it not? *c.* **1609** *Id. Cym.* V. iv. 183–5 I tell thee, fellow, there are none want eyes to direct them the way I am going, but such as wink, and will not use them. **1659** HEYLIN *Animadversions* in FULLER *Appeal* (1840) 506 Which makes me wonder . . . that, having access to those records, . . . he should declare himself unable to decide the doubt. . . . But, 'none so blind as he that will not see'. **1852** E. FITZGERALD *Polonius* 58 'None so blind as those that won't see.' Baxter was credulous and incredulous for precisely the same reason. . . . A single effort of the will was sufficient to exclude from his view whatever he judged hostile to his immediate purpose. **1926** *Times* 12 July 15/3 The most charitable thing that can be said . . . is that none are so blind as those who will not see.

Blind eat (eats) many a fly, The. (B 451)

c. **1430** LYDGATE *Balade* in *Skeat's Chaucer* vii.

295 Men deme hit is right as they see at y; Bewar therfore; the blinde et many a fly. *a.* **1529** SKELTON *Replyc.* 752 The blynde eteth many a flye. **1568** *Jacob & Esau* Hazl.-Dods. ii. 243. **1636** S. WARD *Serm.* (1862) 99 Blind and ignorant consciences . . . swallow many a fly, and digest all well enough.

Blind enough who sees not through the holes of a sieve, He is. (H 523)

1620 SHELTON *Quix* Pt. II. i (ii. 195) How blind is he who sees not light through the bottom of a meal-sieve! **1670** RAY 3 . . . *Hispan.* **1706** STEVENS s.v. Tela.

Blind George of Hollowee, *see* Fain see (That would I).

Blind horse, Ever longer the worse looks the.

c. **1350** *Douce MS. 52* no. 18 Euer lenger þe wors lokys þe blynde hors.

Blind horse is hardiest, The. (H 634)

a. **1628** CARMICHAELL no. 1435. **1641** FERGUSSON no. 830. **1721** KELLY 266 Nothing so bold as a blind Mare.

Blind Hugh, *see* Fain see, (That would I).

Blind in their own cause, Men are. (M 540)

1546 HEYWOOD II. v. H4ᵛ Folk oft tymes are most blind is their owne cause. **1560** SLEIDANUS *Chron.* tr. J. Daus 61ʳ We are all blind in our own cause. **1616** DRAXE no. 1581. **1641** FERGUSSON no. 623. **1678** RAY 384.

Blind lead the blind, If the | both shall fall into the ditch. (B 452)

[MATT. XV. 14]. **1546** HEYWOOD II. v. H1ᵛ Where the blind ledth the blinde, both fall in the dike. **1614** CAMDEN 312 The blind leade the blind and both fall into the ditch. **1678** BUNYAN *Pilgr.* I (1877) 64 That ditch is it into which the blind have led the blind in all ages, and have both there miserably perished. **1868** W. COLLINS *Moonstone* i ch. 10 Mr. Franklin . . . said he had often heard of the blind leading the blind, and now . . . he knew what it meant.

Blind man casts his staff or shoots the crow, As the. (M 74)

1546 HEYWOOD II. ix. L2 Ye cast and coniecture this muche lyke in show, As the blind man casts his staffe, or shootes the crow. **1573** J. BRIDGES *Supremacy of Christian Princes* M2 Not once nor twice neyther, as the blinde man castes his staffe. **1596** WARNER *Albion's Eng.* IX. 44, P2 They hit Capacities, as blinde-man hits the Croe. **1608** ARMIN *Nest Ninnies* Shak. Soc. 15 This was a flat fool; yet, . . . a blind man may hit a crow. **1641** FERGUSSON no. 454 He does as the blind man when he casts his staff.

Blind man may sometimes catch (hit) the hare (crow, mark), A. (M 81)

c. **1384** CHAUCER *Ho. Fame* l. 680 That ben betid, no man wot why, But as a blynd man stert an hare. **1578** WHETSTONE *I Promos and Cass.* v. v. F4ᵛ I see sometime, the blinde man hits a Crowe. **1583** P. STUBBES *Anat. of Abuses* Pt. II New Sh. S. II. 53 *Forte luscus capiat leporem* somtime by chance a blind man may catch a hare. **1616** WITHALS 581 (catch a crow). *a.* **1630** J. TAYLOR *Kicksey Winsey* Wks. 41 A blind man may (by fortune) catch a Hare. **1691** SEWEL 53 (perchange hit the mark).

Blind man's buff, To play at.   (M 494)

1600 S. ROWLANDS *Letting of Humour's Blood* D4ᵛ.   **1639** CLARKE 2 Hide and seek or Blind mans buffe.   **1672** WALKER 57 no. 28 (buffet; to wink and strike).

Blind man's holiday.   (B 452a)

1599 NASHE *Lent. Stuffe* iii. 195 What will not blinde Cupid doe in the night, which is his blindmans holiday?   **1678** RAY 229 Blind-mans holiday, *i.e.* twilight, almost quite dark.   **1738** SWIFT Dial. III. E.L. 324 It is blindman's holiday; we shall soon be all of a colour.   **1866** *Aunt Judy's Mag.* Oct. 358 In blindman's holiday, when no work was to be done.

Blind man's peck should be weel measured, The.

1832 HENDERSON 88.

Blind man's wife needs no painting, The.   (M 446)

[Sp. *c.* **1627** CORREAS *Vocab.* (1906) 188 *La mujer del ciego, para quién se afeita?*]   **1659** HOWELL *Span. Prov.* 4.   **1670** RAY 3 *Hispan.*   **1732** FULLER no. 1597. For whom does the blind Man's Wife paint herself?   **1736** FRANKLIN June Why does the blind man's wife paint her self?

Blind men can (should) judge no colours.   (M 80)

[L. *Caecus non judicat de colore.*]   *c.* **1374** CHAUCER *Troilus* Bk. 2, l. 21 A blynd man kan nat juggen wel yn hewys.   *c.* **1390** GOWER *Conf. Amantis* v. l. 2499 The blinde man no colour demeth.   **1530** PALSGRAVE 511a A blynde man can nat deme no coulours.   **1546** HEYWOOD II. v. H4ᵛ But blinde men shold iudge no colours.   **1590-1** SHAKES. *2 Hen. VI* II. i. 125 If thou hadst been born blind, thou mightst as well have known all our names as thus to name the several colours we do wear.   **1618** BRETON *Courtier & Countryman Wks.* (1879) ii. 5 You cannot but confess that blind men can judge no colours.   ?**1764** J. WESLEY Sermon CXIII *Wks.* vii. 263. When men born blind take upon them to reason concerning light and colours.   **1908** *Christian* 20 Feb. We do not ask the blind their opinion about colours.

Blind man (men), *see also* Kingdom of b. m. (In the) the one-eyed is king; Let me see, as b. m. said.

Blind that eats his marrow,[1] but far blinder he that lets him, He is.   (M 690)

a. **1628** CARMICHAELL no. 691 (his awin marrow).

a. **1641** FERGUSSON MS. no. 546.   **1641** FERGUSSON no. 376. [¹ mate].

Blind, (*adj., adv.*), *see also* Better to be b. than see ill; Better to be half b.; Better to have one eye than be b.; Cat winks a while; Devil is b., (When); Difference between staring and stark b.; Fortune is b.; Gazes upon the sun, (He that) shall at last be b.; Goose that comes to fox's sermon (B.); Hasty bitch brings forth b. whelps; Hatred is b.; Husband must be deaf and the wife b. to have quietness; Love is b.; Man should keep from the b.; Masters should be sometimes b.; Nod is as good . . . to b. horse.

Blind(s), (*verb*), *see* Affection b. reason; Gifts b. the eyes.

Blindworm, *see* Adder could hear and b. could see (If).

Blister will rise upon one's tongue that tells a lie, A. (Report has a blister on her tongue.)   (R 84)

1580 LYLY *Euph. & his Eng.* ii. 21 My tonge would blyster if I should vtter them.   **1584** *Id. Sappho & P.* I. ii. 36 You haue no reason for it but an old reporte.—Reporte hath not alwaies a blister on her tongue.   **1594-5** SHAKES. *L.L.L.* V. ii. 335 Pay him the due of honey-tongu'd Boyet. —A blister on his sweet tongue, with my heart.   **1611** *Id.W.T.* II. ii. 33 If I prove honeymouth'd, let my tongue blister.   **1625** BACON *Ess., Praise* Arb. 355 As we say; That a blister will rise upon one's tongue, that tells a lie.   **1732** FULLER no. 1127 Common Fame hath a Blister on its Tongue.   **1738** SWIFT Dial. I. E.L. 287 I have a blister on my tongue; yet I don't remember I told a lie.

Blithe heart makes a blooming visage, A.   (H 301)

1586 GUAZZO ii. 162 Wee Women commonlie saie, that a merrie heart makes a faire face, and a good complexion.   **1628** CARMICHAELL no. 16 A blyth heart maks a bluming visage.   **1629** *Bk. Mer. Rid.* no. 54 Heart's mirth doth make the face fayre.

Blithe, *see* Robin that herds . . . can be b. as Sir Robert.

Block, Dull (Senseless) as a.   (B 453)

1549 CALVIN *Life or Convers. of a Christian man* G1 (insensible).   **1565** K. *Darius* F3ᵛ.   *a.* **1573** G. HARVEY *Letter-Bk.* 122 (cowlde).   **1590** SPENSER *F.Q.* I. ii. 16 (senseless).   **1599** S. HARSNET *Disc. of practices of Darrel* 209 (senseless).

Block in another's way, To lay a.   (B 454)

c. **1533** J. FRITH *Another Answ. agst. Rastell* B1ᵛ Yet wyl I lay an other blocke in the waye that you shall not be able to remoue.   **1546** HEYWOOD II. v. H3 I haue (quoth she) no blocks in his waie to laie.   *c.* **1550** UDALL *Discourse* F1.

1552 HULOET R6ᵛ Laye a stumblynge blocke in ones way.   **1672** WALKER 18 no. 81 You have thrown a block in my way; put a spoke in my cart.

Block(s), *see also* Beetle and b. (Between); Chip of same b.; Cut b. with razor; Every b. will not make a Mercury; Frog on chopping b., (Sit like).

Blood is alike ancient, All.

1732 FULLER no. 505.

Blood is thicker than water.

[— the tie of relationship.]   [*c.* **1180** HEINRICH DER GLICHESSERE *Reinhart Fuchs.* Ouch hoer ich sagen, daz sippebluot von wassere niht verdirbet.]   **1815** SCOTT *Guy Man.* ch. 38 Weel— Blude's thicker than water—she's welcome to the cheeses.   **1823** GALT *Entail* ch. 2 His mother was sib[1] to mine by the father's side, and blood's thicker than water ony day.   **1882** J. M'CARTHY *Hist. of Own Times* III. 18 An American naval captain . . . declared that 'blood was thicker than water', and that he could not look on and see Englishmen destroyed by Chinese.   **1910** A. M. FAIRBAIRN *Stud. in Rel. & Theol.* 456 Blood is thicker than water; the bond it forms between men is strange and potent and infrangible. [¹ akin.]

Blood of the martyrs is the seed of the church, The.   (B 457)

[TERTULLIAN *Apol.* 50 *Semen est sanguis Christianorum.* The blood of Christians is seed.]   **1560** J. PILKINGTON PS 144 Cyprian writes, that the blood of martyrs is the seed of the church.   **1561** *History of strange wonders* B5 The common Proverbe. The bloode . . . watereth the Garden of the Lorde.   **1562** J. WIGAND *De Neutralibus* M8ᵛ It is a very goodly and a most true saying: Christian mennes bloud is a sede, and in what feldo so euer it is sowed, ther spring vp Christian men most plenteously thick.   **1593** P. STUBBES *Motive to Good Works* 100 Sanguis martyrum semen Ecclesiae, The bloude of martyres is the seede of the Church.   **1596** WARNER *Albion's Eng.* X. 57, R7 Blood of Martyrs well is sayd to be the Churches Seede.   **1619** J. FAVOUR *Antiquity* 469 The bloud of the Martyrs was the seed of the Church.   **1625** PURCHAS *Pilgrims* i, I 168 The seed, the fatning of the Church was the Bloud of her slaine Martyrs.   **1655** FULLER *Ch. Hist.* I. iv. 17 Of all Shires in England, Staffordshire was . . . the largest sown with the Seed of the Church, I mean, the bloud of primitive Martyrs.   *a.* **1697** AUBREY *Life of D. Jenkins* And hanged he had been, had not Harry Martyn told them that sanguis martyrum est semen ecclesiae, and that way would do them more mischief.   **1887** LD. AVEBURY *Pleas. Life* II. xi. The Inquisition has even from its own point of view proved generally a failure. The blood of the martyrs is the seed of the Church.

Blood will have blood.   (B 458)

[*Cf.* GEN. ix. 6 Whoso sheddeth man's blood, by man shall his blood be shed.]   **1559** *Mirr. for Magistrates* (Campbell 99) Blood axeth blood as guerdon dewe.   *Ibid.* Blood wyll haue blood.   **1561** NORTON & SACKVILLE *Gorboduc* IV. ii. 364 Blood asketh blood, and death must

death requite.   *c.* **1589** PEELE *Battle Alcazar* V. E4ᵛ Bloud will have bloud, foul murther scape no scourge.   **1605–6** SHAKES. *M.* III. iv. 122 It will have blood; they say blood will have blood.   **1800** WORDSWORTH *Hart-Leap Well* l. 137 Some say that here a murder has been done, And blood cries out for blood.

Blood(s), *see also* Come of a b. and so is a pudding; Deer is slain (Where) b. will lie; Difference of b. in a basin (No); Flesh and b. as others are, (To be); Good b. makes bad puddings; Like b. . . . makes happiest marriage; Money comes from him like drops of b.; Mouse-trap smell of b. (Let not); Red as b.; Runs in the b. like wooden legs; Scot will not fight till sees own b.; Victory that comes without b. (Great); Virtue is more important than b.; Water (B.) from a stone; Welsh b. is up (His).

Bloody bone, *see* Raw head and b. b.

Bloom is off the peach (plum), The.

1738 SWIFT *Dial.* I. E.L. 287 She was handsome in her time. . . . She has quite lost the blue on the plum.   **1761** A. MURPHY *Old Maid* Wks. (1786) ii. 168 The bloom has been off the peach any time these fifteen years.

Bloom, *see also* Furze is in b. (When the); Gorse is out of b. (When the).

Blooming, *see* Blithe heart makes a b. visage.

Blossom in the spring, That which doth | will bring forth fruit in the autumn.
                                                        (S 784)

1583 B. MELBANCKE *Philotimus* [4] If there be blossoms in the spring, there will be fruite in Autumne.   **1616** DRAXE no. 128.   **1670** RAY 3.   **1732** FULLER no. 3544 No Autumn Fruit without Spring-Blossoms.

Blossom(s), *see also* Autumn fruit without spring b. (No); Beauty is but a b.; Nip in b.; Timely b. timely ripe; Vain-glory b. but never bears.

Blot is no blot unless it be hit, A.
                                                        (B 471)

[Metaphor from backgammon.]   **1599** H. PORTER *Two Angry Women* I. 171 You neuer vse to misse a blot, Especially when it stands so faire to hit.   **1662** FULLER *Yorkshire,* 224 But a Blot is no Blot, if not hit; and an Advantage, no Advantage, if unknown.   **1663** J. WILSON *Cheats* V. iii Provided always, you carry it prudently, for fear of scandal:—a blot, is no blot, till it be hit.

Blot, *see also* Fairer the paper fouler b.; Pens may b. but cannot blush.

Blow first, and sip afterwards.   (B 476)

1615 W. WELDE *Janua Linguarum* no. 259 It is impossible to blow and sup both at once.   **1678**

RAY 103 . . . *Simul sorbere et flare difficile est.*
1706 STEVENS s.v. Sopla.   **1732** FULLER no. 995.

Blow great guns, To.

[= to blow a violent gale.] *a.* **1814** C. DIBDIN
Song; '*The Tar for all Weathers*' (1886) 40 But
sailors were born for all weathers, Great guns
let it blow high or low.   **1840** DICKENS *Barn.
Rudge* ch. 33 It blows great guns indeed.   **1853**
G. J. WHYTE-MELVILLE *Digby Grand* ch. 2.

Blow hot and cold, To.   (M 1258)

[In reference to one of Aesop's Fables.]   **1549**
ERASM. tr. Chaloner *Praise of Folly* G3 Out of
one mouth to blow both hote and colde.   **1562**
J. WIGAND *De Neutralibus* B4 These . . . are in
dede pestilent hypocrites, bycause they blowe
nother hotte nor cold. *Ibid.* 16ᵛ The hermyte
. . . said he could . . . [not] take hym for hys
frende, that coulde breath both hotte and colde
out of all one mouth.   **1577** tr. *Bullinger's
Decades* (1592) 176 One which out of one mouth,
doeth blowe both hoat and colde.   **1638**
CHILLINGWORTH *Relig. of Prot.* I. ii, § 113. 95
These men can blow hot and cold out of the
same mouth to serve severall purposes.   **1897**
M. A. S. HUME *Ralegh* 232 The duplicity of James
himself was marvellous. He blew hot and cold
with equal facility.

Blow in April, If they | you'll have your fill; but if in May, they'll all go away.

1609 HARWARD 103ᵛ Bloe in May bloe all away
Bloe in Aprill thy butts with cider fill.   **1735**
S. PEGGE *Kenticisms, Prov.* E.D.S. 75 *Cherries*:
. . . In the year 1742 it was otherwise. For, tho'
. . . the trees were not in bloom till late in May,
I had a great quantity of White and Black Hearts.

Blow (sound) one's own trumpet, To. *Cf.* Trumpeter is dead, Your.   (T 546)

[CIC. *de Or.* 2. 20. 86 *Domesticum praeconium.*]
1560 W. FULKE *Antiprognosticon* tr. W. Painter
C3 Who shall then be your standard bearer?
or who the trompettour to blare out your praise?
1576 FLEMING *Panopl. Epist.* 59 I will . . . sound
the trumpet of mine own merits.   **1598–9** SHAKES.
M.A. V. ii. 73 It is most expedient for the wise,
. . . to be the trumpet of his own virtues.   **1602** *Id.*
T.C. II. iii. 150 He that is proud eats up himself:
pride is his own glass, his own trumpet, his own
chronicle. *a.* **1625** FLETCHER & MASSINGER
Elder Bro. I. ii. 224 But that modesty forbids,
that I Should sound the trumpet of my own
deserts, I could, &c.   **1751** SMOLLETT *Per.
Pickle* ch. 2 If so be that I were minded to stand
my own trumpeter, some . . . would be taken
all aback.   **1907** A. C. BENSON *Upton Lett.* 251 It
happens too often that biographers of eminent
men . . . do a little adventitious self-advertise-
ment. They blow their own trumpet.

Blow the buck's horn, To.

[= to have his labour for his pains.] *c.* **1386**
CHAUCER *Miller's T.* l. 3387 Absolon may blowe
the bukkes horn.

Blow the gaff, To.

1785 Grose To Blow the Gab, to confess or
impeach a confederate.   [1812] **1819** J. H. VAUX

Vocab. of The Flash language at end of his
Memoirs ii 156 . . . a person having any secret in
his possession, or a knowledge of any thing
injurious to another, when at last induced . . .
to tell it openly . . . is then said to have blown
the gaff upon him.   **1823** JON BEE *Slang, A Dict.
of the Turf, etc.* 12 To 'blow the gaff', or 'gaff
the blow', is to speak of, or let out the fact.
1928 T. S. ELIOT *For Lancelot Andrewes* 65 Only
the pure in heart can blow the gaff on human
nature as Machiavelli has done.

Blow the wind never so fast, it will fall at last.   (W 413)

c. **1475** CAXTON *Hist. Troy* II. 472 Ther is no
wynde so grete ne so rygorous but hit attemperid.
a. **1628** CARMICHAELL no. 329 Blaw the wind
neuers a fast, it will loun at the last. *a.* **1641**
FERGUSSON MS. no. 169.   **1721** KELLY no. 63.
1732 FULLER no. 6306.

Blown up,[1] To be.   (B 477)

1603 CHETTLE, DEKKER, HAUGHTON *Patient
Grissil* IV. iii. 182 Emulo I see will not be seene
without calling. — No faith Madame, he's blowne
vp.   **1605** CHAPMAN, JONSON, MARSTON *Eastward
Ho* II. ii. 220 Tauerns growe dead; Ordinaries
are blowne vp; Playes are at a stand.   **1607**
MIDDLETON *Mich. Term.* I. ii. 43.   **1607** DEKKER
& WEBSTER *Northward Ho* I. ii. 85 I will . . . take
a faire house in the Citty: no matter tho' it be a
Tauerne that has blowne vp his Maister.   **1608**
DEKKER *Belman of London* B4ᵛ.   **1639** CLARKE
176.   **1678** RAY 89. [[1] i.e. a bankrupt.]

Blows best, He that | bears away the horn.   (H 616)

1641 FERGUSSON no. 385.   **1721** KELLY 149 . . .
He that does best, shall have the Reward, and
Commendation.

Blows in the dust, He that | fills his eyes with it.   (D 648)

1640 HERBERT no. 570.   **1660** SECKER *Nonsuch
Prof.* (1880) II. 17 183 He that blows into a heap
of dust is in danger of putting out his own eyes.

Blow(s) (*noun*), *see* Anvil fears no b.; Beast
that goes always never wants b.; First b.; Word
and a b.; Words are but wind, but b. unkind;
Words may pass but b. fall heavy.

Blow, blew, (*verb*), *see also* Cold (Let them that
be) b. at the coal; No man can sup and b.;
Wind b. you hither? (What).

Blow point, *see* Boys' play (To leave).

Bloxham, He was born at.   (B 478)

1662 FULLER *Lincs.* 165 It is a common expression of the Country folk in this County, when
they intend to character a dull, heavy, blundering person, to say of him, he was born at
Bloxham.

Bloxwich[1] bull, Like the.

1867 J. TIMBS *Nooks & Corn. Eng. Life* 261 At

Bloxwich, some wag stole the bull [intended for baiting]. The circumstance gave rise to a local proverb still in use. When great expectations are baffled, the circumstance is . . . likened to 'the Bloxwich bull'. [¹ near Walsall, Staffs.]

Blue and better blue, There may be.

1721 KELLY 58 . . . There may be difference between Things of the same Kind, and Persons of the same Station. L. *Servus servum praestat, & dominus dominum.* 1732 FULLER no. 4940.

Blue coat without a badge, A. (C 471)

1587 *Lett. Philip Gawdy* 29 He vanyshed awaye lyke one that had a blew cote without a couysance. 1597 N. BRETON *Wit's Trenchmour* C2 Olde Ling without musterd, is like a blew coate without a Cognisaunce. 1603 SHAKES. *H.* Q1 F2ᵛ My coate wants a cullison. 1618 *Owl's Almanac* 39 A blew coat without a Cullisan will be like a Habberdine without mustard. 1622 [SHAKES.] *O.* Stationer to Reader The olde English prouerbe, A blew coat without a badge.

Blue, *see also* Beat black and b.; Better b. clothes; Bolt from the b.; Coventry b.; Stafford b.; Three b. beans; True b.

Blunt, *see* John B.

Blush like a black (blue) dog, To.
(D 507)

[= to have a brazen face.] 1579 GOSSON *Sch. Abuse* Arb. 75 We will make him to blush like a blacke Dogge when he is graueled. 1584 R. WILSON *Three Ladies of London* Hazl.-Dods. vi. 293 He has a face like a black dog, and blusheth like the back-side of a chimney. 1592 SHAKES. *T.And.* V. i. 122 What! canst thou say all this, and never blush? — Ay, like a black dog, as the saying is. 1629 T. ADAMS *Serm.* (1861–2) II. 66 A black saint can no more blush than a black dog. 1738 SWIFT *Dial.* I. E.L. 262 You'll make Mrs. Betty blush. — Blush! ay, blush like a blue dog.

Blush, *see also* Bed could tell all it knows; Pens may blot but cannot b.; Women may b. to hear what they were not ashamed to act.

Blushing is virtue's colour (is a sign of grace).   (B 480)

1519 W. HORMAN *Vulgaria* (1926 ed., 308) Often tymes he that is gyltlesse blussheth rather than he that dyd the dede. 1539 R. TAVERNER *Garden* ii F3 Blusshynge is token of an honest nature [Cato]. 1551 CRANMER *Ans. to Gardiner* 331 Better it had ben for you to haue kept such sayings secret vnto your self, which no man may speake without blushyng (except he be past al shame). 1583 G. BABINGTON *Expos. Commandments* 221 Where it hath euer bene held, that blushing in measure, modestie, and silence haue beene commendable tokens in young yeeres, nowe . . . blushing is want of countenance and bringing vp. 1594 SHAKES. *T.G.V.* V. iv. 165 I think the boy hath grace in him: he blushes. 1598–9 *Id. M.A.* IV. i. 35 How like a maid she blushes here . . . Comes not that blood as modest evi-

dence To witness simple virtue? 1605 BACON *Adv. Learn.* I. iii (1900) 20 It was truly said, that *Rubor est virtutis color,* though sometime it come from vice. 1738 SWIFT *Dial.* I. E.L. 269 However, blushing is some sign of grace.

Blustering night, a fair day, A. (N 166)

a. 1609 SHAKES. *Sonnets* 90 Give not a windy night a rainy morrow. 1640 HERBERT no. 307.

Boar, *see* Feeds like a b.; Foam like a b. *See also* Wild boar.

Board, *see* Knock under b.; Stiff as a b.; Swear (look) through an inch b.

Boast, *see* Great b. and small roast.

Boat without the oar, Ill goes the.
(B 490)

1573 SANFORD 102ᵛ.   1578 FLORIO *First F.* 28. 1611 DAVIES no. 229.   1659 HOWELL *Fr. Prov.* 3.

Boat(s), *see also* Burn one's b.; Cornwall without b.; Oar in every man's b.; Row the b., Norman; Same b. (To be in).

Bobtail, *see* Tag, rag, and b.

Bode¹ a robe, and wear it; bode a sack, and bear it.

1721 KELLY 63 . . . Speak heartily, and expect Good, and it will fall out accordingly. [¹ expect.]

Bode good, and get it.

1721 KELLY 63.

Bode(s), *see also* Raven b. misfortune, (The creaking); Weapons b. peace.

Bodkin, To ride (sit).   (B 494)

[= to be wedged in between two others where there is proper room for two only.] 1638 FORD *Fancies* IV. i Where but two lie in a bed, you must be—bodkin, bitch-baby—must ye? 1848 THACKERAY *Vanity F.* ch. 40 He's too big to travel bodkin between you and me. 1872 FLOR. MONTGOMERY *Thrown Together* ii. 62 The three called a hansom outside, and Cecily . . . sat bodkin.

Bodle, *see* Rake hell for a b.

Bodmin, *see* Out of the world and into B.

Body is more (sooner) dressed than the soul, The.   (B 496)

1549 J. CALVIN *Life & Conv. of a Christian man* 17ᵛ–18 It is an olde prouerbe: that whoso euer is much occupyed in caring for the body, for the moste parte, careth lytle or nothynge, for the soule. 1616 DRAXE no. 99 His body is better clothed then his soule. 1640 HERBERT no. 920.

Body is the socket of the soul, The.
(B 498)

1659 HOWELL *New Sayings* 8b (but the Sockett of the Soul). **1664** CODRINGTON 218. **1670** RAY 3.

Body, -ies, *see also* Great b. move slowly; Little b. often harbours great soul; Riches increase (When), b. decreases; Soul needs few things, b. many.

Bog, *see* Frog cannot out of b.

Boil snow or pound it, Whether you | you can have but water of it.
(S 594)

1640 HERBERT no. 180.

Boil stones in butter and you may sup the broth.

1721 KELLY 75 . . . Good Ingredients will make very coarse Meat savoury. **1732** FULLER no. 1003 (sip). **1895** *Westmr. Gaz.* 22 May 6/1 Like the old saying: 'Boil stones in butter and you shall sup the broth.'

Boil the pot (Make the pot boil), To.
(P 505)

[= to provide one's livelihood.] **1577** HARRISON *England* II. ii (1877 i. 63) One of the best paire of bellowes . . . that blue the fire in his [the pope's] Kitchen, wherewith to make his pot seeth. **1657–61** HEYLIN *Hist. Ref.* (1674) 100 So poor, that it is hardly able to keep the Pot boiling for a parson's dinner. **1812** COMBE *Picturesque* xxiii. 18 No fav'ring patrons have I got, But just enough to boil the pot. **1864** CARLYLE *Fredk. Gt.* XVI. ii (1872) VI. 151 A feeling that glory is excellent, but will not make the national pot boil. **1864** TROLLOPE *Sm. H. at Allington* ch. 32 Tell him that if he'll put a little stick under the pot to make it boil, I'll put a bigger one.

Boil, *see also* Money makes the pot b.; Pot's full (When) it will b. over.

Boiling pot, To a | flies come not.
(P 503)

1640 HERBERT no. 123. **1655–62** GURNALL *Chrn. in Armour* (1865) II. 324 Flies will not so readily light on a pot seething hot on the fire as when it stands cold in the window. Baalzebub . . . the god of a fly . . . will not so readily light on thy sacrifice when flaming . . . with zeal.

Boils his pot with chips, Who | makes his broth smell of smoke.

1813 RAY 19. *It.*

Boisterous horse must have a rough bridle, A.
(H 684)

1539 TAVERNER A5 A boysteous horse, a boysteous snaffell. **1616** WITHALS 566. **1616** DRAXE no. 1785. **1639** CLARKE 200.

Bold as a lion, As.
(L 308)

[Prov. xxviii. 1 The righteous are bolde as a lyon.] *a.* **1225** *Ancrene Riwle* 274 Herdi ase leun. *c.* **1430** LYDGATE *Minor Poems* 'Henry VI's Triumphal Entry' l. 75 Of looke and chere sterne as a lyoun. *c.* **1485** *Herod's Killing Children* i 10 For thei be as fers as a lyon in a cage. *c.* **1502** *Robert the Deuil* in *Ancient Eng. Fictions* 30 (proude). **1597** SHAKES. *1 Hen. IV* III. i. 167 Valiant as a lion. **1616** S. S. *Hon. Lawyer* III. F3ᵛ Hee's valiant like a Lyon. **1659** HOWELL *Eng. Prov.* 15b. **1819** SCOTT *Bride Lam.* ch. 11 Caleb, to do him justice, was as bold as any lion where the honour of the family of Ravenswood was concerned.

Bold as Beauchamp, As.
(B 162)

1608 MIDDLETON *Mad World* v. ii Hors'd like a bold Beacham. **1639** CLARKE 152 As bold as Beauchampe. **1662** FULLER *Warwick* 117 . . . I conceive that Thomas [Beauchamp, Earl of Warwick] the first of that name [c. 1346], gave the chief occasion to this Proverbe.

Bold as blind Bayard, As.
(B 112)

c. **1350** CLEANNESS l. 886 Thay blustered as blynd as bayard watz euer. *c.* **1386** CHAUCER *Can. Yeom.* l. 1413 Ye been as boold as is Bayard the blynde. *c.* **1390** GOWER *Conf. Amantis* III. 44 But as Bayard the blinde stede . . . He goth there no man will him bidde. **1532** MORE *Confut. Tyndale* Wks. 500–1 Bee bolde vpon it lyke blynde bayarde. *c.* **1630** JACKSON *Creed* IV. iv. Wks. III. 33 As . . . boldly as blind bayard rusheth into the battle. **1681** BUNYAN *Come & Welcome* Wks. (1855) I. 289 They presume; they are groundlessly confident. Who so bold as blind Bayard? **1732** FULLER no. 5719 Who so bold as blind Baynard [*sic*]?

Bold man that first ate an oyster, He was a.
(M 178)

1655 MOFFETT *Health's Improvem.* vi. 47 Onely Oisters of all fish are good raw (yet he was no Coward that first ventured on them). **1662** FULLER *Essex* 317 King James was wont to say, he was a very valiant man who first adventured on eating of Oysters. **1738** SWIFT *Dial.* II. E.L. 296. **1806** WOLCOT (P. Pindar) *Tristia; Elegy to the Same* 'Who first an oyster eat', was a bold dog.

Bold (wily) mouse that breeds (builds, nestles) in the cat's ear, It is a.
(M 1231)

c. **1430** LYDGATE *Min. Poems* Percy Soc. 167 An hardy mowse, that is bold To breede In cattis eeris. **1522** SKELTON *Why not to Court* 753 Wks. (1843) II. 50 Yet it is a wyly mouse That can bylde his dwellinge house Within the cattes eare. *a.* **1530** R. *Hill's Commonpl. Bk.* E.E.T.S. 140 It ys a sotyll mouse that slepyth in the cattys eare. **1546** HEYWOOD II. v. H3ᵛ I haue ofte herde tell, it had nede to be. A wyly mouse that shuld breede in the cats eare. **1579** LYLY *Euph.* i. 210 Let *Philautus* behaue himselfe neuer so craftely, hee shal know that it must be a wily Mouse that shal breed in the Cats eare. **1640** HERBERT no. 693.

Bold than welcome, More.
(B 506)

c. **1579** MERBURY *Marr. Wit and Wisdom* i. 10

Thou mayest be More welcome and more bolde.
1580 LYLY *Euph. & his Eng.* ii. 162 Where I
thinke my selfe welcome I loue to bee bolde.
1591 FLORIO *Second F.* 53 This house is free, and
you are not so bold as welcome. **1721** KELLY
251 More hamely[1] than welcome. **1738** SWIFT
Dial. I. E.L. 269. [[1] familiar.]

Bold with what is your own, Be.

(B 505)

1604–5 T. HEYWOOD *If you Know not me* l. 490
I hope a man may be bold with his owne.   *c.*
1624 FLETCHER *Rule a Wife* III. iii. 53 Certainly
I may make bold with mine own. **1630**
DAVENANT *Cruel Brother* (1872) II. 136 My good
Lord, the proverb will persuade you To be bold
with what's your own.

Bold with your biggers, or betters, Be not too.

(B 346)

c. **1500** II. NEWTON cited R. II. Robbins *PMLA*
lxv (March 1950) 260 To bold ne to hesy, ne
bourd not to brode.   **1546** HEYWOOD I. xii. E4[v]
Euery wise man staggers, In earnest or boorde to
be busy or bolde With his biggers or betters.
1591 ARIOSTO *Orl. Fur.* Harington XII. 29 Saue
that I see thou doest an helmet want, I would ere
this haue taught thee at the least, Hereafter with
thy betters not to vant. **1659** HOWELL *Eng.
Prov.* 3b.

Bold, *see also* Fortune favours the b.

Bolder than a miller's neck-cloth, What is | which takes a thief by the neck every morning?

(M 959)

1637 *Hist. of Will Sommers* (1676 ed., A 4) The
coller of a Millers shirt . . . every morning it hath
a Thief by the neck.   **1658** *Comes Facundus* 34
In Germany they say, when they speak of a
stout man, that he is as bold as a Millers shirt,
that every morning takes a theef by the neck.
1721 KELLY 34 As wight[1] as a Webster's West-
coat, that every Morning takes a Thief by the
Neck. The Scots have but an ill Opinion of
Weavers' Honesty. Apply'd to them who brag
of their Stoutness.   **1732** FULLER no. 731 As
stout as a Miller's Waistcoat, that takes a Thief
by the Neck every Day.   **1853** TRENCH iv. 79
'The miller tolling with his golden thumb', has
been often the object of malicious insinuations;
and of him the Germans have a proverb: What is
bolder than a miller's neck-cloth, which takes a
thief by the throat every morning?[2] [[1] active]
[[2] Bebel: Dicitur in proverbio nostro: nihil esse
audacius indusio molitoris, cum omni tempore
matutino furem collo apprehendat.]

Boll, *see* Love the b. (If you) you cannot hate
branches.

Bologna, *see* Beggars of B. (Like the blind).

Bolt (Arrow) came never out of your bag (bow, quiver), That.

(B 511)

a. **1530** R. Hill's *Commonpl. Bk.* E.E.T.S. 129
Thys man comyth never owt of thyn owne bow.
1641 FERGUSSON no. 843.   **1659** HOWELL *Fr. Prov.*
16.   **1721** KELLY 305 . . . L. *Ex tua faretra*[1]
nunquam venit ista sagitta. [[1] *pharetra*, quiver.]

Bolt from the blue, A.

[= a complete surprise.] **1837** CARLYLE *Fr.
Revol.* vi. 1 Arrestment, sudden really as a bolt
out of the Blue, has hit strange victims. **1875**
TENNYSON *Q. Mary* V. ii So from a clear sky
falls the thunder-bolt! **1911** W. F. BUTLER
Autobiog. xxi. 380 Like a bolt from the blue
came the news of the Jameson raid.

Bolt, *see also* Fool's b. soon shot; Shaft or a b.
of it (I will make a); Shot my b.

Bolton, *see* Bate me an ace, quoth B.

Bond(s), *see* Busy will have b.; Honest man's
word.

Bondage, *see* Fear is b.

Bone between, To cast a.

(B 518 and D 237)

1530 TYNDALE *Practise of Prelates* P.S. 342
Secretly, by the bishops of the same country,
they cast a bone in the way. [1525–40] **1557**
Merry Dial. 62 In the olde lawe, where the deuill
hadde cast a boone betwene the man and his
wife, at the worste waye, they myght be deuorsed.
1546 HEYWOOD II. ii. G1 The diuell hath caste
a bone (sayd I) to set strife Betwéne you. **1692**
L'ESTRANGE *Josephus' Antiq.* XVI. xi (1733) 439
By this Means she . . . cast in a Bone betwixt the
Wife and the Husband.

Bone in one's leg (throat, mouth, arm, etc.), To have a.

(B 517 and 523)

1542. ERASM tr. Udall *Apoph.* 337b He [Demos-
thenes] refused to speake, allegeyng that he had
a bone in his throte & could not speake. **1596**
SHAKES. *M.V.* I. ii. 47 I had rather be married to
a death's-head with a bone in his mouth.
c. **1640** W. S. *Countrym. Commonw.* 49 (armes).
1672 MARVELL *Rehearsal Transprosed* Gros. ii. 10
(throat). **1678** RAY 67 I have a bone in mine
arm. This is a pretended excuse. **1738** SWIFT
Dial. III. E.L. 321 I can't go, for I have a bone
in my leg. **1845** A. SMITH *Fort. Scattergood* F.
ch. 22 Mr. Joe Jolit . . . stated that he [had] . . .
a bone in his leg, and something green in his eye.

Bone in the leg, Were it not for the | all the world would turn carpenters.

(B 525)

1640 HERBERT no. 1020 . . . (to make them
crutches). **1658** [EDMONDSON] *Comes Fac. in
Via* 184 (all would turn).

Bone of contention, A. *Cf.* Bone between, To cast a, *and* Devil has cast a bone to set strife.

1711 C. M. *Lett. to Curat.* 33 The Liturgie . . . has
been the Bone of Contention in England. **1803**
WELLINGTON. *Disp.* I. 517 A great bone of
contention between Scindiah and Holkar.

Bone to pick (bite, gnaw) on, A.

(B 522)

1533 UDALL *Flowers for Latin Speaking* (1560)

I haue geuen hym a bone to gnawe. *c.* 1533 J.
FRITH *Disput^n. of Purgatory* E6^v (To cast them a
bone to gnawe vppon). 1551 T. WILSON *Rule of
Reason* X. I. 1565 CALFHILL *Ans. Treat. Cross.*
(1846) 277 A bone for you to pick on. 1578
Courtly Controv. N3^v (gaue . . . a bone of repentaunce to chewe vpon). 1602 FULBECKE
Pandectes 69 He . . . gave them a bone to gnawe.
1706 STEVENS s.v. Roer.

Bones bring meat to town.   (B 526)

c. 1622 *Two Noble Ladies* l. 1036 O you know
the bones euer beare the flesh away. *c.* 1640
Berkeley MSS. (1885) iii. 31 . . . meaninge,
Difficult and hard things are not altogether to
bee reiected, or things of small consequence.
1642 FULLER *H. & P. State* v. xviii (1841) 'Bones
bring meat to town'; and those who are desirous
to feast themselves on . . . history, must be
content sometimes . . . to feed on hard words,
which bring matter along with them. 1721
KELLY 337 The Bones bears the Beef home. An
Answer to them that complain that there are
many Bones in the Meat that they are buying.

Bones (No bones) of (about), To make.
                                        (B 527)

1533 UDALL *Flowers for Latin Speaking* (1560)
H3 I will not shrinke to aduenture it . . . I wyll
no bones at it. 1537 *Thersites* A2^v. 1542
ERASM. tr. Udall *Apoph.* (1877) 133. 1548
Id. Par. Luke i. 28 He made no manier
bones ne stickyng, but went in hande to offer
up his ownly son Isaac. 1589 *Whip for Ape*
in LYLY *Wks.* iii. 420 Our *Martin* makes no
bones, but plainlie saies, Their fists shall walke,
they will both bite and scratch. 1642 D. ROGERS
Naaman 579 Who make no bones of the Lord's
promises, but devoure them all. 1850 THACKERAY
Pendennis ch. 64 Do you think that the Government or the Opposition would make any bones
about accepting the seat if he offered it to them?

Bones of a great estate are worth the picking, The.

1721 KELLY 337 . . . Spoken of an Estate under
Burthen, mortgag'd but not sold, that there may
be something made of it.

Bone(s), *see also* Belly is full (When) b. would be
at rest; Better a castle of b. than of stones;
Bred in the b. will not out of the flesh; Breed
young b.; Broken b. well set; Burden makes
weary b. (Too long); Carry a b. in mouth; Cast a
b. in devil's teeth; Child sleep upon b.; Devil has
cast a b. to set strife; Dog gnaws b. (While)
companions would he none; Dog that trots
about finds b.; Dog will not howl if you beat him
with b.; Dogs gnaw b. because cannot swallow;
Fair words break no b.; Feel in one's b.; Flesh is
aye fairest furthest from b.; Give his b. to the
dog (He will not); Gives thee a b.; Gnaw the b.
fallen to thy lot; Grave (In the) dust and b.
jostle not; Hard as a b.; Hard words break no
b.; Joke breaks no b.; Make dice of one's b.;
Nearer the b. sweeter the flesh; Old b. (She will
never make); Old man is bed full of b.; Rod
breaks no b.; St. Hugh's b.; Shirt full of sore b.;
Skin and b.; Throw that b. to another dog;
Tongue breaks b.; White as a whale's b.

Bonnet, *see* Bee in one's b.; Hand twice to your
b. for once to pouch; Head will never fill father's
b.

Bonny bride is soon buskit,[1] and a short
horse is soon wispit, A. *Cf.* Short horse
is soon curried.   (B 662)

a. 1628 CARMICHAELL nos. 78 and 79 A fair
bryde is soone buskit. A fair horse is soone
quhisked. 1641 FERGUSSON no. 34 (and a short
horse soon wispt). 1721 KELLY I . . . What is
of itself beautiful, needs but little adorning: . . .
a little Task is soon ended. 1857 DEAN RAMSAY
Remin. V (1911) 193 Janet replied . . . 'Ay, weel,
a bonny bride's sune buskit.' [[1] dressed,
bedecked.]

Bonny, *see also* Better than she is b. (She is).

Books, To be in (out of) one's.   (B 534)

1509 *Parl. Devils* XLV. ii He is out of our bokes,
and we out of his. 1546 HEYWOOD I. xi. E3^v
I crosse the quite out of my booke. 1549
LATIMER *Serm.* P.S. 124 If you follow them, you
are out of your book. 1565 CALFHILL P.S. 274
Nor marvel if Cross be so deep in your books.
1592 [KYD?] *Murder of John Brewen* (Boas, 288)
No man was so high in her books as Parker.
1594-8 SHAKES. *T.S.* II. i. 221 A herald, Kate?
O! put me in thy books. 1596 NASHE *Saffron W.*
iii. 61 Her frend, that was verie farre in her
books. 1598-9 SHAKES. *M.A.* I. i. 64 I see,
lady, the gentleman is not in your books. 1771
FLETCHER of MADELEY *Wks.* i. 166 You are out
of her books. 1837 J. B. KER 69 In my Books.
To be in favour with.

Book(s), *see also* Author (Like) like b.; Bell, b.
and candle; Beside the b.; Beware of man of one
b.; Black b. (To be in one's); Cards are devil's
b.; Great b. great evil; Lesson without b. (To
con); New b. appears (When) read old one; Old
wood is best to burn . . . old b. to read; Pictures
are the b. of unlearned; Read one like a b.;
Speak without b.; Talk like a b.; Wicked b. is
the wickeder; Worthy to bear his b. (Not);
Years know more than b.

Boose, *see* Cherry's b.

Boot and the better horse, He has gotten the.

1721 KELLY 171 . . . That is, he has gotten the
Advantage in the Exchange.

Boot is on the other leg, The.

[= the case is altered.] 1823 JON BEE *Slang A
Dict. of the Turf* 85 (The boot was placed). 1855
G. J. WHYTE-MELVILLE *Gen. Bounce* ch. 16 'The
young woman as owns that house has got the
boot on the other leg.' 1908 W. S. CHURCHILL
My African J. ch. 3 Here, . . . the boot is on the
other leg, and Civilization is ashamed of her
arrangements in the presence of a savage.

Boots, To give one the.   (B 537)

[In the quotation of 1582 the reference is to the
instrument of torture used in Scotland. In the

other examples it appears to mean to fool, make fun of, a man.] **1582** 19(?) Jan. *H.M.C.* Hatfield House xiii. 202 [Queen Eliz. to the King of Scotland] The poor man who against his will was intercepted with all such epistles as traitors sent and received was for reward put to the boots. **1594** LYLY *Mother B.* IV. ii. 32 What doo you giue me the boots? **1594** SHAKES. *T.G.V.* I. i. 25 You are over boots in love . . . — Over the boots? Nay, give me not the boots! **1606** DEKKER *Seven Deadly Sins: Non-Dram. Wks.*, ii. 60 Polonia gives him the bootes. **1611** COTGRAVE s.v. Bailler To giue one the boots, to sell him a bargaine.

Boot (= aid), *see* Bale is hext (When), b. is next.

Boot(s), *see also* Grease one's b.; Heart is in b.; Jogging while your b. are green; Keep a man out of the mud (To), black his b.; Leg warms (While) b. harms; Over shoes over b.; Too big for one's b.

Booted are not always ready, They that are.   (B 538)

1611 COTGRAVE s.v. Prest Some, though they booted are, vnreadie are. **1640** HERBERT no. 83.

Booted and spurred, *see* Devil run through you b. and s.

Booty, *see* Devil prays, (When) has b. in eye; Play b.

Bopeep, To play. *Cf.* See me and see me not.   (B 540)

1528 TYNDALE *Obed. Chrn. Man* P.S. 214 Mark how he playeth bo-peep with the scripture. **1548** *Answers* tr. G. Bancroft A3 [Believers in the mass] play booe pepe, wyth seste me or seste me not. **1571** J. BRIDGES *Sermon at Paul's Cross* 29 He wil and he will not, this is boe peepe in dede, seest me and seest me not. **1698** DEFOE *Enquiry into the Occasional Conformity of Dissenters* 17 This is playing Bo-peep with God Almighty. **1871** HARDY *Desperate Remedies* ch. 13 They've been playing bopeep for these two or three months seemingly.

Borage, *see* Leaf of b. might buy all they can sell.

Bore a hole through Beacon Hill, You might as well try to.

1855 *N. & Q.* 1st Ser. XI. 223 [Halifax] is overlooked . . . by . . . 'Beacon Hill', and . . . when the inhabitants wished to express the impossibility of any proposal, their reply was, 'You might as well try to bore a hole through Beacon Hill'. . . . A tunnel [now] passes through Beacon Hill.

Bore (Run) him through the nose with a cushion, To. *Cf.* Kill a man with a cushion.   (N 229 and 239)

1560–77 *Misogonus* II. i. 59 That old churle I am sure would haue borde you throughe nose. **1597** T. DELONEY I *Gentle Craft* 129. **1603** *The Bachelor's Banquet* (F. P. Wilson) 66 Thus is he

bored through the nose with a cushen. **1672** WALKER 57 (run).

Born a fool is never cured, He that is.   (F 513)

1609 HARWARD 88. A foole will be a foole still. **1642** TORRIANO 22. **1732** FULLER no. 2391.

Born fair is born married, Who is.   (B 142)

1642 TORRIANO 21 (handsome). **1659** HOWELL *It. Prov.* 2. **1666** TORRIANO *It. Prov.* 4 no. 19 She who is born beautifull, and comely, is born married. Note 13. Meaning, that she will go off without a Portion.

Born for ourselves, We are not.   (B 141)

c. **1525** A. BARCLAY *Mirr. Good Manners* 28 We be not borne for our priuate profite. **1550** R. CROWLEY *One & Thirty Epigrams* E.E.T.S. 51 Ye are not borne to your selfe. **1578** L. LEMNIUS *Touchstone of Complexions* tr. T. Newton 5 One that wel knew himselfe not to be borne only for himselfe. **1590** LODGE *Rosalynde* ed. Greg 4. **1639** CLARKE 264.

Born in a good (ill) hour who gets a good (ill) name, He is.   (H 738 and 740)

c. **1450** *Prouerbis of Wysdom* 12 Yea, well ys hym, þat hath a gwod name. **1540** PALSGRAVE *Acolastus* II. iii. 80 Maye not men . . . thinke, that I was borne in a good howre. **1599** MINSHEU *Span. Gram.* 83. **1616** DRAXE no. 1460 (ill . . . ill). **1659** HOWELL *Span. Prov.* 14 (ill . . . ill). **1706** STEVENS s.v. Horas (evil . . . ill). **1732** FULLER no. 2455.

Born in a mill, He was.   (M 940)

1578 WHETSTONE *Promos and Cassandra* B3 Were you borne in a myll, curtole? you prate so high. **1678** RAY 76 . . . i.e. He's deaf.

Born in August, He was.   (A 397)

1641 FERGUSSON no. 393 Of well skilled persons. . . . **1662** FULLER *Northumb.* 304 He was born in August . . . I am informed by a Scotish man, that it is onely the Periphrasis of a licorish person, and such said to be born in August, whose Tongues will be the Tasters of every thing they can come by.

Born to be hanged, He that is | shall never be drowned.   (B 139)

c. **1503** A. BARCLAY *Castle Labor* B1 He that is drowned may no man hange. **1540** D. LINDSAY *Thrie Estaitis* l. 2096 Quha ever bess hangit with his cord needs never to be drowned. **1593** J. ELIOT *Ortho-Epia Gallica* ed. J. Lindsay 94 He thats borne to be hangd shall neuer be drownde. **1594** SHAKES. *T.G.V.* I. i. 138 Go, go, be gone, to save your ship from wrack; which cannot perish, having thee aboard, Being destin'd to a drier death on shore. **1611** *Id. Temp.* I. i. 26 Methinks he hath no drowning mark upon him; his complexion is perfect gallows. *Ibid.* I. i. 54 He'll be hang'd yet, Though every drop of water swear against it And gape at wid'st to glut him. **1614** CAMDEN 307. **1625** PURCHAS *Pilgrims* (1905–7) xix. 201 Long with two others escaped (the rest drowned). One of the three . . . said nothing, but Gallows claim thy right, which within half a year fell out accordingly. *a.* **1628** CARMICHAELL no. 1454 The water will not reive[1] the widdie.[2] **1723** DEFOE *Col. Jack* vii He had a proverb in his favour, and he got out of the water, . . . not being born to be drowned, as I shall observe afterwards in its place. **1738** SWIFT Dial. I. E.L. 274. **1884** BLACKMORE *Sir Thomas Upmore* ch. 8 Don't tumble into it, . . . though you never were born to be drowned, that I'll swear. [[1] rob. [2] gallows.]

Born under a three-halfpenny (three penny) planet shall never be worth two pence (a groat), He that was. (P 387)

1606 DEKKER *News from Hell* D1[v] All such rich mens darlings are eyther christened by some left-handed Priest, or else borne under a threepenny Planet. [1623] **1635–6** T. POWELL *Art of Thriving* A4[v] He that's borne under a three-penny Planet, shall never be worth a groat. **1670** RAY 64 He that was born under a three half-penny planet, shall never be worth two-pence. **1692** L'ESTRANGE *Aesop's Fab.* ccccxliv (1738) 'No', says Fortune, . . . 'I'll . . . make good the old saying to ye, *That he that's born under a three-penny planet, shall never be worth a groat.*' **1738** SWIFT Dial. I. E.L. 285 If it rained such widows, none of them would fall upon me. Egad, I was born under a three-penny planet, never to be worth a groat. **1882** MRS. CHAMBERLAIN *West. Worc. Words* in NORTHALL *Folkphrases* (1894) 15 He was born under a three-penny planet, i.e. is avaricious, a curmudgeon.

Born under an unlucky planet (star). (P 386)

1572 E. PASQUIER tr. G. Fenton *Monophylo* S4[v] And they borne vnder an vnhappie starre. **1604** DEKKER *Hon. Whore* II. i. 8 ¡Some men I see are borne under hard-fauourd plannets as well as women. **1639** CLARKE 165. **1672** WALKER 10 no. 50 Born under an ill planet; in the wain of the Moon; curs'd in his cradle.

Born when wit was scant, You were. (W 574)

1670 RAY 199.

Born with a caul, He was. (C 197)

1540 PALSGRAVE *Acolastus* 80 May not men . . . thinke, that I was borne in a good howre, or that I was borne with a syly hoffe on myn heed. **1609** JONSON *Alchemist* I. ii. 128 Yo' were borne with a caule o' your head. **1620** J. MELTON *Astrologaster* 46 If a child be borne with a Caule on his head, he shall be very fortunate. **1668** SHADWELL *Sullen Lov.* V. i Sure I was born with a caul on my head, and wrapped in my mother's smock; the ladies do so love me. **1738** SWIFT Dial. I. E.L. 285 I believe you were born with a caul on your head, you are such a favourite among the ladies. **1849** DICKENS *Dav. Cop.* ch. I. **1878** HARDY *Return of Native* ch. 7 'And I was born wi' a caul, and perhaps can be no more ruined than drowned.'

Born with a silver spoon in his mouth, He was. (S 772)

1639 CLARKE 39 He was borne with a penny in 's mouth. **1721** KELLY 101 Every Man is no born . . . Every man is not born to an estate, but must labour for his support. **1762** GOLDSMITH *Cit. World* cxix (Globe) 274 But that was not my chance: one man is born with a silver spoon in his mouth, and another with a wooden ladle. **1814** 3 Aug. Byron *Lett.* Prothero iii. 120 If I was born, as the nurses say, with a 'silver spoon in my mouth', it has stuck in my throat, and spoiled my palate. **1849** LYTTON *Caxtons* II. iii I think he is born with a silver spoon in his mouth. **1906** G. W. E. RUSSELL *Soc. Silhouettes* ch. 17 The youth who is born with a silver spoon in his mouth, the heir to entailed acres and accumulated Consols.

Born within the sound of Bow bell, To be. *Cf.* London cockney. (S 671)

1571 J. BRIDGES *Sermon at Paul's Cross* 104 We are thorough out all the Realme called cockneys that are borne in London, or in the sounde of Bow bell. **1593** NASHE *Christ's Tears* ii. 95 Some graue Auntients (within the hearing of Bow-bell) would be out of charity with mee. **1600** ROWLANDS *Lett. Hum. Blood* iv. 65 I scorne . . . To let a Bow-bell Cockney put me downe. **1617** MINSHEU *Ductor* s.v. A Cockney . . . applied only to one borne within the sound of Bow-bell, that is, within the City of London. **1617** MORISON *Itin.* iii. 53 Londiners, and all within the sound of Bow-bell, are in reproch called Cocknies. **1638** J. TAYLOR *Bull, Bear, and Horse* B7 A Young Shee Citizen borne . . . having never in her life beene a Traveller further than she could heare the sound of Bow Bell. **1662** FULLER *London* 197 He was born within the Sound of Bow-Bell. This is the Periphrasis of a Londoner at large, born within the Suburbs thereof. . . . It is called *Bow-bell*, because hanging in the Steeple of *Bow-Church*, and *Bow-Church* because built on *Bows* or Arches. **1738** SWIFT Dial. II. E.L. 301. **1842–3** W. H. MAXWELL *Hector O'H* ch. 15 An artiste . . . born and indoctrinated within sound of Bow bells. **1926** *Times* 2 Aug. 11/5 Israel Zangwill . . . was born, as he boasted, within the sound of Bow Bells.

Born yesterday, I was not.

1836 HALIBURTON *Clockmaker* i. 126 I guess I wasn't born yesterday. **1837** MARRYAT *Snarl.* ch. 12 The widow read the letter and tossed it into the fire with a 'Pish! I was not born yesterday, as the saying is'. **1871** GILBERT *Pygm. and Galatea* To a suspicious visitor's 'I wasn't born yesterday' Galatea replies 'But I was'.

Born, *see also* Bloxham (He was b. at); First b., first fed; Fools . . . among his kindred, (Who has neither) was b. of a stroke of thunder; Know where they were b. (Men); Little Witham (He was b. at); Maid (This) was b. odd; Naked as he was b.; Natural to die as to be b.; Once b. once must die; Parsley before it is b. is seen by the devil nine times; Poet b. not made; Skill of man (You have), b. between the Beltanes; Soon as man is b. begins to die; Wept when I was b.; Women are b. in Wiltshire.

Borrow, Not so good to | as to be able to lend.   (B 543)

1546 HEYWOOD I. X. C3ᵛ.

Borrow when he has not, Who would | let him borrow when he has.   (B 544)

1659 TORRIANO no. 198.   **1659** N.R. 118.

Borrowed garments never fit well.

1732 FULLER no. 1008.

Borrowed loan should come laughing home, A.   (L 402)

c. **1300** *Provs. of Hending* 25 Selde cometh lone lahynde hom. *c.* **1350** *Douce MS. 52* no. 82 Seldun comyth lone law3yng home. **1641** FERGUSSON no. 29 A borrowed len should come laughing hame. **1721** KELLY 6 ... What a Man borrows he should return with Thankfulness. **1732** FULLER no. 6314.

Borrowed thing will home again.
                                                            (T 125)

c. **1350** *How the Gd. Wife* l. 149 Borowed þing wole hom. *a.* **1500** *Prov. Wisdom* (1892) l. 32. *c.* **1550** *Parl. Birds*. l. 224 in *E.P.P.* iii. 179 (Borrowed ware wyll).

Borrowing days, *see* Put over the b. d.

Borrows must pay again with shame or loss, He that.   (S 266)

1639 CLARKE 246 He that will borrow must pay. **1678** RAY 104 ... Shame if he returns not as much as he borrowed, loss if more, and it's very hard to cut the hair.

Borrow(s, ing), *see* Better buy than b.; Contented who needs neither b.; Goes a b. goes a sorrowing; Horse of own and b. another; Know the value of a ducat, try to b. one; Know what money is (Would you), b. some; Put over b. days; Rath sower never b. of late; St. George to b.; St. John to b.; World ... at staff's end, that needs not to b.

Bosom, *(adj.), see* Friend to b. friend; ... b. enemy.

Bosom, *(noun), see* Abraham's b.; Bird in my b.; Horns in b.; Snake (viper) in b.; Sure as louse in b.

Bossing, *see* Ossing comes to b.

Botch, *see* Patch and long sit.

Botcher, *see* God is no b.

Both ends (the two ends of the year) meet, To make.   (E 135)

1639 CLARKE 242 I cannot make both ends meet. **1662** FULLER *Cumb*. 219 Worldly wealth he

cared not for, desiring onely to make both ends meet. **1748** SMOLLETT *Rod. Rand*. ch. 10 He made shift to make the two ends of the year meet. **1814** JANE AUSTEN *Mansfield P*. ch. 3 If I can but make both ends meet, that's all I ask for. **1884** *Graphic* 23 Aug. 198/2 Her mother has to contrive to make both ends meet.

Bottle, *see* Drunkard's purse a b.; Wine in b. does not quench thirst.

Bottom, *see* Fish (Best) keep the b.; Spare when b. is bare (Too late to); Truth has always fast b.; Tub must stand on own b.; Venture not all in one b.; Wind up your b.

Bottom of the sea, *see* Great way to.

Boughs that bear most, hang lowest, The.   (B 555)

1655 FULLER *Ch. Hist*. x. iii (1868) III. 257 His humility set a lustre on all (admirable that the whole should be so low, whose several parts were so high) ... like a tree loaden with fruit, bowing down its branches. **1732** FULLER no. 4430. **1856** MRS. BROWNING *Aurora L*. II The vines That bear much fruit are proud to stoop with it.

Boughs, Who trusts to rotten | may fall.
                                                            (B 557)

a. **1542** T. WYATT ed. Muir no. 13 l. 14 Me lusteth no lenger rotten boughes to clymbe. *Ibid.,* no. 154 l. 31 Was never birde tanglid yn lyme That brake awaye yn bettre tyme, Then I that rotten bowes ded clyme, And had no hurte but scaped fre. **1573** GASCOIGNE *Dulce Bellum* i. 162 How soone they fall which leane to rotten bowes. *Id. Flowers* i. 914 Who climeth off on hie, and trusts the rotten bowe: If that how breake may catch a fall. *c.* **1576** *Common Cond*. l. 557 CIᵛ Hee that trusts to a broken bough may hap to fall from the tree.

Bough(s), *see also* Bird on briar (b.), (As merry (light) as); Cut not the b. thou standest upon; Father to b., son to plough; Short b. long vintage.

Bought a brush, He has.

1699 B. E. *Dict. Canting Crew* s.v. Brush To Fly or Run away ... Bought a Brush, c. Run away. **1785** GROSE To brush, to run away. Let us buy a brush and lope; let us go away, or off. **1813** RAY 56 ... i.e. He has run away.

Bought and sold.   (B 787)

[= betrayed.] *c.* **1350** *York Plays* (L. T. Smith) 420 Thus schall þe sothe be bought and solde. *c.* **1497** MEDWALL *Fulgens and Lucres* l. 579 The materis bought and solde. **1546** HEYWOOD I. X. C3 Than will the pik-thanke it tell To your moste enmies, you to bie and sell. **1592–4** SHAKES. *1 Hen. VI* IV. iv. 13 Whither, my lord? from bought and sold Lord Talbot. **1592–3** *Id. C.E.* III. i. 72 It would make a man mad as a buck to be so bought and sold. **1596** *Id. K.J.* V. iv. 10 Fly, noble English; you are bought and sold. **1597** *Id. Rich. III* V. iii. 304 Be not bold, For Dickon thy master is bought and sold. **1602** *Id. T.C.* II. i. 46 Thou art bought and sold among those of any wit. **1639** CLARKE 86 You are bought and sold like sheepe in a market. **1818** SCOTT *Rob Roy* ch. 4 Wise folks buy and sell, and fools are bought and sold.

Bought the fox-skin for three pence, and sold the tail for a shilling, He.

1732 FULLER no. 1814.

Bought wit is best. *Cf.* Wit once bought, etc.; Ounce of wit that's bought.
(W 545 and 567)

c. **1490** H. MEDWALL *Nature* I. 2 Wyt is nothyng worth tyll yt be dere bought. **1546** HEYWOOD I. viii. B4ᵛ But wyt is neuer good tyll it be bought. **1599** PORTER *Two Angry Wom.* l. 2313 Tis an olde Prouerbe, & not so old as true, Bought wit is the best. **1600-1** SHAKES. *M.W.W.* IV. v. 54 One that hath taught me more wit than ever I learn'd before in my life; and I paid nothing for it neither, but was paid for my learning. **1688** BUNYAN *Accept Sacrif.* Wks. (1855) I. 704 We say, Wisdom is not good till it is bought; and he that buys it . . usually smarts for it.

Bought wit is dear. (W 546)

1547 J. HALL *Prov. of Salomon* A5 Wyt bought is of to dere a pryce. **1563** *Mirr. for Mag.* (Campbell 402) I bought my wyt to deare. **1575** GASCOIGNE i. 66 Bought wit is deare, and drest wth sower sauce.

Bought, *see also* Buy.

Boulogne, Our fathers won | who never came within the report of the cannon.
(F 100)

1622 T. ADAMS *Serm.* (1861-2) II. 313 So we make a conquest of peace, as the byword says our fathers won Boulogne; who never came within the report of the cannon.

Bound must obey, They that are.
(B 354)

c. **1205** LAYAMON *Brut.* 1051 Ah heo mot nede beien, þe mon þe ibunden bith. *c.* **1390** GOWER *Conf. Amantis* II, l. 540 For who is bounden, he mot bowe. *c.* **1410** *Towneley Plays* xiii, l. 80 Wo is hym that is bun, ffor he must abyde. **1546** HEYWOOD II. v. H2 **1576** PETTIE ii. 46 Alas, . . . ; he must follow of force his General-Captain. [**1594-1600**] **1615** HEYWOOD *Four Prentices* ii. 169 Bound must obey. **1599** PORTER *Two Angry Wom.* l. 904. **1614** CAMDEN 313.

Bound to see more than he can, One is not. (B 353)

1653 FULLER *Infants Advocate* xxi in *Sermons* (1891) II. 242 Our English proverb, . . . *One is not bound to see more than he can.* And I conceive I am in no error, because I follow my present light, and all the means of your prescription have made no alteration on my understanding.

Bound, *see also* Stake, (To be b. to a).

Bounty, *see* Beauty without b. avails nought; Buy dear is not b.

Bourbons learn nothing and forget nothing, The.

[TALLEYRAND *Album perdu* 147 described the émigrés as 'des gens qui n'ont rien appris ni rien oublié depuis trente ans' (King).] **1861** G. J. WHYTE-MELVILLE *Inside Bar* ch. 6 The race [of stud-grooms] . . . possesses its own language, its own customs, its own traditions. As Napoleon the First said of the Bourbons, it learns nothing, and forgets nothing.

Bourd[1] not with Bawty,[2] lest he bite you. (B 571)

a. **1628** CARMICHAELL no. 314 Bourd not with Batie. **1641** FERGUSSON no. 178. **1721** KELLY 56 . . . Do not Jest too familiarly with your Superiors, lest you provoke . . . a surlish Return. [[1] jest. [2] a watch-dog.]

Bourd[1] wi' cats, They that | maun count on scarts.[2]

1710 PALMER *Moral Essays on Proverbs* 249 He that will play with cats must expect to be scratched. **1832** HENDERSON 141. [[1] jest. [2] scratches.]

Bourd, *see also* Sooth b. is no b.

Bout as Barrow was, To be. (B 95)

1670 RAY 217 . . . *Chesh.* bout, that is without it.

Bow and arrows and go to bed, To take one's.

1589 GREENE *Menaphon* Arber 34; Wks. (Gros.) vi. 54 She blubbered and he sightht [*sic*] . . . so that amongst these swaines there was such melodie, that *Menaphon* tooke his bow and arrowes and went to bedde. **1599** NASHE *Lenten Stuff* iii. 167 Therefore I prayse Yarmouth so rantantingly, because I neuer elsewhere bayted my horse, or tooke my bowe and arrowes and went to bed. **1599** SHAKES. *A.Y.* IV. iii. 3 He hath ta'en his bow and arrows and is gone forth to sleep.

Bow bell, *see* Born within the sound of B. b.

Bow, I have a good | but it is in the castle. (B 564)

a. **1628** CARMICHAELL no. 665. **1641** FERGUSSON no. 509. **1721** KELLY 183 . . . Spoken to them who say that they have a Thing very proper for the Business, but it is not at hand.

Bow long bent at last waxes weak, A. (B 561)

a. **1500** 'Mony man makis ryme' Bannatyne MS. STS iii. 8-10. *c.* **1526** *Dicta Sap.* B1ᵛ The bowe with to moche bendyng breketh. **1539** TAVERNER *Publius* A6ᵛ Bendyng breaketh the bowe, but slackyng breaketh the mynde, . . . a bowe if it be bent to much, it breaketh. **1550** HEYWOOD I. xi. D3ᵛ But a bowe long bent, at length must waxe weake. **1579** LYLY *Euph.* i. 196 Though the Cammocke the more it is bowed the better it serueth, yet the bow the more it is bent and occupied, the weaker it waxeth. **1614** CAMDEN 302.

Bow of Ulysses.   (B 562)

[*Fig.* a task of great difficulty: see HOMER *Od.* xxi.] **1545** ASCHAM *Toxoph.* Arb. 135 Penelope brought Vlixes bowe downe amonges the gentlemen, whiche came on wowing to her, that he which was able to bende it and drawe it, might inioye her. **1678** DRYDEN *All for Love*, Pref. Merm. 9 The death of Antony and Cleopatra . . . has been treated by the greatest wits of our nation . . . and . . . their example has given me the confidence to try myself in this bow of Ulysses. **1830** SIR J. HERSCHEL *Stud. Nat. Phil.* III. iii (1851) 273 The bow of Ulysses, which none but its master could bend.

Bow, To bring to one's. *Cf.* Man of God is better for having his bows.   (B 565)

1530 PALSGRAVE 631a I make to the bowe, as we make a yonge persone to our mynde. **1579** LYLY *Euph.* i. 220 Doe you therefore thinke me easely entised to the bent of your bow? **1584** LODGE *Alarum against Usurers* D1ᵛ Mas vsurer smelling out the disposition of the youth, beginnes to bring him to his bowe after this sort. **1602** WITHALS 74 Well-tamed, broken, broght vnder, as they say, to the bowe, Edomitus. **1605** JONSON etc. *Eastward Ho* II. ii. 358 Draw all my seruants in my Bowe. **1682** BUNYAN *Holy War* 206 (1905) Mansoul being wholly at his beck, and brought wholly to his bow.

Bow (*noun*), *see also* Bent of his b.; Long b.; Man of God better for having his b.; Out-shoot a man in his own b.; Wide at the b. hand; Yew b. in Chester (More than one); Young are not always with b. bent.

Bow (*verb*), *see* Better bend (b.) than break; Sooner break than b., (It will).

Bowdon, *see* Vicar of B.

Bowl down hill, It is easy to.   (H 465)

1614 J. HALL *Contempl.* II: *Recoll. Treat.* 1063 An easie Rhetorick drawes vs to the worse part; yea it is hard not to run downe the hill. **1639** CLARKE 151. **1678** RAY 3 (down hill).

Bowl (*noun*), *see* Comes to hand like b. of pint-stoup.

Bowler, *see* Honest man and good b.

Bowling-green, *see* Three things are thrown away in a b.-g.

Bowls, *see* Play at b. must expect rubbers.

Bowrocks, *see* Build sandy b.

Bows and arrows, *see* Man of God is better for having b. and a.

Bows and bills!

[The cry of alarm raised in the English camp in old times.] *a.* **1572** KNOX *Hist. Ref.* 28 (Jam.) The schout ryises, Bowes and Billis! . . . which is a significatioun of extreim defence.

Bows to the bush he gets bield[1] of, Every man.

1721 KELLY 99 . . . Every Man pays court to him that he gains by. [¹ shelter.]

Box Harry, To.

[A phrase formerly used by commercial travellers, who had to content themselves at inns with a makeshift meal. HAZLITT.] **1862** BORROW *Wild Wales* ch. 33 'I will have the bacon and eggs with tea and bread-and-butter, . . . in a word, I will box Harry'.

Box (*noun*), *see* Butler's b. at Christmas; Health, (The chief b. of) is time; Pandora's b.; Wrong b.

Box (*verb*), *see also* Give (B.) it about.

Box on ear, *see* Billingsgate for b. o. e. (As much favour at).

Boys will be boys.   (C 337)

1589 *Censure of Martin Junior. Marprelate Tracts* ed. Pierce 35 I thought boys would be a-doing. **1597** DELONEY I *Gentle Craft* (Mann 97) Youth are youth. **1600** DEKKER *Old. Fort.* I. iii. 66 Fooles and children are best pleasde with toyes. **1601** A. DENT *Plain Man's Pathway* 64 Youth will be youthfull, when you haue saide all that you can. **1672** WALKER 55 Boys will have toys; children will do like children. **1691** SEWEL 61 Boys will have toys. **1826** T. H. LISTER *Granby* ii. 83 Girls will be girls. **1853** THACKERAY *Newcomes* ch. 25 We used to call your grandfather by that playful epithet (boys will be boys, you know). **1905** *Almond of Loretto* 358 The devil has got a lot of maxims which his adherents . . . use . . . 'Boys will be boys'.

Boys (Lads) will be men.   (L 24)

1611 COTGRAVE s.v. Enfant (As we say) boyes will be men one day. **1641** FERGUSSON no. 590 (Laddes). **1732** FULLER no. 1014. **1905** VACHELL *The Hill* 33 I'm sending you to Harrow to study, not books . . . but boys, who will be men when you are a man.

Boys' play, To leave | and go to blow point.   (B 581)

1616 WITHALS 569. **1639** CLARKE 197. **1681** ROBERTSON *Phraseol. Gener.* 997a (fall to).

Boy(s), *see also* Good will (With as) as e'er b. came from school; Least b. carries greatest fiddle; Manned with b. . . . shall have work undone; Miller's b. said so; Naughty b. good men; White-headed b.; Will is good b.

Brabbling[1] curs never want sore ears.
(C 917)

1611 COTGRAVE S.V. Hargneux A brabling curre is neuer without torne eares. **1640** HERBERT no. 52. [[1] brawling.]

Brack, *see* Seek a b. where hedge whole.

Bracken bush, *see* Hare or the b. b.

Brackley breed, better to hang than to feed.
(B 585)

1636 T. POWELL *Art of Thriving* 141–2 Though wee be Leicestershire-fed, yet we be not Brackley bred, I assure you. **1639** CLARKE 203. **1678** RAY 328 . . . Brackley is a decayed Market town . . . in Northamptonshire, not farre from Banbury, which . . . troubling the countrey about with beggers, came into disgrace with its neighbours.

Bradshaw's windmill? What have I to do with.
(B 586)

1678 RAY 317 (*Leics.*) . . . i.e. What have I to doe with another mans business?

Brag is a good dog.
(B 587)

1580 MUNDAY *Zelauto* Ti[v] Brag is a good Dogge, whyle he will holde out: but at last he may chaunce to meete with his matche. **1599** PORTER *Two Angry Wom.* l. 2337 I, brags a good dog, threatned folkes liue long. **1618** *Barnevelt's Apol.* E iv b Bragge is a good Dog still. **1670** RAY 65 Brag's a good dog if he be well set on.

Brag is a good dog but dares not bite.
(B 590)

1616 DRAXE no. 540 Bragging mastiues seldome bite. **1732** FULLER no. 1015.

Brag is a good dog, but Holdfast is a better.
(B 588)

1583 MELBANCKE F1 As to haue is good happ, so to hould fast is a great vertue. **1599** SHAKES. *Hen. V* II. iii. 52 And Holdfast is the only dog, my duck. **1709** DYKES 123. **1752** JOHNSON *Rambl.* No. 197, par. 3 When I envied the finery of any of my neighbours, [my mother] told me that 'Brag was a good dog, but Holdfast was a better'. **1870** READE *Put Yourself* ch. 29 I wouldn't say a word till it was all settled, for . . .

Brag is a good dog, but that he hath lost his tail.
(B 589)

1618 BRETON *Courtier & Countryman* Wks. (1879) II. 7 Some of you . . . can scarcely see a penny in your purse, and . . . if Brag were not a good dog, I know not how he would hold up his tail. **1678** RAY 105.

Brag of many goodmorrows, To.
(G 334)

1545 *Precepts of Cato* Publius O6 There are some that wyll promyse a man many good morowes. **1616** WITHALS 557. **1670** RAY 178.

Braggers, *see* Great b., little doers.

Brain as a burbolt,[1] As much. (B 598)

a. **1553** UDALL *Royster D.* III. ii Arb. 43 As much braine as a burbolt. **1672** WALKER 11, no. 61 He hath no more wit than a stone; no more brains than a burbout. He is a very Codshead. [[1] bird-bolt.]

Brain sows not corn, If the | it plants thistles.
(B 595)

1640 HERBERT no. 1024. **1659** HOWELL *Eng. Prov.* 6b The brain that sowes not corn plants thistles, viz. *If there be not good thoughts, there are bad.*

Brains are addle, His. (B 599)

1621 R. BURTON *Anat. M.* III. iv. i. 2, 895 Their brains were addle, and their bellies as empty of meat as their heads of wit. **1670** RAY 165.

Brains crow, His. (B 600)

1618 BELCHIER *Hans Beer-Pot* F1 I am pretily well, And soes mine hoast, I thinke his braines doe crow. **1678** RAY 230.

Brains don't lie in the beard, The.

1732 FULLER no. 4431.

Brains of a fox will be of little service, if you play with the paw of a lion, The.

1732 FULLER no. 4432.

Brains will work without barm, His.
(B 601)

1594 LYLY *M. Bombie* II. i. 117 My wits worke like barme, alias yest, alias sizing, alias rising, alias Gods good. *a.* **1625** FLETCHER *Demetrius and Enanthe* fo. 35. **1678** RAY 230. *Yorksh.*

Brain(s), *see also* Believe he's bald till you see his b. (Will not); Cudgel one's b.; Guts in his b.; Guts than b. (More); Heat of affection joined with idleness of b.; Idle b. the devil's shop; Mob has many heads but no b.; Pick (Suck) a person's b.; Salt or b. (Do not offer); Worm in his b.

Brambles, *see* Dowry is bed full of b.

Bran, If it be not | it is Bran's brother.

1814 SCOTT *Waverley* ch. 45 You shout . . . as if the Chieftain were just come to your head. '*Mar e Bran is e a brathair*, If it be not Bran, it is Bran's brother', was the proverbial reply of Maccombich. [Bran was the famous dog of Fingal.]

Bran, *see* Devil's meal all b.; Fancy may bolt b. and call it flour; Much b. little meal.

Branch(es), *see* Highest b. not safest roost; Love the boll (If you) you cannot hate b.

Brasenose, Brasen-Nose, *see* Bred in B. College; Testoons are gone to Oxford.

(Brass) farthing, Not worth a.   (F 71)

1520 R. WHITTINGTON *Vulg.* E.E.T.S. 93. **1591**
ARIOSTO *Orl. Fur.* Harington XXI Moral Neither
of both worth the taking for a farthing. **1591**
R. W. *Martin Mar-Sixtus* A3ᵛ He whose talent
of little wit is hardly worth a farthing. **1605**
S. ROWLEY *When you see me* C4ᵛ As for the
Popes faith (good faith's) not worth a farthing.
1672 WALKER 9 He is not worth a brass farthing.

Brass for gold.

[HOM. *Il.* 6. 236 χρύσεα χαλκείων (exchange of
armour).] **1813** BYRON to Gifford 18 June I
will not return my brass for your gold by expressing more fully these sentiments of admiration.

Brass tacks, To come down to.

1903 *New York Sun* (Supplt. to O.E.D.). **1926**
9 Jan. D. H. LAWRENCE *Lett.* ii. 879 Let us get
down to brass tacks. **1945** *Evening News* 27
Aug. Leader. Europe is a big parish . . . needing
. . . parish capacity to come down to brass tacks.

Brass, *see also* Earthen pot keep clear of b.
kettle; Injuries are written in b.

Brave men before Agamemnon, There
were.

[HORACE *Odes* 4. 9.'25 *Vixere fortes ante Agamemnona Multi.* Many brave men lived before
Agamemnon.] *a.* **1616** JONSON *Forest* no. 12
114 There were braue men before Ajax or
Idomen, or all the store That Homer brought to
Troy. **1819** BYRON *Don Juan* i. 5 Brave men
were living before Agamemnon. **1902** DEAN
HOLE *Then & Now* (ed. 7) ix. 116 *Vixere fortes
ante Agamemnona*—there was splendid cricket
before Grace.

Brawling booteth[1] not.

1546 HEYWOOD II. ii. G1 Braulyng booted not
. . . Alone to bed she went. [1 profiteth.]

Bray, *see* Vicar of B.

Bray(s), (*verb*), *see* All men say you are an ass
(When), time to b.; Ass knows well in whose face
he b.; Ass that b. against another ass; Ass that
b. most eats least.

Braying of an ass does not reach
heaven, The.

1802 WOLCOT (P. Pindar) *Ld. B. & his Motions*
Wks. (1816) IV. 236 There is a certain and true
saying, Of animals inclin'd to *braying*; . . . 'An
ass's voice ne'er reached to Heav'n.'

Brayton bargh, and Hambleton hough,
and Burton bream, were all in thy
belly, If | it would never be team.[1]
                                      (B 608)

1670 RAY 257 (*Yorks.*) . . . It is spoken of a
covetous and unsatiable person, whom nothing
will content. *Brayton* and *Hambleton* and *Burton*
are places between *Cawood* and *Pontefraict* in

this County. Brayton Bargh is a small hill.
[1 full.]

Bread and circuses.

[JUVENAL *Sat.* 10. 80 *Duas tantum res anxius
optat, Panem et Circenses.* Two things only they
earnestly desire, bread and the games of the
circus.] **1930** *Times* 11 Nov. 15/4 Processions
are good things, and there is never a better time
for the circuses than when the bread is dear or
scarce.

Bread, butter, and green cheese, is very
good English, and very good Friese.

1869 HAZLITT 100.

Bread for cake, You give me.   (B 633)

1581 C. MERBURY *Brief Discourse* 'Proverbe
Volgari' 18 M'hauete renduto pan per *foccacia
[margin] *Caakes. **1586** GUAZZO ii. 210 I
beleeve it be lawfull for the wife to give her
Husbande (as Bocace saith) Bread for a Cake.
1592 NASHE *Pierce Penn.* i. 185 Onely poore
England giues him bread for his cake, and holdes
him out at the armes end. **1659** HOWELL *It.
Prov.* 16.

Bread in one hand, and a stone in the
other, You show.   (B 634)

1539 TAVERNER 25. He beareth a stone in the
one hande, and breade in the other. **1609** J.
WYBARNE *New Age of Old Names* 10. **1732**
FULLER no. 5994.

Bread is a binder.   (B 612)

1594 GREENE & LODGE *Looking Glass* I. ii. 249.
1611 CHAPMAN *May Day* I. i. 425. *c.* **1616**
BEAUM. & FL. *Scornful Lady* IV. ii. 77. **1618** *Owl's
Almanack* 51.

Bread is buttered on both sides, His.
                                      (B 623)

1678 RAY 232 . . . i.e. He hath a plentifull estate:
he is fat and full. **1732** FULLER no. 6044. **1837**
LOCKHART *Scott* (1839) i. 206 *note* Wherever
Walter goes he is pretty sure to find his bread
buttered on both sides.

Bread is the staff of life.   (B 613)

1638 PENKETHMAN *Artach.* A j 6 Bread is worth
all, being the Staffe of life. **1704** SWIFT *T. Tub*
iv. Wks. (1856) I. 105 'Bread', says he, 'dear
brothers, is the staff of life.'

Bread men break is broke to them
again, What.   (B 630)

1613 DEKKER *Strange Horse-Race* D2 Such
bread as he brake, was but broken to him againe.
1630 TAYLOR (Water-Poet) *Wks.* 186, no. 55.

Bread (Cake) never falls but on its
buttered side, The.

1871 *N. & Q.* 4th Ser. VIII. 506 Lancashire Proverbs.—Unlucky persons often remark, 'My
cake always falls the butter side down'. **1891**

J. L. KIPLING *Beast & Man* 246 We express the completeness of ill-luck by saying, 'The bread never falls but on its buttered side'.

Bread than need, Who has no more | must not keep a dog. (B 632)

[L. *Teipsum non alens, canes alis.* Unable to keep yourself, you are keeping dogs.] 1492 *Saloman and Marcolphus* ed. Duff 10 The pore had ne breed and yet he bought an hownde. 1640 HERBERT no. 128.

Bread's house skaild never. (B 635)

a. 1628 CARMICHAELL no. 325. 1721 KELLY 20 (A Bread House) . . . Bread is the Staff of Life, and while People have that, they need not give over Houskeeping.

Bread and butter, *see* No other meat (They that have); Quarrel with one's b. and b.

Bread, *see also* Acorns were good till b.; Another's b. costs dear; Ask for b. and be given stone; Bachelors' fare, b. and cheese and kisses; Better b. than is made of wheat; Bit what the b. is (You may see by a); Buckinghamshire b. and beef; Butter will stick to his b. (No); Buying of b. undoes us; Crust is better than no b.; Dogs wag tail in love to b.; Dry b. at home; Eat your brown b. first; Eat white b. (When shall we); Eaten b. soon forgotten; Every day brings its b.; Fasts and . . . spares his b. and goes to hell; Fire is half b.; Griefs with b. are less; Honest a man as ever broke b.; Hope is poor man's b.; Kail spares b.; Knows on which side b. is buttered; Lemster b.; Likes not the drink (Who) God deprives of b.; Loves well sheep's flesh that wets b. in wool; New beer, new b. . . . makes hair grow through hood; Rich enough who lacks not b.; Second side of b. less time to toast; Take the b. out of one's mouth; Threatened men eat b.; Wine by savour, b. by colour. *See also* Brown bread.

Breadth, *see* Cow's thumb (Hair's b.).

Break a butterfly upon the wheel, To.

[To break on the wheel was a punishment for extreme criminals.] 1735 POPE *Prol. Sat.* 308 Who breaks a butterfly upon a wheel? 1889 GOSSE *18th Cent. Lit.* 113 The unfairness of breaking such an exquisite butterfly of art on the wheel of his analysis. 1909 *Times Lit. Sup.* 26 Nov. To dissect in cold blood these specimens of buoyant geniality seems like breaking butterflies upon a wheel.

Break a hog of an ill custom, It is hard to. (H 494)
1678 RAY 154.

Break a horse's back, be he never so strong, You may. (H 712)
1639 CLARKE 311.

Break a pasture makes a man; To | to make a pasture breaks a man.

1922 *Spectator* 28 Oct. Much arable land is unsuitable for pasture, and . . . the work of bringing it down to decent pasture would be long and expensive. . . .

Break his neck as his fast, A man shall as soon. (N 67)

1546 HEYWOOD I. xi. E2 In that house commonly suche is the cast, A man shall as soone breake his necke as his fast. a. 1558 *Wealth & Health* l. 688. 1597–8 BP. HALL *Satires* V. ii Housekeeping's dead, Saturio: wot'st thou where? Forsooth, they say far hence, in Breck-neck shire. And, ever since, they say, that feel and laste, That men may break their neck soon as their fast. 1641 FERGUSSON no. 893 Ye will break your neck and your fast alike in his house.

Break one's head and bring a plaster, To. (H 269)

c. 1430 LYDGATE *Minor Poems* Percy Soc. 56 To heke myn hede, and yeve me an houffe. . . . It may wele ryme, but it accordith nought. 1580 LYLY *Euph. & his Eng.* ii. 97 A plaister is a small amends for a broken head. 1608 ARMIN *Nest. Nin.* Shak. Soc. 48 The . . . jester . . . lay in durance a great while, till Will Sommers was faine, after he broke his head, to giue him a plaister, to get him out againe. [a. 1618] in 1662 FULLER *Essex* 326 Whilst Master of the Colledge, he chanced to punish all the Under-graduates therein. . . . The money . . . was expended in new whiteing the Hall of the Colledge. Whereupon a scholar hung up these verses on the Skreen: Doctor Jegon, Bennet-colledge Master, Brake the scholars head, and gave the walls a plaister. 1639 CLARKE 17 He broke my head, and then gave me a plaister. 1738 SWIFT *Dial.* I. E.L. 286 What! you break my head, and give me a plaister. 1816 J. AUSTEN *Persuasion* ch. 13 'This is breaking a head and giving a plaster, truly!' 1818 SCOTT *Rob Roy* ch. 28 Gin I hae broken the head . . . I sall find the plaister.

Break, or wear out, If things did not | how would tradesmen live? (T 465)

1639 CLARKE 125 Tradesmen live upon lack. 1666 TORRIANO *It. Prov.* 165, note 172 Let us break glasses apace, all trades must live. [re Murano near Venice]. 1738 SWIFT *Dial.* I. E.L. 268.

Break Priscian's head, To. (P 595)

[= to violate the rules of grammar. Priscian was a Latin grammarian of the 6th cent.] a. 1529 SKELTON *Speke, Parrot* in Wks. (Dyce) II. 9 Prisians hed broken now handy dandy. 1589 *Puttenham* Arb. 258 Solecismus . . . the breaking of Priscian's head. 1594–5 SHAKES. *L.L.L.* V. i. 24 Laus Deo bone intelligo. — Bone? bone, for bene: Priscian a little scratched; 'twill serve. 1642 FULLER *Holy State* 'Hildegardis' Throwing words at random she never brake Priscian's head. 1663 BUTLER *Hudibras* II. ii. 225 And hold no sin so deeply red As that of breaking Priscian's head. 1728 POPE *Dunciad* iii. 162 Break Priscian's head and Pegasus's neck. 1785 CUMBERLAND *Observer* No. 22, § 6 Observe, how this . . . orator breaks

poor Priscian's head for the good of his country.
1788 GROSE *Dict. Vulg. T.* Priscian . . . was so
devoted to his favourite study, that to speak
false Latin in his company was as disagreeable
to him, as to break his head. **1883** *Daily Tel.*
10 Jul. 5/4 Does Shakespeare never break
Priscian's head?

Break the egg in anybody's pocket, To.

[= to spoil his plan.] *a.* **1734** NORTH *Exam.* 324
This very circumstance . . . broke the egg . . . in
the Pockets of the Whigs.

Break the ice, To.   (I 3)

c. **1535** *Life Fisher* 40 Whom yt chaunced . . .
to be one of the first that brake the yse. **1540**
PALSGRAVE *Acolastus* 31 Philautus . . . cutteth
asonder that yce . . . breaketh the way before
hym. **1571** L. H. *Dict. French and English* 'To
the Reader' Commendable as either breaketh
the yce vnto the better seeing, or treadeth the
path to the discret and cunning. **1579–80** NORTH
Plutarch (1676) 89 To be the first to break the
Ice of the Enterprize. **1594–8** SHAKES. *T.S.* I. ii.
263 If you break the ice, and do this feat, Achieve
the elder, set the younger free For our access.
1646 J. COOKE *Vind. Prof. Law* To Rdr. I have
attempted to break the Ice in a subject concerning reformation in Courts of Justice. **1678**
BUTLER *Hudibras* III. ii. 493 After he had a while
lookd wise, At last broke silence, and the ice.
1741 RICHARDSON *Pamela* (1824) I. ix. 246 You
see . . . that I break the ice, and begin first in the
indispensably expected correspondence between
us. **1893** EARL DUNMORE *Pamirs* I. 226 The ice
being thus broken, Ching Dolai put aside the
reserve habitual to all Celestials.

Breaks his trust, To him that | let trust be broken.

1589 *The Contre-League* tr. E.A. 73 Frangenti
fidem, fides frangatur eidem. To a breaker of
faith, let faith be broken. **1663** F. HAWKINS
F8ᵛ.

Breaks his word, A man that | bids others be false to him.   (M 300)

1548 HALL (1809, 184) (As the common prouerbe
saieth) he, which is a promise breaker, escapeth
not always free. **1732** FULLER no. 311.

Break(s), broke(n), *see also* Better bend than b.;
Bread men b. is b. to them again, (What); Cord
b. at last by weakest pull; Covetousness (Too
much) b. the bag; Fair words b. no bones;
Flint on a feather bed, (To b. a); Grief pent up
will b. the heart; Hell is b. loose; Hops make or
b.; Pot b. (Your) seems better than my whole;
See you in daylight, (They that) winna b. the
house for you; Sooner b. than bow; Sung well
before he b. shoulder; Thread b. where weakest;
Tom pitcher's b. (When), I shall have shards;
Truth will come to light (b. out); Year will not
b. him (Ill).

Breakfast, *see* Fast for my life (If I were to), I
would take good b.; Hare to b. (He that will
have); Hope is good b.; Huntsman's b., lawyer's

dinner; Laugh before b.; Sing before b.; Sleepy
fox has seldom feathered b.

Breaking, *see* Horse needs b., (The best).

Breams in his pond, He that has | is able to bid his friend welcome.   (B 638)

1653 WALTON *Angler* I. x (1915) 165 The French
esteem this fish highly, and to that end have this
proverb, 'He that hath Breams in his pond, is
able to bid his friend welcome'.

Breard[1] like midding[2] breard, There is no.

1721 KELLY 328 . . . The Grains of Corn that are
carried out unto the Dunghill takes Root and
springs amain; spoken when we see People of
mean Birth rise suddenly to Wealth and Honour.
[[1] young corn. [2] dung-hill.]

Breast, *see* Clean b.; Cross on b., devil in heart;
Learning in the b. of a bad man is as a sword in
the hand of a madman; Love in his b.; Nightingale with a thorn against one's b. (To sit like
a).

Breath, One man's | another's death.   (M 482)

1639 CLARKE 253 *Pestilentia.*

Breath, *see also* Fame is but b. of people; First b.
is beginning of death; Keep your b. to cool;
Mother's b. is aye sweet.

Bred in Brasen-Nose College, You were.

[= a play upon the name of a college at Oxford,
to denote a person of much assurance.] **1732**
FULLER no. 6011.

Bred in the bone will not out of the flesh, What is.   (F 365)

[*c.* **1290** *Wright's Polit. Songs* Camd. Soc. 167
Osse radicatum raro de carne recedit.] [*c.* **1470**]
1485 Malory *Morte d'Arthur* IX. xxxix, l. 404 Syr
launcelot smyled and said hard hit is to take
oute of the flesshe that is bred in the bone. **1481**
CAXTON *Reynard* xii Arb. 29 He coude not
refrayne hym self that whiche cleuid by the bone
myght not out of the flesshe. **1546** HEYWOOD II.
viii. K2 This prouerbe prophecied many 'yeres
agone, It will not out of the fleshe, that's bred in
the bone. **1603** MONTAIGNE (Florio) III. xiii. 250
They are effects of custome and use; and . . .
1719 DEFOE *Crusoe* (1840) II. i. 1 What is bred in
the bone will not go out of the flesh. **1721** KELLY
179 It is ill to bring out of the Flesh, that is bred
in the Bone. It is hard to leave those ill Customs
to which we have been long inured. **1912** ALEX.
MACLAREN *Romans* 231 'You cannot expel nature
with a fork', said the Roman. 'What's bred in
the bone won't come out of the flesh', says the
Englishman.

Bredon-hill puts on his hat, When | ye men of the vale, beware of that.

1869 HAZLITT 474 Bredon-hill is in Worcestershire; the 'hat' is of course . . . the heavy cloud

which covers the apex of the hill previously to heavy rain or a thunderstorm.

Breech makes buttons, His (My).
(A 381)

1562–3 *Jack Juggler* Hazl.-Dods. ii. 121 His arse meketh buttons now, and who lusteth to feel, Shall find his heart creeping out at his heel. **1567** R. B. *Appius and Virginia* 305. **1618–19** J. FLETCHER *Bonduca* II. iii. **1670** RAY 165 . . . This is said of a man in fear. . . . Vehement fear causes a relaxation of the *Sphincter ani* and unvoluntary dejection. **1702** *Mouse grown Rat* 23 My Breech began to make Buttons; I dreamt of nothing but Impeachments.

Breeches of a bare-arsed man, To beg. *Cf.* Naked man is sought after. . . .
(B 644)

1546 HEYWOOD I. ix. CI[v] There is nothyng more vayne, as your selfe tell can, Than to beg a breeche of a bare arst man. **1548** SIR T. ELYOT *Bibliotheca* s.v. Calvum vellis, thou would take a breche from a bare arste man. **1616** WITHALS 554. **1659** HOWELL *Eng. Prov.* 15b.

Breech(es), *see also* Breeze in one's b. (To have a); Knit my dog a pair of b.; Master wears no b. (Most); Scratch my b.; Wears the b.; Wine wears no b.

Breed in the mud, All that | are not efts (eels). *Cf.* Mud chokes no eels.   (T 174)

1577 HOLINSHED 1587 iii. 94b Eeles . . . fatten not in faire running water, but in muddie motes and ponds. **1580** LYLY *Euph. & his Eng.* ii. 89 All things that breede in the mudde, are not Euets. **1732** FULLER no. 549 (eels).

Breed of Lady Mary, You | when you're good you're o'er good.

1721 KELLY 363 . . . A drunken Man beg'd Lady Mary to help him on his Horse, and having made many Attempts to no purpose, . . . at length he jump'd quite over. O Lady Mary (said he) when thou art good, thou art o'er good.

Breed of the chapman, You | you are never out of your gate.[1]

1721 KELLY 363'. . . Spoken to them that make Business wherever they go. [1 way.]

Breed of the good man's mother, You | you are aye in the gate.[1]

a. **1628** CARMICHAELL nos. 742, 1446, 1868. **1721** KELLY 364 . . . Spoken to them that are in our Way. Taken from the ill understanding that is often between Mother's in Law, and Daughter's in Law. **1862** HISLOP 183 The gude man's mither is aye in the gudewife's gait. [1 way.]

Breed of the gowk[1], Ye | ye have not a rhyme but ane.   (G 384)

a. **1628** CARMICHAELL no. 1735 (tune). *Ibid.*, no. 1764 (sang). **1641** FERGUSSON no. 905 (ryme).

1721 KELLY 362 (ay but one Song) Spoken to them that always insist upon one thing. [1cuckoo.]

Breed of the miller's daughter, that speered[1] what tree groats[2] grew on, You.

1721 KELLY 364 . . . Spoken when saucy Fellows, bred of mean Parentage, pretend Ignorance of what they were bred with. [1 inquired. 2 husked oats.]

Breed of the miller's dog, Ye | ye lick your mouth (lips) ere the poke be open.
(M 963)

a. **1628** CARMICHAELL no. 1715. **1641** FERGUSSON no. 911. **1674** RAY *Collection of English Words* 8. **1721** KELLY 361 . . . Spoken to covetous People, who are eagerly expecting a thing, and ready to receive it, before it be proffered.

Breed of the tod's[1] bairns, You | if one be good, all are good. *Cf.* Tod's bairns are ill to tame.

a. **1628** CARMICHAELL no. 1537 (Tods birds). **1721** KELLY 361 . . . Spoken of a bad Family, where there are none to mend another. [1 fox.]

Breed young bones, To.

c. **1565** *Bugbears* IV. v. 45. **1566** SENECA *Agamemnon* tr. J. Studley B2 My doughter . . . Doth brede younge bones, and lades her womb. **1594** *Leir* l. 844. **1633** FORD *Broken Heart* II. i. 142.

Breed, breeding (*noun*), *see also* Beware of b.; Birth is much, b. is more; Brackley b.; St. Giles b.

Breed(s), bred (*verb*), *see also* Beggars b.; Best b. have best portion; Dogs bark as b.; Like b. like; Spins well who b. her children; Weapons bode (b.) peace; Where one is b. but . . . (Not).

Breeks, *see* Petticoats woo (When), b. may come speed; Purse to wife (Sell), give b.; Sits full still that has riven b.; Taking the b. off a Hielandman (Ill); Tarry b. pays no fraught.

Breeze in one's breech, To have a.
(B 651)

1612 WEBSTER *White Devil* I. ii. 155 I will put brees in's tayle, set him gadding presentlie. *c.* **1630** BEAUM. & FL. *Monsieur Thomas* IV. vi. What, is the breeze in your breech? **1678** RAY 232 To have a breez, i.e. a gad-fly, in his breech. Spoken of one that frisks about, and cannot rest in a place.

Breeze, *see also* Whistle for b.

Brevity is the soul of wit.   (B 652)

1600–1 SHAKES. *H.* II. ii. 90. **1612** J. TAYLOR *Laugh and Be Fat: Wks.* F., 237 Shortest writ, the greatest wit affoords, And greatest wit, consists in fewest words. **1647** *Countrym. New Commonw.* 16 Brevity is a great praise of eloquence. Cicero. **1833** M. SCOTT *T. Cring. Log* ch. 16 Brevity is the soul of wit, — ahem. **1853** TRENCH i. 8 Brevity, 'the soul of wit', will be eminently the soul of a proverb's wit.

Brew good ale, blessing of your heart, You. (B 450)

[*c.* **1515**] **1530** BARCLAY *Eclog.* II. 17 God blesse the brewer well cooled is my throate. **1594** SHAKES. *T.G.V.* III. i. 295 She brews good ale.—And thereof comes the proverb, Blessing of your heart, you brew good ale. **1622** JONSON *Masque Augurs* l. 181 *Masques at Court* VII. 635 Our Ale's o' the best, And each good guest Prayes for their souls that brew it.

Brew, As they | so let them bake (drink). *Cf.* Bake (As you) so shall you brew. (B 654)

c. **1300** *Cursor M.* l. 2848 Suilk als þai brued now ha þai dronken. *c.* **1350** *Douce MS. 52* no. 97 So brewe, so drynke. *c.* **1390** GOWER *Conf. Amantis* iii. 161 And who so wicked ale breweth Full ofte he mot the worse drinke. *c.* **1410** *Towneley Plays, 2nd. Shep. Play* 501 Bot we must drynk as we brew. **1545** TAVERNER G1ᵛ The prouerbe which commonly we vse in englysh . . . is this: such ale as he hath brewed, let him drinke him self. **1546** HEYWOOD I. viii. C1 (. . . brewe . . . drynke). **1599** PORTER *Two Angry Wom.* l. 1830 No indeed; euen as they brew so let them bake. **1641** FERGUSSON no. 593 Let him drink as he has browin. **1652** *Proc. Parliament* no. 138, 2162 The Admirall . . . said, that as thy brewed so they should bake. **1721** KELLY 186 If you brew well, you'll drink the better. If what you have done be good, and right, you will find the Effects accordingly. **1808** E. HAMILTON *Cottagers of Glenburnie* ch. 14 As she has brewed sae she maun drink.

Brew, *see also* Bake so shall you b. (eat), (As you); Must be if we b. (This).

Brewer's horse has bit, One whom the. (B 656)

1597 SHAKES. *I Hen. IV* III. iii. 9 An I have not forgotten what the inside of a church is made of, I am a peppercorn, a brewer's horse. **1635** T. HEYWOOD *Philocothonista* 44 To title a drunkard by, wee . . . strive to character him in a more mincing phrase; as thus . . . One whom the Brewer's horse hath bit. **1847** HALLIWELL *Dict.* s.v. Brewer's horse A drunkard was sometimes said to be 'one whom the brewer's horse hath bit'. **1917** BRIDGE 100 . . . One who has had a little too much liquor.

Brewing, *see* Sairy b. that is not good in newing.

Briar(s), *see* Bird on b. (bough), (As merry (light) as); Leave in the briers.

Bribe, nor lose thy right, Neither. (R 125)

1640 HERBERT no. 284. **1706** STEVENS s.v. Cohecho Take no Bribe, nor lose no Due.

Bribe will enter without knocking, A. (B 658)

1612 T. ADAMS *The Gallant's Burden* (1616 ed., 49) Bribery creeping in at the key-hole euen when the door of Iustice is locked vp against her. **1616** DRAXE no. 207 A bribe entreth everywhere without knocking. **1639** CLARKE 220.

Bricks without straw, To make. (B 660)

[Said with allusion to Exodus v.] **1614** T. ADAMS *Heaven and Earth Reconciled* G1ᵛ When we should make Bricke, worke in our profession, we are forced to gather Straw, labour for sustenaunce. **1616** DEKKER *Villainies Discovered* K1ᵛ To compell thy Vassall to make more Bricke when strawe and stuffe is taken from him. **1621** BURTON *Anat. Mel.* I. ii. III. xv (1651) 140 Patrons . . . but (hard task-masters they prove) they take away their straw, and compel them to make their number of brick. **1658** *Verney Mem.* (1907) II. 79 It is an hard task to make bricks without straw. **1661** DK. ORMONDE in *11th Rep. Hist. MSS. Comm.* App. V. 10 If they will not let that [act] passe . . . and yet will have us keepe armys, is it not requiring a tale of bricks, without allowing the straw. **1874** L. STEPHEN *Hours in Library* I. vi. 271 It is often good for us to have to make bricks without straw.

Brick(s), *see also* Cat on hot b.; Mortar, (No more), no more b.; Rome b., (I found).

Bridal, *see* Man be at his own b. (Meet that).

Bride goes to her marriage-bed, The | but knows not what shall happen to her. (B 661)

1651 JER. TAYLOR *Holy Dying* I. i (Bohn) 303 Many brides have died . . . according to the saying of Bensirah, the wise Jew, 'The bride went into her chamber, and knew not what should befall her there'. **1678** RAY *Adag. Hebr.* 412 . . . The meaning is, that we ought not confidently to promise ourselves in any thing any great success.

Bride the sun shines on, and the corpse the rain rains on, Happy is the. (B 663)

1601 SHAKES. *T.N.* IV. iii. 26–35 Plight me the full assurance of your faith . . . and heavens so shine That they may fairly note this act of mine! **1607** *Puritan Widow* I. A3ᵛ If, Blessed bee the coarse the raine raynes vpon, he had it, powring downe. **1648** HERRICK *Hesper.* 284 *A Nupt. Song* Blest is the Bride, on whom the Sun doth shine. **1790** GROSE s.v. Popular Superstitions 44.

Bride, *see also* Bonny b. is soon buskit; Muckhill on my trencher, quoth the b.; Simpers like a b.

Bridge of one's nose, To make a. (B 667)

1678 RAY 231 . . . i.e. to intercept ones trencher, cup, or the like; or to offer . . . kindnesses to one, and then . . . do it to another. *a.* **1700** B. E. *Dict.*

Cant. Crew s.v. You make a Bridge of his Nose, when you pass your next Neighbor in Drinking, or one is preferr'd over another's Head.   **1738** SWIFT *Dial.* II. E.L. 301 Pray, my lord, don't make a bridge of my nose.

Bridge, *see also* Cross the b. (Don't) till you get to it; February makes a b.; Golden b. (For flying enemy); Good turn will meet another . . . at B. of London; Head (He that will be) let him be b.; Praise the b. he goes over (Let every man); Water has run under b.

Bridges were made for wise men to walk over, and fools to ride over.
(B 668)

1678 RAY 106.

Bridle and spur that makes a good horse, It is the.

1581 GUAZZO ii. 71 That he teach them [his children] to govern themselves with the bridle and the spur.   **1642** TORRIANO 15.   **1732** FULLER no. 3021.

Bridle (reins), To give one the. (B 671)

1540 PALSGRAVE *Acolastus* 112 He is suffered to ronne on the brydell, or to do what he liste, withoute any restraynt.   **1546** HEYWOOD II. viii. K2 I gaue hir the bridell at begynnyng. And nowe she taketh the brydle in the teeth.   *c.* **1570** *Marr. Wit. and Science* II. i. B2ᵛ Giue her not the bridle for a yeare or twayne.   [**1587**] **1599** PEELE *David and Bethsabe* l. 573 O prowd reuolt of a presumptuous man, Laying his bridle in the necke of sin.

Bridle, *see also* Bite upon the b.; Prosperity lets go b.; Reason lies between spur and b.; Shake a b. over Yorkshire tike's grave; Take the bit (b.) in the teeth.

Bridport, *see* Stabbed with B. dagger.

Bright rain makes fools fain.

1883 ROPER 24.   **1917** BRIDGE 162 . . . When a rain-cloud is succeeded by a little brightness in the sky, fools rejoice and think it will soon be fair weather.

Bright that shines by himself, He is only.
(S 343)

1640 HERBERT no. 707.

Bright, *see also* Clear (b.) as glass; Iron with use grows b.; Look at b. side.

Brill, *see* Deal, Dover, and Harwich, the devil gave.

Brim, *see* Better spare at b.

Brimmer, *see* Deceit in a b. (No).

Bring a cow to the hall and she'll run to the byre.¹
(C 752)

1621 ROBINSON C8.   **1641** FERGUSSON no. 165 Bring a kow to the hall, and she will to the byre again.   **1721** KELLY 86 Drive a Cow to the Hall and she'll run to the Bayer.   Spoken when People

of mean Breeding . . . do not take to, or become, a more honourable Station.   [¹ cow-shed.]

Bring a noble (shilling) to ninepence, To.
(N 194)

1546 HEYWOOD II. v. H1 He maketh his mares with marchantes lykely, To bryng a shillyng to nyne pence quickely.   **1568** FULWELL *Like Will to L.* Hazl.-Dods. iii. 344 For why Tom Tosspot since he went hence, Hath increased a noble just unto nine-pence.   **1607** H. ESTIENNE *World of Wonders* tr. R.C. 81 Hauing brought their twelue-pence to nine-pence, and their nine-pence to nothing.   **1609** HARWARD 110 Prodigality bringeth a noble to nine pence, a castle to a capcase.   **1668** SHADWELL *Sullen Lov.* v. iii Merm. 112 I should soon bring a noble to ninepence then, as they say.   **1670** RAY 187 . . . and ninepence to nothing.   **1721** KELLY 144 He has brought his Noble to Nine Pence, and his Nine Pence to nothing (English).

Bring an abbey to a grange,¹ To.
(A 3)

c. **1480** *Early Miscell.* Warton Cl. 1855 26 And nowe that abbay is turned to a grange.   *c.* **1548** BALE *K. Johan* 579 *Clargy.* Our changes are soche that an abbeye turneth to a graunge. We are so handled we have scarce eyther horse or male.   **1670** RAY 161 . . . We speak it of an unthrift.   [¹ a country-house.]

Bring but that's no there ben, It is ill to.
(B 675)

a. **1628** CARMICHAELL no. 888 It is euill to bring but, that is not there ben.   **1641** FERGUSSON no. 504 It is ill to bring butte the thing that is not there benne.   **1721** KELLY 194 It is ill to bring Butt, that's no there Benn. One cannot produce what he has not.   [Butt is towards the Door. Benn is into the House.]

Bring haddock to paddock, To. (H 5)

[= to come to destitution.]   **1546** HEYWOOD II. x. L3ᵛ. And thus had he brought haddocke to paddocke. Tyll they bothe were not worth a haddock.   **1577** STANYHURST in HOLINSHED *Descr. Ireland* (1587, 21a) I had bene like to haue brought haddocke to paddocke.

Bring home the wealth of the Indies, He who would | must carry the wealth of the Indies with him.

1778 JOHNSON in *Boswell* (1848) lxv. 597 As the Spanish proverb says, 'He who would bring home the wealth of the Indies must carry the wealth of the Indies with him'. So it is in travelling; a man must carry knowledge with him if he would bring home knowledge.   **1882** J. NICHOL *Amer. Lit.* 6 We can only gather interest on the capital we take with us. 'He that would bring home the wealth of the Indies must carry out the wealth of the Indies.'

Brings good news, He that | knocks hard.
(N 140)

1611 COTGRAVE s.v. Hardiment He that brings good news boldly knocks at doore.   **1623**

WODROEPHE 487 He knockes boldly at the Gate that brings good Newes in there at.   1640 HER-BERT no. 824.

Brings himself into needless dangers, He that | dies the devil's martyr.
(D 36)

1639 FULLER *Holy War* II. xxix (1651) 82 Nor will I listen to the unhappy Dutch Proverb, 'He that bringeth himself into needlesse dangers, dieth the devil's martyr'.   **1678** RAY 18 Who perisheth in needless danger is the Devils martyr.

Brings up his son to nothing, breeds a thief, He that.
1732 FULLER no. 2053.

Bring(s), *see also* Bow, (To b. to one's); Care b. gray hair; Clouds b. not rain, (All); Come with me (If wilt), b. with thee; Covetousness b. nothing home; Evening b. all home; Evils we b. on ourselves; Meat in his mouth, (He b.); One thing b. up another thing; Take what you find or what you b.; Thunders in March, (When it) it b. sorrow; Trouble b. experience; Vine b. forth three grapes: ...; Welcome that b. (They are); Worth of a thing is what it will b.

Brink, *see* Edge of his grave (pit's b.), (He is upon the).

Bristles, *see* Expect of a hog but b. (What can you).

Bristol milk.
(M 932)

1644 PRYNNE & WALKER *Fiennes' Trial* 78 Good store of Bristoll milk, strong wines and waters.   **1662** FULLER *Bristol* 34 . . . Meta-phorical Milk, whereby Xeres or Sherry Sack is intended.   **1848** MACAULAY *Hist. Engl.* I. 335 A rich beverage made of the best Spanish wine and celebrated . . . as Bristol Milk.

Bristol, *see also* Shipshape and B. fashion.

Britain, All countries stand in need of.

1577 W. HARRISON *Descr. of England* New Sh. S. ii. 70 It was not said of old time without great reason, that all countries haue need of Britaine, and Britaine itselfe of none.   **1580** LYLY *Euph. & his Eng.* ii. 196 Whereof there was an olde saying, all countries stande in neede of Britaine, and Britaine of none.

Britain, *see also* Little B.

Brittle, *see* Glass, (As b. as).

Broad as it is long, As.
(B 677)

1678 RAY 67. **1732** FULLER no. 2933. **1821** BYRON *Lett.* Prothero v. 379.

Broadgates in Oxford, *see* Verdingales.

Broadside, To burst at the.
(B 678)

1604 JAMES I *Counterblast to Tobacco* B4ᵛ And therefore are you no wiser in taking *Tobacco* for

purging you of distillations, then if for preuenting the Cholike you would take . . . all kinde of meates and drinkes, that would breede grauell in the kidneyes, and then when you were forced to auoyde . . . much grauell in your Vrine, that you should attribute the thanke thereof to such nourishments as bred those within you, that behoued eether to be expelled by the force of Nature, or you to haue burst at the broad side, as the Prouerbe is.   **1670** RAY 217 . . . Drinking phrase.

Brock, *see* Stink like a b.

Broke his hour that kept his day, He never.
(H 739)

1678 RAY 122.

Broken apothecary, a new doctor, A.
(A 278)

1659 HOWELL *Eng. Prov.* 13b.   **1670** RAY 2.

Broken bones well set become stronger.
(B 515)

1579 LYLY *Euph.* i. 206 Doth not he remember that the broken boane once sette together, is stronger than euer it was?   **1598** SHAKES. *2 Hen. IV* IV. i. 222 Our peace will, like a broken limb united, Grow stronger for the breaking.   **1604** *Id. O.* II. iii. 313 This broken joint between you and her husband entreat her to splinter; and . . . this crack of your love shall grow stronger than 'twas before.   **1612** WEBSTER *White Devil* II. i. Like bones which, broke in sunder, and well set, knit the more strongly.   *a.* **1633** G. HERBERT 'Repentance' l. 36 Fractures well cur'd make us more strong.   **1651** WALTON *Sir H. Wotton* in *Lives* (Dent) i. 156 As broken bones well set become stronger, so Sir Henry Wotton did not only recover, but was much more confirmed in his Majesty's estimation.

Broken friendship may be soldered, but will never be sound, A.
(F 759)

c. **1526** *Dicta Sap.* B3 Frendship is soone broken, but nat lightly reclaymed.   **1613** R. DALLINGTON *Aphorisms* 201 Friendship once broken is hardly peeced, And peeced Enmity neuer surely sodred. **1732** FULLER no. 27.

Broken her elbow, She has.
(L 187)

1650 HEATH *Clarastella* II. 64 And so she broke her elboe 'gainst the bed.   **1678** RAY 241 . . . That is, she hath had a bastard.

Broken her elbow at the church (kirk) door, She has.
(E 99)

1670 RAY 166 *Chesh.* It is spoken of a house-wively maid that grows idle after marriage. **1721** KELLY 293 (Kirk) Spoken of a thrifty Maiden, when she becomes a lazy Wife.

Broken her leg above the knee, She has.
(L 187)

1618 FLETCHER *Loyal Subject* III. v 57 If her foot slip and down fall she, And break her leg above the knee.   **1678** RAY 256 . . . i.e. had a bastard.

Broken reed, To lean upon a (*or* trust to a broken staff). (R 61 and S 805)

[ISAIAH xxxvi. 6 Lo, thou trustest in the staff of this broken reed, on Egypt; whereon if a man lean, it will go into his hand, and pierce it.] **1509** BARCLAY *Ship of Fools* i. 271 That man . . . lenyth his body vpon a rede. **1565** J. CALFHILL *Treatise of the Cross* P.S. 131 Refuse to lean to so weak a staff. **1580** MUNDAY *Zelauto* O1ᵛ Who trusteth to a Womans will, were as good leane on a broken staffe. **1580** H. GIFFORD *Posie* Gros. 71 To trust her lookes . . . Is nothing els but trust a broken staffe. **1757** SMOLLETT *Reprisal* I. i You lean upon a broken reed, if you trust to their compassion.

Broken sack will hold no corn, A. (S 3)

1573 SANFORD 109ᵛ A broken bagge can hold no mill. **1611** COTGRAVE s.v. Sac A sacke that's torne, doth shed its corne. **1639** CLARKE 133.

Broken sleeve holds the arm back, A. (S 531)

c. **1470** *Harl. MS. 3362* For my slefe y broke—*Pro manica fracta manus est mea sepe redacta*. *a.* **1530** R. *Hill's Commonpl. Bk.* E.E.T.S. 132 For my brokyn sleve, men me refuce—*Pro manica fracta, manus mea est sepe retracta*. **1550** HEYWOOD I. ix. C1ᵛ A broken sléeue holdth tharme backe. And shame drawth me backe. **1625** JONSON *Staple of News* I. ii.12 And therefore you haue another answering prouerbe: *A broken sleeue keepes the arme backe*.

Broken, *see also* Oath (unlawful) better b. than kept; Pot b. (Your) seems better than my whole one; Promises are either b. or kept; Ship (As b. a) has come to land; Whole from the b., (Keep the).

Broker, *see* Two false knaves need no b.

Broo, *see* Ill flesh ne'er made good b.

Brood (*noun*), *see* Bastard b. always proud; Bird of same nest (b., egg, feather).

Broom, *see* Bestows his gifts as b. honey; Furze (Under the) is . . ., under the b. is silver and gold; New b. sweeps clean.

Broomstick (Besom), To jump (marry over) the.

[= to go through a *quasi*-marriage ceremony, in which the parties jump over a broomstick.] **1774** *Westmr. Mag.* II. 16 He had no inclination for a Broomstick-marriage. **1824** MACAULAY *Misc. Writ.* (1860) I. 95 They were married over a broomstick. **1876** BLACKMORE *Cripps* ch. 19 Three or four score of undergraduates . . . had offered her matrimony, and three or four newly elected fellows were asking whether they would vacate, if they happened to jump the broomstick.

Brosten, *see* Welly b.

Broth, *see* Beef (Such), such be.; Boils his pot with chips, makes b. smell of smoke; Cold b. hot again; Coloquintida spoils b.; Eat the devil as the b. (As good); Good b. in old pot; No b. no ball; Sup Simon, here's good b.

Brother had rather see the sister rich than make her so, The. (B 685)

1611 COTGRAVE s.v. Frere The brother would haue his sister rich, any way, but at his charges. **1678** RAY 203.

Brother, *see also* Eat well is drink well's b.; Sleep is b. of death; Younger brother.

Brought an ill comb to my own head, I have.

1721 KELLY 204 . . . That is, I have engag'd my self in a troublesome Business.

Brown, *see* Addendum p. 930, (Study, To be in a b.).

Brown bread, *see* Ask of my sire b. b. (I had rather); Eat your b. b. first; Good small beer, good b. b. (No such thing as).

Brown man, *see* Red man (To a) read thy rede.

Brows, *see* Honest as skin between b.; Sweat of other men's b., (To live by the).

Browse, *see* Goat must b. where tied.

Brugh, *see* Round the moon there is a b. (When).

Bruit, *see* Much b. little fruit.

Brummagem, *see* Sutton.

Brush, *see* Bought a b. (He has); Fox is known by b. ; Tarred with same b.

Bubble, *see* Man is but a b.

Buchanan's almanac, long foul, long fair.

1721 KELLY 69 . . . When Weather continues long of one sort, it commonly continues as long of the contrary, when it changes.

Buck of the first head, He is like a. (B 693)

[*a.***1606** *Return from Parnassus* Arb. 30 Now sir, a Bucke the first yeare is a Fawne; the second year a Pricket, The third yeare a Sorell, the fourth yeare a Soare, the fift a Bucke of the first head, the sixt yeare a compleat Buck.] **1584** PARSONS *Copy of a Letter (Leicester's Commonwealth)* 167 And this was euident in this mans father, who being a Buck of the first head . . . was intolerable in contempt of others. **1678** RAY 67 . . . Brisk, pert, forward; Some apply it to upstart Gentlemen.

Buck, *see also* Blow the b's. horn; Wild as a b.

Bucket, *see* Kick the b.; Put not the b. too often in the well; Rope in after b. (Throw).

Buckets in a well, Like.   (B 695)

c. **1386** CHAUCER *Knight's T.* l. 1532 Now in the croppe, now doun in the breres, Now up, now doun, as boket in a welle. **1555** HEYWOOD *Epig. on Proverbs* no. CX As fast as one goth, an other cumth in vre. Two buckets in a well, cum and go so sure. **1596** SHAKES. *Rich. II* IV. i. 188 That bucket down and full of tears am I, Drinking my griefs, while you are up on high. **1606** DAY *Ile of Gulls* C4ᵛ My lord and his friend . . . a couple of waters buckets . . . hope winds the one up, dispaire plunges the other downe. *a.* **1697** AUBREY *Life of Robert Saunderson* Had his memorie been greater, his judgement had been lesse: they are like two well-bucketts.

Bucking, *see* Smocks than shirts in a b. (He that has more).

Buckingham, *see* Old man who weds . . . freeman of B.

Buckinghamshire bread and beef.
                                              (B 616)

1613–22 DRAYTON *Polyolb.* xxiii. 247 Wks. (1876) III. 95 Rich Buckingham doth bear the term of Bread and Beef, Where if you beat a Bush, 'tis odds you start a Thief. **1662** FULLER *Bucks.* 128 Buckinghamshire Bread and Beef. The former is as fine, the latter as fat, in this as in any other County. . . . Here if you beat a bush, it's odds you'ld start a Thief. . . . But this proverb is now Antiquated.

Buckle and bare thong together, He will bring (hold).   (B 696)

[= to be stripped of everything.] **1546** HEYWOOD II. viii. K2ᵛ Little and little he decayde so long, Tyll he at length came to buckle and bare thong. **1577** STANYHURST in HOLINSHED *Descr. Ireland* (1587 21a) I am not yet come to my buckle. **1600** *Weakest to Wall* E2 My Benefice doth bring me in no more But what will hold bare buckle and thong together. **1651** H. OXINDEN to K. Oxinden *Oxinden and Peyton Letters 1642–1670* ed. D. Gardiner 174 If he do not marrie well, I know not how I shall according to the saying keepe buckle and thong together. **1678** RAY 232.

Buckle and thong.   (B 699)

1599 NASHE iii. 168 As the buckle to the thong. **1631** MABBE *Celestina* III. 71 Mother and I were nayle and flesh, buckle and thong.

Buckle and thong, *see also* Hold him to it.

Buckle for it, Let them.   (B 700)

1678 RAY 352. Som.

Buckle, *see also* Angry (If you be) you *now* turn the b.

Bucklers, To give (one) the.

[= to yield.] **1589** NASHE Pref. to Greene's *Menaphon* iii. 323 [Our countrymen] would carry the bucklers full easily from all forraine brauers. **1592** GREENE *Second Pt. of Cony-catching* Harrison 12 His maister laught, and was glad . . . to yeeld the bucklers to his prentise, and to become frends. **1598–9** SHAKES. *M.A.* V. ii. 17 I give thee the bucklers. **1616** T. ADAMS *Diseases of the Soul* 53. He vyes vanities with the Slothful, and it is hard to say, who wins the game; yet giue him the bucklers.

Bucklers, *see also* Take up the cudgels (b.).

Buckles his belt his ain gate,[1] Every man.

1721 KELLY 92 Every Man wears his Belt in his own Fashion. An Apology for a Man's acting differently from others. **1818** SCOTT *Ht. Midl.* ch. 28 Aweel, lass, . . . then thou must pickle in thine own poke-nook, and buckle thy girdle thine ain gate. [1 way.]

Buckson, *see* Muckson up to the b.

Bud, *see* Nip in b.

Budget (= sack), *see* Knacks in one's b., (To have); Tinker's b. is full of necessary tools.

Buff nor baff, He can neither say (knows not whether to say).

1481 CAXTON *Reynard* ed. Arber 106 He wyste not what to saye buff ne haff [sic]. **1542** ERASM. tr. Udall *Apoph.* 1584 ed., 12. **1549** LATIMER 7th Sermon before Ed. VI P.S. 227 Not once buff nor baff to him: not a word. **1572** T. WILSON *Usury* (1925 ed.) 341.

Buffet, *see* Bit and a knock (b.).

Bug(s), *see* Snug as a b.; Swear by no beggars (b.).

Bugbears (Bugs) to scare babes.
                                              (B 703)

1530 TYNDALE *Practise of Prelates* P.S. 250 Like bugs, to make fools and children afraid withal. **1565** J. CALFHILL *Treatise of the Cross* P.S. 70. *c.* **1566** CURIO *Pasquin in a Trance* tr. W.P. 24ᵛ The officers hauing found the Bugs that made men afeard. **1594–8** SHAKES. *T.S.* I. ii. 207 Tush, tush! Fear boys with bugs! **1639** CLARKE 209.

Build sandy bowrocks[1] together, We will never.

1721 KELLY 356 . . . That is, we will never be cordial or familiar together. [1 children's sand-castles.]

Build two chimneys, It is easier to | than to maintain one.   (C 347)

1640 HERBERT no. 893. **1757** FRANKLIN Jan. 'Tis easier to build two Chimneys than maintain one in Fuel.

Building and marrying of children are
great wasters.   (B 704)
1611 COTGRAVE s.v. Abandon The building of
houses and making of feasts, are vnlimitted
wasters of a mans substance. *Ibid.*, s.v. Maison
Much building, and often bridalls make bare
pastures, and naked side-walls. **1640** HERBERT
no. 11. **1721** KELLY 60 Bigging, and Bairns
marrying are great Wasters.

Building churches, *see* Foreheet nothing but
b. c.

Building is a sweet impoverishing.
                                      (B 705)
1640 HERBERT no. 459.

Building is a thief.   (B 706)
1602–3 MANNINGHAM *Diary* Camden Soc. 9 The
proverbe is that building is a theife, because it
makes us lay out more money than wee thought
on.

Building is chargeable.   (B 707)
1609 HARWARD 74 Building wipeth soare. **1616**
DRAXE no. 5. **1659** N. R. 21.

Build(ing, built) (*verb*), *see also* Begins to b. too
soon; Charges of b. are unknown; High b. low
foundation; Patch and long sit, b. and soon
flit; Pull down than b. (Easier to); Rome not b.
in day; Sand, (To b. on); Spirit of b. is come
upon him.

Building(s) (*noun*), *see* Good b. without good
foundation (No); High b. low foundation;
Settling an island, the first b.

Builds his house all of sallows, Who |
and pricks his blind horse over the
fallows, and suffers his wife to go seek
hallows,[1] is worthy to be hanged on the
gallows.
c. **1386** CHAUCER *W. of Bath's Prol.* l. 654 Than
wolde he seye right thus, with-outen doute, 'Who-
so that buyldeth his hous al of salwes, And
priketh his blynde hors over the falwes, And
suffreth his wyf to go seken halwes, Is worthy to
been hanged on the galwes!' **1417** *Relig.
Antiquae* (1841) i. 233 (last line reads, 'God sende
hym the blisse of everlasting galos'). [1 make
pilgrimages to shrines.]

Builds on the people, builds on the dirt,
He that.   (P 225)
a. **1600** MACHIAVELLI *Prince* ch. 9 (*An Eliz. tr.*,
ed. H. Craig, 1944) The olde prouerbe (He
buylds his house on slyme that dependes on the
peoples fauour). **1616** DRAXE no. 1613 (mud).
1641 JONSON *Timber* viii 599 Nor let the common
Proverbe ... discredit my opinion. **1666** TORRIANO
It. Prov. 212, no. 16.

Bujalance, *see* Piper of B. (Like the).

Bull in a china shop, A.
1834 MARRYAT *Jacob Faith.* ch. 15 Whatever it
is that smashes, Mrs. T. always swears it was the
most valuable thing in the room. I'm like a bull
in a china-shop. **1863** KINGSLEY *Water Bab.* ch.
8 On went the giant ... like a bull in a china-
shop, till he ran into the steeple ... and knocked
the upper half clean off.

Bull's feather, *see* Wears the b.'s f.

Bull's foot, *see* Knows not a B. from a b.'s f.

Bull, *see also* Bear a b. that has borne a calf (He
may); Bellows like a b.; Bloxwich b.; Farm full
must keep ... young b.; In time the savage b.
bear yoke; Mad as b. of Stamford; Mad b. ....
tied with packthread; One dog one b.; Play
with a b. till you get horn in eye; Red rag to b.;
Roar like a b.; Sweat like a b.; Take the b. by
the horns; Town b. as much a bachelor as he.

'Bull' [on Stock Exchange], *see* Price is too low
(No).

Bull-horn, *see* Show the b.

Bullet has its billet, Every.   (B 720)
1573 GASCOIGNE *Posies*, i 155 Sufficeth this to
prove my theame withall, That every bullet hath
a lighting place. **1748** T. SMOLLETT *Rod. Ran.*
ch. 32 Every shot had its commission. **1765**
STERNE *Trist. Shandy* VIII. xix He [King
William] would often say to his soldiers, that
'every ball had its billet'. **1765** WESLEY *Jrnl.* 6
June He never received one wound. So true is
the odd saying of King William, that 'every
bullet has its billet'. **1837** DICKENS *Pickwick* ch.
19 It is an established axiom that 'every bullet
has its billet'. **1846** J. GRANT *Rom. of War* ch.
20 'Tis the fortune of war; ...—their fate to-day
may be ours to-morrow.

Bullimong, *see* Play the devil in the b.

Bulls the cow must keep the calf, He
that.   (C 765)
c. **1565** *Bugbears* IV. v. 7 Then if I have the Cow
I must have the Calf too. **1580** LYLY *Euph. &
his Eng.* ii. 175 To muse who should father my
first childe, wer to doubt when the cowe is mine,
who should owe the calfe. **1596** SHAKES. *K.J.*
I. i. 123 In sooth, good friend, your father might
have kept This calf bred from his cow from all the
world. **1659** HOWELL *Eng. Prov.* (Introd.) In
our Common Law there are some Proverbs that
carry a kind of Authority with them, as that
which began in Henrie the Fourths time, He
that bulls the Cow must keep the Calf.

Bully is always a coward, A.
1817 EDGEWORTH *Ormond* ch. 24 Mrs. M'Crule,
who like all other bullies was a coward, lowered
her voice. **1826** LAMB *Elia* (in *New Month.
Mag.*) Wks. (1898) 220 *Pop. Fal.* .... Confront
one of the silent heroes with the swaggerer of
real life, and his confidence in the theory
quickly vanishes. **1909** *Times Wkly.* 16 July Like

many bullies, it is . . . a coward. A wolf . . . will cower and suffer itself to be killed.

Bulrush, *see* Bellows like a bull, weak as b.; Knot in a b. (Seek).

Bumsted, *see* Crack me that nut.

Bunch, *see* Keys in b., (He tries all); Mother B.

Bungay, *see* Castle of B.

Bung-hole, *see* Spare at the spigot.

Bunny, *see* Course be fair (If), quoth B.

Bunting for a lark, To take a. (B 722)

[1589] 1601 LYLY *Love's Met.* I. ii. 31 Forresters thinke all Birds to be Buntings. **1600** BRETON *Pasquil's Foolscap*: i. 23 In taking of a Bunting for a Larke . . . He that doth so his Will to folly fit Doth plainely shewe he hath no perfect wit. **1602** SHAKES. *A.W.* II. v. 6 Then my dial goes not true. I took this lark for a bunting. **1619** BRETON *I Would and would not* C8.

Bunting, *see also* Goshawk beats not at b.

Burbolt, *see* Brain as a b. (As much).

Burd(s), *see* Hen goes to the cock (When), b. may gen a knock.

Burden makes weary bones, Too long. *Cf.* Light burdens far heavy.

1463 T. MULL in *Stonor Letters and Papers* 62 To long burthyn makyth wery bonys.

Burden, It is not the | but the over-burden that kills the beast.

1706 STEVENS s.v. Carga. **1823** COLLINS 231 *No mata la carga sino la sobrecarga.* . . . **1832** HENDERSON 82.

Burdens, The greatest | are not the gainfullest. (B 729)

1611 COTGRAVE s.v. Acquests. **1670** RAY 4. **1721** KELLY 336 . . . That is, they who labour sorest, have not the best Wages.

Burden(s) (Burthen), *see also* Ass endures his b.; Cunning is no b.; God shapes back for b.; Knowledge is no b.; Knows the weight of another's b. (None); Light b. far heavy; Pedlar carry own b. (Let); Respect the b.; Sad b. to carry dead man's child. *See also* Burthen.

Burford bait. (B 730)

[= drink.] **1636** TAYLOR *Cat. of Taverns* 58 in Wks. 4th Coll. (Spens. Soc.) Beware of a Bur-fourd bayt, for it may brew the staggers. **1662** FULLER Oxon. 328 To take a Burford bait. This . . . is a bait, not to stay the stomach but to lose the wit thereby, as resolved at last into drunkenness.

Burn[1] daylight, To. (D 123)

c. **1560** *Apius & Virginia* Hazl.-Dods. iv. 121. *c.* **1566** *Bugbears* IV. iii. 21. **1586** R. CROWLEY *Father John Francis* D1 You thinke that we be foles, because that we light waxcandles at day light. *c.* **1595** SHAKES. *R.J.* I. iv. 43 Come, we burn daylight, ho! . . . I mean, sir, in delay We waste our lights in vain, like lights by day. **1600–1** *Id. M.W.W.* II. i. 47 We burn daylight: here, read, read. **1602** KYD *Span. Trag.* III. xiia. 29 Light me your torches then.—Then we burne day light. **1738** SWIFT Dial. III. E.L. 324 No candles yet, I beseech you; don't let us burn daylight. [1 waste.]

Burn does not babble, When the | it's either ower toom[1] or ower fu'.

1832 HENDERSON 94. [1 empty.]

Burn his house to warm his hands, He will. (H 763)

1481 CAXTON *Reynard* Arb. 78 They retche not whos[e] hows brenneth so that they may warme them by the coles. **1640** HERBERT no. 304.

Burn one candle to seek another, To. (C 47)

1579 GOSSON *Sch. Abuse* Arb. 41 I gaue my self to that exercise in hope to thriue but I burnt one candle to seek another, and lost bothe my time and my trauell, when I had doone.

Burn one house to warm another, To.

1881 JESSOP *Arcady* 28 Such as have pulled down three or four farmhouses and thrown the fields into one large holding . . . may find that it was an evil day for them when they began to 'burn one house to warm another'.

Burn one's boats, To.

1877 V. L. CAMERON *Across Africa* I. 313 When on the other side I intended—metaphorically speaking—to 'burn my boats', so that there should be no retreating or looking back. **1927** *Times* 26 Aug. 8/1 Burning one's boats, which is often quoted as a sign of strength, is, in essence, more a sign of weakness.

Burn one's house to get rid of the mice, To. (H 752)

1615 T. ADAMS *England's Sickness* 76 The Empiricke to cure the feuer, destroyes the patient; so the wise man to burne the mise, set on fire his barne. *a.* **1816** WOLCOT (P. Pindar) *2nd Ep. to Mrs. Clarke* Wks. (1816) IV. 446 Who, but a Bedlamite, would fire his house, To wreak his vengeance on a pilfering mouse? **1865** G. MAC-DONALD *Alec Forbes* ch. 83 But ye needna burn the hoose to rid the rottans.[1] [1 rats.]

Burn (Light) the candle at both ends, To. (C 48)

1592 BACON *Promus* no. 1504 To waste that realm as a candle which is lighted at both ends. **1678** RAY 72 A good fellow lights his candle at both ends. **1730** BAILEY *Dict.* s.v. The

Candle burns at both Ends. Said when Husband and Wife are both Spendthrifts. **1753** HANWAY *Trav.* (1762) II. i. iii. 19 Apt to light their candle at both ends; that is to say, they are apt to consume too much, and work too little. **1857** KINGSLEY *Two Yrs. Ago* ch. 10 By sitting up till two in the morning, and rising again at six. . . . Frank Headley burnt the candle of life at both ends.

Burn the midnight oil, To. (o 31)

1635 F. QUARLES *Emblems* II. 2 (1660 ed.) We spend our mid-day sweat, our midnight oyl, We tire the night in thought, the day in toyl. **1650** G. DANIEL *Trinarch.*, *Crastini Anim.* 16 As were that worth our Braines, and Midnight Oyle. **1727** GAY *Fables* Introd. 15 Whence is thy learning? Hath thy toil O'er books consumed the midnight oil?

Burn you for a witch, They that | will lose their coals. (w 586)

1681 S. COLVIL *Whiggs Sup.* Auth. Apol. I commend their zeal, but not their wisdom; and who ever shall take the pains to burn them for witches, will lose both coals and labour. **1721** KELLY 332 . . . Eng. No Body will take you for a Conjurer. **1732** FULLER no. 4974. **1816** SCOTT *Antiq.* ch. 17 'They would burn me, . . . for one great conjurer'. 'They would cast away their coals then', said Oldbuck.

Burn (*noun*), *see* Drink of the b. when cannot bite of brae; Wish the b. dry because it weets our feet.

Burned one candle to St. Michael and another to the Dragon, Like the old woman who.

1603 MONTAIGNE (Florio) IV. i. 5 I could easily for a neede, bring a candle to Saint Michaell, and another to his Dragon, as the good old woman. I will follow the best side to the fire, but not into it, if I can choose.

Burning, *see* Thole well is good for b.

Burns his house, He that | warms himself for once. (H 758)

1640 HERBERT no. 303.

Burns most, He that | shines most. (B 732)

1640 HERBERT no. 568. **1852** E. FITZGERALD *Polonius* 84 . . . A loving heart is the beginning of all knowledge.

Burn(ed, s), (*verb*), *see also* Bannock should b. (Rather my); Candle b. within socket; Fingers, (To b. one's); Fire that's closest kept b. most of all; Fire which lights us at distance will b. us when near; Freezes who does not b.; House is b. down (When); Neighbour's house is on fire; Turn or b.; Warms too near that b.

Burnt child dreads the fire, The. (c 297)

c. **1300** *Provs. of Hending* 24 Brend child fur dredeth. *c.* **1300** *Cursor M.* l. 7223 Sare man aght to dred the brand, that brint him forwit in his hand. *c.* **1350** *Douce MS.* 52 no. 52 Brende chylde fyre dredis. *c.* **1400** *Rom. Rose* l. 1820 Brent child of fier hath mych drede. *c.* **1450** *Beryn* 78 Brennyd cat dredith feir. *c.* **1470** *Harl. MS.* 3362 f. 1 b Onys ybrend euer dret feer— *Ignem formidat adusta manus.* **1546** HEYWOOD II. ii. F4 By that diete a great disease ons I gat. And burnt chylde fyre dredth. **1553** T. WILSON *Arte of Rhet.* Prol. A v A burnt child feareth the fire, and a beaten dogge escheweth the whippe. **1580** LYLY *Euph. & his Eng.* ii. 92 A burnt childe dreadeth the fire. *a.* **1592** T. WATSON Arb. 120 The child whose finger once hath felt the fire, To play therewith will have but small desire. **1670** RAY 66 . . . Almost all Languages afford us sayings and Proverbs to this purpose, such are Παθών δέ τε νήπιος ἔγνω [Even the fool knows when he has suffered.] *Hesiod.* **1837** F. CHAMIER *Saucy Arethusa* ch. 25 I have had one turn at starvation . . .: a burnt child dreads the fire.

Burr(s), *see* Cleave like b.; Newcastle b. in his throat; Took her for rose, but proved a b.

Burr (= halo), *see* Near b. far rain.

Burst with laughing, To be ready to. (L 94)

c. **1565** *Bugbears* III. i. 40 With laughing he was redy to burst. **1606** *Wily Beguiled* Mal. Soc. l. 1637 Wee wil haue good merry rogues there that wil make you laugh till you burst. **1616** WITHALS 556.

Burst, borsten, *see also* Broadside, (To b. at the); Give him the other half egg and b. him; Smithwick (You been like), either clemmed or borsten.

Burthen of one's own choice is not felt, A.

1707 MAPLETOFT 7.

Burthen, *see also* Burden.

Burton, *see* Brayton.

Bury an abbey, He is able to. (A 2)

1678 RAY 352 . . . (a spendthrift).

Bury the hatchet, To. *Cf.* Hang up one's hatchet.

1794 J. JAY *Corr. & Pub. Papers* (1893) IV. 147 To use an Indian figure, may the hatchet henceforth be buried for ever. **1837** W. IRVING *Capt. Bonneville* III. 219 The chiefs met; the amicable pipe was smoked, the hatchet buried, and peace formally proclaimed. **1890** W. F. BUTLER *Napier* 186 It was usual for the Directors of the [East India] Company to give a banquet. . . . Napier accepted the invitation. The hatchet was to be buried.

Bury (-ies, -ied), *see also* Churchyard so handsome (No); Go after a leech (While men), body is
b.; Kills himself with working, b. under gallows;
Shovelfuls to b. truth.

Bus, *see* Missed the b.

Bush natural; more hair than wit.
(B 736)

c. 1549 HEYWOOD II. vii. I4ᵛ Thy tales (quoth he)
shew long heare, and short wit, wife. 1592–3
SHAKES. *C.E.* II. ii. 80 What he [time] hath
scanted men in hair he hath given them in wit.
— . . . Many a man hath more hair than wit.
1594 *Id. T.G.V.* III. i. 349 Item, she hath more
hair than wit. 1670 RAY 166.

Bush, *see also* Bad b. better than open field;
Beat about the b.; Beats the b. (One), another
catches the birds; Bird in hand worth two in b.;
Birds once snared (limed) fear all b.; Bows to
the b. he gets bield of (Every man); Fears every
b. (He that); Hare or the bracken b.; Robin
sings in b. (If); Rush b. keeps cow; Thief does
fear each b.; Thinks every b. a boggard; Wag as
the b. wags.

Bushel, *see* Hide one's light under b.; Measures
another's corn by own b.; Words will not fill a b.

Busiest men find (have) the most leisure (time), The.

1859 SMILES *Self-Help* ch. I Those who have
most to do . . . will find the most time.
1884 J. PAYN *Canon's W.* ch. 34 It is my experience that the men who are really busiest have the
most leisure for everything. 1911 *Times Lit. Sup.*
6 Oct. 365 The busiest men have always the
most leisure; and while discharging the multi-
farious duties of a parish priest and a guardian
he found time for travelling.

Business before pleasure.

1640 *Grobiana's Nuptials* (MS. Bodley 30, 15a)
Well to the buisnesse. On; buisnesse is senior to
complement. 1837 GORE *Stokeshill Place* (quoted
in *N. & Q.* 188, 283). 1854 SURTEES *Handley
Cross* ch. 22 Business first and pleasure arter-
wards.

Business, Without | debauchery.
(B 756)

1640 HERBERT no. 1009.

Business is business.

1797 G. COLMAN *Heir at Law* III. iii. 1876
BLACKMORE *Cripps* ch. 3.

Business is the salt of life.

1672 CODRINGTON 124. 1732 FULLER no. 1026.

Business of life and the day of death, Between the | a space ought to be interposed.
(B 745)

1651 HERBERT (40b).

Business tomorrow.

[PLUTARCH *Pelop.* 10 Εἰς αὔριον τὰ σπουδαῖα.]
1579 PLUTARCH tr. North *Pelopidas* T.C. iii. 20
Archias laughing said unto him: Weighty matters
to-morrow . . . ever after the Grecians made
this a common proverb among them.

Business, *see also* Citizen is at his b. before he
rise; Drive your b.; Every man as his b. lies;
Every man knows his own b. best; Everybody's
b. nobody's b.; Great b. turns on little pin;
Haste in his b. (Who has no), mountains seem
valleys; Likes not his b., likes not him; Little
b. stands great rest, (In); Love and b. teach
eloquence; Mind your b.; Punctuality is soul of
b.; Thinks his b. below him; Wife and children
(He that has) wants not b.; Wind is in north-
west (Do b. when).

Busy as a bee, As.
(B 202)

c. 1386 CHAUCER *Mercht.'s T.* l. 2422 For ay as
bisy as bees Been they. 1578–80 SIDNEY *Arcadia*
ed. Feuillerat 182 As buysy as a bee to know
any thinge. 1580 LYLY *Euph. & his Eng.* ii. 36
A comely olde man as busie as a Bee among his
Bees. 1818 SCOTT *Rob Roy* ch. 17 As busy as
my bees are. 1834 J. B. KER 37 He is as busy as
a bee with two tails.

Busy as a hen with one chicken, As.
(H 415)

1576 HOLYBAND D8ᵛ Shee is as busie as a hen
with two chickens. 1591 W. STEPNEY *Span.
Schoolmaster* L6ᵛ (two chickins). 1592 G.
DELAMOTHE 19. 1633 SHIRLEY *Witty Fair One*
II. ii It has been a proverb, 'as busy as a hen with
one chicken'. 1776 WALPOLE *Lett.* (Toynbee)
9. 388 According to the expressive old adage, I
am as busy as a hen and one chick. 1914 K. F.
PURDON *Folk of Fury* F. v The same as a hen
with only one chicken. She'll fuss and cluck as
much for it as if she had the whole clutch.

Busy folks are always meddling.

1721 KELLY 72.

Busy, To be too | gets contempt.
(C 621)

1640 HERBERT no. 738.

Busy, He that is | is tempted by but one devil; he that is idle, by a legion.
(D 281)

1659 N. R. 121. 1732 FULLER no. 2171.

Busy, Who is more | than he that has least to do?
(L 164)

1616 DRAXE no. 219. 1639 CLARKE 20.

Busy will have bonds (bands).
(B 759)

1616 DRAXE no. 213 Busie will haue bondes.
1670 RAY 66 . . . Persons that are medling and
troublesome must be tied short.

Busy, *see also* Ever b. ever bare.

But when? quoth Kettle to his mare.
(K 20)

1678 RAY (*Chesh.*) 276.

Butcher does not fear many sheep, One.

1853 TRENCH ii. 38 When some of his officers reported . . . the innumerable multitudes of the Persian hosts . . . the youthful Macedonian hero[1] silenced them . . . with the reply: One butcher does not fear many sheep. [[1]Alexander the Great.]

Butcher looked for his knife and it was in his mouth, The.   (B 761)

1609 HARWARD 75[v] The butcher sought his kniff when he had it in his mouth.   **1616** WITHALS 560. **1639** CLARKE 75.   *a.* **1654** SELDON *Table Talk* Arb. 104 We look after Religion as the Butcher did after his Knife, when he had it in his Mouth. **1738** SWIFT Dial. I. E.L. 274 I'm like the butcher that was looking for his knife and had it in his mouth: I have been searching my pockets for my snuff-box, and, egad, here it is in my hand.

Butcher's horse, I think this is a | he carries a calf so well.   (B 765)

1678 RAY 232.

Butcher, *see also* Ram to kill a b. (Possible for).

Butler's box[1] at Christmas, Like a.
(B 766)

[[1] A box into which players put a portion of their winnings at Christmas-time for the butler.] **1580** S. BIRD *Friendly Communication* 43[v] In dicing. When they [dicers] paie the boxe, or giue to anie that stand by, or spend it in good cheere. **1591** H. SMITH *Exam[n] of Usury* D4[v] [Usurers] are like a Butlers boxe: for as all the counters come at last to the Butler; so all the money at last commeth to the Vsurer. **1607–8** D. BARRY *Ram Alley* Hazl.-Dods. x 299 Law Is like . . .   **1609** J. WYBARNE *New Age of Old Names* 12 We wil rather agree at home, then suffer the Butlers boxe to winne all. **1629** J. TAYLOR *Wit & Mirth* in BRAND *Pop. Ant.* (1870) I. 270 Westminster Hall . . . is like a Butler's Box at Christmas amongst gamesters: for whosoeuer loseth, the Box will be sure to bee a winner.

Butter and cheese, It rains.

1706 STEVENS s.v. Agosto Quando llueve en agosto, llueve miel y mosto: . . . We say, it rains Butter and Cheese.

Butter before the sun, To melt like.
(B 780)

1562 J. WIGAND *De Neutralibus* N6[v] We . . . melt away, as it were butter with the heat of the Sunne. [1591] **1593** PEELE *Ed. I* Bullen i. 109 As plainly seen as a three half-pence through a dish of butter in a sunny day. **1592** H. SMITH *Poor Man's Tears*: Wks. ii. 48 No; it [wealth] will melt and consume away like butter in the Sunne. [a. 1594] **1605** *K. Leir* I 1 These foolish

men are nothing but meere pity, And melt as butter doth against the Sun. **1597** SHAKES. *I Hen. IV* II. iv. 114 Didst thou never see Titan kiss a dish of butter? Pitiful-hearted Titan, that melted at the sweet tale of the sun's. **1600–1** *Id. M.W.W.* III. v. 104 As subject to heat as butter; a man of continual dissolution and thaw. **1687** MIEGE s.v. Butter My Mony melts like Butter against the Sun.

Butter in the black dog's hause,[1] Like.
(B 777)

1621 ROBINSON 11 The Dogge hath gotten the Butter to keepe. **1639** CLARKE 95 (as 1621). **1721** KELLY 236 . . . That is, past Recovery. **1816** SCOTT *Antiq.* ch. 38 'Did Dousterswivel know anything about the . . . bullion?' . . . 'Had Dustansnivel ken'd it was there—it wad hae been butter in the black dog's hause.' [[1] throat.]

Butter is gold in the morning, silver at noon, lead at night.   (B 770)

1588 COGAN *Haven of Health* (1612) 156 According to the old English Prouerbe: . . . **1652** FULLER *Com. on Christ's Temp.* in *Sel. Serm.* (1891) II. 89 Some meats are said to be *Gold in the morning, silver at noon, but lead at night.* **1670** RAY 36.   **1738** SWIFT Dial. I. E.L. 262 They say, butter is gold in a morning, silver at noon, but it is lead at night.

Butter is good for anything but to stop an oven.   (B 771)

1656 L. PRICE *A Map of Merry Conceits* A5[v] P: (= Proverb) Butter is good for anything: C: (= Crossing) But not to stop ovens with. **1659** HOWELL *Eng. Prov.* 12a.

Butter is mad twice a year.   (B 772)

1625 JONSON *Staple of News* Second Intermean, 325 So butter answer my expectation, and be not mad butter; 'If it be, It shall both Iuly and December see!' [a. 1626] **1647** FLETCHER *et al. Noble Gent.* 2 D3 Mad as May-butter. **1678** RAY 50 Butter is said to be mad twice a year; once in Summer . . . when it is too thin and fluid; and once in winter . . . when it is too hard and difficult to spread. **1813** BARRETT *Heroine* ed Raleigh 73 Am I mad? . . .—As butter in May·

Butter is once a year in the cow's horn.
(B 773)

1614 CHAPMAN *Ep. Ded. to Od.* Like winter cows whose milk runs to their horns. **1659** HOWELL *Eng. Prov.* 14a. **1678** RAY 50 . . . They mean when the cow gives no milk.

Butter, That which will not be | must be made into cheese.   (B 779)

1587 J. BRIDGES *Def. of Gov. of C. of E.* 522 If it will bee no butter, make it cheeze. If it will not fadge by one meane, then trie it by any other meanes. **1678** RAY 107.

Butter that the cow yields, It is not all.
(B 775)

1546 HEYWOOD II. ix. L1[v] (shites). **1678** RAY 107 All is not butter the cow shites. Non è tutto butyro che fa la vocca. *Ital.*

Butter will stick to his (my) bread, No.
(B 778)

1546 HEYWOOD II. vii. K1ᵛ But there will no butter cleaue on my breade. **1577** R. STANYHURST in HOLINSHED *Chron. Ireland* (1587) 93b. **1636** CAMDEN 303. **1721** KELLY 267 . . . Spoken when all Means we use to thrive miscarry. **1727** SWIFT *Pastoral Dial.* Wks. (1856) I. 628 But now I fear it will be said, No butter sticks upon his bread. **1824** SCOTT *Redg.* ch. 14 'No,' replied Nanty; 'the devil a crumb of butter was ever churned that would stick upon my bread'.

Butter, (*noun*) *see also* Baker (Be not a) if your head be of b.; Boil stones in b.; Dab, quoth Dawkins, when he hit his wife on the arse with a pound of b.; Demure as if b. would not melt; Fair words b. no parsnips; Fat as b.; Knife, (It is a good) it will cut b. when it is melted; Pound of b. among kennel of hounds; Rope and b.; Store of b. (They that have) may lay it thick; Sure as if sealed with b.; That is for that and b.'s for fish.

Butter(ed), (*adj. adv.*), *see* Bread is b. on both sides; Bread never falls but on b. side; Eat a b. fagot, (He that would); Scold like b. wives.

Butter-cake(s), *see* 'No, thank you', has lost many a b.; Wishes were b. (If).

Buttercup, *see* Fresh as a daisy (b.).

Butterfly, *see* Break a b. upon wheel.

Button, Not worth a.
(B 782)

c. **1320** *Sir Beues* 1004 Hauberk ne scheld ne actoun Ne vailede him nouȝt worþ a botoun. **1603** CHETTLE, DEKKER, HAUGHTON *Patient Grissil* I. ii. 86 Shortly we shall not be worth a button. **1620** SHELTON *Quix.* II. xxii (1908) II. 338 Whose knowledge and remembrance is not worth a button. **1796** EDGEWORTH *Par. Asst., Simple Susan* (1903) 135 The attorney says the paper's not worth a button in a court of justice. **1860** SURTEES *Plain or Ringlets?* ch. 68 The Duke's dogs are not worth a button.

Button(s), *see also* Breech makes b.; Care a b. (Not to); Soul above b.; Thrum caps (b.).

Button-hole, *see* Take one down . . . (*or* a b. lower).

Buy a pig in a poke, To.
(P 304)

c. **1300** *Provs. of Hending* (ed. Schleich) in *Anglia* 51. 263 Wen me bedeþ þe gris, opene þe shet. *c.* **1350** *Douce MS. 52* no. 114 When me profereth þe pigge, opon the pogh. **1520** WHITTINGTON *Vulg.* E.E.T.S. 107 It is sayd comenly whan the pygge is profered: open the poughen. **1546** HEYWOOD II. ix. L2ᵛ Ye loue not to bye the pyg in the poke. **1603** MONTAIGNE (Florio) I. xlii. 154 No man will buy a pig in a poke. If you cheapen a horse, you will take his saddle, and clothes from him, and you will see him bare and abroad. **1890** D. C. MURRAY *J. Vale's G.* ch. 25 I can't buy a pig in a poke. . . . Let me know what you've got to sell, and then maybe I'll make a bid for it. [Fr. *acheter chat en poche.*]

Buy an office, (magistracy) They that | must sell something, (justice).
(M 8)

1549 LATIMER *11th Serm. bef. Edw. VI* P.S. 185 Are ciuile offices bought for monei? . . . If thei bei, thei must nedes sel, for it is wittely spoken. *Vendere iure potest, emerat ille prius*, he may lawefully sel it, he bought it before. **1573** SANFORD 5ᵛ Pope Vrbano the fourthe . . . gaue freely for nothyng all offices and benefices, saying, that he that buyeth an office, must needes sell it. *a.* **1602** W. PERKINS *Treatise of Callings* (Wks. 1608 i. 737) The saying is true; he that buies the seat, must sell iustice. **1642** TORRIANO 18 He who buyeth the seat of Justice, must needs make sale thereof. **1642** FULLER *H. & P. State* IV. vii (1841) 255 Sir Augustine Nicolls, whom King James used to call 'the Judge that would give no money'. Otherwise, they that buy justice by wholesale, to make themselves savers, must sell it by retail. **1732** FULLER no. 4975.

Buy and sell, and live by the loss, To.
(L 459)

1577 GRANGE *Gold. Aphroditis* D1ᵛ Who findeth fire in frost, he finds, but yet he liues by losse. **1600** N. BRETON *Pasquil's Mistress* l. 294 He that buies her, will but liue by losse. **1616** DRAXE no. 226. **1623** W. PAINTER *Chaucer new Painted* C6ᵛ Some doe buy and sell and liue by the losse. **1639** CLARKE 81. **1706** STEVENS s.v. Gasto.

Buy at a fair, but sell at home.
(F 25)

1616 DRAXE no. 230. **1640** HERBERT no. 160. **1706** STEVENS s.v. Casa.

Buy dear is not bounty, To.
(B 558)

1640 HERBERT no. 156. **1706** STEVENS s.v. Franqueza (liberality).

Buy gold too dear, A man may.
(M 257)

1546 HEYWOOD II. vii. I4. **1587** *Letters of Philip Gawdy* 23. **1662** FULLER *Kent* 76 He [Walsingham] thought that Gold might . . . be bought too dear. **1887** LUBBOCK *Pleas. Life* II. ii A wise proverb tells us that gold may be bought too dear.

Buy good cheap that bring nothing home, They.
(C 259)

a. **1628** CARMICHAELL no. 1477. **1641** FERGUSSON no. 788. **1721** KELLY 318 . . . Spoken to them that think our Pennyworth too dear.

Buy in the cheapest market and sell in the dearest, To.

1595 LODGE *Fig for Momus*, Ep. 4 Wks. (1883) III. 59 Buy cheape, sell deare. **1862** RUSKIN *Unto this Last* II (1901) 60 Buy in the cheapest market?—yes; but what made your market cheap? . . . Sell in the dearest? . . . but what made your market dear? **1880** FROUDE *Bunyan* 104 'To buy in the cheapest market and sell in the dearest' was Mr. Badman's common rule in business. . . . In Bunyan's opinion it was knavery in disguise.

Buy no stocks, My son. (s 627)

1678 RAY 348 . . . *Good counsel at Gleek.*[1] [[1] a game at cards.]

Buy the cow, If you | take the tail into the bargain.

1721 KELLY 190 It is a Shame to eat the Cow, and worry on the Tail. It is a Shame to perform a great Task all but a little, and then give over. **1732** FULLER no. 2743. **1824** MOIR *Mansie W.* ch. 22 Peter Farrel was a . . . thorough-going fellow, and did not like half-measures, such as swallowing the sheep and worrying on the tail.

Buy the devil, If we | we must sell the devil.

1838 J. C. APPERLEY *Nimrod's North. Tour* 152 There is a saying amongst horse-dealers . . . namely, 'If we buy the devil, we must sell the devil'; but who was the purchaser of this 'devil' I know not.

Buyer beware, Let the. (B 788)

[L. *Caveat emptor, quia ignorare non debuit quod jus alienum emit.* Law Maxim—Let a purchaser beware, for he ought not to be ignorant of the nature of the property which he is buying from another party.] **1523** FITZHERBERT *Husbandry* § 118 Caueat emptor, beware the byer. **1592** NASHE *P. Penniless* i. 155 Sed caueat emptor, Let the interpreter beware. **1607** E. SHARPHAM *Fleire* II, C 4. They are no prouerb breakers: beware the buyer say they. **1927** *Times* 29 Sept. 10/1 We dislike very much, whether it is put in Latin or in English, the phrase 'Let the buyer beware!'

Buyer needs a hundred eyes, The | the seller but one. (N 85)

[It. *Chi compra ha bisogna di cent' occhi; chi vende n' ha assai di uno.*] **1640** HERBERT no. 390. **1642** TORRIANO 2. **1670** RAY 66 . . . This is an Italian Proverb. **1745** FRANKLIN July He who buys had need have 100 Eyes, but one's enough for him that sells the stuff. **1796** EDGEWORTH *Par. Asst., Lit. Merch.* i. (1903) 375 He taught him . . . to get . . . from customers by taking advantage of their ignorance. . . . He often repeated . . . 'The buyer has need of a hundred eyes; the seller has need but of one'.

Buying of bread undoes us, This. (B 791)

1678 RAY 67. (*Joculatory.*)

Buys a house ready wrought, He that | has many a tyle-pin[1] (pin and nail, tile and pin) for nought. (H 759)

1623 CAMDEN 271. **1639** CLARKE 300. **1670** RAY 106. [[1] A peg of hard wood used to fasten the tiles to the laths of a roof.]

Buys and sells is called a merchant, He that. (M 886)

1678 RAY *Adag. Hebr.* 400 . . . This Proverb is used in derision of those who buy and sell to their loss. **1911** A. COHEN *Anct. Jewish Pr.* 78 Does a man buy and sell just to be called a merchant? . . . The chief aim in trade is to make a profit.

Buys dear and takes up on credit, Who | shall ever sell to his loss. (C 816)

1573 SANFORD 102[v]. **1623** W. PAINTER *Chaucer new Painted* C6[v] Buy not for time those wares that are too deare, For many lose thereby.

Buys land buys many stones; He that | he that buys flesh buys many bones; he that buys eggs buys many shells; but he that buys good ale buys nothing else. (L 52)

[c. 1565] **1595** *Peddler's Proph.* B4[v] You shall be sure to haue good Ale for that haue no bones. **1670** RAY 211. **1721** KELLY 172 He that buys Land, buys Stones; He that buys Beef, buys Bones; He that buys Nuts, buys shells; He that buys good Ale, buys nought else.

Buy(s), bought, *see also* All things are to be b. at Rome; Bark ourselves ere we b. dogs so dear; Better b. than borrow; Blames would b.; Bought wit is best; Dear bought and . . . dainties for ladies; Difference between will you b. and will you sell; Experience good if not b. too dear; Leaf of borage might b. all they can sell; Measure thrice what thou b.; Ounce of wit that's bought; Penny to b. his dog a loaf; Repentance too dear, (To b.); See for your love, b. for your money; Wit b.; Wit once b.; Words are but words, but money b. land.

Buzzard, *see* Hawk and b. (Between); Kite will never be good hawk; Old wise man's shadow better than b.'s sword.

By-and-bye, *see* Two anons and a b. is an hour and a half.

Bygones be bygones, Let. (B 793)

[HOM. *Il.* 18. 112 'Αλλὰ τὰ μὲν προτετύχθαι ἐάσομεν, ἀχνύμενοί περ, But we will allow these things to have happened in the past, grieved as we are.] **1546** HEYWOOD II. ix. K3[v] Let all thyngs past pas. *a.* **1577** PITSCOTTIE *Chron. Scotland* S.T.S., l. c. xliv Byganes to be bygones. **1636** RUTHERFORD *Lett.* lxii (1862) I. 166 Pray . . . that byegones betwixt me and my Lord may be byegones. **1648** NETHERSOLE *Parables* 5 Let bygans be bygans. **1706** LD. BELHAVEN *Speech on Union* 2 Nov. I fear not these Articles . . . if we . . . forgive one another, . . . according to our proverb, 'Bygones be bygones'. **1710** PALMER 290 . . . and Fair Play for Time to Come. **1815** SCOTT *Guy Man.* ch. 51 Let us adopt the Scotch proverb . . . 'Let bygones be bygones, and fair play for the future'. **1882** TENNYSON *Prom. May* III. Wks. (1893) 796 Would you beat a man for his brother's fault? . . . Let bygones be bygones.

By-walkers, Many | many balks.[1]

1549 LATIMER *2nd Serm. bef. Edw. VI* P.S. 112 These men walked by-walks, and the saying is, 'Many by-walkers, many balks':[1] many balks, much stumbling; . . . howbeit there were some . . . that walked in the king's highway. [[1] ridges of earth.]

C

Cabbage twice cooked (sodden) is death.
(C 511)

[Gk. Δὶς κράμβη θάνατος. L. JUVENAL *Sat.* 7. 154 *Crambe repetita.*] **1545** TAVERNER G8ᵛ Crambe bis posita mors est Crambe twyse sod is death . . . Crambe . . . we call Radyshe. **1580** LYLY *Euph. & his Eng.* ii. 154 Which I must omitte, least I set before you, Colewortes twise sodden. **1583** RAINOLDS *Reputation of Whitaker* S6ᵛ Cloy vs with crambe recocta, coleworts twice, yea ten times sodden. **1929** *Times* 12 Oct. 6/6 Their havoc is limited to the cabbages; and you know what the opinion of cabbage was amongst the Greeks: Δὶς κράμβη θάνατος.

Cabinet, *see* Jewel by the casket (c.), (None can guess).

Cable, *see* Mouse in time may bite in two a c.

Cackle like a cadowe,[1] She can.   (C 7)

1549 ERASM. tr. Chaloner *Praise of Folly* L3ᵛ More Kacling than a menie of dawes. **1579** *Marr. of Wit. and Wisdom* (1849) 26. [1 jackdaw.]

Cackle often, You | but never lay an egg. *Cf.* Hen does not prate, If the.
(C 5)

1609 HARWARD 76 Cackle not. Yf thou hast gaygned keepe it to thy self. **1615** T. ADAMS *Two Sons* (1861–2 ed. ii. 86) Here's one that cackles when hee has not laid; and God comming findes his nest empty. This is to fry in words, freeze in deeds. **1732** FULLER no. 5867 You cackle often, but never lay an Egg. **1890** D. C. MURRAY *Jno. V's Guard.* ch. 39 You're one o' that family o' poultry as does the cackling for other hens' eggs.

Cackles, *see* Hen that c. in your house.

Cadbury Castle and Dolbury Hill dolven[1] were, If | all England might plough with a golden share.

1630 T. WESTCOTE *View of Devonshire* (1845) 110 Cadberry, alias Caderbyr. . . . The castle [is] . . . a high . . . hill, . . . anciently fortified. . . . This hidden treasure this rhyming proverb goes commonly and anciently—. . . [1 delved.]

Cadgers[1] are aye cracking o' crook-saddles.[2]   (C 6)

a. **1628** CARMICHAELL no. 45 A cadger speiks ay of lead sadils. **1641** FERGUSSON no. 213. **1721** KELLY 77 Cadgers has ay mind of load Sadles. Spoken when People bring in, by Head and Shoulders, a Discourse of those things they are affected with, and used to. **1817** SCOTT *Rob Roy* ch. 26 Ye ken cadgers maun aye be speaking about cart-saddles. **1857** DEAN RAMSAY *Remin.* v (1911) 204 . . . Professional men are very apt to talk too much of their profession. [1 pedlars. 2 pack-saddles.]

Cadger(s), *see also* King's errand may come c.'s gate; Mickle to do when c. ride.

Cadowe, *see* Cackle like a c.

Caesar or nobody, Either.   (C 8)

1588 *Disc. upon the present state of France* 63 The Duke of Guize . . . is alreadie so farre in, that he must needes either be king, or vndone altogether: there is no meane for him betweene these two extremities . . . Assoone as a man hath aspired vnto Tiranny, *Aut Caesar, aut nihil*. **1624** CAPT. J. SMITH *Virginia* i. 168. **1649** LEICESTER *Jour.* July 10 77 If you say, Cesar or nothing, they say, Republique, or nothing. **1666** TORRIANO *Prov. Phr.* s.v. Cesare 36 . . . not to be a neuter.

Caesar's wife must be above suspicion.

1580 LYLY *Euph. & his Eng.* ii. 101 Al women shal be as *Caesar* would haue his wife, not onelye free from sinne, but from suspition. **1591** ARIOSTO *Orl. Fur.* Harington VIII. 35 margin. **1827** HARE *Gues. at Truth* (1873) i. 187–8 Caesar's wife ought to be above suspicion. . . . Yet most . . . would be slow to acknowledge . . . that Caesar himself ought to be so too.

Caesar, *see also* Render unto C.

Cages for oxen to bring up birds in, He builds.   (C 10)

1678 RAY 352. **1732** FULLER no. 1815.

Cain, *see* Raise C.

Cake and pudding to me, It is.   (C 13)

1585 A. MUNDAY *Two Ital. Gentlemen* l. 1034 This will be cake and pudding to them that are truantly. **1602** DEKKER *Satiro.* l. 1899 By my troth sweet Ladies, it's Cake and pudding to me, to see his face make faces, when hee reades his Songs and Sonnets. **1620** SHELTON *Quix.* Pt. 2. 2. (ii. 203) All that was said hitherto is cakes and whitebread to this. **1721** KELLY 172 He woos for Cake and Pudding. Spoken when People pretend Courtship, to promote another Interest.

Cake has its make,[1] Every.   (C 14)

a. **1628** CARMICHAELL no. 1508 There was never a caik bot there was a maik. **1641** FERGUSSON no. 779 There was never a cake, but it had a make. **1762** SMOLLETT *L. Greaves* ch. 10 There's no cake, but there's another of the same make. [1 mate, fellow.]

Cake has its make; Every | but a scrape cake has two.   (C 14)

1641 FERGUSSON no. 779 There was never a cake but it had a make. **1678** RAY 68 . . . Every wench hath her sweet-heart, and the dirtiest commonly the most: make, i.e. match, fellow.

Cake (Meal) is dough, One's. (c 12)

1559 BECON *Prayers &c.* P.S. 277 Or else your cake is dough, and all your fat lie in the fire. **1594–8** SHAKES. *T.S.* I. i. 110 Our cake's dough on both sides. *Ibid.* V. i. 125 My cake is dough; but I'll in among the rest. Out of hope of all but my share of the feast. **1687** SETTLE *Reflect. Dryden* 4 She is sorry his cake is dough, and that he came not soon enough to speed. **1708** MOTTEUX *Rabelais* IV. vi You shall have rare Sport anon, if my Cake ben't Dough, and my Plot do but take. **1721** KELLY 191 I thought all my Meal dough. I thought all my Pains ill bestowed. Spoken when we are disappointed of our Expectation.

Cake(s), *see also* Banbury zeal, cheese and c.; Bread for c., (You give me); Eat your c. and have it; Find the bean in the c.; Land of c.; Poor man turns his c., another takes away.

Calamity (Extremity) is the touchstone of a brave mind (unto wit). (c 15a)

1602 MARSTON *Antonio's Revenge* l. 2136 Calamity gives man a steddy heart. **1607** JONSON *Volp.* v. ii. 6 Good Wits are greatest in extremities. *c.* **1608** SHAKES. *C.* IV. i. 3 You were us'd To say extremity was the trier of spirits; That common chances common men could bear; That when the sea was calm, all boats alike Show'd mastership in floating. **1732** FULLER no. 1045.

Calendar, *see* Death keeps no c.

Calends, *see* Greek c.; Janiveer's c. be summerly gay (If).

Cales, *see* Knight of.

Calf love, half love; old love, cold love.

1823 GALT *Entail* ch. 14 Put off for a year or twa this calf love connection. **1876** BLACKMORE *Cripps* ch. 33 Calf-love . . . was making a fool of this unfledged fellow.

Calf never heard church-bell, That.

1917 BRIDGE 110 . . . A calf born and killed between two Sundays.

Calf, The | the goose, the bee: the world is ruled by these three.

1635 HOWELL *Lett.* 3 Jul. (1903) II. 103 'Anser, Apis, Vitulus, populos et Regna gubernant.' The goose, the bee and the calf (meaning wax, parchment and the pen), rule the world, but of the three the pen is most predominant.

Calf, The greatest | is not the sweetest veal. (c 17)

1636 CAMDEN 307. **1732** FULLER no. 4569. **1790** WOLCOT (P. Pindar) *Benev. Ep. to S.U.* Wks. (1816) II. 89 Brudenall who bids us all the proverb feel, 'the largest calves are not the sweetest veal'.

Calf with the white face, You would have the. (c 19)

1550 *Answer to Commoners* (Camden Soc. ed. N. Pocock 1884 178) They will cry, as the common proverb of Englande saith, to have the calf with the white face. **1576** SANFORD *Mirror Madness* B6ᵛ They muste have the Calfe wyth the whyte face they muste haue they know not what. **1640** JONSON *Tale Tub* II. iv. 2 You doe not know when yo' are well, I thinke: You'ld ha' the Calfe with the white face, Sir, would you?

Calf, calves, *see also* Bear a bull that has borne c. (He may); Bulls the cow, (He that) must keep the c.; Cow c. as for bull (As well for); Cow (Like) like c.; Eat above the tongue, like a c.; Eats the c. in the cow's belly; Essex c.; Golden c.; Kill the fatted c.; Luck (As good) as the lousy c.; Parson's cow (Come home like), with c. at foot; Quey c. dear veal; Suffer a c. to be laid on thee (If thou); Think a c. a muckle beast that never saw cow; Veal will be cheap, c. fall; Wanton as a c. with two dams; Wise as Waltham's c.

Calf's head, *see* Ways of dressing a c. h.

California fever.

1840 DANA *Two Yrs. bef. Mast* ch. 21 The Americans . . . and Englishmen . . . are indeed more industrious . . . than the Spaniards; yet . . . if the 'California fever' (laziness) spares the first generation, it always attacks the second.

Call a man no worse than unthankful, You can. (M 435)

1639 CLARKE 170.

Call a spade a spade, To. (s 699)

[ERASM. *Ad. Ficus ficus, ligonem ligonem vocat.*] **1519** RASTELL *Four Elements* Hazl.-Dods. i. 49 Say plainly, Give me a spade. **1539** TAVERNER 14ᵛ Plaine and homely men call a fygge, a fygge, and a spade a spade. **1542** UDALL *Erasm. Apoph.* 167 Philippus aunswered, that the Macedonians wer feloes of no fyne witte in their termes, but altogether grosse, . . . whiche had not the witte to calle a spade by any other name then a spade. **1647** TRAPP *Marrow Gd., Authors in Comm. Ep.* 641 Gods people shall not spare to call a spade a spade, a niggard a niggard. **1738** SWIFT Dial. III. E.L. 320. You know, I'm old Telltruth; I love to call a spade a spade. **1862** THACKERAY *Philip* ch. 23 Chesham does not like to call a spade a spade. He calls it a horticultural utensil. **1882** H. A. GILES *Historic China* 55 Chinese prosody is of an extremely complicated character . . . it being an almost unpardonable fault to call a spade a spade.

Call another cause.

1738 SWIFT Dial. I. E.L. 283 Well, so much for that, and butter for fish; let us call another cause.

Call her whore (scold, thief) first. (N 112 and W 319)

1580 LYLY *Euph. & his Eng.* ii. 95 Thou callest me theefe first, not vnlike vnto a curst wife, who

deseruing a check, beginneth first to scolde.
1592–3 SHAKES. *C.E.* IV. i. 50 I should have chid
you for not bringing it, But like a shrew you
first begin to brawl.   **1593** *Id. Rich. III* I. iii. 324
I do the wrong, and first begin to brawl.   [**1600**]
1611 *Tarlton's Jests Shak. Jest-Bks.* ii. 220 A
witty scold, meeting another scold, knowing that
scold will scold, begins to scold first.   **1616**
WITHALS 583 Who more ready to call her neighbour scold, then the rankest scold in the parish.
1623 PAINTER B6 She that's a whore will th'other
whore first call.   *a.* **1628** CARMICHAELL no. 399
Call her hure mother or sche call you.   **1672**
MARVELL *Rehearsal Transprosed* Gros. 184 It is
but crying whore first, and having the last word.
1738 SWIFT Dial. I. E.L. 291 Nay, miss, you cried
whore first, when you talked of the knapsack.

Call me cut, Then.   (C 940)

[**1486–1500**] *c.* **1530** MEDWALL *Nature* I B1ᵛ Yf
thou se hym not take hys owne way Call me cut
when thou metest me a nother day.   **1573**
GASCOIGNE *Supposes* i. 235 If I be not even
with thee, call me cut.   **1597** SHAKES. *I Hen. IV*
II. iv. 185 If I tell thee a lie, spit in my face, call
me horse.   [**1600**] **1659** DAY & CHETTLE *Blind
Beggar* l. 2239 And I do not I'll give you leave
to call me Cut.   **1601** SHAKES. *T.N.* II. iii. 176
If thou hast her not i' th'end, call me Cut.   **1606**
T. HEYWOOD 2 *If you know me* l. 170 And I doe
not shew you the right tricke of a Cosin afore I
leaue England, ile giue you leaue to call me Cut.
a. **1633** JONSON *Tale Tub.* IV. i. 97 Then call me
his curtail.

Call one sir, and something else, To.   (S 486)

1641 W. MOUNTAGU in *Buccleuch MSS.* (Hist.
MSS. Comm.) I. 289 The Bishop saying 'Sir',
was mistaken to have said Sirra, and called to the
bar.   **1678** RAY 269 . . . i.e. Sirrah.¹ [¹ a contemptuous form of address.]

Call the bear 'uncle' till you are safe across the bridge.

1912 *Times Wkly.* 12 Apr. 287 Critics . . . can
quote the excellent Turkish proverb, 'Call the
bear "uncle" till you are safe across the bridge',
to justify their refusal to add to the Government's
difficulties.

Call the king my cousin, I would not.

1721 KELLY 225 . . . Added when we say, Had I
such a Thing, could I get such a Place, or effect
such a Project: I would think myself so happy,
that I would flatter no Body.   **1914** K. F. PURDON
Folk of Furry F. ch. 1 There's the way it is wid
women. When they get a daughter marrit, no
matter to who, they'll be that proud, . . . that
they wouldn't call the King their cousin.

Call, *see also* Servant must come when you c.
him.

Calling for, *see* Mischief comes without c. f.

Calm sea, In a | every man is a pilot.   (S 174)

a. **1592** GREENE *James IV* II. ii The pilot in the
dangerous seas is knowne; In calmer waues the

sillie sailor striues.   *c.* **1594** BACON *Promus* no
431 Tranquillo quilibet gubernator.   **1602**
SHAKES. *T.C.* I. iii. 34 The sea being smooth,
How many shallow bauble boats dare sail Upon
her patient breast, making their way With those
of nobler bulk.¹   **1608** *Id. C.* IV. i. 6 When the
sea was calm, all boats alike Show'd mastership
in floating.   **1670** RAY 4.   **1732** FULLER no. 2808
(can steer).

Calm sough, *see* Keep a c. s.

Calm weather in June sets corn in tune.   (W 213)

1573 TUSSER xlii. 117.   **1732** FULLER no. 6207.

Calm, *see also* After a storm.

Calves are gone down to grass, His.   (C 22)

1678 RAY 232 . . . This is a jeer for men with over-
slender legs.   **1823** GROSE (Pierce Egan) s.v.
Calves.

Calves, *see also* Calf.

Cambridge master, *see* Royston horse.

Cambridgeshire camels.   (C 31)

1662 FULLER *Cambs.* 150 . . . I cannot reconcile
this common saying to any considerable sense.
. . . The Fen-men . . . on their stilts, are little
giants indeed.   **1670** RAY 221 . . . A nickname
. . . perhaps because the three first letters are the
same in *Cambridge* and *camel.*   **1897** BP.
CREIGHTON *Some Eng. Shires* 378 'Cambridgeshire camels' was an expression for the marsh-
men . . . on tall stilts.

Came, saw, and overcame, I.   (C 540)

1542 ERASM. tr. Udall *Apoph.* (1877 ed. 300)
When he [Caesar] had euen at the first choppe of
encountreyng, vanquished Pharnaces, he wrote
briefly to his frendes after this sort: I came, I
looked, I conquered.   **1579** NORTH, Plutarch
Julius Caesar T.T. v 52 Caesar . . . wrote three
words unto Anitius at Rome: *Veni, Vidi, Vici*:
to wit, I came, I saw, I overcame.   **1586** WARNER
Albion's Eng. III. xvii. I3ᵛ I came: I sawe: I ouer-
came.   **1591** ARIOSTO *Orl. Fur.* Harington XLVI.
80.   **1594–5** SHAKES. *L.L.L.* IV. i. 68 'Veni, vidi,
vici'; which to annothanize in the vulgar. . . . He
came, saw, and overcame.   **1598** *Id. 2 Hen. IV*
IV. iii. 40 I may justly say with the hook-nos'd
fellow of Rome—I came, saw, and overcame.
1599 *Id. A.Y.* V. ii. 28 There was neuer anything so sudden but . . . Caesar's thrasonical
brag of 'I came, saw, and overcame'.   **1610**
Id. Cym. III. i. 22 A kind of conquest Caesar
made here; but made not here his brag Of 'came,
and saw, and overcame'.

Camel going to seek horns, lost his ears, The.   (C 27)

[ERASM. *Ad. Camelus desiderans cornua etiam
aures perdidit.* The camel in Aesop's fable asks
horns of Jove. Indignant at the foolish request,

he deprives it of its ears. TRENCH.] **1608** CHAPMAN *Consp. Byron* IV. i. 138 But for a subject to affect a kingdom, Is like the camel that of Jove begged horns. **1621** BURTON *Anat. Mel.* I. ii. III. 14. **1678** RAY *Adag. Hebr.* 399 . . . Against those who being discontented with what they have, in pursuit of more lose what they once had.

Camel(s), *see also* Cambridgeshire c.; Strain at a gnat and swallow c.

Cammock, *see* Crooks the tree.

Camnethen, *see* Woe worth ill company.

Camomile is trodden on, The more the | the faster it grows. (C 34)

1560 J. PILKINGTON *P.S.* 143 As camomile with treading on it and walking waxes thicker. **1576** PETTIE i. 36 As the herb camomile the more it is trodden down the more it spreadeth abroad, so virtue and honesty the more it is spited the more it sprouteth. **1590** H. ROBERTS *Defiance to Fortune* D1ᵛ Cammomill the more it is trodden, the more it springeth. **1597** SHAKES. *1 Hen. IV* II. iv. 387 Though the camomile, the more it is trodden on the faster it grows, yet youth, the more it is wasted the sooner it wears. **1606** MARSTON *Fawn* II. i. **1616** T. ADAMS *Divine Herbal* 69. **1637** SHIRLEY *Hyde Pk.* III. ii. For ne'er was simple camomile so trod on, Yet still I grow in love.

Camp, *see* Victualled my c.

Can, *see* Cup and c.

Candle burns within the socket, His. (C 41)

1589 LYLY *Pap with a Hatchet* iii. 410 Within a while appeared olde Martin with a wit worn into the socket. **1591** SHAKES. *3 Hen. VI* II. vi. 1 Here burns my candle out; ay, here it dies. **1593** SIR JOHN PUCKERING (Neale, *Eliz. & her Parlᵗ 1584–1601*, 246) Hee would spend his candle to the socket, but he would be revenged. **1598** SHAKES. *2 Hen. IV* I. ii. 147 What! you are as a candle, the better part burnt out. **1633** LD. BROOKE *Caelica* lxxxvii. 235 When as mans life. . . . In soacket of his earthly lanthorne burnes. **1670** RAY 167 . . . That is, he is an old man. Philosophers are wont to compare mans life to the burning of a lamp. **1827** SCOTT *Chron. Canongate* ch. 1 The light of life . . . was trembling in the socket.

Candle lights others and consumes itself, A. (C 39)

1584 LYLY *Camp.* ii. 316 Prol. at Court, Torches, which giuing light to others, consume themselues. **1599** MINSHEU *Span. Gram.* A2 With the candle to light others, and burne out my selfe. **1659** N.R. 1. **1742** FRANKLIN Feb. The painful preacher, like a candle bright, consumes himself in giving others light.

Candle, *see also* Burn one c. to seek another; Burn the c. at both ends; Burned one c. to St. Michael (Like woman who); Dance nor hold the c. (Neither); Fly that plays too long in c.; Game is not worth c.; Go out like c.; Heathen went to bed without c.; Hold a c. (Not able to); Hold a c. to the devil; Ill battle where devil carries c.; Punch coal, cut c., neither good housewife; Sun with a c. (Set forth the); *Tace* is Latin for c.; Worst may (He that) shall hold c.

Candle-holder proves a good gamester, A good. (C 51)

1594–5 SHAKES. *R.J.* I. iv. 37 For I am proverbed with a grandsire phrase, I'll be a candle-holder and look on. **1659** HOWELL *Eng. Prov.* 13a. **1670** RAY 4. **1732** FULLER no. 138 A good Candle-Snuffer may come to be a good Player.

Candlemas day[1] be fair and bright, If | winter will have another flight: if on Candlemas day it be shower and rain, winter is gone, and will come not again. (C 52)

1523 SKELTON *Garl. Laurel* l. 1441 Wks., i. 418 How men were wonte for to discerne By candlemes day, what wedder shuld holde. **1576** G. HARVEY *Marginalia* 175 A faire Candlemas, a fowle Lent. **1584** R. SCOT *Witchcraft* XI. xv If Maries purifying-day Be cleare and bright with sunny raie, Then frost and cold shall be much more, After the feast than was before. **1612** WEBSTER *White Devil* (1928) v. vi. 265 Let all that belong to Great men remember th'ould wives' tradition, to be like the Lyons i' th Tower on Candlemas-day, to mourne if the Sunne shine, for feare of the pittifull remainder of winter to come. **1653** T. GATAKER, *A Vindication* 125 On *Candlemas* day . . . if it were a close and gloomy day, they [the deer] would come abroad and be frisking upon the lawn, as presaging that winter was in a manner gone, and litle hard weather behind. **1678** RAY 51 . . . This is a translation . . . of that old Latin Distich; *Si Sol splendescat Maria purificante, Major erit glacies post festum quam fuit ante.* **1847** R. CHAMBERS *Pop. Rhymes Scot.* 366 A frosty Candlemas-day is found to be . . . generally indicative of cold for the next six weeks or two months. [¹ 2nd Feb.]

Candlemas Day, On | if the sun shines clear, the shepherd had rather see his wife on the bier.

1830 FORBY 416.

Candlemas-day is come and gone, When | the snow lies on a hot stone. (C 55)

1678 RAY 43.

Candlemas Day, On | throw candle and candlestick away. (C 53)

1678 RAY 344. **1875** DYER *Brit. Pop. Cust.* (1900) 55 From Candlemas the use of tapers at vespers and litanies, which had continued through the whole year, ceased until the ensuing All Hallow Mass, . . .

Candlemas Day, On | you must have half your straw and half your hay. (c 54)

c. 1640 In *Berkeley MSS.* (1885) iii. 30 At Candlemas a provident husbandman should have halfe his fodder, and all his corne remaininge. 1678 RAY 52. 1732 FULLER no. 6487.

Candlemas, As long as the bird sings before | it will greet after it.

1721 KELLY 43. 1846 DENHAM 27.

Candlemas, *see also* Set trees . . . after C.; Wind's in the east on C. day (When the).

Candlesticks, canstick, *see* Coll under c.; St. Matthew get c. new; St. Matthi lay c. by.

Cannon, *see* Boulogne (Our fathers won); Cursed in his mother's belly that was killed by c.

Canny Newcastle.

1787 GROSE *Glos., Northumb.* 213 . . . Spoken jocularly to Newcastle-men, . . . for their partiality to their native town. 1854 SURTEES *Hand. Cross* ch. 19 'Where d'ye come from?' 'Canny-newcassel', replied Pigg.

Canoe, *see* Paddle one's own c.

Canterbury is the higher rack, but Winchester is the better manger. (c 58)

1608 HARINGTON *Nugae Antiquae* (1804) ii. 87 A bishop of Winchester one day in pleasant talke, comparing his revenew with the archbishops of Canterburie should say—'Your Graces will shew better in the racke, but mine will be found more in the maunger.' 1639 CLARKE 206. 1662 FULLER Hants 3 . . . W. Edington, bishop of Winchester, . . . rendring this the reason of his refusal to be removed to Canterbury. . . . The Revenues of Winchester . . . are more advantagious to gather riches thereon. . . . Applicable to such who prefer a wealthy Privacy before a less profitable Dignity.

Canterbury tale, A. (c 59)

1546 J. BALE *Examn. of Anne Askewe* P.S. 162. 1549 LATIMER *Serm.* 8, P.S. 106 We might as well spend that time in reading of profane histories, of Cantorburye tales, or a fit of Robyn Hode. 1608 TOPSELL *Serpents* (1658) 778 To interpret these to be either fables and Canterbury tales, or true historical narrations. 1709 R. STEELE *Tatler* 22 Dec. no. 110, col. 2 I did not care for hearing a Canterbury tale.

Cap after (at) a thing, (at the moon) To throw one's. (c 60)

(a) = to defy.

1601 BRETON *No Whipping* B8ᵛ He cast his Cap at sinne in generall. 1608 SHAKES. *C. I.* i. 210 They threw their caps As they would hang them on the horns o' th' moon. 1609 R. ARMIN *Ital. Tailor* A4 Every Pen & Ink-horne Boy will throwe up his Cap at the hornes of the Moone in censure.

(b) = to despair of overtaking. (c 62)

1592 NASHE *Strange News* i. 318 Pierce Pennilesse may well cast his cappe after it for euer ouertaking it. 1603 DEKKER *The Wonderful Year* (Wilson) 19 *Platoes Mirabilis Annus* . . . May throw *Platoes* cap at *Mirabilis*, for that title of wonderfull is bestowed vpon 1603. 1605–8 SHAKES. *T. Ath.* III. iv. 100 I perceive our masters may throw their caps at their money. 1670 RAY 168 They may cast their caps at him. When two or more run together, and one gets ground, he that . . . despairs to overtake, commonly casts his hat after the for[e]most, and so gives over the race.

Cap be made of wool, If his. (c 63)

[1590] 1635 *Long Meg Westminster* in *Old Bk. Coll. Misc.* ii. 9 I'll make thee pay every farthing, if thy cap be of wool. 1618 BELCHIER *Hans Beer-Pot,* D2ᵛ You shall not flinch, if that your cap be wool. 1633 JONSON *T. Tub* II. ii. 107 Slip, you will answer it, and your Cap be of wool. 1662 FULLER Herts. 33 [In] the Reign of King Henry the Eighth, . . . velvet caps becoming fashionable for Persons of prime Quality, discomposed the proverb, If his cap be made of Wooll, as formerly comprising all conditions of people how high and haughty soever. 1670 RAY 167 . . . was as much to say . . ., As sure as the clothes on his back.

Cap fits, If the | wear it.

1600 BRETON *Pasquil's Foolscap* A3 Where you finde a head fit for this *Cappe*, either bestowe it vpon him in charity, or send him where he may haue them for his money. 1748 RICHARDSON *Clarissa H.* (1785) VII. x If indeed thou findest . . . that the cap fits thy own head, why then . . . e'en take and clap it on. 1816 'QUIZ' *Grand Master* III. 55 If the cap fits him, he may wear it. 1827 SCOTT *Surg. D.* ch. 10 'If Captain Middlemas,' he said, 'thought the cap fitted, he was welcome to wear it'. 1887 BLACKMORE *Springhaven* ch. 4 Put the cap on if it fits.

Cap in the wind, To throw one's.

1579 TOMSON *Calvin's Serm.* Trin. 824/2 Hauing cast their caps into the winde (as the prouerbe is) thinke no harme can touch them. 1588 TERENCE *Andria* tr. Kyffin E2 Vnlesse you make sute to the olde mans freends, you do but throw your cap in the winde.

Cap is better at ease than my head, My. (c 65)

1546 HEYWOOD II. vii. K1 That aspine leafe, suche spitefull clappyng hath bred, That my cap is better at ease than my hed. 1555 HEYWOOD *Epig. on Prov.* LXIV. 1611 DAVIES Prov. 257 Some Coockolds Cappes haue more ease then their Head.

Cap(s), *see also* Belvoir has c.; Feather in c.; Monmouth c.; Pull c.; Put on considering c.; Red c.; Set one's c. at; Thrum c.

Capers like a fly in a tar-box, He. (F 395)

1659 HOWELL *Eng. Prov.* 19a. 1678 RAY 68.

Capers, *see also* Money and c., (He that has) is provided for Lent.

Capon, If thou hast not a | feed on an onion.   (C 68)

1611 COTGRAVE s.v. Chapon. 1670 RAY 4. 1710 PALMER 201.

Capon(s), *see also* Chickens feed c.; Gives thee a c.; Sairy collop that is off c.

Captain, Such | such retinue.   (C 70)

c. 1390 GOWER *Conf. Amantis* III. 2421 Such Capitein such retenue.

Captain, *see also* Old band is c.'s honour.

Capuch, *see* Beads in hand and devil in c.

Caravan, *see* Dogs bark, but c. goes on.

Carcase is, Wheresoever the | there will the eagles¹ (ravens) be gathered together.   (C 73)

[MATT. xxiv. 28]. 1550 ?N. UDALL *Discourse* 2A3 (Bible cited). *c.* 1566 CURIO *Pasquin in a Trance* tr. W.P. 33 Where the caraine is, thither do the Eagles resort. 1573 BULLEIN *Dial. agst. Fever* E.E.T.S. 19 The Rauen will seeke the carrion. 1853 TRENCH iv. 94 . . . Wherever there is a Church or a nation abandoned by the spirit of life, and so a carcase, tainting the air of God's moral world, around it assemble the ministers and messengers of Divine justice, . . . the scavengers of God's moral world. [¹ i.e. vultures.]

Cards are the devil's books.   (C 76)

1676 *Poor Robins Alm. Prognost.* C4 Cards and dice . . . the devil's books and the devil's bones. 1738 SWIFT Dial. III. E.L. 319 Damn your cards, said he, they are the devil's books. *c.* 1785 BURNS *Twa Dogs* ad fin. Or lee-lang nights, wi' crabbit leuks, Pore owre the devil's pictur'd beuks. 1834 SOUTHEY *Doctor* ii. 249 He thought that cards had not without reason been called the Devil's Books. 1910 *Spectator* 17 Dec. 1073 'The sort that tells you the theatre is the devil's front parlour, and cards is his picture-books.'

Cards to show for it, He has good. (C 77)

1581 CAMPION in *Confer.* II. (1584) U4 I would I might be suffered to shewe my cardes. *c.* 1596 SHAKES. *K.J.* V. ii. 105 Have I not here the best cards for the game, To win this easy match, played for a crown? *a.* 1606 *Nobody and Somebody* l. 1836 My Master hath good cards on his side. [c. 1635] 1655 MASSINGER *Bashful Lover* V. i. 412 I met with a rougher entertainment, yet I had Good cards to shew. 1732 FULLER no. 1887.

Card(s), *see also* Cheat mine own father at c.; Cooling c.; Honest a man as any in c.; Lucky at c., unlucky in love; Outface with a c. of ten; Pack of c. (No) without knave; Pack the c. (Many can), yet cannot play; Patience and shuffle the c.; Play one's c. well; Speak by the c.; Sure c.; Tell thy c., then tell what hast won; Throw up c.

Care a button, Not to. *Cf.* Button, Not worth a.   (B 782)

1519 HORMAN *Vulgaria* 36 I set nat a button by dismolde dayes. 1631 *Celestina* tr. Mabbe T.T. 132. 1861 GEO. ELIOT *Silas M.* ch. 3 He did not care a button for cock-fighting.

Care a pin, Not to.   (P 333)

c. 1410 *Towneley Plays* E.E.T.S. 34 Thi felowship. Set I not at a pyn. 1590 SPENSER *F.Q.* I. v. 4 Who not a pin Does care for looke of liuing creatures eye. 1594–5 SHAKES. *L.L.L.* IV. iii. 15 I would not care a pin if the other three were in. 1777 SHERIDAN *Sch. Scandal* III. i. 'Tis evident you never cared a pin for me.

Care a straw (two, three straws), Not to.   (S 917)

a. 1300 *Havelok* 315 He let his oth al ouer-ga, Þerof ne yaf he nouth a stra. *c.* 1369 CHAUCER *Bk. Duchess* 718 Socrates . . . ne counted nat thre strees Of noght that fortune koude doo. 1497 MEDWALL *Fulgens & Lucres* i. 913 A straw for your mockynge. *a.* 1500 *Play of the Sacrament* 125 ed. Boas and Reed A straw for talis. *c.* 1500 *Everyman* l. 222 Be thy thankes I set not a straw. 1611 SHAKES. *W.T.* III. ii. 108 I prize it not a straw. 1609 HARWARD 127ᵛ I waigh thee not a haire . . . not a rush, not a straw, not a Dodkin. 1834 J. B. KER 23 He does not care two straws for her (them). 1861 HUGHES *Tom B. at Oxford* ch. 3 Drysdale, who didn't care three straws about knowing St. Cloud. 1887 *Spectator* 1 Oct. 1304 The British Government . . . does not care one straw what religion its subjects profess.

Care and diligence bring luck.   (D 338)

1540 TAVERNER *Flores aliquot sententiarum* A4 Cura potest omnia, Diligence & study can do al thinges. 1591 STEPNEY *Span. Schoolmaster* L2ᵛ Diligence is the mother of good fortune. 1591 LODGE *Catharos* Hunt. Cl. ed. 13 The prouerbe is, true care preserueth all things. 1612 SHELTON *Quix.* I. iv. 19 Diligence is the mother of good hap. 1732 FULLER no. 1057.

Care brings grey hair.   (C 82)

1530 PALSGRAVE 418b Thought maketh men age a pace. 1583 G. BABINGTON *Exposⁿ of the Commandᵗˢ* 270 Often . . . haue I hard men say that sorow and care wil shorten our time. 1584 WITHALS M6ᵛ Care makes a man haue hoarie heares, Although he haue not many yeares. 1600 DEKKER *Shoem. Hol.* v. v. 30 Care, and, colde lodging brings white haires. 1609 HARWARD 76 Cares bring hore haires. 1659 N.R. 25.

Care is no cure.   (C 83)

1588 GREENE *Pandosto* ed. Thomas 31 In sores past help salues do not heal but hurt, and in things past cure, care is a corrosive. 1592–4 SHAKES. *1 Hen. VI* III. iii. 3 Care is no cure, but rather corrosive, For things that are not to be remedied. 1678 RAY 108.

Care not would have it.   (C 90)

1670 RAY 67. 1721 KELLY 80 . . . If you ask a Man if he will have such a Thing, and he answers *I care not*, it is a sign that he would have it.

Care will kill a cat. *Cf.* Hang care. (c 84)

1585–1616 *Shirburn Ballads* (1907) 91 Let care
kill a catte, Wee'le laugh and be fatte. **1598–9**
SHAKES. *M.A.* V. i. 133 Though care kill'd a cat,
thou hast mettle enough in thee to kill care. **1601**
JONSON *Ev. Man. in Hum.* I. iii. 84. **1623** W.
PAINTER B3ᵛ Some say, Hang sorrow, care will
kill a Cat. **1682** N. O. tr. BOILEAU'S *Lutrin* iv. 322
Exiling fretting Care, that kills a Cat! **1695**
RAVENSCROFT 56 Cry you mercy, kill'd the cat.
1816 SCOTT *Antiq.* ch. 14 Hang expenses—care
killed a cat. **1890** 'R. BOLDREWOOD' *Miner's
Right* ch. 23 He was always ready to enjoy himself . . . 'care killed a cat'.

Care, A pound of | will not pay an
ounce of debt. *Cf.* Hundred pounds of
sorrow.   (P 518)

1589 L. WRIGHT *Display Duty*, 15 (A pound of
sorrow). **1590** GREENE *Never Too Late* 85 (One
pound of care payes not). **1599** PORTER *Angry
Wom. Abingd.* l. 1057. **1600** DEKKER *Shoem.
Hol.* III. iii. 21 (a dram of debt). **1614** CAMDEN
303.

Care(s) (*noun*), *see also* Behind the horseman
sits c.; Children are certain c.; Crowns have c.;
Hang c.; Little gear less c.; Little wealth little
c.; Much coin much c.; Pains to get, c. to keep;
Past cure past c.; Riches bring c.; Wise fear
begets c.

Care(s) (*verb*), *see also* End goes forward, (He c.
not which); Tint thing c. not. (For a); Wise man
c. not for what he cannot have.

Careless hussy makes many thieves, A.
                                            (H 843)

a. 1628 CARMICHAELL no. 164 (rackles). **1663** P.
STAMPOY 4. **1683** MERITON *Yorkshire Ale* (1897)
83–7.

Careless parting between the old mare
and the broken cart, A.

1721 KELLY 54 . . . Spoken when a Husband or
Wife dies who did not love one another. **1818**
SCOTT *Rob Roy* ch. 27 'Gie me my wages . . . ,
and I'se gae back to Glasgow. There's sma
sorrow at our parting, as the auld mear said to
the broken cart.'

Careless, The more | the more modish.

1738 SWIFT *Dial.* I. E.L. 276 She wears her
clothes as if they were thrown on her with a
pitchfork. . . .—Well, that's neither here nor
there; for, you know, the more careless the more
modish.

Cares not whose child cry, so his laugh,
He.   (c 306)

1585–1616 *Shirburn Ballads* (1907) 22 Some care
not how others' children cry, So they themselves
can prosper well. **1721** KELLY 137 (Bairn greet)
. . . Spoken of selfish People, whose Endeavours
terminate upon, and centre in, themselves. **1732**
FULLER no. 1823.

Cares, *see also* Care(s).

Car(e)y, *see* Mother C.'s chickens.

Cargo, *see* Flag protects the c.

Carl riches he wretches, As (The more)
the.   (c 91)

a. 1628 CARMICHAELL no. 202. **1641** FERGUSSON
no. 79. **1721** KELLY 24 . . . Many Men are found
to grow the more niggardly as their Wealth increase. **1853** TRENCH V. 111 Mammon . . . given
sometimes . . . that under its fatal influence they
may grow worse and worse, for (the more) . . .

Carl(s), *see also* Hair and hair; Kiss a c.; Lairds
break (When), c. get land.

Carleton[1] wharlers[2].

1610 HOLLAND *Camden's Brit.* I. 517 As for
Carleton, . . . wherein . . . all in manner that are
borne . . . have an ill-favoured, untunable, and
harsh manner of speech, . . . with a certaine kind
of wharling. **1650** FULLER *Pisgah-sight of Pal.*
II. ix. par. 3 (1869) 167 It is observed in a village
of Charleton in Leicestershire that the people
therein are troubled with wharling in their utterance. [[1] Carleton Curlieu, near Leicester. [2] Persons who pronounce the letter *r* with a guttural
sound.]

Carpenter, Like (Such) | like (such)
chips.   (c 94)

[*c.* 1530] *a.* 1555 BERNERS *Arthur Little Br.* 319
I knowe well my lorde Arthur hath bene here
. . . he is a good carpenter, for he hath made here
a fayre syght of chyppes. **1546** HEYWOOD II. vii.
I4 Such carpenters, such chips. Quoth she folke
tell. **1609** HARWARD 79ᵛ He is not the best
carpenter that maketh the most chipps. **1670**
RAY 115. **1738** SWIFT Dial. II. E.L. 306 You
have eaten nothing. —. . . See all the bones on
my plate: they say a capenter's known by his
chips.

Carpenter(s), *see also* Best c. makes the fewest
chips; Bone in the leg (Were it not for) all would
turn c.

Carpet knight, A.   (c 98)

1574 E. HAKE *Touchstone* C5ᵛ Carpet knights and
giglots. **1576** G. WHETSTONE *Rock of Regard* ed.
Collins 82 Now he consults with carpet knights
about curious masks, and other delightful
shewes. **1576** U. FULWELL *Ars Adulandi* L3ᵛ.
1598–9 SHAKES. *M.A.* V. ii. 32 A whole book
full of these quondam carpet-mongers. **1604**
DEKKER I *Honest Whore* III. i .229 Now, looks My
Master iust like one of our carpet knights, only
he's somewhat the honester of the two. **1616**
DRAXE no. 2334.

Carps, *see* Heresy and beer . . . came into
England.

Carried down the stream, He that is |
need not row.

1732 FULLER no. 2280.

Carrier, *see* John (Tom) Long the c.

Carries all his wardrobe on his back, He.
(w 61)

1578 T. CHURCHYARD *Discourse of the Queen's Entertainment* (Nichols, *Progresses*, 1823, ii. 196) [Wantonness and Riot] Our wealth is all upon our backe. **1591** LYLY *Endym.* IV. ii. 38 My wardrope [is] on my backe, for I haue no more apparrell then is on my body. **1595** SHAKES. *K.J.* II. i. 70 Fiery voluntaries . . . Bearing their birthrights proudly on their backs. **1616** WITHALS 573. **1659** HOWELL *Eng. Prov.* 16a. **1667** 'Rodolphus' *Fortune's Inconstancy* 1959 ed. 51 They soon understood his chiefest Riches and Merchandize to be on his back.

Carries fire in one hand and water in the other, He.
(F 267)

1412–20 LYDGATE *Troy Bk.* IV. 4988 On swiche folke, platly, is no trist, That fire and water holden in her fist. *c.* **1517** SKELTON *Magnif.* Wks. (1843) I. 248 Two faces in a hood covertly I bear, Water in the one hand, and fire in the other. **1541** M. COVERDALE *The Olde Faith* *6 False teachers . . . carye fyre (as they saye) with the one hande and water in the other. **1579** PLUTARCH, tr. North, 'Demetrius' T.C. viii. 309 As the wicked woman Archilochus speaketh of, who, 'Did in the one hand water show, And in the other fire bestow.' **1579** LYLY *Euph.* i. 247 Whatsoeuer I speake to men, the same also I speke to women, I meane not . . . to carrye fire in the one hande and water in the other. **1605** S. ROWLEY *When you See me* l. 969. **1676** BUNYAN *Strait Gate* Wks. (1855) I. 389. **1732** FULLER no. 5886.

Carries well to whom it weighs not, He.
(C 100)

1640 HERBERT no. 391.

Carrion crows bewail the dead sheep, and then eat them.
(C 847)

1640 HERBERT no. 458 The crow bewailes the sheepe, and then eates it. **1670** RAY 6.

Carrion will kill a crow (kite), No.
(C 99)

1609 HARWARD 76 No caren kill a crow. *c.* **1610** BEAUM. & FL. *Wit at S. W.* III. i Every one knows the state of his own body, No carrion kills a kite. **1650** Feb. 12–19, *Mercurius Pragmaticus*, 2 T2ᵛ Hee will make good the Proverb, . . . **1670** RAY 76.

Carrion, *see also* Kite will never be good hawk.

Carrot, *see* Fine as a c. new scraped.

Carry a bone in the mouth (*or* teeth), To.
(B 521)

[= said of a ship when she makes the water foam before her.] **1627** CAPT. SMITH *Seaman's Gram.* ii. 10 If the Bow be too broad, she will seldom carry a bone in her mouth, or cut a feather, that is, to make a fome before her. **1851** LONGFELLOW *Gold. Leg.* V See how she leaps . . . and speeds away with a bone in her mouth.

Carry a nutmeg in your pocket, If you | you'll be married to an old man.

1738 SWIFT *Dial.* I. E.L. 290 *Miss, searching her pocket for a thimble, brings out a nutmeg.* —O, miss, have a care; for if you carry a nutmeg in your pocket, you'll certainly be married to an old man.

Carry (*or* bear) coals, To.
(C 464)

[= to do dirty or degrading work, to submit to humiliation.] **1522** SKELTON (Dyce) II. 34 Wyll ye bere no coles? *c.* **1595** SHAKES. *R.J.* I. i. 1 Gregory, o' my word, we'll not carry coals. **1599** *Id. Hen. V* III. ii. 50 I knew by that piece of service the men would carry coals. **1600** JONSON *Ev. Man out of Hum.* v. i. 16 Here comes one that will carrie coales, ergo, will hold my dogge. **1611** CHAPMAN *May Day* I. i. 430 Above all things you must carry no coals. *a.* **1683** B. WHICHCOTE *Serm.* Those who are sensible that they carry coals, and are full of ill will.

Carry coals to Newcastle, To.
(C 466)

1583 MELVILLE *Autobiog.* (Wodrow S.) i. 163 Salt to Dysart, or colles to Newcastle! **1662** FULLER *Northumb.* 302 . . . That is to do what was done before; or to busy one's self in a needless imployment. **1661** GRAUNT *Bills Mortality*, Ded. Ld. Truro I should (according to our English Proverb) . . . but carry Coals to Newcastle. **1822** SCOTT *Let. Joanna Baillie* 10 Feb. in LOCKHART *Life* It would be a sending coals to Newcastle with a vengeance. **1787** GROSE *Glos.* (1811) 214 . . . In the environs of Newcastle, are most of the coal mines that supply London, and the coal trade to other places.

Carry guts to a bear, Not fit (worthy) to.
(G 486)

1659 HOWELL *Eng. Prov.* 17a. **1670** RAY 200 Not worthy to carry guts after a Bear. **1786** WOLCOT (P. Pindar) *Lousiad* ii. Wks. (1816) I. 168 George thinks us scarcely fit ('tis very clear) To carry guts, my brethren to a bear. **1840** MARRYAT *Poor Jack* ch. 28 Well, if I'm a bear, you ar'n't fit to carry guts to a bear. **1904** MRS. HUGHES *Recollections of Scott* ch. 6 'So, sir, I hear you have had the impudence to assert that I am not fit to carry guts to a bear.' 'Oh no!— I defended you, I said you were.'

Carry (-ies), *see also* Dog that fetches will c.; Knows how to c. dead cock home; Meat in his mouth, (He brings (c.)).

Carshalton, *see* Sutton.

Cart before the horse, To set (put) the.
(C 103)

[= to reverse the natural or proper order.] **1340** *Ayenb.* 243 Moche uolk of religion ʒetteþ þe ʒuolʒ be-uore þe oksen. *c.* **1520** WHITTINGTON *Vulg.* (1527) 2 That techer setteth the carte before the horse that preferreth imitacyon before preceptes. **1589** PUTTENHAM *Eng. Poesie* Arb. 181 We call it in English prouerbe, the cart before the horse, the Greeks call it Histeron proteron, we name it the Preposterous. **1605–6** SHAKES. *K.L.* I. iv. 223 May not an ass know when the cart draws the horse? **1801**

EDGEWORTH *Belinda* ch. 3 Esteem ever followed affection, instead of affection following esteem. Woe be to all who in morals preposterously put the cart before the horse! **1863** KINGSLEY *Water Bab.* ch. 4 They . . . having, as usual, set the cart before the horse, and taken the effect for the cause.

Cart whemling,[1] If ever I get his | I'll give it a putt.[2]   (C 102)

a. **1628** CARMICHAELL no. 555 Get I your waine at a wolting,[1] I sall len it a put.[2] **1641** FERGUSSON no. 492 If I can get his cairt at a walter,[1] I shall lend it a put. **1721** KELLY 197 . . . If I get him at a Disadvantage, I'll take my Revenge on him. [[1] overturning. [2] push.]

Carts that come to Crowland are shod with silver, All the.   (C 107)

1662 FULLER Lincs. 152 Venice and Crowland, . . . may count their Carts alike; that being sited in the Sea, this in a Morasse and Fenny ground, so that an horse can hardly come to it.

Cart(s), *see also* Best c. may overthrow; Cast at c.'s arse; Glean before c. has carried; Horses draw in c. (As good); Make an end of your whistle, though c. overthrow; Old c. well used; Put at the c. that is aye ganging; Sorrow rode in my c.; Time to yoke when c. comes to caples; Unhappy man's c. eith to tumble.

Carter, *see* Swear like a c.

Cart-load, *see* Fall away . . . to a c.

Cart-saddle, *see* Becomes it as cow doth c.

Cartway, *see* Common as the highway, (c.).

Carver, To be one's own.   (C 110)

c. **1558** 'WEDLOCK' *Image of Idleness* B5[v] Ye may be therin as it were your owne caruer. **1573** GASCOIGNE *Supposes* i. 213 In such cases it is not lawful for a man to be his owne carver. **1579** G. HARVEY to E. Spenser *Letter-Bk.* 59 It is Italian curtesye to give a man leave to bee his own carver. **1579** LYLY *Euph.* i. 203 And in this poynt I meane not to be myne owne caruer. **1594** NASHE *Unfort. Trav.* 257 It is not for a straunger to be his owne caruer in reuenge. **1596** SHAKES. *Rich. II* III. iii. 144 Be his own carver and cut out his way. **1600–1** *Id. H. I.* iii. 19 He may not, as unvalued persons do, Carve for himself. **1604** *Id. O.* II. iii. 165 He that stirs next to carve for his own rage Holds his soul light. **1605–6** *Id. M.* I. ii. 16 Brave Macbeth . . . Disdaining Fortune . . . (Like valour's minion), carv'd out his passage. **1614** RALEIGH *Hist. World* v. v. VII. 595 [He] plainly told them, That the Romans would be their owne Caruers, and take what they thought good. **1666** TORRIANO *Prov. Phr.* s.v. Parti 134 To have been first to take, to have been his own carver or chuser.

Carver, *see also* Worst c. in the world, never make good chaplain.

Case is altered, The.   (C 111)

c. **1568** *Liberality & Prodigality* D3. *c.* **1573** G. HARVEY *Letter-Bk.* 124 The case is quite alterid. **1577** HOLINSHED *Hist. Scot.* (1587 i. 22b) So is the case now altered with vs. **1578** *Promus & Cassandra* F2[v]. **1579** *Proverbs of Sir James Lopez de Mendoza* tr. B. Googe 27. **1594** GREENE *Looking-Glass* II. ii. Merm. 105 Faith sir, the case is altered; you told me it before in another manner: the law goes quite against you. **1609** JONSON *Case Altered* [Title].

Case is altered, The | quoth Plowden.[1]   (C 111)

[*a.* **1585**] **1603** DEKKER *Batch. Banq.* Gros. 1. 235 Then is their long warre come to an end, and the case (as Ployden sayth) cleane altered. **1662** FULLER Shrops. 2 This Proverb referreth its originall to Edmund Plowden, an eminent Native and great Lawyer of this County, though very various the relations of the occasion thereof. [[1] 1518–85.]

Case(s), *see also* Circumstances alter c.; Example to another, (He is in ill c. that gives); Hard c. bad law; No c., abuse attorney; Wisdom counsels (When) well goes c.

Cask savours of the first fill, The.   (L 333)

[HORACE *Ep.* 1. 2. 69 *Quo semel est imbuta recens servabit odorem Testa diu.* A cask will long preserve the flavour with which, when new, it was once impregnated. *c.* **1230** *Contra Avaros* in WRIGHT *Polit. Songs* Camd. Soc. 31 Quo semel est imbuta recens servabit odorem.] **1509** BARCLAY *Ship of Fools* i. 47 But fyll an erthen pot first with yll lycoure And euer after it shall smell somwhat soure. **1552** LATIMER *7th Serm. bef. Edw. VI* P.S. 431 Where children are brought up in wickedness, they will be wicked all their lives after, . . . 'The carthen pot will long savour of that liquor that is first put into it.' *c.* **1645** HOWELL *Lett.* 17 Sept. (1903) III. 87 I am not versed in my maternal tongue so exactly as I should be. . . . Yet the old British is not so driven out . . . (for the cask savours still of the liquor it first took in), &c. **1666** TORRIANO 29 A butt gives such a scent as it hath. **1732** FULLER no. 1473 Every Tub smells of the Wine it holds. **1779–81** JOHNSON *Lives Poets* (Bohn) II. 201 A survey of the life and writings of Prior may exemplify a sentence . . . ; *the vessel long retains the scent which it first receives.*

Cask, *see also* Pirate gets nothing of another but c.; Wine savours of c.

Casket, *see* Jewel by the c. (None can guess).

Cassandra warnings.

1589 *Admonit. given by one of the Duke of Savoy's Council* tr. E. Aggas A2 I . . . doe come with a most humble admonition . . . peradventure as a new Cassandra. **1629** T. ADAMS *Serm.* (1861) I. 216 All the prophecies of ill success have been held as Cassandra's riddles. **1928** *Times* 14 Dec. 10/3 His continual 'delay and vacillation', to use Queen Victoria's own words, caused her the gravest anxiety. . . . All her warnings, like those of Cassandra, were neglected, and, like those of Cassandra, were fulfilled in every instance.

Cast a bone in the devil's teeth.

1721 KELLY 79 . . . Gratify some squeezing Oppressor, or some unconscionable Officer, to save your self from his Harm.

Cast at cart's arse, To be.   (C 106)

[= to be in disgrace; offenders were flogged at the tail of a cart.] **1510**? *Wealth & Health* 230 I am cast out at the cartes arse. **1540** PALSGRAVE *Acolastus* Prol., 18 Cast them out at the cartes ars. **1541** SIR T. WYATT (cited *Life and Lett. of Wyatt* ed. Muir 198) But ye know maisters, yt is a common prouerbe 'I am lefte owte of the cartes ars', and yt is take vpon packinge gere together for carriage. **1546** HEYWOOD I. ix. C1ᵛ I am cast at carts ars. **1611** DAVIES no. 398.

Cast (Hand) be bad, If thy | mend it with good play.

1732 FULLER no. 2723. **1902–4** LEAN IV. 5 If your hand[1] be bad, mend it with good play. [1 i.e. at cards.]

Cast beyond the moon, To.   (M 1114)

[= to indulge in wild conjectures.] *c.* **1516** SKELTON *Magn.* 224 All is without Measure and fer beyonde the mone. *c.* **1533** J. FRITH *Another Answ. agst. Rastell* B2ᵛ Rastell thynketh that I . . . boste my self above the mone because I touche Master More his kynsman. **1546** HEYWOOD I. iv. B1ᵛ Feare may force a man to cast beyonde the moone. **1559** *Mirr. Mag.* 529 Beyond the moone when I began to cast . . . what place might be procur'd. *c.* **1590** SHAKES. *T.And.* IV. iii. 65 My lord, I aim a mile beyond the moon. [**1603**] **1607** T. HEYWOOD *Wom. K. Kindness* sc. XIII. l. 63 But, oh! I talk of things impossible, And cast beyond the moon. **1623** CAMDEN 271 He cast beyond the Moone. **1636** *Ibid.* 298 He casts beyond the Moone that hath pist on a nettle.

Cast, He is at last.   (C 115)

1572 CRADOCKE *Ship of Assured Safety* 73 The good olde man father Abraham, beeing now at the laste caste, perceaued he drue towardes his graue. **1587** J. BRIDGES *Defence* 857 Come they now in almost at the last caste. **1616** DRAXE no. 1557.

Cast (hit) in the teeth, To.   (T 429)

a. **1500** *15c. School-Bk.* ed. W. Nelson 80. **1508**? STANBRIDGE *Vulgaria* 27. 7. 8 Cast me in the tethe withale. **1526** TYNDALE *James* i. 5 Which geveth to all men . . . withouten doubleness, and casteth no man in the teeth. **1530** PALSGRAVE 477b I caste in the tethe, or I caste in the nose, as one doth that reproveth another of a faulte. **1539** TAVERNER I *Garden* F7 One dyd hytte in his teeth, that he [Cleanthes] was very fearfull. **1546** HEYWOOD I. xi. E3 But therto deuiseth to cast in my teeth, Checks and chokyng oysters. **1579** LYLY *Euph.* i. 262 The trecheries of his parents . . . will be cast in his teeth. [*c.* **1584**] **1592** LYLY *Gall.* III. i. 44 How cunninglie . . . you hit me in the teeth with loue. **1599** SHAKES. *J.C.* IV. iii. 98 All his faults observ'd, Set in a notebook, learn'd, and conn'd by rote, To cast into my teeth. **1716** HORNECK *Crucif. Jesus* 33 Strangers cast it in his Teeth so often, Where is now thy God?

Cast ne'er a clout till May be out.

[Sp. *c.* **1627** CORREAS *Vocabulario* (1906) 490 Hasta Mayo no te quites el sayo.[1]] **1706** STEVENS s.v. Mayo, *Hasta passado Mayo no te quites el sayo*, Do not leave off your Coat till May be past. Cf. also s.v. Abril, En *Abril* no quites fil: In April do not take off a Thread. Cf. also *Sayo*, Guarda el sayo, para Mayo, Keep your great Coat for May, that is, do not part with it before May. **1732** FULLER no. 6193 Leave not off a Clout, Till May be out. **1832** HENDERSON 154. [1 *Do not leave off your coat till May.*]

Cast not out the foul water till you bring in the clean.   (W 90)

1623 PAINTER C4ᵛ The wise prouerbe wish all men to saue Their foule water vntill they fayrer haue. *a.* **1628** CARMICHAELL no. 400 Cast not furth the auld water quhill the new come in. **1641** FERGUSSON no. 217. **1710** PALMER 89 Don't throw away Dirty Water till you have got Clean. **1721** KELLY 80 . . . Part not with that way of living you have, till you be sure of a better. **1738** SWIFT *Dial.* III. E.L. 319 Mrs. Giddy has discarded Dick Shuttle. . . . She was a fool to throw out her dirty water before she got clean. **1842** LOVER *Handy Andy* ch. 29 'I'll change my clothes' . . . 'You had better wait. . . . You know the old saying, "Don't throw out your dirty wather until you get in fresh".'

Cast of his office, To give one a.   (C 117)

a. **1553** UDALL *Royster D.* I. iv. Arb. 26 Speake to them: of mine office he shall haue a cast. **1666** TORRIANO *It. Prov.* 79 no. 44 The Devil gives him a cast of his Office.

Cast out nature with a fork, Though you | it will still return.   (N 50)

[HORACE *Epist.* I. 10. 24 *Naturam expellas furca, tamen usque recurret.*] **1539** TAVERNER (1552) 44ᵛ Thrust out nature wyth a croche, yet woll she styll runne backe agayne. **1594** LYLY *Mother B.* I i. 100 Why though your sons folly bee thrust vp with a paire of hornes on a forke, yet being naturall, it will haue his course. **1831** PEACOCK *Crotchet Cas.* ch. 1 Mr. Crotchet . . . seemed . . . to settle down . . . into an English country gentleman. . . . But, though you expel nature with a pitchfork, she will always come back. **1850** FROUDE *Short Stud.* (1890) I. 600 Drive out nature with a fork, she ever comes running back.

Cast (Lay) their heads together.   (H 280)

[*c.* **1517**] **1533** SKELTON *Magn.* B3ᵛ Nay let vs our heddes togyder cast. **1590** ROBERTS *Defiance to Fortune* K4 (casting their heads togither). **1590–1** SHAKES. *2 Hen. VI* IV. viii. 56 I see them lay their heads together to surprise me.

Cast up accounts (*or* reckoning), To.   (A 16)

[= To vomit.] **1594** LYLY *Mother B.* II. i. 127 We shall cast vp out accounts, and discharge our stomackes. *Ibid.* II. iv. 18 I must go and cast this matter in a corner. *c.* 1605 DEKKER 2 *Honest Whore* IV. iii. 103 I ha reckonings to cast up. 1678 RAY 87 *Of one drunk* . . . He's about to cast up his reckoning or accompts.

Cast your net where there is no fish, It is in vain to.

1706 STEVENS S.V. Rio. 1732 FULLER no. 2966.

Cast, *see also* Die is c.; Dust in a man's eyes; Fish is c. away that is c. in dry pools; Kernel and leap at the shell, (To lose (c. away) the); Lost all who has one c. left (Has not); Mist before one's eyes, (To c. a); Rub and a good c.; Shoe after one for luck, (To c. an old).

Cast-off, *see* Shoe (a c. o. glove), (To be thrown aside like an old).

Casticand, *see* Skiddaw, Lauvellin, and C.

Castle of Bungay, Were I in my | upon the river of Waveney, I would not care for the king of Cockney.   (C 123)

[*King of Cockneys*: a kind of Master of the Revels at Lincoln's Inn on Childermas Day (28 Dec.). The name of this mock king is perhaps referred to in the following saw.] *a.* 1577 HARRISON *England* II. xiv (1877) I. 266 As for those tales that go of . . . the brag of . . . [Hugh Bigot] that said in contempt of King Henrie the third . . . 'If I were in my castell of Bungeie, Vpon the water of Waueneie, I wold not set a button by the king of Cockneie', I repute them but as toies. 1659 HOWELL *Eng. Prov.* 21a. Were I near my Castle of *Bungey*, Upon the River of *Wavenley*, I would ne care for the King of *Cockeney*. . . . ; *these places are in* Suffolk.

Castles in Spain, To build.   (C 125)

c. 1400 *Rom. Rose* l. 2573 Thou shalt make castels thanne in Spayne, And dreme of joye, alle but in vayne. 1475 CAXTON *Jason* 19 He began to make castellis in Spaygne as louers doo. *a.* 1628 CARMICHAELL no. 635 He bigs castels in Spaine. 1886 W. BLACK *White Heather* ch. 46 I am less hopeful now; . . . my Highland mansion may prove to be a castle in Spain after all.

Castles in the air, To build.   (C 126)

[AUGUSTINUS *Sermo* 2. 6. 8 *Subtracto fundamento in aere aedificare.*] 1566 PAINTER *Pal. of Pleas.* (Jacobs i. 200) His heade ceased not to builde Castels in the ayre. 1580 NORTH *Plutarch* (1676) 171 They built Castles in the air, and thought to do great wonders. 1612–15 BP. HALL *Contempl.* IV. xi (1825) II. 379 Ye great men, spend not all your time in building castles in the air, or houses on the sand. 1633 MASSINGER *New Way* II. i Merm. 131 Ha! ha! these castles you build in the air Will not persuade me or to give or lend A token to you. 1894 BLACKMORE *Perlycross* ch. 13 His wife . . . had seen Jemmy waltzing . . . with one of her pretty daughters, and been edified with castles in the air.

Castle(s), *see also* Better a c. of bones; Bow (I have a good), but in the c.; City (C.) that parleys; Easy to keep c. never besieged; Fair wife

and frontier c.; House is his c. (A man's); Strong town (c.) is not won in an hour.

Cat, Gloved, Muffled, Muzzled, *see* Cat in gloves.

Cat (kit) after kind.   (C 135)

1559 *Mirr. for Mag.* (Campbell) 121 Cat will after kinde. 1568 *Jacob & Esau* IV. iv Hazl.-Dods. ii. 235 Cat after kind (say 'th the proverb) sweet milk will lap. 1570 BALDWIN *Beware the Cat* (1584, B4). 1573 GASCOIGNE *Hundreth Sundry Flowers* i. 450 Olde proverbes never faill, For yet was never good Cat out of kinde. *c.* 1580 G. HARVEY *Letterbk.* Camd. Soc. 120 Tis god philosophy: Katt will to kinde. 1599 SHAKES. *A.Y.* III. ii. 93 If the cat will after kind, so be sure will Rosalinde. 1670 RAY 183 Kit after kind. A chip of the old block. 1692 L'ESTRANGE *Aesop's Fab.* clv (1738) 170 Cat will to kind, as they say, and wicked men will be true to their principles.

Cat after kind, good mouse-hunt.   (C 136)

c. 1275 *Provs. of Alfred* (Skeat) A 296 For ofte museth the Kat after hire moder. 1540 *Nice Wanton* 52 For a good mouse-hunt is cat after kynd. 1546 HEYWOOD I. xi. D3. 1594–5 SHAKES. *R.J.* IV. iv. 11 Ay, you have been a mouse-hunt in your time . . .—A jealous-hood. 1678 RAY 109 That that comes of a cat will catch mice . . . *Chi da gatta nasce sorici piglia.*

Cat among the pigeons, To put the.

1706 STEVENS S.V. Palomar The Cat is in the Dove-house. They say, when a Man is got among the Women. 1948 DEC. 3 *Spectator* 723 The Government's proposal to let the State run the public houses in the new towns has put the cat among the pigeons.

Cat and dog may kiss, yet are none the better friends, The.

c. 1225 *Trin. MS. O. 11. 45* (ed. Förster) in *Eng. Stud.* 31. 7 Hund and cat kissat, ne beoþ hi no þe bet ifrund.

Cat did it, The.

1872 CALVERLEY *Fly Leaves*, '*Sad Memories*' Should china fall or chandeliers, or anything but stocks—Nay stocks when they're in flowerpots—the cat expects hard knocks. 1902–4 LEAN I. 433. . . . A common shift on puss of unwitnessed smashes.

Cat eats the flickle,[1] Little and little the.   (L 353)

a. 1530 *R. Hill's Commonpl. Bk.* E.E.T.S. 130 A litill and a litill, the cat etith vp the bacon flicke. 1546 HEYWOOD II. vii. I4ᵛ. 1609 HAR-WARD 79ᵛ (flitchin). [1 flitch.]

Cat; He is like a | fling him which way you will, he'll light on his legs.   (C 153)

c. 1398 TREVISA *Bartholomew* XVIII. 76 The catte . . . falleth on his owne fete whan he falleth out of hye places. 1519 HORMAN *Vulgaria* (James)

434 Cattes and dogges when they shal fall from hye so nymbleth therself: that they wyl pitch vpon their fete. *a.* 1616 BEAUM. & FL. *Mons. Thomas* III. iii 94 Not hurt him, He pitcht upon his legs like a cat. 1640 TORRIANO *Italian Tutor* 1st dialogue G 2 Like unto so many Cats, come what will, you fall always on your feet. 1678 RAY 282. 1818 KEATS *Lett.* (Rollins) i. 212 He always comes on his Legs like a Cat.

Cat for lard, Send not a. (c 164)

1640 HERBERT no. 644. 1659 TORRIANO no. 30 Thou buyest lard from the cat. 1659 HOWELL *It. Prov.* 11 To go to the cat for bacon.

Cat from a cony (cowlstaff), To know a. (c 171)

[*c.* 1565] *a.* 1595 *Peddler's Proph.* A4 Thinke not but that I know a Cat from a Cony. 1620 SHELTON *Quix.* Pt. II. xxvi Sell not me a cat for a coney. 1696 DILKE *Lover's Luck* III. 17 I know a Cat from a Cowle staff.

Cat, The lickerish[1] (liquorish[1]) | gets many a rap. (c 155)

1611 COTGRAVE s.v. Chat. 1670 RAY 4. [[1] lustful.]

Cat has nine lives, A. (c 154)

1546 HEYWOOD II. iv. G2[v] No wyfe, a woman hath nyne lyues like a cat. *c.* 1595 SHAKES. *R.J.* III. i. 75 Good King of Cats, nothing but one of your nine lives. 1894 BLACKMORE *Perlycross* ch. 11 If a cat has nine lives, sir; a lie has ninety-nine.

Cat has eaten her count, The. (c 137)

c. 1580 WOODES *Confl. Cons.* III. iv D4 But gyf the Sents war gone, the had eate my mark. 1609 HARWARD 79[v]. 1678 RAY 68 . . . It is spoken of women with child, that go beyond their reckoning.

Cat help it, How can the | if the maid be a fool? (c 151)

1578 FLORIO *First F.* 29 What fault hath the Cat, if the mayd be mad. *c.* 1594 BACON *Promus* no. 575 It is the catts nature and the wenches fault. 1642 TORRIANO 38. 1658 *Comes Facundus* 238 (set things in her way). 1678 RAY 109 . . . Not setting up things securely out of her reach or way.

Cat in gloves (*or* gloved, muffled, muzzled cat) catches no mice, A. (c 145 and 157)

1573 SANFORD 105 A gloued catte can catche no myse. 1591 W. STEPNEY *Span. Schoolmaster* L4[v] A mauling cat was neuer good hunter. 1592 DELAMOTHE 1 A mufled Cat is no good mouse hunter. 1611 DAVIES no. 333 Cuft Catt's no good Mouse-hunt. 1623 WODROEPHE 287 A Museld cat is not meete to take Mice. 1623 CAMDEN 266 A mufled Cat was neuer good mouzer. 1641 FERGUSSON no. 96 A gloved cat was never a good hunter. 1670 RAY 67 A muffled cat is no good mouser. 1758 FRANKLIN in ARBER *Eng. Garner* v. 580 Handle your tools,

without mittens! Remember that *The cat in gloves catches no mice*!

Cat is hungry when a crust contents her, The. (c 138)

1611 COTGRAVE s.v. Chat. 1670 RAY 4.

Cat is in the cream-pot, The. (c 139)

1598 T. DELONEY *Gentle Craft* Pt. II (Mann) 208 As well acquainted . . . as the cat in the creamepan. 1678 RAY 233.

Cat is out of kind that sweet milk will not lap, That. (c 167)

1492 *Dial. of Salomon & Marcolphus* (ed. Duff 6) Who shal fynde a catte trewe in kepyng mylke. 1580 MUNDAY *Zelauto* P2 The Catte will eate no sweete milke, for feare of marring her teeth. 1678 RAY 108.

Cat jumps, To see (watch) which way the. (c 140)

[= what direction events are taking.] 1825 S. WOODWORTH *The Forest Rose* I. ii. I know how the cat jumps. 1826 SCOTT *Journal* 7 October. 1827 SCOTT in *Croker Pap.* (1884) I. xi. 319 Had I time, I believe I would come to London merely to see how the cat jumped. 1863 KINGSLEY *Water Bab.* 289 He . . . understood so well which side his bread was buttered, and which way the cat jumped.

Cat kitten'd? Has the.

[= Something trivial as happened.] 1706 STEVENS s.v. Parida Si esta parida la gata? This Question they ask when there are many Lights more than needs; because the Cats Eyes shining in the Night, many Lights to no Purpose represent many Cats Eyes. 1883 BURNE *Shropsh. Folk-Lore* 596.

Cat knows whose beard (lips) she licks, The. (c 140)

[*c.* 1023 EGBERT V. LÜTTICH *Fecunda Ratis* (Voigt) 4 *Ad cuius ueniat scit cattus lingere barbam.* *c.* 1190 *Li Proverbe au Vilain* (Tobler) 2 Li chaz set bien cui barbe il leche.] *c.* 1225 *Trin. MS. O. II.* 45 (ed. Förster) in *Eng. Stud.* 31. 7 Wel wot hure cat, whas berd he lickat. *c.* 1300 *Provs. of Hending* (ed. Schleich) in *Anglia* 51. 270 Wel wote badde [i.e. *cat*], wose berde he lickith. *c.* 1350 *Douce MS.* 52 no. 78 Welle wotys the catte, whoos berde he lykkys. *c.* 1470 *Harl. MS.* 3362, f. 6 Wel wot þe cat whas berd he [likketh]. *c.* 1500 *Sloane MS.* 747, f. 66 *a* Well wote the cat whos berd he lykt. 1523 SKELTON *Garl. Laurell* 1438 And wele wotith the cat whos berde she likkith. 1546 HEYWOOD II. ix. L3 Kyndly he kyst hir, with woords not tart nor tough. But the cat knowth whose lips she lickth wel enough.

Cat left on the malt-heap, To have what the. (c 177)

1600 T. WILSON *The State of England* (ed. F. J. Fisher, Camden Soc., 24) He must have all . . . the rest that which the catt left on the malt heape. **1607** DOBSON's *Dry Bobs* B1ᵛ To˙expect that which the cat leaueth in the malt. **1616** WITHALS 554. **1639** CLARKE 71.

Cat loves mustard, As a.   (C 150)

a. **1628** CARMICHAELL no. 1772 Ye love her as bonie weil as cats dois mustard. **1639** CLARKE 235. **1678** RAY 287.

Cat may look at a king, A.   (C 141)

1546 HEYWOOD II. v. H3 What, a cat maie looke on a King, ye know. **1590** GREENE *Never too late* (1600) 94 A cat may look at a King, and a swain's eye hath as high a reach as a lord's look. **1638** T. HEYWOOD *Wise W. of Hogs.* II. ii . . . and so may I at her. **1893** STEVENSON *Catriona* ch. I 'There is no harm done', said she. . . . [*Cf.* Fr. *Un chien regarde bien un évêque.*]

Cat on hot bricks (a hot bake-stone), Like a.   (C 131)

1678 RAY 285 To go like a cat upon a hot bake stone. **1836** MARRYAT *Mr. Midshipman Easy* ch. I He . . . danced, like a bear upon hot plates, with delight. **1861** G. J. WHYTE-MELVILLE *Inside the Bar* ch. 2 A well-bred, raking-looking sort of mare . . . Beautiful action she had, stepped away . . . **1883** C. READE *Peril. Secret.* ch. 24 'Is not a racehorse a poor mincing thing until her blood gets up galloping?' . . . 'You are right, . . . she steps . . .'

Cat sees not the mouse ever, The.   (C 142)

1640 HERBERT no. 592. **1670** RAY 67.

Cat shuts its eyes while it steals cream, The.

1853 TRENCH iv. 77 . . . Men become wilfully blind to the wrong which is involved in some pleasing or gainful sin.

Cat, the Rat, and Lovell our Dog, rule all England under an Hog, The.   (C 143)

1516 FABYAN *New Chron. Eng. and Fr.* VII. 672 (Our dogge, Ruleth all). **1548** HALL *Chron.* (1809 ed., 398). [**1484**] **1577** HOLINSHED *Chron.* 1586 ed., iii. 746 [Richard III executed] a poore gentleman called Callingborne, for making a small rime of three of his . . . councellors, . . . lord Louell, sir Richard Ratcliffe . . . and sir William Catesbie . . . The Cat, the Rat, and Louell our dog, Rule all England vnder an hog. Meaning by the hog, the . . . wild boare, which was the King's cognisance. **1816** SCOTT *Antiq.* ch. 2 'His name . . . was Lovel.' 'What! the cat, the rat, and Lovel our dog? Was he descended from King Richard's favourite?'

Cat wink, Let the | and let the mouse run.   (C 152)

1522 *Mundus et Infans* 649 A ha!˙syrs, let the catte wynke! **1546** HEYWOOD II. iv. G3 But further stryfe to shonne, Let the cat wynke, and leat the mous ronne.

Cat winked when (both) her eyes were out, The.   (C 174)

1529 MORE *Wks.* 241 As weomen saye, . . . *a.* **1558** *Jack Juggler* l. 1143. **1659** HOWELL *Eng. Prov.* 2b The Catt winked, when both her eyes were out. **1738** SWIFT *Dial.* I. E.L. 263 I'm told for certain, you had been among the Philistines: no wonder the cat wink'd, when both her eyes were out.

Cat winks, When the | little wots the mouse what the cat thinks.   (C 176)

1678 RAY 109. **1732** FULLER no. 6453.

Cat winks a while, Though the | yet sure she is not blind.   (C 169)

c. **1570** *Maid Will You Marry?* in C. Robinson *et al. Handf. Pleas. Delights* 40 (Although the Cat doth winke a while). **1576** *Parad. of Dainty Devices* in *Brit. Bibliog.* (1812) iii. 59 I am not blinde although I winke. **1609** ROWLANDS *Whole crew of Kind Gossips* Hunt. Cl. 20 The cat ofte winkes, and yet she is not blinde. **1678** RAY 109. **1802** WOLCOT (P. Pindar) *Middl. Elect.* vi. Wks. (1816) 214 I daant tell all I know; But mum, I'm dumb, I'm dumb, and zo—Cats wink that be not blend.

Cat would eat fish and would not wet her feet, The.   (C 144)

[Med. Lat. *Catus amat piscem, sed non vult tingere plantam (plantas).*] *c.* **1225** *Trin. MS. O. II. 45* (ed. Förster) in *Eng. Stud.* 31. 7 Cat lufat visch, ac he nele his feth wete. *Catus amat piscem, sed non vult tangere flumen. c.* **1384** CHAUCER *Ho. Fame* iii. l. 1783 For ye be lyke the sweynte cat, That wolde have fissh; but wostow what? He wolde nothing wete his clowes. *c.* **1390** GOWER *Conf. Amantis* IV. l. 1108 As a cat wolde ete fisshes Withoute wetinge of his cles. *c.* **1470** *Harl. MS. 3362*, f. 7 The cat would ete. . . . *Catus vult piscem sed non vult tangere limpham.* **1539** TAVERNER 47 The catte wyll fyshe eate, but she wyl not her feete wette. **1546** HEYWOOD I. xi. D3ᵛ But you lust not to doo, that longeth therto. The cat would eate fyshe, and wold not wet her feete. **1584** WITHALS A8ᵛ. **1592** DELAMOTHE 27. **1605–6** SHAKES. *M.* I. vii. 44 Letting 'I dare not' wait upon 'I would', Like the poor cat i' the adage. **1641** FERGUSSON no. 904 Ye breid of the cat, ye wald fain eat fish, but yee have na will to weet your feet. **1670** RAY 67 The cat loves fish, but she's loath to wet her feet. Le chat aime le poisson, mais il n'aime pas à mouiller le patte. *Gall.*

Cat's away, When the | the mice will play.   (C 175)

c. **1470** *Harl. MS. 3362* in *Anglia* 42. 201 The mows lordchypyth, þer a cat ys nawt. *Mus debaccatur, ubi catus non dominatur. a.* **1530** R. Hill's *Commonpl. Bk.* E.E.T.S. 132 The mowse goth a-brode, wher þe cat is not lorde. **1573** SANFORD 109 When the Catte is not at home, the Myce daunce. **1599** SHAKES. *Hen. V.* I. ii. 172 Playing the mouse in absence of the cat. [**1603**] **1607** T. HEYWOOD *Wom. K. Kindness* sc. xii l. 5 Mum; there's an old proverb—when the cat's away, the mouse may play. **1670** RAY 68 When the cat is away, the mice play. *Ital.* Les rats se promenent a l'aise là ou il n'y a point des chats. *Gall.*

Cat's ear, *see* Bold mouse that breeds in.

Cat's eyes, To have.   (C 180)

1578 G. WHETSTONE 2 *Promus & Cassandra* III. i. 14 There be learing knaues abroade, haue Cattes eyes . . . they can bothe see and marke . . . in the darke.   **1607** DEKKER & WEBSTER *North. Ho* B3 I could teare out those false eyes, those Cats eyes, that can see in the night.   **1613** MARSTON & BARKSTEAD *Insat. Countess* V. ii. 134 These night works require A cat's eyes to impierce dejected darkness.

Cat's foot, *see* Lives under the sign of c. f.

Cat's paw of, To make a.

1785 GROSE To be made a cat's paw of.   **1823** JON BEE *Slang A Dict. of the Turf* 22 A Cat's Paw—is one who is pressed forward to perform disagreeable or dangerous offices for another. **1831** SCOTT *Journ.* 19 Jan. He [Sir W. S.] will not be made a cat's paw of, look you now.   **1844** JOWETT to B. C. Brodie 23 Dec. You must guard against being made a catspaw of.

Cat's paw, *see also* Chestnuts out of the fire.

Cat(s), *see also* Agree like c. and dogs; Agree like two c. in gutter; Ale will make c. speak; Before the c. can lick her ear; Bell the c.; Bides as fast as c. to saucer; Blate cat proud mouse; Bourd wi' c. (They that) maun count on scarts; Care will kill c.; Every day's no Yuleday—cast the c. a castock; Fight like Kilkenny c.; Grin like Cheshire c.; Horse (c.) laugh, (Enough to make a); Keep no more c. than will catch mice; Keep your thanks to feed your c.; Knit . . . my c. a codpiece; Let the c. out of bag; Lives as a cat (As many); Melancholy as a c.; Mouse against c.; Never was c. or dog drowned that could . . . ; No more of a c. but her skin (You can have); Old c. laps as much milk; Old c. sports not; Old c. to an old rat (Put); Playing with straw before old c.; Rain c. and dogs; Room to swing c.; Rub a c. on rump (The more), higher she sets tail; Scalded c. fears cold water; Scratching and biting c. and dogs come together; Shoot the c.; Singed c., better than likely (He is like); Strip it as Slack stript the c.; Teach the c. way to kirn; Tine c. tine game; True as that the c. crew; Turn the c. in pan; Two c. and a mouse never agree; Wanton kittens make sober c.; Watch one as c. mouse; Ways to kill a dog (c.); Weasel and c. make marriage (When), evil presage; Weel kens the mouse when c.'s out; Whip the c.; Wild c. out of a bush (Like); Woe's to them that have the c.'s dish.

Cat-harrow, *see* Draw at the c.

Catch a Tartar, To.   (T 73)

[= to get hold of one who can neither be control-led nor got rid of, or who proves to be too

formidable.]   **1663** BUTLER *Hudibras* I. iii. 865 Now thou hast got me for a Tartar, To make me 'gainst my will take quarter.   **1678** DRYDEN *Kind Keeper* v. i What a Tartar have I caught! **1720** DEFOE *Capt. Singleton* XVI (1906) 260 Tell him, if he should try, he may catch a Tartar. **1861** LD. DUNDONALD *Autobiog.* v. 63 Off Plane Island, we were very near 'catching a Tartar'. . . . We had fallen into the jaws of a formidable Spanish frigate.

Catch a weasel asleep.

1825 J. NEAL *Brother Jonathan* iii. 269.   **1837–47** BARHAM *Ingol. Leg.* (1898) 182 You must be pretty deep to catch weasels asleep.

Catch at, *see* Never c. at falling knife or friend.

Catch birds to-morrow, We shall.
                                                       (B 398)

1546 HEYWOOD II. viii. K2ᵛ Byr lady, than we shall catche byrds to morow.

Catch not at the shadow and lose the substance.   (S 951)

1548 HALL *Chron.* (1809 169) The Duke . . . (like a wise prince) not myndyng to lease the more for the lesse, nor the accident for the substaunce. **1551** T. WILSON *Art of Reason* (1552 ed. V6) It taketh away all substaunce, and leaueth only the shadow.   **1560** *Lett. to W. Cecil* cited C. Read *Mr. Sec. Cecil* 192 We might have sped like the dog in Aesop's fables, which, having a bone in his mouth and seeing the shadow in the water, gaped to have fetched it and so lost both.   **1579** LYLY *Euph.* i. 201 In arguing of the shadowe, we forgoe the substance.   c. **1590** SHAKES. *T.And.* III. ii. 80 He takes false shadows for true substances.   **1594** *Id. T.G.V.* IV. ii. 120 Since the substance of your perfect self Is else devoted, I am but a shadow.   **1602** *How a Man may Choose* Hazl.-Dods. ix. 14 I'll feed on shadows, let the substance go.   **1612** WEBSTER *White Devil* v. i. 168.   **1818** PEACOCK *Nightmare Abbey* ch. 11 Like the dog in the fable, to throw away the substance in catching at the shadow.

Catch old birds with chaff, You cannot.
                                                       (B 396)

1481 CAXTON *Reynard* xl Arb. 110 Wenest thou thus to deceyue . . . I am no byrde to be locked ne take by chaf I know wel ynowh good corn. **1581–90** *Timon* IV. ii (1842) 62 Tis well.—An olde birde is not caught with chaffe.   **1670** RAY 126.   **1824** SCOTT *Redg.* ch. 4 Men do not catch old birds with chaff, my master. Where have you got the rhino you are so flush of?   **1853** THACKERAY *Newcomes* ch. 53 They sang . . . and . . . ogled him as they sang . . . with which chaff our noble bird was by no means to be caught.

Catch (take) one napping, To.
                                                       (N 36–7)

1562 J. PILKINGTON *Expos. Neh.* (1585) 65 Our mortall enemie . . . hopeth to speed at length and take thee napping.   **1579** LYLY *Euph.* i. 230 Althoughe I see the bayte you laye to catche me, . . . neyther are you more desirous to take me nappinge, then I willinge to confesse my meaninge.

1594-8 SHAKES. *T.S.* IV. ii. 46 Nay, I have ta'en you nappinge, gentle love. **1594-5** *Id. L.L.L.* IV. iii. 125 I should blush, I know, To be o'erheard and taken napping so. **1633** D. DYKE *Six Evangel. Hist.* 42 Christ coming as a Judge and King . . . finds them in the midst of their disorders, and takes them napping as we say. **1909** *Times* 18 Mar. By the admission of the Government the Admiralty have allowed themselves to be caught napping.

Catch (take) one napping, To | as Mosse took his mare.   (M 1185)

1569-70 *Stationers' Register* ed. Arber i. 417 [ballad title]. **1583** MELBANCKE *Philot.* 65 Tooke him napping as Moss did his mare. **1607** *Acc. Christmas Prince* (1816) 40 Now Night growes old, yet walkes here in his trapping Till Daye come catch him, as Mosse his graymare, nappinge. **1611** COTGRAVE s.v. *A desprouveu*, at unawares . . . unlooked for; napping, as Mosse tooke his Mare. **1670** RAY 187. **1917** BRIDGE 127.

Catch that catch may.   (C 189)

c. **1390** GOWER *Conf. Amantis* VII. 394 But cacche who that cacche might. **1555** HEYWOOD *Epigr. upon Prov.* no. 293. **1583** J. PRINCE *Fruitful & Brief Disc.* 151 Katch who catch can. *c.* **1612** BEAUM. &FL. *Scornf. Lady* (1904) I. i. l. 296 Men, women, and all woo; catch that catch may. **1821** SCOTT *Kenilw.* ch. 11 The last words seem to mean 'Catch who catch can'.

Catch the wind in a net, To.   (W 416)

a. **1542** WYATT *Lover Despairing*, Wks. (1858) 16 Since in a net I seek to hold the wind. **1579** J. CALVIN *Thirteen Sermons* tr. J. Field B1 They doe but catch the winde in a net. *c.* **1580** SIDNEY I *Arcadia* Wks. (Feuillerat) IV. 69 [He] hopes the flickering winde with net to holde. **1581** GUAZZO i. 212. **1592** LYLY *Midas* V. i. 24 As impossible it is to staye the rumor, as to catch the wind in a nette. **1623** WEBSTER *Devil's Law-Case* V. iv. Wks. (1857) 143 Vain the ambition of kings, Who seek . . . To leave a living name behind, And weave but nets to catch the wind.

Catch two pigeons with one bean, To.   (P 319)

1557 NORTH *Dial of Princes* f. 56 For the prouerbe sayeth, that with one beane, a man maye take two pigeons. **1573** SANFORD 104 (It is a goodly thing to take). **1580** LYLY *Euph. & his Eng.* ii. 173. **1678** RAY 353.

Catching fish is not the whole of fishing.

1913 *Times Lit. Sup.* 28 Nov. 570 Sportsmen who love sport for the sport's sake: 'Catching fish is not the whole of fishing.'

Catch(ing), caught, *see also* Angle all day and c. gudgeon at night; Bird c. in lime; Craft is in c.; Dog (Hindmost, Foremost) c. hare; Eels (He that will c.); First c. your h.; Fish will soon be c. that nibbles at every bait; Fishes (He still) that c. one; Fox (He has c. a); Fox knows much; Lie at c.; Mocking is c.; Springe to c. woodcock;

Thief to c. thief; Trick to c. the old one; Young one squeak (Make the) and you'll c. the old one.

Cater-cousins, They are (not).   (C 191)

[= they are (not) good friends.] **1519** HORMAN *Vulgaria* Roxb. Cl. 322 They be cater cosyns: and almoste neuer a sonder. **1583** MELBANCKE D1ᵛ Ptolomie and Pompey were nowne cater coosins. **1596** SHAKES. *M.V.* II. ii. 117 His master and he, saving your worship's reverence, are scarce cater-cousins. **1598** R. BERNARD tr. *Terence's Andria* V. vii They are not now cater cousins [*inimicitia est inter eos*]. **1823** GROSE (Pierce Egan) s.v. Cater Cousins.

Cathkin's covenant with you, I will make | let abee for let abee. (*See also* Let-a-be.)

[= mutual forbearance.] **1857** DEAN RAMSAY *Remin.* V (1911) 204 . . . The laird of [Hamilton] had . . . been addicted to intemperance. One of his neighbours, . . . personating the devil, claimed a title to carry him off. . . . The laird showed fight . . . when a parley was proposed, and the issue was, 'Cathkin's covenant, Let abee for let abee.'

Cats and dogs, *see* Agree like c. and d.

Cats are alike grey in the night, All.   (C 50)

1546 HEYWOOD I. v. B2 When all candels be out, all cats be grey. **1611** DAVIES no. 387. **1721** KELLY 9. **1771** SMOLLETT *Humph. Clink.* 7 Sept. Wks. (1871) 556 He knew not which was which; and, as the saying is, all cats in the dark are gray. [Fr. La nuit tous les chats sont gris.]

Cats eat what hussies[1] spare.   (C 181)

c. **1225** *Trin. MS. O. 11. 45* (ed. Förster) in *Eng. Stud.* 31. 6 Hund eet, þat hen man spelat. Sepe uorat gnarus canis id quod seruat auarus. *a.* **1628** CARMICHAELL no. 398 Cats eats that hussie spairis. **1639** CLARKE 242 What the good wife spares, the cat eats. **1721** KELLY 326 The things that Wives hains,[2] Cats eat. What is too niggardly spar'd is often as widely squander'd. [[1] housewives. [2] spares.]

Cats hide their claws.

1609 DEKKER *Raven's Almanac* G1 The Tiger when he meanes to prey, then euer hideth his clawes. **1732** FULLER no. 1072.

Cats, *see also* Cat(s).

Cattle, *see* Hurry no man's c.; Kings are kittle c.; Old c. breed not; Roast meat does c.

Caudle, *see* Dead (When I am) make me a c.

Caught a knave in a purse-net, There I.   (K 138)

1616 WITHALS 555. **1639** CLARKE 127. **1659**

HOWELL *Eng. Prov.* 17b. **1670** RAY 216. **1732** FULLER no. 4870.

Caul, *see* Born with a c.

Cause, Take away the | and the effect must cease. (C 202)

1528 TYNDALE *Obed. Chrn. Man.* P.S. 298 As long as the cause abideth, so long lasteth the effect. **1533–4** UDALL *Flowers* 28 Vbi ea causa, quamobrem haec faciunt, erit adempta, desinent, whan the cause wherfore they do al, this shalbe taken away, they wol leaue or surcease. **1548** HALL 55 If you will heale a malady you must firste remoue the cause. *Ibid.* 159 The cause ceasyng, the effect also ceaseth. **1571** J. BRIDGES *Sermon at Paul's Cross* 81 Take away the cause, else the effect will neuer be taken away. [**1589**] **1594** GREENE *Friar Bacon* III. i. 998 Ablata causa, tollitur effectus: . . . Take him away, and then the effects will faile. **1599** MINSHEU *Span. Gram.* 84 He that taketh awaie the occasion, taketh away the offence, i. He that remooueth the allurements, taketh away the sinne. **1620** SHELTON *Quix.* II. lxvii The cause being removed, the sin will be saved. **1645** A. ROSS *Medicus Medicatus* 39. *c.* **1747** J. WESLEY *Serm.* ii. 30.

Cause is good, One | until the other's understood.

1731 *Poor Robins Alm.* Oct. The Proverb is, one Cause is good, Until the other's understood.

Causes to be done, That which a man | he does himself. (M 387)

[COKE *Qui facit per alium facit per se.* He who does a thing by the agency of another, does it himself.] **1692** L'ESTRANGE *Aesop's Fab.* clxvii (1738) 81 That which a man causes to be done, he does himself, and 'tis all a case whether he does it by practice, precept, or example. **1893** H. P. LIDDON *Serm. O.T.* xv. 217 His acquiescence . . . was virtually a commission, and her acts were, morally, his. . . . What is done through another is done by a man himself. **1916** E. A. BURROUGHS *Val. of Decis.* I. ii His reluctance to give the mobilization order in July, 1870, is . . . a commonplace of history. Still, the consent . . . was given; and *Qui facit per alium, facit per se.*

Cause(s), *see also* Angry without a c., . . . pleased without amends; Bad c. that none speak in; Blind in own c.; Call another c.; Ill c. (He who has), sell it cheap; Judge in own c.; Oxford is home of lost c.; Worse appear better c. (Make).

Causeway, *see* Honesty keeps crown of c.

Cave of Adullam.

[I SAM. xxii. 2 David . . . escaped to the cave Adullam: . . . and every one that was in distress, . . . and every one that was discontented, gathered themselves unto him.] **1866** BRIGHT *Sp.* (1876) 349 The right hon. gentleman . . . has retired into what may be called his political Cave of Adullam, and he has called about him 'every one that was in distress and every one that was discontented'. [The Adullamites led by Lowe, seceded from the Liberal party in 1866.]

Caveat, To put in (enter) a. (C 205)

[= to give a warning; from L. *caveat*, let him beware.] **1577** tr. *Bullinger's Decades* (1592) 405 It pleased the goodnesse of God by giuing the law to put in a caueat . . . for the tranquilitie of mankinde. **1642** FULLER *H. & P. State* I. xii. 37 She enters a silent caveat by a blush. **1755** YOUNG *Centaur* I. Wks. (1757) IV. 116 Putting in a caveat against the ridicule of infidels.

Caveat emptor, see Buyer beware.

Cavil will enter in at any hole, and if it find none it will make one. (C 206)

1616 DRAXE no. 243.

Cedar, As straight as a. (C 207)

c. **1580** SIDNEY I *Arcadia* (Feuillerat 158). **1594–5** SHAKES. *L.L.L.* IV. iii. 84 As upright as the cedar. **1611** CHAPMAN *May Day* I. i. 123 Tall and high, like a cedar.

Cedars fall when low shrubs remain, High. (C 208)

1570 F. THYNNE *Debate betw. Pride & Lowliness* ed. Collier 76 And bring full lowe their cedars high and tall. **1576** W. HUNNIS? *Paradise of Dainty Devises* no. 88 The higher that the Ceder tree vnto the heauens doe growe, The more in danger at the top, when sturdie winde gan blowe. **1588** GREENE *Pandosto* ed. Thomas 17 High cedars are crushed with tempests, when low shrubs are not touched with the wind. **1590** T. LODGE *Rosalynde* ed. Greg 25. **1604** DEKKER I *Honest Whore* IV. i. 108 Cedars are shaken, when shrubs do feel no bruize. *c.* **1640** W. S. *Countrym. Commonw.* 25 For high Cedars are shaken with the wind, when low shrubs are scarcely moued, and men in high places had need to looke to their sure footing.

Cellar, *see* Jack in the low c.

Censure(s), *see* Every man's c. moulded in his nature.

Cerberus, *see* Sop to C.

Ceres and Bacchus, Without | Venus grows cold. (C 211)

[TERENCE *Eunuch.* 4. 5. 6 *Sine Cerere et Libero friget Venus.*] **1539** TAVERNER 36 Wythout meate and drynke the lust of the body is colde. **1578** *Susanna* l. 549. **1593** PEELE *Edw. I.* II. 86–9 Wks. (1888) I. 101 I learned in school That love's desires and pleasures cool Sans Ceres' wheat and Bacchus' vine.

Certain, It is | because it is impossible.

[TERTULLIAN *De Carne Christi* 5.] **1642** SIR T. BROWNE *Religio Med.* I. § ix (1881) 18 Involved Ænigmas and riddles of the Trinity, with Incarnation and Resurrection. I can answer all the Objections of Satan . . . with that odd resolution I learned of Tertullian, *Certum est, quia impossibile est* [generally given as *Credo quia . . .*].

Certain, *see also* Nothing is c. but death;
Nothing is c. but the unforeseen; Nothing is so
c. as the unexpected.

**Certainly (surety) and leans to chance,
He that quits | when fools pipe he may
dance.** (C 212)

[HESIOD Νήπιος ὃς τὰ ἕτοιμα λιπὼν τ' ἀνέτοιμα
διώκει. He is a fool who leaves a certainty to
pursue an uncertainty.] 1546 HEYWOOD II. xi.
83 Who that leaueth suretee and leaneth to
chaunce, whan fooles pipe, by auctoritee he maie
daunce. 1548 HALL (1809, 54) The trite and
common adage saith, leaue not the certain for
the vncertain. 1591 W. STEPNEY L5ᵛ. It is meere
folly to leaue the certaine for the vncertaine.
1670 RAY 68.

**'Ch was bore at Taunton Dean; where
should I be bore else.** (T 77)

['*Ch* represents *Ich*, the southern form of pro-
noun *I*.] 1662 FULLER Somerset 21 Where
should I be bore else than in Tonton Deane?
This is a parcel of Ground round about Tonton,
very pleasant and populous. . . . The Peasantry
therein . . . conceive it a disparagement to be
born in any other place. 1670 RAY 251.

Chad (Saint), *see* First comes David next comes
C. *See also* St. Chad.

Chaff, *see* Catch old birds with c.; King's c.
worth other men's corn; Sift him . . . and he
proves c.

**Chain is no stronger than its weakest
link, The.**

1856 C. KINGSLEY Lett. in *Life and Wks.* ii. 248
The devil is very busy, and no one knows better
than he, that 'nothing is stronger than its weakest part'. 1868 L. STEPHEN *Cornhill* xvii. 295
(*Hours in a Library*, 1892 ed., 5) A chain is no
stronger than its weakest link. 1879 FROUDE
Caesar IX. 93 The strength of a chain is no
greater than the strength of its first link. 1908
W. M. RAMSAY in *Expositor* Jan. 7 The critic
who is accustomed to . . . deductive reasoning
(in which, however, the weakness of even one
link in the chain is fatal to the strength of the
whole) is apt to forget that cumulative reasoning
is not of the same kind.

Chain(s), *see also* Free (He is not) that draws c.;
Old c. gall less than new.

Chalk, By a long.

[= by far, in allusion to the use of chalk in
scoring points, &c.] 1837–40 HALIBURTON
Clockm. (1862) 26 Your factories down East . . .
go ahead on the English a long chalk. *a.* 1859
DE QUINCEY *Syst. Heavens* Wks. III. 171 *note* As
regards the body of water . . . the Indus ranks
foremost by a long chalk. 1926 Oct. D. H.
LAWRENCE *Lett.* ii. 945 I . . . am not through, by
a long chalk.

Chalk and cheese, No more like than. (C 218)

c. 1390 GOWER *Conf. Amantis* Prol. 1. 416 Lo,
how thei feignen chalk for cheese. 1530 PALS-

GRAVE 595a There is difference bytwene chake
and chese. 1541 BARNES *Wks.* (1573) 258 This
deffinition agreeth as well with your key, as
chalke and cheese. *a.* 1555 LATIMER in FOXE
A. & M. (1684) III. 413 As though I could not
discern cheese from chalk. 1600 ROWLANDS *Lett.
Humours Blood* vi. 75 Tom is no more like thee,
then Chalks like Cheese. 1672 W. WALKER
Phras. Anglo-Lat. 56 I talk of chalk and you of
cheese. 1819 HANNAH MORE *Two Wealthy F.*
Wks. (1830) III. 131 Their talk was no more like
that of my ol landlord, who was a Lord . . . ,
than chalk is like cheese. 1849 C. BRONTË
Shirley ch. 5 'You think yourself a clever fellow,
I know, Scott.' 'Ay! I'm fairish; I can tell cheese
fro' chalk.'

**Chamber of sickness is the chapel of
devotion, The.** (C 219)

1616 DRAXE no. 1975. 1670 RAY 24.

Chameleon, *see* Changeable as a c., (As); Live on
air like c.

Chance in the cock's spur, There is. (C 227)

1678 RAY 111. 1732 FULLER no. 4890.

**Chance it, I will | as Parson Horne (Old
Horne) did his neck.**

1878 *N. & Q.* 5th Ser. x. 10 'I'll chance it, as old
Horne did his neck', or, 'as parson Horne did
his neck'. Horne was a clergyman in Nottinghamshire. Horne committed a murder. He
escaped to the Continent. After many years'
residence abroad he determined to return. In
answer to an attempt to dissuade him, . . . , he
said, 'I'll chance it' . . . was tried, condemned,
and executed.

**Chances (happens) in an hour, It | that
happens not in seven years.** *Cf.* Day,
Oft times one. (H 741)

c. 1270 *Rawlinson MS. C. 641*, f. 13c in *Eng. Stud.*
31. 16 On dai bringd, thet al ier ne mai. *Quod
donare mora nequit annua, dat brevis hora. Anno
cura datur, tamen una dies operatur. c.* 1350
Douce MS. 52 no. 44 Oft bryngeth on day, þat all
þe ȝere not may. *c.* 1386 CHAUCER *Knight's T.* l.
1668 Yet somtyme it shal fallen on a day That
falleth nat eft withinne a thousand yeer. 1530
PALSGRAVE 544a It falleth in an houre that
happeneth not after in seven yere. 1546 HEY-
WOOD I. xi. E1 It hapth in one houre that hapth
not in vii. yeere. *a.* 1553 UDALL *Roister D.*
IV. iii Arb. 61 For such chaunce may chaunce
in an houre, do ye heare? — As perchance shall
not chaunce againe in seuen yeare. 1614 CAMDEN
308. 1641 FERGUSSON no. 488 It will come in an
houre that will not come in a year. 1721 KELLY
193 It may come in an Hour, that will not come
in a Year.

Chance, (noun), *see also* Certainty and leans to
c., (He that quits); Grieve when the c. is past
(Too late to); Left to c. (Something must be);
Main c.; Policy prevents c.

Chance(s) (*verb*), *see also* One man, (What c. to) may happen to all men.

Chancery, *see* Hell and c. always open.

Change a cottage in possession for a kingdom in reversion, I will not.

(c 674)

1639 CLARKE 256 (kingdom in hope).   **1678** RAY 116.

Change but the name and the story applies to yourself. *See De te fabula narratur.*

Change his mind, A man will never | if he has no mind to change.

1853 TRENCH iii. 59.

Change his old Mumpsimus for the new Sumpsimus, He will not.   (M 1314)

[In allusion to the story of an illiterate English priest, who when corrected for reading 'quod in ore mumpsimus' in the Mass, replied, 'I will not change my old mumpsimus for your new sumpsimus.'] **1531** SIR T. ELYOT *Governour* III. xiv (1880) II. 289 Them whome nothing contenteth out of their accustomed Mumpsimus. **1545** HEN. VIII *Parl. sp.* 24 Dec. in HALL *Chron.*, *Hen. VIII* (1550) 261b Some be to styff in their old Mumpsimus, other be to busy and curious in their newe Sumpsimus. **1545** W. TURNER *Rescuing of the Romish Fox* G8. **1820** SCOTT *Monast.* Introd. Epist. How many gray heads he hath addled by vain attempts to exchange their old Mumpsimus for his new Sumpsimus. **1862** KEBLE in LIDDON, etc., *Pusey* (1897) IV. i. 25 I still hold to my old mumpsimus that . . . we cannot be unchurched.

Change my mill, I am loth to.   (M 943)

1678 RAY 349 . . . *Som. i.e.* Eat of another dish.

Change of pasture makes fat calves.

(c 230)

1542 H. BULLINGER *Christ. State Matrimony* Pref. by T. Becon A7ᵛ Shyfte of meate is good. **1546** HEYWOOD II. iv. G3 And some say, chaunge of pasture makth fat calues. **1602** MARSTON *Ant.'s Revenge* I. 1220. **1639** CLARKE 191.

Change of weather is the discourse of fools.   (c 231)

1659 HOWELL *Span. Prov.* 2. **1664** CODRINGTON 189. **1670** RAY 28.

Change place but not change the grief (mind), One may.   (P 374)

[HOR. *Ep.* I. xi. 27: Coelum non animum mutant qui trans mare currunt.] **1581** W. AVERELL *Charles and Julia* G4ᵛ Chaunge of place cannot transforme nor alter any minde: Though ayre and soyle he doo exchaunge, his greefe dooth stay by kinde. **1586** R. CROWLEY *Friar John Francis* B4 That saying, Coelum non animum mutant, qui trans mare currunt. They that runne ouer the Sea, doo not change their minde but the ayre.

1597 *Politeuphuia* 122 Change of ayre doth not change the mind. **1604** MARSTON *Malcontent* III. i. 7 Sad souls may well change place, but not change grief. **1633** J. FORD *Broken Heart* (1927, New Sh. S.) I. i. 12 Soules sunke in sorrowes, are never without 'em; They change fresh ayres, but beare their griefs about 'em.

Change (s, changing), *see also* Bad for the better (To c. the); Chop and c.; Coward c. colour; Leopard cannot c. his spots; Times c. and we with them; Wine and wealth c. wise men's manners; Wise man c. his mind; Wise man needs not blush for c. his purpose; Woman's mind and winter wind c. oft.

Changeable as a chameleon, As.

(c 221)

1572 E. PASQUIER *Monophylo* tr. G. Fenton 39 Loue being as a Camelion chaunging diuers coulours according to his sundrie obiectes. c. **1597** JONSON *Case Is Altered* V. i. 17 His thoughts, Cameleon-like, change euery minute.

Changeful as the moon.   (M 1111)

c. **1380** CHAUCER *Rom. Rose* B 3778 And chaunge as the moone. **1588** W. AVERELL *Marvellous Combat of Contrarieties* (STUBBES *Anatomy of Abuses* New Sh. S. I. 253) Women . . . more wauering then the wind, more mutable then the Moone. **1594–5** SHAKES. *L.L.L.* V. ii. 212 Thus change I like the moon. **1596** SPENSER *F.Q.* VII. vii. 50 So that as changefull as the Moone men vse to say.

Changeling, To be no.   (c 234)

1551 CRANMER *Ans. to Gardiner* 51 You . . . beyng so ful of crafte and vntrewth in your owne contrey, shew your self to be no chaungeling, where so euer you become. c. **1573** G. HARVEY *Letter-Bk.* 151 I would not you should thinke me a chaungelinge. **1583** MELBANCKE F4 I am no chaungling, like the broode of the Cameleon. [c. **1597**] **1609** JONSON *Case Is Altered* I. iv. 5 Slid I am no changling. **1608** SHAKES. *C.* IV. vii. 10 Yet his nature In that's no changeling. **1681** ROBERTSON 323 He's no changeling; he is still the same man. **1738** SWIFT *Dial.* I. E.L. 260 I see you are no Change-ling.

Changing of works is lighting of hearts.

(c 235)

a. **1628** CARMICHAELL no. 394 Changeing of warks is lichting of harts. **1641** FERGUSSON no. 214.

Chapel, *see* God has his church (Where), the devil will have c.

Chaplain, *see* Lord (Like), like c.; Worst carver in the world, never make good c.

Chapman, *see* Breed of the c., never out of your gate.

Chapping sticks, *see* Fools should not have c. s.

Chapter, *see* First c. of fools.

Char¹ is charred, That (This).   (C 241)

[= that job's done.]   *c.* **1400** *Seven Sages* (Percy Soc.) 88, l. 2603 'Sire,' scho sayed, 'this char hys heved.'   **1570** *Marriage Wit & Sc.* IV. iv. Hazl.-Dods. ii. 375 This char is char'd well.   **1590–5** *Sir Thos. More* III. i. 118 *Shaks. Apoc.* 398 This charre beeing charde, then all our debt is payd.   [**1591**] **1593** PEELE *Ed. I* Bullen i. 137.   **1670** RAY 168 That char is char'd (as the good wife said when she had hang'd her husband).   **1917** BRIDGE 111 That char's charred, as the boy said when he'd killed his father.   [¹ piece of work.]

Character, *see* Studies pass into c.

Charge look to it, Now you have a.
                                          (C 247)
1609 S. HARWARD 80 Looke to thine owne charg.   **1616** WITHALS 581.   **1639** CLARKE 92.

Charge of souls, He that has | transports them not in bundles.   (C 246)
1640 HERBERT no. 986.

Charge, *see also* Double c. will rive cannon.

Chargeable, *see* Building is c.

Charges of building, and making of gardens are unknown, The.   (C 244)
1640 HERBERT no. 412.

Charily, *see* Chastely, (If not) yet c.

Charing Cross, *see* Old as C. C.

Charing, Smoky.

1736 S. PEGGE *Kenticisms, Prov.* E.D.S. 69 Smoking Charing. [Charing is near Ashford.]

Charitable give out at (the) door and God puts in at the window, The.
                                          (C 248)
1678 RAY 353.

Charity and Pride do both feed the poor.   (C 250)
1597 *Politeuphuia* 211.   **1732** FULLER no. 1084.

Charity begins at home.   (C 251)
c. **1380** WYCLIF *Of Prelates* in Wks. (Matthew) 78 Charite schuld bigyne at hem-self.   **1509** A. BARCLAY *Ship of Fools* i. 277 For perfyte loue and also charite Begynneth with hym selfe for to be charitable.   **1616** BEAUM. & FL. *Wit without M.* v. ii. 16 Charity and beating begins at home.   **1659** FULLER *Appeal Inj. Innoc.* in *Hist. Camb. Univ.* (1840) 317 'Charity begins, but doth not end, at home.' . . . My Church History . . . began with our own domestic affairs, . . . I intended . . . to have proceeded to foreign churches.   **1748** SMOLLETT *Rod. Rand* ch. 6 The world would do nothing for her if she should

come to want—charity begins at home.   **1853** TRENCH V. (1894) 102 . . . It is not for nothing that we have been grouped in families, neighbourhoods, and nations.

Charity construes all doubtful things in good part.   (C 252)

[I COR. xiii. 7 Charity . . . Beareth all things, believeth all things, hopeth all things, endureth all things.]   *a.* **1560** *Impatient Poverty* l. 454 Charytie alwaye wyll saye the beste.   **1599** RAINOLDS *Overthrow Stage Plays* 45 Chari/tie beleeueth all things, hopeth all things.   **1664** CODRINGTON 188 Charity and Industry do take all things doubtfull in the best construction.

Charity covers a multitude of sins.

[I PET. iv. 8 Charity shall cover the multitude of sins.]   *a.* **1633** G. HERBERT *Priest to the Temple* xii.

Charity grows cold.   (C 253)

[MATT. xxiv. 12 The charity of many shall wax cold.]   **1530** TYNDALE *Practise of Prelates* P.S. 257 (love).   **1550** R. CROWLEY *One & Thirty Epigrams* E.E.T.S. 11 The charitie of rich men is nowe thorowe colde.   **1557** R. EDGEWORTH *Sermons* 54 Iniquitie is so aboundaunt that charitie is all colde.   **1571** J. BRIDGES *Sermon at Paul's Cross* Charitie is waxen very cold.   **1572** T. WILSON *Discourse upon Usury* (1925 ed.) 201.   *a.* **1600** NASHE *Summer's Last Will* iii. 263.   **1609** DEKKER *Gull's Horn-book,* ch. 3.   **1642** SIR T. BROWNE *Relig. Med.* II. iv. 'Tis the general complaint . . . that Charity grows cold.   **1837** T. HOOK *Jack Brag* ch. 15 The wind blows . . . about one, and I'm as cold as charity.

Charles's¹ Wain, The four wheels of | Grenville, Godolphin, Trevannion, Slanning slain.

[**1643**] **1911** CROSSING *Folk Rhymes of Devon* 97 . . . [In] the contest at Bristol, between the Royalists and the troops of the Parliament, . . . Sir Nicholas Slanning and Colonel Trevannion were slain, Sir Bevil Grenville and Sidney Godolphin having fallen in previous engagements. . . . Charles['s] . . . 'wain' made no real progress when the 'wheels' were gone.   [¹ Charles I.]

Charm, *see* Third is a c.

Charon waits for all.

1708 PRIOR *Turtle & Spar.* All that wear feathers first or last Must one day perch on Charon's mast.   **1732** FULLER no. 1089.

Charre-folks¹ are never paid.   (C 242)

1678 RAY 112 . . . That is, give them what you will they are never contented.   **1732** FULLER no. 1083 Chare Folks are never paid enough.   [¹ persons hired for jobs.]

Charren, *see* Smoke of C.

Charter, *see* 'If' and 'An' spoil good c.; Possession is worth an ill c.

Charterhouse, *see* Sister of the C.

Charybdis, *see* Scylla.

Chase, *see* Stern c. long c.; Wild goose c.

Chasing, *see* Mind's c. mice (Your).

Chastely, If not | yet charily.   (L 381)

1528 TYNDALE *Obed. Chrn. Man* P.S. 232
As our lawyers say, *Si non caste, tamen caute*;
that is, If ye live not chaste, see ye carry clean,
and play the knave secretly.   **1554** H. HILARIE
(= J. Bale?) *Resurrection of the Mass* A3ᵛ They
maye lyue *Si non caste, tamen caute* Lyke great
common Bulles in euery towne.   c. **1566** C. A.
CURIO tr. W. P. *Pasquin in a Trance* E2.   **1576**
PETTIE i. 32 Do not some men say that women
always live chastely enough, so that they live
charily enough.   **1586** G. WHETSTONE *English
Mirror* M6 The lesson, long before giuen vnto
the Cleargie, *Si non caste, tamen caute*.   **1587**
GREENE *Penelope's Web* in Wks. Gros. v. 209
Offences are not measured by the proportion but
by the secrecie: *Si non caste, tamen caute*: . . .
1604 WEBSTER etc. *Malcontent* IV. i. 23.

Chastens one, chastens twenty, He that.
Cf. Chastises one, etc.   (O 44)

1640 HERBERT no. 356.

Chastens, *see also* Happy is he that c. himself.

**Chastise with scorpions instead of
whips, To.**

[I KINGS xii. 11 My father hath chastised
you with whips, but I will chastise you with
scorpions.]   **1867–77** FROUDE *Short Stud.* (1890)
III. 104 'My father chastised you with whips, and
I will chastise you with scorpions.' So answered
a foolish Hebrew king, and lost an empire for his
pains.   **1879** M. PATTISON *Milton* 153 Prelatry
was now scourging the nonconformists with
scorpions instead of whips.   **1908** *Times Lit.
Sup.* 6 Mar. If the Egyptian Pashas had chastised
their own people with whips, they had chastised
the Sudanese with scorpions.

Chastises one amends many, He that.
Cf. Chastens one, etc.   (O 45)

1616 DRAXE no. 359.   **1642** TORRIANO 19 He
who punisheth one threatneth a hundred.   **1670**
RAY 4.

Chastity, *see* Beauty and c. seldom agree.

Chats, *see* Love of lads and fire of c.

**Chatters *to* you, Who | will chatter *of*
you.**

1853 TRENCH iii. 63 *note*.

**Chatting to chiding is not worth a
chute.¹**   (C 256)

[= scolding is not worth replying to.]   **1546**
HEYWOOD II. v. H2ᵛ [¹ chut, chewet, jackdaw.]

Chawbent, *see* Cheshire.

Cheam, *see* Sutton.

Cheap and nasty.

1831 *Blackw. Mag.* Feb. 416/2 On the top of the
'cheap and nasty', did you never pass through
Birmingham?   **1885** C. LOWE *Prince Bismarck*
(1898) ch. 7 [Bismarck] wished to spare his
countrymen . . . a repetition of the 'cheap and
nasty' verdict which had been pronounced on
their products at Philadelphia.   **1926** *Times* 31
Mar. 15/4 Official rudeness is cheap, though
nasty.

Cheap enough to say, *God help you*, It is.

1732 FULLER no. 2922.

Cheap sitting as standing, It is as.
                                        (S 495)

1666 TORRIANO *It. Prov.* 277 no. 204 The English
say . . .   **1738** SWIFT Dial. I. E.L. 262.   **1858**
SURTEES *Ask Mamma* ch. 47 Let's get chairs and
be snug; . . .

Cheap(er, -est), (*adj.*), *see also* Best is best c.;
Buy good c. that bring nothing home; Buy in c.
market and sell in dearest; Dearer it is the c.;
Friend too c., (Make not); Good c. is dear;
Good cheer and good c.; Good thing c. (He will
never have) that is afraid to ask price; Light c.,
lither yield; Meal c. and shoon dear; Saying goes
good c.

Cheap (*verb*), *see* Heap (The more you), worse
you c.

Cheapen, *see* Never c. unless you mean to buy.

Cheapside is the best garden.   (C 260)

1662 FULLER London 190 Natural Commodities
are not to be expected to growe in this place, . . .
Cheapside being called the best Garden only by
Metaphore.

Cheat, and the cheese will show.

1917 BRIDGE 35 . . . That is, if too much cream
has been extracted or the cows poorly fed.

**Cheat at play, He that will | will cheat
you anyway.**

1721 KELLY 168 (in Play, will not be honest in
earnest).   **1732** FULLER no. 6302.

Cheat'em, *see* Starv'em.

**Cheat mine own father at cards, I
would.**   (F 88)

1580 S. BIRD *Friendly Communication* 40 Are not
these woords vsuall amongst gamesters: At
cardes I will deceiue mine owne Father, if I can:
At Dice I will not trust mine owne brother.

Cheater, *see* Kingdom of a c. (In the) wallet
carried before.

Cheating, *see* Knavery (C.) in all trades.

Check, *see* Sure as c.

Cheek by cheek (jowl).   (C 263)

c. 1300 R. BRUNNE tr. Langtoft's *Chron.* (1810) 223 Vmwhile cheke bi cheke. 1530 PALSGRAVE 834b Cheke by cheke. [*c.* 1530] *c.* 1555 BERNERS *Arthur Little Br.* 352 They made great chere eche to other, and soo rode togyther cheke by cheke tyl they came to theyr tentes. 1533–4 UDALL *Flowers* 188 As we vse to saye in englysshe, cheke by cheke, or at the harde heeles. [*c.* 1570] 1599 *Sir Clyomon* l. 1399 Cheke by ioule. 1576–7 HANMER *Anc. Eccles. Hist. Eusebius* VIII. xxv. 164 He who . . . lived cheeke by iolle with the Emperor. 1595 SHAKES. *M.N.D.* III. ii. 338 I'll go with thee, cheek by jowl. 1638 T. BREWER *Lord Have Mercy Upon Us* A2 Cheeke by joule. 1662 A. WOOD *Life & Times* W.C. 130 Respect to Masters (by bachelaurs) lost; they go cheek by jole with you without any respect. 1684 F. HAWKINS *New Youth's Behaviour* 54 If he be a man of great quality, walk not at all with him cheek by joul.

Cheeks, *see* Little mense o' the c. to bite off nose.

Cheer, *see* Good c. and good cheap; Good c. is lacking, (When); Welcome is best c.; Whipping c., (You shall have).

Cheerful look makes a dish a feast, A.
(L 424)

1611 COTGRAVE s.v. Més A cheerefull looke fills vp halfe-emptie dishes. 1640 HERBERT no. 62.

Cheese, If you will have a good | and have'n old, you must turn'n seven times before he is cold.   (C 272)

1656–91 J. AUBREY *Nat. Hist. Wilts.* (1847) 105. 1678 RAY *Som.* 352.

Cheese and money should always sleep together one night.

1917 BRIDGE 35 . . . Said by farmers in old times, who, immediately the cheese was sold and weighed, demanded payment in gold before the cheese was sent away.

Cheese digests everything but itself.
(C 269)

c. 1566 G. HARVEY *Marginalia* 140 [citing Erasmus *Parabolae*] Caseus est nequam, quia digerit omnia, Se quam. 1584 LYLY *Sappho & Phao* III. ii. 26 It is against the old verse, *Caseus est nequam.*—Yea, but it digesteth all things except it selfe. 1614 T. ADAMS *The Devil's Banquet* Pt. I Wks. i. 161. 1678 RAY 40 Cheese it is a peevish elf, It digests all things but it self. This is a translation of that old rhythming Latin verse, *Caseus est nequàm, quia digerit omnia se quàm.* 1738 SWIFT Dial. II. E.L. 311.

Cheese, *see also* After c. comes nothing; Bachelors' fare, bread and c. and kisses; Banbury zeal, c., and cakes; Bread, butter, and green c. very good Friese; Butter and c., (It

rains); Butter (That which will not be) must be made into c.; Chalk and c.; Cheat and c. will show; Green c. (You see no) but teeth water; Hard c.; Hull c.; King's c. goes away in parings; Moon is made of c.; Mouse in c. (Speak like); Mousetrap smell of c. (Let not); Safe as mouse in c.; See his nose c. first; Suffolk c.; Thin as Banbury c.; Toasted c.

Cheiny, *see* Philip and C.

Cherry year, a merry year: a plum year, a dumb year, A. *Cf.* Pear year, etc., Plum year, etc.   (Y 7)

1664 *Poor Robin's Almanac*, quoted in Lean, i. 419 A cherry year's a merry year, a sloe year's a woe year, a haw year's a braw year, an apple year's a drappin' year, a plum year's a glum year. 1678 RAY 52. 1732 FULLER no. 6139. 1893 INWARDS 5.

Cherry's boose,[1] He has got into.

c. 1791 PEGGE *Derbicisms* E.D.S. 90 When a man weds a second wife, older and perhaps not so handsome as the first, they say 'He has put Browney into Cherry's boose'. 1917 BRIDGE 67 . . . He has got into good quarters. A favourite name for a red cow, . . . the most esteemed for milking. [[1] cow-stall.]

Cherry(ies), *see also* Disgraces are like c.; Peas with the King, c. with beggar; Red as a c.; Two bites of a c.; Woman and c. are painted for harm.

Cherry-tree, One | suffices not two jays.
(C 281)

1567 *Prizes Drawn in Lottery* in *Loseley MSS* 123, 487; 208 What is a tree of cherries worth to foure in a company. 1576 LAMBARD *Peramb. of Kent* (1826) 269 It might wel be verified of them, which was wont to be commonly saide, *Unicum Arbustum, non alit duos Erithacos.* One Cherry tree sufficeth not two Iays. 1869 HAZLITT 306.

Cheshire born and Cheshire bred, strong i' th' arm and weak i' th' head.

1917 BRIDGE 36.

Cheshire cat, *see* Grin like C. c.

Cheshire chief of men.   (C 282)

1603 DRAYTON *The Baron's Wars* Wks. (Hebel) ii. 19 and v. 71 With those of Chesshire, chiefest for their place. 1608 HARINGTON *Brief View Church* (1792) i. 244 He was translated to Chester the chiefe City of that Shire, that some call chiefe of men. 1613–22 DRAYTON *Polyolb.* viii. 8 (1876) II. 67 For which, our proverb calls her, *Cheshire, chief of men.* 1662 FULLER Chesh. 173 . . . The Cestrians have always demeaned themselves right valiantly in their undertakings.

Cheshire nor Chawbent, Neither in.
(C 283)

1678 RAY 301 . . . That is, nither in Kent nor

Christendome. Chawbent is a town in Lancashire. **1917** BRIDGE 96 Neither in Cheshire nor
Chowbent. A peculiar kind of saying which is
hard to describe—neither here nor there, neither
in the greater nor in the less. Chawbent or
Chowbent, near Manchester, was generally supposed to be much behind the times.

**Cheshire, In | there are Lees as plenty
as fleas, and as many Davenports as
dogs' tails.**

1787 GROSE (*Chesh.*) 155 . . . The names of Lee
and Davenport are extremely common in this
county; the former is, however, variously spelt as
Lee, Lea, Leigh, Ley, &c. **1917** BRIDGE 18 As
many Leighs as fleas, Massies as asses, Crewes as
crows, and Davenports as dogs' tails. Four of
the great Cheshire families. . . . Another version:
Egertons and Leighs As thick as flees.

Chess, *see* Play at c. when house on fire.

Chess-board, *see* World on your c. (Had you the).

Chester, *see* Yew bow in C. (More than one).

Chestnut horse, A.

1838 SOUTHEY *Doctor* V. 58 It is a saying founded
on experience that a chestnut horse is always a
good one, and will do more work than any horse
of the same size of any other colour.

**Chestnuts out of the fire with the cat's
(dog's) paw, Take the.**   (c 284)

[LA FONTAINE IX. 17.] **1586** G. WHITNEY *Choice
Emblems* I. 58 The ape, did reach for Chest-
nuttes in the fire, But fearinge muche, the burning of his toes, Perforce was bar'de, longe time
from his desire. **1640** HERBERT no. 584 To take
the nuts from the fire with the dog's foot. **1657**
M. HAWKE *Killing is Murder* These he useth as
the monkey did the Cat's paw to scrape the nuts
out of the fire. **1662** FULLER Surrey 80 The
Fable is well known of an Ape, which, having a
mind to a Chest-nut lying in the fire, made the
foot of a Spanniel to be his tongs, by the proxy
whereof he got out the Nut for himself. **1692**
L'ESTRANGE *Aesop's Fab.* clxxxvi (1738) 200 'Tis a
court master-piece, to draw chestnuts out of the
fire with other peoples fingers. **1868** H. SMART
Breezie Langton ch. 4 You served us all pretty
much the same as the monkey did the cat when
he wanted the hot chestnuts.

Cheverel, *see* Conscience like a c.'s skin.

**Chevin[1] to the trout, Said the | my
head's worth all thy bouk.[2]**   (c 285)

1496 *Bk. St. Alban's Fishing* 28 The cheuyn is a
stately fysshe: and his heed is a deynty morsell.
1678 RAY 52. [[1] chub. [2] belly.]

Chew the cud, To.   (c 896)

1382 WYCLIF *Hosea* vii. 14 Thei chewiden cud
vpon whete, and wyne, and departiden fro me.
1547 *Homilies* 1 *Exhort. Holy Script.* II (1859) 15
Let vs ruminate, and (as it were) chewe the cudde
that wee maye haue the sweete iewse . . . &
consolation of them. **1551** CRANMER *Ans. to*

Gardiner 410 As many as haue a trewe faith and
belefe in hym, chawyng theyr cuddes, and perfectly remembryng the same death and passion.
1749 FIELDING *Tom Jones* XVIII. iii Having left
her a little while to chew the cud, if I may use
that expression, on these first tidings.

Chick(s), *see* January c.; Love like c. (They).

Chicken, To be no.
(*a*) chicken-hearted, a coward.   (c 290)

1633 T. STAFFORD *Ire. Appeased* (1810) I. xix, I.
199 Not finding the Defendants to be Chikins,
to be afraid . . . of every cloud or kite. **1707**
FARQUHAR *Beaux Strat.* IV. ii You assure me that
Scrub is a coward?—A Chicken, as the saying is.

(*b*) = no longer young.

1711 STEELE *Spectator* no. 216 You are now past
a chicken. **1720** SWIFT *Stella's Birthday* Pursue
your trade of scandal-picking, Your hints that
Stella is no chicken. **1761** A. MURPHY *Old Maid*
Wks. (1786) II. 158 Recollect, sister, that you are
no chicken. **1877** E. WALFORD *Gt. Families* I. 207
He must have been well forward in years—or at
all events, as they say, no chicken.

**Chicken is the country's, but the city
eats it, The.**   (c 289)

1640 HERBERT no. 108.

Chickens feed capons.   (c 291)

1678 RAY 111 . . . Chickens come to be capons.
1732 FULLER no. 1056 Capons were at first but
Chickens.

Chicken(s), *see also* Children and c. always
picking; Count one's c. before hatched; Curses,
like c., come home to roost; Fox run (Though
the), c. has wings; Hen, (Like) like c.; Keep
your thanks to feed your c.; Michaelmas c. . . .
never come to good; Mother Cary's c.

Chiding, *see* Chatting to c. not worth a chute;
Woe to the house where there is no c.

Chief, *see* Cheshire c. of men.

Child, To a | all weather is cold. (c 316)

1640 HERBERT no. 732.

**Child for the first seven years, Give me
a | and you may do what you like with
him afterwards.**

1902–4 LEAN III. 472 . . . A Jesuit maxim.

**Child has a red tongue, like its father,
The.**   (c 298)

1678 RAY 234.

**Child is christened, When the | you may
have godfathers enough.**   (c 319)

1623 PAINTER B7[v] The christned child may
Godf'ers haue enow. **1639** CLARKE 283 . . . every
man will be Godfather. **1670** RAY 69 . . . When
a mans need is supplied or his occasions over,

people are ready to offer their assistance or service. **1732** FULLER no. 5573 (When the Christning is over).

Child is father of the man, The.

1802 WORDSWORTH '*My heart leaps up*' l. 7. **1871** SMILES *Character* 33 The influences which contribute to form the character of the child endure through life. . . . 'The child is father of the man'; or, as Milton puts it, 'The childhood shows the man, as morning shows the day.' **1905** MYERS *Wordsworth* 93 'The child is father of the man', . . . and Wordsworth holds that the instincts and pleasures of a healthy childhood sufficiently indicate the lines on which our mature character should be formed.

Child may have too much of his mother's blessing, A.   (c 299)

1609 HARWARD 102ᵛ (A man). **1639** CLARKE 161 (man). **1670** RAY 122 . . . Mothers are oftentimes too tender and fond of their children. Who are ruined and spoiled by their cockering and indulgence.

Child says nothing, but what it heard by the fire, The.   (c 300)

1640 HERBERT no. 300. **1721** KELLY 318 The bairn speak in the Fields what he heard by the Slett.[1] [[1] fireside.]

Child sleep upon bones, Let not a.
                                                    (c 311)

1678 RAY 351 . . . *Som.* i.e. The nurses lap.

Child to hear (see) something, To be with.   (c 317)

1540 PALSGRAVE *Acolastus* 67 They be with chylde tyll they be at this deyntie meates thou speakeste of. **1548** UDALL etc. *Erasm. Par. Luke* xxiii. 8 The man had of long tyme been with chylde to haue a sight of Jesus. **1551** T. WILSON *Rule of Reason* S7 What with the secretenesse of the thyng, and what with the silence of her sonne, she was wonderfull with childe, till she had gotte some what of the boie. *c.* **1578** SIDNEY *Lady of May* (Feuillerat ii. 335) I am gravidated with child, till I have endoctrinated your plumbeous cerebrosities. **1660** PEPYS *Diary* May 14 I sent my boy, who like myself, is with child to see any strange thing.

Child's bird and a knave's (boy's) wife, A.   (c 320)

c. **1400** LYDGATE *Churl & Bird* 374 A childes birrde and a knavis wyfe Have often siethe gret sorrowe and myschaunce. **1523** SKELTON *Garl. Laurel* l. 1452 Wks. i. 419 But who may haue a more vngracyous lyfe Than a chyldes birde and a knauis wyfe? **1678** RAY 351 A child's bird and a boy's wife are well used. *Som.*

Child's pig but father's bacon.   (c 321)

c. **1350** *Douce MS. 52*, no. 113 Childe is pigge, and fader is the flicche. Porcellus nati fit perna patris veterati. **1678** RAY 111 . . . Parents usually tell their children, this pig or this lambe is thine, but when they come to be grown up and

sold, parents themselves take the money for them. **1914** K. F. PURDON *Folk of Furry F.* ch. 2 It would be 'child's pig and Daddy's bacon', . . . with that calf.

Child's service is little, A | yet he is no little fool that despises it.   (c 322)

1640 HERBERT no. 206.

Child(ren), *see* Adam's c. (We are all); Adam's c. (We are all) but silk makes the difference; Ask the mother if c. like father; Bachelors' wives and maids' c.; Better a snotty c.; Better c. weep than old men; Burnt c. dreads fire; Cares not whose c. cry; Cockers his c. (He that) provides for enemy; Devil's c.; Die like a chrisom c.; Give a c. while he craves . . . you'll have foul knave; Happy is he that is happy in c.; Harry's c. of Leigh, never one like; Heaven takes care of c.; Horse (The best) needs . . . and aptest c. needs teaching; Kindness is lost bestowed on c.; Kingdom whose king is c.; Kiss the c. for nurse's sake; Late c. early orphans; Maintains one vice (What) would bring up two c.; *Maxima debetur*; Morning sun, wine-bred c. seldom end well; Old men are twice c.; Past dying of her first c.; Poor man's cow dies, rich man's c.; Praise the c. and make love to mother; Put another man's c. in your bosom; Sad burden to carry dead man's c.; Service a c. does father is to make him foolish; Silly c. is soon ylered; Virtue and a trade best portion for c.; Well for him who has good c.; Wife and c. bills of charges; Wipes the c.'s nose (He that); Wise c. that knows own father; Wise man commonly has foolish c.

Children, He that has | all his morsels are not his own.   (c 339)

1640 HERBERT no. 423.

Children and chicken must be always picking.   (c 327)

1573 TUSSER 178 Yong children and chickens would ever be eating. **1670** RAY 33.

Children (Drunkards) and fools cannot lie (speak truth).   (c 328)

1537 C. HAYES in *St. Papers Hen. VIII* 1283 Addenda, Vol. I, Pt. i 437 [It is] an old saying that a child, a fool and a drunken man will ever show their conditions and the truth. **1545** TAVERNER H6 Oure common prouerbe . . . Children, drunkers and fooles, can not lye. **1546** HEYWOOD I. xi. D4ᵛ Men saie also, childerne and fooles can not ly. **1549** ERASM. tr. Chalenor *Praise Folly* Q4ᵛ That priuilege fooles haue to speake trouthe without offence. **1578** FLORIO *First F.* G1. **1591** LYLY *Endym.* IV. ii. 101 Children and fooles speake true. **1599** SHAKES. *J.C.* (folio) I. iii. 74 Why Old men, Fooles, and Children calculate. **1602** DEKKER *Satiro-Mastix* I. ii. 269 A foole will confesse truth. **1634** *Cacoethes Leaden Legacy* A9 The English Proverbe saith, that truth by fooles is onely told. **1670** RAY 69 (speak truth). **1805** SCOTT *Lett. to Ellis* in Lockhart *Life* xiii. It is a proverb, that children and fools talk truth.

Children and fools have merry lives.

(c 329)

1639 CLARKE 298. **1670** RAY 69 . . . They are not concern'd either for what is past, or for what is to come. **1813** BARRETT *Heroine* ed. Raleigh 10 Only fools, children, and savages, are happy.

Children and fools must not play with edged tools. *Cf.* Jesting with edged tools.

(J 45)

a. **1568** ASCHAM *Schoolmaster* (Wks. ed. Wright 266) . . . but fine edge tooles in a fole or mad mans hand. **1642** MILTON *Apol. Smect.* Prose Wks. (1904) III. 114 That he may know what it is to be a child, and yet to meddle with edged tools, I turn his antistrophon upon his own head. **1839** DICKENS *N. Nickleby* ch. 47 'Oh dear, what an edged tool you are!' 'Don't play with me then', said Ralph impatiently, 'You know the proverb.'

Children are certain cares, but uncertain comforts.

(c 330)

1639 CLARKE 240. **1670** RAY 4. **1886** E. J. HARDY *How to be Happy* ch. 17 Children are *not* 'certain sorrows and uncertain pleasures' when properly managed.

Children are poor men's riches.

(c 331)

1541 H. BULLINGER *Christ. State Matrimony* tr. Coverdale 1543 ed., K6 Children are wemens best Iewels. **1582** WHETSTONE *Hept. Civil Disc.* X2ᵛ Children are the most rich Iuelles in the worlde. **1602** SHAKES. *A.W.* I. iii. 26 And I think I shall never have the blessing of God till I have issue o' my body; for they say barnes are blessings. **1611** COTGRAVE s.v. Enfant. **1670** RAY 4. **1732** FULLER no. 1094.

Children are to be deceived with comfits and men with oaths.

[PLUTARCH, *Lysander*, and ERASM. *Ad.*, substituting 'dice' for 'comfits'. HOR. *Sat.* I. 1. 25 *Ut pueris olim dant crustula blandi Doctores,* As enticing teachers are wont to give pastry to boys.] **1589** *The Contre-Guyse* F2ᵛ This maxime of Lisander: Wee must deceiue children with small bones, and men with cates. **1605** BACON *Adv. Learn.* II. xxiii (1900) 246 That other principle of Lysander, That children are to be deceived with comfits, and men with oaths: and the like evil and corrupt positions.

Children, He that has no | brings them up well (feeds them fat).

(c 340)

1573 SANFORD 103 He that hath no children doth bring them vp well. **1578** FLORIO *First F.* 28ᵛ (feedeth them wel). **1611** DAVIES no. 236. **1616** DRAXE no. 634.

Children hear at home, What | soon flies abroad.

(c 344)

1611 COTGRAVE s.v. Enfant. **1670** RAY 4. **1732** FULLER no. 5482. **1818** SCOTT *Rob Roy* ch. 27 Bairns and fules speak at the Cross what they hear at the ingle-side.

Children in Holland, The | take pleasure in making What the children in England take pleasure in breaking.

1822 SCOTT *Nigel* Introd. Ep. For the critics, they have their business, and I mine; as the nursery proverb goes—'The children in Holland take pleasure in making What the children in England take pleasure in breaking.'

Children, He that has no | knows not what is love.

(c 341)

1591 SHAKES. *3 Hen. VI* V. v. 62 How sweet a plant have you untimely cropp'd! You have no children, butchers! If you had, The thought of them would have stirr'd up remorse. **1595** *Rich. Duke York* H2 You haue no children Deuells, if you had, The thought of them, would then haue stopt your rage. **1595** SHAKES. *K.J.* III. iv. 90 You hold too heinous a respect of grief.— He talks to me that never had a son. *c.* **1595** *Edmond Ironside* l. 1512 None feeles a mothe[r]s sorrow but a mother. **1605–6** SHAKES. *M.* IV. iii. 204 Your castle is surpris'd; your wife and babes Savagely slaughter'd . . .—My children too?—Wife, children, servants, all That could be found . . .—Be comforted . . .—He has no children. **1639** CLARKE 240 None knowes the affection of Parents but they that have Children. **1666** TORRIANO *It. Prov.* 89, no. 34.

Children learn to creep ere they can go. *Cf.* First creep and then go.

(c 332)

c. **1350** *Douce MS.* 52, no. 116 Fyrst the chylde crepyth and after gooth. *c.* **1435** WAKEFIELD PLAYS 'First Shepherds' l. 100. **1546** HEYWOOD I. xi. D4ᵛ Children lerne to crepe er they can lerne to goe. **1561** SENECA *Herc. Furens* tr. Jasper Heywood Ded. A3 Tech the little children to goe that yet canne but creepe.

Children nowadays, There are no.

1902–4 LEAN IV. 145 . . . This was said 200 years ago: Ah! il n'y a plus d'enfans.—MOLIÈRE, *Mal. Im.* xi.

Children pick up words as pigeons peas, and utter them again as God shall please.

(c 333)

1594–5 SHAKES. *L.L.L.* V. ii. 315 This fellow picks up wit as pigeons peas, and utters it again when God doth please. **1670** RAY 213.

Children (Maidens) should be seen, and not heard.

(M 45)

c. **1400** *Mirk's Festial* E.E.T.S. I. 230 For hyt ys an old Englysch sawe: 'A mayde schuld be seen, but not herd'. **1560** T. BECON *Catechism* P.S. 369 A maid should be seen, and not heard. **1596** SHAKES. *M.V.* III. ii. 8 A maiden hath no tongue but thought. **1670** RAY 51 (Maidens must). **1733** SWIFT Dial. I. E.L. 264 (maids). **1772** R. GRAVES *Spiritual Quix.* III. 18 It is a vulgar maxim that a pretty woman should rather be seen than heard. **1857** G. ELIOT *Scenes Cler. Life* 'Janet's Repentance' ch. 8 (Little gells must be). **1866** E. J. HARDY *How to be Happy* ch. 17 'Little people should be seen and not heard' is a stupid saying.

Children stand quiet, When | they have done some ill.   (c 345)

1640 HERBERT no. 504.   1642 TORRIANO 88 When children whist and say nothing, then have they done some mischief.

Children suck the mother when they are young, and the father when they are old.   (c 334)

1602 J. MANNINGHAM *Diary* 12 An old child sucks hard; i. children when they growe to age prove chargeable.   1678 RAY 112.   1732 FULLER no. 1099 (and the Father, when grown up).

Children to bed and the goose to the fire.   (c 335)

1670 RAY 168.   1710 STEELE *Tatler* No. 263 (1899) IV. 339 We have all of us heard in our infancy, of 'putting the children to bed, and laying the goose to the fire'. This was one of the jocular sayings of our forefathers.

Children when they are little make parents fools, when they are great they make them mad.   (c 336)

1640 HERBERT no. 939.   1670 RAY 4.

Children, *see also* Child(ren).

Chimneys, Many | little smoke. (c 348)

1583 STUBBES *Anat.* (New Sh. S.) 105 Many Chimnies, but little smoke.   1603 H. CROSSE, *Virtue's Commonwealth* (Gros.) 89.   1616 DRAXE no. 1009.

Chimney(s), *see also* Build two c. (Easier to) than maintain one; Think there is bacon (Where you), there is no c.

Chin, *see* Swim, (He needs must).

China orange, *see* Lombard Street.

China shop, *see* Bull in a c. s.

Chin-cough, *see* Tail will catch the c.

Chink, So we get the | we'll bear with the stink.   (c 350)

[L. *Non olet*. 'It doesn't smell'; founded upon a remark of Vespasian after applying to his nose a handful of the gold brought in by his tax on urine. SUET. *Vesp.* 23. JUV. 14. 204. Fr. *L'Argent n'a pas d'odeur*. cf.   1628 EARLE *Microcosm.*, *Phisitian* Arb. 25 Of al odors he likes best the smel of Vrine, and holds *Vespatians* rule, that no gain is vnsauory.]   1596 HARINGTON *Metam. of Ajax* (1814) 68 So we get the chinks, We will bear with the stinks.   1639 CLARKE 293.   1692 DRYDEN *To Mr. Southern* 8 But the gain smells not of the excrement.   1721 KELLY 359 We will bear with the Stink, when it brings in the Clink.   1888 J. E. T. ROGERS *Econ. Interp. Hist.* (1894) II. xxi. 464   Defoe . . . was ready to take a brief from either of the contending factions. He had

accepted as his guide in literary life the adage of Vespasian, *Non olet*.   1902 A. LANG *Hist. Scot.* II. xiii. 335 It did not follow that James need continue to take money from hands dipped in his mother's blood. Of money, however, from whatever quarter, James thought *non olet*.

Chip in a pottage pot, Like a | doth neither good nor harm.   (c 353)

1619 J. FAVOUR *Antiquity* 234 *Hierome* . . . is made but as a chip in a Keale pot.   1659 N. R. 74.   1670 RAY 168.   1688 *Vox Cleri Pro Rege* 56 A sort of Chip in Pottage, which (he hopes) will not do Popery much good, nor the Church of England much harm.   1880 *Church Times* 25 June (D.) The Burials Bill . . . is thought . . . to resemble the proverbial chip in porridge, which does neither good nor harm.   1910 JOYCE *Eng. as we Speak it in Ireld.* 141 A person who does neither good nor harm . . . is 'like a chip in porridge'; almost always said as a reproach.

Chip of the (same) old block, A.
                                                          (c 352)

c. 1626 *Dick Dev.* IV. i Why may not I be a Chipp of the same blocke out of which you two were cutt?   1627 SANDERSON *Serm.* I. 283 Am not I a child of the same Adam, a vessel of the same clay, a chip of the same block, with him?   1642 MILTON *Apol. Smect.* Prose Wks. (1904) III. 144 How well dost thou now appear to be a chip of the old block, that could find 'Bridge Street and alehouses in heaven'?   1670 RAY 168 . . . He is his father's own son: taken always in an ill sense.   1824 SCOTT *Redg.* ch. 15 My father (God bless the old man!), a true chip of the old Presbyterian block.

Chips, *see* Best carpenter makes the fewest c.; Boils his pot with c.; Carpenter (Like) like c.; Hew not too high lest c. fall in eye; Merry as three c.

Chloe, *see* Drunk as C.

Choice in rotten apples, There is small.
                                                          (c 358)

1594–8 SHAKES. *T.S.* I. i. 129 Faith, as you say, there's small choice in rotten apples.   1622 J. DE LUNA *Gram. Span. & Eng.* tr. I.W. 263 Ther's but small choyce where the whole flocke is bad. [*a.* 1667] 1698 LACY *Sauny the Scot* I. 2.

Choice to begin love, but not to end it, A man has.   (M 234)

c. 1573 I. WHITNEY *Sweet Nosegay* B8 In loving, ech one hath free choyce, or ever they begin, But in their power it lyeth not, to end when they are in.   *c.* 1584 G. HARVEY *Marginalia* ed. Moore Smith 100 A man hath free arbitrage to begin Looue, but not to ende it.   1732 FULLER no. 1374 Enter upon Love when you will; but give over when you can.

Choice, *see also* Burthen of one's own c. not felt; Hobson's c.; Pay your money and take your c.

Choke(s, -ed), *see* Hastens a glutton (Who), c. him; Lie could have c. him; Mote may c. a man; Too much pudding c. a dog.

Choleric drinks, The | the melancholic eats, the phlegmatic sleeps.   (c 360)

1640 HERBERT no. 924.   **1670** RAY 5.

Choleric man withdraw a little; From a | from him that says nothing for ever.   (M 145)

1631 MABBE *Celestina* T.T. 99 That ancient adage: from an angry man get the gone but for a while; but from an enemy for ever. **1640** HERBERT no. 164.

Choose a wife on a Saturday rather than a Sunday.   (W 378)

1659 HOWELL *Span. Prov.* 2 . . . viz. when she is in her fine cloaths.   **1737** FRANKLIN Oct. If you want a neat wife, chuse her on a Saturday.   **1813** RAY 54 If thou desirest a wife, chuse her on Saturday rather than on a Sunday. i.e. see her in an undress.   **1846** DENHAM 2.

Choose for yourself and use for yourself.   (c 361 and M 134)

1616 DRAXE no. 2392 Euery man must chuse and vse his owne wife.   **1639** CLARKE 230.

Choose neither a woman nor linen by candle-light.   (W 682)

1573 SANFORD 51 Choose not a woman, nor linnen clothe by the candle.   **1611** DAVIES no. 79 Choose neither Women nor Lynnen by Candle. **1678** RAY 64 Neither women nor linnen by candle-light. **1737** FRANKLIN May Fine linen, girls and gold so bright Choose not to take by candle-light. **1738** SWIFT Dial. III. E.L. 324 They say women and linen show best by candle-light.

Choose none for thy servant who has served thy betters.   (S 230)

1640 HERBERT no. 1014.   **1852** E. FITZGERALD *Polonius* 76 A proverb bids us beware of taking for servant one who has waited on our betters.

Choose not a house near an inn, or in a corner.   (H 753)

1640 HERBERT no. 286 . . . an Inne (viz. for noise); or in a corner (for filth).

Choose not a wife by the eye only.   (W 344)

1543 G. COUSIN *Office of Servants* A4 [In choosing a servant] we must make our choise not onely throughe our eyes, and not to content oure eares. **1581** TILNEY *Duties in Marriage* B4ᵛ We seeke to feede our eyes, and not to content oure eares. Why? . . . shal a man choose his wyfe with his eares.   **1581** GUAZZO ii. 14 Olympias the mother of Alexander, whose saying . . . was, that women are to be married with the eares, before they are with the eyes.   **1603** PLUTARCH *Morals* tr. Holland 319 And in trueth we ought not to goe about for to contract marriage by the eie or the fingers.   **1666** TORRIANO *It. Prov.* 268, no. 25 A woman ought to become a spouse, rather with her ears, than with her eyes. **1732** FULLER no. 462.

Choose thy company before thy drink.   (c 563)

1621 ROBINSON 14.   **1639** CLARKE 24.

Choosers, *see* Beggars must be no c.

Choosing a wife, and buying a sword, we ought not to trust another, In.   (c 362)

1640 HERBERT no. 490.

Choos(e -ing), *see also* Best or worst to man is c. good or ill wife; Evils, (Of two) c. least; Horse made and wife to make (C.); Pays the lawing c. the lodging (Let him that); Wink and c.

Chop and change, To.   (c 363)

[The meaning of *chop* has passed from that of 'to barter' to that of to 'change, alter'.]   *c.* **1460** *Digby Myst.* 'Wisdom' (1882) v. 642 I . . . choppe and chaunge with symonye, and take large yiftes. **1525**? TYNDALE tr. *2 Cor.* ii. 17 Choppe and change with the worde of God.   **1540** COVERDALE *Confut. Standish* Wks. II. 419 Even as ye pervert the words of holy scripture . . . as ye chop and change with it.   *a.* **1547** SURREY ed. Padelford (1928) 43. 12.   **1570** TUSSER 7ᵛ Chopping and changing I can not commende. **1635** QUARLES *Embl.* I. ix (1718) 38 O, who would trust this world . . . That . . . chops and changes ev'ry minute.   **1888** *Poor Nellie* 299 It is to be hoped he knows his own mind this time, and does not intend chopping and changing again.

Chop logic, To.   (L 412)

[= to bandy logic, argue.]   *c.* **1525** SKELTON *Replyc.* 118 Wolde . . . That wyse Harpocrates Had your mouthes stopped . . . Whan ye logyke chopped.   **1528** TYNDALE *Obed. Chrn. Man* P.S. 307 The sophisters with their anagogical and chopological sense.   **1577** STANYHURST *Descr. Irel.* in HOLINSHED VI. 49 You charge me . . . that I presume to chop logike with you . . . by answering your snappish Quid with a knappish Quo.   **1594–5** SHAKES. *R.J.* III. v. 150 Choplogic? What is this?   **1611** BEAUM. & FL. *Kt. Burn.* P. I. 51 Harke how he chops Logicke with his Mother.

Chopped hay, It goes down like.   (H 234)

1678 RAY 235.   **1725** ERASM. *Fam. Colloquies* tr. N. Bailey (1733, 512) He was as hard as a Flint, he could have lived upon chopt Hay.   **1746** GRAY to Wharton 11 Sept. It [Aristotle] tastes for all the world like chopped hay.

Chough, *see* Cornish c.

Chrisom, *see* Die like a c. child.

Christ (The church) takes not, What | the exchequer carries away.   (c 364)

1659 HOWELL *Span. Prov.* 21 That which Christ hath not, the Exchequer carrieth.

Christen the bairn, When you | you (should) know what to call it.

1721 KELLY 347 . . . Spoken in Bargain making when we agree on express Terms, we know not what to give, and what to expect. 1862 HISLOP 211 When ye christen the bairn ye should ken what to ca't.

Christened with pump water, He was.
(W 94)

1678 RAY 79 . . . It is spoken of one that hath a red face.

Christen(s, -ed), *see also*' Child is c. (When), godfathers enough; Parson always c. own child first.

Christendom, *see* Kent nor C.

Christian, A complete | must have the works of a Papist, the words of a Puritan, and the faith of a Protestant.
(C 366)

1635 HOWELL *Fam. Lett.* 25 Aug. (1655) II. xi. 23 One who said, That to make one a compleat Christian, he . . .

Christians to the lions! The.

[TERTULLIAN *Apolog.* xl in RAMSAY *Ch. in Rom. Emp.* (1894) 327 'If the Tiber rises, if the Nile does not rise, if the heavens give no rain, if there is an earthquake, famine, or pestilence, straightway the cry is, . . .] 1629 T. ADAMS *Serm.* (1862) I. 466 The Christians . . . made Aurelius's army to prosper . . .; yet *Christianos ad leones,—* Throw the Christians to the lions.

Christian(s), *see also* Jews spend at Easter; Rain (There is no), the C. are cause.

Christmas all the year, They keep.
(C 370 and 372)

1557 TUSSER B2ᵛ When Christmas is done, kepe not Christmas time still. [*c.* 1602] 1608 *Merry Devil of Edmonton* I. i. 66 The riotous old knight Hath overrun his annual revenue In keeping jolly Christmas all the year. 1639 CLARKE 233 Christmas lasts not all the yeare. 1672 WALKER no. 83, 25.

Christmas comes but once a year.
(C 369)

1573 TUSSER 28 At Christmas play and make good cheere, for Christmas comes but once a yeere. 1622 WITHER 'A Christmas Carroll' in *Faire-Virtue*. And what they want they take in beer, For Christmas comes but once a year. 1931 *Times* 24 Dec. 13/2 'Christmas comes but once a year,' said the old rhyme, 'but when it comes it brings good cheer.' . . . There was a time when Christmas 'good cheer' meant principally a succession of massive meals.

Christmas, *see also* After C. Lent; Coming and so is C.; Talk of C. so long that it comes.

Christmas-pies, *see* Devil makes C. p.

Church-bell, *see* Calf never heard c. b., (That).

Church is an anvil which has worn out many hammers, The.

1908 ALEX. MACLAREN *Acts Apost.* I. 136 . . . and the story of the first collision is, in essentials, the story of all.

Church is not so large but the priest may say service in it, The. (C 377)

1678 RAY 113.

Church mis-went, If you would go to a | you must go to Cuckstone in Kent.

1736 S. PEGGE *Kenticisms, Prov.* E.D.S. 69 . . . 'Or very unusual in proportion, as Cuckstone church in Kent, of which it is said—"if you would goe", &c.'. Dr. Plot's Letter to Bp. Fell, in LELAND *Itin.* ii. 137. [. . . It refers to Cuxton, near Rochester.]

Church mouse, *see* Mouse (Mice).

Church (Kirk) stand in the churchyard (kirkyard), Let the. (C 379)

1678 RAY 113. 1832 HENDERSON 130 . . . Everything in its place.

Church will lose nothing, and defend nothing, The. (C 378)

1626 OVERBURY *Obs. in Trav.* Wks. (1890) 242 The unproportionable part of the land which the church holds, all which is likewise dead to militarie uses. For, as they say there, *The church will lose nothing, nor defend nothing.*

Church work goes on slowly. (C 383)

1629 T. ADAMS *Visitat. Serm.* Wks. 935 If the Ouerseers looke not well to the busenesse, too many will make Church-worke of it; for such loytering is now fallen into a Prouerbe. 1639 FULLER *Holy War* III. i. (1840) 117 Guy . . . besieged Ptolemais . . . But this siege was church-work, and therefore went on slowly. 1712 ADDISON *Spect.* No. 383 Wks. (1902) III. 361 The fifty new churches will . . . mend the prospect; but church-work is slow!

Church(es), *see also* All are not saints that go to c.; Bells call others but enter not c.; Christ (The c.) takes not (What), exchequer carries away; Fashion's sake, as dogs go to c.; Flaming figure in country c.; Foreheet nothing but building c.; God has his c. (Where), the devil . . . ; Good dog who goes to c.; Houses than parish c. (More); Itch of disputing is scab of c.; Nearer the c., farther from God; New c. old steeple; Parsons than parish c. (More); *Pater noster* built c.; See a churchman ill (Though you), continue in c.; Spitting in c. (Some make conscience of), yet . . . ; Suffolk is land of c.; Three ways, the c., sea, court; Visible c.; Wonders of England.

Churchman, *see* See a c. ill (Though you), continue in church.

Churchyard, A piece of a | fits everybody. (P 290)

1640 HERBERT no. 1027.

Churchyard is so handsome, No | that a man would desire straight to be buried there. (C 385)

1640 HERBERT no. 969.

Churchyard, *see also* Church stand in the c.; Green winter fat c.; Green Yule . . . fat c.; Hot May fat c.; Young physician fattens the c. *See also* Kirkyard.

Churl fall out of the moon, Have a care lest the.

c. **1380** CHAUCER *Troilus* Bk. I, l. 1023 Quod Pandarus, 'Thow hast a ful gret care Lest that the cherl may falle out of the moone!' **1846–59** *Denham Tracts* ii. 57 F.L.S. (as an 'old, very old proverb').

Churl, *see also* Put a c. upon a gentleman.

Churl's feast is better than none at all, A. (C 388)

1592–3 SHAKES. *C.E.* III. i. 24 Good meat, sir, is common; that every churl affords. [*c.* **1590**] **1594** GREENE & LODGE *Looking Glass* III. ii. 1018 (We must feed vpon prouerbes now; as . . . a Churles feast is). **1609** HARWARD 77 Churles feast.

Churm, *see* Swarm of bees in a c.

Churning days, I will make him know. (D 117)

1678 RAY 235.

Cipher in arithmetic, Like a. (C 391)

1399 LANGLAND *Rich. Redeless* iv. 53 Than satte summe, as siphre doth in awgrym, That noteth a place, and no thing availith. **1547** J. HARRISON *Exhort. Scottes* 229 Our presidentes . . . doo serue but as Cyphers in Algorisme, to fill the place. [**1591**] **1593** PEELE *Edward I* I. i. 172 (but a poore cipher in agrum). **1599** SHAKES. *Hen. V* Prol. 17 Since a crooked figure may Attest in little place a million; . . . Let us, ciphers to this great accompt, On your imaginary forces work. **1611** *Id. W.T.* I. ii. 6 Like a cipher, Yet standing in rich place, I multiply. **1613** T. ADAMS *Heaven & Earth Reconcil'd* D1ᵛ Like a meere Cypher, which fills vp a place, and increaseth the number, but signifies nothing.

Circe, *see* Cup of C.

Circumstances alter cases.

[*Cf.* **1600** DRAYTON *Idea* (Wks. ed. Hebel ii. 324) The Circumstance doth make it good or ill. **1642** TORRIANO 60 Conditions break laws.]

1678 T. RYMER *Tragedies of the Last Age* (1692, 117) There may be circumstances that alter the case. **1870** C. DICKENS *E. Drood* ch. 9 But circumstances alter cases. **1895** J. PAYN *In Market Overt* ch. 39 Circumstances alter cases even with the best of us, as was shown in a day or two in the conduct of the Bishop.

Circuses, *see* Bread and c.

Cities are taken by the ears. (C 402)

[= by propaganda.] **1640** HERBERT no. 970.

Cities seldom change religion only. (C 403)

1651 HERBERT no. 71a.

Cities, *see also* City (-ies).

Citizen is at his business before he rise, The. (C 393)

1640 HERBERT no. 958.

Citizens of Cork are all akin, The.

1574 R. STANYHURST *Descr. of Ireland* in Holinshed 25 C1 They [the citizens of Cork] trust not the countrie adioining, but match in wedlocke among themselves onlie, so that the whole citie is welnigh linked one to the other in affinitie. **1654** FULLER *Comment. Ruth* in *Sermons* (1891) I. 100 Camden reports of the citizens of Cork, that all of them . . . are of kindred one to the other: but I think, that all wealthy men will hook in the cousin, and draw in some alliance.

City is in a bad case, whose physician has the gout, That. (C 401)

1678 RAY *Adag. Hebr.* 397. **1911** A. COHEN *Anct. Jew. Prov.* 107 Unhappy the province whose chancellor of the exchequer is one-eyed.

City (Castle, Valour, Virtue, Woman) that parleys is half gotten, A. (C 122 and V 14)

1548 W. PATTEN *Exped*ⁿ *into Scotland* (Tudor Tracts 143) A prophecy among the Frenchmen, which saith *Chateau qui parle, et femme qui ecout L'un veut rendre, et l'autre* and so forth. **1549** *Complaynt of Scotland* E.E.T.S. xiii. 108 Ther is ane ald prouerb that says, that ane herand damysele, and ane spekand castel, sal neuyr end vith honour. **1567** PAINTER (Jacobs) iii. 48 A Citty is halfe won when they within demaunde for parle. **1637** HOWELL *Lett.* 4 Dec. (1903) II. 106 Others . . . will endure . . . a siege; but will incline to parley at last, and . . . fort and female which begins to parley is half won. **1640** HERBERT no. 586 Valour that parlies is neare yealding. **1651** HERBERT no. 1097. **1721** BAILEY s.v. Virtue Virtue which parleys is near a Surrender. **1734** FRANKLIN 40 Neither a fortress nor a m—d will hold out long after they begin to parley.

City (-ies), *see also* Chicken is country's but c. eats it; Gate wider than c., (Make not); Great c. great solitude; Men, not walls, make c. safe; No gates no c.; Reward and punishment are the walls of a c.; See the c. for the houses (Cannot).

Civility costs nothing.

1706 STEVENS S.V. Cortesía Mouth civility is worth much and costs little. **1841** S. WARREN *Ten Thousand a Year* ch. 3 It may be as well . . . to acknowledge the . . . fellow's note—. . . **1873** ALLINGHAM *Rambles* I. 207 . . . nothing, that is, to him that shows it; but it often costs the world very dear.

Civility, *see also* Loses anything by c. (One never).

Clap, *see* Lawton gate a c.; Thunderbolt has its c.

Clapper, *see* Tongue runs like c. of mill.

Clartier[1] the cosier, The.

1816 SCOTT *Antiq.* ch. 26 There was dirt good store. Yet . . . an appearance of . . . comfort, that seemed to warrant their old sluttish proverb, . . . **1913** A. & J. LANG *Highw. & By.* in Border ix. 239 In an arctic climate, there may perhaps be some excuse for the proverb: . . . [[1] dirtier.]

Claw me, and I'll claw thee.   (c 405)

[Used of mutual flattery.] **1530** TYNDALE *Practise of Prelates* P.S. 260. As the manner of scalled horses, the one to claw the other. **1530** PALSGRAVE 486a Clawe my backe, and I wyll clawe thy toe. **1531** TYNDALE *Expos.* I *John* (1537) 72 We saye, clawe me, clawe the. **1545** TAVERNER Ii. **1567** J. JEWEL *Def. of the Apology* 413 The Prouerbe is common, One hande claweth an other. **1629** T. ADAMS *Serm.* (1861–2) I. 186 'Claw me and I will claw thee'; wink at mine, and I will not see thy faults. **1738** SWIFT *Dial.* III. E.L. 318. **1825** *Blackw. Mag.* XVII. 461 I do not object to Jeffrey's clawing his . . . brother Editor, who so regularly claws him in his New Monthly.

Claw the back of (*or* claw by the back), To.   (B 17)

[= to 'stroke down', flatter.] *c.* **1394** LANGLAND *P. Pl.* Crede 365 Whou þey curry Kinges, & her back claweþ. *a.* **1541** WYATT *Poet. Wks.* (1868) 158 'Take heed of him that by thi back thee claweth'; For none is worse than is a friendly foe. *a.* **1575** PILKINGTON *Nehemiah* P.S. 400 One jade claweth another by the backe.

Claw the elbow, To. *Cf.* Rub the elbow.

[To flatter.] **1589** GREENE *Euphues his censure* Gros. vi. 161 How clarkely Achilles began to claw hir [Polixena] by the Elbowe. **1592** *Id. Defence of Cony-catching* 59 This clawed this Glorioso by the elbow. **1594** *King Leir* IV. vii. 79 'Sblood how the old slave claws me by the elbow.

Claws it as Clayton clawed the pudding when he eat bag and all, He.   (c 407)

1678 RAY 282. **1732** FULLER no. 1826.

Claw(s), *see also* Cats hide c.; Devil is known by his c.; Jaws outrun your c. (Don't let); Lion is known by his c.; Scratch (C.) where itches not.

Clay, *see* Cleveland in c.; Cold (pale) as c.; Sand feeds the c. (Where the).

Clayton, *see* Claws it as C. clawed pudding.

Clean as a penny.   (p 188)

1681 W. ROBERTSON *Phraseol. Generalis* 338. **1720** GAY *Poems* ii. 279 (Underhill) Clean as a penny drest. **1834** J. B. KER 39.

Clean as a whistle, As.

1825 J. NEAL *Brother Jonathan* He smacks him thro' the ribs—clean as a whistle. **1828** *Craven Gloss.* S.V. As clean etc. a proverbial simile, signifying completely, entirely. **1849** W. S. MAYO *Kaloolah* (1850) V. 41 A first rate shot, . . . head taken off as clean as a whistle.

Clean breast, To make a.

1752 CAMERON in *Scots Mag.* (1753) Oct. 508/1 He pressed him . . . to make a clean breast, and tell him all. **1869** C. READE *Foul Play* ch. 66 I've got a penitent outside, . . . he'll make a clean breast. **1891** A. LANG *Ess. in Lit.* 107 The pagan Aztecs only confessed once in a lifetime—. . . then they made a clean breast of it once for all.

Clean heels, light meals.

1917 BRIDGE 38 . . . Refers to the superiority of clay land over sandy land for yielding milk . . . On sandy land, cows come to be milked with clean feet; but on clay land the gate places are very muddy.

Clean, *see also* Conscience is cumbered and stands not c.; Foul (He that has to do with) never comes away c.; Water makes all c., (Fair); Wrap up in c. linen.

Cleanliness is next to godliness.

1605 BACON *Adv. of Learning* II Cleanness of body was ever deemed to proceed from a due reverence to God. *a.* **1791** WESLEY *Serm.* lxxxviii *On Dress* (1838) III. 15 Slovenliness is no part of religion . . . 'Cleanliness is indeed next to godliness'. **1876** BURNABY *Ride to Khiva* ch. 10 . . . The latter quality, as displayed in a Russian devotee, is more allied with dirt than anything else.

Clear (bright) as glass.   (G 135)

1481 CAXTON *Reynard* (ed. Arber, 11) As clere as ony glas. **1579** SPENSER *Shep. Cal.* August, l. 80 A scleare as the christall glasse. **1584** WITHALS F1 (bright). **1591** ARIOSTO *Orl. Fur.* Harington I. 36 She . . . dranke the riuer water cleere as glasse. **1599** SHAKES. *Pass. Pilgr.* 7, l. 3 Brighter than glass. **1608** J. DAY *Law Tricks* I. i She was Pure as the diamond, cleere as christall glasse.

Clear as the day, As.   (D 56)

1562 G. LEGH *Accidence of Armoury* B4ᵛ (the none daye). **1566** L. WAGER *Mary Magd.* E4 (day). **1587** J. BRIDGES *Defence* 113 (noone day). **1590–1** SHAKES. *2 Hen. VI* II. i. 106 Thou seest not well. — Yes, master, clear as day. **1671** CLARKE *Phras. Puer.* 212 (noon day).

Clear as the sun, As.   (S 969)

1528 TYNDALE *Obed. Chrn. Man* P.S. 213
Clearer than the sun. **1539** TAVERNER 56ᵛ The
thyng that is apparant, and whiche noman
denyeth: we cal as cleare as the sonne. **1557**
EDGEWORTH *Serm.* 2H1ᵛ (bright). **1562** J.
WIGAND *De Neutralibus* D3ᵛ It is clearer than the
sunne lyght at none dayes, that a man maye not
. . . bee a Neutre. **1574** W. FULKE *Serm. at
Hampton Court* G1ᵛ (Sunne at noone dayes).
1599 SHAKES. *Hen. V* I. ii. 86 So that, as clear as
is the summer's sun, King Pepin's title. **1639**
CLARKE 252 (the Sunne at noone). **1688** BUNYAN
Jerusalem Sinner Saved, Wks. i. 70 The text is as
clear as the sun. **1813** BARRETT *Heroine* ed.
Raleigh 116.

Clear, *see also* Conscience fears not . . . (A c.).

Cleave the pin, To.   (P 336)

[= in archery, to hit the pin in the centre of the
white of the butts.] *c.* **1450** *Coventry Myst.*
Shaks. Soc. 138 Now, be myn trowthe, ȝe hytte
the pynne. **1586** MARLOWE *1 Tamburl.* II. iv 8
For kings are clouts that every man shoots at,
Our crown the pin that thousands seek to cleave.
1594–5 SHAKES. *L.L.L.* IV. i. 129 Then will she
get the upshoot by cleaving the pin. *c.* **1595**
Id. R.J. II. iv. 15 The very pin of his heart
cleft with the blind bow-boy's butt-shaft.

**Cleave to the crown though it hang on a
bush.**

1851 STRICKLAND *Lives of Q. of Eng.* II. 419 The
crown [of Richard III] was hidden by a soldier in
a hawthorn-bush, but was soon found. . . . To the
same circumstance may be referred the loyal
proverb of—'Cleave to the crown though it hang
on a bush'.

**Cleave (Hang, Hold) together like
burrs, They.**   (B 723)

c. **1330** *Arth. & Merl.* 8290 Togider thei cleued
. . . So with other doth the burre. [*c.* **1515**]
c. **1530** BARCLAY *Eclog.* II. l. 873. Together they
cleaue more fast then do burres. **1546** HEYWOOD
II. v. H4 They cleaue togither like burs; that
waie I shall Pike out no more, than out of the
stone wall. **1639** CLARKE 63 (hold). **1678** RAY
250 (hang). **1721** ARBUTHNOT *John Bull* (1727)
59 When a fellow stuck like a bur, that there was
no shaking him off.

**Clemency is cruelty, and cruelty clem-
ency, Sometimes.**

1853 TRENCH ii. 43 Catherine de Médicis . . .
urged on him . . . a proverb, . . . one of the most
convenient maxims for tyrants that was ever
framed: . . .

Clemmed, *see* Smithwick (You been like) either
c. or borsten.

**Clent,[1] The people of | are all Hills,
Waldrons, or devils.**

1894 NORTHALL *Folk-phrases* E.D.S. 24 . . .
Worc. . . . Before 1600, 30 entries of Hills, 18 of
Waldron, . . . are registered in the parish books.

Afterwards the Hills and Waldrons multiplied
exceedingly. [¹ Clent Hills, near Birmingham.]

Clergy, *see* Kittle shooting at c.; Ounce of
discretion worth a pound of c.; Three classes of
c., Nimrods. . . .

Clergymen's sons always turn out badly.

1886 E. J. HARDY *How to be Happy* ch. 19 . . .
Because the children are surfeited with severe
religion, *not* with the true religion of Christ.
1922 DEAN INGE *Outspoken Ess.* 2nd Ser. 264 An
Eton boy . . . when asked why the sons of Eli
turned out badly, replied 'The sons of clergymen
always turn out badly'.

Clerk makes the justice, It is the.
                                              (C 408)

1660 A. BROME *Poems* 'The Leveller' 'Tis we
commons make the lords, and. . . . **1678** RAY
114. *a.* **1697** J. AUBREY *Country Revell* (A.
Powell, *Aubrey*, 291).

Clerk of the weather, The.

1841 F. CHAMIER *Tom Bowl.* ch. 41 The wind
died away, and . . . Lanyard, who longed for the
action . . . cursed the clerk of the weather.

**Clerks, The greatest | are not the wisest
men.**   (C 409)

[Med. L. *Magis magni clerici non sunt magis
sapientes.* The greatest scholars are not the
wisest men. RABELAIS I. xxxix.] *c.* **1386** CHAUCER
Reeve's T. l. 4054 The gretteste clerkes ben
noght wisest men, As whilom to the wolf thus
spake the mare.¹ **1481** CAXTON *Reynard* xxvii
(Arb.) 63 It is true that I long syth haue redde
and herde that the best clerkes ben not the wysest
men. *a.* **1603** Q. ELIZABETH in CREIGHTON *Q.
Eliz.* (1896) 284 When the Bishop of St. Davids
preached . . . on . . . 'Lord teach us to number
our days . . .', Elizabeth . . . told him that 'he
might have kept his arithmetic for himself: but I
see that . . .'. **1655** FULLER *Ch. Hist.* III. i (1868)
I. 331 Henry Beauclerc . . . crossed the common
proverb, . . .; being one of the most profound
scholars and most politic princes in his generation.
[¹ 'The fable of the Wolf and the Mare is found in
the Latin Esopean collections.' WRIGHT.]

Clerk(s), *see also* Clock goes as pleases c.; Devil
be vicar, (If), you will be c.; Parish c.; Priest
(Such as the), such c.; St. Nicholas' c.; Schools
make subtle c.

**Cleveland in the clay, bring in two soles
and carry one away.**   (C 410)

1670 RAY 257 . . . Cleveland is that part of Yorkshire, which borders upon the bishoprick of
Durham, where the ways in winter time are very
foul and deep.

Cleveland, *see also* Roseberry Topping.

Clever, *see* Too c. by half.

Clew, *see* Labyrinth (In) take c.; Wimple in
lawyer's c.

Climate(s), *see* Travellers change c.

Climb the ladder must begin at the bottom, He who would.

1710 PALMER 1 He that wou'd tread a Ladder true must begin at the first step. **1756** J. WESLEY *Lett.* iii. 364 Am I then to step first on the highest round of the ladder? **1821** SCOTT *Kenilw.* ch. 7 I was the lowest of the four in rank—but what then?—he that climbs a ladder must begin at the first round.

Climb(s, ed), see also Ass c. a ladder (When), may find wisdom in women; Never c. never fell.

Climbers, see Hasty c. have sudden falls.

Clink, see Kiss the c.

Clip the wings of, To.   (w 498)
1578 *Courtly Controv.* P2 You clipped his [Love's] wings, so that nauer since it could flye but about you. **1581** MERBURY *Brief Discourse* H. Unton to Reader 4ᵛ Seeke to spurre others to treade these his good steppes: then by your discommendation to clippe their winges, which else of them selues would make the like flight. **1590** MARLOWE *Mass. Paris* III. ii Away to prison with him! I'll clip his wings. **1591** ARIOSTO *Orl. Fur.* Harington XXXIII. 37 Now clipped are their wings. **1592** NASHE *Piers Penniless* i. 179. **1596** *Estate of Eng. Fugitives* 24 He began to suspect his greatnes, & wold haue clipt his wings. **1657** W. LONDON *Cat. of most vendible Books* D1ᵛ To clip the Wings of Industry. **1697** DRYDEN *Virg. Georg.* IV. 161 To clip the Wings Of their high-flying Arbitrary Kings. **1874** BLACKIE *Self-cult.* 10,To clip the wings of our conceit.

Clips, see also King's English (He c.).

Cloak for his knavery, He has a.
                                             (c 419)
1566 J. BARTHLET *Pedegrew of Popish Heretiques* 8 These two persons . . . alwayes seeking to haue a cloke for their follie, and manifest errors. **1578** G. WHETSTONE 2 *Promos & Cassandra* III. iii K1 To deuise a cloke to hyde a knaue? *c.* **1633** CLAVELL & MARMION *Soddered Citizen* I. iii. Mee thinkes I haue, a Cloake for my knavery. **1678** RAY 235.

Cloak for the rain, It is good to have a.
                                             (c 417)
c. **1520** SKELTON *Magnif.* in Wks. (Dyce) I. 225 Ye, for your wyt is cloked for the rayne. **1545** TAVERNER H3ᵛ A cloke for the rayne. . . . As if a man beynge taken in the house of a fayre woman whiche hath no good name, fayneth that he came thyther to haue a shyrte made of her, or for other affayres. This is a clooke for the rayne. **1548** HALL 701. **1599** PORTER *Angry Wom. Abingd.* Mal. Soc., 2411 Tis good to haue a cloake for the raine, a bad shift is better then none at all. **1611** DAVIES no. 85 A Queane hath euer a Cloke for the rayne.

Cloak to make when it begins to rain, Have not thy.   (c 418)
a. **1595** *Edw. III* III. ii. 20–4. **1639** CLARKE 267 Hee that provides not a cloak before the raine,

may chance to be wet to his cost. **1372** FULLER no. 1808.

Cloak, see also Although the sun shine leave not thy c.; Hector's c.; Old c. makes new jerkin; Plymouth c.; Pride may lurk under threadbare c.

Clock goes as it pleases the clerk, The.
                                             (c 425)
1612 T. ADAMS *The Gallant's Burden* (1616 ed. 47) Take heed you stay not too long; the Diuell is a false Sexton, and sets the Clocke too slow, that the Night comes ere wee be aware. **1678** RAY 114. **1732** FULLER no. 4451.

Clock(s), see also Agree like the c. of London; Belly is the truest c.; Colne c. always at one; Put back the c.

Clog(s), see Jack-an-Ape be merry; Nought is to wed with (Where), wise men flee the c.; Twice c., once boots.

Cloister, see Go old to the court, young to c.; Monk out of c.

Close as cockles, As.   (c 499)
1601 JONSON *Cynthia's Revels* V. iv. 534 Shee kisses as close as a cockle. **1613** SHAKES.? & FLETCHER *Two Noble Kinsmen* IV. i. 13 Close as a cockle. **1632** RANDOLPH *The Jealous Lovers* II. xii These eyes are witnesse that descried 'um kissing Closer then cockles.

Close (hard) as oak, As.   (o 1)
1552 HULOET P2ᵛ (Hard). **1604** SHAKES. *O.* III. iii. 214 To seal her father's eyes up close as oak. **1763** COLMAN *Deuce is in Him* II. I am close as oak, an absolute freemason for secresy.

Close mouth catches no flies, A (Into a shut mouth flies fly not).   (M 1247)
1599 MINSHEU *Span. Gram.* 83 In a closed vp mouth a flie cannot get in. **1617** MORYSON *Itin.* (1907–8) III. 400 I must remember the traveller of two good Italian proverbs: *In bocca serrata mai non entrò mosca.* Keep close lips and never fear, Any flies should enter there. **1623** CAMDEN 265. **1640** HERBERT no. 219. **1659** FULLER *Appeal Inj. Innoc.* (1840) 302 The Spanish proverb . . . is necessary in dangerous . . . times: 'where the mouth is shut, no fly doth enter'. **1700** DRYDEN *Fables, Cock & Fox* Not flattering lies shall soothe me more to sing with winking eyes, And open mouth, for fear of catching flies. **1897** 'H. S. MERRIMAN' *In Kedar's T.* ch. 23 Concha, remembering . . . that no flies enter a shut mouth, was silent.

Close(ly), see also Lives safely that lives c.; Lives well that well has lurked (that lives c.); Thoughts c. and countenance loose (Keep).

Closet, see Skeleton in c.

Cloth, see Ale is meat, drink, and c., (Good); Bad c. that take no colour; Best c. may have moth in it; Cut out of whole c., (To); Northern c., shrunk in the wetting, (Like); Self-edge makes show of c.

Cloth-market, He is in the.   (c 438)

1678 RAY 235 . . . i.e. in bed.   **1738** SWIFT Dial. I. E.L. 261 I hope your early rising will do you no harm. I find you are but just come out of the cloth-market.

Clothe thee in war: arm thee in peace.   (w 40)

1640 HERBERT no. 386.

Clothe thee warm, eat little, drink enough, and thou shalt live.   (L 343)

1573 SANFORD 110ᵛ.   **1578** FLORIO First F. 34. **1629** Bk. Mer. Rid. Prov. no. 129.

Clothes, *see* Better blue c. (He is in his); Craft must have c.; Critics like brushers of noblemen's c.; Easter let your c. be new; God sends cold after c.; Mend your c. and you may hold out; Put off his c. before goes to bed (He will not); Truth has good face but bad c.; Wear c. (Ever since we), we know not one another.

Cloud, To be under a.   (c 441)

[= in trouble; out of favour; under a slur.]   *c.* **1500** *Song Lady Bessy* Percy Soc. 79 Then came he under a clowde That some tyme in England was full hee.   **1662** FULLER Norfolk 251 When he [Coke] was under a cloud at Court, and ousted of his Judge's place, the lands . . . were . . . begged by a Peer.   **1705** STRYPE *Life of Cheke* (1821) vi. § 1. 138 Thus died Cheke in a cloud; and his name, once most honoured, much eclipsed by his infirmity.

Cloud has a silver lining, Every.   (c 439)

1634 MILTON *Comus* 221 Was I deceived, or did a sable cloud Turn forth her silver lining on the night?   **1871** SMILES *Charac.* viii (1876) 218 While we see the cloud, let us not shut our eyes to the silver lining.   **1885** GILBERT *Mikado* II. Orig. Plays Ser. III. (1895) 198 Don't let's be downhearted! There's a silver lining to every cloud.

Clouds are upon the hills, When the | they'll come down by the mills.   (c 445)

1678 RAY 49.

Clouds bring not rain, All.   (c 443)

1584 WITHALS A4 Non stillant omnes quas cernis in aëre nubes, All the clowdes which thou seast in the ayre do not yeeld rayne.   **1591–2** SHAKES. *3 Hen. VI* V. iii. 13 Every cloud engenders not a storm.   **1660** TORRIANO *It. Prov.* 208, no. 33.

Clouds look as if scratched by a hen, If | get ready to reef your topsails then.

1883 ROPER 12.   **1893** INWARDS 92.

Clouds, To speak in the.   (c 444)

1560 *Cont. betwixt Churchyard & Camell* C1 Your boasts and braggs . . . Haue doone no harme thogh Robyn Hood, spake with you in a cloud.   **1581** C.T. *Short Inventory* A6ᵛ If by chance they wright or speake, it is alwayes in clowds, in libel manner, and to the defamation, and discredite of some one . . . man.   **1587** J. BRIDGES *Defence* 101 Raysing of mystes, dazeling of eyes, walking in cloudes.   **1587** T. HUGHES *et al. Misf. of Arthur* IV. ii. 29 You speake in cloudes, and cast perplexed wordes.   **1671** CLARKE *Phras. Puer.* 319 He speaks i'th clouds, few can understand him.

Cloud(s), *see also* After black c. clear weather; Day so clear; Pries into every c. (He that); Red c. in the east.

Cloudy mornings turn to clear afternoons (evenings).   (M 1178)

[BK. OF TOBIT iii. 22: post tempestatem tranquillitatem facis.]   *c.* **1200** *Ancrene Riwle* (Morton) 376 Louerd, þet makest stille after storme.   *c.* **1374** CHAUCER *Troilus* Bk. 3, l. 1060 For I have seyn of a ful misty morwe Folowen ful ofte a myrie someris day.   **1539** VIVES *Introd. to Wisdom* E7ᵛ Mery euentides do often times folowe carefull mornynges.   **1546** HEYWOOD II. ix. L3 Thus cloudy mornyngs turne to clere after noones.   *c.* **1595** *Edmond Ironside* l. 1060 A lowringe morninge proves a fayer daye.   **1655** FULLER *Ch. Hist.* I. iv. par. 1 (1868) I. 35 Dark . . . was the morning of this century, which afterward cleared up to be a fair day.   **1678** RAY 48 I'th' old o'th' moon A cloudy morning bodes a fair afternoon.   **1721** KELLY 48 A misty Morning may prove a good Day.   **1732** FULLER no. 327 (misty).   **1841** CHAMIER *Tom Bowl.* ch. 2 Though it's cloudy in the morning, the sun may shine bright enough at noon.

Clout a man will not wipe his nose on, It is a foul.

1551 CRANMER *Answer to Gardiner* 17 It is a foule cloute that you wold refuse to wype your nose withall.

Clouts, A husband (lord, etc.) of.   (w 387)

[1486–1500] *c.* **1530** MEDWALL *Nature* l. 194 (lorde).   [1525–40] **1557** *Merry Dial.* (husband).   **1542** UDALL 106 (wiues).   **1582** *Love and Fortune* C3 I were as good serue a maister of clowtes.   [1597] **1599** CHAPMAN *Hum. Day's Mirth* sc. 7, l. 6 A king of clouts.   *a.* **1603** SHAKES. First Quarto III. iv. 102 To leaue him that bare a Monarkes minde, For a king of clowts, of very shreads.

Clout(ed), *see also* Alike every day makes c. on Sunday; Better a c. than a hole; Cast ne'er a c. till May be out; Cobble and c.; Cow is in the c. (When), she's soon out; Craft lies in c. shoes; Hertfordshire c. shoon; Money is welcome though in dirty c.; Pale as a c.

Cloven (hoof) foot, To show the.

[= to manifest Satanic agency or temptation.]
1594 GREENE *Looking Glass for London* Gros.
xiv. 83 Hath neuer a clouen foote: a diuell,
quoth he. **1604** SHAKES. *O.* V. ii. 289 I look
down towards his feet: but that's a fable. **1639**
The Sophister F1 They say a man may know the
Divell by his cloven Foote. **1662** BUTLER
Hudibras I. i. 184 Whether the serpent, at the fall,
Had cloven feet or none at all. **1822** SCOTT *Nigel*
ch. 14 Pleasant communings we had . . . until
she showed the cloven foot, beginning to confer
with me about some wench. **1822** GALT *Provost*
ch. 3 The cloven hoof of self-interest was . . . to
be seen aneath the robe of public principle.
1910 *Spectator* 19 Nov. 848 Only when [St.
Bernard] speaks of household discipline does the
in cloven hoof of monastic tyranny show.

Cloven, *see also* Devil is known by his claws (c.
feet, horns).

Clover, To live (*or* be) in.

1699 A. BOYER *Compleat French Master* 142 Do
you think to live in Clover thus all your life-
time? **1710** *Brit. Apollo* II. No. 105. 3/1 I liv'd
in Clover. **1813** RAY 57 He's in clover. **1856**
R. VAUGHAN *Mystics* (1860) II. VIII. ix. 102 He
has been sometimes in clover as a travelling
tutor, sometimes he has . . . fared hard. **1864–5**
DICKENS *Our Mut. F.* Bk. I, ch. 15 A man with
coals and candles and a pound a week might be
in clover here.

Clown(s), *see* Give a c. your finger; Middlesex c.

Club law.

1599–1600 [G. RUGGLE?] *Club Law* [title]. **1624**
BURTON *Anat. Mel.* 3.4.1.5,3Z3 Clubbe law, fire
and sword for Hereticks. **1691** SEWEL 104 All
things are carried by Club-law.

Clubs are trumps.   (C 453)

[= physical force is to decide the matter.] **1588**
GREENE *Pandosto* (1843) 27 Taking up a cudgel
. . . sware solemnly that she would make clubs
trump if hee brought any bastard brat within her
dores. **1594** *Selimus* l. 1884. **1607** *Widow of
Watl. St.* III. i Aye, I knew by their shuffling,
clubs would be trump.

Clubs, *see also* Hertfordshire c.

Clude, *see* Escape C. and be drowned in Conway.

Coach and four (six) may be driven through any Act of Parliament, A.
(C 457)

a. **1686** SIR STEPHEN RICE in MACAULAY *Hist. Eng.*
III. xii (1898) 426 What . . . the law . . . gave
them, they could easily infer from a saying which,
before he became a Judge, was often in his
mouth, 'I will drive', he used to say, 'a coach and
six through the Act of Settlement'. **1817** EDGE-
WORTH *Ormond* ch. 18 King Corny . . . has
ended . . . by being his own lawyer; he has drawn
his will so that any lawyer could drive a coach
and six through it. **1962** 9 Feb. *Times* Coach
and four driven through Trades Disputes Act.

Coaches won't run over him, The.

1813 RAY 186 . . . i.e. He is in jail.

Coach(es), *see also* Fifth wheel to c.; Horses (As
good) draw in carts as in c.

Coals of fire on the head, To heap, (cast, gather).
(C 468)

[Rom. xii. 20: to produce remorse by requiting
evil with good.] **1377** LANGLAND *P. Pl.* B. xiii.
144 To louye . . . þine enemye in al wyse euene
forth with þi-selue, Cast coles on his hed. *c.*
1605 *Ratsey's Ghost* E4ᵛ You may heape more
coales vpon your head, then you can wel tell
how to put off. **1846** DICKENS *Let.* to Landor
22 Nov. I forgive you your reviling of me:
there's a shovelful of live coals for your head.
1874 CARLYLE *Let.* to John Carlyle '[Disraeli] . . .
I almost never spoke of without contempt . . .
and . . . here he comes with a pan of hot coals
for my guilty head'.

Coal(s), *see also* Carry c.; Carry c. to Newcastle;
Cold (Let them that be) blow at c.; Cold c. to
blow at; Cuckold and conceals it, (Who is a)
carries c. in bosom; Glowing c. sparkle; Haul
over the c.; Hot as c.; Punch c., cut candle,
neither good housewife; Treasure consisted of c.

Coast is clear, The.   (C 469)

1530 PALSGRAVE 486b The kynge intendeth to go
to Calays, but we muste first clere the costes.
[*a.* **1525**] *c.* **1545** SKELTON *Colyn Cloute* l. 1259
Wks. i. 359 Tyll the cost be clere. *c.* **1566** *The
Bugbears* V. v. 4 Are the Costes clere abowte?
1567 HARMAN *Caveat* (ed. Furnivall) 30 Where
these rufflares might well beholde the coaste
about them cleare. **1590** LODGE *Rosalynde* Wks.
(1883) I. 52 Seeing the coast cleare, . . . he sate
him downe . . . and there feasted. **1592–4**
SHAKES. *1 Hen. VI* I. iii. 88 See the coast clear'd,
and then we will depart. **1612–15** BP. HALL
Contempl. I. vi (1825) II. 192 Herod is now sent
home. The coast is clear for the return of that
holy family. **1872** C. READE *Wand. Heir* ch. 4
The coast was no sooner clear than Philip ran
out and invited James into his office.

Coat, He who has but one | cannot lend it.

1706 STEVENS s.v. Sayo.

Coat is on one's back, As sure as the.
(C 470)

1575 GASCOIGNE *Glass Govt.* IV. iii. I will be as
true to thee as thy coate is to thy backe. **1579**
G. HARVEY *Letter-Bk.* 60 Am not I as sure as of
the shirte or gowne on my backe to heare and
putt up these . . . odious speeches. **1601** A.
DENT *Plain Man's Pathway* 128 As sure as the
coate of our backe. **1607** *Dobson's Dry Bobs*
C3 Predestinate vnto him before either coat or
shert. **1639** CLARKE 209 (coats on your back).
1670 RAY 208 [as 1639].

Coat that makes the gentleman, It is not the gay.
(C 474)

1615 W. GODDARD *Nest of Wasps* no. 57 Nowe

tis cloathes the gentleman doth make. **1616**
WITHALS 581. **1639** CLARKE 124. **1670** RAY 11.
1732 FULLER no. 3002 It is not the fine Coat,
that makes the fine Gentleman.

Coat, Under a ragged_(threadbare) | lies wisdom. (C 476)

1581 GUAZZO i. 162 Oft times under a clownishe
coate is hidden a noble and lively understanding.
1616 DRAXE no. 1687 Many times wisedome
lieth vnder a threed-bare cloth. **1623** WOD-
ROEPHE 276 Often under a poore Wead, Is
found a Man that is well-bred. **1666** TORRIANO
It. Prov. 311, no. 4 Under greasie clothes, are
oft found rare virtues.

Coat, *see also* Blue c. without a badge; Cut your
c. according to cloth; Honour without maintenance; Jacket (c.), (To baste); Learn to shape
Idle a c.; Lost the large c. for the hood; Near is
my c. but nearer my skin; Refer my c. and lose a
sleeve; Shape a c. for the moon; Shape c. for
them, but not their weird; Turn one's c.

Cob a hat and pair of shoes, Give | and he'll last for ever.

1869 HAZLITT 142 ... *S. Devon.* Provide a stone
foundation and a slate coping for a cob (*mud*)
wall.—SHELLY.

Cob's pound, *see* Lob's pound.

Cobble and clout, They that can | shall have work when others go without. (W 849)

1670 RAY 72. **1732** FULLER no. 6454.

Cobbler deals with all [awl], The. (C 479)

1626 BRETON *Soothing* B3ᵛ. **1639** CLARKE 32.

Cobbler go beyond his last, Let not the. (C 480)

[PLINY THE ELDER *Nat. Hist.* 35. 36 (10) *Ne supra
crepidam iudicaret (sutor).*] **1539** TAVERNER f. 17
Let not the shoemaker go beyond hys shoe.
1579 LYLY *Euph.* i. 180 The Shomaker must not
go aboue his latchet, nor the hedger meddle
with anye thing but his bill. *c.* **1595** SHAKES.
R.J. I. ii. 40 It is written that the shoemaker
should meddle with his yard, and the tailor with
his last. **1605** T. HEYWOOD *If you know not me*
Wks. (1874) I. 210 Shoomaker, you goe a little
beyond your last. **1608** J. DAY *Law Tricks* A2
If the Cobler wold look no further then the shoe
latchet, we should not haue so many corrupt
translations. **1692–4** L'ESTRANGE *Aesop's Fab.*
ccxxv (1708) 245 The Cobler is not to go beyond
his last. **1721** KELLY 242 ... This is from the
Latin, Ne sutor ultra [Erasmus is responsible for
the bad *ultra*] *crepidam.* Taken from the famous
Story of *Apelles,* who could not bear that the
Cobler should correct any part of his Picture
beyond the Slipper. **1875** JOWETT *Plato* (ed. 2)
III. 53 Great evil may arise from the cobbler
leaving his last and turning into ... a legislator.
1908 LECKY *Hist. & Pol. Ess.* 21 In this, as in
most other cases, the proverb was a wise one
which bids the cobbler stick to his last.

Cobbler's law; he that takes money must pay the shot. (C 481)

1678 RAY 90.

Cobblers and tinkers are the best ale-drinkers. (C 482)

1659 HOWELL *Eng. Prov.* 17a. **1670** RAY 5.
1732 FULLER no. 6229.

Cobbler(s), *see also* Higher the plum-tree ...
richer the c., blacker his thumb; Mock not a c.

Cock a hoop (the cock on the hoop), To set (be). (C 493)

[app. to turn on the tap and let the liquor flow;
hence, to drink without stint. By extension: to
become reckless, to set all by the ears. Later, to
be in a state of elation.] **1519** HORMAN *Vulgaria*
(James) 436 He setteth al thyngs at cocke in the
hope. **1529** MORE *Comf. agst. Trib.* II. Wks.
1177/2 They ... set them downe and dryncke
well for our sauiours sake, sette cocke a hoope,
and fyll in all the cuppes at ones, and then lette
Chrystes passion paye for all the scotte. **1538**
BALE *Three Lawes* 1806 Cheare now maye I
make & set cocke on the houpe. Fyll in all the
pottes, and byd me welcome hostesse. **1565**
OSORIUS *Pearl of Princes* tr. Shacklock 46ᵛ To set
cocke on hoope, and crye care away. *c.* **1595**
SHAKES. *R.J.* I. v. 78 You 'll make a mutiny among
my guests! You will set cock-a-hoop. **1621**
MOLLE *Camerar. Liv. Libr.* III. i. 147 Resolued ...
to set cock in hoope, and in guzling and good
cheere spent all that was left. **1663** BUTLER
Hudibras I. iii. 14 Hudibras ... having routed
the whole Troop, With Victory was Cock-a-
hoop. **1719** *Cordial Low Spirits* 162 The church
was very cock-a-hoop, and held up its head and
crow'd. **1817** EDGEWORTH *Love & L.* ii. i. To
make Catty cockahoop, I told her that, &c.
1834 GREVILLE *Men. Geo. IV* (1875) III. xxiii. 104
The Tories have been mighty cock-a-hoop.

Cock-and-bull story, A. (S 910)

1608 DAY *Law Trickes* IV. ii. What a tale of a
cock and a bull he tolde my father. **1621**
BURTON *Anat. Mel.* II. ii. IV. (1651) 274 Some
mens whole delight is ... to talk of a Cock and
Bull over a pot. **1681** *Trial S. Colledge* 36 You
run out in a story of a Cock and a Bull, and I
know not what. **1796** BURNET *Mem. Metastasio*
II. 77 Not to tire you with the repetition of all
the cock and bull stories which I have formerly
told you, &c. **1863** KINGSLEY *Water Bab.* ch. 6
They invented a cock-and-bull story, which ...
I never told them.

Cock crows on going to bed, If the | he's sure to rise with a watery head.

1584 R. SCOT *Disc. Witchcraft* XI. 19 When the
cocke crow manie times together, a man may
ghesse that raine will followe shortlie. **1846**
DENHAM 18 ... i.e. it will be rain next morning.

Cock is bold (crouse) on his own dung-hill (midden), A. (C 486)

[SENECA *De Morte Claudii: Gallus in sterquilinio
suo plurimum potest.* The cock is master on his

own dunghill.] *c.* 1023 EGBERT VON LÜTTICH
Fecunda Ratis I. l. 239 Confidens animi canis
est in stercore noto. *c.* 1200 *Ancrene Riwle*
(Morton) 140 As me seith: Thet coc is kene on
his owune mixenne. 1387 TREVISA in HIGDEN's
Polychron. vii. 5 As Seneca seiþ, a cock is most
myzty on his dongehille. *c.* 1430 LYDGATE *Pilgr.
Life of Man.* l. 10048 How that every wyht ys
bold upon hys owne (erly and late) at the dongel
at hys gate [= DEGUILEVILLE, *Pèlerinage* ed.
Stürzinger l. 6351: *Chascun est fort sur son
fumier et en sa terre se fait fier.*] 1546 HEYWOOD
I. xi. D2 But he was at home there, he myght
speake his will. Euery cocke is proude on his
owne dunghill. 1579 SPENSER *Shep. Cal.* Sept.
46 As cocke on his dunghill crowing cranck.
1591 STEPNEY L3ᵛ (is bragge). *c.* 1600 DAY
Blind Beggar II Thou durst not thus in scorn to
old Strowd prate, But cock on thine own hill,
thus near thy Gate. 1641 FERGUSSON no. 75 A
cock is crouse in his own midding. 1771
SMOLLETT *Humph. Clink.* 13 July Wks. (1871)
534 Insolence . . . akin to the arrogance of the
village cock, who never crows but upon his own
dunghill.

Cock moult before the hen, If the | we shall have weather thick and thin: but if the hen moult before the cock, we shall have weather hard as a block.

(C 488)

1656–91 J. AUBREY *Nat. Hist. Wilts* (1847) 16.
1670 RAY 43.

Cock of hay, The first | frights the cuckoo away.

1846 DENHAM 52.

Cock of the walk.

1688 HOLME *Armoury* II. 251/2 The Cocks Walk
is the place where he is bred, which usually is a
place that no other Cock comes to. 1823 GROSE
Dict. Vulg. T. (Egan) Cock, or Chief Cock of the
Walk. The leading man in any Society or body;
the best boxer in a village or district.

Cock won't fight, That.

1822 SCOTT *Pirate* ch. 34. 1836 DAVID CROCKETT
Exploits 99. The captain . . . went ashore in the
hope of persuading them to refund — but, . . .
1850 THACKERAY *Pendennis* ch. 67 'Tell that to the
marines, Major', replied the valet, 'that cock
won't fight with me'. 1888 'R. BOLDREWOOD'
Robbery under Arms ch. 1 My lawyer . . . argued
that . . . no proof had been brought . . . that I had
wilfully killed any one . . . . But that cock wouldn't
fight. I was found guilty . . . and sentenced to
death. 1906 W. DE MORGAN *Jos. Vance* ch. 2 I
heard Father say that cock wouldn't fight.

Cock's spur, *see* Chance in the c.

Cock(s) (*noun*), *see also* Barley-corn better than
diamond to c.; Eats his c. alone; Farm full must
keep old c.; Fighting c., (Live like); Forward c.
that crows in shell; Full flock . . . young c.; Hen
goes to c., (When); Jump at it like c. at gooseberry; Knows how to carry dead c. home; Old c.
crows, so crows young; Red c. (The); Servant

and a c. must be kept but a year; Teague's c.,
that fought one another; True as that . . . c.
rocked cradle; Young c. love no coops.

Cock (*verb*), *see* Time to c. your hay and corn.

Cocker, According to.

[= exact, correct: Edw. Cocker (1631–75) published his *Compleat Arithmetician* before 1669.]
1764 A. MURPHY *Apprentice* I. i. I have *Cocker's*
Arithmetic below stairs . . . I'll . . . get it for him.
1817 17 Sept. BYRON *Lett.* Prothero iv. 170
Making six hundred and thirty pounds . . .
according to my Cocker. 1854 DICKENS in
Forster *Life* Bk. 7, ch. 1, as suggested title for
Hard Times.

Cockers his child, He that | provides for his enemy.

(C 308)

1640 HERBERT no. 789.

Cockle and corn grow in the same field.

(C 497)

[1600] 1659 DAY & CHETTLE *Blind Beggar* G2ᵛ I
ha seen Wheat and Barley grow amongst cockell
and darnell, and many an honest man keep
Knaves company. 1602 *Poet. Rhap.* 129, I. 187
The self same ground both corne and cockle
breeds. 1685 DRYDEN *Thren. Aug.* l. 351, 78
Our isle indeed, too fruitful was before; But all
uncultivated lay . . . With rank Geneva Weeds
run o'er, And cockle, at the best, amidst the corn
it bore.

Cockle(s), *see also* Close as c.; Corn is some c.
(In much); Sowed c. reaped no corn.

Cockles of the heart, To warm (rejoice) the.

(C 498)

1671 EACHARD *Observ. Answ. Enquiry* (1685) 26
This Contrivance of his did inwardly . . . rejoice
the Cockles of his heart. 1747 WARBURTON on
Hamlet III. ii. 136 The common people say: You
rejoice the cockles of my heart, for muscles of
my heart; an unlucky mistake of one shell fish for
another. 1792 SCOTT *Let.* 30 Sept. in LOCKHART
Life An expedition . . . which would have de-
lighted the very cockles of your heart. 1834
MARRYAT *Jacob Faith.* ch. 12 There's a glass of
grog for you. . . . See if that don't warm the
cockles of your old heart. 1858 DARWIN in *Life
& Lett.* (1888) II. 112 I have just had the inner-
most cockles of my heart rejoiced by a letter
from Lyell. 1910 *Brit. Wkly.* 27 Oct. Poor
mothers who gave their babies gin . . . 'to warm
the cockles of their hearts'.

Cockloft is unfurnished, His.   (C 500)

1621 J. HOWELL *Lett.* 2 Feb. (1903) I. 102 'Sir',
said Bacon, 'Tall men are like high houses of
four or five storys, wherein commonly the uppermost room is worst furnished.' 1662 FULLER
Westminster 236 Edward the First. . . was very
high in stature. And though oftimes such . . . are
observed to have little in their cock-loft, yet was
he a most judicious man. 1663 BUTLER *Hud.* I.
i. 162 Such as take lodgings in a head That's to
be let unfurnished. 1678 RAY 235 . . . *i.e.* He
wants brains. 1873 22 Oct. KILVERT *Diary* ii.

386 To have attics to let unfurnished. **1896** F.
LOCKER-LAMPSON *My Confid.* (Nelson) 56 Tall
men are like tall houses—often poorly furnished
on the top story.

Cockney, *see* Castle of Bungay; London c.

Cockpit, *see* Netherlands are c. of Christendom.

Codpiece, *see* Hold or cut c.; Knit . . . my cat a c.

Coelum non animum mutant, see Travellers
change climates, etc.

Coffin, *see* Mahomet's c.; Nail into c. (Drive).

Coggeshall, *see* Jeering C.

Coil, To keep a.   (C 505)

1566 ERASMUS *Diversoria* tr. E.H. ed. de Vocht
l. 421 They keepe like a coile with their singinge,
theire chatting, their hoopinge and hallowinge,
. . . theire bounsinge, . . . **1598–9** SHAKES. *M.A.*
V. ii. 82 Yonder's old coil at home. **1613** *Id.*
T.N.K. II. iv. 18 What a coil he keeps. **1659**
HOWELL *Fr. Prov.* 18 To keep a foul horrible
coyl.

Coin is not common, Where | commons[1] must be scant. *Cf.* Wine is not common.   (C 508)

1546 HEYWOOD II. i. F2. **1639** CLARKE 113.
[1 provisions.]

Coin, *see also* Much c. much care; Pay one in
own c.

Colchester, *see* Weavers' beef of C.

Cold April the barn will fill, A.

1659 HOWELL *Span. Prov.* 21 A cold April, much
bread, and little wine. **1706** STEVENS s.v. *Abril*
A cold April, much Corn and little Wine. *Ibid.*,
A cold April fills the Granary, or Barn; and a
wet one the Granary, and the Field. **1732** FULLER
no. 6356.

Cold as a key.   (K 23)

c. **1390** GOWER *Conf. Amantis* VI. 244 Was nevere
Keie Ne posen ys upon the wal More inly cold.
1501 DOUGLAS *Pal. Honour* sig. D ii st. 61 With
quakand voce and hart cald as a key. **1546**
HEYWOOD II. i. F3ᵛ Hotte as a toste, it grew cold as
a kaie. **1593** SHAKES. *Rich. III* I. i. 5 Poor key-
cold figure of a holy king! **1594** *Id. Lucr.*
l. 1774 And then in key-cold Lucrece' bleeding
stream He falls. **15—** R. PARSONS (cited 1581
W. Fulke, *Brief Confutⁿ of Popish Disc.* 52) If
wee . . . shalbe yet kea cold in our maister his
seruice.

Cold (pale) as clay.   (C 406)

c. **1600** *Death's Summons* l. 11 in *Roxb. Bal.* IV. 27
His face was pale as any clay. **1602** [T. HEY-
WOOD?] *How a Man may Choose* ix. 65 She is
this day as cold as clay. *c.* **1680** *Careful Wife's
Counsel* l. 47 in *Roxb. Bal.* iii. 480 Will find the
world as cold as clay.

Cold as ice.   (I 2)

1481 CAXTON *Reynard* ed. Arb. 37 As colde as
Ise. *c.* **1600** *Charlemagne* l. 1804 Thys goulde
has made my Chollor as colde as snowe watter.
1672 WALKER 23, no. 41.

Cold, Let them that be | blow at the coal.   (C 460)

c. **1380** *Sir Ferumbras* in *Engl. Charlemagne
Romances* E.E.T.S. I, l. 2230 þan saide Lucafere.
'We haue a game in this contray: to blowen atte
glede.' **1546** HEYWOOD I. x. Dᵛ Aunt, leat
theim that be a colde blowe at the cole. **1670**
RAY 72 Let him that is cold blow the coal. **1721**
KELLY 235 . . . Let them drudge about Business,
that want it, and expect Benefit by it.

Cold broth hot again, that loved I never; old love renewed again, that loved I ever.

1721 KELLY 79. **1732** FULLER no. 6429.

Cold coal to blow at, A.   (C 459)

a. **1628** CARMICHAELL no. 35 A cald cole to blaw
at. **1641** FERGUSSON no. 548. **1708** M. BRUCE
Lect. 33 (Jam.) If I had no more to look to but
your reports, I would have a cold coal to blow at.
1816 SCOTT *Old Mort.* ch. 7 'Aweel', said Cuddie
. . . 'I see but ae gate for 't, and that's a cauld coal
to blow at, mither'.

Cold comfort.   (C 542)

c. **1325** *E. E. Allit. P.* C 264 Lorde! Colde watȝ
his cumfort. **1571** GOLDING *Calvin on Ps.* x. 14
We receive but cold comfort of whatsoever the
Scripture speaketh. **1594–8** SHAKES. *T.S.* IV. i.
33 Shall I complain on thee to our mistress,
whose hand . . . thou shalt soon feel, to thy cold
comfort. **1596** *Id. K.J.* V. vii. 42 I beg cold
comfort. **1612–15** BP. HALL *Contempl.* IV. xi
(1825) II. 380 The cripple . . . looked up, it was
cold comfort that he heard, 'Silver and gold have
I none'.

Cold hand and a warm heart, A.

1902–4 LEAN III. 380.

Cold iron, To hammer on.   (I 98)

1620 SHELTON *Quix.* II. vi. ii. 223 To preach in a
desert, or to beat cold iron. **1659** HOWELL *Span.
Prov.* 5.

Cold May and a windy makes a full barn and a findy,[1] A.   (M 764)

1573 TUSSER (1580) 46 Cold Maie, and windie
Barne filleth vp finelie. **1628** 3 May T. CROS-
FIELD *Diary* ed. Boas 22. **1670** RAY 41. **1750**
ELLIS *Mod. Husb.* III. iii. 9 A cold May and a
windy, Makes a full barn and a findy; because a
cold and dry May prevents . . . weeds. [1 solid,
full, substantial.]

Cold of complexion, good of condition. (C 580)

1573 G. HARVEY *Letter Bk.* 124 Cowldist of

complexion, And best of condition, complayne of extreame heate. **1678** RAY 116.   **1732** FULLER no. 1119.

Cold pudding will settle your love.

(P 622)

1685 WESLEY *Maggots* 41 Settle the Wit, as Pudding settles Love.   **1738** SWIFT Dial. II. E.L. 304.   **1848** A. SMITH *Christ. Tadpole* ch. 60 The cold plum-pudding too, was a wonder . . . and . . . there was enough of it to settle everybody's love.

Cold shoulder, To give (show) the.

1816 SCOTT *Antiq.* ch. 33 'The Countess's dislike didna gang farther at first than just showing o' the cauld shouther'.   **1840** DICKENS *Old C. Shop* ch. 66.   **1853** SURTEES *Sponge's Sport. T.* ch. 36 Jack . . . was more used to 'cold shoulder' than cordial receptions.   **1860** THACKERAY *Lovel* ch. 1 (show).

Cold weather and knaves come out of the north.

(W 214)

1659 HOWELL *Fr. Prov.* 8b Cold weather and crafty knaves come from the North.   **1670** RAY 19.

Cold wind reach you through a hole, If | say your prayers, and mind your soul.

1736 FRANKLIN July If wind blows on you through a hole, Make your will and take care of your soul.   **1846** DENHAM 16.

Cold, *see also* Blow hot and c.; Charity grows c.; Child (To a) all weather is c.; Day lengthens c. strengthens; Gaining, c. gaming (No); God sends c. after clothes; Have to say (What you) will keep c.; Hour's c. will spoil seven years' warming; Hunger and c. deliver man to enemy; Ladyday comes c. on water; May c. thirty days c.; Old and c.; Over hot over c.; Pepper is hot in mouth but c. in snow; Pride feels no c.; Salt water never gives c.; Soon hot, soon c.; Stuff a c. starve fever.

Coldest flint there is hot fire, In the.

(F 371)

1579 LYLY *Euph.* i. 224 I, but in the coldest flinte there is hotte fire.   **1593–4** SHAKES. *Lucr.* l. 181 As from this cold flint I enforc'd this fire, So Lucrece must I force to my desire.   **1602** *Id. T.C.* III. iii. 256 It lies as coldly in him as fire in a flint, which will not show without knocking. **1605–8** *Id. T.Ath.* I. i. 24 The fire in the flint shows not till it be struck.   **1616** DRAXE no. 2004. **1732** FULLER no. 2822.   **1837** S. LOVER *Rory O'More* ch. 6 Perhaps . . . John Bull is like his own flint-stones, with fire enough in him, only you must strike him hard.

Coldingham common, *see* Conscience like C. c.

Cole-prophet, To play.

(C 510)

1543 G. COUSIN *Office of Servants* B 6 [The

slothful servant] beinge sente on an errante fyndeth many barres in the same with colpropheting, as, a lion is in the way.   **1546** HEYWOOD I. ix. C1[v] Ye plaie coleprophet (quoth I) who takth in hande, To knowe his answere before he doo his errande.   **1565** AWDELEY *Frat. Vagabonds* 15 Cole Prophet is he, that when his Maister sendeth him on his errand, he wyl tel his answer therof to his Maister as he depart from hym.   **1584** R. SCOT *Disc. Witchcr.* IX. iii. 170 To plaie the cold prophet, as to recount it good or bad lucke, when salt or wine falleth on the table.

Colewort, *see* Cabbage (1580 quotn.).

Coll[1] under canstick.[2]

(C 512)

[a Christmas game; used fig.] **1546** HEYWOOD I. x. C3 Coll vnder canstyke she can plaie on bothe hands, Dissimulacion well she vnderstands.   *c.* **1553** T. BECON *Displaying Popish Mass* P.S. 260 Can ye not play cole under candlestick.   **1562** J. WIGAND *De Neutralibus* M2[v] Paules mynde is not to haue the truth hidden, nor to play cole vnder candlesticke.   **1573** J. BRIDGES *Supremacy of Christ. Princes* R2 He hath plaied Cole vnder the candlestick.   **1659** HOWELL *Eng. Prov.* 4b.   [[1] to embrace. [2] candlestick.]

Collar, *see* After a c. a halter; Neck out of the c.

Collier, *see* Like will to like, quoth devil to c.; Melancholy as a c.'s horse.

Collier's sack, bad without and worse within, Like a.

1706 STEVENS s.v. Costal.   **1732** FULLER no. 3221.

Collop, *see* Dear c. cut out of own flesh; Sairy o. that is off capon.

Colne clock, always at one, Like.

1873 HARLAND & WILKINSON *Lancashire Leg.* 194 A steady person is said to be 'like Colne clock— always at one': *i.e.* always the same.

Coloquintida spoils all the broth, A little.

1565 J. CALFHILL *Treatise of the Cross* P.S. 210 They will haue a crop of Colocyntida, to mar a whole pot full of pottage.   **1579** LYLY *Euph.* i. 189 One leafe of Colliquintida marreth and spoyleth the whole potte of porredge.   **1616** DRAXE no. 691 A little Coloquintida marreth a whole pot of pottage.   **1630** T. ADAMS *Wks.* 711.   *a.* **1677** P. WARWICK *Memoirs* (1701) 84 The Romanists . . . having the policy of flinging coloquintida into one pott.

Colours of the rainbow, All the.

(C 519)

1562 G. LEGH *Accidence of Armoury* 171 A flower de luse . . . hath all the colours of a Rainebowe.   **1586** J. CASE *Praise of Music* 12 The painters shop may vie with the rainebow for colors.   [*c.* **1589**] **1601** LYLY *Love's Metam.* IV. i. 27 This Garland of flowers . . . hath all colours of the Rainebowe.   **1596** SHAKES. *K.J.* IV. ii. 13

To . . . add another hue Unto the rainbow. **1600–1** *Id. M.W.W.* IV. v. 106 I was beaten myself into all the colours of the rainbow.   **1607** G. MARKHAM *Cavelarice* 43 Horses of all maner of colours in the Rainbow.

Colour(s), *see also* Black (Above) there is no c.; Blind men can judge no c.; Blushing is virtue's c.; Coward changes c.; Horse of another c.; Kythe in your own c.; Lie all manner of c. but blue; Nail one's c. to the mast; Sail under false c.; Truth fears no c.; Truth needs no c.

Colouring, *see* Coral needs no c.

Colt's tooth, A.   (C 525)

c. **1386** CHAUCER *W. of Bath's Prol.* l. 602 But yet I hadde alwey a coltes tooth.   *c.***1565** *Bugbears* III. i. 25 As yf hys coltes teeth in his head were yet stiking.   **1576** LEMNIUS *Touchstone of Complexions* tr. T. Newton 98 Not to haue shedde all theyr Calues teeth [Dutch].   **1588** GREENE *Perimides* Wks. Gros. VII. 91 Hee hath beene a wag, but nowe age hath pluckt out all his Coltes teeth.   **1613** SHAKES. *Hen. VIII* I. iii. 48 Your colt's tooth is not cast yet.   **1709** STEELE *Tatler* no. 151, par. 4 My Aunt Margery had again a Colt's-Tooth in her Head.   **1800** WOLCOT (P. Pindar) *Ld. Auck. Tri.* Wks. (1812) IV. 317 His Majesty . . . Had a Colt's tooth and loved another Dame.

Colt(s), *see also* Kick of dam hurts not c.; Ragged as a c.; Ragged c. may make good horse; Ride a young c. (When you), see saddle be girt; Trick the c. gets at first backing; Young c. will canter.

Comb (a person's) head with a three-legged stool, etc., To.   (H 270)

[= to beat, thrash.] [1525–40] **1557** *A merry dialogue* 60 I gat me a thre foted stole in hand, and he had but ones layd his littell finger on me, he shuld not haue founde me lame.   **1555** HEYWOOD A 4 Home is homely: yea, and too homely some tyme. Where wyues footestoles, to their husbandes heads clyme.   **1567** *Mery Tales* (SKELTON *Wks.*, ed. Dyce I. lix) Hys wife woulde diuers tymes in the weeke kimbe his head with a iii-footed stoole.   **1591** NASHE *A wonderful Prognostication* iii. 389.   **1594–8** SHAKES. *T.S.* I. i. 64 To comb your noddle with a three-legg'd stool.   **1785** GROSE *Dict. Vulg. T.* s.v. Comb She combed his head with a joint-stool; she threw a stool at him.   **1896** LOCKER-LAMPSON *My Confid.* 390 The mother . . . would . . . shy the furniture about. To use her own words of homely vigour, she combed her husband's head with a three-legged stool.

Comb your head backward yet, Somebody will.

1721 KELLY 286 . . . Spoken by Mothers to stubborn Daughters; intimating they will come under the Hands of a Step Mother, who, it is likely, will not deal too tenderly with them.

Comb, *see also* Brought an ill c. to my head; Cut the c. of; Scabby heads love not c.

Come after with salt and spoons, To.

1590 R. HARVEY *Plain Percival* B1ᵛ Sith Martin and his brood hath furnished the first course . . . and againe his . . . frinds . . . haue counter coursd him, . . . I follow like a plaine dunstable Groome, with salt and spoones on a trencher.   **1611** DRAYTON *Wks.* (Hebel) i. 500 And I come after bringing Salt and Spoones.   **1639** CLARKE 304.   **1699** B.E. *Dict. Cant. Crew*, s.v. Salt . . . of one that is none of the Hastings.

Come again, They will | as Goodyer's pigs did.   (G 344)

1678 RAY 235 . . . *i.e.* never.

Come and welcome; go by, and no quarrel.   (Q 2)

1678 RAY 236.

Come, but come stooping.

1642 TORRIANO 99.   **1813** RAY 93.

Come by, *see* Hard to c. b. are much set by (Things).

Come cut and longtail. *Cf.* Tag, rag, and bobtail.   (C 938)

1590 R. HARVEY *Plain Perceval* A3ᵛ Come cut and longe taile.   *c.* **1591** [1599] GREENE ? *George a Green* F3 Call all your towne forth, come cut and longtaile.   **1594** NASHE *Christ's Tears* i 186 Raile vpon me till your tongues rotte, short cut and long taile, for groats a peece euery quarter.   **1600–1** SHAKES. *M.W.W.* III. iv. 47 Ay, that I will, come cut and long-tail, under the degree of a squire!   **1601–2** *2 Return from Parnassus* l. 1469 As long as it [tobacco] lasts, come cut and longe-taile, weele spend it as liberally for his sake.   **1613** SHAKES. & FLETCHER ? *T.N.K.* V. ii. 49 And, for a jig, come cut and long-tail to him! He turns ye like a top.   **1630** D'AVENANT *Cruel Brother* IV. I will have 'em all; come cut and longtail.

Come day, go day, God send Sunday.   (D 61)

1616 DRAXE no. 2011 Come day, goe day, the day is long enough.   **1721** KELLY 77 . . . Spoken to lazy, unconscionable Servants, who only mind to serve out their Time, and get their Wages.   **1846** DENHAM 15 Come day, gang day, God send Sunday. The sluggard's daily prayer.

Come home, *see* Cows c. h., (Till the); Duck in the mouth (C. h. with); Parson's cow (C. h. like).

Come in at the window (back door), To.   (W 456)

[Said of a bastard.]   **1551** CROWLEY *Pleasure and Pain* l. 348 Wks. 119 And youe were gladde to take them in, Bycause you knewe they dyd knowe That youe came in by the wyndowe.   **1551** T. WILSON *Rule of Reason* (1552 ed., O8ᵛ) Some by thrustyng on, choppe in at a wyndowe when the dore is shitte vppe.   **1581** GUAZZO ii. 62 Those which come in at the backe doore . . . doe often . . . avaunce themselves.   **1596** SHAKES.

K.J. I. i. 171 In at the window, or else o'er the hatch. . . . I am I, howe'er I was begot. **1605** CHAPMAN *All Fools* III. i. 422 Though he came in at the window, he sets the gates of your honour open. **1629** SHIRLEY *The Ball* II. i. I came in at the wicket, some call it the window. **1664** COTTON *Scarron.* (1715) 20 She [Venus] came in at the Window.

Come not to counsel uncalled.   (C 678)

1539 TAVERNER 13 Ad consilium ne accesseris antequam uoceris. Come not to counsayle afore thou be called. *a.* **1585** MONTGOMERIE *Cherrie & Slae* lxxviii (1821) 42 Thair is a sentence said be sum, 'Let nane uncalled to counsell cum, That welcum weins to be.' **1591** ARIOSTO *Orl. Fur.* Harington XLI. 42 A madnesse meere it is . . . Will counsell and aduise men what to do, Not being cald of counsell thereunto. [**1591**] **1593–4** *Jack Straw* l. 770 I haue read this in Cato [in corrupt Latin]. **1641** FERGUSSON no. 220.

Come of a blood and so is a pudding, You are.   (B 467)

a. **1641** MS. no. 1553 in FERGUSSON 113 Ye ar sib[1] to a pudding ye ar com of a blood. **1721** KELLY 368 . . . Spoken to them who boast of their genteel Blood. [[1] kin.]

Come right in the wash, It will all.

1612 *Don Quixote* III. vi (i. 157) All will away in the bucking. **1706** STEVENS s.v. Colada It will all out in the Buck. *Ibid.* s.v. Mancilla The Spot will come out in the washing. Or, as we say, It will rub out when it is dry. **1876** S. BUTLER in H. Festing Jones *S.B.* 1920 i. 243 As my cousin's laundress says, 'It will all come right in the wash'.

Come, If they | they come not; if they come not, they come.   (C 531)

1662 FULLER *Northumberland* 303 The cattle of people living hereabout, turn'd into the common pasture, did by instinct and custome return home at night, except violently intercepted by the Free-booters, and Borderers, who living between two Kingdomes, owned no King, whilst Vivitur ex rapto, Catch who catch may. . . . If therefore these Borderers came, their cattle came not; if they came not, their cattle surely returned. **1670** RAY 248 (Northumb.).

Come to, *see* See what we must c. to if we live.

Come to himself, Let him | like Mac-Kibbon's crowdy.[1]

1721 KELLY 237 . . . Spoken when People are angry without a Cause. **1818** SCOTT *Rob Roy* ch. 25 Ye'll cool and come to yourself, like Mac-Gibbon's crowdy, when he set it out at the window-bole. [[1] brose; porridge.]

Come(s) to light, *see* Nothing c. fairer to l. than long hid.

Come to mickle, It is | but it's no come to that.

1721 KELLY 207 . . . Spoken when we reject the Proffer of a mean Service, Match, or Business, we are not come so low as that yet.

Come(s) to pass, *see* Forehets (That which one most) soonest c. to p.

Come what come may.

(C 529 and H 137)

c. **1475** MALORY Bk. XX Falle whatsumever falle may. [**1486–1500**] *c.* **1530** MEDWALL *Nature* I C3 Hap what hap may. **1530** PALSGRAVE 453a Betyde what maye betyde. *Ibid.* 578b Happe what happe shal. **1545** R. ASCHAM *Toxophilus* 35 Tide what maye betide. [*a.* **1563**] **1661** *Tom Tyler and His Wife* l. 804, 22 Hap good hap, will, hap good, hap evil; Even hap as hap may. **1590–1** SHAKES. *2 Hen. VI* III. ii. 402 O, let me stay, befall what may befall! **1591** ARIOSTO *Orl. Fur.* Harington XXII. 49 Hap good or ill, fall what may fall. **1603** T. HEYWOOD *Woman killed with kindness*, Wks. ii. 118 Fall what may fall. **1605–6** SHAKES. *K.L.* IV. i. 49 I'll bring him the best 'parel that I have, Come on't what will. **1605–6** *Id. M.* I. iii. 146 Come what come may, Time and the hour runs through the roughest day.

Come wind, come weather.   (W 414)

c. **1569** W. WAGER *The Longer thou Livest* F2 We will neither passe of wind nor wether. **1581** W. AUEVELL *Charles & Julia* K3 They . . . once were sau'd, in spight of winde and weather. **1684** BUNYAN *Pilgrim's Progress* Pt. 2 Who would true Valour see . . . One here will constant be, come Wind, come Weather.

Come with me, If thou wilt | bring with thee.   (C 532)

1573 SANFORD 109ᵛ. **1578** FLORIO 33ᵛ. **1732** FULLER no. 6286 Bring something, Lass, along with thee, If thou intend to live with me.

Come with the wind, go with the water.

[Things ill-gotten will be ill-spent.] **1721** KELLY 83 . . . Lat. *Male parta, male dilabuntur.* **1892** HENLEY & STEVENSON *Deac. Brodie* I. ii Onyway, Deacon, ye'd put your ill-gotten gains to a right use: they might come by the wind but they wouldna gang wi' the water.

Comely (Nimble) as a cow in a cage, As.

(C 747)

1399 LANGLAND *Rich. Redeless* iii. 262 As becometh a kow to hoppe in a cage! **1546** HEYWOOD II. i. F3 She is in this marriage As comely as is a cowe in a cage. **1678** RAY 287 (nimble) **1828** LYTTON *Pelham* ch. 77 I have made them as nimble as cows in a cage—I have not learned the use of my fists for nothing.

Comes first to the hill, may sit where he will, He that.   (H 463)

a. **1628** CARMICHAELL no. 748. **1641** FERGUSSON no. 347. **1721** KELLY 142 (Midding) . . . He that comes first has commonly the best Choice. [[1] dunghill.]

Comes in with his five eggs, He.   (E 92)

[= to break in fussily with an i dle story.] **1542** ERASM. tr. Udall. *Apoph.* 272 Persones comyng in with their fiue egges, how that Scylla had

geuen ouer his office of Dictature. **1546** HEY-
WOOD II. i. F3 In came the thyrde, with his V.
egges. **1596** NASHE *Saffron W.* iii. 128 (tale of
ten egs . . . and nine of them rotten). **1639**
CLARKE 19 He comes in with his five egges, and
foure be rotten. **1738** SWIFT Dial. I. E.L. 270
What! and you must come in with your two
eggs a-penny, and three of them rotten.

Comes nought out of the sack, There | but what was there. (N 326)

1581 J. CARTIGNY *Voyage of the Wandering
Knight* tr. W. Goodyear B4 Out of a sacke
nothing come, but such as is in it. **1611** COT-
GRAVE s.v. Sac On ne peut tirer du sac que ce
qu'y est . . . there can come no more (no other
stuffe) from a man then is in him. **1640** HERBERT
no. 833.

Comes of a hen, He that | must scrape. (H 420)

1591 FLORIO 179 What is hatcht by a hen, will
scrape like a hen. **1640** HERBERT no. 415. **1659**
TORRIANO no. 75 (Who is of a hen-brood). **1852**
E. FITZGERALD *Polonius* 92 Let him who would
know how far he has changed the old Adam,
consider his Dreams. . . .

Comes to (the) hand like the bowl of a pint-stoup, It.

[= is acceptable or opportune.] **1819** SCOTT
Bride Lam. ch. 11 The thunderbolt . . . only
served to awaken the . . . inventive genius of the
flower of Majors-Domo . . . Caleb exclaimed,
'Heavens be praised!—this comes to hand like
the boul of a pint stoup'.

Comes uncalled, He who | sits unserved. (C 537)

a. **1585** MONTGOMERIE *Cherrie & Slae* lxxviii
(1821) 42 Zea, I haif hard another zit, 'Quha
cum uncallt, unservd suld sit'. *a.* **1628** CAR-
MICHAELL no. 747. **1721** KELLY 77 . . . They
have no reason to expect good Usage, who go to a
Feast uncall'd.

Comes from above, That which | let no man question. (M 388)

1662 FULLER Leics. 137 Henry Noel . . . was of
the first rank in the Court. And though his
Lands and Livelyhood were small, . . . yet in
State . . . and expences, did ever equalize the
Barons of great worth. If any demand whence
this proceeded, the Spanish Proverb answers
him, 'That which cometh from above, let no man
question'.

Comes last to the pot, He that | is soonest wroth. (P 496)

a. **1536** R. HILL E.E.T.S. no. 42, 132 He that
commeth last to the pot, ys sonnest wrothe.
1546 HEYWOOD II. x. L3ᵛ Than was it proued
true, as this prouerbe gothe, He that commeth
last to the pot, is soonest wrothe. **1611** DAVIES
no. 43 The last at the Pot is the first wroth.

Comes late, Who | lodges ill. (L 408)

1573 SANFORD 103ᵛ. **1578** FLORIO *First F.* 5.
1659 TORRIANO no. 119 (fares ill). **1732** FULLER
no. 2381.

Come(s), came, *see also* Beginnings c. great
things, (From small); Cut and c. again; Easy c.;
First c., first served; Everything c. to him who
waits; Good luck c. by cuffing; In time c. whom
God sends; Legs, (How c. you hither?; Lightly c.;
Lost (It is not) that c. at last; Mischief c. without
calling for; Never do evil that good may c. of it;
Never long that c. at last; Old soldier (To c. the);
Quickly c. quickly go; Servant must c. when
you call him, (A good); Shires (To c. out of the);
Staff and wallet, (To c. to the); Take things as
they c.; Thick sown thin c. up; Weather, (Take
the) as it c.; Weeping c. into world; Wit enough
to c. in from rain; Yorkshire on one (To c.).

Comfits, *see* Children deceived with c.

Comfort, *see* Children certain cares but uncertain c.; Cold c.; Evils have their c.; Want of
money want of c.

Comforter's head never aches, The. (C 545)

1590 GREENE *Never Too Late* Gros. viii. 84 The
old adage is not alwayes true, consulenti numquam caput doluit. **1590** LODGE *Rosalynde*
Hunt. Cl. i. 34 Being such a good Phisition to
others, wilt thou not minister receipts to thy
selfe? But perchance thou wilt say: Consulenti
numquam caput doluit. **1640** HERBERT no. 392.

Comforter, *see also* Job's c.

Coming, and so is Christmas.

1738 SWIFT Dial. I. E.L. 273 'She's coming,
madam.' . . . 'Coming! ay, so is Christmas.'
1854 SURTEES *Hand. Cross* ch. 62. Miss always
reported that she saw the offer was coming, but
Mama . . . observed that 'Christmas was coming
too'.

Coming events cast their shadows before them.

1803 CAMPBELL *Lochiel's Warn.* And coming
events cast their shadows before. **1857** TROL-
LOPE *Barch. Tow.* ch. 24 The coming event of
Mr. Quiverful's transference to Barchester
produced a delicious shadow in the shape of a
new outfit for Mrs. Quiverful.

Coming to heaven with dry eyes, No. (C 549)

1614 T. ADAMS *Fatal Banquet*, Wks. (1861), i. 173
The Prouerbe is too true for many; No man
comes to heauen with drie eyes. **1629** *Id.
Serm.* (1861–2) ii. 373 Many saints have now
reaped this crop in heaven, that sowed their
seed in tears. David, Mary Magdalene, Peter; as
if they had made good the proverb, No coming
to heaven with dry eyes'.

Command of custom is great, The. (C 551)

1616 WITHALS 541 The force of custome and
Antiquity auaileth much. **1640** HERBERT no.
590.

**Command others, He is not fit to | that
cannot command himself.**   (c 552)

c. 1510 STANBRIDGE *Vulg.* E.E.T.S. 56 It becometh hym euyll to be a mayster vpon seruauntes
that cannot ordre hymselfe. 1621 FLETCHER
Pilgrim II. ii How vilely this shows, In one that
would command anothers temper, And hear
no bound in's own. 1669 PENN *No Cross, No
Crown* (1726) xix. 383 Cato . . . would say, No
Man is fit to Command another, that cannot
Command himself.

Command your man, and do it yourself.
                                   (M 84)

1666 TORRIANO *It. Prov.* 60 note 127 (as the
English say). 1670 RAY 169. 1692 L'ESTRANGE
Aesop's Fab. liii (1738) 66 Men are more sensible
in their own case than in another's; . . . according to the old saying, Command your man, and
do't yourself. 1706 STEVENS s.v. Cuydado.

Command(s), *see also* Counsel is no c.; Do as thy
master c. thee . . .; Force hidden in a sweet c.;
Pay well, c. well, hang well; Will, (As I) so I c.

**Commandment: The Eleventh | thou
shalt not be found out.**

1860 WHYTE-MELVILLE *Holmby H.* ch. 14 Who
wink . . . at the infraction of every commandment
in the Decalogue, provided we are scrupulous
to keep the eleventh, . . . which says, 'thou shalt
not be found out!' 1894 DEAN HOLE *More Mem.*
ch. 12 They stand in awe of but one commandment, 'Thou shalt not be found out'.

Commandments, The ten.   (c 553)

[= the ten finger-nails, esp. of a woman.] *c.*
1520–2 J. HEYWOOD *Four P's* Hazl.-Dods. i. 381
I beseech him that high sits, Thy wife's ten
commandments may search thy five wits. 1542
ERASM. tr. Udall *Apoph.* (1877), 27. 1590–1 SHAKES.
2 Hen. VI I. iii. 140 Could I come near your
beauty with my nails, I could set my ten commandments in your face. [*c.* 1590] 1594 *Taming
of a Shrew* B3 Hands off I say, and get you
from this place; Or I will set my ten commandments in your face. 1814 SCOTT *Wav.* ch. 30
I'll set my ten commandments in the face o'
the first loon that lays a finger on him.

**Commands enough that obeys a wise
man, He.**   (M 160)

1640 HERBERT no. 547. 1642 TORRIANO 12. 1650
JER. TAYLOR *Holy Liv.* II. iv (1850) 84 The humble
man . . . in all things lets God chose for him . . .
He does not murmur against commands. Assai
commanda, chi ubbidisce al saggio.

**Commend not your wife, wine, nor
horse.**   (W 345)

1597 *Politeuphuia* 91ᵛ Neyther flatter nor chide
thy wife before him that is a stranger. 1642
TORRIANO 77. 1659 TORRIANO no. 149 (adding
'a good store of mony'). 1732 FULLER no. 1126
with 'house' for 'horse'.

**Commits a fault, He that | thinks every-
one speaks of it.** *Cf.* Fault, Who is in:
Faulty stands on his guard.   (F 111)

1509 A. BARCLAY *Ship of Fools* ii. 256 He that is
gylty thynketh all that is sayde Is spokyn of hym.
1545 *Precepts of Cato* Bk. 1. no. 17, E7ᵛ He
that is gyltie in any maner thynge Thynketh that
only of him is all their whysperynge. 1615
WELDE *Janua Linguarum* tr. W. Welde 23 A man
knowing himselfe to be guiltie, thinketh all things
to be spoken of him. 1640 HERBERT no. 554.

Commodity, *see* Every c. has its discommodity.

**Common a good thing is the better, The
more.**   (T 142)

1576 PETTIE i. 89 Of good things I think the more
common the more commendable. 1596 HARING-
TON *Met. Ajax* ed. Donno 192 As the old saying
is, (bonum quo communius eo melius) . . . Goodnesse is best, when it is common showne. 1605
MARSTON *Dutch Courtesan* I, i. 149 Since then
beauty, love, and woman are good, how can the
love of woman's beauty be bad? and, Bonum,
quo communius eo melius. 1656 CULPEPER
Concl.: Aurum Pot. O3ᵛ Wee confesse it's an
old saying, That better is the good the more
common it is.

Common as a barber's chair, As.
                                   (B 73)

1554 H. HILARIE *Resurrection of the Mass* A3ᵛ
I am as common as the Barbours chayre. 1579
GOSSON *Sch. Abuse* Arb. 66 Venus . . . that made
her self as common as a Barbars chayre. 1602
SHAKES. *A.W.* II. ii. 17 It is like a barber's chair
that fits all buttocks. 1796 WOLCOT (P. Pindar)
Orson & Ellen Wks. (1816) IV. 72 Unlike some
lasses, common known As is a barber's chair.

Common as coleman hedge.   (c 509)

1585 HIGGINS *Nomenclator* 532 An arrant whore;
a coleman hedge. 1616 WITHALS 563. 1639
CLARKE 191.

Common as the highway (cartway).
                         (c 109 and H 457)

c. 1377 LANGLAND *P. Pl.* A. iii. 127 As
Comuyn as the Cart-wei to knaues and to alle.
c. 1460 *Wisdom* 655 Lust ys now comun as the
way. 1493 [H. PARKER] *Dives and Pauper* 4ᵛ
Other wickednesses ben as common as the carte-
way. 1593 P. FOULFACE *Bacchus' Bounty* C4
As common . . . as cartway. 1598 SHAKES. *2
Hen. IV* II. ii. 160 This Doll Tearsheet should be
some road.—I warrant you, as common as the
way between Saint Alban's and London. 1678
RAY 90 . . . A whore.

Common fame is a liar.   (F 44)

1594 LYLY *Mother B.* III. iii. 30 Reports are no
truths. *c.* 1606 SHAKES. *A.C.* I. i. 60 The common liar, who Thus speaks of him at Rome. 1614
W. BROWNE *Shepherd's Pipe* vii Wks. (1869) II.
236 Fame is a liar, and was never other. 1822
SCOTT *Pirate* ch 39 But common fame, Magnus
considered, was a common liar.

Common fame is seldom to blame.
(F 43)

1597 LOK *Son. Conscience* (Gros.) 83: *Ecclesiastes*, 299 Though prouerbe truely say, by fame's affect, God's judgement lightly doth a truth detect. **1639** CLARKE 227. **1670** RAY 88 . . . A general report is rarely without some ground. **1721** KELLY 80 Common Fame sindle[1] to blame. A Man will seldom be under an universal ill Report, unless he has given some occasion for it. [[1] seldom.]

Common horse is worst shod, The.
(H 637)

1546 HEYWOOD I. xi. E2ᵛ. **1639** CLARKE 170.

Common servant is no man's servant, A.
(S 231)

1573 SANFORD 103ᵛ He that serueth the Common Wealthe, serueth none. **1590** SIR ROGER WILLIAMS *Brief Discourse of War* 49 True it is, those that serues many, serues nobodie. **1629** *Bk. Mer. Rid.* Prov. no. 85.

Common (*adj.*), *see also* Coin is not c. (Where), commons must be scant; Death is sure (c.). to all; Homo is c. name to all men; Wine is not c. (Where), commons must be sent.

Common (*noun*), *see* Held together, as men of Marham when they lost their c.

Communications, *see* Evil c. corrupt.

Companion in a long way and a little inn, A man knows his.

1706 STEVENS s.v. Camino. **1732** FULLER no. 284. **1908** *Times Lit. Sup.* 25 Dec. 487 When one's brother mortal has stood the searching test of the long road and the little inn, it is a duty . . . to regard him with gratitude.

Companion like the penny, There is no.
(C 560)

1659 HOWELL *Span. Prov.* 13. **1670** RAY 21. *Hispan.*

Companion(s), *see also* Dog gnaws bone (While), c. would he none; Hunchback sees not own hump but c.'s; Louse is man's c.; Merry c. a wagon in the way.

Company, As a man is, so is his.
(M 248)

1541 BULLINGER *Christian State of Matrimony* tr. Coverdale (1543 ed. H1) So maye much be spyed also, by the company and pastyme that he vseth. For a man is for the moost parte condicioned euen lyke vnto them that he kepeth company wythe all. **1591** H. SMITH *Prep. to Marriage* (1657, 22) If a man can be known by nothing else, then he may be known by his companions. **1601** DENT *Plain Man's Pathway* 336. **1616** DRAXE no. 283. **1610** BRETNOR *Almanac* April (Good days) Like company, like credite. **1622**

c. DUDIN *Grammar Span. and English* 253 Such as a mans company, such his manners. **1710** PALMER 36 Shew me the Company, and I will shew thee the Man.

Company in trouble, It is good to have.
(C 571)

a. 1349 R. ROLLE *Meditations on the Passion* C. Horstmann *Yorkshire Writers* i. 101 It is solace to haue companie in peyne. *c.* 1374 CHAUCER *Troilus* Bk. I. l. 708 Men seyn, to wrecche is consolacioun To have another felawe in his peyne. *c.* 1386 *Id. Canon's Y.T.* (G.) l. 746 For vnto shrewes joye it is and ese To have hir felawes in peyne and disese. **1579** LYLY *Euph.* i. 238 In miserie Euphues it is a great comfort to haue a companion. **1594** SHAKES. *Luc.* l. 790 Fellowship in woe doth woe assuage. *Ibid.* l. 1581 It easeth some, though none it ever cur'd, To think their dolour others have endur'd. **1620** SHELTON *Quix.* II. xiii (1908) II. 269 If that which is commonly spoken be true, that to have companions in misery is a lightener of it, you may comfort me. **1670** RAY 5.

Company makes the feast, The.
(C 572)

1653 WALTON *Angler* v 'Tis the company and not the charge that makes the feast.

Company, *see also* Better be alone than in bad c.; Better to be beaten than in bad c.; Choose not thy c. before thy drink; Crowd is not c.; Dies without c. of good men; Hell for c. (Nobody will go to); John C.; Keep good men c.; Keep not ill men c.; Keeps c. with wolf; Keeps his road who gets rid of bad c.; Kenned folk nae c.; Knaves (The more), worse c.; Meat than guests or c., (Better to want); Room is better than his c.; Sike as thou wald be, draw to sike c.; Two is c., three is none; Want of c. welcome trumpery; Woe worth ill c., quoth the kae of Camnethen.

Comparison that makes men happy or miserable, It is.
(C 575)

1676 T. SHADWELL *Virtuoso* II. No Man's happy but by comparison. **1732** FULLER no. 5071.

Comparison, *see also* Man, woman, and devil three degrees of c.

Comparisons are odious.
(C 576)

c. 1440 LYDGATE *Polit. Relig. & Love Poems* 22 Odyous of olde been comparisonis. *c.* 1566 CURIO *Pasquin in a Trance* tr. W.P. 4ᵛ By vs Canonistes comparisons are counted odious. **1566** J. BARTHLET *Pedegrew of Popish Heretiques* 24 Omnis comparatio odiosa. Euery comparison is odious. **1579** LYLY *Euph.* i. 214 Livia, though shee bee faire, . . . is . . . not so amiable as my Lucilla . . . ; but least comparisons shoulde seeme odious, . . . I will omit that. **1598–9** SHAKES. *M.A.* III. v. 16 Comparisons are odorous. *c.* **1600** DONNE *Elegies* viii She and comparisons are odious. **1724** SWIFT *Drap. Lett.* v. Wks. (1856) II. 30 A judge . . . checked the prisoner . . . taxing him with 'reflecting on the court by such a comparison, because comparisons were odious'. **1859** S. R. HOLE *Lit. Tour Irel.* ch. 14 Many men

... forgetting that ... 'Comparisons are odious', are never happy but in detecting intelicities.

Compass, Live within.   (c 577)

1579 CALVIN *Serm.* tr. L.T. 133a Wee haue need of some order or bridle, to hold vs within our compasse. **1582** WHETSTONE *Heptameron* 12. **1590** R. WILSON *Three Lords* B2ᵛ The prouident forsee to keepe themselues within their owne compasse. **1590–5** MUNDAY *et al. Sir T. More* IV. iv. 25 For keeping still in compass . . . we have sailed beyond our course. **1595** H. CHETTLE *Piers Plainness* E1 I had kept within compass. **1597** SHAKES. *1 Hen. IV* III. iii. 21 [I] lived well, and in good compass. **1732** FULLER no. 914 Better live within Compass, than have large Comings in.

Compelled, *see* Love cannot be c.

Complain, *see* All c.; God c. not.

Complains wrongfully on the sea that twice suffers shipwreck, He.   (s 172)

[PUBL. SYRUS 264 (Ribbeck) *Improbe Neptunum accusat qui iterum naufragium facit.*] *c.* **1526** *Dicta Sapientum* D1ᵛ He that hath ones experience, and perillously aduentereth hym selfe agayne, foolysshely than he accuseth Fortune. **1539** TAVERNER *Publius* D4ᵛ He that the seconde tyme suffreth shipwrake, wyckedly blameth god. **1579** SPENSER *Shep. Cal.* Feb. The Soueraigne of the Seas he blames in vain That, once sea-beate, will to sea again. **1640** HERBERT no. 706. **1670** RAY 23.

Complexion, *see* Cold of c.

Complies against his will, He that | is of his own opinion still.

1678 BUTLER *Hudibras* III. iii. 547.

Complimentary letter asks another, One.

1596 NASHE *Saffron W.* S2 iii. 116 One côplementarie Letter asketh another; & *Gabriell* first writing to him, and seeming to admire him and his workes, hee could doo no lesse . . . but returne him an answere in the like nature.

Con, *see* Lesson without book, (To c.)

Conceal(s), *see* Cuckold and c. it; Soberness. c. (What), drunkenness reveals; Woman c. what she knows not.

Conceited¹ goods are quickly spent.
                                                  (G 300)
1678 RAY 116. [¹ imagined.]

Conditions, *see* Gentleman that has gentle c., (He is a); Proper that has proper c.

Conduct, *see* Advice (We may give) but cannot give c.

Confess and be hanged.   (c 587)

1589 *De Caede et Interitu Gallorum Regis* A2ᵛ Confesse and be hanged man In English some saie. *c.* **1592** MARLOWE *Jew of Malta* IV. ii Merm. 291 Blame not us but the proverb, . . . **1595** *A Pleasant Satire on Poesy* (*A Satire Menippized*) 42. **1604** SHAKES. *O.* IV. i. 37 To confess, and be hanged for his labour. **1665** J. WILSON *Projectors* III. I . . . —I am for none of 't! **1821** SCOTT *Pirate* ch. 39 At the gallows! . . . confess and be hanged is a most reverend proverb.

Confess debt and beg days.

1721 KELLY 79. **1732** FULLER no. 1139.

Confessed, *see* Fault c. half redressed.

Confession, *see* Open c. good for soul; Open c. open penance.

Confessor, *see* Better to be a martyr than c.

Confidence is a plant of slow growth.

1776 EARL OF CHATHAM *Speech* 14 Jan. in LEAN III. 443 Confidence is a plant of slow growth in an aged bosom. **1908** SNEYD-KYNNERSLEY *H.M.I.* ch. 3 Confidence is a plant that for special reasons grows slowly in that land [Wales]; and occasionally there were outbursts of fury.

Confidence, *see also* Skill and c. are unconquered army.

Confuted and yet not convinced, One may be.

1732 FULLER no. 3771.

Congleton rare, Congleton rare, sold the Bible to pay for a bear.

1813 RAY 242 Congleton bears. . . . The clerk of Congleton having taken the old church bible . . . sold it to buy a bear. . . . From this, . . . proceeds the name of Congleton bears. **1917** BRIDGE 39 . . . In the year 1662 the Church Bible was worn out and money was collected to buy another. . . . The town bear, kept for baiting, died, and the keeper applied . . . to the Corporation. They granted him the 'Bible Money', as . . . the bear was wanted immediately for the Town Wakes.

Connaught, *see* Hell or C.

Conquering weapon as the necessity of conquering, There is no such.   (w 203)

1651 HERBERT no. 1064.

Conqueror, He came in with the.
                                                  (c 594)
1593 B.R. *Greene's News* C1ᵛ My auncesters came in with the Conquest. **1594–8** SHAKES. *T.S.* Ind. I. 4 The Slys are no rogues. Look in the chronicles; we came in with Richard Conqueror. **1639** CHAPMAN *The Ball* I Is he not a complete gentleman? his family came in with the conqueror. **1888** J. E. T. ROGERS *Econ. Interp.*

Hist. (1894) II. xix A good many people say now, that their families came here with the Conqueror.

Conqueror, *see also* **Love's wars, (In) he who flies is c.**

Conquers, *see* **Victory, (He gets a double) who c. himself.**

Conscience as large as a friar's sleeve, He has a.   (c 607)

c. 1594 BACON no. 1503 Il a la conscience large come la manche d'un cordelier. *a.* 1628 CAR-MICHAELL no. 1784 Your conscience is lyke a gray freirs sleive. 1645 J. MARSH *Marsh his Mickle Monument* A2 You whose consciences are as large as a Gray Friers sleeve. 1659 N. R. 50 (as large as a Franciscan's sleeve).

Conscience as large as a shipman's hose, A.   (c 599)

1540 *Controv. between Smythe and Gray* (Hazlitt *Fug. Tracts* no. 8) Do ye take the holy scriptures to be lyke a shypmans hose? Nay nay; although a shypmans hose wyll serue all sortes of legges. 1560 *Cont. betwixt Churchyard & Camell* F4ᵛ Ye . . . vse suche termes, as might be made a shipmans hose. 1562 J. WIGAND *De Neutralibus* I3 When he [M. Pompilius] had declared vnto him [Antiochus] such matters as he had in com-maundement, Antiochus shaped him an auns-weare like a shipmannes hose, and referred all to his frendes Counsail. . . . Would to God there were som Pompilius that would compell these Anthiochoes, to say as they thinke. 1565 J. CALFHILL P.S. 209 As for this text it is a shipmans hose with them. 1579 J. CALVIN *Thirteen Sermons* tr. J. Field A3ᵛ They call it [the Word of God] a deade letter, a nose of Waxe, a Shipmans hose, a Schoole mistresse of error. *Ibid.* B1 [God's word] as though it were a Shipmans hose, to be altred and changed at their pleasure. 1581 ESTIENNE 38 Making of the Scriptures a shippe-mans hose, or a tale of Robin Hood. 1639 CLARKE 66.

Conscience fears not (laughs at) false accusations, A clear.   (c 597)

c. 1536–7 ERASM. *Pilgr. Pure Devotion* f. 24ᵛ A giltles mynde puttythe away feare. 1580 LYLY *Euph. & his Eng.* ii. 40 A cleere conscience needeth no excuse, nor feareth any accusation. 1602 J. MANNINGHAM *Diary* Feb. 4, 123 A guiltles conscience needes not feare the lawes. 1607 CHAPMAN *Bussy D'Amb.* II. i. 10 So confident a spotless conscience is, So weak a guilty. 1611 SHAKES. *W.T.* III. ii. 28 I doubt not then but innocence shall make False accusation blush. 1732 FULLER no. 42.

Conscience is a cut-throat.   (c 600)

1616 WITHALS 554.   1639 CLARKE 66.

Conscience is a thousand witnesses.
                                                           (c 601)

1539 TAVERNER 29 (Conscientia mille testes. The conscience is). 1550 *A notable and maruailous epistle* tr. E. Aglionby A7ᵛ. 1567 BALDWIN Bb4 (Socrates). 1578 FLORIO *First F.* 32ᵛ

Conscience serueth in stead of a thousand wit-nesses. 1579 LYLY *Euph.* i. 296. 1592 GREENE *Philomena* Gros. xi. 200 I see, and with trembling I feele, that a guiltye conscience is a thousand witnesses. 1597 SHAKES. *Rich. III* V. ii. 17 Every man's conscience is a thousand men, To fight against this guilty homicide. *Ibid.* V. iii. 194 My conscience hath a thousand several tongues, And every tongue brings in a several tale, And every tale condemns me for a villain. 1624 BURTON *Anat.* 3. 4. 1. 3, 4A4. 1629 *Bk. Mer. Rid.* Prov. no. 33 (serueth for).

Conscience is cumbered and stands not clean, Whose | of another man's deeds the worse will he deem.   (c 611)

c. 1450 in *Reliq. Antiquae* (1841) i. 205 Whos conscience is combred and stondith nott clene, Of anothir manis dedis the wursse woll he deme.

Conscience like a cheverel's skin, He has a.   (c 608)

1583 STUBBES *Anat. Abus.* II. 12 The lawiers have such chauerell consciences. *c.* 1595 SHAKES. *R.J.* II. iv. 79 O! here's a wit of cheveril, that stretches from an inch narrow to an ell broad. 1613 *Id. Hen. VIII* II. iii. 31 The capacity Of your soft cheveril conscience. 1662 FULLER *Wales.* 5 *Cheveral consciences,* which will stretch any way for advantage. 1678 RAY 351 . . . (That will stretch.) A Cheverel is a wild goat. *Somers.*

Conscience like Coldingham[1] common, Ye hae a.

1862 HISLOP 328 . . . 'Coldingham moor, or common, was an undivided waste of above 6,000 acres. The saying is applied to persons of lax principles.' [¹ Berwick.]

Conscience was hanged long ago.
                                                           (c 602)

1596 W. PERKINS *Discourse of Conscience* (1603) 3G4. 1623 PAINTER B7 They say that con-science seuen yeares agoe, Was hang'd, and after buried also. 1656 L. PRICE *Map of Merry Conceits* A5. 1659 N. R. 25.

Conscience, *see also* **Friend as far as c. permits; Good c. a feast; Guilty c. is a self-accuser; Nonconformist c.; Once a year a man may say, on his c.; Quiet c. sleeps; Term time in the court of c.**

Consent, *see* **Silence gives c.**

Consider(ing), *see* **Know what shall be (He that would) must c.; Put on c. cap.**

Constable for your wit, You might be a.
                                                           (c 616)

1598–9 SHAKES. *M.A.* III. iii. 22 You are thought here to be the most senseless and fit man for the constable of the watch. 1599 JONSON *Ev. Man out of Hum.* I. ii. 15 Why, for my wealth I might be a Iustice of Peace. — Ay, and a Constable for your wit. 1622 MIDDLETON *Changeling* I. ii. I'll undertake to wind him up to the wit of constable. 1678 RAY 236.

Constable in midsummer watch, Like a.

1586 *Eng. Courtier & Count. Gent.* (1868) 67 When wee come to . . . London, . . . wee will put on Courtlike garments, and . . . some of vs weare them with a good grace. — I beleeue you, euen like a Constable in Mid-sommer watch.

Constable of Openshaw sets beggars in the stocks at Manchester, The.
(c 617)

1678 RAY (*Ches.*) 301.   **1917** BRIDGE 113 Always given as a Cheshire proverb, but it can only be so because Openshaw was in the old Diocese of Chester. 'Openshaw is a township in the parish of Manchester and about three and a half miles from the Cathedral where the stocks were formerly placed.' [*N. & Q.* iv. 12. 524.]

Constable, *see also* Out-run the c.

Constancy of the benefit of the year in their seasons argues a Deity, The.
(c 619)

1640 HERBERT no. 773.

Constant dropping wears the stone.
(D 618)

[OVID *Epist. ex Ponto* 4. 10. 5 *Gutta cavat lapidem. Cf.* JOB xiv. 19 Little drops pierce the flint upon which they often fall.] *c.* **1200** *Ancrene Riwle* (Morton) 220 Lutle dropen thurleth thene ulint thet ofte ualleth theron. *c.* **1387** USK *Test. of Love* I. iii. 101 So ofte falleth the lethy water on the harde rocke, til it haue thorow persed it. *c.* **1477** CAXTON *Jason* 26 The stone is myned and holowed by contynuell droppyng of water. **1549** LATIMER *7th Serm. bef. Edw. VI* P.S. 232 It is a good wise verse, *Gutta cavat lapidem non vi sed saepe cadendo;* 'The drop of rain maketh a hole in the stone, not by violence, but by oft falling'. **1591** SHAKES. *3 Hen. VI* III. ii. 50 He plies her hard; and much rain wears the marble. **1593–4** *Id.* ¡*Luc.* l. 560 Tears harden lust Though marble wear with raining. *Ibid.* l. 959 Time's office is to . . . waste huge stones with little water-drops.   **1596** *Id. Rich. II* III. iii. 164 Or shall we . . . make some pretty match with shedding tears? As thus; to drop them still upon one place, Till they have fretted us a pair of graves Within the earth. **1602** *Id. T.C.* III. ii. 182 When waterdrops have worn the stones of Troy.   **1874** WHYTE-MELVILLE *Uncle John* ch. 6 Constant dropping wears away a stone; constant flirtation saps the character. **1912** 19 Dec. D. H. LAWRENCE *Lett.* i. 169 . . . as my mother used to say.

Construe(s), *see* Charity c. all doubtful things in good part.

Consult, *see* Advice, (If you wish good) c. an old man; Take counsel of (*or* C. with) pillow.

Consume your own smoke.

1843 CARLYLE Letter to Sterling 4 Dec. in FROUDE, *T. Carlyle, History of his Life in London* I. xii I see almost nobody. I . . . study to consume

my own smoke.   *a.* **1893** JOWETT *Life* i. 371 You know Carlyle's saying 'Consume your own smoke', which has perhaps the advantage of increasing the internal heat.

Consumes, *see* Candle lights others and c. itself; Sloth c.

Contemplates, He that | has a day without night.
(D 78)

1640 HERBERT no. 601.   **1670** RAY 5.   **1732** FULLER no. 2069 (with 'on his bed' after 'contemplates').

Contempt pierces even through the shell of the tortoise.

1842 MACAULAY *Ess., Fred. the Gt.* Wks. vi. 689 Contempt, says the eastern proverb, pierces even through the shell of the tortoise; and neither prudence nor decorum had ever restrained Frederic from expressing his measureless contempt for . . . Lewis.

Contempt, *see also* Busy (To be too) gets c.; Evils are cured by c. (Some); Familiarity breeds c.; Four good mothers have four bad daughters: . . . familiarity, c.

Contending with the master of thirty legions, It is ill.
(c 622)

[SPARTIANUS *Hadr.* 15. 12 *Illum doctiorem omnibus . . . qui habet triginta legiones.*] **1605** BACON *Adv. Learn.* I. iii (1900) 27 Accounted . . . discretion in him[1] that would not dispute his best with Adrianus Caesar; excusing himself, That it was reason to yield to him that commanded thirty legions.   **1629** T. ADAMS *Serm.* (1861–2) III. 285 The philosopher[1] that had shamed himself by weakly disputing with Adrian . . . thus excused himself . . . , 'Would you have me contend with him that commands thirty legions?'   *a.* **1654** SELDEN *Table Talk* Arb. 111 'Tis not seasonable to call a man traitor that has an army at his heels. [[1] Favorinus.]

Content in his poverty, He who is | is wonderfully rich.

1566 G. GASCOIGNE & F. KINWELMERSH *Jocasta* II. i. 446 [margin] Content is riche.   **1613** R. DALLINGTON *Aphorisms* 315 Content is the poore mans riches, and Desire the rich mans povertie. **1623** WODROEPHE 480.

Content is all.
(c 623a)

1581 *Howell his devices* (Raleigh) 58 Contented meane exceedeth all.   **1609** HARWARD 78 A Contented minde is all in all.   **1639** CLARKE 38.

Content is happiness.
(c 624)

c. **1566** *Bugbears* IV. ii. 20 Content is agreed. **1579** E. HAKE *News out of Paul's Churchyard* B1[v] Content is pleased.   **1591** FLORIO *Second F.* 29 Content is pleased. [*c.* **1589**] **1594** LODGE *Wounds* l. 2329 Who so liues content is happy wise.   **1666** TORRIANO *It. Prov.* 52 no. 29.   **1732** FULLER no. 1152.

Content is more than a kingdom.

(c 623)

c. 1560 T. LUPTON *Money* 631 Contentation
makes me as rich as a king. 1586 WARNER
Albion's Eng. IV. xx L3 Content is worth a
Monarchie. 1589 *Ibid.* v. xxvii R3 Content
exceedes a Crowne. 1591 SHAKES. *3 Hen. VI*
III. i. 64 My crown is call'd content; A crown
it is that seldom kings enjoy. 1591 GREENE *Wks.*
Gros. ix 279 Quiet perswaded her that content
was a kingdome. 1597 *Politeuphuia* 204b
Content is more worth then a kingdome. 1607
T. HEYWOOD *Wom. K. Kindness* III. i. 8. 1616
WITHALS (A contented mind). 1639 CLARKE 213.
1732 FULLER no. 1153.

Content is the philosopher's stone, that turns all it touches into gold. (c 625)

1642 FULLER *H. & P. State* III. xvii (1841) 186
Those who seek for the philosopher's stone, . . .
must not do it with any covetous desire to be
rich . . . Whosoever would have this jewel of
contentment, (which turns all into gold . . .)
must come . . . divested of . . . covetous thoughts.
1732 FULLER no. 1154.

Content lodges oftener in cottages than palaces. *Cf.* Love lives in cottages.

(c 626)

1584 LYLY *Sappho and Phao* I i. 15 Sweete life,
seldom found vnder a golden couert, often
vnder a thached cotage. 1595 R. TURNER *Garland of a Green Wit* C4ᵛ I haue heard it sayd,
there is more content in a Country Cottage, then
a Kings Pallace. [1604] 1607 DEKKER & WEBSTER *Sir T. Wyatt* I. ii. 17 What care I though a
Sheep-cote be my Pallace Or fairest roofe of
honour. 1732 FULLER no. 1155.

Content with his own kevel,[1] Let every man be.

1583 MELBANCKE *Philotimus* R1ᵛ Content your
self with your owne lot. 1721 KELLY 232 . . . L.
Sorte tuâ contentus abi. [¹ lot.]

Content (*adj., noun*), *see also* No man is c.;
Rich that possesses much, (He is not) but he
that is c. with what he has; Studies his c. (He
that).

Content(s), (*verb*), *see* Fortune torments me, (If)
hope c. me; Need much whom nothing will c.

Contented mind is a continual feast, A.

(M 969)

1535 COVERDALE *Bible Prov.* XV. 15 A quiet heart
is a continual feast. 1592 WARNER *Albion's Eng.*
VII. 37 X3ᵛ It is a sweete continuall feast to
liue content I see. 1766 *Goody Two-Shoes* V. iii.

Contented who needs neither borrow nor flatter, He may well be. (N 89)

1477 RIVERS *Dictes* (1877) 69 Some axed him of
howe moche goode[s] a man ought to be content,
and he answered to haue so moche as he neded nat
to flatre nor borowe of other. 1670 RAY 5. 1710
PALMER 313.

Contented, *see also* Enough who is c. with little;
Nature is c. with a little; Nothing (He that has)
is not c.; Nothing (He has), that is not c.

Contentibus, quoth Tommy Tomson, kiss my wife and welcome.

1721 KELLY 81 . . . Spoken facetiously when we
comply with a Project. 1738 SWIFT Dial. III.
E.L. 324.

Contention, *see* Bone of c.; Hundred ells of c.
(In) not inch of love; Spreade the table, c. will
cease.

Contentment, *see* Wealth (The greatest) is c.

Contraries being set the one against the other appear more evident. (c 630)

1533 ELYOT *Of Know.* V. 96 For every thinge
sheweth moste perfecetly, and after the common
proverbe of marchantis, best to the sale, whan it
is ioyned or compared with his contrary. c. 1565
R. EDWARDES *Damon & Pythias* l. 353. c. 1577
J. NORTHBROOKE *Treatise agst. Dicing* 26. 1583
G. BABINGTON *Exposⁿ of Commᵗˢ* 461 Easily may
we gather one contrarie by an other. 1592
DELAMOTHE 9 Two contraries, giue light the one
to the other. 1668 DRYDEN *Essay of Dram.
Poesy* (ed. Ker i. 69) The old rule of logic might
have convinced him, that contraries, when placed
near, set off each other.

Contraries, *see also* Dreams go by c.

Control, *see* Corrects not small faults, will not c.
great ones, (He that).

Convenience, *see* Every commodity (1609
quotn.).

Conversation makes one what he is.

(c 632)

1545 *Precepts of Cato* B4 With good men euer
let thi conuersacion be. And then shalte thou
get muche honeste. 1640 HERBERT no. 926.

Converses not, He that | knows nothing.

(M 527 and N 274)

1594-5 SHAKES. *T.G.V.* I. i. 2 Home-keeping
youth have ever homely wits. 1611 COTGRAVE
s.v. Ville He that goes not abroad knowes nothing. 1616 DRAXE no. 642 He that goeth not in
company, knoweth nothing. 1642 TORRIANO 23
He who still keepeth home, knoweth nothing.
1664 CODRINGTON 195 He that converseth not
with Men, knoweth nothing. 1670 RAY 5. 1732
FULLER no. 2070.

Convince(s, d), *see* Confuted and yet not c.;
Good orator who c. himself.

Conway, *see* Escape Clude and be drowned in C.

Cony, *see* Cat from a c. (cowlstaff), (To know a).

Coo, *see* Cow.

Cook any one's goose, To.

1851 *Street Ballad* in MAYHEW *Lond. Labour* I. 243 (Hoppe) If they come here we'll cook their goose, The Pope and Cardinal Wiseman. **1853** SURTEES *Sponge's Sport. T.* ch. 24 'If he's after either of the Jawley girls, he'll be bad to shake off'.... 'I think if he is, I could cook his goose for him.'

Cook-ruffian, able to scald the devil in his feathers. (C 643)

1565 J. CALFHILL *Treatise of the Cross* P.S. 81 Cook ruffian, that mars good meat in the dressing. **1670** RAY 169.

Cook that cannot lick his own fingers, He is a poor (ill). (C 636)

c. **1510** STANBRIDGE *Vulgaria* E.E.T.S. 27 He is an euyll coke that can not lycke his owne lyppes. **1545** TAVERNER C3 He is an euyll cooke that can not lycke his owne fyngers. **1546** HEYWOOD II. viii. K3 A poore cooke that maie not licke his owne fyngers. *c.* **1595** SHAKES. *R.J.* IV. ii. 6 (ill). **1598** PUTTENHAM *Eng. Poesie* Arb. 199 A bad cooke that cannot his owne fingers lick. **1642** FULLER *H. & P. State* IV. viii (1841) 260 Sir Thomas Cook ... had well licked his fingers under queen Margaret (whose wardrobe he was, ...), a man of a great estate. **1721** KELLY 138 He's a sarry[1] Cook that may not lick his own Fingers. Apply'd satyrically to Receivers, Trustees, Guardians, and other Managers. Signifying that they will take a Share of what is among their Hands. [[1] poor, mean.]

Cook's shop, *see* Starve in a c. s.

Cook(s), *see also* French would be best c. in Europe; God sends meat, devil c.; Salt c. bear blame; Too many c. spoil broth.

Cooked, *see* Cabbage twice c. is death.

Cookery, *see* Hunger finds no fault with c.

Cool as a cucumber, As. (C 895)

1615 BEAUM. & FL. *Cupid's Revenge* I. i Young Maids were as cold as Cowcumbers. **1627** [GAY?] *New Song of New Similies* I ... Cool as a Cucumber could see The rest of Womankind. **1838** DE QUINCEY *Greek Lit.* Wks. (1890) X. 318 Thucydides ... is as cool as a cucumber upon every act of atrocity.

Cool mouth, and warm feet, live long, A. (M 1248)

1611 COTGRAVE S.V. Pied A coole mouth and a dry foot preserve a man long time aliue. **1640** HERBERT no. 21.

Cool one's heels, To. (H 391)

[*c.* 1602] **1637** T. HEYWOOD *Royal King* vi. 46 Or else he may coole his heeles without if his appetite be hot. *c.* **1611** CHAPMAN *Il.* iii. 340 The soldiers all sat down enrank'd, each by his arms and horse That then laid down and cool'd their hoofs. **1631** DEKKER *Penny-Wise Pound-Foolish* E3 Didding him ... Stand there still and coole his heeles, and (with that) shut the dores upon him. **1633** ROWLEY *Match at Midnight* Hazl.-Dods. xiii. 52 Let him cool his heels there till morning. **1642** FULLER *H. & P. State* IV. i (1841) 231 O, whilst their heels cool, how do their hearts burn! **1752** FIELDING *Amelia* VI. ix In this parlour Amelia cooled her heels, as the phrase is, near a quarter of an hour.

Cool, *see also* Keep your breath to c.

Cooling card, A. (C 644)

1560–77 *Misogonus* III. ii. 23 Heavy newes for yow I can tell yow of a cowlinge carde. *c.* **1566** *Bugbears* III. i. 51. **1592–4** SHAKES. *I Hen. VI* V. iii. 84 There all is marr'd: there lies a cooling card. **1621** JAS. I *Answ. Commons* in RUSHW. *Hist. Coll.* (1659) I. 51 God sent us a Cooling-card this year for that heat.

Coot, *see* Bald as a c.; Wit than a c. (No more).

Cope, *see* Segging is good c.

Copy of his countenance, It is but a. (C 647)

[= not spoken sincerely.] *c.* **1568** WAGER *Longer thou livest* Cii It is but a coppie of his countenance. **1678** RAY 70. **1760** J. WESLEY *Lett.* iv. 107.

Coral needs no colouring, Right. (C 649)

1579 LYLY *Euph. Ep. Ded.* i. 181 The right Coral needeth no colouring Where the matter it selfe bringeth credit, the man with his glose winneth small commendation. **1732** FULLER no. 4051.

Corbie messenger, You are. (M 903)

c. **1300** *Cursor M.* l. 1892 For-þi men sais on messager þat lengs lang to bring answare, He mai be cald, with right resun An of messagers corbun. *c.* **1480** HENRYSON *Wks.* (S.T.S.) II. 86, l. 1152 Schir Corbie Rauin wes maid Apparitour. **1721** KELLY 385 ... Taken from the Raven sent out of the Ark; apply'd to them who being sent an Errand do not return with their Answer.

Corbies, *see* Kittle shooting at c. and clergy.

Cord breaks at the last by the weakest pull, The. (C 650)

1625 BACON *Ess.*, *Seditions* Arb. 401 Stormes, though they blow ouer diuers times, yet may fall at last; And as the Spanish Prouerb noteth well; ...

Corinth, It is not given to every man to go to. (M 202)

[Gk. Οὐ παντὸς ἀνδρὸς εἰς Κόρινθον ἔσθ' ὁ πλοῦς. HORACE *Epist.* I. 17. 36 *Non cuivis homini contingit adire Corinthum.*] **1542** UDALL *Apoph.* (1877) 379 *Lais* an harlot of *Corinthe* ... was for none but lordes and gentlemen that might well paie for it. Whereof came vp a prouerbe, that it was not for euery man to go vnto *Corinthe*. **1566** PAINTER ed. Jacobs i. 77. **1576** G. GAS-

COIGNE ii. 518. **1597** *Politeuphuia* 252 The Corinthians for their incontinencie, haue been euill spoken of; they were so inchast that they prostrated their own daughters to inrich themselues; hence came the prouerbe, It is not fit for euery man to goe to Corinth; for they payd well for their pleasure. **1706** STEVENS s.v. Corinto It is not every Man's lot to Sail to Corinth. Every Man is not born to be great, or to do his Pleasure. **1911** *Times Lit. Sup.* 24 Nov. 471 It is 'not every man who has the luck to go to Corinth', still less is it every man who is able to describe it when he has been there.

Cork, It is nothing but.

1854 *N. & Q.* 1st Ser. x. 128 In Oxfordshire, when a child exhibits an overweening fondness for a parent, with a view to gaining some coveted indulgence, it is usually denominated 'Cork' . . . 'It is nothing but cork' is a common expression from parent to child.

Cork (city), *see* Citizens of C. all akin; Limerick was, . . . C. shall be finest city.

Cork, *see also* Squeeze a c. little juice; Swim like a c.

Corn and horn go together.   (c 652)

1678 RAY 116 . . . *i.e.* for prices; when corn is cheap cattel are not dear, & vice versa. **1858** SURTEES *Ask Mamma* ch. 25 Foreign cattle . . . were coming in . . . and the old cry of 'down corn, down horn', frightened the 'stout British farmer'.

Corn hides itself in the snow as an old man in furs, The.   (c 653)

1640 HERBERT no. 241.

Corn him well, he'll work the better.

1721 KELLY 79 . . . Taken from Usage given to Horses. Apply'd to the giving of large Fees that you may be the better serv'd.

Corn in Egypt.

[In allusion to *Gen.* xlii. 2.] *a.* **1834** LAMB *Let. in* AINGER *Life* vii There is corn in Egypt while there is cash at Leadenhall.

Corn is cleansed with wind, and the soul with chastenings.   (c 655)

1640 HERBERT no. 154.

Corn is in the shock, When the | the fish are on the rock.

1865 HUNT *Pop. Romances W. of England* (1896) 428. **1869** HAZLITT 528 . . . *Cornwall.* An allusion to the correspondence of the fishing season with the harvest—more especially the pilchard fishery.

Corn, In much | is some cockle.   (c 659)

1528 SIR T. MORE *Dial.* ed. Campbell ii 245 A cockle among the corn. **1600** NASHE *Summers Last W.* Epil., iii. 293 In much Corne is some cockle; in a heape of coyne heere and there a

peece of Copper. **1615** *Janua Linguarum* 29 Among bundles and sheaues of cockle there is wheat.

Corn lies under the straw that is not seen, Much.   (c 661)

1639 CLARKE 145.

Corn, *see also* Acorns better than c. (To esteem); After Lammas c. ripens; Brain sows not c. (If); Cockle and c. grow in the same field.; God sends c. and devil mars sack; Good years c. is hay; King's chaff worth other men's c.; Land has its laugh and every c. its chaff; Look at your c. in May; Measures another's c. by own bushel; Neighbour's ground yields better c. than ours; Sickle into another man's c., (To put one's); Sows good seed (He that) shall reap good c.; Weed amongst c. nor suspicion in friendship (Neither); Weeds overgrow c.; Wind blows not down c., (Every); Wind shakes no c. (All this).

Corner(s), *see* Truth seeks no c.; Wind in that door (c.).

Cornish chough, A.

a. **1587** *Mirror for Mag.* (ed. Campbell 493) The Cornish Choughe did picke them in the face. **1595** *Locrine* v. iii Are the Cornish choughs in such great numbers come to Mercia? **1602** R. CAREW *Surv. of Cornwall* (1769), 36. **1617** MIDDLETON & ROWLEY *Fair Quarrel* II. ii My name is Chough, a Cornish gentleman. **1824** SCOTT *Redg.* ch. 22 Pengwinion, you Cornish chough, has this good wind blown you north?

Cornish gentlemen are cousins, All.   (G 78)

1602 CAREW *Surv. of Cornwall* (1769), 64 The prouerbe, that . . . **1724** DEFOE *Journey to Land's E.* (Morley) 138 They generally intermarry . . . from whence they say that proverb upon them was raised, viz., 'That all the Cornish gentlemen are cousins'.

Cornish hug, A.   (H 804)

1617 MIDDLETON & ROWLEY *Fair Quarrel* II. ii I'll show her the Cornish hug. **1662** FULLER *Cornw.* 197 To give one a Cornish Hugg. . . . The Cornish are Masters of the Art of Wrestling. . . . It is figuratively appliable to the deceitful dealing of such, who secretly design their overthrow whom they openly embrace. *c.* **1802** WOLCOT (P. Pindar) *Invit. to Bonaparte* Wks. (1816) IV. 265 And a warm *Cornish hug*, at thy landing.

Cornish man, men, *see* Tre, Pol, and Pen.

Corns, *see* Horse is troubled with c.

Corntown, *see* Stirling.

Cornwall will bear a shower every day, and two on Sunday. *Cf.* Hampshire, etc.

1864 *N. & Q.* 3rd Ser. v. 208.

Cornwall without a boat, To send a husband into.   (C 666)

c. **1565** *Bugbears* III. i. 29 I hope she wyll not fayle for hys further preferment to send hym in to Corne wayle. **1567** PAINTER *Pal. of Pleasure* (Jacobs) iii. 128 Either of them without shipping sought to send other into Cornouale. **1659** HOWELL *It. Prov.* 17. **1662** FULLER Cornw. 198 . . . This is an Italian Proverb, where it passeth for a *description* (or *derision* rather) of such a Man who is wronged by his Wifes disloyalty. **1670** RAY 223.

Cornwall, *see also* Devil will not come into C.; Saints in C. than in heaven (More).

Cornwallis, *see* Paston poor.

Coronation, *see* Never but once at a c.

Corporations have neither souls to be saved nor bodies to be kicked.

c. **1820** JOHN POYNDER *Literary Extracts* Lord Chancellor Thurlow [*c.* 1775] said that the corporations have neither bodies to be punished nor souls to be damned. **1886** SALA *Amer. Revis.* 360 You know what Lord Eldon said about Corporate Boards—that they had neither souls to be saved nor bodies to be kicked.

Corpse, *see* After a dream of a wedding comes c.; Bride the sun shines on and the c. . . . (Happy the).

Correct *Magnificat*, To.   (M 11)

[A byword for presumptuous fault-finding. *Magnificat* is the hymn of the Virgin Mary, in LUKE i. 46–55, beginning, in the Vulgate, *Magnificat anima mea Dominum*. L. *magnificare* = to magnify.] **1533** ELYOT *Knowledge* Pref. 3 Accomptyng to be in me no lyttell presumption, that I wylie in notynge other mens vices correct Magnificat. **1540** PALSGRAVE *Acolastus* 18 Thou Philyp fynde faute whiche takest vppon the to correct Magnificat. **1659** HEYLIN *Animadv.* in FULLER *Appeal Inj. Innoc.* (1840) 514 This is according to the old saying, to correct *Magnificat*. Assuredly, archbishop Whitgift knew better what he was to write, than to need any such critical emendations.

Correct *Magnificat* before one has learnt *Te Deum*, To.   (M 10)

[= to attempt that for which one has no qualifications.] **1542** ERASM. tr. Udall *Apoph.* 342b Suche . . . yᵗ will take vpon theim to bee doctours in those thynges in whiche theimselfes haue no skille at all, for whiche wee saie in Englyshe, to correcte Magnificat before he haue learned Te Deum. **1583** MELBANCKE E1 (before he can sing Te Deum).

Corrects not small faults, He that | will not control great ones.   (F 122)

c. **1576** WHYTHORNE 142 Of small fawts not let at the beginning often tyms springeth great and mihty mischefs. **1611** COTGRAVE *s.v.* Culot. **1659** N. R. 41.

Corruption of one thing is the generation of another, The.   (C 667)

1576 LAMBARDE *Kent* 2D4ᵛ The olde Maxime of Philosophie, Corruptio vnius, generatio alterius. **1600** *Livy* tr. Holland To Reader The corruption of one thing is the generation of another. **1604** MARSTON *Malcontent* III. i. 155 The corruption of coin is either the generation of a usurer or a lousy beggar. **1646** BROWNE *Vulgar Errors* Keynes ii. 208 That axiom in Philosophy, that the generation of one thing, is the corruption of another. **1693** DRYDEN *Ded. Third Misc.* 55 Thus the corruption of a poet is the generation of a critic. **1738** SWIFT *Dial.* II. E.L. 313 They say, that the corruption of pipes is the generation of stoppers.

Corruption of the best becomes the worst.   (C 668)

[L. *Corruptio optimi pessima*.] **1579** LYLY *Euph.* i. 241 Most true it is that the thing the better it is the greater is the abuse. **1609** SHAKES. *Sonn.* 94 For sweetest things turn sourest by their deeds. *a.* **1612** CHARRON *Of Wisdom* tr. Lennard (1640) 304. **1618** BP. HALL *Contempl.* IV. ix (1825) II. 360 But there is nothing so ill as the corruption of the best. **1856** BRIMLEY *Ess.* on *Angel in the House*. The worst . . . French novels . . . depict a certain kind of real life without reserve . . . *corruptio optimi pessima est*.

Cosier, *see* Clartier the c.

Cost hot water, It will.   (W 97)

1537 *Lisle Papers* XI. 100 (P.R.O.) If they be to be had, I will have of them, or it shall cost me hot water. **1655–62** GURNALL *Chrn. in Armour* (1865) I. 144 If the devil be so mighty, . . . then sure it will cost hot water before we display our banners upon the walls of that new Jerusalem.

Cost, The more | the more honour.   (C 670)

1591 HARINGTON *Orl. Furioso*, Adv. to Reader All their figures are cut in wood, and none in metall, and in that respect inferior to these, at least (by the old prouerbe) the more cost, the more worship. **1639** CLARKE 134. **1641** FERGUSSON no. 835. **1721** KELLY 317 . . . Spoken to them that propose an expensive Thing, when a cheaper would do. **1822** SCOTT *Pirate* ch. 11 'Ay, ay, brother, . . . that 's spoken like your wise sell. The mair cost the mair honour—that 's your word ever mair.'

Costs little, What | is less esteemed.   (L 370)

1620 SHELTON *Quix.* IV. vii (1908) I. 340 'It is also said as well', quoth Camilla, 'that "that which costeth little is less esteemed".'

Costs more to do ill than to do well, It.   (M 1143)

1640 HERBERT no. 262.

Cost(s) (*noun*), *see also* Counts all c. will never plough; Free of another man's c.; Learn at other men's c.; Pottage of a stool-foot (With c. make); Woo but c. (Who may).

Cost(s) (*verb*), *see also* Civility c. nothing; Kind (He has it by), it c. him nought; Nothing c. so much as what is given; Pleasure is not pleasant unless it c. dear; Three things c. dear, caresses of dog. . . . , Wine that c. nothing.

Costlet, *see* After a sort, as C. served.

Cotswold lion, A.   (L 323)

[A humorous name for a sheep.] **1440** Satirical rhymes on Siege of Calais in *Archaeologia* xxxiii. 130 Com renning on him fersly as lyons of Cotteswold. **1537** *Thersites* Hazl.-Dods. i. 400 Now have at the lions on Cots'old. *a.* **1553** UDALL *Royster D.* Arb. iv. vi. 70 Then will he looke as fierce as a Cotssold lyon. **1600** *Sir J. Oldcastle*, Pt. I. ii. i. 228 *Shakes. Apoc.* 138 You olde stale ruffin! you lion of Cotswold!

Cotswold, *see also* Long in coming as C. barley.

Cottage(s), *see* Change a c. in possession; Content lodges oftener in c. than palaces; Love lives in c. as well as in courts.

Couch a hogshead, To.   (H 504)

[= go to sleep.] *c.* **1510** *Cock Lorell's Boat* l. 339 Some couched a hogges heed vnder a hatche. **1546** HEYWOOD II. ii. G1ᵛ In meane tyme my akyng head to ease, I wyll couch a hogs hed. **1570** *Marr. Wit & Science* D1ᵛ Here you couche a coddes head.

Couch like a quail, To.

c. **1386** CHAUCER *Clerk's T.* ll. 1205–6 In jalousie I rede eek thou him bynde, And thou shalt make hym couche as doth a quaille. **1537** *Thersites* Hazl.-Dods. 396 (play couch-quail).

Cough will stick longer by a horse than half a peck of oats, A.   (c 676)

1678 RAY 117.   **1732** FULLER no. 54.

Cough (*noun*), *see also* Dry c. trumpeter of death; Love and a c. cannot be hid.

Cough (*verb*), *see* Drink in your pottage, c. in your grave.

Councils of war never fight.

1867 A. D. RICHARDSON *Beyond the Mississippi* 40 According to the proverb it [a council of war] never fights.   **1891** A. FORBES *Bar. Biv. & Batt.* (1910) 191 Solomon's adage that in the multitude of counsellors there is wisdom does not apply to war. 'Councils of war never fight' has passed into a proverb.

Counsel be good, If the | no matter who gave it.   (c 690)

c. **1640** W. S. *Countrym. Commonw.* 21 Refuse not any mans good counsell . . . though it come from thy inferiour.   **1732** FULLER no. 2704.

Counsel breaks not the head.   (c 679)

1640 HERBERT no. 443.

Counsel (Lawyer), He that is his own | has a fool for a client.

1850 HUNT *Autob.* ch. 11 The proprietor of the *Morning Chronicle* pleaded his own cause, an occasion in which a man is said to have 'a fool for his client' (that is to say, in the opinion of lawyers).   **1911** *Brit. Wkly.* 21 Dec. 386 There is a popular impression, for which there is a good deal to be said, that a man who is his own lawyer has a fool for his client.

Counsel is no command.   (c 681)

c. **1390** CHAUCER *W. of Bath's Prol.* l. 67 Conseil-lyng is no comandement.   **1530** R. WHITFORD *Work for Householders* H2 Whan you giue counseyll vnto a frende: say this semeth best vnto me, not thus you must nedeli do. For you may soner get rebuke or blame for your counsel yf it proue not, than thanke for your good counsel, though it spede well.   **1721** KELLY 76 . . . That is, I advise you so; but you may do as you please.   **1732** FULLER no. 1182.

Counsel must be followed, not praised.

1580 LYLY *Euph. & his Eng.* ii. 149–50 The counsaile of a friend must be . . . followed, not praysed.   **1594** LYLY *Mother B.* II. iii. 26 Vertue is not to be praised, but honored.   **1732** FULLER no. 1183.

Counsel nor court, Neither of his.

1546 HEYWOOD I. xi. E3 I was nother of court nor of counsaile made.   **1580** LYLY *Euph. & his Eng.* ii. 143 Howe he imployed it, he shall him-selfe vtter, for that I am neither of his counsaile nor court.

Counsel of fools, To the | a wooden bell.   (c 699)

1611 COTGRAVE s.v. Bois For woodden consulta-tions woodden bells.   **1640** HERBERT no. 535.

Counsel that has no escape, It is an ill.   (c 693)

1539 TAVERNER *Publius* E2 An euyll counsayle is that which can not be chaunged.   **1640** HER-BERT no. 715.

Counsel thou wouldst have another keep, first keep it thyself, The. *Cf.* Keep one's own counsel.   (c 682)

1566 L. WAGER *Mary Magd.* D2 Ye shal not kepe my counsel, if ye can not kepe your own.   **1598–9** SHAKES. *M.A.* III. iii. 80 Keep your fel-lows' counsels and your own.   **1600–1** *Id. H.* IV. ii. 9 Do not believe it — Believe what? — That I can keep your counsel, and not mine own.   **1623** CAMDEN 279.   **1670** RAY 5 Keep counsel thyself first.

Counsel to give (take) than to take (give), We have better.   (c 700)

1592 DELAMOTHE 37 We can giue alwayes better

counsell to other, then to our selues. **1621**
ROBINSON 32. **1639** CLARKE 22. **1664** CODRING-
TON 226 (to take, than to give).

Counsel will make a man stick his own mare.

1721 KELLY 82 . . . Spoken when we are over
persuaded to do a Thing. **1737** RAMSAY Ill
Counsel will gar a man stick his ain mare.

Counsel, *see also* Come not to c. uncalled; Court
(One of the), but none of the c.; Dog bark (If
old), gives c.; Enemy may chance to give good c.;
Fool may give a wise man c.; Give neither c. nor
salt; Give others good c. . . . (He can); Good c.
has no price; Good c. never comes amiss; Good
c. never too late; Healthful man can give c. to
sick; Ill c. mars all; Keep c. (Three may) if two
away; Keep one's c.; Less of your c. more of
your purse; Lucky men need no c.; Mum is c.;
Night is mother of c.; Take c. of pillow; Wiving
and thriving should take c.; Women's c. is cold.

Counselled, He that will not be | cannot be helped. (c 702)

1621 ROBINSON 24. **1639** CLARKE 22. **1670**
RAY 6. **1747** FRANKLIN Aug.

Counsellor, He that is his own | knows nothing sure but what he has laid out. (c 703)

1640 HERBERT no. 1001.

Counsellor like counsel, Like.

1581 J. CARTIGNY *Voyage of the Wandering
Knight* tr. W. Goodyear B3 There is an olde
Prouerbe, Such as my Counsailour is, such must
needes bee my counsell.

Counsellors, Though thou hast never so many | yet do not forsake the counsel of thy own soul. (c 704)

1678 RAY *Adag. Hebr.* 414.

Counsels in wine seldom prosper. (c 701)

1640 HERBERT no. 810. (Wine-counsels). **1664**
CODRINGTON 190. **1670** RAY 5. **1732** FULLER
no. 1184 Counsel over Cups is crazy.

Count not four, except you have them in a wallet. (F 620)

1640 HERBERT no. 962. **1666** TORRIANO *It. Prov.*
229, no. 23 (till they be in the bag).

Count one's chickens before they are hatched, To. (c 292)

1560–77 *Misogonus* IV. i. 15 My chickings are
not hatcht I nil to counte of him as yet. *a.* **1575**
T. HOWELL *New Sonnets and pretty Pamphlets* 11
Counte not thy Chickens that unhatched be.
1579 GOSSON *Ephem.* 19a I woulde not have him

to counte his chickens so soone before they be
hatcht. **1664** BUTLER *Hudibras* II. iii. 923 To
swallow gudgeons ere they're catch'd, And count
their chickens ere they're hatch'd. **1678** RAY
117 Count not your chickens before they be
hatch't. **1906** SERJT. MEREWETHER in LADY D.
NEVILL *Reminisc.* 306–8 A victory may be
snatched, But never count your little chicks,
Before they're safely hatched.

Count your gains, *see* Ill luck to.

Count, *see also* Angry (When) c. a hundred; Cat
has eaten her c.

Countenance, To be put out of. (c 705)

1544 H. STALBRIDGE [J. BALE] *Epistle Exhortatory*
Appdx. D6 Yf ye thynke Wraghton thus ouerthrowne or yet dasshyd out of countenounce ye are
sore deceyued. **155..** Ballad in Hazlitt in
Halliwell *Nugae Poet.* 49 Everyman lackyng yt
than Is clene owte of countenaunce. **1551**
T. WILSON *Rule of Reason* P6ᵛ Thei will saie, he
speaketh too too babyshelye, and so dashe hym
out of countenaunce, that he shall not well
knowe what to saie. **1589** *Theses Martinianae
Marprel. Tracts* ed. Pierce 328 There be that
affirm the rimers and stage-players to have clean
put you out of countenance. **1594–5** SHAKES.
L.L.L. V. ii. 272 This pert Berowne was out of
count'nance quite. **1659** HOWELL *Fr. Prov.* 19
He was put quite out of countenance.

Countenance, *see also* Copy of his c.; Hospitality
(Sin against) to open doors, shut c.; Thoughts
close and c. loose.

Counter(s), *see* Kiss the clink (c.); Nail to c.;
Slothful is servant of the c.; Words are wise
men's c.

Counting culzies[1] no kindness, Over narrow. (c 707)

a. **1628** CARMICHAELL no. 1216. **1641** FERGUS-
SON no. 669. **1721** KELLY 273 . . . When People
deal in Rigour with us, we think our selves but
little oblig'd to them. [¹ elicits.]

Countries, So many | so many customs (laws). (c 711)

c. **1100** *Anglo-Saxon Gnomic Verses* (Grein) I. 17
Efen-fela bega, þeoda, and þeawa [an equal num-
ber both of countries and customs]. *c.* **1300**
Provs. of Hending 4 Ase fele thedes, ase fele
thewes. *c.* **1374** CHAUCER *Troilus* Bk. 2, l. 28
In sondry londes, sondry ben usages. **1582**
WHETSTONE *Heptameron* V4ᵛ (customes). **1657**
TORRIANO *Choice Ital. Dial.* 71 (fashions). **1670**
RAY 73 Tant de gens tant de guises. *Gall.*

Country for a wounded heart, The.

1907 A. C. BENSON *From Coll. W.* [ed. 4] 107 (says
the old proverb).

Country, right or wrong, My (Our).

1706 STEVENS s.v. Dios Right or wrong, God help
our Council. A saying of obstinate Men of no
Conscience, who would have God prosper their

undertakings, tho' never so unjust. **1816** s. DECATUR *Toast* Our country! . . . may she always be in the right; but our country, right or wrong. **1891** J. E. T. ROGERS *Ind. & Commer. Hist.* I The habit . . . of uttering in the treatment of economical questions . . . 'our country, right or wrong', is not patriotism, . . . but . . . a pestilent, economical heresy. **1927** *Times* 5 Feb. 11/5 I would much prefer to enrol myself among those whose motto is 'My country right or wrong' than among those whose motto is 'My country always wrong'.

Country which has no history, Happy is the.

1740 FRANKLIN *Poor Richard* Happy that Nation, fortunate that age, whose history is not diverting. **1858–65** CARLYLE *Fred. the Gt.* XVI. i Happy the people whose annals are blank in history. **1859** G. ELIOT *Adam Bede* ch. 6 The happiest women, like the happiest nations, have no history. **1871** KINGSLEY *At Last* ch. 3 Trinidad ought to have been . . . a happy place from the seventeenth to the nineteenth century, if it be true that happy is the people who have no history. **1880** BLACKMORE *Mary Aner.* ch. 6 This land, like a happy country, has escaped, for years and years, the affliction of much history.

Country, countries, see also Britain (All c. stand in need of); Chicken is the c.'s but city eats it; Free c.; Go into c. to hear news at London; God made the c.; Smoke of a man's own c.; Sun rises in morning in every c.; Well with me (Where it is), there is my c.; Wise man esteems every place to be his own c.; World (This is the) and the other is c.

Counts all costs, He that | will ne'er put plough in the earth. (C 673)

a. **1628** CARMICHAELL no. 736. **1641** FERGUSSON no. 339. **1721** KELLY 126 . . . He that forcasts all Difficulties, that he may meet with in his Business, will never set about it.

Counts all the pins in the plough, He that | will never yoke her.

1721 KELLY 126.

County Clare payment, A.

1913 LADY GREGORY *New Com.* 96 Only a thank-you job; a County Clare payment, 'God spare you the health!'

Couple are newly married, When a | the first month is honey-moon, or smick smack: the second is, hither and thither: the third is, thwick thwack: the fourth, the Devil take them that brought thee and I together.

1670 RAY 53.

Couple is not a pair, Every.

1875 CHEALES *Proverbial Folk-Lore* 37. **1893** ALLINGHAM *Var. in Prose* III. 318 I'll . . . pass

. . . to Doctor Johnson and Horace Walpole. — Who by no means formed a pair.

Courage, see Despair gives c. to coward; Dutch c.

Course be fair, If that the | again and again quoth Bunny to his bear. (C 717)

1616 WITHALS 553 . . . *Bis ac ter quod pulchrum est.* **1639** CLARKE 179. **1670** RAY 163.

Course of true love never did run smooth, The.

1595 SHAKES. *M.N.D.* I. i. 134 The course of true love never did run smooth. **1836** M. SCOTT *Cruise Midge* ch. 11.

Course, see also Nature will have her c.; Need will have its c.; Tide keeps its c.; Youth will have its c.

Court, One of the | but none of the counsel. (C 727)

1546 HEYWOOD I. xi. E3 I was nother of court nor of counsaile made. **1639** CLARKE 78. **1721** KELLY 272 . . . One of the Party, but not admitted into their Secrets, and Intrigues.

Court, At | every one for himself. (C 718)

c. **1386** CHAUCER *Knight's T.* ll. 1181–2 At the kynges court, my brother, Ech man for hymself. **1611** COTGRAVE s.v. Court In Court men studie onely their owne fortunes. **1640** HERBERT no. 795. **1659** HOWELL *It. Prov.* 10.

Court has no almanac, The. (C 720)

1640 HERBERT no. 894. **1710** S. PALMER *Moral Essays on Prov.* 318 All Europe has consented to the Proverb, that in a Prince's Court there is no Almanack.

Court holy-water. (H 532)

1519 HORMAN *Vulgaria* (Roxb. Cl.) 333 I haue many feyre promessis and halywater of court. **1562** J. WIGAND *De Neutralibus* L6 Gret men seme to fauor their sides, though it be but with court holy water. *a.* **1593** *Jack Straw* Hazl.-Dods. v. 403. **1605–6** SHAKES. *K.L.* III. ii. 10 Court holy-water in a dry house is better than this rain-water out o' door. **1611** COTGRAVE s.v. Eau. **1678** RAY 236 . . . Eau beniste de la cour. *Gall.* Fair words and nothing else.

Court, see also Counsel nor c. (Neither of his); Dover c.; Dwell in c. (Whoso) must curry favour; Far from c. far from care; Friend at c.; Go old to the c.; Highest in c. nearest the widdie; Leave the c. ere c. leave thee; Lives in c. dies upon straw; Long in c., deep in hell; Men in c. (So many), so many strangers; Power seldom grows old at c.; Three ways, the church, sea, c. See also Courts.

Courtesies, He may freely receive | that knows how to requite them.   (C 736)

1664 CODRINGTON 195. 1670 RAY 22.

Courtesy entreated is half recompensed, A.

1642 TORRIANO 99. 1672 CODRINGTON 106.
1732 FULLER no. 57.

Courtesy is cumbersome to them that ken it not.   (C 730)

a. 1628 CARMICHAELL no. 405 (knawis). 1641
FERGUSSON no. 226. 1721 KELLY 156 Heigh
how[1] is heavy some, An old Wife is dowisome,[2]
And Courtesy is cumbersome, To them that
cannot shew it. The whole is for the sake of the
Last, viz. that People who are not used to good
Breeding, and mannerly Behaviour, perform it
very untowardly. [[1] an interjection of sorrow.
[2] tedious.]

Courtesy on one side only lasts not long.
                                          (C 731)

1611 COTGRAVE s.v. Courtoisie Courtesies vn-
requited continue not. 1640 HERBERT no. 809.
1732 FULLER no. 1191.

Courtesy, Where there is o'er mickle | there is little kindness.

1721 KELLY 350.

Courtes(yies), see also Full of c. full of craft;
Less of your c., more of your purse; Rank c.
when forced give thanks for own.

Courtier, see Young c. old beggar.

Courting and wooing bring dallying and doing.   (C 738)

1636 CAMDEN 294. 1732 FULLER no. 6264
(canting).

Courts, It is at | as it is in ponds; some fish, some frogs.

1732 FULLER no. 2912.

Cousin, Call me | but cozen me not.
                                          (C 739)

c. 1552 Manifest Det. Dice & Play C3 Bee they
young be they old that fauleth into our laps, and
be ignorant of our arte, we call them all by the
name of a cosin, as men that wee make as much
of, as if they were of our kinne. 1580 LYLY
Euph. & his Eng. ii. 21 Cassander . . . determined
with him-selfe to make a Cosinne of his young
Neuew. 1589 Letters of Philip Gawdy 46 He
passed it over and called me cosin. c. 1591-4
Thomas of Woodstock l. 13 Would our Cussen
king soe Cussen vs, to poysen us in our meate.
1593 SHAKES. Rich. III IV. iv. 223 Cousins indeed, and by their uncle cozen'd. 1597 Id.
1 Hen. IV I. iii. 254 'Kind cousin' — O, the
devil take such cozeners. 1600-1 Id. M.W.W.
IV. v. 71 There is three cozen-germans that has

cozen'd all the hosts of Readius. 1602 How Man
May Choose Hazl.-Dods. ix. 81 You are a common cozener, everybody calls you cousin. 1655
FULLER Hist. Camb. (1840) 117 Savill . . . , (To
try whether he could make cousens of his aunt's
children). 1678 RAY 118. 1790 TRUSLER Prov.
Exempl. 20 'A truce with your kindness, my
good sir',—. . .

Cousin(s), see also Call the king c.; Cornish
gentlemen c.; Kentish c.; Marry come up, my
dirty c.

Covenant, see Cathkin's c. . . . let abee for let
abee.

Coventry, To send (a person) to.

1765 Club bk. Tarporley Hunt in EG. WARBURTON
Hunting Songs Introd. (1877) 16 Mr. John Barry
having sent the Fox Hounds to a different place
to what was ordered . . . was sent to Coventry,
but return'd upon giving six bottles of Claret to
the Hunt. 1796 EDGEWORTH Par. Asst., Eton
Mont. III. ii. He'd send me to Coventry, . . . did
he but know I was condescending to make this
bit of explanation, unknown to him. 1916 E. A.
BURROUGHS Val. of Decis. II. iv. The 'sportsman-
ship' of the house united against him, and
punished his treason by sending him to Coventry.

Coventry blue. Cf. True blue.   (T 542)

[Blue thread manufactured at Coventry, and used
for embroidery.] 1581 W. STAFFORD Exam. of
Certain Complaints New Sh. S. 89 The chiefe
trade of Couentry was heretofore in making of
blew threde. 1590 T. LODGE Rosalynde ed. Greg
149. 1591 S. SMELLKNAVE Fearful effects of Two
Comets 28 Knit Nettes of Coventry blewe for
Woodcockes. a. 1592 GREENE Jas. IV (Gros.) IV.
iii. 1752 Edge me the sleeues with Couentry blew.
1600 T. HEYWOOD et al. 1 Edw. IV i. 86 As good
Couentry-silk blue thread, as euer thou sawest.
1624 JONSON Masque of Owls vii. 784 And though
his hue Be not Coventrie-blue, Yet is he undone By the thred he has spunne. 1662
FULLER Warwick 118 . . . The best blews . . . are
died in Coventry. It is applied to . . . a fast and
faithfull friend.

Cover your head by day as much as you will, by night as much as you can.
                                          (H 242)

1642 TORRIANO 45. 1678 RAY 41.

Cover yourself with your shield, and care not for cries.   (S 332)

1640 HERBERT no. 161.

Cover (noun), see Cup (Like), like c.

Coverlet, see Honour under c. (Cannot come to).

Covers me with his wings and bites me with his bill, He.   (W 496)

1616 DRAXE no. 1043. 1670 RAY 5. 1710
PALMER 207.

Covers thee discovers thee, He that.
(C 743)

1620 SHELTON *Quix.* II. v (1908) II. 221 'Would you know why, husband?' answered Teresa: 'for the proverb that says he that covers thee discovers thee. Every one passeth his eyes slightly over the poor, and upon the rich man they fasten them.' **1694** BOYER 108.

Cover(s) (*verb*), *see also* Hat c. family; Love c. many infirmities.

Covet, *see* All c. all lose.

Covetous man is good to none and worst to himself, The. (M 86)

1539 TAVERNER *Publius* D1 (The couetouse body). **1597** *Politeuphuia* 240ᵛ (worst friend). **1614** LODGE *Ep.* 108, 443. **1732** FULLER no. 53.

Covetous spends more than the liberal, The. (M 1151)

1639 CLARKE 39 More spends the niggard then the liberall. **1640** HERBERT no. 683.

Covetous was never good, Over.

1481 CAXTON *Reynard* xxxiii Arb. 95 It falleth ofte who that wold haue all leseth alle Ouer couetous was neuer good.

Covetous, *see also* Miserable (C.) man makes a penny of a farthing; Poor man wants some things, a c. man all things.

Covetousness (Too much) breaks (bursts) the bag (sack). (C 744)

c. **1594** BACON *Promus* (Pott) no. 616 Covetousness breaks the sack. **1620** SHELTON *Quix.* III. vi (1908) I. 148 But, as covetousness breaks the sack, so hath it also torn my hopes. **1651** HERBERT no. 1071. **1659** HOWELL *Span. Prov.* 5 (Too much). **1666** TORRIANO 244 (Too much). **1670** RAY 26 . . . *Hispan.* (Too much). **1710** PALMER 34 (breaks the Jack, i.e. the leathern jack). **1821** SCOTT *Kenilw.* ch. 4 Be not over greedy, Anthony. Covetousness bursts the sack and spills the grain. **1853** TRENCH V. 111 (bursts).

Covetousness brings nothing home.
(C 745)

1601 DENT *Pathway to Heaven* 81 (The old Proverb saith . . .). *a.* **1640** J. SMYTH *Lives of the Berkeleys* ii. 414 The comon proverbe, That covetousnes never brought home clear gaines. **1678** RAY 117 Ref. to Fable of dog who saw his shadow in the pond. *Ital.*

Covetousness is (Riches are) the root of all evil. (C 746)

[I TIMOTHY vi. 10 For the love of money is the root of all evil.] *c.* **1387** CHAUCER *Pard. T.* Prol. l. 6 Radix malorum est cupiditas. *a.* **1529** SKELTON *Image Hypocrisy*: Wks. ii. 423 Be ware of covetyse, The rote of all ill vice. **1539** TAVERNER I *Garden*

E8ᵛ [Diogenes] sayde couetyse is the mother . . . and hedde of all euyls. Not moche swaruynge from Salomon whiche calleth it the rote of all euylles. **1549** LATIMER *Serm.* 11, P.S. 184 It is a true saying, Radix omnium malorum avaritia, Covetousness is the root of all wickedness. **1591** ARIOSTO *Orl. Fur.* Harington XXXIV. 19 (the branch and roote of ill). **1616** WITHALS 546 (Riches are).

Covetousness often starves other vices.

1732 FULLER no. 1178.

Covetousness, *see also* Lechery and c. go together; Poverty wants many things, c. all; Sins grow old (When), c. is young.

Cow calf as for the bull, As well for the.

1546 HEYWOOD II. iv. G3 As well for the cowe calfe as for the bull.

Cow (sow) has calved (pigged), His.
(C 756)

[*c.* 1522] *c.* **1545** SKELTON *Why Come Not to Court* ii. 29 Our mare hath cast her fole. [*c.* 1553] **1575** *Gam. Gurt. Needle* IV. i. D1 Hathyour browne cow cast hir calfe, or your sandy sowe her pigs. **1603** S. HARSNET *Decl. of Egregious Popish Impostures* Q2ᵛ His sow hath pigged. **1609** S. HARWARD 79ᵛ. **1616** JONSON *Ev. Man in Humour* IV. ii. 110 How now! whose cow ha's calu'd? **1678** RAY 70 His cow hath calved, or sow pig'd. He hath got what he sought for, or expected.

Cow in a fremit loaning (an uncouth loan),[1] Like a.

1721 KELLY 223 ˙ (an uncouth loan). That is, every Body look'd strange to me. **1821** SCOTT *Let.* 11 June in LOCKHART *Life* lii (1860) 452 To hear . . . a probationer in divinity, preach his first sermon in the town of Ayr, *like a cow in a fremd loaning.* **1837–9** LOCKHART *Scott* ch. 56 (1860) 488 In the glittering . . . assemblages of that season, the elder bard [Crabbe] was . . . very like *a cow in a fremd loaning.* **1862** HISLOP 87 (unco loan). That is, strange or out of place. [¹ strange milking-place.]

Cow is in the clout, When the | she's soon out.

1721 KELLY 342 Eng. Ready Money will away. **1832** HENDERSON 58 Put a cow in a clout and she will soon wear out. (The price of a cow is soon spent.)

Cow knows not what her tail is worth till she has lost it, The. (C 749)

1611 COTGRAVE s.v. Vache Vache ne sçait que vaut sa queue iusques à ce qu'elle l'ait perdue. The want, more then the vse, indeares the worth of good things; we know our friends best when we want them most. **1623** WODROEPHE 523 A Kow knowes not what her Taile may, Vntill shee haue mist it all away. Spend not our Goods but by Measure. **1640** HERBERT no. 870. **1721** KELLY 321 The Cow may want her own Tail yet. You may want my Kindness hereafter, though you deny me yours now.

Cow, Like | like calf.   (c 759)

1564 BULLEIN *Dial. agst. Fever* E.E.T.S. 21
Her son is like the mother . . . , like cow like calf.
1659 HOWELL *Brit. Prov.* 21 As the Cow so the
Calf.

Cow little giveth that hardly liveth, The.

1573 TUSSER (1878 ed., 86) (February Cow).
1732 FULLER no. 6325.

Cow of his own, Who would keep a | when he may have a quart of milk for a penny?   (c 767)

1659 HOWELL *Letter of Advice* ¶2 It is better to
buy a quart of Milk by the penny then keep a
Cow. **1680** BUNYAN *Mr. Badman* (ed. Brown,
154) . . . Meaning, who would be at the charge
of a Wife, that can have a Whore when he
listeth? **1895** S. BUTLER *Note-Books* 285 I knew
one gentleman who asked his [the Archbishop
of Canterbury's] advice . . . He told him that it
was cheaper to buy the milk than to keep a cow.

Cow that gives a good pail of milk, and then kicks it over, Like the. *Cf.* **Goat gives a good milking, etc.**   (M 661)

1546 HEYWOOD II. vii. K1ᵛ Margery good cowe
(quoth he) gaue a good meele, But than she cast
it downe agayne with hir heele. **1599** PORTER
Angry Wom. Abingd. Mal. Soc. l. 2323 Be not
you like the Cowe, that giues a good sope of milke,
and casts it downe with his heeles. **1639** FULLER
Holy War v. xxii (1840) 280 These Italians . . .
as at first they gave good milk, so they kicked it
down with their heel, and by their mutual discord caused the loss of all they helped to gain in
Syria.

Cow that's first up, The | gets the first of the dew.

1721 KELLY 306 . . . Recommending Diligence,
and Industry.

Cow to catch a hare, Set a.   (c 763)

1611 COTGRAVE s.v. Vache A Cow may catch a
Hare. **1678** RAY 342.

Cow with the iron tail, The.

[= the pump.] **1896** J. C. HUTCHESON *Crown &
Anchor* ch. 12 'We'll send ashore for a cow for
you', . . . put in Mr. Stormcock ironically . . .
'Dobbs, you know the sort of cow the young
gentlemen wants—one with an iron tail.'

Cow's horn, *see* Crooked as a c. h.; Tip c. h. with
silver.

Cow's tail, *see* Grow like a c. t.

Cow's thumb (hair's breadth), To a.
                    (c 769 and H 28)

1533 J. HEYWOOD *Play Weather* C1ᵛ The tre
remouyth no here bred from hys place. **1562**

J. WIGAND *De Neutralibus* J4 Wewi ll not shrinke
any heare breadth from the truth. **1670** RAY
216 To a cows thumb. To a hairs breadth.
1681 T. FLATMAN *Heraclitus Ridens* No. 40 (1713)
II. 2 Let him alone, he'll trim their whiskers and
comb their Perukes for them to a Cow's thumb.

Cow-turd, *see* Humble-bee in c.

Cow(s), coo, *see also* Bare moor he . . . gets not a
c.; Barley straw . . . when c. gives water; Beat a
horse . . . and a c. till she be mad; Becomes it as
c. does cart-saddle; Bletherin' c. forgets calf;
Bring a c. to the hall and she'll run to byre;
Bulls the c.; Butter once a year in c.'s horn;
Butter that the cow yields (Not all); Buy the c.
(If you), take the tail; Comely as c. in cage;
Crab in a c.'s mouth (No more than); Crooning
c.; Curst c. short horns; Devil's c. calves twice a
year; Every man as he loves . . . when he kissed
his c.; God gives the c.; Good c. has evil calf
(Many); Grow like a c.'s tail; Hackerton's c.;
Look to the c. and the sow; Looked on me as c.
on bastard calf; Love as . . . between c. and
haystack; Luck as had the c. that stuck herself;
Mackissock's c.; Neighbour's ground (c.) yields
better corn (more milk) than ours; Old brown c.
laid egg; Parson's c. (Come home like) with a
calf; Poor man's c. dies; Red c. good milk; Rush
bush keeps c.; St. Robert gave his c. (Freely
as); Sell the c. and sup the milk; Sell the c.
must say the word (Who will); Sheep and a c.
(Now I have); Slender in the middle as a c.;
Tint a c. (He never) that grat for a needle;
Tune the old c. died of; Welshman's c., little
and good.

Coward changes colour, A.   (c 773)

1545 TAVERNER G4ᵛ The cowarde chaungeth
colours. **1616** DRAXE no. 394 (often changeth
colour).

Coward to his mettle, Put a | and he'll fight the devil.   (c 777)

1648 HERRICK *Hesper., Feare gets force* (O.U.P.)
302 Despaire takes heart, when ther's no hope
to speed: The Coward then takes Armes, and
do's the deed. **1669** WINSTANLEY *New Help
Discourse* 107 Make a Coward Fight, and he
will kill the Devil. **1721** KELLY 281. **1732**
FULLER no. 3980.

Cowards are cruel.   (c 778)

1485 MALORY *Morte d'Arthur* xviii. 24 Ever
wylle a coward shewe no mercy. **1603** MON-
TAIGNE (Florio) II. xxvii. 226 (chap. heading)
Cowardize, the mother of Crueltie. **1616**
DRAXE no. 407 Cruell people are fearefull. **1727**
GAY *Fables* i. 33 Cowards are cruel but the
brave love mercy. **1849** C. BRONTË *Shirley* ch.
21 The magistrates are . . . frightened, and, like
all cowards, show a tendency to be cruel.

Cowards die often.   (c 774)

1596 DRAYTON *Mortimeriados* l. 2723 Every
houre he dyes, which ever feares. **1599** SHAKES.
J.C. II. ii. 32 Cowards die many times before
their deaths.

Cowards, Many would be | if they had courage enough.

a. **1680** ROCHESTER *Sat. agst. Mankind* l. 158 All men would be cowards if they durst. **1695** W. MORGAN *Religio Militis* 19 All men would be Cowards, if they durst. **1732** FULLER no. 3366. **1779–81** JOHNSON *Lives of Poets* (Bohn) I. 224 This was meant of Rochester, whose buffoon conceit was . . . a saying often mentioned, that every Man would be a Coward if he durst.

Coward(s), *see also* Bully is always a c.; Despair gives courage to c.; Necessity and opportunity make c. valiant; Valiant man's look more than c.'s sword; Virtue of c. is suspicion.

Cowl (Habit, Hood) does not make the monk, The.   (H 586)

[L. *Cucullus non facit monachum.* NECKAM *Non tonsura facit monachum, non horrida vestis.* RABELAIS I. Prol. *Vous mesmes dictes que l'habit ne faict poinct le moine.*] *c.* **1200** *Ancr. Riwle* 12 Vrom the worlde witen him clene and unwemmed: her inne is religiun and nout iþe wide hod ne iðe blake. *c.* **1387** USK *Test. of Love* in *Skeat's Chaucer* VII. 91 For habit maketh no monk; ne weringe of gilte spurres maketh no knight. *c.* **1400** *Rom. Rose* l. 6192 Habite ne maketh monk ne frere; But a clean life and devotion Maketh gode men of religion. **1588** GREENE *Pandosto* Pr. Wks. (1881–3) IV. 289 Trueth quoth *Fawnia,* but all that weare Cooles are not Monkes. **1601** SHAKES. *T.N.* I. v. 50 Lady, cucullus non facit monachum; that's as much to say as I wear not motley in my brain. **1604** *Id. M.M.* V. i. 261 Cucullus non facit monachum: honest in nothing, but in his clothes. **1613** *Id. Hen. VIII* III. i. 23 They should be good men. . . . But all hoods make not monks. **1641** FERGUSSON no. 525 It is not the habite that makes the monk. **1820** SCOTT *Abbot* ch. 26 'Call me not doctor, . . . since I have laid aside my furred gown and bonnet.' 'Oh, sir, . . . the cowl makes not the monk.'

Cowlstaff, *see* Cat from a cony (c.), (To know a).

Cowped the mickle dish into the little, He has.

1721 KELLY 144 . . . The Jest is in the different Signification of the Word *Cowp,* which signifies to buy and sell Grain, Cattel, &c., and to turn one Thing upon another. Spoken when People have faln behind in Dealing.

Cows come home, Till the.   (C 772)

1593 J. ELIOT *Ortho-Epia Gallica* ed. J. Lindsay 43 I am tied by the foote till the Cow come home. **1610** A. COOKE *Pope Joan* in *Harl. Misc.* (1745) iv. 125 Drinking, eating, feasting, and revelling, till the Cow come Home, as the Saying is. *c.* **1612** BEAUM. & FL. *Scornf. Lady* II. i. Kiss till the Cow come home. **1738** SWIFT *Dial.* II. E.L. 308 I warrant you lay a-bed till the cows came home.

Cows, *see also* Cow(s).

Coy as a croker's[1] mare, As.   (C 833)

1546 HEYWOOD II. i. F2ᵛ Of auncient fathers she toke no cure nor care, She was to theim as koy as a crokers mare. **1659** HOWELL *Eng. Prov.* 10b. [[1] a saffron-dealer.]

Cozen, *see* Cousin (Call me).

Crab[1] in a cow's mouth, It is no more to him than a.

1732 FULLER no. 2990. *Ibid.* no. 5505 What's a Crab in a Cow's Mouth? **1791** WOLCOT (P. Pindar) *Rights of Kings* Wks. (1816) II. 194 Too soon your band its weakness would deplore! A crab in a cow's mouth—no more! [[1] crab-apple.]

Crab of the wood, The | is sauce very good for the crab of the sea, but the wood of the crab is sauce for a drab, that will not her husband obey. (C 784)

1659 HOWELL *Eng. Prov.* 6a The wood of a Crabbe, is good for a Drabb that will not her Husband obey. **1670** RAY 210.

Crab, To go backwards like the.

1579 LYLY *Euph.* i. 208 To true it is that as the Sea Crabbe swimmeth alwayes agaynst the streame; so wit alwayes striueth agaynst wisedome. **1597** *Politeuphuia* 17ᵛ Louers oft tymes proceede in theyr sutes as Crabs, whose paces are alwaies backward. **1600–1** SHAKES. *H.* II. ii. 203 You yourself, sir, shall grow old as I am, if, like a crab, you could go backward. [1601–2] **1606** *2 Return from Parnassus* l. 1584 [The instruction is to read 'metulas' backwards.] Mitto tibi metulas, cancros imitare legendo. **1820** PEACOCK *Four Ages of Poetry* Percy Reprints iii. 16 The march of his intellect is that of a crab, backward. **1860** PEACOCK *Gryll Grange* ch. I.

Crab, *see also* Runner (Look like a) quoth devil to c.; Sillier than a c.; Sour as a c.

Crabs, The greatest | be not all the best meat.   (C 786)

1546 HEYWOOD I. xi. E2 We had . . . a chese very greate. But the greattest crabs be not all the best meate. **1639** CLARKE 180.

Crab-tree, The older the | the more crabs it bears.

1856 ABP. WHATELY *Annot. on Bacon's Ess.* 42 (1876) 452 (says the proverb).

Crab-tree where you will, Plant the | it will never bear pippins.   (C 788)

1579 LYLY *Euph.* i. 191 Plante and translate the crabbe tree where and whensoeuer it please you and it will neuer beare sweete apple.

Crab-tree, *see also* Hang a dog on a c.

Crack me that nut (quoth Bumsted). Cf. Hard nut to crack.   (N 359)

1545 ELYOT *Def. Gd. Wom.* B4ᵛ Nowe knacke me that nut, Maister Candidus. **1546** HEYWOOD II. vii. J3ᵛ Knak me that nut. **1600** DEKKER *Old*

Fort. I. i. 53 My tongue speakes no language but
an Almond for Parrat, and cracke me this Nut.
1678 RAY 69 . . . (quoth Bumsted).

Crack(s), *see also* Ape can c. a nut (Before an);
Hen c. nuts (As fast as a); Strings high stretched
soon c.

Cracked bell can never sound well (is never sound), A. (B 274)

1629 T. ADAMS *Serm.* (1861) I. 73 A wicked man's
tongue discovers him. A bell may have a crack,
though invisible; take the clapper and strike, and
you shall soon perceive it. **1732** FULLER no.
6358. **1823** COLLINS 77 *Campana cascada,
nunca sana.* 'A cracked bell is never sound.'—It
has a reference to persons of weak minds, arising
from natural infirmity or some bodily accident.

Cracked nuts with her tail, She goes as if she. (N 364)

1678 RAY 291.

Crackling, *see* Thorns make greatest c.

Cradle straws are scarce out of his breech. (C 795)

1678 RAY 346.

Cradle(s), *see also* Between the c. and the grave;
Fair in the c., foul in saddle; Foot on c. . . . sign
of good housewife; Hand that rocks the c.;
Knock in the c. (He got a); Plough going (Better
have one) than two c.; Shod in c., barefoot in
stubble.

Craft against craft makes no living. (C 797)

1640 HERBERT no. 890.

Craft brings nothing home. (C 798)

1616 DRAXE no. 401. **1670** RAY 6. **1732** FULLER
no. 1199 Craft counting all things, brings nothing home.

Craft, He that has not the | let him shut up shop. (C 802)

1640 HERBERT no. 860.

Craft in daubing, There is. (C 803)

1454 *Paston Letters* (1900) I. 269 Her moder . . .
seyth to her that ther is gode crafte in dawbyng.
c. **1530** *Hyckescorner* 259, 260 If my handes
were smyten of, I can stele with my tethe;
For ye knowe well there is crafte in daubynge.
a. **1575** PILKINGTON P.S. 465 (even in daubing).
1623 CAMDEN 278. **1678** RAY 120 There is more
craft in daubing then throwing dirt on the wall.

Craft is in the catching, All the. (C 796)

c. **1570** *Juli and Julian* l. 761 All the craft is in
the chatchinge. **1608** DEKKER *The Dead Term*

G2ᵛ All the craft was in the catching. **1616**
DRAXE no. 1093. **1631** MABBE *Celestina* T.T. 163.
1639 CLARKE 146.

Craft lies in clouted shoes. (C 800)

1563 *Mirror for Mag.* ed. Campbell 402 Where is
more craft than in the clowted shoen? **1581**
C. THIMELTHORPE *Short Inventory* F4ᵛ No craft
to the clouted shoo. **1594** *Knack to Know an
Honest Man.* l. 193 Craft often lurketh in a
shepheards coate. [1635] **1655** MASSINGER
Bashful Lover v. i. There's craft In the clouted
shoe.

Craft must have clothes, but truth loves to go naked.

1597 *Politeuphuia* 30b Craft hath neede of
cloaking, where truth is euer naked. **1732**
FULLER no. 1200.

Craft, *see also* Full of courtesy, full of c.; Gentle
c.; Mariners' c.; No man c.'s master first day.

Crafty knave needs no broker, A. *Cf.* Two false knaves. (K 122)

1584 R. WILSON *Three Ladies of London* Hazl.-
Dods vi. 257 A couple of false knaves together,
a thief and a broker. **1590–1** SHAKES. *2 Hen. VI*
I. ii. 100 They say,—A crafty knave does need no
broker; yet am I Suffolk, and the cardinal's
broker. **1591** GREENE *Disc. Coz.* Gros. 185.
1598 JONSON *Ev. Man in Hum.* III. ii. 32 That
cannot be, if the prouerbe hold; a craftie knaue
needs no broker. **1623** CAMDEN 266 (A false
knaue).

Crafty man, To a | a crafty and a half. (M 393)

1599 MINSHEU *Span. Gram.* 83 To one traitor,
two traitors, i. To ouer reach one craftie knaue,
set two craftie knaues to him and they will cony
catch him. **1640** HERBERT no. 796.

Crambe repetita, see Cabbage twice cooked.

Cranes of Ibycus, The.

[*c.* 540 B.C. Gk. Αἱ Ἰβύκου γέρανοι. Ibycus, a
Greek poet, attacked by robbers, called on a
flight of cranes to avenge his death. The subsequent sight of these cranes called forth a
remark which led to the arrest and execution of
the murderers. ERASM. *Ad. Ibyci grues.*] **1853**
TRENCH ii. 36 *The Cranes of Ibycus* passed into a
proverb, very much as our Murder will out, to
express the wondrous leadings of God whereby
. . . secret things of blood are brought to the open
light of day. **1905** ALEX. MACLAREN *Genesis* 19
According to the fine old legend of the cranes of
Ibycus, a bird of the air will carry the matter.

Crave, *see* Nothing c. nothing have; Nothing
have nothing c.; Youth knew what age would c.
(If).

Cravers are aye ill payers, Sore. (C 807)

a. **1628** CARMICHAELL no. 198. **1721** KELLY 286
. . . This Proverb, and the Reverse, *viz.* Ill Payers

are sore Cravers, I have never yet seen fail. **1737** RAMSAY III. 186 Ill payers are ay guid cravers.

Craving, *see* Shameful (Shameless) c. must have shameful nay.

Crawley brook, *see* Crooked as C. b.

Creaking door (gate) hangs long on its hinges, A.

1776 T. COGAN *John Buncle, Junior* i. 239 But they say a creaking gate goes the longest upon its hinges; that's my comfort. **1880** BARING GOULD *Mehalah* ch. 22 Your mother ... may live yet a score of years. Creaky gates last longest.

Cream of the jest, That is the. (C 811)

1666 TORRIANO *Prov. Phras.* s.v. Coda 41 To leave out the cream of the jest. **1678** RAY 69.

Cream, *see also* Cat shuts eyes while steals c.

Creampot love, *see* Cupboard love.

Cream-pot, *see* Cat is in the c. p.

Credit (honour), No man ever lost his | but he who had it not. (M 326)

c. **1526** *Dicta Sap.* C2 None loseth mony saue he that had it. But he is sayde to haue lost his fidelite that had it nat, that is to saye, he that hath bene vnfaythfull. *a.* **1571** R. EDWARDS *Damon & Pythias* G2 Where can you say I euer lost mine honestie?—You neuer lost it, for you neuer had it, as farre as I know. **1599** SHAKES. *A.Y.* I. ii. 68 But if you swear by that that is not, you are not forsworn. No more was this knight, swearing by his honour, for he never had any. **1664** CODRINGTON 206. **1670** RAY 6.

Credit decayed, and people that have nothing, Take heed of. (H 377)

1599 MINSHEU 84. **1651** HERBERT no. 1150.

Credit lost is like a Venice-glass broken. (C 814)

1614 T. ADAMS *Fatal Banquet* II Wks. 193 A mans name is like a glasse, if it be once crack'd, it is soone broken. **1633** SHIRLEY *Witty Fair One* II. ii And if she chance any way to crack her Venice glass, it will be not so easily soldered. **1659** HOWELL *New Sayings* 4a Reputation like a Venice-glasse easily crackd. **1664** CODRINGTON 189. **1670** RAY 6. **1796** EDGEWORTH *Par. Asst.* (1903) 411 He found the truth of the proverb, 'that credit lost is like a Venice glass broken—it can't be mended again'.

Credit, *see also* Buys dear and takes up on c. (Who); Honesty (C.) keeps crown of causeway; Lost his c., dead to the world; Religion, c., are not to be touched.

Creditors have better memories than debtors. (C 818)

1659 HOWELL *Span. Prov.* 8 The Creditor hath a better memory then the Debtor. **1758** FRANK-

LIN in ARB. *Eng. Garner* V. 585 When you have got your bargain; you may, perhaps, think little of payment, but. . . .

Creed, *see* Judicare came into the c. (To know how); Paternoster (He may be in my) but never in my c.

Creel, *see* Put your hand in c. and take out adder or eel.

Creep, *see* Children begin to c. ere they go; Find some hole to c. out at; First c. then go; Kind (Love) will c. where it may not go; Speak as if you would c. into my mouth (You).

Cress, Not worth a.

c. **1387** USK *Test. of Love* in *Skeat's Chaucer* vii. 73 Their might is not worth a cress. **1393** LANGLAND *P. Pl.* C. xii. 14 Wysdom and wit now · is nat worth a carse.[1] [[1] cress.]

Cricket, *see* Merry as a c.

Cries wine and sells vinegar, He. (W 463)

1659 HOWELL *Span. Prov.* 3. **1732** FULLER no. 1831.

Criffel, *see* Skiddaw.

Crimes (Mischiefs) are made secure by greater crimes (mischiefs). *Cf.* Sin plucks on sin. (C 826)

1566 SENECA *Agamemnon* tr. J. Studley 115 The safest path to mischief is by mischiefe open still. **1588** T. HUGHES *Misfortunes of Arthur* I. iv. 77 The safest passage is from bad to worse. *c.* **1592** KYD *Span. Trag.* III. xii. H4ᵛ Per scelus semper tutum est sceleribus iter. For euils unto ils conductors be. **1604** MARSTON *Malcontent* V. ii. 208 Black deed only through black deed safely flies. **1605-6** SHAKES. *M.* III. ii. 55 Things bad begun make strong themselves by ill. **1633** GOFFE *Orestes* II. iv. C4ᵛ Mischiefe by mischiefe findes the safest way.

Crime, *see also* Greater the man the greater the c.

Criminal, *see* Mercy to c.

Criminate, *see* No man is bound to c. self.

Cripple, *see* Crooked carlin, quoth the c.; Dwells next door to c. will learn to halt; Halting before a c. (Hard); Mocks a c. ought to be whole.

Cripplegate, *see* Lame as St. Giles, C.

Critics are like brushers of noblemen's clothes. (C 829)

1625 BACON *Apophthegms* no. 64. **1651** HERBERT no. 1157.

Croaking, *see* Raven bodes misfortune (The c.).

Croaks, *see* Crow c. before the rain (The hoarse).

Crock, *see* Part with the c. as the porridge (As soon).

Crocodile tears.   (C 831)

[ERASM. *Ad. Crocodili lacrimae.*] **1548** COOPER s.v. Crocodilus . . . A prouerbe, applied unto them, which hatyng an other man, whom they would destroie, or haue destroied, thei wil seme to bee sorye for hym.   **1563** BISHOP GRINDAL to Earl of Leicester (Strype *Grindal* 77) I begin to fear, lest his Humility in Words be a counterfeit Humility, and his Tears, Crocodile Tears.   **1563** *Mirror for Mag.* ed. Campbell 403 Set forth wyth syghes and teares of Crocodyle.   **1573** J. BRIDGES *Supremacy of Christian Princes* R2 (quoting T. Stapleton & adding parenthesis) Your vntruthes . . . be so notorious and so many, that it pitieth me in your behalf (Crocodili lachrymae) to remember them. *Ibid.* 12 The fained teares of such wel wishing Crocodiles.   **1579** LYLY *Euph.* i. 220 The Crocodile shrowdeth greatest treason vnder most pitifull teares.   **1590** SPENSER *F.Q.* I. v. 18.   **1590–1** SHAKES. *2 Hen. VI* III. i. 226 Gloucester's show Beguiles him as the mournful crocodile With sorrow snares relenting passengers.   **1604** *Id. O.* IV. i. 241 If that the earth could teem with woman's tears Each drop she falls would prove a crocodile.   **1625** BACON *Ess., Of Wisdom* Arb. 187 It is the Wisedome of Crocodiles, that shed teares, when they would deuoure.   **1912** *T.L.S.* 29 Mar. 128 [Maria Theresa's] crocodile tears over Poland, . . . alienate much of the sympathy which would attach to a good woman.

Croesus, *see* Rich as C.

Croft, *see* Hallamshire shall be God's c.

Croker's mare, *see* Coy as a c. m.

Cromwell, *see* Curse of C.

Crook[1] in the lot of every one, There is a.

a. **1732** T. BOSTON *The Crook in the Lot* (1767) 14 The crook in the lot is the special trial appointed for every one.   **1818** SCOTT *Ht. Midl.* ch. 12 I trust to bear even this crook in my lot with submission.   **1880** BLACKMORE *Mary A.* ch. 11 In every man's lot must be some crook, since this crooked world turned round. [[1] affliction, trial.]

Crook, *see also* Hook or by c.

Crooked as a cow's horn, As.

1804 Dec. EDW. JENNER in D. Fisk's *Dr. Jenner of Berkeley* 218 (I am grown as).

Crooked as Crawley brook, As.   (C 809)

1662 FULLER *Beds.* 114 . . . a nameless brook . . . running by Crawley, and falling . . . into the Ouse.

Crooked carlin, quoth the cripple to his wife. *Cf.* Mocks a cripple.

1639 CLARKE 80 The creeple blames his neighbour for halting.   **1721** KELLY 78.

Crooked logs make straight fires.

(L 411)

1584 WITHALS G8[v] Both the crooked and the streighte parte of the wood serue indifferentlye for the fire.   **1611** COTGRAVE s.v. Busche.   **1640** HERBERT no. 45 A crooked log makes a strait fire.   **1670** RAY 6.

Crooked[1] man should sow beans, A | and a wud[2] man peas.

1721 KELLY 42 . . . The one agrees to be thick sown, and the other thin. [[1] lame. [2] mad.]

Crooked, *see also* Staff be c. (If), shadow not straight.

Crooks the tree, Timely (Soon) | that will good cammock[1] (gambrel[2]) be.

(T 493)

c. **1450–1500** *The Gd. Wife wd. a Pilgrimage* l. 72 The tre crokethe son that good cambrel wyll be.   **1546** HEYWOOD II. ix. L1 Tymely crookth the tree, that wil a good camok bee.   **1591** LYLY *Endym.* III. i. 36 But timely, Madam, crookes that tree that wil be a camock.   **1670** RAY 75 (Soon . . . gambrel).   **1721** KELLY 97 Early crooks the tree that in good cammon[3] will be. . . . Children soon shew their Propensities and Inclinations. [[1] a crooked-tree, or bent beam as for the knee of a ship. [2] a crooked stick used by butchers for expanding the carcass of a sheep. [3] a crooked stick for playing at shinty.]

Crooning cow, a crowing hen, and a whistling maid boded never luck to a house, A.

1721 KELLY 33 . . . The two first are reckoned ominous, but the Reflection is on the third.   **1891** J. L. KIPLING *Beast & Man* 40 'A whistling woman and a crowing hen are neither fit for God nor men,' is a mild English saying.   **1917** BRIDGE 28 A whistling wife and a crowing hen will fear the old lad[1] out of his den. [[1] the devil.]

Crop, *see* Neck and c.

Cross and (or) pile.   (C 835)

[Fr. *Croix et* (ou) *pile*. The obverse and (or) reverse side of a coin, the *pile* being the under iron of the minting apparatus. *Fig.* The two sides of anything; one thing and its opposite.] *c.* **1390** GOWER *Conf. Amantis* II. 390 Whos tung neither pyl ne crouche mai hyre.   *c.* **1450** *Pol. Poems* (1859) II. 240 Crosse and pyle standen in balaunce.   *a.* **1613** OVERBURY *Newes, Countrey Newes* Wks. (1856) 175 That good and ill is the crosse and pile in the ayme of life.   **1706** STEVENS s.v. Canto Fortune is so inconstant that good or bad Luck is but Cross and Pile.

Cross as two sticks, As.

1831 SCOTT *Journ.* 2 Nov. Wind as cross as two sticks, with nasty squalls of wind and rain.   **1834** J. B. KER 12.   **1842** S. LOVER *Handy Andy* ii. 24 The renowned O'Grady was according to her account as cross as two sticks.   **1855** LD. HOUGHTON in *Life* I. xi. 518 [He] has been as cross as two sticks at not having been asked to dinner at court.

Cross has its inscription, Each. (c 838)

1639 CLARKE 16 Each crosse has it's inscription.
1670 RAY 75 . . . Crosses and afflictions come
not by chance, . . . but are laid on men for some
just reason. . . . Many times we may read the sin
in the punishment. **1853** TRENCH vi. 140 . . .
the name . . . inscribed upon it, of the person for
whom it was shaped.

Cross on anything, To make a. (c 842)

[= to reckon as specially happy.] **1546** HEY-
WOOD I. xi. E3ᵛ Come, go we hens frend (quoth
I to my mate). And now will I make a crosse on
this gate.

**Cross on the breast, and the devil in the
heart, The.**   (c 837)

c. **1566** CURIO *Pasquin in a Trance* tr. W.P. 58
Wherefore wear they [Knights of Rhodes] that
crosse in the vpper garmentes? Bicause they can
not cary it in their heartes. **1598** SIR R. BARCK-
LEY, *Of the Felicity of Man* 551 *Cruzes de fuera,
& diablo de dentro*: crosses without, and the
diuell within. **1616** DRAXE no. 1038. **1732**
FULLER no. 4462.

Cross the bridge till you get to it, Don't.

1851 LONGFELLOW *Golden Legend* vi Don't cross
the bridge till you come to it, Is a proverb old, and
of excellent wit. **1866** C. H. SMITH *Bill Arp* 179
(before). **1895** ADDY *Househ. Tales* 144 One
who anticipates difficulty is told not to cross the
bridge till he gets to it.

Cross the stream where it is ebbest.[1]
                                            (s 926)

1603 HOLLAND tr. *Plutarch's Morals* 747 There
is still a Lancashire proverb. . . . **1615** BRATH-
WAIT *Strap. for Div.* 222 O let me now perswade,
be not extreame, (Its easie saies the Prouerb) to
wade the streame, Where th' foord's at lowest,
recollect to minde. **1859** TRENCH *Sel. Gloss.*
(1873) 80 as 1603. [¹ shallowest.]

**Cross (Penny) to bless himself with, He
has never a.** *Cf.* **Penny to buy, etc.**
                                            (c 836)

1540 PALSGRAVE *Acolastus* 91 He shal be pollyd
and shauen by vs, tyl he shal not haue a halfe-
penye lefte to blesse hym with. *Ibid.* 140 The
moneylesse knaue, (that hath neuer a crosse lefte
him to blesse him with). **1546** HEYWOOD II. viii.
K3 (peny). **1568** FULWELL *Like Will to L.*
Hazl.-Dods. iii. 346 Not a cross of money to
bless me have I. [*c.* 1604] **1638** T. HEYWOOD
Wise W. of Hogs. Wks. (1874) V. 281 Ile play the
Franck gamester . . . I will not leave my selfe one
Crosse to bless me. **1670** RAY 170. **1766** GOLD-
SMITH *Vic. W.* ch. 21 To come and take up an
honest house, without cross or coin to bless
yourself with. **1819** SCOTT *Bride Lam.* ch. 5 The
Lord Keeper has got all his estates; he has not a
cross to bless himself with.

Crosses are ladders that lead to heaven.
                                            (c 840)

1616 DRAXE no. 406 The Crosse is the ladder of
heauen. **1670** RAY 6. **1859** SMILES *Self-Help*

341 If there be real worth in the character, . . .
it will give forth its finest fragrance when pressed.
'Crosses', says he old proverb, . . .

Cross, *(adv.), see also* **Bear with sore head** (as c.
as).

Cross(es), *(noun) see also* **Cry at the c.; Devil
himself must bear c.; Devil lurks behind c.;
Heads (C.) I win; No c. no crown.**

Cross-bow, *see* **Fish with a c.** (No sure rule to.)

Crouse, *see* **Nothing so c. as new washen louse.**

Crow croaks before the rain, The hoarse.
                                            (c 854)

1615 *Janua Linguarum* tr. W. Welde 51. **1616**
DRAXE no. 1970.

Crow flies, When the | her tail follows.
                                            (c 858)

a. **1628** CARMICHAELL no. 1289 (craw). **1641**
FERGUSSON no. 713 (craw). **1832** HENDERSON
97 (craw).

Crow in a gutter, Like a.   (c 852)

1579 FULKE *Confut. Sanders* 675 He triumpheth
like a crow in a gutter. **1582** *Love and Fortune*
l. 273 They are set a sunning like a Crow in a
gutter. **1659** HOWELL *Eng. Prov.* 1b. **1662** J.
WILSON *Cheats* (1693) III. iv. G1 It should be a
Sweetheart (forsooth)—how it strutts, like a
Crow in a Gutter!

**Crow is never the whiter for washing
herself often, A.**   (c 850)

1578 *Courtly Controv.* N4 It profited as muche
as if he had washed a Crow to make hir white.
1584 WITHALS M3ᵛ A harlot is not made cleane
Nor a crow made white with water. **1678** RAY
121. **1732** FULLER no. 1210.

Crow is white, To say the.   (c 853)

c. **1497** MEDWALL *Fulgens & Lucres* ll. 163–4 Ye,
goth the worlde so now a day That a man must
say the crow is white. **1509** A. BARCLAY *Ship of
Fools* ii. 212. **1546** HEYWOOD II. v. H2ᵛ As good
than is to say the crow is whight. **1576** *Princely
Pleasures at the Court at Kenilworth* in Gascoigne
i. 119 His eloquence can serue to make the
Crowe seeme white. **1578** *Courtly Controv.* N4.

**Crow thinks her own bird(s) fairest
(whitest), The.**   (c 851)

1513 DOUGLAS *Æneis* ix. Prol. 78 The blak craw
thinkis hir awin byrdis quhite. **1546** HEYWOOD
II. iv. G3 The crow thynkth hir owne byrds
fairest in the wood. **1621** BURTON *Anat. Mel.*
III. i. II. iii (1651) 421 Another great tye or cause
of love, is consanguinity; . . . every crow thinks
her own bird fairest. **1670** RAY 76 . . . So the
Ethiopians are said to paint the Devil white.
Every one is partial to . . . his own compositions,
his own children, his own country. **1823** GALT
Entail ch. 29 'The craw thinks its ain bird the
whitest', replied the Leddy.

Crow to pluck (pull) with one, To have a.

(c 855)

[= to have fault to find.]   c. **1460** *Towneley
Myst.* xviii. 311 Na, na, abide, we haue a craw
to pull.   **1509** A. BARCLAY *Ship of Fools* ii. 8 A
wrathfull woman . . . He that hir weddyth hath
a crowe to pull.   **1546** HEYWOOD II. v. H3 If he
leaue it not, we haue a crow to pull.   **1592–3**
SHAKES. *C.E.* III. i. 80 Well, I'll break in. Go
borrow me a crow [i.e. bar of iron]. . . . — If a
crow help us in, sirrah, we'll pluck a crow together.   **1665** J. WILSON *Project.* v. Wks. (1874)
266 I've a crow to pluck w' ye. Where's my
coach and the eight horses you talk'd of?   **1849**
Tait's Mag. XVI. 385/1 If there be 'a crow to
pluck' between us and any contemporary, we
shall make a clean breast of it at once.

Crow(s) (*noun*), *see also* Black as a c.; Blind man
casts staff or shoots c.; Blind man may sometimes hit c.; Carrion c. bewail dead sheep;
Carrion will kill c. (No); Evil c. evil egg; Hawks
(C.) will not pick out c.'s eyes; High for the pie
(Not too) nor too low for c.; Killing a c. with
empty sling; Make the c. a pudding; March kill
c., pie, . . . and raven; Safe as a c. in a gutter;
White c.

Crow(s) (*verb*), *see also* Brains c.; Cock c. on going
to bed; Hen c. louder than cock (Sad house
where).

Crow-trodden, You look as if you were.

(L 436)

[= subjected to ignominious treatment.]
1560–77 *Misogonus* III. i. 199 Thart a crowe-
trodden houre Ile not suffer the an thou wert my
grandum.   **1592** NASHE *Strange News* i. 288
Thou art such a crow trodden asse.   c. **1620**
FLETCHER *Custom of the Country* IV. iv. 54 I
look as if I were crow-trodden.   **1678** RAY 237.

Crowd is not company, A.   (c 861)

1625 BACON *Ess., Friendship* Arb. 165 For a
crowd is not company; and faces are but a
gallery of pictures; . . . where there is no love.
1732 FULLER no. 62.

Crowdy, *see* MacKibbon's c.

Crowing hen, *see* Crooning cow.

Crowland, *see* Carts that come to C.; Ramsey.

Crown is no cure for the headache, A.

(c 862)

c. **1580** SIDNEY *Arcadia*, Wks. IV. 81 Kinges
Crownes do not help them, From the Cruell
heade ache.   **1612–26** BP. HALL *Contempt.* XVIII.
iv (1825) I. 565 Yet could not that misgotten
crown of his keep his head always from aching.
1640 HERBERT no. 576.   **1757** FRANKLIN Aug.
The royal crown cures not the headache.

Crown, *see also* Cleave to the c.; Right, master,
four nobles a year's a c. a quarter.

Crowns have cares.   '(c 863)

1576 PETTIE i. 101 In greatest charge are greatest
cares. *Ibid.* ii. 136 Kingdoms, they say, are but
cares.   **1590** LODGE *Rosalind* ed. Greg 33 Crowns
have crosses.   **1591** *Troublesome Reign of K.
John* Pt. I A3 The heauie yoke Of pressing
cares, that hang vpon a Crowne.   **1595** SHAKES.
Rich. II IV. i. 194 Part of your cares you give me
with your crown.   **1598** *Id. 2 Hen. IV* III. i. 31
Uneasy lies the head that wears a crown.   **1639**
CLARKE 137. *Ibid.* 272 (Kingdomes).

Croydon, *see* Sutton.

Cruelty is a tyrant that's always attended with fear.   (c 866)

1616 DRAXE no. 407 Cruell people are fearefull.
1664 CODRINGTON 190.   **1670** RAY 6.   **1732**
FULLER no. 1213.

Cruelty is more cruel, if we defer the
pain.   (c 867)

1592 DELAMOTHE 5.   **1651** HERBERT no. 1110.

Cruelty, *see also* Clemency is c. (Sometimes);
Mercy to criminal, c. to people.

Crumb(s), *see* Musician has forgot note (When),
c. in throat; Pick up (Gather) one's c.

Crupper, *see* Marriage rides upon the saddle and
repentance upon the c.; Old mare would have
new c.

Crust is better than no bread, A. (c 869)

1577 BRETON *Wks. of a Young Wit* (ed. J. Robertson 29).   **1609** HARWARD 75 Better one shive
then no bread.   **1616** BRETON *Cross. Prov.* A5.
1626 *Id. Soothing* A5ᵛ.

Crust, *see* Cat is hungry when c. contents her;
Ill dog that deserves not c.; Leap at a c.

Crusty, You need not be so | you are
not so hard-baked.   (N 88)

1594 LYLY *Mother B.* II. iii. 67.   **1678** RAY 352
She is as crousty as that is hard bak'd. *Som.*
(One that is surly and loath to doe any thing.)
1695 RAVENSCROFT 57 [as 1594].

Crutch of time does more than the club
of Hercules, The.

1732 FULLER no. 4464.

Crutch(es), *see also* Literature is . . . bad c.; One
foot is better than two c.

Cry at the cross, To.   (c 841)

[The market-cross, at which public announce-
ments were made.]   a. **1529** SKELTON *Dyuers
Balettys* 36 Wks. (1843) I. 24 It can be no counsell
that is cryed at the cros.   **1533** SIR T. MORE
Debellation 1127a It is no counsayle ye wote
well that is cryed at the crosse.   **1611** COTGRAVE
s.v. Sing Thou hast not cried it at the crosse.

1823 GALT *Entail* ch. 21 As we need na cry sic things at the Cross, I'm mindit to hae you and him for the witnesses.

Cry 'Barley',¹ To.

[= to ask for truce, in children's games in Scotland.] *c.* **1400** *Sir Gawain and the Green Knight* l. 295 And I schal stonde hym a strok, stif on þis flet; Elleȝ þou wilt diȝt me þe dom to dele hym an oþer barley. **1757** SMOLLETT *Reprisal* II. x I'se no be the first to cry barley. **1814** SCOTT *Waverley* ch. 42 A proper lad o' his quarters, that will not cry barley in a brulzie.² [¹ ? without resistance shown. ² fray.]

Cry (out) before one is hurt, To. (c 873)

1548 *Reliq. Antiquae* (1843) II. 16 Ye may the better understand that I cry not before I am pricked. **1611** COTGRAVE s.v. Anguille Such as . . . crie before their paine approch them. **1678** RAY 237 You cry before you're hurt. **1721** KELLY 204 It is time enough to cry, Oh, when you are hurt. Spoken to dissuade People from groundless Fears. **1850** THACKERAY *Pendennis* ch. 69 I . . . took up a pistol. You see it is not loaded, and this coward cried out before he was hurt. **1908** *Spectator* 6 June The gull's rule is to cry out before he is hurt.

Cry 'Chuck', *see* Soon enough to c. 'C.'

Cry for the moon, To.

1550 *Answer to Commons* (Camden Soc. ed. N. Pocock 1884, 178) They will cry to have a piece of the moon. **1852** DICKENS *Bleak Ho.* ch. 6 He was a mere child in the world, but he didn't cry for the moon. **1910** *Spectator* 5 Feb. A large section of the Liberal Party are crying for the moon.

Cry hem and have him.

1599 SHAKES. *A.Y.* I. iii. 20 Hem them away. — I would try, if I could cry 'hem', and have him. **1690** *Dict. Cant. Crew* F7 *Hem.* to call after one with an inarticulate Noise.

Cry (one) Notchel, To. (N 247)

[= to proclaim publicly that one will not be responsible for debts incurred by the person named.] **1681** *Dial. btw. Sam. & Will.* in *Harl. Misc.* (1744) II. 101 The King's Majesty, . . . him they cryed Nochell. — What, as Gaffer Block of our Town cryed his Wife? **1859** in *N. & Q.* 3rd Ser. (1866) X. 108 On Wednesday there was at Accrington an extraordinary instance of the disgraceful practice of 'notchel crying'.

Cry (weep) one's eyes out, To. (E 269)

1611 COTGRAVE s.v. Appaiser He may weepe his eyes out that hath none to still him. *Ibid.* s.v. Pleurer (appease). **1613** CHAPMAN *Rev. Bussy* v. i. 144 Those loveliest eyes . . . she wept quite out. **1640** HERBERT no. 17 (as Cotgrave). **1704** CIBBER *Careless Husb.* I. i I could cry my Eyes out.

Cry peccavi, To. (P 170)

[L. *Peccavi*, 'I have sinned', hence an acknowledgement of guilt. TER. *Ad.* 2. 4. 12.] **1509**

FISHER *Fun. Serm. Hen. VII* Wks. (1876) 272 Kynge Dauid that wrote this psalme, with one worde spekynge his herte was chaunged sayenge *Peccaui.* **1553** T. WILSON *Arte of Rhet.* (1580) 65 Much soner shall al other be subiect vnto him, and crie *Peccaui.* **1730** SWIFT *Sheridan's Submission* Wks. (1755) IV. I. 259 Now lowly crouch'd, I cry peccavi.

Cry quits (quittance), To. (Q 18)

1578 *Courtly Controv.* Q2ᵛ She . . . cried quittance for hir husbands death, and hir own defamation. **1580** LYLY *Euph. & his Eng.* ii. 187 Euphues cryed quittance, for he saide thinges that are commonly knowne it were folly to repeat. **1585** A. MUNDAY *Fedele & Fortunio* F4ᵛ I'le teache thee a way, to crye quittance with her before it be long. **1594** *Wars of Cyrus* V. i. 1413 Crie quittance with the couetous king. **1639** FULLER *Holy War* III. xi (1840) 134 This opportunity was lost by the backwardness . . . of . . . the English, say the French writers. To cry quits with them, our English authors impute it to the envy of the French. **1837** MARRYAT *Perc. Keene* ch. 19 I should have fired at you, so we may cry quits on that score.

Cry roast meat, To. (M 849)

[= to be foolish enough to announce to others a piece of private luck or good fortune.] **1611** GRUTER 188. *c.* **1612** BEAUM. & FL. *Scornf. Lady* v. i. Wks. (1905) I. 297. Cannot you fare well, but you must cry roast meat? — He that fares well, and will not bless the founders, is either surfeited or ill taught. **1614** CAMDEN 315 You cannot fare well but you must cry rost meate. **1638** SIR T. HERBERT *Trav.* (ed. 2) 209 At length the home-bred Chyna cryes roast-meat. **1670** RAY 88 You can't fare well, but you must cry roast-meat. Sasse bonne farine sans trompe ny buccine. *Gall.* Boult thy fine meal, and eat good past, without report or trumpets blast. **1673** WYCHERLEY *Gent. Dancing-Master* I. ii. Hark you, madame, can't you fare well but you must cry 'Roast meat'? **1820** LAMB *Elia.* I *Christ's Hosp.* The foolish beast, not able to fare well but he must cry roast meat. **1827** SCOTT *Journ.* I Jan. My life has been spent in such day-dreams. But I cry no roast-meat.

Cry with one eye, and laugh with the other, To. (E 248)

c. **1369** CHAUCER *Bk. Duch.* l. 633 She ys fals; and ever laughynge With oon eye, and that other wepynge. *c.* **1460** HENRYSON *Test. of Cresseid* 230 Thus variant sho was, quha list tak keip, With ane eye lauch, and with the uther weip. **1600–1** SHAKES. *H.* I. ii. 11 With an auspicious and a dropping eye. **1621** BURTON *Anat. Mel.* III. ii. III. iv (1651) 498 They . . . weep with the one eye, laugh with the other; or . . . they can both together. **1678** RAY 242. **1732** FULLER no. 4737 The rich Widow cries with one Eye, and laughs with the other.

Cry 'Wolf', To. (W 609)

[= to raise a false alarm; in allusion to the fable of the shepherd boy who deluded people with false cries of 'Wolf!'] **1692** L'ESTRANGE *Aesop's Fab.* ccclx. 332 The Boy . . . would be Crying *a Wolf, a Wolf,* when there was none, and then could not be Believed when there was. **1858** MRS. CRAIK *Woman's Th.* 281 After crying 'Wolf' ever since . . . seventeen—as some young ladies are fond of doing . . . the grim wolf, old age, is actually showing his teeth in the distance. **1887** BLACKMORE *Springhaven* ch. 53 In a matter like that French invasion, . . . 'the cry of wolf' grows stale at last, and then the real danger comes.

Cry you mercy; I | I have killed your cushion.   (M 896)

1530 PALSGRAVE 501b I kry you mercy, I kylled your cussheyn. **1594** LYLY *Mother B*. IV. ii. 66. On thy conscience tell me what tis a clock ? — I cry you mercy, I have killed your cushion.

Cry you mercy; I | I took you for a joint-stool.¹   (M 897)

[*Cf*. **1670** RAY 68 Cry you mercy, kill'd my cat . . . spoken to them who do one a shrewd turn, and then make satisfaction with asking pardon or crying mercy.] **1594** LYLY *Mother B*. IV. ii. 28 You neede not bee so lustye, you are not so honest. — I crie you mercy, I tooke you for a ioynd stoole. [*Note*. Proverb for an unfortunate apology or a pert reply.] **1605–6** SHAKES. *K.L.* III. vi. 51 Cry you mercy, I took you for a joint-stool. **1616** WITHALS 553 Ante hoc te cornua habere putabam, I cry you mercy, I tooke you for a joynd stoole. **1639** CLARKE 160. [¹ A stool made of parts joined or fitted together.]

Cry Yule at other men's cost, It is easy to.   (Y 53)

a. **1500** BANNATYNE MS. STS iii. 8 It is eith to cry zule on ane vder manis cost. *c*. **1549** HEYWOOD I. xi. D3ᵛ To flee charge, and fynde ease, ye wold now heere oste. It is easy to cry vle at other mens coste. *a*. **1628** CARMICHAELL no. 897 (under ane other mannis stule). **1641** FERGUS-SON no. 495.

Cry (*noun*), *see* Far c. to Lochow; Great c. little wool.

Cry, cries, cried (*verb*), *see also* Laugh and c. with a breath; Laugh before breakfast, c. before supper; Sing before breakfast, c. before night; Wife c. five loaves a penny.

Crying over spilt milk, It is no use.
                                                         (M 939)

[**1484** CAXTON *Aesope* (Jacobs) ii. 270 The thyrd [doctrine] is that thow take no sorowe of the thynge lost whiche may not be recouered.] **1659** HOWELL *Brit. Prov*. 40 No weeping for shed milk. **1738** SWIFT Dial. I. E.L. 268 'Tis a folly to cry for spilt milk. **1884** J. PAYN *Canon's W*. ch. 15 There would be a row, . . . ; but he would say, like a wise man, 'There's no use in crying over spilled milk'.

Cuckold and conceals it, Who is a | carries coals in his bosom.   (C 885)

1659 HOWELL *Span. Prov*. 14. **1670** RAY 6. *Hispan*. **1706** STEVENS s.v. Cornudo.

Cuckold come, If a | he'll take away the meat, if there be no salt on the table.
                                                         (C 880)

1590 R. HARVEY *Plain Percevall* 9 Service without salt, by the rite of England, is a Cuckholds

fee, if he claime it. **1678** RAY 69 If a Cuckold come he'll take away the meat. *viz*. If there be no salt on the table. **1738** SWIFT Dial. II. E.L. 298 Here's no salt; cuckolds will run away with the meat.

Cuckold is the last that knows of it, The.   (C 877)

1604 MARSTON *What You Will* I. iii A Cuckold . . . he must be the last must know it. **1636** CAMDEN 306. **1706** STEVENS s.v. Cornudo (knows it). **1712** ARBUTHNOT *John Bull* I. viii It is a true saying, that the last man of the parish that knows of his cuckoldom is himself. It was observed by all the neighbourhood that Hocus had dealings with John's wife that were not so much for his honour; but this was perceived by John a little too late.

Cuckold wear his own horns, Let every.
                                                         (C 882)

1659 HOWELL *Eng. Prov*. 3a. **1670** RAY 6. **1762** SMOLLETT *Sir Launcelot Greaves* ch. 13.

Cuckolds go to heaven, In rain and sunshine.   (R 12)

1591 FLORIO *Second F*. 143 All cuckolds shall obtaine Paradise. **1623** WODROEPHE 299 Al Cuckolds shal go to Heauen. **1659** HOWELL *Eng. Prov*. 12b.

Cuckold(s), *see also* A-cold than a c. (Better be); Hope better, quoth Benson; Mock not, quoth Mumford; Strand on the Green, thirteen houses, fourteen c.

Cuckoo comes, When the | he eats up all the dirt.

[i.e. the mire of winter dries up. LEAN.] **1680** *Yea and Nay Alm*. April. Ladies . . . may walk abroad to take their pleasure, for any old woman will tell you that when the Cuckow comes he eats up all the dirt. **1830** FORBY 430 I will come when the cuckoo has pecked up the dirt. *i.e.* In the spring. **1876** MRS. BANKS *Manch. Man* ch. 8 Bush and tree put out pale buds. . . . The cuckoo —to use a village phrase—has 'eaten up the mud'; and the town was alive with holiday-makers.

Cuckoo comes in April, and stays the month of May; sings a song at midsummer, and then goes away, The.

1869 HAZLITT 363.

Cuckoo comes to (sits on) the bare (dry) thorn, When the | sell your cow and buy you corn: but when she comes to the full bit, sell your corn and buy you sheep.   (C 893)

1659 HOWELL *Eng. Prov*. 16b When the Cuckow sitteth on a dry thorn, Sell thy Cow, and sow thy corn. **1670** RAY 43.

Cuckoo goes to Beaulieu Fair to buy him a greatcoat, The.

1863 J. R. WISE *New Forest* ch. 16 (1895) 180 . . . referring to the arrival of the cuckoo about the

15th of April, whilst the day on which the fair is held is known as the 'cuckoo day'.

Cuckoo has but one song, The. (c 894)

1530 TYNDALE *Ans. to More* P.S. 119 Ye reply not, but keep your tune, and unto all things sing cuckoo, cuckoo, 'We be the church and cannot err'. *a.* **1550** *Parliament of Birds* Harl. Misc. 1745 v. 479 I synge, sayde the Cuckowe, euer one Songe. **1551** T. WILSON *Rule of Reason* T4 Petitio principii, the cuckowes song, that is, a repeting of that wholly in the conclusion, whiche before was onely spoken in the first proposition. **1552** HULOET G5 Cuckowes note by circumlocution, when one can synge but one tune, or tel one tale. **1563** J. PILKINGTON P.S. 639. **1595** F. SABIE *Pan's Pipe* ed. Bright and Mustard 25 Each bird sent merrily musicall harmonie: The Cuckow flew abroad with an ode vniforme. **1639** CLARKE 303.

Cuckoo sings all the year, The. (c 891)

1541 *Sch. Ho. Wom.* B2 Allbeit that fewe men do hym here The kucko syngeth euery yere. [*c.* 1605] **1630** DEKKER *2 Hon. Whore* II. i. 259 Ile trust neither Lord nor Butcher with quicke flesh for this tricke; the Cuckoo I see now sings all the yeere.

Cuckoo, *see also* Breed of the gowk (c.); Cock of hay frights c.; March the c. starts; Nightingale and c. sing both in one month; Third of April comes c.; Three flails and c.; Turn the money when you hear the c.

Cuckstone, *see* Church mis-went.

Cucullus non facit monachum, *see* Cowl (Habit, Hood) does not make the monk.

Cucumber, *see* Cool as a c.

Cud, *see* Chew the c.

Cudgel (beat) one's brains, To. (B 602)

1560 *Contention Betwixt Churchyard and Camell* †ii[v] Thus beating thair brains in vain they do toyle. **1569** *Marr. Wit & Science* A3 l. 83 But thou must take another way to woe, And beate thy brayne and trauayle too and froe. **1573** GASCOIGNE i. 152 Beate my braynes about Geometrie. **1577** BEZA *Abraham's Sacrifice* tr. A. Golding B4 I beate my braynes, that by no kind of way My labour be in any wise misspent. **1600–1** SHAKES. *H.* V. i. 56 Cudgel thy brains no more about it. **1849** THACKERAY *Pendennis* ch. 15 When a gentleman is cudgelling his brain to find any rhyme for sorrow besides borrow and to-morrow.

Cudgels, *see* Take up c.

Cuffing, *see* Good luck comes by c.

Cumber, John à, *see* Devil and J. à C.

Cumbered, *see* Conscience is c.

Cumbersome, *see* Courtesy is c.

Cunning as a dead pig, As | but not half so honest. (P 297)

c. **1579** MERBURY *Marr. Wit and Wisdom* (1846) ii. 16 I am as wise as my mothers sowe. **1672** W. WALKER 16, no. 51 As subtle as a dead pig. *Non plus sapit quam occisa sus.* **1738** SWIFT Dial. III. E.L. 317.

Cunning is no burden. (c 899)

1520 WHITTINGTON *Vulg.* E.E.T.S. 40 Connynge . . . semeth no burden to hym yt hath hit. **1539** TAVERNER 22[v]. **1636** CAMDEN 294. **1642** FULLER *H. & P. State* II. xxv (1841) 138 Cunning is no burden to carry, as paying neither porterage by land, nor pondage by sea. **1732** FULLER no. 4182 Skill is . . .

Cunning wife makes her husband her apron, The. (w 346)

1659 HOWELL *Span. Prov.* 4. **1664** CODRINGTON 215. **1670** RAY 29. *Hispan.*

Cunning (*noun*), *see also* God and my c., (I thank).

Cup and can. (c 903)

[= constant or familiar associates.] **1546** HEYWOOD II. iii. G2[v] Mery we were as cup and can coulde holde. **1584** MUNDAY *Fidele & Fortunio* E2[v]. **1594** NASHE *Unfort. Traveller* ii. 248. **1639** CLARKE 47. **1729** SWIFT *Libel on Dr. Delany* You and he are cup and can. **1738** *Id.* Dial. III. E.L. 320 (as great as cup and can).

Cup and the lip, Many things fall (Many a slip) between the. (T 191)

[Gk. Πολλὰ μεταξὺ πέλει κύλικος καὶ χείλεος ἄκρου. CATO in *Aul. Gell.* 13. 17. 1 *Inter os atque offam multa intervenire posse.* ERASM. *Ad. Multa cadunt inter calicem supremaque labra.*] **1539** TAVERNER 15 Many thynges fall betwene the cuppe and the mouth. *Ibid.* 16 (the cuppe and the lyppes). **1580** LYLY *Euph. & his Eng.* ii. 223. **1591** ARIOSTO *Orl. Fur.* Harington XVIII. 47 Much falls between the challice and the chin. **1633** JONSON *T. Tub.* III. vii. 16. **1712** ARBUTHNOT *John Bull* II. xiii Many things happen between the cup and the lip—witnesses might have been bribed, juries managed, or prosecution stopped. **1824** MOIR *Mansie W.* ch. 22 (many a slip). **1853** TRENCH ii. 37 Setting down the untasted cup, . . . the master went out to meet the wild boar, and was slain in the encounter; and thus . . . , the proverb, (find place between). **1887** T. A. TROLLOPE *What I Remember* I. xii. 256 A whole series of slips . . .

Cup in the pate is a mile in the gate, A. (c 904)

1656 F. OSBORNE *Advice to Son* I. li Especially when they have got a pot in their pate. **1694** MOTTEUX *Rabelais* IV. ch. 65. **1738** SWIFT Dial. II. E.L. 312.

Cup is fullest, When the | then bear her fairest. (c 910)

c. **1300** *Provs. of Hending* xvi When the coppe is follest, thenne ber hire feyrest. *a.* **1628**

CARMICHAELL no. 269 Beare the cap eaven quhill it is full. *Ibid.*, no. 1286 Quhen the cup is ful, beare it equale. **1641** FERGUSSON no. 708 (euinest). **1721** KELLY 346 When the cup's full carry it even. When you have arrived at Power and Wealth, take a care of Insolence, Pride, and Oppression. **1732** FULLER no. 122. **1820** SCOTT *Monast.* Introd. Ep. 'It is difficult,' saith the proverb, 'to carry a full cup without spilling.' The wealth of the community ... was ... a snare to the brethen. **1903** G. H. KNIGHT *Master's Qns.* 145 All hands are not steady enough to carry a full cup.

Cup, Like (Such) | like (such) cover.
(C 906)

1532 T. MORE *Conf. Tyndale's Ans.* Pref., 2B1 A very mete couer for such a cuppe. **1549** LATIMER *5th Serm. bef. Edw. VI* P.S. 181 She was a rich woman, she had her lands by the sheriff's nose. He was a gentleman of a long nose. Such a cup, such a cover! **1655** FULLER *Ch. Hist.* IX. ii, § 20 (1868) II. 552 John Story, ... a cruel persecutor in the days of Queen Mary, ... great with the Duke de Alva (like cup, like cover!).

Cup of Circe, The.

[HOMER *Od.* X.; VIRGIL *Aen.* vii.] **1581** GUAZZO i. 246 Wee have been in the very jawes of Scilla, and drunke of Cyrces cup. **1592–3** SHAKES. *C.E.* V. i. 271 I think you all have drunk of Circe's cup. **1861** G. J. WHYTE-MELVILLE *Inside the Bar* ch. 1 I did not even mistrust the cup of Circe. Ah! she made a pig of her admirer, that ancient enchantress; and in Miss Lushington's presence the admirer makes an ass of himself.

Cup, *see also* Drink of the same c.; Kiss the c.; No sooner up but ... nose in c.; Poison is poison though in golden c.; St. Giles' c.

Cupar,[1] He that will to | maun to Cupar.

1721 KELLY 141 He that will to Cowper, will to Cowper.[1] A Reflection upon obstinate Persons, that will not be reclaim'd. **1818** SCOTT *Rob Roy* ch. 28 The Heccate ... ejaculated, 'A wilfu' man will hae his way: ... !' **1893** STEVENSON *Catriona* ch. 13. [1 Cupar, a town in Fife.]

Cupboard (*or* Cream-pot) love.
(C 912)

c. **1594** BACON no. 697. *c.* **1665** *Roxb. Ball.* VI. 529 And all for the love of the cubbard. **1678** RAY 69 Cream-pot love. Such as young fellows pretend to dairymaids, to get cream and other good things of them. **1757** *Poor Robin* (N.) A cupboard love is seldom true. **1874** DASENT *Tales from Fjeld* 184 To have such a cupboard lover.

Cupboard(s), *see also* Belly cries c.; Love locks no c.

Cur will bite before he bark, A.
(C 915)

1623 CAMDEN 265.

Cur(s), *see also* Brabbling c. sore ears; Curst c. must be tied short; Yelping c. will raise mastiffs.

Curate's egg, good in parts, Like the.

1895 *Punch* cix. 222 'I'm afraid you've got a bad egg, Mr. Jones.' 'Oh no, my Lord, I assure you! Parts of it are excellent!' **1926** *Times* 24 Dec. 11/6 London is architecturally like the curate's egg, 'good in parts'.

Cured her from laying in the hedge,[1] I have | quoth the good man, when he had wed his daughter.
(L 132)

1678 RAY 56. [1 As hens are inclined to do if allowed free range.]

Cured, What can't be | must be endured.
(C 922)

1377 LANGLAND *P. Pl.* B. x. 439 For *qant* OPORTET *vyent enplace . il ny ad que* PATI. [For when MUST comes forward, there is nothing for it but to SUFFER.] **14 . .** *Grammat. Rules in Reliq. Antiq.* (1843) II. 14 And when *oportet* cums in plas, Thou knawys *miserere*[1] has no gras. *c.***1407** LYDGATE *Reson & Sensuality* l. 4757 For the thyng that may nat be eschewed But of force mot be sywed. **1579** SPENSER *Shep. Cal.* Sept. Wks. (Globe) 474 And cleanly cover that cannot be cured: Such ill, as is forced, mought nedes be endured. **1591** SHAKES. *3 Hen. VI* V. iv. 37 What cannot be avoided 'Twere childish weakness to lament or fear. **1592** *Id. T.G.V.* II. ii. 1 Have patience, gentle Julia.—I must, where is no remedy. **1763** CHURCHILL *Proph. of Famine* 363 Patience is sorrow's salve: what can't be cured, So Donald right areads, must be endured. **1870** KINGSLEY *Madam How* ch. 1 That stupid resignation which some folks preach . . . is merely saying— . . . [1 have mercy.]

Cure(s) (*noun*), *see* Bewails himself that has c. in hands; Care is no c.; Desperate cuts desperate c.; Past c. past care; Pays the physician does the c. (Who); Prevention better than c.

Cure(s, d) (*verb*), *see also* Born a fool is never c.; Crown no c. for headache; Disease known half c.; Doctor c., (If) sun sees it; Evil sare c. by contempt; Fancy may kill or c.; Ground sweat c. all disorders; Hand that gave the wound must give the c.; Herb will c. love (no); Kill or c.; Like c. like; Physicians kill more than they c.; Sick of a fever lurden must be c. by hazel gelding; Time c. all things.

Curiosity is ill manners in another's house.

1622 C. OUDIN *Grammar in Spanish and English* 271 Curiosity is ill beseeming in an other's house. **1732** FULLER no. 1220.

Current, *see* Stream (c.) stopped swells the higher.

Curry, *see* Jacket, (To baste (c. etc.)).

Curry favour, *see* Dwell in court.

Curse, Not worth a.

c. 1390 GOWER *Conf. Amantis* III. 1652. 1820 BYRON *Letters*, etc. v. 57 (Prothero) The Neapolitans are not worth a curse and will be beaten.

Curse of Cromwell, The.

1818 SCOTT *Ht. Midl.* ch. 8. 1827 *Id. Two Drovers* ch. 2 Then the curse of Cromwell on your proud Scots stomach. 1845 CARLYLE *Cromw. Lett. & Sp.* Lett. 85 Such is what the Irish common people still call the 'Curse of Cromwell'; this is the summary of his work in that country.

Cursed in his mother's belly that was killed by a cannon, He was. (C 57)

1609 R. ARMIN *Two Maids of More-clacke* H3 They say hees curst that by a cannon dies. 1636 CAMDEN 204 Now he is thought the most unfortunate, and cursed in his mother's wombe, who dyeth by great shotte. 1662 FULLER Sussex 99 Yet do I not believe what Souldiers commonly say, that he was curs'd in his Mother's belly, who is kill'd with a Cannon. 1670 RAY 110 Who was kill'd by a cannon bullet, was curst in his mothers belly.

Curses, like chickens, come home to roost. (C 924)

c. 1275 *Prov. of Alfred* (Skeat) A 84 Eueryches monnes dom [judgement] to his owere dure churreth. *c.* 1386 CHAUCER *Parson's T.* l. 620 And ofte tyme swich cursynge wrongfully retorneth agayn to hym that curseth, as a bryd that retorneth agayn to hys owene nest. 1592 *Arden of Fevers* IV. iv. 40 For curses are like arrowes shot upright, which falling down light on the shuter's head. 1810 SOUTHEY *Kehama* Motto Curses are like young chickens; they always come home to roost. 1880 SMILES *Duty* 89 Their injustice will return upon them. . . .

Curst cow has short horns, A. (C 751 and G 217)

[L. *Dat Deus immiti cornua curta bovi.*] *c.* 1475 *Eight Goodly Questions* in BELL'S *Chaucer* viii. 189 God sendeth a shrewd cow a short horne. 1509 BARCLAY *Ship Fools* i. 182 To a wylde cowe god doth short hornys sende. 1546 HEYWOOD I. x. C4ᵛ How be it lo'god sendth the shrewd cow short hornes. 1588 GREENE *Pandosto* Wks. (1881–3) IV. 247 A curst cow hath oftentimes short hornes, and a willing minde but a weake arm. 1598–9 SHAKES. *M.A.* II. i. 21 It is said 'God sends a curst cow short horns'; but to a cow too curst he sends none. 1641 FERGUSSON no. 93 An ill willy kow should have short hornes. 1670 RAY 74 . . . Providence so disposes that they who have will, want power or means to hurt.

Curst cur (dog) must be tied short, A. (D 447)

1592 DELAMOTHE 3 (dogge). 1612 WEBSTER *White Devil* I. ii. 188 Women are like curst dogges, civilitie keepes them tyed all day time, but they are let lose at midnight. 1623 CAMDEN 265 (dog).

Curtain lectures. (C 925)

1632 *The Pinder of Wakefield* B1ᵛ Then [after marriage] is the time for curtaine sermons.

1633 T. ADAMS *Exp. 2 Pet.* ii. 5 Often have you heard how much a superstitious wife, by her curtain lectures, hath wrought upon her Christian husband. 1710 ADDISON *Tatler* no. 243 He was then lying under the Discipline of a Curtain-Lecture.

Cushion, *see* Beside the c. (Set); Bore him through nose with a c.; Cry you mercy . . . killed your c.; Idle person devil's c.; Kill a man with c.; Miss the c.

Custom (Habit) is a second nature. (C 932)

[CICERO *De Finibus* 5. 25. 74 *Consuetudine quasi alteram quandam naturam effici.* Custom produces a kind of second nature.] *c.* 1390 GOWER *Conf. Amantis* VI. 664 Usage is the seconde kinde. 1422 J. YONGE *Gov. of Prynces* E.E.T.S. 238 For as Ypocras sayth, 'costome is the seconde nature or kynde'. 1547 BALDWIN N6ᵛ. 1629 T. ADAMS *Serm.* (1861–2) I. 263 That custom, being a second nature, the heart hath lost the name of heart. 1712 ADDISON *Spect.* no. 447 Wks. (1902) III. 453 Custom is a second nature. It is indeed able to form the man anew. 1817 SCOTT *Rob Roy* ch. 10 Habit has become a second nature.

Custom without reason is but ancient error. (C 935)

1542 T. BECON *Invective agst. Swearing* (n.d., H6) S. Ciprian [Epist. ad pomp. contra Steph. Dist. VIII] sayth . . . a custome without trueth, is an olde errour. 1551 T. WILSON *Rule of Reason* (1552 ed., X8) Custom is the mother . . . vnto all error. 1567 BALDWIN Y4. 1597 *Politeuphuia* 58 Custome, though neuer so auncient, without truth is but an old error; *Ibid.* 144ᵛ (without credite). 1732 FULLER no. 1226.

Customs, With | we live well, but laws undo us. (C 937)

1640 HERBERT no. 973.

Custom(s), *see also* Bad c. is like a good cake; Command of c. is great; Countries (so many), so many c.; Once a use, ever a c.

Cut a feather, To. (F 160)

[= to make fine distinctions.] 1599 H. PORTER *Two Angry Wom.* l. 1030 What though that honest *Hodge* haue cut his finger heere? or as some say, cut a feather? [= drunk]. *a.* 1633 AUSTIN *Medit.* (1635) 169 Nor seeke . . . with nice distinctions, to cut a Feather [with the Schoolemen]. 1684 T. GODDARD *Plato's Demon* 317 Men who . . . have not the skill to cut a feather.

Cut and come again.

1699 *New Dict. Cant. Crew* s.v. Cut and come again, of Meat that cries come Eat me. 1738 SWIFT Dial. II. E.L. 297. 1823 BYRON *D. Juan* 8. 35 But Johnson was a clever fellow, who Knew when and how 'to cut and come again'. 1824 MAGINN *Misc.* 2. 206 A small additional slice of the same genuine honest cut and come again dish. 1853 SURTEES *Sponge's Sport T.* ch. 5 Its being all in the funds . . . keeps him constantly in cash, and enables him to 'cut and come again'.

Cut blocks with a razor, To.

[= to waste ingenuity, etc.] **1774** GOLDSMITH *Retal.* 42 'Twas his fate unemployed or in place, sir, To eat mutton cold and cut blocks with a razor.

Cut down an oak and set up a strawberry, To.   (O 2)

1662 FULLER Devon 246 I would not wish this County the increase of these Berries, according to the Proverb; . . .

Cut down the woods, If you | you'll catch the wolf.

1732 FULLER no. 2747.

Cut Falkland wood with a penknife, Long ere you.   (F 36)

1641 FERGUSSON no. 596. **1662** FULLER Northumb. 303 . . . It is spoken of such who embrace unproportionable and improbable means to effect the means propounded to themselves . . . Falkland . . . in Fife, having a bonny wood . . . about it. **1721** KELLY 241 . . . Spoken when People set about a Work without proper Tools.

Cut for the simples, To be.   (S 463)

[A play upon the words, *simples* being medicinal herbs.] **1650** in SIMPSON *Documents of St. Paul's* Camd. Soc. 148 The Witts of Pauls, Or a Catalogue of those Book-sellers Apprentices, . . . which are to be cut of the simples this next spring. **1699** *New Dict. Cant. Crew* s.v. He must be cut of the Simples, Care must be taken to cure him of Folly. **1738** SWIFT *Dial.* I. E.L. 265. **1828** CARR *Craven Gloss.* s.v. 'Wants cutting for t' simples', is a ludicrous expression applied to one who has been guilty of some foolish act. **1846** *Jerrold's Shil. Mag.* III. 431 'Get cut for the simples before thou takes promissory notes without dates again'.

Cut large shives of another's loaf, To. *Cf.* Shive of a cut loaf.   (S 360)

1590 *The Cobbler of Canterbury* (1608) 13 The Prior perceived that the scull had cut a shiue on his loafe. **1670** RAY 162 To cut large thongs of another man's leather. . . . It may pass for a sentence thus, Men cut large shives of others loaves.

Cut large thongs of other men's leather, Men.   (T 229)

[L. *Ex alieno tergore lata secantur lora.*] *c.* **1300** *Provs. of Hending* st. 28 Of un-boht hude men kerueth brod thong. **1456** MARG. PASTON in *P. Lett.* II. 226 Men cut large thongs here of other mens lether. *c.* **1549** HEYWOOD II. v. H1 Whyle they cut large thongs of other mens lether. **1584** WITHALS F8. *Ibid.*, 11 (large latchets). **1586** G. WHETSTONE *Eng. Mirror* 49 See what large coates, Pope Gregory the 7. cut of other mens cloath. **1605** CHAPMAN *All Fools* IV. i. 147 What huge large thongs he cuts Out of his friend

Fortunio's stretching leather. **1641** FERGUSSON no. 672 Of other mens lether, men takes large whanges. **1655–62** GURNALL *Chrn. in Armour* (1865) I. 251 They then live . . . putting off . . . till the winter of old age. . . . Who gave thee leave to cut out such large thongs of that time which is not thine but God's? **1670** RAY 162. **1853** TRENCH V. 105 The comparative wastefulness wherewith that which is another's is too often used: *Men cut broad thongs from other men's leather.*

Cut not the bough that thou standest upon.   (B 554)

1528 TYNDALE *Obed. Chrn. Man* P.S. 304 We say, . . . 'Cut not the bough that thou standest upon': whose literal sense is, 'Oppress not the commons'; and is borrowed of hewers.

Cut oats green, If you | you get both king and queen.

1889 E. PEACOCK *Lincolnshire Glos.* E.D.S. 379 That is, if *oats* be not cut before they seem fully ripe, the largest grains which are at the top of the heads will probably fall out and be lost.

Cut off a dog's tail and he will be a dog still.   (D 520)

1573 SANFORD 109ᵛ. **1578** FLORIO *First F.* 33ᵛ. **1629** *Bk. Mer. Rid.* Prov. no. 122.

Cut off one's nose to spite one's face, To.

[*a.* **1200** PETER OF BLOIS *Male ulciscitur dedecus sibi illatum, qui amputat nasum suum.*] *a.* **1561** *Deceit of Women.* I1 He that byteth his nose of, shameth his face. **1788** GROSE *Dict. Vulg. T.* (ed. 2) s.v. Noso He cut off his nose to be revenged of his face, said of one who, to be revenged of his neighbour, has materially injured himself. **1853** SURTEES *Sponge's Sport. T.* ch. 27 At first I thought of going home, taking the hounds away too. . . . Then I thought that would be only like cutting off my nose to spite my face. **1926** *Times* 25 June 14/4 It was no use cutting off the nose of a Trade Agreement worth £34,000,000 . . . in order to spite the face of a *régime* we did not approve of.

Cut off with a shilling, To.

[= to disinherit by bequeathing a shilling.] **1700** FARQUHAR *Constant Couple* IV. iii. 43 When I die, I'll leave him the Fee-Simple of a Rope and a Shilling. **1762** COLMAN *Mus. Lady* II. 27 I'll disinherit him—I won't leave him a groat— I'll cut him off with a shilling. **1823** GALT *Entail* ch. 17.

Cut one's own throat (with one's own knife), To.

[= to be the means of one's own defeat or destruction.] **1583** MELBANCKE I4 Some . . . haue bene daggers to their own throat. *Ibid.* K4ᵛ Thou . . . settest a dagger to thyne owne throate. **1583** GOLDING *Calvin on Deut.* lxxx. 490 They cut their own throtes with their own knife. **1867–77** FROUDE *Short Stud.* (1890) I. 172 They . . . believed that Elizabeth was cutting her own throat, and that the best that they could do was to recover their own queen's favour.

Cut one's thong according to one's leather, To. (T 229)

1484 CAXTON *Fab. Avian* (1889) 220 Ne also it is not honeste to make large thonges of other mennes leder. **1530** R. WHITFORD *Werk for Housholders* G4ᵛ Then (after the commune prouerbe) cut your thonges: after or accordynge vnto your ledder. **1605** CHAPMAN, JONSON, MARSTON *Eastw. Ho.* V. v. 119 Seeke not to goe beyonde your Tether, But cut your Thongs vnto your Lether.

Cut out of whole cloth, To. (C 433)

c. **1516** J. SKELTON *Magnificense* l. 145 It were a shame to God I make an othe, without I myght cut it out of the brode clothe. **1546** GARDINER *Letters* 11 Jan., Crymsen damaske . . . as we saye, cut owte of the hol cloth. c. **1606** SHAKES. *A.C.* II. ii. 56 If you 'll patch a quarrel, As matter whole you have not to make it with, It must not be with this.

Cut the comb of, To. (C 526)

1542 BECON *Nosegay Early Works* P.S. 205 This shall pluck doun your comb, as they use to say. **1548** HALL *Chron.* 1 Hen. IV 12ᵛ My combe was clerely cut. **1565** OSORIUS *Pearl for a Prince* tr. R. Shacklock C7ᵛ There is nothing of more powre then the feare of God, . . . to cutt the combe of bragging and lightnes. **1591** ARIOSTO *Orl. Fur.* Harington XXXVII. 94 His combe now cut, his furie now is tamed. c. **1607** MIDDLETON *Trick* IV. iv. 32 'Twill cut his comb, i faith. **1644** JESSOP *Angel of Eph.* 58 The one cuts the combe of Episcopall Dominion. **1670** RAY 169 To cut ones comb. As is usually done to cocks when gelded. **1896** CONAN DOYLE *Rodney S.* ch. 10 'That's Dick 'Umphries, the same that was cock of the middleweights until Mendoza cut his comb for 'im'.

Cut the grass (ground) (from) under a person's feet, To. (G 419)

[= to foil, thwart, trip him up.] **1567** FENTON *Bandello* T.T. ii. 10 I find a greater falt in myself in suffring an other to cut the earthe frome under my feete. **1572** E. PASQUIER *Monophylo* tr. G. Fenton 51 Cutte the grasse from vnder their feete. **1576** PETTIE i. 121 The other wooer . . . thought the grass had been cut from under his feet. **1659** HOWELL *Fr. Prov.* 9. **1672** MARVELL *Reh. Transp.* i. 278 You are all this while cutting the grass under his feet. **1777** MORGAN *Dram. Char. Falstaff* 44 If we desert this principle we cut the turf from under us.

Cut (split) the hair, To. (H 32)

[= to make fine or cavilling distinctions.] **1594–5** SHAKES. *L.L.L.* V. ii. 259 The tongues of mocking wenches are as keen As is the razor's edge invisible, Cutting a smaller hair than may be seen, Above the sense of sense. **1652** SANCROFT *Mod-Policies* in D'OYLY *Life* (1821) II. 241 Machiavel cut the hair when he advised, not absolutely to disavow conscience, but to manage it with such a prudent neglect, as is scarce discernible from a tenderness. **1692** L'ESTRANGE *Josephus, Philo's Emb. to Caius* x (1702) 901 To cut a Hair betwixt Satyr and Flattery. **1732** FULLER no. 6457 It's hard to split the Hair, That nothing is wanted, and nothing to spare.

Cut (slip) the painter, To.

[= to sever a connection.] **1699** *New Dict. Cant. Crew* s.v. I'll cut your Painter for ye, I'll prevent ye doing me any Mischief. **1867** SMYTH *Sailor's Word-bk.* s.v. Cut your painter, make off. **1888** T. W. REID *Life W. E. Forster* II. 99 The sooner we 'cut the painter' and let the Greater Britain drift from us the better it would be for Englishmen.

Cut to unkindness, No. (C 942)

1599 SHAKES. *J.C.* III. ii. 183 This was the most unkindest cut of all. **1621** BURTON *Anat. Mel.* I. ii. IV. vii (1651) 169 No cut, to unkindness, as the saying is: a frown and hard speech, . . . especially to courtiers, or such as attend upon great persons, is present death. **1659** HOWELL *Eng. Prov.* 13a.

Cut your coat according to your cloth. (C 472)

1546 HEYWOOD I. viii. C1 I shall Cut my cote after my cloth. **1580** LYLY *Euph. & his Eng.* ii. 188 Be neither prodigall to spende all, nor couetous to keepe all, cut thy coat according to thy cloth. **1592** DELAMOTHE 19. **1902** *Spectator* 19 Apr. A Prime Minister who will make the financial condition of the nation his prime care . . . will insist on . . . 'cutting his coat according to his cloth'.

Cut, (*noun*), *see also* Call me c.; Desperate c., desperate cures; First c.

Cut(s), (*verb*), *see also* Better c. the shoe; Come c. and long tail; Hold or c. codpiece point; Knife, (It is a good) it will c. butter when it is melted; Knife, (Man may slay (c.) himself with his own); Laugh in one's face and c. his throat, Measure thrice . . . c. but once; Score twice before c. once; Sword of lead, (to slay (c. one's throat) with a); Work c. out, (To have one's).

Cut-purse is a sure trade, A | for he has ready money when his work is done. (C 945)

1659 HOWELL *Eng. Prov.* 18b. **1670** RAY 6.

Cutter's[1] law.

1816 SCOTT *Old Mort.* ch. 8. **1826** *Id. Woodst.* ch. 29 I see, sir, you understand cutter's law—when one tall fellow has coin, another must not be thirsty. [[1] cutter = cut-throat, desperado.]

Cutting, *see* Tailor's shreds are worth the c.

Cut-throat, *see* Conscience is a c.

Cutty, *see* Sup with a c. than want a spoon (Better to).

Cutwell (*proper noun*), *see* Knife . . . made five miles beyond C.

D

Dab, quoth Dawkins, when he hit his wife on the arse with a pound of butter.
(D 54)

1659 HOWELL *Eng. Prov.* 12a. **1670** RAY 215. **1823** GROSE ed. Pierce Egan s.v. Dab.

Dabo tibi, see Better is one *Accipe.*

Daft that has to do, and spares for every speech, He is but.

a. **1585** A. MONTGOMERIE *Cherrie & Slae* xxvii (1821) 16 He is bot daft that hes ado, And spairis for euery speiche. **1721** KELLY 167.

Dagger hand, see Hold up your d. h.

Daggers drawn (drawing), To be at.
(D 9)

1540 PALSGRAVE *Acolastus* 46 We neuer mete togyther, but we be at daggers drawynge. **1553** GRIMALDE *Cicero's Offices* 12a They . . . among themselues are wont to bee at daggers drawing. **1565** OSORIUS *Pearl for Princes* tr. R. Shacklock 60 (at dagger drawing with Godlynes). **1668** L'ESTRANGE *Vis. Quev.* (1708) 214 Upon this point were they at Daggers-drawn with the Emperor. **1801** EDGEWORTH *Belinda* ch. 16 Lady Delacour and she are at daggers-drawing. **1813** BARRETT *Heroine* ed. Raleigh 7 (at daggers drawn). **1870** R. B. BROUGH *Marston Lynch* xxiv. 257 Was Marston still at daggers drawn with his rich uncle?

Dagger(s), see also All is gone (When), what avails d.?; Look d.; Playing with short d. (Ill); Swear d. out of sheath; Wear the wooden d.

Daimport, see Talk as Dutch as D.'s (Darnford's) dog.

Dainties love, Who | shall beggars prove.
(D 13)

1573 TUSSER 33 (1878) 72 Who dainties loue, a begger shall proue.

Dainties of the great are the tears of the poor, The. *Cf.* Pleasures of the mighty, etc.
(D 11)

1640 HERBERT no. 937.

Dainty, dainties, see also At ease (He that is) seeks d.; Dear bought . . . are d. for ladies; Dinners cannot be long where d. want; Plenty is no d.; Plenty makes d.

Daisy (-ies), see Dock to a d. (As like as); Fresh as a d.; Leap at a d.; Tread on nine d., spring.

Dallies with his enemy, He that | dies by his own hand (by his hand). (E 138)

c. **1576** WHYTHORNE 117 Hee who seeketh the Kompany or fellowship of hiz enemiez seeketh hiz own distruksion. **1591** STEPNEY L3ᵛ He that will to his enemy yeeld, may like a coward die in the field. **1599** MINSHEU *Span. Gram.* 82 Whosoeuer disdainfully dallies with his enimie, dies by his owne hande. i. by making no reckoning of his enimie, receaues dammage. **1659** HOWELL *Span. Prov.* 14 Who dallies with enemy dies betwixt his hands. **1732** FULLER no. 2073 (gives him leave to kill him). *Ibid.* no. 2304 He that slights his Enemy, dies by his Hand.

Dally not with women or money.
(M 1038)

1640 HERBERT no. 150.

Dam leaps over, Where the | the kid follows.

1732 FULLER no. 5662.

Dam of that was a whisker,¹ The. (D 15)

1678 RAY 89 *A great Lie* . . . **1681** HICKERINGILL *News fr. Colchester* Wks. (1716) I. 394 With what astonishment the People . . . were struck, when they read . . . this whisking Lye. [¹ something great, excessive.]

Dam, see also Devil and his d.; Devil, (Bring you the) and I'll bring out his d.; Kick of d. hurts not colt; Looks as if he had sucked d. through hurdle.

Dame, see Dorty d. may fa' in the dirt; Holiday d.; Ruled by own d.; Tocherless d. sits long.

Dance, They who | are thought mad by those who hear not the music.

1575 H. C. AGRIPPA *Vanity of Arts and Sciences* tr. Sanford 30ᵛ Daunsing litle differing from madnes . . . excepte it were tempered with the sounde of instrumentes. **1576** G. GASCOIGNE *Grief of Joy* ii. 553 For daunce allone, (I meane withowt some noyse,) And that woulde seeme, a very madde mans parte. **1581** GUAZZO i. 164. **1927** *Times* 16 Feb. 15/4 (an old proverb).

Dance attendance, To. (A 392)

1519 W. HORMAN *Vulgaria* (1926 ed., 303), I am wery of . . . daunsynge attendaunce at his gate. **1522** SKELTON *Why not to Court* 626 And Syr ye must daunce attendance, . . . For my Lords Grace, Hath now no time or space, To speke with you as yet. **1590–1** SHAKES. *2 Hen. VI* I. iii. 169 Last time I danc'd attendance on his will Till Paris was besieg'd, famish'd, and lost. **1593** *Id. Rich. III* III. vii. 56 Welcome, my

lord: I dance attendance here; I think the duke
will not be spoke withal. **1613** *Id. Hen. VIII*
V. ii. 30 Not thus to suffer A man of his place
. . . To dance attendance on their lordships'
pleasures. **1883** GILMOUR *Mongols* xxxi. 362
After dancing attendance on the court for a
month or two they receive their dismission.

Dance barefoot, To. (D 22)

[Said of an elder sister when a younger one was
married before her.] **1594–8** SHAKES. *T.S.* II. i.
33 She must have a husband; I must dance barefoot on her wedding day. **1742** MRS. DELANY
Life & Corr. (1861) II. 188 The eldest daughter
was much disappointed that she should dance
barefoot, and desired her father to find out a
match for her.

Dance Barnaby, To. (B 91)

[= to dance to a quick movement, move
expeditiously.] **1664** COTTON *Scarron.* (1715) 7
Bounce cryes the Port-hole, out they flie And
make the World dance Barnaby. **1664** ETHER-
EDGE *Com. Revenge* v. ii Widow, here is music;
send for a parson, and we will dance Barnaby
within this half-hour.

Dance (*or* march) in a net, To. (N 130)

[= to act without concealment, while expecting
to escape notice.] **1528** TYNDALE *Obed. Chrn.
Man* P.S. 247 In case like unto them which, when
they dance naked in nets, believe they are invisible. **1532** MORE *Confut. of Tyndale* cxxvii.
I go so bare dawnsyng naked in a net. **1573**
GASCOIGNE *Adv. of Master F.J.* i. 490 Sutch as
. . . do yet conjecture that they walke unseene in
a net. **1583** FULKE *Def. Tr. Script.* vi (1843) 242
Now you have gotten a fine net to dance naked
in, that no ignorant blind buzzard can see you.
[*c.* **1587**] **1592** KYD *Span. Trag.* IV. iv. 118 Whose
reconciled sonne Marcht in a net, and thought
himself vnseene. *c.* **1599** CHAPMAN *All Fools* II.
i. 252 Think not you dance in nets. **1659**
HOWELL *Eng. Prov.* 11a You dance in a nett, and
you think no body sees you. **1679** DRYDEN
Limberham II. i I have danced in a net before my
father, . . . retired to my chamber undiscovered.
1822 SCOTT *Nigel* ch. 14 You must not think to
dance in a net before old Jack Hildebrod.

Dance nor hold the candle, You will neither.

1721 KELLY 367 . . . That is, you will neither do,
nor let do. **1732** FULLER no. 6013.

Dance, When you go to | take heed whom you take by the hand. (H 386)

1621 ROBINSON 24. **1639** CLARKE 24. **1721**
KELLY 320 . . . Spoken to them who have impru-
dently engag'd with some who have been too
cunning, or too hard for them.

Dance the Tyburn jig, To. (J 56)

[= to be hanged.] **1697** VANBRUGH *Relapse*
(1708) Epil. 73 Did ever one yet dance the
Tyburn Jigg, With a free Air, or a well-pawdered
Wigg?

Dance to (after) (a person's) pipe (whistle, etc.), To. (M 488)

[MATT. xi. 17 We piped unto you, and ye did not
dance.] *c.* **1480** *Early Eng. Misc.* ed. Halliwell
25 I wylle dance whylle the world wylle pype.
1546 HEYWOOD II. vi. 11 That to daunce after
her pipe, I am ny led. **1598**? STOW *Survey* 1603
ed. Kingsford ii. 215 London neuer led the dance,
but euer followed the pipe of the Nobilitie.
1604 MIDDLETON *Father Hubb. Tales* Wks. (1886)
VIII. 65 Till the old devourer . . . death, had
made our landlord dance after his pipe. **1670**
RAY 170 To dance to every mans pipe or whistle.
1823 SCOTT *Peveril* ch. 7 I thought I had the
prettiest girl in the Castle dancing after my
whistle. **1845** S. AUSTIN *Ranke's Hist. Ref.* I. 523
That most of these councillors . . . will 'dance to
Rome's piping', if they do but see her gold.

Dance to every fool's pipe, I will not. (F 522)

1732 FULLER no. 2644.

Dance upon nothing, To.

[= to be hanged.] **1833** S. SMITH *Life . . . of Major
Jack Downing* 174 He must dance upon nothing,
with a rope round his neck. **1839** H. AINSWORTH
Jack Sheppard ch. 31 (Farmer), 'You'll dance
upon nothing presently', rejoined Jonathan
brutally.

Dance without a fiddle (pipe), I will make him. (P 343)

1517–27 J. RASTELL *Four Elements* Hazl.-Dods.
i. 47 That is the best dance without a pipe, That
I saw this seven year. **1567** PAINTER *Palace
Pleas.* (Jacobs) iii. 334 Do you not see how cun-
inge I am to make men daunce without Taber,
or Pipe? **1616** T. ADAMS *Divine Herbal* 119 (pipe).
[**1625**] **1647** J. FLETCHER *Chances* I. viii. 2 Are ye
well arm'd?—Never fear us. Here's that will make
'em dance without a fiddle. **1678** RAY 71 . . . *i.e.*
I'll do him an injury, and he shall not know how.

Dances well to whom fortune pipes, He. (F 611)

c. **1390** CHAUCER *Reeve's Prol.* l. 22 We hoppen
alwey whil the world wol pype. **1573** SANFORD 102
(well inough). **1636** CAMDEN 297. **1796** EDGE-
WORTH *Par. Asst.* (1903) 410 No doubt of that . . .
He always dances well to whom fortune pipes.

Dancing (fighting) days are done, His (My). (D 118)

1573 GASCOIGNE *Adv. of Master F.J.* i. 397–8
My dauncing dayes are almost done. **1582** C.
FETHERSTON *Dial. agst. Dancing* B1ᵛ How many
mens seruauntes being set to woorke, do after
their dauncinge dayes lie snorting in hedges,
because they are so weary that they cannot
worke? **1591** ARIOSTO *Orl. Fur.* Harington
VIII. 44 His youthful dayes were done, he could
not daunce. **1595** SHAKES. *R.J.* I. v. 29 You
and I are past our dancing days. **1603** JONSON
Entertainment at Althorp vii. 129 l. 264 All those
dauncing dayes are done. **1604** R. DALLINGTON
View of Fraunce V Iᵛ My dancing dayes are done.
1721 KELLY 256. **1816** J. AUSTEN *Emma* ch. 38.
1818 SCOTT *Rob Roy* ch. 28 (fighting).

Dance, (*noun*), *see* Hop whore! . . . Hangman lead the d.

Dance(s, d, -ing), (*verb*) *see* Devil d. in empty pocket; I will make one . . . when he d. in clogs; Love d. well that d. among thorns; Maids in Wanswell may d. in an eggshell; Merry that d. (All are not); Shaking of the sheets, (To d. the); Take a spring of his fiddle and d. (Let him).

Danes, *see* Kill the D. (It would).

Danger is next neighbour to security. *Cf.* Secure is not safe.

1607 *Dobson's Dry Bobs* G1 No man so much in daunger as he who dreadeth none. **1647** *Countryman's New Commonwealth* 5 Security hath perill. **1732** FULLER no. 1233.

Danger itself the best remedy for danger. *Cf.* Danger, Without | we cannot, etc. (D 30)

c. **1526** ERASM. *Dicta Sap.* A4ᵛ He that vnderstandeth perell, knoweth howe to auoyde perell. Truely folehardynesse peryllously gothe in hande with a thyng, bycause it knoweth nat feare. **1577** HOLINSHED (1587) iii. 98a Nunquam periculum sine periculo vincitur. *c.* **1580** SIDNEY *First Arcadia* iv. 122 With Daunger to avoyde Daunger. **1586** GUAZZO ii. 144 One danger is expelled by an other, As one nayle is driven out by an other. **1651** HERBERT no. 1054. **1666** TORRIANO *It. Prov.* 202 no. 21 One danger is not overcome without another.

Danger makes men devout.

c. **1552** W. BALDWIN *Beware the Cat* (1584) D2. **1639** CLARKE 273.

Danger once, Better pass a | than be always in fear. (D 27)

1542 UDALL *Apoph.* 275ᵛ He [Caesar] answered, that better it was ons for all together to dye, then to bee in perpetuall care of takyng heede. **1598** BARCKLEY *Fel. Man* V. 416 Were it not better (said Iulius Caesar) to die once, then to liue in such continuall feare and suspition? **1631** HEYWOOD 2 *Fair Maid* ii. 356 The very doubt of what the danger is, Is more then danger can be. **1659** HOWELL *It. Prov.* 14. **1664** CODRINGTON 231. **1670** RAY 9.

Danger (River) past and God forgotten, The. (D 31)

1571 SIR T. SMITH to Burghley cited C. Read *Ld. Burghley and Q. Elizabeth* 48 If her Majesty do still continue in extremities to promise, in recoveries to forget, what shall we say but as Italians do, Passato il pericolo, gabbato il santo. **1591** ARIOSTO *Orl. Fur.* Harington XLI. Moral Scampato il pericolo giabbato il santo, When danger is scaped, the Saint is—mocked. **1611** COTGRAVE s.v. Sainct The danger past our vowes are soone forgotten. **1640** HERBERT no. 207 (river). **1670** RAY 6 (danger). *a.* **1685** T. JORDAN *Epigram* in *Epigrammatists* (1876) 261 The danger past, both are alike requited; God is forgotten, and the soldier slighted. **1721** KELLY 88 . . . In time of Danger and Affliction Men will

address themselves earnestly to God for Relief; but too often when relieved forget to be thankful. **1732** FULLER no. 1234. **1853** TRENCH iii. 71 (river).

Danger, Without | we cannot get beyond danger. *Cf.* Danger itself, etc. (D 37)

1539 TAVERNER *Publius* E3 Peryl is neuer ouercom with out peryll. **1631** MABBE *Celestina* T.T. 179 Without danger no danger is overcome. **1640** HERBERT no. 1010.

Danger(s) *see also* Brings himself into needless d. (He that); Lost (All is not) that is in d.; Nought is never in d.; Out of debt . . . ; Out of office . . . ; Post of honour is post of d.; Sail without d. (He that would); Seeks trouble (d.); Wars (He that is not in) is not out of d.; Wisdom (What is not) is d.

Dangerous fire begins in the bed straw, It is a. (F 272)

c. **1386** CHAUCER *Merch. T.* l. 1783 O perilous fyr, that in the bedstraw bredeth! **1651** HERBERT no. 1070.

Dangerous, *see also* Experience sometimes d.; Wound that bleeds inwardly most d.

Darby and Joan.

[= an attached couple, espec. in advanced years and in humble life.] **1735** *Gent. Mag.* v. 153 has a copy of verses: 'Old Darby, with Joan by his side, You've often regarded with wonder: He's dropsical, she is sore-eyed, Yet they're never happy asunder.' **1773** GOLDSMITH *She Stoops to C.* I. i You may be a Darby, but I'll be no Joan, I promise you. **1857** MRS. MATHEWS *Tea-Table Talk* I. 50 They furnished . . . a high-life illustration of Derby and Joan. **1932** *Daily Mail* 25 Feb. 7/7 Mr. & Mrs. Joseph Ball, both aged more than 80, . . . were regarded as the village 'Darby and Joan'.

Dare not for his ears (eyes), He. (E 15)

1520 WHITTINGTON *Vulg.* E.E.T.S. 91 He durste not for all yᵉ eyen in his head speke to me after that. **1545** W. TURNER *Rescuing of the Romish Fox* 13. *c.* **1570** *Sir Clyomon & Sir Clamydes* i. 2084 Not for the eares of my head with him I dare trie. **1678** RAY 240.

Dare not show his head, He. (H 246)

1551 T. WILSON *Rule of Reason* (1580) 49 This manne . . . durst not once for his life shewe his hedde, for feare. **1616** DRAXE no. 451 Hee dareth not shew his head for debt. **1678** RAY 89 . . . A Bankrupt.

Dare, *see also* May if you list, but do if you d.; Sair dung bairn that d. not greet; Soul is my own, (I d. not say).

Dark as a wolf's mouth.

1706 STEVENS s.v. Boca *Escuro como boca de lobo*, as dark as a Dungeon, literally, as a Wolf's Mouth, because their Mouths are black. **1828**

scott *Fair Maid* ch. 24 The moon is quite obscured, and the road as black as a wolf's mouth.

Dark in Dover, When it's | 'tis dark all the world over.

1736 s. pegge *Kenticisms, Prov.* E.D.S. 70.

Dark, *see also* Destiny always d.; Drive black hogs in the d.; Fair and the foul, by d. are like store; Good name keeps lustre in d.; Good to be in d. as without light; Gropes in the d. (He that); Joan is as good as my lady in the d.; Leap in the d.

Darkest hour is that before the dawn, The.   (D 84)

1650 fuller *Pisgah Sight* II. xi. 229 It is always darkest just before the day dawneth. **1760** j. wesley *Journal* iv. 498. **1849** c. brontë *Shirley* ch. 20 This is a terrible hour, but it is often that darkest point which precedes the rise of day. **1900** j. mccarthy *Hist. Own Times* v. 41 Ayoob Khan now laid siege to Candahar. . . . As so often happens in the story of England's struggles in India, the darkest hour proved to be that just before the dawn. **1906** alex. maclaren *Expos. Deut.*—1 *Sam.* 270.

Darling(s), *see* Better be an old man's d.; Mothers' d. milksop heroes.

Darnford, *see* Daimport.

Dart, *see* River of Dart.

Dartford, *see* Sutton.

Dartmouth, *see* Kingswear.

Dash, At first.   (D 42)

[1525–40] 1557 *A merry dialogue* ed. de Vocht 57 Gyue you me a mocke at first dash. **1562** j. wigand *De Neutralibus* I4ᵛ This thy shrynking, and thy relenting and goyng at the first dash to the papistes part. **1581** guazzo ii. 106. **1583** p. stubbes *Anat. of Abuses* ed. Furnivall (1882) ii. 29 The poore man, if hee haue scraped any little thing togither, is forced to disburse it at the first dash. *c.* **1591** shakes. *1 Hen. VI* I. ii. 71 She takes upon her bravely at first dash. **1672** Walker 59, no. 65 To be out at the first dash.

Dasnell[1] dawcock[2] sits among the doctors, The.   (D 52)

1634 withals 558 The dosnell Dawcocke come dropping in among the Doctors. **1639** clarke 297. **1659** howell *Eng. Prov.* 15b (as 1634). [¹ stupid, clownish. ² jack-daw, *i.e.* simpleton.]

Date is out, The.

1587 g. whetstone *Censure of loyal Subj.* C3 The date . . . is out. **1587** j. bridges *Defence* 1212 Their date was out. **1594** o.b. *Questions* K1ᵛ The date of such wasters were out. **1597** shakes. *1 Hen. IV* II. iv. 483 A true face and a good

conscience—Both which I have had: but their date is out. **1603** *Batchelor's Banquet* ed. F. P. Wilson 67 The date of these delights is out. **1614** jonson *Barth. Fair* v. 497 The date of my Authority is out.

Date of the devil, The.

[Is opposed to the date of our Lord.] **1362** langland *P. Pl.* A. II. 81 In þe Date of þe deuel þe Deede was a-selet.¹ *a.* **1529** skelton *Sp. Parrot* 439 Yet the date of ower Lord And the date of the Devyll dothe shrewdlye accord. [¹ sealed, signed.]

Daub(ing), *see* Craft in d.; Wine washes off d.

Daughter and eat fresh fish betimes, Marry your. *Cf.* Marry your daughters betimes.   (D 45)

1659 howell *Span. Prov.* 23. **1721** kelly 86 Daughters and dead Fish are no keeping Wares. If so! let the Daughters be dispos'd of, and the Fish eaten as soon as conveniently you can; lest the one miscarry and the other stink. **1796** wolcot (P. Pindar) *Orson & Ellen* Wks. (1816) IV. 68 For daughters and dead fish, we find, Were never keeping wares.

Daughter-in-law, *see* Mother-in-law.

Daughter is stolen, When the | shut Pepper Gate.   (D 46)

1662 fuller *Chester* 188 Peppergate was a postern of this City. . . . The Mayor . . . had his daughter (as she was playing at ball with other Maidens in Pepper-street) stoln away by a Young man, through the same gate; whereupon, . . . he caused it to be shut up.

Daughter of the horse-leech, The.

[**1560** prov. xxx. 15 (1586) The horse leache hath two daughters *which crie,* Giue giue.] **1662** fuller *Staffs* 43 These two wicked Instruments, who, with the two 'daughters of the horse leach', were always crying, give give. **1823** scott *Peveril* ch. 38 Such . . . were the morning attendants of the Duke of Buckingham—all genuine descendants of the daughter of the horse-leech, whose cry is 'Give, give'. **1882** besant *All Sorts* ch. 28 The habit of demanding remained, because the reformer is like the daughter of the horse-leech, and still cries for more.

Daughter (mistress) win, He that would the | must with the mother (maid) first begin.   (D 43)

1578 *Courtly Controversy* T4ᵛ If you will seeke a shorte and assured way . . . court the mother . . . for hauing once gayned place in the good opinion of the mother, the good will of the daughter is alreadie wonne. **1591** ariosto *Orl. Fur.* Harington v. 12 margin A pollicie vsed sometime to woo the maid to win the mistres. **1611** l. barry *Merry Tricks* l. 848 Doe not you know That he which would be inward with the Mistris, Must make a way first through the waiting mayde? *c.* **1620** massinger *Fatal Dowry* II. iii Courting my woman?—As an entrance to The fauour of the mistris. **1670** ray 49. **1904** 'h. s. merriman'

Tomaso's Fortune ix Felipe was wooing the daughter through the mother, as men have often done before him.

Daughter(s), *see also* Dawted d. daidling wives; Four good mothers have four bad d. . . . ; Married to a gunner's d.; Marry your d. betimes; Marry your son when you will, your d. when you can; Michaelmas chickens and parsons' d.; Mother (Like), like d.; Mother trot, (If the) how can the d. amble?; Son is my son; Tent thee . . . if I can't rule my d.; Truth is God's d.; Truth is time's d.; Two d. and back door are thieves; Vine of a good soil and d. of good mother (Take).

Davenport, *see* Cheshire (In) there are . . . D.

David (Saint), *see* First comes D.

David[1] and Chad[2]: sow peas good or bad.   (D 49)
1659 HOWELL *Eng. Prov.* 21b David and Chad sow good or bad.   1670 RAY 43.   1846 DENHAM 40. [¹ 1 March. ² 2 March.]

David's sow, *see* Drunk as D. s.

Davy do all things, You are.
1721 KELLY 392 . . . Spoken to them that pretend that nothing can be right done unless they be about it.

Davy Jones's locker.
[1760–2 SMOLLETT *Sir Launcelot Greaves* ch. 7 I have seen Davy Jones in the shape of a blue flame, d'ye see, hopping to and fro on the sprit-sail yardarm.]   1785 GROSE *Dict. Vulg. T.* David Jones's locker, the sea.   1803 *Nav. Chron.* x. 510 The . . . seamen would have met a watery grave; or, to use a seaman's phrase, gone to Davy Jones's locker.   1837 CHAMIER *Saucy Areth.* ch. 14 The boat was capsized, . . . and . . . all hands are snug enough in Davy Jones's locker.

Daw, *see* Wise as a d.

Dawcock, *see* Dasnell d.

Dawkin, *see* Dab, quoth D.; Strike, D.

Dawted daughters make daidling wives.
1862 HISLOP 47 . . . Daughters . . . much indulged or petted at home before marriage make but indifferent wives.

Day after the fair, A.   (D 112)
[Gk. Κατόπιν ἑορτῆς ἥκεις. L. *Post festum venisti.* You have come after the feast.]   1530 PALSGRAVE 802a A day afore [*sic*] the fayre, whiche we use for an adage, meanyng that one . . . cometh too late.   1546 HEYWOOD I. viii. C1.   1548 HALL *Chron.* 2186 A daie after the faire, as the common proverb saieth.   1616 BRETON *Cross. Prov.* A4ᵛ He is a fond Chap-man that comes after the fayre.   1676 ETHEREGE *Man of Mode* III. i. You came a day after the fair.   1900 LANG *Hist. Scot.* I. 277 The king was willing to accept the truce, though it came 'a day after the fair'.

Day has eyes, the night has ears, The.   (D 62)
a. 1628 CARMICHAELL no. 1437.   1641 FERGUSSON no. 810 The day hes eyne, the night hes ears.   1721 KELLY 336.

Day, Oft times one | is better than sometimes a whole year.   (D 83)
1481 CAXTON *Reynard* xxvii Arb. 66 Oftymes one day is better than somtyme an hole yere.

Day is short, and the work is much, The.   (D 63)
c. 1400 *Beryn* Chauc. Soc. l. 3631 The day is short, the work is long.   1678 RAY *Adag. Hebr.* 414 . . . *Ars longa vita brevis.*   1740 WESLEY *Works* viii. 374.

Day lengthens the cold strengthens, As the.   (D 58)
1631 PELLHAM *God's Power* 818 The New Year now begun, as the Days began to lengthen, so the Cold began to strengthen.   1639 CLARKE 18.   1639 *Berkeley MSS.* (1885) iii. 30 When the daies begin to lengthen the cold begins to strengthen.   1670 RAY 43.   1721 KELLY 52 . . . February and March are much more cold and piercing than December or January.   1899 SIR A. WEST *Recollect.* ch. 21 Bearing out the old adage, . . .

Day may bring, What a | a day may take away.   (D 109)
1592 DELAMOTHE 5 What one day giues vs, another takes away from vs.   1597 *Politeuphuia* 130 [as 1592].   1651 HERBERT no. 1111 (as 1592).   1732 FULLER no. 5475.

Day never so long, Be the | at length comes evensong.   (D 59)
c. 1390 GOWER *Conf. Amantis* VI. 578 Bot hou so that the dai be long, The derke nyht comth ate laste.   1509 HAWES *Pastime of Pleas.* ch. 42, l. 5479 For though the day be neuer so longe, At last the belles ryngeth to euensonge.   1546 HEYWOOD II. vii. I4ᵛ Yet is he sure be the daie neuer so longe, Euermore at laste they ryng to euensonge.   1587 HOLINSHED J. Hooker to Raleigh before 'The Conquest of Ireland' A3 (according to the old countrie saieng . . . it will ring to euensong).   1612 T. ADAMS *The Gallant's Burden* (1616 ed., 39).   1916 SAINTSBURY *Eng. Lit.* 165 We owe to him [Hawes] one of the oldest forms . . . of the beautiful saying—Be the day weary, or be the day long, At length it draweth to evensong.

Day passes without some grief, No.   (D 91)
1616 WITHALS 543.   1664 CODRINGTON 206.   1670 RAY 6.

Day so clear but has dark clouds, No.   (D 92)
1590–1 SHAKES. *2 Hen. VI* II. iv. i Thus sometimes hath the brightest day a cloud.   1592

DELAMOTHE 17 There is no day neuer so cleare, but it hath some darke cloudes. **1597** SERJEANT HARRIS (Neale *Eliz. I & her Parl*[ts] *1584–1601*, 343) The fairest day hath a cloud to shadow it. **1651** HERBERT no. 1123.

Day still while the sun shines, It is.

(D 85)

1528 TYNDALE *Obed. Chrn. Man* P.S. 298 It is always day so long as the sun shineth. **1639** CLARKE 294. **1670** RAY 77.

Day that you do well there will be seven moons in the lift,[1] and one in the midden,[2] The.

1721 KELLY 327 . . . Intimating that such a one will never do well. **1732** FULLER no. 4468 The Day that you do a good Thing, there will be seven new Moons. [[1] sky. [2] dung hill.]

Day will pay for all, One.   (D 97)

1581 T. LUPTON *Siuqila* 15 A common saying, A day will come shall pay for all. **1616** DRAXE no. 1855.

Day without a line, No.   (D 93)

[L. *Nulla dies sine linea.* No day without a line. *Cf. Pliny* 35. 10. 36, § 84.] **1573** L. LLOYD *Pilg. of Princes*** I[v] If your worship do folowe but *Apelles* sayinges vnto his schollers, that no day shoulde passe without the reading of one line. **1578** *Courtly Controv.* R2[v] According to the examples of the most excellent painters, who suffered no day to escape without the drawing of some line at the least. **1579** LYLY *Euph.* i. 285 Follow Apelles that cunning and wise Painter, which would lette no day passe ouer his head, without a lyne, without some labour. **1616** T. ADAMS *Divine Herbal* 19 Line must be added to line. **1825** SCOTT *Journ.* 1 Dec. *Nulla dies sine linea.* But never a being, from my infancy upwards, hated task-work as I hate it. **1905** A. VAMBÉRY *Story of Strug.* I. iv. 148 True to my principle . . . 'Nulla dies sine linea', I had not one lost day to record.

Day(s), *see also* All in the d.'s work; Bad d. that has good night (Never); Barnaby bright longest d. shortest night; Better d. better deed; Blustering night fair d.; Broke his hour that kept his d. (Never); Churning d.; Clear as d.; Come d. go d.; Contemplates (He that) has d. without night; Cover your head by d.; Devil bides his d.; Discourse makes short d.; Dog has his d.; Drunken days have their tomorrows; Evening crowns d.; Ever and a d.; Every d.; Fair d. in winter; February has one and thirty d.; Fowl of a fair d.; Halcyon d.; Life and a d. longer (All one's); Longest d. has end; Lucy light shortest d.; Man may learn wit every d.; Merry (Happy) as d. is long; Never is long d.; Night (d.) of it (Make); One d. was three till liberty was borrow; One of these d. is none of these d.; Praise a fair d. at night; Promise more in a d. than fulfill in year; Rainy d. (Lay up for); Rise early (Though you) yet d. comes at his time; St. Thomas . . . shortest d.; Say no more till d. be longer; See d. at little hole; Sees thee by d.

will not seek by night; Sleeps all the morning (Who) may go begging all the d. after; Summer's d. (As good as one shall see in a); Tomorrow is new d.; Twelfth D. the d. are lengthened; Twenty-four hours in d. (Only); Two dismal d., d. of death and d. of doom.

Daylight, *see* Burn d.; Drink less and go home by d.; Fair fall truth and d.; See you in d. (They that) winna break the house.

De mortuis nil nisi bonum, see Speak well of the dead.

De te fabula narratur.

[HORACE *Sat.* I. I. 69 *Mutato nomine de te Fabula narratur*: Change but the name and the story applies to yourself.] **1853** G. J. WHYTE-MELVILLE *Digby G.* ch. 26 The reader has probably had quite enough of Digby Grand and his autobiography; but to some . . . he may say, *Mutato nomine, de te fabula narratur.* **1929** *Times* 12 June 17/4 The eye of fancy catches every seaside place in England pointing the finger at some other with a '*De te fabula*', for fear itself should be accused.

Dead (Deaf, Dumb) as a door-nail (door-tree), As.   (D 567)

[A beam used for fastening the door. *Cf.* OE. næзl.] *c.* **1350** *Will. Palerne* 628 For but ich haue bote[1] of mi bale[2] I am ded as dorenail. **1362** LANGLAND *P. Pl.* A i. 161 Fey[3] withouten fait[4] is febelore þen nou3t, And ded as a dore-nayl. **1377** *Ibid.* B i. 185 As ded as a dore-tre. *a.* **1400–50** *Alexander* l. 4747 Dom as a dorenayle & defe was he bathe. **1590–1** SHAKES. *2 Hen. VI* IV. x. 39 If I do not leave you all as dead as a door-nail. **1598** *Id. 2 Hen. IV* V. iii. 126 What, is the old King dead?—As nail in door. **1639** CLARKE 301 (deafe). **1843** DICKENS *Christ. Car.* ch. 1 Old Marley was as dead as a door-nail. **1855** MRS. GASKELL *North and South* ch. 17 (dour as). **1884** *Pall Mall G.* 29 May 5/2 The Congo treaty may now be regarded as being as dead as a door-nail. [[1] relief, remedy. [2] trouble. [3] faith. [4] deed.]

Dead as a herring, As.   (H 446)

1600–1 SHAKES. *M.W.W.* II. iii. 8 By gar, de herring is no dead, so as I vill kill him. **1603** *Bachelor's Banquet* ed. F. P. Wilson 95. **1664** BUTLER *Hudibras* II. iii. 1148 Hudibras, to all appearing, Believ'd him to be dead as Herring. **1727** [GAY?] 'New Song of new Similies' *Poems* ed. Faber 646.

Dead as mutton, As.

c. **1770** BICKERSTAFFE *Spoiled Child* II. ii Thus let me seize my tender bit of lamb—(*aside*) there I think I had her as dead as mutton. **1812** J. & H. SMITH *Rejected Addresses* Motto. **1914** SHAW 'Parents and Children', in *Misalliance, etc.* vii The old Bernard Shaw is as dead as mutton.

Dead as Queen Anne, As.

1722 LADY PENNYMAN *Miscell.* (1740) 97 He's as dead as Queen Anne the day after she dy'd.

1837–47 BARHAM *Ingol. Leg.* (1898) 40 Mrs. Winnifred Pryce was as dead as Queen Anne!

Dead avails not and revenge vents hatred, To lament the.   (D 125)

1591 ARIOSTO *Orl. Fur.* Harington IX. 41 By teares no good the dead is done, And sharpe reuenge asswageth malice cheefe. **1598–9** SHAKES. *M.A.* V. i. 39 Yet bend not all the harm upon yourself. Make those that do offend you suffer too. **1666** TORRIANO *It. Prov.* 205, no. 10.

Dead bee makes no honey, A.   (B 206)

1492 *Dialogue of Salomon & Marcolphus* ed. Duff 11. **1573** SANFORD 102. **1611** DAVIES no. 227 . . . But from dead Bees it's had for money. **1659** HOWELL *Brit. Prov.* 3 Neither for peace nor for warre, will a dead Bee gather honey.

Dead dogs bark (bite) not.   (D 448)

1571 R. EDWARDS *Damon and Pithias* D3ᵛ A dead dogge can not bite. **1596** A. COPLEY *Fig for Fortune* (Spens. S.) 23 Dead dogges barke not. *a.* **1622** J. FLETCHER *Custom of Country* IV. ii. 26 A dog that's dead, The Spanish proverb says, will never bite.

Dead, When I am | make me a caudle¹.   (C 196)

1297 R. GLOUC. (1824) 561 As me seiþ, wan ich am ded, make me a caudel. *a.* **1628** CARMICHAELL no. 1276 Quhen I am deid mak me caddell. **1637** NABBES *Microcosmus* (1887) IV. 198 By that time you are dead I will have made you a cawdle. **1721** KELLY 351 . . . Be kind to me when I am alive, for I shall not value, or be better for your Presents, when I am dead. [¹ a warm drink.]

Dead man, *see* Fart out of a d. m. (You will as soon get a); Sad burden to carry d. m.'s child; Speak not of a d. m. at table.

Dead men and absent there are no friends left, To.   (M 591)

c. **1300** *Provs. of Hending* 37 Frendles ys the dede. **1599** MINSHEU *Span. Gram.* 83. **1611** COTGRAVE s.v. Ami The dead haue no friends, the sicke but faint ones. *c.* **1640** W. S. *Countrym. Commonw.* 2 (and absent are). **1659** HOWELL *Fr. Prov.* 8 The dead hath no friend, the sick but half a one.

Dead men don't bite (do no harm).   (M 510)

[Gk. Νεκρὸς οὐ δάκνει. ERASM. *Ad. Mortui non mordent.*] **1548** HALL *Chron.* 128 A prouerbe . . . saith, a dead man doth no harme. *a.* **1593** *Jack Straw* Hazl.-Dods. V. 412 I trow they cannot bite, when they be dead. **1611** BEAUM. & FL. *Kt. Burn.* P IV. i. Yet am I glad he's quiet, where I hope He will not bite again. **1655** FULLER *Ch. Hist.* IX. iv (1868) III. 24 The dead do not bite; and, being despatched out of the way, are forgotten. **1882** STEVENSON *Treas. Is.* ch. 11. **1902** LANG *Hist. Scot.* II. 327 The story that Gray 'whispered in Elizabeth's ear, The dead don't bite', is found in Camden.

Dead men have no friends.

XVc. *Early English Carols* (ed. R. L. Greene) 366 Dede men haue no frond. **1605** J. HALL *Medit. and Vows* 2nd century no. 69 The Spanish proverb is too true; Dead men and absent finde no friends. **1674** J. SMITH 197 (as Hall).

Dead men tell no tales.   (M 511)

c. **1552** T. BECON *Of Fasting* P.S. 548 He that hath his body loaden with meat and drink, is no more meet to pray unto God than a dead man is to tell a tale. **1663** J. WILSON *Andron. Comn.* I. iv. 'Twere best To knock them i' th' head. . . . The dead can tell no tales. **1703** FARQUHAR *Inconstant* V. Ay, ay, dead men tell no tales. **1850** KINGSLEY *Alton Locke* ch. 4 Where are the stories of those who have not risen— . . . who have ended in desperation? . . . Dead men tell no tales.

Dead men's shoes, He goes long barefoot that wears (waits for). *Cf.* Iron shoes.   (M 619)

1530 PALSGRAVE 644a Thou lokest after deed mens shoes. *c.* **1549** HEYWOOD I. xi. C5 Who waitth for dead men shoen, shal go long barfote. *c.* **1641** FERGUSSON MS. no. 542 He should hav Iron shoon quho byds his neighbors dead. **1670** RAY 78 He that waits for dead mens shooes, may go long enough barefoot. A longue corde tire qui d'autruy mort desire. He hath but a cold suit who longs for another mans death. **1721** KELLY 148 . . . Spoken to them who expect to be some Man's Heir, to get his Place, or Wife, if he should dye. **1771** J. WESLEY *Lett.* V. 293. **1815** SCOTT *Guy Man.* ch. 37 That's but sma' gear, puir thing; she had a sair time o't with the auld leddy. But it's ill waiting for dead folk's shoon. **1870** C. READE *Put Yourself* ch. 29 What, go into his house, and wait for dead men's shoes! Find myself some day wishing . . . that noble old fellow would die!

Dead mouse feels no cold, A.   (M 1227)

a. **1628** CARMICHAELL no. 892 It is not cold to a slaine mouse. **1678** RAY 123.

Dead, or teaching school, He is either.

[Gk. ˚Η τέθνηκεν ἢ διδάσκει γράμματα.] **1655** FULLER *Hist. Univ. Camb.* (1840) 237 Nicias, . . . (having many scholars in his army,) had fought unfortunately against the Sicilians, and when such few as returned home were interrogated, what became of their companions, this was all they could return, 'They were either dead, or taught school'.

Dead shot at a yellow-hammer, A.

1796 EDGEWORTH *Par. Asst., Eton Mont.* (1903) 188 I always took you for 'a deadshot at a yellow-hammer'. [*Note.* Young noblemen at Oxford wore yellow tufts at the tops of their caps. Hence their flatterers were said to be dead-shots at yellow-hammers.]

Dead woman will have four to carry her forth, A.   (W 622)

1599 SANDYS *Europae Spec.* (1629) 194 Seeing as the Proverbe is, a dead woman will haue foure to carry her forth. **1678** RAY 354.

Dead, *see also* Baldwin's d. (My Lord); Devil is d.; Died half a year ago (Who) d. as Adam; Dog's d. since you were whelp; Ewe is drowned (When) she's d.; Gape long enough; Gives his goods before he be d. (He that); Giving is d.; King is d.; Praise no man till he is d.; Prince hates (He whom a) is as good as d.; Speak well of the d.; Stark d.; Trumpeter is d. (Your); Trust is d., ill payment killed it; Turns lie d. . . . (Ten good).

Deadly disease neither physician nor physic can ease, A. (D 356)

1573 SANFORD 101ᵛ. 1629 *Bk. Merry Rid.*, Prov. no. 56.

Deadly, *see* Beasts, The most d. of wild is a backbiter (tyrant).

Deaf (mute, silent, etc.) as a post. *Cf.* Post, As good speak to the. (P 490)

1540 PALSGRAVE *Acolastus* 47 He wotteth ful lyttel howe deffe an eare I intende to gyue him, . . . he were as good to tell his tale to a poste. 1551 CROWLEY *Pleas. & Pain* Ye deafe dorepostis, Coulde ye not heare? 1612 SHELTON *Quix.* III. xi (i. 207) Mute like a post. *a.* 1845 HOOD *Tale of a Trumpet* She was deaf as a post.

Deaf as an adder, As. (A 32)

[*Cf.* PSALM lviii. 4.] 1545 W. TURNER *Rescuing of the Romish Fox* L2 Ye will not hear the Scripture but as an aspis stop your eares lest ye should heare the Scripture. *c.* 1590–1 SHAKES. *2 Hen. VI* III. ii. 76 Art thou like the adder waxen deaf? 1590 LODGE *Rosalynde* ed. Greg 45 All adder-like I stop mine ears. 1591 ARIOSTO *Orl. Fur.* Harington XXXII. 19 To giue me hearing of my plaint he feares, As to the charme the Adder stoppes his eares. 1591 GREENE *Farewell to Folly* Gros. ix. 273 The noble men plaide like the deafe Addar that heareth not the sorcerers charme. *Ibid.* 310 No adder so deafe, but had his charme. 1822 SCOTT *Pirate* ch. 28.

Deaf as those who will not hear, None so. (H 295)

1546 HEYWOOD II. ix. K4 Who is so deafe, or so blynde, as is hee, That wilfully will nother here nor see? 1551 CRANMER *Ans. to Gardiner* 58 There is no manne so deafe as hee that will not heare, nor so blynd as he that will not see, nor so dull as he that wyll not vnderstande. *c.* 1560 INGELEND *Disobed. Child* Hazl.-Dods. ii. 285 I perceive by this gear, That none is so deaf as who will not hear. 1598 SHAKES. *2 Hen. IV* I. ii. 62 Boy, tell him I am deaf.—You must speak louder, my master is deaf.—I am sure he is, to the hearing of anything good. 1824 BENTHAM *Bk. of Fallacies* Wks. (1843) II. 412 None are so completely deaf as those who will not hear.

Deaf ear, To turn a. (E 13)

c. 1440 HYLTON *Scala Perf.* (W. de W. 1494) II. xxii Make deef ere to them as though thou herde haue not. 1508 J. FISHER *Sayings of David* 2 G7ᵛ We . . . wyl not here the prevy gyle hyd vnder that bodyly pleasure, but goo by with a defe eare.

1540 SIR T. ELYOT *Pasquill the Plain* B5ᵛ He . . . wyll leane a defe eare towarde you. 1548 HALL *Chron.* (1809 ed., 406). 1607 H. ESTIENNE *World of Wonders* 104.

Deaf gains the injury, The, *or* Deaf men go away with the blame. (D 127)

1640 HERBERT no. 927. 1664 CODRINGTON 222. 1670 RAY 6. 1732 FULLER no. 1243.

Deaf man, *see* Hae will a d. m. hear; Knock at a d. m.'s door; Sing at a d. m.'s door.

Deaf nuts. (N 365)

[= nuts with no kernel. ERASM. *Ad. Vitiosa nuce non emam.*] 1613 BP. HALL *Serm. I Sam.* xii. 24 He is but a deaf nut therefore, that hath outward service without inward fear. 1637 RUTHERFORD *Lett.* (1862) I. 331 I live upon no deaf nuts, as we use to speak. 1721 KELLY 395 You are not fed on deaf Nuts. Spoken to those who are plump and in good liking. 1808 SCOTT to C. K. Sharpe 30 Dec. in LOCKHART *Life* The appointments . . . are £300 a year—no deaf nuts. 1858 DE QUINCEY *Autob. Sk.* Wks. I. 88 A blank day, yielding absolutely nothing—what children call a deaf nut.

Deaf, *see also* Husband must be d. . . . to have quietness; Mad words d. ears (For); Masters should be . . . sometimes d.; Tale to a d. man, (You tell a).

Deal, Dover, and Harwich, the devil gave with his daughter in marriage; and, by a codicil to his will, he added Helvoet and the Brill.

1787 GROSE *Kent* 184 . . . A satyrical squib thrown at the inn-keepers of those places, in return for the many impositions practised on travellers.

Deal fool's dole, To. (F 524)

1670 RAY 171 . . . To deal all to others and leave nothing to himself.

Deal, *see* Dover shark, D. savage.

Deal with a fox, If you | think of his tricks.

1732 FULLER no. 2717.

Deal wi' the deil, They that | get a dear pennyworth.

1862 HISLOP 302.

Dealing, *see* Plain d.

Deals in dirt has aye foul fingers, He that.

1737 RAMSAY III. 183.

Deals in the world needs four sieves, He that. (W 868)

1640 HERBERT no. 899.

Deal(s), *see also* Fool that the fool is, (He is not the), but he that with the fool d.; Sits above that d. acres.

Dean, *see* Devil and the d. begin with ae letter.

Dear bought and far fetched are dainties for ladies. (D 12)

c. 1350 *Douce MS. 52* no. 7 Ferre ifet and dere i-bow3t is goode for ladys. Res longe lata bene fit dominabus amata.   *c.* 1470 *Harl. MS. 3362* no. 22 Thyng fer ybrowt ys wel ylouyd.   *a.* 1530 *R. Hill's Commonpl. Bk.* E.E.T.S. 132 A thyng ferre fett is good for ladyes.   1546 HEYWOOD I. xi. E1 But though we get little, dere bought and far fet Are deinties for ladies.   1550 LATIMER *Last Serm. bef. Edw. VI* P.S. 253 We must have our power from Turkey, of velvet . . . ; far fetched, dear bought.   1596 SHAKES. *M.V.* III. ii. 314 Since you are dear bought, I will love you dear. 1609 JONSON *Silent Wom.* Prol. When his cates are all in brought, Though there be none far-fet, there will dear-bought, Be fit for ladies.   1641 FERGUSSON no. 272 Far sought and dear bought, is good for Ladies.   1738 SWIFT Dial. I. E.L. 278 But you know, farfetch'd and dear-bought is fit for ladies.   1876 MRS. BANKS *Manch. Man* ch. 42 'Where did these beautiful things come from?' . . . 'India, . . . they are "far-fetched and dear-bought", and so must be good for you, my lady.'

Dear bought, *see also* Hengston Down; Honesty may be d. b.

Dear collop that is cut out of thine own flesh, It is a. (C 517)

1546 HEYWOOD I. x. D1 I haue one of myne owne, whom I must loke to.   Ye aunte (quoth Ales) . . . I haue heard saie, it is a deere colup That is cut out of thowne fleshe.   1590 GREENE *Never Too Late* 44 It is a neere collop, saies he, is cut out of the owne flesh.   1592–4 SHAKES. *I Hen. VI* V. iv. 18 God knows thou art a collop of my flesh.   1611 *Id. W.T.* I. ii. 134 Yet were it true To say this boy were like me . . . Most dear'st! my collop!   *c.* 1641 FERGUSSON MS. no. 908 It is a neir collop is cut of thy owin flesh.

Dear ship stands (stays) long in the haven (harbour), A. (S 345)

a. 1628 CARMICHAELL no. 48 A deir schip stands lang in the heaven.   1641 FERGUSSON no. 14. 1721 KELLY 50 . . . Apply'd often to nice Maids.

Dear year(s), *see* Longer lives good fellow than d. y.; Three d. y. will raise a baker's daughter.

Dear, *see also* Buy d. is not bounty; Know what would be d. (He that could); Pleasure is not pleasant unless it cost d.; Repentance too d., (To buy); Thing which is rare is d.

Dearer it is the cheaper, The.
(D 130)

1642 TORRIANO 88 . . . Means, I shall save by not buying any at all of that commodity.   1730 FULLER no. 4472.

Dearth, *see* Drought never bred d.; Wicked thing to make d. one's garner.

Death and marriage make term day.
(D 137)

a. 1628 CARMICHAELL no. 455.   1641 FERGUSSON no. 232.   1721 KELLY 84 . . . Marriage frees a Man from his Service in Scotland; and Death in all Countries.

Death come to me from Spain, May my.

1625 BACON *Ess. Despatch* Arb. 245 The . . . Spaniards, haue been to be noted of Small Dispatch; Mi venga la Muerte de Spagna; Let my Death come from Spaine; For then it will be sure to be long in comming.   1853 TRENCH iii. 53 The Italians have a proverb . . . of the tardiness of the despatch of all business in Spain.

Death defies the doctor.

[L. *Contra vim mortis non est medicamen in hortis.*]   1721 KELLY 89.

Death devours lambs as well as sheep.
(D 139)

1620 SHELTON *Quix.* II. xx (1908) II. 326 There is no trusting in the Raw-bones, I mean Death, that devours lambs as well as sheep.   1732 FULLER no. 1245.

Death in your house, You have | and do bewail another's. (D 160)

1640 HERBERT no. 376.

Death is a plaster (remedy) for all ills.
(D 141)

1616 BRETON 2 *Crossing of Prov.* B1ᵛ What is a remedy for all diseases? Death.   1631 KNEVET *Rhodon and Iris* II. ii. D3ᵛ.

Death is sure (common) to all. (D 142)

1579 J. CALVIN *Thirteen Sermons* 135 Death (as it is said in the common prouerb) is sure to all. 1597 *Politeuphuia* 216ᵛ Death is common to all persons, though to some one way, and to some another.   1600 T. HEYWOOD *et al. I Edw. IV* i. 51 Death's an honest man; for he spares not the King.   1600–1 SHAKES. *H.* I. ii. 72 Thou know'st 'tis common.   All that lives must die, Passing through nature to eternity.   1609 HARWARD 82 Death is common to all men, this we must all comme to.   1631 DEKKER *Match* III. i. 200 Death is a common fate.

Death is the end of all.

1584 WITHALS K3 Death is . . . the ende of all thinges.   1587 HOLINSHED iii. 835 Death . . . is the last end of all things.   *c.* 1591 MARLOWE *Edward II* l. 2275 Death ends all, and I can die but once.   *c.* 1594 SHAKES. *R.J.* III. iii. l. Death's the end of all.   *c.* 1595 *Edmond Ironside* l. 1300 (of woe).   [1603] 1607 T. HEYWOOD *Woman Killed with Kindness* sc. x. l. 20 Death is th' end of all calamity.   1631 HEYWOOD 2 *Fair Maid* ii. 410 Death will end all.

Death is the grand leveller. (D 143)

1578 FLORIO *First F.* 88ᵛ We are all in all subiect vnto death, and when wee are deade, there is no difference betwixt vs. **1591** *2 Troublesome Reign K.J.* E2ᵛ The fierce inuade of him [Death] that conquers kings. **1604** SHAKES. *M.M.* III. i. 40 Death we fear, That makes these odds all even. **1610** *Id. Cym.* IV. ii. 252 Thersites' body is as good as Ajax, When neither are alive. **1620** SHELTON *Quix.* Pt. II. ii. 261 At their burial they are equal. **1732** FULLER no. 1250.

Death keeps no calendar. (D 144)

1640 HERBERT no. 908. **1666** TORRIANO *It. Prov.* 159, no. 27 (hath). **1670** RAY 6. **1732** FULLER no. 1251.

Death of a bairn is not the skailing¹ of a house, The.

1706 STEVENS s.v. Muerte The House is not unfurnish'd for the Death of Children. **1721** KELLY 329 . . . The Death of a Child bears no Proportion to the Death of a Husband, or Wife. [¹ breaking up.]

Death of a young wolf never comes too soon, The. (D 145)

1592 DELAMOTHE 23. **1651** HERBERT no. 1131.

Death of the wolves is the safety of the sheep, The. (D 146)

1573 SANFORD 106ᵛ (safetie of the beastes). **1578** FLORIO *First F.* 31ᵛ The death of the woolfe, is the health of the sheepe. **1651** HERBERT no. 1086. **1913** A. C. BENSON *Along Road* 270 The Ouseleys have a very curious motto, '*Mors lupi agnis vita*', 'The death of the wolf is life to the lambs'.

Death pays all debts. (D 148)

[**1592**] **1597** SHAKES. *Rich. III* IV. iv. 21 Edward for Edward pays a dying debt. **1597** *Id. I Hen. IV* III. ii. 157 The end of life cancels all bands. **1603** MONTAIGNE (Florio) I. vii. 38 The common saying is, that *Death acquits us of all our bonds.* **1610** SHAKES. *Cym.* V. iv. 159 Are you ready for death? . . . The comfort is, you shall be called to no more payments. **1611** *Id. Temp.* III. ii. 126 He that dies pays all debts. **1827** SCOTT *Two Drovers* ch. 2 Death pays all debts; it will pay that too.

Death upon wires, Like.

1910 P. W. JOYCE *Eng. as We Speak in Ireld.* 138 An extremely thin emaciated person is . . . ; alluding to a human skeleton held together by wires.

Death's day is doom's day. (D 161)

1579 LYLY *Euph.* i. 308 Euery ones deathes daye is his doomes daye. *a.* **1609** SHAKES. *Sonn.* 14, l. 14 Thy end is truth's and beauty's doom and date. **1732** FULLER no. 1255.

Death's door, To be at. (D 162)

1515 A. BARCLAY *Life of St. George* E.E.T.S. l. 822. **1519** W. HORMAN *Vulg.* H4ᵛ He is at dethis dore. **1542** ERASM. tr. Udall *Apoph.* (1877 ed., 221). **1550** COVERDALE *Spir. Perle* xviii To bring unto deaths door, that he may restore unto life again. **1591** SHAKES. *3 Hen. VI* III. iii. 105 Even in the downfall of his mellow'd years, When nature brought him to the door of death? **1860** TROLLOPE *Framley P.* ch. 43.

Death(s), *see also* After d. the doctor; Age is jocund (When), it makes sport for d.; Breath (One man's) another's d.; Business of life and day of d. (Between); Cabbage twice cooked is d.; Door may be shut (Every) but d.'s; Dry cough trumpeter of d.; Enter this life (But one way to), but gates of d. without number; Fair d. honours; Fazarts (To) hard hazards are d.; Fear d. as children the dark; Fear of d. is worse than d. itself; Fears d. lives not (He that); First breath is beginning of d.; Good life makes good d.; Hold on like grim d.; Iron shoes, (He should wear) that bides his neighbour's d.; Life (Such a) such a d.; Life you loved me not (In), in d. you bewail me; Lightening before d.; Lived that lives not after d. (He has not); Nothing is certain but d.; Nothing so sure as d.; Old man's staff rapper at d.'s door; Old men go to d., d. comes to young; Old men . . . make much of d.; Owe God a d.; Pale as d.; Peace and patience and d. with repentance; Pulls with a long rope that waits another's d.; Raven bodes misfortune (d.), (The croaking); Remedy for all but d.; Silent as d; Sleep is brother of d.; — image of d.; Sure as d.; Swan sings when d. comes; Two dismal days, day of d. and day of doom; Welcome d., quoth the rat.

Debauchery, *see* Business (Without), d.

Debt(s), *see* Better go to bed supperless than rise in d.; Better to pay and have little than have much and to be in d.; Care will not pay ounce of d.; Confess d. and beg days; Death pays all d.; Hundred pounds of sorrow pays not d.; Lying rides upon d.'s back; Names are d.; Old d. better than old sores; Old thanks pay not new d.; Out of d., out of danger; Pay one's d. to nature; Poind for d. but not for kindness; Promise is d.; Sins and our d. often more than we think; Sorrow will pay no d.; Speak not of my d.; Sturt pays no d.

Debtor's pillow, *see* Sleeps too sound (Let him that) borrow d. p.

Debtors are liars. (D 172)

1640 HERBERT no. 165.

Debtors, Of ill | men take oats. (D 173)

1579 GOSSON *Sch. Abuse* Arb. 63 If Players get no better Atturnie to plead their case, I will holde mee contented where the Haruest is harde, too take Otes of yl debters in parte of payment. **1583** B. MELBANCKE *Philotimus* R3ᵛ For wante of better Haruest, to take oates in parte of payment. **1609** S. HARWARD 82 Of a badd debter take broaken coyne. **1641** FERGUSSON no. 676 Of ill debtours, men takes eattes [sic].

Deceit in a bag-pudding, There is no.
(D 175)

1584 RICHARD WILSON *Three Ladies of London*
D1 Sirra there is no deceite in a bagge pudding,
is there? 1678 RAY 193.

Deceit in a brimmer, There is no.
(D 176)

1659 HOWELL *Eng. Prov.* 5b.

Deceit, *see also* Trust is mother of d.

Deceive a deceiver is no deceit, To.
(D 182)

[a. 1550] 1626 *Jests Scogin* in Shak. *Jest-Bks* ii. 63
To deceive him that goeth about to deceive is no
deceit.   c. 1566 W. WAGER *The Cruel Debtor* T4ᵛ
To deceive such one as is known deceiuable Is
no deceyte.   1575 H. C. AGRIPPA *Vanity of Arts
and Sciences* tr. Sanford 160 It is no deceipte to
deceiue him that deceiueth.   1576 U. FULWELL
Ars Adulandi L2ᵛ To deceiue a deceiuer is no
disceit.   1590–1 SHAKES. *2 Hen. VI* III. i. 264 For
that is good deceit Which mates him first that
first intends deceit.   1591 ARIOSTO *Orl. Fur.*
Harington IV. 2 (no guile).   1607 MIDDLETON
Mich. Term IV. iii. 23 No sin to beggar a deceiver's heir.

Deceive oneself is very easy, To.
(D 178)

1640 HERBERT no. 632.   1659 HOWELL *Span.
Prov.* 18.   1710 PALMER 290.

Deceive the fox must rise betimes, He
that will.   (F 645)

1580 MUNDAY *Zelauto* P2ᵛ You must rise somewhat more early, if you goe beyond me.   1616
DRAXE no. 792.   1640 HERBERT no. 351.   1646
J. HOWELL *Lett.* 20 Feb. (1903) III. 4 They must
rise betimes that can put tricks upon you.   1721
KELLY 130 He must rise early, that deceives the
Tod. Spoken to those that think to out wit a
cunning Fellow.   1896 J. C. HUTCHESON *Crown
& Anchor* ch. 2 You'd have to get up precious
early in the morning to take me in, as you know
from old experience of me.

Deceives me once, He that | shame fall
him; if he deceives me twice, shame fall
me.   (F 121)

a. 1600 *Tarlton's Jests* Pt. I Sh. Soc. 11 Who
deceives me once, God forgive him; if twice,
God forgive him; but if thrice, God forgive him,
but not me, because I could not beware.   1650
A. WELLDON *Secret History of James I* (Scott 1811)
i. 475 The Italians having a proverb, He that
deceives me once, it's his fault, but if twice, it's
my fault.   1659 N. R. 54.   1721 KELLY 134.
1738 SWIFT *Dial.* I. E.L. 280 Well, miss, if you
deceive me a second time, 'tis my fault.

Deceive(s, d), *see also* Children are to be d. with
comfits, men with oaths; Hope d., (Too much);
Married, (He that goes far to be) will either d. or
be d.; No man so wise but he may be d.; Once d.

ever suspected (He that); Trusts not is not d.;
Women naturally d.

December, *see* May and January (D.).

Declaim against pride, It is not a sign of
humility to.

1732 FULLER no. 2994.   1749 FRANKLIN Sept.

Dee mills, Rent of D. m. (If you had).

Deeds are fruits, words are but leaves.
(D 186)

1616 DRAXE no. 457.   1670 RAY 7.

Deeds are males, and words are females.
(D 187)

1573 SANFORD 52ᵛ The deeds are manly, and the
words womanly.   1585 WHETSTONE *Hon. Reputation of a Soldier* A3 Le parole son femine, & i
fatti son maschi.   1592 DELAMOTHE 35 [as 1573].
1598 FLORIO *Worlde of Wordes* Ep. Ded. Our
Italians saie, Le parole sono femine, & i fatti
sono maschij, Wordes they are women, and
deeds they are men.   1621 HOWELL *Lett.* I Oct.
(1903) I. 86 The Neapolitans . . . make strong,
masculine promises, but female performances
(for deeds are men, but words are women).   1659
TORRIANO no. 165.   1796 EDGEWORTH *Par. Asst.*
(1903) 415 He does more than he says. Facts are
masculine, and words are feminine.

Deeds, not words.   (W 820)

1592–4 SHAKES. *1 Hen. VI* III. ii. 49 O! let no
words, but deeds, revenge this treason!   1602 *Id.
T.C.* III. ii. 56 Words pay no debts, give her
deeds.   1613 *Id. Hen. VIII* III. ii. 155 'Tis a kind
of good deed to say well: And yet words are no
deeds.   1616 DRAXE no. 461 Doing is better then
saying.   1663 BUTLER *Hudibras* I. i. 868 Where
we must give the world a proof Of deeds, not
words.   1812 EDGEWORTH *Absentee* ch. 6 'Sir
James . . . added, "Deeds not words" is my
motto'.   1895 PAYN *In Market Overt* ch. 20 It is
deeds and not words that are required of you.

Deed(s), *see also* Difference between word and d.,
(There is great); Fair words and foul d.; Few
words and many d.; Ill d. cannot honour;
Italians wise before d.; Turns lie dead and one
ill d. report abroad does spread, (Ten good);
Will for d.; Word to d. greet space; Words and
not of d. (Man of).

Deem(s, -ed), *see* Ill d. half hanged; Soon d.
soon repents.

Deep as a well, As.

1595 SHAKES. *R.J.* III. i. 93 'Tis not so deep as a
well, nor so wide as a church-door, but 'tis
enough.   1606 T. HEYWOOD *2 If you Know not
Me* l. 2501.

Deep as hell, As.

[1599] 1601 JONSON *Ev. Man Out* III. vii. 66 I
haue hid it as deep as hel, from the sight of

heauen. **1600–1** SHAKES. *M.W.W.* III. v. 13 If
the bottom were as deep as hell, I should down.
1604 *Id. M.M.* III. i. 95 His filth within being
cast, he would appear A pond as deep as hell.
[1610] **1612** DEKKER *If It Be Not Good* Pearson
ed. iii. 269. **1620** CERVANTES *Don. Q.* tr. Shelton
Pt. II. ch. 22 (ii. 338).

Deep drinks the goose as the gander, As.   (G 345)

c. **1549** HEYWOOD II. vii. E6ᵛ.   **1580** LYLY *Euph.
& his Eng.* ii. 55.   **1611** DAVIES no. 247.

Deeper the sweeter, The.   (D 188)

1580 LYLY *Euph. & his Eng.* ii. 219 The honny
that lieth in the bottome is the sweetest.   **1588**
GREENE Wks. (Gros.) vi. 165 Thoughts, the
farther they wade, the sweeter.   **1596** J. HARRING-
TON *Met. of Ajax* (Lindsay) 98 The deeper is the
sweeter.   **1601** JONSON *Ev. Man in Hum.* II. i. 40.
1622 MIDDLETON *Changeling* I. ii.   **1639** CLARKE
46.

Deep(er), *see also* Farther in, the d.; Long in
court, d. in hell.

Deepest (troubled) water is the best fishing, In the.   (W 96)

1616 DRAXE no. 724.   **1631** MABBE *Celestina* T.T.
67 It is an ancient and received Rule; That
it is best fishing in troubled waters.   **1636** CAM-
DEN 300 (troubled).   **1659** N. R. 67 (troubled).
1664 CODRINGTON 201.   **1670** RAY 9.

Deer is slain, Where the | some of her blood will lie.   (D 190)

a. **1628** CARMICHAELL no. 1268.   **1641** FERGUSSON
no. 703.   **1721** KELLY 346 . . . Spoken when some
of what we have been handling is lost, or when
there is some indication of what has been a doing.
1732 FULLER no. 5663.

Deer, *see also* Run like a d.; Stricken d. withdraws to die.

Defects of his qualities, Every man has the.

1887 SYMONS *Introd. to Browning* 19 Mr. Browning has the defects of his qualities.   **1911** *Times
Wkly.* 6 Oct. 804 But Lord Curzon, like every
other mortal, cannot escape from the defects of
his qualities.

Defend (Deliver) me from my friends; God | from my enemies I can (will) defend myself.   (F 739)

[OVID *A. A.* I. 751 *Non est hostis metuendus
amanti. Quos credis fidos effuge: tutus eris.*]
1477 RIVERS *Dictes and Sayings* (1877) 127 Ther
was one that praied god to kepe him from the
daunger of his frendis.   **1585** QUEEN ELIZABETH
(J. E. Neale, *Eliz. I & her Parliaments* 70) There
is an Italian proverb which saith, From my
enemy let me defend myself; but from a pre-
tensed friend, good Lord deliver me.   **1595** A.
COPLEY *Wits, Fits, etc.* (1614) 50 A fained friend
God shield me from his danger, For well I'le

saue my selfe from foe and stranger.   **1604**
MARSTON *Malcontent* IV. iv. Now God deliver me
from my friends . . . for from my enemies Ile
deliver myself.   **1647** J. HOWELL *Lett.* 14 Feb.
(1903) II. 257 There is a saying that carrieth with
it a great deal of caution, 'From him whom I
trust God defend me, for from him whom I trust
not, I will defend myself.' **1666** TORRIANO *It. Prov.*
7, no. 27.   **1821** SCOTT *Let.* 20 Apr. in LOCKHART
Life ch. 51 (1860) 446 The Spanish proverb
says, 'God help me from my friends, and I will
keep myself from my enemies'; and there is much
sense in it.   **1850** C. BRONTË *Let. to G. H. Lewes*
Jan. I can be on my guard against my enemies,
but God deliver me from my friends!   **1904** SIR
H. HAWKINS *Reminisc.* ch. 23 The person a
prisoner has most to fear when he is tried is too
often his own counsel . . . called the *friend* of the
prisoner; and I should conclude . . . that the
adage 'Save me from my friends' originated in
this connexion.

Defend, *see also* Spend me and d. me.

Deferred, *see* Hope d.

Deil, *see* Devil.

Deity(-ies), *see* Constancy of benefit of year
argues D.; Feet of the d. shod with wool.

Delay comes a let, After a.   (D 194)

a. **1628** CARMICHAELL no. 107.   **1641** FERGUSSON
no. 259.   **1721** KELLY 52.

Delays are dangerous.   (D 195)

c. **1300** *Havelock* l. 1352 Dwelling haueth ofte
scathe wrought.   *c.* **1374** CHAUCER *Troilus* iii.
l. 852 Thus wryten clerkes wyse, That peril is with
drecching in y-drawe.   *c.* **1457** *Paston Letters*
(Gairdner) I. 414 Taryeng drawyth parell.   **1579**
LYLY *Euph.* i. 212 Delayes breede daungers,
nothing so perillous as procrastination.   **1591**
SHAKES. *1 Hen. VI* III. ii. 33 Defer no time, delays have dangerous ends.   **1620** SHELTON *Quix.*
Pt. II. xxii. ii. 338 'Tis ordinarily said that
delay breeds danger.   **1678** OTWAY *Friendship in
F.* 39 Come, come, delayes are dangerous.

Delays are (not) denials.

1586 WARNER *Albion's Eng.* IV. xxi. MI Delay,
he sayeth, breedeth doubts, but sharpe denyall
death.   **1611** COTGRAVE s.v. Vouloir A delay
imports a deniall; and he that driues one off
with words, doth meane to let him haue nought
but words.   **1907** W. H. G. THOMAS *Comment.* on
Gen. i–xxv. 183 God's delays to Abraham were
not denials.

Delays (noun), *see also* Desires are nourished by
d.

Deliberates, *see* Woman that d. is lost.

Delight (noun), *see* Every man has his d.

Delilah, The lap of.

[Samson disclosed the secret of his strength
while dallying with Delilah, a Philistine women.
Judges xvi. 4–20.]   **1616** T. GATACRE *Balm from*

Gilead (1862) 99 Ease and prosperity slay some fools; wealth and hearts-ease, like Delilah, rock them asleep on her lap. **1872** G. J. WHYTE-MELVILLE *Satanella* ch. 18 But who, since the days of Samson, was ever able to keep a secret from a woman resolved to worm it out? As the strong man in Delilah's lap, so was Bill in the boudoir of Mrs. Lushington.

Deliver, *see* Defend (D.) from my friends; Hunger and cold d. a man up to his enemy.

Deludes, *see* Hope often d. foolish man.

Deluge, *see* After us the d.

Delved, *see* Adam d.

Demand is a jest, Where the | the fittest answer is a scoff.   (D 199)

1597 *Politeuphuia* 168ᵛ. **1639** CLARKE 86. **1670** RAY 109.

Demands, He that | misses not, unless his demands be foolish.   (D 200)

1640 HERBERT no. 359.

Demure as if butter would not melt in his (her) mouth, As.   (B 774)

1530 PALSGRAVE 620a He maketh as thoughe butter wolde nat melte in his mouthe. **1626** J. FLETCHER *Fair M. of Inn* IV. i. A spirit shall look as if butter would not melt in his mouth. **1670** RAY 171. **1850** THACKERAY *Pendennis* ch. 60 She smiles and languishes, you'd think that butter would not melt in her mouth.

Denial, *see* Asks faintly begs d.; Delays are not d.

Denies, *see* Gives to all (Who), d. all.

Denshire (*or* Devonshire) land, To.   (L 55)

[= to clear or improve land by paring off turf, etc., burning them, and then spreading the ashes.] **1607** NORDEN *Surv. Dial.* 228 They . . . call it . . . in the South-East parts, Devonshiring. **1662** FULLER *Devon.* 248 To Devon-shire land . . . may be said to Stew the land in its own liquor. **1799** *Trans. Soc. Encourag. Arts* XVII. 160 The land . . . was denshired, and one crop of oats taken from it.

Depends on another dines ill and sups worse, He who.

1707 MAPLETOFT 57. **1813** RAY 164 Who depends upon another man's table often dines late.

Derby ale, *see* Dunmow bacon.

Derby's bands.   (D 203)

1570 *Marriage of Wit and Science*, Hazl.-Dods. ii. 362. **1572** T. WILSON *Discourse upon Usury* 227 The poore man, the more he dealeth wyth

usurie, the more he is wrapped in Darbyes bandes, as they say. **1576** GASCOIGNE *Steele Gl.* ii. 163 To binde such babes in father Derbies bands. **1602** R. CAREW *Survey of Cornwall* (1769 ed., 15ᵛ).

Descend than to ascend, It is easier to. *Cf.* Sooner fall than rise.   (D 204)

1611 GRUTER 179. **1614** CAMDEN 308. **1639** CLARKE 260.

Descend(s), *see also* Fire d. not.

Descent to hell (Avernus[1]) is easy, The.   (D 205)

[VIRGIL *Aen.* 6. 126 *Facilis descensus Averno.*] **1513** G. DOUGLAS tr. *Aeneid* It is rycht facill and eith gait, I the tell, For to descend and pas on down to hell. *c.* **1536–7** ERASM. *Pilgr. Pure Devotion* f. 44ᵛ The goynge downe to hell is easy and leyght, but the commynge frome thens of greate dyffyculty. **1559** J. FERRARIUS *Good Ordering of a Commonwealth* tr. W. Bavande Ep. Ded. So easie is the waie that leadeth manne to perdicion: so harde is the passsage that bryngeth hym to saluacion. *c.* **1566** CURIO *Pasquin in a Trance* tr. W.P. 82ᵛ It is an easie matter to goe to Hell, as euery man knoweth, as Virgil sayth. Facilis descensus Auerni. *a.* **1640** J. SMYTH *Lives of the Berkeleys* i. 26 The way downe to hell is easy. **1697** DRYDEN tr. *Aeneid* vi. 192–3 The gates of hell are open night and day; smooth the descent, and easy is the way. **1922** DEAN INGE *Outspoken Ess.* 58 If ever a Church alienates from itself not only the best intellect but the best conscience of the nation, . . . the descent to Avernus is easy and the return very difficult. [1 the entrance to the infernal regions.]

Descent, *see also* Higher the mountain the greater the d.

Desert and reward be ever far odd (seldom keep company).   (D 206)

1546 HEYWOOD I. xi. E2ᵛ (be oft tymes thyngs far od). **1611** DAVIES no. 33 Desart and Reward be euer farre od. **1670** RAY 7 . . . seldom keep company.

Desert, *see* Get money in a d.; Ship of the d.

Deserve, *see* First d. then desire.

Deservers grow intolerable presumers, Great.   (D 210)

1651 HERBERT no. 1167.

Deserves not the sweet that will not taste the sour, He.   (S 1035)

1533–4 N. UDALL *Flowers* 140 He that suffereth and manfully endureth the sowre, shal afterwarde haue the swete. **1535** *Dial. Creatures* II D1 Who that desyryth the swete to Assaye, muste taste byttyr. **1545** TAVERNER H3 He hath not deserued the swet, which hath not tasted the sowre. **1576** PETTIE i. 78 He is not worthy to suck the sweet who hath not first savoured the sour. **1659** HOWELL *Eng. Prov.* 13b.

Design, *see* Shirt knew my d. (If).

Desire has no rest. (D 211)

1551 W. BALDWIN *Beware the Cat* (1584) C2ᵛ Ernest desier banisheth sleep. **1621** BURTON *Anat. Mel.* I. ii. III. 11.

Desires are nourished by delays. (D 213)

[c. **1594**] **1601** LYLY *Love's Met.* III. i. 78 Disdaine increaseth desire. **1596** WARNER *Albion's Eng.* IX. 47 P7ᵛ Delay giues men Desier. *c.* **1600** *Merry Devil of Ed.* II. iii. 13 Experience says, That love is firm that's flatter'd with delays. **1615** *Janua Linguarum* 29. **1616** DRAXE no. 468. **1670** RAY 7.

Desires but little has no need of much, He that. (L 347a)

1588 SIDNEY *Arcadia* (Feuillerat) i. 14 Wanting little, because they desire not much. **1614** SENECA tr. Lodge *Epist.* cviii. 443 He that coueteth little, hath not need of much. **1732** FULLER no. 2077.

Desires honour, He that | is not worthy of honour. (H 566)

1539 VIVES *Introd. to Wisdom* C1 Honour commonly fastest flyeth from hym, that moste seketh it, and gothe to them, that lest regarde it. **1599** SHAKES. *Hen. V* IV. iii. 28 But if it be a sin to covet honour, I am the most offending soul alive. **1659** TORRIANO no. 211 He is least worthy of honour who most seeks it. **1660** W. SECKER *Nonsuch Prof.* II. (1891) 55 The old maxim is worthy to be revived; . . .

Desire(s) (*noun*), *see also* Begins to die that quits d.; Fortune (d.) torments me, (If) hope contents me; Humble hearts, humble d.

Desire(s) (*verb*), *see also* Believe what we d.; First deserve then d.; Market of his ware, (He that d. to make) must watch an opportunity to open his shop; More a man has, the more he d.; Poor that has little (Not), but that d. much.

Despair gives courage to a coward. (D 216)

1576 PETTIE i. 182 Consider the force of love which maketh . . . the most cowards most courageous. **1579** NORTH *Plutarch's Julius Caesar* T.C. vii. 164 A desperate man feareth no danger, come on. **1591** SHAKES. *3 Hen. VI* I. iv. 40 Cowards fight when they can fly no further. **1591** ARIOSTO *Orl. Fur.* Harington XIII. 3 Dispaire hath euer danger all contemned. **1612** CHAPMAN *Widow's Tears* V. ii. 190 Despair, they say, makes cowards turn courageous. **1732** FULLER no. 1272.

Despair(ed), *see* Nothing is to be . . . d. of.

Despatch, *see* Hatch, match, d.

Desperate cuts (diseases) must have desperate cures. (D 357)

[L. *Extremis malis extrema remedia.*] **1539** TAVERNER f. 4 Stronge disease requyreth a

stronge medicine. *c.* **1595** SHAKES. *R.J.* IV. i. 68 I do spy a kind of hope, Which craves as desperate an execution As that is desperate which we would prevent. **1598–9** *Id. M.A.* IV. i. 252 To strange sores strangely they strain the cure. **1600–1** *Id. H.* IV. iii. 9 Diseases desperate grown By desperate appliance are reliev'd, Or not at all. **1639** CLARKE 200. **1655** FULLER *Ch. Hist.* IX. ii (1868) II. 559 Seeing desperate diseases must have desperate cures, he would thunder his excommunication against her. **1713** DEFOE *Reas. agst. Suc. Ho. of Han.* Wks (1912) vi. 514 A proverbial saying in physic, desperate diseases must have desperate remedies.

Despise pride with a greater pride, There are those who.

1546 ERASM. tr. Udall *Apoph.* (1877) 82 To Diogenes, saiyng I trede the pride of Plato vnder my feete: So thou doest in deede (quoth Plato) but it is with an other kinde of pride, as greate as mine. **1853** TRENCH iv. 81 A proverb founded . . . on the story of Diogenes . . . treading under his feet a rich carpet of Plato's.

Despises his own life is soon master of another's, He who.

[SENECA *Ep.* 4. 8 *Quisquis vitam suam contempsit, tuae dominus est.*] **1621** BURTON *Anat. Mel.* III. iv. II (1651) 694 How many thousands . . . have made away themselves, and many others! For he that cares not for his owne, is master of another mans life. **1642** D. ROGERS *Naaman* X. 295 As one said of a traitor whoso despiseth his own life may easily be master of anothers. **1648** HERRICK *Hesp.* (Muses' Lib.) 488 He's lord of thy life who contemns his own. **1666** TORRIANO *It. Prov.* 312 no. 1 He is Master of anothers life, who slighteth his own. **1708** SWIFT *Remarks upon 'Rights of Church'* Wks. (1856) II. 183 He that hath neither reputation nor bread hath very little to lose, and hath therefore as little to fear. . . . 'Who ever values not his own life, is master of another man's'; so there is something like it in reputation.

Destiny is always dark, A man's. (M 469)

1621 ROBINSON 35 No man knoweth his destiny. **1651** HERBERT no. 1180.

Destiny, *see also* Hanging and wiving go by d.; Marriage is by d.

Destroy the lion while he is yet but a whelp.

1732 FULLER no. 1276.

Destroy the nests and the birds will fly away. (N 124)

1655 FULLER *Ch. Hist.* VI. v. (1868) II. 318 Thacker, being possessed of Repingdon [Repton] abbey . . . plucked down . . . a . . . church belonging thereunto, adding he would destroy the nest, for fear the birds should build therein again. **1721** KELLY 88 Ding down the Nests, and the Rooks will flee away. Destroy the places where villains shelter, and they will disperse. **1837–47** BARHAM *Ingol. Leg.* (1898) 361 I hear the sacrilegious cry, 'Down with the nests, and the rooks will fly!'

Destroys, *see* Writing d. the memory.

Destruction, *see* Dicing, drabbing, and drinking bring men to d.; Pride goes before d.

Deuce ace, *see* Size cinque.

Devil always leaves a stink behind him, The.   (D 224)

a. **1591** HY. SMITH *Serm.* (1866) II. 36 Into every shop he [*i.e.* the devil] casts a short measure, or a false balance. . . . Thus in every place where he comes . . . he leaves an evil savour behind him. **1650** FULLER *Pisgahsight Pal.* IV. vii (1869) 552 The rabbins say he was represented as a he-goat. . . . Indeed, both devils and goats are said to go out in a stink.

Devil always tips at the biggest ruck,[1] The.

1886 R. HOLLAND *Chesh. Gloss.* E.D.S. 454. **1917** BRIDGE 113. [1 heap.]

Devil among the tailors, The.

[= a row going on.]   **1834** LD. LONDONDERRY *Let.* 27 May in *Court Will. IV & Victoria* (1861) II. iv. 98 Reports are various as to the state of the enemy's camp, but all agree that there is the devil among the tailors.

Devil and all, The.   (D 284)

[= everything right or wrong, especially the wrong.] **1528** ROY & BARLOW *Rede me & be not Wroth* ed. Arber 39 Some saye he [Wolsey] is the devill and all. **1543** BALE *Yet a Course* Baptyzed bells, bedes, organs . . . the devyll and all of soche idolatrouse beggery. *c.* **1566** CURIO *Pasquin in a Trance* tr. W.P. 59 To do the deuill and all of mischiefe. **1586** G. WHETSTONE *English Mirror* 178 That same learning . . . in stubborne wits . . . doth the diuell and all of lust. **1811** EARL GOWER 18 Dec. in *C. K. Sharpe's Corr.* (1888) I. 508 I begin to fear that the rheumatism has taken possession of your right arm . . . which would be the devil and all, as the vulgar would say.

Devil (and all) to do, The.

[= much ado.]   **1708** MOTTEUX *Rabelais* V. iii. There was the Devil and all to do. **1712** ARBUTHNOT *John Bull* III. v. Then there was the devil and all to do; spoons, plates, and dishes flew about the room like mad.

Devil and Dr. Faustus (Foster), The.

1706 DEFOE *Review* iii, no. 81, 323. **1726** *Id. History of the Devil* It is become a proverb, 'as great as the Devil and Dr. Foster:' whereas poor Faustus was no doctor, and knew no more of the Devil than another body. **1749** FIELDING *Tom Jones* Bk. xviii, ch. 8.

Devil and his dam, The.   (D 225)

[*The devil's dam*: applied opprobriously to a woman.] **1393** LANGLAND *P. Pl.* C. xxi. 284 Rys vp ragamoffyn and reche me alle þe barres, That belial þy bel-syre beot with þy damme. **1528**

ROY & BARLOW *Rede me & be not Wroth* ed. Arber 52 He playeth the devill and his dame. **1538** BALE *Thre Lawes* D I[v] The deuyll or hys dam. *c.* **1590** SHAKES. *T.And.* IV. ii. 63 Well, God give her good rest! What hath he sent her? — A devil. — Why, then she is the devil's dam: a joyful issue. [*c.* 1592] **1604** MARLOWE *Faustus* II. ii. Think on the Devil. — And his dam too. **1592–4** SHAKES. *I Hen. VI* I. v. 5 Devil, or devil's dam, Ill' conjure thee: Blood will I draw on thee, thou art a witch. **1592–3** *Id. C.E.* IV. iii. 45 It is the devil.—Nay, she is worse, she is the devil's dam. **1594–8** *Id. T.S.* III. ii. 152 Why, she's a devil, a devil, the devil's dam. **1600–1** *Id. M.W.W.* IV. v. 97 The devil take one party and his dam the other. **1604** *Id. O.* IV. i. 146 Let the devil and his dam haunt you. **1707** J. STEVENS tr. *Quevedo's Com. Wks.* (1709) 350 Such . . . Sayings are a Discredit to your self. As for Instance . . . the Devil and his Dam.

Devil, Bring you the | and I'll bring out his dam.   (D 223)

1616 WITHALS 581.   **1639** CLARKE 209.

Devil and John a Cumber, The.   (D 226)

1590 A. MUNDAY *John a Kent & John a Cumber* 999 This John a Cumber . . . that went beyond the deuill, And made him serue him seuen yeares prentiship. **1659** HOWELL *Eng. Prov.* 18a The Devil and John of Cumberland. **1660** TATHAM *Rump* IV. i (1879) 253 The devil and John à Cumber go with him.

Devil and the dean begin with a letter; The | when the devil gets (has) the dean, the kirk will be the better.

                                         (D 227)

1641 FERGUSSON no. 862 (hes).   **1832** HENDERSON 12.

Devil and the deep (Dead) sea, Between the.   (D 222)

1621 ROBINSON 21 Betwixt the Deuill and the dead sea. *a.* **1628** CARMICHAELL no. 369 (deip). **1637** MONRO *Exped.* II. 55 (Jam.) I with my partie, did lie on our poste, as betwixt the devill and the deep sea. **1672** WALKER II. no. 60 Betwixt the devil and the dead sea. **1691** SEWEL 48 (and the red sea). **1721** KELLY 58 . . . That is, between two Difficulties equally dangerous. **1822** SCOTT *Pirate* ch. 18 Between the Udaller . . . and Captain Cleveland, a man is, as it were, atween the deil and the deep sea. **1859** H. KINGSLEY *Geof. Ham.* ch. 39.

Devil be a vicar, If the | you will be his clerk.   (D 285)

1670 RAY 171. **1721** KELLY 196 . . . Spoken of Trimmers, Turn-coats, and Time-servers.

Devil bides his day, The.

1721 KELLY 303 . . . Taken from a Supposition that the Devil, when he enters into a Covenant with a Witch, sets her a Date of her Life which he stands to. Spoken when People demand a Debt or Wages before it be due.

**Devil can cite Scripture for his purpose,
The.** (D 230)

[MATT. iv. 6 And saith [the devil] unto him, If
thou be the Son of God, cast thyself down for it is
written...] **1573** BRIDGES *Supremacy of Christian
Princes* P3ᵛ Here M.Stapleton standeth altogither
on the terme of the Scripture ... he dothe it euen
as the deuill obiected scripture vnto Christ. **1583**
MELBANCKE R4 Thou imitates the Deuill in his
alleadging of Scriptures, for he neuer bringes
out an whole text, but so much as is for his owne
enorm intended purpose. [**1589**] **1633** MARLOWE
Jew of Malta I. ii. III What, bring you Scripture
to confirm your wrongs. **1595** PIERRE LE ROY
A Pleasant Satire (*A Satire Menippized*) 135 The
diuel will alleadge scripture but yet not rightly.
1596 SHAKES. *M.V.* I. iii. 93 The devil can cite
Scripture for his purpose. An evil soul, producing holy witness, Is like a villain with a smiling
cheek...**1612–15** BP. HALL *Contempl.* II. iii (1825)
II. 213 Let no man henceforth marvel to hear
heretics or hypocrites quote Scriptures, when
Satan himself hath not spared to cite them.
1821 SCOTT *Kenilw.* ch. 4 A sort of creeping
comes over my skin when I hear the devil quote
Scripture.

**Devil cannot come, Where the | he will
send.**

1853 TRENCH vi. 150 . . . sets out to us the
penetrative character of temptations, and the
certainty that they will follow and find men out in
their most secret retreats.

Devil dances in an empty pocket, The.
(D 233)

c. **1412** HOCCLEVE *De Regim. Princ.* (1897) st. 98
The feend, men seyn, may hoppe in a pouche,
Whan that no croys[1] there-inne may a-pere.
a. **1500** *15c. School Bk.* ed. Nelson 89. *a.* **1529**
SKELTON *Bowge of Court* 365 The deuyll myghte
daunce therein for any crowche.[2] *c.* **1549**
ERASM. *Two Dial.* tr. E. Becke f. 15ᵛ The Deuyll
(god saue vs) maye daunce in thy purse for euer
a crosse that thou hast to kepe him forthe. **1580**
LYLY *Euph. & his Eng.* ii. 24 My Barrell of golde
... ranne so on the lees, that the Diuell daunced
in the bottome, where he found neuer a crosse.
1636 MASSINGER *Bash. Lov.* III. i. The devil sleeps
in my pocket; I have no cross To drive him from
it. **1823** GROSE ed. Pierce Egan s.v. Devil. [[1] coins
bore a cross on the reverse. [2] cross.]

Devil ding[1] another, Let one. (D 287)

c. **1641** FERGUSSON MS. no. 457 Gar ane deuill
ding ane other. **1721** KELLY 234 . . . Spoken
when two bad Persons quarrel. **1857** DEAN
RAMSAY *Remin.* v. (1911) 195. [[1] beat.]

**Devil divides the world between
atheism and superstition, The.** (D 234)

1651 HERBERT no. 1107.

**Devil drives, He that the | feels no lead
at his heels.**

1606 DEKKER *News from Hell* D3. **1732**
FULLER no. 2331.

**Devil find a man idle, If the | he'll set
him to work.**

c. **1386** CHAUCER *Mel.* B² l. 2785 Therfore seith
Seint Ierome: 'Dooth somme goode dedes, that
the devel which is oure enemy ne fynde yow nat
unoccupied.' **1647** *Countrym. New Commonw.*
30 Be alwaies doing of somewhat, that the
Divell find thee not idle. Hierom. **1715** WATTS
Divine Songs 20 For Satan finds some mischief
still for idle hands to do. **1721** KELLY 221.
1887 LD. AVEBURY *Pleas. of Life* II. x. An old
saying tells us that the Devil finds work for those
who do not make it for themselves.

**Devil gets up to the belfry by the
vicar's skirts, The.** (D 235)

1659 HOWELL *Span. Prov.* 20 By the skirts of the
Vicar the Devil climes up to the Steeple. **1706**
STEVENS s.v. Halda. **1732** FULLER no. 4476.

Devil go with thee down the lane, The.
(D 236)

c. **1549** HEYWOOD II. vii. I4ᵛ.

**Devil goes (Deil's gane) ower Jock
Wabster, The.**

1725 A. RAMSAY *Gent. Shep.* I. ii. The 'Deil gaes
ower Jock Wabster', hame grows hell; When
Pate misca's ye waur than tongue can tell. **1818**
SCOTT *Rob Roy* ch. 26 They will turn desperate
—five hundred will rise that might hae sitten at
hame—the deil will gae ower Jock Wabster.
1857 DEAN RAMSAY *Remin.* v. (1911) 196 The
deil's gane ower Jock Wabster . . . expresses
generally misfortune or confusion, but I am
not quite sure . : . who is represented by Jock
Wabster. **1878** *N. & Q.* 5th ser. vi. 64.

Devil goes shares in gaming, The.

1707 MAPLETOFT 12.

Devil has cast a bone to set strife, The.
(D 237)

[**1525–40**] **1557** *Merry Dial.* 62 In the olde lawe,
where the deuill hadde cast aboone betwene the
man and the wife, at the worste waye, they myght
be deuorsed. **1546** HEYWOOD II. ii. G1 (to set
stryfe Betwene you). **1616** DRAXE no. 2055.

**Devil himself must bear the cross,
Where none will, the.** (D 309)

1579 LYLY *Euph.* i. 201 Where none will, the
Diuell himselfe must beare the crosse. **1732**
FULLER no. 5652 (none else).

**Devil in every berry of the grape, There
is a.** (D 296)

1634 HOWELL *Lett.* 17 Oct. (1903) II. 194 The
Turk...will...drink water,...for Mahommed
taught them that there was a devil in every berry
of the grape. **1649** T. WEAVER *Commend. Verses*
in WALTON *Angler* Make good the doctrine of
the Turks, That in each grape a devil lurks.

Devil is a busy bishop in his own diocese, The.   (D 240)

1548 LATIMER *Serm. of Plough* P.S. 70 Who is the most diligentest bishop and prelate in all England . . . ? . . . It is the devil. He is the most diligent preacher of all other he is never out of his diocess. **1641** FERGUSSON no. 814. **1857** DEAN RAMSAY *Remin.* V (1911) 196.

Devil is a hog, When the | you shall eat bacon.   (D 306)

1678 RAY 70. [*Joculatory*.]

Devil is an ass, The.   (D 242)

1607 DEKKER & WILKINS *Jests to Make You Merry* (Gros. ii. 175). **1616** JONSON *Devil is an Ass* Prol. The DIVELL is an Asse: That is, to-day, The name of what you are met for, a new Play. **1620** SHELTON *Quix.* Pt. II. XXXV. iii. 72. **1891** A. LANG *Ess. in Little* 186 Their best plan (in Bunyan's misery) is to tell Apollyon that the Devil is an ass. **1905** ALEX. MACLAREN *Matthew* I. 83 The title . . . would be coarse if it were not so true, 'The Devil is an Ass'.

Devil is at home, The.   (D 243)

1620 MIDDLETON *World Tost at Tennis* Wks. (Bullen) vii. 185 Why, will he have it in 's house, when the proverb says, The devil's at home? **1738** SWIFT *Dial.* I. E.L. 262 I must needs go home for half an hour. — Why, colonel, they say the devil's at home. **1810** CRABBE *Borough* xix (Oxf.) 184 A foolish proverb says, 'the devil's at home'; But he is here and tempts in every room.

Devil is blind, When the.   (D 295)

[**1639–61**] **1662** *Song* in *Rump Songs* I. 8 The Scots in despite shall please their own mind, And do what they please when the Devil is blind. **1659** HOWELL *Eng. Prov.* 12b. **1678** RAY 70. [*Joculatory*.] **1692** L'ESTRANGE *Aesop's Fab.* xcix (1738) 114 It happened . . . one day to be just such a flattering tempting sea again as that which betrayed him before: Yes, yes, says he, When the Devil's blind. **1738** SWIFT *Dial.* I. E.L. 272 I'll make you a fine present one of these days. — Ay; when the devil's blind, and his eyes are not sore yet. **1823** GROSE ed. Pierce Egan s.v. Devil.

Devil is busy in a high wind, The.

1790 BURNS *Tam O' Shanter* The wind blew as 'twad blawn its last; . . . That night, . . . The Deil had business on his hand. **1825–6** PEACOCK *A Mood of Mind* 'The devil in a gale of wind is as busy as a bee'. **1866** BLACKMORE *Cradock N.* ch. 31 The parlour chimney-stack had fallen . . . Miss Rosedew . . . was reading . . . the 107th Psalm . . . as the devil is ever so busy in a gale of wind.

Devil is dead, The.   (D 244)

c. **1470** *Mankind* in MANLY *Spec. of Pre-Shakesp. Drama* i. 37 Qwyst, pesse! The deull ys dede! *a.* **1529** SKELTON *Col. Cloute* 36 The deuyll, they say, is dede. **1546** HEYWOOD II. ix. K4 The diuell is dead wife (quoth he) for ye see, I loke lyke a lambe in all your words to mee. **1616** WITHALS 576 The Deuill is dead in a ditch.

1619 FLETCHER *M. Thomas* III. i. 222 Bear up, man! Diavalo morte! **1670** RAY 80 In the mouths of the French and Italians. . . . The Devil is dead [signifies] that a difficulty is almost conquered, a journey almost finished, or as we say, The neck of a business broken. **1709** *Brit. Apollo* II. No. 56, 3/2 At Play 'tis often said, When Luck returns—The Devil's dead. **1861** H. KINGSLEY *Ravenshoe* ch. 11 I will have my say when I am in this temper. . . . The devil is not dead yet. . . . Why do you rouse him? **1861** READE *Cloist. & Hearth*, Denys's catchword, 'The devil is dead'.

Devil is dead, and buried in Kirkcaldy, The.

1837 *Tales of the Borders* III. 379 But the deil's no buried i' Kirkaldy, if I wadna hae a blink through Cubby Grindstane's skylicht. **1842** R. CHAMBERS *Pop. Rhymes Scot.* 72 A JACOBITE RHYME Some say the deil's dead, and buried in Kirkaldy!

Devil is dead, When the | he never lacks a chief mourner.

1853 TRENCH iv. 77 When the devil is dead, he never lacks a chief mourner; . . . there is no abuse so enormous, no evil so flagrant, but that the interests or passions of some will be so bound up in its continuance that they will lament its extinction.

Devil is dead, When the | there's a wife for Humphrey.   (D 307)

1678 RAY 84. [*Joculatory*.] **1732** FULLER no. 5580 (widow).

Devil is God's ape, The.   (D 247)

1579 TOMSON *1st Ep. Paul to Tim.* iv: *Serm. Calvin* 343 But see howe the diuell . . . playeth the Ape, and counterfeteth what so euer God hath ordeined for our saluation. **1595** *Polimanteia* B1 Satan desiring in this to bee Gods ape. **1629** T. ADAMS *Serm.* (1862) I. 206 Observe how the devil is God's ape, and strives to match and parallel him, both in his words and wonders. **1639** FULLER *Holy War* IV. xxi. These took . . . the name and habit of *Pastorelli*, poor shepherds; in imitation belike (as the devil is God's ape) of those in the gospel. **1905** ALEX. MACLAREN *Matthew* II. 236 'The devil is God's ape'. His work is a parody of Christ's.

Devil is good (kind) to his own, The.   (D 245)

1606 DAY *Isle of Gulls* III. ii. You were worse then the devil els; for they say hee helps his Servants. *c.* **1607** MIDDLETON *Trick to catch the Old One* I. iv. 31 The devil has a care of his footmen. **1721** KELLY 310 . . . Spoken when they whom we affect not, thrive and prosper in the World; as if they had their Prosperity from the Devil. **1738** SWIFT *Dial.* III. E.L. 317. **1804** S. T. COLERIDGE *Notebks.* ed. K. Coburn ii. 1962 no. 2060 The Devil has help'd him to a Commodore's Share Aye! aye! the Devil knows his Relations. **1837** F. CHAMIER *Saucy Areth.* ch. 14 Weazel was the only midshipman saved besides myself; the devil always takes care of his own.

Devil is good to some (somebody), The.
(D 248)

1659 HOWELL *Eng. Prov.* 16b. (some body).
1678 RAY 70.

Devil is good when he is pleased, The.
(D 249)

1581 WOODES *Conflict of Conscience* III. iii. The
devil is a good fellow, if one can him please.
1639 CLARKE 214. 1684 BUNYAN *Seasonable
Counsel* Wks. (Offor) II. 707 The devil, they
say, is good when he is displeased. 1721 KELLY 333
. . . Spoken to People who readily take every
thing amiss. 1732 FULLER no. 1916 He is good
as long as he's pleas'd; and so is the Devil.
1738 SWIFT Dial. II. E.L. 295 She is very good-
humoured. — Ay, my lord; so is the devil when
he's pleased. 1813 1 Sept. BYRON *Corr.*
Prothero ii. 257 (amusing when pleased).

Devil is in the dice, The. (D 250)

c. 1604 T. HEYWOOD *Wise Woman of Hogsdon* I. i.
Now if the Devill have bones, these Dyce are
made of his. 1678 RAY 70.

Devil is known by his claws (cloven feet, horns), The. (D 252)

[c. 1592] 1604 MARLOWE *Faustus* I. ivA 57 I'll tell
you how you shall know them; all he-devils has
horns, and all she-devils has clifts and cloven
feet. 1600–1 SHAKES. *M.W.W.* V. ii. 15 No
man means evil but the devil, and we shall know
him by his horns. 1604 *Id. O.* V. ii. 289 I
look down towards his feet—but that's a fable.
If that thou be'st a devil, I cannot kill thee.
1612 WEBSTER *White Devil* V. iii. 103 'Tis the
Devill. I know him by a great rose he weares on's
shooe To hide his cloven foot. 1802 4 Jan. C.
LAMB *Morning Post* It has been the policy of that
antient and grey simulator, in all ages, to hide his
horns and claws.

Devil is never far off, The.

1642 D. ROGERS *Matr. Hon.* 335 The divell is
never farre off: but presents this butter in so
Lordly a dish, that the soule spies not the hammer and naile in his hand.

Devil is never nearer than when we are talking of him, The.

1670 RAY 80.

Devil is not always at one door, The.
(D 254)

1592 G. DELAMOTHE 27 The Deuill is not alwayes
at a poore mans doore. 1639 CLARKE 244.
1640 HERBERT no. 31.

Devil is not so black as he is painted, The. (D 255)

1592 *History of Dr. Faustus* A4ᵛ He thought
the diuel was not so black as they vse to paynt
him, nor hell so hote as the people say. 1596

LODGE *Margarite Amer.* 84 Devils are not so
black as they be painted . . . nor women so wayward as they seem. 1642 HOWELL *For. Trav.*
xiv. Arb. 65 The Devill is not so black as he is
painted, no more are these Noble Nations and
Townes as they are tainted. 1820 SCOTT *Monast.*
ch. 24 Answer . . . whatever the Baron asks you
. . . and . . . show no fear of him—. . . 1833
MARRYAT *Peter S.* ch. 29 Fear kills more people
than the yellow fever. . . . The devil's not half
so black as he's painted—nor the yellow fever
half so yellow, I presume.

Devil is not so ill as (no worse than) he's called, The.

1721 KELLY 306 (no worse than). Apply'd to
those who speak worse of bad Men than they
deserve. 1815 SCOTT *Guy Man.* ch. 32 'Well',
said the deacon . . . , 'the deil's no sae ill as he's
ca'd. It's pleasant to see a gentleman pay the
regard to the business o' the county that Mr.
Glossin does.'

Devil is subtle, yet weaves a coarse web, The.

1853 TRENCH iii. 57 The ways of falsehood and
fraud are so perplexed and crooked, that . . .
the wit of the cleverest rogue will not preserve
him from being entangled therein. . . .

Devil knows many things because he is old, The. (D 246)

1586 GUAZZO i. 168 Young men for lacke of
yeeres and experience, cannot bee wise: And
thereof commeth the Proverbe, That the Divell
is full of knowledge, because hee is olde. 1871
C. KINGSLEY *At Last* ch. 7 It may have taken ages
to discover the Brinvilliers, and ages more to
make its poison generally known. . . .

Devil loves no holy water, The.
(D 220)

c. 1500 *Life Robt. Devil* l. 174 in *Early Pop.
Poetry* i. 226 They dyd flee fro hym, as the
deuyll fro holy water. 1537 W. TURNER *Old
Learn. and New* E5ᵛ The deuyl is afrayed of
holy water. 1576 LAMBARDE *Peramb. Kent*
(1826) 301 The olde Proverbe how well the
Divell loveth holy water. 1629 T. ADAMS *Serm.*
(1862) I. 165 You wrong Rome's holy water, to
think it the devil's drink, when the proverb says,
the devil loves no holy water. 1678 RAY 287 To
love it as the Devill loves holy water. 1738
SWIFT Dial. II. E.L. 305.

Devil lurks (sits) behind the cross, The.
(D 256)

1612 SHELTON *Quix.* Pt. I. vi. i. 36 Then was
another book opened, . . . *The Knight of the Cross.*
. . . Quoth the curate, '. . . it is a common
saying, "The devil lurks behind the cross";
wherefore let it go to the fire'. 1710 PALMER 373.

Devil made askers, The.

1738 SWIFT Dial. II. E.L. 308 Sir John, will you
taste my October? . . . — My lord, I beg your
pardon; but they say, the devil made askers.

Devil makes his Christmas-pies of lawyers' tongues and clerks' fingers, The. (D 258)

1591 FLORIO *Second F.* 179 Of three things the Deuill makes his messe, Of Lawyers tongues, of Scriueners fingers, you the third may gesse. [*i.e.* women]. **1616** T. ADAMS *Three Divine Sisters* 26 (pie of lewd Tongues). **1629** T. ADAMS *Serm.* (1862) II. 482 Corrupt and conscienceless lawyers you will confess to be sharp and wounding brambles. The Italians have a shrewd proverb against them: . . . **1669–96** J. AUBREY *Brief Lives* (1898) I. 422 Sir Robert Pye, attorney of the court of wards, . . . happened to die on Christmas day: the news being brought to the serjeant, said he 'The devil has a Christmas pie'.

Devil never assails a man except he find him either void of knowledge, or of the fear of God, The. (D 259)

1651 HERBERT no. 1176.

Devil never sent a wind out of hell, but he would sail with it, The.

1721 KELLY 333 . . . Spoken of Trimmers and Time-servers.

Devil on Dun's back, The. (D 260)

a. **1634** HEYWOOD & BROME *Late Lancashire Witches* II. i. The Divell on Dun is rid this way. **1639** CLARKE 197.

Devil on sale, To set the. (D 303)

1546 HEYWOOD II. vii. I2 Here is a tale, For honestee, meete to set the dyuell on sale.

Devil over Lincoln, He looks as the. (D 277)

1546 HEYWOOD II. ix. K4 Than wold ye loke ouer me, with stomake swolne, Lyke as the deuill lookt ouer Lyncolne. **1566** ERASM. *Diversoria* tr. E.H. ed. de Vocht l. 349 They bee eye hym with suche a bigge an[d] frowning countenaunce as if the Dueyl should loke ouer Lincoln (as they doe saye). **1592** GREENE *Def. of Cony-catching* (Harrison) 58. **1602** WITHALS 92 Sternlie, sowerlie, grimlie, as the Diuell should looke ouer Lincoln, Torue. **1662** FULLER *Linc.* 153 . . . Lincolne Minister is one of the statelyest Structures in Christendome . . . The Devil . . . is supposed to have overlookid this Church . . . with a torve and tetrick countenance, as maligning mens costly devotion. *Ibid.* Oxon. 328 Some fetch the original of this Proverb from a stone picture of the Devil, which doth (or lately did) over-look Lincoln Colledge. . . . Beholders have since applied those ugly looks to envious persons. **1738** SWIFT *Dial.* I. E.L. 286 She looked at me as the devil looked over Lincoln.

Devil owed me a good turn, The. (*Cf.* D 261)

1665 J. WILSON *Projectors* v (1874) 267 I was finely helpt up when I married you. . . . But the devil ow'd me a good turn!

Devil prays, When the | he has a booty in his eye.

1706 STEVENS s.v. Diablo (he designs to deceive). **1707** MAPLETOFT 73 (he means to cheat you). **1732** FULLER no. 5576.

Devil rides on (upon) a fiddle-stick, The. (D 263)

[= here's a fine commotion.] **1597** SHAKES. *1 Hen. IV* II. iv. 470 Heigh, heigh! the devil rides upon a fiddle-stick: what's the matter? *a.* **1625** BEAUM. & FL. *Hum. Lieut.* (1905) IV. iv, 176 For this is such a gig, for certain, gentlemen, The fiend rides on a Fiddle-stick.

Devil run through you booted and spurred with a scythe at (on) his back, The. (D 264)

a. **1625** BEAUM. & FL. *Wom. Prize* V. iii. Wks. (C.U.P.) viii. 85 A Sedgly[1] curse light on him, which is, 'Pedro; The Fiend ride through him booted, and spurr'd, with a Sythe at 's back. **1659** HOWELL *Eng. Prov.* 2b. [1 near Dudley, Staffs.]

Devil sets his foot (casts his club) on the blackberries on Michaelmas-day, The.

1727 C. THRELKELD *Synop. Stirp. Hibernicarum* RUBUS MAJOR . . . The Fruit of the Bramble is reputed infamous, for causing sore Heads; . . . but I look upon this as a vulgar Error, and that after Michaelmas the D—— casts his Club over them, which is a Fable. **1852** SIR W. R. WILDE *Irish Pop. Super.* 14 It is a popular belief—kept up probably to prevent children eating them when over ripe—that the pooca, as he rides over the country, defiles the blackberries at Michaelmas and Holly-eve. **1902–4** LEAN I. 488 . . . In the Midlands children won't touch them after, because then they are 'gubby', . . . i.e. flies have deposited their eggs in the ripe fruit.

Devil sometimes speaks the truth, The. (D 266)

[**1592**] **1597** SHAKES. *Rich. III* I. ii. 73 O wonderful, when devils tell the truth. **1597** *Politeuphuia* 258[v] The deuils ofttimes spake truth in oracles, to the intent they might shadow theyr falshoods the more winningly. **1631** WILLIAM FOSTER *Hoplocrisma Spongus* 20 The Divell is a lyer . . . yet sometimes he tels the truth. **1732** FULLER no. 5308 Truth may sometimes come out of the Devil's Mouth.

Devil take the hindmost, The. (D 267)

[HORACE *De Arte Poet.* 417 *Occupet extremum scabies.*] **1608** BEAUM. & FL. *Philas.* (1904) V. iii. 139 What if . . . they run all away, and cry . . . **1725** DEFOE *Everybody's Bus.* Wks. (Bohn) II. 513 In a few years the navigation . . . will be entirely obstructed. . . . Every one of these gentlemen-watermen hopes it will last his time, and so they all cry, . . . *a.* **1797** NELSON in SOUTHEY *Life* (1813) iii. 'From that moment, not a soldier stayed at his post—it was the devil take the hindmost. Many thousands ran away who had never seen the enemy.' **1906** G. W. E. RUSSELL *Social Silh.* xlv. He starts in life with a definite plan of absolute and calculated selfishness. . . . His motto is *Extremum occupet scabies—* . . .

Devil tempts all, The | but the idle man tempts the devil.

1707 MAPLETOFT 110. **1840** MRS. CARLYLE *Let.* (Autumn) to Mrs. C. I am always as busy as possible; on that side at least I hold out no encouragement to the devil. **1887** LD. AVEBURY *Pleas. Life* I. vi. There is a Turkish proverb that the Devil tempts the busy man, but the idle man tempts the Devil.

Devil the friar but where he was? Where had the. (D 308)

1581 T. LUPTON *Too Good to be True* Pt. 2 S4ᵛ I maruel where he had it (where gote the Divel the Friar, said the King?). **1612** J. TAYLOR *Sculler* Epig. 7: Wks. 18. **1738** SWIFT *Dial.* I. E.L. 405 Where did you get it?—Why, where 'twas to be had; where the devil got the friar.

Devil to pay, The. (D 268)

[Supposed to refer to alleged bargains with Satan, and the inevitable payment to be made to him in the end.] *c.* **1400** *Douce MS. 104* in *Reliq. Antiquae* (1841) I. 257 Beit wer be at tome for ay, Than her to serve the devil to pay. **1711** 28 Sept. SWIFT *Jrnl. to Stella* The Earl of Strafford is to go soon to Holland, and let them know what we have been doing; and then there will be the devil and all to pay. **1820** 4 Nov. Byron *Lett.* Prothero v. 108 There will be shortly the devil to pay and . . . there is no saying that I may not form an Item in his bill.

Devil to pay and no pitch hot, The.

[Alluding to the difficulty of 'paying' or caulking the seam near a ship's keel called the devil.] **1788** GROSE s.v. Pay. **1822** SCOTT *Pirate* ch. 36 If they hurt but one hair of Cleveland's head, there will be . . . **1872** BLACKMORE *Maid of Sker* ch. 48.

Devil was sick, The | the devil a monk would be; the devil was well, the devil a monk was he. (D 270)

[Med. Lat. *Aegrotavit daemon, monachus tunc esse volebat; Daemon convaluit, daemon ut ante fuit.*] **1586** L. EVANS *Withals Dict. Revised* K8 The diuell was sicke and crasie; Good woulde the monke bee that was lasie. **1629** T. ADAMS *Serm.* (1862) I. 111 God had need to take what devotion he can get at our hands in our misery, for when prosperity returns, we forget our vows. . . . **1692** L'ESTRANGE *Aesop's Fab.* xci (1738) 127 . . . This . . . applies . . . to those that promise more in their adversity than they either intend, or are able to make good in their prosperity. **1881** D. C. MURRAY *Joseph's C.* ch. 17 A prisoner's penitence is a thing the quality of which is very difficult to judge until you see it . . . tried outside. 'The devil was sick.'

Devil will not come into Cornwall, for fear of being put into a pie, The.

1787 GROSE (*Cornw.*) 160 . . . The people of Cornwall make pies of almost every thing eatable,

as squab-pie, herby-pie, pilchard-pie, mugetty-pie, etc.

Devil wipes his tail with the poor man's pride, The. (D 271)

1659 HOWELL *Fr. Prov.* 10b (wipes his arse). **1670** RAY 21.

Devil would have been a weaver but for the Temples, The. (D 272)

1678 RAY 91.

Devil's back, *see* Got over the d. b. spent under his belly.

Devil's child (children) the devil's luck, The. (D 312)

1678 RAY 126. **1721** KELLY 333 The Dee'ls bairns have Dee'ls luck. Spoken enviously when ill People prosper. **1798** NELSON in SOUTHEY *Life* ch. 5 He . . . obtained everything which he wanted at Syracuse. . . . 'It is an old saying', said he in his letter, 'that the devil's children have the devil's luck.' **1841** F. CHAMIER *Tom Bowl.* ch. 29 The luck of the fellow! . . . not a leg or an arm missing. . . . The devil's children have the devil's luck.

Devil's cow calves twice a year, The.

1721 KELLY 310 . . . Spoken when they whom we affect not, thrive and prosper in the World; as if they had their Prosperity from the Devil.

Devil's guts, The. (D 313)

1678 RAY 72 . . . The surveyours chain.

Devil's martyr, *see* Brings himself into needless dangers (He that).

Devil's meal is all (half) bran, The. (M 784)

1592 DELAMOTHE 29 (is halfe turned into branne). **1611** DAVIES no. 222 The Meale of the deuill turnes all to branne. **1611** COTGRAVE s.v. Diable Halfe of the deuils meale turnes vnto branne. **1639** CLARKE 326 (halfe). **1670** RAY 80 (half). **1853** TRENCH vi. 151 . . . unrighteous gains are sure to disappoint the getter.

Devil's mouth is a miser's purse, The. (D 314)

1589 L. WRIGHT *A Summons for Sleepers* A3 A couetous mans purse is called the diuels mouth. **1593** NASHE *Christ's Tears* ii. 99.

Devil's teeth, *see* Cast a bone in d. t.

Devil(s), deil, *see also* Atheist one point beyond the d.; Away goes the d. when door shut; Beads in hand and d. in capuch; Belle giant or d. of Mountsorrel; Better fleech d. than fight him; Better keep the d. at the door; Better the d. you know; Black as the d.; Black (Though I am), I am not d.; Busy (He that is) is tempted by one d.; Buy the d. (If we), must sell d.; Cards are the d.'s books; Cook-ruffian, able to scald d.; Cross on breast and d. in heart; Date of the d.; Deal wi' the d. get dear pennyworth; Ding the d. into a wife (You may); Do little for God if d. were dead; Eat the d. as the broth (As good); Every man for himself and d. take hindmost; Garby whose soul neither . . . d. would have; Give a thing; Give the d. his due; God by the toe, (When they think they have), they have the d. by the fist; God has church (Where), d. will have chapel; God made white man, d. made mulatto; God sends corn and d. mars sack; God sends meat and d. sends cooks; God will give (That which) d. cannot reave; Good to fetch d. a priest; Got over the d.'s back; Great as the d. and Earl of Kent; Happy is that child whose father goes to d.; Harrow hell and scum the d.; Hold a candle to the d.; Holyrood day d. goes a-nutting; Hug one as d. hugs witch; Idle brain the d.'s shop; Ill battle (procession) where d. carries colours; Imps follow when the d. goes before, (No marvel if); Innocent as a d. of two years old; Knows one point more than d.; Leave her . . . and let d. flit her; Lie against d. (Sin to); Like will to like, quoth d. to collier; Long spoon that sups with d.; Man is a . . . d. to man; Man, woman, and d., three degrees; Marriage (He has a great fancy to) that goes to d. for wife; Marrying the d.'s daughter (As bad as); More like the d. than St. Laurence; Needs must when d. drives; Never go to d. dish-clout in hand; Once a d. always a d.; Parsley before it is born is seen by the d. nine times; Patter the d.'s paternoster; Physician is . . . d. when one must pay; Play the d. in the bullimong (*or* horologe); Pull d., pull baker; Pull the d. by the tail; Rains when sun is shining (If it), d. is beating wife; Raise no more d. than you can lay; Raise the d. than lay him (Easier to); Rise betimes that will cozen d.; Runner (Look like a), quoth d. to crab; Saint abroad, d. at home; Saint but the d. he is, (He looks like a); Seldom lies d. dead by gate; Serve the d. for God's sake; Shipped the d. (He that has) must make best; Spite of the d. and Dick Senhouse; Strike, Dawkin, d. is in the hemp; Swallowed the d. swallow his horns; Swear the d. out of hell; Takes the d. into his boat (He that), must carry; Talk of the d.; Tell truth and shame d.; Wite God (You need not) if d. ding you over; Woman is flax . . . the d. comes; World, the flesh, and the d.; Young saint, old d.

Devonshire dumplings.

a. 1812 WOLCOT (P. Pindar) *Add. to my Bk.* Wks. (1816) II. 250 A servant of Sir Francis Drake, . . . a true Devonshire dumplin. 1902–4 LEAN I. 63 A Devonshire dumpling. A short, thick, and plump young woman.

Devonshire, *see also* Denshire.

Devotion, *see* Chamber of sickness chapel of d.; Ignorance is mother of d.; Prayer but little d. (Has much); Sharp stomach makes short d.

Devour(s, -ed), *see* Hare (He has d. a); Little cannot be great unless he d. many; Time d. all things.

Devout, *see* Danger makes men d.

Dew, *see* Cow that's first up gets first of d.; St. Bartholomew brings cold d.

Diamonds cut diamonds.   (D 323)

[Used of persons well matched in wit or cunning.] 1593 NASHE *Christ's Tears* ii. 9 An easie matter is it for anie man to cutte me (like a Diamond) with mine own dust. 1604 MARSTON *Malcontent* IV. iii. None cuttes a diamond but a diamond. *c.* 1612 WEBSTER *Duchess of Malfi* V. v. 91 Whether we fall by ambition, blood, or lust, Like Diamonds, we are cut with our owne dust. *c.* 1613 BEAUM. & FL. *Bonduca* V. i Thou rich diamond cut with thine own dust. 1628 FORD *Lover's Mel.* I. iii. We're caught in our own toils. . . . 1738 SWIFT Dial. III. E.L. 320. 1863 READE *Hard Cash* ch. 25.

Diamond, *see also* Barley-corn better than d. to cock; Hard as a d.; Rough d.

Dicing, drabbing and drinking bring men to destruction.   (D 324)

c. 1577 J. NORTHBROOKE *Treatise agst. Dicing* Sh. Soc. 115 Dyce, wine and venerie . . . did hasten all my woe, and brought to me great neede. 1607 DEKKER *Knight's Conjuring* iii. 28 Dycing, drinking, and drabbing . . . were the ciuil plagues that very vnciuily destroied the sonnes (but not the sinnes) of the cittie. 1616 BRETON *Cross. of Prov.* A7ᵛ Dicing, drabbing, and drinking, are the three Ds. to destruction.

Dice, *see* Devil is in the d.; Make d. of one's bones; Throw of the d. (Best) is to throw them away.

Dick's (Nick's) hatband, As queer (tight, odd) as.

1796 GROSE *Dict. Vulg. T.* s.v. Dick . . . that is, out of spirits, or don't know what ails me. [*Newcastle form c.* 1850. As queer as Dick's (Nick's) hatband, that went nine times round and wouldn't meet.] 1837 SOUTHEY *Doctor* iv. 252 Who was that other Dick who wore so queer a hat-band that it has ever since served as a standing comparison for all queer things? 1902–4 LEAN II. ii. 865 As queer as Dick's hatband, made of a pea-straw, that went nine times round and would not meet at last.

Dick, *see also* Tom, D., and Harry.

Dickins *or* Dickson, *see* Gets by that, as D. did.

Die a dog's death (like a dog), To.
                                           (D 509)

1529 RASTELL *Pastime* (1811) 57 He lyved lyke a lyon, and dyed lyke a dogge. 1591 I *Troublesome Reign K.J.* F2 To my conscience a clog to dye like a dog. 1593 *Jack Straw* Fı In strangling cords die like dogs. 1594 NASHE *Unfort.*

Trav. ii. 241 He dyde like a dogge, he was hangd and the halter paid for. **[1600] 1659** DAY & CHETTLE *Blind Beggar* C2ᵛ Shall I betray his life that sav'd me from the death of a Dog? *Ibid.* H2ᵛ Let me dye like a Dog on a Pitchfork. **1605–8** SHAKES. *T.Ath.* II. ii. 91 Thou wast whelped a dog, and thou shalt famish a dog's death. **1699** B.E. *Dict. Canting Crew* Die like a Dog, to be hang'd. **1894** FENN *In Alpine Valley* I. 22 To die this dog's death, out here under these mountains.

Die by inches, To.

1791 WOLLSTONECRAFT *Original Stories* ch. I Allow the poor bird to die by inches. **1836** MARRYAT *Midsh. Easy* ch. 16 Hanging they thought better than dying by inches from starvation.

Die in harness, To.

1776 FLETCHER OF MADELEY *Wks.* i. 197. **1834** MARRYAT *Jacob Faith.* ch. 40 I am like an old horse . . . in a mill, that . . . cannot walk straight forward; and . . . I will die in harness.

Die in one's shoes, To.   (S 381)

[To be hanged.] **1666** TORRIANO *Prov. Phr.* S.V. Piedi, 147: To dye with ones feet in ones shooes, viz. to dye a sudden death. **1699** *Dict. Canting Crew* Die like a Dog, to be hang'd, . . . Die on a Fish-day or in his shoes, the same. **1725** GAY *Newgate's Garland* l. 4 Ye honester poor Rogues, who die in your Shoes. **1834** J. B. KER 36.

Die is cast, The.   (D 326)

[L. *Alea iacta est* The die is cast, founded upon *Iacta alea esto* (SUETONIUS *Caes.* l. 32) Let the die be cast! said to have been uttered by Caesar, at the Rubicon, 49 B.C.] **1548** W. PATTEN *Expedⁿ into Scotland* (*Tud. Tr.* 154) The chance is cast, and the word thus uttered cannot be called again. **1558** QUEEN ELIZABETH (Earl of Northampton, *Defensative*, 1594, ch. 16, as cited by Hakewill in his *Apology*, 1635 ed., 136). *c.* **1612** JONSON *Epicoene* IV. ii. 43 Iacta est alea. **1616** DEKKER *Artillery Garden* C3ᵛ The Die is throwne to the last chance. **1627** G. HAKEWILL *Apol. of Power and Providence of God* 120 Iacta est alea; the dice are throwne. **1634** SIR T. HERBERT *Trav.* A iii b Is the die cast, must At this one throw all thou hast gaind be lost? **1712** 31 May. SWIFT *Jrnl. to Stella* I never wished so much as now that I had stayed in Ireland; but the die is cast. **1887** S. COLVIN *Keats* 181 He writes . . . 'I should like to cast the die for Love or Death' . . . It was for death that the die was cast.

Die (*noun*), *see also* Smooth as a d.

Die like a chrisom[1] child, To. *Cf.* Innocent as a new-born babe.   (B 4)

1599 SHAKES. *Hen. V* II. iii. 12 'A made a finer end and went away an it had been any christom child. **1680** BUNYAN *Life Badman* 566 Mr. Badman died like a lamb; or as they call it, like a chrisom-child, quietly and without fear. [¹ a child newly baptized, still wearing the chrisomer, or christening robe. In the bills of mortality children dying within a month of birth were **called** *chrisoms.*]

Die well that live well, They.   (L 391)

1506 *Cal. Shep.* II. 169 He that leuyth well maye not dye amys. **1530** R. WHITFORD *Work for Householders* H3ᵛ The most sure waye to dye well, is well to lyue. **1557** EDGEWROTH *Sermons* 3P1ᵛ Non potest male mori qui bene vixerit, he can not die ill that hath liued well. **1616** DRAXE no. 445 He dieth well, that liueth well. **1639** CLARKE 215.

Die, When I | the world dies with me.   (W 891)

1584 WITHALS K6 When I do die, the worlde doth die, and both together buried lie. **1615** BRATHWAIT *Strap. for Devil* 225 Since as the Prouerbe is, when he is gone, The world's gone with him, as all in One. **1621** ROBINSON 27. **1639** CLARKE 264.

Died half a year ago is as dead as Adam, He that.

1732 FULLER no. 2079.

Dies for age, When he | you may quake for fear.

1721 KELLY 357 . . . Intimating that you are not much younger. **1762** GOLDSMITH *Cit. of World,* Lr. 123 Wks. (Globe) 279 'Who is old, sir? when I die of age, I know of some that will quake for fear.'

Dies like a beast who has done no good while he lived, He.   (B 154)

1640 HERBERT no. 993 Hee a beast doth die, that hath done no good to his country. **1707** MAPLETOFT 112.

Dies this year is excused for the next, He that.

1578 THOS. WHITE *Sermon at Paul's Cross* 3 Nov. 1577, 81 That Heathen prouerb . . . too common among Christians: He that dieth this yere is scused for the next.

Dies without the company of good men, puts not himself into a good way, He that.   (C 567)

1640 HERBERT no. 995.

Die(d, s), *see also* Afraid of him who d. last year; All men must d.; Anger d. quickly with good man; Begins to d. that quits desires; Better d. with honour than live with shame; Cowards d. often; Dallies with his enemy (Who) d. by own hand; Do or d.; Envy never d.; Fools live poor to d. rich; Gives thee a bone; Gods love d. young (Whom the); Happy till he d. (Call no man); Heathen, when they d., went without candle; Horse must d. in some man's hand; King never d.; Know not who lives or d.; Know where they were born, not where shall d.; Leave more to do when we d. than have done; Like to d. mends not kirkyard; Live as they would d.; Live longest must d. at last; Lives most, d. most;

Lives wickedly hardly d. honestly; Love too much that d. for love; Man can d. but once; Marries ere he be wise will d. ere he thrive; Natural to d. as to be born; Never say d.; No man d. of an ague; No man knows when shall d.; Old be, or young d.; Old man, when thou d., give me double; Prettiness d. first (quickly); Sick (Who never was) d. first fit; Soon as man is born begins to d.; Take it with you when you d. (You can't); Wife that kept her supper . . . and d. ere day; Young men d. many; Young men may d. but old must d.

Diet, *see* Father of disease (Whatsoever was), ill d. was mother; Little with quiet; Physicians are Dr. D. (Best).

Dieu-gard, *see* Beck is as good.

Difference between Peter and Peter, There is some.   (D 332)

1620 SHELTON *Quix.* Pt. IV. xx. ii. 136 Master barber, you should take heed how you speak; for . . . there is some difference between Peter and Peter. **1732** FULLER no. 4937.

Difference between staring and stark blind (mad), There is.   (D 334)

1546 HEYWOOD II. vii. I4 The difference betwene staryng and starke blynde, The wyse man at all tymes to folow can fynde. **1579** LYLY *Euph.* i. 189 Consider wyth thy selfe, the greate difference betweene staringe and starke blinde. **1616** DRAXE no. 495. **1629** FORD *Lover's Melan.* II. ii. Am I stark mad?—No, no, you are but a little staring—there's difference between staring and stark mad. You are but whimsied yet. **1670** RAY 79 . . . If you read it stark mad, it signifies, that we ought to distinguish, and not presently pronounce him stark mad that stares a little. . . . If you read it stark blind, then it . . . is a reprehension to those who put no difference between extremes, as perfect blindness and *Lynceus* his sight. **1787** WOLCOT (P. Pindar) *Ode upon Ode* Wks. (1816) I. 322 Peter, there's odds 'twixt staring and stark mad.

Difference between Will you buy? and Will you sell? There is a.

1721 KELLY 317 . . . When People proffer their Goods, Buyers will be shy: and when People ask to buy, Sellers will hold their Wares the dearer. *c.* **1790** Ayreshire song collected by Burns. The man at the fair that wad sell, He maun learn at the man that wad buy.

Difference between word and deed, There is great.   (D 333)

1578 *Courtly Controv.* T2ᵛ O what difference is betwixt wel doing and wel saying. **1581** J. CARTIGNY *Voyage of the Wand. Knight* I2 There is no difference betweene his [God's] saieng and doing. For what he saith, he doth. **1600** BLOUNT *Hist. Uniting Portugal* I. 21 Not knowing the difference betwixt saying and doing. **1666** TORRIANO *It. Prov.* 71, no. 23 There's a great deal of difference twixt doing and saying.

Difference is wide that the sheets will not decide, The.   (D 330)

1582 WHETSTONE *Hept. Civil Disc.* F4 Among the married, quarrels in the day, are qualified with kisses in the night. **1611** W. VAUGHAN *Spirit Detrac.* 310 According to which agrees that Italian saying; . . . the heate of the bed thawes oftentimes the ice of secrecie or Taciturnitie. **1678** RAY 201. **1732** FULLER no. 6155 (very wide).

Difference of bloods in a basin, There is no.   (D 335)

1560 T. BECON *Wks.* II. 18 (LEAN IV. 85). **1562** J. PILKINGTON *Proph. Haggai* P.S. 125 If the poor and rich man's blood were both in one basin, how should the one be known to be better than the other, seeing we crack so much of it? **1580** LYLY *Euph. & his Eng.* ii. 67 You talke of your birth, when I knowe there is no difference of blouds in a basen. **1602** SHAKES. *A.W.* II. iii. 116 Strange is it that our bloods, . . . pour'd all together, Would quite confound distinction. **1732** FULLER no. 4907.

Difference, *see also* Adam's children (We are all) but silk makes the d.; Tweedledum and Tweedledee.

Dig a pit (make a snare) for another and fall into it oneself, To.   (P 356)

[PSALM vii. 15. ECCLES. X. 8.] **1509** BARCLAY *Ship of Fools* ii. 40. *c.* **1532** *Tales* no. 16 Some tyme one fallethe in the dytche, that he him selfe made. **1559** R.P. in J. BRADFORTH *Godly Meditation* D4ᵛ In the same pyt they haue digged for other, let them be taken. **1566** PAINTER i. 216. **1571** R. EDWARDS *Damon & Pithias* Incidi in foveam quam feci. **1576** PETTIE ii. 103. *a.* **1628** CARMICHAELL no. 798 (ditch). **1630** DEKKER *London Look Back* (Wilson *Plague Pamphlets* 182). *a.* **1633** JONSON *Tale of a Tub* IV. iii. 13. **1659** HOWELL *Span. Prov.* 9.

Dig one's grave with one's teeth, To.   (E 53)

[Fr. DE LINCY *Prov. Franc.* I. 214 Les gourmands font leurs fosses avec leurs dents.] **1616** T. ADAMS *Sacrifice of Thankfulness* 53 As the French prouerbe sayes, They haue digged their Graue with their Teeth. **1655** FULLER *Ch. Hist.* IV. iii (1868) I. 608 King Edward . . . by intemperance in his diet, in some sort, digged his grave with his own teeth. **1854** SURTEES *Hand. Cross* ch. 2 More people dig their graves with their teeth than we imagine.

Dig (*or* take) up the hatchet, To.

[= to take up arms, or declare hostilities, from the custom of the N. Amer. Indians.] **1753** G. WASHINGTON *Jrnl. Writ.* (1889) I. 21 Three Nations of French Indians . . . had taken up the Hatchet against the English. **1861** H. KINGSLEY *Ravenshoe* ch. 45 For Lord Saltire's landed property I shall fight. . . . We will dig up the tomahawk, and be off on the war-trail in your ladyship's brougham. **1898** STEVENSON *Mast. Ball.* ch. 11 A dreadful solitude surrounded our steps. . . . 'They must have dug up the hatchet', he said.

Digests, *see* Cheese d. everything but itself; Victuals (Of all) drink d. quickest.

Dighton is pulled down, When | Hull shall become a great town.   (D 337)

1670 RAY 257 Yorkshire. . . . Dighton is a small Town not a mile distant from Hull, and was in the time of the late wars for the most part pull'd down.

Dilemma, *see* Horns of a d.

Diligence, *see* Care and d. bring luck.

Diligent scholar, and the master's paid, A.   (S 133)

1640 HERBERT no. 183.

Dim Sarsnick with him, It is.

1917 BRIDGE 84 It's Dim Sarsnick with him. 'DymSassenach = 'I don't understand English': used by the Welsh when they do not understand, or pretend not to understand, what is said to them in English. . . . In Cheshire the saying superseded . . . 'None so deaf as those who won't hear.'

Dine with Duke Humphrey, To.

     (D 637)

[= to go dinnerless.]   **1590–5** *Sir T. More* III. iii. 343 He may chance dine with Duke Humphrey to-morrow. **1591** ?NASHE *Wonderfull . . . Prognostication* iii. 393 Sundry fellowes in their silkes shall be appointed to keep Duke Humfrye company in Poules, because they know not wher to get their dinner abroad. **1592** G. HARVEY *Four Lett.* (Nares s.v. *Duke Humphrey*) To seek his dinner in Poules with duke Humphrey. **[1592] 1597** SHAKES. *Rich. III* IV. iv. 175 What comfortable hour canst thou name That ever grac'd me in thy company?—Faith, none but Humphrey Hour, that call'd your Grace To breakfast once forth of my company. **1599** BP. HALL *Sat.* III. vii. 6 Trow'st thou where he din'd to-day? In sooth I saw him sit with Duke Humphray. **1604** *Penniless Parl. Threadbare Poets* (Farmer) Let me dine twice a week at Duke Humphrey's table. **1662** FULLER Lond. 198 After the Death of good Duke Humphrey . . . to Dine with Duke Humphrey [imported] to be Dinnerlesse. **1748** SMOLLETT *Rod. Rand.* ch. 55 (Farmer) My mistress and her mother must have dined with Duke Humphrey, had I not exerted myself. **1790** GROSE s.v. London This proverb, Fuller says, has altered its meaning. At first it meant dinner at another man's table: for Humphrey . . . commonly called the good Duke, kept an open table, where any gentleman was welcome to dine. After his decease, to dine with Duke Humphrey meant to go dinnerless. . . . Fuller says, that persons who loitered about in St. Paul's church during dinner-time, were said to dine with Duke Humphrey, from a mistaken notion that he was buried there. **1843** DICKENS *M. Chuz.* ch. 1 He will have no choice but to dine again with Duke Humphrey.

Dine with St. Giles and the Earl of Murray, To.

[The Earl of Murray was interred in St. Giles's Church, Edinburgh.] **1680** FR. SEMPILL *Banishm. Prov.* 87 I din'd with saints and noblemen, Even sweet St. Giles and the Earl of Murray.

Dined as well as my Lord Mayor of London, I have.   (L 449)

1577 WM. HARRISON *Description of England* (Furnivall i. 151) They thinke . . . themselves to have fared so well, as the lord Maior of London. **1580** LYLY *Euph. & his Eng.* ii. 194 Hauing halfe dyned, they say as it were in a prouerbe, that they are as well satisfied as the Lorde Maior of London. **1602** J. MANNINGHAM *Diary* 40 [Fleetwood the Recorder] imprisoned one for saying he had supt as well as the Lord Maior, when he had nothing but bread and cheese. **1662** FULLER Lond. 199 . . . That is, as comfortably, as contentedly, according to the Rule, Satis est quod sufficit, enough is as good as a Feast. **1738** SWIFT Dial. II. E.L. 306.

Dines and leaves, He that | lays the cloth twice.   (C 430)

1599 MINSHEU *Span. Gram.* 82 (and leaueth for another time, couers the table twice). **1640** HERBERT no. 347.

Dine(s), *see also* Depends on another, d. ill; Rich man may d. when he will.

Ding[1] doun Tantallon, big[2] a brig[3] to the Bass.

1907 HENDERSON & WATT *Scotland of To-day* xi. James V attacked [Tantallon Castle] in 1528 . . . but to no purpose, and so to 'Ding doun Tantallon Big a brig to the Bass', became a Scots proverb for things impossible. [[1] beat. [2] build. [3] bridge.]

Ding[1] the Deil into a wife, You may | but you'll never ding him out of her.

1721 KELLY 360 . . . That is, a Wife is seldom mended by being beaten. [[1] beat.]

Ding, *see also* Devil d. another (Let one); Wand d. him (Let his own).

Dinner, At | my man appears.   (D 341)

1640 HERBERT no. 37.

Dinners cannot be long where dainties want.   (D 344)

1546 HEYWOOD II. i. F2 Diners can not be long, where deyntees want. **1614** CAMDEN 305. **1639** CLARKE 136.

Dinner(s), *see also* After d. sit awhile; Eat a good d. (He that would); Eaten your d. off floor; God send us of our own when rich men go to d.; Half an hour soon lost at d.; Hunger makes d.; Huntsman's breakfast, lawyer's d.; Saves his d. will have more supper.

Diocese, *see* Devil busy bishop in own d.

Dirk, *see* Never draw d. when dunt will do.

Dirt enough, Fling | and some will stick.
(D 349)

[L. *Calumniare fortiter, aliquid adhaerebit.*]
1656 *Trepan* 33 She will say before company,
Have you never had the French Pox? speak as
in the sight of God: let them Reply what they
will, some dirt will stick. 1660 T. HALL *Funebria
Florae* 38 Lye lustily, some filth will stick. 1678
B. R. *Letter Pop. Friends* 7 'Tis a blessed Line in
Matchiavel—If durt enough be thrown, some
will stick. 1706 E. WARD *Hud. Rediv.* I. II. 11
Scurrility's a useful trick, Approv'd by the most
politic; Fling dirt enough, and some will stick.
1856–70 FROUDE *Hist. Eng.* xii. 438 No dirt
sticks more readily than an accusation of this
kind when boldly and positively insisted on.

Dirt into the well that has given you water, Cast no.
(D 345)

1590 SHAKES. *T.And.* V. ii. 171 Here stands the
spring whom you have stain'd with mud. 1593–4
Id. Lucr. l. 577 Mud not the fountain that
gave drink to thee. 1678 RAY *Adag. Heb.* 404
Never cast dirt into that fountain of which thou
hast sometime drank. 1707 MAPLETOFT 116.
1732 FULLER no. 1067.

Dirt, The more | the less hurt.

1832 HENDERSON 13 The mair dirt, the less hurt.
1854 SURTEES *Handley Cross* ch. 32.

Dirt, *see also* Builds on the people, (He that)
builds on d.; Cuckoo comes, (When) eats all the
d.; Deals in d. has aye foul fingers (He that);
Ducks have eaten up d., (Not till); Eat a peck of
d. (Every man must); Falls into the d. (He that);
Go through d. (How does he); What serves d.
for if it do not stink.

Dirt-bird (Dirt-owl) sings, The | we shall have rain.
(D 351)

1678 RAY 80 . . . When melancholy persons are
very merry, it is observed that there usually
followes an extraordinary fit of sadness; they
doing all things commonly in extremes.

Dirten arse dreads aye.
(A 326)

a. 1628 CARMICHAELL no. 434. 1721 KELLY 85
. . . When People are sensible that they have done
amiss, they are still apprehensive of Discovery.

Dirty, *see* Hungry dogs [*also* Scornful dogs]
will eat d. puddings; Little, (He that has) is
less d.

Disarmed peace is weak, A.
(P 151)

1640 HERBERT no. 628.

Discloses, *see* Time d. all things.

Discontent is his worst evil, A man's.
(M 470)

1640 HERBERT no. 298.

Discontented man knows not where to sit easy, A.
(M 90)

1640 HERBERT no. 345.

Discord, *see* Apple of d.

Discourse makes short days and nights, Sweet.
(D 352)

1611 COTGRAVE s.v. Long Long discourses make
short dayes. 1640 HERBERT no. 727.

Discovers, *see* Covers thee d. thee.

Discreet advise, While the | the fool does his business.
(D 353)

1640 HERBERT no. 273.

Discreet women have neither eyes nor ears.
(W 683)

c. 1595 SHAKES. *R.J.* III. iii. 62 Wise men have
no eyes. 1640 HERBERT no. 482. 1670 RAY 7.
1732 FULLER no. 1295 (Discreet Wives have sometimes).

Discretion is the better part of valour.
(D 354)

[EUR. *Suppl.* 510 Καὶ τοῦτό τοι τἀνδρεῖον ἡ
προμηθία.] *c.* 1477 CAXTON *Jason* E.E.T.S. 23
Than as wyse and discrete he withdrewe him
sayng that more is worth a good retrayte than a
folisshe abydinge. 1595 SHAKES. *M.N.D.* V. i.
226 This lion is a very fox for his valour.—True;
and a goose for his discretion [&c.] 1597 *Id.
I Hen. IV* V. iv. 121 The better part of valour is
discretion; in the which better part, I have saved
my life. 1608 *Id. C.* I. i. 200 For though
abundantly they lack discretion, Yet are they
passing cowardly. 1611 BEAUM & FL. *A King*
IV. iii. 60 My sword lost, . . . for discreetly I
rendered it. . . .—It showed discretion the best
part of valour. 1885 C. LOWE *Prince Bismarck*
ch. 3 Napoleon . . . had vowed that he would
free Italy 'from the Alps to the Adriatic', but . . .
he acted on the maxim that . . .

Discretion, *see also* Offices may be given, not d.;
Ounce of d. worth pound of wit; Valour can do
little without d.; Valour would fight but d.
would run away.

Disdainfulness, *see* Abundance of things.

Disease known is half cured, A.
(D 358)

1569 *Amorous Tales* tr. J. Sanford C3 Euery
sickenesse which is soone knowen, may easily be
cured. 1581 T. LUPTON *Siuqila Too Good to be
True* M3ᵛ When the disease is knowne, it is
sooner cured. 1616 T. ADAMS *Diseases of the
Soul* 56 The knowledge of the disease is halfe the
cure. 1631 *Celestina* tr. Mabbe (Tud. Tr.) 26
The first recovery of sicknesse, is the discovery
of the disease. 1694 JAMES WRIGHT *Country
Contentments* sect. III. Faults, like Diseases,
when perfectly discover'd are half cured. 1732
FULLER no. 75.

Disease, The chief | that reigns this year is folly.
(D 355)

1640 HERBERT no. 765.

Diseases are the interests of pleasures.
(D 359)

1616 WITHALS 542 (interest). **1664** CODRINGTON 190. **1670** RAY 7. **1732** FULLER no. 1297 (Price of ill Pleasures).

Disease(s), *see also* Agues (D.) come on horseback; Deadly d. neither physician can ease; Desperate cuts (d.) must have desperate cures; Doctor is often more to be feared; Father of a d. (Whatsoever was), ill diet was mother; Many dishes many d.; Remedy is worse than d.; Sun rises (When) d. will abate.

Disgrace, *see* Poverty is no d.

Disgraces are like cherries, one draws another.
(D 361)

1640 HERBERT no. 487.

Disguised, He is.
(D 362)

1562 HEYWOOD *Fifth Hundred of Epigr.* no. 34 Three cuppes full at once shall oft dysgyse thee. **1607** DELONEY *Strange Hist.* (1841) 14 The saylors and the shipmen all, through foule excesse of wine, Were so disguisde that at the sea they shewed themselves like swine. **1678** RAY 87.

Dish, To lay (cast, throw) (a thing) in one's.
(T 155)

[= to reproach or taunt him with it.] **1551** T. WILSON *Logike* (1580) 62b When wee charge hym with a like fault, and laye some greater matter in his dishe. **1559** T. BECON *Prayers* P.S. 390 Let no man object and lay in my dish old custom. **1587** J. BRIDGES *Defence* 770 Why did not Salomon lay that in her [the Q. of Sheba's] dish, and tell her, that she could not be a Queene, because she could not . . . gouerne an armie? **1596** NASHE *Saffron W.* iii. 57 Hee casts the begger in my dish at euerie third sillable. **1615** SWETNAM *Arraignm. Women* (1880), 18 Hir dowrie will be often cast in thy dish if shee doe bring wealth with her. **1722** SEWEL *Hist. Quakers* (1795) I. 8 Under the bloody reign of Queen Mary, this was laid in his dish.

Dish while I shed my pottage, Hold the.
(D 369)

1588 'MARPRELATE' *Epitome* ed. Pierce 120 Your dealing therein is but to hold my dish, while I spill my pottage. **1602** MARSTON *Antonio and Mell.* v. i. 21. **1670** RAY 218.

Dish(es), *see also* Beggar knows his d.; Better are small fish than empty d.; Cowped the mickle d. into the little; First d. aye best eaten; First d. pleases all; Gets by that as Dickins by d.; Hog is never good but in d.; Liar, lick d.; Lick your d.; Lost that is put into riven d.; Mair in a mair d.; Many d. many diseases; Pay with same d. you borrow; Revenge is a d. that should be eaten cold; Speaks as if every word would lift d.; Spoon in every man's d., (To have a).

Dish-clout my table-cloth, I will not make my.
(D 380)

1678 RAY 125. **1732** FULLER no. 2646.

Dish-clout, *see also* Never go to devil d. in hand; Thing in it (There is a), quoth . . . when he drank d.

Disorderly, *see* God is made master of family (When), he orders d.

Dispraise, *see* Praise by evil men is d.; Praise nor d. thyself (Neither).

Disputants, Of two | the warmer is generally in the wrong.

1826 LAMB *Elia; Pop. Fallacies* Wks. (1898) 223 . . . Warmth and earnestness are a proof at least of a man's own conviction of the rectitude of that which he maintains. Coolness is as often the result of . . . indifference to truth . . . , as of . . . confidence in a man's own side in a dispute.

Dispute, *see* Truth is lost (In too much d.).

Disputing, *see* Itch of d. is scab of church.

Dissemble, *see* Knows not how to d. (Who).

Distaff, *see* Foot on cradle, hand on d. . . . good housewife; Hercules with d.; Philosophy of the d.; St. D.'s day; Spider lost her d.; Spindle and thy d. ready (Get thy); Spun (If it will not be), bring not to d.; Tow on one's d. (To have).

Distance, *see* Fire that lights us at a d.; Friends agree best at d.; Manners know d.

Distrust, *see* Remember to d.

Ditch, *see* Better to go about than fall into d.; Blind lead blind, both fall in d.; Winter never died in d.

Ditchwater, *see* Dull as d.

Dived deep into the water, You have | and have brought up a potsherd.
(W 127)

1678 RAY *Adag. Hebr.* 407.

Divide and rule.
(D 391)

[L. *Divide et impera.*] **1588** *Disc. upon the present state of France* 44 It hath been alwaies her [Catherine de Medici's] custome, to set in France, one against an other, that in the meane while shee might rule in these diuisions. **1605** J. HALL *Medit.* I. 93 For a Prince . . . is a sure Axiome, Diuide and rule. **1633** PH. FLETCHER *Purple Isl.* VII. lxv. In which two swords he [sedition] bore: his word, Divide and reign. *a.* **1640** J. SMYTH *Lives of the Berkeleys* i. 275 The truth of divide et impera; seuer the conspirators and their devices are confounded. **1775** FLETCHER OF MADELEY *Wks.* V. 232. **1907**

20 Apr. *Spectator* 605 The cynical maxim of 'Divide and rule' has never . . . clouded our relations with the daughter-States.

Divided, *see* Fears are d. in the midst; Kingdoms d. soon fall.

Divine ashes are better than earthly meal.   (A 340)

1640 HERBERT no. 684. **1666** TORRIANO *It. Prov.* 44 no. 20 Heavenly ashes is more worth, than worldly flower [flour].

Divine grace was never slow (late).
(G 390)

1640 HERBERT no. 710. **1666** TORRIANO *It. Prov.* 108 no. 37 Divine favours were never too late.

Diviner, *see* Make me a d. and I will make you rich.

Divinity, *see* Good husbandry good d.; No d. is absent if Prudence present.

Do a foolish thing once in one's life, One cannot | but one must hear of it a hundred times.

1738 SWIFT Dial. II. E.L. 299 You have stolen a wedding, it seems?—Well; one can't do a foolish thing once in ones life, but one must hear of it a hundred times.

Do as he would, He that may not | must (will) do as he may.
(M 554, 769, 769a)

c. **1530** *Terence in English* (Andria) C6ᵛ It is comenly told we must do as we may when we may not as we wold. **1539** TAVERNER 48ᵛ Whan that thynge can not be done that thou woldest, woll that thou cannest. **1546** HEYWOOD II. v. H2 Who that maie not as they wolde, will as they maie. **1592** SHAKES. *T.A.* II. i. 106 And so must you resolve That what you cannot as you would achieve, You must perforce accomplish as you may. **1616** DRAXE no. 3 Who that may not as they will, must will as they may. **1659** HOWELL *Eng. Prov.* 10 (must will). **1721** KELLY 169.

Do as I say, not as I do.   (D 394)

[MATT. xxiii. 3.] *a.* **1100** Homily in MS. Cotton Tiberius C1 ed. N. R. Ker in *The Anglo-Saxons. Studies presented to Bruce Dickins* (1959) 277 ll. 8–9. Ac þeah ic wyrs do þonne ic þe lære, ne do þu na swa swa ic do, ac do swa ic þe lære gyf ic þe wel lære. *c.* **1514** BARCLAY *Eclogues* I. 489 Liue as they teach, but liue not as they do. **1546** HEYWOOD II. v. H4ᵛ It is as folke dooe, and not as folke saie. **1689** SELDON *Table-talk* (1887) 145 Preachers say, Do as I say, not as I do. **1911** 24 June *Spectator* 957 It has always been considered allowable to say . . . to children, . . .

Do as the friar says, not as he does.
(F 673)

1659 HOWELL *Span. Prov.* 14. **1670** RAY 7.

Do as thy master commands thee and sit down at table.   (M 711)

1611 COTGRAVE s.v. Maistre He needs not wait thats bid sit downe by his maister. **1620** SHELTON *Don Quix.* Pt. II. xxix. iii. 218. **1694** BOYER 108 (tho' it be to sit at his Table).

Do as you're bidden and you'll never bear blame.   (B 444)

c. **1550** *Howleglas* (F. Ouvry 1868) 47–8 They that do as the be bid: they be worthy to haue thanke. **1678** RAY 101.

Do as you would be done by.   (D 395)

[LUKE vi. 31.] *c.* **1470** MALORY (Vinaver) iii. 1114 Allwayes a good man will do ever to another man as he wolde be done to hymself. *a.* **1500** *Ratis Raving* E.E.T.S. 35 l. 337 Bot that þow pres to do, my sone Rycht as þow wald to the war done. [c. **1550**] **1641** CAVENDISH *Wolsey* ed. Morley n.d. 159 Let us do to him [Wolsey] as we would be done unto. **1551** T. WILSON *Rule of Reason* M7 Suche sentences as by the lawe of nature are graffed in man. As . . . Do as thou wouldest be done vnto. **1590–5** *Sir T. More* II. iv. A says true: let's do as we may be done by. **1641** FERGUSSON no. 229 Do as ye wald be done to. **1863** KINGSLEY *Water Bab.* ch. 5.

Do better, He that cannot | must be a monk.

1827–30 SCOTT *Tales Grandf.* ch. 21 Douglas was then[1] ordained to be put into the abbey of Lindores, to which sentence he submitted calmly, only using a popular proverb, . . . [[1] 1484.]

Do good: thou doest it for thyself.

1642 TORRIANO 51. **1658** *Comes Facundus* 176 Do good to yourselves (the Italian beggars word). **1732** FULLER no. 1306 Do good, if you expect to receive it.

Do good, *see also* Silly man that can neither d. g. nor ill; Swine never d. g. while he lives.

Do ill, Who would | ne'er wants occasion.   (I 37)

1640 HERBERT no. 116.

Do little for God if the devil were dead, You would.   (L 371)

1641 FERGUSSON no. 909. **1721** KELLY 364 . . . That is, you would do little for Love, if you were not under Fear.

Do much ill, He may | ere he can do much worse.   (I 25)

c. **1549** HEYWOOD I. xi. E1. **1594** BACON *Promus* no. 956. **1611** DAVIES no. 163. **1639** CLARKE 150.

Do no ill, If you | do no ill like. *Cf.* Evil do, Whoso will no, etc.   (I 29)

1641 FERGUSSON no. 489.

Do not all you can; spend not all you have; believe not all you hear; and tell not all you know.

1609 HARWARD 84 Do not all thou maist. **1707** MAPLETOFT 36.

Do on the hill as you would do in the hall. (H 462)

1509 BARCLAY *Ship of Fools* ii. 266. **1570** *Id. Mirrour of Good Manners* 25 Liue thou vpon hill as thou would liue in hall. **1641** FERGUSSON no. 228. **1721** KELLY 85 . . . Accustom yourself to act with Discretion and good Manners at all times. **1732** FULLER no. 1307 Do in the Hole as thou would'st in the Hall.

Do or die.

c. **1577** PITSCOTTIE S.T.S. ed. i. 316 He knew weill thair was no remedie but ether to do or die. **1621** ROBINSON 12 I must either do or dye. **1639** CLARKE 225.

Do right nor suffer wrong, He will neither. (R 126)

1678 RAY 266.

Do the likeliest, and God will do the best (hope the best). (L 291)

a. **1628** CARMICHAELL no. 456 (pray God to do the best). **1641** FERGUSSON no. 234 (do the best). **1721** KELLY 90 (hope the best). **1732** FULLER no. 1310 (as 1721).

Do the next thing.

1907 A. C. BENSON *Upton Lett.* 322 One's immediate duty is happily, as a rule, clear enough. 'Do the next thing', says the old shrewd motto.

Do these things in a green tree, If they | what shall be done in the dry?

[LUKE xxiii. 31.] **1612** SHELTON *Quix.* Pt. III. xi i. 211 If dry I could do this, what should I have done being watered? **1926** *Times* 12 July 15/4 That is the view . . . which the Labour Party would be wise to accept. 'If they do these things in the green tree, what shall be done in the dry?'

Do well and doubt no man, and do well and doubt all men. (M 91)

XVIc. *Early English Carols* (ed. R. L. Greene) 354 Do well, and drede no man. *a.* **1628** CAR-MICHAELL no. 452. **1641** FERGUSSON no. 242. **1721** KELLY 89 Do well and doubt No man. But rest satisfied in the Testimony of a good Conscience.

Do well and have well. (D 398)

c. **1350** *Douce MS. 52*, no. 32 Do welle and haue welle. **1377** LANGLAND *P. Pl.* B. vii. 113 Dowel, and haue wel . . . and god shal haue thi sowle. **1530** PALSGRAVE 523b & 525b. *Ibid.* 832b Best do best have. **1546** HEYWOOD II. ix. K3ᵛ Doo well, and haue well, men saie also. **1576** J. CAIUS *Of English Dogs* tr. A. Fleming To the Reader

A watchword . . . Do well and fare well. **1721** KELLY 90 . . . Be a good Man, and you will be kindly dealt by. **1732** FULLER no. 1311.

Do well than to say well, It is better to. *Cf.* Say well and do well. (D 402)

1539 TAVERNER I *Garden* A4ᵛ It is moche more excellent and gloriouse for a man to do worthy thynges, then to haue a tonge ready and swyfte to talke of worthy thynges. **1567** *Say Well* in *Good and Godly Bal.*, 208 Say weill in wordis is wonderous trick, Bot do weill in deidis is nimbill and quick. **1592** DELAMOTHE 15 (then to speake well). **1597** *Politeuphuia* 158ᵛ (then speake well). *Ibid.* 168ᵛ. **1613** SHAKES. *Hen. VIII* III. ii. 153 'Tis a kind of good deed to say well; And yet words are no deeds. **1666** TORRIANO *It. Prov.* 84, no. 28.

Do well, *see also* Day that you d. w. there will be seven moons; Never too late to d. w.; Say w. and d. w. . . . d. w. is better.

Do what one's own self wills, It is easy to. (D 407)

a. **1593** MARLOWE *Eleg.* I. ii. 10 A burden easly borne is light. **1596** LODGE *Wit's Misery* Hunt. Cl. iv. 102 A good will winneth all things. **1605–6** SHAKES. *M.* II. iii. 48 The labour we delight in physics pain. **1606–7** *Id. A.C.* IV. iv. 20 To business that we love we rise betime And go to't with delight. **1611** *Id. Temp.* III. i. 29 I should do it With much more ease; for my good will is to it, And yours it is against. **1641** FERGUSSON no. 484 It is eith till, that the awn self will.

Do what we like with our own, May we not? (O 99)

[MATT. xx. 15 Is it not lawful for me to do what I will with mine own?] **1550** R. CROWLEY *One & Thirty Epigrams* E.E.T.S. 47 Full certayne he wyste, That with hys owne he might alwayes do as he lyste. *c.* **1594** R. WILSON *The Cobbler's Prophesy* I. 381 What hath any man to doe what I doe with mine owne? **1594** *King Leir* v. iv. 134 'Tis always known, A man may do as him list with his own. **1596** SHAKES. *M.V.* I. iii. 108 And [you do this] all for [my] use of that which is mine own. **1629** T. ADAMS *Serm.* (1861–2) II. 364 'Relieve the poor', saith the Lord: thou . . . wilt give nothing. Why, may we not do with our own what we list? **1867–77** FROUDE *Short Stud.* (1890) II. 545 These evicting gentlemen claimed the right of all men to do as they would with their own, and they turned the tenants . . . out into the roads. **1891** J. E. T. ROGERS *Ind. & Commer. Hist.* II. ii. 208 That . . . a man may not in the case of land, as the Duke of Newcastle thought, 'do what he wills with his own', is no mere antiquarian utterance.

Do what you ought, and come what can. (D 400)

1583 G. BABINGTON *Exposn. of the Commandts.* 268 Better is the warrant euer of this ought to be done, then of this is doone. *c.* **1594** BACON no. 1507 Fais que tu dois, advient que pourra. *a.* **1633** HERBERT *Priest to Temple* 270 Do well and right, and let the world sinke. **1640** HERBERT no. 818. **1721** KELLY 90 . . . Men

193 *Do | Doe*

should act upon a steady Principle of Vertue, Justice, and Honesty, not out of Fear, Interest, or Shame. [Fr. Fais ce que dois, advienne que pourra.]

Do wrong once and you'll never hear the end of it. *Cf.* Turns lie dead, Ten good. (w 943)

1609 HARWARD 123ᵛ Twise I did well and that heard I never Once I did ill and that heare I ever. **1618** D. DYKE *Philemon* Wks. 201 To hit men in the teeth with that base estate wherein once they were . . . is the common practice of many, insomuch, that the proverb is true, Once I did ill, etc.

Do(es, ne), *see also* Advice comes too late (When thing d.); Answer (To be (d.) more than he can); Causes to be d. he d. himself; Easily d. soon believed; Evil d. (Whoso will no); First as last, (As good d. it); God complains not but d. what is fitting; Have what he has not (He that would) should d. what he d. not; I d. what I can, quoth . . . when he threshed in cloak; Lawfully d. which cannot be forborne; Leave more to d. when we die; Man has d. (Whatever) man may d.; No man can d. two things at once; Pain to d. nothing than something (More); Self d., self love; Sooner begun, sooner d.; Sport is to d. deed and say nothing; Thing that's d. is not to d.; Thou thyself canst d. it (If); Want a thing d. (If you); Well d. is twice d.; Well is that well d.

Dock to a daisy, As like as a. (D 420)

1621 ROBINSON 13 An odious comparison, a Docke to a Dazie. **1639** CLARKE 96. **1670** RAY 204 . . . That is very unlike. **1823** GALT *Entail* ch. 65 Will ye compare a docken till a tansie?

Dock, *see also* In d., out nettle.

Dockyard stroke, *see* Work with d. s.

Doctor cures, If the | the sun sees it; but if he kills, the earth hides it. (D 424)

1547 BALDWIN *Treatise Moral Philosophy* (1550) D 6 [Anacharsis] to a paynter that was become a physician . . . sayd: The faultes that thou madest before in thy workes might sone bee espyed, but them that thou makest nowe, are hyd under the yearthe. **1579** 17 July T. WOTTON *Lett. Bk.* 29 Yf where ye wolde and sholde cure, (for lacke of Skyll), ye kyll,—towarde the partys that sufferethe yt—remedye ys ther none. By the partye that dothe yt (howe great soever he be), just recompence can be made none. The untimely practice of Lawyers and Phisitians seemethe to be the cause that this Realme hathe fewe good Lawyers and fewer good Phisitians. **1595** A. COPLEY *Wits, Fits, and Fancies* (1614) C2ᵛ The faultes you made before (when a painter) might easily be seene, but those you commit now (you arc a physician) are hidden under the earth. **1597** *Politeuphuia* 161 Nicocles called Phisitions happy men, because the sun made manifest what good successe so euer happened in their cures, and the earth buried what fault soeuer they committed. **1603** MONTAIGNE (Florio) II. xxxvii. 356

(as 1597). **1623** WEBSTER *Devil's Law Case* II. iii. You that dwell neere these graves and vaults, Which oft doe hide Physicians faults. *a.* **1626** SIR J. DAVIES *Yet other twelve Wonders* The earth my faults doth hide, the world my cures doth see. **1642** TORRIANO 55 Physicians errours are covered over with earth, and rich mens errours with moneyes. **1721** KELLY 184 . . . Spoken to dissuade ignorant People from Quacking, because they cannot kill with License, as Doctors may.

Doctor Doddypoll[1]. (D 429)

c. **1410** *Towneley Plays* E.E.T.S. 173 Ffy, dottypols, with your bookys! *c.* **1510** *Hyckescorner* 695 What, mayster doctour Dotypoll, Can you not preche well in a blacke boll, Or dispute ony dyvynyte? **1562** J. WIGAND *De Neutralibus* M2 It is their bely that maketh them . . . such dottie Polles. **1659** HOWELL *Eng. Prov.* 17b. [1 a blockhead.]

Doctor is often more to be feared than the disease, The. (P 267a)

1615 *Janua Linguarum* tr. W. Welde 15 A prattling Physician is more troublesome then the disease. **1621** BURTON *Anat. Mel.* II. iv. I. i (1651) 364 As he said of Adrian, . . . a multitude of physicians hath killed the emperour; *Plus a medico quam a morbo periculi;* more danger there is from the physician, than from the disease. **1660** W. SECKER *Nonsuch Prof.* II. (1891) 257 Most that perish, it is not their disease which kills them but their physician. They think to cure themselves, and this leaves them incurable. **1861** READE *Cloist. & Hearth*, ch. 73 Paupers got sick and got well as Nature pleased; but woe betided the rich in an age when, for one Mr. Malady killed three fell by Dr. Remedy.

Doctor, One | makes work for another.

1902–4 LEAN IV. 73.

Doctor's opinion, That is but one. (D 426)

c. **1552** *Manifest Detection of Dice-play* (Percy Soc., 14). **1578** THOS. WHITE *Sermon at Paul's Cross* 3 Nov. 1577, 32 You will say . . . it is but one doctours opinion. **1592** GREENE *Quip* Gros. xi. 291 The Doctors doubt of that, quoth Clothbreeches for I am of a different opinion. **1600–1** SHAKES. *M.W.W.* V. v. 167 Doctors doubt that. **1659** HOWELL *Eng. Prov.* 17b. **1721** KELLY 335 . . . Spoken with Resentment to them that offer their Advice contrary to our Interest.

Doctor(s), *see also* After death the d.; Broken apothecary, new d.; Dasnell dawcock sits among d.; Death defies d.; Scoggin is a d.; Sun enters (Where), d. does not. *See also* Physician.

Dodkin (Doit), Not worth a. (D 430)

1594 LYLY *Mother B.* II. ii. 28 **1605–8** SHAKES. *T.Ath.* I. i. 214 Plain-dealing which will not cost a man a doit. *c.* **1609** J. HEALEY (tr. J. HALL) *Discovery of a New World* (Huntington Brown) 25 Not worth a doit. **1660** BEAUM. & FL. *Faithful Friends* IV. v. If my trade then prove not worth a dodkin.

Doe, *see* John D.; Trip like a d.

Doers, *see* Ill d. ill deemers; Talkers (Greatest) least d.

Does evil, He that | never weens good.
(E 199)

c. 1386 CHAUCER *Reeve's T.* l. 4320 Him thar nat wene wel that yvel dooth. 1492 *Dial. of Salomon & Marcolphus* ed. Duff 9 He that doth euyll and hopyth good, is disceyued in thaym bothe. 1641 FERGUSSON no. 337.

Does ill, He that | hates the light.
(I 26)

[JOHN iii. 20 For every one that doeth evil hateth the light.] *c.* 1250 *Owl & Nightingale* l. 229 Vor everich thing that schuniet right Het luveth thuster and hatiet light. 1509 BARCLAY *Ship of Fools* i. 297 For often all yll doers hatyth the day lyght. 1629 *Bk. Mer. Rid.* Prov. no. 77. 1641 FERGUSSON no. 310.

Does most at once, He that | does least.
1707 MAPLETOFT 42.

Does no good, He who | does evil enough.

1616 T. ADAMS *Divine Herbal* 41 That man doth ill, that doth nothing; and he looseth, whiles hee gaines not. 1853 TRENCH vi. 147 The world's confession that he who hides his talent is guilty . . . utters itself in the following proverb: . . .

Does nothing, He that | does ever amiss.
(N 265)

1629 *Bk. Mer. Rid.* Prov. no. 75. 1865 Lancs. Prov. in *N. & Q.* 3rd Ser. VIII. 494 Those who are doing nothing are doing ill.

Does you an ill turn, He that | will never forgive you.

1721 KELLY 169 . . . The Sense and Conscience of his Injustice, or Unkindness, will make him still jealous of you, and so hate you.

Does well, He that | wearies not himself.
(D 413)

1616 DRAXE no. 355. 1663 F. HAWKINS *Youth's Behaviour* F8. 1670 RAY 28.

Does what he should not, He that | shall feel what he would not.
(D 412)

1578 FLORIO *First F.* 26 Who doth that he ought not, chanseth hym he thinks not. 1592 DELAMOTHE 45 (finde). 1629 *Bk. Mer. Rid.* Prov. no. 13 He that doth not that which he ought that haps to him which he neuer thought. 1640 HERBERT no. 783.

Does what he will, He that | does not what he ought.
(D 414)

1640 HERBERT no. 350. 1747–8 RICHARDSON *Clar. Harlowe* iv. let. 24 He who does what he will seldom does what he ought.

Dog at it, To be (old).
(D 506)

1590 NASHE *An Almond for a Parrot* iii. 351 Oh, he is olde dogge at expounding, and deade sure at a Catechisme. 1596 LODGE *Wit's Misery* F1 He is dog at recognisances and statutes. 1594 SHAKES. *T.G.V.* IV. iv. 14 To be, as it were, a dog at all things. 1601 *Id. T.N.* II. iii. 60 I am dog at a catch. 1602 *How a Man May Choose* Hazl.-Dods. ix. 28 (old dog at). 1699 B. E. s.v. Old Old-dog-at-it, good or expert.

Dog at the Nile, Like a.

[ERASM. *Ad. Ut canis e Nilo. i.e.* lapping as they run for fear of crocodiles.] 1580 LYLY *Euph. & his Eng.* ii. 56. Wine should be taken as the Dogs of Egypt drinke water, by snatches. 1606 MARSTON *Sophonisba* I'le . . . trust her as our dogs drinke dangerous Nile. 1791 I. DISRAELI *Curios. Lit.* (1858) I. 11 He[1] read many of these, but not with equal attention—'Sicut canis ad Nilum, bibens et fugiens;' like a dog at the Nile, drinking and running. *a.* 1884 PATTISON *Essay on F. A. Wolf* Hayne said of himself that he prelected 'as a dog drinks from the Nile'. [[1] D. Ancillon 1617–92.]

Dog bark, If the old | he gives counsel.
(D 484)

[L. *Prospectandum vetulo latrante.* When the old dog barks it is time to look out.] 1640 HERBERT no. 197. 1885 E. P. HOOD *World of Prov. & Par.* 229 Some scamp of a fellow . . . might learn something . . . from another old proverb, . . .

Dog (wolf) barks in vain at the moon, The.
(D 449)

1520 WHITTINGTON *Vulgaria* 72 They playe as the dogge doeth that barketh at the moone all nyght. 1551 CRANMER *Ans. to Gardiner* 73 Dogges barke at the moone without any cause. 1580 LYLY *Euph. & his Eng.* ii. 90 As lykely to obtain thy wish, as the Wolfe is to catch the Moone. 1595 SHAKES. *M.N.D.* V. i. 361 The wolf behowls the moon. 1599 *Id. J.C.* IV. iii. 27 I had rather be a dog and bay the moon Than such a Roman. 1630 MASSINGER *Picture* (1813) I. ii. 138 The wolf But barks against the moon, and I contemn it.

Dog bites the stone, not him that throws it, The.

1546 W. HUGH *Troub. Man's Med.* (1831) 5 I would not have thee . . . [ascribe] worldly miseries to the stars, to fate and fortune; playing therein the part of the dog, which bites the stone that is hurled at him . . . ; but rather imitate . . . David, who blamed not Shimei . . . but imputed his despite unto the Lord. 1580 LYLY *Euph. & his Eng.* ii. 11 They . . . wil[l] not stick to teare Euphues, bicause they do enuie Lyly: Wherein they resemble angry Dogges, which byte the stone, not him that throweth it.

Dog (etc.) does not eat dog (etc.).
(W 606)

1534 POLYDORE VERGIL on the barons rallying to young Henry III Canis caninam non est [= edit]. 1543 W. TURNER *Hunting of the Romish Fox* A2ᵛ The prouerbe . . . one dog will not eat of an other dogges flesh. **1576** PETTIE ii. 81 Wolves neuer prey upon wolves. **1598–9** SHAKES. *M.A.* III. ii. 70 The two bears will not bite one another when they meet. **1602** *Id. T.C.* V. vii. 19 One bear will not bite another, and wherefore should one bastard? *a.* **1603** G. FENTON cited R. L. Douglas in *Tragical Discourses* (1890), xxxviii Dogs will not eat dogs' flesh. **1651** HERBERT no. 1125 A wolfe will never make war against another wolfe. **1659** TORRIANO no. 45 One wolfe devours not another. **1790** WOLCOT (P. Pindar) *Comp. Epist. to Bruce* Wks. (1816) II. 171 Dog should not prey on dog, the proverb says. **1866** KINGSLEY *Hereward* ch. 30 . . . and it is hard to be robbed by an Englishman, after being robbed a dozen times by the French.

Dog doff his doublet, It would make a.

(D 490)

1678 RAY 239. *Chesh.*

Dog for your friend, and in your other hand a stick, Keep a.

c. **1192** W. MAP *De Nugis Curialium* Dist. v, cap. iv, Prouerbium Anglicum de seruis est, Haue hund to godsib, ant stent[1] in thir oder hond, quod est, Canem suspice compatrem, et altera manu baculum. [[1] stick.]

Dog (Hound) gnaws bone, While the | companions would he none. (D 518)

[Med. L. *Dum canis os rodit, sociari pluribus odit.* *Li Proverbe au Vilain* (Tobler) no. 10 Chiens en cuisine son per n'i desire.] *c.* **1225** *Trin. MS. O.* 11. 45 (ed. Förster) in *Eng. Stud.* **31.** 8 Wil ðe hund gnagþ bon, ifere nele he non. Dum canis os rodit, sociari pluribus odit. *c.* **1470** *Harl. MS. 3362* in *Anglia* 42. 202 Whyl þe dogge gnaweth [bone, companion wold he haue non]. *Dum canis os rodit, sociari pluribus odit.* **1584** WITHALS C3 Whiles a dogge gnawes a bone, he hateth his fellow, whom otherwise he loues.

Dog has his (a) day, A (Every).

(D 464)

[*a.* **1525–9**] **1561** *Godly Qu. Hester* l. 636 A prouerbe as men say a dogge hath a day. **1545** TAVERNER H7 A dogge hath a day. **1546** HEYWOOD I. xi. D4 A dog hath a daie. **1550** Q. ELIZ. in STRYPE *Eccl. Mem.* II. xxviii. 234 Notwithstanding, as a dog hath a day, so may I perchance have time to declare it in deeds. **1600** DEKKER *Old Fort.* II. ii. 195 Theres nothing impossible: a dog has his day, and so haue you. **1600–1** SHAKES. *H.* V. i. 286 The cat will mew, and dog will have his day. **1633** JONSON *T. Tub* II. i. 4 A man ha' his houre, and a dog his day. **1670** RAY 80. **1726** POPE *Od.* xxii. 41 Dogs, ye have had your day. **1837** CARLYLE *Fr. Rev.* III. I. i How changed for Marat, lifted from his dark cellar. . . ! All dogs have their day; even rabid dogs. **1851** BORROW *Lavengro* iii. 291 Every dog has his day, and mine has been a fine one.

Dog in a doublet, A. (D 452)

c. **1549** ERASM. *Two' Dial.'* tr. E. Becke f4 This is a dogge in a doblet, a sowe with a sadle, of all that euer I se it is a non decet. **1577** HARRISON *Desc. Eng.* New Sh. S. 1. 168 Except it were

a dog in a doublet, you shall not see anie so disguised, as are my countrie men of England. **1577** GRANGE *Gold. Aphroditis* F1 As seemely as . . . a dogge in a dublet. **1581** C. THIMELTHORPE *Short Inventory I* 3 As good a sight as to see a curre dogge in a satten doublet. **1600** DEKKER *Shoem. Hol.* II. iii. 99 My maister wil be as proud as a dogge in a dublet. **1620** SHELTON *Quix.* Pt. II. i. iii. 173 'And what care I', quoth Sanchica, 'what he says that sees me stately and majestical? "There's a dog in a doublet", and such-like.' **1659** HOWELL *Eng. Prov.* 1b A dogg in a dublett, bitch in a baskett. **1778** BOSWELL *Johnson* lxvi (1848) 607 'I think it is a new thought . . . in a new attitude.' . . .—'It is the old dog in the new doublet.'

Dog in a fair: Like a | here, there, and everywhere. (D 494)

c. **1540?** SKELTON ed. Dyce *Poems attrib.* ii. 445 Ye come among vs plenty By coples in a peire, As sprites in the heire, Or dogges in the ffayre. **1840** BARHAM *Ingoldsby Legends* 'Jackdaw of Rheims' That little jackdaw kept hopping about; Here and there Like a dog in a fair.

Dog in the manger, Like a. (D 513)

[LUCIAN *Tim.* 14 ἡ ἐν τῇ φάτνῃ κύων. In allusion to Aesop's fable.] *c.* **1390** GOWER *Conf. Amantis* II. 84 Thogh it be noght the houndes Kinde to ete chaf, yit wol he werne An Oxe which comth to the berne, Therof to taken eny fode. **1559** J. FERRARIUS *Good Ordering of a Commonwealth* tr. W. Bavande 17 Lucians Dogge . . . liyng in the maunger, neither would eate oates hymself, ne yet suffer the horses ones to laie their lippes on theim. **1564** BULLEYN *Dial. agst. Fever* (1888) 9 Like vnto cruell Dogges liyng in a Maunger, neither eatyng the Haye theim selues ne sufferyng the Horse to feed thereof hymself. **16.** . CHAPMAN (?) *Charlemagne* III. i. 271 Have ye not hearde of Aesopp's dog, that once lay snarling in the oxes maunger? **1621** BURTON *Anat. Mel.* I. ii. III. xii (1651) 115 Like a . . . dog in the manger, he doth only keep it, because it shall do nobody else good, hurting himself and others. **1706** STEVENS s.v. Escaño.

Dog in the morning, A | sailor take warning; a dog in the night is the sailor's delight.

1883 ROPER 6 . . . (A sun-dog in nautical language is a small rainbow near the horizon.)

Dog in the well, There is a. (D 504)

1641 FERGUSSON no. 849. **1721** KELLY 305 . . . There is something amiss.

Dog is a lion at home, Every. (D 465)

1659 N. R. 29. **1659** TORRIANO no. 220. **1666** TORRIANO *It. Prov.* 36 no. 33.

Dog is allowed his first bite, Every.

1902–4 LEAN I. 439 . . . i.e. is not punished. **1913** *Spectator* 15 Mar. 440 Every dog is allowed by the law one free bite.

Dog is drowning, When a | every one offers him drink. (D 516)

1611 COTGRAVE s.v. Chien. **1640** HERBERT no. 77.

Dog is hanged for his skin, Many a | and many a man is killed for his purse.

(D 497)

1626 BRETON *Soothing* B4.   **1639** CLARKE 97.

Dog is made fat in two meals, A.

1863 WISE *New Forest* xvi (1895) 180 ... is applied to upstart or purse-proud people.

Dog is valiant at his own door, Every.

(D 465)

1568 TILNEY *Duties in Marriage* D8ᵛ ˙Dogs barke boldely at their owne maisters doore.   **1666** TORRIANO *It. Prov.* 127 no. 14 Every dog is stout upon his own dunghill.

Dog (man) of wax, A.   (D 453)

c. **1595** SHAKES. *R.J.* I. iii. 75 A man, young lady! lady, such a man As all the world—why, he's a man of wax.   [**1599**] **1600** MUNDAY *et al. Oldcastle* II. ii. 32 (dogge).   **1607** G. WILKINS *Miseries Enf. Marr.* B3 But me a Dog of wax, come kisse, and agree.   **1640** JONSON *Tale Tub* II. ii. 62 You'll clap a dog of waxe as soone, old Blurt?

Dog, The hindmost (foremost) | may catch (catches) the hare.   (D 480)

1580 LYLY *Euph. & his Eng.* ii. 178 The last dogge oftentimes catcheth the Hare, though the fleetest turne him.   **1635** QUARLES *Div. Emb.* IV. iv. Be wisely patient; . . . The hindmost hound oft takes the doubling hare.   **1659** HOWELL *Eng. Prov.* 16a The hindmost hound may catch the hare.   **1662** FULLER *Derb.* 234 As the last Dog most commonly catcheth the Hare which other Dogs have turned and tired before; so such who succeed in dangerous and difficult enterprises, generally reap the benefit of the adventures of those who went before them.   **1664** CODRINGTON 212 (foremost).   **1670** RAY 10 The foremost dog catcheth the hare.   **1721** KELLY 306 The foremost hound grips the hare. Recommending Diligence, and Industry.

Dog returns to his vomit, The.

(D 455)

[2 PETER ii. 22.]   *c.* **1400** *Rom. Rose* C. 7285 He is the hound, . . . That to his castyng goth ageyn.   **1534** TYNDALE *2 Peter* ii. 22 It is happened vnto them according to the true proverbe: The dogge is turned to his vomet agayne.   **1575** GASCOIGNE ii. 5.   **1580** LYLY *Euph. & his Eng.* ii. 92 With what face Euphues canst thou returne to thy vomit, seeming with the greedy hounde to lap vp that which thou diddest cast vp.   **1598** SHAKES. *2 Hen. IV* I. iii. 99 Thou common dog . . . now thou wouldst eat thy dead vomit up.   **1599** *Id. Hen. V* III. vii. 63 Le chien est retourné à son propre vomissement.   **1832–8** S. WARREN *Diary of Late P.* ch. 22 His infatuated wife betook herself—'like the dog to his vomit . . .'—to her former . . . extravagance and dissipation.

Dog that fetches, will carry, The.

1830 FORBY 429 . . . *I.e.* A talebearer will tell tales *of* you, as well as *to* you.

Dog that has lost his tail, To look like a.

(D 511)

1573 G. HARVEY *Letter-Bk.* 42 (He . . . looketh like).   **1583** MELBANCKE *Philotimus* D3 (To go like).   **1639** CLARKE 259 (He loundge's as).   **1678** RAY 286.

Dog that is idle barks at his fleas, The | but he that is hunting feels them not.

1894 DEAN HOLE *More Mem.* ch. 11 Honest work is the best cure for all the ills that flesh is heir to, because, according to the Chinese proverb, . . .

Dog that licks ashes trust not with meal, The.   (D 457)

1640 HERBERT no. 389.

Dog that trots about, The | finds a bone.

1843 BORROW *Bible in Sp.* ch. 47 (As the gipsies say).

Dog to bite him, A man may cause his own.   (M 258)

1550 HEYWOOD II. vii. E8 A man maie handle his dog so, That he may make him bite him, though he wold not.   **1670** RAY 7.   **1710** PALMER 335.

Dog to follow you, If you would wish the | feed him.   (D 485)

1611 COTGRAVE s.v. Chien He that will haue a good dog must feed him well; he that desires a good seruant must vse him well.   **1659** HOWELL *Span. Prov.* 17.   **1706** STEVENS s.v. Can If you would have the Dog follow you give him Bread.

Dog under a door, He looks like a.

(D 475)

1530 PALSGRAVE 551b The knave fleareth lyke a dogge under a doore.   *Ibid.* 575a He grynneth lyke a dogge under a doore.   **1678** RAY 70.

Dog who hunts foulest, hits at most faults, The.   (D 460)

1659 HOWELL *Eng. Prov.* 1b.   **1732** FULLER no. 1318 Dogs, that hunt foulest, hit off most Faults.

Dog will bark ere he bite, A.   (D 461)

c. **1549** HEYWOOD II. vii. K1 A dog will barke er he bite, and so thow, After thy barkying wilt bit me.

Dog will not howl if you beat him with a bone, A.   (D 463)

1659 HOWELL *Brit. Prov.* 24 The dog will not bite, for being struck with a Bone.   **1721** KELLY 42 . . . People will bear easily some rough usage, . . . if they see their Advantage in it.   **1826** SCOTT *Woodst.* ch. 20 'I can bide the bit and the buffet, . . . a hungry tyke ne'er minds a blaud with a rough bane.'

Dog worry my uncle, If I do.

1847 HALLIWELL *Dict.* s.v. Dog (1889) I. 308 . . .
a phrase implying refusal on being asked to do
anything contrary to one's wishes.

**Dog's bark, At every | seem not to
awake.** (D 525)

c. **1532** SIR ADRIAN FORTESCUE no. 56 At every
dogge that barkes, one ought not to be anoyd.
1550 HEYWOOD II. v. H2 For little more or lesse
no debate make, At euery dogs barke, seeme
not to awake.

**Dog's dead since you were a whelp,
Many a.**

1721 KELLY 255. **1732** FULLER no. 3336.

Dog's life, hunger and ease, A.

(D 521)

1542 ERASM. tr. Udall (1877, 142) The most
parte of folkes calleth it a miserable life, or a
dogges life, that is . . . in present daunger of . . .
sicknesse or diseases. *c.* **1570** *Marr. Wit and
Science* IV. i. C3 A life wythall my hart I would
not wyshe a dogge. **1607** TOMKIS *Lingua* II. iv.
D4 Here's a Dogges life. **1666** TORRIANO *It.
Prov.* 276 note 157 The English say, Hunger and
ease is a Dogs life. **1670** RAY 172. **1721** KELLY
18 A dog's Life, mickle Hunger, mickle Ease.
Apply'd to careless, lazy Lubbers, who will not
work, and therefore have many a hungry Meal.
1913 KIPLING 'The Village that Voted' Politics
is a dog's life without a dog's decencies.

**Dog's nose and a maid's knees are
always cold, A.** (D 522)

1639 CLARKE 72 A dog's nose is ever cold. **1670**
RAY 51.

Dog's tail, *see* Cut off a d. t.

Dog's trick, That is a. (D 546)

c. **1540** POLYDORE VERGIL *Eng. Hist.* (trans.
Camden Soc.), viii. 284 I will heere, in the way
of mirthe, declare a prettie dog tricke or gibe as
concerninge this mayden. **1639** *Oxinden Letters*
1607–42 ed. D. Gardiner 160 Her dogge tricke
to bee most busie and present when frends are
most in adversitie. **1678** RAY 344. **1699** B. E.
s.v. Dog'd He play'd me a Dog-trick, he did
basely and dirtily by me.

Dogged that does it, It is.

1867 TROLLOPE *Last Chron. Barset* ch. 61. Mr.
Crawley . . . repeated . . . Giles Hoggett's words.
'It's dogged as does it. It's not thinking about
it.' **1877** J. R. GREEN *Lett.* to Miss Stopford 30
Mar. I found that 'dogged does it' had got into
my blood, and I knuckled to at my work with
a resolve to get it done.

Dogs are fine in the field. (D 529)

1640 HERBERT no. 941.

Dogs bark as they are bred.

1721 KELLY 84 . . . Spoken when People, vilely
educated, behave themselves accordingly. **1732**
FULLER no. 1313.

**Dogs bark, but the caravan goes on,
The.**

1930 *Times* 4 July 17/4 I was struggling to explain the situation to an old Moor. . . . After
thinking it over he murmured: . . .

**Dogs bark not (No dogs shall bark) at
him, All.** (D 526)

1540 PALSGRAVE *Acolastus* 79 There shall no
dogges barke at myne ententes. **1546** HEYWOOD
II. v. H3ᵛ All dogs barke not at hym. **1584** R.
WILSON *Three Ladies of London* Hazl.-Dods. vi.
336 All the dogs in the town shall not bark at your
doings. **1589** T. COOPER *Admon. People Eng.* E3
If he shall by any cunning bee able to pull away
the reward of learning, hee right well seeth that
hee shall farre fewer dogges to barke at
him. **1595** SHAKES. *M.V.* I. i. 94 When I ope my
lips let no dogs bark. **1605** S. ROWLEY *When
You See Me* l. 1071 All the Dogges in the towne
must not barke at it. **1650** T. FULLER *Pisgah-
sight* 409 No dog durst bark against him.

**Dogs (Fools) begin in jest and end in
earnest.** (D 532)

1612–15 BP. HALL *Contempl.* x. iii (1825) I. 269
As fools and dogs use to begin in jest, and end
in earnest, so did these Philistines. **1659** N. R.
27.

Dogs bite, In every country. (C 709)

1640 HERBERT no. 620. **1666** TORRIANO *It. Prov.*
36, no. 19.

**Dogs gnaw bones because they cannot
swallow them.** (D 451)

1640 HERBERT no. 457 The dog gnaws the bone
because he cannot swallow it. **1670** RAY 7.

Dogs in dough, Like.

1894 NORTHALL *Folk-phrases* 19 . . . *i.e.* unable
to make headway.

Dogs run away with whole shoulders.

(D 534)

1622 WITHER *Christm. Car.* Poems (1891) 121
Rank misers now do sparing shun, . . . And dogs
thence with whole shoulders run. **1670** RAY 172
. . . Not of mutton, but their own, spoken in
derision of a miser's house.

**Dogs that bark at a distance bite not at
hand.** (D 531)

1592 DELAMOTHE 5 A dogge that barkes farre
of, dares not come neare to bite. **1611** DAVIES
no. 28. **1623** CAMDEN 268 Dogges barking
aloofe, bite not at hand. **1670** RAY 59.

Dogs that put up many hares kill none.

1732 FULLER no. 1319.

**Dogs wag their tails not so much in
love to you as to your bread.** (D 459)

1611 COTGRAVE s.v. Amour Dogs fawne on a
man no longer then he feeds them. **1666**

TORRIANO *It. Prov.* 36 no. 27 A dog wags not his tail for thee, but for the bread. **1706** STEVENS s.v. Cola (not for your sake, but for the bread).

Dogs, Like | when one barks all bark.
(D 539)

[L. *Latrante uno, latrat statim et alter canis.*] **1612** WEBSTER *White Devil* v. iii. Merm. 99 That old dog-fox, that politician, Florence! . . . I'll be friends with him; for, mark you, sir, one dog Still sets another a-barking. *c.* **1612** SHAKES. *Hen. VIII* II. iv. 159 Village curs, Bark when their fellows do. **1639** CLARKE 148. **1732** FULLER no. 3736 One barking Dog, sets all the Street a barking.

Dogs will redd[1] swine.
(D 535)

a. **1628** CARMICHAELL no. 451. **1641** FERGUSSON no. 238. **1721** KELLY 85 . . . A third Opposite will make two contending Parties agree. [[1] to put in order; to part combatants.]

Dog(s), *see* Bad d. (Into mouth of) falls good bone; Bad d. never sees wolf; Bark ourselves ere we buy d. so dear (We will); Barking d. seldom bite; Beat the d. before lion; Best d. leap stile first; Better to have d. fawn than bite; Beware of silent d.; Black d. on one's back (To have); Blush like a black d.; Brag is a good d.; Bread than need (Who has no more) must not keep d.; Butter in the black d.'s hause (Like); Cat and d. may kiss; Curst cur (d.) tied short; Cut off a d.'s tail, will be d. still; Dead d. bark not; Die a d.'s death; Dry as a d.; Eat a pudding . . . d. shall have skin; Everybody's d. that whistles; Expect a good whelp from an ill d.; Fashion's sake, as d. go to church; Fast as a d. can trot (*or* will lick); Fells two d. with one stone; Fiddlers, d., and flies come uncalled; Fight d., fight bear; Flesh stands never so high but d. will venture; Folk's d. bark worse than themselves; Folly is a bonny d.; Gardener's d. that neither eats cabbages; Give a child while . . . and a d. while tail wave; Give a d. an ill name; Give his bone to the d. (He will not); Go to the d.; Good d. deserves good bone; Good d. who goes to church; Hair of d. that bit you; Hang a d. on a crab-tree; Hang his d. (He that would); Help the d. over stile; Horse (d.) laugh, (Enough to make a); Hungry as a d.; Hungry d. will eat dirty puddings; Hunt's (Wood's) d. that will neither go to church; Illbred d. that beat bitch; Ill d. that deserves not crust; Keep a d. and bark myself; Keeps another man's d. (He that); Kennel is lodging good enough for a d.; Knit my d. a pair of breeches; Knows not a pig from a d.; Lazy as Ludlam's d.; Lean d. for hard road; Lean d. to get through hedge; Lies down with d. rises with fleas; Little d. have long tails; Little d. start the hare; Living d. better than dead lion; Love me love my d.; Mad d. bites his master; Make a hog or a d. of it; Man has his hour and d. his day; Many d. worry one hare; Melancholy as a d.; Miller's d.; Moon does not heed barking of d.; Never d. barked against crucifix but . . . ; Never was cat or d. drowned that could . . . ; Old d. barks; Old d. bites; One d. one bull; Open doors d. come in; Poor d. that

doesn't know 'Come out'; Poor d. that is not worth whistling; Proud as a d. with two tails; Quarrelling d.; Quarrelsome d.; Scalded cat (d.) fears cold water; Scarce of horseflesh where two ride a d.; Scorn a thing as a d. tripe; Scratching and biting cats and d. come together; Sirrah your d., not me; Sleeping d. lie (Let); Sleeps as d. when wives sift meal; Smith's d. that sleeps at sound of hammer; Staff (Stick) to beat d.; Straw to his d., bones to ass; Strikes my d. (He that) would strike me; Taking wall of a d.; Talk as Dutch as Daimport's d.; Teach an old d. tricks; Thieves (All are not) that d. bark at; Three things cost, caresses of d.; Thrift of you and wool of d.; Throw that bone to another d.; Toiling d. comes halting; Toils like a d. in a wheel; Too much pudding will choke d.; Trust not horse's heel nor d.'s tooth; Trust to d. (While you), wolf in sheepfold; Two cats . . . two d. and a bone never agree; Two d. strive for bone, third runs away with it; Use one like a d.; Vex a d. to see pudding creep; Want a pretence to whip a d. (If you); Ways to kill d. than hanging (More); Wolf for his mate (Who has) needs d. for his man; Women and d. set men by the ears; Word to throw at a d.; Worst d. that is wags tail.

Doing nothing we learn to do ill, By.
(D 547)

[CATO MAJOR *Nilne agendo homines male agere discunt.*] **1531** ELYOT *Governor* ed. Croft i. 270 In doing nothinge men lerne to do iuel. **1567** FENTON *Bandello* T.T. ii. 63 Plato, who affirmeth that in doynge nothyng men lerne to do evill. **1640** HERBERT no. 757.

Doing we learn, In.
(D 548)

[SENECA *Epist.* 98. 17.] **1589** NASHE *Anat. of Absurd.* i. 43 Quid faciendum sit, a faciente discendum est. **1640** HERBERT no. 803.

Doing(s), *see also* Great d. at Gregory's; Saying and d. are two things; Saying is one thing, d. another; Shortest answer is d.; Worth d. at all worth d. well.

Doit, *see* Dodkin (D.).

Dolbury Hill, *see* Cadbury Castle.

Dole, *see* Happy man; Scrambling at a rich man's d.

Dominy(-ies), *see* Mickle to do when d. ride; Pigeons and priests (Doves and d.) make foul houses.

Doncaster daggers, *see* Dunmow bacon.

Done, Lady, *see* Fair as L. D.

Done at any time, What may be | will be done at no time.
1721 KELLY 355.

Done by night appears by day, What is.
(N 179)

c. 1390 GOWER *Conf. Amantis* v. l. 4597 Thing
don upon the derke nyht I after knowe on daies
liht. 1593–4 SHAKES. *Lucr.* l. 747 Day . . .
night's scapes doth open lay. 1666 TORRIANO
It. Prov. 263 no. 2 That which is done in the
dark, appears in the sun-shine. 1706 STEVENS
s.v. Noche.

Done cannot be undone, Things. *Cf.*
Past cannot be recalled, (Things).
(T 200)

c. 1460 *The Gode Wyfe wold a Pylgremage*
E.E.T.S. I. 119 When dede is doun, hit ys to late.
1541 N. UDALL Letter to Sir T. Wriothesley
(*Roister Doister* ed. Scheurweghs xxxii) If ye
possibly maye to forget that is past and cannot
nowe bee again vndone. 1546 HEYWOOD I. x. C4.
1548 HALL 575. *c.* 1590 SHAKES. *T.And.* IV. ii.
73 Villain, what hast thou done? — That which
thou canst not undo. [1592] 1597 *Id. Rich. III*
IV. iv. 292 Look what is done cannot be now
amended. 1605–6 *Id. M.* III. ii. 12 Things
without all remedy Should be without regard:
what's done is done. *Ibid.* V. i. 65 What's done
cannot be undone. 1608 *Id. P.* IV. iii. 1–6 Why
are you foolish? Can it be undone? . . . — Were
I chief lord of all this spacious world, I'd give it
to undo the deed. 1632 MASSINGER *City Madam*
v. iii. I care not where I go: what's done, with
words Cannot be undone. 1818 MISS FERRIER
Marriage ch. 67 I hope you will think twice
about it. Second thoughts are best. . . .

Done ill once, He that has | will do it
again.

1707 MAPLETOFT 53.

Done no ill the six days, If you have |
you may play the seventh.

1732 FULLER no. 2757.

Done twice, If things were to be | all
would be wise. (T 185)

1640 HERBERT no. 700. 1659 HOWELL *Span.
Prov.* 18.

Done, *see also* Do(es).

Donkey between two bundles of hay,
Like a.

[Known as Buridan's ass, but not to be found in
his works.] *a.* 1763 BYROM *Fight bet. Figg &
Sutton* Dame Victory . . . remain'd like the ass
'twixt two bottles of hay, Without ever moving
an inch either way. 1824 MOIR *Mansie W.* ch.
25 I swithered,[1] and was like the cuddie[2] between the two bundles of hay. 1850 KINGSLEY
Alton Locke ch. 27 You've been off and on
lately between flunkeydom and The Cause, like
a donkey between two bundles of hay. 1886
E. J. HARDY *How to be Happy* ch. 2 Some men
. . . have almost died of indecision, like the donkey between two exactly similar bundles of hay.
[[1] hesitated. [2] ass.]

Donkey, *see also* Hurry no man's cattle; Talk
the hind leg off a d.; Time to cock hay when d.
blows his horn. *See also* Ass.

Doom, *see* Two dismal days, day of death and
day of d.

Doomsday we shall see whose arse is
blackest, At.

a. 1628 CARMICHAELL no. 225. *a.* 1685 BURNET
Hist. of my own Time ed. Airy ii. 300 He [Charles
II] complained with great scorn of the imputation
of subornation that was cast on himself. He
said he did not wonder that the earl of Shaftesbury, who was so guilty of those practices, should
fasten them on others; and he used upon that a
Scotch proverb very pleasantly, 'At doomsday
we shall see whose arse is blackest.' 1721 KELLY
313 (There is a Day coming that will shew)
Meaning the Day of Judgment.

Doomsday, *see also* Death's day is d.; Thousand
pounds and . . . all one at d.

Door, Here is the | and there is the way.
(D 556)

c. 1475 *Mankind* 154 Nought. Her ys the dore,
her ys the wey! 1546 HEYWOOD I. xi. D4 Nowe
here is the doore, and there is the wey, and so . . .
farewell. 1594–8 SHAKES. *T.S.* III. ii. 205 The
door is open, sir, there lies your way. 1601 *Id.
T.N.* I. v. 187 If you be not mad, be gone . . . —
Will you hoist sail, sir? Here lies your way.
1602 R. CAREW 'Excellency of Eng. Tongue'
(1769 ed. of *Survey*, 11). 1625 JONSON *Staple of
News* III. iv. 76 There lies your way, you see the
doore. 1639 CLARKE 70.

Door may be shut but death's door,
Every. (D 554)

1610 SHAKES. *Cym.* V. iv. 196 Thou shalt be then
freer than a jailer. No bolts for the dead. 1666
TORRIANO *It. Prov.* 317 no. 31. 1853 TRENCH i.
17 What is 'All men are mortal', as compared
with the proverb: . . .

Door must either be shut or open, A.

[Fr. *Il faut qu'une porte soit ouverte ou fermée.*
1691 BRUEYS ET DE PALAPRAT, *Grondeur* l. 6.]
1762 GOLDSMITH *Cit. World* li There are but the
two ways; the door must either be shut, or it
must be open. 1896 SAINTSBURY *19th Cent. Lit.*
361 Fiction . . . pleads in vain for detailed treatment. For all doors must be shut or open; and
this door must now be shut.

Door of gold, Who will make a | must
knock a nail every day.

1640 HERBERT no. 1004. 1707 MAPLETOFT 107.

Door(s), *see also* Beggar, (One) enough at a d.;
Creaking d.; Death's d.; Devil is not always at
one d.; Dog under d. (Looks like); Hatch
before the d. (Good to have); Hospitality (Sin
against) to open d., shut countenance; Love at
d., leave at hatch; Love comes in at window,
goes out at d.; One d. shuts (Where) another

opens; Open d. dogs come in; Open d. may tempt saint; Open the d. with an axe; Postern d. makes thief and whore; Servant must . . . shut the d. after him; Stoop that has low d.; Sweep before his own d. (If each); Wind in that d. *See also* Back door, Stable door.

Door-nail, *see* Dead (Deaf, Dumb) as a d.

Dorty[1] dame may fa'[2] in the dirt, The.

1832 HENDERSON 89. [[1] saucy to her suitors. [2] fall.]

Dot the i's, To.

1528 TYNDALE *Obed. Chrn. Man* 15[v] Haue . . . so narowlye loked on my translatyon, that there is not so much as one I therin if it lacke a tytle ouer his hed, but they haue noted it. **1849** THACKERAY in *Scribner's Mag.* I. 557/1 I have . . . dotted the i's. **1896** *Daily Chron.* 20 Apr. 4/7 [He] dotted our 'i's' and crossed our 't's' with a vengeance.

Dote more on it than a fool on his bauble, To.   (F 509)

1659 HOWELL *Fr. Prov.* 14 He is more besotted then a fool with his bable. **1670** RAY 172.

Double charge will rive a cannon.

a. **1628** CARMICHAELL no. 463 (charges). **1721** KELLY 86 . . . Spoken when People urge upon you more than you can bear, be it Meat, Drink, Work, or so.

Double, *see also* Holiness is d. iniquity, (Pretended); Victory, (He gets a d.) who conquers himself; Work d. tides.

Doublet, *see* Dog doff his d. (Would make); Dog in a d.; Near is my coat (d.) but nearer my shirt; Old man, when thou diest, give me d.

Doubt, When in | do nowt.

1917 BRIDGE 389 . . . This shows the cautious Cheshireman at his best.

Doubt(s), *see also* Do well and d. no man; Knows nothing, d. nothing.

Doubtful, *see* Charity construes all d. things in good part; Persuasion of fortunate sways d.

Dough, *see* Cake is d. (One's); Dogs in d., (Like).

Dove's flood is worth a king's good, In April.   (A 308)

1610 CAMDEN *Britannia* tr. Holland 587 If it chance to swel above the bankes and overflow the Medowes in April . . . the inhabitants use commonly to 'chant this joyfull note. In Aprill Doves floud, Is worth a Kings good. **1662** FULLER Staffs. 40 Dove, a River parting this and Derbyshire, when it overfloweth its Banks in April, is the *Nilus* of Staffordshire.

Dove(s), *see also* Eagles do not breed d.; Innocent as a d.; Noah's d.; Pigeons and priests (D. and dominies); Serpent than d. (To have more of).

Dovecots have most doves, Fair. *Cf.* Pigeons and priests.

[OVID *Tristia* I. ix. 7 Adspicis, ut veniant ad candida tecta columbae.] **1545** ERASM. *Precepts of Cato* tr. Burrant 'Seven Wise Men' C2 Ouid compareth suche flatterynge frendes vnto Piggions who as longe as the doufehouse is freshe and newe, they abyde and haunt there, but yf it begynne ones to wexe olde and rotten, they wyll flee way from it to another. **1580** G. HARVEY *Letters between Spenser and Harvey* (Gros. i. 89) Tyle me the Doouehouse trimly, and gallant, where the like storehouse? Fyle[1] me the Doouehouse: leaue it vnhansome, where the like poorehouse? **1589** GREENE *Menaphon* (Gros. vi. 47) Doves delight not in foule cottages. **1660** H. PETERS *Dying Father's Last Legacy* (1684 ed. 49) Fair dovecots have most pigeons. **1663** F. HAWKINS *Youth's Behaviour* F7 Ad candida tecta columbam. Doves flock to fair houses. [[1] Defile].

Dovecots, *see also* Flutter the d.

Dover court: all speakers, and no hearers.   (D 575)

1662 FULLER *Kent* 64 . . . The proverb is applyed to such irregular conferences, wherein the People are all Tongue and no Eares. **1706** STEVENS s.v. Behetrias. **1888** QUILLER-COUCH *Troy Town* ch. 19 Then for up ten minutes 'twas Dover to pay, all talkers an' no listeners.

Dover shark and a Deal savage, A.

1787 GROSE (*Kent*) 183 Dover-men have obtained the nickname of shark. The appellation of Deal savage, probably originated from the brutality and exaction of the boatmen.

Dover, *see also* Berwick to D.; Dark in D. (When it's), dark all world over; Deal, D., and Harwich, the devil gave; Jack of D.

Dowb, *see* Take care of D.

Down, He that is | down with him.   (M 194)

1530 PALSGRAVE 757a Whan a man is throwen under the foote ones, than every man gothe'upon hym. **1596** M. B. *Trial of true Frdship.* B2[v] If we are once downe, there are few that wil lend vs their hands to help vs up againe. *c.* **1632** *Pepysian Garland* (Rollins) 411 If a man be once downe, the world cryes downe with him still. **1639** CLARKE 68 If a man once fall, all will tread on him. **1678** RAY 129. **1721** KELLY 199 If a Man be once down, down with him. If Fortune frown upon a Man, his Friends will lessen, and his Enemies multiply. **1910** JOYCE *Eng. as We Speak* 109 'When a man is down, down with him': a bitter allusion to the tendency of the world to trample down the unfortunate and helpless.

Down the wind, To go.   (w 432)

[*c. 1597*] **1609** JONSON *Case is Altered* IV. v. 6
[For I goe downe the wind, and yet I puffe.   **1600**
N. BRETON *Pasquils Passe and Passeth not* Wks.
(Gros.) I. 11   Want and vertue must go downe
the wind.   **1601** CHETTLE & MUNDAY *Downfall of
Earl of Huntington* Hazl.-Dods. viii. 140   He is
down the wind, as all such shall. That revel,
waste and spend, and take no care.   **1604**
SHAKES. *O.* III. iii. 264   If I do prove her haggard
. . . I'ld whistle her off and let her down the wind
To prey at fortune.   **1613** FLETCHER etc.
Honest Man's Fortune II. iv. 34.   **1663** PEPYS
Diary 25 Jan.   So that I perceive he goes down
the wind in honor as well as every thing else,
every day.   **1706** STEVENS s.v. Capa   To go
down the Wind, to decline.

Down, *see also* Fallen (He that is) cannot help
him that is d.; First up, last d.; Haste when you
come d.; Hit a man when he is d.; Nought lay
d., nought take up.

Downs, *see* Ups and d., (To have many).

Downham, *see* Rising was, Lynn is.

Down hill, *see* Bowl d. h. (Easy to).

**Dowry is a bed full of brambles, A
great.**   (D 577)

1640 HERBERT no. 758.   **1659** HOWELL *Span.
Prov.* 18 (brabbles).

Dozen, *see* Thirteen of you may go to d.;
Tongue runs nineteen to d.

Drabbing, *see* Dicing, d. and drinking bring men
to destruction.

Draff[1] is good enough for swine. (D 580)

a. **1529** *Gentlenes & Nobility* l. 943   Thou sayst
trew, drafe is good Inough for swyne.   *c.* **1566**
CURIO *Pasquin in a Trance* tr. W.P. 65ᵛ   Draffe
good enough for Hogges.   **1614** TAYLOR (Water-
P.) *Nipping of Abuses* B4 (A Prouerb old) draffs
good enough for hogges.   **1623** CAMDEN 268.
1670   RAY 82.   **1721** KELLY 85   . . . Spoken
jocosely when People refuse what is good, and
fine, and feed upon that which is more course.
[1 hogwash.]

**Draff is your errand, but drink ye
would.**   (D 581)

1546 HEYWOOD I. xi. D2ᵛ.   **1580** LYLY *Euph. &
his Eng.* ii. 221   Draffe was mine arrand, but
drinke I would.   **1623** CAMDEN 267   Draft was
his errand, but drinke he would.   **1721** KELLY
88   Draff he sought, but Drink was his errand.
Spoken of them who make a sleeveless Errand
into a House where they know People are at
Dinner.

Dragon's teeth, To sow.

[= the dragon's teeth fabled by Hyginus (fab.
178) to have been sown by Cadmus, from which
sprang armed men.]   **1853** MARSDEN *Early Purit.*
290   Jesuits . . . sowed the dragon's teeth which

sprung up into the hydras of rebellion and
apostasy.

Dragon, *see also* Serpent, unless . . . , does not
become d.

Drank, *see* Drink.

Draught, *see* Air of a window stroke of cross-
bow; Cold wind reach you (If).

Draw at the cat-harrow,[1] They.
                                              (C 187)

a. **1555** SIR DAV. LINDSAY *Complaynt to K.* 305 8
Wks. (1879) I. 54   For every lord, as he thocht
best, Brocht in ane bird to fyll the nest; To be ane
wacheman to his marrow, Thay gan to draw at
the cat harrow.   **1721** KELLY 329   They draw the
cat harrow; that is, they thwart one another.
[1 A nursery game, played by pulling crossing
loops of thread.]

**Draw (Pull, Shrink) in (*or* Shoot out)
one's horns, To.**   (H 620)

13 . . *Coer de L.* 3835   They . . . gunne to drawen
in her hornes, As a snayl among the thornes.
c. **1374** CHAUCER *Troilus* i, l. 300   He was tho
glad his hornes in to shrinke.   **1430–40** LYDGATE
Bochas I. xx (Bodl. MS.) f. 83/1   Who is knowe
outrewe . . . Shrynkith his hornis whan men
speake of falsheede.   **1589**? LYLY *Pap w. Hatchet*
iii. 404   Now the old cuckold hath puld in his
hornes.   **1662** FULLER *Kent.* 95   The Kentish
Gentry acquitted themselves so valiant . . . that
Perkin shrunk his horns back again into the shell
of his ships.   **1678** A. WOOD *Life & Times* W.C.
228   When the parliament was prorogued he
plucked in his horne.   **1818** SCOTT *Rob Roy* ch.
14   The fallow . . . drew in his horns, and . . .
acknowledged he might hae been mista'en.
1832 M. SCOTT *Tom Cring. Log* ch. 13   She
had no sooner gone, than Bang began to shoot
out his horns a bit. 'I say, Tom, let us have the Don to
let us have . . . a tumbler of hot brandy and water.'
1891 *Sat. Rev.* 19 Dec. 682/2   They are imploring
the Council to draw in its horns.

Draw the line somewhere, One must.

1750 J. WESLEY *Lett.* iii. 48   How carefully would
he have drawn the line.   **1887** BLACKMORE *Springhaven* ch. 18   One must draw the line somewhere,
or throw overboard all principles; and I draw it
. . . against infidels and against Frenchmen.
1896 J. BEALBY *Daughter of Fen* ch. 29   Vulgar,
presuming, low-bred upstarts must be kept in
their places. . . . The line must be drawn somewhere.

Draw water to (one's) mill, To.
                                              (M 952)

[= to seize every advantage.]   **1573** SANFORD
110.   **1578** FLORIO *First F.* 14   Euery man
draweth water to hymselfe.   **1641** FERGUSSON no.
250   Every man wishes the water to his own
mylne.   **1649** HOWELL *Pre-em. Parl.* 10   Lewis the
eleventh . . . could well tell how to play his game,
and draw water to his owne Mill.   **1670** RAY 121
Every miller draws water to his own mill.   **1706**
STEVENS s.v. Agua.

Drawlatch, *see* John D.

Drawn wells are seldom dry. (w 262)

1597 GERARD *Herbal* 287 A Well doth neuer yeelde such store of water as when it is most drawne and emptied. **1611** TOURNEUR *Ath. Trag.* IV. iii. Your want of vse should rather make your body like a Well; the lesser t'is drawne, the sooner it growes dry. **1639** CLARKE 107. **1648** HERRICK *Hesper.* 832 Wks. (1893) II. 77 Milk stil your Fountains, and your Springs, for why? The more th'are drawn, the lesse they will grow dry. **1670** RAY 83 . . . Puteus si hauriatur melior evadit. . . . All things, especially mens parts, are improved and advanced by use and exercise. **1732** FULLER no. 1327.

Drawn wells have sweetest water. (w 263)

1602 SIR JOHN BEAUMONT *Met. of Tobacco* E4 The sweetest water is in deepest wells. **1639** CLARKE 107.

Draws his sword against his prince, Who | must throw away the scabbard. (s 1055)

1604 R. DALLINGTON *The View of France* F3ᵛ His King, against whom yee drawe the sword, ye must throw the scabberd into the riuer. **1613** *Id. Aphorisms* 331 When the sword of iustice is drawne, . . . throw the scabberd into the fire. **1659** HOWELL *Eng. Prov.* 17a. **1843** MACAULAY *Ess., Hampden* Wks. v. 583 Hampden . . . was for vigorous and decisive measures. When he drew the sword, as Clarendon has well said, he threw away the scabbard.

Draw(s), *see also* Salt beef d. down drink apace; Well worth aw, makes plough d.

Dread(s), *see* Dirten arse d. aye.

Dream of a dry summer, To. (s 966)

1578 W. FULWOOD *Enemie of Idleness* 250 I thinke you dreamed of a drie Summer. **1589** [NASHE?] *Pasquil* i. 102 (You tel me a tale of). **1602** MARBECK *Def. of Tobacco* F2. **1670** RAY 172.

Dream of a funeral and you hear of a marriage.

1766 GOLDSMITH *Vicar of Wakefield* ch. 10 My wife had the most lucky dreams in the world. It was one night a coffin and cross-bones, the sign of an approaching wedding. **1883** BURNE *Shrops. Folk-Lore* 263. **1909** *Brit. Wkly.* 8 July 331 'Dream of a funeral and you hear of a marriage' . . . has probably been verified many times in the experience of ordinary people.

Dreamed (*verb*), *see* Know all (Since you), tell what I d.

Dreams are lies. (D 587)

1584 LYLY *Sappho and Phao* IV. iii. 44 Dreams are but dotings, which come either by things wee see in the day, or meates that we eate. **1610–15** *Stonyhurst Pag.* vii. 52. 7 Dreames be seldome to be trusted. **1659** HOWELL *Fr. Prov.* 9 Dreams are dotages or lyes.

Dreams go by contraries. (D 588)

c. 1400 *Tale of Beryn* prol. 108 Comynly of these swevenys the contrary man shul fynde. **1548** W. PATTEN *Exped. into Scotland* (Tud. Tr. 83) My Lord's Grace dreamt one thing, and the contrary came to pass. **1584** LYLY *Sappho & Phao* IV. iii. 24 I dreamed last night, but I hope dreams are contrary, that . . . all my hair blazed on a bright flame. **1673** WYCHERLEY *Gent. Dancing Master* IV. i. Never fear it: dreams go by the contraries. **1818** FERRIER *Marriage* ch. 24 Everybody knows dreams are always contrary. **1909** *Brit. Wkly.* 8 July 331 The old saying, 'Dreams go by contraries', is established on a much surer basis of evidence than the telepathic premonitions which find a corresponding fulfilment.

Dream(s) (*noun*), *see also* After a d. of a wedding; Friday night's d.; Hope is but d. of those that wake; Morning d. come true.

Dress an egg and give the offal to the poor, To. (E 74)

1678 RAY 90 *A covetous person.* He'll dress . . .

Dress up a stick and it does not appear to be a stick. (s 849)

[Span. *Palo compuesto no parece palo.* A stick dressed up does not look like a stick.] **1620** SHELTON *Quix.* Pt. II. li. iii. 178 Go well clad, for a stake well dressed seems not to be so. **1640** HERBERT no. 101 Dresse a stick, and it seemes a youth. **1666** TORRIANO *It. Prov.* 187 no. 21 Clothes set forth poles, and cloth[e] but a pillar, and it shall look like a Lady.

Dress (*noun*), *see* Whore in a fine d.

Dressed, *see* Body more d. than soul; Rises first is first d.

Dressing, *see* Fine d. is a foul house swept.

Drift is as bad as unthrift. (D 595)

1659 HOWELL *Eng. Prov.* 6a. **1678** RAY 71.

Drink and drought come seldom together. (D 597)

1641 FERGUSSON no. 240. **1721** KELLY 88 (not always). **1732** FULLER no. 1329 (as 1721).

Drink and whistle at once, One cannot. (D 606)

1581 GUAZZO ii. 36 It is a common saying, that one cannot drinke and whistle at once. **1666** TORRIANO *Prov. Phr.* s.v. Bere 13 Not to be able to drink and whistle at one and the same instant time, viz. not to be able to do two things at once.

Drink as much after an egg as after an ox, One should. (M 1271)

1608 HARINGTON *Sch. of Salerne* A7 Remember . . . For every egge you eate you drink as oft. **1659** HOWELL *Eng. Prov.* 13a. **1670** RAY 36 This is . . . fond and ungrounded. **1738** SWIFT *Dial.* II. E.L. 310.

Drink between meals, Do not.

1609 HARWARD 84.

Drink in your pottage, If you | you'll cough in your grave. (P 511)

1653 URQUHART *Gargantua* II. xii. i. 248 That antick Proverb, which saith, Who in his pottage-eating drinks will not When he is dead and buried see one jot. **1670** RAY 133. **1738** SWIFT Dial. II. E.L. 306 I have been just eating soup; and they say, if one drinks with one's porridge, one will cough in one's grave.

Drink less, and go home by daylight.

c. **1300** *Provs. of Hending* 38 in *Reliq. Antiquae* i. 116 Drynk eft lasse, and go by lyhte hom.

Drink like a fish, To. (F 325)

c. **1614** FLETCHER *Night-Walker* iv. i. Give me the bottle, I can drink like a Fish now, like an Elephant. **1619** JONSON *Pleas. Reconciled* vii. 481 I haue drunck like a frogge to-day. **1646** SHIRLEY *Triumph of Beauty* (Dyce, vi. 321) I can drink like a fish. **1744** THOS. GRAY *Let. to Dr. Wharton* 26 Apr. Mr. Trollope and I are in a course of tarwater . . . I drink like a fish. **1822** SCOTT *Nigel* ch. 35 He retained the gravity of a judge, even while he drank like a fish.

Drink nettles in March, and eat mugwort in May, If they would | so many fine maidens wouldn't go to the clay.

[**1747** WESLEY *Prim. Physick* (1762) 35 Take an ounce of Nettle juice. **1753** CHAMBERS *Cycl. Supp.* Mugwort has long been famous as an uterine and antispasmodic.] **1846** DENHAM 38.

Drink of the burn, We can | when we cannot bite of the brae. (B 731)

a. **1628** CARMICHAELL no. 150 Ane may drink of the burne but not byte of the brey. **1641** FERGUSSON no. 908. **1721** KELLY 344 . . . Spoken when People want Bread, for none complain for want of Drink.

Drink of the same cup, To. (C 908)

a. **1547** J. REDFORD Fragment of Interlude *Wit & Science* (MSR reprint) 47 Syns we haue droonke all of one cup shake handes lyke freendes. **1570** *Several Confessions of T. Norton & C. Norton* (*Phoenix Britannicus* 1732, 420). **1579** LYLY *Euph.* i. 238 Nowe shalt not thou laugh Philautus to scorne, seeing you haue both druncke of one cup. **1596** SPENSER *F.Q.* V. i. 15 That I mote drinke the cup whereof she dranke. **1640** JONSON *Magn. Lady* V. i. 7 There's your errour now! Yo' ha' drunke o' the same water.

Drink of this water, Don't say, I'll never | how dirty so ever it be. *Cf.* **Cast not out the foul water.** (W 98)

1710 S. PALMER 236. **1732** FULLER no. 5016. **1906** CUNNINGHAME GRAHAM *His People* 'Dagos' *fin.* It is not good to say fountain—out of your basin I shall never drink . . . eh, no señor.

Drink only with the duck.

[i.e. drink only water.] **1362** LANGLAND *P. Pl.* A. v. 58 He schulde . . . Drinken bote with þe Doke and dyne but ones.

Drink the ocean dry, To. (O 9)

1550 *A notable & marvellous Epistle* B2ᵛ He . . . was . . . troubled wyth an vnsacyable thyrste, as though he woulde haue dronke vp Hister and Nilus. **1587** MARLOWE 2 *Tamb.* III. i In number yet sufficient To drinke the river *Nile* or *Euphrates*. *c.* **1589** MARLOWE *Jew of Malta* V. v. 121 As sooner shall they drink the ocean dry, Than conquer Malta. **1595** SHAKES. *Rich. II* II. ii. 144 The task he undertakes Is numb'ring sands and drinking oceans dry.

Drink water, Let none say, I will not. (W 98)

1620 SHELTON *Quix.* Pt. II. lv. iii. 209 Let . . . no man say, I'll drink no more of such a drink; for where we think to fare well, there is oft ill usage. **1640** HERBERT no. 310.

Drink wine, and have the gout; drink no wine, and have the gout too. (W 458)

1584 COGAN *Haven of Health* Ep. Ded. I have heard many gentlemen say ere now: Drink wine, and have the gout: drink none, and have the gout. As who should say, that it maketh no matter what a man eateth or drinketh. **1670** RAY 38 . . . With this saying, intemperate persons that have or fear the gout, encourage themselves to proceed in drinking wine notwithstanding.

Drink(ing), (noun), *see also* Ale is meat, d., and cloth (Good); Choose not thy company before thy d.; Dicing, drabbing and d. bring men to destruction; Garlic makes a man d.; Hanged that left his d.; Likes not the d. (Who) God deprives of bread; Meat and d. to one, (To be); Meat and good d.; Salt beef draws down d. apace; Speak of my d. that never consider my drouth; Speaks in his d. what he thought in drouth; Tale of two d.; Victuals (Of all) d. digests quickest; Want in meat (What they), take out in d.; Words would have much d.

Drinking at the harrow when he should be following the plough, He is. (H 179)

1639 CLARKE 47.

Drinking, *see also* Eating and d., (Ingenious man that found out); Eating and d. takes away stomach; Eating and d. wants but a beginning; Speak of my great d. (Many).

Drinks not wine after salad, He that | is in danger of being sick. (W 464)

1611 COTGRAVE s.v. Salade A Sallet without wine is raw, unwholesome, dangerous. **1670** RAY 39 Qui vin ne boit apres salade est en danger estre malade, i.e. He that drinks not wine after salade, is in danger to be sick. **1706** STEVENS s.v. Ensalada.

Drinks, The more one | the more one may. (M 1149)

1557 T. NORTH *Dial. Princes* (1582) Bk. III, ch. 20, 269 I finde, that the more I eate, the more I dye for hunger, the more I drinke, the greater thirst I haue. **1577–87** HARRISON *Descr. of Eng.* ed. Furnivall i. 161 The more the drinker tipleth, the more he may. **1616** DRAXE no. 553. **1666** TORRIANO *It. Prov.* 25 no. 24 (would).

Drink(s), drank, drunk, (verb), see also Brew (As they), so let them d.; Choleric d.; Clothe thee warm . . . d. enough; Deep d. the goose as the gander; Draff is your errand, but d. ye would; Eat and eat but do not d. (You); Eat at pleasure, d. by measure; Eat thy meat and d. thy d.; Horse d. when he will (Let); Husband d. to the wife (When); Ill guest that never d. to host; Never d. was never athirst; Old man will not d. (When), go to him in another world; Penny in purse will bid me d.; Pisses more than he d., (He); Run as you d. might catch hare; Stay and d. of your browst; Thing in it, quoth . . . when he d. dish-clout; Up hill spare me . . . let me not d. when hot; Walk groundly . . . d. roundly; Wine is drawn, must be d.

Drive a snail to Rome, Ye. (S 582)
1641 FERGUSSON no. 897.

Drive a top over a tiled house, As soon. (T 438)
1546 HEYWOOD II. v. H3ᵛ I shall as soone trie hym or take hym this waie, As dryue a top ouer a tyeld house. **1659** HOWELL *Eng. Prov.* 3a.

Drive black hogs in the dark, It is ill to. (H 500)
1583 MELBANCKE *Philotimus* 2A3ᵛ To see a blacke Swine before the Sun rise, is a signe of euill lucke that present day and this hath his originall from a prouerb of Empodocles. **1678** RAY 103. **1732** FULLER no. 2963. **1748** FRANKLIN July How can they advise, if they see but a part? 'Tis very ill driving black hogs in the dark.

Drive out the inch as you have done the span. (I 48)
1589 8 Jan. *H.M.C.* Hatfield House xiii I will abide the inshes as I haue done the spane. *a.* **1628** CARMICHAELL no. 244 (Do *or* drive). **1641** FERGUSSON no. 235. **1721** KELLY 84 . . . Spoken to encourage People to continue in ill Service, or bear ill Circumstances, whose end is near at hand.

Drive the nail that will go. (N 14)
1655 FULLER *Ch. Hist.* II. iv. (1868) I. 201 Thus he drave that nail . . . which would go best for the present. It was *argumentum ad hominem*. **1738** GAY *Fables* Ser. II. ix. Hence Politicians, you suggest, Should drive the nail that goes the best.

Drive the nail to the head. (N 15)
1585 A. DENT *Sermon of Repentance* B3ᵛ See

then the force of Repentance, when God striketh it into the hart of man, and driueth the naile to the head as they say. **1639** CLARKE 3.

Drive your business, do not let it drive you.
1672 CODRINGTON 124 Let every one be sure to drive his own business, rather than to let it drive him. **1736** FRANKLIN *Way to Wealth* Wks. (Bigelow) I. 443.

Driver, see Know your d. (I will make you).

Drives a subtle trade, He. (T 458)
1678 RAY 91.

Drives an ass and leads a whore, Who | has toil and sorrow evermore. (A 368)
1611 COTGRAVE s.v. Mener He that beleeues a woman, and leads an Asse, hath brought his bodie (and mind) t'an euill passe. **1617** MORYSON *Itin.* III. i. 26 (1907–8) III. 403 It is proverbially said, Chi asini caccia e donne mena, Non è mai senza guai & pena.[1] . . . **1639** CLARKE 259. **1642** TORRIANO 21 He that driveth an asse, mans a whore, and runneth upon the sand, is never out of toil, and pain. [1 GIUSTI 87 Chi asino caccia e p . . . mena, non esce mai di pena.]

Drive(s, n), see also Devil d.; Gently over the stones; Grief d. out the less, (The greater); Lead nor d. (Neither); New love d. out the old love; One fire (heat) d. out another; One nail (love) d. out another; One poison d. out another; Shifts, (He is put (d.) to his); Three things d. out of house, smoke . . .

Driving a flock than one, It is better.
1664 J. WILSON *Andron. Comn.* III. v. Wks. (1874) 172 The people are like sheep—'tis better driving A flock than one.

Driving his hogs over Swarston Bridge,[1] He is.
1787 GROSE (*Derbysh.*) 162 . . . This is a saying used in Derbyshire, when a man snores in his sleep. [1 Swarkeston Bridge, over the Trent.]

Driving his hogs (pigs) to market, He is. (H 501)
1738 SWIFT *Dial.* II. E.L. 315 He fell asleep, and snored so hard that we thought he was driving his hogs to market. **1903** S. HEDIN *Centr. Asia* II. 318 The sleeping men . . . went on driving their pigs to market for all they were worth.

Driving turkeys to market, He is.
1869 HAZLITT 165 He is driving turkeys to market. i.e. He cannot walk straight.

Drogheda, see Ross was, Dublin is, D. shall be.

Drop of water in the sea, As lost as a. (D 613)
c. **1548** J. BALE *Image of both Churches* Pt. 3 P.S. 623 Scarce is it in comparison . . . as one drop

of water to the whole sea, or as an handful of sand is to the whole earth. **1589** ?NASHE *Pasquil of Marforius* i. 97 For Pasquil to come in now with any aduice . . . were to cast (God wot) one little droppe of water into the Sea. **1592–3** SHAKES. *C.E.* I. ii. 35 I to the world am like a drop of water That in the ocean seeks another drop, Who, falling there to find his fellow forth (Unseen, inquisitive), confounds himself. *Ibid.* II. ii. 124 For know, my love, as easy mayst thou fall A drop of water in the breaking gulf And take unmingled thence that drop again Without addition or diminishing As take from me thyself, and not me too.

Drop(s), *see* Gangs up i' sops (When it), it'll fau in d.; Last d. makes cup run over; Many d. make shower.

Dropping(s), *see* Constant d. wears stone; Lose the d. of his nose (He will not).

Dross, *see* No silver without d.

Drought never bred dearth in England.
(D 622)

1533 HEYWOOD *Play of Weather* l. 364 And it is sayd syns afore we were borne That drought doth neuer make derth of corne. **1640** HERBERT no. 749 Drought never brought dearth. **1659** HOWELL *Fr. Prov.* 21 A dry year never beggars the Master. **1670** RAY 42. *c.* **1685** AUBREY *Nat. Hist. Wilts.* 33 (1847) 'Tis a saying in the West, that a dry yeare does never cause a dearth. **1721** KELLY 8 A dry Summer never made a dear Peck. . . . Though the Straw in such Years be short, yet the Grain is good and hearty. **1917** BRIDGE 52 . . . 'It has been proved . . . by practical farmers that in the fine hot years they do the best.'

Drought, Drouth, *see also* Drink and d. seldom together; Mouth (Whoso has) shall ne'er in England suffer d.; Pedlar's d.; Speak of my drink that never consider my d.

Drowned mouse (rat), Like a. (M 1237)

c. **1425** *Castle of Perseverance* 3080 Thou schalt lye drenkelyd[1] as a mous. **1542** ERASM. tr. Udall *Apoph.* 180b An hedde he had . . . Three heares on a side, like a drouned ratte. **1578** T. CHURCHYARD *Discourse of the Queen's Entertainment* Nichols *Progresses* 1823 ii. 201 We were all so dashed and washed, that it was a . . . pastime to see us looke like drowned rattes. **1592–4** SHAKES. *1 Hen. VI* I. ii. 12 Or piteous they will look, like drowned mice. **1678** RAY 286 To look like a droun'd mouse. **1697** DAMPIER *Voy.* I. iv. 70 The storm drencht us all like so many drowned Rats. **1778** FRANCES BURNEY *Evelina* ch. 19 You hadn't a dry thread about you . . . and poor Monseer French, here, like a drowned rat, by your side! [[1] drowned.]

Drowning man will catch at a straw, A.
(M 92)

1534 MORE *Dial. of Comfort* E.L. 134 Lyke a man that in peril of drowning catcheth whatsoever cometh nexte to hande, . . . be it neuer so simple a sticke. **1566** PAINTER i. 141 We see them that feare to be drowned, do take hold of

the next thinge that commeth to hande. **1583** J. PRINCE *Fruitful & Brief Disc.* 30 We do not as men redie to be drowned, catch at euery straw. [**1603**] **1631** CHETTLE *Hoffman* l. 1858 Men that dye by drowning, in their death, Hold surely what they claspe, while they haue breath. **1612–15** BP. HALL *Contempl.* XIX. i (1825) I. 609 The drowning man snatches at every twig; . . . the messengers . . . catch hastily at . . . , 'Thy brother Benhadad'. **1748** RICHARDSON *Clarissa* VII. 12 A drowning man will catch at a straw, the proverb well says. **1848** THACKERAY *Vanity F.* ch. 18 'You fool, why do you catch at a straw?' calm good sense says to the man that is drowning.

Drown(ed, ing), *see also* Bacchus has d. more men than Neptune; Dog is d. (When), every one offers him drink; Drunk than d. (Better); Ewe is d. (When the) she's dead; Never was cat or dog d. that could see shore; Pour not water on d. mouse; Safe from the East Indies, d. in Thames; Water where the stirk d. (There was aye some).

Drug in the market, A.

1662 FULLER Monmouthsh. 54 [He] made such a vent for Welsh Cottons, that what he found Drugs at home, he left Dainties beyond the Sea. **1760** MURPHY *Way to Keep Him* I A wife's a drug now; mere tar-water, with every virtue under the sun, but nobody takes it. **1840** HOOD *Up Rhine* 163 Quite a drug in the market.

Drum, Jack *or* Tom, *see* J. D.'s entertainment.

Drums beat, Where | laws are silent.
(D 624)

[CICERO *Pro Milone* 4. 10 *Silent enim leges inter arma.* For the laws are dumb in the midst of arms.] **1549** H. BULLINGER *Treatise concerning magistrates* C2ᵛ This prouerbe is of the deuyll, not of god . . . *Sileant inter arma leges.* Lawes kepe silence in warre. **1577** HOLINSHED 1587 ed. vi. 148 Good lawes amongst the clinking noise of armor are oftentimes put to silence. **1579** NORTH's Plutarch 'Julius Caesar' (T.C. vii. 168) Time of war and law are two things. **1586** G. WHETSTONE *English Mirror* M5 In the time of peace Arms giue place to Lawes [Socrates]. **1592** DELAMOTHE 43. Amongest the sound of trompets and drommes, the voyce of the good lawes cannot be heard. **1655–62** GURNALL *Chrn. in Armour* (1865) I. 553 The church is intended by Christ into his house. . . . It is his kingdom; and how can his laws be obeyed, if all his subjects be in a hubbub one against another? *Inter arma silent leges*—laws are silent amid arms. **1658** C. HOOLE *Sententiae Pueriles* 13 Laws are silent amongst weapons. **1721** KELLY 358. **1888** J. E. T. ROGERS *Econom. Interp. Hist.* (1894) II. xiii. The laws . . . of economical progress, are as silent during warfare as those of the constitution are.

Drunk as a beggar. (B 225)

1609 J. HALL *Discovery of a new world*, tr. J. Healey (ed. H. Brown) 55 As foxt as forty beggers. **1612** DEKKER *Oper se O*. M2ᵛ 25. **1616** DRAXE no. 555 As drunken as a Rat or Beggar. **1639** CLARKE 47.

Drunk as a fiddler.

1607 *The Puritan* v. i. 56 As drunck as a common fiddeler. **1834** MARRYAT *Peter Simple* ch. 14 As drunken as a Gosport fiddler.

Drunk as a fish.   (F 299)

1629 JONSON *New Inn* III. i. 210. **1700** CONGREVE *Way of World* IV. ix.

Drunk as a lord, As.   (L 439)

1654 E. GAYTON *Festivious Notes on Don Quixote* 17 Drunke—as any Lord. **1659** SOMERS *Tracts* (1811) VII. 184 The proverb goes 'As drunk as a lord'. **1731** COFFEY *Devil to pay* I. ii I . . . am now come with a firm Resolution, . . . to be as richly drunk as a Lord. **1837** J. B. KER 233.

Drunk as a mouse (rat), As.   (M 1219)

a. 1310 in WRIGHT *Lyric P.* xxxix. 111 When that he is dronke as ase a dreynt mous, thenne we shule borewe the wed ate bayly. *c.* 1386 CHAUCER *W. of Bath's Prol.* l. 246 Thou comest hoom as dronken as a Mous. **1553** T. WILSON *Arte of Rhet.* (1580) 128 As if one had . . . kepte the Tauerne till he had been as dronke as a Ratte. **1607** *Dobson's Dry Bobs* ch. 8 (Rats). **1837** J. B. KER 77 (rat).

Drunk as a wheelbarrow, As.   (W 290)

1675 C. COTTON *Burlesque upon Burlesque* 128 Drunk as Drum, or Wheelbarrow. **1678** RAY 87. **1694** MOTTEUX *Rabelais* V. xxxix A . . . sottish Fellow, continually raddled, and as drunk as a Wheelbarrow.

Drunk as Chloe.

1823 JON BEE *Slang A Dict. of the Turf etc.* 71. **1837** J. B. KER 108. **1906** Q. COUCH *Mayor of Troy* ch. 9.

Drunk as David's sow, As.   (S 1042)

1652 *A Notable and pleasant History of . . . Hectors, Or, St. Nicholas Clerkes*, 11 As drunk as *David's* Sow. **1671** SHADWELL *Miser* IV I am as drunk . . . as David's sow, as the saying is. **1720** GAY *New Similes* For though as drunk as David's sow, I love her still the better. **1836** MARRYAT *Midsh. Easy* ch. 14.

Drunk than drowned, You had better be.

1830 FORBY 430 . . . *i.e.* It is better to exceed in wine now and then, than to be constantly drinking largely of weak liquors.

Drunk, *see also* Ape d.; Ever d. ever dry; Kills a man when he is d.

Drunkard alone, Let but the | and he will fall of himself.   (D 628)

1678 RAY *Adag. Hebr.* 407.

Drunkard's purse is a bottle, A.   (D 629)

1640 HERBERT no. 143.

Drunkard(s), *see also* Children (D.) and fools cannot lie.

Drunken days have all their tomorrows.

1875 SMILES *Thrift* 181 (as the old proverb says).

Drunken folks seldom take harm.   (M 94)

1591 ARIOSTO *Orl. Fur.* Harington XXX. 13 If fortune that helpe frantike men and drunke Had not him safe conueyd. **1605** CHAPMAN, JONSON, MARSTON *Eastw. Ho* III. ii. They say yet, 'drunken men never take harm'. This night will try the truth of that proverb. **1670** RAY 83.

Drunken man is always dry, A.

1560 J. PILKINGTON *P.S.* 51 (according to the proverb).

Drunken man (men), *see* Heaven takes care of . . . d. m.; Stagger like d. m.

Drunkenness, *see* Soberness conceals, d. reveals; Vine brings forth three grapes: . . . second of d.

Dry as a biscuit.   (B 404)

1599 SHAKES. *A.Y.* II. vii. 39 As dry as the remainder biscuit After a voyage. [1599] **1600** JONSON *Every Man Out* Ind. 176 A gallant . . . who . . . (now and then) breakes a drie bisket jest. **1620** J. C. *Two Mer. Milk-Maids* V. i. O1 Set my lips to a Flagon of Beere . . . and drunke it as dry as a Bisket.

Dry as a dog, As.   (D 433)

[*c.* 1591] **1592** *Arden of Fev.* II. ii. 199 Come, let's go drinke: choller makes me as drye as a dog. [*c.* 1592] **1616** MARLOWE *Faustus* II. iiib 34. **1672** LACY *Old Troop* V. i.

Dry as a kex,[1] As.   (K 22)

1533 UDALL *Flowers for Latin speaking* (1560) U2 As drie as a kixe. **1550** HEYWOOD *100 Epigrams* no. 47 Light as a kix. **1553** *Respublica* V. x. **1578** LEMNIUS tr. T. Newton 28. **1891** T. HARDY *Tess.* ch. 17 I should be dry as a kex with travelling so far. [1 The dry stem of certain herbaceous plants.]

Dry as dust, As.   (D 647)

[*c.* 1500 *Ludus Coventriae* xiv. 21 (1841) 123 Davy dry dust.] **1581–90** *Timon* II. v. I am as dry as duste. **1600** DEKKER *Shoem. Holiday* II. iii. **1640** HERBERT 135 Death is drie as dust.

Dry August and warm does harvest no harm.   (A 396)

1573 TUSSER 128. **1732** FULLER no. 6209.

Dry bread at home is better than roast meat abroad.   (B 618)

1640 HERBERT no. 681. **1659** HOWELL *It. Prov.* 5.

Dry cough is the trumpeter of death, A.
(c 677)

1654 HOWELL *Lett.* (1903) III. 77 Mr. Watts is still troubled with coughing, and . . . as the Turk hath it, 'A dry cough is the trumpeter of death'. **1670** RAY 5.

Dry feet, warm head, bring safe to bed. *Cf.* Keep your feet dry.   (F 576)

1640 HERBERT no. 402.

Dry light is the best.

1625 BACON *Ess., Friendship* Arb. 175 Heraclitus saith well, in one of his Ænigmaes; . . . The Light, that a man receiueth, by Counsell from Another, is Drier, and purer, then that which commeth from his own Vnderstanding. **1907** S. LEE *Gt. Englishmen of 16th C.* 247 The dry light of reason is the only illuminant which permits men to see clearly phenomena as they are.

Dry May and a dripping June bring all things into tune, A.

1742 *An Agreeable Companion* 35 A dripping June Brings all Things in Tune. **1846** DENHAM 50 A good leak in June sets all in tune. **1883** ROPER 22. **1893** INWARDS 29. **1912** *Spectator* 28 Dec. 1094 'A dripping June sets all in tune', and on sandy soils not only farm crops but garden flowers do best in a wet summer.

'Dry meat, It is' | said the country fellow when he lost the hare.

1659 HEYLIN *Animadv.* in FULLER *Appeal* (1840) 496 . . . and so let Calais pass for 'a beggarly town', and 'not worth the keeping', because we have no hope to get it.

Dry (*adj.*), *see also* Drink the ocean d.; Drunken man is always d.; Hard (d.) as a bone; High and d.; Keep your feet d.; Sorrow is always d.; Sow d. and set wet; Turnips like d. bed; Wish the burn d. because it weets our feet (We maunna).

Dry(-ies), (*verb*), *see* Nothing d. sooner than tears.

Dublin, *see* Limerick was, D. is, Cork shall be finest city; Ross was, D. is, Drogheda shall be.

Ducat, *see* Know the value of d. (If you would).

Duck in the mouth, To come home with a.

a. **1656** R. CAPEL in SPURGEON *Treas. Dav. Ps.* ix. 18 Money, which lying long in the bank, comes home at last with a duck in its mouth.

Duck swim? Will a.

1842 S. LOVER *Handy Andy* ch. 4 'What do you say, . . . will you dine with me?' 'Will a duck swim?' chuckled out Jack Horan. **1872** G. J. WHYTE-MELVILLE *Satanella* ch. 29 'Are you game for a day with the stag?' 'Will a duck swim!' was the answer.

Duck will not always dabble in the same gutter, A.

1721 KELLY 45. **1732** FULLER no. 82.

Ducks and drakes of (with), To make.
(D 632)

[= to throw away idly or carelessly.] *c.* **1581–90** *Timon* V. v. I will make duckes and drakes with this my gold. . . . Before your fingers touch a piece thereof. **1605** CHAPMAN, JONSON, MARSTON *Eastward Ho* I. i. 120 Be idle, . . . make Duckes and Drakes with shillings. **1768–74** TUCKER *Lt. Nat.* (1852) II. 164 A miser has it in his power to make ducks and drakes of his guineas. **1810** WELLINGTON in GURW. *Desp.* VII. 32 His Majesty's Government never intended to give over the British army to the Governors of this Kingdom to make ducks and drakes with.

Ducks fare well in the Thames, The.
(D 631)

1670 RAY 83.

Ducks have eaten up the dirt, Not till the.

1710 (23 Dec.) SWIFT *Journal to Stella* Other things . . . you shall know one day, when the ducks have eaten up all the dirt. **1712** ARBUTHNOT *Lewis Baboon turned Honest* ch. 3. **1738** SWIFT *Dial.* II. E.L. 314 When may we hope to see you again in London?—Why, madam, not till the ducks have eat up the dirt, as the children say.

Duck(s), *see also* Drink only with d.; (Dying) d. in thunder (Like a); Like a duke? like a d.; More rain . . . more water will suit d.; Nibbled to death by d. (As good be); Swim like a fish (d.); Take to . . . like d. to water; 'Time enough' lost the d.

Dudgeon-heft, *see* All is gone . . . (When), what avails dagger with d.?

Dudman[1] and Ramehead[2] meet, When.
(D 633)

[i.e. never.] **1602** R. CAREW *Survey of Cornwall* (1769) 141 Amongst sundrie prouerbs, allotting an impossible time of performance, the *Cornish men* haue this one, When Ramehead and Dudman meet. **1662** FULLER *Cornwall* 198 These are two forelands, well known to Sailers, well nigh twenty miles asunder; and the Proverbe passeth for the Periphrasis of an impossibility. [[1] Dodman Point, S.W. of St. Austell. [2] Rame Head, the W. horn of Plymouth Bay.]

Due, *see* Give everyone his d.; Loses his d. gets not thanks.

Duke Humphrey, *see* Dine with D. H.

Duke of Exeter's daughter.

[A rack invented by the Duke of Exeter in the reign of Henry VI.] **1642** FULLER *H. & P. State* IV. xiii (1841) 284 A daughter of the duke of

Exeter invented a . . . cruel rack . . . often used, in the Tower of London, and commonly called . . . 'the duke of Exeter's daughter'. **1822** SCOTT *Nigel* ch. 25 They threatened to make me hug the Duke of Exeter's daughter. **1878** J. GAIRDNER *Rich. III* iv. 125 Being . . . a prisoner in the Tower, in the severe embrace of 'the Duke of Exeter's daughter'.

Duke, *see also* Like a d. ? like a duck.

Dulcarnon,[1] I am at.   (D 638)

c. **1374** CHAUCER *Troilus* iii. 930 I am, til God me bettre mynde sende, At dulcarnoun, right at my wittes ende. **1852** *N. & Q.* 1st Ser. v. 180 The other day . . . a person . . . declaring he was at his wit's end, exclaimed, 'Yes, indeed I am at Dulcarnon'. [[1] From Arabic *two-horned*, applied to Euclid i. 47; hence a problem, difficulty.]

Dull as a beetle.   (B 220)

1520 WHITTINGTON *Vulg.* E.E.T.S. 36. **1620** SHELTON *Quix.* Pt. II. xiii. ii. 269. **1670** RAY 204.

Dull (Flat, Dead) as ditchwater, As.

1725 ERASM. *Fam. Colloquies* tr. N. Bailey (1733, 512), (dead). **1772** *Garrick Corr.* (1831) i. 465 'The Grecian Daughter's' being as dead as dishwater after the first act. **1837–8** DICKENS *O. Twist* ch. 39 As dull as swipes. **1865** *Id. Mut. Friend* III. ch. 10 He'd be sharper than the serpent's tooth, if he wasn't as dull as ditchwater.

Dull, *see also* Ass, as d. as an; Block, (D. as a); Lead, (As heavy (d.) as); Work and no play makes . . . d. boy.

Dull-edge, *see* Knife . . . made at D.

Dumb men get no lands.

c. **1390** GOWER *Conf. Amantis* vi. 318 For selden get a domb man londe, Take that proverbe, and understonde. **1406** HOCCLEVE *La Male Règle* 433 The prouerbe is 'the doumb man no lond getith'. *a.* **1628** CARMICHAELL no. 52 A dum man wan never land. **1670** RAY 83 . . . This is parallel to . . . Spare to speak and spare to speed.

Dumb, *see also* Speak with your gold and make other tongues d.

Dumpling(s), *see* Devonshire d.; Norfolk d.

Dumps, To be in the.   (D 640)

1529 MORE *Comf. agst. Trib.* I Wks. 1140/2 What heapes of heauynesse, hath of late fallen amonge vs already, with whiche some of our poore familye bee fallen into suche dumpes. **1534** LUPSET *Treat. Dying Well* ed. Gee 268 He stode styll in a musynge dumpte. **1555** J. PHILPOT

Sixth Exam[n]. P.S. 55 To the great grief of the lord bishop . . . , as it appeared by the dumps he was in. **1557** EDGEWORTH *Serm.* 3H2 He . . . would be in his dumps when he were among his louing friendes and good felowes at a feast. **1580** LYLY *Euph. & his Eng.* ii. 174 Frauncis . . . seeing Philautus all this while to be in his dumpes, beganne thus to playe with him. **1581** GUAZZO i. 22 At the first I was in my dumpes. [1589] **1633** MARLOWE *Jew of Malta* I. ii. 374 How now, Don Mathias? in a dump? **1590** H. ROBERTS *Defiance to Fortune* H2[v] Elenora . . . striken in a dumpe, began to studie an answere. *Ibid.* K2 Andrugio . . . thus standing in dumpes. **1594–8** SHAKES. *T.S.* II. i. 276 How now, daughter Katharine! in your dumps? **1612** CHAPMAN *Widow's Tears* II. iv. 56. **1659** HOWELL *Fr. Prov.* 21 You put me to my dumps, or my wits end. **1785** GROSE s.v. Dumps Down in the dumps.

Dun [*i.e.* the horse] is in the mire.

                                  (D 642 and 643)

[(*a*) Things are at a standstill or deadlock; (*b*) *Dun in the Myre*, an old Christmas game in which a heavy log was lifted and carried off by the players.] *c.* **1386** CHAUCER *Maniple's Prol.* l. 5 Sires, what! Dun is in the myre. *c.* **1440** CAPGRAVE *Life St. Kath.* II. 1046 For as wyth me, dun is in the myre, She hath me stoyned and brought me to a bay. *c.* **1529** SKELTON *Garland of Laurell* (Dyce) l. 1433 Dun is in the myre, dame, reche me my spur. **1541** *Schoolhouse of Women* B4 Lytell ye [women] care So ye maye haue, that ye desyre Though dun, and the packe, lye in the myre. *c.* **1595** SHAKES. *R.J.* I. iv. 41 If thou art Dun, we'll draw thee from the mire. **1599** TASSO *Marr. and Wiving* E4[v] She hath made Iacke a Gentleman, and hath drawne Dunne out of the mire. **1605–6** SHAKES. *K.L.* II. ii. 3 Where may we set our horses?—I' the mire. **1613** T. FITZHERBERT *Supplement to the Discussions of M. D. Barlowe's Answere* [attacking Donne's *Pseudo-Martyr*] 106 You see into what a quicksand (as I may say) or quagmire of absurdityes M. Dunne hath plunged himselfe ouer head and eares, . . . insomuch that now he hath need of some good help to draw Dunne out of the mire. **1640** SHIRLEY *St. Patk. for Ireld.* (N.), Then draw Dun out of the mire, And throw the clog into the fire. **1905** *N. & Q.* 10th Ser. III. 11 An old proverb 'Dun's in the mire' . . . 'Dun' is evidently the name of a horse, and the saying no doubt had its origin in the dreadful state of the roads in early days.

Dun's the mouse.   (D 644)

[A quibble on the word *done*.] *c.* **1595** SHAKES. *R.J.* I. iv. 40 The game was ne'er so fair, and I am done.—Tut! dun's the mouse, the constable's own word. **1600** *Sir John Oldcastle* III. ii. Dunne is the mouse. **1620** *Two Merry Milkmaids* Why then 'tis done, and dun's the mouse, and undone all the courtiers.

Dun, *see also* Devil on D.'s back.

Dunder do gally[1] the beans, The.

                                            (D 645)

1678 RAY 347 . . . *Somers.* Beans shoot up fast after thunder-storms. [[1] affright.]

Dunghill, *see* Cock is bold on own d.; Sun is never the worse for shining on d.

Dunmow bacon, and Doncaster daggers, Monmouth caps and Lemster wool, Derby ale and London beer.

(A 101. B 22. M 1105)

1589 'MARPRELATE' *Just Censure* ed. Pierce 380 A draught of Darby ale. **1659** HOWELL *Eng. Prov.* 14a. **1670** RAY 258.

Dunmow, *see also* Flitch of bacon from D.

Dunstable (road), Downright (As plain as). (D 646)

1546 HEYWOOD II. v. H2ᵛ For were ye as playne as dunstable hye waie. **1549** LATIMER *2nd Serm. bef. Edw. VI* P.S. 113 Some that walked in the kynges highe waye ordinarilye, vprightlye, playne Dunstable waye. **1662** FULLER Beds. 114 'As plain as Dunstable Road'. . . . Applyed to things plain and simple . . . Such this Road being broad and beaten. **1718** PRIOR *Conversation* 49 Sometimes to me he did apply; But Down-right Dunstable was I. **1790** GROSE s.v. Beds As plain as Dunstable road. Downright Dunstable. **1824** SCOTT *Redg.* ch. 24 If this is not plain speaking, there is no such place as downright Dunstable in being.

Dunt(s), *see* Never draw dirk when d. will do; Words are but wind but d. the devil.

Dursley, You are a man of. (M 635)

c. **1640** *Berkeley MSS.* iii. 26 Hee'l proove, I thinke, a man of Durseley. **1662** FULLER *Glouc.* 352 . . . It is taken for one that breaks his word, and faileth in performance of his promises; parallel to Fides Graeca, or Fides Punica. Duresley is a Market and cloathing Town in this County. **1902-4** LEAN I. 88 . . . Murray refers this to the sharping qualities of the clothier hereabouts.

Dust in a man's (people's) eyes, To throw (cast). (D 650)

[= to mislead by misrepresentation.] *c.* **1450** 'Pluk of her bellys and let her fly' (Poem in *Rel. Ant.* i. 27) Wene ye that I loue hym? Nay. let be!—Yet for to dryve the dowste yn hys eye! *c.* **1527** J. RASTELL *Calisto and Mel.* A6ᵛ Se ye not this smoke In my maisters eyes that they do cast. **1581** GUAZZO i. 67 They doe nothing els but raise a dust to doe out their owne eyes. **1612** *Crt. & Times Jas. I* (1849) I. 169 To countermine his underminers, and, as he termed it, to cast dust in their eyes. **1616** DRAXE no. 205. **1767** FRANKLIN *Wks.* (1887) IV. 79 It required a long discourse to throw dust in the eyes of common sense. **1926** *Times* 22 Feb. 11/2 The remedies proposed in the French report are only an attempt to throw dust in people's eyes.

Dust is on your feet, While the | sell what you have bought. (D 653)

1678 RAY *Adag. Hebr.* 401 . . . The meaning is that we should sell quickly (though with light gaines) that we may trade for more.

Dust raised by the sheep does not choke the wolf, The.

1706 STEVENS s.v. Polvo. **1732** FULLER no. 4491. **1865** TRENCH *Poems; Proverbs* xxii. 303 There is no ointment for the wolf's sore eyes, Like clouds of dust which from the sheep arise.

Dust, (*noun*), *see also* Blows in the d. (He that); Dry as d.; Fly sat on axletree; Grave (In the) d. and bones jostle not; Kiss (Lick) the d.; March d.; March sun causes d.; Play off your d.; Rain lays great d. (Small); Shake the d. off one's feet.

Dust (*verb*), *see* Jacket, (To baste (curry, d. etc.)).

Dutch courage.

[= bravery induced by drinking.] **1824** SCOTT *Redg.* ch. 16 'Not the twentieth part of a drop', said Nanty. 'No Dutch courage for me.' **1873** H. SPENCER *Stud. Sociol.* viii. 188 A dose of brandy, by stimulating the circulation, produces 'Dutch courage'.

Dutch uncle, To talk to one like a.

[= to reprove sharply.] **1837** J. C. NEAL *Charcoal Sk.* 201 If you keep a cutting didoes, I must talk to you both like a Dutch uncle. **1853** *N. & Q.* 1st Ser. VII. 65/2 In some parts of America, when a person has determined to give another a regular lecture, he will often be heard to say 'I will talk to him like a Dutch uncle'. **1897** CONRAD *Nigger of N.* ch. 4 To-morrow I will talk to them like a Dutch Uncle. A crazy crowd of tinkers!

Dutch, *see also* Talk as D. as Daimport's dog.

Dutchman, I am a.

1848 A. SMITH *Chris. Tadpole* ch. 58 If that don't do it, I'm a Dutchman! **1866** LES. STEPHEN in MAITLAND *Life & Lett.* (1906) X. 184 If I don't come out to the United States next year, I'm a Dutchman.

Dutchman's anchor, It is like the | he has got it at home. Cf. Bow (I have a good).

1823 COLLINS 67 'I have a good doublet in France' . . . is said to ridicule persons who boast of having something which they cannot use or come at. We say, 'It is like the Dutchman's anchor, he has got it at home.'

Dutchman, *see also* Irishman for a hand.

Dwarf on a giant's shoulders sees further of the two, A. (D 659)

[L. *Pygmaei gigantum humeris impositi plus quam ipsi gigantes vident.*] *c.* **1327** HIGDEN *Polychronicon* 14 *nanus residens in humeris gigantis*, trs. **1387** TREVISA As a dwerf sittynge on a geauntis nekke. **1611** COTGRAVE s.v. Genta We, hauing the aid of our auncestors knowledge, vnderstand somewhat more then they did. **1621** BURTON *Anat. Mel.* Democ. to Rdr. (1651) 8 I say with Didacus Stella (in Luc. 10, tom. 2) . . . I may . . . see farther than my predecessors. **1640** HERBERT no. 50. **1642** FULLER *Holy State* (1841) II. 6 Grant them [the moderns] dwarfs, yet stand they on giants' shoulders and may see further. **1895** STEPHENS *Life E. A. Freeman* II. 467 Arnold disparaged by men who . . . had by climbing upon Arnold's shoulders been enabled to see a little farther than Arnold himself.

Dwell at Rotheras, Every one cannot.
(R 190)

1659 HOWELL *Eng. Prov.* 21b ... A delicate seat
of the Bodmans in Herefordshire. **1790** GROSE
s.v. Herefordshire.

Dwell, Wherever a man | he shall be
sure to have a thorn-bush near his door.
(M 415)

1639 CLARKE 165. **1678** RAY 209 ... No place,
no condition is exempt from all trouble. *Nihil
est ab omni parte beatum.* [HORACE *Odes* 2. 16.
27 There is nothing that is blessed in every
respect.] **1912** *Spectator* 27 July 137 *The
Thorn Bush near the Door.* . . . This book is . . .
[a] description of every day life in London.

Dwell in court must needs curry favour,
Whoso will.   (C 724)

c. 1400 *Beryn* E.E.T.S. 1. 362 As þouȝe she had
lernyd cury fauel, of som old ffrere. *c.* 1450
Provs. of Wysdom 91 Who so wyll in cowrt
dwell, Nedis most he cory fauell.[1] *c.* 1510
BARCLAY *Mirr. Gd. Manners* (1570) F6 Flatter
not as do some, With none curry fauour. **1545**
TAVERNER F7ᵛ Oure englyshe prouerbe . . . He
that woll in court dwell, must nedes currye
fauel . . . fauell is an olde englyshe worde, and
signifieth as moch fauour doth nowe a dayes.
1557 N. T. (Geneva) *Matt.* viii. 20 *note* He
thoght by this meanes to courry fauour with
the worlde. *c.* 1561 UNDERHILL *Narr. Reform.*
Camden Soc. 159 Accordynge to the olde
provearbe . . . He thatt wylle in courte abyde
Must cory favelle bake and syde, for souche gett
moste gayne. **1616** DRAXE no. 736 Hee that
will in Court dwell, must speake Hauell. **1691**
WOOD *Ath. Oxon.* ii. 470 [It] was then by him
published to curry favour with the Royalists.
[1 favel = a chestnut horse, and to curry favel
came to mean to employ deceit. Later, favel was
transformed into favour and to curry favour took
its present meaning.]

Dwells next door to a cripple, He that |
will learn to halt.   (C 828)

c. 1535 ELYOT *Educ.* B3 This prouerbe is vsed:
He that dwelleth by a crepyll, shall lerne to halte.
c. 1577 J. NORTHBROOKE *Treatise agst. Dicing* ed.
Collier 80 According to the old saying: If thou
with him that haltes doest dwell, To learne to

halt thou shalt full well. **1579** LYLY *Euph.* i. 267
It is an olde Prouerbe that if one dwell the next
dore to a cr[e]ple he wil learne to hault, if one be
conuersant with an hypocrite, he wil soone
endeuour to dissemble.

(Dying) duck in thunder (a thunderstorm), Like a.

1785 WOLCOT (P. Pindar) *Lyric Odes* vii. Wks.
(1816) I. 68 Gaping upon Tom's thumb, with
me in wonder, The rabble rais'd its eyes—like
ducks in thunder. **1832** M. SCOTT *Tom Cring.
Log* ch. 9. **1863** KINGSLEY *Water Bab.* ch. 5.
1880 J. PAYN *Confid. Agent* III. 161 Look less like
a duck in a thunderstorm. *a.* **1911** GILBERT
Lost Bab Ballads (1932) 59 He ... rolled his eyes
of blue As dying ducks in thunderstorms Are
often said to do.

Dying men speak true (prophesy).
(M 514)

1595 COPLEY *Wits, Fits* VII. 204 Yes, it is best
telling a truth in the houre of death. **1596**
SHAKES. *K.J.* V. iv. 26 What in the world should
make me now deceive, Since I must lose the use
of all deceit? Why should I then be false, since
it is true That I must die here, and live hence, by
truth? **1596** *Id. M.V.* I. ii. 24 And holy men
at their death have good inspirations. **1596** *Id.
Rich. II* II. i. 5 O, but they say the tongues
of dying men Enforce attention like deep har-
mony. Where words are scarce, they are seldom
spent in vain, For they breathe truth that breathe
their words in pain. **1597** *Id. 1 Hen. IV* V. iv.
83 O, I could prophesy, But that the earthy
and cold hand of death Lies on my tongue.
1607 DEKKER & WEBSTER *Sir Th. Wyatt* i. 451
G1 Oft dying men are fild with prophesies, But
ile not be a prophet of your il. **1610** SHAKES.
Cym. V. v. 40 She alone knew this; And, but
she spoke it dying, I would not Believe her lips in
opening it. **1630** T. D. *Bloody Banq.* v. i. G3
Dying men Prophesie, faith tis our last end; Nor
I must tell you brother, that I hate you, In that
you have betray'd my lov'd Mazeres.

Dying, *see also* Past d. of her first child.

Dyke, *see* February fill d.; Earth big the d. (Let
the); Leaps over the d. where lowest (Every one);
Sheep (If one) leaps over d.; Steal not my kail,
break not my d.

Dysart, *see* Salt to D. (Carry).

E

Eagle can gaze at the sun, Only the.
(E 3)

1562 G. LEGH *Accidence of Armoury* 104 The
Eagle ... is brightest of sight of all other fowles,
so that, if his yong ones will not looke against
the sunne, without watering eyen, then he
killeth them, thinkyng that they are not hys
owne, but misbegotten. **1581** H. GOLDWELL

Brief Declarⁿ B5 The Eagle beholding the sunne,
coueteth to build her nest in the same, and so
dimmeth her sight. **1591** SHAKES. *3 Hen. VI* II.
i. 91 Nay, if thou be that princely eagle's bird,
Show thy descent by gazing 'gainst the sun.
1594–5 *Id. L.L.L.* IV. iii. 222 What peremptory
eagle-sighted eye Dares look upon the heaven
of her brow? **1613** *Id. T.N.K.* II. ii. 34 And like
young eagles teach 'em Boldly to gaze against
bright arms.

Eagle's eye, To have an.   (E 6)

1583 J. PRIME *Faithful & Brief Discourse* 26
Eagles eyes haue we till we looke into the sunne.
c. **1595** SHAKES. *R.J.* III. v. 221 An eagle, madam,
Hath not so green, so quick, so fair an eye.
1603 CHETTLE, DEKKER, HAUGHTON *Patient
Grissil* I. ii. 211 Women haue eagles eyes, To
prie euen to the heart. *c.* **1605** *Life and Death
Ratsey* A4 For as hee had an Eagles eye to
espie aduauntage, so had he a Lions heart to
effect his purpose.

Eagle's old age, An.   (E 5)

1533–4 N. UDALL *Flowers* 158ᵛ Aquilae senectus,
the old age of an egle, is a latin prouerbe vsed
to be spoken of old men, or others that liue
more by drynk than by mete. For [Pliny] . . .
egles dyen . . . neither for age, nor by reson of any
sycknes, but for hungre and lacke of meate [by
reason of growth of upper bill or bebe ouer the
nether]. **1548** COOPER s.v. Aquila. **1672**
WALKER 31, no. 63 A fresh hearty old man.

Eagles catch no flies.   (E 1)

[ERASM. *Ad. Aquila non captat muscas.*] **1563**
Mirr. for Magistr. ed. Campbell 405 The iolly
Egles catche not little flees. **1581** PETTIE i. 200
That is the right act of a Prince, and therefore it
is well saide, That the Egle catcheth not flies.
1586 J. FARNE *Blazon of Gentry* ii. 21. **1655**
FULLER *Ch. Hist.* III. viii (1868) I. 481 When any
bishopric, . . . or good living, (*aquila non capit
muscas!*) was like to be void, the pope . . . predisposed such places . . . as he pleased. **1786** MRS.
PIOZZI *Anec. of S. Johnson* (1892) 76 With regard
to slight insults . . . : 'They sting one (says he)
but as a fly stings a horse; and the eagle will not
catch flies.'

Eagles do not breed doves.   (E 2)

[HOR. *Carm.* 4. 4. 31 *Neque imbellem feroces
progenerant aquilae columbam.*] **1578** *Courtly
Controv.* Lıᵛ The auntient prouerbe, that the
Egle hatcheth not a pigeon. **1581** GUAZZO ii. 15
Remembring the saying, that the Eagle breedeth
not the Pigeon. **1592** SHAKES. *T.And.* II. iii. 149
'Tis true! the raven doth not hatch a lark. **1613**
BEAUM. & FL. *Hon. Man's F.* III. i. Doves beget
doves; and eagles, eagles, Madam: a citizen . . .
seldom at the best proves a gentleman.

Eagles fly alone.   (E 7)

c. **1580** SIDNEY *First Arcadia* (Feuillerat) iv. 12
Egles wee see flye alone, and they are but sheepe
which allway heard together. *a.* **1623** WEBSTER
Duch. of M. v. ii. Eagles commonly fly alone:
they are crows, daws, and starlings that flock
together.

Eagles, *see also* Carcase is (Wheresoever), **e.**
gathered together.

Early bird catches the worm, The.   (B 368)

1636 CAMDEN 307. **1670** RAY 84. **1859** H.
KINGSLEY *Geof. Ham.* ch. 31. **1891** J. L. KIPLING
Beast & Man 125 Where we should say, 'The
early bird catches the worm', the Indian rustic
says, 'who sleeps late gets the bull-calf, he who
rises early the cow-calf'—which is more valuable.

Early master, long (soon) knave.

(M 712)

c. **1350** *Douce MS.* 52 no. 68 Erly master, longe
knave. *c.* **1450** *Provs. of Wysdom* l. 33 To erly
mayster, the sonner knave. **1641** FERGUSSON
no. 245. **1721** KELLY 95 (soon) . . . When a
Youth is too soon his own Master, he will
squander his Patrimony, and so must turn
Servant.

Early pricks that will be a thorn, It.

(T 232)

c. **1350** *Douce MS.* 52 no. 137 Hit is sone
sharpe þat schal be a thorne. *c.* **1450** *Coventry
Plays* E.E.T.S. 56 Yt ys eyrly scharp thatt wol
be thorne. **1523** SKELTON *Garl. of Laurell* 1437
Wks. (Dyce) I. 418 It is sone aspyed where the
thorne prikkith. **1546** HEYWOOD II. ix. L1 It
priketh betymes, that will be a good thorne.
c. **1557** *Jacob & Esau* Hazl.-Dods. ii. 196 Young
it pricketh (folks do say), that will be a thorn,
Esau hath been naught, euer since he was born.
1590 LODGE *Rosalynde* Wks. (1883) I. 18 What
sirha, well I see earlie prickes the tree that will
prooue a thorne. **1591** SHAKES. *3 Hen. VI* V. v.
13 What! can so young a man begin to prick?
1636 CAMDEN 295. **1721** KELLY 97 . . .Children
soon shew their Propensities and Inclinations.

Early sow, early mow.   (S 688)

1639 CLARKE 233. **1721** KELLY 96 . . . The
sooner a Man sets about a Business, the sooner
he finds the Effects of it.

Early to bed and early to rise, makes a man healthy, wealthy, and wise.

(B 184)

1496 *Treatise of Fishing with an Angle* hi As the
olde englysshe prouerbe sayth in this wyse, who
soo woll ryse erly shall be holy helthy and zely.
1523 FITZHERBERT *Husbandry* E.D.S. 101 At
grammer-scole I lerned a verse, . . . Erly rysyng
maketh a man hole in body, holer in soule, and
rycher in goodes. **1599–1601** SHAKES. *T.N.* II.
iii. 3 Not to be a-bed after midnight is to be up
betimes; and *diluculo surgere*, thou knowest,
——. **1602** [T. HEYWOOD?] *How a Man may
Choose* Hazl.-Dods. ix. 27 Diluculo surgere est
saluberrimum. **1639** CLARKE 91. **1766** *Goody
Two-Shoes* (3 ed.) II. i. Ralph, the raven, composed the following verse, . . . 'Farly to bed, and
early to rise, Is the way to be healthy, and
wealthy, and wise.' **1853** SURTEES *Sponge's
Sport. T.* ch. 9 Early to bed and early to rise
being among Mr. Sponge's maxims, he was
enjoying the view . . . shortly after daylight.

Early up and never the nearer.   (E 27)

1546 HEYWOOD I. ii. A3 They were earely vp,
and neuer the nere. **1601** MUNDAY & CHETTLE
Death of Earl of Huntington F4 Y'are earely up
and yet are nere the neare. **1629** T. ADAMS *Serm.*
(1861–2) I. 505 He is early up and never the
nearer; saluting Christ in the morning but none
of those that stayed with him.

Early wed, early dead.

1615 *The Cold Year, 1614* (*Old Bk. Collector's
Miscellany* ed. Hindley ii. 8) Early bridals, make
early burials. **1895** *N. & Q.* 8th Ser. VIII. 516.

Early, *see also* God's help is better than e. rising; Plaints e. that plaints on his kail; Rises over e. that is hanged ere noon.

Earnest, *see* Mows may come to e.

Ears (on either ear), To sleep securely on both. (E 24)

[ERASM. *Adagia* 307b: In utramvis dormire aurem, est animo ocioso, securo, vacuoque esse.] **1540** PALSGRAVE *Acolastus* 25 I lyke one that sleapeth on bothe his eares. i. than had I noth-thynge to breake my slepe with. **1571** R. EDWARDS *Damon & Pithias* C1 At night secure dormiunt in vtranque aurem. **1572** CRADOCKE *Ship of Assured Safety* 178 Sleeping soundly and quietly on bothe the eares. **1602** *Poet. Rhap.* II, i. 51 Thy store will let thee sleepe on either eare. **1672** MARVELL *Reh. Trans.* Gros. 121 As to any answer to Bayes his second Book or his third, for ought I can see, J. O. sleeps on both ears.

Ears glow, If your | someone is talking of you. (E 14)

c. **1374** CHAUCER *Troilus* Bk. 2, l. 1021 And we shal speek of the somwhat, I trowe, Whan thow art gon, to don thyn eris glowe! **1546** HEYWOOD II. i. F3 Hir eares might well glow, For all the towne talkt of hir. **1584** R. SCOT *Disc. of Witch-craft* xii. 16. **1602** *Ent. at Harefield* (Bond's Lyly i. 491) All this day my left eare glowed . . . allwaies a signe of Strangers, if it be in Summer; . . . if . . . in the Winter, 'tis a signe of Anger. **1673** MARVELL *Reh. Trans.* Pt. II. Gros. 321 My ears, Mr. Bayes, do not so much as glow for all your talking of them.

Ear(s), *see also* Ass is known by his e.; Belly wants e.; Cities are taken by e.; Dare not for his e.; Deaf e., (To turn a); Fear has a quick e.; Fields have eyes, woods e.; Flea in e.; Harvest e. thick of hearing; Hear on that e., (He cannot); In at one e.; Kings have many e.; Lead one by e.; Lend me your e. awhile; Little pitchers have great e.; Music eye of e.; Nature has given two e., one tongue; Pair of e. draws hundred tongues; Play with the e. than tongue (Better); Set by the e.; Shake your e.; Sow by the e. (To have); Spies are e. and eyes of princes; Tell you a tale and find you e.; Up to the e.; Walls have e.; Wide e. and short tongue; Wolf by e.

Earth big[1] the dyke,[2] Let the. (E 34)

a. **1628** CARMICHAELL no. 1225 Of the earth the dyke mon be bigged. **1641** FERGUSSON no. 678 Of the earth mon the dyke be biggit. **1721** KELLY 235 . . . Let the Expense that attends a Thing, be taken out of the Profit that it yields. [[1] build. [2] ditch.]

Earth, *see also* Pomp the e. covers; Six feet of e. make all equal; Wots not whether he bears the e.

Earthen pot must keep clear of the brass kettle, The. (P 495)

[= the weaker must avoid a collision with the stronger.] **1586** APOCRYPHA *Eccles.* ch. 13, v. 2 For how agree the kettle and the earthern pot together? for if the one be smitten against the other, it shall be broken. **1612–15** BP. HALL *Contempl.* XXI. v (1825) II. 133 Now see, what it is for thine earthen pitcher to knock with brass. Now, where is the man that would needs contest with Haman? **1732** FULLER no. 4494. **1822** SCOTT *Nigel* ch. 11 Buckingham is Lord of the Ascendant . . . ; You are the vase of earth; be-ware of knocking yourself against the vase of iron. **1909** *Spectator* 8 May 745 A dispassionate explanation of the unfortunate consequences that would inevitably happen should the cracked earthen pot [Russia] come into contact with the iron vessel [Germany].

Ease who has enough, He is at. (E 36)

c. **1350** *How the Gd. Wife* l. 94 At ese he is þat selde þonket.[1] *c.* **1460** *Wisdom* E.E.T.S. l. 70, 54 Farewell, consyens! I know not yow; I am at eas, hade I inow. **1493** [H. PARKER] *Dives & Pauper* I[v] It is an olde prouerbe: He is wel at ease that hath inough. [[1] gives thanks.]

Ease, If you would be at | all the world is not. (E 39)

1640 HERBERT no. 1019.

Ease makes thief.

c. **1180** *Hali Meidenhad* 17 Eise makeð þeof. *c.* **1300** *Provs. of Hending* (ed. Schleich) in *Anglia* 51. 272 Wrothelich endit, þat liþir doth. *c.* **1350** *Douce MS. 52* no. 35 Ese makyth thefe.

Ease (*noun*), *see also* All men will please (He that) shall never find e.; Angry (He that is) is seldom at e.; Cap is better at e. than head; Honour and e. seldom bedfellows; Itch and e. can no man please; Pennyworth of e.; Suffer-ance (Of) comes e.; Take one's e. in one's inn; Think of e. but work on; World's wealth (If we have not) have world's e. *See also* At ease.

Ease (*verb*), *see* Nothing is (Where), little thing doth e.

Easier (sooner) said than done. (S 116)

c. **1450** *Religious and Love Poems* [E.E.T.S. cited in Arden ed. of *3 Henry VI* III. ii. 90] Better saide thanne doon. **1483** *Vulg.* (1529) C8 *Facilius multo est dictu quam factu* It is easyer to saye than to do. **1519** HORMAN *Vulg.* (James) 119. **1546** HEYWOOD II. v. H4[v] That is (quoth she) sooner saiyd than done, I drede. **1681** ROBERTSON 471 'Tis more difficult then you think for; sooner said then done. **1824** MOIR *Mansie W.* ch. 9. **1884** BLACKMORE *Tommy Up.* ch. 18.

Easier to commend poverty than to endure it, It is.

1666 TORRIANO *It. Prov.* 214 no. 26.

Easier to, *see under significant words following.*

Easily done is soon believed, That which is. (D 419)

1664 CODRINGTON 216. **1670** RAY 8.

East Indies, *see* Safe from the E. I. and drowned in Thames.

East or west, home is best.

1869 SPURGEON *John Ploughman's Talk* ch. 13.

East, *see also* Longer e. shorter west; North for greatness, e. for health; Rain from e.; Too far e. is west; Wind's in the e. (When), neither good for man nor beast; Wind's in the e. on Candlemas Day (When). . . .

Easter, At | let your clothes be new, or else be sure you will it rue.

c. **1595** SHAKES. *R.J.* III. i. 27 Didst'thou not fall out with a tailor for wearing his new doublet before Easter? **1875** DYER *Brit. Pop. Cust.* (1900) 160 Poor Robin says: . . .

Easter day, If it rains on | There shall be good grass but very bad hay.

1686 A. WOOD *Life & Times* W.C. 288.

Easter day lies in our Lady's lap, When | then, O England, beware of a clap.

(E 48)

1614 T. ADAMS *Soul's Sickn.* Wks. 472 He dreams . . . of a popish curse. And Our Lord lights in our Ladies lappe, and therefore England must haue a clappe. **1616** *Id. Diseases of the Soul* 64 [The Busy-body is a dangerous Prognosticator as] Our Lord lights in our Ladies lappe, and therefore England must haue a clappe. **1654** E. GAYTON *Pleasant Notes upon Don Quixote* 47 Those yeares most joyfull where our Ladies day (being Rent-day) fals out late, when the Lady lies in the Lords lap. **1659** HOWELL *Eng. Prov.* 16b When Christ falleth in our Ladies lapp, Then lett England look for a clapp. **1662** FULLER Berks. 83 'When our Lady falls in our Lord's lap Then let England beware a sad clap/ mishap', *alias*, 'Then let the Clergy-man look to his cap' . . . It . . . would intimate . . . as if the blessed Virgin . . . watcheth an opportunity of Revenge on this Nation. And when her day (being the five and twentieth of March . . .) chanceth to fall on the day of Christs Resurrection, then . . . some signal judgment is intended to our State, and Church-men especially. **1910** *Times Wkly.* 13 May How strange Good Friday should have fallen on Lady Day[1] this year! The old proverb has come too true: 'If our Lord falls on our Lady's lap, England shall have a great mishap.' [1 Feast of Annunciation, 25 Mar.]

Easter so longed for is gone in a day.

(E 47)

1611 COTGRAVE s.v. Pasques The long-desired Passeouer is in a day past ouer. **1642** TORRIANO 84. **1658** *Comes Facundus* 193. **1659** HOWELL *Eng. Prov.* 20b.

Easter, *see also* Jews spend at E.; Short Lent that must pay at E.; Warrant you for egg at E.

Easterly winds and rain bring cockles[1] here from Spain.

1846 DENHAM 12. [1 A weed of the cornfields, or a disease which turns the corn black.]

Easy as an old shoe.

1825 BROCKETT *N. C. Gloss* s.v. Old-Shoe. **1894** NORTHALL *Folk Phrases* 8 (E.D.S.).

Easy as kiss my hand, As.   (H 64)

1665 C. COTTON *Scarron.* (1715) IV. 61 But you may make em, at Command, As eas'ly stay as kiss your Hand. **1666** TORRIANO *Prov. Phr.* s.v. Terra 214 To be like spitting on the ground, viz. an easy matter; the English say, As easie as to kiss ones hand. **1878–9** A. TROLLOPE *John Caldigate* ch. 38 It's as easy as kiss.

Easy as lying, As.

1600–1 SHAKES. *H.* III. ii. 347 'Tis as easy as lying. **1890** J. PAYN *Burnt Million* ch. 40 'As easy as lying', is a common proverb, but it must have been invented by an optimist.

Easy come, easy go. *Cf.* Lightly come; Quickly come.

1832–8 S. WARREN *Diary of L. Phys.* ch. 22 . . . characteristic of rapidly acquired commercial fortunes. **1861** H. SPENCER *Education* ch. 2 . . . a saying as applicable to knowledge as to wealth.

Easy to fall into a trap, but hard to get out again, 'Tis.   (T 468)

1580 LYLY *Euph. & his Eng.* ii. 157 It is easie to fall into a Nette, but hard to get out. **1732** FULLER no. 5072.

Easy to keep the castle that was never besieged.

a. **1628** CARMICHAELL no. 901. **1721** KELLY 96 Eith[1] to keep the Castle that was never beseeg'd. [1 easy.]

Easy to, *see also* under *significant words following.*

Eat a buttered fagot, He that would (must) | let him go to Northampton.   (F 22)

1662 FULLER Northampt. 281 (must) . . . Because it is the dearest Town in England for fuel, where no Coles can come by Water, and little Wood doth grow on Land. **1678** RAY 328.

Eat a good dinner, He that would | let him eat a good breakfast.   (D 343)

1605 *Fair Maid Bristow* C1 For as the old saying is, He that hath a good dinner, knowes better the way to supper. **1666** TORRIANO *It. Prov.* 60 no. 121. **1678** RAY 124.

Eat a hen in Janivere; If one knew how good it were to | had he twenty in the flock, he'd leave but one to go with the cock.   (H 422)

1630 CROSFIELD *Diary* Jan. 29, ed. Boas 40 He that will live another yeare must eate a hen in Januvere. **1659** HOWELL *Eng. Prov.* 21a. **1670** RAY 213.

Eat a peck of dirt (ashes, salt) before he dies, Every man must. (M 135)

1603 CHETTLE, DEKKER, HAUGHTON *Patient Grissil* I. ii. 15 I thinke I shall not eate a pecke of salt: I shall not liue long sure. **1639** CLARKE 165 (ashes). **1659** HOWELL Letter of Advice I You and I having eaten a peck of salt together. **1670** RAY 57. **1738** SWIFT Dial. I. E.L. 274. **1819** J. KEATS *Letters* (ed. M. B. Forman) 315 This is the second black eye I have had since leaving school . . . we must eat a peck before we die. **1883** PAYN *Thicker than Water* ch. 49 It is a sin of omission, . . . a portion of that peck of dirt which we are all said to eat in our lives without knowing it.

Eat a pudding at home, If you | the dog shall have the skin. (P 625)

1623 CAMDEN 272. **1639** CLARKE 102.

Eat above the tongue, like a calf, You. (T 410)

1678 RAY 348.

Eat and eat, You | but you do not drink to fill you. (E 51)

1670 RAY 33 . . . That much drinking takes off the edge of the Appetite to meat, we see by experience in great drinkers, who for the most part do (as we say) but pingle[1] at their meat and eat little. [[1] trifle.]

Eat, and welcome; fast, and heartily welcome. (E 49)

1678 RAY 84. **1721** KELLY 98 (twice) . . . A jocose Invitation to our known Friend to eat. **1732** FULLER no. 1355.

Eat another yard of pudding first, You must.

1830 FORBY 428 . . . *i.e.* You must wait till you grow older.

Eat at pleasure, drink by measure. (P 409)

c. **1532** SIR ADRIAN FORTESCUE no. 24 Eate & drink by measor, and defye thy leche. **1611** COTGRAVE s.v. Pain. **1670** RAY 38 . . . This is a French Proverb, Pain tant qu'il dure, vin à mesure, and they themselves observe it.

Eat gold, If she would | he would give it her.

1576 PETTIE i. 146 If you would eat gold, as they say, you might have it. **1708** CENTLIVRE *Busy Body* III. iv. If . . . eating gold, as the old saying is, can make thee happy, thou shalt be so. **1738** SWIFT Dial. I. E.L. 288.

Eat his part on Good Friday, He may. (P 75)

1546 HEYWOOD I. xi. D4 He maie his parte on good fryday eate, And fast neuer the wurs, for ought he shall geate. **1596** SHAKES. *K.J.* I. i.

234 Sir Robert might have eat his part in me Upon Good Friday and ne'er broke his fast.

Eat me without salt (with garlic), He could. (s 78)

c. **1425** *Castle of Perseverance* l. 1372 We haue etyn garlek euerychone. **1580** BARET *Alveary* O33 Odium agreste . . . A Prouerbe vsed, when a man hateth one euen with a deadlie hate, and as our phrase of speach is, He could willingly eate his heart with salt. **1624** JONSON *Neptune's Triumph* vii. 689 They are fishes. But ha' their garlick, as the Prouerb sayes. **1639** CLARKE 71 You must not think to eat me up without salt. **1670** RAY 173 He could eat my heart with garlick. That is, he hates me mortally. **1721** KELLY 157 He could eat me bul[1] salt . . . . The Man hates me vehemently. **1738** SWIFT Dial. I. E.L. 277 Does not miss look as if she could eat me without salt? [[1] without.]

Eat of the goose that shall graze on your grave, He hopes to. (G 353)

1509 BARCLAY *Ship of Fools* ii. 170 Suche as they moste gladly dede wolde haue Etyth of that gose that graseth on theyr graue. **1599** PORTER *Angry Wom. Abingd.* l. 496 The goose that grazeth on the greene, quoth he, May I eate on, when you shall buryed be!' **1639** CLARKE 236.

Eat one's heart (out), To. (H 330)

[*Il.* 6. 202 *Ὃν θυμὸν κατέδων.* ERASM. *Ad. Cor ne edito.*] *c.* **1535** ELYOT *Educ.* F2 Eate no harte, what doth it els signifie, but accombre not thy mynde with thoughtes, ne do not fatigate the with cares? **1539** TAVERNER 54[v] Eate not thy harte (that is to saye) consume not thy selfe wyth cares. **1579** LYLY *Euph.* i. 281 Not to eate our heartes: that is, that wee shoulde not vexe our selues with thoughts. **1596** SPENSER *F.Q.* I. ii. 6 He could not rest; but did his stout heart eat. **1600** J. PERROTT *Consideration of Human Condition* Pt. I 19 That olde Adage, which adviseth a man not to eate up his hearte, signifying that such as are troubled with much sorowe, consume away, even as if they had eaten up their owne heartes. **1616** DRAXE no. 1348 He eateth his owne heart. **1621** BURTON *Anat. Mel.* I. ii. II. vi. (1836) 159 Achilles eating of his own heart in his idleness, because he might not fight. **1625** BACON *Ess., Friendship* Arb. 171 The Parable of Pythagoras is darke, but true; Cor ne edito; Eat not the Heart. [Quoted by PLUTARCH *De Educ. Puer.* 17.] **1850** TENNYSON *In Mem.* cviii. 3 I will not eat my heart alone.

Eat one's words, To. (W 825)

1551 CRANMER *Ans. to Gardiner* 172 Brynge you forthe some place in my booke, where I saye, that the lordes supper is but a bare signification withoute anye effecte or operation of god in the same, or else eate your woordes. **1571** GOLDING *Calvin on Ps. lxii. 12,* I. 236[v] God eateth not his word when he hath once spoken. **1580** BARET *Alveary* M136. **1598–9** SHAKES. *M.A.* IV. i. 276 Will you not eat your word? **1599** *Id. A.Y.* V. iv. 143 I will not eat my word, now thou art mine. *a.* **1618** RALEIGH *Rem.* (1644) Nay wee'le make you confesse . . . and eat your own words. **1670** RAY 173.

Eat (a person) out of house and home, To. (H 784)

c. **1410** *Towneley Plays* E.E.T.S. xiii. l. 244 Bot were I not more gracyus and rychere befar, I were eten outt of howse and of harbar. **1509** BARCLAY *Ship of Fools* ii. 93 And ete theyr mayster out of hous Deuourynge his good tyll he be pore and bare. **1527** TYNDALE *Parable of Wicked Mammon* P.S. 122 Eat the poor out of house and harbour. [*c.* **1591**] **1598** *Famous Vict. of Hen. V* B4ᵛ (out of doores). **1598** SHAKES. *2 Hen. IV* II. i. 70 All I have. He hath eaten me out of house and home. **1712** ARBUTHNOT *John Bull* (1755) 53 John's family was like to be eat out of house and home. **1832** HT. MARTINEAU *Life in Wilds* iv. 54.

Eat the devil as the broth he is boiled in, As good. (D 291)

1545 BRINKLOW *Lamentacyon* E.E.T.S. 89 If it be so that God, through the kynge, hath caste out the deuell out of this realme, and yet both he and we soppe of the broth in which the deuell was soden. **1670** RAY 80. **1738** SWIFT *Dial.* II. E.L. 306.

Eat (Have) the fruit, He that would | must climb the tree.

1721 KELLY 141. **1732** FULLER no. 2366.

Eat the kernel, He that will | must crack the nut. (K 19)

[PLAUTUS *Curc.* I. I. 55 *Qui a nuce nucleum esse vult, frangit nucem.*] *c.* **1500** in *Antiq. Repertory* (1809) iv. 416 And yf ye wolde the swetnes haue of the kyrnell, Be content to byte vpon the harde shell. **1539** TAVERNER 47 He that woll eate the carnell out of the nutte, breaketh the nutte. He that loke for profyte, maye not flee labours. **1584** WITHALS D5. **1670** RAY 84 ... No gains without pains. **1831** MACAULAY *Ess., Johnson* (1872) 183 It is certain that those who will not crack the shell of history will never get at the kernel.

Eat the (*or* one's) leek, To.

1599 SHAKES. *Hen. V* V. i. 10 He is come to me ... and pid me eat my leek. **1835** DISRAELI *Let.* 20 Aug. in *Cor. Sister* (1886) 43 It was whispered the Whigs meant to swallow the Corporation leek. **1859** *All Year Round* No. 29. 61 The Welshmen very humbly ate their leek. **1902** G. W. E. RUSSELL *Coll. & Recol.* 2 Ser. (1909) 118 A politician who had once professed Republicanism was made to eat the leek in public before he could be admitted to the Cabinet.

Eat thy meat, and drink thy drink, and stand thy ground, old Harry. (M 813)

1678 RAY 343.

Eat till you sweat and work till you freeze.

a. **1570** *Marriage of Wit and Science* Shakes. Soc. 12. **1579** LYLY *Euph.* i. 251 Neyther was I much vnlike these Abbaie lubbers in my lyfe ... which laboured till they were colde, eat till they sweate,

and lay in bed til their boanes aked. **1721** KELLY 100 ... An upbraiding Speech to lazy Servants who love Meat better than Work. **1732** FULLER no. 2424.

Eat to live and not live to eat. (E 50)

c. **1410** *Secreta Secret.* E.E.T.S. 67 I will ete so that y leue and noght lyf that y ete. **1539** TAVERNER I *Garden* B2ᵛ Socrates sayde, many lyued to eate and drynke, but he contrarily dyd eate and drynke to lyue. *c.* **1552** T. BECON *Treatise of Fasting* P.S. 545 We live not to eat, but we eat to live. *c.* **1577** NORTHBROOKE *Dicing, etc.* Shakes. Soc. 40 Thou lyuest not to eate, butte eat as thou mayest lyue. **1621** BURTON *Anat. Mel.* II. ii. I. ii (1651) 235 Eat and live, as the proverb is, ... that only repairs man which is well concocted, not that which is devoured. **1733** FRANKLIN *Poor Richard* 'May' Eat to live, and not live to eat.

Eat well is drink well's brother. (D 658)

1659 HOWELL *Span. Prov.* 23 Who eats well and drinks well doth do his duty. **1721** KELLY 95 ... Spoken when we have eaten well, and taken a large Draught after. **1732** FULLER no. 1357.

Eat white bread? When shall we | When the puttock is dead.

[*Puttock* = a kite; hence, a greedy fellow.] **1629** T. ADAMS *Serm.* (1861–2) II. 329 We may sing, or rather sigh one to another, as little children chant in the streets: 'When shall we eat white bread? When the puttock is dead': when there is not a sacrilegious lawyer left.

Eat your brown bread first, It is a good thing to.

1830 FORBY 429 ... *i.e.* If you are unfortunate in the early part of life, you may hope for better success in future.

Eat your cake and have your cake (it), You cannot. (C 15)

1546 HEYWOOD II. ix. L2 I trowe ye raue, Wolde ye bothe eate your cake, and haue your cake? **1611** DAVIES no. 271 A man cannot eat his cake and haue it stil. *a.* **1633** HERBERT *The Size* 138 Wouldst thou both eat thy cake and have it? **1738** SWIFT *Dial.* I. E.L. 287 She was handsome in her time; but she cannot eat her cake and have her cake. *a.* **1763** SHENSTONE *Detached Thoughts* 'A person cannot eat his cake and have it' is, as Lord Shaftesbury observed, a proper answer to many splenetic people. **1907** A. C. BENSON *From Coll. Window* (ed. 4) 35 There still remains the intensely human instinct, which survives all the lectures of moralists, the desire to eat one's cake and also to have it.

Eat your nails, You had as good.

1678 RAY 241. **1738** SWIFT *Dial.* I. E.L. 265.

Eaten a bear-pie, He that has | will always smell of the garden.[1] (B 148)

1659 HOWELL *Eng. Prov.* 18a. **1678** RAY 66. [¹ bear-garden.]

Eaten a horse, and the tail hangs out at his mouth, He has. (H 651)

[1596] 1605 *Stukeley* l. 1314. 1678 RAY 74.

Eaten a snake, She has. (S 584)

1519 HORMAN *Vulg.* (James) 50 Thou hast eate an edders skyn. 1580 LYLY *Euph. & his Eng.* ii. 134 Therefore, hath it growen to a Prouerb in *Italy*, when one seeth a woman striken in age to looke amiable, he saith she hath eaten a Snake. *c.* 1605 DEKKER 2 *Hon. Whore* I. ii. 44 Scarce can I read the Stories on your brow, which age hath writ there; you looke youthfull still.—I eate Snakes, my Lord. 1639 CLARKE 166 (He).

Eaten (swallowed) a stake, He has. (S 810)

1530 PALSGRAVE 461a Haste thou eaten a stake, I shall make the [= thee] bowe. 1546 HEYWOOD I. xi. D3ᵛ How be it for any great courtesy he doth make, It seemth the gentyll man hath eaten a stake. 1611 DAVIES no. 340 Some Lasses haue eaten a stake to the end. *a.* 1637 JONSON *Underwoods* viii. 141 Drest, you still for man should take him, And not think h' had eat a stake. 1678 RAY 271 He hath swallowed a stake, he cannot stoop.

Eaten bread is (soon) forgotten. (B 620)

1599 MINSHEU *Span. Gram.* 80. 1623 CAMDEN 268. 1639 CLARKE 169. 1890 CHADWICK *Comment. on Exod.* ch. 16 The bitter proverb that eaten bread is soon forgotten must never be true of the Christian.

Eaten his bed straw, To look as if he had. (B 201)

1678 RAY 286.

Eaten the hen's rump, He has.

1642 TORRIANO 58 . . . That is, he is full of talk, for in Italy the rump is . . . presented to . . . the most talkative. 1659 HOWELL *It. Prov.* 16 Ha mangiato del culo della gallina. He is full of talk, it being the custome in Italy to give the greatest talker the rump of the hen. 1813 RAY 191.

Eaten your dinner off the floor, You might have.

1843 T. C. HALIBURTON *Attaché* I. 201 You might eat off the floor a'most, all's so clean. 1848 DICKENS *Dombey & Son* ch. 2 The cleanest place, my dear! You might eat your dinner off the floor. 1864 J. PAYN *Lost Sir Massingb.* ch. 32 [A] spotless kitchen, so exquisitely clean that you might, as the phrase goes, 'have eaten your dinner off the floor'.

Eaters, *see* Nice e. seldom meet with good dinner.

Eating and drinking, He was an ingenious man that first found out.

1738 SWIFT Dial. II. E.L. 304.

Eating and drinking takes away one's stomach. (E 54)

1611 COTGRAVE s.v. Mangeant Eating and drinking will take away any mans stomack. 1670 RAY 84. 1738 SWIFT Dial. II. E.L. 299. 1785 GROSE *Dict. Vulg. T.* s.v. Damper Eating and drinking being, as the proverb wisely observes, apt to take away the appetite.

Eating and drinking wants but a beginning.

1721 KELLY 98.

Eating and scratching wants but a beginning. (S 166)

c. 1641 FERGUSSON MS. no. 382 (and clawing). 1666 TORRIANO *It. Prov.* 141 no. 3 (all lyes in the beginning). 1721 KELLY 286 (Scarting and eating) Spoken when People eat more than they thought they could, or to persuade People of weak Stomachs to begin. 1732 FULLER no. 5158 To eat and to scratch a man need but begin. 1738 SWIFT Dial. II. E.L. 297.

Eats his cock alone, Who | must saddle his horse alone. (C 490)

1599 MINSHEU *Span. Gram.* 84. 1640 HERBERT no. 348. 1706 STEVENS s.v. Gallo.

Eats least eats most, He that. (L 163)

1586 GUAZZO ii. 135 The lesse one eates, the more he eates. I meane he liveth longer to eat more. *a.* 1633 HERBERT 295 He that will eat much, let him eat little; because by eating little he prolongs his life. 1659 HOWELL *Span. Prov.* 23 Who eats much eats little. 1707 MAPLETOFT 53 He who eats most eats least.

Eats leaves and voids silk, He. (L 142)

1642 TORRIANO 50. 1659 HOWELL *It. Prov.* 11 (and shites silk).

Eats most porridge, He that | shall have most meat.

1706 STEVENS s.v. Duro (Pottage). 1732 FULLER no. 2092.

Eats the calf in the cow's belly, He. (C 18)

1642 FULLER *H. & P. State* III. ix (1841) 163 The law of good husbandry forbids us to eat a kid in the mother's belly,—spending our pregnant hopes before they be delivered. 1721 KELLY 138 . . . Applied to them who spend their Rent before it be due. 1875 SMILES *Thrift* 277 Interest . . . goes on increasing until . . . it reaches . . . one hundred per cent. This is what is called 'eating the calf in the cow's belly'.

Eats the hard shall eat the ripe, He that. (H 146)

1640 HERBERT no. 210. 1706 STEVENS s.v. Duro.

Eats the king's goose shall be choked with the feathers, He that. (K 77)

1611 COTGRAVE s.v. Roy He that eateth a Goose of the Kings doth spue vp her feathers a hundred yeares after. *Ibid.* s.v. Oye . . . viz. He that

purloynes the Princes treasure payes in th'
arrerage (by himselfe, or his heires) one time or
another. **1629** T. ADAMS *Serm.* (1861–2) II. 507
What family, that hath had but a finger in these
sacrileges, hath not been ruinated by them? . . .
Remember the proverb: 'He that eats the king's
goose shall have the feathers stick in his throat
seven years after.' **1670** RAY 15.

Eats the meat, let him pick the bone, He who.

1706 STEVENS s.v. Carne Where they eat your
Flesh, let them gnaw the Bones.

Eat(s, en, ing, ate) *see also* Angler e. more than
he gets; Appetite comes with e.; Apple going to
bed; Ass that brays most e. least; Bake (As you)
so shall you brew (e.); Bit that one e. no friend
makes; Bitten (Though he be) he's not all e.;
Blind e. many a fly; Blind that e. his marrow;
Cats e. what hussies spare; Clothe thee warm, e.
little; Dog does not e. dog; Friars observant;
Humble pie; Hungry he could e. horse; Leeks in
Lide; Looks as big as if e. bull beef; Never a.
flesh (He that); Never be ashamed to e.; Often
and little e. makes fat; Peas with king; Shameful
leaving worse than shameful e.; Simonds sauce
(To e. of); Simpers like a mare when she e.
thistles; Stomachs to e., (He has two) one to
work; Sups ill who e. all at dinner; Thresher
(To e. like a); Trees e. but once; Work (He that
will not) shall not e.

Ebb will fetch off what the tide brings in, The. *Cf.* Flow has its ebb.   (T 284)

1587 *Mirror for Mag.* Churchyard 'Wolsey'
511 This weltring world, both flowes and ebs
like seas. **1664** CODRINGTON 216. The tide will
fetch away what the ebb brings. **1670** RAY 26
(as 1664). **1732** FULLER no. 4495.

Ebb(s), *see also* Flood but there is as low an e.,
(There is not so great a); Floods have low e.,
(High); Flow has its e.; Low e. at Newgate.

Ecce signum.   (S 443)

c. **1475** *Mankind* 609 The halter brast asondur
(Ecce signum). **1583** ELIZABETH to Burghley
(T. Wright *Eliz. & her Times* 1838 ii. 201) I have
of late seen an ecce signum, that if an ass kicke
you, you feele it too soone. [*c.* **1590**] **1594**
SHAKES. *Taming of A Shrew* B4. *c.* **1590** T. LODGE
& R. GREENE *Looking-Glass* l. 2250. *c.* **1591**
MARLOWE *Faustus* III. iii. *c.* **1592–5** *Thomas of
Woodstock* l. 1537. **1597** SHAKES. *1 Hen. IV*
II. iv. 161 My sword hack'd like a hand-saw—
ecce signum! I never dealt better since I was a
man. **1631** HEYWOOD 2 *Fair Maid* ii. 168.

Eden (river), *see* Uther-Pendragon.

Edenhall, *see* Luck of E.

Edge of his grave (pit's brink), He is upon the.   (E 57)

1574 WITHALS I 1ᵛ An old manne at the pittes
brinke. **1623** WODROEPHE 497. **1657** LEIGH
264 To be upon the brink of the pit. Alterum
pedem in cymba charonti habere.

Edge, *see also* Fall back fall e.

Edged tools, *see* Children and fools must not
play with e. t.; Jesting with e. t. (Ill).

Educate our masters, We must.

1867 ROBERT LOWE *Sp. in H. of Commons*, 15
July I believe it will be absolutely necessary that
you should prevail on our future masters to
learn their letters [popularized as above]. **1871**
FROUDE *Short Stud.* Ser. II, on Progress III 'We
must educate our masters', said Mr. Lowe
sarcastically.

Eels, He that will catch | must disturb the flood.

1594 LIPSIUS *6 Books of Politicks* tr. Jones R 1
As Aristophanes saith, it is good catching of
Eeles, when the water is stirred. **1607** *Lingua*
I. i.

Eel(s), *see also* Breed in the mud (All that) not
e.; Hide an e. in sack (Cannot); Hold of his word
as of a wet e. (As much); Holds a wet e. by the
tail, (He); Mud chokes no e.; Nimble as e.;
Nothing when you are used to it, as e. said; Put
your hand in creel and take out adder or e.;
Slippery as e.; Witham e.; Woman has an e. by
the tail, (Who has a).

Eelskins, *see* Merchant of.

Effect speaks, the tongue needs not, The.   (E 64)

1546 HEYWOOD ii. v. H4ᵛ But it is as folke dooe,
and not as folk say. **1640** HERBERT no. 709.

Effect, *see also* Cause (take away) and e. must
cease.

Efts, *see* Breed in the mud (All that) not e.

Egg and the hen, To have both the.   (E 80)

1573 SANFORD 109ᵛ There are men in the worlde,
that woulde haue the egge and the hen. **1578**
FLORIO *First F.* f. 33ᵛ There be many that wyl
. . . **1629** *Bk. Mer. Rid.* Prov. no. 118.

Egg, and to bed, An.   (E 68)

1639 CLARKE 113. **1732** FULLER no. 594.

Egg, But one | and that addled.

1659 HOWELL *Span. Prov.* 20 God gave me but
one Egge, and that was addle. **1706** STEVENS
s.v. Huevo. **1732** FULLER no. 1031. **1823**
COLLINS 14 Praise thyself chick, thou hast laid
an egg, and that a bad one.

Egg to the apples, From the.   (E 85)

[HORACE *Sat.* I. 3. 6 *Ab ovo usque ad mala*: i.e.
from the first to the last dish.] **1559** COOPER s.v.
Ouum Ab ouo vsque ad mala, prouerbially from
the begynnyng to the endyng. **1580** LYLY *Euph.*

& *his Eng.* ii. 216 To talke of other thinges in that Court wer to bring Egges after apples. **1584** WITHALS O7 From the beginning to the ende, *Ab ouo usque ad mala.* **1589** *Letters of Philip Gawdy* 31. **1619** J. FAVOUR *Antiquity* 595 Let vs repeate, not *ab ouo, ad malum*, from the egge to the apple, but *a nido ad malum.* **1639** CLARKE 3. **1848** BROS. MAYHEW *Image of his Father* ii. 16 'Let me hear all about it, as the Latin phrase runs, *ab ovo usque ad mala*—from beginning to end', said the doctor.

Egg will be in three bellies in twenty-four hours, An. (E 71)

1678 RAY 131. **1732** FULLER no. 1361.

Egg without salt, As an. (E 65)

1580 LYLY *Euph. & his Eng.* ii. 98 A wit ... without loue is lyke an Egge with-out salte. **1666** TORRIANO *Prov. Phr.* s.v. Cappari 29 To be as savoury as Capers without salt; the English say, as an egge without salt.

Egging, *see* Ill e. ill begging.

Eggs, To tread (walk) upon. (E 91)

[= to walk warily.] **1591** ARIOSTO *Orl. Fur.* Harington XXVIII. 63 So soft he treds, . . . As though to tread on eggs he were afraid. **1607** T. HEYWOOD *Wom. K. Kindness* sc. xiii. l. 21 Tread softly, softly.—I will walk on eggs this pace. *a.* **1734** NORTH *Ld. Guilford* (1808) I. 245 This gave him occasion . . . to find if any slip had been made (for he all along trod upon eggs). **1862** CALVERLEY *Verses & Transl.* Charades vi Each treading carefully about, as if he trod on eggs.

Eggs come to be fried, When the.

1620 SHELTON *Quix.* IV. x. ii. 26 It shall be perceived at the frying of the eggs, I mean that you shall see it when master inkeeper's worship . . . shall demand the loss and damage. **1823** COLLINS 26 'You will find it out when you are about to fry the eggs'.—A thief, . . . having stolen a frying-pan, was met by the master of the house . . . who asked him his business there; he answered, 'You will know it when you go to fry the eggs'.

Eggs for money, To take. (E 90)

[= to be put off with something worthless.] **[1571]** **1633** E. CAMPION *Hist. Ire.* II. ix. 113 Notwithstanding his high promises, having also the Kings power, he is glad to take eggs for his money, and bring him in at leysure. **1577** R. STANYHURST in Holinshed *Chron. Ireland* (1587) 94a Thomas . . . was soone intreated, hauing so manie irons in the fire, to take eggs for his monie. **1604** R. DALLINGTON *View of France* M I ᵛ The [French] Cauallery giues a furious onset at the first charge: but after that first heate, they will take egges for their money. **1611** SHAKES. *W.T.* I. ii. 161 Mine honest friend, Will you take eggs for money? **1670** G. H. *Hist. Cardinals* II. i. 130 Contented to take Eggs (as it were) for their money.

Eggs in one basket, To have (put) all your. Cf. Venture not all in one bottom. (E 89)

[= to risk all on a single venture.] **1666** TOR-RIANO *Prov. Phr.* s.v. Ova 125 To put all ones

Eggs in a Paniard, viz. to hazard all in one bottom. **1710** S. PALMER *Moral Essays on Prov.* 344 Don't venture all your Eggs in One Basket. **1874** WHYTE-MELVILLE *Uncle John* ch. 27 'May I carry your basket all my life?' 'If you'll put all your eggs in it, yes', answered Annie boldly. **1894** LD. AVEBURY *Use of Life* ch. 3 Do not put too many eggs in one basket. However well you may be advised, . . . something may occur to upset all calculations.

Eggs, He that would have | must endure the cackling of hens. (E 82)

1659 TORRIANO no. 206. **1670** RAY 120 Erasmus saith, they commonly say . . . It is I suppose a Dutch proverb. **1721** KELLY 223 I would not have your Cackling, for your Egg. I would not have your Trouble and Noise for all the Advantage you bring me.

Eggs on the spit, I have. (E 86)

[1598] 1601 JONSON *Ev. Man in Humour* III. iii. 42 I haue egges on the spit; I cannot go yet sir. **[1614] 1631** *Id. Barth. Fair* I. iv. 15 I haue both egges o' the Spit, and yron i' the fire. **1678** RAY 241 . . . I am very busie. Egges if they be well roasted require much turning. **1711** SWIFT *Jrnl. to Stella* 27 Dec. We have eggs on the spit, I wish they may not be addle. **1818** SCOTT *Rob Roy* ch. 28 (other eggs).

Eggs to fry, I have other. (E 87)

1659 HOWELL *Eng. Prov.* 12b.

Egg(s), *see also* Addled e. as idle bird (As good be); Apple, an e., and a nut; Better an e. to-day; Bird of the same nest (brood, e., feather); Bird such nest (e.), (Such); Break the e. in pocket; Cackle often but never lay e; Comes in with his five e.; Curate's e. (Like the); Dress an e. and give the offal; Drink as much after e. as after ox; Erasmus laid e. of Reformation; Evil crow, evil e.; Fool to roast e. (Set a); Full as an e. of meat; Give him the other half e.; Good e. nor bird (Neither); Half an e. is better than an empty shell; Hen e. goes to the ha' to bring goose e.; Never take a stone to break e.; Omelets; Peeled e. (Come to a); Reason in roasting of e.; Set my house on fire to roast e.; Shave an e. (Hard to); Steal an e. will steal an ox; Sure as e. is e.; Warrant you for an e. at Easter; Won with the e. and lost with shell.

Egg-pie, *see* Lancashire man.

Eggshell, Not worth an. (E 95)

1481 CAXTON *Reynard* 40, 110 Thou woldest not sette by me an egge shelle. *c.* **1500** T. MORE *These Four Things* 4 Wks. I. 340 This toye and that, and all not worth an egge. **1600–1** SHAKES. *H.* IV. iv. 53. Exposing what is mortal and unsure To all that fortune, death and danger dare, Even for an egg-shell. **1659** HOWELL *Eng. Prov.* 14a.

Egg-shell, *see also* Maids in Wanswell may dance in an e., (All the); Sail over the sea in e. (Hard to); Truss up his wit in e. (You may).

Eglinton, Earl of, *see* God send us some money.

Egypt, *see* Corn in E.; Enchantments to E.; Riches of E. are for foreigners.

Egyptians, *see* Spoil the E.

Eighth of June it rain, If on the | it foretells a wet harvest men sain.

1732 FULLER no. 6204.

Elbow-grease, It smells of.   (E 103)

1616 WITHALS 562. 1639 CLARKE 92. 1670 RAY 173.

Elbow grease gives the best polish.

1672 MARVELL *Reh. Trans.* I. v. Two or three brawny fellows in a corner with meer ink and elbow-grease do . . . harm. 1823 GALT *Entail* ch. 8 He has . . . dintit ma . . . table past a' the power o' bees-wax and elbow grease to smooth. 1830 FORBY 431 . . . i.e. hard rubbing makes furniture look brighter; generally industry is the surest road to success.

Elbow(s), *see also* Broken her e. (She has); Claw the e.; Eye nor my e. (Neither my); Out at e.; Pillows under the e. (To sew); Rub the e.; Scratch my breech, I'll claw your e.; Shake the e.; Spring in his e.; Touch your eye but with your e. (Never).

Elden Hole needs filling.   (E 105)

1670 RAY 173 . . . Spoken of a lier. Eldenhole is a deep pit in the Peak of Darbyshire.

Elder's white, When | brew and bake a peck; when elder's black, brew and bake a sack.   (E 106)

1678 RAY 352. *Somerset.*

Element, Out of one's.   (E 107)

1599 BROUGHTON'S *Lett.* viii. 26 You are in for all day . . . it is your element. 1600–1 SHAKES. *M.W.W.* IV. ii. 154 She works by charms, by spells, by th' figure, and such daub'ry as this is, beyond our element. 1601 *Id. T.N.* III. i. 54 Who you are and what you would are out of my welkin—I might say 'element' but the word is overworn. *Ibid.* III. iv. 118 I am not of your element. 1603 MONTAIGNE (Florio) III. ix. 78 They thinke themselves out of their element, when they are out of their Village. 1772 R. GRAVES *Spiritual Quixote* V. 14.

Element, *see also* Speak ill of others is fifth e.

Elephant, *see* Fly into an e. (Changes a).

Ell[1] and tell[2] is good merchandise.

1721 KELLY 95 . . . The best Market is to get ready Money for your Wares. [[1] ell-wand. [2] to count out money.]

Ell,(s), *see also* Hundred e.; Ill comes in by e.; Inch in a miss; Inch is as good as e.; Measure with long (short) e.

Elm has its man, Every.

1928 *Times* 29 Nov. 10/5 Owing to the frequency with which this tree sheds its branches, or is uprooted in a storm, it has earned for itself a sinister reputation. 'Every elm has its man' is an old country saying.

Elm, *see also* Ask pears of an e.; Vine embraces the e.

Eloquence, *see* Love and business teach e.

Embrace(s), *see* Fortune smiles (When) e. her; Greater e. the less; Vine e. the elm.

Emperor of Germany, The | is the King of kings; the King of Spain, king of men; the King of France, king of asses; the King of England, the king of devils.
                 (E 110)

1647 WARD *Simple Cobler* 51 There is a quadrobulary saying, which passes current in the Westerne World, That the Emperour is King of Kings, the Spaniard, King of Men, the French, King of Asses, the King of England, King of Devils. 1786 WOLCOT (P. Pindar) *Lousiad* iii. Wks. (1816) I. 191 I do not vish myself more greater efils— A king of Englis be a king of defils.

Emperor, *see also* Pope by voice . . . e. by force.

Empty hands no hawks allure.   (H 111)

[c. 1175 J. OF SALISBURY *Polycraticus* v. x *Veteri celebratur proverbio: Quia vacuae manus temeraria petitio est.*] c. 1386 CHAUCER *Reeve's T.* l. 4134 With empty hand, men may na haukes tulle [allure]. c. 1430 LYDGATE *Minor Poems* Percy Soc. 174 With empty hand may noon haukys lure, And lyke the audience, so uttir the language. c. 1549 HEYWOOD II. v. H1 He hath his haukes in thine mew but make ye sure, With empty hands men maie no haukes allure. 1612 WEBSTER *White Devil* III. ii 'Tis gold must such an instrument procure; With empty fist no man doth falcons lure. *a.* 1628 CARMICHAELL no. 1653.

Empty leech (tick) sucks sore, An.
                 (L 175)

1639 CLARKE 38 (tick). 1672 WALKER 36 no. 14.

Empty purse causes a full heart, An. *Cf.* Light purse makes a heavy heart.

1600 DEKKER *Old Fortunatus* I. ii. If his belly be emptie, his heart is full. 1734 FIELDING *Don Quix. in Eng.* I. vi.

Empty purse fills the face with wrinkles, An.   (P 648)

1616 DRAXE no. 1679. 1670 RAY 22. 1736 BAILEY *Dict.* s.v. Purse.

Empty purse that is full of other men's
money, That is but an. (P 662)
1678 RAY 194. **1732** FULLER no. 4352 (folks).

Empty sack (bag) cannot stand upright,
An. (B 30)
1642 TORRIANO 90 *Sacco vuoto non può star in
piedi.* An emptie sack cannot stand upright:
NOTA. Applied to such as either pinch themselves, or are pincht by hard fortune. **1758**
FRANKLIN *P. Rich. Alm.* in ARBER *Eng. Garner* v.
584 Poverty often deprives a man of all spirit
and virtue. 'Tis hard for an Empty Bag to stand
upright! **1788** B. FRANKLIN *Autobiog.* E.L. 114
(empty sack). **1896** LOCKER-LAMPSON *My
Confid.* 395 Gibbs . . . by this artifice . . . made
a hundred per cent . . . Gibbs was a needy man,
and . . . would often say, 'It's hard for an empty
sack to stand upright'.

Empty the baby with the bath, To.
1908 [1911] G. B. SHAW *Getting Married* Pref. 186
We shall in a very literal sense empty the baby
out with the bath by abolishing an institution
which needs nothing more than a little . . .
rationalizing to make it . . . useful. **1937**
MAISIE WARD *Insurrection versus Resurrection*
(T.L.S. 1 Jan. 1938 4b). **1944** G. B. SHAW
Everybody's Political What's What? 172 When
changing we must be careful not to . . . in mere
reaction against the past.

Empty vessels make the greatest
sound. (V 36)
1547 BALDWIN (1550, Q 4ᵛ) As emptye vesseles
make the lowdest sounde, so they that haue the
leaste wyt, are the greatest babblers. **1579** LYLY
Euph. i. 194 The emptie vessell giueth a greater
sownd then the full barrell. **1599** SHAKES. *Hen. V*
IV. iv. 64 I did never know so full a voice
issue from so empty a heart: but the saying is
true, 'The empty vessel makes the greatest
sound'. **1603** HOLLAND tr. *Plut. Morals* 159
Like empty vessels, void of sense and full of
sound. **1612–15** BP. HALL *Contempl.* XIII. i.
(1825) I. 370 Those vessels yield most sound,
that have the least liquor. **1707** SWIFT *Facult. of
Mind* Wks. (1856) II. 285 I have always observed
that your empty vessels sound loudest.

Empty (*adj. adv.*), *see also* Better an e. house;
Fill the mouth with e. spoon; Full of himself
(So) that he is e.; Half an egg is better than an
e. shell; Killing a crow with e. sling.

Empty (*verb*), *see also* Sea with a spoon, (To e.
the).

Enchantments to Egypt.
1853 TRENCH III. 68 The Rabbis [said]: *Enchantments to Egypt,* Egypt being of old accounted
the head-quarters of all magic.

Encounters, *see* Goes far (Who), has many e.

End before you begin, Think on the.
Cf. Look to the end. (E 128)
c. **1405** *The Castle of Perseverance* l. 3648 Euyr
at the begynnynge Thynke on your last endynge.

c. **1500** *Everyman* A 2 This story sayeth man in
the begynnynge Loke well and take good hede
to the endynge. **1592** DELAMOTHE 17 We must
thinke vpon, before we execute. **1692** R.
L'ESTRANGE *Fables* 83, I. 81 It is Wisdom to
Consider the End of Things before we Embark,
and to Forecast Consequences.

End crowns all (*or,* the work), The.
(E 116)
[L. *Finis coronat opus.*] *a.* **1548** REDFORD *Wit
and Science* l. 31 Thende of hys jornay wyll
aproue all. **1552** TAVERNER f. 74 The ende
declareth all. **1590–1** SHAKES. *2 Hen. VI* V. ii.
28 La fin couronne les œuvres. [*c.* **1589**] **1592**
KYD *Span. Trag.* II. vi. Thou talkst of haruest,
when the corne is greene: The end is crowne of
euery worke well done. **1592** DELAMOTHE 29
The end doth crowne the worke (La fin couronne
l'œuure). **1602** SHAKES. *T.C.* IV. v. 223 The
end crowns all, And that old common arbitrator,
Time, Will one day end it. **1602** *Id. A.W.* IV.
iv. 35 All's well that ends well: still the fine's
the crown; What e'er the course, the end is the
renown. **1614–16** *Times Whistle* E.E.T.S. 130
Successe by the event is knowne, the end Doth
every action praise, or discommend. **1615**
CHAPMAN *Od.* v. 58 But th' end shall crown all.

End goes forward, He cares not which.
(E 130)
[*c.* **1497**] *a.* **1520** MEDWALL *Fulgens* C1 For he
carith not whiche ende goth before. **1596** M. B.
Trial True Frdship B4 An idle . . . magistrate,
which cares not (as they say) which end goes
formost. **1616** DRAXE no. 2297. **1666** TOR-
RIANO *It. Prov.* 133 note 29 Prodigals . . . care
not which end goes formost.

End justifies the means, The. (E 112)
[**1650** JESUIT HERMANN BUSENBAUM *Medulla theol.
Cum finis est licitus, etiam media sunt licita.*]
1583 G. BABINGTON *Exposn. of the Commandments* P.S. 260 The ende good, doeth not by and
by make the meanes good. [**1624**] **1647** FLET-
CHER *Wife for Month* IV A little evil may well be
suffered for a general good, Sir. **1721** PRIOR
Hans. C. (1858) 88 What if to spells I had recourse, 'Tis but to hinder something worse! The
end must justify the means. **1820** SCOTT *Abbot*
ch. 12 It is in the cause of Heaven that I command them to embrace, . . . the end, sister, sanc-
tifies the means we must use. **1897** C. C. KING
Story Brit. Army 341 The districts annexed, and
righteously governed, had recently . . . been
'huge cockpits of slaughter'. The end here un-
questionably justified the means. **1907** W. H. G.
THOMAS *Genesis I–XXV* 198 How frequently this
remarkable combination of good motive and
bad conduct occurs in history and daily life! The
end does *not* justify the means, whatever people
may say.

End makes all equal, The. (E 117)
1573 SANFORD 106. **1611** DAVIES Prov. no. 66.
1732 FULLER no. 4496.

End of an old song, There is an.
(E 126)
1596 T. NASHE *Saffron W.* iii. 96 And so make an
end of an old song. **1603** DEKKER *Wonderful*

Year (*Plague Pamph*. ed. Wilson 61). **1675** C.
COTTON *Burlesque upon Burlesque* 160. **1721**
KELLY 331 . . . That is, you have all that I can
tell you of it.

End of one's tether, To reach the.

1523 FITZHERBERT *Husb*. § 148 (As long as thou
eatest within thy tedure, that thou nedest not to
begge nor borowe of noo man.) **1549** LATIMER *2nd
Serm. bef. Ed. VI*, To Rdr. (Arb.) 51 Learne to eat
within thy teather. **1690** LOCKE *Hum. Underst.*
I. i § 4 To prevail with the busy Mind . . . to stop,
when it is at the utmost Extent of its Tether.
a. **1734** NORTH *Exam*. III. viii § 57 (1740) 627 As
to the last Order . . . which properly belongs to
the next Reign and so beyond my Tedder. **1809**
MALKIN *Gil Blas* X. ii. 8 At length she got to the
end of her tether, and I began. **1858** TRELAWNY
Recollections ch. 6 (I am nearly at). **1873** J. S.
MILL *Autobiog*. 182 I had come to the end of my
tether; I could make nothing satisfactory of
Induction, at this time.

End of passion is the beginning of repentance, The.   (E 119)

1623 O. FELTHAM *Resolves* viii (Dent) 18 It often
falls out, that the end of passion is the beginning
of repentance. **1630** DEKKER *London Look Back*
(*Plague Pamph*. ed. Wilson 175) Repentance is
the Mother of Amendment.

End of the rainbow, Go to the | and you'll find a crock of money.

1836 W. D. COOPER *Glos. of Provin. in Sussex*
(1853) 40.

End of the staff (stick), To have (*or* get) the better (*or* worse *or* wrong).   (E 132)

1387 TREVISA *Higden* (Rolls) II. 29 Men of þat
side schal haue the wors ende. **1533** UDALL
Flowers (1560) S6 As we halfe prouerbially saie
in englishe, to geue one the worse ende of the
staffe. **1534** *Two Coventry C.C. Plays* E.E.T.S.
45 He schal be sure, asse God me saue, Eyuer
the worse yend of the staff to haue. **1542** ERASM.
tr. Udall *Apoph*. (1877) 340 As often as thei see
theim selfes to haue the wurse ende of the staffe
in their cause. **1626** JACKSON *Creed* VIII. viii. 71
He having gotten (as wee say) the better end of
the staffe, did wrest our wills at his pleasure.
1753 RICHARDSON *Grandison* (1754) II. ii. 12 Miss
Byron, I have had the better end of the staff, I
believe? **1890** 'ROLF BOLDREWOOD' *Colon.
Reformer* ch. 20 You will rarely find that the
apparently impassive countryman has 'got the
wrong end of the stick'.

End tries all, The.   (E 116)

c. **1390** GOWER *Conf. Amantis* VI. 2383 An ende
proveth every thing. **1509** BARCLAY *Ship of
Fools* i. 207 Byde the ende, that onely prouyth
all. *c.* **1566** *The Bugbears* II. v. The end shall
trulye try. [*c.* **1591**] **1599** [GREENE?] *George a
Green* D3. **1597** *Wit's Commonwealth* 129 The
end of euery thing is the tryall of the action.
1598 SHAKES. *2 Hen. IV* II. ii. 45 Let the end try
the man. *a.* **1628** CARMICHAELL no. 1618.

Ending, *see* Ill beginning ill e.; Somerton e.

Ends ill which begins in God's name, That never.   (G 273)

1639 CLARKE 109.

End(s) (*noun*), *see also* Better e. of string; Both
e. meet (Make); Death is e. of all; Everything
has an e.; Fingers' e.; Fool does in e.; Game's
e. (At the) shall see who gains; Land's e.;
Longest day has e.; Longest night has e.; Look
to the e.; Love without e. has no e.; Make an e.
of your whistle though cart overthrow; See no
further than e. of nose; Staff's e., (To hold at);
Stay a while . . . e. the sooner; Tongue's e. (To
have at); Wills e. wills means; Wit's e.; World
still he keeps at his staff's e.

End(s) (*verb*), *see* Bairns o' Falkirk (Like) they'll
e. ere they mend; Mend or e.; War, (All may
begin a) few can e. it; Well that e. well; Wrong
comes to wrack (will e.).

Endure labour in this world, He that will not | let him not be born.   (L 2)

1573 SANFORD 50. **1629** *Bk. Mer. Rid.* Prov.
no. 7.

Endure to itch, He that will not | must endure to smart.   (I 105)

c. **1549** HEYWOOD I. x. D1 He whom in ytchyng
no scratchyng will forbeare, He must beare the
smartyng that shall folowe there. **1678** RAY 162.

Endure(d), *see also* Ass e. burden; Cured (What
can't be) must be e.; Mickle maun good heart e.;
No man better knows good than he who has e.
evil.

Endures is not overcome, He that.

(E 136)

[VERG. *Aen*. 5. 710 *Superanda omnis fortuna
ferendo*.] *c.* **1374** CHAUCER *Troilus* IV. 1. 1584
Men seyn 'the suffrant overcom'th', parde.
c. **1382** (?) GOWER *Vox Clam*. iii. 409 *Nobile
vincendi genus est pacientia*. **1629** *Bk. Mer.
Rid.* Prov. no. 28 He that can quietly endure
ouercommeth. **1640** HERBERT no. 854. **1641**
FERGUSSON no. 331 He that tholes overcomes.

Enemies, If you have no | it's a sign fortune has forgot you.   (E 145)

[PUBL. SYRUS (Ribbeck) 315 *Miserrima est
fortuna quae inimico caret*.] **1666** TORRIANO *It.
Prov.* 169, no. 11 He hath never a friend, who
hath never an enemie. **1670** C. HOOLE *Catonis
Disticha* 48 That fortune is most miserable that
wants an enemy. **1732** FULLER no. 2759.

Enemy, There is no little.   (E 142)

c. **1386** CHAUCER *T. Mel*. 1. 2512–13 Ne be nat
necligent to kepe thy persone, nat only fro thy
gretteste enemys but fro thy leeste enemy. Senek
seith: 'a man that is wel avysed, he dredeth his
leste enemy'.[1] **1659** HOWELL *Fr. Prov.* 8. **1733**
FRANKLIN Sept. **1887** LD. AVEBURY *Pleas. of
Life* I. v. Unfortunately, while there are few great
friends there is no little enemy. [[1] PUB. SYRUS
Sent. 255 *Inimicum, quamvis humilem, docti est
metuere*.]

Enemy, One | can do more hurt than ten friends can do good.

1711 SWIFT *Jrnl. to Stella* 30 June I have been gaining enemies by the scores, and friends by the couples, which is against the rule of wisdom, because they say . . .

Enemy, His own | is no one's friend.

1768 GOLDSMITH *Good-nat. Man* iv (Globe) 633 I see that it is in vain to expect happiness from him, who has been so bad an economist of his own; and that I must disclaim his friendship who ceases to be a friend to himself.

Enemy, If you would make an | lend a man money, and ask it of him again.

1813 RAY 7. *Lusit.*

Enemy may chance to give good counsel, An.

[ARISTOPHANES *Aves* 376 ’Αλλ’ ἀπ’ ἐχθρῶν δῆτα πολλὰ μανθάνουσιν οἱ σοφοί. And yet wise men learn much from enemies. OVID *Metamorph.* iv. 428 *Fas est et ab hoste doceri*; it is lawful to learn even from an enemy.] **1663** F. HAWKINS *Youth's Behaviour* F8ᵛ Fas est et ab hoste doceri. Instruction is good, though it come from an enemy. **1732** FULLER no. 600. **1911** *Spectator* 21 Sept. 594 It is lawful, declares the old Latin proverb, to be taught by one's foe.

Enemy seem a mouse, Though thy | yet watch him like a lion.

1732 FULLER no. 5015.

Enemy, In an | spots are soon seen.

1732 FULLER no. 2813.

Enemy your friend, Make your.

1639 CLARKE 189. **1641** FERGUSSON no. 325 He is wise that can make a friend of a foe.

Enemy's mouth seldom speaks well, An. (E 144)

1481 CAXTON *Reynard* iv Arb. 7 Sir Isegrym that is eyul sayd it is a comyn prouerbe An Enemyes mouth saith seeld wel.

Enemy (-ies), *see also* Art has no e. but ignorance; Bashfulness e. to poverty; Believe no tales from e.; Best is oftentimes e. of good; Better an open e.; Better go by your e.'s grave than his gate; Dallies with his e., (He that) dies by his own hand; Defend me from my friends; Forgive an e. (If we are to), not bound to trust; Friend to a bosom friend (No), no e. to bosom e.; Gifts from e. dangerous; Gives honour to his e. (He that); Golden bridge (For flying e.); Good is e. of the best; Hunger and cold deliver a man up to his e.; Keep yourself from . . . reconciled e.; Mickle power makes many e.; No man's e. but his own; Nothing worse than familiar e.; One e. is too many; Passes a winter's day (He that) escapes an e.; Reconciled e. (Take heed of);

Science has no e. but the ignorant; Servants (So many), so many e.; Speak well of friend, of e. say nothing; Strike the serpent's head with e.'s hand; Trust not . . . old e.; War is not done so long as e. lives; Wind that comes in . . . and reconciled e.

Engine(s), *see* Great e. on small pivots.

England a good land, and a bad people. (E 146)

1659 HOWELL *Fr. Prov.* 20 England's a good Countrey, but ill people. **1662** FULLER Berks. 87 . . . This is a French Proverb; and we are glad that they . . . will allow any goodness to another Country.

England is the paradise of women, the hell of horses, and the purgatory of servants. (E 147)

[**1583** R. D. *The Mirrour of Mirth* K1ᵛ Paris is a paradise for women, a hel for mens Horses, and a Purgatorye for those that followe suits of Law.] **1617** MORYSON *Itin.* iii. 53 England . . . is said to be the hell of horses, the purgatory of servants, and the paradise of women. **1630** DEKKER *Hon. Whore* Pt. II. iv. i. England, they say, is the only hell for horses, and only paradise for women. *c.* **1641** FERGUSSON MS. no. 1699 England is said to be a hel for horses a purgatorie for servantis ane paradice for wemen. **1662** FULLER Berks. 85 . . . For the first, *Bilia vera* . . . For the next, . . . *Ignoramus* . . . For the last, . . . we cast it forth as full of falshood.

England is the ringing island. (E 148)

1655 FULLER *Church Hist.* VI. ii. 288 This in England (commonly called the ringing Island) was done with tolling a bell. **1662** FULLER Berks. 84 ‘England is the ringing island.’ Thus it is commonly call'd by Foreigners, as having greater, moe, and more tuneable Bells than any one Country in Christendom.

England were but a fling, save for the crooked stick and the greygoose wing. (E 149)

1662 FULLER Berks. 85 . . . ‘But a fling’, . . . not to be valued. . . . ‘But for the crooked stick’, &c. That is, use of Archery. **1874** GREEN *Short Hist. Eng. P.* 261 [At Agincourt] his archers bared their arms . . . to give fair play to ‘the crooked stick and the grey goose wing’, but for which—as the rime ran—‘England were but a fling’.

England win, He that will | must with Ireland first begin. (E 150)

1567 DIEGO ORTIZ quoted in FROUDE, *Hist. of England* x. 480 There is an English proverb in use among them which says—... **1596** WARNER *Albion's Eng.* x. 54, R1ᵛ It is a saying auncient (not autenticall, I win) That who-so Englande will subdew, with Ireland must begin. **1617** MORYSON *Itin.* (1907) II. 170 Incouraged by the blind zeale . . . or animated by an olde Prophesie He that will England winne, Must with Ireland first beginne, did also raise two rebellions. **1662** FULLER Berks. 87 . . . England . . . is too great a morsel for a forreign foe to be chopped up at once; and therefore it must orderly be attempted, and Ireland be first assaulted.

England wrings, When | Thanet sings.

1892 *Murray's Handbk. Kent* (ed. 5) 219 The Isle of Thanet.—The soil is generally light and chalky, and a wet summer, elsewhere a great evil, is here rather longed for. Hence a local proverb—'When England wrings The island sings'.

England's difficulty is Ireland's opportunity.

1902–4 LEAN I. 35. **1914** *Spectator* 8 Aug. 190 That chapter in our history when it could be said that 'England's danger was Ireland's opportunity'.

England's wooden walls.

1576 LAMBARDE *Kent* 2 M2ᵛ Highe Ioue doeth giue thee walles of wood, appointed to Minerue, The which alone inuincible, may thee, and thine, preserue. **1585** SIR WALTER MILDMAY (cited J. E. Neale, *Eliz. & her Parliaments 1584–1601*, 55) The navy, being justly termed the wall of England. [*c.* 1587] **1594** MARLOWE & NASHE *Dido* I. i. 65 Epeus horse, to Aetnas hill transformed, Prepared stands to wracke their wooden walles. **1605** JONSON etc. *Eastw. Ho* II. ii. 100 Expose other mens substances to the mercie of the windes, under protection of a wooddden wall. *a.* **1607** DEKKER *Whore of Babylon* I. ii. 64 Weele build about our waters wooden walles. *c.* 1650 G. GOODMAN in *Court of James I* (1839, i. 53) The old saying was, that England was ditched about with the sea, and had wooden walls. **1662** FULLER *Cumberland* 215 Our wooden walls (so our ships are commonly called). **1703** *The Levellers* (*Harl. Misc.* v (1745), 416) Some say, That our Ships are the Walls of our Island.

England, *see also* Antwerp pistol pointed at heart of E.; Famine in E. begins at horse-manger; Gluttony is sin of E.; Heart of E.; Hempe is spun (When), E. is done; Little E. beyond Wales; Long beards heartless ... makes E. thriftless; Merry E.; Sand feeds the clay (When the); Victuals in E. (More good) than in other kingdoms; War with world, peace with E.; Wonders of E.

Englanders, *see* Little E.

English archer beareth under his girdle twenty-four Scots, Every.

1545 ASCHAM *Toxoph.* Arb. 84 The Scottes them selues ... gyue the whole prayse of shotynge honestlye to Englysshe men, saying thus: that euery Englysshe Archer beareth vnder hys gyrdle. xxiiii. Scottes.

English are a nation of shop-keepers, The.

1766 J. TUCKER *Four Tracts* III (1774) 132 A shop-keeper will never get the more Custom by beating his customers; and what is true of a Shop-keeper, is true of a Shop-keeping Nation. **1776** ADAM SMITH *Wealth Nat.* IV. vii (1828) III.

41 To found a great empire for the sole purpose of raising up a people of customers, may at first sight appear a project fit only for a nation of shopkeepers. **1848** THACKERAY *Vanity Fair* ch. 28. **1896** 'H. S. MERRIMAN' *Flotsam* ch. 9 We are shop-keepers. ... But at times we ... put up the shutters and lock the door—and then there is usually the devil to pay. **1911** *Times Wkly.* 17 Feb. Napoleon ... described the English as a nation of shopkeepers. Uttered in a sneering spirit, it embodied ... the profound truth that our prosperity is based upon our trade.

English are the swearing nation, The.

1713 DEFOE *Reasons agst. Suc. of H. Hanover* Wks. (Bohn) vi. 518 Nay, have we not been called in the vulgar dialect of foreign countries 'the swearing nation'?

English never know when they are beaten, The.

1853 G. J. WHYTE-MELVILLE *Digby G.* ch. 4 The name of Englishman [is] a type of all that is resolute, daring, and invincible. We have a high authority in the expression of Napoleon, that 'they never know when they are beaten'. **1911** J. H. A. MACDONALD in *Spectator* 30 Sept. 489 The British subject has a repute for not knowing when he is beaten, and it is a valuable quality for a martial race. ... But it has often been an injurious hindrance where the question was [one] ... of progress in things practical, especially in mechanical developments.

English summer, An | three (two) hot days and a thunderstorm.

1853 G. J. WHYTE-MELVILLE *Digby G.* ch. 5 The three fine days of an English summer too surely end with their proverbial thunderstorm. **1854** SURTEES *Hand. Cross* ch. 51 Summer was merely inserted as a sort of compliment,—three hot days and a thunderstorm being the general amount of an English summer. **1909** *Times* 28 May People speak of the English summer as consisting of three fine days ending in a thunderstorm.

English, *see also* King's E.; Wardour-street.

Englishman, One | can beat three Frenchmen.   (E 155)

1599 SHAKES. *Hen. V.* III. vi. 145 When they were in health, ... I thought upon one pair of English legs Did march three Frenchmen. **1745** HOR. WALPOLE *Let.* to G. Montagu 13 Jul. We, who formerly ... could any one of us beat three Frenchmen, are now so degenerated, that three Frenchmen can evidently beat one Englishman. **1748** BOSWELL *Johnson* (on the French Academy) This is the proportion ... As three to sixteen hundred, so is the proportion of an Englishman to a Frenchman. **1762** GOLDSMITH *Cit. World* cxx (Globe) 274 We had no arms; but one Englishman is able to beat five Frenchmen at any time. **1833** MARRYAT *P. Simple* ch. 46 My men, ... there are three privateers ... it's just a fair match for you—one Englishman can always beat three Frenchmen. **1851** BORROW *Lavengro* ch. 26 In the days of pugilism it was no vain boast to say, that one Englishman was a match for two of t'other race [i.e. the French].

Englishman is never happy but when he is miserable, An | a Scotchman never at home but when he is abroad, and an Irishman never at peace but when he is fighting.

1865 ABP. WHATELY *Commonpl.-Bk.* 293 (It has been said).

Englishman Italianate is a devil incarnate, The.   (E 154)

[Ital. *Inglese italianato è un diavolo incarnato.*] **1570** ASCHAM *Scholemaster* Arb. 78 The *Italian* sayth of the English Man, ... *Englese Italianato è un diabolo incarnato*, that is to say, you remaine men in shape and facion, but becum deuils in life and condition. **1580** LYLY *Euph. & his Eng.* ii. 88. **1591** GREENE *Disc. Coosnage* 6 I am Englishe borne, and I have English thoughts; not a Devill incarnate because I am Italianate. **1659** HOWELL *It. Prov.* I An Englishman Italianate is a Devil incarnate. **1873** J. R. GREEN *Lett.* 7 Feb. Don't think I am getting 'Italianate', which according to Ascham is pretty much the same as 'a devil incarnate'.

Englishman knows not when a thing is well, A right.   (E 156)

1545 S. GARDINER to Sir Wm. Paget (*Lett.* ed. Muller 180) They saye that an Englishe man in al feates excellith if he coulde leave whenne it is wel, which they cal tollere manum de tabula. **1591** ARIOSTO *Orl. Fur.* Harington XXXIII [History] Protogenes ... was noted for somewhat too much curiositie and tediousnesse (a fault our countrimen be much noted of, that they know not when their worke is well). **1597** SHAKES. *2 Hen. IV* I. ii. 200 It was alway yet the trick of our English nation, if they have a good thing, to make it too common. **1616** WITHALS 567 You are a right Englishman, you cannot tell when a thing is well. **1642** *A Presse full of Pamphlets* The right Nature, or Stampe of English-men, who think a thing to be never well enough done till it be overdone, and prove uselesse or hurtfull. **1670** RAY 85. **1672** DRYDEN *Def. of the Epilogue* (*Essays* ed. Ker i 172) Fletcher ... does not well always; and, when he does, he is a true Englishman; he knows not when to give over. **1738** SWIFT *Dial.* II. E.L. 307 I find you are a true Englishman; you never know when you are well.

Englishman loves a lord, An.

1909 *Spectator* 3 July 9 It is always said that an Englishman loves a lord. It would be more exact to say that he is in love with lordliness.

Englishman weeps, The | the Irishman sleeps; but the Scottishman gangs while[1] he gets it.

1721 KELLY 323 ... A pretended Account of the Behaviour of these three Nations, when they want Meat. [[1] till.]

Englishman's (Briton's) privilege to grumble, It is an.

1866 BLACKMORE *Cradock N.* ch. 64 Sir Cradock grumbles ... now and then, because, like all of us Englishmen, he must have his grievance. **1871** C. KINGSLEY *At Last* ch. 3 Trinidad is loyal (with occasional grumblings, of course, as is the right of free-born Britons). **1881** W. WESTALL *Old Factory* ch. 37 We are like to grumble a bit sometimes—it is an Englishman's privilege, you know.

Englishman, *see also* Heart of an E. towards Welshman; House is his castle; Irishman for a hand ... the E. for a face; Peerage is E.'s Bible; Settling an island, the first building ... by an E. an alehouse; Way to an E.'s heart.

Enjoy, *see* Goods are theirs that e. them; Name (He that has the) may e. the game; So much is mine as I e.

Enough, and none to spare, Like Madam Hassell's feast.

1856 *N. & Q.* 2nd Ser. I. 313. *Ibid.* II. 339 This proverb is changed only in name in Ireland. In Dublin ... it originated at the table of a Mrs. Casely, who ... was accustomed to say, 'Well, I declare; just enough and none to spare'. [*Cf.* **1917** BRIDGE 54 Enough and no more, like Mrs. Milton's feast.]

Enough for one is enough for two, What's.

1902–4 LEAN IV. 178.

Enough is as good as a feast.   (E 158)

[EURIPIDES *Phoen.* 554 ἐπεὶ τά γ' ἀρκοῦνθ' ἱκανὰ τοῖσι σώφροσιν.] *c.* **1375** BARBOUR *Bruce* xiv. 363–4 He maid thame na gud fest, perfay, And nocht-for-thi yneuch had thai. *c.* **1420** LYDGATE *Ass. Gods* E.E.T.S. 59 I. 2035 As good ys ynough as a gret feste. **1546** HEYWOOD II. xi. M1. **1594–5** SHAKES. *L.L.L.* V. i. 1 Satis quod sufficit. **1662** FULLER Lond. 199. **1738** SWIFT *Dial.* I. E.L. 264. **1826** LAMB *Ess., Pop. Fallacies* Wks. (1898) 223 That enough is as good as a feast. Not a man, woman, or child in ten miles round Guildhall, who really believes this saying.

Enough is enough.   (E 159)

1546 HEYWOOD II. xi. M1. **1562** G. LEGH *Accidence of Armoury* B3ᵛ What nedeth more then Inoughe? **1570** *Marr. Wit and Science* D4. **1834** SOUTHEY *Doctor* i. 199 As for money, enough is enough.

Enough, Of | men leave. *Cf.* Enough where nothing left.   (E 167)

a. **1628** CARMICHAELL no. 1221 Of aneuch men beirs[1]. **1641** FERGUSSON no. 666. **1721** KELLY 272 ... They who leave no Scraps can hardly be said to have enough. [[1] leaves]

Enough one day, He will have | when his mouth is full of mould.   (E 166)

1583 P. STUBBES *Anatomy of Abuses* Pt. II!New Sh. S. ii. 27 Greedy gentlemen, who will neuer have inough, till their mouths be full of clay, and their bodie full of grauell. **1670** RAY 173. **1721**

KELLY 161 (full of Mools) Spoken of covetous People, who will never be satisfied while they are alive.

Enough where nothing [was] left, There was never. *Cf.* Enough (Of) men leave.
(E 168)
1639 CLARKE 38.   1659 TORRIANO no. 228.

Enough who is contented with little, He has. (E 162)
c. 1560 T. LUPTON *Money* 1. 630 I euer haue ynough wherewith I am content.   1570 W. BALDWIN *Beware the Cat* (1584) B3 A little suffiseth him that hath inough.   1658 E. PHILLIPS *Mysteries of Love and Eloquence* 159 He hath enough that's pleased.   1659 N. R. 41 (as 1658).   1779 19 Oct. JOHNSON *Lett.* (Chapman) ii. 309 You have enough, if you are satisfied.

Enough, *see also* Ease who has e., (He is at); More than e. too much; Soon e. if well e.

Enough to, *see* Saint swear.

Enriched, *see* Envy never e. any man; Pension never e. young man.

Ensign, *see* Old band (e.) is captain's honour.

Enter into a house, When you | leave the anger ever at the door. (H 788)
1640 HERBERT no. 896.

Enter into Paradise must have a good key, He that will. (P 47)
1616 DRAXE no. 960 It is a good Key that must open Paradise.   1639 CLARKE 186 'Tis a good key that opens heaven.   1640 HERBERT no. 895.   1732 FULLER no. 2347 (must come with a right Key).

Enter this life, There is but one way to | but the gates of death are without number. (D 140)
[VIRGIL: Mille viae mortis.]   *c.* 1390 GOWER *Confessio Amantis* IV. l. 2246 Althogh ther be diverse weie To deth, yit is ther bot on ende.   1539 VIVES *Introd. to Wisdom* F1 Death may com to vs, by an infinite sort of wayes.   1581 SENECA *Thebais* tr. T. Newton T.T. i. 107 Death ech where is: and wayes to death in thousand corners are.   1588 HUGHES *Misfortunes of Arthur* I. iii.   1603 MONTAIGNE (Florio) II. iii. 32 Nature ... hath left us the key of the fields. She hath appointed but one entrance unto life, but many a thousand wayes out of it.   1616 T. ADAMS *Diseases of the Soul* 72 One meanes of comming into the world, infinite of going out.   *c.* 1628 FULKE GREVILLE, LD. BROOKE *Alaham* IV. i. Wks. (Gros.) III. 257 If Nature saw no cause of suddaine ends, She that but one way made to draw our breath, Would not haue left so many doores to Death.

Enter(s), *see also* Nothing e. into close hand.

Enterprise, *see* Examined e. goes boldly.

Entertainment, *see* Jack Drum's e.

Entreated, *see* Courtesy e. half recompensed.

Envied, envies, *see* Better be e. than pitied; Potter (One) e. another.

Envious man grows lean (shall never want woe), The. (M 96)
c. 1350 *How the Gd. Wife* l. 87 Enuious herte Himself fret.[1]   *a.* 1500 *Harl MS. 3362* 309 A envyows man wexit lene.   1598 BARCKLEY *Fel. Man* v. 626 The envious man growes leane to see others fat.   1599 SHAKES. *J.C.* I. ii. 194–208 Yond Cassius has a lean and hungry look . . . Such men as he be never at heart's ease Whiles they behold a greater than themselves.   1636 CAMDEN 307.   *c.* 1640 W. S. *Countrym. Common.* 6 An envious man repines at the prosperity of another. [[1] frets, fretteth.]

Envy never dies. (E 172)
1523–5 BERNERS tr. *Froissart* ch. 428 There is a Comune proverb, the whiche is true, and that is, howe envy never dyeth.   1616 DRAXE no. 586 Enuie is neuer dead.   1624 BURTON *Anat. Mel.* 91 Hatred hath an end, envy never ceaseth (*from* Cardan).   1658 C. HOOLE *Sententiae Pueriles* 15 Envy ceaseth after death.

Envy never enriched any man. (E 173)
1616 DRAXE no. 585 A man shall neuer bee enriched by enuie.   1670 RAY 8.

Epsom, *see* Sutton.

Equal, *see* End makes all e.; Turf, (On and under) all men e.

Equality, *see* Friendship cannot be without e., (Perfect).

Erasmus laid the egg of the Reformation, and Luther hatched it.
1547 S. GARDINER to Somerset *Letters* ed. Muller 403 (Now I agre with them that said).   1563 J. FOXE *Bk. Martyrs.* vi. 47 (19 c. edn.).   1877 TRENCH *Mediev. Ch. Hist.* XXVI (1879) 399 [Erasmus] had too earnestly denounced the corruptions of the Church not to be regarded with dislike and suspicion by all who clung to these;—it was he, they said, who laid the egg which Luther hatched.

Erasmus, *see also* Hang between heaven and hell, like E.

Ermine, In an | spots are soon discovered. *Cf.* In an enemy.
1586 J. CASE *Praise of Music* *3ᵛ A blemish is soonest perceiued in a comely body.   1642 TORRIANO 78 (soon seen).   1732 FULLER no. 2814.

Err is human, To. (E 179)
[L. *Humanum est errare.*]   1539 VIVES *Introd. to Wisdom* D7 It is naturally gyuen to al men to

erre, but to no man to perseuer . . . therin. **1542** ERASM. tr. Udall *Apoph.* (1877) xiii Bothe wer men, and might erre. **1575** C. AGRIPPA *Vanity of Arts and Sciences* tr. Sanford ¶3ᵛ Tullie . . . in the first of his *Offices* . . . sayth . . . to erre . . . is mans propertie. **1576** PETTIE i. 6 *Errare humanum est; in errore perseverare, belluinum.* **1578** *Courtly Controv.* E3 To offend is humaine, to repent diuine, and to perseuere diuelish. **1594** HOOKER *Eccles. Polity,* Preface, ch. ix Think ye are men, deem it not impossible for you to err. **1596** WARNER *Albion's Eng.* X. 59, Sıᵛ To erre is proper then to Men, but brutish to persist. **1631** *Celestina* tr. Mabbe 57 (as Pettie, but English). **1655–62** GURNALL *Chrn. in Armour* (1865) I. 298 The first shows thee a weak man—*humanum est errare,* to err is human. **1659** HOWELL *Fr. Prov.* 12 To erre is humane, to repent is divine, to persevere is Diabolicall. **1711** POPE *Ess. Crit.* 525 To err is human; to forgive, divine. **1908** *Times Lit. Sup.* 27 Mar. The modern moralist pardons everything, because he is not certain of anything, except that to err is human.

Err(ed), *see also* Talk much and e. much; War (In) it is not permitted twice to e.; Wise e. not (If) hard for fools.

Errand, *see* Draff is your e., but drink ye would; Go twenty miles on your e.; King's e. may come cadger's gate; Sleeveless e.; Tod never sped better than . . . own e.; Wise man on an e. (Send).

Error, *see* Custom without reason ancient e.; Show a good man his e. he turns it to virtue.

Errs and mends, Who | to God himself commends. (G 232)

1599 MINSHEU *Span. Dial.* 67 (and amends). **1620** SHELTON *Quix.* (1900) iii. 20 Pardon me, sir, and pity my youth . . . 'Who errs and mends, to God himself commends.' **1659** HOWELL *Span. Prov.* 15. **1719** DE ALVARADO 152.

Escape a scouring, To. (s 163)

1560 T. PALFREYMAN *A Mirror or clear glass* D5 Thou hast escaped a scouringe, or passed thorough the pykes. **1639** CLARKE 80. **1721** DEFOE *Mem. Cavalier* x (1840) 187 Aylesbury escaped a scouring for that time.

Escape Clude, and be drowned in Conway, To. (c 455)

1662 FULLER Carnarvon 30 . . . Scylla [and] Charibdis . . . were neer, . . . whereas the two Rivers of Clude and Conway are twenty miles a-sunder.

Escape, *see also* Counsel that has no e. (Ill).

Escaped mouse ever feels the taste of the bait, The. (M 1228)

1640 HERBERT no. 679.

Escaped the thunder, and fell into the lightning, I. (T 276)

1599 MINSHEU *Span. Gram.* 80. **1612** N. POWNOLL *The Yg. Divine's Apology* A5 For so to shunne

shame, and seeke glorie, what were it else, but (as the Spaniard speaketh) to escape the thunderbolt, and fall into the lightning's flash. **1651** HERBERT no. 1084.

Essex calves. (c 21)

1573 G. HARVEY *Letter-Book* Camden Soc. 135 Foes must be frende, quoth an Essex kalfe. **1605** CHAPMAN, JONSON, MARSTON *Eastw. Ho* II. ii. 244 These women Sir, are like Essex Calues. **1617** MORYSON *Itin.* III. i. 53 (1907–8) III. 463 Essex men are called calves (because they abound there). **1662** FULLER Essex 320 . . . Essex . . . producing Calves of the fattest, fairest and finest flesh in England, (and consequently in all Europe,) and let the Butchers in Eastcheap be appealed vnto as the most Competent Judges therein. **1719** D'URFEY *Pills* IV. 43 It prov'd an Essex Calf. **1909** *Times Lit. Sup.* 26 Nov. As a rule these men have been Scots or Cornishmen rather than 'Essex calves'.

Essex (Suffolk) stiles, Kentish miles, Norfolk wiles, many a man beguiles. (s 857)

16th c. in *Reliq. Antiquae* i. 269 Suffolk full of wiles, Norffolk full of giles. **1573** TUSSER *500 Points* (1878 ed. 209) Norfolke wiles, so full of giles. **1606** DEKKER *News from Hell* B4ᵛ The miles are not halfe so long as those betweene Colchester and Ipswich. *c.* **1608** D. BARRY *Ram Alley* Hazl.-Dods. X. 356 Learn'd in Norfolk wiles. **1617** MORYSON *Itin.* III. i. 53 (1907–8) III. 463 Norfolk wiles (for crafty litigiousness): Essex stiles (so many as make walking tedious); Kentish miles (of the length). **1662** FULLER Suffolk 55 Suffolk stiles. It is a measuring cast, whether this Proverb pertaineth to Essex or this County . . . both . . . abound with high stiles troublesome to be clambred over. **1670** RAY 86 . . . For stiles *Essex* may well vie with any County of England. . . . Length of miles I know not what reason *Kent* hath to pretend to . . . but for cunning in the Law and wrangling, *Norfolk* men are justly noted.

Estate, He has a good | but that the right owner keeps it from him. (E 185)

1678 RAY 78. **1738** SWIFT Dial. I. E.L. 279.

Estate in two parishes is bread in two wallets. (E 184)

1640 HERBERT no. 231.

Estate(s), *see also* Bones of a great e. worth the picking; Gentleman without e.; Hard thing to have great e. and not love it; Many e. are spent in the getting; Near of kin to an e. (Good to be.)

Esteem(ed, s), *see* Costs little (What) less e.; Wise man e. every place his own country.

Ethiop, *see* Wash an E. white.

Ettle, *see* Oft e. whiles hit.

Eve, *see* Adam delved and E. span; Say to pleasure, Gentle E.

Even hand to throw a louse in the fire, He has an.

1706 STEVENS s.v. Ojo Ironically spoke; as we say . . .   **1738** SWIFT *Dial.* I. E.L. 279.

Even reckoning makes long friends. *Cf.* Short reckoning.   (R 54)

1546 HEYWOOD II. iv. G4ᵛ Euen recknyng makth longe freends.   **1670** RAY 136 (keeps).   **1760** COLMAN *Polly Honeycombe* 16 Right Reckoning makes long friends, you know.

Evening brings all home, The.

[SAPPHO Ἔσπερε πάντα φέρων ὄσα φαίνολις ἐσκέδασ' Αὔως, / φέρεις οἶν, φέρεις αἶγα, φέρεις ἀπυ μάτερι παῖδα.]   **1857** DEAN RAMSAY *Remin.* v (1911) 200 *The e'ening brings a' hame* is an interesting saying, meaning that the evening of life, or the approach of death, softens many of our political and religious differences.

Evening crowns (praises) the day, The. *Cf.* Praise a fair day at night.   (E 190)

1545 TAVERNER G5ᵛ Our englyshe prouerbe —At euen men shulde the fayre day preisen. **1612–15** BP. HALL *Contempl.* XIX. v (1825) I. 633 The evening praises the day, and the chief grace of the theatre is in the last scene. 'Be faithful to the death, and I will give thee a crown of life.' **1615** M. R. *President for Young Pen. Men* B1ᵛ It is the Euening praiseth the Day, and he is only happy that holds out to the end.   *a.* **1619** DANIEL *A Funeral Poem* 380 For 'tis the evening crowns the day.   **1692** L'ESTRANGE *Aesop's Fab.* ccxciv (1738) 307 'Tis matter of humanity . . . to be tender one of another: for no man living knows his end, and 'tis the evening crowns the day. **1721** KELLY 336 . . . For as our Success appears then, it is good or bad.

Evening orts are good morning fodder.   (O 79)

a. **1628** CARMICHAELL no. 468.   **1639** CLARKE 114.   **1721** KELLY 96 . . . Spoken when a Man Breakfasts upon what he left for Supper.   **1732** FULLER no. 1401 (oats).

Evening praises the day, and the morning a host, The.   (E 190)

1640 HERBERT no. 635.   **1642** TORRIANO 70 The evening commendeth the morning, but the morning commendeth mine hoste.

Evening red and morning grey help the traveller on his way: evening grey and morning red bring down rain upon his head.   (E 191)

1584 *Withals* N7ᵛ The euening red, the morning gray, Foreshewes a cleare and summers day. **1611** COTGRAVE s.v. Matin . . . presage a faire succeeding day.   **1639** CLARKE 263 An evening red and a morning gray, Are sure signes of a faire day.   **1846** DENHAM 8 An evening red and morning grey, Will set the traveller on his way; But if the evening's grey, and the morning red, Put on your hat or you'll wet your head.   **1893** INWARDS 54.

Evening words are (not) like to morning.   (W 787)

c. **1390** CHAUCER *Prol.* 830 If euensong and morwe-song accorde.   *a.* **1450** RYLANDS Latin MS. 394 3ᵛ (W. A. Pantin in *Bulletin of John Rylands Lib.* Jan. 1930) Euen songe and morn songe beth not both on.   *c.* **1594** BACON no. 1478 Les paroles du soir ne sembles a celles du matin. **1601** DEACON & WALKER *Spirits & Devils* (R.E.S. viii. 4. 47) His Euen-song and Morne-song they are one and the same.   **1611** COTGRAVE s.v. Parole The evening chat is not like the mornings tattle.   **1640** HERBERT no. 65.

Evening, Eve, see also Hour in morning worth two in e.; Promising is the e. of giving; Tib's e.; Yule is good on Yule e.; Yule is young in Yule e.

Evensong, see Day never so long cometh e.

Event(s), see Coming e. cast their shadows; Wise after the e.

Ever and a day, For.   (D 74)

c. **1528** TYNDALE *Parable of Wicked Mammon* P.S. 38 I took my leave and bade him farewell for our two lives and (as men say) a day longer. **1530** PALSGRAVE 855.   **1533** J. FRITH *Answ. agst. Rastell* D5 Then saye they adieu for euer and a daye.   **1594–8** SHAKES. *T.S.* IV. iv. 93 I have no more to say, But bid Bianca farewell for ever and a day.   **1599** *Id. A.Y.* IV. i. 129 Now tell me how long you would have her after you have possess'd her.—For ever and a day.   **1639** CLARKE 279.

Ever busy, ever bare.

1721 KELLY 91 . . . It is not always found that they who pursue the World most eagerly, gets the greatest Share of it.

Ever drunk, ever dry.   (D 625)

1509 BARCLAY *Ship of Fools* i. 51 The more that some drynke: the more they wax drye.   **1605** CHAPMAN, JONSON, MARSTON *Eastw. Ho* I. ii. He that's most drunken may soonest be athirst. **1614** CAMDEN 305.   **1639** CLARKE 37 (drinke).

Ever, see also Blind horse (E. the worse looks the); Wear clothes (E. since we).

Every beggar is descended from some king, and every king is descended from some beggar.   (B 232)

1602 *Thomas Lord Cromwell* I. ii There's legions now of beggars on the earth, That their original did spring from kings: And many monarchs now whose fathers were the riff-raff of their age. **1631–59** FULLER *Infants Advoc.* xix in *Collected Serm.* (1891) II. 222 We have a saying, . . .

Every block will not make a Mercury.   (M 893)

[L. *Ex quovis ligno non fit Mercurius.*]   **1586** T. BRIGHT *Treat. of Mel.* 9 (As it was wont to be said) Mercurie is not made of euerie tree.   **1587** BRIDGES *Defence of Gvt. of C. of E.* 1274

Mercurius non fit ex quolibet ligno, there are not many of such excellency. **1629** T. ADAMS *Serm.* (1861–2) II. 300 It was wont to be said, Ex quolibet ligno non fit Mercurius,—Every block is not fit to make an image. **1689** SHADWELL *Bury Fair* II. i. Ex quovis ligno, &c. Mercury's statue is not made of every wood. **1732** FULLER no. 1410. **1860** PEACOCK *Gryll Grange* ch. 19 This is not the way to discover the wood of which Mercuries are made.

Every commodity has its discommodity. Cf. Suffer the ill. (C 555)

1565 J. HALL *Court of Virtue* Q1 No commoditie is without a discommoditie. [**1576**] **1577** GASCOIGNE *Grief of Joy* ii. 514 Well wrott hee whiche said: Omnis commoditas, sua fert incomoda secum. **1576** PETTIE 76. **1581** GUAZZO i. 29. **1616** DRAXE no. 272. **1672** WALKER 36 no. 26 No convenience without its inconveniency. **1706** STEVENS s.v. Atajo (as 1672).

Every day braw[1] makes Sunday a daw.[2]

1851–63 *Ulster Jrnl. Arch.* ii in LEAN I. 347. [¹ fine. ² a drab.]

Every day brings its bread with it. (D 65)

1640 HERBERT no. 5. **1659** HOWELL *Fr. Prov.* 6.

Every day comes night. (D 70)

1573 SANFORD 108ᵛ. **1578** FLORIO *First F.* 33. **1579** CALVIN *Four Sermons* tr. J. Field Ep. Ded. There is no sommer but bringeth a Winter, no day but hath a night. **1659** TORRIANO no. 82 There is no day but night follows.

Every day is holiday with sluggards. (S 548)

1539 TAVERNER 40 Wyth sluggers or vnhardy persons, it is alwayes holydaye. **1611** DAVIES *Epigr.* 42.

Every day is not yesterday. (D 69)

1621 ROBINSON 39. **1639** CLARKE 124.

Every day of the week a shower of rain, and on Sunday twain. (D 67)

1659 HOWELL *Eng. Prov.* 11b ... a Proverb in many Shires of England.

Every day of thy life is a leaf in thy history.

1902–4 LEAN III. 455.

Every day's no Yule-day—cast the cat a castock.[1]

a. **1628** CARMICHAELL no. 840. **1721** KELLY 94. **1846** DENHAM 62. [¹ = kale stock, cabbage stump.]

Every evil under the sun, For | there is a remedy or there is none: if there be one, try and find it; if there be none, never mind it.

1869 HAZLITT 135.

Every extremity is a fault. (E 224)

1573 SANFORD H3ᵛ. **1583** P. STUBBES *Anatomy of Abuses* New Sh.S. i. 33 *Omne extremum uertitur in uitium*, every extreme is turned into vice. **1597** MONTGOMERIE *Cherrie and Sloe* l. 1426: *Poems*, 49 Sturt [trouble] follows all extreams. **1603** H. CROSSE *Virtue's Commonw.* (Gros.) 16 Extremes are ever hurtful. **1608** MIDDLETON *Family of Love* (Bullen) III. v. i. Extremes are perilous. **1616** DRAXE no. 650 All extremitie is euill. **1629** *Bk. Mer. Rid.* Prov. no. 30. **1721** KELLY 286 (as 1597).

Every fault, In | there is folly. (F 113)

c. **1641** FERGUSSON MS. no. 435 Faultis in affection ar but slight follies. **1659** HOWELL *Br. Prov.* 34. **1707** MAPLETOFT 126. **1878** J. PLATT *Morality* 34.

Every hand fleeces, Where | the sheep goes naked. (H 103)

1597 *Politeuphuia* 166. **1639** CLARKE 187. **1732** FULLER no. 5645.

Every light has its shadow. (L 272)

1578 FLORIO *First F.* P1 Ther is no light without darknesse, . . . no shadowe without a bodye. **1586** L. LLOYD *Pilg. of Princes* 991 Plini most truelie saith, that there is no light without shadow, nor no vertue without enuie. **1592** DELAMOTHE 17 There was neuer any light, but it had some shadow.

Every light is not the sun. (L 273)

1659 HOWELL *Eng. Prov.* 13a. **1670** RAY 15.

Every little helps. Cf. Everything helps.

1791 O'KEEFFE *Wild Oats* V. iii. Here—it's not much! but every little helps. **1840** MARRYAT *Poor Jack* ch. 13 That's a very old saying, that every little helps.

Every maid is undone. (M 15)

1678 RAY 172.

Every man a little beyond himself is a fool. (M 99)

1677 YARRANTON *Engl.'s Improvement* 105 Every Man is a Fool when he is out of his own way. **1732** FULLER no. 1421.

Every man as he loves, quoth the good man when he kissed his cow. (M 103)

1546 HEYWOOD II. i. F3 And in this case euery man as he loueth Quoth the good man, whan that he kyst his cowe. **1675** COTTON *Poet. Wks.* (1715) *Scoffer Scoft* 162 Why each one as he likes, you know, quo'th good Man when he kissed his Cow. **1721** KELLY 91 Every Man to his Mind, quoth the Carle when he kiss'd his Cow. **1738** SWIFT *Dial.* I. E.L. 260 Why, every one as they like, as the good woman said when she kiss'd her cow. **1741** CHESTERFIELD 25 July. **1842** E. FITZGERALD *Lett.* 22 Sept. (1901) I. 136 Every one to his taste, as one might well say to any woman who kissed the cow pastured there.

Every man as his business lies. *Cf.* Every man must walk in his own calling.
(M 104)

1597 SHAKES. *1 Hen. IV* II. ii. 75 Every man to his business. **1600–1** *Id. H.* I. v. 128 I hold it fit that we shake hands and part; You, as your business and desire shall point you. For every man hath business and desire, Such as it is. **1678** RAY 107.

Every man cannot be a master (lord).
(M 107)

1545 TAVERNER G7 Oure englyshe prouerbe ... Euerye man may not be a lorde. **1546** HEYWOOD I. xii. E4ᵛ Euery man maie not syt in the chayre. **1592** DELAMOTHE 55. **1604** SHAKES. *O.* I. i. 43 We cannot all be masters. **1732** FULLER no. 537. All Men can't be Masters.

Every man for himself, and God (the devil) for us all (take the hindmost).
(M 113)

c. **1386** CHAUCER *Knight's T.* l. 1182 At the Kynges court, my brother, Ech man for hym-self, ther is noon oother. [*c.* 1515] *c.* 1530 BARCLAY *Eclog.* i. 1009 Eche man for him selfe, and the fiende for all. **1546** HEYWOOD II. ix. L2 Euery man for hym selfe, and god for vs all. **1572** SANFORD *Houres of Recreation* 219 Euery man for him self, and the Deuill for all. **1629** T. ADAMS *Serm.* (1861–2) II. 90 That byword, 'Every man for himself, and God for us all', is uncharitable, ungodly. **1830** MARRYAT *King's Own* ch. 53 The captain ... ordered the sailor to leave the boat. 'Every man for himself, and God for us all!' was the cool answer of the refractory seaman. **1858** D. MULOCK *A Woman's Thoughts* 39 The world is hard enough, for two-thirds of it are struggling for the dear life—'each for himself, and de'il tak the hindmost'. [Fr. *Chacun pour soi et Dieu pour tous.*]

Every man gets his own, When | the thief will get the widdie.[1]

1721 KELLY 352. [¹ gallows.]

Every man has his delight.   (M 115)
1609 HARWARD 84. **1616** DRAXE no. 478.

Every man has his faults.   (M 116)

[1525–40] **1557** *A merry dialogue* 63 There liueth no man without faulte. **1578** *Courtly Controv.* Q3ᵛ As there is no Saint in Paradise but hath his feast, so is there no creature liuing but hath some fault. **1582** WHETSTONE *Heptameron* I2 No man so faultlesse, but that somewhat in him may be amended. **1583** MELBANCKE *Philot.* 2C3ᵛ But no man is borne without a blemishe. **1590** W. SEGAR *Bk. Honour and Arms* III. ix. 148 There is no man liuing faultles. **1592** DELAMOTHE 51 Any man whosoeuer, whether he be borne of a high or of a low degree, hath some fault in him. **1593** *Tell-Trothes New Year's gift* New Sh. S. 32 I knowe that euery one hath his faulte. **1600–1** SHAKES. *M.W.W.* I. iv. 13 He is something peevish that way, but nobody but has his fault. **1605–8** *Id. T.Ath.* III. i. 28 Every man hath his fault, and honesty is his. **1639** CLARKE 80. **1666** TORRIANO *It. Prov.* 68 no. 8. *a.* **1774** J. WESLEY *Wks.* vi. 163 (his infirmity).

Every man has his (proper) gift.
(M 117)

1563 *Mirror for Mag.* (Campbell 144) Every man hath his gyft. **1621** ROBINSON 26 (owne). **1639** CLARKE 89. **1640** J. D. *Knave in Grain* D3ᵛ Every one has his gift.

Every man has his price.

a. **1745** WALPOLE in W. COXE, *Memoirs of Sir R. W.* (1798) i. 757 All those men have their price. *a.* **1761** J. RICH *Corr.* v. 308 It is said, but not to the credit of human nature, that every man has his price. **1790** WESLEY *Serm.* 123 That politician ... whose favourite saying was, 'Do not tell me of your virtue. . . . : I tell you, every man has his price'. **1845** JAMES *Smuggler* ch. 10. **1892** LIDDON *Some Words of Christ* 23 That shallow maxim of worldly cynicism, which tells us that 'every man has his price'.

Every man (thing) in his (its) way.
(M 100)

c. **1497** MEDWALL *Fulgens & Lucres* II. 36 Euery man must haue hys mynde. [*c.* 1517] *c.* 1545 SHELTON *Speak Parrot* l. 92: Wks. II. 6 Euery Man after his maner of wayes. **1546** HEYWOOD I. xi. E1. **1550** BECON *Fortress* P.S. 617 Every man in his vocation. **1577** R. STANYHURST in Holinshed *Conquest of Ireland* (1587 55b) It is an old saying, that euerie man in his owne art is best of credit and most to be beleeued. **1611** COTGRAVE s.v. Tour Chascun à son tour Euerie one in his time, ranke, or turne. **1620** SHELTON *Quix.* Pt. II. lix (iii. 236) Every man in his ability. **1653** A. WILSON *History of Gt. Britain* 185 Every man in his Profession! **1678** RAY 84. **1693** W. FREKE *Select Essays* A6 Every thing in its way.

Every man is a king (master) in his own house.   (M 123)

1587 J. BRIDGES *Defence* 249 (As wee commonlie saye) euerie man is a Bishop ouer his owne familie. **1592** DELAMOTHE M6ᵛ Euery clowne is king at home. **1629** MASSINGER *Roman Actor* I. ii. I in mine own house am an emperor.

Every man is best known to himself.
(M 124)

1616 DRAXE no. 305. **1639** CLARKE 65.

Every man is mad on some point.

a. **1721** PRIOR *Dialog. of Dead* (1907) 267 As you were saying, every man is mad, but in a different manner, and upon some particular objects.

Every man is master, Where | the world goes to wrack.[1]   (M 412)

1539 TAVERNER 46 Where one hedde and ruler is not, but euerie man as a lorde doth what hym lusteth, there is no thynge well done. 1616 WITHALS 566. 1639 CLARKE 218. [¹ wreck.]

Every man is the architect of his own fortune.   (M 126)

[SALLUST *De Rep.* I. I *Faber quisque fortunae suae.*] 1533 UDALL *Flowers* (1560) 24 A prouerbiall speakyng: Fortunam sibi quisque fingit, Every man maketh . . . is causer of his own fortunes. 1539 TAVERNER f. 37 A man's owne maners do shape hym hys fortune. 1594 NASHE *Terrors of the Night* i. 377 There is an olde philosophicall common Prouerbe Vnusquisque fingit fortunam sibi, Euerie one shapes hys owne fortune as he lists. 1605 BACON *Adv. of Learn.* Bk. II It grew to an adage, Faber quisque Fortunae propriae. 1613 BROWNE *Brit. Past.* iii. 585 Each man the workman of his fortune is. 1620 SHELTON *Quix.* II. lxvi (1908) III. 285 Hence 'tis said that every man is the artificer of his own fortune. 1649 MILTON *Eikon.* xxi Architects of their own happiness. 1687 DRYDEN *Hind and Panther* iii. 1268 Smiths of their own foolish fate. 1818 FERRIER *Marriage* ch. 52 As every man is said to be the artificer of his own fortune, so every one . . . had best be the artificer of their own friendship.

Every man knows his own business best.   (M 130)

1567 PAINTER iii. 206 Euery man knoweth his owne affayres. 1616 BRETON *Cross. of Prov.* B1 (what is best for himselfe). 1742 FIELDING *Andrews* II. v. The gentleman stared . . . and, turning hastily about, said, 'Every man knew his own business'.

Every man likes his own thing best.   (M 131)

[1525–40] 1557 *A merry dialogue* 63 Euery man . . . thinkes hys owne way best. 1539 TAVERNER 6ᵛ Euery man thynketh hys owne thynge fayre. 1581 C. MERBURY *Brief Discourse* 32 All men . . . thinke alwayes their owne religion best, their owne customes commendablest, their owne lawes soundest. 1599 SHAKES. *A.Y.* V. iv. 55 A poor virgin, sir, an ill-favour'd thing, sir, but mine own.

Every man mend (amend) one, If | all shall be mended (amended).   (M 196)

1541 *Schoolhouse of Women* D4 God graunt vs all, we may do this, Euery man to amende one, in that is amys. 1555 HEYWOOD *Epigr. upon Prov.* no. I If euery man mende one, all shall be mended. 1579 LYLY *Euph.* i. 276 Let vs endeauour euery one to amend one, and we shall all soone be amended. 1641 FERGUSSON no. 511 Ilk man mend ane, and all will be mendit. 1670 RAY 20. 1852 E. FITZGERALD *Polonius* cxi To two bad verses which I write Two good shall be appended: If every man would mend a man, Then all mankind were mended.

Every man must walk (labour) in his own calling (trade, vocation). *Cf.* Every man in his way: Every man as his business lies.   (C 23)

[I COR. vii. 20 Let every man abide in the same calling wherein he was called.] 1539 TAVERNER E1 Let euerye man exercise hym selfe in the facultie that he knoweth. 1549 LATIMER *6th Serm.* P.S. 215 Labour in thy vocation. *a.* 1550 *Parl. of Birds* Harl. *Misc.* v, 1745, 480 Euery Man must lyue by his Crafte. 1590–1 SHAKES. *2 Hen. VI* IV. ii. 17 And yet it is said, 'Labour in thy vocation'; which is as much to say as 'Let the magistrates be labouring men'; and therefore should we be magistrates. 1597 *Id. 1 Hen. IV* I. ii. 101 Why, Hal, 'tis my vocation, Hal. 'Tis no sin for a man to labour in his vocation. 1605 MARSTON *Dutch Courtesan* I. i. Every man must follow his trade. 1605 S. ROWLEY *When You See Me* l. 982 Euery man according to his calling. 1608 MIDDLETON *Family Love* III. ii. 25 'Tis my vocation, boy: we must never be weary of well-doing. *a.* 1721 PRIOR *Dialog. of Dead* (1907) 221 Every man to his trade, Charles, you should have challenged me at long pike or broad sword. 1721 KELLY 97 Every Man to his Trade, quoth the Boy to the Bishop. A Bishop ask'd a Cabbin Boy if he could say his Prayers, he ask'd the Bishop if he could say his Compass, the Bishop said no; why then, says the Boy, . . .

Every man should take his own.
                                                                            (M 209)

1590 SHAKES. *T.And.* I. i. 280 Suum cuique is our Roman justice. This prince in justice seizeth but his own. 1595 *Id. M.N.D.* III. ii. 458 And the country proverb known, That every man should take his own. 1596 SPENSER *F.Q.* v. iv. 20 So was their discord by this doome appeased, And each one had his right. 1651 HOBBES *Leviathan* I. xv. 72 Justice is the constant Will of giving to every man his own.

Every man to his taste. *Cf.* Every man as he loveth, etc.   (M 101)

1580 LYLY *Euph. & his Eng.* ii. 161 Euery one as he lyketh. 1611 COTGRAVE s.v. Chascun Every one as hee likes. 1849 LYTTON *Caxtons* XVII. i. Every man to his taste in the Bush.

Every man will have his own turn served.   (M 139)

1539 S. GARDINER to Bonner (*Letters* ed. Muller 86) Every man seeketh his owne. 1616 DRAXE no. 835.

Every man's censure is first moulded in his own nature.   (M 447)

1651 HERBERT no. 1181.

Every man's man had a man, and that made the Treve fall.

1721 KELLY 94 . . . The Trave was a strong Castle built by black Douglas. The Governour left a Deputy, and he a Substitute, by whose Negligence the Castle was taken and burn'd: spoken when Servants employ other Servants to do the Business that they were entrusted with, and both neglect it.

Every man('s), see also under significant words following.

Every man (one) after his fashion.
(M 100)

[c. 1517] c. 1545 SKELTON *Speak Parrot* l. 92 Wks. ii. 6 Euery Man after his maner of wayes. [1523–40] 1557 *A merry dialogue* 63 Euery man hath hys maner and euery man hath his seueral aptite or mynde. 1546 HEYWOOD I. xi. E1. 1578 THOS. WHITE *Sermon at Paul's Cross* 3 Nov. 1577 45 Trahit sua quenque voluptas, Euery man followeth his owne fansie. 1614 CAMDEN 305. 1621 ROBINSON 4. 1639 CLARKE 89.

Every one is weary: the poor in seeking, the rich in keeping, the good in learning.
(P 466)

1640 HERBERT no. 678.

Every one is witty for his own purpose.
(P 641)

1616 DRAXE no. 834.   1640 HERBERT no. 754.

Every one puts his fault on the times.
(F 101)

1640 HERBERT no. 675.   1872 BLACKMORE *Maid of Sker* i I pray you to lay the main fault thereof on the badness of the times.

Every one (horse) thinks his sack (pack) heaviest.
(S 4)

Cf. 1573 GASCOIGNE *Hundreth Sundry Flowers* i. 427 Every body thinketh their own greif greatest. 1611 COTGRAVE s.v. Fardeau Euerie one finds his owne burthen heauie enough. 1640 HERBERT no. 748. 1732 FULLER no. 1420 Every Horse thinks his own Pack heaviest.

Every one's faults are (are not) written in their foreheads.
(F 120)

1609 HARWARD 90 Your owne faults are not written in your forehead. 1659 HOWELL *Fr. Prov.* 24 Au vis le vice. Every ones fault is writ in his forehead. 1678 RAY 141. 1721 KELLY 214 It is well, that all our Faults are not written in our Face. Spoken to them who upbraid us with some Faults that we have been guilty of; alledging if theirs were as well known, they would look as black.

Every one, see also under significant words following.

Every wind is ill to a crazy (broken) ship.
(S 353)

1616 DRAXE no. 1780 (broken). 1640 HERBERT no. 395. 1670 RAY 6. 1732 FULLER no. 5126. 1869 SPURGEON *John Ploughman* ch. 7 Every wind is foul for a crazy ship.

Every, see also under significant words following.

Everybody's business is nobody's business.
(W 843)

[AR. *Pol.* 2. 1. 10 ἥκιστα γὰρ ἐπιμελείας τυγχάνει τὸ πλείστων κοινόν.] 1611 COTGRAVE s.v. Ouvrage Euerie bodies worke is no bodies worke. 1653 WALTON *Angler* I. ii. 1725 DEFOE *Everybody's business is nobody's business*, Title. 1829 COBBETT *Adv. to Y. Men* vi (1906) 294 Public property is never so well taken care of as private property; ...

Everybody's dog that whistles, I am not.
(D 481)

1616 WITHALS 570. 1639 CLARKE 232. 1826 SCOTT *Woodstock* ch. 9 'You are sure he will come, like a dog at a whistle,' said Wildrake.

Everybody, see also Fault suspects e., (Who is in).

Everything comes to him who waits.
[c. 1515] c. 1530 BARCLAY *Eclog.* ii. 843 Somewhat shall come who can his time abide. 1642 TORRIANO 26 He who can wait, hath what he desireth. 1847 DISRAELI *Tancred* IV. viii. Everything comes if a man will only wait. 1863 LONGFELLOW *Wayside Inn* ii. All things come round to him who will but wait. 1894 LD. AVEBURY *Use of Life* XV (1904) 93 Do not expect too much, and do not expect it too quickly. 'Everything comes to those who know how to wait.' 1908 S. PAGET *Confes. Med.* 114 Nature ... is not in any hurry ... ; everything comes to her, who waits [Fr. *Tout vient à point à qui sait attendre.*]

Everything has an end.
(E 120)

c. 1374 CHAUCER *Troilus* Bk. 3. l. 615 But at the laste, as every thyng hath ende. c. 1490 *Partonope* E.E.T.S. l. 11144 Ye wote wele, of all thing moste be an ende. 1530 PALSGRAVE 527/2 Every thynge at the laste draweth to his ende. 1548 HALL *Chron.* 94 As all thinges ende, so sorow asswageth. 1562 G. LEGH *Accidence of Armoury* 182 All worldly thinges haue an ende (excepte the householde wordes, betwene man and wife which some yere hath iii. endes). 1563 *Mirror for Mag.* ed. Campbell 343 Euery thinge hath ende. 1616 BRETON *Cross. Prov.* A6. 1841 DICKENS *B. Rudge* ch. 20.

Everything has an end, and a pudding has two.
(E 121)

1592 NASHE *Strange News* i. 281 Every thing hath an end, and a pudding hath two. 1611 BEAUM. & FL. *Kt. Burn. P.* i. i. As writers say, all things have end, And that we call a pudding, hath his two. a. 1628 CARMICHAELL no. 216 (staff). *Ibid.* no. 850 (pudding). 1738 SWIFT *Dial.* I. E.L. 286. 1826 SCOTT *Woodst.* ch. 10.

Everything has its seed.
1616 DRAXE no. 125.

Everything helps, quoth the wren, when she pissed into the sea.
(W 935)

[1590 G. MEURIER *Deviz. familier.* 'Peu aydc' disçoit le formy, pissant en mer en plein midy.]

1542 H. BRINKLOW *Lamentation* E.E.T.S. 90 As greate neade of your feastes as hath the see . . . of the pissynge of the wrenne. 1602 *Letters of Philip Gawdy* 118 The wrenn sayde all helpte when she . . . in the sea. 1623 CAMDEN 268. *a.* 1628 CARMICHAELL no. 217. 1706 STEVENS s.v. Grano. 1721 KELLY 13.

Everything in turn, except scandal, whose turn is always.

1887 BLACKMORE *Springhaven* ch. 18 You know the old proverb— . . .

Everything is as it is taken.   (T 31)

c. 1525 J. RASTELL *Four Elements* Hazl.-Dods. i. 8 Wisdom and folly is as it is taken. 1531 ELYOT *The Governor* i. 278 Euerything is to be estemed after his value. 1542 A. BORDE *Dietary* E.E.T.S. 260 Euery thyng as it is handled. 1580 MUNDAY *Zelauto* P1 All is well that is well taken. 1587 J. BRIDGES *Defence* 239 We must not thinke, to scape heere with this saying, euery thing as it is vsed, or taken. 1589 [LYLY] *Pap with a Hatchet* iii. 401 (Alls). 1616 BRETON *Cross. of Prov.* B3ᵛ. 1639 CLARKE 180.

Everything is good in its season.

(S 190)

1492 *Dial. of Salomon & Marcolphus* ed. Duff 13 Alle thinges haue theyre seasons and tyme. [*c.* 1515] 1521 BARCLAY *Éclog.* v. l. 87 Eche tyme and season hath his delyte and Joyes. 1591 W. STEPNEY *Span. Schoolmaster* L3ᵛ Euery thing in his season, & after pescods come peasen. 1616 DRAXE no. 1916. 1639 CLARKE 237. 1659 HOWELL *Span. Prov.* 21 Every thing in its season, and Turnips in Autumn. 1706 STEVENS s.v. Cosa (in Advent).

Everything is of use to a housekeeper.

(U 21)

1611 COTGRAVE s.v. Poinct He that keepes house makes vse of euerie thing. 1640 HERBERT no. 70.

Everything is the worse for wearing.

(W 207)

c. 1520 SKELTON *Magnyf.* I. 456 All thynge is worse whan it is worne. 1600 *Weakest to Wall* D3 It will not be much the worse for the wearing. 1639 CLARKE 190. 1670 RAY 159. 1823 GALT *Entail* ch. 38 Baith you and me, Grippy, are beginning to be the waur o' the wear.

Everything is yours, You think | but a little the king has.

1738 SWIFT *Dial.* II. E.L. 316 I'm sure 'tis mine. —What! you think everything is yours, but a little the King has.

Everything must have a beginning.

(B 257)

c. 1374 CHAUCER *Troilus* Bk. 2, l. 671 For every thyng a gynnyng hath it nede. 1575 GASCOIGNE *Gl. Govt.* ii. 37 All thinges have a beginning, shee is a woman, and nothing is unpossible. *a.* 1627 MIDDLETON *Mayor of Queenb.* IV. iii. I'll be the first then: Everything has beginning. 1641

FERGUSSON no. 1 All things hath a beginning (God excepted). 1840 MARRYAT *Poor Jack* ch. 31 'You've never been to sea before.' 'No . . . ; but there must be a beginning to everything.'

Everything new is fine.   (E 193)

c. 1595 SHAKES. *Rich. II* II. i. 24 Where doth the world thrust forth a vanity—So it be new, there's no respect how vile—That is not quickly buzz'd into his ears? 1611 COTGRAVE s.v. Nouveau Euery new thing looks fair. 1639 CLARKE 228 Every thing's pretty, when 'tis new. 1640 HERBERT no. 76.

Everything would fain live.   (E 193a)

[*c.* 1587] 1594 MARLOWE & NASHE *Dido* II. i. 238 Yet who so wretched but desires to live. 1616 DRAXE no. 1229. 1670 RAY 116. 1721 KELLY 94 . . . Spoken in excuse of Man or Beast, who make their best Endeavour to get a Living. 1732 FULLER no. 1469.

Everything, *see also* Fool believes e.; Little of e., and nothing in the main; Nose into e., (To put one's).

Evil communications corrupt good manners.   (C 558)

[I COR. XV. 33.] 1530 PALSGRAVE 499a (Foule wordes). 1533 T. MORE *Debell. Salem* xiv; Wks. 1557, 960 For (as saynt Paule speaketh of such heresies) euill communicacion corrupteth good maners. 1558 J. FISHER *Three Dialogues* C1 Corrumpunt etiam Sanctos commercia praua, Euyll company dooth corrupte alway. [1570] (1584 E3ᵛ) BALDWIN *Beware the Cat* Euil communication confoundeth good vertues. 1583 G. BABINGTON *Exposⁿ. of Commandments* 307 (Euill words). 1587 G. WHETSTONE *Censure of a loyal Subject* C1 Euill companie corrupt good manners. 1599 H. PORTER *Angry Wom. Abing.* l. 2309. (Ill words).

Evil crow, An | an evil egg.   (B 376)

1536 LATIMER *2nd Serm. bef. Conv.* P.S. 42 Ye know this is a proverb much used: 'An evil crow, an evil egg'. Then the children of this world . . . cannot choose but be evil. 1560 BECON *Cat.* P.S. 347 Of an evil crow cometh an evil egg. 1581 GUAZZO ii. 15 An ill byrde, layeth an ill egge. 1706 STEVENS s.v. Cuervo As is the Crow, so is the Egg.

Evil do, Whoso will no | shall do nothing that belongs thereto. *Cf.* Do no ill, If thou, etc.   (I 28)

1537 R. WHITFORD *Werke for Householders* D7 The olde prouerbe sayth, who so wyll none euyll do, shulde do nothynge that longeth therto. 1539 TAVERNER (1545) G8 Oure Englishe prouerbe He that woll no hurte do, muste do nothynge that longe there to. 1546 HEYWOOD II. v. H3. *c.* 1577 J. NORTHBROOKE *Treat. agst. Dicing*, Shaks. Soc. 173 Come you away from it, and vse it no more, . . . : as the olde saying is, He that will none euill do, Must do nothing belonging therto. 1732 FULLER no. 6305 . . . must do nought that's like thereto.

Evil for good, To render.   (E 204)

[I SAM. XXV. 21.]   **1481** CAXTON *Reynard* Arber 69   Thus doth he euyl for good.   *c.* **1489** *Id. Sons Aymon* X. E.E.T.S. 265   The proverbe may well be reherced for a trouth, that sayth Often happeth evill for a good torne.   **1623** WODROEPHE 512   And Ill for Good is greatest Wickednesse.

Evil grain, Of | no good seed can come.
                                         (G 405)

a. **1522** DOUGLAS *Aeneid* 4 Prol. 14   Of wikkyt grayn quhou sal gude schaif beschorn?   **1559** *Mirror for Mag.* Campbell 169   Vicious grayne must cum to fowl endes barne.   **1616** DRAXE no. 130.   **1670** RAY 8.

Evil (Naught) is soon learned, That which is.   (L 154)

1639 CLARKE 260 (naught).   **1670** RAY 8.

Evil (ill) manners, Of | spring good laws.   (M 625)

[MACROBIUS 3. 7. 10 *Vetus verbum est; leges inquit, ex malis moribus procreantur.* ERASM. *Ad. Bonae leges ex malis moribus procreantur.*]   **1539** TAVERNER 28   Good lawes be gendred of euyll maners.   **1578** TIMME *Caluine on Gen.* 70   According to the common Proverb . . .   **1619** J. FAVOUR *Antiquity* 406   Good laws proceed from euill manners.   **1655** FULLER *Hist. Camb.* iii. 54   Ill Manners occasion Good laws, as the Handsome Children of Ugly Parents.

Evil that comes out of thy mouth flieth into thy bosom.

1616 DRAXE no. 1994   The euill that commeth out of the mouth, returneth (or falleth) into the bosome.   **1670** RAY 8.

Evil there is odds, In.   (E 201)

1616 DRAXE no. 605.   **1639** CLARKE 197.

Evils are cured by contempt, Some.
                                         (E 208)

1651 HERBERT no. 1052.   **1732** FULLER no. 1906   He is above his Enemies, that despises their Injuries.

Evils (Harms, Ills, Mischiefs), Of two | choose the least.   (E 207)

c. **1374** CHAUCER *Troilus* Bk. 2 l. 470 'Of harmes two the lesse is for to chese'.   **1461** *Paston Lett.* (Gairdner) II. 73   Of ij. harmys the leste is to be take.   **1485** *Paris and Vienne* tr. Caxton E.E.T.S. 39   It byhoueth to eschewe of two euyls the werse.   **1546** HEYWOOD I. v. B2   Of two yls, choose the least whyle choyse lyth in lot.   **1549** *Complaynt of Scotland* E.E.T.S. 163   3e suld cheis the smallest of thir tua euillis.   **1580** LYLY *Euph. & his Eng.* ii. 108   Of two mischiefes the least is to be chosen.   [*c.* **1590**] **1592** *Soliman and Perseda* IV. i. 237 (extremes).   [1592] **1602** *Thos. Ld. Cromwell* III. ii. 91   Of two euils, 'tis best to shun the greatest.   [1600] **1657** *Lust's Dominion* Hazl.-Dods. xiv. 131 (In extremities).   **1891** A. FORBES *Bar. Biv. & Bat.* (1910) 187   Either the Turks would

make a prisoner of me . . . or I must . . . take my chance of the Russian fire as I galloped for . . . shelter. . . . 'Of two evils choose the less', says the wise proverb.

Evils have their comfort; good none can support (to wit) with a moderate and contented heart.   (E 206)

1640 HERBERT no. 208.

Evils we bring on ourselves are the hardest to bear, The.

1902–4 LEAN IV. 119   . . . Bien est malheureux qui est cause de son malheur.—Cordier, 1538.

Evil (*adj. adv.*), *see* Helps the e. hurts the good (He that); Ill (E.) gotten ill (e.) spent; Ill (E.) will never said well; Praise by e. men is dispraise; Put off the e. hour.

Evil(s) (*noun*), *see also* Bear with e.; Covetousness is . . . the root of all e.; Discontent worst e.; Does e. (He that) never weens good; Does no good, does e. enough; Every e. under the sun (For) there is remedy; Good against e. (Set); Good is to be sought out and e. attended; Hopes not for fears not e.; Idleness is root of all e.; Mischief (E.) comes without calling for; Never do e. that good may come of it; Sucked e. from dug; Sufficient unto the day is e. thereof; Welcome e. if alone; Women (Wives and wind) are necessary e.

Evil, *see also* Ill.

Ewe and a lamb, Now I have got an | every one cries, Welcome Peter. *Cf.* **Sheep and a cow.**

1706 STEVENS s.v. Oveja.   **1732** FULLER no. 3690.

Ewe is drowned, When the | she's dead.

a. **1628** CARMICHAELL no. 1275.   **1721** KELLY 354   . . . Spoken when a thing is gone, and past Recovery.

Ewe(s), Yowe(s), *see also* Lamb where it's tipped, the e. where she's clipped; Many frosts . . . make rotten y.; Old e. lamb fashion; Silly flock where e. bears bell; Stamps like a e.

Ewell, *see* Sutton.

Examined enterprise goes on boldly, An.   (E 170)

1640 HERBERT no. 618.

Example is better than precept.
                                         (E 213)

c. **1400** *Mirk's Festival* E.E.T.S. 216   Then saythe Seynt Austeyn that an ensampull yn doyng ys mor commendabull then ys techyng other prechyng.   *a.* **1568** ASCHAM *Schoolmaster* Mayor 61   One example is more valiable . . . than twenty preceptes written in bookes. **1586** J. CASE *Praise of Music* 80 Examples stick deeper than precepts. *a.* **1594** J. AYLMER (1701 Strype *Aylmer* 274) Good example is ofttimes better than a great deal of Preaching. **1706** STEVENS S.V. Predicar He preaches well who lives well. That is, a good Example is the best Sermon. **1708** PRIOR *Turtle & Spar.* Example draws where precept fails, And sermons are less read than tales. **1824** MOIR *Mansie W.* ch. 19 Example is better than precept, as James Batter observes. **1894** LD. AVEBURY *Use of Life* ch. 19 Men can be more easily led than driven: example is better than precept.

Example to another, He is in ill case that gives. (C 112)

1573 SANFORD 110 (Naught is he). **1629** *Bk. Mer. Rid.* Prov. no. 125.

Example, *see also* Laws not by e., (We live by); Like me, God bless the e.

Exception proves the rule, The. (E 213a)

[*Exceptio firmat regulam in non exceptis,* shortened from CIC. *pro Balbo* 14. 32.] **1663** J. WILSON *Cheats* To Rdr. A2ᵛ I think I have sufficiently justified the brave Man, even by this Reason, That the Exception proves the Rule. **1765** JOHNSON 'Preface' to his ed. of *Shakespeare* C2ᵛ The exception only confirms the rule. **1827–48** HARE *Gues. at Truth* ii. (1859) 510.

Exception, *see also* Rule without some e. (No general).

Exchange (A fair exchange) is no robbery. (C 228)

1546 HEYWOOD II. iv. G4 Though chaunge be no robbry for the chaunged case. *c.* **1590** *John of Bordeaux* l. 213. **1609** HARWARD 120ᵛ (Swoppery). *a.* **1628** CARMICHAELL no. 540 (Fair shifts). **1655** FULLER *Ch. Hist.* I. v (1868) I. 61 In lieu of what he left behind him, (exchange is no robbery), he carried along with him some of St. Alban's dust. **1748** SMOLLETT *Rod. Rand.* ch. 41 Casting an eye at my hat and wig, . . . he took them off, and clapping his own on my head, declared that a fair exchange was no robbery. **1819** SCOTT *Leg. Mont.* ch. 14 This sword is an Andrew Ferrara, and the pistols better than my own. But a fair exchange is no robbery.

Exchequer, *see* Christ takes not (What), the e. carries away.

Excuses himself, accuses himself, He who. (E 215)

[HIERONYMUS *Ep.* 4 *ad virginem* c. 3 *Dum excusare credis, accusas.* Fr. *Qui s'excuse, s'accuse.*] **1596** SHAKES. *K.J.* IV. ii. 30 And oftentimes excusing of a fault Doth make the fault the worse by the excuse. **1611** COTGRAVE S.V. Excuser Some when they meane to excuse, accuse, themselues. **1616** DRAXE no. 625 To excuse is to accuse. **1664** CODRINGTON 191 Excusing is oftentimes accusing. **1884** J. PAYN *Canon's Ward* ch. 31 It is very difficult for a person in my position to excuse without accusing himself.

Excuse(s) (*noun*), *see also* Absent without fault, present without e.; Bad e. better than none; Find a woman without e.; Idle folks lack no e.; Ill paymaster never wants e.; Naught is that muse that finds no e.; Woman need but look on apron-string.

Excuse(d) (*verb*), *see also* Dies this year is e. for the next, (He that).

Exeter, *see* Duke of E.'s daughter.

Exon, *see* Kirton.

Expect a good whelp from an ill dog, We may not. (W 292)

1678 RAY *Adag. Hebr.* 398.

Expect from a hog but a grunt? What can you.

1731 *Poor Robins Alm.* If we petition a Hog, what can we expect but a grunt. **1827** SCOTT *Two Drovers* ch. 1 If he had not . . . been but a Dumfriesshire hog . . . he would have spoken more like a gentleman, But you cannot have more of a sow than a grumph. **1910** P. W. JOYCE *Eng. as we Speak* 137 Of a coarse, ill-mannered man, who uses unmannerly language: 'What could you expect from a pig but a grunt.'

Expect of a hog but his bristles? What can you.

1813 RAY 201.

Expect(s, ed), *see also* Bear with evil, e. good; Blessed is he who e. nothing; Gift much e. paid not given; Pleasure long e. is dear sold; Suffer and e.

Experience is good, if not bought too dear.

1721 KELLY 91 (but often). **1732** FULLER no. 1479.

Experience is sometimes dangerous. (E 218)

1573 SANFORD 105. **1578** FLORIO *First F.* f. 30 Experience sometymes is perilous. **1629** *Bk. Mer. Rid.* Prov. no. 110.

Experience is the mistress of (teaches) fools. (E 220)

a. **1568** ASCHAM *Scholem.* Erasmus . . . saide wiselie that experience is the common schole-house of foles. **1579** LYLY *Euph.* i. 260 It is commonly said, yet doe I thinke it a common lye, that Experience is the Mistresse of fooles, for . . . they be most fooles that want it. **1579** *North's Plutarch* Amyot to Reader TC i. 16 (school-mistress). **1618** BRETON *Courtier & Countryman* Wks. (1879) II. 8 Let ignorance be an enemy to wit, and experience be the mistress of fools. **1641** FERGUSSON no. 255 Experience may teach a fool. **1670** RAY 86 Experientia stultorum magistra. Wise men learn by others harms, fools by their own. **1874** WHYTE-MELVILLE *Uncle John* ch. 10 Experience does not make fools wise. . . . Most proverbs are fallacious. None greater than that which says it does.

Experience is the mother (father) of wisdom (knowledge) (and memory the mother). (E 221)

1539 TAVERNER *Garden* 2 C8ᵛ Experience is mother of prudence. **1548** HALL 383 Experience the very mother and mastres of wisedome. **1573** SANFORD H4ᵛ Experience is the mother of things. **1578** FLORIO *First F.* f. 32ᵛ Tyme is the father of truth, and experience is the mother of al things. **1581** GUAZZO i. 33 Experience is the father of wisdome, and memorie the mother. **1590** SIR JOHN SMYTHE *Certain Discourses* *2ᵛ Experience is the mother of Science. **1594** LIPSIUS 6 *Bks. of Politics* tr. Jones 12 Vse begot me, and Memorie my mother brought me forth [Afranius on Wisdom]. **1616** DRAXE no. 632 Experience the mother of wisedome. **1707** MAPLETOFT 34. **1732** FULLER no. 1480 Experience is the Father of Wisdom, and Memory the Mother.

Experience keeps a dear school, but fools learn in no other.

[*Cf.* **1604** DRAYTON *Owle* l. 1088 Fooles still too deare have sound Experience bought.] **1758** FRANKLIN *Way to Wealth* (Crowell) 24 *Experience keeps a dear school, but fools will learn in no other,* as Poor Richard says. **1897** C. C. KING *Story of Brit. Army* 112 But the British leaders were to learn the fact, they might have foreseen, in the 'only school fools learn in, that of experience'.

Experience without learning is better than learning without experience.

1707 MAPLETOFT 77.

Experience, *see also* Trouble brings e. and e. brings wisdom.

Explained, *see* Judge knows nothing unless it has been e. to him three times.

Express, *see* Modest words to e. immodest things, (It is hard to find).

Extreme law (justice, right) is extreme wrong (injustice, injury). (R 122)

1508 J. FISHER *Sayings David in Psalms* 261 The lawe is [if?] vsed extremely after the wordes as they be wryten shall be many tymes grete wronge. **1539** TAVERNER 28 *Summum ius summa iniuria* Extreme lawe is extreme wronge. **1548** HALL *Chron.* 499 The Adage, the extremitie of Iustice, is extreme iniurie. **1569** GRAFTON *Chron.* (1809) II. 228 The extremitie of iustice is extreme iniustice. **1580** LYLY *Euph. & his Eng.* ii. 214 Iustice without mercie were extreame iniurie. **1597** *Politeuphuia* 86 Extreame Law, is extreame wrong. *a.* **1634** CHAPMAN *Chabot* II. iii. 17 Extreme justice is . . . the extreme of injury. **1639** CLARKE 172.

Extreme will hold long, No. (E 222)

1586 WARNER *Albion's Eng.* III. xvii. 13ᵛ Perpetuitie doth fayle in euery thing extreeme. **1592** DELAMOTHE 55 An extreme grief cannot continue long. **1605** MARSTON *Dutch Courtezan* II. i. Nothing extreame lives long. **1616** BRETON *Cross. Prov.* 3, B3. **1624** CAPT. JOHN SMITH *Virginia* i. 44. **1639** CLARKE 321.

Extremes meet.

1606 SHAKES. *A.C.* III. iv. 19 No midway 'Twixt these extremes at all. **1780** WALPOLE *Letters* (Cunningham) vii. 395 We seem to be plunging into the horrors of France . . . yet, as extremes meet, there is at this moment amazing insensibility. **1809** MALKIN *Gil Blas* I. v. Gentlemen, extremes are said to meet. **1822** SCOTT *Nigel* ch. 27 This Olifaunt is a Puritan?—not the less likely to be a Papist, . . . for extremes meet. **1853** TRENCH iv. 96 *Extremes meet* . . . Roman Emperors would one day have blasphemous honours paid to them, . . . on the next day . . . to be flung at last into the common sewer.

Extremity, *see also* Calamity (E.) is the touchstone of a brave mind (unto wit); Every e. a fault; Man's e., God's opportunity.

Eye behind him (or in the back of his head), He has an. (E 236)

[PLAUT. *Aul.* I. I. 25 *In occipitio quoque oculos habet.*] *c.* **1575** *Gammer Gurton's Needle* II. ii. She hath an eie behind her. **1616** WITHALS 559. **1721** KELLY 170 He has an Eye in his Neck. Spoken of wary and cautious People.

Eye is a shrew, The. (E 229)

a. **1591** HY. SMITH *Serm.* (1866) I. 283 It is a true proverb, The eye is a shrew; although it shew light, yet it leadeth many into darkness. If Eve had not seen, she had not lusted. **1678** RAY 354.

Eye is bigger than the belly, The. *Cf.* Better fill a man's belly. (E 261)

1580 LYLY *Euph. & his Eng.* ii. 99 Thou art like the *Epicure,* whose bellye is sooner filled then his eye. **1603** MONTAIGNE (Florio) I. xxx. 33 I feare me our eies be greater than our bellies. **1640** HERBERT no. 1018. **1726** SWIFT *Gulliver* II. viii. Wks. (1856) I. 40 The captain . . . replied with the old English proverb, 'That he doubted mine eyes were bigger than my belly'. **1738** *Id.* Dial. II. E.L. 306 I thought I could have eaten this wing of a chicken; but my eye's bigger than my belly. **1823** GROSE ed. Pierce Egan s.v. Belly.

Eye is the window of the heart (mind), The. *Cf.* Forehead and the eye, In the | the lecture of the mind doth lie. (E 231)

1545 PHAER *Reg. Life* I. C4 The eyes . . . are the windowes of the mynde, for both ioy and anger . . . are seene . . . throughe them. *c.* **1577** NORTHBROOKE *Treatise* (1843 ed., 156) The eyes are . . . called, fores et foenestrae animae; the doores and windowes of the minde. **1595** SHAKES. *Rich. II* I. iii. 208 Uncle, even in the glasses of thine eyes I see thy grieved heart. **1666** TORRIANO *It. Prov.* 175, no. 32.

Eye nor my elbow, Neither my.

1894 NORTHALL *Folk-phrases* 20 . . . i.e. neither one thing nor the other.

Eye, One | of the master sees more than ten of the servants. (E 243)

1640 HERBERT no. 687. **1732** FULLER no. 3749 (ten of the Man's).

Eye of the master will do more work than both his hands, The.

1758 FRANKLIN *Poor Rich. Alm.* in ARBER *Eng. Garner* v. **1876** MRS. BANKS *Manch. Man* ch. 14.

Eye sees not, What the | the heart rues not. *Cf.* Far from eye, etc. (E 247)

a. **1153** ST. BERNARD *Sermon v All Saints* Quod non videt oculus cor non dolet. *a.* **1181** *Serlo of Wilton* (ed. Oberg, Stockholm 1965) 116, no. 55. **1545** TAVERNER B5 That the eye seeth not, the hart rueth not. **1546** HEYWOOD II. vii. I3 That the eie seeth not, the hert rewth not. **1548** HALL *Chron.* 867 That the iye seeth, the harte rueth. **1603** MONTAIGNE (Florio) III. xiii. 286 I never desire or find fault with that I see not: That Proverb is verified in me; What eye seeth not, the heart rueth not. **1620** SHELTON *Quix.* II. lxvii (1908) iii. 293 The heart dreams not of what the eye sees not. **1669** PENN *No Cross, no Crown* v What the eye views not, the heart craves not, as well as rues not. **1706** STEVENS s.v. Ojo. **1721** KELLY 341 . . . Men may have Losses, but if they be unknown to them they give them no Trouble. **1853** TRENCH vi. 146 On the danger of overlooking and forgetting all the suffering of others . . . which is not actually submitted to our eyes: . . .

Eye that sees all things else sees not itself, The. (E 232)

a. **1591** HY. SMITH *Serm.* (1866) I. 284 As the eye seeth all things and cannot see itself; so we can see other men's faults, but not our own. **1594** NASHE *Unf. Trav.* ii. 201 Ded. 3 How wel or ill I haue done in it, I am ignorant: (the eye that sees round about it selfe, sees not into it selfe).

Eye will have his part, The. (E 234)

1640 HERBERT no. 466.

Eyes about him, He has all his.
(E 266)

1666 TORRIANO *Prov. Phr.* s.v. Biggio 15 . . . To be no fool. **1764** H. BROOKE *Fool of Quality* Preface. **1766** GOLDSMITH *Vicar of Wakefield* ch. 14 My wife . . . called me back to advise me . . . to have all my eyes about me. **1813** RAY 60 . . . i.e. He looks well after his affairs.

Eyes are upon the king, Many.

1616 DRAXE no. 1150.

Eyes as Argus, As many. (E 254)

[Argus, in fable, had a hundred eyes.] *c.* **1374** CHAUCER *Troilus* Bk. 4, l. 1459 Youre fader is in

sleght as Argus eyed. *c.* **1535** W. CALVERLEY *Dialogue* CI [of Henry VIII] Eyed as Argus. *c.* **1548** BALE *K. Johan* 244 Nay, ye can not, thowgh ye had Argus eyes. **1575** GASCOIGNE i. 199 If I had as many eyes as Argus, I coulde not have sought a man more narrowly.

Eyes as red as a ferret's. (E 255)

1530 PALSGRAVE 457/2 His eyes be so bleared with drinkyng that they be as reed as a fyrret. **1599** SHAKES. *J.C.* I. ii. 185 And Cicero Looks with such ferret and such fiery eyes As we have seen him in the Capitol, Being cross'd in conference by some senators. **1699** B. E. s.v. Ferreted.

Eyes draw (gather, pick) straws, His.
(E 263)

[= to be sleepy.] *c.* **1641** FERGUSSON MS. no. 1046 My eyes is gathering straes. **1691** MRS. D'ANVERS *Academia* 36 Their Eyes by this time all drew straws. **1738** SWIFT Dial. III. E.L. 324. **1796** WOLCOT (P. Pindar) *Orson & Ellen* v. 125 Their eyelids did not once pick straws. **1824** MOIR *Mansie W.* ch. 24 As I had been up since five in the morning . . . my een were gathering straws.

Eyes have one language everywhere, The. (E 256)

1640 HERBERT no. 959.

Eyes on letters nor hands in coffers, Neither. (E 264)

1573 SANFORD 108 Neither the eye in the letter, nor the hande in the purse of an other. **1578** FLORIO *First F.* f. 33. **1609** HARWARD 85ᵛ Eys from other mens writings, eares from other mens secretts, and hands from other mens coyne. **1640** HERBERT no. 288. **1659** HOWELL *It. Prov.* 12.

Eye(s), *see also* All my e. and Betty Martin; All's out is good for prisoners; All that you get you may put in your e.; Basilisk's e. is fatal; Better e. out; Better e. sore; Better fill man's belly than e.; Better to have one e.; Bird to pick out his own e. (Brought up); Black in any one's e. (To say); Blessed is e. betwixt Severn and Wye; Buyer needs hundred e.; Cat shouts its e. while it steals cream; Cat's e.; Choose not a wife by e. only; Cry one's e. out; Cry with one e., laugh with other; Day has e., night has ears; Dust in e.; Eagle's e.; Fair wife (Who has) needs more than two e.; Far from e. far from heart; Fields have e.; Finger in e.; Forehead and e. (In) lecture of mind; Gifts blind e.; Greedy e. to have leal heart (Hard for); Green in e.; Handful of dust will fill e.; Hawks will not pick hawk's e. out; Heart's letter is read in e.; Hit the bird in e.; I was by . . . when my e. was put on; Ignorant has eagle's wings and owl's e.; Jaundiced e. all things look yellow (To); Jest not with the e.; Keep your e. open before marriage; Keep your mouth shut and e. open; Kings have many e.; Learning is e. of mind; Light is naught for sore e.; Little troubles e., less soul; London Bridge had fewer e. (If); Master's e. makes horse fat; Miller's e.; Mist before one's e.; Mote in another's e.; Music e. of ear; Nature has given two e.; Needle's e.; One e. (He that has but) sees better; One e. (He that has but) must be afraid to lose it; Pipe one's e.; Plays more than sees forfeits e.; Please your e. and plague heart; Proud e., open purse . . . bring mischief; Religion, credit, the e. not to be touched; Rolling e. roving heart; See with one's own e.; Sheep's e.; Sight for sore e.; Sleep with one e. open; Surgeon must have eagle's e.; Suspicion has double e.; Touch your e. but with elbow; Twinkling of an e.; Two e. see more than one; War and physic governed by e.; Wash their throats before they washed their e.; Water is the e. of landscape; Whirl the

e. shows kite's brains; Winks with one e. (He that) I will not trust; Woman has an e. more than man; Wool over e. *See also* Jew's e.; Weather-eye.

Eyewitness, One | is better than two (ten) hear-so's.   (E 274)

1519 HORMAN *Vulgaria* 299 One wytnes that sawe the dede: is worthe . x . that herde of it. **1539** TAVERNER 43ᵛ Pluris est oculatus testis unus q auriti decem. One eye wytnesse, is of more value, then ten eare wytnesses. **1616** G. HAKEWILL *Answer to Dr. Carier* 251. **1639** CLARKE 309.

F

Face as long as a fiddle, To have a.

[= to look dismal.]   **1903** A. T. QUILLER-COUCH *Hetty Wesley* II. iv. All looked at her; even Johnny Whitelamb looked, with a face as long as a fiddle.

Face is no index to the heart, The.   (F 1)

1567 *A pleasant disport* (*Filocolo* tr. H. G.) *2ᵛ Deme not by viewe of face Least hast makes wast.   **1573** SANFORD 98ᵛ Iuuenal in his seconde Satyre sayeth: Fronti nulla fides, that is, Trust not the face.   [*c.* **1589**] **1592** KYD *Span. Trag.* III. i. Ther's no credit in the countenance.   **1601** SHAKES. *T.N.* I. ii. 48 Though that nature with a beauteous wall Doth oft close in pollution, yet of thee I will believe thou hast a mind that suits With this thy fair and outward character. **1605–6** *Id. M.* I. iv. 11 There's no art To find the mind's construction in the face.

Face is the index of the heart (mind), The.   (F 1)

[L. *Vultus est index animi.*]   *a.* **1575** J. PILKINGTON *Nehemiah* P.S. 292 The affections of the mind declare themselves openly in the face and behaviour of man.   **1576** LEMNIUS *Touchstone of Complexions* tr. T. Newton F1 The countenance . . . is the Image of the mynde.   **1584** *Withals* L7 Your face doth testifie what you be inwardly.   **1605–6** SHAKES. *K.L.* IV. vi. 52 And here's another, whose warp'd looks proclaim What store her heart is made on.   **1605–6** *Id. M.* I. iv. 11 There's no art To find the mind's construction in the face.   **1614–16** *Times Whistle* ii. 630–2 Man is to man a subject of deceite; And that olde saying is vntrue, 'the face Is index of the heart'.   **1666** TORRIANO *It. Prov.* 317, no. 5 (image of the mind).   **1837** LOVER *Rory O'More* ch. 42 'Your brow and your mouth are playing at cross purposes; for while gloom sits on the one, mirth is twitching at the other.' 'The face is the index of the mind . . . : it is a true saying.'

Face made of a fiddle, To have one's.   (F 11)

[= to be irresistibly charming.]   **1678** RAY 243 I think his face is made of a fiddle, every one that

looks on him loves him.   **1762** SMOLLETT *Sir L. Greaves* (1780) I. viii. 84 Your honour's face is made of a fiddle; every one that looks on you loves you.   **1816** SCOTT *Old Mort.* ch. 37 How could I help it? His face was made of a fiddle.

Face the music, To.

[= to face boldly the consequences of one's actions, to accept the inevitable.]   *a.* **1851** J. F. COOPER in SCHELE DE VERE *Americanisms* (1872) 601 Rabelais' unpleasant 'quarter' is by our more picturesque people called *facing the music.* **1897** RHODES in *Westm. Gaz.* 6 Jan. 5/1 I will not refer to the vulgar colloquialism that I was afraid to face the music.

Face to face, the truth comes out.

1706 STEVENS s.v. Barba (shame appears).   **1732** FULLER no. 1485.   **1852** E. FITZGERALD *Polonius* 53 'Face to face truth comes out apace.' (If you have but an eye to find it by.)

Face to God, He has one | and another to the devil.   (F 10)

1641 FERGUSSON no. 468.   **1721** KELLY 152. **1732** FULLER no. 1878.

Face(s), *see also* Ass knows well in whose f. he brays; Calf with the white f.; Fair f. cannot have crabbed heart; Fair f. foul heart; Fair f. half a portion; Foul f. (Never a) but there's foul fancy; Friday f.; Gallows in f.; God or a painter; Good f. needs no band; Good f. on a thing (Put); Good f. recommendation; Good fame better than good f.; Joy of the heart makes f. merry; King's f. should give grace; Laugh in one's f. and cut one's throat; Looks in a man's f. (He that) knows what money in purse; Put a blithe f. on ill heart (Ill to); Set one's f. like a flint; Truth has a scratched f.; Truth has good f., bad clothes; Two f. in one hood; Visor to hide ill-favoured f.; Wipes his nose . . . forfeits his f.

Facilis descensus Averno, see Descent to Avernus.

Fact, *see* Truth (f.) is stranger than fiction.

Facts, So much the worse for the.

1902–4 LEAN IV. 96.

Facts are stubborn things.

1749 SMOLLETT *Gil Blas* X. i.   1756–66 AMORY *John Buncle* 124 Facts are things too stubborn to be destroyed by laughing and doubting.   1866 BLACKMORE *Cradock N.* ch. 51.   1867 FROUDE *Short Studies* I 'Homer' Facts, it was once said, are stubborn things; but in our days we have changed all that.

Fade(s), *see* Beauty f. like a flower; Flowers soonest f., (The fairest).

Fagot, *see* Eat a buttered f. go to Northampton.

Fail(s, ed), *see* Friends f. fliers; Good that f. never; Love f., (Where) we espy all faults; Mickle f. that fools think.

Failure teaches success.

1902 G. BALFOUR *Life of Stevenson* I. 101 It is an old . . . saying that failure is the only high-road to success.

Failures, *see* Three f. and a fire make a Scotsman's fortune.

Fain see, That would I | said blind George of Hollowee (blind Hugh).

(G 84)

1533 J. HEYWOOD *Pardoner & Friar* B3 Mary that wolde I se quod blynde hew.   1633 JONSON *T. Tub* II. ii. 25 That would I fain zee, quoth the blind George of Holloway.   1678 RAY 268. 1738 SWIFT *Dial.* I. E.L. 272 O! 'tis the prettiest thing. . . . Would I could see it, quoth blind Hugh.

Fain, *see also* Fowl of a fair day (As f. as).

Faint at the smell of a wallflower, He will.

1787 GROSE (London) 198 . . . Intimating that the person so spoken of had been confined in the goal of Newgate; formerly styled the wall-flower, from the wall-flowers growing up against it.

Faint heart never won fair lady (castle).

(H 302)

c. 1390 GOWER *Conf. Amantis* V. 6573 Bot as men sein, wher herte is failed, Ther schal no castell ben assailed.   1545 TAVERNER B2 A coward verely neuer obteyned the loue of a faire lady.   1569 W. ELDERTON *Ballad, Brittain's Ida* v. i. Faint hearts faire ladies neuer win.   1580 LYLY *Euph. & his Eng.* ii. 131 Faint hart, Philautus, neither winneth Castell nor Lady. 1592–3 SHAKES. *V.A.* l. 569 Affection faints not like a pale-fac'd coward But then woos best when most his choice is froward.   1614 CAMDEN 306 Faint heart neuer wonne fair Lady.   1753 RICHARDSON *Grandison* I. xvi (1812) 28 Then,

madam, we will *not* take your denial. . . . Have I not heard it said, that . . .   1802 EDGEWORTH *Irish Bulls* ch. 11.   1839 DICKENS *N. Nickleby* ch. 53.

Faintly, *see* Asks f. begs denial.

Fair and the foul, by dark are like store, The.

1546 HEYWOOD I. v. B2.

Fair and sluttish (foolish), black and proud, long and lazy, little and loud.

(F 28)

c. 1641 FERGUSSON MS. no. 1424 Of the culloris of women. Fair & foolish, litil & loud, Long & lusty, black & proud. Fat & merry, lean & sad, Pale & pettish, Red & bad, High cullo*ur* (in a woman) choler showes; And shee's unholsome that lyk sorrell growes. Nought ar the peeuish, proud, malitious, But worst of all the Red shrill, jealious.   1670 RAY 51.   1732 FULLER no. 6409.

Fair and softly, as lawyers go to heaven.

(L 128)

1670 RAY 193.   1845 A. SMITH *Scatterg. Fam.* ch. 15 You buy as slowly as lawyers go to heaven, and that takes a long time for 'em to do.

Fair and softly goes far. *Cf.* Soft pace goes far.

(S 601)

c. 1350 *Douce MS.* 52 no. 50 Fayre and softe me ferre gose.   *c.* 1374 CHAUCER *Troilus* Bk. 5 l. 347 Thei take it wisly faire and softe.   *c.* 1400 *Tale of Beryn* E.E.T.S. 28 But feir and sofft with ese, homward they hir led.   *c.* 1450 *Coventry Plays* E.E.T.S. 50 For soft and essele men goo far. 1530 PALSGRAVE 835a Fayre and soft, or softly. 1576 HOLYBAND E1 Softe passe goeth farre. 1578 FLORIO *First F.* D2 Who goeth softly, goeth well.   1598–9 SHAKES. *M.A.* V. iv. 72 To the chapel let us presently.—Soft and fair, friar.   1607 TOPSELL *Four-f. Beasts* (1673) 210 The proverb is old and true, . . .   1639 CLARKE 3 Soft and faire goes far.   1641 FERGUSSON no. 359 Hulie[1] and fair men rides far journeys. 1670 RAY 87 . . . He that spurs on too fast at first setting out, tires before he comes to his journey's end. *Festina lente.*   1818 SCOTT *Ht. Midl.* ch. 45. 1914 K. F. PURDON *Folk of Furry F.* ch. 2 I'm slow, but fair and easy goes far in a day. [[1] softly.]

Fair as Lady Done, As.

(L 30)

1670 RAY 208.   1678 RAY 283 . . . *Chesh.* The Dones were a great family in Cheshire, living at Utkinton . . .: Nurses use there to call their children so if girls.   1917 BRIDGE 12 . . . The wife of Sir John Done (*d.* 1629), of Utkinton, hereditary bow-bearer of Delamere Forest.

Fair chieve[1] all where love trucks.[2]

(A 177)

1670 RAY 47. [[1] See quotation under next proverb. [2] = deals.]

Fair chieve good ale, it makes many folks speak as they think.

(A 102)

1678 RAY 93 . . . Fair chieve is used in the same

sense here as . . . Good speed, Good success have it. **1710** PALMER 18 (Well fare).

Fair day in winter is the mother of a storm, A.   (D 72)

1639 CLARKE 171 A faire day is mother of a storme. **1651** HERBERT no. 1145.

Fair day, To a | open the window, but make you ready as to a foul.   (D 105)

1640 HERBERT no. 119.

Fair death honours the whole life, A.
(D 151)

1578 FLORIO *First F.* 34 A gallant death, doth honour a whole life. **1581** GUAZZO i. 182 (worthy). **1640** HERBERT no. 522. **1657** TORRIANO *Introd. to Ital. Tongue* 251 A noble death crowns a mans whole life.

Fair face foul heart, A.   (F 3)

1584 LYLY *Camp.* II. ii. 56 Women [have] faire faces, but false hearts. **1592–3** SHAKES. *C.E.* III. ii. 13 Bear a fair presence, though your heart be tainted. **1596** *Id. M.V.* I. iii. 174 I like not fair terms and a villain's mind. **1598** JONSON *Ev. Man in Humour* IV. iii. 95 I haue knowne fayre hides haue foule hartes eare now. **1605–6** SHAKES. *M.* I. vii. 82 False face must hide what the false heart doth know. *a.* **1628** CARMICHAELL no. 99 (taill). **1659** HOWELL *Brit. Prov.* 3. **1866** READE *G. Gaunt* ch. 40 A mob . . . shouting, 'Murderess . . . Fair face but foul heart!'

Fair face cannot have a crabbed heart, A.   (F 5)

c. **1572** T. RICHARDSON *Proper New Song* in C. Robinson et al *Handf. Pleas. Delights* 11 For good conditions do not lie, where is a pleasant face. **1581** GUAZZO ii. 8 It sildome falleth out, that a good mind is lodged in a mishapen body. [*c.* **1589**] **1601** LYLY *Love's Metam.* III. i. 52 Faire faces should haue smoothe hearts. **1592** DELAMOTHE 39 When the face is faire, the hart must be gentle. **1593** *Passionate Morrice* New Sh. S. 92 Building vpon the prouerbe, . . .

Fair face is half a portion, A.   (F 4)

1530 PALSGRAVE 358 She that is good and fayre nede none other dowrie. **1616** DRAXE no. 157 Shee that is faire, hath halfe her portion. **1639** CLARKE 120.

Fair fall truth and daylight.   (T 564)

1678 RAY 211.

Fair field (stage) and no favour, A.

1695 CONGREVE *Love for Love* Epil. Then pray continue this your kind Behaviour, For a clear Stage won't do, without your Favour. **1829** T. CARLYLE *Novalis* Centenary ed. 1899 xxvii 55 (. . ., and the right will prosper). **1836–7** DICKENS *Pickwick* ch. 28 A clear stage and no favour for the goblins. **1853** C. KINGSLEY *Hypatia* ch. 2 I promise you a clear stage and—

a great deal of favour. **1864** J. H. NEWMAN *Apologia* pt. iv (stage). **1883** E. PENNELL-ELMHIRST *Cream Leicestersh.* 202 He . . . asked only for a fair field and a clear course.

Fair gainings make fair spendings. (G 9)

1573 SANFORD 104. **1629** *Bk. Mer. Rid.* Prov. no. 99. **1659** TORRIANO no. 212 Ones gettings orders ones spendings.

Fair in love and war, All is.   (A 139)

[**1592**] **1594** *Knack to Know a Knave* Hazl.-Dods. vi. 544 Deceit in love is but a merriment To such as seek a rival to prevent. **1606** MARSTON *The Fawn* IV. i. 716 An old saw hath bin, Faith's breach for love and kingdoms is no sin. **1620** SHELTON *Quix.* Pt. II. xxi (ii. 332). *c.* **1630** BEAUM. & FL. *Lovers' Progress* v. ii. All stratagems In love, and that the sharpest war, are lawful. **1801** EDGEWORTH *Belinda* ch. 20 In love and war, you know, all stratagems are allowable. **1845** G. P. R. JAMES *Smuggler* ch. 17 But after all, in love and war, every stratagem is fair, they say. **1884** J. PAYN *Canon's Ward* ch. 18 When she reminded him of his solemn promise . . . , he hinted that 'all things were fair (lies included) in love or war'.

Fair in the cradle, and foul in the saddle (or vice versa).   (C 792)

1614 CAMDEN 306 Foule in the cradle, prooueth faire in the sadle. **1670** RAY 87. **1706** STEVENS s.v. Potro As we say, Foul in the Cradle and fair in the Saddle. **1732** FULLER no. 6119.

Fair is not fair, but that which pleases.
(F 24)

1594–5 SHAKES. *L:L.L.* IV. i. 23 A giving hand, though foul, shall have fair praise. **1605–8** *Id. T.Ath.* I. ii. 13 Faults that are rich are fair. [**1635**] **1655** MASSINGER *Bashful Lover* I. i. I guess the reason; A giving hand is still fair to the receiver. **1640** HERBERT no. 492. **1670** RAY 9.

Fair lasts all the year, The.   (F 26)

1541 *Schoolhouse of Women* B2ᵛ The fayre is here Bye when ye lyst, it lasteth ouer yere. **1546** HEYWOOD II. ii. G1. **1611** DAVIES no. 1. **1639** CLARKE 233 (lasts not).

Fair offer is no cause of feud, A.

1721 KELLY 109 . . . Spoken when one refuses what we proffer them. **1818** SCOTT *Ht. Midl.* ch. 26.

Fair (Good) pawn never shamed his master, A.   (P 124)

1609 HARWARD 110ᵛ (good). **1623** CAMDEN 265. **1631** BRATHWAITE *Whimzies. A Wine-soaker* (1859) 103 Howsoever, a good pawn never sham'd his master. **1670** RAY 130. **1721** KELLY 7 . . . It is no Shame for a man to borrow on a good Pawn.

Fair play's a jewel.

1823 J. F. COOPER *Pioneers* ch. 17. **1824** SCOTT *Redg.* ch. 21. **1837** CHAMIER *Saucy Areth.* ch. 9.

Fair play, *see also* Hands off and f. p.; Turn about is f. p.

Fair shop and little gain, A.   (w 139)

1573 SANFORD 102ᵛ Waxe, linnen cloath, and Fustaine, A fayre shoppe and little gayne. 1629 *Bk. Mer. Rid.* Prov. no. 69.

Fair thing full false, There is many a.
(T 198)

[*a.* 1511] 1570 HENRYSON *Paddock and Mouse*: *Fab.*, 210 That prouerb is nocht trew; For fair thing is oft tymes ar fowll fakin. 1546 HEYWOOD II. ix. L4 In pure peynted processe, as false as fayre. *a.* 1628 CARMICHAELL no. 1142. 1641 FERGUSSON no. 801.

Fair things, Of | the autumn is fair.
(T 194)

1640 HERBERT no. 572.

Fair way, To be in a.

a. 1618 RALEIGH *Ess.* (1650) E. v. The Caliphes . . . obtained . . . a mighty Empire. which was in faire way to have enlarged. 1814 D. H. O'BRIEN *Captiv. & Escape* 101 Being in a fair way of succeeding.

Fair weather after foul.

1645 HERRICK *Hesperides* ed. Martin 188.

Fair weather after you.   (w 217)

1497 MEDWALL *Fulgens & Lucres* l. 944 Ye god sende vs mery wether! 1540 PALSGRAVE *Acolastus* 57 Fare well it, or fayre wether after it. [*c.* 1591] 1592 *Arden of Fev.* IV. i. 44. 1594–5 SHAKES. *L.L.L.* I. ii. 136 And so farewell.—Fair weather after you! 1599 PORTER *Angry Wom. Abing.* l. 926 Shal II fling an olde shooe after ye?—No, you should saye God send faire weather after me! 1605 S. ROWLEY *When You See Me* K2ᵛ.

Fair weather in winter on one night's ice, Expect not.   (w 215)

1640 HERBERT no. 453 Trust not one night's ice. 1670 RAY 28.

Fair weather prepare for foul, In.

1732 FULLER no. 2818.

Fair weather should do any harm, It is a pity that.   (P 368)

1616 DRAXE no. 506. 1639 CLARKE 79. 1738 SWIFT Dial. II. E.L. 295.

Fair weather when the shrews have dined, It will be.   (w 218)

1546 HEYWOOD I. xiii. F2 Whan al shrews haue dynd, Chaunge from foule wether to faire is oft inclind. 1678 RAY 243.

Fair wife and a frontier castle breed quarrels, A.   (w 348)

1591 ARIOSTO *Orl. Fur.* Harington XII, Notes The

common originall of all quarrels, namely honour and women. 1640 HERBERT no. 103. 1658 *Comes Fac. in Via* 234.

Fair wife, Who has a | needs more than two eyes.   (w 377)

1545 *Precepts of Cato* Publius O3ᵛ It is harde to saue and kepe that whiche many men desyre, as money and a fayre wyfe. 1658 *Comes Fac. in Via* 234 (she is not all your own). 1659 HOWELL *Span. Prov.* 14. 1664 CODRINGTON 226. 1670 RAY 9.

Fair without, false (foul) within. *Cf.* **Fair face and a foul heart.**   (F 29)

c. 1200 *Old Eng. Homilies* (Morris) I. 25 Als swa is an eppel . . . wið-uten feire and frakel wið-innen. *c.* 1275 *Provs. of Alfred* (Skeat) 30 Mony appel is bryht wiþ-vte And bitter wiþ-inne. *c.* 1386 CHAUCER *Canon's Yeoman's T.* l. 964 Ne every appul that is fair at eye Ne is nat good, what so men clappe or crye. *c.* 1430 LYDGATE *Minor Poems* Percy Soc. 43 Appeles and peres that semen very gode, Ful ofte tyme are roten by the core. 1541 *Schoolh. of Women* B2ᵛ [Women] Fayre without, and foule within. 1598–9 SHAKES. *M.A.* IV. i. 99 What a Hero hadst thou been If half thy outward graces had been plac'd About thy thoughts and counsels of thy heart! But fare thee well, most foul, most fair! 1605–6 *Id. M.* I. i. 10 Fair is foul, and foul is fair. *Ibid.* I. iii. 38 So foul and fair a day I have not seen. 1621 BRATHWAITE *Omphale* (1877) 277 As spotted as the Ermine, whose smooth skin, Though it be faire without, is foule within.

Fair woman and a slashed gown find always some nail in the way, A.
(w 624–5)

1642 TORRIANO 14 A fair woman and a pinckt garment is ever meeting with some tenter-hook. 1658 *Comes Fac.* 234. 1670 RAY 9.

Fair woman without virtue is like palled wine, A.

1707 MAPLETOFT 5.

Fair word in flyting,[1] There was never a.
(w 773)

a. 1628 CARMICHAELL no. 1510. 1641 FERGUSSON 96 no. 804. 1683 MERITON *Yorks. Ale* (1697) 83–7 Neay, faire words in flighting. 1721 KELLY 303 . . . An Excuse for what a Man might say in his Passion, upon Provocation. [1 scolding.]

Fair words and foul deeds cheat wise men as well as fools. *Cf.* **Good words and ill deeds, etc.**   (w 788)

1573 SANFORD 102 Fayre wordes and wicked deedes, deceyue wyse men and fooles. 1578 FLORIO *First F.* 27ᵛ. 1589 L. WRIGHT *A Summons for Sleepers* C3 Faire words and wicked deeds deceive both wise men and fooles. 1616 DRAXE no. 730 (deceiue many).

Fair words and foul play cheat both young and old.

1707 MAPLETOFT 69. **1710** PALMER 154 Fair Words and Foul Deeds, cheat Wise Men as well as Fools.

Fair (Soft) words break no bones.

(W 789–90)

c. 1450 *How the Good Wife* l. 43 Ne fayre wordis brake neuer bone. **1592** DELAMOTHE 5. **1598** J. LYLY? *Ent. at Mitcham* ed. Hotson 21 If wordes breake no bones, colors cannot. **1611** DAVIES no. 52. **1641** FERGUSSON no. 270 Faire words brake neuer bane, foule words breaks many ane. **1662** FULLER York 230 Expounding Scripture in a typicall way . . . crouded his Church with Auditors, seeing such soft preaching breaks no bones. **1670** RAY 158 (Soft).

Fair (Fine) words butter no parsnips.

(W 791)

1639 CLARKE 169. **1676** WYCHERLEY *Pl. Dealer* V. iii. Fair words butter no cabbage. **1692** L'ESTRANGE *Aesop's Fab.* cccxl (1738) 353 Relations, friendships, are but empty names of things, and *Words butter no parsnips.* **1797** G. COLMAN *Heir at Law* III. iii. Business is business, and fine words, you know, butter no parsnips. **1847–8** THACKERAY *Vanity F.* ch. 19 Who . . . said that 'fine words butter no parsnips?' Half the parsnips of society are served and rendered palatable with no other sauce.

Fair words did fet gromwell[1] seed plenty.

(W 792)

1546 HEYWOOD II. i. F3ᵛ His wife was set In suche dotage of hym, that fayre woordes dyd fet, Gromelseede plentee. [1 hard seeds used in medicine.]

Fair words fill not the belly.

(B 287)

1571 R. EDWARDS *Damon and Pythias* C2 I neuer heard that a man with wordes could fill his belly. **1580** LYLY *Euph. & his Eng.* ii. 227 Fayre words fatte few. **1670** RAY 61 The belly is not filled with fair words. **1732** FULLER no. 1491.

Fair words hurt not the mouth (tongue).

(W 793)

c. 1549 HEYWOOD I. ix. C2 It hurteth not the tounge to geue fayre wurdis. **1605** CHAPMAN, JONSON, MARSTON *Eastw. Ho* IV. ii. 147 O Madam, Faire words neuer hurt the tongue. **1614** CAMDEN 306. **1659** HOWELL *Eng. Prov.* 5b Smooth Language grates not the toung. **1670** RAY 158 Soft words hurt not the mouth. Douces *or* belles paroles ne scorchent pas la langue. *Gall.* Soft words scald not the tongue.

Fair words make fools fain.

(W 794)

[*c.* 1023 EGBERT V. LÜTTICH *Fecunda Ratis* (Voigt) 116 Promissis uacuis spes luditur irrita follis.] *c.* 1225 *Trin. MS. O. 11.* 45 (ed. Förster) in *Eng. Stud.* 31. 5 Beau premettere e poy doner fet le fol conforter. *c.* 1390 GOWER *Conf. Amantis* VII. 1564 Word hath beguiled many a man.

c. 1400 *Rom. Rose* l. 4446 Fair biheeste desceyveth feele. **1471** RIPLEY *Comp. Alch.* v. in *Ashm.* (1652) 157 Fayre promys makyth folys fayne. **1546** HEYWOOD II. v. H2ᵛ. **1599** SHAKES. *J.C.* III. i. 42 That which melteth fools, I mean sweet words. **1641** FERGUSSON no. 261 Fair heghts[1] makes fooles fain. **1829** SCOTT *Anne of G.* ch. 4 Fine words to make foolish maidens fain. [1 promises.]

Fair words make me look to my purse.

(W 795)

1640 HERBERT no. 548.

Fair words will not make the pot play.[1] *Cf.* Keep the pot boiling.

1721 KELLY 106. [1 boil.]

Fair words, *see also* Keep off and give f. w.

Fair(est), (*adj. adv.*), *see also* Blustering night, f. day; Born f. is born married, (Who is); Farewell frost, f. weather next; Fat, f., and forty; Flowers soonest fade, (The f.); Fowl of a f. day (As fain as); Full moon brings f. weather; New things are f.; Owl thinks own young f.; Plays you as f. as if picked pocket; Praise a f. day at night; Smoke follows f.

Fair (*noun*), *see also* Buy at f. but sell at home; Day after the f.; Dog in a f., (Like); Speak of the f. as things went with them.

Fairer the hostess, the fouler the reckoning, The.

(H 730)

1611 COTGRAVE s.v. Bourse A faire hostesse brings in a foule reckoning. *a.* **1635** CORBET *Poems* in CHALMERS V. 579 A handsome hostess makes the reckoning deare. **1659** HOWELL *Eng. Prov.* 2b.

Fairer the paper, the fouler the blot, The.

1732 FULLER no. 4513.

Fairest flower in his crown (garden, garland), It is the.

(F 387)

1546 HEYWOOD II. viii. K2ᵛ And she is scand Not onely the fayrest floure in your garlande, But also she is all the fayre floures therof. **1592** KYD *Span. Trag.* (Boas) I. iv. 4 Don Andreas . . . Who, liuing was my garlands sweetest flower. **1670** RAY 176 . . . (in his crown or garden).

Fairy (-ies), *see* Scythe cuts (Where), no more f.

Faith with heretics, No.

(F 33)

1555 J. PROCTOR *Hist. of Wyatt's Rebellion* (*Antiq. Rep.* iii (1808), 93) They thinking no part of theyr worshippe stained in breaking promise with a traitoure. *c.* **1566** CURIO *Pasquin in a Trance* tr. W.P. 68ᵛ Their [the papists'] curssed lawes which saye, that promise must not be kept with Heretiques. **1568** HENRY CHARTERIS Preface to Lindsay's *Wks.* ed. Hamer i. 400. **1571** J. BRIDGES *Sermon at Paul's Cross* 153 Shall

I trust his [a papist's] false faithe? . . . Example their faithe to John Husse, and their generall rule, *Nulla fides haereticis est habenda*, No faith must be kepte with heretikes. **1587** MARLOWE 2 *Tamb.* II. i. 33. [1589] **1633** *Id. Jew of Malta* II. iii. 310 It's no sin to deceive a Christian; For they themselves hold it a principle, Faith is not to be held with heretics. **1596** SHAKES. *K.J.* III. i. 174 And blessed shall he be that doth revolt From his allegiance to a heretic. ? *a.* **1630** J. TAYLOR *Kicksey Winsey* (1630), 2D3 They being Romists, I a Protestant: Their Apostatical injunction saith, To keepe their faith with me, is breach of faith. **1753** RICHARDSON *Grandison* (1812) VII. iii. 562 I remember the hint he gave to Father Marescotti; but would even *that* good man have thought himself bound to observe faith with heretics in such a case?

Faith, *see also* Love ask f. and f. asks firmness; Love is (Where) there is f.; Money, wisdom, and good f. less than men count upon; Pins his f. upon another's sleeve; Punic f.

Faithful friend is hard to find, Remember man and keep in mind, A.

1721 KELLY 285.

Falcon, *see* Kite will never be good hawk.

Falconer, *see* Swear like a f.

Falkirk, *see* Bairns o' F. (Like the).

Falkland, *see* Cut F. wood with a penknife.

Fall away from a horse-load to a cart-load, To. (H 720)

1630 DEKKER 2 *Hon. Whore* V. i. 18 Any woman that has falne from a Horse-load to a Cart-load,[1] . . . can direct you to her. [*Note.* [1] An allusion to the carting of prostitutes.] **1738** SWIFT *Dial.* I. E.L. 282 Don't you think the colonel's mightily fall'n away of late? — Ay, fall'n from a horseload to a cartload.

Fall back, fall edge. (B 12)

[= Whatever may happen.] **1552** LINDSAY *Three Estates* l. 403 We sall neuer sleip one wink till it be back or eadge. **1553** *Respublica* V. v Fall backe fall edge I am ons at a poincte. **1622** MABBE tr. *Aleman's Guzman d'Alf.* I. 9 Fall back, fall Edge, goe which way you will to work. **1830** SCOTT *Jrnl.* 22 Dec. Fall back, fall edge, nothing shall induce me to publish what [etc.].

Fall into sin is human, To | to remain in sin is devilish.

[ST. CHRYSOST. *Adhortatio ad Theod. lapsum*, I. 14: 'Humanum enim est peccare, diabolicum uero perseuerare.'] *c.* **1386** CHAUCER *Mel.* l. 2457 The proverbe seith: that 'for to do synne is mannysh, but certes for to perseuere longe in synne is werk of the devel'. **1655–62** GURNALL *Chrn. in Armour* (1865) I. 298 It is bad enough to fall into an error, but worse to persist. The first shows thee a weak man . . . but the other makes thee too like the devil, who is to this day of the same mind he was at his first fall.

Fall not out with a friend for a trifle. (F 689)

1621 ROBINSON 33. **1639** CLARKE 25. **1670** RAY 9.

Fall on his back and break his nose, He would.

1642 TORRIANO 91 If I should fall backwards I should break my nose: Nota, That is, I am so crost in every thing that I undertake. **1659** HOWELL *It. Prov.* 2 If I fell backward, I should break my nose, I am so unlucky. **1853** TRENCH i. 21 Of the man . . . to whom the most unlikely calamities . . . befall, they say: . . . **1912** *Spectator* 18 May 788 'He who is born to misfortune falls on his back and fractures his nose' says a misanthropic humorist.

Fallen, He that is | cannot help him that is down. (F 39)

1640 HERBERT no. 753.

Falling master makes a standing servant, A.

1721 KELLY 15 . . . Men fall behind in the World by Negligence . . . which knavish Servants will be sure to take their Advantage of; It is no new thing to see a Receiver buy his Master's Estate.

Falling out of lovers is the renewing of love, The. (F 40)

[TERENCE *Andria* 3. 3. 23 *Amantium irae amoris integratio est.*] **1520** WHITTINGTON *Vulg.* E.E.T.S. 39 The variaunce of louers (sayth Terence) is the renuynge of loue. *c.* **1530** *Terens in English* (*Andria*) C1. **1539** TAVERNER *Publius* B6. **1578** R. EDWARDES *Parad. D. Deuises* 49 *Amantium irae amoris redintigratio est.* . . . I have found, this prouerbe true to proue, The falling out of faithfull frends, renuing of loue. **1602** SHAKES. *T.C.* III. i. 96 Falling in after falling out may make them three. **1621** BURTON *Anat. Mel.* III. ii. III. iv (1651) 489 She would . . . pick quarrels upon no occasion, because she would be reconciled to him again. *Amantium irae amoris redintegratio,* . . . the falling out of lovers is the renewing of love. **1753** RICHARDSON *Grandison* III. xviii. (1812) 229.

Falling, *see also* Never catch at f. knife or f. friend.

Falls into the dirt, He that | the longer he stays there the fouler he is. (D 348)

a. **1628** CARMICHAELL no. 1638 The mair in merdis[1] ye tramp into, the fouler will com out your schone. **1640** HERBERT no. 409. **1721** KELLY 130 . . . Spoken to those who lye under a Slander, urging them to get themselves clear'd as soon as they can. **1732** FULLER no. 2096. [[1] excrement.]

Falls today may rise to-morrow, He that. (F 38)

1620 SHELTON *Quix.* II. lxv (1908) III. 282 He that falls to-day may rise to-morrow, except it be that he mean to lie a-bed. **1732** FULLER no. 2097 (may be up again).

Fall(s) (*noun*), *see* Higher standing lower f.; Higher the fool greater the f.; Highest tree has greatest f.; Pride will have f.; Stumble may prevent f.

Fall(s), fell (*verb*), *see also* All that shakes f. not; Arrow shot upright f. on the shooter's head; Ass f. (Wherever), there will never f. again; Better sit still than f.; Better to go about than f.; Boughs, (Who trusts to rotten)/may f.; Cedars f. when low shrubs remain, (High); Cup and the lip (Many things f. between); Descend (F.) than to ascend (Easier to); Dig a pit for another and f. into it oneself, (To); Kingdoms divided soon f.; Never climbed never f.; Never rode never f.; Rides sure that never f.; Sky f.? (What if the); Smoke, (Shunning the) they f. into the fire; Sooner f. than rise (One may); Struck at Tib, down f. Tom; Take me not up before I f.; Wisest man may f.

False as a Scot, As.   (s 154)

1548 HALL *Chron.* 584 When the kyng hearde that the erle of Angus her husband was departed, he sayd, it was done like a Scot. **1587** SIR JOB THROCKMORTON (J. E. Neale *Eliz. I & her Parl[ts] 1584–1601*, 172) As a boy, I heard it said that falsehood was the very nature of a Scot. **1670** RAY 204. **1701** DEFOE *True-born Englishman* ii. Wks. (1911) V. 444 False from the Scot, and from the Norman worse.

False (True) as God is true, As. (G 173)

1543 W. TURNER *Hunting of the Romish Fox* C7[v] Thys sayenge is as false as God is trewe. **1546** HEYWOOD II. vii. I2[v]. **1581** G. ELLIOTT *True Report of taking of E. Campion* Arber, *Eng. Garner* VIII. 220 So false as God is true. **1596** SHAKES. *Rich. II* IV. i. 64 As false, by heaven, as heaven itself is true! **1601** CHETTLE & MUNDAY *Death of Earl of Huntington* Hazl.-Dods. viii. 270 true as God is true. **1616** DRAXE no. 663.

False as hell, As.   (H 398)

1604 SHAKES. *O.* IV. ii. 39 Heaven truly knows that thou art false as hell. **1611** BEAUM & FL. *A King and No King* III. i. 147. **1680** D'URFEY *Virtuous Wife* IV. iii. **1813** BARRETT *Heroine* ed. Raleigh 279.

False tongue will hardly speak truth, A.   (T 383)

1616 DRAXE no. 110.

False with one can be false with two.

1604 SHAKES. *O.* I. iii. 294 She has deceived her father and may thee. **1902–4** LEAN III. 463.

False, *see also* Breaks his word, (A man that)/ bids others be f. to him; Conscience fears not . . . f. accusations, (A clear); Fair thing full f. (Many a); Fair without f. within; Sail under f. colours; Two f. knaves need no broker.

Falsehood (flattery, fraud) in fellowship, There is.   (F 41)

c. **1470** G. ASHBY *Poems* E.E.T.S. 26 Be wele ware of falsehode in felawship. [*c.* **1517**] **1533** SKELTON *Magn.* C1[v] Falshode in felowshyp is my sworne brother. **1539** TAVERNER 47[v] Flatery and folowing of mens myndes getteth frendes, where speakyng of trouth gendreth hatred. **1546** HEYWOOD II. v. H2[v] If he plaie falsehed in felowshyp, plaie ye. **1576** PETTIE i. 101 Alas! my Germanicus, are you to know . . . the falsehood in friends? **1579** LYLY *Euph.* i. 197 Haue I not also learned that . . . there is falshood in fellowship? **1594** NASHE *Unf. Trav.* ii. 300. **1598–9** SHAKES. *Hen. V* III. vii. 111 I will cap that proverb with 'There is flattery in friendship.' **1614** CAMDEN 313.

Falsehood never made a fair hinder end.

c. **1380** BARBOUR *Bruce* XV. 122 Bot I trow falsat evirmar Sall have unfair and evill ending. *a.* **1628** CARMICHAELL no. 508 (Falset). *Ibid.* no. 536 Frost and falset hes ay a foule hinderend. **1641** FERGUSSON no. 263.

Fame is a magnifying glass.   (F 45)

[**1583** MELBANCKE L2 Fame in Virgill . . . is euer the stronger the farther it goeth.] **1642** FULLER *Holy State* III. xxiii Fame generally overdoes. **1732** FULLER no.1495.

Fame is but the breath of the people.
                                                  (F 46)

1611 CORYAT *Crudities* (1905) i. 60 Fame is but winde. **1650** JER. TAYLOR *Holy Liv.* I. ii (1875) 17 That which would purchase heaven for him he parts with for the breath of the people; which at best is but air, and that not often wholesome. **1732** FULLER no. 1497 . . . and that often unwholesome.

Fame, *see also* Common f. a liar; Common f. seldom to blame; Good f. better than good face; Sows virtue shall reap f.; Ways to f. (Many).

Familiarity breeds contempt.   (F 47)

[PUB. SYRUS 102 *Parit contemptum nimia familiaritas.* AUGUSTINE (?) *Scala Paradisi* cap. 8 (Migne 40. 1001) *Nimia familiaritas parit contemptum.*] 12th cent. ALANUS DE INSULIS in Wright *Minor Anglo-Latin Satirists* Record Scr. ii. 454. *c.* **1386** CHAUCER *Mel.* l. 1685 Men seyn that 'overgreet hoomlynesse engendreth dispreisynge'. *c.* **1449** PECOCK *Repr.* 184 Ouermyche homlines with a thing gendrith dispising toward the same thing. **1539** TAVERNER 2 *Garden* 4[v] Hys [Alfonsus's] specyall frendes counsailled him to beware, least his ouermuche familiaritie myght breade him contempte. **1548** UDALL, etc. *Erasm. Par. John* 34a Familiarity bringeth contempt. **1600–1** SHAKES. *M.W.W.* I. i. 226 I hope upon familiarity will grow more contempt. **1641** FERGUSSON no. 667 Over great familiaritie genders despite. **1654** FULLER *Comment on Ruth* in *Serm.* (1891) I. 86 With base and sordid natures familiarity breeds contempt. **1869** TROLLOPE *He Knew He Was Right* ch. 56 Perhaps, if I heard Tennyson talking every day, I shouldn't read Tennyson. Familiarity does breed contempt.

Familiarity, *see also* Four good mothers have bad daughters: . . . f., contempt.

Family, families, *see* Accidents will happen; Fool of f.; Hat covers f.; Poor kin (f.) that has neither whore nor thief.

Famine in England begins at the horse-manger, A. *Cf.* **After a famine in the stall.**   (D 131. F 51)

1636 CAMDEN 303 No dearth but breeds in the horse-manger. **1662** FULLER *Berks.* 85 (begins first). **1670** RAY 44 . . . In opposition to the rack: for in dry years when hay is dear, commonly corn is cheap: but when oats . . . is dear, the rest are seldom cheap.

Famine, *see also* After a f. in the stall; Under water, f.

Fan, *see* Fog cannot be dispelled with f.

Fancy flees before the wind.

1721 KELLY 105 . . . Love and liking are not always well grounded.

Fancy may bolt¹ bran and think it flour.   (F 54)

1546 HEYWOOD II. iv. G3ᵛ Fancy may boult bran, and make ye take it flowre. **1587** J. BRIDGES *Defence* 13. **1611** DAVIES no. 359 (till it be). **1670** RAY 88. [¹ sift.]

Fancy may kill or cure.

1721 KELLY 111 . . . There are many Stories of the Power of Imagination to do Good or Evil, and . . . the Efficacy of these Things that they call Charms depend[s] intirely upon it. **1732** FULLER no. 1500.

Fancy passes beauty.   (F 55)

1678 RAY 136. **1732** FULLER no. 1501 (surpasses).

Fanned fires and forced love never did well yet.

1721 KELLY 108 . . . Both Flames burn brightest when they come freely. **1824** FERRIER *Inheritance* ch. 34 There's an old byword, 'Fanned fires and forced love ne'er did weel'; and some people will maybe not crack quite so crouse by and by.

Far about, *see* Go f. a. seeking the nearest.

Far behind must follow the faster.

1721 KELLY 107 . . . People whose Business and Labour is behind their Neighbours, must be the more busy and industrious.

Far behind that may not follow, They are.

1721 KELLY 324 . . . Spoken when People do not despond, though behind others.

Far cry to Lochow, It is a.

1819 SCOTT *Leg. Mont.* ch. 12 A proverbial expression of the tribe, meaning that their [Campbell's] ancient hereditary domains lay beyond the reach of an invading army. **1890** 'ROLF BOLDREWOOD' *Miner's Right* ch. 23 Because it was 'a far cry to Lochow', or, in other words, a long way from the Oxley to Pekin, no protest on the part of his Celestial Highness reached us.

Far fetched, *see* Dear bought and f. f. are dainties.

Far folk fare best.   (F 413)

1616 DRAXE no. 501. **1639** CLARKE 177. **1678** RAY 136 Far folkes fare well, and fair children die. People are apt to boast of the good and wealthy condition of their far-off friends, and to commend their dead children.

Far fowls have fair feathers.   (F 625)

c. **1508** DUNBAR *Schir, yit remimbir* 21 (1907) 129 Ay farest faderis hes farrest fowlis Suppois thay haif no sang but youlis. **1721** KELLY 102 (Fat Fowls) . . . Spoken when People extol what they have heard or seen elsewhere, as giving little Credit to them. **1789** BURNS *Five Carlins* For far aff fowls have feathers fair.

Far from court, far from care.   (C 722)

1639 CLARKE 205. **1732** FULLER no. 1503.

Far from eye, far from heart. *Cf.* **Eye sees not, What the, etc.**

c. **1300** *Provs. of Hending* 27 Fer from eye, fer from herte. *c.* **1300** *Cursor M.* l. 4508 Hert sun for-gettes that ne ei seis. *c.* **1386** CHAUCER *Miller's T.* l. 3392 Men seyn right thus 'Alwey the nye slye Maketh the ferre leeve to be looth'. *c.* **1400** *MS. Latin no. 344, J. Rylands Libr.* (ed. Pantin) in *Bull. J. R. Libr.* XIV. 24 Ferre from ye, ferre from hert. **1706** STEVENS s.v. Ausencia As far from the Eyes, So far from the Heart.

Far from home, near thy harm.

a. **1561** *Deceit of Women* C3ᵛ (It is a comon prouerbe . . .).

Far from Jupiter, far from thunder.
                                                    (J 81)

1580 LYLY *Euph. & his Eng.* ii. 120 My dealyngs about the Courte shall be fewe, for I loue to stande aloofe from *Ioue* and lyghtning. **1629** T. ADAMS *Serm.* (1861–2) III. 43 *Procul a Jove, Procul a fulmine* [ERASM. *Ad.*] was the old saying: Far from Jupiter, far from his thunder. **1692** L'ESTRANGE *Aesop's Fab.* xi (1738) 14 *Far from Jupiter* (says the adage) *far from the thunder.* What signifies the splendour . . . of courts . . . , considering the . . . frowns of princes.

Far shooting never killed bird.   (S 389)

1640 HERBERT no. 405 (Faire).

Far (farthest, further), *see also* Best loved f. off; Foot f. than the whittle (He that stretches) . . . ; Go f. fare worse; Goes f. (He that) has many encounters; See no f. than the end of one's nose; So f. so good.

Fare (*noun*), *see* Bachelors' f.; Fiddler's f.;
Hard f. makes hungry bellies.

**Fared worse than when I wished for
my supper, I never.**   (s 1001)

1623 CAMDEN 272. **1670** RAY 157.

Fare(s, d), (*verb*), *see also* Banquet (There is no
great) but some f. ill; Far folk f. best; Fox f.
best when banned; Go farther f. worse; Welcome
(He that is) f. well; Well f. nothing once a year.

Farewell and be hanged.

1575 G. HARVEY *Letter-Book* Camden Soc. 95
Farewell and be hanged, good man cowe. **1577**
R. STANYHURST in Holinshed *Chron. Ireland*
(1587, 95b) This cold salutation of Farewell and
be hanged. **1584** R. WILSON *Three Ladies* E3.
a. **1593** PEELE *Edward I* (Bullen i. 138). **1608**
MIDDLETON *Trick to Catch* IV. i. **1670** RAY 174
. . . friends must part.

Farewell, fieldfare!

c. **1374** CHAUCER *Troilus* Bk. 3, l. 861 The harm
is don, and far-wel feldefare! *c.* **1400** *Rom. Rose*
5510 And synge 'Go fare-wel, feldefare'. All
suche freendis I beshrewe. **1878** *N. & Q.* 5th
Ser. IX. 136–7 in LEAN IV. 225 That the fieldfare
is a migrant seems to have been accepted in
Chaucer's time from the proverbial phrase,
'Farewell, fieldfare!'

**Farewell, forty pence! Jack Noble is
dead (a-bed).**   (F 618)

[= contemptuous dismissal.] *c.* **1500** MEDWALL
Nature in '*Lost*' *Tudor Plays* (1907) 98 She
opened a window and put forth her head—
Hence, Forty Pence! quo' she, Jack Noble is a-
bed. *c.* **1575** *Clyomon* F2ᵛ l. 1417 Farewell
forty pence. [1600] **1659** DAY & CHETTLE *Blind
Beggar* v. K2 Why farewell 40 pence. **1631** F.
LENTON *Characters* (1663) no. 17 Her Purse . . .
seldome exonerats its selfe till the Maulster
appeares, and then farwel forty pence. **1639**
CLARKE 68.

Farewell frost.   (F 769)

c. **1560** *Misogonus* I. iii. 97. **1564** BULLEIN *Dial.
agst. Fever* (1888) 72 Hitherto hath not been
found neither cow nor man, and all the milk is
gone. Farewell frost! **1573** GASCOIGNE *Dulce
Bellum.* i. 146. **1594** LYLY *Mother B.* II. iii. 97.
1596 SHAKES. *M.V.* II. vii. 75 Cold indeed, and
labour lost, Then farewell, heat, and welcome,
frost. **1670** RAY 174 . . . nothing got, nor
nothing lost.

Farewell frost, fair weather next.

1721 KELLY 104 . . . Spoken when they go off,
whom we are glad to part with.

Farewell, gentle Geoffrey!   (G 81)

c. **1475** *Mankind* l. 155. *c.* **1520** J. RASTELL *Four
Elements* C5 Farewell gentyll John. **1546** HEY-
WOOD I. xi. D4. **1565** *King Darius* F3 Fare-
well gentle Hary.

Farewell, *see also* Welcome (Such), such f.

**Fare-ye-weel, Meg Dorts, and e'en's ye
like.**

1725 A. RAMSAY *Gentle Shep.* I. 1. **1862** HISLOP
94 . . . A jocose adieu to those who go away
in the sulks.

Farlie(s), *see* Fault (If it be), it is no f.; Longer
we live more f. we see. *See also* Ferlies.

**Farm full, He that will have his | must
keep an old cock and a young bull.
But cf. Full flock,** etc.

1750 W. ELLIS *Mod. Husbandman* III. 94 When a
bull comes to be four, he is heavy and sluggish.
. . . The old verse says, . . .

Farm(s), *see also* Flitting of f. makes mailings
dear; Hold the greatest f. (They that) pay least
rent.

Farmer(s), *see also* Feed like a f.; Pigeons go a
benting (When), f. lie lamenting.

**Fart out of a dead man, You will as
soon get a.**   (F 63)

1546 HEYWOOD I. xi. D4ᵛ. **1605** CHAPMAN,
JONSON, MARSTON *Eastw. Ho* IV. ii. 142. **1625**
JONSON *Staple of News* III. ii. 98. **1659** HOWELL
Eng. Prov. 14a (horse). **1672** WALKER 8.

Farther in, the deeper, The.

1721 KELLY 324 . . . Spoken to People engag'd
into an intricate Business: The more they struggle
the more they are intangled. **1824** MOIR *Mansie
W.* ch. 20 This astonished us more and more,
and . . . I though there surely must be some
league and paction with the Old One; but the
further in the deeper.

**Farther the sight the nearer the rain,
The.**

1883 ROPER 23. **1893** INWARDS 105.

**Farthest (Longest) way about is the
nearest way home, The.**   (W 158)

1580 LYLY *Euph. & his Eng.* ii. 96 Thou goest
about (but yet the neerest way) to hang me vp
for holydayes. **1600** KEMP *Nine Days' Wonder*
(*Social England*, Lang 156) Getting so into
Master Mayor's gates a nearer way, But, at last,
I found it the further way about. **1635** QUARLES
Emblems IV. ii. 2 The road to resolution lies by
doubt: The next way home's the farthest way
about. **1642** FULLER *H. & P. State* IV. ix. 11
When . . . he privately tells his prince of his
faults, he knows, by Nathan's parable, to go the
nearest way home by going far about. **1670**
RAY 95 . . . What is gained in the shortness, may
be lost in the goodness of the way. **1905** ALEX.
MACLAREN *Matthew* i. 166 The longest way
round is sometimes the shortest way home.

Farthing(s), *see* Brass f. (Not worth); Four f.
and a thimble; Miserable man makes a penny
of a f., and the liberal of a f. sixpence; Thinks
his penny (f.) good silver.

Fash one's thumb, To.

[= to give oneself trouble.] **1786** BURNS *Earnest Cry & Prayer* v Speak out, an' never fash your thumb. **1818** SCOTT *Ht. Midl.* ch. 16 It was lang syne, . . . and I'll ne 'er fash my thumb about it.

Fashion's sake, For | as dogs go to church (the market). (F 76)

1599 SHAKES. *A.Y.* III. ii. 240 I had as lief have been myself alone.—And so had I; but yet, for fashion' sake, I thank you too for your society. **1721** KELLY 109 . . . Spoken when we see People declare for a Party, or make a Profession, which we suppose they would not do, if it were not in Vogue. **1732** FULLER no. 1590.

Fashion, *see also* Every one after his f.; Out of the world out of f.; Plain f. is best; Tailors and writers must mind f.

Fast and loose is no possession. (F 78)

1621 ROBINSON 39. **1639** CLARKE 159.

Fast and loose, *see* Play f. and l.

Fast as a dog can trot, As. (H 660)

1530 PALSGRAVE 610 Truste hym nat, he wyll lye as fast as a dogge wyll trotte. **1678** RAY 89 He lies as fast as a dog can trot. **1695** RAVENSCROFT 30 (They both lie faster, than).

Fast as a dog will lick a dish, As. (D 478)

1546 HEYWOOD II. vii. I2ᵛ She will lye as fast as a dogge will lycke a dishe. **1721** KELLY 151 (He can lie).

Fast (thick) as hops, As. (H 595)

1590 NASHE *Pasquil's Apol.* I c They must be throwne ouer the Pulpit as thicke as hoppes. **1599** PORTER *Angry Wom. Abingd.* l. 2306 The water drops from you as fast as hops. **1607** MIDDLETON *Mich. Term Induction* Come . . . up thick . . . like hops and harlots. **1690** D'URFEY *Collin's Walk* i. 7 To make him sprout as fast as hops.

Fast as one goes another comes, As. (G 161–2)

1546 HEYWOOD I. iii. A4.

Fast (Safe, Sure) bind, fast (safe, sure) find. (B 352)

1546 HEYWOOD I. iii. A4 Than catche and holde while I may, fast bind, fast fynde. *c.* **1548** BALE *K. Johan* l. 1897 As the saynge is, he fyndeth that surely bynde. **1573** TUSSER 83 *Washing* (1878) 173 Drie sunne, drie winde, safe binde, safe finde. **1596** SHAKES. *M.V.* II. v. 53 Shut doors after you: 'Fast bind, fast find', A proverb never stale in thrifty mind. **1622** J. FLETCHER *Span. Cur.* II. ii. So, so, fast bind, fast find. **1655** FULLER *Ch. Hist.* IV. iv. (1868) I. 611 Because 'sure bind, sure find', he [Richard III] is said, and his queen, to be crowned again in York with great solemnity.

1824 SCOTT *Redg.* ch. 13. **1890** D. C. MURRAY *J. Vale's Guard* ch. 6.

Fast for [fear of] breaking your shins (falling), Not too. (F 141)

1580 BARET *Alveary* C59 A Prouerbe applyed vnto those, that take no deliberation in bringing any thing to passe: and as we say, not to[o] fast for breaking your shinnes. *c.* **1591–4** *Thomas of Woodstock* v. i. 225 Not too fast for falling. **1599** PORTER *Angry Wom. Abingd.* l. 874 Haste makes waste; softe fire make sweete malt; not too fast for falling. **1616** WITHALS (1634, 63) As we say, to breake their shinnes for hast. **1624** T. BREWER *A Knot of Fools* C4.

Fast for my life, If I were to | I would take a good breakfast in the morning. (L 246)

1678 RAY 67. **1738** SWIFT *Dial.* II. E.L. 303 If I were to fast for my life, I would take a good breakfast in the morning, A good dinner at noon, and a good supper at night.

Fast(-er, -est), (*adj. adv.*), *see also* Bird caught in lime strives, (The more the) the f. he sticks; Hen cracks nuts, (As f. as a); Last makes f.; Mistress is the master, (Where the) the parsley grows the f.; Over f. over loose; Play f. and loose; Runs f. gets most ground; Runs f. gets the ring.

Fast (*noun*), *see* Break his neck as his f. (As soon); Feast or a f.; St. Stephen, no f.

Fastens where there is gain, Every one. (G 2)

1640 HERBERT no. 496.

Fasting, *see also* Belly is full (He whose) believes not the f.; Full man and a f. (It is ill speaking between); Never well, full nor f.; Speak to a f. man (Never).

Fasts and does no other good, Who | spares his bread and goes to hell. (G 323)

1642 TORRIANO 22 (saveth his bread, but hieth himself to the devil). **1650** JER. TAYLOR *Holy Liv.* IV. v (Bohn) 190 The devil . . . will be as tempting with the windiness of a violent fast as with the flesh of an ordinary meal. . . . Fasting alone will not cure this devil. Chi digiuna ed altro ben non fa, Sparagna il pane, ed al inferno va. **1659** HOWELL *It. Prov.* I.

Fasts enough that has had a bad (slender) meal, He. (M 787)

1611 COTGRAVE s.v. Assez He that feeds barely fasts sufficiently. **1650** JER. TAYLOR *Holy Liv.* IV. v (1850) 190 A diet of fasting, a daily lessening of our portion of meat and drink, . . . which may make the least preparation for the lusts of the body. Digiuna assai chi mal mangia. **1732** FULLER no. 1844.

Fat as a fool.   (F 443)

1575 *Apius and Virginia* B1 l. 228.   1579 LYLY
Euph. i. 256.   1678 RAY 283.

Fat as a hen in the forehead, As.
                                            (H 416)
[Ironical.]   1594 LYLY *Mother B.* IV. ii. 9 Ile
warrant tis to as much purpose as a hem [*for
hen?*] in the forehead.—There was an auncient
prouerbe knockt in the head.   1611 COTGRAVE
s.v. Pie We say . . . as fat as a Henne's on the
forhead.   1618–19 J. FLETCHER *Bonduca* I. ii.
Will feed ye up as fat as hens i' th' foreheads.
1738 SWIFT Dial. III. E.L. 320.

Fat as butter, As.   (B 767)

1584 LYLY *Camp.* I. ii. 76 I would make mine
eyes fatte as butter.   1597 SHAKES. *I Hen. IV* II.
iv. 492 A gross fat man.—As fat as butter.   1604
DEKKER *News from Gravesend* (*Plague Pamphlets*,
ed. Wilson 72).   1621 BURTON *Anat. Mel.* II. ii.
v. Alpine mice . . . sleeping under the snow . . . as
fat as butter.   1727 [GAY?] 'New Song of new
Similies' *Poems* ed. Faber 645.

Fat drops from fat flesh.   (D 616)

1597 SHAKES. *I Hen. IV* II. ii. 104 Falstaff sweats
to death And lards the lean earth as he walks
along.   1600–1 *Id. M.W.W.* IV. v. 90 They
would melt me out of my fat drop by drop.
1678 RAY 137.

Fat, fair, and forty.

1795 O'KEEFFE *Irish Minnie* II. iii. Fat, fair, and
forty were all the toast of the young men.   1824
SCOTT *Redg.* ch. 7.

Fat housekeepers make lean executors.
                                            (H 793)
1611 COTGRAVE s.v. Testament Great house-
keepers often die beggars.   1721 KELLY 111 . . .
Because they spend all in their Lifetime.   1732
FULLER no. 1505.   1758 FRANKLIN *Poor Rich.
Alm.* in ARBER *Eng. Garner* V. 582 A fat kitchen
makes a lean Will.

Fat is in the fire, (All) the.   (F 79)

[In early use expressing failure, but now meaning
there will be an explosion.]   c. 1374 CHAUCER
Troilus Bk. 3, l. 710 This night shal I make it
wel, Or casten al the gruwel in the fyre.   1399
LANGLAND *Rich. Redeles* II. 51 That shente all
the browet, And cast adoun the crokk the colys
amyd [ruined the pottage and cast down the pot
amidst the coals].   1546 HEYWOOD I. iii. A4
Then farwell ryches, the fat is in the fyre.   1578
SIDNEY *Lady of May Rhombus the schoolmaster.
O tace, tace,* or all the fat will be liquefied.   1633
JONSON *Entertainm. at Welb.* vii. 798 Else all the
Fat i' the Fire were lost.   1797 WOLCOT (P.
Pindar) *Livery of London* Wks. (1812) III. 449
Should we once complain The fat will all be in
the fire.   1902 *Autobiog. of W. Besant* 164
Ganneau asked permission to see the MS., and
then all the fat was in the fire.

Fat land grow foulest weeds, On.
                                            (W 241)
1393 LANGLAND *P. Pl. C.* xiii. 224 On fat londe
and ful of donge foulest wedes groweth.   1579

LYLY *Euph.* i. 251 Doth not common experience
make this common vnto vs, that the fattest
grounde bringeth foorth nothing but weedes if
it be not well tilled? That the sharpest wit
enclineth onely to wickednesse, if it bee not
exercised? *Ibid.* 263 The fertill soyle if it bee
neuer tilled doth waxe barren, and that which is
most noble by nature is made vyle by negligence.
1598 SHAKES. *2 Hen. IV* IV. iv. 54 Most subject
is the fattest soil to weeds; And he, the noble
image of my youth, is overspread with them.

Fat paunches have lean pates.
                                     (B 293. P 123)
[Gk. Παχεῖα γαστὴρ λεπτὸν οὐ τίκτει νόον. JEROME
Pinguis venter non gignit sensum tenuem. (A fat
paunch does not produce fine sense.)]   1576
HOLYBAND F2ᵛ He which seeketh after those
thinges loseth his labour. . . . A fine wit in a fatt
bellie.   1580 BARET *Alveary* P388 Pinguis venter
. . . A Prouerbe to be applied to those, which riot
and abound in bellie cheere, and yet would seeme
to excell Pallas in reason, which things are quite
contrarie: for riotousnesse doth dull the wit.
1584 LYLY *Camp.* I. ii. 79 An old saw of abstin-
ence, Socrates': The belly is the heads graue.
1586 GUAZZO ii. 142 This Prouerbe is as true as
common. That a fat bellie doth not engender a
subtill witte.   1594–5 SHAKES. *L.L.L.* I. i. 26 Fat
paunches have lean pates, and dainty bits Make
rich the ribs, but bankrupt quite the wits.   1639
CLARKE 192 Fat paunches and lean pates.   1721
KELLY 106 (bode). A groundless Reflection upon
fat Men.   1732 FULLER no. 1506 (make).

Fat sorrow is better than lean sorrow.
                                            (S 650)

1662 N. ROGERS *Rich Fool* 253 But as some
women say that covet rich Husbands, Better a
fat Sorrow, then a leane.   1678 RAY 137 . . .
Better have a rich husband and a sorrowfull life
then a poor husband and a sorrowfull life with
him; spoken to encourage a maid to marry a
rich man, though ill conditioned.   1732 FULLER
no. 1507.   1902 DEAN HOLE *Then & Now* [7 ed.]
ch. 8 They forget awhile the 'mighty difference'
which one of them suggested, when told by a
rich neighbour that we all had our troubles,
'between fat sorrow and lean'.

Fat, *see also* Bastes the f. hog, (Every man);
Laugh and be f.; Lick the f. from the beard;
Little knows the f. man what lean thinks;
Little knows the f. sow what lean does mean;
Swine over f. cause of own bane; Take the f. with
the lean; Too free to be f.

Fatal, *see* Basilisk's eye is f.; Sexton is a f.
musician.

**Fate leads the willing, but drives the
stubborn.**   (F 82)

[SENECA *Epist.* 107. 11 *Ducunt volentem fata,
nolentem trahunt.* From a quatrain by Cleanthes,
quoted by Epictetus at the end of his *Enchiridion.*]
1629 T. ADAMS *Serm.* (1861–2) II. 94 What thou
must do, do willingly. Fata volentem ducunt,
nolentem trahunt. God gently leads thee coming,
but drags thee on withdrawing.   *a.* 1657 LOVE-
LACE E.L. 369 Fates lead the willing, but the
unwilling draw.   1732 FULLER no. 1508.

Fate, *see also* Flying from f. (No); Sure as f.

Father, That is for the | but not for the son.

a. 1628 CARMICHAELL no. 938.   1721 KELLY 322 . . . Spoken when a Thing is done with slight Materials, and consequently will not be lasting.

Father buys, The | the son bigs,[1] the grandchild sells, and his son thigs.[2]

1721 KELLY 312 . . . A Proverb much used in *Lowthian*, where Estates stay not long in one Family.   1862 HISLOP 280 The grandsire buys, the father bigs, the son sells, and the grandson thigs. [[1] builds. [2] begs.]

Father, One | is enough to govern one hundred sons, but not a hundred sons one father.   (H 89)

1640 HERBERT no. 404.   1706 STEVENS s.v. Padre.

Father is judge, He whose | goes safe to his trial.   (F 87)

1620 SHELTON *Quix.* II. xliii. For according to the proverb, 'He that hath the judge to his father, &c.' and I am governor, which is more than judge.   1706 STEVENS s.v. Padre.   1732 FULLER no. 2400.

Father, One | is more than a hundred schoolmasters.   (F 90)

1640 HERBERT no. 686.

Father, Like | like son.   (F 92)

[ERASM. *Ad. Hodie vulgo dicitur ex Athanasii symbolo detortum, Qualis pater, talis filius.*] 1362 LANGLAND *P. Pl.* II. 934 (Wright) I. 29 And Mede is manered after hym, Right as kynde asketh *Qualis pater talis filius.*   c. 1386 CHAUCER *Leg. Good Women* l. 2448 It com hym of nature As doth the fox Renard, [so doth] the foxes sone.   1509 BARCLAY *Ship of Fools* i. 236 An olde prouerbe hath longe agone be sayde That oft the sone in maner lyke wyll be Vnto the Father.   1581 SENECA *Thebais* tr. T. Newton T.T. i. 116 Like Syre, like Sonnes.   1616 DRAXE no. 1571.   1708 DYKES *Mor. Reflect. Provs.* 30. . . .   1841 S. WARREN *Ten Thous. a Year* ch. 26 Two such bitter Tories . . . for, like father, like son.

Father of a disease, Whatsoever was the | an ill diet was the mother.   (F 93)

1651 HERBERT no. 1048.

Father to the bough, the son to the plough, The.   (F 84)

1576 LAMBARDE *Peramb. of Kent* (1826) 497.   1662 FULLER *Kent* 64 . . . That is, though the Father be executed for his Offence, the Son shall neverthelesse succeed to his Inheritance.   1787 GROSE (*Kent*) 182 . . . One of the privileges of gavel-kind, . . . whereby . . . only the goods and chattels, but not the lands, are forfeited to the crown, on the execution of a criminal.

Father was a bad (no) glazier, Your.
                                  (F 95)

1560–77 *Misogonus* IV. i. 127 Lets see to I pray yow what were your father a glacier letes haue some rome to or else I may chaunch giue the an arsebutt.   1738 SWIFT *Dial.* I. E.L. 263 You stand in your own light. . . .—I'm sure he sits in mine. Pr'ythee, Tom, sit a little further; I believe your father was no glazier.   1910 P. W. JOYCE *Eng. as We Speak* 113 'Your father was a bad glazier': said to a person who is standing in one's light.

Father, *see also* Cheat mine own f. at cards; Child f. of man; Give it about . . . come to f. at last; Happy is he whose friends (f.) born before him; Happy is that child whose f. goes to devil; Head will never fill f.'s bonnet; Lime makes rich f., poor son; Love to a f.'s, (No); Speak good of archers for your f. shot; Speak good of pipers, your f. was fiddler; Teach your f. to get children.

Fattens, *see* Young physician f. the churchyard.

Fault confessed is half redressed, A.
                                  (C 589)

1558 *Wealth & Health* l. 804 Yf thou haue doone amisse, and be sory therfore, Then halfe a mendes is made, for that is contrission.   1592 *Arden of Fevers.* IV. iv. *Shaks. Apoc.* A fault confessed is more than half amends.   1622 BEAUM. & FL. *Prophetess* v. iii. For faults confess'd, they say, are half forgiven.   1732 FULLER no. 1140 Confession of a Fault makes half amends.   1822 SCOTT *Nigel* ch. 29 Indeed, to confess is, in this case, in some slight sort to redress.

Fault, He has but one: | he is nought.
                                  (F 108)

1546 HEYWOOD I. xi. D3ᵛ.   1732 FULLER no. 6054 Your main Fault is, you are good for nothing.

Fault is as great as he that is faulty, The.   (F 102)

1640 HERBERT no. 369.

Fault is, Where no | there needs no pardon.   (F 116)

1579 LYLY *Euph.* i. 324 There is no priuiledge that needeth a pardon.   1613 MARSTON & BARKSTEAD *Insat. Countess* III. ii. 55 There needs no pardon where there's no offence.   1616 DRAXE no. 315.   1617 *Machivels Dugge* f. 8 (excuse). 1639 CLARKE 208.

Fault, If it be a | it is no farlie.[1]

1721 KELLY 190 . . . Spoken in Excuse for doing a Thing, bad indeed, but common, and usual. [[1] miracle, wonder.]

Fault, Like | like punishment.   (F 114)

1530 PALSGRAVE 378 Telz crimes telz paynes, suche faultes suche paynes.   1542 BECON *Policy War: Early Wks.* P.S. 243 What shall we then say but as the common proverb is, like fault, like punishment? **1591** ARIOSTO *Orl. Fur.* Harington XXXI. 41.

Fault of a wife, He has | that marries mam's pet. *Cf.* Dawted daughters, etc.

1721 KELLY 153 . . . Maids that have been much indulged by their Mothers, and have had much of their Will, seldom prove good Wives.

Fault (guilty) suspects everybody, Who is in. *Cf.* Commits a fault. Faulty stands on guard. (F 117)

1591 SHAKES. *3 Hen. VI* V. vi. 11 Suspicion always haunts the guilty mind. **1593–4** *Id. Luc.* l. 1342 But they whose guilt within their bosoms lie Imagine every eye beholds their blame. **1596** *Id. M.V.* I. iii. 156 Christians . . . Whose own hard dealings teaches them suspect The thoughts of others. **1603** SIR W. ALEXANDER *Darius* l. 1964 They think all faultie, who themselves are vitious. **1607** JONSON *Volp.* III. viii. 20 Guilty men Suspect, what they deserue still. **1666** TORRIANO *It. Prov.* 48, no. 15.

Faults are theirs that commit them, The first | the second theirs that permit them. *Cf.* Deceives me once. (F 121)

1592 DELAMOTHE 55 A second fault ought not to be pardonned. **1707** MAPLETOFT 10. **1732** FULLER no. 4528.

Faults are thick where love is thin. *Cf.* Love fails (Where) we espy all faults. (L 550)

1616 DRAXE no. 1295 Where Loue is not, there is hatred. **1659** HOWELL *Brit. Prov.* 2. **1886** E. J. HARDY *How to be Happy* ch. 6.

Faults on both sides, There are.

1710 J. TRAPP *Most Faults on One side: or the Shallow Politicks . . . of the Author of a late Pamphlet entitled Faults on Both Sides Considered and Expos'd. [Title].* **1902** DEAN HOLE *Then & Now* [ed. 7] ch. 13 My convictions are, after sixty years of intercourse with clergy and laity . . ., that there are faults on both sides.

Fault(s), Fauts, *see also* Absent without f.; All f. to mend (Hard for any man); Commits a f. (He that); Corrects not small f., will not control great ones, (He that); Every f. there is folly (In); Every man has his f.; Every one puts his f. on times; Every one's f. not written in foreheads; Find f. if you knew how; Find f. that cannot mend; Find f. with fat goose; Find f. with my shoes; Finds f. with others and does worse himself, (He); Foolish in the f., wise in punishment; Great men have great f.; Hantle o' f. (Some hae); Hunger finds no f. with cookery; January commits f.; Love fails (Where), we espy f.; Men's years and f. more than they own; Punishment (Many without), but none without f.; Spy f. if eyes were out (You would); Wants a mule without f. (He who); Wink at small f. *See also* Mend-fault.

Faultless, *see* Lifeless that is f.

Faulty stands on his guard, The. *Cf.* Commits a fault. Fault (Who is in). (F 125)

1640 HERBERT no. 793. **1670** RAY 9.

Faustus, *see* Devil and Dr. F.

Favour, Without | none will know you, and with it you will not know yourself. (F 127)

1640 HERBERT no. 159. **1706** STEVENS s.v. Favor.

Favour will as surely perish as life. (F 126)

1651 HERBERT no. 1055.

Favour(s) (noun), *see also* Grace will last,'f. blast; Great men's f. uncertain; Kissing goes by f.

Favours (verb), *see* Fortune f.; Fortune f. fools; Fortune f. the bold.

Fawn like a spaniel, To. *Cf.* Flattering as a spaniel. (S 704)

[**1589**] **1633** MARLOWE *Jew of Malta* II. iii. We Jews can fawn like spaniels when we please. **1596** NASHE *Saffron W.* iii. 33. **1599** SHAKES. *J.C.* III. i. 43 That which melteth fools; I mean sweet words, Low-crooked curtsies, and base spaniel fawning. **1611** MIDDLETON *Roar. Girl* V. i. He hath been brought up in the Isle of Dogs, and can both fawn like a spaniel, and bite like a mastiff, as he finds occasion. **1613** SHAKES. *Hen. VIII* V. iii. 126 You play the spaniel, And think with wagging of your tongue to win me. **1841** DICKENS *B. Rudge* ch. 35 He looked patient . . . and fawned like a spaniel dog.

Fawn, *see also* Better to have dog f. than bite; Spaniels that f. when beaten.

Fazarts,[1] To | hard hazards are death ere they come there. (F 129)

a. **1585** MONTGOMERIE *Cherrie & Slae* l. 377 To fazarts, hard hazarts Is deid or they cum thair. **1721** KELLY 332 . . . Cowardly People are almost kill'd at the sight of Danger. [[1] cowards.]

Fear death as children to go in the dark, Men. (M 547)

1607–12 BACON *Ess., Death* Arb. 382 Men feare death as Children feare to goe in the darke. **1670** RAY 7.

Fear gives wings. (F 133)

1586 WARNER *Albion's Eng.* II. viii. D4ᵛ Then fled the Giant night and day (for feare did lend him wings). **1590** SPENSER *F.Q.* III. vii. 26 Thereto fear gaue her wings. **1631** DRUB *Duch. Suffolk* II D1ᵛ Oh feare what art thou! lend me wings to flie. **1666** TORRIANO *It. Prov.* 60, n. 146

For fear hath wings, as the Latin hath it, Timor addidit alas. **1889** R. L. STEVENSON *Mast. of Ball.* ch. 12 Greed and fear are wings.

Fear has a quick ear. (F 134)

1609 JONSON *Silent Woman* IV. v. 98. **1654** GAYTON *Pleasant Notes Don Q.* 65.

Fear is bondage, All. (F 130)

1573 SANFORD 52. **1629** *Bk. Mer. Rid.* Prov. no. 35.

Fear (suspicion) is one part of prudence. (F 135)

1604 DEKKER I *Hon. Whore* V. ii. 11 Wisely to feare, is to be free from feare. **1604** SHAKES. *O.* I. iii. 382 I know not if't be true; Yet I, for mere suspicion in that kind, Will do as if for surety. **1605** CHAPMAN *All Fools* II. i. 273 Suspicion is (they say) the first degree Of deepest wisdom. **1616** DRAXE no. 698 Feare casteth perils. *c.* **1626** J. SMYTH *Lives of the Berkeleys* i. 275 The proverbe That to abstaine and distrust are two mayne sinewes of wisdome. **1707** MAPLETOFT 8 Wise Distrust is the Parent of Security. **1732** FULLER no. 1300 Distrust is the Mother of Safety, but must keep out of Sight. *Ibid.* no. 1512. *Ibid.* no. 2099 He that fears Danger in time, seldom feels it.

Fear is stronger than love. (L 556)

1567 tr. XENOPHON *Cyropaedia* IV. Q3 Fear and law is sufficient to restraine loue. **1621** ROBINSON 20 He cannot loue me that is afraid of me. **1624** BURTON *Anat. Mel.* III. ii. v. 4 note in margin, Vehement Feare expells Loue. **1732** FULLER no. 1513.

Fear keeps and looks to the vineyard, and not the owner. (F 136)

1599 MINSHEU *Span. Gram.* 83. **1651** HERBERT no. 1072.

Fear keeps the garden better than the gardener. (F 136)

1640 HERBERT no. 268.

Fear not the loss of the bell more than the loss of the steeple. (L 464)

[*a.* 1618] **1628** RALEIGH *Prerog. Parl.: Remains* 116 To fear that, were to fear the losse of the bell, more then the losse of the steeple. **1678** RAY 351.

Fear nothing but sin. (N 252)

1616 DRAXE no. 1123 (Be afraid of). **1639** CLARKE 268 (Be ashamed of). **1640** HERBERT no. 299.

Fear of death is worse than death itself.

1594 *Leir* IV. vii. 34. **1594** NASHE *Terrors of the Night* i. 376 The feare of anie expected euill, is worse than the euill it selfe. **1594** KYD *Cornelia* IV. ii. 166 The feare of euill doth afflict vs more Then th' euill it selfe, though

it be nere so sore. **1621** BURTON *Anat. of Mel.* (1624, 1.2.4.7) A true saying, *Timor mortis, morte peior*, the feare of death is worse than death it selfe. **1631** HEYWOOD 2 *Fair Maid* (ii. 356) (danger). **1641** S. MARMION *The Antiquary* Hazl.-Dods. xiii. 485 The fear of evil is worse than the event.

Fear, the beadle of the law. (F 137)

1650 STAPYLTON *Strada's Low-C. Wars* ii. 33 Fear, the beadle of the law, terrified them from the beginning. **1651** HERBERT no. 1056.

Fear the Greeks, even when bringing gifts, I. *Cf.* Gifts from enemies.

[VIRGIL *Aen.* 2. 49 *Timeo Danaos, et dona ferentes.*] **1777** JOHNSON *Let.* 3 May in *Boswell* (1848) lvii. 530 Tell Mrs. Boswell that I shall taste her marmalade cautiously at first. Timeo Danaos et dona ferentes. Beware, says the Italian proverb, of a reconciled enemy. **1929** *Times* 26 Oct. 13/3 MR. MOSES . . . must now be reflecting on the wisdom of the advice to 'fear the Greeks even when they bring gifts'.

Fear the worst, It is good to. (W 912)

[*c.* 1486–1500] *c.* **1530** MEDWALL *Nature* II, H1 I dout and drede The wurst as wyse men do. [*c.* 1553] **1566–7** UDALL *Ralph Roister D.* II. iii. 10 It is good to cast the wurst. **1574** J. HIGGINS *Mirr. for Mag.* 'Locrinus' 37 Wise men alwayes vse to dreade the worste. **1590–5** MUNDAY *et al. Sir Thomas More* IV. i. 42 To doubt the worst is still the wise man's shield That arms him safe. *c.* **1591** MARLOWE *Edw. II* l. 2521 Tis good to feare the worst. [1592] **1597** SHAKES. *Rich. III* II. iii. 31 Come, come, we fear the worst. All will be well. **1639** CLARKE 66.

Fear (Provide for) the worst; the best will save itself. (W 913)

1528 SIR T. MORE *Wks.* (1557) 105b . . . deme the best . . . prouide for the worst. **1546** HEYWOOD I. v. B2 To prouide for the worst, while the best it selfe saue. **1599** SHAKES. *J.C.* V. i. 97 But since the affairs of men rest still uncertain, Let's reason with the worst that may befall. **1659** HOWELL *Eng. Prov.* 17a (Provide for). **1670** RAY 89 (It's good to). **1885** E. P. HOOD *World of Prov.* 477 'Provide for the worst, and the best will look after itself', says caution.

Fearful as Plutus, As.

1621 BURTON *Anat. Mel.* I. ii. III. 13 (1651) 116 *Timidus Plutus*, an old proverb, As fearful as Plutus; . . . trusting no man. **1853** TRENCH V. 112 A Latin proverb on the moral cowardice which it is the character of riches to generate, Timidus Plutus.

Fearful as the hare, As. (H 147)

[*c.* 1591] **1592** *Arden of Fev.* III. v. 126 Thou hast . . . heard as quickly as the fearefull hare. **1601** SHAKES. *T.N.* III. iv. 368 A very dishonest paltry boy, and more a coward than a hare. **1606** CHAPMAN *Sir G. Goosecap* I. i. 70. **1666** TORRIANO *Prov. Phr.* s.v. Poltrone 152 To be a greater Coward than a hare, viz. which immediately at the least noise, makes away, and betakes her self to her heels.

Fears are divided in the midst.
(F 142)

1640 HERBERT no. 639.

Fears death lives not, He that.
(D 155)

1534 LUPSET *Treat. Dying Well* ed. Gee 284 It is a true sayinge, that who so euer feareth death, he shal neuer do a dede worthy for a lyuyng man. **1545** ERASM. *Precepts of Cato* F1ᵛ He that so sore feareth his death, . . . it were as good to haue no lyfe at all. **1640** HERBERT no. 781.

Fears every bush must never go a-birding, He that.
(B 737)

c. **1526** *Dicta Sap.* D3ᵛ He that is agast or afrayd of eche bushe may nat go through the wodde. **1580** LYLY *Euph. & his Eng.* ii. 123 He that feareth euery bush must neuer goe a birding, he that casteth all doubts, shall neuer be resolued in any thing. **1584** WITHALS D2ᵛ Hee is a bad hunter and a madde, that feareth euery bough. *c.* **1641** FERGUSSON MS. no. 680 He that is afrayd of every bush wil never proue good huntsman.

Fears every grass must not walk (piss) in a meadow, He that.
(G 416)

c. **1412** HOCCLEVE *Reg. of Princes* (Furnivall) l. 1887 Men seyn, who-so of every grace hath drede, let hym beware to walk in any mede. *c.* **1566** *The Bugbears* (ed. Bond) I. iii. 14 He shall never piss in medow that fearethe every grasse. **1614** CAMDEN 307 (pisse). **1710** PALMER 195 He that's afraid of every Nettle must not Sleep on the Grass.

Fears leaves, He that | let him not go into the wood.
(L 143)

1592 DELAMOTHE 47 Hee that is afriad of leaues, must not goe to the wood. **1611** COTGRAVE. s.v. Peur Let him thats skar'd by leaues keepe from the Wood. **1616** DRAXE no. 702 (as 1592). **1640** HERBERT no. 1092. **1670** RAY 55 . . . This a French Proverb englished. Qui a peur de feuilles ne doit aller au bois.

Fears you present will hate you absent, He that.

1732 FULLER no. 2101.

Fear(s) (*noun*), *see also* Danger once (Better pass) than be always in f.; Dies for age (When he) you may quake for f.; Gold (When we have) we are in f.; Guilty conscience . . . feels continual f.; Lives ill (He that) f. follows; Medicine for f. (No); Pains to get . . . f. to lose; Riches bring cares and f.; Travels not by sea knows not f.; Weapons of war will not arm f.; Wise f. begets care.

Fear(s) (*verb*), *see also* Anvil f. no blows (The); Birds once snared (limed) f. all bushes; Conscience f. not . . . false accusations, (A clear); Hopes not for good f. not evil; Lion when he is

absent, (Who takes a) f. a mouse present; Love is full of f.; Many f. (Whom) must needs f. many; Right (He that has) f.; Truth f. no colours; Truth loves (f. no) trial.

Feast and a bellyful, Little difference between a.
(D 331)

1659 HOWELL *Eng. Prov.* 13b. **1678** RAY 100. **1790** TRUSLER *Prov. Exempl.* 169 When hunger is satisfied, even the sight of meat is disgusting.

Feast or a fast, Either a.

1732 FULLER no. 3113 Is there no Mean, but Fast or Feast? **1912** *Daily Tel.* 26 July 12 Dock labour has been graphically described as 'either a feast or a fast'. Good wages may be earned in a short time. . . . On the other hand, work is not always obtainable.

Feast to a miser's (churl's), No.
(F 145)

1611 DAVIES no. 350. 'A Man shall as soone breake his necke as his fast In a miser's house': Yet stay, . . . it is confest That there is no cheare to a Miser's feast. **1639** CLARKE 39 No feast to a misers. *Ibid.* 192 No feast to a churles. **1678** RAY 137 No feast to a Misers. Il n'est banquet que d'homme chiche. *Gall.*

Feast(s), *see also* Better come at end of f.; Cheerful look makes f.; Churl's f. is better than none at all; Company makes f.; Contented mind; Enough is as good as a f.; Fools make f.; Good conscience; Skeleton at f.; War is death's f.; Yule f. done at Pasch.

Feather by feather, the goose is plucked.
(F 151)

1666 TORRIANO *It. Prov.* 174, no.'1 Quill by quill, is a goose pluck'd. **1732** FULLER no. 1514. **1790** TRUSLER *Prov. Exempl.* 183 The weak man . . . hair by hair . . . got off the whole tail without much labour. **1856–70** FROUDE *Hist. Eng.* XII. 414 Howard, whose notion was to 'pluck the feathers of the Spaniards one by one', sent his own launch . . . to take her.

Feather in hand, A | is better than a bird in the air.
(F 152)

1640 HERBERT no. 578.

Feather in one's cap, A.
(F 157)

1596 NASHE *Saffron W.* iii. 30 Caualier flourishing with a feather in my cappe . . . in the face of enuie and generall Worlds opinion. **1602** WITHALS 17. **1657** W. LONDON *Cat. of the most vendible Books* I2 It's recorded that Solomons Library was the feather in the Plume of his glorious Enjoyments. **1661** DR. DENTON to Sir R. Verney *Verney Memoirs* iv (1899) 7 A feather in my capp. **1678** RAY 342 He put a fine feather in my cap, i.e. Honour without profit. **1699** *Dict. of the Canting Crew* He has a Feather in his Cap, a Periphrasis for a Fool. **1808** SCOTT in LOCKHART *Life* (1860) xvii 163 Literary fame, he always said, was a bright feather in the cap.

1824 L. HUNT in *Examiner* 28 Mar. Gresset wrote other poems, . . . but the Parrot is the feather in his cap.

Feather one's nest, To.   (N 125–6)

[= enrich oneself.]   **1553** *Respublica* in '*Lost' Tudor Plays* (1907) 183 Now is the time come . . . to feather my nest.   **1583** STUBBES *Anat. Abus.* II (1882) 38 By this meanes . . . they feather their nests well inough.   **1612** T. TAYLOR *Comm. Titus* i. 7 Yet all this worke is neglected, that his owne neast may be well feathered.   **1680** BUNYAN *Mr. Badman* (1929) 142 When *Mr. Badman* had well feathered his Nest with other mens goods and money, after a little *he breaks*.   **1721** KELLY 161 He has feathered his Nest, he may flye when he will. Spoken of them who have had a good Place so long, that they have gotten Estates. **1753** SMOLLETT *Ct. Fathom* (1784) 41/2 His spouse . . . was disposed to feather her own nest, at the expense of him and his heirs.   **1884** J. PAYN *Canon's Ward* I Adair . . . had feathered his nest . . . , had laid his hands upon everything that could be realized, and turned it into portable property.

Feathers, To be shot with one's own.   (F 166)

1545 TAVERNER H2ᵛ We be taken with our owne fethers. This prouerbe ryseth of the fable, that sheweth howe the egle whiche was striken through with an arowe when she sawe the arrowe made of byrdes fethers wherewith she was wounded, sayde. We be now caught not of others, but euen of oure owne fethers. It is applyed vpon them which minister and trouble, like to the englyshe prouerbe: hath made a rod for his owne arse.   **1569** UNDERDOWNE *Aethiop. Hist.* T.T. II. 74 That which greeveth me most, is that, (as the Proverbe saith) shee useth mine owne Fethers against me.   **1710** PALMER 332 We are often Shot with Our Own Feathers.

Feather(s), *see also* Afraid of the wagging of f.; Anvil should have a hammer of f. (An iron); Ask a kite for a f.; Bird of the same nest (brood, egg, f.); Bird take back own f. (If every); Birds of a f. flock together; Cut a f.; Fine f. make fine birds; Fly, (He would fain) but wants f.; Fool and his f.; Fools wore f. (If); Knocked me down with a f. (Might have); Light as a f.; Meet-mate and you meet (If your) . . . two men bear a f.; Peacock has fair f.; Wears the bull's f.; White f.; Words and f. wind carries away.

Featherbed, *see* Flint on a f., (To break a); Go to heaven in f.

February fill dyke.   (F 167)

1557 TUSSER DI Feuerell fill dyke, doth good with his snowe.   **1670** RAY 40 February fill dike Be it black or be it white: But if it be white, It's the better to like.   **1721** KELLY 107 February fill dike either with black or white. February brings commonly rough Weather, either Snow or Rain.   **1879** R. JEFFERIES *Wild Life South. Co.* ch. 17 February 'fill ditch', as the old folk call it, on account of the rains.

February has one and thirty days, Reckon right, and.   (F 170)

1640 HERBERT no. 229.   **1670** RAY 9.

February makes a bridge, and March breaks it.   (F 169)

1640 HERBERT no. 739.   **1732** FULLER no. 1516. **1914** *Brit. Wkly.* 12 Mar. 690 The wintry weather of Tuesday . . . did its best to justify the old English saying, . . .

Februeer doth cut and shear.   (F 171)

1633 JONSON *T. Tub.* I. i. 1 Februere Doth cut and sheare.

February (Februeer), *see also* Months in the year curse a fair F.; Welshman had rather see . . . than fair F.

Fed at another's hand (table), He that is | may stay long ere he be full.   (H 76)

1640 HERBERT no. 439.   **1813** RAY 164 Who depends upon another man's table often dines late.

Fed, *see also* Better f. than taught.

Fee, *see* Lean f. fit reward for lazy clerk.

Feed by measure and defy the physician.   (M 802)

c. **1549** HEYWOOD II. vii. I4.   *a.* **1628** CARMICHAELL no. 473 Eat measurelie and defye the mediciners.   **1670** RAY 39 Feed sparingly, and defie the Physician.   **1721** KELLY 236 Live in measure, and laugh at the Mediciners. Nothing contributes more to Health, than a temperate Diet. Whereas, Nimia gula morborum Mater.

Feed like a farmer, To.   (F 62)

1618 J. TAYLOR *Penniless Pilgrimage* (Wks. 1630, 123) We drew like Fidlers, and like Farmers fed. *a.* **1641** T. HEYWOOD *Rich. Whittington* A2ᵛ As the Proverb goeth, he fed like a farmer.   **1655** FULLER *Ch. Hist.* VI. ii (V. 13) On which the abbot fed as the farmer of his grange.   **1670** RAY 202. **1738** SWIFT Dial. II. E.L. 312 I have fed like a farmer: . . . my jaws are weary of chewing.

Feeding out of course makes mettle out of kind.

1721 KELLY 103 . . . Good Pasture will make a small Breed of Cattel larger.

Feeds like a boar in a frank,[1] He.   (B 483)

1598 SHAKES. *2 Hen. IV* II. ii. 140 Where sups he? doth the old boar feed in the old frank?   **1631** F. LENTON *Characters* (1663) no. 15 His greatest study is how he may . . . feed at ease like a Boar in a Frank. [¹ sty.]

Feeds like a freeholder of Maxfield (*or* Macclesfield) who has neither corn nor hay at Michaelmas, He. (F 669)

1670 RAY 208. **1678** *Id.* (*Chesh.*) 301 . . . *Maxfield* is a market town . . . , where they drive a great trade of making and selling buttons. When this came to be a Proverb, it should seem the inhabitants were poorer or worse husbands then now they are.

Feed(s), fed, *see also* Beggars breed and rich men f.; Better f. than taught; Dog to follow you, (If you wish) f. him; First born, first f.; Gape long enough; Smoke, (To f. oneself with); Strike as ye f.; Well for him who f. a good man; Where one is bred (Not), but where f.

Feel in one's bones, To.

1605–8 SHAKES. *T.Ath.* III. vi. 113 Lord Timon's mad.—I feel't upon my bones. **1841** DICKENS *Barn. Rudge* ch. 53 I seem to hear it, Muster Gashford, in my very bones. **1875** HOLLAND *Sevenoaks* ch. 23 I can feel the thing in my bones.

Feel, *see also* Does what he should not shall f. what he would not; Guilty conscience . . . f. continual fear.

Feeling has no fellow. (F 175)

1678 RAY 138. **1725** *Matchless Rogue* 56. **1732** FULLER no 1518.

Feet of the (avenging) deities are shod with wool, The. *Cf.* God comes with leaden feet. (G 182)

[MACROB. *Proverbium . . . deos laneos pedes habere. Cf.* PETRON. *Dii pedes lanatos habent.*] **1578** *Courtly Controv.* 2G2ᵛ Her feet were made of wool. [Of a cat after a rat]. *c.* **1592** MARLOWE *Dr. Faustus* III. i. Thus, as the Gods creepe on with feete of wool, Long ere with Iron hands they punish men. **1592** DELAMOTHE 7 Goth hath his feete of woollen, his armes be iron. **1616** DRAXE no. 1849. **1853** TRENCH vi. 148 . . . Here . . . is introduced—the noiseless approach and advance of these judgements, as noiseless as the steps of one whose feet are wrapped in wool.

Feet (legs) under another man's table, To thrust one's. (F 572)

1545 *Precepts of Cato* Publius O3 (legges). **1573** J. CARR *Larum Bell for London* D1ᵛ [The beggared prodigal] gladde to set his feete vnder other mens tables. **1589** L. WRIGHT, *A Summons for Sleepers,* *2ᵛ The prelacie which these new devising church-founders are now so desirous to have established . . . must liue popularly with their feet vnder other mens tables, and their tongues tyed to other mens purses. *c.* **1594** SHAKES. *T.S.* II. i. 394 (set foot). **1623** PAINTER C7 Whose foote is alwaies his friends table vnder, If he grow prouident it is a wonder. **1678** RAY 272. **1732** FULLER no. 5247.

Feet, *see also* Foot.

Fell (*noun*), *see* Fleece and f.

Fell swoop, *see* Swoop (At one fell).

Felled, *see* Oak is not f. at one stroke.

Fellow-ruler, He that has a | has an over-ruler. (F 184)

1611 COTGRAVE s.v. Avoir. **1670** RAY 9.

Fellow(s), *see* All f. at football; Feeling has no f.; Giff gaff was a good f.; Good f. costly name; Hail f. well met; King of good f.; Longer lives good f. than dear year; Stone-dead has no f.

Fellowship, *see* Falsehood in f.; Poverty parts f.

Fells two dogs with one stone, He. *Cf.* Kills two birds.

1721 KELLY 131 . . . Spoken when a Man with one and the self same Pains effects two different Businesses.

Fence against a flail, No. (F 185)

1666 TORRIANO *Prov. Phras.* s.v. Botte 19b. **1670** RAY 89 . . . Some evils and calamities assault so violently, that there is no resisting of them. **1710** S. PALMER 140. **1730** SWIFT *On Stephen Duck*[1] Wks. (1856) I. 637 The thresher Duck[1] could o'er the queen prevail, The proverb says, 'no fence against a flail'. [[1] a farm-labourer, advanced by Queen Caroline; rector of Byfleet, 1752.]

Fence against ill fortune, No. (F 186)

1623 CAMDEN 279 Ther's no fence for ill fortune. **1670** RAY 89 . . . Some evils and calamities assault so violently, that there is no resisting of them.

Fence, *see also* Nigger in the f.

Fencer has one trick in his budget more than ever he taught a scholar, A. (F 187)

1616 WITHALS 566. **1639** CLARKE 127.

Ferlies[1] make fools fain.

1821 SCOTT *Pirate* ch. 4 'I had only some curiosity to see the new implements he has brought.' 'Ay, ay, ferlies make fools fain.' [[1] wonders.]

Ferlie(s), *see also* Farlie.

Fern grows red, When | then milk is good with bread. (F 189)

1584 T. COGAN *Haven Health* (1612) 194, 152 According to that old saying; When fearne waxeth red, then is milke good with bread. **1659** HOWELL *Eng. Prov.* 11b. **1670** RAY 35 When Fern begins to look red Then milk is good with brown bread. It is observed by good housewives, that milk is thicker in the Autumn then in the Summer.

Fern is as high as a ladle, When the | you may sleep as long as you are able. (F 190)

1670 RAY 35.

Fern is as high as a spoon, When the | you may sleep an hour at noon. (F 191)

1670 RAY 34. **1732** FULLER no. 6186.

Fern-bush, *see* Fox from a f. (Know a).

Ferret, *see* Eyes as red as a f.'s; Rabbit hunting with dead f.

Festina lente, *see* Make haste slowly.

Fetch fire, You are come to. (F 283)

c. **1374** CHAUCER *Troilus* Bk. 5, l. 485 'Be we comen hider To fecchen fir, and rennen hom ayein?' **1579** LYLY *Euph.* i. 218 Comming to *Naples* but to fetch fire, as the byword is, not to make my place of abode. **1721** KELLY 374 . . . Spoken to them who make short Visits.

Fetch the five pounds? When do you.

[A man of Poole, it is said, may claim £5, if he gets a certificate of honesty at the end of his apprenticeship.] **1787** GROSE (*Dorset.*) 169 It is a common water joke to ask the crew of a Pool ship, whether any one has yet received that five pounds.

Fetch(ed, es), *see also* Dear bought and far f. are dainties for ladies; Dog that f. will carry; Good to be sent for (or f.) sorrow; Lives longest (He that) must f. wood farthest; Send and f.

Fetters, *see* Loves his f. be they gold (No man).

Feud, *see* Friar forgot f., (Never); What rake the f. where friendship dow not?

Fever, *see* California f.; Scarlet f.; Stuff a cold and starve f.

Few lawyers die well, few physicians live well. (L 129)

1569 C. AGRIPPA *Vanity of Arts and Sciences* tr. Sanford (1575) 179ᵛ It is growne to a prouerbe: *Neither the Phisition lyueth well, nor the Lawer dyeth well.* **1598** SIR R. BARCKLEY *Of the Felicity of Man* 384 There is a common prouerbe, that neither a Phisition liueth well, nor a lawyer dieth well. **1636** CAMDEN 295.

Few words and many deeds. (W 797)

1592 DELAMOTHE 41. **1600** *Look about You* l. 1236 This fellow is of the humour I would chuse my wife, Few words and many paces, a word and a way. **1616** DRAXE no. 460.

Fewer his years, The | the fewer his tears.

1732 FULLER no. 6233.

Few(-er, -est), *see also* Best carpenter makes the f. chips; Jupiter has loved (F. there be whom just); More the merrier, f. the better cheer; One's too f., three's too many; War, (All may begin a) f. can end it.

Fickle, *see* Fortune is variant (f.); Praise none too much, for all f.

Fiction, *see* Truth is stranger than f.

Fiddle, but not the stick, He has got the. (F 203)

[*c.* 1591] **1595** PEELE *O.W.T.* l. 297 Why this goes rounde without a fidling stick. **1653** WALTON *Angler* 106 I lent you indeed my Fiddle, but not my Fiddlestick. **1678** RAY 86 . . . i.e. The books but not the learning, to make use of them, or the like.

Fiddle for shives,[1] Go | among old wives. (S 361)

1639 CLARKE 68 (good). **1670** RAY 175. [¹ slices of bread.]

Fiddle while Rome is burning, To.

[= to be occupied with trifles in face of a crisis.] **1649** G. DANIEL *Trinarch.* To Rdr. 163 Let Nero fiddle out Rome's Obsequies. **1855** KINGSLEY *West. Ho!* ch. 10 It is fiddling while Rome is burning, to spend more pages over the sorrows of . . . Rose Salterne, while the destinies of Europe are hanging on the marriage between Elizabeth and Anjou. **1926** *Times* 28 June 10/5 I should like to remind . . . Liberals . . . that 'Nero fiddled while Rome burned'.

Fiddle, *see also* Agree like f. and stick; Dance without f.; Face as long as f.; Face made of a f. (To have one's); Fit as a f.; Good tune on old f.; Least boy carries greatest f.; Play first (second) f.; Sow to a f.; Take a spring of his own f.

Fiddlers, dogs, and flies, come to feasts uncalled. (F 206)

1585 ROBSON *Choice Change* L2 Three guests which are first at a banquet. Flatterers. **1594** LYLY *Mother B.* v. iii. 382 You need no more send for a fidler to a feast, than a begger to a fayre. **1641** FERGUSSON no. 206. **1721** KELLY 111 . . . Fidlers for Money, the Flies for a Sip, and the Dogs for a Scrap.

Fiddler's fare; meat, drink, and money. (F 204, 205)

1586 J. CASE *Praise of Music* 21 Meate, drink and mony, which they cal fidlers wages. **1592** NASHE *Pierce Penniless* i. 242 I know . . . a gentleman that bestowed much cost in refining of musicke, and had scarse Fidlers wages for his labor. **1592** *Soliman and Perseda* I. iv. 52 Giue him a Fidlers fee, and send him packing. **1606** *Return from Parn.* I. i. 380 Fiddlers' wages. **1608** *Dumb Knight* Hazl.-Dods. x. 169 You have had more than fidler's fare, for you have meat, money, and cloth. **1639** CLARKE 161 Meat, drinke, and money, a fidler's life. **1659**

HOWELL *Eng. Prov.* 16b.   **1721** KELLY 111 . . .
Spoken often when we have din'd with our
Friend, and after won some Money from him at
Play.   **1738** SWIFT *Dial.* III. E.L. 319 Did your
Ladyship play?—Yes, and won; so I came off
with Fidlers fare, Meat, Drink, and Money.

Fiddler(s), *see also* Drunk as a f.; Fools and f.
sing at their meat; House of a f. (In the) all
fiddle; More fool than f.

Fiddlestick, *see* Devil rides on f.

Fiddlestrings, *see* Fret one's self to f.

Fidging mare should be well girded, A.

1721 KELLY 8 . . . A cunning tricky Fellow
should not be trusted without great caution.

Fie upon hens! quoth the fox, because he could not reach them.

1678 RAY 142.

Field requires three things; A | fair weather, sound seed, and a good husbandman.

1642 TORRIANO 96.   **1846** DENHAM 3.

Field, *see also* Cockle and corn grow in the same
f.; Dogs fine in f.; Fair f. and no favour; Game
cheaper in market; Harborough f.; Hard-
fought f. where no man escapes.

Fieldfare, *see* Farewell f.

Fields (Hedges) have eyes, and woods (walls) have ears. *Cf.* Walls have ears.

(F 209)

c. **1225** *Trin. MS. O 11. 45* (ed. Förster) in *Eng.
Stud.* 31. 8 Veld haued hege, & wude haued
heare—Campus habet lumen et habet nemus
auris acumen.   *c.* **1386** CHAUCER *Knight's T.*
l. 1522 But sooth is seyd, go sithen many yeres,
That 'feeld hath eyen and the wode hath eres'.
c. **1430** *K. Edward & the Shep.* (Hartshorne,
A.M.T.) 46 Wode has erys, felde has siȝt.   *c.*
1470 *Harl. MS. 3362* (ed. Förster) in *Anglia* 42.
202 Feld haþ eye, wode haþ ere.   **1546** HEYWOOD
II. v. H3 But feelds haue eies, and woodes haue
eares, ye wot.   **1611** COTGRAVE s.v. Bois (as 1546).
1664 J. HOWELL *Dodona's Grove* A4ᵛ Hedges
have eares, the rurall Proverb sayes.   **1738**
SWIFT *Dial.* III. E.L. 320 They say hedges have
eyes, and walls have ears.   **1822** SCOTT *Nigel*
ch. 6 It is not good to speak of such things . . . ;
stone walls have ears.   **1905** WEYMAN *Starvecrow F.* ch. 28 Heedful of the old saying, . . .

Fierce(r), *see* Mastiff grows the f. for being tied
up.

Fifteen, *see* Pease has its veaze, (Every) and a
bean f.

Fifth wheel to a coach, A.   (W 286)

1513 DOUGLAS *Eneados* Prol. XIII, l. 117–18 As
to the text accordyng neuer a deill Mair than
langis to the cart the fift quheill.   **1631** DEKKER
Match me in London I ad fin. Thou tyest but

wings to a swift gray hounds heele, And addest
to a running charriot a fift wheele.   **1913** *Spectator* 22 Mar. 499 These local bodies are . . .
useless, a fifth wheel in a coach which runs none
too smoothly . . . at the best.

Fig for him (it), A.   (F 210)

1575 *Churchyard's Chips* H7ᵛ A figge for
chaunce.   **1576** WAPULL *Tide Tarries No Man*
A4.   **1578** W. FULWOOD *Enemy of Idleness* 249
Sir, if you be so short, a fig for you.   **1589** LYLY
Pap with an Hatchet. Alias, A fig for my Godson
[title].   **1590–1** SHAKES. *2 Hen. VI* II. iii. 67 A
fig for Peter!   **1600–1** *Id. M.W.W.* I. iii. 27
'Convey' the wise it call. 'Steal'? foh! a fico
for the phrase!   **1618** BRETNOR *Almanac* April
(Evil days) A fig for my god sonne.   **1619** N.
BRETON '*World of Wishes*' in *I would & would
not* C8ᵛ I would I were an excellent Grocer:
for then I would neuer be with out a fig for my
Godson.

Fig, Not worth a.   (F 211)

1528 MORE *Wks.* (1557) 241.   **1600** ROWLANDS
Let. Humours Blood i. 7 All Beere in Europe is
not worth a figge.   **1852** THACKERAY *Esmond*
III. ch. 2 Nor . . . is the young fellow worth a fig
that would.

Fig, To give one a.   (F 213)

1565–6 CHURCHYARD *Churchyard's Farewell
Ballads & Broadsides* ed. H. L. Collmann 1912
no. 30, l. 26 Whose nature gives the Court a
figg when worldly happe is gone.   **1585** A.
MUNDAY *Fedele and Fortunio* E4ᵛ Giue her a
Fico [= poison] out of hande.   *c.* **1589** THESES
MARTINIANAE C3 Haue you strangled him?
Haue you giuen him an Italian figge?   *c.* **1594**
SHAKES. *K.J.* II. i. 162 It grandam will Give it a
plum, a cherry, and a fig.   **1594** NASHE *Unfort.
Trav.* ii. 299 So haue the Italians no such sport
as to see poore English asses, how soberlie they
swallow Spanish figges, deuoure anie hooke
baited for them.   **1600** *Sheepheards Slumber* in
Bodenham *Eng. Helicon* ed. J. P. Collier 210
With scowling browes their follies check and so
give them the Fig.

Figs after peace (Pasch).   (F 214)

1584 WITHALS D3ᵛ Thy deedes are as figges
when Easter is past: that is, thy labour is lost,
. . . for figges are then out of season.   **1641**
FERGUSSON no. 278.

Fig(s), *see also* Grapes of thorns or f. of thistles,
(One cannot gather); Peach will have wine and
f. water; Peel a f. for friend; Thorn springs
not a f., (Of a).

Fight against the wind, To.   (W 431)

c. **1500** *Melusine* XIX. 107 Wel fole is he that
fighteth ayenst the wynd, wenyng to make hym
be styll.   [*c.* 1537] *c.* **1560** UDALL *Thersytes* B3ᵛ
Do not set your mynde To fyghte with the wynde.
1551 CRANMER *Ans. to Gardiner* 220 I shuld do
nothing else but spend wordes in vaine, and beat
the wynd to no purpose.   [1587] **1599** PEELE
David and Bethsabe l. 181 He . . . makes their
weapons wound the sencelesse winds.

Fight dog, fight bear.   (D 467)

1583 STUBBES *Anat. of Abuses* New Sh. S. 178
Some . . . will not make anie bones of xx . . .
pound at once to hazard at a bait, with 'fight
dog, feight beare (say they), the deuill part all!'
1600 *Weakest to Wall* B4ᵛ Come dogge, come
diuell, he that scapes best Let him take all.   **1623**
MIDDLETON *Span. Gip.* IV. iii. A match; we'll
fight dog, fight bear. *a.* **1642** SIR W. MONSON
Naval Tracts III. (1704) 350/2 You must fight
according to the old saying, Fight Dog, Fight
Bear; that is, till one be overcome.   **1678** RAY
244 . . . Ne depugnes in alieno negotio. [Fight
not in another person's concerns.]   **1831** SCOTT
Diary 5 Mar. A resolution to keep myself clear
of politics, and let them 'fight dog, fight bear'.

Fight for one's own hand, To.

1818 SCOTT *Rob Roy* ch. 26 Rob is for his ain
hand, as Henry Wynd feught [with note].
1828 *Id. F. M. Perth* ch. 34 'I fought for my
own hand', said the Smith indifferently; and the
expression is still proverbial in Scotland.   **1879**
FROUDE *Cæsar* ix. 92 Lesbos was occupied by
adventurers, who were fighting for their own
hand. **1900** A. LANG *Hist. Scot.* IX. 291 The
Celt recognized no part in Lowland patriotism.
. . . He fought, like Hal of the Wynd, for his own
hand.

Fight like Kilkenny cats, To.

[= to engage in a mutually destructive struggle.]
[*a.* 1850] in LEAN I. 276 The Kilkenny cats, who
fought till there was nothing but their tails left
of either.   **1864** *N. & Q.* 3rd Ser. V. 433 It has
become a proverb, 'as quarrelsome as the Kilkenny cats'—two of the cats in which city are
asserted to have fought so long and so furiously
that nought was found of them but two tails!
1866 BLACKMORE *Cradock N.* ch. 51 When shall
we men leave off fighting, cease to prove . . . the
legends of Kilkenny (by leaving only our tails
behind us, a legacy for new lawsuits) . . . ?

Fight with (one's own) shadow, To.
(S 262)

[Gk. *Σκιαμαχία.* A fighting with shadows.]   **1565**
J. CALFHILL *Treatise of the Cross* P.S. 63 Ye
might . . . fight with a shadow.   **1570** JOHN DEE
Preface to H. Billingsley's *Elements of Geometry*
A 4–A 4ᵛ I will not . . . fight against myne owne
shadowe.   **1580** WILLIAM CHARKE *An answer to
a seditious pamphlet lately cast abroad by a Jesuit*
C 8 The prouerbe maketh it a uayne fight to
fight with a shadowe.   **1596** SHAKES. *M.V.* I. ii.
55 He will fence with his own shadow.   **1608**
R. WOODCOKE *Goodly Answer* B2.   **1659** FULLER
Appeal Inj. Innoc. in *Hist. Camb. Univ.* (1840)
592 To fight with a shadow (whether one's own
or another's) passeth for the proverbial expression of a vain and useless act.   **1670** RAY 175 . . .
To be afraid of his own fancies, imagining danger
or enemies, where there are none.

Fight(s), *see also* Better fleech a fool than f.
him; Cock won't f., (That); Councils of war
never f.; Full belly neither f.; Kernel and leap
at (f. for) the shell, (To lose); Law, logic, and the
Switzers f. for anybody; Sore f. wrens as cranes;
Speaks well f. well (He that).

Fighting cocks, To live like.

1826 COBBETT *Rur. Rides* (1885) II. 107 [They]
live like fighting-cocks upon the labour of the
rest of the community.   **1858** SURTEES *Ask
Mamma* ch. 24 The servants here seem to live
like fighting-cocks, . . . breakfasts, luncheons,
dinners, teas, and suppers.

Fighting, *see also* Dancing (f.) days done;
Painting and f. look aloof (On).

Fights and runs away, may live to fight another day, He that.   (D 79)

[Gk. 'Ανὴρ ὁ φεύγων καὶ πάλιν μαχήσεται.]   *a.*
1250 *Owl & Night.* 176 'Wel fiзt þat wel fliзt',
seiþ þe wise.   *?a.* **1300** *Salomon & Sat.* (1848)
272 Wel fyþt þat wel flyþ quoþ Hendyng.   *c.*
1440 *Gesta Rom.* lvii. 420 (Add. MS.) It is an
olde sawe, He feghtith wele that flcith faste.   *c.*
1532 *Tales* no. 56 Demosthenes sayde: he that
fleeth cometh agayne to batayle.   **1591–2** SHAKES.
2 Hen. VI V. ii. 86 But fly you must; . . . Away,
for your relief, and we will live To see their
day and them our fortune give.   **1602** *Id.
A.W.* III. ii. 37 Your son will not be killed so
soon as I thought he would.—Why should he
be killed?—So say I, madam, if he run away . . . ;
the danger is in standing to't.   **1621** BURTON
Anat. Mel. II. iii. VII (1651) 357 He that runs
away in a battle, as Demosthenes said, may fight
again.   **1656** MENNES & SMITH *Musarum Deliciae*
He that fights and runs away May live to fight
another day.   **1678** BUTLER *Hudibras* III. ii. 243
For those that fly may fight again, which he can
never do that's slain.   **1750** J. RAY *Hist. Rebell.*
50 The Dragoons . . . thought proper . . . a
sudden retreat; as knowing that, He that fights
and runs away, May turn and fight another Day.

Figures, *see* Truth has no need of rhetoric (f.).

File, *see* Time is a f. that wears.

Fill the mouth with an empty spoon, To. *Cf.* Gives fair words, etc.   (M 1262)

1581 GUAZZO ii. 86 According to the proverbe,
I went about to fil your mouth, with an empty
spoone.   **1639** CLARKE 314.   **1664** CODRINGTON
230.   **1670** RAY 175.   **1721** KELLY 384 You
have put a toom[1] Spoon in my Mouth. You have
rais'd, and disappointed my Expectation.
[[1] empty.]

Fills, *see also* Little and often f. purse.

Filth under the white snow the sun discovers, The.   (F 218)

1640 HERBERT no. 495.

Find a woman (you) without an excuse, and find a hare without a meuse.[1]
(H 156. W 654)

c. **1548** *The Will of the Devil* A4ᵛ Item, I gaue
to all Women, souereygntee, which they most
desyre; & that they neuer lacke excuse.   **1592**
GREENE *Disp. bet. Conny-Catch.* Bodley Hd. 22
Come but to the olde Prouerbe . . . 'Tis as hard

to find a Hare without a Muse, as a woman without a scuse. **1659** HOWELL *Eng. Prov.* 12a Take a Hare without a muse, and a Knave without an excuse, and hang them up. **1670** RAY 174 Find you without an excuse, and find a hare without a muse. [¹ A gap through which a hare is wont to pass.]

Find ease, *see* All men will please (He that) shall never f. e.

Find fault if you knew how, You would.
(F 119)

1639 CLARKE 80.

Find fault that cannot mend, He may.
(F 110)

1528 PAYNELL *Reg. San.* A3ᵛ It is farre more easie to carpe at, then to cure a fault. **1577** *Art of Angling* A3ᵛ I haue spied a fault which I had need to mend. **1580** LYLY *Euph. & his Eng.* ii. 205 More wil enuie me then imitate me, and not commende it though they cannot amende it. **1609** HARWARD 113 Reprehend they will that cann not amend. **1721** KELLY 171. **1732** FULLER no. 1985 He may find Fault, but let him mend it if he can.

Find fault with a fat goose, You.
(F 118)

1678 RAY 248. **1732** FULLER no. 5902.

Find fault with my shoes, and give me no leather, I never loved them that.

1721 KELLY 224 . . . Apply'd to them that find fault with some part of our Habit, yet contribute nothing to make it better.

Find guilty Gilbert¹ where he had hid the brush, To.
(G 114)

1608 ARMIN *Nest Nin.* Shakes. Soc. 39 Not I, says another; but by her cheeks you might find guilty Gilbert, where he had hid the brush. [¹ a N. country name for a dog.]

Find it where the Highlandman found the tongs, To.

1721 KELLY 383 A Highland Man being challenged for stealing a pair of Tongs, said he found them; and being asked where? He said, Hard by the Fire side, Spoken when Boys have pick'd something, and pretend they found it.

Find not that you do not seek, Take heed you.
(H 385)

1546 HEYWOOD II. v. H3ᵛ But whan she semed to be fixed in mynde, Rather to seeke for that she was lothe to fynde. **1596** HARINGTON *Metam. of Ajax* (1814) 122 If a man had no light to work, yet he would feel, to seek that he would not find, for fear lest they should find that they did not seek. **1670** RAY 9. *Ital.*

Find (Found) out, *see* Eating and drinking (Ingenious man that first f. o.).

Find some hole to creep out at, He will.
(H 518)

c. **1533** J. FRITH *Disputⁿ of Purgatory* F6 Theyr maner is when they are in a strayte euer to seke a startynge hole. **1572** CRADOCKE *Ship of assured Safety* 40 Was there neuer any Momus in a corner, that could espye an hole to creepe oute at. **1672** WALKER 15 no. 35 To find some creeping hole; starting hole; hole to creep out at. **1678** RAY 253. **1687** MIÈGE s.v. Hole (To have a Hole to).

Find the bean in the cake, To.

1578 *Courtly Controv.* 2A1 Othersome to be thought they had founde (as the Prouerbe sayth) the beane in the cake, and that they were more able than men accompted them. **1592** NICHOLS *Prog. of Q. Eliz: Speech at Sudely* 8 Cut the cake: who hath the beane shall be kinge. (i.e. Who finds the bean in the cake on Twelfth Night shall be king of the company). **1611** COTGRAVE s.v. Febve Trouver la febve au gasteau To find what one looks for, to meet with a thing for his purpose.

Find what was never lost, To.
(T 182)

1536 LATIMER *2nd Serm. bef. Conv.* P.S. 51 This, to pray for dead folks, this is not found, for it was never lost. How can that be found that was not lost. **1546** HEYWOOD I. xi. D3 If ye seke to fynde thynges er they be lost, Ye shall fynde one daie you come to your cost. **1609** ARMIN *Two Maids* A4ᵛ How can ye find the gloue was neuer lost? **1732** FULLER no. 5918 You have found what was never lost.

Finds fault with others and does worse himself, He.
(F 107)

c. **1425** *Wakefield Play* 'Judgement' l. 562 Ye tolde ilk mans defawte and forgate your awne. **1481** CAXTON *Reynard* ed. Arber 89 Whoo that wyl chyde or chastyse see that he be clere hym selfe. [*c.* 1530] *c.* **1545** H. RHODES *Bk. Nurture* (1577 ed.) *in Babies Bk. etc.*, 93 Correct not faults in other, and thy selfe do vse the same. **1594–5** SHAKES. *L.L.L.* IV. iii. 127 As his your case is such. You chide at him, offending twice as much. **1605–8** *Id. T.Ath.* V. i. 36 Wilt thou whip thine own faults in other men? **1609** *Id. Son.* 152, l. 5 But why of two oaths' breach do I accuse thee When I break twenty?

Find(s), found, *see also* Better lost than f.; Grind or f.; Hides (He that) can f.; Lost all, f. myself; Modest words to express immodest things, (It is hard to f.); Nothing seek nothing f.; Seek that which may be f.; Seek till you f.; Seeks f. (He that); Speak as one f.; Take one as you f. him; Take things as you f. them; Take what you f. or what you bring.

Finder(s), *see* Fox is f.; Losers seekers, f. keepers.

Finding's keeping.

1863 SPEKE *Discov. Source Nile* ch. 5 The scoundrels said, 'Findings are keepings by the laws of our country; and as we found your cows, so we will keep them'.

Fine as a carrot new scraped, As.

1834 J. B. KER 43 Said in ridicule . . . of some jack-in-office. **1886** R. HOLLAND *Cheshire Gloss.* E.D.S. 445.

Fine (proud) as a lord (lord's bastard), As.   (L 443)

1530 PALSGRAVE 446a Thou arte as prowde as if thou were a lorde. **1678** RAY 284 As fine [or proud] as a Lords bastard.

Fine as fivepence, As.   (F 341)

1564 BULLEIN *Dial. agst. Fever* E.E.T.S. 62 Out of the countree . . . as fine as fippence! **1575** *App. & Virginia* Mal. Soc. l. 225 As fine as phippence, as proude as a Pecocke. [**1600**] **1662** *Grim the Collier of Croydon* Hazl.-Dods. viii. 414 Finer than fivepence. **1659** HOWELL *Eng. Prov.* 11a As fine as fippence, as neat as ninepence. **1778** BURNEY *Evelina* Lett. 50. (You are all). **1837** J. B. KER 48.

Fine as if you had a whiting hanging at your side, or girdle, You are as.   (W 317)

1678 RAY 345.

Fine dressing is a foul house swept before the doors.   (D 594)

1640 HERBERT no. 243. **1732** FULLER no. 1538 (is usually).

Fine (Fair) feathers make fine birds (fair fowls).   (F 163)

[SPONDANUS (1557–95) on *Od.* 6. 29 quotes *proverbium apud meos Vascones 'speciosae plumae avem speciosam constituunt'*.] **1592** DELAMOTHE 29 The faire feathers, makes a faire foule. **1611** DAVIES no. 219 The faire Feathers still make the faire Fowles. But some haue faire feathers that looke but like Owles. **1670** RAY 87 Fair feathers make fair fowls. Fair clothes, ornaments and dresses set off persons . . . God makes and apparel shapes. **1714** MANDEVILLE *Fab. Bees* (1725) I. 130 Fine feathers make fine birds. **1858** SURTEES *Ask Mamma* ch. 10 Mrs. . . . essayed to pick her to pieces, intimating that she was much indebted to her dress—that fine feathers made fine birds. **1917** BRIDGE 57 · · · but they don't make *lady*-birds.

Fine words dress ill deeds.   (W 800)

c. **1303** BRUNNE *Handl. Synne* 4179 Wyth feyre wurdys he shal the grete; But yn hys herte he shal thynke For to do the a wykked blynke. **1640** HERBERT no. 479.

Fine words, *see also* Fair words.

Fine, *see also* Makes a thing too f., breaks it; Whore in a f. dress.

Finger and thumb, They are.   (T 645)

[= on intimate terms.] **1579** LYLY *Euph.* i. 214 In that thou crauest my aide, assure thy selfe I wil be the finger next the thumbe. **1659** HOWELL

Eng. Prov. 13b You two are finger and thumb. **1730–6** BAILEY s.v. Thumb They are Finger and Thumb, that is, they are so great together, there is no parting them.

Finger in one's mouth, With one's.

[= (*a*) helplessly inactive, (*b*) with nothing accomplished, 'looking foolish'.] *c.* **1577** J. NORTHBROOKE *Treatise agst. Dicing* 163 If I can declare this to you, then your beliefe . . . is vayne . . . otherwise you would haue set your finger vpon your mouth. **1596** NASHE *Saffron W.* iii. 124 I would not . . . be won to put my finger in my mouth & crie mumbudget. **1621** ROBINSON 39 You should not come for an errand and goe home with your finger on your cheeke. **1649** CROMWELL *Lett.* 14 Nov. To stand with our fingers in our mouths. **1706** STEVENS s.v. Dedo. **1874** *Spectator* (1891) 28 Mar. 443 He returned to Ireland with his finger in his mouth.

Finger in the eye, To put.   (F 229)

[**1525–40**] **1557** *A Merry Dialogue* 71 She put the finger in the eye, and wepte. **1534** HEYWOOD *Play Love* C1 She set the fynger in the eye. **1592–3** SHAKES. *C.E.* II. ii. 205 No longer will I be a fool, To put the finger in the eye and weep. **1594–8** *Id. T.S.* I. i. 78 It is best Put finger in the eye. **1640** BRATHWAITE *Art Asleep Husb.* 20 If shee have cause to put finger ith' eye, she will chuse rather to dye than discover it to any other. **1867** TROLLOPE *Last Chron. Bars.* ch. 32 He may have put his finger into my eye; but, if so, why not also into the eyes of a jury?

Finger in the pie, To have a.   (F 228)

1553 *Republica* in '*Lost' Tudor Plays* (1907) Bring me in credit that my hands be in the pie. **1587** J. BRIDGES *Def. of Gvt. of C. of E.* 383 Haue their finger in this pye. **1613** SHAKES. *Hen. VIII* I. i. 52 No man's pie is freed From his ambitious finger. **1659** B. HARRIS *Parival's Iron Age* 75 Lusatia . . . must needs, forsooth, have her Finger in the Pye. **1678** RAY 244 He had a finger in the pie when he burnt his nail off. **1886** MISS TYTLER *Buried Diamonds* ch. 12 Susie . . . liked to have a finger in every pie.

Fingers are all thumbs, His.   (F 233)

[**1534**] **1557** T. MORE *Passion Christ*, Wks. 1299 Euery fynger shalbe a thombe, and we shall fumble it vp in hast. **1546** J. HEYWOOD II. v. H1 Whan he should get ought, eche fynger is a thumbe. [*c.* **1553**] **1566–7** UDALL *Roister D.* I. iii. Arb. 22 Ah, eche finger is a thombe to day me thinke. **1899** A. T. QUILLER-COUCH *Ship of Stars* ch. 13 I think my fingers must be all thumbs.

Fingers are lime twigs, His.   (F 236)

a. **1500** J. SKELTON *The Bowge of Courte* l. 509 Lyghte lyme fynger, he toke none other wage. *c.* **1510** *Hickscorner* 651, 2 All my fyngers were arayed with lyme, So I conuayed a cuppe manerly. **1543** G. COUSIN *Office of Servants* A8 Some men . . . leaue abrode money . . . for profe if their seruauntes be limefingered. **1596** HARINGTON *Metam. Ajax* (1814) 65 A certain gentleman that had his fingers made of lime-twigs, stole a piece of plate. **1611** SHAKES. *Temp.* IV. i. 246 Come, put some lime upon your fingers. **1670** RAY 175 . . . Spoken of a thievish person.

Fingers (hands) in mortar, To have one's. (F 241)

[= to have building going on.] **1665** GERBIER *Brief Disc.* 3 Those who say, That a wise man never ought to put his finger into Morter. **1738** SWIFT *Dial.* II. E.L. 295 You are come to a sad dirty house; I am sorry for it, but we have had our hands in mortar.

Fingers itch to be at it, His. (F 237)

1565 OSORIUS *Pearl for Princes* tr. R. Shacklock 43ᵛ Is there any thing els that your fyngers itche at, tyll you haue it donne? **1622** DEKKER & MASSINGER *Virgin Martyr* IV. ii. 51 For now my fingers itch to bee at her.

Fingers on thy lips, Lay thy. (F 239)

1509 BARCLAY *Ship of Fools* ii. 232 . . . layeth his fynger before hys lyp. [c. **1590**] **1598** GREENE *James IV* v. iv. 2106 Good Merchant, lay your fingers on your mouth. **1600-1** SHAKES. *H.* I. v. 188 Still your fingers on your lips, I pray.

Fingers, To burn one's. (F 240)

1551 CRANMER *Ans. to Gardiner* 116 Smithe as soone as he had touched it, felte it so scawlding hotte, that he durst not abyde it, but shranke awaye by and by for feare of burning his fyngers. **1595** HARTWELL *War betw. Turks and Persians* Ep. Ded. A 2 Wherewithall I list not to meddle for feare of burning my fingers. **1656** *Trepan* 31 She has . . . burnt both fingers and her thumbe. **1929** 6 Aug. D. H. LAWRENCE *Lett.* ii. 1173 I expect . . . they'll burn the four books just to show that they can burn something—their own fingers also, I hope.

Fingers were made before forks, and hands before knives. (F 235)

1567 *Loseley MSS.* (ed. Kempe 1836) 212 As God made hands before knives, So God send a good lot to the cutler's wives. **1738** SWIFT *Dial.* II. E.L. 301.

Fingers' ends, At one's. (F 245)

1528 ROY & BARLOW *Rede me* Arber 110. c. **1533** J. FRITH *Disputⁿ of Purgatory* A3ᵛ We maye now wel tast at our fingers endes that we haue longe bene in that miserable case that Paule prophesyed vppon vs. **1542** ERASM. tr. Udall *Apoph.* (1877) 39. **1549** *Id.* tr. Chaloner *Praise of Folly* C1ᵛ. **1550** W. HARRYS *The market or fair of Usurers* A6 Judas lesson . . . what wyll ye gyue, is learned at the fyngers endys. **1594-5** SHAKES. *L.L.L.* V. i. 65 Thou hast it ad dunghill, at the fingers' ends, as they say. **1601** *Id. T.N.* I. iii. 73 I have them at my fingers' ends. **1711** STEELE *Spect.* no. 156 Names which a man of his learning has at his Fingers-Ends. **1862** CARLYLE *Fredk. Gt.* (1865) III. IX. ii. 82 All manner of Military Histories . . . are at his finger-ends.

Finger(s), *see also* Better a f. off; Devil makes Christmas pies of clerks' f.; Fish on one's f. (To find); Fools cut f.; German's wit in f.; God strikes with f.; Give a clown your f.; Look through one's f.; Love his little f. more . . . ; Put one's f. in fire; Put your f. in fire and say

it was fortune; Sailors' f. all fish-hooks; Sucked not this from f.'s ends; Turn round one's f.; Wet f. (With a); Wit in his little f. (He has more).

Finglesham Church, *see* Married at F. C.

Finishes, *see* Begins many things f. few.

Fire and tow. (F 268, 278)

c. **1303** BRUNNE *Handl. Synne* 7924 But of wymmen hyt ys grete wundyr, Hyt fareth wyth hem as fyre and tundyr. c. **1450-1500** *Gd. Wife wd. a Pilgrimage* l. 40 Feyr and towe ileyde togeder, kyndoll hir woll. **1603** H. CROSSE *Virtue's Commonwealth* ed. Grosart 63 Some petty fogger . . . forward enough to put fier to towe. **1616** DRAXE no. 1517 There is no quenching of fire with towe. c. **1635** BEAUM & FL. *Elder Brother* I. ii. For he is fire and tow; and so have at him. **1670** RAY 175. **1813** *Id.* 153 (as 1616).

Fire and water, To go through. (F 285)

c. **825** *Vesp. Psalter* lxv[i]. 12 We leordun ðorh fyr & weter. **1530** PALSGRAVE 653b He shall passe thorowe fyre and water or he get it. **1534** HERVET tr. *Xenophon's Householde* 61b They wolde gladly folowe theym through fire and water, and throughe all maner of daunger. **1600-1** SHAKES. *M.W.W.* III. iv. 100 A woman would run through fire and water for such a kind heart. *Ibid.* III. v. 112 Master Brook, I will be thrown into Etna, as I have been into Thames, ere I will leave her thus.

Fire and water are good servants, but bad masters. (F 253)

1562 BULLEIN *Bulwarke of Defence* f. 12 Water is a very good seruaunt, but it is a cruell maister. **1615** T. ADAMS *England's Sickness* 20 The world, like fire, may be a good seruant, will bee an ill Master. **1662** FULLER *Cornw.* 203 Philosophy being in Divinity as Fire and Water in a Family, a good Servant, but bad Master. **1738** SWIFT *Dial.* II. E.L. 315 Why, fire and water are good servants, but they are very bad masters.

Fire and water have no mercy. (F 254)

1577 PEACHAM *Garden of Eloquence* (1593) 87. **1585** A. MUNDAY *Two Italian Gentlemen* G1ᵛ They say fire and water hath no mercy. **1599** NASHE *Lenten Stuff* iii. 164. **1626** BRETON *Soothing* A5ᵛ. **1639** CLARKE 203.

Fire away, Flanagan!

1841 S. WARREN *Ten Thous. a Year* ch. 31 And you won't be angry? . . . Then fire away, Flannagan!' cried Titmouse joyfully.

Fire cannot be hidden in flax (straw). (F 255)

1557 EDGEWORTH 2X3 It [a venemous heat] will no more be kept in, then fyre couered vnder strawe, whiche must neades burst out in one place or an other. **1580** LYLY *Euph. & his Eng.* ii. 184 Fire can-not be-hydden in the flaxe with-out smoake. **1590** LODGE *Rosalynde* 15 Fire cannot bee hid in the straw, nor the nature of man so concealed, but at last it will haue his course. **1597** *Politeuphuia* 20 Neither fire in the strawe, nor loue in a womans lookes, can be concealed. **1613** SHAKES. *T.N.K.* V. iii. 97 It could No more be hid in him than fire in flax.

Fire descends not. (F 256)

1576 PETTIE ii. 27 The earth draweth downward because it is heavy, the fire flieth upward because it is light. **1579** LYLY *Euph.* i. 191 Doe you not knowe that which al men doe affirme and knowe . . . That fire cannot be forced downewarde? That Nature will haue course after kinde? **1579** GOSSON *Sch. Abuse* 43 Fire and Ayre mount vpwards, Earth and Water sinke downe. [1594–1600] **1615** T. HEYWOOD *Four Prentices* ii. 200 All our spirits are fire, Which burnes not downward, but is made t' aspire. **1666** TORRIANO *It. Prov.* 321, n. 105.

Fire from ice (snow), To strike. (F 284)

1594 SHAKES. *T.G.V.* II. vii. 19 Thou wouldst as soon go kindle fire from snow As seek to quench the fire of love with words. **1611** *Second Maiden's Tragedy* l. 885 Would you haue me worke by wonders to strike fire out of yce.

Fire is as hurtful as healthful. (F 258)

1579 GOSSON *Sch. Abuse* Arb. 23 Fyre is as hurtfull, as healthie. **1597** *Politeuphuia* 166b. **1639** CLARKE 211.

Fire is good for the fireside.

1862 HISLOP 96 . . . All things are good in their proper places.

Fire is half bread.

1908 C. M. DOUGHTY *Wand. in Arabia* I. x. 196 Cheerful is the gipsy fire of . . . bushes: there is a winter proverb of the poor in Europe, 'Fire is half bread!'

Fire is never without heat, The. (F 261)

1583 MELBANCKE *Philot.* C2ᵛ It is no fyre that giues no heate. **1592** DELAMOTHE 29. **1597** *Politeuphuia* 152ᵛ Fire were not to be counted fire, if it wanted heate, nor vertue to be knowne with repetition. **1611** DAVIES no. 220.

Fire of London[1] was a punishment for gluttony, The.

1787 GROSE (*London*) 206 The fire of London was a punishment for gluttony. For Iron-monger-lane was red-fire-hot, Milk-street boiled over; it began in Pudding-lane, and ended at Pye-corner. [[1] 1666.]

Fire of straw (hay), A. (F 270)

1573 SANFORD 102ᵛ. **1577** PEACHAM *Garden of Eloquence* (1593) 30 He that maketh his fire with hay, hath much smoke and little heate. **1578** FLORIO *First F.* 28ᵛ. **1629** *Bk. Mer. Rid.* Prov. no. 71 A fire of straw yields naught but smoke. **1666** TORRIANO *It. Prov.* 97, no. 4. **1732** FULLER no. 2236 He that maketh a Fire of Straw, hath much Smoke and but little Warmth.

Fire, Make no | raise no smoke. (F 275)

1546 HEYWOOD II. v. H2ᵛ There is no fyre without some smoke, we see. Well well, make no fyre, reyse no smoke, (sayd shee).

Fire so low, You cannot make the | but it will get out. (F 293)

1640 HERBERT no. 965.

Fire that's closest kept burns most of all. (F 265)

[OVID *Met.* 4. 64 *Quoque magis tegitur, tectus magis aestuat ignis.*] *c.* **1374** CHAUCER *Troilus* Bk. 2, l. 538 Wel the hotter been the gledes rede, That men hem wryen with asshen pale and dede. *c.* **1385** *Id. Leg. Good Women* l. 735 Wry the glede and hotter is the fyr. **1565** SACKVILLE & NORTON *Gorboduc* III. i. 101. **1578** *Courtly Controv.* G3ᵛ The heate of glowing brondes couered with ashes, are more feruente and violent when they breake out, than the flames of blazing brushe discouered and dispersed in the open ayre. **1579** LYLY *Euph.* i. 210 The fire kepte close burneth most furious. **1591–2** SHAKES. *1 Hen. VI* III. i. 190 This late dissension grown betwixt the peers Burns under feigned ashes of forged love And will at last break out into a flame. **1592** *Id. T.And.* II. iv. 36 Sorrow conceal'd, like to an oven stopp'd, Doth burn the heart to cinders where it is. **1594–5** *Id. T.G.V.* I. ii. 30 Fire that's closest burns most of all. *Ibid.* II. vii. 21 I do not seek to quench your love's hot fire, But qualify the fire's extreme rage . . .—The more thou damm'st it up, the more it burns. **1592–3** *Id. V.A.* l. 331 An oven that is stopp'd, or river stay'd Burneth more hotly, swelleth more with rage. **1611** COTGRAVE s.v. *Feu* The more that fire's kept downe the more it burns.

Fire, that's God's angel, By this.

[EX. iii. 2: The Angel . . . appeared unto him in a flame of fire; PS. civ 4; HEB. i. 7.] *c.* **1570** *Misogonus* III. i. 240 By this fier that bournez thats gods aungell. **1597** SHAKES. *1 Hen. IV* III. iii. 32 If thou wert any way given to virtue, I would swear by thy face; my oath should be, 'by this fire, that's God's angel'. **1598** CHAPMAN *Blind Beggar of Alexandria* l. 1044 By pistol which is Gods angell. **1602** DEKKER *Satiro-Mastix* I. ii. 67 By this Candle (which is none of Gods Angels). *c.* **1605** DEKKER & WEBSTER *N.Ho* II. i. 183 By this Iron (which is none a Gods Angell).

Fire to flax, Put not. (F 278)

c. **1386** CHAUCER *W. of Bath's Prol.* l. 89 For peril is bothe fyr and tow t'assemble. **1530** PALSGRAVE 417b Adde fyre to towe and you shal sone have a flame. **1545** TAVERNER G3ᵛ *Ignem igni ne addas.* Put not fyer to fyer. . . . This prouerbe is touched in Englyshe where it is sayde, that we ought not put fyre to towe. **1577** STANYHURST in Holinshed *Chron. Ireland* (1587) 89b Putting fire to flax. **1588** GREENE *Pandosto* ed. Thomas 6. **1590** SHAKES. *2 Hen. VI* V. ii. 54 And beauty, that the tyrant oft reclaims, Shall to my flaming wrath be oil and flax. **1639** CLARKE 197.

Fire which lights (warms) us at a distance will burn us when near, The.

c. 1374 CHAUCER *Troilus* Bk. I, l. 448 And ay the ner he was, the more he brende. For ay the ner the fir, the hotter is. **1580** LYLY *Euph. & his Eng.* ii. 120 Fire giueth lyght to things farre off, and burneth that which is next to it. The Court shineth to one that come not there, but singeth those that dwell there. **1584** *Id. Camp.* IV. iv. 21 The love of kings is like . . . fire, which warmeth afar off, and burneth near hand. **1642** TORRIANO 63 That fire which does not warm me, will I never permit to scorch me. **1869** HAZLITT 368 The fire which lighteth us at a distance will burn us when near.

Fire(s), *see also* Better a wee f. to warm us; Carries f. in one hand; Chestnuts out of f.; Child says nothing but what it heard by f.; Coals of f. on the head (Heap); Coldest flint there is f.; Dangerous f. begins in bedstraw; Even hand to throw a louse in the f., (He has an); Fanned f. and forced love; Fat is in the f.; Fetch f. (You are come to); Flax from f. and youth from gaming, (Keep); Freets fail (When), f.'s good for fiercy; Frying-pan into f.; Fuel to the f., (To add more); Gold is tried in the f.; Green wood makes hot f.; Heart is on f. (When); House, a wife, and a f. to put her in; House on f., (Like a); Kentshire, hot as f.; Kindle not a f. you cannot extinguish; Little f. burns deal of corn; Little sticks kindle f.; Little wind kindles, much puts out f.; Longest at f. soonest finds cold; Love of lads and f. of chats soon out; Make a f. (He that can) can end quarrel; Mix water with f.; Much smoke, little f.; Neighbour's house is on f.; No f., no smoke; No smoke without f.; Oil on the f. is not way to quench; Oil to f. (Add); One f. drives out another; Own f. is pleasant (*under* Own hearth); Play at chess when house on f.; Play with f.; Poke a man's f. after known him seven years; Pudding in the f., (There is a) . . . ; Put one's finger in f.; Set my house on f. to roast eggs; Ships fear f. more than water; Silks and satins put out the f.; Sit near the f. when chimney smokes; Skeer your own f.; Skirts of straw (Who has) fear the f.; Smell f. (Well may he) whose gown burns; Smoke of a man's own country, better than f. of another; Smoke (Shunning the) they fall into the f.; Soft f., sweet malt; Spark a great f., (Of a small); Spend much (If you can), put the more to the f.; Three failures and a f. make fortune; Three removes as bad as f.; Water afar quenches not f.; Water f., quickly make room; Well to work and make a f. care and skill require; Woman is flax, man is f.

Fireside, *see* Fire is good for f.

Firm as a rock, As.   (R 151)

1541 H. BULLINGER *Christ. State Matrimony* tr. Coverdale 1543 ed., L3ᵛ The worde and promyse of an occupyer must be as ferme and fast as the rocke of stone. **1598** SHAKES. *2 Hen. IV* IV. i. 188 Our peace shall stand as firm as rocky mountains. **1603** CHETTLE, DEKKER, & HAUGHTON *Patient Grissill* D1ᵛ Thy faith . . . I haue

found it sollid as the rocke. **1611** DAVIES no. 329 (sure).

First advice of a woman and not the second, Take the.   (w 668)

1576 GASCOIGNE *Philomene* Wks. ii. 192 No remedie remaynde But onely womans witte, Which sodainly in queintest chance, Can best it selfe acquit. **1611** CHAPMAN *May Day* II. i. 166 Women do best when they least think on't. **1639** CLARKE 22 A womans counsell is sometime good. Primo crede mulieris consilio, secundo noli. **1659** HOWELL *Span. Prov.* 16 Take thy wifes first counsel, not the second. **1853** TRENCH iv. 89 . . . for in processes of reasoning, out of which the second counsels spring, women may and will be inferior to us. [Fr. Prends le premier conseil d'une femme, et non le second.]

First as last, As good do it.   (F 294)

c. **1592–5** *Thomas of Woodstock* l. 1622. **1593** G. HARVEY *Pierce's Super.,* Gros. ii. 247 (at-first as at-last).

First, I am not the | and shall not be the last.   (F 295)

c. **1200** *Ancrene Riwle* 86 Nert tu nout, i þisse þinge, þe uorme,[1] ne þe laste. **1678** RAY 74. [¹ first.]

First blow is as much as two, The.
                                         (B 472)

1640 HERBERT no. 913.

First blow is half the battle, The.

1773 GOLDSMITH *She Stoops to C.* II. i. I have been thinking, George, of changing our travelling dresses. . . .— . . . The first blow is half the battle. I intend opening the campaign with the white and gold. **1790** BURNS *Prol. at Dumfries* He bids you mind, amid your thoughtless rattle, That the first blow is ever half the battle.

First blow makes the wrong, The | but the second makes the fray.   (B 475)

1589 BACON *Advert. Controv. Church* ed. Burgoyne, 37 . . . The prouerbe that the second blow maketh the fray. **1590** *Mar Mar-Martin* I If all be true that Lawyers say, The second blowe doth make the fray. *a.* **1631** DONNE *Serm.* xl (Alford) 306 The first blow makes the Wrong, but the second makes the Fray. **1676** HALE *Contempl.* I. 242 It is a true Proverb, It is the second blow makes the fray. **1898** A. J. C. HARE *Shropshire* ch. 8 'It takes two blows to make a battle', is a local proverb.

First born, first fed.   (B 138)

1616 DRAXE no. 1523. **1659** HOWELL *Fr. Prov.* 4.

First breath is the beginning of death, The.

1576 PETTIE i. 62 Even in our swathe-clouts death may ask his due. **1732** FULLER no. 4524.

First catch your hare.

[*c.* **1300** BRACTON *De legibus et consuetudinibus Angliae* IV. xxi. §4 (Rolls ed. III. 234) *Et vulgariter dicitur quod primo oportet cervum capere, et postea, cum captus fuerit, illum excoriare.* (quot. in 1931 A. TAYLOR *The Proverb* 79).] **1853** BRIMLEY *Ess.* '*My Novel*' The sagacious Mrs. Glasse prefaces her receipt for hare-soup by the pithy direction, first catch your hare. **1854** SURTEES *Handley Cross* ch. 44 As Mrs. Glasse would say, however, 'first catch your horse'. **1855** THACKERAY *Rose & Ring* ch. 14 'To seize wherever I should light upon him—' ' First catch your hare! . . .' exclaimed his Royal Highness. **1896** *Daily News* 20 July 8/2 The familiar words, 'First catch your hare', were never to be found in Mrs. Glasse's famous volume.[1] What she really said was, 'Take your hare when it is cased.' [1 *Art of Cookery*, 1747.]

First chapter of fools is to hold themselves wise, The. (C 239)

1573 SANFORD 104ᵛ (is to be helde as accompted wise). **1581** GUAZZO i. 93. **1659** HOWELL *Eng. Prov.* 1a.

First chapter of fools magnifies themselves, The. (C 240)

1611 DAVIES no. 61. **1616** DRAXE no. 737 (magnifie themselues).

First come, first served. (C 530)

[ERASM. gives as modern proverb Qui primus venerit, primus molet.] *c.* **1386** CHAUCER *W. of Bath's Prol.* l. 389 'Whoso that first to mille comth, first grynt.' **1599** PORTER *Angry Wom. Abingd.* Mal. Soc. l. 2295 So, first come, first seru'd; I am for him. **1608** ARMIN *Nest Nin.* (1842) 25 He found the sexton . . . making nine graves, . . . and whoso dies next, first comes, first served. **1819** SCOTT *Leg. Mont.* ch. 20 All must . . . take their place as soldiers should, upon the principle of—first come, first served.

First comes David,[1] next comes Chad,[2] and then comes Winneral (Winnold)[3] as though he was mad.

1846 DENHAM 34. [1 1st March, 2 2nd March, 3 3rd March. A corruption of Winwaloe.]

First creep, and then go. *Cf.* Children learn to creep. (C 820)

c. **1410** *Towneley Plays* E.E.T.S. 103 Fyrst must vs crepe and sythen go. **1639** CLARKE 116. **1670** RAY 75 You must learn to creep before you go. **1854** SURTEES *Hand. Cross* ch. 17 But we must all creep afore we can walk, and all be bitten afore we can bite.

First cut, The | and all the loaf besides. (C 941)

1662 FULLER Kent. 63 Kent and Christendome (parallel to Rome and Italy) is as much as the First cut, and all the Loafe besides. **1732** FULLER no. 4526.

First degree of folly, The | is to hold one's self wise, the second to profess it, the third to despise counsel. *Cf.* First chapter of fools, etc. (D 193)

1598 BARCKLEY *Fel. Man* IV. 362 Patrarke saith, To beleeve that thou art wise, is the first degree to foolishnesse: the next is to professe it. **1640** HERBERT no. 460.

First deserve, and then desire. (D 208)

a. **1575** J. PILKINGTON *Nehemiah* P.S. 447 Deserve, and then desire. **1622** ELIZ. WATSON OF YORK (J. Evans *English Posies* 1931, xxv) Desire & Deserve. **1636** CAMDEN 296.

First dish is aye best eaten, The.

1721 KELLY 336.

First dish pleases all, The. (D 367)

1640 HERBERT no. 744. **1732** FULLER no. 4527.

First glass for thirst, The | the second for nourishment, the third for pleasure, and the fourth for madness.

1586 GUAZZO ii. 152 A certaine wise man was wont to saie: That the first cup of Wine was of thirst: The second of merrinesse: The third of temptation: The fourth of foolishnesse. **1621** BURTON *Anat. Mel.* Democr. to Rdr. (1651) 44 The first pot quencheth thirst. . . secunda Gratiis, Horis, et Dionysis—the second makes merry: the third for pleasure: quarta ad insaniam, the fourth makes them mad.

First impressions are half the battle (most lasting).

1700 CONGREVE *Way of the World* iv. 1 There is a great deal in the first impression. **1759** FRANKLIN *Wks.* (1840) iii. 407 First impressions given him . . . to our disadvantage. **1843–4** DICKENS *M. Chuz.* ch. 5 First impressions, you know, often go a long way, and last a long time.

First learn, What we | we best can.

1721 KELLY 340.

First of April, On the | hunt the gowk another mile.

1846 DENHAM 41. [April gowk = April fool.]

First of April, On the | you may send a fool (gowk[1]) whither you will.

1732 FULLER no. 6135. **1869** HAZLITT 304 On the first of Aperill, you may send a gowk[1] whither you will. [1 *i.e.* a fool.]

First of March, On the | the crows begin to search.

1846 DENHAM 39 . . . Crows are supposed to begin pairing on this day.

First of July, If the | it be rainy weather, 'twill rain more or less for four weeks together.

1732 FULLER no. 6467.

First of November, On the | if the weather holds clear, an end of wheat-sowing do make for this year. (F 296)

1573 TUSSER 90 (1878) 181 Seede cake. Wife, some time this weeke, if the wether hold cleere, an end of wheat sowing we make for this yeare. **1846** DENHAM 61.

First pig, but the last whelp (puppy) of the litter, is the best, The. (P 300)

1659 HOWELL *Ital. Prov.* 2 The first pig, the last puppy is best. **1678** RAY 53 Primo porco, ultimo cane. i.e. The first pig, but the last whelp of the litter is the best. **1732** FULLER no. 4530.

First think, and then speak. (T 219)

1557 EDGEWORTH *Sermons Repertory* A6ᵛ Thinke well and thou shalt speake well. **1597** *Politeuphuia* 148 Wise men think more then they speake. **1600-1** SHAKES. *H.* I. iii. 59 Give thy thoughts no tongue, Nor any unproportion'd thought his act. **1609** HARWARD 103ᵛ Meditate before thou speak. **1616** DRAXE no. 2045 (A man must). **1623** PAINTER B1ᵛ Thinke twise, then speak, the old Prouerbe doth say. *a.* **1628** CARMICHAELL no. 543 (and last fulfill). **1639** CLARKE 133.

First thrive and then wive. (T 264)

1577 N. BRETON *Works of a Young Wit* (Poems ed. J. Robertson 65) And now I thinke thou seest, how I beginne to thryue, and thryuing now you may suspecte, that I would seeke to wyue. [1598] **1616** HAUGHTON *Englishmen for my Money* l. 1940 Will you be wiu'de? first . . . Learne to be thriftie. **1594-8** SHAKES. *T.S.* I. ii. 55 And I have thrust myself into this maze, Haply to wive and thrive as best I may. **1608** *Id. P.* V. ii. 9 So he thriv'd That he is promis'd to be wiv'd To fair Marina. **1639** CLARKE 230.

First try and then trust. *Cf.* Try your friend before you trust him. (T 595)

1448 FASTOLF Paper 43 Neuer trust ontryed qᵈ Spirlyng. **1639** CLARKE 305.

First up, last down.

1602 WITHALS 21 . . . as we commonly say, goe to bed with the Lambe, and rise with the Larke: as some interpret, downe with the first, and vp with the last.

First wife is matrimony, the second company, the third heresy, The. (W 350)

1569 HOWELL *Span. Prov.* 1.

First word of flyting,[1] You have got the.

1721 KELLY 374 . . . Spoken to them that blame us lest we should blame them. [¹ scolding.]

First word stand, Let the.

1599 PORTER *Angry Wom. Abingd.* Mal. Soc. l. 1053 Shall we be merry? and we shall, say but we shall, and let the first word stand.

First, *see also* Best go f.; Better be f. in a village; Call her whore (scold, thief) f.; Comes f. to the hill may sit where he will; Dash, (At f.); Let your house to your enemy (F. year); Love like the f. love, (No); Rises f. is f. dressed. *See also under significant words following 'First'.*

Fish (fair, well) and catch a frog, To. *Cf.* Fond fisher that angles for frog.

(F 767)

1530 PALSGRAVE 602a I have layde for a pickrell, but I wene I shall catche a frogge. **1546** HEY-WOOD I. xi. D2ᵛ But now he hath well fisht and caught a frog. *a.* **1555** LATIMER in FOXE *A. & M.* (1684) III. 413 Well, I have fished and caught a frog; brought little to pass with much ado. **1565** J. CALFHILL *Treatise of the Cross* P.S. 210 Have they not fair fished, think you, to make such ado to bring in the Devil? **1605** CHAPMAN, JONSON, MARSTON *Eastw. Ho* IV. i (1889) 474 Your ladyship hath 'fished fair, and caught a frog' as the saying is. **1678** RAY 245.

Fish begins to stink at the head.

(F 304)

[Gk. Ἰχθὺς ἐκ τῆς κεφαλῆς ὄζειν ἄρχεται. ERASM. gives as vulgar proverb *Piscis primum a capite foetet.*] **1581** GUAZZO ii. 102. **1585** J. PRIME *Sermon at St. Mary's* B2 If the eie be sound, the fish is sweet. **1611** COTGRAVE s.v. Poisson The head of a fish is euer tainted first.

Fish do (to) the water, To love (take to) it as well as (no more than). (F 327)

1576 GUAZZO i. 19 And love solitarinesse so wel, as fishes doe the water. **1602** SHAKES. *A.W.* III. vi. 76 I love not many words.—No more than a fish loves water. *a.* **1894** J. A. FROUDE *Autobiog.* (Dunn) 27 I . . . took to it [Greek] as a fish takes to the water.

Fish follow the bait. (F 306)

1598-9 SHAKES. *M.A.* II. iii. 100 Bait the hook well! This fish will bite. **1631** JONSON *Staple News* III. ii. 121 Baites, Sir, for the people! And they will bite like fishes. **1640** HERBERT no. 607 (adores). **1670** RAY 9.

Fish for a herring and catch a sprat, To. (H 450)

1639 CLARKE 2. **1670** RAY 180. **1732** FULLER no. 5165 (with a herring).

Fish in the sea as ever came out of it, There are as good. *Cf.* Sea has fish for every man.

Cf. c. **1573** G. HARVEY *Lett. Bk.* 126. **1816** T. L. PEACOCK *Headlong Hall* ch. 14 There never was a fish taken out of the sea, but left another as good behind. **1822** SCOTT *Nigel* ch. 35. **1881** GILBERT *Patience* (Dragoons' chorus) There's fish in the sea, no doubt of it, As good as ever came out of it. **1905** HOUSMAN ed. *Juvenalis Saturae* Pref. xxi But there are as bad fish in the sea as ever came out of it.

Fish is cast away that is cast in dry pools. (F 307)

c. **1374** CHAUCER *Troilus*, Bk. 4, l. 765 How sholde a fissh withouten water dure? *c.* **1390** LANGLAND *P. Pl.* C. vi. 149 Right as fishes in flood . . . whanne hem faileth water, Deyen for drouthe whenne thei drye liggen. *c.* **1549** HEY-WOOD I. xi. D3ᵛ. **1605** CHAPMAN, JONSON, MARSTON *Eastw. Ho* v. ii. 70. **1670** RAY 90 Fishes are cast away, that are cast into dry ponds.

Fish is caught, When the | the net is laid aside. (F 330)

1615 T. ADAMS *Serm.* (1861–2) II. 112 On a sudden, these 'sons of thunder' are as mute as fishes. What is the matter? . . . Oh, sir, they have the promotion already. You may perceive the fish is caught, by their hanging aside their nets. [1641–8] **1699** HOLLES *Mem.* 99 And now they think they have all in there own hands, the Fish is catcht, they may throw away the net.

Fish, The best (greatest) | keep (swim near) the bottom. (F 302)

c. **1566** CURIO tr. W. P. *Pasquin in a Trance* 33 Into the deepe waters, the great fishe alwayes goeth. **1616** BRETON *Cross Prov.* A3 The greatest sort of fish keep the bottome. **1639** CLARKE 212 (swim neare).

Fish mars water, and (but) flesh mends it. (F 308)

1573 SANFORD 104ᵛ. **1578** FLORIO *First F.* 29ᵛ Fish marreth the water, and flesh doth dresse it. **1629** *Bk. Mer. Rid.* Prov. no. 104 Fish marreth water, and flesh mendeth it. **1678** RAY 41 Fish spoils water, but flesh mends it.

Fish must swim thrice. (F 309)

[*a.* **1550**] **1630** *Mer. Tales Madmen Gotham* 20 in *Shakes. Jest-Bks.* iii. 25 The Priest said: in Lent, thou shouldest Most refraine from drunkennesse, and abstaine from drinke. Not so, said the fellow: for it is an old Prouerbe, that fish must swim. **1609** HARWARD 89ᵛ Fish would swimme. **1611** COTGRAVE s.v. *Poisson* We say, fish must ever swimme twice. **1638** BRAITH-WAIT *Barnabees Jrnl.* iii. With carouses I did trimme me, That my fish might swim within me. **1670** RAY 38 . . . Once in the water, a second time in the sawce, and a third time in wine in the stomach. Poisson, gorret & cochin vie en l'eau, & mort en vin. *Gall.* Fish and young swine live in water and die in wine. **1738** SWIFT *Dial.* II. E.L. 297 Tom, they say fish should swim thrice. . . . First it should swim in the sea, (do you mind me?) then it should swim in butter; and at last, sirrah, it should swim in good claret.

Fish nor flesh (nor good red herring), Neither. (F 319)

1528 TYNDALE *Obed. Chrn. Man* P.S. 299 We know not . . . whether they be fish or flesh,

for they do nought for us. **1528** *Rede me & be nott wrothe* I. iij b Wone that is nether flesshe nor fisshe. **1546** HEYWOOD I. x. C3ᵛ She is nother fishe nor fleshe, nor good red hearyng. **1597** SHAKES. *1 Hen. IV* III. iii. 128 Why? she's neither fish nor flesh; a man knows not where to have her. **1600** HOLLAND *Livy* xxiv, xlv (1609) 540 He had the party himselfe in jelousie and suspition, as one neither fish nor flesh, a man of no credit. **1682** DRYDEN *Dk. Guise* Ep., Poems O.U.P. 247 Damn'd Neuters, in their middle way of steering, Are neither Fish nor Flesh nor good Red-Herring. **1816** SCOTT *Old Mort.* ch. 30 Langcale cannot be suitably or preceesely termed either fish, flesh, or gude red herring; whoever has the stronger party has Langcale. **1902** DEAN HOLE *Then & Now* (7 ed.) ch. 6 Behold an hermaphrodite, neither 'fish, flesh, fowl, nor good red herring', the demolition of a woman, the caricature of a man, ridiculed as 'our friend from Middle Sex'.

Fish of one and flesh (fowl) of another, To make. (F 314)

[to make an invidious distinction; to show partiality.] **1639** CLARKE 182 I will not make flesh of one and fish of the other. **1670** RAY 9 (I'll not). **1725** DEFOE *Everybody's Business* Wks. Bohn II. 510 The complaints alleged against the maids are . . . very applicable to our gentlemen's gentlemen; I would, therefore, have them under the very same regulations, and . . . would not make fish of one and flesh of the other. **1885** *Manch. Exam.* 21 May 5/2 This is making fish of one and fowl of another with a vengeance.

Fish on one's fingers, To find. (F 326)

1583 GREENE *Wks.* Gros. II. 85 Pharicles . . . found fish on his fingers, that he might be the last should take his leave of Publia. **1590** LODGE *Rosalynde* 122 Hunt, Cl. Ganimede rose as one that would suffer no fish to hang on his fingers.

Fish out of water, Like a. (F 318)

[attrib. to St. Athanasius: not later than A.D. 373. *See* SKEAT *Early Eng. Prov.* 89.] *c.* **1374** CHAUCER *Troilus* Bk. 4, l. 765 How sholde a fissh withouten water dure? *c.* **1386** *Id. Prol.* l. 180 Ne that a Monk whan he is reccheless Is likned til a fissh that is waterlees. *c.* **1390** LANGLAND *P. Pl.* C. vi. 149–50 Right as fishes in flod whanne hem faileth water, Deyen for drouth whenne thei drye liggen. **1613** PURCHAS *Pilgrimage* VI. xii. 636 The Arabians out of the desarts are as Fishes out of the Water. **1655–62** GURNALL *Chrn. in Armour* (1865) I. 215 A tradesman out of his shop . . . is as a fish out of the water, never in his element till he be in his calling again. **1851** KINGSLEY *Yeast* ch. 11 A navvy drops into a church by accident, and there he has to sit like . . . **1876** BURNABY *Ride to Khiva* ch. 2 A diplomatist in a land where he cannot read the newspapers or converse with all classes of society . . . is rather like a fish out of water. **1913** 1 Feb. D. H. LAWRENCE *Lett.* i. 184 (Gaping . . .).

Fish that comes to net, All is. (A 136)

c. **1520** in *Ballads from MSS.* B.S. i. 95 Alle ys ffysshe that commyth to the nett. **1523** LD. BERNERS *Froiss.* I. ccccxvi. 727 Such as came after toke all . . . for all was fysshe that came to net. **1578** BULLEIN *Dial. agst. Fever* (1888) 90

Taking up every commodity, refusing nothing: all is fish that cometh to the net. **1680** BUNYAN *Mr. Badman* i. Wks. (1855) III. 598 What was his father's could not escape his fingers, all was fish that came to his net. **1826** LAMB to J. B. Dibdin, 14 July All jests were fish that to his net came.

Fish that will not some time or other bite, It is rare to find a.

1732 FULLER no. 5114.

Fish to fry, I have other.   (F 313)

1603 S. HARSNET *Decl. of egreglous popish impostures* N3 I haue other Cod-fish in water, that must not be forgotten. **1660** EVELYN *Mem.* (1857) III. 132 I fear he hath other fish to fry. **1710–11** SWIFT *Jrnl. to Stella* 8 Feb. I have other fish to fry; so good morrow my ladies all. **1889** MRS. OLIPHANT *Poor Gent.* ch. 44 I've got other things in hand ... I've got other fish to fry.

Fish will soon be caught that nibbles at every bait, That.   (F 324)

1580 LYLY *Euph. & his Eng.* ii. 104 Philautus, who euer as yet but played with the bait, was now stroke with the hooke. [c. 1612] **1633** P. FLETCHER *Pisc. Eclog.* V : *Poems*, ii. 287 The fish long playing with the baited hook, At last is caught: thus many nymph is took. **1616** DRAXE no. 1854 The fish playeth so long with the hooke, vntill she be caught. **1660** W. SECKER *Nonsuch Prof.* II (1891) 241 If you ... be found nibbling at the bait, you may justly expect the hook to enter into your bowels! **1732** FULLER no. 4342.

Fish with a cross-bow, It is no sure rule to.   (R 204)

1640 HERBERT no. 293.

Fisherman's walk: A | three steps and overboard.

1836 M. SCOTT *T. Cringle's Log* ch. 1. **1853** G. J. WHYTE-MELVILLE *Digby Grand* ch. 2. **1896** F. LOCKER-LAMPSON *My Confid.* 77 The riverpilots ... at anchor, taking a fisherman's constitutional ('three steps and overboard').

Fishes that catches one, Still he.   (O 59)

1592 DELAMOTHE 53 Still fisheth he that catcheth one. **1611** COTGRAVE S.V. Pescher And yet he fishes who catches one. **1639** CLARKE 294. **1670** RAY 91 ... Tousjours pesche qui en prend un. *Gall.*

Fish(es) (noun), *see also* Affairs, like salt f., ought to be a good while a-soaking; Better are small f. than empty dish; Cast your net where no f. (Vain to); Cat would eat f.; Catching f. not whole of fishing; Corn is in shock (When), f. are on rock; Courts (It is at) as in ponds, some f.; Daughter and eat fresh f., (Marry your); Drink like a f.; Drunk as a f.; Fools lade water, but wise men catch f.; Fresh f. and new-come guests; Fresh f. and poor friends; Good f. if it were caught; Gravest f. is oyster; Great f. eat up small; Great river great f. (In a); Gut no f. till

you get; Had I f. is good without mustard; Had I f. never good with garlic; Herring is king (Of all f. in sea); Kettle of f.; Little f. are sweet; Little f. slip through nets; Loaves and f.; Mute as f.; News are like f.; No man cries stinking f.; Old f. and young flesh; Old f., old oil, old friend; Raw pulleyn ... and f. make churchyards fat; Sea has f. for every man; Silly f. caught twice; Swear (If you) you'll catch no f.; Swim like a f.; Taken by a morsel, says the f.; Unsonsy f. gets unlucky bait; Venture a small f. to catch great one; Wind is south (When) ... bait into f.'s mouth. Wind is west (When) f. bite best. *See also* Salt fish.

Fish (*verb*), *see also* Angle (F.) with golden hook.

Fisher, *see* Fond f. that angles for frog; March whisker never good f.; Mock no pannier men; Wind's in north (When), f. goes not forth.

Fisher's folly, *see* Kirkbie's castle.

Fish-guts, *see* Keep your ain f.

Fish-hooks, *see* Sailors' fingers all f. h.

Fishing before the net, It is ill.   (N 127)

c. **1410** *Towneley Plays* E.E.T.S. 104 Ye fysh before the net. *c.* **1480** HENRYSON *Wks.* S.T.S. II. 130, l. 1755 The Lark ... said, 'Scho fischit lang befoir the Net.' **1546** HEYWOOD I. xi. E1. **1641** FERGUSSON no. 379 He that fishes afore the net, lang or he fish get. **1721** KELLY 148 He that fishes before the Net, long e'er he Fish get. Spoken to those who devour by Expectation, what they have not in Possession, for the Fish are not gotten till the Net be drawn ashore.

Fishing in troubled waters, It is good.   (F 334)

[PETER OF BLOIS (Migne) 154 *Vulgo enim dicitur, Aqua turbida piscosior est.* MAP *De Cur. Nug.* (Camden Soc.) 242 *In aqua turbida piscantur uberius.*] **1568** GRAFTON *Chron.* II. 102 Their persuasions whiche alwayes desyre your unquietnesse, wherby they may the better fishe in the water when it is troubled. *c.* **1580** SIDNEY *First Arcadia* (Feuillerat) 242 The waters beeying as the Proverb saythe trubled and so the better for his fisshing. **1595** DANIEL *Civ. Wars* i. st. 82 They thought best fishing still in troubled streams. **1611** COTGRAVE S.V. Trouble. **1612–15** BP. HALL *Contempl.* XVIII. i (1825) I. 548 Jeroboam had secretly troubled these waters, that he might fish more gainfully. **1624** T. HEYWOOD *The Captives* l. 1656. **1641** FERGUSSON no. 521 It is góod fishing in drumling[1] waters. **1670** RAY 90. **1682** DRYDEN *Abs. & Achit.* II. 314 Who Rich and Great by past Rebellions grew, and long to fish the troubled Waves anew. **1722** SEWEL *Hist. Quakers* (1795) I. iv. 276 You delight to fish in troubled waters. **1902** A. LANG *Hist. Scot.* II. 335 Arran had been trying to fish in the troubled waters. [1 turbid, muddy.]

Fishing, The end of | is not angling, but catching.   (E 113)

1580 LYLY *Euph. & his Eng.* ii. 159. **1732** FULLER no. 4497. **1910** *Spectator* 5 Nov. 723 Mr.

Sheringham recognizes that the business of fishing is to catch fish if possible.

Fishing to fishing in the sea, No.
(F 336)

1575 CHURCHYARD *Chippes* 41 (Collier) Some say there is no fishing to the seas.   **1577** PEACHAM *Garden of Eloquence* (1593) 87 I haue heard my father say, and eke my mother sing, There is no fishing to the sea, nor service to the King.   *c.* **1580** HARVEY *Marginalia* (1913) 142 No fisshing to the Sea, nor service to A King.   **1591** LYLY i. 428 [as Harvey].   *c.* **1591** GREENE *James IV* i. ii. 436 [as Harvey].   **1602** BRETON *Wonders w. Hearing* Wks. Gros. II. 9 Oh sir, nothing venture nothing have, there is no fishing to the sea, the gain of one voyage will bear the loss of many.   **1625** PURCHAS *Pilgrims* (1905–7) XIX. 251 I am none of Neptune's secretaries; yet know this, that there is no fishing to the sea, and no country so strong by sea as that which findeth most employment in this kind.   **1659** HOWELL *Eng. Prov.* 18b There is no fishing to the Sea, nor service to the Kings.   **1670** RAY 90 . . . Il fait beau pescher en eau large. *Gall.* It's good fishing in large waters.

Fishing, see also Deepest water best f.

Fishing-rod has a fool at one end and a fish at the other, A.

1819 L. HUNT in *The Indicator*, 17 Nov. *Angling* The good old joke . . . that angling is . . . 'a stick and a string, with a fly at one end and a fool at the other'.

Fish-pool, see Poole was a f., (If).

Fist, see Fool that makes a wedge of f.; God by the toe, (When they think they have), they have the devil by the f.; Grease a man in the f.

Fit (fine) as a fiddle, As.
(F 202)

1596 NASHE iii. 113 As right as a fiddle.   [**1598**] **1616** HAUGHTON *Eng. for my Money* IV. i. This is excellent, i' faith; as fit as a fiddle.   **1603** *Batchelor's Banquet* (ed. Wilson) 28 As fine as a farthing fiddle.   **1882** MISS BRADDON *Mt. Royal* III. xi. 253 'Is Salathiel pretty fresh?' asked the Baron. 'Fit as a fiddle.' See also, for a discussion of this proverb, *N. & Q.,* vol. 192, no. 8, 159.

Fit(s, ted) (verb), see All things f. not all persons; Cap f. (If the) wear it; Suit is best that best f.; Well f. abide (Things).

Fitting, see God complains not, but does what is f.; Suffered to do more than is f. (He that is) will do more than is lawful.

Five pound note, There never was a | but there was a ten pound road for it.

1862 HISLOP 287 There ne'er was a five pound note but there was a ten pound road for't. Such was the reply of a lady . . . when asked what she did with all the money she got.

Five, see Fetch the f. pounds? (When do you); Follow him long ere f. shillings fall from him; Four and spends f., (He that has but) has no need of a purse.

Fivepence, see Fine as f.

Flag protects the cargo, The.

1902–4 LEAN IV. 122 The flag protects the cargo. —(Sea.) Le pavillon couvre la marchandise.

Flag, see also Trade follows f.

Flail(s), see Fence against a f. (No); November take f.; Three f. and cuckoo; Thresher take f.

Flame, see Fuel (Take away), take away f.

Flaming figure (Fair show) in a country church, It will make a.
(S 409)

1670 RAY 192 (fair show).   **1721** KELLY 207 It will make a bra[1] show, in a Landward[2] Kirk. A Jest upon a Girl when we see her fond of a new Suit.   **1738** SWIFT *Dial.* II. E.L. 296 Your ladyship has a very fine scarf.—Yes, my lord; it will make a flaming figure in a country church. [[1] braw, fine. [2] country.]

Flanagan, see Fire away, F.!

Flanders mares, fairest afar off, Like.

1717 *Six N. Count. Dairies* Surtees Soc. 82 Uncle told me now we are to see yon damsel of Mr. Collingwood's. She's like a Flanders mare.   **1732** FULLER no. 3229.

Flap with a foxtail, He gave him a.
(F 344)

c. **1530** TYNDALE *Expos. Matt.* P.S. 127 They either look through the fingers, or else give thee a flap with a fox-tail for little money.   **1530** PALSGRAVE 563a I flatter hym to begyle him, or I gyve one a slappe with a foxe tayle.   **1553** T. WILSON *Arte of Rhet.* (1909) 37 So that he gaineth alwaies, . . . whereas the other get . . . a flappe with a Foxe taile.   **1602** *Thos. Lord Cromwell* IV. ii. 33 *Shakes. Apoc.* 181 I, we shall haue now three flappes with a Foxe taile.   **1633** JONSON *T. Tub.* II. iv. 33 But a man may breake His heart out i' these dayes, and get a flap With a fox-taile, when he has done.   **1670** RAY 176 . . . That is, to cozen or defraud.   **1808** SCOTT *Let.* 19 Nov. in LOCKHART *Life* ch. 18 (1860) 172 I owe Jeffrey a flap with a fox-tail on account of his review of Marmion.

Flat, That is.
(F 345)

[(*a*) formerly = that's the undeniable truth; (*b*) a defiant expression of one's determination.] **1576** *Common Conditions* C2 I can do it, this is plaine and flat.   **1577** BEZA *Abraham's Sacrifice* tr. A. Golding Prol. But yit you must, or else I tell you flat, That both of vs our labour lose togither.   [*c.* **1587**] **1592** KYD *Span. Trag.* III. vi. 47 Hang-man, nowe I spy your knauery, Ile not change without boot, that flat.   [*c.* **1590**] **1592** *Soliman and Perseda* II. ii. 75 I must haue a bout with you, sir, thats flat.   [*c.* **1590**] **1598** *Famous Vict. of Hen. V.* D4ᵛ Ile clap the law on your

backe, thats flat. *a.* 1594 PEELE *David & Bethsabe*
l. 569 I will not goe home sir, thats flat. **1594–5**
SHAKES. *L.L.L.* III. i. 95 The boy hath sold him
a bargain, a goose, that's flat. *a.* 1595 PEELE
Old Wives Tale l. 897 Ile serve you, that is flat.
1597–8 SHAKES. *I Hen. IV* I. iii. 218 Nay, I will;
that's flat. *Ibid.* IV. ii. 43 I'll not march through
Coventry with them, that's flat. **1665** *Surv.
Aff. Netherl.* 120 Its the greatest Bogg of Europe
. . . that's flat. **1716** ADDISON *Drummer* I. i. I'll
give Madam warning, that's flat. **1852** SMEDLEY
L. Arundel i. 15 'I won't then, that's flat', exclaimed Rachel.

Flat as a flounder, As.   (F 382)

1611 COTGRAVE s.v. Nez A nose as flat as a Flooke
(say we). *c.* 1625 BEAUM. & FL. *Women pleased*
II. iv. **1659** HOWELL *Eng. Prov.* 5a. **1720** GAY
New Similes Flat as a flounder when I lie.

Flat as a pancake, As.   (P 39)

1542 ERASM. tr. Udall *Apoph.* (1877) 250 His
nose as flat as a cake, bruised or beaten to his
face. **1571** J. BRIDGES *Sermon at Paul's Cross*
125. **1599** PORTER *Angry Wom. Abingd.* Mal. Soc.
l. 1080 And makes him sit at table Pancake
wise, Flat, flat. **1836** LEIGH HUNT *Visit to
Zoolog. G.* in *New Month. Mag.* Aug. One tread
of his foot would have smashed the little per-
tinacious wretch as flat as a pancake.

Flatter, *see* Contented who needs neither borrow
nor f.

Flatterer as a man's self, There is no such.

1612 BACON Essay 'Of Love' It hath beene well
said [by Plutarch], that the Arch-flatterer with
whom al the petty-flatterers have intelligence, is
a Mans selfe. **1732** FULLER no. 4922.

Flatterer's throat is an open sepulchre, A.   ₍F 346)

1640 HERBERT no. 588.

Flatterer, *see also* Beasts, The most deadly of
wild is a backbiter (tyrant), of tame ones a f.;
Foe to a f. (No); Friend and your f. (I cannot be).

Flattering as a spaniel. *Cf.* Fawn like a spaniel.   (S 704)

1585 GREENE *Wks.* Gros. v. 103 Like Spanyels
flattering with their tayles. **1599** SHAKES. *J.C.*
III. i. 42 That which melteth fools—I mean,
sweet words, Low-crooked curtsies, and base
spaniel fawning. **1606–7** *Id. A.C.* IV. xii. 20
The hearts That spaniel'd me at heels . . . do
discandy. **1613** *Id. Hen. VIII* V. iii. 126 You
play the spaniel And think with wagging of your
tongue to win me. **1616** WITHALS 553. **1639**
CLARKE 285. **1670** RAY 204. **1748** SMOLLETT
Rod. Random ch. 45 As supple as a spaniel.

Flattery, *see* Imitation is sincerest f.

Flavour, *see* Nothing has no f.

Flax from fire and youth from gaming, Keep.   (F 351)

1600 SHAKES. *M.W.W.* III. i. 37 Keep a gamester
from the dice and a good student from his book,
and it is wonderful. **1642** TORRIANO 70. **1659**
HOWELL *It. Prov.* 12. **1666** TORRIANO *It. Prov.*
271, no. 1.

Flax, *see* Fire cannot be hidden in f.; Fire to f.
(Put not); Leisure, as f. grows, (At); Spindle and
distaff ready, God will send f.; Woman is f.

Flay a louse for its skin (flea for the hide and tallow), To.   (L 473)

1591 FLORIO *Second F.* 117 He was such a
couetous miser, that he would haue fleade a
louse to saue the skin of it. **1659** WODROEPHE
285 He would haue flayed a Louse for her skin,
he was so couetous. **1623** HOWELL *It. Prov.* 16
He would flay a louse to sell the skin. **1820**
SCOTT *Abbot* ch. 19 The falconer observed, that
. . . it had got harder and harder . . . to the poor
gentlemen and yeoman retainers, but that now it
was an absolute flaying of a flea for the hide and
tallow. **1837** CHAMIER *Saucy Areth.* ch. 21
'Well', said the boatman, as he looked at the
money, '. . . you would skin a flea for its hide
and tallow!'

Flay (Skin) a flint (groat), To.   (F 373)

[= to act meanly in order to get or save money.]
1640 HERBERT no. 764 You cannot flea[1] a stone.
1659 *Burton's Diary* (1828) IV. 398 Some of them
were so strict that they would flea a flint. **1678**
RAY 245 He would flay a flint, or flay a groat,
spoken of a covetous person. **1884** BESANT
Childr. Gibeon II. xxxi. Just as the toper squeezes
the empty bottle and the miser skins the flint.
[1 flay.]

Flay, *see also* No man can f. a stone.

Flea, a fly, and a flitch of bacon, A.

1902–4 LEAN (*York*) I. 219 (Arms of the County.)
A flea, a fly, and a flitch of bacon. The flea will
suck any one's blood; the fly drink out of any
one's cup; and the bacon is no good till it is
hung.

Flea in March, If you kill one | you kill a hundred.

1902–4 LEAN III. 512.

Flea in one's ear, A.   (F 354)

[= a stinging reproof, which sends one away dis-
comfited. Fr. *avoir la puce en l'oreille*, in the
sense of being tormented by the desires and cares
of love, occurs in *a.* 1465 CHARLES D'ORLÉANS
Chanson I and in 1546 RABELAIS III. vii.] *c.* 1430
Pilgr. Lyf. Manhode (1869) II. xxxix. 91 And
manye oothere grete wundres . . . whiche ben
fleen in myne eres. **1546** HEYWOOD I. xi. D3ᵛ
He standth now as he had a flea in his eare.
1577 tr. *De L'Isles Legendarie* B vj 6 Sending
them away with fleas in their eares, vtterly disappointed of their purpose. *a.* 1625 BEAUM. &
FL. *Love's Cure* III. iii. He went away with a flea
in 's ear, Like a poor cur. **1712** ARBUTHNOT

John Bull III. vi. We being stronger than they, sent them away with a flea in their ear. **1887** RIDER HAGGARD *Jess* ch. 13 I sent him off with a flea in his ear, I can tell you.

Flea (Fly) stick in the wall, Let that.

1757 SMOLLETT *Reprisal* II. iii. Let that flie stick i' the wa'—when the dirt's dry it will rub out. **1818** SCOTT *Rob Roy* ch. 23 'It will be a shame . . . to me and mine, . . . for ever.' 'Hout tout, man! let that flee stick in the wa', answered his kinsman; 'when the dirt's dry it will rub out.' **1824** MOIR *Mansie W.* ch. 26. **1866** READE *G. Gaunt* ch. 16.

Flea(s), *see also* Dog that is idle barks at f., hunting feels not; Flay a f. for hide and tallow; Lies down with dogs, rise with f.; Nothing must be done hastily but killing f.

Flea-bitten horse never tires, A.

(H 640)

1577 *Heresbach's Husb.* (1586) ii. 116b The fleabitten horse prooveth alwaies good in travell. **1614** JONSON *Barthol. Fair* IV. iv. 16 Why, well said, old Flea-bitten; thou'l't neuer tyre, I see.

Flee never so fast you cannot flee your fortune.

1721 KELLY 108 . . . Spoken by them who believe that all Things come by Fatality.

Flee, *see also* Nought is to wed with (Where) . . . f. the clog.

Fleece and fell, To have both. *Cf.* Good shepherd must fleece his sheep, etc.

(F 357)

1639 CLARKE 39 Will you have both fleece and fell?

Fleech(s), *see* Better f. a fool than fight him; Every hand f. (Where), sheep go naked.

Fleet, *see* Whet his knife on . . . the F.

Flemings, *see* Shoulder of mutton and English beer make F. tarry.

Flesh is aye fairest that is farthest from the bone, The. [*But cf.* Nearer the bone the sweeter the flesh.]

a. **1628** CARMICHAELL no. 1585 They are ay fair that is far fra the bane. **1721** KELLY 325 . . . Spoken to them who are plump and look well.

Flesh, All | is not venison.

(F 360)

1592 DELAMOTHE 55. **1651** HERBERT no. 1096. **1659** HOWELL *Fr. Prov.* 10 . . . Venison nor Feasant. **1670** RAY 91.

Flesh and blood as others are, To be.

(F 367)

1541 BULLINGER *Christian State of Matrimony* tr. Coverdale (1543 ed., F6ᵛ) Thou wilt saye:

Halas we are but flesh and bloud. I aunswere: Were not our fore fathers flesh and bloud also? *c.* **1564** *Bugbears* I. i. 18 You are master, I am servant, but else of flesh and bone I ame as well made as you. **1565** OSORIUS *Pearl for a Prince* tr. R. Shacklock 38 They so speake . . . as though they were not made of fleshe and bone as other men be. **1584** LYLY *Camp.* II. ii. 68 Though she haue heauenly giftes, vertue and bewtie, is she not of earthly mettall, flesh and bloud? **1593–4** SHAKES. *T.S.* Ind. ii. 125 I will therefore tarry in despite of the flesh and the blood. **1598–9** *Id. M.A.* V. i. 34 I will be flesh and blood. [**1599**] **1600** MUNDAY *et al. Oldcastle* IV. i. 165 I confesse I am a frayle man, flesh and bloud as other are. **1599** SHAKES. *J.C.* III. i. 67 Men are flesh and blood. **1600** T. HEYWOOD *et al.* 2 *Edw. IV* i. 127 You are flesh and blood as we, and we as you. **1601** SHAKES. *T.N.* V. i. 28 Put your grace in your pocket, sir, for this once, and let your flesh and blood obey it. **1666** TORRIANO *Prov. Phr.* s.v. Mano 98a To be made no better than other folks, to be flesh and bloud as others are. **1920** M. BEERBOHM *And Even Now* 201 Goethe . . . was not made of marble. He started with all the disadvantages of flesh and blood, and retained them to the last.

Flesh is frail.

(F 363)

[MATT. xxvi. 41: The flesh is weak.] *c.* **1390** GOWER *Confessio Amantis* VIII. 289 The fleisch is frele and falleth ofte. **1565** J. HALL *Court of Virtue* O7ᵛ My flesh is fraile, and shakes for feare. *c.* **1594** MUNDAY *John a Kent* l. 1057 Sometimes ye knowe fleshe and bloode will be frayle. **1597** SHAKES. *I Hen. IV* III. iii. 167 I have more flesh than another man, and therefore more frailty. **1613** *Id. Hen. VIII* V. iii. 10 We all are men, In our own natures frail and capable Of our flesh.

Flesh stands never so high but a dog will venture his legs.

(F 364)

1678 RAY 139.   **1732** FULLER no. 1553.

Flesh, *see also* Fat drops from fat f.; Fish mars water, f. mends it; Fish nor f. (Neither); Fish of one and f. of another (Make); Ill f. ne'er made good broo; Never ate f. thinks pudding dainty; Old fish and young f.; Spirit is willing, f. weak; Take away the salt, throw f. to dogs; Way of all f.; World, the f., and the devil.

Fletcher, *see* Like than Jack f. and his bolt (No more); Mends as the f. mends bolt.

Flies haunt (go to) lean horses.

(F 401)

1573 SANFORD 101ᵛ (go to). **1592** DELAMOTHE 35 (as 1573). **1611** DAVIES no. 45 (haunt). **1640** HERBERT no. 73 (are busiest about).

Flies, You hunt after.

(F 405)

c. **1516** J. SKELTON *Magnificence* l. 503 We haue made Magnyfycence to ete a flye. *c.* **1558** J. BALE *K. Johan* (B text) l. 2396 Vsurped power may goo a birdynge for flies. **1591** *True History of Civil Wars of France* 419 Sixtus . . . hunting flies ouer their heads, blessed them. **1595** V. *Saviolo his Practice* B [Men must not] catch (as

they saie) at euerie flie that passeth by. **1659**
HOWELL *Fr. Prov.* 18 . . . You trifle away time.

Fling at the brod[1] was ne'er a good ox.

1721 KELLY 107 . . . Taken from a drawing Ox,
who kicks when he is prick'd by the Goad.
Apply'd to them who spurn at Reproof. [[1] goad.]

Fling, (*noun*), *see also* After your f. watch for
sting; England were but a f.

Fling, (*verb*), *see* Handkerchief (F.).

Flint (blade) on a feather bed, To break a.   (F 372)

1579 LYLY *Euph.* i. 193 Is it not common . . .
That the softe fetherbed breketh the hard blade?
1596 SHAKES. *M.V.* II. ii. 150 To be in peril of my
life with the edge of a feather-bed.   **1607** DEKKER
& WEBSTER *North. Ho* II. D2ᵛ I have known as
tough blades as any are in England broke upon a
feather bed.   **1666** TORRIANO *It. Prov.* 32, no. 35
As they say, a mud-wall deads a Canon-bullet,
and no way to break a flint-stone so well, as on
a feather-bed, Humility overcomes Pride.

Flint, *see* Coldest f. there is fire (In); Flay a f.;
Hard as a f.; Set one's face like a f.; Water from
a f.

Flitch of bacon from Dunmow, He may fetch a.   (F 375)

1362 LANGLAND *P. Pl.* ix. 5515 (Wright) I. 169
And though thei do hem to Dunmowe, But if the
devel me helpe, To folwen after the flicche, Fecche
thei it nevere.   *c.* **1386** CHAUCER *W. of Bath's
Prol.* l. 217 The bacoun was nat fet for hem, I
trowe, That som men han in Essexe at Dunmowe.
1662 FULLER *Essex* 321 This proverb dependeth
on a custome practiced in the Priory of Dunmow.
. . . Any person . . . might demand . . . a Gammon
or Flitch of Bacon, upon the solemn taking of the
ensuing oath [that husband and wife had not
quarrelled since marriage].   **1708** PRIOR *Turtle
& Sparrow* 233 Few married folk peck Dunmow-
bacon.   **1815** 2 Feb. BYRON *Correspondence* ed.
J. Murray 1922, i. 350 She does as she likes,
and don't bore me, and we may win the Dunmow
flitch of bacon for anything I know.   **1912** *Daily
Tel.* 6 Aug. 3 Six years have been passed since the
Dunmow flitch of bacon has been bestowed on
any couple who could truthfully take oath that
neither had 'offended each other in deed or word,
Or in a Twelvemonth and a Day repented not in
thought any way'.

Flitch, *see also* Cat eats the f.; Flea, a fly, and a f.

Flitting of farms makes mealings dear.

1721 KELLY 8 As one flits, another sits, and that
makes the Mealings [farms] dear.   **1846** DEN-
HAM 3.

Flitting(s), *see also* Fools are fain of f.; Moonlight f. (Make a); Saturday f. light sittings.

Flock follow the bell-wether, The.

                                            (F 376)
1655 FULLER *Ch. Hist.* IV. ii. (1868) I. 567 I am
little moved with what T. Walsingham writes,

(whom all later authors follow, as a flock the
bell-wether).   **1709** SWIFT in *Tatler* no. 66
Daniel can . . . grow fat by voluntary subscription, while the parson of the parish goes to law
for half his dues. Daniel will tell you, it is not
the shepherd, but the sheep with the bell, which
the flock follows.   **1896** 'H. S. MERRIMAN' *Flotsam* ch. 23 Others soon followed her ladyship,
. . . for most women are like sheep in their visits,
especially if the bell-wether carries a title.

Flock, *see also* Birds of a feather f. together;
Driving a f. than one (Better); Full f. (He who
will have); Sheep in f.; Silly f. where ewe bears
bell.

Flodden, *see* Mair tint at F.

Flog (*also* to mount on) a dead horse, To.

1770 J. WESLEY *Letters* v. 178 All is well. We
have no need to 'dispute about a dead horse'.
1879 TRENCH *Med. Ch. Hist.* [ed.] x. 145 The
passion . . . never embodied itself in the shape of
an eighth Crusade; and those who tried to
quicken it again . . . were doomed to discover the
truth . . . that it is no use to flog a dead horse.
1926 *Times* 19 July 13/6 By this time, however,
Count Metternich was flogging a dead horse.

Flog (a person) within an inch of his life, To.

1854 B. P. SHILLABER *Life and Sayings of Mrs.
Partington* 81 I'll be tempered to whip you
within an inch of your skin.   **1872** C. READE
Wand. Heir ch. 5 They . . . bound Regulus to a
tree, and flogged him within an inch of his life.

Flood but there is as low an ebb, There is not so great a.   (F 380)

1509 BARCLAY *Ship of Fools* i. 128 For whyle the
Se floweth and is at Burdews hye It as fast ebbeth
at some other place.   **1616** DRAXE no. 48.

Floods have low ebbs, High.   (F 381)

1545 TAVERNER C8 The english prouerbe After
a low ebbe commeth a floode.   **1576** R. EDWARDS
Par. Dainty ₍Dev. 96 l. 30 Ded'st ebbe hath
highest flowe.   **1579** GOSSON ed. Arber 50.   *c.*
1592 NASHE *Summer's Last Will* l. 403.   **1592–
1602** W. S. *Cromwell* II. iii. 34 A mighty ebbe
followes a mighty floud.

Flood(s), *see* April f. carries away frog; Dove's f.
worth a king's good; May f. never did good;
Michaelmas Day (So many days old the moon is),
so many f.; Old as the f.; Winter's thunder and
summer's f. never boded good.

Floor, *see* Eaten your dinner off f. (Might have).

Flounder, *see* Flat as a f.

Flour, *see* Fancy may bolt bran and call it f.

Flow (ebb) has its ebb, (flow), Every.

                                            (F 378)
c. **1420** LYDGATE *Troy Bk.* II. l. 2013 After a
flowe, an ebbe folweth ay.   **1545** TAVERNER C8

The english prouerbe . . . After a lowe ebbe commeth a floode. **1576** PETTIE ii. 91 The sun being at the highest, declineth: and the sea being at full tide ebbeth. [**1587**] **1599** GREENE *Alphonsus* Prol. 69 When the surgent seas Haue ebde their fill, their waues do rise againe And fill their bankes vp to the very brimmes. **1639** CLARKE 123 A flow will have an ebbe. **1721** KELLY 97 . . . There is a time when Families, and single Persons thrive, and there is a time when they go backward.

Flowers in May, As welcome as.

(F 390)

1540 PALSGRAVE *Acolastus* 122 Howe do al thinges shewe pleasantly (as do flowres in May, or in the sprynge tyme)? **1591** FLORIO *Second F.* 55 Welcome Maie with his flowres. **1623** WODROEPHE 251. **1645** HOWELL *Lett.* 28 Apr. (1903) II. 97 Yours of the fifth of March, . . . was as welcome to me as flowers in May. **1840** DICKENS *Old C. Shop* ch. 48.

Flowers soonest fade, The fairest.

(F 391)

1573 GASCOIGNE *Flowers* i. 90 No Flower is so freshe, but frost can it deface. **1576** PETTIE ii. 2 As the freshest colours soonest fade the hue . . . so . . . the finer wit he was endued withal, the sooner was he made thrall and subject to love. *c.* **1595** SHAKES. *R.J.* IV. v. 28 Death lies on her like an untimely frost Upon the sweetest flower of all the field. **1637** MILTON *Death Fair Inf.* I. i. O Fairest flower, no sooner blown but blasted.

Flower(s), *see also* Beauty fades like a f.; Bee sucks honey out of the bitterest f.; Beetle flies over many a sweet f.; Fairest f. in his crown; Fresh as f. in May; One f. makes no garland.

Flutter the dovecotes, To.

1608 SHAKES. *C.* V. vi. 115 Like an eagle in a dove-cote, I fluttered your Volscians in Corioli. **1864** FROUDE *Short Stud. Sc. Hist.* (1867) 2 A work which . . . fluttered the dovecotes of the Imperial Academy of St. Petersburg.

Fly, Not worth a.

(F 396)

1297 R. GLOUCESTER (1724) 428 Wat was þy strengþe worþ? . . . ywys noȝt worþ a flye. *c.* **1352** LAU. MINOT *Songs K. Ed. Wars* in WRIGHT *Pol. Poems* (1859–61) I. 59 And all thaire fare noght wurth a flye. *c.* **1470** HENRYSON *Mor. Fab.*, '*Fox, Wolf. Cadg.*' (1917) 97 For he that will not laubour and help himself, . . . he is not worth ane fle.

Fly and eke a friar will fall in every dish and matter, A.

c. **1386** CHAUCER *W. of Bath's Prol.* l. 835 Lo, goode men, a flye, and eek a frere, Wol falle in every dysshe and eek mateere.

Fly, He would fain | but he wants feathers.

(F 164)

c. **1549** HEYWOOD I. xi. D3ᵛ He would fayne flee, but he wanteth fethers. **1592** DELAMOTHE 39 One can not flye, before he hath wings. **1592–4**

SHAKES. *1 Hen. VI* I. i. 75 Another would fly swift, but wanteth wings. **1611** DAVIES no. 345 Some would faine flie but feathers they want. **1670** RAY 91 . . . Sine pennis volare haud facile est. PLAUT. in *Poenulo*. Nothing of moment can be done without necessary helps, or convenient means.

Fly, If you must | fly well.

(F 406)

1640 HERBERT no. 1021.

Fly follows the honey, A.

c. **1412** HOCCLEVE *De Reg. Princ.* 110 A flye folowethe the hony. **1547** SENECA *De Remediis Fortuitorum* B4 Flyes folowe honny, wolfes carren.

Fly has her spleen, The | and the ant her gall.

(F 393)

[L. *Habet et musca splenem.* Even a fly has anger. ERASM. *Ad. Formicae inest sua bilis.*] **1580** LYLY *Euph. & his Eng.* ii. 90 The Flye his splene, the Ant hir gall. **1584** *Id. Camp.* v. iv. 130 Sparkes haue their heate, Antes their gall, Flyes their splene. **1584** R. WILSON *Three Ladies of London* Hazl.-Dods. vi. 386 Have ye not heard that the fly hath her spleen, And the ant her gall? **1590** T. LODGE *Rosalynde* ed. Greg 77. **1623** CAMDEN 265. **1662** FULLER Rutl. 349 [Jeffrey] shewed to all, that *Habet musca suum splenum*; and they must be little indeed that cannot do mischief.

Fly in amber, A.

1735 POPE *Ep. Arbuthnot* 169 Pretty! in amber to observe the forms Of hairs, or straws, or dirt, or grubs, or worms! **1778** WALPOLE *Letters* (Toynbee) x. 319 A line of yours [Mason] will preserve me like a fly in amber. **1847** BLACKWELL Mallet's *North. Antiq.* 374 Byron caught him up, and . . . preserved him, like a fly in amber, for future generations to wonder at.

Fly in the face of Providence, To.

1706 STEVENS s.v. Puñada To fly in the face of Heaven. **1860** G. ELIOT *Mill on Floss* ch. 2. **1894** BARING-GOULD *Queen of L.* II. 59 I am not one to fly in the face of Providence. **1911** *Spectator* 3 June 840 Knox . . . says: 'God hath determined that His Kirk . . . should be taught not by angels but by men.' That being so, we do but fly in the face of Providence when we provide not for men but for angels.

Fly in the ointment, A.

[ECCLES. X. 1. Dead flies cause the ointment of the Apothecary to send forth a stinking savour.] **1833** LAMB *Poor Relations* A fly in your ointment, a mote in your eye. **1920** 25 Jan. D. H. LAWRENCE *Lett.* i. 616 (There is always . . .).

Fly into an elephant, He changes a.

(F 398)

1548–9 N. UDALL *Paraphr. of Erasmus* 2nd ded. to Q. Katherine A6 The Sophistes of Grece coulde through their copiousnes make an Elephant of a flye, and a mountaine of a mollehill. **1549** ERASM. tr. Chaloner *Praise of Folly* A2

Labour of a sely fly to make an Elephante.   **1560**
T. BECON *Catechism* P.S. 338.   **1573** HARVEY
Lett. Bk. 32 Thai made of a gnat an elephant.
1578 *Courtly Controv.* 2D1 Making of an
Elephant, a mouse.   **1581** GUAZZO i. 133.   **1596**
LODGE *Wit's Misery* B2ᵛ (mouse).   **1736**
BAILEY s.v. Elephant To make of a fly an ele-
phant.   **1813** RAY 75.

Fly, The | sat upon the axletree of the chariot-wheel and said, What a dust do I raise!   (D 652)

1581 GUAZZO i. 153 According to the example of
the Flye, whiche sitting uppon a Carte that was
driven on the way, saide, hee had raysed a verie
great dust.   **1612** BACON *Ess., Vain-glory* Arb.
462 It was pretily deuised of Æsop, . . . So there
are some vaine persons, that whatsoeuer goeth
alone, or moues vpon greater meanes, they
thinke it is they that carry it.   *a.* **1721** PRIOR *The
Flies* (Says t' other, perched upon the wheel)
Did ever any mortal Fly Raise such a cloud of
dust as I!   **1823** SYD. SMITH Speech at Thirsk 24
Mar. 'Here we are, a set of obscure country
clergymen, . . . like flies on the chariot-wheel;
perched upon a question of which we can neither
see the diameter, nor control the motion, nor
influence the moving force.'

Fly, The | that plays too long in the candle, singes his wings at last.   (F 394)

1565 J. HALL *Court of Virtue* R6ᵛ As flyes oft
tymes in candle flame, Doo play tyll they be
burnt and dye.   **1566** SENECA *Medea* tr. Studley
l. 383 The candell blase delyghtes with burnyng
trym, The Flye, tyll she be burned in the flame.
1571 J. BRIDGES *Sermon at Paul's Cross* 38 The
flie that flittereth too neare the flame of the candell, burneth her selfe.   **1579** LYLY *Euph.* i. 212.
a. **1591** HY. SMITH *Serm.* (1866) I. 279 As the fly,
by often dallying with the candle, at last scorcheth
her wings with the flame; so taking, he¹ was taken,
and at last was drunk.   **1596** SHAKES. *M.V.* II.
ix. 79 Thus hath the candle sing'd the moth.
1618 BRETON *Wks.* ed. Gros. i. ii. 11. [¹ Noah.]

Fly that (the) pleasure which pains afterward (bites tomorrow).   (P 410)

1573 SANFORD 51ᵛ Flee that present pleasure.
whiche afterwarde maketh thee sory.   **1629** *Bk.
Mer. Rid.* Prov. no. 29.   **1640** HERBERT no. 444
Fly the pleasure that bites to-morrow.   **1710** S.
PALMER 347.

Fly up with Jackson's hens, I will make him.   (J 24)

c. **1560** *Misogonus* IV. ii. 31 Ye may fly vp toth
roust with Jacksons hens.   **1678** RAY 86 . . . i.e.
undo him.   **1887** T. DARLINGTON *Folk-Speech of
S. Chesh.* E.D.S. 192 Fly up . . . to be bankrupt.
The full phrase 'to *fly up* with Jackson's hens' is
more frequently heard.

Fly with the owl, To.   (O 95)

1622 MALYNES *Anc. Law-Merch.* 426 There is a
Custome that no Officer may arrest after Sun
set; such therefore as goe abroad at those times,
are said to Fly with the Owle, by a common
prouerbe.

Fly, flies (*noun*), *see also* Blind eats many a f.;
Boiling pot (To a) f. come not; Capers like a f. in
a tar box; Close mouth catches no f.; Eagles
catch no f.; Fiddlers, dogs, and f. come uncalled;
Flea, a f. and a flitch; Flea (f.) stick in the wall
(Let that); Honey (Make yourself) and f. will
devour; Hungry f. bite sore; Kill two f. with
one flap; Laws catch f. but let hornets free;
Light as a f.; Lose a f. to catch trout; Swallowed
a f.

Fly, flies, flown (*verb*), *see also* Beetle f. over
many a sweet flower; Bird must flighter that f.
with one wing; Birds were f.; Pigs may f.; Owl f.

Flying enemy, *see* Golden bridge.

Flying from fate, No.   (F 83)

1573 GASCOIGNE *Jocasta* III. i. What heauen hath
done, that cannot I vndo.   **1587** [**1599**] GREENE
Alphonsus l. 118 In vaine it is, to striue against
the streame, Fates must be followed.   **1591**
Locrine I. i. 32 But what so ere the fates deter-
mind haue, It lieth not in vs to disanull.   **1591–2**
SHAKES. *3 Hen. VI* IV. iii. 58 What fates impose,
that men must needs abide.   **1592** LYLY *Gall.* I.
i. 69 Destinie may be deferred, not preuented.
[**1592**] **1597** SHAKES. *Rich. III* IV. iv. 218 All un-
avoided is the doom of destiny.   **1604** MARSTON
What You Will I. iv. Hopelesse to strive with fate.
1659 HOWELL *It. Prov.* 5 That which heaven
sends we cannot avoid.   **1732** FULLER no. 3568.
1910 *Spectator* 17 Dec. 1074 'All went well
enough till a circus come to the town, and then I
was mad to join it. . . . I was called to it, and
you can't go against your fate'.

Flying without wings, No.   (F 407)

[PLAUTUS *Poenulus* 4. 2. 49 *Sine pennis volare
haud facile est.* It is not easy to fly without
feathers.]   **1605** CHAPMAN, JONSON, MARSTON
Eastw. Ho II. i. (1889) 459 We must have trades
to live withal; for we cannot stand without legs,
nor fly without wings.   **1670** RAY 91 . . . Nothing
of moment can be done without necessary helps,
or convenient means.   **1721** KELLY 267 . . . A
Man cannot thrive and prosper in the World,
that has no Stock, or Support.

Flyting, *see* Fair word in f. (Never a); First word
of f. (Got the).

Foal amble if the horse and mare trot? How can the.   (F 408)

c. **1549** HEYWOOD I. xi. D3 The litter is lyke to
the syre and the damme. Howe can the fole
amble, yf the hors and mare trot?   **1553** T.
WILSON *Arte of Rhet.* 61 Trotte sire and trotte
damme, how should the fole amble?   **1621**
BURTON *Anat. Mel.* III. iii. IV. ii (1651) 628 If the
dam trot, the foale will not amble.   **1641** FERGUS-
SON no. 806 Trot mother, trot father, how can
the foal amble?

Foam like a boar, To.   (B 484)

1546 HEYWOOD I. xi. E3ᵛ She fometh lyke a bore.

Fodder, *see* Barley straw good f. when cow gives
water.

Foe to a flatterer, No. (F 411)

1576 R. EDWARDS *Par. Dainty Dev.* (1868) 97 [Title]. **1629** T. ADAMS *Serm.* (1861–2) I. 188 Plus nocet lingua adulatoris quam manus persecutoris.[1] There is no foe to the flatterer. [1 AUGUST. in Ps. lxvi.]

Foe(s), *see also* Friend thy f., (Make not); Misfortune makes f. of friends; One enemy (f.) is too many; Secret f. gives sudden blow; Tell thy f. that thy foot acheth (Never); Truth finds f.; Woes unite f.

Fog cannot be dispelled with a fan, A.

1846 DENHAM I.

Fog, *see also* March, (F. in) frost in May.

Folk's dogs bark worse than themselves.

1721 KELLY 102 . . . Spoken when our Neighbour's Servants resent a Thing we have done, worse than they would do themselves.

Folks grow old, When | they are not set by. (F 430)

1639 CLARKE 280.

Folk(s), *see also* Beating proud f., (It is good); Busy f. always meddling; Drunken f. seldom take harm; Far f. fare best; Greedy f. have long arms; Mad f. in narrow place, (Heed); Poor f.

Follow him long ere five shillings fall from him, You will. (S 339)

c. **1641** FERGUSSON MS. no. 1633 Ye will follow him long or 5s. fall from him. **1721** KELLY 378 . . . Discouraging from paying Court and Attendance upon those by whom you will never be bettered. **1732** FULLER no. 5944 You may follow him long e're a Shilling drop from him.

Follow love (pleasure, glory) and it will flee thee: flee love (pleasure, glory) and it will follow thee. (L 479)

c. **1400** *Rom. Rose* B. 4783 If thou flee it [love], it shal flee thee; Folowe it, and folowen shal it thee. *c.* **1549** HEYWOOD I. xi. B7[v] Folowe pleasure, and than will pleasure flee. Flee pleasure, and pleasure will folow thee. **1592** SHAKES. *T.G.V.* V. ii. 49. Why, this it is to be a peevish girl That flies her fortune when it follows her! **1641** FERGUSSON no. 277. **1670** RAY 21 Fly pleasure and it will follow thee. **1678** *Id.* 55 Follow love and it will flee, Flee love and it will follow thee. This was wont to be said of glory, Sequentem fugit, fugientem sequitur. Just like a shadow.

Follow one like one's shadow, To. (S 263)

1545 *Precepts of Cato* L8[v] Death dothe folowe a man . . . none otherwyse, then the shadowe foloweth the body. **1548–9** N. UDALL *Paraphrase of Erasmus* 2nd ded. to Queen Katherine A1[v] 'Lyke as the shadow doth remedileese folowe and accumpanie the body in the sunne light, so . . . **1550** *Id. Discourse* (tr. Peter Martyr) F4 Folow after, euen as a shadow is wonte to go with the body in the Sunshyne. *Ibid.* F4[v]. **1551** WILSON *Rule of Reason* K6[v] Prayse foloweth vertue, as the shadow doth the bodie. **1581** GUAZZO ii. 25 She will follow her head, as the shadowe doth the body. **1636** T. BREWER *Lord Have Mercy Upon Us* A2 Although (like a man and his mate) they [punishment and sin] doe not goe cheeke by joule, like a man and his shadow they doe. **1697** W. POPE *Seth* [*Ward*] 78 As constant to him as the Shadow to the Body.

Follow not truth too near the heels, lest it dash out thy teeth. (T 592)

1614 SIR W. RALEIGH *Hist. of the World* Preface Who-so-ever in writing a moderne Historie, shall follow truth too neare the heeles, it may happily strike out his teeth. *a.* **1634** S. ROWLEY *The Noble Soldier* C3[v] I will follow Truth at the heeles, tho her foot beat my gums in peeces. *a.* **1640** J. SMYTH *Lives of the Berkeleys* ii. 431 I . . . know that truth is not to bee followed too near the heeles. **1651** HERBERT no. 1138. **1655** FULLER *Ch. Hist.* IX. viii (1868) III. 166 I know how dangerous it is to follow truth too near to the heels; yet better it is that the teeth of an historian be struck out of his head for writing the truth, than that they . . . rot in his jaws, by feeding . . . on the sweetmeats of flattery. **1827** HARE *Gues. at Truth* (1873) ch. I 283 Circumstantial accuracy with regard to facts is a very ticklish matter . . . As Raleigh says in a different sense . . . 'if we follow Truth too near the heels, it may haply strike out our eyes'.

Follow one's nose, To. (N 230)

[= to go straight on, without reflection or preconceived plan.] *c.* **1350** *Cleanness* l. 978 in *Allit. Poems* E.E.T.S. 67 Loth and tho lulywhite his lefly two de3ter, Ay fol3ed 3ere face bifore her bothe y3en. *c.* **1508** STANBRIDGE *Vulgaria* E.E.T.S. 24 Ryght forthe on thy nose. Recta via incede. [1598] **1616** HAUGHTON *Englishmen for my Money* l. 1529 The best way . . . is to follow your nose. **1635** SHIRLEY *Lady of Pleas.* II. ii. Merm. 291 Give him leave To follow his nose, madam, while he hunts In view—he'll soon be at fault. **1650** B. *Discolliminium* 19 I'le follow Providence, or my Nose, as well as I can. **1772** R. GRAVES *Spiritual Quixote* VI. i. Follow your nose, and your arse will tag after. **1823** GROSE ed. Pierce Egan s.v. Nose.

Follow the old fox, It is good to.

1639 CLARKE 268.

Follow the river and you'll get to the sea. *Cf.* Rivers run into the sea, All. (R 137)

c. **1594** BACON no. 875 He who does not know the way leading down to the sea should follow a river. *a.* **1595** *Edward III* v. i. 92 All riuers haue recourse vnto the Sea. **1604** R. CUDWORTH in W. Perkins *Commentary upon Galatians* 575 He that follows a riuer, must needes at length come to the Sea. **1608** J. HALL *Epistles* I. v. 37 Euen little streams empty themselues into great rivers, and they againe into the sea. **1732** FULLER no. 1556.

Follow (Looks) to freits, He that | freits will follow him.

? 17 . . *Adam o' Gordon* xxvii in PINKERTON *Select. Sc. Ballads* (1783) I. 49 Wha luik to freits, my master deir, Freits will ay follow them. **1721** KELLY 128 . . . He that notices superstitious Observations (such as spilling of Salt, . . .) it will fall to him accordingly. **1804** MUNGO PARK in LOCKHART's *Scott* ch. 13 (1860) 117 He answered, smiling, '*Freits* (omens) follow those who look to them' . . . . Scott never saw him again. **1914** *Times Lit. Sup.* 10 Apr. 178 The Kings of Scots have always been beset by omens, and . . . to him who follows freits, freits follow.

Followers, *see* Money wants no f.

Follows Nature, He that | is never out of his way.   (N 41)

1576 PETTIE i. 14 and 83. **1579** LYLY *Euph.* i. 192 Doth not Cicero conclude and allowe that if wee followe and obey Nature we shall neuer erre? **1597** *Politeuphuia* 180 The man that lyueth obedient to nature, can neuer hurt himselfe thereby. **1732** FULLER no. 2108.

Follows the Lord, He that | hopes to go before.   (L 441)

1640 HERBERT no. 994.

Follow(s, -ed), *see also* Counsel must be f.; Dam leaps over (Where), kid f.; Far behind that may not f.; Imps f. when the devil goes before, (No marvel if the); Sheep (One) f. another.

Folly is a bonny dog.   (F 432)

a. **1628** CARMICHAELL no. 513 Folie is a bonie dodge[1]. **1641** FERGUSSON no. 269. **1857** DEAN RAMSAY *Remin.* v (1911) 200 . . . Meaning, I suppose, that many are imposed upon by the false appearances and attractions of vicious pleasures. [[1] subterfuge.]

Folly of one man is the fortune of another, The.

1607 BACON *Ess., Fortune* in Wks. (1858) VI. 472.

Folly to being in love, No.   (F 437)

1659 HOWELL *Br. Prov.* 27 No Folly, to Love. **1710** S. PALMER 137. **1768** RAY 50 No folly to being in love, or where loves in the case, the Doctor is an Ass.

Folly were grief, If | every house would weep.   (F 434)

1640 HERBERT no. 370.

Folly (-ies), *see also* Disease (Chief) that reigns is f.; Every fault (In) there is f.; First degree of f. is to hold self wise; Ignorance is bliss; Knowledge is f. except grace guide it; Jollity but has smack of f. (No); Short f. are best; Wisdom to find out own f.

Fond[1] fisher that angles for a frog, He is a. *Cf.* Fish and catch a frog.   (F 333)

1616 BRETON 2 *Cross.* A3. [[1] foolish.]

Fond of barter that niffers with Old Nick, He is.

1834 A. CUNNINGHAM *Wks. of Burns* VIII. 278 *Glossary.* (Scot. Say.)

Fond of gape-seed, She is.   (G 32)

1598 FLORIO *World of Words* s.v. Anfanare To go seeking for a halfepeny worth of gaping seede. **1600** NASHE *Summers Last Will* iii. 275. Buy gape-seede. **1602** *Entertainment at Harefield* (NICHOL's *Progresses* 1823 iii. 586) You come to buy gape seed. **1603** MONTAIGNE (Florio) III. ix. 2 Such as gather stubble (as the common saying is) or looke about for gape-seed. **1830** FORBY 431 . . . i.e. Of staring at everything that passes.

Fool always rushes to the fore, A.

1853 TRENCH iii. 59.

Fool and his feather. *Cf.* Feather in his cap. Fools wore white caps (feathers), If all.

[*c.* 1553] 1566–7 N. UDALL *Roister D.* I. iv. 97 It was a fooles feather had light on your coate . . . a haire that was fall from your hed. *c.* **1569** W. WAGER *The Longer thou Livest* F2. **1604** MARSTON *Malcontent* v. ii. No foole but has his feather. **1611** DEKKER & MIDDLETON *The Roaring Girl* C4[v] One fether, the foole's peculiar still. **1613** SHAKES. *Hen. VIII* I. iii. 25 Those remnants Of fool and feather that they got in France. **1615** BRETNOR *Almanac* Dec. A feather for a foole.

Fool and his money are soon parted, A.   (F 452)

1573 TUSSER ch. x. no. 11 A foole and his monie be soone at debate, which after with sorrow repents him too late. **1587** J. BRIDGES *Def. of Govt. of C. of E.* 1294 A foole and his money is soone parted. **1629** HOWELL *Fam. Lett.* 20 Oct. T.B. intends to give money for such a place . . . I fear it will be verified in him that a fool and his money is soon parted. **1670** RAY 91. **1748** SMOLLETT *Rod. Rand.* ch. 11 Well, fools and their money are soon parted. **1816** SCOTT *Antiq.* ch. 39 A fool and his money is soon parted, nephew.

Fool as he looks, Not such a.

1888 MRS. OLIPHANT *Second Son* ch. 9 Oh, I am not such a fool as I look. My father always said so. **1905** VACHELL *The Hill* 70 I shan't forget either that you're not half such a fool as you look.

Fool asks much, The | but he is more fool that grants it.   (F 453)

1616 DRAXE no. 231. **1640** HERBERT no. 282.

Fool at forty is a fool indeed, A.   (F 454)

1557 EDGEWORTH *Sermons* 4G1 When he [Rehoboam] begonne hys raigne he was one and fortye yeares of age, and then of lyke age must hys mates bee. . . . And he that hath not learned some experience or practice and trade of the world by that age wil neuer be wise. *c.* 1670 COTTON *Visions* No. 1 He who at fifty is a fool, Is far too stubborn grown for school. 1725 E. YOUNG *Satires* no. ii Be wise with speed; A fool at forty is a fool indeed.

Fool believes everything, A.　　(F 456)

[PROV. xiv. 15 The simple believeth every word.] 1579 CALVIN *Sermons* tr. L.T. 1241/1 It is true that men must needes first inquire, before they can haue the certein doctrine: and it is sayd in the prouerb, that a foole casteth no doubt in any thing. 1599 RAINOLDS *Overthrow Stage Plays* 54 But you should haue marked that the scripture saith also, A foole beleeueth euery thing. 1610 A. COOKE *Pope Joan* in *Harl. Misc.* iv. 130 Florimundus justified the Proverb, A Fool believeth every Thing.

Fool does in the end, What the | the wise man does at the beginning.

(F 512)

1535 *Dial. Creatures* 207, 212 A foole beholdith but onely the begynnynge of his workys but a wiseman takyth hede to the ende. 1659 HOWELL *Fr. Prov.* 6 The fool ends alwayes at the beginning. 1853 TRENCH V. 121 . . . the wise with a good grace what the fool with an ill. 1866 KINGSLEY *Hereward* ch. 5 'It's a fool's trick', answered the stranger. . . , 'to put off what you must do at last.'

Fool finds a horseshoe, When a | he thinks aye the like to do.

1721 KELLY 348 . . . Spoken when they, who have had some Fortune, think always to be as successful. 1732 FULLER no. 6415.

Fool has bethought himself, When a | the market's over.

1706 STEVENS s.v. Necio.　1732 FULLER no. 5530.

Fool, He has great need of a | that plays the fool himself.　(N 72)

1611 COTGRAVE s.v. Fol.　1640 HERBERT no. 46. 1721 KELLY 161 He would fain have a Fool that makes a Fool of himself.

Fool: I am a | I love anything (everything) that is good.　(F 491)

1678 RAY 247.　1738 SWIFT Dial. I. E.L. 268 I'm like all fools; I love everything that's good.

Fool in hand, You have not a.　(F 514)

1576 *Common Conditions* F1ᵛ Thinke not you haue a foole in hand I waraunt yee. [*c.* 1592] 1615 T. HEYWOOD *Four Prent. Lond.* 226 You thinke you haue a foole in hand. 1601 SHAKES. *T.N.* I. iii. 61 Fair lady, do you think you have fools in hand?—Sir, I have not you by th' hand. 1607 DEKKER & WEBSTER *West. Ho* IV. ii. F2ᵛ What do you think you haue Fops in hand? 1671 CLARKE *Phras. Puer.* s.v. Discern 95.

Fool in his sleeve, Every one has a.

(F 451)

1640 HERBERT no. 881.　1659 HOWELL *Span. Prov.* 18.　1710 S. PALMER 55.

Fool is fulsome, A.　(F 463)

1594 LYLY *Mother B.* II. iii. 75 Nothing so fulsome as a shee foole. 1659 HOWELL *Eng. Prov.* 10b.　1670 RAY 10.

Fool knows more in his own house than a wise man in another's, A.　(F 467)

1567 PAINTER (Jacobs) iii. 206 The Foole knoweth better what hee hath, than hys neighbors do, be they neuer so wise. 1620 SHELTON *Quix.* II. xliii.　1640 HERBERT no. 257.　1659 TORRIANO no. 129 A fool knows better his own businesse than a wise man anothers.

Fool, One | makes many (a hundred).

(F 501)

[L. *Unius dementia dementes efficit multos.* The madness of one makes many mad.] 1617 J. SWETNAM *School of Defence* 11 The olde Prouerbe, One foole makes many. 1640 HERBERT no. 525 (a hundred). 1659 HOWELL *Eng. Prov.* 9a (maketh many fools). 1738 SWIFT Dial. I. E.L. 271.　1813 SCOTT *Let.* to Byron 6 Nov. in LOCKHART's *Life* As to those who . . . take my rhapsodies for their model . . . they have exemplified the ancient adage, 'one fool makes many'.

Fool may ask more questions in an hour than a wise man can answer in seven years, A.　(F 468)

1666 TORRIANO *It. Prov.* 249, no. 10. One fool may ask more than seven wise men can answer. 1670 RAY 91.　1738 SWIFT Dial. II. E.L. 307 They say a fool will ask more questions than the wisest body can answer. 1822 SCOTT *Pirate* ch. 18 Bryce Snailsfoot is a cautious man . . .; he knows a fool may ask more questions than a wise man cares to answer.

Fool may give a wise man counsel, A.

(F 469)

c. 1374 CHAUCER *Troilus* Bk. 1, l. 630 A fool may eek a wis-man ofte gyde. *c.* 1375 *Ywain and Gawain* ed. Schleich 1887, ll. 1477–8 Bot 3it a fole þat litel kan May wele cownsail anoþer man. 1509 BARCLAY *Ship of Fools* (1874) i. 58 Oft a folys counsayle Tourneth a wyse man to confort and auayle. 1721 KELLY 25 . . . An Apology of those who offer their Advice to them who may be supposed to excel them in Parts and Sense. 1818 SCOTT *Ht. Midl.* ch. 45 If a fule may gie a wise man a counsel, I wad hae him think twice or he mells wi' Knockdunder.

Fool may sometimes speak to the purpose (tell the truth), A.　(F 449)

[Gk. Πολλάκι τοι καὶ μωρὸς ἀνὴρ κατακαίριον εἶπε. L. *Interdum stultus benè loquitur.*] 1545 TAVERNER 57 Oftentymes euen the fole hytteth the nayle on the head and speaketh thynges in place. This prouerbe therfore admonysheth vs not to reiecte ne despyse an holsome and ryght sentence spoken otherwhiles out of a rude felowes mouth. **1549** T. CHALONER *Pr. Folly* T3ᵛ Remember the Greeke prouerbe, that oftentimes a foole maie speake to purpose. [1598] **1616** HAUGHTON *Englishmen for my Money* l. 351 Fooles tell the truth men say. **1668** J. WILSON tr. *Moriae Encomium* 160 Remembering in the mean time, that Greek proverb . . . Sometimes a fool may speake a word in season.

Fool may throw a stone into a well, A | which a hundred wise men cannot pull out. (F 470)

1640 HERBERT no. 527.

Fool of the family: The | make a parson of him.

1545 ASCHAM *Toxoph.* Arb. 154 This boye is fit for nothynge els, but to set to lerning and make a prest of. **1648** JOHN HALL *Sat.* i. 133–6 But if it chance they have one leader sone Born for to number eggs, he must to school; Especiall' if some patron will engage Th' advowson of some neighbouring vicarage. **1905** J. OXENHAM *White Fire* ch. 9 I was at Eton with B— and at Oxford. He always was a fool. . . . He ought to have gone into the Church.

Fool of thyself, Make not a | to make others merry.

1621 BURTON *Anat. Mel.* II. iii. VII (1651) 360.

Fool or a physician, Every man is a. (M 125)

[TAC. *Ann.* 6. 46 [*Tiberius*] *solitus eludere medicorum artes atque eos, qui post tricesimum aetatis annum ad internoscenda corpori suo utilia vel noxia alieni consilii indigerent.*] **1592** GREENE *Quip* xi [cancelled passage] A Physitian or a foole. **1592** LYLY *Midas* II. ii. 39 Spoken like a Physicion. Or a foole of necessitie. **1594** O. B. *Questions* G1 This old prouerbe; Either a foole or a Phisition. **1600–1** SHAKES. *M.W.W.* III. iv. 83 I seek you a better husband.—That's my master, Master Doctor . . . 'Nay,' said I, 'will you cast away your child on a fool and a physician?' **1601** HOLLAND tr. *Pliny* xxviii. 5 [ii. 304] Every man is to be his owne Physician: whereupon might rise this proverbe, *A foole or a Physician.* **1601** JONSON *Poetaster* III. iv. 8–10. **1607** BARNES *Divils Charter* L3 Eyther mere fooles or good physitions all. **1659** HOWELL *Eng. Prov.* 6b Every one a fool or a Physitian to himself after thirtie. **1670** RAY 35 Every man is either a fool or a Physician after thirty years of age. **1721** KELLY 101 Every man at thirty is a fool or a physician. He is a Fool who at that Age knows not his Constitution. **1742** GRAY to West Jan. quoting Cheyne [Dr. George, 1671–1743] Every man after fourty is either a fool or a physician. **1851** HELPS *Compan. of Sol.* ch. 10 A man learns certain rules of health, so that it is said that at forty he is either a fool or a physician.

Fool praises another, One.

1740 FRANKLIN Nov. Who knows a fool must know his brother; For one will recommend another.

Fool says, The | Who would have thought it? (P 77)

1540 TAVERNER B2ᵛ Indecora sapienti vox est. Non putaram, aut non expectaram. It is an uncourtly sayeing for a wise man to say, I wold not have thought it, or I wolde not have loked that it should have come so to passe. **1594** LYLY *Mother B.* IV. ii. 38. **1608** J. DAY *Law Tricks or Who would have thought it?* **1616** DRAXE no. 136 It is the part of a foole to say, I had not thought. **1639** CLARKE 320 Who would have thought it? **1732** FULLER no. 4539.

Fool sometimes, Every man is a | and none at all times. (F 499)

1640 HERBERT no. 163 None is a fool alwaies, every one sometimes. **1721** KELLY 99 . . . An Apology for an imprudent Action, in ourselves, or others.

Fool that forgets himself, He is a. (F 480)

c. **1374** CHAUCER *Troilus* Bk. 5, l. 98 I have herd seyd ek tymes twyes twelve, 'He is a fool that wole foryete hymselve.' **1596** SHAKES. *K.J.* III. iv. 48 I am not mad; I would to heaven I were! For then, 'tis like I should forget myself. **1641** FERGUSSON no. 344.

Fool that is not melancholy once a day, He is a. (F 481)

1642 J. HOWELL *For. Trav.* VIII. 55 He is accounted little lesse a foole, who is not melancholy once a day. **1678** RAY 346.

Fool that kisses the maid when he may kiss the mistress, He is a. (M 1021)

1659 HOWELL *Eng. Prov.* 15b. **1670** RAY 111 If you can kiss the mistress, never kiss the maid.

Fool that makes a wedge of his fist, He is a. (F 482)

1611 COTGRAVE s.v. Coing. **1640** HERBERT no. 585. **1659** HOWELL *Fr. Prov.* 11 (hammer).

Fool that marries his wife at Yule, He is a | for when the corn's to shear the bairn's to bear.

1721 KELLY 167 . . . If a Woman be got with Child in Christmas, it is like that she may lye in in Harvest, the throngest time of the Year.

Fool that the fool is, He is not the | but he that with the fool deals. (F 486)

1586 *Maitland Folio MS.* S.T.S. i. XIV. l.15 Thou art ane fule gif thow with fulis dalis. a. **1628** CARMICHAELL no. 89. **1721** KELLY 146 . . . Spoken against wanton Boys, when they are playing upon an Ideot.

Fool that thinks not that another thinks, He is a. (F 484)

1640 HERBERT no. 287.

Fool thinks, As the | so the bell clinks.
(F 445)

c. **1390** GOWER *Conf. Amantis* i. 75 For as it
seemeth that a bell Like to the wordes that men
tell Answereth right so. **1607** *Lingua* III. vii. As
the fool thinketh, so the bell clinketh. I protest
I hear no more than a post. **1621** BURTON *Anat.
Mel.* I. iii. III (1651) 211 He that hears bells, will
make them sound what he list, *As the fool thinketh, so the bell clinketh.* **1732** FULLER no. 6121.
1850 CARLYLE *Latter-Day Pamph.* viii (1885)
285–6 It is a true adage, . . .

Fool to roast eggs, Set a | and a wise man to eat them.
(F 504)

1678 RAY 241.

Fool to the market (far, to France), Send a | and a fool he will return again. *Cf.* Home as wise.
(F 503)

1586 G. WHITNEY *Emblems* 178 The foole that
farre is sente some wisedome to attaine; Returnes
an idiot, as he wente, and bringes the foole againe.
a. **1628** CARMICHAELL no. 646 He came hame
mair fule nor he raid a feild. *Ibid.* no. 1354 (a
foole commes hame). **1678** RAY 140 . . . The
Italians say, Chi bestia va a Roma bestia retorna.
He that goes a beast to Rome returns thence a
beast. Change of place changes not men's minds
or manners. **1738** SWIFT *Dial.* I. E.L. 280 You
may go back again, like a fool, as you came.
1772 R. GRAVES *Spiritual Quix.* X. 2 He that goes
abroad a fool, will come home a coxcomb.
1832 HENDERSON 22 Send a fool to France and
he'll come a fool back.

Fool to the old fool, No.
(F 506)

1546 HEYWOOD II. ii. F4ᵛ But there is no foole
to the olde foole, folke saie. **1594** LYLY *Mother
B.* IV. ii. 96 In faith I perceiue an olde sawe and
a rustie, no foole to the old foole. **1614** CAMDEN
313. **1721** KELLY 256 . . . Spoken when Men of
advanc'd Age behave themselves, or talk youth-
fully, or wantonly. **1859** TENNYSON *Grandmother* Wks. (1893) 226 I . . . spoke I scarce
knew how; Ah, there's no fool like the old one—
it makes me angry now. **1893** H. P. LIDDON
Serm. on O.T. xi. 162 'No fool is so bad as the
old fool', for . . . he is less capable of improvement than a young one.

Fool, A | unless he knows Latin, is never a great fool.

1853 TRENCH iv. 78 The Spaniards [have] . . .
on the folly of a pedant as the most intolerable
of all follies: ∴ . .

Fool wanders, The | the wise man travels.

1732 FULLER no. 4540. **1887** LD. AVEBURY *Pleas.
Life* I. vii. 'He that would make his travels
delightful must first make himself delightful'
(Seneca). According to the old proverb, . . .

Fool who makes his physician his heir (executor), He is a.
(F 483)

[PUB. SYRUS *Male secum agit aeger, medicum qui
haeredem facit.* A sick man does badly for himself who makes the physician his heir.] **1539**
TAVERNER *Publius* D4ᵛ That sycke body dothe
naught for him selfe, that maketh his physician
his executour. For he prouoketh him to kyll
him. **1553** *Precepts of Cato* (1560) Ff4ᵛ He is
not lyke long to prosper, Who maketh a phisicion
his heyer. **1584** LYLY *Camp.* V. iv. 47 If one be
sick, what wouldest thou haue him do?—Be sure
that he make not his Phisition his heire. **1648**
HERRICK *Hesper.* 316 *On Leech.* Wks. (1893) I.
161 He knows he must of Cure despaire, Who
makes the slie Physitian his Heire. **1733** FRANK-
LIN Feb. He's a fool that makes his doctor his
heir.

Fool will not give his bauble for the Tower of London, A.
(F 476)

1509 BARCLAY *Ship of Fools* i. 256 For it is oft
sayd of men both yonge and olde A foole wyll
nat gyue his Babyll for any golde. a. **1530**
R. Hill's *Commonpl. Bk.* E.E.T.S. 130. **1577**
GRANGE *Gold. Aphrod.* Ep. Ded. (Being somewhat wedded as most fools are) to mine owne
opinion, who would hardly forgoe their bable
for the Tower of London. **1599** PORTER *Angry
Wom. Abingd.* Mal. Soc. l. 2391 (will not leave).
1641 FERGUSSON no. 118.

Fool's bell is soon rung, A.

c. **1400** *Rom. Rose* 5266 And fooles can not
holde his tunge; A fooles belle is soone runge.

Fool's bolt is soon shot, A. *Cf.* Shot one's bolt.
(F 515)

c. **1225** *South. Legendary* E.E.T.S. I. 93 Ouwer
[ʒoure al] bolt is sone ischote. c. **1275** *Provs. of
Alfred,* A. 421 Sottes bolt is sone i-schote. c.
1300 *Provs. of Hending* xi Sottes bolt is sone
shote. **1375** *Ywain & Gawain* (Ritson) I. l. 2168
For fole bolt es sone shot. c. **1450** *Proverbis of
Wysdom* in HERRIG's *Archiv.* 90 l. 113 A fole is
bolt is sone i-shote. **1493** H. PARKER *Dives &
Pauper* A2ᵛ. **1546** HEYWOOD II. iii. G1ᵛ She
maie saie (quoth I) a fooles bolte soone shot.
1599 SHAKES. *Hen. V* III. vii. 119 You are the
better at proverbs, by how much—A fool's bolt
is soon shot. **1599** *Id. A.Y.* V. iv. 60 By my
faith, he is very swift and sententious.—According to the fool's bolt, sir. c. **1628** (?) FORD *The
Queen* (ed. Bang) in *Mat. zur Kunde des Eng.
Dramas* XIII l. 1012 A wise mans bolt is soon
shot. **1748** SMOLLETT *Rod. Rand.* ch. 53 'Your
bolt is soon shot, according to the old proverb',
said she.

Fool's bolt may sometimes hit the mark, A.
(F 516)

1580 FULWELL *Ars Adul.* Dial. 7 Fools bolts
(men say) are soonest shot yet oft they hit the
mark. **1732** FULLER no. 107 (hit the white).

Fool's haste is no speed.
(F 518)

1481 CAXTON *Reynard* Arb. 110 Men fynde many
fooles that in hete hasten hem so moche that
after they repent hem and thenne it is to late.
1641 FERGUSSON no. 266. **1721** KELLY 102 . . .
Spoken when People make a great Bustle, and
. . . often by their too much Haste spoil what they
are about.

Fool's paradise, A.   (F 523)

1462 *Paston Lett.* (Gairdner 1904) iv. 49 I wold
not be in a folis paradyce. **1528** ROY *Rede
Me* Arb. 86 Thus my lady, not very wyse,
Is brought in to foles paradyse. *c.* **1595** SHAKES.
R.J. II. iv. 161 If ye should lead her into a fool's
paradise, as they say, it were a very gross kind of
behaviour. **1728** POPE *Dunc.* iii. 9. **1856** MRS.
BROWNING *Aur. Leigh* iv. 341 Love's fool-para-
dise Is out of date, like Adam's.

Fool's tongue is long enough to cut his own throat, A.   (F 521)

1673 DARE *Counsellor Manners* 51 Many a man
doth with his Tongue cut his own throat. **1732**
FULLER no. 108.

Fool(s), *see also* All the wit in the world (If you
had), f. would fell you; Ass (F.) that brays
against other ass; Barber learns shaving f.;
Begged for a f.; Better be a f. than knave;
Better fleech a f. than fight him; Born a f. is
never cured, (He that is); Bridges were made
for . . . f. to ride over; Change of weather the
discourse of f.; Child's service . . . f. that
despises; Children and f. cannot lie; —— have
merry lives; —— must not play with edged
tools; Counsel (He that is own) has f. for client;
Counsel of f. (To) wooden bell; Deal f.'s dole;
Discreet advise (While), f. does his business;
Dogs (F.) begin in jest; Dote more on it than f.
on bauble; Every man a little beyond himself a
f.; Experience is mistress of f.; Experience
keeps a dear school . . .; Fair words make f.
fain; Fat as a f.; Ferlies make f. fain; First
chapter of f.; Fishing-rod has f. at one end;
Fortune favours f.; God help the f.; God sends
fortune to f.; Higher the f. greater fall; Hood
for this f.; Knave and a f. never take thought;
Knave than f., (I'd rather have); Knaves and f.
divide the world; Lawyers' houses built on f.;
Lend and lose, so play f.; London Bridge was
made for f. to go under; Love makes a wit of
the f.; Mad f. in narrow place, (Heed); Man at
five, f. at fifteen; Many a one for land takes f. by
hand; Mickle fails that f. think; More f. than
fiddler; More knave than f.; More know Tom F.;
No play without f.; Nod for a wise man, rod for
f.; Nod from a lord breakfast for f.; Oil of f.;
Play with a f. at home; Promise and give nothing, comfort to f.; Reason governs wise man and
cudgels f.; Riches serve wise man, command f.;
Sends a f. expects one (*or* means to follow);
Success makes f. seem wise; Talks to himself
speaks to a f.; Teaches himself has f. for master;
Too much of nothing but f.; Travel makes a f.
worse; Two f. in one house too many; Two f.
met; Vicar of f. is his ghostly father; Want of a
wise man (For) f. set in chair; Whip for a f.;
White wall is f.'s paper; Who's the f. now; Wise
(None is so) but f. overtakes; Wise erred not
(If), go hard with f.; Wise man by day no f. by
night; Wise man changes his mind, f. never; Wise
man must carry the f.; Wise men have their
mouth in their heart, f. . . . ; —— learn by other
men's harms, f. . . . ; —— make proverbs, f.
repeat; —— propose, f. determine; —— silent,

f. talk; Wit (He has some) but f. has keeping;
Woman she is fair (Tell a); Woman's advice . . .
who won't take is f.; Words are money of f.;
World is full of f.; Young men think old men f.
See also Fools, Play the fool.

Fooleries, *see* Truths too fine spun are subtle f.

Foolish in the fault, He that is | let him be wise in the punishment.   (F 112)

1640 HERBERT no. 555.

Foolish (Peevish) pity mars a city.   (P 366)

1556 J. HEYWOOD *Spider & Flie* Farmer 307 This
. . . Is either not pity, or peevish pity, which (as
th'old saying saith) marreth the city. *a.* **1567**
T. BECON *Catechism* P.S. 310. **1580** S. BIRD
Friendly Communication ¶ 1. **1623** CAMDEN 275
(Peevish). **1639** CLARKE 181.

Foolish sheep that makes the wolf his confessor, It is a.   (S 303)

1642 TORRIANO 53 That is a silly sheep that goeth
to the wolf to shrive her self. **1664** CODRINGTON
222. **1670** RAY 23.

Foolish tongues talk by the dozen.   (T 414)

c. **1400** *Rom. Rose* l. 5265 Fooles can not hold
hir tunge. **1640** HERBERT no. 645.

Foolish, *see also* Do a f. thing once (One cannot)
but one must hear of it; Hope often deludes the
f. man; Judge, (From a f.) a quick sentence;
Least f. is wise; Service a child does his father
(The first) is to make him f.; Wise man commonly has f. children.

Fools and bairns should not see half-done work.

1721 KELLY 108 (Fools should not). **1818**
SCOTT in LOCKHART'S *Life* ch. 43 (1860) 386
'Bairns and fools' . . . according to our old canny
proverb, should never see half-done work. **1913**
A. & J. LANG *Highw. & By. in the Border* ch. 9.

Fools and fiddlers sing at their meat, None but.

1813 RAY 9.

Fools are fain of flitting.   (F 529)

[HOR. *Ep.* I. 14. 43 *Optat ephippia bos: piger
optat arare caballus.* The ox covets the horse's
trappings, the lazy horse wishes to plough.]
1641 FERGUSSON no. 262. **1721** KELLY 105 . . .
and wise Men of sitting. Spoken to them who
are fond of altering their Place, Station, or Condition, without good Reason.

Fools are fain of nothing (right nought).   (F 530)

1586 J. MAXWELL *Some Resounes and Proverbs*
(Motherwell 1832) 86 A lytle thing pleseth a

foole. *a.* **1628** CARMICHAELL no. 105 A foole is
fain of richt nocht. **1641** FERGUSSON no. 275
(right nought). **1721** KELLY 111 . . . Spoken
when we see People much taken up with fair
Promises, or improbable Expectations.

Fools are wise as long as silent.

(F 531)

[PROV. xvii. 28 Even a fool, when he holdeth his
peace, is counted wise.] **1596** SHAKES. *M.V.* I.
i. 95 I do know of these That therefore only are
reputed wise For saying nothing. **1611** COT-
GRAVE s.v. Sage Fooles are held wise as long as
they are silent. **1659** N. R. 33.

**Fools bite one another, but wise men
agree together.** (F 532)

1640 HERBERT no. 452.

**Fools build houses, and wise men buy
(live in) them.** (F 533)

1670 RAY 91. **1721** KELLY 110 Fools Big[1] Houses
and wise Men buy them. I knew a Gentleman
buy £2000 worth of Land, build a House upon
it, and sell both House and Land to pay the
Expences of his building. **1732** FULLER no. 1573
(enjoy). **1911** SIR W. F. BUTLER *Autobiog.* ch. 19
The adage says that fools build houses for other
men to live in. Certainly the men who build the
big house of Empire for England usually get the
attic or the underground story in it for their own
lodgment. [[1] Build.]

**Fools cut their fingers, but wise men
cut their thumbs.**

1738 SWIFT *Dial.* I. E.L. 266. **1902-4** LEAN III.
467 Fools cut their fingers, but wise men cut
their thumbs . . . i.e. the follies of the wise are
prodigious.

Fools give to please all but their own.

(F 534)

1640 HERBERT no. 735.

**Fools grow (Folly grows) without
watering.** (F 431)

1640 HERBERT no. 581 (Folly growes). **1642**
TORRIANO 55 . . . Nota. An evil weed groweth
apace. **1707** MAPLETOFT 43. **1732** FULLER no.
1574. **1853** TRENCH (1905) 73.

**Fools had baubles, If all | we should
want fuel.** (F 548)

c. **1350** *Douce MS.* 52 no. 109 A fole sholde
neuer haue a babulle in hande. **1611** COTGRAVE
s.v. Fol If all fooles bables bore, wood would
be verie deere. **1640** HERBERT no. 63. **1659**
HOWELL *Span. Prov.* 17 (want wood).

**Fools lade the water, and wise men
catch the fish.** (F 538)

c. **1450** *Babees Bk.* Furnivall 332 Folus lade
polys,[1] wisemenn ete þe fysshe. *c.* **1520** SKELTON
Magnif. I. 300 Wel, wyse men may ete the fysshe,
when ye [i.e. Fancy] shal draw the pole.[1] **1636**
CAMDEN 296. [[1] pools.]

Fools live poor to die rich. (F 539)

1659 N.R. 32.

**Fools make feasts, and wise men eat
them.** (F 540)

1573 SANFORD 106 Fooles make feastes, and
wyse menne enioye them. **1611** DAVIES no. 65
(the banquets). **1639** CLARKE 186. **1721** KELLY
110 . . . This was once said to a great Man in
Scotland, upon his giving an Entertainment.
Who readily answer'd, Wise Men make Proverbs
and Fools repeat them. **1832-8** S. WARREN
Diary of Late Phys. ch. 22. Her trembling husband . . . suggested . . . the old saying, . . .

**Fools nor beggars nor whores among his
kindred, Who has neither | was born of a
stroke of thunder.**

1642 TORRIANO 36 (begot of a flash of thunder).
1659 HOWELL *It. Prov.* 11.

Fools one to another, We are. (F 556)

1640 HERBERT no. 381.

Fools set far (long) trysts. (F 542)

a. **1628** CARMICHAELL no. 512. **1641** FERGUSSON
no. 267. **1721** KELLY 102 . . . Spoken when
People promise to do a Thing a good while hence.

**Fools set stools for wise folks to stumble
at.** (F 543)

1605 S. ROWLEY *When You See Me* F2[v] Yee
know what the old Prouerbe saies . . . When
fooles set stooles, and wise men breake their
shinnes. **1623** CAMDEN 269. **1623** PAINTER B2
Take heed when fooles Set stooles, that you
thereat breake not your shins. **1670** RAY 91.

**Fools should not fool it, If | they shall
lose their season.** (F 550)

1640 HERBERT no. 703.

Fools should not have chapping sticks.[1]

(F 544)

a. **1628** CARMICHAELL no. 521 Fooles sould have
na chopping stiks. **1641** FERGUSSON no. 279.
1681 S. COLVIL *Whigs Sup.* I. 68 It is the simplest
of all tricks To suffer fools have chopping sticks.
1721 KELLY 104 . . . Spoken when we take a
Stick from a Child, or when others are doing
Harm with what they have taken up. **1818**
SCOTT *Rob Roy* ch. 34 Deil tak him . . . that gies
women either secret to keep or power to abuse
—fules shouldna hae chapping sticks. [[1] dangerous tools or weapons.]

**Fools tie knots, and wise men loose
them.** (F 545)

1639 CLARKE 88. **1721** KELLY 107 . . . Spoken
when People . . . have spoil'd and entangled a
Business, which will require Wisdom to set right
again.

Fools went not to market, If | bad wares would not be sold.   (F 551)

1611 COTGRAVE s.v. Marché . . . (So fooles are sometimes good for something.) **1640** HERBERT no. 66 Were there no fooles, badd ware would not passe. **1670** RAY 10. *Hispan.*

Fools will be fools still.   (F 547)

1575 *Gam. Gurton's N.* I. iv. Might ha kept it when ye had it! but fooles will be fooles styll. **1577** *A merry and pleasant Prognostication* A4 Naturall fooles, will be fooles still. **1609** HARWARD 88 A foole will be a foole still. **1659** HOWELL *It. Prov.* 7 Who is born a fool is never cured.

Fools will be meddling.   (F 546)

[PROV. XX. 3 Every fool will be meddling.] *c.* **1380** CHAUCER *Parl. of Fowles* l. 574 But sooth is seyd, 'a fool can noght be stille.' **1599** SHAKES. *A.Y.* III. ii. 105 Peace, you dull fool! . . . I'll graff it with you, and then I shall graff it with a medlar. **1616** DRAXE no. 214. **1670** RAY 91. **1738** SWIFT *Dial.* I. E.L. 276 Why, madam, fools will be meddling; I wish he may cut his fingers.

Fools wore feathers (white caps), If all | we should seem a flock of geese. (F 549)

1640 HERBERT no. 513. **1658** *Comes Fac.* 308.

Foot a man halts, To know on which.

c. **1530** *Calisto and Melibea* l. 143. **1586** *Lazarillo de Tormes* ed. Crofts 40. **1659** HOWELL *Fr. Prov.* 16.

Foot further than the whittle,[1] He that stretches | will stretch into the straw.

a. **1300** *Walter of Henley's Husb.* (1890) 4 Wo þat stretchet forþerre þan his wytel wyle reshe in þe straue his fet he mot streche. **1393** LANGLAND *P.Pl.* C. XVII. 76 When he streyneþ hym to strecche, þe straw is hers whitel. [[1] blanket.]

Foot on the cradle and hand on the distaff is the sign of a good housewife, The.   (F 563)

1659 HOWELL *Span. Prov.* 2. **1670** RAY 14. *Hispan.* **1721** KELLY 307 The Foot at the Cradle, and the Hand at the Roke[1] is the Sign of a good House-Wife. Spoken jocosely when we see a Woman spinning, and rocking the Cradle with her Foot. **1737** RAMSAY III. 195 The foot at the cradle an' the hand at the reel, Is a sign o' a woman that means to do weel. [[1] distaff.]

Foot out of the langel,[1] You have aye a.

1721 KELLY 392 . . . Spoken to them that perversely oppose every Thing. [[1] a tether.]

Foot, feet, *see also* All f. tread not in one shoe; Ball at one's f.; Best f. foremost; Better a bare f.; Better the f. slip; Bishop has put his f. in it; Cat would eat fish but not wet f.; Cool mouth and warm f.; Devil is known by his claws

(cloven f., horns); Dry f. warm head bring safe; Dust on f., (While); Foul f. makes full wame; Foul f. (You have o'er) to come so far ben; God comes with leaden f.; Going (Walking) f. aye getting; Hand and f., (With); Hand like a f.; Head and f. keep warm; Keep something for sore f.; Keep your f. dry and head hot; Length of person's f. (Find); Measure yourself by own f.; One f. in grave (To have); One f. in straw; One shoe not fit all f.; Open your mouth but you put your f. in it (Never); Peacock has fair feathers but foul f.; Seek in a sheep five f.; Shoe fits not every f.; Steal a hog and give the f.; Tell thy foe that thy f. acheth (Never); Thinks his f. be where his head; White f. (One), buy him; Will is ready (Where), f. is light; Wisdom has one f. on land, another on sea. *See also* Feet, Hind foot.

Football, *see* All fellows at f.

Footsteps, *see* Master's f. fatten soil.

Forbear not sowing because of birds.   (S 694)

1581 GUAZZO i. 21 Wee must not leave to sowe corne for feare least the byrdes eate it up. **1640** HERBERT no. 670.

Forbear, forborne, *see also* Bear and f.; Lawfully done which cannot be f.

Forbearance (Omittance, Sufferance) is no acquittance.   (F 584)

[L. *Quod defertur non aufertur.* What is deferred is not relinquished.] **1546** HEYWOOD II. iv. G4ᵛ But suffrance is no quittance in this dayment. **1548** HALL *Chron.* (1809, 100) The olde prouerbe sayeth, long sufferaunce is no acquittance. [1591] **1592** *Arden of Fevers.* II. ii. 87 Arden escap'd vs. . . . But forberance is no acquittance; another time wele do it. **1596** SPENSER *F.Q.* IV. iii. 11 But to forbeare doth not forgiue the det. **1599** SHAKES. *A.Y.* III. v. 133 But that's all one; omittance is no quittance. **1667** MILTON *P.L.* X. 52 But soon shall find Forbearance no acquittance ere day end.

Forbid a thing, and that we (women) will do.   (F 477. F 585. W 650)

[ov. *Am.* 3. 4. 17 *Nitimur in vetitum semper, cupimusque negata.*] *c.* **1386** CHAUCER *W. of Bath's Prol.* l. 519 Forbede us thyng, and that desiren we. **1567** *Merry Tales* no. 120 The more yee forbydde some women a thynge, the greater desyre they haue to do it. **1573** SANFORD 21 Mans desire is kindled through things forbidden. [c. 1587] **1592** KYD *Span. Trag.* III. v. That, they [women] are most forbidden, they will soonest attempt. [1591] **1592** *Arden of Fevers.* I. i. 52 Women, when they may, will not, But, beeing kept back, straight grow outragious. **1641** FERGUSSON no. 276. **1721** KELLY 107 Forbid a Fool a Thing, and that he will do.

Forbidden fruit is sweet.   (F 779)

[GEN. iii. 6.] *c.* **1386** CHAUCER *Parson' T.*s I. 332 The flessh hadde delit in the beautee of the fruyt defended. **1629** T. ADAMS *Serm.* (1861–2)

1. 53 But as the proverb hath it, apples are sweet when they are plucked in the gardener's absence. Eve liked no apple in the garden so well as the forbidden. **1661** *The Wandering Whore* Pt. v. 11 The forbidden fruit is sweetest.

Force hidden in a sweet command, There is great. (F 586)

1581 GUAZZO ii. 108 Threatning words, wherewith they make all the house to shake: not knowing that (as the Poet sayth) Great force lies hid in gentle Soveraigntie. **1640** HERBERT no. 589.

Force without forecast is of little avail.

1721 KELLY 106. **1732** FULLER no. 1589.

Force, *see also* Pope by voice, . . . emperor by f.; Subtlety is better than f.

Force put, He is at a. (P 668)

1657 G. STARKEY *Helmont's Vind.* 328 In expectation that Nature being forced to play a desperate game, and reduced to a forc't put, may [&c.]. **1678** RAY 79. **1772** NUGENT *Hist. Friar Gerund* I. 526 He thought that it might pass for a case of necessity, or forced-put. **1876** in *N. & Q.* 5th Ser. v. 266 A tradesman [of Torquay] told me . . . that he had left his house very early . . . 'but not from choice, 'twas a force-put'.

'Ford', In | in 'ham', in 'ley', and 'ton', the most of English surnames run.

1605 R. VERSTEGAN *Restit. of Dec. Intell.* (1673) 326 Ton . . . I take to be one of the greatest terminations we have, and . . . [it] may be said, . . . **1879** C. W. BARDSLEY *Rom. of Lond. Direct.* 32 The rhyme . . . is true, that . . . All names with this termination are local, and comprise a large proportion of our national nomenclature.

Ford, *see also* God strikes not with both hands; Praising a f. till a man be over (Not good).

Forecast is better than work-hard. (F 588)

1612 CHAPMAN *Widow's Tears* II. iv. Acknowledge forecast is better than labour. **1670** RAY 92. **1695** RAVENSCROFT 17 (as good as Work). **1721** KELLY 106 Force, without Forecaste, is little worth. Strength, unless guided by Skill and Discretion, will avail but little. **1732** FULLER no. 1588.

Forecasts all perils, He that | will never sail the sea.

a. **1585** MONTGOMERIE *Cherrie & Slae* xxxviii (1821) 22 'And I haif hard', quod Hope, 'that he Sall nevir schaip to sayle the se, That for all perrils castis'. **1659** HOWELL *Span. Prov.* 17 Who dares not adventure, let him not pass the Sea.

Forecasts all perils, He that | will win no worship.

1721 KELLY 167 . . . Because he will be frightened from any noble Attempt.

Forecast(s), *see also* Force without f. of little avail; Lie in bed and f.

Forego, *see* All have and naught f., (He would).

Forehead and the eye, In the | the lecture of the mind doth lie. *Cf.* Eye is the window of the heart. (F 590)

1611 JONSON *Cat.* IV. 434 In short, let it be writ in each mans fore-head What thoughts he beares the publike. **1616** DRAXE no. 654 (heart is read). **1639** CLARKE 269. **1670** RAY 92. **1710** PALMER 113.

Forehead, *see also* Penny in the f.

Foreheet[1] nothing but building churches and louping[2] over them, I will. (N 278)

1678 RAY (*Northern*) 355 I'll foreheet . . . nothing but building Churches and louping over them. **1738** SWIFT *Dial.* II. E.L. 314 I hear . . . you have foreswore the town.—No, madam; I never foreswore anything but the building of churches. [[1] forbid. [2] leaping.]

Foreheets,[1] That which one most | soonest comes to pass. (F 591)

1678 RAY 71. [[1] forbids.]

Fore-horse, *see* Ride the f.

Forelock, *see* Time by the f. (Take).

Foremost, *see* Dog (Hindmost, F.) may catch (catches) hare; Worst goes f.

Forenoon(s), *see* Longer f. shorter afternoon; Two f. in the same day (Cannot have).

Fore-rooms, *see* Lies backward and lets out her f.-r., (She).

Foreswear, *see* Foreheet (F.) nothing but building churches.

Foretold, *see* Long f. long last.

Forewarned, forearmed. (H 54)

[L. *Praemonitus, praemunitus.*] *a.* **1530** R. Hill's *Commonpl. Bk.* E.E.T.S. 132 He that is warned ys half armed. **1530** PALSGRAVE 417b He that is admonisshed is halfe armed. *c.* **1530** REDFORD *Wit & Sci.* 1021 'Once warne[d], half-armed' folk say. **1546** HEYWOOD II. vi. I2 Half warnd half armd. **1591** SHAKES. *3 Hen. VI* IV. i. 113 I will arm me, being thus fore-warn'd. [1591] **1592** *Arden of Fevers.* I. 583 Fore-warned, forearmed; who threats his enemy, Lends him a sword to guard himself withal. **1662** FULLER *Devon* 272 Let all ships passing thereby be forearmed because forewarned thereof. **1883** PAYN *Thicker than W.* ch. 12 But she was forewarned and forearmed.

Forewit, One good | is worth two afterwits. (F 595)

1545 TAVERNER A3 Better is one fore thought than two after. **1546** HEYWOOD I. viii. C1 Howbeit when bought wits to best price bee brought,

Yet is one good forewit woorth two after wits.
1588 A. MARTEN *Exhortation Harl. Misc.* 1744,
i. 171b Have hereafter as good a Fore-wit, as . . .
After-wit. **1609** HARWARD 109 Be philipp
forewitt and not Adam Afterwitt.

Forfeits, *see* Plays more than he sees (He that)
f. his eyes; Wipes his nose . . . f. his face.

Forge, *see* Water in a smith's f.

Forget(s), forgot(ten), *see* Bourbons learn nothing and f. nothing; Fool that f. himself; Forgive
and f.; Friar f. feud (Never); Learns young f.
not; Long absent soon f.; Musician has f. his note
(When), crumb in throat; Seldom seen, soon f.;
Soon learnt, soon f.

Forgive an enemy, If we are bound to |
we are not bound to trust him.
1732 FULLER no. 2728.

Forgive and forget.   (F 597)
a. **1225** *Ancrene Riwle* 124 Al þet hurt and al
þet sore were uorȝiten and forȝiuen uor gled-
nesse. **1377** LANGLAND *P. Pl.* B. xvii. 241 So wil
Cryst of his curteisye · and men crye hym mercy,
Bothe forȝiue and forȝete. **1546** HEYWOOD II.
ix. K3ᵛ Prayng hir, to forgeue and forget all
free. **1591** SHAKES. *3 Hen. VI* III. iii. 200 I forgive and quite forget old faults. **1595–6** *Id. Rich.*
II I. i. 156 Forget, forgive; conclude and be
agreed. **1602** *Id. A.W.* V. iii. 9 I have forgiven
and forgotten all. **1605–6** *Id. K.L.* IV. vii. 84
Pray you now, forget and forgive: I am old and
foolish. **1621** BURTON *Anat. Mel.* Democr. to
Rdr. (1651) 78 If . . . I have said amiss, let it be
forgotten and forgiven. **1775** SHERIDAN *Rivals*
v. iii. Give me your hand, Sir Lucius, forget and
forgive. **1894** LD. AVEBURY *Use of Life* ch. 2
Individuals often forget and forgive, but Societies
never do.

Forgive (pardon) all but (any sooner
than) thyself.   (A 199)
c. **1526** *Dicta Sap.* A3 Be mylde to other to
thyne owne selfe roughe. **1539** TAVERNER 2
Garden 42ᵛ Cato also sayde, that he forgaue al
men that offended saue him selfe. **1545** *Precepts
of Cato* Cleobulus 4 L4ᵛ Forgeue other, to
thee ofte offendynge, But thy selfe forgeue not
in any euyl doynge. **1581** GUAZZO ii. 102 By
the example of Cato, who sayd, He pardoned
everyone but hymselfe. *a.* **1593** PEELE *Edward I*
(Bullen 165) Pardon me and pardon all. **1611**
COTGRAVE s.v. Pardonner. **1640** HERBERT no.
677. **1664** CODRINGTON 192. **1670** RAY 10.

Forgive(n), *see also* Fristed is not f.; Vengeance
is to f. (Noblest).

Fork is commonly the rake's heir, The.
1732 FULLER no. 4536.

Fork(s), *see also* Better with a rake than a f.;
Fingers were made before f.

Form, *see* Hare always returns to f.

Forsake not the market for the toll.
                                              (M 671)
1623 CAMDEN 269. **1670** RAY 119.

Forsakes measure, He that | measure
forsakes him.   (M 803)
a. **1628** CARMICHAELL no. 724. **1641** FERGUSSON
no. 315 He that forsakes missour, missour forsakes him. **1721** KELLY 158 . . . That is, he who
is immoderate in any-Thing, Design, or Action,
shall meet with Treatment accordingly.

Forth bridles the wild Highlandman.
[The River Forth was a restraint upon Highland
raids.] **1818** SCOTT *Rob Roy* ch. 28 Bailie
Jarvie suggested, in his proverbial expression,
that 'Forth bridles the wild Highlandman'.
1886 STEVENSON *Kidnapped* ch. 26 Forth is our
trouble; ye ken the saying, . . .

Fortunate, If you are too | you will not
know yourself; if you are too un-
fortunate, nobody will know you.
1732 FULLER no. 2733.

Fortunate, *see also* Persuasion of f. sways
doubtful; Wicked (The more), more f.

Fortunatus' purse.
[= the inexhaustible purse of a fairy tale hero.]
1600 DEKKER *Old Fortunatus* III. i. 388 If this
strange purse his sacred vertues hold, Weele
circle England with a wast of Gold. **1626**
JONSON *Fortun. Isles* vii. 713, l. 184 Where
would you wish to be now, or what to see, Without the Fortunate Purse to bear your charges.
1910 *Times Wkly.* 8 July 515 The Chancellor of
the Exchequer . . . regards it as the bag of
FORTUNATUS in which he has only to dip his hand
to draw out as much as he pleases.

Fortune can take from us nothing but
what she gave us.   (F 599)
[PUB. SYRUS *Nihil eripit Fortuna nisi quod et
dedit.*] **1566** *Medea* tr. J. Studley C1 Full
well may fortunes weltying whele to beggyng
brynge my state, As for my worthy corage that
she neuer shall abate. **1592** DELAMOTHE 11
Fortune can take away our goods, but neuer our
vertue. **1640** BRATHWAITE *Art Asleep Husb.* 221
Fortune can but take from us what is hers. **1666**
TORRIANO *It. Prov.* 93, no. 26. **1732** FULLER no.
1598.

Fortune favour I may have her, If | for
I go about her: if fortune fail, you may
kiss her tail, and go without her.
                                              (F 613)
1659 HOWELL *Eng. Prov.* 15b. **1670** RAY 212.

Fortune favours fools.   (F 600)
[L. *Fortuna favet fatuis.*] *c.* **1560** L. WAGER *The
Longer thou Livest* D4 Fortune can exalte fooles.
1563 GOOGE *Epytaphes* Arb. 74 But Fortune
fauours Fooles as old men saye. **1603** N. BRETON
Pkt. of Letters in Wks. Gros. II *h* 33 Because

Fortune fauors few fooles this yeare, wee must tarry longer to play our game. **1643** T. BROWNE *Religio Medici* pt. i. § 18 That contemptible Proverb, That fools only are Fortunate.

Fortune favours the bold (brave).
(F 601)

[VIRGIL *Aen.* 10. 284 *Audentes fortuna iuvat.*] *c.*|1374 CHAUCER *Troilus* Bk. 4 l. 600 Thenk eek Fortune, as wel thiselven woost, Helpeth hardy man to his enprise. *c.* **1390** GOWER *Conf. Amantis* VII. 400 And saith, 'Fortune unto the bolde|Is favorable for to helpe'. **1481** CAXTON *Reynard* Arb. 66 Who that is hardy th[e] auenture helpeth hym. **1539** TAVERNER 9ᵛ Audaces fortuna iuuat. Fortune helpeth men of good courage. **1622** FLETCHER *Prophetess* IV. vi He is the scorn of Fortune: but you'll say, That she forsook him for his want of courage, But never leaves the bold. *c.* **1724** A. RAMSAY *The Widow can Bake* For fortune aye favours the active and bauld. **1841** CHAMIER *Tom Bowl.* ch. 11 Fortune, they say, favours the brave; . . . and Bowling . . . ran the vessel close to the fort.

Fortune is blind.
(F 604)

c. **1500** Proverbs at Leconfield (*Antiq. Rep.* 1809, iv. 418) Fortune is fykill fortune is blynde. **1583** MELBANCKE A1ᵛ Fortune is blinde and cannot see. **1586** LA PRIMAUDAYE 468 They are very blind, who, calling Fortune blind, suffer themselues to be guided and ledde by hir. *c.* **1587** KYD *Span. Trag.* l. 330 Fortune is blinde and sees not my deserts. **1587** *Mirror for Mag.* ed. Campbell 315. **1588** GREENE *Pandosto* Prose Wks. (1881-3) vi. 245 Fortune although blind, . . . sent them . . . a good gale of winde. **1596** SHAKES. *M.V.* II. i. 36 So may I, blind fortune leading me, Miss that which one unworthier may attain. **1598-9** *Id. Hen. V.* III. vi. 33 Fortune is painted plind, with a muffler afore her eyes, to signify to you that Fortune is plind. **1601** JONSON *Poetaster* V. i. 54 All humane businesse fortune doth command Without all order; and with her blinde hand, Shee, blinde, bestowes blinde gifts. *a.* **1607** MARSTON *What you Will* I. i.

Fortune is made of glass.
(F 607)

c. **1500** Proverbs at Leconfield (*Antiq. Rep.* 1809, iv. 418) Fortune is bretall and of a glassy metall. **1539** TAVERNER *Publius* C4 Fortune is brykle as glasse, when she glystereth, she breaketh. **1540** PALSGRAVE *Acolastus* 159 Men saye trewely herein, Fortune is made of glasse, whiche whyle it shineth moste glorious, is broken a sonder.

Fortune is variant (fickle).
(F 606)

c. **1390** GOWER *Conf. Amantis* VIII. 585 Fortune hath euer been muable and mai no while stande stable. *c.* **1420** LYDGATE *Assembly of Gods* st. 46 10 E.E.T.S. Varyaunt |she [Fortune] was. **1509** BARCLAY *Ship of Fools.* i. 126 Fortune euer hath an incertayne ende. **1592-1602** W. S. *Cromwell* II. i. 56 Fickle is fortune and her face is blinde.

Fortune knocks once at least at every man's gate.
(F 608)

1567 FENTON *Bandello* T.T. ii. 148 Fortune once in the course of our life dothe put into our handes

the offer of a good torne. **1869** HAZLITT 136. **1889** W. F. BUTLER *C. G. Gordon* 51 Fate, it is said, knocks one at every man's door . . . Gordon had just passed his thirtieth year when Fortune . . . knocked at . . . the door which was to lead him to fame.

Fortune smiles, When | embrace her.
(F 615)

1611 COTGRAVE s.v. Heur Good fortune quickly slips from such as heed it not. **1616** WITHALS 539 (take the advantage of it). **1620** SHELTON *Quix.* ii. v ii. 220 It is not fit that whilst good luck is knocking at our door we shut it: let us therefore sail with this prosperous wind. **1664** CODRINGTON 224. **1670** RAY 10 When Fortune smiles on thee, take the advantage. **1694** BOYER 110 When Fortune knocks, be sure to open the door. **1732** FULLER no. 5553.

Fortune to be pictured on a wheel, Not only ought | but every thing else in the world.

1651 HERBERT no. 1077.

Fortune to one is mother, to another is stepmother.
(F 609)

[*c.* **1515**] **1521** BARCLAY *Ecl.* v. l. 153 Fortune to them [towndwellers] is moche more fauorable, Fortune to them, is lyke a moder dere, As a stepmoder she dothe to vs [countrydwellers] apere. **1573** SANFORD A3 True it is as Hesiodus saith, time is otherwhile a mother, otherwhile a stepdame. **1578** *Courtly Controv.* G1 Fortune a continuall stepmother to suche, as she aduaunceth. **1581** T. HOWELL *Devices* (1906) 52 My stepdame strange, I Fortune yet doe finde. **1592** DELAMOTHE 11. **1651** HERBERT no. 1118.

Fortune (desire) torments me, If | hope contents me.
(F 614)

1592 DELAMOTHE 35 Desire tormentcth vs, and hope comforteth vs. **1598** SHAKES. *2 Hen. IV* II. iv. 171 'Si fortune me tormente, sperato me contento.' *Ibid.* V. v. 97 'Si fortuna me tormenta, spero contenta.' **1614** A. COPLEY *Wits, Fits and Fancies* 35 Hanniball Gonsago being in the low Countries ouerthrowne from his horse by an English Captaine, and commanded to yeeld himselfe prisoner: kist his sword and gaue it the English man saying: Si Fortuna me tormenta, Il speranza me contenta. **1622** SIR RICH. HAWKINS *Voyage into the S. Sea* 13 Si fortuna me tormenta; Esperanca me contenta: Of hard beginnings, many times come prosperous and happie events.

Fortune(s), see also Dances well to whom f. pipes; Enemies, (If you have no); Every man is the architect of own f.; Fence against ill f. (No); Flee never so fast, cannot flee f.; Folly of one man f. of another; Gains enough whom f. loses; Give a man f.; God sends f. to fools; Good man whom f. makes better; Great f. brings misfortune; Industry is f.'s right hand; Manners make often f.; Ounce of good f.; Put your finger in fire and say it was f. See also Good fortune, Ill fortune.

Forty, forties, *see* Farewell f. pence; Fool at f. is a fool indeed; Hungry f.

Forward cock that crows in the shell, It will be a.

1591 LYLY *Endym.* II. ii. 14 Away, peeuish boy, a rodde were better vnder thy girdle, than loue in thy mouth: it will be a forward Cocke that croweth in the shell.

Forward, *see also* End goes f., (He cares not' which); Go f. and fall.

Foster, *see* No longer f., no longer lemman.

Foul dirty ways, and a long sickness, Take heed of.   (H 379)

1599 MINSHEU *Span. Dial.* 84. **1651** HERBERT no. 1153.

Foul face, There is never a | but there's a foul fancy.

1917 BRIDGE 119 There's never a fou' face but there's a fou' fancy. Ugly people have ugly thoughts.

Foul feet, You have o'er | to come so far ben.[1]   (F 580)

c. **1641** FERGUSSON MS. no. 1608. **1721** KELLY 372 . . . That is, you are too mean to pretend to such a Courtship. [[1] into the house.]

Foul foot makes a full wame, A.
                                        (F 564)
1641 FERGUSSON no. 119. **1721** KELLY 27 . . . Industry will be sure of a Maintenance. A Man that carefully goes about his Business will have foul Feet.

Foul morning may turn to a fair day, A. *Cf.* Cloudy mornings.

1624 BURTON *Anat. Mel.* II. iii. III. 275 A lowring morning may turne to a faire after noone. **1732** FULLER no. 115.

Foul, He that has to do with what is | never comes away clean. *Cf.* Touches pitch, etc.

c. **1250** *Owl & Night.* 299 Alured seide an oþer side a word þat is isprunge wide: 'þat wit þe fule haueþ imene, ne cumeþ he neuer from him cleine.'

Foul water as soon as fair will quench hot fire.   (W 92)

1546 HEYWOOD I. v. B2. **1594** LYLY *Mother B.* III. iv. 24. *a.* **1628** CARMICHAELL no. 523 (slokins[1] fyre). **1639** CLARKE 44. [[1] quenches.]

Foul (*adj.*), *see also* Clout . . . nose on, (It is a f.); Fair and f., by dark are like store; Love (No) is f.

Foul(s) (*verb*), *see* No man f. hands in own business.

Found you and here (As I found you) I leave you, Here I.   (F 224)

c. **1513** MORE *Richard III* 1821 ed. 14 Such as I leaue you, suche bee my children lyke to fynde you. [*c.* 1550] **1560** *Nice Wanton* B1ᵛ A knaue I found the, a knaue I leaue the here. [*c.* 1553] **1566–7** UDALL *Ralph Roister D.* I. iii. 80 Here I founde you, and here I leave both twaine. *c.* **1590** *John of Bordeaux* l. 407 Fooles I found you and foull I leu ye. **1602** SHAKES. *A.W.* V. ii. 45 O my good lord, you were the first that found me.—Was I, in sooth? And I was the first that lost thee. **1636** W. SAMPSON *Vow Breaker* I. ii Fooles I found you, and so I must leave you in spite of my hart.

Found out, *see* Commandment (Eleventh); Eating and drinking (Ingenious who f. o.).

Foundation, *see* Good building without good f. (No); High buildings low f.

Four and spends five, He that has but | has no need of a purse.   (F 622)

1609 HARWARD 90ᵛ He that gayneth fower and spendeth six needeth no purse. **1623** WODROEPHE 278 Who hath but Foure, and spendeth Seauen, Needeth no Purse to put his Money in. **1732** FULLER no. 2134.

Four farthings and a thimble, will make a tailor's pocket jingle.   (F 72)

1659 HOWELL *Eng. Prov.* 15b. **1670** RAY 215.

Four good mothers have four bad daughters: truth, hatred; prosperity, pride; security, peril; familiarity, contempt.   (M 1206)

1647 *Countrym. New Commonw.* 5. **1659** N. R. 35 Four good Mothers beget four bad Daughters, Great familiarity contempt, Truth hatred, Virtue envy, Riches ignorance. **1666** TORRIANO *It. Prov.* 135 no. 21 (Security, danger).

Four pence to a groat, As like as.
                                        (F 623)
c. **1555** *Jack Juggler* E1ᵛ In euery thing as iust as. iiii. pens to a grote. **1678** RAY 286.

Four(s), *see also* Count not f. except in wallet; Simile (No) runs on all f.; Two and two make f.

Fowey, The gallants of.   (G 13)

1587 HARRISON'S *Descr. of Britain* in HOLINSHED i. 62 The ships of Fawy sailing on a time by Rhie and Winchelseie in the time of king Edward the third, refused stoutlie to vale anie bonet there, . . . Herevpon the Rhie and Winchelseie men made out vpon them with cut and long taile: but so hardlie were they interteined by the Fawy pirates (I should saie adventurers) that they were driven home againe . . . in token of their victorie . . . the Foyens were called the gallants of Fawy or Foy. **1602** R. CAREW *Survey* *of Cornwall* (1769) 135. **1787** GROSE (*Cornwall*) 161 The gallants of Foy. The inhabitants of Foy were, in the time of King Edward IV, famous for their privateers, and their gallant behaviour at sea; whence they obtained that denomination. **1920** F. MUIRHEAD *England* 179 It was . . . one of the foremost seaports of the kingdom, and the achievements of the 'Gallants of Fowey' rank with those of the 'Sea-Dogs of Devon'.

Fowl of a fair day, As fain (glad) as a. (F 624)

1377 LANGLAND *P. Pl.* B. x. 153 Thanne was I also fayne, as foule of faire morwe. **1678** RAY 285 (glad). **1862** HISLOP 40 As fain as a fool[1] o' a fair day. [[1] fowl.]

Fowl(s), *see* Far f. fair feathers; Fish of one and f. of another (Make).

Fowler's pipe sounds sweet till the bird is caught, The.

1617 R. BRATHWAIT *Solemn Disputation* 20 (while th' bird is caught). **1732** FULLER no. 4542.

Fox, He has caught a. (F 651)

1599 MINSHEU *Span. Dial.* 18 Some of vs may suffer himselfe to be turned into a foxe. i. To be drunk. **1620** SHELTON *Quix.* Pt. II. xxvi (iii. 8) *Note* As we say, to catch a fox. **1661** 23 April Coronation Day PEPYS *Diary* E.L. i. 159 My head began to turn, and I to vomitt, and if ever I was foxed, it was now. **1699** *New Dict. Canting Crew* E7 He has caught a fox, he is very drunk.

Fox fares best when he is banned (cursed), The. (F 632)

1548 A. BORDE *Introduction* E.E.T.S. 166 The more the fox is cursed, the better he doth fare. *c.* **1565** W. WAGER *Enough is as good as a feast* E4ᵛ. **1592** CHETTLE *Kindhartes Dreame* (1874) 70 But I perceiue you fare as the Fox, the more band, the better hap. **1602** *Thomas Ld. Cromwell* II. iii *Shakes. Apoc.* 173 Praie thy worst; The Fox fares better still when he is curst. **1605** JONSON *Volpone* V. iii. 119 The Foxe fares euer best, when he is cursed. **1614** CAMDEN 312 The Fox fareth well when he is cursed. **1655** FULLER *Ch. Hist.* III. v (1868) I. 411 These Caursines[1] were generally hated for their extortions. . . . [They] cared not what they were called, being akin to the cunning creature, which fareth best when cursed. **1721** KELLY 331 The tod[2] never fares better than when he's ban'd. Spoken when we are told that such People curse us, which we think the effect of Envy, the Companion of Felicity. The Fox is cursed, when he takes our Poultry. [[1] Lombard bankers of Cahors. [2] fox.]

Fox for his mate, He that has a | has need of a net at his girdle. (F 644)

1640 HERBERT no. 428.

Fox from a fern-bush, He does not know a. (F 630)

1580 LYLY *Euph. & his Eng.* ii. 92 It is a blynde Goose that knoweth not a Foxe from a Fearne-bush. **1587** BRIDGES *Def. of Govt.* 99 It seemed (as the saying is) either a foxe or a fearne brake. **1616** WITHALS 574 He spake of a Foxe but . . . it was but a ferne brake. **1639** CLARKE 143. **1846–59** *Denham Tracts* F.L.S. ii. 107.

Fox has once got in his nose, When the | he'll soon find means to make the body follow. (F 655)

1578 THOS. WHITE *Sermon at Paul's Cross* 3 Nov. (1577) 29 If his [the serpent's] head be once in he will shifte for himselfe, and soone winde in his whole body. **1591** SHAKES. *3 Hen. VI* IV. vii. 25. **1607** DEKKER & WEBSTER *Sir T. Wyatt* D1ᵛ. **1612** WEBSTER *White Devil* IV. i. 136. **1629** FORD *Lover's Melancholy* IV. ii.

Fox is brought to the furrier, At length the. (L 200)

1611 COTGRAVE s.v. Regnard Enfin les regnards (viz. their skinnes) se trouvent chez le pelletier: Prov. The craftie are at length surprised. **1640** HERBERT no. 81. **1796** EDGEWORTH *Par. Asst., Lit. Merchts.* iii (1903) 409 Still at your old tricks . . . No fox so cunning but he comes to the furrier's at last. **1818** SCOTT *Rob Roy* ch. 27 They'll be upsides wi' Rob at the last . . . the fox's hide finds aye the flaying knife.

Fox is known by his brush (furred tail), The. (F 633)

1545 BRINKLOW *Compl.* xxiv As yᵘ mayest knowe a foxe by his furred taile. **1607** WALKINGTON *Opt. Glass* 38 A fox is known by his brush.

Fox is the finder, The. (F 634a)

1587 J. BRIDGES *Defence of Govt.* A4 [The civil war in the Church of England] might haue bene ended long ago, had it not bene more by the importunity of our brethren themselues, who, (as the old saying accordeth, the Foxe the first fynder,) haue both made and continually receiued this ciuil warre. [1642] **1647** CLEVELAND *To Prince Rupert* l. 137 Who's doubly paid (fortune or we the blinder?) For making plots, and then for Fox the Finder. **1738** SWIFT *Dial.* I. E.L. 279. **1914** K. F. PURDON *Folk of Furry F.* ch. 7 'Dan Grennan . . . had a great deal to say . . . about a bullock that is missing. But I can't help thinking of a saying . . . how that the fox always smells his own smell!'

Fox knows much, The | but more he that catcheth him. (F 637)

1631 MABBE *Celestina* T.T. 207 If the fox be crafty, more crafty is he that catches him. **1640** HERBERT no. 280. **1706** STEVENS s.v. Zorro.

Fox lick a lamb, It is an ill sign to see a. (S 442)

1678 RAY 142.

Fox may grow grey, but never good, The. (F 638. W 616)

1572 J. PARINCHEF *Extract of Examples* 18 The Foxe may change his cote, but neuer will leaue

his crafte (From Brusonius lib. I. cap. 1.).   **1631**
MABBE *Celestina* T.T. 207 Though the fox change
his haire, yet he never changeth his nature.   **1659**
TORRIANO no. 7 A wolfe casts his haire, but not
his malice.   **1721** KELLY 361 You breed of the
tod, you grow gray before you grow good.
Spoken to old gray headed Sinners who will not
reform their Lives.   **1749** FRANKLIN Mar. Many
foxes grow grey, but few grow good.

Fox preaches, When the | then beware your geese.   (F 656)

a. **1450** *Castle of Perseverance* l. 804. (kepe wel
yore gees).   *c.* **1460** *Towneley Myst.* E.E.T.S. 12
Let furth youre geyse, the foxe wille preche.
c. **1502** *Robert the Deuil* in *Ancient Eng. Fictions*
23 Take hede the foxe wyll be an aunker for he
begynneth to preche.   **1546** HEYWOOD II. vii. I4ᵛ
For though this appeere a propre pulpet peece,
Yet whan the foxe preacheth, than beware our
geese.   **1614** CAMDEN 304.   **1721** KELLY 344
When the Tod[1] preaches, look to the Geese.
When wicked Men put on a Cloak of Religion,
suspect some wicked Design. [1 fox.]

Fox (Wolf) preys farthest from his home (den), The.   (F 639)

1585 E. SANDYS *Serm.* 3, 64 The fox will not
worry near his bele [shelter, refuge].   **1592**
DELAMOTHE M4ᵛ A good wolfe will neuer hunt
too neare his denne.   **1597** *Politeuphuia* 169
(as 1592).   **1629** T. ADAMS *Serm.* (1861–2) II. 317
The fox seldom preys near home, nor doth Satan
meddle with his own.   **1659** HOWELL *Eng. Prov.*
2b.   **1670** RAY 31 The fox preys furthest from's
hole. Crafty thieves steal far from home.   **1706**
STEVENS s.v. Lobo.

Fox run, Though the | the chicken has wings.   (F 650)

1640 HERBERT no. 549.   **1732** FULLER no. 5008.

Fox should not be of the jury at a goose's trial, A.

1732 FULLER no. 116.   **1802** WOLCOT (P. Pindar)
Middl. Elect. i A fox should not be of the jury
Upon a goose's trial.

Fox that had lost its tail would persuade others out of theirs, The.   (F 646)

a. **1581** N. WOODES *Conflict of Conscience* G3ᵛ
The Foxe . . . caught in snare, and scapt with
losse of tayle, To cut off theirs, as burthenous,
did all the rest counsayll.   **1658** FLECKNOE
Enigm. Characters 78 Like the fox, who having
lost his own taile, would needs perswade all
others out of theirs.

Fox to keep the (his) geese (hens), He sets the.   (F 643)

1589 *The Contre-League* tr. E.A. 40 A wolfe to
keepe the sheepe, and a foxe to looke to the
hennes.   **1639** CLARKE 9.   **1672** WALKER 31 no.
52.   **1709** O. DYKES *Eng. Prov.* 45 He sets the
Fox to keep his Geese . . . reflects upon . . . men
. . . intrusting either *Sharpers* with their *money*,
Blabs with their *Secrets*, or *Enemies* . . . with

their *Lives*.   **1822** SCOTT *Nigel* ch. 29 Come,
damsel, now I will escort you back to the Lady
Mansel, and pray her . . . that when she is again
trusted with a goose, she will not give it to the
fox to keep.

Fox turns monk, At length the.   (F 640)

1611 COTGRAVE s.v. Moine.   **1640** HERBERT no.
72.

Fox was sick, The | and he knew not where: he clapped his hand on his tail, and swore it was there.   (F 641)

1659 HOWELL *Eng. Prov.* 12a The Fox had a
wound he knew not where, He look'd in his
arse and found it there.   **1678** RAY 71.   **1738**
SWIFT Dial. II. E.L. 300 I have cut my finger . . .
this finger: no, 'tis this: I vow I can't find which
it is.—Ay; the fox had a wound, and he could
not tell where, &c.   **1830** LYTTON *Paul C.* ch. 18
'The fox had a wound, and he could not tell
where'—we feel extremely unhappy, and we
cannot tell *why*.

Fox's wiles will never enter the lion's head, The.   (F 659)

1580 LYLY *Euph. & his Eng.* ii. 108 The Foxes
wiles shal neuer enter into ye Lyons head, nor
Medeas charmes into *Philautus* heart.

Fox(es), *see also* Best among them (Never a),
as fellow said by f. cub; Bought the f.-skin for
three pence; Brains of a f. of little service if . . .
paw of lion; Deal with a f. (If you); Deceive the
f. must rise betimes; Fie upon hens, quoth f.;
Flap with a f.'s tail, (Give one a); Follow the old
f.; Goose that comes to f.'s sermon (Blind); Isle
of Wight has no f.; Lion's skin cannot (If), the
f.'s shall; Long runs the f. as he has feet; No
more of the f. than the skin (You can have);
Old f. not easily snared; Old f. want no tutors;
Red as a f.; Sleepy f. has seldom feathered
breakfasts; Tail does often catch f.; Take hares
with f.; Wolf and f. of one counsel. *See also
under* Tod.

Frail, *see* Flesh is f.

France is a meadow that cuts thrice a year.   (F 662)

[Fr. France est un pré qui se tond trois foys
l'année.]   **1640** HERBERT no. 892.

France (England) win, He that will | must with Scotland first begin.   (F 663)

1548 HALL *Chron.* (1890) 55 The old auncient
prouerbe . . . whiche saieth he that will Fraunce
wynne, muste with Scotlande firste beginne.
1577 HOLINSHED *Chron.* (1808) 66 Rafe Neuill
. . . thought good to mooue the King to begin
first with Scotland; . . . concluding . . . with this
old saieng; that who so will France win, must
with Scotland first begin.   **1599** SHAKES. *Hen. V.*
I. ii. 166 But there's a saying . . . ; If that you
will France win, Then with Scotland first begin.

1902 A. LANG *Hist. Scot.* II. 363 Father Creighton and other Scots held that 'He who would England win Must with Scotland first begin', and credulously believed that James would be converted.

France's ruin, The day of | is the eve of the ruin of England.

1626 SIR T. OVERBURY *Obs. Trav.* Wks. (1890) 245 Now the only entire body in Christendome that makes head against the *Spanish* monarchy, is *France*; and therefore they say in *France*, that the day of the ruine of *France*, is the eve of the ruine of England.

France, *see also* King of F.

Franciscans' hackney, *see* Go upon F. h.

Fraud, *see* Frost and f. end in foul.

Fray, *see* Better come at end of feast than beginning of f.; First blow makes . . . the second makes a f.; Thrift and he are at f.

Free and easy.

1699 LISTER *Journ. Paris* 41 In a very free and easy posture. **1711** *Spectator* no. 119 ¶ 3 The fashionable world is grown free and easy. **1764** COWPER to Mrs. Hill 5 Jan. Reading over what I have written, I find it perfectly free and easy. **1864** NEWMAN *Apol.* ch. 2. I had a lounging free-and-easy way of carrying things on.

Free as a bird in air. (B 357)

1533 J. HEYWOOD *Pardoner and Friar* A1 As free As be the byrdes that in the ayre flee. **1631** T. POWELL *Tom of all Trades* New Sh. S. 166 He may trade as free as bird in ayre.

Free as air (the wind). (A 88)

[*c.* 1592] **1596** *Edward III* II. i. 286 Religion is austere and bewty gentle; To strict a gardion for so faire a ward! O, that shee were, as is the aire, to mee! **1599** SHAKES. *A.Y.* II. vii. 48 I must have liberty Withal, as large a charter as the wind, To blow on whom I please. **1604** *Id. O.* (Q) V. ii. 220 Liberall as the ayre. **1604** MARSTON *What You Will* I. iii. Free as ayre. **1607** HEYWOOD *Fair Maid of the Exchange* (1874) ii. 18 As free as aire. **1608** SHAKES. *C. I.* ix. 88 Were he the butcher of my son, he should Be free as is the wind. **1608–9** FLETCHER *Faithful Shep.* I. i Be ye fresh and free as Air. **1820** S. ROGERS cited Byron *Lett.* Prothero v. 138 As free as air.

Free country, This is a.

1833 J. NEAL *The Down-Easters* I. 102 Free country, neighbor. **1889** WESTALL *Birch Dene* (1891) 243 It would never do to make th' cottages too comfortable. . . . And this is a free country. Them as doesn't like 'em can leave 'em. **1911** *Spectator* 2 Sept. 339 I can leave off work when I please, and so can Smith, Brown, Jones, and Robinson. . . . This is a free country!

Free (liberal) of another man's cost (pottage), To be. (M 613)

1551 R. CROWLEY *Philargyrie* C2ᵛ I wyll, though he Liberall be Of that which coste me nought.

1583 MELBANCKE P2ᵛ It is an easie matter, but most wicked, to bee liberall of that whiche is not mine owne but my husbands. **1584** A. MUNDY *Watchword to England* 376 Largiuntur ex alieno, they be liberall of that, which is not their owne to giue. **1600** T. HEYWOOD *et al.* *I Edw. IV* i. 71 You can be frank of another mans cost. **1623** J. LEICESTER no. 83 (Liberal of). **1732** FULLER no. 5861 You are very free of another Man's Pottage.

Free of fruit that wants an orchard, He is.

1721 KELLY 134 . . . Spoken to them who tell how free and liberal they would be, if they had such Things, or were such Persons.

Free of her lips, free of her hips. (L 325)

1576 PETTIE ii. 32 They are as loose of their lips and as free of their flesh. **1678** RAY 62. **1732** FULLER no. 6269.

Free of his gift as a poor man is of his eye, He is as. (G 96)

1546 HEYWOOD I. xi. D4ᵛ As fre of gyft as a poore man of his eye. **1584** WITHALS D4ᵛ (blinde man). **1639** CLARKE 242 (a Jew of the eye). **1659** HOWELL *Eng. Prov.* 14a.

Free of horse that never had one, He is. (H 695)

c. 1300 *Provs. of Hending* xxvii He is fre of hors þat ner nade non, quoþ Hendyng. **1641** FERGUSSON no. 828. They are good willie of their horse that hes nane.

Free, He is not | that draws his chain. (C 213)

1592 DELAMOTHE 15 The horse that draws after him his halter is not altogether escaped. **1640** HERBERT no. 830. **1659** HOWELL *It. Prov.* 6.

Free(r), *see also* Ape is of his tail (As f. as an); Love is f.; Nothing f. than a gift; Thought is f.; Too f. to be fat.

Freedom is a fair thing. (F 668)

1375 BARBOUR *Bruce* I. l. 225 A! fredome is A noble thing! **1641** FERGUSSON no. 264.

Freemen, *see* Mountaineers always f.

Freets[1] fail, When all | fire's good for the fiercy.[2] (F 259)

a. 1628 CARMICHAELL no. 1304 Quhen althings failes, fyre is gude for the fairsie. **1641** FERGUSSON no. 282 Fire is good for the farcie. **1721** KELLY 353 . . . Spoken when after ordinary Attempts, we betake ourselves to extraordinary. [1 charms. 2 glanders.]

Freezes who does not burn, He.

1907 *Brit. Wkly.* 19 Dec. 321 That old saying, 'Alget qui non ardet'—'he freezes who does not burn', is true . . . , and wherever we find . . . success, it has been attained as the result of . . . whole-hearted enthusiasm.

Freight, *see* Many ventures make full f.

Freit(s), *see* Follows f. (He that).

French leave, To take.

[= to depart, act, without asking leave or giving notice.] **1771** SMOLLETT *Humph. Clink.* (1895) 238 He stole away an Irishman's bride, and took a French leave of me and his master. **1816** SCOTT *Antiq.* ch. 3 I began to think you had . . . taken French leave, as . . . MacCribb did, when he went off with one of my Syrian medals. **1841** CHAMIER *Tom Bowl.* ch. 2 I kept thinking of Susan, and . . . made up my mind to take French leave and visit her.

French soldier carries a marshal's baton in his knapsack, Every.

[*Tout soldat français porte dans sa giberne le bâton de maréchal de France.* Attributed (in a slightly different form) to Louis XVIII (*Moniteur Univ.* Aug. 8, 1819) and to Napoleon (E. BLAZE, *La vie militaire sous l'Empire* (1837) I. v).] **1867–77** FROUDE *Short. Stud.* (1890) III. 204 It was said a few years ago that every French drummer-boy knew that he carried a marshall's baton in his knapsack.

French would be the best cooks in Europe if they had got any butcher's meat, The.

1874 BAGEHOT *Biog. Stud., Guizot* 358 Parisian literature . . . generally reminds its readers of the old saying, . . .

French, *see also* Jack would be gentleman if could speak F.; Pedlar's F.; Tottenham is turned F.

Frenchmen, *see* Englishman (One) can beat three F.

Frenzy, heresy, and jealousy, seldom cured.   (F 672)

a. **1529** SKELTON *Replycacion* l. 406 For be ye wele assured That frensy nor ielousy nor heresy wyll neuer dye. **1591** ARIOSTO *Orl. Fur.* Harington XXXI [moral] Our old English Prouerbe: From Heresie, Phrenesie, and Iealousie, good Lord deliuer me. **1651** HERBERT no. 1049.

Frequent (*verb*), *see* Well used (Where men are) they'll f.

Fresh as a daisy (buttercup).

1813 BARRETT *Heroine* ed. Raleigh 236 (oyster) 261 (daisy). **1857** G. ELIOT *Scenes of Clerical Life* 'Janet's Repentance' ch. 7. **1964** *Times* 21 Oct. [Olympic Games] Miss Packer . . . World record, yet fresh as a buttercup.

Fresh as a rose.   (R 176)

c. **1390** CHAUCER *W. of Bath's Prol.* l. 448 As fressh as is a rose. **1412–20** LYDGATE *Troy Book* v. 2897 With swetenes freshe as any rose.

1580 MUNDAY *Zelauto* P3 As fresh as the redolent Rose. **1590** SPENSER *F.Q.* II. ix. 36 That was right faire and fresh as morning rose. **1678** RAY 284 . . . in June.

Fresh as flowers in May.   (M 763)

c. **1370** CHAUCER *Knights T.* l. 1037 Fressher than the May with floures newe. *c.* **1380** *Id. Troilus & Cressida* Bk. 5, l. 844 As fressh as brauche in May. *c.* **1440** *Lyf of our Lady* G2 (Caxton) Fayrer than Floure in maye. **1631** HEYWOOD *Fair Maid of West* II. I. You shall meete some of them sometimes as fresh as flowers in May.

Fresh as paint.

1850 THACKERAY *Pendennis* ch. 7.

Fresh fish and new-come guests smell in three days.   (F 310)

1580 LYLY *Euph. & his Eng.* ii. 81 As we say in *Athens,* fishe and gestes in three dayes are stale. **1584** WITHALS B2ᵛ After three dayes fish is vnsauorie, and so is an ill guest. **1611** COTGRAVE s.v. Poisson. **1648** HERRICK *Hesper.* 378 Wks. (1893) I. 189 Two dayes y'ave landed here; a third yee know, Makes guests and fish smell strong; pray go. **1670** RAY 90 Fresh fish and new come guests, smell by they are three days old.

Fresh fish and poor friends become soon ill savoured.

1721 KELLY 106 . . . Spoken when we see poor Relations slighted.

Fret like gummed taffeta (velvet), To.   (T 8)

[The material being stiffened with gum, quickly rubbed and fretted itself out.] **1597** SHAKES. *I Hen. IV* II. ii. I I have removed Falstaff's horse, and he frets like a gummed velvet. **1604** DEKKER *News from Graves-end* (*Plague Pamphlets* ed. Wilson 67) Fret not worse than gumd Taffety. **1604** MARSTON *What You Will* I. ii. **1629** T. ADAMS *Serm.* (1861–2) II. 361 Shall the black coat carry away the tithe-shock? The gummed taffeta gentlemen would fret out at this. **1738** SWIFT *Dial.* II. E.L. 312 Smoke miss; faith, you have made her fret like gum taffeta.

Fret one's self to fiddlestrings, To.

1834 J. B. KER 6 He frets his guts to fiddle strings. **1835** MRS. CARLYLE *Lett.* I. 43 I do but . . . fret myself to fiddlestrings. **1876** MRS. BANKS *Manch. Man* ch. 43 She was fretting herself to fiddle-strings for a fellow younger than herself.

Friar, a liar, A.   (F 674)

1381 WALSINGHAM *Historia Anglicana* (Rolls Ser.) II. 13. *Nota Contra Fratres Mendicantes.* . . . In diebus istis . . . bonum [erat] argumentum. . . . 'Hic est Frater, ergo mendax.' *c.* **1568** CURIO *Pasquin in a Trance* tr. W. P. 65ᵛ Fryers and lyers shaped both in one moulde. **1647** TRAPP *Comm.* I. *Tim.* iv. 2 It was grown to a common proverb, A friar, a liar.

Friar forgot feud, Never.

1820 SCOTT *Monast.* ch. 10 The devil was in me when I took this road—I might have remembered the proverb, 'Never Friar forgot feud'.

Friar never loved, What was good the.
(F 676)

c. **1605** DAVIES *Wit's Pilg.*, 18 There was a time (to speak whereof I faint Sith That that was, nere lou'd the ducking Frir'e). **1619** J. FAVOUR *Antiquity* 412 It is an old said saw, *Was good, neuer loued the Frier.* a. **1633** JONSON *T. Tub* III. vii. 13 What should have beene, that never lov'd the Friar. **1662** FULLER Cardigan 26. **1670** RAY 94.

Friar preached against stealing, and had a goose (pudding) in his sleeve, The.
(F 675)

c. **1525** *Hundred Mer. Tales* 68 in *Shakes. Jest-Bks.* i. 97 In his sermon there he [the friar] rebuked . . . them that met to breke theyr faste . . . and said it was called the deuyls blacke brekefast. And with that worde spekynge . . . there fell a podyng out of his sleue which he hym selfe had stolen. **1640** HERBERT no. 737. **1659** HOWELL *Eng. Prov.* 2a . . . when he had a pudding in his sleeve.

Friar's beaten, When the | then comes James.
(F 677)

1639 CLARKE 282. **1695** RAVENSCROFT 62 (Jack).

Friars observant spare their own and eat other men's.
(F 678)

1573 SANFORD 105. **1578** FLORIO *First F.* 30. **1629** *Bk. Mer. Rid.* Prov. no. 112.

Friar(s), *see also* Conscience as large as a f.'s sleeve, (He has a); Devil the f. but where he was? (Where had the); Do as the f. says; Fly and eke a f. will fall in every dish; Pudding for a f.'s mouth.

Friday and the week is seldom alike.

c. **1386** CHAUCER *Knight's T.* l. 1539 Selde is the Friday al the wowke y-like. **1874** W. PENGELLY in *N. & Q.* 5th Ser. II. 184 [Corn.] Friday and the week are seldom aleek.

Friday look (face), A.
(F 681)

1583 MELBANCKE *Philotimus* E1ᵛ Friday faced scoulds. **1592** GREENE *Wks.* Gros. xii. 120 The foxe made a Friday face, counterfeiting sorrow. **1846** DENHAM 6 Has a Friday look (sulky, downcast).

Friday night's dream on the Saturday told, is sure to come true be it never so old.

Cf. **1615** SIR T. OVERBURY etc. 'Character of a Milkmaid' A Frydayes dreame is all her superstition: that shee conceales for feare of anger. **1846** DENHAM 11. **1898** HARE *Shropshire* ch. 2

Friday, in this neighbourhood, is still called Cross Day. . . .

Friday will be either king or underling.

1587 W. HARRISON *Description of England* New Sh. S. ii. 90 The fridaie being commonlye called among the vulgar sort either King or worling, because it is either the fairest or foulest of the seauen. **1875** A. B. CHEALES *Proverb Folk-Lore* 19.

Friday's hair, and Saturday's horn, goes to the D'ule[1] on Monday morn.
(F 682)

[i.e. unlucky to cut hair on Friday and nails on Saturday.] **1678** RAY 294. [1 devil.]

Friday's moon, come when it will comes too soon.

1790 GROSE s.v. Popular Superstitions 47. **1869** HAZLITT 138.

Friday, *see also* Sings on F. will weep Sunday.

Friend and your flatterer too, I cannot be your.
(F 709)

1550 R. CROWLEY *One & Thirty Epigrams* E.E.T.S. 30 A Flatteryng frende is worse than a foe. **1584** WITHALS 16ᵛ The flatterer doth praise and commend, but yet for all that hee is no true frend. **1592** DELAMOTHE 29 The frend that doth flatter, is a foe. **1596** WARNER *Albion's Eng.* x. 61, S6ᵛ We cannot also loue our Friends, and flatter their A-misse. **1669** PENN *No Cross, No Crown* II. xix Phocion . . . was honest and poor . . . Antipater, pressing him to submit to his sense, he answered, 'Thou canst not have me for thy friend and flatterer too'. **1732** FULLER no. 2592. **1744** FRANKLIN Sept. The same man cannot be both friend and flatterer.

Friend as far as the altar (conscience permits), A.
(F 690)

1536 ELYOT *Lett.* to Cromwell in *Governour* ed. Croft cxxx The amity betwene me and sir Thomas More, which was but *usque ad aras*, as is the proverb. **1539** TAVERNER I *Garden* E5ᵛ Pericles . . . to his frend requyrynge hym to beare false witnesse for hym, . . . aunswered: he wolde be his frende but vnto the aultre. Signifieng, that so farre forth a man may do pleasure to his frende, as he go not beyonde the boundes of religion and honestye. **1547** BALDWIN *Treatise Moral Philosophy* P4ᵛ It is lawfull to be a frende, but no farther then to the aulter: that is we ought not for our frendes sake to transgresse our religion. **1583** G. BABINGTON *Exposn. of Commandments* P.S. 446 Pericles an heathen man could say, we must be a friende to our friende no further than the altar. **1612** SHELTON *Quix.* IV. vi (i. 318) . . . usque ad aras . . . **1736** BAILEY *Dict.* s.v. Conscience.

Friend asks, When a | there is no to-morrow.
(F 722)

1611 COTGRAVE s.v. Demain. **1640** HERBERT no. 32. **1710** PALMER 367.

Friend at a sneeze; He is a | the most you can get of him is a *God bless you.*
(F 703)

c. 1450 SHIRLEY'S MS. Addit. 16165 fol. 244 Balade Yit might I seyne, cryst se 'eyne [= save] as whan men sneese. 1530 PALSGRAVE 866a Christ helpe, as we say to one, when he neseth. *c.* 1566 *The Bugbears* I. ii. 71-2 When he happnethe to sneese in the nighte hath he not ned of on to saie Christe helpe. 1651-3 JER. TAYLOR *Sunday Serm.* XIII (1850) 162 'A friend at a sneeze and an alms-basket full of prayers', a love that is lazy . . . and a pity without support, are the images and colours of that grace, whose very constitution and design is beneficence and well-doing. 1659 TORRIANO no. 171 (God help thee). 1686-7 J. AUBREY *Remains of Gent. and Jud.* ed. J. Britten 103 We haue a Custome, that when one sneezws, every one els putts off his hatt, and bowes, and cries God bless you Sir. 1732 FULLER no. 2436.

Friend at (in) court, A.

1655 DICKSON *On Ps.* cv. 16 When the Lord was to bring his people into Egypt He provided so as they should have a friend at court before they came. 1848 DICKENS *Dombey* ch. 38 I shouldn't wonder—friends at court you know.

Friend in court is better than (worth) a penny in purse, A. (F 687)

c. 1400 *Rom. Rose* l. 5541 For freend in court ay better is Than peny in [his] purs. *a.* 1534 *Hyckescorner* 659 [Frewyll] But a frende in courte is worth a peny in purse. 1580 LYLY *Euph.* & *his Eng.* ii. 227 I know that a friende in the court is better then a penney in the purse. 1598 SHAKES. *2 Hen. IV* V. i. 29 I will use him well: a friend i' the court is better than a penny in purse. 1670 RAY 73 . . . is worth a penny in a man's purse.

Friend in need is a friend indeed, A.
(F 693)

c. 1275 *Provs. of Alfred* Skeat 50 A such fere þe is help in mode. *c.* 1430 LYDGATE *Minor Poems* E.E.T.S. ii. 755 Ful weele is him that fyndethe a freonde at neede. 1460 WILLIAM WORCESTER *Paston Letters* (1901) i. 507 A very frende at nede experience will schewe be deede. 1530 R. WHITFORD *Werke for Housholders* H2 A true frende loueth at all tymes and neuer feyleth at nede. 1572 CRADOCKE *Ship of assured Safety* 97 Faire fare a good freend at neede. 1599 [SHAKES.] *Pass. Pilgr.* 20, l. 51 He that is thy friend indeed, He will help thee in thy need. 1641 FERGUSSON no. 815 There is no friend to a friend in mister.[1] 1678 RAY 142. 1802 EDGEWORTH *Rosanna* ch. 4. 1866 READE *G. Gaunt* ch. 46. [¹ need.]

Friend in the market is better than money in the chest, A.

1664 CODRINGTON 184 A Friend in the way is better than a penny in the Purse. 1706 STEVENS s.v. Amigo. 1732 FULLER no. 119.

Friend is another self, A. (F 696)

[ARIST. *Eth.* 4.4 ἔστι γὰρ ὁ φίλος ἄλλος αὐτός.] 1539 TAVERNER I *Garden* F1ᵛ Demaunded, what a frend is, One soule, quoth he [Aristotle], in two bodyes. *Ibid.* F6 Demaunded what is a frende, he [Zeno] aunswered on other I. 1542 ERASM. tr. Udall *Apoph.* (1877) 233 The prouerbe *amicus alter ipse* . . . two frendes are one soul and one body. 1567 BALDWIN *Treatise of Moral Phil.* P6ᵛ A frende is properlye named thother I. 1576 PETTIE i. 157 Of all griefs it is most griping when friends are forced to part each from other . . . when own's self is separated from himself, or at least his second self. 1579 LYLY *Euph.* i. 197 A friend is . . . at all times an other I. 1579 *Proverbs* of Sir James Lopez de Mendoza tr. B. Googe 101ᵛ We reade in the Cronicle of the Philosophers that Aristotle beeing demaunded what hee accounted a friende to be; made answere, that it was one minde in two bodyes. 1596 M.B. *Trial of true Friendship* B1ᵛ My friend . . . is another my selfe. *Ibid.* B2 A frend is called alter idem, another moity, or another selfe. 1631 F. LENTON *Characters* (1663) sig. H *A true friend,* . . . He is a mans second selfe.

Friend is my nearest relation, A good.
(F 701)

1611 COTGRAVE s.v. Parenté A sound friend is a second kinsman. 1732 FULLER no. 151.

Friend is never known till a man have need, A. (F 694)

[ENN. ap. Cic. *Am.* 17. 64 *Amicus certus in re incerta cernitur.* *c.* 1190 *Li Proverbe au Vilain* (Tobler) 32 Au besoing voit on qui amis est, ce dit li vilains.] *c.* 1300 BRUNNE *Handl. Synne* l. 2251 At nede shul men proue here frendys. *c.* 1340 DAN MICHEL *Ayenbite* (Morris) 186 Ate niede: me y3i3þ huet þe urend is. 1380 GOWER *Conf. Amantis* v. 4912 Thou schalt finde At nede fewe frendes kinde. *c.* 1489 CAXTON *Sonnes of Aymon* xix. 433 It is sayd, that at the nede the frende is knowen. 1546 HEYWOOD I. xi. E4. 1567 W. LILY *Short Introd. of Grammar* C5 A true friende, is tried in a doubtful matter. 1594 *Knack to Know an Honest Man* i. 281 When is the time for friends to shew themselues, But in extremitie. 1599 PORTER *Angry Wom. Abing.* Mal. Soc. l. 2312 Amicus certus in re [in] certa cernitur. 1614 CAMDEN 302. 1860 PEACOCK *Gryll Grange* ch. 34 Friends are shown in adversity.

Friend is not so soon gotten as lost, A.
(F 695)

1567 PAINTER *Pal. of Pleasure* Jacobs ii. 177 As the common prouerbe and wise sayinge reporteth, that the vertue is no lesse to conserue frendship gotten, than the wisedome was great to get and win the same. 1599 PORTER *Angry Wom. Abingd.* Mal. Soc. l. 1835 By lady, an friend is not so soone gotten as lost. 1732 FULLER no. 1612.

Friend that grinds at my mill, He is my.
(F 705)

1616 DRAXE no. 801. 1639 CLARKE 26. 1773 VIEYRA s.v. Amigo.

Friend thy foe, Make not thy.

c. 1327 *Chester Plays, Crucifixion* Shaks. Soc. II. 63 Ah! man, be still, I thee praye, . . . Make not thy frende thy foe.

Friend to a bosom friend; No | no enemy to a bosom enemy.

1721 KELLY 261.

Friend to everybody is a friend to nobody, A. (F 698)

1623 WODROEPHE 475 All Men's Friend, ne Man's Friend. **1642** TORRIANO 9. **1645** FULLER *Gd. Thts. Bad T.; M. Cont.* xii I cannot conceive how he can be a friend to any, who is a friend to all. **1727** GAY *Fables, Hare & many Fr.* Friendship, like love, is but a name, Unless to one you stint the flame. **1778** JOHNSON in *Boswell* lxiv (1847) 593 An old Greek said, 'He that has *friends* has *no friend*'.[1] [¹ οὐθεὶς φίλος ᾧ πολλοὶ φίλοι. ARISTOTLE, *Eud. Eth.* 7. 12.]

Friend to thyself, Be a | and others will befriend thee. (F 684)

xvc. Early Eng. Carols (Greene) 382 Be thi own freynd. **1545** *Precepts of Cato* i, no. 40, G2 Be a frende to thy frend, but yet se thou most of al, be thine owne frend. **1611** COTGRAVE s.v. Valoir As thou of thine owne selfe doest deeme, so other men will thee esteeme. **1721** KELLY 57 ... Men's Friends commonly bear a proportion to their Circumstances in the World. **1732** FULLER no. 847.

Friend too cheap to thee nor thyself too dear to him, Make not thy. (F 711)

1601 SHAKES. *T.N.* III. ii. 50 This is a dear manikin to you, Sir Toby.—I have been dear to him, lad—Some two thousand strong, or so. **1659** HOWELL *Eng. Prov.* 18b.

Friends agree best at a distance. (F 734)

1592 DELAMOTHE 45 He that will keepe his frend, let him haue nothing to doe with him. **1611** COTGRAVE s.v. Entretenir He that loues to continue a friend must haue but little to doe with him. **1621** J. TAYLOR (Water-P.) *Trav. Twelvepence* 1630 ed. 71 But there's no great loue lost 'twixt them and mee, We keepe asunder, and so best agree. **1721** KELLY 103.

Friends all things are common, Among. (F 729)

[PYTHAGORAS Κοινὰ τὰ τῶν φίλων.] **1483** TERENCE *Vulgaria* S.T.C. 23904 P8ᵛ It is an olde byworde All thyngys are comon amonge frendys. **1539** TAVERNER 52ᵛ Amicorum omnia sunt communia. Amonges frendes all thynges be commune. **1546** W. HUGH *Troub. Man's Med.* (1831) I. i. 3 As all things are common among them which are trusty and faithful friends, so, doubtless, are the very affections of the mind. **1771** FLETCHER OF MADELEY *Wks.* ii. 319 (are or should be common). **1853** TRENCH vi. 134 ... Where does this find its exhaustive fulfilment, but in the communion of saints?

Friends are thieves of time. (F 735)

1605 BACON *Adv. Learn.* II. xxiii (1900) 218 We use to advise young students from company keeping, by saying, Amici fures temporis. *a.*

1612 CHARRON *Of Wisdom* (1640) 217 Friends steal away time. **1783** BOSWELL *Johnson* lxxv (1848) 727 He may love study, and wish not to be interrupted by his friends: Amici fures temporis.

Friends both in heaven and hell, It is good to have some. (F 749)

1592 DELAMOTHE 19. **1651** HERBERT no. 1127.

Friends fail fliers. (F 737)

c. **1513** SIR. T. MORE *Richard III* (1821) 75. **1577** HOLINSHED *Chron.* (1808) III. 381 We might ... make them true by our going, if we were caught and brought back, as friends fail fliers. **1623** CAMDEN 269. **1639** CLARKE 25.

Friends in general, Many | one in special. (F 754)

1640 HERBERT no. 281.

Friends may meet, but mountains never greet. (F 738)

1530 PALSGRAVE 635a Hylles do never mete, but acquayntaunce dothe often. **1568** FULWELL *Like will to L.* (1906) 13 It is an old saying, that mountains and hills never meet; But I see that men shall meet, though they do not seek. **1594** LYLY *Mother B.* v. iii. 229 Then wee foure met, which argued we were no mountaines. **1599** SHAKES. *A.Y.* III. ii. 171 It is a hard matter for friends to meet; but mountains may be removed by earthquakes, and so encounter. **1618** TAYLOR (Water P.), cited in Southey *Uneducated Poets* O.U.P. 61 I found the proverb true, that men have more priviledge than mountains in meeting. **1670** RAY 94 ... Mons cum monte non miscebitur. Pares cum paribus. Two haughty persons will seldom agree together. **1757** SMOLLETT *Rehearsal* II. ii But, he and I sall meet before mountains meet. **1848** GASKELL *Mary Barton* ch. 2.

Friends (The best of friends) must part. (F 733)

c. **1380** CHAUCER *Troilus* Bk. 5, l. 343 Alwey freendes may nat ben y-feere. *c.* **1602** CHAPMAN *May-Day* IV. iv. 51. **1620** Roxb. *Ballads* (Hindley) I. 253. For friends, you know must part. **1731** SWIFT *On Death of Dr. Swift* But dearest friends, they say, must part. **1821** SCOTT *Kenilw.* ch. 11 The best friends must part, Flibbertigibbet. **1910** G. W. E. RUSSELL *Sketch & Snap.* 212 But the best of friends must part, and it is time to take our leave of this ... high-souled cavalier.

Friends round the Wrekin, All. (F 756)

1700 CONGREVE *Way of World* III. xv You could intreat to be remember'd then to your friends round the Rekin. **1706** FARQUHAR *Recruit. Off.* Ded. To all Friends round the Wrekin. **1787** GROSE 220 To all friends round the Wrekin. A mode of drinking to all friends, wheresoever they may be, taking the Wrekin as a centre. The Wrekin is a mountain in the neighbourhood of Shrewsbury. **1813** RAY 72 ... not forgetting the trunk-maker and his son Tom.

Friends, All are not | that speak us fair. (A 112)

c. **1350** *How the Gd. Wife* l. 69 Al is no3t trewe þat faire speket. **1580** LYLY *Euph. & his Eng.* ii. 95 Nor [are] all friends that beare a faire face. **1639** CLARKE 128.

Friends, Have but few | though many acquaintances. (F 741)

c. **1565** W. WAGER *Enough Good as Feast* D2ᵛ Be not rash in taking a freend Aristotle dooth say. **1659** HOWELL *Eng. Prov.* 5b. **1670** RAY 11.

Friends tie their purse with a cobweb thread. (F 736)

1659 HOWELL *It. Prov.* 2.

Friend(s), *see also* Admonish your f.; Among f. all things common; Before you make a f. eat . . . with him; Better an open enemy; Better lose a jest than a f.; Bit that one eats no f. makes; Breams in his pond, f. welcome; Cat and dog may kiss, yet none the better f.; Dead men and absent no f. left; Dead men have no f.; Defend me from my f.; Dog for your f., (Keep a) . . .; Enemy (His own) no man's f.; Enemy your f. (Make your); Even reckoning long f.; Faithful f. is hard to find; Fall not out with a f.; Fresh fish and poor f. become soon ill savoured; Full purse never wanted f.; Go down ladder . . . up when you choose f.; Good cheer is lacking (When) f. will be packing; Good f. that speaks well of us; Grow howbackit bearing your f. (You will never); Happy is he whose f. born before him; Hatred with f. succour to foes; Hit him hard: he has no f.; Hunger knows no f.; Kindred (Wheresoever you see), make much of your f.; Kiss and be f.; Knave is in plum-tree (When) he has neither f. nor kin; Lawsuits consume f.; Lend your money lose f.; Lend (When I), I am his f.; Life without f. is death; Little intermeddling makes good f.; Live without our f. (We can), but not our neighbours; Lost (It is not) that f. (neighbour) gets; Love your f. but look to yourself; Love your f. with his fault; Many f. (He that has); Many kinsfolk few f.; Marriages and funerals (At) f. are discerned; Merry when f. meet; Mirror (Best) is an old f.; Misfortune makes foes of f.; Never catch at falling f.; No longer foster, no longer f.; No man has a worse f. than he brings; Old f. are best; Old fish, old oil, old f.; One enemy is too many, a hundred f. too few; One God, no more, but f.; Physician like f. (No); Poor folks' f. soon misken them; Prosperity (In time of) f. will be plenty; Prosperity makes f.; Prove thy f. ere need; Purse is his best f., (His); Put off the person of a judge . . . of a f., Quits his place well that leaves f.; Rich folk have many f.; Rich knows not who is f.; See your f. (Whensoever you), trust to yourself; Short reckonings long f.; Speak well of f., of enemy nothing; Strength enough to bear misfortunes of f.; Thunder lasted (While), bad men f.; Trencher f. are seldom good neighbours; Trust not new f.; Try your f. before you trust; Two f. have a common purse (When); Two f. with one gift (Make); Wanted me and your meat (If you) would want one good f.

Friended, *see* Man is f. (As a), so law ended.

Friendship cannot be without equality, Perfect. (F 761)

c. **1526** ERASM. *Dicta Sapientum* A4 Most sure amyte is, that resteth bitwene equals. **1539** TAVERNER 53 Amicitia aequalitas. Frendship (sayeth pythagors) is equalitie, and al one mynde or wyll. **1580** LYLY *Euph. & his Eng.* ii. 150 In friendeship there must be an equalitie of estates. **1666** TORRIANO *It. Prov.* 305, no. 2 Where there is no equality, never will there be perfect amity. **1697** W. POPE *Seth* [*Ward*] 100 Where there is no Equality there can be no Friendship.

Friendship cannot stand always on one side. (F 760)

1641 FERGUSSON no. 280 Friendship stands not in one side. **1721** KELLY 103 . . . Friendship is cultivated by mutual good Offices; spoken to urge some Instances of Kindness on them, to whom we have been formerly oblig'd.

Friendship, *see also* Broken f. may be soldered; Falsehood in f.; Hedge between keeps f. green; Love puts in (When) f. is gone; Sudden f. sure repentance; Weed amongst corn nor suspicion in f., (Neither); What rake the feud where f. dow not?

Friese, *see* Bread, butter, and green cheese.

Fright a bird is not the way to catch her, To. (B 373)

c. **1594** BACON no. 1543 Qui veut prendre un oiseau, qu'il ne l'effarouche. **1611** COTGRAVE s.v. Oiseau Deale gently with the bird thou mean'st to catch. **1616** DRAXE no. 14. **1639** CLARKE 311. **1640** HERBERT no. 42 He that will take the bird must not skare it. **1670** RAY 95. **1721** KELLY 106 Flaying[1] a Burd is no the way to grip it. A vile Intimation! that a Man should conceal his ill Intentions upon any, lest they provide against it, and so prevent it. **1732** FULLER no. 1627. [[1] frightening.]

Frighted, frightened, *see* Lived too near a wood to be f. by owls; More afraid (f.) than hurt.

Fristed[1] is not forgiven, The thing that's. (T 150)

[L. *Quod differtur non aufertur.* That which is deferred is not relinquished.] *a.* **1628** CARMICHAELL no. 1462. **1641** FERGUSSON no. 782. **1721** KELLY 305. **1824** SCOTT *Redg.* ch. 12 He was murdered in cold blood, with many a pretty fellow besides.—Well, we may have our day next—what is fristed is not forgiven. [[1] delayed, or sold on credit.]

Frog cannot out of her bog, The. (F 763)

1659 TORRIANO no. 6. **1659** N.R. 13. **1670** RAY 95. **1732** FULLER no. 6113.

Frog on a chopping block, To sit like a.
(F 765)

1678 RAY 289. **1732** FULLER no. 723 As pert as a Frog upon a Washing-Block.

Frog, *see also* April flood carries away f.; Fish and catch f.; Fond fisher that angles for f.; Gossips are f.; Look to him, jailer . . . f. in stocks; Naked as f.; Toad (f.) said to harrow.

Froize, *see* Pudding (If it won't) it will f.

Frost and fraud both end in foul (have always foul ends).
(F 770)

1607 *A True Report of the . . . Murder . . . in the house of Sir Jerome Bowes* C3. **1614** CAMDEN 306 Frost and fraud haue alwaies foule ends. **1621** BURTON *Anat. Mel.* I. ii. III. xv (1651) 138 They do manifestly perceive, that (as he said) frost and fraud come to foul ends. **1662** FULLER Chesh. 177 It was an ordinary Speech in his Mouth to say, Frost and Fraud both end in Foul. **1721** KELLY 103 Frost and Falshood has ay a foul hinder end.

Frost never lasts more than three days, A white.

1883 ROPER 17 adding 'A long frost is a black frost'. **1893** INWARDS 114.

Frosts, The first and last | are the worst.
(F 773)

1640 HERBERT no. 954.

Frosts in March, So many | so many in May.
(F 775)

1659 HOWELL *Eng. Prov.* 16a If frost in March there will be some in May. **1678** RAY 344.

Frost(s), *see also* Farewell f.; God will (What) no f. can kill; Hail brings f. in tail; Hunger in f. that will not work in heat; Many f. and many thowes make rotten yowes; March, (Fog in) f. in May; Surprised with the first f.

Frugality is the mother of liberality.

1596 *Estate of English Fugitives* 131 It is an old saying, Frugalitie is the mother of Liberalitie, and Warinesse of Securitie.

Frugality, *see also* Industry is fortune's right hand, f. her left.

Fruit fails, When all | welcome haws.

1721 KELLY 350 . . . Spoken when we take up with what's coarse, when the good is spent. **1914** K. F. PURDON *Folk of Furry F.* ch. 17 'Lame of a leg, and grey in the head! . . . that's a fancy man for a girl to take!' 'Marg was none too young herself, . . . and when all fruit fails welcome haws! She wanted someone'.

Fruit have, If you would | you must bring the leaf to the grave.
(F 778)

1678 RAY 53 . . . That is, you must transplant your trees just about the fall of the leaf, . . . not sooner, because of the motion of the sap, not later, that they may have time to take root before the deep frosts.

Fruit ripens not well in the shade.

1732 FULLER no. 1632.

Fruit, *see also* Autumn f. without spring blossoms (No); Beauty may have fair leaves, yet bitter f.; Deeds are f.; Eat the f. (He that would) must climb tree; Forbidden f.; Free of f. that wants orchard; Good f. of a good tree; Husbandman ought first to taste of the new grown f.; Love is the f. of idleness; No root no f.; Tree but bears some f. (No); Tree is known by its f.; Tree (Like) like f.; Tree loaded with f. people throw stones; Tree often transplanted bears not much f.

Fruitfulness, *see* Moist hand argues amorous nature (f.).

Fry (Stew) in one's own grease (juice), To.
(G 433)

13 . . *Coer de L.* Better it is that we out renne, Thenne . . . frye inne oure owne gres! *c.* **1386** CHAUCER *W. of Bath's Prol.* l. 486 I made folk swich chere, That in his owene grece I made hym frye For angre, and for verray yalousye. [*c.* 1525–9] **1561** *Queen Hester* l. 1044 He fried him in his grease. **1546** HEYWOOD I. xi. E3ᵛ She fryeth in hir owne grease, but as for my parte, If she be angry, beshrew her angry harte. **1600–1** SHAKES. *M.W.W.* II. i. 59 Entertain him with hope till the wicked fire of lust have melted him in his own grease. *Ibid.* III. v. 100 Stinking clothes that fretted in their own grease. **1656** EARL MONM. tr. *Boccalini's Advts. Parnass.* (1674) 204 [He] could not better discover Hypocrites, than by suffering them (like Oysters) to stew in their own water. *Cf.* **1662** FULLER Devon 248 Stew the land in its own liquor, to make the same ground to find compost to fatten its self. **1664** COTTON *Scarron.* (1715) 89 I stew all Night in my own Grease. **1885** SIR W. HARCOURT *Sp. at Lowestoft* 14 Dec. Liberals must not be in a hurry to turn the Tories out. He would let them for a few months stew in their own Parnellite juice.

Fry, *see also* Eggs to f., (I have other); Fish to f., (I have other).

Frying-pan into the fire, Out of the. *Cf.* Shunning the smoke.
(F 784)

[*c.* 1515] *c.* **1530** BARCLAY *Eclog.* I E.E.T.S. Out of the water thou leapest into the fyre. **1528** MORE *Wks.* (1557) 179 col. 2 Lepe they lyke a flounder out of a frying-panne into the fyre. **1546** HEYWOOD II. v. H4 As the flounder dothe, Leape out of the frying pan into the fyre. **1577** J. BISHOP *Beautiful Blossoms* N4ᵛ (much like vnto Aesopes fishe, that foolishly leaped). **1591** ARIOSTO *Orl. Fur.* Harington XIII. 28 But I was sau'd, as is the flounder when He leapeth from the dish into the fire. **1623** CAMDEN 273. **1625** PURCHAS *Pilgrims* (1905–7) I. 14 Out of the frying-pan of Paynim rites, into the fire of Mahometry. **1875** SMILES *Thrift* 275 The man in debt . . . tries a money-lender; and, if he succeeds, he is only out of the frying-pan into the fire.

Frying-pan said to the kettle, The | 'Avaunt, black brows!' *Cf.* Kettle calls the pot. Kiln calls oven.   (F 782)

1620 SHELTON *Quix.* II. lxvii (1908) III. 293 'Methinks, sir, . . . you are like what is said that the frying-pan said to the kettle, "Avaunt, blackbrows"; you reprehend me for speaking of proverbs, and you thread up yours by two and two.' **1659** HOWELL *Span. Prov.* 3 The Frying-pan told the Kettle, get thee hence thou black ars. **1732** FULLER no. 4551.

Fuel, Take away | take away flame.   (F 786)

1639 CLARKE 192. **1670** RAY 95 . . . Remove the tale-bearer, and contention ceaseth.

Fuel to the fire, To add more.   (F 785)

1566 P. BEVERLEY *Ariodanto and Jenevra* ed. Prouty 111. *c.* **1589** KYD *Spanish Tragedy* III. x. That were to adde more fewell to the fire. *a.* **1674** CLARENDON *Life* (1759, iii. 611).

Fuel, *see also* Fools had baubles, (If all) we should want f.; Laid in his f. before St. John (Never rued that).

Fulfill, *see* Promise more in a day than they will f. in a year, (Men may).

Full as an egg is of meat (oatmeal), As.   (K 149)

1520 WHITTINGTON *Vulgaria* 96 He that may haue your company maye be glad therof: for ye be as ful of good maner as an egge is of oote mele. [*c.* **1553**] **1575** *Gammer Gurton's N.* v. ii. 57 An egge is not so ful of meate, as she is ful of lycs. *c.* **1590** R. GREENE *Friar Bacon* l. 2027 Another saith my head is as full of Latine as an egs full of oatemeale. *c.* **1595** SHAKES. *R.J.* III. i. 24 Thy head is as full of quarrels as an egg is full of meat. **1639** CLARKE 69 As full of knavery as an egge of meat. **1719** PRIOR *Bivo & Charon* Wks. (1858) 419 As full of champagne as an egg's full of meat.

Full belly neither fights nor flies well, A.   (B 295)

1592 NASHE *Pierce Penniless* i. 201 *Plenus venter nil agit libenter.* **1611** COTGRAVE s.v. Tripe (He thats full bellied). **1640** HERBERT no. 88. **1844** E. FITZGERALD *Lett.* 22 Aug. (1901) I. 173 It is a grievous thing to grow poddy: the age of chivalry is gone then . . . 'a full belly neither fights nor flies well'.

Full flock, He who will have a | must have an old stag[1] and a young cock. *But cf.* Farm full, etc.

a. **1697** J. AUBREY in HALLIWELL *Dict. Arch. & Prov. Wds.* (1889) II. 794 Aubrey gives the following Lancashire proverb. . . . He that will have a full flock Must have an old *stagge* and a young cock. *MS. Royal Soc.* 298. [[1] gander.]

Full man and a fasting, It is ill speaking between a. *Cf.* Belly is full.

a. **1641** FERGUSSON MS. no. 1349 Thair is nothing betuix a bursten body and a hungered. **1824** SCOTT *Redg.* Lett. 11 Ye maun eat and drink, Steenie, . . . for we do little else here, and it's ill speaking between a fou man and a fasting.

Full moon, Like a.

1882 BESANT *All Sorts & C.* ch. 1 This ornament of the Upper House was a big, fat man, with a face like a full moon.

Full moon brings fair weather, The.

1893 INWARDS 64.

Full of courtesy, full of craft.   (C 732)

1576 PETTIE I. 116 In fairest speech is . . . feigning rifest. **1594** NASHE *Unfort. Trav.* ii. 210 Much companie, much knauery, as true as that olde adage, Much curtesie, much subtiltie. **1608** SHAKES. *P.* I. iv. 75 Who makes the fairest show means most deceit. **1609** HARWARD 81 Much curtesy much craft. **1639** CLARKE 13. **1670** RAY 73 . . . Sincere and true hearted persons are least given to complement and ceremony. It's suspicious he hath some design upon me, who courts and flatters me. **1796** EDGEWORTH *Par. Asst.* (1903) 392 We have been finely duped. . . . Full of courtesy, full of craft!

Full of himself that he is quite empty, He is so.

1732 FULLER no. 2472.

Full purse, He that has a | never wanted a friend.

xvc. *Early Eng. Carols* (Greene) 391 My purse is my owne frende. **1721** KELLY 161.

Full(est), *see also* Belly is f. . . . believes not who is fasting; Belly is f., bones would be at rest; Belly is f., mind among maids; Cup is f. (When), bear her fairest; Farm f.; Foul foot makes f. wame; Hell will never be f. till you be in it; Never well, f. nor fasting; Son f. and tattered; Well is f. (When), it will run over.

Fulsome, *see* Fool is f.

Funeral, One | makes another (many).

1894 BLACKMORE *Perlycross* ch. 7 It has been said, and is true too often . . . that one funeral makes many. A strong east wind . . . whistled through the crowd of mourners.

Funeral(s), *see also* Dream of f., hear of marriage; Marriages and f. (At) friends are discerned.

Fur (= furrow), *see* Whip and whirr never made good f.

Furmity kettle, *see* Simpers like a f. k.

Furred, *see* Bare arse than a f. hood, (Better a).

Furrier, *see* Fox is brought to f.

Further than the wall he cannot go.
                                        (W 12)

1528 MORE *Wks.* (1557) 187 col. 1 I am in this matter euen at the harde walle, and se not how to go further. **1546** HEYWOOD II. v. H3ᵛ That dede without words shal dryue him to the wal. And further than the wall he can not go. **1565** CALFHILL *Treatise of the Cross* P.S. 62. **1611** DAVIES no. 366.

Further we (you) go, The | the further behind.   (G 151)

c. **1430** LYDGATE *Minor Poems* E.E.T.S. II. 382 The more I go, the further I am behynde. **1477** RIVERS *Dicts and Sayings* (1877) 144 He that goth owte of his weye, the more he goth, the ferther he is behinde. **1546** HEYWOOD II. viii.

K2ᵛ Ye maie walke this waie, but sure ye shall fynde, The further ye go, the further behynde. **1659** HOWELL *Eng. Prov.* 5b. **1607** DEKKER *Whore of Babylon* Lectori The streame of her Vertues is so immensurable, that the farther they are waded into, the farther it is to the bottom.

Further(est), *see also* Far.

Fury, *see* Patience provoked turns to f.

Furze, Under the | is hunger and cold; under the broom is silver and gold.
                                        (F 790)

1678 RAY 348.

Furze is in bloom, When the | my love's in tune.

1752 *Poor Robin Alm.* August Joan says: 'Furze in bloom still', and she'll be kiss'd if she's her will. **1908** *Spectator* 9 May At almost any season of the year gorse can be found in ... flower ...'.

G

Gab, *see* Gift of g.

Gabriel blows his horn, When | then this question will be decided.   (G 1)

? a. **1384** (?) WYCLIF *Eng. Wks.* E.E.T.S. XXVI. vii. 382 And I wote wel þat gabriel schal blow his horne or þai han preuyd þe mynor. **1659** HOWELL *Eng. Prov.* 21b When *Gabriel* blowes his horn, then this question will be decided; *viz.* Never.

Gad, *see* Tribe of Levi ... tribe of G.

Gaff, *see* Blow the g.

Gain is to lose, Sometimes the best.
                                        (G 5)

c. **1607** A. BREWER *The Lovesick King* ed. Swaen l. 1895 We get by losing it. **1640** HERBERT no. 224.

Gain teaches how to spend, To.   (G 8)
1640 HERBERT no. 455.

Gain, All is not | that is put in the purse.   (A 151)

1609 HARWARD 71 (gotten). **1626** BRETON *Soothing* B4 (got). **1639** CLARKE 187. **1678** RAY 194 All is not won that is put in the purse. **1761** STERNE *T. Shandy* III. XXX.

Gain savours sweetly from anything.
                                        (G 3)

[JUVENAL *XIV.* 204-5.] **1542** BECON *Nosegay:*

Early Wks., P.S. 222 Savour of lucre is good, howsoever a man come by it. **1551** CROWLEY *Philargyrie* A7 Gayne doeth smell Excedynge well In euery thyng. **1581** H. ESTIENNE *Stage of Popish Toys* 9.They kept this prouerbe .... lucri bonus odor ex re qualibet, that is, *The smel of gain is good of euery thing.* **1603** H. CROSSE *Virtue's Commonwealth* H4 Gaine is sweete of whatsoeuer it commeth. **1628** EARLE *Micro.* Arb. 4, 25 Of al odors he likes best the smel of Vrine, and holds Vespatians rule, that no gaine is unsauory. **1638** *A Description of Time* A8 The smell of gain is sweete, though from a Iakes.

Gains enough whom fortune loses, He.

1573 SANFORD 102. **1611** COTGRAVE s.v. Gaigner Assez gaigne qui malheur perd; He gets ynough that misses an ill turne. **1629** *Bk. Mer. Rid.* Prov. no. 60. **1659** HOWELL *Fr. Prov.* 6 ('scapes a mischance).

Gains well and spends well, He that | needs no account book.   (A 19)

1640 HERBERT no. 853.

Gains will quit the pains, The.   (G 6)

1583 MELBANCKE Q3ᵛ Thinking that gaines would recompense paines ... I came againe. **1586** J. HARRISON *Mal. Soc. Collections* iii. 162 By your leave I would measure my paynes accordynge to my gaynes if I weare as he is. **1595** LODGE *Fig for Momus* Hunt. C. iii. 59 Buy cheape, sell deare, thy profit quites thy paine. **1734** FRANKLIN 7 Hope of gain lessens pain.

Gain(s) (*noun*), *see also* Fastens where there is g.; Great g. makes work easy; Great pain and little g.; Ill luck to count your g.; Ill-gotten goods (g.); Lacks a stock (Who), his g. not worth chip; Light g. heavy purses; Lose your time (If you). cannot get g.; Loss is another man's g., (One man's); No pains, no g.; Pain forgotten when g. follows; Pain is g.

Gain(ed, s), (*verb*), *see also* Gear is easier g. than guided; Gives discreetly g. directly; Knows what may be g. never steals (He that); Merchant that g. not, loses.

Gainfullest, *see* Burdens (Greatest) are not g.

Gaining, cold gaming, No.

1623 J. BALMFORD *Reply to Gataker* 11 The common saying is, Sine lucro friget lusus, No gaining, cold gaming.

Gaining(s), *see also* Fair g. make fair spendings; Sparing is first g.

Galen, *see* Suppers (By) more have been killed than G. cured.

Gall, *see* Fly has spleen, ant g.; Honey and g. in love there is store, (Of); Honey tongue, heart of g.

Gallants, *see* Fowey (G. of).

Galley-slave, *see* Work like g.

Gallop, *see* Beggar on horseback . . . ride a g.; Kick in one's g.; Snail's g.

Gallows groans for him (you), The.
(G 15)

1577 *Misogonus* I. iv The gallowes grones for this wage [= wagge] as iust rope ripe. **1585–1616** *Shirburn Ballads* xxxii (1907) 131 Thus, then he scaped hanging, And made no more moan; But yet for his presence the gallows did groan. *a.* **1628** CARMICHAELL no. 1429 (quhill it get yow). **1738** SWIFT *Dial.* I. E.L. 288 Well, go hang yourself in your own garters, for I'm sure the gallows groans for you.

Gallows in his face, He has the.

1611 SHAKES. *Temp.* I. i. 32 His complexion is perfect gallows. **1768** GOLDSMITH *Good-nat. Man.* v. (Globe) 637/1 Hold him fast, the dog: he has the gallows in his face. **1891** SCOTT *Bride Lam.* ch. 6 As to Craigie, . . . he had gallows written on his brow in the hour of his birth.

Gallows will have its own at last, The.
(G 20)

c. **1592** WM. PERKINS *Salve for a Sick Man* (1603) f. 528b In the daies of King Edward . . . one . . . desperately minded to . . . cried out saying, O gallowse claime thy right. *a.* **1624** CAPT. J. SMITH *Virginia* 'Hist. of Bermudas' (MacLehose) i. 366 One of them being asked what hee thought in the worst of that extremity,

answered, he thought nothing but gallowes claime thy right. **1707** MAPLETOFT 72.

Gallows, *see also* Builds his house all of sallows; Hanged (If), I'll choose g.; Kills himself with working . . . buried under g.; Save a thief from g.; Sea and the g. refuse none; Thieves and whores meet at the g.

Galt, *see* Try your skill in g. first.

Gambrel, *see* Crooketh the tree.

Game is cheaper in the market than in the fields and woods.

1706 STEVENS s.v. Caca Talk of Game, and buy it in the Market. **1732** FULLER no. 1641.

Game is not worth the candle, The.
(S 776)

1602 *The Jesuits' Catechism* 27b As good fellowes vse to say, The sport is worthy of a candle. **1603** MONTAIGNE (Florio) II. xvii. 153 The horror of a fall doth more hurt me, than the blow. The play is not worth the candle. **1640** HERBERT no. 752 It is a poore sport that's not worth the candle. **1668** COWLEY *Ess.* x (1904) 105 When the light of life is so near going out, and ought to be so precious, *le jeu ne vaut pas la chandelle*, the play is not worth the expense of the candle. **1874** P. BAYNE in *Contemp. Rev.* Oct. 706 The game would not be worth the candle.

Game that two can play at, That is a.

1819 BYRON in IRIS ORIGO *The Last Attachment* 90 Two can play at that. **1845** E. FITZGERALD *Lett.* 12 June (1901) I. 193 I . . . told him two could play at that game. **1864** J. H. NEWMAN *Apologia* Pt. v (ed. W. Ward 1931) 'Two can play at that' was often in my mouth. **1896** J. C. HUTCHESON *Crown & Anchor* ch. 20.

Game's end, At the | we shall see who gains.
(G 23)

1640 HERBERT no. 538. **1642** TORRIANO 6 (is seen who is the winner).

Games, In all | it is good to leave off a winner.

1732 FULLER no. 2812.

Game(s), *see also* Perseverance kills the g.; Play small g. before he will sit out (He will); Play the g.; Tine cat tine g.

Gamester, The better | the worser man.
(G 24)

1568 TILNEY *Duties in Marriage* C1 A daylie gamester, a common blasphemer. **1639** CLARKE 96.

Gamesters and race-horses never last long.
(G 25)

1640 HERBERT no. 751. **1642** TORRIANO 4 The credit of a race-horse, a gamester, and a whore, lasteth but a short time.

Gamester(s), see also Candle-holder good g.; Hasty g. oversee.

Gaming, women, and wine, while they laugh, they make men pine.　　　(G 27)

c. 1576 *Common Cond.* l. 238 B1 Weeman, dise and drinke, lets him nothing keepe. 1579 LYLY *Euph.* i. 256 It is play, wine, and wantonnesse, that feedeth a louer as fat as a foole. 1640 HERBERT no. 604.

Gaming, see also Devil goes shares in g.; Flax from fire and youth from g., (Keep); Gaining, cold g., (No).

Gander, see Goose, g., gosling, three sounds; Goose so grey that cannot find g.; Man among the geese when g. away; Sauce for the goose.

Gangs up i' sops, When it | it'll fau down i' drops.

1828 CARR *Craven Dialect* ii. 147. **1869** HAZLITT 458 . . . A North Country proverb, the sops being the small detached clouds hanging on the sides of a mountain.—HALLIWELL.

Gap(s), see Hap (Some have); Stop g. with rushes; Stop two g. with one bush.

Gape for a benefice, To.　　　(B 308)

1605 S. ROWLEY *When You See Me* l. 222 Euery bodie thinks that if the Pope were dead, you gape for a benefice. **1616** WITHALS 557. [1631] **1639** R. ZOUCHE *The Sophister* G4ᵛ Yawn like one that gapes for a Benefice. **1639** CLARKE 38. **1670** RAY 246. **1738** SWIFT *Dial.* II. E.L. 316 What, Mr. Neverout, do you gape for Preferment.

Gape like an oyster, To.　　　(O 114)

1550 HEYWOOD *100 Epigrams* no. 67 On whom gape thine oysters so wyde, oyster wife? **1594** *Knack to know a Knave* Hazl.-Dods. vi. 567 At your request I will . . . lay myself open to you, like an oyster. *c.* **1608** D. BARRY *Ram Alley* Hazl.-Dods. x. 369 Of all meats I love not a gaping oyster. **1614** JONSON *Barth. Fair* v. v. 23 I haue gaped as the oyster for the tide, after thy destruction. **1618–19** J. FLETCHER *Bonduca* I. ii Thou want'st drink. Did I not find thee gaping like an oyster For a new tide,.

Gape long enough ere a bird fall in your mouth, You may. *Cf.* Larks will fall into mouth.　　　(B 390)

1540 PALSGRAVE *Acolastus* 77 Do thou but gape, and I shall make larkes fall in to thy mouthe. **1621** ROBINSON 23. **1639** CLARKE 153. **1670** RAY 96. **1732** FULLER no. 5945 (fly into your mouth).

Gape-seed, see Fond of g.

Gapes until he be fed, He that | well may he gape until he be dead. *Cf.*

Gape long enough. Larks will fall into mouth.　　　(G 31)

c. 1549 HEYWOOD I. ix. C2 Nay, he that gapeth tyll he be fed, Maie fortune to fast and famishe for honger. 1611 DAVIES no. 400. 1721 KELLY 119. 1738 SWIFT *Dial.* II. E.L. 316 Do you gape for preferment?—Faith, I may gape long enough, before it falls into my mouth.

Gaping against (before) an oven, It is ill.　　　(G 33)

a. 1250 *Owl & Night.* 292 (1922) 28 Ne wit¹ þan ofne² me ne 30nie.³ 1577–87 HOLINSHED *Chron.* (1807–8) II. 389 A man ought not to chide with a foole, nor gape over an oven. 1659 HOWELL *Eng. Prov.* 12a (before). 1670 RAY 96 (No gaping). [¹ against. ² oven. ³ yawn.]

Garby whose soul neither God nor the devil would have, He is like.

1732 FULLER no. 2461.

Garden without its weeds, No.　　　(G 37)

1579 LYLY *Euph.* i. 322 No doubt it is in the courte . . . as in all gardeins, some flowers, some weeds. **1618** J. TAYLOR *Penniless Pilgrimage* (*Wks.* 1630, 126) The fairest Garden hath some weedes. **1621** BURTON *Anat. Mel.* III. iv. I. iii. (1651) 676 The divel . . . will never suffer the church to be quiet or at rest: no garden so well tilled but some noxious weedes grow up in it. **1732** FULLER no. 3576. *Ibid.* no. 152 A good Garden may have some weeds. **1826** SOUTHEY *Lett.* (to daughters) 19 July (1912) 414 But the best dispositions require self-watchfulness, as there is no garden but what produces weeds.

Garden(s), see also Charges of building and . . . g. are unknown; Cheapside is best g.; Fear keeps the g. better than gardener; Land (You may be on), yet not in g.; Market is best g.; Patience grow in g. (Let).

Gardener's dog, that neither eats cabbages himself, nor lets anybody else, Like the.　　　(G 38)

[**1640** OUDIN *Curios. franç.* 97 Comme le chien du jardinier qui ne mange pas des choux et ne veut pas que personne en mange.] **1642** TORRIANO 52 To play the gardners dog: Nota, That is, dogs will eat no hearbs themselves, nor permit any other creature to eat any by them. **1659** HOWELL *It. Prov.* 16. **1706** STEVENS s.v. Perro. **1732** FULLER no. 3235.

Garlands are not for every brow.

1642 TORRIANO 10 Although a garland stand not in a farthing, yet it doth not become every bodies head. **1732** FULLER no. 1642.

Garland, see One flower makes no g.

Garlic makes a man wink, drink, and stink.　　　(G 40)

c. 1510 STANBRIDGE *Vulgaria* B3 Garlyke maketh a man to slepe. 1594 NASHE *Unfort. Trav.* ii.

249. **1607** SIR J. HARINGTON *Englishman's Doctor* (1922) 86 And scorne not Garlicke like to some that thinke It onely makes men winke, and drinke, and stinke.

Garlic, *see also* Eat me without g.; Smell of g. takes away the smell of onions.

Garment(s), *see* Borrowed g. never fit; Last g. made without pockets.

Garner, *see* Says his g. is full (None).

Carters of a man's guts, To make.

c. **1591** R. GREENE *James IV* l. 1289 Ile make garters of thy guttes. **1596** *Knack to know an Honest Man* l. 1016 Keepe out I say, least I make garters of your guttes. **1601** JONSON *Cynthia's Revels* IV. iii. 359 I will garter my hose with your guts. **1704** J. WALKER *Sufferings of the Clergy* s.v. Richard Raynolds, Stoke Fleming, Devon. **1937** 18 Sept. J. LINDSAY, Letter in T.L.S.

Garters, *see* Hang himself in own g.

Gate of horn, The. *Cf.* Ivory gate.

[In classical legend (*Od.* 19. 562 ff.; *Aen.* 6. 893) that through which true dreams came forth.] *c.* **1587** KYD *Span. Trag.* l. 85 The gates of Horn: Where dreames haue passage in the silent night. [**1662** FULLER Cornw. 195 Dreams have two Gates: one made (they say) of horn; By this Port pass true and Propheticks Dreames. **1831** MACAULAY *Ess., Hampden* Wks. V. 557 [Archbishop Laud] dreamed that he had turned Papist; of all his dreams the only one, we suspect, which came through the gate of horn.

Gate wider than the city (door wider than the house), Make not the. (D 557)

[DIOG. LAERTIUS VI. ii. 57.] **1584** LYLY *Camp.* Prol. at Blackfriars. Least like the Mindyans, we make our gates greater then our towne. **1597** BRETON *Wit's Trenchmore* Dedn. To make a large gate of a little Towne. **1599** R. LINCHE *Fountain of Ancient Fiction* A4ᵛ It is an absurd part in an architector to frame a long and vast entry for a little house. **1603** H. CHETTLE *England's Mourning Garment* (Harl. Misc. 1745, iii. 501) My Epistle to you is like the little Town that the Cynick would have persuaded the Citizens was ready to run out at the great Gates. **1608** G. WILKINS *Painfull Adventures of Pericles* Preface. Not willing to make a great waie to a little house. **1616** T. ADAMS *Three Divine Sisters* 30 It is absurd in building, to make the Porch bigger then the House. **1635** E. LEIGH *Selected . . . Observations* *8ᵛ Least I should bee vp-brayded with the city of Myndus, for making my porch too bigge. **1639** CLARKE 11 (doore wider then the house). **1659** G. EVERARD *Panacea* A6 Lest the portal prove too great for the house. **1697** W. POPE *Seth* [Ward] 3 I fear the Gate is too great for this little City.

Gate(s), *see also* Better go by your enemy's grave than his g.; Breed of the chapman, never out of your g.; Breed of the good man's mother, aye in the g.; Creaking door (g.); Gold goes in at any g.

except heaven's; Ivory g.; Lies not in your g., breaks not your shins; No g. no city; Speers the g. he knows well; Stone that lies not in your g.; Withy tree would have new g. (Old). *See also* Yate.

Gath, Tell it not in.

[**1382** WYCLIF *2 Sam.* i. 20 Woleth ʒe not telle in Geth, ne telle ʒe in . . . Aschalon.] **1745** J. WESLEY *Lett.* v. 351. **1751** RICHARDSON 11 July (*Corresp.* iii. 169) A wise man to be in love! Tell it not in Gath. **1904** MARIE CORELLI *God's Gd. Man* ch. 20 The fact is—but tell it not in Gath—I was happier without them!

Gather(s, ed), *see* Grapes of thorns . . . (One cannot g.); Hand that gives g.; Narrow g. widely spent; Pick up (G.) one's crumbs; Scatter with one hand, g. with two; World is unstable, therefore g. in time.

Gathering, *see* Little good comes of g.

Gaudy morning bodes a wet afternoon, A.

a. **1595** *Edward III* iv. ix. 17 The proverbe . . . Too bright a morning breeds a lowring daie. **1624** BURTON *Anat. Mel.* 96 A fair morning turns to a lowring afternoone. **1893** INWARDS 50.

Gaudy, *see also* Neat but not g.

Gauntlet, To throw (cast, fling) down the.

1590 *Pasquil's Apol.* I. D iv 6 I cast them my Gauntlet, take it vp who dares. **1806** SURR *Winter in Lond.* (ed. 3) II. 204 The duchess of Drinkwater appeared upon the field of fashion, and threw down the gauntlet of defiance to Belgrave. **1867** TROLLOPE *Last Chron. Barset* ch. 67. [She] had thrown down her gauntlet to him, and he had not been slow in picking it up.

Gauntlet of a hedging glove, Make not a. (G 49)

1639 CLARKE 5. **1732** FULLER no. 3318.

Gauntlet, *see also* Run the g.

Gave, *see* Give(s).

Gay, *see* Merry (G.) as a lark.

Gaze (glower) at the moon (stars) and fall in the gutter (ditch), To. (S 827)

c. **1532** *Tales* no. 25 Laertius writes, that Thales Milesius went out of his house . . . to beholde the starres . . . and so longe he went backewarde that he fell plump into a ditch. **1547** BALDWIN C3ᵛ As he went forth . . . to beholde the starres, he fell doune sodaynlye into a pit. **1598** DELONEY *Thomas of Reading* (1623 ed. Mann) 250. While Thales gazed on the starres, he stumbled in a pit. **1625** BACON *Apophthegms* no. 25. **1721** KELLY 377 You look'd at the Moon, and fell on the Midding. Spoken to them, who pretended and design'd great things, but afterwards took up with less. **1732** FULLER no. 5904.

Gaze, *see also* Eagle can g. at the sun, (Only the).

Gazes upon the sun, He that | shall at last be blind.

1528 TYNDALE *Obed. Chrn. Man* P.S. 307 Now if thou leave the natural use of the sun, and will look directly on him to see how bright he is, and suchlike curiosity, then will the sun blind thee. **1579** S. GOSSON *School of Abuse* Arb. 53. **1580** LYLY *Euph. & his Eng.* ii. 40. **1590** GREENE *Never Too Late* ed. Gros. viii. 139. *c.* **1590** MARLOWE *Mass. at Paris* sc. ii, l. 106. **1590** LODGE *Rosalynde* ed. Greg 3.

Gear[1] is easier gained than guided.

1721 KELLY 115 (gotten) ... It may be gotten by Chance, or Inheritance, but must be guided by Discretion. [[1] wealth, property.]

Gear that is gifted[1] is never so sweet as the gear that is won, The.

1875 SMILES *Thrift* 177 A penny earned honestly is better than a shilling given. A Scotch proverb says, ... [[1] given.]

Gear, *see also* Good g. that lasts aye; Kindness cannot be bought for g.; Leal folks never wanted g.; Little g. less care; Shame fall the g. and the blad'ry.

Geese are swans, All (his).   (G 369)

a. **1529** SKELTON *Magnyfycence* l. 302 In faythe, els had I gone to long to scole, But yf I coulde knowe a gose from a swanne. **1573** GASCOIGNE *Dan B. of Bath* i. 132 To make a Swan of that which was a Crowe. **1589** *Pasquil's Ret.* C1 Euery Goose ... must goe for a Swan, and whatsoeuer he speakes, must be Canonicall. **1594–5** SHAKES. *R.J.* I. ii. 86 Compare her face with some that I shall show, And I will make thee think thy swan a crow. **1621** BURTON *Anat. Mel.* Democ. to Rdr. 29 All his Geese are Swannes. **1777** BOSWELL *Johnson* lxi (1848) 558 Taylor, who praised every thing of his own to excess, ... 'whose geese were all swans', ... expatiated on ... his bull-dog.

Geese slur on the ice, To as much purpose as the.   (P 642)

1670 RAY 190. *Chesh.*

Geese, *see also* Goose.

General, *see* Best g. who makes fewest mistakes; One bad g. better than two good.

Generations to make a gentleman, It takes three.

1598 ROMEI *The Courtier's Academy* 187. **1625** F. MARKHAM 11 The sonne [of an ignoble father ascending to honour] ... is more noble; for hee hath both his owne, and his fathers glories. ... But the third running the same race without any disparagement, here is the perfection and praise of true Honor. *Ibid.* 48 These three perfit descents do euer so conclude a perfit Gentleman of Blood. **1857** BAGEHOT *Biograph. Stud.* (1899) 47 (It is said that Sir Robert Peel observed). **1902** DEAN HOLE *Then & Now* ch. 3 Whatever may be the causes ... the dictum, 'It takes three generations to make a gentleman', is no longer in quotation.

Generation, *see* Corruption of one is the g. of another.

Generous, *see* Just before g.

Genoa has mountains without wood, sea without fish, women without shame, and men without conscience.   (G 59)

1642 HOWELL *For. Trav.* viii. Arb. 41 It is proverbially said, there are in Genoa, Mountaines without wood, Sea without fish, Women without shame, and Men without conscience, which makes them to be termed the white Moores. **1666** TORRIANO *It. Prov.* 102 no. 31 Genoua Sea without fish, Air without fouls, Mountains without woods, and Women without shame.

Gentility without ability is worse than plain beggary.   (G 62)

1580 MUNDAY *Zelauto* F1 Vertulesse Gentillytie is wurse then Beggerie. **1639** CLARKE 226 (as 1580). **1670** RAY 96.

Gentility, *see also* Honour (G.) is but ancient riches.

Gentle (meek, mild, etc.) as a lamb, As.   (L 34)

c. **1362** LANGLAND *P. Pl.* A. VI. 43 He is as louh as a lomb . louelich of speche. *c.* **1440** LYDGATE *Fall. Princes* I. 6934 Stille as a lamb, most meek off his visage. *c.* **1502** *Robert the Devil* in *Ancient Eng. Fictions* 32 (tame). [*c.* 1515] **1521** BARCLAY *Ecl.* V. l.446(Humble). **1520** WHITTINGTON *Vulg.* E.E.T.S. 99 I shall make hym as styll as a lambe or euer I haue done with hym. **1577** R. STANYHURST in Holinshed *Descr. Ireland* 1587 35a (meeke). **1585** A. DENT *Sermon of Repentance* D7ᵛ He died as quiet as a Lambe. [*c.* 1590] **1598** *Famous Vict. of Hen. V* E1ᵛ (tame). *c.* **1595** SHAKES. *R.J.* II. v. 45 I'll warrant him, as gentle as a lamb. **1595** *Id. Rich. II* II. i. 175 In peace was never gentle lamb more mild. **1670** RAY 206.

Gentle craft, The.   (C 801)

[= the trade of shoemaking.] **1592** R. GREENE *Quip for an Upstart Courtier* Wks. Gros. xi 264. **1592** NASHE *Pierce Penilesse* i. 201. *a.* **1593** *George-a-Greene* (1599) F4b You shall be no more called Shoomakers. But you and yours to the worlds ende, Shall be called the trade of the gentle craft. **1688** R. HOLME *Armoury* III. 99/1 A Man on a Seat [a Shooe-maker] ... exercising of the Gentle Craft. **1845** LONGFELLOW *Poems* 90 Hans Sachs, the cobbler-poet, laureate of the gentle craft.

Gentle hawk half mans herself,[1] The.
(H 225)

1611 COTGRAVE s.v. Oiseau The gentle Hawke (halfe) makes, or mannes, her selfe. 1640 HERBERT no. 30. [[1] i.e. becomes tractable.]

Gentle heart is tied with an easy thread, A.
(H 304)

a. 1633 HERBERT *The Glimpse* l. 20. 1640 *Id.* no. 726. 1666 TORRIANO *It. Prov.* 58, no. 1 A gentle heart is tied with a twine threed.

Gentle horse that never cast his rider, He is a.

1721 KELLY 166 He's a gentle Horse that never cust[1] his Rider. He is a good Servant that never disobliged his Master. [[1] threw.]

Gentle housewife mars the household, A.
(H 799)

1611 COTGRAVE s.v. Femme The ouer gentle huswife marres her household. *Ibid.*, s.v. Teigneux A tender housewife makes a tainted houshold. 1640 HERBERT no. 44.

Gentle puddocks[1] have long toes.

1721 KELLY 114 Spoken to dissuade you from provoking Persons of Power and Interest; because they can reach you, though at a distance. [[1] probably = puttocks = kites.]

Gentle, *see also* Gentleman that has g. conditions, (He is a); Mastiff be g., (Though).

Gentleman but his pleasure, What's a.
(G 75)

1573 G. HARVEY *Letter-Book* Camden Soc. 15. 1584 R. WILSON *Three Ladies* E3[v] An Emperour for all his wealth can have but his pleasure. [c. 1600] 1631 T. HEYWOOD I *Fair Maid* ii. 312 What's the style of King Without his pleasure? 1670 RAY 96. 1732 FULLER no. 5506.

Gentleman, He that would be a | let him go to an assault (storm a town).
(G 73)

1640 HERBERT no. 878. 1664 CODRINGTON 230 (storm a Town). 1670 RAY 11 (as 1664).

Gentleman of the first head, A. (G 66)

1509 BARCLAY *Ship of Fools* i. 36 A fox furred Jentelman: of the fyrst yere or hede. *c.* 1550 *Parliament of Birds* (Harl. Misc. 1745, v. 482) And called hym a Page of the fyrst Heed. 1552 HULOET *Abced.* N 5 Gentleman of the first head, or *ironice* to be applyed to such as would be estemed a gentleman, having no poynt or qualitie of a gentleman, nor gentleman borne. 1584 COOPER *Thesaurus* s.v. Homo Noui homines, Cic. Gentlemen of the first heade. 1611 COTGRAVE s.v. Gentilhomme de ville A Gentleman of the first head, an vpstart Gentleman. 1616 T. ADAMS *Diseases of the Soul* 62.

Gentleman that has gentle conditions, He is a.
(G 71)

c. 1532 *Tales* no. 70 Goodes and riches do not make a gentyl man, but noble and vertuous conditions do. 1555 *Second Exam of John Philpot* P.S. 12. 1609 HARWARD 90[v] A gentleman should have gentlemanlike conditions. 1616 DRAXE no. 841.

Gentleman that pays the rent, The.

[= the pig.] 1837 LOVER *Rory O'More* ch. 23 A pig wallows on a dunghill . . . until a starved cur . . . drives him for shelter into the house, whose mistress protects 'the gintleman that pays the rint'. 1907 G. B. SHAW *John Bull's Other Island* IV They call a pig that in England. That's their notion of a joke.

Gentleman will do like a gentleman, A.
(G 67)

c. 1390 CHAUCER *W. of Bath's T.* l. 1168 He is gentil that dooth gentil deedis. 1570 TUSSER K4 But gentlemen will gently do, where gentlenesse is shewed. 1599 MINSHEU *Span. Gram.* 83. 1600 DEKKER *Shoem. Hol.* I. i. 49 He is proper that proper doth. 1630 BRATHWAIT *Eng. Gent.* 266. 1706 STEVENS s.v. Hidalgo He is a Gentleman who behaves himself like one. 1854 J. W. WARTER *Last of Old Squires* 43 His common saying was 'Gentle is that gentle does'.

Gentleman without an estate is like a pudding without suet, A.
(G 68)

1602 J. MANNINGHAM *Diary* 117 (like a leane pudding without fatt). 1659 HOWELL *Eng. Prov.* 12a (money). 1670 RAY 96 (living). 1732 FULLER no. 129.

Gentleman's greyhound and a salt box, seek them at the fire, A.
(G 77)

1640 HERBERT no. 205.

Gentleman (-men), *see also* Adam delved . . . (When) who was then the g.; Coat that makes the g. (Not); Cornish g. cousins; Generations to make g. (Takes three); Jack-an-apes is no g.; Jack would be a g. if could speak French; —— if he had money; Jack-out-of-doors (Not) nor yet g.; King can make . . . not a g.; Little g. in black velvet; Manchester men and Liverpool g.; Manners and money make g.; Meant for a g. but spoilt; Put a churl upon a g.; Swear like a g.; Thief passes for g.

Gentleness, *see* Husband (In) wisdom in wife g.; Severity is better than g., (Sometimes).

Gentles, Where there are | there are aye off-fallings.
(G 63)

c. 1641 FERGUSSON MS. no. 1438. 1721 KELLY 348 . . . Spoken jocosely to our Children, when they have forgot something where they were last; as their Gloves, Knives, &c. 1862 HISLOP 322 . . . There is such abundance of good prepared, that something may be reasonably expected for the poor. It may also be a delicate allusion to the failings of the aristocracy.

Gently over the stones, Drive.

1711 SWIFT *Jrnl. to Stella* 30 June A gallop! sit fast, sirrah, and don't ride hard upon the stones. **1843–4** DICKENS *M. Chuz.* ch. 29 Gently over the stones, Poll. Go a-tiptoe over the pimples. **1886** E. J. HARDY *How to be Happy* ch. 11 . . . This piece of advice, . . . given to inexperienced whips, may be suggested metaphorically to the newly-married.

Gentry sent to market will not buy one bushel of corn. (G 80)

a. **1598** LORD BURGHLEY in PECK *Desid. Curiosa* (1779) 47 For a man can buy nothing in the market with gentility. **1662** FULLER Yorks. 216 Seeing Gentry alone . . . (as the plain Proverb saith) sent to Market will not buy a bushell of Wheat, it is good even for those of the best birth to acquire some Liberall quality. **1670** RAY 96. **1721** KELLY 119 (a Peck of Meal.) Spoken when a bare Gentlewoman is proffered in Marriage to the Son of a wealthy Yeoman. *Ibid.* 293 Send your gentle Blood to the Market and see what it will buy. **1858** SURTEES *Ask Mamma* ch. 10 Marry him to some . . . young woman in his own rank of life, . . .: gentility is all very well to talk about, but it gets you nothin' at the market.

Geoffrey, *see* Farewell, gentle G.

Geometry, *see* Hangs by g.

George-a-Green, As good as. (G 83)

1590 *Tarlton's News out of Purgatory* (1844 ed. J. O. Halliwell, 56). **1597** DELONEY *Jack of Newbury* Wks. (Mann) 16. *a.* **1599?** GREENE *George-a-Greene* IV. i Many in manner of a proverb say, 'Were he as good as George-a-Greene, I would strike him sure'. **1648** HERRICK *Hymn to Bacchus* Wks. (1893) II. 60 Yet he'le be thought or seen, So good as *George-a-Green*.

Gerard's bailiff, Here is | work or you must die with cold. (G 85)

1678 RAY 355 *Somerset.*

German's wit is in his fingers, The. (G 88)

1605 SYLVESTER *Du Bartas* Week II, Day ii, Pt. 3, l. 616 The Northern man, whose wit in's fingers settles. **1640** HERBERT no. 36.

German, *see also* Jump as G.'s lips.

Get him where you left him, You will.

1721 KELLY 388 . . . Spoken of even tempered People.

Get money in a desert, He would.

1813 RAY 196 . . . He would thrive where another would starve.

Get the poor man's answer, He will.

1721 KELLY 165 . . . That is, a flat Denial; spoken when it is said that such a Man will court a Woman, whom we suspect he will not get.

Gets by that, He | as Dickins (Dickson) did by his dishes (distress). (T 154)

['Distress', first found in Clarke, appears to be an error.] **1579** R. GALIS *A Brief Treatise containing the cruelty of Elizabeth Style* (*Library*, 1938, xviii. 278) I was constrained to take half the money they cost mee gaining by them as Dickins did by his Dishes Who bying fiue for twopence solde six for a peny. *c.* **1599** MIDDLETON *Old Law* v. i No more is got by that than William Dickins got by his wooden dishes. **1621** ROBINSON 35 (Dickins . . . dishes). **1639** CLARKE 82 (Dickons . . . distres). **1670** RAY 171 To get by a thing as Dickson did by his distress. That is, over the shoulders, as the vulgar usually say. **1837** SOUTHEY *Doctor* iv. 251 Who was William Dickins, whose wooden dishes sold so badly that when any one lost by the sale of his wares, the said Dickins and his dishes, were brought up in scornful comparison?

Gets does much, He who | but he who keeps does more. (K 12)

c. **1374** CHAUCER *Troilus* Bk. 3, l. 1634 As gret a craft to kepe wel as winne. *c.* **1526** *Dicta Sap.* C1 Greater vertue it is to kepe and defende thynges gotten, than to gete them. **1548** HALL *Chron.* (1809 ed. 415) If wyse men say trew, there is some pollycie in gettyng, but much more in kepyng. *Ibid.* 112. Experience teacheth that there is no lesse praise to be geuen to the keper then to the getter, for verely gettyng is a chaunce and kepyng a wit. *a.* **1576** WHYTHORNE 100 It iz not so easy A matter for on to gett A frend az it iz to keep A frend. **1581** GUAZZO i. 187 The vertue is no lesse to keepe, then for to get. **1592** DELAMOTHE 43 He that doth get, doth much, he that doth keepe, doth more. **1664** W. CONYERS *Hemerologicum Astronicum* May 11 He that doth get, doth much, but he that doth keep doth more. **1707** MAPLETOFT 113.

Gets little thanks for losing his own, A man.

1721 KELLY 53 . . . If a Man do not exact those Perquisites that he has a Title to, People will think them not due.

Get(s), got, gotten, *see also* All that you g. you may put in your eye; Friend not so soon g. as lost; Give as good as one g.; Man may lose more in an hour than he can g. in seven; Poor man g. a poor marriage; Seek mickle, g. something; So g. so gone; Soon g., soon spent; Spend as you g.; Sun of one (To g. the). *See also significant words following* 'get'.

Giant(s), *see* Belle g.; Dwarf on g.'s shoulders.

Giblets, *see* Hare's head against goose g.; Steal a goose and give the g. *See also* Goose giblets.

Giddy, He that is | thinks the world turns round. (W 870)

1594–8 SHAKES. *T.S.* V. ii. 20. **1621** BURTON *Anat. Mel.* III. iv. I. (1651) 672 Though . . .: the whole world contradict it, they care not, . . .: and as Gregory well notes of such as are vertiginous, they think all turns round and moves.

Giff gaff was a good fellow, but he is soon weary. (G 94)

1549 LATIMER *3rd Serm. bef. Edw. VI* P.S. 140 Somewhat was given to them before, and they must needs give somewhat again, for Giffe-gaffe was a good fellow. **1624** BP. R. MONTAGU *New Gagg* 92 Giff-gaff is a good fellow. **1636** CAMDEN 296 Give gave was a good man. **1670** RAY 96 Giff gaff was a good man, but he is soon weary. **1721** KELLY 122 (Give is a good Man, but). Men are soon weary of always giving, and receiving no Return. **1818** SCOTT *Ht. Midl.* ch. 16 Gif-gaf makes gude friends, ye ken. **1895** *Dundee Advertiser* in *Daily News* 22 Mar. 7/2 The 'giff-gaff' principle of making friends. *Cf.* **1861** G. ELIOT *Silas Marner* ch. 11 Before I said 'sniff' I took care to know as she'd say 'snaff' . . . I wasn't a-going to open *my* mouth . . . and snap it to again, wi' nothing to swaller.

Gift (Given) horse in the mouth, Look not a. (H 678)

[*a.* 420 ST. JEROME *Comment Epist. Ephes.*, Praef. Noli (ut vulgare est proverbium) equi dentes inspicere donati. Med. Lat. Si quis dat mannos, ne quaere in dentibus annos. RABELAIS I. xi De cheval donné tousjours reguardoit en la gueulle.] *c.* **1510** STANBRIDGE *Vulg.* E.E.T.S. 27 A gyuen hors may not [be] loked in the tethe. **1539** TAVERNER 49ᵛ A gyuen horse (we saye) maye not be loked in the mouth. **1546** HEYWOOD I. v. B2ᵛ Where gyfts be geuen freely, est west north or south, No man ought to loke a geuen hors in the mouth. **1620** SHELTON *Quix.* II. iv (1908) II. 215 I am not so very an ass as to refuse it, according to the proverb, 'Look not a given horse in the mouth'. **1659** N.R. 80 (guift Horse). **1710** PALMER 40 (Gift Horse). **1826** LAMB *Pop. Fallacies* Wks. (1898) 227 THAT WE MUST NOT LOOK A GIFT-HORSE IN THE MOUTH. . . . Some people have a knack of putting upon you gifts of no real value, to engage you to substantial gratitude. **1873** ALLINGHAM *Rambles* Wks. II. 74 The policy of not looking a gift horse in the mouth may easily be carried too far . . . and the guardians of . . . York Minster ought to be particular.

Gift makes room for him, A man's. (M 472)

[PROVERBS xviii. 16 A man's gift maketh room for him, and bringeth him before great men.] **1732** FULLER no. 308.

Gift much expected is paid, not given, A. (G 98)

1597 WARNER *Albion's England* v. 26 To loiter well deserued Gifts, is not to giue but sell, When to requite ingratitude, were to do euill well. **1640** HERBERT no. 574. **1666** TORRIANO *It. Prov.* 76, no. 24 A gift long look'd for, is sold, not given. **1732** FULLER no. 130 A gift long waited for is sold, not given.

Gift of the gab, The. (G 99)

1695 COLVIL *Whigs Supplic.* To Rdr. A v [Pretended quot. from Z. Boyd]. There was a Man called Job, . . . He had a good gift of the Gob.[1] **1794** GODWIN *Caleb Williams* 29. **1853** G. J. WHYTE-MELVILLE *Digby G.* ch. 10. [1 mouth.]

Gift, Who receives a | sells his liberty. (G 104)

c. **1350** *How the Gd. Wife* l. 75 Bunden is þat ʒiftes takitz. **1539** *Precepts of Cato* Publius A7 To take a benefite is to sell thy libertie. He is not his owne man, that vseth another mans benefite. **1642** TORRIANO 8. That is a bitter gift, that depriveth one of his liberty. **1666** *Id. It. Prov.* 76, no. 19. *Ibid.* 216, no. 29 Who receives from another, selleth his liberty.

Gifted, *see* Gear that is g. never so sweet.

Gifts blind the eyes. (G 105)

[DEUT. xvi. 19.] *c.* **1350** *How the Gd. Wife* l. 73 Gode wise men with ʒiftes men maÿ ouergon. **1583** STUBBS *Anat. Abuses* New Sh. S. ii. 16 Remembring what the wise man saith: Gifts blinde the eies of the wise, and peruert iudgement. **1630** T. ADAMS *Spiritual Eye-Salve*, Wks. 662. **1664** CODRINGTON 193.

Gifts (bribes) enter everywhere without a wimble.[1] (G 107, 108)

1612 T. ADAMS *The Gallant's Burden* (1616 ed., 49) Bribery creeping in at the key-hole euen when the door of Iustice is locked vp against her. **1616** DRAXE no. 207 A bribe entreth euery where without knocking. **1620** SHELTON *Quix.* Pt. II. xxxv (iii. 71) Gifts do enter stone walls. **1639** CLARKE 220 (as 1616). **1640** HERBERT no. 955. [1 gimlet.]

Gifts from enemies are dangerous. (G 109)

1545 TAVERNER G5 *Hostium munera, non munera*. The gyftes of enemyes be no gyftes. **1580** WM. CHARKE *An answer to a seditious pamphlet* D 1 If the giftes of enemies be giftlesse gifts (as the prouerbe noteth) . . . **1614** D. DYKE *Mystery of Self-Deceiving* 15 As in the prouerbe, there are giftlesse gifts. **1732** FULLER no. 1650.

Gift(s), *see also* Bestows his g. as broom honey; Every man has his (proper) g.; Free of his g. as poor man of eye; Gives me small g.; Great g. from great men; Little given seasonably excuses great g.; Nothing freer than a g.; Takes g. (She that), herself she sells; Throw no g. at giver's head; Wicked man's g.

Giglot, *see* Peas (The smaller the) . . . the fairer the woman the more the g.

Gilbert, *see* Find guilty G.

Gild(ing), *see* Pills were pleasant, (If), they would not want g.; Sugar (g.) the pill.

Gilead, *see* Balm in G.

Gileynour, *see* Greedy man and g. soon agreed.

Gill, *see* Herring must hang by own g.

Gilt, *see* Take the g. off gingerbread.

Gimmingham, Trimmingham, Knapton and Trunch, North Repps and South Repps are all of a bunch. (G 116)

1670 RAY (Norfolk) 245. **1678** RAY (*Norfolk*) 327 . . . These are names of Parishes lying close together.

Gingerbread, *see* Take the gilt off.

Gip with an ill rubbing, quoth Badger, when his mare kicked.

1678 RAY 85 . . . A ridiculous expression, used to persons that are pettish and froward.

Girdle, *see* Angry (If you be) you may turn buckle of g.; Fox for mate; Head under one's g. (To have a man's); Hen on hot g.; Honey in the mouth, (He has) and a razor at the g.; Keys hang not at one man's g.; M under one's g. (To have an).

Girl worth gold, A.

1585 MUNDAY *Fedele & Fortunio* l. 1703 Such a girle is worth golde in a deare yeere. **[1600] 1631** T. HEYWOOD I *Fair Maid of West* or *A Girl Worth Gold* [title] *Ibid.* ii. 332 Thou art a Girle worth gold.

Gist of a lady's letter is in the postscript, The.

1801 EDGEWORTH *Belinda* ch. 20 The substance of a lady's letter, it has been said, always is comprised in the postscript. **1887** BLACKMORE *Springhaven* ch. 54 Watching . . . the last communication of the sun, and his postscript (which, like a lady's, is the gist of what he means).

Give a child while he craves, and a dog while his tail doth wave, and you'll have a fair dog, but a foul knave.

(C 304)

1303 *Handlyng Synne* 7240 (SKEAT *E. E. Prov.* 39) Yyue thy chylde when he wyl kraue, And thy whelpe whyl hyt wyl haue, Than mayst thou make, yn a stounde, A foule chylde and a feyre hounde. **1623** PAINTER B8 The Prouerb saith, Giue children while they craue, And Dogges so long as they their tailes will waue, And in the morning you shall plainly she [*sic*], Your dogges will cleaner then your children be. *a.* **1628** CARMICHAELL no. 591. **1670** RAY 82. **1721** KELLY 112 Give a bairn his Will, and a Whelp his fill, and none of these two will thrive. The Whelp will be fat and lazy; and the Child will be perverse and froward.

Give a clown your finger, and he will take your hand. (C 449)

1640 HERBERT no. 111. **1706** STEVENS s.v. Aldeano (foot). **1721** KELLY 118 (Carle) . . . Suffer an unmannerly Fellow to intrude upon you, and he will intrude more and more.

Give a dog an ill name and hang him. *Cf.* Ill name.

1706 STEVENS s.v. Perro (and his work is done). **1721** KELLY 124 . . . Spoken of those who raise an ill Name on a Man on purpose to prevent his Advancement. **1815** SCOTT *Guy Man.* ch. 23 It is pithily said, 'Give a dog an ill name and hang him,' and . . . if you give a man, or a race of men, an ill name, they are very likely to do something that deserves hanging. **1888** MRS. OLIPHANT *Second Son* ch. 41 Give a dog an ill name and hang him, they say; call a woman a mother-in-law, and it's the same thing.

Give a groat for an owl, He is in great want of a bird that will. (W 32)

1678 RAY 101. **1706** STEVENS s.v. Gana. **1802** WOLCOT (P. Pindar) *Pitt & his S.* Wks. (1816) IV. 230 'A man must be hard driv'n to find a bird, Who offers two-pence for an owl.'

Give a lie twenty-four hours' start, and you can never overtake it.

1902–4 LEAN III. 471.

Give a loaf, and beg a shive.[1] (L 399)

1631 WEEVER *Anc. Funeral Mon.* 112 The religious Order . . . could by no means be brought in . . . to giue a loafe, and beg a shiue, to turne themselues out of actuall possession, and lie at the Kings mercie. **1678** RAY 247. [[1] slice.]

Give a man an annuity and he'll live for ever.

1824 BYRON *Juan* II. lxv 'Tis said that persons living on annuities Are longer lived than others, . . . Some . . . *do* never die. **1851** G. OUTRAM *The Annuity* She's some auld Pagan mummified, Alive for her annuity.

Give a man fortune (luck) and cast (throw) him into the sea. (M 146)

1576 *Parad. of Dainty Devices*, no. 27 Geve me good Fortune all men sayes, and throw me in the seas. *c.* **1600** *Edmond Ironside* l. 1737 Give a man luck and cast him over the gallous. **1620** SHELTON *Quix.* II. xlii (1908) III. 108 Here the proverb comes in, and joins well, that 'Give a man luck, and cast him in the sea'. **1639** CLARKE 125. **1721** KELLY 113 (Luck) . . . Spoken when a Man is unexpectedly fortunate.

Give a slave a rod, and he'll beat his master. (S 524)

1639 CLARKE 193.

Give a thing, and take a thing, to wear the devil's gold ring. (T 128, 129)

1571 J. BRIDGES *Sermon at Paul's Cross* 29 Shal we make God to say the worde, and eate his worde? to giue a thing, and take a thing, little children say, This is the diuels goldring, not Gods gifte. **1601** SHAKES. *T.N.* V. i. 7 This is to give a dog, and in recompense desire my dog again. **1611** COTGRAVE s.v. Retirer To giue a thing, and take a thing; to weare the diuell's goldring. **1629** T. ADAMS *Serm.* (1861–2) II. 288 Things dedicated to God are not to be transferred to the uses of men; . . . [it is] a proverb

among our children. To give a thing and take
a thing is fit for the devil's darling. **1642** FULLER
Holy State III. xxv (1841) 220 Plato saith, that
in his time it was a proverb amongst children:
Τῶν ὀρθῶς δοθέντων, οὐκ ἔστιν ἀφαίρεσις. 'Things
that are truly given must not be taken away
again.' **1721** KELLY 120 . . . Is the ill Man's
Goud¹ Ring. A Cant among Children, when
they demand a Thing again, which they had
bestowed. [¹ gold.]

Give a thing and take again, and you shall ride in hell's wain. (T 129)

1601 SHAKES. *T.N.* V. i. 7 This is to give a dog,
and in recompense desire my dog again. **1678**
RAY 146.

Give a Yorkshireman a halter, and he'll find a horse.

1869 HAZLITT 141.

Give and take. (G 121)

1519 HORMAN *Vulg.* (James) 98 A man muste
somtyme gyue and somtyme take. [**1592**] **1597**
SHAKES. *Rich. III* V. iii. 6 We must both give and
take, my loving lord. **1662** FULLER Surrey 96 The
King, who in this kind would give and not take,
being no Good Fellow in tart Repartees, was . . .
highly offended. **1778** FRANCES BURNEY *Evelina*
ch. 25 Give and Take is fair in all nations. **1832**
MARRYAT *N. Forster* ch. 47 Give and take is fair
play. All I say is, let it be a fair stand-up fight.

Give as good as one gets, To.

1738 SWIFT Dial. I. E.L. 276. **1791** BOSWELL
Johnson iv. 276.

Give everyone his due. *Cf.* Give the devil his due. (D 634)

[**1582** ROM. xiii. 7 (Rhem.) Render therfore to al
men their dew (1611 their dues).] **1583** MEL-
BANCKE B2ᵛ Art thou such a louinge woorme to
succourles creatures, to robb God of his due.
1590 R. HARVEY *Plain Percival* B1 Giue euery
man his right. **1597** SHAKES. *1 Hen. IV* I. ii.
51 I'll give thee thy due, thou hast paid all
there. **1599** PORTER *Angry Wom. Abing.* l. 1025
Giue euery man his due. **1602** SHAKES. *T.C.* II.
ii. 173 Nature craves All dues be rend'red to
their owners. *a.* **1633** DONNE Elegy xiii I blush
to give her half her due; Yet say, No poyson's
halfe so bad as Iulia. **1641** JONSON *Timber* 66
Let Aristotle and others have their dues. **1654**
WHITLOCK *Zootomia* 184 They study not Men
for any other end, than to give every one their
Due. **1691** SEWEL 157 To give every one his
Due.

Give gave, *see* Giff gaff.

Give him an inch and he'll take an ell. (I 49)

1546 HEYWOOD II. ix. L1ᵛ Whan I gaue you an
ynche ye tooke an ell. **1599** PORTER *Angry Wom.
Abingd.* l. 2344 Giue an inche, and youle
take an elle. **1612–15** BP. HALL *Contempl.* IV.
ix (1825) III. 358 It is the fashion of our bold
nature, upon an inch given to challenge an ell.
1798 CANNING & FRERE *Anti-Jacobin* XXXV

Though they still took an ell, when we gave them
an inch, They would all have been loyal—like
Ballynahinch. **1841** DICKENS *B. Rudge* ch. 30
A troublesome class of persons who, having an
inch conceded them, will take an ell. **1953** T. S.
ELIOT *Confidential Clerk* (Faber 1962, 225) If
you give Miss Angel an inch She'll take an ell.

Give him one and lend him another, I thought I would. (O 46, 47)

1670 RAY 177 . . . i.e. I would be quit with him.

Give him the other half egg and burst him. (E 72)

1678 RAY 241.

Give his bone to the dog, He will not.

1721 KELLY 154 . . . Spoken of sturdy People,
who will not readily part with their Interest, or
be bullied out of it.

Give (Box) it about, it will come to my father at last. (F 85)

[*c.* **1680** The story is told of young Ralegh and
his father in a passage omitted from A. Clark's
edition of Aubrey's *Brief Lives* ii. 194: 'Box
about, 'twill come to my Father anon.']
1693 LUTTRELL *Brief Rel. State Affairs* 19
Oct. (1857 iii. 207) One health was, Box it about,
it will come to my father, meaning king James.
1721 KELLY 121 . . . A young Fellow was sitting
in Company with his Father, who . . . gave him a
Blow; who immediately gave his left Hand Man
as much, and bad[e] him give it about. Spoken
when we would have some ill Turn done to some
body, but not immediately by our self. **1738**
SWIFT Dial. III. E.L. 323 Methinks you are very
witty upon one another: come, box it about;
'twill come to my father at last.

Give little to his servant, He can | that licks his knife (trencher). (L 345)

c. **1400** *Rom. Rose* C. l. 6502 What shulde he
yeve that likketh his knyf? **1640** HERBERT no.
846. **1813** RAY 14 (*Ital.*) (own trencher).

Give neither counsel nor salt till you are asked for it.

1707 MAPLETOFT 8.

Give one's head for the washing (nought), To. (H 252)

c. **1500** MEDWALL *Nature* l. 721 in *'Lost' Tudor
Plays* (1907) 66 A well-drawn man is he; and
a well-taught, That will not give his head
for nought. **1542** H. BULLINGER *Christ. State
Matrimony* (1543, A5) Pref. by T. Becon Like
a ioly ruffelare, lyke a fellowe, that wyll not
gyue his head for the wasshynge. **1578** *Courtly
Controv.* 201ᵛ. **1596** NASHE *Saffron W.* iii. 73
But the time was, when he would not haue
giuen his head for the washing. **1663** BUTLER
Hudibras I. iii. 256 For my Part it shall ne'er be
sed, I for the washing give my Head. **1721**
KELLY 154 He will not give the head for the
washing. Spoken of sturdy People, who will not
readily part with their Interest, or be bullied out
of it. **1738** SWIFT Dial. I. E.L. 270.

Give others good counsel but will take
none himself, He can.   (c 688)

1533–4 N. UDALL *Flowers* 189 Thou canst gyue
counsaylle vnto others, and . . . be wyse in other
mennes mattiers, and not . . . be able to helpe
or ease thyne owne selfe. **1575** GASCOIGNE *Glass
of Govt* M2 Se how euerye man can geue good
counsell, and few can followe it. **1616** DRAXE
no. 383. **1624** J. HEWES *Perfect Survey* N2
Many men counsell others better then themselues.
1664 J. WILSON *Cheats* I. ii Most men can counsel
others, few, themselves.

Give the devil his due. *Cf.* Give everyone his due.   (D 273)

1589 LYLY *Pap w. Hatchet* D ij Giue them
their due though they were diuels. **1596** NASHE
Saffron W. iii. 36 Giue the diuell his due. **1597**
SHAKES. *1 Hen. IV* I. ii. 114 He was never yet a
breaker of proverbs: he will give the devil his due.
1598–9 *Id. Hen. V* III. vii. 114 I will take that
up with 'Give the devil his due'. **1618** J.
FLETCHER *Loyal Subj.* I. iii Whose doubts and
envies—But the Devil will have his due. **1642**
Prince Rupert's Declarat. 2 The Cavaliers (to
give the Divell his due) fought very valiantly.
1751 SMOLLETT *Per. Pick.* ch. 15 You always
used me in an officer-like manner, that I must
own, to give the devil his due.

Give what he hasn't got, A man cannot.

1586 *Lazarillo de Tormes* tr. Rowland, ed.
Crofts 48 No man can give that which he hath
not. **1775** JOHNSON in *Boswell* I. (1848) 455
This is an old axiom which no man has yet
thought fit to deny. Nil dat quod non habet.

Given him turnips, She has.

1845 FORD *Handb. Spain* i. 27 *note.* This gourd
forms a favourite metaphor . . . she has refused
him; it is the 'giving cold turnips' of Suffolk.
1869 HAZLITT 346 . . . *Devonshire*, i.e. Jilted him.

Given them green stockings, She has.

1862 HISLOP 259 . . . Spoken when a young
woman marries before her elder sisters.

Gives discreetly (to another) gains
directly (bestows on himself), He who.
                                         (G 124)

1611 COTGRAVE s.v. Donné He that giues dis-
cretly gaines directly. **1664** CODRINGTON 197
(as 1611). **1684** RYCAUT tr. *Gracian's Critick*
240. **1732** FULLER no. 2114 He that gives to a
worthy Person bestows a Benefit upon himself.

Gives fair words, He who | feeds you
with an empty spoon. *Cf.* Fill the
mouth with empty spoons.

1659 TORRIANO no. 166.

Gives his goods before he be dead, He
that | take up a mallet and knock him
on the head.   (A 187. G 308)

1605–6 SHAKES. *K.L.* I. iv. 104 Would I had two
coxcombs and two daughters!—Why, my boy?—

If I gave them all my living, I 'ld keep my coxcombs myself. **1623** WODROEPHE 486 This last
is the greatest Folie; meaning to giue away his
Goods to vngratefull Children before hee dye.
1640 HERBERT no. 855 He that gives all before
hee dies provides to suffer. **1641** FERGUSSON
no. 382 He that takes all his geir fra himself, and gives to his bairns, it were weill ward
to take a mell and knock out his harmes.[1] **1670**
RAY 78 Who gives away his goods before he is
dead, Take a beetle and knock him on the head.
1710 PALMER 27 (beetle). **1721** KELLY 156 He
that gives all his Geer to his Bairns, Take up a
Beetle, and knock out his Harns[1] . . . John Bell,
. . . having given his whole Substance to his
Children, was by them neglected; after he died
there was found . . . a Mallet with this Inscription, I John Bell, leaves here a Mell, the Man to
fell, who gives all to his Bairns, and keeps nothing to himsell. **1912** *T.L.S.* 31 May 222 The
rhyme on an almshouse in the Bargates at
Leominster[2]—He that gives away all before he
is dead, Let 'em take this hatchet and knock
him on y⁰ head. [[1] brains. [2] founded 1735.]

Gives honour to his enemy, He that |
is like to an ass.   (H 567)

1678 RAY *Adag. Hebr.* 413.

Gives me small gifts, He that | would
have me live.   (G 113)

[*c.* **1190** *Li Proverbe au Vilain* (Tobler) 8 Qui
petit me done, il veut que je vive.] *c.* **1300** *Provs.
of Hending* no. 20 That me lutel yeueth, he my
lyf ys on. **1640** HERBERT no. 1000.

Gives thee a bone, He that | would not
have thee die.   (B 519)

1640 HERBERT no. 355. **1642** TORRIANO 34.
1650 JER. TAYLOR *Holy Liv.* IV. § 8 (1850) 219
A cup of water, if it be but love to the brethren,
. . . shall be accepted. Chi ti da un' ossa, non
ti verrebbe morto.

Gives thee a capon, He that | give him
the leg and wing.   (c 67)

1640 HERBERT no. 109.

Gives to all, denies all, Who.   (A 213)

1597 *Politeuphuia* 81 To be kinde to all, is to be
kinde to none. **1611** COTGRAVE s.v. Donner
Hee that giues me all denies me all; viz. He that
offers me all meanes to giue me nothing. **1640**
HERBERT no. 38. **1659** HOWELL *Span. Prov.* 17.

Gives to be seen, He that | will relieve
none in the dark.

1732 FULLER no. 2115 He that gives to be seen,
would never relieve a Man in the dark.

Gives twice who gives quickly, He.
                                         (G 125)

[PUBL. SYRUS 235 (Ribbeck) *Inopi beneficium bis
dat qui dat celeriter. Cf.* SENECA *Ep.* 108. 9.]
c. **1385** CHAUCER *Leg. Good Wom.* Prol. l. 441
For whose yeveth a yifte, or doth a grace, Do
it by tyme, his thank is wel the more. *c.* **1526**

Dicta Sap. C4ᵛ The gyft that quicke and promptely is gyuen to him that hath nede, is twyse more thanke worthie. **1553** T. WILSON *Arte of Rhet.* (1909) 119 He giueth twise, that giueth sone and cherefully. **1612** SHELTON *Quix.* IV. vii (1908) I. 340 It is an old proverb, 'that he that gives quickly, gives twice'. **1670** RAY 11. He giveth twice that gives in a trice. **1775** JOHNSON 19 Jan., in *Boswell* (1848) xlvii. 427 I did really ask the favour twice; but you have been even with me by granting it so speedily. *Bis dat qui cito dat.* **1907** *Spectator* 22 June 979 The Union Jack Club ... needs £16,000. ... He gives twice who gives quickly.

Give(n, s, gave), *see also* Better g. a shilling than lend; Better g. than take; Better g. wool than sheep; Boots (To g. one the); Bread for cake (You g. me); Bridle (reins) (To g. one the); Charitable g. out at door; Counsel to g. ... (We have better); Eat gold (If she would) he would g. it her; Fear g. wings; Fig (To g. one a); Gift much expected paid not g.; Good mother says not ... but g.; Grateful man (To) g.; Hand that g. gathers; Hand that g. the wound must g. cure; Handsome head ... pray g. tester; Hard g. more than he that has nothing; Lends (He that) g.; Long a giving knows not how to g.; Losers leave to speak (G.); Piper a penny to play (G. the); Spent we had (What we), what we g. we have. *For* To give, *see also under significant words following.*

Giving and taking, In | There may be mistaking.

1694 BOYER 110.

Giving is dead, restoring very sick.
(G 127)

1573 SANFORD 50 Giuen is dead, and restored is nought. **1611** DAVIES no. 62 (Restoring is dying). **1640** HERBERT no. 573.

Giving much to the poor, doth enrich (increase) a man's store.   (G 128)

c. **1350** *How the Gd. Wife* l. 12 Wel hat þat þe pouere ȝiueȝ. *c.* **1400–50** *Ibid.* l. 12 Tresour he hath þat pouere fedith. **1613** CHAPMAN *Rev. Bussy D'Amb.* I. ii. 91 What ye give, ye have. **1640** HERBERT no. 191. **1670** RAY 96 (increase). **1710** PALMER 156.

Glad, *see* Sad because I cannot be g.

Gladness, A man of | seldom falls into madness.   (M 290)

1659 HOWELL *Eng. Prov.* 17a. **1670** RAY 11.

Gladness, *see also* Sadness and g. succeed each other.

Glasgow people, Greenock folk, and Paisley bodies.

1842 R. CHAMBERS *Pop. Rhymes of Scot.* 20 ... These words imply gradations of dignity, the Paisley bodies being ... at the bottom of the scale.

Glass, As brittle as.   (G 134)

1412–20 LYDGATE *Troy Bk.* v. 854 Brotel as glas. **1539** TAVERNER *Publius* C4 Fortune is brykle as glasse, when she glystereth, she breaketh. **1553** BECON *Jewel Joy* P.S. 437 Beauty ... is more brittle than glass. **1590** GREENE *Mourn. Garm.* Gros. ix. 217 She is fickle as the brittle glasse. **1599** SHAKES. *Pass. Pilg.* 7, l. 3 And yet as glass is brittle. **1672** WALKER 9 no. 33 As brittle as a Venice glass.

Glass is run, His.   (G 132)

1590 LODGE *Rosalynde* ed. Greg 2 His glass was run. **1591–2** SHAKES. *3 Hen. VI* I. iv. 25 The sands are numbered that make up my life. **1592–4** *Id. 1 Hen. VI* IV. ii. 35 Ere the glass that now begins to run Finish the process of his sandy hour, These eyes ... Shall see thee withered. **1611** *Id. W.T.* I. ii. 305 She would not live The running of one glass.

Glass tells you, What your | will not be told by counsel.   (G 133)

1592 DELAMOTHE 45 He that beholdes himselfe in a glasse, may see himselfe well. **1640** HERBERT no. 255.

Glass, *see also* Clear (bright) as g.; Fame is magnifying g.; First g. for thirst; Fortune is made of g.; Grey as g.; Head of g. (He who has) must not throw stones; Loves g. without G. (He that); Luck of Edenhall (If g. break); Wine is g. of mind; Woman and g. in danger; Women look in their g. (The more).

Glastonbury Tor, *see* Old as G. T.

Glazier, *see* Father was a bad g.

Glean before the cart has carried, To.
(G 140)

c. **1549** HEYWOOD I. xi. D3ᵛ Thou goest a-gleinyng er the cart haue caried. **1616** DRAXE no. 1814 (before that the Cart haue caried).

Gled[1] whistled, It was never for nothing that the.

1721 KELLY 199 ... People who officiously offer their Service may be suspected to have some selfish End in it. [1 kite.]

Glimmer in the touch-box,[1] There is a.
(G 141)

1678 RAY 247. [1 a musketeer's box for priming-powder.]

Glitters, *see* Gold (All is not) that g.

Gloucestershire kindness.

1894 NORTHALL *Folk-phrases of Four Co.* 14 Gloucestershire kindness, giving away what you don't want yourself.

Gloucestershire, *see also* Sure as God's in G.

Glove(s), *see* Cat in g.; Gauntlet of a hedging g. (Make not); Hand and g.; Iron hand in velvet g.; Shoe (a cast-off g.), (To be thrown aside like an old); Shoeing-horn to help on g.

Glowing coals sparkle oft.   (c 463)

1615 *Janua Linguarum* tr. W. Welde 17 Glowing coales sparkle often. **1616** DRAXE no. 1340. **1670** RAY 72 . . . When the mind is heated with any passion, it will often break out in words and expressions, *Psalm* 39.

Glow-worm lights her lamp, When the | the air is always damp.

1883 ROPER 31. **1893** INWARDS 145.

Glue did not hold, The.

1813 RAY 196 . . . i.e. You were baulked in your wishes: you missed your aim.

Glutton, *see* Hastens a g. (Who), chokes him; Meals (Two hungry) make third a g.

Gluttony is the sin of England. (G 147)

a. **1547** *Apol. Eng. Gluttony* in *Reliq. Antiq.* i. 326 He sayd that Englysshemen ar callyd the grettyste fedours in the worlde. **1640** FULLER *Joseph's Parti-col. Coat* Sermons (1891) I. 203 Gluttony is the sin of England; for though . . . we may entitle ourselves to the pride of the Spanish, jealousy of the Italian, wantonness of the French, drunkenness of the Dutch, and laziness of the Irish; . . . yet our ancientest carte is for the sin of gluttony.

Gluttony kills more than the sword. *Cf.* Suppers (By).   (G 148)

a. **1384** WYCLIF *Wks.* ed. T. Arnold iii. 158 As clerkes seyn commynly, glotonie slees mo men then dos swerde. **1509** BARCLAY *Ship of Fools* ii. 266 Mo dye By glotony, excesse and lyuynge bestyall Than by hunger, knyfe, or deth naturall. **1522** SIR T. MORE *De quatuor novissimis* (1557, col. 100). **1528** *Regimen sanitatis Salerni* A2ᵛ Truely the prouerbe sayth, that there dye many mo by surfet, than by the sworde. **1601** T. WRIGHT *Passions of the Mind* 206 Gluttonie must be the nursse of Physitians, since, plures occidit gula quam gladius. **1617** MORYSON *Itin.* I. i. i (1907–8) I. 20 A round table . . . with many inscriptions persuading temperance, such as . . . Plures crapula quam ensis. Gluttony kills more than the sword. **1641** FERGUSSON no. 763 Surfeit slayes mae nor the sword. **1721** KELLY 299 Surfeits slay more than Swords. Plures necat gula quam gladius.

Gluttony, *see also* Belly full of g. will never study; Fire of London punishment for g.

Gnat, *see* Strain at a g.

Gnaw the bone which is fallen to thy lot.   (B 516)

1678 RAY *Adag. Hebr.* 411 . . . That is, He that hath an ill wife must patiently beare with her: It may also be applyed to other things.

Go a long way after one is weary, One can (may).

1853 TRENCH iv . . . [has] the poetry of an infinite sadness about it, so soon as one gives it that larger range of application which it is capable of receiving. **1913** *Brit. Wkly.* 2 Jan. 454 In a paragraph on the Austrian Emperor . . . the words occur, 'We keep going a long time after we are tired'.

Go about, *see* Better to g. a. than to fall.

Go after a leech, While men | the body is buried.

a. **1388** USK *Test. Love* III. vii. 79 While men gon after a leche, the body is buryed.

Go but *Gaw*, Do not say.   (s 110)

c. **1569** FORREST *Hist. Joseph* I. 171 This woorde, Gawe me and goynge with them too, Dyd six tymes more good then Goo yee shoulde doo. *c.* **1582** *Love and Fortune* l. 745 Ile goe with thee I faith, gaw lets be gone. **1659** HOWELL *Eng. Prov.* 4a Do not say go, but gaw, viz. go thy self along. **1669** DUDLEY NORTH *Obs. and Adv. Oeconom.* 50 In small families especially in the country, the master may say Gow (as we phrase it in East England) or go we, implying that he will accompany them. **1830** FORBY 432 'There is a deal of difference between go and gow'. *i.e.* between ordering a person to do a thing, and going with him to see him do it, or doing it with him. [Gow, *v.* let us go; an abbrev. of 'go we'.]

Go down the ladder when you marry a wife; go up when you choose a friend.   (L 25)

1678 RAY *Adag. Hebr.* 400 . . . The meaning isᵎ that we should not marry a wife above our rank, though we choose such a friend.

Go far about seeking the nearest, You.

1721 KELLY 370 . . . Spoken to them who, out of Design, speak not directly to the Business, or who take an improper Course to obtain their end.

Go farther and fare worse.   (G 160)

1546 HEYWOOD II. iv. G3ᵛ And might haue gon further, and haue faren wurs. **1614** BP. HALL *Recoll. Treat.* 412 That ancient check of going far and faring worse. **1738** SWIFT *Dial.* II. E.L. 299. **1847–8** THACKERAY *Vanity F.* ch. 4.

Go forward and fall, go backward and mar all.   (G 152)

1580 MUNDAY *Zelauto* P2 I am not so farre ouer shoes: but I may returne yet drie, but I am not so far in, but I may easily escape out. **1599** MINSHEU A2 I had waded so farre in it, as without helpe I could not get ouer, nor without danger and shame returne backe. **1605–6** SHAKES. *M.* III. iv. 136. I am in blood Stepp'd in so far that, should I wade no more, Returning were as tedious as go o'er. **1614** 31 March J. CHAMBERLAIN (ed. McClure i. 521) When a man

307 *Go | Go*

is halfe way over he were as goode go forward as turn backe. **1616** WITHALS 552. **1639** CLARKE 250.

Go here away, go there away, quoth Madge Whitworth when she rode the mare in the tedder. (M 4)
1678 RAY 85.

Go home, and say your prayers.
1637 SHIRLEY *Hyde Pk.* I. ii Go home, and say your prayers, I will not look For thanks till seven years hence.

Go in God's name, so ride no witches. (G 265)
1678 RAY 247.

Go into the country to hear what news at London, You must. (C 712)
1678 RAY 345. **1887** HARDY *Woodlanders* ch. 4 As the saying is, 'Go abroad and you'll hear news of home'.

Go not for every grief to the physician, nor for every quarrel to the lawyer, nor for every thirst to the pot. (G 445)
1586 G. WHETSTONE *The English Mirror* 14 This olde and approoued Prouerb, Honor (and vse) the Phisition, for necessities sake: Which importeth extreame daunger, and not euery trifling distemperature. **1640** HERBERT no. 290.

Go old to the court, and young to a cloister, A man must | that would go from thence to heaven. (M 275)
1678 RAY 117.

Go out and kill? What shall we.
1896 'H. S. MERRIMAN' *The Sowers* ch. 21 'The Prince', continued De Chauxville, ... 'is a great sportsman, ... a mighty hunter. I wonder why Englishmen always want to kill something.' **1902–4** LEAN I. 19 What shall we go out and kill? (The after-breakfast inquiry.) An Englishman's idea of happiness is to find something he can kill and to hunt it.

Go out like a candle in a snuff (the snuff of a candle), To. (C 49)
[*a.* 1535] **1553** T. MORE *Dial. Comf.* II. iii, Wks. 1557, 1172 I cannot licken my life more metely now than to the snuffe of a candle that burneth within the candlestickes nose. **1589** LYLY *Pap with Hatchet* iii. 410 Within a while appeared olde Martin with a wit worn into the socket, twinkling and pinking like the snuffe of a candle. *a.* **1618** SYLVESTER (1621) 1162 Forgotten all their Storie . . . Went out in Snuffe and left ill sent behind. *a.* **1618** RALEIGH in HANNAH, *Poems of Wotton and Raleigh* 74 Cowards [may] fear to die; but Courage stout, Rather than live in Snuff, will be put out. **1654** WARREN *Unbelievers* 252 His Arguments should go out like a snuffe of a candle in the socket. **1687** WINSTANLEY *Eng.*

Poets (Milton) in GOSSE *Gossip in Lib.* (1893) 110 But his Fame is gone out like a Candle in a Snuff, and his Memory wil always stink. **1841** S. WARREN *Ten Thous. a Year* ch. 9 'Bess dropped off sudden, like, at last, didn't she?' . . . 'She went out, as they say, like the snuff of a candle.'

Go over the stile, He that will not | must be thrust through the gate. (S 855)
1678 RAY 206.

Go snacks, To. (S 578)
[= to have a share; divide profits.] **1693** DRYDEN etc. *Juvenal* vii. 135 If one piece thou take, That must be cantled, and the Judge go snack. **1701** FARQUHAR *Sir H. Wildair* IV. ii. Well, monsieur! 'tis about a thousand pounds; we go snacks. **1778** BURNEY *Evelina* Lett. 62. *Ibid.* Lett. 82. **1809** MALKIN *Gil Blas* X. xi. You shall go snacks in all that we can squeeze out of the old fellow. **1884** BLACKMORE *Tom. Upmore* ch. 16 If John Windsor would go snacks, I should feel half inclined to consider about consulting a Solicitor.

Go the whole hog, To.
1830 GALT *Lawrie T.* II. i (1849) 43 I reckon Squire Lawrie may go the whole hog with her. **1837** TH. HOOK *Jack Brag* ch. 5 He determined to 'go the whole hog', and follow up this feint . . . which might . . . be turned into a real attack. **1905** VACHELL *The Hill* 147 You're not prepared to go the whole hog? You want to pick and choose.

Go through dirt? How does he.
1917 BRIDGE 75 .'.. How does he bear suffering or temptation?

Go to a goat (ass) for wool, You. (G 170)
[ERASM. *Ad. De lana caprina.*] **1548** T. ELYOT *Bibliotheca* Asinum tondes, thou shearest an asse . . . of one that attempteth a vayne, foolyshe, and unprofitable enterpryse. **1579** A. HALL *Quarrel betw. Hall and Mallorie* in *Misc. Antiq. Angl.* 37 De lana caprina was the contention. **1592** GREENE *Quip* ed. Hindley 8 Others striving whether it were wool or hair the goat bare. **1623** JOHN LEYCESTER no. 12 Thou seekest wool of an Asse (Ab Asino lanam quaeris). **1629** T. ADAMS *Serm.* (1861–2) I. 330 He shall hardly get from his patron the milk of the vicarage; but if he looks for the fleeces of the parsonage, he shall have, after the proverb, *lanam caprinam.*[1] **1721** KELLY 364 You come to the Goat's House to thig[2] Wool. **1802** WOLCOT (P. Pindar) *Middle. Elect.*, Let. ii. Wks. (1816) IV. Vor he that goeth vor *manners* there, Goeth to a goat vor *wool*. [[1] goats' wool. [2] beg.]

Go to bed at noon, Ye would make me. (B 197)
1546 HEYWOOD II. vii. K1 It semeth ye wolde make me go to bed at noone. **1605–6** SHAKES. *K.L.* III. vi. 84. We'll go to supper i' the morning.—And I'll go to bed at noon. **1622** DRAYTON *Polyolbion* xxiii. l. 250.

Go to heaven in a featherbed, To. *Cf.*
Going to heaven in a sedan. (H 352)

c. **1520** SIR THOS. MORE in HARPSFIELD *Life*
E.E.T.S. 75 If his wife or any of his children
had beene diseased or troubled, he would say
vnto them: 'We may not looke at our pleasures
to goe to heauen in Fether-beddes.' **1630**
BRATHWAIT *Eng. Gent.* (1641) 152 Wee cannot
goe to heaven on beds of down. **1678** RAY 243
. . . Non est e terris mollis ad astra via. [Not
easy is the passage from the earth to the stars.]

Go to heaven in a string, To. (H 353)

[= to be hanged: referred originally to the
Jesuits who were hanged in the reign of Elizabeth.]
1583 MELBANCKE K2ᵛ He was gone to heauen in
a halter. **1592** GREENE *2nd Pt. Conny-catching*
(Bodley Head Q.) 19 The quest went vpon him
and condemned him, and so the priggar went to
heauen in a string. *a.* **1708** T. WARD *England's
Reform.* II (1710) 47 Then may he boldly take
his Swing, and go to Heaven in a string.

Go to heaven in a wheelbarrow, To.
(H 354)

[= to go to hell.] **1629** T. ADAMS *Serm.* (1861–2)
I. 144 This oppressor must needs go to heaven.
. . . But it will be, as the byword is, in a wheelbarrow: the fiends, and not the angels, will take
hold on him.

Go to hell for the house profit, He will.
(H 402)

1641 FERGUSSON no. 473 *Of hypocrites.* **1721**
KELLY 156 . . . Spoken of them that will do any
Thing for Gain.

Go to pot (to the pot), To. (P 504)

[= to be cut in pieces like meat for the pot; to be
ruined or destroyed.] **1530** TYNDALE *Answ. to
More* P.S. 110 And then goeth a part of little
flock to pot, and the rest scatter. **1531** ELYOT
Governor (Croft) i. 196 Kylling of dere . . .
serueth well for the potte (as is the commune
saynge). **1542** ERASM. tr. Udall *Apoph.* (1877)
129 The ryche . . . went daily to the potte. **1546**
HEYWOOD II. v. H2 The weaker goth to the
potte. **1670** RAY 190. **1757** SMOLLETT *Reprisal*
I. viii. Wks. (1871) 610 All our fine project gone
to pot! *a.* **1812** WOLCOT (P. Pindar) *Peter's
Pension* Wks. (1816) I. 417 What if *my* good
friend Hastings goes to pot?

Go to the dogs, To. (D 543)

[= to be ruined.] **1549** ERASM. *Pr. Folly* tr.
CHALONER M1 Rather shoulde we let all the
worlde goe to wreke bothe with dogge and catte
(as thei saie) than ones to make a lesyng. **1619**
R. HARRIS *Drunkard's Cup* A2b One is coloured,
another is foxt, a third is gone to the dogs. **1865**
LES. STEPHEN *Let.* to Lowell 13 Jan. An elderly
Tory . . . added that we were all going to the dogs
in consequence of that . . . Reform Bill. **1909**
E.PHILLPOTTS *The Haven* I. xiv None agreed together save in this: that Brixham was going to
the dogs a good deal quicker than the rest of
the world.

**Go to the well against his will, If the
lad | either the can will break or the
water will spill.**

1721 KELLY 185 . . . Spoken when People mis-
manage a Business, that they were forc'd to go
about against their Mind.

**Go twenty miles on your errand first,
I will.** (M 927)

1670 RAY 177.

**Go up like a rocket and come down like
the stick, To.**

1838 R. H. BARHAM in R. H. D. Barham's *Life* ii.
48 Poor man, he has gone up like a rocket and
is coming down like the stick. **1909** *Brit. Wkly.*
7 Jan. We know the talk about a man going up
like a rocket and coming down like a stick. . . .
It is generally the man's own fault.

Go up the ladder to bed, You will.
(L 27)

c. **1550** *Nice Wanton* B1 By the masse ye wyl
clyme the ladder. **1678** RAY 256 . . . *i.e.* be
hang'd. **1823** GROSE ed. Pierce Egan s.v. Bed.

**Go upon the Franciscans' hackney;
i.e. on foot, To.** (F 664)

1651 HERBERT no. 1035.

Go, goes, gone, *see also* All are not saints that g.
to church; All is g. (When), what avails dagger;
Beast that g. always never wants blows;
Bedfordshire, (To go to); Better g. by your
enemy's grave than his gate; End g. forward,
(He cares not which); Expect to g. when you
die (Where do you); Fast as one g. another comes;
First creep then g.; House and land are g.
(When), learning is excellent; Lechery and
covetousness g. together; Love will g. through
stone walls; Married, (He that g. far to be) will
either deceive or be deceived; Peel straws, (G.);
Policy . . . (g. beyond strength); Servant must
. . . g. when you bid him (A good); Tell me with
whom thou g.; Thither as I would g. I can g.
late; Touch and g.; Way to be g. is not to stay;
Welcome when thou g.; *For* To go, To go
through, To go to, *see also under significant
words following.*

**Goat gives a good milking, but she
casts it all down with her foot, The.**
Cf. **Cow that gives a good pail of milk,**
etc.

a. **1628** CARMICHAELL no. 1586 (. . . al day . . . at
evin). **1721** KELLY 310 . . . Spoken when they
who do a piece of good Service, by their after
Behaviour spoil the good Grace of it.

**Goat must browse (bleat) where she is
tied, The.** (G 168)

1611 COTGRAVE s.v. Chevre. **1640** HERBERT no.
56. **1721** KELLY 343 Where the Buck is bound

there he must bleat. Men must bear these Hardships to which they are bound, either by Force or Compact. **1852** E. FITZGERALD *Polonius* 59 'The goat must browse where she is tied'. Poverty . . . surrounds a man with ready-made barriers, which, if they do mournfully gall and hamper, do at least prescribe for him, and force on him, a sort of course and goal.

Goats, You have no | and yet you sell kids.

1706 STEVENS s.v. Cabra. **1732** FULLER no. 5922.

Goat(s), *see also* Beard were all (If), g. might preach; Go to a g. for wool; Stink like a g.

God and my cunning, I thank.

a. **1576** WYTHORNE 83 (az the old proverb saith).

God, and parents, and our master, can never be requited.   (G 210)

1611 COTGRAVE s.v. Dieu No man can sufficiently requite his Father, Maister, Maker. **1640** HERBERT no. 805. **1658** *Comes Fac.* 237. **1659** N. R. 38. **1670** RAY 12.

God bless the Duke of Argyle!

1859 HOTTEN *Slang Dict.* (1874) 178 God bless the Duke of Argyle! A Scottish insinuation made when one shrugs his shoulders . . . Said to have been the thankful exclamation of the Glasgow folk, at finding . . . iron posts, erected by his grace in that city to mark . . . his property, very convenient to rub against. **1877–80** E. WALFORD *Tales of Gt. Fam.* (1890) 36 A Scotchman has good reason occasionally to cry out 'God bless the Duke of Argyll', for reasons best known north of the Tweed.

God bless you, *see* Friend at a sneeze.

God by the toe, When they think they have | they have the devil by the fist.   (G 260)

1548 HALL 462 The duches thinkyng to haue gotten God by the foote, when she had the deuell by the tayle. *Ibid.* 762 The Bishop thinking that he had God by the too, when in dede he had (as after he thought) the Deuell by the fiste. **1556** J. POYNET *Pol. Power* L4ᵛ. **1584** LODGE *Alarum for Usurers* Hunt. Cl. B2ᵛ (God by the heel).

God comes at last (is at the end) when we think he is farthest off.   (G 180)

1640 HERBERT no. 598 God is at the end, when we thinke he is furthest off it. **1659** HOWELL *It. Prov.* 7. **1670** RAY 11.

God comes to see without a bell.   (G 181)

1640 HERBERT no. 384. **1659** HOWELL *Span. Prov.* 2. (to visit us). **1706** STEVENS s.v. Dios. **1823** COLLINS 385 'God came to visit him without a bell'.—It intimates, that a man has had some unexpected good fortune. It is the custom in Spain, when a person is dying, to carry the

viaticum to the house, preceded by an attendant ringing a bell; . . . which gave rise to the proverb of God paying a visit.

God comes with leaden feet, but strikes with iron hands. *Cf.* Feet of the deities.   (G 182)

1579 LYLY *Euph.* i. 302 Though God haue leaden handes which when they strike paye home, yet hath he leaden feet which are as slow to ouertake a sinner. **1579** J. DYOS *Sermon* D8 It is sayd that he [God] hath leaden feete: but he hath iron handes. **1596** DU BARTAS *Babilon* 21–2 (woolen feete). **1609** J. WYBARNE *New Age of Old Names* 27 Iustice . . . with Iron hand, though with leaden feet. **1616** T. ADAMS *A Divine Herbal* 48. **1629** *Id. Serm.* (1861–2) I. 214 Though these punishments fall not suddenly, yet certainly, if repentance step not between . . . God hath leaden feet, but iron hands. **1670** RAY 11.

God complains not, but does what is fitting.   (G 183)

1640 HERBERT no. 182.

God gives his wrath by weight, and without weight his mercy.   (G 186)

1592 DELAMOTHE 7. **1597** *Politeuphuia* 132 (mercy without measure). **1647** *Countrym. New Commonw.* 31 (his judgements . . . without measure). **1651** HERBERT no. 1115.

God gives the cow, but not by the horn.

c. **1400** *Cloud of Unknowing* E.E.T.S. 1944 For þei sey þat God sendeþ þe kow, bot not by þe horne. *A ladder of foure Rongys (Douce MS. 322¹, f. 55 b)* quoted in preceding, p. 57 n. He yeveth the Oxe by the horne . . . when he not called offerth hys grace. [¹ said to be tr. of the *Scala Claustralium* of Guigo II, Prior of the Grande Chartreuse towards the end of the 12th cent.]

God gives the milk, but not the pail.

1912 *Spectator* 18 May 788 In the wisdom of the West, the necessity for hard work and for initiative is continually emphasised. 'God gives the milk, but not the pail', is typical of many sayings of the people.

God has his church (temple), Where | the devil will have his chapel.   (G 259)

1560 BECON *Catechism* P.S. 361 For commonly, wheresoever God buildeth a church, the devil will build a chapel just by. **1621** BURTON *Anat. Mel.* III. iv. I. i (1651) 640 Blind zeale . . . is religions ape. . . . For where God hath a temple, the divel will have a chappel. **1670** RAY 70. **1701** DEFOE *True Born Englishman* Wherever God erects a House of Prayer, The Devil always builds a Chapel there: And 'twill be found upon Examination, The latter has the largest Congregation. **1903** G. H. KNIGHT *Master's Questions* 90 Nowhere does the devil build his little chapels more cunningly than close under the shadow of the great temple of Christian liberty. A thing in itself completely right and good, may be, in its effects on others, completely evil.

God have mercy, horse, *see* Godamercy, etc.

God heals, and the physician has the thanks. (G 190)

1640 HERBERT no. 169. **1659** HOWELL *Span. Prov.* 20 (gets the silver). **1736** FRANKLIN Nov. God heals and the doctor takes the fee.

God help the fool, quoth Pedley. (G 191)

1678 RAY 72 . . . This Pedley was a naturall fool himself, and yet had usually this expression in his mouth. Indeed none are more ready to pity the folly of others, than those who have but a small measure of wit themselves.

God help the poor, for the rich can help themselves. (G 192)

1609 DEKKER *Work for Armourers*, title-page God helpe the Poore, The rich can shift. **1721** KELLY 124 . . . Spoken in case of Famine or Scarcity of Bread.

God help the rich, the poor can beg. (G 193)

1623 PAINTER B7 God helpe rich men they all say, If poore men want they goe abegging may. **1659** HOWELL *Eng. Prov.* 16a. **1721** KELLY 124 . . . Spoken . . . in case of public Disturbances.

God help us (*or* you), *see* Cheap enough to say, *G. h. y.*; Lie down and cry, *G. h. u.*

God (Heaven) helps them that help themselves. (G 236)

[L. *Dii facientes adjuvant.*] **1545** TAVERNER H1ᵛ Dii facientes adiuuant. The goddes do helpe the doers. **1551** T. WILSON *Rule of Reason* S1ᵛ Shipmen cal to God for helpe, and God will helpe them, but so not withstandyng, if they helpe them selfes. **1580** BARET *Alveary* s.v. Induce God doth helpe those in their affaires, which are industrious: according to *Homere*. **1640** HERBERT no. 537 Helpe thy selfe, and God will helpe thee. **1736** FRANKLIN June God helps them that help themselves. **1841** S. WARREN *Ten Thous. a Year* ch. 21 Never, never despair, Mr. Aubrey! Heaven helps those who help them-selves. **1892** LIDDON *Serm. Wds. of Christ* 43 As the proverb most truly says, He helps them that help themselves.

God is a good man. (G 195)

a. **1519** *Lit. Gest Robin Hood* IV C5ᵛ God is holde a ryghtwys man. *c.* **1525** *Hundred Merry Tales* no. 83 Ther cam one whych sayd that God was a good man. [**1547–53**] *c.* **1565** WEVER *Lusty Juventus* Hazl.-Dods. ii. 73 He will say that God is a good man. **1579** J. CALVIN *Thirteen Sermons* 169 Loe those merry Greekes, when they shall be exhorted to returne from their wickednesses: o I muste yet a good while vse it: and God is a good fellow. **1598–9** SHAKES. *M.A.* III. v. 36 Well, God's a good man.

God is a sure paymaster. (G 197)

1613 T. ADAMS *The White Devil* 1862 ed. ii. 232 God is made his debtor, and he is a sure pay-master. **1639** CLARKE 325.

God is better pleased with adverbs than with nouns. (G 198)

[ARISTOTLE *Eth.* 5. 8.] **1607** DEKKER *Whore of Babylon* III. ii. 152 All good must not be done, but onely that—Quod bene et legitime fieri potest: For Sir I know, that Deus magis amat aduerbia quam nomina. **1607** J. HALL *Holy Obs.* 14, Wks. iii. 167 God loveth adverbs; and cares not how good, but how well. **1612** T. ADAMS *Gallant's Burden* 1616 ed. 47 (Mane, is the Lords Aduerbe, the Diuels Verbe:) The Lord sayth, Early; the Diuell sayth, Tarry. **1613** R. DALLINGTON *Aphorisms* 87 Vices are stronger in the Aduerbe, then in the Adiectiue: and so be vertues. To do that is well, is better then to do that is good: for, a man may do what is honest sometimes, against his will: whereas in all vertuous actions, there is a free election. That Iudge therefore, who giueth sentence before both Parties be heard, may iudge the right, but not aright. **1620** J. FORD *Line Life* 64 This man not only liues, but liues well, remembring always the old adage, that God is there warder of aduerbes, not of nownes.

God is made the master of a family, When | he orders the disorderly. (G 255)

1640 HERBERT no. 983.

God (Nature) is no botcher. (G 199)

1546 HEYWOOD II. i. F3 God is no botcher syr, saide an other. He shapeth all partes, as eche parte maie fitte other. *a.* **1567** T. BECON *Catechism* P.S. 174 (according to this old saying). **1616** BRETON *Cross. of Prov.* A7 (Nature). **1639** CLARKE 224 (Nature).

God is where He was (still in heaven). (G 201, 202)

1530 PALSGRAVE 519a (still in heaven) Never dispayre, man, God is there as he was. **1546** HEYWOOD I. xii. E4ᵛ Take no thought in no casc, god is where he was. **1600** *Weakest to Wall* C2 Heauen is where it was. *a.* **1602** KYD *Span. Trag.* additions l. 1902 Well, heauen is heauen still. **1612** SHELTON *Quix.* IV. iii (i. 290) God is in heauen. **1678** RAY 147 . . . Spoken to encourage People in any distress. **1841** BROWNING *Pippa Passes* God's in his heauen, all's right with the world.

God keep me from four houses, a usurer's, a tavern, a spital, and a prison. (G 203)

1640 HERBERT no. 816.

God keep me from the man that has but one thing to mind.

1706 STEVENS s.v. Dios God deliver you from a Man of one Book: that is, that knows but one Book, because he has read it often and having it in his head, alwaysₐtires and torments you with it. **1721** KELLY 115 . . . Because he will mind that Thing to purpose. Spoken by great Men, when poor People importune them about some special Interest, which they have at Heart.

God knows well which are the best
pilgrims.   (G 204)

1611 COTGRAVE s.v. Pelerin God knowes who's
a good Pilgrim. **1678** RAY 147.

God loathes aught, When | men
presently loathe it too.

1853 TRENCH vi. 141 That ancient German
proverb: . . . He who first uttered this must have
watched long . . . how it ever came to pass that
even worldly honour tarried not long with them
from whom the true honour whereof God is the
dispenser had departed.

God loves, Whom | his bitch brings
forth pigs.   (G 261)

1659 HOWELL *Span. Prov.* 16. **1706** STEVENS
s.v. Dios. **1813** RAY 45 . . . Under the blessing
of heaven all things co-operate for his good, even
beyond his expectations. [Span.]

God made me, I am as.

1599 PORTER *Angry Wom. Abing.* l. 2285 My
Maister is not so wise as God might haue made
him. **1620** SHELTON *Quix.* II. iv (ii. 213) Euery
man is as God hath made him, and sometimes a
great deal worse. **1738** SWIFT Dial. I. E.L. 281.
They said that you were a complete beauty.
—My lord, I am as God made me. **1766**
GOLDSMITH *Vicar of Wakefield* ch. 1 They are as
Heaven made them.

God made the country, and man made
the town.

[VARRO *Nec mirum, quod divina natura dedit
agros, ars humana aedificavit urbes.*] **1783**
COWPER *Task* I. 749. **1869** LECKY *Hist. Europ.
Mor.* (1905) I. ii. 265 Varro expressed an
eminently Roman sentiment in that beautiful
sentence which Cowper has introduced into
English poetry, 'Divine Providence made the
country, but human art the town.' [1870] **1897**
H. TENNYSON *Tennyson: Memoir* II. 96 [T. said]
'there is a saying that if God made the country,
and man the town, the devil made the little
country-town'.

God make me great and big, for white
and red I can make myself.

1573 SANFORD 105ᵛ (will make).   **1642**
TORRIANO 56 . . . Nota, A custome of Venetian
courtezans, or Buona roba's, so to say.

God makes and man (apparel) shapes.
                                                      (G 206)

1621 BURTON *Anat. Mel.* III. ii. III. iii (1651) 473
The greatest provocations of lust are from our
apparel; God makes, they say, man shapes, and
there is no motive like unto it. **1650** BULWER
Anthropomet. 256 God makes, and the Tailor
shapes. **1678** RAY 177 God makes and apparel
shapes; but money makes the man. Pecunia vir.
Χρήματα ἀνήρ· Tanti quantum habeas sis. Horat.

God never sends mouth but He sends
meat.   (G 207)

1377 LANGLAND *P. Pl.* B. xiv. 39 For lente
neuere was lyf but lyflode were shapen. **1546**

HEYWOOD I. iv. B1 God neuer sendeth mouthe,
but he sendeth meat. *c.* **1612** FLETCHER *Scornf.
Lady* I. i They say nature brings forth none
but she provides for them. **1641** FERGUSSON
no. 293 God sends never the mouth but the
meat with it. **1894** LD. AVEBURY *Use of Life*
ch. 12 Children are sometimes spoken of as
'sent', and improvident parents excuse themselves by saying that 'if God sends mouths, He
will send food to fill them'. **1905** A. MACLAREN
Expos. of Script., Matt. I. 103 God never sends
mouths but He sends meat to fill them. Such
longings prophesy their fruition.

God oft has a great share in a little
house.   (G 208)

1611 COTGRAVE s.v. Maison God hath a great
share in a small house. **1640** HERBERT no. 60.

God or a painter, He is either a | for he
makes faces.   (G 230)

1557 EDGEWORTH *Sermons* 3D2ᵛ Some [women]
can not be contente with their heere as God made
it, but dothe painte it and set it in an other hue,
. . . 3D4 This adulteration and chaunging of
gods handyworke by painting womans heere to
make it seme faire and yelow, or of their leers of
their chekes to make them loke ruddy or of their
forehed to hide the wrinkles and to make them
loke smoth, is of the deuils inuention and neuer
of gods teaching. **1594–5** SHAKES. *L.L.L.* V. ii.
635 He's a god or a painter; for he makes faces.
1598–9 *Id. M.A.* II. iii. 31 Her hair shall be
of what colour it please God. **1600** DEKKER
Old Fort. v. ii. 7 Ile teach you to liue by the
sweate of other mens browes.—And to striue to
be fairer then God made her. **1609** *Id.
Gull's Horn Bk.* Proem: Gros. ii. 202 You
Courtiers . . . will screw forth worse faces then
those which God and the Painter has bestowed
vpon you. **1732** FULLER no. 1914.

God provides for him that trusts.
                                                      (G 211)

1601 CHETTLE & MUNDAY *Death of Earl of
Huntington* Hazl.-Dods. viii. 296 Our sovereign
. . . Hath scatter'd all our forces. . . . Yet God
provides. **1640** HERBERT no. 728.

God reaches us good things by our own
hands.

1732 FULLER no. 1683.

God save the mark.

[prob. originally a formula to avert an evil
omen, hence used by way of apology when
something horrible, etc., has been mentioned.]
c. **1595** SHAKES. *R.J.* III. iii. 53 I saw the wound,
I saw it with mine eyes, God save the mark.
1761 STERNE *T. Shandy* III. xxxiii My father . . .
had no more nose, my dear, saving the mark,
than there is upon the back of my hand. **1815**
HOGG *Pilgrims of the Sun*, Dedⁿ to Byron Not
for . . . thy virtues high (God bless the mark!) do
I this homage plight.

God say Amen, *see* All good, and G. say Amen.

God, The most high | sees, and bears: my neighbour knows nothing, and yet is always finding fault.

1813 RAY 324. *Per.*

God send us of our own when rich men go to dinner. (G 213)

1639 CLARKE 37.

God send us some money, for they are little thought of that want it, quoth the Earl of Eglinton at his prayers.

1721 KELLY 113.

God send you joy, for sorrow will come fast enough. (G 215)

1605 *London Prodigal* III. iii God give you joy, as the old zaid proverb is, and some zorrow among. **1616** DRAXE no. 1306. **1639** CLARKE 185.

God send you more wit, and me more money. (G 216)

1599 PORTER *Angry Wom. Abing.* l. 1968 Well said wisdome, God send thee wise children.— And you more mony. **1616** WITHALS 555. **1659** HOWELL *Eng. Prov.* 15b. **1721** KELLY 120 . . . Silver, for we have both need of it. Spoken when People propose, or say, what we think foolish and improper. **1732** FULLER no. 1689. **1738** SWIFT Dial. III. E.L. 319 A dull unmannerly brute! well, God send him more wit, and me more money.

God send you readier meat than running hares.

1721 KELLY 113 . . . Spoken to those who have improbable Expectations.

God sends cold after clothes. (G 218)

1546 HEYWOOD I. iv. B1 God sendth colde after clothes. **1603** MONTAIGNE (Florio) III. vi. 190 God sends my cold answerable to my cloths. **1641** FERGUSSON no. 289 God sends men cauld as they have clothes to. **1706** STEVENS s.v. Dios. **1721** KELLY 113 God sends Men Cloth, according to their cold. God supports and supplies Men, according to their Circumstances.

God sends corn and the devil mars the sack. (G 219)

1616 DRAXE no. 34 (asketh). **1664** CODRINGTON 193 (giveth). **1670** RAY 97.

God sends fortune to fools. (G 220)

1546 HEYWOOD II. vi. I1ᵛ That they saie as ofte, God sendeth fortune to fooles. **1592** KYD *Soliman* (Boas) II. ii. 1 God sends fortunes to fools. **1599** SHAKES. *A.Y.* II. vii. 19 'Call me not fool till heaven hath sent me fortune.' **1614** CAMDEN 306. **1706** STEVENS s.v. Bobo Fools have Fortune.

God sends meat and the devil sends cooks. (G 222)

1542 BOORDE *Dyetary* E.E.T.S. 260 It is a common prouerbe, 'God may send a man good meate, but the deuyll may send an euyll coke to dystrue it'. **1545** ASCHAM *Toxoph.* II Arb. 132 He maye . . . haue cause to saye so of his fletcher, as . . . is communelye spoken of Cookes; . . . that God sendeth vs good fethers, but the deuyll noughtie Fletchers. **1617** TAYLOR *Trav.* (1630) 85 Such dyet we had, that the Prouerbe was truly verified *God sent meat, and the Diuel sent Cookes.* **1738** SWIFT Dial. II. E.L. 307. **1822** SCOTT *Nigel* ch. 27 That homely proverb that men taunt my calling with, —'God sends good meat, but the devil sends cooks.'

God shapes the back for the burthen.

1822 COBBETT *Rur. Rides* 2 Jan. (1914) 55 As 'God has made the back to the burthen', so the clay and coppice people make the dress to the stubs and bushes. **1838–9** DICKENS *N. Nickleby* ch. 18 Heaven suits the back to the burden. **1883** BARING-GOULD *John Herring* ch. 6 The sisters worried these men a good deal. They all took it in good part. Their backs were made to bear their burden.

God stays long, but strikes at last. (G 224)

1591 ARIOSTO *Orl. Fur.* Harington XXII Morall If God stay long ear he to strike beginne, Though long he stay, at last he striketh sure. **1611** SHAKES. *Temp.* III. iii. 72 For which foul deed The powers, delaying (not forgetting), have Incens'd the seas and shores, yea, all the creatures, Against your peace. **1613** *Id. T.N.K.* I. iv. 4 Th' impartial gods . . . behold who err, And in their time chastise. **1659** HOWELL *Br. Prov.* 19.

God stint all strife. (G 225)

1546 HEYWOOD II. viii. K2ᵛ I can no more herein, but god stynt all stryfe.

God strikes not with both hands, for to the sea he made havens, and to rivers fords. (G 226)

1640 HERBERT no. 315. **1659** HOWELL *Span. Prov.* 7.

God strikes with his finger, and not with all his arm. (G 227)

1592 DELAMOTHE 7. **1605** J. SYLVESTER *Bartas* 390. **1651** HERBERT no. 1114.

God take the sun out of the heaven, Though | yet we must have patience. (G 252)

1640 HERBERT no. 980.

God tempers the wind to the shorn lamb. (S 315)

[Cf. **1594** H. ESTIENNE *Premices* 47 Ces termes, *Dieu mesure le froid à la brebis tondue,* sont les propres termes du proverbe. Vray est qu'on le dit encore en deux autres sortes: (dont l'une est, *Dieu donne le froid selon la robbe*).] **1640** HERBERT no. 867 To a close shorne sheepe, God gives wind by measure. **1768** STERNE *Sent. Journ.* II. 175 God tempers the wind, said Maria, to the shorn lamb. **1880** GOLDW. SMITH *Cowper* 59 It seems that the book found its way into the dictator's hands, . . . and that he even did something to temper the wind of criticism to the shorn lamb.

God when all is done, There is.
(G 250)

1546 HEYWOOD I. vii. B4 Ye there was God (quoth he) whan all is doone.

God will give, That which | the devil cannot reave.[1]
(G 239)

1641 FERGUSSON no. 544. **1721** KELLY 320 . . . Spoken when we have attain'd our End in spite of Opposition. [1 rob us of.]

God will have see, That | shall not wink.
(G 248)

1560 *Nice Wanton* Hazl.-Dods. ii. 182 But it is an old proverb, you have heard it, I think: That God will have see, shall not wink.

God will help, Where (Whom) | nothing does harm (none can hinder).   (G 263)

c. **1300** *Havelock* 647 Soth it is, þat men seyt and suereth:[1] 'þer god wile helpen, nouth no dereth'.[2] *c.* **1450** MERLIN 524 Ther-fore is seide proverbe, that god will haue a saued, no man may distroye. *a.* **1533** LD. BERNERS *Huon.* cxxx. 480 It is a commune prouerbe sayde, 'whome that god wyll ayde, no man can hurt'. **1721** KELLY 357 Whom God will help none can hinder. [1 swear. 2 injures.]

God will, What | no frost can kill.
(G 254)

1621 ROBINSON 8. **1639** CLARKE 225. **1732** FULLER no. 6106.

God will, When | no wind but brings rain.
(G 256)

1616 DRAXE no. 900 When God will, at all windes it will raine. **1640** HERBERT no. 332. **1706** STEVENS s.v. Dios When God pleases it Rains with all Winds.

God will punish, he will first take away the understanding, When.   (G 257)

[SOPHOCLES *Ant.* 622 Τὸ κακὸν δοκεῖν ποτ' ἐσθλὸν τῷδ' ἔμμεν ὅτῳ φρένας θεὸς ἄγει πρὸς ἄταν. LYCURGUS 159. 20 Οἱ θεοὶ οὐδὲν πρότερον ποιοῦσιν ἢ τῶν πονηρῶν ἀνθρώπων τὴν διάνοιαν παράγουσι. PUB. SYRUS *Sentent.* (Orelli) 741 *Stultum facit Fortuna quem vult perdere.* **1611** JONSON *Catiline* III. 392 It is a madnesse, Wherewith heauen blinds 'hem, when it would confound 'hem, That they should thinke it. **1694** JOSHUA BARNES *Euripides* Index Prior, letter D Deus quos vult perdere dementat

prius. Ibid. 515, l. 436 Ὅταν δὲ δαίμων ἀνδρὶ πορσύνῃ κακὰ τὸν νοῦν ἔβλαψε πρῶτον = Trag. adesp. 455 N².] **1640** HERBERT no. 688. **1687** DRYDEN *Hind & Panther* iii. 1093 For those whom God to ruine has design'd, He fits for Fate, and first destroys their Mind. **1783** BOSWELL *Johnson* ch. 75 (1848) 718 I once talked to him of some of the sayings which every body repeats, but nobody knows where to find, such as *Quos* DEUS *vult perdere, prius dementat.* **1817** 2 Ap. BYRON *Lett.* Prothero iv, 93 God maddens him whom 'tis his will to lose. And gives the choice of death or phrenzy— choose. **1885** C. LOWE *Bismarck* (1898) ch. 4 Either driven mad by the gods who meant to destroy them, or deluded with hopes of succour from friends who could do nothing but leave them in the lurch, the Danes remained stone-deaf to the moderate proposals of the allies.

God will send time to provide for time.
(G 228)

1546 HEYWOOD I. xii. E4ᵛ Well (quoth I) God will sende Tyme to prouide for tyme. *a.* **1750** WESLEY *Sermons* ii. 40 God's time is the best time.

God's bairn is eith[1] to lear.

1721 KELLY 112 . . . A Child endowed with grace and good Nature will be easily taught. [1 easy.]

God's blessing make my pot boil, or my spit go? Will.

1721 KELLY 351 . . . A great Oppressor . . . when poor People offered him all that they could get, and bid him take it with God's blessing, . . . would stormingly say, *Will God's Blessing make my Pot play, or my Spit go?*

God's grace and Pilling Moss[1] are boundless.   (G 267)

1662 FULLER *Lancs.* 124 Pyllyn-Mos is the Fountain of Fewell (Turfe) in this County, and is conceived inexhaustible by the Vicinage. . . . May God's grace (which the vulgar, in their profane Proverb, unequally yoak therewith) . . . never be drained . . .! [1 Near Fleetwood; in 1920 a breeding-ground for vast flocks of sea-gulls.]

God's help is better than early rising.
(G 268)

1620 SHELTON *Don Quix.* Pt. II. xxxiv (iii. 63). **1732** FULLER no. 1685.

God's help is nearer than the fair éven.
(G 269)

a. **1628** CARMICHAELL no. 565. **1641** FERGUSSON no. 290. **1721** KELLY 117 . . . God's immediate Providence may sooner Assist us, than any second Causes that we can propose.

God's lambs will play.

1830 FORBY 432 . . . An apology for riotous youth.

God's mill grinds slow but sure.
(G 270)

[SEXTUS EMPIRICUS 'Οψὲ θεῶν ἀλέουσι μύλοι, ἀλέουσι δὲ λεπτά. The mills of the gods grind slowly, but they grind small. PLUT. *De sera num. vind.* Οὐχ ὁρῶ τί χρήσιμον ἔνεστι τοῖς ὀψὲ δὴ τούτοις ἀλεῖν λεγομένοις μύλοις τῶν θεῶν. I don't see any use in these 'late-grinding' mills of the Gods.] **1640** HERBERT no. 747. **1870** LONG-FELLOW tr. *von Logau, Retribution* Though the mills of God grind slowly, yet they grind exceeding small. **1899** A. WHITE *Modern Jew* 98 [The] capture and destruction of the Spanish fleet . . . satisfied them that though the mills of God grind slowly the ruin of Spain was an equitable adjustment of her debt to the Jews.

God's poor and the devil's poor, There are.
(G 274)

1613 T. ADAMS *The White Devil* (1861–2) II. 232 There are God's poor and the devil's poor: those the hand of God hath crossed; these have forced necessity on themselves by a dissolute life.

Gods love die young, Whom the.
(G 251)

[MENANDER *Dis Exapaton, Frag.* 4 'Ον οἱ θεοὶ φιλοῦσιν ἀποθνῄσκει νέος. PLAUTUS *Bacchides* 4. 7. 18 *Quem di diligunt Adolescens moritur, dum valet, sentit, sapit.* Whom the gods love dies young, while still he can enjoy health, tastes and senses.] **1546** W. HUGH *Troub. Man's Med.* II (1831) 46 But among all others, saith the Greek poet Menander, most happy are they, and best beloved of God, that die when they are young. **1553** T. WILSON *Arte of Rhet.* (1909) 73 Whom God loueth best, those he taketh soonest. *c.* **1591** MARLOWE *Edw. II* III. ii. 79 Ah, boy! this towardnes makes thy mother fear Thou art not mark'd to many days on earth. **1651** HERBERT no. 1094 Those that God loves do not live long. **1821** BYRON *Juan* IV. xii 'Whom the gods love die young', was said of yore.

God, gods, *see also* All must be as G. will; Afflictions are sent to us by G. for our good; Charitable give out and G. puts in; Danger past, G. forgotten; Do little for G. if devil were dead; Do the likeliest, G. will do best; Ends ill which begins in G.'s name (Never); Every man for himself and G. for all; Face to G. (He has one), another to devil; False as G. is true; Fire (By this) that's G.'s angel; Garby whose soul neither G. would have; Go in G.'s name; Grace of G. is enough; —— is worth a fair; Guided that G. guides (They are well); Have G. have all; Heaven (G.) is above all; In time comes whom G. sends; Knees of the g.; Like me, G. bless the example; Likes not the drink, G. deprives of bread; Loses nothing who keeps G. for friend; Lost be for G. (Let that which is); Make a poor man knight (Little of G.'s might); Man does what he can, G. what He will; Man is a g. to man; Man is to man a g.; Man of G.'s making, (He is a); Man punishes action, G. intention; Man's extremity G.'s opportunity; Nearer the church, farther from G.; Not G. above gets all men's love; Nothing is impossible to G.; One G., no more, but friends; Out of G.'s blessing into the

warm sun; Owe G. a death; Peace (Where there is) G. is; Pleases not G. (When it); Poor that G. hates; Serves G. for money (He that); Serves G. (He who) serves good master; Sooth as G. is king; Sows (He that) trusts in G.; Spender (To good) G. is treasurer; Spindle and distaff ready, G. will send flax; Sure as G.'s in Gloucestershire; Thrives he whom G. loves; True as G. is in heaven; Trust in G. but keep powder dry; Wite G. (You need not) if Deil ding you over.

Godalming rabbits.

[**1762** C. CHURCHILL *Ghost* i. 435–8 But if such things no more engage The taste of a politer age, To help them out in time of need Another Tofts must rabbits breed.] **1787** GROSE (*Surrey*) 226 Godalmin rabbits. A term of reproach to the inhabitants of this place, . . . for the well-known deception practised by a Mrs. Tofts, who pretended to be delivered of live rabbits.

Godamercy (Gramercy) horse.
(G 276)

1546 HEYWOOD II. vii. Iiʳ God a mercy, hors! **1595** J. PAYNE *Royal Exchange* As the hostes reckonyng with her gest less willing to lodge in her hows then his tyred horse, made a low curtesy . . . to the beaste, and seyd 'Gathamercy horse'. *c.* **1600** COLLIER *Roxb. Ballads* 29 (1847) The hostler, to maintaine himself with money in 's purse, Approves the proverbe true, and sayes, gramercy horse. **1659** HOWELL *Eng. Prov.* 14a (Gramercy). **1710** *Brit. Apollo* III. no. 118. 3/1 I find I'm whole, God a mercy Horse.

Godfathers oft give their blessings in a clout.
(G 277)

[= money wrapped up in a cloth.] **1546** HEY-WOOD II. ix. L2 Well (quoth he) if ye lyst to bryng it out, Ye can geue me your blessyng in a clout. **1611** DAVIES no. 267.

Godfathers, *see also* Child is christened (When) g. enough.

Godliness, *see* Cleanliness next to g.

Godly, *see* Peter is so g. that God don't make him thrive.

Godolphin, *see* Charles's Wain; Never a Granville wanted.

Goes a borrowing, goes a sorrowing, He that.
(B 545)

c. **1470** *Harl. MS. 116* (*Rel. Antiq.* I. 316) f. 125a He that fast spendyth must nede; borowe but whan he schal paye aȝen, then ys al the sorowe. **1545** TAVERNER F6. **1573** TUSSER XV. 31. **1678** RAY 104. **1836** MARRYAT *Midsh. Easy* ch. 8 You had made your request for the loan . . . fully anticipating a refusal (from the feeling that he who goes a borrowing goes a sorrowing). **1894** LD. AVEBURY *Use of Life* ch. 3 Debt is slavery. 'Who goes a-borrowing goes a-sorrowing.'

Goes and comes, He that | makes a good voyage. (v 98)

1573 SANFORD 103ᵛ. **1578** FLORIO *First F.* 29 (returneth). **1629** *Bk. Mer. Rid.* Prov. no. 90. **1659** TORRIANO no. 99 (goes and returns).

Goes far, He that | has many encounters. (E 111)

1640 HERBERT no. 608.

Goes not out of his way that goes to a good inn, He. (W 159)

1611 COTGRAVE s.v. Fourvoyer. **1640** HERBERT no. 831.

Goes (walks) softly (plainly) goes (walks) safely (surely), He that.
(G 165. W 9)

1549 LATIMER *Serm.* 7, P.S. 89 For, as they say commonly, Qui vadit plane, vadit sane; that is, He that walketh plainly, walketh safely. **1592** DANIEL *Complaint of Rosamond* l. 285. **1600** BODENHAM *Belvedere* Spens. Soc. 49 He wisely walketh that doth safely goe. **1616** BRETON I *Cross.* A4ᵛ He that goes softly goes safely. **1659** HOWELL *It. Prov.* 7 Who goeth soft, goeth safe. **1681** ROBERTSON 672 He that goes softly, goes surely.

Goes to bed supperless, Who | all night tumbles and tosses. (B 196)

1567 PAINTER *Pal. of Pleasure* (Jacobs) iii. 215 Accordynge to the prouerbe: He that goeth to bed supperlesse, lyeth in his bed restlesse. **1578** FLORIO *First F.* H1. **1670** RAY 37 . . . This is an Italian Proverb. Chi va à letto senza cena Tutta notte si dimena.

Goes to bed thirsty, He that | rises healthy. (B 187)

1640 HERBERT no. 1003. **1678** RAY 37. . . . Qui couche avec la soif se leve avec la santé.

Goes, *see also* Go.

Going (Walking) foot is aye getting, A.
(F 565)

c. **1300** *Cursor M.* 28939 (Cott. Galba) Gangand fote ay getes fode. *a.* **1628** CARMICHAELL no. 126 A gangand fute is ay gettand and it were a thrissel. **1670** RAY 262 (walking). **1721** KELLY 11 . . . if it were but a thorn. A Man of Industry will certainly get a Living: Though this Proverb is often applied to those who went abroad, and got a Mischief. **1914** PURDON *Folk of Furry F.* ch. 6 It's better for a body to be moving somewhere, even if it's only to get you a prod of a thorn in the toe!

Going to grass with his teeth upwards, He is.

1813 RAY 196 . . ., i.e. He is going to be buried.

Going to heaven in a sedan, There is no. *Cf.* Go to heaven in a featherbed.

1732 FULLER no. 4910.

Gold do? What cannot. *Cf.* Money do, etc. (M 1102)

1592 LYLY *Midas* I. i. 89 What is it that gold cannot command, or hath not conquered? *a.* **1594** R. WILSON The *Cobbler's Prophesy* l. 772 For what cannot the golden tempter do? **1604** DEKKER I *Honest Whore* IV. iv. 143 What can golde not doe? **1631** HEYWOOD 2 *Fair Maid* ii. 366 The King is wondrous bountifull, and what is't gold cannot. **1639** CLARKE 221.

Gold goes in at any gate except heaven's. (G 282)

1629 T. ADAMS *Serm.* (1861–2) I. 143 Philip was wont to say that an ass laden with gold would enter the gates of any city; but the golden load of bribes and extortions shall bar a man out of the city of God. **1639** CLARKE 220. **1660** W. SECKER *Nonsuch Prof.* ii (1891) 134 The gates of heaven . . . are not unlocked with a golden key. **1670** RAY 97.

Gold is an orator. (G 285a)

[**1592**] **1597** SHAKES. *Rich. III* IV. ii. 38 Gold were as good as twenty orators. **1594** BARNFIELD *Affect Shep.* Percy Soc. 48 Gold is a deepe-perswading orator.

Gold is but muck.

1592 LYLY *Midas* II. ii. 5 Gold is but the earths garbadge. **1594** NASHE *Terrors of Night* i. 352 Yron and golde which are carths excrements. *c.* **1598** JONSON *Case is altered* IV. ix. 20 The old proverb's true, I see. . . .

Gold is tried in the fire. (G 284)

[ZECH. xiii. 9; I PET. i. 7; etc.] *a.* **1500** *15c. School-Bk.* ed. W. Nelson 44 As golde is provyde by fire, so is a trusty frende knowne in trouble. **1504** ATKYNSON *Imit. Christ* I. xvii in *Imit. Christi* E.E.T.S. 165 For as golde is proued in the fournes, so man by tribulacion. **1557** EDGEWORTH *Sermons* 2H4 Gold when it is cast into the fire to be tried taketh no hurt by the fyre but rather muche good. **1592** DELAMOTHE N7ᵛ Gold is approued in the fournace, and the frend in troubles. **1666** TORRIANO *It. Prov.* 179, no. 9 The furnace trys gold, and gold a woman.

Gold, The purest | is the most ductile.
(G 291)

1593 NASHE *Christ's Tears* ii. 56 Golde which is the soueraigne of Mettals bends soonest, onely Iron (the pesant of all) is most inflexible. **1620–8** FELTHAM *Resolves, Humility* (1904) 285 I will (in things not weighty) submit freely; the purest gold is most ductile: it is commonly a good blade that bends well.

Gold knew what gold is, If | gold would get gold, I wis. (G 288)

1640 HERBERT no. 1012.

Gold may buy land, He that has.
(G 286)

a. **1628** CARMICHAELL no. 752. *c.* **1641** FERGUS-
SON MS. no. 526. **1683** MERITON *Yorks. Ale*
(1697) 83–7.

Gold mines, *see* Parnassus has no g. m.

Gold of Toulouse.

1548 SIR T. ELYOT *Bibliotheca Aurum Tolosanum
habere,* A prouerbe, which had this begynnynge,
when Quintus Cepio tooke by assaulte the citie
of Tolosa in Italy: there was founde in the
temples greate plenty of golde, whiche beyng
taken awaye, all that had any parte therof died
miserably, wherof happened this prouerbe,
whan anye man fynyshed his lyfe in miseyrie,
men would say, that he had golde of Tolosa.
1621 BURTON *Anat. Mel.* I. ii. III. xv (1651) 138
It is *aurum Tholosanum,* and will produce no
better effects. **1629** T. ADAMS *Serm.* (1861–2) II.
507 What family, that hath had but a finger in
these sacrileges, hath not been ruinated by them?
They have been more unfortunate to the gentry
of England than was the gold of Tholossa to the
followers of Scipio. **1871** LIDDELL *Stud. Hist.
Rome* I Q. Servilius Caepio . . . gained an evil
reputation by the sack of Tolosa. . . . The
plunder he took was immense: but the greater
part was seized by robbers on the way to Marseilles, and 'Toulouse gold' became a proverbial
expression for ill-gotten but unprofitable gains.

Gold, All is not | that glitters. (A 146)

[L. *Non omne quod nitet aurum est.*] *c.* **1220**
Hali Meidenhad E.E.T.S. 9 Nis hit nower neh
gold al þat ter schineþ. *c.* **1300** *Provs. of
Hending* no. 18 Hit nis nout al gold, þat shineþ.
c. **1386** CHAUCER *Can. Yeom. Prol. & T.* l. 962
But al thyng which that shyneth as the gold, Nis
nat gold, as that I have herd it told. *c.* **1430**
LYDGATE *Fall Princes* IV. 15 All is not gold that
shineth bright. **1553** BECON *Reliques of Rome*
(1563) 207 All is not golde that glistereth. **1596**
SHAKES. *M.V.* II. vii. 65 All that glisters is not
gold; Often have you heard that told. **1614**
CAMDEN 303 (glisters). **1638** DRUMM. OF HAWTH.
Biblioth. Edinb. Lectori Wks. (1711) 222 All is
not gold which glittereth. **1784** JOHNSON 2 Oct.
in *Boswell* (ed. 2) All is not gold that glitters, as
we have been often told.

Gold (money), When we have | we are in fear; when we have none we are in danger.
(G 293)

1616 DRAXE no. 500 . . . when we haue it not, wee
are troubled. **1642** TORRIANO 99 To have gold is
a fear, to have none is a grief. **1664** CODRING-
TON 226 (in trouble). **1670** RAY 12.

Gold which is worth gold, That is.
(G 292)

1611 COTGRAVE s.v. Or. **1640** HERBERT no. 841.
1655–62 GURNALL *Chrn. in Armour* (1865) I. 531
We say, 'That is gold which is worth gold'—
which we may anywhere exchange for gold.
1706 STEVENS s.v. Oro.

Gold, *see also* Ass loaded with g.; Balance
distinguishes not between g. and lead; Brass for

g.; Butter is g. in morning; Buy g. too dear;
Door of g. (Who will make) must knock nail
every day; Eat g., (If she would), he would give
it her; Girl worth g.; Good as g.; Good name
better than riches (g.); Labours and thrives (He
that) spins g.; Liberty is more worth than g.;
Lock will hold against g. (No); Look to a gown
of g.; No silver (g.) without dross; Old friends
. . . and old g. are best; Ounce of state requires
pound of g.; Pour g. on him, he'll never thrive;
Speak with your g. (You may); Touchstone tries
g. (As the); Trust him with untold g. (You may);
Try your skill . . . then in g.; Win g. and wear g.

Golden age never was the present age, The.

1732 FULLER no. 4556. **1880** BLACKMORE *Mary
Anerley* ch. 44 She began . . . to contemplate the
past as a golden age . . . and to look upon the
present as a period of steel.

Golden (silver) bridge, For a flying enemy make a.
(B 665)

[ERASM. *Apoph.* viii. 14, quoting Alphonso of
Aragon, *Hostibus fugientibus pontem argenteum
exstruendum esse.* **1534** RABELAIS I. xliii.] **1576**
LAMBARDE *Kent* 2S2 It was well sayde of one . . .
If thine enemie will flye, make him a bridge of
Golde. **1578** J. YVER *Courtly Controv.* tr.
H. Wotton U1 Oh how wise was the Captayne,
who said, that to constraine the enemy too
much, was the meane to giue him weapon to
defende him selfe: but also thoughte it moste
expedient to make hym a golden bridge to flye
awaye. **1592** DELAMOTHE 47. *a.* **1601** NASHE
Christ's Tears ii. 179 I thought to make my
foe a bridge of golde, or faire words, to flie by.
1620 SHELTON *Quix.* II. lviii (1908) III. 231 One
only knight expects you, who is not of that mind
or opinion of those that say, To a flying enemy a
silver bridge. **1633** MASSINGER *Guardian* I. i For
a flying foe, Discreet and provident conquerors
build up A bridge of gold. **1889** STEVENSON
Mas. of Ball. ch. 4 A military proverb: that it
is a good thing to make a bridge of gold to a
flying enemy.

Golden calf, The.

[EXODUS xxxii.] **1732** FULLER no. 4704 The
People will worship even a Calf, if it be a
Golden one. **1827** HARE *Guesses at Truth* ch. I
(1859) 164 Millions . . . who fancy that happiness
may be attained by riches, . . . may be numbered
among the idolaters of the golden calf. **1902**
G. W. E. RUSSELL *Col. & Recol.* 2 Ser. (1909) ii
The worship of the Golden Calf is the characteristic cult of modern Society.

Golden life in an iron age, We must not look for a.
(L 267)

a. **1591** H. SMITH *Trial of the Righteous* (1657, 245)
Seeing then your Kingdom is not here, look not
for a golden life in an Iron world. **1616** DRAXE
no. 2177 A golden life is not to be expected in
an yron world. *Ibid.* no. 2503 A man must not
looke for a golden life in an yron world. **1639**
CLARKE 124. **1670** RAY 14. **1732** FULLER no.
5450.

Golden mean, The.   (M 792)

[HOR. *Od.* 2. 10. 5 *Aurea mediocritas.*] *c.* **1200**
Ancrene Riwle 336 Þe middel weie of mesure is
euer guldene. **1587** *Mirror for Mag.* ed.
Campbell 331 Golden meane is best in euery
trade of life. *a.* **1591** HY. SMITH *Serm.* (1886) I.
162 The golden mean is good for all things.
Solomon doth not forbid to eat honey, but eat
not too much, lest thou surfeit. **1642** MILTON
Apol. Smect. Prose Wks. (Bell) III. 164 If they,
for lucre, use to creep into the church undis-
cernibly, ... provide that no revenue there may
exceed the golden mean. **1901** R. G. MOULTON
Shaks. as Dram. Art. 46 Proverbs like 'Grasp
all, lose all', ... express moral equilibrium, and
the 'golden mean' is its proverbial formula.

Golden, *see also* Angle with g. hook; Poison is
poison though in g. cup.

Goldfinch, *see* Makes his mistress a g.

Golgotha are skulls of all sizes, In.
                                          (G 297)

a. **1591** HY. SMITH *Serm.* (1866) I. 261 As many
little skulls are in Golgotha as great skulls.
1660 W. SECKER *Nonsuch Prof.* II. (1891) 294 As
there are none too old for eternity, so there are
none too young for mortality. In Golgotha there
are skulls of all sizes.

**Gone over Asfordby Bridge backwards,
He has.**

1678 RAY (*Leics.*) 317 ... Spoken of one that is
past learning. **1881** EVANS 299 ... In modern
usage it is applied to one who 'sets the cart
before the horse' in word or deed.

Gone, *see also* Go.

**Good advisement, There came never ill
of.**   (I 34)

1597 *Politeuphuia* 134ᵛ Take good aduisement
ere thou begin, but the thing once determined,
dispatch with all diligence. *a.* **1628** CAR-
MICHAELL no. 1217. **1721** KELLY 334 ... A
Persuasion to consider well of a thing before you
go about it.

Good against evil, Set.   (G 318)
1640 HERBERT no. 823.

Good and quickly seldom meet.
                                        (G 311)
1640 HERBERT no. 580. **1790** TRUSLER *Prov.
Exempl.* 138 According to the Italians, Hastily
and well never met. A man of sense may be
expeditious, but is never in a hurry.

Good apple on a sour stock, No.

1393 LANGLAND *P. Pl.* C. xi. 206 For god seith
hit hym-self ... 'shal neuere good appel Thorw
no sotel science on sour stock growe'.[1] [1 *Matt.*
vii. 18.]

Good as a play, As.   (P 392)
1579 GOSSON *Sch. Abuse* Arb. 35 It is a right
Comedie, to marke their behauiour. **1606**

DEKKER *News from Hell* Prose Wks. Gros. ii 118
It was a Comedy, to see what a crowding ...
there was. **1638** TAYLOR (Water-Poet) *Bull,
Beare,* etc. 43 in *Wks.* 3rd coll. Spens. S. It was
as good as a comedy to him to see the trees fall.
1837–8 DICKENS *O. Twist* ch. 5.

Good as gold, As.

1841 DICKENS *Old Cur. Shop* ch. 29 There was
the baby, too [at Astley's], who had never
closed an eye all night, but had sat as good as
gold, trying to force a large orange into its
mouth. **1868** W. COLLINS *The Moonstone* ch. 14.

Good as one's word, To be as.   (M 184)

1577 STANYHURST *Chron. Ireland* i. 104a.
c. **1594** MUNDAY *John a Kent* l. 1053 Ye seeme an
honest man, and so faith, could ye be as good as
your woord, there be that perhaps would come
somewhat roundly to ye. **1598** SHAKES. *2 Hen.
IV* V. v. 86. Sir, I will be as good as my word.
1599 *Id. Hen. V* IV. viii. 32 I met this man with
my glove in his cap, and I have been as good as
my word. **1600–1** *Id. M.W.W.* III. iv. 104
So I have promised, and I'll be as good as my
word. **1601** *Id. T.N.* III. iv. 306 And for that
I promis'd you, I'll be as good as my word.
1610 BRETNOR *Almanac* 'August' Good Days.
1673 MARVELL *Rehearsal Transprosed* Gros. ii.
345.

**Good bargain (pennyworth), At a |
make a pause (think twice).**   (B 79)

1640 HERBERT no. 529 On a good bargain think
twice. **1642** TORRIANO 1 At a great penniworth
pawse a while. **1666** TORRIANO *It. Prov.* 65 no.
35 At a good penyworth pause a little while.
1710 PALMER 29 (think twice). **1758** FRANKLIN
P. Rich. Alm. in ARBER *Eng. Garner* v. 583 At a
great pennyworth, pause a while! ... perhaps
the cheapness is apparent only. **1796** EDGE-
WORTH *Par. Asst., Lit. Merchts.* ii (1903) 391
'Think twice of a good bargain', says the
proverb.

Good bearing begins worship, In.

c. **1350** *How the Gd. Wife* 17 In þi god beringe
biginnet þi wvschipe.

**Good (Hard) beginning makes a good
ending, A. *Cf.* Well begun, etc.** (B 259)

c. **1300** *Provs. of Hending* ii God beginning
maketh god endynge. *c.* **1350** *Douce MS. 52,*
no. 22 Of a gode begynnyng comyth a gode
endyng. *c.* **1390** GOWER *Conf. Amantis* Prol.
l. 86 But in proverbe I have herd seye That
who that wel his werk begynneth The rather a
good ende he wynneth. **1546** HEYWOOD I. iv.
B1 A harde begynnyng maketh a good endyng.
Ibid. I. x. C3ᵛ of a good begynnyng comth a
good ende. **1614** CAMDEN 302 A hard beginning hath a good ending. **1710** PALMER I.

**Good blood makes bad puddings with-
out groats or suet. *Cf.* Gentleman without estate.**   (B 460)

c. **1622** *Two Noble Ladies* l. 986 Bloud without
fat makes leane puddings: and gentry without
money is not halfe so good as rich yomanrie.

1665 J. WILSON *Projectors* II. i I have so often heard him protest against your great matches, as he calls 'em, and compares 'em to an ill pudding—all blood and no fat. **1678** RAY 66 ...Χρήματα ἀνήρ. Nobility is nothing but ancient riches: and money is the idol the world adores. *Ibid.* 230 He hath good blood in him if he had but groats to it. **1869** *Lonsdale Glos.*, *Groats* . . . The proverb current in Lonsdale, 'Blood without groats is nowt', meaning that family without fortune is of no consequence.

Good broth may be made in an old pot. (s 644)

1601 J. CHAMBER *Treatise agst. Judicial Astrologie* B1ᵛ As good broth may come out of a woodden ladle, as out of siluer spoone. **1611** COTGRAVE s.v. Vieil No pot makes so good pottage as the old one. **1666** TORRIANO *It. Prov.* 111 no. 9 (sops). **1880** SPURGEON *Ploughman's Pictures* 84.

Good building without a good foundation, No. (F 619)

1493 H. PARKER *Dives & Pauper* R7 Debile fundamentum fallit opus: A feble grounde disseyueth the werke. *c.* **1560** *Impatient Poverty* l. 932 Make a sure foundacyon, or yet set up the rofe. **1597** *Politeuphuia* 166 Where the foundation is weake, the frame tottereth. **1599** MINSHEU *Span. Dial.* X. x. 2ᵛ Vpon a good foundation a good building is made. **1620** SHELTON *Quix.* II. xx. ii. 320. **1732** FULLER no. 3578.

Good cheap is dear. (C 257)

[good cheap = a bargain.] *c.* **1375** *Cato Major* I. xxix in *Anglia VII* ƿat is a good chep may beo dere, And deore good chep also. **1563** J. PILKINGTON *Confutation* P.S. 506 A good thing cannot be too dear. **1640** HERBERT no. 261.

Good cheap, *see also* Buy g. c. that bring nothing home; Good cheer and g. c. gars many haunt the house; Saying goes g. c. *See also* Good thing cheap.

Good cheer and good cheap gars[1] many haunt the house. (C 264)

a. **1628** CARMICHAELL no. 573. **1641** FERGUSSON no. 288. [1 causes.]

Good cheer is lacking, When | our friends will be packing. (C 266)

1616 WITHALS 557. **1639** CLARKE 12. **1732** FULLER no. 6299.

Good conscience is a continual feast, A. (C 605)

[*Cf.* PROV. xv. 15 But he that is of a merry heart hath a continual feast.] **1605** BACON *Adv. Learn.* II Whereunto the wisdom of that heavenly leader hath signed, also hath affirmed that a good conscience is a continual feast. **1616** DRAXE no. 316. **1621** BURTON *Anat. Mel.* II. iii. VII (1651) 358 When they have all done, *a good conscience is a continual feast.* **1655** WILL ROADES to Sir Ralph Verney, *Verney Memoirs*

(1894) iii. 234. **1834** PROUT *Fraser's Mag.* Dec. A good conscience was the *juge convivium* of his mind.

Good counsel has no price. (C 683)

1606 J. DAY *Isle Gulls* E4 Good counsell is worth good monie, Madame. **1659** HOWELL *Span. Prov.* 10 No value can be put upon good counsel.

Good counsel never comes amiss. (C 684)

1616 DRAXE no. 381 Good counsell will doe no harme. **1732** FULLER no. 1708.

Good counsel never comes too late. (C 685)

1633 JONSON *T. Tub* III. vii. 22 Good counsels lightly never come too late.

Good cow has an evil (bad) calf, Many a. (C 761)

1520 WHITTINGTON *Vulg.* E.E.T.S. 72 It is comenly sayd: many a good kowe bryngeth forthe a sory calfe. **1546** HEYWOOD I. x. D1. **1605** CHAPMAN, JONSON, MARSTON *Eastw. Ho* IV. ii. 164 Thou art not the first good Cow hast had an ill Calfe. **1670** RAY 74 Many a good cow hath but a bad calf. Ἀνδρῶν ἡρώων τέκνα πήματα. Heroum filii noxii. . . . Men famous for learning, vertue, valour, success have for the most part either left behind them no children, or such as that it had been more for their honour and the interest of humane affairs, that they had died childless. **1721** KELLY 7 An ill cow may have a good calf. Bad People may have good Children.

Good dog deserves a good bone, A. (D 470)

1611 COTGRAVE s.v. Bon. **1633** JONSON *T. Tub* II. iv. 10 A good dog Deserves, Sir, a good bone of a free Master.

Good dog who goes to church, He is a.

1826 SCOTT *Woodst.* ch. 1 Bevis . . . fell under the proverb which avers, 'He is a good dog which goes to church'; for . . . he behaved himself . . . decorously. **1896** F. LOCKER-LAMPSON *My Confid.* 44 'Tis said, by men of deep research, He's a good dog who goes to church.

Good egg nor bird, Neither (Never). (E 77)

1591 STEPNEY *Span. Schoolmaster* 154 Neither good egge nor good bird. **1629** T. ADAMS *Serm.* (1861–2) I. 170 But sin of itself is good neither in egg nor bird, neither in root nor branch. **1670** RAY 173. **1678** *Id.* 355 He'll never dow (i.e. be good) egg nor bird. **1721** KELLY 262 Never good egg, or burd.[1] Spoken of bad boys, when they become worse Men. [1 chicken.]

Good enough for the parson unless the parish were better, It is. (P 64)

1678 RAY 187 . . . It's here supposed that if the Parish be very bad the Parson must be in some fault, and therefore any thing is good enough for that Parson whose Parishioners are bad, either by reason of his ill example, or the neglect of his duty.

Good enough is never ought.   (G 326)

1678 RAY 148.

Good even, good Robin Hood.   (E 188)

1522 SKELTON *Why not to Court* 192–4 Wks. (1843) ii. 32 He sayth, How saye ye, my lords? Is nat my reason good? Good euyn, good Robyn Hood! **1573** GASCOIGNE i. 171 Yea Robyn Hoode. **1879** C. W. BARDSLEY *Rom. Lond. Direct.* 61 'Good even, Robin Hood', . . . implied civility extorted by fear.

Good face is a letter of recommendation, A.

[PUBL. SYR. 169 *Formosa facies muta commendatio est.*] **1620** SHELTON *Quix.* II. lxiii (1908) III. 270 His beauty giving him in that instant, as it were, a letter of recommendation. **1768** STERNE *Sent. Journ.* Amiens. There was a passport in his very looks. **1771** SMOLLETT *Humph. Clink.* 11 Oct. Wks. (1871) 580 His honest countenance was a good letter of recommendation.

Good face needs no band, and a bad one deserves none, A.   (F 6, 7)

1579 LYLY *Euph.* i. 181 Where the countenaunce is faire, ther neede no colours. **1612** T. HEYWOOD *Apol. for Actors* A3 A good face needs no painting, and a good cause no abetting. **1639** CLARKE 131. A good face needs no band. **1678** RAY 97 . . . Some make a rhyme of this, by adding, And a pretty wench no land. **1738** SWIFT Dial. I. E.L. 274.

Good face on a thing, To put a.   (F 17)

1387 TREVISA tr. Higden Rolls S. vii. 25 And made good face to þe eorle and semblant. *c.* **1489** CAXTON *Sons of Aymon* ix. 227 Lete vs . . . bere oute a good face as longe as we ben alyve. **1540** *Acolastus* 35 (fayre face) & 69. **1566** PAINTER i. 184 (bold face). **1567** *Id.* iii. 199 (good face). **1659** HOWELL *Eng. Prov.* 6a To put a good face on an ill game. **1867** FREEMAN *Norm. Conq.* (1876) I. iv. 231 Richer puts as good a face as he can on Hugh's discomfiture.

Good fame is better than a good face.

1721 KELLY 71. **1732** FULLER no. 150.

Good fellow is a costly name, A.

1721 KELLY 16, 17 . . . Because it requires a great deal to procure it, and more to uphold it; spoken when People urge us to spend, that we may be reckoned good Fellows.

Good finds good.   (G 312)

1640 HERBERT no. 456.

Good fish if it were but caught, It is   (F 317)

1659 HOWELL *Eng. Prov.* 12a Good fish, but all the craft is in the catching. **1678** RAY 71 . . . It's spoken of any considerable good that one hath not, but talks much of, sues for, or endeavours after. **1732** FULLER no. 2936.

Good for nothing, He is.   (N 258)

1533–4 N. UDALL *Flowers* 172ᵛ Nequam is he that is good for nothynge, but euen a very naughty vnthryfte. **1593** *Tom Tell-troth's New Year's gift* New Sh. S. 11 An olde trott . . . good nothing but to keepe the cat out of the ashes. **1639** CLARKE 70. **1666** TORRIANO *Prov. Phr.* s.v. Cervello 36 The English say, Who is good for nothing but to shell pease.

Good for the back, That which is | is bad for the head.

1670 RAY 58. **1721** KELLY 330.

Good fruit of a good tree.   (F 777)

c. **1525** TYNDALE *Pathway* P.S. 22 A good tree bringeth forth good fruit, and an evil tree evil fruit. **1581** GUAZZO ii. 15 It is sieldome seene that a good tree bringeth forth ill fruites. **1586** R. CROWLEY *Father John Francis* I2 The good tree is neuer without good fruites. **1659** N. R. 6 A sweet tree yeeldeth savoury fruit.

Good for the head, That which is | is evil for the neck and the shoulders.   (H 267)

1604 JAMES I *Counterblaste* Arb. 107 There is almost no sort either of nourishment or medicine, that hath not some thing in it disagreeable to mans bodie, . . . according to the olde prouerbe, That which is good for the head, is euill for the necke and the shoulders. *a.* **1628** CARMICHAELL no. 572 (evil for the shoulders).

Good for the liver may be bad for the spleen.

1706 STEVENS s.v. Higado (bad for the milt). **1732** FULLER no. 1711.

Good fortune, *see* Ounce of g. f. worth pound of forecast.

Good Friday, *see* Eat his part on G. F.

Good friend that speaks well of us behind our backs, He is a.   (F 704)

1602 JONSON *Poetaster* III. i. 239 Thou should'st find a good sure assistant of mee: one, that would speake all good of thee in thy absence. **1678** RAY 143. **1710** PALMER 59. **1732** FULLER no. 2465 He's my Friend that speaks well of me behind my Back.

Good gear that lasts aye, It is.   (G 58)

c. **1384** CHAUCER *Ho. Fame* l. 1147 Men seyn, what may ever laste. *c.* **1602** SHAKES. *A.W.* II. ii. 53 Things may serve long but not serve ever. *a.* 1628 CARMICHAELL no. 864 It is gude geir that serves the turne. *c.* 1641 FERGUSSON MS. no. 896 (quhilk lasts ay).

Good goose (bear), do not bite. (G 349)

1571 *Life & Death of J. Story* A3ᵛ A kyndly beare wyll bite by tyme. 1592 LYLY *Midas* I. ii. 106 Who wil take vs to be Foxes, that stand so nere a goose, and bite not? 1592 NASHE *Strange News* i. 307 Good Beare, bite not. 1593 G. HARVEY *Gros.* ii. 244 Good Beare bite not. *c.* 1595 SHAKES. *R.J.* II. iv. 76 Nay good goose, bite not. 1599 PORTER *Angry Wom. Abingd.* l. 2394 Good Goose, bite not.

Good goose that's ay dropping, It is a. (G 360)

a. 1628 CARMICHAELL no. 912. 1641 FERGUSSON no. 524. 1721 KELLY 190 . . . It is a good Friend that is always giving; spoken to dissuade us from too much importuning a Friend.

Good hand, good hire. (H 69)

1611 COTGRAVE s.v. Servir Good seruice, of it selfe, demaunds reward. 1639 CLARKE 92.

Good harvest, He that has a | may be content with some thistles. (H 183)

1639 CLARKE 198. 1721 KELLY 150 He that has a good Crop, may be doing with some Thistles. If a Man hath had a great deal of good Conveniencies, he may bear with some Misfortunes.

Good harvests make men prodigal, bad ones provident. (H 185)

1611 COTGRAVE s.v. Année. 1670 RAY 13.

Good health, He who has | is young; and he is rich who owes nothing.

1664 W. CONYERS *Hemerologicum Astronomicum* 15 Oct. He is young enough that is in Health— and old enough that is not in Debt. 1707 MAPLETOFT 12.

Good heart cannot lie, A. (H 316)

1611 COTGRAVE s.v. Coeur An honest heart cannot dissemble. 1640 HERBERT no. 800.

Good heart conquers ill fortune, A. (H 305)

1571 R. EDWARDS *Damon and Pythias* D1ᵛ Multum iuuat in re mala animus bonus. 1591–2 SHAKES. *2 Hen. VI* III. i. 100 A heart unspotted is not easily daunted. 1591–2 *Id. 3 Hen. VI* IV. iii. 46–7 Though fortune's malice overthrow my state, My mind exceeds the compass of her wheel. 1598 *Id. 2 Hen. IV* II. iv. 31 A good heart's worth gold. 1599 MINSHEU *Span. Gram.* 84 A good hart breaketh ill hap. 1604 SHAKES. *O.* I. iii. 206 What cannot be preserv'd when fortune takes, Patience her injury a mock'ry makes. 1620 SHELTON *Quix.* II. xxxv (1908) III. 72 A good heart conquers ill fortune, as well thou knowest.

Good heed has good hap. (H 370)

[*Cf. c.* 1566 N. UDALL *Ralph Roister D.* III. iii. 104 Good happe is not hastie.] 1638 J. CLARKE *Phraseol. Puerilis* C7 Good heed hath as good hap. 1681 ROBERTSON 718.

Good horse cannot be of a bad colour, A. (H 646)

a. 1628 CARMICHAELL no. 1621 There is gude horse of all hewis. 1653 WALTON *Angler* v It is observed by some, that 'there is no good horse of a bad colour'. 1721 KELLY 126 Horses are good of all Hues. 1891 J. L. KIPLING *Beast & Man* 179 'A good horse is never of a bad colour' . . . is wildly irreverent from the Oriental point of view. 1912 *Spectator* 28 Dec. 1094 Virgil . . . did not hold that 'a good horse cannot be of a bad colour'.

Good horse oft needs a good spur, A. Cf. Spur and whip for dull horse. Spurring free horse (Ill). Untimeous spurring spills horse. (H 648)

1592 DELAMOTHE 25. 1639 CLARKE 93.

Good horse that never stumbles, It is a. (H 670)

1530 PALSGRAVE 742a He is a good horse that stumbleth nat sometyme. 1546 HEYWOOD I. viii. C1 Though it be a good hors That neuer stumbleth. 1599 PORTER *Angry Wom. Abingd.* l. 1058 Well, 'tis a good horse neuer stumbles. 1670 RAY 105 . . . and a good wife that never grumbles. 1721 KELLY 126 . . . And a better Wife that never grumbled. Both so rare, that I never met with either.

Good horses make short miles. (H 714)

1640 HERBERT no. 935.

Good house, In a | all is quickly ready. (H 776)

1595 COPLEY *Wits, Fits* III. 81 For in a kitchen well burnish'd supper is soone furnish'd. 1611 COTGRAVE s.v. Maison. 1640 HERBERT no. 58.

Good hurler[1] that's on the ditch, He is a.

1856 ABP. WHATELY *Annot. Bacon's Ess.* (1876) 495 'Lookers-on many times see more than gamesters' . . . has a parallel in an Irish proverb: 'He is a good hurler that's on the ditch.' [1 hockey-player.]

Good (bad) husband makes a good (bad) wife, A. Cf. Good Jack, Good wife, etc. (H 831)

1492 *Salomon & Marcolphus* ed. Duff 12 Of a good man cometh a good wyf. *Cf.* 1542 C. AGRIPPA *Treatise of Nobility of Womankind* D8 Yll wyues neuer chaunce, but to yll husbandes. 1591 FLORIO *Second F.* 193. 1616 DRAXE no. 2398. 1621 BURTON *Anat. Mel.* III. iii. IV. i. (1836) 648 For as the old saying is, a good husband makes a good wife. 1702 FARQUHAR *Inconstant* II. i A good Husband makes a good Wife at any time. 1706 STEVENS s.v. Trato A bad Husband makes a bad Wife.

Good husbandry is good divinity.
1707 MAPLETOFT 108.   **1846** DENHAM 2.

Good is good, but better carries it.
(G 313)

1609 BRETNOR *Almanac* November Good Days Better would do well.   **1640** HERBERT no. 454. **1678** RAY 148 Though good be good, yet better is better *or* better carries it.

Good is the enemy of the best, The. *Cf.* Best is enemy of good.

1912 J. KELMAN *Thoughts on Things Eternal* 108 Every respectable Pharisee proves the truth of the saying that 'the good is the enemy of the best'. . . . Christ insists that we shall not be content with a second-best, though it be good.

Good is to be sought out and evil attended.
(G 314)

1572 CRADOCKE *Ship of Assured Safety* a6ᵛ It is a Prouerbe amongst the Grekes . . . that if in euils any good may be founde, the same must be sifted oute.   **1640** HERBERT no. 112.   **1710** PALMER 148 Seek Good, and be ready for Evil.

Good Jack makes a good Jill, A. *Cf.* Good husband, etc.
(J 1)

1623 PAINTER C8 A good Iacke alwaies maketh a good Gyll.   **1636** CAMDEN 291.   **1670** RAY 108 . . . Inferiours imitate the manners of superiours; . . . wives of their husbands.   **1876** MRS. BANKS *Manch. Man* ch. 47 Justifying her daughter's flight with . . . 'A good Jack makes a good Jill'.

Good judgement that relies not wholly on his own, He has a.
(J 96)

1642 TORRIANO 57.   **1707** MAPLETOFT 1.   **1732** FULLER no. 1882.

Good kail is half a meal (half meat).
(K 2)

1670 RAY 36 (keal).   **1721** KELLY 118 (half meat). Good Broth will, in some measure, supply the want of Bread.   **1732** FULLER no. 6252.

Good land: evil (foul) way.
(L 50)

a. **1633** DONNE *Poems* (Grierson) i. 81 There is best land where there is foulest way.   **1640** HERBERT no. 802.   **1653** WALTON *Angler* II. i (1915) 256 The foul way serves to justify the fertility of the soil, according to the proverb, 'There is good land where there is foul way'.

Good language which all understand not, That is not.
(L 64)

1640 HERBERT no. 302.

Good lasses, All are | but whence come the bad wives?

1721 KELLY 19 All are good lasses, but, where comes the ill Wives from? No body can blame young Women for putting the best Side outmost, and concealing their bad Humours 'till they get Husbands.

Good life, A handful of | is better than a bushel of learning.
(H 126)

1534 TYNDALE *Parable of Wicked Mammon* Arber's ed. of Joy's Apology xi In my mynde therfore a little vnfayned loue after the rules of Christ is worth moche hie learning.   **1623** WODROEPHE 503 A Handfull of Godly Living, Is better then a Tunne of Learning.   **1640** HERBERT no. 3.   **1659** HOWELL *Fr. Prov.* 11.

Good life makes a good death, A.
(L 245)

1561 T. BECON *Sick Man's Salve* P.S. 190 Of a good life cometh a good death.   **1592** DELA-MOTHE 57 A good life engendreth good death. **1616** DRAXE no. 444 An honourable death followeth an honourable life.   **1629** *Bk. Mer. Rid.* Prov. no. 27.

Good luck comes by cuffing.

1706 STEVENS s.v. Puñada . . . That is, a Man must struggle and take pains to be fortunate. **1813** RAY 136.

Good luck, More by | than by good guiding (management).
(C 225)

c. **1576** WHYTHORNE 21 Mor by good hap then by kunning.   [*c.* **1590**] **1594** *Taming of a Shrew* B3ᵛ Twas more by hap then any good cunning. **1616** DRAXE no. 779 More by chance then any good cunning.   *a.* **1628** CARMICHAELL no. 342 Better thro hap, nor gude hussieskep.   **1621** ROBINSON 13 It is more through hap then good husbandry.   **1721** KELLY 248 . . . Spoken when a Thing, ill managed, falls out well.   **1852** MRS. CARLYLE *Lett.* to T.C., 10 Aug. Mazzini . . . made my hair stand on end with his projects. If he is not shot, or in an Austrian fortress within the month, it will be more by good luck than good guiding.

Good maid, but for thought, word, and deed, She is a.
(M 25)

[**1666** TORRIANO *Prov. Phr.* s.v. Peccato 137 The English usually say of a young childe or girl under age, She is a Maid, i'll swear for her, Thought, word and deed.]   **1678** RAY 258.

Good man can no more harm than a sheep (she-ape), A.
(M 149)

c. **1549** HEYWOOD I. x. C4ᵛ She can no more harm than can a she ape.   **1614** CAMDEN 302. **1616** DRAXE no. 2464 (a shee ape).   **1639** CLARKE 77.

Goodman is from home, When the | the good wife's table is soon spread.
(G 333)

a. **1628** CARMICHAELL no. 1292 (the buird claith is tint).   **1641** FERGUSSON no. 725 (the board-cleaths tint).   **1678** RAY 61.   **1721** KELLY 352 When the good Man's away the Board Cloth is tint.[1] Because the Commons will then be short. [1 lost.]

Goodman is the last who knows what's amiss at home, The. (G 332)

1658 *Comes facundus* 21. **1670** RAY 52. **1707** MAPLETOFT 106.

Goodman says, As the | so say we; but as the good woman says, so must it be. (G 331)

1623 PAINTER C8ᵛ (as the good wife saith, so all must be). *a.* **1628** CARMICHAELL no. 176 (al mon be). **1670** RAY 51.

Good man thrive, If a | all thrive with him.

1640 HERBERT no. 695.

Good man whom fortune makes better, He is a.

1732 FULLER no. 2438.

Good man (men), *see also* Amongst g. m. two men suffice; Breed of g. m.'s mother; God is a g. m.; Learning makes g. m. better; Praise makes g. m. better; Show a g. m. his error; Well for him who feeds g. m.

Good manners to except my Lord Mayor of London. (M 624)

[**1655** FULLER *Church Hist.* III. vi (14) The richest and proudest (always good manners to except Cardinal Wolsey).] **1662** FULLER Lond. 199 . . . This is a corrective for such, whose expressions are of the largest size, and too general in their extent. . . . It is not civil to fill up all the room in our speeches of our selves, but to leave an upper place voyd . . . for our betters.

Good manners to show your learning before ladies, It is not. (M 627)

1694 *Let. Love* Ep. Ded. II. A3 Nay, some, tho' they were Addressing to you, would have the impertinence to bring in Latin and Greek. **1738** SWIFT Dial. II. E.L. 308 *Tace* is Latin for a candle.—Is that manners, to show your learning before ladies?

Good (ill) master a good (ill) scholar, A. (M 721)

1568 D. ROWLAND *Comfortable Aid for Scholars* K3ᵛ The good gouerner maketh a good subiect, and the good master a good scoler. **1639** CLARKE 238 An ill master makes bad schollers.

Good master shall have good wages, He that serves a. (M 718)

c. **1502** *Robert the Devil* in *Ancient Eng. Fictions* 25 Whosoeuer serueth a good mayster he is lyke to haue good wages. **1611** COTGRAVE s.v. Bon (looks for a good reward). **1616** DRAXE no. 1932.

Good memories have ill judgements.

1721 KELLY 119 . . . Spoken to them who call to Mind a past Thing, at an unseasonable time, or before improper Company.

Good memory, He that has a | gives few alms. (M 869)

1662 FULLER Devon 254 The Welch have a Proverb . . . 'He that hath a good memory, giveth few Alms'; because he keepeth in mind what and to whom he had given before.

Good men (folks) are scarce. *Cf.* Make much of one. (M 521)

1616 DRAXE no. 1806 A good man is hard to be found. **1638** D. TUVIL *Vade Mecum* (3rd ed.) 96. **1660** TATHAM *Rump* II. i. Could you find no better company?—Good men were scarce. **1721** KELLY 124 Good Folks are scarce, you'll take care of one. Spoken to those who carefully provide against ill Weather, or cowardly shun Dangers. **1738** SWIFT Dial. I. E.L. 269 Come, come, miss, make much of nought; good folks are scarce. **1822** SCOTT *Pirate* ch. 5 Triptolemus . . . knew good people were scarce, . . . and had . . . that wisdom which looks towards self-preservation as the first law of nature.

Good morrow, *see* Brag of many g. m.; Sheep and a cow (Now I have) everybody bids g. m.

Good mother says not, Will you? but gives, The. (M 1195)

1640 HERBERT no. 467. **1706** STEVENS s.v. Madre.

Good name is better than riches (gold), A. (Take away my good name and take away my life.) (N 22, 25)

[PROV. xxii. I: A good name is rather to be chosen than great riches.] *c.* **1350** *How the Gd. Wife* I. 81. **1477** RIVERS *Dictes* (1877 ed. 64) Good renomme is bettir than richesse. *c.* **1526** *Dicta Sap.* B2ᵛ It is better to haue a good name, than richesse. **1583** G. BABINGTON *Expos. of Commandᵗˢ* P.S. 438 A mans name is dearer than either life or goods. **1593** T. CHURCHYARD *Challenge* P1ᵛ They thought it a double death to loose their good name. **1604** SHAKES. *O.* III. iii. 161 Who steals my purse steals trash . . . But he that filches from me my good name Robs me of that which not enriches him And makes me poor indeed. **1614** T. ADAMS *Fatal Banquet* II, Wks. 193 It robs man of his good name, which is above all riches. **1670** RAY 124. Take away my good name and take away my life. **1732** FULLER no. 4306 (as 1670). **1790** TRUSLER *Prov. Exempl.* 60 What is life without a character? *Take away my good name, and take away my life.*

Good name keeps its lustre in the dark, A. (N 23)

[PUBL. SYRUS Bona fama in tenebris proprium splendorem obtinet.] **1539** TAVERNER *Publius* B2 A good fame euen in darckenes loseth not her due beuty and renoume. *a.* **1593** MARLOWE *Hero & Leander* II. 240 Rich jewels in the darke are soonest spide. *c.* **1610** WEBSTER *White Devil* III. ii. 305 Through darknesse Diamonds spred their ritchest light. *a.* **1632** DEKKER [ROWLEY] *Noble Soldier* F3 Dangers (like Starres) in dark attempts best shine. **1664** CODRINGTON 184. **1670** RAY 18.

Good neighbour, A | a good morrow.
(N 106)

c. 1470 *Harl. MS. 116* in *Rel. Antiq.* I. 316 He that hath a good neyghboure hath a good morowe. 1576 HOLYBAND D8ᵛ. 1594 *Mirr. Policy* (1599) Oiij The common proverb ·saith, That who so hath a good neighbour, hath a good morrow. 1599 SHAKES. *Hen. V* IV. i. 6 Our bad neighbour makes us early stirrers. 1670 RAY 124 (good good-morrow).

Good news may be told at any time, but ill in the morning.
(N 139)

1640 HERBERT no. 877.

Good night, landlady (Nicholas).

[1600] 1659 DAY & CHETTLE *Blind Beggar* K2 I'll take my leave on thee with an oh good night Land-lady the Moon is up. 1659 HOWELL *Eng. Prov.* 11b Good night Nicholas, the Moon is in the Flockbedd.

Good night(s), *see also* Many G. n. is loth away.

Good or ill hap of a good or ill life, is the good or ill choice of a good or ill wife.

1721 KELLY 331. 1732 FULLER no. 6413.

Good orator who convinces himself, He is a.

1707 MAPLETOFT 16.

Good painter can draw a devil as well as an angel, A.
(P 27)

1592 DELAMOTHE 55. 1639 CLARKE 311.

Good payer is master of another's purse, A.
(P 130)

1640 HERBERT no. 595. 1659 HOWELL *It. Prov.* 12. A good paymaster is Lord of another mans purse.

Good paymaster needs no surety, A.
(P 131)

1620 SHELTON *Quix.* II. xiv (1908) II. 274 A staid voice answered and said: 'A good pay-master needs no surety.' 1640 HERBERT no. 113 A good pay-master starts not at assurances. 1706 STEVENS s.v. Pagadór (is not in pain for his Pawn).

Good pedigrees, In | there are governors and chandlers. *Cf.* Poor kin that has neither whore nor thief.
(P 178)

1640 HERBERT no. 222.

Good reason and part cause.

1721 KELLY 122. Good reason, and part of cause. An ironical Approbation of some foolish Saying, Action, or Design. 1862 HISLOP 108. 1902–4 LEAN III. 475 Good reason and part

cause.—Quoted by Dean Church . . . (1887) as a subtle Scotch proverb, meaning that the good reasons for a decision are often only part of the cause of its being adopted.

Good riddance to bad rubbish.

1848 DICKENS *Dombey & Son* ch. 44. 1944 L. P. HARTLEY *The Shrimp & the Anemone* ch. 11.

Good riding at two anchors, men have told, for if one break the other may hold.
(R 119)

[PROPERTIUS 3. 13. 41 *Nam°melius duo¯defendunt retinacula navim.*] *c.* 1549 HEYWOOD II. ix. K4ᵛ Good ridyng at two ancres men haue tolde, For if the tone faile, the tother maie holde. 1579 LYLY *Euph.* i. 255 It is safe riding at two ancres. 1601 SHAKES. *T.N.* I. v. 21 I am resolved on two points.—That if one break, the other will hold.

Good ruler, No man can be a | unless he has first been ruled.
(S 246)

1539 TAVERNER 2 *Nemo bene imperat, nisi qui paruerit imperio.* No man can be a good ruler, onles he hath bene fyrste ruled. 1563 *Mirror for Mag.* ed. Campbell 407. 1581 GUAZZO ii. 97–8 Impossible . . . he should . . . play the mayster well, who never had mayster. *Ibid.* 98 Those onlye knowe well how to commaund, which know well howe to obaye. 1620 SHELTON *Quix.* Pt. II. xxxiii (iii. 54) He that cannot govern himself will ill govern others. 1671 MILTON *P.R.* III. 194 [He can] best reign who first Hath well obeyed. 1841 CHAMIER *Tom Bowl.* ch. 44 Many instances of oppression and tyranny . . . had originated in Curlew's ignorance, both of the duties of a seaman and of an officer. It was evident he had never learnt to obey, and thus was unfit for command.

Good saver is a good server, A.
(S 105)

1598 R. CLEAVER *A Godly Form of Household Government* 76–90 A good saver is as good as a good getter [L. B. WRIGHT *Middle-class Culture* 212]. 1678 RAY 350.

Good service is a great enchantment.
(S 250)

1616 DRAXE no. 1933 No such enchantment as a good seruice. 1640 HERBERT no. 291.

Good shape is in the shears' mouth, A.
1721 KELLY 46.

Good shepherd must fleece his sheep, not flay them, A.
(S 329)

[SUET. *Tib.* 32 fin. *Boni pastoris est tondere pecus, non deglubere.*] 1539 TAVERNER 48ᵛ It is the parte of a good shepherde or pastor to sheare the shepe and not to plucke of theyr skinnes. 1616 WITHALS 553 A good shepheard must take the fleece, and not the fel. 1616 DRAXE no. 1564.

Good small beer, good brown bread, or a good old woman, There is no such thing as. *Cf.* Good things I do not love.

1738 SWIFT Dial. II. E.L. 302 Pray, friend, give me a glass of small beer, if it be good.—Why, colonel, they say there is no such thing as good small beer, good brown bread, or a good old woman.

Good spear, He that has a | let him try it. (s 732)

1573 SANFORD 28ᵛ (proue it against a wal). **1578** FLORIO *First F.* 103 (proueth him against the wall). **1629** *Bk. Mer. Rid.* Prov. no. 74.

Good sport that fills the belly, That is.

1721 KELLY 190. **1732** FULLER no. 4354.

Good swimmers at length are drowned. (s 1041)

1585 ROBSON *Choice Change* Lɪᵛ We may take example by 3 sorts of men which hazard themselues in daunger, and often perish. The best swimmers are drowned. The best climbers do fall. The best fencers are wounded. **1611** COTGRAVE s.v. Nageur Good swimmers at the length feed Haddocks. **1640** HERBERT no. 801. **1907** *Illust. Lond. News* 1 June He was a strong swimmer; but, as the Eastern proverb has it, 'The fate of the swimmer is to be taken by the sea'.

Good that are away, They are aye.

1721 KELLY 338 . . . Spoken when People lavishly commend those of their Friends that are abroad or dead.

Good that does me good, That is my. (G 319)

1639 CLARKE 109 That's good that doth us good. **1678** RAY 148.

Good that failed never, He is. (F 23)

a. **1628** CARMICHAELL no. 687. **1641** FERGUSSON no. 367. **1721** KELLY 163 . . . A Persuasion to bear the Neglects of a Friend, who has, on other Occasions, been beneficial to you.

Good that he is good for nothing, So. (N 324)

c. **1594** BACON no. 908 Tanto buon che val niente. **1607–12** BACON *Ess., Goodness* Arb. 200 The Italians haue an vngracious prouerbe Tanto buon che val niente, So good that he is good for Nothinge. **1639** CLARKE 78 So good as good for nothing. **1738** SWIFT Dial. II. E.L. 309. How do you like these preserved oranges? —. . . They are too good.—O, madam, I have heard 'em say, that too good is stark naught. **1871** SMILES *Character* 301 It is still . . . the practice to cultivate the weakness of woman rather than her strength. . . . She incurs the risk of becoming the embodiment of the Italian proverb—'so good that she is good for nothing'.

Good that knows not why he is good, He cannot be. (K 181)

c. **1580** SIDNEY 1 *Arcadia* (Feuillerat) iv. 5 Hee can not bee good, that knowes not whye hee ys good. **1602** CAREW *Survey of Cornwall* (1769) 87. **1732** FULLER no. 1819.

Good that mends, It is.

1721 KELLY 205 . . . Spoken when we hear that a Person, or Thing, is better, or does better.

Good thing cheap, He will never have a | that is afraid to ask the price. (T 132)

1611 COTGRAVE s.v. Demander Let no man thinke to haue, that asks not, things good cheape. **1616** DRAXE no. 38. **1670** RAY 56 Il n'aura ja[mais] bon marché qui ne le demande [pas]. *Gall.*

Good thing is soon caught up, A. (T 131)

1611 COTGRAVE s.v. Beau A goodly thing is quickly snatched up. **1664** CODRINGTON 184 (snatch'd). **1670** RAY 12 (as 1664). **1732** FULLER no. 181.

Good things are hard. (T 181)

[Gk. Χαλεπὰ τὰ καλά. Attributed to Solon and Pittacus; Socrates quotes as an old proverb (PL. *Crat.* 1. 384 A).] *c.* **1535** ELYOT *Educ.* 6, C3ᵛ For it is said in a prouerbe: Good thinges are difficile. **1539** TAVERNER 29ᵛ Harde or difficile be those thynges that be goodly or honeste. This sentence of the wyse man Solon declarethe vnto vs that the waye of honestie, of vertue, of renowm, is vneasye, paynful, ieopardouse, harde. **1603** HOLLAND tr. *Plutarch's Morals* 6 Whatsoever is faire and goodly, the same also is hard and difficult. **1664** JOS. MEDE Wks. I. Gen. Pref. That all excellent things are hard, is so confessed a truth, that it has passed into a vulgar proverb. **1853** TRENCH vi. 136 With the proverb, Good things are hard, [Socrates] continually rebuked their empty pretensions; and made suspicious at least their delusive promises.

Good things I do not love; Some | a good long mile, good small beer, and a good old woman. (T 195)

1678 RAY 148.

Good time coming, There is a.

1818 SCOTT *Rob Roy* ch. 32 'I could have wished it had been . . . when I could have better paid the compliments I owe your Grace;—but there's a gude time coming'. **1846** CHARLES MACKAY *The Good Time Coming* There's a good time coming, boys, A good time coming. **1851** KINGSLEY *Yeast* ch. 17 Your very costermonger trolls out his belief that 'there's a good time coming'.

Good tither, a good thriver, A. (T 358)

1573 TUSSER *500 Points* s.v. Good husbandlie lessons ch. 10, no. 52 Ill tithers, ill thriuers, most commonlie bee. **1678** RAY 352. *Somerset.*

Good to be good in your time, for you know not how long it will last, It is.

1721 KELLY 193 . . . Spoken to those who are now in Credit, Power, and Authority; that they should not be proud or insolent; for they may meet with a Change.

Good to be in the dark as without light, It is as. (D 40)

1659 N. R. 63.   1670 RAY 77.

Good to be sent for sorrow (to fetch sorrow), You are. (M 151)

1670 RAY 194 Good to fetch a sick man sorrow and a dead man wo. *Chesh.* 1721 KELLY 379 . . . Spoken to them who tarry long when they are sent an Errand. *Ibid.* 122 Good to fetch sorrow to a sick Wife. 1738 SWIFT Dial. I. E.L. 294 You are fit to be sent for sorrow, you stay so long by the way. 1917 BRIDGE 70 He's good to fetch a sick man sorrow and a dead man woe. There are plenty of people ready to convey sorrowful tidings. It also applies to anyone going about his business in a lazy or slovenly manner.

Good to fetch the devil a priest, You are. (D 275)

c. 1641 FERGUSSON MS. no. 595. 1721 KELLY 379 . . . Spoken to them who tarry long when they are sent an Errand.

Good tongue is a good weapon, A.

1721 KELLY 8.   1732 FULLER no. 180.

Good tongue, Who has not a | ought to have good hands.

1813 RAY 166.

Good tongue that says no ill, and a better heart that thinks none, It is a.

1721 KELLY 222 . . . Used when we have no Inclination to speak our mind freely, concerning Courts, or great Men.

Good trade, He that has no | it is to his loss. (T 459)

1640 HERBERT no. 560.

Good tree is a good shelter, A. (T 487)

1599 MINSHEU *Span. Gram.* 84 Whosoeuer leaneth to a good tree, getteth a good shadow, i. whosoeuer hath a sure man to trust vnto, hath a great pleasure. 1620 SHELTON *Quix.* Pt. II. xxxii (iii. 41) Lean to a good tree and it will shadow thee. 1674 J. SMITH, *Grammatica Quadrilinguis* 205 He that leans on a good Tree, a good shadow covers him. *i.e.* It is good to have a great mans Protection. 1732 FULLER no. 182.

Good tree that has neither knap[1] nor gaw,[2] It is a.

1721 KELLY 218 . . . There is nothing altogether perfect. [[1] knob. [2] want, blemish.]

Good tune played on an old fiddle, There's many a.

1903 S. BUTLER, *Way of All Flesh,* ch. 61. 1917 BRIDGE 117.

Good (Ill, Shrewd) turn asks (deserves, requires) another, One. (T 616, 617)

c. 1400 MS. *Latin 394, John Rylands Libr.* (ed. Pantin) in *Bull. J. R. Libr.* XIV 92 O good turne asket another. 1509 BARCLAY *Ship of Fools* ii. 38 One yll turne requyreth, another be thou sure. 1545 *Precepts of Cato* F8 (asketh). c. 1549 HEYWOOD I. xi. E2ᵛ Onc good tourne askth an other. 1552 HULOET B2ᵛ Aske one good turne for an other. 1579 (1607 ed. D1ᵛ) J. FOXE to R. Day *Christ Jesus Triumphant* One shrewd turne for an other. 1589 SPENSER *F.Q.* II. viii. 56 What need Good turnes be counted, as a seruile bond? 1602 *Lord Cromwell* II. ii *Shaks. Apoc.* 172 As indeede one good turn asketh another. 1612–15 BP. HALL *Contempl.* XIV. ii (1825) I. 408 One good turn requires another. . . . David's soldiers were Nabal's shepherds; . . . justly should they have been set at the upper end of the table. 1654 H. L'ESTRANGE *Chas. I* (1655) 15 One good turn deserves another. 1670 RAY 20 (shrewd). 1824 SCOTT *St. Ronans* ch. 17 But one good turn deserves another—in that case, you must . . . dine with me. 1894 STEVENSON & OSBOURNE *Ebb-Tide* ch. I 'One good turn deserves another. . . . Say the word and you can have a cruise upon the carpet.'

Good turn for it, I will watch you a. (T 615)

[1598] 1616 HAUGHTON *Englishmen for my Money* l. 602 Ile watch him a good turne I warrant him. 1599 PORTER *Angry Wom. Abing.* l. 2293 Ile watch her a good turne for it. 1639 CLARKE 209 I'le watch you a good turne.

Good turn, He that will do thee a | either he will be gone or die. (T 614)

1599 MINSHEU *Span. Gram.* 80.   1651 HERBERT no. 1083.

Good turn, One | will meet another, if it were at the Bridge of London.

a. 1628 CARMICHAELL no. 129 A gude turne meits ane other and it were at the brig of Lun. 1721 KELLY 275 . . . Spoken by them who make a Return for former Favours.

Good ware makes quick markets. (W 62)

[PLAUTUS *Poenulus* I. 2. 128 *Proba merx facile emptorem repperit.* Good wares easily find a buyer.] 1611 COTGRAVE s.v. Marchand Good chaffer cannot want a chapman. 1616 DRAXE no. 2337 (good markets). 1616 BRETON *Cross. Prov.* B3. 1639 CLARKE 106.

Good watch prevents misfortune. (W 83)

1592–4 SHAKES. *1 Hen. VI* II. i. 58 Had your watch been good, This sudden mischief never could have fall'n. 1611 COTGRAVE s.v. Bon. 1664 CODRINGTON 194. 1670 RAY 28.

Good wife and health is a man's best wealth, A.

1591 H. SMITH *Preparative to Marriage* (1657) 17, margin A Wife is a poor mans riches. **1721** KELLY 31. **1732** FULLER no. 6313.

Good wife in the country, There is one | and every man thinks he has her. (w 374)

1620 SHELTON *Quix.* II. xxii (1908) II. 334 It was an opinion of I know not what sage man, that there was but one good woman in the world; and . . . that every man should think, that was married, that his wife was she. **1670** RAY 49. **1738** SWIFT *Dial.* I. E.L. 291 They say, that every married man should believe there's but one good wife in the world, and that's his own.

Good wife makes a good husband, A. (w 351)

[**1525–40**] **1557** *Mer. Dial.* 63 It lieth great parte in the women, for the orderinge of theyr husbandes. **1546** HEYWOOD II. viii. K2ᵛ A good wife makth a good husbande, (they saie). **1614** CAMDEN 302. **1758** 9 Jan. Johnson *Lett.* (Chapman) i. 113 Good Wives make good husbands.

Good wife's a goodly prize, saith Solomon the wise, A.

1678 RAY 58.

Good wife's away, When the | the keys are tint.¹ (w 375)

1668 R.B. 44 (Quhen the good-wife is fra hame the). **1721** KELLY 352 . . . For if she be not at home you'll get no Drink. [¹ lost.]

Good will and welcome is your best cheer. *Cf.* Welcome is the best cheer. (G 338)

c. **1477–8** *Bk. Courtesy* l. 258 E.E.T.S. 27 The poete saith how that a poure borde Men may enriche with cheerful wil and worde. *a.* **1530** *R. Hill's Commonpl. Bk.* 31 E.E.T.S. 131 In a thyn table, good chere is best sawse. **1575** WHETSTONE *Promos and Cassandra* (Nichol i. 69) Where good wyll the welcome geves, provysion syld is scant. **1584** WITHALS Consider the countenance, not the fare, the good will not the good cheare of him which bids thee to his table. **1639** CLARKE 222.

Good will, With as | as e'er boy came from school. (w 398)

1573 GASCOIGNE i *Fruits War* 175, no. 171 And home we came as children come from schoole. **1591** W. STEPNEY 90 Will you pledge me?—Yea, with as good will as euer I came from schoole. **1594–8** SHAKES. *T.S.*¹ III. ii. 145 Signior Gremio, came you from the church? —As willingly as e'er I came from school. **1639** CLARKE 186. **1659** HOWELL *Eng. Prov.* 6a.

Good wind that blows a man to the wine, It is a. (w 420)

1594 LYLY *Mother B.* II. v. 5 It was an olde prouerbe, when his greate grandfather was a childe, that it was a good winde that blew a man to the wine.

Good wine engenders good blood. (w 461)

a. **1530** *R. Hill's Commonpl. Bk.* E.E.T.S. 'Is this wyn good?' 'That is it . . . It chereth the hert and comforteth the blod.' **1568** W. TURNER *Of Wines* E3 Wine . . . will . . . increase bloud and norish. **1568** G. B. GELLI *Fearful Fancies of the Florentine Cooper* tr. W. Barker C7ᵛ (Good drink). **1584** LYLY *Camp.* v. iii. 12 Good drinke makes good bloud. **1594** NASHE *Unfort. Trav.* ii. 308 Good drinke makes good blood. **1598** SHAKES. *2 Hen. IV* IV. iii. 86 This . . . sober-blooded boy doth not love me; . . . he drinks no wine. **1598–9** *Id. M.A.* I. i. 216 Prove that ever I lose more blood with love than I will get again with drinking. *c.* **1602** *Id. A.W.* II. iii. 97 I am sure thy father drank wine. [**1604**] **1607** DEKKER & WEBSTER *Sir T. Wyatt* II. iii. 70 (Good victailes makes). **1616** DRAXE no. 2430. **1719** DE ALVORADO 63 (creates).

Good wine needs no bush. (w 462)

[A bunch of ivy was the sign of a vintner's shop.] *c.* **1426** LYDGATE *Pilgr. Life of Man* l. 20415 And at tavernys (with-oute wene) Thys tooknys nor thys bowys grene, . . . The wyn they mende nat. **1539** TAVERNER F2ᵛ Wyne that is saleable and good nedeth no bushe or garland of yuye to be hanged before. **1545** *Id.* F2ᵛ [as above, adding] The english prouerbe is thus Good wyne neadeth no signe. **1579** LYLY *Euph.* i. 181 When the Wyne is neete, there needeth no Iuie-bush. **1599** SHAKES. *A.Y.* Epil. If it be true that good wine need no bush, 'tis true, that a good play needs no epilogue. **1623** CAMDEN 269 (no Iuy-bush). **1641** FERGUSSON no. 287 (not a wispe). **1674** R. GODFREY *Inj. & Ab. Physic* 168 As good Wine needs no Bush, no more do good Medicines a printed Bill. **1845** FORD *Handbk. Spain* I. 30 Good wine needs neither bush, herald, nor crier.

Good winter brings a good summer, A. (w 507)

1616 DRAXE no. 118. **1670** RAY 29.

Good wit, Such a one has a | if a wise man had the keeping of it. *Cf.* Wit is folly unless wise man has keeping of it. (w 562)

1636 CAMDEN 305.

Good wits jump. (w 578)

1594–8 SHAKES. *T.S.* I. i. 184 I have it, Tranio.— Master, for my hand, Both our inventions meet and jump in one. **1618** BELCHIER *Hans Beer-Pot* D1 Good wits doe jumpe. **1620** SHELTON *Quix.* Pt. II, ch. xxxvii (iii. 81) Good wits will soon meet. **1659** HOWELL *Eng. Prov.* 17a Good wits commonly jump. **1688** SHADWELL *Squire Als.* III. i Say'st thou so my girl! good wits jump.

I had the same thought with thee. **1738** SWIFT
Dial. I. E.L. 285. **1760–7** STERNE *T. Shandy*
ch. 53 Great wits jump.

Good word costs no more than a bad
one, A.   (w 807)
1579 *Proverbs* of Sir James Lopez de Mendoza
tr. B. Googe 13ᵛ Good woordes coste but a
litle. **1692** L'ESTRANGE *Aesop's Fab.* (1738)
cclxxvi. 292 *A good word*, they say, *costs no more
than a bad.* **1732** FULLER no. 1735.

Good words and ill deeds deceive wise
and fools. *Cf.* Fair words and foul
deeds.   (w 788)
1601 T. WRIGHT *The Passions of the Mind* 141
Wordes good, and workes ill, Makes fooles and
wisemen leese their skill. **1611** DAVIES no. 228.

Good words anoint us, and ill do
unjoint us.   (w 803)
1573 SANFORD 107 Good wordes do annointe,
the shrewde do pricke. **1578** FLORIO *First F.* 31ᵛ
Good woords annoynt a man, the yl woordes kyl
a man. **1611** DAVIES no. 72.

Good words are good cheap.   (w 804)
1639 CLARKE 194.

Good words cool more than cold water.
                                                 (w 806)
1616 DRAXE no. 2481 A good word doeth coole
more then a cauldron of water. **1640** HERBERT
no. 263 Good words quench more then a
bucket of water. **1670** RAY 158. **1706** STEVENS
s.v. Palabra (kettle of water).

Good words cost nought.   (w 808)
1542 SIR T. WYATT *Throughout the World* Fair
words . . . be good cheap, they cost right
nought. **1599** PORTER *Angry Wom. Abingd.* l. 2309
Good words cost nought. **1640** HERBERT no.
155 Good words are worth much, and cost little.
1721 KELLY 124 . . . And therefore may be the
freelier given.

Good words fill not a sack.   (w 809)
a. **1628** CARMICHAELL no. 1132 Manie words
fillis not the firlot,[1] or sck. **1641** FERGUSSON no.
627 (Mony words . . . furlot). **1678** RAY 220.
1732 FULLER no. 1737. [[1] Vessel for measuring
corn.]

Good words without deeds are rushes
and reeds.   (w 812)
1659 HOWELL *Eng. Prov.* 17a. **1670** RAY 30.
1732 FULLER no. 6247.

Good workmen are seldom rich.
                                                 (w 861)
1640 HERBERT no. 756.

Good world, if it hold, It is a.
1721 KELLY 191 . . . Spoken to them who take
their Ease and Pleasure now, without respect to
their future Condition.

Good world, It is a | but they are ill that
are on it.
1721 KELLY 191 . . . The word World is sometimes taken for the Universe, and sometimes for
Mankind; in the first Sense it is good, in the
second bad.

Good years corn is hay, In | in ill years
straw is corn.   (c 654)
1640 HERBERT no. 216. **1706** STEVENS s.v. Año.

Good (*adj.*, *adv.*), *see also* All g., and God say
Amen; All things are g. unseyit; All things in
their being are g. for something; All women are
g.; Breed of Lady Mary, when you're g. you're
o'er g.; Every one is weary, the g. in learning;
Everything is g. in season; Evil manners (Of) g.
laws; Friar never loved what was g.; George-a-
Green (G. as); Give as g. as one gets; Grey before he is g.; Medlars are not g. till rotten;
Nothing but is g. for something; Presumed g.
till found in fault; Some g., some bad, as
sheep; Soon as syne (As g.); Summer's day (As
g. as one shall see in a); Tale ill told (G.) is
marred; Tale (G.) is none the worse twice told;
Too g. is stark naught; Too g. to be true; Year
(A g.) will not make him.

Good(s) (*noun*), *see also* Afflictions are sent to us
by God for our g.; Bear with evil and expect g.;
Better g. afar off; Bode g. and get it; Conceited
g. quickly spent; Do g., thou doest it for thyself;
Does no g. (He who) does evil; Evil for g., (To
render); Evils have their comfort, g. none can
support; Gives his g.; Hopes not for g. fears not
evil; Ill that does not hurt (So great is) as the g.
that does not help; Ill-gotten g.; Little g. comes
of gathering; Little g. soon spent; Little g. to
stark nought; Lose his g.; Man far from his g. is
near harm; Man has no more g. than gets g. of;
Never do evil that g. may come of it; No man
better knows what g. is; Nothing so bad but
something of g.; Pardoning bad is injuring g.;
Plenty of g. (He that has) shall have more;
Poverty is hateful g.; See no g. near home (Some
can); Stolen g. never thrive; Swine (He is like),
never do g. while he lives.

Good, It is, *see also under significant words
following.*

Goodman, *see* Learn your g. to make milk kail.

Goodness is not tied to greatness.
                                                 (G 336)
1611 COTGRAVE s.v. Acquests The goodnesse of a
thing rests not in the greatnesse of it. **1626**
BRETON *Soothing* B1 Greatnesse and goodnesse
goe not ever together. **1631** WM. FOSTER
Hoplocrisma Spongus A4 Better is goodnesse
without greatnesse, than greatnesse without
goodnesse. **1639** CLARKE 226 Greatnesse and
goodnesse goe not alway together. **1655** T.
MUFFETT *Healths Improvement* 161 As the Greek
proverb saith, Goodness is not tied to greatness,
but greatness to goodness.

Goodness, *see also* Idleness (Of) comes no g.; Wine is master's, g. butler's.

Goods are theirs that enjoy them.

(G 302)

1578 FLORIO *First F.* 31ᵛ The ware is not his that gathers it, but his that enjoyes it. **1579** SPENSER *Shep. Cal.* May Wks. Globe 459 Good is no good, but if it be spend. **1603** MONTAIGNE (Florio) I. xlii. 161 Whatsoever the goods of fortune are, a man must have a proper sense to savour them: it is the enjoying and not the possessing of them, that makes us happy. **1640** HERBERT no. 850.

Goods in the window, To keep (put) all one's.

1658 [EDMONDSON] *Comes Facundus* 288 They had all their furniture of their house in the Portell. **1911** H. G. WELLS *New Machiavelli* bk. 3, ch. 1 §1.

Goods, *see also* Good(s).

Goodwin Sands,[1] To set up shop upon.

(S 393)

c. **1549** HEYWOOD II. ix. K4ᵛ But you leaue all anker holde, on seas or lands. And so set vp shop vpon Goodwyns sands. **1678** RAY 72 Let him set up shop on Goodwins sands. This is a piece of Countrey wit; there being an equivoq; in the word *Good-win*, which is a surname, and also signifies gaining wealth. **1748** FRANKLIN May Sell-cheap kept shop on Goodwin Sands, and yet had store of custom. [1 Sandbanks off the coast of Kent, exposed at low water.]

Goodwin Sands, *see also* Tenterden steeple.

Goodyer's pig, Like | never well but when he is doing mischief.

(G 343)

1670 RAY 209. *Cheshire.*

Goodyer, *see also* Come again, as G.'s pigs did.

Goose and gander and gosling, are three sounds but one thing.

(G 351)

1659 HOWELL *Span. Prov.* 20. **1678** RAY 148.

Goose cannot graze after him, A.

(G 352)

1611 CHAPMAN *May-Day* III. i. Plays (1889) 290 The pasture is so bare with him that a goose cannot graze upon 't. **1670** RAY 178.

Goose so grey in the lake, There is no | that cannot find a gander for her make.[1]

(G 362)

c. **1386** CHAUCER *W. of Bath's Prol.* l. 269 Ne noon so grey goos gooth ther in the lake, As, seïstow, wol been withoute make. **1594** LYLY *Mother B.* III. iv. 13 He loues thee well that would runne after.—Why, *Halfpenie*, there's no goose so gray in the lake, that cannot finde a gander for her make. **1883** J. PAYN *Thicker than W.* ch. 1 She was ... by no means averse to a third experience in matrimony. 'There swam no goose so gray', they were wont to quote. [1 mate.]

Goose that comes to the fox's sermon, It is a blind (silly).

(G 358)

1580 LYLY *Euph. & his Eng.* ii. 99 It is ... a blinde Goose that commeth to the Foxes sermon, *Euphues* is not entangled with *Philautus* charmes. **1583** MELBANCKE Y1ᵛ Woe to the Geese that haue the Fox for their priest. **1584** GREENE *Arbast's Anatomy of Fortune* Wks. Gros. iii. 208 It is ... a blind goose that runneth to the foxe's sermon. **1732** FULLER no. 2881 (silly).

Goose that will eat no oats, Young (Old) is the.

(G 368)

1580 LYLY *Euph. & his Eng.* ii. 133. **1591** *Id.* *Endym.* V. ii. 27 Why shee is so colde, that no fyre can thawe her thoughts.—It is an olde goose, Epi, that will eate no oates. **1732** FULLER no. 6037.

Goose that will not baste herself, It is a sorry.

(G 361)

1670 RAY 218. **1732** FULLER no. 2886.

Goose, He that has a | will get a goose.

1721 KELLY 132 ... A Man that is wealthy, will be sure to get Gifts, whereas he that is poor will remain so.

Goose, geese, *see also* Before St. Chad every g. lays; Calf, the g., bee, world is ruled by; Children to bed and g. to fire; Cook anyone's g.; Deep drinks g.; Eat of the g. that shall graze on your grave; Eats the king's g. (He that); Feather by feather g. is plucked; Find fault with fat g.; Fools wore feathers, (If all) we should seem flock of g.; Fox preaches (When), beware g.; Fox should not be of jury at g.'s trial; Fox to keep the g. (Sets); Good g., do not bite; Good g. that's ay dropping; Goslings lead the g. to grass; Hare's head against the g. giblets (Set the); Kill the g. that lays golden eggs; Know a g. from a gridiron; Macfarlane's g. that liked play better than meat; Man among the g. when gander away; Many women, many words, many g. ...; Meat in the g. eye; Meddles in all things (Who) may shoe g.; Rain raineth and g. winketh (When), little wots gosling ...; Reason pist my g. (Such a); Sauce for the g.; Say bo to a g.; See a woman weep (No more pity) than g. go barefoot; Shoe the g.; Skill in horseflesh to buy g.; Steal a g. and give giblets; —— and stick down feather; Tittle-tattle, give the g. more hay; Valentine's Day will good g. lay; Walsall man's g.; Widecombe folk are picking g.; Winchester g.; Wise as a g.; Women and g. (Where) wants no noise.

Gooseberry, *see* Jump at it like cock at g.

Gordian knot, To cut the (a).

(G 375)

[An intricate knot tied by Gordius, a Phrygian king. Whoever loosed it was to rule Asia, so

Alexander the Great cut it through with his sword. The phrase means to get rid of a difficulty by force or by evading the supposed conditions of solution. ERASM. *Ad.* I. 9. 48.] **1561** T. NORTON *Inst. Chr. Rel* IV. xix. 610 It is like the Gordian; which it is better to breake in sunder, than to labor so much in vndoinge it. **1572** CRADOCKE *Ship of Assured Safety* 140 Thus farre I haue trauelled metely wel in loosing this same knot of Gordius. **1579** FULKE *Heskin's Parl.* 396 Hee had found out a sworde to cutt in sunder this Gordian knot. **1581** GUAZZO ii. 89. **1591** ARIOSTO *Orl. Fur.* Harington XIX. 50. **1599** SHAKES. *Hen. V* I. i. 46 Turn him to any cause of policy, The Gordian knot of it he will vnloose. **1682** SIR T. BROWNE *Chr. Mor.* II, § 13 Death will find some ways to vnty or cut the most Gordian knots of Life. **1841** S. WARREN *Ten Thous. a Year* ch. 3 Suicide . . . is a way . . . of cutting the Gordian knot of the difficulties of life.

Gordon(s), *see* Miscall a G. in raws of Strathlogie; Tender G. that dow not be hanged.

Gorse is out of bloom, When the | kissing's out of fashion. *Cf.* Furze is in bloom, etc.

c. **1225** *Trin. MS. O. 11. 45* (ed. Förster) in *Eng. Stud.* 31. 5 Whanne bloweþ þe brom, þanne wogeþ grom; Whanne bloweþ þe furs, þanne wogeþ þe he wurs. *Lixa uel opilio procus est florente mirica; Rusco florente minus hic gaudebit amica.* **1752** *Poor Robin's Alm.* Aug. Dog-days are in he'll say's the reason why kissing now is out of season: but *Joan* says furz in bloom is still, And she'll be kissed if she's her will. **1847** DENHAM 12 When whins are out of bloom, kissing's out of fashion. Whins are *never* out of bloom. **1860** G. J. WHYTE-MELVILLE *Holmby H.* ch. 2 'When the gorse is out of bloom, young ladies', quoth Sir Giles, 'then is kissing out of fashion!' . . . There is no day in the year when the blossom is off the gorse.

Goshawk beats[1] not at a bunting,[2] A. (G 376)

1616 WITHALS 556. **1639** CLARKE 69. [[1] flies. [2] woodlark.]

Goslings lead the geese to grass (water). [(G 377)

[**1640** OUDIN *Curios. franç.* 398 Les oisons veulent mener paistre leur mère (The goslings would lead their mother out to grass).] **1642** TORRIANO 60 Goslings have the geese to watering. **1732** FULLER no. 1740 (water).

Gosling(s), *see also* Goose, gander, g., three sounds; May-day is . . . gone, thou art a g.; Rain raineth (When the) . . . little wots the g.; Shoe the g.

Gospel, With the | one becomes a heretic. (G 380)

1659 HOWELL *It. Prov.* 6 The Gospel makes Heretiques. **1666** TORRIANO *It. Prov.* 81 no. 24 With the Gospel sometimes a body becomes an Heretick. **1853** TRENCH iii. 56 How curious . . . the confession . . . that the maintenance of the

Roman system and the study of Holy Scripture cannot go together. . . . *With the Gospel one becomes a heretic.*[1] [[1] *Con l'Evangelo si diventa eretico.*]

Gospel, All is (is not) | that comes out of (his) mouth. (A 147)

a. **1250** *Owl & Night.* 1268. For thi seide Alfred swithe wel And his worde was goddspel, That [etc.]. *c.* **1374** CHAUCER *Troilus* Bk. 5 l. 1265 God wot I wende . . . That every word was gospel that ye seyde. *c.* **1386** *Id. Leg. Good Women* l. 326 Al ne is nat gospel that is to yow pleyned. *c.* **1400** *Rom. Rose* l. 7609 Alle is not gospel oute of doute, that men seyn in the towne aboute. *c.* **1532** *Tales* no. 37 All is nat gospell that suche wanderers about saye, nor euerye word to be beleued. **1546** HEYWOOD II. ii. G1 All is not gospell that thou dooest speake. **1579** LYLY *Euph.* i. 214 Philautus thincking . . . all to bee gospell that *Euphues* vttered. **1601** SHAKES. *T.N.* V. i. 280 As a madman's epistles are no gospels, so it skills not much when they are deliver'd. **1611** DAVIES *Prov.* no. 324 (clawbacks speakes). **1670** RAY 178 (is not). **1880** E. A. FREEMAN in *Life & Lett.* (1895) II. 467 I . . . don't take as Gospel either all that you say or all that the *Beamish boys* say.

Gospel, *see also* True (Sooth) as g.

Gossips are frogs, they drink and talk. (G 381)

1640 HERBERT no. 275.

Gossip(s), *see also* Merry when g. meet; Up to one's g.

Got over the devil's back is spent under his belly, What is. (D 316)

1582 S. GOSSON *Plays Confuted* G7ᵛ That which is gotten over the deuils backe, is, spent vnder his belly. **1600** J. BAXTER *A Toile for Two-Legged Foxes* 188 As it hath been gotten ouer the deuills backe, so shall it be spent vnder his dammes belly. **1607** MIDDLETON *Mich. Term* IV. i What's got over the devil's back (that's by knavery), must be spent under his belly (that's by lechery). **1670** RAY 80 What is gotten over the Devils back, is spent under his belly. Malè *parta malè dilabuntur.* What is got by oppression or extortion is many times spent in riot and luxury. **1822** SCOTT *Pirate* ch. 31 You shall not prevail on me to go farther in the devil's road with you; for . . . what is got over his back is spent—you wot how.

Gotham, *see* Wise as a man of G.

Gout, To the | all physicians are blind. (G 386)

1586 WHETSTONE *The English Mirror* 14 The Physitions . . . can not cure as well as giue ease to the Gowt. **1611** COTGRAVE s.v. Goutte A la goutte le medecin ne voit goutte: As they find (by the little helpe they find) they haue it, and take Physick for it. **1659** HOWELL *It. Prov.* 14. **1666** TORRIANO *It. Prov.* 107 no. 36 In the gout the Physician sees no cure.

Gout, *see also* Drink wine and have the g.; Pain like g. (No).

Government stroke, *see* Work with G. s.

Gowk, *see* Breed of the g. (cuckoo), ye have not a rhyme but ane; See the g. in your sleep.

Gown is his that wears it, and the world his that enjoys it, The. (G 387)

1573 SANFORD 107 The gowne is not his that maketh it, but his that enioyeth it. **1640** HERBERT no. 476. **1736** BAILEY *Dict.* s.v. World.

Gown(s), *see also* Best g. that goes up and down house; Fair woman and a slashed g.; Green g.; Lawyers' g. lined with wilfulness of clients; Look to a g. of gold; Maid oft seen and g. oft worn; Puts on a public g. (He that); Tailor must cut three sleeves to woman's g.

Grace is best for the man. (G 392)

1621 ROBINSON 24 (good). **1641** FERGUSSON no. 285. **1670** RAY 270.

Grace of a gray bannock is in the baking of it, The.

1721 KELLY 303 . . . The setting out of an ordinary Thing to best Advantage will make it look well.

Grace of God is (gear) enough, The. (G 393)

1377 LANGLAND *P. Pl.* B. ix. 176 And thanne gete ȝe the grace of god . and good ynogh to lyue with. **1590** SPENSER *F.Q.* I. x. 38 The grace of God he laid up still in store . . . He had enough. **1596** SHAKES. *M.V.* II. ii. 136 The old proverb is very well parted between my master Shylock and you, sir: you have the grace of God, sir, and he hath enough. **1641** FERGUSSON no. 859 (gear).

Grace of God is worth a fair, The. (G 394)

c. **1350** *Douce MS.* 52 no. 41 The grace of God is better þen. iii. feyrys. **1546** HEYWOOD I. xii. E4ᵛ Though euery man maie not syt in the chayre. Yet alway the grace of God is woorth a fayre. **1616** DRAXE no. 901.

Grace of God, *see also* O Master Vier . . . we had no g. of G., no shipwreck upon our coast.

Grace will last, favour (beauty) will blast. (G 395)

c. **1450** *Prouerbis of Wysdom* 28 Owte take grace all thyng shall passe. **1576** PETTIE ii. 38 Beauty and comeliness continue not, whereas courtesy and clemency remain for ever. **1732** FULLER no. 6292 (beauty).

Grace, *see also* Diving g. never slow; Heart of g.; Knowledge is folly except g. guide it; Pride and

g. dwelt never in one place; Seek g. at graceless face; Space cometh g. (In); Whoredom and g. ne'er in one place.

Grafting on a good stock, It is good. (G 397)

1591 H. SMITH *Preparative to Marriage* (1657 ed. 20) They say, it is good grafting vpon a good stock. **1678** RAY 354. **1732** FULLER no. 5082.

Grain by grain, and the hen fills her belly. (G 398)

[**1623**] **1653** MIDDLETON & ROWLEY *Span. Gipsy* II. i Grain picked up after grain makes pullen fat. **1706** STEVENS s.v. Grano (Craw). **1732** FULLER no. 1744.

Grain, One | fills not a sack, but helps his fellow. (G 399)

c. **1542** A. BORDE *Dietary of Health* E.E.T.S. 240 Many cornes maketh a great hepe. **1640** HERBERT no. 226. **1706** STEVENS s.v. Grano.

Grain of salt, To take a thing with a. (G 402)

[mod. L. *cum grano salis* = to accept a statement with a certain amount of reserve.] **1599** RAINOLDS *Overthrow Stage Plays* 79 Thinke you that you had spoken with any graine of salt? **1647** TRAPP *Comm. Rev.* vi. 11 This is to be taken with a grain of salt. **1908** *Athenaeum* 1 Aug. 118/1 Our reasons for not accepting the author's pictures of early Ireland without many grains of salt.

Grains of allowance, He must have his. (G 403)

1678 RAY 248.

Grain(s), *see also* Against the g.; Evil g. (Of) no good seed; Sift him g. by g.

Gramercy, *see* Godamercy.

Grampus, To puff and blow like a.

1826 SCOTT *Woodst.* ch. 34 The bulky Corporal . . . puffed and blew like a grampus that has got into shoal water. **1851** MELVILLE *Moby Dick* ch. 31 This fish, whose loud sonorous breathing, or rather blowing, has furnished a proverb to landsmen.

Grandame, *see* Jack Sprat would teach g.; Teach your g. to grope ducks; ——to sup sour milk.

Grandfather's servants are never good.

1706 STEVENS s.v. Criado. **1732** FULLER no. 1745.

Grandmother, *see* Teach your g.

Grange, *see* Bring an abbey to a g.

Grantham gruel, nine grits and a gallon of water.   (G 472)

c. 1624 *Marvelous Medicine* in *Roxb. Bal.* VIII. 427 Some gruel of Grantham, boyl'd for the nonce.   1662 FULLER Lincs. 153... The Proverb is applicable to those who in their Speeches or Actions multiply what is superfluous.

Grantham steeple stand awry, It is height[1] makes.   (H 396)

1591 *Simon Smell-Knave* CI *Grantam* steeple by the assistance of learned Masons, may perhappes be taught to holde uppe his head manly againe. 1596 LODGE *Wit's Misery* Hunt. Cl. iv. 14 His beard is cut like the spier of Grantham steeple. 1638 BRATHWAIT *Barnabees Jrnl.* iii Thence to Grantham I retiring, Famous for a Spire aspiring.   1647 CLEVELAND *Elegy on Archb. of Canterbury.* 'Tis height makes Grantham steeple stand awry.   1662 FULLER Lincs. 152 This Steeple seems crooked unto the beholders ... though some conceive the slendernesse at such a distance is all the obliquity thereof. Eminency exposeth the uprightest persons to exception; and such who cannot find faults in them, will find faults at them, envying their advancement.   1732 FULLER no. 5086. [[1] 280 ft.]

Granville, *see* Never a G. wanted loyalty.

Grapes are sour, The.   (F 642)

[Said proverbially with allusion to Æsop's fable of 'The Fox and the Grapes'.]   1484 CAXTON *Fables of Æsop* iv. 1 [The fox] sayd these raysyns ben sowre.   1602 SHAKES. *A.W.* II. i. 68 O! will you eat no grapes, my royal fox? Yes, but you will My noble grapes, an if my royal fox Could reach them.   1629 T. ADAMS *Works* 69 The foxe dispraiseth the grapes he cannot reach.   1640 HERBERT no. 130 The fox, when hee cannot reach the grapes, saies, they are not ripe.   1721 KELLY 287 Soure Plumbs quoth the Tod,[1] when he could not climb the Tree.   1857 TROLLOPE *Barch. Tow.* ch. 46 Mr. S. . . . said, as plainly as a look could speak, that the grapes were sour. [[1] fox].

Grapes of thorns or figs of thistles, One cannot gather.   (G 411)

[MATT. vii. 16 Do men gather grapes of thorns, or figs of thistles?]   1537 W. TURNER *Old Learn. and New* B3ᵛ How can a thorne tre brynge forth a grape.   1577 A. GOLDING *Late Murther of Geo. Sanders* ed. L. T. Golding 179 Such as the roots is, such are the braunches, and the twigges of a thorne or bramble can beare no grapes.   1586 J. OVERTON *Jacob's Journey* 67 Where Jacob looked for nothing, but thistles, he gathered figges.   1609 HARWARD 91ᵛ You cann not gather grapes of thornes.   1666 TORRIANO *It. Prov.* 268 no. 14 Thorns produce no figs. 1867 TROLLOPE *Last Chron. Bars.* ch. 23 You do not look to gather grapes from thistles, after you have found that they are thistles.   1878 HARDY *Return of Native* Bk. 4 ch. 6 I have certainly got thistles for figs in a worldly sense.

Grape(s), *see also* Black plum (g.) sweet as white; Devil in every berry of g.; Thorn springs not a fig, (g.), (Of a); Vine brings forth three g.: . . .; Woman that loves to be at window like bunch of g.

Grasp all, lose all.   (M 1295)

c. 1205 LAYAMON *Brut* (Madden) I. 278 For þe mon is muchel sot: Þe nimeð to himseoluen Mare þonne he maȝen walde.   *c.* 1386 CHAUCER *Mel.* B² l. 2405 For the proverbe seith, He that to muche embraceth, distreyneth litel.   1573 SANFORD 52 He that embraceth too much, bindeth nothing.   1611 DAVIES Prov. 278 Who too much gripeth, the lesse he holdeth. *Ibid.* 279 Who too much embraceth still the lesse closeth.   1659 TORRIANO no. 13 Who imbraceth all, nothing grasps.   1790 TRUSLER *Prov. Exempl.* 189 *Grasp all, lose all.* The known fable of the Dog and the Shadow is a true emblem of covetousness.   1901 R. G. MOULTON *Shaks. as Dram. Art.* 46 Proverbs like 'Grasp all, lose all', . . . exactly express moral equilibrium. [Fr. *Qui trop embrasse mal étreint.*]

Grass and hay, we are all mortal.   (G 413)

a. 1451 LYDGATE *Minor Poems* E.E.T.S. ii. 809 That nowe is heye some tyme was grase. 1631 BRAITHWAITE *Whimzies* ed. Halliwell 14, 73 Which makes him conclude in his owne element; Grasse and hay, we are all mortall.   *a.* 1640 J. SMYTH *Lives of the Berkeleys* ii. 96 The grasse that grows, to-morrow's hay, And man that's now, assoone is clay.   1666 TORRIANO *It. Prov.* note 214, 277 Good fellows, or rather Hectors and Ranters who say, Grass and Hay, we are mortal, let's live till we dye.

Grass grows not upon the highway (at the market cross).   (G 415)

1659 HOWELL *Brit. Prov.* 24 In market growes no grass nor grain.   1678 RAY 149.   1721 KELLY 309 There grows no Grass at the Market Cross. An Invective against the Barrenness of Whores.

Grass grows on (under) his (my) heel (foot), No.   (G 421)

[*c.* 1553] 1566–7 UDALL *Royster D.* IV. v. Arb. 67 Ye are as low goer sir . . . Maistresse since I went no grasse hath growne on my hele. 1580 LYLY *Euph. & his Eng.* ii. 17 Neither Grasse will growe, nor Mosse cleaue to thy heeles.   1607 TOPSELL *Four-footed Beasts* 210 The hare . . . leaps away again, and letteth no grasse grow under his feet.   1737 RAMSAY 24 He'll no let Grass grow at his Heels.   1857 TROLLOPE *Barch. Tow.* ch. 15 He was not a man who ever let much grass grow under his feet.

Grass grows, While the | the horse starves.   (G 423)

[Simeon of Chieti 1243: *Timemus ne illius vulgaris proverbii locus adveniat: . . . Dum herba crescit equus moritur, & dum fugans canis mingit fugiens lupus evasit.*]   *c.* 1350 *Douce MS.* 52 no. 20 While þe grasse growes, þe goode hors sterues.   *c.* 1440 CAPGRAVE *Life St. Kath.* II. 253 The gray hors, whyl his gras growyth, May sterue for hunger, þus seyth þe prouerbe.   *a.* 1530 R. *Hill's Commonpl. Bk.* (1858) 140 Whyle the grasse growyth the hors stervyth. 1600–1 SHAKES. *H.* III. ii. 333 Ay, sir, but 'While the grass grows'—the proverb is something musty.   1614 CAMDEN 314.   1697 W. POPE *Seth* [Ward] 6 The Saying is, The Horse does

not die, before the Grass is grown. **1820** GALT
Ayrshire Leg. ch. 10 I understand, sir, . . . that
you have a notion of Miss Bell Tod, but that
until ye get a kirk there can be no marriage.
But the auld horse may die waiting for the new
grass. **1884** J. PAYN *Canon's Ward* ch. 50
What's to become of me . . . while our schemes
are ripening? While the grass grows the steed
starves. **1896** FROUDE *Counc. of Trent* ii. 27
Thinkers are a minority in this world. Thought
works slowly, and while the grass grows the
steed starves.

Grass look green (grow) in Janiveer, If | 'twill look (grow) the worser all the year. (G 417)

1670 RAY 40 If the grass grow in Janiveer, It
grows the worse for't all the year. **1732**
FULLER no. 6147.

Grass (Summer) on the top of the oak tree, Look for. (G 424)

1670 RAY 44 . . . Because the grass seldom springs
well before the oak begins to put forth. **1882**
CHAMBERLAIN 38 Look for summer on the top of
an oak tree.

Grass, *see also* Calves are gone down to g.; Cut
the g. under feet; Easter day, (If it rains on),
There shall be good g. but very bad hay; Fears
every g. (He that); Going to g. with teeth
upwards; Green as g.; Higher the hill, lower the
g.; March g. never did good; Pluck the g. to
know the wind; St. Matthias both leaf and g.;
Snake in g.; Turk's horse doth tread (Where), g.
never grows.

Grateful man, To a | give money when he asks. (M 394)

1622 HOWELL *Lett.* I. ii. 9, I 107 Sir, Thanks for
one Courtesy is a good Usher to bring on
another. **1640** HERBERT no. 115. **1706** STEVENS
s.v. Agradecido To a grateful Man more than is
ask'd.

Grave, In the | dust and bones jostle not for the wall.

1732 FULLER no. 2826.

Grave(s) (*noun*), *see also* Better go by your
enemy's g. than his gate; Between the cradle and
g.; Dig one's g. with one's teeth; Eat of the
goose that shall graze on your g.; Edge of his
g., (He is upon the); Lie all alike in our g.;
More thy years nearer thy g.; One foot in g. (To
have); Parsley fried will bring woman to g.;
Sleeping enough in g. (There will be); Sundial in
g. (What good); Turn in his g.; Walking over my
g.; White man's g.

Gravel pit, *see* Live in a g. p.

Gravest fish is an oyster; the gravest bird's an owl; the gravest beast's an ass; and the gravest man's a fool, The.

1737 RAMSAY III. 194.

Gray (*adj.*), *see* Grey.

Gray's Inn for walks, Lincoln's Inn for a wall, the Inner Temple for a garden, and the Middle for a hall. *Cf.* Inner Temple rich, etc. (G 432)

[The four great Inns of Court, in London, are
legal societies having the exclusive right of
calling persons to the English Bar.] **1659**
HOWELL *Eng. Prov.* 21b.

Gray's Inn, *see also* Inner Temple.

Graze on the plain, To. (P 380)

[= to be turned out of doors.] **1546** HEYWOOD
II. x. L3[v] He turnde hir out at durs, to grase on
the playne. **1605** CHAPMAN, JONSON, MARSTON,
Eastw. Ho IV. ii. 26 Or else go graze o' the
common. **1611** COTGRAVE s.v. Sac and Soleil
He is turned out to grazing. **1869** HAZLITT A 18.

Graze, *see also* Eat of the goose that shall g. on
your grave; Goose cannot g. after him.

Grease a man in the fist (hand), To. (M 397)

a. **1529** SKELTON *Magnyf.* 437–8 Wyth golde and
grotes they grese my hande, In stede of ryght
that wronge may stande. **1583** STUBBES *Anat.
Abus.* Furnivall I. 117 If you have argent . . . to
grease them in the fist withall, than your sute
shall want no furtherance. **1604** 27 Nov.
Guildhall Repertory xxvi, Pt. 2 474–5b The
sayd Wright sayd the matter cold neuer haue
bene soe carryed against the goldsmithes if my
Lord Maior had not been greased in the hand,
rubbing the palme of one hande with the other.
1670 RAY 178 . . . That is to put money in his
hand, to fee or bribe him. **1690** D'URFEY
Collin's Walk iii. 93 Where many a Client
Verdict miss'd, For want of greazing in the fist.

Grease a fat sow in the tail, To. *Cf.* Bastes the fat hog. (s 682)

c. **1549** HEYWOOD I. xi. E1 What should we
(quoth I) grease the fat sow in thars. **1583**
MELBANCKE F1[v] Fulsum huswiues greasing the
fatt sowe in the tayle to make better bacon.
1611 DAVIES no. 18 (All men do). *a.* **1628**
CARMICHAELL no. 475. Everie man flammes[1] the
fat sowis erss. **1721** KELLY 93 . . . They will be
sure to get most Gifts that least want them.
1786 WOLCOT (P. Pindar) *Lousiad* iii. Wks.
(1816) I. 199 To greaze a vat ould pig in the tail.
[[1] bastes.]

Grease one's boots, To.

1813 RAY 198 To grease one's boots. *Ungere gli
stavile [stivali]. Ital.* To cajole or flatter.

Grease, *see also* Fry in one's own g.; Knave's g.

Greases his wheels helps his oxen, He who. (W 288)

1666 TORRIANO *It. Prov.* 241 no. 2 Grease the
wheel, if thou intend the cart shall go. **1732**
FULLER no. 2384.

Great and the little have need one of another, The.

1732 FULLER no. 4564.

Great as beggars, As.

1639 Letter of EDMUND VERNEY, *Verney Memoirs* (1892) i. 170 My Colonel and I are as great as two beggers. **1682** BUNYAN *Holy War* 260 When Cerberus and Mr. Profane met, they were presently as great as beggers.

Great as the devil and the Earl of Kent,[1] As.

a. **1704** T. BROWN Wks. (1760) II. 194 We became as great friends as the Devil and the Earl of Kent. **1738** SWIFT *Dial.* III. E.L. 320. [1 Earl Godwin, *d.* 1053.]

Great birth is a very poor dish at table.

1707 MAPLETOFT 37.

Great boast and small roast (makes unsavoury mouths).   (B 488)

c. **1532** R. COPLAND *Spyttel House* l. 978 Grete boost and small roost. **1546** HEYWOOD I. xi. D4 I thanke you (quoth I) but great bost and small roste, Maketh vnsauery mouthes, where euer men oste. *a.* **1591** HY. SMITH *Poor Man's Tears* 1657 ed. 512 Every one is good to the poor, . . . but they will give them nought but words. Then I say, great boast and small roast makes unsavoury mouthes. **1614** CAMDEN 306. **1648** HERRICK *Hesper.* 221 *Great Boast, Small Roast* Wks. (1893) I. 115 Of flanks and chines of beef doth Gorrel boast He has at home; but who tastes boiled or roast? **1670** RAY 64 . . . Grands vanteurs petits faiseurs. *Gall.* **1907** *Spectator* 16 Nov. 766 As a matter of fact boasting is joined to meagre performance. . . . 'Much boast, small roast', is both English and Italian.

Great bodies move slowly.   (B 503)

1612–15 BP. HALL *Contempl.* XXI. ii (1825) II. 102 Great bodies must have slow motions: as Jerusalem, so the church of God, whose type it was, must be finished by leisure. **1721** KELLY 124 . . . Spoken of the Deliberations of Parliaments, and other great Assemblies; or in Jest to them that go slowly on in their Business.

Great book is a great evil, A.   (B 530)

[CALLIM. Μέγα βιβλίον μέγα κακόν.] **1621** BURTON *Anat. Mel.* Democ. to Rdr. (1651) 7 Oftentimes it falls out (which Callimachus taxed of old) a great book is a great mischief. **1909** *Brit. Wkly.* 8 Apr. 13 It may be . . . said in reference to this unhappy production that a great book is indeed a great evil.

Great braggers, little doers.   (B 591)

1539 TAVERNER 49[v] Great braggers commonly be least fyghters. **1597** DELONEY *Gentle Craft* II. vi. **1611** COTGRAVE s.v. Langue. Those that promise most performe least. **1623** W. PAINTER *Chaucer New Painted* C3 Drauling Knaues will euen as seldome fight. **1732** FULLER no. 1753.

Great businesses turn on a little pin. *Cf.* Great engines.   (B 757)

1640 HERBERT no. 720.

Great city, a great solitude, A.   (C 398)

[Gk. Μεγάλη πόλις μεγάλη ἐρημία. ERASM. *Magna civitas magna solitudo.*] *c.* **1594** BACON *Promus* no. 268 Magna civitas, magna solitudo. **1625** BACON *Ess., Friendship* Arb. 165 The Latin adage meeteth with it a little; Magna ciuitas, magna solitudo; because in a great town, friends are scattered. **1732** FULLER no. 191. **1845** A. SMITH *Scatterg. Fam.* ch. 15 There is no solitude so terrible and dreary as that felt in the very heart of a vast, unsympathizing city.

Great cry and little wool.   (C 871)

c. **1475** FORTESCUE *Govt. of Eng.* (Plummer) X. 132 His hyghnes shall haue þeroff, but as hadd þe man þat sherid is hogge, much crye and litil woll. **1579** GOSSON *Sch. Abuse* Arb. 28 As one said at the shearing of hogs, great cry and little wool, much adoe and smal help. **1659** HOWELL *Eng. Prov.* 13b (quoth the Devil when he sheard the hogg). **1663** BUTLER *Hudibras* I. i. 852 Or shear swine, all cry and no wool. **1678** RAY 237 . . . (as the fellow said when he shear'd his hogs). Assai romor & poca lana. *Ital.* **1711** ADDISON *Spect.* no. 251 Wks. (1902) III. 150 Those . . . make the most noise who have least to sell, . . . to whom I cannot but apply that old proverb of 'Much cry, but little wool'. **1721** KELLY 165 Humph, quoth the Dee'l, when he clip'd the Sow, A great Cry, and little Woo. Spoken of great Pretences, and small Performances. **1804** WOLCOT (P. Pindar) *Lyric Odes* iii Exclaim, 'Great *cry*, and little wool!' As Satan holla'd, when he shaved the pig. **1827** SCOTT *Journ.* 24 Feb. As to the collection, it was much cry and little woo', as the deil said when he shore the sow. **1891** J. L. KIPLING *Beast & Man* 93 For 'great cry and little wool' rustics say, 'The goat bleated all night and produced only one kid',—two being the usual number.

Great doings at Gregory's; heat the oven twice for a custard.   (D 550)

1678 RAY 72. **1732** FULLER no. 1755.

Great engines turn on small pivots. *Cf.* Great businesses.

1658 *Comes Facundus* 183 Great engines turn on little pins.

Great fish eat up the small, The. (F 311)

c. **1410** *Pride of Life (Non-Cycle Mystery Plays,* ed. O. Waterhouse 100). *c.* **1440** *Castle of Perseverance* l. 2821 Þe grete fyschys ete þe smale. **1509** BARCLAY *Ship of Fools* I. 101 The wolfe etis the shepe, the great fysshe the small. **1608** SHAKES. *P.* II. i. 27 Master, I marvel how the fishes live in the sea.—Why, as men do a-land; the great ones eat up the little ones. **1616** DRAXE no. 1511.

Great fortune brings with it great misfortune.   (F 610)

1642 TORRIANO 6.   **1651** HERBERT no. 1144.
1659 N. R. 37.

Great gain makes work easy.

1721 KELLY 119 (gains).   **1732** FULLER no. 1756.

Great gifts are from great men. (G 111)

1639 CLARKE 187.   **1670** RAY 98.

Great honours are great burdens.

(H 582)

1547 BALDWIN *Treatise Moral Philosophy* P1ᵛ
He that desyreth great charges, desyreth great
troubles.   **1576** PETTIE i. 101 In greatest charge
are greatest cares.   **1611** JONSON *Catiline* III. i
Great honors are great burdens.   **1670** FLECK-
NOE *Epigrams* 53.

Great journey to the world's end, It is a.
(J 78)

1639 CLARKE 3.   **1670** RAY 158.

Great loss but¹ some small profit, No.
(L 463)

c. **1641** FERGUSSON MS. no. 1408.   **1670** RAY 117.
[¹ without.]

**Great man and a great river are often
ill neighbours, A.**

1657 E. LEIGH *Select Observations* 276 A great
Lord, A great Bell, A great River are three ill
Neighbours.   **1732** FULLER no. 198.   **1813** RAY
117 A great lord is a bad neighbour.

**Great memory without learning, A man
of a | has a rock¹ and a spindle, and no
stuff to spin.**   (M 292)

1599 MINSHEU *Span. Gram.* 81.   **1651** HERBERT
no. 1085 (no staffe). [¹ distaff.]

Great men have great faults.   (M 524)

1616 DRAXE no. 1383.   **1639** CLARKE 160 Great
mens faults are never small.

**Great men would have care of little
ones, If | both would last long.** (M 532)

1640 HERBERT no. 697.

Great men's favours are uncertain.

1584 WITHALS I7ᵛ The fauoure of Princes,
Peeres and greate men, hath no certaine state
but flits now and then.   **1612** A. STAFFORD
Meditations 104 A great mans fauor is hardly
got, & easily lost.   **1736** BAILEY *Dict.* s.v.
Favour.

Great men's sons seldom do well.

(M 611)

[**1508** Eras. *Adagia* Chil. i, cent. vi, no. 32.]
1539 TAVERNER 58 Heroum filii noxæ. The

chyldren of most renowned and noble personages
be for most part destructious to the common
wealth.   **1621** BURTON *Anat. Mel.* III. ii. VI. iii
(1651) 568 Think but of that old proverb,
Ἡρώων τέκνα πήματα, Heroum filii noxæ, great
men's sons seldome do well.   **1642** TORRIANO 61
Great men, either they have no children, or they
are none of the wisest . . . alluding to that of
Franciscus Petrarcha, in his book, De remediis
utriusque fortunæ.

Great men (man), *see also* Great gifts are from
g. m.; Keep yourself from anger of g. m.;
Serve a g. m. you will know sorrow.

**Great nose, He that has a | thinks
everybody is speaking of it.**

1721 KELLY 127 (mickle) . . . People that are
sensible of their Guilt, are always full of
Suspicion.   **1826** SCOTT *Diary* 24 Jan. I went to
the Court for the first time to-day, and, like the
man with the large nose, thought everybody was
thinking of me and my mishap.

**Great ones if there were no little ones,
There would be no.**   (O 63)

c. **1513** SIR T. MORE *Rich. III* 1821 ed. 37 Sometime withoute smal thinges greatter cannot
stande.   **1640** HERBERT no. 292.   **1732** FULLER
no. 4868.

**Great pain and little gain will make a
man soon weary.**   (P 16)

15 c. Early Eng. Carols (Greene) 393 Small
geynes and much payne.   *a.* **1548** HALL *Chron.*
(1809 ed., 236) Much payne and no gayn.   **1616**
DRAXE no. 2302.   **1639** CLARKE 154.

Great pains quickly find ease.   (P 21)

1640 HERBERT no. 534.

**Great pedigrees, In | there are gover-
nors and chandlers.**   (P 178)

1640 HERBERT no. 222.

Great put the little on the hook, The.
(G 434)

1640 HERBERT no. 945.

**Great river, In a | great fish are found:
but take heed lest you be drowned.**
(R 138)

1640 HERBERT no. 167.

Great ship asks deep waters, A.

(S 346)

1640 HERBERT no. 449.   **1732** FULLER no. 203
(must have deep water).

Great shoe fits not a little foot, A.

(S 366)

1548 COOPER s.v. Herculis Cothurnos: Herculis
cothurnos, was vsed for a prouerbe, wherein a
thynge of lyttelle importaunce was set foorthe

with great eloquence or other thynge, solemne, more apte for a greatter mattier. **1579** GOSSON *School of Abuse* Arb. 21 Draw . . . Hercules shoes on a childes feete. **1581** GUAZZO i. 133 Agesilaus finding fault [with over-emphasis of small matters] saide hee liked not of that Shoomaker, who made a great shoo for a little foote. **1596** SHAKES. *K.J.* II. i. 143 It [a lion's robe] lies as sightly on the back of him As great Alcides' shoes upon an ass. **1616** DRAXE no. 21. **1639** CLARKE 138.

Great strokes make not sweet music.

(S 940)

1580 LYLY *Euph. & his Eng.* ii. 224 Instruments sound sweetest when they be touched softest. **1592** DELAMOTHE 39 One can not with great blowes, make sweete Musicke. **1611** COTGRAVE s.v. Vielle (Not great, but apt, stroakes). **1640** HERBERT no. 26. **1670** RAY 12 The greatest strokes make not the best musick.

Great thieves hang the little ones, The.

(T 119)

1539 TAVERNER I *Garden* E7ᵛ When Diogenes sawe the officers lede one, taken for stelynge a cuppe, out of the treasorie: Lo, quoth he, the great theues leade the lyttell thefe. **1597** SHAKES. *I Hen. IV* I. ii. 60 Do not thou, when thou art king, hang a thief.—No; . . . Thou shalt have the hanging of the thieves. **1607** H. ESTIENNE *World of Wonders* tr. R.C. 81 How is it . . . (according to the old saying) that the greater [thieves] hang the lesse? *Ibid.* 81 Great theeues rob the lesse, as great fishes deuoure the yong frie. *c.* **1611** JONSON *Catiline* III. 506 Th'are petty crimes are punish'd, great rewarded. **1616** DRAXE no. 2116 The greater thiefe leadeth the lesser to the gallows. **1639** CLARKE 172 Little thieves are hang'd, but great ones escape. **1660** SECKER *Nonsuch Prof.* iii (1891) 276 It was formerly the complaint of a certain person, 'That the greatest thieves did execution upon the least'. **1692** L'ESTRANGE *Aesop's Fab.* ccccxcviii (1738) 545 Thus goes the world, the little thieves hang for't, while the great ones sit upon the bench.

Great trees are good for nothing but shade.

(T 505)

1640 HERBERT no. 546.   **1642** TORRIANO 11.

Great trees keep down (under) the little ones.

(T 507)

1642 FULLER *H. & P. State* IV. iii (1841) 240 Most of the clergy (more pitying his profession than person) were glad, that the felling of this oak would cause the growth of much underwood. **1732** FULLER no. 1769 (under).

Great way (voyage) to the bottom of the sea, It is a.

(W 146)

1616 WITHALS (1634, 43) This is drawne from the bottom of the sea. **1639** CLARKE 4. **1732** FULLER no. 1850 He goes a great Voyage, that goes to the Bottom of the Sea.

Great weights hang on small wires.

(W 255)

1639 CLARKE 109.   **1642** FULLER *H. & P. State* IV. viii (1841) 260 The counsel for the king, hanging as much weight on the smallest wire as it would hold, aggravated each particular. **1732** FULLER no. 1773 (Great weight may hang). **1898** ALEX. WHYTE *Bib. Char., Gid. to Abs.* 34 They have suspended excellent New Testament sermons on these adapted texts; hanging great weights on small wires.

Great winds blow upon high hills.

(W 450)

c. **1200** *Ancrene Riwle* (Morton) 178 Euer so the hul is more and herre, so the wind is more theron. **1563** CHURCHYARD *Mirr. Mag.*, l. 253 The wynde is great vpon the hyghest hilles, The quiete life is in the dale belowe. **1670** RAY 107 (Huge winds).

Great wits have short memories.

(W 577)

[*Cf.* **1584** WITHALS E7ᵛ A dull wit doth hold that fast which is put into it.] **1592** NASHE *Strange News* i. 304 The sharpest wits, I perceiue, haue none of the best memories. **1600** I *Ret. Parnassus* III. 1013 Its verie true, good wittes haue badd memories. **1668** DRYDEN *Sir M. Mar-all* IV. i Good wits, you know, have bad memories. *a.* **1763** SHENSTONE *Detached Thoughts on Writing and Books* 'Great wits have short memories' is a proverb; it undoubtedly has some foundation.

Great would have none great, and the little all little, The.

(G 435)

1640 HERBERT no. 946.

Great, *see also* Barkers are no biters (G.); Beginnings come g. things, (From small); Dainties of g. are tears of poor; Flood . . . (There is not so g. a); God make me g. and big, for white and red I can make myself; Grooms and householders are alike g. (Where) disastrous for houses; Little cannot be g. unless devour many; Promises and small performances, (G.); Spark a g. fire, (Of a small); Wise and g. (He that is truly) lives too early. *See also under significant words following* 'Great'.

Greater embraces (includes, hides) the less, The.

(G 437)

1581 C. MERBURY *Brief Discourse* H. Unton to Reader *4ᵛ I haue burst out into these few rude lines, not to th'Ende I am able to purchasse praise vnto th'Author, (Because the lesse can not authorize the greater) but that I may gaine commendation to my selfe. **1593–4** SHAKES. *Luc.* l. 663 The lesser thing should not the greater hide. **1594** *Id. T.G.V.* III. i. 349 'Item. She hath more hair than wit'—. . . for the greater hides the less. *c.* **1594** BACON no. 132 Omne majus continet in se minus. **1605** JONSON *Sejanus* III. 104 The greater doth embrace the lesse. **1633** DU BARTAS tr. Sylvester *Weeks* I. iii. 484 And sith (in reason) that which is included, Must be less than that which doth include it.

Greater the man the greater the crime, The. (M 153)

[1592] 1596 *Edw. III* II. i. 434 The greater man, the greater is the thing, Be it good or bad, that he shall vndertake. **1600** *Look about You* L I[v] The greater man the greater his transgression. **1732** FULLER no. 4566.

Greater the sinner, the greater the saint, The.

1772 R. GRAVES *Spiritual Quix.* VII. It was a maxim with Mr. Whitfield . . . *Ibid.* VIII. 17 The blacker the sinner, the brighter the saint. **1856** E. HINCHCLIFFE *Barthomley* 29 (the old proverb).

Greater the truth, The | the greater the libel.

c. **1787** BURNS *Lines etc.* Wks. (Globe) 150 Dost not know that old Mansfield, who writes like the Bible, Says the more 'tis a truth, sir, the more 'tis a libel? **1828** LYTTON *Pelham* ch. 25. **1882** S. A. BENT *Fam. Short Say.* (ed. 8) 371 . . . A maxim of the law in vogue . . . while Mansfield[1] presided over the King's Bench. . . . The maxim is said to have originated in the Star Chamber. [[1] 1705–93.]

Greatest hate springs from the greatest love, The. (H 210)

1579 LYLY *Euph.* i. 197 Ye deepest loue tourneth to the deadliest hate. **1581** GUAZZO ii. 85 Knowe you not that where is great love, from thence proceedeth great hate? **1732** FULLER no. 4573.

Greatest, *see also under significant words following.*

Greatness, *see* Goodness is not tied to g.; North for g.

Greed, *see* Need makes g.

Greedy eating horse. To a | a short halter. (H 696)

1599 MINSHEU *Span. Gram.* 83. **1651** HERBERT no. 1106.

Greedy eye to have a leal[1] heart, It is hard for a.

1721 KELLY 209 . . . Because such act against the bent of their Inclinations. [[1] loyal, honest.]

Greedy folks have long arms.

1721 KELLY 122 . . . People will make strange shifts to get what they have a Desire for.

Greedy is the good-less.

c. **1300** *Provs. of Hending* 15 Greedy is the godles.

Greedy man and the gileynour[1] are soon agreed, The.

1721 KELLY 307 . . . The covetous Man will be glad of a good Offer, and the Cheat will offer well, designing never to pay. [[1] cheat.]

Greedy, *see also* Kirk is aye g.

Greek Calends, At (On) the. *Cf.* Latter Lammas. (G 441)

[L. *Ad Graecas kalendas,* humorous for 'never', since the Greeks used no calends in their reckoning of time. Due to the Emperor Augustus; SUET. *Div. Aug.* 60.] **1540** PALSGRAVE *Acolastus* 142 At the Grekish calendes . . . or a daye after domes day. *a.* **1649** DRUMM. OF HAWTH. *Consid. Parlt.* Wks. (1711) 185 That gold, plate, and all silver, given . . . in these late troubles, shall be paid at the Greek Kalends. **1860** PEACOCK *Gryll Grange* ch. 7 That question is adjourned to the Greek kalends.

Greek meets Greek, When | then comes the tug of war. (G 440)

[The now usual perversion of Lee's line.] **1677** LEE *Rival Qu.* IV. 240 When Greeks joyn'd Greeks, then was the tug of War. **1824** SCOTT *St. Ronans* ch. 18 Mowbray had . . . some reason to admit that, When Greek meets Greek, then comes the tug of war. The light skirmishing betwixt the parties was ended, and the serious battle commenced. **1863** C. READE *Hard Cash* ch. 35 Meantime, . . . Greek was meeting Greek only a few yards off. Mr. Hardie was being undermined by a man of his own calibre.

Greek to me (him), It is (was). (G 439)

c. **1566** CURIO *Pasquin in a Trance* tr. W.P. 63[v] He spake Greeke, I vnderstoode him not well. **1573** GASCOIGNE *Hundreth Sundry Flowers* 'Adventures passed by Master F.I.' i. 397 Gentlewoman (quod he) you speake Greeke, the which I haue nowe forgotten. **1575** *Id. Supposes* I. i This gear is Greek to me. [*c.* **1590**] **1594** LODGE & GREENE *Looking-Glass* I. iii. 304 Thou speakest Hebrew to him when thou talkest to him of conscience. *a.* **1599** *George a Greene* sc. vii. l. 632 (Hebrue). **1599** SHAKES. *J.C.* I. ii. 282–7 Did Cicero say anything?—Ay, he spoke Greek . . . but, for mine own part, it was Greek to me. **1688** SHADWELL *Squire of Als.* iv. i All this fine language had been heathen Greek to me. **1705** STRYPE *Life Sir J. Cheke[1]* (1821) i, § 2. 14 This language was· little known or understood hitherto in this realm. And if any saw a piece of Greek they used to say, *Graecum est; non potest legi,* i.e. 'It is Greek, it cannot be read'. **1840** DICKENS *Barn. Rudge* ch. 1 I am a stranger, and this is Greek to me. [[1] Prof. of Greek, Cambridge, 1540–51.]

Greek(s), *see also* Fear the G.; Merry G.; Tale if it were told in G., (A good).

Green as a leek, As. (L 176)

c. **1370** CHAUCER *Romaunt of the Rose* l. 212 Al-so grene as ony leek. **1573** GASCOIGNE *Dan B. of Bath* i. 130 Pale and greene as leekes. **1585** HIGGINS *Nomenclator* I. 180 A colour as greene as a leeke. **1595** SHAKES. *M.N.D.* V. i. 326 His eyes were green as leeks.

Green as grass, As. (G 412)

1387 TREVISA tr. Higden i. 123 (Rolls ser.) þe þridde [third] þre monþes grene as gras. **1533–4**

UDALL *Flowers* 50. **1552** HULOET O4ᵛ As freshe as grasse. *Ibid.* O5ᵛ (Grene). **1573** GASCOIGNE i. 150. **1678** RAY 285.

Green cheese, You see no | but your teeth must water. (c 275)

1546 HEYWOOD II. ix. L2ᵛ Haue ye'not herde tell all couet all leese: Ah syr, I se, ye maie see no greene chese But your teeth muste water. **1639** CLARKE 39 He sees no green cheese but his mouth waters after it.

Green gown, To give a woman a.

[= to roll her in sport on the grass; hence euphemistically, see quot. 1825–80.] *a.* **1586** SIDNEY *Arcadia* I (1598) 84 Then some greene gownes are by the lasses worne In chastest plaies. *a.* **1593** PEELE *Edw. I* I. ii. **1599** GREENE *Geo. a Greene* Wks. Gros. ₍xiv. 140 Madge pointed to meet me in your wheate-close. . . . And first I saluted her with a greene gowne and after fell as hard a-wooing as if the Priest had been at our backs, to haue married vs. **1699** B. E. *Dict. Cant. Crew, Green Gown,* a throwing of young lasses on the grass and kissing them. **1825–80** JAMIESON *Green Gown,* the supposed badge of the loss of virginity, Roxb.

Green¹ in my eye? Do you see any.

1851 MAYHEW *Lond. Labour* II. 41 'I'm not a tailor, but I understands about clothes, and I believe that no person ever saw anything green in my eye.' **1894** BLACKMORE *Perlycross* ch. 21 Serjeant, do you see any green in my eye? [¹ gullibility.]

Green winter (Yule) makes a fat churchyard (kirkyard), A. *Cf.* Green Yule and a white Pasch. (w 508)

1635 SWAN *Spec. Mundi* V. vi. 160 (They also say, that a hot Christmas makes). **1642** FULLER *Holy State* III. xix. 202 A green Christmas is neither handsome nor healthfull. **1659** N. R. 11 A hot Winter makes a full Churchyard. **1670** RAY 42 . . . This Proverb was sufficiently confuted *anno* 1667, in which the winter was very mild; and yet no mortality . . . ensued the Summer or Autumn following. **1721** KELLY 30 (yule) . . . This, and a great many proverbial Observations upon the Seasons of the Year, are groundless. **1816** SCOTT *Antiq.* ch. 23 It cam a green Yule, and the folk died thick and fast—for ye ken a green Yule makes a fat kirkyard. **1857** G. ELIOT *Scenes of Clerical Life* 'Amos Barton' ch. 6 (Yule).

Green wood makes a hot fire. (w 735)

1477 RIVERS *Dictes* (1877) 65 The grene wode is hotter than the other whan it is wel kyndeled. **1553** R. WILSON *Arte of Rhet.* (1909) 84 In greene wood we may see, that where as the fuell is not most apt for burning, yet the fire lasteth longer. **1640** HERBERT no. 862.

Green wound is soon healed, A. (w 927)

c. **1532** SIR ADRIAN FORTESCUE no. 43 A wound when it is grene, is best to be healid. **1566** P. BEVERLEY *Ariodante and Jenevra* ed. Prouty 81

The pacient, when the wound is greene, a salve doth soonest finde. **1579** LYLY *Euph.* i. 249 Searche the wounde while it is greene; too late commeth the salue when the sore festereth. **1590–1** SHAKES. *2 Hen. VI* III. i. 287 Stop the rage betime, Before the wound do grow uncurable; For, being green, there is great hope of help. **1593** *Tell Truth's New Years Gift* New Sh. S. 34 It is easy to cure a greene wound. **1670** RAY 31.

Green Yule and a white Pasch¹ make a fat churchyard, A. *Cf.* Green winter.

1931 *Times* 8 Jan. 8/3 If fully stated, 'A green Yule and a white Pasch make a fat churchyard', there is no fallacy, as a mild winter followed by a severe spring is so often fatal to old and delicate people. [¹ Easter.]

Green, *see also* Do these things in a g. tree, (If they); Given them g. stockings, (She has); Grey hairs are nourished with g. thoughts; Hills are g. far away; Grey and g. worst medley; Hoar head and a g. tail; Lincoln g.; Marry in green . . . sorrow; Moon is made of g. cheese; Strew g. rushes for stranger; Thraw the wand while g.; Truth is always g.; Wigs on g.; Yellow's forsaken and g.'s foresworn.

Greenland, *see* Northerly wind and blubber.

Greenock, *see* Glasgow people, G. folk.

Greet(s) (i.e. weep), *see* Laugh at leisure, you may g. ere night; No play where one g. and another laughs; Sair dung bairn that dare not g.; See a woman g. (No more pity) than goose go barefoot.

Gregory, *see* Great doings at G.'s.

Grenville, *see* Charles's Wain.

Grey (*proper name*), *see* John G.'s bird.

Grey and green make the worst medley. *Cf.* Hoar head and green tail. (G 430)

c. **1386** CHAUCER *Reeve's Prol.* l. 3877 For in oure wyl ther stiketh evere a nayl, To have an hoor heed and a grene tayl, As hath a leek. **1597–8** BP. HALL *Satires* IV. iv The maidens mock, and call him withered leek, That with a green tail hath an hoary head. **1678** RAY 149 . . . Turpe senex miles, turpe senilis amor. Ovid.

Grey as a badger, As.

1707 THOS. BROWN *Letters from the Dead to the Living,* 'Lilly to Cooley' (*Amusements,* ed. A. L. Hayward, 1927, 413). **1720** SWIFT Wks. (Scott) xiv. 134 Though she lives till she's grey as a badger all over.

Grey as glass, As.

c. **1390** CHAUCER *C. T. Prol.* l. 152 Hir eyen greye as glas. *c.* **1560** L. WAGER *Mary Magdalene* D3ᵛ. [1590] **1600** *Cobbler of Canterbury* 7. **1592** SHAKES. *T.G.V.* IV. iv. 188 Her eyes are grey as glass; and so are mine.

Grey before he is good, He is. (G 431)

1678 RAY 249. **1706** STEVENS s.v. Cabeça.

Grey (White) hairs are death's blossoms. (H 31)

c. **1386** CHAUCER *Reeve's Prol.* l. 3869 This whyte top wryteth myne olde yeres. **1588** GREENE *Pandosto* Prose Wks. (1881–3) IV. 271 Thou seest my white hayres are blossoms for the grave. **1678** RAY 149.

Grey hairs are nourished with green thoughts.

1582 WHETSTONE *Heptameron* S4ᵛ To proue an olde mans sufficiencie, there is a common Prouerbe: Gray haires are nourished, with greene thoughts.

Grey head is often placed on green shoulders, A.

1766 J. WESLEY *Standard Lett.* v. 10 Grey heads stand upon green shoulders. **1814** *Intrigues of a Day* III. iii As the proverb says, a grey head is often placed on green shoulders.

Grey mare is the better horse, The.
(M 647)

[= the wife rules the husband.] **1546** HEYWOOD II. iv. G4. *c.* **1645** HOWELL *Lett.* I. iv. ix To suffer the Gray-mare sometimes to be the better Horse. **1726** *Adv. Capt. R. Boyle* 2 She began to tyrannize over my master, . . . and soon prov'd, as the Saying is, The grey Mare to be the better Horse. **1847** TENNYSON *Princ.* v. 441 The gray mare Is ill to live with, when her whinny shrills From tile to scullery.

Grey (*adj.*), *see also* Care brings g. hair; Evening red and morning g.; Fox may grow g.; Horns and g. hair do not come by years.

Greyhound, *see* Gentleman's g. and a salt box; Head like a snake. [The shape of a good g.]

Grice(s), *see* Barren sow was never good to pigs (g.); Lay the head of sow to tail of g.

Grief (sorrow) drives out the less, The greater. (G 446)

[ERASM. *Similia* 572c Major dolor obscurat minorem.] **1593–4** SHAKES. *Luc.* l. 1821 Why, Collatine, is woe the cure for woe? Do wounds help wounds, or grief help grievous deeds? *c.* **1595** SHAKES. *R.J.* I. ii. 47 One pain is less'ned by another's anguish. **1598** MERES *Pall. Tamia* 2Rᵛ The greater sorrow obscureth the lesser. **1604** SHAKES. *O.* I. iii. 55 For my particular grief Is of so floodgate and o'erbearing nature That it engluts and swallows other sorrows, And it is still itself. **1606–7** *Id. A.C.* II. i. 42 I know not, Menas, How lesser enmities may give way to greater. **1631** MABBE *Celestina* XXI. 280 One griefe drives out another; and sorrow expelleth sorrow.

Grief is lessened when imparted to others. (G 447)

1540 PALSGRAVE *Acolastus* 136 It greueth men lesse, whan they haue other in peyne or trouble with them. **1559** SENECA *Troas* tr. Jasper Heywood III. ii D8ᵛ Oft tymes the weping of the eyes, the inward grief out weares. **1561** T. BECON *Sick Man's Salve* P.S. 155 Inward trouble is the greatest grief in the world. Declare . . . what it is; and we will do the best we can to quiet your mind. **1566** P. BEVERLEY *Ariodanto and Jenevra* ed. Prouty 110 By disclosing of his griefe, he findes to ease his smart. [c. **1587**] **1592** KYD *Span. Trag.* I. iii. 32 Complaining makes my greefe seeme lesse. [**1592**] **1597** SHAKES. *Rich. III* IV. iv. 126 Why should calamity be full of words? . . . —Let them have scope: though what they will impart Help nothing else, yet do they ease the heart. **1599** *Id. A.Y.* I. iii. 98 And do not seek to take your charge upon you, To bear your griefs yourself and leave me out. **1599** *Pass. Pilgr.* 20, l. 55 Thus of every grief in heart He with thee doth bear a part.

Grief of the head is the grief of griefs, The. (G 448)

1659 HOWELL *Eng. Prov.* 10b.

Grief pent up will break the heart. *Cf.* **Grief is lessened.** (G 449)

1589 *Triumphs Love and Fort.* IV. ii. F1 O Gods that deepest greefes are felt in closest smart. **1592** SHAKES. *T.And.* II. iv. 36 Sorrow concealed, like an oven stopp'd, Doth burn the heart to cinders where it is. **1594–8** *Id. T.S.* IV. iii. 77–8 My tongue will tell the anger of my heart, Or else my heart, concealing it, will break. **1597** *Politeuphuia* 162ᵛ Sorrowes concealed are the more sower, and smothered griefes, if they burst not out, will breake the hart. **1605–6** SHAKES. *M.* IV. iii. 209 Give sorrow words. The grief that does not speak Whispers the o'erfraught heart and bids it break. **1609** HARWARD 126 Yf it were not for weeping the heart would burst. **1732** FULLER no. 1775 (will burst).

Griefs with bread are less, All. (G 452)

1620 SHELTON *Quix.* II. xiii (1908) II. 266 And yet not so bad if we might eat at all, for good fare lessens care. **1640** HERBERT no. 377.

Grief(s), *see also* Change place but not change the g. (mind), (One may); Day passes without some g. (No); Folly were g. (If); Honour (Where no), there is no g.; Secrets (If you would know) look for them in g.; Sudden joy kills sooner than excessive g.; Time (and thinking) tame g.; Whither goest, g.

Grieve for that (what) you cannot help, Never. (G 453)

1592 SHAKES. *T.G.V.* III. i. 241 Cease to lament for that thou canst not help. **1600** HEYWOOD *et al.* 1 *Edw. IV* i. 5 Seem you but sorry for what you haue done, And straight shele put the finger in the eye, With comfort now, since it cannot be helped. **1611** SHAKES. *W.T.* III. ii. 219 What's gone and what's past help Should be past grief. **1619** DRAYTON *Idea* no. 61 Since ther's no helpe, Come let us kisse and part, Nay, I have done: You get no more of Me, And I am glad, yea glad withall my heart, That thus so cleanly, I my Selfe can free. **1621** ROBINSON 19 Greeue neuer your selfe, for that cannot bee amended. **1639** CLARKE 292.

Grieve when the chance is past, It is too late to.   (C 224)

1616 WITHALS 544 It is too late to repent to-morrow. **1636** CAMDEN 300. **1639** CLARKE 95 'Tis too late to repent when the day's lost.

Grig, *see* Merry as a g.

Grim, *see* Hold on like g. death.

Grin and abide (bear it), To.

a. **1775** W. HICKEY *Memoirs* I. 196 'I recommend you to grin and bear it' (an expression used by sailors after a long continuance of bad weather). **1794–6** E. DARWIN *Zoon.* (1802) II. 114 Thus we have a proverb where no help could be had in pain, 'to grin and abide'. **1834** MARRYAT *P. Simple* ch. 54 The best plan is to grin and bear it. **1876** BLACKMORE *Cripps* ch. 10 All things are dead against me; I must grin, as you say, and bear it. **1910** Mar. 9 D. H. LAWRENCE *Lawrence in Love* (1968) 50 I must grin and abide till then.

Grin like a Cheshire cat, To.

1808 C. LAMB *Let.* to Manning 26 Feb. I made a pun the other day, and palmed it upon Holcroft, who grinned like a Cheshire cat. **1855** THACKERAY *Newcomes* ch. 24 Mamma is smiling with all her might. In fact Mr. Newcome says . . . , 'That woman grins like a Cheshire cat'. **1865** DODGSON *Alice* ch. 6.

Grind or find, I will either.   (G 455)

1639 CLARKE 246 If yu'l find, I'le grind. *Ibid.* 177 He will neither find nor grinde. **1670** RAY 178.

Grind(s), *see also* Axe to g.; Friend that g. at my mill; Mill always going g. coarse and fine; Mill cannot g. with water that is past; Miller g. more men's corn than one; Mills will not g. if you give them not water; Millstone (Lower) g. as well as upper.

Grindstone, *see* Nose to the g. (To hold); Scot, a rat, and a Newcastle g.

Grisel(l), *see* Mars in the wood than g. (More); Patient G.

Grist to the (one's) mill, To bring.
                                                          (A 122)

1583 GOLDING *Calvin on Deut.* cxxiii. 755 There is no lykelihoode that those thinges will bring gryst to the mill. **1655** FULLER *Ch. Hist.* III. vi (1868) I. 444 And here foreign casuists bring in a bundle of mortal sins, all grist for their own mill. **1822** GALT *Provost* ch. 4 By which . . . no little grist came to his mill.

Grist, *see also* Horse next to mill.

Groaning horse and a groaning wife never fail their master, A.   (H 649)

1546 HEYWOOD II. iv. G2v A gronyng horse, and a gronyng wyfe, Neuer fayle theyr maister. **1670** RAY 51 (grunting horse). **1706** STEVENS s.v. *Bestia* We have a Beastly saying, That a grunting Horse, and a groaning Wife never forsake the Rider.

Groans, *see* Gallows g. for him.

Groat, Not worth a (grey).   (G 458)

1509 BARCLAY *Ship of Fools* i. 159 Skant worth a grote. **1546** HEYWOOD I. xi. D4v And I knew hym, not woorth a good grey grote. . . . Poore as the poorest. **1694** *The Brothers* in *Terence made English* 189 The woman's not worth a Groat.

Groat is ill saved that shames the master, The.   (G 457)

1623 CAMDEN 278. **1670** RAY 23. **1853** TRENCH 110 Others . . . forbid this frugality from degenerating into a sordid and dishonourable parsimony; such . . . as . . . *The groat is ill saved which shames its master.*

Groat, *see also* Be still is worth a g.; Flay (Skin) a g.; Four pence to a g. (As like as); Give a g. for owl; Hole in the g. to-day (Will be a); Kens his g. among other folk's kail; Light as the Queen's g.; Nippence; Penny is well spent that saves g.; Pin a day is g. a year.

Groby pool, For his death there is many a wet eye in.   (D 152)

1678 RAY (*Leics.*) 317. **1902–4** LEAN I. 124 . . . *i.e.* eyot or little isle, implying that no tears are shed by his friends. [It is the largest sheet of water in the county.]

Groby Pool, *see also* Thatch G. P. with pancakes.

Groin, *see* Hang the g.

Cromwell seed, *see* Fair words did fet.

Groom is a king at home, Every.

1592 DELAMOTHE 7 Euery clowne is king at home. **1611** DAVIES no. 52.

Grooms and householders are all alike great, Where | very disastrous will it be for the houses and all that dwell in them.

1399 LANGLAND *Rich. Redeles* i. 65–7 Ffor, as it is said . by elderne[1] dawis,[2] 'Ther gromes and the goodmen . beth all eliche grette, Well wo beth the wones[3] . and all that woneth ther-in!' [[1] ancestors. [2] days. [3] dwellings.]

Gropes in the dark finds that he would not, He that.   (D 39)

1659 HOWELL *Eng. Prov.* 13a. **1670** RAY 12.

Ground, He is on the. (G 463)

1641 FERGUSSON no. 442 *Of weasters and divers.*[1] **1642** TORRIANO 57 Hc hath light on the ground with his breech: Nota, That is, he hath paid all his debts: A custome in Italy for bankrupts when all is lost, after some imprisonment, they hoist them up by a pully, strapado like, thrice, and so let them light on a stone . . . and so they clear the world with that public disgrace, and no man can challenge any thing of them ever after. [[1] bankrupts.]

Ground sweat cures all disorders, A.

c. **1816** FARMER *Musa Pedestris* 81 We . . . sent him to take a ground-sweat [buried him]. **1830** FORBY 434 'A ground sweat cures all disorders', i.e. In the grave all complaints cease from troubling.

Ground, *see also* Balk of good g., (Make not a); Cut the grass (g.) under feet; Kiss (Lick) the g.; Lies upon the g. (He that) can fall no lower; Love the g. he treads on; Neighbour's g. yields better corn than ours; Remedy against ill man is much g. between; Tom Tiddler's g.

Groundsel[1] speaks not, The | save what it heard at (of) the hinges. (G 471)

1640 HERBERT no. 295. **1670** RAY 12 (of). [[1] threshold.]

Grow howbackit[1] bearing your friends, You will never. (F 742)

1639 CLARKE 177 He may bear all his friends on his backe. **1862** HISLOP 334 . . . From this we can infer that the person addressed does not allow himself to be troubled by his friends. [[1] hump-backed.]

Grow like a cow's tail, To. (C 770)

1609 HARWARD 114ᵛ He is a roper. He getteth his living by going backward. He groweth like a cows tayle. *c.* **1641** FERGUSSON MS. no. 1592. Ye breid of a tyks taill ye grow ay backward. **1678** RAY 249 To grow like a cows tail, i.e. downwards. **1721** KELLY 361 (as *c.* 1641) . . . Spoken to Boys who do not improve at School. **1829** G. GRIFFIN *Collegians* ch. 12 'Grew?—If she did, it's like the cow's tail, downwards.'

Grow(s), *see also* Camomile is trodden on, (The more) the faster it g.; Charity g. cold; Cockle and corn g. in the same field; Fools g. without watering; Leisure, as flax g., (At); Many things g. in garden never sown; Mastiff g. the fiercer for being tied up; Mistress is the master, (Where the) the parsley g. the faster; One for the mouse . . . and one to g.; Straighter g. the palm; Strings high stretched . . . quickly g. out of tune; Tree that g. slowly.

Growed by night, This. (N 176)

1678 RAY 72 . . . Spoken of a crooked stick or tree, it could not see to grow. (*Joculatory.*)

Growing youth has a wolf in his belly, A. (Y 49)

[*Cf.* **1886** JOWETT *Life* III. 220 No man will be pacified when he hath the wolf in his belly. (Said of the Irish.)] **1607** *Jests of George Peele* Bullen ii. 400 The feather-bed . . . his friend slily conveyed away, hauing as villanous a wolf in his belly as George. **1611** COTGRAVE s.v. Ieune A youth in growing hath a Wolfe in his guts. **1666** TORRIANO *It. Prov.* 56 no. 12 A young man who still groweth, hath a woolf in his belly. **1823** COLLINS 214 . . . That is, he is a great eater.

Growth, *see* Confidence is plant of slow g.

Gruel, *see* Grantham g.

Grumble, *see* Englishman's privilege.

Grunt, *see* Expect from a hog but a g. (What can you).

Grunting horse, *see* Groaning horse.

Guard, (*noun*), *see* Faulty stands on his g.; Welt or g. (Without).

Guard (*verb*), *see* Teeth g. the tongue, (Good that the).

Gudgeon(s), *see* Angle all day and catch g.; Swallow g.

Guess, *see* Jewel by the casket, (None can g.).

Guest(s), *see* Fresh fish and new-come g.; Ill g. that never drinks to host; Meat than g. or company, (Better to want); Unbidden g. knows not where to sit.

Guide (*noun*), *see* No man before his g.; Takes the raven for g. (He that).

Guided that God guides, They are well.

1721 KELLY 337 . . . Spoken when some Person has committed some Malefice.

Guide(d), (*verb*), *see also* Gear is easier gained than g.

Guilty conscience is a self-accuser (feels continual fear), A. *Cf.* Conscience is a thousand witnesses.

(C 606)

1545 *Precepts of Cato* E7ᵛ He that is gyltie in any maner thynge, Thynketh that only of him is all their whysperynge. **1562** J. WIGAND *De Neutralibus* A7 Conscius ipse sibi, de se putat omnia dici. He that hath a giltye conscience thinketh euery thinge spoken by hym. **1590** H. ROBERTS *Defiance to Fortune* P1 Guiltie consciences be timorous. [1592] **1597** SHAKES. *Rich. III* V. iii. 179 O coward conscience, how dost thou afflict me! **1597** *Politeuphuia* 10ᵛ A Guilty conscience is a worme that bites and neuer ceaseth . . . A guiltie conscience is neuer without feare. **1600–1** SHAKES. *H.* III. i. 83 Conscience does make cowards of us all. **1604** DRAYTON *Owl* (1619 ed.) l. 174, Wks. ii. 484 A guiltie Conscience feeles continuall feare. **1666** TORRIANO *It. Prov.* 154 no. 2 Who is guilty of any misdeed, thinks that every body is speaking of his fact. **1744** *Life & Adv. Mat. Bishop* 106 It is an old saying, a guilty conscience needs no accuser. **1881** D. C. MURRAY *Joseph's Cl.* ch. 8 'Where are *you* off to?' asked George with a great effort . . . a guilty conscience needs no accuser.

Guilty, *see also* Fault (g.) suspects everybody, (Who is in); Find g. Gilbert; Innocent until proved g.; Truest jests sound worst in g. ears.

Guise, *see* Sluggards' g.

Gull comes against the rain, The.
(G 478)

1616 DRAXE no. 1969 The Gull commeth not, but against a tempest. **1664** CODRINGTON 214 The Gull is alwayes seen against a tempest. **1670** RAY 98.

Gull(ed), (*verb*), *see* World will be g. (If).

Gummed taffeta (velvet), *see* Fret like g. t.

Gun(s), *see* Blow great g.; Highlandman's g. that needed new lock; Shoot with silver g.; Stand to one's g.; Sure as a g.

Gunner to his linstock, The | and the steersman to the helm.

1748 SMOLLETT *Rod. Rand.* ch. 42 I meddle with nobody's affairs but my own; the gunner to his linstock,[1] and the steersman to the helm, as the saying is. **1894** SIR H. MAXWELL *Life W. H. Smith* 262 He . . . never showed any disposition to trespass on the province of science or literature. . . . There is sound sense in the adage, 'The cobbler to his last and the gunner to his linstock'. [[1] a staff with a forked head to hold a lighted match.]

Gunner, *see also* Married to g. daughter.

Gunshot, *see* Out of g.

Gut no fish till you get them.

1721 KELLY 114 . . . Spoken to them who have pregnant Expectations, and boast of them as if they had them in Possession. **1824** MOIR *Mansie*

W. ch. 20 The doing so might not only set them to the sinful envying of our good fortune, . . . but might lead away ourselves to be gutting our fish before we get them.

Guts (No guts) in his brain, He has.
(G 484)

1602 SHAKES. *T.C.* II. i. 70 This lord . . . who wears his wits in his belly, and his guts in his head. **1663** BUTLER *Hudibras* iii. 1091 Truly that is no Hard Matter for a Man to do, That has but any Guts in's Brains. **1678** RAY 249 (no guts). The *anfractus* of the brain, look'd upon when the *Dura mater* is taken off, do much resemble guts. **1694** MOTTEUX *Rabelais* v. Prol. (1737) 53 One without Guts in his Brains, whose Cockloft is unfurnish'd. **1738** SWIFT Dial. I. E.L. 284 The fellow's well enough, if he had any guts in his brains. **1823** GROSE ed. Pierce Egan s.v. Brains To have some brains in his guts; to know something.

Guts than brains, He has more.
(G 485)

1678 RAY 249.

Guts uphold the heart, The | and not the heart the guts.

1620 SHELTON *Quix.* Pt. II. xlvii. iii. 142. **1706** STEVENS s.v. Tripas Let the Guts be full, for it is they that carry the Legs. **1719** DE ALVORADO 58 The Guts carry the Feet, and not the Feet the Guts. **1732** FULLER no. 4585.

Guts, *see also* Carry g. to a bear (Not fit to); Devil's g.; Garters of a man's g., (To make).

Gutter Lane, All goes down.   (A 132)

1628 RICHARD RAWLIDGE *A Monster Late Found Out and Discovered* C2v An hundred Kanns of Beere . . . were filled in a trice, and almost as sodainly turned downe Guttur lane. **1662** FULLER Lond. 200 . . . A small lane, . . . leading out of Cheapside, . . . which Orthography presents . . . [as] *Guthurun*-lane, from him the once Owner thereof. . . . The Proverb is applicable to those who spend all in Drunkennesse and Gluttony. **1670** RAY 243 . . . Guttur being Latine for the throat.

Gutter, *see also* Crow in g.; Duck will not always dabble in same g.; Gaze at moon and fall in g.; Repairs not his g. (Who) repairs whole house; Safe as a crow (sow) in a g.

Gyges, *see* Ring of G.

H

Hab or nab. (H 479)

[= get or lose, hit or miss, at random.] **1530**
PALSGRAVE 833a By habbe or by nabbe. **1542**
UDALL *Apoph.* 186 Putte to the plounge of . . .
habbe or nhabbe, to wynne all, or to lese all.
c. **1565** *The Pedlar's Prophecy* l. 1174 Hab or
nab, away the mare. **1580** LYLY *Euph. & his
Eng.* ii. 123 Philautus determined, hab, nab, to
sende his letters. **1601** SHAKES. *T.N.* III. iv. 227
Hob, nob, is his word: give't or take't. **1664**
BUTLER *Hudibras.* II. iii. 990 Cyphers, Astral
Characters . . . set down Habnab at random.
1831 SCOTT *Jrnl.* II. 388 It is all hab-nab at a
venture.

Habit(s), *see* Custom (H.) is second nature;
Holy h. cleanses not foul soul; Pursuits become
h.

Hackerton's cow, That is.

[Hackerton was a lawyer who when told that his
heifer had been gored by an ox, claimed the ox
in recompense; but when told that the reverse of
this had happened, replied, 'The case alters
there'.] **1721** KELLY 326 . . . Spoken when
People alter their Opinions when the Case
comes home to themselves.

Hackney mistress, hackney maid. (M 1019)

1616 WITHALS 579. **1639** CLARKE 217. **1670**
RAY 99 . . . Ὁποία ἡ δέσποινα τοῖαι καὶ θερα-
παινίδες. CIC. *Epist. Att.* 5. Qualis hera tales
pedissequæ. [Like mistress, like maid.] **1732**
FULLER no. 1780.

Had I fish, is good without mustard (butter). (H 7)

1623 CAMDEN 271 (butter). **1670** RAY 99. **1721**
KELLY 145 Had I fish was never good to eat with
Mustard. An Answer to them that say, had I
such a Thing, I would do so, or so.

Had I fish, was never good with garlic. (H 7)

a. **1628** CARMICHAELL no. 623. **1641** FERGUSSON
no. 300.

'Had I wist', Beware of. (H 8)

c. **1350** *Douce MS.* 52 no. 98 Holde þy thombe
in thi fyst. And kepe þe welle fro 'Had I wyst'.
c. **1390** GOWER *Conf. Amantis* II. 102 And is all
ware of *had I wist.* *c.* **1400** *Arthur* (Furnivall)
l. 545 Ther nys no man wel nye, y tryste, þat
can be waar of hadde wyste. *c.* **1500** *Percy
Provs.* in *Anglia* XIV. 486 Of had I wyst all way
beware. **1526** SKELTON *Magnyf.* Wks. (1843) I.
232 Hem, syr, yet beware of Had I wyste! **1546**
HEYWOOD I. ii. A3 And that deliberacion dothe
men assyst, Before they wed, to beware of had I
wist. **1732** FULLER no. 976.

Had I wist, comes too late. (H 9)

c. **1400** *Beryn* E.E.T.S. l. 2348 But nowe it is to
late to speke of had-I-wist. **1639** CLARKE 281.

Had I wist, was a fool. (H 10)

[L. *Stultum est dicere, Non putarem.*] *c.* **1425**
Wakefield Second Shepherds 93 Had I wyst
is a thyng it seruys of noght. **1533** SIR T. ELYOT
Of the Wisdom which maketh a wise man 100
In the office of a wise man, (Peraduenture) is
neuer herde spoken: No more than is . . . these
wordes: Had I wist. **1545** TAVERNER A3 Had I
wyst, is a foles worde. **1599** BRETON *Anger &
Pat.* Wks. Gros. ii. 60. **1721** KELLY 131
(quoth the fool) . . . Spoken when People say,
Had I wist what would have been the Consequence of such an Action, I had not done it.

Haddock, Not worth a. (H 4)

1546 HEYWOOD II. x. L3ᵛ And thus had he
brought haddocke to paddocke. Till they bothe
were not worth a haddocke.

Haddock, *see also* Bring h. to paddock; Leaped
a h.

Hae¹ lad and run lad. (L 22)

c. **1641** FERGUSSON MS. no. 613. Have lade and
go lad maks ane speidy ladde. **1721** KELLY 131
. . . Give ready Money for your Service, and you
will be sure to be well served. [¹ Here, take.]

Hae¹ will a deaf man hear.

a. **1628** CARMICHAELL no. 618. **1721** KELLY 133.
[¹ Here, take.]

Hail brings frost in the tail. (H 12)

1639 CLARKE 197. **1670** RAY 42. **1882** CHAMBER-
LAIN 38.

Hail fellow well met (with one), To be. (H 15)

[= to be intimate (too intimate) with.] **1519**
HORMAN *Vulg.* f. 148 He made so moche of his
servaunt that he waxed hayle felowe with hym.
1581 GUAZZO ii. 105 The maister . . . being as
you say haile fellow well met with his servant.
1586 J. HOOKER *Girald. Irel.* in *Holinshed* ii.
105/2 He . . . placed himselfe . . . hard at the
earle of Ormond his elbow, as though he were
haile fellow well met. **1616** WITHALS 567 *Ne
cuivis porrigas dextram.* Bee not haile fellowe
well met with euery one. **1670** EACHARD
Cont. Clergy 74 The multitude did not go haile
fellow well met with Him. **1888** RIDER HAG-
GARD *Col. Quaritch* I. i. 4 He was popular . . .
though not in any hail-fellow-well-met kind of
way.

Hair, Not worth a. (H 19)

1509 BARCLAY *Ship of Fools* i. 177 Skantly
worth a here. **1565** *King Darius* A4 Not worth
the valour of a heare. **1590** SPENSER *F.Q.* II. x.
28 In his crowne her [Leir] counted her no haire.
1613 WITHER *Abuses Stript* Epigr. 10 To call you
best, or the most faire . . . is now not commendations worth a haire.

Hair and hair makes the carl's head bare.   (H 21)

[HOR. *Ep.* 2. l. 45.] **1548** COOPER s.v. Cauda To pluck the heares of an horse tayle, a prouerbe spoken of hym, that by littell and lytell atcheueth that he coulde not do immediatly all togither. **1621** ROBINSON 24 (will make the carle bald). *a.* **1628** CARMICHAELL no. 628 (maks the cairle beld). **1639** CLARKE 10 Pull haire and haire and you'll make the carle balde. **1641** FERGUSSON no. 326. **1721** KELLY 136 . . . An Estate may be ruined by small Diminutions.

Hair grows through his hood, His.
                                                                      (H 17)

c. **1450** in *Rel. Antiq.* (1843) II. 67 He that lovyth welle to fare, Ever to spend and never spare But he have the more good His here wol grow throw his hood. *c.* **1550** INGELEND *Disob. Child* Hazl.-Dods. ii. 301 Therefore let him look his purse be right good, That it may discharge all that is spent, Or else it will make his hair grow through his hood. **1554** H. HILARIE (= J. Bale?) *Resurrection of the Mass* A8ᵛ If I [the Mass] were not, their hayre [the masspriests' hair] should grow thorow their cappes. **1587** FULWELL *Like Will to L.* Hazl.-Dods. iii. 325 So that my company they think to be so good, That in short space their hair grows through their hood. **1611** COTGRAVE s.v. Saffran It hath made him bankrupt, his haire is thereby growne through his hat. **1678** RAY 73 . . . He is very poor, his hood is full of holes.

Hair in one's neck, A.

[= a cause of trouble or annoyance.] *a.* **1450** *Ratis Raving* III. 199 Think one the har is in thi nek. **1818** SCOTT *Rob Roy* ch. 23 An Bailie Grahame were to get word o' this . . . it wad be a sair hair in my neck!

Hair of the dog that bit you, A. (H 23)

1546 HEYWOOD I. xi. E4 I praie the leat me and my felowe haue A heare of the dog that bote vs last nyght. **1611** COTGRAVE s.v. Beste Our Ale-knights often . . . say, Giue us a haire of the dog that last bit us. **1661** PEPYS April 3 Up among my workmen, my head akeing all day from last night's debauch . . . . At noon dined with Sir W. Batten and Pen, who would needs have me drink two good drafts of sack to-day, to cure me of my last night's disease, which I thought strange but I think find true. **1738** SWIFT *Dial.* II. E.L. 310 Our way is, to take a hair of the same dog next morning. **1824** SCOTT *Redg.* ch. 14 He took a large glass of brandy. 'A hair of the dog that bit me', he continued.

Hair so small but has his shadow, No.
                                                                      (H 25)

[PUBLIUS SYRUS 138 *Etiam capillus unus habet umbram suam.* Even a single hair has its shadow. ERASM. *Ad.* (1508) iii. iii. 32 Etiam capillus unus habet umbram suam.] *c.* **1526** *Dicta Sap.* C1 [As in Erasm.] Nothynge is so lytell, but that it maye somwhat do. **1539** TAVERNER *Publius* B8ᵛ Euen one heare of the head hath his shadowe, that is to wete, there is nothyng so symple and vile, but can do sumwhat. **1579** S. GOSSON *Sch. of Abuse* ed. Arber 16 Little heares haue their shadowes. **1584** LYLY

Sappho & Phao Prol. 372 There is no needles point so smal, which hath not his compasse: nor haire so slender, which hath not his shadowe. **1590** LODGE *Rosalynde* Wks. (1883) I. 130 Affirming, that as . . . the smallest haires have their shadowes: so the meanest swaines had their fancies. **1596** *Id. Wits Miserie* Wks. (1883) IV. 24 If you say that (as PUBLIUS MIMUS saith) the smallest haire hath his shadow (and with Rabin BEN-AZAI) that no man liuing is to bee contemned. **1651** HERBERT no. 1124. **1659** TORRIANO no. 62.

Hair (thread), To hang by a.   (T 250)

[Often with reference to Dionysius of Syracuse (405–367 B.C.) who allowed a courtier named Damocles to take his place at a banquet, but had a sword hung over him by a hair, to illustrate the insecurity of place and power.] **1528** TYNDALE *Obed. Chrn. Man* P.S. 194 Look on him as thou wouldest look on a sharp sword that hanged over thy head by a hair. **1545** *Precepts of Cato* 'Sage Sayings' Thales D3ᵛ There are that fayneth it [life] to hange by an heere or a twynned threde. **1563** *Mirr. for Mag.* Lord Hastings (Campbell) 288 By syngle heare deaths sworde hong over my head. **1571** TIGURINUS *Instit. of a Christian Prince* 10 Euill men . . . are alwayes euen as though their liues hung vpon a thred. **1581** C. MERBURY *Brief Discourse* 15 The tyrant hath the pointe of a sworde hanging ouer his head: always languishing in continuall feare. **1581** SENECA *Ten Trag. Hercules Octaeus* tr. Studley T.T. ii. 216 The swerde will fall that hanges but by a twyne. **1586** WHETSTONE *Eng. Mirr.* 214 Dionisius caused a naked sword with the point directly vppon Damocles head, to bee fastned only with the hayre of a horse tayle. **1591** *True Hist. of Civil Wars of France* 302 Theyr liues and state . . . did hang on a rotten thread. *c.* **1595–6** SHAKES. *K.J.* V. vii. 53 All the shrouds wherewith my life should sail Are turned to one thread, one little hair. **1706** STEVENS s.v. Cabello (hair) . . . to stand upon very ticklish Circumstances. **1882** 'F. ANSTEY' *Vice Versa* ch. 1 He was an old gentleman . . . of irreproachable character . . . ; no Damocles' sword of exposure was swinging over his bald but blameless head.

Hair to make a tether of, A.

[= a slight pretext of which to make a great deal.] **1809** SCOTT *Let. to G. Ellis* 3 Nov. in LOCKHART *Life* Those who wish to undermine it want but, according to our Scotch proverb, a hair to make a tether of.

Hair(s), *see also* Against the h.; Bush natural, more h. than wit; Cow's thumb (h.'s breadth); Care brings gray h.; Cut (Split) the h.; Friday's h. and Saturday's horn; Grey h. are nourished with green thoughts; Grey h. death's blossoms; Horns and grey h.; Horse lies down (Where), h. will be found; Maidens (All are not) that wear bare h.; Shame is past shedd of your h.; Whelp of the same litter (h.).

Hake, *see* Lose in h. (What we), shall have in herring.

Halcyon days.   (D 116)

1540 HYRDE tr. *Vives' Instr. Chr. Wom.* (1592) P1 Wherefore those daies be called in Latine

Halcionii, that is as you would say, the Halcion birdes daies. **1562** J. WIGAND *De Neutralibus* N4ᵛ God of hys great goodnesse doth some-tymes spare hys churche some Halcione dayes, whiche men should make much of. **1587** LAMBARDE to Burghley Nichols *Progresses* (1823) iii. 558 These few halcyon dayes I haue enjoyed at my ferme. **1587** J. BRIDGES *Defence of the Govt.* 5 Her Maiesties raigne hath bene the daies of the Alcions sitting in the neste, most free from tempests, of all other parts of Gods church. **1592–4** SHAKES. *1 Hen. VI* I. ii. 131 Expect Saint Martin's summer, halcyon days. **1673** MARVELL *2 Rehearsal Trans.* Gros. ii. 365 If this course were once effectually taken, the whole year would consist of halcyon holidayes.

Haldon[1] has a hat, When | let Kenton beware of a skatt.[2]

1759 BRICE *Top. Dict.* s.v. Kenton. **1790** GROSE s.v. Scatt. **1893** INWARDS *Weather Lore* 101. [1 In Devonshire. 2 Shower of rain.]

Hale pow,[1] He should have a | that calls his neighbour nitty know.[2] (P 532)

1621 ROBINSON 8 (nitty now). *a.* **1628** CAR-MICHAELL no. 656. **1641** FERGUSSON no. 354. **1721** KELLY 133 . . . A Man ought to be free of these Faults that he throws up to others. [1 head. 2 hillock.]

Half a crown, *see* Lubberland.

Half a loaf is better than no bread. (H 36)

1546 HEYWOOD I. xi. D4ᵛ For better is halfe a lofe then no bread. *a.* **1548** HALL (1809 ed., 236) Some bread is better to the hungry person, then no bread. **1567** *Appius & Virg.* Mal. Soc. l. 1109 And well this prouerb commeth in my head, Birlady halfe a loafe is better then nere a whit of bread. **1609** HARWARD 115ᵛ One shive is better then no bread. **1642** D. ROGERS *Naaman* to Rdr. He is a fool who counts not half a loaf better than no bread, or despiseth the moonshine because the sun is down. **1850** KINGSLEY *Alton L.* ch. 10 We must live somehow, and half a loaf is better than no bread.

Half a word (tale) is enough for a wise man. (H 39)

1573 SANFORD 101ᵛ To a good vnderstander halfe a woorde is inough. **1611** COTGRAVE s.v. Mot A good wit's well inform'd by halfe a Word. *a.* **1628** CARMICHAELL no. 626 (gude aneuch). **1659** HOWELL *Fr. Prov.* 8 Half a word to a good understander. **1721** KELLY 169 Half a Word to a wise Man.

Half an acre is good land. (H 40)

1659 HOWELL *Eng. Prov.* 2a. **1670** RAY 99. **1721** KELLY 143 Half Acres bears good corn. Alluding to the half Acre given to the Herd, and commonly spoken in gaming, when we are but half as many as our Antagonists.

Half an egg is better than an empty shell. (H 37)

1621 ROBINSON 19. **1628** CARMICHAELL no. 289 Better half eg nor tume[1] dowp.[2] **1639** CLARKE 86 (empty shell). [1 empty. 2 shell.]

Half an hour is soon lost at dinner.

1738 SWIFT Dial. II. E.L. 298 Sir John, fall to: you know half an hour is soon lost at dinner.

Half an hour's hanging hinders five miles' riding. (H 42)

1678 RAY 150.

Half an hour, *see also* Hour.

Half-done work, *see* Fools and bairns.

Half is more than the whole, The. (H 43)

[HESIOD *Works & Days* 40. Πλέον ἥμισυ παντός. ERASM. *Ad. Dimidium plus toto.*] **1550** LATIMER *Serm. Stamford* P.S. 277 There is a proverb . . ., *Dimidium plus toto*; 'The half sometimes more than the whole.' The mean life is the best life and the most quiet life of all. **1791** I. DISRAELI *Cur. Lit.* (1858) III. 35 The admonition of the poet . . . to prefer a friendly accommoda-tion to a litigious lawsuit, has fixed a paradoxical proverb . . . Πλέον ἥμισυ παντός, The half is better than the whole! **1907** A. C. BENSON *From Coll. W.* (ed. 4) 80 It is true of conversation as of many other things, that the half is better than the whole. People who are fond of talking ought to beware of being lengthy.

Half-seas over, To be. (H 53)

[= half-drunk.] **1671** J. BALTHARPE *Straights Voyage* ed. Bromley 38 Some were quite Drunk, and some were Sober, And some were also half Seas over. **1692** DRYDEN *Cleom.* v. ii I'm half-seas o'er to death. *a.* **1700** B.E. *Dict. Cant. Crew* Half Seas over, almost Drunk. **1714** *Spectator* No. 616, par. 4 Our friend the alderman was half seas over before the bonefire was out. **1730** FIELDING *T. Thumb* I. ii I already half-seas over am. **1816** PEACOCK *Headlong Hall* ch. 14.

Half shows what the whole means, The. (H 44)

c. **1530** *Calisto and Meliboea* C1ᵛ Now know ye by the half tale what the hole doth meane. **1546** HEYWOOD II. vii. K1. **1602** MANNINGHAM *Diary* ed. Bruce Judge the whole by part, as merchants sell their wares. **1616** DRAXE no. 853.

Half the battle, *see* First blow.

Half the truth is often a great lie.

1758 FRANKLIN July. **1859** TENNYSON *The Grandmother* VIII That a lie which is half a truth is ever the blackest of lies, That a lie which is all a lie may be met and fought with outright, But a lie which is part a truth is a harder matter to fight.

Half the way to know the way. (H 45)

1659 HOWELL *Brit. Prov.* 11.

Half (One half of) the world knows not how the other half lives. (H 46)

[**1532** RABELAIS II. xxxii *La moytié du monde ne sçait comment l'autre vit.*] **1607** J. HALL *Holy*

Obs. 17, Wks. ii. 168 One half of the World knows not how the other lives. **1633** R. ASHLEY *Cochin-China* A1 The one moity [of the world] is in a maner vnknowne to the other. **1640** HERBERT no. 907. **1721** KELLY 274 Men bred to Ease and Luxury are not sensible of the mean Condition of a great many. **1755** FRANKLIN Pref. It is a common saying, that . . . **1816** J. AUSTEN *Emma* ch. 9 One half of the world cannot understand the pleasures of the other. **1830** MARRYAT *King's Own* ch. 10 It is an old proverb that 'one half of the world do not know how the other half live'. Add to it, nor *where* they live.

Half, halves, *see also* Better h.; Never do things by h.; Take h. in hand (Best to); Woman kissed is h. won.

Halfpenny (ies, ce), *see* Hand on another h. (To have); Hand on one's h.; Hap and h. goods enough; Know by a h. if priest will take offering; Look twice at a h.; Nothing for nothing, and little for h.; Put two h. in a purse; Thinks his penny (h.) good silver; Three halfpence.

Halfpennyworth, Ha'porth, *see* Hang saving, bring us a h. of cheese; Ship (To lose) for h. of tar.

Halgaver, *see* Summoned before Mayor of H.

Halifax law. *Cf.* Lidford law. (L 590)

1577 HARRISON *Desc. England* in Holinshed (1586 ed.) 185 At Halifax . . . if it [a felony] be valued by foure constables to amount to the sum of thirteene pence halfe penie, he is forthwith beheaded. **1586** LEICESTER in MOTLEY *United Netherlands* (1860) i. 444 I have had Halifax law—he is condemned first and inquired upon after. **1609** J. WYBARNE *New Age of Old Names* 61.

Halifax, *see also* Heading H.; Hell, Hull, and H.

Hall benches (binks) are slippery (sliddery). (B 355)

c. **1450** HENRYSON *Mor. Fab.* 154 (1845) 209 Be war in welth, for hall-benkis ar rycht slidder. *a.* **1628** CARMICHAELL no. 627 (sliddery). **1641** FERGUSSON no. 335 Hall binkes are sliddrie. **1721** KELLY 133 Hall binks are sliddery. Great Men's Favour is uncertain.

Hall into the kitchen, Out of the. (H 56)

1540 PALSGRAVE *Acolastus* 153 From the horses to the asses. i. from the halle in to the kitchin. **1545** TAVERNER H6ᵛ Promoted or descended out of the hall into the kytchen. **1596** NASHE *Saffron W.* iii. 102.

Hall, *see also* Bring a cow to the h.; Do on the hill as in the h.

Hallamshire[1] shall be God's croft, When all the world shall be aloft, then.
(W 890)

1678 RAY 340 (Yorks.). [¹ Sheffield and its surroundings.]

Halloo (Whistle) until one is out of the wood, Not to.

1792 D'ARBLAY *Diary* (1876) iii. 473 Mʳ Windham says we are not yet out of the wood, though we see the path through it. **1801** W. HUNTINGTON *Bank of Faith* 85 But, alas! I hallooed before I was out of the wood. **1866** KINGSLEY *Hereward* ch. 3 Don't halloa till you are out of the wood. This is a night for praying rather than boasting. **1876** FAIRBAIRN in *Contemp. Rev.* June 137 He halloos, not only before he is out of the wood, but before he is well into it. **1922** MRS. MEYNELL Feb. I whistled before I was out of the wood when I said my cold was better.

Halt before you are lame, You. (H 57)

1670 RAY 179. **1710** PALMER 295.

Halt(s), *see also* Foot a man h., (To know on which).

Halter to hang himself, He has made a.
(H 58)

1575 GASCOIGNE *Glass of Gvt.* ii. 68 They . . . founder and cast themselues in their own halter. **1616** WITHALS 582. **1626** JONSON *Staple of News* v. iii. 16 In mine owne halter, I haue made the *Noose.* **1639** CLARKE 200.

Halter, *see also* After a collar comes a h.; Better a lean jade than empty h.; Give a Yorkshireman a h.; Hang together like pebbles in h.; Horse that draws his h.; Rope (H.) (Name not) in his house that hanged himself; Stretch without a h.

Halting (To halt) before a cripple, It is hard. (H 60)

c. **1374** CHAUCER *Troilus* Bk. 4, ll. 1457-9 'It is ful hard to halten unespied Byfore a crepel, for he kan the craft: Youre fader is in sleght as Argus eyed.' **1546** HEYWOOD II. v. H3ᵛ It is harde haltyng before a cripple ye wot. **1581** B. RICH *Farewell to the Militarie Prof.* Sh. Soc. 44 Wee haue a proverbe—it is ill haultyng before a creeple. **1655** FULLER *Ch. Hist.* IV. iv (1868) I. 614 Buckingham . . . pretending very fair in his behaviour. But, hard it is to halt before a cripple, and dissemble before King Richard. **1710** PALMER 319.

Hambleton, *see* Brayton.

Hamlet without the Prince of Denmark, Like.

1793 W. WORDSWORTH *Lett. to Bishop Watson* (*Prose Wks.* ed. Gros. i. 21) Your Lordship's conduct may bring to mind the story of a company of strolling comedians, who gave out the play of *Hamlet* as the performance of the evening. The audience was not a little surprised to be told, on the drawing up of the curtain, that from the circumstances of particular convenience it was hoped they would dispense with the omission of the character of—Hamlet. **1818** Aug. 20 BYRON *Lett.* Prothero iv. 251 My autobiographical Essay would resemble the tragedy of Hamlet at the country theatre, recited 'with the part of Hamlet left out by particular desire'. **1859** MEREDITH *Richard Feverel*, ch. 4, 'What have you been doing at home, Cousin Rady?' 'Playing Hamlet, in the absence of the Prince of Denmark.' **1910** *Times Wkly.* 17 June 452 The Army without Kitchener is like *Hamlet* without the Prince of Denmark. **1932** A. HUXLEY in *Letters of D. H. Lawrence* Introd. x His book is *Hamlet* without the Prince of Denmark. **1941** R. R. MARETT *A Jerseyman at Oxford* viii But all this sounds like Hamlet with its leading part [Jowett] left out.

Hammer and the anvil, Between the.
(H 62)

[ERASM. *Ad. Inter malleum et incudem.* Jerome's Latin of Origen's saying.] **1534** LD. BERNERS *Gold Bk. M. Aurel.* (1546) Eij, My spyrite is betwene the harde anuielde and the importunate hammer. **1548** ZWINGLI *Certain Precepts* A7ᵛ We being here betwixt the hammer and the stithe. **1659** HOWELL *It. Prov.* 8. **1892-3** J. A. FROUDE *Council of Trent* (1896) v. 110 Fate had dealt hardly with [Pope Clement VII]. For half his reign, as he said, he had been between the anvil and the hammer. **1927** 23 Jan. D. H. LAWRENCE *Lett.* ii. 961 One can only do one's best and then live and die. One is between the hammer and the anvil.

Hammer and tongs.

1708 *Brit. Apollo* no. 56 3/2 I'm now coming at you, with Hammer and Tongs. **1958** LEIGH FERMOR *Mani* ch. 8.

Hammer, *see also* Anvil should have a h. of feathers, (An iron); Anvil (When you are) . . . , when you are h., strike; Church is anvil which has worn out many h.; Cold iron, (To h. on).

Hampden, *see* Tring, Wing, and Ivinghoe.

Hampshire ground requires every day in the week a shower of rain, and on Sunday twain. *Cf.* Cornwall, etc. (H 63)

1678 RAY 353. **1790** GROSE s.v. Hants. **1813** RAY 248.

Hampshire hog.
(H 488)

[= a native of Hampshire.] **1622** DRAYTON *Polyolb.* II. xxiii. 240 As Hamshire long for her, hath the term of Hogs. **1720** *Vade Mecum for Malt-worms* (1850?) I. 50 Now to the sign of Fish let's jog, There to find out a Hampshire Hog, A man whom none can lay a Fault on, The Pink of Courtesie at *Alton*. **1866** BLACKMORE *Cradock N.* ch. 7 'Naw oose Hampshire hogs, But to zhow the way in bogs.' So John Rosedew quoted . . . from an old New Forest rhyme.

Hand and foot, With.

1533-4 UDALL *Terence* 1560 A3 He doeth all thinges with hand and foote [manibus pedibusque] or with tooth and nayle. *Ibid.* C4ᵛ. **1562** J. WIGAND *De Neutralibus* D4ᵛ The Papistes stryue with hande and fote (as they say) that the perfite fulfilling of the lawe is our owne doyng.

Hand and glove.
(H 92)

c. **1630** *The Soddered Citizen* l. 2352 Like the hand vnto the glove, Y'are ioyn'd, in sweete vnitinge loue. **1654** E. GAYTON 129 . . . had been Hand and Glove. **1680** R. MANSEL *Narr. Popish Plot* 103 Mrs. Collier, to whom Mr. Willoughby was such a Croney, that they were hand and glove. **1780** COWPER *Table T.* 173 As if the world and they were hand and glove. **1881** BESANT & RICE *Chapl. of Fleet* I. iv The Doctor is . . . hand-in-glove with the bishop.

Hand is in, His.
(H 67)

c. **1460** *Towneley Myst.* (Surtees) 220 Yit efte, whils thi hande is in, Pulle ther at with som kyn gyn. **1586** A. DAY *Eng. Secretary* i (1625) 44 There was no rake-hell . . . but his hand was in with him, and that he was a copesmate for him. *c.* **1594-5** SHAKES. *L.L.L.* IV. i. 126 Wide o' the bow-hand! I' faith, your hand is out. . . . An if my hand be out, then belike your hand is in. **1613** *Id. T.N.K.* IV. i. 139 He'll tickle't up In two hours, if his hand be in.

Hand in the lion's mouth, He that has his | must take it out as well as he can. *Cf.* Lion's mouth.
(H 82)

[*Cf.* PS. xxii. 21; 2 TIM. iv. 17.] **1696** *Cornish Comedy* I. v. My hand is in the lion's mouth; I must agree with him. **1721** KELLY 171 . . . He that is under the Distress of a severe Person, must extricate himself as well as he is able. **1819** SCOTT *Ivanhoe* ch. 44 Thy hand is in the lion's mouth.

Hand like a foot, You have made a.

1721 KELLY 386 . . . Spoken to those who are disappointed of their Expectations. **1738** SWIFT *Dial.* I. E.L. 268 Who'er writ it [a letter], writes a hand like a foot.

Hand of man, Whatever is made by the | by the hand of man may be overturned.
(H 102)

1651 HERBERT no. 1184.

Hand on another half-penny, To have one's.

[= to have another object in view.] **1577** GASCOIGNE *Posies* i. 432 But his Mistresse (having hyr hand on another halfpenny) gan thus say unto him.

Hand (Heart) on one's halfpenny, To have one's.
(H 80, 315)

[= to have a particular object in view.] **1541** BULLINGER *Chr. State Matrimony* tr. Coverdale (1543 ed., D7ᵛ) Theyr harpynge is vpon theyr halfepeny, theyr mynd is to be riche with mariage. **1542** ERASM. tr. Udall *Apoph.* (1877) 72 Aristippas . . . whose mind was more on his halfpenie, then Pluto had set his. **1546** HEYWOOD I. vi. B3 So hard is your halfpeny, That my reasonyng your reason setteth nought by. **1550** LATIMER *Serm.* 14 P.S. 270 (mind). **1583** MELBANCKE *Philotimus* 2C4ᵛ Thy heart must be on thy halfpenye. **1589** GREENE *Menaphon* Arb. 49 Twere necessarie he tolde us how

his heart came thus on his halfepence.   *c.* **1612**
JONSON *Ev. Man In Hum.* II. i. 79 (hand).   **1639**
CLARKE 36 (heart).

Hand over head.   (H 70)

[= recklessly.] *c.* **1440** *Bone Florence* 475 Than
they faght hand ovyr hedd.   **1549** LATIMER *7th
Serm. bef. Edw. VI* P.S. 218 These doctors we
. . . thank God for . . . but yet I would not have
men to be sworn to them, and so addict, as to
take hand over head whatsoever they say.
1655–62 GURNALL *Chrn. in Armour* (1865) I. 293
The Bereans . . . did not believe hand over head,
but their faith was the result of a judgment . . .
convinced by scripture evidence.   **1760** WESLEY
Lett. IV. 126.   **1839** G. JAMES *Louis XIV* III. 240
A lavish guardian, who . . . spent the estate
hand-over-head.

Hand over head, as men took the Covenant.   (H 71)

1678 RAY 250.   **1697** POPE *Life of Seth* [Ward]
ed. Bamborough 101 You do not choose your
Friends hastily and hand over head.   **1791–1823**
I. DISRAELI *Curios. Lit.* (Chandos) III. 59 . . . preserves the manner in which the Scotch covenant
. . . was violently taken by above sixty thousand
persons about Edinburgh, in 1638.

Hand play, churls' play.

[Span. *Juego de manos juego de villanos.* Sport
with the hands is the sport of peasants.]   **1689**
SHADWELL *Bury Fair* II. i (Merm.) 389. Is not
that a pretty clinch, Jack? [*He gives him a rap
on the back.*]—Sir, let me tell you, there is a
Spanish proverb, which says, *Whego*[1] *de manos,
whego de Vilanos.* [[1] Phonetic for *juego,* 'joke'
or 'play'.]

Hand that gave the wound must give the cure (salve), The.   (H 90)

1576 PETTIE i. 178 As the same hand which did
hurt me, did help me.   **1579** LYLY *Euph.* i. 215
Such a wound must be healed wher it was first
hurt.   **1579** CALVIN *Four Sermons* tr. J. Field
E1 Seeking the medicine at his [God's] hande
who hath giuen vs the wound.   **1591–2** *Troublesome Reign K.J.* B3 That hand that gaue the
wound must giue the salue To cure the hurt, els
quite incurable.   **1641** HENRY OXINDEN (to
Elizabeth Dallison) in *Oxinden Let.* no. 228, 293
I doe find that noe hand is soe like to curc the
wound but that which made it.

Hand that gives, gathers, The.   (H 72)

1659 HOWELL *Brit. Prov.* 34.

Hand to mouth, *see* Live from h. to m.

Hand that rocks the cradle rules the world, The.

a. **1881** W. R. WALLACE *John o'London's Treasure
Trove.* The hand that rocks the cradle Is the
hand that rules the world.

Hand twice to your bonnet for once to your pouch,[1] Put your.

1737 RAMSAY III. 192. [[1] purse.]

Hand, One | washes another (the other) and both the face. *Cf.* following proverb.
                                          (H 87)

[ERASM. *Ad. Manus manum lavat,* quoting
χεὶρ χεῖρα κνίζει.]   **1573** SANFORD 110ᵛ.   **1578**
FLORIO *First F.* 34.   **1580** LYLY *Euph. & his Eng.*
ii. 9 (but they both wash the face).   **1584** WITHALS
F4 Both hands are cleansed when the one is washed
with the other.   **1596** SPENSER *F.Q.* IV. i. 40
Myself will for you fight, As ye have done for me,
The left hand rubs the right.   **1617** MORYSON
Itin. I. ii. 17 He that writes often, shall often
receive letters for answere: for one hand
washeth another.   **1640** HERBERT no. 239.   **1719**
DE ALVARADO 151.   **1881** DEAN PLUMPTRE
Eccles. iv. 9 Two are better than one. . . . So
the Greek proverb ran as to friends χεὶρ χεῖρα
νίπτει, δάκτυλός τε δάκτυλον. 'Hand cleanseth
hand, and finger finger helps.'

Hand, One | will not wash the other for nothing.

1721 KELLY 275.

Hand(s), *see also* At h. (All is not); Bark and tree
(Put not h. between); Beads in the h.; Bear one
in h.; Better h. loose than in ill tethering; Bird
in h.; Bite the h. that feeds you; Bread in one's
h.; Burn his house to warm h.; Cold h. warm
heart; Dallies with enemy dies by own h.; Easy
as kiss my h.; Empty h. no hawks allure; Even
h. to throw louse in fire; Feather in h.; Fed at
another man's h.; Fight for one's own h.;
Fingers were made . . . and h. before knives;
Fool in h.; God reaches us good things by our
own h.; Good h. good hire; Good tongue (Who
has not) ought to have good h.; Grease a man in
h.; Heart and h.; Help, h., for I have no lands;
Iron h. in velvet glove; Kings have long h.;
Kiss the h. they wish cut off; Many h. light
work; Moist h. argues amorous nature; Mouth
has beguiled your h. (Your); Nothing enters
into close h.; Nothing is stolen without h.;
Pleased (If you be not) put h. in pocket; Refuse
with the right h.; Right h. from left (Knows
not); Right h., (He is his); Scatter with one h.,
gather with two; Sow with the h.; Spit on his h.;
Stretch your arm (h.) no further than sleeve;
Surgeon must have lady's h.; Two h. in dish,
one in purse; Upper h. (To have); Wash my h.
and wait on you; Wash one's h. of a thing;
Wash your h. often; Washing his h. (For) none
sells lands; Wide at the bow h.; Wise behind the
h.; Wise h. does not all foolish mouth speaks;
Writes a h. like a foot.

Hand (at cards), *see* Cast (H.) be bad (If), mend
by good play.

Handful of trade is an handful of gold, An.

1721 KELLY 13.   **1732** FULLER no. 603.

Handkerchief, To fling (throw) one's.

[= to express condescending preference for a
person.]   **1622** J. FLETCHER *Sea-Voyage* III. i

Like the Grand Signior ... then draw I forth My handkercher, and having made my choice, I thus bestow it. **1718** (O.S.) LADY M. W. MONTAGU *Let.* Countess of Mar 10 Mar. The Sultana ... assured me, that the story of the Sultan's throwing a handkerchief is altogether fabulous. **1850** THACKERAY *Pendennis* ch. 65 'And so, ... you condescend to fling to me your royal pocket handkerchief', said Blanche.

Handle without mittens, To.   (M 1028)

[= to treat unmercifully.] **1631** WEEVER *Anc. Funeral Mon.* 300 This merry deuill ... would have handled with rough Mittins, as the prouerbe is. **1659** HOWELL *Fr. Prov.* 16 They will not be caught without mittains. **1678** RAY 76. **1699** R. L'ESTRANGE *Erasm. Colloq.* (1711) 178 He handled the Reverend Fathers without Mittens.

Handles a nettle tenderly is soonest stung, He that.   (N 133)

1579 LYLY *Euph.* i. 212 True it is *Philautus* that he which toucheth the nettle tenderly, is soonest stoung. **1660** W. SECKER *Nonsuch Prof.* II. (1891) 158 Sin is like a nettle, which stings when it is gently touched, but hurts not when it is roughly handled. **1732** FULLER no. 2126. **1753** AARON HILL *The Nettle's Lesson* Tender-handed stroke a nettle, And it stings you for your pains; Grasp it like a man of mettle, And it soft as silk remains. **1830** FORBY 430 'Nip a nettle hard, and it will not sting you'—*i.e.* Strong and decided measures prevail best with troublesome people.

Handles thorns shall prick his fingers, He that.   (T 236)

1611 COTGRAVE s.v. Haye He that makes hedges often prickes his fingers. **1616** BRETON *Wks.* Gros. ii. E6. **1670** RAY 148.

Handle(s), *see* Most things have two h.

Hands full, To have one's.   (H 114)

[*c.* 1470] **1485** MALORY *Morte d'Arthur* XX. xxii. 837 Sythen that ye so unknyghtelye calle me of treson Ye shalle haue bothe your handes ful of me. **1546** HEYWOOD II. v. H4ᵛ. *c.* 1566 C. A. CURIO *Pasquin in a Trance* tr. W.P. 72ᵛ Let eache man crye for warre, let euery man haue his hands full. **1819** May 6 BYRON *Lett.* Prothero iv. 295 Like Rob Roy, I shall have my hands full. **1927** 13 May D. H. LAWRENCE *Lett.* ii. 977.

Hands off and fair play.   (H 112)

a. **1628** CARMICHAELL no. 624 (is). **1639** CLARKE 273. **1815** SCOTT *Guy Man.* ch. 40 (is).

Hands off other folks' bairns, Hold your | till you get some of your own.   (H 112)

1586 WARNER *Albion's Eng.* II. xii. G3 Hands of, commaunded Hercules, for Horse I am no hay. *a.* **1628** CARMICHAELL no. 625 Hald af your hands af other folks bairnes. **1721** KELLY no. 174 . . . Spoken by a Girl, when a young Man offers to teaze her.

Hands, With unwashed.   (H 125)

[ERASM. *Adagia* 354c Illotis manibus.] **1540** PALSGRAVE *Acolastus* 63 Why be these holy thynges, to be medled with, with vnwashed handes? **1562** J. WIGAND *De Neutralibus* F8ᵛ Those mennes rashnesse ... whiche as it were with vnwashen hands meddle with these controuersies. **1597** SHAKES. *I Hen. IV* III. iii. 182 Rob me the exchequer the first thing thou doest, and do it with unwash'd hands too.

Hands, *see also* Hand(s).

Handsaw is a good thing, but not to shave with, A.

1732 FULLER no. 210. **1746** FRANKLIN Dec. Tim and his handsaw are good in their place, Tho' not fit for preaching or shaving a face. **1802** WOLCOT (P. Pindar) *Middl. Elect.* i A handsaw is a useful thing, But never made for shaving.

Handsel, *see* Thieves' h. ever unlucky.

Handsome at twenty, He that is not | nor strong at thirty, nor rich at forty, nor wise at fifty, will never be handsome, strong, rich, or wise.   (T 631)

1591 FLORIO *Second F.* 101 And who is not at twentie, and knowes not a thirtie, And hath not at fortie in store, Will not be while he liues. **1640** HERBERT no. 349. **1741** S. RICHARDSON *Familiar Lett.* LXV.

Handsome head of hair; You have a | pray give me a tester.[1]   (H 277)

1678 RAY 73 . . . When Spendthrifts come to borrow money they commonly usher in their errand with some frivolous discourse in commendation of the person they would borrow of, or some of his parts or qualities: The same be said of beggers. [¹ sixpence.]

Handsome is that handsome does.   (D 410)

1580 MUNDAY *Sunday Examples* Sh. S. 78 But as the ancient adage is, goodly is he that goodly dooth. **1670** RAY 99 He is handsome that handsome doth. **1766** GOLDSMITH *Vicar of W.* ch. 1 They are as heaven made them, handsome enough if they be good enough; for handsome is that handsome does. **1829** COBBETT *Adv. to Y. Men* iii (1906) 122 'Handsome is that handsome does', used to say to me an old man, who had marked me out for his not over-handsome daughter.

Handspike, *see* Purser's shirt on a h. (Like a).

Handwriting, *see* Writing (H.) on the wall.

Hang a dog on a crab-tree, and he'll never love verjuice.[1]   (D 473)

1659 HOWELL *Eng. Prov.* 5b He that is hang'd in a Crabb tree, will never love Verjuyce. **1670** RAY 81 . . . This is a ludicrous and nugatory saying, for a dog once hang'd is past loving or hating. But generally men and beasts shun those things, by or for which they have smarted. **1692** L'ESTRANGE *Aesop's Fab.* lix (1738) 74 Affliction makes a man both honest and wise; for the smart brings him to a sense of his error, and the experiment to the knowledge of it. . . . [¹ The juice of sour fruit, formerly much used in cooking.]

Hang a nose, To. (N 231)

[= to have an inclination or hankering.] **1649** G. DANIEL *Trinarch. Hen. V* cxxv Chuse his Bread, And hang a Nose to Leekes, Quaile-Surfetted. **1655** tr. *Sorel's Com. Hist. Francion* VIII. 19 If there be in my Kitchin any thing better than another . . . this Gallant wil hang a nose after it.

Hang all my bells upon one horse, I must (will) not. (B 279)

1659 HOWELL *Eng. Prov.* 14b . . .; *viz. Give all away to one son.* **1732** FULLER no. 1786 Hang not all your bells upon one horse.

Hang between heaven and hell like Erasmus, To.

1590 R. HARVEY *Plain Percival* B3 Say not thou as an olde Pasquill said . . . of that famouse and modest Clarke Erasmus, that I hang houering in the mid way betwixt heauen and hell. **1706** STEVENS s.v. Alma We have a saying, he hangs betwixt Heaven and Hell like Erasmus. *a.* **1734** R. NORTH *Life of John North* 1744 ed. 268 So diffident of the Event, that, between Impulse and Despair, he was like Mahomet in his Tomb, or, as they say, Erasmus hung.

Hang by the heels, Let him. (H 388)

1678 RAY 353 Let him hang by the heels. *Som.* (Of a man that dies in debt: His wife leaving all at his death, crying his goods in three markets and three Parish Churches is so free of all his debts.)

Hang care (sorrow). *Cf.* Care will kill a cat. (C 85)

c. **1600** I *Ret. from Parn.* i. 40. Hange sorrow! [1598] **1601** JONSON *Ev. Man In Hum.* I. iii. 83 Hang sorrow. **1604** *Wit Woman* C4ᵛ Why? hang sorrow, twill not buy a Pipe. **1639** CLARKE 292. **1666** TORRIANO *It. Prov.* 162, note 24 As the English say, Hang sorrow, cast away care.

Hang him that has no shift (shifts) and him that has one too many. (S 336)

1678 RAY 346. **1721** KELLY 128 . . . He that has no Shift, is not worth hanging; and he that has too many, may be hanged in time. **1732** FULLER no. 1785. **1738** SWIFT Dial. I. E.L. 288. The loop of my hat is broke, how shall I mend it? [*He fastens it with a pin.*] Well, hang him, say I, that has no shift.—Ay, and hang him that has one too many.

Hang him that has no shifts. (S 335)

1606 *Wily Beguiled* sc. viii E1ᵛ. **1616** WITHALS 584. **1639** CLARKE 42.

Hang himself in his own garters, He may go. (G 42)

1591 ARIOSTO *Orl. Fur.* Harington X. 37 But burned maist thou be, or cut in quarters, Or driuen to hang thy selfe in thine owne garters. **1595** SHAKES. *M.N.D.* V. i. 348 If he that writ it had played Pyramus and hang'd himself in Thisby's garter. **1596** T. LODGE *Wit's Misery* E4 I will make the moule warpe hang himselfe in his owne garters. **1597** SHAKES. *I Hen. IV* II. ii. 42 Hang thyself in thine own heir apparent garters. [1599] **1660** SIR B. RUDYERD *Le Prince d'Amour* 71 Go hang thee in thy Garters. **1601** SHAKES. *T.N.* I. iii. 10 These clothes are good enough to drink in, and so be these boots too: an they be not, let them hang themselves in their own straps. **1605** JONSON *Volp.* V. iii. 20. **1611** TOURNEUR *Ath. Trag.* II. v And as I ran, indeed I bid him hang himself in his own garters. **1652** 'G. ALBUMAZAR' *Mercurius Phreneticus* 2 Potes pendere in tuo Gartero, you may hang yourself in your own Garters. **1678** RAY 246. **1692** T. D'URFEY *The Marriage-Hater Match'd* V. iii. **1738** SWIFT *Dial.* I. E.L. 288 Well, go hang yourself in your own garters.

Hang his dog, He that would | gives out first that he is mad. (D 477)

1530 PALSGRAVE 450b He that wyll kyll his neyghbours dogge beareth folkes in hande he is madde. **1591** *Hist. of Civil Wars of France* 430 (kill). **1670** RAY 81. . . . He that is about to do any thing disingenuous, unworthy, or of evil fame, first bethinks himself of some plausible pretence. **1732** FULLER no. 2362.

Hang in your light, *see* Lips; Maidenhead.

Hang one's harp on the willows, To. (H 174)

[PS. cxxxvii. 1, 2 We wept, when we remembered Zion. We hanged our harps upon the willows.] **1431** LYDGATE 'A Defence of Holy Church' *Minor Poems* E.E.T.S., 10, ll. 24–5 And on the salwys olde foule and thikk To hang hir orgnes. [1610] **1620** BEAUM. & FL. *Philaster* II. ii. 61 If there be but two such more in this Kingdom, and near the Court, we may even hang up our Harps. **1633** P. FLETCHER *Pisc. Eclog.* iv No marvel if I hate my jocund rhymes, And hang my pipe upon a willow bough. **1757** SMOLLETT *Reprisal* I. 8 All our fine project gone to pot!—We may now hang up our harps among the willows. [*Cf.* **1840** J. B. KER *Supplement* 168 He hangs his fiddle up with his hat. The complaint of the patient dependent of his arrogant patron.]

Hang saving: bring us a ha'porth of cheese. (P 337)

c. **1630** *Hang Pinching* [title of ballad] in *Roxb. Ballads* B.S. iii. 255. **1642** TORRIANO 75 Do, lay on more wood; hang it, the ashes will yield money. Nota. Vsed by way of Irony, when we see one laying of too much wood on the fire. **1738** SWIFT *Dial.* II. E.L. 311 Come, hang saving; bring us up a half-p'orth of cheese.

Hang than to hold, Better to. (H 129)

1567 HARMAN *Caveat* (Viles & Furnivall) 76 He is better to hang then to drawe forth. **1624** T.

BREWER *A Knot of Fools* A 4 Better to hang, then to feed. **1635** MERITON *Yorks. Ale* 48 Sike fowkes are fitter to hang than hawd. **1639** CLARKE 86.

Hang the groin (an arse, a leg), To.
(A 384)

[= to hesitate or hold back; also to grumble.] **1546** HEYWOOD II. vi. Ii Suche an olde wytche . . . As euermore lyke a hog hangeth the groyne, On her husband, except he be hir slaue. **1577–87** HOLINSHED *Chron.* (1807–8) III. 163 At this answer The duke hoong the groin. **1596** HARINGTON *Metam. Ajax* 54 Some of our rude contrimen English this (obtorto collo) hanging arse. **1681** BEHN 2 *Rover* III. i, 155 Think of a Million, Rogue, and do not hang an Arse thus. **1883** STEVENSON *Treas. Isl.* I. v. You have your hands on thousands, you fools, and you hang a leg!

Hang together like pebbles in a halter, They.
(P 169)

1551 WILSON *Rule Reason* S5 This geare hangeth together like a broken potte sheerd. **1639** CLARKE 155 It hangs together as pebles in a wyth.[1] **1678** RAY 250. [1 basket.]

Hang up one's hatchet (axe), To.
(H 209)

[= to cease from one's labours, to rest.] *c.* **1200** *Owl and Nightingale* (Cotton MS. *c.* 1250) l. 658 Hong up þin ax! *a.* **1327** *Pol. Songs* Camden Soc. 223 Hang up thyn hachet ant thy knyf Whil him lasteth the lyf with the long shonkes. *c.* **1430** *Hymns Virg.* (1867) 69 Hang up þin hatchet & take þi reste. *a.* **1500** *Sir Gawain and the Green Knight* l. 477 Now sir, heng vp þyn ax, þat hatz in-nogh hewen. *a.* **1530** *R. Hill's Common Pl. Bk.* (1858) 140 When thou hast well done hang up thy hatchet. **1555** HEYWOOD *Epig. on Proverbs* CXLVII I haue hangde vp my hatchet, and scapte thy [*for* my] selfe. **1659** HOWELL *Eng. Prov.* 6b I have hang'd vp my hatchet and scap'd my self.

Hang yourself for a pastime.
(P 92)
1678 RAY 73.

Hanged for a sheep as a lamb, As good (well) be.
(S 293)
1678 RAY 350 (an old sheep) *Somerset.* **1721** KELLY 46 . . . Used at a Game at Tables, when I venture high in order to recover my Game which otherwise would be lost. **1836** MARRYAT *Midsh. Easy* ch. 17 We may as well be hanged for a sheep as a lamb, . . . I vote that we do not go on board.

Hanged for leaving his liquor, like the saddler of Bawtry,[1] He will be. *Cf.* Hanged that left his drink.
1790 GROSE s.v. Yorkshire. **1818** S. PEGGE *Curialia Mix.* 340 This saying, often applied . . . to a man who quits his friends too early, and will not stay to finish his bottle. [1 Yorks.]

Hanged, If I be | I'll choose my gallows.
(G 18)
1631 SHIRLEY *Love Tricks* v. ii. I hope I shall choose my own gallows then. *a.* **1633** JONSON *T. Tub* IV. vi. 97–8 Hang'd . . .? yes sure; unlesse, as with the Proverbe, You meane to make the choice of your own gallowes. **1659** HOWELL *Eng. Prov.* 16b If I be hang'd Ile chuse my gallowes. **1738** SWIFT *Dial.* II. E.L. 296. Well, miss, if I must be hanged, I won't go far to choose my gallows; it shall be about your fair neck.

Hanged in May, He that is | will eat no flannes[1] in midsummer.
1820 SCOTT *Abbot* ch. 33 He that is hanged in May will eat no flannes in Midsummer. [1 custards, pancakes.]

Hanged, He that has had one of his family | may not say to his neighbour, Hang up this fish. *Cf.* Rope, Name not.
(F 48)
1678 RAY *Adag. Hebr.* 408 . . . The meaning is, we must abstain from words of reproach, . . . especially when we are not free from the crimes which we reproach others for.

Hanged that left his drink behind him, He was. *Cf.* Hanged for leaving his liquor.
(D 601)
c. **1640** *Roxb. Ballads* B.S. 416 He was hang'd that left his drinke behinde. **1659** HOWELL *Eng. Prov.* 5b He was hangd who left his drink behind him; A thief being pursued to an Alehouse, left suddenly his drink behind, and so was discover'd and hang'd. **1678** RAY 71 . . . Good fellows have a story of a certain malefactour, who came to be suspected upon leaving his drink behind him in an Alehouse, at the News of an Hue and cry. **1738** SWIFT *Dial.* II. E.L. 312 Stay till this bottle's out; you know, the man was hang'd that left his liquor behind him.

Hanging and wiving (wedding) go by destiny. *Cf.* Marriage is destiny.
(W 232)
1519 W. HORMAN *Vulgaria* ed. M. James 37 It is my destenye to be hanged. **1541** *Schoolhouse of Women* Bi[v] Some men . . . saye it goeth by destenye To hange or wed . . . I am well sure Hangynge is better of the twayne Sooner done, and shorter payne. **1546** HEYWOOD I. iii. A4[v] Be it far or ny, weddyng is desteny, And hangyng lykewise, sayth that prouerbe, sayd I. **1596** SHAKES. *M.V.* II. ix. 82 The ancient saying is no heresy: 'Hanging and wiving goes by destiny.' **1600** DEKKER *Shoem. Hol.* IV. ii. Well, God sends fooles fortune, and . . . he may light vpon his matrimony by such a deuice, for wedding and hanging goes by destiny. *a.* **1628** CARMICHAELL no. 630 Hanging gois be hap, bot coms to yow be heritage. **1664** BUTLER *Hudibras* II. i. 839 If matrimony and hanging go By dest'ny, why not whipping too? **1738** SWIFT *Dial.* I. E.L. 284 'Twas her fate; they say, marriage and hanging go by destiny.

Hanging's stretching; mocking's catching. *See also* Mocking is catching.

(H 131)

1678 RAY 200.

Hanging, *see also* Agree like bells, want but h.; Half an hour's h. hinders . . . riding; Hemp for h.; Thieves and rogues have the best luck, if they but scape h.; Ways to kill dog than h. (More).

Hangs by geometry, It.   (G 82)

1581 H. GOLDWELL *Brief Declarⁿ* B4ᵛ Some there were and so manifold, that Geometrie whercon the body of man hangeth coulde not beare being intollerable, nor the minde which consisteth in Arithmetique, number being infinite. **1583** MELBANCKE *Philot.* X4 With more griefe, then can be borne with Geometry. [**1622**] **1647** FLETCHER *Spanish Curate* III. ii. **1738** SWIFT Dial. I. E.L. 286 My petticoat! how it hangs by jommetry!

Hangs himself on Sunday, He that | shall hang still uncut down on Monday.

(S 993)

1546 HEYWOOD I. xi. 27 Well, he that hangth hym selfe a sondaie (saied he) Shall hang styll vncut downe a mondaie for me.

Hang(s, ed), *see also* Almost was never h.; Born to be h. never be drowned; Boughs that bear most h. lowest; Confess and be h.; Conscience was h. long ago; Dog is h. for his skin, (Many a); Farewell and be h.; Hair (thread), (To h. by); Halter to h. himself; Haste to h. true men (No); Herring must h. by own gill; Ill deemed half h.; Ill name, half h.; Kill a man in jest and be h. in earnest; Kills a man when drunk shall be h.; Lincoln shall be h. for London's sake; Live to be old (If you would not), be h. young; Luck goes on (If your), you may hope to be h.; Men of all trades (Of), they especially h. thieves; Messengers should not be h.; Mumchance . . . h. for saying nothing; Over holy man h.; Pay well . . . h. well; Rich before night, h. before noon; Rich man's money h. him; Rises over early that is h. ere noon; Rope enough . . . h. himself (h. his mare); Rope (Name not) in his house that h. himself; Scant of news that told father was h.; Sheep h. by his own shank (Let every); Steal for others shall be h.; Suits h. half a year in Westminster Hall; Tender Gordons that dow not be h.; Worst use can put man to is h. him.

Hangman, *see* Hop whore! . . . h. lead the dance.

Hankering and hinging on is a poor trade.

1721 KELLY 142 . . . Spoken of the miserable Condition of those who depend upon great Men's Promiscs for Places and Preferments.

Hans-in-kelder.

[Dutch, lit. Jack-in-cellar: an unborn child.] **1635** BROME *Sparagus Garden* III. iv. Wks.

(1873) III. 159 Come here's a health to the Hans in Kelder, and the mother of the boy, if it prove so. **1816** SCOTT *Let.* 12 Nov. in LOCKHART *Life* ch. 37 (1860) 337 I think of sending you one day . . . a little drama. . . . It is yet only in embryo—a sort of poetical Hans in Kelder.

Hantle[1] o' fauts, Some hae a | ye're only a ne'er-do-weel.

1862 HISLOP 264 . . . Some, though very bad, still have some redeeming qualities; the party addressed has none. [[1] a considerable number.]

Hap and halfpenny goods enough.

(H 135)

1621 ROBINSON 24. *a.* **1628** CARMICHAELL no. 633 (warlds geir aneuch). **1639** CLARKE 126. **1641** FERGUSSON no. 374 Hap and a half-pennie, is warlds geir enough. **1670** RAY 100 . . . i.e. Good luck is enough, though a man hath not a penny left him.

Hap, Some have the | some stick in the gap.   (H 136)

1639 CLARKE 125. **1721** KELLY 296.

Hap, *see also* Good or ill h. of a good or ill life; No man can make his own h.

Happen(s), *see* Chances (H.) in an hour that h. not in seven years; Many things h. unlooked for; One man, (What chances to) may h. to all men; Unforeseen that h.

Happiness, *see* Content is h.; Talks much of his h. (He that).

Happy for a day, Let him that would be | go to the barber; for a week, marry a wife; for a month, buy him a new horse; for a year, build him a new house; for all his life time, be an honest man.

1662 FULLER Wales 6 Italian.

Happy is he that chastens himself.

(C 255)

1640 HERBERT no. 137.

Happy is he that is happy in his children.

1732 FULLER no. 1787.

Happy is he whose friends were (father was) born before him.   (F 740)

1666 TORRIANO *Prov. Phr.* s.v. Ricchi The English . . . say of a rich man that never purchas'd his Estate, His Father was born before him. **1670** RAY 99 i.e. Who has *rem non labore parandum sed relictam.* **1721** KELLY 379 You may thank God that your Friends were born before you. Spoken to unactive thriftless People, who, if their Parents had left them nothing must have begg'd. **1732** FULLER no. 1790. **1738** SWIFT *Dial.* III. E.L. 317 Why, madam, 'tis happy for him that his father was born before him. **1833** MARRYAT *Peter Simple* ch. 39 (father).

Happy is she who marries the son of a dead mother. *Cf.* Well married who has neither.

1721 KELLY 162 . . . There is rarely a good understanding between a Daughter in Law, and her Husband's Mother.

Happy is that child whose father goes to the devil. (C 305)

1549 LATIMER *Serm.* 9 P.S. 146 (The old saying is, Happy). **1552** *Id. Serm. Lord's Prayer* V. P.S. 410 There is a common saying amongst the worldlings, Happy is that child whose father goeth to the devil. . . . Many a father goeth to the devil for his child's sake; in that he . . . scraped for his child, and forgat to relieve his poor miserable neighbour. **1591** SHAKES. *3 Hen. VI* II. ii. 47 And happy always was it for that son Whose father for his hoarding went to hell? **1670** RAY 100 Happy is the child whose father went to the devil. For commonly they who first raise great estates, do it either by usury and extortion, or by fraud and cozening, or by flattery and ministering to other men's vices.

Happy is the, *see* Bride the sun shines on; Country which has no history; Wooing that is not long.

Happy man cannot be harried,[1] The.

1721 KELLY 313 . . . Spoken when a fear'd Misfortune happen'd for the best. [1 ruined.]

Happy man, happy dole (be his dole). (M 158)

[= may happiness be his portion.] **1546** HEYWOOD I. iii. A4ᵛ Than wed or hang (quoth he) what helpth in the whole To haste or hang a loofe, happy man happy dole. **1594–8** SHAKES. *T.S.* I. i. 135 Sweet Bianca! Happy man be his dole. **1597** *Id. 1 Hen. IV* II. ii. 73 Now my masters, happy man be his dole, say I. **1600–1** *Id. M.W.W.* III. iv. 62 If it be my luck, so; If not, happy man be his dole. **1611** *Id. W.T.* I. ii. 163 No, my lord, I'll fight.—You will? Why, happy man be his dole. **1660** TATHAM *Rump.* I. i A short life and a merry life, I cry. Happy man be his dole. **1809** MALKIN *Gil Blas* VIII. ix Happy man be his dole who can get them to dinner or supper.

Happy man, happy kevel.[1] (M 157)

a. **1628** CARMICHAELL no. 632 (cavill). **1721** KELLY 159 . . . Jocosely spoken when People are drawing Lots, or when it has faln out well with us, or our Friend. [1 lot.]

Happy, Call no man | till he dies. (M 333)

[AESCH. *Ag.* 928. SOPH. *Oed. Rex*, last words. EUR. *Androm.* 100. HDT. 132 (Solon and Croesus). OV. *Met.* 3. 135.] **1545** TAVERNER G5ᵛ Salon aunswered kynge Cresus, that no man coulde be named happy, tyl he had happely and prosperouslye passed the course of his lyfe. [1562] **1565** NORTON & SACKVILLE *Gorboduc* III. i. 11 Oh no man happie, till his ende be seene. **1591** ARIOSTO *Orl. Fur.* Harington XXIII. Morall Ovid said of Cadmus . . . Our onely dying day, and end doth show If that a man haue happie beene or no. **1596** SPENSER *F.Q.* IV. iv. 43 So nought may be esteemed happie till the end. **1603** MONTAIGNE (Florio) I. xviii. 83 We must expect of man the latest day, Nor e'er he die, he's happy, can we say. **1891** *Times* 5 Dec. Call no man happy till he dies is the motto . . . suggested by the career of Dom Pedro [of Brazil].

Happy, *see also* Better be h. than wise; Comparison that makes men h.; Hour wherein a man might be h. could he find it; Merry (H.) as the day is long; Merry (H.) as a king; Misery enough to have once been h.; Sickle . . . love I not to see, but the good ale tankard, h. might it be.

Harborough field, I will throw you into. (H 143)

1678 RAY (*Leics.*) . . . A threat for children, Harborough having no field.

Harbory, *see* Ill of his h. is good of waykenning.

Harbour, *see* Rogue's wardrobe is h. for a louse.

Hard (dry) as a bone. (B 514)

1552 HULOET P2ᵛ. *c.* **1555** *Songs and Bal. Philip and Mary* 5, 14 Also the congars, as dry as a bonne. **1678** RAY 283 (dry).

Hard as a diamond, As.

c. **1380** *Rom. of Rose* B l. 4385. **1552** HULOET s.v. Diamond.

Hard as a flint (stone), As. (H 311. S 878)

c. **1390** CHAUCER *Merchant's T.* l. 1990 An herte as hard as any stoon. *c.* **1400** *Pety Job* 318 in *26 Pol. Poems* 131 Me thynketh myn hert ys harder than a ston. **1530** PALSGRAVE 624a As harde as a stone. **1565** NORTON & SACKVILLE *Gorboduc* IV. i. 38 Such hard hart of rocke and stonie flint. **1601** SHAKES. *T.N.* I. v. 270 Love make his heart of flint that you shall love. *Ibid.* v. i. 118 Live you the marble-breasted tyrant. **1720** GAY *Poems* (Underhill) ii. 278 Hard is her heart as flint or stone.

Hard as nails.

1837–8 DICKENS *O. Twist* ch. 9. **1896** SHAW *You Never Can Tell* I. My landlord is as rich as a Jew and as hard as nails.

Hard baked, *see* Crusty (You need not be so).

Hard cases make bad law.

[SALL. *Cat.* 51. 27 *Omnia mala exempla ex bonis* (i.e. good special cases) *orta sunt.*] **1902–4** LEAN III. 479 Hard cases make bad law, i.e. lead to legislation for exceptions. **1909** *Spectator* 809 Even so bad a case . . . does not . . . alter our attitude . . . 'Hard cases make bad law', and also bad policy. **1945** CHURCHILL (Premier) 12 June (in H. of Commons) Hard cases do not make good law.

Hard cheese.

1876 MRS. BANKS *Manch. Man* ch. 42 It's hard cheese for a man to owe everything to his father-in-law.

Hard fare makes hungry bellies. (F 56)

1616 BRETON *Wks.* Gros. ii. E6 Hard fare makes hungry stomackes. **1639** CLARKE 241. **1732** FULLER no. 1796.

Hard-fought field, where no man escapes unkilled, A. (F 207)

1546 HEYWOOD I. xi. E4 Olde men saie that are skyld, A hard foughten feeld, where no man scapeth vnkyld. **1639** CLARKE 103 'Tis an hard battel where none scape. **1641** FERGUSSON no. 549 It's a sair field where all are dung[1] down. [1 beaten.]

Hard gives more than he that has nothing, The. (H 144)

1599 MINSHEU *Span. Gram.* 80 More giueth the hard than the naked. **1640** HERBERT no. 259. **1706** STEVENS s.v. Dar (than the naked).

Hard heart against hard hap (Stout heart to a stey[1] brae), Set. (H 326)

a. **1585** ALEX. MONTGOMERIE *Cherrie & Slae* xxxvi (1821) 21 So gets ay, that sets ay, Stout stomackis to the brae. **1639** CLARKE 15. **1721** KELLY 287 Set a stout heart to a stay Brea. Set about a difficult Business with Courage and Constancy. **1821** GALT *Annals of Par.* ch. 1 I began a round of visitations; but oh, it was a steep brae that I had to climb, and it needed a stout heart. For I found the doors . . . barred against me. **1830** CARLYLE *Let. to Brother John* 11 Feb. 'Stout heart to a stay brae' then, my brave boy! There is nothing in this world to frighten a clear heart. [1 steep.]

Hard-hearted as a Scot of Scotland, As. (S 155)

1678 RAY 285.

Hard nut to crack, A. *Cf.* Crack me that nut.

1745 FRANKLIN *Lett.* Wks. 1887 II. 16 Fortified towns are hard nuts to crack. **1888** J. PAYN *Myst. Mirbridge* ch. 21 You will find Robert Morris a hard nut to crack.

Hard task to be poor and leal, It is a.

1721 KELLY 211 . . . Because Poverty is a great Tentation to steal.

Hard thing to have a great estate, and not fall in love with it, It is a.

1721 FULLER no. 2862.

Hard to come by are much set by, Things that are. (T 201)

c. **1400** *Rom. Rose* l. 2737 May no man have good, but he it by. A man loveth more tendirly The thyng that he hath bought most dere. *a.* **1567** T. BECON *Catechism* P.S. 142 Things soon given wax vile; but things long desired, and at the last obtained, are highly esteemed and had in great price. **1582** WHETSTONE *Heptameron* VI (As the Prouerbe goeth) things that are dearely bought, are of vs intirely belooued. **1587** GREENE *Wks.* Gros. iv. 101 Hardlie come by, warilie kept. *c.* **1590** *John of Bordeaux* l. 101 The harder goote the swetter in the tast. **1629** T. ADAMS *Serm.* (1861-2) II. 545 Benefits common to all . . . are little regarded: but *quæ rarissima carissima*—things hard to come by are much set by. **1639** CLARKE 101 Things hardly atteined are long reteined.

Hard to please a knave as a knight, It is as. (K 126)

1639 CLARKE 275. **1670** RAY 111.

Hard winter when one wolf eats another, It is a. (W 509)

1579 LYLY *Euph.* i. 223 Men themselues haue by vse obserued, that it must be a hard winter, when one Wolfe eateth an other. **1584** WITHALS C2 I neuer see one Woolfe eate another before. **1651** HERBERT no. 1125 A wolfe will never make war against another wolfe. **1670** RAY 156 . . . Mauvaise est la saison quand un loup mange l'autre. **1710** PALMER 327.

Hard with hard makes not the stone wall. (H 145)

[Med. L. *Durum et durum non faciunt murum.*] **1573** SANFORD 104 Harde with harde neuer made good wall. **1629** T. ADAMS *Serm.* (1861-2) II. 317 The Italians have a proverb, 'Hard without soft, the wall is nought'. Stones . . . without mortar . . . make but a tottering wall. . . . The society that consists of nothing but stones, intractable and refractory spirits, . . . soon dissolves. **1655** FULLER *Ch. Hist.* II. iii. (1868) I. 143 'Hard with hard', saith the proverb, 'makes no wall'; and no wonder if the spiritual building went on no better, wherein the austerity and harshness of the pastor met with the ignorance and sturdiness of the people.

Hard words break no bones.

c. **1450** Towneley Play of *Noah* 380 E.E.T.S. 34 Thise grete wordis shall not flay me. **1683** MERITON *Yorkshire Ale* 83 Foul words break neay bones. **1867** TROLLOPE *Last Chron. Bars.* ch. 42 I often tell 'em how wrong folks are to say that soft words butter no parsnips, and hard words break no bones. **1882** BLACKMORE *Christow.* ch. 49 'Scoundrel, after all that I have done—'. 'Hard words break no bones, my friend.'

Hard, *see also* Beginning is h., (Every); Close (h.) as oak; Eats the h. shall eat the ripe; Good things are h.; Row to hoe (H.); Sweet is the nut, but bitter (h.) the shell; Three things . . . h. to be known; Work h., live h. . . . . would be h. indeed.

Hard, It is; Hard to make, It is. *See also under significant words following.*

Hardships, *see* Misfortunes (H.) never come alone.

Hare, He has devoured a. *Cf.* Hare is melancholy meat. (H 159)

1576 LEMNIUS *Touchstone of Complexions* tr. T. Newton 154 They . . . are neuer requested vnto any such pleasurable assembly . . . being reputed . . . such as neuer (according to the prouerbe) tasted or eate an Hare. [Margin] To eate a Hare, a Prouerbe. **1577** T. KENDALL *Flowers of Epigrams* B2 Thou didst neuer eate an hare. **1599** H. BUTLER *Diet's Dry Dinner* K2 It is a receiued opinion, that vse of Hares fleshe procureth beautie, fresh colour, and cheerfull countenance, for a seuenight space: in so much as the Italians haue a by-word, which speaketh thus of a faire man, He hath eaten an Hare.

Hare always returns to her form, The.

1659 HOWELL *Span. Prov.* 10 At the end of 1000. years the Hare returns to her first form. **1818** SCOTT *Ht. Midl.* ch. 34 I have no thought of stirring from the house I was born in; like the hare, I shall be worried in the seat I started from.

Hare away, There goes the. (H 157)

[= here or there the matter ended.] *c.* **1500** MEDWALL *Nature* pt. II, l. 589 (BRANDL *Quellen* 134) There went the hare away. **1528** ROY & BARLOW *Rede me and be not wroth* ed. Arber 63 There goeth the hare quyte away. **1546** HEYWOOD II. v. H4 And here goth the hare awaie. **1579** GOSSON *Sch. Abuse* Arb. 70 *Hic labor, hoc opus est*, there goeth the hare away. [*c.* **1587**] **1592** KYD *Span. Trag.* III. xii. 24 Here's the king . . . there goes the hare away. **1600** HOLLAND *Livy* XXXV. xlv. 914 And here went the hare away. **1620** SHELTON *Quix.* II. xxx. iii. 31 But where we least think there goes the hare away. **1659** HOWELL *Fr. Prov.* 16 (lies).

Hare is melancholy meat. *Cf.* Hare, He has devoured a. (H 151)

1558 BULLEIN *Govt. of Health* 90 The fleshe of hares be hoote and drye, ingenderers of melancholye. **1576** LEMNIUS *Touchstone of Complexions* tr. T. Newton 153ᵛ. **1597-8** SHAKES. *1 Hen. IV* I. ii. 76 What sayest thou to a hare, or the melancholy of Moorditch? **1621** BURTON *Anat. Mel.* I. ii. II. 1 (1651) 67 Hare, a black meat, melancholy, and hard of digestion. **1738** SWIFT *Dial.* II. E.L. 303 Will your ladyship have any of this hare?—No, madam, they say 'tis melancholy meat.

Hare (Tod¹) or the bracken bush, Either the.

1659 T. PECKE *Parnassi Puerp.* 143 He can't discern a hare from a brake-bush. **1670** RAY 179 It's either a hare or a brake-bush . . . something if you knew what. **1721** KELLY 97 (tod) . . . Spoken to silly People when they speak with Uncertainty. [¹ fox.]

Hare to breakfast, He that will have a | must hunt over-night. (H 154)

1636 CAMDEN 297. **1732** FULLER no. 2365.

Hare's foot, *see* Kiss the h. f.

Hare's head (foot) against the goose giblet(s), Set the. (H 161)

1545 TAVERNER E4ᵛ As I say in our englyshe prouerbe: Set the hares head against the gose gyblet. **1546** HEYWOOD II. iv. G4. **1599** DEKKER *Shoem. Hol.* II. i (Merm.) 17 I'd set my old debts against my new driblets, And the hare's foot against the goose giblets. **1633** ROWLEY *Match. Midn.* Hazl.-Dods. v. 88 As I have been bawd to the flesh, you have been bawd to your money, so set the hare-pie against the goose-giblets. **1670** RAY 179 . . . That is, balance things, set one against another. **1732** FULLER no. 4109.

Hares may pull dead lions by the beard. (H 165)

[ERASM. *Ad.* IV. vii. 82 *Mortuo leoni et lepores insultant.*] **1580** BARET *Alveary* M487 [as in Erasm.] . . . A proverbe vsed when any take libertie in the absence of their gouernour. **1581** GUAZZO i. 73 Of these, this saying rose, That the Lion being dead, the verie Hares triumph over him. [*c.* **1587**] **1592** KYD *Span. Trag.* I. ii. 172 So hares may pull dead lions by the beard. **1592** T. NASHE *Strange News* i. 271. **1596** SHAKES. *K.J.* II. i. 138 You are the hare of whom the proverb goes Whose valour plucks dead lions by the beard. **1609** J. WYBARNE *New Age of Old Names* 41 Why doe these sillie Hares thus insult vpon a dead Lyon? **1639** CLARKE 216. **1697** W. POPE *Seth* [Ward] 187 These flock of Hares had the boldness to insult, and pull by the Beard the dying, or rather dead Lion.

Hare(s), *see* Blind man may sometimes catch h.; Cow to catch a h. (Set a); Dog (Hindmost) may catch h.; Dogs that put up many h. kill none; Dry meat . . . when he lost the h.; Fearful as the h.; Find a woman . . . and a h. without meuse; First catch your h.; God send you readier meat than running h.; Hunt for a h. with tabor; Mad as a h.; Run after two h. (If you); Run with the h. and hunt with hounds; Seek a h. in a hen's nest; Take h. with foxes; Tortoise to catch h. (Set); Tortoise wins race while h. is sleeping.

Harlot, *see* Silk and scarlet (In).

Harm watch, harm catch. (H 167)

1481 CAXTON *Reynard* XX Arb. 50 I shal vnbynde my sack. yf he wil seche harm he shal fynde harme. **1614** JONSON *Barthol. Fair* V. iv. 180. **1663** J. WILSON *Cheats* II. v And to our seeming, it said again—Harm watch, harm catch. **1706** STEVENS s.v. Caça.

Harm(s), *see also* Better the devil (h.) you know; Beware by other men's h.; Far from home, near thy h.; Good man can do more h.; Hate not at first h.; Silence does seldom h.

Harmless, *see* Innocent (h.) as a dove.

Harness, *see* Die in h.

Harp and harrow, To agree like.

[= things entirely different, though their names alliterate.] **1563** BECON *Displ. Pop. Masse* (1637) 299 The Lords Supper and your peevish, popish private masse do agree together . . . as the common proverbe is, like harpe and harrow, or like the hare and the hound. **1624** GATAKER *Transubst.* 203 These things hang together like harp and harrow, as they say. **1639** CLARKE 94. **1700** T. BROWN tr. *Fresny's Amusem. Ser. & Com.* 34 [Bethlehem] Bedlam . . . whether the Name and Thing be not as disagreeable as Harp and Harrow.

Harp on (upon) one (another) string, To. (s 936)

c. **1374** CHAUCER *Troilus* Bk. 2, l. 1033 For though the beste harpour upon lyve Wolde on the beste sowned joly harpe . . . Touche ay o streng. . . . It sholde maken every wight to dulle. c. **1513** SIR T. MORE *Rich. III* 1821 ed. 54 The Cardinall made a countinance to the tother Lord, that he should harp no more vpon that string. c. **1533** J. FRITH *Answ. agst. Restell* D1ᵛ Se howe he harpeth all of one strynge. **1579** LYLY *Euph.* i. 272 He sholde more ouer talke of manye matters, not alwayes harp vpon one string. **1587** BRIDGES *Defence* 1192 They harping on an other string. [**1592**] **1597** SHAKES. *Rich. III* IV. iv. 365 Harp not on that string, madam; that is past. **1600–1** *Id. H.* II. ii. 185 How say you by that? Still harping on my daughter. **1608** *Id. C.* II. iii. 249 Say you ne'er had done 't—Harp on that still—but by our putting on. **1662** FULLER *Somers.* 24 Which harping on that one string of his fidelity . . . was harmonious to queen Elizabeth.

Harp on the string that gives no melody, You. (s 935)

1546 HEYWOOD II. iv. G4 Ye harpe on the stryng, that giueth no melody. Your tongs ron before your wits. **1580** LYLY *Euph. & his Eng.* ii. 151 Thou harpest on that string, which long since was out of tune, but now is broken. **1639** CLARKE 179 (makes no good musick).

Harp, *see also* Ass play upon a h.; Hang one's h. on willows.

Harper(s), *see* Blind as a h.; Have among you, blind h.

Harquebuze, *see* Spectacles are death's h.

Harried, *see* Happy man cannot be h.

Harrington (i.e. a farthing), Not worth a. (H 178)

[A patent to coin farthings was granted in 1613 to Lord Harrington of Exton, hence the name.] **1628** SIR H. WOTTON *Let.* 12 Aug. in *Reliq. Wott.* (1672) 558 I have lost four or five friends, and yet I thank God, not gotten the value of one *Harrington*.

Harrogate Wells, Said the Devil when flying o'er | I think I am getting near home by the smells.

1902–4 LEAN I. 222. [Harrogate, in Yorkshire, is noted for its sulphurous, chalybeate, and saline springs.]

Harrow (Rake) hell, and scum the devil. (H 400)

1603 S. HARSNET *Decl. Egreg. Popish Impostures* 160 If hell it selfe had beene raked (as they say) and 13 of the deuils most deuilish Ministers fetched from thence, they could not haue passed *Weston*, and his twelue deuilish tragedians, in any degree. **1670** RAY 180 (Harrow or rake hell, and). **1699** B.E. s.v. Scumm Rake Hell and Skim the Devil. **1732** FULLER no. 1798 (and rake up the Devil).

Harrow (*noun*), *see* Drinking at the h.; Harp and h.; Ox is never woe, till he to h. go; Toad said to h., cursed be so many lords.

Harry's children of Leigh, never a one like another. (H 181)

1670 RAY 217 (*Cheshire*).

Harry, *see also* Box H.; King H.; Tom, Dick, and H.

Hartlepool, *see* Mayor of H. (Like the).

Harvest ears, thick of hearing. (H 186)

1546 HEYWOOD II. ix. K3ᵛ You had on your haruest eares, thicke of hearyng. **1602** WITHALS 46 Thine eares be on pilgrimage . . . as they say commonly, Thou hast on thy haruest eares.

Harvest follows seed-time. (H 182)

1639 CLARKE 183.

Harvest(s), *see also* Eighth of June it rains (If on) wet h.; Good h. (He that has) may be content with some thistles; Good h. make men prodigal; Help, for help in h.; Long h. of little corn; Short h. make short adlings; Sickle into another man's corn, (h.), (To put one's); Snow in h. (Welcome as).

Harwich, *see* Deal, Dover, and H., the devil gave.

Has it and will not keep it; He that | he that wants it and will not seek it; he that drinks and is not dry, shall want money as well as I. (M 1041)

1659 HOWELL *Eng. Prov.* 21a. **1670** RAY 211.

Hassell's feast (Madam), *see* Enough and none to spare.

Haste and wisdom are things far odd. (W 523)

1546 HEYWOOD I. ii. A3 Than seeth he haste and wisdome thyngs far odde. **1616** DRAXE no. 930.

Haste but good (speed), No. (H 199)

c. **1534** BERNERS *Huon* ch. 99, 320 It is a saynge that an yll haste is not good. **1546** HEYWOOD II. ix. L2ᵛ. a. **1553** UDALL *Ralph Roister D.* I. iii.

Arb. 20 No haste but good, Madge Mumble-crust, for whip and whurre[1] The olde prouerbe doth say, neuer made good furre.[2]   **1639** CLARKE 115 No hast but good speed.   **1721** KELLY 261 No more haste than good speed. . . . Spoken when we are unreasonably urged to make haste. [[1] hurry. [2] furlong.]

Haste comes not alone.   (H 188)

1611 COTGRAVE s.v. Haste Hast neuer comes alone, viz. hath euer some trouble or other t'accompanie it.   **1640** HERBERT no. 826.

Haste in his business, Who has no | mountains to him seem valleys.   (H 202)

1640 HERBERT no. 997.

Haste is from hell (the devil).

1633 HOWELL *Fam. Lett.* 5 Sept. (1903) II. 140 As it is a principle in chemistry that *Omnis festinatio est a Diabolo*, All haste comes from Hell, so in . . . any business of State, all rashness and precipitation comes from an ill spirit.   **1929** *Times* 12 Sept. 14/3 Listening patiently to the views . . . [f]or he understood the East; he knew that for an Intelligence officer 'haste is from the devil'.

Haste makes waste.   (H 189)

c. **1386** CHAUCER *Melibee* l. 2244 The prouerbe seith . . . 'in wikked haste is no profit'.   **1546** HEYWOOD I. ii. A3 Show after weddyng, that hast maketh waste.   **1663** BUTLER *Hudibras* iii. 1253 *Festina lente*, Not too fast; For haste (the proverb says) makes waste.   **1853** TRENCH i. 16 Many excellent proverbs, such as Haste makes waste . . . have nothing figurative about them.

Haste makes waste, and waste makes want, and want makes strife between the goodman and his wife.   (H 190)

1678 RAY 151.

Haste, The more | the less (worse) speed.   (H 198)

c. **1350** *Douce MS.* 52 no. 86 The more hast, þe worse spede.   *c.* **1430** LYDGATE *Minor Poems* Percy Soc. 75 The slowar paas, the further in rennyng; The more I renne, the more wey I lese.   **1546** HEYWOOD I. ii. A3ᵛ Moste times he seeth, the more haste the lesse speede.   *c.* **1595** SHAKES. *R.J.* II. iii. 94 Wisely and slow; They stumble that run fast.   **1595** *Locrine* I. ii (*Shakes. Apoc.*) 43 My penne is naught; gentle-men, lend me a knife. I thinke the more haste the worst speed.   **1611** DAVIES no. 48 The more haste, the worse speede.   **1887** BLACKMORE *Springhaven* ch. 57 Some days had been spent by the leisurely Dutchman in providing fresh supplies, and the stout bark's favourite maxim seemed to be, 'the more haste the less speed'.   **1894** LD. AVEBURY *Use of Life* xii (1904) 77 Do nothing in a hurry. Nature never does. 'Most haste, worst speed.'

Haste, The more | the worse speed, quoth the tailor to his long thread.

1721 KELLY 313.

Haste to hang true men, No.   (H 201)

c. **1550** *Jacke Juggeler* Hazl.-Dods. ii. 120 I fear hanging, whereunto no man is hasty.   **1599** PORTER *Angry Wom. Abingd.* l. 875 There's no hast to hang true men.   **1662** FULLER London 195 As if Londoners . . . aim more at dispatch than Justice; and, to make quick Riddance (though no hast to hang true men), acquit half, and condemn half.   **1695** RAVENSCROFT 56 (true Folk).

Haste trips up its own heels.

1732 FULLER no. 1801.

Haste when you come down than when you went up, Make no more.   (H 195)

1567 *Merry Tales* (HAZLITT *Shakes. Jest Bks.* i. 44) Take hede, that thou go neuer downe faster than thou wentest vp.   **1604** *Pasquils Jests* (1864) 42 Take heed that you never goe faster downe then you go up.   **1678** RAY 151 As the man said to him on the tree top, Make no more haste when you come down then when you went up.   **1692** L'ESTRANGE *Aesop's Fab.* ccclxix (1738) 388 Have a care . . ., whenever you climb another tree, that you come no faster down than you went up.

Haste, *see also* Anger and h. hinder good counsel; Fool's h. no speed; Make h. slowly; Make h. to an ill way; Marry in h.; More h. than speed; No man makes h. to the market; Thrive in all h. (You would).

Hastens a glutton, Who | chokes him.   (G 145)

1640 HERBERT no. 858.

Hastes well that wisely can abide, (He), *see* Make haste slowly.

Hastily, *see* Nothing must be done h. but killing fleas.

Hastings, He is none of the.   (H 203)

1546 HEYWOOD I. xi. E2ᵛ Toward your work (quoth he) ye make such tastings, As approue you to be none of the hastyngs.   **1662** FULLER Sussex 100. . . . There is a Noble and Antient family of the Hastings . . . Earls . . . of Hunting-don. Now men commonly say, They are none of the Hastings, who being slow and slack go about business with no agility.

Hasty bitch brings forth blind whelps, The.   (B 425)

[ERASM. *Ad.* (quoting Aristotle and Galen) *Canis festinans caecos parit catulos*.]   **1556** R. ROBINSON tr. *More's Utopia* 2nd ed. To Reader Arb. 19 But as the latin prouerbe sayeth: the hastye bitche bringeth forth blind whelpes. For when this my worke was finished, the rudenes thereof shewed it to be done in poste haste.   **1575** GASCOIGNE *Posies* i. 68 The swiftest bitche brings foorth the blyndest whelpes.   **1755** FRANKLIN Mar. The hasty Bitch brings forth blind Puppies.

Hasty (The highest) climbers have sudden (the greatest) falls. *Cf.* Higher standing, lower fall.   (C 413, 414)

a. **1300** *Prov. Hendyng* ed. Schleich 18 Clymb not to hye, lest þou falle. *a.* **1449** LYDGATE *Minor Poems* II. 477 (*The Churl and the Bird*) And whoo disireth to clymbe to hih aloftt Bi sodeyn torn felith often his fal vnsoftt. *c.* **1460** *Wisdom* 444 Who clymyt hye, hys fall gret ys. **1509** BARCLAY *Ship of Fools* i. 140 He that coueytys hye to clym aloft If he hap to fall, his fall can nat be soft. **1563** *Mirr. for Mag.* ed. Campbell 370 Hasty rising threatneth sodayne fall. **1566** GASCOIGNE *Jocasta* Epil. 28 Who climbes too soone, he oft repentes too late. **1579** SPENSER *Shep. Cal.* Jul., Wks. Globe 466 Great clymbers fall unsoft. **1581** SENECA *Ten Trag.* 'Hercules Oetaeus' tr. J. Studley T.T. ii. 217 Hasty climers oft in haste doe reele. [**1598**] **1616** HAUGHTON *Englishmen for my Money* H4ᵛ They say, high climers haue the greatest falles. **1659** HOWELL *Fr. Prov.* 11 A high climbing, a great coming down. **1670** RAY 71 (as . . . many Court-favourites).

Hasty gamesters oversee.   (G 26)
1678 RAY 151. **1732** FULLER no. 1803 (oversee themselves).

Hasty (angry) man never wants woe, A.
                                                    (M 159)

c. **1374** CHAUCER *Troilus* Bk. 4, l. 1568 For hastif man ne wanteth nevere care! *c.* **1390** GOWER *Conf. Amantis* III. 1861 Folhaste is cause of mochel wo. *c.* **1420** *Peter Idle's Instructions to his son* (Miessner) l. 238 An hasty man wanteth neuer woo. *c.* **1450** *Prov. of Wysdom* in HERRIG's *Archiv.* 90 l. 125 Hastye man lackyþe no sorow. **1546** HEYWOOD I. ii. A3ᵛ. **1614** CAMDEN 302. **1616** DRAXE no. 87 The angry man neuer wanteth woe. **1640** HERBERT no. 536 (choleric). **1721** KELLY 2 (willful). **1732** FULLER no. 801 Angry Men seldom want Woe.

Hasty meeting, a hasty parting, A.
1721 KELLY 19. **1736** BAILEY *Dict.* s.v. Woo.

Hasty people will never make good midwives.   (P 224)
1659 HOWELL *Eng. Prov.* 3b. **1670** RAY 101.

Hasty to outbid another, Be not too.
                                                    (O 89)
1664 CODRINGTON 188. **1670** RAY 3.

Hasty, see also Too h. to be parish clerk.

Hat covers his family, His.
1858 SURTEES *Ask Mamma* ch. 16 His hat had so long covered his family, that he hardly knew how to set about obtaining his own consent to marry. **1894** BLACKMORE *Perlycross* ch. 40 Jakes . . . sat down, thanking the crown of his hat that it covered the whole of his domestic interests.

Hat is not made for one shower, A.
                                                    (H 204)
1640 HERBERT no. 673.

Hat, see also Bredon-hill puts on h.; Cob a h. and a pair of shoes (Give); Haldon has a h., (When); Head (He that has no) needs no h.; Nothing old but shoes and h.; Pull down your h. on wind side.

Hatband, see Dick's h. (Queer as).

Hatch¹ before the door, It is good to have (keep, set) a.   (H 207)
[= to keep silence.] **1546** HEYWOOD I. xi. D2ᵛ Well I will no more sturre. It is good to haue a hatche before the durre. **1555** R. SMITH in FOXE *A. & M.* (1684) III. 336/2 Seeing God hath given a Tongue, And put it under power: The surest way it is to set A hatch before the door. **1579** GOSSON *Sch. Abuse* Arb. 53 I wish that euery rebuker shoulde place a hatch before the door. **1584** R. WILSON *Three Ladies of London* Hazl.-Dods. vi. 343. [*c.* **1592**] **1594** *Knack to know a Knave* Hazl.-Dods. vi. 535. **1611** DAVIES *Prov.* no. 188. [¹ a half-door; small gate or wicket.]

Hatch, match, and despatch.
1878 J. PAYN *By Proxy* ch. 19 First came the Births, Deaths, and Marriages, . . . the female mind . . . takes an interest in the 'Hatch, Match, and Despatch' of its fellow-creatures.

Hatch, (noun), see also Love at door, leave at h.

Hatch(es), (verb), see also Mischief h. (He that).

Hatchet, To throw (fling, sling) the.
[= to make exaggerated statements.] **1780** G. PARKER *Life's Painter* xii. 85 Many . . . habituate themselves by degrees to a mode of the hatchet-flinging extreme. **1893** T. B. FOREMAN *Trip to Spain* 97 The ladies titter, knowing, as we do the skipper's habit of slinging the hatchet.

Hatchet, see also Bury the h.; Dig up the h.; Hang up one's h.; Helve after h. (Throw); Pap with a h.

Hate (one) like poison, To.   (P 459)
1530 PALSGRAVE 579b He hateth me lyke poyson. **1594** *King Leir* II. iv. 147 These foppets . . . by this hand, I hate them ten times worse than poison. **1812** EDGEWORTH *Absentee* ch. 13 I know she hates me like poison. **1838-9** DICKENS *N. Nickleby* ch. 9 I hate him worse than poison.

Hate not at the first harm.   (H 168)
1639 CLARKE 235.

Hate(s), see also Greatest h. from greatest love; Love as in time you should h.; Love me for little that h. me for nought; Prince h., (He whom a) is as good as dead; Toad, (To h. one like a).

Hated man, *see* Seldom does the h. m. end well.

Hated of his subjects, He that is | cannot be counted a king. (s 950)

1641 FERGUSSON no. 373.

Hates not the person, but the vice, One. (p 238)

1533 TYNDALE *Enchiridion* N2ᵛ We must defye and abhorre the vices, but not the man. **1597** BODENHAM *Wit's Commonw.* 222ᵛ We ought not to hate the man but his vices. **1604** SHAKES. *M.M.* II. ii. 37 Condemn the fault, and not the actor of it? **1666** TORRIANO 313 no. 4.

Hatred is blind, as well as love.

1732 FULLER no. 1805. **1903** MERRIMAN *Barlasch* ch. 21 Love, it is said, is blind. But hatred is as bad.

Hatred with friends is succour to foes. (H 212)

1573 SANFORD 109. **1578** FLORIO *First F.* 33 Hatred among friendes is succour vnto strangers. **1616** DRAXE no. 343.

Hatred, *see also* Dead avails not and revenge vents h., (To lament the); Four good mothers have four bad daughters: truth, h.; . . .

Hatter, *see* Mad as a h.

Hatteras, *see* Bermudas.

Haul (Fetch, Bring, *or* **Call) over the coals, To.** (c 467)

[= to call to account: originally in reference to the treatment of heretics.] **1565** CDL. ALLEN in FULKE *Confut.* (1577) 372 S. Augustine, that knewe best how to fetche an heretike ouer the coles. **1639** FULLER *Holy War* v. ii (1840) 243 If they should say the Templars were burned wrongfully, they may be fetched over the coals themselves. **1658** J. SMITH *Wit Restor'd* (Hotten) 283 Your Smith can fetch em over the coales. **1804** EDGEWORTH *Pop. Tales; Contrast* ch. 1 'This is by way of calling me over the coals for being idle, I suppose!' said Sally. **1832** MARRYAT *Newton F.* ch. 13 Lest he should be 'hauled over the coals' by the Admiralty.

Have among you, blind harpers. (H 176)

[= a drinking pledge.] **1546** HEYWOOD II. vii. I3. I came to be mery. wherwith meryly, Proface. Haue among you blynd harpers (sayd I). **1608** DAY *Hum. out of B.* iv. iii Are you blind, my lord?—As a purblind poet: have amongst you, blind harpers. **1664** COTTON *Scarronides* (1715, i. 7) Quoth he, blind Harpers, have among ye.

Have at it, and have it.

1852 E. FITZGERALD *Polonius* 112 'Have at it, and have it'. One might add many capital English proverbs of this kind, all so characteristic of the activity and boldness of our forefathers.

Have God and have all. (G 229)

1641 FERGUSSON no. 377.

Have his muck for his meat, You will. (M 1300)

1639 CLARKE 170. **1670** RAY 186.

Have is have. (H 215)

1596 SHAKES. *K.J.* I. i. 173 Have is have, however men do catch. **1599** *Id. A.Y.* V. i. 37 Learn this of me: to have, is to have.

Have to say, What you | will keep cold, I warrant.

1738 SWIFT Dial. II. E.L. 315 Don't ask questions with a dirty face: I warrant, what you have to say will keep cold.

Have what he has not, He that would | should (would) do what he does not. (H 216)

1546 HEYWOOD II. ix. L1ᵛ Ye (quoth she) who had that he hath not, wolde Doo that he dooth not, as olde men haue tolde. **1611** DAVIES *Prov.* 275 [as 1546]. **1640** HERBERT no. 559.

Have, has, *see also* All h. and nought forego, (He would); Ask and h; Better to h. than wish; Knows not where to h. you, (One); Nothing crave, nothing h.; Nothing h., nothing crave; Want when I h.; What is he, but what h. he (Not).

Have, To, *see also under significant words following.*

Havens, *see* God strikes not with both hands.

'Haves' and the 'have nots', The.

1620 SHELTON *Quix.* II. xx. ii. 325 But two lineages in the world, Have-much and Have-little. **1742** JARVIS *D. Quix.* II. xx. The Haves and Have-nots. **1911** W. F. BUTLER *Autobiog.* ch. 9 The have's and the have-not's were always face to face, ready to shoot down or to rush in. **1927** *Daily Mail* 26 Apr. 8/3 People . . . argue that society is divided by a kind of wicked, cunning provision into the 'haves' and the 'have nots'.

Haw, Not worth a. (H 221)

c. **1280** *Castle of Love* in *Vernon MS.* E.E.T.S. 368 Ne wisdam nis not worth an hawe. **1297** R. GLOUC. (1724) 254 Al nas wurth an hawe. *c.* **1386** CHAUCER *W. of Bath's Prol.* l. 659 I sette noght an haw Of his proverbes. *a.* **1399** *Complaint of Ploughman* in WRIGHT *Pol. Poems* (1861) I. 312 An harlots sonne not worth an hawe. **1593** *Jack Straw* Hazl.-Dods. v. 394 We'll not leave a man of law, Nor a paper worth a haw.

Haw(s), *see also* Fruit fails (When) welcome h.; Many h. many snaws.

Hawk and buzzard, Between.　(H 223)

1611 BRETNOR *Almanac* August Evil Days. *c.* **1613** MIDDLETON *No Wit, No Help* I. i. 263. **1631** DEKKER *Match me in London* IV. ii. 5 Whether to recoyle or aduance on, I am betweene Hawke and Buzzard. **1638** BRATHWAIT *Barnabees Jrnl.* (1876) M2 Like a semidormant, and semivigilant, betwixt hawke and buzzard. **1692** L'ESTRANGE *Aesop's Fab.* ccclii (1738) 365 A fantastical levity that holds us *off and on, betwixt hawk and buzzard*, as we say. **1832** J. P. KENNEDY *Swallow B.* (1860) 17 I entered Richmond between hawk and buzzard.

Hawk of the right nest, He's a.

1721 KELLY 138.　**1732** FULLER no. 2439.

Hawking, The first point of | is hold fast.　(P 453)

c. **1450** *Booke of Hawkyng* in *Reliq. Antiq.* (1841) I. 296 In the begynnyng of termes of hawkyng. . . . The first is holde fast when abatith. **1546** HEYWOOD II. iv. G4. **1579** LYLY *Euph.* i. 236. **1583** MELBANCKE R1ᵛ. **1665** J. WILSON *Projectors* II. i. 'Tis the first point of falconry to hold fast; and if the young master has that good quality, I dare trust him for the rest.

Hawks (Crows) will not pick out hawks' (crows') eyes.　(C 856)

1573 SANFORD 104 One crowe neuer pulleth out an others eyes. **1818** SCOTT *Rob Roy* ch. 30 I wadna . . . rest my main dependence on the Hielandmen—hawks winna pike out hawks' een. They may quarrel amang themsells, . . . but they are sure to join . . . against a' civilised folk. **1883** PAYN *Thicker than W.* ch. 41 Members of his profession . . . while warning others of the dangers of the table, seem to pluck from them the flower safety. Is it . . . that, since 'hawks do not peck out hawks' een', they know they can be cured for nothing?

Hawk(s), *see also* Empty hands no h. allure; Gentle h. half mans herself; Highflying h. fit for princes; Kite will never be good h.; Know a h. from a handsaw; One point of a good h. (She has); Ware h.

Hawse-hole, To come (creep) in through the.

1850 MELVILLE *White Jacket* Wks. 1922, 30 In sea parlance, 'they come in at the hawse-holes.' **1889** R. L. STEVENSON *Master of Ball.* ch. 9 The mates [were] ignorant rough seafarers, come in through the hawsehole. **1898** W. C. RUSSELL *Romance of Midsh.* ch. 11 Bowser . . . had come in through the hawsepipe, by which is signified he had begun his career in the forecastle. . . . But he was . . . a safe . . . commander. **1902** A. B. LUBBOCK *Round the Horn* ch. 6 The mate . . . [is] a man who came through the hawsehole, and has seen some very hard times.

Hay in (on) one's horns, To carry.　(H 233)

[= to be ill-tempered or dangerous. HORACE *Sat.* I. 4. 34 *Faenum habet in cornu*, from an ox

apt to gore, whose horns were bound about with hay.] **1563** J. PILKINGTON *Confutation* P.S. 584 As the Latin proverb says of unruly beasts, that they were wont to be known by hanging hay on their horns, foenum habet in cornu. **1601** JONSON *Poetaster* IV. iii. 109 A sharpe thornie-toothed satyricall rascall, flie him; hee carries hey in his horne. **1648** HERRICK *Hesper., Oberon's Pal.* (1869) 176 He's sharpe as thorn, And fretfull carries hay in's horne. **1769** BOSWELL *Johnson* xxii (1848) 202 Horace . . . compares one who attacks his friends . . . to a pushing ox, that is marked by a bunch of hay put upon his horns: '*Faenum habet in cornu.*'

Hay, *see also* Chopped h.; Cock of h. frights cuckoo; Donkey between two bundles of h.; Easter day, (If it rains on), there shall be good grass but very bad h.; Grass and h., we are all mortal; Lim h.; Make h. while sun shines; Money like h., (Make); Needle in bottle of h.; Orts of good h. (Make not); Time to cock h.; Web of a bottle of h. (Hard to make).

Hazards, *see* Fazarts (To) hard h. are death.

Hazel, *see* Sick of a fever lurden cured by h.

Hazelnuts, The more | the more bastard children.

1844 NORTHALL *Folk-phrases* E.D.S. 24. *Glouc.*

He can ill (be), *see* Master that never was scholar; Pipe that lacks lip.

He cannot (be), *see under significant words following.*

He that, He that cannot, He that has (no), He that is, He that will, He who, He will (not), He would (have), He would not, *see under significant words following.*

Head aches, When the | all the body is the worse.　(H 275)

[L. *Si caput dolet, omnia membra languent.* If the head aches, all the members languish.] *c.* **1230** WRIGHT *Pol. Songs John to Edw. II* Camden Soc. 31 *Cui caput infirmum cetera membra dolent.* *c.* **1399** GOWER *Pr. of Peace* in SKEAT *Chaucer* vii. 212 Of that the heed is syk, the limmes aken. **1521** CHRISTINE DE PISAN *Body of Polcye* a 2ᵛ And the hed be sycke all the body shall feele it. **1546** HEYWOOD II. vii. K1ᵛ God sende that hed (saied she) a better nurs. For whan the head aketh, all the bodie is the wurs. *c.* **1592-5** *Thomas of Woodstock* l. 152. *c.* **1595** *Edmond Ironside* l. 1090 Kinges are the heades and yf the head but ache the little finger is distempered. **1620** SHELTON *Quix.* II. ii. ii. 201 According to the saying, 'Quando caput dolet', . . . I mean . . . that when the head aches, all the body is out of tune; . . . I, being thy lord and master, am thy head.

Head and feet keep warm, The | the rest will take no harm.　(H 253)

1603 MONTAIGNE (Florio) II. xii. 242 This common saying is alwais in the peoples mouth:

Tenez chauds les pieds et la teste, Au demeurant vivez en beste. **1611** COTGRAVE s.v. Demeurant The foot and head kept warme, no matter for the rest. **1670** RAY 39. **1832** HENDERSON 128 Keep the head and feet warm, and the rest will take nae harm.

Head and shoulders, To thrust out by.
(H 274)

1577–87 R. STANYHURST in Holinshed *Descr. Ireland* (1587, 21a) Tom Drum's entertainment, which is, to bale a man in by the head, and thrust him out by both shoulders. **1587** J. BRIDGES *Defence* 516 We thinke not, that by and by they must bee thrust out by head and shoulders. [c. 1582] **1595** SIDNEY *Def. Poetry* 39 All their Playes . . . thrust in the Clowne by head and shoulders. **1600–1** SHAKES. *M.W.W.* V. v. 141 We would have thrust virtue out of our hearts by the head and shoulders. [1602] **1637** T. HEYWOOD *Royal King* vi. 32 I shall be forc't to turne you out by the head and shoulders. **1699** B.E. s.v. Fetch (brought in by).

Head, You have a | and so has a pin (nail).

1709 STEELE *Tatler* No. 83 My boy breaks glasses and pipes; and . . . I only say, 'Ah, Jack! thou hast a head, and so has a pin'. **1738** SWIFT Dial. I. E.L. 273 Madam, I can't go faster than my legs will carry me.—Ay, thou hast a head, and so has a pin. **1823** GALT *Entail* ch. 8 Girzy, t'ou has a head, and so has a nail.

Head is down, When my | my house is theekit (thatched).

a. **1628** CARMICHAELL no. 539 Fra your heid beis doun your house is theiked. **1721** KELLY 342 . . . Spoken by those who are free from Debts, Concerns, or future Projects; as common Tradesmen, Day Labourers, and Servants who work . . . and get their Wages.

Head is full of bees, His. *Cf.* Bee in bonnet.
(H 255)

1513 DOUGLAS *Æneis* viii. Prol. 120 Quhat bern be thou in bed with heid full of beis? *c.* **1549** HEYWOOD I. xii. E4ᵛ Their heddes be full of bees. *a.* **1553** UDALL *Ralph Roister D.* I. iv. Arb. 29 Who so hath suche bees as your maister in hys head, Had neede to haue his spirites with Musike to be fed. **1611** DAVIES *Prov.* no. 319 (Poore Poets heads are euer). **1641** FERGUSSON no. 461. Of drunkards.

Head is screwed on the right way, His.

1843 MANDELL CREIGHTON *Life & Lett.* ch. 1 [He] had a contempt for those . . . who had not their head screwed on the right way.

Head, He that will be a | let him be a bridge.
(H 251)

1662 FULLER *Cardig.* 26 He that will be a Head, let him be a Bridge . . . is founded on a Fictitious tradition [that] . . . Benigridran, a Briton, . . . came to a River over which neither was Bridg nor Ferrey; hereupon he was fain to carry all his men over . . . on his own back.

Head like a snake, A | a neck like a drake, a back like a beam, a belly like a bream, a foot like a cat, a tail like a rat.

1670 RAY 212. [The shape of a good greyhound.]

Head may never ache till that day, I wish my.

1738 SWIFT Dial. I. E.L. 271 Miss is in love. —I wish my head may never ache till that day.

Head, He that has no | needs no hat.
(H 250)

1611 COTGRAVE s.v. Chaperon (hood). **1616** DRAXE no. 1486 (cap). **1640** HERBERT no. 996. **1670** RAY 101 . . . Qui n'a point de teste n'a que faire de chaperon. *Gall.*

Head nor tail, It has neither.
(H 258)

1573 GASCOIGNE *Supposes* i. 202 I find neither head nor foote in it. **1575** *Id. Glass of Govᵗ* ii. 34 This order of teaching . . . hath in it neither head nor foote. **1587** HOLINSHED A. Fleming before Bk. I It is not a worke for euerie capacitie, naie it is a toile without head or taile euen for extra-ordinarie wits. **1616** WITHALS 578. **1639** CLARKE 231.

Head (House) of glass, He that has a | must not throw stones at another.
(H 789)

c. **1374** CHAUCER *Troilus* Bk. 2, l. 867 And forthi who that hath a hed of verre, For cast of stones war him in the werre! **1640** HERBERT no. 196. **1660** SECKER *Nonsuch Prof.* II (1891) 183 What do you get by throwing stones at your enemys windows, while your own children look out at the casements? **1666** TORRIANO 45 no. 6 Who hath his brains of glass let him not go into a battel of stones. **1754** SHEBEARE *Matrimony* (1766) II. 102 Thee shouldst not throw stones, who hast a Head of Glass thyself. **1891** J. E. T. ROGERS *Ind. & Commerc. Hist.* 36 I am not sure that we in modern times can decently charge the Roman people with the lust of conquest, for . . . most of the European monarchies would be throwing stones from glass houses.

Head of hair, *see* Handsome h. of h., pray give me a tester.

Head of wax, He that has a | must not walk in the sun.
(H 249)

1640 HERBERT no. 425. **1659** HOWELL *It. Prov.* 7. **1749** FRANKLIN July If your head is wax, don't walk in the Sun.

Head under one's girdle, To have a man's.
(H 248)

[To have him in subjection, under control.] **1528** ROY & BARLOW *Rede me* Arb. 114 [Wolsey] sayth, vnder his girthell, He holdeth Kynges and Princes. **1546** HEYWOOD II. v. H3ᵛ And if ye chance in aduoutrie to catche hym, . . . Then haue ye his head fast vnder your gyrdell. **1554–7** CAVENDISH *Wolsey* ed. Morley 70. **1629** T.

ADAMS *Serm.* (1861–2) I. 330 If he may not have his head under his girdle, and his attendance as servile as his livery-groom's, he thinks himself indignified. **1639** CLARKE 177.

Head will never fill your father's bonnet, Your.

1721 KELLY 372 . . . That is, you will never be so wise a Man as your Father.

Headache, *see* Crown no cure for h.

Heading Halifax. *Cf.* Halifax law.

1613–22 DRAYTON *Polyolb.* xxvii. 59 And travelling along by Heading-*Halifax*. [**1787** GROSE (*Yorks.*) 231 At Halifax persons taken in the act of stealing cloth, were instantly, and without any process, beheaded, with an engine called a maiden.]

Head's running upon Jolly Robins, Your.

1596 T. LODGE *Wit's Misery* Hunt. Cl. E2ᵛ He [the usurer] casts Jolly Robbins in his head how to cousin the simple fellow. **1629** *Merchandise of Popish Priests* Of him whom we see very lively and pleasantly disposed, we say, his head is full of jolly Robins [cited in Mann's ed. of Deloney 537]. **1917** BRIDGE 159.

Heads as Hydra, As many. (H 278)

[A fabulous monster with a hundred heads.] **1575** CHURCHYARD *Chips* (Nichols *Progresses* 1833 ed. i. 400) She haleth Hidras heads. [c. **1591**] **1592** *Arden of Fev.* III. i. 12 Reprehension makes her vice to grow As Hydraes head that flourished, by decay. **1597** SHAKES. *I Hen. IV* V. iv. 25 Another king? They grow like Hydra's heads. **1604** *Id. O.* II. iii. 294 Had I as many mouths as Hydra. *a.* **1647** BEAUM. & FL. *Lawes of Candy* I. ii. 260 Supposing that their adversaries grew Like *Hydra's* head. **1690** DRYDEN *Don Sebas.* I. i (Merm.) II. 306 The fruitful heads of Hydra.

Heads (Cross) I win, tails (pile) you lose. (C 834)

[From deciding a matter by spinning a coin in the air and seeing whether the obverse or reverse falls uppermost.] **1673** T. SHADWELL *Epsom Wells* (1927 ii. 123) Worse than cross I win, pile you lose. *a.* **1677** SIR P. WARWICK *Memoir* (1701, 187) Cross you lose, and pile I win. **1678** BUTLER *Hudibras* III. iii. 685 For matrimony, and hanging here, Both go by destiny so clear. That you as sure may pick and choose, As cross I win, and pile you lose. **1846** DK. RUTLAND in *Croker Papers* (1884) III. xxiv. 59 A game which a sharper once played with a dupe, intitiled, 'Heads I win, and tails you lose.' **1926** *Times* 28 May 14/7 A better exposition of the un-businesslike principle of 'heads you win; tails we lose', would be hard to conceive.

Head(s), *see also* Arrow shot upright falls on shooter's h.; Baker (Be not a) if your h. be of butter; Bald h. soon shaven; Bear with sore h.; Better be h. of a dog (ass, pike, yeomanry); Break one's h, and bring plaster; Bring an old house on h.; Buck of first h.; Cap is better at ease than h.; Cast (Lay) their h. together; Coals of fire on h.; Comb h. with three-legged stool; Comb your h. backwards; Comforter's h. never aches; Counsel breaks not h.; Cover your h. by day; Dare not show his h.; Drive the nail to the h.; Dry feet warm h. bring safe; Fish begins to stink at h.; Gentleman of first h.; Give one's h. for the washing (for naught); Good for back bad for h.; Good for h. evil for neck; Grey h. green shoulders; Grief of h.; Hand over h.; Hare's h. against goose giblets; Hit the nail on h.; Hoar h. and green tail; Hold up your h., for there is money bid for you; Holds up her h. like a hen drinking (a hundred pound aver); Idle h. box for wind; Keep one h. for reckoning; Keep one's h. above water; Keep your feet dry and h. hot; King Charles' h.; Lapwing that runs away with shell on h.; Man is h., woman turns it; Medusa's h.; Men (H.) (So many); Mickle h. little wit; Mob has many h.; Noon on one's h., (To ring); Old h. and young hands; Old h. young shoulders; Over h. and ears; Raw h. and bloody bones; Red beard and black h.; Rises betimes (Who) has something in h.; Run one's h. against wall; Scabby h. love not comb; Scald h. soon broken; Scratches his h. with one finger; Soft place in one's h.; Sound h. that has not soft piece; Spite of one's teeth (h.); Spur in h. worth two in heel; Stoop when the h. is off (No time to); Strange beast that has neither h.; Swearing came in at the h.; Tongue in one's h. (To keep a good); Tongue talks at h.'s cost; Two faces (h.) in one hood; Two h. better than one; Windmills in the h.; Wise h. close mouth; Wit in his h. (He has no more); Woman's tongue in his h.

Heal[1] (soaking) sail is good sail. (S 72)

a. **1628** CARMICHAELL no. 1371 Sokane seall is best. **1641** FERGUSSON no. 765 (sokand). **1721** KELLY 143 . . . It is good merchandising when we can put off all our Wares in one Bulk. Spoken jocosely when we take all that is before us. [[1] whole.]

Healed as hurt, A man is not so soon. (M 252)

1599 PORTER *Angry Wom. Abingd.* l. 2327 A man is not so soone whole as hurt. **1614** CAMDEN 302. **1721** KELLY 48 . . . Misfortunes come suddenly, but their Remedies by more slow degrees.

Healer, *see* Time cures all things (is a h.).

Healing of an old sore, It is ill. (H 283)

1509 BARCLAY *Ship of Fools* i. 164 In olde sores is grettest ieopardye. **1546** HEYWOOD II. viii. K2 She hath (they say) bene styffe necked euermore. And it is yll healyng of an olde sore. **1579** LYLY *Euph.* i. 249 Searche the wounde while it is greene, to late commeth the salue when the sore festereth. **1732** FULLER no. 3727 Old Sores are hardly cured.

Heal(s), *see* God h.; Physician, h. thyself.

Health and money go far. (H 286)
1640 HERBERT no. 447.

Health and sickness surely are men's double enemies. (H 287)
1640 HERBERT no. 1011.

Health is better than wealth. (H 289)
[Eccles. xxx. 15 Health and strength is above all gold (Geneva).] **1578** L. LEMNIUS *Touchstone of Complexions* tr. T. Newton A2 Health passeth gold. **1584** COGAN *Hav. of Health*, Ep. Ded. Health and strength is above all gold (as saith Jesus Syrach). **1678** RAY 153.

Health is great riches (a jewel, a treasure). (H 288)
c. **1510**? *Wealth and Health* l. 185 If he [a poor man] haue helth, that is a treasure. **1530** PALSGRAVE 358 He that hath his helth is ryche ynough. **1603** MONTAIGNE (Florio) II. xxxvii. 351 Health is a very precious jewell. **1615** T. ADAMS *England's Sickness* 57 Health is precious. Cara est cuique salus, Euery mans health is deare to him. **1639** CLARKE 314 (a jewell).

Health is not valued till sickness comes. (H 290)
1553 *Respublica* l. 1344 Health after sickness is sweeter euermore. **1578** *Courtly Controv.* 2H2 It is oure peruerse nature to make none accompte of the good, vntill wee haue loste it, and that sorrowe for the wante of it teacheth vs the value thereof. **1581** R. MULCASTER *Positions* ch. 35 What a treasure health is, they that haue it do finde, though they feele it not till it faile. **1600** *Maid's Metamorphosis* E4ᵛ They know the want of health that haue bene sick. **1631** DEKKER *Penny-wise, Pound-foolish* A3 Life . . . knowes not her owne pretious value, till Sicknesse layes it in the Ballance. **1666** TORRIANO 119 no. 4 In sickness health is known. **1732** FULLER no. 2478.

Health, The chief box of | is time. (B 574)
1640 HERBERT no. 911.

Health without money is half an ague. (H 291)
1640 HERBERT no. 509. **1642** TORRIANO 90 (a sicknesse). **1659** HOWELL *It. Prov.* 14 (as 1642).

Health, *see also* Best men when in worst h.; Good h. (He that has); Good wife and h.; Kent (Some places of) have h. and no wealth; Little labour much h.; North for greatness, east for h.; Pledge your own h. (Must not); Poverty is the mother of h.

Healthful man can give counsel to the sick, The. (M 182)
1539 TAVERNER 19 Facile cum valemus recta consilia ægrotis damus. When we be hayle, we

easely gyue good counsayles to the sycke. This sentence of Terence. . . . **1550** *A notable and maruailous epistle* C3 He that is hole, can sone geue counsaile too the sycke. *a.* **1581** N. WOODES *Conflict of Conscience* I i. **1592** DELAMOTHE 23. **1651** HERBERT no. 1130.

Healthful, *see also* Fire is as hurtful as h.; No man was made more h. by sickness.

Heap, The more you | the worse you cheap. (M 1154)
1670 RAY 102 . . . The more you rake and scrape, the worse success you have.

Heap (*noun*), *see* Strike all of a h.

Hear a toll or knell, When thou dost | then think upon thy passing bell. (T 375)
1624 DONNE *Devotions* xvii. 98 Never send to know for whom the bell tolls; It tolls for thee. **1659** HOWELL *Eng. Prov.* 6a.

Hear all parties (both sides). (P 87)
[ST. AUGUSTINE *De Duabus Animabus*, XIV. ii *Audi alteram partem.*] **1481** CAXTON *Reynard* Arb. xxv. 57 There ben many that complayne on other and ben in the defaute them self. Audi alteram partem, here that other partye. **1546** HEYWOOD I. xiii. Fiᵛ A man shold here all parts, er he iudge any. **1641** FERGUSSON no. 327. **1692** L'ESTRANGE *Aesop's Fab.* xi (1738) 14 'Tis against common justice to pass sentence without hearing both sides. **1883** READE *Peril. Secret* ch. 6 I should wish you to hear both sides.

Hear and see and say nothing (little). Cf. Hear much. (N 275)
c. **1430** LYDGATE *Minor Poems* Percy Soc. 155 Here al thyng and kepe thy pacience. *c.* **1450** *Prov. of Wisdom* 99 Hyre and se, and be styll. *Ibid.* 95 Hyre and se, and say nowght. *Ibid.* 119 Hyre and se, and say but lyte. *a.* **1451** LYDGATE *Minor Poems* E.E.T.S. ii. 800 See myche, say lytell, and lerne to soffer in tyme. *c.* **1470** HARL. MS. 3362 in Anglia 42 199 Here þe and sey nawt. **1509** BARCLAY *Ship of Fools* i. 200 They that wyll liue in quyetnes and rest must here and se and hasty wordes refrayne. **1546** HEYWOOD I. xi. E2 I see muche, but I saie littell, and doo lesse. **1578** EDWARDES *Par. D. Devises* (1927, 94, l. 9) Wherefore in all as men are bent, Se all, saie nought, holde thee content. **1583** MELBANCKE C2ᵛ Thus you hearing, and seing and saying nothing. **1584** R. WILSON *Three Ladies of London* D2 Audeo et taceo, I see and say nothing. **1659** HOWELL *Fr. Prov.* 11 Hear, see, and hold thy peace, if thou wilt live in peace.

Hear much, speak little. (M 1277)
c. **1420** *Peter Idel's Instructions* E.E.T.S. l. 59 Telle neuer the more, though þou moche hire. *c.* **1526** ERASM. *Dicta Sap.* A2 Here moche and speke lytell. **1539** TAVERNER I *Garden* F6ᵛ [Zeno] We shuld heare very moch, and speake very lytle. **1562** HEYWOOD *Epigr.* (1867) 96 Who hereth oft, And speaketh seeld,

Be witte aloft, He wynth the feeld. **1600–1**
SHAKES. *H.* I. iii. 68 Give every man thy ear, but
few thy voice. **1621** BURTON *Anat. Mel.* II. iii.
VII (1651) 360 Out of humane authors take these
few cautions . . . *Hear much: speak little.*

Hear on that ear, He cannot. (E 11)

1533–4 UDALL *Flowers* 128 Surdo narrare
fabulam, to tel a tale to a deife body, is a prouerbe
to be sayd of them that labour in vayne. And it
is the same that we vse to speke prouerbially,
whan we here a thyng that lyketh vs not, saying
thus. I can not here on that side. **1546** HEY-
WOOD II. ix. K3ᵛ Than were ye deafe; ye coulde
not here on that syde. **1548** HALL *Chron. Hen.
IV* 16b The kyng was required to purchase his
deliverance . . . but he could not heare on that
side. **1563** *Mirror for Mag.* 173 Being deaf (as
men say) on that eare. *a.* **1617** BAYNE *On Eph.* i
If he haue no mind to perform it, we say, hee
cannot heare on that side. **1641** FERGUSSON
no. 396 He hears not at that ear. **1670** RAY 180.
1721 KELLY 150 He is deaf on that side of his
Head. Spoken of those who like not, and therefore take no Notice of, your Proposals.

Hear(s), *see also* Adder could h.; All men speak
(When), no man h.; Believe not half what you
h.; Child says nothing but what it h.; Child to h.
something (To be with); Children h. at home
(What) soon flies abroad; Deaf as those who will
not h. (None so); Do a foolish thing once (One
cannot) but one must h. of it; Listeners h. no
good of themselves; Love to h. well of themselves (Men); Speaks the thing he should not;
Strike but h.; Women may blush to h. what
they were not ashamed to act; Wrong h., wrong
answer gives.

Heard a pin drop, You might have.

1824 SUSAN FERRIER *Inheritance* II. xiv You might
have heard a pin drop in the house while that
was going on. **1838–9** DICKENS *N. Nickleby* ch. 2
(fall—a pin! a feather). **1893** MONT. WILLIAMS
Leaves of a L. ch. 30 Mr. Gladstone began to
speak. That great crowd . . . became . . . profoundly silent. You actually might have heard
the proverbial pin drop.

Heard where he is not seen, He may be.
(H 296)

c. **1607** MIDDLETON *Trick* III. iv. 6 One may hear
you before they see you. **1639** CLARKE 58
(when). **1670** RAY 180.

Hearers, Were there no | there would be
no backbiters. (H 297)

1640 HERBERT no. 69.

Hearing, From | comes wisdom; from
speaking, repentance.

1707 MAPLETOFT 31.

Hearing, *see also* Ill h. ill rehearsing; Worth the
h.

Hearken to reason, or she will be heard.
(R 42)

1611 COTGRAVE s.v. Mettre Let reasons rudder
steere thy prow, least thou make wrecke on woes
enow. **1640** HERBERT no. 74. **1758** FRANKLIN
Way to Wealth (Crowell) 24 Remember . . .
further, that If you will not hear Reason, she will
surely rap your knuckles.

Hearken to the hinder end of it.

1721 KELLY 144 Spoken when we suspect that
such a Project, or Action, will have an ill
Consequence.

Hears much and speaks not at all, He
that | shall be welcome both in bower
and hall. (M 1274)

1586 G. WHITNEY *Emblems* 191 Heare much; but
little speake. **1670** RAY 102.

Heart and hand, With. (H 339)

1593 [A.] *A pleasant fancie called The passionate
morris dance* New Sh. Soc. 102 [In those days]
hand and heart went together. [**1600**] **1659** DAY
& CHETTLE *Blind Beggar* v. 13 Give me thy hand,
and with thy hand thy heart. [**1602**] **1611**
CHAPMAN *May Day* v. i. 19 Both my hand and
heart . . . ever at your service. **1604** SHAKES.
O. III. iv. 43 The hearts of old gave hands; but
our new heraldry is hands not hearts. **1608**
DAY *Humour* 313 They haue . . . our hearts and
hands. **1616** WITHALS 563. **1632** FLETCHER
Beggar's Bush IV. vi. 18 Hand and heart, man.
1639 CLARKE 92.

Heart has its own ache, Every.

[PROV. xiv. 10 The heart knoweth his own
bitterness.] **1732** FULLER no. 1418.

Heart is a fire, When the | some sparks
will fly out of the mouth. *Cf.* Heart
thinks.

1520 WHITTINGTON *Vulg.* E.E.T.S. 77 Whan the
herte is full of pryde, yᵉ tongue is full of boost
and braggynge. **1579** J. CALVIN *Thirteen
Sermons* 121 When the hearts then are thus set
on fire, it is not possible but that the tongues
also must ouerflow too outrageous against the
other. **1732** FULLER no. 5589.

Heart is caught in the rebound, Many a.

1872 G. J. WHYTE-MELVILLE *Satanella* ch. 8
On Satanella's refusal of her veteran admirer,
she calculated. . . . In such an ignominious state
men are to be caught on the rebound. **1902–4**
LEAN IV. 41 Many a heart is caught in the
rebound. *i.e.* after a repulse by another.

Heart is full of lust, When the | the
mouth's full of leasings.

1721 KELLY 352 A Reflection upon these
damnable Lies, enforc'd with horr'd Oaths, by
which poor Maids are deceiv'd.

Heart is in his boots (shoes), His.

1767 *Garrick Corresp.* i. 271 (1831) 6A Whose
soul and spirit . . . are now even in her shoes.

1863 SPEKE *Disc. of Nile* ii With 'my heart in my shoes', I gave what I thought their due . . . and motioned them to be off. **1891** A. FORBES *Barracks Biv. & Bat.* (1910) 2 Cholera was decimating the troop, and the hearts of brave men were in their boots.

Heart is in his heels, His. (H 314)

[HOM. *Il.* 15. 280 πᾶσιν δὲ παραὶ ποσὶ κάππεσε θυμός. Their heels took in their dropping hearts (Chapman).] **1548** ERASM. tr. Udall *Par. Luke* xxii 174 b Petur beeyng feared with this saiyng of a woman . . . as if his herte had been in his hele clene gon. **1548** HALL *Chron.* 1809 ed. 443 Their hartes were in their heeles. **1563–87** FOXE *A. & M.* (1631) III. xi. 253/2 When the Bishop heard this, . . . his heart was in his heeles and . . . he with the rest of the Court betooke them to their legges. **1594** LIPSIUS *Six Bks. of Politics* tr. Jones 140 That saying of Homere, That their heart is in their heele. **1611** COTGRAVE s.v. *Danser* Wee say, his heart is not so light as his heeles.

Heart is in his hose, His. (H 314)

c. **1410** *Towneley Plays* E.E.T.S. 113 A, thy hart is in thy hose! *c.* **1536–7** ERASM. *Pilgr. Pure Devotion* 24ᵛ (As Homere saythe) my harte was almost in my hose. **1546** HEYWOOD I. xi. D4 Your hert is in your hose all in dispayre. *c.* **1600** *Timon* I. v My hart is at the bottome of my hose. **1641** FERGUSSON no. 673 Of fleyit[1] persons. [[1] frightened.]

Heart is in his mouth, His. (H 331)

[HOM. *Il.* 22. 452 πάλλεται ἦτορ ἀνὰ στόμα To my throat my heart bounds (Chapman).] **1537** *Thersites* B4. **1548** ERASM. tr. Udall *Par. Luke* xxiii. 199 Hauyng their herte at their verai mouth for feare. **1549** J. CALVIN *Life and Conv. of a Christian man* H7 Thei tremble, and their hert is at their mouth, as at the naming of a very vnhappy and vnlucky thing. **1716** ADDISON *Drummer* I. i And faith my heart was in my mouth; I thought I had tumbled over a spirit. **1856** WHYTE-MELVILLE *Kate Cov.* ch. 13 A ring at the door-bell brings everybody's heart into everybody's mouth.

Heart (understanding), Who has not a | let him have legs. (H 336)

1573 SANFORD 103. He that hath no heart, hath legges. **1578** FLORIO *First F.* G4ᵛ. **1642** TORRIANO 19 He who hath not a heart, nor memory, let him have legs: . . . For if he be a coward, he may run for't: if no memory, then hauing good legs he may the better run away upon the same errand again, for what hath been forgotten. **1732** FULLER no. 2146 He that has no Heart, ought to have Heels. **1813** RAY 24 (understanding) *Ital.*

Heart of an Englishman towards a Welshman, The. (H 313)

1662 FULLER *Cardig.* 26 The heart of an Englishman (whom they call Saxons) towards a Welchman. It is either applied to such who are possessed with prejudice, or only carry on outward compliance without cordial affection. **1902–4** LEAN I. 233 Calon y Sais wrth Cymro. The heart of an Englishman (or Saxon) towards a Welshman, *i.e.* open or secret hatred.

Heart of England, The.

1897 BP. CREIGHTON *Story Eng. Shires* 309 It was not accidental that Warwickshire produced the greatest of Englishmen. 'The heart of England', as the county has been called, summed up all and was most purely English in its scenery that associations.

Heart of gall, *see* Honey tongue.

Heart of grace, To take. (H 332)

[= to pluck up courage.] **1530** PALSGRAVE 748 They lyved a great whyle lyke cowardes, but at the laste they toke herte a gresse to them. *c.* **1536–7** ERASM. *Pilg. Pure Devotion* f. 24ʳ You haue causyd me to take harte of grasse. **1545** *Precepts of Cato* Publius H2 She takynge a lytle hart of grece. **1546** HEYWOOD II. viii. K2 She taketh such hert of gras. **1548** ERASM. tr. Udall *Par. Matt.* xxii. 106 They takyng hart of grace agayne. **1549** J. CALVIN *Life and Conv. of a Christian Man* G2ᵛ Beinge chered by the consolation of God, they take herte of grace vnto them. **1555** HEYWOOD *Three Hund. Epigrams* no. 92 Thou takest hart of grasse wyfe, not hart of grace. **1712** ARBUTHNOT *John Bull* IV. iv He was afraid to venture himself alone with him. At last he took heart of grace. **1890** *Times* 14 Oct. 6/2 The non-union labourers . . . took heart of grace and applied for work.

Heart of oak, He is. (H 309)

[**1582**] **1589** *Love and Fortune* l. 1677 Why then my noble youths of Oke pluck vp your harts with me. **1591** *The Speeches and Honourable Entertainment at Cowdrey* (LYLY i. 425) All heartes of Oke. **1600–1** SHAKES. *M.W.W.* II. iii. 26 Ha, bully! What says my Aesculapius? my Galen? my heart of elder? **1602** DEKKER *Satiro-Mastix* (1873) i. 265 My tough hearts of Oake that stand too't so valliantly. **1609** *Old Meg of Herefordsh.* Yonkers that have hearts of oake at fourscore yeares. **1691** WOOD *Ath. Oxon.* II. 221 He was . . . a heart of oke, and a pillar of the Land. **1870** DICKENS *E. Drood* ch. 12 A nation of hearts of oak.

Heart thinks, What the | the tongue speaks. *Cf.* Heart is a fire. (H 334)

1477 RIVERS *Dictes* (1877) 26 The mouth sheweth often what the hert thinketh. **1548** HALL (1809, 92) Heart thought not that tong talked. **1583** GREENE *Mamillia* in Wks. Gros. ii. 116 Gonzaga . . . thought, what the heart did think, the tongue would clinck. **1596** M. B. *Trial of True Frdship.* B2ᵛ It is not alwaies true, that what the heart thinks, the tongue clacketh. **1598–9** SHAKES. *M.A.* III. ii. 12 What his heart thinks his tongue speaks. **1599** *Id. A.Y.* III. ii. 234 Do you not know I am a woman? When I think, I must speak. **1614** CAMDEN 314. **1721** KELLY 356 When the Heart is full, the Tongue will speak.

Heart's letter is read in the eyes, The.

1640 HERBERT no. 220.

Hearts may agree, though heads differ. (H 341)

1602 SHAKES. *A.W.* I. iii. 50 Howsome'er their hearts are sever'd in religion, their heads are both one. **1732** FULLER no. 2480.

Heart(s), *see also* Antwerp pistol pointed at h. of England; Blithe h. makes a blooming visage; Changing of works lighting of h.; Cockles of the h.; Cold hand warm h.; Country for wounded h.; Eat one's h. out; Eye is the window of the h.; Eye sees not (What the) h. rues not; Face is no index to the h.; Faint h. never won; Fair face cannot have crabbed h.; Fair face foul h.; Gentle h. is tied; Good h. cannot lie; Good h. conquers fortune; Good tongue that says no ill, better h. thinks none; Grief pent up will break the h.; Guts uphold the h.; Hard (Stout) h. against hard hap (to stey brae); Hope, (If it were not for) h. would break; Humble h., humble desires; Joy of h. makes face fair; Kind h. soonest wronged; Lady's h. and beggar's purse; Lay sorrow to your h. (Never); Leal h. lied never; Long day (Not a), but good h. rids work; Love makes hard h. gentle; Loyal h. . . . Traitors' Bridge; Mickle maun good h. endure; Nearest the h. nearest the mouth; Nothing is impossible to willing h.; Please your eye and plague your h.; Poor h. that never rejoices; Prolong your life, quiet h. loving wife; Put blithe face on black h.; Rolling eye roving h.; Send you away with a sore h.; Set your h. at rest; Short folk's h. soon at their mouth; Spite of one's teeth, (h. etc.); Surgeon must have lion's h.; Tine h. tine all; Velvet true h.; Way to an Englishman's h.; Will may win my h.; Wise men have mouth in h., fools h. in mouth.

Hearth, *see* Keystone under the h.; Own h. is gowd's worth.

Heat nor cold abides always in the sky, Neither.   (H 343)

1678 RAY 47 *Ne caldo, ne gelo resta mai in cielo.* Ital.

Heat of affection, There is no | but is joined with some idleness of brain, says the Spaniard.   (H 344)

1651 HERBERT no. 1050.

Heat (Sunshine) that melts the wax will harden the clay, The same.   (s 980)

1551 CRANMER *Answer to Gardiner* 244 It is one Sonne that shyneth vppon the good and the badde, that melteth butter, and makethe the earthe harde. 1578 *Courtly Controv.* 2G4ᵛ One onely sunne melteth the waxe, and hardeneth the myre. 1579 GASCOIGNE *Hemetes* ii. 476 We see that one self same soonshyne doth both harden the clay, and dissolve the waxe. 1586 LA PRIMAUDAYE *Fr. Academy* 387 One and the same sunne softeneth the waxe, and hardeneth the clay. 1629 T. ADAMS *Serm.* (1861–2) II. 476 As by the heat of the sun wax is softened, and yet clay is hardened; so by the preaching of the word the hearts of such as shall be saved are mollified; but the hearts of the lost are further obdurate. 1660 SECKER *Nonsuch Prof.* II. (1891) 25 The same heat that melts the wax, will harden the clay.

Heat, *see also* Fire is never without h.; One fire (h.) drives out another.

Heathen, when they died, went to bed without a candle, The.

1732 FULLER no. 4589.

Heave, *see* Home (with h. and ho), (To pay one).

Heaven and hell is not known till hereafter, All of.

1732 FULLER no. 540.

Heaven (God) is above all.   (H 348)

1595 SHAKES. *Rich. II* III. iii. 17 The heavens are o'er our heads.—I know it uncle; and oppose not myself Against their will. *c.* 1599 J. MARSTON *Antonio and Mellida* IV. i. 29 Hell is beneath, yet heauen is ouer all. 1604 SHAKES. *O.* II. iii. 95 Well, God's above all; and there be souls must be saved, and there be souls must not be saved. 1613 *Id. Hen. VIII* III. i. 99 Heaven is above all yet; there sits a judge That no king can corrupt.

Heaven takes care of children, sailors, and drunken men.

1861 HUGHES *Tom. B. at Oxford* ch. 12 Heaven, they say, protects children, sailors, and drunken men; and whatever answers to Heaven in the academical system protects freshmen. 1865 G. MACDONALD *A. Forbes* ch. 76 They say there's a special Providence watches ower drunk men and bairns.

Heaven, To be in.

1533–4 N. UDALL *Flowers* 33ᵛ I am in heuen, or I wold neuer desire any other heuen (In coelo esse). *Ibid.* 173 We be euen in heuen, or (as we say in iestynge) we haue apostles lyues, or sayntes lyues. 1672 WALKER 21 no. 5.

Heaven, To be in the ninth (third).   (H 351)

1572 G. FENTON *Monophylo* 2ᵛ I seemed translated and rapt aboue the thirde heauen. *Ibid.* 30ᵛ The pleasure which hir onely societie brings . . . fashions such a fift heauen in you. 1578 *Courtly Controv.* 2D2ᵛ He felt himselfe rapte into the thirde heauen, where loue lodgeth. 1583 MELBANCKE F2 (rapt into the third heauen). 1600 JONSON *Ev. Man out Hum.* IV. viii. 19 Hee will thinke himselfe i' the ninth heauen. 1608 *Mer. Devil Edmon.* D4ᵛ I was last night in the third heauens.

Heaven will make amends for all.

1732 FULLER no. 2483.

Heaven, *see also* Better go to h. in rags; Coming to h. with dry eyes (No); Cuckolds go to h. (In rain and sunshine); Friends both in h. and hell; Go to h. in a feather-bed, (string, wheelbarrow); God (H.) helps them that help themselves; Going to h. in a sedan (No); Gold goes in at any gate except h.'s; Hang between h. and hell; Hell is wherever h. is not; Hell (They that be in); Husbands are in h. whose wives scold not; Marriages are made in h.; Prayer penetrates h.,

(A short); Seventh h.; Spits against h.; Way to
h. is alike; Way to h. is as ready by water as
land; Way to travel is towards h. (Best); Well
since he is in h. (He is).

Heavy purse makes a light heart, A.
(P 655)

1521 A. BARCLAY *Eclog.* IV. Prol. l. 20 Whan
purse is heuy ofttyme the hert is lyght. *a.* **1595**
The Pedlar's Prophecy l. 1591 An heauie purse
maketh a mans heart light. **1631** JONSON *New
Inn* I. i. 14 *A heauy purse makes a light Heart.*
There 'tis exprest.

Heavy, *see also* Bear it away (He will) if not too
h.; Lead, (As h. as).

Hector's cloak, To take.　　　(H 357)

1662 FULLER Northumb. 302 When Thomas
Piercy, earl of Northumberland, Anno 1569, was
routed in the Rebellion . . . against queen
Elizabeth, he hid himself in the house of Hector
Armstrong, of Harlow, . . . who for money
betrayed him to the Regent of Scotland . . . 'To
take Hector's cloak', is continued to this day
. . . , when they would express a man that
betrayeth his friend who trusted him.

Hedge between keeps friendship green, A.

1707 MAPLETOFT 47.　**1710** PALMER 168 A wall
between preserves love.　**1917** BRIDGE 3.

Hedge have, If you would a good | carry the leaves to the grave.　(H 360)

[For meaning *see* Fruit have, etc.]　**1678** RAY
350.

Hedge is lowest, Where the | men may soonest over.　(H 364)

1546 HEYWOOD II. v. H2ᵛ Where the hedge is
lowest, men maie soonest ouer.　**1580** MUNDAY
Zelauto I2ᵛ (the beastes goe ouer soonest).
1639 CLARKE 172.　**1655–62** GURNALL *Chrn. in
Armour* (1865) I. 296 The devil chose rather to
assault Eve than Adam . . . He labours to creep
over where the hedge is lowest, and the resistance
likely to be weakest.　**1721** KELLY 250 Men
loup the Dike where it is leaghest.[1] That is,
oppress and over-run those who are least able to
resist them. [1 lowest.]

Hedge(s), *see also* Common as Coleman h.;
Cured her from laying in the h.; Fields (H.)
have eyes; Leap over h. before come at stile;
Leap over nine h. (Ready to); Love your neighbour, yet pull not down h.; Low h. easily leaped
over; Seek a brack where h. is whole; Sheltering
under an old h. (Good); Side of the h. (To be on
right *or* wrong); Sun does not shine on both
sides of h.

Heed, *see* Dance, (When you); Good h. has good
hap; Mad fools in narrow place, (Take h. of);
Plenty will take no h., (He who of); Take h.
does surely speed; Take h. is fair thing (good
rede); Stepmother (Take h. of); Too much
taking h. is loss; Young wench, (Take h. of a).

Heel of Achilles.

[= the only vulnerable spot (in allusion to the
story of the dipping of Achilles in the river
Styx).]　**1810** COLERIDGE *Friend* 431 Ireland,
that vulnerable heel of the British Achilles.
1864 CARLYLE *Fred. Great* XVII. ii. IV. 522
Hanover . . . the Achilles'-heel to invulnerable
England.　**1944** *Times* 19 June 5/6 Military
observers have dubbed Viipuri the Achilles' heel
of the Finnish defences.

Heels, To kick (turn) up one's.
(H 392)

1580 MUNDAY *Zelauto* K4 My father . . . lookes
that the olde suter will soone turne vp his heels.
1592 T. NASHE *Pierce Penniless* i. 204.　**1611**
FLORIO S.V. Fare il pane 180: To die or kicke vp
ones heels.

Heel(s), *see also* Beat your h. against the ground
(As good); Beef to the h.; Clean h. light meals;
Cool one's h.; Grass grows on his h. (No); Hang
by the h.; Haste trips up own h.; Heart is in his
h. (His); Jack-an-Ape be merry; Kick one's h.;
Lay sorrow to your heart (Never), when others
to their h.; Out at h.; Pair of h. is often worth
two of hands; Scorn with the h.; Show a fair
pair of h.; Spur in the head is worth two in the
h.; Take to one's h.; Touch me not on sore h.;
Trust not a horse's h.

Heifer, *see* Plough with any one's h.

Height, *see* Grantham steeple; Robin that herds
on h.

Heir(s), *see* Fool who makes physician h.; Ill
man lie in thy straw (Let an), looks to be thy h.;
Land was never lost for want of h.; Mouse a
hole . . . has become h.; Usurers live by fall of h.

Held together, They | as the men of Marham when they lost their common.
(M 876)

1662 FULLER Lincs. 153 Some understand it
Ironically; that is, they were divided with several
Factions. . . . Others use this Proverb only as an
expression of ill Successe. . . . Though this Proverb be frequent in this Shire Marham is in
Norfolk.　**1818** SCOTT *Ht. Midl.* ch. 29 'Since
they hae lost Jim the Rat, they hold together no
better than the men of Marsham when they lost
their common'.

Hell (chancery) is always open.

[VERGIL *Aen.* vi. l. 126] *c.* **1566** CURIO *Pasquin in
a Trance* tr. W.P. 83 Hel gate . . . stood daye
and night continually open.　**1732** FULLER no.
2486.

Hell for company, There is nobody will go to.　(H 409)

1613 WITHER *Abuses* Sp.S. I. 16, i 178 For I have
heard them tell, With mates they care not if they
goe to hell.　**1651** HERBERT no. 1177.

Hell, Hull and Halifax, From | good Lord deliver us.   (H 399)

1594 A. COPLEY *Wits, Fits, etc.* (1614) 112 It is proverbiall in our countrie; From Hull, Hell, and Halifax, Good Lord deliver us. **1623** J. TAYLOR (Water-P.) *Mer. Wher. Fer. Voy.* Wks. 1630, 12 There is a Pruuerbe, and a Prayer withall, That we may not to three strange places fall: From *Hull*, from Halifax, from *Hell*, 'tis thus, From all these three, *Good Lord deliuer vs.* **1662** FULLER Yorks. 189 'From Hell, Hull, and Halifax, . . . deliver us.' This is part of the Beggar's and Vagrant's litany. . . . Hull is terrible unto them, as a Town of good government. . . . Halifax is formidable unto them for . . . Theeves . . . stealing cloath, are instantly beheaded with an Engine.

Hell is broke loose.   (H 403)

1570 W. BALDWIN *Beware the Cat* (1584, D1) I thought all the deuils in hel had broken loose. **1573** GASCOIGNE *Fruits of War* i. 160. **1577** *Misogonus* II. v. 15 I thinke hell breake louse when thou gatst the this poste. **1594** GREENE *Friar Bacon* IV. i Merm. 283 Hell's broken loose; your Head speaks; and there's such a thunder and lightning, that I warrant all Oxford is up in arms. **1611** SHAKES. *Temp.* I. ii. 214 Hell is empty, And all the devils are here. **1623** JONSON *Time Vind.* vii. 660 How now! what's here! Is hell broke loose? **1738** SWIFT *Dial.* I. E.L. 280 Hey, what a clattering is here! one would think hell was broke loose. **1821** BYRON *Vis. Judg.* lviii Their . . . cries . . . realised the phrase of 'hell broke loose'. **1857** READE *White Lies* ch. 21 A furious cannonade roared . . . till daybreak. Hell seemed broke loose.

Hell is full of good meanings and wishes.
                                           (H 404)

1574 E. HELLOWES *Guevara's Epistles* 205 Hell is full of good desires. **1616** T. ADAMS *A Divine Herbal* 150 One said, that hell is like to bee full of good purposes, but heauen of good workes. **1640** HERBERT no. 170. **1655–62** GURNALL *Chrn. in Armour* (1865) I. 412 The proverb saith, 'Hell is full of good wishes',—of such, who now, when it is too late, wish they had acted their part otherwise . . . than they did. And do you not think there are . . . good meanings also? **1659** HOWELL *Span. Prov.* 3 Hell is full of good intentions.

Hell is paved with good intentions.

1736 WESLEY *Journ.* 10 July It is a true saying, Hell is . . . **1775** JOHNSON in *Boswell* (1848) xlix. 450 No saint . . . was more sensible of the unhappy failure of pious resolves than Johnson. He said one day, . . . 'Sir, hell is paved with good intentions'. **1819** SCOTT *Bride Lam.* ch. 7. **1839** SIR C. NAPIER in BUTLER *Life* (1890) 96 Hell may be paved with good intentions, but it is assuredly hung with Manchester cottons. **1847** J. A. FROUDE *Shadows of the Clouds* 114 I shall have nothing to hand in, except intentions,—what they say the road to the wrong place is paved with. **1865** RUSKIN *Ethics of Dust* ch. 5 Their best intentions merely make the road smooth for them . . . You can't pave the bottomless pit; but you may the road to it.

Hell is wherever heaven is not.   (H 406)

1592 DELAMOTHE 23 Hell is in euery place, wherein the Lord is not. **1597** *Politeuphuia* 260 Hell is euery where, where heauen is not. **1732** FULLER no. 2489.

Hell or Connaught.

1896 W. O'C. MORRIS *Ireland 1494–1868* 154 Cromwell resolved . . . to compel the 'rebel' owners of land to take refuge in Connaught . . . 'Hell or Connaught', a phrase that has come down to this time. **1911** *Autobiog. of Sir W. F. Butler* ch. 16 The alternative was like that which Cromwell gave, . . . only that Connaught was left out.

Hell, They that be in | ween there is none other heaven.   (H 410)

1546 HEYWOOD I. xi. E1ᵛ They that[be in hell, wene there is none other heuen. **1586** R. CROWLEY *Friar John Francis* A2ᵛ Our English Prouerbe. They that be in hell, doo perswade themselues, that there is none other heauen. **1590** SIR J. SMYTH *Disc. Weapons* Proeme *iiij b They verifie the olde Proverb, which is, That such as were never but in Hell, doo thinke that there is no other Heaven. **1597** BACON *Col. of G. & E.* no. 6 The formes to make it conceyued that that was euill which is chaunged for the better are, He that is in hell thinkes there is no other heauen. *a.* **1628** CARMICHAELL no. 796. **1639** CLARKE 199.

Hell will never be full till you be in it.

1721 KELLY 160 . . . A bitter Reflection upon them who are very covetous, or very malicious.

Hell, *see also* Better go . . . than to h. in embroidery; Deep as h.; Descent to h. easy; False as h.; Fasts and does no other good . . . goes to h.; Friends both in heaven and h.; Go to h. for the house profit; Hang between heaven and h. . . .; Harrow h. and scum devil; Haste is from h.; Heaven and h. not known till hereafter; Hopers go to h.; Lackey comes to h.'s door (When) devils lock gates; Long in court, deep in h.; Rake h. for a bodle; Redemption from h. (No); Sel, sel, has half-filled h.; War begins (When), h. opens; Wicked man his own h.; Work hard . . . and go to h., hard indeed.

Helmet of Pluto, The.

1625 BACON *Ess., Delays* Arb. 525 For the *Helmet of Pluto*, which maketh the Politicke Man goe Inuisible, is, *Secrecy* in the Counsell, and *Celerity* in the Execution.

Help at a dead lift, To.

                                  (F 699. L 271)

1551 RALPH ROBINSON *Utopia* II, *Pol. Govt.* 76 Whiche they graunte to be not so good as horses at a sodeyne brunte, and (as we saye) at a deade lifte. **1578** WHETSTONE I *Promos and Cass.* V. iv F2ᵛ I haue founde a helpe at a dead lyfte. **1599** *Warning to Fair Women* (Simpson *School of Sh.* ii. 301) Try al her friends to helpe at this dead lift. **1616** DRAXE no. 799 He is a friend at a dead lift. **1636** CAMDEN 290 (A friend will helpe . . .). **1639** CLARKE 26 (as 1636). **1749** J. WESLEY *Lett.* ii. 348.

Help, for help in harvest.

1721 KELLY 170 . . . That is, help me now, and I will help you on your throngest[1] Occasions. [[1] busiest.]

Help, hands; for I have no lands.
(H 116)

1565 OVID *Met.* tr. Golding Bk. 3 l. 745 His handes did serve in steade of lands. **1591** B3 *Troub. Raigne K. John* I Help hands, I haue no lands, honour is my desire. **1608** ARMIN *Nest. Nin.* (1842) 47 Fool, says the jester, use thy hands, help hands, for I haue no lands. **1754** FRANKLIN Jan. Help, Hands; For I have no Lands.

Help the (lame) dog over the stile.
(D 479)

1546 HEYWOOD I. xi. E1 As good a dede, As it is to helpe a dogge ouer a style. **1616** WITHALS (1634, 62) To helpe a dogge over a stile, spoken of helpe where is no neede. **1638** CHILLINGWORTH *Relig. Prot.* I. III. § 33. I once knew a man out of courtesy, help a lame dog over a stile, and he for requital bit him by the fingers. **1738** SWIFT *Dial.* I. E.L. 282 I know I shall always have your good word; you love to help a lame dog over the stile. **1857** KINGSLEY *Two Years Ago* ch. 25.

Help (*noun*), *see also* Bale (Need) is hext (When), boot (h.) is next; God's h. is better than early rising; God's h. is nearer than the fair even; Mickle ado and little h.; Thou thyself canst do it (If), attend no other's help.

Helps little that helps not himself, He.
(H 412)

1573 SANFORD H2ᵛ He doth little, that helpes not him selfe. **1576** WAPULL *Tide Tarries No Man* B1 For who helpes not himselfe, before any other, I coumpt him a foole, if he were my brother. **1629** *Bk. Mer. Rid.* Prov. no. 16.

Helps the evil hurts the good, He that.
(E 200)

c. **1526** *Dicta Sap.* B2ᵛ The good men haue wronge, whan the yll are suffred vnpunysshed. **1539** TAVERNER *Publius* B2ᵛ He hurteth the good, whosoeuer spareth the badde. **1547** BALDWIN (1550) P3ᵛ. **1597** *Politeuphuia* 169 Hee that helpeth an euill man, hurteth him that is good. **1732** FULLER no. 2163.

Help(s, ing, ed) (*verb*), *see also* At hand (All is not) that h.; Counselled, (He that will not be) cannot be h.; Everything h. quoth the wren; Fallen, (He that is) cannot h. him that is down; God h. the fool (poor, rich); God h. them that h. themselves; God will h. (Where *or* Whom) nothing does harm (*or* can hinder); Grieve for that you cannot h. (Never); Never be angry at (Two things), what he can h. and what he cannot h.; Three h. one another bear burthen of six.

Helve (axe) after the hatchet (helve). To throw the.
(H 413)

[= to add new loss to that already incurred.] *c.* **1200** MAP *De Nugis Cur.* I. x *Manubrium post securim iacere.* **1546** HEYWOOD II. ix. L2ᵛ For here I sende thaxe after the helue awaie. **1577–87** HOLINSHED *Chron.* (1807–8) IV. 338 Rather throw the helve after the hatchet, and leave your ruines to be repaired by your prince. **1603** MONTAIGNE (Florio) III. ix. 4 I abandon my selfe through despaire, . . . and (as the saying is), cast the haft after the hatchet. **1824** SCOTT *St. Ronan's* ch. 26 Monsieur Martigny will be too much heartbroken to make further fight, but will e'en throw helve after hatchet.

Helvoet, *see* Deal, Dover, and Harwich, the devil gave.

Hem, *see* Cry h. and have him.

Hemp for your hanging begins to bud.

1578 LUPTON *All for Money* B2ᵛ The hempe for your hanging beginnes for to budde.

Hemp is spun, When | England is done.
(H 414)

1625 BACON *Ess., Prophecies* Arb. 536 The triuiall *Prophecie*, which I heard, when I was a Childe, . . . was; *When Hempe is sponne; England's done.* Whereby, it was generally conceived, that after the *Princes* had Reigned, which had the Principiall *Letters*, of that Word *Hempe* (which were *Henry, Edward, Mary, Philip, Elizabeth) England* should come to utter Confusion. **1662** FULLER *Berks.* 83.

Hemp, *see also* Stalk of carl h. in you (You have a).

Hempstead, *see* Raw H.

Hen cracks nuts, As fast as a.

1593 *Letters of Philip Gawdy* 76 Kelly . . . maketh gold as fast as a henne will cracke nuttes. **1603** *Bachelor's Banquet* (ed. Wilson) 104.

Hen crows louder than the cock, It is a sad house where the.
(H 778)

1573 SANFORD 33ᵛ. **1578** FLORIO *First F.* 110 Naught are those houses, where the henns crow and the cocke hold his peace. **1592** DELAMOTHE 27. **1621** QUARLES *Ester* Med. III. Wks. (1880–1) II. 50 Ill thriues the haplesse Family, that showes A Cocke that's silent, and a Hen that crowes. **1625** J. HOWELL *Lett.* 5 Feb. (1903) I. 250 I remember a French proverb: 'La maison est miserable et mechante Ou la poule plus haut que le cocq chante.' 'That house doth every day more wretched grow Where the hen louder than the cock doth crow.' *a.* **1628** CARMICHAELL no. 1080 Litle grace for the gude mannis freinds, quhair the hen crawis before the cock. **1678** RAY 64 . . . *Trista è quella casa dove le galline cantano e 'l gallo tace.* Ital. **1866** C. READE *G. Gaunt* ch. 20 This house is no place for us that be women: . . . where the hen she crows and the cock do but cluck.

Hen does not prate, If the | she will not
lay. *Cf.* Cackle often.

1580 LYLY *Euph. & his Eng.* ii. 4 Hens do not
lay egges when they clucke, but when they
cackle. **1642** TORRIANO 68 That hen that
cackleth, is she that hath laid the eggs. **1659**
N. R. 121 Who means to have the egge must
endure the cackling of the Hen. **1732** FULLER
no. 2799 If you would have a Hen lay, you
must bear with her cackling. **1830** FORBY 427
'If the hen does not prate, she will not lay':
i.e. Scolding wives make the best housewives.

Hen egg goes to the ha',[1] The | to bring
the goose egg awa'.

1721 KELLY 316 . . . Spoken when poor People
give small Gifts to be doubly repaid. [1 hall, the
great house.]

Hen goes to the cock, When the | the
burds[1] may gen a knock.

1721 KELLY 350 . . . Spoken when Widows who
design a second marriage prove harsh to their
Children. [1 chickens.]

Hen, Like | like chicken.   (H 424)

[**1632**] **1659** MASSINGER *City Madam* (1887) I. i.
405 He's grown Rebellious, madam.—Nay, like
hen, like chicken. **1659** HOWELL *It. Prov.* 9
Who comes of a hen, must do like a hen.

Hen live, Let the | though it be with her
pip.   (H 423)

1620 SHELTON *Quix.* II. v. ii. 218 Let the hen
live, though it be with her pip; live you, and
the devil take all the governments in the world.
1694 BOYER 108 Let the Pullet live tho' she ha'
got the pip. **1706** STEVENS s.v. Gallina.

Hen on a hot girdle (griddle), Like a.

1812 W. TENNANT *Anster F.* VI liv As would a hen
leap on a fire-hot griddle. **1824** MOIR *Mansie W.*
ch. 8 I began to be . . . uneasy, and figeted on
the board like a hen on a hot girdle. **1895**
J. BARLOW *Maureen's Fairing* 42 The misthress
had been like a hin on a hot griddle ever since.

Hen that cackles in your house and lays
in another's, It is no good.

1584 WITHALS A7 A badde henne is that which
layeth egges for our neighbours, and not for
them that keepe her. **1706** STEVENS s.v. Gallina.
1732 FULLER no. 2987.

Hen's nest, *see* Seek a hare in a h. n.

Hen(s), *see also* Black h. lays white egg; Busy as
a h. with one chicken; Cock moult before h. (If);
Comes of a h. must scrape (He that); Crooning
cow, a crowing h.; Eat a h. in Janivere; Eaten
the h.'s rump; Egg and the h. (To have both);
Eggs, (He that would have) must endure the
cackling of h.; Fat as a h. in the forehead; Fie
upon h. quoth fox; Grain by grain and the h.
fills; Nice as a nun's h.; Offer your h. for sale
on rainy day (Never); Pecked to death by a h.

(As good be); Poor h. that can't scrat for one
chick; Sell his h. on a rainy day; Son of the white
h.; Thrift goes by the profit of a yeld h. (Your);
Women and h. through gadding are lost. *See
also* Hens.

Hende[1] as a hound in a kitchen, As.

1377 LANGLAND *P. Pl.* B. v. 261 'I am holden',
quod he, 'as hende as hounde is in kychyne'.
[1 well-behaved.]

Hengsten Down well wrought is worth
London town dear bought.   (H 430)

1602 R. CAREW *Survey of Cornwall* (1811) 272
The country people have a bye-word, that
Hengsten Down, well yrought, Is worth London
Town, dear ybought, Which grew from the
store of tin, in former times, there digged up.
1662 FULLER Cornwall 198 . . . [Refers to] the
treasure . . . of Tinne [which] . . . is now fallen to
a scant-saving scarcity.

Henley, *see* More fools in H.

Henry the Eighth pulled down monks
and their cells, Henry the Ninth should
pull down bishops, and their bells.
                                     (H 434)

1608 J. HARINGTON *Brief View State of Ch. Eng.*
(1653) Title page. Written for the private use of
Prince Henry, upon occasion of that Proverb, . . .

Henry VIII, *see also* King Henry.

Henry[1] was the union of the roses,[2] In |
in James[3] of the kingdoms.   (H 431)

1629 T. ADAMS *Serm.* (1861–2) II. 326 We are not
shuffled into a popular government, nor cut into
cantons by a headless, headstrong, aristocracy;
but *Henricus Rosas, Regna Jacobus*—in Henry
was the union of the roses, in James of the
kingdoms. [1 Henry VII. 2 Houses of York and
Lancaster. 3 James I.]

Hens are free of horse corn.

1721 KELLY 170 . . . Spoken of those who are
free of what is not their own.

Hens, *see also* Hen(s).

Heraldry, *see* Metal upon metal false h.

Herb will cure love, No.

[OVID *Met.* I. 523 Hei mihi, quod nullis amor est
sanabilis herbis!] *c.* **1386** CHAUCER *Leg. Good
Women* 1187 Love wol love, for nothing will it
wonde [cease]. *c.* **1590** *John of Bordeaux* l. 108
[in Latin] (medecabeles). **1602** *How a Man may
Choose a Good Wife* Hazl.-Dods. ix. 9 [in Latin]
(medicabilis). **1771** J. WESLEY *Wks.* XIV. 269 [in
Latin] (medicabilis). **1832** HENDERSON 42.

Herb-John,[1] Without | no good pottage.

[**1658** GURNALL *Chrn. in Armour* II. 12 (in DAVIES
Suppl. Eng. Gloss. 309) *Herb-John* in the pot

Hercules could contend against two, Not even. (H 436)

[Gk. Οὐδὲ Ἡρακλῆς πρὸς δύο. L. ERASM. *Ad. Ne Hercules quidem adversus duos.*] **1539** TAVERNER f. 17 Not Hercules agaynst two, that is to saye: Thoughe a man neuer so much excelleth other in strength, yet it woll be harde for hym to matche two or mo at ones. **1576** GASCOIGNE *Grief of Joy* ii 540 But two to one, can be no equal lot, For why? the Latin proverb, saith, you wot, *Sit quisque similis inter suos, Ne Hercules enim contra duos.* **1590** T. LODGE *Rosalynde* ed. Greg 105 But as *Ne Hercules quidem contra duos,* so Rosader could not resist a multitude. **1591** SHAKES. *3 Hen. VI* II. i. 53 But Hercules himself must yield to odds. **1607** CHAPMAN *Rev. of Bus.* III. i Merm. 271 Two are enough to encounter Hercules.

Hercules was not begot in one night.

1674 MILTON *Dec. for Elect. of John III.* Prose Wks. (1890) III. 481 It was not right that a hero . . . should in a moment . . . be made a king, whenas antiqiuty by an ancient proverb has delivered, 'that Hercules was not begot in one night'.

Hercules with the distaff.

1778 JOHNSON in *Boswell* (1848) lxiv. 592 'You shall see what a book of cookery I shall make . . .'— 'That would be Hercules with the distaff indeed'.

Hercules, *see also* Crutch of time . . . club of H.

Herds (= shepherds), *see* Ill h. fat wolves.

Here a little and there a little. (S 611)

1546 HEYWOOD I. xi. D4. **1555** *Id. Epigr. on Proverbs* no. ccxxxvii Here sum and theare sum. **1601** A. DENT *Plain Man's Pathway* 367. **1616** DRAXE no. 1264. By little and little. **1616** T. ADAMS *Divine Herbal* 19. **1702** G. SMALRIDGE *Sermon before House of Commons* 21.

Here to-day and gone to-morrow. (T 368)

1549 J. CALVIN *Life and Conv. of a Christian man* H2ᵛ This prouerbe that man is here to-day and gone to morow. **1562** G. LEGH *Accidence of Armoury* 187 Like as this [a skeleton] is to day, suche shalte thou bee to morowe. **1578** T. BLENNERHASSET *Mirror for Mag.* Campbell 381 Here to day, wee knowe least ourselues, where to morrowe. **1616** DRAXE no. 1428 Aliue to day, and dead to morrow. **1638** J. TAYLOR *Bull Bear̨ and Horse* A6ᵛ. **1721** KELLY 166 Here to Day, and away to Morrow. **1731** *Poor Robins Alm.* The *world is full of Vissitudes, we are here today, and gone to-morrow,* as the Shoe-maker said when he was going to run away.

Here, *see also* Better say, Here it is; Neither h. nor there.

Hereafter comes not yet. (H 439)

a. **1542** *Unpub. Poems from the Blage MS.* ed. Muir XLVI. 7 Syns that hieraufter coums not yet. *a.* **1542** WYATT ed. Muir 1949 no. 162. **1546** HEYWOOD II. vii. 14ᵛ Though hereafter comes not yet. **1611** DAVIES Prov. no. 84 Herafter comes not. **1660** TATHAM *Rump.* III. i. Wks. (1879) 234 We'll think on that hereafter.—Hereafter comes not yet, then, it seems? **1721** KELLY 144 . . . Spoken when we suspect that such a Project, or Action, will have an ill Consequence.

Heresy and beer (turkey, carp, pickerel[1]) came into England both in a year. (H 440)

1599 BUTTES *Dyets Dry Dinner* G4 I know not how it happened (as he merrily saith) that heresie and beere came hopping into England both in a yeere. **1643** Baker *Chron.* (1660) 317 About [1524] it happened that divers things were newly brought into England, whereupon this Rhyme was made: 'Turkeys, Carps, Hoppes, Piccarell,[1] and Beer, Came into England all in one year'. **1646** *Ex-ale-tation of Ale* 6 For with this same beere came up heresies here, the old Catholike drink is a [pot of good Ale]. [1 young pike.]

Heresy is the school of pride. (H 442)

1651 HERBERT no. 1057.

Heresy may be easier kept out than shook off. (H 443)

1651 HERBERT no. 1059.

Heresy, *see also* Frenzy, h., and jealousy seldom cured.

Heretic and a good subject, For the same man to be a | is impossible. (M 144)

1651 HERBERT no. 1058 (incompossible). **1659** N.R. 35.

Heretic, *see also* Faith with h. (No); Gospel (With the) one becomes h.

Hero, *see* No man is a h. to valet.

Herring is the king, Of all the fish in the sea. (F 320)

1583 MELBANCKE *Philot.* K2 Those blooming daies, when in youth red herring was a king. **1601** JONSON *Ev. Man in Humour* I. iii. 12 Herring the king of fish. **1599** NASHE *Lenten Stuff* iii. 149. **1639** CHAPMAN *Chabot* III. ii. 80 Herrings, which some say is the King of fishes. **1659** HOWELL *Eng. Prov.* 21a.

Herring must hang by its own gill, Every. (H 448)

1609 HARWARD 85 (tayle). **1639** CLARKE 20. **1670** RAY 102. **1721** KELLY 240 (head). Every man must stand by his own endeavour, industry, and interest. **1818** SCOTT *Rob Roy* ch. 26 Na, na! let every herring hing by its ain head, and every sheep by its ain shank.

Herrings in a barrel, Like.

1881 D. C. MURRAY *Joseph's Coat* ch. 12 The hall of justice was small . . . and there were fifty or sixty people packed into it like herrings in a barrel.

Herring(s), *see also* Barrel the better h. (Never a); Dead as a h.; Fish for h. and catch sprat; Lean as a shotten h.; Lose in hake (What we), shall have in h.; Poke savour of the h.; Red h.; Sprat nowadays calls itself h.; Sprat to catch h.

Hertfordshire clubs and clouted shoon.

(C 454)

1600 T. HEYWOOD *et al.* *1 Edw. IV* i. 90 Clubs and clouted shoes, there's none enamoured here. **1613–22** DRAYTON *Polyolb.* xxiii. 249, 50 (1876) III. 95 So *Hartford* blazon'd is, *The Club, and clowted Shoone.* **1662** FULLER Herts. 18 Hertfordshire clubs and clouted shoon. Some will wonder how this Shire, lying so near to London, . . . should be guiltie of so much Rusticalness. But the finest Cloth must have a List, and the pure Pesants are of as coarse a thread in this County as in any other place.

Hertfordshire kindness.   (K 44)

1662 FULLER Herts. 18 The people in this County at entertainments drink back to them who drank to them. **1738** SWIFT Dial. II. E.L. 301 This moment I did myself the honour to drink to your lordship—Why, then, that's Hertfordshire kindness.

Hesky's library—all outside, Like.

1917 BRIDGE 90 Like Hesky's library—all outside. Anything pretentious or unreal. A common saying in Cheshire and North Wales in the middle of last century. When Mr. Bamford Hesketh erected Gwrych Castle . . . the owner had not a tithe of the books necessary to fill [the library shelves].

Hew (Climb, Look) not too high lest the chips fall in thine eye.   (C 357)

c. **1330** BRUNNE *Chron.* (Hearne) I. 91 Sorow þan is his pyne, þat he wis ouer his heued, þe chip falles in his ine. *c.* **1350** Douce MS. 52 no. 128 Whoso heweth to hye, þere falle chippis in his ye. *c.* **1370** *Sir Eglamour* (Schleich) l. 70 The man þat hewes ouer-hey, þe chyppis fallis in his eye. *c.* **1390** GOWER *Conf. Amantis* i. 75 Full ofte he heweth up so highe, That chippes fallen in his eye. *c.* **1433** LYDGATE *Edmund & Tremund* iii. 5 I am ferful aboue myn hed to hewe, lyst froward chippis of presumpcioun sholde blynde myn eyen in ther fallyng doon. *a.* **1530** R. Hill's *Commonpl. Bk.* (1858) 140 Clyme not to hye lest chypys fall yn thyn eie. *c.* **1549** HEYWOOD II. vii. I4 Hewe not to hye, lest the chips fall in thine iye. **1580** LYLY *Euph. & his Eng.* ii. 219 In the choyce of a wife . . . one looketh high as one that feareth no chips. **1641** FERGUSSON no. 317. He that hewes over hie, the spaill will fall into his eye. **1670** RAY 102 (Look) . . . *Noli altum sapere.*

Heyden, *see* Paston poor.

Hiccup, To cure one of the.

1635 SHIRLEY *Lady of Pleas.* III. ii Merm. 314 I am not troubled with the hickup, gentlemen, You should bestow this fright upon me. **1744** BIRCH *Life Boyle* in *Boyle's Wks.* I. 83 Some are freed from the hiccough, by being told of some feigned ill news. **1910** JOYCE *Eng. as We Speak* 202 'To cure a person's hiccup' means to . . . bring him to his senses. . . . [It] is the general belief through Ireland that . . . hiccup may be cured by suddenly making some . . . alarming announcement to the person.

Hickledy pickledy, one among another.

(H 452)

1659 TORRIANO no. 179 Fair or brown, so much a peece, higledy pickledy. **1678** RAY 349 . . . We have in our language many the like . . . reduplications to signifie any confusion or mixture.

Hide an eel in a sack, You cannot.

(E 63)

1640 HERBERT no. 762. **1732** FULLER no. 5875.

Hide nothing from thy minister, physician, and lawyer.   (P 261)

1573 SANFORD 50 *Al Medico & Auuocato Non tener il ver' celato,* Conceale not the truthe From the Phisition and Lawyer. **1578** FLORIO *First F.* 27 From the Phisition & Attorney, keepe not the truth hidden. **1640** HERBERT no. 105 Deceive not thy Physitian, Confessor, nor Lawyer. **1670** RAY 103 . . . He that doth so, doth it to his own harm or loss, wronging thereby either his soul, body, or estate. **1748** FRANKLIN July To friend, lawyer, doctor, tell plain your whole case; Nor think on bad matters to put a good face. **1834** EDGEWORTH *Helen* ch. 21 Always tell your confessor, your lawyer, your physician, your friend, your whole case.

Hide one's light (candle) under a bushel, To.   (L 275)

[**1526–34** TINDALE *Matt.* v. 15 Nether do men lyght a candell, and put it vnder a busshell, but on a candelstick, and it lighteth all them which are in the housse.] **1379** HENRY DANIEL *Liber Uricrisiarum* (MS. e Mus. 187 f. 1 l. 49) þat I be noȝt made a lyȝtede lantern hide vnder a busshel. *c.* **1548** J. BALE *Image of both Churches* pt. 2 P.S. 440 The candle that He lit us to see over the house [they must] convey under the bushel. **1548–9** N. UDALL Pref. to *Paraphrase of Erasmus* B3ᵛ As long as the candel light of the gospel was kepte hidden vnder the bushell. *c.* **1550** VERMIGLI *A Disc. concerning the Sacrament* tr. Udall Preface Suche a notable worke . . . to be suppressed or kepte (as it wer) hidden vnder a bushel. *c.* **1607** MIDDLETON *Trick* II. i. 75 Can a man of such exquisite qualities be hid under a bushel? *a.* **1873** LYTTON *Kenelm C.* VII. vii Slothfully determined to hide his candle under a bushel.

Hide (*noun*), *see* Horns go with h. (Let).

Hide, hid, hidden, (*verb*), *see also* Bait h. the hook; Fire cannot be h. in flax; Greater embraces (includes, h.) the less; Misery best, (He bears) that h. it most; Nothing comes fairer to light than long h.; Sin that is h. is half forgiven; Steals can h.; Visor to h. ill-favoured face, (A well-favoured).

Hides can find, He that. (H 453)

c. 1400 *Seven Sages* Percy Soc. 68 He may wel fynde that hyde him selven. 1639 CLARKE III. 1646 FULLER *Wounded Consc.* (1841) 339 Our English proverb saith, he that hath hid can find. 1678 RAY 137 They that feal (i.e. hide) can find. 1842 MARRYAT *Perc. Keene* ch. 3 Yes, yes, those who hide can find.

Hielandman, *see* Taking the breeks off a H. (Ill).

High and dry.

1822 R. G. WALLACE *Fifteen Years in India* 48 Another surf sent [him] high and dry. 1853 BUNSEN in *Life and Wks. of Kingsley* (1901), ii. 112 You know of the persecution of the Evangelicals, and High and dry against Maurice. 1894 DEAN HOLE *More Mem.* ii. 29 The clergy, . . . described by their critics as 'High and Dry', high in their self-esteem, and 'dry as a Monday bun' in their discourses. 1910 *Times Lit. Sup.* 9 Dec. What is usually called the 'High and Dry' section was in fact . . . a 'Low Church or Latitudinarian party, . . . content to leave things as they were'.

High as a hog, all but the bristles, As. (H 484)

1670 RAY 202 . . . Spoken of a dwarf in derision.

High as two (three) horse loaves,[1] As. (H 721)

[A jocular standard of measurement.] 1546 HEYWOOD I. x. C3 As high as twoo horse loues hir persone is. 1573 COOPER *Thesaurus* s.v. *a tenero* (three). 1591 ARIOSTO *Orl. Fur.* Harington VII. 62 Her stature scant three horseloaues did exceed. 1670 RAY 202 (three) . . . spoken of a dwarf in derision. [1 made of beans and wheat.]

High buildings have a low foundation. (B 708)

1623 CAMDEN 265 A high building, a low foundation. 1670 RAY 103 (as 1623).

High for the pie, Not too | nor too low for the crow. (P 283-4)

1546 HEYWOOD II. vii. I4 Measure is a mery meane, as this dothe show, Not to hy for the pye, nor to lowe for the crow. 1639 CLARKE 206.

High in the instep, To be. (I 84)

[= haughty, proud.] 1541 BULLINGER *Christian State of Matrimony* tr. Coverdale B3ᵛ Froward and scoldyng wyues . . . they are so lady lyke and hygh in the ynne steppe. 1546 HEYWOOD I. xi. D4ᵛ He is so hye in thynstep. 1548 BOORDE *Introd.* E.E.T.S. xxvi. 189 They be hyghe in the instep, and stondeth in theyr owne consayte. 1580 LYLY *Euph. & his Eng.* ii. 179. 1617 MORYSON *Itin.* II. 26 Now the Gentleman was

growne higher in the instep, as appeared by the insolent conditions he required. 1828 *Craven Dial.* s.v. 'She is rather high in her instep', she is proud and haughty.

High places have their precipices.

1732 FULLER no. 2501. 1813 RAY 121.

High ropes, To be on the. (R 175)

[= in an elated, disdainful, or enraged mood.] 1694 MOTTEUX *Gargantua* T.T. V. xviii. iii. 299 He was upon the High-Rope, and began to rail at them like mad. 1699 B.E. s.v. Rope Upon the High-ropes, Cock-a-hoop. 1711 SWIFT *Jrnl. to Stella* 6 Dec. The Duke of Marlborough . . . is one day humble, and the next day on the high ropes. 1773 GOLDSMITH *Stoops to Conq.* II. Wks. (Globe) 653/2 All upon the high rope! His uncle a colonel. 1838 DICKENS *N. Nickleby* ch. 31 I went there the night before last, and he was quite on the high ropes about something.

Higher standing, The | the lower fall. (S 823)

c. 1230 *Hali Meid.* 15 Se herre degre se þe fal is wurse. *c.* 1430 LYDGATE *Minor Poems* Percy Soc. 24 Who sitteth highest moost like to fall soon. 1493 H. PARKER *Dives and Pauper* R7ᵛ The higher degre the fal. 1549 *Compl. of Scotland* E.E.T.S. 170 The mair eleuat that ane person be in superfleu digniteis, his fal and ruuyn sal be the hauyar. Quanto gradus altior, tanto casus grauior. 1641 FERGUSSON no. 839 The higher up, the greater fall. 1670 RAY 102. 1721 KELLY 319 The higher up, the lower fall.

Higher the ape goes, The | the more he shows his tail. (A 271)

c. 1594 BACON *Promus* 309, no. 924 He doth like the ape that the higher he clymbes the more he shows his ars. 1603 MONTAIGNE (Florio) II. xvii. 156 The saying of Lord Oliver, whilome Chaunceler of France . . . 1640 HERBERT no. 745. 1670 RAY 57 . . . The higher beggars or base bred persons are advanced, the more they discover the lowness and baseness of their spirits and tempers. 1743 POPE *Scriblerus*' note to *Dunciad* iv. 18 'Vet. Adag. The higher you climb, the more you shew your A—. Verified in no instance more than in Dulness aspiring. Emblematized also by an Ape climbing and exposing his posteriors'. 1861 C. READE *Cloist. & H.* ch. 52 Margaret retorted: '. . . Your speech betrays you. 'Tis not till the ape hath mounted the tree that she shews her tail so plain.'

Higher the fool, The | the greater the fall.

1707 MAPLETOFT 125 (Welsh).

Higher the hill, The | the lower the grass. (H 464)

1509 BARCLAY *Ship of Fools* i. 188 On hyest places most gras doth not ay growe. 1721 KELLY 330 . . . People of the most greatest Fortunes are not the most liberal.

Higher the mountain the greater descent, The. (M 1212)

1584 WITHALS B5ᵛ The higher the hill is, the deeper is the dale, or the valley is the lower. **1616** DRAXE no. 67.

Higher the plum-tree, The | the riper (sweeter) the plum: the richer the cobbler, the blacker his thumb.

(P 441)

1579 GOSSON *Ephemerides* 76 b Rich Coblers, haue blacke Thumbes. **1639** CLARKE 88 (sweeter). **1659** HOWELL *Eng. Prov.* 17 b (... The better the shooe the blacker the thumb). **1659** N.R. 112. **1670** RAY 210. **1732** FULLER no. 6420.

Highest branch is not the safest roost, The.

1563 *Mirr. for Mag.* ed. Campbell 381 Where the tree the smallest braunches bere, The stormes do blowe and have most rigor there.

Highest in court (Nearest the King) nearest the widdie.¹

1621 ROBINSON 7 Neere the King neere the gallowes. *a.* **1628** CARMICHAELL no. 1194 (Neirest the king). **1641** FERGUSSON no. 651 (Nearest the King). **1721** KELLY 126 . . . Witness the fatal Fall of many Courtiers. [¹ gallows.]

Highest tree has the greatest fall, The. (T 489)

c. **1374** CHAUCER *Troilus* Bk. 2, l. 1380–6 Whan that the stordy ook, . . . Receyved hath the happy fallyng strook, The grete sweigh doth it come al at ones. . . . For swifter cours com'th thing that is of wighte, Whan it descendeth, than don thynges lighte. **1566** LINDSAY *Dial. between Experience and a Courtier* Epist. to Reader. **1639** CLARKE 122. **1670** RAY 13.

High(er), *see also* Cedars fall when low shrubs remain, (H.); Floods have low ebb, (H.); Hew (Climb, Look) not too h. lest chips fall in eye; Ride the h. horse; Stream stopped swells the h.

Highflying hawks are fit for princes.

(H 229)

1616 BRETON *Cross. Proverbs* A8ᵛ (are fitted for). **1639** CLARKE 41. **1670** RAY 101.

Highgate, *see* Sworn at H.; Water his horse at H.

Highlandman's gun, Like the | that needed a new lock, stock, and barrel.

1817 SCOTT *Let. to Terry* 29 Oct. in LOCKHART *Life* Like the Highlandman's gun, she wants stock, lock, and barrel, to put her into repair.

Highlandman, *see also* Find it where H. found tongs; Forth bridles the H. *See also* Hielandman.

Highway is never about, The. *Cf.* Highway, He that leaves the. (H 459)

1621 ROBINSON 25 (is the best way). **1623** J. CHAMBERLAIN *Letters* (McClure) ii. 508 Commonly the high way is both safest and shortest. **1639** CLARKE 202.

Highway, He that leaves the | to cut short, commonly goes about. *Cf.* Highway is never about.

1568 'K. James V his Pasquill' Bannatyne MS. i. 134 (Melville 24) Far better's the hie gate Nor the by rod. **1659** HOWELL *Span. Prov.* 16 By no means leave not the high-way for a bypath. **1707** MAPLETOFT 74. **1732** FULLER no. 2213.

Highway, *see also* Common as the h.; Grass grows not upon h.; Man must not leave the king's h. for a pathway; Silent H.; Sows in the h. (He that).

Hilary term, *see* Keep H. t.

Hill¹ belly (back), fill belly.

(*Cf.* B 298)

c. **1529** *Gentleness and Nobility* l. 440 There is no ioy nor pleasure in this world here But hyll fill belly and make good chere. **1570** TUSSER K1 What hilbacke and fill belly maketh away, that helpe to make good, or else looke for a fray. **1573** *Id.* 1878 ed., 23 As interest or vsurie plaieth the dreuil, so hilback and filbellic biteth as euil. *Ibid.* 183 What hilback and filbellie maketh away. **1616** J. DEACON *Tobacco Tortured* 73 Hil-backe, and fil-bellie is now mine hourely care. **1917** BRIDGE *Cheshire Proverbs* 3 A hill² an' a fill³ and an' o'er-neet⁴. [¹ Cover with clothes. ² Bed. ³ Meal. ⁴ Night's lodging.]

Hill in King Harry's day, This was a. (H 468)

1678 RAY 73. (*Joculatory.*)

Hills (proper name), *see* Clent (People of).

Hills are green (blue) far away.

1887 H. CAINE *Deemster* ch. 5 'What's it saying'; they would mutter; 'a green hill when far from me; bare, bare when it is near'. **1914** *Spectator* 6 June, 955 It is the habit of the Celt to create fanciful golden ages in the past—'Blue are the faraway hills', runs the Gaelic proverb.

Hill(s), *see also* Clouds are upon h. (When); Comes first to h.; Do on the h. as in the hall; Higher the h. lower the grass; Hop against h.; Mist comes from the h. (When); Old as the h.; Praise a h. but keep below; Up h. spare me; Up the h. favour me; Vale best discovers h.

Hilt(s), *see* Loose in the h.

Hinckley field, *see* Last man that he killed.

Hind foot, *see* Ill paut with her h. f. (She has).

Hinder end, *see* Falsehood never made a fair h. e.; Hearken to the h. e.

Hindmost, *see* Devil take h.; Dog (H.) may catch hare; Every man for himself.

Hindustan, *see* Pepper to H.

Hinge(s), *see* Creaking door long on h.; Groundsel speaks not save ... heard at h.

Hinging on, *see* Hankering and h. o. is a poor trade.

Hip, To have one on the. (H 474)

[= have one at a disadvantage.] **1546** HEYWOOD II. v. H3ᵛ Then haue ye hym on the hyp, or on the hyrdell. **1564** *Dial. betw. Cap and Head* B6 As fayre a tonged man as any in England, till hee haue catched them on the hippe. **1596** SHAKES. *M.V.* IV. i. 329 Now, infidel, I have thee on the hip. **1604** *Id. O.* II. i. 299 I'll have our Michael Cassio on the hip. **1639** FULLER *Holy War* II. viii (1840) 59 Arnulphus ... fearing to wrestle with the king, who had him on the hip, and could out him at pleasure. **1837** J. B. KER 91.

Hip, *see also* Bite out of your own h. (Take a).

Hire, *see* Good hand good h.; Labourer worthy of h.

Hired horse tired never, A. (H 661)

a. **1641** FERGUSSON MS. no. 98. **1683** MERITON *Yorks. Ale* 83-7 (1697).

Hires the horse, He that | must ride before. (H 659)

1639 CLARKE 99. **1670** RAY 106.

History repeats itself.

1553 QUINTUS CURTIUS tr. J. Brend (1561 ed., A3ᵛ) There is nothing new vnder the Sunne (as the wise man saith) and it is impossible for any thing to chaunce either in the war or in common policie, but there the like maye be found to haue chaunced in times past. **1570** DEMOSTHENES tr. T. Wilson [Thucydides says (I. xxii):] Like time bringeth forth lyke examples. **1583** MELBANCKE A2ᵛ Auncient antiquities canne afford like examples. **1597** *Politeuphuia* 152 Time is the repeater of all things. **1857** G. ELIOT *Scenes of Clerical Life* 'Janet's Repentance' ch. 10 History, we know, is apt to repeat itself. **1885** A. JESSOPP *Daily Life in a Med. M.* 163 That age has passed away for ever. History repeats itself, it is true, but history will not bear mimicry. **1902** J. K. LAUGHTON in *Lect. Hist. 19th Cent.* 87 Should we again be at war with France, history would repeat itself in many of its phases.

History, *see also* Ale and h.; Country which has no h.; Every day of thy life is a leaf.

Hit (Kick) a man when he is down, To.

1551 CRANMER *Ans. to Gardiner* 339 It bee but a small peece of manhoode to strike a manne

whan he is downe. *a.* **1607** TOMKIS *Lingua* Fi Fie fie fie Heuresis, beate him when hee's downe? **1712** SWIFT *Jrnl. to Stella* 8 Jan. The Duke of Marlborough says there is nothing he now desires so much as to ... soften Dr. Swift. ... Now he is down, I shall not trample on him. **1853** THACKERAY *Newcomes* ch. 29 I don't know whether it is very brave in you to hit a chap when he is down. **1870** J. R. GREEN *Let.* to Freeman 31 Aug. I can't kick France now she's down, as Jupiter does.

Hit (Strike) below the belt, To.

1890 S. BARING-GOULD *Arminell* II. xxxiv. 265 You have behaved infamously towards your benefactor, you have hurt him where he is most sensitive—hitting, you contemptible little coward, below the belt. **1926** *Times* 13 Jul. 10/3 In England we did not believe in stabbing a man in the back or hitting him below the belt.

Hit him hard: he has no friends.

1850 D. M. MULOCK *Woman's Thoughts* 156 The poor costermonger, who shouts after the little pugilistic sweep the familiar tragio-comic saying: 'Hit him hard; he's got no friends!'

Hit one over the thumbs, To. (T 274)

[= to punish, or reprove sharply.] **1540** PALSGRAVE *Acolastus* 20 Haue men hytte the vpon the thombes? **1548** HALL 33 In the later ende of hys oracion, he a little rebuked the lady Margaret and hyt her of [*Grafton* on] the thombes. **1553** T. WILSON *Arte of Rhet.* (1580) 3 The Philosopher ... did hit a yong man ouer the Thumbes verie handsomely, for vsyng ouer old, and ouer straunge woordes. [entered 1587]. **1591** GREENE *Farewell to Folly* Gros. ix. 285 Peratio ... thought to crosse Benedetto ouer the thumbs. [*c.* **1590**] **1594** LODGE & GREENE *Looking-Glass* I. ii. 206 Well said, Smith, that crost him ouer the thumbs. *c.* **1590** *Plain Percival* 1860 ed. 33 A washing blow of this ... can wipe a fellow over the thumbs.

Hit or miss. (H 475)

[1547-53] *c.* **1565** WEVER *Lusty Juventus* A2ᵛ I will go seeke them, whether I hyt or mysse. **1553** T. WILSON *Arte of Rhet.* (1909) 87 Which shot in the open and plaine fields at all adventures hittie missie. **1602** SHAKES. *T.C.* I. iii. 384 But, hit or miss, Our project's life this shape of sense assumes. **1678** RAY 73 Hit or misse for a cowheel. **1705** HICKERINGILL *Priest-cr.* I. (1721) 14 Do we all march towards Heaven hit or miss, and by guess? **1873** OUIDA *Pascarèl* II. 42 It is not the happy-go-lucky hit-or-miss sort of thing that you may fancy.

Hit the bird in the eye, To. (B 387)

1639 CLARKE 210. **1670** RAY 181.

Hit the nail on the head, To. (N 16)

[= to come at the point of the matter.] **1508** STANBRIDGE *Vulg.* B5 Thou hyttest the nayle on the head. *c.* **1520** *Terence in English* (Andria) B2ᵛ Thou hyttist the nayle on the head. *a.* **1529** SKELTON *Col. Cloute* 34 And yf that he hyt The nayle on the hede, It standeth in no stede. **1599** H. BUTTES *Dyets Drie Dinner* E vj His chiefe pride resteth in hitting the nayle on the head with

a quainte Epithite. **1614** CAMDEN 305 Euery
man cannot hit the naile on the head. **1662**
FULLER Linc. 169 James Yorke . . . set forth a
Book of Heraldry. . . . And although there be
some mistakes (no hand so steady as always to
hit the nail on the Head) [&c.]. **1852** E. FITZ-
GERALD *Polonius* 15 Where the writer has gone to
the heart of a matter, the centre of the circle, hit
the nail on the head and driven it home. **1903**
BRYCE *Stud. Contemp. Biog.* 461 Mr. Gladstone
showed in argument a knack of hitting the nail
not quite on the head.

Hit (Shoot nigh) the prick (mask, pin, white, etc.), To. *Cf.* Shoot nigh the p.
                                               (P 336 and P 571)

c. **1400** *Sowdone Bab.* 2260 Thou kanste welle
hit the prikke.[1] *c.* **1425** *Wakefield Plays* 'Judgement' l. 370 I trowd it drew nere the prik.
a. **1500** *Ludus Coventriae* 'Trial of Joseph and
Mary' Now be myn trowthe ye hytte the pynne.
1546 HEYWOOD I. vi. B3 Ye mary (quoth he)
nowe ye shoote ny the pricke. **1586** GUAZZO, ii.
158 I have not so neerelie hit the white, as my
meaning was. **1590** MARLOWE *1 Tamburlaine* II.
iv. 8 For kings are clouts that every man shoots
at, Our crown the pin that thousands seek to
cleave. **1594–5** SHAKES. *L.L.L.* IV. i. 127 Indeed
'a must shoot nearer, or he'll ne'er hit the clout
. . . Then will she get the upshoot by cleaving the
pin. *c.* **1595** *Id. R.J.* II. iv. 15 The very pin
of his heart cleft with the blind bow-boy's butt-
shaft. **1624** J. HEWES *Survey Eng. Tongue* K1
Who is it that shooting all the day, doth not
sometimes hit the marke? [1 mark in shooting
with bow.]

Hit(s), *see also* Oft ettle, whiles h.; Once h. (He
that) is ever bending; Shoots oft at last shall h.
mark; Vulgar will keep no account of your h.

Hitch your wagon to a star.

1870 EMERSON *Society and Solitude* 'Civilization'.

Hither, *see* Legs, (How came you h. ?)

Ho with him, There is no. *Cf.* Out of all whooping.
                                               (G 264. H 477)

1560–77 *Misogonus* II. iii. 55 Thoughe you
thinke him past whoo, He may yet reduce him.
1569 J. PHILLIP *Patient Grissill* l. 1155 This
youncar is one of them that God bad whoe.
1577 LEMNIUS *Touchstone of Complexions* 101ᵛ
They keepe neither ho, nor measure in their
affections.

Ho, *see* Heave and h., (To pay one home with);
Out of all whooping (*or* h.).

Hoar head and a green tail, To have a. *Cf.* Grey and green make the worst medley.
                                               (L 177)

c. **1386** CHAUCER *Reeve's Prol.* l. 3878 To have an
hoor heed and a grene tayl, As hath a leek; for
thogh oure myght be goon, Oure wyl desireth
folie evere in oon. **1566** PAINTER i. 124 Olde
men . . . that for loue like the grene stalkes or
graye heades of Lekes, doe desire to sauer your
mouthes. **1591** GREENE *Farewell to Folly*
Grosart ix. 323 Respect and experience had

taught him, that olde men were like leekes gray
headed and often greene tailde. **1608** DEKKER
Lanthorn and Candlelight K3ᵛ [of old men] to see
white heads growing vpon green stalkes. **1706**
STEVENS s.v. Cabeca We say, . . . a grey Head and
a green Tail. **1721** KELLY 363 (white Head).

Hoarse, *see* Crow croaks before the rain, (The h.).

Hoards up money, He that | takes pains for other men.
                                               (M 1044)

1567 BALDWIN *Treatise Moral Philosophy* A5ᵛ.
1597 *Politeuphuia* R1ᵛ. **1732** FULLER no. 2165.

Hob's pound, *see* Lob's pound.

Hobby runs away with him, His.

1834 EDGEWORTH *Helen* ch. 17 Beauclerc's
hobbies, I plainly see, will always run away with
him headlong.

Hobby, *see also* Ride a h. to death.

Hobby-horse, Every man has his.

1676 HALE *Contempl.* I. 201. Almost every
person hath some hobby horse or other wherein he
prides himself. *a.* **1791** WESLEY *Serm.* lxxxiii.
II. 2 Wks. (1811) IX. 434 Every one has (to use the
cant term of the day . . .) *his hobbyhorse!* Something that pleases the great boy for a few hours.

Hobson's choice.
                                               (H 481)

[Tobias Hobson, the Cambridge carrier, who let
out horses, compelled customers to take the
horse which happened to be next the stable-door,
or go without. *c.* **1599** *Pilgrimage to Parnassus*
l. 630 Woulde it not greeue a man of a good
spirit to see Hobson finde more money in the
tayles of 12 Jades, than a scholler in 200 bookes?
1604 MIDDLETON *Father Hubburd's Tales* viii.
101 Not on horseback, but in Hobson's
waggon? **1617** R. COCKS *Diary* I Oct., II. 294
Once we are put to Hodgsons choise to take
such previlegese as they will geve us, or else goe
without. **1649** *Somers Tracts* (1811) vii. 87 I
had Hobson's choice, either be a Hobson or
nothing. **1660** S. FISHER *Rustick's Alarm* Wks.
(1679) 128 If in this Case there be no other (as
the Proverb is) then Hobson's choice . . . which is,
chuse whether you will have this or none.
a. **1708** T. WARD *Eng. Ref.* (1716) 326 Where to
elect there is but one, 'Tis Hobson's choice,
Take that or none. **1714** *Spectator* 509. **1858**
R. SURTEES *Ask Mamma* ch. 43 It was a case of
Hobson's choice with them.

Hoe, *see* Row to h. (Hard); Tickle it with a h.

Hog has its Martinmas, Every. (H 486)

1620 SHELTON *Quix.* II. lxii. iii. 265 I thought . . .
it had been . . . turned to ashes for an idle
pamphlet; but it will not, like hogs, want its
Saint Martin. [*Note.* That saint's day is hogs'
searing.] **1659** HOWELL *Span. Prov.* 21 (his
Saint Martin). **1706** STEVENS s.v. Puerco.

Hog his own apple, Every.

1748 SMOLLETT *Rod. Rand.* ch. 41 I let them have
share and share while it lasted. Howsomever,

I should have remembered the old saying, *Every hog his own apple.*

Hog in armour, A.   (H 489)

[= a stiff clumsy person.] **1659** HOWELL *Eng. Prov.* 19a He looketh like a Hogg in armour. **1706** STEVENS s.v. Mona (is still but an Hog). **1774** *Westmr. Mag.* II. 457 I never see Alderman —— on horseback, but he reminds me of an hog in armour. **1857** TROLLOPE *Three Clerks* ch. 25 But he did not carry his finery like a hog in armour, as an Englishman so often does when an Englishman stoops to be fine.

Hog is never good but when he is in the dish, The.

1587 MASCALL *Govt. Cattle* (1627) 270 Where fore the common saying is, the hog is never good but when he is in the dish.

Hog never looks up to him that threshes down the acorns, The.   (H 492)

1623 PAINTER B6ᵛ Like the Hogge[s] that Acornes feed vpon, And neuer looke vp from what tree they come. **1654** FULLER *Comment. on Ruth in Serm.* (1891) I. 9 In prosperity, we are commonly like hogs feeding on the mast, not minding his hand that shaketh it down. **1732** FULLER no. 4599.

Hog that's bemired endeavours to bemire others, A.

1599 MINSHEU (1623) *Span. Dial.* 39 One hog that hath wallowed in the mire will beray another. **1706** STEVENS s.v. Puerco. **1732** FULLER no. 214.

Hogs Norton, where pigs play on the organ. *Cf.* Pigs play on the organ.   (H 505)

c. **1520**? *Interlude of Youth* Hazl.-Dods. II. 31 Were thou born in Trumpington, And brought up at Hoggesnorton? **1573** J. BRIDGES *Supremacy of Christian Princes* H4 Ye haue bene brought vp neyther at courte nor mannour, but at Hogges norton as they say. **1592** NASHE *Strange News* i. 323. **1640** *Wits Recreation* (Hotten) 88 You your garden may Hogs Norton call, here Pigs on organs play. **1659** HOWELL *Eng. Prov.* 16a I think thou wast born at *Hoggs-Norton*, where piggs play upon the Organs. **1662** FULLER Oxf. 327 You were born at Hogs-Norton. This is a Village, properly called Hoch-Norton, whose inhabitants (it seems formerly) were so rustical in their behaviour, that boorish and clownish people are said born at *Hogs-Norton*. **1881** EVANS 301 'Hogs Norton, where Pigs play on the Organ'. . . . To say that a man comes from Hog's Norton is simply equivalent to saying that he snores.

Hogs to a Banbury market, He has brought his.

1639 CLARKE 201.

Hogs (Pigs) to a fair (fine) market, He has brought his.   (H 503)

[**1600**] **1659** DAY & CHETTLE *Blind Beggar* v. K1ᵛ I have brought my hogs to a fair Market. **1600** *Look about You* l. 961 My fa fa father has brought his ho ho hoges to a fa fa faire m m market. **1618–19** J. FLETCHER *Bonduca* v. ii You have brought your hogs to a fine market; you are wise, Sir. **1638** CLARKE *Phraseol. Puer.* 76 *Triticum advexi & hordeum vendo* . . . I have brought my hogges to a faire market. **1659** HOWELL *Eng. Prov.* 5a You have brought your hogs to a fair market. Spoken in derision when a business hath sped ill. **1748** SMOLLETT *Rod. Rand.* ch. 15 Strap . . . observed that we had brought our pigs to a fine market. **1805** LAMB *Mr. H——.* II. Wks. (1898) 641 Your Honour has had some mortification . . .; you have brought your pigs to a fine market. **1890** D. C. MURRAY *John Vale's G.* ch. 16 Mr. Orme . . . felt that he had brought his pigs to a poor market.

Hogs (dogs) to the honey pots (porridge-pot), The.   (H 491)

1560–77 *Misogonus* II. iv. 180 Is the preist hande ith honye pott yet? *c.* **1579** MERBURY *Marr. Wit and Wisdom* sc. iii The cook is not so sone gone As the doges hed is in the porigpot. *a.* **1604** MARLOWE *Faustus* III. iii. A52 And I must be a dog.—I' faith, thy head will never be out of the pottage-pot. **1678** RAY 354.

Hog(s), *see also* Bastes the fat h. (Every man); Better my h. dirty home; Break a h. of ill custom (Hard to); Devil is a h. (When); Drive black h. in dark; Driving his h. . . . (He is); Expect of a h. but bristles (a grunt) (What can you); Go the whole h.; Hampshire h.; High as a h.; Kill h. (He who does not) will not get black puddings; Last man he killed keeps h.; Make a h. or a dog of it; One h. (He that has) makes him fat; Routing like a h.; Steal a h. and give feet; Worst h. gets best pear.

Hogshead, *see* Couch a h.

Hoist with his own petard.

1600–1 SHAKES. *H.* III. iv. 207 For 'tis the sport to have the enginer Hoist with his own petar. **1826** SCOTT *Woodst.* ch. 33 'Tis sport to have the engineer Hoist with his own petard, as our immortal Shakespeare has it. **1885** C. LOWE *Bismarck* (1898) 322 The Chancellor had been caught in his own trap, hoist, so to speak, with his own petard.

Hoist your sail when the wind is fair.   (S 23)

1583 MELBANCKE *Philotimus* C4ᵛ Yt is well, therefore, to make hay while the sunne shines, when winde is at will to hoyse vp saile. **1599** TASSO *Marr. and Wiving* F2ᵛ If they [thy sons] venter on the seas, thou likewise hoysest vp the sailes of the winds of thy thoughts, lest their ship by tempest should runne vpon some rocke. **1732** FULLER no. 2518. **1822** SCOTT *Nigel*, Introd. Ep. A man should strike while the iron is hot, and hoist sail while the wind is fair.

Hoistings, or Hustings, You are all for the. (H 506)

1662 FULLER *Lond.* 200 It is spoken of those who by Pride or Passion are mounted or elated to a pitch above the due proportion of their Birth, Quality, or Estate. . . . It cometh from the Hustings, the Principal and highest Court in London.

Holborn, *see* Ride backwards up H. Hill.

Hold a candle to, Not able (fit) to.
(C 44)

1562 G. LEGH *Accidence of Armoury* 231 Not worthy to vnlace the buskynn of Parmenides, or to holde the candell to many herehaughtes that he could name. **1641** DERING *Virtues Carmelite* 43 Though I be not worthy to hold the candle to Aristotle. **1861** G. J. WHYTE-MELVILLE *Market Harbor.* ch. 18 The Reverend . . . always declared . . . that Cissy could not hold a candle to what her mother had been in her best days. **1882** BLACKMORE *Christowell* ch. 36 Some one . . . intending ill to my poor pears. . . . That man . . . who . . . had nothing fit to hold a candle to my *Léon Leclerc.* **1883** W. E. NORRIS *No New Thing* I. vii. 175 Edith is pretty, very pretty; but she can't hold a candle to Nellie.

Hold a candle to the devil, To. (C 42)

[= to assist in wrong-doing.] **1461** *Paston Lett.* (Gairdner) II. 73 It is a common prouerbe, 'A man must sumtyme set a candel before the Devyle.' **1520** WHITTINGTON *Vulg.* E.E.T.S. 107 Thou art aboute to please a shrewe (I haue espyed) as a man that offereth a candell to the deuyll. **1546** HEYWOOD I. x. C3ᵛ I fearyng She wolde spit her venym, thought it not euyll To set vp a candell before the deuyll. **1599** PORTER *Angry Wom. Abingd.* l. 2329 Yet Ile giue him good words, 'tis good to hold a candle before the deuill. **1649** HOWELL *Pre-em. Parl.* 20 According to the Italian Proverb, That one must sometimes light a candle to the Devil. **1828** SCOTT *F. M. Perth* ch. 29 Here have I been holding a candle to the devil, to show him the way to mischief.

Hold fast when you have it. (H 513)

c. **1460** *Towneley Plays* 'Killing of Abel' l. 142 It is better hold that I haue then go from doore to doore to craue. *c.* **1515** *Bugbears* IV. iv. 18 Now I have him I will hold him. **1546** HEYWOOD I. x. D1 Hold fast whan ye haue it (quoth she) by my lyfe. **1562** *Id. Epig.* 294, 171 Holde fast when ye haue it, if it be not thyne. **1576** WAPULL *Tide* G3ᵛ Hold me when you haue me. **1611** COTGRAVE s.v. Tenir He that holds let him hold still; or, let him that hath a hold keepe it. **1621** ROBINSON 6. **1639** CLARKE 233. **1876** MRS. BANKS *Manch. Man* ch. 10 Then . . . rang, clear and distinct, Humphry Chetham's motto— 'Quod tuum tene!' (What you have, hold!)

Hold him to it buckle and thong.
(B 697)

1658 *Wit Restor'd* in *Mus. Deliciae* (Hotten) i. 280 When one is held to it hard, buckle and thong. **1678** RAY 73.

Hold hook and line. (H 589)

[*c.* **1597**] **1609** JONSON *Case Is Altered* I. v. 42 Ile giue you a health I faith; for the heauens you mad Capriccio, hold hooke and line. **1598** SHAKES. *2 Hen. IV* II. iv. 150 Hold hook and line, say I. **1607** SHARPHAM *Fleir* E2 Caught I hope, hold hooke and line, he's fast by heaven. **1613** J. D. *Secrets of Angling* A2 Hold hooke and line then all is mine.

Hold my peace, Although I | I gather up stones. (P 144)

1599 MINSHEU *Span. Dial.* 20 . . . He that is silent gathereth reasons to confute his aduersarie. **1659** HOWELL *Span. Prov.* 19 I that do hold my peace do gripe stones. **1903** A. T. QUILLER-COUCH *Hetty Wesley* I. iii These Hindus are the devil . . . for nursing a grudge. 'Keep a stone in your pocket seven years: turn it, keep it for another seven; 'twill be ready at your hand for your enemy'—that's their way.

Hold nor to bind, Neither to.

1824 SCOTT *St. Ronan's* ch. 15 A lord! . . . a lord come down to the Waal—they will be neither to haud nor to bind now. **1824** MOIR *Mansie W.* ch. 2 The old lady was neither to hold nor bind, and nothing would serve her but having . . . the old woman . . . committed to the Tolbooth. **1900** J. MCCARTHY *Hist. Own Times* V. 144 King Theebaw was . . . a madman, . . . like Caligula. . . . He was a man, . . . 'Neither to haud nor to bind.'

Hold of his word as of a wet eel by the tail, As much. Cf. Holds a wet eel by tail: *also* **Who has a woman.** (H 508)

1546 HEYWOOD I. x. C3 Hir promise of frendshyp, for any auayle Is as sure to holde, as an eele by the tayle. **1567** *Trial of Treasure* D3 As trusty as is a quicke ele by the tayle. **1639** CLARKE 247.

Hold on like grim death, To.

1837 TH. HOOK *Jack Brag* ch. 20 'Delightful breeze!' said Mr. Buckthorne to Jock, who was holding on, like grim death, by the companion. **1861** READE *Cloist. & Hearth* ch. 4 He would seize it with his teeth, and . . . hold on like grim death by his huge ivories.

Hold one's tongue in an ill time, One may. (M 260)

1616 DRAXE no. 42. **1670** RAY 103.

Hold or cut codpiece point. (C 502)

1595 SHAKES. *M.N.D.* I. ii. 98 Hold or cut bowstrings. **1678** RAY 73.

Hold that will away? Who can (may).
(H 515)

c. **1374** CHAUCER *Troilus* Bk. 4, l. 1628 For who may holde a thing that wol awey? *c.* **1465** MARGERY HAMPDEN *Stonor Letters* i. 70 Ther may no man hold þat woll awaye. **1546** HEYWOOD II. vi. I1ᵛ Saieth an other, who maie holde that will awaie. **1548** HALL 568. **1592** *History of Dr. John Faustus* A2ᵛ. **1614** JONSON *Barth. Fair* I. v. 109 Who can hold that will away? I had rather loose him then the Fayre, I wusse. **1721** KELLY 352 . . . Spoken when our friends will not be prevail'd upon to tarry with us.

Hold the ass by the bridle, It is good to. (A 364)

1592 DELAMOTHE 23. **1611** DAVIES no. 218. **1639** CLARKE 161.

Hold the greatest farms, They that | pay the least rent. (F 61)

1651 HERBERT no. 1100 . . . applied to rich men that are unthankful to God.

Hold up your head, for there is money bid for you.

1706 STEVENS s.v. Cesto (We say). **1736** SWIFT *Dial.* I. E.L. 265 Well, methinks here's a silent meeting. Come, miss, hold up your head, girl: there's money bid for you.

Hold up your dagger hand. (D 8)

1639 CLARKE 46. **1678** RAY 88 *Phrases . . . belonging to . . . drinking.*

Hold your tongue, husband, and let me talk that have all the wit. (T 390)

1678 RAY 84. **1732** FULLER no. 2521.

Hold his tongue, *see* Knows not how to h. h. t. (He that); Leave to speak (Must have) who cannot h. h. t.; Speak well (He cannot) that cannot h. h. t. *See also* Hold one's t.

Holdfast, *see* Brag is a good dog but H. better.

Holds a wet eel by the tail, He. *Cf.* Hold of his word: *also* Who has a woman. (E 61)

[ERASM. *Adagia* 179 F: Cauda tenes anguillam.] **1576** R. EDWARDS *Par. Dainty Dev.* (1927) 70, l. 12 Thus while I helde the Ele by the taile, I had some hope, yet neuer wanted feare. **1593** *Pass. Morrice* in *Tell-Trothes New Yeare's Gift, etc.*, New Sh. S. 88 Is it not folly to striue to keepe a wet Eele by the taile? **1608** DEKKER *Bellman* H2. **1721** KELLY 141 He has a sliddery Gripe that has an Eel by the Tail. Spoken to them who have to do with cunning Fellows, whom you can hardly bind sure enough.

Holds up her head like a hen drinking (a hundred pound aver[1]), She.

1721 KELLY 294 Spoken of a Woman who affectedly holds her Head high. [¹ horse.]

Hold(s), *see also* Bag to h. (To give); Dance nor h. candle (Neither); Dish while I shed my pottage (H. the); Glue did not h.; Hang than to h. (Better); Hawking (First point of) is h. fast; Knows enough that knows how to h. peace; No

man h. you; Speaks sows (He that) . . . h. his peace gathers; Staff's end (To h. at); Sun with a candle (To set forth).

Hole calls the thief, The. (H 519)

1640 HERBERT no. 204.

Hole in the groat today, and the supper to seek, There will be a.

1721 KELLY 325 . . . A Saying of Labourers, when they fear a rainy Afternoon.

Hole in the house, There is a. (H 521)

c. **1641** FERGUSSON MS. no. 1321. **1721** KELLY 315 . . . Spoken when some are present, before whom it is not proper to speak our Mind.

Hole in the water, To make a.

[= to commit suicide by drowning.] **1813** RAY 201. **1853** DICKENS *Bleak Ho.* ch. 46 Why I don't go and make a hole in the water I don't know.

Hole under his nose that all his money runs into, He has a. (H 517)

1611 COTGRAVE s.v. Soulier The hole too open under the nose, breeds tattered shooes, and ragged hose. **1659** HOWELL *Fr. Prov.* 10 The hole too ope under the nose, breeds ragged shoes and tattered hose. **1732** FULLER no. 1858.

Hole(s), *see also* Blind enough who sees not through h. of sieve; Cavil will enter at any h.; Find some h. to creep out at; Mouse a h. (Gave); Mouse that has one h. quickly taken; Peeps through h.; Pick a h.; Proud tod that will not scrape own h.; See day at a little h.; Tell how many h. be in a scummer; Tinkers who in stopping one h. make three; Wind that comes in at h. (Take heed of); Wish your skin full of h. (Long ere you).

Holiday dame, She is an. (D 20)

1542 BULLINGER *Christ. State Matrimony* Pref. by T. Becon (1543, A7ᵛ) Therfore must the sely poore wyues . . . be kept for holy dayes, teyed vp at hard meate. **1546** HEYWOOD II. x. L4 In condicion they differd so many waies That lyghtly he layde hir vp for holy daies. **1580** LYLY *Euph. & his Eng.* ii. 96 Thou goest about . . . to hang me vp for holydayes, as one neither fitting thy head nor pleasing thy humor. **1678** RAY 73 She's an holy-day dame. (*Joculatory.*)

Holiday(s), *see also* Blind man's h.; Every day is h. with sluggards; Necessity has no h.

Holiness is double iniquity, Pretended. (H 525)

1539 TAVERNER *Publius* A4ᵛ Counterfeyted holynes (they saye) is double wickednes. **1589** *Mar-Martin* C1 This old said sawe . . . Seem'd sanctitie is trecherie. **1616** DRAXE no. 521. **1647** *Countrym. New Commonw.* 12 (Dissembled).

Holland, *see* Children in H. take pleasure in making.

Holloway, Blind George of, *see* Fain see (That would I).

Holmesdale, The vale of | never won nor never shall.   (v 8)

1576 W. LAMBARDE *Peramb. of Kent* (1596) 520, 904 The Danes were ouerthrowne and vanquished. This victorie, . . . begate, as I gesse, the common bywoord, vsed amongst the inhabitauntes of this vale, . . . The vale of Holmesdale, Neuer wonne, nor neuer shale. **1659** HOWELL *Eng. Prov.* 21a . . . Holmesdale is near Rigat[1] in Surrey. [[1] Reigate.]

Holy habit cleanses not a foul soul, A.   (H 1)

1640 HERBERT no. 669.

Holy I'll be, I, marry will I.   (H 528)

1616 WITHALS 560. **1639** CLARKE 139.

Holy, *see also* Over h. was hanged; Sunday comes (When) it will be h. day.

Holyrood Day[1] the devil goes a-nutting, On.   (H 530)

1693 *Poor Robin* Sept. 14, 26 in LEAN II. i. 242 The devil, as some people say A-nutting goes Holy Rood Day; Let women, then, their children keep At home that day. **1830** FORBY 418. [[1] 14 Sept.]

Holy-water, *see* Court h.; Devil loves no h.; Parish priest forgets he was h. clerk.

Home as wise as one went, To return (come). *Cf.* **Fool to the market.** (F 460)

c. **1528** HEYWOOD *Four PP* A2 Yet welcome home as wyse as ye went. **1587** BRIDGES *Defence* 1237 The most part of them came home as wise, or perhaps wiser than they went out. [*c.* **1591**] **1595** PEELE *Old Wives Tale* l. 762 Goe thy waies home as wise as thou camst.

Home is home, though it be never so homely.   (H 534)

1546 HEYWOOD I. iv. B1 And home is homely, though it be poore in syght. **1569-70** STATIONERS' REG. Ballad entry Home is home, be it never so ill. **1591** ARIOSTO *Orl. Fur.* Harington XXXIX. 61 Home though homely twere, yet it is sweet, And natiue soile is best. **1611** COTGRAVE s.v. Pouvoir When all is done home's homelie. **1670** RAY 103. **1692** L'ESTRANGE *Aesop's Fab.* clxxxv (1738) 198 'Why truly', says the tortoise, 'I was at home, . . . and . . .' **1721** KELLY 132 Hame is a hamely word. Eng. Home is seemly, if it was never so homely. **1826** LAMB *Pop. Fallacies* no. 12. **1832** MOTHERWELL Introd. to Henderson's *Scot. Prov.* (1881) xix Nothing more bitter was ever uttered . . . against our Supreme Court of Judicature, than the saying

. . . Hame is hamely, quo' the Deil, when he fand himself in the Court of Session.

Home Rule, Rome Rule.

1911 *Spectator*, Suppt. 29 Apr. 628 Ireland is now ruled partially by the priests, and may be so entirely in the near future if it is true that 'Home Rule is Rome Rule'.

Home (with heave and ho), To pay one.   (H 346)

1550 R. HUTCHINSON *Image of God* P.S. 22 If he [the shooter] draw it [his shaft] far and up to the iron, then it payeth home, as they say, then it giveth a mighty stroke. **1557** EDGEWORTH 3B3 He payde theym home eueri halfpeny vt in prouerbio. **1566** SENECA *Octavia* tr. T. Nuce E4[v] Poppoea and Nero Whom mothers griefe, and hand reuenging wracke, Shall send with heaue and hoe, to funerall stacks. **1583** MELBANCKE 2B4 Hector at length with his heaued codgill, paide him home with heaue and how. **1601** JONSON *Ev. Man in Hum.* I. ii. 23 Horson Scanderbag rogue, oh that I had a horse; by Gods lidde i'de fetch him backe againe, with heaue and ho. **1616** WITHALS 560 Their owne knauery, will pay them home at the length. **1666** TORRIANO *Prov. Phr.* s.v. Pegola 138 Fowly to abuse one, to pay one home, and soundly.

Home, *see also* Borrowed thing will h. again; Charity begins at h.; Covetousness brings nothing h.; Devil is at h.; Dry bread at h. better than; East or west, h. is best; Far from h., near thy harm; Farthest way about nearest way h.; Fox preys farthest from h.; Go h. and say prayers; Good man is from h. (When) . . . table soon spread; Husband be not at h. (If) there is nobody; Little journeys . . . bring safe h.; Long h.; Place like h. (No); See no good like h.; Ship comes h.; Tarry-long brings little h.; Weeping Cross (To go h. by).

Homer sometimes nods.   (H 536)

[HORACE *Ars P.* 359 *Quandoque bonus dormitat Homerus.*] **1530** PALSGRAVE 897 And ther where they shall se the good Homer have ben aslepe to be wyllyng by good maner to wake him, in correctyng the fautes in the whiche by cause of the same he is fallin. **1621** BURTON *Anat. Mel.* Democr. to Rdr. (1651) 78 The very best may sometimes err; *aliquando bonus dormitat Homerus.* **1674** DRYDEN *Apol. Heroic Poetry* Horace acknowledges that honest Homer nods sometimes: he is not equally awake in every line. **1887** HUXLEY in *19th Cent.* Feb. 196 Scientific reason, like Homer, sometimes nods.

Homo homini lupus, see Man is to man a wolf.

Homo is a common name to all men.

[W. LILY *Introd. of Grammar* 1567 ed., A5.] **1567** HARMAN *Caveat* New Sh. S. ed. 73 A Doxe . . . is commen and indifferent for any that wyll vse her, as homo is a common name to all men. **1581** WITHALS L4 Homo is indifferent to man woman or childe. **1607** *The Puritan* I. i. 18 Know that death is as common as Homo, a common name to all men. **1612** *Cornucopiae* Gros. 119.

Honest a man as any is in the cards if (when) the kings are out, As. (M 67)

1583 MELBANCKE Bb 2. **1678** RAY 291. **1732** FULLER no. 697. **1823** GROSE ed. Pierce Egan s.v. Honest Man.

Honest a man as ever broke bread (lived by bread), As. (M 68)

1585 A. DENT *Sermon of Repentance* B4 I haue knowen . . . men, which before their conuersion and inward chang, were counted as honest men as euer brake bread. **1599** PORTER *Angry Wom. Abing.* l. 2318 As good a man . . . as ere broke bread, or drunke drinke. **1598–9** SHAKES. *M.A.* III. v. 36 An honest soul . . . as ever broke bread. **1600–1** *Id. M.W.W.* I. iv. 135 An honest maid as ever broke bread. [1600] **1631** T. HEYWOOD I *Fair Maid* ii. 277. My father was a Baker, . . . as honest a man as ever lived by bread.

Honest a man as ever trod on neat's (shoe-) leather, As. (M 66)

1545 TAVERNER H7 The starkest knaue that goeth on two legges. *a.* **1577** *Misogonus* IV. i. 158 As vp right a fellowe as ere trod on netes lether. *c.* **1590** PEELE *O.W.T.* l. 582 As good a fellow as euer troade vppon Neats leather. **1594** LYLY *Mother B.* II. iii. 19 I haue as fayre a face as euer trode on shoo sole. **1599** SHAKES. *J.C.* I. i. 26 As proper men as ever trod upon neat's leather. **1608** MIDDLETON *Mad World* III. ii. 195 As comfortable a man to woman as ever trod shoe leather. *c.* **1610** SHAKES. *Temp.* II. ii. 68. A present for any emperor that ever . . . **1622** MABBE tr. *Aleman's Guzman d'Alf.* II. 163 As arrent a villaine as ever trode vpon a shooe of leather.

Honest as the skin between his brows, As. (S 506)

a. **1575** *Gammer Gurton's Needle* v. ii. 121 I am as true . . . as skin betwene thy browes. **1598–9** SHAKES. *M.A.* III. v. 10 An old man, . . . but, in faith, honest as the skin between his brows. **1614** JONSON *Barthol. Fair* IV. v. 47. **1633** *A Banquet of Jests* Pt. II. 126.

Honest (Sober) by Act of Parliament, You cannot make people. (P 229)

1631 JONSON *Devil is an Ass* IV. i This act may make him honest.—If he were To be made honest, by an act of Parliament, I should not alter, i' my faith of him. **1905** ALEX. MACLAREN *Expos. Math.* II. 185 The people who do not believe in certain . . . restrictions of the liquor traffic say, 'You cannot make people sober by Act of Parliament'.

Honest look covers many faults, An.

1642 TORRIANO 99 (covers an infinite faults). **1732** FULLER no. 609 (An honest good Look).

Honest man and a good bowler, An. (M 183)

1594–5 SHAKES. *L.L.L.* V. ii. 577 He is a marvellous good neighbour, faith, and a very good bowler. **1635** QUARLES *Emb.* I. x The vulgar proverb's crost, he hardly can Be a good bowler and an honest man. **1639** CLARKE 72.

Honest man's word is as good as his bond, An. *Cf.* Good as one's word; King's word. (M 458)

a. **1400** CHAUCER *Bk. of Duchess* l. 935 Hir simple recorde Was founde as trewe as any bonde. *c.* **1500** *Lancelot* l. 1673 A kingis word shuld be a kingis bonde. **1594** SHAKES. *T.G.V.* II. vii. 75 His words are bonds, his oaths are oracles. *a.* **1606** *No-Body and Some-Body* l. 485 *Nobodies* word is as good as his bond. **1642** FULLER *H. & P. State* v. xiii (1841) 382 *He hath this property of an honest man, that his word is as good as his bond.* **1753** RICHARDSON *Grandison* Let. v I am no flincher . . . the word of Sir Rowland Meredith is as good as his bond. **1859** SMILES *Self-Help* ix David Barclay . . . was a mirror of . . . honesty; . . . his word was always held to be as good as his bond.

Honest men marry soon, wise men not at all. (M 529)

1659 HOWELL *It. Prov.* I Honest men use to marry, but wise men not. **1670** RAY 17 *Ital.*

Honest, *see also* Name of an h. woman is mickle worth; North-west wind (H. man and a); Poor but h.; Thread will tie an h. man better than a rope will do a rogue; Turn the (an h.) penny; Wise that is h.

Honesty is the best policy. (H 543)

1599 SANDYS *Europae Spec.* (1632) 102 Our grosse conceipts, who think honestie the best policie. **1608** SHAKES. *C.* III. ii. 42 I have heard you say, Honour and policy, like unsever'd friends, I' the war do grow together. **1657** W. LONDON *Cat. of most vendible Books* F3ᵛ Charles the great used to set his Crown upon the Bible, concluding, that Piety was the best Policy. **1662** FULLER *Warwicks.* This his [St. Wolstan] plain-dealing so wrought on his adversaries (Honesty at long running is the best Policy) that he was . . . continued . . . in his Bishoprick. **1773** BYROM *Poems (The Nimmers)* I. 75 I'll filch no filching;—and I'll tell no lye; Honesty's the best Policy—say I. **1904** *Spectator* 18 June 953 Archbishop Whately's saying that 'honesty is the best policy, but he is not an honest man who is honest for this reason'.

Honesty (Credit) keeps the crown of the causeway.

1721 KELLY 155 . . . An honest Man has nothing to be asham'd of, and so cares not whom he meets. *Ibid.* 317 Truth and honesty, &c. **1832** HENDERSON 9 Credit keeps the crown o' the causey.

Honesty may be dear bought, but can never be an ill pennyworth.

1721 KELLY 162 . . . For it will be sure to make a Man a Gainer at the last.

Honesty, see also Beauty and h. seldom agree; Knavery may serve, but h. is best; Surfeits of too much h. (A man never).

Honey and gall in love there is store, Of. (H 557)

1580 G. HARVEY *Three Proper Letters* Oxford Spenser 627 Of Honny, and of Gaule, in Loue there is store, The Honny is much, but the Gaule is more. **1616** DRAXE no. 1307 (as 1580). **1664** CODRINGTON 207.

Honey in the mouth, He has | and a razor at the girdle. (H 547)

1581 C. MERBURY *Discourse of Royal Monarchy* I. 2 Vi sono di quelli, che secondo il prouerbio hanno il mele in bocca e'il rasaio a cintolo. **1581** GUAZZO i. 68 Hony in their mouth, and a knife in their hand. *Ibid.* i. 137 He hath Honie in his mouth, and a Rasor at his girdle. **1659** HOWELL *It. Prov.* 10.

Honey, Make yourself all | and the flies will devour you. (H 545)

1620 SHELTON *Quix.* II. xlix. iii. 157 Ay, ay, cover yourselves with honey, and you shall see the flies will eat you. **1694** BOYER 110 Daub your self with honey, and you'll never want Flies. **1706** STEVENS s.v. Miel Turn honey and the Flies will eat you, that is, If you are mealy-mouth'd, or too sweet-temper'd, People will insult over you. **1791–1823** I. DISRAELI *Curios. Lit.* (Chandos) III. 51 The Italian proverbs have taken a tinge from their deep and politic genius . . . **1853** TRENCH iii. 69 We say: Daub yourself with honey, and you'll be covered with flies.

Honey cloys the stomach, (maw), Too much. (B 204. H 560)

[PROVERBS XXV. 27.] **1377** LANGLAND *P. Pl.* B. 54–6 Salomon . . . seith, *sicut qui mel comedit multum, non est ei bonum*: . . . To Englisch-men this is to mene. . . . The man that moche hony eteth. . . . his mawe it engleymeth.[1] *c.* **1386** CHAUCER *Mel.* l. 1415 And Salomon seith, 'If thou hast founden hony, ete of it that suffiseth; for if thou ete of it out of mesure, thou shalt spewe'. **1539** CRANMER Preface to 'Great Bible' A man may eate to much of hony be it neuer so sweete. **1545** R. ASCHAM *Toxophilus* ed. Wright 13. **1548** N. UDALL *Paraphrase* A5ᵛ Honey is waloweish and ouercasteth the stomake, yf it be plenteously taken by it selfe alone: but if with vinegre it be made eagredoulce, than is it not onely delectable and plesaunt of relice, but also comfortatiue and holesome too. **1580** LYLY *Euph. & his Eng.* ii. 191 Honnie taken excessiuelye cloyeth the stomache. **1595** SHAKES. *M.N.D.* II. ii. 137 A surfeit of the sweetest things The deepest loathing to the stomach brings. [¹ cloys.]

Honey in his pot, He that has no | let him have it in his mouth. (H 550)

1616 DRAXE no. 1677 (hath none in his mouth). **1640** HERBERT no. 360. **1642** TORRIANO 26 He who hath not money in his purse, let him have honey in his mouth.

Honey is not for the ass's mouth. (H 552)

1612 SHELTON *Quix.* IV. xxv. ii. 177 'Honey is not made for the ass's mouth', quoth Sancho; 'wife, thou shalt know it in good time'. **1694** BOYER 108 'Tis not for Asses to lick honey'. **1706** STEVENS s.v. Miel. **1732** FULLER no. 2537.

Honey is sweet, Every bee's. (B 209)

1640 HERBERT no. 609.

Honey is sweet, but the bee stings. (H 553)

c. **1535** W. CALVERLEY C3 Though the honey be swete the stinge is greuance. **1576** G. WAPULL *Tide Tarrieth No Man* A3 In the Bee . . . we see, Sweete honey and sting. **1640** HERBERT no. 212. **1670** RAY 13.

Honey that is licked from the thorn, Dear bought is the. (H 554)

c. **1175** *Old Eng. Homilies* (Morris) I. 185 Nis nan blisse . . . thet ne beo To bitter aboht; thet et huni ther-in, beoth licked of thornes. *c.* **1240** *Ureisun* Huni þer-in beoþ liked of þornes. *c.* **1300** *Provs. of Hending* 31 Dere is boht the hony that is licked of the thorne. *c.* **1350** *Douce MS.* 52 no. 79 Hit is harde to lykke hony fro the thorne. *Ibid.* no. 80 Dere is þe hony bou3t þat on thornes is sou3t. *c.* **1390** GOWER *Conf. Amantis* vi. 324 And thus as I have said a-forn, I licke hony on the thorn. **1592** DELAMOTHE 53. **1597** GERARD *Herbal* 408. **1678** RAY 379. **1732** FULLER no. 2215 He that licks Honey from a Nettle pays too dear for it.

Honey tongue, a heart of gall, A. (H 561. T 391)

c. **1300** *Cursor M.* l. 25729 Hony þai bede and gif us gall. *c.* **1510** SKELTON *Bowge Court* l. 131: Wks. i 35 Vnder hony ofte tyme lyeth bytter gall. **1580** LYLY *Euph. & his Eng.* ii. 148 A dissembler hath evermore honey in his mouth, and gall in his mind. *a.* **1581** MARBECK *Bk. of Notes* 675 citing J. Poynet They promise honny with a poysoned mouth. **1582** T. WATSON *Passionate Century* xii O bitter sweete, or hunny mixt with gall. **1597** *Politeuphuia* 30ᵛ Hee is a mortall enemy that carryeth gall in his hart, and honey in his tongue. **1602** SHAKES. *T.C.* II. ii. 144 You have the honey still, but these the gall. **1614** CAMDEN 302. **1706** STEVENS s.v. Miel Under the Honey there is Gaul.

Honey, see also Bee sucks h. out of the bitterest flowers; Bee sucks h. (Where) spider sucks poison; Bees are old (When) yield no h.; Bees are (Where), there is h.; Bees that have h. in mouths; Bestows his gifts as broom h.; Fly follows h.; Lick h. through cleft stick; Lick h. with little finger; Milk and h.; Saying H. (Not with) sweetness comes; Shares h. with bear (He who); Steals h. should beware of sting; Sweet as h.; Wine (Of) the middle, of h. the bottom.

Honey-bird, see 'Sweet-heart' and 'H.' keeps no house.

Honey-moon, It is but (will not always be). (H 563-4)

1546 HEYWOOD I. vii. B4 It was yet but hony moone. **1580** LYLY *Euph. & his Eng.* ii. 49 It being now but Honnie Moone, I endeauoured to courte it with a grace. **1584** WITHALS A2ᵛ The pleasant moneth of May, doth not last alway. **1605** CHAPMAN, JONSON, & MARSTON *Eastw. Ho* IV. ii. 154 It's but Honey-moone yet with her Ladiship. **1639** CLARKE 123. **1706** STEVENS s.v. Bodas.

Honey-moon, *see also* Couple are newly married (When) first month is h.

Honey-pot(s), *see* Bear to a h. (Like a); Hogs to the h. p.

Honi soit qui mal y pense, see Ill be to him, etc.

Honour a physician before thou hast need of him. (P 264)

1678 RAY *Adag. Hebr.* 411 . . . That is, we must honour God in our health and prosperity that he may be propitious to us in our adversity.

Honour among thieves, There is.

c. **1630** *The Soddered Citizen* l. 305 Theeues haue betweene themselues, a truth, And faith, which they keepe firme, by which they doe subsist. **1703** MOTTEUX *Quixote* II. lx The old proverb still holds good, Thieves are never rogues among themselves. **1823** JON BEE 98 'There is honour among thieves but none among gamblers' is very well authentically spoken, but not true in fact. **1828** LYTTON *Pelham* ch. 69 I have often heard . . . that there is *honour* among thieves. **1891** A. LANG *Ess. in Little* 140 [Capt. Morgan[1]] was indeed a thief, and bilked his crews . . . Who would linger long when there is not even honour among thieves? [[1] the buccaneer, *c.* 1635-88.]

Honour and ease are seldom bedfellows. (H 568)

[*a.* **1465**] **1543** J. HARDYNG *Eng. Chronicle in Metre* Honour and ease together may not been. **1639** CLARKE 137.

Honour and profit lie not in one sack. (H 569)

1599 MINSHEU *Span. Gram.* 84 Honour and profit are not contained together in one sacke. **1640** HERBERT no. 232. **1659** HOWELL *Span. Prov.* 17 (bag). **1706** STEVENS s.v. Honra (as 1659).

Honour buys no beef in the market.

1668 SHADWELL *Sullen Lov.* v. iii I am not ambitious of that. As the excellent proverb says, 'Honour will buy no beef'.

Honour ceases, Where | there knowledge decreases. *Cf.* Honours nourish arts. (H 580)

1616 WITHALS 558. **1639** CLARKE 137. **1670** RAY 104.

Honour (Gentility) is but ancient riches. (G 60)

c. **1386** CHAUCER *W. of Bath's T.* l. 1117 Crist wole, we clayme of hym oure gentillesse, Nat of oure eldres for hire old richesse. *a.* **1598** LD. BURGHLEY *Ten Precepts* (1637, 7) For gentility is nothing else but antient riches. **1618** N. BRETON *Courtier & Countryman* Roxb. rep. 190 Another of an excellent worlds wit, . . . would say, that honour was but ancient riches. **1625** F. MARKHAM *Bk. of Honour* 22-3. **1651** HERBERT no. 1033.

Honour is the reward of virtue. (H 571)

1501-2 Pageant for Princess Katherine on marriage with Arthur (*Antiq. Rep.* ii, 1808, 280) Honour ye wott well the rewarde of vertue is. **1510** SIR T. MORE *Life of Picus. a.* **1568** U. FULWELL *Like Will to Like* C4ᵛ *Virtutis premium honor* Tully dooth say: Honour is the guerdon for vertue due. **1576** PETTIE i. 36. *c.* **1596** R. ASHLEY *Of Honour* ed. Heltzel 62 Oftentymes ys Honor called by Philosophers the reward of vertue.

Honour, (Authority, Place) shows the man. (A 402)

[BIAS (*Ar. Eth.* 5. 3.) ἀρχὴ ἄνδρα δείκνυσι] *a.* **1500** *Prov. Wisdom* l. 167 When man hath, what his wyll is, Then shewyth he, what he is. **1530** PALSGRAVE 674b A man is never knowen tyll he be put in auctorite. **1539** TAVERNER D4ᵛ *Magistratus virum indicat* Authoritie declareth a man. **1540** *Id. Flores* A2 *Magistratus virum arguit.* Authoritie or office vttereth what the man is. **1544** H. STALBRIDGE *Epistle Exhortatory* Appdx. D6 Auctoryte (they saye) maketh fooles bolde. **1597** BACON *Essays* no. 11 A place sheweth the man. **1612-15** BP. HALL *Contempl.* xiii. v (1825) i. 389 Honour shows the man; and if there be any blemishes of imperfection, they will be seen in the man that is unexpectedly lifted above his fellows. **1642** D. ROGERS *Matrim. Honour* 45 The old speech is, Magistracy makes not the man, but discovers what mettell is in him. **1659** TORRIANO no. 207 A place or office discovers what a man is.

Honour, Where there is no | there is no grief. (H 581)

1616 DRAXE no. 989. He that hath no honour, hath no sorrow. **1640** HERBERT no. 186.

Honour under coverlet, We cannot come to. (H 579)

1640 HERBERT no. 533.

Honour without maintenance is like a blue[1] coat without a badge. (H 574)

1660 TATHAM *The Rump* III. i (1879) 239 I have heard some say, that honour without maintenance is like a blew coat without a badge. [[1] blue was the common colour for a servant's livery.]

Honour without profit is a ring on the finger. (H 575)

1611 COTGRAVE s.v. Seigneurie Honour without profit is like a six-pennie rent to one that hath nothing else to liue on. **1631** *Celestina* tr. Mabbe (1894 ed., 140). **1640** HERBERT no. 230. **1706** STEVENS s.v. Honra.

Honourable, *see* Marriage is h.

Honours change manners.   (H 583)

[L. Honores mutant mores.] **1528** ROY & BARLOW *Rede me and be not Wroth* ed. Arb. 47 I perceaue wel nowe that honores, As it is spoken, mutant mores. **1548** HALL *Chron.* (1809) 387 But when he [Rich. III] was once crouned king . . . he cast a way his old con-dicions as ye adder doeth her skynne, verefieng ye old prouerbe, honoures chaunge maners. *a.* **1628** CARMICHAELL no. 1054 (Lordships). **1629** T. ADAMS *Serm.* (1861–2) ii. 418 Honours change manners; and we will not know those in the court who often fed us in the country. **1641** FERGUSSON no. 580 (as *a.* 1628). **1670** RAY 104 . . . As poverty depresseth and debaseth a man's mind. So great place and estate advance and enlarge it; but many times corrupt and puff it up. **1721** KELLY 237 . . . When People grow rich, and powerful, they grow proud. **1757** JOHNSON 21 June in *Boswell* (1848) xii. 108 You might write to me now and then, . . . But honores mutant mores. Professors forget their friends.

Honours nourish arts. *Cf.* Honour ceases.   (H 584)

[CICERO *Tusc.* I. 2. 4. *Honos alit artes.*] **1539** TAVERNER 26 *Honos alit artes.* Honoure mayteineth kunnynge. *c.* **1570** F. THYNNE *Pride and Lowliness* Sh. S. 22 Sayeth not the proverbe, honors norishe artes? **1592** R. GREENE *Quip* ed. Hindley 18.

Honour(s), *see also* Better die with h. than live with shame; Cost (The more), more h.; Credit (h.), No man lost; Desires h. (He that) is not worthy; Gives h. to his enemy (He that); Great h. great burdens; Ill deed cannot bring h.; Jest not with . . . h.; Modesty sets off one newly come to h.; No profit to h.; Post of h. is post of danger; Praise (H.) is reflexion of virtue; Prophet not without h. save in own country. *See also* Lip-honour.

Hoo, Kent.

1587 HARRISON *Descr. of Britain* (in HOLINSHED, i. 30) There goeth an old prouerbe in rime . . . He that rideth into the hundred of How, Beside pilfering sea-men shall find durt ynow. **1735** PEGGE *Kent. Prov.* in E.D.S. [no. 12, 73 (as 1587).

Hood for this fool, A.   (H 585)

1509 BARCLAY *Ship of Fools* i. 38 To kepe you from the rayne, ye shall haue a foles hode. *a.* **1548** R. COPLAND *Jyl of Brentford's Testament* l. 325 For he that worketh, vnknowing whan to haue, Not half a fart is worthi for to craue, And besyde that, a hood full of bels. *c.* **1566** COLLMAN *Ball. and Broadsides* Roxb. Cl. 93 A hood, a hood, for such a foole.

Hood, *see also* Bare arse than a furred h., (Better a).; Hair grows through his h; Lost the large coat for the h.; Rivington Pike; Two faces in one h.

Hoof, To beat it on the.   (H 587)

15961–633 JONSON *Tale Tub* III. iii. 22 I'll leaue to beat it on the broken hoofe, And ease my pastures. **1600–1** SHAKES. *M.W.W.* I. iii. 79 Trudge, plod away i' the hoof. **1623** 'J. DAW' *Vox Graculi* D2 Some Players (if Fortune turned Phoenix, faile not of her promise) . . . are in danger to meet with a hard Winter, and be forced to trauell softly on the hoofe. **1699** B. E. s.v. Hoof: Hoof it, or Beat it on the Hoof, to walk on Foot.

Hoof, *see also* Cloven h.

Hook, On one's own.

1834 DAVIS *Lett. of J. Downing* 35 We was all on our own hook. **1845** *N. Y. Herald* Oct. (Bartlett) The time is fast approaching when we shall have our American Pope . . . and American Catholic everything, on our own hook. **1849** THACKERAY *Pendennis* ch. 69 Do we come out as Liberal Conservative, or as Government men, or on our own hook? **1861** HUGHES *Tom B. at Oxford* ch. 2 I thought today I would go on my own hook, and see if I couldn't make a better hand of it.

Hook or by crook, By.   (H 588)

[= by fair means or foul.] *c.* **1380** WYCLIF *Eng. Wks.* E.E.T.S. 250 Comynly thei schulle bie hem with pore mennes goddis with hook or with crook. *c.* **1390** GOWER *Conf. Amantis* V. 251 So what with hoke and what with croke They make her maister ofte winne. **1542** T. BECON *Invect. agst. Swearing* n.d. F4ᵛ. *c.* **1549** HEYWOOD I. xi. E3ᵛ By hoke or croke nought could I wyn there. **1649** MILTON *Eikonoklastes* Prose Wks. (1904) I. 397 Master of almost two millions yearly, what by hook or crook, was still in want.

Hook's well lost to catch a salmon, A.
                                            (H 590)

1616 DRAXE no. 2225. **1639** CLARKE 41. **1670** RAY 104.

Hook(s), *see also* Bait hides the h.; Great put the little on the h.; Hold h. and line; Off the h.

Hoop, *see* Knock on the h. another on barrel; Round as a ball (h.).

Hop against the hill, To.   (H 469)

[= to strive against an unsurmountable obstacle. HAZL.] *c.* **1450** 'Ever thank God of all' in MS. Trin. Coll. Camb. O.9.38 (a variant of Carleton Brown, C14 *Lyrics* no. 105) l. 12 Hyt is not to stryve ayens the hyll. **1573** GASCOIGNE *Hundreth Sundry Flowers* i. 55. **1576** PETTIE i. 27.

Hop the twig, To.

[= to go off, die.] **1785** GROSE *Dict. Vulg. T.* Hop the twig, to run away (*cant*). **1797** MARY ROBINSON *Walsingham* IV. 280 [He] kept his bed three days, and hopped the twig on the fourth. **1828** *Craven Dial., Hop*, to die. *Ibid.*, *Hop*, 'to hop the twig', to run away in debt. **1870** MISS BRIDGMAN *R. Lynne* II. iv. 289 If old Campbell hops the twig.

Hop whore, pipe thief.   (w 320)

1546 HEYWOOD II. vii. K1ᵛ Now go to thy derlyngis, and declare thy greefe. Where all thy pleasure is, hop hoore, pipe theefe. *a.* **1558** *Wealth and Health* l. 679.

Hop whore! Pipe thief! Hangman lead the dance.   (H 134. w 320)

1546 HEYWOOD II. vii. K1ᵛ Hop hoore, pype theefe. **1611** DAVIES no. 258. **1615** J. STEPHENS *Essays* II. 28 in *Bks. Char.* 254 He [the hangman] hath many dependant followers: for (as the proverb saith) hangman leades the dance.

Hops, *see* Ladybirds (Plenty of) plenty of h.

Hope (well) and have (well).   (H 611)

1540 PALSGRAVE *Acolastus* 114 Hope welle and haue well. *c.* **1566** *The Bugbears* IV. v. 28. **1576** W. HUNIS in *Paradise Dayntie Deuises* (1810) 57 Hope well and haue well (Title). **1600** A. FRAUNCE in *Eng. Parnassus* (1913) 107 Hope and haue, in time a man may gaine any woman. **1614** CAMDEN 307 Hope well, and haue well. **1721** KELLY 290 *Spee¹ well and hae well* . . . That is, hope and expect good Things, and it will fall out accordingly. [¹ bode.]

Hope better, I | quoth Benson, when his wife bade him, Come in, cuckold.
     (B 312)

1678 RAY 86 (hope a better). **1732** FULLER no. 2608.

Hope deceives, Too much.   (H 608)

1573 SANFORD 110. **1578** FLORIO *First F.* 33ᵛ. **1629** *Bk. Mer. Rid.* Prov. no. 126.

Hope deferred maketh the heart sick.
     (H 600)

[Prov. xiii. 12.] *c.* **1529** J. RASTELL *Calisto and Mel.* A5ᵛ For long hope to the hart mych troble wyll do. **1557** EDGEWORTH *Sermons* 2K2ᵛ The hope that is deferred, prolonged, and put of, vexeth the minde. **1616** DRAXE no. 474 Long hope is the fainting of the soule. **1836** MARRYAT *Midsh. Easy* ch. 29 How true it is that hope deferred maketh the heart sick! . . . the buoyant calculations of youth had been . . . crushed, and now, . . . he dared not hope.

Hope for the best. *Cf.* Fear the worst.
     (B 328)

1565 NORTON & SACKVILLE *Gorboduc* I. ii. C1 Good is I graunt of all to hope the best, But not to liue still dreadlesse of the worst. **1571** J. BRIDGES *Sermon at Paul's Cross* 41 I haue good cause to hope the beste, where I know not the worste. **1581** W. AVERELL *Charles & Julia* D7 To hope the best, and feare the worst, (Loe, such is Loouers gaines). [*c.* **1587**] **1592** KYD *Span. Trag.* III. i. 35 Yet hope the best. **1590** SPENSER *F.Q.* IV. vi. 37 Its best to hope the best, though of the worst affrayd. **1592** DELAMOTHE 15 We must feare the worste, and also hope the best. **1726** *Adv. Capt. R. Boyle* 16 Come, hope for the best, said I.

Hope is a good breakfast but a bad supper.   (H 601)

1625 BACON *Apoph.* in *Mor. & Hist. Wks.* (1894) 170 Saith the fisherman, 'We had hope then to make a better gain of it'. Saith Mr. Bacon, . . . 'Hope is a good breakfast, but it is a bad supper'. **1963** 9 April *Times* 1 col. (Agony) 3.

Hope is but the dream of those that wake.

[ARISTOTLE in DIOG. LAERT. 5. 18 ἐρωτηθεὶς τί ἐστιν ἐλπίς; 'Εγρηγορότος, εἶπεν, ἐνύπνιον.] **1718** PRIOR *Solomon* iii. 102.

Hope is the poor man's bread.   (H 603)

1640 HERBERT no. 477. **1650** JER. TAYLOR *Holy Liv.* II. vi (1850) 98 Please thyself with hopes of the future. La speranza è il pan de' poveri.

Hope of long life beguileth many a good wife.

c. **1300** *Provs. of Hending* 39 Hope of long lyf Gyleth mony god wyfe.

Hope often deludes the foolish man.

c. **1300** *Havelock* 307 E.E.T.S. 10 Hope maketh fol man ofte blenkes.

Hope, If it were not for | the heart would break.   (H 605)

c. **1200** *Ancrene Riwle* 80 Ase me seið, ʒif hope nere, heorte to breke. *c.* **1350** *Douce MS.* 52 no. 127 Hope ne were, hert brostun were. *c.* **1440** *Gesta Rom.* E.E.T.S. 228 Yf hope were not, hert shulde breke. *c.* **1470** *Harl. MS. 3362* f. 4a ʒyf hope nere hert wolde toberste. **1614** CAMDEN 314 (Without hope). **1636** S. WARD *Serm.* (1862) 60 Were it not for hope in small pressures, we say heart would burst. **1660** TATHAM *The Rump* II. i (1879) 222. **1894** LD. AVEBURY *Use of Life* ch. 15 There is an !old proverb that if it were not for Hope the heart would break. Everything may be retrieved except despair.

Hope keeps man alive.   (H 604)

1584 WITHALS H7ᵛ Hope maynteineth mans life. **1672** WALKER 44 no. 97 . . . Spes alit. **1732** FULLER no. 2544 Hope keeps a Man from hanging, and drowning himself.

Hopers go to hell.

1721 KELLY 164 . . . Spoken when they, whom we are reproving for their Carelessness, and Negligence, say they hope to do well enough.

Hopes not for good, He that | fears not evil.   (G 317)

[1604] **1607** DEKKER & WEBSTER *Sir T. Wyatt* IV. iv. 41 I hope for nothing, therefore nothing feare. **1640** HERBERT no. 563. **1732** FULLER no. 2166 He that hopes no Good fears no Ill. **1854** SURTEES *Handley Cross* ch. 72 Where no hope is left, is left no fear.

385

Hope(s) (*noun*), *see also* Life (While there is) there is h.; Lives by h. will die by hunger; Lives in h. (He that) dances.

Hope(s) (*verb*), *see also* Do the likeliest, h. the best.

Hopper, *see* St. Mattho take h. and sow; St. Valentine, set thy h. by mine.

Hops make or break.

1869 HAZLITT 208. 1902–4 LEAN I. 419 . . . The yield is most uncertain and the cultivation most expensive; the value of the land may be won in a single year or its whole expenditure lost.

Hops, *see also* Fast as h.; Ladybirds (Plenty of), plenty of h.; St. James's Day be come . . . you may have h.

Horn mad (wood). (H 628)

[1525–40] 1557 *Merry Dial.* 73 He loked soureli ypon his doughter, as though he had bene horne woode with her. 1546 HEYWOOD II. x. L3ᵛ She was (as they sai) horne wood. 1592–3 SHAKES. *C.E.* II. i. 57 Why, mistress, sure my master is horn-mad. . . . I mean not cuckold-mad; but, sure, he is stark mad. 1598–9 *Id. M.A.* I. i. 233 If this should ever happen, thou wouldst be horn-mad. 1600–1 *Id. M.W.W.* I. iv. 44 If he had found the young man, he would have been horn-mad. *Ibid.* III. v. 134 If I have horns to make one mad, let the proverb go with me; I'll be horn-mad. 1639 CLARKE 178.

Horn of a pig's (ape's) tail, You cannot make a. (H 619)

[1591] 1593 PEELE *Edw. I* Bullen i. 145 Never made man of a woman born A bullock's tail a blowing horn. 1616 WITHALS 568 It is hard makeing a horne of an apes taile. 1636 CAMDEN 302 Make a pipe of a pigges taile. 1639 CLARKE 168 (apes tale). 1670 RAY 104.

Horn spoon holds no poison, A.

1721 KELLY 43 . . . They who cannot procure better Spoons are not worth poisoning.

Horne (Old *or* Parson), *see* Chance it, as P.H. did his neck.

Horner, Popham, Wyndham, and Thynne, when the abbot went out, then they went in. (H 614)

1669–96 AUBREY *Lives* (Clark) i. 279 Hopton, Horner, Smyth, and Thynne, when abbots went out, they came in. 1902–4 LEAN I. 187 Horner, Popham, Wyndham, and Thynne, when the Abbot went out, then they went in.—Higson [*MSS. Coll.*] 173.—The four families to whom Glastonbury Abbey estate was granted at the Dissolution. 1927 *Times* 1 Apr. 16/3 John Horner, traditionally said to have been steward to the Abbot of Glastonbury. . . . An old local rhyme records that—'Wyndham, Horner, Popham, and Thynne, When the Abbot went out, they came in'.

Hornet, *see* Wasp's (h.'s) nest, (To stir a).

Horns and grey hairs do not come by years. (H 626)

1599 MINSHEU *Span. Dial.* 3 As they say in my Country, Hoare haires, and hornes come not by age. 1678 RAY 156. 1719 DE ALVARADO 5.

Horns go with the hide, Let the.

1862 HISLOP 209 Let the horns gang wi' the hide. The horns bearing but insignificant value in comparison with the hide, they should be thrown into the purchase of the latter free of charge.

Horns in his bosom, He that has | let him not put them on his head. (H 624)

1624 BURTON *Anat. Mel.* III. iii. IV. i. (1638) 620 *Sapientes portant cornua in pectore, stulti in frone,* saith *Nevisanus,* wise men beare their hornes in their hearts, fooles on their foreheads. 1640 HERBERT no. 567. 1670 RAY 104 . . . Let a man hide his shame, not publish it. 1732 FULLER no. 5704 (forehead).

Horns in his pocket than wind them, He had better put his. (H 623)

1678 RAY 74. 1732 FULLER no. 1852 (blow them).

Horns of a dilemma, To be on the.

[Each of the alternatives of a dilemma—in scholastic Lat. *argumentum cornutum*—on which one is figured as liable to be caught or impaled.] 1647 COWLEY *Mistr., Agst. Hope* i And both the Horns of Fates Dilemma wound. 1836 MARRYAT *Midsh. Easy* ch. 13 Between the master and me I am on the horns of a dilemma. 1887 FOWLER *Deduct. Logic* v. 121 In disputation, the adversary who is refuted by a dilemma is said to be 'fixed on the horns of a dilemma'.

Horn(s), *see also* April blows his h.; Blows best (He that) bears away h.; Butter is once a year in cow's h.; Camel going to seek h. lost ears; Corn and h. go together; Crooked as a cow's h.; Cuckold wear his own h. (Let every); Curst cow short h.; Devil is known by his h.; Draw in one's h.; Friday's hair and Saturday's h.; Gabriel blows his h. (When); Gate of h.; God gives cow; Hay in one's h. (Carry); Hunters (All not) that blow h.; Lips (h.) hang in your light; Make a spoon or spoil h.; New tout in old h.; Nicks in her h. (She has many); Old oxen have stiff h.; Ox is taken by the h.; Play with a bull till get h. in eye; Right as a ram's h.; Wear a h. and blow it not. *See also* Buck's horn, Cow's horn.

Horologe, *see* Play the devil in the h.

Horse, a wife, and a sword may be shewed, but not lent, A. (W 381)

1568 TILNEY *Duties in Marriage* C6 The olde saying, that a man may shewe his wife, and his sworde to his friende, but not to farre to trust them. 1574 E. HELLOWES *Guevara's Epistles* 509

It is an old prouerb that the wife and the sword may bee shewed, but not lent. **1576** HOLYBAND E7ᵛ One lendeth not willingly these three things. I. His wife. 2. His horse. 3. His armes. **1591** W. STEPNEY *Span. Schoolmaster* M6ᵛ Four things cannot be lent, a good horse, a wise woman . . . a faithful seruant . . . a good sword. **1623** CAMDEN 279 (The wife and the sword).

Horse and man (foot).   (H 655)

[= completely.] **1562** G. LEGH *Accidence of Armoury* 230 As Syr Iohn Froysart sayeth, lett Englishe archers shoote wholye together, that those Swart Rutters, maye be ouer throwen horse and man. [**1594–1600**] **1615** T. HEYWOOD *Four Prentices* ii. 200 We straight should ouerthrow you Horse and Foote. c. **1595** W. PERKINS *Govt. of Tongue* (Wks. 1608, i. 451a) Horse and man and all to the deuill. [**1596**] **1605** *Stukeley* l. 311 She's mine, horse and foot. **1599** CHAPMAN *Hum. Day's Mirth* vi. 51 Then is he ouerthrown both horse and foot. **1603** DEKKER *Wonderful Year* (*Plague Pamphlets* ed. Wilson 35) It . . . ouer-turnd them . . . horse and foote. **1607** MIDDLETON *The Phœnix* Wks. (Bullen) I. 180 I hope I shall overthrow him horse and foot. **1639** CLARKE 86. **1666** TORRIANO 134, no. 43.

Horse cast a shoe, Your.   (H 709)
1678 RAY 349.

Horse corn, *see* Hens are free of h. c.

Horse drink when he will, not what he will, Let a.   (H 676)
1678 RAY 157.

Horse in a mill, Like a.   (H 697)
1607 DEKKER & WEBSTER *Northward Ho* B3ᵛ I that like a horse Ran blind-fold in a Mill (all in one circle). **1611** DEKKER & MIDDLETON *Roaring G.* I. i. i My thoughts must run As a horse runs that's blind round in a mill. **1645** J. MARSH *Marsh his Mickle Monument* M1ᵛ They travelled all night, (like horses in a Mill blindfold). **1679** SHADWELL *True Widow* I had rather suffer, by venturing to bring new things upon the stage, than go on like a mill-horse in the same round. [Note by Shadwell, in first ed., at the back of the 'Dramatis Personæ'.]

Horse is troubled with corns, That.   (H 694)
1663 S. BUTLER *Hud.* I. i. 433 That Caesar's horse . . . who as fame goes, had corns upon his feet and Toes. **1678** RAY 74 . . . *i.e.* foundered.

Horse (cat, dog, etc.) laugh, It would have made a. *Cf.* Ale will make a cat speak.   (H 673)
1546 HEYWOOD II. i. F3ᵛ To see his sweete lookes, and here hir sweete wurdes. And to thinke wherfore they bothe put both in vre, It wolde haue made a hors breake his halter sure. **1563** J. PILKINGTON *Confutation* P.S. 587 To read those miracles would make a horse to laugh. **1593** *Tell-Troth's New Year's Gift* New Sh. S. 4 An

Oration that would haue made a mastie to haue broke his collor with girning thereat. [**1598**] **1616** HAUGHTON *Englishmen for my Money* l. 1256 It would make any Mouse, Ratte, Catte, or Dogge, laugh to thinke, what sport we shall haue. **1626** JONSON *Staple of News* First Intermean One *Smug*, a Smith, would haue made a horse laugh, and broke his halter, as they say. **1670** RAY 165 'Twould make a horse break his bridle, or a dog his halter. **1879** J. R. PLANCHÉ 'The Queen of the Frogs' I. iv. It would have made a cat laugh.

Horse lies down, Where the | there some hair will be found.   (H 704)
a. **1530** R. *Hill's Commonpl. Bk.* E.E.T.S. 129 Whan the hors waloweth, som heris be loste. c. **1549** ERASM. *Two Dial.* tr. E. Becke f. 22ᵛ The prouerbe . . . where the horse walloweth there lyeth some heares. **1639** CLARKE 216 Where the horse rubbs some haire is left behind. **1662** FULLER *Cornw.* 193 Foraigners . . . sometimes are driven hither against their will, but never without the profit of the Inhabitants, according to the Common Proverbe, . . .

Horse loaves, *see* High as two h. l.

Horse made and a man to make, A. *Cf.* the following proverb.   (H 635)
1611 COTGRAVE s.v. Valet Chuse a horse made, a seruant to be made. **1640** HERBERT no. 22.

Horse made, and a wife to make, Choose a.   (H 636)
1640 HERBERT no. 871.

Horse, Who has no | may ride on a staff.
1444 LYDGATE in *Pol. Poems* (1859) II. 219 Whoo hath noon hors on a staff may ride. **1492** *Dial. of Salomon and Marcolphus* ed. Duff 11 He that hath no horse muste go on fote.

Horse may stumble that has four legs, A.   (H 663)
1640 HERBERT no. 740. *a.* **1641** FERGUSSON MS. no. 101 (snapper[1]). **1678** RAY (Scottish) 360 A horse may stumble on four feet. **1721** KELLY 26 (as *a.* 1641) . . . An Excuse for those who inadvertently misplace their Words. [¹ stumble].

Horse must die in some man's hand, The old.   (H 680)
a. **1628** CARMICHAELL no. 847 In some mannis aucht[1] mon the auld horse die. **1641** FERGUSSON no. 477. **1721** KELLY 312. [¹ ownership.]

Horse, The best | needs breaking, and the aptest child needs teaching.   (H 632)
1639 CLARKE 100.

Horse next the mill carries all the grist, The.   (H 664)
1623 CAMDEN 279. **1670** RAY 121. **1732** FULLER no. 4601.

Horse of another (the same) colour, A.
(H 665)

[*a.* 1563] 1661 *Tom Tyler* l. 414 But I bridled a Colt of a contrarie hare. 1599 SHAKES. *A.Y.* III. ii. 379 Boys and women are, for the most part cattel of this colour. 1601 *Id. T.N.* II. iii. 157 My purpose is indeed a horse of that colour. *c.* 1610–40 *The Telltale* l. 1145 I haue neuer a horse of that Cullor. 1867 TROLLOPE *Last Chron. Bars.* ch. 24 What did you think of his wife? That's a horse of another colour altogether.

Horse of your own, Have a | and you may borrow another.
(H 650)

1659 HOWELL *Brit. Prov.* 34 Have a horse of thy own, thou maist borrow another.

Horse, One | stays for another. (H 698)

1666 TORRIANO *Prov. Phr.* 1 s.v. Abbate To fall too, and not to stay at all, the English say, to stay, as one horse stays for another. 1738 SWIFT *Dial.* II. E.L. 298. You see, sir John, we stayed for you as one horse does of another.

Horse that draws after him his halter, The | is not altogether escaped. (H 666)

1592 DELAMOTHE 15. 1639 CLARKE 250. 1651 HERBERT no. 1120. 1732 FULLER no. 4602. 1853 TRENCH vi. 147 . . . so long as any remnant of a sinful habit is retained by us, so long as we draw this halter, we make but an idle boast of our liberty.

Horse that was foaled of an acorn (a wooden horse), (To ride on a). (H 708)

c. 1547 *Pore Helpe* l. 255 in *Early Pop. Poetry,* iii. 261 Your happe may be to wagge upon a wooden nagge. 1678 RAY 253 (You'll ride on). That is the gallows. 1708 MOTTEUX *Rabelais* v. xxviii. (1737) 128 May I ride on a horse that was foal'd of an acorn. 1828 LYTTON *Pelham* III. xviii. 296 As pretty a Tyburn blossom as ever was brought up to ride a horse foaled by an acorn.

Horse that will not carry a saddle must have no oats, A.

1642 TORRIANO 9 . . . By carrying a saddle is meant labour, and so applied to idle drones in the world, such as are not worthy of their meat and drink, at least not of any choise meat. 1659 *Id.* no. 19 To a horse that carries not a saddle, oats are not to be sifted. 1732 FULLER no. 218.

Horse will not void oats, A.

1721 KELLY 84 It is hard to make a Horse shite Oats that never eat any [given as an English proverb]. 1745 FRANKLIN *Wks.* (Bigelow) II. 35–6 If, as the proverb says, it is unreasonable to expect a horse should void oats, which never eat any.

Horse's head is swollen so big that he cannot come out of the stable, His.
(H 710)

[= He can't pay the ostler.] *c.* 1515 BARCLAY *Eclog.* I. 10 His horse is so fat, that playne he

is not able To get his body nor head out of the stable. 1659 HOWELL *Eng. Prov.* 6a.

Horses, As good | draw in carts, as coaches.

1621 BURTON *Anat. Mel.* II. iii. VII. (1651) 350.

Horse(s), *see also* Ass goes a-travelling, he'll not come home h.; Ass thinks himself worthy to stand with the king's h.; Beat a h. till he be sad; Beat the ass (h.) (He that cannot) beats the saddle; Best thing for inside of man is outside of h.; Blind h. (Ever the worse looks); Blind h. is hardiest; Boisterous h. must have rough bridle; Boot and the better h. (He has gotten); Break a h.'s back (You may); Brewer's h. has bit (One whom); Bridle and spur makes good h.; Butcher's h., he carries calf; Cart before h.; Chestnut h.; Common h. is worst shod; Cough will stick by a h.; Eaten a h. and tail hangs out; Every one (h). thinks his sack heaviest; Flea-bitten h. never tires; Flies haunt lean h.; Flog a dead h.; Foal amble if h. trot (How can); Free of h. that never had one; Galled h. not endure comb; Gentle h. that never cast rider; Gift h. in the mouth (Look not); Give a Yorkshireman halter, he'll find h.; Good h. cannot be bad colour; Good h. good spur; Good h. make short miles; Good h. should be seldom spurred; Good h. that never stumbles; Grass grows (While) the h. starves; Greedy eating h. (To) short halter; Groaning h. . . . never fail master; High h.; Hired h. tired never; Hires the h. (He that) must ride before; Hounds and h. devour masters; Hungry (So) he could eat h.; Hungry h. makes clean manger; Ill h. that can neither whinny nor wag tail; Jade eats as much as good h.; King's h.; Kindly aver never good h.; Know the h. by his harness (You may); Latin, a h., and money (With) you will pass; Lead a h. to water; Lend thy h. for long journey, return with skin; Lets his h. drink at every lake (He that); Life in it, (the old h.) yet, (There is); Like to like, scabbed h. to old dike; Live h. and you'll get grass; Loader's h. that lives among thieves (Like a); Luck in h. . . . kiss parson's wife; Man is not a h. because born in stable; Melancholy as a collier's h.; Mettle is dangerous in a blind h.; Mule (h.) scrubs another (One); Nod is as good . . . to blind h.; Old wood is best . . . old h. to ride; One thing thinks the h.; Ox before, of a h. behind (Take hold of); Proud h. that will not bear provender; Ragged colt . . . good h.; Ride a h. and mare on shoulders; Royston h.; Rub a galled h., he will wince; Run before h. to market; Running h. open grave; Saddle on right h.; Scabbed h. cannot abide comb; Scald h. for scabbed squire; Scholar as my h. Ball (As good); Set their h. together (They cannot); Short h. soon curried (*also under* Bonny bride); Shortly as a h. will lick; Shoulder of mutton for a sick h.; Spur a free h. (Do not); Spur a hamshackled h. (Idle to); Spur and whip for dull h.; Steal a h. (One man may); Steal the h. and carry home bridle; Strong as a h.; Swap h. when crossing; Taken my h. and left me the tether; Tale of roasted h.;

Trust not h.'s heel; Turk's h. treads (Where); Walking with a h. in hand (Good); Water his h. at Highgate (Make him); White h.; White h. and a fair wife (He that has); Wild h. will not drag the secret from me; Willing h. (All lay load on); Win the h. or lose the saddle; Wishes were h. (If); Work for a dead h.; Work like a h.; Wrong h.; Young trooper, old h.

Horse, *see also* Fore-horse, Jade, Mare, Nag, White h.

Horse(d) (*verb*), *see* Manned with boys and h. with colts.

Horseback, When one is on | he knows all things. (H 718)
1640 HERBERT no. 982.

Horseback, *see also* Agues (Diseases) come on h.; Beggar on h.; Knave on h.; St. George, always on h. and never rides (Like).

Horseflesh, *see* Scarce of h. where two ride on dog; Skill in h. to buy a goose.

Horse-leech, *see* Daughter of h.

Horse-load, *see* Fall away from a h.

Horseman, *see* Behind the h. sits care.

Horse-manger, *see* Famine in England begins at h. m.

Horseshoe, *see also* Fool finds a h. (When) he thinks like to do; Tomorrow morning I found a h.; Wear like a h. (She will).

Horse-turd, *see* Apples swim (See how we).

Hose, In my other (tother). (H 723)
[Ironical: 'not if I know it'.] *c.* **1591–4** *Thomas of Woodstock* I. iii. 100. In your tother hose, uncle? **1594** LYLY *Mother B.* II. iii. 49 I have loued thee long, Silena.—In your tother hose. **1598** FLORIO s.v. Zoccoli Zoccoli Tush tush, awaie, in faith sir no, yea in my other hose. **1602** [MIDDLETON?] *Blurt* II. ii. 270 I'll play, sir. [*aside*] But in my t'other hose. **1640** JONSON *Tale Tub* II. iii. 40 Wee rob'd in Saint Iohn's wood? I' my tother hose!

Hose (*proper name*), *see* Whores in H. than . . . in Long Clawson (More).

Hose, *see also* Conscience as large as a shipman's h.; Heart is in h.; Man is a man though h. on his head; Welshman's h.

Hosed and shod, He came in. (C 539)
1678 RAY 74 . . . He was born to a good estate. He came into the world as a Bee into the hive: or into an house, or into a trade, or employment.

Hospital, *see* Suit at law and urinal bring to h.

Hospitality, It is a sin against | to open your doors and shut up your countenance. (S 469)
1605 BACON *Adv. Learn.* II. xxiii. 3 (1900) 218 Saith Cicero, . . . ; *Nil interest habere ostium apertum, vultum clausum*; it is nothing won to admit men with an open door, and to receive them with a shut and reserved countenance. **1732** FULLER no. 2883. **1746** FRANKLIN Dec. Half Hospitality opens his Door and shuts up his Countenance.

Host's invitation is expensive, An.
1642 TORRIANO 66 An hosts invitation is not without expence. **1732** FULLER no. 612.

Host, *see also* Ask mine h. whether he have good wine; Reckons without his h.

Hostages, *see* Wife and children . . . h. to fortune.

Hostess, *see* Fairer the h. fouler the reckoning.

Hot as coals, As. (C 462)
1533 UDALL *Flowers for Latin Speaking* (1560) E4. **1540** PALSGRAVE *Acolastus* 104 He loueth ye as hot as coles. **1542** ERASM. tr. Udall *Apoph.* (1877) 38. **1563** FOXE *Actes* (1846) V. 19 The bishop and all his doctors were as hot as coals.

Hot love, hasty vengeance. (L 482)
a. **1628** CARMICHAELL no. 639. **1721** KELLY 163 . . . The love that's too violent will not last long.

Hot love is soon cold. (L 483)
1530 WHITFORDE *Wk. Householders* E3ᵛ (As the comune prouerbe saythe) hote loue is soone colde. **1546** HEYWOOD I. ii. A3 Than perceyue they well, hotte loue sone colde. *a.* **1547** J. REDFORD *Wit and Science* l. 709 Hastye love is soone hot and soone cold. **1579** LYLY *Euph.* i. 197 Hot loue waxed soone colde. **1670** RAY 46. **1732** FULLER no. 2549.

Hot May makes a fat churchyard, A. (M 766)
1609 HARWARD 103ᵛ. **1659** HOWELL *Eng. Prov.* 11b. **1670** RAY 42.

Hot sup, hot swallow. (S 997)
c. **1400** *MS. Latin no. 394*, J. Rylands Libr. (ed. Pantin) in *Bull. J. R. Libr.* XIV 26 Drynke hoot and swolow hoot. **1559** COOPER s.v. Intero Selfe doe, selfe haue, hote suppe, hote swallow. **1639** CLARKE 239.

Hot, *see also* Bear it away if not too h. or too heavy; Blow h. and cold.; Cost h. water; Kentshire, h. as fire; Over h., over cold; Pepper is h. in mouth but cold in snow; Seek h. water under ice; Soon h., soon cold; Toast (As h. as); Too h. to hold.

Hounds and horses devour their masters. (H 715)

1616 DRAXE no. 1726. Horses, dogges, and seruants deuoure many. **1639** CLARKE 325.

Hound(s), *see also* Bear's (h.'s) tooth, (As white as a); Dog (H.) gnaws bone (While), companion would be none; Hende as a h. in a kitchen; Masterless h. (Like a); Pound of butter among kennel of h.; Run with hare and hunt with h.; We h. slew the hare.

Hour in a day between a good housewife and a bad, There is but an.
(H 743)

1678 RAY 74 . . . With a little more pains, she that slatters might do things neatly.

Hour in the morning is worth two in the evening, An.

1827 HONE *Ev. Day Book* ii. 477 [Cited as 'an old and a true saying'].

Hour to-day, One | is worth two to-morrow.

1732 FULLER no. 3761.

Hour wherein a man might be happy all his life could he find it, There is an.
(H 742)

1651 HERBERT no. 1143.

Hour's cold, One | will spoil seven years' warning.

1721 KELLY 276.

Hour's sleep before midnight, One | is worth three (two) after. (H 744)

1640 HERBERT no. 882. **1670** RAY 37 (two). **1829** COBBETT *Adv. to Y. Men* i (1906) 35 It is said by the country-people that one hour's sleep before midnight is worth more than two are worth after midnight; and this I believe to be a fact.

Hour, *see also* Born in good (ill) h.; Broke his h. that kept day (He never); Chances in an h.; Darkest h. is that before dawn; Evil h.; Half an h. soon lost at dinner; Half an h.'s hanging hinders . . . riding; Man has his h.; Man may lose more in an h. than he can get in seven; Put off the evil h.; Strong town not won in an h.

House, a wife, and a fire to put her in, A.

1721 KELLY 264 Never look for a wife, till you have a house, and a fire to put her in. The Jest is in *a Fire to put her in*, a House to put her in, and a Fire to set her by. **1738** SWIFT *Dial.* I. E.L. 291 But, colonel, when do you design to get a house, and a wife, and a fire to put her in?

House and home, *see* Eat out of h. and h.

House and land are gone and spent, When | then learning is most excellent.

1753 S. FOOTE *Taste* (ed. 2) I. i. 12 It has always been my Maxum . . . to give my Children Learning enough; for, as the old saying is, . . . **1896** S. BARING-GOULD *Broom-Squire* ch. 26 I have . . . got Simon to write for me, on the fly-leaf. . . . When land is gone, and money is spent, Then learning is most excellent.

House built by the wayside is either too high or too low, A. (H 766)

1642 TORRIANO 29 (in the open street). Meaning every one will be passing their censure upon it as they go along. **1658** *Comes Fac.* 181. **1659** TORRIANO no. 118 (in the open street). **1670** RAY 106. **1732** FULLER no. 220.

House goes mad when women gad.

1822 SCOTT *Nigel* ch. 4 Let your husband come to me, good dame, . . . The proverb says, 'House goes mad when women gad'.

House is a fine house when good folks are within, The. (H 769)

1640 HERBERT no. 952.

House is burned down, When the | you bring water.

1575 GASCOIGNE *Glass of Government* ii. 71 All too late the water comes, when house is burned quite. **1706** STEVENS s.v. Casa. **1732** FULLER no. 5592.

House is his castle, A man's (Englishman's). (M 473)

1581 H. ÉTIENNE *Stage of Popish Toys* tr. G.N. 88 [The English papists owe it to the Queen that] youre house is youre Castell. **1581** MULCASTER *Positions* 40, 225 He is the appointer of his owne circumstance, and his house is his castle. *cf.* **1640** HERBERT no. 413 My house, my house, though thou art small, thou art to me the Escuriall. **1642** FULLER *Fast Serm., Innoc. Day* Sermons (1891) I. 260 It was wont to be said *A man's house is his castle*; but if this castle of late hath proved unable to secure any, let them make their conscience their castle. **1670** RAY 106 . . . This is a kind of law Proverb, *Jura publica favent privato domus.* **1779** JOHNSON in *Boswell* (1848) lxviii. 626 In London, . . . a man's own house is truly his *castle,* in which he can be in perfect safety from intrusion. **1836–7** DICKENS *Pickwick* ch. 24 Some people maintain that an Englishman's house is his castle. That's gammon. **1893** R. HEATH *Eng. Peasant* 33 The popular notion of every Englishman's house being his castle was conspicuously demonstrated to be a fallacy, by 22 and 23 Car. 2.15.

House of a fiddler, In the | all fiddle.
(H 777)

a. **1633** HERBERT *Priest to the Temple* Wks. 240 In the house of those that are skill'd in Musick, all are Musicians. **1640** *Id.* no. 223. **1732** FULLER no. 2809 In a fidlers house all are dancers.

House on fire, Like a.

[Very fast, vigorously.] **1809** W. IRVING *Knickerb.* (1824) 291 At it they went like five hundred houses on fire. **1837** DICKENS in Forster *Life* I. vi. 107 I am getting on . . . like a house o' fire, and think the next Pickwick will bang all the others.

House out of the windows, To throw (fling) the. (H 785)

[= to put everything into confusion.] **1562** BULLEIN *Bulwarke of Defence* f. xxviii Haue at all, . . . caste the house out at the window. **1604** DEKKER I *Hon. Whore* V. ii. 28 To throw the house out at window will be the better and no man will suspect that we lurke here to steale mutton. **1611** BEAUM. & FL. *Kt. Burn. P.* III. v We are at home now; where, I warrant you, you shall find the house flung out of the windows. **1766** GOLDSMITH *Vicar* ch. 21. **1844** W. H. MAXWELL *Sport & Adv. Scott.* vi (1855) 77 Would not . . . Stubbs throw the house out of the windows?

House shows the owner, The. (H 772)

1597 *Politeuphuia* 168ᵛ A maister ought not to bee knowne by the house, but the house by the maister. **1611** COTGRAVE s.v. *Maison* The house discovers the owner. **1640** HERBERT no. 8.

House stands on my lady's ground, His. (H 764)

1678 RAY 75.

House well-furnished makes a woman wise, A. (H 773)

1642 TORRIANO 16 (room). **1658** *Comes Fac.* 232. **1732** FULLER no. 223 (a good housewife).

Houses than parish churches, There are more. (H 791)

1579 GOSSON *Sch. Abuse* Arb. 37 There are more houses then Parishe Churches.

House(s), *see also* After the h. is finished leave it; Back door robs h.; Best gown that goes up and down h.; Better an empty h.; Better one h. filled; Better one h. troubled; Bread's h. skaild never; Burn his h. to warm his hands; Burn one h. to warm another; Burn one's h. to rid of mice; Burns his h., (He that) warms himself for once; Buys a h. ready wrought (He that); Choose not a h. near an inn; Commend not your . . . h.; Curiosity ill manners in another's h.; Eat out of h. and home; Enter into a h. (When); Fools build h.; God keep me from four h.; God oft has share in h.; Good h. (In a) all quickly ready; Head is down (When my) h. is thatched; Head (H.) of glass; Hole in the h. (There is a); Justice pleases few in own h.; Lawyers' h. built on fools; Let your h. to your enemy (First year); Little h. has wide mouth; Little h. well filled; Love his h. yet ride on ridge; Marries a widow and two children . . . has three backdoors to h.; Master absent and h. dead; Neighbour's h. on fire; Old man in h. good sign; Play at chess when h. on

fire; Pulls an old h. on head; Put nothing into h., take nothing out; Rats desert falling h.; Safe as h.; Savers in a h. do well (Some); See the city for the h. (Cannot); See your h. in flames (When) warm yourself; Set one's h. on fire to roast eggs; Small h. has wide throat; Thatched his h.; Thatches his h. with turds (He that); Well (He that would be) needs not go from own h.; Woe to the h. where there is no chiding. *See also* Glass house.

House-going parson makes a church-going people, A.

1913 *Brit. Wkly.* 2 Jan. 445 If anyone was missed at church, the next morning he went to the truant's house. . . . He firmly believed that a house-going parson makes a church-going people.

Household, *see* Woeful is the h. that wants a woman.

Householders, *see* Grooms and h. are all alike great (Where); Wishers and woulders no good h.

Housekeeper(s), *see* Everything is of use to h.; Fat h. make lean executors; Noble h. need no doors.

Housekeeping, *see* Marriage is honourable, but h. a shrew.

House-top in anger, To be on the. Cf. Three words. (H 797)

[1525–40] **1557** *A Merry Dialogue* 78 I wolde haue flowen to the hores [*sic*] toppe and I wolde haue crowned myne husbande . . . with a pysbowle. [*a.* 1550] **1626** *Jests Scogin* in *Shakes. Jest-Bks.* ii. 91 I defie thee, said Scogin's wife (and was up in the house top). **1599** PORTER *Angry Wom. Abingd.* l. 1261 In troth I shall growe angrie, if you doe not,—Growe to the house topwith your anger sir. **1611** DAVIES no. 290 On the house top in anger, soone is a foole.

Housewife, (wives), *see* Bare walls . . . giddy h.; Foot on cradle . . . sign of good h.; Gentle h. mars household; Hour in a day between good h. and bad; Punch coal, cut candle . . . neither good h.; Rouk-town seldom good h.; Sweet in the bed . . . was never good h.

Housewifery, *see* Patch by patch good h.

How does your Whither go you? (W 316)

1678 RAY 346 . . . (*Your wife.*)

How, *see also* No matter h.

Howbackit, *see* Grow h. bearing your friends (You will never).

Howl with the wolves, One must.

1578 TIMME *Calvin on Gen.* vi. 181 This diuelishe prouerbe . . . we must howle among the Wolues. **1649** BP. HALL *Cases Consc.* (1650) 187 What do you howling amongst Wolves, if you be not one? **1853** TRENCH v. 107 . . . when a general cry is raised against any, it is safest to join it, lest we be supposed to sympathize with its object. . . . In the whole circle of proverbs there is scarcely a baser or more cowardly than this. **1897** A. C. DOYLE *Uncle Bernac* ch. 1 Napoleon's power is far too great to be shaken. This being so, I have tried to serve him, for it is well to howl when you are among wolves.

Hue, *see* Black will take no other h.

Hug one as the devil hugs a witch, To. (D 299)

1640 GLAPTHORNE *Wit in Constable* (1874) II. 193 As the Divell hug'd the witch. **1678** RAY 286. **1738** SWIFT *Dial.* I. E.L. 292. Why she and you were as great[1] as two inkle-weavers. I've seen her hug you as the devil hugged the witch. **1823** GROSE ed. Pierce Egan s.v. Hug. [1 intimate.]

Hug, (*noun*), *see* Cornish h.

Hugger-mugger,[1] In. (H 805)

a. **1529** SKELTON *Magnyf.* 392 As men dare speke it hugger mugger. **1589** [? LYLY] *Pappe w. Hatchet* iii. 401 He woulde not smoother vp sinne, and deale in hugger mugger against his Conscience. **1600–1** SHAKES. *H.* IV. v. 80 We have done but greenly, In hugger-mugger to inter him. **1678** BUTLER *Hudibras* III. iii. 123 Where I, in hugger-mugger, hid, Have noted all they said or did. **1762** C. CHURCHILL *The Ghost* III. Wks. (1868) 289 It must not, as the vulgar say, Be done in hugger-mugger way. **1882** BLACKMORE *Christowel* ch. 46 By assenting to a hugger-mugger style of slapdash. [1 secretly.]

Hull cheese. (C 276)

1678 RAY 340 You have eaten some Hull cheese. *i.e.* Are drunk, Hull is famous for strong Ale.

Hull, *see also* Dighton is pulled down (When), H. great town; Hell, H., and Halifax; Oxford for learning . . . H. for women.

Humble hearts have humble desires. (H 328)

1611 COTGRAVE s.v. Coeur Little things content low thoughts; or, an humble heart is humble in desires. **1640** HERBERT no. 6.

Humble pie, To eat.

[= to submit to humiliation.] **1823** GROSE ed. Pierce Egan s.v. Sing Small. **1830** FORBY App. 432 'To make one eat humble pie'—*i.e.* To make him lower his tone, and be submissive. **1855** THACKERAY *Newcomes* ch. 14 'You drank too much wine last night, and disgraced yourself. . . . You must get up and eat humble pie this morning.' **1861** H. KINGSLEY *Ravenshoe* ch. 30 He had . . . to eat humble pie, to go back . . . and accept their offers.

Humble, *see also* Noble (The more), more h.

Humble-bee in a cow-turd thinks himself a king, An. (H 806)

1576 PETTIE ii. 124. **1659** HOWELL *Eng. Prov.* 1b. **1670** RAY 14.

Humble bee, *see also* H. b. in a churn, *under* Swarm of bees all in a churn.

Humility, *see* Declaim against pride; Pride that apes h.

Humours, *see* Stillest h. are the worst.

Hump, *see* Hunchback does not see own h.

Humphrey, *see* Devil is dead (When), there's a wife for H.

Hunchback does not see his own hump, but sees his companion's, The.

1659 HOWELL *Span. Prov.* 3 The crumpshouldered sees not his hunch, yet he sees that of his companions. **1758** FRANKLIN *Mar.* Happy Tom Crump ne'er sees his own Hump. **1905** ALEX. MACLAREN *Expos. Matthew* I. 327 Every body can see the hump on his friend's shoulders, but it takes some effort to see our own.

Hundred ells of contention, In an | there is not an inch of love. (E 109)

1640 HERBERT no. 817.

Hundred, He that owes an | and has an hundred and one, need not fear; he that has an hundred and one, and owes an hundred and two, the Lord have mercy upon him. (H 808)

1659 HOWELL *Span. Prov.* 17 (I recommend him to God) [Wrongly translated]. **1706** STEVENS s.v. Ciento . . . In short, he that has more than he owes is safe, but he who owes more than he has is in a desperate condition. **1732** FULLER no. 2132 [the second half only]. **1849–50** DICKENS *Dav. Cop.* ch. 12 Annual income twenty pounds, annual expenditure nineteen nineteen six, result happiness. Annual income twenty pounds, annual expenditure twenty pounds ought and six, result misery.

Hundred pounds of sorrow pays not one ounce of debt, An. (P 518)

1640 HERBERT no. 414 A hundred loade of thought will not pay one of debts. **1642** TORRIANO 18 (as 1640). *a.* **1704** T. BROWN *Wks.* (1760) III. 247 [cited as 'the country proverb'].

Hundred, *see also* All one a h. years hence; Lost in the h. found in the shire; One man is worth h.; Sluggard takes an h. steps.

Hung, *see* Tongue is ill h., (His).

Hunger and cold deliver a man up to his enemy.

1706 STEVENS s.v. Hambre.   **1813** RAY 126.

Hunger breaks (pierces) stone walls.

(H 811)

c. **1350** *Douce MS.* 52 no. 28 Hungur brekyth stone and walle. **1546** HEYWOOD I. xii. E4ᵛ Some saie, and I feele hungre perseth stone wall. **1608** SHAKES. *C.* I. i. 204 They said they were anhungry; sigh'd forth proverbs: That hunger broke stone walls. **1634** *P.R.O. State Papers Dom.* CCLXXI, July 1, no. 3, 128 Capt. Henry Bell to Abp. Laud . . . Beseeches the Archbishop to . . . consider the old proverb 'Hunger breaketh stone walls'. **1677** YARRANTON *England's Improvement* 179 Hunger will brake stone walls. **1787** GROSE (*Glos., Suff.*) 224 Hunger will break through stone walls, or any thing except a Suffolk cheese. Suffolk cheese is, from its poverty, the subject of much low wit. It is by some represented as only fit for making wheels for wheelbarrows. **1839** T. C. CROKER *Pop. Songs of Ireld.* 38 A facetious essayist . . . observes . . . 'the Irish might have attempted to satisfy hunger with trefoil,[1] . . . for hunger will break through a stone wall'. [¹ shamrock.]

Hunger drives the wolf out of the woods.

(H 812)

1567 PAINTER *Pal. of Pleasure* (Jacobs) III. 216 Now I well perceiue that Hunger forceth the Woulf oute of his Denne. **1666** TORRIANO 83 no. 35 Hunger drives the woolf out of the forest. **1748** SMOLLETT tr. *Gil Blas* XII. vii (1907) II. 385 This one . . . I own is the child of necessity. Hunger, thou knowest, brings the wolf out of the wood.

Hunger drops out of his nose. (H 813)

[*c.* **1517**] **1533** SKELTON *Magn.* G2ᵛ I gyue hym Crystys curse with neuer a peny in his purse . . . Ye, for requiem aeternam groweth forth of his nose. **1546** HEYWOOD I. xi. E1ᵛ Hunger droppeth euen out of bothe theyr noses. **1575** *A notable Discourse* Preface (Southern, 172) They be nowe a dayes called Pinche penyes, and such that hunger droppeth out of their noses. **1605** CHAPMAN, JONSON, MARSTON *Eastw. Ho* IV. i Come away, I say, hunger drops out at his nose. **1611** COTGRAVE s.v. Chiche-face A . . . wretched fellow, one out of whose nose hunger drops.

Hunger finds no fault with the cookery.

(H 814)

1577 *Art of Angling* C2 Hunger findeth no fault. **1659** N. R. 50 Hunger hath alwaies a good Cook. **1732** FULLER no. 2566.

Hunger in frost that will not work in heat, They must.

(F 722)

c. **1540** BANNATYNE MS. S.T.S. i. 134. *c.* **1549** HEYWOOD I. xi. D3ᵛ. **1691** W. SEWEL 239. **1639** CLARKE 144.

Hunger is good kitchen[1] meat. (H 815)

a. **1540** MELVILLE 22 'King James the Fyft his Pasquil' (and Bannatyne MS. i. 134). *a.* **1628** CARMICHAELL no. 649. **1641** FERGUSSON no. 298. **1721** KELLY 127 . . . The same with the English, *Hunger is good Sauce*. [¹ anything eaten with bread as a relish.]

Hunger is sharper than thorn (the sword).

(H 818)

1550 BECON *Fortr. Faithful*: P.S., 601 (Ye know the common proverbs . . . Hunger is). **1553** *Id. Jewel of Joy* P.S. 465 Hunger is a sharp thorn. **1613** FLETCHER *et al. Honest Man's Fortune* II. ii. 1 (the sword).

Hunger is the best sauce. (H 819)

[CICERO *Fames optimum condimentum.*] **1362** LANGLAND *P. Pl.* VI. 4324 (Wright) I. 133 Er hunger thee take, And sende thee of his sauce. [*c.* **1515**] *c.* **1530** BARCLAY *Ecl.* II, l. 743 Make hunger thy sause be thou neuer so nice, For there shalt thou finde none other kinde of spice. **1539** TAVERNER 1 *Garden* B1 He [Socrates] sayd, the beste sawce is hungre. **1555** EDEN *Decades* 62 marg. **1564** ERASM. tr. Udall *Apoph.* (1877) 2 Socrates said, the best sauce in the world for meates, is to bee houngrie. **1642** FULLER *H. & P. State* II. xix (1841) 109 God is not so hard a Master, but that he alloweth his servants sauce (besides hunger) to eat with their meat. **1659** HOWELL *Fr. Prov.* 5 There's no sauce to appetite. **1850** KINGSLEY *Alton L.* ch. 9 If hunger is, as they say, a better sauce than any Ude invents.

Hunger knows no friend.

1719 DEFOE *Crusoe* II. ii Hunger knows no friend.

Hunger makes dinners, pastime suppers.

(H 821)

1640 HERBERT no. 819. **1659** HOWELL *Fr. Prov.* 12. Hunger makes us dine, and pleasure makes us to sup.

Hunger makes hard beans sweet.

(H 822)

c. **1350** *Douce MS.* 52 no. 29 Hungur makyth harde benys swete. *a.* **1530** R. *Hill's Commonpl. Bk.* E.E.T.S. 133 Hungre maketh hard bones [read *benes*] softe. Dura licet faba denti sic salus esurienti. *c.* **1549** HEYWOOD I. x. D1. **1670** RAY 107 Hunger makes hard bones sweet beans. Erasmus relates as a common Proverb . . . Hunger makes raw beans rellish well or taste of Sugar. **1691** W. SEWEL 239 (as 1670).

Hunger waits only eight days.

1837 A. LEIGHTON in *Tales of Borders* III. 239 'Hunger waits only eight days, as the sayin' is', replied he, 'an' ye'll live mair than that time, I hope'.

Hunger, *see also* Lie down for love (They that) should rise for h.; Lives by hope will die by h.

Hungry as a dog.

c. **1590** SIR J. DAVIES Epigram no. 19.   **1607**
DEKKER *Jests to make you merry* CI[v].   **1862**
Dialect of Leeds 405.

Hungry as a hunter, As.

1581 R. MULCASTER *Positions* ch. 26 Is his
appetite better then the Archers is though the
prouerbe helpe the hungrie hunter?   *c.* **1621** *The
Welsh Ambassador* 1. 1536 As hungry as a
huntsman.   **1650** TRAPP *Comm. Lev.* xvii. 13
Though hee bee as hungrie as a hunter.   **1818**
LAMB to Mrs. Wordsworth 18 Feb. Up I go,
mutton on the table, hungry as a hunter.   **1855–7**
MAGINN *Misc.* i. 358.

Hungry dogs will eat dirty puddings.

(D 538)

1538 J. BALE *Three Laws* B4.   **1546** HEYWOOD
I. v. B2[v] What, hungry dogges will eate durty
puddyngs man.   **1600** DEKKER *Old Fort.* II. ii. 72
The horse . . . has his head ever in the manger;
. . . and a hungry dog eats dirty puddings.
1670 RAY 82 . . . *Jejunus raró stomachus vulgaria
temnit.*   **1709** MANDEVILLE *Virgin Unmask'd*
(1724) 32 Dirty puddings for dirty dogs.   **1738**
SWIFT Dial. I. E.L. 267. I scorn your words.—
Well, but scornful dogs will eat dirty puddings.
1816 SCOTT *Antiq.* ch. 43 The messenger (one of
those dogs who are not too scornful to eat dirty
puddings) caught in his hand the guinea which
Hector chucked at his face.   **1830** G. COLMAN
(Jr.) *Random Rec.* I. 37 'Hungry dogs eat dirty
pudding', which is a satire upon the distress of
epicures, during the scarcity of provisions.   **1832**
HENDERSON 34 Hungry dogs are blythe o'
bursten puddins.

Hungry enough to eat nails.   (N 19)

1540 PALSGRAVE *Acolastus* 128 So . . . strong a
stomake, that I can digeste . . . horse shoo nayles
(and nede were).   **1661** *Pr. Blacksm.* 1. 93 in
Roxb. Bal. ii. 130 Your roaring-boy . . . Could
never yet make the Smith eat his nails.

Hungry flies bite sore.   (F 402)

1546 HEYWOOD II. ix. K4 On suche as shewe, that
hungry flyes byte sore.   **1611** DAVIES no. 88.
1678 RAY 159 . . . The horse in the Fable with a
gall'd back desired the flies that were full might
not be driven away, because hungry ones would
then take their place.

Hungry forties, The.

1911 *Times Wkly.* 25 Aug. 683 A . . . complete
refutation of the legend that the food prices of
the 'hungry forties' were immediately reduced
by the abolition[1] of the Corn Laws. [[1] 1846.]

**Hungry he could eat a horse behind the
saddle, He is so.**   (H 654)

c. **1641** FERGUSSON MS. no. 666.   **1678** RAY 253.

**Hungry horse makes a clean manger,
A.**   (H 668)

1659 HOWELL *Eng. Prov.* 2b.

**Hungry, If thou be | I am angry; let
us go fight.**   (G 155)

1678 RAY 65.

Hungry man, an angry man, A.

(M 187)

1594 SHAKES. *T.G.V.* I. ii. 67 Is it near dinner
time?—I would it were, That you might kill
your stomach on your meat And not upon your
maid.   **1608** *Id. C. V.* i. 50 He [Coriolanus]
had not din'd. The veins unfill'd, our blood is
cold, and then We pout upon the morning, are
unapt To give or to forgive; but when we have
stuff'd These pipes and these conveyances of our
blood . . . we have suppler souls Than in our
priest-like fasts.   **1613** FLETCHER *et al. Honest
Man's Fortune* IV. i. 239 I am never angrye
fasting.   *c.* **1641** FERGUSSON MS. no. 553
Hungry men ar angry.   **1659** HOWELL *Eng. Prov.*
13b.   **1694** *Plautus's Comedies Amphit.* 53 'Tis
an old Proverb, That an empty Belly and a slack
Guest, makes one as mad as the Devil.   **1738**
SWIFT Dial. II. E.L. 296 I'm hungry.—And I'm
angry, so let us both go fight.   **1909** *Spectator*
22 May 824 The *Acharnians* . . . made fun of the
Athenians. . . . 'A hungry man is an angry
man' . . . and the Athenians were certainly
hungry.

Hungry man smells meat afar off, A.

(M 188)

a. **1641** FERGUSSON MS. no. 19 Ane hungrie man
sies far.   **1721** KELLY 3 A hungry Man sees
Meat far.   **1732** FULLER no. 224.

Hungry, *see also* Cat is h. when crust contents
her; Hard fare h. bellies; Meals, (Two) h. make
fourth glutton; Poor (H.) as a church mouse.

**Hunt for (Catch) a hare with a tabor,[1]
To.**   (H 160)

[= to seek to do something almost impossible.]
1399 LANGLAND *Rich. Redeles* I. 58 Men
my3tten as well haue hunted an hare with a
tabre As aske ony mendis ffor þat þei mysdede.
c. **1430** LYDGATE *Minor Poems* Percy Soc. 154
Men with a tabour may lyghtly catche an hare.
1546 HEYWOOD I. ix. CI[v] And yet shall we
catche a hare with a taber, As soone as catche
ought of them.   **1579** LYLY *Euph.* i. 193 You
shal assone catch a Hare with a Taber as you
shal perswade youth . . . to such seueritie of lyfe.
1624 CAPT. J. SMITH *Virginia* IV. 155 Will any
goe to catch a Hare with a Taber and a Pipe?
[[1] a small drum.]

Hunt(s), *see also* Dog who h. foulest; Flies, (You
h. after); Hare to breakfast (He that will have)
must h. overnight.

**Hunt's (Wood's) dog that will neither
go to church (out) nor stay at home,
Like.**   (H 823)

1666 TORRIANO *Prov. Phr.* s.v. Tenere The
English say, Neither go to Church, nor yet stay
at home.   **1678** RAY 291.   **1732** FULLER no. 3241
(Wood's).   **1880** *N. & Q.* 6th Ser. II. 166 'Why',
said the old man, 'it has been a say as long ago as
I was a child, Contrary as Wood's dog, that
wouldn't go out nor yet stop at home.'   **1917**

BRIDGE 90 ... *Impossible to please* ... 'Hunt was a Shropshire labourer, whose dog when shut up at home during service-time howled . . .; but when his master took him with him . . . the dog would not enter the church'.

Hunters, All are not | that blow the horn. (A 113)

[Med. Lat. *Non est venator quivis per cornua flator.*] **1586** L. EVANS *Withals Dict. Revised* E6 Every horne blower is not a hunter. **1678** RAY 160.

Hunter(s), *see also* Hungry as a h.

Hunting, hawking, and paramours, for one joy a hundred displeasures. (H 824)

a. **1628** CARMICHAELL no. 647. **1641** FERGUSSON no. 362.

Hunting morning, *see* Southerly wind.

Hunting, *see also* Dog that is idle barks at fleas; War, h. . . . full of trouble.

Huntsman's breakfast, the lawyer's dinner, The. (H 826)

1573 HOLYBAND *Cit. at Home* in *Elizabethan Home*, St. Clare Byrne, 1930. 48 Did you never heare speak of hunters breakfast, lawiers dinner, marchants supper and drinkyng of Moonkes? **1576** *Id. The French Littelton* C8ᵛ We say in our country that hunters breakfast, lawyers dinner, supper of marchauntes, and Monkes drinking is the best chere that one can make, and to liue like an Epicure. **1659** N. R. 111.

Hurdle, *see* Looks as if he sucked dam through h.

Hurleburle-swyre, *see* Little kens the wife.

Hurler, *see* Good h. that's on the ditch.

Hurry no man's cattle; you may come to have a donkey of your own.

1822 SCOTT *Pirate* ch. 9 'A' in gude time, replied the jagger, 'hurry no man's cattle'. **1854** SURTEES *Handley Cross* ch. 32. **1869** HAZLITT (1907) 236 Hurry no man's cattle; you may come to have a donkey of your own. Sometimes said to an impatient child.

Hurry, *see also* Old man in h.

Hurts another hurts himself, He that. (H 830)

1573 SANFORD 103ᵛ. **1578** FLORIO *First F.* 29. **1629** *Bk. Mer. Rid.* Prov. no. 84.

Hurt(s), *see also* Cry out before one is h.; Dirt (The more), less h.; Enemy (One) can do more h.; Healed as h. (Not so soon); Helps the evil (He that) h. the good; Ill that does not h. me (So great is); Kills that thinks but to h.; Malice h. itself most; No man, though never so little, but can h.; Offended (H.) but by himself (None is); Threatens many that h. any.

Hurtful, *see* Fire is as h. as healthful.

Husband be not at home, If the | there is nobody. (H 836)

1640 HERBERT no. 1016.

Husband, don't believe what you see, but what I tell you.

1706 STEVENS s.v. Marido. **1732** FULLER no. 2577.

Husband drinks to the wife, When the | all would be well; when the wife drinks to the husband, all is well. (H 838)

1659 HOWELL *Eng. Prov.* 7b When the good Wife drinketh to the Husband all is well in the House. **1670** RAY 53. **1732** FULLER no. 5593.

Husband, In the | wisdom, in the wife gentleness. (H 837)

1640 HERBERT no. 658.

Husband must be deaf and the wife blind to have quietness, A. (H 834)

1578 FLORIO *First F.* 26 There neuer shal be chiding in that house, where the man is biynd, and the wife deafe. **1637** HEYWOOD *Pleas. Dial.* 334 Then marriage may be said to be past in all quietnesse, when the wife is blind, and the husband deafe. **1710** S. PALMER 338 The Husband must not See, and the Wife must be Blind.

Husbandman ought first to taste of the new grown fruit, The. (H 842)

1548 HALL *Chron.* (1809 ed., 262) The old auncient adage which saith, that the husbandman ought first to taste of the new growen frute. **1568** GRAFTON *Chron.* Edw. IV, II. 5.

Husbandry, *see* Good h. good divinity.

Husbands are in heaven whose wives scold (chide) not. (H 814)

c. **1549** HEYWOOD II. vii. E8. **1670** RAY 14.

Husband(s), *see also* Clouts, (A h. of); Cornwall without a boat (Send h. into); Cunning wife makes h. her apron; Good h. good wife; Good wife good h.; Ill h. who is not missed; Lewd bachelor jealous h.; Maids want nothing but h.; Marriage (In) the h. should have two eyes; Usurers good h.; Wives make rammish h., (Rutting); Workman (The better), the worse h.; Wrongs of a h. not reproached.

Hussy (-ies), *see* Careless h. makes many thieves; Cats eat what h. spare.

Hustings, *see* Hoistings (You are for the) or H.

Hydra, *see* Heads as H. (As many).

Hyena, *see* Laugh like a h.

I

I do what I can (my endeavour, good will), quoth the fellow, when he threshed in his cloak.   (G 342)

1602 MANNINGHAM *Diary* Camd. Soc. 131 'I will doe myne endeavor' quoth he that thrasht in his cloke. **1639** CLARKE 155. **1678** RAY 247 I'll do my good will, as he said that thresht in's cloak. This was some Scotchman, for I have been told, that they are wont to do so.

I proud (stout) and thou proud (stout), who shall bear the ashes out?   (A 341)

c. **1549** HEYWOOD I. x. B4ᵛ I proud, and thou proud, who shall beare thasshes out. **1639** CLARKE 33. **1706** STEVENS s.v. Bamba (stout . . . dirt). **1853** TRENCH iv. 83 The Gallegas proverb, You a lady, I a lady who shall have the hogs a-field? . . . So too our own: I stout and you stout, who will carry the dirt out?

I to-day, you to-morrow.   (T 371)

[L. *Hodie mihi, cras tibi.* To-day it is my turn, to-morrow yours. Lady Jane Grey scratched, when imprisoned in the Tower, *Sors hodierna mihi cras erit illa tibi.*] *c.* **1200** *Ancrene Riwle* 278 'Ille hodie, ego cras'; þet is, 'He to daie, ich to morwen.' *c.* **1592** MARLOWE *Jew of Malta* IV. iv. 20 Whom I saluted with an old hempen proverb, *Hodie tibi, cras mihi.* **1596** SPENSER *F.Q.* VI. i. 41 What haps to-day to me, to-morrow may to you. **1639** CLARKE 124. **1721** KELLY 350 What is my turn to Day, may be yours to-morrow. **1927** E. V. LUCAS in *Times* 11 Mar. 15/6 To-morrow . . . hardly occupies the Jamaican mind at all. . . . There is even a native proverb: To-day fo' me; tomorrow fo' you.' **1927** *Times* 15 Mar. 16/5 The Upper House of Congress . . . when the dignity and privileges of a Senator are concerned . . . can translate *Hodie mihi, cras tibi* as well as any Latinist.

I was by, quoth Pedley, when my eye was put out.   (P 179)

1678 RAY 242 . . . This Pedley was a natural fool, of whom go many stories.

I will make one, quoth Kirkham, when he danced in his clogs.   (K 103)

1670 RAY 182. *Chesh.*

Ibycus, *see* Cranes of I.

Ic, *see* Words ending in *i.* mock physician.

Ice, *see* Break the i.; Cold as i.; Fire from i., (To strike); Geese slur on i.; Injuries don't use to be written on i.; Seek hot water under i.

Iceland, *see* Snakes in I.

Idle, Be not | and you shall not be longing.   (I 6)

1640 HERBERT no. 308.

Idle brain is the devil's shop, An.
                                                       (B 594)

a. **1602** W. PERKINS *Treat. of Callings* (Wks. 1608, i. 729) The idle body and the idle brain is the shop of the deuill. **1629** T. ADAMS *Serm.* (1861–2) II. 450 The slothful person is the devil's shop, wherein he worketh engines of destruction. **1678** RAY 161. **1859** SMILES *Self-Help* ch. 9 Steady employment . . . keeps one out of mischief, for truly an idle brain is the devil's workshop.

Idle (lazy) folks (people) have the most labour (take the most pains, have the least leisure).   (F 420)

1678 RAY 161. **1706** STEVENS s.v. Moco We say, Lazy People make themselves Work. **1707** MAPLETOFT 112 Idle lazy Folks have most labour. **1732** FULLER no. 3056 Idle People take the most Pains. **1853** SURTEES *Sponge's Sport. T.* ch. 53 'Got a great deal to do', retorted Jog, who, like all thoroughly idle men, was always dreadfully busy. **1890** D. C. MURRAY *J. Vale's Guard.* ch. 19 It is as true in morals as it is in business that lazy people take the most pains. **1908** *Spectator* 10 Oct. The difference between leisureliness and laziness runs parallel with that between quickness and haste. 'Idle people', says the proverb, 'have the least leisure'.

Idle folks lack no excuses.   (F 421)

1616 WITHALS 559 Idlenes is neuer to seeke for an excuse. **1639** CLARKE 234.

Idle head is a box for the wind, An.
                                                       (H 257)

1640 HERBERT no. 651.

Idle man, *see* Devil tempts all, but i. m. tempts devil.

Idle person is the devil's cushion (playfellow), An.   (I 10)

c. **1577** J. NORTHBROOKE *Treatise agst. Dicing* 58 Idlenesse is Sathans fetheᵈbed and pillowe. **1597** *Politeuphuia* (1598 ed.) 246ᵛ Sloth is the deuils cushion or pillow. **1614** T. ADAMS *Fatal Banquet* II. Wks. 197 The Idle man is the Deuils Cushion, whereupon he sits and takes his ease. **1624** BURTON *Anat. Mel.* 73 Idleness . . . the Diuells cushion, as Gualter calls it, his pillow, and chiefe reposall. **1732** FULLER no. 620 (playfellow).

Idle youth, An | a needy age.   (Y 38)

1564 W. BULLEN *Dialogue* (1888 ed., 90) Yong and folishe, olde and beggerlie. **1583** G. BABINGTON *Commandments* 383 Gette nothing in youth, and haue nothing in age. **1611** COTGRAVE s.v. Jeunesse An idle youth a needie age. **1642** TORRIANO 54 A young man idle, an old man needy. **1651** HERBERT no. 1042. **1657** E. LEIGH *Select Observations* 266. **1659** N. R. 16. **1672** CODRINGTON 107. **1706** STEVENS s.v. Mocedad An idle Youth is follow'd by a troublesome Old Age. **1736** BAILEY *Dict.* s.v. Youth.

Idle(s), *see also* Devil find a man i.; Dog that is i. barks at fleas; Learn to shape I. a coat; Sick of the i.; Sick of the i. crick.

Idleness, Of | comes no goodness.
(I 15)

1611 COTGRAVE s.v. Gueule. **1678** RAY 161. **1732** FULLER no. 3698 Of Idleness never comes any good. **1780** 27 July JOHNSON *Lett.* (Chapman) ii. 382.

Idleness (Sloth) is the key of beggary (poverty).
(I 12)

1597 *Politeuphuia* (1598 ed.) 246ᵛ Sloth is the Mother of pouerty. **1616** BRETON *Crossing of Prov.* B1 Of idlenesse comes naught but ignorance.—Yes, Beggery. **1659** HOWELL *Span. Prov.* 8. **1670** RAY 14. **1706** STEVENS s.v. Pereza Sloath is the Key to Poverty.

Idleness is the root (mother) of all evil (sin, vice). *Cf.* Covetousness root of all evil.
(I 13)

1205 LAYAMON *Brut* Madden II. 624 Idelnesse maketh mon His monscipe leose. Idelnesse maketh cnihte For-leosen his irihte. *c.* **1386** CHAUCER *Sec. Nun's Tale* l. 1 The ministre and the norice unto vices. Which that men clepe in Englissh ydelnesse. *c.* **1430** LYDGATE *Fall of Princes* E.E.T.S. I. ii. 2249 First this kyng ches to been his guide Moodir off vices, callid idilnesse. *c.* **1550** REDFORD *Wyt & Sci.* Sh. S., 16 For that common strumpet, Idellnes, The verye roote of all vyciousnes? **1599** JAMES VI *Basil. Dor.* Arb. 155 For banishing of idleness (the mother of all vice). **1856** FROUDE *Hist. Eng.* I. 54 Every child . . . was to be trained up in some business or calling, 'idleness being the mother of all sin'.

Idleness must thank itself if it go barefoot.
1813 RAY 126.

Idleness (Sloth) turns the edge of wit.
(I 14. S 542)

1579 LYLY *Euph.* i. 263 Sloth tourneth the edge of wit, Study sharpeneth the minde. **1583** MELBANCKE *Philot.*, T2ᵛ Your wittes will rust for wante of good vsage. **1616** DRAXE no. 1046. **1650** TAYLOR *Holy Living* (1861) I. i. 13 Idleness is the rust of time. **1670** RAY 14.

Idleness, *see also* Love is the fruit of i.

'If' and 'An' spoils many a good charter.

[L. *Suppositio nihil ponit in re.*] **1721** KELLY 209 . . . Spoken when a Thing is promised upon such a Condition, If they can, If they have time. Taken from the Clauses Irritant in a Conveyance.

If ifs and an's were pots and pans, there'd be no trade for tinkers.

1850 KINGSLEY *Alton Locke* ch. 10 'If a poor man's prayer can bring God's curse down . . .'

'If ifs and ans were pots and pans.' **1886** *N. & Q.* 7th Ser. I. 71 There is also the old doggerel—If ifs and ands Were pots and pans Where would be the work for Tinkers' hands?

'Ifs' and 'ands'. *Cf.* If ifs and an's.
(I 16)

1513 MORE *Rich. III* (1883) 47 What, quod the protectour, thou seruest me, I wene, with iffes and with andes. **1592** KYD *Span. Trag.* Boas II. i. 77 What, Villaine, ifs and ands? **1678** CUDWORTH *Intell. Syst.* 723 Absolutely, and without any ifs and ands.

Ignorance is bliss, Where | 'tis folly to be wise.
(I 17)

1742 GRAY *Ode Prospect Eton Coll.* 98–9 Thought would destroy their paradise! No more; where ignorance is bliss, 'Tis folly to be wise. **1900** E. J. HARDY *Mr. Thos. Atkins* 291 Never did soldiers set out for a war in better spirits than did ours for this . . . against the Boers. They . . . afforded a pathetic illustration of the proverb: 'Where ignorance is bliss 'tis folly to be wise.'

Ignorance is the mother of devotion.
(I 17)

1559 BP. JEWELL *Wks.* P.S. III. ii. 1202 *Ignorantia enim, inquit, mater est verae pietatis quam ille appellavit devotionem.* **1573** *New Custom* Hazl.-Dods. iii. 10 That I, Ignorance, am the mother of true devotion. **1590** SIDNEY I *Arcadia* (Feuillerat) 5 Yt comes of a very yll grounde, that ignorance should bee ye mother of faithfullnes. **1621** BURTON *Anat. Mel.* III. iv. I. ii (1651) 653 The best meanes . . . is to keep them still in ignorance: for *Ignorance is the mother of devotion*, . . . This hath been the divels practice. **1629** T. ADAMS *Serm.* (1861–2) II. 411 Sing not, thou Roman siren, that ignorance is the dam of devotion, to breed it.

Ignorance is the mother of impudence.
(I 18)

1573 SANFORD B1ᵛ Socrates . . . helde, that Ignoraunce was the mother of presumption. **1589** L. WRIGHT *A Summons for Sleepers* G2ᵛ Ignorance hath alwayes the boldest face. **1597** *Politeuphuia* 56 Ignorance hath euer the boldest face. **1666** TORRIANO 116 no. 14 Ignorance the Mother of presumption. **1732** FULLER no. 3067.

Ignorance of the law excuses no man.
(I 19)

[Law Maxim *Ignorantia iuris neminem excusat.*] **1530** SAINT GERMAN *Dial. betw. Dr. Div. and Stud. Laws Eng.* II. xlvi. 154 Ignorance of the law though it be inuincible doth not excuse. **1586** G. WHETSTONE *Eng. Mirror* 233 In all good gouernments there is a common *Maxime, Non excusat ignorantia iuris.* The ignorance of the Lawe exceedeth not. **1592** DELAMOTHE I Ignorance doth not excuse the faultie. **1629** T. ADAMS *Wks. Med. upon Creed* 1099 But if the King make speciall lawes, . . . euery subject is bound to know that. *Ignorantia Iuris* will excuse no man.

Ignorance, *see also* Art has no enemy but i.;
Wonder is daughter of i.

Ignorant have an eagle's wings and an owl's eyes, The. (I 20)

1616 DRAXE no. 298 [The ignorant] is Eagle
eyed in other mens matters, but as blind as a
buzzard in his owne. *Ibid.* no. 1076 The ignorant
hath the wings of an Eagle, and the eyes of an
Owle. **1640** HERBERT no. 902.

Ignorant, *see also* Science has no enemy but the i.

Ill (lean) agreement is better than a good (fat) judgement, An. (A 78)

1573 SANFORD 107ᵛ A leane agreement is better
than a fatte sentence. **1640** HERBERT no. 264.
1659 HOWELL *It. Prov.* I (as 1573). **1666**
TORRIANO I, no. 17 A sorry agreement is better
than a good sute in Law. **1753** FRANKLIN Aug.
A lean award is better than a fat judgment.

Ill air slays sooner than the sword. (A 93)

a. **1450** *Ratis Raving* I. 167 (1870) 30 Tras weil
the philosophur *is* word, Than sonar slais ill air
na suord. **1576** PETTIE ii. 52 The air whereby
we live, is death to the diseased or wounded man.

Ill bargain where no man wins, It is an. (B 78)

1578 G. WHETSTONE *Promos and Cassandra* H3
The match goes harde, which rayseth no mans
gaine. **1599** DRAYTON *Sonnets* (no. 63 in 1619
ed.). **1721** KELLY 182.

Ill battle (procession) where the devil carries the colours (candle, cross), It is an. (P 596)

1608 BEAUM. & FL. *Philas.* IV. i. O there 's a
Rank Regiment where the Devil carries the
Colours, and his Dam Drum major. **1616**
DRAXE no. 947 It is an euill procession, where the
Deuill beareth the Crosse. *Ibid.* no. 2204 It is an
euill countrey where the deuill rules, or carieth
the Crosse. **1627** DRAYTON *Agincourt* 82 Ill's
the procession (and foreruns much loss),
wherein men say the devil bears the cross. **1670**
RAY 7. *Ibid.* 22 It is an ill procession where the
devil holds the candle. **1678** *Id.* 192 It's an
ill procession where the Devil carries the cross.
1853 TRENCH iv. 77 When rogues go in procession, the devil holds the cross;[1] when evil men
have all their own way, . . . in the inverted
hierarchy which is then set up, the foremost in
badness is foremost also in such honour as is
going. **1909** *Spectator* 2 Oct. 488 Colet . . .
warned the King . . . that they who were fighting
through hatred and ambition were warring
under the banner . . . of the Devil. [¹ It. *Quando
i furbi vanno in processione, il diavolo porta la
croce.*]

Ill be to (Shame take) him that thinks ill. (S 277)

[*Honi soit qui mal y pense.*] *c.* **1460** SIR R. ROS
La Belle Dame in SKEAT *Chaucer* VII. 397 Who

thinketh il, no good may him befal. **1546** HEY-
WOOD I. ix. C2 And shame take him that shame
thinkth, ye thinke none. **1589** PUTTENHAM
Arb. 116 Commonly thus Englished, Ill be
. . ., but in mine opinion better thus, Dis-
honoured is he who meanes dishonorably. **1596**
SPENSER *F.Q.* IV. 66 Shame be his meede, quoth
he, that meaneth shame. **1600–1** SHAKES.
M.W.W. V. v. 67 And, *Honi soit qui mal y
pense* write In emerald tufts, flowers purple, blue,
and white. **1650** COTGRAVE Howell's Ep. Ded.,
. . . We english it, Ill be to him who thinks ill;
though the true sense be, let him be beray'd who
thinks any ill, being a metaphor taken from a
child that hath berayed his clouts, and in
France ther's not one in a hundred who understands this word nowadayes. **1668** DENHAM in
DRYDEN, *Misc.* v. 76 Who evil thinks, may evil
him confound.

Ill (bad) beginning an ill (bad) ending, An. (B 261)

1562 A. BROKE *Romeus and Juliet* To the Reader
The evil man's mischief warneth men not to be
evil. To this good end serve all ill ends of ill
beginnings. **1571** J. BRIDGES *Sermon at Paul's
Cross* 106 This wicked beginning must nedes
haue a wretched endyng. **1576** INNOCENT III
Mirror of Man's Life tr. H. Kerton F2 It is a
iust iudgement, that wealth of euil beginning
should haue a worser ending. **1580** LYLY
Euph. & his Eng. ii. 149 Commonly there
commeth an yll ende where there was a naughtie
beginning. *a.* **1593** *Jack Straw* Hazl.-Dods. v.
383 After so bad a beginning, what's like to
ensue? **1596** SHAKES. *K.J.* III. i. 94 This day
all things begun come to ill end. **1639** CLARKE
109 (ill).

Ill (Foul) bird that bewrays (defiles, fouls) its own nest, It is an. (B 377)

[*c.* **1023** EGBERT V. LÜTTICH *Fecunda Ratis*
(Voigt) l. 148 *Nidos commaculans inmundus
habebitur ales: Pelex nec factis claret nec
nomine digna.*] *a.* **1250** *Owl & Night.* 99–100
(1922) 10 'Dahet habbe þat ilke best þat fuleþ his
owe nest'. *c.* **1320** N. BOZON *Contes Moralisés*
205 Hyt ys a fowle brydde that fylyȝth hys
owne nest. *c.* **1378** GOWER *Mir. de l'Omme*
l. 23413 Trop est l'oisel de mesprisure Q'au son
ny propre fait lesure. *c.* **1440** CAPGRAVE *Life St.
Kath.* v. 1594 It is neyther wurshipful ne honest
On-to mankeende to foule soo his nest. **1509**
BARCLAY *Ship of Fools* i. 173 It is a lewde birde
that fyleth his owne nest. **1546** HEYWOOD II.
v. H3 It is a foule byrd, that fyleth his owne nest.
I wold haue him . . . leaue lewde tickyng.
a. **1591** HY. SMITH *Serm.* (1866) I. 26 It becometh not any woman to set light by her
husband, nor to publish his infirmities: for they
say, That is an evil bird that defileth her own
nest. **1599** SHAKES. *A.Y.* IV. i. 182 We must
have your doublet and hose plucked over your
head, and show the world what the bird hath
done to her own nest. **1614** CAMDEN 308 It is a
fowle bird that fileth his owne nest. **1670** RAY
62. **1701** DEFOE *Trueborn Englishman* Explan.
Pref. I am taxed with bewraying my own nest,
and abusing our nation, by discovering the
meanness of our original. **1818** SCOTT *Rob Roy*
ch. 26 Where's the use o' vilifying ane's country,
and bringing a discredit on ane's kin, before
southrons and strangers? It's an ill bird that
files its ain nest. **1926** *Times* 7 Sept. 17/5

Nothing . . . can excuse the bad taste of Samuel Butler's virulent attack upon his defenceless family . . . It's an ill bird that fouls its own nest.

Ill bird that pecks out the dam's eyes, It is an. (B 378)

1639 CLARKE 272.

Ill cause, He who has an | let him sell it cheap.

1707 MAPLETOFT 59.

Ill, Of one | come many.

a. **1628** CARMICHAELL no. 1219 (commes mae). **1641** FERGUSSON no. 679.

Ill comes in by ells, and goes out by inches. *Cf.* **Mischief comes by pound.**

(I 30)

1640 HERBERT no. 194.

Ill (Ill news) comes often on the back of worse. (M 1013)

1721 KELLY 201 . . . (upon worse Back). Spoken when one Misfortune succeeds another. **1737** RAMSAY III. 186 Ill comes upon waur's back.

Ill counsel mars all. (C 692)

1616 WITHALS 579 Ill counsaile is the Deuill and all. **1639** CLARKE 22.

Ill deed cannot bring honour, An. (D 184)

1640 HERBERT no. 806.

Ill deemed, half hanged. *Cf.* **Ill name, He that has.**

a. **1628** CARMICHAELL no. 729. **1641** FERGUSSON no. 312. **1721** KELLY 195 . . . A Man that is vehemently suspected, will soon be found guilty.

Ill doers are ill deemers (dreaders). (D 432)

1509 BARCLAY *Ship of Fools* i. 297 Yll doers alway hate the lyght. *a.* **1568** ASCHAM *Schoolmaster* Wks. Wright 230 Ill doinges, breed ill thinkinges. **1576** PETTIE ii. 119 For *mala mens, malus animus*, an evil disposition breedeth an evil suspicion! **1721** KELLY 176. **1737** RAMSAY III. 186 Ill doers are ay ill dreaders. **1738** SWIFT Dial. I. E.L. 287. **1815** SCOTT *Guy Man.* ch. 50 It is the ill-doers and ill-dreaders. **1824** FERRIER *Inheritance* II. xxxiv 'They say ill-doers are ill-dreaders', retorted his antagonist. **1828** SCOTT *Fair Maid* ch. 17 Put me not to quote the old saw, that evil doers are evil dreaders. **1886** STEVENSON *Kidnapped* ch. 27 If you were more trustful, it would better befit your time of life. . . . We have a proverb . . . that evil doers are aye evil-dreaders.

Ill dog that deserves not a crust, It is an. (D 487)

1580 BARET *Alreary* D 697 Digna canis pabulo . . . A Prouerbe declaring that the laborer is worthie

of his hire, it is taken as well of the labour of the mind, as of the bodie. **1639** CLARKE 91 (bad). **1670** RAY 81 . . . *Digna canis pabulo.* Ἀξία ἡ κύων τοῦ βρώματος. *Eras. ex Suida.*

Ill egging[1] makes ill begging. (E 94)

1623 CAMDEN 272. **1670** RAY 84 . . . Evil persons by enticing and flattery, draw on others to be as bad as themselves. [1 urging on.]

Ill flesh (beef) ne'er made good broo[1].

a. **1628** CARMICHAELL no. 479 Evill flesh never gude bruse. **1721** KELLY 198 Ill flesh was never good Bruise.[1] Signifying that ill natur'd People seldom do a good Thing: The Scots call an ill natured Boy, Ill Flesh. **1862** HISLOP 172 Ill flesh ne'er made gude broo, Bad meat never made good soup; or, a bad man cannot be expected to do a good act. [1 broth.]

Ill for the rider, good for the abider. (R 118)

1611 COTGRAVE s.v. Bon In a fruitfull ground there is filthie going; in the best soyle the worst way. *c.* **1620** J. SPEED *Eng. Wales Scot. and Ire. Described* 11. E2ᵛ What is worst for the Rider, is best for the Abider. **1630** T. WESTCOTE *View of Devonsh.* 1845. 36 For the ill travel for horses, our common English proverb maketh full amend; which is versified and says this—The country is best for the bider That is most cumbersome to the rider. **1639** CLARKE 18 . . . The best ground's the dirtiest. **1670** RAY 43 The worse for the rider, the better for the bider. *Bon pais* [i.e. pays] *mauvais chemin. Gall.* Rich land, bad way.

Ill fortune, He that has no | is troubled with good. (F 612)

1640 HERBERT no. 358. **1670** RAY 10 (cloyed).

Ill fortune, *see also* Fence against i. f. (No); Good heart conquers i. f.; Ill marriage is a spring of i. f.

Ill-gotten (Evil-gotten) goods (gains) never (seldom) prosper. *Cf.* **Thieves' handsel.** (G 301)

[HESIOD *Opera et Dies* l. 349 Κακὰ κέρδεα ἶσ' ἄτῃσι. Dishonest gains are losses.] **1519** HORMAN *Vulg.* f. 77 Euyll gotten ryches wyll neuer proue longe. *c.* **1526** ERASM. *Dicta Sap.* A3 Felix criminibus nullus erit diu. Welthe yuell gotten dureth nat longe. **1539** TAVERNER 25 Male parta male dilabuntur.[1] Euyll gotten good go euyll away. It is commonly sene by the hygh prouydēce of God that goodes vnlaufully gotten vanysh awaye, no man knoweth how. **1575** GASCOIGNE *Dulce Bellum* ii. 146 Since goods ill got, so little time endure. *c.* **1577** J. NORTHBROOKE *Treat. agst. Dicing* 125 As the poet sayth, De bonis male quaesitis, vix gaudebit haeres tertius; euill gotten goods shall neuer prosper. **1591** SHAKES. *3 Hen. VI* II. ii. 45 Didst thou never hear That things ill got had ever bad success? **1609** JONSON *Case Altered* v. xii. 90 Ill-gotten goods ne'er thrive; I plaied the thiefe, and now am robd my selfe. **1761** A. MURPHY *The Citizen* I. ii. Wks. (1786) II.

233 The moment young master comes to possession, 'Ill got, ill gone', I warrant me. **1826**
LAMB *Elia, Pop. Fallacies* ii THAT ILL-GOTTEN
GAIN NEVER PROSPERS. . . . It is the trite consolation administered to the easy dupe, when he has
been tricked out of his money or estate. [¹ CICERO
Phil. 2. 27. 65.]

Ill-gotten goods thrive not to the third heir. (G 305)

[L. *De male quaesitis non gaudet tertius haeres.*
A third heir does not enjoy property dishonestly
got.] *c.* **1303** BRUNNE *Handl. Synne* l. 9477 For
thys men se, and sey alday, 'The threde eyre
selleþ alle away'. **1542** T. BECON *Invective agst.
Swearing* n.d., F5 The goodes, which are
wrongefully gotten, the thyrde heyre shall
scasely enioye. **1564** BULLEIN *Dial. agst. Fever*
(1888) 72 They had no power in law to be-will
unto their children that which was gotten in
serving the Devil, which would not prosper to
the third heir. **1593** NASHE *Christ's Tears* ii. 97.

Ill (Evil) gotten, ill (evil) spent (gone). (G 90)

[*Quot. by* CICERO *Phil.* 2. 27. 65. *Male parta male
dilabuntur.*] **1481** CAXTON *Reynard* Arb. 8
Male quesisti et male perdidisti; hit is ryght that
it be euil lost that is evil wonne. *c.* **1500** *Harl.
MS. 2331,* f. 147 *a* (*Rel. Ant.* I. 20) Euil gotten,
wors spent. **1555** HEYWOOD *Epig. upon Prov.*
no. 126 Ill gotten ill spent. **1564** BULLEIN *Dial.
agst. Fever* (1888) 72 For evil gotten goods are
evil spent. **1614** CAMDEN 305 Euill gotten,
euill spent. **1641** FERGUSSON no. 481 Ill win, ill
warit.¹ **1659** TORRIANO no. 231 Ill got, soon
consumed. [¹ laid out.]

Ill guest that never drinks to his host, He is an. (G 474)

c. **1576** WYTHORNE 88 I hav hard say dyverz
tyms when I waz beyond the seaz in the low
kuntrey or Duchland, that hee waz but an
vnmanerly and an vnthankfull gest who wold
not drink to hiz host ons in A feast tym. **1678**
RAY 86.

Ill (Wrong) hearing makes ill (wrong) rehearsing. *Cf.* Understands ill: Wrong hears. (H 299)

c. **1641** FERGUSSON MS. no. 1477 (Wrong . . .
wrong). **1721** KELLY 187 . . . Spoken when we
hear one give a wrong Account of a matter of
fact. **1820** SCOTT *Monast.* ch. 35.

Ill herds make fat wolves (foxes). (H 437)

a. **1628** CARMICHAELL no. 496 (Evil). *c.* **1641**
FERGUSSON MS. no. 821. **1721** KELLY 220 . . .
It signifies that careless Keepers give Thieves
occasion to steal. **1737** RAMSAY III. 186 (foxes).

Ill horse can neither whinny nor wag his tail, It is an. (H 671)

1593 B.R. *Greene's News* McKerrow E1ᵛ It is
a tyred Iade that cannot cry weehee, and a
sorry Mare that cannot wag her taile. **1594**
LYLY *Mother B.* IV. ii. 193. And 1 restored

him so gently, that hee neither would cry
wyhie, nor wag the taile. **1670** RAY 105. **1732**
FULLER no. 2882 (silly horse).

Ill husband who is not missed, He is an. (H 832)

1614 Letter to John Hoskyns (*Life* by L. B.
OSBORN 41) 'Tis a bad husband that a wife and
child . . . not miss. **1616** DRAXE no. 8. *a.* **1641**
MELVILLE 5.

Ill language, There were no | if it were not ill taken. (L 65)

1598–9 SHAKES. *M.A.* III. iv. 32 An bad thinking
do not wrest true speaking, I'll offend nobody.
1640 HERBERT no. 294. **1732** FULLER no. 4945.

Ill layers up make many thieves.

1721 KELLY 196.

Ill life, An | an ill end. (L 247)

c. **1300** *King Alisaunder* (Weber) 753 Soth hit is,
in al[le] thyng, Of eovel lif comuth eovel
eyndyng. **1574** J. HIGGINS *Mirror for Mag.* ed.
Campbell III Ill life: worse death, doth after
still insue. **1591** ARIOSTO *Orl. Fur.* Harington
XXIII. 3. **1600** DEKKER *Old Fort.* V. ii. 156 A
foule life makes death to looke more foule.
a. **1628** CARMICHAELL no. 61. **1670** RAY 261.

Ill look among lambs, He has an.

1721 KELLY 155 . . . Applied to wanton young
Fellows casting an Eye to the Girls; alluding to a
superstitious Fancy among the Scots, that an ill
Eye may do harm. **1732** FULLER no. 1861.

Ill luck? What is worse than. (L 584)

1639 CLARKE 166. **1641** *Organ's Echo* in
WILKINS *Polit. Ballads* (1860) I. 5 The proverb
says, *What's worse than ill luck.* **1659** HOWELL
Eng. Prov. 3b. **1664** WILSON *Projectors* II. i Wks.
(1874) 234 Then our business is done already.
What's worse than ill luck? **1721** KELLY 354
. . . Spoken when a thing miscarries purely by
Misfortune.

Ill luck is good for something. (L 576)

1636 CAMDEN 300. **1732** FULLER no. 3074.

Ill luck is worse than found money. (L 577)

1591 GREENE *Art of Coney-Catching* (Harrison)
21 Tis ill luck to keep founde money. **1670**
RAY 110.

Ill luck to count your gains during the game.

1773 BYROM *Misc. Poems,* 'The Pond' I. 72 He
knew a wise old Saying, which maintain'd, That
'twas bad Luck to count what one had gain'd.

Ill man has his ill day, Every. (M 98)

1640 HERBERT no. 92. **1710** PALMER 123 Every
Ill Man will have an Ill Time.

Ill man lie in thy straw, Let an | and he looks to be thy heir. (M 208)

1640 HERBERT no. 271.

Ill marriage is a spring of ill fortune, An. (M 679)

1616 DRAXE no. 2378.

Ill name, He that has an | is half hanged. *Cf.* Give a dog ill name: Ill deemed. (C 817. N 25)

1546 HEYWOOD II. vi. I2 He that hath an yll name, is halfe hangd, ye know. **1596** M. B. *Trial True Frdship.* B4 A man that hath lost his credit, is halfe hanged. **1629** T. ADAMS *Serm.* (1861–2) I. 224 It is a very ominous and suspicious thing to have an ill name. The proverb saith, he is half-hanged. **1641** FERGUSSON no. 312 He that is evil deemed is half hanged. **1897** M. A. S. HUME *Raleigh* 270 'Were not *fama malum gravius quam res*, and an ill name half hanged, . . . he would have been acquitted.'

Ill natures, the more you ask them, the more they stick. (N 39)

1640 HERBERT no. 106.

Ill news comes apace (unsent for, too soon, never comes too late). (N 145, 147, 148)

1530 PALSGRAVE 466a He knocketh to soone at the dore that bringeth yvell tydynges. **1539** TAVERNER *Publius* A4 Sad and heuy tydynges be easily blowen abroade be they neuer so vaine and false and they be also sone beleued. But suche thynges as be good, ryght, and honest, are hardly beleued. **1547** S. GARDINER to Somerset (*Lett.* ed. Muller 292) Evil thinges be oversone knowen. **1574** HELLOWES *Guevara's Ep.* (1577) 58 Euil newes neuer comes too late. [*c.* **1587**] **1592** KYD *Span. Trag.* I. iii Euill newes will flie faster still than good. **1592** DELAMOTHE 57 An ill word is quickly spread abroad. **1603** DRAYTON *Barons Wars* (ed. Hebel 1932) II. xxviii. 233, 34, Ill Newes hath Wings, and with the Wind doth goe. **1639** CLARKE 123 (comes unsent for). **1666** TORRIANO *It. Prov.* 171 no. 13 (flyes apace). **1670** FULLER no. 3077. **1671** MILTON *Samson Ag.* l. 1538 For evil news rides post, while good news baits. **1685** DRYDEN *Thren. Aug.* l. 49 Ill news is winged with fate, and flies apace. **1706** STEVENS s.v. Sonarse Good News is rumour'd but bad News flies. **1838** 9 DICKENS *N. Nickleby* ch. 33 Ill news travels fast.

Ill news is too often true. (N 144)

1592 DELAMOTHE 37 (be commonly to true). **1611** DAVIES no. 47 Ill newes are commonly true. **1639** CLARKE 228. **1721** KELLY 221 Ill news are ay o'er true.

Ill of his harbory is good of his way-kenning, He that is. (H 142)

a. **1628** CARMICHAELL no. 740 (waygang). **1641** FERGUSSON no. 341. **1721** KELLY 143 (lodging). Spoken when I ask my Neighbour a Loan, and he tells me that he cannot, but such an one can.

Ill paut[1] with her hind foot, She has an.

1721 KELLY 297 . . . Signifying that such a Woman is stubborn. Taken from Cows who kick when they are milked. [[1] back stroke.]

Ill paymaster never wants excuse, An.

1622 CÉSAR BUDIN *Grammar Span. and Eng.* tr. I. W. 217 An ill paymaster neuer wants excuses. **1732** FULLER no. 627.

Ill plea should be well pleaded, An.

1721 KELLY 20.

Ill said that was not ill taken, It was never. *Cf.* Ill language, There were no.

1721 KELLY 189 . . . Intimating that we had no ill Design in what we said, only the Man took it ill.

Ill servant will never be a good master, An. (S 235)

1621 ROBINSON 13 A good Prentice will be a good Master. *a.* **1628** CARMICHAELL no. 65 Ane evil servand will never be a gude maister. *c.* **1641** FERGUSSON MS. no. 97. **1683** MERITON *Yorks. Ale* 83–7.

Ill spun weft[1] will out either now or eft,[2] An. (W 249)

c. **1300** *Provs. of Hending* 35 Euer out cometh euel sponne web. *c.* **1350** *Douce MS.* 52 no. 31 Euyl spunnen ȝerne comyth euyll oute. *c.* **1460** *Towneley Myst. 2nd. Shep. Play* 587 Ill spon weft, iwys, ay commys foull owte. **1670** RAY 154 . . . This is a Yorkshire proverb. [[1] web. [2] afterwards.]

Ill that does not hurt me, So great is the | as is the good that does not help me.

1573 SANFORD 50. **1578** FLORIO *First F.* 32. **1629** *Bk. Mer. Rid.* Prov. no. 1.

Ill to himself will be good to nobody, He that is. (I 39)

1583 MELBANCKE *Philot.* 2C3 Ill to all, and worst to my selfe. **1623** WODROEPHE 495 He is neither good for him selfe, nor for others. **1721** KELLY 125. **1732** FULLER no. 2284.

Ill tongue may do much, An.

1583 G. BABINGTON *Expos[n] of Comm[ts]* 456 There is no mischiefe to the mischiefe of the tongue. **1710** 25 Dec. SWIFT *Journal to Stella* An ill tongue may do much. And 'tis an old saying.

Ill turn is soon done, An.

1721 KELLY 43. **1732** FULLER no. 631.

Ill vessels seldom miscarry. (V 38)

1611 COTGRAVE s.v. Vaisseau A course glasse neuer falls vnto the ground. **1640** HERBERT no. 87.

Ill ware is never cheap.   (w 64)

1611 COTGRAVE s.v. Mauvais Bad ware is neuer cheape ynough. **1623** PAINTER C6 Bad ware's alwaies deare. **1640** HERBERT no. 61.

Ill weed (Crop of a turd) mars a whole pot of pottage, One.   (w 240)

1546 HEYWOOD II. vi. I2 For were ye . . . The castell of honestee in all thyngs els. Yet shoulde this one thyng . . . Defoyle and deface that castell to a cotage. One crop of a tourde marrth a pot of potage. **1571** J. BRIDGES *Sermon at Paul's Cross* 161 This one euill herbe, that I thinke is able' to marre all their pot of porrage, (For I tell ye it is *Mors in olla*, Death in the porrage pot & that no lesse than damnation) had they twenty good herbes besides. **1579** LYLY *Euph.* i. 189 One leafe of *Colloquintida*, marreth and spoyleth the whole potte of por-redge. **1614** CAMDEN 310. *a.* **1628** CAR-MICHAELL no. 210 A tuird will spil a potful of bruse.

Ill weeds grow apace (fast).   (w 238)

c. **1470** *Harl. MS.* 3362 (ed. Förster) in *Anglia* 42. 200 Wyl[d] weed ys sone y-growe. *Creuerat herba satis, que nil habet utilitatis.* **1546** HEY-WOOD I. x. C4ᵛ Ill weede growth fast Ales: wherby the corne is lorne. **1578** FLORIO *First F.* 31ᵛ An yl weede groweth apace. [**1592**] **1597** SHAKES. *Rich. III* II. iv. 13 'Ay,' quoth my uncle Gloucester, 'Small herbs have grace, great weeds do grow apace': And since, methinks, I would not grow so fast, Because sweet flowers are slow and weeds make haste. *Ibid.* III. i. 103 You said that idle weeds are fast in growth. **1614** CAMDEN 308 (fast). **1641** FERGUSSON no. 476 Ill weids waxes weill. **1660** TATHAM *The Rump* I. i. **1738** SWIFT Dial. I. E.L. 266. **1905** A. MACLAREN *Matt.* II. 208.

Ill (Evil) will never said well.   (I 41)

c. **1400** *Rom. Rose* B. 3802 For Wikkid-Tunge seith never well. **1536** J. LEYLAND to Cromwell (H. McCusker *John Bale*, 1942, 13). **1548** HALL 744 Euil wil said neuer well. *Ibid.* 709 Euill tongues neuer saied well. **1566** L. WAGER *Mary Magdalene* (1902) Prol. l. 22 For euill will neuer said well, they do say. **1599** SHAKES. *Hen. V* III. vii. 109 'Tis a hooded valour; and when it appears, it will bate.—'Ill will never said well.' **1623** CAMDEN 268 Euill will, neuer sayes well. **1721** KELLY 176 Ill will never spoke well. When People are known to have an Aver-sion to any Person, or Party, what they say of them, must be received with some Abatement.

Ill wind that blows nobody (no man) good (to good), It is an.   (A 94. w 421)

1546 HEYWOOD II. ix. L1 An yll wynde that blowth no man to good, men saie. **1573–80** TUSSER 29 It is an ill winde turnes none to good. **1591** SHAKES. *3 Hen. VI* II. v. 55 Ill blows the wind that profits nobody. **1598** *Id. 2 Hen. IV* V. iii. 88 What wind that blew you hither, Pistol?—Not the ill wind which blows no man to good. **1640** HERBERT no. 872 It's an ill aire where wee gaine nothing. **1655** FULLER *Ch. Hist.* II. ii (1868) l. 157 It is an ill wind which bloweth no man profit. He is cast on the shore of Friezland · . . , where the inhabitants . . . were by his

preaching converted to Christianity. **1660** TATHAM *Rump* II. i. Wks. (1879) 220 'Tis an ill wind, they say, bloughs nobody good. **1832–8** s. WARREN *Diary of Phys.* i My good fortune (truly it is an ill wind that blows *nobody* any good) was almost too much for me. **1839** DICKENS *N. Nickleby* ch. 56 But it's a ill wind as blows no good to nobody. **1928** *Times* 7 Jan. 6/2 It is an ill wind that blows nobody any good, and cannot we all learn a lesson from the recent great snowstorm?

Ill word, One | asks another.   (w 770)

c. **1549** HEYWOOD I. ix. C2 One yll woord axeth an other, as folks speake. **1614** CAMDEN 310 One ill word asketh another.

Ill word meets another, One | and it were at the Bridge of London. (w 771)

1641 FERGUSSON no. 41. **1662** FULLER Lond. 196.

Ill workers are aye guid to-putters[1] (onlookers).

1737 RAMSAY III. 186. **1862** HISLOP 176 Ill workers are aye gude onlookers. [[1] task-masters.]

Ill wound is cured, An | not an ill name.   (w 928)

1640 HERBERT no. 245. **1664** CODRINGTON 218 The evil wound is cured, but not the evil name. **1670** RAY 18 (as 1664).

Ill, (*adj., adv.*), see also Cook that cannot lick (I.); Devil is not so i. as called; Does you an i. turn (Who) never forgive you; Ends i. which begins in God's name (That never); Give a dog an i. name; Good (i.) master a good (i) scholar; Good news may be told any time, i. in morning; Good or i. hap of good or i. life; Keep yourself from . . . man of i. fame; Learning makes i. man worse; Lives i., fear follows; Make haste to an i. way; Neighbour (An i.) is an i. thing; Nothing between poor man and rich but . . . i. year; Nothing to be got without pain (but i. name); Picture of i. luck; Remedy against i. man; Sorrow (and i. weather) come unsent for; Speaks i.; Stomach (An i.) makes all the meat bitter; Tongue is i. hung; Toothache is more ease than to deal with i. people; Trust is dead, i. payment killed it; Understands i., answers i.; Well and them cannot, i. and can.

Ill(s), (*noun*), see also Costs more to do i.; Death is a plaster for all i.; Do i. (Who would) ne'er wants occasion; Do much i. (He may) ere he can do worse; Do no i. (If thou) do no i. like; Does i. hates light (He that); Doing nothing we learn to do i.; Done i. once will do it again; Done no i. the six days, play the seventh; Evils (I.) (Of two) choose the least; North (Out of) all i. comes forth; Say no i. of the year till past; Suffer the i., look for the good; Three i. come from north.

Ill, It is, *see under significant words following.*

Ill-bred dog that will beat a bitch, It is an.

1732 FULLER no. 2898.

Ill-favoured, *see* Visor to hide i. f. face.

Image of rye-dough, To look like an. -
(I 42)

1686–7 J. AUBREY *Remains of Gent. and Jud.* ed.
J. Britten 107 We have a sayeing, She lookes
(He stands) like an image of rye-dough. . . .
In the old time the little Images that did adorn
the Altars were made of Rye-dough.

Image, *see also* Sleep is i. of death.

Imitation is the sincerest flattery.

1820 COLTON *Lacon* ccxvii Imitation is the
sincerest of flattery. **1901** S. LANE-POOLE *Sir H.
Parkes* viii. 138 No sincerer flattery exists than
imitation.

Immodest, *see* Modest words to express i. things,
(It is hard to find).

Impossibilities, *see* No one is bound to i.

Impossible, *see also* Certain because it is i.;
Heretic and good subject; Naught's i. as t'auld
woman said; Nothing is i. to God; Nothing is i.
to willing heart.

Impoverishing, *see* Building is a sweet i.

Impression(s), *see* First i.; Soft wax will take any
i.

Improve(s), *see* Havocks (He that) may sit, i.
must flit.

**Imps follow when the devil goes before,
No marvel if the.** (M 706)

a. **1591** H. SMITH 'The way to walk in' 1657 ed.
163. **1616** DRAXE no. 926.

Impudence, *see* Ignorance is mother of i.

In and out, like Billesdon I wote.
(B 349)

1678 RAY (*Leic.*) 317. **1848** EVANS 115 . . .
A scattered irregular village [between Leicester
and Uppingham].

In at one ear and out at the other.
(E 12)

c. **1374** CHAUCER *Troilus* Bk. 4, l. 434 Oon ere it
herde, at tothir out it wente. **1546** HEYWOOD
II. ix. K4ᵛ Thaduyse of all freends I saie, one and
other Went in at the tone eare, and out at the
tother. **1641** FERGUSSON no. 532. **1738** SWIFT
Dial. III. E.L. 323.

In by the week, He is. (W 244)

1533–4 N. UDALL *Flowers* A2 He is in for a
birde, or he is in by the weke. Captus est.
c. **1553** UDALL *Ralph Roister D.* I. ii. 4. **1555**
HEYWOOD *Epig. on Prov.* no. LX. **1594–5**
SHAKES. *L.L.L.* V. ii. 61 O that I knew he were
but in by th' week! **1616** DRAXE no. 1312.

In dock, out nettle. (D 421–2)

[Originally a charm uttered to cure nettlestings
by dock-leaves, became a proverbial expression
for changeableness and inconstancy.] *c.* **1374**
CHAUCER *Troilus* Bk. 4, 460 But canstow pleyen
raket, to and fro, Nettle in, dok out, now this,
now that. **1546** HEYWOOD II. i. F4 For in one
state they twayne could not yet settyll But
waueryng as the wynde, in docke out nettyll.
a. **1553** UDALL *Ralph Roister D.* II. iii. Arb. 34
I cannot skill of such chaungeable mettle, There
is nothing with them but in docke out nettle.
1655 FULLER *Ch. Hist.* I. v, §§ 47, 48 (1868) I.
246 'Monks for their insolency were driven out
of their seats, and secular clerks brought into
their room.' Thus was it often, 'in dock, out
nettle', as they could strengthen their parties.
1861 T. HUGHES *Tom B. at Oxford* ch. 23 The
constable . . . found some dock leaves, . . .
rubbed her hands with the leaves, repeating the
old saw Out nettle, In dock: Dock shall ha' A
new smock; Nettle shan't Ha' narrun.

In for a bird, To be. (B 384)

1533–4 UDALL *Flowers* A2 He is in for a birde,
or he is in by the weke. Captus est. *c.* **1579**
MERBURY *Marr. Wit and Wisdom* Sh.S. ii. 14
And afaith, then, he is in for a berd. **1598**
R. BERNARD *Andria* I. i. 11 He is taken, he is
in by the snare; he is in for a bird, he is in by the
weeke.

In for a penny, in for a pound. (P 196)

1695 RAVENSCROFT *Canterbury Guests* v. i Well,
than, O'er shooes, o'er boots. And In for a
penny, in for a Pound. **1815** SCOTT *Guy Man.*
ch. 46 'I will', quoth Sampson . . . for he
thought to himself, in for a penny, in for a
pound; and he fairly drank the witch's health in
a cup of brandy. **1827** HARE *Gues. at Truth* i
(1859) 230 No propagation or multiplication is
more rapid than that of evil. . . . He who is in for
a penny, . . . will find he is in for a pound. **1839**
DICKENS *N. Nickleby* ch. 57 If you're in for a
penny, you're in for a pound. **1894** BLACKMORE
Perlycross ch. 15 In for a penny, in for a pound.
Throw the helve after the hatchet. . . . These and
other reckless maxims . . . were cited.

**In time comes he (she) whom God
sends.** (T 299)

1640 HERBERT no. 397. **1670** RAY 51 (she).
1732 FULLER no. 2831.

**In time the savage bull does bear the
yoke.** (T 303)

[OVID *Ars Amatoria* 2. 472 *Tempore lenta pati
frena docentur equi. Ibid.* 2. 184 *Rustica paulatim
taurus aratra subit.*] **1557** NORTH *Dial Princes*
App. vii. 748 Bee the beasts never so wilde, at
length . . . the Oxe contented to yeelde to the
yoake: onelie a woman is a beast, which will

neuer bee tamed. **1576** R. EDWARDS *Par. Dainty Dev.* 23 l. 21 The Oxe dooth yeelde vnto the yoke. **1582** T. WATSON *Hecatompathia* XLVII In time the Bull is brought to weare the yoake. [*c.* **1587**] **1592** KYD *Span. Trag.* (Boas) II. i. 3 In time the sauage Bull sustains the yoake. **1598–9** SHAKES. *M.A.* I. i. 226 In time the savage bull doth bear the yoke.

In vain he craves advice that will not follow it. (v 2)

1611 COTGRAVE s.v. Croire. **1670** RAY I.

In vain is the mill-clack, if the miller his hearing lack. (v 1)

1631 MABBE *Celestina* XVI T.T. 244 To what use serves the clapper in the Mil, if the Miller be deafe? **1640** HERBERT no. 328. **1706** STEVENS s.v. Citola There is no need of a Clapper in the Mill, if the Miller is Deaf.

In vain the net is spread in the sight of any bird. (v 3)

[*Prov.* i. 17] **1581** GUAZZO i. 52 In vaine (as the Prouerb sayth) The net is pitcht in the sight of the birdes. **1888** J. E. T. ROGERS *Econ. Interp. Hist.* (1894) II. xxi. 473 The landowners in Pitt's time foresaw this. . . . They would certainly be caught, and the net was spread in vain in sight of the bird.

In vain, *see also* Nature does nothing i. v.; Rise early.

Inch a man (king), To be every. (M 161)

1576 *Comm. Cond.* 907 Rome for a cutter is euery ynche a man. **1600** DEKKER *Shoem. Hol.* v. ii. 31 Shoemakers are . . . men euery inch of them, al spirite. **1605–6** SHAKES. *K.L.* IV. vi. 109 Ay, every inch a king.

Inch breaks no square, An. (I 54)

1555 HEYWOOD *Epigr. upon Prov.* no. 4 An inche breakth no square. **1636** S. WARD *Serm.* (1862) 104 A good conscience . . . says not, an inch breaks no square, and small faults must be winked at. **1760** STERNE *T. Shandy* II. v. This fault in Trim broke no squares with them. **1771** SMOLLETT *Humph. Clink.* 17 May Wks. (1871) 492 Eastgate understood the hint; and told him that one day should break no squares.

Inch in a miss is as good as an ell, An. (I 56)

1614 CAMDEN 303. **1659** HOWELL *Eng. Prov.* 7b (as bad as). **1721** KELLY 35 *An inch of a miss is as good as a span.* Spoken when a thing was near the effecting, and yet did not hit. **1732** FULLER no. 635. An Inch is missing, is as bad as an Ell.

Inch is as good as an ell, An. (I 47)

1546 HEYWOOD II. ix. LI[v] As good is an ynche As an ell. **1611** DAVIES no. 269. **1818** SCOTT *Ht. Midl.* ch. 43 His great surprise was, that so small a pistol could kill so big a man . . . an inch was as good as an ell.

Inch of a nag is worth a span of an aver,[1] An. (I 57)

a. **1628** CARMICHAELL no. 145 (inch of ane horse). **1641** FERGUSSON no. 150. **1721** KELLY 28 . . . A little Man, if smart and stout, is much preferable to an unwieldy Lubber. [[1] work-horse.]

Inch of his will, for a span (an ell) of his thrift, He will not give an. (I 50)

1520 R. WHITTINGTON *Vulg.* E.E.T.S. 91 Many a man setteth more by an ynche of his wyl than an ell of his thryfte & thou art one of them. **1580** *Letters of Philip Gawdy* 3. **1641** FERGUS-SON no. 398. **1721** KELLY 150 . . . Spoken of wilful and obstinate People, who will not comply with your most advantageous Proposals, if contrary to their perverse Humours.

Inch(es), *see also* Die by i.; Drive out the i. as you have the span; Flog (a person) within i. of his life; Give him an i. and he'll take ell; Ill comes in by ells and goes out by i.; Ready at an i.; Ride an i. behind tail; Sees an i. before his nose.

Includes, *see* Greater embraces (i., hides) the less, (The).

Inconvenience, *see* Better a mischief.

Indentures, To make. (I 63)

[= to stagger as when drunk.] *c.* **1548** *An Invective Agst. Drunkenness* B1 Must he go anye whyther, his legges stacker, so he reeleth, and maketh indentures. **1598** I. M. *A Health to the Gentlemanly Profession of Servingmen* (W. C. Hazlitt) 138 Making Indentures all along the ditches. **1603** DEKKER *The Wonderful Year* E4[v] His legges drew a paire of Indentures, betweene his bodie and the earth. **1611** COTGRAVE s.v. Tournoyer. **1681** *Roxb. Ballads* B.S. vi. 3 Being so drunk that he cutteth indentures.

Index, *see* Face is no i. to heart; Face is i. to heart.

Indian summer.

[A period of calm, dry, mild weather, with hazy atmosphere, occurring in the late autumn in the Northern United States.] **1794** E. DENNY *Milit. Journ.* (1859) 198, Oct. 13th Pleasant weather. The Indian summer here [near Presque Isle]. **1830** DE QUINCEY *Bentley* Wks. VI. 180 An Indian summer crept stealthily over his closing days. **1898** BOLDREWOOD *Rom. Canvass Town* 71 Mild Indian-summer-like days.

Indies, *see* Bring home wealth of the I.

Industry is fortune's right hand, and frugality her left. (I 64)

1651 HOBBES *Phil. Rud. Govt. and Society* (1841), XII. 159 Riches are gotten with industry, and kept by frugality. **1664** CODRINGTON 201. **1670** RAY 14. **1799** EDGEWORTH *Pop. Tales; Lame Jervas* ii . . . a proverb which has been worth ten times more to me than all my little purse contained.

Infirmities, *see* Love covers many i.

Ingleborough,[1] Pendle,[2] and Peny-ghent,[3] are the highest hills between Scotland and Trent.   (P 184)

1586 CAMDEN *Britannia* 430–1 Horum libentius meminerim, quod in Apennino nostro sunt eminentissimi; inde vulgo vsurpatur, Ingleborrow, Pendle, and Penigent, Are the highest hils between Scotland and Trent. **1613–22** DRAYTON *Polyolb.* xxviii. 115 (1876) III. 189 That *Ingleborow* Hill, *Pendle*, and *Penigent*, Should named be the high'st betwixt our *Tweed* and *Trent.* **1670** RAY 256 Pendle, Penigent *and* Ingleborough, Are the three highest hills all England thorow. These three hills are in sight of each other, Pendle on the edge of Lancashire, Penigent and Ingleborough near Settle in Yorkshire, and not far from Westmorland. [[1] Yorks. 2,373 ft. [2] Lancs. 1,830 ft. [3] Yorks. 2,273 ft.]

Inheritance, *see* Beauty is no i.; Service is no i.

Iniquity, *see* Holiness is double i., (Pretended).

Injuries are written in brass.   (I 71)

c. **1513** SIR T. MORE *Rich. III* 1821 ed. 86 Men vse if they haue an euil turne, to write it in marble: and whoso doth vs a good tourne, we write it in duste. **1586** R. CROWLEY *Friar John Francis* A3 All the benefites . . . bestowed vpon you, haue beene written in duste and not in Marble. **1591** ARIOSTO *Orl. Fur.* Harington XXIII. 1 Men say it, and we see it come to passe, Good turns in sand, shrewd turns are writ in brasse. **1592** SHAKES. *T.And.* IV. i. 102 I will go get a leaf of brass, And with a gad of steel will write these words, And lay it by. **1613** *Id. Hen. VIII* IV. ii. 45 Men's evil manners live in brass; their virtues We write in water. **1623** MASSINGER *Duke Milan* V. i For injuries are writ in brass, kind Graccho, And not to be forgotten.

Injuries don't use to be written on ice.
1732 FULLER no. 3096.

Injury is to be measured by malice.
1732 FULLER no. 3099.

Injury (-ies), *see also* Deaf gains the i.; Insult to i.; Neglect will kill an i. sooner than revenge; Patience under old i. invites; Pocket an i.; Remedy for i. is not to remember.

Ink, *see* Black as i.; Wash out i. with i.

Inkhorn, *see* Smell of the i.

Inn, *see* Companion in a . . . little i. (A man knows his); Goes not out of way . . . to good i.; Take one's ease in one's i.

Inner Temple rich, the Middle Temple poor; Lincoln's Inn for law, and Gray's Inn for a whore, The. *Cf.* Gray's Inn for walks, etc.
1813 RAY 237.

Inner Temple, *see also* Gray's Inn.

Innocence is no protection.
1605 JONSON *Sejanus* IV. i. 40 No innocence is safe, When power contests. **1732** FULLER no. 3100.

Innocent actions carry their warrant with them.   (I 81)
1573 SANFORD 106[v] Innocencie bringeth with hir, hir owne defence. **1578** FLORIO *First F.* 31[v] Innocencie beareth her defence with her. **1732** FULLER no. 3102.

Innocent as a devil of two years old, As.   (D 219)
1678 RAY 286. **1695** RAVENSCROFT 48 (harmless). **1738** SWIFT *Dial.* I. E.L. 287 I meant no Harm. —No, to be sure, my Lord! you are as innocent as a Devil of Two Years old.

Innocent (harmless, simple) as a dove, As.   (D 572)
[MATT. X 16: Be ye therefore wise as serpents, and harmless as doves.] **1560** J. PILKINGTON P.S. 45 Ware as a serpent and simple as a dove. **1580** *Pet and Jackman* in Hakluyt *Principal Navig.* iii. 255 Innocent as doves, yet wilie as serpents. **1590–1** SHAKES. *2 Hen. VI* III. i. 69 As innocent . . . As is the sucking lamb or harmless dove. **1659** HOWELL *Eng. Prov.* 15b.

Innocent as a lamb.   (L 33)
1526 *Great Herbal* 6 A4 For it kepeth a man chast as a lambe. [**1589**] **1633** MARLOWE *Jew of Malta* II. iii. 22. **1590–1** SHAKES. *2 Hen. VI* III. i. 69 As innocent . . . As is the sucking lamb or harmless dove.

Innocent as a new-born babe (as child unborn). *Cf.* Die like a chrysom child.   (B 4)
1538 BALE *K. Johan* l. 858 As clere, as that daye thow wert borne. **1559** *Mirror for Mag.* 'George D. of Clarence' (Campbell) 232 As innocent, As is the babe that lacketh kindely breth. **1578** T. CHURCHYARD *Discourse of the Queen's Entertainment* (Nichols *Progresses* 1823 ii. 197) Chast life is pure as babe new borne. **1606** O. ORMEROD *The Picture of a Papist* 191 As innocent as the childe newelie borne. **1608** MIDDLETON *The Family of Love* Wks. (Bullen) iii. 115 I am as innocent in this as the child new-born. **1745** SWIFT *Dir. to Servants* 'Chambermaid', offering to take her oath . . . that she was innocent as the child unborn.

Innocent until he is proved guilty, Every one is held to be. *Cf.* Presumed good, All are.
1772 JUNIUS *Letters* no. 67 Where the guilt is doubtful, a presumption of innocence should in general be admitted. **1910** *Spectator* 6 Aug. 205 The rule that a man must be assumed to be innocent till proved guilty is thoroughly sound.

Insatiable, *see* Three things are i.

Inscription, *see* Cross has its i., (Each).

Inside, *see* Best thing for i. of a man.

Instep, *see* High in the i.

Insult to injury, To add.

1748 E. MOORE *The Foundling* v. ii This is adding insult to injuries. **1805** *Ann. 8th Cong.* 2 Sess 1072 It was adding insult to injury, and expenses to both. **1837** DICKENS *Pickwick* ch. 35 'Not content with writin' up Pickwick, they puts "Moses" afore it, vich I call addin' insult to injury.'

Intent, *see* Bashful mind hinders good i.

Intentions, *see* Hell is paved with good i.; Man punishes action, God i.

Intents and purposes, To all.

1546 *Act* 37 *Hen. VIII,* c. 9, § 1 To all intents, constructions, and purposes. **1629** STRATFORD *Let.* in *Slingsby's Diary* (1836) 321 Your self [being] as formerly vice president to all intentts. **1716** ADDISON *Drummer* i Sir George is as dead at present, to all Intents and Purposes, as he will be a Twelve-month hence. **1879** M. ARNOLD *Mixed Ess. Porro unum* 162 The rest of the nation consists, for all intents and purposes, of one immense class.

Interest will not lie.   (I 86)

1677 YARRANTON *Eng. Improvem.* I. 110 Interest will not lie, every Man will be for his own Interest. **1682** DRYDEN *The Medal* l. 88 Int'rest never lyes. **1688** BUNYAN *Work of Jesus Christ* Wks. (1855) i 164 Our English proverb is, Interest will not lie; interest will make a man do that which otherwise he would not do.

Intermeddling, *see* Little i. good friends.

Invented the Maiden first hanselled it, He that.   (M 41)

[OVID *Ars Am.* l. 655 *Neque enim lex aequior ulla, Quam necis artifices arte perire sua.*] **1652** TATHAM *Scots. Fig.* II. Wks. (1879) 141 I'm sworn to cheat my father, and 'tis fit He that first made the gin should hansell it. **1721** KELLY 140. **1853** TRENCH ii. 37 . . . The Regent Morton, the inventor of . . . 'The Maiden', a sort of . . . guillotine, was himself the first upon whom the proof of it was made. Men felt . . . that 'no law was juster than that the artificers of death should perish by their own art'.

Invitation, *see* Host's i. is expensive; Small i. will serve beggar.

Invite not a Jew either to pig or pork.
                                                         (J 50)

[**1596** SHAKES. *M.V.* I. iii. 28 If it please you to dine with us.—Yes, to smell pork . . . I will buy with you, sell with you, . . . and so following; but I will not eat with you.] **1732** FULLER no. 3106.

Invited you to the roast? Who.

1721 KELLY 351 . . . Spoken when People put their Hand uninvited to what is not theirs.

Invite(s), *see also* Sign i. you in, money redeem you out.

Ipswich, a town without inhabitants, a river without water, streets without names, where asses wear boots.

1787 GROSE (*Suffolk*) 224 . . . This description of Ipswich was given to King Charles II by the Duke of Buckingham. . . . The town, having no manufactory, was thinly inhabited; the streets at that time were not named; at low water the bed of the river is left dry; and the bowling-green of Christ-church priory . . . was rolled by asses, in a sort of boots, to prevent their feet sinking into the turf.

Ira furor brevis est, see Anger is a short madness.

Ireland, *see* England win (He that will) must with I. begin; England's difficulty I.'s opportunity.

Irish, *see* More I. than the I.; Weep I.

Irishman before answering a question always asks another, An.

1910 P. W. JOYCE *Eng. as We Speak* 109 . . . he wants to know why he is asked.

Irishman for a hand, The | the Welshman for a leg, the Englishman for a face, and the Dutchman for a beard.
                                                         (I 89)

1605 DEKKER 2 *Hon. Whore* I. i. 58 There's a saying when they commend Nations: It goes, the Irishman for his hand, Welshman for a leg, the Englishman for a face, the Dutchman for beard.

Irishman on the spit, Put an | and you can always get another Irishman to baste him.

1907 G. B. SHAW *John B.'s Other Is.* (1912) Pref. xxxiii To thump the Nationalist or Orange tub . . . puts a premium on the rancour or callousness that has given rise to the proverb . . .

Irishman's obligations, Like an | all on one side.

1894 NORTHALL *Folk-phrases* 19.

Irishman, *see also* Englishman is never happy . . . I. never at peace; Englishman weeps, I. sleeps.

Iron age, *see* Golden life in i. a. (Not look for).

Iron entered into his soul, The.   (I 90)

[L. *Ferrum pertransiit animam ejus, Ps.* civ (cv) 18, a mistranslation in the Vulgate of the Heb.

(lit. 'his person entered into the iron', i.e. fetters, chains).] *c. 825 Vesp. Psalter* civ. 18 Iren ðorhleorde sawle his. *a.* **1340** HAMPOLE *Psalter* civ. 17 Yryn passid thorgh his saule. **1539** BIBLE (Great) *Ps.* cv. 18 Whose fete they hurt in the stockes: the yron entred in to hys soule. **1768** STERNE *Sent. Journ.* (1778) II. 32 (*Captive*), I saw the iron enter into his soul. **1843** MACAULAY *Ess., Mad. D'Arblay* (1865) II. 304/2 She was sinking into a slavery worse than that of the body. The iron was beginning to enter into the soul.

Iron hand in a velvet glove, An.

1850 CARLYLE *Latter-Day Pamph.* ii (1885) 48 Soft of speech and manner, yet with an inflexible vigour of command . . . 'iron hand in a velvet glove', as Napoleon defined it. **1882** PIDGEON *Engineer's Holiday* (1883) 167 Whose hand of iron was never ungloved with velvet.

Iron nails that scratches a bear, He must have. (N 9)

1678 RAY 98. **1801** WOLCOT (P. Pindar) *Out at Last* A man must have, the proverb says, Good iron nails that scratches a bear. **1828** LYTTON *Pelham* ch. 77 He must have iron nails who scratches a bear. You have sent me a challenge, and the hangman shall bring you my answer.

Iron not used soon rusts. (I 91)

1576 F. PATRICIUS *Civil Policy* B4 Marcus Cato wrote . . . that mannes lyfe was as Iron, whych if a man do . . . putte in vse, is in wearinge made bryghte, but being not put in vse, is withe Ruste consumed and cankered. **1579** LYLY *Euph.* i. 251 Doth not the rust fret the hardest yron if it bee not vsed? **1608** SHAKES. *C.* IV. v. 220 This peace is nothing but to rust iron. **1609** HARWARD 96ᵛ Iron vnoccupyed will soone gather rust.

Iron shoes, He should wear | that bides his neighbour's dead.[1] Cf. Dead man's shoes. (S 375)

c. **1576** WHYTHORNE 12 Hee that looketh to wear dead folks shows had need to bee shod with iron. *a.* **1628** CARMICHAELL no. 652. **1668** R.B. 25. [¹ death.]

Iron whets iron. (I 91a)

1545 TAVERNER Iiᵛ Yron whetteth yron. *c.* **1594** BACON no. 549 Iron sharpeth against iron.

Iron with use grows bright. (I 93)

1576 F. PATRICIUS *Civil Policy* B4 Marcus Cato wrote . . . that mannes lyfe was as Iron, whych if a man do . . . putte in vse, is in wearinge made bryghte, but being not put in vse, is withe Ruste consumed and cankered. **1579** LYLY *Euph.* i. 195 Yron the more it is vsed the brighter it is. **1598** MARLOWE *Hero and Leander* I. 231 Vessels of brass oft handled, brightly shine. **1607** DEKKER & WEBSTER *Westw. Ho* IV. F3ᵛ Beautie (like gold) being vs'd becomes more bright.

Iron(s), *see also* Anvil should have hammer of feathers, (An i.); Cold i., (To hammer on); Cow with i. tail; Golden life in i. age; Many i. in the fire; Strike while i. hot.

Isis, *see* Ass of I.

Island, *see* England is ringing i.; Settling an i., the first building.

Isle of Saints, The.

1875 KILLEN *Eccles. Hist. Ireland* I. 40 In the seventh century Ireland was known by the designation of 'The Isle of Saints'. . . . Its missionaries laboured with singular success in France, Germany, Switzerland, and Italy, as well as in Great Britain.

Isle of Wight has no monks, lawyers, or foxes, The. (I 102)

1586 CAMDEN *Britannia* 551 Wight. . . . Incolae facete gloriari solebant, quasi reliquis beatiores essent, quod cucullatos monachos, causidicos, et lupos non habuerint. **1607** DEKKER & WEBSTER *West. Ho* III. i. E1ᵛ Though the Isle of Wight could not of long time neither in dure Foxes nor Lawyers, yet it could brook the more dreadful Cockatrice. **1610** P. HOLLAND *Brit.* Wight i. 274 The inhabitants of this Isle were wont merrily to make their boast, that their case was happier than all others, because they had neither hooded monks, nor cavilling Lawyers, nor yet crafty foxes. **1662** FULLER Hampshire 3 (nor Foxes). This Speech hath more Mirth than Truth in it. That they had Monks, I know . . . That they have Lawyers they know, when they pay them their Fees; and that they have Foxes their Lambs know.

Italianate, *see* Englishman I.

Italians are wise before the deed, The | the Germans in the deed, the French after the deed. (I 103)

1604 DALLINGTON *View France* R4ᵛ The Italian is wise beforehand; the Almayne, in the doing; and the French, after the thing is done, saith one of their owne Writers. **1640** HERBERT no. 947. **1659** HOWELL *Lett. of It. Prov.* 2 Whereas the *French* is wise after the Fact, the *Dutch* and *English* in the Fact, the *Italian* is wise before.

Italy, *see* Live in I.

Itch and ease can no man please. (I 106)

1546 HEYWOOD II. iv. G3ᵛ But all thyng maie be suffred sauyng welth. An olde saide sawe, itche and ease, can no man please. **1587** J. BRIDGES *Def. of Gov. of C. of E.* 536 Itch and ease cannot please. **1659** HOWELL *Eng. Prov.* 3a. **1732** FULLER no. 6237.

Itch of disputing is the scab of the church, The. (I 108)

[*c.* **1639**] **1651** *Reliquiae Wottonianæ* (1672) I. 135 *Panegyrick to K. Charles. Disputandi pruritus fit*

Ecclesiarum Scabies. 147 In my opinion (if I may have pardon for the phrase) *The Itch of disputing, will prove the Scab of Churches.* 1651 HERBERT no. 1137 [transln. of the saying *Disputandi prurigo est ecclesiae scabies*].

Itch(es), *see also* Endure to i. (He that will not); Fingers i. to be at it, (His); Scratch where it i. not.

Ithuriel's spear.

[A touch of the angel Ithuriel's spear exposed deceit.] 1667 MILTON *Par. Lost* iv. 810 Him thus intent Ithuriel with his spear Touched lightly; for no falsehood can endure Touch of celestial temper. 1926 A. CLUTTON-BROCK *Ess. on Relig.* vi. 157 The new weapon of psychology . . . may become for us an Ithuriel's spear. When the Devil within us pretends to be an angel . . . at a touch of that spear the disguise will fall away.

Ivinghoe, *see* Tring.

Ivory gate, The. *Cf.* Gate of horn.

[In classical legend that through which false dreams came forth; *Od.* 19. 564; *Aen.* 6. 895.] 1590 SPENSER *F.Q.* I. i. 40 *Morpheus* house . . . Whose double gates he findeth locked fast, The one faire fram'd of burnisht Iuory, The other all with siluer ouercast. 1870 MORRIS *Earthly Par.* I. Apol., Let it suffice me that my murmuring rhyme Beats with light wing against the ivory gate.

Ivory, *see also* White as i.

Ivy bush, *see* Owl in i. b.

Ivy-leaf, Not worth an.

c. 1390 GOWER *Conf. Amantis* IV. 586 That all nys worth an yvy lef.

Ivy leaf, *see also* Pipe in an i. l.

J

Jack-a-lent, A.   (J 9)

1553 H. MACHYN *Diary* Camden Soc. 33 And then shreyffing Jake-of-lent on horssbake, and a doc[tor] ys fezyssyoun, and then Jake-of-lent[s] wyff. *c.* 1560 WRIGHT *Songs etc. Philip and Mary* Roxb. Cl. 191 Then Jacke-a-lent comes justlynge in, with the hedpeece of a herynge. [1594–1600] 1615 T. HEYWOOD *Four Prentices* ii. 186 You old Jack a lent, sixe weeks and vpwards. 1600–1 SHAKES. *M.W.W.* V. v. 124 See now how wit may be made a Jack-a-Lent when 'tis upon ill employment. 1633 JONSON *T. Tub* IV. ii. 47 Thou . . . Travaild'st to Hamsted Heath on a Ash-we'nsday, Where thou didst stand six weekes the Jack-of-Lent for boyes to hoorle three throwes a penny, at thee. 1706 STEVENS s.v. Dominguillo. . . . a Figure of Straw cover'd with old Rags. 1813–49 *Brand's Pop. Antiq.* I. 101. 1863 *Chambers' Bk. of Days* I. 240/2.

Jack among the maids.

[= a gallant, a ladies' man.] 1785 J. TRUSLER *Mod. Times* I. 160 The Mayor . . . was a pleasant man, and Jack among the maids.

Jack-an-Ape be merry, Can | when his clog is at his heel?   (J 10)

c. 1440 *Book of Curtasye* Furnivall l. 108 Thou art like an ape tey3ed with a dogge. *c.* 1450 *Polit. Poems* Wright II. 232 Jac Napes wolde one the see a maryner to ben, with his cloge and his cheyn. 1636 CAMDEN 294.

Jack-an-apes is no gentleman.   (J 2)

1626 BRETON SOOTHING A8ᵛ. 1639 CLARKE 226. 1693 ROBERTSON *Phras. Gen.* 752 (Jack).

Jack-an-apes than all the bears, More ado with one.   (A 41)

c. 1569 J. PHILLIP *Patient Grissell* l. 543 C4ᵛ Heares more a do with Jacke Napes, then twenty Beares. 1616 DRAXE no. 756. 1639 CLARKE 73. 1732 FULLER no. 3464.

Jack and Gill (Jill). *Cf.* Jack has, etc.; Jack shall have, etc.

14 . . LYDGATE *London Lyckpeny* 83 Some songe of lenken and Iulyan for there mede. *c.* 1450 *Cov. Myst.* Shakes. Soc. 340 And I wole kepe the feet this tyde Thow ther come both Iakke and Gylle. 1577 R. STANYHURST in Holinshed *Descr. Ireland* 11 By beating Iacke for Gill. 1661 NEEDHAM *Hist. Eng. Rebell.* 74 Princes are brav'd by Jack and Jill. 1706 STEVENS s.v. Ollaza Every Jack must have his Jill. 1852 LYTTON *My Novel* III. 10 If Gill was a shrew, it was because Jack did not . . . stop her mouth with a kiss.

Jack at a pinch.   (J 11)

c. 1610–40 *The Telltale* l. 1059 I am faigne to bee Jack at a pinch still. 1622 MABBE tr. *Aleman's Guzman d'Alf.* I. 130 When there was neede of my seruice . . . I was seldome or neuer wanting; I was Iacke at a pinch. 1699 B. E. *Dict. Cant. Crew, Jack at a Pinch,* a poor Hackney Parson. 1883 WHITCHER *Widow Bedott Papers* ch. 2 Miss Coon . . . knows that the Major took her [to wife] 'Jack at a pinch'— seein' he couldent get such as he wanted, he took such as he could get.

Jack (Tom) Drum's entertainment.
                                              (J 12)

[= a rough reception, turning an unwelcome guest out of doors.] 1577 HOLINSHED *Desc.*

Irel. 1587 ed., 21a Tom drum his interteinment, which is, to hale a man in by the head, and thrust him out by both the shoulders. 1579 GOSSON *Sch. Abuse* Arb. 22 Plato when he sawe the doctrine of these Teachers, . . . gaue them all Drummes entertainment, not suffering them once to shew their faces in a reformed common wealth. 1583 MELBANCKE DⅠᵛ Hee had scarce Iacke drummers enterteynement, for Jacke was shut out. 1587 J. BRIDGES *Defence* 525 Another curteous intertainment of Tom Drumme, by the heade and shoulders to thrust out . . . the heades of Colleges. 1602 SHAKES. *A.W.* III. vi. 34 If you give him not John Drum's entertainment, your inclining cannot be removed. 1607 DAY *Parl. of Bees* V With Jack Drum's entertainment he shall dance the jig called Beggar's Bush. 1649 J. TAYLOR (Water-P.) *Wand. to West* 16 The Hostess being very willing to give the courteous entertainment of Jack Drum, commanded me very kindly to get me out of doors.

Jack has (must have) his Jill, Every. *Cf.* Bad a Jill; Jack shall have Jill.

(J 6)

1611 COTGRAVE s.v. Demander Like will to like; a Jacke lookes for a Gill. 1619 *Satyricall Epigr.*, in BARDSLEY'S *Puritan Nomen.* (1897) 104 The proverb is, each *Jacke* shall have his *Gill.* 1670 RAY 108 Every Jack must have his Gill. *Chascun demande sa sorte. Gall.* Like will to like. It ought to be written *Jyll.* 1738 SWIFT Dial. I. E.L. 282 You are a saucy Jack, to use such expressions.—Why, then, miss, . . . I must tell you there's ne'er a Jack but there's a Gill. 1855 G. J. WHYTE-MELVILLE *Gen. Bounce* ch. 2 'Every Jack has his Gill', if he and she can only find each other out at the propitious moment.

Jack-hold-my-staff.

(J 15)

[= a servile attendant.] 1540 PALSGRAVE *Acolastus* 160. 1542 UDALL *Apoph.* 4 Thou shouldest not in this maner haue been a Ihon hold mystaf. 1625 BP. MOUNTAGU *App. Cæsar* II. xvi. 217 As if . . . the man [were not] to be made any more account of than *Iack hold my staffe,* by these Rabbies. 1678 MRS. BEHN *Sir Patient Fancy* v Madam, in plain English I am made a . . . Jack-hold-my-staff, . . . to give Leander time to marry your Daughter.

Jack in a box.

(J 16)

1570 *Satir. Poems Reform* xxii. 78 Jak in the bokis, for all thy mokis a vengeance mot the fall! 1577 *Misogonus* III. i Its no tale of Iacke a male [= Jack in the male or trunk.] 1583 MELBANCKE *Philotimus* (British Bibliographer ii. 446). 1690 *New Dict. Cant. Crew* G2 Jack in a box, a Sharper or Cheat.

Jack in office.

(J 17)

[= a consequential petty official.] 1608 SHAKES. *C. V.* ii. 59 You shall perceive that a jack guardant cannot office me from my son Coriolanus. *c.* 1610–40 *The Telltale* l. 1170 Who made yow Iack in office among vs. 1670 RAY 214 To be Jack in an office. 1699 B. E. *Dict. Cant. Crew* G2 *Jack in an Office,* of one that behaves himself Imperiously in it. 1742 FRANKLIN *Mar.* Two upstart Jacks in Office, proud and vain. 1732 FULLER no. 3050 Jack in an office is a great man. 1895 D. C. MURRAY *Martyred Fool* II. ii.

169 A jack in office of the average *juge d'instruction* type, who barked at him in the common imperative way of his tribe.

Jack in the low cellar.

(J 18)

[a rendering of Dutch *Hans-in-Kelder,* an unborn child.] 1640 R. BROME *Asparagus* III. iv Come here's a health to the Hans in Kelder, and the mother of the boy, if it prove so. 1751 SMOLLETT *Per. Pick* ch. 10 When his companions drank to the *Hans en Kelderr,* or Jack in the low cellar, he could not help displaying an extraordinary complacence of countenance.

Jack is as good as his master.

1706 STEVENS s.v. Pedro Peter is as good as his Master. Like Master, like Man. 1869 C. READE *Foul Play* ch. 40 Is it the general opinion of seamen before the mast? Come, tell us. Jack's as good as his master in these matters. 1895 R. GARNETT *Age of Dryden* 245 The simple discovery that for the novelist's purpose, Jack was as good as his master. 1905 W. C. RUSSELL *Old Harb. T.* ch. 11 If the crew are to be carried away to an unbeknown place, they all go below to a man, for Jack's as good as his master when it comes to his having to do something which they didn't agree for.

Jack's in love, If | he's no judge of Jill's beauty.

1732 FULLER no. 2681.

Jack (John) of all trades.

(J 19)

1618 MYNSHUL *Ess. Prison* 24 Some broken Citizen, who hath well plaid Iack of all trades. 1639 MAYNE *City Match* II. v You mungrel, you John of all Trades. 1712 ARBUTHNOT *John Bull* iv Old Lewis Baboon was a sort of Jack of all trades, which made the rest of the tradesmen jealous. 1813 SCOTT *Let. to Joanna Baillie* 21 Mar. in LOCKHART *Life* Being a complete jack-of-all-trades, from the carpenter to the shepherd, nothing comes strange to him.

Jack of all trades, and master of none.

1732 FULLER no. 3051 (is of no Trade). 1770 *Gent. Mag.* xl. 61 Jack at all trades, is seldom good at any. 1800 EDGEWORTH *Pop. Tales, Will* i 'How comes it that I am so unlucky?' 'Jack of all trades, and master of none!' said Goodenough, with a sneer. 1878 S. WALPOLE *Hist. Eng.* I. 311 It would be unfair to say of Lord Brougham that he was 'Jack of all trades and master of none'.

Jack of (on) both sides.

(J 21)

1562 [Title] A Godly and necessary Admonition concerning Neutres, such as deserve the grosse name of Iack of both sydes. 1656 EARL MONM. *Advt. fr. Parnass.* 338 That he hath won this universal good will by the vice of playing Jack of both sides. 1759 DILWORTH *Pope* 59 That he was a papist, a jack o' both sides. 1882 BLACKMORE *Christowell* ch. 23 Rose Arthur . . . wondered at his impartiality about a gentleman whom he had longed so lately to put upon a bonfire. Somehow or other, . . . now he seemed a Jack of both sides.

Jack of Dover.   (J 20)

['The name of some dish, probably a pie that had been cooked more than once.' (Skeat.)] *c.* 1386 CHAUCER *Cook's Prol.* l. 4346 Many a Iakke of Douere hastow soold That hath been twies hoot and twies coold. **1604** *Jack of Dover* [Title]. **1670** RAY 234 . . . This he [Chaucer] makes parallel to Crambe bis cocta; and appliable to such as grate the eares of their Auditours with ungrateful tautologies, of what is worthless in it self, tolerable as once uttered in the notion of novelty, but abominable if repeated.

Jack-out-of-doors, Not | nor yet gentleman.   (J 22)

1616 WITHALS 569.   **1639** CLARKE 206.

Jack (John) out of office.   (J 23)

1546 HEYWOOD II. iii. G2 And Iak out of office she maie byd me walke. **1560** T. BECON *Catechism* P.S. 65 Make the Holy Ghost, as they used to say, Jack out of office. **1592–4** SHAKES. *I Hen. VI* I. i. 175 I am left out; for me nothing remains. But long I will not be Jack-out-of-office. **1667** L'ESTRANGE *Vis. Quev.* ii (1668) 79 We should be but so many Jacks out of Office.

Jack Robinson, *see* Before one can say.

Jack shall have Jill, All shall be well. *Cf.* Jack and Jill; Jack has his Jill.
                                    (A 164)

c. 1516 SKELTON *Magn.* l. 287 What auayleth Lordshyp yourself for to kyll With care and with thought how Jacke shall haue Gill? **1546** HEYWOOD II. iii. G1ᵛ Com chat at home, al is wel. Iak shall haue gill. **1595** SHAKES. *M.N.D.* III. ii. 461 Jack shall haue Jill; Naught shall go ill; . . . And all shall be well. **1623** CAMDEN 266.   **1639** CLARKE 63.

Jack Sprat (Archdeacon Pratt) he loved no fat, and his wife she loved no lean: And yet betwixt them both, they licked the platters clean.   (J 25)

c. 1570 *Marr. Wit and Science* v. v F1 Ye are but Jack Sprot to mee.—Haue houlde heare is a morsell for thee to eate. **1639** CLARKE 17 Jack will eat no fatt, and Jill doth love no leane. Yet betwixt them both they lick the dishes cleane. **1659** HOWELL *Eng. Prov.* 20a Archdeacon Pratt would eat no fatt, His wife would eat no lean; Twixt Archdeacon Pratt and Joan his wife, The meat was eat up clean. **1670** RAY 211.

Jack Sprat would teach his grandame.
                                    (J 26)

1639 CLARKE 4 Jack sprat teacheth his grandame. **1670** RAY 108 . . . *Ante barbam doces senes.*

Jack would be a gentleman if he could speak French.   (J 3 and 4)

1482 CAXTON *Polychronicon* (in N.S. Aurner, *Caxton* 144) It is sayd by a comyn proverbe Jack wold be a gentleman if he coude speke frensshe.   *c.* 1515 SKELTON *Coyst.* in Wks. (Dyce) I. 16 For Jak wold be a jentylman that late was a grome.   *c.* 1549 HEYWOOD I. xi. B8ᵛ Iacke wold be a gentilman, yf he could speke frenche.   **1580** MUNDAY *Zelauto* Q3 Then Gyll would be a Gentlewoman, if she could but Parle vn petit de Francoys. [1592] **1597** SHAKES. *Rich. III* I. iii. 72 Since every Jack became a gentleman, There's many a gentle person made a Jack. **1662** FULLER Berks. 86 We ape the French . . . in their language (which if Jack could speak, he would be a Gentleman). **1670** RAY 108 . . . This was a Proverb, when the gentry brought up their children to speak French. **1713** DYKES Jack will never make a Gentleman . . . In short, every one is not a Gentleman, that is vulgarly call'd so now-a-days. **1721** BAILEY Jack will never make a Gentleman . . . let a Man get never so much Money to buy an Estate, he cannot purchase one grain of GENTILITY with it, but he will discover himself one Time or other, in Point of Behaviour, to be of a mean Extract, awkward, ungenteel, and ungenerous, a Gentleman at Second-hand only, or a vain-glorious Upstart. **1732** FULLER no. 3052.

Jack would be a gentleman if he had money.   (J 5)

1639 CLARKE 98.

Jack would wipe his nose if he had it.

1659 HOWELL *Fr. Prov.* 8b (John).   **1670** RAY 108.

Jack, *see also* Good J. good Jill; Play the J.; Work and no play makes J. dull boy; Yellow J.

Jackal, *see* Lion's provider.

Jacket (coat), To baste (curry, dust etc.) one's.   (J 13)

1553 UDALL *Ralph Roister D.* l. 340 The worst is but a curried cote. **1582** *Love and Fortune* C4 I was bolde to brushe the dust out of your geere. *a.* **1610** *Histriomastix* ed. R. Simpson II. l. 282 The dust out of your coat I intend for to beat. **1639** CLARKE 76 Hee'l curry your coat. **1670** WALKER *Idiom. Ang.-Lat.* 154 I'll dust your coat for you. **1687** T. BROWN *Saints in Uproar*: Wks. i. 84 I'll substantially thrash your Jacket for you.

Jacks¹ are common to all that will play.

1598 JONSON *Ev. Man in Hum.* II. iii. 184 I can compare him to nothing more happely then a Barber's virginals; for euery one may play vpon him. **1611** DAVIES no. 174 [¹ The parts of virginals which twanged the wires; used for the keys of a musical instrument.]

Jackson, *see* Fly up with J.'s hens.

Jade eats as much as a good horse, A.
                                    (J 29)

1640 HERBERT no. 519.

Jade, *see also* Better a lean j.; Spur a j. a question.

James, *see* Friar's beaten (When the), then comes J.; Henry was union of roses, J. of kingdoms.

Janiveer[1] freeze the pot by the fire.
(J 34)

1557 TUSSER D1 As Janeuer fryse pot, bidth corne kepe hym lowe. **1659** HOWELL *Span. Prov.* 21. **1670** RAY 40. [[1] January.]

Janiveer sows oats, Who in | gets gold and groats; who sows in May, gets little that way. (J 35)

1557 TUSSER B4 In January husbandes, that powcheth the grotes: will breake vp their lay, or be sowing of otes. **1573** *Id.* (1878 ed. 75) Who now [January] sowes otes, gets gold and grotes. Who sowes in May gets little that way. **1732** FULLER no. 6149. **1813** RAY 36.

Janiveer's calends be summerly gay, If | 'twill be winterly weather till the calends of May. (J 36)

1686-7 J. AUBREY *Rem. Gent. & Jud.* (1881) 7 There is a proverb in Welsh of great antiquity, sc. Haf hyd gatan Gaiaf hyd Fay. That is, if it be somerly weather till the Kalends of January, it will be winterly weather to the Kalends of May. **1732** FULLER no. 6483. **1893** INWARDS 10.

January chicks, To have.

1813 RAY 202 To have January chicks. [Ital.] *Aver i pulcini di gen[n]aio.* To have children in old age.

January commits the fault, and May bears the blame.

1659 HOWELL *It. Prov.* 14. **1893** INWARDS 11.

January, Janiveer, Janivere, *see also* Eat a hen in J.; Grass look green in J. (If); March in J., J. in March; May and J.

Jardines, *see* Johnstons.

Jaundiced eye, To the | all things look yellow. (A 160)

c. **1386** CHAUCER *Mel.* B[2] 2891 The prophete seith that 'troubled eyen han no cleer sighte'. *c.* **1580** SIDNEY *Arcadia* Wks. IV. 338 Like them that have the yellow jaunders everything seeming yealow unto them. **1612** WEBSTER *White Devil* I. ii Merm. 12 The fault . . . is not in the eyesight. —True; but they that have the yellow jaundice think all objects they look on to be yellow. **1660** W. SECKER *Nonsuch Prof.* II. (1891) 184 Nero thought no person chaste, because he was so unchaste himself. Such as are troubled with the jaundice see all things yellow. **1709** POPE *Ess. Crit.* II. 359 All looks yellow to the jaundic'd eye.

Jaup, *see* Ride fair and j. none.

Jaw (= rush of water), *see* Jouk and let the j. gae by.

Jaws outrun your claws, Don't let your.

1577 W. HARRISON *Description of Eng.* New Sh. S. i. 151 The artificers in cities and good townes . . . some of them doo suffer their iawes to go oft before their clawes. **1917** BRIDGE 50.

Jay(s), *see* Cherry-tree suffices not two j.

Jealous, *see* Love being j.

Jealousy, *see* Frenzy, heresy, and j., seldom cured; Love is never without j.

Jedwood *or* Jeddart[1] justice.

[= trial after execution.] **1605-9** in P. H. BROWN *Hist. Scot.* (1902) ii. 263 In association with the Earl of Dunbar, who in 1606 was appointed chief Commissioner, [Cranstoun] plied his task so effectually that . . . their work is significantly commemorated in the Border phrase 'Jeddart Justice'—hang first and try afterwards. **1706** A. SHIELDS *Eng. Ch. Commun.* Pref. 8 Guilty of Couper Justice and Jedburgh Law as the proverb is. **1828** SCOTT *F. M. Perth* ch. 32 We will have Jedwood justice—hang in haste and try at leisure. **1831** MACAULAY *Essay on Byron's Life* True Jedwood justice was dealt out to him. [[1] Jedburgh.]

Jeering Coggeshall. (C 504)

1662 FULLER *Essex* 321 . . . How much truth herein, I am as unable to tell, as loth to believe. . . . No Town in England, of its bigness, afforded more Martyrs in the raign of queen Mary, who did not jeer or jeast with the fire.

Jenny, *see* Silly Jockey (Never was) but there was as silly J.

Jeopardy, *see* Joy (With all your) join your j.

Jerdans, *see* Johnstons.

Jericho, Go to. (J 39)

[= get away!] **1542** R. MORS [= H. Brinkelow] *Lamentation of a Christian Printed at Jericho in the land of Promes* [Title]. **1545** S. GARDINER to Paget (*Letters* ed. J. A. Muller 1933 159) I bad, soo we might have peace, send me to Jherico . . . howe fondly it cam in to my penne to wryte, 'Send me to Jherico'. **1575** *Appius and Virginia* D1 Haue with ye to Jerico. *a.* **1633** JONSON *Tale Tub* II. iv. 30 An' you say the word, send me to *Ierico.* **1635** HEYWOOD *Hierarch.* iv. 208 Who would . . . I know. Bid such young boyes to stay in Iericho Vntill their Beards were growne, their wits more staid. **1694** *Terence made English* 146 Ay let him be jogging to Jericho for me. **1837-46** BARHAM *Ingol. Leg., Mis. at Margate* (1898) 389 She with her apron wiped the plates, and, as she rubb'd the delf, Said I might 'go to Jericho, and fetch my beer myself!'

Jericho, *see also* Wish one at J.

Jerusalem, *see* Way to Babylon.

Jest not with the eye, or with religion (honour).   (E 242. R 64)

1587 BRIDGES *Defence* 763 It is an old saying, Non est bonum ludere cum sanctis. **1597** BACON *Essays* 'Discourse' (Arber, 16) Some thinges are priuiledged from iest, namely Religion, matters of state, great persons. **1612** T. ADAMS *The Gallant's Burden* (1616, 30) We say, (*Non bonum ludere cum sanctis*) It is no safe iesting with holy thinges. **1616** T. ADAMS *A Divine Herball* 81 A mans name, his faith, and his eye must not be iested withall. *a.* **1628** CARMICHAELL no. 313 Bourde neither with me nor with my honour. **1640** HERBERT no. 157. **1659** TORRIANO no. 205. **1674** RAY *Collection of English Words* 7 Burd neither with me nor with my honour, *Prov. Scot.* **1721** KELLY 64 Bourd[1] not with my Eye, nor with my Honour. Both these are too tender Points to be jested with; and the Honour often more nice than the Eye. [1 jest.]

Jest, If you give (make) a | you must take a jest.

1706 STEVENS s.v. Burlador He that gives a jest must take a jest. **1738** SWIFT *Dial.* I. E.L. 276 I'll give you as good as you bring: what! if you give a jest you must take a jest.

Jest(s), *see also* Back broad enough to bear blame (j.); Better lose a j.; Cream of the j.; Demand is a j., (Where the) . . . ; Dogs begin in j. end in earnest; Joke breaks no bones; Kill another in j.; Leave a j. when pleases; Nose will abide no j.; True word spoken in j.; Truest j. sound worst in guilty ears. *See also* Bourd.

Jesting with edged tools, It is ill. *Cf.* Children and fools must not, etc.   (J 45)

c. **1510** STANBRIDGE *Vulg.* E.E.T.S. 20 It is shrewed to iape with naked swords. *a.* **1568** ASCHAM *Schoolmaster* (Wks. ed. Wright 266) . . . but fine edge tooles in a fole or mad mans hand. **1588** GREENE *Pandosto* Pr. Wks. (1881–3) IV. 293 It is ill iesting with edged tooles, and bad sporting with kinges. **1613** BEAUM. & FL. *Honest M. Fort.* II. i. I do not love to see a sword drawn in the hand of a man that looks so furious, there's no jesting with edge tools. **1623** CAMDEN 272 Its not good iesting with edg'd toolcs. **1642** MILTON *Apol. Smect.* Prose Wks. (1904) iii. 114 That he may know what it is to be a child, and yet to meddle with edged tools, I turn his antistrophon upon his own head. **1662** FULLER *Westmr.* 236 A place . . . by the Exchequer Court commonly called Hell; I could wish it had another name, seeing it is ill jesting with edge-tools, especially such as are sharpened by Scripture. **1721** KELLY 267 No jesting with edg'd Tools. It is no safe jesting with powerful Men, or sacred Things. **1839** DICKENS *N. Nickleby* ch. 47 'Oh dear, what an edged tool you are!' 'Don't play with me then', said Ralph impatiently, 'You know the proverb.' **1860** PEACOCK *Gryll Grange* ch. 19 Science is an edged tool with which men play like children and cut their fingers.

Jesting, *see also* Long j. never good.

Jew, To look like a.   (J 51)

1611 CORYAT *Crudities* (1776) I. 299 Our English prouerbe: To looke like a Iewe (whereby is meant sometimes a weather beaten warp-faced fellow, sometimes a phrenticke and lunaticke person, sometimes one discontented).

Jewel by the casket (cabinet), None can guess the.   (J 55)

a. **1450** *Gesta Romanorum* E.E.T.S. ch. 66 The Emperour late made iij vessels, and þe first was of clene goolde, and full of precious stonys owtewarde, And withinne full of deede bonys; And it had a superscripcion in theise wordis, Thei þat chese me shull fynde in me þat þei seruyd'. The secunde vessel was all of cleene siluer, and full of precious stonys; and outwarde it had þis superscripsion, Thei þat chesith me, shull fynde in me þat nature and kynde desirith. And þe thirde vessell was of leed, And with inne was full of precious stonys, And with oute was sette þis scripture, thei þat chese me shull fynde [in] me þat god hath disposid . . . þe dowter . . . byhelde þe first vessell, . . . and þenne she thowte, what haue I deseruid for to haue so precious a vessel, And þoȝ it be neuer so gay with oute, I not howe fowle it is with Inne; . . . she lokid to þe secunde . . . and . . . saide, ' My nature & kynde askith but dilectacions of þe flessh; . . . she lokid to þe third, . . . and . . . saide 'Sothly, god disposid neuer Ivill; Forsoth þat which god hath disposid woll I take and chese.' **1586** J. CASE *Praise of Music* 29 A precious stone may be set in ledde. **1596** SHAKES. *M.V.* III. ii. [Bassanio, to win Portia, chooses among the caskets of gold, silver, and lead]. **1596** M.B. *Trial of True Friendship* C2 Critius sometimes wil choose a gilden boxe full of bones, before a leaden one ful of pretious gems, for men iudge onely by the outward appearance and protestations of men, and so . . . beleeue subtil Rodeyan because she can tel the smoother tale before simple Cordeill. **1616** ADAMS *Divine Herbal* Third Sermon 95. **1639** FULLER *Holy War* III. iv. 114 (So true it is, none can). **1732** FULLER no. 4606 The Jewel is not to be valued for the Cabinet.

Jew's eye, *see* Worth a J. e.

Jews spend at Easter, The | the Moors at marriages, the Christians in suits.   (J 54)

1640 HERBERT no. 242. **1642** TORRIANO 61 (Christians at law). **1651–3** JER. TAYLOR *Sunday Serm.* xxi. (1850) 585 Is it not a sad thing that . . . it should become a proverb that 'the Jew spends all in his passover, the Moor in his marriage, and the Christian in his lawsuits'? **1659** HOWELL *It. Prov.* 18.

Jew(s), *see also* Invite not a J. to pig; No J., no wooden shoes; Use one like a J.

Jewel, *see also* Black man is pearl (j.) in fair woman's eye; Fair play's a j.; Health is great riches (a j.); Liberty is more worth than gold (a j.); Plain dealing is a j.; Virtue is a j.

Jill, *see* Bad a J. (There is not so); Jack and J.; Jack shall have J.

Joan is as good as my lady in the dark.
(J 57)

[Gk. Λύχνου ἀρθέντος, γυνὴ πᾶσα ἡ αὐτή. ERASM. *Ad. Sublata lucerna nihil interest inter mulieres.* When the light is removed, every woman is the same.] *c.* 1530 *Of Gentleness and Nobility* Cᶦᵛ As good is the foule as the fayre in the dark. 1546 HEYWOOD I. v. B2 The faire and the foule, by darke are lyke store. 1594–5 SHAKES. *L.L.L.* III. i. 195 Some men must love my lady, and some Joan. 1596 *Id. K.J.* I. i. 184 Now can I make any Joan a lady. 1599 A. MUNDAY *Joan as good as my Lady* (play-title, Henslowe's *Diary* ed. Greg i. 102). 1601 A. DENT *Plain Man's Pathway* 59. 1620 SHELTON *Quix.* II. xxxiii. iii. 55 Here is as good bread made as in France; and in the night Joan is as good as my lady. 1648 HERRICK *Hesper.* 865 Wks. (1893) II. 86 Night makes no difference 'twixt the Priest and Clark; *Jone* as my Lady is as good i' th' dark.

Joan, *see also* Darby and J.

Job's comforter, A.
(J 62)

[= a comforter who aggravates distress.] [JOB xvi. 1: Then Job answered . . . miserable comforters are ye all.] 1615 T. ADAMS *England's Sickness* 58 Miserable Comforter (as Jobs friend were iustly called). 1630 BRATHWAIT *Eng. Gent.* (1641) 132 Iob called his friends miserable comforters. 1654 FULLER *Serm., Comfort in Calamity* This *If*, . . . is likely to prove with Job's friend, but a miserable comforter. 1738 SWIFT Dial. III. E.L. 321 Your ladyship looks thinner than when I saw you last.—Your ladyship is one of Job's comforters. 1836 MARRYAT *Midsh. Easy* ch. 29 You are one of Job's comforters, Martin. 1927 18 Dec. D. H. LAWRENCE *Lett.* ii. 1027.

Job, *see also* Patient as J.; Poor as J.

Jock the laird's brother, He is but.

1721 KELLY 139 . . . The Scottish Lairds' Concern and Zeal for the Stᵃnding and Continuance of their Families, mᵃkes the Provision for their younger Sons very small.

Jock's news, That is.

1721 KELLY 339 . . . Spoken when People tell that for News which every body knows.

Jock, *see also* Little J. gets the little dish.

Jockey, *see* Silly J. (Never was) but there was as silly Jenny.

Jogging while your boots are green, Be.
(B 536)

1594–8 SHAKES. *T.S.* III. ii. 207 You may be jogging whiles your boots are green. 1777 C. DIBDIN *Quaker* I. i. You may as well be jogging, Sir, While yet your boots are green.

Jogging, *see also* Plough be j. (If).

John à Cumber, *see* Devil and J.

John-a-dreams (John-a-nods).
(J 64)

[= a dreamy fellow.] 1600 BRETON *Pasquil's Pass* Gros. i. 11a When John a Noddes will be a Gentleman because his worship weares a veluet coate. 1600–1 SHAKES. *H.* II. ii. 561 I . . . peak, Like John-a-dreams, unpregnant of my cause, And can say nothing. 1602 BRETON *Old Madcaps New Gallymaufry* Robertson 116 (John a Nods). 1603 HARSNET *Pop. Impost.* xxiii. 160 Hee would say The Apostle wrote like a good plain Iohn a nods. 1876 HENLEY *Bk. Verses* (1888) 91 Kate-a-Whimsies, John-a-Dreams, Still debating, still delay.

John-a-droyne.
(J 65)

c. 1525 *Hundred Merry Tales* no. 4 One callyd John adroyns. 1562 HEYWOOD *Epig.* no. 88 Yet hogis head in hogstowne is no Iohn a droyne, Pigs dare not quich there, if hogis head hang the groyne. 1596 NASHE *Saffron Walden* iii. 95 That poor Iohn a Droynes his man, . . . a great big-boand thresher.

John-a-nokes and John-a-Stiles.
(J 66)

[Fictitious names for parties in a legal action; hence sometimes used indefinitely for any individual person.] 1531 *Dial. on Laws Eng.* I. vi. 12 If a man be outlawed, and after by his wyll byqueth certayne goodes to Iohn at Style. *Ibid.* II. ix. 19 If a man haue lande for terme of lyfe of Iohan at Noke and make a lease. 1577 STANYHURST in Holinshed *Chron. Ireland* (1587) 100b Such a simple John a Stile . . . no wiser than Patch the late lord cardinall his foole. 1581 SIDNEY *Apol. Poetrie* Arb. 53 Doth the Lawyer lye then, when vnder the names of Iohn a stile and John a noakes [Wks. (1622) 520 Iohn of the Stile, & Iohn of the Nokes] hee puts his case? 1678 MRS. BEHN *Sir Patient Fancy* v. Madam, in plain English I am made a John-A-Nokes of. 1714 *Spectator* no. 577, par. 6 The humble Petition of John a Nokes and John a Stiles, Sheweth, That your Petitioners have had Causes depending in Westminster-Hall above five hundred years. 1815 SCOTT *Guy Man.* ch. 42 Adventurers who are as willing to plead for John o' Nokes as for the first noble of the land.

John Barleycorn.
(J 67)

[= the personified spirit of malt liquor.] *c.* 1620 [Title] in Pepysian Library, A pleasant new ballad . . . of the bloody murther of Sir John Barleycorn. 1670 RAY 59 Sr John *Barley-corn's* the strongest knight. 17. . *John Barleycorn* in PERCY'S *Reliques*, John Barleycorn has got a beard Like any other man. 1786 BURNS *Scotch Drink* iii John Barleycorn, Thou king o' grain.

John (Jack) Blunt.

[= a blunt fellow.] 1508 DUNBAR *Twa mariit wemen* 142 For all the buddis of Iohne Blunt, quhen he abone clymis. 1898 *Daily News* 17 Nov. 5/4 He was at once a Jack Blunt and equal to a trick.

John Bull.

[= Englishmen collectively, or the typical Englishman.] 1712 ARBUTHNOT [Title] Law is a Bottomless Pit. Exemplified in the Case of the Lord Strutt, John Bull, Nicholas Frog and Lewis

Baboon: who spent all they had in a Lawsuit. *a.* 1791 BOSWELL *Johnson* xxx. (1848) 269 [Johnson] was, indeed, if I may be allowed the phrase, at bottom much of a John Bull: much of a blunt true-born Englishman. **1898** G. W. E. RUSSELL *Coll. & Recoll.* ch. 5 The typical John Bull—Lord Palmerston's 'Fat man with a white hat in the twopenny omnibus'. **1910** *T.L.S.* 29 July Our peculiarly English and prosaic idol of John Bull . . . is a creation of the English mind in its grossest mood.

John Company.

[A humorous appellation of the East India Company, taken over from the name *Jan Kompanie*, by which the Dutch E.I.C., and now the Dutch Government, are known to natives in the East.] **1785** tr. *Sparrmann's Voy. Cape G. Hope*, &c. x. II. 21 I ordered my interpreter to say farther, that we were the children of *Jan Company*, who had sent us out to view this country. **1808** *Life Ld. Minto in India* (1880) 184 (Y.) Preparations to save Johnny Company's cash. **1893** W. C. RUSSELL *Emigr. Ship* ch. 3 One of the handsomest of John Company's ships. **1910** *Times Wkly.* 21 Jan. Great Moguls who sat on the peacock throne at Delhi . . ., till the Mutiny ended them and 'John Company' together.

John Doe and Richard Roe.

[John Doe (*Eng. Law*), the name given to the fictitious lessee of the plaintiff, in the (now obsolete) mixed action of ejectment, the fictitious defendant being called *Richard Roe*.] **1768** BLACKSTONE *Comm.* III. xviii. 274 The security here spoken of . . . is at present become a mere form: and John Doe and Richard Roe are always returned as the standing pledges for this purpose. **1790** BURKE *Reflections on the Fr. Rev.* E.L. 227 The patriotic donations were to make good the failure of the patriotic contribution. John Doe was to become security for Richard Roe. **1841** S. WARREN *Ten Thous. a Year* ch. 8 John Doe further says that one Richard Roe (who calls himself—'a Casual Ejector') came and turned him out, and so John Doe brings his action against Richard Roe.

John Drawlatch.   (J 68)

[= thief, loafer, ne'er-do-well.] **1543** G. COUSIN *Office of Servants* B2ᵛ In Hecyra [Terence] faigneth Parmeno slaue vnto Pamphilus to be somdeale geuin to vices, and a verye drawlatche. **1546** HEYWOOD II. viii. K2ᵛ Why will ye (quoth he) I shall folowe hir will? To make me Iohn drawlache, or such a snekebill.¹ [¹ *sneakbill*, a word of contempt.]

John Grey's bird.   (J 69)

c. 1575 GASCOIGNE i. 167 The Greene knight was amongst the rest Like John Greyes birde that ventred with the best.

John (Tom) Long the carrier.   (J 71)

c. 1549 HEYWOOD I. xi. D3ᵛ I will send it him by John Long the carrier. **1602** WITHALS 4 (Tom Long). *c.* 1654 HOWELL *Lett.* 5 June (1903) III. 116 That yours should be a whole month in making scarce 100 English miles . . . is strange to me, unless you purposely sent it by John Long

the carrier. **1834–7** SOUTHEY *Doctor* iv. 136 Who was Tom Long the carrier? . . . what road did he travel?

John o'Groats, *see* Land's End to J. o' G.

John Roper's window, To look in at.

1552 HULOET 2C3ᵛ s.v. Roper. Schœnoplocos, Restio is he that loketh in at John ropers window by translation, he that hangeth him selfe.

John¹ Thomson's man.   (J 73)

[= a man who is guided by his wife.] **1500–20** DUNBAR *Poems* lxii. 4 God gif ȝe war Johne Thomsounis man. **1637** R. MONRO *Exp. Scots Regim.* II. 30 Some will allege, he was Iohn Thomsons man. . . . All stories esteeme them happie, that can live together, man and wife, without contention. **1681** S. COLVIL *Whiggs Supp.* I. 18 So the imperious Roxalan, made the Great Turk John Thomson's man. **1721** KELLY 72 Better be John Tomson's man, than Ring and Dinn's, or John Knox's. John Thomson's Man is he that is complaisant to his Wife's Humours, Ring and Dinn's is he whom his Wife scolds, John Knox's is he whom his Wife beats. **1816** SCOTT *Old Mort.* ch. 38 D'ye think I am to be John Tamson's man, and maistered by women a' the days o' my life? [¹ Joan.]

John Trot.

[= an uncultured person, bumpkin.] **1753** FOOTE *Eng. in Paris* Epil. The merest John Trot in a week you shall zee *Bien poli, bien frizé*. **1762** COLMAN *Mus. Lady* II. i. Our travelling gentry . . . return from the tour of Europe as mere English boors as they went—John Trot still. **1827** HOOD *John Trot* (Ballad) John Trot he was as tall a lad As York did ever rear.

Johnny Newcome.

1837 CHAMIER *Saucy Areth.* ch. 15 You always know a Johnny Newcome by his getting his back to the breeze.

Johnny Raw.

1813 COL. HAWKER *Diary* (1893) I. 68 A grand attack was made on the Johnny raws of Blandford. **1823** in HONE *Every-day Bk.* II. 1395. There were some Johnny Raws on board. **1886** STEVENSON *Kidnapped* (1888) 39 You took me for a country Johnnie Raw, with no more mother-wit or courage than a porridge-stick.

Johnson, *see* Venture it, as J. did his wife.

Johnstons, We are as many | as you are Jerdans (Jardines).

1721 KELLY 347 . . . Taken from two Families who were always on one side; though now the Proverb signifies that we have as many to take our Part, as you have to take yours, yet I am inclined to believe that at first it signified that we contribute as much to the common Cause as you do. **1832** HENDERSON 140 There's as mony Johnstones as Jardines. (As many on one side as on the other.)

Joint, To be out of. (J 75)

c. 1516 SKELTON *Magn.* l. 2414 Specyally to redresse that were out of ioynte. *c.* 1565 *Bugbears* III. iii. 76 Though it be out of Ioynt yet . . . I will bryng a redy answere. 1600–1 SHAKES. *H.* I. v. 189 The time is out of joint. 1611 DONNE *First Anniv.* l. 191 So is the worlds whole frame Quite out of joynt, almost created lame.

Joint, *see also* Nose out of j.

Joint-stool, *see* Cry you mercy, I took you for j.

Joke breaks no bones, A.

1781 JOHNSON in Boswell *Life* (Hill) iv. 129 (jest). 1819 BYRON *Letters* Prothero iv. 466. A joke, the proverb says, breaks no bones; but it may break a bookseller.

Jollity but has a smack of folly, There is no. (J 76)

1616 DRAXE no. 758 Neuer was there great spirit without some mixture of folly. 1640 HERBERT no. 493.

Jolly, *see* Over j. dow not.

Jolly Robins, *see* Head's running upon J. R.

Jouk[1] and let the jaw[2] gae (gang) by.

1721 KELLY 189 Juck, and let a jaw go o'er you. That is, prudently yield to a present Torrent. 1818 SCOTT *Rob Roy* ch. 25 Gang your ways hame, like a gude bairn—jouk[1] and let the jaw[2] gae by. [[1] stoop. [2] rush of water.]

Journey(s), *see* Begin a j. on Sunday; Great j. to world's end; Little j. . . . bring safe home; Long j. (In a) straw weighs; Prayers and provender hinder no j.; Sports and j. men are known (In); World is long j.

Jove (Jupiter) laughs at lovers' perjuries. (J 82)

[TIBULLUS 3. 6. 49 *Periuria ridet amantum Jupiter.* OVID *A.A.* l. 633 *Jupiter ex alto periuria ridet amantum.*] *c.* 1565 *Bugbears* III. iv. 31 I have hard that god on hye doth lawgh when lovers breake there vowes. 1567 *Lady Lucres* in *Plasidas,* etc. Roxb. Cl. 143 Jupiter rather laughethe then takethe angerlye the periurynge of louers. 1580 GREENE *Mamillia* in Wks. Gros. ii. 92 Dooe not the Gods, saye the Poets, laugh at the periurie of Louers? and that Iupiter smyles at the crafte of Cupyd. *c.* 1595 SHAKES. *R.J.* II. ii. 92 At lovers' perjuries, They say Jove laughs. 1621 BURTON *Anat.* 3. 2. 2. 4, (1638 ed. 492) When Louers sweare, Venus laughes . . . And Iuppiter smiles. 1700 DRYDEN *Pal. & Arcite* II. 140 And Jove but laughs at lovers' perjury!

Jowl, *see* Cheek by cheek (j.).

Joy, With all your | join all your jeopardy.

1546 HEYWOOD II. xi. L4ᵛ.

Joy of the heart makes the face fair, The. (J 84)

1573 SANFORD 101ᵛ The merynesse of the heart, causeth a fayre colour in the face. 1578 FLORIO *First F.* 27ᵛ The gladnes of the hart, causeth a faire colour in the face. 1586 GUAZZO ii. 162 Wee women commonlie saie, that a merrie heart makes a faire face, and a good complexion. 1601 T. WRIGHT *The Passions of the Mind* 50 According to the old prouerb, *Cor gaudens exhilerat faciem,* a rejoycing heart maketh merry the face. 1611 DAVIES no. 224 The ioy of the heart coulors the face. 1629 *Bk. Mer. Rid.* Prov. no. 54 The heart's mirth doth make the face fayre. 1616 DRAXE no. 1395 (merry).

Joy without annoy (alloy), No. (J 85)

[L. *Extrema gaudii luctus occupat.* Grief borders on the extremes of gladness.] *c.* 1386 CHAUCER *Nun's Priest's T.* B² l. 3205 For evere the latter ende of joye is wo. 1565 J. HALL *Court of Virtue* Q1ᵛ No Ioy without some care. 1592 DELAMOTHE 1 After a little ioye, we feele the greater annoy. 1616 WITHALS 575 Your inconstant ioy, preports annoy. 1639 CLARKE 134.

Joy(s), *see also* God send you j.; Hunting, hawking . . . for one j. hundred displeasures; One year of j.; Sorrow (Of thy) be not . . . of thy j. be not too glad; Sudden j. kills sooner than excessive grief; Weep for j. is kind of manna.

Judas kiss, A. (J 92)

[LUKE xxii. 48 Jesus 'said unto him, Judas, betrayest thou the Son of man with a kiss?] *c.* 1523 BARCLAY *Mirr. Good Manners* 75 Of a flattering foo to haue a Iudas kisse. *c.* 1548 BALE *K. Johan* l. 2109 A false Judas kysse he hath gyven and is gone. 1599 SHAKES. *A.Y.* III. iv. 8 Marry, his kisses are Judas's own children. 1618 J. FLETCHER *Loy. Subj.* IV. vi. The Judas way, to kiss me, bid me welcome, And cut my throat. 1865 DICKENS *Our Mut. Fr.* iii, ch. 5 Sophronia . . . found it necessary to . . . give Bella a kiss. A Judas order of kiss.

Judas might have repented before he could have found a tree to have hanged himself upon, had he betrayed Christ in Scotland. (J 91)

1659 HOWELL *Eng. Prov.* 21a.

Judge but himself, He who will have no | condemns himself.

1707 MAPLETOFT 12.

Judge conceives quickly, judges slowly, A good. (J 95)

c. 1386 CHAUCER *Mel.* B² l. 2221 And eek men seyn that thilke juge is wys that soone understandeth a matiere and juggeth by leyser. 1640 HERBERT no. 599.

Judge, from a foolish | a quick sentence. (J 94)

1573 GASCOIGNE *Flowers* i. 88 The sentence sone is sayde, when will it selfe is Judge. 1578

Courtly Controv. 2B2ᵛ From a foolishe iudge proceedeth shorte sentence. **1592** DELAMOTHE 9 (rash sentence). **1659** HOWELL *Span. Prov.* 11 (short sentence).

Judge from appearances, Never.

(A 285)

1526 TYNDALE *John* vii. 24 Judge not after the vtter aperaunce, but iudge rightewes iudgement. **1890** MONTAGU WILLIAMS *Leaves of a L.* xx. (1893) 144 Little did the audience know what subsequently transpired as to her character. . . . She wore . . . every appearance of innocence, but in her person she illustrated the truth of the old adage that one should not judge by appearances. **1896** J. C. HUTCHESON *Crown & Anchor* ch. 15 I learnt . . . not to judge by appearances and from hasty conclusions as to the character of my messmates.

Judge in his own cause, No man ought to be.

(M 341)

1528 TYNDALE *Obed. Chrn. Man* P.S. 241 No man is a right judge in his own cause. **1578** *Courtly Controv.* N1ᵛ Bycause (you men) are in this place Iudges in your own cause, suffer not your selues to be surmounted by particular affection. **1592-3** SHAKES. *V. & A.* l. 220 Being judge in love, she cannot right her cause. **1604** *Id. M.M.* V. i. 166 Be you judge Of your own cause. **1639** CLARKE 180 No man must be his own judge. **1775** J. WESLEY *Lett.* vi. 186 No man is a good judge in his own cause. **1845** H. BROOM *Legal Maxims* 418 It is unreasonable, that, if wrong be done to a man, he should be his own judge thereof, according to the maxim, *nemo debet esse judex in propriâ causâ.* **1928** *Times,* 22 Aug. 9/4 The principle that no judge could be a judge in his own cause was generally accepted. The chairman of a meeting was in a quasi-judicial capacity.

Judge knows nothing unless it has been explained to him three times, A.

1962 *Times* 12 May 12/3 [The Lord Chief Justice] (It is always said that).

Judge not, that ye be not judged.

[MATT. vii. 1 Judge not, that ye be not judged.] **1481** CAXTON *Reynard* ed. Arber 73 Deme ye noman, and ye shal not be demed. **1925** A. CLUTTON-BROCK *Ess. on Life* x. 109 The saying, 'Judge not, that ye be not judged', is . . . a statement of fact. Nothing makes us dislike a man so much as the knowledge that he is always judging us and all men.

Judgement as he runs, He that passes | overtakes repentance.

(J 97)

1539 TAVERNER *Publius* A6 He hasteneth to repente him selfe whiche iudgeth lyghtly. Be not to quicke in iudgement. Of heady sentence gyuing, oftentymes foloweth repentaunce. **1666** TORRIANO *It. Prov.* 105 no. 27 Who suddenly will judge, hastens himself to repentance. **1732** FULLER no. 2244.

Judgement, *see* Actions are our security (Our own) not others' j.; Good j. that relies not on his own.

Judges' wigs.

1823 COBBETT *Rural Rides* 2 Aug. I saw . . . several parcels of those white, curled clouds that we call *Judges' Wigs.*

Judge(s), *see also* Father is j. (He whose) goes safe to trial; Put off the person of a j.; Sober (grave) as a j.

Judicare came into the creed, To know how.

(J 98)

c. **1350** *Speculum* ed. Utley xxi. 196 Now wot I qwou judicare was set in the crede. **1546** HEYWOOD I. viii. C4. **1611** DAVIES *Prov.* no. 410.

Juice, *see* Fry (Stew) in their own grease (j.); Orange hard squeezed yields bitter j.

July, *see* Bathes in May; First of J. it be rainy (If); No tempest, good J.; Shower in J. . . . worth plow of oxen.

Jump[1] (*or* Just) as German's lips, As.

(G 87)

1546 HEYWOOD II. ii. F4ᵛ The hen (quoth she) the cock (quoth he) iust (quoth she) As Iermans lips. **1549** J. PROCTOUR *Fall of the late Arian* O6ᵛ (iuste). **1551** WILSON *Rule of Reason* G5 [The argument] hangeth together like germaines lyppes as we vse to saye. **1579** GOSSON *Sch. Abuse* Arb. 27 Shall see them agree like Dogges and Cattes, and meete as iump as Germans lippes. *a.* **1584** D. FENNER *Counter-Poison* (quotᵃ) 58 They . . . come iust as nere the text as Iarmans lips are said to come together. **1587** J. BRIDGES *Def. of Gov. of C. of E.* 534 These things hang together like Germaines lippes. **1659** HOWELL *Eng. Prov.* 3a As just as Jerman's lipps; *spoken in Derision.* [[1] exactly (here used in sarcasm).]

Jump (*or* leap) at it like a cock at a gooseberry (blackberry), To.

(C 489)

1670 RAY 209 . . . at a black-berry. Spoken of one that endeavours, but can do no harm. **1813** SCOTT *Let. to Southey* 4 Sept. in LOCKHART *Life* ch. 26 I . . . beg you think before you reject the offer . . . I should have jumped at it like a cock at a gooseberry. **1824** *Id. St. Ronan's* ch. 2 He just jumped at the ready penny, like a cock at a grosert.[1] **1836** M. SCOTT *Cruise of Midge* ch. 8 Ancient maidens, who at forty loup like a cock at a grousart[1] . . . at the *homo* they turned up their noses at twenty. [[1] gooseberry.]

Jump(s), *see also* Broomstick (To j. the); Cat j., (To see which way).

June, *see* Bathes in May; Calm weather in J. sets corn in tune; Dry May and dripping J.; Eighth of J. it rain (If) foretells wet harvest.

Jupiter has loved, Few there be whom just. (F 198)

1550 *A notable and marvellous epistle* C3. **1601** JONSON *Cynthia's Revels* V. i. 37 Did it not liue vnblemisht in some few, Whom equall Ioue hath lou'd. **1616** *Id. Ev. Man in Hum.* III. i. 21 Oh, Mr. Matthew, that's a grace peculiar but few; quos aequus amauit Ivpiter.

Jupiter, *see* Far from J. far from thunder.

Jury, *see* Fox should not be of j.; London j. hang half, save half.

Just as a square, As.

[= as exact as a measuring-square.] *c.* **1386** CHAUCER *Sum. T.* l. 2090 Thou shalt me fynde as just as is a squyre.

Just before you are generous, Be.

1777 SHERIDAN *Sch. for Scandal* IV. i. 'Be just before you're generous'.—Why, so I would if I could. **1833** MARRYAT *P. Simple* ch. 11 I owe every farthing of my money. . . . There's an old proverb—be just before you're generous. **1908** *Spectator* 4 Apr. A likeable man is tempted to be generous before he is just.

Just war is better than an unjust peace, A. (P 154)

[TAC. *Ann. Miseram pacem vel bello bene mutari.* For the opposite see CIC. *ad Fam.* 6. 6. 5 *Vel iniquissimam pacem iustissimo bello antiferrem.*] **1545** S. GARDINER to Paget (*Lett.* ed. Muller 189) The sentence of oon that said the worst peace is better thenne the best warre. **1555** *Instit. Gentlem.* E7ᵛ I allow (sayeth he [Tully]) an vnjuste peace to bee better than a moste rightefull warre. **1595** DANIEL *Civ. Wars* I. 73 Since wise men ever have preferred farre Th' unjustest peace before the justest warre. **1605** DANIEL *Ulys. & Siren* For oft we see a wicked peace To be well chang'd for war. **1629** T. ADAMS *Serm.* (1862) II. 87 There is enough in every man to keep him from idleness; if at least he do not prefer an unjust peace to a just war.

Justice pleases few in their own house. (J 107)

1640 HERBERT no. 396.

Justice, *see also* Basket-justice will do j.; Buys an office must sell j.; Clerk makes the j.; Jedwood j.; Mercy surpasses j.; Much law little j.; Poetical j.

K

Ka me, ka thee. (K 1)

[= implies mutual help, or mutual flattery.] *c.* **1549** HEYWOOD I. xi. E2ᵛ Ka me ka the, one good tourne askth an other. **1565** J. HALL *Court of Virtue* T4ᵛ Ca me ca thee. **1603** MONTAIGNE (Florio) III. v. 139 Nature stood ever on this point, Kae mee Ile kae thee. *c.* **1608** D. BARRY *Ram Alley* Hazl.-Dods. X. 335 Ka me, ka thee; one thing must rub another. **1608** ARMIN *Nest Nin.* Shak. Soc. 34 Kay me I'll kay thee; give me an inch to-day I'll give thee an ell to-morrow. *a.* **1658** FORD, &c. *Witch Edmonton* II. i If you'll be so kind to ka me one good turn, I'll be so courteous to kob you another. **1721** KELLY 227 Kae me, and I'll kae thee. Spoken when great People invite and feast one another, and neglect the Poor. **1821** SCOTT *Kenilw.* ch. 5 Bear this in upon her . . . and let me alone for extolling you in her ear . . . *Ka me, ka thee.* **1823** BYRON *Juan* XI. lxxviii. Caw me, caw thee.

Kae, *see* Woe worth ill company, quoth the k.

Kail spares bread. (K 5)

a. **1528** CARMICHAELL no. 1006. **1641** FERGUSSON no. 557. **1721** KELLY 227 *Kail hains¹ bread.* Good Broth will, in some measure, supply the want of Bread. [¹ saves.]

Kail through the reek, To give one his.

[= to let a person 'have it'.] **1757** SMOLLETT *Reprisal* II. i. Guid faith! you and I man ha' our

kail through the reek. **1816** SCOTT *Old Mort.* ch. 14 When my mither and him forgathered they set till the sodgers, and I think they gae them their kale through the reek! **1836** M. SCOTT *Cruise of Midge* ch. 11 Was it not a proud thing for a parritch-fed laddie . . . to gie them their kail through the reek, and cry 'anathema marantha' against the vices of the rich.

Kail, *see also* Good k. is half a meal; Learn your goodam to make milk k.; Plaints early that plaints on k.; Steal not my k.; Sup k. with him (He would not).

Kalends, *see* Calends.

Keep a calm sough.

[= say little or nothing.] **1820** SCOTT *Abbot* ch. 17 Keep a calm sough, as the Scots say— hear every man's counsel, and keep your own. **1823** J. GALT *Entail* ch. 20 I'll keep a calm sough—least said's soonest mendit—I'll haud my tongue. **1880** MRS. LYNN LINTON *Rebel Family* ch. 13 Keeping a calm sough was the best wisdom.

Keep a dog and bark myself, I will not. (D 482)

1583 MELBANCKE Q2ᵛ It is smal reason you should kepe a dog, and barke your selfe. **1670** RAY 81 . . . That is, must I keep servants, and do my work myself. **1721** KELLY 203 . . . If I keep

servants, they shall do my work for me. **1738**
SWIFT *Dial.* I. E.L. 264 Good miss, stir the
fire. . . . —Indeed, your ladyship could have
stirred it much better. — . . . I won't keep a dog
and bark myself.

Keep (bear) a low sail, To.

1557 EDGEWORTH *Serm.* 4G4 All for to geue vs
example to kepe a low saile. **1578** *Courtly
Controv.* 2F3ᵛ A poore disinherited Princesse
. . . I beare so lowe a sayle. **1579** GOSSON *Sch.
Abuse* Arb. 24 I will beare a lowe sayle, and
rowe neere the shore. **1605** HEYWOOD *If it be
not good* l. 59 When our state did beare the
lowest saile.

Keep a man out of the mud, The way to | is to black his boots.

1909 M. LOANE *An Englishman's Cas.* ch. 7
Mothers firmly believe in the old saying, 'The
way to keep a man out of the mud is to black
his boots', and always dress their sons as well as
they possibly can.

Keep a penny, Who will not | never shall have many.   (P 213)

1541 BULLINGER *Chr. State Matr.* tr. Coverdale
64ᵛ Who so spareth not the penye shall neuer
come by the pownde. *c.* **1625** *Pepys Bal.* 51, ii.
33 For such as haue no care, a penny for to
keepe: Shall neuer be worth a pound. **1639**
CLARKE 129.

Keep a thing seven years and you will find a use for it. *Cf.* Lay things by.
(T 141)

1541 BULLINGER *Chr. State Matr.* tr. Coverdale
1543 ed. L4ᵛ Lette it not be lost, that maye do
any good in tyme to come. **1623** PAINTER C5
Things of small value the old proverb say, Wise
men seuen yeares will carefully vp lay. **1642**
TORRIANO 75 Lay up thy goods in a corner,
there will be a time, they will be usefull. **1663**
KILLIGREW *Parson's Wedding* II. vii. According to
the Proverb; Keep a thing seven years, and then
if thou hast no use on't throw't away. **1826**
SCOTT *Woodst.* ch. 28 Two lines of Horace,
which I have carried in my thick head several
years, . . . have come pat to my purpose. . . . If
you keep a thing seven years you are sure to
find a use for it at last. **1863** C. READE *Hard
Cash* ch. 29 It is the very thing . . . I . . . put it
away, and forgot it. They say if you keep a
thing seven years.

Keep Bayard¹ in the stable, To.
(B 111)

c. **1400** *Beryn* E.E.T.S. l. 3183 Ful trewe is that
byword, 'a man to seruesabill, Ledith offt[e]
beyard [Bayard] from his owne stabill'. **1546**
HEYWOOD I. xii. E4ᵛ Their landlorde came to
theyr howse to take a stresse For rent, to haue
kept bayard in the stable. **1623** CAMDEN 273.
[¹ a (bay) horse.]

Keep counsel, Three (Two) may | if two (one) be away.   (T 257)

c. **1400** *Rom. Rose* 2529 For tweyne of noumbre
is bet than thre In every counsell and secre.

c. **1530** HENRY VIII (Cavendish *Life of Wolsey*
ed. Singer 1827, 394. 399) Three may keep
counsel if two be away. **1546** HEYWOOD II. v. G4ᵛ
We twayne are one to many (quoth I) for men
saie, Three maie keepe a counsell, if two be
awaie. *c.* **1558** W. WEDLOCKE *Image of Idleness*
(1574) F1ᵛ The common Prouerb . . . two may
chaunce to keep councel but the third neuer.
1578 WHETSTONE *Promos & Cassandra* E3ᵛ.
1579 LYLY *Euph.* i. 213 I wold haue swalowed
mine own sorrow in silence, knowing . . . that
two may keep counsel if one be away. **1592**
SHAKES. *T.And.* IV. ii. 144 Two may keep
counsel when the third's away. *c.* **1595** *Id. R.J.* II.
iv. 190 Is your man secret? Did you ne'er hear
say, Two may keep counsel, putting one away?
1640 HERBERT no. 714 Three can hold their
peace if two be away. **1670** RAY 148 . . . The
French say, Secret de Deux secret de Dieu,
secret de trois secret de tous.

Keep good men company, and you shall be of the number.   (M 535)

1477 RIVERS *Dictes* (1877) 26 Acompanye the
with good people, and thou shalt be on of hem.
1553 T. WILSON *Rhet.* 5 According to the
Prouerbe by companying with the wise, a man
shall learne wisedome. **1620** SHELTON *Quix.*
II. xxxii. iii. 41 Keep company with good men,
and thou shalt be as good as they. **1640**
HERBERT no. 120. **1694** BOYER 108 Keep
honest Company, and honest thou shalt be.

Keep Hilary term, To.   (H 461)

[= to be cheerful or merry.] **1629** T. ADAMS
Serm. (1861–2) I. 68 This joy . . . overcomes the
world, nonsuits the devil, and makes a man
keep Hilary-term all his life.

Keep my mind to myself, and tell my tale to the wind, I will.

1721 KELLY 182 . . . I will . . . conceal my Resentments; but I will watch an Opportunity for
Retaliation.

Keep no more cats than will catch mice, I will.   (C 183)

1673 DARE *Counsellor Manners* 84 (kill Mice).
1678 RAY (*Somerset*) 350 . . . (*i.e.* no more in
family then will earn their living). **1861** READE
Cloist. & Hearth ch. 52 Now, Martin, you
must help. I'll no more cats than can slay mice.
1898 F. T. BULLEN '*Cachalot*' 25 In the ordinary
merchantman there are decidedly 'no more
cats than can catch mice'.

Keep not ill men company, lest you increase the number.   (M 536)

1581 GUAZZO i. 44 According to the proverbe,
A friend of fooles wil become like unto them.
1598 SHAKES. *2 Hen. IV* V. i. 72 It is a wonderful
thing to see the semblable coherence of his
men's spirits and his. They, by observing of
him, do bear themselves like foolish justices; he,
by conversing with them, is turned into a justice-
like servingman. **1640** HERBERT no. 314. **1659**
HOWELL *Span. Prov.* 18 (Keep not ill company).

Keep off and give fair words.

1756 WESLEY *Lett.* iii. 175 Will you leap into the
fire with your eyes open? Keep off. What else

have you to do? **1818** SCOTT *Rob Roy* ch. 26 He tried if Mac Vittie and Co. wad gie him siller on them—but . . . they keepit aff, and gae fair words.

Keep one head for the reckoning, It is good to. (H 260)

1573 *New Custom* Hazl.-Dods. iii. 43 But, as the proverb saith, it is good to keep still One head for the reckoning, both sober and wise.

Keep one's head above water, To.

[= to avoid ruin by a continued struggle.] **1742** FIELDING *J. Andrews* III. xiii If I can hold my head above water it is all I can. **1809** MALKIN *Gil Blas* v. i, par. 7 To carry me discreetly through the world, and keep my head above water. **1860** SURTEES *Plain or Ring?* ch. 39 I'm . . . just able by the greatest caution and prudence to keep my head above water and no more.

Keep one's own counsel, To. *Cf.* Counsel thou would'st have. (C 694)

1598–9 SHAKES. *M.A.* III. iii. 80 Keep your fellows' counsels and your own. **1600–1** *Id. H.* IV. ii. 9 That I can keep your counsel and not mine own. **1639** CLARKE 67 Keep counsell first thy selfe. **1711** ADDISON *Spect.* No. 12, par. 1 I am the best Man in the World to keep my own Counsel. **1855** MACAULAY *Hist. Eng.* IV. 584 William kept his own counsel so well that not a hint of his intention got abroad.

Keep one's tongue within one's teeth, To. (T 392)

a. **1561** *Deceit of Women* H4[v] Alas what haue I doone, for it is not wel now, but yf I had kept my tethe before my tongue: than had I done wel. **1660** TATHAM *Rump.* I. i (1879) 212 You know, my lord, I can keep my tongue within my teeth sometimes. **1721** KELLY 225.

Keep sheep by moonlight, To.

[= to be hanged in chains.] **1898** A. E. HOUSMAN *Shropsh. Lad* ix [Lads] That shepherded the moonlit sheep A hundred years ago.

Keep some till furthermore come. (K 11)

1639 CLARKE 129. **1670** RAY 110.

Keep something for the sore foot.

1721 KELLY 226 . . . Preserve something for Age, Distress, and Necessity. **1830** CARLETON *Traits &c., Three Tasks* Jack would feel a little consarn for not being able to lay past anything for the *sore foot.*

Keep the keepers? Who shall. (K 13)

[JUVENAL *Sat.* 6. 347 *Quis custodiet ipsos custodes?*] *c.* **1550** POPE PIUS II, *Goodly History of the Lady Lucres* (1560) D2 (cited in E.E.T.S. ed. of Boorde's *Introduction*, 342) In vayne doth the husband set kepers ouer her; for who shal kepe those kepers? **1567** *Plasidas, &c.* Roxb.

Cl. 132 (as 1550). **1611** JONSON *Catiline* III. i. 108 And watch the watcher. **1732** FULLER no. 5718 Who shall keep the keepers?

Keep the pot boiling. *Cf.* Fair words will not make . . .: Money makes the pot boil.

1825 BROCKETT *N. C. Gloss., Keep-the-pot-boiling,* a common expression among young people, when they are anxious to carry on their gambols with spirit. **1837** DICKENS *Pickwick* ch. 30 Mr. Pickwick . . . went slowly and gravely down the slide . . . 'Keep the pot a bilin', sir!' said Sam.

Keep the staff in your own hand.

1710 PALMER 27. **1737** RAMSAY ch. 21, no. 15.

Keep the wolf from the door, To. (W 605)

[= to avert starvation.] *a.* **1529** SKELTON *Col. Cloute* 152–5 Lyke Aaron and Ure,[1] The wolfe from the dore To werryn[2] and to kepe From theyr goostly shepe. **1546** HEYWOOD II. vii. J4[v] I wold haue ye stur Honestly, to kepe the wulfe from the dur. **1645** HOWELL *Lett.* 28 Apr. (1903) I. 99 *He or she* should have wherewith to support both, . . . at least to keep the wolf from the door, otherwise it were madness to marry. **1885** J. ORMSBY *Don Quixote* I Introd. 30 [Cervantes] married . . . a lady . . . who brought him a fortune which may possibly have served to keep the wolf from the door, but if so, that was all. **1915** 12 Feb. D. H. LAWRENCE to B. Russell *Lett.* i. 317 No man amongst us . . . shall have any fear of the wolf at the door, for all wolves are dead. [[1] Hur. [2] guard.]

Keep your ain fish-guts to your ain sea-maws.[1]

1721 KELLY 118 Give your own sea maws your own fish guts. If you have any Superfluities give them to your poor Relations, Friends, or Countrymen, rather than to others. **1816** SCOTT *Antiq.* ch. 15 My gude man likes to ride the expresses himsell: we maun gie our ain fish-guts to our ain sea-maws. It's a red half-guinea to him every time he munts his mear. **1857** DEAN RAMSAY *Remin.* v (1911) 197 . . . This was a favourite proverb with Scott when he meant to express the policy of first considering the interests that are nearest home. [[1] gulls.]

Keep (Save) your breath (wind) to cool your broth (porridge). (W 422)

1580 MUNDAY *Zelauto* T2. **1581** BELL *Agst. Osorius* 483 But you come to late gentle Symon with these fables and bables: and may keepe your breath to keale your potage. **1599** PORTER *Angry Wom. Abingd.* ll. 917–19. You may speake when ye are spoken to, and keepe your winde to coole your pottage. **1605** CHAPMAN, JONSON, MARSTON *Eastw. Ho* III. ii My speeches were ever in vain . . .; and therefore, . . . I will save my breath for my broth anon. **1721** KELLY 229 (brose). Spoken to them who talk much to little purpose. **1738** SWIFT *Dial.* I. E.L. 275. **1796** EDGEWORTH *Par. Asst.* (1903) 262 None of your flummery stuff will go down with his worship . . .; so you may . . . spare your

breath to cool your porridge. **1813** J. AUSTEN
Pride & Prej. ch. 6 There is a very fine old
saying, . . . 'Keep your breath to cool your
porridge', and I shall keep mine to swell my
song. **1816** SCOTT *Old Mort*. ch. 35 Hold
your peace and keep your ain breath to cool
your ain porridge.

Keep your eyes wide open before marriage, and half shut afterwards.

1738 FRANKLIN June.

Keep your feet dry, and your head hot; and for the rest live like a beast. *Cf.* Dry feet: Head and feet.   (F 579)

1603 MONTAIGNE (Florio) II. xii. 242 This common saying is always in the people's mouth:
*Tenez chauds les pieds et la teste, Au demeurant
vivez en beste*. (With marginal gloss: JOUBERT
Err. Pop. [1570] pur. ii. pag. 140 Keepe warme
(t'is meete) thy head and feete: In all the rest,
live like a beast). **1642** TORRIANO 12 (eat like a
beast). **1659** HOWELL *It. Prov*. 15 . . . *viz.*
temperately. **1678** RAY 42.

Keep your mouth shut and your eyes (ears) open.

1581 GUAZZO i. 120 Keepe the mouth more
shut, and the eares more open. **1710** PALMER
143. **1737** RAMSAY III. 188 Keep your mouth
close an' your een open.

Keep your pecker[1] up.

1853 'C. BEDE' *Verdant Green* I. xii. Keep your
pecker up. **1857** DICKENS *Lett*. 17 Aug. Keep
your pecker up with that. **1927** 28 May D. H.
LAWRENCE *Lett*. ii. 980 One must keep one's
pecker up. You've never fought enough. I,
perhaps, too much. [[1] courage, resolution.]

Keep your shop and your shop will keep you.   (S 392)

1605 CHAPMAN, JONSON, MARSTON *Eastw. Ho* I. i. I
. . . garnished my shop . . . with thrifty sentences;
as, 'Touch-stone, keep thy shop, and thy shop will
keep thee'. **1712** *Spectator* 14 Oct. [He, Sir W.
Turner] would say, *Keep your Shop, and your
Shop will keep you*. **1759** GOLDSMITH *Bee* vii
I would earnestly recommend this adage to
every mechanic in London, 'Keep your shop,
and your shop will keep you'. **1823** 9 Jan.
C. LAMB to B. Barton *Lett*. Keep to your Bank,
and the Bank will keep you. **1831** MACAULAY
Ess., Boswell's Johnson Richardson, like a man
of sense, kept his shop; and his shop kept him.

Keep your thanks to feed your chickens (cat).   (T 96)

1681 ROBERTSON 784. **1709** DYKES Pref. iii Let
'em keep their Thanks to feed their Chickens.
1862 HISLOP 176 Tak your thanks to feed your
cat.

Keep your weather-eye open.

1851 MELVILLE *Moby Dick* (1922) I. 197. **1867**
ADML. SMYTH *Sailor's Word-Bk*. 724 'Keep your
weather-eye open', be on your guard; look
out for squalls.

Keep yourself from the anger of a great man, from the tumult of a mob, from a man of ill fame, from a widow that has been thrice married, from a wind that comes in at a hole, and from a reconciled enemy.

1707 MAPLETOFT 67.

Keeps another man's dog, He that | shall have nothing left him but the line.   (M 454)

1623 CAMDEN 270. **1670** RAY 81 . . . This is a
Greek Proverb. Ὅς κύνα τρέφει ξένον τούτῳ
μόνον λίνος μένει. The meaning is, that he who
bestows a benefit upon an ungrateful person
loses his cost. For if a dog break lose, he
presently gets him home to his former master,
leaving the cord he was tied with. **1710**
PALMER 275.

Keeps company with the wolf, Who | will learn to howl.   (C 574)

1579 TOMSON *2 Tim. iii: Serm. Calvin* 873 Is it to
giue vs leaue to doe euill, and for euery one of vs
to say, he maye goe houle amongest the wolues?
1591 FLORIO *Second F*. 57 Who is bread among
wolfes will learne to houle. **1670** RAY 30.

Keeps his own, He that | makes war.   (W 41)

1640 HERBERT no. 848.

Keeps his road well enough who gets rid of bad company, He.

1707 MAPLETOFT 2.

Keep(ing, s), kept, *see also* Better k. now than
seek anon; Christmas all the year (They k.);
Coil (To k. a); Counsel thou wouldest another
k., k. thyself; Cow of his own (Who would k. a);
Dog for your friend (K. a); Finding's k.; Flax
from fire and youth from gaming (K.); Gets
doth much, . . . k. doth more; Goods in the
window (To k. all one's); Has it and will not k.
it; Have to say (What you) will k. cold; Heresy
easier k. out; Hope k. man alive; Life and soul
together (To k.); Man should k. from the blind;
Men get wealth and women k. it; Servant and
cock must be k. but a year; Staff's end (To k.
at); Tongue in one's head (To k. a good); Who
wots who may k. sheep; Whole from broken
(K.); Wife that k. her supper . . . died ere day;
World still he k. at his staff's end.

Keer, *see* Kent and K.

Kelly, *see* King may come to K.

Kenned folks are nae company.

1737 RAMSAY III. 128.

Kenned, *see also* Little k. less cared for.

Kennel is lodging good enough for a dog, A. (K 14)

1626 BRETON *Soothing* A8ᵛ (is fit for). 1639 CLARKE 138.

Kennel, *see* Look not for musk in a k.

Kennington, *see* Naughty Ashford.

Kens his groats among other folk's kail, He. (G 459)

a. 1628 CARMICHAELL no. 1814. 1641 FERGUSSON no. 423 *Of weillie persons.* . . . 1721 KELLY 153 . . . Spoken of those who are sharp and sagacious in knowing their own. 1857 DEAN RAMSAY *Remin.* vi (1911) 238 An old lady . . . from whom the 'Great Unknown'[1] had derived many an ancient tale, . . . protested, 'D'ye think, sir, I dinna keen my ain groats in ither folk's kail?' [1 Scott.]

Kent and Keer[1] have parted many a good man and his mare.

1873 HARLAND & WILKINSON *Lancashire Leg.* 193 . . . Many have perished in fording both rivers when swollen, and in crossing the adjacent sands. [1 Two rivers flowing into Morecambe Bay.]

Kent, Some places of | have health and no wealth, some wealth and no health, some health and wealth, some have neither health nor wealth. (K 15)

1576 LAMBARDE *Peramb. Kent* 200 Very reasonable is their conceite, which doe imagine that Kent hath three steps, or degrees, of which the first (say they) offereth Wealth without health: the second, giveth both Wealth and health: and the thirde affoordeth Health onely, and little or no Wealth. 1586 CAMDEN *Brit., Kent* 164 [in Latin]. 1610 *Ibid.,* tr. Holland I 324 The Inhabitants distinguish it . . . into three . . . portions, the upper wherof, lying upon Tamis, they say is healthy, but not so wealthy: the middle . . . both healthfull and plentifull: the lower . . . wealthy, but not healthy [= Romney Marsh]. 1659 HOWELL *Eng. Prov.* 20b. 1678 RAY 315 Some part of *Kent* hath *health and no wealth,* viz. East *Kent.* Some *wealth and no health,* viz. The weald of *Kent.* Some both *health and wealth,* viz. the middle of the Countrey and parts near *London.*

Kent nor Christendom, Neither in. (K 16)

c. 1492 Carol (R. L. GREENE *Early English Carols* 4) Come thou no more here nor in Kent. *a.* 1542 SIR T. WYATT *Satire* I But here I am in Kent and Christendom. 1579 SPENSER *Shep. Cal.* Sept. Kelmscott 69 Sith the Saxon king Never was woolfe seene, many nor some, Nor in all Kent, nor in Christendome. 1662 FULLER *Kent* 63. . . . This home Proverb . . . ought to be restrained to English Christendome, whereof Kent was first converted to the Faith. So then Kent and Christendome (parallel to Rome and Italy) is as much as the First cut, and all the Loafe besides. 1876 W. W. SKEAT in PEGGE

Kenticisms E.D.S. 62 [*Neither in Kent nor Christendom.*] Kent is obviously singled out as containing the metropolis (Canterbury) of all English Christendom.

Kentchester Hill, *see* Sutton Wall.

Kentish cousins.

1736 S. PEGGE *Kenticisms, Prov.* E.D.S. 64 *Kentish Cousins.* The sense of this is . . . cousins germans quite remov'd. . . . The inhabitants are kept at home more than they are in the inland counties. This confinement naturally produces intermarriages amongst themselves.

Kentish Longtails. (K17)

1560 ed. BALE *Acts of Engl. Votaries* E5. Polydorus applieth it vnto kentish men at Stroud by Rochester, for cuttinge of Thomas Beckets horsses tail. 1576 LAMBARDE *Kent* 2R2. A name, or familie of men, sometime inhabiting Stroude [in Kent] (saith Polydore) had tailes clapped to their breeches by Thomas Becket, for reuenge and punishment of a dispite done to him, in cutting of the taile of his horse. [margin] The beginning of this scoffing by word, Kentishe tailes. 1592 NASHE *Strange News* i. 287 Thy long Kentish-tayld declaration against *Greene. c.* 1600 DELONEY *Wks.* Mann 383 The valiant courage and policie of the Kentishmen with long tayles. 1622 DRAYTON *Polyolb.* XXIII. 237 *Kent* first in our account, doth to it selfe apply, (Quoth he) this Blazon first, *Long Tayles and Libertie.* 1617 MORYSON *Itin.* III. i. 53 (1907-8) III. 463 The Kentish men of old were said to have tails, because trafficing in the Low Countries, they never paid full payments of what they did owe, but still left some part unpaid. 1662 FULLER *Kent* 63 . . . To come closer to . . . this. Proverb, I conceive it first of outlandish extraction, and cast by foreigners as a note of disgrace on all the English, though it chanceth to stick only on the Kentish at this Day.

Kent(-ish), *see also* Essex stiles, K. miles; Great as the devil and the Earl of K.; Hoo, K.; Knight of Cales; Lithe as a lass of K.; Men of K.

Kentshire, hot as fire.

1736 S. PEGGE *Kenticisms, Prov.* E.D.S. 61 . . . This country is remarkably hot on account of its chalk hills and chalky as well as gravelly roads.

Kerchief, *see* White as a k.

Kernel and leap at (fight for) the shell, To lose (cast away) the. (K 18)

1560 W. CECIL cited C. Read *Mr. Sec. Cecil* 189 We, content with the kernel, yielded to them the shell to play withall. 1566 T. HESKYNS *Parl. of Christ* M5 Ye cast awaie the kernell, and fight for the shale. 1572 CRADOCKE *Ship of Assured Safety* a7 If any sweetenesse may be piked out of that that is soure, we must not by and by refuse, and cast away either the nutkernell for the huske, or the corne for the chaffe, or the rose for the prickes that growe about it. 1583 MELBANCKE I2ᵛ To prefer the barke before the tree, to take the shell and leaue the nutt. 1639 CLARKE 81.

Kernel, *see* Eat the k. must crack nut.

Kettle calls the pot black-brows (burnt-arse), The.   (K 21)

[= equally black.] **1620** SHELTON *Quix.* II. lxvii.
iv. 227 You are like what is said that the frying-pans aid to the Kettle, 'Avant, blacke-browes'.
1639 CLARKE 8 The pot calls the pan burnt-arse.
1699 *Dict. Cant. Crew* s.v. 'The Pot calls the
kettle black A—', when one accuses another of
what he is as Deep in himself. **1706** STEVENS
s.v. Sarten (black Arse). **1841** S. WARREN *Ten
Thous. a Year* ch. 2 'Come, you know you're a
liar, Huck . . .' 'The pot and kettle, anyhow, Tit,
as far as that goes.'

Kettle of fish, A pretty (fine).

[= a muddle, or awkward state of things.]
1742 FIELDING *J. Andrews* I. xii 'Here's a
pretty kettle of fish', cries Mrs. Tow-wouse.
1800 WELLINGTON *Let. to Close* 2 Oct. in GURW.
Desp. (1837) I. 245 If so, we shall have a fine
kettle of fish at Seringapatam. **1921** 2 Mar.
D. H. LAWRENCE *Lett.* ii. 643 Your letter was a
nice little kettle of old fish.

Kettle, *see also* Frying-pan said to k., 'Avaunt
. . .'; Medea's k.; Simpers like a furmity k.
See also Brass kettle.

Kettle (*proper name*), *see* But when? quoth K.

Kevel, *see* Content with own k.; Happy man,
happy k.

Kex, *see* Dry as a k.

Keys hang not at one man's girdle, All the.   (K 29)

c. **1400** *MS. Latin no. 394, J. Rylands Libr.* (ed.
Pantin) in *Bull. J.R. Libr.* XIV f. 3ᵛ Not all
keyes hongen atte oo wyues gyrdell. **1546**
HEYWOOD I. xi. D4 The kays hang not all by one
mans girdill man. **1579** GOSSON *Sch. Abuse* B.
45 But all the keyes hang not at one man's
girdle. **1641** FERGUSSON no. 63 All the keys of
the countrey hangs not at ane belt. **1721**
KELLY 11 All the Keys of the World hings not at
your belt. Spoken to those who refuse us their
Help, . . . intimating that others may afford
what they deny us.

Keys in the bunch, He tries all the.   (K 28)

1616 DRAXE no. 1961. **1639** CLARKE 60.

Key(s), *see also* Cold as a k.; Good wife's away
(When) k. are tint; Idleness k. of beggary;
Kisses are k.; Kit hath lost her k.; Like punish-ment . . . k. and keyhole sustain; Prayer should
be k. of day; Silver k. open iron lock; Used k.
always bright; Wife is k. of house.

Keystone under the hearth, keystone under the horse's belly.

1863 J. R. WISE *New Forest* ch. 15 The smuggler's
local proverb, . . . That is to say, the smuggled

spirits were concealed either below the fireplace
or in the stable, just beneath where the horse
stood.

Kick against the prick(s)[1] (wall), To.   (F 433)

[ACTS ix. 5: It is hard for thee to kick against the
pricks.] *c.* **1300** *Cursor M.* l. 19626 Hit is to þe
ful harde & wik for to wirk a-gaine þe prik.
c. **1380** CHAUCER *Truth* l. 11 Be war also to
sporne ayeyns an al. *c.* **1390** GOWER *Conf.
Amantis* III. 16 And thus myn hand agein the
pricke I hurte. *c.* **1430** LYDGATE *Pilgr. Life of
Man* E.E.T.S. 390, l. 14459 Hard ys to sporne
ageyn an hal. **1539** TAVERNER 14 (gode). **1546**
HEYWOOD II. v. H2 Foly it is to spurne against a
pricke. **1555** *Id. Epig. on Prov.* CCLIV Folly
to spurne or kyck ageynst the harde wall. **1576**
OXFORD to Burghley cited C. Read *Ld. Burghley
& Q. Elizabeth* 133 I see it but in vain calci-trare contra li busse. **1592** ARIOSTO *Orl. Fur.*
Harington XIV. 40 They learned had vnto their
paine, It was in vaine against the wall to
kicke. **1641** FERGUSSON no. 510 It is hard to
fling at the brod[1] or kick at the prick. *a.* **1677**
BARROW *Serm.* III. 394 To blow against the
wind, to kick against the pricks. **1926** *Times*
29 June 17/3 The West Ham Board of Guar-dians persist in kicking against the pricks.
[¹ goad.]

Kick an attorney downstairs and he'll stick to you for life.

1902–4 LEAN IV. 24. (A Bar proverb.)

Kick down the ladder, To.   (L 26)

1599 SHAKES. *J.C.* II. i. 22 Lowliness is young
ambition's ladder, Whereto the climber-upward
turns his face; But when he once attains the
upmost round, He then unto the ladder turns his
back. [1600] **1657** *Lust's Dominion* Hazl.-Dods.
xiv. 159 Philip Makes you his ladder, and being
climb'd so high As he may reach a diadem, there
you lie. **1655** FULLER *Ch. Hist.* v. iii (1868) II.
65 [Polydore Virgil] is said to have burned all
those rare authors, which he could compass into
his possession. Thus . . . he cut down those
stairs whereby he ascended the throne of his
own knowledge. **1659** 'JOHN IRETON' *Oration* 2
Tis heart-breaking when any person can hit us in
the teeth that they raised us; oh those steps must
be pulled down. **1749** FIELDING *Tom Jones* I. 13
When you are got up, to kick the stool from
under you. **1794** NELSON in NICOLAS *Disp.* (ed.
2) I. 449 Duncan is, I think, a little altered;
there is nothing like kicking down the ladder a
man rises by. **1848** THACKERAY *Book of Snobs*
ch. 7 She has struggled so gallantly for polite
reputation that she has won it: pitilessly kicking
down the ladder as she advanced degree by
degree. **1882** S. R. GARDINER *Introd. Eng. Hist.*
68 The Great Council . . . might be inclined, if
they proved successful, to kick over the ladder
by which they had risen to power.

Kick in one's gallop, To have a.

1809 MALKIN *Gil Blas.* III. x. My fairy queen, . . .
you have an ugly kick in your gallop. I have
observed you with the players. **1836** M. SCOTT
Cruise of Midge ch. 1 A grapeshot . . . had
shattered his left thigh, and considerably
shortened it, thereby giving him a kick in his
gallop.

Kick of the dam (mare) hurts not the colt, The.   (K 30)

1599 MINSHEU *Span. Gram.* 83 The kicke of the mare hurteth not the colt *i.* A freinds reproofe neuer doth ill. **1609** HARWARD 102 (The mares kick). **1642** TORRIANO 16 (hurteth not the stallion). **1732** FULLER no. 4611.

Kick one's heels, To.

[= to stand waiting idly or impatiently.] **1760** FOOTE *Minor* II (1781) 51 To let your uncle kick his heels in your hall. **1833** MARRYAT *P. Simple* ch. 13 I'll trouble him [not] to . . . leave me here kicking my heels.

Kick over the traces, To.

[= to throw off the usual restraints.] **1844** STEPHENS *High Life in New York.* II. 174 Kick in the traces. **1861** H. KINGSLEY *Ravenshoe* ch. 42 I'll go about with the rogue. He is inclined to kick over the traces. **1876** L. STEPHEN *Hours in England* II. 354 The effervescence of genius which drives men to kick over the traces of respectability.

Kick the beam, To.

1667 MILTON *Par. Lost* IV. 1004 The latter quick up flew and kickt the beam. **1712** ADDISON *Spect.* No. 463 The latter, to show its comparative lightness, immediately flew up and kickt the Beam. **1748** T. SMOLLETT *Roderick Random* ch. 9 A straw thrown into either scale would make the balance kick the beam.

Kick the bucket, To.

[The beam on which a slaughtered pig is suspended by the heels is called in Norfolk a 'bucket', hence the phrase signifies 'to die'.] **1785** GROSE *Dict. Vulg. T.* **1806** WOLCOT (P. Pindar) *Tristia* Wks. (1816) IV. 309 Pitt has kick'd the bucket. **1810** TANNAHILL *Poems* (1846) 57 Till time himsel' turn auld and kick the bucket. **1899** W. P. RIDGE *Son of the State* ch. 11 A man that's getting near to kicking the bucket can't be too cautious of what he says.

Kick the wind, To.

1598 FLORIO *Worlde of Wordes* 96/1 *Dar de' calci a Rouaio*, to be hang'd, to kicke the winde.

Kick(ed, s), *see also* Ass k. you (When), never tell; Corporations have not bodies to be k.; Monkey's allowance, more k. than halfpence.

Kid in her kilting,[1] She has got a.

1721 KELLY 300 . . . That is, she has got a Bastard about her. [[1] trussed-up petticoats.] '

Kid that keeps above is in no danger of the wolf, The.

1732 FULLER no. 4612.

Kid(s), *see also* Dam leaps over (Where), k. follows; Goats (You have no) yet sell k.; Piece of a k. worth two of a cat.

Kilkenny cats, *see* Fight like K. c.

Kill a man for a mess of mustard, He will.   (M 180)

1555 HEYWOOD *Epigr. on Prov.* no. CCVII. **1659** HOWELL *Eng. Prov.* 7a.

Kill a man with a cushion, To.

(M 398)

1609 ROWLANDS *Whole Crew Kind Gossips* Hunt. Cl. 12 Go to (quoth I) y' are best beat out my braines With Cushions now, to make the prouerbe true. **1616** WITHALS 575. **1639** CLARKE 310. **1670** RAY 218.

Kill a pig every day, We don't.

1877 E. PEACOCK *Gloss. of Lincolnshire Wds.* (1889) 403 'We don't kill a *pig* every day', that is, we have not every day a merry-making.

Kill another in jest and be hanged in earnest, A man may.

1599 PORTER *Angry Wom. Abingd.* ll. 2791–2 Heare, and make an end, you may kill one another in jist, and be hanged in earnest.

Kill but whoave,[1] We will not.

1674 RAY *Coll. of Eng. Words* 53 . . . *Prov. Chesh.* **1917** BRIDGE *Cheshire Proverbs* 150 . . . Spoken of a pig or fowl which has been covered by some utensil in readiness to kill.   [[1] cover.]

Kill hogs, He who does not | will not get black puddings.

1706 STEVENS s.v. Puerco.

Kill or cure.

1624 CAPT. J. SMITH *Virginia* 'Hist. of the Bermudas' MacLehose ed. i. 384 Some there were that died presently after they got ashore, it being certainly the quality of that place, either to kill, or cure quickly.

Kill the Danes, It would.

1842 LEVER *Jack Hinton* ch. 48 Comfortable! The ways of this place would kill the Danes! Nothing but ringing bells from morning till night: carriages drivin' like wind up to the door.

Kill the fatted calf, To.

1526 TYNDALE *Luke* xv. 23 And brynge hidder that fatted caulfe, and kyll hym, and lett vs eate, and be mery. **1647** COWLEY *Mistress, The Welcome,* i. Go, let the fatted calf be kill'd. **1810** J. MOORE *Post-Captain* (ed. 4) viii. 34 The whole family crowded round him: the fatted calf was killed; and all was joy, mirth, and jubilee.

Kill the goose that lays the golden eggs, To.   (G 363)

1484 CAXTON *Æsope* (Jacobs) II. 245 This fable sayeth of a man whiche had a goos that leyd euery day an egge of gold. [The whole fable is given.] **1589**? LYLY *Pap w. Hatchet* iii. 404 A man . . . had a goose, which euerie daie laid him a golden egge, hee . . . kild his goose, thinking to haue a mine of golde in her bellie, and finding nothing but dung, . . . wisht his goose aliue. **1824** SCOTT *St. Ronan's* ch. 11 You must draw the neck of the goose which lays the golden eggs; you must lend me the whole stock. **1911** *Spectator* 22 Apr. 592 Capital already committed to an industry can sometimes be 'held up' by the State and forced to accept, not the market price, but a price artificially fixed. . . . Such treatment soon kills the goose that lays the golden eggs. **1925** *Times* 19 Dec. M. Bratiano, the Finance Minister, is 'killing the goose that lays the golden eggs'.

Kill two birds with one stone (bolt, sling), To. *Cf.* Fells two dogs. (B 400)

[OVID *A.A.* 3. 358 *Unus cum gemino calculus hoste perit.*] **1590** SIR JOHN SMYTHE *Certain Discourses**** 2ᵛ To the intent that they might hit two markes at one shoote. **1609** HARWARD 97ᵛ (It is good killing). **1611** COTGRAVE s.v. *Coup D'une pierre faire deux coups.* . . . **1656** HOBBES *Liberty*, etc. (1841) 117 T. H. thinks to kill two birds with one stone, and satisfy two arguments with one answer. **1659** HEYLIN *Animadv.* in FULLER *Appeal Inj. Innoc.* (1840) 656 That two birds might be killed with the same bolt, no sooner was Dr. Price deceased, but the bishop of Lincoln . . . calls the prebends together. **1662** FULLER *Kent* 81 Thus have I (not killed two Birds with one bolt, but) revived two men's memories with one Record. **1670** RAY 197 (one shaft [or stone.] . . . Gall. . . . Ital.) **1843** DICKENS *M. Chuz.* ch. 6 It was their custom, . . . whenever such a thing was practicable, to kill two birds with one stone. **1902** *Spectator* 11 Jan. It will be convenient and economical to kill two birds with one stone and to use the same men for garrisoning the country and for settling on the land.

Kill two flies with one flap, To. (F 404)

1678 RAY 275.

Kill with kindness (as fond apes do their young), To. (K 51)

a. **1557** *Wealth and Health* D1ᵛ With kindnes my her ye do kyll. **1580** LYLY *Euph. & his Eng.* ii. 5 I should resemble the Ape, and kill it by cullyng it. **1582** WHETSTONE *Heptameron of Civil Discourses* T4. **1583** GREENE *Wks.* Gros. ii. 26 Jason . . . in lieu of her loue, killed her [Medea] with kindnesse. **1593** *Tell-Truths New Years Gift* New Sh. S. 43 Thou kilst by kindnesse, if thou kilst. **1594–8** SHAKES. *T.S.* IV. i. 192 This is a way to kill a wife with kindness. **1601** LYLY *Love's Met.* IV. ii. That young cruell resembleth old Apes, who kill by culling:[1] . . . neuer smiling but when shee meaneth to smite. **1607** T. HEYWOOD *Woman killed with Kindness* [title]. **1629** T. ADAMS *Serm.* (1861–2) II. 57 These are Satan's white boys, or rather black boys, whom he kills, like the ape her young, with kindness, and damns with indulgence. **1670** RAY 2 The Ape so long clippeth her young that at last she killeth them. **1698** FRYER *Acc. E. India & P.* 100 Tom Coriat . . . was killed with kindness by the English Merchants. [1 hugging.]

Killed her for good will, I | said Scot, when he killed his neighbour's mare.

(G 341)

1678 RAY 85.

Killed the blue spider in Blanch powder land, This is he that.

a. **1553** UDALL *Ralph Roister D.* I. iv. Arb. 28 This is hee vnderstand, That killed the blewe Spider in Blanchepouder lande.

Killing a crow with an empty sling, It is ill.

1678 RAY 120.

Killing no murder.

1657 SEXBY & TITUS *Killing no Murder* [Title of a pamphlet to prove that the assassination of the Protector, Cromwell, was lawful and laudable.] **1836** MARRYAT *Mldsh. Easy* ch. 18 In this case killing's no murder . . . by the laws of society, any one who attempts the death of another has forfeited his own. **1908** *Times Lit. Sup.* 5 June The exception is the share which he took in the conspiracy of Orsini against Napoleon III. . . . It was probably a case to which Holyoake would have applied the doctrine of 'killing no murder'.

Kills a man when he is drunk, He that | shall be hanged when he is sober.

(M 175)

a. **1538** T. STARKEY *Dialogue* i. 31 He that kyllyth a man dronk, sobur schalbe hangyd. *c.* **1549** HEYWOOD I. x. D1 He that kylth a man, whan he is dronke (quoth she) Shalbe hangd whan he is sobre. *c.* **1590** LYLY *Mother B.* V. iii. 367 Thinges done in drinke may be repented in sobernes, but not remedyed. **1659** HOWELL *Eng. Prov.* 13b. **1721** KELLY 344 . . . The law makes Drunkenness no Excuse, but rather an Aggravation.

Kills himself with working, He that | must be buried under the gallows.

(W 853)

1658 E. PHILLIPS *Myst. Love and Eloq.* 175 He that loves another better then himself, starves in a Cooks shop . . . And ought to be buried under the Gallows. **1678** RAY 221. **1854** A. E. BAKER *Northants. Glos.* 264 Those who kill themselves with hard work, it is said, 'will be buried under the gallows'.

Kills that thinks but to hurt, He often.

1607 H. ESTIENNE *World of Wonders* tr. R.C. 160 He often killeth who thinkes but to hurt. *c.* **1645** MS. proverbs in *N. & Q.* 154, 27. **1659** HOWELL *Fr. Prov.* 24.

Kill(s, ed), *see also* Burden (It is not) that k. the beast; Cursed in his mother's belly that was k. by cannon; Dog is hanged . . . and man is k. for his purse (Many a); Fancy may k. or cure; Gluttony k. more than sword; Go out and k. (What shall we); Last man that he k. keeps hogs; Leeches k. with licence; March, k. crow, pie, and cadow; Pace that k.; Perseverance k. the game; Physicians k. more than they cure; Sudden joy k. sooner than excessive grief; Trust is dead, ill payment k. it; Ways to k. dog than hanging (More).

Kiln call the oven burnt-house (burnt-tail), Ill may the. *Cf.* Frying-pan said to the kettle: Kettle called the pot black-arse. (K 33)

1603 MONTAIGNE (Florio) III. v. 186 Which some say proverbially 'Ill may the Kill call the Oven burnt taile!' **1609** HARWARD 107 The oven calleth the peele burnt tayle. **1639** CLARKE 79. **1853** TRENCH iii. 67.

Kiln of malt is on fire, My. (K 34)

1579 A. HALL *Quarrel betw. Hall and Mallorie* in *Misc. Antiq. Angl.* 19 Well what will you have more? the kyll is a fire. **1636** CAMDEN 302. **1818** SCOTT *Rob Roy* ch. 37 The kiln's on fire— she's a' in a lowe.[1] [[1] blaze].

Kiln, *see also* Peck of malt (For my) set k. on fire.

Kilting, *see* Kid in her k. (She has got a).

Kim Kam arsie versie. (A 328. K 35)

1542 UDALL *Apoph.* 6ᵛ Many persones dooe arsee versee, in that thei take the losse of a lytle money more greuously at the hert, then the losse of a frende. **1550** TAVERNER 62ᵛ Thynges done preposterously, cleane contrarily, and arsy versy as they say. **1608** SHAKES. C. III. i. 304 This is clean Kam.—Merely awry. **1609** HARWARD 97ᵛ Kim-kam. **1616** DRAXE no. 23. **1639** CLARKE 7.

Kin, *see* Bear all his k. (A man cannot); Knave is in plum-tree (When) he has . . . nor k.; Man should keep from the blind and give to his k.; Near of k. to land (Good to be); Poor k. that has neither whore nor thief.

Kind as a kite, As | all you cannot eat you'll hide. (K 113)

1610 BRETNOR *Almanac* February As kind as a kite. **1623** PAINTER C1 He is no kinder then a Kite, For what he cannot eate hee'll always hide. **1639** CLARKE 287 (as 1610). **1670** RAY 202.

Kind hearts are soonest wronged. (H 342)

1616 BRETON 2 *Cross. Prov.* A2ᵛ. **1639** CLARKE 27.

Kind, He has it by | it costs him nought. (K 42)

c. **1374** CHAUCER *Boethius* Bk. iv, l. 98 'Thou nilt nat thanne denye', quod sche, 'that the moevement of goynge nys in men by kynde?' **1572** J. PARINCHEF *Extract of Examples* 86 When he was a yong man he beat his father (quod he) and this my sonne when he commeth

to age wil beate me, for it commeth to vs by kind. **1587** *Mirr. for Mag.* ed. Campbell 465. **1616** DRAXE no. 1471 It commeth to him by kind, it cost him nought. **1623** CAMDEN 272. *a.* **1628** CARMICHAELL no. 1798 (ye coft[1] it not). **1639** CLARKE 111. **1670** RAY 182. **1732** FULLER no. 5484 What cometh by kind costeth nothing. [[1] bought.]

Kind (Kindness, Love) will creep where it may not go. (K 49)

[Kind (= nature) was mistaken variously for Kinship and Kindness or Love. *See* quotations.] *c.* **1350** *Douce MS. 52* no. 85 Kynde crepus ther hit may no go. **1460** *Towneley Myst., 2nd Shep. Play* 591, I *Pastor* I trow, kynde will crepe Where it may not go. *c.* **1500** *Everyman* l. 316 To my kynnesmen I wyll truely, prayenge them to helpe in my necessyte. I beleve that they wyll do so, for kynde will crepe where it may not go. **1546** HEYWOOD I. xi. D3 Men say, kynde wyll creepe where it can not go. **1548** E. HALL *Chron.* f. 190. He . . . rode in poste to his kinsman . . . verefying the old proverbe kynne [*sic*] will crepe where it maie not go. **1594** SHAKES. *T.G.V.* IV. ii. 20 You know that love Will creep in service where it cannot go. **1614** CAMDEN 309 (Kindnesse). **1635** QUARLES *Div. Emb.* IV. iii. 3 Thy thoughts are swift, although thy legs be slow; True love will creep, not having strength to go. **1641** FERGUSSON no. 555 (kindnesse). **1753** RICHARDSON *Grandison* II. xvi. (1812) 132 Lean upon me, my dear, and *creep*: love will creep, they say, where it cannot go. **1857** DEAN RAMSAY *Remin.* v. (1911) 203 *Kindness creeps where it canna gang* prettily expresses that where love can do little, it will do that little though it cannot do more.

Kind, *see* Cat after k.; Cat is out of k. that sweet milk will not lap.

Kindle not a fire that you cannot extinguish. (F 273)

1584 B. R. *Euterpe* (Lang) 136 I will kindle no moe coales then I may well quenchc. **1664** CODRINGTON 203.

Kindle(d), *see also* Wood half-burnt is easily k.

Kindly[1] aver[2] will never make a good horse, A. (A 403)

1599 JAMES VI *Basil. Doron* Arb. 128 It is an old and true saying, that a kindly aver will never become a good horse: for . . . it is evil to get out of the flesh that is bred in the bone. **1678** RAY 95 . . . In our ancient writings *Averium* signifies any labouring beast. **1721** KELLY 40 A kindly aver was never a good nag. Those who are naturally of a low, mean Mind, will make but a sorry Figure in a higher Station. [[1] natural; [2] work-horse.]

Kindness cannot be bought for gear. (K 45)

a. **1628** CARMICHAELL no. 1011 (not be bocht). **1641** FERGUSSON no. 556. **1721** KELLY 227 . . . But rather by mutual good Offices.

Kindness comes of will.   (K 46)

a. **1628** CARMICHAELL no. 1010. **1641** FERGUS-
SON no. 554. **1721** KELLY 226 (awill). That is,
Love cannot be forc'd.

Kindness is lost that's bestowed on children and old folks (men).   (K 47)

1509 BARCLAY *Ship of Fools* II. 182 All is lost
that thou dost gyue to fynde. Four sortis of
people: the first is a vylayne. Or chorle, for
agayne thou shalt hym proue vnkynde. The
seconde a childe, for his forgetfull mynde
Expellyth kyndnes, the thirde a man in age
The fourth a woman varyable as the wynde.
1581 GUAZZO i. 236 Favours are not to bee
done either to a childe or to an olde man. For
the one forgetteth them, the other dyeth before
he have occasion to requite them. **1616** ADAMS
Sacr. of Thankfulness 42 We have a saying
from Aristotle, *Nec in puerum, nec in senem
collocandum esse beneficium*,—That our beneficence should not be fixed upon a child or an old
man; for the child, before he comes to age will
forget it, and the old man will die before he can
requite it. **1639** CLARKE 45. **1641** FERGUSSON
no. 475 It is tint[1] that is done to childe and auld
men. [[1] lost.]

Kindness lies not aye in one side of the house.   (K 48)

a. **1628** CARMICHAELL no. 1016 Kindnes can not
lest (*or* stand) on a syde. **1641** FERGUSSON no.
564. **1721** KELLY 227 Kindness cannot stand
ay on one side. Spoken when you offer an
Instance of Kindness to them who have been
formerly kind to you.

Kindness, *see also* Courtesy (Where o'er mickle),
little k.; Gloucestershire k.; Hertfordshire k.;
Kill with k.; Kind (K.) will creep where it may
not go; Poind for debt, not for k.

Kindred, Wheresoever you see your | make much of your friends.   (K 53)

1659 HOWELL *Eng. Prov.* 11b. **1732** FULLER no.
5660.

Kindred, *see also* Fools . . . among his k. (Who
has neither), was born of a stroke of thunder;
Shame in a k.

King and pope, the lion and the wolf, The.   (K 60)

1659 HOWELL *Eng. Prov.* 12b . . . A Proverb
used in King Johns time, in regard of the great
exactions.

King Arthur did never violate the refuge of a woman.   (K 88)

1605 CHAPMAN, JONSON, MARSTON *Eastw. Ho*
v. i. 29 Would the Knight o' the Sunne, or
Palmerin of England, haue vsd their Ladies
so . . .? or sir Lancelot? or sir Tristram?
. . . They would helpe poore Ladies, Ours
make poore Ladies. **1662** FULLER Cardigan 26
Ne thorres Arthur Nawad gwraig. That is,
King Arthur did never violate the refuge of a

Woman. Arthur is . . . the mirrour of manhood. By the Woman's Refuge, many understand her Tongue, and no valiant man will
revenge her words with his blows.

King can do no wrong, The.   (K 61)

c. **1538** T. STARKEY *Dialogue* I. iv. 35 *Eng. in
Reign Hen. VIII* II. 101 Hyt ys comyngly sayd
. . . a kyng ys aboue hys lawys. **1569** HOWELL
Ded. to *Eng. Prov.* 2. **1682** DRYDEN *The Medal*
l. 135 That Kings can doe no wrong we must
believe. **1689** SELDEN *Table-Talk* Arb. 61 The
King can do no wrong, that is no Process can be
granted against him. **1763** BOSWELL *Johnson*
xvi. (1848) 144 Goldsmith . . . disputed . . .
against the well-known maxim of the British
constitution, 'the King can do no wrong'.
1765 BLACKSTONE *Comm.* I. vii. 246 . . . The
prerogative of the crown extends not to do any
injury: it is created for the benefit of the people,
and therefore cannot be exerted to their prejudice. **1908** E. M. SNEYD-KYNNERSLEY *H.M.I.*
ch. 19 The Canons were appointed by the
Crown. The King can do no wrong, but he may
be misguided.

King can (may) make a knight, but not a gentleman, The.

1689 SELDEN *Table-Talk* Arb. 52 The King cannot make a Gentleman of Blood . . . but he can
make a Gentleman by Creation. **1902–4** LEAN
IV. 128 The king may make a knight, but not a
gentleman.

King can make a serjeant,[1] but not a lawyer, The.

1732 FULLER no. 4613. [[1] Serjeant-at-law.]

King Charles's head.

[The type of an obsessing notion.] **1849–50**
DICKENS *Dav. Cop.* ch. 14 As I looked along
the lines [of Mr. Dick's Memorial] I thought
I saw some allusion to King Charles the First's
head again in one or two places.

King comes to Wogan, It shall be done when the.   (K 59)

1659 HOWELL *Eng. Prov.* 21a . . . a little Village;
viz. An impossibility. **1787** GROSE (*Worcs.*) 231
. . . Wogan is a small village, . . . quite out of any
thoroughfare, and therefore very unlikely to be
ever visited by the king.

King goes as far as he can, and not so far as he would, The.

1706 STEVENS s.v. Rey.

King Harry loved a man.   (K 92)

c. **1600** *Return from Parnassus* I. 735 *Ficus pro
diabolo* Kinge Harrie loued a man! **1605**
S. ROWLEY *When you See Me* l. 1099 (loues).
a. **1635** NAUNTON *Fragm. Reg.* Arb. 28 The
people hath it to this day in proverb, King
Harry loved a man. **1636** CAMDEN 301. **1662**
FULLER Sussex 113 These Three were knighted
for their valour by King Henry the Eighth (who
never laid his sword on his shoulders who was
not a Man). **1845** CARLYLE *Cromwell* Introd. iii

Tourneying successfully before King Harry, who loved a man.

King Harry[1] robbed the church, and died a beggar. (K 93)

1678 RAY 354. [[1] Henry VIII.]

King Harry, *see also* Hill in K. H.'s day (This was a).

King is dead. The | Long live the King!

1859 LD. DUFFERIN *Lett. from High Lat.* (1895) 116 The last fiery segment had disappeared beneath the purple horizon, and all was over. 'The King is dead . . . the King is dead! Long live the King!' And up from the sea . . . rose the young monarch of a new day.

King (Prince), Like | like people. (K 70)

c. 1548 J. BALE *Image of both Churches* P.S. 357 Such people, such governor; such swarms, such stinking leader. 1548 HALL (1809, 47) It is daily seen, that as princes change, the people altereth, and as kynges go, the subiectes folowe. 1579 J. DYOS *Sermon* L6 Such Prince such subiectes. 1593 P. STUBBES *Motive to Good Works* 149 An olde prouerbe and verie true, Quales Principes, Nobiles, et Gubernatores, tales populi, et subditi, Such as the Prince, Nobles, and Gentlemen are, such are commonly the people and subiects also. 1616 DRAXE no. 1234 (Priest, Prince). 162! BURTON *Anat. Mel.* Democr. to Rdr. (1651) 49 As the princes are, so are the people; *qualis rex, talis grex.* 1648 HERRICK *Hesper.* No. 760 Like Prince, Like People. Examples lead us, and wee likely see, Such as the Prince is, will his people be. 1706 STEVENS s.v. Rey. Such as the King is, such is the Flock, or his People.

King (prince) loves the treason but hates the traitor, A. (K 64)

[TACITUS *Annals* l. 58 *Proditores etiam iis quos anteponunt invisi sunt.* Traitors are hated even by those whom they prefer.] 1583 MELBANCKE *Philot.* D3[v] I commende that sentence, though I hate the traytour that spoke it. 1586 *La Primaudaye* tr. T. Bowes 422 Caesar Augustus . . . drinking to others, said with a loud voyce: I loue treason well, but I loue not traitors. 1588 GREENE *Pandosto* ed. Thomas 9. [1591] 1594 *Selimus* l. 2115 O sir, I loue the fruite that treason brings, But those that are the traitors, them I hate. *a.* 1627 MIDDLETON *Women Beware* II. ii. Merm. 305 I'm like that great one, Who making politic use of a base villain, He likes the treason well, but hates the traitor. 1692 L'ESTRANGE *Aesop's Fab.* cxciv. (1738) 209 *We love the treason, but we hate the traitor.* 1706 STEVENS s.v. Rey.

King may come to Kelly yet, and when he comes he'll ride, The.

1721 KELLY 323 . . . The Time may come, that I may get my Revenge upon such People; and then I will do it to purpose.

King of a molehill, To be. (K 55)

a. 1578 T. STUKELEY in T. Westcote *Hist. Devonshire in 1630* (1845 ed.), 271 He projected

to people Florida, . . . having this proverb often in his discourse, 'I had rather be king of a molehill than subject to a mountain'. 1583 MELBANCKE *Philot.* D4[v] It is better to be king of a mould hil, then to be subiecte to a mountaine. 1585 J. PRIME *Sermon* B1 Their minds, whose whole life is a worldly glory and whose only desire is to be aloft, to be the monarks, if it be but of a mole-hill. 1594 PEELE *Battle Alcazar* II. ii. C1[v] King of a mole-hill had I rather be, Than the richest subiect of a monarchie. 1659 HOWELL *Eng. Prov.* 10b (then a Keysars slave).

King never dies, The.

[L. *Rex nunquam moritur.* Law Max.] 1588 *Discourse upon the present estate of France* tr. E. Aggas 11 In France a king neuer dieth, because that so soon as one is gone, there is an other straightway in his place. 1589 *The Contre-Guise* H4[v]. 1659 HOWELL Ded. to *Eng. Prov.* 2 The King cannot die. 1760 H. WALPOLE *Let.* 25 Oct. I had already begun to think that the lawyers for once talked sense, when they said the *King never dies.* He[1] probably got his death . . . by viewing the troops. 1911 H. BROOM *Legal Max.* (ed. 8) 36 . . . 'It is true', said Lord Lyndhurst, 'that the king never dies; the demise is immediately followed by the succession; . . . The sovereign always exists; the person only is changed.' [[1] Geo. II.]

King of England (of France, of Spain), *see* Emperor of Germany.

King of France and twenty thousand men went up the hill, and so came home again, The.

1649 J. TAYLOR (Water-P.) *Wonders of West* (1872) 28 *In imitation of a mighty king, Whose warlike acts, good fellows often sing.* The King of France and twenty thousand men, Went up the hill, and so came home again.

King of France get wot of that, Long ere the.

1721 KELLY 231 . . . Spoken when People make a great Talk of some little Accident.

King of good fellows is appointed for the queen of beggars, The. (K 66)

c. 1565 *Bugbears* I. ii. 4 The king of good felowes that didst lie with the queene of beggars. 1636 CAMDEN 307. 1732 FULLER no. 4616.

King of your word, You should be a. (K 74)

1641 FERGUSSON no. 906. 1816 SCOTT *Old Mortality* ch. 14 King's blood must keep word.

King over the water, The.

[= the representative of the exiled Stuart dynasty.] 1749 FIELDING *Tom Jones* VII. iv. From these meals she retired about five minutes after the other servants, having only staid to drink, 'the king over the water'. 1824 SCOTT *Redg. Let.* v. He so far compromised his loyalty, as to announce merely 'The King', as his first toast. . . . Our guest made a motion with his glass so as to pass it over the water-decanter . . . , and added, 'Over the water'.

King, Whosoever is | thou wilt be his man.   (K 73)

1670 RAY 183.

Kings' chaff is worth other men's corn.
(K 78)

1612 SHELTON *Quix.* IV. xii. ii. 40 A king's crumb is more worth than a lord's loaf. *a.* 1628 CARMICHAELL no. 1459. 1641 FERGUSSON no. 563. 1721 KELLY 226 . . . The Perquisites that attend Kings Service is better than the Wages of other Persons. 1788 BURNS *Lett.* Fergusson i. 245 King's caff is better than ither folks' corn. 1818 SCOTT *Rob Roy* ch. 34 They say . . . that kings' chaff is better than other folk's corn; but I think that canna be said o' kings' soldiers, if they let themselves be beaten wi' a wheen auld carles.

King's cheese goes half away in parings, The.   (K 79)

1659 HOWELL *Eng. Prov.* 1a . . . *viz. among so many Officers.* 1709 DYKES 299 . . . The courts of princes . . . are seldom free from pilferers, pick-pockets, and thieves . . . in places of trust. 1735 FRANKLIN June The King's cheese is half wasted in parings; but no matter, 'tis made of the peoples milk.

King's coat, *see* Wear the k. c.

King's English, He clips the.   (K 75)

[= is drunk.] [1598] 1616 HAUGHTON *Englishmen for my Money* l. 319 A clipper of the Kings English. 1600 *Look about You* C2 Marry heares a stammerer taken clipping the Kings English. 1603 DEKKER *The Wonderful Year* E4ᵛ If he [a drunkard] had clipt but a quarter so much of the King's siluer, as he did of the Kings English, . . . 1745 FRANKLIN *Drinker's Dict.* in Wks. (Bigelow) II. 24.

King's English, The.   (K 80)

1391 CHAUCER *Astrolabe* Prol. l. 56 And preie God save the king, that is lord of this langage. 1553 T. WILSON *Arte of Rhet.* (1909) 162 These fine English clerkes will say, they speake in their mother tongue, if a man should charge them for counterfeiting the Kings English. 1592 NASHE *Strange News* i. 261 Still he must be running on the letter, and abusing the Queenes English without pittie or mercie. 1600–1 SHAKES. *M.W.W.* I. iv. 5 Abusing of God's patience, and the King's English. 1714 *Spectator* 3 Nov. Mrs. Mayoress clip'd the King's *English.* 1876 MRS. BANKS *Manch. Man* ch. 15 In her attempt to appear . . . a lady, she 'clipped the King's English', and made almost as glaring errors as Mrs. Malaprop.

King's errand may come the cadger's[1] gate[2] yet, The.

1721 KELLY 311 . . . A great Man may want a mean Man's service. 1827 SCOTT *Let.* 30 Nov.

in LOCKHART *Life* ch. 74 Would to God the King's errand might lie in the cadger's gait, that I might have some better way of showing my feelings than merely by a letter of thanks. [[1] pedlar, gipsy, beggar. [2] way.]

King's face should give grace, A.

1827–30 SCOTT *Tales Grandf.* ch. 26 Henry VIII . . . blamed the implacability of James . . . , and quoted an old proverb—A king's face should give grace.

King's horse, He shall have the. (K 76)

1678 RAY 89 *A lier* . . .

King's horses, *see* Ass thinks himself worthy.

King's word, The | is more than another man's oath.   (K 82)

a. 1500 *Lancelot* l. 1673 O Kingis word shuld be a kinges bonde. 1554 PRINCESS ELIZ. (to Qu. Mary) in *Original Let. II* (1827) 155, ii. 255: (This olde saynge, that a Kinge's worde was more). 1608 H. FITZSIMON *Reply to M. Rider's Rescript* 103 For the woord of a King, sayd Isocrates to K. Nicocles, is more to be trusted then the oath of another. *a.* 1674 CLARENDON *Hist. of Rebellion* 1707, iii. 583 Let all our Subjects . . . rely upon the word of a King. [MS. note by Swift: 'Usually good for Nothing.']

King(s), *see* Call the k. cousin; Cat may look at a k.; Eats the k.'s goose (He that); Emperor of Germany is the K. of k.; Every beggar descended from some k.; Every man is a k. in his own house; Every thing is yours (You think) but a little the k. has; Eyes are upon the k.; Friday will be k.; Groom is a k. at home; Hated of his subjects cannot be counted k.; Highest in court (Nearest the k.), nearest the widdie; Inch a man (k.), (To be every); Kingdom whose k. a child (Woe to); Man must not leave the k.'s highway for a pathway; Merry (Happy) as a k.; Must is for the k.; Nothing is (Where) k. must lose his right; Owl is k. of night; Peas with k., (Eat); Pope by voice, k. by birth . . . ; Rich as a k.; Sail, quoth the k.; Service to the k.'s (No); Subject's love is k.'s lifeguard; Two suns (k.); What the k. wills; Wipes his nose . . . forfeits his face to the k.

Kingdom come.

[From the clause *Thy kingdom come* in the Lord's Prayer.] 1785 GROSE *Dict. Vulg. T.* s.v. He is gone to Kingdom come, he is dead. 1789 WOLCOT (P. Pindar) *Subj. Paint.* Wks. (1812) II. 180 Sending such a Rogue to Kingdom-come. 1836 MARRYAT *Midsh. Easy* ch. 30 They will all be in Kingdom come tomorrow morning, if the breeze comes more on the land. 1870 MISS BRIDGMAN *R. Lynne* I. xii. 184 So old aunt Duncan has gone to kingdom come at last.

Kingdom of a cheater, In the | the wallet is carried before.   (K 91)

1640 HERBERT no. 465.

Kingdom of blind men, In the | the one-eyed is king. (E 240)

[ERASM. *Ad.* 2.4.96.] **1522** SKELTON *Why not to Court* 529–32 But haue ye nat harde this, How an one eyed man is Well syghted when He is amonge blynde men? **1609** HARWARD 117 (a squinteyd man is). **1640** HERBERT no. 469. **1665** MARVELL *Satires, Char. of Hol.* Among the blind the one-eyed blinkard reigns, So rules among the drowned he that drains. **1779–81** JOHNSON *Lives of Poets, Milton* (1908) I. 147 He might still be the giant of the pygmies, the one-eyed monarch of the blind. **1871** A. B. MITFORD *Tales of Old Japan* (1886) 26 I know but one warbler whose note has any music in it, the *uguisu*, . . . at best, a king in the kingdom of the blind.

Kingdom whose king is a child, Woe to the. (W 600)

[Ecclesiastes x. 16.] **1509** BARCLAY *Ship of Fools* ii. 14. *c.* **1513** SIR T. MORE *Rich. III* (1821 ed.) 113 Veh regno cuius rex puer est. Woe is that Realme, that hathe a chylde to theyre Kynge. **1548** HALL *Chron.* (1809 ed. 371). *Ibid.* 386 Often ruith the realme where chyldren rule, and women gouerne. **1563** *Mirror for Mag.* ed. Campbell 391. [1592] **1597** SHAKES. *Rich. III* II. iii. 11 Woe to that land that's govern'd by a child.

Kingdoms divided soon fall. (K 89)

?*a.* **1439** LYDGATE *Fall of Princes* E.E.T.S. 1924, i, l. 3822 Kyngdamys deuyded may no while endure. **1562** NORTON & SACKVILLE *Gorboduc* First Dumb Show A state knit in vnitie doth continue strong against all force. But being diuided, is easely destroyed. **1595** GARNIER *Cornelia* tr. Kyd I. 35 A state deuided cannot firmely stand. **1666** TORRIANO *It. Prov.* 233, no. 22.

Kingdom, *see also* Change a cottage in possession for k. in reversion; Content is more than k.; Love rules k. without sword; Mind to me a k. is.

Kings and bears oft worry their keepers. (K 85)

1641 FERGUSSON no. 561. **1721** KELLY 226 . . . Witness the tragical End of many Courtiers.

Kings are kittle cattle to shoe behind.

[*Kittill to scho behind* = Not to be depended upon.] **1818** SCOTT *Ht. Midl.* ch. 38 'Kings are kittle cattle to shoe behind, as we say in the north', replied the Duke; 'but . . . the matter is quite certain'.

Kings are out of play. (K 86)

1571 R. EDWARDS *Damon and Pythias* C2ᵛ But Kynges matters passyng our reache, pertayne not to vs. *a.* **1628** CARMICHAELL no. 1009. **1641** FERGUSSON no. 560. **1721** KELLY 225 . . . It is not right, in Subjects, to jest upon Kings, or to pry narrowly into their Determinations, and Actions.

Kings have long arms (hands, many ears and many eyes). (K 87)

[Gk. Μακραὶ τυράννων χεῖρες. L. OVID *Heroides* 17 166 An nescis longas regibus esse manus? Knowest thou not that kings have long arms?] **1539** TAVERNER A4ᵛ Longae regum manus. Kynges haue longe handes. They can brynge in men, they can pluck in thinges, though they be a great weye of. *Ibid.* A4 Multae regum aures, atque oculi. Kynges haue many eares and manye eyes, as who shulde saye, nothynge can be spoken, nothynge doon so secretly agaynst kynges and Rulers, but by one meanes or other at lengthe it wol come to their knowledge. **1541** ELYOT *Image of Gouernaunce* (1556 ed., f. 40ᵛ) Suche abuses can not be long hydde from princes, that haue theyr eares perforate (as is the prouerbe). **1548** HALL (1809, 43). **1579** LYLY *Euph.* i. 221 Knowest thou not Euphues that kinges haue long armes, and rulers large reches? **1586** G. WHETSTONE *Eng. Mirr.* 204 (wide ears, and out-streatched hands). **1641** FERGUSSON no. 562 Kings hes long ears. **1642** FULLER *H. & P. State IV* xxi (1840) 326 They stand in daily fear lest Darius Longimanus (such a one is every king) should reach them, and revenge himself. **1752** FRANKLIN Jan. **1823** SCOTT *Peveril* ch. 45.

Kings, *see also* King(s).

Kingswear[1] was a market town When Dartmouth[1] was a furzy down.

1926 *Times* 4 Feb. 13/4 Some little local jealousy, as in the old rhyme: Kingswear was a market town When Dartmouth was a furzy down. [[1] in Devon.]

Kink-cough, *see* Tail will catch the chin-cough.

Kinsfolk, *see* Many k. few friends; Marriages and funerals (At) friends discerned from k.

Kinsman helps kinsman, but woe to him that has nothing. (K 98)

1573 SANFORD 51 (Kinsman with kinsman). **1578** FLORIO *First F.* 32ᵛ Kinsfolkes with kinsfolke, wo to hym that hath nothing. **1629** *Bk. Mer. Rid.* Prov. no. 19.

Kinsman, *see also* Near neighbour better than far k.; Servant (If you would have good), take neither k. nor friend.

Kippen, *see* Out of the world and into K.

Kirby, *see* Sutton.

Kirk and a mill of it, Make a.

1721 KELLY 252 . . . That is, make your best of it. **1823** J. GALT *Entail* ch. 18 The property is my own . . . and surely I may mak a kirk and a mill o't an I like.

Kirk is aye greedy, The. (K 102)

c. **1641** FERGUSSON MS. no. 1366. **1721** KELLY 314 . . . Clergymen have Perquisites and Tythes due from every Man in the Parish, and because they demand these small sums they are called covetous.

Kirk is mickle, The | but you may say mass in one end of it.

a. **1628** CARMICHAELL no. 1630. **1721** KELLY 314 . . . Spoken when People say something is too much, intimating that they need take no more than they have use for. **1824** SCOTT *Redg.* Let. xiii. 'Better have a wine-glass, Mr. Peebles, . . .' 'If the kirk is ower muckle we can sing mass in the quire', said Peter, helping himself in the goblet out of which he had been drinking the small beer.

Kirk, *see also* Church (K.) stand in churchyard (Let the); Love his house (k.) yet not ride on ridge; Physic do not work, prepare for k.; Rives the k. to theek the quire.

Kirkbie's castle, and Fisher's folly; Spinola's pleasure, and Megse's glory.

(K 100)

1598 STOW *Survey of London* 128 Bishopsgate Ward. . . . This house, being so largely and sumptuously builded by a man[1] of no greater calling or possessions, was mockingly called Fishers Folly, and a Rithme was made of it, and other the like in this manner, Kirkebies Castle, and Fishers Folly, Spinilas Pleasure, and Megses glorie. [[1] Iasper Fisher free of the Goldsmithes. STOW 128.]

Kirkcaldy, *see* Devil is dead and buried in K.

Kirkham, *see* I will make one, quoth K.

Kirkyard, *see* Let the church stand in the k.; Like to die mends not k.

Kirtle, *see* Near is my coat (k.) but nearer is.

Kirton was a borough town When Exon was a vuzzy down.

1876 *N. & Q.* 5th Ser. VI. 364 When Kirton wuz a borough town, Ex'ter was a vuzzydown. **1911** CROSSING *Folk Rhy. of Devon* 13 . . . Crediton, or Kirton as it is still frequently called, was once of greater importance than it is to-day.

Kiss (Knock) a carle, and clap (ding[1]) a carle, and that's the way to tine[2] (win) a carle.

(C 92)

c. **1641** FERGUSSON MS. no. 923. **1721** KELLY 228 . . . People of mean breeding are rather to be won by harsh Treatment, than civil. *Ibid.* 228 Knock a Carle, and ding a Carle; and that's the way to win a Carle. [[1] beat. [2] lose.]

Kiss and be friends.

(F 753)

c. **1300** BRUNNE *Chron.* (Hearne) 64 Kisse and be gode frende in luf and in a wille. **1419** *Twenty-six Poems* E.E.T.S. 69 Make hem kyssen and be frende, þat were fou [foes] feynt. **1635** QUARLES *Div. Emb.* II. viii. Come, buss[1] and friends; . . . what ails my babe to cry? **1689** SELDEN *Table-Talk, Money* Arb. 76 The People and the Prince kist and were Friends, and so things were quiet for a while. **1738** SWIFT *Dial.* I. E.L. 286. **1778**

FRANCES BURNEY *Evelina* Lett. 82 He'll do you no harm, man!—come, kiss and be friends! [[1] kiss.]

Kiss and tell, To.

(K 106)

1616 JONSON *Forest* no. 5 'Tis no sinne loues fruit to steale, But the sweet theft to reueale. **1675** C. COTTON *Scoffer Scoft* 67 And if he needs must kiss and tell, I'll kick him headlong into Hell. [*c.* **1800**] **1856** H. COCKBURN *Memorial* 59 Up she of fourscore sat, and said with an indignant shake of her shrivelled fist and a keen voice—'the dawmed villain! does he kiss and tell!' **1816** 22 July BYRON *Corr.* Prothero iii. 339 The old reproach against their admirers of 'Kiss and tell'.

Kiss than spin, She had rather.

(K 105)

1678 RAY 255. **1732** FULLER no. 4123.

Kiss the child for the nurse's sake, Many.

(C 312)

13th cent. MS. quoted in **1846** WRIGHT *Essays on the Middle Ages* i. 150 *Osculor hunc ore natum nutricis amore.* *c.* **1470** *Harl. MS. 3362* (ed. Förster) in *Anglia* 42. 199 Ofte me kessyt þe chil(d) for [the nurse's sake]. *Osculor hunc ore puerum nutricis amore.* **1492** *Dial. of Salomon and Marcolphus* ed. Duff 12 He that kyssyth the lambe lovyth the shepe. **1546** HEYWOOD II. vii. K1. **1594** BACON *Promus* (Pott) 216, no. 495. **1655–62** GURNALL *Chrn. in Armour* (1865) I. 82 Some will kiss the child for the nurse's sake, and like the present for the hand that brings it. **1721** KELLY 243 Many one kisses the Bairn for Love of the Nurrish. That is, shows their Kindness to the Companions, Friends, or Relations, of those upon whom they have a Design, which they hope by their Influence to effect. **1823** SCOTT *Peveril* ch. 8 Among men, dame, many one caresses the infant that he may kiss the child's maid.

Kiss the clink[1] (counter[1]), To.

(C 416)

[= to be confined in prison.] *c.* **1560** HUTH *Ancient Ballads, &c.* (1867) 227 Then some the Counter oft doo kisse, If that the money be not paid. **1588** J. UDALL *Diotrephes* Arb. 22 I will make thee kiss the Clinke for this geare. **1620** ROWLANDS *Night Raven* (1872) 11 You kisse the Counter sirra. [[1] prison.]

Kiss the cup, To.

(C 909)

[= to drink.] *c.* **1412** HOCCLEVE *De Reg. Princ.* 3815 More is . . . honurable, a man compleyne of thirst, Than dronken be, whan he þe cuppe haþ kist. **1579** GOSSON *Sch. Abuse* Arb. 25 Kissing the cupp too often. **1706** STEVENS s.v. Jarro To kiss the Pot often.

Kiss (Lick) the dust (ground), To.

(D 651)

1535 COVERDALE *Bible* Psalms LXXI. i. 24 His enemies shal licke the dust. **1589** *Pasquil's Ret.* B Ouerthrow the state, and make the Emperiall crowne of her Maiestye kisse the ground. **1605–6** SHAKES. *M. V.* viii. 28 I will not yield To kiss the ground before young Malcolm's feet. **1611** *Id. W.T.* V. i. 199 They kneel, they kiss the earth. **1782** COWPER *Boadicea* 19 Soon her pride shall kiss the ground. **1835** I. TAYLOR *Spir. Despot.* x. 410 To kiss the dust before monstrous superstitions. **1867** TROLLOPE *Last Chron. Barset* ch. 56 She had yielded and had kissed the dust.

Kiss the hand they wish cut off, Many. (H 85)

1599 MINSHEU *Span. Dial.* 50 The Prouerbe saith, A man kisseth those hands that he would see cut off. **1634** HOWELL *Lett.* 28 Feb. (1903) II. 135 An Italian . . . will tell you that he kisseth your hand a thousand times over, when he wisheth them both cut off. **1640** HERBERT no. 283. **1657** TORRIANO *Introd. to It. Tongue* 59. **1897** 'H. S. MERRIMAN' *In Kedar's Tents* ch. 24 'A Carlist . . . rag whose readers are scarcely likely to be interested for a good motive in . . . the Queen Regent. . . . Many kiss the hands they would fain see chopped off.'

Kiss the hare's foot, To. (H 162)

[= to be late *or*, to starve.] **1598** *Servingmans Comfort* in *Inedited Tracts* (Hazlitt, 1868) 112 Vpon payne to dyne with Duke Humfrie or kisse the Hares foote. **1613–16** W. BROWNE *Brit. Past.* II. ii We had need Make haste away, unlesse we meane to speed With those that kisse the Hares foot. **1738** SWIFT *Dial.* II. E.L. 298. **1818** SCOTT *Let. to Croker* 5 Feb. in LOCKHART *Life* ch. 40 The poor clergyman [got] nothing whatever, or, as we say, *the hare's foot to lick.*

Kiss the post, To. (P 494)

[= to be shut out in consequence of being too late.] [*c.* 1515] *c.* **1530** BARCLAY *Eclog.* II, l. 1001 Shalt thou lose thy meat and kisse the post. **1600** T. HEYWOOD *1st Pt. Edw. IV*, Wks. (1874) IV. 47 Make haste thou art best, for feare thou kiss the post. **1681** W. ROBERTSON *Phraseol. Gen.* (1693) 475 You must kiss the post, or hare's foot, *Sero venere bubulci.*

Kiss the rod, To. (R 156)

[As children formerly had to do before chastisement.] **1528** TYNDALE *Obed. Chrn. Man* P.S. 196 If he knowledge his fault and take the correction meekly, and even kiss the rod. **1572** CRADOCKE *Ship of Assured Safety* 95 Neither will I studie to treade in their malitious steps . . . But rather kisse the rod with submission, wherwith I am scourged by Gods hande. **1580** MUNDAY *Zelauto* O4ᵛ. *a.* **1586** SIDNEY *Arcadia* II. (1867) 190 Yet he durst not but kiss his rod and gladly make much of his entertainment. **1594** *King Leir* l. 611 I do willingly embrace the rod. **1594** SHAKES. *T.G.V.* I. ii. 57 Foolish love That, like a testy babe, will scratch the nurse And presently all humbled kiss the rod! **1595–6** *Id. Rich. II* V. i. 32 Wilt thou, pupil-like, Take thy correction mildly, kiss the rod. **1628** SHIRLEY *Witty Fair One* I. iii. Come, I'll be a good child, and kiss the rod. **1800** I. MILNER in *Life* xii (1842) 209 When the fits of illness come, I do not, I believe, properly kiss the rod.

Kisses are keys. (K 104)

1616 N. BRETON *Cross. Prov.* A3ᵛ Wanton kisses are the keyes of sinne. **1639** CLARKE 28.

Kisses his wife (Sits to work) in the market-place, He that | shall have many teachers. (W 358)

1636 CAMDEN 297. **1659** HOWELL *Eng. Prov.* 13a He that kisseth his wife in the market-place shall have many teachers. **1670** RAY 110 (shall have enough to teach him). **1706** STEVENS s.v. Plaça We have an old saying, He that lies with his Wife. . . . **1721** KELLY 173 . . . *at the Market Cross, will have many to teach him.* Spoken when People are officiously instructing us in doing what we are about. **1732** FULLER no. 2303 (sits to work).

Kiss(es), (*noun*), see Bachelors' fare: bread and cheese and k.; Judas k.

Kiss(ed, es), (*verb*), see also Better k. a knave; Contentibus . . . k. my wife; Easy as k. my hand; Every man as he loves . . . when he k. his cow; Fool that k. the maid; Luck in horses must k. parson's wife; Never k. a man's wife; Wipes the child's nose (He that) k. mother; Woman k. is half won.

Kissing goes by favour. (K 108)

1616 DRAXE no. 693 Kissing commeth by fauour. **1621** BURTON *Anat. Mel.* II. iii. VII. footnote. **1639** CLARKE 28. **1659** HEYLIN *Animadversions* in FULLER *Appeal Inj. Innoc.* (1840) 618 But 'kissing goes by favour', as the saying is; and therefore let him favour whom he pleases, and kiss where he favoureth. **1721** KELLY 225 . . . Men shew Regard, or do Service, to People as they affect. **1880** BLACKMORE *Mary Aner.* ch. 21 'I should like . . . to give you one kiss, Insie' . . . Before he could reason in favour of a privilege which goes proverbially by favour, the young maid was gone.

Kissing, see also Gorse is out of bloom (When), k. out of fashion.

Kit¹ has lost her key. (K 109)

1533 MORE *Apol.* xxiv. Wks. 888/2 Certaine letters which some of the brethrene let fall of late, and lost theim of likelyhedde as some good kitte leseth her kayes. **1564** *Scott.* Pref. in *Eng. Garner* III. 71 Oblations and offerings . . . for deliverance of bad husbands . . ., to keep down the belly, and when 'Kit had lost her key'. [¹ Catherine or Kate.]

Kit, see Cat (K.) after kind.

Kitchen boys, see Laird slight lady (If), so will k. b.

Kitchen physic is the best physic. (P 260)

1542 A. BORDE *Dietary* E.E.T.S. 277 The chefe physycke . . . dothe come from the kytchyn. **1562** BULLEIN *Bulwark of Def.* (*Bk. of Comp.*) 48 With kitchin phisicke: whiche kitchin, I assure thee, is a good Poticaries shop. **1738** SWIFT *Dial.* II. E.L. 307.

Kitchen, *see also* Hall into the k., (Out of the); Hunger is good k. meat; Little k. makes large house; Said in the k. should not be heard in hall; Take tea in the k.

Kite will never be a good hawk, A carrion. (One cannot make a falcon of a buzzard.)   (K 114)

c. **1300** *King Alis.* l. 3047 Nultow never, late ne skete A goshawk maken of a Kete, No faucon mak[en] of busard, No hardy knyht mak of coward. *c.* **1400** *Rom. Rose* l. 4031 Man [ne] may, for no daunting, Make a sperhauke oI a bosarde. *c.* **1576** HOLYBAND D8ᵛ (A Carreine kite). *c.* **1558** 'WEDLOCK' *Image of Idleness* A5 Lyke as yf the Tercell wolde saye that his Eeryer or dame were a Puttocke or Kyte, which argueth him selfe neuer lykly to proue good hauke. **1578** FLORIO *First F.* 30ᵛ (A Bytter). **1611** DAVIES Prov. 64 (A Bittur). **1614** CAMDEN 302. **1820** SCOTT *Monast.* ch. 19 For seldom doth a good hawk come out of a kite's egg.

Kite, *see also* Ask a k. for a feather; Carrion will kill k. (No); Kind as a k.; Leg of a lark better than a k.; Whirl the eyes shows k.'s brain; Yellow as k.'s foot.

Kitten(s), (*noun*), *see* Playful as a k.; Wanton k. make sober cats.

Kittened, (*verb*), *see* Cat k.? (Has the).

Kittle cattle, *see* Kings are k. c. to shoe behind.

Kittle[1] shooting at corbies and clergy, It is.

1737 RAMSAY III. 187.   **1787** BURNS *Brigs of Ayr* As for your Priesthood I shall say but little, Corbies and Clergy are a shot right kittle.   **1855** STIRLING-MAXWELL in *Misc. Ess. & Addr.* (1891) 28 Against our divines I shall say but little, A mark to know a knave by. not met with any but these three—'It's kittle shooting at corbies and clergy'. [[1] difficult.]

Kitty Sleitchock's[1] bannock, You have gotten a piece of.

1721 KELLY 373 . . . Spoken when young ones flatter us for something. [[1] Kate the Flatterer.]

Knack to know a knave, A.

1579 E. HAKE *News out of Paul's Churchyard* 1872 ed. F3ᵛ Haue ye not seene the knacke to know knaues by, compiled by many knaues? *c.* **1580** *Hist. MSS. Comm.* 11th Report Appdx. vii. (1888) 281 [Inquiries about the hearing mass, the having popish books, including one called A knacke to knowe a knave.] **1592** [Play title]. **1593** *The Passionate Morrice* New Sh. S. 91 It is great pittie we should not haue many knackes to know knaues by. **1594** *Knack to Know an Honest Man* l. 475 (an arrant knaue). **1596** M. B. *The Triall of true Friendship*; . . . *Otherwise, A knacke to know a knaue from an honest man* [Title]. *c.* **1614** J. FLETCHER *Wit without Money* III. vi. A mark to know a knave by.

Knacks in one's budget, To have.   (K 118)

1546 HEYWOOD II. vi. Ii.   *c.* **1566** CURIO *Pasquin in a Trance* tr. W.P. 62ᵛ These knaues haue manye such knackes in their Bougets.   **1573** J. BRIDGES *Supremacy of Christian Princes* K1ᵛ. **1659** HOWELL *Eng. Prov.* 14a.

Knapton, *see* Gimmingham.

Knave is in a plum-tree, When a | he has neither friend nor kin.   (K 141)

1640 HERBERT no. 507.

Knave than a fool, I'd rather have a.

1659 N. R. 15 A man had better have a Knave, than a fool, to his Servant.   **1913** *Folk-Lore* xxiv. 77.

Knave, The more (worse) | the better luck.   (K 130)

1550 LATIMER *Sermons* P.S. 280 It is an old proverb, the more wicked, the more fortunate. **1579** J. DYOS *Sermon* 13 Accordyng to the Prouerbe: Quo peior, eo fortunatior: the worser man the better lucke.   **1609** HARWARD 101ᵛ (The woorse man) . . . but it is· but for a tyme.   **1636** CAMDEN 307.   **1660** TATHAM *Rump* IV. i. (1879) 250 What says Pluck?—The worser knave, the better luck!

Knave to the learned (old) knave, No.   (K 131)

1571 R. EDWARDS *Damon & Pythias* Hazl.-Dods. iv. 78 You are a-wily collier and a brave, I see now there is no knave, like to the old knave. **1617** MORYSON *Itin.* III. i. 5 (1907–8) III. 358 Thus the English Proverb saith. No knave to the learned knave.

Knave(s), *see also* Better be a fool than k.; Better kiss a k.; Caught a k. in a purse-net; Cold weather and k. come out of the north; Crafty k. needs no broker; Knack to know a k.; Know a k. (If ye would); Merry when k. meet; More k. than fool; Mortar (No more) . . . cunning k. has cunning trick; Old k. no babe; Once a k. ever a k.; Pack of cards without k. (No); Stool in the sun (Put), when one k. rises . . .; Two false k. need no broker; Walk, k., walk; Ware, k., quoth Tomkins to his shadow; World is full of fools (k.).

Knavery (Cheating) in all trades, but most in tailors, There is.   (K 152)

1632 MARTIN PARKER *Knavery in all Trades* (title).   **1654** 12–19 July *Mercurius Fumigosus* 49 If there be not Knavery in *All Trades*, I shrewdly am mistaken.   **1658** *Comes Facundus* 192.   **1666** TORRIANO 19 no. 91 As the English in Drollery will say, There's cheating in all Trades, but ours.   **1692** L'ESTRANGE *Æsop's Fab.* clxxxiii. (1738) 195 Jupiter appointed Mercury to make him a composition of fraud and hypocrisy, and to give every artificer his dose on't. . . . Mercury . . . gave the tailors the whole quantity that was left, and from hence comes the old saying, . . . **1719** DE ALVARADO 64 (in all things, except old Cloaths).

Knavery may serve for a turn, but honesty is best at long run.   (K 150)

1678 RAY 164.

Knavery, *see also* Cloak for his k.

Knave and a fool never take thought, A.
(K 127)

1626 BRETON *Soothing* A5. **1639** CLARKE 292.

Knave as amongst knaves, As good be a.

1645 *The old Proverbe* . . . [title, WING C6009].

Knave on horseback.

1577 B. GOOGE *Heresbach's Husb.* (1586) 47 As the Prouerbe in Englande is, Set a Knaue on horsebacke, and you shall see him shoulder a Knight.

Knave's grease.

1569 J. PHILLIP *Patient Grissell* l. 534 All the place sauoreth of thy knaues grease I see well. **1602** WITHALS 73 Mastigophorus, . . . that is worthy to be beaten, or scourged, they call it knaues grease.

Knaves and fools divide the world.
(K 144)

1659 N. R. 71. **1670** RAY 111.

Knaves, The more | the worse company.   (K 146)

1519 *Four Elements* Hazl.-Dods. i. 35 What, art thou here? I see well, I, The mo knaues the worse company. *c.* **1549** HEYWOOD I. xi. D3ᵛ But the mo knaues the woorse company to greete.

Knaves, *see also* Knave(s).

Knees of the gods, On the.

[= beyond human control. HOM. *Il.* 17. 514; *Od.* l. 9 θεῶν ἐν γούνασι.] **1879** BUTCHER & LANG *Odyssey* 1. 9 Howbeit these things surely lie on the knees of the gods, whether he shall return or not. **1886** FROUDE *Oceana* ch. 7 If the several provinces continue to increase their numbers at the present rate, there will be more than fifty millions then. There is a proverb that 'nothing is certain but the unforeseen'. . . . ταῦτα θεῶν ἐν γούνασι κεῖται. **1900** *Daily News* 17 Aug. 6/5 Such things are yet upon the knees of the gods. **1922** 10 Apr. D. H. LAWRENCE *Lett.* ii. 700 I hope I shall arrive in Taos with ten cents left in my pocket. . . . Knees of the Gods.

Knee(s), *see also* Broken her leg above the k.; Dog's nose and maid's k.

Knell, *see* Hear a toll or k. (When dost), think on passing bell.

Knife into a person, To have one's.

1890 D. C. MURRAY *John V's. Guard.* ch. 36 I reckon you've got your knife into Mr. Jousserau. **1911** *Spectator* 3 June 854 The dislike of the Socialists for Mr. John Burns . . . has never been disguised, and they seldom lose an opportunity of 'getting their knife' into him.

Knife, It is a good | it will cut butter when it is melted (it was made at Dulledge, it was made five miles beyond Cutwell).   (K 155)

1602 R. MARBECK *Def. of Tabacco* D2ᵛ Giue me a sharpe fine edged, cutting knife, to eate my meate withall, rather then a dull penny whittle, fit to cut butter withall, when it is warme, as the common Prouerbe is. **1678** RAY 255. *Ibid.* A good knife, it was made five miles beyond Cutwell. **1732** FULLER no. 2857 ('twas made at Dull-edge).

Knife, A man may slay (cut) himself with his own.

c. **1387** CHAUCER *Parson's T.* l. 858 A man may sleen hymself with his owne knyf. *Id. Merchant's T.* l. 1839 (ironical) A man may do no sinne with his wyfe Ne hurte hymselven with his owne knyfe. **1611** COTGRAVE S.V. Couper He wounds himselfe with his owne weapons; as does a learned Diuine that fals into heresie; . . . a wealthie man that becomes either a miser, or an vnthrift, etc.

Knife whets another, One.   (K 156)

1576 *Courtly Controv.* 2A2 Like as two kniues sharpen eche other. **1616** DRAXE no. 811. **1666** TORRIANO *It. Prov.* 48, no. 30.

Knife, knives, *see also* Butcher looked for his k.; Never catch at falling k.; Oxford draws k.; Oxford k. and London wives; Same k. cuts bread and fingers; Say true, will you swallow my k.?; Smith forges weak k. (Often); Stuck a k. to my heart (If you had); War to the k.; Whet a k. for own throat; Whet his k. on Fleet.

Knight of Cales, A | and a gentleman of Wales, and a laird of the north countree; a yeoman of Kent, with his yearly rent, will buy them out all three.
(K 163)

[Cadiz was captured by Essex in 1596.] *a.* **1658** F. OSBORNE *Tradit. Memoirs* (*Secret History of James I*, 1811, i. 41). **1659** HOWELL *Eng. Prov.* 17a. **1662** FULLER *Kent* 62 . . . *Cales Knights* were made in that voyage, by Robert Earle of Essex, anno Dom. 1596, to the number of sixty, whereof . . . some were of low fortunes.

Knight of the post.   (K 164)

[= a perjurer; one who got his living by giving false evidence.] **1559** *Mirr. for Mag.* 'Jack Cade' (Campbell) 175. **1560** *Contr. betwixt Churchyard and Camell* G3 There bee knightes of the post, whiche will them selues forswere. **1576** PETTIE i. 159. **1578** WHETSTONE *Promos*

and Cassandra K1. **1580** E. KNIGHT *Trial Truth*
39 b Men, . . . who will not let to sweare vpon a
booke, . . . beyng hyred therevnto for money
. . . called Knightes of the poste. **1599** KYD
Sol. & Pers. v. iii Faith, two great Knights of
the post swore vpon the Alcaron that he would
haue firde the Turkes Fleete.

Knight, *see also* Carpet k.; King can make a k.;
Make a poor man k. (Little of God's might to).

Knit my dog a pair of breeches and my cat a codpiece. (D 492)

1678 RAY 255.

Knit, *see also* Know well ere thou k.

Knock at a deaf man's door, To. *Cf.* Sing at deaf man's door. (M 499)

1601 A. DENT *Plain Man's Pathway* 55 It is but
euen to plough the Sea, or knocke at a deafe
mans doore. **1616** B. RICH *Ladies Looking
Glasse* 3. **1639** CLARKE 7 You knock at a
deafeman's doore—wrong doore.

Knock in the cradle, He got a. (K 166)

1611 DONNE *Anat. of World*; *First Anniv.* 195
Poems (1896) II. 111 Then first of all The
world did in her cradle take a fall, And turn'd
her brains. **1678** RAY 255.

Knock on the hoop, and another on the barrel, He gives one.

1813 RAY 13 . . . *Ital.* i.e. he speaks now to the
purpose, now on matters wholly extraneous.

Knock under the board (table). (B 487)

[= succumb in a drinking-bout.] **1599** PORTER
Angry Wom. Abingd. ll. 1064-5 Sbloud yee
shall take more then will do yee good, Or Ile
make yee clap vnder the table. **1666** TORRIANO
Prov. Phr. 127a To have got soundly drunk,
a cup too much, . . . fox, so¯as to knock under
the table. **1678** RAY 74. . . . He must do so that
will not drink his cup. **1691-2** *Gentl. Jrnl.* 10
Mar. He that flinches his glass and to Drink is
not able, Let him quarrel no more, but knock
under the Table.

Knock, *(noun), see also* Bit and a k.; Young
men's k. old men feel.

Knocked me down with a feather, You might have.

[= overcome with surprise.] **1740** S. RICHARD-
SON *Pamela* Letter VII I was so confounded at
these words, you might have beat me down with
a feather. **1821** COBBETT *Rural Rides* 6 Nov.
I asked the ostler the *name* of the place; and, as
the old women say, 'you might have knocked me
down with a feather', when he said, 'Great
Bedwin'. **1855** MRS. GASKELL *North and South*
ch. 43 Yo' might ha' knocked me down wi' a
straw. **1891** A. FORBES *Barracks, Biv. & Bat.*
(1910) 95 You might have knocked him down
with a 'feather—he was stricken absolutely
dumb.

Knock(ed, s, ing), *(verb), see also* Bribe will
enter without k.; Fortune k. at every man's
gate; Kiss (K.) a carle and ding a carle.

Knot in a (bul)rush, To seek (find) a. (K 168)

[TER. *And.* 5.4.38 *Nodum in scirpo quaerere* =
to find difficulties where there are none.] **1340**
Ayenbite 253 þet zekþ þet uel ine þe aye oþer
þane knotte ine þe resse. **1533** T. MORE *Confut.
Barnes in Confut. Tyndale* VIII: Wks. 1557, 778
Thys wer but finding of a knot in a rushe. **1581**
J. BELL *Haddon's Answ. Osor.* 436 Myne opposed
aduersary will seeke after a knott in a Bullrush
as the Prouerbe is. **1584** Withals E3ᵛ You
seeke a knot in a rush, that is, you finde faulte
where none is. (*c.* **1590**) **1598** GREENE *James IV*
III. ii. 1198 They seeke a knot in a ring that
would wrong my master or his seruants in this
Court. *a.* **1601** NASHE i. 373 Cares enough the
ordinarie course of our life tythes of his own
accord to us, though we seeke not a knot in
a bulrush. **1748** EDWARDS *Can. of Criticism*
8 Ex. 30 Here our profess'd Critic . . . is Can.
searching after knots in a bulrush.

Knot is loose, Where the | the string slips. (K 169)

1579 GOSSON *Ephemerides* 28 Where the Knot
is loose the string slippes. **1597** *Politeuphuia*
166 Where the knot is loose, the string slyppeth.
1639 CLARKE 248.

Knot(s), *see also* Fools tie k.; Gordian k.; Tailor
that makes not a k. loses stitch; Tied a k. with
his tongue.

Knotty timber must have sharp wedges. (P 289)

1539 TAVERNER 4ᵛ To a crabbed knot muste be
sought a crabbed wedge. A stronge disease
requyreth a strong medicine. A shrewed wyfe, a
shrewed husbande to tame her. A boysteous
horse, a boysteous snaffel. **1577** R. STANYHURST
in Holinshed *Descr. Ireland* (1587 18b) Good
policie now and then to cleave knurd knobs with
crabbed wedges. **1585** A. DENT *Serm. of
Repentance* C2 Hard knobbie Timber must haue
hard Wedges, and hard strokes with a beetle.
1589 T. WHITE *Serm. preached 17 Nov.* 32 Harde
and knottie wood must haue Iron Wedges.
1597 GERARD *Herbal* 287 Many . . . haue been
sustained to haue vnto such an hard knot, a
crabbed wedge, or else had vtterly perished.
1601-2 SHAKES. *T.C.* I. iii. 316 Blunt wedges
rive hard knots. **1611** DAVIES *Epig.* no. 137
A crabbed knot a crabbed wedge must haue.
1616 DRAXE no. 1949. **1664** CODRINGTON 203.
1670 RAY 15.

Know a goose from a capon (gridiron), To.

1548 HALL *Chron.* (1809 ed. 490) He coulde not
descerne a Goose from a Capon. **1896** J. C.
HUTCHESON *Crown & Anch.* vi He's quite a
contrast to the sucking Nelsons . . . who don't,
as a rule, know a goose from a gridiron!

Know a hawk from a handsaw, To.
(H 226)

[In the following, *handsaw* is generally explained
as a corruption of *heronshaw*, or *hernsew*, dial.
harnsa, heron.] 1600–1 SHAKES. *H.* II. ii. 374
I am but mad north, north-west; when the wind
is southerly, I know a hawk from a handsaw.
1850 KINGSLEY *Alton L.* ch. 4 Wasn't there
enough in that talk . . . to show anybody that,
who can tell a hawk from a hand-saw?

Know a knave, If ye would | give him
a staff. (K 125)

1640 HERBERT no. 19. 1659 HOWELL *Fr. Prov.*
2 (a true Clown).

Know all, Since you | and I nothing,
tell me what I dreamed last night.
(A 201)

1640 HERBERT no. 336.

Know by a halfpenny if the priest will
take an offering, They will. (H 51)

1641 FERGUSSON no. 792. 1721 KELLY 321 . . .
A small Experiment will discover a covetous
Inclination.

Know by a penny how a shilling
spends, You may. (P 214)

1678 RAY 78. [*Joculatory*.]

Know by your nose (looks) what
pottage (porridge) you love, One may.
(N 227)

1556 T. HILL *Brief and Pleas. Epit. Physiog.* D3ᵛ
That face . . . declareth that man to be a drinker
of good wyne after the choyse of the nose, as the
prouerbe is. 1564 BULLEIN *Dial. agst. Fever*
1888) 79 I see by his nose that of al potage
he loueth good Ale. 1590 LODGE *Rosalynde*
Wks. (1883) I. 42 Her colour chaungde, and
she said to Aliena, See, Mistresse, where our iolly
Forester comes. And you are not a little glad
thereof, quoth Aliena; your nose bewrayes what
porredge you loue. 1610 FIELD *Woman is a W.* I.
ii. Merm. 351 One may see by her nose what pottage she loves. 1639 CLARKE 179 (lookes . . .
porridge). 1670 RAY 125.

Know good manners, You | but you use
but a few. (M 631)

1520 R. WHITTINGTON *Vulg.* E.E.T.S. 95 Ye have
seen more good maners then ye have borne
awaye. 1639 CLARKE 2. 1670 RAY 185. 1732
FULLER no. 5919 You have good manners, but
never carry them about you.

Know him as well as if I had gone
through him with a lighted link (as if I
were within you), I. (K 171. T 246)

1599 PORTER *Angry Wom. Abingd.* l. 2315 I
know your mind as well as though I were within
you. 1721 KELLY 202 (candle). 1732 FULLER
no. 2611. 1738 SWIFT *Dial.* III. E.L. 318

Madam, I fancy I know your thoughts, as well
as if I were within you.

Know him not, I | should I meet him in
my pottage dish. (P 484)

1590 *Almond for a Parrot* McKerrow Nashe iii.
348 I giue you but a tast of them by the waie,
that you may knowe them the next time you
meete them in your dish. 1608 ARMIN *Nest of
Ninnies* Sh. Soc. 27 You heare . . . how he is
markt: if ye mette him in your pottage-dish, yet
know him. 1672 WALKER 13 no. 94. 1678
RAY 265. 1732 FULLER no. 2613 (porridge).

Know how the market goes, You may |
by the market folks. (M 676)

1545 *Precepts of Cato* 'Sage Sayings' Bias B6ᵛ
If thou wylte knowe howe the market goeth,
thou must lerne that of them that boughte and
soulde in the market. 1546 HEYWOOD I. xi. D4ᵛ
Men know (quoth I) I haue herde nowe and
then, Howe the market gothe by the market
men. *a.* 1591 HY. SMITH *Serm.* (1866) I. 11 If
thou wilt know a godly man, . . . mark . . .
report, because as the market goes, so they
say the market-men will talk. 1639 CLARKE
63.

Know no more than the Pope of Rome
about it, I.

1664 BUTLER *Hudibras* II. iii. 195 That durst
upon a *truth* give doom He knew no more
then th' *Pope of Rome.* 1678 RAY 255 To
know one no more than he does the Pope of
Rome. 1863 *N. & Q.* 3rd Ser. III. 470 Persons
when professing entire ignorance of any subject,
exclaim, 'I know no more than the Pope of
Rome about it'; . . . the expression [is] especially
current . . . in Pembrokeshire.

Know not me, If you | you know
nobody. (K 174)

1575 GASCOIGNE *Glass of Govᵗ* ii. 36 Know you
not Eccho? Why then you know no man.
c. 1584 R. WILSON *Three Ladies of London*
Hazl.-Dods. vi. 397. 1598 *Mucedorus* I. iv.
65. 1605–6 T. HEYWOOD I and 2 *If You Know
Not Me, You Know Nobody.* [Title: also i. 42.]

Know not who lives or dies, We.
(K 179)

1640 HERBERT no. 966.

Know nothing except that I know not,
I. (N 276)

1542 UDALL *Apoph.* 15ᵛ Of all the saiynges of his
[Socrates] there is none so muche taken vp, as
that he saied, that he knewe nothyng, sauyng
onely this, that he knewe no thyng. 1581
C. THIMELTHORPE *Short Inventory* H7ᵛ The wise
and learned wil say, hoc solum scio quod nihil
scio. I only know this that I know nothing at al.
1583 MELBANCKE *Philot.* N2 If yow be inquisitiue
of any crime in Florence, which is rather to bee
amended priuatelye, then reprehended pub-
licklye, my aunswere is Nihil scio, nisi nescio.
1604 SHAKES. *M.M.* II. iv. 76 Let me be ignorant,
and in nothing good But graciously to know I

am no better.—Thus wisdom wishes to appear most bright When it doth tax itself. **1633** J. FORD *Broken Heart* IV. i. Maids know onley that they know not.

Know one another, They that | salute afar off.   (K 177)

1640 HERBERT no. 185.

Know one from Adam, Not to.

1844 STEPHENS *High Life in New York* I. 191 He don't know me from Adam. **1861** G. J. WHYTE-MELVILLE *Market Harbor.* ch. 7 'Who's that fellow? Is he staying with you at Harborough? . . . 'Don't know him from Adam,' he replied.

Know the horse by his harness, You may.   (H 707)

1581 GUAZZO i. 161 (As the saying is) judging the horses by the sadles and furnyture. **1621** ROBINSON 25. **1639** CLARKE 64. **1670** RAY 105. [But *cf.* **1732** FULLER no. 5883 You can't judge of the horse by the harness.]

Know the ropes, To.

[= to be acquainted with ways of doing things.] **1840** R. H. DANA *Bef. Mast* ch. 9 The captain, who . . . 'knew the ropes', took the steering oar. **1874** *Slang Dict.* 271 'To know the ropes', is to be conversant with the minutiae of metropolitan dodges. **1892** STEVENSON *Wrecker* ch. 22 Anywhere from Tonga to the Admiralty Isles, he knew the ropes and could lie in the native dialect.

Know the value of a ducat, If you would | try to borrow one. *Cf.* Know what money is, etc.

1659 HOWELL *Span. Prov.* 13 (Crown). **1706** STEVENS s.v. Ducado. **1732** FULLER no. 2801.

Know the worst is good, To.   (W 915)

c. **1558** 'WEDLOCK' *Image of Idleness* D1 It shalbe wysedome to cast the worst before it fall. **1595** SHAKES. *M.N.D.* I. i. 62 I beseech your Grace that I may know The worst that may befall me in this case. **1597** *Politeuphuia* 123ᵛ It is some comfort in misery, to know the worst of our mishaps. **1605–6** SHAKES. *M.* III. iv. 134 For now I am bent to know By the worst means [witches] the worst. **1639** CLARKE 199.

Know the worth of water till the well is dry, We never.   (W 922)

a. **1628** CARMICHAELL no. 1140 Manie wats not quhairof the wel sauris[1] quhill it fall drie. **1659** HOWELL *Brit. Prov.* 24 Of the Well we see no want, till either dry, or Water skant. **1721** KELLY 351. **1758** FRANKLIN *Poor Rich Alm.* in ARBER *Eng. Garner* v. 583 Always taking out of the meal tub, and never putting in, soon comes to the bottom. Then, as *Poor* DICK says, When the well's dry, they know the worth of water! [¹ tastes.]

Know thyself.   (K 175)

[THALES in DIOGENES LAERTIUS, I. I. 13, 40. Γνῶθι σαυτόν. JUVENAL 11. 27 *E coelo descendit*

γνῶθι σεαυτόν.] **1481** CAXTON *Reynard* ed. Arb. 73 Late euery man knowe hym self, that is my counseyl. *c.* **1526** ERASM. *Dicta Sap.* A3ᵛ *Nosce te ipsum.* Knowe thy selfe. **1531** SIR T. ELYOT *Governour* (Croft) III. iii 203 The words be these in latine, *Nosce te ipsum*, whiche is in englysshe, know thy selfe. **1545** ASCHAM *Toxoph.* Arb. 155 That wise prouerbe of Apollo, *Knowe thy selfe*: that is to saye, learne to knowe what thou art able, fitte, and apt vnto, and folowe that. **1660** W. SECKER *Nonsuch Prof.* II (1891) 186 The heathen tell us that 'know thyself' was an oracle that came down from heaven. Sure I am it is this oracle that will lead us to the God of heaven. **1737** RAMSAY III. 188 Ken yoursel, and your neighbours winna misken you. **1850** LYTTON *Caxtons* XVI. x 'Know thyself', saith the old philosophy. 'Improve thyself', saith the new. **1905** A. MACLAREN *Exposn., Matthew* I. 113 The proud old saying of the Greeks, 'Know thyself', if it were followed out unflinchingly . . . would result in this profound abnegation of all claims. [See more in *N. & Q.* Vol. 180, 177.]

Know well ere thou knit.

c. **1450** *Prouerbis of Wysdom* 39 Know well, ore þou knyt to fast; Fore ofte rape[1] rewyþe at last. [¹ haste.]

Know what I know, I.   (K 173)

1546 HEYWOOD II. vii. K1 I wot what I wot. **1570** [**1584**, A4ᵛ] W. BALDWIN *Beware the Cat* Argument I know what I know. *c.* **1592** MARLOWE *Jew of Malta* IV. vi. 14 I know what I know; he's a murderer. **1592–3** SHAKES. *C.E.* III. i. 11 Say what you will, sir, but I know what I know. **1594–5** *Id. L.L.L.* V. ii. 490 I can assure you, sir, we know what we know. **1605–6** *Id. K.L.* I. v. 15 Yet I can tell what I can tell. **1659** HOWELL *Span. Prov.* 18 I know what I know, but I will keep it to myself. **1905** WEYMAN *Starvecrow F.* ch. 28 Therefore I'll spare speech, But—I know what I know.

Know what money is, Would you | go borrow some. *Cf.* Know the value of a ducat.   (M 1104)

1640 HERBERT no. 374. **1841** S. WARREN *Ten Thous. a Year* ch. 4 'If you want to learn the value of money, try to borrow some', . . . and Titmouse was now going to learn that useful but bitter lesson.

Know what shall be, He that would | must consider what has been.   (K 170)

1641 Nov. HENRY OXINDEN (to Margaret Lady Oxinden), in *Oxinden Let.* 230 Hee who will see what shall bee let him consider what hath bene. **1666** TORRIANO *It. Prov.* 81 no. 18 If thou wilt know what must be, look at what is past. **1732** FULLER no. 2367.

Know what would be dear, He that could | need be a merchant but one year.   (M 887)

1546 HEYWOOD I. i. A2 Who so that knewe, what wolde be dere, Shulde nede be a marchaunt but one yeere. *a.* **1585** MONTGOMERIE *Cherrie & Slae* xciv (1821) 50 Quha wist quhat wald be cheip or deir, Sould neid to traffique but a ȝeir, Gif things to cum were kend. **1670** RAY 78 . . . Such a merchant was the Philosopher Thales . . . he foreseeing a future dearth of Olives, the year following, bought up at easie rates all that kind of fruit then in mens hands.

Know what you can do till you try, You never.

1829 MARRYAT *Frank Mild.* ch. 7 I have often heard my poor old uncle say that no man knows what he can do till he tries. **1893** MONT. WILLIAMS *Leaves of a Life* ch. 13 On hearing the verdict he . . . shouted out: 'I told you so . . . ! You never know what you can do till you try.'

Know what's o'clock, To.   (O 10)

a. **1525** SKELTON *Colyn Cloute* i. 319 To knowe whate ys a clocke Vnder her surfled smocke, And her wanton wodicocke. [**1589**] **1594** LYLY *Mother B.* IV. ii. 65 On thy conscience tell me what tis a clocke? **1823** JON BEE *Slang A Dict. of the Turf* 19 He who knows 'which way the Bull ran, is up to snuff' and may be considered as 'one who knows what o'clock 'tis'. **1837** DICKENS *Pickwick* ch. 43 I know what's o'clock, Sir. Wen I don't, I'll ask you, Sir. **1878** BROWNING *Two Poets of Croisic* xciv You've learnt your lesson, found out what's o'clock.

Know when one is well (well off), To.   (K 183)

1553 *Respublica* IV. iv Thow canst not see, thow wretch canst thow whan thow art well? **1640** JONSON *Tale Tub* II. iv. 2 You doe not know when yo' are well, I thinke. **1836** MARRYAT *Midsh. Easy* ch. 12 (well off). **1869** M. TWAIN *Innocents Abroad* ch. 26 (well off).

Know when to spend and when to spare, and you need not be busy; you'll ne'er be bare.   (K 176)

1633 T. STAFFORD *Ire. Appeased* III. xiii (1810), iii. 610 And knoweth when to spend, and when to spare. **1664** CODRINGTON 203 (is great wisdom). **1721** KELLY 225. **1732** FULLER no. 6437.

Know where they were born, Men | not where they shall die.   (M 550)

1580 MUNDAY *Zelauto* T1ᵛ. **1639** CLARKE 108.

Know which way the wind blows, To.   (W 144)

1546 HEYWOOD II. ix. K4 I know, And knew, whiche waie the wynde blew, and will blow. **1548** HALL *Chron.* (1809 ed., 475) The Scottish kynge . . . beganne to perceaue whiche waye the wynde blewe. **1577** R. STANYHURST in Holinshed *Desc. Ireland* (1587, 18) I weigh not two chips which waie the wind bloweth. [**1625**] **1647** FLETCHER *Chances* III. v. 49 I know where the wind sits.

Know your driver, I will make you.   (D 612)

1678 RAY 345 (*Somerset*).

Know your meaning by your mumping (gaping),[1] I.   (M 797)

1639 CLARKE 64 (your winking). **1659** HOWELL *Eng. Prov.* 21a You may know his meaning by his gaping. **1670** RAY 186 (gaping). **1721** KELLY 183 . . . I know by your motions and gestures what you would be at, and what you design. *a.* **1734** NORTH *Exam.* I. iii. § 46 We are to understand his Meaning by his Mumping. [1 grimacing.]

Know(n, s), *see also* Better k. than trusted; Better the devil you k.; Black sheep (To k. one from a); Cat from a cony (cowlstaff) (To k. a); Converses not (He that) k. nothing; Devil is k. by his claws; Devil k. many things because old; Every man is best k. to himself; Every man k. his own business best; Favour (Without) none will k. you; Fool k. more in own house; Foot a man halts (To k. on which); Fox k. much; Friend never k. till man have need; Good man is last who k. what's amiss; Horseback (When on) k. all things; Judge k. nothing unless explained three times; Judicare came into creed (To k. how); Knack to k. a knave; Little k. the fat sow what lean doth mean; No man better k. what good is; No man k. when he shall die; Pay what you owe and you'll k. what you're worth; Shirt k. my designs (If my); Shuns the man that k. him; Sins are not k. till acted; Speers the gate he k. (Many); Spies (Life of) is to k., not to be k.; Sports and journeys men are k. (In); Tell not all you k.; Three things there be hard to be k.; Travels (He that) k. much; Twyford my name is, I k. nothing of matter; Way to turn him (He k. not which); Wicked (Hard to be) but worse to be k. so; Workman is k. by his work.

Knowing, *see* Thinking is far from k.

Knowledge is folly, except grace guide it.   (K 189)

1640 HERBERT no. 248.

Knowledge is no burthen.

1616 WITHALS 582. **1640** HERBERT no. 692. **1641** FERGUSSON no. 559 Knowledge is eith[1] borne about. [1 easily.]

Knowledge is power.

[PROV. xxiv. 5 A wise man is strong; yea, a man of knowledge increaseth strength.] **1590–1** SHAKES. *2 Hen. VI* IV. vii. 69 Ignorance is the curse of God, Knowledge the wing wherewith we fly to heaven. **1620** BACON *Nov. Organ.* Aphor. iii Scientia et potentia humana in idem coincidunt, quia ignorati causae destituit effectum. [Knowledge and human power are synonymous, since the ignorance of the cause frustrates the effect.] **1822** BYRON *Corres.* ed. J. Murray 1922, ii. 214 They say 'Knowledge is power'. **1853** LYTTON *My Novel* I. iii. **1859** SMILES *Self-Help* ch. 11 'Knowledge is power'; but . . . knowledge of itself, unless wisely directed, might merely make bad men more dangerous. **1907** S. LEE *Gt. Englishmen 16th Cent.* 4 [Bacon's] Latin apophthegm, 'nam ipsa scientia potestas est'[1]—'for knowledge is power'—might be described as the watchword of the intellectual history of England . . . in the sixteenth century. **1908** J. A. SPENDER *Com. Bagshot* ix. 84 Women understand men . . . better than any man understands women. Since knowledge is power, woman has a control over man which man never has over her. [[1] *De Haeresibus* x. 329.]

Knowledge makes one laugh, but wealth makes one dance. (K 190)

1640 HERBERT no. 957.

Knowledge without practice makes but half an artist. (K 191)

1551 T. WILSON *Rule of Reason* (1552 ed., P6ᵛ) After knowledge atteined, exercise is mooste necessarie . . . learnyng is best confirmed, when knowledge is put in vre. **1616** DRAXE no. 2493 (is nothing). **1732** FULLER no. 3141.

Knowledge, *see also* Devil never assails man unless void of k.; Honour ceases (Where), k. decreases; Zeal without k.

Knows enough that knows nothing if he knows how to hold his peace, He. (E 164)

1573 SANFORD 51 He knoweth inough that knoweth nought, if he knoweth how to holde his peace. **1581** GUAZZO i. 121 It is likewise sayd, That hee knoweth ynough who knoweth nothing if he knowe how to holde his peace. **1629** *Bk. Mer. Rid.* Prov. no. 21 (as 1573).

Knows how many (blue) beans make five, He.

1612 SHELTON *Quix.* IV. v. i. 309 As though I knew not how many numbers are five. *a.* **1628** CARMICHAELL no. 1766 Ye ken how many beins maks five. **1659** HOWELL *It. Prov.* 2 I know well how many loafs make a couple, and how many pair three oxen make. **1706** STEVENS s.v. Cinco He knows not how many make five. **1830** GALT *Laurie T.* (1849) II. i. 42 Few men who better knew how many blue beans it takes to make five. **1894** NORTHALL *Folk-phrases* 16 To say of a man that 'He knows how many beans make five' is to speak highly of his shrewdness. **1909** *Times Wkly.* 11 June 377 But the Bishop . . . knew how many beans make five, and he soon found out about Margaret.

Knows how to carry the dead cock home, He.

1869 HAZLITT 193 A correspondent of *Notes and Queries* says: . . . This . . . was in common use in the Derbyshire village where I was born. It was said of lads and men who . . . in . . . games, trials of strength, or fights, knew how to bear defeat manfully. . . .

Knows little, He that | often (soon) repeats it.

1659 HOWELL *Span. Prov.* 1 Who knows little tells it quickly. **1706** STEVENS s.v. Saber (soon). **1707** MAPLETOFT 22 He who knows but little

presently outs with it. **1732** FULLER no. 2209. **1813** RAY 124 *Quien poco sabe presto lo reza.* He that knows little soon repeats it.

Knows most, Who | speaks least.

1666 TORRIANO 189 no. 10.

Knows not a B from a battledore,[1] He. *Cf.* Say B to a battledore. (B 1)

1563–87 FOXE *A. & M.* II. 474 He knew not a B from a battledore nor ever a letter of the book. **1565** J. HALLE *Hist. Expostulat.* (1844) 16 He had no learnyng in the world, nor coulde reade Englishe (and as I suppose knewe not a letter, or a b from a bateldore). **1587** J. BRIDGES *Def. of Govᵗ C. of E.* 112 They know not a B from a battle-dore. **1609** DEKKER *Guls Horne-Bk.* 3 You shall not neede to buy bookes, no, scorne to distinguish a B from a battle dore. **1639** CLARKE 297. [[1] A horn-book.]

Knows not a B from a bull's foot, He.

[= entirely illiterate.] **1401** *Polit. Poems* (Wright) II. 57 I knew not an A from the wyndmylne, ne a B from a bole foot. **1721** KELLY 159 He knows not a B by a Bull's Foot. That is, he is illiterate. **1824** MOIR *Mansie W.* ch. 21 One who . . . could distinguish the difference between a B and a bull's foot. **1887** BLACKMORE *Springhaven* ch. 5 But the opinion of the men was different, because they knew a bee from a bull's foot.

Knows not a pig from a dog, He. (P 302)

1666 TORRIANO *Prov. Phr.* 173a The English say, He knows not a Pig from a Dog. **1678** RAY 264.

Knows not how to dissemble, Who | knows not how to live. (D 386)

1573 E. VARAMUND *Furious Outrages of France* 66 The oldc saying of Lewes the eleuenth . . . which was wont to say that he knew neuer a Latin sentence but this one, *Qui nescit dissimulare nescit regnare*, He that can not skill to dissemble can not skill to be a king. **1576** PETTIE i. 116 He which knoweth not how to dissemble knoweth not how to live. **1577** HOLINSHED (1587) iii. 105b Qui nescit fingere nescit regere. **1589** G. PUTTENHAM *Art of English Poesy* III. xviii The great Emperour [Vespasian] that had it vsually in his mouth to say, *Qui nescit dissimulare nescit regnare.* **1654** E. GAYTON *Pleasant Notes on Don Quixote* 163. **1892** SIR H. MAXWELL *Meridiana* 61 THE ART OF COMPLAISANCE . . . (London, 1697) . . . bears on the title the forbidding aphorism—'Qui nescit dissimulare nescit vivere'.

Knows not to swim goes to the bottom, In the world, who. (W 877)

1599 MINSHEU *Span. Gram.* 84 Round world, he that cannot swim, let him sinke to the bottome. **1640** HERBERT no. 285. **1659** TORRIANO no. 183. The world is round, and he that cannot swim sinks to the bottome. **1706** STEVENS s.v. Mundo This World is a round Sea, or Gulph, and he that cannot swim, goes to the bottom.

Knows not where to have you, One.
(K 186. M 228)

a. **1576** WHYTHORNE 42 I kowld not yet assiur my self to be siur to know wher and how to hav her. **1576** LEMNIUS *Touchstone of Complexions* 140 They . . . aunsweare so doubtfullye and perplexedlye, that a man cannot tel where to haue them. **1578** T. GARTER *Susanna* 253 You know where to haue me [= find me]. **1597** SHAKES. *1 Hen. IV* III. iii. 128 Why, she's neither fish nor flesh; a man knows not where to have her.—. . . Thou or any man knows where to have me. [1602] **1637** T. HEYWOOD *Royal King* vi. 60 I knew where I should have you. **1616** DRAXE no. 2264. **1672** WALKER 14 no. 17 You are as unconstant as the wind, as wavering as the weathercock. . . .

Knows nothing, He that | doubts nothing.
(N 268)

1611 COTGRAVE s.v. Rien. **1640** HERBERT no. 861. **1853** TRENCH iv. 78.

Knows on which side his bread is buttered, He.
(S 425)

1546 HEYWOOD II. vii. K1ᵛ I knowe on whiche syde my breade is buttred. **1564** BULLEIN *Dial. agst. Fever* (1888) 112 He knoweth upon which side his bread is buttered well enough. **1819** SCOTT *Bride Lam.* ch. 18 No man knows so well as Bittlebrains on which side his bread is buttered. **1882** BLACKMORE *Christowell* ch. 9 You know . . . upon which side your bread is buttered. And you think to make a good thing of what you have got out of me.

Knows one point more than the devil, He.
(P 455)

1599 MINSHEU *Span. Dial.* 29 (A mulitter). **1620** SHELTON *Quix.* II. xxviii. iii. 214 I know that you know an ace more than the devil in all you speak or think. **1659** HOWELL *Span. Prov.* 2. **1813** RAY 204.

Knows the weight of another's burden, None.
(W 252)

1640 HERBERT no. 880.

Knows what may be gained in a day, He that | never steals.
(D 80)

1640 HERBERT no. 445.

Knows who's a good maid? Who.
(M 30)

1678 RAY 172.

Knows, *see also* Know(n, s).

Kythe[1] in your own colours, that folk may ken you.

1832 HENDERSON 129 Kythe in your ain colours. **1862** HISLOP 202. [¹ appear.]

Kythe, *see also* Love me (If you), k. that.

L

Labour as long lived, pray as ever dying.
(L 11)

1640 HERBERT no. 480.

Labour for one's pains, To have nothing but one's.
(L 1)

1589 NASHE *Pref. to Greene's Menaphon* iii. 314 They haue nought but . . . (to bring it to our English Prouerbe) their labour for their trauell. **1602** SHAKES. *T.C.* I. i. 69 I have had my labour for my travail. **1655–62** GURNALL *Chrn. in Armour* (1865) I. 224 ‖They are but few that carry away the prize in the world's lottery; the greater number have only their labour for their pains. **1670** RAY 183.

Labour in vain, To.
(V 5)

[PS. cxxvii. 1: Except the Lord build the house, they labour in vain.] **1528** ROY & BARLOW *Rede me* Arb. 110 Bestowynge his laboure in vayne. **1540** PALSGRAVE *Acolastus* 51 Thou laborest al for nought, or spendest thy labour in vayne. **1581** N. WOODES *Conflict of Conscience* l. 660 Then were my labour done but in vaine. **1639** CLARKE 153.

Labour is light where love doth pay.

1539 FRONTINUS *Stratagems of War* tr. R. Morysine a2ᵛ Love hath no leaden heles, and as he is quicke, so is al labour light, where loue hyreth the workman. **1582** T. WATSON Ἑκατομπαθία Arb. 138 The Labour is light, where Loue is the Paiemistres. **1600** DRAYTON *Idea* ii. 340.

Labour overcomes all things.
(L 5)

1567 *Amorous Tales* tr. J. Sanford D8ᵛ Care and great labour can do al things. **1568** D. ROWLAND *Comfortable Aid for Scholars* K4 Labor may doo any thing. **1585** ROBSON *Choice Change* N2 Labour is very strong because it ouercommeth all things. **1616** DRAXE no. 1175.

Labour, *see also* Endure l. in this world (He that will not); Idle folks have most l.; Land (He that has some) must have l.; Little l. much health; Lose one's l.; Ox go where he shall not l. (Whither shall); Pride of rich makes l. of poor; Six days shalt thou l. and the seventh . . .; Think no l. slavery.

Labourer is worthy of his hire, The.
(L 12)

[LUKE X. 7.] **1508** J. FISHER *Sayings David in Psalms* 167 The werke man that hath done his labour without murmure or grudge is worthy to haue his hyre, his rewarde. **1606** HEYWOOD 2 *If You Know Not Me* (1874) 275. **1659** MILTON *Means to Remove Hirelings*: Wks. (1931–8) vi. 48 As when our Saviour saith, the laborer is worthy of his hire. **1824** SCOTT *St. Ronans* ch. 10 Your service will not be altogether gratuitous, my old friend, the labourer is worthy of his hire. **1880** MYERS *Wordsworth* 100 Wordsworth . . . was far from expecting . . . to make a rapid fortune; but he felt that the labourer was worthy of his hire.

Labours and thrives, He that | spins gold.
(G 287)

1640 HERBERT no. 341. **1706** STEVENS s.v. Oro He who plows, and breeds Cattle, spins Gold.

Labyrinth, If you go into a | take a clew with you.
(L 14)

1580 LYLY *Euph. & his Eng.* ii. 156 Theseus woulde not goe into the Laborinth without a threede that might shew him the way out. **1732** FULLER no. 2752.

Laced, *see* Mutton, (He loves l.)

Lachrymae, see Sing l.

Lack[1] what they would fain have in their pack, Many men.
(M 537)

a. **1628** CARMICHAELL no. 1125. **1641** FERGUSSON no. 612. **1721** KELLY 249 . . . Men will seem to discommend what they have a great Mind to, in order to get it cheaper. [[1] discommend.]

Lack, (*noun*), *see* Love (In) no l.; Tradesmen live upon l.

Lack, (*verb*), *see also* Better leave than l.; What d'ye l.

Lackey comes to hell's door, When a | the devils lock the gates.
(L 21)

1640 HERBERT no. 984.

Lacking[1] breeds laziness, praise breeds pith.[2]

1721 KELLY 237 . . . Discommend a Boy and you discourage him, but commend him and it will spur him on. [[1] discommending. [2] force.]

Lackland, Sir John.

[= one who has no landed possessions.] **1594** GREENE *Looking Glass* Wks. Gros. xiv. 40 How cheere you, gentlemen? you crie 'no lands' too; the Judge hath made you a knight for a gentleman, hath dubbed you sir John Lackland.

Lack-latin, Sir John.

[= a name for an ignorant priest.] *c.* **1535** SIR F. BYGOD *Treat. concern. impropriations* C vj Is it nat great pitye to se a man to haue thre or foure benefyces . . . which he neuer cometh at, but setteth in euery one of them a syr John lacke latin, that can scarce rede his porteus.[1] **1537** W. TURNER *Comparison between the Old Learning and the New* H2ᵛ Ihon lack latyne shall suffice for that office wel ynough. **1614** JACKSON *Creed* III. iii. § 5 We are bound to believe the Church's decisions read or explained unto us (by the pope's messenger though a Sir John Lack-latin). [[1] breviary.]

Lacks a stock, Who | his gain is not worth a chip.
(S 866)

1546 HEYWOOD II. ix. L1ᵛ. **1614** CAMDEN 314. **1639** CLARKE 92.

Lacqueys, *see* Pride rides, (When) shame l.

Ladder(s), *see* Climb the l. must begin at bottom; Crosses are l. to heaven; Go down the l. when you marry; Go up the l. to bed; Kick down the l.; Step after step l. is ascended; World is a l.

Ladies, *see also* Lady(-ies).

Ladle, *see* Fern is as high as a l. (When); Sceptre is one thing, l. another; Wife that never cries for l. till pot runs over.

Lads love[1] is lassies' delight, and if lads won't love, lassies will flite.[2]

1828 W. CARR *Dial. of Craven* I. 273 'Lads love[1] is lassies delight', a vulgar phrase common in Craven, to which is frequently added . . . 'And if *lads* don't *love*, lassies will flite.'[2] [[1] The Shrub Southernwood: *Artemisia Abrotanum*, also known as 'Old Man'. [2] scold.]

Lad's love's a busk of broom, hot awhile and soon done.
(L 23)

1670 RAY 46 *Chesh.*

Lad(s), *see* Boys (L.) will be men; Hae l. and run l.; Love of l.; Royet l. make sober men.

Lady Day the latter,[1] On | the cold comes on the water.

1732 FULLER no. 6217. [[1] Formerly 'Lady Day' was used to denote not only the Annunciation (25 Mar.) but also other festivals of the Virgin, including her Conception (8 Dec.).]

Lady's (Lord's) heart and a beggar's purse, Nothing agrees worse than a.

[*c.* 1515] **1521** BARCLAY *Eclog.* v, l. 20 His pursys linynge was symple, poore, and thynne: But a lordes stomake and a beggers pouche Full ill accordeth. **1546** HEYWOOD I. x. C4ᵛ There is nothing in this worlde that agreeth wurs, Than doethe a ladies hert and a beggers purs. **1555** *Id. Epig.* 47 There is nothyng in this worlde that agreeth wurse, Then doth a lordes harte and a beggers purse.

Lady(-ies), *see also* Amends for l. (all); Easter day lies in our L.'s lap, (When) England beware; Gist of l.'s letter in postscript; House stands on my l.'s ground; Joan is as good as my l. in dark; Laird slight the l. (If the); Prayers are done (When) my l. is ready.

Ladybirds, Plenty of | plenty of hops.
1869 HAZLITT 317.

Laid in his fuel before St. John,[1] Never rued the man that.
1732 FULLER no. 6205. [1 Dec. 27.]

Laird of pity, He looks like the. (L 32)
1641 FERGUSSON no. 406. *Of fleyit[1] persons.* . . . [1 frightened.]

Laird slight the lady, If the | so will all the kitchen boys.
1721 KELLY 185 . . . If People despise their own so will other Persons.

Lairds break, When | carles get land.
1721 KELLY 348 . . . When a great Estate is sold, mean People, who have a little Money, will buy each a Share.

Laird's brother, *see* Jock the l. b.

Lamb where it's tipped, and the ewe where she's clipped, The.
1721 KELLY 307 . . . A proverbial Rule about Tythes; signifying that the Lamb shall ˙pay Tythes in the Place where the Ewe was when she took the Ram, but the old Sheep where they were shorn.

Lambs, Like | you do nothing but suck and wag your tail.
1721 KELLY 386 . . . Taken from young Lambs; spoken to them who have got a plentiful Condition, Place, or Station. **1732** FULLER no. 3230.

Lamb(s), *see also* Bed with the l.; Death devours l. as well as sheep; Ewe and a l. (Now I have) . . . Welcome Peter; Fox lick a l. (Ill sign); Gentle as˙a l.; God tempers the wind; God's l. will play; Ill look among l.; Innocent as a l.; Life of wolf is death of l.; March comes in . . . goes out like l.; Old ewe l. fashion; Soon goes the young l.'s skin to market.

Lambskin, *see* Lap in a l.

Lame as St. Giles, Cripplegate, As.
(s 43)
1600 JONSON *Ev. Man out Hum.* Ind. 72 As lame As Vulcan, or the founder of Cripple-gate. **1662** FULLER Lond. 200 . . . This proverb . . . is spoken . . . of such who for some light hurt lagg behind, and sometimes is applied to those who out of Lazinesse . . . counterfeit Infirmity.

Lame goes as far as your staggerer, The.
(L 41)
1640 HERBERT no. 517. **1670** RAY 15.

Lame post brings the truest news, The.
(P 489)
1640 HERBERT no. 331. Stay till the lame messenger come, if you will know the truth of the thing. **1659** N. R. 115. **1732** FULLER no. 4620.

Lame tongue gets nothing, The. (T 393)
1636 CAMDEN 307.

Lame traveller should get out betimes, A.
1732 FULLER no. 235.

Lame, *see also* Halt before you are l. (You); Punishment is l. but comes; Retreat (In a) the l. are foremost; See which leg you are l. of.

Lament, *see* Dead avails not, . . . (To l. the); Short pleasure long l.

Lammas, *see* After L. corn ripens; Latter L.

Lammermoor lion,[1] You look like a.
1721 KELLY 380 . . . Lammermoor is a large Sheep Walk in the East of Scotland. The English say, An Essex Lyon. [1 i.e. a sheep.]

Lamp, *see* Glowworm lights l.; Oil left in the l., (There is); Smells of the l.

Lancashire fair women.   (L 45)
1547 S. GARDINER to Somerset (*Letters* ed. Muller 1933 386) By the Paraphrasis [of Erasmus] the keping of a concubyne ys called but a light fault. And that were good for Lankeshire. **1609** DEKKER *The Raven's Almanack* G1 A wench of a good bone and a lusty complexion, much like to Lancashire breed. **1613–22** DRAYTON *Polyolb.* xxvii. 65 (1876) III. 175 Ye lusty⸗lasses then, in *Lancashire* that dwell, For beauty that are said to bear away the bell. **1662** FULLER Lancs. 107 . . . God . . . having given fair complections to the Women in this County, Art may save her pains . . . in endeavouring to better them.

Lancashire law—no stakes, no draw.
1828 W. CARR *Dial. of Craven* I. 274 '*Lancashire* law, no stakes, no draw', a saying whereby a person who loses a wager endeavours to evade payment when the wager was merely verbal and no stake deposited.

Lancashire man at any time, or tide, He that would take a | must bait his hook with a good egg-pie, or an apple with a red side.   (M 177)
1599 H. BUTTES *Dyets Dry Dinner* A2 Here are neither eg-pies for the Lancashire-man, nor

Wag-tailes for the Kentish-man. **1607** DEKKER & WEBSTER *Northward Ho* B4. **1613** DRAYTON *Polyolb.* xxvii. 65, 68 (1876) III. 175 Ye lusty lasses then, in *Lancashire* that dwell, . . . As ye the Egg-pie love, and Apple cherry-red. [Footnote: He that will fish for a *Lancashire* man, at any time or tide, Must bait his hook with a good Egg-pie, or an Apple with a red side.] **1617** FYNES MORYSON *Itinerary* iii. 54. **1678** RAY 316 (egge-pie).

Lancashire thinks today, What | all England will think to-morrow.

1902–4 LEAN I. 116 . . . This was in the days of the Anti-Corn-Law League. Since then the initiative in political movements proceeds from Birmingham.

Lancashire witches.[1]

1634 T. HEYWOOD & BROME *Lancashire Witches*[1] (Title of Play). **1787** GROSE (*Lancs.*) 186 Lancashire witches . . . at the same time as it records the beauty of the Lancashire females, carries with it a kind of reflection on the males, for . . . executing a number of poor innocent people, under the denomination of witches. **1809** 11 Aug. BYRON *Lett. and Jour.* I. 239 The Cadiz belles being the Lancashire witches of their land. [[1] In 1612 nine witches were hanged in Lancashire; and in 1633 seventeen were sentenced, but not executed.]

Land has its laugh,[1] Every | and every corn has its chaff.   (L 48)

a. **1628** CARMICHAELL nos. 469–70 Everie land hes the laich. Everie corne hes the cafe.[2] **1641** FERGUSSON no. 249 (as *a.* 1628). **1721** KELLY 92 . . . Every Country hath its own Laws, Customs, and Usages. **1916** *Brit. Wkly.* 2 Nov. 84 'Every land', says the old Scottish proverb, 'has its ain lauch'. And every class has its own mode of thought and expression. [[1] ill-drained area. [2] chaff.]

Land, He that has some | must have some labour.   (L 53)

1639 CLARKE 59. **1670** RAY 112. **1732** FULLER no. 2161.

Land of cakes, The.

[Refers to the *oatcakes* of Scotland and is applied (originally in banter) to Scotland or the Scottish Lowlands.] **1669** SIR R. MORAY in *Lauderdale Papers* (1885) II. cxiv. 171 If you do not come out of the land of cakes before New Year's day. *c.* **1730** BURT *Lett. N. Scotl.* (1760) II. xxiv. 271 The Lowlanders call their part of the Country the Land of Cakes. *a.* **1846** J. IMLAH *Song, Land o' Cakes*, An' fill ye up and toast the cup, The land o' cakes for ever.

Land of Nod, The.

[= sleep. A pun on the biblical place-name, GEN. iv. 16.] **1738** SWIFT *Dial.* III. E.L. 325. **1818** SCOTT *Ht. Midl.* ch. 30 There's queer things chanced since ye hae been in the land of Nod. **1863** READE *Hard Cash* ch. 18 [It] had my lady into the land of Nod in half a minute.

Land, To see.

[ERASM. *Ad.* 1126E: Terram video.] **1672** WALKER 20 no. 16. **1755** 1 Feb. JOHNSON *Lett.* (Chapman) i. 61 I now begin to see land.

Land was never lost for want of an heir.
                                        (L 54)

1678 RAY 165 . . . Ai ricchi non mancano parenti. *Ital.* The rich never want kindred.

Land, You may be on | yet not in a garden.   (L 58)

1640 HERBERT no. 964.

Land's end.   (L 62)

c. **1549** HEYWOOD II. vii. I4[v] Thou gossepst at home to mete me at lands ende. **1553** T. WILSON *Rhet.* 147 Some newe fellowes when they thinke one a Papist, they will call him streight a Catholique, and be euen with him at the lands end.

Land's End to John o' Groat's, From the.

[= through Great Britain.] **1823** SCOTT *St. Ronan's* ch. 10 I can beat Wolverine from the Land's-End to Johnnie Groat's. **1827** HARE *Gues. at Truth* (1873) i. 232 From the Land's End to John of Groat's House, scarcely a man any longer remembers that the business of governors is to govern. **1890** PAYN *Burnt Mil.* ch. 14 If you laid it down in sovereigns, . . . it would have reached from the Land's End to John o' Groat's.

Lands, He that has | has quarrels (war).
                                        (L 59)

1579 J. CALVIN *Thirteen Sermons* 97[v] The common Prouerbe is: He that hath land, hath warre at hand. **1592** DELAMOTHE 45 He that hath some land, must haue also warre and debat. **1611** COTGRAVE s.v. Guerre No land without warre: he that hath land is seldome out of law. **1640** HERBERT no. 1002. **1666** TORRIANO 284 no. 32 Who buies land buies war.

Land(s), *see also* Buys l. buys many stones; Dull men get no l.; England good l., bad people; Fat l. grow foulest weeds; Gold may buy l. (He that has); Good l., evil way; Good l. where there is foul way; Little house well filled, little l. well tilled; Many a one for l. takes a fool by the hand; Near of kin to l. (Good to be); No Man's L.; Occupation is as good as l.; Words are but words, but money buys l.

Landlady, *see* Good night, l.

Landscape, *see* Water is eye of a l.

Lane, *see* Devil go with thee down l.; Long l. that has no turning; Turnagain l.

Langel, *see* Foot out of the l. (You have a).

Language(s), *see* Billingsgate l.; Eyes have one l.; Good l. which all understand not (That is not); Ill l. if not ill taken (No); Nothing so necessary for travellers as l.

Lank, *see* After a l. a bank.

Lanthorn, *see* Night (To great) a great l.

Lap in a lambskin,[1] To.   (L 40)

1546 HEYWOOD II. vi. I2 She must obeie those lambs, or els a lambs skyn, Ye will prouide for hir, to lap her in. **1595** R. TURNER *Garland of a Green Wit* E1ᵛ Wishing if she would auoyd his displeasure, to be packing, least he furred his Mandilion with a few Lamb-skinnes. [[1] To lam, beat.]

Lap, *see* Delilah, (l. of).

Lapped (Wrapped) in his mother's smock, He was.   (M 1203)

1585 A. MUNDAY *Fidele and Fortunio* D4ᵛ He euer made my Mother to wrap mee in her smocke. **1590** GREENE *Never too Late* in Wks. viii. 198 How should I be vsed: but as one that was wrapt in his mothers smock when hee was borne. **1606** MARSTON *What You Will* v. i. **1639** CLARKE 49 (lapt). **1668** SHADWELL *Sullen Lov.* v. i Sure I was born with a caul on my head, and wrapped in my mother's smock; the ladies do so love me. **1670** RAY 184. **1704** STEELE *Lying Lover* II. ii I can't believe there's anything in that old whim of being wrapt in one's mother's smock. . . . But . . . I have strange luck with the women. **1721** KELLY 139 He was wrap'd in his Mother's Sark Tail. **1738** SWIFT Dial. II. E.L. 308 Indeed, miss, I believe you were wrapt in your mother's smock, you are so well beloved.

Lapwing cries farthest from her nest, The.   (L 68)

1580 LYLY *Euph. & his Eng.* ii. 4 In this I resemble the Lappwing who . . . flyeth with a false cry farre from their nestes. **1581** C. THIMELTHORPE *Short Inventory* I4 This leads vs with the Lapwing cleane from our matter. **1592** GREENE *Art Conny Catching* II. 4 Who . . . cry with the Lapwing farthest from their nest. **1592–3** SHAKES. *C.E.* IV. ii. 27 Far from her nest the lapwing cries away: My heart prays for him, though my tongue do curse. **1607** CHAPMAN *Rev. of Bus.* v. i (1874) 210 Trust not his oath. He will lie like a lapwing, when she flies Far from her sought nest, still 'here 'tis', she cries. **1678** RAY 256.

Lapwing that runs away with the shell on its head, Like a. *Cf.* Shell, To be in the.   (L 69)

1598 MERES *Pall. Tamia* 44 As the Lapwing runneth away with the shell on her head, as soone as she is hatched. **1600–1** SHAKES. *H.* V. ii. 181 This lapwing runs away with the shell on his head. **1631** JONSON *Staple News* III. ii. 195 And Coachmen, To . . . driue, Like Lapwings, with a shell vpo' their heads, Thorow the streets. **1678** BUNYAN *P.P.* ed. Wharey 1960 ed. 127 Thou talkest like one, upon whose head is the Shell to this very day.

Lard, *see* Cat for l.

Larder but has its mice, No.

1732 FULLER no. 3587.

Large as life, As (and twice as natural).

1799 EDGEWORTH *Lame Jervas* ch. 2 I see the puppets, the wheelbarrows everything as large as life! **1836** HALIBURTON *Clockmaker* As large as life and twice as natural. **1853** C. BEDE *Verdant Green* ch. 61 An imposing-looking Don, as large as life and quite as natural. **1894** BLACKMORE *Perlycross* ch. 21 To be sure I was, as large as life, and twice as natural!

Large, *see also* Conscience as l. as a friar's sleeve (He has a); Conscience as l. as a shipman's hose.

Larks will fall into one's mouth ready roasted, To think that.

(B 390. G 31. L 71)

[Fr. **1640** OUDIN *Curios. franc.* 10 *Les allouetes luy tomberont toutes rosties dans la bouche.*] **1540** PALSGRAVE *Acolastus* 77 Do thou but gape, and I shall make larkes fall in to thy mouthe. **1659** HOWELL *Fr. Prov.* . . . spoken of a sluggard.

Lark(s), *see also* Bed with the lamb, rise with l.; Bunting for a l. (To take a); Leg of a l. better than; Lovers live by love as l. by leeks; Merry (Gay) as a l.; Sing like a l.; Sky falls we shall catch l.

Lass in the red petticoat shall pay for all, The.   (L 75)

1662 J. WILSON *Cheats* I. ii Come—the red petticoat must piece up all. **1678** RAY 80 . . . Young men answer so when they are chid for being so prodigal and expensive, meaning, they will get a wife with a good portion, that shall pay for it.

Lass with the tear in her eye, Take a.

1823 GALT *Entail* ch. 98 'Bell Fatherlans', resumed the Leddy, 'I'll tak you wi' the tear in your ee'. **1827** SCOTT *Surg. Dau.* ch. 4 'I may be brought up by a sabre, . . . then your road to Menie will be free and open, and . . . you may take her "with the tear in her ee", as old saws advise.'

Lasses are lads' leavings.   (L 77)

1670 RAY 217 (*Chesh.*).

Lass(es), Lassy (-ies), *see also* Good l. (All are), but whence bad wives?; Lads love is l. delight; Lisping l. good to kiss; Lithe as a l. of Kent.

Last, but not least.   (L 82)

1580 LYLY *Euph. & his Eng.* ii. 113 Of these three but one can stand me in steede, the last, but not the least. **1599** SHAKES. *J.C.* III. i. 189 Though last, not least in love. *a.* **1627** MIDDLETON *Mayor of Queenb.* III. iii Though I speak last, my lord, I am not least. **1853** SURTEES *Sponge's Sport. T.* ch. 67 Though last not least, here's Facey Romford.

Last drop makes the cup run over, The.
(D 615)

1655 FULLER *Ch. Hist.* XI. ii (1868) III. 449 When the cup is brimfull before, the last (though least) super added drop is charged alone to be the cause of all the running over. **1876** J. PAYN *Halves* ch. 10 An application of her brother-in-law for a five-pound note . . . was the last drop that caused Mrs. Raeburn's cup of bitterness to overflow.

Last garment is made without pockets, Our.

1853 TRENCH v. 113 This Italian . . . teaches . . . with an image Dantesque in its vigour, that 'a man shall carry nothing away with him when he dieth', *Our last robe,* that is, our winding sheet, *is made without pockets.*[1] **1909** ALEX. MACLAREN *Expos., Ephesians* 41 There is nothing that is truly our wealth which remains outside of us, and can be separated from us. 'Shrouds have no pockets.' [[1] *L'ultimo vestito ce lo fanno senza tasche.*]

Last legs, To be (go) on one's.
(L 193)

[= the end of one's life; fig. the end of one's resources.] *c.* **1618** MASSINGER, etc. *Old Law* v. i. My husband goes upon his last hour now.—On his last legs, I am sure. **1678** RAY 89 *A Bankrupt.* He goes on's last legs. **1846** DE QUINCEY *Syst. Heavens* Wks. (1854) iii. 174 If the Earth were on her last legs. **1857** TROLLOPE *Barch. Tow.* ch. 1 The bishop was quite on his last legs.

Last make fast.
(A 186)

c. **1350** *Douce MS.* 52 no. 48 Who-so comyth late to his in, shall erly forthynke. **1555** HEYWOOD *Epig. on Prov.* no. CCII He that cumth last make all fast. **1576** HOLYBAND D8[v] He that cometh last, maketh the dore fast. **1578** FLORIO *First F.* 29 He that commeth last, let hym shut the doore. **1659** HOWELL *Eng. Prov.* 6b . . . viz. shut the dore. **1881** A. B. EVANS *Leicest. Wds.* E.D.S. 302 'Last make fast'. . . . It is a recognized rule in passing through a gate that has been opened.

Last man that he killed keeps hogs in Hinckley field, The.
(M 206)

1678 RAY 317 (*Leics.*) . . . Spoken of a coward that never durst fight. **1881** A. B. EVANS *Leicest. Wds.* E.D.S. 301. . . . It is now, and I imagine always was, applied rather to a boaster of the 'Ancient Pistol' type.

Last my time, It will.

1856 FROUDE *Hist. Eng.* I. 222 Such thoughts . . . were thrust aside as an uneasy dream, . . . or with the coward's consolation, 'It will last my time'.

Last prayers, She is at her.
(P 558)

1678 RAY 79 (*Joculatory*).

Last straw breaks the camel's back, The.
(F 158)

1655 ABP. BRAMHALL *Wks.* IV. 59 in LEAN IV. 20 It is the last feather that breaks the horse's back.

1706 STEVENS s.v. Bestia (as 1655). **1848** DICKENS *Dombey* ch. 2 As the last straw breaks the laden camel's back, this piece of underground information crushed the sinking spirits of Mr. Dombey. **1881** D. C. MURRAY *Joseph's Coat* ch. 4 Young Joe's resolve to emigrate . . . had been the last straw which broke the camel's back, and they were now irreconcilable. **1902** G. W. E. RUSSELL *Coll. & Recoll.* (1909) 116 Palmerston's contumacy was the last straw, and he was . . . dismissed from the Foreign Office.

Last suitor wins the maid, The.
(S 693)

1611 COTGRAVE s.v. Aimé (wench). **1670** RAY 15. **1732** FULLER no. 4624.

Last word (though one talk bilk for it), To have the. *Cf.* Women will have.
(W 764)

1555 J. PHILPOT *Examinations* P.S. 82 My lord of Lincoln . . . said that thou wert a frantic fellow, and a man that will have the last word. **1633** JONSON *T. Tub* I. i. 60 He will have the last word, though he talk bilk for 't.—Bilk! What's that?—Why, nothing: a word signifying Nothing; and borrowed here to express nothing. **1678** RAY 228. **1738** SWIFT *Dial.* I. E.L. 276 Miss, you have shot your bolt: I find you must have the last word.

Last (*adj., adv.*), see also Better the l. smile; Cast, (He is at l.); Comes l. to the pot soonest wroth; First (I am not the) and shall not be the l.; First as l., (As good do it); First up, l. down; Pays l. never pays twice; Women will have the l. word. See also At last.

Last (*noun*), see Cobbler go beyond his l. (Let not).

Last(s) (*verb*), see Courtesy on one side l. not long; Good gear that l. aye; World will not l.

Latchet, see Lie with a l.

Latch-key, see Liberty but no l.

Late children, early orphans.
(C 310)

1659 HOWELL *Span. Prov.* 10 A late Child an early Orphan. **1742** FRANKLIN *Mar.* Late Children, early Orphans.

Late-comers are shent.[1]

1599 PORTER *Angry Wom. Abingd.* ll. 1176–7 Tushe, there is no good luck in this delaye . . .; late commers man are shent. **1657** TORRIANO *It. Dial.* 142 The common saying . . . late come, ill lodged. [[1] ruined.]

Late repentance is seldom true.
(R 77)

1552 LATIMER *Wks.* P.S. II. 193 It is a common saying, *Pœnitentia sera raro vera.* **1639** CLARKE 255. **1732** FULLER no. 3145.

Late, see also Better l. than never; Comes l. lodges ill; Marries l. marries ill; Marry l. or never; Never too l. to do well; Never too l. to mend; Never too l. to repent; Repentance comes too l.; Rises l. must trot; Too l. aware. *See also* Too late to.

Latin, a horse, and money, With | you may travel the world. (L 89)

1611 COTGRAVE s.v. Florin Qui a Florin, latin, roussin, par tout il trouve chemin: (Wherin, by florin, store of coyne is vnderstood). **1659** HOWELL *Span. Prov.* 10 With Latine, a good Nag, and Money, thou mayst travel the world. *Id. It. Prov.* 6. **1666** TORRIANO 91 no. 11 With a Florin, Latin and a good Nag, one may find out the way in any Country. **1809** MALKIN *Gil Blas* x. x Those who can talk Latin may always find their way to Rome.

Latin, *see also* Fool, unless he knows L.; Morning sun and a L. bred woman; Speak false L.; *Tace* is L. for candle; Young wench, (Take heed of a) . . . and a L. woman.

Latter Lammas, At. *Cf.* Greek Calends. (L 90)

[= never.] **1553** *Respublica* III. v Faith youer Mars-ship will thrive att the latter Lammas. **1567** GASCOIGNE i. 472 Many writers . . . draw their sentences in length, & make an ende at latter Lammas. **1642** FULLER *Holy & Prof. St.* IV. xv. 316 This your will At latter lammas wee'l fulfill [his translation of *Ad Graecas, bone rex, fient mandata, Calendas*, a line by Q. Elizabeth]. **1857** KINGSLEY *Two Yrs. Ago* ch. 7 A treatise . . . which will be published probably . . . in the season of Latter Lammas, and the Greek Kalends.

Laugh and be (grow) fat. (L 91)

1596 HARINGTON *Metam. of Ajax* (1814) 68 Many of the worshipful of the city, that make sweet gains of stinking wares; and will laugh and be fat. **1599** JONSON *Ev. Man out Hum.* III. i. 10. When shall we sup together, and laugh and be fat with those good wenches, ha? **1682** N. O. tr. *Le Lutrin* iv. 40 There will we . . . laugh, grow fat. **1737** GREEN *Spleen* 93 Laugh and be well. Monkeys have been extreme good doctors for the spleen. **1823** SCOTT *Peveril* ch. 33 He seems to have reversed the old proverb of 'laugh and be fat'. **1844** T. HOOD *Lett. to a Child*, Apr. I mean . . . to laugh till I grow fat, or at least streaky.

Laugh and cry both with a breath (at once, like rain in sunshine), To.
(B 640. L 92a)

1531 ELYOT *Governor* ii. 145 She all blusshing with an eye halfe laughinge halfe mourninge. **1578** *Courtly Controv.* 2M1 Who hathe viewed in the Spring time, raine and Sunneshine in one moment, might beholde the troubled countenaunce the of gentlewoman, after she had read, and ouerread the letters of hir *Floradin* wyth an eye, nowe smilyng, then bathed in teares. **1582** WHETSTONE *Heptameron* Z1ᵛ Who so in the Spryngtime, in one Moment had seene rayne and Sunshine, might againe beholde the lyke chaunge in Pierias troubled countenaunce. **1592–3** SHAKES. *V. & A.* l. 413 For I have heard it

[love] is a life in death, That laughs and weeps, and all but with a breath. **1594** *Id. T.G.V.* I. iii. 84 O, how this spring of love resembleth The uncertain glory of an April day, Which now shows all the beauty of the sun, And by-and-by a cloud takes all away. **1605–6** *Id. K.L.* IV. iii. 17 You have seen Sunshine and rain at once: her smiles and tears Were like, a better way. **1616** DRAXE no. 515 He doeth laugh and weepe with one breath. **1616** WITHALS 581 It is a hard thing. . . . **1639** CLARKE 147. **1670** RAY 184 He can laugh and cry and both in a wind. **1732** FULLER no. 4120 She can laugh and cry both in a Wind.

Laugh and lay (lie) down. (L 92)

[An obsolete game at cards.] **1522** SKELTON *Why not to Court* 928 Now nothynge but pay, pay, With, laughe and lay downe, Borowgh, cyte, and towne. **1591** FLORIO *Second F.* 67 What game doo you plaie at cardes? At primero, at trump, at laugh and lie downe. **1606** CHAPMAN *Gent. Usher* IV. ii. 83 Sweet lady, if you will laugh and lie down, I am pleased. **1634** S. R. *Noble Soldier* II. ii. in BULLEN *O. Pl.* I. 268 Sorrow becomes me best. A suit of laugh and lye downe would wear better. *a.* **1825** FORBY *Laugh-and-lay-down*, a childish game at cards.

Laugh at leisure, you may greet[1] ere night.

1721 KELLY 240 . . . A Reprimand to them that laugh intemperately. [¹ weep.]

Laugh before breakfast, you'll cry before supper. *Cf.* Sing before breakfast.
(M 1176)

1530 PALSGRAVE 776 You waxe mery this morning, God gyve grace you wepe nat or nyght. **1611** COTGRAVE s.v. Soir Some laugh amornings who ere night shed teares. **1721** KELLY 332 They that laugh in the Morning may greet e'er Night. **1902–4** LEAN IV. 28 . . . Tel rit au matin qui pleure au soir.

Laugh (smile) in one's face and cut one's throat, To. (F 16)

1390 CHAUCER *Knight's T.* l. 1141 The smyler with the knyf under the cloke. **1562** SACKVILLE & NORTON *Gorboduc* IV. ii. 122 Then saw I how he smiled with slaying knife Wrapped vnder cloke. **1583** MELBANCKE E2ᵛ The fashion of the worlde (saith Plutarch) looke a man in the face, and cut his throate. **1587** RANKINS *Mirr. Monsters* 11ᵛ Beware of such pernitious Gnatonists who taking vs friendlie by the one hand, haue in the other a naked blade to shed our bloud, and smiling in our faces, seeke to betraie our soules. **1591** SHAKES. *3 Hen. VI* III. ii. 182 Why, I can smile, and murder whiles I smile. **1600–1** *Id. H.* I. v. 107 Meet it is I set it down That one may smile, and smile, and be a villain. **1616** WITHALS 563 Hee laughes you in the face, but he could wish you at the deuill. **1629** T. ADAMS *Serm.* (1861–2) iii. 267 It is a dissembling falsehood in man to smile and betray, as Judas began his treachery with a kiss. Such are likened to those bottled windy drinks, that laugh in a man's face, and then cut his throat. **1670** RAY 184. **1738** SWIFT *Dial.* II.

E.L. 300 I have some excellent cider . . . How is it treacherous?—Because it smiles in my face, and cuts my throat.

Laugh in one's sleeve, To.   (s 535)

[= to be secretly amused.] **1546** HEYWOOD II. v. H3 To that I said nought, but laught in my sleeue. **1560** DAUS tr. *Sleidane's Comm.* 64 If I coveted nowe to avenge the injuries that you have done me, I myght laughe in my slyve. **1600** DEKKER *Old Fort.* III. i. 123 (smile). **1642** D. ROGERS *Naaman* 228 Thou . . . hast fleerd and laught in the sleeve at the sincere. **1799** WOLCOT (P. Pindar) *Nil Admirari* Wks. (1816) III. 443 With smiles her eulogy Miss Hannah hears; Laughs in her sleeve at all thy pompous praise. **1836** MARRYAT *Midsh. Easy* ch. 23 Mr. Hicks laughed in his sleeve, so did Jack.

Laugh like a hyena, To.   (H 844)

a. **1594** R. WILSON *Cobbler's Prophecy* E2 l. 1061 You laugh Hiena like. **1599** SHAKES. *A.Y.* IV. i. 139 I will laugh like a hyen, and that when thou art inclined to sleep. **1837** TH. HOOK *Jack Brag* ch. 14 The purser of the ship—a great coarse creature, who used to laugh all day long like a hyæna. **1857** TROLLOPE *Barch. Tow.* ch. 33 Mrs. Proudie smiled as a hyena may probably smile before he begins his laugh. . . . And then the hyena laughed out.

Laugh (smile) on the other (wrong) side (of one's face, mouth), To.   (s 430)

1606 *Wily Beguiled* xiii Ile haue a rumpe of beefe for thee, shal make thy mouth stand oth tother side. **1666** TORRIANO 173 no. 34 The English say, when one hath conveniently reveng'd ones self on another; Now you can laugh but on one side of your mouth, friend. **1809** MALKIN *Gil Blas* II. v, par. 2 We were made to laugh on the other side of our mouths by an unforeseen occurrence. **1834** EDGEWORTH *Helen* ch. 26 Ladies may smile, but they would smile on the wrong sides of their pretty little mouths if they had been treated as I have been. **1842** s. LOVER *Handy Andy* ch. 3 'I'll make him laugh at the wrong side of his mouth', thought the Squire . . . and began a very smart horse-whipping of the attorney. **1905** WEYMAN *Starvecrow F.* ch. 7. He'll drub you . . . till you smile on the other side of your face!

Laughed at, He is not | that laughs at himself first.

1732 FULLER no. 1936. **1786** MRS. PIOZZI *Anec. of S. Johnson* (1892) 99 Thinking I suppose that the old maxim, of beginning to laugh at yourself first where you have anything ridiculous about you, he . . . called his girl *Trundle* when he spoke of her. **1927** *Times* 17 Sept. 11/4 Any man who laughs at his own misfortunes has . . . saved himself from being laughed at by others.

Laughing matter, To be no.

1530 R. WHITFORD *A Werke for Housholders* F2 It [confession] is no laughynge game. [c. **1591**] **1599** GREENE? *George a Green* l. 466 My masters, said I, it is no laughing matter. **1861-2** THACKERAY *Philip* ch. 16 Starvation is no laughing matter.

Laughing to girn[1] in a widdy,[2] It is nae.

1737 RAMSAY III. 187. [[1] grin. [2] gallows.]

Laughing, *see also* Burst with l., (To be ready to).

Laughs (best) who wins (laughs last), He. *Cf.* Better the last smile, etc.   (L 93)

1546 HEYWOOD I. v.'B2 He laugheth that winneth. **1591** I *Troublesome Reign K. John* C3 Let them reioyce that at the ende doo win. **1604-5** SHAKES. *O.* IV. i. 125 Ha, ha, ha!—So, so, so! Laugh that wins! **1607-8** *The Christmas Prince* (Mal. Soc. 109) Hee laugheth best that laugheth to the end. **1659** N. R. 54 He laugheth that winneth. **1715** VANBRUGH *Country House* II. v. But mum, he laughs best that laughs last. **1823** SCOTT *Peveril* ch. 38 Your Grace knows the French proverb, 'He laughs best who laughs last'. **1904** 'H. S. MERRIMAN' *The Last Hope* ch. 16 Men must have . . . laughed at the astounding simplicity of the French people. But he laughs best who laughs last.

Laughs ill that laughs himself to death, He.   (D 154)

1616 DRAXE no. 1401. **1639** CLARKE 201. **1670** RAY 15. **1732** FULLER no. 1962.

Laugh(s), *see also* Bachelors l. and show our teeth (We); Conscience fears not (l. at) false accusations, (A clear); Horse l., (Enough to make a); Jove l. at lovers' perjuries; Knowledge makes one l.; Maid that l. half taken; No play where one greets and another l.; Women l. when they can, and weep when they will.

Laughter, *see* Better the last smile than first l.

Laurence bids wages, *see* Lazy Laurence.

Lauvellin, *see* Skiddaw.

Lavender, *see* Lay (up) in l.

Lavishly, *see* Speaks l. shall hear knavishly.

Law for lying, No.   (L 110)

1678 RAY 172 . . . A man may lie without danger of the law.

Law for the rich, One | and another for the poor.

1830 MARRYAT *King's Own* ch. 11 Is there nothing smuggled besides gin? Now, if the husbands and fathers of these ladies—those who have themselves enacted the laws—wink at their *infringement*, why should not others do so? . . . There cannot be one law for the rich and another for the poor. **1888** J. E. T. ROGERS *Econ. Interp. Hist.* (1894) II. xxi There is an objection to the taxation of the inheritance of personal property of a very serious kind. It is that it is one law for the rich and another for the poor. **1913** *Spectator* 8 Nov. 757 The idea prevails abroad that there is one law for the 'rich' Englishman and another for the 'poor' foreigner.

Law for wagging of a straw, He will go to. (L 99)

1548 A. BORDE *Introduction* E.E.T.S. 122. [*c.* 1555] *c.* 1563 *Jack Juggler* l. 1194 He . . . woll sone pike a quarell be it wrong or ryght To the inferior and weker for a cople of strawes. **1615** W. GODDARD *Nest Wasps* 16. C2ᵛ Thou knowst a barlie strawe Will make a parish parson goe to lawe. **1616** WITHALS 563. **1670** RAY 184.

Law grows of sin, and chastises it, The. (L 102)

1573 SANFORD 52. **1578** FLORIO *First F.* 32ᵛ. **1639** *Bk. Mer. Rid.* Prov. no. 39.

Law is a bottomless pit.

1712 ARBUTHNOT *John Bull* vi Law is a bottomless pit; it is a cormorant, a harpy, that devours everything. **1823** J. GALT *Entail* ch. 92 But what lawyer would laugh, even in his own 'bottomless pit'?

Law is a lickpenny. *Cf.* Agree, for the law is costly.

1621 HOWELL *Lett.* 20 Mar. (1903) i. 109 Law is a pickpurse. **1818** SCOTT *Ht. Midl.* ch. 38 But aw licks up a', as the common folk say. **1824** *Id. St. Ronans* ch. 28 You talked of a lawsuit —law is a lick-penny, Mr. Tyrrel.

Law is an ass, The.

a. **1634** CHAPMAN *Revenge for Honour* III. ii I am ashamed the law is such an ass. **1838** DICKENS *O. Twist* ch. 51 'If the law supposes that', said Mr. Bumble . . . 'the law is a ass—a idiot.'

Law is not the same at morning and at night, The. (L 105)

1640 HERBERT no. 905.

Law, logic, and the Switzers fight for anybody. (L 108)

1593 NASHE *Christ's Tears* ii. 99 Law, Logique, and the Suizers may be hir'd to fight for any body. **1598** MERES *Palladis Tamia* 2G5ᵛ As the Switzers and Logicke fight for euery body: so do Lawyers. *a.* **1651** R. DAVENPORT *Survey Sciences* 327 (fight on any side).

Law makers should not be law breakers. (L 118)

c. **1386** CHAUCER *Introd. Man of Law's T.* ll. 43–4 For swich lawe as man yeveth another wight He sholde hym-selven usen it by right. **1659** TORRIANO no. 208 He deserves not to give lawes who cannot indure to receive them. **1669** PENN *No Cross, No Crown* xix Xenophanes being jeered for refusing to play at a forbidden game, answered, '. . . They that make laws, must keep them.' **1721** KELLY 232 . . . Lat. *Patere legem quam tulisti.* **1830** MARRYAT *King's Own* ch. 11

You'll allow also that law-makers should not be law-breakers.

Law of the Medes and Persians, The. (L 113)

[Often used, with allusion to DANIEL vi. 12, as the type of something unalterable.] **1382** WYCLIF *Dan.* vi. 15 The lawe of Medis and Persis. **1614** ADAMS *Soul's Sickness* 1616 ed. 6 His will is like the Persian law, vnalterable. [*a.* 1657] **1693** J. HACKET *Mem. Williams* Pref. b4 The Laudean Faction (like the Laws of the Medes and Persians) altereth not. **1762** CHURCHILL *Ghost* ii. 657 For what his greatness hath decreed, Like laws of Persia and of Mede, . . . Must never of repeal admit. **1853** 'C. BEDE' *Verdant Green* I. ii His word is no longer the law of the Medes and Persians, as it was at home.

Law(s), *see also* Abundance of l. breaks no l.; Agree for the l. is costly; Club l.; Cobbler's l.; Customs (With) we live well, but l. undo us; Cutter's l.; Drums beat (Where) l. are silent; Evil manners (Of) good l.; Extreme l. wrong; Fear, the beadle of l.; Halifax l.; Hard cases bad l.; Ignorance of the l. excuses no man; Lancashire l.; Love is without l.; Loves l. (He that) will get his fill; Man is friended (As a) so l. is ended; Many lords many l.; Much l. little justice; Nature true l.; Necessity has no l; Pennyweight of love worth pound of l.; Pleaing at the l. is like fighting through whin; Possession is nine points of l.; Show me the man and I'll show the l.; Stafford l.; Stopford l.; Suit at l. and urinal; Suit of l. (One) breeds twenty; Take the l. into own hands; Thousand pounds of l. not ounce of love; Uncertainty of l. (Glorious); Vengeance of the l.; War, hunting, and l. full of trouble; Will, (As I) . . . (Will is his l.); Worst people have most l.; Wrong l. make short governance.

Lawful, *see* Suffered to do . . . will do more.

Lawfully done which cannot be forborne, That may be.

1779–81 JOHNSON *Lives of Poets, Pope* (Bohn) III. 183 It must be remembered that *necessitas quod cogit defendit*; that may be lawfully done which cannot be forborn. Time and place will always enforce regard.

Lawing, *see* Pays the l. choose the lodging.

Lawless, *see* Love is l.

Lawn, *see* Sell l. before he can fold it (He that will).

Lawrence, *see* Laurence.

Laws catch flies but let hornets go free. (L 116)

c. **1412** HOCCLEVE *De Reg. Princ.* (1860) 101 Right as lop-webbes flyes smale and gnattes Taken, and suffren grete flyes go, For alle this world lawe is reulede so. **1567** *Amorous Tales* tr. J. Sanford E8 [attrib. to Anacharsis]. **1578** PRUDENTIUS tr. R. Robinson *Moral Method* 4a [attrib. to Anacharsis and Solon]. **1586** G. WHETSTONE *English Mirror* 226 [attrib. to the sage Cleobulus]. *a.* **1591** HY. SMITH *Serm., Mem. for Mag.* (1657) 531 Our laws have been a long time like to Spiders' webs, so that the great buzzing Bees break through, and the little feeble flies hang fast in them. **1625** BACON *Apoph.* Wks. (Chandos) 381 One of the Seven [Solon, *Diog. La.* l. 57] was wont to say; That laws were like cobwebs; where the small flies were caught, and the great break through. *a.* **1628** FULKE GREVILLE *Treatise of Monarchie* I. st. 10 All laws like cobwebs catching little flies, but never great ones without princes' eyes. **1707** SWIFT *Facult. of Mind* Wks. (1856) II. 285 After which, laws are like cobwebs, which may catch small flies, but let wasps and hornets break through.

Laws not by examples, We live by.
(R 206)

1577 J. NORTHBROOKE *Treatise agst. Dicing* ed. Collier 148 It is sayde, Legibus enim vivimus, non exemplis: we liue by lawes, and not by examples. **1623** J. BALMFORD *Reply to Gataker* 18 We must liue by precepts, not by examples. **1630** T. ADAMS *Physic from Heaven* Wks. 300 Examples are good furtherances, but ex praeceptis viuitur; we must liue by precepts.

Laws, The more | the more offenders (sins).
(L 117)

[TACITUS *Annals* 3. 27 *Corruptissima republica plurimae leges.* The more corrupt the state, the more numerous the laws.] **1573** SANFORD 4 Where there are many lawes, there be also or else haue ben many vices. **1593** FULKE GREVILLE (Neale, *Eliz. I and her Parlts. 1584–1601*) 307 The more laws we make the less liberty we leave ourselves. **1614** T. ADAMS *Devil's Banquet* Wks. 1861, i. 170 Ex malis moribus oriuntur plurimae leges—to meet with the multiplicity of sins there is required a multitude of laws. *c.* **1620** MIDDLETON & ROWLEY *World Tost at Tennis* (Wks. ed. Bullen vii. 176) The more laws you make The more knaves thrive by't. **1667** MILTON *Par. Lost* xii. 283 So many Laws argue so many sins Among them. **1732** FULLER no. 4663. **1766** GOLDSMITH *Vicar of W.* ch. 27 The multitude of laws produce new vices.

Laws, *see also* Law(s).

Lawsuit, *see also* Suit at law.

Lawsuits consume time, and money, and rest, and friends.
(L 122)

1640 HERBERT no. 776.

Lawton gate a clap, She has given.
(L 123)

1678 RAY (*Chesh.*) 300 . . . Spoken of one got with child and going to London to conceal it. *Lawton* is in the way to *London* from several parts of *Cheshire*.

Lawyer, A good | an evil neighbour.
(L 124)

1604 R. DALLINGTON *The View of Fraunce* B4 I haue heard some poore Countreyman say, He loues not to haue his house too neere a Lawyer. It should seeme they bee ill Neighbours. **1611** COTGRAVE s.v. Advocat. **1670** RAY 15.

Lawyer must be a great liar, A good.

1674 J. SMITH *Grammatica Quadrilinguis* (Fr.-Eng.), 65 Lawyers are oftentimes lyars. **1703** E. WARD *Writings* ii. 319 ('a common saying').

Lawyer never goes to law himself, A.

1666 TORRIANO *It. Prov.* 206 no. 1 No good Attorney will ever go to law. **1902–4** LEAN III. 393.

Lawyer's opinion is worth nothing unless paid for, A.
(L 125)

c. **1460** *Wisdom* l. 669 Wo Wytt haue law, must haue monye. [*c.* **1581**] **1584** R. WILSON *Three Ladies of London* C1ᵛ Thou art akinne to the Lawyer, thou wilt doo nothing without a fee. **1597** HARVEY *Trim. Nashe* (1885) 26 No fee, no lawe. **1605–6** SHAKES. *K.L.* I. iv. 127. This is nothing, fool.—Then 'tis like the breath of an unfee'd lawyer, you gave me nothing for't. **1616** DRAXE no. 276 A Lawyer will not pleade but for money. **1657** W. LONDON *Cat. of the most vendible Books* 12 A Lawyers lips are lockt without a fee. **1902–4** LEAN III. 393.

Lawyers' gowns are lined with the wilfulness of their clients.

1707 MAPLETOFT 17.

Lawyers' houses are built on the heads of fools.
(L 130)

1622 MIDDLETON *Changeling* III. iii Just at the lawyer's haven we arrive, By madmen and by fools we both do thrive. **1640** HERBERT no. 951.

Lawyer(s), *see also* Counsel (L.) (He that is his own) has fool for client; Fair and softly as l. to heaven; Few l. die well; Go not for every . . . quarrel to l.; Hide nothing from thy l.; Huntsman's breakfast, l.'s dinner; Isle of Wight has no l.; King can make . . . not a l.; Old physician, young l.; Wimple in a l.'s clew.

Lay (up) in lavender, To.
(L 96)

[= (*a*) to lay aside carefully for future use, (*b*) *slang* to pawn, (*c*) to put out of the way of doing harm.] **1592** GREENE *Upst. Courtier* (1871) 34 He is ready to lend . . . upon rings . . . or any other good pawn, but the poor gentleman pays so dear for the lavender it is laid up in that . . . **1600** JONSON *Ev. Man out Hum.* III. iii. 40 Which sute . . . new lies in lauander. **1605** CHAPMAN, JONSON, MARSTON *Eastw. Ho* V. i. 56 Rather then thou shouldest pawne a ragge more I'ld lay my Ladiship in lauender. *a.* **1628** EARLE *Microcosm., Yng. rawe Preacher* Arb. 23 He . . . ha's a jest still in lavender for Bellarmine. *a.* **1639** WOTTON *Let. to Walton* in *Relig.* (1651) 512 Yours hath lyen so long by me (as it were in lavender) without an answer. **1664** COTTON *Scarron.* 1715 ed. 49 She laid him [Julus] up in Lavender. *a.* **1700** B.E. *Dict. Cant. Crewe* s.v. *Laydup-in Lavender,* when any Cloaths or other Moveables are pawn'd or dipt for present Money. **1822** SCOTT *Nigel* ch. 23 Lowestoffe is laid up in lavender only for having shown you the way into Alsatia.

Lay it on with a trowel, To.   (T 539)

[= to express a thing coarsely; now *spec.* to flatter grossly.] **1599** SHAKES. *A.Y.* I. ii. 94 Well said, that was laid on with a trowel. **1650** FULLER *Pisgah-sight* II. vi (1869) 142 Flattery of the Roman emperors, . . . so gross that it seems . . . daubed with a trowel. **1694** CONGREVE *Double Dealer* III. X. **1732** FULLER no. 5930 You lay on your Butter, as with a Trowel. **1898** G. W. E. RUSSELL *Coll. & Recoll.* ch. 23 He [Lord Beaconsfield] said to Mr. Matthew Arnold . . . 'Every one likes flattery; and when you come to Royalty you should lay it on with a trowel.'

Lay on more wood; ashes give money.
                                             (W 738)

1642 TORRIANO 75. Do, lay on more wood, hang it, the Ashes will yeeld money. **1658** *Comes Fac.* 194 (as 1642). **1678** RAY 65.

Lay sorrow to your heart when others lay it to their heels, Never.

1871 *N. & Q.* 4th Ser. VIII. 506 LANCASHIRE PROVERBS.—. . . This is said when any one is grieved by the desertion of children or friends.

Lay the head of the sow to the tail of the grice.[1]

1721 KELLY 62 . . . That is, balance your Loss with your Gain. **1818** SCOTT *Rob Roy* ch. 24 An I am to lose by ye, I'se ne'er deny I hae won by ye mony a fair pund sterling—Sae, an it come to the warst, I'se e'en lay the head o' the sow to the tail o' the grice. [1 pig.]

Lay the reins on the neck, To.

1581 GUAZZO ii. 24 Let the reine lye too loose on the womans neck, and referre the care of her and his owne honour, onely to her small discretion. *c.* **1600** *Edmund Ironside* l. 157 Yf you lay the teame vppon theire neckes and lett them have but any scope to runne . . . **1607** R. C[AREW] tr. *Estienne's World of Wonders* 58 Youth is set at libertie, and haue the reine laid in their necks to runne at random. **1807** OPIE *Lect. on Art* iv (1848) 332 No man ever more completely laid the reins on the neck of his inclinations.

Lay the stool's foot in water, To.

1830 FORBY 433 . . . To make preparation for company. It is derived from the custom of washing brick floors.

Lay the sweet side of your tongue to it.

1721 KELLY 239 . . . An Answer to them that ask what they will get to their Hasty-Pudding.

Lay things by, they may come to use. *Cf.* Keep a thing seven years.

a. **1500** *15c. School Bk.* ed. W. Nelson 61 Ther is nothynge but it wyle serue for sumwhat . . . lay hym upe ageynst another tyme. **1541** BULLINGER tr. Coverdale *Christ. State Matrimony* (1543 ed.) L4ᵛ Lette it not be lost, that maye do any good in tyme to come. **1642** TORRIANO 75 Lay up thy goods in a corner, there will be a time, they will be usefull. **1732** FULLER no. 3154.

Lay your wame to your winning.

1832 HENDERSON 16 . . . Let not your household expenditure exceed your income. **1862** HISLOP 247 Poor folk maun fit their wame to their winning.

Lay(ing), *see also* Block in another's way (To l. a); Cast (L.) their heads together; Cured her from l. in hedge; Fingers on thy lips (L. thy); Laugh and l. down; Lick and l. down; Nought l. down nought take up; Rainy day (L. up for).

Layer(s) up, *see* Ill l. u. make thieves.

Layton, *see* Prayers (They shall have) . . . quoth vicar of L.

Laziness, *see* Lacking breeds l.; Pride and l. would have mickle upholding.

Lazy as Ludlam's dog, As | that leaned his head against a wall to bark.
                                             (L 587)

1670 RAY 202. **1801** WOLCOT (P. Pindar) *Out at Last* Wks. (1816) III. 385 Lazy as Ludlam's lazy dog, That held his head against the wall to bark. **1891** J. & L. KIPLING *Beast & Man* 287 English rustics talk of a man 'as lazy as Ludlam's dog that leaned his head against the wall to bark'.

Lazy-bones.

[= a lazy person.] **1592** G. HARVEY *Pierce's Super.* (1593) 185 Was . . . legierdemane a sloweworme, Viuacitie a lasie-bones. **1809** MALKIN *Gil Blas* II. i. par. 6 Master lazy-bones did not like sitting up!

Lazy Laurence.

[= an idle person; possibly mere alliteration, or in allusion to the heat prevalent about St. Laurence's day, Aug. 10.] **1784** *Gent. Mag.* II. 349 When a person in hot weather seems lazy, it is a common saying that Lawrence bids him high wages. **1796** EDGEWORTH *Par. Asst.*, 'Lazy Lawrence' (1903) 53 He was found early and late at his work, established a new character, and . . . lost the name of 'Lazy Lawrence'. **1796** PEGGE *Anonym.* VIII. xix (1809) 348 *Laurence bids wages;* a proverbial saying for *to be lazy;* because St. Laurence's day is the 10th of August within the dog-days. **1821** CLARE *Vill. Minstr.* II. 23 When . . . the warm sun smiles And 'Lawrence wages bids' on hills and stiles. **1836** W. D. COOPER *Glos. Sussex Provinc.* 24 'I ha'e got a touch o' ol' Laurence todae, I be troubled to git ane wud me work'. **1863** J. R. WISE *New Forest* ch. 16 If a peasant is lazy, it is proverbially said, 'Laurence has got upon him', or, 'He has got a touch of Laurence'. **1880** *E. Cornwall Gloss.* He's as lazy as Larence. One wad think that Larence had got hold o'n.

Lazy ox is little better for the goad, A.

1706 STEVENS s.v. Buey. **1732** FULLER no. 236.

Lazy sheep thinks its wool heavy, A.

1727 GAY *Fables, Hare & Friends* The sheep was feeble, and complain'd His sides a load of wool sustain'd. **1732** FULLER no. 237.

Lazy, *see also* Lean fee fit reward for l. clerk; Long and l.

Lea, *see* Leave her on a l.

Lead a horse to the water, A man may | but he cannot make him drink.
(M 262)

c. **1175** *Lambeth Hom.* (Morris) 9 Hwa is þet mei þet hors wettrien þe him self nule drinken? **1546** HEYWOOD I. xi. D3 A man may well bryng a horse to the water, But he can not make hym drynke without he will. **1647** FULLER *C. Wounded Consc.* One may bring them down to the spring of life, but cannot make them drink of the waters thereof. **1763** JOHNSON in *Boswell* xvi. (1848) 146 You need not be afraid of his forcing you to be . . . a lawyer; . . . 'One man may lead a horse to the water, but twenty cannot make him drink.' **1857** TROLLOPE *Barch. Tow.* ch. 35 'Well,' said she . . . , 'one man can take a horse to water, but a thousand can't make him drink.'

Lead, As heavy (dull) as.
(L 134)

1481 CAXTON *Reynard* Arb. 37 As heuy as leed. *c.* **1550** BALE *K. Johan* l. 2138. [*c.* **1553**] **1560–7** UDALL *Ralph Roister D.* II. i. 22 As heavie as lead lumpes. *c.* **1595** SHAKES. *R.J.* II. v. 17 Unwieldy, slow, heavy and pale as lead. **1597** *Id. 1 Hen. IV* V. iii. 34 I am as hot as molten lead, and as heavy too. [**1600**] **1657** *Lust's Dominion* Hazl.-Dods. xiv. 98 Dull as lead. **1836** MARRYAT *Midsh. Easy* ch. 7.

Lead nor drive, Neither.
(L 138)

1667 L'ESTRANGE *Quevedo's Visions* (1668) iii. 92 Another . . . would neither Lead nor Drive. **1678** RAY 75 . . . An untoward, unmanageable person.

Lead one by the ear (nose), To.
(N 233)

[LUCIAN, *Hermos.* 168: οὐδὲν κωλύσει σε τῆς ῥινὸς ἕλκεσθαι ὑφ' ἑκάστου = L. *naribus trahere*, as was done with bears.] *c.* **1486–1500** MEDWALL *Nature* I. 960 (ear). *c.* **1497** *Id. Fulgens* II. 150 (ear). *c.* **1516** J. SKELTON *Magn.* 712 (eyre). **1540** SIR T. ELYOT *Pasquil the Plain* B3 (nose). *c.* **1566** CURIO *Pasquin in a Trance* tr. W. P. Not suffer our selues to be led by the nose. **1581** T. LUPTON *A Persuasion from Papistry* 149 T3 He maye leade them by the noses whiche waye he liste. **1598** FLORIO *Worlde of Wordes* s.v. *Menar per il naso*, to leade by the nose, to make a foole of one. **1604**

SHAKES. *O.* I. iii. 395 The Moor . . . will as tenderly be led by the nose As asses are. **1611** *Id. W.T.* IV. iv. 790 Though authority be a stubborn bear, yet he is oft led by the nose with gold. **1621** BURTON *Anat. Mel.* III. iv. I. ii. (1651) 648 They will make others most devout and superstitious, . . . and lead them by the nose like so many bears in a line. **1639** FULLER *Holy War* II. xxxi (1840) 90 Manasses, . . . under pretence of opening the queen's eyes, did lead her by the nose, captivating her judgment instead of directing it. *a.* **1687** COTTON *Poet. Wks.* (1765) 198 He master is of thee indeed, and thee still by the nose does lead. **1721** 28 July BOLINGBROKE to Swift Mystery will lead millions by the nose.

Lead (*noun*), *see* Balance distinguishes not between gold and l.; Devil drives . . . no l. at heels; Pale as l.; Sword of l., (To slay with a).

Lead(s) (*verb*), *see also* Fate l. the willing; Hop whore! . . . Hangman l. the dance.

Leaden (wooden) sword in an ivory (a painted) sheath, A.
(S 1048)

[L. *In eburna vagina plumbeus gladius.*] **1533–4** UDALL *Flowers for Latin Speaking* (1560) Z2 A latine prouerbe: *Plumbeo iugulare gladio*, to cutte ones throte with a sworde of lead, that is to saie, to goe about . . . to conuince a man with a vayne . . . argument. **1540** TAVERNER tr. *Erasm. Flores sententiarum* O1 *Qui forma decorus indecore loquitur, ex eburnea uagina plumbeum educit gladium* A goodlye person that speaketh vngoodly wordes, draweth forth a leaden swerd out of an Iuery skaberd. **1542** ERASM. tr. Udall *Apoph.* (1877) 163 Hearyng a young strieplyng, of a verie well fauoured and honeste face, vsyng vnhonest communicacion Art thou not ashamed, quoth he, to drawe a sword of lead out of an ieuorie sheathe? [**1589**] **1592** LYLY *Midas* I. ii. 41 That's a leaden dagger in a veluette sheath, to haue a black tongue in a faire mouth. **1590–5** MUNDAY *et al. Sir T. More* IV. iv. 135 They are like golden flies on leaden hooks. **1612** T. ADAMS *The Gallant's Burden* (1616 ed. 56) A Woodden Dagger in a faire Sheath. **1616** WITHALS 560 A wooden dagger in a painted sheath. **1639** CLARKE 6 (as **1616**). **1706** STEVENS s.v. Vayna A Leaden Knife in a Golden Sheath. A fair outside, and foul within.

Leaden, *see also* God comes with l. feet.

Leaf of borage might buy all the substance that they can sell, A.
(L 141)

1546 HEYWOOD I. x. C3ᵛ But wed of corage They must in all haste, though a leafe of borage Myght bye all the substaunce that they can sell.

Leaf (-ves), *see also* Aspen l., (To quake like an); Beauty may have fair l.; Deeds are fruits, words but l.; Eats l. and voids silk; Every day of . . . a l. in thy history; Fears l. (He that) . . . not go into wood; Fruit have, (If you would) you must bring l. to grave; Hedge have, (If you would) carry l. to grave; St. Matthias both l. and grass; Take a l. out of book; Turn a new l.

Leak will sink a great ship, A small.
(L 147)

1616 T. ADAMS *Three Divine Sisters* 28 It is a little leake that drowneth a shippe. **1642** FULLER *Holy State* I. viii Many little leaks may sink a ship. **1732** FULLER no. 407. **1745** FRANKLIN Jan. Beware of little expenses, a small leak will sink a great ship.

Leak, *see also* Old vessels must l.; Sieve, (To be (l.) like a).

Leal folks never wanted gear.
1721 KELLY 231.

Leal heart lied never.

1768 A. ROSS *Helenore* (1778) 89 Her dowie pain she could no more conceal; The heart, they'll say, will never lie that's leal. **1862** HISLOP 206.

Leal, *see also* Hard task to be poor and l.

Lean as a rake, As.
(R 22)

c. **1386** CHAUCER *Prol.* l. 287 As lene was his hors as is a rake. [**1503**] *c.* **1545** SKELTON *Phyllyp Sparrowe* l. 913: Wks. i. 79 His bones crake, Leane as a rake. **1555** HEYWOOD *Epig. on Prov.* no. xlii Skyn and bone, leane as a rake. **1589** SPENSER *F.Q.* II. xi. 22 His body leane and meagre as rake. **1608** SHAKES. *C.* I. i. 23 Let us revenge this with our pikes ere we become rakes; for the gods know I speak this in hunger for bread. **1659** HOWELL *Eng. Prov.* 10b. *a.* **1732** GAY *New Song New Sim.* Songs, etc. (1784) II. 115 Lean as a rake with sighs and care.

Lean as a shotten herring.
(H 447)

1588 W. AVERELL *Combat of Contrarieties* B1ᵛ This yeere bumbd like a Barrell, the next shottend like a Herring, nowe your hose hang loose like a bowe case, the next daie as straite as a pudding skinne. **1590** GREENE *Never Too Late* Gros. viii. 187 Thou hadst alate . . . a louely fat paire of cheekes, and now thou lookest like a shotten herring. **1593** G. HARVEY Wks. Gros. ii. 130 His conceit is as lank, as a shotten herring. **1597** SHAKES. *I Hen. IV* II. iv. 120 Go thy ways, old Jack, die when thou wilt; if manhood, good manhood, be not forgot upon the face of the earth, then am I a shotten herring. **1607** T. W. *The Optic Glass of Humours* C6. **1659** HOWELL *Fr. Prov.* 18.

Lean dog for a hard road, A.
1917 BRIDGE 4.

Lean dog to get through a hedge, A.
1902–4 LEAN III. 393 . . . Spare people most easy to pull through an illness. (Lancashire.)

Lean fee is a fit reward for a lazy clerk, A.
(F 172)

1579 GOSSON *Ephemerides* (*Sch. Abuse* Arb. 11) A leane fee is fitte for a lazie Clarke. **1583** MELBANCKE *Philot.* E3ᵛ Indeede a leane fee befits a lazye clarke. **1597** *Politeuphuia* 166. **1639** CLARKE 221.

Lean liberty is better than fat slavery.

1605 T. HEYWOOD I *If You Know Not Me* l. 1184 Better be a Milk-maid free, then a Madame in bondage. **1732** FULLER no. 3158.

Lean to the wrong shore, To.
(S 395)

1546 HEYWOOD II. ii. G1 Ye leane (quoth he) to the wrong shore.

Lean, *see also* Envious man grows l.; Snapping so short makes you look so l.

Leap an inch from a slut (shrew), She cannot.
(I 59)

1648 25 Jan.–3 Feb. *Mercurius Aulicus*, Numb. 1, A2ᵛ Not one of 'em are able to leap three foot from a knave. **1678** RAY 256 She doth not leap an inch from a shrew. **1732** FULLER no. 4121 (slut).

Leap at a crust, To.
(C 870)

1582 WHETSTONE *Heptameron* 14 Want wyll so quicken them, as the Husband wyll leape at a Cruste, and the Wife trot for her Dinner. **1600** DEKKER *Old Fort.* II. ii. 94 [Hunger] Sheele make a man leape at a crust. **1612** T. JAMES *Jesuits Downfall* 23 You shall see them all leape at a crust, ere it be long. **1616** WITHALS 566. **1616** DRAXE no. 1026.

Leap at a daisy, To.
(D 14)

[= to be hanged.] **1553** *Respublica* v. ii Some of vs erelong maie happe leape at a daisie. **1575** *Gammer Gurton N.* v. ii. 235 I will go neare for this to make ye leape at a dasye.

Leap in the dark, A.
(L 148)

1697 VANBRUGH *Prov. Wife* v. vi Now I am in for Hobbes' voyage; a great leap in the dark.[1] **1721** DEFOE *Moll Flanders* (1840) 75 Make matrimony, like death, a leap in the dark. **1903** BRYCE *Biograph. Stud.* 57 The Act of 1867 was described at the time as 'a leap in the dark'. [1 referring to traditional last words of Thomas Hobbes (d. 1679), 'I am going to take a great leap into obscurity'. Cf. traditional last words of Rabelais (d. 1553) *Je m'en vais chercher un grand peut-être*.]

Leap into a well, If you | Providence is not bound to fetch you out.

1732 FULLER no. 2795.

Leap over nine hedges, He is ready to.
(H 365)

1678 RAY 353.

Leap over the hedge before you come at the stile (*or vice versa*), To. *Cf.* Over the stile.
(H 363)

1553 *Respublica* I. iii (You will over the hedge ere ye). **1560** *Contention betwixt Churchyard and Camell* A2ᵛ You leape ore the hedge, and seeith not the gate. **1566** GASCOIGNE *Supposes* ii. 202 You would fayne leape over the stile before you come at the hedge. **1670** RAY 184.

Leap year is never a good sheep year, A.

1601 J. CHAMBER *Treatise against Judicial Astrology* 110 Shepheards and heardsmen . . . report that their flocks and cattell those yeares [in leap years] either conceiue not at all, or if they do, yet go not out their time, or if they go out, yet they bring forth certain weake and crossed ware. *a.* **1628** CARMICHAELL no. 1075. **1846** DENHAM 17.

Leaped a haddock (whiting), There.

(W 318)

[= an opportunity was missed.] **1546** HEYWOOD II. vii. 13 There lepte a whityng (quoth she). *c.* **1612** BEAUM. & FL. *Scornf. Lady* IV. I My little Levite hath forsaken me . . . : well fool, you leapt a Haddock when you left him. **1670** RAY 199 To let leap a whiting, *i.e.* To let slip an opportunity.

Leaps over the dyke where it is lowest, Every one.

(M 549)

1610 ROWLANDS *Martin Mark-All* Hunt. Cl. 19, ii. 14 You will verifie the old saying, where the ditch is lowest, there men goe ouer thicke and three-fold. **1621** ROBINSON 20. *a.* **1628** CARMICHAELL no. 1113 (at the neirest). **1641** FERGUSSON no. 629 (at the laichest). **1721** KELLY 97 Every one loups o'er the Dike where it is laighest. . . . Signifying that poor People are run down by every Body.

Leap(s), *see also* Dam l. over (Where), kid follows; Kernel and l. at the shell, (To lose); Look before you l.; Recoil a little . . . l. the better; Stumble at straw and l. over block.

Learn at other men's cost, It is good to. *Cf.* Beware by other men's harms.

(M 615)

c. **1526** *Dicta Sapientum* B2 What shulde be eschewed lerne nat of thyne owne yll, but by the yuels of other take ensample. **1559** *Mirr. for Mag.* (Campbell) 192 To learne by others griefe sum haue the grace. **1573** TUSSER *Husb.* X (1878) 23 Then happie is he by example that can take heede by the fall of a mischieued man. **1574** *Mirr. for Mag.* (Campbell) 118 If we could lerne by others to be wise. **1659** HOWELL *It. Prov.* 8 He is happy who learns at another mans cost.

Learn to pray, He that will (would) | let him go to sea.

(S 173)

1576 GASCOIGNE *Steele Glas* ii. 170 For towarde shipwracke, many men can pray. *a.* **1631** DONNE *Sat.* vii Poems (1896) II. 209 Friends, like land soldiers in a storm at sea, Not knowing what to do, for him did pray. **1640** HERBERT no. 84. **1655–62** GURNALL *Chrn. in Armour* (1865) I. 577 The proverb indeed is, 'He that would learn to pray, let him go to sea'. **1659** N. R. 42. **1678** BUTLER *Hudibras* III. ii. 537 (As carnal seamen, in a storm, Turn pious converts, and reform). **1694** R. SOUTH *Twelve Sermons* 199 Ia. **1908** *Spectator* 13 Aug. 452 These sailors . . . can only call upon the Most High. . . .

There is a Basque proverb, 'Let him who knows not how to pray, go to sea'.

Learn to say before you sing.   (L 150)

1639 CLARKE 116.

Learn to shape Idle a coat, You will soon.   (I 5)

1602 CAREW *Surv. of Cornwall* (1769) f. 56 To reproue one of laziness, they will say, Doest thou make Idle a coate? that is, a coate for idlenes? **1678** RAY 254.

Learn weeping, and you shall gain laughing.   (L 151)

1640 HERBERT no. 127.

Learn young, learn fair.   (L 152)

a. **1628** CARMICHAELL no. 1034.   **1641** FERGUSSON no. 570.

Learn your goodam to make milk kail.

1721 KELLY 233 . . . Spoken to them who officiously offer to teach them who know more than themselves.

Learned timely to steal (beg) that could not say 'Nay', He.   (N 53)

c. **1460** *Towneley Myst., 2nd Shep. Play* 524 He lernyd tymely to steyll that couth not say nay. *a.* **1628** CARMICHAELL no. 659 (deny). **1641** FERGUSSON no. 349 He gangs earlie to steal, that cannot say na. **1721** KELLY 170 He gangs early to beg that cannot say nay. Because Men will make a Prey of his liberal Disposition.

Learned (*adj.*), *see also* Lives well is l. enough.

Learning in the breast of a bad man (a prince) is as a sword in the hand of a madman.   (L 156)

1508 J. FISHER *Three Dialogues* A4ᵛ Arte and learnyng Are as a sworde in a mad mans hande. Doctrina scolisti est gladio insani similis. **1569** W. WAGER *The Longer thou Livest* G3ᵛ A wicked man hauing learning and cunning . . . is like one whose wittes are running, I meane a madde man hauing a sword in his hand. **1591** HARINGTON *Allegory of Orl. Fur.* 413 The chiefe fault commonly is, in those counsellors that put a sword into a madmans hand, by putting such conceits into Princes heads. **1629** TUVILL *Vade Mecum* Of Learning 16 Learning . . . in a Prince . . . is like a dangerous knife in the hands of a mad-man.

Learning is the eye of the mind. (L 157)

1616 DRAXE no. 1192.

Learning makes a good man better and an ill man worse.

c. **1612** P. CHARRON *Of Wisdom* tr. S. Lennard (1640) 507 One . . . hath said . . . That learning marreth weake wits, and spirits, perfiteth the strong and naturall. **1707** MAPLETOFT 96. **1732** FULLER no. 3162.

Learning, *see also* Experience without l.; Good life better than bushel of l. (Handful of); Good manners to show l. before ladies (Not); Great memory without l.; House and land are spent (When), l. is excellent; Love of money and of l. rarely meet; Much l. makes a man mad; Much science (l.) much sorrow; Ounce of discretion worth pound of l.; Oxford for l.; Pay more for schooling than l. is worth; Wit without l. tree without fruit.

Learns a trade (an art), He that | has a purchase made. *Cf.* Art, He who has an.
(T 460)

1559 *A Woorke of Ioannes Ferrarius* tr. W. Bavarde 79ᵛ The Prouerbe saith that a craftesman neuer dyeth a begger. **1578** FLORIO *First F.* 31 Learne thou an art and lay it aside, for tyme wil come thou shalt haue neede of it. **1584** R. WILSON *Three Lords* C2 Better . . . learne a trade to liue another day. **1611** COTGRAVE s.v. Mestier He that hath a good trade hath a goodlie reuenue. **1640** HERBERT no. 978.

Learns young, Whoso | forgets not when he is old.
(Y 42)

c. **1275** *Provs. of Alfred* (Skeat) A 100–5 The mon þe on youhþe yeorne leorneþ . . . he may beon on elde wenliche lorþeu. [The man who learns eagerly in youth . . . may be an excellent teacher when he is old.] *c.* **1300** *Provs. of Hending* 6 Whose yong lereth,[1] olt[2] he ne leseth.[3] *c.* **1400** *Beryn* E.E.T.S. l. 938 For thing I-take in [youthe, is] hard to put away. **1567** *Amorous Tales* tr. Sanford F1 Learne in thy youth that which shall be profitable for thee in thy olde age. **1623** PAINTER B1 What in youth a man hath most in vre, The same to keepe till death hee shall bee sure. **1659** HOWELL *Fr. Prov.* 5 What's learnt in youth doth last to the grave. [[1] learneth. [2] old. [3] loseth.]

Learn(s, t, ed), *see also* Anchor of a ship . . . never l. to swim; Better l. by neighbour's skaith; Bourbons l. nothing; Doing nothing we l. to do ill; Doing we l.; Evil is soon l.; *Fas est et ab hoste doceri*; First l. (What we) we best can; Live and l.; Man may l. wit every day; Never too old to l.; News, (You must go to the oven or the mill if you will l.); Nothing questions nothing l.; Soon l., soon forgotten; Wise men l. by other men's harms; Writing you l. to write.

Lease, *see* New l. of life; No man has l. of his life.

Least boy always carries the greatest fiddle, The.
(B 577)

1670 RAY 112 . . . All lay load upon those that are the least able to bear it. For they that are least able to bear, are least to resist the imposition of the burden. **1710** PALMER 146. **1732** FULLER no. 4629 (omitting 'always').

Least foolish is wise, The.
(F 559)

1640 HERBERT no. 910.

Least in sight, To play.
(S 440)

1590 R. HARVEY *Plain Perceval* A3ᵛ Martin . . . plaies least in sight. [*c.* 1590] **1592** *Soliman and Perseda* V. iii. 95. **1591** ARIOSTO *Orl. Fur.* Harington XLIII. 71. **1603** S. HARSNET 2 Himselfe and his actors doe play least to be seene. **1616** J. CHAMBERLAIN (McClure ii. 31). **1631** *Celestina* tr. Mabbe 24.

Least, *see also* Last but not l.

Leather, Nothing like.
(N 310)

1692 L'ESTRANGE *Aesop's Fab.* ccccxlviii (1738) 484 There was a council of mechanics called to advise about the fortifying of a city. . . . Up starts a currier; Gentlemen, says he, when y'ave said all that can be said, there's nothing in the world like leather. **1837** SIR F. PALGRAVE *Merch. & Friar* (1844) 147 Depend upon it, Sir, there is nothing like leather. **1905** WEYMAN *Starvecrow F.* ch. 2 'My lords would not sleep in their beds . . . if it were not for the yeomanry and the runners.' . . . Mrs. Gilson coughed drily. 'Leather's a fine thing', she said, 'if you believe the cobbler.'

Leather, *see also* Cut large thongs of other men's l.; Cut one's thong according to one's l.; Find fault with my shoes and give no l.; Raw l. will stretch; Shoes are made of running l.; Tongue is made of loose l. (Your); Tough as l.

Leave a jest when it pleases lest it turn to earnest.
(J 46)

1591 ARIOSTO *Orl. Fur.* Harington XII. *Moral* We may see that things done in iest, oft turne to earnest. **1592–3** SHAKES. *C.E.* II. ii. 24 Hold, sir, for God's sake! Now your jest is earnest. [1603] **1607** T. HEYWOOD *Woman Killed with Kindness* I. iii. 58 Unhappy jest that in such earnest ends. **1640** HERBERT no. 104. Leave jesting whiles it pleaseth, lest it turne to earnest. **1706** STEVENS s.v. Burlas. **1732** FULLER no. 6357 (pleases you best).

Leave her on a lea and let the devil flit her.
(L 133)

1599 PORTER *Angry Wom. Abingd.* ll. 2291–2 But and they would be ruld by me, they should set her on the Ieland, and bid the Diuell split her. **1639** CLARKE 12 Now they leave me on a lea-land. **1659** HOWELL *Eng. Prov.* 16b . . . A Lincolnshire Proverb spoken of a scolding wife; viz. Tye her to a Plow-ridge, and lett the Devill remove her to a better Pasture.

Leave in the briers, To.
(B 673)

[in troubles, difficulties.] **1520** WHITTINGTON *Vulg.* E.E.T.S. 98 Thou art a sure spere at nede. that leues a man stykkynge in the breres. **1563** FOXE *A. & M.* I. 208/1 Leaving the Bishops, and such others, in the Briers. **1670** RAY 166 To leave one in the briers (or suds).

Leave in the lurch, To.
(L 588)

[= to leave in adverse circumstances, or unexpected difficulty.] **1576** G. HARVEY *Lett.-Bk.* Camden Soc. 163 Lest he fail in his reckning . . . and so leave himself in the lurch. **1600**

HOLLAND *Livy* 222 The Volscians seeing themselves abandoned and left in the lurch by them, . . . quit the campe and field. **1705** STRYPE *Life of Cheke* v. ii (1821) 94 The Lords . . . proclaimed Mary Queen, . . . and thus was poor Sir John Cheke left in the lurch. **1879** BROWNING *Martin Relph* 66 He has left his sweetheart here in the lurch.

Leave is light.   (L 170)

1546 HEYWOOD I. x. C3ᵛ Ye might haue knokt or ye came in; leaue is lyght. **1611** GRUTER 180. **1614** CAMDEN 309. **1631** JONSON *New Inn* V. v. 82 But you must aske my leaue first, . . . Leaue is but light. **1670** RAY 113 . . . It's an easie matter to ask leave. **1721** KELLY 230 . . . A Reproof to them who intrude upon your Interest, without your Permission.

Leave more to do when we die, We | than we have done.   (M 1164)

1640 HERBERT no. 972.

Leave neither stick nor stone standing, To.

1553 T. BECON *Jewel of Joy* P.S. 434 (. . . as they use to say).

Leave no stone unturned, To.   (S 890)

[= to try every possible means. EUR. *Heracl.* 1002 πάντα κινῆσαι πέτρον. PLINY *Ep.* l. 20. 15 . . . *omnia pertempto, omnia experior, πάντα denique λίθον κινῶ.* ERASM. *Ad. Omnem movere lapidem.*] **1545** S.· GARDINER to W. Paget (*Lett.* ed. Muller 195) The French men be so ernest to haue Bolen as they undowtedly *movere omnem lapidem.* **1548** W. PATTEN *Exped^n into Scotland* (*Tudor Tracts* 68) What policy hath he left unproved? What shift unsought? Or what stone unturned? **1550** CRANMER *Def. of Doct. of Sacrament* 68 We must turne euery stone (as the prouerbe sayth) to seke out the truthe. *c.* **1552** *Dice-Play* B6 He will refuse no labour nor leaue no stone vnturned, to pick up a penny. **1655** FULLER *Ch. Hist.* XI. iii (1868) III. 471 They did whatsoever good men could, . . . leaving no stone unturned which might advantage them herein. **1926** *Times* 17 Apr. 14/3 The Government . . . would leave no stone unturned to avoid the catastrophe of a stoppage.

Leave off while the play is good.
                                                              (P 399)

c. **1350** *Douce MS.* 52 no. 58 When game is best, Hit is tyme to rest. *c.* **1390** GOWER *Conf. Amantis* VIII. 3087 In his proverbe seith the wise, whan game is best, is best to leaue. *c.* **1450** *Provs. of Wisdom* (ed. Zupitza) in *Archiv. f. d. Stud. d. Neueren Sprachen* 90. 245 When game is best, is tyme to lete. **1594–5** SHAKES. *R.J.* I. iv. 39 The game was ne'er so fair, and I am done. *Ibid.* I. v. 117 Away, be gone; the sport is at the best. **1721** KELLY 233 . . . Lest, if it be continued, it may come to earnest. Spoken also by People of Age and Gravity, when young People jest upon them, intimating that they will not bear it. **1820** SCOTT *Monast.* ch. 13 When I saw our host break ranks, . . . I e'en pricked off with myself while the play was good. **1882** W. BATES *Maclise Port. Gal.* (1898) 280 James Smith . . .

laid down the principle . . . that when a man had played a good game, he should retire from the tables, and leave off a winner.

Leave off, *see also* Piper of Bujalance who got . . . ten [maravedi] to l. o.

Leave the court ere the court leave thee.
                                                              (C 726)

a. **1628** CARMICHAELL no. 1053. **1641** FERGUSSON no. 577. **1710** PALMER 61. **1721** KELLY 234 . . . A good Advice in its literal Sense, if Courtiers would take it, but it signifies that we should mortify our vicious Inclinations, by Consideration and Religion, before old Age make them forsake us.

Leave to speak who cannot hold his tongue, He must have.   (L 168)

a. **1522** DOUGLAS *Aeneid* 3 Prol. 20 Quha kan not hold thar peice are fle to flyte. *a.* **1628** CARMICHAELL no. 698. **1641** FERGUSSON no. 301. **1683** MERITON *Yorks. Ale* (1697) 83–7. **1721** KELLY 145 . . . Spoken against impertinent and indefatigable Baublers.

Leave to thrive for throng,[1] You cannot get.

1721 KELLY 365 . . . That is, your too much haste spoils your Business. [[1] press of business.]

Leave (Let) well alone.   (W 260)

c. **1396** CHAUCER *Envoy to Bukton* l. 27 Unwys is he that kan no wele endure. If thow be siker, put the nat in drede. [*c.* **1565–6**] **1626** *Jests of Scoggin* (*Sh. Jest Bks.* ii. 143) When it was well. you could not let it alone. **1577** HOLINSHED (1587 ed., i. 162b) Ye iudged well once, but ye may not change well againe. *c.* **1595–6** SHAKES. *K.J.* IV. ii. 28 When workmen strive to do better than well, They do confound their skill in covetousness. [1597] **1599** CHAPMAN *Hum. Day's Mirth* Sc. v. l. 87 I'll leave when I am well. **1605–6** SHAKES. *K.L.* I. iv. 347 Striving to better, oft we mar what's well. **1609** *Id. Son.* 103, l. 9 Were it not sinful then, striving to mend, To mar the subject that before was well? **1834** MARRYAT *Jacob Faith.* ch. 33 You're well off at present, and 'leave well alone' is a good motto. **1849** LYTTON *Caxtons* VI. vi We have been happy for more than eighteen years without them, Kitty! . . . To leave well alone is a golden rule worth all in Pythagoras. **1863** C. READE *Hard Cash* ch. 53 Colt cast a glance of triumph, and declined to re-examine. He always let well alone.

Leave (off) with an appetite.   (A 289)

1551 [R. CROWLEY] *Fable of Philargyrie* Cᵛ 1l shall, quoth he / Ryght healthfull be / To leaue wyth Appetite. **1558** BULLEIN *Govt. of Health* 37 And so leue w[ith] an appetite, passinge the time wyslie betwene dinner and supper. **1586** GUAZZO ii. 136 Saint Augustine saith, Eat alwaies so, that thou still have an appetite.

Leave, leavings, (*noun*), *see also* French l. (Take); Lasses with lad's l.; Losers l. to speak (Give).

Leaves the old way for the new, Who | will find himself deceived.   (w 161)

1573 SANFORD 50 (oftentimes is found to go astray). **1629** *Bk. Mer. Rid.* Prov. no. 2 (as 1573). **1666** TORRIANO *It. Prov.* 271 no. 9. **1808** E. HAMILTON *Cottagers of Glenburnie* ch. 13 Auld ways are aye the best.

Leave(s), leaving, left (*verb*), *see also* Better l. than lack; Cat l. on the malt-heap, (To have what the); Dines and l. lays cloth twice; Enough (Of) men l.; Found you and here . . . I l. you, (Here I); Get him where you l. him; Highway, (He that l.); Like it or l. it; Man must not l. the king's highway for a pathway; Mire, (To l. in the); Oil l. in the lamp, (There is); Shameful l. worse than shameful eating; Take it or l. it.

Lecher, *see* Old man l.

Lechery and covetousness go together.   (L 173)

1590 SPENSER *F.Q.* I. iv. 26–7 Such one was *Lecherie*, the third of all this traine. And greedy *Auarice* by him did ride. [1621–39] **1653** [J. FORD] *Queen* IV. 30 'Tis an old proverbe that leachery and covetousnes go together, and 'tis a true one too.

Lecture(s), *see* Curtain l.; Forehead and eye (In) l. of mind.

Lee(s) (*proper name*), *see* Cheshire there are L. (In).

Leech, *see* Empty l. (tick) sucks sore; Go after a l. (While men), body is buried.

Leeches kill with licence.

1721 KELLY 232 . . . An Argument dissuading People of no Skill from Quacking; for if any that they administer to die, they will be blam'd; But if any die under the Hands of a Physician, no notice is taken of it.

Leeful[1] man is the beggar's brother, The.

1721 KELLY 315 . . . Spoken when we have lent something that we now want, and must be forced to borrow. [1 The man that is ready to lend.]

Leek, Not worth a.

c. **1350** *Alexander* l. 4229 And your lare of a leke suld nevir the less worth. c. **1400** *Rom. Rose* B. 4830 Sich love I preise not at a lek. c. **1412** HOCCLEVE *De Reg. Princ.* (1860) 60 Love on luste groundede is not worthe a leeke. a. **1529** SKELTON *Col. Cloute* 183 Wks. (1843) I. 318 But it is not worth a leke. **1555** HEYWOOD *Epig. on Prov.* CLXXXII Not the value of a good greene leeke.

Leeks in Lide, and ramsins[1] in May, Eat | and all the year after physicians may play.   (L 178)

1558 BULLEIN *Gov[t] Health* 45 Leekes doe purge the blood in March. **1686–7** AUBREY *Rem. Gent. & Jud.* 13 The vulgar in the West of England doe call the month of March, Lide [= O.E. Hlȳde]. A proverbiall rhythme—. . . [1 Garlic.]

Leek(s), *see also* Eat the l.; Green as a l.; Smell of garlic (l.) takes away smell of onions.

Leeward for fine weather, Look not, like the Dutchman, to.

1883 ROPER 13.

Left his purse in his other hose (breeches), He has.   (P 652)

1616 WITHALS 584. **1639** CLARKE 244. **1721** KELLY 138 *He left his money in his other breeks.* A Taunt to him that wants Money to pay his Reckoning.

Left to chance, Something must be.

1903 W. C. RUSSELL *Overdue* ch. 2 'Something must be left to chance', was a condition of Lord Nelson's tactics, and a clear recognition of the limits of human penetration.

Left (*adj.*), *see* Over the l. shoulder; Refuse with the right hand and take with the l.

Leg bail, To give (take).

[= to run away, decamp.] **1774** FERGUSSON *Poems* (1807) 234 They took leg-bail and ran awa With pith and speed. **1775** ADAIR *Amer. Ind.* 277 I had concluded to use no chivalry, but give them leg-bail instead of it, by . . . making for a deep swamp. **1785** GROSE *Dict. Vulg. T.* s.v. Leg To give leg bail and land security, to run away. **1842–3** W. H. MAXWELL *Hector O'Hal.* ch. 4 The priest and my lady will hear all in the morning, and, faith, I'll give them leg-bail in the mean time.

Leg of a lark is better than the body of a kite, A.   (L 186)

1546 HEYWOOD I. iv. B1 She, by lacke of substance seemyng but a sparke, Steynth[1] yet the stoutest, For a leg of a larke Is better than is the body of a kyght. **1605** CHAPMAN, JONSON, MARSTON *Eastw. Ho* V. i. 151. **1666** TORRIANO *It. Prov.* 242, note 13 A pestle of a lark, is better worth than the leg of a kite. **1670** RAY 112 One leg of a lark's worth the whole body of a kite. **1684** BUNYAN *Pilgr.* II (1867) 192 Yea, with delight, Say my lark's leg is better than a kite. [1 checks.]

Leg warms, While the | the boot harms.   (L 188)

a. **1500** R. *Hill's Commonpl. Bk.* E.E.T.S. 128 While the fote warmith, the sho harmith. **1546** HEYWOOD II. ii. F4[v] Long liyng warme in bed is holsome (quoth shee) While the leg warmeth, the boote harmeth (quoth hee). **1721** KELLY 251 Mickle sorrow comes to the screa,[1] e'er the heat come to the tea.[2] [[1] shoe.   [2] toe.]

Legs, How came you hither ? On my.
(L 191)

c. **1590** MUNDAY *John a Kent* l. 325. But will they come?—They will, if you goe.—But how? —Why on their feet, I knowe no other way. [1592] **1597** SHAKES. *Rich. III* I. iv. 86 I would speak with Clarence, and I came hither on my legs. [1598] **1616** HAUGHTON *Eng. for My Money* G1[v] How come we to Wesmistere?— Why on your Legges fooles, how should you goe ? **1632** SHIRLEY *Love in Maze* (ed. Dyce) ii. 297 How came you hither?—Why, upon my feet.

Leg(s), *see also* Baker by his bow l. (He should be a); Belly carries the l.; Best foot (l.) forward; Bone in the l. (Were it not for); Boot is on other l.; Broken her l. above knee; Cat (He is like a) light on l.; Gives thee a capon; Heart (Who has not) let him have l.; Last l.; Lies have short l.; Long be thy l. and short thy life; Lose a l. rather than life; Marriage (More belongs to) than four bare l.; Northampton stands on other men's l.; Old use and wont, l. about the fire; Right as my l.; Runs in the blood like wooden l.; See which l. you are lame of; Set a person on his l.; Shake a loose l.; Stand on one's own l.; Stretch your l. according to coverlet; Talk the hind l. off a donkey; Thought has good l.; Use l. and have l.; White l. would aye be rused.

Legion(s), *see* Contending with master of l. (Ill).

Leicestershire, *see* Shake a L. man . . . beans rattle.

Leigh, *see* Harry's children of L.

Leighton Buzzard, *see* Tring, Wing, and Ivinghoe.

Leisure, as flax grows, At.   (L 196)

1621 ROBINSON 30.   *a.* **1628** CARMICHAELL no. 203 At lazer as lint growis.   **1639** CLARKE 304.

Leisure, *see* Busiest men have most l.; Laugh at l.; Luck in l.; Time stays not fool's l.

Leman *or* Lemman, *see* No longer foster no longer l.; Tender as a parson's l.

Lemster [Leominster] bread and Weabley ale.   (B 624)

1586 CAMDEN *Britannia* 352 *Frumento item ideo est fœlix, & pane e purissimo polline, vt huius panis & Weabliæ potus . . . in prouerbium cesserint.* **1610** *Ibid.* tr. Holland 620 So renowned also it is for wheat, and head of the finest floure, that Lemster bread and Weabley Ale . . . are growne unto a common proverbe.   **1700** J. BROME *Trav.* 102 Hence it is grown Proverbial among the Inhabitants, For Lempster Bread and Weobley Beer, none can come near.

Lemster [Leominster] wool (ore[1]).
(W 753)

[*c.* **1515**] **1521** BARCLAY *Eclog.* IV. l. 316 Cornewayl hath tynne and Lymster wolles fyne. *a.* **15.** . SKELTON 'Elynour Rumming' Some fyll theyr pot full of good Lemster woll.   [1589] **1594** GREENE *Friar Bacon* l. 1450 Such woole As Lempster cannot yelde more finer stuffe. **1613–22** DRAYTON *Polyolb.* vii. 145 (1876) I. 176 At *Lemster*, for whose wool whose staple doth excell. *Ibid.* vii. 151 Where lives the man so dull, Britain's further shore, To whom did never sound the name of *Lemster* Ore? That with the silkworm's web for smallness doth compare. **1648** HERRICK *Hesper., Oberon's Pal.* (1901) I. 215 A bank of mosse . . . farre more Soft then the finest Lemster Ore.   **1662** FULLER Herefordshire 33 As for the Wooll in this County, it is best known to the honour thereof by the name of Lempster Ore. [[1] wool.]

Lemster wool, *see also* Dunmow bacon.

Lend and lose; so play fools.   (F 552)

1678 RAY 347.

Lend me your ears awhile.   (E 18)

1581 R.S. in C. THIMELTHORPE *Short Inventory* L1[v] Come lend your Eares to hear a word or twayne.   **1586** R. CROWLEY *Father John Francis* D1[v] But first, wee must lende you our eares a while.   **1599** SHAKES. *J.C.* III. ii. 73.   **1599** MARSTON *Antonio and Mellida* l. 1796 Lende me your eare.   **1662** *The Wits* ed. Elson 166.

Lend your horse for a long journey, you may have him return with his skin.
(H 675)

1659 HOWELL *Eng. Prov.* 1b.   **1670** RAY 14.

Lend your money and lose your friend.
(F 725)

c. **1594** BACON no. 1569 Qui prest a l'ami perd au double.   **1597** *Politeuphuia* 77 He that lends, must loose his friend, or els his mony without heede.   **1600–1** SHAKES. *H.* I. iii. 75 Neither a borrower nor a lender be; For loan oft loses both itself and friend.   **1611** COTGRAVE s.v. *Ami Qui preste à l'ami perd au double*: Prov. viz. both friend and money. To which purpose we haue a . . . Ryme, which begins with, I lent my money to my friend, and ends with I lost both money, and my friend. *a.* **1640** MELVILLE 'Ane ABC' 41 'I had a penny and freind . . . I lend my penny to my freind . . . I crav'd my penny at my freind . . . I lost my penny and my freind. . . .   **1721** KELLY 240 . . . It is not the lending of our Money that loses our Friend; but the demanding it again.

Lenders, *see* Spenders are bad L.

Lends, gives, He that.   (L 199)

1640 HERBERT no. 787.

Lends his pot may seethe his kail in his loof,[1] He that.

1737 RAMSAY III. 184. [[1] palm of hand.]

Lend(s), *see also* Better give a shilling than l.; Borrow (Not so good to) as to l.; Coat (He who has but one) cannot l. it; Enemy (If you would make), l.; Give him one and l. him another; World still . . . at staff's end, that . . . never will l.

Length begets loathing.

1742 JARVIS *Don Quixote* II. xxvi Length begets loathing. 1896 F. LOCKER-LAMPSON *My Confid.* 43 'Length begets loathing'. I well remember the sultry Sunday evenings when . . . we simmered through Mr. Shepherd's long-winded pastorals.

Length of a person's foot, To find (know) the.   (L 202)

1580 LYLY *Euph. & his Eng.* ii. 68 You shal not know the length of my foote, vntill by your cunning you get commendation. a. 1591 HY. SMITH *Serm. Satan's compassing* (1657) 491 [Satan] marks how every man is inclined, . . . and when he hath the measure of his foote, then he fits him. 1594–5 SHAKES. *L.L.L.* V. ii. 475 Do not you know my lady's foot by the squier? [i.e. square, measure.] 1616 DRAXE no. 1169 I know the length of his foot. a. 1617 BAYNE *On Eph.* I. 15 (1643) 156 Persons who can humour them, and find the length of their foot. 1826 SCOTT *Woodst.* ch. 19 I think I know the length of this man's foot. We have had a jollification or so together.

Lenson Hill, *see* Akin as L. H. to Pilsen Pen.

Lent, When I | I was a friend; and when I asked, I was unkind. So of my friend I made a foe; therefore I will no more do so.   (F 723)

c. 1450 *Provs. of Wysdom* 163 When I lent, I had a frend; But when I askyd, he was vnkynd. 1545 *Precepts of Cato* C3ᵛ. 16th c. *Old Eng. Prov. in Reliq. Antiq.* i. 208 When I lent I was a frend, When I asked I was unkinde. 1639 CLARKE 169 When I lend I am his friend, when I ask I am unkind.

Lent (*noun*), *see* After Christmas comes L.; Marry in L., live to repent; Money and capers, (He that has) is provided for L.; Short L. that must pay at Easter.

Lent (*verb*), *see also* Lippens to l. ploughs, his land will lie ley.

Leominster, *see* Lemster.

Leopard cannot change his spots, A.   (L 206)

[JER. xiii. 23.] 1546 J. BALE *Examⁿ Anne Askewe* P.S. 177 Their old conditions will change when the blackamorian change his skin, and the cat a mountain her spots. 1579 LYLY *Euph.* i. 191 Can the Aethiope chaunge or alter his skinne? or the Leoparde his hewe? 1596 SHAKES. *Rich. II* I. i. 174 Lions make leopards tame.—Yea, but not change his spots.

Leopard, In a | the spots are not observed.   (L 205)

1640 HERBERT no. 660.

Less, *see* Greater embraces the l.; Grief drives out the l., (The greater).

Less of your counsel (courtesy) and more of your cost (purse).   (L 208)

1629 T. ADAMS *Serm.* (1861–2) II. 407 With a show of spiritual counsel, they neglect corporal comfort; and . . . the poor might well reply, More of your cost, and less of your counsel. 1639 CLARKE 43. 1670 RAY 74 Less of your courtesie and more of your purse. *Re opitulandum non verbis.*

Lessened, *see* Grief is l. when imparted to others.

Lesson without book, To con (say).

1530 PALSGRAVE 739 My father . . . dyd stryke my heed by cause I had conned my lesson without the booke. 1549 J. PROCTOUR *Fall of the late Arian* H8ᵛ The woman now saithe her lesson without boke. 1571 J. BRIDGES *Sermon at Paul's Cross* 136 This lesson was so well conde without booke, that there was nothing but money would fetch it. c. 1600 SHAKES. *T.N.* II. iii. 139 An affectioned ass, that cons state without book, and utters it by great swarths. 1607 H. ESTIENNE *World of Wonders* 102.

Let-a-be for let-a-be. *Cf.* Cathkin's covenant, etc.

[= mutual forbearance.] 1822 SCOTT *Pirate* ch. 37 I am for let-a-be for let-a-be, as the boys say. 1836 M. SCOTT *Cruise Midge* ch. 2 The Scotch corporal . . . took the liberty of putting in his oar . . . 'Beg pardon, Mr. Brail, but let abee for let abee with mad dogs and daft folk, is an auld but very true adage.'

Let anybody lie by him, He will not.   (L 211)

1678 RAY 89 *A Liar* . . .

Let me see, as the blind man said.

1612 SHELTON *Quix.* IV. xxii. ii. 160 Let us behold ourselves, as one blind man said to another. 1864–5 DICKENS *Our Mut. Fr.* Bk. II. ch. 2 'What's the news in-doors?' . . . 'Let me see, said the blind man. Why the last news is, that I don't mean to marry your brother.'

Let sleeping dogs lie. *Cf.* Wake not a sleeping lion.   (W 7)

c. 1374 CHAUCER *Troilus* Bk. 3, l. 764 It is nought good a slepyng hound to wake. c. 1386 *Id. Franklin's T.* l. 1472 Lat slepen that is stille. 1546 HEYWOOD I. x. DIᵛ. 1597–8 SHAKES. *2 Hen. IV* I. ii. 145 Wake not a sleeping wolf. 1647 *Countryman's New Commonw.* 22 Wake not a sleeping Lyon. 1681 S. COLVIL *Whiggs Sup.* II. 27 It's best To let a sleeping mastiff rest. 1824 SCOTT *Redg.* lett. xi Take my advice, and speer as little about him as he does about you. Best to let sleeping dogs lie. 1882

BLACKMORE *Christowell* ch. 26 He laughed at the maxim of antiquity, *quieta noli movere*; which is, in our vernacular, 'let sleeping dogs lie'. **1902** A. LANG *Hist. Scot.* II. 509 It was the error of James that in ecclesiastical matters he could not obey the proverb, 'Let sleeping dogs lie'.

Let the cat out of the bag, To.

[= to disclose a guarded secret.] **1760** *Lond. Mag.* xxix. 224 We could have wished that the author . . . had not let the cat out of the bag. **1796** EDGEWORTH *Par. Asst., Eton M.* III. ii I forgot, I was nigh letting the cat out o' the bag again. **1836** MARRYAT *Midsh. Easy* ch. 21 Gascoigne closed his chair to Jack's, who, he was afraid, being a little affected with wine, would 'let the cat out of the bag'. **1847–8** THACKERAY *Vanity F.* ch. 19 Letting the cat of selfishness out of the bag of secrecy.

Let your house to your enemy; The first year | the second, to your friend; the third, live in it yourself.

1869 HAZLITT 382.

Let (= hindrance), *see* Delay comes l., (After); Little l. lets ill workman; Whet brings no l.

Let(s), *see* Lies backward and l. out her fore-rooms, (She).

Let (a, every, him, &c.), *see also under the significant words following.*

Lets his horse drink at every lake, and his wife go to every wake, He that | shall never be without a whore and a jade. (w 359)

1591 FLORIO *Second F.* 41 Who lets his wife go to euerie feaste, And lets his horse drinke at euerie puddle, Shall haue of his horse, a starke iadish beast And of his best wife, a twang with a huddle. **1640** HERBERT no. 434 Who letts his wife goe to every feast, and his horse drinke at every water, shall neither have good wife nor good horse. **1678** RAY 29.

Letter stay for the post, Let your | not the post for the letter. (L 213)

1642 TORRIANO 14 It behoveth the letter to wait upon the messenger, not the messenger upon the letter. **1664** CODRINGTON 203. **1670** RAY 15. *Ital.*

Letter(s), *see also* Complimentary l. asks for another; Eyes on l. (Neither) nor hands in coffers; Gist of a lady's l. in postscript; Heart's l. read in eye; *Littera scripta manet*; Money will do more than lord's l.; R is dog's l.; Three l., (Man of).

Lettuce, *see* Lips (Like), like l.

Level, *see* Line and l. (By).

Leveller, *see* Death is the grand l.

Levi, *see* Tribe of L.

Lewd bachelor makes a jealous husband, A.

1707 MAPLETOFT 26.

Lewisham, long, lazy, lousy.

1787 GROSE (*Kent*) 183 . . . Lewisham is certainly a very long town or village, and, . . . was once a very poor one. . . . The alliteration of this proverb, rather than the truth of it, has preserved it to the present time.

Liar is not believed when he speaks the truth, A. (L 217)

[CICERO *De Div.* 2. 71. 146 *Mendaci homini, ne verum quidem dicenti, credere solemus.* We are accustomed to give no credit to a liar, even when he tells the truth.] **1477** RIVERS *Dictes, &c.* (1877) 117 The reward of a lyar is that he be not beleuid of that he reherseth. **1573** J. BRIDGES *Supremacy of Christian Princes* 4 Mendaci non creditur ne iurato quidem. A lyer is not beleeued, no thoughe he sweare. **1692** L'ESTRANGE *Aesop's Fab.* (1738) lxxiv A common liar (says the old moral) shall not be believed even when he speaks true.

Liar is worse than a thief, A. (L 218)

1545 *Precepts of Cato* D1 There is no man that knoweth what a thefe and a lyer meaneth, and what their qualities be, but wyll with al his heart be rydde of a lier to take a thefe, for of the thefe he maye beware, of the other he cannot. **1547** S. GARDINER to Somerset (*Lett.* ed. J. A. Muller 1933, 293) We saie a man were better haue a thief in his house then a lier. **1623** PAINTER B5 A Lyar is counted in a common-wealth, Worse then a thiefe that liueth vpon stealth. **1626** BRETON *Soothing* A6. **1639** CLARKE 150.

Liar, lick dish. (L 222)

1575 *Gammer Gurton N.* v. ii. 252 Thou lier lick-dish, didst not say the neele wold be gitten? [**1603**] **1631** CHETTLE *Hoffman* 1. 2046 Lyer, lyer, licke dish.

Liars begin by imposing upon others, but end by deceiving themselves. (L 221)

1611 SHAKES. *Temp.* I. ii. 101 Made such a sinner of his memory, To credit his own lie. **1622** BACON *Hen. VII* Wks. (Chandos) 446 Perkin . . . with oft telling a lie, was turned by habit almost into the thing he seemed to be; and from a liar to a believer. **1718** PRIOR *Alma* iii As folks, quoth Richard, prone to leasing, Say things at first because they're pleasing, . . . Till their own dreams at length deceive 'em, And, oft repeating, they believe 'em.

Liars have need of good memories.   (L 219)

[QUINT. 4. 2. 91 *Mendacem memorem esse oportet.*] *c.* **1531** LATIMER *Let.* 4: *Serm. and Rem.* 312 You may learn how necessary it is for a liar to have a good memory. *a.* **1542** WYATT *Defence*: Wks. ed. Gilfillan, 37 For they say He that lie well must have a good remembrance, that he agree in all points with himself, lest he be spied. **1565** J. CALFHILL *Treatise of the Cross* P.S. 88. **1589** ?NASHE *Ret. of Pasquil* i. 102 A lyer must haue no shetle memory. **1692** L'ESTRANGE *Aesop's Fab.* cccliii (1738) 366 Wherefore parasites and liars had need of good memories. **1710-11** SWIFT *Examiner* There is one essential point wherein a political liar differs from others of the faculty, that he ought to have but a short memory. **1721** KELLY 50 . . . Lest he tell the same Lye different ways.

Liar(s), *see also* Common fame is a l.; Debtors are l.; Friar a l.; Lawyer must be great l.; Show me a l. and I will show thief; Vaunter and l. near akin.

Libel, *see* Greater the truth.

Liberal [man], *see* Covetous spends more than l.; Free (l.) of another man's pottage; Miserable man makes a penny of a farthing; Poor and l.

Liberality, *see* Frugality is the mother of l.

Liberty, but no latch-key.

1902 A. R. COLQUHOUN *Mastery of Pacific* 129 In the Philippines . . . finances are to be controlled by the Americans . . . But that a man . . . fit for self-government . . . cannot be entrusted with public funds is . . . equal to 'liberty, but no latch-key'!

Liberty hall.

1773 GOLDSMITH *Stoops to C.* II (Globe) 652/1 This is Liberty-hall, gentlemen. You may do just as you please here. **1845** G. J. JAMES *Smuggler* ch. 7 Let every man do as he likes. Have I not heard you, a thousand times, call your house Liberty Hall?

Liberty is more worth than gold (is a pearl, is a jewel). (L 223)

1484 CAXTON *Fab. Aesop* ed. Jacobs III. 15, 91 There is no rychesse gretter than lybete for lyberte is better than alle the gold of the world. **1584** WITHALS B7 Libertie better then gold or siluer. **1609** HARWARD 99 Liberty is a iewell. **1639** CLARKE 188 Libertie is a peerelesse pearle.

Liberty is not licence. (L 226)

[**1623**] **1640** JONSON *Time Vind.* vii. 662 Ther's difference 'twixt liberty, and licence. *a.* **1645** MILTON *Sonnet* vii Licence they mean when they cry liberty. *a.* **1720** SHEFFIELD (Dk. Buckhm.) *Wks.* (1753) I. 272 They are for licence, not for liberty. **1852** DAVIES & VAUGHAN tr. *Republic of Plato* Analysis of Bk. viii Liberty, degenerating into licence, is the chief feature of such a state [democracy].

Liberty, *see also* Bean in liberty . . . comfit in prison; Gift, (Who receives a) sells his l.; Lean l. better than fat slavery; Loses his l. loses all; Marries for wealth sells l.; One day was three till l. was borrow; Too much l. spoils all.

Library, *see* Hesky's l.

Lice, *see* Nits will be l.

Licence, *see* Liberty is not l.; Poetic l.

Lick and lay down.

1824 SCOTT *St. Ronans* ch. 14 What for suld I no have a Corpus delicti, . . . or any other Corpus that I like, sae lang as I am willing to lick and lay down the ready siller? **1862** HISLOP 210 . . . A proverbial form of expression of a man's being able to pay his way.

Lick honey through a cleft stick, To.
(H 559)

1670 RAY 184. **1732** FULLER no. 5197.

Lick honey with your little finger.
(H 555)

1581 GUAZZO i. 245 That olde saying, that wee must taste honie but with our fingers end. **1639** CLARKE 306.

Lick (a person or thing) into shape, To.
(S 284)

[= to give form and regularity to; to mould, make presentable. DONATUS *Life of Virgil* Carmen se more ursae parere dicens, et lambendo demum effingere.] **1413** *Pilgr. Sowle* (Caxton 1483) IV. xxiv. 70 Beres ben brought forthe al fowle and transformyd and after that by lyckynge of the fader and the moder they ben brought in to theyr kyndely shap. **1562** A. BROKE *Romeus and Juliet* 'To the Reader' The mountain bear Brings forth unformed . . . her young, . . . her often-licking tongue Giue them . . . shape. **1576** J. CAIUS *Of English Dogs* tr. A. Fleming (*Social England* ed. A. Lang 44) I hope, having, like the bear, licked over my young, I have waded in this work to your contentation. **1576** 1 June W. LAMBARDE to Sir Henry Sidney (MS., letter before Rawlinson copy of *Peramb. of Kent.* Bodl. Lib.). Alle this haue I recounted . . . to thend that yow may see, by what myshap and mydwife this Bearwhelp and vntymely byrthe of myne was brought into open lyghte, which otherwise I ment . . . to haue kept from straying farre, tille suche tyme as it had bene lycked to some better shape and seemlyness. **1591** SHAKES. *3 Hen. VI* III. ii. 161 Like to a chaos, or an unlick'd bearwhelp. [**1600**] **1657** *Lust's Dominion* Hazl.-Dods. xiv. 161 This chaos, This lump of projects, ere it be lick'd over, 'Tis like a bear's conception. **1621** BURTON *Anat. Mel.* Democr. to Rdr. (1676) 7b Enforced, as a Bear doth her Whelps, to bring forth this confused lump, I had not time to lick it into form. **1738** 23 Feb. GRAY *Corr.* ed. Toynbee and Whibley 80 One must be lick'd; . . . Bear I was born, and bear, . . . I'm like to remain. **1780** WESLEY *Wks.* (1872) IX. 509. **1862** MRS. CARLYLE *Lett.* III. 132.

Lick it up like Lim hay, To. (L 298)

1670 RAY 206 . . . *Lim* is a village on the river *Mersey*, that parts *Cheshire* and *Lancashire*, where the best hay is gotten.

Lick the fat from the (a person's) beard, To. (F 80)

[= to forestall the results of (a person's) enterprise or industry.] **1542** T. BECON *Invective agst.*

Swearing C5ᵛ He hath lycked the fatte from hys paryshners berdes, and hath taken his iourney. **1546** HEYWOOD I. iii. A4 And therby the fat cleane flyt fro my berde. **1548** HALL *Chron.* 169b Other . . . merchants . . . sore abhorryng the Italian nacion for lickyng the fat from their beards, and taking from them their accustomed livyng. **1579** SPENSER *Shep. Cal.* Sept. 123 But they that shooten neerest the pricke Sayne, other the fat from their beards doen lick. **1888** DOUGHTY *Arabia Deserta* (1923) i. 311 It irked the lean Beduin souls to see the parasite grow fat of that which he licked vilely from their beards.

Lick whole, To.   (L 227)

[= to heal of wounds or sores by licking.] *c.* **1550** *Disc. Common Weal Eng.* (1893) 32 If anie men haue licked theim selues whole youe be the same. **1596** BP. W. BARLOW *Three Serm.* i. 129 Who vnder a show of licking them whole, suck out euen their hart blood. **1670** RAY 184 To lick ones self whole again. **1712** ARBUTHNOT *John Bull* IV. vi He would quickly lick himself whole again, by his vails.

Lick with the rough side of one's tongue, To give a.

c. **1685** R. NORTH *Lives* Bohn i. 288 He [Judge Jeffries] called it 'giving a lick with the rough side of his tongue'. **1857** G. ELIOT *Scenes o, Clerical Life* 'Mr. Gilfil's Love-Story' ch. I.

Lick your dish.   (D 370)
1678 RAY 88.

Lick(s, ed), *see also* Cat knows whose beard she l.; Cook that cannot l. his fingers; Dog that l. ashes; Fox l. lamb, (Ill sign if); Give little to his servants that l. his knife (He can); Kiss (L.) the dust; Liar, l. dish; Lockerby l.; Loved mutton well that l.; Loves bacon well that l.; Loves roast meat well that l.; Ox, when loose, l. himself with pleasure.

Lickerish of tongue, light of tail.
                                          (T 395)
c. **1386** CHAUCER *W. of Bath's Prol.* l. 466 For al so siker as cold engendreth hayl, A likerous mouth moste han a likerous tayl. **1530** PALSGRAVE 535a If the comen people speake wysely, so sure as froste engendreth hayle, a lycorouse mouthe, a lycorouse tayle. **1545** TAVERNER E4ᵛ Our Englysh prouerbe . . . sayeth A lycourouse mouthe, a lycourouse tayle. **1553** T. WILSON *Arte of Rhet.* 66 Likeryshe of tongue, lighte of taile.

Lickerish (liquorish), *see also* Cat (The l.) gets many a rap.

Lickpenny, *see* Law is l.; London l.

Lide, *see* Leeks in L. (Eat).

Lidford[1] (Lydford) law. *Cf.* Halifax law.   (L 590)
1399 LANGLAND *Rich. Redeless* iii. 145 Be the lawe of Lydfford. **1565** JEWEL *Repl. Harding*

(1611) 356 But heere he thought . . . to call vs Theeues, and wicked Judges, and to charge vs with the Law of Lydford. **1629** T. ADAMS *Serm.* (1861–2) II. 120 As it is reported of a judge of the Stannery at Lydford, in Devonshire, who having hanged a felon among the tinners in the forenoon, sat in judgment on him in the afternoon. *c.* **1644** W. BROWNE *Lidford Journey* Wks. (Roxb.) II. 352 I ofte haue heard of Lidford Lawe, How in the Morne they hang & drawe, And sitt in iudgment after. **1710** *Brit. Apollo* II. No. 3, 5/2 First Hang and Draw, Then hear the cause by Lidford Law. [¹ A village between Tavistock and Okehampton.]

Lie abed, *see* Name is up (His), he may l. a.

Lie against (on) the devil, It is a sin to.
                                          (S 470)
c. **1513** SIR T. MORE *Richard III.* 1821 ed. 85 (belie the deuil). **1548** HALL *Chron.* 363 (1809) It wer synne to lye on the deuil. *a.* **1555** RIDLEY *Wks.* 10 It is also a true common proverb, that it is euen sin to lie upon the deuil. **1587** J. BRIDGES *Def. of Govt. of C. of E.* 71 Belye not (as they saye) the diuell. **1641** FERGUSSON no. 483. **1678** RAY 125 (belie).

Lie all alike in our graves, We shall.
                                          (G 428)
c. **1570** T. PRESTON *Cambyses* A3 Your grace therein may hap receiue with others for your part, The dent of death in those affaires, all persons are alike. **1591** H. SMITH *Magistr. Script.*: Wks. i. 367 This is some comfort to the poor, that once he shall be like the rich; one day he shall be as wealthy, as mighty, and as glorious as a king; One hour of death will make all alike. **1606** 2 *Ret. from Parn.* I. iv. B4 We all are equall in our latest graue. **1639** CLARKE 13. **1670** RAY 56. **1732** FULLER no. 5455.

Lie all manner of colours but blue, Thou'lt | and that is gone to the litting.
                                          (M 632)
1678 RAY 75 . . . *i.e.* dy[e]ing. (*Joculatory.*)

Lie at (the) catch (upon the catch), To.
                                          (C 188)
[= to set oneself to entrap a person, to be captious.] **1605** T. RYVES *Vicar's Plea* (1620) 141 That hee seeme not to lie at catch for an aduantage against his inferiour fellow minister. **1659** FULLER *Appeal Inj. Innoc.* in *Hist. Camb. Univ.* (1840) 405 I have to do with an adversary who lieth at catch for the least advantage. **1678** BUNYAN *Pilgr.* I. (1877) 88 You lie at the catch, I perceive.—No, not I; I am only for setting things right.

Lie be well drest, Though a | it is ever overcome.   (L 239)
1640 HERBERT no. 133.

Lie could have choked him, If a | that would have done it.   (L 233)
1678 RAY 89.

Lie down, and cry, *God help us*, We must not. *Cf.* **God helps them.** (D 388)

1594 *Knack to know Knave* sc. 8, l. 47 If you be downe, and bid God help you vp, and do not help yourself, you may fortune lie and perish. **1611** CHAPMAN *May-Day* I. i (1889) 278 Do not lie in a ditch, and say God help me; use the lawful tools he hath lent thee. **1706** STEVENS s.v. Ayudar and Cura. **1710** PALMER 95. **1732** FULLER no. 5449.

Lie down[1] for love, They that | should rise for hunger.

1721 KELLY 339 . . . Alledging if they had not been too well fed, they would not be troubled with that Disease. Lat. *Sine Cerere & Baccho, friget Venus.* [[1] fall sick.]

Lie had worried you, If a | you had been dead long since.

1721 KELLY 201.

Lie in bed and forecast, To. (B 193)

1678 RAY 75.

Lie in bed till meat falls in one's mouth, To. *Cf.* **Gapes until he be fed: Larks fall.**

c. **1549** HEYWOOD I. ix. C2 Tyl meate fall in your mouth, will ye ly in bed.

Lie in one's throat, To. (T 268)

1576 G. GASCOIGNE *Grief of Joy* ii. 528 Thow lyest in thy throte. **1589** *Hay any Work for Cooper* (Marprelate Tracts ed. Pierce 272). **1594–5** SHAKES. *L.L.L.* IV. iii. 12 Well, I do nothing in the world but lie, and lie in my throat. **1599** *Id. Hen. V* IV. viii. 15 That's a lie in thy throat. **1666** TORRIANO *Prov. Phr.* s.v. Gola 76 To lye in ones throat, to tell gross lyes.

Lie, One | makes (calls for) many. (L 236)

1533–4 UDALL *Flowers* 25ᵛ One falshode or subtiltie bringeth in an other. **1572** E. PASQUIER *Monophylo* tr. G. Fenton 11 The olde saying, that one fable drawes on another. **1642** FULLER *H. & P. State* v. xii (1841) 379 Having made one lie, he is fain to make more to maintain it. **1732** FULLER no: 3766 (calls for).

Lie or two may escape, In many words a.

1548 HALL *Chron. Ded. to Edw. VI* (1809) vi I might beleue all written in his greate volumes to bee as trewe as the Gospell. But I haue redde an olde Prouerbe, which saithe, that in many woordes, a lye or twayne sone maie scape.

Lie upon roses when young, If you | you'll lie upon thorns when old. (R 186)

1635 QUARLES *Emblems* I. vii And he repents in thorns, that sleeps in beds of roses. **1732** FULLER no. 2764.

Lie where he was slain, He will not. (L 243)

a. **1585** MONTGOMERIE *Cherrie & Slae* xxiv (1821) 20 He will not ly quhair he is slaine, That douttis befoir he dies. **1721** KELLY 135 . . . Spoken of timorous People, as if their Corpse would flee from the Place where they should be kill'd.

Lie will steal, He that will. *Cf.* **Show me a liar.**

1607 R. WEST *Court of Conscience* F1ᵛ (as the Prouerbe saith) He that will lie will steale. **1607** DEKKER & WILKINS *Jests to make you Merry* F1 Lyers, and such commonly are theeues. **1630** J. TAYLOR *Wks.* R1 He that will lie will steale. **1656** L. PRICE *Map of Merry Conceits* A4.

Lie with a latchet (witness), That is a. (L 238)

[= a great lie.] **1594–8** SHAKES. *T.S.* V. i. 105 Here's packing, with a witness, to deceive us all. **1610** A. COOKE *Pope Joane* 20 He writes, that, in as much as she was a Germaine, no Germaine could euer since be chosen Pope. Which is a lie with a latchet. **1678** RAY 89 *A great Lie.* That's a lie with a witness. *Ibid.* 257 That's a lie with a latchet, All the dogs i' th' town cannot match it. **1694** MOTTEUX *Rabelais* V. xxx. 152 That's a Lye with a Latchet.

Lief go to mill as to mass, Ye had as. (M 950)

1636 CAMDEN 310. **1732** FULLER no. 5909 You had rather go to Mill than to Mass.

Lies backward and lets out her fore-rooms, She. (F 594)

1611 TOURNEUR *Ath. Trag.* V. ii She's forc'd To let her fore-roomes out to others, and Her selfe contented to lie backwards. **1612** (1630) J. TAYLOR *The Sculler* 3C4ᵛ She brake the Lawes: In letting out her formost Roome for pelfe, And (for her pleasure) backward lay her selfe. **1639** *Con. Clinches, Flashes and Whimsies* in *Shakes. Jest-Bks.* iii. 72 She lay backwards, and did let out her fore-roomes. **1666** TORRIANO *Prov. Phr.* s.v. Valentino 224 in drollery spoken of such Women as love to be doing; which the English express by Lying Backwards, and Letting out their Fore-Rooms.

Lies down (Sleeps) with dogs, He that | must rise up with fleas. (D 537)

[SENECA *Qui cum canibus concumbunt cum pulicibus surgent.*] **1573** SANFORD 103ᵛ *Chi va dormir con i cani, si leva con i pulici.* He that goeth to bedde with Dogges, aryseth with fleas. **1612** WEBSTER *White Devil* V. i. 162 They have a certain spice of the disease; For they that sleep with dogs shall rise with fleas. **1640** HERBERT no. 343 He that lies with the dogs, riseth with fleas. **1670** RAY 82 . . . Chi con cane dorme con pulce se leva. *Ital.* Qui se couche avec les chiens se leve avec des puces. *Gall.* **1721** KELLY 129 . . . If you keep Company with base and unworthy Fellows, you will get some Ill by them. **1791** WOLCOT (P. Pindar) *Rights of Kings* viii

To this great truth, a universe agrees, '*He who lies down with dogs, will rise with fleas*'. **1842** LEVER *Jack Hinton* ch. 22 If you lie down with the dogs, you'll get up with fleas, and that's the fruits of travelling with a fool.

Lies have short (no) legs (wings).
(L 241)

1573 SANFORD (1576) 216 A lye hath one lame legge. *Ibid.* Lies haue short legs. **1578** FLORIO *First F.* 31ᵛ Lyes have short legges. **1611** DAVIES no. 73 Lyes haue short wings. **1666** TORRIANO 30, no. 33 A lye hath no feet. *Ibid.* 30, no. 35 Lyes haue short legs. **1732** FULLER no. 263 A lie hath no leg, but a scandal has wings. **1853** TRENCH vi. 128.

Lies like truth, He.

1841 CHAMIER *Tom Bowl.* ch. 5 He lied so much like truth that she was deceived.

Lies long abed, He that | his estate feels it.
(B 188)

1640 HERBERT no. 179. **1761** A. MURPHY *Citizen* I. ii He that lies in bed, his estate feels it.

Lies not in your gate, It that | breaks not your shins.
(G 44)

a. **1628** CARMICHAELL no. 1606 (your tais). **1641** FERGUSSON no. 505.

Lies upon the ground, He that | can fall no lower.
(G 464)

[ALAIN DE LILLE (1114–1203) *Doctrinale Altum* 8 *Qui jacet in terrâ, non habet unde cadat.*] *a.* **1523** BARCLAY *Mirr. of Good Manners* Spens. S. 46 A man on grounde resting can not much lower fall. [*c.* 1587] **1592** KYD *Span. Trag.* I. iii. 15 [Latin only]. **1608** SHAKES. *P.* I. iv. 78 Our ground's the lowest, and we are half-way there. **1614** RALEIGH *Hist. World* Pref., C4ᵛ I am on the Ground already; and therefore haue not far to fall. **1629** T. ADAMS *Serm.* (1861–2) II. 192 We say, *Qui jacet in terris, non habet unde cadat,*— He that lies on the ground hath no lower descant to fall to. **1663** BUTLER *Hudibras* I. iii. 877 I am not now in Fortune's power, He that is down can fall no lower. **1678** BUNYAN *Pilgr.* II (Shepherd's Boy's Song) He that is down needs fear no fall.

Lie(s) (*noun*), *see also* Almost and very nigh saves many a l.; Ask no questions told no l.; Blister . . . upon tongue that tells a l.; Dreams are l.; Give a l. start; Long ways long l.; Misunderstanding brings l.; Slander (It may be) but no l.; Tell a l. and find a truth; 'They say so' is half a l.; Trusts in a l. (He that) shall perish in truth.

Lie(s, d) (*verb*), *see also* All (Love) l. a-bleeding; Better speak truth rudely than l. covertly; Dummie cannot l.; Horse l. down (Where); Interest will not l.; Leal heart l. never; Let anybody l. by him (He will not); Old enough to l. without doors; Mire, (To leave (l.) in the); Old men and travellers l. by authority; Painters and poets have leave to l.; Pigs love that l. together;

Stye, (The worse their) the longer they l.; Swear (He that will) will l.; Tongue l. that speaks in haste; Traveller may l. with authority.

Life and a day longer, All one's.

1526 TYNDALE *Wicked Mammon* Pref. P.S. 38 I . . . bode him farewel for oure two liues and as men saye a daye longer.

Life and soul together, To keep.

1591 FLORIO *Second F.* 27. We haue as much as wil serue to keepe life and sowle together. **1642** TORRIANO 47. **1775** 3 July MRS. THRALE in Johnson *Lett.* (Chapman) ii. 55.

Life for a living man, There is aye.

1721 KELLY 323 . . . Spoken when we are disappointed of something that we expected; intimating that we can, and will, live without it. **1834** CARLYLE *Lett.* to John C. 22 July This being my task *till* the end of the year, why should I curiously inquire what is to become of me next? 'There is aye life for a living body.'

Life in it (the old horse) yet, There is.

1639 CLARKE 294 There's some life in't yet. **1948** *The Times* 13 Nov. 5 col. 4 (old horse still).

Life is a pilgrimage.
(L 249)

1539 VIVES *Introd. to Wisdom* B5ᵛ What other thynge is oure lyfe, but a certayne peregrination? **1557** EDGEWORTH 2V4 We . . . be come into this vale of misery and sorowe, . . . not to settle our selues on worldly Wealth and pleasures here, . . . we seke for another [city], the citie of heauen aboue. **1576** PETTIE i. 81 The pilgrimage of this my short life. **1579** LYLY *Euph.* i. 252, 308. **1595–6** SHAKES. *Rich. II* II. i. 155 His time is spent; our pilgrimage must be. **1599** *Id. A.Y.* III. ii. 119 How brief the life of man Runs his erring pilgrimage. **1604** *Id. M.M.* II. i. 36 See that Claudio Be executed by nine to-morrow morning: . . . For that's the utmost of his pilgrimage. *a.* **1626** SIR J. DAVIES version of *Ps.* xxxix. 12 On earth a pilgrim as my fathers were (*Vulg. peregrinus*). *a.* **1633** G. HERBERT *The Church* 113 The Pilgrimage (title).

Life is a shadow (smoke).

1549 J. CALVIN *Life and Conv. of a Christian Man* H1ᵛ Mans lyfe, to be lyke a smoke or shadowe, is not onely knowen to learned men, but also the common people vse no prouerbe more in their mouthes.

Life is a shuttle.
(L 250)

[JOB vii. 6: My days are swifter than a weaver's shuttle.] **1600–1** SHAKES. *M.W.W.* V. i. 25 I know also life is a shuttle.

Life is a span.
(L 251)

[PS. xxxix. 6 (Prayer-Book) Behold, thou hast made my days as it were a span long.] **8th** *c.* *Beowulf* 2727 ða wæs eall sceacen dogor-gerimes. [Now the span (*lit.* the number) of his days was all run out.] **1578** LYLY *Euph.* i. 252 Our lyfe is . . . of such shortnesse that Dauid sayth it is

but a spanne long. **1599** SHAKES. *A.Y.* III. ii. 119
How brief the life of man Runs his erring
pilgrimage, That the stretching of a span
Buckles in his sum of age. **1599** DAVIES *Immort.
Soul* Introd. xlv (1742) 12 I know my Life's a
Pain, and but a Span. **1604** SHAKES. *O.* II. iii. 67
Man's life's but a span. **1605-8** *Id. T.Ath.* V.
iii. 3 Timon is dead, who hath outstretch'd his
span. **1836** O. W. HOLMES *My Aunt* in *Poems*
(1846) 86 Her waist is ampler than her life, For
life is but a span.

Life is half spent before we know what it is. (L 252)

1600 W. CORNWALLIS *Essays* 2, B6 We begin not
to liue before we are ready to die. **1640** HERBERT
no. 917. **1732** FULLER no. 3208.

Life is not all beer and skittles.

1836-7 DICKENS *Pickwick* ch. 41 It's a regular
holiday to them—all porter and skittles. **1857**
T. HUGHES *Tom Brown* I. ii. Life isn't all beer and
skittles. **1888** R. KIPLING *Drums Fore & Aft*
The men . . . fell in for their first march, when
they began to realize that a soldier's life was not
all beer and skittles.

Life is sweet. (L 254)

c. **1350** *Patience* l. 156 in *Allit. Poems* E.E.T.S. 96
For be monnes lode neuer so luther, the lyf is ay
swete. *c.* **1390** GOWER *Conf. Amantis* V. 239
Crist diede him self for the feith; But now our
ferful prelate saith; 'The life is swete'. *c.* **1450**?
York plays *Abraham's Sac.* l. 279 Isaac. A! dere
fadir, lyff is full swete. **1574** J. HIGGINS *Mirror
for Mag.* ed. Campbell 201. [*c.* **1589**] **1601** LYLY
Love's Metam. III. ii. 6 Life is sweete, hunger
sharpe; betweene them the contention must bee
short. **1659** HOWELL *Eng. Prov.* 4a Life is
sweet though it alway sweat. **1668** J. WILSON tr.
Moriae Encomium 49 Old women . . . ever
mumbling in their mouths (φῶς ἀγαθòν) *Life is
sweet.* **1863** C. READE *Hard Cash* ch. 31 He
came up gurgling . . . and swimming for his life
. . . Life is sweet.

Life lies not in living, but in liking. (L 255)

1589 GREENE *Menaphon* Gros. vi. 55 Hee that
liues without loue, liues without life. **1639**
CLARKE 322. **1670** RAY 113 . . . Martial saith,
Non est vivere, sed valere vita.

Life of man is a winter's day and a winter's way, The. (L 256)

1640 HERBERT no. 914 (a winter way). **1664**
CODRINGTON 222 (a winters way, and a winters
day). **1670** RAY 16.

Life of the wolf is the death of the lamb, The. (L 258)

1616 DRAXE no. 1102. **1639** CLARKE 325.

Life, Such a | such a death. (L 263)

1573 SANFORD 109 Such as the life is, such is the
end. **1576** LAMBARDE *Kent* 2H2 I report me to
all indifferent and Godly leaders, whether suche
a lyfe deserued not suche a death. **1585** T.

SPARKE *Sermon at Cheanies* 30 *Qualis vita, finis
ita,* such life such death. **1592** DELAMOTHE 53
(an end). **1639** CLARKE 322.

Life, While there is | there is hope. (L 269)

[CICERO *Ad Atticum* 9. 10. 3 *Aegroto, dum
anima est spes esse dicitur.* As the saying is,
while there is life there is hope. ERASM *Ad.
Aegroto, dum anima est spes est.*] **1539** TAV-
ERNER 37ᵛ The sycke person whyle he hath lyfe,
hath hope. **1670** RAY 113. **1727** GAY *Fables* I.
xxvii. 49 'While there is life, there's hope', he
cried; 'Then why such haste?' so groaned and
died. **1841** CARLYLE *Heroes* V (1896) 248 One
should have tolerance for a man, hope of him.
. . . While life lasts, hope lasts for every man.
1869 C. READE *Foul Play* ch. 11 They lost, for a
few moments, all idea of escaping. But, . . .
while there's life there's hope: and . . . their
elastic minds recoiled against despair.

Life without a friend, is death without a witness. (L 259)

1640 HERBERT no. 385. **1706** STEVENS s.v. Vida.
1732 FULLER no. 3211 (. . . death with a vengeance).

Life you loved me not, In | in death you bewail me. (L 248)

1640 HERBERT no. 218.

Life, lives, *see also* Art is long, l. short; Business
of l. and day of death (Between); Cat has nine l.;
Despises his own l. master of another's; Dog's
l.; Enter this l. (But one way to); Golden l. in
iron age; Good l. better than learning; Good l.
makes good death; Hope of long l. beguileth;
Ill l. ill end; Large as l.; Long be thy legs,
short thy l.; Long l. has long misery; Lose a leg
rather than l.; Lucky in l., unlucky in love;
Money or your l.; New lease of l.; No man has
lease of his l.; Prolong your l. (Two things), quiet
heart loving wife; Short l. and merry; Speaks ill
(Of him that) consider the l.; Spies (The l. of);
Time (He that has) has l.; Unworthy of l. that
causes not l.

Lifeguard, *see* Subject's love is king's l.

Lifeless that is faultless, He is. (L 270)

1546 HEYWOOD I. xi. D3ᵛ He is liueles, that is
fautles, olde folkes thought. **1639** CLARKE 80.
c. **1641** FERGUSSON MS. no. 416 Faultles lifles.
1649 TORRIANO 89.

Lift, *see* Help at a dead l., (To); Lout so low and
l. so little; Woman's advice best at dead l.

Light a torch gives, The more | the shorter it lasts.

1732 FULLER no. 4664 (the less while).

Light as a feather. (F 150)

c. **1535** SIR D. LYNDSAY *Three Estates* l. 3527
Lichter nor ane fidder. **1548** HALL *Chron.* (1809

ed., 474). **1629** SHIRLEY *Wedding* II. iii. Light as a feather, hanging will never kill you. **1841** MARRYAT *Mast. Ready* ch. 32.

Light as a fly.   (F 392)

1509 BARCLAY *Ship of Fools* ii. 290 Light as fle. *c.* **1560** *Tom Tyler* l. 112. **1616** WITHALS 580. **1670** RAY 206.

Light as the Queen's groat.   (Q 6)

1621 ROBINSON 35. **1639** CLARKE 159.

Light burdens far heavy. *Cf.* Burden, Too long.   (B 727)

1546 HEYWOOD II. ix. L2ᵛ A syr lyght burdeyn far heuy (quoth she) This lyght burdeyn in longe walke welny tierth me. **1611** DAVIES *Prov.* no. 40 A Light Lode is heauy to carry farre. **1640** HERBERT no. 15 Light burthens, long borne, growe heavie. **1670** RAY 114 . . . Petit fardeau poise à la longue, or, Petite chose de loing poise, *Gall.* **1682** BUNYAN *Greatness of the Soul* Wks. (1855) I. 124 We use to say, light burdens far carried are heavy.

Light cheap, lither¹ yield.   (C 258)

[i.e. That which is cheaply bought brings a poor return.] *c.* **1300** *Provs. of Hending* 30 Lyht chep, luthere yeldes. *c.* **1400** *MS. Latin no. 394 John Rylands Libr.* (ed. Pantin) in *Bull. J. R. Libr.* XIV. 103 Ly3t chepe, lyther for3eldes. *c.* **1460** *Towneley Myst., 2nd Shep. Play* 170 And men say 'Lyght chepe Letherly foryeldys'. **1670** RAY 114 . . . That that costs little, will do little service; for commonly the best is best cheap. [¹ bad.]

Light gains (winnings) make heavy purses.   (G 7)

1546 HEYWOOD I. xi. D4ᵛ Euer more light gaynes make heuy purses. **1594** BACON *Promus* f. 89a. **1614** CAMDEN 309. **1641** FERGUSSON no. 767 Small winning makes a heavie purse.

Light is naught for sore eyes, The.   (L 274)

c. **1548** J. BALE *Image of Both Churches* pt. 2 P.S. 391 The light is hateful unto sore eyes. **1579** GOSSON *Ephemerides* 19 Sore eyes maye not view the light, without a scarfe. **1580** LYLY *Euph. & his Eng.* ii. 157 He that hath sore eyes must not behold the candle. **1639** CLARKE 161. **1670** RAY 114 . . . A l'œil malade la lumière nuit, *Gall.* He that doth evil hateth the light, &c.

Light, In your own | like the Mayor of Market-Jew.

1864 *N. & Q.* 3rd Ser. v. 275 . . . The pew of the Mayor of Marazion¹ (or Market-Jew) was so placed, that he was in his own light. [¹ Cornwall.]

Light (heavy) purse makes a heavy (light) heart, A.   (P 659)

c. **1514** BARCLAY *Eclog.* iv. 20 When purse is heauy oftetime the heart is light. **1555** HEYWOOD *Epig. on Proverbs* no. CL Lyght purses Make

heuy hartes. **1584** R. WILSON *Three Ladies of London* Hazl.-Dods. vi. 282 I had many clients, and many matters that made my purse light, and my heart heavy. **1595** H. CHETTLE *Piers Plainnes* E1ᵛ They made manie light purses and heavye hearts. **1609** T. RAVENSCROFT *Deuteromelia* F3 It is a light heart and a heauie purse which makes a man so merry. **1732** FULLER no. 241.

Light (*adj. adv.*), see also Bird on briar (bough), (As merry (l.) as); Leave is l.

Light (*noun*), see also Does ill (He that) hates l.; Dry l.; Every l. has its shadow; Every l. is not the sun; Hide one's l. under a bushel; Lips hang in your l.; Little is the l. seen far in the night; Lucy l.; Maidenhead hangs in your l.; Nothing comes sooner to l. than long hid; Stand in one's own l.; Summer can be seen by own l.; Truth will come to l.

Light(s), (*verb*), see Candle l. others and consumes itself; Glow-worm l. lamp.

Lighted upon a lime¹ twig, He.

1732 FULLER no. 1964. [¹ bird-lime.]

Lightening before death, A.   (L 277)

1584 COGAN *Haven of Health* (1612) 135 A Lating prouerbe, *Cygnea cantio*, which among the common people is termed, a lightning before death. **1594-5** SHAKES. *R.J.* V. iii. 90 How oft when men are at the point of death Have they been merry! which their keepers call A lightning before death. **1615** CHAPMAN *Od.* xviii. 230 Th'utmost lightning that still ushers death. **1641** BROME *Jov. Crew* v. Wks. (1873) III. 441 If it be a lightning before death, the best is, I am his heir. **1678** RAY 76 . . . A little before they dye . . . their understanding and memory return to them; as a candle just before it goes out gives a great blaze. **1712** ADDISON *Spect.* No. 517, par. 2 We were once in great Hopes of his Recovery . . . but this only proved a light'ning before Death. **1785** WALPOLE *Lett.* (Toynbee) 13. 322 I hope this revival of wit is not lightning before death. **1840** HOOD *Up Rhine* 7 The old saying about a lightening before death. **1876** TENNYSON *Harold* 3. 1 This lightning before death plays on the word.

Light-heeled mother makes a heavy-heeled daughter, A.   (M 1198)

a. **1628** CARMICHAELL no. 154 Ane olied¹ mother makes a sueir² daughter. **1670** RAY 53 . . . Because she doth all her work herself, and her daughter the mean time sitting idle, contracts a habit of sloth. **1721** KELLY 22 An olight¹ Mother makes a sweir² Daughter. [¹ nimble. ² lazy.]

Lightly come, lightly go. *Cf.* Easy come; Quickly come.   (C 533)

c. **1374** CHAUCER *Troilus* Bk. 2, l. 1238 For-why men seith, 'Impressiounes light Ful lightly ben ay redy to the flighte'. *c.* **1386** *Id. Pard. T.* l. 781 And lightly as it comth so wol we spende. *c.* **1518** *Virgilius* in *Ancient English Fictions* 36 He wolde haue made the peny to be

as lyghtely gat as spente. **1546** HEYWOOD II.
ix. L1 Lyght come lyght go. **1576** U. FULWELL
Ars Adulandi E4ᵛ Experience taught me that
easely woone was lightly loste. **1616** R. C.
Times' Whistle vi. 2828 E.E.T.S. 89 'But
lightly come', we say, 'doth lightly goe'. **1712**
ARBUTHNOT *John Bull* II. iv A thriftless wretch,
spending the goods and gear that his forefathers
won with the sweat of their brows: light come,
light go. **1861** READE *Cloist. & Hearth* ch. 37
Our honestest customers are the thieves ... with
them and with their purses 'tis lightly come, and
lightly go.

Lightning lightly¹ before thunder, There is. (L 281)

1545 *Precepts of Cato* [Publius] K2 As the
lyghtnynge goeth before thunder So. . . .
1581 MERBURY *Brief Discourse* 45 The Lightening goeth before the thunder. **1611** SHAKES.
Temp. I. ii. 201 Jove's lightnings, the precursors
O' the dreadful thunder-claps. **1616** DRAXE
no. 2351 Lightly before thunder, lightening.
1639 CLARKE 209. c. **1660-8** ANNE BRADSTREET
(Wks. 1867) Meditations no. 29 Lightening doth
usually preceed thunder and stormes, raine; and
stroaks do not often fall till after threat'ning.
[¹ commonly].

Like a duke? like a duck. (D 636)

[1523] **1568** SKELTON *How Doughty Duke
Albany* l. 222: Wks. ii. 74 Syr duke, nay, syr
ducke ... for small lucke Ye haue in feates of
warre. **1546** HEYWOOD II. vii. K1ᵛ Then euery
daie to fare lyke a duke with thee. Lyke a duke,
lyke a duck (quoth she) thou shalt fare, except
thou wilt spare.

Like blood, like good, and like age, make the happiest marriage. (B 465)

1579 *The Proverbs of Sir James Lopez de Mendoza*
tr. B. Googe 65 Accordinge to tholde Prouerbe,
Like good, like blood, like age, maketh a good
mariage. **1579** LYLY *Euph.* i 283 Yet let his
wife be such a one as is neither much more noble
in birth, or farre more richer in goodes, but
according to the wyse saying: choose one euery
way, as neere as may bee equall in both. **1601**
SHAKES. *T.N.* I. iii. 101 She'll none o' th' Count.
She'll not match above her degree, neither in
estate, years, nor wit. **1639** CLARKE 28. **1710**
PALMER 269.

Like breeds like. (L 282)

1557 EDGEWORTH *Sermons* 2Y2ᵛ With the holy a
man shalbe holy, and wyth a frowarde synner, a
man shall be naughtye and synnefull, for lyke
maketh lyke. **1577** *Misogonus* Ii 79 The like
bredes the like (eche man sayd). **1583** J. PRINCE
Fruitful and Brief Disc. 2 In all things naturally
like cometh of like.

Like cures like.

[L. *Similia similibus curantur.* KING quotes
SAMUEL HAHNEMANN, *Organon der Heilkunst*,
1810.] **1850** MELVILLE *White Jacket* (1922 ed.)
284 The grand maxim Mr Similia Similibus
Curantur Hahneman does not hold true, since,
with them, *like cures* not *like*. **1853** 'C. BEDE'
Verdant Green ch. 8 On the homœopathic
principle of 'like cures like', a cigar was the best
preventative against ... smoke.

Like is the same, No. (A 167, L 288)

[L. *Nullum simile est idem.*] **1587** BRIDGES
Defence 1387 It is an old and a true prouerbe,
Nullum simile est idem, Nothing that is the like
is the same. **1591** I *Troublesome Reign of K.
John* B1ᵛ Know you not, Omne simile non est
idem. **1599** SHAKES. *J.C.* II. ii. 128 Every like
is not the same, O Caesar. **1600** THYNNE *Embl.
and Epig.* 94 But what is like is not the same, as
all menn well doe finde. **1621** ROBINSON 12
They are very like, but not the same. **1638**
ROWLEY *Shoemaker a Gent.* II Why wouldst not
have her like me?—Because no like's the same.
1706 STEVENS s.v. Pedro Every like is not the
same.

Like it or leave it.

1602 N. BRETON *Olde Mad-cappes new Gallymawfrey* To the Reader I ... referre it to the
Worlde, to like it, or leaue it. **1631** W. SALTON-
STALL *Picturae Loquentes* A6 Like it or leave it.
1738 SWIFT *Dial.* I. E.L. 267 I don't much like
the colour of that ribbon. — ... If you don't
much like it, you may look off it.

Like it, or lump¹ it.

1828 NEAL *Rachel* 70 If you don't like it, you
may lump it. **1833** *Id. Down Easters* I. vii. 104
Let 'em lump it if they don't like it. **1864-5**
DICKENS *Our Mut. Fr.* Bk. IV. ch. 3 'I'm a-going
to call you Boffin, for short, . . . If you don't
like it, it's open to you to lump it.' [¹ put up with.]

Like me, God bless the example. (G 240)

1670 RAY 184.

Like one as if he had been spit out of his mouth, As. (M 1246)

c. **1400** *Beryn* E.E.T.S. 97 l. 3232 Be-hold thy
sone! it semeth crope out of þy mowith. **1602**
BRETON *Wonders worth Hear.* (1879) 8/1 Twoo
girles, ... the one as like an Owle, the other as
like an Urchin, as if they had been spitte out of
the mouthes of them. [1625] **1647** FLETCHER
Chances I. ix. 62 Your own eyes, signior, and
the nether lip As like ye as ye had spit it. **1738**
SWIFT *Dial.* III. E.L. 318 She's as like her
husband as if she were spit out of his mouth.
1837 J. B. KER 64.

Like punishment and equal pain, both key and keyhole do sustain. (P 637)

1584 WITHALS G1ᵛ. **1639** CLARKE 239.

Like than Jack Fletcher¹ and his bolt,² No more. (J 14)

a. **1522** DOUGLAS *Aeneid* I Prol. 143 Na mair
like than the devill and Sanct Austyne. [a. 1567]
1571 R. EDWARDS *Damon and Pythias* B2 We are
as like in condicions, as Iacke Fletcher and his
Bowlt. **1576** L. TWYNE *Pat. of Painefull Adv.*
(1903) 75 There is no more likenesse betweene
them sauing that the childe hath the generall
shape and proportion of a man, than is betweene
Jack fletcher and his bolt. [¹ arrow-maker.
² arrow.]

Like that they are the worse for it, They are so. (L 290)

1611 SHAKES. *W.T.* II. iii. 95 Might we lay th' old proverb to your charge, So like you 'tis the worse. **1616** OVERBURY *Sergeant Char.*, ed. Paylor 163 He is so like him, that hee is the worse for it, and hee takes after his father. **1678** RAY 354.

Like to die mends (fills) not the kirkyard. (L 295)

1641 FERGUSSON no. 594. **1721** KELLY 233. Long e'er like to die fill the Kirkyerd. **1906** W. DE MORGAN *Joseph Vance* 457 Half-dead never filled the churchyard.

Like to like, a scabbed horse to an old dike. (L 284)

1621 ROBINSON 12. **1639** CLARKE 287. **1721** KELLY 231.

Like to like, and Nan for Nicholas. (L 285)

1611 COTGRAVE s.v. Demander Like will to like; a Iacke lookes for a Gill. **1659** HOWELL *Span. Prov.* 9. **1670** RAY 15.

Like will to like. (L 286)

[HOM. *Od.* 17. 218 ὡς αἰεὶ τὸν ὁμοῖον ἄγει θεὸς ὡς τὸν ὁμοῖον. CICERO *De Senect.* 3. 7 Pares autem vetere proverbio cum paribus facillime congregantur.] *c.* **1375** *Scottish Legendary* (Horstmann) *Matthias* xii. 134 Lyke to lyk draw ay. *c.* **1386** CHAUCER *Squire's T.* l. 608 I trowe he hadde thilke text in mynde, That 'alle thyng, repeirynge to his kynde, Gladeth hymself'. *c.* **1430** LYDGATE *Minor Poems* (Percy Soc.) 55 Alle thynge in kynde desirith thynge i-like. *c.* **1460** *Provs. of Good Counsel* (Furnivall) 70 This proverbe dothe specify: Lyke wyll to lyke in eche company. **1509** BARCLAY *Ship of Fools* ii. 35 For it is a prouerbe and an olde sayd sawe that in euery place lyke to lyke wyll drawe. **1539** TAVERNER 8ᵛ Simile gaudet simili. The lyke delyteth in the lyke. Similitude (as Aristotle sayth) is mother of loue. **1579** LYLY *Euph.* i. 197 Doth not the simpathy of manners make the coniunction of mindes? Is it not a by woord like will to like? **1648** HERRICK *Hesper.* No. 1044 Wks. (1893) II. 138 Like will to like, each Creature loves his kinde. **1823** SCOTT *Peveril* ch. 14 How could I help it? like will to like—the boy would come—the girl would see him.

Like will to like, quoth the devil to the collier. (L 287)

1559? T. BECON *Lord's Supper and Pope's Mass* P.S. 383 Like will to like quod the Deuil when he danced with the collier. **1568** FULWELL *Like Will to L.* (1906) 24 Like will to like, quoth the Devil to the Collier. **1591** ARIOSTO *Orl. Fur.* Harington xvi. 6 margin (Dignum patella operculum Or as the English Prouerbe saith). **1680** BUNYAN *Mr. Badman* xii. Wks. (1855) III. 647 Hang them rogues . . . Like to like, quoth the Devil to the collier, this is your precise crew.

Like (a, the), Like as, *see also under significant words following.*

Like(s) (*verb*), *see* Do what he l. with his own; Every man l. his own thing best.

Like (likeliest, liking), *see* Do the l., and hope the best (*or* God will do best); Life lies not in living but in l.; Likeness causes l.; Marry your l.; Somewhat l., (That is).

Likely lies in the mire, and unlikely goes by it (gets over). (L 292)

a. **1628** CARMICHAELL no. 1213 Oftymes liklie lyis in the myre. **1641** FERGUSSON no. 592 (and unliklie goes by it). **1721** KELLY 238 (gets over). Good Likelihood is not always an infallible token of great Strength, Skill, or Fortune. **1732** FULLER no. 3242 (gets over).

Likeness causes liking. (L 294)

1539 TAVERNER A8 *Æqualis æqualem delectat* Lyke delyteth the lyke. *Ibid.* A8ᵛ Simile gaudet simili. The lyke delyteth in the lyke. Similitude (as Aristotle sayth) is mother of love. [Margin: Similitudo mater amoris.] **1586** J. CASE *Praise of Music* 34 Similitudo parit amicitiam saith Boetius. **1593** SIDNEY *Arcadia* To the Reader (Feuillerat) i. 524 Likeness is a great cause of liking. **1605** *The Countess of Lincoln's Nursery* A4ᵛ Likenesse is Mother & Nurse of liking. **1639** CLARKE 27. **1732** FULLER no. 3243. Likeness begets Love, yet proud Men hate one another.

Likes not his business, Who | his business likes not him.

1846 T. WRIGHT *Essays on Middle Ages* i. 140 We have the saying 'Who likes not . . .', &c. **1869** HAZLITT 471.

Likes not the drink, Who | God deprives him of bread. (D 605)

1640 HERBERT no. 394. **1664** CODRINGTON 228. **1670** RAY 11.

Likes, *see also* Like(s).

Lim hay, *see* Lick it up like L. h.

Lime makes a rich father and a poor son.

1846 DENHAM 6. **1917** BRIDGE 92 Lime enriches the father and beggars the son. Lime is not . . . a manure, but it renders available the inert matter in the soil, and it is therefore necessary to follow it up with manure.

Lime, *see also* Bird caught in l. strives, (The more the) faster he sticks; Fingers are l. twigs; Lighted upon l. twigs.

Limed, *see* Birds once snared (l.) fear all bushes.

Limerick was, Dublin is, and Cork shall be, the finest city of the three.

1859 DEAN HOLE *Lit. Tour in Ireld.* xviii To my fancy the old prophecy is fulfilled—'Limerick

was, Dublin is, and Cork shall be The finest city
of the three.'

Lincoln green.   (L 301)

[= a bright green stuff made at Lincoln.]
c. **1510** *Gest R. Hode* ccccxxii in CHILD *Ballads* III.
77 Whan they were clothed in Lyncolne grene,
They kest away theyr graye. **1613–22** DRAYTON
Polyolb. XXV. 262 (1876) III. 150 Whose swains in
shepherds' gray, and girls in *Lincolne* green.
a. **1845** HOOD *Forge* I. xiii With little jackets . . .
Of Lincoln green.

Lincoln shall be hanged for London's
sake.   (L 299)

c. **1590** *Sir Thomas More* III. i. *Shakes. Apocr.* 397
This the olde prouerbe now compleate dooth
make, That Lincolne should be hangd for
London's sake.

Lincoln was, London is, and York
shall be.   (L 300)

1588 J. HARVEY *Discursive Prophecies* 56. **1607**
DEKKER & WEBSTER *Northward Ho* A2. **1623**
J. TAYLOR (Water-P.) *Mer. Wher. Fer. Voy.*
Wks. (1630) 11 There is a Prouerbe, part of
which is this, They say that *Lincolne was, and
London is.* **1662** FULLER York 226 . . . That
Lincoln was, namely a far Fairer, Greater,
Richer City . . . doth plainly appear by the ruins
thereof . . . That *London is,* we know; that
York shall be, God knows.

Lincoln's Inn, *see* Gray's Inn; Inner Temple.

Lincoln, *see also* Devil over L. (He looks as);
Tom of L.

Lincolnshire bagpipes. *Cf.* Bagpipe, He
is like a.   (B 35)

c. **1545** J. BALE *Examⁿ of Cobham and Thorpe*
P.S. 102 Well spoken, mylord, for Lincolnshire
bag-pipes. **1577** *Art of Angling* C5ᵛ. **1584**
Three Ladies of London Hazl.-Dods. vi. 393 The
sweet ballad of the Lincolnshire bagpipes. **1597**
SHAKES. *1 Hen. IV.* I. ii. 72 I am as melancholy as
a gib cat, . . . or the drone of a Lincolnshire
bagpipe. **1617** MORYSON *Itin.* III. i. 54 (1907–8)
III. 463 Lincolnshire bells and bag-pipes . . . are
proverbially spoken of.

Lincolnshire, where hogs shit soap, and
cows shit fire.   (L 302)

1659 HOWELL *Eng. Prov.* 21a. **1670** RAY 236
Lincolnshire . . . The inhabitants of the poorer
sort washing their clothes with hogs dung, and
burning dried cow-dung for want of better fuel.

Line and level, By.   (L 305)

c. **1420** LYDGATE *Troy-Bk.* Now they put instede
of mortar In the joyntures coper gilt ful dere;
To make them joyne by levell and by line. **1530**
PALSGRAVE 833 By lyne and by square. **1552**
HULOET R6ᵛ Lay by line, or rule, or to direct.
1556 W. BALDWIN to Sir T. Cawarden (Revels
Docs. Ed. VI and Mary ed. Feuillerat 26) Line
and levell Iustice. **1573** GASCOIGNE *Flowers*
i. 68 By line and Leysure. **1573** TUSSER (1580)

42 Through cunning with dible, rake, mattock,
and spade, by line and by leauell, trim garden is
made. **1583** MELBANCKE E1ᵛ We must worke
by lyne and leisure, and not leape ouer the stile.
1611 COTGRAVE s.v. A Pied By line and leuell, by
compasse and measure, proportionably. **1611**
SHAKES. *Temp.* IV. i. 238 We steal by line and
level, an't like your grace. **1639** CLARKE 92.
1892 *see quot. under* Silk and scarlet.

Line one's pockets, To.   (P 664)

[= to amass a comfortable fortune.] *c.* **1514**
A. BARCLAY *Cyt. & Uplondyshm.* Percy Soc. lxi
He had a pautner with purses manyfold And
surely lined with silver and with golde. **1604**
SHAKES. *O.* I. i. 53 Others there are Who, . . .
throwing but shows of service on their lords, Do
well thrive by them, and when they have lin'd
their coats Do themselves homage. **1731**
W. BOWMAN *Serm.* xxix Tho' such change
would line our breeches.

Line to the wall, Bring your | not the
wall to the line.   (L 304)

[ERASM. *Ad.* II. v. 36 *Ad amussim applica
lapidem, non ad lapidem amussim*]. **1604**
CHAPMAN *Bussy* III. i. 70 To the line the stone,
Not to the stone, the line should be oppos'd.
1732 FULLER no. 1021.

Line, *see also* Day without a l. (No); Draw the l.
somewhere; Hold hook and l.; Peace beyond
the l. (No); Straight as a l.; Stricken the ball
under the l.

Linen often to water, soon to tatter.

(W 101)

1678 RAY 347 Often to the water often to the
tatter (*of linnen*). **1732** FULLER no. 6378.

Linen, *see also* Choose neither a woman nor l. by
candle-light; Wash dirty l. in public.

Lining, *see* Cloud has silver l.

Link, *see* Chain no stronger than weakest l.;
Know him as if through him with lighted l.

Linstock, *see* Gunner to l.

Lion among sheep and a sheep among
lions, A.   (L 309)

a. **1576** WHYTHORNE 64 Thei bee az lyons wher
thei fynd hiumilite, and wher thei fynd lyons,
thei do bekum in koraӡ az sheep. **1589**
PUTTENHAM *Art Eng. Poesy* III. xxiv, ed. Willcock
and Walker, 293 (As the prouerbe goeth . . . a
Lyon).

Lion in the way (path), A.   (L 312)

[PROV. xxvi. 13 The slothful man saith, There is
a lion in the way.] **1543** G. COUSIN *Office of
Servants* B6 The slothful servant beinge sente
on an errante fyndeth many barres in the same
with colprophesing, as, a lion is in the way.
1560 J. PILKINGTON P.S. 43. **1641** MILTON
Reform. II. Wks. (1847) 18/1 They fear'd not

the bug-bear danger nor the lion in the way that the sluggish and timorous politician thinks he sees. **1868** BRIGHT *Sp. Ireland* I Apr. You have always . . . lions in the path. ?**1913** 14 July D. H. LAWRENCE *Lett.* i. 213 (path).

Lion is known by his claws (paw), The.
(L 313)

[Gk. Ἐκ τῶν ὀνύχων τὸν λέοντα γιγνώσκειν. To judge of the lion from his claws. ERASM. *Ad.* I. ix. 34 *Leonem ex unguibus aestimare.*] **1548** W. PATTEN *Exped*[n] *into Scotland* (Tudor Tracts 71) Their acts . . . are not less certainly known . . . than is the lion, as they say, by the paw. **1574** J. BALE *Pageant of Popes* tr. J. Studley 84[v] Shall we not knowe the father by the childe, or the Lion by his talentes? **1579–80** LODGE *Def. Poetry* Shakes. Soc. 3 The Rubie is discerned by his pale rednes; and who hath not hard that the Lyon is known by hys clawes? **1639** CLARKE 131 (pawe). **1642** D. ROGERS *Naaman* 158 By the paw we may judge of the lion, and perceive how far sanctification lies above self. **1861** DEAN STANLEY *Eastern Ch.* ch. 3. Many more stories might be told of him [Spyridion], but (to use the words of an ancient writer who has related some of them) 'from the claws you can make out the lion'.

Lion is not so fierce as he is painted (as they paint him), The.
(L 314)

1599 MINSHEU *Span. Gram.* 83 (as they paint him). **1639** FULLER *Holy War* V. xxx (1840) 300 But the lion is not so fierce as he is painted, nor this empire so formidable as fame giveth it out. **1640** HERBERT no. 289 (as 1599). **1670** RAY 114 The lion's not half so fierce as he is painted. . . . Things are represented at a distance . . . beyond their just proportion and merit. Fame is a magnifying glass.

Lion may come to be beholden to a mouse, A.
(L 315)

1484 CAXTON *Fab. Aesop* ed. Jacobs I. 13. 26. **1563** *Mirr. for Mag.* 'Lord Hastings' (Campbell) 274 The mouse may somtyme help the Lyon in nede. **1613** BEAUM. & FL. *Honest Man's Fort.* III. i. Pray you accept My will to do you service: I have heard The mouse once saved the lion in his need. **1732** FULLER no. 264. **1842** MARRYAT *Perc. Keene* ch. 17. A mouse may help a lion, as the fable says.

Lion spares the suppliant, The. (L 316)

1554–7 G. CAVENDISH *Wolsey* ed. Morley 140 The noble and gentle lion . . . when he hath vanquished any beast, and seeth him yielded, . . . then will he show most clemency. **1580** LYLY *Euph. & his Eng.* ii. 142 Lions spare those that couch to them, the Tygresse biteth not when shee is clawed. [**1592**] **1596** *Edw. III* IV. ii. 33 The Lion scornes to touch the yeelding pray. **1594–5** SHAKES. *L.L.L.* IV. i. 81 Thus dost thou hear the Nemean lion roar 'Gainst thee, thou lamb, that standest as his prey. Submissive fall his princely feet before, And he from forage will incline to play. **1595** SPENSER *Amoretti* 20 And yet the lyon, that is lord of power . . . In his most pride disdeigneth to devoure The silly lambe that to his might doth yield.

Lion when he is absent, Who takes a | fears a mouse present. (L 318)

1642 TORRIANO 22 (mole). **1659** HOWELL *It. Prov.* 11 (mouse).

Lion's mouth, The. *Cf.* Hand in lion's mouth.

[**1560** GENEVA BIBLE *Ps.* xxii. 21 Saue me from the lyons mouth. *2 Tim.* iv. 17 I was deliuered out of the mouth of the Lion.] **1601** DENT *Pathw. Heaven* 62 What doth hee else, but (as it were) put his finger into the Lion's mouth. **1720** DEFOE *Mem. of a Cavalier* iv. 289 He wou'd not lay down his Arms, saying it was better to die, than to run into the Lion's mouth. **1906** W. DE MORGAN *Jos. Vance* ch. 42 If I had to live my life over again, . . . should I dare to put my head into the lion's mouth, as I did?

Lion's provider, The.

[= jackal, *lit. & fig.*] [The jackal was formerly supposed to go before the lion and hunt up his prey for him.] **1667** DRYDEN *Ann. Mir.* st. 82 Their fireships like jackals appear, Who on their lions for the prey attend. **1672** W. DE BRITAINE *Dutch Usurp.* 33 They must not be like the Joecaul, which provides food for the Lyon. **1808** SCOTT *Let. to W. Gifford* 25 Oct. in LOCKHART *Life* If you will accept of my services as a sort of jackal or lion's provider. *a.* **1822** SHELLEY *Daemon of World* 426 There man was long the train-bearer of slaves . . . The jackal of ambition's lion-rage.

Lion's share, The.

[Fable of Aesop, PHAEDR. l. 5.] **1790** BURKE *Fr. Rev. Wks.* V. 252 Nor when they were in partnership with the farmer . . . have I heard that they had taken the lion's share. **1823** SCOTT *Peveril* ch. 21 'The goodman has . . . come to wait on you himself. He always does so when company drink wine.' 'That he may come in for the host's, that is, the lion's share.' **1897** M. A. S. HUME *Ralegh* 42 The confiscated lands of the departed Desmonds in Munster were to be scrambled for, and Ralegh naturally came in for the lion's share.

Lion's skin cannot, If the | the fox's shall. (L 319)

[ERASM. *Ad. Si leonina pellis non satis est, vulpina addenda.*] **1573** SANFORD 58[v] If the Lions skin be not enough, take the Wolfes too. *Erasmus* attributeth this last saying also to *Lysander* Captaine of the *Lacedemonians* [Here given to King Antigonus]. **1579** NORTH *Plutarch's Alexander & Caesar* (T.C. vii. 231) He might haue sewed (as they say the case of the fox with the skin of the lion). **1594** *Selimus* 1733 I like Lysander's counsel passing well; 'If that I cannot speed with lion's force, To clothe my complots in a fox's skin'. **1621** HOWELL *Lett.* 30 Nov. (1903) I. 95 The Duke of Savoy . . . though he be valiant enough, yet he knows how to patch the lion's skin with a fox's tail. **1670** RAY 184 . . . *Si leonina pellis non satis est, assuenda vulpina.* . . . To attempt or compass that by craft, which we cannot obtain by force. **1700** TYRRELL *Hist. Eng.* II. 847 When the Lyon's Skin alone would not serve turn, he knew how to make it out with that of the

fox. **1906** ALEX. MACLAREN *Expos., Deut.* I *Sam.*
359 He had a streak of oriental craft, and stood
on the moral level of his times and country, in
his readiness to eke out the lion's skin with the
fox's tail.

Lion's skin is never cheap, A. (L 320)

1611 COTGRAVE s.v. Lion *Il n'y eut iamais bon
marché de peaux de lions, . . .* a Lyons skinne
was neuer bought good cheape. **1640** HERBERT
no. 55.

Lions, To see (show) the. (L 322)

[= the sights worth seeing, from the practice of
taking visitors to see the lions which used to be
kept in front of the present entrance to the
Tower of London.] **1590** GREENE *Wks.* Gros.
viii. 6 This countrey Francesco was no other
but a meere nouice, and that so newly, that to vse
the old prouerb, he had scarce seene the lions.
1630 CAPT. J. SMITH *True Trav.* xviii Arb. 872
After, one Master John Bull . . . , with divers of
his friends, went to see the Lyons [in the Tower].
1709 STEELE *Tatler* No. 30 16 June I took three
lads, . . . to show them . . . the lions, the tombs,
Bedlam, and the other places which are entertainments to raw minds. **1840** HOOD *Up Rhine*
96 The rest of the day was spent in seeing the
Lions—and first the Cathedral.

Lion(s), *see also* Army of stags led by l.; Ass in
l.'s skin; Ass to be called a l. (What good can it
do); Bear wants tail and cannot be l.; Beard the
l.; Beat the dog before the l.; Bold as a l.;
Brains of fox of little service if . . . paw of l.;
Christians to the l.; Cotswold l.; Destroy the l.
while a whelp; Dog is l. at home; Fox's wiles
never enter l.'s head; Hand in the l.'s mouth
(He that has); Hares may pull dead l.; Lammermoor l.; Living dog . . . dead l.; Man is a l.
in own cause; March comes in like l.; One, but
a l.; Sell the bear's (l.'s) skin before; Sight of a
man has force of a l.; Wake not a sleeping l.

Lip-honour costs little, yet may bring in much. (L 331)

1642 TORRIANO 82 Lip-honour may do much
good, and stand a man but in a little. **1732**
FULLER no. 3245.

Lippens[1] to lent ploughs, He that | his land will lie ley.[2] (P 436)

a. **1628** CARMICHAELL no. 704 (to bone plewis).
1641 FERGUSSON no. 302 (bon plowes). **1721**
KELLY 145. He that trusts to bon Ploughs, will
have his Land lye lazy. **1862** HISLOP 146
(land lang lea). He that relies on favours being
granted is liable to disappointment. [[1] trusts.
[2] unploughed.]

Lips hang in your light, Your. (L 330)

a. **1529** SKELTON *Magn.* l. 1050 Tusshe! thy
lyppes hange in thyne eye. **1546** HEYWOOD
II. iv. G3ᵛ Your lyps hang in your light, but this
poore man sees Bothe howe blyndly ye stande in
your owne lyght. **1581** N. WOODES *Conflict of
Conscience* C2ᵛ Ye purblinded fooles, dco your
lyps blinde your eyes? **1593** B.R. *Green's News*
G2 (hang . . . in theyr own lights). *c.* **1594**
BACON *Promus* (Pott) 119, no. 107.

Lips, Like (Such) | like (such) lettuce (meat). (L 326)

[L. *Similem habent labra lactucam,* an alleged
saying of M. Crassus, when he heard a description of an ass eating thistles. *See* JEROME *Ep.*
l. 7 and at length *N. & Q.* 175. 99.] *a.* **1540**
BARNES Wks. (1573) 189/1 No doubt the prouerbe is true, such lippes, such lectuce, such
saintes such miracles. *a.* **1548** HALL (1809 ed.,
233). **1568** FULWELL *Like will to L.* Hazl.-Dods.
iii. 330 And as the wise man said, such letuce
such lips. **1587** FLEMING *Contn.* Holinshed III.
1017/2 Like lips, like lettice, as is their cause so
are the rulers. *a.* **1628** CARMICHAELL no. 1359
(quo the kw eating thrissils). **1631** JONSON *New
Inn* II. vi. 19 Lætitia! a faire omen! And I take it.
Let me haue still such Lettice for my lips. **1640**
CAREW *To . . . Davenant* Like lips, meet like meat.
1670 RAY 114 . . . *Similes habent labra lactucas . . .*
As when a dull scholar happens to a stupid or
ignorant master; a froward wife to a peevish
husband.

Lip(s), *see also* Cat knows whose beard (l.) she
licks; Cup and l.; Fingers on thy l., (Lay thy);
Free of her l.; Pipe that lacks his upper l.
(He can ill); Stiff upper l. (Keep).

Liquor, *see* Ale (L.) will make cat speak;
Hanged for leaving his l.; Mix your l., (Never);
Wine is best l. to wash glasses.

Lisping lass is good to kiss, A. (L 76)

1639 FORD *Lady's Trial* IV. ii. Your lips are
destined to a better use, Or else the proverb fails
of lisping maids.—Kithing you mean. **1678**
RAY 349.

List, *see* Believe it (me) if you l.; May if you l.,
but do if you dare; Take it as you will (l.).

Listeners hear no (never hear) good of themselves. (L 336)

1647 26 Jan.-2 Feb. *Mercurius Elencticus* 76
The old Proverb is, Hearkners never heare good
of them selves. **1678** RAY 75. **1692** L'ESTRANGE
Aesop's Fab. clxx (1738) 183 'Tis an old saying,
that *Listeners never hear well of themselves;* and
Mercury's curiosity sped accordingly in this
fable. **1836** MARRYAT *Midsh. Easy* ch. 17 'If I
mistake not, . . . your conversation refers to me'.
'Very likely it does,' replied the boatswain.
Listeners hear no good of themselves.' **1839**
DICKENS *N. Nickleby* ch. 42 'If it is fated that
listeners are never to hear any good of themselves', said Mrs. Browdie, 'I can't help it and
I am very sorry for it'.

Literature is a good staff but a bad crutch.

1830 SIR W. SCOTT Lockhart's *Life* E.L. 136 I
determined that literature should be my staff but
not my crutch. **1835** *Poor Scholar* in WILSON
Tales of Borders I. 199 I found that literature
was a good staff but a bad crutch; and . . . I used
it accordingly. **1859** SMILES *Self-Help* iv (as
1830).

Lith[1] and selthe[2] are fellows.

c. **1300** *Havelok* 1338 E.E.T.S. 41 Lith and selthe felawes are. (*Note* 141: Goldborough tells him to avoid delay, since rest may accompany success, but cannot precede it.) [[1] rest. [2] success.]

Lithe as a lass of Kent.   (L 73)

1579 SPENSER *Shep. Cal.* Feb. 74 His dewelap as lythe, as lasse of Kent. **1593** DRAYTON *Dowsabell* Her features all as fresh above, As is the grass that grows by Dove; And lyth as lasse of Kent.

Lither, *see* Long as he is l., he might thatch.

Litter is like to the sire and the dam, The.   (L 337)

c. **1549** HEYWOOD I. xi. D3 Commenly all thyng shewth fro whens it camme. The litter is lyke to the syre and the damme.

Litter, *see also* First pig . . . of l. is the best; Whelp of the same l.

Littera scripta manet.

[The written letter remains.]   *a.* **1347** MURIMUTH *Chron.* I quotes *Res audita perit, littera scripta manet.* **1581** C.T. *Short Inventory* A5 Litterae scriptae manent, . . . writinges remayne a long time. **1642** HOWELL *For. Trav.* iii Arb. 20 For the Penne maketh the deepest furrowes, and doth fertilize, and enrich the memory more than any thing else, Littera scripta manet.

Little and good fills the trencher, A.   (L 365)

1640 HERBERT no. 505. **1670** RAY 16 That little which is good fills the trencher.

Little and little, By.   (L 340)

[EXOD. xxiii. 30: By little and little I will drive them out.] *c.* **1380** WYCLIF *Sel. Wks.* I. 358 Crist wole teche his disciplis bi litel and litel alle þes. **1530** PALSGRAVE 833a. **1548** HALL *Chron.* 30 By litle and litle, the Englishemen recouered again many tounes. **1612** BACON *Essays* (1864) xii. 134 Custom of profane scoffing in holy matters; which doth by little and little deface the reverence of religion. **1682** DRYDEN *Religio* Pref., ed. Saintsbury, x. 12 Their descendants lost, by little and little, the primitive and purer rites.

Little and loud.

c. **1640** *The Four Complexions* [print sold by Tho. Jenner.] *c.* **1641** FERGUSSON MS. no. 1424 Of the culloris of women. Fair and foolish, litil and loud, Long and lusty, black and proud. Fat and merry, lean and sad, Pale and pettish, Red and bad, High cullour (in a woman) choler showes; And shee's unholsome that lyk sorrell growes. Nought ar the peeuish, proud, malitious, But worst of all the Red shrill, jealious. **1648** HERRICK *Hesper.*, No. 601 '*Little and Loud*' Wks. (1893) I. 277 Little you are; for Womans sake be proud; For my sake next, (though little) *be not loud.* **1659** HOWELL Letter of Advice before *Eng. Prov.* 2.

Little and often fills the purse.   (L 372)

1582 S. GOSSON *Plays Confuted* The ignorant . . . are to be fed like children, with a litle and often. **1658** *Comes Facundus* 23. **1666** TORRIANO *It. Prov.* 211, no. 10. **1732** FULLER no. 3249. **1790** TRUSLER *Prov. Exempl.* 183 . . . he who begins to save, will soon find himself rich.

Little bird is content with a little nest, A.   (B 379)

1616 DRAXE no. 1260 For a little bird, a little nest. **1732** FULLER no. 244.

Little birds that can sing and won't sing should be made to sing.   (B 366)

1678 RAY 343 The bird that can sing and will not sing must be made to sing. **1721** KELLY 320 . . . Spoken when we use rough Means to perverse People. **1845** DICKENS *Cricket on H.* ch. 2 'The bird that can sing and won't sing, must be made to sing, they say,' grumbled Tackleton. **1890** D. C. MURRAY *J. Vale's Guard.* ch. 7 Your uncle is very little pleased with the progress you have been making. . . . Little birds that can sing and will not sing will have to be made to sing.

Little body often harbours a great soul, A.   (B 501)

1599 SHAKES. *Hen. V* 2nd Prol. 16 England . . . like little body with a mighty heart. **1611** COTGRAVE s.v. Lievre A little bush may hold a great Hare, a little bodie a great heart. **1670** RAY 16. **1888** QUILLER-COUCH *Troy Town* ch. 6. She bore a great soul in a little body.

Little Britain.

[L. *Britannia minor* (Geoff. of Monmouth) = Brittany, in France.] **1662** FULLER Wales The Danes wofully harassed the Land, which caused him to ship himself over into little Britain in France; the inhabitants whereof may be termed Cosin-Germans to the Welch.

Little business stands great rest, In.   (B 751)

a. **1400** CHAUCER *Truth* l. 10 Gret reste stante in litel besinesse. *c.* **1465** AGNES PASTON *Paston Letters* ed. N. Davis no. 44 Youre fadyr sayde, 'In lityl bysynes lyeth ryche rest.' **1523** SKELTON *Garl. Laurel* l. 1410 Wks. i. 417 With litell besynes standith moche rest.

Little can a long tongue lein.[1]

1721 KELLY 240 . . . Spoken as a Reproof to a Baubler [*i.e.* babbler]. [[1] conceal.]

Little cannot be great unless he devour many, The.   (L 354)

1616 DRAXE no. 1566 A little body cannot be great, except he eate many. **1640** HERBERT no. 922.

Little dogs have long tails.

1721 KELLY 233.

Little dogs start the hare, the great get her. (D 540)

1640 HERBERT no. 593.   **1732** FULLER no. 3254 (but great ones catch it).

Little England beyond Wales. (E 151)

1586 CAMDEN *Britannia* 373 [margin].   **1610** P. HOLLAND *Brit.* Pembroke I. 652 This tract was inhabited by Flemings . . . [and] is tearmed by the Britains Little England beyond Wales. **1662** FULLER Pembrokeshire 56. A part of this Country is peopled by Flemmings, placed there by King Henry the first, . . . and their Country is called little England beyond Wales.   **1670** RAY 258 . . . so called because the inhabitants speak good English.

Little Englanders.

1895 *Westm. Gaz.* 1 Aug. 2/2 The error so often made by Little Englanders.   **1910** *Times Wkly.* 10 June 420 Goldwin Smith was . . . a Little Englander of the Little Englanders. He saw nothing in the Empire . . . but a burden on England and an obstacle to the full civic development of the Colonies.

Little fire burns up a great deal of corn, A. (F 274)

1557 EDGEWORTH *Sermons* 3I2 A little fire burneth a whole groue, or a greate wodde.   **1586** *La Primaudaye* 130 A little fire consumeth a great wood.   **1592** DELAMOTHE 41 A small fire, makes often a great smoke. c. **1592** SHAKES. *3 Hen. VI* IV. viii. 7 A little fire is quickly trodden out, Which being suffered rivers cannot quench.   **1595** *A pleasant Satyre* (*A Satyre Menippized*) 99 A little fire maketh a great flame.   **1678** RAY *Adag. Hebr.* 413 . . . To be understood of the mischief which an evil and slandring tongue does, and is exemplified in Doeg who by this means brought destruction upon the Priests.

Little fish are sweet.

1830 FORBY 434 . . . It means small gifts are always acceptable.   **1914** K. F. PURDON *Folk of Furry F.* ch. 7 'They'll sell at a loss', he went on, with a sigh, 'but sure, little fish is sweet! and the rent has to be made up'.

Little fishes slip through nets, but great fishes are taken.

1509 BARCLAY *Ship of Fools* i. 191.   **1598** MERES *Palladis* f. 246.

Little for the rake after the besom, There is. (L 366)

a. **1628** CARMICHAELL no. 1070.   **1641** FERGUSSON no. 787.   **1721** KELLY 319 . . . There is little to be gotten of such a Thing, when covetous People have had their Will of it.

Little gear, less care. *Cf.* **Little wealth little care.**

1721 KELLY 236.

Little gentleman in black velvet, The.

[= a mole.] [A Jacobite phrase, referring to the belief that the death of William III was caused by his horse's stumbling over a molehill.]   **1814** SCOTT *Wav.* ch. 11 The little gentleman in black velvet who did such service in 1702.   **1928** *Times* 11 Oct. 19/6 One may recognize him as 'the little gentleman in black velvet' of Jacobite toasts, whose hillock gave William III his fatal fall from his horse.

Little given seasonably, excuses a great gift, A. (L 355)

1640 HERBERT no. 834.

Little good comes of gathering.

a. **1450** *Tale of Colkelbie Sow* 19–21 in HAZLITT *Pop. Poetry of Scot.* (1895) I. 185 For in old prouerbe we sing Cumis littill gud of gaddering Quhair wrechit awerice birnis.

Little good (gear) is soon spent. (G 299)

1555 HEYWOOD *Epigr. upon Proverbs* no. 169 Lyttel good, soone spended.   **1639** CLARKE 242.   **1641** FERGUSSON no. 931.   **1721** KELLY 231.

Little good to stark nought, To come from. (G 320)

1639 CLARKE 83.   **1670** RAY 178.

Little house has a wide mouth, A.

1721 KELLY 6 A wie House has a wide Throat.   **1865** *Lancs. Proverbs* in *N. & Q.* 3rd Ser. viii. 494 (as 1721).   **1883** BURNE *Shropsh. Folk-Lore* 589.

Little house well filled, a little land well tilled, and a little wife well willed, A. (H 779)

1545 TAVERNER I2ᵛ The english . . . sayeth in this wyse.
A lyttle house well fylled
A lytle ground well tylled } is best.
And a little wife well wylled
1670 RAY 53.   **1738** SWIFT Dial. II. E.L. 307 What do you think of a little house well filled? —And a little land well tilled?—Ay; and a little wife well willed?

Little intermeddling makes good friends (fair parting). (I 87)

a. **1628** CARMICHAELL no. 1044 Litle intrometting maks gude freinds.   **1641** FERGUSSON no. 929 (as *a.* 1628).   **1721** KELLY 233 (fair parting).

Little, He that has | is the less dirty. (L 348)

1640 HERBERT no. 436.

Little is the light will be seen far in a mirk night.

1819 SCOTT *Bride Lam.* ch. 26 'But the . . . blaze which might have been seen ten miles off . . .?' 'Hout awa! it's an auld saying and a true,— . . .

Little Jock gets the little dish, and it holds him aye long little.

1721 KELLY 230 . . . Poor People are poorly serv'd, which prolongs their Poverty. **1862** HISLOP 216.

Little journeys and good cost bring safe home.   (J 80)

1640 HERBERT no. 502.

Little kenned, less cared for.

1721 KELLY 237 . . . Spoken of such of our Relations as dwell at a Distance. Lat. *Non sunt amici, amici qui vivunt procul.*

Little kens the wife that sits by the fire, how the wind blows cold in Hurleburle-swyre.   (W 366)

a. **1628** CARMICHAELL no. 1087 (Hurle Brough swyre). **1641** FERGUSSON no. 600. **1721** KELLY 229 . . . *Hurle-burle-swyre* is a Passage through a Ridge of Mountains, that separate Nithsdale from Twadale,[1] and Clydsdale[2]: Where . . . there is a perpetual blowing . . . They who are at Ease, know little of the Trouble that others are expos'd to. **1819** SCOTT *Bride Lam.* ch. 6 Keep you the cheek of the chimney-nook till I come back. . . . Little kens the auld wife that sits by the fire, How cauld the wind blaws in hurle-burle swire. [1 Tweeddale. 2 Clydesdale.]

Little kitchen makes a large house, A.   (K 111)

1581 GUAZZO i. 188 The steward answered . . . that that small kitchin had made the house so great. **1614** SIR T. OVERBURY *Characters* Wks. (1890) 144 A *French cooke.* He is the prime cause why noblemen build their houses so great: for the smalnesse of their kitchin, makes the house the bigger. **1640** HERBERT no. 470.

Little knows the fat sow (man) what the lean does mean (thinks).   (S 676)

c. **1350** *Douce MS.* 52 no. 115 Lytyl wote þe full what þe hungry aylyz. *c.* **1480** *The lytylle Childrenes lytil Boke* in *Babees Book* (Furnivall) 16 For the fulle wombe without any faylys wot fulle lytyl what the hungry ayly3. **1546** HEYWOOD I. x. D1ᵛ Litle knoweth the fat sow, what the leane doth meane. **1550** BECON *Fort. Faith* Prol. A ii According to the common Prouerbe, Lyttel wote the ful sow that is in yᵉ stye, What the hungrye sow ayleth, that goeth by. **1640** HERBERT no. 605 The fatt man knoweth not what the leane thinketh. **1852** E. FITZGERALD *Polonius* ch. 11 'The Fat Sow knows not what the Lean one thinks' . . . Swollen Wealth is well enacted from the fat Sow reclining in her sty, as a Dowager in an opera-box, serenely unconscious of all her kindred's leanness without.

Little labour, much health, A.   (L 6)

1640 HERBERT no. 689.

Little let[1] lets an ill workman, A.   (L 209)

1640 HERBERT no. 755. [1 hindrance.]

Little London beyond Wales.

1670 RAY 258 . . . i.e. *Beaumaris* in the Isle of *Anglesey*: so called because the inhabitants speak good *English.*

Little losses amaze, great tame. (L 465)

1640 HERBERT no. 1013.

Little mead, little need.   (M 779)

1678 RAY 352 . . . *Somerset.* (A mild winter hoped for after a bad summer.)

Little meddling makes much rest.

                                    (M 858)

c. **1386** CHAUCER *Manciple's T.* l. 350 That litel janglyng causeth muchel reste. *c.* **1450** *Prouerbis of Wysdom* 128 Lytyll medlyng makyþe mych rest. **1546** HEYWOOD II. ii. G1ᵛ To medyll lytle for me it is best. For of lytle medlyng comth great rest. *c.* **1591** *Fair Em* l. 1500 He is best at ease that medleth least. **1635** SWAN *Spec. Mundi* (1670) 368 In little medling is much rest. **1659** HOWELL *Eng. Prov.* 9a Of little medling cometh great ease.

Little mense[1] o' the cheeks to bite off the nose.

1862 HISLOP 216 . . . It is bad policy for a person to injure another with whom he is intimately connected, or upon whom he is depending. [1 discretion.]

Little money as you have manners, If you had as | you would be the poorest man of your kin.

1721 KELLY 205 . . . Spoken to wealthy People, when they behave themselves rudely, haughtily, or insolently. **1732** FULLER no. 2754.

Little of everything, and nothing in the main, A.

1706 STEVENS s.v. Cosa. **1732** FULLER no. 247.

Little (Small) pitchers have great (long, wide) ears.   (P 363)

1546 HEYWOOD II. v. G4ᵛ Auoyd your children, smal pitchers haue wide eares. [1592] **1597** SHAKES. *Rich. III* II. iv. 37 Good madam, be not angry with the child.—Pitchers have ears. **1594-8** *Id. T.S.* IV. iv. 52 Not in my house, Lucretio; for you know Pitchers have ears, and I have many servants. **1640** HERBERT no. 380 (wide). **1837-47** BARHAM *Ingol. Leg., St. Dunstan* A truth Insisted on much in my earlier years, To wit, 'Little pitchers have very long ears!' **1915** *Lit. Digest* 4 Sept. 475/1 The little pitchers with big ears have been taking in a good deal of war talk.

Little pot is soon hot, A.   (P 497)

1546 HEYWOOD I. xi. D2 It is wood[1] at a woorde, little pot soone whot. **1594-8** SHAKES. IV. i. 6 Now were not I a little pot and soon hot, my very lips might freeze to my teeth. **1606** DAY *Isle of Gulls.* III. ii Nay, though I be but a little

pot, I shall be as soon hot as another. **1670**
RAY 115 . . . Little persons are commonly
cholerick. **1883** READE *Peril. Secr.* ch. 15
Cheeky little beggar, But . . . 'a little pot is soon
hot'. [¹ mad, furious.]

Little (Least, Nothing) said is soon (soonest) amended (mended).   (L 358)

c. **1460** *Parl. of Birds* E.E.P.P. iii. 169 Who
sayth lytell he is wyse . . . And fewe wordes are
soone amend. **1555** HEYWOOD *Epig. upon Prov.*
no. 169 Lyttle sayde, soone amended. **1599**
PORTER *Angry Wom.Abing.* l. 1832. **1634** FORD *Per.
Warb.* IV. ii. **1635** SWAN *Spec. Mundi* (1670) 368
In little medling is much rest; and 'nothing said
is soonest amended'. **1721** KELLY 231 Little
said soon mended. **1776** T. COGAN *John Buncle,
Junior* i. 237–8 But mum's the word; least said is
soonest mended. **1818** SCOTT *Rob Roy* ch. 29
About treason and all that, it's lost time to speak
of it—least said is sunest mended. **1837**
DICKENS *Pickwick* ch. 48 The old lady . . . ventured to approach Mr. Benjamin Allen with a
few comforting reflections, of which the chief
were that . . . the least said the soonest mended.
1917 BRIDGE 89 Least said soonest mended, but
nowt said needs no mending. **1929** 10 Aug.
D. H. LAWRENCE *Lett.* ii. 1175 Least said, soonest
mended.

Little sap in dry pease hulls, There is.   (S 93)

a. **1628** CARMICHAELL no. 1081 (widered). **1641**
FERGUSSON no. 842 There [is] little sap in dry
peis hooles.

Little, He that has | shall have less.

1639 CLARKE 82.

Little sticks kindle the fire; great ones put it out.   (S 851)

c. **1300** BRUNNE *Handle. Synne* l. 12438 Thou
seest stykkes that are smale, They brenne fyrsk
feyre. **1640** HERBERT no. 323.

Little stream drives a light mill, A.   (S 928)

1579 GOSSON *Ephemerides* (*Sch. Abuse* Arber
10–11) A little streame serves to drive a light
Mill. **1597** *Politeuphuia* 166. **1639** CLARKE
129.

Little take a little, Of a.   (L 363)

1580 MUNDAY *Zelauto* N2ᵛ Thus of a little take a
little when you come thereto: and of a little
leaue a little how euer you doo. **1609** HARWARD
128ᵛ Of a litle you must take a litle. **1721**
KELLY 276.

Little thing, Of a | a little displeases.   (T 143)

1640 HERBERT no. 814.

Little things are great to little men.

1764 O. GOLDSMITH *The Traveller* l. 42 These
little things are great to little men. **1765**
JOHNSON *Preface to Shakespeare* (*Johnson on

Shakespeare, ed. Raleigh 51) Small things make
mean men proud. *a.* **1792** SIR JOSHUA REYNOLDS
Two Dialogues (*Johnsonian Miscellanies*, Birk-
beck Hill ii. 235). **1827** HONE *Table-Book* 110.

Little things are pretty.   (T 188)

1539 TAVERNER 50ᵛ Unto lyttel thynges is a
certayne grace annexed. **1609** HARWARD 112
Every thing is prety when it is yong. **1678** RAY
169 . . . Χάρις βαιοῖσιν ὀπηδεῖ.

Little things please (affect, attract) little minds.   (T 189)

[OVID *Ars Amatoria* l. 159 *Parva leves capiunt
animos.*] **1576** PETTIE ii. 33 A little thing pleaseth
a fool. **1584** LYLY *Sappho & Phao* II. iv. 60
Litle things catch light mindes. **1845** DISRAELI
Sybil III. ii Little things affect little minds.
Lord Marney . . . was kept at the station which
aggravated his spleen.

Little tit,¹ all tail.   (T 355)

1546 HEYWOOD I. x. C3 But little titte all tayle,
I haue herde er this. [¹ a small animal or object.]

Little to sew, when tailors are true.   (T 25)

a. **1628** CARMICHAELL no. 1297 Quhen tailours
aw there is litle to sew. **1641** FERGUSSON no. 719
Quhen taylours are true, there little good to
shew. **1721** KELLY 235 . . . Lat. *Raro, ad
tempus, fidem præstant artifices.*

Little troubles the eye, but far less the soul.   (L 359)

1641 FERGUSSON no. 599.

Little wealth little care. *Cf.* Little gear, less care.   (W 198)

1616 DRAXE no. 144 Little goods, little cares.
1640 HERBERT no. 501.

Little wind kindles, much puts out the fire, A.   (W 424)

1586 GUAZZO ii. 149. **1594–8** SHAKES. *T.S.* II. i.
135 Though little fire grows great with little
wind, yet extreme gusts will blow out fire and all.
1640 HERBERT no. 680. **1646** H. ESTIENNE *Art of
Making Devices* tr. T. Blount 59 Ovid's verses,
Lenis Alit Flammas, Grandior Aura Necat, An
easie winde nourisheth the fire, but a greater
destroyes it.

Little wit, You have a | and it does you good sometimes.   (W 571)

1639 CLARKE 298. **1664** CODRINGTON 230.
1670 RAY 30.

Little wit in the head makes much work for the heel (feet). *Cf. the following proverb.*

1832 HENDERSON 83 Little wit in the head maks
muckle travel to the heel. **1895** S. O. JEWETT
Life of Nancy 253 You'd ought to set her to
work, and learnt her head to save her heels.

Little wit makes meikle travel. *Cf. the
preceding proverb.*   (w 559)

1641 FERGUSSON no. 569.   **1707** MAPLETOFT 121.
1721 KELLY 230 *Little wit as mickle travell.*
Spoken when People for want of Skill, put
themselves to more Trouble than they need.

Little wit will serve a fortunate man,
A.   (w 560)

1573 SANFORD 109 A little wit is inough for him
to whom fortune pipes.   **1707** MAPLETOFT 27.

Little with quiet is the only diet, A.
                                             (L 361)

c. **1300** *King Alis.* (Weber) l. 7365 Better is,
lyte to have in ese Then muche to have[n] in
malese. *a.* **1500** *15c. School-Bk.* ed. W. Nelson
59 He that hath but litell and be content is
better at ease than he that is riche and alwaye
careth for more.   **1611** COTGRAVE s.v. Peu A
little with quietnesse is Gods owne gift. *Ibid.* s.v.
Paix A little with peace is a great blessing.
1640 HERBERT no. 327.

Little Witham, He was born at. (L 373)

1560 HEYWOOD *Fourth Hund. of Epig.* no. 19
Whens come great breeches? from little wittam.
1662 FULLER Lincs. 153 . . . This Village in this
County by Orthography is Witham. . . . But
such nominal Proverbs take the advantage of all
manner of Spelling as due unto them. It is
applyed to such people as are not overstock'd
with acutenesse.

Little wood will heat a little oven, A.

1642 TORRIANO 4 For a little oven, a little wood
will serve.   **1732** FULLER no. 254.

Little, *see also* Ask much to have l.; Better to
pay and have l. than have much and to be in
debt; Cat eats flickle, l. by l.; Every l. helps;
Fair and sluttish . . . l. and loud; Great and l.
need one another; Great ones (No) if no l.;
Here a l. there a l.; Love me l. and love me long;
Many a l. makes a mickle; Nature is content with
a l.; Nothing is (Where), a l. thing does ease;
Poor that has l., (He is not); Secret is too l. for
one . . . ; Stone in the way overturns a great wain,
(A l.); Tarry-long brings l. home; Woman were
as l. as she is good (If a), peascod would make
her a gown.

Live a little while, If you will | go to
Bapchild; if you'd live long, go to
Tenham or Tong.

1736 S. PEGGE *Kenticisms Prov.* E.D.S. 67 . . .
Bapchild is indeed a bad and unhealthy situation.
[It is adjacent to Tong, which adjoins Teynham.]

Live and learn.   (L 379)

1575 GASCOIGNE *Glass of Government* ii. 88 We
live to learne, for so Sainct Paule doth teach.
1579 LYLY *Euph.* i. 193 You haue lyued long and
learned lyttle.   **1639** CLARKE 267.   **1659** HOWELL
Eng. Prov. 13b One may live and learn, and be
hang'd and forget all.   **1662** J. WILSON *Cheats*

III. iii I see a man may live and learn every day.
1704 STEELE *Lying Lov.* I. i Don't stand gaping,
but live and learn, my lad.   **1894** LD. AVEBURY
Use of Life ch. 6 No doubt we go on learning as
long as we live: Live and learn.

Live and let live.   (L 380)

1622 MALYNES *Anc. Law-Merch.* 229 According
to the Dutch prouerbe . . . Leuen ende laeten
leuen, to liue and to let others liue.   **1641**
FERGUSSON no. 582.   **1678** RAY 170 . . . *i.e.*
Do as you would be done by. Let such pennyworths as your Tenants may live under you.
1692 L'ESTRANGE *Aesop's Fab.* cxxxix (1738) 154
Live and let live, is the rule of common justice.
1854 SURTEES *Handley Cross* ch. 37 (as the criminal said to the hangman).   **1902** J. H. ROSE in
Lect. Hist. 19th Cent. 77 Napoleon had no conception of the maxim—'Live and let live'. His
commercial ideas were narrowly national.   **1906**
HERBERT PAUL *Stray Leaves* Bp. Creighton, 'Live
and let live' was his motto.

Live, I | and lords (the best) do no
more.   (L 444)

1599 PORTER *Angry Wom. Abingd.* ll. 1042–3
Well, how dooth thy maister?—Forsooth liue,
and the best dooth no better.   **1721** KELLY 400
Even living, and Lairds do no more.   **1732**
FULLER no. 2616.

Live, He will (would) | as long as old
Rosse (Russe) of Pottern,[1] who lived
till all the world was weary of him.
                                             (R 188)

1659 HOWELL *Eng. Prov.* 14b (Russe).   **1678**
RAY 80 (would). . [[1] near Devizes, Wilts.]

Live as they would die, Let all. (A 196)

1576 H. KERTON *Mirror of Man's Life* ded. to
Innocent III A1ᵛ I hold him therefore most
wisest, that so liueth as though he shoulde always
die. *Ibid.* D5 We should stil so liue, as thogh we
shuld alwaies die.   **1579** LYLY *Euph.* i. 308 So
shouldest thou lyue as thou mayst dye, and
then shalt thou dye to lyue.   **1581** GUAZZO ii.
70 They learne to live as if they were stil at the
point to dye. *a.* **1628** CARMICHAELL no. 1069.
1640 HERBERT no. 725.

Live by selling ware for words, One
cannot.   (w 65)

1616 WITHALS 568.   **1639** CLARKE 156.   **1670**
RAY 154.   **1732** FULLER no. 3741 (goods).

Live by the quick (living), not by the
dead, We must.   (Q 12)

1545 TAVERNER B3 Oure Englyshe prouerbe—we
ought to lyue by the quycke and not by the
deade.   **1576** PETTIE i. 109 You are to know
that we must live by the living, not by the dead.
1605 T. HEYWOOD *If you know not me* Shakes.
Soc. 52 'Twere fit To spend some funeral tears
upon her hearse. . . .—Ay, but do you not
know the old proverb? We must live by the
quick, and not by the dead.   **1614** SIR T.
OVERBURY *Characters* Wks. (1890) 145 *A Sexton.*

Of all proverbs, hee cannot endure to heare that which sayes, We ought to live by the quick, not by the dead. **1738** SWIFT Dial. II. E.L. 315.

Live ever, If you would | you must wash milk from your liver. (M 934)

1609 HARWARD 89ᵛ Wash milk from thy liver. **1611** COTGRAVE s.v. Laict Wash thy milke off thy liuer (say we). **1678** RAY 36 . . . Vin sur laict c'est souhait, Laict sur vin c'est venin. *Gall.* This is an idle old saw, for which I can see no reason but rather the contrary.

Live for aye, He that would | must eat sage in May. (S 22)

1588 COGAN *Haven of Health* (1612) xi. 32 In *Schola Salerni* it is demanded *Cur moriatur homo cui saluia crescit in horto*? As who should say, such is the vertue of sage, that if it were possible, it would make a man immortall. **1678** RAY 36 . . . That Sage was by our ancestours esteemed a very wholesome herb, and much conducing to longevity appears by that verse in *Schola Salernitana, Cur moriatur homo cui Salvia crescit in horto*? **1732** FULLER no. 6253 (butter and sage).

Live from hand to mouth, To. (H 98)

[= to live improvidently.] **1549** ERASM. tr. Chalenor *Praise of Folly* G1 Lyue from hande to mouthe. **1557** EDGEWORTH *Sermons* 3H2ᵛ Veluet and other silkes be as commonly on the pore mans backe, that liueth from hand to mouth, as on the gentleman. **1580** J. CONYBEARE *Adagia* 50 They liue from hande to mouthe. **1603** MONTAIGNE (Florio) III. iv. 68 I live from hand to mouth, and . . . I live but to my selfe. **1712** ARBUTHNOT *John Bull* xv Poor Frog . . . is in hard circumstances, he has a numerous family, and lives from hand to mouth. **1910** *Spectator* 6 Aug. 199 Other women . . . waste by living in a needlessly hand-to-mouth fashion.

Live, horse, and you'll get grass.

1738 SWIFT Dial. I. E.L. 292 I hope to have a rich . . . wife yet before I die.—Ay, Tom; live, horse, and thou shalt have grass.

Live in a gravel pit, He would. (G 429)

1678 RAY 72 . . . Spoken of a wary, sparing, niggardly person.

Live in Italy, A man would | but he would choose to die in Spain. (M 308)

1651 HERBERT no. 1047 A man would live in Italy (a place of pleasure), but he would chuse to dye in Spain, (where they say the Catholic Religion is professed with greatest strictness).

Live in peace and rest, He that would (will) | must hear, and see, and say the best. *Cf.* Hear and see and be still. (P 140)

c. **1450** *Prov. of Good Counsel* E.E.T.S. l. 52 Yf thou wylte leve in peas and reste, here, and see, and sey the beste. **1611** DAVIES no. 69.

1623 PAINTER B3 Heare and see and alwaies say the best. **1639** CLARKE 102. **1670** RAY 130 . . . Oy, voy, & te tais, si tu veux vivre en paix, *Gall.* Ode, vede, tace, Se vuoi viver in pace, *Ital.* **1796** EDGEWORTH *Par. Asst.* (1903) 410 Let him make himself happy his way, and we ours. . . .

Live longest, They that | must die at last. (L 81)

1616 DRAXE no. 1423. **1639** CLARKE 323. **1670** RAY 116.

Live longest, They who | will see most.

1605–6 SHAKES. *K.L.* V. iii. 325 We that are young shall never see so much nor live so long. **1620** SHELTON *Quix.* II. liii. iv. 118 My Mother was used to say, That it was needfull to live long, to see much. **1837** TH. HOOK *Jack Brag* ch. 17 I'll watch her pretty closely. . . . Never mind; them as lives longest sees the most.

Live on air like the chameleon, To. (M 226)

1557 *Lover Shows Death* l. 34 in *Tottel's Misc.,* i. 168 A fishe on lande to whom no water flowes, As Chameleon that lackes the ayer so sote. **1562** G. LEGH *Accidence of Armoury* 143 His liuing is onely of the Ayer, and neuer eateth anye thinge, which I haue sene halfe a yeare proued. **1578–80** SIDNEY I *Arcadia* ed. Feuillerat 190. **1589** NASHE *Anat. of Absurdity* i. 36 As the Chamelion which is fed with the ayre. **1594** SHAKES. *T.G.V.* II. i. 160 The chameleon Love can feed on the air. **1600–1** *Id. H.* III. ii. 91 Of the chameleon's dish: I eat the air, promise-crammed. **1629** T. ADAMS *Serm.* (1862) I. 361 Is he ever the fuller or fatter for our word? Not unless, like a chameleon, he can live by air. **1670** RAY 56 A man cannot live by the air. *a.* **1812** WOLCOT (P. Pindar) *Lyric Odes* v. (1816) I. 18 No matter, verily, how slight their fare; Nay, though camelion-like, they fed on air.

Live peaceably with all breeds good blood, To. (A 205)

1640 HERBERT no. 963.

Live to be old, If you would not | you must be hanged when you are young. (L 377)

1670 RAY 126.

Live well for a week, If you would | kill a hog; if you would live well for a month, marry; if you would live well all your life, turn priest. (M 1107)

1662 FULLER *Wales* 6 The Italian-humor, who have a merry Proverb, Let him that would be happy for a Day, go to the Barber; for a Week, marry a Wife; for a Month, buy him a New-horse; for a Year, build him a New-house; for all his Life-time, be an Honest-man. **1666** TORRIANO *It. Prov.* 151, no. 18 Who intends to have a good month, let him to the bath, a good year, let him marry, a good week, let him kill a hog, who will be happy alwaies, let him turn

Priest. **1809** s. PEGGE *Anonymiana* II. xix. 64 If you would live well for a week, kill a hog; if you would live well for a month, marry; if you would live well all your life, turn priest. . . . Turning priest . . . alludes to the celibacy of the Romish Clergy, and has a pungent sense, as much as to say, do not marry at all.

Live without our friends, We can | but not without our neighbours.

1721 KELLY 348.   **1732** FULLER no. 5435.

Live(s), *see also* Altar (He that serves at) ought to l. by altar; Ask (He that cannot) cannot l.; Better die with honour than l. with shame; Clover (L. in); Compass (L. within); Die well that l. well; Eat to l.; Everything would l.; Fighting cocks (L. like); Gives me small gifts would have me l.; Hen l. (Let the) though with her pip; Know not who l. or dies (We); Laws not examples (We l. by); Long (Not how) but how well we l.; Longer l. a good fellow than dear year; Longer we l. more farlies we see; Lover is not where he l. but where he loves; Man l. (As a) so shall he die; Mind what you must l. by; Preaches well who l. well; See what we must come to if we l.; Soul is not where it l. but where loves; Sure as you l.; Sweat of other men's brows (L. by); Threatened folk l. long; Too wise to l. long; Trades l. (Let all); Tradesmen l. upon lack; Unworthy to l. who l. for himself; Warned folks may l.

Lived that lives not after death, He has not. (D 153)

1640 HERBERT no. 873.

Lived too near a wood to be frightened by owls, I have.

1738 SWIFT Dial. III. E.L. 323 Never fear him, miss.— . . . Do you think I was born in a wood, to be afraid of an owl?

Liver, *see* Good for the l. bad for spleen.

Liver (= who lives), *see* Longer l. take all, (Let the).

Liverpool, *see* Manchester men and L. gentlemen.

Lives as a cat, As many.

c. **1625** BEAUM. & FL. *Mons. Thomas* III. i. 238 There be as many lives in't, as a cat carries. **1684** BUNYAN *Pilgr.* II (1862) 331 He had, as they say, as many lives as a cat. **1738** SWIFT Dial. I. E.L. 291 They say a woman has as many lives as a cat.

Lives by hope will die by hunger, Who. (H 598)

1616 DRAXE no. 992 Hope will make a man neither eat nor drinke. **1623** WODROEPHE 302 Hee who lives of Hope makes a thinne Belly. **1689** SHADWELL *Bury Fair* III. i Hope is a very

thin diet, fit for love in a fever. **1699** A. BOYER *Compleat French Master* 145 What do'st generally live vpon, prithee?—Hopes and ill Words.—I should think that but very slender Diet. **1711** ADDISON *Spect.* No. 191 Wks. (Bohn) III. 63 The man who will live above his present circumstances, is in great danger of living in a little time much beneath them; or, as the Italian proverb runs, The man who lives by Hope will die by Hunger. **1721** KELLY 129 (hath a slender diet).

Lives by love, and lumps in corners (the cupboard), She. (L 541)

1678 RAY 75 (*Joculatory*). **1738** SWIFT Dial. I. E.L. 282 Miss lives upon love.—Yes, upon love and lumps of the cupboard.

Lives ill, He that | fear follows him. (F 139)

1640 HERBERT no. 110.

Lives in court dies upon straw, He that. (C 723)

1573 SANFORD 103ᵛ. **1579** LYLY *Euph.* i. 312. **1629** *Bk. Mer. Rid.* Prov. no. 91. **1659** HOWELL *It. Prov.* 11.

Lives in hope, He that | dances without music. (H 599)

1591 FLORIO *Second F.* 149 He that dooth liue in hope, dooth dance in narrowe scope. **1640** HERBERT no. 1006. **1670** RAY 13 *Hispan.* (without a minstrel).

Lives long suffers much, He that. (L 388)

1611 COTGRAVE s.v. Souffrir The longer we liue the more we haue t'indure. **1620** SHELTON *Quix.* II. xxxii. iii. 45 'Tis good to live long, to see much; although 'tis said also that he that lives long suffers much.

Lives long that lives well, He. (L 386)

1545 TAVERNER B3ᵛ This prouerbe in englishe is thus. Begyne betyme for to be sage, yf thou woll leade longe olde age. **1553** T. WILSON *Arte of Rhet.* (1909) 83 They liued long enough, that haue liued well enough. **1623** DRUMMOND *Cypress Grove* (Kastner ii. 97) Who liueth well, liueth long. **1642** FULLER *H. & P. State* I. vi (1841) 15 If he chance to die young, yet he lives long that lives well. **1721** KELLY 168 He that liveth well, liveth long.

Lives longest, He that | must fetch his wood farthest. (W 737)

1608 J. NORDEN *Surveyors Dialogue* (Harrison, *Description of England*, New Sh. S. iii. 191) As the Prouerbe is, Let them that liue longest, fetch their wood farthest. **1623** CAMDEN 271. **1625** PURCHAS *Pilgrims* (1905–7) xix. 247 Herein we may verify the old proverb, That he which liveth longest, shall fetch his wood furthest. **1670** RAY 116.

Lives most, dies most, He that.

(L 389)

1640 HERBERT no. 437.

Lives not well one year, He that | sorrows seven after. (Y 9)

1640 HERBERT no. 562. **1748** RICHARDSON *Clarissa* iv, let. 24 He that lives ill one year will sorrow for it seven.

Lives under the sign of the cat's foot, He. (S 441)

1678 RAY 68 . . . He is hen-peckt, his wife scratches him.

Lives unsafely that looks too near on things, He. (T 183)

1611 COTGRAVE s.v. Esplucher (to matters). **1640** HERBERT no. 43.

Lives well is learned enough, He that.

(L 390)

1611 COTGRAVE s.v. Vivre He that liues well enough hath skill enough. **1640** HERBERT no. 86.

Lives well that well has lurked (that lives closely), He.

[OVID *Tristia* III. iv. 25: Bene qui latuit bene vixit.] **15. .** *Life of Fisher* MS. Harl. 6382 E.E.T.S. 14 It is an old saying and trewe: well hath he liued that well hath lurked. *c.* **1581–90** *Timon Shakes. Lib.* ed. W. C. Hazlitt 1875 II. ii. 403 Who hath lurk'd close hath liu'd well. **1613** R. DALLINGTON *Aphorisms* 103 He liueth safely, that liueth closely.

Lives wickedly can hardly die honestly, He that. (L 392)

1616 DRAXE no. 1232. **1664** CODRINGTON 198. **1670** RAY 16.

Living dog is better than a dead lion, A.

(D 495)

[ECCL. ix. 4.] **1566** J. BARTHLET *Pedigrew of Heretiques* A2ᵛ. **1595** DANIEL *Civ. Wars* 4. st. 3 Their wisedom . . . Live dogges before dead Lyons estimates. **1655** FULLER *Ch. Hist.* III. i (1868) I. 322 Doth not Solomon say true, 'A living dog is better than a dead lion'; when such a little cur durst snarl at the corpse of a king? **1664** J. WILSON *Andronicus Comnenius* IV. iii. (A living mouse). **1855** MRS. GASKELL *North and South* ch. 46 (A living ass). **1906** IAN HAMILTON *Staff-Off. Scrap-Bk.* I. 197 To the Japanese soldier . . . the dead lion is one thousand times more enviable than the live dog.

Living man all things can, No. (M 315)

[VIRGIL *Eclog.* 8. 63 Non omnia possumus omnes. We cannot any of us do all things.] **1539** TAVERNER 36 All men can not do all thynges. Thys is the sayenge of the poete Vergill. **1616** WITHALS 544. **1639** CLARKE 147. *Ibid.* 97 No man is good at all things.

Living well is the best revenge. (L 397)

1579 LYLY *Euph.* i. 285 The greatest harme that you can doe vnto the enuious, is to doe well. **1640** HERBERT no. 524. **1659** HOWELL *It. Prov.* 12 Wilt thou be revenged of thy enemy? carry thy self well.

Living, *see also* Almsgiving lessens no man's l.; Life for l. man; Life lies not in l.; Live by the l. (We must); Remember the l.

Lizard(s), *see* Rock l.; Serpent has bitten (Whom a), l. alarms.

Load, *see* Willing horse (All lay l. on).

Loader's horse that lives among thieves, Like a. (L 398)

[Loader = carrier; carriers were not noted for honesty.] **1678** RAY 350 . . . (The countrey man near a town.) *Som.*

Loadstone, *see* Love is l.

Loaf (-ves), *see* Cut large shives of another's l.; First cut and all l. besides; Give a l. and beg shive; Half a l. better than . . .; Penny to buy his dog a l.; Set not your l. in till oven hot; Shive of a cut l. (Safe taking); Shive of my own l.; Traitors at the table; Wife cries five l. a penny.

Loan, *see* Borrowed l. should come laughing home.

Loaning, *see* Cow in a fremit l. (Like a).

Loathe(s), Loathing, *see* Better go away longing than l.; God l. aught, (When) men l. it too; Length begets l.

Loaves and fishes. (L 401)

[= material benefits rather than spiritual blessings.] **1389** WYCLIF *John* vi. 9, 26 O child is here, that hath fyue barley looues and fyue fysches. . . . ʒe seken me, not for ʒe syʒ the tokenis, but for ʒe eeten of looues, and ben fillid. **1614** BP. HALL *Recoll. Treat.* 954 If it were not for the loaves and fishes, the traine of Christ would bee lesse. **1905** G. O. TREVELYAN *Interludes* 124 A Mohammedan foundation, something between a college and a monastery. . . . It is very richly endowed, and the loaves and fishes are kept strictly among the founder's kin.

Loaves, *see also* Loaf (-ves).

Lob's (Cob's, Hob's) pound. (L 403)

[= prison, lock-up; also *fig.* an entanglement, difficulty.] **1597** E. S. *Discov. Knights of Post* B1 Knights of the Poste, Lords of lobs pound, and heires apparant to the pillory. **1639** CLARKE 188 Hee's in Cobs pound. **1663** BUTLER *Hudibras* I. iii. 910 Crowdero, whom in Irons bound, Thou basely threw'st into Lob's pound. **1796** MME. D'ARBLAY *Camilla* IV. iii What! are you all in Hob's pound? **1829** BENTHAM *Justice & Cod. Petit.* Wks. (1843) V. 494

Pass on to the dependant, when the time came for his finding himself in Lob's pound. **1895** *E. Angl. Gloss.* Lobs-pound, to be in any difficulty or perplexed state.

Lobster, *see* Runner (Look like a), quoth devil to l.

Lochaber axe, He looks like a. (A 410)

a. **1628** CARMICHAELL no. 1818. **1641** FERGUSSON no. 407 *Of fleyit*[1] *persons.* . . . **1721** KELLY 373 You look like a Lochaber Ax new come from the Grindstone. Us'd when People look sillily, demurely, foolishly, or wildly. [[1] frightened.]

Lochow, *see* Far cry to.

Lock will hold against the power of gold, No.   (L 406)

1580 LYLY *Euph. & his Eng.* ii. 71 And who is so ignorant that knoweth not, gold be a key for euery locke? **1640** HERBERT no. 317.

Lock, (*noun*), *see also* Highlandman's gun that needed l., stock, and barrel; Prayer should be l. of night; Silver key open iron l.; Stock, l., and barrel.

Locker, *see* Davy Jones's l.

Locks, (*verb*), *see* Love l. no cupboards.

Lockerby lick, A.

[= a face-blow.] [**1593**] in HUME BROWN *Hist. Scot.* (1902) II. 219 The two forces met at Dryfe Sands, near Lockerby;[1] and . . . the Johnstones gained a decisive victory. . . . From the number of face-wounds given in the battle, a 'Lockerby lick' passed into the common speech of the country. **1882** A. CUNNINGHAM *Tradl. Tales* (1887) 232 If ye lay a hand . . . on the poor demented lassie, I'se land ye a Lockerby lick. [[1] Dumfries.]

Lockington, *see* Put up your pipes and go to L.

Lockit, Bessie, *see* Rynt you witch, quoth B. L.

Locksmiths, *see* Love laughs at l.

Lodges, *see* Comes late l. ill (Who); Content l. oftener in cottages than palaces.

Lodging, *see* Kennel is l. good enough for a dog; Wine ever pays for l.

Log nor a stork, Neither a | good Jupiter.   (L 409)

[In allusion to Æsop's fable of the frogs who appealed to Jupiter for a king, and being dissatisfied with the log given them found him replaced by a stork.] **1566** J. BARTHLET *Pedegrew of Popish Heretiques* X3[v] Neyther doe the Popistes misseresemble their brother Mahomete whose religion . . . hath . . . ruled the poore sely soules, as Iupiters blocke amongst a number of frogges. **1615** T. ADAMS *England's Sickness* 95

Like the Log which Iupiter (in the Fable) threw downe to the frogs Regem petentibus, to be their king. **1620–8** FELTHAM *Resolves* (Dent) 169 I like neither a devouring Stork, nor a Jupiter's log. **1732** FULLER no. 3521. **1907** *Spectator* 16 Nov. 744 The rise of the Mahdi in 1881, and the subsequent liberation of . . . the Soudan from Egyptian rule, was only a substitution of King Stork for King Log.

Log, To sleep like a.   (L 410)

1584 WITHALS G8[v] Thou liest like a logge without life or soule. **1666** TORRIANO *Prov. Phr.* s.v. Ciocco 40 . . . To sleep soundly.

Log(s), *see also* Crooked l. straight fires.

Logic, *see* Chop l.; Law, l., and the Switzers fight for anybody.

Lombard Street to a China orange, All.

[Lombard Street, in London, has many banks.] **1752** MURPHY *Gray's Inn Journ.* No. xi 30 Dec. I'll lay all Lombard-Street to an egg-shell that it is true. **1832** MARRYAT *N. Forster* ch. 47 'All Lombard Street to a China orange, 'tis Surcœuf', replied Captain Oughton. **1848–9** LYTTON *Caxtons* IV. iii 'It is Lombard Street to a China orange', quoth Uncle Jack. 'Are the odds . . . so great?' **1962** 12 May *Evening Standard* 4 Mr. George Woodcock . . . says it is all England to a china orange that the strike will take place.

Lombard, *see also* Sick of the L. fever.

London Bridge had fewer eyes, If | it would see better.

1869 HAZLITT 246 . . . In allusion to the numerous and narrow openings for vessels.

London Bridge was built upon woolpacks. *Cf.* Salisbury cathedral. (L 416)

1607 BEAUMONT *K. Burn. P.* Induction The rearing of London Bridge upon woolsacks. **1659** *London Chaunticleers* Hazl.-Dods. xii. 341 When we kept the Whitson ale, when we danced *The Building of London Bridge upon woolpacks.* **1812** J. BRADY *Clavis Calendaria* I. 194 'That London Bridge was built upon wool-sacks'; that is, the expense of the fabric . . . about the end of the 12th century, was defrayed by an impost, . . . upon the wool brought to the metropolis.

London Bridge was made for wise men to go over, and fools to go under. (L 417)

1591 FLORIO *Second F.* 19 Wherefore were bridges made I pray you?—To goe ouer then.— Why would you haue vs goe vnder them?—Oh oh I knowe your meaning then. **1639** CLARKE 249. **1670** RAY 16 (to pass over and for fools to pass under). [LEAN I. 140 The present bridge was built in 1825. The danger to light wherries in shooting the bridge was appreciable.]

London Bridge, *see also* Good turn (One) will meet another.

London cockney, A. *Cf.* Born within the sound of Bow bell. (c 501)

[In the earliest references 'cockney' means 'a mother's darling', a 'milksop'. *Cf.* **1552** Huloet 2Z^v Playe the cockeney, delicias facere. See also Fuller, below.] **1564** BULLEIN *Dial. agst. Feuer Pest* ed. Bullen 59 [London citizen's wife at Barnet] Why, is Charcole made? I had thought all thynges had been made at London, yet I neuer see no Charcoles made there: by my trouth, I had thought that thei had growen vpon trees, and had not been made. [*Margin*] A wise cockney. **1571** J. BRIDGES *Sermon at Paul's Cross* 104 We are thoroughout all the Realme called cockneys that are borne in London, or in the sounde of Bow bell. **1600** ROWLANDS *Lett. Hum. Blood* iv. 65 I scorne ... To let a Bow-bell Cockney put me downe. **1617** MINSHEU *Ductor* s.v. *A Cockney* ..., applied only to one borne within the sound of Bow-bell, that is, within the City of London. **1617** MORYSON *Itin.* III. 53 Londiners, and all within the sound of Bow-bell, are in reproch called Cocknies, and eaters of buttered tostes. **1662** FULLER Lond. 196 ... I meet with a double sense of this word Cockeney ... I. One coaks'd or cockered, made a wanton or Nestle-cock of ... so that ... they can endure no hardship ... 2. One utterly ignorant of Husbandry ... so that they may be perswaded any thing about Rural Commodities.

London jury; A | hang half, and save half. (J 104)

1608 MIDDLETON *Trick Catch Old One* IV. v. 178 Thou that goest upon Middlesex juries, and wilt make haste to give up thy verdict because thou wilt not lose thy dinner. **1662** FULLER Lond. 195 ... as if Londoners, frequently impannelled on Juries, ... to make quick Riddance ..., acquit half, and condemn half. **1732** FULLER no. 231 (A Kentish jury).

London lickpenny. (L 228)

14.,? [*Title*] *London Lyckpeny.* [1600] **1659** DAY & CHETTLE *Blind Beggar* D2 London lick penny ... t' as lick'd me with a witness. **1602** S. ROWLANDS *Green's Ghost* i. 23 London is a lickpenie. **1662** FULLER Lond. 196 ... The Countryman coming up hither, by his own experience, will easily expound the meaning thereof. **1710–11** SWIFT *Jrnl. to Stella* 15 Jan. It has cost me three guineas to-day for a periwig. ... Well, London lickpenny; I find it true.

London, She has been at | to call a strea a 'straw', and a waw a 'wall'. (L 415)

1670 RAY 218 ... *Chesh.* This the common people use in scorn of those who having been at London are ashamed to speak their own country dialect.

London, *see also* Dunmow bacon ... L. beer; Fire of L. punishment for gluttony; Lincoln shall be hanged for L.'s sake; Lincoln was, L. is; Little L. beyond Wales; Nobody's nails can reach L.; Oxford for learning, L. for wit; Oxford knives and L. wives; Which way to L.? A poke full of plums. *See also* Clocks, Lord Mayor of London.

Londoner like, ask as much more as you will take. (L 418)

1678 RAY 349.

Lone sheep (man) is in danger of the wolf, The. (M 213. S 306)

1592 DELAMOTHE 23. **1611** COTGRAVE s.v. Homme seul The lone man is Wolues meat. **1639** CLARKE 117.

Long (*proper name*), *see* Beggar that goes by the way can't beg through L.; John (Tom) L. the carrier.

Long a giving knows not how to give, He that is. (G 129)

1640 HERBERT no. 494.

Long a widow weds with shame. (W 337)

1659 HOWELL *Brit. Prov.* 19.

Long absent, soon forgotten. *Cf.* Seldom seen. (F 596)

[*c.* 1547–53] **1565** WEVER *Lusty Juventus* C3^v By longe absence brought out of memory. [**1554**] **1565** *Wealth and Health* l. 200 Absence is cause of strangeness. *a.* **1576** WHYTHORNE 83 An old prouerb ... absens kawzeth forgetfulnes. **1611** COTGRAVE s.v. Ami Long absence alters affection. **1616** DRAXE no. 9. **1670** RAY 55 ... Parallel to this are, *Out of sight, out of mind*, and *Seldom seen, soon forgotten.* **1710** PALMER 65 Far absent soon Forgotten.

Long and lazy, little and loud; fat and fulsome, pretty and proud. (L 421)

a. **1576** WHYTHORNE 23 Hy women be layzy and low be lowd, fair be sluttish, and fowll be prowd. **1591** FLORIO *Second F.* 189 If long, she is lazy, if little, she is lowde. **1639** CLARKE 118 Long be lither, and little be loud. **1648** HERRICK *Hesper.* no. 358 Long and Lazy. That was the Proverb. Let my mistress be Lasie to others, but be long to me. **1659** HOWELL *Eng. Prov.* 10b ... *in point of women.* **1872** BLACKMORE *Maid of Sker* ch. 13 You are long enough, and lazy enough; put your hand to the bridle.

Long (short) and the short (long) of it, The. (L 419)

c. **1330** BRUNNE *Chron.* (Hearne) 222 To say longly or schorte, alle [that] armes bare. [*a.* 1567] **1571** R. EDWARDES *Damon and Pythias* l. 778 This is the short and longe. **1589** *Martin's Month's Mind* in NASHE *Wks.* Gros. I. 185 This is the short and the long, and the somme of all. **1599** SHAKES. *Hen. V* III. ii. 110 That sal I surely do, that is the breff and the long. [*a.* 1660] **1693** URQUHART *Gargantua* III. xxviii. II. 146 This is in truth, the long and the short on't. **1681** W. ROBERTSON *Phraseol. Gen.* 837b *The* LONG *and the short of a business*; Summa rei. **1837–8** DICKENS *O. Twist* ch. 20 (the short and the long).

Long as a Welsh pedigree, As.   (P 176)

1614 SIR T. OVERBURY *Characters* 'A Welchman' Above all men he loves a Herrald, and speakes pedigrees naturally.   **1615** J. STEPHENS *Essays and Characters* 'A Welsh Client' He beleeues himselfe to be a kins man of Cadwallader, though he deriues his pedegree from the dust of ninety nine generations.   **1639** R. WILLIS *Mount Tabor* 120–1 In a Towne within the Marches of Wales . . . when wee came into the parlour . . . I observed a table . . . with two columns of Pedegrees . . . with the name of the goodman of the house, as lineally descended from . . . two ancient Princes.   **1662** FULLER *Wales* 7 Any Welsh gentleman . . . can presently clime up, by the stairs of his pedigree, into princely extraction.   **1846** J. GRANT *Rom. of War* ch. 18 Señor Sancho . . . has a name as long as a Welsh pedigree.

Long as he is lither,[1] If he were as | he might thatch a house without a ladder.   (H 775)

1678 RAY *Chesh.* 257.   [1 lazy.]

Long as I live, I'll spit in my parlour, As.

1721 KELLY 53 As long as I live I'll fart at my own Fire-side.   **1732** FULLER no. 710.

Long as Meg of Westminster, As.   (M 865)

c. **1589** LYLY *Pap with a Hatchet* iii. 403.   **1590** 18 Aug. *Stationers' Register Life of Long Meg of Westminster*.   **1593** G. HARVEY *Pierce's Supererogation* (cited Deloney, ed. Mann 532).   **1662** FULLER *Westmr.* 236, . . . Applyed to persons very tall, especially if they have hop-pole heighth, wanting breadth proportionable thereunto. That such a gyant woman ever was in Westminster, cannot be proved. [A cannon in Dover Castle and a flagstone in Westminster Abbey were called after her. LEAN II. 850.]

Long a-tuning your pipes, You are as | as another would play a spring.[1]

1721 KELLY 371 . . . You are as long a setting about a thing, as another would actually do it.   [1 tune.]

Long be thy legs and short be thy life.   (L 192)

c. **1549** HEYWOOD II. vii. I4ᵛ Thy tales (quoth he) shew long heare, and short wit, wife. But long be thy legs, and short be thy lyfe.

Long beards heartless; painted hoods witless; gay coats graceless; makes England thriftless.   (B 145)

1577 HOLINSHED *Edw. III* (1587 ed.) 347a The Scots in derision . . . made a rime. . . .   **1580** STOW *Chron. of Eng., Edw. III.* 359 The Scottes made manye taunting rimes against the *English-men* . . . amongst the which was. . . .

Long, It is not how | but how well we live.   (L 378)

1574 GUEVARA *Familiar Epistles* tr. Hellowes (1584, 192) The honest care not to liue long, but well.   **1664** CODRINGTON 200 It is not how long we live, but how well we live.   **1670** RAY 16.

Long bow, To draw (pull) the.   (B 570)

[= to exaggerate, to lie.]   **1678** RAY 89 *A Lier*. He's a long-bow-man.   **1824** BYRON *Juan* xvi. i They . . . draw the long bow better now than ever.   **1853** THACKERAY *Newcomes* ch. 52 It was not much of a fib that Barnes had told. . . . But if he had recollected . . . [he] would not have pulled that unlucky long-bow.   **1908** C. M. DOUGHTY *Wand. in Arabia* I. ii. 13 Pity Mohammed had not seen Petra! he might have drawn another long-bow shot in Wady Mûsa.

Long Clawson, *see* Whores in Hose than . . . in L. C. (More).

Long day, Not a | but a good heart rids work.   (D 94)

1611 COTGRAVE s.v. Grand Not long dayes, but strong hearts, dispatch a worke.   **1640** HERBERT no. 24.

Long day that never pay, They take a.   (D 102)

1678 RAY 188.

Long foretold, long last; short notice, soon past.

1866 A. STEINMETZ *Man. of Weathercasts* 155 Old saws about the barometer.   **1889** JEROME *Three Men in Boat* ch. 5 The barometer is . . . misleading. . . . Boots . . . read out a poem which was printed over the top of the oracle, about 'Long foretold, long last; Short notice, soon past'. The fine weather never came that summer.

Long harvest of (for) a little corn, A.   (H 184)

c. **1549** HEYWOOD I. xii. E4 Surely . . . ye haue in this tyme thus worne, Made a long haruest for a little corne.   **1579** LYLY *Euph.* i 239 *Euphues* (quoth shee) you make a long haruest for a lyttle corne, and angle for the fishe that is already caught.   **1614** CAMDEN 302.   **1670** RAY 180.   **1786** *Har'st Rig* cxlii (1794) 43 Lang was the har'st and little corn!

Long (last) home, To go to one's.   (H 533)

[= the grave.]   [ECCLES. xii. 5 Man goeth to his long home.]   **1303** BRUNNE *Handl. Synne* l. 9195 And thy traueyle shalt thou sone wende, For to thy long home sone shalt thou wende.   **1573** GASCOIGNE *Dan B. of Bath* i. 112 To my long home thus my life it hasteth.   **1576** L. LEMNIUS *Touchstone of Complexions* 30 Then [at the age of 63 or 65] Age hasteneth on apace, and draweth towarde his long home. *Ibid.* 51.   **1590** H. ROBERTS *Defiance to Fortune* E2 The very remembrance of your disobedience . . . will bring his white head with sorrow to his last home. **1594** *True Trag. Richard III* l. 1638 (longest). **1662** FULLER Warwickshire 119 Some think she went her own pace to the grave, while others suspect a grain was given her, to quicken her in her journy to her long home.

Long in coming as Cotswold barley, It is as. (C 546)

1662 FULLER Glos. 353 . . . It is applied to such things as are slow but sure. The Corn, in this cold County on the Wowlds, . . . is very backward at the first; but afterwards overtakes the forwardest in the County. **1670** RAY 228 *Gloucestershire.*

Long in court, deep in hell.

1559 J. FERRARIUS *Good Ordering of a Commonwealth* tr. W. Bavande 32ᵛ This saiyng . . . true: Long in court, depe in hell.

Long jesting was never good. (J 47)

1640 HERBERT no. 694.

Long journey, In a | straw weighs. (J 77)

1640 HERBERT no. 820. **1659** HOWELL *Span. Prov.* 15 (is heavy).

Long lane (run) that never turns (has no turning), It is a. *Cf.* Runs far. (R 207)

1633 8 July *Stationers' Register* Arb. iv. 299 (ballad) Long runns that neere turnes. **1659** HOWELL *It. Prov.* 8 Every streight thing hath its turning. **1670** RAY 117 (run). **1732** FULLER no. 2863. **1778** FOOTE *Trip Calais* II. Wks. (1799) II. 355 It is a long lane that has no turning. **1827** SCOTT *Chron. Canongate* ch. 5 It is a long lane that has no turning. . . . He has sown his wild oats, . . . and has settled into a steady respectable man. **1894** LD. AVEBURY *Use of Life* iii (1904) 24 If money comes in slowly at first, do not be discouraged; it is a long lane which has no turning; . . . lay up some for a rainy day, remembering that good lanes have their turnings as well as bad ones.

Long life has long misery. (L 260)

1539 TAVERNER *Publius* C7 Oh into howe miserable thinges and full of repentaunce do men run by lyuyng longe? In a longe lyfe, do many thynges happen, that a man wolde not haue. **1597** *Politeuphuia* 183 A long lyfe, hath commonly long cares annexed with it. **1611** COTGRAVE s.v. Vivre The longer life the greater griefe. **1732** FULLER no. 3270.

Long lives a merry man as a sad, As. (M 71)

[PUB. SYRUS 438: *O vita misero longa, felici brevis.*] *c.* **1300** *Vernon MS.* E.E.T.S. 347 A Lenger liueth a glad mon then a sori. *c.* **1350** *Douce MS.* 52, no. 57 As long leuyth a mery man as a sory. *a.* **1553** UDALL *Ralph Roister D.* I. i Arb. 11 As long lyueth the mery man (they say) As doth the sory man, and longer by a

day. **1594–5** SHAKES. *L.L.L.* V. ii. 18 She might ha' been a grandam ere she died; And so may you, for a light heart lives long. **1598** *Id. 2 Hen. IV.* V. iii. 48 A merry heart lives long-a. **1602** D. LYNDSAY *Thrie Estaits* l. 106 Als lang leifis the mirrie man As the sorie for ocht he can. **1614** CAMDEN 302.

Long looked for comes at last. (L 423)

c. **1483** *Quatuor Sermones* Roxb. Cl. 53 A thynge that is long desyred at the last it comyth **1548** N. UDALL *Paraphrase* A5ᵛ The birth of your Maiestie was the more swete, because it was so long wished for, so long loked for, and so long craued ere it came. **1594–8** SHAKES. *T.S.* II. i. 325 Now is the day we long have looked for. **1608** ARMIN *Nest Ninnies* Shakes. Soc. 15 Though long lookt for comes at last, yet they shoot short that aim to hit this mark. **1655** FULLER *Ch. Hist.* II. ii (1868) I. 130 Long-looked-for-comes at last. King Edwin, almost three years a candidate-at-large of Christianity, embraceth the same. **1846** DICKENS *Bat. of Life* II A gay day . . . for us. . . . Long looked forward to, dearest, and come at last.

Long man, *see* Seldom is l. m. wise.]

Long mint, little dint. (M 983)

a. **1628** CARMICHAELL no. 104 After lang mint lidder[1] dint. *c.* **1641** FERGUSSON MS. no. 135. After long mint never Dint. **1721** KELLY 237 . . . Spoken when Men threaten much, and dare not execute. **1832** HENDERSON 129 . . . (Long attempted or threatened, little executed.) [¹ feeble.]

Long pull, a strong pull, and a pull all together, A.

1822 BYRON *Vision of Judg.* st. 1 The devils had ta'en a long, strong pull, and a pull all together, as they say at sea. **1834** MARRYAT *Jacob Faith.* ch. 12.

Long run, In (At) the.

[= in the end.] **1627** J. CARTER *Plain Exposition* (F. Hall) 117 At the long run. **1656** CROMWELL *Speech* 17 Sept. They [the discontented] must end at the interest of the Cavalier at the long run. **1804** EDGEWORTH *Contrast* ch. 9 At the long run, these fellows never thrive. **1842** MRS. CARLYLE *Lett.* I. 156 Compromises never are found to answer, I think, in the long run.

Long runs the fox as he has feet, As. (F 627)

c. **1450** HENRYSON *Mor. Fab.* 29 Aye runnes the Foxe as long as hee feete hes. **1641** FERGUSSON no. 8.

Long spoon, He should have a | that sups with the devil. (S 771)

c. **1386** CHAUCER *Sqr.'s T.* 1. 602 Therefore bihoueth hire a ful long spoon that shal ete with a feend. **1545** TAVERNER B1ᵛ He had nede to haue a longe spone that shulde eate with the deuyl. **1592–3** SHAKES. *C.E.* IV. iii. 59 Marry, he must have a long spoon that must eat with the devil. **1611** *Id. Temp.* II. ii. 90 This is a devil, and no monster: I will leave him; I have no long spoon. **1641** FERGUSSON no. 350 He should have a long shafted spoon that sups kail with the devil. **1818** SCOTT *Ht. Midl.* ch. 45 I wad hae him think twice or he mells wi' Knockdunder. He suld hae a lang-shankit spune that wad sup kail wi' the deil. **1853** TRENCH vi. 151 *He had need of a long spoon that eats with the devil* . . . men fancy . . . they can cheat the arch-cheater, . . . being sure in this to be miserably deceived. **1948** GRAHAM GREENE *Heart of the Matter* Pt. 3, ch. 1 One needs a long spoon to sup with you, Yusef.—My enemies do, Not my friends. **1966** MACMILLAN *Winds of Change* ch. 17 Having no understanding of the man [Hitler] with whom he [Chamberlain] tried to sup, he never provided himself with the necessary length of spoon.

Long standing and small offering makes poor parsons. (S 824)

1546 HEYWOOD II. ix. L3 Men saie (saied he) long standyng and small offring Maketh poore parsons. *a.* **1628** CARMICHAELL no. 1032 (a pure [= poor] preist). **1641** FERGUSSON no. 575 Lang standing, and little offering makes a poore prise. **1721** KELLY 235 Long standing, and little offering, makes a poor priest. Spoken by Hucksters, Pedlars, and the like, when they have an ill Market.

Long-tail, *see* Come cut and l. t.

Longtails, *see* Kentish L.

Long tarrying takes all the thanks away. *Cf.* He loses his thanks. (T 72)

c. **1500** *Melusine* xx. 387 Long taryeng quenchith moch the vertu of the yefte. *c.* **1526** *Dicta Sap.* B2 A benyfyte gote with great sekyng loseth a great part of the thanke. **1539** TAVERNER *Publius* A6ᵛ If thou offre thy frende the thing that he nedeth, vnasked, it is worthe double thanke. A benefite extorted by crauing hath loste a greate parte of the thanke. **1559** CATHERINE OF SUFFOLK to W. Cecil cited C. Read *Mr. Sec. Cecil* 67 A good turn quickly done is twice done and when it is so long tarried for, it loses half the grace of the benefit. **1587** BRIDGES *Defence* 1114 citing Bullinger in *Rom.* 12 That excellent saying of Seneca, in his second book *De benefic.* That is an vnthankfull good turne, that stricketh long fast between the hands of the giuer. **1616** DRAXE no. 473 He looseth his thankes that promiseth and delaieth. *a.* **1628** CARMICHAELL no. 1026. **1641** FERGUSSON no. 566. **1670** RAY 7 (as 1616). **1706** STEVENS s.v. Gracias He loses his Thanks, who promises and delays.

Long time to know the world's pulse, There needs a. (T 318)

1612 SHELTON *Quix.* III. 1. i. 105. They say well, that one must haue a long time to come to the knowledge of bodies. **1640** HERBERT no. 886.

Long tongue is a sign of a short hand, A. (T 397)

1640 HERBERT no. 251. **1659** HOWELL *Portugal Prov.* (*Span. Prov.*) 26. Ibid., *Fr. Prov.* 9. **1721**

KELLY 43 (*has*). . . . They who are lavish in their Promises are often short in their Performances.

Long-tongued wives go long with bairn. (W 385)

1670 RAY 49. **1721** KELLY 239 . . . Baubling Wives will tell every tattling Gossip that they have conceived; which makes them long expect their lying in. Apply'd to those who discover their Projects, Designs, and Intentions, long before they are put in Execution.

Long ways, long lies. (W 175)

1614 CAMDEN *Rem., Art.* (1870) 224 Some have sailed . . . as far as China, . . . to fetch the invention of guns from thence, but we know the Spanish proverb, 'Long ways, long lies'. **1659** HOWELL *Span. Prov.* 11 From long wayes, large lyes. **1699** A. BOYER *Compleat French Master* 136 Great Lyes commonly come afar off. **1706** STEVENS s.v. Via.

Longer east, the shorter west, The. (E 45)

1546 HEYWOOD I. xiii. F2 Alwaie the longer east the shorter west. **1639** CLARKE 17.

Longer forenoon, the shorter afternoon, The. (F 592)

1546 HEYWOOD I. xiii. F2.

Longer (longest) liver take all, Let the. (L 395)

c. **1565** W. WAGER *Enough is as good as a feast* B2 The longest liuer. pay all. **1577** *A merry and pleasant Prognostication* C7ᵛ For this is true and euer shall, The longest liuer shall haue all. *c.* **1594** SHAKES. *R.J.* I. v. 13 Be brisk awhile, and the longer liver take all. **1616** DRAXE no. 1233. *a.* **1628** CARMICHAELL no. 1037 (¹ bruke all). [¹ enjoy.]

Longer lives a good fellow than a dear year. (G 330)

1678 RAY 170.

Longer the worse, The.

1481 CAXTON *Reynard* ed. Arber 90 I am seke and fele me the lenger the werse. *c.* **1526** *Dicta Sap.* D4 Euer the longer the worse / that is / mennes maners degenerate dayly more and more. **1530** PALSGRAVE 858b. **1621** B. ROBINSON 8 The longer the worse, like to my old shooes.

Longer we live, the more farlies¹ we see, The. (F 60)

a. **1628** CARMICHAELL no. 1447. **1641** FERGUSSON no. 798. **1721** KELLY 313. [¹ wonders.]

Longer you look at it the less you will like it, The.

1854 SURTEES *Handley Cross* ch. 32. **1872** G. J. WHYTE-MELVILLE *Satan.* ch. 23 It's no use being shifty about it. You've got to jump, and the longer you look, the less you'll like it.

Longest at the fire soonest finds cold.

1721 KELLY 238 . . . Those who are used to Ease, Softness, and Plenty, will soon be sensible of a contrary Condition.

Longest day has an (his) end (must have an end), The. (D 90)

c. **1390** GOWER *Conf. Amantis* I. 578 Bot hou so that the dai be long. The derke nyht comth ate laste. **1580** LYLY *Euph. & his Eng.* ii. 35 The longest Summers day hath his euening. **1599** SHAKES. *J.C.* V. i. 125 But it sufficeth that the day will end. **1612–15** BP. HALL *Contempl.* XX. v (1825) II. 33 The longest day must have his evening. Good Elisha, that had lived some ninety years, . . . is now cast upon the bed of his . . . death. **1614** CAMDEN 313 (his end). **1659** HOWELL *Eng. Prov.* 10a. **1670** RAY 77 (must have an end). **1721** KELLY 337 (*will have an end*) Spoken when Men now in Power oppress us, signifying that there may be a Turn. **1841** CHAMIER *Tom Bowl.* ch. 2 The longest day will have an end, and though it's cloudy in the morning, the sun may shine bright enough at noon. *Cf.* **1848** GASKELL *Mary Barton* ch. 10 The weariest day draws to an end.

Longest night will have an end, The. *Cf.* Every day comes night. (N 164)

c. **1475** CAXTON *Hist. Troy* II. 473 Ther is no nyght so derke but that hit is surmounted wyth the day. **1504** ATKYNSON *Imit. Christ* II. viii in *Imit. Christi* 186 For after wynter foloweth somer, after the night the day. **1509** BARCLAY *Ship of Fools* ii. 319 After the day cometh the nyght So after pleasour oft comys payne. *c.* **1606** SHAKES. *M.* IV. iii. 239 The night is long that never finds the day. **1613** WITHER *Abuses* I. xvi. *Sorrow* Calmes doe the roughest stormes that are attend, And th' longest night that is will haue an end.

Long(er, est), (*adj., adv.*), see also Art is l., life is short; Barnaby bright; Broad as l.; Buchanan's almanac, l. foul l. fair; Burden makes weary bones (Too l.); Extreme will hold l. (No); Fair and sluttish l. and lazy; Farthest (L.) way about is nearest way home; God stays l. but strikes at last; Life and a day l, (All one's); Live l.; Lives l.; Never is l. day; Never l. that comes at last; Old l. (He that would be); Row to hoe (L.); St. Thomas gray; Stye (The worse) l. they lie.

Longing, see Better go away l. than loathing; Idle, (Be not) and you shall not be l.

Look at (on) the bright side.

1726 J. WESLEY *Serm. Wks.* CXXXV. vii. 468 Let us immediately recur to the bright side. **1864** J. PAYN *Lost Sir Mas.* XX No news is good news, you know, . . . We should always look upon the bright side of things. **1905** G. O. TREVELYAN *Interludes* 150 Englishmen are always inclined to look at the bright side of things, as long as there is a bright side at which to look.

Look at your corn in May, If you | you'll come weeping away; if you look at the same in June, you'll come home in another tune. (C 660)

1639 CLARKE 307 They that go to their corn in May may come weeping away: they that go in June may come back with a merry tune. **1670** RAY 41. **1846** DENHAM 46.

Look babies, To. (B 8)

[i.e. the small image of oneself reflected in the pupil of another's eye.] *c.* **1566** *The Bugbears* IV. v. 40 Some one or other lookt babies in here eie. **1580** T. CHURCHYARD *Churchyard's Chance* E1 And loe amid my laughing ¡eyen, twoo pretie babes did plaie. **1589** T. LODGE *Glaucus and Scilla* Hunt. Cl. C2ᵛ She lookes for babies in his eies. [*c.* 1589] **1594** *Id. Wounds* l. 1396 Why stand you looking babies in my face? **1599** BRETON *Wit's Will* (1860) 44 Chinning and embracing, and looking babies in one anothers eyes. **1621** BURTON *Anat. Mel.* III. ii. VI. v (1651) 576 They may kiss and coll, lye and look babies in one anothers eyes.

Look before (ere) you leap. (L 429)

c. **1350** *Douce MS.* 52, no. 150 First loke and aftirward lepe; Avyse the welle, or thow speke. **1528** TYNDALE *Obed. Chrn. Man* P.S. 304 We say, . . . 'Look ere thou leap': whose literal sense is, 'Do nothing suddenly, or without advisement'. **1546** HEYWOOD I. ii. A3ᵛ Ye may learne good cheape, In weddyng and al thing, to looke or ye leape. **1567** PAINTER (Jacobs) iii. 53 He that loketh not before he leapeth, may chaunce to stumble before he sleepeth. **1579** LYLY *Euph.* i. 319 In thinges of great importaunce, wee commonly looke before we leape. **1597** MONTGOMERIE *Cherrie & Slae* xxiv (1821) 20 Luik quhair to licht, before thou loup. **1664** BUTLER *Hudibras* II. ii. 503 (1854) I. 156 And look before you ere you leap. **1836** MARRYAT *Midsh. Easy* ch. 6 Look before you leap is an old proverb. . . . Jack . . . had pitched into a small apiary, and had upset two hives of bees.

Look daggers, To.

1622 MASSINGER & DEKKER *Virgin Martyr* IV. i. Thine eyes shoot daggers at that man. **1833** MARRYAT *P. Simple* ch. 52 Lord Privilege . . . looked daggers at me as he walked upstairs.

Look in your mouth to know how old you are, A man need not. (M 287)

[JUVENAL *Sat.* 6. 199 *Facies tua computat annos.* Your face shows your years.] **1616** WITHALS 557. **1639** CLARKE 280. **1670** RAY 188. **1721** KELLY 359 Eng. They need not look in your Mouth to know your Age.

Look nine ways, To. (W 145)

[= asquint, askew.] **1542** ERASM. tr. Udall *Apoph.* (1877) 203 Squyntied he was, and looked nyne wayes. **1649** G. DANIEL *Trinarch., Rich. II*, 326 Passion flyes Squinting, and, as wee say, Nine wayes at Thrice. **1653** *Verney Memoirs* iii (1894) 58 When I told her of your question, she looked nine waies at once, and gave you noe answer.

Look not for musk in a dog's kennel.
(M 1329)

1611 COTGRAVE s.v. Chien (ciuet). **1640** HERBERT no. 23. **1655–62** GURNALL *Chrn. in Armour* (1865) I. 468 Who would look for musk in a dog's kennel? That thou mayest sooner find there than any true sweetness . . . in unholiness.

Look not on pleasures as they come but as they go.

a. **1633** G. HERBERT 'The Church Porch' l. 458. **1707** MAPLETOFT 103.

Look on the wall, and it will not bite you.
(W 14)

1678 RAY 83 . . . Spoken in jeer to such as are bitten with mustard.

Look through the (one's) fingers (at, upon), To.
(F 243)

1481 CAXTON *Reynard* (Arber 65) How lawhe thise false subtyl shrewis that . . . teche men see thurgh their fyngres. And alle for to wynne money. **1528** TYNDALE *Obed. Chrn. Man* P.S. 169. **1532** Id. *Expos. St. Matthew* P.S. 127 They either look through the fingers, or else give thee a flap with a fox-tail, for a little money. **1549** LATIMER *4th Serm. bef. Edw. VI* P.S. 152 If the kynge . . . shoulde loke through his fingers, and wynke at it. **1691** J. WILSON *Belphegor* III. i. Enough to make a modest woman look through her fingers.

Look to a gown of gold, and you will at least get a sleeve of it.

1824 SCOTT *Redg.* Let. ii My visions of preferment, . . . are . . . capable of being realised. . . . What says my father's proverb? 'Look to a gown of gold, and you will at least get a sleeve of it.' **1859** SMILES *Self-Help* 386 He who has a high standard . . . will certainly do better than he who has none at all. 'Pluck at a gown of gold', says the Scotch proverb, 'and you may get a sleeve o't.'

Look to him, jailer; there's a frog in the stocks.
(J 31)

1678 RAY 72. **1732** FULLER no. 3274.

Look to the cow, and the sow, and the wheat mow, and all will be well enow.
(C 760)

1678 RAY 347. *Somerset.*

Look to (Mark) the end.
(E 125)

[L. *Respice finem. Gesta Rom.* ch. 103 *Quidquid agas, prudenter agas, et respice finem.*] *c.* **1300** *Cursor M.* l. 4379 For qua bigin wil ani thing He aght to thinc on the ending. *c.* **1350** *Royal MS. 8 E xvii* f. 107a Er þu do eny þing, þenk one þe ending. **1550** LATIMER *Serm. Stamford* P.S. 294 'Respice finem, mark the end'; look upon the end. The end is, all adversaries of the truth must be confounded and come to nought. **1592–3** SHAKES. *C.E.* IV. iv. 38 Mistress, *respice finem*, respect your end; or rather, . . .

'Beware the rope's end'. *c.* **1593** MARLOWE *Edw. II* II. i. 16 He is banish'd . . . Ay, for a while; but, Baldock, mark the end. **1816** SCOTT *Antiq.* ch. 8 A pedigree of a hundred links is hanging on a tenpenny tow; . . . , *respice finem—* look to your end.

Look to (in) (a person's) water, To.
(W 109)

[To scrutinize a person's conduct rigorously, in reference to the inspection of a patient's urine as a means of diagnosis.] **1377** LANGLAND *P. Pl.* B. II. 223 Thanne loured leches. and lettres thei sent, That he sholde wonye with hem . wateres to loke. **1530** TYNDALE *Practice of Prelates* P.S. 266 When one holy father had seen his water, and spied what complexion he was. **1546** HEYWOOD I. xi. E2 By my faith you come to loke in my water. **1598** SHAKES. *2 Hen. IV* I. ii. 1 Sirrah, . . . what says the doctor to my water? —He said, sir, the water itself was a good healthy water; but for the party that owed it, he might have more diseases than he knew for! **1600** ROWLANDS *Lett. Humours Blood* vi Heele looke vnto your water well enough. **1700** T. BROWN *Amusem. Ser. & Com.* Wks. (1720) III. 36 I . . . judged he had been whipping it in with the Gentlewoman before mentioned, tho' 'twas not convenient to tell him so, lest his Wife should watch his Waters more narrowly than she had done.

Look twice at (both sides of) a penny (halfpenny), To.

1824 MOIR *Mansie W.* ch. 20 He was . . . Aberdeen-awa like, and looking at two sides of a halfpenny; but . . . he behaved to me like a gentleman. **1861** READE *Cloist. & Hearth* ch. 36 Gerard . . . always looked at two sides of a penny, and he tried to purchase this mass a trifle under the usual terms. **1863** Id. *Hard Cash* ch. 12 I look twice at a penny; but she looks twice at both sides of a halfpenny before she will let him go.

Look where it is not, as well as where it is, You must.

1732 FULLER no. 5964.

Looked for, *see* Long l. f. comes at last.

Looked on me as a cow on a bastard calf, She.
(C 764)

1678 RAY 353 . . . *Somerset.* [*i.e.* coldly, suspiciously.]

Lookers-on (Standers-by) see more than players (most of the game).
(S 822)

c. **1529** PALSGRAVE (cited *Acolastus* Introd. xxxviii) It fareth between thee and me as it doth between a player at the chess and a looker on, for he that looketh on seeth many draughts that the player considereth nothing at all. **1569** DAMIANO *Play of the Chests* tr. Rowbotham A3 The bystanders . . . commonly see more then the players. **1575** T. CHURCHYARD *Chips* (Nichols *Progresses* 1823, i. 395). **1578** G. WHETSTONE *Promus and Cassandra* I2 As at Cheastes, though skylfull players play, Skyllesse vewers may see what they omyt. **1589** PUTTENHAM *Art of Poetry* (*Eliz. Crit. Essays* Gregory Smith ii. 184) No lesse then doth the looker on or beholder of a game better see into all points of auantage, then the player himselfe. *c.* **1595** BACON *Promus* no. 145 (standers by). **1597–8** *Id. Ess., Followers* Arb. 38 To take aduise of friends is euer honorable: *For lookers on many times see more then gamesters.* **1635** HOWELL *Lett.* I May (1903) II. 138 There is a true saying, that the spectator ofttimes sees more than the gamester. **1748** RICHARDSON *Clar. Harlowe* ch. 7 A stander-by may see more of the game than one that plays. **1884** J. PAYN *Canon's Ward* ch. 24 In love affairs, . . . when the love is . . . on one side, it is the looker-on who sees most of the game.

Looks as big as if he had eaten bull beef, He. (B 719)

1579 GOSSON *Ephemerides* They haue eaten bulbief. **1580** BARET *Alveary* 270 Such as haue a terrible and frowning countenance, and (as our common byword saith) which looke as though they had eaten Bulbeefe. **1670** RAY 164.

Looks as if he had neither won nor lost, He. (L 437)

1590 LODGE *Rosalynde* Hunt. Cl. 190 The shepheard stoode as though hee had neither won nor lost. **1678** RAY 257 . . . He stands as if he were mop't, in a brown study, unconcern'd. **1738** SWIFT *Dial.* I. E.L. 282.

Looks as if (though) he had sucked his dam through a hurdle, He. (D 16)

1670 RAY 170.

Looks as the wood were full of thieves, He.

1641 FERGUSSON no. 405 *Of fleyit¹ persons.* . . . [¹ frightened.]

Looks breed love. *Cf.* Love comes by looking. (L 501)

[ERASM. Ad. *Amor ex oculo*.] **1539** TAVERNER 11ᵛ Ex aspectu nascitur amor. Of syght is loue gendred. *c.* **1577** NORTHBROOKE *Treat. agst. Dicing* (1843) 89 She must needes fire some . . . According to the olde prouerbe, ex visu amor. *a.* **1579** F. MERBURY *Marr. Wit & Wisdom* 27 Ubi animus ibi oculus Where he loves there he lookes. *c.* **1587** MARLOWE I *Tamb.* II. v. 63. **1590** H. ROBERTS *Defiance to Fortune* D2 Lookes (men say) are the messengers of loue. *c.* **1594–5** SHAKES. *R.J.* I.ⁱⁱⁱ. 98 I'll look to like, if looking liking moue. **1596** *Id. M.V.* III. ii. 63 Tell me where is fancy bred? . . . It is engender'd in the eyes, With gazing fed. **1601** *Id. T.N.* I. v. 280 Methinks I feel this youth's perfections With an invisible and subtle stealth To creep in at mine eyes. **1624** J. HEWES *Perfect Survey* H4 Love doth spring vp by the Eye. **1639** CLARKE 28. **1695** RAVENSCROFT 19 Looking breeds liking.

Looks in a man's face, He that | knows not what money is in his purse. (M 455)

1609 HARWARD 86ᵛ It is hard to look a man in the face and to tell what he hath in his purse. **1616** DRAXE no. 655.

Looks not before, He that | finds himself behind. (L 433)

1640 HERBERT no. 200.

Looks not well to himself that looks not ever, He. (L 432)

1611 COTGRAVE s.v. Garder He lookes not, that still lookes not, to himselfe. **1640** HERBERT no. 835.

Looks one way and rows another, He. (W 143)

1579 GOSSON *Ephemerides Sch. Abuse*, Arb. 87 Hee shewed him selfe a cunning sculler that rowes his Bote forwarde, thoughe hee haue turned his face too the sterne. **1583** MELBANCKE *Philot.* P1ᵛ I will not double withe you in driuinge you of withe faire language, when my meaninge is nothinge more then to disappoynte my appoyntment, and so Imitate the waterman, whiche lookethe one waye, and roweth another. **1621** BURTON *Anat. Mel.* Democr. to Rdr. (1651) 29 Teach others to fast, and play the gluttons themselves; like watermen, that row one way and look another. **1650** FULLER *Pisgah-sight* 384 It is proper for Spies (like Water-men and Rope-makers) for surety sake to look one way and work another. **1655** *Id. Ch. Hist.* III. iv (1868) I. 389 The clergy looking at London, but rowing to Rome, carrying Italian hearts in English bodies. **1858** TROLLOPE *Dr. Thorne* ch. 25 No workman was ever worth his salt who looked one way while he rowed another. **1867–77** FROUDE *Short Stud.* (1890) I. 155 Bunsen . . . could not get inside the English mind. He did not know that some people go furthest and go fastest when they look one way and row the other.

Look (noun), *see also* Cheerful l. makes a feast; Friday l.; Honest l. covers faults; Ill l. among lambs; Love not at first l.; Pitiful l. asks enough; Valiant man's l.

Look(s, ed, ing), (*verb*), *see also* Ashamed to l. one in the face; Charge l. to it, (Now you have a); Fool as he l., (Not such a); John Roper's window, (To l. in at); Leeward for fine weather (L. not to); Longer you l. the less you will like; Show me not (L. not on) the meat; Trust me, but l. to thyself; Women l. in their glass (The more).

Look(s) as (or like), *see under significant words following.*

Loose in the hilts, She is. (H 472)

[= conjugally unfaithful.] *c.* **1555** *Songs and Bal. Philip and Mary* Roxb. Cl. 21, 68 For, alas! she was nat sur in the hafte. **1590** GREENE *Never Too Late* Gros. viii 199 It made me loose in the haft like a dudgin dagger. **1623** WEBSTER *Duch. of M.* II. v. Merm. 168 Read there—a sister damned: she's loose i' the hilts; Grown a notorious strumpet. **1650** HOWELL *Cotgrave's Dict.* Ep. Ded. In French *Cocu* is taken for one who's wife is loose in the hilts. **1682** VILLIERS (Dk. Buckhm.) *Chances* Wks. (1714) 136 It's no matter, she's loose i' th' Hilts, by Heaven.

Loose, *see* Better hand l. than in ill tethering; Fast and l. is no possession.

Lord, Like | like chaplain.   (L 442)

c. **1550** BALE *K. Johan* Camden Soc. 73 Lyke Lorde, lyke chaplayne.

Lord(s), *see also* Accord (No) where every man would be l.; Clouts, (A husband (l.) of); Drunk as a l.; Englishman loves a l.; Fine as a l. (l.'s bastard); Follows the L. (He that); Lady's (L.'s) heart and beggar's purse; Live (I), and l. do no more; Many l. many laws; New l. new laws; Nod from a l. breakfast for fool; Rich as a l.; Swear like a l.

Lord Mayor of London, *see* Dined as well as; Good manners to except.

Lordship, One good | is worth all his manners.[1]   (L 453)

1639 CLARKE 168. [1 manors.]

Lordship(s), *see also* Love and l. like no fellowship; Wears a whole l. on his back.

Lose a fly to catch a trout, You must. *Cf.* **Venture a small fish.**   (F 399)

1640 HERBERT no. 827.

Lose a leg rather than a life.

1607 DAY &c. *Travels of three English Brothers* Wks. (Bullen) 65 To saue the body we must loose a lim. **1732** FULLER no. 3278.

Lose a Scot, We will not.   (S 157)

1662 FULLER *Northumb.* 303. . . . That is, 'we will lose nothing, however inconsiderable soever, which we can save or recover. . . .' This proverb began in the English borders, when . . . they had little esteem of, and less affection for, a Scotchman.

Lose his goods for want of demanding them, A man may.   (M 264)

1616 DRAXE no. 192. **1670** RAY 7.

Lose in hake, What we | we shall have in herring.   (H 33)

1602 R. CAREW *Survey of Cornwall* (1769) 34 The Hakes . . . haunted the coast in great abundance; but now, being depriued of their wonted baite, are much diminished; verifying the prouerb, . . . **1639** CLARKE 17 What I lost i'th salt fish I gained i'th red herrings.

Lose nothing for asking.   (A 346)

1586 GUAZZO ii. 196 Nothing is lost for asking. **1640** HERBERT no. 968 Manie things are lost for want of asking. **1670** RAY 58. **1721** KELLY 381 You'll let nothing be tint[1] for want of craving. [1 lost.]

Lose one's labour, To.   (L 9)

[*c.* **1515**] *c.* **1530** BARCLAY *Eclog.* II. l. 1103 Should wise men suppose in court so to preuayle? Lost is their labour, their study and trauayle. **1539** VIVES *Introd. to Wisdom* D6 Thou lesest both tyme and laboure, if thou be not attente vppon suche thinges, as thou doest rede and here. **1542** H. BRINKLOW *Complaint of R. Mors* E.E.T.S. 67 All their labour is lost. **1549** T. CHALENOR *Praise of Folly* H4 [His wife] loste both hir labour and cost about it. *c.* **1566** CURIO tr. W. P. *Pasquin in a Trance* 42 He might haue gone thither, and haue lost his labour. **1579** LYLY *Euph.* i. 248 If she be a modest matrone my labour is lost. *c.* **1591-2** SHAKES. *3 Hen. VI* III. i. 32 Your labour is but lost.

Lose the droppings of his nose, He will not.   (D 619)

1564 Pleasant *Dial. of Cap and Head* (1565 ed., B7) He . . . is so hard, that he wil not leese the dropping of his nose. *c.* **1565** W. WAGER *Enough* E2. **1567** PAINTER *Pal. Pleas.* iii. 299 Vsurers . . . Who cannot spare the dropping of their nose. **1594** NASHE *Unfort. Trav.* ii. 306. **1659** HOWELL *Eng. Prov.* 12a.

Lose what you never had, You cannot.

1653 WALTON *Angler* I. v (1915) 108 He has broke all; there's half a line and a good hook lost.—Aye, and a good Trout too.—Nay, the Trout is not lost; for . . . no man can lose what he never had. **17** . . WESLEY *Sermon* XC *Wks.* vii. 41.

Lose your time, If you | you cannot get money or gain.   (T 295)

1577 N. BRETON *Wks. of a Young Wit* ed. J. Robertson 62 Who lettethe slippe conuenient tyme, is litle like to winne. **1613** [N. BRETON] *Uncasing of Machiavel's Instructions* ed. J. Robertson 155 Time was ordain'de to get and not to loose. **1616** DRAXE no. 2148 In loosing time, a man getteth no money. **1640** HERBERT no. 320.

Lose(s), losing, *see also* All covet all l.; Ambition l. many a man; Better l. jest than friend; Bleating sheep l. her bit, (A); Gain is to l. (Sometimes); Gets little thanks for l. his own; Grasp all l. all; Kernel and leap at the shell, (To l. the); Lend and l.; Lend your money, l. friend; Man may l. more in an hour than he can get in seven; Merchant that gains not, l.; Play well if you l. (It signifies nothing to); Tale never l. in telling; Win at first, l. at last.

Losers leave to speak (talk), Give.   (L 458)

1533 MORE *Wks.* (1557) 1018 Hit is an olde curtesye at the cardes perdy, to let the leser haue hys wordes. **1546** HEYWOOD II. vi. I1[v] And where reason and custome (they say) afoords, Alwaie to let the loosers haue theyr woords. **1590-1** SHAKES. *2 Hen. VI* III. i. 185 And well such losers may have leave to speak. **1592** NASHE *Pierce Pen.* i 160 I, I, weele giue loosers leauue to talke. **1592** SHAKES. *T.And.* III. i. 232 Losers will have leave To ease their stomachs

with their bitter tongues. **1655** FULLER *Ch. Hist.*
IV. i. (1868) I. 540 Give winners leave to laugh,
and losers to speak, or else both will take leave
to themselves. **1665** J. WILSON *Projectors* IV
You've saved your money, and the loser may be
allow'd the liberty of speaking. **1721** KELLY 123
Give losing Gamesters leave to talk. Suffer
Men who have had Losses and Wrongs, to express their Resentments. **1818** SCOTT *Ht. Midl.*
ch. 48 The captain, who had lost . . . at backgammon, was in the pouting mood not unusual
to losers, and which, says the proverb, must be
allowed to them.

Losers seekers, finders keepers.

1824 MOIR *Mansie W.* ch. 11 According to the
auld Scotch proverb of 'He that finds keeps,
And he that loses seeks'. **1856** C. READE
Never Too Late ch. 65 I told them we have a
proverb—'Losers seekers, finders keepers'.

Loses anything by politeness (civility), One never. *Cf.* Civility costs nothing.

1659 TORRIANO no. 224 Civility gains more then
strength of arms. **1902–4** LEAN IV. 75.

Loses by doing a good turn, One never.

1642 TORRIANO 78. **1664** CODRINGTON 207.
1670 RAY 12. **1721** KELLY 275 . . . Spoken by
them who make a Return for former Favours.

Loses his due gets not thanks, He that.
(D 635)

1640 HERBERT no. 363.

Loses his liberty loses all, Who.

c. **1430** LYDGATE *Churl & Bird* 92–5 And thowe
my cage forged were with golde, . . . I remembre
a proverb said of olde, 'Who lesethe his fredam,
in faith! he loseth all'.

Loses his thanks who promises and delays, He. *Cf.* Long tarrying takes all the thanks away. (T 95)

1616 DRAXE no. 473. **1670** RAY 7 . . . *Gratia ab
officio, quod mora tardat, abest.* **1706** STEVENS
s.v. Gracias.

Loses his wife and sixpence, He that | has lost a tester.[1] (W 360)

1611 COTGRAVE s.v. Femme (hath some losse by
the money). **1666** TORRIANO *It. Prov.* 154 no. 31
Who loseth a wife, and a farthing hath a great
loss of the farthing. **1670** RAY 49. **1678** *Id.* 58
(as 1666 and also as 1670). **1738** SWIFT Dial. I.
E.L. 291 They say, he that has lost his wife and
sixpence, has lost a tester. [1 sixpence.]

Loses indeed that loses at last, He.

1732 FULLER no. 1975.

Loses is merchant, He that | as well as he that gains. (M 888)

1640 HERBERT no. 518. **1659** HOWELL *It. Prov.* 4.

Loses nothing who keeps God for his friend, He. (N 263)

1611 COTGRAVE s.v. Perdre Hee that keepes God
to friend can nothing loose. **1640** HERBERT
no. 35 He loseth nothing that loseth not God.
1670 RAY 16.

Loss embraces shame. (L 462)

1640 HERBERT no. 603.

Loss | He that is not sensible of his | has lost nothing. (L 461)

c. **1526** *Dicta Sap.* B4 It is no domage that thou
parceyuest nat. **1576** PETTIE ii. 77 So long as I
know it not, it hurteth me not. **1604** SHAKES. *O.*
III. iii. 346 He that is robb'd, not wanting what
is stol'n, Let him not know't, and he's not
robb'd at all. **1732** FULLER no. 2186.

Loss is another man's gain, One man's. (M 337. R 136)

c. **1526** *Dicta Sap.* B2 There is no lucky fortune,
whiche chaunceth nat to anothers yll. *Ibid.* D1ᵛ
Lyghtly whan one wynneth, an other loseth.
1605–6 SHAKES. *M.* I. ii. 67 What he hath lost
noble Macbeth hath won. **1625** BACON *Ess.*
Seditions Arb. 405 Whatsoeuer is some where
gotten, is some where lost. **1666** TORRIANO *It.
Prov.* 314 no. 31 It's never for one, but that it
proves well for another. **1733** LORD MAYOR
BARBER to Swift (*Corr.* ed. Ball v. 24) Your loss
will be our gain, as the proverb says. **1890**
A. LANG ed. *Hypnerotomachia* vi. **1918** 21 Feb.
D. H. LAWRENCE *Lett.* i. 544 One man's gain is
another man's loss.

Loss(es), *see also* Better a little l.; Buy and sell
and live by l.; Fear not l. of bell more than l. of
steeple; Great l. but some profit (No); Little l.
amaze.

Lost all and found myself, I have. (A 195)

1639 CLARKE 198.

Lost all who has one cast left, He has not. (A 180)

1611 COTGRAVE s.v. Failli He hath not mist that
hath one throw to cast. **1659** HOWELL *Fr. Prov.*
15 He hath not yet lost, that hath once to throw
more. **1664** CODRINGTON 197 He hath not lost
all who hath one throw to cast. **1670** RAY 16
(as 1664). **1732** FULLER no. 1876.

Lost be for God, Let that which is.

1853 TRENCH ii. 39 The father of a family,
making his will . . . , ordained concerning a
certain cow which had strayed, . . . that, if it was
found, it should be for his children, if not found,
for God: and hence the proverb,[1] . . . arose.
[1 Spanish.]

Lost his credit, He that has | is dead to the world. (C 817)

1519 HORMAN *Vulgaria* ed. James 119 Yf a man
haue lost his credence: he is halfe vndon. **1590**
GREENE *Francesco's Fortunes* Gros. viii. 154 She

which hath crackt her credite is hanged. **1616**
DRAXE no. 1455 What is a man, when his good
name is gone? **1640** HERBERT no. 357. **1670**
RAY 6. *Ibid.* 124 Take away my good name and
take away my life.

Lost his taste, To him that has | sweet is sour. (T 75)

1576 PETTIE i. 172 The sight of meat is very
loathsome to him whose stomach is ill, or hath
already eaten his fill. **1579** LYLY *Euph.* i. 194
To the stomacke quatted with daynties all
delycates seeme quesie. **1580** *Id. Euph. & his
Eng.* ii. 101 A sick man's mouth, who can
realish nothing by the taste, not that the fault is
in the meat, but in his malady. **1616** DRAXE
no. 320. **1670** RAY 26. **1732** FULLER no. 5182
To him that has a bad Taste, sweet is bitter.

Lost (Won) in the hundred[1] will be found (lost) in the shire, What is. (H 809)

1520 WHITTINGTON *Vulg.* E.E.T.S. 93 For what
so euer thou wynnes in the shyre Thou shall
lese it in the hondreth. **1546** HEYWOOD II. ix.
K4ᵛ But towne or feelde, where most thryfte
dyd apeere, What ye wan in t' hundred ye lost in
the sheere. **1629** T. ADAMS *Serm.* (1861–2) II. 531
Some have objected . . . that . . . this sitting of
Antichrist in Rome proves them to be a true
church. But I am sure, . . . what they get in the
hundred they lose in the shire. **1662** FULLER
Northants 301 He had not one foot of land . . .
in the whole County . . . [but] had a very fair
estate elsewhere. And, as our English proverb
saith, 'What is lost in the Hundred will be found
in the Shire'; so what was lost in the shire
would be found in the Land. **1670** RAY 169
What is got in the county, is lost in the hundred.
What is got in the whole sum is lost in particular
reckonings; or . . . What is got one way, is lost
another. **1732** FULLER no. 5522 What they lose
in the Hundred they gain in the County.
[¹ subdivision of a county.]

Lost (Tint), It is not | that a friend (neighbour) gets. (F 751)

[**1558**] **1566** L. WAGER *Mary Magdalene* D4ᵛ
There is nothyng lost that is done for such a
friende. *a.* **1628** CARMICHAELL no. 904 It is no
tint that is done to freinds. **1641** FERGUSSON
no. 518 (as *a.* 1628). **1721** KELLY 198 It is no
tint, a friend gets. **1891** J. L. KIPLING *Beast &
Man* 188 'The public at large have reaped much
of the crop sown by Government for its own
army, but, . . . What a neighbour gets is not
lost'.

Lost, It is not | that comes at last.

1612 SHELTON *Quix.* IV. iv. i. 297 But it is not
lost that comes at last; I will see her, and
then all things shall be amended. **1648** HERRICK
Hesper. no. 655 Wks. (1893) II. 118 Though
long it be, yeares may repay the debt; None
loseth that, which he in time may get. **1721**
KELLY 12.

Lost, All is not | that is in danger. (A 148)

c. **1500** *Melusine* E.E.T.S. XXII. 147 All is not
yet lost that lyeth in parell. **1611** COTGRAVE

s.v. *Gesir.* **1639** CLARKE 294. **1670** RAY 117
. . . As for instance, he whose sheep die of the
rot, saves the skins and wooll. **1694** A. BOYER
Compl. Fr. Master 108 All is not lost that is
delay'd. **1721** KELLY 12 All in not tint¹ that's
in peril. . . . Our Affairs may come to a better
Effect than is now expected. [¹ lost.]

Lost that is put into a riven dish, All is. (A 143)

1611 MIDDLETON *Roaring Girl* IV. ii When we
have done our best, all's but put into a riven
dish; we are but frumped at and libelled upon.
a. **1628** CARMICHAELL no. 1842 Ye sal get your
kaill in a revin dish. **1639** CLARKE 154. All you
doe for him is put into a riven dish. **1670** RAY
137 . . . All is lost that is bestowed on an
ungrateful person.

Lost that is unsought, It is. (L 455)

1546 HEYWOOD I. xi. E1. **1659** HOWELL *Eng.
Prov.* 14a.

Lost the large coat for the hood, Oft times for sparing of a little cost a man has.

c. **1390** GOWER *Conf. Amantis* V. 4785 For
sparinge of a litel cost Fulofte time a man hath
lost The large cote for the hod.

Lost (Tint) the tongue of the trump,[1] You have.

1721 KELLY 389 . . . That is, you want the main
Thing. [¹ Jew's harp.]

Lost with an apple and won with a nut (or vice versa). (A 295)

1546 HEYWOOD I. x. C3 She is lost with an
appull, and woon with a nut. **1579** LYLY
Euph. i. 206 If he perceiue thee to be wonne with
a Nut, he will imagine that thou wilt be lost with
an Apple. [**1600**] **1659** DAY & CHETTLE *Blind
Beggar* F4 Hee's won with a Apple, and lost
again with a nut. **1623** SANDERSON *Serm.*
(1681) I. 95 Of a wavering and fickle mind; as
we say of children: won with an apple, and lost
with a nut. **1659** HOWELL *Eng. Prov.* 15b He
may be gott by an Apple, and lost by a Nutt.
1732 FULLER no. 2201.

Lost, see also All is l. that goes beside your
mouth; Better l. than found; Drop of water
in the sea, (As l. as a); Find what was
never l.; Love l., (No); Lucky John Toy, l. a
shilling; Money often l. for want of money;
Occasion l. cannot be redeemed; Tint (L.) thing
(For a) care not.

Lot, see Crook in the l. of everyone; No man
content with l.

Loth to bed, see Sick of the slothful guise.

Lottery, see Marriage is a l.

Loud as Tom of Lincoln,[1] As. (T 377)

a. **1625** J. FLETCHER *Woman's Prize* III. iv Mixt
with a learned lecture of ill language, Louder than

Tom o' Lincoln. **1662** FULLER *Lincs.* 152. . . . Tom of Lincoln may be called the Stentor (fifty lesser bells may be made out of him) of all in this County. **1818** SCOTT *Ht. Midl.* ch. 30 Madge, who is as loud as Tom of Lincoln, is somewhat still. [[1] the great cathedral bell.]

Loud one, That is a.   (O 60)

1678 RAY 89 *A great Lie.* . . .

Loud, *see also* Little and l.

Louse, Not worth a.   (L 472)

c. **1380** *Sir Ferumbras* E.E.T.S. l. 439 Him semede it nas noght worth a lous batayl with him to wage. *c.* **1492** *Selection of Carols* ed. R. Greene 53. *c.* **1540** *E.P.P.* iii. 308 Then seke an other house; This is not worth a louse. **1586** R. CROWLEY *Friar John Francis* B3 Not worth the leanest Lowse, that euer crawled in the cowle of a Franciscan Fryer. **1698** *Elegy on Death of Trade* in *Harl. Misc.* ii. 276a But, Faith, I'm scarce worth a Louse.

Louse is a man's (beggar's) companion.
(L 471)

c. **1532** *Tales* no. 24 [A servant finds a louse on the king's robe.] Oh quod the kynge, it is good lucke. For this declareth me to be a man. For that kynde of vermyne principally greueth mankynde. **1594** R. WILSON *Coblers Proph.* l. 836 What thinke ye as the Prouerb goes that beggers haue no lice? **1594** NASHE *Unfort. Trav.* ii. 226 (anie gentlemans companion). **1600–1** SHAKES. *M.W.W.* I. i. 16 The dozen white louses do become an old coat well . . . It is a familiar beast to man and signifies loue. **1616** BRETON 2 *Cross. of Prov.* B1 (Begger's). **1706** STEVENS s.v. Piojo (a Gentleman's Companion). **1736** SWIFT *Dial.* I. E.L. 279 A Louse is a Man's Companion, but a Flea is a Dog's Companion.

Louse, lice, *see also* Beggar pays benefit with a l.; Better a l. in a pot; Even hand to throw a l. in the fire; Flay a l. for skin; Nits will be l.; Nothing so crouse as a new washen l.; Rogue's wardrobe is harbour for a l.; Skin a l. and send hide to market; Sure as a l. in Pomfret; Sure as l. in bosom; Three skips of l. (Not worth).

Lout[1] so low and lift so little, I will never.

1721 KELLY 184 . . . Returns of a haughty Maid to them that tell her of an unworthy Suitor. [[1] stoop.]

Love a woman, He that does not | sucked a sow.   (W 627)

1667 L'ESTRANGE *Quevedo's Visions* (1668) v. 166 'My Officious Friend', said I, 'he that does not Love a Woman suck'd a Sow.' **1732** FULLER no. 2083. **1738** SWIFT *Dial.* I. E.L. 291 And they say he that hates woman, sucked a sow.

Love and a cough (light) cannot be hid.
(L 490. 500)

[L. *Amor tussisque non celantur.*] *c.* **1300** *Cursor M.* l. 4276 Luken luue at the end wil

kith. **1551** T. WILSON *Rule of Reason* M5[v] Loue . . . is so hote of it selfe that it must nedes breake out into flames, and shewe it selfe at one tyme, or other. **1573** SANFORD 98[v] Foure things cannot be kept close, Loue, the cough, fyre, and sorowe. **1592** DELAMOTHE 55 A perfect loue can not be disguised. **1595** R. TURNER *Garland of a Green Wit* B1[v] Loue cannot be hidden. **1600** DEKKER *Old Fort.* II. ii. 118 Age is like loue, it cannot be hid. **1601** SHAKES. *T.N.* II. i. 145 A murd'rous guilt shows not itself more soon Than love that would seem hid: love's night is noon. **1611** COTGRAVE s.v. Amour Loue, and the Cough cannot be hidden. **1640** HERBERT no. 49. **1642** TORRIANO 9 (Love, the Itch, and the Cough). **1670** RAY 47 . . . The French and Italians add to these two the itch. **1721** KELLY 242. Love and Light cannot be hid. **1737** FRANKLIN April Love, cough, and a smoke, can't well be hid. **1863** G. ELIOT *Romola* ch. 6 If there are two things not to be hidden—love and a cough—I say there is a third, and that is ignorance.

Love and be wise, One cannot (To be wise and eke to love is granted scarce to God above).   (L 558)

[PUBL. SYRUS 22 *Amare et sapere vix Deo conceditur.*] *c.* **1526** *Dicta Sap.* B1[v] To haue a sadde mynde & loue is nat in one person. **1539** TAVERNER *Publius* A5 To be in loue and to be wyse is scase graunted to god. **1553** *Precepts of Cato* (1560) T1[v]. **1579** LYLY *Euph.* i. 210 To loue and to lyue well is not graunted to Iupiter. **1580** G. HARVEY *Three Letters* (Oxford Spenser, 627), To be wise, and eke to Love, Is graunted scarce to God aboue. **1602** SHAKES. *T.C.* III. ii. 153 To be wise and love Exceeds man's might; that dwells with gods above. **1605** BACON *Adv. of Learning* II. Wks. (J. M. Robertson) 79 It is not granted to man to love and to be wise. **1605** MARSTON *Dutch Courtezan* II. ii. 104 The Gods themselues cannot be wise and love. *a.* **1612** CHARRON *Of Wisdom* tr. Lennard (1640) 239 It was impossible even for *Iupiter* himselfe to love, . . . and to be wise at one time.

Love and business teach eloquence.
(L 491)

1606 MARSTON *Fawne* v. i Love is very eloquent, makes all men good orators. **1640** HERBERT no. 704.

Love and lordship like no fellowship.
(L 495)

(1) In the sense that they brook no rivals: *c.* **1386** CHAUCER *Knight's T.* l. 1625 Ful sooth is seyd that love ne lordshipe Wol nought, his thankes, have no felaweshipe. **1545** TAVERNER Ii Loue ne lordeshyp, woll no fellashyp. **1562** J. WIGAND *De Neutralibus* F5[v] The Germanes, haue a common saying of loue: Either loue me alone, or meddle not with me at all. Allein mein, oder lass gar sein. And in England we haue an olde said sawe: Loue and Lordshippe loueth no felowship. **1591** SPENSER *M. Hubberd* 1026 But either (algates[1]) would be Lord alone; For Love and Lordship bide no paragone. **1639** CLARKE 27. **1670** RAY 46 . . . Lovers and Princes cannot endure rivals or partners. **1721** KELLY 242 Love and lordship like no marrows.[2] **1773** Vieyra s.v. Amor (never like fellowship). [[1] always. [2] partners.]

(2) In the sense that they agree not together: [OVID *Metam.* 2. 846 *Non bene conueniunt nec in una sede morantur Maiestas et Amor.* Love and high Majestie agree not well, nor will together in one bosom dwell (Sandys), of Jupiter as a bull.] **1591** ARIOSTO *Orl. Fur.* Harington XIII. 5 He that in art of loue did show his skill Saith loue and maiestie agrees but ill. **1859** LEIGH HUNT in Blunden (1930) 195, on Shelley's style, It disproves the adage of the Latin poet. Majesty and love do sit on one throne in the lofty buildings of his poetry.

Love and pease-pottage will make their way (are two dangerous things). (L 496)

1654 E. GAYTON *Pleasant Notes upon Don Quixote* 46 Love and Pease-pottage are a dangerous surfet. **1670** RAY 47 . . . Because one breaks the belly, the other the heart. **1721** KELLY 231 Love, and raw Pease, are two ill Things, the one breaks the Heart, and the other brusts the Belly. **1738** SWIFT Dial. I. E.L. 282 (are two dangerous things).

Love as in time to come you should hate, and hate as you should in time to come, love. (T 309)

[Gk. Old men, according to the counsel of Bias, καὶ φιλοῦσιν ὡς μισήσοντες καὶ μισοῦσιν ὡς φιλήσοντες, ARIST. *Rhet.* 2. 13.4, both love as if they were going to hate, and hate as if they were going to love. L. PUBL. SYRUS 245 *Ita amicum habeas, posse ut facile fieri hune inimicum putes.* Regard your friend as if you thought that he might easily become your enemy.] **1481** CAXTON *Reynard* 29, 75 A man shal loue his frende by mesure and not his enemye hate ouermoche. **1539** TAVERNER 31 *Ama tanquam osurus, oderis tanquam amaturus.* Loue as in tyme to come thou shuldest hate, & hate as thou shuldest in tyme to come loue. **1592** DELAMOTHE 17. **1605** BACON *Adv. Learn.* II. xxiii (1900) 245 That ancient precept of Bias, construed not to any point of perfidiousness but only to caution and moderation, *Et ama tanquam inimicus futurus, et odi tanquam amaturus.* **1625** *Id. Apoph.* Wks. (Chandos) 359 Bias gave in precept, 'Love as if you should hereafter hate: and hate as if you should hereafter love'. **1651** HERBERT no. 1126 We must love as looking one day to hate. **1844** KINGLAKE *Eothen* ch. 25 Treat your friend, says the proverb, as though he were one day to become your enemy, and your enemy as though he were one day to become your friend.

Love as there is between the old cow and the haystack, As much.

1738 SWIFT Dial. III. E.L. 320.

Love asks faith, and faith (asks) firmness. (L 497)

1640 HERBERT no. 544. **1670** RAY 16. *Ital.*

Love at the door and leave at the hatch, To. (D 562)

1678 RAY 258. **1732** FULLER no. 5200 To love the Door and leave the Hatch.

Love begets love.

[L. *Amor gignit amorem.*] **1648** HERRICK *Hesper.* no. 47. Wks. (1900) II. 51 Love love begets; then never be Unsoft to him who's smooth to thee. **1812** E. NARES *I'll Consider of It* iii. 82 'Love' says the proverb, 'produces love'. **1909** A. MACLAREN *Ephesians* 275 Love begets love, and . . . if a man loves God, then that glowing beam will glow whether it is turned to earth or turned to heaven.

Love being jealous, makes a good eye look asquint. (L 498)

1591 FLORIO *Second F.* 83 To much loue makes a sound eye oftentimes to see a misse. **1640** HERBERT no. 543 Love makes a good eye squint. **1670** RAY 16.

Love best, Whom we | to them we can say least. (L 165)

1576 PETTIE ii. 29 As I have heard, those that love most speak least. **1594** SHAKES. *T.G.V.* I. ii. 32 They love least that let men know their love. **1595** *Id. M.N.D.* V. i. 104 Love, therefore, and tongue-tied simplicity In least speak most, to my capacity. **1598–9** *Id. M.A.* II. i. 275 Silence is the perfectest herald of joy. I were but little happy, if I could say how much. Lady, as you are mine, I am yours. **1605–6** *Id. K.L.* I. i. 61 What shall Cordelia speak? Love, and be silent. **1670** RAY 47.

Love cannot be compelled. (L 499)

c. **1390** CHAUCER *Franklin's T.* l. 36 Love wol nat ben constreyned by maistrye. *a.* **1534** J. HEYWOOD *Love* D1 Wyll wyll not be Forced in loue. **1539** TAVERNER *Publius* A4 Loue can not be wroung out, but fall away it may . . . sodenly and perforce thou canst not expelle it, but by lytle and lytle it may slyde awaye. **1590** SPENSER *F.Q.* III. i. 25 Ne may loue be compeld by maisterie. **1591** LYLY *Endym.* v. iii. 231 I will not commaund loue for it cannot be enforced: let me entreat it. **1592** SHAKES. *T.G.V.* V. ii. 7 Love will not be spurr'd to what it loathes. *Ibid.* V. iv. 57 I'll . . . love you 'gainst the nature of love,—force ye. **1621** BURTON *Anat. Mel.* III. ii. VI. v. (1651) 577 You must consider that *Amor cogi non potest*, love cannot be compelled, they must affect as they may.

Love comes as goes, As good. (L 475)

c. **1470** HENRYSON *Mor. Fab.* III. xvii in Harvey Wood 512 The prouerb sayis 'als gude lufe cummis as gais'. [*c.* 1535] **1602** LINDSAY *Three Estates* l. 1726.

Love comes in at the window and goes out at the door. (L 502)

1611 GRUTER 181. **1614** CAMDEN 309. **1670** RAY 47.

Love covers many infirmities. (L 503)

[I PET. iv. 8: Charity shall cover the multitude of sins.] *c.* **1607** MIDDLETON *Trick to Catch* II. i. 50 Love covers faults, you know. *c.* **1641** FERGUSSON MS. no. 974. **1645** J. MARSH *Marsh his*

Mickle Monument N4 Loue couers ev'ry fault. **1666** TORRIANO 226, note 197 Love covers a multitude of faults.

Love dancing well that dance among thorns, They. (D 26)

1623 CAMDEN 279 (will dance). **1670** RAY 77.

Love does much, money does everything (more). (L 504)

[Fr. **1612** GRUTER *Floril.* III. 186 Amour peut moult; argent peut tout. Sp. *c.* **1627** CORREAS *Vocab.* (1906) 68 Amor faz molto, argen faz todo.] *c.* **1534** GILLES DUWES 1048 Love dothe moche. **1584** GREENE *Morando* Pt. I. iii. 61. **1593** J. ELIOT *Ortho-Epia Gallica* ed. J. Lindsay 58 Loue doth much, and monie doth all. **1666** TORRIANO *It. Prov.* 9 no. 18 Love can do much, but gold can do more. **1732** FULLER no. 3286.

Love expels another, One. (L 538)

1577 GRANGE *Gold. Aphroditis* E1 Sith Socrates vs byd deuide one Venus into two, In two likewise Dan Cupid God, loue tormentes to abate. **1579** LYLY *Euph.* i. 255. **1624** BURTON *Anat. Mel.* III. ii. v. ii. (1638) 551 Driue out one loue with another . . . one loue driues out another. **1666** TORRIANO *It. Prov.* 10 no. 36.

Love fails, Where | we espy all faults. *Cf.* Faults are thick where love is thin. (L 550)

1659 HOWELL *Brit. Prov.* 5. **1670** RAY 16.

Love his house (the kirk) well, and yet not ride on the ridge,[1] A man may. (M 266)

1546 HEYWOOD II. iv. G2ᵛ. **1553** T. WILSON *Arte of Rhet.* (1580) 192 A man maie love his house well, and yet not ride vpon the ridge. **1614** CAMDEN 302. **1721** KELLY 37 (the kirk) . . . A Man may love a Thing, or Person, very well, and yet not show too much Fondness. **1738** SWIFT Dial. II. E.L. 314 A man may love his house very well without riding on the ridge. **1824** SCOTT *Redg.* ch. 13 One may love the Kirk, and yet not ride on the rigging of it; and one may love the king, and yet not be cramming him eternally down the throat of . . . folk that may . . . like another king better. **1853** TRENCH iv. 76 *A man may love his house well, without riding on the ridge;* it is enough for a wise man to know what is precious to himself, without . . . evermore proclaiming it to the world. **1857** DEAN RAMSAY *Remin.* v. (1911) 202 *He rides on the riggin o' the kirk.* The rigging being the top of the roof, the proverb used to be applied to those who carried their zeal for church matters to the extreme point. [¹ top of the roof.]

Love his little finger more than thy whole body, I. (F 227)

1546 HEYWOOD II. v. H3 He loueth hir better at the sole of the foote, Than euer he loued me at the herte roote. **1659** HOWELL *Eng. Prov.* 15a.

Love in his breast, He that has | has spurs in his sides. (L 481)

1605–6 SHAKES. *M.* I. vi. 22 But he rides well, And his great love, sharp as his spur, hath holp him To his home before us. **1640** HERBERT no. 426. **1659** N. R. 56 (on his breast hath Spurres on his sides). **1659** HOWELL *It. Prov.* 2 (a spur in his flank).

Love is a sweet torment (bitter-sweet). (L 505a)

1533 HEYWOOD *Love* C1ᵛ Loue . . . drynketh bytter swete. **1580** LYLY *Euph. & his Eng.* ii. 80 You see what Loue is . . . A paine full of pleasure, a ioye replenished with misery. **1586** *Id. Endym.* v. ii. 13 Viandes, some sweete and some sowre; which proueth loue to bee, as it was saide of in olde yeeres, *Dulce venenum.* **1616** DRAXE no. 1310. *a.* **1637** JONSON *Underwoods* viii. 197 Love's a bitter-sweet.

Love is blind. (L 506)

c. **1386** CHAUCER *Merch. T.* l. 1598 For love is blynd al day, and may nat see. *c.* **1390** GOWER *Conf. Amantis* i. 47 ffor loue is blind and may noght se. **1583** MELBANCKE *Philotimus* G2 Loue is blind. **1594** SHAKES. *T.G.V.* II. i. 61 If you love her you cannot see her—Why?—Because Love is blind. *c.* **1595** *Id. R.J.* II. i. 33 If love be blind, love cannot hit the mark. *Ibid.* III. ii. 9 If love be blind, It best agrees with night. **1596** *Id. M.V.* II. vi. 36 But love is blind, and lovers cannot see The pretty follies that themselves commit. **1599** *Id. Hen. V* V. ii. 295 Yet they [maids] do wink and yield, as love is blind and enforces. **1855** G. BRIMLEY *Ess.,* 'Tennyson' (1882) 52 There is profound beauty and truth in the allegory that represents love as a blind child.

Love is blind, Though | yet 'tis not for want of eyes.

1732 FULLER no. 5004.

Love is foul, No | nor prison fair. (L 545)

1592 DELAMOTHE 17. **1611** DAVIES no. 215 There was never fair prison nor love with foul face. **1640** HERBERT no. 829.

Love is free.

c. **1386** CHAUCER *Knight's T.* l. 1606 Thynk wel that love is fre! And I wol love hire maugree al thy myght.

Love is full of fear (trouble). (L 507)

[ov. *Her.* l. 12 *Res est solliciti plena timoris amor.*] *c.* **1374** CHAUCER *Troilus* Bk. 4, l. 1644 For I am evere a-gast, for-why men rede That love is thyng ay ful of bisy drede. **1578** *Susanna* l. 201 Love is full of feare. **1591** ARIOSTO *Orl. Fur.* Harington XLVI. 97 Loue is euer fearfull. **1592–3** SHAKES. *V. & A.* l. 1021 Fie, fie, fond love! thou art so full of fear. **1599** PORTER *Angry Wom. Abing.* l. 2570 (feares). **1616** DRAXE no. 1322 (trouble).

Love is lawless.   (L 508)

c. **1380** CHAUCER *Troilus* Bk. 4, l. 618 Thorugh love is broken al day every lawe. *c.* **1386** *Id. Knights T.* ll. 1163-6 Wostow nat wel the olde clerkes sawe,[1] That who shal yeve a lovere any lawe; Love is a grettor lawe, by my pan, Than may be yeve of any erthely man? *c.* **1390** GOWER *Conf. Amantis* I. 18 For loves lawe is out of reule. **1576** PETTIE i. 177 If . . . love had law. **1579** LYLY *Euph.* i. 228 As loue knoweth no lawes. **1581** RICH *Farewell to Militarie Prof.* Shakes. Soc. 131 As love is without lawe, so it is without respect, either of friende or foe. **1639** CLARKE 27. **1700** DRYDEN *Pal. & Arcite* I. 326 (Globe) 519 And knowst thou not, no law is made for love? [[1] BOETHIUS, *De Consolatione Philosophiae*, lib. III. met. xii. 47 *Quis legem det amantibus? Maior lex amor est sibi.*]

Love is never without jealousy.   (L 510)

1576 PETTIE ii. 102 Love, they say, is light of belief, and jealousy is grounded upon love. **1592-3** SHAKES. *V. & A.* l. 1137 It [love] shall be waited on with jealousy. **1594** *Id. T.G.V.* II. iv. 174 For love, thou know'st, is full of jealousy. **1603** N. BRETON *Pkt. Mad Lett.* Wks. (1879) II. 21 I perceive it is true, . . . that love is not without jealousy. **1721** KELLY 241 . . . Lat. *zelotypiam parit amor.* **1732** FULLER no. 4731 The Reward of Love is Jealousy. **1837** TH. HOOK *Jack Brag* ch. 3 None who have not felt jealousy— and, since there never can be love without it, who has not?

Love is no lack, In.   (L 485)

c. **1400** *Mirk's Festial* E.E.T.S. 165 For loue haþe no lake. **1546** HEYWOOD I. iv. BI One shewth me openly in loue is no lacke. **1593** *Tell-trothes New-Yeares Gift* (1876) 7 Contentment in loue . . . according to the saying, *Loue hath no lacke.* **1614** CAMDEN 308. **1650** BROME *Jov. Crew* III. (1708) 36. That's a most lying proverb that says, Where love is there's no lack: I am faint, and cannot travel further without meat. **1721** KELLY 240 Love has no lack, if the Dame was ne'er so black.

Love is not found in the market.
(L 511)

1640 HERBERT no. 401. **1642** TORRIANO 9.

Love is sweet in the beginning but sour in the ending.   (L 513)

1579 LYLY *Euph.* i. 248 Though the beginning of loue bring delyght, the ende bringeth destruction. **1592-3** SHAKES. *V. & A.* l. 1138 It [love] shall . . . Find sweet beginning, but unsavoury end. **1616** DRAXE no. 1309.

Love is the fruit of idleness.

1540 TAVERNER *Flores Sententiarum* Amor ociosorium est negotium Loue is the busyness of loyterers. [**1551**] **1584** W. BALDWIN *Beware the Cat* D8 Loue is loiterers occupation. **1647** *Countryman's New Commonwealth* 21 Love (in Iamblicus sensure) is the fruit of idlenesse. **1748** SMOLLETT *Rod. Random* ch. 64.

Love is the loadstone of love.   (L 514)

1594-5 SHAKES. *R.J.* II. ii. 157 Love goes toward love. **1666** TORRIANO *It. Prov.* 10 no. 22 (is wont to be). **1732** FULLER no. 3288.

Love is the true price (reward) of love.
(L 515)

c. **1250** *Ancrene Wisse* ed. M. Day E.E.T.S. 225 1952 181 Me sulleþ wel luue uor luue (One fitly sells love for love). *c.* **1420** *Twenty-six Poems* E.E.T.S. 76 Loue for loue is euenest boughte. **1539** VIVES *Introd. to Wisdom* II[v] The rediest waye to be loued is fyrste to loue. For loue is allured by nothyng so moche as by loue. **1569** E. FENTON *Wonders of Nature* 66 Loue . . . can not be payed but wyth loue. **1640** HERBERT no. 540. **1700** DRYDEN *Pal. & Arcite* II. 373 (Globe) 533 For 'tis their maxim, Love is love's reward. **1852** E. FITZGERALD *Polonius* ch. 19 Healthy, happy English labourers . . . Not, however, to be bought wholly by money wages—'Love is the true price of love.'

Love is, Where | there is faith. (Where there is no trust there is no love).
(L 551)

a. **1536** R. *Hill's Commonpl. Bk.* E.E.T.S. 56, 47 An old said sawe . . . Wher is lytyll love ther is lytill tryste. **16th c.** *Balliol, Oxf.* 346 in *Early Eng. Carols* 235 Wher is lytyll love, ther is lytill tryste. **1586** PETTIE ii. 201 According to the common saying, where love is there is faith. **1599** CHAPMAN *Hum. Day's Mirth* ed. Parrott xiv. 148, 93 Where there is no trust, there is no love. **1639** CLARKE 90 They never love us, whom we mistrust.

Love is without reason (law).   (L 517)

1509 BARCLAY *Ship of Fools* i. 81 He that louyth is voyde of all reason. **1581** B. RICH *Farewell to Militarie Prof.* Shakes. Soc. 191 Love is without lawe, so it maketh the pacientes to bee as utterly voide of reason. **1595** SHAKES. *M.N.D.* III. i. 132 Reason and love keep little company nowadays. **1597** *Politeuphuia* 15[v] Love is without law, and therefore aboue law. **1600-1** SHAKES. *M.W.W.* II. i. 5 Though Love use Reason for his precision, he admits him not for his counsellor. **1616** DRAXE no. 1316 Loue an vnruly passion.

Love lasts as long as money endures.

1474 CAXTON *Chesse* III. iii. Hereof men say a comyn proverbe in englond, that loue lasteth as longe as the money endurith.

Love laughs at locksmiths.

1592-3 SHAKES. *V. & A.* l. 576 Were beauty under twenty locks kept fast, Yet love breaks through and picks them all at last. **1803** C. COLMAN (Jun.) *Love Laughs at Locksmiths* [Title]. **1877** E. WALFORD *Tales of Our Gt. Fam.* (1890) 261 Dorothy [Vernon] was . . . Kept almost a prisoner . . . Love, however, laughs at locksmiths.

Love like chick, They.   (C 286)

[*Chick* = a term of endearment.] **1648** HERRICK *Hesper., For Duke of Yorke* 8 And so dresse him up with love, As to be the chick of Jove. **1678** RAY 347. *Somerset.*

Love like pig and pie (pudding), They.

1621 BURTON *Anat. Mel.* III. ii. III. iii. (1651) 478 If she be rich, . . . they love her dearly, like pig and pye, and are ready to hang themselves if they may not have her. **1678** RAY 349 I love thee like pudding, if thou wert pie I'de eat thee. **1738** SWIFT *Dial.* II. E.L. 305 I love him like pie, I'd rather the devil had him than I.

Love like the first love, No. (L 478)

a. **1487** *Thewis of Gd. Women* l. 156 The fyrst luf ay be lowyt best. **1576** PATRICIUS *Civil Policy* tr. R. Robinson L3 First loue is most steadfast. *c.* **1604** T. HEYWOOD *Wise Woman of H.* V. 352 First loue and best beloued. **1606** G. NEWTON *Sermon of Nobility* A3ᵛ First affections makes deep impressions. **1659** N. R. 111 The first love is the fastest. **1659** HOWELL *Fr. Prov.* 22 There is no love like to the first.

Love lives in cottages as well as in courts. *Cf.* Content lodges. (L 519)

1590 LODGE *Rosalynde* Hunt. Cl. 95 Loue lurkes assoone about a Sheepcoate as a Pallaice. **1591** ARIOSTO *Orl. Fur.* Harington XIV. 52 Curtesie oftimes in simple bowres Is found as great as in the stately towres. **1670** RAY 16. **1721** KELLY 236 . . . Conjugal Love much more, for they who live in Cottages . . . seldom marry for Interest, Wealth, or Court Favour.

Love locks no cupboards. (L 520)

1639 CLARKE 26.

Love lost between them, There is no. (L 544)

(*a*) Their affection is mutual. *a.* **1592** *Fair Em* l. 1443 Nor was there any loue betweene vs lost, But that I held the same in high regard. *c.* **1640** R. DAVENPORT *Surv. Sci.* Wks. (Bullen 1890) 327 Oh my sweete! Sure there is no loue lost when you two meete. **1823** LAMB *Elia* Ser. II. *New Year's Coming of Age, Shrove Tuesday* was helping the *Second of September* . . . which courtesy the latter returned . . .—so that there was no love lost for that matter. (*b*) They have no love for each other. *c.* **1609** MIDDLETON *The Witch* IV. iii. 10 I am resolu'd There's no hate lost betweene vs: for I know She do's not love me now, but painefully. **1620** SHELTON *Quix.* II. xxii. ii. 335 'There's no love lost', quoth Sancho, 'for she speaks ill of me too when she list.' ?**1622** J. TAYLOR (Water-P.) *Trav. Twelve-pence* Wks. (1630) I. 71 But there's no great loue lost 'twixt them and mee, We keepe asunder and so best agree. **1889** T. A. TROLLOPE *What I remember* III. 91 Between Italian and French radicals there is really no love lost.

Love makes a wit of the fool.

1624 BURTON *Anat. Mel.* III. ii. III. iii. I4 As it [love] makes wisemen fooles, so many times it makes fooles become wise. **1774** C. DIBDIN *Quaker* I. viii. According unto the proverb, love maketh a wit of the fool.

Love makes all hard hearts gentle. (L 521)

1584 WITHALS N6ᵛ Hard harts are broken at leastwise bowde, By soft intreating, which is alowde. **1640** HERBERT no. 542.

Love makes one fit for any work. (L 523)

1640 HERBERT no. 646.

Love makes the world go round.

[JACOPONE DA TODI *Cielo e terra per te [amor] si conduce.* DANTE, *Paradiso* fin. Love . . . that moves the sun in heaven and all the stars (Cary).] **1656** COWLEY *David.* 'Tis thou that mov'st the world through every part. **1712** BLACKMORE *Creation* [Refers the belief to Aristotle.] **1865** DODGSON *Alice in W.* ch. 9. **1882** GILBERT *Iolanthe* In for a penny, in for a pound, 'Tis love that makes the world go round.

Love me for little that hate me for naught, They.

1813 RAY *Scot. Prov.* 310.

Love me, If you | kythe¹ that.

1721 KELLY 187 . . . If you have a Value for me, show it by your Deeds. When one professeth Kindness for another, he will Answer, *What says the Bird?* alledging that there is a Bird whose Note is *Kythe that.* [¹ make it appear.]

Love me little, (and) love me long. (L 559)

1546 HEYWOOD II. ii. G1 Old wise folke saie: loue me lyttle, loue me long. *a.* **1548** HALL *Chron.* (1809) 444 The olde Proverbe love me little and love me longe. *c.* **1595** SHAKES. *R.J.* II. vi. 14 Therefore love moderately; long love doth so. **1629** T. ADAMS *Serm.* (1861–2) II. 418 Men cannot brook poor friends. This inconstant charity is hateful, as our English phrase premonisheth: 'Love me little and love me long'. **1721** KELLY 229 . . . A Dissuasive from shewing too much, and too sudden Kindness. **1907** *Times Lit. Sup.* 8 Mar. Mrs. Bellew is a lady who cannot love either little or long. She . . . tires very quickly of the men who are irresistibly drawn to her.

Love me, love my dog. (D 496)

[*a.* **1153** ST. BERNARD *Serm., In Festo S. Mich.*, iii. *Qui me amat, amat et canem meum.*] *c.* **1480** *Early Miscell.* Warton Cl. 62 He that lovythe me lovythe my hound. **1546** HEYWOOD II. ix. K4ᵛ Ye haue bene so veraie a hog, To my frends. What man, loue me, loue my dog. **1612** CHAPMAN *Widow's Tears* I. ii Love me? love my dog.—I am bound to that by the proverb, madam. **1692** L'ESTRANGE *Aesop's Fab.* cvi. (1738) 122 . . . For there are certain decencies of respect due to the servant for the master's sake. **1826** LAMB *Pop. Fallacies* Wks. (1898) 231 THAT YOU MUST LOVE ME, AND LOVE MY DOG . . . We could never yet form a friendship . . . without the intervention of some third anomaly, . . .—the understood *dog* in the proverb.

Love most are least set by, They who. (L 561)

1659 HOWELL *Eng. Prov.* 12b. **1670** RAY 16.

Love needs no teaching. (L 524)

a. **1618** RALEIGH *Rem.* (1664) 35 Love needs no teaching.

Love not at the first look (Love at first sight).   (L 426)

[*a.* 1593] 1598 MARLOWE *Hero & L.* I. 174 Where both deliberate, the love is slight; Who ever lov'd, that lov'd not at first sight? 1599 SHAKES. *A.Y.* III. v. 81 'Who ever lov'd that lov'd not at first sight?' 1611 *Id. Temp.* I. ii. 440 At the first sight They have chang'd eyes. 1639 CLARKE 28.

Love of lads and fire of chats[1] is soon in and soon out.   (L 526)

c. 1460 *Good Wyfe wold a Pylgr.* in *Q. Eliz. Acad.* E.E.T.S. 41 A fyre of sponys, and louve of gromis, Full soun woll be att a nende. 1670 RAY 46 *Derbyshire.* [[1] chips.]

Love of money and the love of learning rarely meet, The.

1651 HERBERT no. 1168.

Love of the wicked is more dangerous than their hatred, The.

1732 FULLER no. 4636.

Love or money, For.   (L 484)

a. 1561 CAVENDISH *Wolsey* E.E.T.S. 68. 8–9 The fynnest vyandes that they cowld gett other for mony or frendshyppe. *c.* 1566 C. A. CURIO *Pasquin in a Trance* tr. W.P. 69 They were treating howe they might bring Germany into the lappe of the Romish Church, eyther for loue, money, or by force. 1590 C. S. *Right Relig.* 18 Then should not men eyther for loue or money have pardons. 1712 SWIFT *Jrnl. to Stella* 7 Aug. No more ghosts now for love or money. 1801 EDGEWORTH *Cas. Rackrent* (1890) 13 Many gentlemen . . . made it their choice . . . when there was no room to be had for love or money, to sleep in the chicken-house.

Love puts in, When | friendship is gone.   (L 549)

1576 PETTIE ii. 96 Where love leadeth . . . no friend is forced of. 1579 LYLY *Euph.* i. 209 Where loue beareth sway, friendshippe can haue no shew. 1592 SHAKES. *T.G.V.* V. iv. 54 In love Who respects friend? 1598–9 *Id. M.A.* II. i. 182 Friendship is constant in all other things Save in office and affairs of love. *a.* 1625 BEAUM. & FL. *Lovers' Progress* I. i.

Love, Next to | quietness.   (L 536)

1678 RAY 194.

Love rules his kingdom without a sword.   (L 528)

1640 HERBERT no. 541.   1834 EDGEWORTH *Helen* ch. 6 What a pretty proverb that was, . . .—'Love rules his kingdom without a sword.'

Love the babe for her that bare it. (B 5)

1639 CLARKE 285.

Love the boll, If you | you cannot hate the branches. *Cf.* Loves the tree.
                                                       (B 508)

1639 CLARKE 285.

Love (Worship) the ground he (she) treads on, To.   (G 468)

c. 1529 *Calisto and Melibea* l. 442 Yet worship I the ground that thou gost on. *c.* 1598 DELONEY 2 *Gentle Craft* ed. Mann 195 (love). *c.* 1612 BEAUM. & FL. *Scornf. Lady* V. i. 'Tis a shame you should use a poor Gentlewoman so untowardly; she loves the ground you tread on. 1856 DICKENS, &c. *Wreck Golden Mary* ii. 19 I worshipped the very ground she walked on! 1889 R. L. STEVENSON *Master of Ball.* ch. 2 Loving, as folks say, the very ground she trod on.

Love to a father's, No.   (L 537)

1640 HERBERT no. 121.

Love to hear well of themselves, Men.
                                                       (M 551)

1639 CLARKE 12.

Love too much that die for love, They.
                                                       (L 546)

1611 COTGRAVE s.v. Mourir.   1670 RAY 16.

Love what nobody else loves, I.

1738 SWIFT *Dial.* II. E.L. 299 Prithee, Tom, send me the two legs . . . of that pigeon; for, you must know, I love what nobody else loves.

Love will find a way.   (L 531)

1625 BACON *Essay* 'Of Love' Love can finde entrance, not only into an open Heart; but also into a Heart well fortified; if watch be not well kept. *c.* 1598 DELONEY 1 *Gentle Craft* ed. Mann 136 Thus loue you see, can finde a way, To make both Men and Maids obey. 1661 T. B. *Love Will Find out the Way* [Title]. *a.* 1765 PERCY *Reliques* III. iii. (1857) 517 Over the mountains, And over the waves; . . . Love will find out the way.

Love will go through stone walls.
                                                       (L 532)

1594–5 SHAKES. *R.J.* II. ii. 67 Stony limits cannot hold love out. 1616 BRETON 2 *Crossing* B3ᵛ.

Love without end has no end.   (L 533)

1625 BACON *Apoph.* Wks. (Chandos) 358 There is a Spanish adage, 'Love without end hath no end': meaning, that if it were begun not upon particular ends it would last. 1651 HERBERT no. 1160 . . . says the Spaniard: (meaning, if it were not begun on particular ends, it would last).

Love your friend, but look to yourself. *Cf.* See your friend.

1721 KELLY 238.

Love your friend with his fault. (F 710)

1539 TAVERNER 40 Mores amici noueris, non oderis. Know the fascions of thy frende, but hate them not. **1581** GUAZZO i. 104 According to the saying, we must love a freend with his imperfection. **1650** JER. TAYLOR *Holy Liv.* II. iv. (1850) 78 Cyrus, . . . amongst his equals in age, . . . would never play at any sport . . . in which he knew himself more excellent than they. Ama l'amico tuo con il difetto suo. **1852** E. FITZGERALD *Polonius* ch. 104 A modern Greek proverb says, 'Love your friend with his foible'. **1853** TRENCH iii. 49 The Latin proverb, Mores amici novens, non oderis [see HORACE, *Sat.* I. 3. 24–93] . . . finds its grateful equivalent in the Italian, Ama l'amico tuo con il difetto suo (*Love your friend with his fault*).

Love your neighbour, yet pull not down your hedge. (N 109)

1640 HERBERT no. 141. **1761** A. MURPHY *The Citizen* I. ii. You have taught me to be cautious in this wide world. Love your neighbour, but don't pull down your hedge. **1889** MRS. OLIPHANT *Neighb. on Green* ch. 1 They were so friendly that it was once proposed to cut it down, . . . but . . . the end of it was that the hedge remained.

Loved mutton well that licked where the ewe lay, He. *Cf.* Loves well sheep's flesh. (M 1339)

a. **1628** CARMICHAELL no. 726. **1721** KELLY 125 . . . Spoken to them who will sip the bottom of a Glass where good Liquor was, or scrape a plate, after good Meat. **1816** SCOTT *Antiq.* ch. 44 That German devil was glowering at the lid of the kist (they liked mutton weel that licket whare the yowe lay).

Love's (Lover's)-knot, A true. (L 571)

1565 OSORIUS *Pearl for Princes* tr. R. Shacklock 43 The holy ordynaunces which Christ hath ordeined . . . with the which we haue fastened our selues vnto hym as it were with a true loue knott. **1583** MELBANCKE D1ᵛ Frendships . . . knitt with a true-loues knot made of siluer copper. **1588** T. CHURCHYARD *A Spark of Friendship* Nichols *Progresses* 1823, ii. 589 Friendship is (without comparison) the only true-love-knot, that knits, in conjunction, thousands together. **1592** SHAKES. *T.G.V.* II. vii. 45 I'll knit it [hair] up in silken strings With twenty odd-conceited truelove knots. [1603] **1631** CHETTLE *Hoffman* l. 1442 I wrought it in a sampler, 'Twas heart in hand, and true loues knots and words. **1639** CLARKE 320 (The true). **1651** H. OXINDEN to K. Oxinden *Oxinden and Peyton Letters 1642–1670* ed. D. Gardiner 175 True love and true lover's knot beetwene man and wife continues indissoluble.

Love's wars, In | he who flies is conqueror. (L 554)

1642 TORRIANO 77. **1732** FULLER no. 2819.

Love (*noun*), *see also* Absence sharpens l.; All (L.) lies a-bleeding; Best smell is bread . . . best l. of children; Calf l. half l.; Children, (He that has no) knows not what is l.; Choice to begin l. (A

man has); Cold broth . . . old l. renewed again; Course of true l. never run smooth; Cupboard l.; Fair chieve all where l. trucks; Fair in l. and war; Fanned fires and forced l.; Faults are thick where l. thin; Fear is stronger than l.; Follow l. and it will flee; Folly to being in l. (No); Furze is in bloom (When), l. in tune; Herb will cure l. (No); Honey and gall in l. there is store, (Of); Hot l. hasty vengeance; —— soon cold; Hundred ells of contention (In) not inch of l.; Jack's in l. (If) he's no judge; Kind (L.) will creep where it may not go; Labour is light where l. doth pay; Lad's l. a busk of broom; Lie down for l. (They that) should rise for hunger; Lives by l. and lumps; Looks breed l.; Lovers live by l.; Lucky at cards, unlucky in l.; Lucky in life, unlucky in l.; Marries for l. without money (Who); Marry first and l. will follow; Merry as be can, for l. ne'er delights in sorrowful man; New l. drives out the old l.; Off with the old l. (Best to be); Old l. not forgotten; One nail (l.) drives out another; Pennyweight of l. worth pound of law; Pity is akin to l.; Poverty comes in (When) l. leaps out; Presents of l. fear not to be ill taken; See for your l., buy for your money; Salt water . . . wash away l.; Sound l. not soon forgotten; Soup and l. (Of) first is best; Subject's l. is king's lifeguard; Thousand pounds of law (In a) not ounce of l.; True l. kythes in need; War, hunting, and l. full of trouble; Wine and youth increase l.

Love(s, d) (*verb*), *see* Best l. furthest off; Every man as he l.; Fish do the water, (To l. it as well as); Fool (I am a), I l. anything good; Good things I do not l.; Jupiter has l., (Few there be whom just); Life you l. me not (In), in death bewail; Mutton, (He l. laced); Soul is . . . where it l.; Speaks me fair and l. me not; Truth l. trial; Woman l. in extremes; World wags (I wot how), best l. that has most bags.

Lovell, *see* Cat, the Rat, and L.

Lover is not where he lives but where he loves, The. (L 565)

1577 GRANGE *Gold. Aphroditis* E4ᵛ The hart [of a lover] being more where he loueth, than where he giueth life. **1580** LYLY *Euph. & his Eng.* ii. 48 For you may perceiue that he is not where he liues, but wher he loues. **1594–5** SHAKES. *L.L.L.* V. ii. 804 Hence hermit then—my heart is in thy breast. *a.* **1609** *Id. Son.* no. 22 l. 5 For all that beauty that doth cover thee Is but the seemly raiment of my heart, Which in thy breast doth live, as thine in me. **1662** FULLER *Westmorland* 140 The Proverb is, Homo non est ubi animat, sed amat, One is not to be reputed there where he lives, but where he loves.

Lovers live by love, as larks live by leeks. (L 569)

1546 HEYWOOD I. x. C3ᵛ Louers lyue by loue, ye as larkes liue by leekes Saied this Ales, muche more then halfe in mockage. **1670** RAY 46 . . . This is I conceiue in derision of such expressions as living by love. **1721** KELLY 367 You live on Love as Laverocks[1] do on Leeks. A Jest upon them that eat little. [[1] larks.]

Lover(s), *see also* Falling out of l. is renewing of l.; Jove laughs at l.'s perjuries; Poor beauty finds more l.

Loves bacon well that licks the swine-sty door, He. (B 23)

1678 RAY 96. 1732 FULLER no. 1978 (licks the Sow's Breech).

Loves glass without G, He that | take away L and that is he. (G 138)

1669 *New Help to Discourse* 265. 1678 RAY 55. 1746 FRANKLIN Jan. He that whines for Glass without G Take away L and that's he.

Loves his fetters, No man | be they made of gold. (M 338)

c. 1549 HEYWOOD I. viii. CI . . . Were I loose from the louely lynkes of my chayne, I would not daunce in such fayre fetters agayne. 1573 GASCOIGNE *Master F.J.* i. 490 I . . . sit and smile at the fond devices of such as have enchayned them selves in the golden fetters of fantasye. 1605 CHAPMAN, JONSON, MARSTON *Eastw. Ho* IV. ii. 151. 1611 DAVIES no. 395 (Gyues). 1894 LD. AVEBURY *Use of Life* iii. (1904) 27 All fetters are bad, even if they be made of gold.

Loves law, He that | will get his fill of it.

1721 KELLY 165 . . . For such are sure of two Things, an uneasy Life, and a broken Fortune.

Loves noise, He that | must buy a pig.

1706 STEVENS s.v. Ruydo. 1813 RAY 143 . . . *Quien quiere ruydo, compre un cochino. Hisp.*

Loves roast meat well that licks the spit, He. (M 819)

[1619] 1647 FLETCHER *Mad Lover* II. i. 183 He loves roast well That eats the Spit. 1666 TORRIANO *It. Prov.* 101 no. 26 To a cat that licks the spit, trust not roast-meat. 1670 RAY 137.

Loves the poor well, She | but cannot abide beggars. (P 470)

1678 RAY 350 . . . *Somerset. (of pretenders to charity).*

Loves the tree, He that | loves the branch. *Cf.* Love the boll. (T 488)

1591 SHAKES. 3 *Hen. VI* V. vii. 31 And that I love the free from whence thou sprang'st, Witness the loving kiss I give the fruit. 1639 CLARKE 285 If you love the boll you cannot hate the braunches. 1640 HERBERT no. 857.

Loves well sees afar off, He that.

1640 HERBERT no. 352 He that liues [*sic*] well sees a farre off. 1659 HOWELL *Span. Prov.* 19 *Quien bien quiere, de lexos vee.*

Loves well sheep's flesh, He | that wets his bread in the wool. *Cf.* Loved mutton well. (M 1339)

c. 1450–1500 *Gd. Wife wd. a Pilgrimage* l. 36 Witt a O and a I, þe mon ys at þe foll, That he wyll low ys scheppys flesche, that wettytt his bred in woll. a. 1530 *R. Hill's Commonpl. Bk.* E.E.T.S. 131 He loveth well moton, þat weteth his bred in woll—Optat eius carnem tangens in vellere panem. 1546 HEYWOOD II. v. H3 He loueth well sheeps flesh, that wets his bred in the wul. 1670 RAY 123 He loves mutton well that dips his bread in the wooll.

Loves, *see also* Love(s).

Low ebb at Newgate, He that is at a | may soon be afloat at Tyburn. (E 56)

1555 HEYWOOD *Three Hundred Epigrams* no. lvi Thou art at an ebbe in Newgate, thou hast wrong. But thou shalt be a flote at Tyburne ere long. 1597 SHAKES. *1 Hen. IV* I. ii. 37 Now in as low an ebb as the foot of the ladder, and by-and-by in as high a flow as the ridge of the gallows. 1662 FULLER *Middlesex* 178 . . . I allow not this Satyricall Proverb, as it makes mirth on men in Misery. 1670 RAY 238.

Low hedge is easily leaped over, A. (H 361)

1611 GRUTER 172. 1614 CAMDEN 302. 1670 RAY 16. 1732 FULLER no. 259.

Low, *see also* Cedars fall when l. shrubs remain, (High); Flood but there is as l. an ebb, (There is not so great a); Floods have l. ebbs, (High); Seldom is . . . l. man lowly.

Lower, *see* Mill-stone (The l.) grinds as well.

Lowly sit, richly warm. (S 492)

1609 HARWARD 101ᵛ. 1639 CLARKE 205 (Poorely sit and). 1670 RAY 117 . . . A mean condition is both more safe and more comfortable, then a high estate.

Loyal heart may be landed under Traitors' Bridge, A. (H 320)

1662 FULLER *Lond.* 199 . . . This is a Bridge under which is an Entrance into the Tower. . . . Passive Innocence, . . . may be accused without cause, and disposed at the pleasure of others.

Lubberland, where the pigs run about ready roasted, and cry, Come eat me!

1614 JONSON *Barthol. Fair* III. ii. 75 Good mother, how shall we finde a pigge, if we doe not looke about for't? will it run off o' the spit, into our mouths thinke you? as in Lubberland? and cry, *we, we*?

Lubberland, where they have half-a-crown a day for sleeping.

1813 RAY 64 You would do well in lubberland, where . . .

Lucifer, *see* Proud as L.

Luck, As good | as had the cow that stuck herself with her own horn. (L 573)

1678 RAY 287. **1828** LYTTON *Pelham* ch. 55 Things . . . grew worse with me, who have had 'as good luck as the cow that stuck herself with her own horn'.

Luck, As good | as the lousy calf, that lived all winter and died in the summer. (L 574)

1678 RAY 287.

Luck goes on at this rate, If your | you may very well hope to be hanged.

1706 STEVENS s.v. Dicha By the luck you have Father, you will dye on the Gallows or Hang'd. **1732** FULLER no. 2806.

Luck in horses, He that would have good | must kiss the parson's wife. (L 575)

1621 JONSON *Gipsies Met.* l. 842, variant read. You'll have good luck to horseflesh, o' my life, You ploughed so late with the vicar's wife. **1678** RAY 86. **1738** SWIFT *Dial.* II. E.L. 300 I have had devilish bad luck in horseflesh of late. —Why, then, Sir John, you must kiss a parson's wife.

Luck in leisure, There is.

1683 G. MERITON *Yorks. Dialogue* 9.

Luck in odd numbers, There is. (L 582)

[VERG. *Ecl.* 875 *Numero deus impare gaudet.*] **1590** SPENSER *F.Q.* III. iii. 50 Spitt thrise upon me, thrise upon me spitt; Th' uneven nomber for this business is most fitt. **1600–1** SHAKES. *M.W.W.* V. i. 3 This is the third time: I hope good luck lies in odd numbers. **1826** S. LOVER *Rory O'More* 'Then here goes another', says he, 'to make sure, For there's luck in odd numbers', says Rory O'More. **1883** J. PAYN *Thicker than W.* ch. I She was . . . by no means averse to a third experiment in matrimony. . . . 'There was luck in odd numbers.'

Luck of Edenhall, If that glass either break or fall, farewell the.

[See LONGFELLOW's tr. of UHLAND *Das Glück von Edenhall*; also SCOTT *Border Minstrelsy* ii. 196.] **1794** W. HUTCHINSON *Hist. Cumberland* I. 269 An old painted drinking glass, called the Luck of Edenhall, is preserved with great care [in the Musgrave family]. . . . The legendary tale is, that the butler, going to draw water, surprised a company of fairies . . . near the well: he seized the glass . . . they tried to recover it; but, after an ineffectual struggle, flew away, saying: If that glass either break or fall, Farewel the luck of Edenhall.

Luck, *see also* Better l. next time; Care and diligence bring l.; Devil's child, devil's l.; Give a man l.; Good l. comes by cuffing; Good l., (More by); Knave (The more), better l.; Muck there is l., (Where there is); Picture of ill l.; Properer man, worse l.; Rice for good l.; Shitten l. is good l.; Shoe after one for l., (To cast an old); Thieves and rogues have best l.; Voyage never has l. where each has vote; Worse l. now, the better another time. *See also* Good luck, Ill luck.

Lucky at cards, unlucky in love.

1738 SWIFT Dial. III. E.L. 324 Well, miss, you'll have a sad husband, you have such good luck at cards. **1865** T. W. ROBERTSON *Society* II. ii. I'm always lucky at cards! — Yes, I know an old proverb about that . . . Lucky at play, unlucky in ——. **1925** Aug. D. H. LAWRENCE *Lett.* ii. 851 Perhaps it's really true, lucky in money, unlucky in love.

Lucky in life, unlucky in love.

1908 E. PHILLPOTTS *The Mother* II. xiii. One might almost think the old saying 'Lucky in life, unlucky in love' was true.

Lucky men need no counsel.

1642 TORRIANO 78 It is to no purpose to counsel him who is lucky. **1707** MAPLETOFT 12.

Lucky pudding, If ever you make a | I shall eat the prick.[1] (P 624)

1641 FERGUSSON no. 543. **1721** KELLY 198 . . . That is, I am much mistaken if ever you do good. [¹ skewer.]

Lucky, *see also* Third time's l.; Wicked (The more), more l.

Lucy light, the shortest day and the longest night. (L 585)

1611 DONNE *Anat. of World. Prog. of S.*, 2nd *An.* 119 (1896) II. 131 Think that they bury thee, and think that rite Lays thee to sleep but a Saint Lucy's night. **1629** T. ADAMS *Med. Creed* Wks. (1861–2) III. 239 Under the law they had short days and long nights. . . . Theirs was a St Lucy's day, short and cloudy, ours is a St Barnaby's day. **1678** RAY 52.

Ludlam, *see* Lazy as L.'s dog.

Lugs, *see* Pint stoups hae lang l.

Lump(s), *see* Head is all of a l.; Like it or l. it; Lives by love and l.

Lurch, *see* Leave in the l.

Lurden, *see* Sick of a fever l.

Lurk(ed), *see* Devil l. behind cross; Lives well that well has l.

Lust, *see* Heart is full of l. (When), mouth's full of leasings; Man is known mortal by . . . l.

Lustful as a sparrow.   (s 715)

c. **1390** CHAUCER *Prol.* l. 626 As hoot he was, and lecherous, as a sparwe. [*c.* **1580**] **1590** SIDNEY *Arcadia* Feuillerat i. 134 The Sparrow lust to playe. **1594** NASHE *Unfort. Trav.* ii. 225 The sparrow for his lechery liueth but a yeare. **1604** SHAKES. *M.M.* III. ii. 185 Sparrows must not build in his house-eaves, because they are lecherous.

Lustre, *see* Good name keeps l. in dark.

Lute, *see* Ass play on l.; Ship, woman and l. ever repairing.

Luther, *see* Erasmus laid egg of Reformation.

Lydford, *see* Lidford.

Lying rides upon debt's back.

1758 FRANKLIN *Way to Wealth* (Crowell) 22 If you cannot pay . . . you will make . . . sneaking excuses, and . . . sink into . . . lying; for, . . .

Lying, *see also* Easy as l.; Law for l. (No); Whispering there is l. (Where).

Lynn, *see* Rising.

M

M under one's girdle, To have (*or* carry) an.   (M 1)

[= to use a respectful prefix (Mr., Mrs.) when addressing or mentioning a person.] [*a.* **1553**] **1566–7** UDALL *Roister D.* III. iii. Arb. 48 Ralph Royster Doister were hir owne I warrant you. —Neare an M by your girdle? **1605** CHAPMAN, JONSON, MARSTON *Eastw. Ho* IV. ii. 184 Must Goulding sit vpon vs?—You might carry an M vnder your girdle to Maister Deputis worship. **1738** SWIFT *Dial.* I. E.L. 268 What, plain Neuerout! methinks you might have an M under your girdle, miss. **1816** SCOTT *Old Mort.* ch. 29 Ye might hae had an M under your belt for Mistress Wilson of Milnwood.

Macclesfield, *see* Feeds like a . . . of M. *See also* Maxfield.

Macfarlane's geese, Like | that liked their play better than their meat.

a. **1628** CARMICHAELL no. 1714 (that tuke mair tent to). **1721** KELLY 361 You breed of Mac-Farlan's geese, you have more mind of your play, than your meat. Spoken to our Children, when their Earnestness upon their Play, keeps them from Dinner. **1820** SCOTT *Monast.* ch. 13 The Miller . . . intimating . . . some allusion to the proverb of MacFarlane's geese, which 'liked their play better than their meat'. [*Note.*—Wild geese . . . in Loch Lomond . . . were supposed to have some connection with the ancient family of MacFarlane . . . James VI . . . had been much amused by the geese pursuing each other . . . When one which was brought to table, was found to be tough and ill-fed, James observed— 'that MacFarlane's geese liked their play better than their meat'.]

Mackerel is in season when Balaam's ass speaks in church.

1902–4 LEAN I. 442 . . . The lesson in the old Lectionary (Numbers xxii) for 2nd Sunday after Easter.

Mackerel sky.   (M 2)

1669 WORLIDGE *Syst. Agric.* (1681) 295 In a fair day, if the sky seem to be dapled with white Clouds, (which they usually term a Mackarel-sky) it usually predicts rain. **1895** ADDY *Househ. Tales, &c.* 119 Yorkshire farmers . . . call a sky which is flecked with many small clouds a 'mackerel sky': A mackerel sky Is never long dry.

Mackerel sky and mares' tails make lofty ships carry low sails.

1869 INWARDS 59.

Mackerel, *see also* Mute as m.; Sprat to catch m.

MacKibbon's crowdy, *see* Come to himself (Let him).

Mackissock's cow did, I will do as | I'll think more than I say.

1721 KELLY 183 I . . . will . . . conceal my Resentments; but I will watch an Opportunity for Retaliation.

Macwhid, *see* Make a shift.

Mad action, One | is not enough to prove a man mad.

1732 FULLER no. 3767.

Mad as a (March) hare, As.   (H 148)

c. **1386** CHAUCER *Friar's T.* l. 1327 For thogh this Somonour wood were as an hare. **1529** MORE *Supp. Soulys* Wks. 299/2 As mad not as a march hare, but as a madde dogge. **1602** DEKKER I *Hon. Whore* V. ii. 131 They are madder then march haires. **1863** KINGSLEY *Water Bab.* ch. 5 A very clever old gentleman: but . . . as mad as a March hare.

Mad as a hatter.

1837–40 HALIBURTON *Clockm.* (1862) 109 Sister Sal . . . walked out of the town as mad as a hatter. **1857** HUGHES *Tom Brown* II. iii. He's a very good fellow, but as mad as a hatter. **1865** DODGSON *Alice in W.* ch. 6.

Mad as Ajax, As.　　　　　　　(A 95)

1594–5 SHAKES. *L.L.L.* IV. iii. 7 This love is as mad as Ajax: it kills sheep; it kills me. **1607** CHAPMAN *Bussy d'Amb.* III. i. Quarrel with sheep, and run as mad as Ajax.

Mad as the baiting bull of Stamford, As.　　　　　　　　　　　　　(B 721)

1662 FULLER Lincs. 152 . . . Earl Warren . . . gave all those Meadows . . . on condition that they find a Mad Bull . . . Six weeks before Christmas day, for . . . that sport every year.

Mad bull is not to be tied up with a packthread, A.

1732 FULLER no. 266. **1746** FRANKLIN Oct. Mad kings and mad bulls are not to be held by treaties and packthread.

Mad dog bites his master, The.

1706 STEVENS s.v. Perro. **1732** FULLER no. 4644.

Mad fools (folks) in a narrow place, Take heed of.　　　　　　　(H 381)

1599 MINSHEU *Span. Gram.* 84. **1651** HERBERT no. 1149 (folks).

Mad parish must have a mad priest, A.　　　　　　　　　　　　　　　(P 53)

1642 TORRIANO 5 (as mad a). **1732** FULLER no. 268.

Mad words deaf ears, For.　　　(T 56)

[Fr. **1558** MEURIER *Colloq. A folles paroles oreilles sourdes.* Sp. *c.* **1627** CORREAS *Vocab.* (1906) 17 *A palabras locas, orejas sordas.*] *c.* **1594** BACON no. 1564 A paroles lourdes aureilles sourdes. **1611** COTGRAVE s.v. Parole Let th'eares be deafe when words grow rude. **1616** DRAXE no. 753 For foolish talke deafe eares. **1732** FULLER no. 1593. **1853** TRENCH vi. 140.

Mad world, my masters, A.　　　(W 880)

[1603] **1635** BRETON *A Mad World My Masters*: Wks. ii. [Title]. *a.* **1606** *Nobody and Somebody* l. 777 Tis a mad world, Maister. **1608** MIDDLETON *A Mad World, My Masters* [Title]. **1649** J. TAYLOR *Wand. to West.*: Wks. I. B1. 'Tis a mad world (my masters) and in sadnes I travail'd madly in these dayes of madnes.

Mad, You will never be | you are of so many minds.　　　　　　　(M 978)

1580 LYLY *Euph. & his Eng.* ii. 185 Loue quoth Euphues will neuer make thee mad, for it commeth by fits, not like a quotidian, but a tertian. **1670** RAY 118. **1738** SWIFT Dial. I. E.L. 276.

Mad, *see also* Dance (They who) are thought m.; Difference between staring and stark m.; Every man is m. on some point; Horn m.; House goes m. when women gad; Money makes one m., (Too much); Much learning makes a man m.; Oppression makes wise man m.

Madame Parnell,[1] crack the nut and eat the kernel.　　　　　　　(M 3)

1659 HOWELL *Eng. Prov.* 21b . . . This alludes to labor. [[1] *Parnel*, M.E. *Peronelle*, a Christian name from St. *Petronilla*, came to signify a wanton young woman.]

Made a song of, She is not to be.

1721 KELLY 296 . . . An Abatement to a Woman's Commendation for Beauty. **1818** SCOTT *Rob Roy* ch. 4 I think it nae great thing to make a sang about.

Made, *see also* Fortune is m. of glass; God m. me, (I am as); Knife . . . m. at Dull-edge.; Many a thing's m. for money.

Madge Whitworth, *see* Go here away.

Madman (men), *see* Learning in breast of bad man as sword in hand of m.; Sword in m.'s hand; Welshman (The older the) the more m.

Madness, *see* Anger is short m.; Gladness (A man of) seldom falls into m.; Midsummer moon (m.); Mirth without measure is m.

Maggot[1] bites, When the.　　(M 5)

1683 R. L'ESTRANGE *Observator* 470, i. Prethee, where Bites the Magot to day, Trimmer? **1687** MIÈGE *Gt. Fr. Dict.* II. s.v. Magget I shall do it, when the magget bites. [[1] a whimsical or perverse fancy.]

Magnificat at matins, Like.　(M 9)

1559 COOPER s.v. Lens In lente vnguentum, a prouerbe signifiing the thynge to be absurde, as farre from the purpose as Magnificat from mattens. *c.* **1580** J. CONYBEARE 45 As farre from the purpose ·as Magnificat from mattines. **1588** BP. ANDREWES *Serm. at Spital* (1629) 24 Their note comes in like magnificat at Matins. **1611** COTGRAVE s.v. Magnificat Chanter Magnificat à matines. To doe things disorderly, or use a thing unseasonably. **1659** HOWELL *Fr. Prov.* 3 To sing Magnificat in the morning; which should be at Vespers. *Ibid.* 7 As proper as the Magnificat in the morning.

Magnificat, *see also* Correct M. (To).

Magpie, *see* One [m.] for sorrow.

Mahomet's coffin (tomb),[1] Like.　(M 13)

1589 Letter of SIR H. WOTTON (ed. Pearsall Smith i. 231) The Polonians are sospesi in aria come l'archo di Machometo. [1598] **1616** HAUGHTON *Englishmen for my Money* l. 2111 Haue your Adamants . . . left you hanging Twixt Heauen and Earth like Mahomets Sepulchre? **1649**

MILTON *Eikon*. Prose Wks. (1904) I. 394 We meet next with a comparison . . . , 'that the parliament have hung the majesty of kingship in an airy imagination of royalty, between the privileges of both houses, like the tomb of Mahomet.' **1718** PRIOR *Alma* ii. 719 The balance always would hang even, Like Mahomet's tomb, 'twixt earth and heaven. **1818** SCOTT *Rob Roy* ch. 30 Would not suffer the honest Bailie to remain suspended, like the coffin of Mahomet, between heaven and earth. **1894** STEVENSON & OSBOURNE *Ebb-Tide* ch. 7 Birds whisked in the air above, . . . fishes in the scarce denser medium below; between, like Mahomet's coffin, the boat drew away on the surface. [¹ fabled to be kept in suspension by loadstones.]

Mahomet, *see also* Mountain will not come to M.

Maid and a virgin is not all one, A.
(M 19)

1626 BRETON *Soothing* A8ᵛ. **1639** CLARKE 152.

Maid oft seen, A | and a gown oft worn, are disesteemed and held in scorn.
(M 20)

1611 COTGRAVE s.v. Fille. **1670** RAY 17. **1732** FULLER no. 6395.

Maid that laughs is half taken, A.
(M 22)

1664 CODRINGTON 183. **1670** RAY 16. **1732** FULLER no. 269.

Maid was born odd, This.
(M 27)

1678 RAY 77 Spoken of a maid who lives to be old, and cannot get a husband.

Maid, wife, nor widow, She is neither.
(M 26)

1578 G. WHETSTONE I *Promos and Cassandra* IV. iii. E2ᵛ I monster now, no mayde nor wife, haue stoupte to Promos lust. **1591** *True History of Civil Wars of France* 403 This Lady is of such holynes, that she is neither a maide, nor wife, nor widow. **1596** WARNER *Albion's Eng.* IX. 47 P7ᵛ Such match we made, that Maide, nor Wife, nor Widowe, left he me. **1600** T. HEYWOOD et al. *I Edw. IV* i. 84 [to Jane Shore] Now thou art nor widow, maide, nor wife. **1602** *How a Man may choose a Good Wife from a Bad* Hazl.-Dods. ix. 76. **1604** SHAKES. *M.M.* V. i. 179 My lord, she may be a punk; for many of them are neither maid, widow, nor wife. **1678** RAY 90.

Maiden (The), *see* Invented the M. (He that).

Maiden with many wooers often chooses the worst, A.

1721 KELLY 32 . . . Often true literally, but applied to those who having many things in their Proffer, choose the worst.

Maidenhead hangs in your light, Your.

1675 C. COTTON *Burlesque upon Burlesque: Or, The Scoffer Scoft* (*Wks.*, 1715, 228) Your Maiden-

head hangs not in your light. **1738** SWIFT *Dial.* II. E.L. 308 Where's my knife? sure I ha'n't eaten it. . . .—No, miss; but your maidenhead hangs in your light.

Maidenhood, *see* Malkin's m.

Maidens must be mild and meek, swift to hear and slow to speak.

1721 KELLY 247 . . . A Rhyme much canted by Mothers to their Daughters in former Times; but now almost antiquated. **1732** FULLER no. 6410.

Maidens should be meek (mim) till (while) they be married.
(M 44)

1599 SHAKES. *A.Y.* IV. i. 132 Maids are May when they are maids, but the sky changes when they are wives. *a.* **1628** CARMICHAELL no. 1120. **1641** FERGUSSON no. 994. **1721** KELLY 253 Maidens should be meek till they be married, and then burn Kirks. Spoken often by way of Reflection, when we say that such a one is a good humour'd Girl, as if you would say, observe how she'll prove when she is married. **1855** W. STIRLING-MAXWELL *Prov. Philos. Scot.* Wks.(1891) vi. 31 Our own country . . . is hardly . . . less cynical . . . 'Maidens should be mim till they're married, and then they may burn kirks'. **1917** BRIDGE 93 (mim).

Maidens, All are not | that wear bare hair.
(A 115)

1641 FERGUSSON no. 146 All are not maidens that wears bair hair. **1721** KELLY 4 All is not gold that glitters, nor maidens that wear their hair. It was the Fashion some Years ago for Virgins to go bare headed; . . . every thing is not so good as its appears.

Maidens' tochers and ministers' stipends are aye less than they are called.

1721 KELLY 248 . . . Maidens Portions are magnified to procure them Suiters. And Ministers Livings are call'd larger, by them who grudge that they are so large.

Maids in Wanswell may dance in an eggshell, All the.
(M 32)

a. **1640** J. SMYTH *Hundred of Berkeley* iii. 372 [Wanswell, Gloucestershire] A well . . . nowe called Holy well, . . . From the concurrence and confluence of all ages and sexes, meetinge at this vnholy well, The proverbe arose, which yet continueth; That. . . .

Maids say 'Nay' and take it.
(M 34)

1534 J. HEYWOOD *Play Love* C3ᵛ Your payne is most if she say nay and take it. *c.* **1535** LYNDSAY *Three Estates* l. 305 We will tak it . . . Howbeit that wee say nay. **1562** HEYWOOD *Three Hundr. Epig.* no. 223 Say nay and take it. [**1590**] **1594** GREENE & LODGE *Looking-Glass* II. ii. 452 Tut, my Remilia, be not thou so coy, Say nay, and take it. [**1592**] **1597** SHAKES. *Rich. III* III. vii. 50 And be not easily won to our requests; Play the maid's part, still answer nay, and take it. **1648** HERRICK *Hesper.* 676 Wks. (1893) II. 28 Women, although they ne'er so goodly make it, Their fashion is, but to say no, to take it. **1738** SWIFT *Dial.* I. E.L. 264 Give her a dish; for they say maids will say no, and take it. **1896** F. LOCKER-LAMPSON *My Confid.* 16 Maids, in modesty, say 'No' to that which they would have the profferer construe 'Ay'.

Maids than Malkin, There are more | (and more men than Michael). (M 39)

1546 HEYWOOD I. xi. D2ᵛ Tushe, there was no mo maydens but malkyn tho. **1579** GOSSON *Sch. Abuse* Arb. 37 There are . . . more maydes then Maulkin. *a.* **1625** FLETCHER *Woman's Prize* I. iii. Well there are more Maides than Maudlin, that's my comfort.—Yes, and more men than Michael. **1636** CAMDEN 308 There's more Maids than Maukins. **1678** RAY 172 There are more maids then Maukin, and more men then Michael.

Maids want nothing but husbands, and when they have them they want everything. (M 35)

1678 RAY 347. *Somerset.*

Maid(s), maiden(s), *see* All meats . . . all m. to be wed; Belly is full (When the); Cat help it (How can) if m. a fool; Children (M.) should be seen not heard; Crooning cow . . . and whistling m. boded never luck; Every m. is undone; Good m. but for thought, word, and deed; Jack among the m.; Knows who's a good m. (Who); Mealy-mouthed m. stands long at the mill; Meeterly as m. in fairness; Merry as the m.; Mope eyed by living a m.; Nineteen nay-says of a m. half a grant; Old m. lead apes in hell; Old wives are good m.; Suffolk fair m.; Tall m. is stooping (While), little one hath swept; Will not (If one), another will; Worst store, m. unbestowed.

Main-brace, *see* Splice the m.

Main chance, Look (Have an eye) to the. (E 235)

1579 LYLY *Euph.* i. 245 Let me stand to the maine chaunce. **1580** *Id. Euph. & his Eng.* ii. 188 Alwayes haue an eye to the mayne, what soeuer thou art chaunced at the buy. **1584** R. WILSON *Three Ladies Lond.* I. E ij b Trust me thou art as craftie to haue an eye to the mayne chaunce: As the Taylor that out of seuen yardes stole one and a halfe of durance. **1590–1** SHAKES. *2 Hen. VI* I. i. 203 Then let's make haste away, and look unto the main . . .—. . . Main chance, father, you meant; but I meant Maine. **1625** HOWELL *Lett.* 6 Jan. (1903) I. 247 Bacon . . . scarce left money to bury him, which, . . . did argue no great wisdom, it being . . . essential . . . to provide for the main chance. **1670** RAY 117. **1843–4** DICKENS *M. Chuz.* ch. 8 The education of Mr. Jonas had been conducted . . . on the strictest principles of the main chance. The very first word he learnt to spell was 'gain'. **1879** W. MINTO *Daniel Defoe* 135 [Defoe] was a man of business, and practised the profession of letters with a shrewd eye to the main chance.

Main (noun), *see* Little of everything, and nothing in the m.; Might and m., (With).

Maintains one vice, What | would bring up two children.

1758 FRANKLIN in Arber *Eng. Garner* v. 582 Away, then, with your expensive follies! . . . For, as *Poor* DICK says, . . . *What maintains one vice, would bring up two children.*

Maintenance, *see* Honour without m.

Mair[1] in a mair[2] dish.

1721 KELLY 247 . . . That is, a great deal more; an Answer to them who ask you if you will have any more, when you have gotten but very little. [[1] more. [2] bigger.]

Mair lost at Sherramuir, There was | where the Hielandman lost his faither and his mither, and a gude buff-belt worth baith o' them.

1814 SCOTT *Waverley* ch. 47 His death was lamented by few. Most . . . agreed in the pithy observation . . . that there 'was mair *tint* (lost) at Sheriff-Muir'.[1] [[1] where a battle was fought, near Stirling, in the Jacobite rebellion of 1715.]

Mair tint[1] at Flodden,[2] There was.

1820 SCOTT *Monast.* ch. 10 The Fife men say, an the whole pack of ye were slain, there were more lost at Flodden. [[1] lost. [2] Battle of Flodden, 1513.]

Make a fire well, He that can | can end a quarrel. (F 269)

1640 HERBERT no. 557.

Make a hog or a dog of it (a thing). (H 496)

1670 RAY 217. **1721** KELLY 252 . . . means, bring it either to one use, or another.

Make a poor man a knight, It is little of God's might to. (L 352)

[JUVENAL *Sat.* 7. 197 *Si fortuna volet, fies de rhetore consul.*] *a.* **1628** CARMICHAELL no. 918. **1641** FERGUSSON no. 522. **1721** KELLY 182.

Make a shift, I will | as Macwhid did with the preaching.

1721 KELLY 188 . . . Alexander Macwhid was a knowing Countryman. . . . At the Restoration, Clergymen being scarce, Bishop Taylor ask'd him if he thought he could preach, he answered that he could *Make a shift.* . . . The Proverb is spoken when we promise to do as well as we can.

Make a spoon or spoil a horn, He will.

[= achieve success or be a failure.] **1818** SCOTT *Rob Roy* ch. 22 Mr. Osbaldistone is a gude honest gentleman; but I aye said he was ane o' them wad make a spune or spoil a horn. **1820** 23 Apr. BYRON *Letters* v. 16 I can't cobble. I must either make a spoon or spoil a horn—and there's an end. **1892** *Boys Own Paper* Dec. 87/1 Your son . . . will turn out something some day. He'll make a spoon or spoil a horn.

**Make ab or warp of the business as soon
as you can.** (A 1)

c. **1640** SMYTH *Berkeley MSS. 30,* no. 39 Il'e
make abb or warp of it. If not one thinge yet
another. **1659** HOWELL *Eng. Prov.* 17a . . . *A
metaphor taken from weavers.*

Make ado and have ado. (A 35)

a. **1550** *Parliament of Birds* (*Harl. Misc.* v. (1745),
480) He must haue a do, that a do doth make.
1678 RAY 70.

Make all sure, To. (A 206)

1597 SHAKES. *1 Hen. IV* V. iii. 47 I have paid
Percy; I have made him sure. *Ibid.* V. iv. 126
I'll make him sure; yea, and I'll swear I kill'd
him. **1601** MUNDAY & CHETTLE *Death of Robert
Earl of Huntington* Hazl.-Dods. viii. 227 What,
has thou made him sure?—It's dead-sure he is
dead, if that be sure. **1612** CHAPMAN *Widow's
Tears* III. i. 74 We made all short, and sweet,
and close, and sure. **1639** CLARKE 278.

**Make an end of your whistle, though
the cart overthrow, You will.** (E 129)

1678 RAY 276.

Make dice of one's bones, To.

1582 WHETSTONE *Heptameron* H4 A man can
haue . . . of a begger, but his scrip: vnles he
will sel . . . the dice maker, the bones. **1621**
BURTON *Anat. Mel.* III. i. 3, 3 We will not relent
till we . . . have made dice of his bones, as they
say, see him rot in prison. **1646** J. COOKE
Vindic. of the Law 22 We say proverbially 'make
dice of his bones', the meaning whereof is, that
if a prisoner die in execution, after the Crowner
has viewed his body, the creditor hath dice
delivered to him at the Crowne Office as having
all that he is likely to have.

Make haste slowly. (H 192)

[Gk. Σπεῦδε βραδέως. L. *Festina lente.* AUGUSTUS
in *Suet.* 2. 25.] *c.* **1374** CHAUCER *Troilus* Bk. I,
l. 956 He hasteth wel that wisly kan abyde.
1590 LODGE *Rosalynde* Wks. (1883) I. 123
Festina Lente, especially in Loue: for momen-
tarie fancies are ofttimes the fruites of follies.
1663 BUTLER *Hudibras* I. iii. 1253 (1854) 107
Festina lente, Not too fast; For haste (the
proverb says) makes waste. **1694** SOAME in
Dryden Misc. 4. 157 Gently make haste. **1744**
FRANKLIN Apr. Make haste slowly. **1907**
Spectator 12 Jan. 43 'Hasten slowly' is a very
good motto in Imperial politics.

**Make haste to an ill way, that you may
get out of it.** (H 193)

1640 HERBERT no. 124. **1659** N. R. 76.

Make hay while the sun shines. (H 235)

1509 BARCLAY *Ship of Fools* ii. 46 Who that in
July whyle Phebus is shynynge About his hay is
nat besy labourynge . . . Shall in the wynter his
negligence bewayle. **1546** HEYWOOD I. iii. A4
Whan the sunne shynth make hey. **1583** MEL-
BANCKE *Philotimus* 24 Yt is well therefor to
make hay while the sunne shines. **1591** SHAKES.
3 Hen. VI IV. viii. 61 The sun shines hot; and,
if we use delay, Cold biting winter mars our
hop'd-for hay. **1636** CAMDEN 302 Make hay
while sunne shines. **1835** MRS. CARLYLE *Lett.*
July 'It is good to make hay while the sun
shines', which means, in the present case, . . .
to catch hold of a friend while she is in the
humour. **1853** TRENCH iii. 64 . . . is truly
English, and could have had its birth only under
such variable skies as ours.

**Make me a diviner and I will make thee
rich.** (D 392)

1573 SANFORD 105. **1578** FLORIO *First F.* 30. **1629**
Bk. Mer. Rid. Prov. no. 111. **1659** HOWELL *It.
Prov.* 7 (Prophet). **1732** FULLER no. 3315
(Soothsayer).

Make much of nought. (M 1280)

1639 CLARKE 314. **1678** RAY 347 You love to
make much of naught (*your self*). **1738** SWIFT
Dial. I. E.L. 269 Come, come, Miss, make
much of nought; good folks are scarce.

**Make much of one, good men are scarce.
Cf. Good men are scarce.** (M 1281)

1631 PHIN. FLETCHER *Sicelides* III. iv. Wks. (1908)
I. 224 Good men are scanty, make much of one.
1670 RAY 118.

Make much of what you have. (M 1282)

1616 WITHALS 573. **1639** CLARKE 129.

Make one's mouth water, To.

1555 R. EDEN *Decades of New World* 143 These
craftie foxes [cannibals] . . . beganne to swallowe
theyr spettle as their mouthes watered for
greediness of theyr prey. **1594** LYLY *Mother B.*
I. iii. 40 He is able to make a Ladies mouth
water if she winke not. **1738** SWIFT Dial. III.
E.L. 324.

Make or mar. Cf. Hopes make or break. (M 48)

c. **1420** LYDGATE *Assembly of Gods* 556
Neptunus, that dothe bothe make & marre.
1542 ERASM. tr. Udall *Apoph.* 267b Declaring
that he was vtterly mynded to put al in hasards
to make or marre. [*c.* **1550**] **1641** CAVENDISH
Wolsey ed. Morley n.d. 133 He would either
make or mar . . . which was always his [Crom-
well's] common saying. **1594–5** SHAKES. *L.L.L.*
IV. iii. 187 Nay it makes nothing, sir.—If it
mar nothing neither. **1599** *Id. A.Y.* I. i. 27 I
am not taught to make anything.—What mar
you then Sir? **1604** *Id. O.* V. i. 4 It makes us,
or it mars us. **1613** DAY *Festivals* vii. (1615) 206
That Part of a Woman which either makes all,
or marres all, I meane her Tongue. **1885** MRS. C.
PRAED *Affinities* II. xii. 5 As for Lady Romer's
scheme, it is not my business to make or mar it.

**Make sport, He that cannot | should
mar none.** (S 775)

1662 J. WILSON *Cheats* II. ii. (1874) 37 If I can
make no sport, I'll mar none. **1721** KELLY 143.

Make the crow a pudding, You look as if you would. (C 860)

c. **1598** DELONEY *Gentle Craft* II. iii. Let no man . . . say thou gauest the crow a pudding, because loue would let thee liue no longer. **1599** SHAKES. *Hen. V* II. i. 84 By my troth, he'll yield the crow a pudding one of these days. **1678** RAY 237 You look as if you would make the crow a pudding, *i.e.* die. **1721** KELLY 167 He owes a pudding to the glade.¹ Spoken of a poor weak Beast which we suspect to be a dying. [¹ kite.]

Make up one's mouth, To. (M 1263)

1546 HEYWOOD I. xi. E3 Here withall his wife to make vp my mouthe, Not onely hir husbandes tauntyng tale auouthe, But therto deuiseth to cast in my teeth, Checks and chokyng oysters. **1553** *Respublica* I. i. And nowe is the tyme come . . . to make vp my mouth, and to feather my neste. **1584** COGAN *Haven Health* (1636) 170 Commonly at great feasts . . . they use to serve vp sturgeon last, as it were to make up the mouth. **1659** HOWELL *Fr. Prov.* 16.

Make up, *see also* Market, (To m. one's).

Make your bed, As you | so you must lie on it. (B 189)

c. **1590** G. HARVEY *Marginalia* (1913) 88 Lett them . . . go to there bedd, as themselves shall make it. **1640** HERBERT no. 340 He that makes his bed ill, lies there. **1721** KELLY 16 As you make your bed, so you lie down. According to your Conditions you have your Bargain. **1881** D. C. MURRAY *Joseph's Coat* ch. 30 'You have made your bed', says the . . . proverb '. . . lie upon it.' But it is no easier to lie upon it because the briars between the sheets were put there by your own hands.

Make, To, *see also under significant words following.*

Make (a, the, your), *see also under significant words following.*

Make not (a, the, thy), *see also under significant words following.*

Makes a good war, He that | makes a good peace. (W 42)

[*c.* **1580**] **1590** SIDNEY *Arcadia* Feuillerat i. 188 They beget of a just war, the best child, peace. **1640** HERBERT no. 420. **1732** FULLER no. 2230.

Makes a thing too fine, He that | breaks it. (T 133)

1640 HERBERT no. 440. **1642** TORRIANO 28.

Makes himself a sheep, He that | shall be eaten by the wolf. (S 300)

1583 MELBANCKE *Philotimus* 2B4ᵛ He . . . that needes be a sheepe, cannot greatly grudge to be bitten with a fox. **1592** DELAMOTHE 45. **1611** DAVIES no. 53 'If men become Sheepe, the Wolfe will deuoure them'. **1617** MORYSON *Itin.* III. i. 25 (1907-8) III. 400 According to the Italian

proverb: *Chi pecora si fa, il Lupo se la mangia.* The man who makes himself a sheep, The wolf will eat, whilst he doth sleep. **1651** HERBERT no. 1089. **1670** RAY 141 . . . Qui se fait brebis le loup le mange. *Gall.* He that is gentle and puts up affronts and injuries shall be sure to be loaden. **1710** PALMER 360.

Makes (not) his mistress a goldfinch, He that | may find her a wagtail. (M 1020)

1589 LYLY *Midas* I. i. 82 If therfore thou make not thy mistres a goldfinch, thou mayst chance to find her a wagtaile. **1597** *Politeuphuia* 17 (perhaps in time). **1604** E. GRYMESTON *Miscellanea* H2 (wife). **1647** *Countrym. New Commonwealth* 8 He that makes his Mistresse a goldfinch, may perhaps finde her a wagtaile. **1832** HENDERSON 61 Mak your wife a goodspink and she'll turn a water-wagtail.

Makes much of his painted sheath (sheets), He. (S 291)

c. **1520** WHITTINGTON *Vulg.* E.E.T.S. 105 He is not a lytle proude of his paynted sheythe and loketh of a heyght. **1555** HEYWOOD *Epig. on Prov.* no. lxxi. Thou makste much of thy peynted shethe, and wylt do, It hauynge not one good knyfe longyng therto. **1560** July *Lett.* to W. Cecil cited C. Read *Mr. Sec. Cecil* 192 They that make most of their painted sheath will never do such service to the realm as you have done. **1567** PAINTER (Jacobs) iii. 199. **1641** FERGUSSON no. 446 *Of proud persons.* He makes meikle of his painted sheits.

Makes no mistakes, He who | makes nothing.

1868 BISHOP W. C. MAGEE *Sermon* (at Peterborough) The man who makes no mistakes does not usually make anything. **1896** J. CONRAD *Outcast of the Islands* ch. 3 It's only those who do nothing that make no mistakes, I suppose. **1911** *Times Wkly.* 3 Nov. 883 Of course, he has made mistakes such as all men make who ever make anything. **1925** *Times* 9 Nov. 17/4 The comforting assurance that 'a man who never makes mistakes never makes anything'.

Make(s), making, *see also* God or a painter, for he m. faces; Man of God's m.; Stomach an apothecary's shop, (M. not thy).

Malady, *see* Much meat much m.

Males, *see* Deeds are m.

Malice hurts itself most. (M 51)

1572 HARVEY *Marginalia* 103 Malice drinkith upp the greatist part of her owne poyson. **1597** *Politeuphuia* 23ᵛ (as 1572). **1639** CLARKE 197. **1732** FULLER no. 3327 (as 1572).

Malice is mindful. (M 52)

c. **1600** *Edmund Ironside* l. 1387 Remember this, malice hath a perfect memory. **1639** CLARKE 196. **1721** KELLY 249 . . . Spoken when People rip up old Sores, and think, with Resentment, upon old Disobligations. **1732** FULLER no. 3329.

Malice, *see also* Injury is measured by m.; More m. than matter; Well well is word of m.

Malkin's[1] maidenhood.

1377 LANGLAND *P. Pl.* B. I. 181–2 ӡe ne haue na more meryte. in masse ne in houres,[2] Than Malkyn of hire maydenhode. that no man desireth. *c.* **1386** CHAUCER *Man of Law's T.* l. 30 Tyme . . . wol nat come agayn, withouten drede, Namoore than wole Malkynes maydenhede. [[1] a wanton slattern. [2] services of the church.]

Malkin, *see also* Maids than M. (More).

Malt is above meal (wheat) with him.
(M 58)

[= he is drunk.] **1546** HEYWOOD I. xi. D2 Malt is aboue wheate with hym market men saie. **1626** BRETON *Fantastickes* B3 Haruest. Malt is now aboue wheat with a number of mad people. **1641** FERGUSSON no. 850 The malt is above the beir. **1824** SCOTT *Redg.* ch. 12 'Come, Provost,' said the lady rising, 'if the maut gets abune the meal with you, it is time for me to take myself away.' **1891** A. FORBES *Bar. Biv. & Bat.* (1910) 62 As he marched home from the little public-house . . . with 'the malt abune the meal', his effort to appear preternaturally sober was quite a spectacle.

Malt, *see also* Kiln of m. is on fire; Merry as mice in m.; Peck (part) (For my) of m., set kiln on fire; Sit in the chair that have m. to sell; Soft fire sweet m.

Malt-heap, *see* Cat left on the m., (To have what the).

Malt-man comes on Monday, The.
(M 59)

1600 DRAYTON *Oldcastle* III. iii. 27 Be mery, wench, the mault-man comes on munday. ?**1622** J. TAYLOR (Water-P.) *Trav. Twelvepence* (1630) 70 The Malt-man came on Munday, & would haue me. **1659** HOWELL *Eng. Prov.* 9b.

Malt-man (men), *see also* Merry when m. meet; Worst world that ever was, m. got his sack again.

Malvern Hill, Go dig at.
(M 762)

1564–5 *Stationers' Register* Arb. i. 270 . . . to men of suche Willes that are so Redy to Dygge vp Malbron hilles [a ballad]. **1659** HOWELL *Eng. Prov.* 20b. Spoken of one whose wife wears the breeches. **1790** GROSE s.v. Worcestershire.

Malvern, *see also* Sip up the Severn and swallow M.

Mammering, I stand in a.
(M 61)

1532 T. MORE *Conf. Tyndale* Pref.: Wks. 1557, 343 He was in a mamering whether he would retourne agayn ouer the sea. **1540** PALSGRAVE *Acolastus* 157. **1578** *Courtly Contro.* A4 My quill remayned long (as men say) in a mamorie. **1581** H. GOLDWELL *Brief Declaration* A2 I stande . . . in a mammering maze like Alexanders men. **1587** BURGHLEY to Walsingham cited C.

Read *Ld. Burghley & Qu. Elizabeth* 385 Resting this night in a mammering whether to go unsent for or no. **1591** ARIOSTO *Orl. Fur.* Harington XLV. History. **1616** WITHALS 561.

Man among the geese when the gander is away, You are a.
(M 433)

1670 RAY 177. *Chesh.*

Man assaulted (surprised) is half taken, A.
(M 218)

1573 SANFORD 51ᵛ. **1629** *Bk. Mer. Rid.* Prov. no. 22. **1642** TORRIANO 59 (set upon). [*Cf.* A man surprised is half beaten. **1732** FULLER no. 310.]

Man at five may be fool at fifteen, A.

1721 KELLY 10 . . . A pregnant, pert, witty Child, may prove but a heavy worthless Man.

Man at the wheel, *see* Speak to.

Man be at his own bridal, It is meet that a.
(M 201)

c. **1390** LANGLAND *P. Pl.* C. III. 56 And al the riche retynaunce . that roteth hem on fals lyuynge Were bede to that brudale. **1546** HEYWOOD I. vi. B3 Ye know well it is, ... Meete, that a man be at his owne bridale. **1579** LYLY *Euph.* i. 228 But mee thincs it is good reason, that I shoulde be at mine owne brydeall, and not giuen in the Church, before I knowe the Bridegrome. **1611** DAVIES *Prov.* no. 390.

Man before his mother, He will be a.
(M 179)

[1625] **1647** MASSINGER *et al. Love's Cure* II. ii. Thou wilt scarce be a man before thy Mother. *c.* **1641** FERGUSSON MS. no. 566. **1721** KELLY 174 . . . Spoken to ill grown Children. **1888** STEVENSON *Black Arrow* ch. 3 'I do but jest', said Dick. 'Ye'll be a man before your mother, Jack.'

Man but his mind? What is a. (M 405)

[*Cf.* **1578** *Mirr. for Mag.* 478 The minde and not the Man dooth make or marre.] **1639** CLARKE 16.

Man can die but once, A. (M 219)

c. **1425** *Towneley Plays* 'Resurrection' 481. We dy bot oones. **1549** H. BULLINGER *Treatise or Sermon* A6ᵛ What thynge can a man reproue in warre? because men do dye which must dye once, wherby peace may follow? **1563** FOXE *Acts and Monuments* (Hebel–Hudson–F. R. Johnson, 192) To the most miserable man in the world this one thing is granted, that he can die but once. **1598** SHAKES. *2 Hen. IV* III. ii. 228. **1606** *Id. A.C.* IV. xiv. 27 Death of one person can be paid but once. **1616** DRAXE no. 489 (but one maner of death). **1708** PRIOR *Turtle & Spar.* With great submission I pronounce, That people die no more than once. **1840** MARRYAT *Olla Pod.* ch. 12 'A man cannot die more than once', is an old apophthegm, . . . but . . . a man can die . . . once professionally or legally, and once naturally.

Man can do no more than he can, A.
(M 220)

1530 PALSGRAVE 474b No man can do above his power. *c.* **1530** HEN. VIII to Ann Boleyn (*Harl. Misc.* 1808, i. 198) Ultra posse non est esse. **1591** STEPNEY L2ᵛ The king can do no more then he is able. **1594** NASHE *Unfort. Trav.* ii. 210 Men can doe no more than they can do. **1670** RAY 67.

Man does what he can, and God what he will.
(M 231)

1616 DRAXE no. 893. **1639** CLARKE 87.

Man far from his good is near his harm, A.
(M 232)

c. **1350** *Douce MS. 52* no. 12 Who is ferre from his disshe is nyhgh his harme. *c.* **1400** *MS. Latin no. 394* J. *Rylands Libr.* (ed. Pantin) in *Bull. J. R. Libr.* XIV f. 6ᵛ Who so is fer from his disch is nyȝe his harm. **1546** HEYWOOD II. ix. K4. **1614** CAMDEN 302. **1641** FERGUSSON no. 299 He that is far from his geir, is neir his skaith.

Man has done, Whatever | man may do.

1863 C. READE *Hard Cash* ch. 29 'Whatever man has done man may do', said Dr. Sampson stoutly.

Man has his hour, and a dog his day, A. *Cf.* Dog has his day.

c. **1525–9** *Godly Queen Hester* (Greg) 26. **1633** JONSON *T. Tub* II. i. 4 Right! vor a man ha' his houre, and a dog his day.

Man has his mare again, All is well, and the.
(A 153)

a. **1548** R. COPLAND *Jyl of Brentford's Testament* l. 62 The poore mare shal haue his man agayn. **1595** SHAKES. *M.N.D.* III. ii. 463 The man shall haue his mare again, And all shall be well. **1647** J. FLETCHER *Chances* III. iv. Why, the man has his mare again, and all's well. **1678** RAY 259. **1712** ADDISON *Spect.* no. 481 I am pleased with a porter's decision . . . upon . . . a virtuous woman's marrying a second husband, while her first was yet alive. . . . [He] solves it . . . by the old proverb, that if his first master be still living, 'The man must have his mare again.'

Man has no more goods than he gets good of, A. *Cf.* Goods are theirs that enjoy them.
(M 236)

1621 ROBINSON 24. **1641** FERGUSSON no. 86. **1721** KELLY 25 . . . What a Man enjoys of his Substance is really his, the rest he has only the keeping of.

Man in the moon.
(M 240)

a. **1310** in WRIGHT *Lyric P.* xxxix. 110 This ilke mon upon heh when er he were, wher he were ythe mone boren ant y-fed. *c.* **1374** CHAUCER *Troilus* Bk. I, l. 1023 Thou hast a ful gret care Lest that the cherl may falle out of the moone. *c.* **1449** PECOCK *Repr.* II. iv. (Rolls) 155 A man which stale sumtyme a birthan of thornis war

sett in to the moone there forto abide for euere. *a.* **1548** HALL *Chron. Rich. III* 37 When the quene had heard this frendely mocion (which was as farre from her thought as the man that the rude people saie is in the moone). **1584** HERODOTUS *Euterpe* tr. B.R. ed. Lang 127 This is as true as the man in the moone. **1587** (?1577) HOLINSHED iii. 872a This . . . I will adde (least I might seeme to tell a tale of the man in the moone). **1594–5** SHAKES. *L.L.L.* V. ii. 215 Yet still she is the moon, and I the man. **1595** *Id. M.N.D.* V. i. 238 Myself the man i' the moon do seem to be. **1611** *Id. Temp.* II. i. 240 The man i' the moon's too slow. *Ibid.* II. ii. 129 I was the man in the moon, when time was. **1621** LAUD *Serm.* 19 June 24 These conuerted Iewes must meet out of all Nations: the ten Tribes as well as the rest . . . Men in the Moone. **1778** FRANCES BURNEY *Evelina* (1920) I. 202 'He'd no more right to our money than the man in the moon'. **1811** E. NARES *Thinks-I-To-Myself* i. 54 I cared no more about it, than the man in the moon. **1866** *John Bull* I Sept. 584/1 Mr. Mum, the man in the moon, who, he said was a necessary consequence of a Totnes election.

Man in the oak.

[= a spirit supposed to inhabit an oak.] **1584** R. SCOTT *Discov. Witchcr.* VII. xv. (1886) 122 Robin Goodfellow, the spoorne,[1] the mare, man in the oke. **1604** MIDDLETON *Witch* I. ii. Dwarfes, Imps, . . . the Man i' th' oake. [1 spectre, phantom.]

Man in the street, The.

1831 GREVILLE *Mem.* 22 Mar. (1874) II. 131 The other [side affirms] that the King will not consent to it, knowing, as 'the man in the street' (as we call him at Newmarket) always does, the greatest secrets of kings. **1844** EMERSON *Essays* II. Self-reliance. But the man in the street, finding no worth in himself which corresponds to the force which built a tower or sculptured a marble god, feels poor when he looks on these. **1850** *Id. Representative Men* VI. Napoleon. The man in the street finds in him [Napoleon] the qualities and powers of other men in the street. **1854** *Id. Lett. and Soc. Aims.* Wks. (Bohn) III. 192 The speech of the man in the street is invariably strong. **1909** *Spectator* 22 May 808 The Socialist party . . . are concerned only with the facts which meet the eye of 'the man in the street'.

Man is a lion in his own (a good) cause, A.
(M 242)

1641 FERGUSSON no. 120. **1721** KELLY 6 . . . No Man so zealous for, or assiduous in, a Man's Business, as himself. **1732** FULLER no. 1907 He is a lion in a good cause.

Man is a man though he have but a hose on his head, A.
(M 244)

c. **1386** CHAUCER *Can. Yeom. T.* l. 726 Now may I were an hose upon myn heed. **1588** 'MARPRELATE' *Epitome* ed. Pierce 135 A man is a man, though he go naked. **1590** R. HARVEY *Plain Perceval* A3 A man is a man, though have but a hose on his head. **1592** NASHE *Strange News* i. 307. **1599** PORTER *Angry Wom. Abingd.* ll. 902–3 I am your fathers man, and a man's a man an a haue but a hose on his hed. **1612** SHELTON *Quix.* iii. xi. i. 209 'No more of that, sir,' said Sancho; 'a man is a man, though he have but a hose on his head.' **1708** DYKES *Mor. Reflect. Prov.* 255 A man is a man still, if he hath but a hose on his head. . . . We may sometimes chance to meet with a Diogenes in rags. **1738** SWIFT *Dial.* II. E.L. 315 A man's a man, if he has but a nose on his face.

Man is as old as he feels, and a woman as old as she looks, A.

1907 *Illus. Lond. News* 25 May The adage that a man is as old as he feels, and a woman as old as she looks, may be said to contain much inherent truth.

Man is but a bubble.   (M 246)

[Gk. Πομφόλυξ ὁ ἄνθρωπος. ERASM. *Ad. Homo bulla.*] **1539** TAVERNER 34ᵛ Man is but a bubble, or bladder of the water. **1545** *Precepts of Cato* 'Sage Sayings' Thales D3 Some compare the lyfe of man to a bubble, some to the lightnes of a feyther, some other to the glydynge of a shadowe. **1597** SHAKES. *Rich. III* IV. iv. 83 I call'd thee then . . . A dream of what thou wast . . . a breath, a bubble. **1651** JER. TAYLOR *Holy Dying* (1850) I. i. 299 A man is a bubble, (said the Greek proverb) which Lucian represents . . . saying, that all the world is like a storm, and men rise up in their several generations, like bubbles descending *à Jove pluvio*, from God and the dew of heaven, from a tear and a drop of rain, from nature and Providence.

Man is either a god (saint) or a devil (wolf) to man. *Cf.* **Man is to man a god; Man is to man a wolf (devil).**   (M 247)

1603 MONTAIGNE (Florio) III. v. 106 It is a match whereto may well be applied the common saying . . . Man unto man is either a God or a Wolfe. **1612** WEBSTER *White Devil* IV. ii. 92 Woman to man Is either a God or a wolfe. **1616** WITHALS 558 Man to man, is either a Saint, or a Diuell. **1639** CLARKE 137 (to his neighbour).

Man is friended, As a | so the law is ended.   (M 63)

1538 T. STARKEY *England* (Cowper) I. iii. 86 For (as hyt ys commynly and truly also sayd) 'materys be endyd as they be frendyd'. **1586** G. WHETSTONE *English Mirror* 237. **1614** CAMDEN 303.

Man is known to be mortal by two things, sleep and lust, A.   (M 249)

1625 BACON *Apophthegms* no. 123. **1651** HERBERT no. 1159.

Man is not a horse because he was born in a stable, A.

1836 M. SCOTT *T. Cring. Log* ch. 4 An Englishman . . . born in Buenos Ayres . . . having joined the patriots, this brought treason home to him. . . . 'Truly, . . . a man does sometimes become a horse by being born in a stable.' **1906** *Times Lit. Sup,* 27 Apr. Except on the principle that the man who is born in a stable is a horse, [Lever] was not an Irishman at all.

Man is the head, but woman turns it.

1875 A. B. CHEALES *Prov. Folk-Lore* 12. **1917** BRIDGE 93.

Man is the measure of all things.

[PLATO *Cratylus* 4. Πάντων χρημάτων μέτρον εἶναι ἄνθρωπον.] **1547** W. BALDWIN O7ᵛ. **1615** H. CROOKE *Microcosmographia* (1631 ed., B2). **1627** G. HAKEWILL *Apology* 177 A memorable saying of Protagoras, reported and repeated by Plato, that man was *rerum omnium mensura*, the measure of all things. **1631** CHAPMAN *Caesar & Pompey* II. iv. 117 As of all things man is said the measure, So your full merits measure forth a man.

Man is a wolf to man (*Homo homini lupus*).   (M 245)

[PLAUTUS *As.* 2. 4. 88. ERASM. *Ad.*] **1545** *Precepts of Cato* Bias 'Sage Sayings' B5ᵛ One man semeth to deuoure another lyke rauenynge wolues. c. **1554** W. TURNER *Hunting of the Romish Wolf* E5 It is a common prouerbe amongest learned men, *Homo homini lupus*, a man is a Wolfe vnto a man. a. **1567** T. BECON *Catechism* P.S. 333 Euery one of us ought to be to other not a wolf but a god. **1569** C. AGRIPPA *Vanity of Arts & Sciences* tr. Sanford (1575) 124 Man (as the Prouerbe saith) is a woulfe to man. **1596** T. LODGE *Wit's Misery* B1 The old Prouerbe . . . that Homo est homini dæmon, Man vnto man is a deuill. **1621** BURTON *Anat. Mel.* I. i. I. i. (1651) 4 The greatest enemy to man is man, who, by the devil's instigation, is . . . a wolf, a devil to himself and others. **1662** FULLER *Merioneth* 44 It is my desire, that . . . the people . . . give no longer occasion to the Proverb, 'Homo Homini Lupus'. **1785** COWPER *The Task* iv. Wks. (1836) VII. 38 I mourn the pride and avarice that make man a wolf to man. **1888** J. E. T. ROGERS *Econ. Interp. Hist.* (1894) II. xvi. 341 '*Homo homini lupus*', said Plautus. . . . This is the comment in which the historical relations of man to man have been . . . condensed.

Man is to man a god.   (M 241)

[Gk. Ἄνθρωπος ἀνθρώπῳ δαιμόνιον. CAECILIUS STATIUS *Fragment* 16, *Homo homini deus est, si suum officium sciat*, Man is a god to his fellowman, if he know his duty.] **1548** HALL *Chron.* (1809) 324 The olde Greke prouerbe . . . that a man, to a man shall sometyme be as a God, for the young erle Henry[1] . . . by the labor of Ihon Cheulet, . . . was preserued, saved, and deliuered. **1559** J. FERRARIUS *Good Ordering of a Commonwealth* tr. W. Bavande 2ᵛ Man is a God to man. **1581** GUAZZO i. 43. [[1] Henry of Richmond.]

Man lives, As a | so shall he die, as a tree falls, so shall it lie.   (M 64)

[ECCLES. xi. 3 If the tree fall toward the south, or toward the north, in the place where the tree falleth, there it shall be.] **1549** LATIMER *Seven Sermons* Arb. 118 Wheresoeuer the tree falleth . . . there it shall rest. c. **1550** *Howleglas* (Ouvry) 84 As men liue so is their end. **1669** PENN *No Cross, No Crown* ch. 12 As the tree falls, it lies; and as death leaves men, judgment finds them. **1678** RAY 296. **1836** M. SCOTT *Cruise of Midge* ch. 14 It is of no use, . . . as the tree falls, so must it lie—it is a part of my creed.

Man may learn wit every day, A.

(M 263)

1609 HARWARD 81ᵛ (learne somewhat). **1616** DRAXE no. 2445.

Man may lose more in an hour than he can get in seven, A.　(M 265)

1583 MELBANCKE D2ᵛ The merchaunt loseth more in an houre then he gaineth in 20 yeres. **1616** DRAXE no. 1723.

Man must not leave the king's highway for a pathway, A.　(M 281)

1562 J. WIGAND *De Neutralibus* M8 It is the best, the surest, and moste holsome waye for vs all to abyde still in the kinges highe waye or the most sure beaten path, and to leaue and forsake all to by walkes and rounde aboutes which crafty wittes inuent. **1616** DRAXE no. 2325. **1659** HOWELL *Span. Prov.* 16 By no means leave not the high-way for a by-path.

Man of God is better for having his bows and arrows about him, The.

(M 291)

1659 HOWELL *Eng. Prov.* 2a.

Man of God's making, He is (is not) a.

(M 162)

[1591] 1593 PEELE *Edw. I* ii. B4 I am a poore Friar, a man of Gods making, and a good fellow as you are. **1594–5** SHAKES. *L.L.L.* V. ii. 524 'A speaks not like a man of God his making. **1596** *Id. M.V.* I. ii. 50 God made him, and therefore let him pass for a man. **1599** *Id. A.Y.* III. ii. 191 Is he of God's making? What manner of man? Is his head worth a hat? or his chin worth a beard? **1599** PORTER *Angry Wom. Abingd.* l. 976. **1600–1** SHAKES. *H.* III. ii. 33 I have thought some of Nature's journeymen had made men, and not made them well, they imitated humanity so abominably. **1630** MASSINGER *Picture* IV. ii He was once a creature, It may be, of God's making, but long since He is turn'd to a druggist's shop.

Man of straw is worth a woman of gold, A.　(M 294)

1591 FLORIO *Second F.* 173 (more worth). **1615** DANIEL *Hymen's Tri.* Idolatrize not so that sex but hold A man of straw more than a wife of gold. **1670** RAY 49 . . . *Un homme de paille vaut une femme d'or.*

Man of, *see also* Beware of m. o. one book; Gladness seldom falls into madness; Great memory without learning; Many trades begs on Sunday; Three letters; Words and not deeds is like a garden full of weeds.

Man or mouse.　(M 297)

1541 *Schoolhouse of Women* B3 Feare not she sayeth vnto her spouse A man or a mouse, whyther be ye. **1542** ERASM. tr. Udall *Apoph.* 267b He was vtterly mynded to put al in hasard to make or marre, & to bee manne or mouse. *c.* **1542** BORDE *Dietary of Health* E.E.T.S. 240

Not able to kepe man nor mowse. *c.* **1622** FLETCHER *Love's Cure* II. ii. I will make a man, or a mouse on you. **1639** CLARKE 41 A man or a mouse, a king or a begger. **1869** TENNYSON *North. Farmer* ii Dosn't thou knaw that a man mun be either a man or a mouse?

Man proposes, God disposes.　(M 298)

[PROV. xvi. 9 (Vulgate) *Cor hominis disponit uiam suam; sed Domini est dirigere gressus eius.*—*De Imitatione Christi,* Rib. i. c. 19 *Homo proponit, sed Deus disponit.*] **1377** LANGLAND *P. Pl.* B. xi. 36, 37 *Homo proponit,* quod a poete . and Plato he hyght, And *Deus disponit,* quod he . lat God done his wille. *c.* **1450** tr. *De Imitatione* I. xix. For man purposiþ & god disposiþ. **1530** PALSGRAVE 670b Man purposeth and God disposeth. **1612** SHELTON *Quix.* II. lv. iv. 139 But man purposeth and God disposeth. **1625** PURCHAS *Pilgrims* (1905–7) XIX. 506, 7 The Zelanders . . . coined . . . money . . . with this sentence: Man purposeth God disposeth. **1641** FERGUSSON no. 625 Man propons, but God dispons. **1655–62** GURNALL *Chrn. in Armour* (1865) II. 360 Whatever will thou makest, God is sure to,be thy executor. Man may propose and purpose, but God disposeth. **1853** TRENCH iii. 66.

Man punishes the action, but God the intention.

1732 FULLER no. 3332.

Man should keep from the blind and give to his kin, A.

1461 *Paston Lett.* ed. Gairdner (1904) iv. 13 It is a comon proverbe, A man xuld kepe fro the blynde and gevyt to is kyn. **1721** KELLY 118 Give your own Sea Maws your own Fish Guts. If you have any Superfluities give them to your poor Relations, Friends, or Countrymen, rather than to others. **1816** SCOTT *Antiquary* ch. 15 We maun gie our ain fish-guts to our ain sea-maws.

Man sleeps, When a | his head is in his stomach.　(M 409)

1640 HERBERT no. 981.

Man that sought his mare, and he riding on her, You are like the.

1721 KELLY 363 . . . Spoken to them that are seeking what they have about them.

Man without money is no man at all, A.

(M 305)

1592 DELAMOTHE 55 . . . (is a body without the soule). **1659** N. R. 17 A man without money is a body without life. **1732** FULLER no. 317.

Man without money than money without a man, Rather a.　(M 361)

1529 HYRDE *Instr. Chr. Wom.* XVI. 110 I had leaver have a man without money than money without a man. **1539** TAVERNER I *Garden* E1ᵛ. [Themistocles.] **1592** DELAMOTHE 21 We must rather seeke for a man that wantes wealth, then for a wealth that wantes a man. **1608** J. DAVIES

Minor Poems 71 Tithes and lands I like, yet rather fancy can, A man that wanteth gold, then gold that wants a man.

Man without reason is a beast in season, A.   (M 306)

1659 HOWELL *Eng. Prov.* 11b.   **1670** RAY 22.
1732 FULLER no. 6244.

Man without religion is like a horse without a bridle, A.   (M 307)

[L. *Homo sine religione, sicut equus sine freno.*]
1621 BURTON *Anat. Mel.* III. iv. I. ii. (1651) 646 Justice and religion are the two chief props . . . of a . . . commonwealth: . . . as Sabellicus delivers.

Man, woman, and devil, are the three degrees of comparison.

1732 FULLER no. 3335.

Man's extremity is God's opportunity.   (M 471)

1602 WARNER *Albion's Eng.* Bk. 13, ch. 76, 315 Thus sensuall Epicure, thy selfe gainsaiste it [a Godhead] not for shame: Yea, Atheist, in Extremeties, thou touchest on his Name.
1605–6 SHAKES. *K.L.* IV. vi. 73 Think that the clearest gods, who make them honours Of men's impossibilities, have preserv'd thee.
1629 T. ADAMS *Serm.* (1861–2) I. 96 Here is now a delivery fit for God, a cure for the almighty hand to undertake, Man's extremity is God's opportunity.   **1706** LD. BELHAVEN *Speech in Scot. Parl. on Union* 2 Nov.   **1916** E. A. BURROUGHS *Valley of Decis.* (1920) viii. 197 This was . . . a typical case of 'Man's extremity, God's opportunity'.

Man's meat, To be.   (M 490)

a. **1576** WHYTHORNE 76 A yoong ʒentilwoman . . . for her gifts of natiur waʒ mans meat.   **1666** TORRIANO *Prov. Phr.* s.v. Starvi o Starci, 203: To be Marriageable; spoken of a Maid grown up, as the English say, to be Mans-meat.

Man's praise in his own mouth stinks, A.   (M 476)

[L. *Laus in proprio ore sordescit.* Praise in one's own mouth is offensive.]   **1484** CAXTON *Fab. Avian* no. 11, 229 No fowler a thyng is to the man than with his mouth to preyse hym self.   **1596** SHAKES. *M.V.* III. iv. 22 This comes too near the praising of myself. Therefore no more of it.   **1612** SHELTON *Quix.* III. ii. i. 111. Men say that proper praise stinks.   **1614–16** *Times Whistle* iii. 1088–9 Hast thou that auncient, true saide sawe forgot, That 'a man's praise in his owne mouth doth stinke'?   **1832** HENDERSON 47 Self-praise comes aye stinking ben.[1]   **1854** SURTEES *Hand. Cross* ch. 45 'Self-praise is no commendation', muttered our Master.   **1864–5** DICKENS *Our Mut. Fr.* Bk 4, ch. 2 'Mr. and Mrs. Boffin will remind you of the old adage, that self-praise is no recommendation.'   [[1] home.]

Man, men, *see also* Ambition loses many a m.; Breaks his word (A m. that) bids others be false; Danger makes m. devout; Dog (m.) of wax; Grace is best for the m.; Greater the m. greater the crime; Hand of m. (Whatever is made by) . . . may be overturned; Homo is common name to all m.; Hope keeps m. alive; Horse and m.; Inch a m. (Every); Learning in the breast of bad m.; Living m. (No) all things can; Master (Like) like m.; Mind is the m.; Money makes the m.; North-west wind (Honest m. and a); Remember thou art but a m.; Show me not (Look not on) the meat but the m.; Show me the m., and I'll show the law; Style is the m.; Tailor makes the m.; Thread will tie an honest m. better; Today a m., tomorrow a mouse; Woman confusion of m.

Man (men), *see also these preceded by one of the following adjectives*: All, Angry, Another, Black, Blind, Bold, Brown, Busiest, Choleric, Cornish, Covetous, Crafty, Crooked, Dead, Deaf, Discontented, Drowning, Drunken, Dumb, Dying, Envious, Every, Fat, Foolish, Full, Good, Grateful, Gravest, Great, Greedy, Happy, Hasty, Hated, Healthful, Honest, Hungry, Idle, Ill, Ingenious, Last, Leeful, Liberal, Long, Low, Manchester, Married, Mercenary, Merry, Mighty, Miserable, Moneyless (Silverless), Naked, Nine, No, Old, One, Other, Pale, Patient, Poor, Properer, Red, Rich, Sick, Silent, Silly, Simple, Singing, Slothful, Sober, Solitary, Sullen, Threatened, True, Two, Unhappy, Valiant, Waking, White, Wicked, Wight, Wilful, Wise, Wisest, Wrong, Young.

Man (cannot, had, has, is, may, must, never, shall as soon, were, will never, would), *see also under significant words following.*

Man's, A, *see* Destiny always dark; Discontent his worst evil; Gift makes room for him; House is his castle; Studies pass into character.

Manchester bred: long in the arms, and short in the head.

1869 HAZLITT 273.   **1902–4** LEAN I. 119 Higson (*MS. Coll.*) 51.

Manchester men and Liverpool gentlemen.

1881 *N. & Q.* 6th Ser. III. 148 There is a common saying in Lancashire: 'A Liverpool gentleman, a Manchester man, a chap fra' Bought'n (Bolton), and a fella fra' Wiggin' (Wigan).   **1908** E. M. SNEYD-KYNNERSLEY *H.M.I.* ch. 28 The commercial travellers, and others, speak of Manchester *men*, and Liverpool *gentlemen*.

Manchester, *see also* Constable of Openshaw.

Manful, *see* Mickle but not m.

Manger, *see* Canterbury higher rack, but Winchester better m.; Dog in m.; Hungry horse clean m.; Rack and m.

Manned with boys, and horsed with colts, He that is | shall have his meat eaten, and his work undone.   (B 582)

1623 CAMDEN 270.   **1670** RAY 118.   **1721** KELLY 169 . . . Because the Boy will neglect his Business, and the Horse will throw him.

Manners and money make a gentleman.
(M 1051)

1659 HOWELL *Span. Prov.* 9 Money and good manners makes Cavelleers.   **1706** STEVENS s.v. Costumbre (make Sons Gentlemen).   **1732** FULLER no. 3333.

Manners know distance.

1648 HERRICK *Hesper., To Sir L. Pemb.* Wks. (Aldine) I. 189 Manners knowes distance, and a man unrude, Wo'd soon recoile, and not intrude His Stomach to a second Meale.

Manners make often fortunes.   (M 630)

1539 TAVERNER 37[v] *Sui cuique mores fingunt fortunam.* A mans owne maners do shape hym hys fortune.   **1597** *Politeuphuia* 166b A mans owne manners doth shape him his fortunes.   **1664** CODRINGTON 206.   **1670** RAY 17.

Manners maketh (make the) man.
(M 629)

c. **1350** *Douce MS. 52* no. 75 Maner makys man. *c.* **1460** *Prov. of Wisdom* (ed. Zupitza) in *Archiv f. d. Stud. d. neueren Sprachen* 90. 245 Euer maner and clothyng makyth man.   **1487** CAXTON *Bk. Good Manners* Prol. According to an olde prouerbe, he that is not manerd is no man. for maners make man.   **1509** BARCLAY *Ship of Fools* i. 282 An olde prouerbe . . . Sayth that good lyfe and maners makyth man.   **1605** *London Prodigal* I. ii. *Shaks. Apoc.* 196 For thers an old saying: . . . Be he borne in barne or hall, Tis maners makes the man and all.   **1662** FULLER *Hants* 3 'Manners make a man' quoth William Wickham'.[1] This generally was his Motto, inscribed frequently on the places of his Founding.   **1701** DEFOE *True-born Eng.* II. Wks. (Bohn) V. 444 Now, Satire, if you can, Their temper show, for manners make the man.   **1721** KELLY 246 Meat feeds, cloth cleeds, but manners makes the man . . . Good Meat, and fine Cloaths, without good Breeding, are but poor Recommendations.   **1902** A. R. COLQUHOUN *Mastery of Pacif.* 252 It is the gravest mistake to . . . introduce the freedom of speech and laxity of manners characteristic of modern Europe and America into the East, whose people are still under the impression that 'manners makyth man'.   [1 Bishop of Winchester, 1367–1404, founder of Winchester College and New College, Oxford.]

Manners, *see also* 'After you' is good m.; Curiosity ill m. in another's house; Evil m. (Of) spring good laws; Good m. to except Lord Mayor; Good m. (Not) to show learning before ladies; Honours change m.; Know good m. but use few (You); Little money as m. (If you had); Lordship (One good) is worth all his m.; Meat is much, m. is more; Men (Like) like m.; Mend his m. (Let him); Nurture and good m. maketh man; Other times, other m.; Wine and wealth change wise men's m.

Manors, *see* Lordship (One good) is worth all his manners [= manors].

Many a little makes a mickle. *Cf.* Many small make a great.   (L 362)

c. **1200** *Ancrene Riwle* 54 Thus ofte, ase me seith of lutel wacseþ muchel.   **1545** TAVERNER G5 We commonly say in englyshe: Many a lyttle maketh a great.   **1614** CAMDEN 310.   **1655** FULLER *Ch. Hist.* VI. v (1868) II. 311 Vast was the wealth accruing to the crown by the dissolution of chantries. 'Many a little', saith the proverb, 'make a mickle'. These foundations, though small in revenue, yet being many in number, mounted up a great bank.   **1712** *Spectator* 14 Oct.   **1721** KELLY 254 Many littles make a mickle. *Lat. Ex granis fit acervus.*   **1758** FRANKLIN *Way to Wealth* (Crowell) 19.   **1844** CARLYLE to his mother, 24 Apr., in FROUDE, *Carlyle's Life in London* xii.

Many a man (one) serves a thankless master.   (M 310)

1620 SHELTON *Quix.* II. lxvi. iii. 286 That it may not be said, So a good servant, an ungrateful master.   *a.* **1628** CARMICHAELL no. 1129.   **1641** FERGUSSON no. 626.   **1721** KELLY 248.

Many a man sings that wife home brings; wist he what he brought, weep he might.

c. **1275** *Provs. of Alfred* A 15 264–7 (1907) 26 Monymon singeþ þat wif hom bryngeþ; wiste he hwat he brouhte, wepen he myhte.   *c.* **1300** *Provs. of Hending* 18 Monimon syngeth, When he hom bryngeth Is yonge wyf; Wyste [he] whet he broghte, Wepen he mohte.

Many a one for land takes a fool by the hand.   (L 49)

c. **1300** *Provs. of Hending* 36 Monimon for londe, Wyueth to shonde.   **1639** CLARKE 99 For a little land, take a fool by the hand.   **1678** RAY 56 Many an one for land takes a fool by the hand, *i.e.* marries her or him.   **1732** FULLER no. 6263.

Many a one says well that thinks ill.

1738 SWIFT *Dial.* I. E.L. 266 Well, miss— Ay, ay; many a one says well that thinks ill.

Many a thing's made for money (the penny).   (T 215)

1590 R. HARVEY *Plain Percevall* (1846) 19 He spide a Iacke an apes, in a gaie cote . . . Good Lord what knacks are made for money, now adaies?   **1591** LYLY *Endym.* II. ii. 139 Why it is a Squirrel.—A Squirrel? O Gods, what things are made for money!   **1732** FULLER no. 5503 What pretty Things Men will make for Money, quoth the old Woman, when she saw a Monkey?   **1857** DEAN RAMSAY *Remin.* V (1911) 203 *Mony a thing's made for the pennie, i.e.* Many contrivances are thought of to get money. *Ibid.* A ridiculous addition used to be made to the common Scottish saying, *Mony a thing's made for the pennie,* . . . 'As the old woman said when she saw a black man'—taking it for granted that he was an ingenious and curious piece of mechanism made for profit.

Many dishes make many diseases. *Cf.* Much meat, much malady.   (D 378)

1592 DELAMOTHE 29 The diuersitie of meates doth hinder digestion. **1622** H. PEACHAM *The Complete Gentleman* (1634, ed. G. S. Gordon) 228 Many dishes breed many diseases. **1655** T. MUFFETT *Healths Improvement* 272 (quoted as proverb).

Many dogs may easily worry[1] one hare.   (D 541)

1592 DELAMOTHE 9 Two little dogges, make a mastif affrayd. **1639** CLARKE 56 (Woorie one). **1721** KELLY 245 (Hounds) . . . Spoken when a potent Family, with their Friends, Relations, and Followers, bear hard upon a poor Man. [1 kill.]

Many drops make a shower (flood).   (D 617)

1559 *Mirror for Mag.* (Campbell) 126 Drops engendre mighty fluds. **1576** PETTIE i. 171 Small drops of rain engender great floods. [1592] **1596** *Edw. III* IV. iv. 59 The drops are infinite, that make a floud. **1600** *The Maid's Metamorphosis* Prol. Drops not diminish, but encrease great floods. **1624** BURTON *Anat. Mel.* I. ii. IV. vii. 151 (make a flood). **1846** DENHAM I.

Many estates are spent in the getting, since women, for tea, forsook spinning and knitting; and men, for punch, forsook hewing and splitting.

1758 FRANKLIN in ARBER *Eng. Garner* V. 582.

Many fair promises in marriage making, but few in tocher[1] paying.   (w 823)

1641 FERGUSSON no. 838 There are many fair words in the marriage making, but few in the tochergood paying. **1721** KELLY 246 . . . People will flatter you with fair Promises and Proposals; till they get you engag'd in some Project for their Interest, but after alter their Tune. [1 portion, dowry.]

Many fear, Whom | must needs fear many.

c. **1526** *Dicta Sapientum* A2 Whom many dredeth must nedes feare many.

Many friends, He that has | eats too much salt with his meat.   (F 744)

1616 DRAXE no. 798 Amongst friends much salt is eaten. **1659** HOWELL *Eng. Prov.* 19a.

Many frosts and many thowes[1] make many rotten yowes.[2]

1864 DENHAM 62. [1 thaws. 2 ewes.]

Many 'Good nights' is loth away.

a. **1628** CARMICHAELL no. 1170. *a.* **1721** PRIOR *Thief & Cord.* Wks. (1858) 190 And often took

leave; but was loth to depart. **1721** KELLY 251 . . . Spoken by those who, by reason of some Accident, return after they had taken their Leave.

Many hands make light (quick, slight) work.   (H 119)

[ERASM. *Ad. Multae manus onus levius reddunt.* Many hands make a burden lighter.] *c.* 1350 *Douce MS.* 52 no. 70 Many hondys makyn lyghth worke. *c.* 1350 *How the Gd. Wife* l. 131 Many honden maken li3t werk. 14.. *Sir Beues* 3012 (MS. M.) Though Ascaparde be neuer so starke, Many handes make lyght warke! *c.* 1470 *Harl. MS. 3362*, f. 76. Many handis makith lyth werk—*Multorum manibus alleuiatur opus.* **1539** TAVERNER 36 Many handes make a lyghte burthen. **1546** HEYWOOD II. v. H1 Many handis make light warke. **1599** JAMES VI *Basil. Dor.* (Roxb.) II. 60 Establish honest, diligent, but few searchers (for manie handes make slight worke). **1614** CAMDEN 309. **1616** BRETON *Cross. Prov.* B3 (quick). **1663** F. HAWKINS *Youth's Behav.* 90. **1678** BUTLER *Hudibras* III. ii. 261 Most hands dispatch apace, and make light work (the proverb says). **1721** KELLY 244 (slight). Because, while every one trusts to another, the Work is neglected. **1830** W. CARLETON *Irish Peasantry* (1864) I. 37 Many hands make light work, and . . . it wasn't long till they had cleared a way for themselves.

Many haws, many snaws.

1842 R. CHAMBERS *Pop. Rhymes Scot.* 37 Mony hawes, Mony snaws. It is thus inferred that, when there is a great exhibition of blossoms on the hedgerows, the ensuing winter will be remarkable for snowstorms. . . . A providential object, . . . to supply food for the birds in the coming season. **1846** DENHAM 24 Many hips and haws, many frosts and snaws.

Many-headed beast [= the multitude], The.   (M 1308)

[HOR. *Ep.* I. i. 76 Bellua multorum es capitum.] **1531** ELYOT *The Governor* (Croft) i. 9 A monstre with many heedes. **1539** R. TAVERNER 2 *Garden* F5ᵛ That beast of manye heddes I meane . . . the people, for so . . . Horace calleth them. **1542** ERASM. tr. Udall *Apoph.* 109 The multitude of the grosse people, beeyng a beaste of many heddes. **1586** WHETSTONE *English Mirror* 208 (attrib. to Socrates). **1598** SIDNEY *Arc.* II, Bk. ii. 199 O weak trust of the many-headed multitude. **1608** SHAKES. *C.* II. iii. 17 He himself stuck not to call us the many-headed multitude. **1734** POPE *Imit. Horace* Ep. I. i. 121 The people are a many-headed beast.

Many irons in the fire, part (some) must cool.   (I 99, 100)

1549 SIR W. PAGET *Let. to Somerset* 7 July (P.R.O., St. Pap. Dom. Edw. VI. viii. No. 4) Put no more so many yrons in the fyre at ones. **1621** ROBINSON 12 He that hath many Irons in the fire, some will coole. **1624** CAPT. SMITH *Virginia* iv. 159 They that have many Irons in the fire, some must burne. **1641** FERGUSSON no. 601 Mony yrons in the fire part mon coole. **1721** KELLY 255 . . . When Men have too many Works in hand, too many Offices, or Imployments, some must be neglected. **1881** WESTALL *Old Factory* ch. 3 Dr. Leatherlad was . . . by no means a bad teacher, but having many irons in the fire . . . he had to leave his scholars . . . pretty much to their own devices.

Many kinsfolk and few friends. (K 97)

1546 HEYWOOD I. xi. E4 Many kynsfolke and few freends, some folke saie. But I fynde many kynsfolke, and freende not one. **1621** BURTON *Anat. Mel.* III. i. II. ii. (1651) 421 The love of kinsmen is grown cold, 'many kinsmen (as the saying is) few friends'. **1670** RAY 94 . . . Ones kindred are not always to be accounted ones friends. **1710** PALMER 252 (relations). **1721** KELLY 251 Many aunts, many emms,[1] many kinsfolk, few friends. Spoken by them that have many rich Friends, and are little the better for them. [1 relations.]

Many lords, many laws. (L 445)

1616 DRAXE no. 70.

Many means to get money. (M 795)

1639 CLARKE 191.

Many rains, many rowans;[1] many rowans, many yawns.[2]

1846 DENHAM 54 [1 Rowans are the fruit of the mountain ash; and an abundance thereof is held to denote a deficient harvest. [2] Light grains of wheat, oats, or barley.]

Many small make a great. *Cf.* Many a little makes a mickle. (S 554)

c. **1386** CHAUCER *Parson's T.* l. 362 For the proverbe seith that 'manye smale maken a greet'. **1546** HEYWOOD I. xi. D4 Here some and there some, many small make a great. **1602** R. CAREW *Survey of Cornwall* 1769 ed., 68ᵛ. *a.* **1628** CARMICHAELL no. 1127.

Many strike on an anvil, When | they must strike by measure. (A 260)

1640 HERBERT no. 551. **1642** TORRIANO 14 (keep time). **1670** RAY 17.

Many things grow in the garden that were never sown there. (T 190)

[Sp. *c.* **1627** CORREAS *Vocab.* (1906) 207 Nace en la güerta lo que el hortelano no siembra. (*In the garden more grows than the gardener sows.*)] **1659** HOWELL *Span. Prov.* 6. **1670** RAY 12. **1709–10** ADDISON *Tatler* no. 146 (1899) III. 174 That spurious crop of blessings and calamities which were never sown by the hand of the Deity, but grew of themselves. **1853** TRENCH iv. 92 More springs in the garden than the gardener ever sowed . . . is a proverb . . . for parents and teachers, that they lap not themselves in a false dream of security.

Many things happen unlooked for. (T 192)

1548 HALL (1809 ed. 392) This ioyefull message . . . was the more pleasaunte because yt was vnloked for. **1578** *Courtly Controv.* N3ᵛ Happily one good houre maye chaunce vnlooked

for. **1592** DELAMOTHE 15 Oft some good happeneth to vs, when we least looke for it. **1639** CLARKE 123.

Many trades, A man of | begs his bread on Sunday. (M 293)

1606 2 *Ret. from Parnassus* v. iv We haue run through many trades, yet thriue by none. *a.* **1628** CARMICHAELL no. 136 A man of manie crafts thrave never. **1721** KELLY 5 . . . A Man of many Trades seldom thrives so well, as he that sticks closely to one. **1862** HISLOP *Proverbs of Scotland* 16 (may beg his bread on Sunday).

Many ventures make a full freight. (V 30)

1616 DRAXE no. 44. **1670** RAY 17.

Many wells, many buckets. (W 264)

c. **1549** HEYWOOD II. vii. E7ᵛ But well wyfe well. Well well (quoth she) many wels, many buckets. **1611** DAVIES *Prov.* 253 (as *c.* 1549). **1616** DRAXE no. 2454.

Many women, many words; many geese, many turds. (W 687)

c. **1350** *Douce MS. 52* no. 69 There ben women, there ben wordis; there ben gese, there ben tordys. *c.* **1425** *Castle of Perseverance* ll. 2650–1 Ther wymmen arn, are many wordys: . . . ther ges syttyn, are many tordys. **1541** *Schoolhouse of Women* B4ᵛ Where many geese be, are many tordes And where be women, are many wordes. **1581** C. THIMELTHORPE *Short Inventory* I6 It hath bene an old sainge, many geese many birdes, many women many words. *a.* **1628** CARMICHAELL no. 1302. **1678** RAY 64 Where there are women and geese there wants no noise.

Many words, many buffets. (W 816)

c. **1549** HEYWOOD II. vii. E7ᵛ Ye (quoth he) and many woords, many buffets. Had you some husbande, and snapte at hym thus, I wys he would geue you a recumbentibus.[1] **1616** DRAXE no. 2483. [1 knockdown blow.]

Many words, In | the truth goes by. (W 828)

1545 TAVERNER B5ᵛ Oure *Englyshe* prouerbe . . . where many wordes be, the trueth goeth by. **1548** HALL *Chron.* Dedn. I haue redde an olde proverbe, whiche saithe, that in many woordes, a lye or twayne sone maie escape. *a.* **1550** *Parl. of Birds Harl. Misc.* 1745, v. 479. **1616** DRAXE no. 2047 Where many words are the truth goeth by.

Many (a, a man, a one, can, have been, men); *see also under significant words following.*

Mar, marred, *see* Fish m. water; Make or m.; Market is m.; Marriage makes or m. a man; May makes or m. wheat.

Marble, *see* Rome brick (I found), I leave it m.

March borrowed from April three days, and they were ill.   (A 307)

1646 BROWNE *Pseudo. Epi.* VI. iv So it is usual among us . . . to ascribe unto March certain borrowed days from April. **1670** RAY 41 April borrows three days of March and they are ill. **1721** KELLY 252 . . . It is alleg'd that the first three Days of *April* are commonly rough and intemperate, and these we call the borrowing Days. **1731** *Poor Robin's Alm.* Obs. on April . . . There is an old proverb . . . viz. March borrow'd of April three Days and they were ill, They kill'd three Lambs were playing on a hill. **1847** R. CHAMBERS *Pop. Rhymes Scot.* 368 March borrowed from April Three days, and they were ill: The first o' them was wind and weet; The second o' them was snaw and sleet; The third o' them was sic a freeze, It froze the birds' nebs to the trees.

March comes in like a lion and goes out like a lamb.   (M 641)

c. 1620–35 *The Telltale* l. 336 (as mild as a lamb). **1624** J. FLETCHER *Wife for Month* II. i. I would chuse March, for I would come in like a Lion.— But you'ld go out like a Lamb, when you went to hanging. **1640** HOWELL *Dodona's G.* 10 Like the moneth of March, which entreth like a Lion, but goeth out like a Lamb. **1670** RAY 41 March hack ham comes in like a lion, goes out like a lamb. **1849** C. BRONTË *Shirley* ch. 15 Peter . . . had sense to feel that . . . he had better be civil. Like March, having come in like a lion, he purposed to go out like a lamb.

March comes in with adder heads, and goes out with peacock tails.

1721 KELLY 251.

March dust, A peck of | and a shower in May, makes the corn green and the fields gay.

1721 KELLY 43.   **1732** FULLER no. 6476.

March dust (wind) and May sun, makes corn (clothes) white and maids dun.

1670 RAY 41 (wind . . . clothes).   **1846** DENHAM 39.

March dust is worth a king's ransom, A bushel (peck) of.   (B 743)

c. 1530 HEYWOOD *Play of Wether* 622 (Brandl) One bushell of march is worth a kynges raunsome. **1557** TUSSER D1 A bushel of Marche dust, worth raunsomes of gold. [*c.* 1598] 1609 JONSON *Case is Altered* V. xiii. 67 March faire al, for a faire March is worth a king's ransome. **1639** CLARKE 307 (A coome [= four bushels]). **1662** FULLER *Berks.* 87 (In England). . . . A general good redounds to our Land by a dry March. **1885** D. C. MURRAY *Rainbow G.* V. iv. A neighbour . . . quoted the proverb that a peck of March dust is worth a king's ransom.

March, Fog in | frost in May.

1612 A. HOPTON *Concordancy of Years* 103 Some say, so many mistes in March, so many hoare frosts after Easter. **1944** *The Times* 26 May 6 In this part of Surrey there is a saying: 'Fog in March frost in May', in which everyone believes.

March grass never did good.   (G 418)

1678 RAY 44. **1732** FULLER no. 6475. **1908** *Sphere* 14 Mar. 233 Weather saws which the wintry weather has brought home . . . to us. 'March grass', says one of them, 'never did good'.

March in Janiveer, Janiveer in March I fear.   (M 642)

1678 RAY 44. **1908** *Sphere* 14 Mar. 233 'Janiveer in March I fear'. . . . This reminds one of . . . saws which the wintry weather has brought home . . . to us.

March, In | kill crow, pie,[1] and cadow,[2] rook, buzzard, and raven; or else go desire them to seek a new haven.

1846 DENHAM 35. [[1] magpie. [2] jackdaw.]

March many weathers.   (M 643)

1678 RAY 44. **1732** FULLER no. 6475 March many-Weathers rain'd and blow'd, But March Grass never did good.

March sun causes dust, The | and the winds blow it about.   (S 974)

1664 CODRINGTON 220.   **1670** RAY 17.

March sun raises, but dissolves not, The.   (S 975)

1640 HERBERT no. 614.   **1659** HOWELL *It. Prov.* 14 (heats but does not melt).

March, In | the birds begin to search; in April the corn begins to fill; in May, the birds begin to lay.

1869 HAZLITT 233.

March, In | the cuckoo starts; in April, a' tune his bill; in May, a' sing all day; in June, a' change his tune; in July, away a' fly; in August, away a' must; in September, you'll *allers* remember; in October, 'ull never get over.

1849 HALLIWELL *Pop. Rhymes & Nurs. T.* 160 In April the cuckoo shows his bill; in May, he sings all day; in June, he alters his tune; in July, away he'll fly; in August, away he must. **1869** *N. & Q.* 4th Ser. III. 94. [East Anglia.]

March whisker[1] was never a good fisher.   (W 309)

1641 FERGUSSON no. 643. **1721** KELLY 254 . . . A windy March is a Token of a bad Fish Year. **1732** FULLER no. 6127. **1842** R. CHAMBERS *Pop. Rhymes Scot.* 74 March whisker Was ne'er a gude fisher—. . . A blustering March is unfavourable to the angler, although good for the farmer. [[1] blusterer.]

March wind kindles (wakes) the adder and blooms the thorn (whin).

1846 DENHAM 39 March wind, kindles the ether,[1] and blooms the whin. [[1] adder.]

March, *see also* February makes bridge, M. breaks it; First of M. crows begin to search; Flea in M.; Frosts in M., so many in May; Mad as a M. hare; Steal a m.; Thunders in M., (When it) it brings sorrow; Windy M. and rainy April.

Mare has a bald face, When the | the filly will have a blaze.[1]   (M 656)

1659 HOWELL *Eng. Prov.* 2b. **1732** FULLER no. 5596. [[1] white mark on face.]

Mare's nest, To find a.   (M 658)

[= an illusory discovery.] **1576** R. PETERSON *Galateo* (1892) 111 Nor stare in a mans face as if he had spied a mares nest. **1582** N. BRETON in *Works* Gros. 16 To laughe at a horse nest, and whine too like a boy. *a.* **1619** FLETCHER *Bonduca* v. ii. Why dost thou laugh? What Mares nest hast thou found? **1721** KELLY 385 You have found a horse nest. Spoken to them who laugh without a Cause. **1738** SWIFT *Dial.* I. E.L. 275 What! you have found a mare's nest, and laugh at the eggs? **1892** *Times Wkly.* 21 Oct. 18/2 Colonel S.'s discovery is a mere mare's nest.

Mare's shoe and a horse's shoe are both alike, A.   (M 659)

1641 FERGUSSON no. 147 A mache and a horse shoe are both alike. **1721** KELLY 34. **1732** FULLER no. 318.

Mare's tails, *see* Mackerel sky and m. t.

Mares in the wood than Grisell, There are more.   (M 660)
1678 RAY 173.

Mare(s), mear (*Scot.*), *see also* Bites the m. by the thumb; Careless parting . . . m. and broken cart; Counsel will make a man stick his own m.; Coy as a croker's m.; Fidging m. should be well girded; Flanders m.; Gip . . . quoth Badger, when his m. kicked; Grey m. is better horse; Man has his m. again; Man that sought his m., and he riding on her; Miller's m. (Like a); Money makes m. go; Nag with a weamb, m. with nean; Old m. leave flinging (Hard to make); Old m. would have new crupper; Proo naunt your m. puts; Put the man to the m. that can manage; Ride who will, the m. is shod; Shank's m.; Shoe the wild (mockish) m.; Simpers like a m. when she eats thistles; Speaks ill of my m. would buy her; Whose m. is dead?

Marham, *see* Held together, as the men of M.

Mariners' craft is the grossest, yet of handicrafts the subtillest.   (M 663)
1573 SANFORD 104[v]. **1629** *Bk. Mer. Rid.* Prov. no. 101.

Mariners, *see also* St. Paul's m.

Marines, *see* Tell that to the m.

Mark after her mother, She has a.   (M 665)

1678 RAY 259 . . . That is, she is her mother's own daughter. *Patris est filius.*

Mark with a white stone, To.   (S 891)

[= to reckon as specially fortunate or happy, in allusion to the use of a white stone among the ancients as a memorial of a fortunate event. ERASM. *Ad. Creta notare, carbone notare.*] **1540** PALSGRAVE *Acolastus* 74 O Festyuall daye . . . worthye to be marked with a stone as whyte as snowe. *c.* **1645** HOWELL *Lett.* I. I. xiii (1890) 38 You are one . . . whose Name I haue mark'd with the whitest Stone. **1748** SMOLLETT *Rod. Rand.* ch. 52 'God be praised! a white stone!' . . . he alluded to the *Dies fasti* of the Romans, *albo lapide notati.* **1885** HORNADAY *Two Yrs. in Jungle* ch. 27 I have marked that day with a white stone as being the one on which I ate my first durian.

Mark, *see also* Ball does not stick to the wall (If) it will at least leave m.; Bigger the man, better the m.; Blind man may sometimes hit m.; Fool's bolt may sometimes hit m.; God save the m.; Hit the prick (m.); Scotsmen take m. from a mischief; Shoot wide of the m.; Shoots oft shall hit m.; Shoots well that hits m.

Marked, *see* Person m. (Take heed of).

Market cross, *see* Grass grows not at the m. c.

Market days, *see* Mickle between m. d.

Market goes, As the | wives must sell.   (M 670)

1545 *Precepts of Cato* B3[v] Accordynge to the prouerbe and common saying, Take thy market whyle tyme is, least of thy pryce thou do mysse. **1546** HEYWOOD I. xi. D4[v] Men know . . . Howe the market gothe by the market men. *c.* **1590** LYLY *Love's Met.* I. ii. 32 Take your penniworth whiles the market serues. **1599** SHAKES. *A.Y.* III. v. 59 Sell when you can. You are not for all markets. *c.* **1602** *Id. A.W.* I. i. 144 Off with't [virginity] while 'tis vendible; answer the time of request. **1659** N.R. 78 Men must make there market as the time serves. **1721** KELLY 52 (Wares must sell). **1732** FULLER no. 734.

Market is marred, The.

1547 J. BALE *Exam[n] Anne Askewe* P.S. 244 They are like to mar all their market. **1554** H. HILARIE (= J. Bale?) *Resurrection of the Mass* B1 Their market will be altogether marred. **1587** J. BRIDGES *Defence* 1372 The market is well fallen, and perhaps mard, for the vtterance of these wares. **1616** DRAXE no. 2065 His markets are marred. **1632** *Holland's Leaguer* C4 Had he amplified . . . vpon this Text, he had mar'd his owne market.

Market is the best garden, The. (M 675)

1640 HERBERT no. 743. **1670** RAY 17 . . . *At London they are wont to say*, Cheapside is the best garden.

Market of his ware, He that desires to make | must watch an opportunity to open his shop. (M 674)

1597 *Politeuphuia* 166. **1639** CLARKE 237.

Market, To make up one's. (M 672)

1559 T. BECON *Disp. Popish Mass Prayers* P.S. 274 Pope Urban . . . made up all the market; for he ordained a feast, called Corpus Christi. **1590** LODGE *Rosalynde* 104 Well sir, if your market may be made no where els, home again. **1594** NASHE *Unfort. Trav.* ii. 263 I stepping to her with a dunstable tale made vp my market. **1672** WALKER 34 no. 10 He knows how to make his market (make use of his time) well enough.

Market(s), *see also* Abide a bad m. (He that cannot); Buy in cheapest m.; Driving hogs (pigs, turkeys) to m.; Drug in m.; Fool has bethought himself (When), m.'s over; Fool to m., (Send); Fools went not to m. (If) bad wares not sold; Forsake not m. for the toll; Friend in the m.; Game cheaper in m.; Gentry sent to m. will not buy . . . corn; Good ware quick m.; Hogs to a fair m. (He has brought); Honour buys no beef in m.; Know how the m. goes; Love is not found in m.; Moneyless man goes fast through m.; No man makes haste to m. where nothing . . . but blows; Run before one's horse to m.; Sell his ware after the m.; Three women make m.

Market-Jew, *see* Light (In your own), like the Mayor of M.

Market-place, *see* Kisses his wife (*or* Sits to work) in the m. (He that).

Marls sand, He who | may buy the land.

1753 *Gent. Mag.* 120 We have an old saying [Lancs.]: He that marls sand may buy land. **1917** BRIDGE 72 . . . The marl acted as manure and was . . . of most value on sandy soil. . . . The whole proverb stands thus: 'He that marls sand may buy the land, He that marls moss, shall have no loss, He that marls clay, flings all away.'

Marriage halves our griefs, doubles our joys, and quadruples our expenses.

1902–4 LEAN IV. 44.

Marriage is a lottery. (M 681)

1605 MARSTON *The Dutch Courtesan* III. i. 73 Husbands are like lots in the lottery: you may draw forty blanks before you find one that has any prize in him. **1633** JONSON *T. Tub* I. i. 97. I smile to think how like a lottery These weddings are. **1642** FULLER *H. & P. State* III. xxii (1841) 203 Marriage shall prove no lottery to thee, when the hand of Providence chooseth for thee;

who, if drawing a blank, can turn it into a prize, by sanctifying a bad wife unto thee. **1875** SMILES *Thrift* 266 'Marriage is a lottery'. It may be so if we abjure the teachings of prudence. *a.* **1898** BURNE-JONES in his *Life* Isn't marriage a lottery? . . . Then shouldn't it be prohibited by law?

Marriage (Matrimony) is (comes by) destiny. *Cf.* Hanging and wiving. (M 682)

1548 HALL *Chron.* (1809) [Edw. IV] 264 Bot now consider the old prouerbe to be true yt saieth: that marriage is destinie. **1576** PETTIE i. 123 Marriages are guided by destiny. **1602** SHAKES. *A.W.* I. iii. 59 Your marriage comes by destiny. **1605** CHAPMAN *All Fools* V. i (1874) 74. Give me your hand, there is no remedy, Marriage is ever made by destiny.

Marriage is honourable. (M 683)

[HEBREWS xiii. 4 Marriage is honourable in all, and the bed undefiled.] **1576** PETTIE i. 11 As amongst all the bonds of benevolence and good-will there is none more honourable, ancient, or honest than marriage. **1598–9** SHAKES. *M.A.* III. iv. 27 Is not marriage honourable in a beggar? *Ibid.* V. iv. 30 This day to be conjoin'd In the state of honourable marriage. **1616** BRETON 2 *Cross.* A3ᵛ.

Marriage is honourable, but house-keeping is a shrew. (M 684)

1609 HARWARD 94ᵛ (a gentleman). **1639** CLARKE 328 (A wife is a fine thing). **1670** RAY 48. **1738** SWIFT *Dial.* I. E.L. 285.

Marriage makes or mars a man. (M 701)

1546 HEYWOOD I. viii. B4ᵛ And sens our one mariyng or marryng daie, Where any of theim se vs, they shrinke awaie. **1589** PUTTENHAM *Art Eng. Poesy* (ed. Willcock and Walker 1936) III. xix. 207 The maide that soone married is, soone marred is. *c.* **1595** SHAKES. *R.J.* I. ii. 13 And too soon marr'd are those so early made [i.e. married]. **1600–1** *Id. M.W.W.* I. i. 24 I may quarter coz.—You may, by marrying.—It is marring indeed, if he quarter it. **1602** *Id. A.W.* II. iii. 291 A young man married is a man that's marr'd. **1625** HOWELL *Lett.* 5 Feb. (1903) I. 248 You are upon a treaty of marriage. . . . A work of such consequence that it may make you or mar you. **1666** TORRIANO *It. Prov.* 143 no. 30 Who marries, either makes himself, or mars himself. **1841** CAPT. MARRYAT *Poacher* ch. 28 Neither my Ophelia nor Amelia should marry . . . without I was convinced the gentleman considered it a very serious affair. It makes or mars a man, as the saying is.

Marriage, More belongs to | than four bare legs in a bed. (M 1146)

c. **1549** HEYWOOD I. viii. C1 In house to kepe housholde, whan folks wyll wed, Mo thyngs belong, than foure bare legs in a bed. *a.* **1628** CARMICHAELL no. 1092 Mor belongs to a bed nor four bair legs. **1631** JONSON *New Inn* V. v. 136 Foure thousand pound! that's better Then sounds the prouerbe, foure bare legs in a bed.

1721 KELLY 234 Long e'er four bare legs heat in a bed. To dissuade People who have no Stock from marrying. **1738** SWIFT Dial. I. E.L. 286 Consider, Mr. Neverout, four bare legs in a bed: and you are a younger brother. **1823** J. GALT *Entail* ch. 7 Now-a-days it's no the fashion for bare legs to come thegither—The wife maun hae something to put in the pot as well as the man.

Marriage rides upon the saddle and repentance upon the crupper. (M 685)

1604 E. GRYMESTON *Miscellanea* H3ᵛ. **1659** HOWELL *Fr. Prov.* 24.

Marriage, He has a great fancy to | that goes to the devil for a wife.

1732 FULLER no. 1856.

Marriage, In | the husband should have two eyes, and the wife but one.

1580 LYLY *Euph. & his Eng.* ii. 62 In mariage, as market folkes tel me, the husband should haue two eies, and the wife but one.

Marriages and funerals, At | friends are discerned from kinsfolk. (M 687)

1573 SANFORD 101ᵛ. **1629** *Bk. Mer. Rid.* Prov. no. 55 (and burials). **1642** TORRIANO 8 (At weddings and burials). **1732** FULLER no. 829.

Marriages are made in heaven. (M 688)

1567 PAINTER *Pal. of Pleasure* (Jacobs) iii. 24 True it is, that marriages be don in heauen and performed in earth. **1578** *Courtly Controv.* Q2ᵛ The Prouerbe saith, the firste marriages are made in Heauen, and the seconde in Hell. **1580** LYLY *Euph. & his Eng.* ii. 223 Mariages (as they say) are made in heauen, though consumated in yearth. **1662** FULLER *Westmr.* 237 But that Motion died with her father, Heaven (wherein marriages are made) reserving that place for Margaret. **1721** KELLY 183 If marriages be made in heaven, some had few friends there. **1738** SWIFT Dial. I. E.L. 284 They say, marriages are made in heaven; but I doubt, when she was married, she had no friend there. **1853** TRENCH iii. 48.

Marriage(s), *see also* Bride goes to m. bed; Death and m. make term day; Ill m. spring of ill fortune; Keep your eyes open before m.; Like blood . . . makes happiest m.; Money makes m.; Motions are not m.; Poor man gets a poor m.; Weasel and cat make m. (When), evil presage.

Married at Finglesham Church, To be.

1736 PEGGE *Kenticisms, Prov.* E.D.S. 71 . . . There is no church at Finglesham; but a chalk-pit celebrated for casual amours; of which kind of rencounters the saying is us'd.

Married, He that goes far to be | will either deceive or be deceived.

1642 TORRIANO 37 (will either be cozened, or doth intend to cozen). **1659** HOWELL *Span. Prov.* 17.

Married man turns his staff into a stake, A. (M 312)

c. **1620** MASSINGER *Fatal Dowry* IV. i But married once, A man is stak'd, or pown'd, and cannot graze Beyond his own hedge. **1640** HERBERT no. 366. **1670** RAY 17 (must turn).

Married men, *see* Bachelors laugh.

Married to the gunner's daughter, To be.

[= to be lashed to a ship's gun for punishment.] **1785** GROSE s.v. Gunner's Daughter. **1821** BYRON in MOORE *Lett.* (1833) 139 As . . . Captain Whitby . . . used to say to his seamen (when 'married to the gunner's daughter')—'two dozen, and let you off easy'. **1833** MARRYAT *P. Simple* ch. 32 I'll marry some of you young gentlemen to the gunner's daughter.

Married woman has nothing of her own but her wedding-ring and her hair-lace, A.

1738 SWIFT Dial. III. E.L. 322 They say a married woman has nothing of her own but her wedding-ring and her hair-lace: but if women had been the law-makers, it would have been better.

Marries a widow and two children (daughters) marries three thieves (has three back doors to his house) | He that. (W 335)

a. **1576** WHYTHORNE 98 It iz an old saieng that hee who weddeth with A widow who hath ij children, hee shalbe kumbred with iij theavs, bekawz that the mother . . . will purloin and filch from her husband to bestow it vpon her children. **1623** PAINTER C8ᵛ (with children three, . . . of foure theeues sure shall be). **1670** RAY 51 (three children marries four thieves). **1721** KELLY 137 no. 84 He that marries a Widow, and two Daughters, has three back Doors to his House. *Ibid.* no. 85 He that marries a Widow, and two Daughters, marries three stark Thieves. Because his Wife will put Things away to them, or for them.

Marries a widow, He that | will often have a dead man's head thrown in his dish. (W 336)

1546 HEYWOOD II. vii. I3ᵛ For I neuer meete the at fleshe nor at fishe, But I haue sure a deade mans head in my dyshe. **1813** RAY 15 *Hisp.* **1884** J. PAYN *Canon's Ward* ch. 27 It is always dangerous to marry a widow, because of the unpleasant comparisons which she may make.

Marries between the sickle and the scythe, Who | will never thrive. (S 422)

1678 RAY 352.

Marries ere he be wise, He that | will die ere he thrive. (W 229)

1546 HEYWOOD I. viii. CI. **1641** FERGUSSON no. 361. **1721** KELLY 148 . . . For want of Skill

to manage a Family, he will put himself so far
behind, that he will not easily recover.

Marries for love without money, Who | has good nights and sorry days. (L 552)

1623 WODROEPHE 486 Fy on Loue without
Mony! **1642** TORRIANO 37. **1664** CODRINGTON
226. **1670** RAY 17. **1732** FULLER no. 5710.

Marries for wealth, He that | sells his liberty. (W 195)

1581 GUAZZO ii. 7 Where entereth in the riche
dowrye, there goeth out the free libertye. **1640**
HERBERT no. 784. **1732** FULLER no. 2238.

Marries late, He that | marries ill. (M 697)

1589 NASHE *Anat. of Absurdity* i. 13 Thys common prouerbe, he that marrieth late marrieth
euill. **1640** HERBERT no. 863. **1706** STEVENS
s.v. Casar. **1898** G. B. SHAW *Plays Pleasant and
Unpleasant* Pref. There is an old saying that if a
man has not fallen in love before forty, he had
better not fall in love after.

Marrow, *see* Blind that eats his m.

Marry a beggar, and get a louse for your tocher-good[1]. *Cf.* Beggar pays; See a b.

1721 KELLY 245 . . . A Dissuasive from joining
in Trade, or Farm, with a poor Man, where the
whole Loss must lye on you. [[1] portion.]

Marry a widow before she leaves mourning. (W 338)

1640 HERBERT no. 252. **1659** HOWELL *Span.
Prov.* 17. **1706** STEVENS s.v. Viuda, . . . and a
Maid before he can see her own Nose.

Marry a widow, Never | unless her first husband was hanged.

1721 KELLY 260 . . . Lest she upbraid you with
him, and sing you an old Scottish Song: *You
will never be like our old good Man.*

Marry come up.

c. **1595** SHAKES. *R.J.* II. v. 64 Marry, come up,
I trow; Is this the poultice for my aching bones?
1608 *Id. P.* IV. vi. 150 Marry, come up, my dish
of chastity with rosemary and bays! **1642** J.
EATON *Honey-c. Free Justif.* 14 Taunting and
reproachfull terms, as, *Marry come up.* **1862**
BORROW *Wild Wales* I. xxiv. 276 Unworthy?
marry come up! I won't hear such an expression.

Marry come up, my dirty cousin. (C 740)

1674 T. DUFFET *Empress of Morocco* 4
Marry come up, my durty Cozen, He may have
such as you by th' Dozen. **1678** RAY 68 . . .
Spoken by way of taunt, to those who boast
themselves of their birth, parentage, or the like.
1706 STEVENS s.v. Hermano. **1721** KELLY 82
. . . A Reprimand to mean People, when they
propose a Thing that seems too saucy. **1738**
SWIFT Dial. II. E.L. 305.

Marry first, and love will come after-wards (follow). (L 534)

1600–1 SHAKES. *M.W.W.* I. i. 224 Can you love
the maid?—I will marry her, sir, at your request;
but if there be no great love in the beginning, yet
heaven may decrease it. **1601** MARSTON *Jack
Drum* III. E3ᵛ Love should make marriage, and
not marriage love. **1607** G. WILKINS *Miseries
Enf. Marr.* B1 You stray from the steps of
Gentility, the fashion among them is to marry
first, and loue afterwards by leisure. **1699** *Poor
Robin's Alm.* Jan. O this Devilish thirst of Gold,
which shall cause many to Marry where they do
not fansie, relying upon the *Sunday-Penny's
Proverb,* . . . **1780** MRS. H. COWLEY *Belle's
Strat.* III. i. Wks. (1813) 265 Then you wont
trust to the good old Maxim—'Marry first, and
Love will follow'?

Marry in green, They that | their sorrow is soon seen.

1847 R. CHAMBERS *Pop. Rhymes Scot.* (1870)
341 Green . . . [has] been connected by superstition with calamity and sorrow. . . . They that
marry in green, Their sorrow is soon seen. . . .
In the north of Scotland, no young woman would
wear such attire on her wedding day.

Marry in haste, and repent at leisure. (H 196)

[PHILEMON *Fab. Incertae, Frag.* 105 Γαμεῖν
ὃς ἐθέλει, εἰς μετάνοιαν ἔρχεται. He who would
marry is on the road to repentance.] **1566**
TILNEY *Duties in Marriage* B4 Some haue loued
in post haste, that afterwards haue repented
them at leysure. **1566** PAINTER i. 29 Leaste in
making hastie choise, leasure for repentaunce
shuld folow. **1576** PETTIE ii. 61 Bargains made
in speed are commonly repented at leisure.
1577 *A merry and pleasant prognostication* C2
Who this yere loueth in hast: Maie hap to
repent ere the yere be past. **1591** SHAKES. *3
Hen. VI* IV. i. 18 Hasty marriage seldom
proveth well. **1598–9** *Id. M.A.* II. i. 62 Wooing,
wedding, and repenting, is as a Scotch jig, a
measure, and a cinque-pace: the first suit is hot
and hasty, . . . the wedding, mannerly-modest, as
a measure, . . . and then comes Repentance, and,
with his bad legs, falls into the cinquepace faster
and faster, till he sink into his grave. **1614**
DAY *Festivals* (1615) 282 Marrying in hast, and
Repenting at leisure. **1670** RAY 47 *Ital.* **1734**
FRANKLIN May Grief often treads upon the
heels of pleasure, Marry'd in haste, we oft
repent at leisure. **1872** SIR W. STIRLING-
MAXWELL *Rector. Addr.* in Wks. (1891) VI. 425
'Marry in haste and repent at leisure' is a proverb
that may be borne in mind with advantage in the
choice of a party as well as of a wife. **1883**
J. PAYN *Thicker than W.* ch. 31 She had married
in haste, and repented, not at leisure, but with
equal rapidity.

Marry in Lent, and you'll live to repent.

1876 MRS. G. L. BANKS *Manch. Man* ch. 18 The
double fees of Lent, and the ill-luck supposed
to follow a couple united during the penitential
forty days. **1929** *Daily Mail* 6 March 11/5
A London registrar told a *Daily Mail* reporter
yesterday: The fixed idea that marriages should
not take place in Lent seems to have disappeared.

Marry in May, repent alway (bairns decay).

[OVID *Fasti* 5. 490 *Mense malum Maio nubere vulgus ait.* To marry in the month of May is unlucky, they say.] **1675** *Poor Robin's Alm.* May The proverb saies . . . Of all the moneths 'tis worst to wed in May. **1821** GALT *Annals of Par.* ch. 6 [We] were married on the 29th day of April . . . on account of the dread that we had of being married in May, for it is said, 'Of the marriages in May, The bairns die of a decay'. **1841** CHAMIER *Tom Bowling* ch. 57. Mrs. Talbot, in this month, in spite of Ovid's declaration, that 'the girls were good for nought who wed in May', was to be married.

Marry late or never, It is good to.

(M 693)

1616 DRAXE no. 2382 It is good to marry late. **1639** CLARKE 329. **1670** RAY 47.

Marry not an old crony, or a fool, for money.

1621 BURTON *Anat. Mel.* II. iii. VII. (1651) 428.

Marry your daughters betimes, lest they marry themselves. *Cf.* **Daughter (Marry your) and eat fresh fish.** (D 47)

a. **1598** LORD BURLEIGH *Precepts* (1637) 9. **1621** BURTON *Anat. Mel.* III. ii. VI. v. (1651) 577 'Tis good to get them husbands betimes . . . ; they perchance will marry themselves else, or do worse. **1651** HERBERT no. 1171. **1659** N.R. 79.

Marry your like (equal, match). (E 178)

[OVID *Heroides* 9. 32 Siqua voles apte nubere, nube pari. If you would marry fitly, marry your equal.] *c.* **1535** ELYOT *Educ.* 14 F3ᵛ For it is a prouerbe replensyed with wysdome: Seke the a wyfe pareile vnto the. **1539** TAVERNER 25 Seke the an egal wyfe. *Id.* 1 *Garden* F4ᵛ [Pittacus] was wont to saye to suche as went about to be maryed. Equalem tibi ducito, Marie thy matche or felowe. **1568** TILNEY *Duties in Marr.* B2 Equalitie is principally to be considered in thys matrimoniall amitie, as well of yeares, as of the giftes of nature, and fortune. For equalnesse herein, maketh friendlynesse . . . take to thee thy peere. Marry not a superiour, sayth Plutarch. **1577** *Bullinger's Decades* (1592) 228 That vsuall Prouerbe: Marrie a wife of thine owne degree. **1639** CLARKE 230 (with your match). **1659** HOWELL *Span. Prov.* 15 Mary and converse with your equal. **1721** KELLY 252 Marry above your match, and you get a master. A Wife, above our Station and Condition, will be apt to despise us, think herself disgrac'd, and prove insolent.

Marry your son when you will, your daughter when you can. (S 626)

1640 HERBERT no. 149. **1659** HOWELL *Span. Prov.* 9. **1706** STEVENS s.v. Hijo.

Marry (-ies, -ied), *see* Advise none to m.; Always say 'No' (If you), never be m.; Before you m. be sure of a house; Born fair is born m., (Who is); Broomstick (To m. over the); Carry a nutmeg (If you), m. to old man; Couple are newly m. (When a), first month is; Fool that m. wife at Yule; Happy is she who m. son of dead mother; Honest men m. soon, wise not at all; Live well for a . . . month (If you would), m.; Maidens should be meek till m.; Needles and pins, when a man m.; Needy when he is m. shall be rich when buried; No man is a match for woman till m.; Promising and performing (Between) man may m. his daughter; Shrew than a sheep (Better to m.); Two bachelors drinking to you . . . soon be m.; Well m. who has neither mother-in-law; Young man should not m. yet.

Marry the devil's daughter, and living with the old folks, As bad as.

1830 FORBY 434 . . . Commonly applied to a person who has made unpromising connexions in marriage.

Marrying, *see also* Building and m. of children are great wasters.

Marshal's bâton, *see* French soldier carries.

Marshland (The), *see* Bailiff of the M.

Martin, *see* Robin and the wren.

Martinmas, *see* Hog has its M. (Every); Wind is on M. Eve (Where the).

Martyr(s), *see* Better to be a m. than confessor; Blood of the m. is seed of Church; Devil's m.; Religion but can boast m. (No); Suffering (Not the) but the cause makes m.

Marvel, *see* Imps follow when the devil goes before, (No m. if the).

Mary (Lady), *see* Breed of L. M., when you're good you're o'er good.

Mass nor matins, Neither. (M 708)

[= nothing of very serious import.] [*a.* **1450**] **1468** *Doomsday* in *Coventry Myst.* 404 Mass nor mateynes. **1528** SIR T. MORE *Dial. conc. Heresyes* I. xx. Wks. 145/2 It maketh no matter they saye, ye may beginne agayne and mende it, for it is nother masse nor mattyns.

Mass, *see also* Kirk is mickle but you may say m.; Lief go to mill as to m.; Meat and m. never hindered; No priest no m.

Master absent and the house dead, The. (M 725)

1640 HERBERT no. 940.

Master and servant, Every one is a. *Cf.* **Master must serve, etc.** (M 713)

1609 HARWARD 103 The maister of the howse is indeed the only servant. He cares for all and pays for all. **1640** HERBERT no. 1026.

Master in an house, One | is enough.
(M 729)

[ERASM. *Ad.* 614E Multitudo imperatorum Cariam perdidit.] **1539** TAVERNER 43ᵛ [As in Erasm.] This prouerbe aduertiseth vs that nothynge is more noysome nor more pestiferous to a common weale, then the ouermoche libertye of a multitude. **1621** ROBINSON 13. **1639** CLARKE 218.

Master, Like | like man.   (M 384, 723)

[ERASM. *Ad. Qualis hera, talis pedissequa*, from CIC. *ad Att.* 5. 11. *Qualis dominus, talis et servus*, PETRONIUS ARBITER *Satyricon* 58.] **1530** PALSGRAVE 378 Suche maystre suche man. **1533–4** UDALL *Flowers* 69ᵛ Suche a maistre suche man. **1548** ERASM. tr. Udall *Par. Luke* xxiii. 177 Beeyng lyke men lyke maister accordyng to the prouerbe. **1568** FULWELL *Like Will to L.* (1906) 24. **1620** SHELTON *Quix.* II. x. ii. 248 This master of mine . . . is a bedlam . . . , and I . . . am the greater coxcomb of two, . . . if the proverb be true that says, 'like master, like man'. **1706** STEVENS s.v. Señor A bad Master makes a bad Servant. **1840** MARRYAT *Poor Jack* ch. 1 They say, 'Like master, like man'; and I may add, 'Like lady, like maid'. Lady Hercules was fine, but her maid was still finer.

Master must serve (another), He that is a. *Cf.* Master and servant, etc.
(M 717)

1557 EDGEWORTH *Serm.* 3V2ᵛ He that is maister of much, is compelled to be seruaunt to many. **1640** HERBERT no. 991.

Master of himself, He that is | will soon be master of others.

1597 *Politeuphuia* 168ᵛ He is vnworthy to be a maister ouer others that cannot master himselfe. **1732** FULLER no. 2182.

Master of straw eats a servant of steel, A.   (M 726)

1640 HERBERT no. 1029.

Master one than engage with ten, Better.

1721 KELLY 72 (fight with). **1732** FULLER no. 916.

Master that never was scholar, He can ill be.   (M 714)

1530 PALSGRAVE 447b It behoveth a man first to be a scoler and than a maister. **1587** J. BRIDGES *Defence* 924 [citing Jerome in epist. ad Rusticum] Bc not a Maister before thou haste bin a scoler. **1616** WITHALS 567 Hee can ill play the master, that hath not been a scholler. **1639** CLARKE 284.

Master wears no breech, Most. *Cf.* Wear the breeches.   (M 727)

a. **1500** *Early Eng. Carols* 272 The most mayster of the hows weryth no brych. **1546**
HEYWOOD II. iii. G1ᵛ Shall the maister weare a breeche, or none, sey you. **1553** T. WILSON *Arte of Rhet.* 89 As though the good man of the house weare no breeches or that the Graye Mare were the better horse. **1588** GREENE *Pandosto* Prose Wks. (Huth) IV. 267 His wife . . . taking up a cudgel (for the most maister went breechles) sware solemnly that shee would make clubs trumps. **1590–1** SHAKES. *2 Hen. VI* I. iii. 144 Though in this place most master wear no breeches, She shall not strike Dame Eleanor unreveng'd. **1623** CAMDEN 274.

Master's eye makes the horse fat, The.
(M 733)

[PLUTARCH *Moralia*, Bk. I. Οὐδὲν οὕτω πιαίνει τὸν ἵππον ὡς βασιλέως ὀφθαλμός. Nothing fattens the horse so much as the master's eye.] **1530** R. WHITFORD *Werke for Housholders* H1 The slepe [for 'step'] of the housbande [husbandman] maketh a fatte donghyll. And the eye of the mayster a fast hors. That is to meane that the presence of the mayster in euery corner is moche profytable. **1552** LATIMER *5th Serm. Lord's Prayer* P.S. 394 A fellow asked a philosopher. . . . 'How is a horse made fat?' The philosopher made answer, . . . 'With his master's eye' . . . meaning . . . that the master should . . . take heed to the horse-keeper, that the horse might be well fed. **1579** LYLY *Euph.* i. 245 It is the eye of the maister that fatteth the horse, and the loue of the woman, that maketh the man. **1631** BRAITHWAIT *Whimzies* (1859) 69 The masters eye feeds his horse; but the ostlers starves him. **1706** STEVENS s.v. Pienso.

Master's footsteps fattens the soil, and his foot the ground, The.   (M 733–4)

1530 R. WHITFORD *Werke for Housholders* H1 The slepe [for 'step'] of the housband [husbandman] maketh a fatte donghyll. **1547** BALDWIN *Moral Philosophy* N6 Nether is there ought better to make lande fertyle, than the steppes of the owner. **1576** LEMNIUS *Touchstone of Complexions* 54ᵛ. **1640** HERBERT no. 486. **1648** HERRICK *Hesper., Country Life* 23 Wks. (1921) 226 The best compost for the Lands Is the wise Masters Feet, and Hands. **1659** HOWELL *Eng. Prov.* 10b. **1721** KELLY 308 The master's foot is the best foulzie[1] . . . The other asked, what was the best gooding[1] for Ground? and was answered, The Master's Foot. . . . The Care and Concern of a Man will make his Business prosper. [[1] manure.]

Master-blow, *see* Reserve the m.-b.

Masterless hound, Like a.

c. **1530** REDFORD *Play Wit & Sci.* 542 (1903) 440 Lyke a masterles hownde Wandryng all abowt seakyng his master.

Masters should be sometimes blind, and sometimes deaf.   (M 737)

1666 TORRIANO *It. Prov.* 41 no. 10 In the house the Master should be blind, and the Woman deaf. **1732** FULLER no. 3376. **1895** J. PAYN *In Market O.* ch. 9 He . . . well knew when to be deaf, as it behoves a good tutor, above all men to know.

Master(s), *see also* Art (In every) it is good to have m.; Ass must be tied where m. will have him; Diligent scholar, m.'s paid; Do as thy m. commands thee and sit down at table; Early m. long knave; Educate our m.; Every man cannot be a m.; Every man is king (m.) in his own house; Every man is m. (Where) world to wrack; Eye of the m. sees more (One); Eye of the m. will do more work; Falling m. standing servant; God and parents and our m. never requited; God is made m. of family (When), he orders disorderly; Good m. a good scholar; Good m. shall have good wages, (He that serves a); Jack is as good as his m.; Jack of all trades, m. of none; Mad world, my m.; Meat for your m., (She is); Mistress is the m., (Where the) the parsley grows the faster; Mistress (Such) . . . such m. such man; No man is his craft's m. first day; Purse be your m.; Scholar may waur the m.; Servant before m., (One must be); Servant known by m.'s absence; Servants make worst m.; Share not pears with your m.; Sleepy m., servant a lout; Trim tram, like m. like man; Want will be my m.; Wife (He that has) has m.; Wrongs of a . . . m. not reproached.

Mastery mows the meadows down.
(M 741)
a. 1628 CARMICHAELL no. 1091. 1641 FERGUS-SON no. 615. 1721 KELLY 251 . . . Spoken when People of Power and Wealth effect a great Business in a short Time. 1818 SCOTT *Ht. Midl.* ch. 45 The Captain . . . keeps a high hand over the country, . . . and maistry, ye ken, maws the meadows doun.

Mastery, *see also* Use makes m.

Mastiff be gentle, Though the | yet bite him not by the lip. (M 744)
1640 HERBERT no. 132. 1710 PALMER 335.

Mastiff grows the fiercer for being tied up, A. (M 742)
c. 1554 W. TURNER *Hunting of the Romish Wolfe* E1 Great masties do more harme that ar commonly tied, when as they breake lose, then other do that commonly roue abrod at liberty. 1732 FULLER no. 320.

Mastiff(s), *see also* Spit in his mouth and make him m.; Yelping curs will raise m.

Match, *see* Hatch, m., despatch; Marry your m.; Meddle with your m.; No man is a m. for woman till married.

Mate, *see* Fox for m.; Wolf for m.

Matins, *see* Magnificat at m.; Mass nor m., (Neither).

Matrimony, *see* Marriage (M.) is destiny; Pulse beats m. (Her).

Matter(s), *see* Laughing m., (To be no); Meddle not with another man's m.; Mince m.; More malice than m.; Much m. of wooden platter.

Maw, *see* Sweet in mouth, sour in m.

Maxfield[1] measure, heap and thrust (thrutch). (M 799)
1670 RAY 217 *Chesh.* 1787 GROSE (*Ches.*) 156 Maxfield measure, heap and thrutch (thrust). At some places the measure is . . . heaped above the top. . . . That of Maxfield was of this kind. 1878 *N. & Q.* 5th Ser. x. 284 We have an old colloquial saying; . . . 'Maxfield measure, upyeped and thrutched', that is, it is heaped up and pressed down. [1 Macclesfield.]

Maxfield, *see also* Feeds like a freeholder of M.

May, The merry month of. (M 1106)
1412–20 LYDGATE *Troy. Bk.* I. 1293 And May was com, þe monyth of gladnes. 1577 GRANGE *Gold. Aphroditis* K4 It mighte be the merry moneth of May. 1579 SPENSER *Shep. Cal.* May Wks. (Globe) 458 Is not thilke the mery moneth of May. 1598 BARNFIELD *Ode* As it fell vpon a Day, In the merrie Month of May.

May and January (December). (M 768)
c. 1386 CHAUCER *Merch. T.* l. 1693 That she, this mayden, which that Mayus highte, . . . Shal wedded be unto this Januarie. 1565 *Bugbears* III. i. 9 Hys whyte beard . . . With her . . . golden lokes are even as fytt to wead As march with lusty may shuld match. 1581 T. HOWELL *Devises* I ij In fayth doth frozen Ianus double face, Such fauour finde, to match with pleasant Maye. 1606 DEKKER *Sev. Sins* Arb. 44 You doe wrong to Time inforcing May to embrace December. 1620 BOCCACCIO *Decameron* tr. IV. x. G2ᵛ When freezing December will match with flouring May. 1891 R. BUCHANAN *Coming Terror* 267 When asthmatic January weds buxom May.

May be has a may not be, Every. (M 770)
1678 RAY 174. 1721 KELLY 358 What may be, may not be.

May-bee was ne'er a gude honey bee.
1832 HENDERSON 131.

May bees don't fly this month.
1721 KELLY 252 May bees fly not this time o' the year. A Return to them that say, *May be*, such a Thing will come to pass. 1738 SWIFT *Dial.* I. E.L. 265 Maybe there is, colonel.—Ay, but May bees don't fly now, miss.

May birds come (are aye) cheeping.
1862 HISLOP 223 . . . This refers to the popular superstition against marrying in . . . May, the children of which marriages are said to 'die of decay'. 1895 S. O. ADDY *Househ. Tales, etc.* 116 Children born in the month of May require great care in bringing up, for 'May chickens come cheeping'.

May cold is a thirty-day cold, A.

1876 BLACKMORE *Cripps Carrier* ch. 35 This is the worst time of year to take cold, 'A May cold is a thirty-day cold'.

May-day is come and gone; thou art a gosling and I am none.

1846 DENHAM 44 . . . Should an attempt be made, to make any one a May-gosling [the equivalent of an 'April fool'] on the 2nd of May, this rhyming saying is retorted upon them.

May-day, pay-day, pack rags and go away.

1883 C. S. BURNE *Shropshire Folk-Lore* 465 A good deal of hiring is still done . . . on the first of May. . . . The saying runs—. . .

May flood never did good, A.   (M 771)

1639 CLARKE 307.   **1678** RAY 45.

May-hill, If he can climb over | he'll do.
(M 772)

1619 2 Jan. J. CHAMBERLAIN *Letters* (McLure) ii. 197 We cannot be out of the feare [of the safety of the Queen] till we see her past the top of May-hill.   **1666** TORRIANO *Prov. Phr.* s.v. Poggiolino 151 The English say of one Convalescent, To do what one can to get up May Hill.   **1846** DENHAM 43 He'll never climb May-hill; or, If he can climb over May-hill he'll do. May is considered a *trying month* for health.

May if you list, You | but do if you dare.
(L 335)

1678 RAY 350.

May makes or mars the wheat.

1822 COBBETT *Rural Rides* 19 June (1914) 79 The old remark of the country people in England, that '*May* makes or mars the wheat'; for it is May that the ear and the grains are *formed.*

May never goes out without a wheat-ear.

1830 FORBY 417.

May (*noun*), *see also* April showers M. flowers; Bathes in M., (He who) will soon be laid in clay; Beans blow before M.; Cast ne'er a clout till M. be out; Cold M. and windy; Dry M. and dripping June; Flowers in M. (Welcome as); Hanged in M.; Hot M., fat churchyard; January commits fault, M. bears blame; Leeks in Lide and ramsins in M.; Look at your corn in M. (If you); March dust and a shower in M.; March dust and M. sun, corn white maids dun; March, (Fog in) frost in M.; March (In) the birds . . . in M. the birds; March (In) the cuckoo . . . in M. a' sing; Marry in M. repent; Sage in M. (Set); Shear your sheep in M.; Town in M. (He that is in).

Maynooth, *see* Pardon of M.

Mayor of Altrincham, The | and the mayor of Over; the one is a thatcher, the other a dauber.[1]   (M 773)

1678 RAY 301 *Cheshire* . . . These are two petty Corporations whose poverty makes ₁them ridiculous to their neighbours.'   **1917** BRIDGE 115 . . . A good thatcher was a very skilled workman. . . . The Mayoralty of Altrincham (. . . created by Charter in 1290) has been held by members of the best families in the district. [1 a plasterer, builder of clay walls.]

Mayor of Altrincham, lies in bed while his breeches are mending, The.   (M 774)

1678 RAY 301 *Cheshire.*   **1787** GROSE (*Ches.*) 157 . . . As the mayor of every other town must do, if he had but one pair, as is said to have been the case with this worshipful magistrate.   **1818** SCOTT *Ht. Midl.* ch. 45 'I was like the Mayor of Altringham, who lies in bed while his breeches are mending, for the girl did not bring up the right bundle to my room till she had brought up all the others by mistake.'

Mayor of Hartlepool, Like the | you cannot do that.   (M 776)

1678 RAY 317.   **1787** GROSE (*Leics.*) 190 . . . It seems to belong to Durham, Hartlepool being within that bishopric. The sense of it is, you cannot work impossibilities. . . . A mayor of a poor corporation, . . . told them, that though he was mayor of that corporation, he was still but a man, there being many things that he could not do.

Mayor of London (Lord), *see*‿Dined as well as; Good manners to except.

Mayor of Northampton opens oysters with his dagger, The.   (M 777)

1600–1 SHAKES. *M.W.W.* II. ii. 3 Why, then the world's mine oyster, Which I with sword will open.   **1662** FULLER *Northants* 281 This Town being eighty miles from the Sea, Sea-fish may be presumed stale therein.

Maypole, He that will have a | shall have a maypole.

1695 CONGREVE *Concerning Humour in Comedy* Spingarn ii. 252 They have a Proverb among them. . . .

Mead, *see* Little m. little need.

Meadow(s), *see* France is a m.; Mastery mows m. down; Thin m. soon mowed.

Meal cheap and the shoon dear, The | quoth the souter's wife, that would I hear.

1721 KELLY 317.

Meals, Two (Three) hungry (ill) | make the third (fourth) a glutton.   (M 789)

1546 HEYWOOD I. xi. E3ᵛ At breakfast and dyner I eete lyttle meate. And two hongry

meales make the thyrde a glutten. **1607** G.
MARKHAM *Cavelarice* 48. **1623** CAMDEN 278
Three hungry meales, makes the fourth a glutton.
1640 HERBERT no. 575 (ill). **1655** FULLER
Ch. Hist. VI. ii. (1868) II. 218 At last a sirloin of
beef was set before him, on which the abbot fed
. . . and verified the proverb, that 'two hungry
meals make the third a glutton'. **1721** KELLY
302 . . . Spoken when one eats greedily after
long fasting. Applied also to other Things of the
like nature, where long wanting sharpens the
Appetite.

Meal(s), *see also* Baking beside m. (It is good);
Better are m. many than one too merry; Cake
(M.) is dough; Devil's m. is all bran; Dog is
made fat in two m.; Drink between m., (Do not);
Fasts enough that has bad m.; Malt is above m.;
Much bran little m.

Meal-tub, *see* Always taking out of the.

Mealy-mouthed maidens stand long at the mill.

1737 RAMSAY III. 190.

Mean is the best, The. *Cf.* Golden mean is best. Measure is merry mean. Measure is treasure. (M 793)

c. **1500** PROVERBS at Leconsfield (*Antiq. Repert.*
iv. 414) Meane is best. **16th c.** *Mean is Best*
348 in *Early Eng. Carols* 236 The mene ys beste.
1540 PALSGRAVE *Acolastus* 156 The meane is
beste or . . . measure is a mery meane. **1639**
CLARKE 213 A meane is best. Ne quid nimis.

Mean (*noun*), *see* Golden m.; Measure is a merry
m.; Virtue is found in the middle (m.).

Meaning, *see* Hell is full of good m.; Know your
m. by your mumping.

Means, Use the | and God will give the blessing. (M 796)

1580 LYLY *Euph. & his Eng.* ii. 67 Vse the meane,
if you desire to haue the ende. **1633** DRAXE
no. 1178. **1670** RAY 17. **1732** FULLER no. 5413
(trust to God for the blessing).

Means, *see* End justifies m.; Many m. to get
money.

Meant for a gentleman, He was | but was spoilt in the making.

1738 SWIFT *Dial.* I. E.L. 276 I think she was cut
out for a gentlewoman, but she was spoil'd in
the making. **1830** FORBY 434.

Meant, *see also* Take things as m.

Mear, *see* Mare.

Measure everyone by your own yard, To. (Y 1)

1579 LYLY *Euph.* i. 210 Did not *Gyges* cut
Candaules a coate by his owne measure? **1678**
RAY 260. To measure his cloth by anothers yard.

Measure for measure. (M 800)

[MATT. vii. 2 With what measure ye mete it shall
be measured unto ye.] **1530** PALSGRAVE 635a.
1553 *Precepts of Cato* (1560, E6). **1559** *Mirr.
for Mag.* (Campbell) 99 For looke what
measure we other awarde, The same for vs
agayne is preparde. **1576** PETTIE i. 134. **1577**
HOLINSHED (Furnivall i. 127). **1591-2** SHAKES.
3 Hen. VI II. vi. 55 Measure for measure must
be answered. **1592** *Id. T.And.* V. iii. 66 There's
meed for meed, death for a deadly deed! **1599**
Warning Fair Women G3 Measure for measure,
and lost bloud for bloud. **1604** SHAKES. *M.M.*
[Title]. *Ibid.* V. i. 409 Like doth quit like, and
Measure still for Measure.

Measure in all things, There is a. (M 806)

c. **1380** CHAUCER *Troilus* Bk. 2, l. 715 In every
thyng, I woot, there lith mesure. *c.* **1450-1500**
The Gd. Wife wd. a Pilgrimage l. 45 Kepe a
mese for allys. **1509** BARCLAY *Ship of Fools* i.
97. *c.* **1526** ERASM. *Dicta Sap.* A4ᵛ To moche is
nought, for measure in all thynges is best. **1547**
BALDWIN L6 Vse a meane in all thynges. **1580**
LYLY *Euph. & his Eng.* ii. 152 In all things I
know there must be a meane. **1594** NASHE
Unfort. Traveller ii. 212 (moderation). **1598-9**
SHAKES. *M.A.* II. i. 59 If the prince be too
important, tell him there is measure in everything. **1616** DRAXE no. 1406.

Measure is a merry mean. (M 804)

1399 *Richard Redeles* II. 139 Mesure is a meri
mene. *a.* **1529** SKELTON *Magnyf.* 385 Wks.
(1843) I. 238 Yet mesure is a mery mene.
1546 HEYWOOD II.vii. I4 Measure is a mery meane
as this dothe show, Not to hy for the pye, nor to
lowe for the crow. **1553** MORE *Dial. Comfort*
E.L. 211 But yet you wote wel to much is to
much, and measure is a mery meane. **1563**
NEWBERY *Dives Pragmaticus* st. 74 Honest
myrth in measure, is a pleasaunt thyng. **1575**
GASCOIGNE i. 73 Thus learne I by my glasse, that
merrie meane is best. **1616** SURFL. & MARKH.
Country Farm 580 So greatly . . . is the merrie
meane commended. **1639** CLARKE 206.

Measure is medicine.

1362 LANGLAND *P. Pl.* A. I. 33 Measure is
Medicine þauh þou muche ȝeor[n]e.

Measure is treasure. (M 805)

c. **1200** *Ancrene Riwle* 286 Euerich thing me mei
ouerdon. Best is euer i-mete. *c.* **1350** *Douce
MS.* 52 no. 81 Mesure is tresure. *a.* **1451**
LYDGATE *Minor Poems* E.E.T.S. ii. 776 Men
wryte of oold how mesour is tresour. *a.* **1529**
SKELTON *Sp. Parrot* 64 In mesure is tresure.
1641 FERGUSSON no. 611.

Measure the meat by the man, To. *Cf.* Show me not the meat. (M 844)

1678 RAY 354 (i.e. The message by the messenger).

Measure thrice what thou buyest; and cut it but once. (M 807)

1591 FLORIO *Second F.* 97 Alwaies measure
manie, Before you cut anie. **1670** RAY 17 *Ital.*

1721 KELLY 255 Measure twice, cut but once. Take good Deliberation before you fall to actual Execution. 1853 TRENCH iv. 88 A word of timely caution . . . lies in the . . . Russian proverb: Measure thy cloth ten times; thou canst cut it but once.

Measure with the long ell (with the short ell), To.

[= to measure unfairly as buyer or seller respectively.] 1474 CAXTON *Chesse* 119 In hys right hand an elle for to mesure wyth. 1580 SIDNEY *Arcadia* (1622) 62 The night measured by the short ell of sleepe. 1637 R. MONRO *Exped.* II. 46 Sometimes the Souldiers (the worst sort of them) measured the packes belonging to the Marchants with the long ell.

Measure yourself (not another) by your own foot.   (E 217. F 567)

1541 BULLINGER *Christ. State Matrimony* tr. Coverdale 1543 ed., L4ᵛ Spende no more than thou wottest how to get it. When thyne expences and receytes be alyke, a lytle losse maye ouerthrow the. 1545 TAVERNER H4 By this prouerbe we be therefore warned that we dylate not our selues beyond our condition and state, neyther yet esteme our selues by the prayses of flatterours, or opinion of the people, or by fauoure of false fortune, but only by our propre and true qualities. 1562 J. WIGAND *De Neutralibus* B1ᵛ I measure my selfe by myne owne fote. 1580 LYLY *Euph. & his Eng.* ii. 219 [They] can be likened to nothing els so well, then as if a man should be constrayned to pull on a shooe by an others last, not by the length of his owne foote. 1589 *Id. Pap with a Hatchet* To the Reader iii. 396 They measure conscience by their owne yard. 1600–1 SHAKES. *H.* I. iii. 70 Costly thy habit as thy purse can buy. 1620 SHELTON *Quix.* II. v. ii. 219 'Measure yourself by your means,' said Teresa. 1666 TORRIANO *It. Prov.* 72 no. 13 According to ones means, one makes ones expense. 1694 BOYER 108 Let every one measure himself with his own Ell. 1732 FULLER no. 3319 Make not another's Shoes, by your Foot.

Measure (noun), *see also* Eat at pleasure, drink by m.; Feed by m. and defy physician; Forsakes m. (He that); Man is the m. of all; Maxfield m.; Mete and m. make men wise; Mirth without m. is madness; Sin to sell dear (It is no) but to give ill m.; Vessel (The greatest) has but its m.; Weening is not m.; Weight and m. take away strife.

Measure(d) (verb), *see also* Men are not to be m. by inches.

Measures another's corn by his own bushel, He.   (C 663)

1623 PAINTER B6 They that be nought the old Prouerb doth tell, Will measure others by their owne bushell. 1631 W. SALTONSTALL *Picturae Loquentes* F1ᵛ Her corne stands not long for the sellers sake, and she crosses the proverbe, for shee measures it out by anothers bushell. 1644 MILTON *Areop.* Arb. 72 We shall know nothing but what is measur'd to us by their bushel? 1670 RAY 186 You measure every

ones corn by your own bushel. 1738 SWIFT *Dial.* I. E.L. 293 You measure my corn by your bushel. 1881 TYLOR *Anthropology* (1889) 410 The student of history must avoid that error which the proverb calls measuring other people's corn by one's own bushel.

Measures not himself is measured, He that.   (M 808)

1640 HERBERT no. 432.

Measures oil shall anoint his fingers, He that.   (O 26)

1611 COTGRAVE s.v. Huile (besmeares his fingers). 1616 DRAXE no. 1762 (anointeth). 1670 RAY 126 . . . Qui mesure l'huile il s'en oingt les mains. *Gall.*

Meat and drink to one, To be.   (M 842)

a. 1500 *15c. School Book* ed. W. Nelson 15 When I receyue enythyng from hym [my father] . . . it doth me more goode then mete or drynke. 1533 FRITH *Ans. More* E1 It ys meate and drinke to this childe to plaie. 1599 SHAKES. *A.Y.* V. i. 11 It is meat and drink to me to see a clown. 1600–1 *Id. M.W.W.* I. i. 268 That's [bearbaiting] meat and drink to me now. 1672 WALKER 14 no. 3.

Meat and good drink, If it wasn't for | the women might gnaw the sheets.

1539 TAVERNER 36 *Sine Cerere et Baccho friget Venus.* Without meate and drynke the lust of the body is colde. 1598 R. BERNARD *Terence in English* 96 (2nd ed.) [quoted as 'the old saying'].

Meat and mass never hindered any man.   (M 825)

a. 1628 CARMICHAELL no. 134 A mease of meat hinderit never man. 1639 CLARKE 273 Meat and mattens hinder no mans journey. 1641 FERGUSSON no. 644. 1670 RAY 120 (as 1639) . . . In other words, Prayers and provender, &c. 1721 KELLY 253. 1818 SCOTT *Rob Roy* ch. 29 'What the deevil are ye in sic a hurry for?' said Garschattachin; 'meat and mass never hindered wark'. 1893 STEVENSON *Catriona* ch. 19 Meat and mass never hindered man. The mass I cannot afford you, for we are all good Protestants. But the meat I press on your attention. 1900 R. B. CUNNINGHAME GRAHAM *Thirteen Stories* 'A Hegira.' Not that the halt lost time, for travellers all know that 'to hear mass and to give barley to your beasts loses no tittle of the day'.

Meat (morsel) for mowers, No.   (M 832)

[= unsuitable to, or unobtainable by, people of low degree.] 1542 ERASM. tr. Udall *Apoph.* 342 Lais an harlot of Corinthe . . . so dere & costely that she was no morsel for mowers. 1580 LYLY *Euph. & his Eng.* ii. 153 And sure I am shee did not hang for thy mowing. 1581 MULCASTER *Positions* ch. 38 (1887) 179 To hope for hie mariages, is good meat, but not for mowers. 1583 MELBANCKE *Philotimus* 2E2 Marmalet is no meat for mowers. 1616 DRAXE no. 1092 It is not for your mowing. 1639 CLARKE 72.

Meat for your master, She is. (M 837)

1592 NASHE *Pierce Penniless* i. 195 As if they were no meate but his Maisterships mouth. **1598** SHAKES. *2 Hen. IV* II. iv. 118 Away, you mouldy rogue, away! I am meat for your master. **1738** SWIFT Dial. III. E.L. 323 Hands off! that's meat for your master. **1876** J. PAYN *Halves* ch. I He was wholly unsuspicious of her design, imagining her to be meat for his masters.

Meat in a goose's eye, There's. (M 840)

1621 J. TAYLOR (Water-P.) *Taylor's Goosey* (1630) pagin. I, 105 For the old Prouerbe I must here apply, Good meate men may picke from a Gooses eye. **1641** FERGUSSON no. 854 There is meickle hid meat in a goose eye. **1678** RAY 148.

Meat in his mouth, He brings (carries). (M 816)

1578 *Courtly Controv.* 2C2 Perswading him selfe . . . that the King woulde delaye no tyme . . . nor forslowe thys new loue (which carryed meate in the mouth). **1582** R. STANYHURST *Virgil* A3ᵛ. **1670** RAY 186.

Meat, One man's | is another man's poison. (M 483)

[*Quod cibus est aliis, aliis est acre venenum*, from LUCR. 4. 637. What is food for some is black poison to others.] *a.* **1576** WHYTHORNE 58 On bodies meat iz an otherz poizon. **1603** MONTAIGNE (Florio) II. xii. 73 What to one is meate, t'another poison brings. **1604** *Platoes Cap* B4 That ould moth-eaten Prouerbe . . . One mans meate, is another mans poyson. **1614** W. BARCLAY *Nepenthes, or the Vertues of Tobacco* in ARBER *Counterblaste* 116 As concerning the hatred of Princes, one mans meate is another mans poyson. *a.* **1721** PRIOR *Dial. of Dead* (1907) 246 May I not nauseate the food which you covet; and is it not even a proverb, that what is meat to one man is poison to another. **1908** ALEX. MACLAREN *Acts Apos.* I. 382 It is we ourselves who settle what God's words and acts will be to us. The trite proverb, 'One man's meat is another man's poison', is true in the highest regions. **1912** 29 June D. H. LAWRENCE *Lett.* i. 133.

Meat is in, When | anger is out. (M 846)

1621 ROBINSON 16. **1639** CLARKE 178.

Meat is much, but manners (mense[1]) is more (better). (M 826)

a. **1628** CARMICHAELL no. 1095 (menss). **1639** CLARKE 93. **1641** FERGUSSON no. 608 Meat is good, but mense is better. **1721** KELLY 244 (as 1641) . . . Let not one's Greediness on their Meat intrench upon their Modesty. [¹ modesty.]

Meat pleases not all mouths, All. (M 810)

1546 HEYWOOD II. ii. F4ᵛ That one loueth not, an other doth. **1607** R. WILKINSON *The Merchant Royal* 29 Euerie meate was not made for euerie mouth; only bread was made for all. **1732** FULLER no. 535 All Meat is not the same in every Man's Mouth. *Ibid.* no. 3560 No Dish pleases all Palates alike.

Meat than guests or company, It is better to want. (M 822)

1602 JONSON *Poetaster* II. ii. 207 Sweetly was it said of a good olde house-keeper, I had rather want meate, then want ghests. **1609** HARWARD 80 (then good company). **1616** DRAXE no. 711.

Meat(s), *see* After m. mustard; Ale is m., (Good); All m. to be eaten; Bones bring m. to town; Crabs (Greatest) be not all best m.; Dry m. . . . when he lost the m. let him pick bone; God send you readier m. than hares; God sends m. and the devil sends cooks; Hare is melancholy m.; Hunger is good kitchen m.; Hungry man smells m.; Lie in bed till m. falls in mouth; Loves roast m. that licks; Man's m., (To be); Measure the m. by the man; Medicines are not m.; Merry at m. (Good to be); Mind is on his m.; Morn come and m. with it (Let); Much m. much malady; New m. new appetite; No other m. (They that have), bread eat; Poor men seek m. for their stomach; Quick at m., quick at work; Reconciled enemies and m. twice boiled (Take heed of); Roast m. does cattle; Roast m. (Give dog); Show me not (Look not on) the m. but the man; Stomach (To have) and lack m.; Stomach makes all the m. bitter, (An ill); Sweet m. . . . sour sauce; Tripe's good m. if wiped; Want in m. (What they) let them take in drink; Wanted me and your m.; Wholesomest m. at another man's cost.

Medal has its reverse, Every. (M 851)

1603 MONTAIGNE (Florio) III. xii. 164 *Ogni medagalia ha il suo riverscio; Each outside hath his inside*, saith the Italian. **1659** TORRIANO no. 81 Every medall hath its right side and its wrong. **1842** LEVER *Jack Hinton* ch. 2 Happily, there is a reverse to the medal. **1908** W. S. CHURCHILL *My African J.* ch. 3 That there is a rude reverse to the East African medal . . . cannot be disputed.

Meddle nor make,[1] I will neither (not). (M 852)

1564 *Child Marr.* (1897) 123 I will neither make nor medle with her. **1593** NASHE *Christ's Tears* ii. 101. **1598–9** SHAKES. *M.A.* III. iii. 48 The less you meddle or make . . . the more is for your honesty. **1600–1** *Id. M.W.W.* I. iv. 98 I vil teach a . . . priest to meddle or make. **1602** *Id. T.C.* I. i. 14 I'll not meddle nor make no further. *Ibid.* I. i. 82 I'll meddle nor make no more in the matter. **1661** PEPYS *Diary* 7 Nov. Pegg kite now hath declared she will have the beggarly rogue the weaver; and so we are resolved neither to meddle nor make with her. **1678** RAY 68 Quoth the young Cock, I'll neither meddle nor make. When he saw the old cocks neck wrung off, for taking part with the master, and the old hens, for taking part with the dame. *Ibid.* 260 I will neither meddle nor make, said Bill Heaps, when he spilled the buttermilk. **1849** C. BRONTË *Shirley* ch. 21 Moore may settle his own matters henceforward for me; I'll neither meddle nor make with him further. [¹ interfere.]

Meddle not with another man's matter.
(M 493)

1584 WITHALS G5 You may meddle with no mans matter except you be desired. **1602** *Ibid.* 331 Ab alieno abstinere, To forbeare, or not to meddle with other mens goods. **1609** HARWARD 96 Meddle not with high matters, matters above thy reach. **1611** FLORIO *New World of Words* s.v. Aia 17 To meddle with what belongs not to him. **1659** HOWELL *Span. Prov.* 7 Meddle not with what does not belong unto thee. **1672** WALKER 9 no. 32 Meddle not with that which nothing concerns you. Meddle with that you have to do with.

Meddle with your match.
(M 747)

c. **1590** MUNDAY *John a Kent* III. l. 195 (Shakes. Soc. 37) Let him heerafter meddle with his mates. **1598** JONSON *Ev. Man in Hum.* III. v. 121 Nay, he will not meddle with his match. **1612–15** BP. HALL *Contempl.* VI. ii. (1825) l. 140 We meddle not with our match, when we strive with our Maker. **1721** KELLY 246 . . . Spoken by People of Age, when young People jest upon them too wantonly: Or by weak People, when insulted by the more strong and robust. **1738** SWIFT *Dial.* III. E.L. 323 Miss, you are too severe; you would not meddle with your match.

Meddle with your old shoes.
(S 377)

c. **1547** BALE *Three Laws* IV Go meddle thee with olde shone. *c.* **1547** *Id. John Baptist* (*Harl. Misc.* 1808, i. 24) Go teache thy olde shoes. **1577** *Misogonus* II. v. What, are you his spoksman? Meddle you with your old showes. **1639** CLARKE 21 Goe fiddle-medle with your old shoes. **1670** RAY 186.

Meddles in all things may shoe the gosling, Who. *Cf.* Shoe the goose.
(T 218)

[*To shoe the goose, gosling* = to spend one's time in trifling or unnecessary labour.] *c.* **1434** Whoso melles of wat men dos, Let hym cum hier and·shoo the ghos. *Inscription* in Whalley Church cited in Farmer's ed. of Heywood's *Proverbs.* **1546** HEYWOOD II. iii. G2. **1659** HOWELL *Eng. Prov.* 3a Who medleth with all things. may goe and shooe Goslings. **1804** EDGEWORTH *Pop. Tales, Lame Jervas* ch. 3 A blacksmith once said to me, when . . . asked why he was not both blacksmith and white-smith, 'The smith that will meddle with all things may go shoe the goslings'.

Meddlesome Matty.

1804–5 ANN & J. TAYLOR *Orig. Poems* (1877) 169 'Meddlesome Matty' (Title) In vain you told her not to touch, Her trick of meddling grew so much. **1927** *Times* 17 Aug. 11/5 My warning was addressed to those who would make of the League 'a kind of international Meddlesome Matty'.

Meddling, *see* Busy folks always m.; Fools will be m.; Little m. much rest.

Medea's[1] kettle.

a. **1616** JONSON *Mercury Vind.* l. 88 To haue Medea's kettle hung vp, that they may souse into it when they will, and come out renewed. **1695** CONGREVE *Love for L.* IV. iii. Merm. 279 Change the shape and shake off age; get thee Medea's kettle, and be boiled anew. [[1] a sorceress of Colchis.]

Medes, *see* Law of M. and Persians.

Medicine (remedy) for fear (but cut off the head), There is no.
(M 860)

a. **1628** CARMICHAELL no. 1520 There is na medicine for feare. **1721** KELLY 319 There is no remedy for fear but cut off the head. For a panic Fear is beyond all Arguments.

Medicines are not meat to live by.
(M 861)

1545 ASCHAM *Toxoph.* Arb. 60 Aristotle him selfe sayeth, that medicines be no meate to lyue withall. **1597** *Politeuphuia* 160.

Medicine, *see also* Measure is m.

Medlars are never good till they be rotten.
(M 863)

1584 LYLY *Sappho and Phao* II. i. 101 The Medler, which in the moment of his full ripeness is known to be in a rottennes. **1599** SHAKES. *A.Y.* III. ii. 107 I'll graff it with you and then I shall graff it with a medlar. Then it will be the earliest fruit i' th' country; for you'll be rotten ere you be half ripe, and that's the right virtue of the medlar. **1678** RAY 52.

Medlar(s), *see also* Time and straw make m. ripe.

Medusa's head.

1726 J. ARMSTRONG *Imit. of Shaks.* So . . . wrought the grisly aspect Of terrible Medusa, . . . When wandering through the woods she frown'd to stone Their savage tenants. **1900** L. STEPHEN *Lett.* in MAITLAND *Life* (1906) ix. 150 When I introduced theological topics . . . my 'Medusa's head' petrified the company. **1908** SIR F. TREVES *Cradle of Deep* iii. 14 She can see in the lazar-house, . . . the future of her days. . . . The fresh young face will become the Medusa's head.

Meek, *see* Maidens must be m.

Meet troubles half-way, Don't.

1598–9 SHAKES. *M.A.* I. i. 99 Are you come to meet your trouble? The fashion of the world is to avoid cost, and you encounter it. **1732** FULLER no. 3200, Let your Trouble tarry till its own Day comes. **1896** HUTCHESON *Crown & Anch.* ch. 16 I can't see the use of anticipating the worst and trying to meet troubles half-way.

Meet (*verb*), *see also* Extremes m.; Know him not should I m. him; Merry m., merry part; Thieves and whores m. at the gallows.

Meet as, *see* Rope for a thief; Sow to bear saddle; Thief for the widdy.

Meeterly as maids are in fairness.

(M 36)

1678 RAY 355 *Northern Proverbs* . . . Meeterly (*indifferently*) as maids are in fairness.

Meeting, *see* Hasty m. hasty parting; Sorrow is at parting if at m. laughter.

Meet-mate and you meet together, If your | then shall we see two men bear a feather.

1546 HEYWOOD I. xi. E2ᵛ [Of means employed altogether disproportionate to the end in view. Farmer's ed. of Heywood, 140.]

Meg Dorts, *see* Fare-ye-weel, M. D.

Meg of Westminster, *see* Long as M.

Megse's glory, *see* Kirkbie's castle.

Melancholic, *see* Choleric drinks, m. eats.

Melancholy as a cat, As.   (C 129)

[*c.* **1580**] **1590** SIDNEY *Arcadia* Feuillerat i. 135 The Cat [gave] his melancholie. **1592** LYLY *Midas* V. ii. 100. **1597** SHAKES. *I Hen. IV* I. ii. 72 I am as melancholy as a gib cat. **1659** HOWELL *Eng. Prov.* 10b. **1720** GAY *New Similes* I melancholy as a cat, am kept awake to weep. **1837** J. B. KER 13 (gib cat).

Melancholy as a collier's horse, As.

(C 515)

c. **1602** *Return from Parnassus* IV. i. 1512. **1659** HOWELL *Eng. Prov.* 10b.

Melancholy as a dog, As.   (D 438)

1592 FLEETWOOD (to Ld. Burghley) in *Qu. Eliz. Times* ii. 417 Mr. John Amersan . . . is as malinchoy as a curre dogge, according to the Bysshopricke proverb. **1594** NASHE *Unf. Trav.* ii. 218 The dice of late are growen as melancholy as a dog. **1662** *The Wits* ed. Elson 175.

Melancholy, *see also* Fool that is not m. (He is a).

Melody, *see* Harp on string that gives no m.

Melt like wax, To.   (W 137)

[PS. xxii. 14 My heart is like wax; it is melted in the midst of my bowels. PS. xcvii. 5 The hills melted like wax at the presence of the Lord.] **1562** J. PILKINGTON *Aggeus and Abdias* P.S. 246 Their hearts melted in their bodies like wax. **1580** LYLY *Euph. & his Eng.* ii. 111 I haue melted like wax against the fire. **1586** J. HARRISON (Mal. Soc. Collections iii. 164) All our paynes in Learning . . . will melt away as waxe before the sonne. **1596** SHAKES. *K.J.* V. iv. 24 Life, Which bleeds away, even as a form of wax Resolveth from his figure 'gainst the fire? **1866** KINGSLEY *Hereward* ch. 31 It made their hearts . . . melt like wax within them.

Melt(ed, s), *see also* Butter before the sun, (To m. like); Heat that m. wax harden clay; Knife, (It is a good) it will cut butter when it is m.

Melverley¹, { God help me. / and what do you think?

1850 *N. & Q.* 1st Ser. I. 325 Melverley, by Severn side . . . is frequently inundated in winter, and, consequently, very productive in summer. . . . If a Melverley man is asked in winter where he belongs, the . . . reply is, 'Melverley, God help me'; but . . . in summer, . . . Melverley, and what do you think?' [¹ 11 m. from Shrewsbury.]

Memory (-ies), *see* Creditors have better m. than debtors; Good m. (He that has) gives few alms; Good m. have ill judgements; Great m. without learning; Great wits, short m.; Liars need good m.; Wolf may lose teeth but not. m.; Writing destroys the m.

Men are not angels.   (M 544)

1548 HALL (1809 ed., 783) You knowe well that we be men frayle of condicion and no Angels. *c.* **1565** *The Pedlar's Prophecy* l. 922 We are men of flesh and blood, and no Angels. **1583** BP. BABINGTON *Exposition of the Commandments* 401 Wee are men, and no Angels. **1589** T. COOPER *Admon. People Eng.* D2 They [bishops] are men, and no Angels . . . He is an Angell that neuer falleth, hee is no man. *c.* **1598** T. DELONEY 2 *Gentle Craft* (Mann 148) Women are not Angels, though they haue Angels faces. **1612–13** SHAKES. *Hen. VIII* V. iii. 10 But we all are men . . . few are angels. **1639** CLARKE 80.

Men are not to be measured by inches.

(M 546)

1603 MONTAIGNE (Florio) I. xix. 113 A little man is a whole man as well as a great man. Neither men nor their lives are measured by the Ell. **1659** TORRIANO no. 199 Men are not measured by the yard or ell. **1721** KELLY 116 God doth not measure men by inches. People of small Stature may have stout Hearts. **1732** FULLER no. 3390. **1858** C. READE *Jack of All T.* ch. 8 Five feet four . . . did not come up to her notion . . . I should have . . . told her the pluck makes the man, and not the inches.

Men get wealth and women keep it.

(M 548)

1642 TORRIANO 55 Men purchase wealth, and women have it in keeping. Nota. They are commonly best at saving. **1666** TORRIANO *It. Prov.* 238, no. 24 Men procure wealth, and women lay it up.

Men in court, So many | and so many strangers.   (M 582)

1640 HERBERT no. 874.

Men, Like | like manners.

1842 TENNYSON *Walking to the Mail* 55 Like men, like manners: like breeds like, they say.

Men, not walls, make a city safe. (M 555)

[THUCYD. *Hist.* 7. 77. 7. Ἄνδρες γὰρ πόλις καὶ οὐ τείχη, οὐδὲ νῆες ἀνδρῶν κεναί. It is men who make a city, not walls, or ships without crews.] **1489** CAXTON *Fates Arms* E.E.T.S. II. 143 For as a prouerbe saith The walles maken not the stronge castelles but the deffense of good folke maketh hit imprenable. **1539** TAVERNER I *Garden* A8ᵛ Lycurgus beyng asked why he forbadde that the citie shulde be fensed with walles, Aunswered: Bycause that citye wanteth no walles, whiche is fenced not with stones but with men. **1542** ERASM. tr. Udall *Apoph.* 1877 ed. 217 A castle or any stronghold is not so sure and safe from enemies, by the sense of diches and walles, as by valiaunte and hardie mennes bodies. [**1576**] **1577** R. DAVIES *Funeral Sermon Walter Earl of Essex* D4 They say the realme is walled about bycause it is enuirroned with the sea: but I holde rather with their iudgements, that make the fidelitie and true hearts of thy subiectes, and especially . . . the Nobilitie . . . , the strong towers of defence. [*c.* **1576?**] **1594** *Wars of Cyrus* I. i. 135 An armie of vnited hearts Is stronger then a fort of brazen walles. **1587** HARRISON *Desc. of Eng.* Furnivall i. 216 If . . . any forren inuasion should be made, . . . then . . . a wall of men is farre better than stacks of corne and bags of money. **1591** LYLY *Endym.* v. iii. 181 I account more strength in a true hart, then in a walled Cittie. **1608** SHAKES. *C.* III. i. 199 What is the city but the people? **1666** TORRIANO *It. Prov.* 115, no. 11 Walls make not a City, but men. **1732** FULLER no. 5121 'Tis the Men, not the Houses, that make the City. **1927** *Times* 13 Oct. 15/2 In the old Greek saying it is the men who make a city: so with a public school.

Men of all trades, Of the | they especially hang thieves.

c. **1300** *Provs. of Hending* 34 Of alle master¹ men, mest me[n] hongeth theues. [¹ trade, occupation.]

Men of Kent, The.

1662 FULLER *Kent* 63 A man of Kent. This may relate either to the Liberty or to the courage of this County men. **1787** GROSE (*Kent*) 181 All the inhabitants of Kent, east of the river Medway, are called Men of Kent, from the story of their having retained their ancient privileges, particularly those of gavelkind, by meeting William the Conqueror, at Swanscomb-bottom. . . . The rest of the inhabitants of the county are stiled Kentish men. **1861** C. BEDE *New Rector* X. 104 The 'Men of Kent', you know, were never conquered! **1926** *Times* 5 July 24/7 Handley Cross Spa . . . lay . . . in the heart of the country of Men of Kent and Kentish Men.

Men (Heads), So many | so many minds (wits). (M 583)

[TERENCE *Phorm.* 2. 4. 14 *Quot homines tot sententiae.*] *c.* **1386** CHAUCER *Squire's T.* l. 203 As many heddes, as manye wittes ther been. **1483** TERENCE *Vulgaria* S.T.C. 23904 Q3ᵛ Many men many opinyons Euery man has his guyse. *c.* **1532** *Tales* no. 59 As Cicero, Persius. and Flaccus say: As many men so many myndes: as many heedes so many wyttes. **1539** TAVERNER 13 Quot homines, tot sententiæ.

So many heades, so many judgementes. **1546** HEYWOOD I. iii. A4ᵛ All this no further fits, But to shew, so many heds so many wits. **1579** LYLY *Euph.* i. 190 But so many men so many mindes, that may seeme in your eye odious, which in an others eye may be gratious. **1590** TARLTON *News Purgat.* Shakes. Soc. 73 I could not learn for whom this torment was provided, for that so many men, so many censures. **1616** GREENE *Mourning Garm.* Wks. Huth. ix. 174 So many heads, so many censures, euery fancy liketh a sundry friend. **1621** BURTON *Anat. Mel.* Democr. to Rdr. (1651) 9 So many men, so many minds: that which thou condemnest, he commends. **1641** S. MARMION *The Antiquary* Hazl.-Dods. xiii. 436 (humours). **1692** L'ESTRANGE *Aesop's Fab.* ccclviii (1738) 374 . . . and this diversity of thought must necessarily be attended with folly, vanity, and error.

Men's years and their faults are always more than they are willing to own.

1707 MAPLETOFT 20.

Men, *see also* Man (men).

Men, Men are, Men use to, *see also under significant words following.*

Mend his manners, Let him | 'twill be his own another day. (M 628)

[*c.* **1550**] **1560** *Nice Wanton* C2 Apply your lerning and your Elders obay, It wil be your proffit an other day. **1594–5** SHAKES. *L.L.L.* IV. i. 100 Here, sweet, put up this; 'twill be thine another day. **1602** [w.s.] *Ld. Cromwell* C2 Tom, or Maister Thomas, learne to make a Horse-shooe, it will be your owne another day. **1640** JONSON *Tale Tub* II. ii. 68 Let 'hun mend his manners then, and know his betters: It's all I aske 'hun: and 'twill be his owne; And's Masters too, another day. **1678** RAY 76.

Mend or end, Either. (M 874)

1578 T. WHITE *Serm. at Paul's Cross* 3 Nov. 1577. 74. It [the plague] hathe mended, as manye it hathe ended. **1592** T. LODGE 'Deaf man's dialogue' in *Euphues' Shadow* (Hunt. Club 81) Neyther may we mend it till God end it. **1598** BURGHLEY to R. Cecil cited C. Read *Ld. Burghley & Q. Elizabeth* 541 I will prove all good means, either to amend, or to make a good end. **1599** TASSO *Of Marr. and Wiving* G3ᵛ For his great mercies sake, either (soone) to mend them [women], or quickly to end them. **1602** SHAKES. *T.C.*|I. ii. 74 Time must friend or end. **1603** FLORIO Dedn. of his *Montaigne* to Lady Rich Your all praise-exceeding father . . . lived not to mend or end it [the Arcadia]. **1605** DANIEL *Queen's Arcadia* IV. iv All extremities must end or mend. **1605–6** SHAKES. *M.* III. i. 111 I would set my life on any chance, To mend it or be rid on't. **1611** *Id. W.T.* II. iii. 181 Commend it [an infant] strangely to some place Where chance may nurse or end it. **1639** CLARKE 223. **1759** WESLEY *Journ.* 30 Aug. I took knowledge what manner of teachers they had been accustomed to, and determined to mend them or end them. **1884** J. MORLEY in *Times* 31 July 11/4 The . . . question of mending or ending the H. of L.

Mend your clothes, and you may hold
out this year. (C 437)

1640 HERBERT no. 100. 1706 STEVENS s.v. Sayo.

Mend-fault, One | is worth twenty spy-
faults.

1882 CHAMBERLAIN 39.

Mends as sour ale mends in summer, He.
(A 106)

1546 HEYWOOD II. ix. K4 Than wold ye mende,
. . . as sowre ale mendthe in sommer. 1579
J. DYOS *Sermon* D7 We amend . . . as sower ale
in sommer; we become euery day worse and
worse. 1639 FULLER *Holy War* v. xvi (1840) 271
They lost none of their old faults, and got many
new, mending in this hot country as sour ale
in summer. 1738 SWIFT *Dial.* III. E.L. 321
Manners, indeed! I find you mend like sour ale
in summer.

Mends as the fletcher[1] mends his bolt,
He. (F 370)

1530 PALSGRAVE 634b He mendeth as the
fletcher dothe his bolte. 1546 HEYWOOD II. ix.
K4 Than wold ye mende, as the fletcher mends
his bolt. [1 arrowmaker.]

Mends is worth misdeeds. (M 873)

a. 1625 *New Poems by James I* ed. A. F. West-
cott no. LI l. 110 The prouerbe sayes that
mends is for misdeed. *a.* 1628 CARMICHAELL
no. 1101. 1641 FERGUSSON no. 631. 1721
KELLY 320 There is nothing but 'mends for
misdeeds. If I have done you harm, I will make
reparation.

Mend(s, ed), *see also* All faults to m. (Hard for any
man); Bairns o' Falkirk (Like) they'll end ere
they m.; Best go first, rest remain to m.; Cast be
bad, (If thy) m. it by good play; Errs and m.
(Who) to God commends; Every man m. one
(If); Find fault that cannot m.; Good that m.
(It is); Little said soon m.; Never too late to m.;
Stumbles and falls not, m. his pace; Things at
worst m.; Young enough to m.

Mens sana in corpore sano, see Sound mind in a
sound body.

Mercenary man, *see* Virtue flies from heart of
m. m.

Merchandise, *see* Ell and tell good m.

Merchant bare, He is not a | that has
money, worth or ware. (M 884)

1623 PAINTER C6ᵛ The prouerbe saith, hee's
neuer chapman bare, That either ready money
hath, or ware. 1664 CODRINGTON 200. 1670
RAY 17. 1721 KELLY 171 . . . A good Merchant
may want ready Money. 1732 FULLER no. 6240
(money-worth and).

Merchant of eelskins, A. (M 882)

1545 ASCHAM *Toxoph.* Arb. 151 He that wyll . . .
vse the seas knowinge no more what is to be
done in a tempest than in a caulme, shall soone
becumme a marchaunt of Eele skinnes. 1546
HEYWOOD II. v. H1. 1624 T. HEYWOOD *Captives*
IV. i. 39 Who knowes but I In tyme may prooue
a noble marchant?—Yes, of eele skinnes.
1659 HOWELL *Fr. Prov.* 14 A pedling Merchant,
or . . . 1659 *Id. Eng. Prov.* 15a.

Merchant that gains not, loses, A.
(M 889)

1607 H. ESTIENNE *World of Wonders* tr. R. C. 114
The merchant that is no gainer, is a loser. 1611
COTGRAVE s.v. Gaigner The marchant loses
when he gaines not. 1640 HERBERT no. 47.

Merchant[1] with us, To play the. (M 891)

1573 J. BRIDGES *Supremacy of Christian Princes*
A3 The Bishop playeth not the opponent, but
you playe the Marchant. 1576 *Common Conditions* E3ᵛ l. 1262 They were not contented to
make me captain to serue them abord But they
must make a Marchant of me with target and
sword. 1593 NASHE *Christ's Tears* ii. 159.
1632 W. ROWLEY *New Wonder* Hazl.-Dods. xii.
165 I doubt Sir, he will play the merchant with
us. [1 to rob, cheat.]

Merchant, *see also* Buys and sells (He that)
called m.; Know what would be dear (He that
could) need be m. but one year; Loses (He that)
is m. as he that gains; Promises like a m.

Merciful, *see* Stout be m. (As you are).

Mercury, *see* Every block will not make M.

Mercy surpasses justice.

c. 1374 CHAUCER *Troilus* Bk. 3, l. 1282 'Here
may men see that mercy passeth[1] right'. 1387-8
T. USK *Test. Love* III. i. 137 Mercy bothe right
and lawe passeth.[1] [1 surpasses.]

Mercy to the criminal may be cruelty to
the people.

[COKE *Minatur innocentibus qui parcit nocentibus.*
He threatens the innocent who spares the
guilty.] 1711 ADDISON *Spect.* No. 169 In the
public administration of justice, mercy to one
may be cruelty to others.

Mercy, *see also* Cry you m.; God gives his wrath
by weight.

Mere scholar, a mere ass, A. (S 135)

1606 MARSTON *What You Will* IV. i I am a
meere Scholler, that is a meere sot. 1621
BURTON *Anat. Mel.* I. ii. III. xv. (1836) 202
Because they cannot ride an horse, . . . they are
. . . accounted silly fools . . .: a meer scholar, a
meer ass. 1639 CLARKE 152. 1657 W. LONDON
Cat. of most vendible books D1 I had rather be
no Scholar, than a meer Scholar. 1732 FULLER
no. 322 A mere Scholar at Court is an Ass
among Apes.

Merry (witty) and wise, It is good to be.
(G 324)

1546 HEYWOOD I. ii. A3 Whan hasty witlesse myrth is mated weele, Good to be mery and wyse, they thynke and feele. [*c.* 1553] 1566–7 UDALL *Ralph Roister D.* I. i. 6. **1567** *Trial of Treasure* Hazl.-Dods. iii. 272 Therefore it is good to be witty and wise. **1611** BEAUM. & FL. *Kt. Burn. P.* II. i Come, come, George, let's be merry and wise. **1662** L'ESTRANGE *A Whipp* 21 You are merry, sir; be wise too; and do not mind the King too much of the Act of Oblivion. **1721** KELLY 123 . . . Spoken when Peoples Mirth border[s] too much upon Folly.

Merry as a cricket, As.
(C 825)

1530 PALSGRAVE 873b. **1546** HEYWOOD I. xi. D2. **1597** SHAKES. *I Hen. IV* II. iv. 86 As merry as crickets, my lad. **1659** HOWELL *Eng. Prov.* 3a. **1857** KINGSLEY *Two Yrs. Ago* ch. 4 I have not had all the luck I expected; but am . . . as merry as a cricket. **1860** PEACOCK *Gryll Grange* ch. 6 As happy as three crickets.

Merry as a grig,[1] As.
(G 454)

1566 DRANT *Horace Sat.* I. iii A merry grig, a iocande frende. **1720** GAY *New Similes* She . . . merry as a grig is grown. **1760** GOLDSMITH *Ess.* vi Globe 304 I grew as merry as a grig, and laughed at every word that was spoken. **1887** BLACKMORE *Springhaven* ch. 39 'General', cried Charron, now as merry as a grig. [[1] small eel.]

Merry (Happy) as a king.
(K 54)

c. **1512** *Hickscorner* C3ᵛ. *c.* **1530** *Youth* A4ᵛ I wyll make as mery as a kynge. **1595** PEELE *Old Wives Tale* A3 This Smith leads a life as merrie as a king. **1600** DEKKER *Shoem. Hol.* v. v. 143 I liude as merry as an emperor. *c.* **1727** [GAY?] 'New Song of new Similies' *Poems* ed. Faber 646 Full as an Egg was I with Glee; And happy as a King. **1840** LEVER *Chas. O'Mal.* ch. 75 My father mixed a jug of . . . punch, and sat down as happy as a king.

Merry (Gay, Happy) as a lark, As.

1606 CHAPMAN *Sir Giles Goosecap* IV. i. 221 Merry as the morning lark. **1811** E. NARES *Thinks-I-To-Myself* i. 170 I was now as happy as a lark. **1813** BARRETT *Heroine* ed. Raleigh 278 As blithe as larks. **1835** SOUTHEY *Doctor* iii. 57 Always gay as a lark and busy as a bee. **1838** THACKERAY *Yellowplush Papers* (Oxford ed. 240) As merry as a lark. *Ibid.* 197 Gay as a lark.

Merry as a pie.
(P 281)

c. **1386** CHAUCER *Shipman's T.* l. 209 And forth she gooth as jolif as a pye. **1546** HEYWOOD II. iii. G2ᵛ And she for hir parte, made vs cheere heauen hye. The fyrst parte of diner mery as a pie. **1576** LEMNIUS *Touchstone of Complexions* 138ᵛ. **1605** S. ROWLEY *When You See Me* C3 (a magge pie). **1611** DAVIS *Prov.* no. 364 (Pies).

Merry as be can, Aye be as | for love ne'er delights in a sorrowful man.
(L 476)

1678 RAY 55.

Merry as beggars.
(B 243)

1641 S. MARMION *The Antiquary* Hazl.-Dods. xiii. 493 As jovial as twenty beggars. **1659** HOWELL *Eng. Prov.* 11a (fourty beggars). **1681** E. RAWLINS *Heraclitus Ridens* March 1 You'l be as merry as forty Beggars I find.

Merry as mice in malt, As.
(M 1242)

1639 CLARKE 185. **1659** HOWELL *Eng. Prov.* 3a.

Merry (happy) as the day is long, As.
(D 57)

1566 ERASM. *Diversoria* l. 427 They liue as well as hearte canne thinke, or, as the day is broad and longe to. **1594** LYLY *Mother B.* I. iii. 48 As proud as the day is long. *c.* **1595** SHAKES. *K.J.* IV. i. 18 I should be as merry as the day is long! *c.* **1598–9** *Id. M.A.* II. i. 41. **1631** *Celestina* tr. Mabbe 54 (merry). **1705** A. CHAVES *Cares of Love* 17 We'll live happy as the Day is long. **1772** GRAVES *Spirt. Quix.* Bk. XI, ch. 8 They were married in a fortnight's time; and are now as happy as the day is long. **1836** MARY HOGARTH *Lett. T.L.S.* 1960 833 (happy).

Merry as the maids, As.
(M 33)

1630 *Roxb. Ballads* B.S. i. 448 For with joviall blades I'm as mery as the maids. **1684** BUNYAN *Pilgr. P.* II. (1877) 210 At Madam *Wanton's*, where we were as merry as the maids. **1818** SCOTT *Rob Roy* ch. 9 We will . . . have old Cobs the fiddler, and be as merry as the maids.

Merry as three chips, As.
(C 356)

1546 HEYWOOD I. vii. B4 So plaied these tweyne, as mery as thre chipps.

Merry at meat, It is good to be.
(M 815)

a. **1500** *Prov. Wisdom* l. 75 Make mery at mete. **1616** DRAXE no. 718. **1670** RAY 18.

Merry companion is a waggon in the way, A.
(C 559)

c. **1526** *Dicta Sapientum* B3ᵛ A mery felowe yt can commune well by the waye, auoydeth so the werynesse therof, lyke as though thou rodest in a wagayne. **1539** TAVERNER *Publius* B4ᵛ A pleasount felowe to talke with by the way is as good as a chariot. **1553** *Precepts of Cato* (1560) X4ᵛ A mery companion that can talke and clatter, Vpon the highewaye, is insteade of an horse lytter. **1579** LYLY *Euph.* i. 323 A pleasant companion is a bayte in a iourney. **1583** STUBBES *Anat. of Abuses* New Sh. S. i. 22 *Comes facundus in via, pro vehiculo est* . . . A good Companion to trauayle withall is insteade of a Wagon or Chariot. **1616** BRETON 2 *Cross. of Prov.* A3 A merry Companion is a Wagon in the way. **1621** BURTON *Anat. Mel.* II. ii. VI. iv. (1651) 302 A merry companion is better than music, and, . . . *comes jucundus in viâ pro vehiculo,*[1] as a wagon to him that is wearied on the way. **1639** CLARKE 291 Good company is a good coach. **1766** GOLDSMITH *Vicar* ch. 18 'Good company upon the road' says the proverb, 'is the shortest cut.' **1838** APPERLEY

Nimrod's North T. 10 A pleasant companion is said to shorten the road, and . . . I always endeavour to find the 'comes jucundus', which the facetious Publius Syrus says, is as good as a coach itself. [¹ Pub. Syrus.]

Merry England.

c. 1300 *Cursor M.* 8 First conquerour of meri Ingland. **1436** *Siege Calais* in *Pol. Poems* (Rolls) II. 156 The crown of mery Yngland. **1552** J. CAIUS *Wks.* ed. Roberts 29 The old world, when this countrie was called merry England. **1590** SPENSER *F.Q.* I. x. 61 Saint George of mery England the signe of victoree. **1819** SCOTT *Ivanhoe* ch. 37 It cannot be that in merry England, the hospitable, the generous, the free . . . there will not be found one to fight for justice. *a.* **1830** HAZLITT *Merry England* (Title of an essay) Pleasures in the open air 'were sufficient to justify the well-known appellation of Merry Sherwood' and in like manner we may apply the phrase to Merry England.

Merry Greek.   (M 901)

c. 1549 *Two Dial.* tr. E. Berke f. 25ᵛ Such gaye grekes, lusty brutes and ionkers. [*c.* 1553] **1566–7** UDALL *Ralph Roister D.* Mathewe Merygreeke [the name of a character in the play]. **1602** SHAKES. *T.C.* I. ii. 102 I think Helen loves him better than Paris.—Then she's a merry Greek indeed! **1665** C. COTTON *Scarron.* (1715 ed.) IV. 64 Merry as Greeks and drunk as Lords.

Merry in hall when beards wag all, It is.   (H 55)

a. 1300 *King Alis.* 1164 Swithe mury hit is in halle. When the burdes wawen alle! **1546** HEYWOOD II. vii. I3ᵛ. **1550** BECON *Fort. Faith.* Prol. A ii They remember thys olde sayinge: It is mery in hal, Whĕ berdes wag al. **1593** PEELE *Edw. I* xiii. 41–3 Wks. Bullen i. 180 Set these lords and ladies to dancing; so shall you fulfil the old English proverb, ''Tis merry in hall when beards wag all'. **1598** SHAKES. *2 Hen. IV* V. iii. 35. **1616** JONSON *Masque of Christmas* vii. 437 l. 9 Let me be brought before my Lord Chamberlaine, . . . : 'tis merrie in hall, when beards wag all. **1738** SWIFT *Dial.* II. E.L. 311 Come, they say, 'tis merry in the hall when beards wag all. **1858** TROLLOPE *Dr. Thorne* ch. 1 They poured the liquor in, . . . but the beards did not wag as they had been wont to wag.

Merry is the feast-making till we come to the reckoning.   (F 149)

1678 RAY 175. **1732** FULLER no. 3409 (Company).

Merry man, *see* Long lives a m. m. as a sad.

Merry meet, merry part.   (M 864)

1678 RAY 175. **1695** RAVENSCROFT 52. **1732** FULLER no. 3410.

Merry monarch.¹

? *c.* 1665 ROCHESTER *Sat. on King* 19 Restless he rolls about from Whore to Whore. A merry Monarch, scandalous, and poor. **1712** STEELE

Spect. no. 462, par. 5 This very Mayor afterwards erected a statue of his merry Monarch in Stocks-Market. [¹ Charles II.]

Merry pin,¹ To be in a.   (P 335)

c. 1386 CHAUCER *Merchants T.* l. 1516 Youre herte hangeth on a joly pyn. *c.* 1475 *Macro Plays, Wisdom* v. 492 I woll sett my soule on a mery pynne. *c.* 1486–1500 MEDWALL *Nature* i. 865 To set hys hart on a mery pyn And byd hym make good chere. [1525–40] **1557** *A merry dialogue* 89 Be neyther in your dumpes, nor alwayes on your mery pinnes. **1530** PALSGRAVE 830b. Apon a mery pynne. **1661** BLOUNT *Glossogr.* (ed. 2) s.v. He is in a merry Pin. **1670** RAY 189 . . . Probably this might come from drinking at pins. The Dutch and English . . . were wont to drink out of a cup marked with certain pins. **1782** COWPER *Gilpin* 178 Right glad to find His friend in merry pin. **1887** A. RILEY *Athos* 210 Our prelate was in merry pin. [¹ humour.]

Merry that dance lightly, All are not.   (D 23)

1380 CHAUCER *Parl. Fowls* l. 592 Daunseth he murye that is myrtheles? *c.* **1425** LYDGATE *Daunce Macabre* 392 Alle be not mery wich that men se daunce. **1611** COTGRAVE s.v. Aise. **1640** HERBERT no. 808.

Merry Wakefield.   (W 6)

[*c.* 1591] **1599** [GREENE?] *George a Green* E4 My friend, this is the towne of merry Wakefield. **1615** R. BRATHWAIT *Strappado for Div.* 203 The first whereof that I intend to show, Is merry *Wakefield* and her *Pindar*¹ too. **1662** FULLER *Yorks.* 190 . . . What peculiar cause of mirth this Town hath above others I doe not know. [¹ George-a-Green.]

Merry when friends meet, It's.   (F 750)

1564 W. BULLEIN *Dial. agst. Fever* E.E.T.S. (1578) 66 Marie when frendes dooe meete. **1600** BRETON *Pasquil's Foolscap* E3ᵛ. **1616** DRAXE no. 797. **1639** CLARKE 26.

Merry when gossips meet, 'Tis.   (G 382)

1602 S. ROWLAND [Title]. **1639** CLARKE 184.

Merry when knaves meet, It is.   (K 143)

c. 1520 *Cock Lorells Bote* Percy Soc. 14 But mery it is whan knaues done mete. **1540** PALSGRAVE *Acolastus* 129 It is merye . . . whan knaues in graine mete. *c.* **1549** HEYWOOD I. xi. D3ᵛ. **1602** S. ROWLAND *Tis Merrie when Gossips Meet* in Wks. Hunt. Cl. I Ther's a Booke cal'd *T'is merry when Knaues meete.* And ther's a Ballad, *'T'is merry when Malt-men meete*: and besides, there's an old Prouerbe, The more the merrier.

Merry when maltmen meet, It is.   (M 60)

1601 B. BARNES *The Devil's Charter* l. 1555. **1602** *see quotation under preceding proverb.* *c.* **1630** *Roxb. Ballads* B.S. i. 59.

Merry (-ier), *see also* Bird on briar (bough), (As m. (light) as; Happy (M.) as a king; Jack-an-Ape

be m. (Can); More the m. (The); Sing so m. a
note (Who can) as who cannot change groat.

Merryman, *see* Physicians are . . . Dr. M. (Best).

Messan, *see* We hounds . . . quoth the m.

Messengers should neither be headed nor hanged.   (M 905)

1519 HORMAN *Vulgaria* 380 No man shulde do
an harolde harmc. **1599** SHAKES. *A.Y.* IV. iii.
11 It bears an angry tenure. Pardon me; I am
but as a guiltless messenger. *a.* **1628** CAR-
MICHAELL no. 1135. **1641** FERGUSSON no. 622.
1721 KELLY 246 . . . An Excuse for carrying an
ungrateful Message. L. *Legatus nec violatur,
nec læditur.*

Messenger(s), *see also* Corby m.; Lame m.

Messmate before a shipmate; shipmate before a stranger; stranger before a dog.

1824 COOPER *Pilot* 259 . . . —but a dog before a
soldier. **1867** ADML. W. H. SMYTH *Sailor's
Word-Bk.* 478 Comrades in many ways;
whence the *saw* . . . **1898** W. C. RUSSELL
Rom. of Midsh. ch. 14 There's no love lost
between you . . . I remember a sailor reciting
. . . : 'A messmate before a shipmate, a shipmate
before a stranger, a stranger before a dog, but a
dog before a soldier'.

Metal upon metal is false heraldry.
(M 906)

1643 CLEVELAND *Upon Sir Thos. Martin* l. 24
Metal upon metal is ill armoury. **1650** T.
FULLER *Pisgah Sight* 6 Fat upon Fat is false
Heraldry in husbandry. **1659** *Id. Appeal
Inj. Innoc.* in *Hist. Camb. Univ.* (1840) 400
What? Doth he[1] allege himself to prove his own
opinion? My bad heraldry was never guilty
of such a fault,—metal upon metal! **1673**
MARVELL 323 Brass upon brass is false heraldry.
c. **1725** SWIFT *Poem upon W. Wood*[2] *Wks.*
(1856) I. 718 I cannot agree; For metal on
metal is false heraldry. Why that may be true;
yet Wood[2] upon Wood,[3] I'll maintain with my
life, is heraldry good. [[1] P. Heylin. [2]W. Wood
obtained a patent for coining halfpence for
Ireland. [3] i.e. the gallows.]

Mete and measure make men wise.
(M 907)

c. **1641** FERGUSSON MS. no. 1039. **1721** KELLY
247 . . . Spoken when People would have what
they buy weighed, or measured.

Methusalah, *see* Old as M.

Mettle is dangerous in a blind horse.
(M 909)

1636 S. WARD *Serm.* (1862) 76 It would grieve
a man, indeed, to see zeal misplaced, like
mettle in a blind horse. **1670** RAY 18. **1721**
KELLY 244 . . . And so is Bigotry, and blind
Zeal, in an ignorant Fellow. **1832** HENDERSON
83 Mettle is kittle in a blind horse.

Mettle, *see also* Coward to his m.; Feeding out of
course makes m. out of kind.

Meum and *tuum.*   (M 910)

[L. = Mine and Thine.] **1550** POLYDORE VERGIL
438 *Illae duae semper religiosi pestiferae voces,
Meum et Tuum.* **1594** GREENE & LODGE *Looking-gl.* (1598) C ii j What, wooe my subjects
wife that honoureth me?—Tut, kings this
meum, tuum should not know. **1606** DANIEL
Queen's Arc. 1001 These proprieties of *meum*
and *tuum.* *a.* **1667** J. TAYLOR *Serm.* 17 Let the
husband and wife infinitely avoid a curious
distinction of mine and thine. **1820** LAMB *Two
Races of Men* in *Lond. Mag.* Dec. Wks. (1898) 20
What a careless, even deportment hath your
borrower! . . . What a liberal confounding of
those pedantic distinctions of *meum* and *tuum.*
1827 HARE *Gues. at Truth* (1873) i. 3 The first
thing we learn is *Meum*, the last is *Tuum.*
None can have lived among children without
noticing the former fact; few have associated
with men and not remarkt the latter. **1876**
BURNABY *Ride to Khiva* ch. 7 My friend and
self . . . brought up the rear, with a careful eye
upon our effects, as the people . . . were said to
have some difficulty in distinguishing between
meum and *tuum.*

Meum, Tuum, Suum, set all the world together by the ears.

[L. = mine, thine, his.] *a.* **1628** CARMICHAELL
no. 31 About mine and thyne ryses meikle
stryfe. **1902–4** LEAN IV. 48.

Mice, *see* Mouse.

Michael, *see* Maids than Malkin (More) and more
men than M.

Michaelmas chickens and parsons' daughters never come to good.

1894 NORTHALL *Folk Phrases* E.D.S. 19.

Michaelmas Day, So many days old the moon is on | so many floods after.
(D 120)

1612 A. HOPTON *Concordancy of Years* 109 . . .
So many flouds will happen that Winter. **1661**
M. STEVENSON *Twelve Moneths* 44 They say so
many dayes old the Moon is on *Michaelmas*
day, so many Floods after.

Michaelmas moon rises aye alike soon, The.

1721 KELLY 334 . . . The Moon . . . rising more
Northerly, rises more early. My Country
People believe it to be a particular Providence
of God that People may see to get in their Grain.

Michaelmas rot comes never in the pot.
(R 189)

1639 CLARKE 307. *c.* **1640** J. SMYTH *Berkeley
MSS.* 31 no. 50 Sheepe . . . Rottinge at Michaelmas, dye in Lent after, when that season of the
yeare permitted not the poore husbandman to
eat them.

Michaelmas, *see also* Spends his M. rent in midsummer.

Mickle ado, and little help.   (A 36)

1579 GOSSON *Sch. Abuse* Arb. 28 Much adoe, and smal help. **1670** RAY 120.

Mickle between market days, There is.

1721 KELLY 325 . . . Times, Modes, Prices, and other Circumstances are mutable.

Mickle, but not manful.

1721 KELLY 253.

Mickle fails that fools think.

c. **1374** CHAUCER *Troilus* Bk. I. · l. 217 But alday faileth thing that fooles wenden. **1721** KELLY 243.

Mickle head, little wit.   (H 245)

c. **1470** *Mankind* i. l. 47 Yowr wytt ys lytyll, yowr hede ys mekyll. **1562** HEYWOOD *Epig.* no. 56, 209 Thy head is great . . . and without wit within. **1641** FERGUSSON no. 632. **1721** KELLY 253 . . . A groundless Reflection; an eminent Instance to the contrary was John, Duke of Lauderdale.

Mickle maun (must) a good heart thole[1].   (M 915)

a. **1628** CARMICHAELL no. 1098 (thole). *a.* **1641** FERGUSSON MS. no. 1010 Meikle must ane good heart tholl. **1721** KELLY 253 (as *a.* 1641). [1 suffer.]

Mickle power makes many enemies.

1721 KELLY 253 . . . Occasion'd partly by Envy, partly by Fear. L. *Necesse est ut multos timeat, quem multi timent.*

Mickle spoken, part maun spill. (M 916)

a. **1628** CARMICHAELL no. 1100. **1641** FERGUSSON no. 621.

Mickle to do when cadgers (dominies[1]) ride, There is.

1721 KELLY 315 (Domine's) . . . For such are not well provided for riding, nor expert at it. **1836** MRS. CARLYLE *Let.* to Mrs. Welsh 5 Sept. The proverb says 'there is much ado when cadgers ride'. . . . I do not know precisely what 'cadger' means, but . . . the friends . . . of cadgers should therefore use all soft persuasions to induce them to remain at home. [1 pedagogues.]

Mickle, *see also* Come to m. (It is), but no to that; Kirk is m.; Many a little makes a m.; Moyen does m.; Seek m. and get something.

Midden, *see* Cock is bold on own m.

Middle, *see* Virtue is found in the m.

Middle Temple, *see* Gray's Inn; Inner Temple.

Middlesex clowns.   (C 450)

a. **1633** JONSON *Tale Tub* I. iii. 45 (As they zay) a Clowne of Midlesex. **1662** FULLER Middx. 177 A Middlesex Clown. . . . The multitude of Gentry here . . . discover the *Clownishness* of others, and render it more Conspicuous. However, . . . there are some of the Yeomanry in this County as completely Civill as any in England.

Midnight oil, *see* Burn the m. o.

Midshipman's half-pay.

1856 C. KINGSLEY *Lett.* May in DAVIES *Sup. Eng. Glos.* 406 You fellows worked like bricks, spent money, and got midshipman's half-pay (nothing a-day and find yourself).

Midst, *see* Worst piece in the m.

Midsummer moon (madness).

1555 HEYWOOD *Epig. on Proverbs* XCV As mad as a marche hare: where madnes compares: Are not mydsomer hares, as mad as march hares? **1588** *Martin Marprelate Epitome* (*Tracts*, Pierce 129) You may demand whether it be midsummer moon with him or no. **1590** *An Almond for a Parrot* Nashe iii. 363. **1596** NASHE *Saffron W.* iii. 38 Ere hee bee come to the full Midsommer Moone, and raging Calentura of his wretchednes. **1601** SHAKES. *T.N.* III. iv. 53 Why, this is very midsummer madness. **1678** RAY 76 'Tis midsummer moon with you *i.e.* You are mad. **1691** DRYDEN *Amphitryon* IV. Plays (1701) II. 428 What's this Midsummer-Moon? Is all the World gone a madding? **1706** STEVENS s.v. Luna. **1889** R. L. STEVENSON *Master of Ball.* ch. 4 This is Midsummer madness.

Midsummer, *see also* Mile to m. (To have but a); Spends his Michaelmas rent in m.

Midwife (-ves), *see* Hasty people never good m.; Ride as if to fetch m.

Might and main, With.   (M 923)

c. **1425** *Wakefield Plays* 'Resurrection' l. 505 With mayn and might. *c.* **1500** *Mundus et Infans* ll. 243 and 278. **1513** H. BRADSHAW *St. Werburge* E.E.T.S. I. 33, 16 With herte mynde and harneys redy day and nyght Theyr enemyes to subdue, by power, mayne and myght. **1579** SPENSER *Shep. Cal.* March, l. 86 I . . . shott at him with might and maine. **1672** WALKER 53, no. 61 Tooth and nail; with might and main.

Might is (makes, overcomes) right.
            (M 922)

[PLATO *Rep.* l. 338 Φημὶ γὰρ ἐγὼ εἶναι τὸ δίκαιον οὐκ ἄλλο τι ἢ τὸ τοῦ κρείττονος ξυμφέρον. For I [Thrasymachus] say that justice is nothing else than the interest of the stronger. LUCAN l. 174 *Mensuraque iuris vis est.*] *a.* **1327** *Pol. Songs* (Camden) 254 For miht is right, the lond is laweles. *c.* **1390** GOWER *Conf. Amantis* V. 2021 ffor wher þat such on is of myht, His will schal stonde in stede of riht. **1546** HEYWOOD II. v. H2ᵛ We see many tymes, myght ouercomth ryght. **1598** SHAKES. *2 Hen. IV* V. iv. 24 O God, that right should thus overcome might!

1639 CLARKE 172 (overcomes). 1790 TRUSLER *Prov. Exempl.* 78 The law is so expensive, . . . that those who have not sufficient money to support perhaps a just cause, must give it up . . . ; for *might* too often overcomes right. 1876 TENNYSON *Showday at Battle Abbey* We stroll and stare Where might made right eight hundred years ago. 1892 J. NICHOL *Carlyle* 77 [In] *Chartism* . . . he clearly enunciates 'Might is right'—one of the few strings on which . . . he played through life.

Might or by sleight, Either by. (M 921)

1621 ROBINSON 8. 1639 CLARKE 127. 1670 RAY 186. 1721 KELLY 179 If I cannot do by Might, I'll do by Slight. If I dare not attack my Enemy openly, I'll do him an Injury in a private, and clandestine Way.

Mighty, mightier, *see* Pen is m. than the sword; Truth is m. and will prevail; Wrath of a m. man (Take heed of).

Mighty, *see also* Pleasures of m., tears of poor.

Mild, *see* Gentle (M.) as a lamb; Maidens must be m.

Mile is two in winter, Every. (M 924)

1640 HERBERT no. 949.

Mile to midsummer, To have but a.

[= to be somewhat mad.] *c.* 1465 *Eng. Chron.* Camden Soc. 92 Tho bestys that thys wroughte to mydsomer have but a myle.

Mile(s), *see also* Cup in pate worth m. in gate; Go twenty m. on errand; Good things I do not love, good long m.; Knife . . . made five m. beyond Cutwell; Miss as good as m.; Robin Hood's m.; Sit awhile and go a m.; Welsh m.

Milk and honey.

[EXODUS iii. 8.] 1783 J. KING *Th. on Difficulties*, &c. ii. 28 America is now the fancied land of milk and honey. 1826 DISRAELI *Viv. Grey* II. i The milk and honey of the political Canaan.

Milk bowl, *see* Wheamow (I am very), quoth old woman when she stepped into m. b.

Milk is white, and lies not in the dyke, but all men know it good meat. (M 935)

1546 HEYWOOD II. iv. G3ᵛ.

Milk kail, *see* Learn your goodam to make m. k.

Milk says to wine, Welcome friend. (M 936)

1640 HERBERT no. 184. 1659 HOWELL *Span. Prov.* 23. . . . Friend, thou art come in good time. 1706 STEVENS s.v. Leche. The Milk said to the Wine you are welcome Friend. The Milk said to the Water Shame light on you Sister.

Milk sod[1] over, Their. (M 938)

1678 RAY 354. 1732 FULLER no. 2510 His milk boil'd over. [1 boiled.]

Milk, *see also* Bristol m.; Cat is out of kind that sweet m. will not lap; Cow of his own, . . . quart of m. for a penny; Cow that gives good pail of m., and kicks it over; Crying over spilt m.; Fern grows red (When), m. good with bread; God gives the m., not the pail; Live ever (If you would), wash m. from liver; Neighbour's ground (cow) yields better corn (more m.) than ours; Nothing turns sourer than m.; Suffolk m.; Wine is old men's m.

Milking, *see* Goat gives a good m. but casts it down.

Milksop, *see* Mothers' darlings m. heroes.

Mill cannot grind with the water that is past, The. (M 944)

1616 DRAXE no. 1589 The water that is past, cannot make the mill goe. 1640 HERBERT no. 153. 1865 ABP. TRENCH *Poems, Proverbs* xix. 303 Oh seize the instant time; you never will With waters once passed by impel the mill.

Mill gets by going, The. (M 945)

1640 HERBERT no. 122. 1706 STEVENS s.v. Azena. 1897 'H. S. MERRIMAN' *In Kedar's T.* ch. 30 'The mill gains by going, and not by standing still,' he said, and added, ... 'But it is always a mistake to grind another's wheat for nothing.'

Mill that is always going grinds coarse and fine, The.

1910 P. W. JOYCE *Eng. as We Speak* 115 A person who talks too much cannot escape saying things now and then that would be better left unsaid.

Mill will go with all winds, His. (M 942)

1625 JONSON *Staple of News* III. ii. 295 He . . . is turned The Churches Miller, grinds the catho-lique grist With euery wind. 1689 SELDEN *Table-Talk* Arb. 32 Collonel Goring serving first the one side and then the other, did like a good Miller that knows how to grind which way so ever the Wind sits. 1732 FULLER no. 2511.

Mill(s), *see also* Born in a m.; Change my m.; Draw water to m.; God's m. grinds slow; Grist to m.; Horse in m. (Like); Horse next to m.; Kirk and a m. of it (Make a); Lief go to m. as to mass; Little stream drives light m.; Mouse in m., (Safe as); News, (You must go to the oven or the m. if you will learn); No m. no meal; Sacks to the m. (More); Safe as a thief in a m.; Water goes by m. that miller knows not of (Much).

Mill-clack, *see* In vain is the m.

Miller got never better moulter[1] than he took with his own hands, The.

(M 954)

1641 FERGUSSON no. 634 Millers takes ay the best multar with their own hand. 1721 KELLY 313 . . . Spoken to them who have a Thing at their own taking. [1 toll.]

Miller grinds more men's corn than one, The.

1596 NASHE *Saffron W.* To Reader iii 18 O! good brother *Timothie*, rule your reason; the Miller gryndes more mens corne than one.

Miller has a golden thumb, An honest.

(M 953)

c. 1386 CHAUCER *Prol.* l. 562 Wel coude he stelen corn and tollen thries, And yet he hadde a thombe of gold, pardee. 1576 GASCOIGNE *Steel Glass* ii. 171. 1678 RAY 354 (*Som.*) Every honest miller hath a golden thumb. They reply, None but a cuckold can see it. 1820 SCOTT *Monast.* ch. 13 Beside that which the miller might have amassed by means of his proverbial golden thumb, Mysie was to inherit . . . land.

Miller, Many a | many a thief.　(M 955)

1533 J. HEYWOOD *Play of Weather* B4ᵛ Who wolde be a myller as goode be a thefe. 1634 T. HEYWOOD & BROME *Late Lancashire Witches* (1874) iv. 195 They say we Millers are theeves. 1673 *Vinegar & Mustard* 19 in HINDLEY, *Old Book Coll. Miscell.* iii.

Miller's boy said so, The.

1830 FORBY 431 . . . It was matter of common report.

Miller's daughter, *see* Breed of the m. d. who speered. . . .

Miller's dog, *see* Breed of the m. d. (Ye).

Miller's eye, *see* Put out m. e.

Miller's mare, Like a.　(M 960)

1606 BRETON *Choice* 68 Can seeme as sober as a Millers Mare. 1620 BEAUM. & FL. *Lit. Fr. Law.* IV. v. 26 I can jump yet. Or tread a measure.— Like a Millers Mare.

Miller's thumb,[1] No bigger than a.

(M 961)

1599 COUNTESS OF SOUTHAMPTON (cited L. Hotson's *Shakes. Sonnets Dated*, 156) Sir John Falstaf . . . made father of a goodly milers thumb, a boye thats all heade and vere litel body. 1675 C. COTTON *Scoffer Scoft* 18 A groom no bigger than a Millers Thumb. [1 A small fish.]

Miller's neck-cloth, *see* Bolder than a m. n. (What is).

Miller(s), *see also* Draw water to one's mill (1670 *quotation*); In vain is mill-clack if m. hearing lack; Put a m. . . . in bag, first that comes out will be a thief; Sure (Good to be), toll it again, quoth m.

Millpond, *see* Smooth as a m.

Mill-post, *see* Thwitten a m.-p. to pudding prick.

Mills and wives are ever wanting.

(M 951)

1581 GUAZZO ii. 36 Women, though never so honest, are insatiable of such trifles. Whereupon it is said, that mills and women ever want something. 1640 HERBERT no. 388 Mills and wives ever want. 1670 RAY 18. 1721 KELLY 249 . . . It requires much to keep a Mill useful, and a Wife fine.

Mills will not grind if you give them not water.

(M 946)

1636 S. WARD *Serm.* (1862) 128 Such mercenary lawyers . . . only keep life in the law so long as there is money in the purse, and when this golden stream ceaseth the mill stands still. 1642 TORRIANO 64 A mill will not grind without wind or water. 1659 HOWELL *Brit. Prov.* 33 The mill stands that wants water. 1732 FULLER no. 3414.

Mills, *see also* Mill(s).

Millstone, I can see as far into a | as another man.　(M 965)

[= to display acuteness; but it is often used ironically.] 1540 PALSGRAVE *Acolastus* 17 We . . . wolde seme to see farther in a myll stone, than excellent auctours haue done before vs. 1546 HEYWOOD I. x. C4 She thought Ales, she had seene far in a mylstone, Whan she gat a husband. 1549 J. PROCTOUR *Fall of the late Arian* I3ᵛ. 1577 STANYHURST *Descr. Irel.* in HOLINSHED (1586) ch. 2 18 He would needs see further in a milstone than others. 1625 HART *Anat. Ur.* II. vii. 92 They . . . could see as farre into a milstone as any of our . . . Physitians. 1668 SHADWELL *Sullen Lov.* IV. i He's resolved to have satisfaction . . . ; and, if I can see as far into a millstone as another, he's no bully Sandy. 1738 SWIFT *Dial.* I. E.L. 276 I'd hold a wager there will be a match between her and Dick Dolt: and I believe I can see as far into a millstone as another man.

Mill-stone, The lower | grinds as well as the upper.　(M 966)

1519 HORMAN *Vulgaria* f. 153 The lower stone can do no good without the hyar. 1678 RAY 172.

Millstone(s), *see also* Seaman, if he carries m., will have a quait; Trusted with a house full of m.; Weep m. *See also* Stone.

Mim[1] as a May puddock[2], As.

1823 GALT *Entail* III. viii. 76 You sitting as mim as a May puddock, when you see us . . . met for a blithesome occasion. [1 demure. 2 frog.]

Mince matters (the matter), To.
(M 755)

[= to extenuate.] **1533** T. MORE *The debellacyon of Salem and Bizance* 992 Though them selfe . . . fall not by such bokes to the myncyng of suche maters, and dyspute howe farre they maye go forwarde in theym. **1604** SHAKES. *O.* II. iii. 239 Thy honesty and love doth mince this matter, Making it light to Cassio. **1606** *Id. A.C.* I. ii. 102 Speak to me home, mince not the general tongue. **1649** BP. HALL *Cases Consc.* (1650) 160 Some Doctors . . . would either excuse, or mince the matter. **1741** RICHARDSON *Pamela* II. 82 Well, Tom, said he, don't mince the matter. Tell me, before Mrs. Andrews, what they said. **1840** CARLYLE *Heroes* ii (1858) 239 A candid ferocity, if the case call for it, is in him; he does not mince matters.

Mind is on his meat, His.

1540 PALSGRAVE *Acolastus* 88 My mynd is al redy in the platters . . . my mynde is in the maunger. **1579** LYLY *Euph.* i. 224. **1616** WITHALS 552 (in the Ambrey). *a.* **1628** CAR-MICHAELL no. 793.

Mind is the man, The.

[CICERO *Rep.* 6. 24. 26 *Mens cuiusque is est quisque.* Each man's mind is himself.] **1616** T. ADAMS *Sacrifice of Thankfulness* 20 Mens cuiusque, is est quisque: As the Minde is, so is the Man. **1642** D. ROGERS *Naaman* 163 The mind of every man is the man: the spirit of the miser, the mind of the drunkard . . . they are more precious to them than life itself!

Mind other men, but most yourself.
(M 563)

a. **1500** *Prov. Wisdom* l. 110. **1639** CLARKE 217.

Mind to me a kingdom is, My. (M 972)

[SENECA *Thyestes* 380 *Mens regnum bona possidet.*] **1588** DYER [Title of Poem.] **1606** CHAPMAN *Mons. d'Olive* II. ii. 21 His mind is his kingdom. **1609** JONSON *Case Altered* I. ii. 41 I am no Gentleman borne, I must confesse; but *my mind to me a kingdome is truly.*—Truly a very good saying.

Mind what you must live by. (M 979)

1639 CLARKE 21. **1672** WALKER 29 no. 18 My mind is upon my meat, I am minding what I must live by.

Mind (Meddle with) your (own) business.
(B 752. M 854)

1530 PALSGRAVE 634a. Medyll with the thynge that you have a do. **1583** G. BABINGTON *Expos*[n]. *of Comman*[u]. 278 They woulde haue euerie fat, they say stand on his owne bottome, and euerie man to medle with himself. [c. **1591**] **1592** *Arden of Fev.* V. i. 214 I pray you meddle with that you haue to do. **1616** T. ADAMS *Diseases of the Soul* 66 [The Busy-body] let him apply this vnction, That he meddle with owne businesse. **1621** ROBINSON 32 Meddle with your owne businesse. **1639** CLARKE 11. **1882** H. H. ALMOND in R. J. MACKENZIE *Life* (1905) 358 The Devil has got a lot of maxims which his adherents . . . are not slow to use—'Mind your own business'. . . . You can't do more good than by putting down . . . evil . . . without being too nice as to whether you have a right to interfere or not. **1890** J. PAYN *Burnt Mil.* ch. 25 When people ask me . . . what is the meaning of this reformation, I shall tell them . . . to mind their own business.

Mind's chasing mice, Your.

1721 KELLY 384 . . . Eng. Your wit's a wool gathering.

Mind(s) (*noun*), *see also* Bashful m. hinders intent; Calamity (Extremity) is the touchstone of a brave m. (unto wit); Change his m. if he has no m. to change (Will never); Change place but not change the grief (m.) (One may); Contented m. continual feast; Eye is the window of the heart (m.); Forehead and eye (In) lecture of m.; Keep my m. to myself (I will); Mad (You will never be), you are of so many m.; Man (What is a) but his m.; Men (So many), so many m.; Month's m. (To have a); Proud m. and beggar's purse; Resolved m. has no cares; Sound m. in sound body; Time out of m.; Unsound m. . . . if you feed you poison; Virtue is the beauty of the m.; Woman's m. change oft.

Mind (*verb*), *see also* God keep me from the man that has but one thing to m.

Mindful, *see* Malice is m.

Mine is yours (mine own), What's | and what is yours is mine. (M 980)

1591 H. SMITH *Prep. to Marriage* (1657 ed., 31) He may not say as Husbands are wont to say, That which is thine is mine, and that which is mine is mine own: but that which is mine is thine, and my self too. **1576** PETTIE i. 116 But that which is mine should be yours, and yours your own. **1604** SHAKES. *M.M.* V. i. 532 Dear Isabel, 'I have a motion . . . Whereto if you'll a willing ear incline, What's mine is yours, and what is yours is mine. **1606** *Id. A.C.* V. i. 150 O, behold, How pomp is follow'd; mine will now be yours; And, should we shift estates, yours would be mine. **1666** TORRIANO 278 no. 238 A Man may make bold with what's ones own, one would think: The English ever say, That which is mine, is my own. **1738** SWIFT *Dial.* II. E.L. 316 Why, what's yours is mine, and what's mine is my own. **1813** BARRETT *Heroine* ed. Raleigh 44 So that's that, and mine's my own, and how do you like my manners, Ignoramus?

Mine, *see also* So much is m. as I enjoy.

Minerva, *see also* Sow teaching M.

Minister(s), *see* Hide nothing from thy m.; Maidens' tochers and m.' stipends aye less than called.

Mint[1] ere you strike. (M 986)

a. **1628** CARMICHAELL no. 1105. **1641** FERGUSSON no. 610. **1721** KELLY 251 . . . Spoken to them that threaten us; give me fair warning, and do your best. [[1] warn.]

Mint (= threatened), *see also* Long m. little dint.

Mint (*noun*), *see* New out of the m.

Mire, To leave (lie) in the. *Cf.* Likely lies in the mire. (M 989)

c. 1492 *Selection of Carols* ed. R. L. Greene 54 For them thou maiste lye in the myre. 1546 HEYWOOD I. iii. A3ᵛ Than my beautyfull mariage lythe in the dyke, And neuer for beautie, shall I wedde the lyke. 1594–5 SHAKES. *L.L.L.* II. i. 120 Your wit's too hot, it speeds too fast, 'twill tire. —Not till it leave the rider in the mire. 1605–8 *Id. T.Ath.* I. ii. 58 Here's that which is too weak to be a sinner, honest water, which ne'er left man i' th' mire. 1608 J. DAY *Law Tricks* I. ii. 19 Take heed; for, if you tire, Sheele keepe her pace and leaue you in the mire.

Mire, *see also* Dun is in the m.; Likely lies in the m.; Peat-pot (Out of) into m.; Town but had a m. (Never a good).

Mirror, The best | is an old friend. (M 990)

1611 COTGRAVE s.v. Miroir An old friend an excellent looking-glasse. 1640 HERBERT no. 296. 1659 HOWELL *Span. Prov.* 7. There is not so clear a mirror as an old friend. 1902–4 LEAN IV. 149 There is no better looking-glass than an old true friend. [Span.] No ay mejor espejo que el amigo viejo.—NUNEZ. 1555.

Mirth of the world dureth but a while, The. (J 90)

1573 SANFORD 50ᵛ. 1613 T. HEYWOOD *Silver Age* (1874) II. 96 Alacke! earths joyes are but short-liv'd, and last But like a puffe of breath, which (thus) is past. 1629 *Bk. Mer. Rid.* Prov. no. 11.

Mirth without measure is madness. (M 993)

1626 BRETON *Soothing* B 4. 1639 CLARKE 185.

Mirth, *see also* Ounce of m. worth pound of sorrow.

Miscall a Gordon in the raws of Strathbogie, Never.

1832 HENDERSON 6 . . . Strathbogie was the district of the Gordons. Never speak ill of a man on his own ground.

Mischief comes by the pound and goes away by the ounce. (M 998)

1573 SANFORD 104ᵛ. 1589 L. WRIGHT *Display of Dutie* 29 Though mischiefe and misery do come by pounds, and go away by ounces: yet a pound of sorrow will not pay an ounce of debt. 1639 CLARKE 165 Mischiefs come by the pound but go away by ounces. 1670 RAY 121. 1732 FULLER no. 3417.

Mischief comes (Evils come) without calling for. (M 999)

1587 BURGHLEY to Walsingham cited C. Read *Ld. Burghley & Q. Elizabeth* 378 Evils will come unsought for. *c.* 1606 R. WILLIAMS *Acclam. Pat.* l. 256 in *Bal. from MSS.* ii, pt. 1, 47 It hathe bene oftymes tolde, Myscheife is ever in all things to bolde. 1666 TORRIANO *It. Prov.* 138 no. 16.

Mischief has swift wings.

1604 J. MARSTON *The Malcontent* IV. i. 210 Good deedes crawle, but mischiefe flies. 1605 *Sir T. Smith's Voyage into Russia* L2ᵛ Mischeife hath the winges of Thought and Resolution. 1609 J. MELTON *Six-fold Politician* 13 Mischiefe is well saide to haue swift winges.

Mischief hatches, mischief catches, He that. (M 996)

1609 HARWARD 104 Mischeeff devised doth often fall upon the contrivers head. 1623 CAMDEN 271. 1639 CLARKE 127.

Mischief, The more | the better sport.

1721 KELLY 337 . . . A common, but wicked and foolish Saying. 1747 LD. LOVAT in CHAMBERS *Hist. Rebel. Scot.* (1828) II. xii. 265 When informed . . . that a scaffold had fallen near the place of execution, by which many persons were killed . . . , he only remarked, 'The mair mischief, the better sport.'

Mischief, With a. (M 1003)

1533 J. HEYWOOD *John* B2ᵛ Now go chafe the wax with a myschyfe. 1538 ELYOT s.v. Abi Abi in malam rem, go hens with a mischefe. 1541 *Schoolh. Wom.* B1ᵛ And nowe god gyue the shame at laste, Commest dronken home, with a myschefe. *a.* 1555 LINDSAY *Squire Meldrum* Wks. ed. Chalmers, ii. 250. For to the teith he did him cleif. Lat him ly thare with ane mischeif. *a.* 1580 *Wife in Morel's Skin* E.P.P. IV. 187 Your comming I would disdayne, And bid you walke with a wylde mischiefe.

Mischief(s), *see also* Better a m. than inconvenience; Crimes (M.) are made secure by greater crimes (m.); Money for m. (They can find); Mother of m. no bigger than midge's wing; No m. but a woman . . . at bottom; Women in m. are wiser.

Misdeeds, *see* Mends is worth m.

Miser, *see* Feast to a m.'s (No).

Miserable (Covetous) man makes a penny of a farthing, and the liberal of a farthing sixpence, The. (M 313)

1640 HERBERT no. 211. 1707 MAPLETOFT 55.

Miserable, *see also* Comparison that makes men m.; Englishman never happy but when m.

Miserere, see Oportet comes in place (When).

Misery best, He bears | that hides it most.   (M 1006)

c. **1584** HARVEY *Marginalia* 95. **1597** *Politeuphuia* 145ᵛ. **1732** FULLER no. 1810.

Misery enough to have once been happy, It is.   (M 1010)

1556 HEYWOOD *Spider and Fly* Sp. S. II. 33 Of pleasure past, remembraunce doth alwaie The pinche of present payne, right much augment. **1562** BULLEIN *Bulwark Def.* Use Sick Men, f. 76 There is no greater aduersitie then in miserie to remember prosperitie. **1563** SACKVILLE *Induction (Mirror for Mag.* ed. Campbell 309) With swete remembraunce of his pleasures past . . . how would he sob and shrike? **1576** PETTIE i. 28 Adversity is ever most bitter to him who hath long time lived in prosperity. **1587** T. HUGHES *et al. Misf. of Arthur* v. i. 188–9 Of all misfortunes and vnhappy Fates, The unhappiest seemes, to haue beene hapie once. [**1592**] **1597** SHAKES. *Rich. III* IV. iv. 118 Forbear to sleep the nights, and fast the days; Compare dead happiness with living woe. **1596** NASHE *Saffron W.* iii. 116 *Miserum est fuisse foelicem.* It is a miserable thing for a man to be said to haue had frends, and now to haue nere a one left. **1619** J. FAVOUR *Antiquity* 413. **1624** BURTON *Anat. Mel.* II. iii. III. *Miserum est fuisse felicem* . . . it is a great miserie to have beene happy. **1639** CLARKE 166. [See the sentiment illustrated at large in *N. & Q.* 174. 436.]

Misery (Adversity) makes (acquaints men with) strange bedfellows.

1611 SHAKES. *Temp.* II. ii. 37 My best way is to creep under his gaberdine; there is no other shelter hereabout: misery acquaints a man with strange bedfellows. **1837–9** LOCKHART *Life Scott* xii (1860) 112 Literature, like misery, makes men acquainted with strange bed-fellows. **1861** DEAN STANLEY *Hist. East. Ch.* ch. 5 (1862) 160 As increasing troubles made strange bed-fellows, the Melitian schismatics and the Arian heretics, once deadly enemies, became sworn allies against . . . Athanasius. **1927** *Times* 27 Aug. 12/1 The . . . alliance of 1923–5 was an illustration of the adage that adversity makes strange bedfellows.

Misery may be mother where one beggar is driven to beg of another.
                                                         (M 1007)

1546 HEYWOOD II. x. L3 But as men saie, misery maie be mother, Where one begger is dryuen to beg of an other. **1664** CODRINGTON 205 Misery must be the Mother when one Beggar begets another.

Misery, *see also* Battle lost (Next to) greatest m. battle gained; Long life has long m.

Misfortune makes foes of friends.

c. **1386** CHAUCER *Monk's T.* ll. 3434–6 For what man that hath freendes thurgh Fortune Mishap wol maken hem enemys, I gesse; This proverbe is ful sooth and ful commune.

Misfortunes (Hardships) never (seldom) come alone (single).
                                     (M 1004, 1012–13)

[EZEKIEL vii. 5.] *c.* **1300** *King Alisaunder* l. 1282 Men telleth in olde mone, 'The qued¹ comuth nowher alone'. *c.* **1350** IPOMADON l. 1350 Come never sorow be it one, But there come mo full gryme. *c.* **1490** *Partonope* E.E.T.S. I. l. 5542 For efter won euylle comythe mony mo. **1509** BARCLAY *Ship of Fools* ii. 251 For wyse men sayth, and oft it fallyth so . . . That one myshap fortuneth neuer alone. *c.* **1526** *Dicta Sap.* C2 There is none iuell that commeth alone without an other in the necke of it. *c.* **1580** SPELMAN *Dial.* Roxb. Cl. 3 A man cannot have one losse, but more will ffollowe. [*c.* **1591**] **1595** *Locrine* v. iv. 242 One mischiefe followes on anothers necke. **1591–2** WILMOT *Tancred and Gism.* v. iii H3ᵛ One mischiefe brings another on his neck, As mighty billowes tumble in the seas. **1594** GARNIER *Cornelia* tr. Kyd v. 293 One mischiefe drawes another on. **1596** SHAKES. *Rich. II* II. ii. 97 A tide of woes Comes rushing on this woful land at once! **1600–1** *Id. H.* IV. v. 75 When sorrows come, they come not single spies, But in battalions. *Ibid.* IV. vii. 164 One woe doth tread upon another's heel. **1622** MABBE tr. *Aleman's Guzman d'Alf.* I. iii. 29 *marg.* Misfortunes seldome come alone. **1721** KELLY 143 Hardships sindle (i.e. seldom) come single. **1837** MARRYAT *Diary on Con.* ch. 32 People will agree in the trite observation that misfortunes never come single. **1894** BLACKMORE *Perlycross* ch. 25 As misfortunes never come single, the sacred day robbed him of another fine resource. **1905** HOUSMAN ed. *Iuvenalis Saturae* (1931) Pref. xvi Misfortunes never come single, and the prattlers about P's authority are afflicted not only with lack of understanding but with loss of memory. [¹ harm.]

Misfortune(s), *see also* Raven bodes m., (The croaking); Strength enough to bear m. of friends; Worst m. are those which never befall.

Misreckoning (Wrong reckoning) is no payment.   (M 1014)

1546 HEYWOOD II. iv. G4ᵛ No (quoth she) nor mysreckning is no paiement. **1573** J. BRIDGES *Supremacy of Christ. Princes* E4 True reckeners do say misreckoning is no payment. **1639** CLARKE 126 (Wrong reckoning). *Ibid.* 156. **1721** KELLY 349 Wrong count is no Payment. And therefore all Accounts pass, Errors excepted.

Miss is as good as a mile, A.

[Formerly *An inch in a miss is as good as an ell.*] **1655** FULLER *Hist. Cambridge* 37 An hair's breadth fixed by a divine finger shall prove as effectual a separation from danger as a mile's distance. **1821** COOPER *Spy* 218 A miss was as good as a mile. **1825** SCOTT *Jrnl.* 3 Dec. (1890) I. 32 He was very near being a poet—but a miss is as good as a mile, and he always fell short of the mark. **1872** BLACKMORE *Maid Sker* ch. 32 A miss is as good as a mile, your reverence. Many a cannon ball has passed me nearer than your horse's hoof.

Miss the bus, To.

[= to miss an opportunity. The Oxford legend to which Morley refers is that Pattison missed the omnibus which would have taken him to Newman and might have taken him to Rome.] **1886** J. MORLEY *Miscellanies* iii. 147 It was probably his [Pattison's] constitutional incapacity for heroic and decisive courses that made him, according to the Oxford legend, miss the omnibus. **1915** C. J. DENNIS *Sentimental Bloke* 118 The deeds and words of some un'appy bloke Who's missed the bus. **1922** *Daily Mail* 28 Oct. 3/3 The Prime Minister has missed the bus . . . He has thrown away the greatest opportunity ever offered . . . to any statesman. **1940** 4 April N. CHAMBERLAIN [on the German invasion of Norway] Hitler has missed the bus. **1945** *Evening Standard* 4 Aug. All Spaniards I spoke to realized that their government had missed the bus.

Miss the cushion, To.   (C 928)

[= to miss the mark, err.] *c.* **1525** SKELTON *Col. Cloute* l. 998 And whan he weneth to syt Yet maye he mysse the quysshyon. **1535** G. JOY *Apol. to Tyndale* Arb. 48 For al his grete diligence . . . yet hath he missed the kushen in many places. **1571** HANMER *Chron. Irel.* (1623) 168 He was elected Archbishop of St. Davids, but at Rome he was outbid, by him that had more money, and missed the Cushin. **1608** HIERON *Defence* II. 157 He hath missed the cushen and sitteth bare.

Miss, *see also* Hit or m.; Inch in a m. as good as ell.

Mist before one's eyes, To cast a.
                                                 (M 1017)

1539 TAVERNER 2 *Garden* 28 He [Xerxes] abused the assemblie of hys lordes for a coloure, to cast a myste before mens eyes. **1551** CRANMER *Answer to Gardiner* 243 All this is spoken quyte besides the mattier, and serueth for nothing but to caste a myst before mens eyes. **1562** J. WIGAND *De Neutralibus* D6ᵛ Albeit nowe and then (to cast a myst before the eyes of the vnlearned) [they] cloke their errours with som textes of Scripture. **1579** GOSSON *Sch. Abuse* Arb. 20 The Iuggler casteth a myst to worke the closer. **1611** *Sec. Maiden's Trag.* IV. i, l. 1636 She trustes me now to cast a mist forsooth before the servauntes eyes. **1672** WALKER 13 no. 85 We will cast a mist before his eyes.

Mist comes from the hill, When the | then good weather it doth spill: when the mist comes from the sea, then good weather it will be.

1846 DENFAM 18.

Mist, *see also* Scottish m. will wet Englishman.

Mistakes, *see* Makes no m. makes nothing.

Mistaking, *see* Giving and taking there may be m.

Mrs. Grundy say? What will.

[*Mrs. Grundy* is an imaginary personification of the tyranny of conventional propriety.] **1798** T. MORTON *Speed the Plough* II. iii (1801) 29 If shame should come to the poor child [her daughter]—I say, Tummas, what would Mrs. Grundy say then? [First appearance, an off-

stage character]. **1813** *Examiner* 15 Mar. 170/2. **1857** LOCKER *Lond. Lyrics* (1874) 102 And many are afraid of God—And more of Mrs. Grundy. **1875** SMILES *Thrift* 249 Custom, habit, fashion, use, and wont, are all represented in her . . . 'What will Mrs. Grundy say?' quells many a noble impulse, hinders many a self-denying act.

Mrs. Partington mopping up the Atlantic, Like.

1831 SYD. SMITH *Speech at Taunton on Reform Bill* The attempt of the Lords to stop the progress of reform, reminds me of . . . Mrs. Partington . . . trundling her mop, . . . and vigorously pushing away the Atlantic Ocean [during an inundation of sea-water at Sidmouth, in 1824]. **1894** F. COWAN *Sea Prov.* 60 Like Mrs. Partington mopping against the tide of the Atlantic.

Mistress is the master, Where the | the parsley grows the faster.

1905 *Folk-lore* xvi. 67 (Mon.).

Mistress, Such | such Nan; such master, such man.   (M 1022)

1557 T. TUSSER C2 Such maister suche man, and such mistres such mayde. **1573** *Id.* 47 E.D.S. 103.

Mistress, *see also* Experience m. of fools; Hackney m. hackney maid; Makes his m. a goldfinch.

Misunderstanding brings lies to town.
                                                 (M 1025)

1639 CLARKE 2. **1670** RAY 121 . . . Lies and false reports arise most part from mistake and misunderstanding.

Mitcham, *see* Sutton.

Mittens, *see* Handle without m.

Mix water with fire, To.   (W 110)

1530 PALSGRAVE 593a All the worlde can nat joyne fyre and water togyther. **1580** BARET A—511 Aquam igni miscere. A Prouerbe to be vsed when we seeme to make things which be in nature contrarye one to the other to agree togither, which is impossible: as fire with water. [1596] **1605** *Stukeley* l. 472 Such a match, what were it but to join Fire and water?

Mix your liquor, Never.

a. **1831** C. DIBDIN JR. *Ben the Boatswain* (1886) 266 By drinking grog I lost my life; so, lest my fate you meet, Why, never mix your liquor, lads, but always drink it neat.

Mixture, *see* Right m. good mortar.

Mob has many heads, but no brains, The.   (M 1029)

1666 TORRIANO *It. Prov.* 210 no. 9 The multitude is a brute with many legs, and without a head. **1732** FULLER no. 4653. **1747** FRANKLIN Nov. A mob's a monster; heads enough but no brains.

Mob, *see also* Keep yourself from . . . tumult of
m.

Mobberley hole, *see* Rain always comes out of.

Mock no pannier men; your father was
a fisher.   (P 41)
1678 RAY 78. **1732** FULLER no. 3425 (if your
father).

Mock not a cobbler for his black
thumbs.
1642 FULLER *H. & P. State* III. ii. (1841) 146
Neither flout any for his profession, if honest,
though poor and painful. Mock not a cobbler
for his black thumbs.

Mock not, quoth Mumford, when his
wife called him cuckold.   (M 1313)
1659 HOWELL *Eng. Prov.* 9a. **1732** FULLER no.
3426.

Mocking (Scorning) is catching.   (S 152)
1670 RAY 140. **1678** *Id.* 200 *Scorning* is
catching. He that scorns any condition, action
or employment, may come to be . . . driven upon
it himself. **1721** KELLY 255. Spoken to discourage People from mimicking any Man's
Imperfections, lest you contract a Habit of them.
1738 SWIFT *Dial.* I. E.L. 282.

Mocks a cripple, ought to be whole, He
that.   (C 827)
1581 GUAZZO i. 163 For as the Proverbe is,
Hee that mocketh the lame, must take heede
that he him selfe goe upright. **1640** HERBERT
no. 565.

Mocks shall be mocked, He who.
                                                      (M 1031)
[JOB xiii. 9: As one man mocketh another, do ye
so mocke him?] **1484** CAXTON *Fab. Poggio* (ed.
Jacobs, 1889) 7, 307 Alle the sallary or payment
of them that mokken other is for to be mocqued
at the last. **1509** BARCLAY *Ship of Fools* i. 213
They that on mockes alway theyr myndes cast
Shall of all other be mocked at the last. **1534**
J. HEYWOOD *Play Love* B4ᵛ For who so that
mocketh shall surely stur This olde prouerbe
mockum moccabitur. **1587** BRIDGES *Defence*
50 . . . As Dauid sayth, Psalm 2. Hee that
dwelleth in the Heauens shall laugh them to
scorne. **1599** PORTER *Angry Wom. Abingd.*
ll. 888–90 It seemes to me, that you maister
Phillip mocke me, do you not know qui mocat
mocabitur, mocke age and se how it will
prosper?

Mock(ing), *see also* Hanging's stretching, m.'s
catching; Toy to m. an ape.

Modest words to express immodest
things, It is hard to find.   (W 814)
1607 H. ESTIENNE *World of Wonders* 262 For (as
the Greeke prouerbe saith) . . . **1645** E. BROOKE
Commonpl. Bk. 27.

Modesty be a virtue, Though | yet
bashfulness is a vice.
1639 CLARKE 268 Bashful modesty is the lack of
chastity. **1732** FULLER no. 5006.

Modesty sets off one newly come to
honour.   (M 1032)
1651 HERBERT no. 1062.

Modish, *see* Careless (The more), more m.

Moist hand argues an amorous nature
(fruitfulness), A.   (H 86)
[*c.* 1602] **1608** *Merry Devil of Edmonton* I. i.
49 Two tedious winters have past o'er since first
This couple lov'd each other, and in passion
Glued first their naked hands with youthful
moisture. **1604** SHAKES. *O.* III. iv. 36 Give me
your hand. This hand is moist, my lady.—It
yet hath felt no age nor known no sorrow.—
This argues fruitfulness and liberal heart.
1606–7 *Id. A.C.* I. ii. 48 If an oily palm be not
a fruitful prognostication, I cannot scratch
mine ear. **1673** D'AVENANT *News* (1872) IV. 174
A moist palm, which assures me that she will not
Be satisfied with a kickshaw.

Mole, *see* Argus abroad, m. at home; Blind as a
m.

Molehill, *see* King of a m., (To be); Mountain
of m.

Moment, *see* Spur of the m.

Monarch, *see* Merry m.

Monday for wealth, Tuesday for health,
Wednesday the best day of all;
Thursday for crosses, Friday for losses,
Saturday no luck at all.
1850 *N. & Q.*, 1st Ser. II. 515. [*Days of the Week.
—Marriage.*]

Monday, *see also* Maltman comes on M.; St. M.;
Saturday is working day, M. holiday of preachers.

Money, All things are obedient to.
                                                       (T 163)
[ECCLES. X. 19: Money answereth all things.]
1390 CHAUCER *Tale of Melibee* B. l. 2740 Salomon seith that alle thynges obeyen to moneye.
c. **1390** GOWER *Conf. Amantis* V. 244 All the
world to gold obeieth. **1539** TAVERNER 14ᵛ.
1581 GUAZZO i. 186 (in subjection to). **1615**
Janua Linguarum tr. W. Welde 5 All things
obey money.

Money and capers, He that has | is
provided for Lent.   (M 1047)
1642 TORRIANO 32. **1659** N. R. 126 (is well
furnisht for). **1732** FULLER no. 2388.

Money answers all things. (M 1052)

[ECCLES. X. 19.] **1630** T. ADAMS *Cosmopolite*: Wks. 678 What quality beares vp so braue a head but money giues it the checkmate! It answereth all things, saith Salomon. A feast is made for laughter, and wine maketh merry: but Money answereth all things. **1659** N. R. 75.

Money begets (breeds, gets) money.

(M 1053)

1572 T. WILSON *Discourse upon Usury* (1925) 248 Money getteth money. **1593** SHAKES. *V. & A.* l. 767 Gold that's put to use more gold begets. **1666** TORRIANO 64 no. 4 Moneys beget moneys. **1689** SELDEN *Table-Talk* Arb. 114 'Tis a vain thing to say, Money begets not Money; for that no doubt it does. **1841** MARRYAT *Poacher* ch. 37 Seven hundred pounds; eh, youngster? . . . Money breeds money. **1861** TRAFFORD *City & Suburb* ch. 14 Money makes money, it is said. **1872** BESANT & RICE *Ready-m. Mort.* ch. 2 Money gets money. If you have but much, you must, in spite of yourself, have more.

Money burns (a hole) in your pocket, Your. (M 1048)

[= clamours to be spent.] *c.* **1530** MORE *Wks.* (1557) 195 A little wanton money which . . . burned out the bottom of his purse. **1573** TUSSER X. E.D.S. 19 Sonne, think not thy monie purse bottom to burn, but keepe it for profite, to serue thine owne turn. **1591** *Troublesome Reign K. John* Pt. 1 B3ᵛ Some money matter, which you suppose burns in the bottome of my chest. **1846** MARRYAT *Privateersman* ch. 8 How could I get rid of my money, which burns in my pocket, if I did not spend as much in one day as would suffice for three weeks? **1875** SMILES *Thrift* 139 A man who has more money about him than he requires . . . is tempted to spend it. . . . It is apt to 'burn a hole in his pocket'.

Money comes from him like drops of blood, His. (M 1049)

1678 RAY 90 *A covetous person.* . . . **1688** BUNYAN *Jer. Sinner Saved* Wks. (1855) I. 87 Niggardly rich men, whose money comes from them like drops of blood.

Money do? What will not. *Cf.* **Gold do; Money will do anything.** (M 1102)

1563 *Mirror for Mag.* ed. Campbell 366 What thing so hard but money can obtayne? **1567** HARMAN *Caveat* (Viles & Furnivall) 60 What can not be hadde for money, as the prouerbe sayth (*Omnia venalia Romæ*). **1578** WHETSTONE 2 *Promos and Cassandra* I. vi. H1 But O, O, quid non pecunia? **1591** ARIOSTO *Orl. Fur.* Harington XXXVII. 78 What cannot gaine and hope of mony worke? **1681** ROBERTSON *Phraseol. Generalis* 892.

Money draws money.

1666 TORRIANO 239 no. 7 Wealth goes to wealth. **1880** MRS. OLIPHANT *Greatest Heir* ch. 2 Others . . . insisted on leaving their money to Lucy on the . . . principle that to those who have shall be given . . . 'Money draws money', the proverb says.

Money for mischief, They can find | when they can find none to buy corn.

(M 1094)

1678 RAY *Adag. Hebr.* 409.

Money has what he wants (most things), He that has. (M 1041*a*)

1528 W. TYNDALE *Parable of the Wicked Mammon* P.S. 69 After the common prouerb, he that hath money hath what him listeth. **1611** COTGRAVE s.v. Argent (most things). **1659** HOWELL *Span. Prov.* 1 Who hath money hath what he will. **1664** T. KILLIGREW 2 *Thomaso* IV. xi. 441 He that hath money hath all.

Money, He for my. (M 1040)

1566 ERASM. *Diversoria* tr. E. H. ed. de Vocht l. 124 This behaviour doth well beseme Frenchmen peraduenture, how be it the fashions of Duche lande shall go for my monye when all is done. **1595** R. HARVEY *Plain Percival* C4 Some earnest protestants are precise in correcting their owne corrupt affections, and in aduertising their brother kindly of his faults as they fall: he goes for my money. [**1598**] **1616** HAUGHTON *Englishmen for My Money* [Title]. **1598–9** SHAKES. *M.A.* II. iii. 56 Well, a horn for my money, when all's done. **1606** T. HEYWOOD 2 *If You Know not Me* l. 1767 Why then the Englishman for thy money. **1668** DRYDEN *Martin Mar-All* V. i They may talk what they will of Oxford for an university, but Cambridge for my money. **1864** TROLLOPE *Small House at Allington* ch. 53 The man as pitched into him would be the man for my money.

Money in his purse, He that has | cannot want a head for his shoulders.

(M 1042)

1659 HOWELL *Eng. Prov.* 13b.

Money in thy purse, Put (Keep).

(M 1090)

1604 SHAKES. *O.* I. iii. 345, &c. **1659** HOWELL *Eng. Prov.* 17a My friend keep money in thy purse; *'Tis one of Solomon's Proverbs said one.* **1659** 'JOHN IRETON' *Oration* Therefore saith the wiseman, My Child get money in thy purse.

Money is a good servant, but a bad master. *Cf.* **Money be not thy servant.**

(M 1055)

1616 WITHALS 541 Money doth either serue as a slaue, or commaund as a Maister. **1633** MASSINGER *New Way* IV. i Merm. 173 I must grant, Riches, well got, to be a useful servant, But a bad master. *a.* **1640** J. SMYTH *Lives of the Berkeleys* ii. 386. **1666** TORRIANO *It. Prov.* 64, no. 27 Money is a Servant to him who can make use of it, otherwise it is a Master. **1887** LD. AVEBURY *Pleas. of Life* II. ii This is of course on the supposition that you are master of money, that the money is not master of you.

Money is often lost for want of money.

(M 1062)

1616 DRAXE no. 744.

Money is round, and rolls away.

(M 1063)

1619 *Helpe to Discourse* (1640) 120 Why is the forme of money round? Because it is to runne from every man. **1659** HOWELL *It. Prov.* 2 Money is round, and so quickly trills away. **1902–4** LEAN I. 424 Bawbees are round and rin away: a grip o' th' ground is gude to hae. [*N. Fife F. L. Journal*, ii. 91.] **1905** A. MACLAREN *Expos.*, *Matt.* II. 256 It is not for nothing that sovereigns are made circular, for they roll very rapidly, and 'riches take to themselves wings and fly away'.

Money is that which art has turned up trump.

(M 1064)

1659 HOWELL *Eng. Prov.* 18a. **1670** RAY 18.

Money is the sinews of (love as well as of) war.

(M 1067)

[LIBANIUS orat. 46 τὰ νεῦρα τοῦ πολέμου. CIC. *Philippica* 5. 2. 5 *Nervos belli pecuniam* (*largiri*).] [1549] **1581** [HALES] *Dis. Commonweal Eng.* II. 86 These coines and treasures be not without cause called of wise men . . . The senowes of warre. **1573** SANFORD 68 *Timotheus* affirmeth, that money is the sinewes of all things. *c.* **1589** PEELE *Battle of Alcazar* l. 221 Gold is the glue, sinewes, and strength of war. *c.* **1590** G. HARVEY *Marginalia* 101. **1592** BACON in Parliament (H. TOWNSHEND *Historical Collections* (1680) 60) Laws are the sinews of peace, money of war. **1592** LYLY *Midas* I. i. 38 I would wish that eueuything I touched might turne to gold: this is the sinewes of warre. **1599** JAMES VI *Basil. Dor.* II Roxb. Cl. 68 Before ye take on warres, . . . remember, that money is *Nervus belli*. **1625** BACON *Ess., Greatness of K.* Arb. 473 Neither is Money the Sinewes of Warre, (as it is trivially said) where the Sinewes of Mens Armes, in Base and Effeminate People, are failing. **1642** FULLER *H. & P. State* II. XX (1841) 114 (*The Good Soldier*) Moneys are the sinews of war; yet if these sinews should chance to be shrunk, and pay casually fall short, he takes a fit of this convulsion patiently. **1732** FULLER no. 3442 Money is the sinew of love as well as of war. **1836** M. SCOTT *T. Cring. Log* ch. 7 A stream of gold and silver flowing into the Bank of England, . . . thus supplying the sinews of war to the government. **1890** J. PAYN *Burnt Mil.* ch. 22 These debts . . . must be prejudicial indeed to any matrimonial project. Yet here was this young fellow actually offering to supply his rival with the sinews of war—and love.

Money is welcome though it come in a dirty clout.

(M 1069)

1629 HOWELL *Lett.* 3 Aug. (1903) I. 309 Nor would I receive money in a dirty clout, if possibly I could be without it. **1659** *Id. Eng. Prov.* 13b Money is welcome, though it come in a shitten clout. **1721** KELLY 249 Money is welcome in a dirten clout. L. *Dulcis odor lucri ex re quâlibet.* **1723** DEFOE *Col. Jack* ii. Wks. (1912) I. 280 People say, when they have been talking of money that they could not get in, I wish I had it in a foul clout.

Money is wise, it knows its way.

(M 1070)

1678 RAY 352 . . . (*Som.*) Sayes the poor man that must pay as soon as he receives.

Money like hay, To make.

1835 J. M. WILSON in the *Tales of Borders* I. 17 Robin Paterson rented a farm . . . of fifty acres, in which, as his neighbours said, he was 'making money like hay'.

Money makes a man free (recommends a man) everywhere.

1542 BECON *Nosegay* P.S. 223 Whosoever hath money may go where he list, and do whatsoever he will at his own pleasure. **1731** *Poor Robin's Alm.* Expln. of Alm. Eat boil'd or roast, or drink good Wine or Beer, But, Money recommends you every where. **1737** RAMSAY III. 190 Money maks a man free ilka where.

Money makes marriage (the match).

(M 1074)

a. **1500** *15c. School-Bk.* ed. W. Nelson 18 Nowadais money maketh mariage with sum menn rather then love or bewtye. **1592** GREENE *Groatsworth of Witte* (Harrison) 26 Money now a dayes makes the match, or else the match is marde. **1607** R. WILKINSON *The Merchant Royal* 25 Let her then be as obedient as Sarah, as deuout as Anna, as vertuous as the Virgin Mary, yet al this is nothing, Quaerenda pecunia primum est, other things may mend it, but monie makes the match. **1609** HARWARD 127ᵛ Wedding goeth by welth. **1621** BURTON *Anat. Mel.* III. ii. III. iii (1651) 478 There is another great allurement, . . . and that is mony; *veniunt a dote sagittae*, mony makes the match. **1732** FULLER no. 3445.

Money makes one mad, Too much.

(M 1101)

1626 BRETON *Soothing* B4 (will make a man). **1659** HOWELL *Eng. Prov.* 13a.

Money makes the man.

(M 1076)

[L. *Divitiae virum faciunt.*] *a.* **1500** *Early Eng. Carols* (Greene) 393 Money makythe the man. **1542** BECON *Nosegay* P.S. 222. **1605** S. ROWLEY *When You See Me* l. 1440 Monie will make vs men. **1616** DRAXE no. 1410 (a man). **1662** FULLER *Hants.* 3 We commonly say, . . . I meet in the *Change*; 'Money makes a man', which puts him in a solvable condition. **1828** LYTTON *Pelham* ch. 35 The continent only does for us English people to see. . . . Here, as you know, 'money makes the man'. **1850** KINGSLEY *Alton L.* ch. 2 Money most truly and fearfully 'makes the man'. A difference in income, as you go lower, makes more and more difference . . . in all which polishes the man. **1920** 7 May D. H. LAWRENCE *Lett.* i. 629 Money maketh a man.

Money makes the mare to go.

(M 1077)

15th c. *Money, Money* 393 in *Early Eng. Carols*, 262 In the heyweyes ther joly palfreys yt [money] makyght to lepe and praunce. **1573** SANFORD 105ᵛ Money makes the horsse to goe. **1670** RAY 122. **1690** T. D'URFEY *Collin's Walk* iii. 96 As Money makes the Mare to go, Even so it makes the Lawyer too. **1809** MALKIN *Gil Blas* I. viii My business on the high road is not to hear sermons. Money makes my mare to go. **1914** K. F. PURDON *Folk of Furry F.* ch. 3.

Money makes the pot boil. *Cf.* Keep the pot boiling. (M 1086)

[1663] 1673 D'AVENANT *Playhouse* V. 101 We'll find out rich husband to make you the pot boil. 1699 *Fables of Aesop* tr. R. L'Estrange 305 'Tis that [Money] which makes the Pot Boyl (as the Proverb says) though the Devil Piss in the Fire.

Money, He that has no | needs no purse. (M 1043)

1616 DRAXE no. 1087. 1666 TORRIANO 63 no. 33. 1813 RAY 139.

Money never comes out of season. (M 1079)

[c. 1591] 1623 SHAKES. *2 Hen. VI* I. ii. 92 Gold cannot come amiss. 1616 DRAXE no. 910. 1639 CLARKE 220.

Money or your life! Your.

1848 16 May J. A. FROUDE to C. Kingsley (W. H. Dunn *Froude* 1961 118) Nothing will open rich John Bull's understanding but a hand at his throat and 'Your money or your life'. 1864 J. PAYN *Lost Sir Massingb.* ch. 29 A pistol was protruded into the carriage. 'Your money or your life! . . . ,' said a rough voice.

Money refused loses its brightness. (M 1080)

1640 HERBERT no. 446.

Money wants no followers. (M 1082)

1651 HERBERT no. 1182.

Money will do anything. *Cf.* Money do? (M 1084)

1584 WITHALS F5 Monie prouideth all things. 1593–4 SHAKES. *T.S.* I. ii. 80 Nothing comes amiss, so money comes withal. 1602 BRETON *Old Madcap's Gallimaufry* (Robertson 129) Hee that hath Money, may do many thinges. 1609 HARWARD 103 Mony doth all. 1613 W. GAMAGE *Linsey-Woolsey* C1 The prouerbe is, Dame Mony can do All. 1616 DRAXE no. 208 . . . in these dayes. 1623 WODROEPHE 475 Mony doth all Things. *c.* 1624 FLETCHER *Rule a Wife* IV. i. 160 Money may do much. [1625] 1647 *Id. Chances* I. xi. 48 Men say gold Does all . . . Now I say beauty can do more. 1706 STEVENS s.v. Dinero Money does all things.

Money will do more than my lord's letter. (M 1085)

c. 1609 JONSON *Ev. Man in Hum.* II. v. 50. 1678 RAY 177. 1732 FULLER no. 3447.

Money, wisdom, and good faith, Of | there is commonly less than men count upon.

1605 BACON *Adv. Learn.* II. xxiii. O.U.P. 232 It is an error frequent for men to shoot over, and to suppose deeper ends and more compass reaches than are: the Italian proverb being . . . for the most part true: Di danari, di seno, e di fede, Cè nè manco che non credi:[1] There is commonly less money, less wisdom, and less good faith, than men do account upon. [[1] GIUSTI *Proverbi Toscani* 263 Danari, senno e fede, ce n'è manco l'uom crede.]

Money, wit, and virtue, Of | believe one-fourth of what you hear.

1707 MAPLETOFT 8.

Money would be gotten if there were money to get it with.

1721 KELLY 250 . . . Intimating that the Man would thrive, if he had a Stock.

Money you refuse will never do you good, The.

1707 MAPLETOFT 2.

Money, *see also* Abundance of m. ruins youth; Bad m. drives out good; Beauty is potent, m. omnipotent; Cheese and m. should sleep together; Dally not with women or m.; Eggs for m. (Take); Fool and his m. soon parted; Get m. in a desert; God send us some m. quoth Earl of Eglinton; God send you . . . and me more m.; Grateful man (To a) give m.; Has it and will not keep it (He that), . . . shall want m.; Health and m. go far; Health without m. half ague; Hoards up m.; Hold up your head, for there is m. bid for you; Hole under his nose that his m. runs into; Know what m. is (Would you), borrow; Latin, a horse, and m. (With), thou wilt pass; Lawsuits consume m.; Lend your m., lose your friend; Little m. as manners (If you had); Looks in a man's face, (He that) knows not what m. is in his purse; Lose your time (If you), you cannot get m.; Love does much, m. everything; Love lasts as m. endures; Love of m. and of learning rarely meet; Love or m. (For); Man without m. no man at all; Man without m. than m. without a man, (Rather a); Manners and m. make gentleman; Many a thing's made for m.; Many means to get m.; Marries for love without m. (Who); Marry not . . . for m.; Merchant bare that has m. (He is not); Moyen does mickle but m. does more; Much m. makes a country poor; Muck and m. go together; No m. no Swiss; Patience, time, and m. accommodate; Pay your m. and take your choice; Plays his m. ought not to value it (He that); Put one's m. on wrong horse; Rag of m.; Ready m.; Rich man's m. hangs him; Sailors get m. like horses; See for your love, buy for your m.; Sign invites you in, m. redeem you out; Skilfullest wanting m. is scorned; Talk is but talk, m. buys lands; Tell m. after your father; Throw good m. after bad; Time is m.; Trade is mother of m.; Travel through world (To) . . . m. and patience; Trust him with untold m. (You may); Turn the m. when hear cuckoo; Want of m. want of comfort; Whores affect not you but your m.; Will buys, m. pays; Words are but words, m. buys lands.

Moneyless (Silverless) man goes fast through the market, A.

1721 KELLY 10 (silverless). . . . Because he does not stay to cheapen or buy. **1732** FULLER no. 330.

Monk out of his cloister is like a fish out of water, A.

[L. *Sicut piscis sine aqua caret vita, ita sine monasterio monachus.* Decretal of Gratian.] *c.* **1386** CHAUCER *Prol.* ll. 179–81 Ne that a monk whan he is recchelees Is likned til a fissh that is waterlees; This to seyn, a Monk out of his cloystre. **1587** J. BRIDGES *Def. of Gvt. of C. of E.* 1258 (As Chaucer sayth) a Monke out of his cloyster, is not worth an oyster.

Monk's hood, *see* Bean in a m. h. (Like a).

Monk(s), *see also* Cowl does not make m.; Devil was sick.; Do better (He that cannot) must be m.; Fox turns m.; Henry VIII pulled down m.; Isle of Wight has no m.; Ox before . . . m. on all sides (Take heed of); Runaway m. never praises convent; Three things are insatiable.

Monkey's allowance, more kicks than halfpence.

1785 GROSS s.v. Monkey. **1824** SCOTT *St. Ronan's* ch. 34 'Which is like monkey's allowance, I suppose', said the traveller, 'more kicks than halfpence'. **1833** MARRYAT *P. Simple* ch. 2 When you get on board, you'll find monkey's allowance—more kicks than halfpence. **1900** E. J. HARDY *Mr. Thomas Atkins* 297 On active service kicks are more plentiful than halfpence. **1917** J. CONRAD *The Shadow-Line* ch. 1 The kicks and the halfpence, as the saying is.

Monkeys, *see* Women in state affairs.

Monmouth caps.   (M 1105)

[= a flat round cap.] **1585–1616** *Shirburn Ballads* xxix (1907) 118 'The miller in his best array'.—He puts on His Monmouth cap. **1598** W. RANKINS *Seven Satires* C1ᵛ Vpon his head a Monmouth cap he wore, With a greene parrats feather broucht before. **1599** SHAKES. *Hen. V* IV. vii. 96 Welshmen . . . wearing leeks in their Monmouth caps. **1662** FULLER *Monmouthshire* 50 The best Caps were formerly made at Monmouth. . . . The trade was . . . removed hence to Beaudly . . . yet . . . they are called Monmouth Caps unto this day.

Monmouth caps, *see also* Dunmow bacon.

Month of Sundays, A.

1832 MARRYAT *Newton Forster* 5 It may last a month of Sundays. **1836** HALIBURTON *Clockmaker* I. 73 They didn't see such a beautiful face once in a month of Sundays. **1842–3** W. H. MAXWELL *Hector O'Hal.* ch. 18 If she's

not married till she marries me, she'll be single for a month of Sundays.

Month's mind to a thing, To have a.
                                                    (M 1109)

[= a strong inclination.] **1575** GASCOIGNE *Glass of Govt.* ii. 40 She hath a monethes minde vnto Phylosarchus. **1584** HERODOTUS *Euterpe* tr. B.R. ed. Lang 130 Aesope the inuenter of fables, to whom this smooth minion [Rhodope] had a monethes mind and more. **1594** SHAKES. *T.G.V.* I. ii. 137 I see you have a month's mind to them. **1598** HALL *Virgidemiarum The Three last Bookes. Of byting Satyres* Lib. 4 Sat. 4 sig. D 1 *b.* He thaws like Chaucer's frosty Ianiuere, And sets a Months minde vpon smyling May. **1605** *London Prodigal* I. ii. 143 (*Shaks. Apoc.*) 197 He hath a moneths mind here to mistresse *Francesse.* **1631** BRATHWAITE *Whimzies* (1859) 118 This hath made him sometimes to have a month's mind to go for Virginia. **1670** RAY 186 . . . In ancient wills we find often mention of a moneths mind. . . . The meaning was, because the party deceased, used to appoint a second lesser funeral solemnity for remembrance of him. **1738** SWIFT *Dial.* I. E.L. 289 She had a month's mind to Dick Frontless, and thought to run away with him.

Months in the year curse a fair Februeer, All the.   (M 1110)

1670 RAY 40. **1706** STEVENS s.v. Febrero. When it does not rain in February, there's neither good Grass nor good Rye. **1847** R. CHAMBERS *Pop. Rhymes Scot.* 364 Good weather in February is regarded as an unfavourable symptom of what is to come.

Month, *see also* May, (Merry m. of).

Moon does not heed the barking of dogs (wolves), The. (The dog (wolf) barks in vain at the moon).   (D 449. M 1119)

[L. *Latrantem curatne alta Diana canem?* Does Diana on high care for the dog that barks at her?] **1520** WHITTINGTON *Vulgaria* 72 They playe as the dogge doeth that barketh at the moon all nyght. **1530** PALSGRAVE 443b This dogge barketh agaynste the moone. **1580** LYLY *Euph. & his Eng.* ii. 90 As lykely to obtain thy wish, as the Wolfe is to catch the Moone. *Ibid.* 150 Eager Wolues bark at ye Moone, though they cannot reach it. **1591** FLORIO *Second F.* Ep. Ded. A3 The moone keeps her course for all the dogges barking. **1595** SHAKES. *M.N.D.* V. i. 361 The wolf behowls the moon. **1599** *Id. A.Y.* V. ii. 102 Pray you, no more of this; 'tis like the howling of Irish wolves against the moon. **1599** *Id. J.C.* IV. iii. 27 I had rather be a dog and bay the moon Than such a Roman. **1599** MINSHEU 4 i 2ᵛ For all the dogs barking the moone will stand where it did. **1621** BURTON *Anat. Mel.* II. iii. VII (1651) 358 Doth the moon care for the barking of a dog? They detract, scoffe, and raile (saith one), and bark at me on every side; but I . . . vindicate myself by contempt alone. **1660** W. SECKER *Nonsuch Prof.* II (1891) 74 Believers resemble the moon, which emerges from her eclipse by keeping her motion; and ceases not to shine because the dogs bark at her.

Moon is made of green cheese, He thinks (would make me believe) the. (M 1116)

c. 1528 ROY & BARLOW *Rede me* Arb. 114 Yf they saye the moone is blewe We must beleve that it is true. *a.* 1529 FRITH *Antith.* (1829) 315 They would make men believe . . . that the moon is made of green cheese. 1530 PALSGRAVE 627a I make hym byleve the moone is made of a calves skynne. 1546 HEYWOOD II. vii. K1 Ye fet circumquaques to make me beleue Or thynke, that the moone is made of a greene cheese. 1611 COTGRAVE s.v. Arain (Wee say of such an Idiot) hee thinkes the Moone is made of greene cheese. 1641 FERGUSSON no. 413 *Of false persons* . . . He wald gar a man trow that the moon is made of green cheis, or thet the cat took the heron. 1783 AINSWORTH *Lat. Dict.* (Morell) I. s.v. *Moon*, Tell me the moon is made of green cheese! 1863 KINGSLEY *Water Bab.* ch. 4 Writing a great book, . . . in which he proved that the moon was made of green cheese.

Moon's in the full, When the | then wit's in the wane.

c. 1621 DEKKER, &c. *The Witch of Edmonton* (*Dramatic Wks.* 1873 IV. 367). 1846 DENHAM 4.

Moon is (Stars are) not seen where the sun shines, The. (M 1120. S 826)

1576 PETTIE ii. 109 When sun shineth, the light of the stars is not seen. 1577 GRANGE *Garden* P3 The brightnesse of the Sunne daseth the light of the Moone. 1579 LYLY *Euph.* i. 199 As the Sunne dimmeth the Moone . . . so this gallant gyrle . . . eclipsed the beautie of them all. 1594–5 SHAKES. *L.L.L.* IV. iii. 226 My love, her mistress, is a gracious moon; She, an attending star, scarce seen a light. 1616 DRAXE no. 1381 Where the Sunne shineth, the Moone hath nought to doe. 1678 RAY 178.

Moon shows a silver shield, If the | be not afraid to reap your field; but if she rises haloed round, soon we'll tread on deluged ground.

1555 L. DIGGES *Prognostication* B1 The Moone . . . bent to red colour, prouoketh wynde. The Moone pale, or some what inclined to blacke, obscure or thicke, threatnith rayne. 1883 ROPER 8. 1893 INWARDS 64.

Moon(s), *see* Bald m. . . . another pint; Bark against m.; Beans in the wane of the m., (Set); Cap after a thing, (at the m.) (To throw one's); Cast beyond the m.; Changeful as the m.; Churl fall out of m. (Care lest); Cry for the m.; Day that you do well there will be seven m.; Dog barks in vain at the m.; Friday's m. comes too soon; Full m. (Like a); Full m. brings fair weather; Gaze at m. and fall in gutter; Man in the m.; Michaelmas Day (So many days old the m. is); Michaelmas m. rises soon; Midsummer m.; No m. no man; Old of the m. (In the) cloudy morning broke; Once in a blue m.; Pale m. does rain; Round the m. there is a brugh (When); Saturday's m. . . . comes too soon; Shape a coat for the m.; Shoot the m.; Sun, m. . . . against us; Sussex m.

Moonlight flitting, To make a.

[= to remove by night, or by stealth.] 1622 W. JAGGARD *Apology* A3 That post-hast, to make the Presse walke by moone-light. 1721 KELLY 145 . . . to signify that a Man has run away for fear of his Creditors. 1821 GALT *Annals of Par.* ch. 31 He was fain to make a moonlight flitting, leaving his wife for a time to manage his affairs. 1824 MOIR *Mansie W.* ch. 17 The whole covey of them, no better than a set of swindlers, . . . made that very night a moonlight flitting. 1892 STEVENSON *Wrecker* ch. 5 I made a moonlight flitting, a thing never dignified.

Moonlight, *see also* Keep sheep by m.

Moonrakers, *see* Wiltshire m.

Moonshine in the mustard-pot. (M 1129)

1639 CLARKE 68. *Ibid.* 154 (water-pot). 1678 RAY 76 Thou shalt have moonshine i' th' mustard-pot for it, *i.e.* nothing.

Moonshine in the water. (M 1128)

1468 *Paston Letters* (Gairdner) iv. 305 If Sir Thomas Howys wer . . . made byleve and put in hope of the moone shine in the water and I wot nat what. 1530 PALSGRAVE 865a. 1546 HEYWOOD I. xi. E3ᵛ I wyll as sone be hylt, As wayte agayne for the moneshyne in the water. 1588 LYLY *Endym.* II. ii. 2. 1594–5 SHAKES. *L.L.L.* V. ii. 207 O vain petitioner! beg a greater matter; Thou now request'st but moonshine in the water. 1818 SCOTT *Rob Roy* ch. 14 It just a' gaed aff like moonshine in water.

Moonshine, *see also* Mouthful of m.

Moor, *see* Bare m. that he goes over and gets not cow.

Moore, *see* Scratch a M.

Moors, The more | the better victory. (M 1131)

1578 *Courtly Controv.* N3ᵛ The victorie is so muche more glorious, as the fight is painefull and dangerous. 1618 SIR ROGER WILLIAMS *Actions of Low Countries* 80 There can bee no braue encounter without men slaine on both sides. True it is, the fewer the better conduct; but the more dyes, the more honour to the fight. 1631 *Celestina* tr. Mabbe (1894 ed., 140) (As it is in the Prouerbe) the more Moores, the better market. 1678 RAY 351. 1813 *Id.* 140 A saying used by the Spaniards, when the Moors were in Spain.

Moors, *see also* Jews spend at Easter; Three M. to a Portuguese.

Mope-eyed[1] by (with) living so long a maid, You are. (L 396)

1648 HERRICK *Hesper., Upon Himselfe* Mopey'd I am, as some have said, Because I've liv'd so long a maid. 1678 RAY 346. 1721 KELLY 394 . . . Spoken to those who overlook a Thing before them. [[1] purblind.]

Moraoh downs, hard and never ploughed, Like.

1864 *N. & Q.* 3rd Ser. v. 275. *Cornish Provs.*

More a man has, the more he desires, The.   (M 1144)

c. **1425** *Castle of Perseverance* l. 3268. **1509** BARCLAY *Ship of Fools* i. 158. **1576** PETTIE i. 126 The more she had, the more she desired to have. **1605–6** SHAKES. *M.* IV. iii. 81 And my more-having would be as a sauce To make me hunger more. **1666** TORRIANO *It. Prov.* 66 no. 9 The more one hath, the more one desires.

More afraid (frightened) than hurt.
                                    (A 55)

1530 PALSGRAVE 558 a He was sorer frayed than hurt. **1546** HEYWOOD I. iv. B1ᵛ All perils that fall may, who feareth they fall shall, Shall so feare all thyng, that he shall let fall all, And be more frayd than hurt. **1579** LYLY *Euph.* i. 316 Certeynly thou art more afrayde then hurte. **1596** WARNER *Albion's Eng.* x. 59 S3ᵛ More skar'd then hurt. **1641** FERGUSSON no. 403 He is war fleyit[1] nor he is hurt. **1725** A. RAMSAY *Gent. Shep.* v. i Bauldy's more afraid than hurt. **1827** LAMB *Lett.* to Patmore 19 Jul. Down went my sister through a crazy chair . . . Mary was more frightened than hurt. [¹ frightened.]

More bare (Worse shod) than the shoemaker's wife and the smith's mare, None.   (S 387)

1546 HEYWOOD I. xi. E1ᵛ But who is wurs shod, than the shoemakers wyfe, With shops full of newe shapen shoes all hir lyfe? **1603** MONTAIGNE (Florio) I. xxiv. 197 When we see a man ill shod, if he chance to be a Shoomaker, wee say . . . commonly none goes worse shod than they. Even so . . . experience doth often shew us, a Physitian lesse healthy, a Divine lesse reformed, . . . a Wiseman lesse sufficient than another. **1641** FERGUSSON no. 790 The Sowter's wife is worst shod. **1678** RAY 202. **1721** KELLY 258 (worse sho'd). **1876** SMILES *Scotch Naturalist* 380 His large family . . . were all . . . well shod, notwithstanding the Scottish proverb to the contrary. 'The Smith's mare and the shoemaker's bairns are aye the worst shod.'

More folks are wed than keep good houses.

1683 MERITON *Yorks. Ale* 17.

More fool than fiddler.   (F 498)

1678 RAY 245.

More fools in Henley.

1894 NORTHALL *Folk-phrases* 19 . . . Used by natives of Henley-in-Arden, co. *Warw.*, when strangers of remarkable appearance tarry in the main street. It might be made to cut both ways certainly.

More haste than good speed.   (H 197)

c. **1513** SIR T. MORE *Richard III* (1821) 23 Broughte the Kynge vppe in greate haste, not in good speede. **1542** ERASM. tr. Udall *Apoph.*

(1877) 41 Soᵗhe persones, as do make moste haste in the beginning, haue commonly (accordyng to our Englishe prouerbe) worst spede toward the endyng. **1546** HEYWOOD I. viii. C1ᵛ I am taught to know, in more haste than good speede How *iudicare* came into the Creede. **1548** HALL (1809, 21) In greate haste and slowe spede. **1642** FULLER *H. & P. State* v. xviii (1841) 438 Anna . . . made more haste than good speed, marrying Andronicus some weeks after the death of Alexius.

More Irish than the Irish themselves.

1843 R. H. BARHAM in R. H. D. Barham's *Life* ii. 166 Hibernicis ipsis Hibernior. **1855** MACAULAY *Hist. Eng.* XII. iii. 204 His ancestors . . ., though originally English, were among those early colonists who were proverbially said to have become more Irish than Irishmen. **1860** RILEY *Dict. Lat. Quot.* (Bohn) 146 *Hibernicis ipsis Hibernior.*—'More Irish than the Irish themselves'. A specimen of modern dog Latin, quoted against those who are guilty of bulls or other absurdities. **1871** C. M. YONGE *Cameos from Eng. H.* 2nd Ser. xviii (1899) 189 In the . . . fourteenth century . . . the great feudal chiefs, descended usually from the Norman and English conquerors, . . . greatly contemning . . . 'the mere Irish', though other people pronounced them . . . '*Hibernis ipsis Hiberniores*' (more Irish than the Irish). **1929** *Times* 30 Jan. 10/3 The Norman-Irish de Burghs, often 'more Irish than the Irish themselves'.

More knave than fool.   (K 129)

c. **1589** [1633] MARLOWE *Jew of Malta* II. iii. 37. **1605** SHAKES. *K.L.* I. iv. 315 You, sir, more knave than fool, after your master. **1620** SHELTON *Quix.* II. xiii. ii. 269. **1624** T. BREWER *A Knot of Fools* More Knaue than foole. *c.* **1630** in *Roxburghe Ballads* (Hindley) I. 72 This man's more knaue than foole. **1738** SWIFT *Dial.* II. E.L. 315.

More know Tom Fool than Tom Fool knows.

1656 S. HOLLAND *Wit and Fancy in a Maze* 63 In all Comedies more know the Clown, then the Clown knows. **1723** DEFOE *Col. Jack* xvii. Wks. (Bohn) I. 506 It was no satisfaction to me that I knew not their faces, for they might know mine . . . , according to the old English proverb, 'that more knows Tom Fool, than Tom Fool knows'. **1896** J. C. HUTCHESON *Crown & Anchor* ch. 33 Some fellow . . . accosts me . . . as if I were an old friend . . . illustrating the truth of the adage, . . . 'More people know Tom Fool than Tom Fool knows'!

More like the devil than St. Laurence.
                                    (D 289)

a. **1522** DOUGLAS *Aeneid* I Prol. 143 Na mair like than the devill and Sanct Austyne. **1678** RAY 256.

More malice than matter.   (M 54)

1678 RAY 352. (*Som.*).

More nice than wise.   (N 158)

1581 B. RICH *Farewell to Militarie Prof.* Shakes. Soc. 139 I warrant you, thei can make it more nice then wise. **1670** RAY 187. **1682** BUNYAN *Greatness of Soul* Wks. (1855) I. 128 Calling those that cry out so hotly against it, men more nice than wise. **1721** KELLY 249 . . . Spoken when people out of bashfulness leave a thing unsaid, or a person unspoken to, which would have contributed to their interest.

More rain, more rest; more water will suit the ducks best.

1864 *N. & Q.* 3rd Ser. V. 208. *Cornish Provs.*

More royalist than the king.

1881 H. JAMES *Portrait of a Lady* ch. 12, 1883 ed. i. 122 You needn't be a better royalist than the king. **1904** 'H. S. MERRIMAN' *The Last Hope* ch. 35 The Duchess of Angoulême, . . . who had despised . . . Louis XVIII and Charles X, for the concessions they had made—who was more Royalist than the King.

More sauce than pig. (s 95)

1624 28 June *Ballad* entered in Stationers' Register Arb. iv. 119. **1659** N.R. 77, (than meat). **1738** SWIFT Dial. II. E.L. 302.

More than enough is too much. (M 1152)

1546 HEYWOOD II. vii. I4ᵛ Here is ynough and to muche. c. **1550** *Robin Conscience* (Hazlitt, *Early Pop. Poetry* iii. 229) You haue enough, if you haue not too much. **1550** HEYWOOD *Epigr.* no. lii More then enough were wast. **1573** SANFORD 105 Superfluitie, or that whiche is more than is inough, breaketh the couer. **1629** *Bk. Mer. Rid.* Prov. no. 107 (breaks the Couer). **1732** FULLER no. 3461.

More than he is worth does spend, Who | he makes a rope his life to end. (M 1165)

1611 COTGRAVE s.v. Corde. **1670** RAY 24.

More the merrier; The | the fewer the better cheer (fare). (M 1153)

[Temp. H. VII MS. Ashmole f. 56 extra verse to Lydgate's *Resoun of a Rammes Horne* And when þei (mynstrels) mete togedere, þer as festis es The more þe meryere- þerfor þei wyll not mourne.] **1530** PALSGRAVE 885a The mo the meryer; the fewer, the better fare. **1546** HEYWOOD II. vii. I3 The mo the merier, we all daie here and see. Ye, but the fewer the better fare (saied hee). **1614** JONSON *Barth. Fair* I. vi. 87 Ay, and Solomon too, Win, the more the merrier. **1629** T. ADAMS *Serm.* (1862) I. 244 The company is . . . all the patriarchs, prophets, saints. . . . Here, the more the merrier, yea, and the better cheer too. **1738** SWIFT Dial. II. E.L. 298. **1855** KINGSLEY *Westw. Ho!* ch. 24.

More there's in it, The | the more there's of it.

1738 SWIFT Dial. I. E.L. 274 There's some dirt in my teacup.—Come, come, the more there's in't, the more there's on't.

More thy years, The | the nearer (nigher) thy grave. (Y 23)

1611 GRUTER 185 (nigher). **1614** CAMDEN 313. **1639** CLARKE 308.

More words than one go to a bargain. *Cf.* **Two (words) to make bargain.** (W 819)

1580 MUNDAY *Zelauto* III. 119 There goeth more woordes to a bargayne then one, and other prayers to be vsed beside the Pater noster. **1590** LODGE *Rosalynde* (Greg) 92 There goes more words to a bargain than one. **1670** RAY 58. **1732** FULLER no. 3465.

More, There are more, *see also under significant words following.*

Morn come and the meat with it, Let the.

1721 KELLY 231 . . . Spoken to them who are solicitous for to-Morrow's Provision.

Morning dreams come true. (D 591)

[HORACE *Sat.* l. 10 *Post mediam noctem visus, cum somnia vera.* He appeared to me after midnight, when dreams are true.] **1540** PALSGRAVE *Acolastus* 66 After mydnyght men saye, that dreames be true. **1681** DRYDEN *Span. Friar* III. ii. Wks. (1701) II. 281 At break of Day, when Dreams, they say, are true. **1810** W. B. RHODES *Bombas. Fur.* This morn, . . . I dreamt (and morning dreams come true, they say). **1912** A. MACLAREN *Exposn., Romans* 87 Our highest anticipations and desires are not unsubstantial visions, but morning dreams, which are proverbially sure to be fulfilled.

Morning mountains, In the | in the evening fountains. (M 1173)

1609 HARWARD 104ᵛ. **1640** HERBERT no. 473. **1659** HOWELL *Fr. Prov.* 12 In the morning to the hills, in the evening to the rills, or fountains.

Morning sun, A | and a wine-bred child, and a Latin-bred woman, seldom end well. (s 977)

1599 MINSHEU *Span. Gram.* 84 Take heede Of a yoong wench a prophetesse, and a latin woman. **1611** COTGRAVE s.v. Soleil A glaring morne, a woman Latinist, and wine-fed child, make men crie had I wist. **1640** HERBERT no. 866.

Morning sun never lasts a day, The. (s 978)

1640 HERBERT no. 375. **1659** HOWELL *Span. Prov.* 22 Too early a Sun lasts not a whole day. **1706** STEVENS s.v. Sol. The Sun that rises very early in the morning lasts but little . . . Apply'd to those who are very early Risers, and are soon weary of Work, or do little. **1754** FRANKLIN Nov. For age and want save while you may; No morning sun lasts a whole day.

Morning sun, *see also* Save while you may, no m. s. lasts whole day.

Morning(s), see also Butter is gold in m.; Cloudy m. turn to clear; Evening praises the day, m. a frost; Evening red and m. grey; Foul m. fair day; Gaudy m. wet afternoon; Hour in m. worth two in evening; Law not same at m. and night; Old of the moon (In the), cloudy m. bodes; Pride of the m.; Rainbow in m.; Sleeps all the m., (He who) may go a begging all the day after; Sun rises in m. in every country; Work in the m. may trimly be done.

Morsel(s), see Children, (He that has) all his m. are not his own; Revenge is a m. for God; Taken by a m.

Mortal, see All men are m.; Grass and hay, we are all m.; Man is known m. by two things.

Mortar, No more | no more brick, a cunning knave has a cunning trick.

(M 1181)

1678 RAY 296.

Mortar, see also Apothecary's m. spoils music; Beat water in a m.; Fingers in m. (To have); Right mixture good m.

Mortimer, see Backare, quoth M.

Morton's[1] Fork (or Crutch).

[a. 1500] **1874** J. R. GREEN *Short Hist.* 296 'Mortons fork', extorted gifts to the exchequer from men who lived handsomely on the ground that their wealth was manifest, and from those who lived plainly on the plea, that economy had made them wealthy. **1894** *Dict. Nat. Biog.* XXXIX. 152 [Morton] has been traditionally known as the author of 'Morton's Fork' or 'Morton's Crutch', but . . . he and Richard Foxe . . . did their best to restrain Henry's[2] avarice. **1932** *Times* 11 Apr. 13/5 There is no alternative but to pay this 'benevolence' . . . Nothing is said as to any payment by the Commissioners [of Inland Revenue] by way of interest . . . Could 'Morton's fork' be more sharply pronged than this? [[1] Lord Chancellor, 1487. [2] Henry VII.]

Mort-stone, see Remove M.

Moses, see Stand M.

Moss, see Wood in a wilderness, m. in a mountain, are little thought of.

Mosse (*proper noun*), see Catch one napping, as M. did his mare.

Most take all.   (M 1186)

1599 *Warning for Fair Women* II. 686 You have no Counters.—Yes, but I have as many as you.— Ile drop with you; and he that has most, take all. *a.* **1633** HERBERT 'The Quidditie' *Wks.* 70. **1678** RAY 347.

Most things have two handles.   (T 193)

[EPICTETUS *Ench.* 63 Πᾶν πρᾶγμα δύο ἔχει λαβάς.] **1650** TAYLOR *Holy Living* II. § 6 There is nothing but hath a double handle, or at least we have two hands to apprehend it. *a.* **1657** J. HACKET *Scrinia Reserata* (1693, 79) The Stoicks said well, that from all Words and Actions, there were two Handles to be catch'd hold of, a Good and a Bad. **1661** J. FELL *Life of Dr. Hammond* 176 Every thing has two handles; if the one prove hot, and not to be touch'd, we may take the other that's more temperate. **1732** FULLER no. 3472 . . . and a wise man takes hold of the best. *a.* **1734** R. NORTH *Lives* (Bohn) i. 361 The public . . . seldom or never takes such matters by the right handles. **1791–1823** I. DISRAELI *Curios. Lit.* (Chandos) III. 334 But everything hath two handles, saith the ancient adage. **1881** CANON AINGER *Chas. Lamb* 176 Lamb . . . loved paradox. . . . As Hartley Coleridge adds, it was his way always to take hold of things 'by the better handle'.

Mote in another's eye but cannot see a beam in your own, You can see a.

(M 1191)

[MATT. vii. 3; LUKE vi. 41.] *c.* **1387** CHAUCER *Reeve's T.* prol. l. 3920. He can wel in myn yë seen a stalke, But in his owene he kan nat seen a balke. **1481** CAXTON *Reynard* ed. Arb. 74 Ther be many that see a strawe in an others eye that can not see a balke in his owne. **1551** CRANMER *Ans. to Gardiner* 201 You can spye a litle moote in a nother mans eye, that cannot see a great blocke in your owne. **1594–5** SHAKES. *L.L.L.* IV. iii. 157 You found his mote; the King your mote did see; But I a beam do find in each of three. **1672** WALKER 21, no. 8 (spie a mote).

Mote may choke a man, A.   (M 1190)

1534 LUPSET *Treat. Dying Well* ed. Gee 269 Euery mote choketh a worldly man. **1639** CLARKE 164. **1670** RAY 122.

Motes in the sun, As many as there are.

(M 1192)

c. **1375** *Sc. Leg. Saints* xxviii. 494 ed. Horstmann, 1882, Sa fele feyndis out caue pas þat þai fulfillit sa þe are As motis ar in sowne-beme fare. *a.* **1500** Cited in G. R. OWST *Literature and Pulpit in Med. Eng.* 1933, 112 As thyke as motis in the sonne. **1594** NASHE *Terrors of Night* i. 349 As thick as moates in the sunne. **1594** GARNIER *Cornelia* tr. Kyd v. 170 The shyuered Launces . . . Fly forth as thicke as moates about the Sunne. **1620** SHELTON *Quix.* II. xliii. iii. 116. **1653** WALTON *Complete Angler* E.L. X. 188 As thick as motes are said to be in the Sun.

Mote, see also Self-love is m. in every man's eye.

Moth, see Best cloth may have m. in it.

Mother Bunch.

1592 NASHE *Pierce Penniless* i. 173 Mother Bunches slimie ale. **1602** DEKKER *Satiro-Mastix* III. i. 162 Mother Bunch how dost thou? **1604** *Pasquil's Jests To the Reader* The . . . most delightful hostesse in England, she was squared into inches, being in height twenty thousand and a halfe . . . in bredth eleven thousand and two inches and a nayles bredth just. **1861** G. J. WHYTE-MELVILLE *Market Harb.* ch. 8 I have seen mammas whom the fairest of Eve's daughters might be proud to resemble; but it is sometimes hard upon the young Phœbe to have perpetually at her side the shapeless Mother Bunch, into the facsimile of which she must eventually grow.

Mother Car(e)y's chicken(s).

[A name given by sailors to the Stormy Petrel; also (in *pl.*) applied to falling snow.] **1767** CARTERET in HAWKSWORTH *Voy.* (1773) I. 318 The peterels, to which sailors have given the name of Mother Carey's chickens. **1836** MARRYAT *Midsh. Easy* ch. 26 'You ought to be thrown overboard', said Gascoigne; 'all this comes from your croaking—you're a Mother Carey's chicken'. **1864** *Athenaeum* 558/2 'Mother Carey's Chickens'.

Mother, Like | like daughter (child).
(M 1199)

[EZEK. xvi. 44: this proverb . . . As is the mother, so is her daughter.] **1509** BARCLAY *Ship of Fools* i. 236 An olde prouerbe hath longe agone be sayde That oft . . . the mayde Or doughter, vnto the mother wyll agre. **1835** MARRYAT *Jacob Faith.* ch. 23 But like mother like child, they say.

Mother of mischief is no bigger (more) than a midge's wing, The. (M 1200)

a. **1628** CARMICHAELL no. 1468. **1641** FERGUSSON no. 840 The mother of mischief is na mair nor a midge wing. **1721** KELLY 310 . . . Spoken when a great Quarrel has risen from a small Occasion. **1796** EDGEWORTH *Par. Asst.*, ' Barring Out ' (1903) 307 (an old proverb). **1858** MRS. CRAIK *A Woman's Thoughts* 177.

Mother says, It is not as thy | but as thy neighbours say. (M 1197)

1678 RAY *Adag. Hebr.* 398 . . . The meaning is that we are not to regard the praises of a near relation, but to listen to what is said by the neighbourhood.

Mother trot, If the | how can the daughter amble?

1614 RICHE *Honesty of this Age* Percy Soc. 32 The old prouerbe is: If the mother trot, how should the daughter amble. **1639** CLARKE 224 Father trot mother trot, how can the daughter amble?

Mother wit, *see* Ounce of discretion (m. w.) worth pound of wit (clergy).

Mother's breath is aye sweet, The.

1721 KELLY 332 . . . Spoken of the tender Affection of Mothers.

Mother's (Woman's) side is the surest, The. (M 1205)

1548 HALL *Chron.* (1809) 101 Was not my great grandmother . . . of the noble house of Valoys? . . . if the old and trite prouerb be true that the woman's side is the surer side and that the child followeth the womb, . . . the surer part is French. **1590** SHAKES. *T.And.* IV. ii. 126 Nay, he is your brother by the surer side, Although my seal be

stamped in his face. **1607** MIDDLETON *Mich. T.* I. i. Wks. (1885) I. 222 Yet the mother's side Being surer than the father's, it may prove, Men plead for money best, women for love.

Mother's smock, *see* Lapped in his m. s.

Mother's son, Every. (M 1202)

c. **1300** *King Alisaunder* (Weber) l. 2098 For mekely ilka modir soun. **1485** MALORY *Morte d'Arthur* II. x And there were slain many mothers' sons. **1545** ASCHAM *Toxoph.* Arb. 69 The Romaynes . . . slewe them euery mother son. **1595** SHAKES. *M.N.D.* I. ii. 69 That would hang us, every mother's son. *Ibid.* III. i. 64 Come, sit down, every mother's son. [**1603**] **1607** T. HEYWOOD *Woman Killed with Kindness* I. i. 82 (child). **1675** C. COTTON *Burlesque upon Burlesque: Or, The Scoffer Scoff't* (Wks. 1715 220) Ev'ry Mothers Daughter. **1837** MARRYAT *Snarl.* ch. 9 I'd have flogg'd each mother's son.

Mother, *see also* Anglesea m. of Wales; Ask the m. if child like father; Child may have too much m.'s blessing; Daughter win, must with m. begin; Fortune is m. to one; Four good m. have four bad daughters . . . ; Frugality is the m. of liberality; Good m. says not, Will you? but gives; Ignorance m. of devotions; Ignorance m. of impudence; Light-heeled m.; Man before his m.; Mark after her m. (She has a); Misery may be m.; Necessity m. of invention; Night is m. of counsel; Pitiful m. . . . . scald head; Poverty is m. of arts; Poverty is m. of health; Snow for a se'nnight is m. to earth; Trade is m. of money; Trust is m. of deceit.

Mothering Sunday, On | above all other, every child should dine with its mother.

1854 A. E. BAKER *Northamptonshire Glos.* 33. **1875** DYER *Brit. Pop. Cust.* (1900) 116 In the *Gent. Mag.* (vol. liv, p. 98) a correspondent tells us that whilst he was an apprentice the custom was to visit his mother on Mid-Lent Sunday (thence called Mothering Sunday) for a regale of excellent furmety.

Mother-in-law and daughter-in-law are a tempest and hail storm.

1707 MAPLETOFT 30.

Mother-in-law remembers not that she was a daughter-in-law, The. (M 1208)

1584 WITHALS L6 This will not acknowledge a mother in lawe, that she her selfe hath bene a daughter in law. **1659** HOWELL *Brit. Prov.* 36 The mother in law doth not remember that she hath been a daughter in law by her Lease. **1732** FULLER no. 4675.

Mother-in-law, *see also* Well married who has neither m.

Mothers' darlings make but milksop heroes.

1732 FULLER no. 3474.

Motions are not marriages.   (M 1210)

1579 A. HALL *Quarrel betw. Hall and Mallorie* in *Misc. Antiq. Angl.* 40 Motions be no lawes. **1678** RAY 56.

Mould, *see* Enough one day (He will have) when mouth full of m.

Moult, *see* Cock m. before hen.

Moulter, *see* Miller got never better m. than he took with own hands.

Mountain and a river are good neighbours, A.   (M 1214)
1640 HERBERT no. 274.

Mountain (out) of a molehill, To make a.   (M 1216)

1548–9 N. UDALL *Paraphr. of Erasmus* 2nd ded. to Q. Katherine A6 The Sophistes of Grece coulde through their copiousnes make an Elephant of a flye, and a mountaine of a molle-hill. *c.* **1557** ROPER *Life of More* (Hitchcock) 63 Thus was the great mountayne turned scant to a litle mole hill. **1570** FOXE *A. & M.* (ed. 2) II. 1361/1 Too much amplifying thinges yᵗ be but small, makyng mountaines of Molehills. **1633** P. FLETCHER *Purple Is.* vii. 65 (1908) II. 101 And molehill faults to mountains multiply. **1778** T. HUTCHINSON *Diary* 5 May I told him his nerves were affected: every mole-hill was a mountain. **1861** DEAN STANLEY *Hist. East. Ch.* Introd. iii The higher and wider is the sweep of vision, the more difficult it is to stumble at trifles, and make mountains out of mole-hills.

Mountain will not come to Mahomet, If the | Mahomet must go to the mountain.
                                         (M 1213)
c. **1594** BACON no. 925 Se no va el otero a Mahoma vaya Mahoma al otero. **1625** BACON *Ess., Boldness* Arb. 519 *Mahomet* cald the Hill to come to him, . . . And when the Hill stood still, he was neuer a whit abashed, but said; *If the Hill will not come to Mahomet, Mahomet wil go to the hil.* **1732** FULLER no. 2707. **1757** GOLDSMITH *Lett. to D. Hodson*, 27 Dec. As the mountain will not come to Mahomet, why Mahomet shall go to the mountain; . . . as you cannot . . . pay me a visit, . . . next summer . . . I shall spend three [weeks] among my friends in Ireland. **1849** LYTTON *Caxtons* VI. iv Neither Kitty nor I can change our habits, even for friendship. . . . Mountains cannot stir, . . . but Mahomet can come to the mountain as often as he likes.

Mountaineers are always freemen.
1803 WORDSWORTH *To Highland Girl* Thou wear'st upon thy forehead clear The freedom of a mountaineer. **1921** M. HEWLETT *Wiltshire Ess.* 41 That last . . . sentiment has disappeared in Kentucky. As my correspondent says, 'Montani semper liberi', Class-distinctions are not effective in the art of the freeborn.

Mountains have brought forth a mouse, The.   (M 1215)
[HORACE *De Arte Poet.* 139 *Parturiunt montes, nascetur ridiculus mus.* The mountains are in

labour, a ridiculous mouse will be born. (An allusion to Æsop's fable of the Mountain in Labour.)] *c.* **1390** GOWER *Conf. Amantis* VII. 3553–75 For so it fell that ilke day, This hell [hill] on his childinge lay, . . . The nerr this hell was upon chance To taken his deliverance, The more unbuxumliche he cride; . . . And ate laste it was a Mous, The which was bore. **1533** SIR T. MORE *Debellation* 1557 ed. 930b When these gret hilles had thus trauailed longe . . . the good houre came on as god would, that one was brought a bedde, with sore labour at last deliuered of a dead mouse. **1549** LATIMER *1st Serm. bef. Edw. VI* P.S. 92 For all their boasts, little or nothing was done; in whom these words of Horace may well be verified, . . . 'The mountains swell up, the poor mouse is brought out.' **1589** NASHE *Pref. to Greene's 'Menaphon'* iii. 312 Let other men . . . praise the Mountaine that in seauen yeares bringeth forth a Mouse . . . ; but giue me the man whose extemporall veine . . . will excell our greatest Art-maisters deliberate thoughts. **1885** D. C. MURRAY *Rainbow G.* III. i After the mountain has been in labour, the kindliest commendations the mouse can deserve can hardly be satisfactory to the mountain.

Mountain(s), *see also* Behind the m. there are people; Friends may meet, but m. . . .; Haste in his business (Who has no), m. to him seem valleys; Higher the m. greater the descent; Morning m. (In the); Promises m. performs molehills.

Mountsorrel, *see* Belle giant or devil of M.

Mouse a hole, I gave the | and she is become my heir.   (M 1230)
1640 HERBERT no. 94.

Mouse [do] against the cat, What may the.
c. **1390** GOWER *Conf. Amantis* III. 1643 What mai the Mous ayein the Cat?

Mouse in a cheese, To speak like a.
                                         (M 1238)
[**1598**] **1616** HAUGHTON *Eng. for My Money* D4 Nay, but your Monsieur's but a Mouse in cheese Compared with my Signor, hee can tell of Lady Venus, and her Sonne blind Cupid. **1599** PORTER *Angry Wom. Abing.* l. 1587 Hush then, mum, mouse in cheese, cat is neare. **1602** WITHALS 144 Rauus . . . signifieth also dull, or blunt, or soft, as Raua vox, that soundeth like a mouse in a cheese. **1608** *Christmas Prince* Mal. Soc. 149 Hee will neuer speake lowder then a mouse in a cheese. **1659** HOWELL *Eng. Prov.* 4a. **1670** RAY 186. **1686** EDMUND VERNEY to his son Edmund, *Verney Memoirs* (1899) IV. 381 I pray when you speak in the [Sheldonian] Theatre doe not speak like a mouse in a chees for that will be a great shame instead of an honour, but speak out your words boldly and distinctly. **1812** E. NARES *I'll Consider of It* ii. 162 She was as silent . . . as a mouse in a cheese.

Mouse in a mill, As safe as a. *Cf.* Safe as a thief in a mill.   (M 1223)
1584 R. WILSON *Three Ladies of London* Hazl.-Dods. vi. 392 Nor I need sell no ballads, but

live like a mouse in a mill, and have another grind my meal for me. **1600** *Weakest to Wall* B4. [1625] **1639** R. DAVENPORT *New Trick* III. i (as Mouse in Mill).

Mouse in pitch, A. (M 1234)

[HERODAS 2. 63 μῦς ἐν πίσσῃ. ERASM. *Mus picem gustans*.] *c*. **1522** ERASMUS in FROUDE *Counc. of Trent* (1892–3) iii 'Alas! that I in my old age should have fallen into such a mess, like a mouse into a pot of pitch.' **1603** MONTAIGNE (Florio) III. xiii. 221 She doth but quest and firret, . . . turning, winding, building, and entangling herselfe in hir owne worke . . . Mus in pice. A Mouse in pitch.

Mouse in time may bite in two a cable, A. (M 1235)

1546 HEYWOOD II. vii. I4ᵛ Littell losse by length maie growe importable. A mouse in tyme, maie byte a two, a Cable. **1605–6** SHAKES. *K.L.* II. ii. 68 Rogues . . . Like rats, oft bite the holy cords a-twain Which are too intrinse t' unloose. **1758** FRANKLIN in ARBER *Eng. Garner* v. 580 Stick to it steadily! and you will see great effects, for . . . *By diligence and patience, the mouse ate in two the cable.*

Mouse that has but one hole is quickly taken, The. (M 1236)

[ERASM. *Mus non uni fidit* quotes PLAUTUS: 'mus . . . Aetatem qui uni cubili nunquam committit suam'. *Epp. Obsc. Vir.* i. 3 *Mus miser est antro qui tantum clauditur uno.*] *c*. **1386** CHAUCER *W. of Bath's Prol.* ll. 572–4 I holde a mouses herte nat worth a leek, That hath but oon hole for to sterte to; And if that faille, thanne is al y-do. **1584** WITHALS C3 The mouse is in an ill case that hath but one hole to lurke in. **1592** DELAMOTHE 27. *a.* **1628** CARMICHAELL no. 1343 Sche is a sarie mowse has bot ane hole. **1651** HERBERT no. 1135. **1659** TORRIANO no. 22 That is a sad mouse that hath but one hole to make her escape at. **1866** BLACKMORE *Craddock N.* ch. 17 Biddy . . . took to her brogue as a tower of refuge. Bilingual races are up to the tactics of rats with a double hole. **1897** 'H. S. MERRIMAN' *In Kedar's T.* ch. 17 The house seemed to have two staircases of stone and two doors. There is a Spanish proverb which says that the rat which has only one hole is soon caught. Perhaps the architect . . . had built his house to suit his tenants.

Mouse (Mice), *see also* Better a louse (m.) in the pot; Blate cat, proud m.; Bold m. that breeds in cat's ear; Burn one's house to get rid of m.; Cat in gloves catches no m.; Cat sees not the m. ever; Cat's away m. will play; Cat wink (Let the) and m. run; Cat winks (When) little wots m. what cat thinks; Dead m. feels no cold; Drowned m. (Like a); Drunk as a m.; Dun's the m.; Enemy seem a m. (Though); Escaped m. feels taste of bait; Hungry as a church m.; Larder but has m. (No); Lion may come to be beholden to m.; Lion when he is absent, (Who takes a) fears a m. present; Man or m.; Merry as m. in malt; Mind's chasing m. (Your); Mountains have brought forth m.; One for m.; Peace and catch a m.; Plough stand to catch a m.

(Let); Poor as a church m.; Pour not water on drowned m.; Safe as a m. in a cheese; Scatter her m. (To); Today a man, tomorrow a m.; Weel kens the m. when cat's out of house.

Mouse-hunt, *see* Cat after kind.

Mouse-trap smell of blood (cheese), Let not the. (M 1245)

1659 HOWELL *Eng. Prov.* 11a (cheese). **1732** FULLER no. 3189. **1802** J. WOLCOT (P. Pindar) *Middl. Elect.* ch. 1 He made poor work o' Cold-bath howze. The trap that wishth to catch a mowze, Shud never smell of *blood*.

Mouth, One | does nothing without another. (M 1257)

1640 HERBERT no. 1028 (month). **1659** N. R. 83.

Mouth has beguiled your hands, Your. (M 1268)

1678 RAY 260. **1732** FULLER no. 6057.

Mouth of his own, He that has a | must not say to another, blow. (M 1251)

1640 HERBERT no. 353. **1732** FULLER no. 2130.

Mouth runs over, His. (M 1252)

[1587] **1594** GREENE *Alphonsus* II. i. 524 Stay there, sir King, your mouth runnes ouer much. **1616** DRAXE no. 363. **1639** CLARKE 133.

Mouth, Whoso has but a | shall ne'er in England suffer drouth. (M 1266)

1670 RAY 85 . . . For if he doth but open it, its a chance but it will rain in. . . . We seldome suffer for want of rain.

Mouth(s), *see also* All is lost that goes beside one's own m.; Bees that have honey in m.; Bitter in m.; Butcher looked for folk . . . in his m.; Close m. catches no flies; Cool m. and warm feet; Crab in a cow's m.; Dark as a wolf's m.; Devil's m. is miser's purse; Duck in the m. (Come home with); Enemy's m. seldom speaks well; Enough one day (He will have) when m. full of mould; Evil that comes out of thy m.; Fair words hurt not m.; Fill the m. with empty spoon; Finger in m.; God never sends m. but sends meat; Good in the maw that is sweet in the m.; Hand in lion's m.; Heart is a fire, sparks out of m.; Heart is full of lust (When) m.'s full of leasings; Heart is in m.; Honey in the m.; Honey is not for ass's m.; Keep your m. shut; Larks will fall into m.; Lie in bed till meat falls in m.; Lion's m.; Look in your m. to know your age; Make one's m. water; Make up one's m.; Man's praise in his own m. stinks; Meat in his m. (He brings); Meat pleases not all m. (All); Muzzle not the oxen's m.; Nearest the heart, nearest the m.; Nurses put one bit in child's m., two in own; Open one's m. wide; Open your m. but you put foot in it; Pepper is hot in m. but cold in snow; Ready m. for

cherry; Speak as if you would creep into my m.;
Speak (You never) but your m. opens; Spit in
your m. (Let me); Stop every man's m. (He
who will); Stop one's m.; Stop two m. with one
morsel; Sweet in the m., bitter in the maw;
Tale (word) out of one's m. (To take the); Wise
hand does not all foolish m. speaks; Wise head
makes close m.; Wise men have their m. in their
heart; Word is in your m. (While); Wry m.
(Make a).

Mouthful of moonshine, To give one a.

1785 GROSE *Dict. Vulg. T.* s.v. A matter or
mouthful of moonshine, a trifle, nothing.

Mower(s), *see* Meat for m. (No).

Mows[1] may come to earnest.

1721 KELLY 254 . . . What you speak in Jest, may
come to be done in Reality. [[1] jesting.]

Mow(s), *(verb)*, *see* Mastery m. the meadows;
Oats will m. themselves; Sow thin and m. thin.

Moyen[1] does mickle, but money does more.

1721 KELLY 243. [[1] interest.]

Much ado about nothing.   (A 38)

1529 HYRDE *Instr. Chr. Wom.* v. 58 They make
great ado about many small matters. **1553**
T. WILSON *Rhet.* (1585 ed. Mair), 191 (about a
little matter). **1598–9** SHAKES. [Title]. **1599**
PORTER *Angry Wom. Abingd.* l. 1313 Heres
a doe about a thing of nothing. **1602** T. A.
Massacre of Money E2 Heer's much adoe about a
thing of noughts. **1607** GRESHAM *Almanac* May
Much adoe about nothing. **1624** T. BREWER *A
Knot of Fools* B1ᵛ Much adoe about nothing.
1828 T. H. LISTER *H. Lacy* i, ch. 16 It [Reading]
saves women from tittle-tattle, and much ado
about nothing.

Much ado to bring beggars to stocks; and when they come there, they'll not put in their legs.   (A 39)

1616 DRAXE no. 140 Much a doe to bring Beggars to the stockes. **1670** RAY 60.

Much bran and little meal.   (B 604)

1616 DRAXE no. 182. **1670** RAY 65. **1732**
FULLER no. 3477 (little flour).

Much bruit, little fruit.   (B 690)

1612 BACON *Essays* 261 But according to the
French proverb, Beaucoup de bruit, peu de
fruit; . . . *c.* **1621** DEKKER, FORD, *et al. Witch of
Edmonton* II. ii (Pearson IV. 358) Much noise to
little purpose. **1639** CLARKE 134. **1639** FULLER
Holy War II. xxix (1840) 87 The French proverb
was verified by this voyage, 'Much bruit and
little fruit'. They not only did no good in the
Holy Land . . . but also did much harm.

Much coin, much care.   (C 506)

[HORACE *Odes* 3. 16 *Crescentem sequitur cura
pecuniam.* Care follows increasing wealth.]
c. **1526** *Dicta Sap.* A2 The richer one is, the
more thoughtfull be lyueth. **1578** FLORIO *First
F.* 32 The plenty of things dooth ingender care.
1597 [BODENHAM] *Wit's Commonw.* f. 153ᵛ.
1639 CLARKE 292. **1691** SEWEL 107.

Much law, but little justice.

1732 FULLER no. 3482.

Much learning makes men mad.   (L 161)

[ACTS xxvi. 24.] **1591** ARIOSTO *Orl. Fur.*
Harington XXIII. 85 And yet we see much
knowledge makes men mad. **1680** R. L'ESTRANGE
Twenty Select Colloq. no. 16, 212 But much
learning makes a man mad.

Much matter of a wooden platter.   (M 754)

1616 WITHALS 565 Much matter of a treene
platter. **1639** CLARKE 133. **1670** RAY 185 . . .
Δεινὰ περὶ φακῆς. [Terrible talk about a lentil.]
Mira de lente, A great stir about a thing of
nothing.

Much meat, much malady (many maladies). *Cf.* Many dishes make many diseases.   (M 829)

1597 *Politeuphuia* 250 It is an old prouerbe,
much meate, much maladie. **1603** H. CROSSE
Virtue's Commonwealth Gros. 146 As the
prouerbe saith, much meate much maladie.
1619 *Keepe within Compasse* C7ᵛ. **1629** T.
ADAMS *Serm.* (1861–2) II. 28 *Multa fercula,
multos morbos*,—Many dishes, many diseases.
1647 TRAPP *Marrow Gd. Authors in Comm. Ep.*
614 Q. Elizabeth . . . knew, that much meat,
much malady. **1670** RAY 120 . . . Our nation
. . . hath been noted for excess in eating, and it
was almost grown a Proverb, That *English* men
dig their graves with their teeth.

Much money makes a country poor, for it sets a dearer price on every thing.   (M 1087)

1651 HERBERT no. 1178.

Much of a muchness.

1727 VANBRUGH & CIBBER *Prov. Husb.* I. i.
I hope at least, you and your good woman agree
still.—Ay, ay! much of a muchness. **1837** T.
HOOK *Jack Brag* ii. I never had two horses that
suited me better. I have . . . nine—much of a
muchness. **1912** SIR EVELYN WOOD *Midsh. to F.
Marshal* ch. 34 The Commander-in-Chief . . .
said more than once, 'Men are much of a muchness; I find officers very much on a par'.

Much science (learning), much sorrow.   (S 141)

1607–40 *Politeuphuia* s.v. Proverbs Much
learning much sorrow. **1639** CLARKE 101.

Much smoke (fire), little fire (smoke). (s 568)

1575 BURGHLEY to Walsingham cited C. Read *Ld. Burghley & Q. Elizabeth* 147 There was great and long talk . . . but I fear there will be more smoke arise than fire. **1580** LYLY *Euph. & his Eng.* ii. 65 Where the least smoake is, there to be the greatest fire. **1592** DELAMOTHE 41 A small fire makes often a great smoke. *a.* **1640** SMYTH 32 no. 84 . . . much adoe about nothinge.

Much would (shall) have more. (M 1287)

c. **1350** *Douce MS.* 52 no. 65 Mykulle wulle more. **1509** BARCLAY *Ship of Fools* i. 101 Though he haue all yet wolde he haue more. **1594** SHAKES. *Luc.* l. 98 Cloy'd with much, he pineth still for more. **1613–22** DRAYTON *Polyolb.* xv. 293 (1876) II. 191 Then *Loddon* next comes in, contributing her store; As still we see, 'The much runs ever to the more'. **1639** CLARKE 99 (shall). **1721** KELLY 245 *Mickle would ay have more.* . . . Spoken of the insatiable Desire that rich Men have after Wealth. **1900** J. MCCARTHY *Hist. Own. T.* v. 94 Expedition after expedition has been sent out to extend the Egyptian frontier. . . . 'Much will have more'; but in this case . . . much is compelled, for the sake of . . . security, to try to have more.

Much, *see also* Make m. of; Rich that possesses m., (He is not); Speak m. who cannot speak well.

Much, *see also under significant words following.*

Muck, Not worth his. (M 1299)

1639 CLARKE 70.

Muck and money go together. (M 1297)

1678 RAY 179 . . . Those that are slovenly and dirty usually grow rich, not they that are nice and curious in their diet, houses, and clothes.

Muck of the world. (M 1298)

c. **1390** GOWER *Conf. Amantis* v. 4854 Bot forto pinche and forto spare, Of worldes muk to gete encress. **1530** PALSGRAVE 582b It is a great folye for a man to hazarde his lyfe for the mucke of this worlde. **1546** HEYWOOD I. xi. E3ᵛ To disdeigne me, who much of the world hordth not. As he dooth. **1606** T. HEYWOOD 2 *If you Know not Me* l. 2446 Though I haue not the mucke of the world I haue a great deale of good Loue. **1608** SHAKES. *C.* II. ii. 123 He . . . look'd upon things precious as they were The common muck o' the world.

Muck there is luck, Where there is.

a. **1628** CARMICHAELL no. 1173 Muk is luk, dame dryte there ben. *c.* **1641** FERGUSSON MS. no. 1062 Muck bods luck dame dryt ye ther ben.

Muck, *see also* Gold is but m.; Have his m. for his meat; Riches are like m. . . . spread abroad.

Muck-hill at his door, He has a good. (M 1301)

1678 RAY 261 . . . i.e. he is rich.

Muck-hill on my trencher, You make a | quoth the bride. (M 1302)

1678 RAY 77 . . . You carve me a great heap. **1732** FULLER no. 5936.

Muck-hill(s), *see also* Old m. will bloom.

Muckson up to the buckson.

1674 RAY *Coll. of Eng. Words* 72 . . . *Devon* Dirty up to the Knucles. **1889** *Folk-Lore Journal* vii. 293 Darby.

Mud chokes no eels.

1732 FULLER no. 3488.

Mud, *see also* Breed in the m. are not efts (All that); Keep a man out of the m. (Way to) is black his boots.

Mugwort, *see* Drink nettles in March, eat m. in May.

Mulatto, *see* God made the white man . . . the devil made m.

Mulberry-tree, *see* Time and art (With) leaf of m. becomes satin.

Mule, As obstinate as a.

1820 31 Mar. BYRON *Letters* iv. 428. **1956** A. L. ROWSE *Early Churchills* 209.

Mule (ass, horse), One | scrubs another. (M 1306)

[ERASM. *Ad. Mutuum muli scabunt.*] **1540** PALSGRAVE *Acolastus* 129 Mules scratche of eche other scabbes or scurffes. **1545** TAVERNER Iᵛ One moile claweth another. **1549** ERASM. tr. Chaloner *Pr. of Folly* 13. **1580** J. CONY-BEARE 25 Mules do gnap or rubbe one another. **1584** COGAN *Haven of Health* (1636) 6 Why (quoth the Emperor[1]) one of you might claw and rub anothers back well enough. So wisely did he delude the practise of parasites, according to the old proverb, Muli mutuum scabunt. **1614** OVERBURY *Characters. An Ostler* Hee puffes and blowes ouer your horse, . . . and leaues much of the dressing to the prouerbe of *Muli mutuo scabunt*, one horse rubs another. **1616** CORYAT *Traueller for Eng. Wits* 37 In Latine, *Mulus mulum scabit*, one Mule scratcheth another; by which the Ancients signified, that courtesies done vnto friends, ought to be requited with reciprocall offices of friendship. **1635** RANDOLPH *Muses Looking-Gl.* III. iv I need not flatter these, they'le do't themselves, And crosse the Proverb that was wont to say One Mule doth scrub another. **1738** SWIFT *Dial.* III. E.L. 318 She and Tom Gosling were banging compliments backward and forward: it looked like two asses scrubbing one another. [1 Augustus.]

Mule, *see also* Wants a m. without fault (He who).

Mulligrubs, *see* Sick of the m.

Mullingar heifer, *see* Beef to the heels.

Multitude, *see* Charity covers a m. of sins.

Mum is counsel (the word). *Cf.* No word but mum.   (M 1310. W 767)

c. 1374 CHAUCER *Troilus* Bk. 3, l. 294 These wyse clerkes that ben dede Han ever yet pro-verbed to us yonge, That 'firste vertu is to kepe tonge'. 1540 PALSGRAVE *Acolastus* Prol. 16 I dare not do so moche as put my hande to my mouthe, and saye mum, is counseyle. 1546 HEYWOOD II. v. G4ᵛ I will saie nought but mum, and mum is counsell. 1687 MONTAGUE & PRIOR *Hind & P. Transv.* 7 It has cost mc some pains to clear Her Title. Well but Mum for that, Mr. Smith. *a.* 1704 T. BROWN *Walks round Lond.*, *Coffee-Houses* Wks. (1709) III. III. 39 But Mum's the Word—for who wou'd speak their Mind among Tarrs and commissioners. 1837 T. HOOK *Jack Brag* ch. 12 All quiet and snug—mum's the word, and no mistake. 1894 BLACK-MORE *Perlycross* ch. 21 Mum's the word.

Mum, *see also* No word but m.

Mumbo Jumbo.

1738 F. MOORE *Trav. Afr.* 40 A dreadful Bugbear to the Women, call'd Mumbo-Jumbo, which is what keeps the Women in awe. 1837 HOOD *Ode to Rae Wilson* xxiv You might have been High Priest to Mumbo-Jumbo. 1876 GEO. ELIOT *Dan. Der.* ch. 28 The name of Mompert had become a sort of Mumbo-Jumbo. 1907 A. C. BENSON *Upton Lett.* 259 Erudition . . . a hideous idol, a Mumbo-Jumbo, a Moloch in whose honour children have still to pass through the fire in . . . dark academic groves.

Mumbudget, To play.   (M 1311)

1559 T. BECON *Displ. Popish Mass Prayers* P.S. 276 Now ye play mum-budget and silence-glum. 1562 J. WIGAND *De Neutralibus* I3ᵛ God . . . doth earnestly reprehend them that play mumme budget or denye them, as he saieth in the thirde Commaundement. 1600 1 SHAKES. *M.W.W.* V. v. 186 I went to her in white, and cried 'mum', and she cried 'budget', as Anne and I had appointed. 1611 COTGRAVE s.v. *Court* To play at Mum-budget, or be at a Nonplus.

Mumchance (Mumphazard) that was hanged for saying nothing, He looks like.   (M 1312)

1550 (1560 ed., S4) J. BALE *Acts of Eng. Votaries* He played momme chance, and woulde make none aunsweare. 1579 GOSSON *Ephemerides* 7 Ready as a man desperate . . . to forsweare my country, to sette the hares heade to the goose gyblettes, and al that I haue at a mumme chaunce. 1670 RAY 209 (Mumphazard) *Chesh.* 1699 B. E. *Dict. Cant. Crew* 'Mumchance', One that sits mute. He looks like Mumchance that was Hang'd for saying of nothing. 1738 SWIFT *Dial. I. E.L.* 267 Methinks you look like Mum-chance, that was hanged for saying nothing.

Mumford, *see* Mock not, quoth M.

Mumphazard, *see* Mumchance.

Mumpsimus, see Change his old *M.*

Murder is out, The.

[Said when something is suddenly revealed or explained.] 1706 FARQUHAR *Recruit. Off.* III. i Now the murder's out. 1831 MACAULAY *Let.* 29 June Barnes . . . pretended that all the best strokes were his. I believed that he was lying. . . . And now the murder is out. 1837 DICKENS *Pickwick* ch. 43 fin. Now the murder's out, and, damme, there's an end on't.

Murder will out (cannot be hid).   (M 1315)

c. 1300 *Cursor M.* 1084 (Gött) For-þi sais into þis tyde, Is no man þat murthir may hide. *c.* 1386 CHAUCER *Nun's Pr. T.* l. 4242 Mordre wol out that se we day by day. 1433 LYDG. *St. Edmund* II. 225 in Horstm. *Altengl. Leg.* (1881) 400 Moordre wil out, though it abide a while. 1592 KYD *Span. Trag.* (Boas) II. vi. 58 The heauens are iust, murder cannot be hid. [1592] 1597 SHAKES. *Rich. III* I. iv. 278 Well, I'll go hide the body in some hole, . . . And when I have my meed, I will away; For this will out. 1596 *Id. M.V.* II. ii. 73 Truth will come to light; murder cannot be hid long. 1600–1 *Id. H.* II. ii. 588 For murder, though it have no tongue, will speak With most miraculous organ. 1604 *Id. O.* V. i. 109 Nay, guiltiness will speak, Though tongues were out of use. 1664 COTTON *Scarron.* (1715 ed.) I. 26 Murther at some odd time will out.

Murder, *see also* Killing no m.

Murray, Earl of, *see* Dine with St. Giles and E. of M.

Muscles, *see* Bear picks m.

Muse as they use, Men.   (M 1318)

1583 MELBANCKE *Philotimus* G3ᵛ Use not, as you muse, and good inough. 1670 RAY 123.

Muse (*noun*), *see* Nought is that m. that finds no excuse.

Music helps not the toothache. (M 1320)

1640 HERBERT no. 532.

Music is the eye of the ear.   (M 1322)

1616 DRAXE no. 1448.

Music on a wheelbarrow, You may make as good.   (M 1323)

1678 RAY 276.

Music, *see also* Apothecary's mortar spoils luter's m.; Face the m.; Great strokes make not m.; Tinker and a piper make bad m. together; Voice is best m.; Women and m. should never be dated.

Musician has forgot his note, When a | he makes as though a crumb stuck in his throat.   (M 1325)

[Gk. Ἀπορία ψάλτου βήξ. The musician slurs his mistake with a cough.] 1616 WITHALS 558

(singer). **1639** CLARKE 108. **1670** RAY 123 . . .
When a singing-man or musician is out or at a
loss, to conceal it he coughes.

Musician, *see also* Sexton is a fatal m.

Musk, *see* Look not for m. in a kennel.

Musselbrogh[1] was a brogh when Edinbrogh was nane; and Musselbrogh 'ill be a brogh, when Edinbrogh is gane.

1842 R. CHAMBERS *Pop. Rhymes of Scot.* 14 This
is a pun or quibble. *Brogh* is a term for a
mussel bed, one of which exists at the mouth of
the Esk and gives name to the burgh. [[1] Musselburgh in Midlothian.]

Must be if we brew (sell ale), This. (B 653)

1678 RAY 87 . . . That is if we undertake mean
and sordid, or lucrative employments, we must
be content with some trouble, inconvenience,
affronts, disturbance, &c. **1721** KELLY 295
Sik things will be, if we sell drink. **1738** SWIFT
Dial. III. E.L. 322 Well, thus it must be, if we
sell ale.

Must (shall, will) be must (shall, will) be, What. (M 1331)

c. **1386** CHAUCER *Knight's T.* l. 1466 As whan a
thyng is shapen it shal be. **1519** W. HORMAN
Vulgaria (1926, 38) That the whiche muste be
wyll be. **1546** HEYWOOD II. i. F3 That shalbe,
shalbe. **1591** H. SMITH *Wedding Garment* A1ᵛ
That which must be, let be. *c.* **1592–3** MARLOWE
Faustus I. i. 75 What doctrine call you this, Che
sera, sera, What will be, shall be? *a.* **1593**
PEELE *Edw. I* sc. xii What will be shall be.
a. **1594** *Selimus* l. 115 What must be, cannot
chuse but be done. *c.* **1595** SHAKES. *R.J.* IV. i.
21 What must be shall be.—That's a certain
text. **1601** *Id. T.N.* I. v. 296 Fate, show thy
force! Ourselves we do not owe. What is
decreed must be—and be this so! **1659** HOWELL
It. Prov. 13 That which will be, will be. **1768**
J. WESLEY *Standard Lett.* v. 85 What must be,
must be. **1841** S. WARREN *Ten Thous. a Year*
ch. 1 It's really very inconvenient . . . for any of
my young men to be absent . . . but—I suppose—
what must be must be.

Must is for the king. (M 1330)

a. **1593** MARLOWE *Edw. II* IV. vi. 81 Your
majesty must go to Killingworth.—Must! 'tis
somewhat hard, when kings must go. **1599**
CHAPMAN *Hum. Day's M.* (1889) 26 Must she
sir; have you brought the king's warrant for it?
1603 DEKKER *et al. Grissil* IV. ii Must is for
Kings, And loe obedience for loe vnderlings.
1659 FULLER *Appeal Inf. Innoc.* (1840) 354 'Must
is for a king', and seeing the doctor and I are
both kings alike, I return, 'He *must not* be so
understood'. **1681** BUNYAN *Come and Welcome*
Wks. (1855) l. 257 'Must is for the king'.
If they shall come, they shall come. **1738**
SWIFT Introd. to *Dial.* E.L. 255 I have taken
care to enforce Loyalty by an invincible Argument, . . . Must is for the King.'

Mustard, *see* After meat m.; Cat loves m. (As a);
Kill a man for a mess of m.; Tewkesbury m.

Mustard-pot, *see* Moonshine in m.

Mute as a fish. (F 300)

c. **1450** BURGH (& LYDGATE) *Secrees* E.E.T.S.
st. 330. 73 Dowmbe as þe ffysh. **1580**
WHETSTONE *Hept. Civil Disc.* D1ᵛ. **1601**
JONSON *Poetaster* IV. iii. 133 What, mute?—Ay,
as fishes. **1616** BRETNOR *Almanac* Sept. As
mute as a herring. **1688** BUNYAN *Build. Ho.
God* ix. Wks. (1855) II. 586 Meek as a lamb,
mute as a fish. **1772** R. GRAVES *Spiritual Quix.*
ii. 8. **1841** DICKENS *B. Rudge* ch. 56 Mute as a
stock-fish.

Mute as a mackerel.

1760 FOOTE *Minor* I. Wks. (1799) I. 238 You
can be secret as well as serviceable? . . . Mute as
a mackrel. **1819** *Metropolis* III. 154 We were
as mute as mackarel for exactly seven minutes
and a half.

Mutton, He loves laced. (M 1338)

[An old word for a whore. JOHNSON *Dict.* 1755.]
1528 ROY & BARLOW *Rede me and be not wroth*
ed. Arber 39 [Wolsey] is not fedd so ofte with
rost befe As with rawe mutton. **1563** NEWBERY
Dives Pragmaticus st. 36 I haue . . . Mylke
Butter Eggs, and one principall dish : Called fine
laced mutton, or what you can wish. *c.* **1570**
July and Julian l. 297 A fine pice of laced mutton.
1578 WHETSTONE I *Promos and Cass.* I. iii. B3
He lou'd lase mutton well. **1594** SHAKES.
T.G.V. I. i. 93 I, a lost mutton, gave your letter
to her, a lac'd mutton; and she, a lac'd mutton,
gave me, a lost mutton, nothing. **1678** RAY 89
. . . A wencher.

Mutton is sweet, and gars folk die ere they be sick.

1721 KELLY 250 . . . That is, makes People steal
Sheep and so be hang'd.

Mutton of a sow, It is hard to make. (M 1340)

1626 BRETON *Soothing* B3ᵛ. **1639** CLARKE 147.

Mutton, *see also* Dead as m.; Loved m. well that
licked; Shoulder of m. and beer make Flemings
tarry; Shoulder of m. draws down another;—is
going (When), good to take slice;—for a sick horse;
Sow is good m. (Your). *See also* Sheep's flesh.

Muxy, He got out of the | and fell into the pucksy. (M 988)

1616 DRAXE no. 604 He is gotten out of the myre
and is fallen into the riuer. **1869** HAZLITT 158
. . . i.e. He got out of the dunghill and fell into
the slough.

Muzzle not the oxen's mouth. (O 113)

[DEUT. xxv. 4.] **1583** G. BABINGTON *Expos. of
the Commandmonies* 234 Testimonies manie are
there in number both in the old and new Testament, as Thou shalt not mussel the mouth of the
Oxe that treadeth out the corne. **1584** WITHALS
C6ᵛ (as 1583). **1641** FERGUSSON no. 636.

Myrtle among nettles, A | is a myrtle still. (M 1344)

1640 BRATHWAITE *Art Asleep Husb.* 166 A
mirtle will shew it selfe a mirtle amongst nettles.
1678 RAY *Adag. Hebr.* 397.

N

Nab[1] me, I'll nab thee.   (N 1)

1678 RAY 351.   **1678** BUTLER *Hudibras* III. ii.
1457 To nab the itches of their sects, as jades
do one another's necks. [[1] to bite gently.]

Nab, *see* Hab or n.

Naboth's vineyard.

[= the coveted possession of a neighbour.]
[I KINGS xxi. 2 Ahab spake unto Naboth,
saying, Give me thy vineyard, . . . because it is
near unto my house.]   **1679** [J. CARYLL] [*title*].
1709 SWIFT *The Garden Plot* Wks. (1856) I. 701
When Naboth's vineyard look'd so fine, The
king cried out, 'Would this were mine!'

Nag with a weamb[1] and a mare with nean,[2] A.   (N 3)

1670 RAY 44. [[1] belly. [2] none.]

Nag, *see also* Bleed your n. on St. Stephen's day;
Inch of a n. worth span of aver.

Nail, On the.   (N 18)

[= on the spot, at once; chiefly used of making
money payments.]   **1596** NASHE *Saffron W.* iii.
40 Tell me, haue you a minde to anie thing in
the Doctors Booke! speake the word, and I will
helpe you to it vpon the naile.   **1600** HOLLAND
Livy VI. xiv. 225 [He] paid the whole debt downe
right on the naile, unto the creditour.   **1720**
SWIFT *Run of Bankers* Wks. (1755) IV. i. 22 We
want our money on the nail.   **1804** EDGEWORTH
Pop. T., *Will* ch. 2 The bonnet's all I want, which
I'll pay for on the nail.

Nail into any one's coffin, To drive (put) a.

[= to do a thing that tends to shorten his life.]
1789 WOLCOT *Wks.* (1795) ii. 100 Care to our
coffin adds a nail, no doubt.   **1836** A. FON-
BLANQUE *Eng. under 7 Administr.* (1837) III. 321
A dram which . . . drives nails into the victim's
coffin, according to the expressive vulgar saying.
1885 LOWE *Prince Bismarck* (1898) iii. 51
Frederick William IV renounced all his sovereign
rights over Neuchâtel. . . . But the incident
preyed deeply on the sensitive spirit of the King.
It drove a nail into his coffin.

Nail one's colours to the mast, To.

[= to adopt an unyielding attitude.]   **1841**
CHAMIER *Tom Bowl.* ch. 55 If ever we get athwart
hawse of a Frenchman, Captain Bowling need
not nail his colours to the mast, for there will
not be one man on board who would haul them
down.   **1848** DICKENS *Dombey* ch. 5 Mrs. Chick
had nailed her colours to the mast and repeated
'I know it isn't'.   **1926** *Times* 28 May 16/5 The
present negotiators . . . had nailed their colours
to the mast, and it was very difficult . . . to take
out any of the nails.

Nail to the counter, To.

[= to expose as false, in allusion to the practice
of dealing thus with spurious coins.]   **1573** C.
DESAINLIENS *French Schoolmaster* (1615) N3ᵛ
There is a counterfet shilling: nayle it at the
threshold of the door.   *a.* **1590** LYLY *Mother B.*
II. i. 52 I shall goe for siluer though, when you
shall bee nailed vp for slips.   **1601–2** *Blurt
Master Constable* (Middleton Wks. (Bullen) i.
40) If he be counterfeit, nail him vp upon one of
your posts.   **1842** O. W. HOLMES *Med. Ess.* Wks.
(1891) IX. 67 A few familiar facts . . . have been
suffered to pass current so long that it is time
they should be nailed to the counter.   **1890**
Spectator 9 Aug. It was a good deed to nail all
this to the counter.

Nail(s), *see also* Drive the n. that will go; Drive
the n. to the head; Hard as n.; Hit the n. on the
head; One n. drives out another; Want of a n.
the shoe is lost.

Nails (*of fingers*), *see* Better ne'er been born as
have n. Sunday shorn; Eat your n. (Had as
good); Iron n. that scratches bear; Naked as my
n.; Nobody's n. can reach London; Paring of his
n. (Part with); Pearl on your n.

Naked as a frog.

1626 J. FLETCHER *Fair M. of Inn* IV. i. Wks.
(C.U.P.) IX. 201 I will make you dance a new
dance call'd leap-frog. . . . And as naked as
a frog.

Naked as a needle.   (N 94)

1350 *Alexander* l. 4027 And aye is naked a
nedill as natour tham schapis.   **1377** LANGLAND
P. Pl. B. XI. 162 Take two stronge men, and
in themese[1] caste hem, And bothe naked as a
nedle.   **1470–85** MALORY *Morte d'Arthur* XI. i.
572 There syr launcelot toke the fayrest lady
by the hand . . . and she was naked as a nedel.
[[1] Thames.]

Naked as a robin.

1883 BURNE *Shropsh. Folk-Lore* 595.   **1890** D. C.
MURRAY *J. Vale's Guard.* xxxviii Time was I
wouldn't ha' married her . . . without her lands.
You can send her now as naked as a robin, if
you like.

Naked as a worm.

c. **1400** *Rom. Rose* l. 454 For naked as a worm
was she.   *a.* **1467** *Gregory's Chron.* (Camd. Soc.)
211 The Lorde Schalys . . . was slayne at Synt
Mary Overeyes . . . , and laye there dyspoyly
nakyd as a worme.

Naked as he was born.   (B 137)

c. **1400** *Sir Isumbras* l. 102 His wyfe and his
childer three . . . Alle als nakede als they were
borne.   *a.* **1500** *15c. School-Bk.* ed. W. Nelson 3.
a. **1530** R. *Hill's Commonplace Bk.* 126.   **1542**
ERASM. tr. Udall *Apoph.* (1877) 59 Either of

them as naked as euer thei wer borne. **1621**
BURTON *Anat. Mel.* III. ii. III. iii (1651) 469 At
our coming to Brazil, we found both men and
women naked as they were born. **1829–30** M.
SCOTT *T. Cring. Log* ch. 12 There lay the canoe
. . . with her crew . . . as naked as the day they
were born.

Naked (bare) as my nail. (N 4)

1533 HEYWOOD *Play of Wether* l. 922 Thou
myghtest go as naked as my nayle. **1540**
PALSGRAVE *Acolastus* 144. **1563** *Mirr. Mag.*
ed. Campbell We . . . Were led in prysoners
naked as my nayle. **1596** NASHE *Saffron W.* iii.
6 As bare as my nayle. **1633** T. HEYWOOD
Eng. Trav. II. i. C iij b He . . . did . . . so Plucke
them and Pull them till hee left them as naked
as my Naile.

Naked man is sought after to be rifled, No. *Cf.* Breeches of a bare-arsed man. (M 345. N 331)

[L. *Nemo potest nudo vestimenta detrahere.* No
one can strip a naked man of his garment.]
1492 *Dialogue of Salomon & Marcolphus* ed.
Duff 9 A nakyd ars no man kan robbe or
dispoyle. **1611** COTGRAVE s.v. Nud A naked
man cannot be stript of clothes. **1612** SHELTON
Quix. III. xi. i. 209 Seeing I . . . am now naked,
I can neither win nor lose. **1651** HERBERT no.
1063.

Naked, *see also* Need makes the n. man run;
Truth shows best n.

Name for nothing, You had not your. (N 24)

1616 DRAXE no. 1458 He hath not his name for
naught. **1678** RAY 261.

Name is up; His | he may lie abed till noon. (N 26, 28)

1611 COTGRAVE s.v. Bruit He that is thought
to rise betime, may lye abed till noone. **1617**
SWETNAM *School of Defence* 41 Hee which is
accounted for an early riser, may lie a bed till
eleauen of the clocke. **1659** HOWELL *Eng. Prov.*
3b Who hath once the fame to be an early
riser, may sleep till noon. **1659** N. R. 47 He
that hath a fame of rising early may sleep till
dinner. **1672** CODRINGTON 379 Get a good
name and go to sleep. **1688** BUNYAN *Jer.
Sinner Saved* Wks. (1855) I. 75 He that can do
thus, . . . he shall have the name and fame he
desires; he may lie a-bed till noon. **1721** KELLY
112 . . . I would not have a Man depend too
much upon this Proverb; for a good Name is
soon lost, and hardly to be retriev'd. **1729**
SWIFT *An Epistle (Christmas-Box for Dr. Delany)*
Wks. (1856) I. 667 How different is this from
Smedley! (His name is up, he may in bed lie.)

Name no names, I. (N 31)

1612 CHAPMAN *The Widow's Tears* II. iv 152
Whom mean you Sir?—Sir, I name none but
him who first shall name himself. *c.* **1614**
BEAUM. & FL. *Wit at S.W.* II. i. So serving-man
Pompey Doodle may be respected as well with
ladies (though I name no parties) as Sir Gregory

Fop. **1633** SHIRLEY *Witty Fair One* v. iii. Somebody hath been cozened, I name nobody. **1858**
C. READE *Jack of All T.* ch. 5 Mr. Yates, who
could play upon the public ear better than
some fiddles (I name no names).

Name of an honest woman is mickle worth, The.

1721 KELLY 334 . . . A Reason given for a
Woman, who has borne a Bastard, for marrying
an inferior Person.

Names and natures do often agree. (N 32)

[I SAM. XXV. 25 As his name is, so is he; Nabal[1]
is his name, and folly is with him.] **1581** N.
WOODES *Conflict of Conscience* Prologue (first
issue) l. 54 Names to natures must agree, as
euery man do knowe. **1639** CLARKE 287. **1762**
STERNE *T. Shandy* I. xix. **1791** I. D'ISRAELI
Curios. Lit. (1858) II. 68 Milton . . . condescends
to insinuate that their barbarous names are
symbolical of their natures,—and from a man
of the name of *Mac Collkittok*, he expects no
mercy. [[1] i.e. fool.]

Names are debts.

1827–48 HARE *Gues. at Truth* (1859) I. 134, 5
No people . . . ever had so lively a feeling of the
power of the names as the Romans. . . . Every
member of a great house had a determinate
course markt out for him . . .: his name ad-
monisht him of what he owed to his country.
1901 ALEX. WHYTE *Bib. Char., Stephen* 15 *Nomina
debita*, says John Donne; that is to say, 'Every
man owes to the world the signification of his
name, and of all his name. Every new addition
of honour or of office lays a new obligation
upon him, and his Christian name above all.'

Name(s), (*noun*), *see also* Born in good hour who
gets good n.; De te fabula narratur; Go in
God's n.; Good fellow is costly n.; Good n. better
than riches; Good n. keeps lustre in dark; Homo
is common n. to all men; Ill n.; Ill wound cured,
not ill n.; Sticks and stones . . . but n. never
hurt; Take away my good n. take away life.

Name (*verb*), *see also* Rope (N. not) in his house
that hanged himself.

Named, *see* Sooner n. sooner come; Worthy to be
n. same day (Not).

Nan, *see* Like to like and N. for Nicholas; Such
mistress, such N.

Naples, *see* See N. and die.

Napping, *see* Catch one n. (as Mosse did his
mare).

Narrow gathered, widely spent.

1721 KELLY 257 . . . Wealth, gotten by too much
sparing, comes often to be widely squander'd.

Narrow, *see also* Mad fools in n. place (Heed);
Turn a n. adlant; Wide will wear, but n. tear.

Nasty, *see* Cheap and n.

Nation, *see* English are swearing n.

Natural to die as to be born, It is as.
(D 327)

[1592] 1596 *Edw. III* IV. iv. 133 To die is all as
common as to liue. 1626 J. TAYLOR *Elegy on
Lancelot Andrewes* (Wks. 1630 3K1) Tis naturall
to dye, as borne to be. 1732 FULLER no. 2911.
1910 *Spectator* 7 May 'Men fear death', says
Bacon, '. . . but the fear of it, as a tribute due
unto nature, is weak'. . . . It is as natural to die
as to be born.

Nature abhors a vacuum.
(N 42)

[PLUT. *De Plac. Phil.* l. 18]. *c.* 1550 K. SMITH
Confutation 62ᵛ Natural reason abhorreth
vacuum. 1584 WITHALS N8 The Philosophers
maintaine that no place is voyde or emptie in
all the world. 1585 DYER *Praise Nothing* 109
Where as the schole men haue this ground that
Natura abhorret vacuum, which is the natural
element or residence of nothing, it consequently
followeth, that she also abhorreth nothing.
1603 HOLLAND *Plutarch's Mor.* 1021 There is
no voidness or vacuity in nature. 1606–7
SHAKES. *A.C.* II. ii. 220 The air . . . but for
vacancy Had gone to gaze on Cleopatra too,
and made a gap in nature. 1642 FULLER *H. & P.
State* V. ii (1841) 340 Queen Joan . . . (hating
widowhood as much as nature doth *vacuum*)
married James King of Majorca. 1771 JOHNSON
20 June in *Boswell* (1848) xxv. 224 Whatever
philosophy may determine of material nature,
it is certainly true of intellectual nature, that it
abhors a vacuum: our minds cannot be empty.
1841 ABP. TRENCH *Notes on Par.* xxi (1889) 368
Since grace will as little as nature endure a
vacuum, he receives a new . . . commission: Go
out . . . and compel them to come in that my
house may be filled.

Nature does nothing in vain.
(N 43)

[AR. *Pol.* l. 2. 10 Οὐθὲν γάρ, ὡς φαμέν, μάτην ἡ
φύσις ποιεῖ, For, as we say, Nature does nothing
in vain.] 1481 CAXTON *Mir. World* I. xiv. 44
Nature fourmeth nothing in vayn. *c.* 1573 G.
HARVEY *Letter-Bk.* 123 Nature, they tell us,
Doth nothinge in vayne. 1575 GASCOIGNE
Posies i. 18 Natures Art, nothing hath made in
vaine. *c.* 1580 G. HARVEY *Marginalia* 128 . . .
Naturam: quae . . . nihil facit frustra. 1605
BACON *Adv. of Learning* (Robertson) 163 Nature
which doth nothing in vain. 1642 SIR T. BROWNE
Relig. Med. I. XV *Natura nihil agit frustra*, is the
only indisputable Axiome in Philosophy. There
are no putable Axiome in Philosophy. There are
no Grotesques in Nature; not anything framed
to fill up empty Cantons, and unnecessary spaces.
1645 J. MARSH *Marsh his Micle Monument* A3
The God of Nature made nothing in vain. 1822
ABP. WHATELY *Use Ab. of Party F.* (1859) 8 No
. . . inherent principle of our nature is in itself
either mischievous or useless. The maxim that
Nature does nothing in vain, is not more true
in the material, than in the moral world.

Nature draws more than ten teams.
1640 HERBERT no. 777. 1670 RAY 18 (oxen).

Nature has given us two ears, two eyes, and but one tongue; to the end we should hear and see more than we speak.
(N 44)

1535 *Dialogues of Creatures* (1816) cclvi To
euery creature longith but oon tongue and two
erys. 1539 TAVERNER I *Garden* F6ᵛ A yonge
man whose tongue neuer stinted babblyng, he
[Zeno] toke vp with this propre sayenge: For
this purpose we haue two eares and but one
tonge, that we shuld heare very moch, and speake
very lytle. 1568 TILNEY *Duties in Marriage* C3
(Xenophon sayeth). 1581 GUAZZO i. 119. 1586
J. CASE *Praise of Music* *3 Nature hath . . . giuen
thee two eares, that thou shouldest aswell applie
the one to the defendant, as the other to the
plaintife. 1605 *London Prodigal* III. ii (*Shakes.
Apoc.*) 205 Euery man hath one tongue, and
two eares: nature, in her building, is a most
curious worke-maister.—That is as much (as)
to say, a man should heare more then he should
speake. *c.* 1635 HOWELL *Lett.* to G. G. (1903)
II. 109 You have two eyes and two ears, but one
tongue. You know my meaning. 1669 PENN
No Cross, No Crown (1726) 378 Demosthenes
. . . had these sentences: 'That wise men speak
little, and that therefore nature hath given men
two ears and one tongue, to hear more than they
speak.'

Nature hates all sudden changes.

[1613 TISSOT *Natura nihil facit per saltum*, applied
by Coke to the law, by Linnaeus to vegetation.]
a. 1633 HERBERT *Providence* 121. l. 133 Thy
[Nature's] creatures leap not. 1721 KELLY 267
. . . It is not safe for a Man to change in his Diet,
Behaviour, or way of living suddainly, from one
extreme to another. 1924 R. W. LIVINGSTONE
Greek Genius 206 We have watched the obscure
beginnings of philosophy, and now we must
pass over nearly two centuries; remembering,
however, that though we can take leaps, nature
nihil facit per saltum.

Nature is conquered (governed) by obeying her.

1827–48 HARE *Gues. at Truth* (1859) I. 166 Bacon
has declared it: *Natura non nisi parendo vincitur*:
and the triumphs of Science since his days have
proved how willing Nature is to be conquered
by those who will obey her. 1916 E. A. BUR-
ROUGHS *Val. of Decis.* (1920) II. iv. 285 'God
resisteth the proud but giveth grace unto the
humble' is only a theological version of the
scientific truism, 'To conquer Nature you must
obey her'.

Nature is content with a little.
(N 45)

1557 EDGEWORTH *Sermons* 2K4 Nature is content with a very litle. *a.* 1567 T. BECON *Catechism* P.S. 102. 1572 T. WILSON *Discourse
upon Usury* ed. Tawney 202 A verye litle
thyng satisfieth nature. 1579 *Proverbs of Sir
James Lopez de Mendoza* tr. B. Googe f. 93ᵛ
Boethius in his second booke of Consolation
saith, that nature contenteth herselfe with a
very smal thing. 1584 LYLY *Campaspe* I. ii. 5
Natura paucis contenta. 1591 W. PERKINS
Treat. of Callings (Wks. 1608, i. 745a). *c.* 1592
NASHE *Summer's Last Will* iii. 243 Nam natura
paucis contenta, none so contented as the
poore man. 1654 GAYTON *Pleasant Notes on
Don Quix.* 194.

Nature is the true law. (N 46)

1573 SANFORD 52. **1578** FLORIO *First F.* 32ᵛ (right). **1629** *Bk. Mer. Rid.* Prov. no. 34 (the true law).

Nature of the beast, It is the.

1678 RAY 77. **1683** JOHN VERNEY to his wife, *Verney Memoirs* (1899) iv. 254 I'me very Sorry John my Coachman Should be soe greate a Clowne to you . . . but t'is the nature of the Beast.

Nature passes[1] nurture (art). *Cf.* Nurture is above nature. (N 47)

1492 *Dial. of Salomon & Marcolphus* ed. Duff 21 Nature goth afore lernyng. **1519** HORMAN *Vulg.* X. 4 No craft can make a thynge so plesaunt as nature. *c.* **1534** GILES DUWES 894 Arte is folower of nature folowyng her right nygh, yet neuerthelesse can not she ouertake her. **1579** LYLY *Euph.* i. 191 Education can have no shew where the excellencie of Nature doth beare sway. **1606** CHAPMAN *Gentleman Usher* I. i. 231 Nature yields more than Art. **1641** FERGUSSON no. 645. [1 surpasses.]

Nature, time, and patience are the three great physicians.

1707 MAPLETOFT 15.

Nature will have her course. (N 48)

c. **1400** *Beryn* E.E.T.S. 105 ffor kynde woll have his cours. **1579** LYLY *Euph.* i. 191 Nature will haue course after kinde. **1590** *Id. Mother B.* I. i. 101 Your son's folly . . . being naturall; it will haue his course. **1616** DRAXE no. 1473. **1666** TORRIANO *Prov. Phr.* s.v. Pani 130 Let nature take her own course.

Nature, *see also* Art improves n.; Cast out n. with a fork, will return; Follows n. (He that); God (N.) is no botcher; Ill n., the more you ask, more they stick; Moist hand argues amorous n.; Names and n. often agree; Nurture is above n.; Pay one's debt to n.; Pope by voice, king by birth (n.); Self-preservation is first law of n.

Naughty Ashford, surly Wye, poor Kennington hard by.

1736 S. PEGGE *Kenticisms, Prov.* E.D.S. 67.

Naughty boys sometimes make good men. (B 580)

1548 HALL (1809, 12) Experience teacheth, that of a rugged colte, commeth a good horse, and of a shreude boye, proueth a good man. **1662** *Life and Death of Mrs. Mary Frith* 7 This Prouerb . . . That an unhappy Girl may make a good Woman. **1662** FULLER Surrey 81 Nicholas West[1] was born at Putney. . . . In him the Proverb was verified, 'Naughty Boyes sometimes make good Men'. He seasonably retrenched his wildness, turned hard Student, became an eminent Scholar and most able States-man. [1 Bishop of Ely, 1515–33.]

Nay-says, *see* Nineteen n. of a maiden half a grant.

Nay, stay, quoth Stringer, when his neck was in the halter. (S 938)

1678 RAY 82. **1732** FULLER no. 3512.

Ne supra crepidam, see Cobbler go beyond his last (Let not).

Neapolitan shrug, To give one the. (S 417)

1594 NASHE *Unfort. Trav.* ii. 298 It is growen to a common prouerbe, Ile giue him the Neapolitan shrug, when one intends to play the villaine, and make no boast of it.

Near as bark to tree, As. (B 83)

1580 LYLY *Euph. & his Eng.* ii. 87 As neere is Fancie to Beautie, . . . as the stalke to the rynde, as the earth to the roote. **1639** CLARKE 286.

Near burr, far rain. *Cf.* Round the moon there is a burr. (B 733)

1631 BRATHWAIT *Whimzies Xantipp.* 104 A burre about the moone is . . . a presage of a tempest. **1699** B. E. Bur, a Cloud, or dark Circle about the Moon, biding Wind and Rain. **1830** FORBY 417 'Near bur, far rain.' The 'bur' is the halo round the moon, and . . . when it appears near the moon there will be fine weather.

Near is my coat (doublet, kirtle, petticoat) but nearer is my shirt (smock). (P 250)

[PLAUTUS *Trin.* 5. 2. 30 *Tunica propior pallio est.*] **1461** *Paston Lett.* (Gairdner) iii. 251 Nere is my kyrtyl, but nerre[1] is my smok. **1539** TAVERNER 15 My cote is nerer me than my robe or gowne. **1545** *Id.* B7ᵛ The Englysshe prouerbo sayethe thus: nere is my cote, but nerer is my shyrt. **1546** HEYWOOD I. X. D1 Though ny be my kyrtell, yet nere[1] is my smocke. I haue one of myne owne whom I must loke to. **1576** HOLYBAND D8ᵛ (peticoate . . . smocke). **1609** HARWARD 105ᵛ (doublet . . . shirt). **1612** JONSON *Alchem.* III. v. 9 And though to Fortune neere be her petticote, Yet, nearer is her smock, the Queene doth note. **1622** HOWELL *Lett.* I May (1903) I. 125 That king . . . having too many irons in the fire at his own home, . . . answered them that his shirt was nearer to him than his doublet. **1641** FERGUSSON no. 657 Neir is the kirtle, but neirer is the sark. **1732** FULLER no. 4745 The Shirt is nearer than the Coat. **1894** NORTHALL *Folk-phrases* E.D.S. 25 The smock is nearer than the petticoat. [1 nearer.]

Near is my coat (shirt) but nearer is my skin. (S 356)

c. **1570** *Ballads* Percy Soc. I. 99 Neerer is my skin then shirte. **1596** LODGE *Marg. Amer.* 103 My shirt is neare me, my lord, but, my skin is nearest. **1614** CAMDEN 305 Close sitteth my shirt, but closer my skin. **1636** HENSHAW *Horae Sub.* 72 His charity begins at home, and there it ends: neare is his coat, but neerer is his skin.

1712 ARBUTHNOT _John Bull_ II. xix 'My shirt', quoth her, 'is near me, but my skin is nearer. Whilst I take care of the welfare of other folks, nobody can blame me to apply a little balsam to my own sores.' 1817 LAMB to Kenneys, Oct. Dear is my shirt, but dearer is my skin.

Near neighbour is better than a far-dwelling kinsman, A. (N 110)

1545 TAVERNER G1 An englysshe prouerbe . . . A nere neyghbour is better than a farre frende. 1597 _Politeuphuia_ 166ᵛ (farre dwelling friend). 1609 HARWARD 105 (a coosin a farre of).

Near of kin to land (an estate), It is good to be. (K 37)

1662 FULLER _Leics._ 127 Our English Proverb, 'It is good to be near a-kin to Land', holdeth in private patrimonies, not Titles to Crowns. 1670 RAY 110 (an estate). 1721 KELLY 197 It is something to be sib¹ to a good estate. Because at the long run it may fall to us. [¹ akin.]

Nearer the bone, The | the sweeter the flesh. _Cf._ The flesh is aye fairest that is farthest from the bone. (B 520)

1559 _Ballads_ Percy Soc. I. 21 The nigher the bone, the flesh is much sweeter. 1584 WITHALS M1ᵛ The fleshe which to the bones stickes nearer, is commonly the sweeter. 1639 CLARKE 163. 1662 FULLER _Wales_ 2 As the sweetest flesh is said to be nearest the bones, so most delicious valleys are interposed betwixt these Mountains. 1824 LAMB _Lond. Mag._ Nov. in _Elia_, 'Capt. Jackson' (1921) 255 Sliding a slender ratio of Single Gloucester upon his wife's plate, . . . he would convey the remanent rind into his own, with a merry quirk of 'the nearer the bone', &c.

Nearer the church, The | the farther from God. (C 380)

_c._ 1303 BRUNNE _Handl. Synne_ l. 9242 Tharfor men seye, an weyl ys trowed, 'þe nere þe cherche, þe fyrþer fro God'. _c._ 1350 _MS. Douce_ 52 no. 15 The nerer the chyrche the fer fro Crist. 1546 HEYWOOD I. ix. C1ᵛ The nere to the churche, the ferther from God. 1579 SPENSER _Shep. Cal._ Jul. Wks. (Globe) 467 To Kerke the narre, from God more farre, Has bene an old-sayd sawe. 1611 TOURNEUR _Ath. Trag._ I. iv Come, set forward to the church. . . .—And verify the proverb —. . . 1620 SHELTON _Quix._ II. xlvii. iii. 142 Eat nothing of all this meat . . . for this dinner was presented by nuns, and it is an old saying, 'The nearer the church, the farther from God'. 1641 FERGUSSON no. 650 Neirest the kirk, farrest fra God. 1819 SCOTT _Ivanhoe_ ch. 20 It makes good the old proverb, The nearer the church. . . .

Nearest himself, Every man is. (N 57)

[ERASM. _Ad._ 147 A: _Heus proximus sum egomet mihi._] _c._ 1570 T. PRESTON _Cambyses_ A3ᵛ He is a man that to himselfe is nie. 1578 BESTE _Voyages of Frobisher_ Hakluyt Soc. 270 Everye manne in that cause is nexte himselfe. 1594 SHAKES. _T.G.V._ II. vi. 23 I to myself am dearer than a friend; For love is still most precious in itself. 1601 JONSON _Cynthia's Revels_ V. vii. 27

As euery one is neerest to himselfe, so this . . . allowable selfe-loue . . . are none without it. 1643 CAWDREY _Good Man_ 27 It is a common and received Proverbe . . . proximus egomet mihi.

Nearest the heart, nearest the mouth. (H 321)

1580 LYLY _Euph. & his Eng._ ii. 170 Euery one talketh of that most he liketh best. _a._ 1628 CARMICHAELL no. 1195. 1641 FERGUSSON no. 654. 1721 KELLY 265 . . . Spoken to them who, designing to name one Person, by Mistake names another, perhaps a Mistress or Sweetheart.

Nearest way is commonly the foulest, The.

_c._ 1595 BACON _Promus_ no. 1247 In actions as in wayes the nearest the fowlest. 1605 _Id. Advancement of Learning_ ii (J. M. Robertson) 164. 1625 _Id. Apophthegms_ no. 245. 1732 FULLER no. 4921 There is no short Cut of a Way, without some ill Way.

Near(er, est), _see also_ Devil is never n. than when we are talking of him; Farthest way about n. way home; Go far about seeking the n.; Lives unsafely that looks too n.

Neat as a new pin, As.

1796 WOLCOT _Orson & Ellen_ Wks. (1816) IV. 71 How neat was Ellen in her dress! As neat as a new pin! 1849–50 THACKERAY _Pendennis_ I. xii Major Pendennis, whom Miss Costigan declared to be a proper gentleman entirely . . . as neat as a pin.

Neat (comely) but not gaudy. (C 541)

1600–1 SHAKES. _H._ I. iii. 71 Costly thy habit as thy purse can buy, But not express'd in fancy; rich, not gaudy. 1615 WELDE _Janua Ling._ 12 no. 179 Let thy attire be comely, and not gorgeous. 1631 BRATHWAIT _Eng. Gentlewoman_ (1641) 399 Making this her Impreze: _Comely not gaudy._ 1850 THACKERAY _Pendennis_ ch. 13.

Neatness, _see_ North for greatness, south for n.

Necessity and opportunity may make a coward valiant. (N 62)

1590 SPENCER _F.Q._ III. vii. 26 Thereto feare gaue her wings, and neede her courage taught. 1611 COTGRAVE s.v. Necessité Necessitie addes mettall to the meacocke; makes the coward grow couragious. 1613 R. DALLINGTON _Aphorisms_ 120 Necessitie makes the most cowards valiant. 1732 FULLER no. 3514.

Necessity has no holiday.

_c._ 1440 _Palladius on Husbandry_ ed. B. Lodge E.E.T.S. i. 176 Necessity nath never haliday.

Necessity (Need) has (knows) no law. (N 76)

[SIMONIDES 8. 20 Ἀνάγκᾳ δ' οὐδὲ θεοὶ μάχονται. Even the gods war not with necessity. PLUTARCH _De Def. Orac._ Ἅπαντα τἀναγκαῖα συγχωρεῖ θεός. _Law Max.—Necessitas non habet legem._] 1377

LANGLAND *P. Pl.* B. xx. 10 Nede ne hath no lawe, ne neure shal falle in dette. *c.* 1440 *Jacob's Well* 206 þanne nede hath no lawe. *a.* 1529 SKELTON *Col. Cloute* 864 Wks. (1843) I. 344 But it is an olde sayd sawe, That nede hath no lawe. 1530 TYNDALE *Answer to More* P.S. 18 Two things are without law, God and necessity. 1546 HEYWOOD I. x. C3ᵛ But neede hath no lawe, neede maketh hir hither iet. *a.* 1555 RIDLEY *Lament. Ch.* (1566) D iv The latter reason . . . includeth a necessitie which, after the common sayinge, hathe no law. 1653 H. COGAN *Pinto's Trav.* xlvi. 268 Necessity, which hath no law, compelled us thereunto. 1837 CARLYLE *Fr. Rev.* III. I. iii Your Hessian forager has only 'three sous a day': . . . women . . . are robbed; . . . for Necessity, on three half-pence a day, has no law.

Necessity is a hard weapon (dart). (N 58)

1539 TAVERNER f. 34ᵛ *Ingens telum necessitas.* Necessitie is a sore weapon. 1540 PALSGRAVE *Acolastus* 61. 1553 T. BECON *Jewel of Joy* P.S. 465 (dart). 1567 PAINTER iii. 213 Remembryng what a harde Weapon Necessitye is. 1615 WELDE *Janua Ling.* 27 Necessity is a mighty weapon.

Necessity is coal black. (N 59)
1678 RAY 180.

Necessity is the mother of invention. *Cf.* Poverty is the mother of all arts. (N 61)

1519 HORMAN *Vulg.* f. 52 Nede taught hym wytte. 1545 *Precepts of Cato* Publius L2 Pouertie is wyttye and ful of inuention. 1545 ASCHAM *Toxoph.* Arb. 134 Necessitie, the inuentour of all goodnesse (as all authours in a maner, doo saye) . . . inuented a shaft heed. [*c.* 1587] 1594 MARLOWE and NASHE *Dido* I. i. 169 See what strange arts necessity finds out. 1608 CHAPMAN *Byron* IV. ii. 35 The great mother of all productions, grave Necessity. 1630 DRAYTON *Muses' Elysium* x. 54 What cannot strong necessity finde out? 1641 FERGUSSON no. 617 Mister¹ makes men of craft. 1726 SWIFT *Gul. Trav.* IV. x. Wks. (1856) I. 75 I sold my shoes with wood, which I cut from a tree. . . . No man could more verify the truth. . . . 'That necessity is the mother of invention'. *a.* 1763 SHENSTONE *Detached Thoughts on Writing* Necessity may be the mother of lucrative invention, but is is the death of poetical invention. 1891 J. E. T. ROGERS *Indust. & Com. Hist. Eng.* v We have got an old proverb, . . . for the extension of it in detail is the substance of a good part of the Plutus of Aristophanes, 'that necessity is the mother of invention'. Take away the necessity and the invention goes with it. [¹ Necessity.]

Necessity, *see also* Conquering weapon as n. of conquering (No such); Virtue of n. (Make).

Neck and crop.

[= bodily, completely.] 1816 HONE *Ev. Day Book* i. 461 Explain the terms . . . neck and crop. . . . 1833 M. SCOTT *T. Cring. Log* ch. 16 Chuck them neck and crop . . . down a dark staircase. 1890 S. BARING-GOULD *Arminell* ch. 29 So he is turned out of the house, neck and crop.

Neck or nothing (nought). (N 66)

1678 RAY 347. 1715 M. DAVIES *Athen. Brit.* I. 321 Worth venturing Neck or nothing for. 1738 SWIFT *Dial.* I. E.L. 290 [*The Footman . . . falls down stairs*]. Neck or nothing; come down or I'll fetch you down. 1782 COWPER *Gilpin* 89 Away went Gilpin, neck or nought. 1810 CLARKE *Trav. Russia* 333 She rides, to use the language of English sportsmen, 'neck or nothing'. 1834 EDGEWORTH *Helen* ch. 25 But, neck or nothing. I am apt to go through with whatever I once take into my head. 1892 A. DOBSON *S. Richardson* 121 Miss Mulso . . . was not one of Richardson's neck-or-nothing flatterers. 1908 W. S. CHURCHILL *My African Journey* ch. 2 Three or four daring Britons . . . gallop . . . neck or nothing—across rocks, holes, tussocks, nullahs.

Neck out of the collar, To slip one's. (N 69)

1563 FOXE *A. and M.* (1631 ed. ii. 253a). *c.* 1566 C. A. CURIO *Pasquin in a Trance* tr. W. P. 71 Doubting least they whould slip their heads out of the coller. 1571 J. BRIDGES *Sermon at Paul's Cross* 28 Here they [the Papists] would slippe the coller with a shift of descant. 1581 GUAZZO ii. 95 He hadde shrunke his heade oute of the coller of those insupportable paynes. 1583 GOLDING *Calvin on Deut.* cxxv 772 Albeit we . . . would slippe our heades out of the coler seeking to shift off yᵉ matter. [1592] 1597 SHAKES. *Rich. III* IV. iv. 112 Now thy proud neck bears half my burden'd yoke; From which even here, I slip my wearied head. 1616 DRAXE no. 1963 He draweth his necke out of the coller. 1633 D. DYKE Wks. *Philemon* 242 Religion . . . will not teach thy servant to slip his neck out of the collar, and to deny thee service and subjection. 1655 FULLER *Ch. Hist.* IX. viii. 30 (1868) III. 168 [Parsons] having got his neck out of the collar, accused others for not drawing weight enough.

Neck, *see also* Break his n. as his fast (As soon); Chance it, as Horne did his n.; Good for the head evil for n.; Hair in n.; See thy n. as long as my arm.

Neck-cloth, *see* Bolder than miller's n. (What is).

Need makes greed.

1721 KELLY 265 . . . Want is a Temptation to Covetousness.

Need makes the naked man run (and sorrow makes websters spin). (N 77)

[*c.* 1517] 1533 SKELTON *Magn.* C2 Tusche he that hath nede man let him rynne. *a.* 1628 CARMICHAELL no. 1191 Neid garris naiked men rin and sorrow gars wobsters [*sic*] spin. 1639 CLARKE 225. 1641 FERGUSSON no. 656 (as Carmichaell but with 'websters'). 1670 RAY 124 (or the naked quean spin).

Need makes the old wife trot. (N 79)

c. 1225 *Trin. MS. O.* 11. 45 (ed. Förster) in *Eng. Stud.* 31. 8 Neode makad heald wif eorne. *c.* 1470 *Harl. MS. 3362*, f. 3a Nede makyth an old wyfe [rame]. *a.* 1530 *R. Hill's Commonpl.*

Bk. (1858) 140 Nede makyth the old wyffe to trotte. **1546** HEYWOOD II. x. L3ᵛ Neede makth the olde wyfe trot. **1608** TOPSELL *Serpents* (1658) 780 Hunger breaketh stonewalls, and hard need makes the old wife trot. **1822** SCOTT *Pirate* ch. 24 Stimulated by the spur which maketh the old woman proverbially to trot, Swertha posted down to the hamlet, with all the speed of threescore.

Need much whom nothing will content, They. (M 1291)

1639 CLARKE 38. **1670** RAY 124. **1732** FULLER no. 4969.

Need of a besom that sweep the house with a turf, They have. (N 82)

1678 RAY 101.

Need of a blessing who kneel to a thistle, They have. (N 83)

1580 MUNDAY *Zelauto* VI Theyr courtesie is ouermuch that will kneele to a Thystle. **1623** CAMDEN 279 (will kneele). **1664** CODRINGTON 223 (who pray to a Thief). **1678** RAY 103. **1732** FULLER no. 4964. [See *N. & Q.* 180. 237.]

Need will have its course. (N 81)

?**1475** *Assembly of Ladies Chaucerian and other Pieces* ed. Skeat l. 665 But nede wol have his cours in every thing. **1598** JONSON *Ev. Man in Hum.* II. ii. 53. **1678** RAY 180.

Need, *see also* Bale (N.) is hext (When) boot is next; Bread than n.; Fool (He has great n. of a); Four and spends five, (He that has but) has no n. of a purse; Friend in n.; Great and little have n. one of another; Necessity (N.) has no law; Once in ten years man has n. of another; See him n. but not see him bleed; Truth has no n. of rhetoric; Two false knaves n. no broker.

Needham. (H 460)

1575 GASCOIGNE *Posies* i. 73 Saint needam be their speede. **1580** TUSSER *500 Points* 78ᵛ At needhams shore, to craue the beggars bone. **1592** GREENE *Quip* ed. Hindley 28 Saint Needam's-cross. **1603** H. CROSSE *Virtue's Commonwealth* Gros. 63 Come home by Needham-crosse, not fooles aere. **1616** T. ADAMS *Diseases of the Soul* 53 Idlnesse is the coach to bring a man to Needome. **1662** FULLER Suffolk 55 'You are in the highway to Needham'. Needham is a Market-Town in this County. . . . They are said to be in the highway to Needham who hasten to poverty.

Needingworth, It comes from. (N 91)

1639 CLARKE 68.

Needle, Not worth a.

c. **1200** *Ancrene Riwle* 400 And alle þeos þinges somed, agean mine bode, ne beoð nout worð a nelde.[1] *a.* **1399** *Complaint of Ploughman* in WRIGHT *Pol. Poems* (1861) I. 327 Soche willers witte is not worth a nelde.[1] *c.* **1425** *Wakefield Plays* 'Abel' l. 123. [¹ needle.]

Needle in a bottle[1] of hay, Like a. (N 97)

1532 MORE *Wks.* (1557) I. 837 To seke out one lyne in all hys bookes wer to go looke a nedle in a medow. **1565** J. CALFHILL *Treatise of the Cross* P.S. 173 To find a pin's head in a cartload of hay. **1592** GREENE *Upst. Courtier* (1871) 4*b* He . . . gropeth in the dark to find a needle in a bottle of hay. **1610** FIELD *Woman is a W.* I. ii Merm. 351 That little old dried neat's tongue. . . . Methinks he in his lady should show like a needle in a bottle of hay. **1690** W. WALKER *Idiom. Anglo. Lat.* (1695) pref. A labour much like that of seeking a needle in a Bottle of Hay. **1711** SWIFT *Jrnl. to Stella* 22 Oct. I must rout among your letters, a needle in a bottle of hay. **1742** GRAY *Lett.* (1900) I. 105 A coach that seem'd to have lost its way, by looking for a needle in a bottle of hay. [¹ bundle.]

Needle's eye. (C 26)

[MATT. xix. 24 It is easier for a camel to go through a needle's eye, than for a rich man to enter into the kingdom of God.] **1534** LUPSET *Treat. Dying Well* 286 For as harde a thynge it is to plucke through the small nedels eie a greatte caboull rope, as to brynge a rich man in at heuens wycket. **1579** GOSSON *Sch. Abuse* Arb. 27 Euerie one of them may . . . daunce the wilde Morice in a Needles eye. **1595–6** SHAKES. *Rich. II* V. v. 17 It is hard to come as for a camel To thread the postern of a small needle's eye. **1622** FITZGEFFREY *Elisha* 46 He had learned also how to make the Camell passe through the needles eye, namely by casting off the bunch on the back. **1872** BESANT & RICE *Ready-m. Mort.* ch. 46 A single-hearted . . . rich man, for whom the needle's eye is as easy to pass, as for the poorest pauper.

Needles and pins, needles and pins: when a man marries his trouble begins.

1843 HALLIWELL *Nursery Rhymes* 122. **1876** BLACKMORE *Cripps* lii Cripps . . . was sadly singing . . . that exquisite elegiac— . . . .

Needles' points, To stand (walk) on. (N 100)

1600 DEKKER *Shoem. Hol.* IV. i. 58 Come Hans, I stand vpon needles. **1613** CHAPMAN *Rev. Bussy D'Amb.* I. i. 107 For so on needles' points My wife's heart stands with haste of the revenge. **1664** KILLIGREW *Pandora* V. 75 State Affairs, where the wisest ever walk on needles points.

Needle(s), *see also* Naked as n.; Pins and n.; Put it together with hot n. and burnt thread; St. Peter's n. (Go through); Sharp as a n.; Steel in my n. eye, though little; Tine n. tine darg; Tint a cow that grat for n. (He never).

Needs must.

c. **1330** *Seven Sages of Rome* E.E.T.S. (1933) l. 1597 O nedes he sschal, þat nedes mot. *c.* **1390** GOWER *Conf. Amantis* I. 291 For it is seid thus overal, That nedes mot that nede schal. [c. **1591**] **1598** GREENE *James IV* Ind. l. 40 Needs must, needs sal. **1604** E. GRIMSTONE *Hist. Siege*

Ostend 195 We beleeue them no more then needs must. **1871** BROWNING *Balaustion* 2287 She shall go, if needs must.

Needs must when the devil drives.
(D 278)

c. **1420** LYDGATE *Ass. of Gods* E.E.T.S. l. 20 For hit ys oft seyde by hem that yet lyues He must nedys go that the deuell dryues. **1523** SKELTON *Garl. Laurel.* 1434 Nedes must he rin that the deuyll dryuith. **1546** HEYWOOD II. vii. I3 And that he must needes go, whom the diuel doth driue. **1592** KYD *Span. Trag.* III. xii. 81 For needs must he go that the devils driue. **1602** SHAKES. *A.W.* I. iii. 29 He must needs go that the devil drives. **1613** PURCHAS *Pilgrimage* I. xv. 71 Needs must they goe whom the diuell driueth. **1664** COTTON *Scarron.* 1715 ed. i. 1 He needs must go, the Devil drives. **1839** DICKENS *N. Nickleby* ch. 5 Needs must, you know, when somebody drives. Necessity is my driver and that is only another name for the same gentleman. **1853** R. S. SURTEES *Sponge's Sport.* T. ch. 25 'Well', said he, 'needs must when a certain gentleman drives'.

Needy when he is married, He that is | shall be rich when he is buried. (M 699)

1616 DRAXE no. 2380. **1670** RAY 48. **1707** MAPLETOFT 112 (He that is poor).

Ne'er-do-weel, *see* Hantle o' fauts (Some hae), ye're only n.

Negatives, *see* Positive (One) weighs more than twenty n.; Two n. make affirmative.

Neglect will kill an injury sooner than revenge. (*Cf.* Remedy for injuries).
(N 102)

1607 JONSON *Volp.* II. ii. 20 Sir, calumnies are answer'd best with silence. **1620–8** FELTHAM *Resolves* (Dent) 213.

Neighbour-quart is good quart. (N 121)
1678 RAY 180 . . . *i.e.* Giffe gaffe is a good fellow.

Neighbour's house is on fire, Look to thyself when thy. (N 116)

[VIRGIL *Aen.* 2. 311 *Proximus ardet Ucalegon.* Your neighbour Ucalegon is on fire. HORACE *Ep.* I. 18. 84 *Tua res agitur, paries cum proximus ardet.* Your own property is at stake, when your neighbour's house is on fire.] **1519** HORMAN *Vulg.* Roxb. Cl. 184 Whan my neybours house is a fyre: I can nat be out of thought for myn owne. **1572** CRADOCKE *Ship of Assured Safety* b5 Here I remembred one of Virgils verses, Who saythe in one of his Ecloges these wordes. When fired is thy neighbours wall, Surely thy daunger is not small. [**1590**] **1594** LODGE & GREENE *Looking-Glass* V. v. 227 O proud adulterous glorie of the West! Thy neighbour burns, yet dost thou feare no fire. **1636** CAMDEN 299. **1639** CLARKE 250. **1662** FULLER Cumberland 217 'When thy neighbour's house doth burn, Take heed the next be not thy turn.' **1891** J. E. T. ROGERS *Ind. & Com. Hist.* ch. 4 The true cause . . . of a credit panic is the close interlacing of monetary interests. If Ucalegon's house catches fire, his neighbours are in extreme risk of the conflagration extending.

Neighbour's scathe is my present peril My next. *Cf. preceding proverb.*

1721 KELLY 245 . . . L. [*Nam*] *tua res agitur paries quum proximus ardet.*

Neighbours, He dwells far from (or has ill) that is fain to praise himself. (N 117)

1492 *Dial. of Salomon & Marcolphus* (ed. Duff 6) He that hath euyll neighborys praysyth himself. **1509** BARCLAY *Ship of Fools* ii. 68 Men . . . In theyr olde prouerbes often comprehende That he that is amonge shrewyd neyghbours May his owne dedes laufully commende. **1591–2** SHAKES. *T.And.* V. iii. 118 When no friends are by, men praise themselves. **1598–9** *Id. M.A.* V. ii. 65 There's not one wise man among twenty that will praise himself.—An old, an old instance, Beatrice, that lived in the time of good neighbours. **1599** PORTER *Angry Wom. Abingd.* l. 2400 You dwell by ill neighbours Richard, that makes yee praise your selfe. **1659** HOWELL *Eng. Prov.* 16a Who commendeth himself, wanteth good neighbours. **1670** RAY 125 . . . *Proprio laus sordet in ore.* Let another man praise thee, and not thine own mouth; a stranger, and not thine own lips. [*Prov.* xxvii. 2.] **1721** KELLY 375 You live beside ill Neighbours. Spoken when People commend themselves. **1738** SWIFT Dial. I. E.L. 275 I find you live by ill neighbours, when you are forced to praise yourself.

Neighbour is an ill thing, An ill. (N 108)
1545 TAVERNER G1 Euyll betydeth bicause of an euyll neighbour. **1639** CLARKE 317.

Neighbour's ground (cow) yields better corn (more milk) than ours, Our.
(N 115)

[*Fertilior seges est alieno semper in arvo.*] **1545** TAVERNER H3ᵛ The corne in an other mans ground semeth euer more fertyll and plentifull then doth oure owne. **1583** G. BABINGTON *Expos. of Commandments* 511 Vicinum pecus grandius vber habet: Our neighbours kowe doeth giue more milke than ours. **1584** WITHALS C1 Wee thinke alwayes the corne that growes in another bodies ground to be better then our own. **1623** J. LEYCESTER no. 119. **1659** HOWELL *Span. Prov.* 4 My neighbours goat gives more milk then mine. **1956** PLAY-TITLE *The Grass is Greener* [the other side of the hedge].

Neighbour(s), *see also* Ask of my fire (Rather) than borrow of n.; Ask your n. if you shall live in peace; Better learn by n.'s skaith; Danger next n. to security; God sees and bears, n. finds fault; Good n. good morrow; Hale pow that calls n. nitty know; Iron shoes, (He should ware) that bides his n. dead; Lawyer (Good), evil n.; Live without our friends but not our n.; Lost (It is not) that a friend (n.) gets; Love your n., yet pull not down hedge; Mother says (It is not as), but as n. say; Near n. better than far-dwelling kinsman; Trencher friends seldom good n.; Way is an ill n.; Well with him beloved of n.

Neither here nor there.   (H 438)

1543 G. COUSIN *Office of Servants* B7 Better . . .
to do a thing neither here, ne there, then that
through idlenes they shuld intend to worse
occupations. 1581 A. MANUTIUS *Phrases Linguae
Latinae* 62 It is neither here nor there, or I
passe not what you thinke of me. 1594 NASHE
Unfort. Trav. ii. 210. 1600–1 SHAKES. *M.W.W.*
I. iv. 96 But notwithstanding that, I know Anne's
mind, that's neither here nor there. 1604 *Id.
O.* IV. iii. 59 Doth that bode weeping?—'Tis
neither here nor there. 1722 STEELE *Consc. Lov.*
IV. 1 Merm. 349. 1762 STERNE *T. Shandy* VI. vi
But this is neither here nor there: why do I
mention it? 1815 SCOTT *Guy Man.* ch. 4 And
I had a wee bit of law business besides, but that's
neither here nor there.

Neither (a, in, my, of his, to), see *under significant
words following.*

Nemo repente fuit turpissimus, see No man ever
became thoroughly bad all at once.

Neptune, see Bacchus has drowned more than N.

**Nertown was a market town, when
Taunton was a furzy down.**

1851 *N. & Q.* 1st Ser. IV. 149 . . . This Nertown
is a village adjoining Taunton. . . . It's name is
. . . a corruption of . . . Nethertown.

Nessus, see Shirt of N.

Nest(s), see Bird loves her n.; Bird of the same n.
(brood, egg, feather); Bird such n. (egg), (Such);
Birds of this year in last year's n. (No); Destroy
the n., birds fly away; Feather one's n.; God
builds the n. of blind bird; Hawk of right n.; Ill
bird that bewrays own n.; Lapwing cries
farthest from n.; Little bird content with little
n.; Mare's n., (To find a); Wasp's (hornet's) n.,
(To stir a).

Net of the sleeper catches fish, The.
                                              (N 128)

[Gk. Εὕδοντι κύρτος αἱρεῖ. ERASM. *Ad. Dormientis
rete trahit.*] 1549 ERASM. tr. Chaloner *Folly*
P4ᵛ [of Timotheus] Slepe he neuer sa fast, his
nette catcheth for hym. *c.* 1594 BACON *Promus*
no. 515 Dormientis rete trahit. 1683 WHITE-
KENNETT tr. *Erasm. Pr. of Folly* (8th ed.) 135
Thus Timotheus, the Athenian commander, in
all his expeditions was a mirror of good luck,
because he was a little underwitted; from him
was occasioned the proverb, *The net fills though
the fisherman sleeps.* 1853 TRENCH V. 119 The
following [is] often quoted or alluded to by
Greek and Latin authors: *The net of the sleeping
(fisherman) takes.*

Net (trap), To be taken in one's own.
                                              (F 626)

1481 CAXTON *Reynard* ed. Arber 86 See how the
horse . . . was taken in his owne nette. 1530
Supper of the Lord Tyndale P.S. 230 This old
holy upholder . . . is brought euen to be taken
in his own trap. 1550 CRANMER *Def. of Doct.*

of Sacrament 69 Thou art taken with thyne
owne nette. 1551 *Id. Ans. to Gardiner*
57 Let the reader now iudg, whether you bee
caughte in youre owne snare or no. 1564 Jan.
WM. CECIL cited C. Read *Mr. Sec. Cecil* 287
God amend them that, meaning to make traps
of malice, are for the most part trapped themselves. 1576 PETTIE i. 125 She may be taken in
the net which she layeth to entangle other. 1581
GUAZZO i. 39 You shall bee then taken in your
owne net.

Net(s), see also Cast your n. where no fish (Vain
to); Dance in a n.; Fish is caught (When) n. is
laid aside; Fish that comes to n. (All is); Fishing
before n., (Ill); Fox for mate, (Who has) has need
of n.; In vain the n. is spread; Rough n. not best
catcher of birds; Women are the devil's n.

**Netherlands are the cockpit of Christen-
dom, The.**

1612 T. ADAMS *The Gallant's Burden* (1616 ed. 19)
Behold France made a Cocke-pitte for Massacres
for the vnciuill ciuill Warres thereof: Thinke
of the vnquiet bread long eaten in the Low-
Countries. 1642 HOWELL *For. Trav.* xiii. Arb.
60 For the *Netherlands* have been for many
yeares, . . . the very Cockpit of Christendome,
the Schoole of Armes, and Rendezvous of all
adventurous Spirits.

Nettle(s), see Drink n. in March; Handles a n.
tenderly (He that); In dock out n.; Myrtle
standing among n.; Pissed on a n.; Stung by a n.
(Better to be).

**Neust (Newst) of a neustness (newst-
ness).**

1813 RAY 274 . . . *i.e.* Almost the same. An
expression very current in Berkshire, about
Binfield.

**Never a Granville[1] wanted loyalty, a
Godolphin wit, or a Trelawny courage.**

1869 HAZLITT 290 *Cornw.* [1 Sir Rich. Grenville,
d. Azores, 1591; and Sir Bevil Grenville, *d.*
Lansdowne, 1643, belonged to this family.]

**Never a whit as never the better, As
good.**   (W 314)

1546 HEYWOOD II. xi. L4ᵛ. 1599 BRETON *Anger
& Patience* Wks. Gros. II. 60. 1652 FULLER *Com.
on Christ's Temp.* in *Sel. Serm.* (1891) II. 73
. . . and in effect it was never shown which was
so soon removed. 1732 FULLER no. 687.

**Never answer a question until it is
asked.**

1492 *Dialogue of Salomon & Marcolphus* ed.
Duff 11 He that answeryth afore he is de-
maunded shewyth hym selfe a fole. 1902–4
LEAN IV. 56.

**Never ate flesh, He that | thinks a
pudding a dainty.**

1721 KELLY 126 . . . A Man not us'd to what is
good, thinks much of what is indifferent.

Never be angry at, Two things a man should | ; what he can help, and what he cannot help.

1721 KELLY 322.   **1732** FULLER no. 5335.

Never be ashamed to eat your meat.
(M 830)

1639 CLARKE 269.   **1670** RAY 57 . . . *Apud mensam verecundari neminem decet. Erasmus* takes notice, that this Proverb is handed down to us from the Ancients. . . . Yet some there are who out of a rustick shamefacedness or over-mannerliness are very troublesome at table, expecting to be . . . often invited to eat, and refusing what you offer them.

Never be weary of well doing.   (w 268)

[GALAT. vi. 9 Let us not be weary in well-doing.]   **1609** HARWARD 127ᵛ (You are soone weary of).   **1616** DRAXE no. 356 Neuer wearie of that which is good.   **1670** RAY 154.   **1771** J. WESLEY *Lett.* V. 120.

Never bite, unless you make your teeth meet.

1721 KELLY 258 . . . This . . . savour[s] too much of Malice and Revenge. . . . The more noble Way is to forget and to forgive.

Never but once at a wedding (coronation).   (w 230)

[a. **1600**]**1611** *Tarlton's Jests* in *Shakes. Jest-Bks.* ii. 235 Did you see the like before?—Never but once, in London.   a. **1640** J. DAY *Pereg.* ed. Bullen, xvi. 70 But being a scoller, and a poore one to, they had noe vse for him except it were once in a coronation to make a speech for the entertainment of a prince.   **1678** RAY 263. Once at a Coronation. *Ibid.* 346 I never see't but once and that was at a wedding.   **1738** SWIFT Dial. I. E.L. 270.

Never catch at a falling knife or a falling friend.

1864 J. H. FRISWELL *Gentle Life* 79 The Scotch . . . have a like proverb. . . .

Never cheapen unless you mean to buy.

1563 T. NEWBERY *Dives Pragmaticus* st. 22 Fyrst cheape, and then bye.   **1578** *Courtly Controv.* F1 Suttle marchants . . . euer dispraise the wares they determine to buy, to the ende they may bargaine at their owne price.   **1659** TORRIANO no. 153 Who findes fault means to buy. **1902–4** LEAN IV. 56.

Never climbed never fell, He that.
(C 412)

1546 HEYWOOD I. xii. E4ᵛ.   **1611** DAVIES *Prov.* no. 373.   **1659** HOWELL *Eng. Prov.* 15a.   **1719** DE ALVARADO 135 (mounted).

Never do evil that good may come of it.
(E 203)

1578 WHETSTONE *Promos and Cassandra* A4 Doyng good, that euill might come thereof.

1582 *Id. Heptameron* Ii Men doo euill . . . that good may come of it, and it is allowed. And men doo good . . . that euill may come of it, and it is forbidden.   **1583** G. BABINGTON *Exposn. of the Commandments* 263 To doe euill that good may come of it, wee may not.   **1596** SHAKES. *Rich. II* II. iii. 145 To find out right with wrong—it may not be.   **1607** DEKKER *Whore Bab.* III. ii. 147 And this I find—Quod non sunt facienda mala, vt veniant bona. For good; (how great soeuer) must be don, No ill how small soeuer.

Never do things by halves.

1753 HANWAY *Trav.* (1762) II. xiv. i. 343 Nadir, who did nothing by halves, was determined to pull off the mask.   **1883** C. READE *Peril Secr.* ch. 8 'Oh, never do things by halves', said the ready girl.

Never dog barked against the crucifix but he ran mad.

1642 FULLER *H. & P. State* V. vi. (1841) 355 *He scoffs . . . at sacred things.*—This . . . ulcers men's hearts with profaneness. The Popish proverb, well understood, hath a truth in it: . . .

Never drank was never athirst, He that.
(D 607)

1611 COTGRAVE S.V. Soif Hee's not athirst that water drinkes not.   **1659** HOWELL *Eng. Prov.* 13b.

Never draw your dirk when a dunt[1] will do.

1832 HENDERSON 51. [[1] blow.]

Never go to the devil and a dishclout in your hand.

1721 KELLY 264 . . . If you will be a Knave, be not in a Trifle, but in something of Value.

Never good that mind their belly so much.   (B 302)

1678 RAY 347. *Somerset.*

Never is a long day (term).

c. **1386** CHAUCER *Canon's Yeoman's T.* l. 1411 Nevere to thryve were to long a date.   **1721** KELLY 260 (Term) . . . Spoken to them that say they will never get such a Thing effected.   **1884** J. PAYN *Canon's Ward* ch. 25 I will never, never marry again.' 'Never is a long day . . .', said Jeanette cheerfully.   **1887** BLACKMORE *Springhaven* ch. 17 She never could pay her rent. But 'never is a long time,' . . . and . . . she stood clear of all debt now.

Never kiss a man's wife, nor wipe his knife, for he will be likely to do both after you.   (M 492)

1621 ROBINSON 10 To kisse a mans Wife, or wipe his knife, is a thankless office: or, it is a thanklesse thing to feed another mans dogge. **1639** CLARKE 45 To kiss a man's wife, or wipe his knife, is a thankless office.   **1721** KELLY 263

Never long that comes at last, He (It) is.
(L 79)

1611 COTGRAVE s.v. Venir He that comes at the length stayed not too long. **1626** BRETON *Soothing* B2 (It is neuer long). **1639** CLARKE 295 (as 1626).

Never-mass, At.
(N 136)

[= never.] **1537** *Thersites* D4. **1618** BRETNOR *Almanac* Aug. At Nihilmas. **1639** CLARKE 229.

Never rode never fell, He that.
(R 117)

a. **1628** CARMICHAELL no. 762. **1641** FERGUSSON no. 655. **1721** KELLY 139.

Never say die.

[= never give in.] **1837** DICKENS *Pickwick* ch. 2 Never say die—down upon your luck. **1838** *Wilson's Tales of Borders* IV. 142 Never say 'die', while there's a shot[1] in the locker, Bill; we'll weather many a Friday's sailing yet. **1848** A. SMITH *Christ. Tadpole* I Never say die, mother: that's the line of business. **1926** 21 May D. H. LAWRENCE *Lett.* ii. 915. [[1] money.]

Never sigh, but send.
(S 436)

1678 RAY 348. *Ibid.* 81 Sigh not, but send, He'll come if he be unhang'd. **1721** KELLY 89 Do not sigh for him, but send for him; if he be unhang'd he'll come. Spoken when a young Maid sighs, alledging that it is for a Sweetheart. **1738** SWIFT Dial. I. E.L. 271 Come, miss, never sigh, but send for him.

Never take a stone (forehammer) to break an egg, when you can do it with the back of your knife.

1721 KELLY 266. **1737** RAMSAY III. 191 Ne'er tak a forehammer to break an egg when ye can do it wi' a pen knife.

Never take the tawse[1] when a word will do the turn.

1721 KELLY 266 . . . Severity ought never to be used where fair Means will prevail. [[1] a leather strap with a fringed end, used instead of a rod.]

Never the nearer, *see* Early up.

Never too late to do well.
(D 403–4)

c. **1577** J. NORTHBROOKE *Treatise agst. Dicing* 78 Nunquam serum est, quod verum est, that is, neuer to late done, which is truly done. **1590** GREENE *Never Too Late* Gros. viii. 6 Numquam sera est ad bonos mores via. **1664** CODRINGTON 207 Never too late to be good.

Never too late to mend.
(M 875)

1590 GREENE *Never too Late* [Title]. [c. **1590**] **1594** LODGE & GREENE *Looking-Glass* V. v. 2220 Amends may neuer come too late. *c.* **1645** HOWELL *Lett.* 9 Nov. (1903) III. 139 We have both of us our failings that way: . . . but it is never over late to mend. **1837** T. HOOK *Jack Brag* ch. I Ah, Johnny, . . . you never will mend till it is too late. **1883** J. PAYN *Thicker than W.* ch. 10.

Never too late to repent.
(R 80)

c. **1230** *Ancrene Wisse* ed. Tolkien E.E.T.S. no. 249, 173 Nunquam sera penitentia si tamen uera. Nis neauer to leete penitence þat is goðliche imaket. *a.* **1591** HY. SMITH *Serm.* (1866) I. 218 It is an old saying, Repentance is never too late; but it is a true saying, Repentance is never too soon. **1670** RAY 112 . . . *Nunquam sera est, &c.*

Never too old (late) to learn.
(L 153)

[SENECA *Epist.* 76. 3. *Tamdiu discendum est quamdiu nescias: si proverbio credimus, 'quamdiu vivis'.* We must go on learning as long as we are ignorant; or, if we believe the proverb, as long as we live.] [c. **1515**] *c.* **1530** BARCLAY *Ecl.* II. l. 538 Coridon thou art not to olde for to lere. **1555** *Institution of a Gentleman* B7ᵛ No man can be to olde to learne. **1572** J. PARINCHEF *Extract of Examples* 72–3 Salinus Julianus, . . . was woont to say that he would be glad to learne, albeit one of his feete were in the graue . . . in these days we haue an other sentence common in most mens mouthes, I am now too olde to learne. **1596** SHAKES. *M.V.* III. II. 160 Happy in this, she is not yet so old But she may learn. **1607** MIDDLETON *Mich. Term* I. i. 325 There's no woman so old but she may learn. *a.* **1627** *Id. Mayor Queenb.* v. i. Merm. II. 383 A man is never too old to learn. **1670** RAY 112. **1712** ARBUTHNOT *John Bull* I. vii. A lawyer I was born, and a lawyer I will be; one is never too old to learn. **1721** KELLY 266 (late). L. *Nunquam sera est ad bonos mores via.*

Never was cat or dog drowned, that could but see the shore.
(C 159)

c. **1594** BACON *Promus* no. 590 A catt will never drowne if she sees the shore. **1642** TORRIANO 77. **1666** *Id. It. Prov.* 36 no. 28 Neither dog nor cat ever drown, so long as they can discern the shore. **1732** FULLER no. 3532.

Never was strumpet fair.
(S 942)

1640 HERBERT no. 431.

Never well (pleased) full nor fasting.
(W 265)

1598 J. HALL *Virgidemiarum* 4. 5. 30 Nor full nor fashing can the Carle take rest. **1603** *The Bachelor's Banquet* (F. P. Wilson) 77 You were never other . . . never pleased full nor fasting. **1608** J. HALL *Characters* 'Malcontent' He is neither well full nor fasting. **1617** J. SWETNAM *School of Defence* 13 Some are neuer well full nor fasting. **1621** ROBINSON 10. **1639** CLARKE 34 Neither pleased full nor fasting. **1670** RAY 176. **1692** L'ESTRANGE *Aesop's Fab.* ccxcv (1738) 307. **1721** KELLY 376 You are never pleas'd fow[1] or fasting. [[1] full.]

Never, *see also* Now or n.

Never, *see also under significant words following.*

New beer, new bread and green wood, will make a man's hair grow through his hood.

1750 W. ELLIS *Mod. Husbandm.* I. 91 For as the Verse or Proverb says—New Beer, new

Bread, and green Wood will make a Man's Hair grow through his Hood. [i.e. reduce him to poverty.]

New book appears, When a | read an old one.

1907 A. C. BENSON *From Coll. Window* (ed. 4) 297 What [Walter Pater] is condemning is the . . . encrusting of the mind with prejudices and habits, the tendency, as Charles Lamb wittily said, whenever a new book comes out, to read an old one.

New broom sweeps clean, A.   (B 682)

?*a.* **1542** *Unpub. Poems from the Blage MS.* ed. Muir XLVI. 19 What tho nu broum suype very clyne. **1546** HEYWOOD II. i. F3ᵛ Some thereto said, the greene new brome swepith cleene. **1579** LYLY *Euph.* i. 232 Ah well I wotte that a newe . . . broome sweepeth cleane. **1721** KELLY 15 (besom). . . . Spoken of new servants, who are commonly very diligent; and new officers, who are commonly very severe. **1867** FROUDE *Short Stud.* III. 77 New brooms sweep clean. Abbot Thomas, like most of his predecessors, began with attempts at reformation.

New church, old steeple: poor town and proud people.

1873 HARLAND & WILKINSON *Lancashire Leg.* 202 As to the prosperous and beautiful village of Bowness, on Windermere—. . . .

New College, *see* Thrive as N.C. students.

New is not true, What is | and what is true is not new.

[**1772** J. H. VOSS in *Vossischer Musenalmanach* 71 (King), Dein redseliges Buch lehrt mancherlei Neues und Wahres: Wäre das Wahre nur neu, ware das Neue nur wahr.] **1639** CLARKE 228 The newest things, not alwayes truest. **1779** JOHNSON in *Boswell Life* I found that generally what was new was false.   *a.* **1861** CLOUGH *Consider it again* 'Old things need not be therefore true', O brother men, nor yet the new!   **1880** J. NICHOL *Byron* 167 We are told . . . that he knew little of art or music. . . . It is true but not new. Hunt proceeds to say that Byron had no sentiment . . .; it is new enough, but is manifestly not true. **1928** *Times* 4 Feb. 8/2 Sir Arthur Evans has fallen a victim . . . to the old slogan 'What is new cannot be true'.

New lease of life, To take out a.

1809 SCOTT *Lett. to Ellis* 8 Jul. in LOCKHART *Life* ch. 19 My friend has since taken out a new lease of life, and . . . may . . . live as long as I shall;—such odious deceivers are these invalids. **1865** FROUDE *Short Stud.* (1890) I. 161 Had the popes and cardinals been wise they would have . . . cleared their teaching of its lumber, and taken our a new lease of life both for it and for themselves.

New lords, new laws.   (L 446)

1548 HALL *Chron., Hen. VI* 169 Tholde spoken proverbs, here toke place: New Lordes, new

lawes. **1613** J. STEVENS *Cinthia's Revenge* B2ᵛ From the succession of new Kings, new lawes Take their originall. **1721** KELLY 260 . . . L. *Novus Rex, nova lex.* **1824** SCOTT *St. Ronans* ch. 14 But new lords new laws—naething but fine and imprisonment, and the game no a feather the plentier.

New love drives out the old love, The.
(L 538)

c. **1380** CHAUCER *Troilus* Bk. 4, l. 414 The newe loue out chaceth ofte the olde.   *c.* **1558** WEDLOCK *Image of Idleness* B4ᵛ The common prouerbe, . . . that new loue dryueth away olde sorowes. **1562** A. BROOKE *Romeus and Juliet* (Munro) l. 208 So novel loue out of the mind the ancient love doth rive. **1706** STEVENS s.v. Amor (makes the Old be forgot).

New meat begets a new appetite.
(M 831)

1616 DRAXE no. 254 New meats prouoke the appetite. *Ibid.* no. 268 New meate bringeth a new appetite. **1670** RAY 18.

New nothing, A.   (N 253)

1578 W. FULWOOD *Enemy of Idleness* 250 I owe you a newe nothing to hange vppon your sleeue. **1678** RAY 342 A fine new nothing.

New prince, Of a | new bondage.
(P 590)

1592 DELAMOTHE 9.   **1651** HERBERT no. 1116.

New out of the mint.   (M 985)

1593 NASHE *Christ's Tears* ii. 15 Newe mynt my minde to the likenes of thy lowlines. **1594-5** SHAKES. *L.L.L.* I. i. 175 Armado is . . . a man of fire-new words, fashion's own knight. **1601** *Id. T.N.* III. ii. 19 You should then have accosted her; and with some excellent jests, fire-new from the mint, you should have bang'd the youth into dumbness. **1639** CLARKE s.v. *Novitas* 228. **1666** TORRIANO *Prov. Phr.* s.v. Zecca 239 To be Mint-new, viz. just newly coyn'd; the English say, Bran-new, or spick and span new.

New Testament, *see* Testament.

New (green) things are fair (gay).
(T 161)

c. **1380** CHAUCER *Leg. of Good Women* l. 1077 To som folk ofte newe thyng is sote.   *c.* **1386** *Id. Squire's T.* l. 610 Men loven of propre kynde newefangelnesse.   *c.* **1412** LYDGATE *Troy Bk.* IV. 572 Here men may se how it is natural then to delite in þing[e] þat is newe. **1546** HEYWOOD II. i. F3ᵛ All thyng is gay that is greene. **1592** DELAMOTHE 9.   **1611** DAVIES *Prov.* no. 321 All greene things are gay. **1651** HERBERT no. 1117.

New tout[1] in an old horn, A.   (T 449)

a. **1628** CARMICHAELL no. 143.   **1678** RAY 361 A new sound in an old horn. **1721** KELLY 28 An old tout in a new Horn. Spoken when we hear (perhaps in other words) what we have heard before. **1822** SCOTT *Nigel* ch. 27 There are . . . Puritans of papistical principles—it is just a new tout on an old horn. [¹ blast.]

New, *see also* Everything n. is fine; Nothing n. under sun.

Newcastle burr in his throat, He has the.

1760 FOOTE *Minor* (1781) Introd. 9 An Aunt just come from the North, with the true New Castle bur in her throat. **1787** GROSE (*Northumb.*) 212 . . . The people of Newcastle, Morpeth, and their environs, have a peculiar guttural pronunciation.

Newcastle, *see also* Canny N.; Carry coals to N.; Scot, a rat, and a N. grindstone.

Newcome, *see* Johnny N.

Newer is truer.   (N 137)

1546 HEYWOOD II. iv. G3ᵛ Thy ryme (quoth he) is muche elder then myne. But myne beyng newer is trewer then thyne.

Newgate, *see* Low ebb at N. (He that is at).

News are like fish.   (N 149)

1616 BRETON 2 *Cross. Prov.* A4ᵛ . . . Not so, for then they would stinke when they are stale.

News, you must go to the oven or the mill, If you will learn.   (N 143)

1589 *Temporis Filia Veritas* A2 Men say all newes are to be heard of at a Smythe Forge, a Barbers shoppe, or at a mill. **1611** COTGRAVE s.v. Moulin An Ouen, and Mill are nurseries of newes. **1659** HOWELL *Fr. Prov.* 11.

News, *see also* Brings good n. (He that) knocks hard; Go into country to hear n.; Good n. may be told any time, ill in morning; Ill (Ill n.) comes on back of worse; Ill n. is often true; Jock's n.; Lame post brings truest n.; No n. is good n.; Scant of news that told his father was hanged; Stay a little and n. will find you; Tell me n.

Next, *see* Do the n. thing; Thank you for the n. (I will).

Next to (a, no), *see under significant words following.*

Niagara, *see* Shoot N.

Nibbled to death by ducks, One had as good be.   (D 156)

1678 RAY 240.

Nice as a nun's hen, As.   (N 353)

15th cent. *Reliq. Antiq.* (1841) i. 248 Some [women] be nyse as a nonne hen. **1546** HEYWOOD II. i. F3 She toke thentertainment of the yong men All in dalyance, as nyce as ·a nun's hen. **1553** T. WILSON *Rhet.* (1580) 223 I knewe a Prieste that was as nice as a Nonnes Henne, when he would saie Masse.

Nice eaters seldom meet with a good dinner.

1732 FULLER no. 3540.

Nice wife, A | and a back door oft do (will soon) make a rich man poor.
                                             (W 370)

c. **1450** *Prov. of Good Counsel* (Furnivall) l. 33 A nyse wyfe & A backe dore, Makyth oftyn tymus A ryche man pore. **1551** W. BALDWIN *Beware the Cat* (1584) E7ᵛ A wanton wife and a back-door wil soon make a rich man poor. **1639** CLARKE 218. **1640** HERBERT no. 474 The back-doore robs the house. **1721** KELLY 45 . . . The Wife will spend, and the Servants purloyn.

Nice, *see also* More n. than wise.

Nichils in nine pokes.   (N 159)

[*Nichil* (med. L.) or *Nihil* (class. L.) = nothing is 'a word which the Sheriff answers, that is opposed concerning Debts illeviable, and that are nothing worth, by reason of the insufficiency of the Parties from whom they are due'. See **1684** MANLEY *Cowell's Interpreter.*] **1530** PALSGRAVE 850 Nyfels in a bagge. **1584** R. SCOT *Discov. Witches* (1886) XVI. vi. 406 The witches . . . that . . . give their soules to the divell . . . and their bodies to the hangman to be trussed on the gallows, for nichels in a bag. **1670** RAY 188 . . . *Chesh. i.e.* Nothing at all. **1678** *Id.* 261 *Nichils* in nine pokes *or* nooks. **1917** BRIDGE 97 Nichills in nine holes. Nothing at all. Absolutely empty. . . . There are two variants, the first of which is fairly common in Cheshire:— Nichills in nine pokes (sacks or bags). Nichills in nine nooks.

Nicholas, *see* Good night, landlady, (N.).

Nick (of time), In the.   (N 160)

1565 GOLDING *Metam.* (ed. Rouse) Bk. III. 314, 69 And for to fierce hir ire, Another thing cleane overthwart there commeth in the nicke. **1569** J. PHILLIP *Patient Grissell* l. 915 These yonkers . . . are come in the nicke. **1577** HANMER *Anc. Eccl. Hist.* VI. vi. The Romane navie . . . arrived at the very pinch, or as commonly we say, in the nicke. **1594** LYLY *Mother B.* III. ii. 18 My deuice was, . . . that he should come in the nicke when she was singing. **1604** SHAKES. *O.* V. ii. 320 Iago in the nick came in and satisfied him. [Ff. 'interim'.] **1642** *Declar. Lords & Comm. to Gen. Assembly Ch. Scot.* 12 In this nick of time. **1681** DRYDEN *Span. Friar* I. i. A seasonable girl, just in the nick now. *a.* **1707** S. PATRICK *Autobiogr.* (1839) 179 I look upon it as a singular providence of God, that Dr. Harris . . . should come in at that nick of time. **1775** SHERIDAN *Rivals* IV. iii. To be sure I'm just come in the nick. **1877** BESANT & RICE *Son of Vulcan* Prol. ii. This grand-uncle had 'gone over to the majority' in the very nick of time.

Nick, *see* Dick's (N.'s) hatband; Fond of barter that niffers with Old N.; Old N.

Nicks (Wrinkles) in her horn, She has a good many.

[JUVENAL *Sat.* 6. 199 *Facies tua computat annos.* Your face reckons your years.] **1721** KELLY 359 We may know your Age by the Wrinkles of your Horn. Spoken to old Maids when they pretend to be young. **1910** P. W. JOYCE *Eng. as We Speak* 113 'She has a good many nicks in her horn': said of a girl who is becoming an old maid. A cow is said to have a nick in her horn for every year.

Nigger in the wood-pile (fence), A.

[= a private reason or motive for action, which is not divulged. *Cf.* **1636** F. LENTON *Lentons Leisures Described* C2 Obseruing how like so many Kites they lay wayt for the Chicken in the Wood-pile.] **1852** cited in *Kans. Hist. Quart.* xi (1942), 235 No 'nigger in the wood pile here'...; white men are at the bottom of this speculation. **1862** *Congress. Globe* 3 June 2527/1 [These gentlemen] spoke two whole hours . . . in showing—to borrow an elegant phrase, the paternity of which belongs, I think, to their side of the House—that there was 'a nigger in the wood-pile'. **1888** BRET HARTE *Phyllis of Sierras* I. iii. 90 There's another Englishman coming up from 'Frisco . . . he'll guess there's a nigger in the fence somewhere. **1911** WOODROW WILSON in *Outlook* 11 Aug. 944 If you go through the schedules you will find some nigger in every wood pile. **1919** SIR W. OSLER in CUSHING *Life* 1946 ed. 1362 The influenza bacillus had just been isolated from his sputum and he was pleased about this. 'I knew', said he, 'there was a nigger in the wood-pile'.

Nigh, *see* Almost and very n. saves many a lie; Shoot n. the prick.

Night, As secret (silent) as the. (N 165)

1602 [T. HEYWOOD] *How a Man May Choose* G3 She blusht and said that long tongu'd men would tell, I seem'd to be as secret as the night, and said, on sooth I would put out the light. [**1603**] **1607** T. HEYWOOD *Woman Killed with Kindness* sc. vi. l. 147 I will be secret, lady, close as night. **1611** JONSON *Cat.* III. l. 432 Be secret as the night. **1648** J. S. *Wits Labyrinth* 13.

Night comes, The | when no man can work.

1526 TYNDALE *John* ix. 4 The nyght commeth, when no man can worke. **1791** BOSWELL *Johnson* xxi. (1847) 192 I observed upon the dial-plate of his watch a short Greek inscription . . . Νὺξ γὰρ ἔρχεται, . . . 'the night cometh when no man can work'. **1902** FAIRBAIRN *Philos. Chrn. Rel.* (ed. 2) I. iv. 143 Men thought of themselves more worthily and of their deeds more truly when they saw that a night came when no man could work.

Night is the mother of counsel. (N 174)

[MENANDER *Monosticha* 150 Ἐν νυκτὶ βουλὴ τοῖς σοφοῖσι γίγνεται. By night counsel comes to the wise. ERASM. *Ad. In nocte consilium.*] **1573** SANFORD 106ᵛ (of thoughts). **1590** SPENSER *F.Q.* I. i. 291 Untroubled night, they say, gives

counsell best. **1608** D. BARRY *Ram Alley* Hazl.-Dods. x. 336 Night is the mother of wit. **1640** HERBERT no. 746 (of Councels). **1660** DRYDEN *Astraea Red.* 93 Well might the ancient poets then confer On Night the honoured name of Counseller.

Night (day) of it, To make a. (N 178)

1580 S. BIRD *Friendly Communication* 50 When ther is a meting pitched, wher they make a daie of it (as they saie) and sit by it, that is accounted a gamesters feast. **1602** *Narcissus* l. 88 Youle make as good a night of it heere as if you had beene at all the houses in the towne. **1607** DEKKER & WEBSTER *Northw. Ho.* v. G2 Weel make a night of it. **1626** JONSON *Staple of News* II. v. 129 (day). **1693** CONGREVE *Old Bachelor* (ed. Summers) iv. 204 I'm resolv'd to make a Night on't. **1843** DICKENS *Martin Chuzzlewit* ch. 6 (heavy night).

Night, To a great | a great lanthorn. (N 177)

1640 HERBERT no. 731.

Night, *see also* Barnaby bright: longest day and shortest n.; Blustering n., fair day; Cats alike grey in n.; Cover your head . . . by n. as much as you can; Day has eyes, n. ears; Done by n. appears by day; Every day comes n.; Growed by n. (This); Longest n. will have end; Lucy light . . . longest n.; Rich before n.; Runs in the n. stumbles; St. Thomas . . . longest n.; Sun has set, no n. followed.

Nightingale and the cuckoo sing both in one month, The. (N 181)

1626 BRETON *Soothing* A8. **1639** CLARKE 106.

Nightingale with a thorn against one's breast, To sit (sing) like a. (N 183)

c. **1510** B.M. MS. Royal Appen. 58 8ᵛ, printed in *Anglia* xii. 264 She syngyth in the thyke And under hur brest a prike To kepe her fro slepe. **1563** J. HALL *Poesie in Form of a Vision* A3 For as they fayne the thorne so sharpe dyd seme to touch hyr [Philomela's] breast. **1576** GASCOIGNE *Complaint of Philomene* ii. 179. *c.* **1587–92** KYD *Span. Trag.* l. 806 The gentle Nightingale . . . singing with a prickle at her breast. [*c.* 1592] **1596** *Edw. III* I. i. 109 Feruent desire . . . Is farre more thornie pricking than this blade; That with the nightingale, I shall be scard, As oft as I dispose my selfe to rest. *a.* **1593** GREENE *Friar Bacon* l. 1623. **1593–4** SHAKES. *Lucrece* l. 1135. **1599** *Id. Pass. Pilg.* 20, l. 7 Everything did banish moan, Save the nightingale alone. She poor bird as all forlorn, Lean'd her breast up-till a thorn. **1610** G. FLETCHER *Christ's Victory* Gros. 194 But leaning on a thorn her dainty chest, For feare soft sleepe should steale into her breast, Expresses in her song grief not to be expressed. **1630** T. ADAMS *Fire Content.* Wks. (1861), ii. 155 The godly must be fain to sit, like the nightingale, with a thorn against her breast.

Nightingale, *see also* Owl sings (When), n. hold her peace; Third of April comes . . . n.

Nightwork.   (N 184)

1594 PLAT *Jewel-House* 67 My purpose is onely to put some in minde of their grosse night-woorkes. **1598** SHAKES. *2 Hen. IV* III. ii. 194 Ha, 'twas a merry night. And is Jane Nightwork alive? [**1599**] **1600** JONSON *Every Man Out* O3ᵛ (v. viii. 30) I mar'le what peece of nightworke you haue in hand now. **1639** CLARKE s.v. Nox 227 Night-works. Clandestina scelera.

Nil admirari (Wonder at nothing).

[HORACE *Epist.* I. 6. I *Nil admirari, prope res est una, Numici, Solaque, quae possit facere et servare beatum.* To wonder at nothing is about the one and only thing, Numicius, which can make a man happy, and keep him so.] *a.* **1626** SIR JOHN DAVIES *Acrostic on Q. Elizabeth* Brave spirit, large heart, admiring naught. **1821** BYRON *Juan* v. 100 I ne'er could see the very Great happiness of the 'Nil Admirari'. **1855** TENNYSON *Maud* iv. 7 Not to admire or desire. **1881** DEAN PLUMPTRE *Ecclesiastes* v. 8 The words 'wonder not' tells us . . . who had been his teachers. In that counsel we have a distinct echo from one of the floating maxims of Greek pro-verbial wisdom, from the Μηδὲν θαυμάζειν ('wonder at nothing') of Pythagoras . . . which has become more widely known through the *Nil admirari* of Horace. **1883** J. PAYN *Thicker than W.* ch. 14 The Aglaia Club, which . . . was a somewhat 'used up' and *nil admirari* society.

Nile, *see* Dog at the N. (Like a); Throw him into N. . . . fish in his mouth.

Nimble (quick) as an eel (in a sandbag), As.   (E 59)

1594-5 SHAKES. *L.L.L.* I. ii. 28 An eel is quick. *c.* **1595** *Thomas of Woodstock* l. 295 As nimble as an Eele. **1601** JONSON *Cynthia's Revels* II. v. 23 They are all (as a youth would say) no better then a few trowts cast a-shore, or a dish of eeles in a sand-bagge. **1606** T. HEYWOOD 2 *If you Know not Me* l. 909 Knauery as quick as Eeles. **1732** FULLER no. 719 As nimble as an Eel in a Sand-Bag.

Nimble ninepence.

1851 MAYHEW *Lond. Labour* (1864) II. 263/1 'The nimble ninepence' being considered 'better than the slow shilling'. **1894** ASTLEY *50 Years Life* II. 68 Not a bad instance of the nimble ninepence.

Nimble, *see also* Comely (N.) as cow in cage; Quick and n.

Nimrod(s), *see* Three classes of clergy, N.

Nine tailors make a man.   (T 23)

c. **1600** *2 Tarlton's Jests* Sh. Soc. ed. 21 Two tailors goe to a man. **1607** DEKKER & WEBSTER *Northw. Ho* II They say three taylors go to the making vp of a man. **1615** CLEVELAND *Poems* 23 Like to nine Taylors, who if rightly spell'd, Into one man, are monosyllabled. **1663** BUTLER *Hudibras* I. ii. 22 Compos'd of many Ingredient Valors Just like the Manhood of nine Taylors. **1771** SMOLLETT *Humph. Clink.* 18 Jul. Wks. (1871) 539 Made her believe I was a tailor, and

that she was going to marry the ninth part of a man. **1819** SCOTT *Lett.* 26 July in LOCKHART *Life* They say it takes nine tailors to make a man—apparently, one is sufficient to ruin him. **1908** H. B. WALTERS in *Church Bells* 96 'Nine Tailors make a man', is *said* to be really 'nine tellers', 'tellers' being the strokes for male, female, or child, in a funeral knell or passing bell. 3 × 3 for male. [In Dorset these strokes are said to be called tailors: *Acad.* 11 Feb. 1899, 190/1.]

Nine words at once, To talk.   (W 826)

1509 BARCLAY *Ship of Fools* i. 96 Some speketh IX. wordes at thryse. **1528** TYNDALE *Obed. Chrn. Man* P.S. 302 If thy wife giue thee nine words for three, go to the Charterhouse, and buy of their silence. **1611** COTGRAVE s.v. Tost To speak thicke, or fast, or (as we say) nine words at once.

Nine, *see also* Parsley, . . . seen by devil n. times; Run to work as if n. men held you; Wonder, (N. days).

Nine-pence to the shilling.

1889 E. PEACOCK *Glos. Lincs.* E.S.D. 370 Nine-pence-to-the-shilling.—Below the average in common sense. 'How's Mr. . . . ? Thaay do saay as he's nobut nine-pence-to-th'-shilling.'—M. F., Scotton, 1876.

Ninepence, *see* Bring a noble to n.; Nimble n.

Nineteen bits of a bilberry, He will make.   (B 422)

1678 RAY 229 . . . Spoken of a covetous person.

Nineteen nay-says of a maiden are a half a grant.

1721 KELLY 268 . . . Spoken to encourage those who have had a Denial from their Mistress to attack them again.

Nineteen, *see also* Tongue runs n. to dozen.

Nip in the bud (blossom).   (B 702)

1565 OSORIUS *Pearl for a Prince* tr. R. Shacklock 31ᵛ Princes doe vnwisely which doo not nyp wickednes in the hed, So sone as it doth begin. **1590** T. LODGE *Rosalynde* ed. Greg 58 And now, through the decree of the unjust stars, to have all these good parts nipped in the blade. **1590-1** SHAKES. *2 Hen. VI* III. i. 89 Thus are my blossoms blasted in the bud. **1594-5** *Id. L.L.L.* V. ii. 789 If frosts and fasts, hard lodging and thin weeds Nip not the gaudy blossoms of your love. *c.* **1605** DEKKER *2 Hon. Whore* II. ii. 23 Now it [love] is but in the bud.—Well, say she's nipt. **1613** DALLINGTON *Aphorisms* 100 If they be not nipped in the bud. **1721** KELLY 211 . . . It is good to prevent, by wholesome Correction, the vicious Inclinations of Children. **1732** FULLER no. 3543. **1786** J. WESLEY *Wks.* xi. 336.

Nippence, nopence, half a groat wanting twopence.   (N 188)

1659 HOWELL *Eng. Prov.* 12a.

Nits will be lice. (N 191)

a. **1700** *New Dict. Cant. Crew* H7 Nitts will be Lice. **1791** I. DISRAELI *Curios. Lit.* (1858) III. 44 Oliver Cromwell's coarse but descriptive proverb conveys the contempt which he felt for some of his mean and troublesome coadjutors: 'Nits will be lice!'

'**No**', *see* Say 'No' till you are asked (Don't).

No better than she (they) should be. (B 335)

[= of doubtful moral character.] **1604** *Pasquils Jests* (1864) 35 A man whose wife was no better then she should be. **1606** J. DAY *Isle of Gulls* G3ᵛ Some of it is no better than it should be. **1611** COTGRAVE s.v. Putte. **1712** STEELE *Spect.* No. 503 Some say, 'A very fine lady'; others, 'I'll warrant you, she is no better than she should be.' **1882** J. C. MORRISON *Macaulay* 105 He goes up to the dignified dames ... and finishes by telling them roundly that in his opinion they are all no better than they should be.

No bishop, no king. (B 408)

1589? LYLY *Whip for Ape* iii. 420 Yes, he that now saith. Why should Bishops bee? Will next crie out, Why Kings? The Saints are free. **1604** JAMES I in FULLER *Ch. Hist.* (1655) x. i. (1868) III. 201 *His Majesty.*—I approve the calling and use of bishops in the church; and it is my aphorism, 'No bishop, no king'. **1641** 'SMECTYMNUUS' *Vind. Answ.* § 16, 208 King James of blessed memory said, *no Bishop no King*: it was not he, but others that added, *No Ceremony, no Bishop.*

No broth, no ball; no ball, no beef.

1853 MRS. GASKELL *Cranford* ch. 4 We used to keep strictly to my father's rule, 'No broth, no ball; no ball, no beef'; and always began dinner with broth. Then we had suet puddings, boiled in the broth with the beef; and then the meat itself. If we did not sup our broth, we had no ball.

No case: abuse the plaintiff's attorney.

1662 J. WILSON *Cheats* I. iv. Wks. (1874) 28 Then, if at any time you find you have the worst end of the staff, leave off your cause and fall upon the person of your adversary. **1890** *Times* 6 Dec. [Biog. notice] Mr. Huddleston ... attacked the police as severely as if his instructions had been similar to the time-honoured 'No case, abuse the opposing attorney'. **1913** *Times Lit. Sup.* 5 Sept. 365 All kinds of irrelevancies of the proverbial 'abuse-the-plaintiff's-attorney' type, are calmly brushed aside by such Judges as the Lords of Appeal in Ordinary.

No cross, no crown. (C 839)

1609 BRETNOR *Almanac* March Good days A crosse before a Crowne. **1621** QUARLES *Ester Med.* ix, The way to Blisse lyes not on beds of Downe, And he that had no Crosse, deserues no Crowne. **1669** W. PENN [title] No Cross no Crown; a Discourse shewing ... that the ... daily bearing of Christ's Cross, is the alone way to the rest and kingdom of God. **1910** ALEX. MACLAREN *Expos., Hebrews* xiii. 10, 15 Jesus Christ, and Jesus Christ's servants ... obey the same law, and that law is, no cross, no crown.

No devil so bad as a she-devil.

a. **1576** WHYTHORNE 75 (It iz an old saing emong vs that there iz).

No divinity is absent if Prudence is present.

[JUVENAL *Sat.* 10. 365 and 14. 315. *Nullum numen abest si sit prudentia.* Sandys, OVID *Met.* 11 (Comm.) Where wisdom, there the God; quoted by Chesterfield, Letter 28.] **1783** JOHNSON in *Boswell* lxxv. (1848) 717 Though the proverb *Nullum numen abest, si sit prudentia,* does not always prove true, we may be certain of the converse of it, *Nullum numen adest, si sit imprudentia.* *Note.* Mrs. Piozzi gives a more classical ... variation: *Nullum numen adest ni sit prudentia*—CROKER. **1837** LOCKHART *Life Scott* ch. 37 (1860) 333 Scott ... seldom failed to introduce some passing hint of caution—such as *Nullum numen abest si sit prudentia.* **1880** BLACKMORE *Mary Aner.* ch. 49 'If prudence be present, no divinity is absent', according to high authority; but the author of the proverb must have first excluded love from the list of divinities.

No fire, no smoke (without smoke). *Cf.* No smoke without some fire. (F 282)

1386 CHAUCER *Mel.* B² l. 2375 'It may nat be' seith he [Seneca] 'that, where greet fyr hath longe tyme endured, that ther ne dwellth som vapour of warmnesse.' **1546** HEYWOOD II. v. H2ᵛ There is no fyre without some smoke. **1580** LYLY *Euph. & his Eng.* ii. 100 No fire made of wood but hath smoake. **1641** WENTWORTH *Ld. Strafford Speech bef. Ho. of Lords,* 13 April Where hath this fire lain hid for so many hundred years, without smoke to discover it? **1659** HOWELL *Eng. Prov.* 15a (without smoak). **1869** TROLLOPE *He knew he was right* ch. 15 Mrs. MacHugh said that there was never fire without smoke.

No gates, no city. (G 43)

1662 FULLER *Worc.* 183 The great and ancient Gates of London Town (No Gates, no City) now are voted down, And down were cast.

'**No, I thank you**', *see* Would *No, I t. you* had never been made.

No Jews, no wooden shoes.

[*c.* **1754**] **1861** H. MAYHEW *Lond. Labour* II. 117 'No Jews! No wooden shoes!!' Some mobleader ... had in this distich cleverly blended the prejudice against the Jews with the easily excited but vague fears of a French invasion.

No longer foster,[1] no longer lemman[2] (friend). (F 714)

c. **1412** HOCCLEVE *De Regim. Princ.* (1860) 60 Ne lenger forster, ne lenger lemman. Love on luste groundede is not worth a leeke. **1546** HEYWOOD II. ix. 79 I saie to suche (saied she) no longer foster, No longer lemman. **1639** CLARKE 33 (freind). [[1] nourish, support. [2] lover, mistress.]

No longer pipe, no longer dance.
(P 346)

1620 SHELTON *Quix.* II. vii. ii. 233 It shall not be said, master, for me, 'No longer pipe no longer dance.' **1623** CAMDEN 274. **1641** Letter of EDMUND VERNEY, *Verney Memoirs* (1892) ii. 131. **1721** KELLY 257 ... A Reflection on those who have been advantaged by us heretofore, whose Kindness continues no longer than they are getting by us. **1796** EDGEWORTH *Par. Asst., Lit. Merchts.* ch. 3 (1903) 410 'He always dances well to whom fortune pipes.' 'Yes, no longer pipe, no longer dance', replied Francisco; and here they parted.

No man before his guide.
(B 666)

1561 T. HOBY *Courtier* ii. 173 Whan the Duke was passing over a very swift river, he said to the trompetter: Goo on. The trumpetter tourned him backe with his cappe in his hande and after a reverend maner, saide: It shalbe youres my lorde. **1595** COPLEY *Wits, Fits* v. 137 A Nobleman being to passe through a water, commaunded his Trumpetter to goe before, and sound the depth of it: Who to shew himselfe very mannerly, push'd this encharge, and push'd the Noble-man himself forward, saying. No (sir) not I, your L. shall pardon me. **1611** COTGRAVE s.v. Pont Ore waters deepe, and bridges weake or hollow, the man must lead the way, the maister follow. **1639** CLARKE 6.

No man better knows what good is than he who has endured evil.
(M 317)

1576 PETTIE i. 190 Trouble and adversity makes quiet and prosperity far more pleasant. **1592** DELAMOTHE 19 Good shall neuer be found to be good, Vnlesse it haue bene first proued by the euill. **1597** *Politeuphuia* 4 None Knoweth better how great is the losse of Hauen, then they that are iudged to lyue continually in Hel. **1616** DRAXE no. 643. **1659** TORRIANO no. 134 He knows not what good is who hath not tried what evil is. **1670** RAY 8.

No man can do two things at once. *Cf.* A man cannot be in two places at once; No man can sup and blow together.
(M 318)

1547 W. BALDWIN L8ᵛ Attempte not two thynges at ones, for the one will hynder the other. **1548** ELYOT s.v. Flo Simul flare et sorbere, a prouerbe signifiyng to dooe two contrary thynges together.

No man can flay a stone.
(S 895)

1640 HERBERT no. 764. **1670** RAY 9.

No man can make his own hap.
(M 320)

a. **1628** CARMICHAELL no. 1200. **1641** FERGUSSON no. 659. **1721** KELLY 267.

No man can play the fool so well as the wise man.
(M 321)

[HORACE *Odes* 4. 12. 27 *Misce stultitiam consiliis brevem; Dulce est desipere in loco.* And be for once unwise. While time allows, 'Tis sweet the fool to play.—Conington. *Don Quix.* II. iii. He must not be a fool that would well counterfeit to be so.] **1545** *Precepts of Cato* H2ᵛ Some tyme to playe the foole, is a poynt of wyt. **1581** GUAZZO i. 159 Gonella noteth ... That to playe the foole well, it behooveth a man first to be wise. **1592** DELAMOTHE 11 To play the foole well, is signe of wisedome. **1601** SHAKES. *T.N.* III. i. 57 This fellow's wise enough to play the fool, And to do that well craves a kind of wit. **1601** JONSON *Poetaster* v. 46 I haue read in a booke, that to play the foole wisely, is high wisdome. **1611** DAVIES Prov. no. 54 None plaies the foole well without wit. **1641** FERGUSSON no. 662. **1721** KELLY 267. **1732** FULLER no. 2849 It is a cunning Part to play the Fool well. **1860** PEACOCK *Gryll Grange* ch. 14 The fool he looked for was one which it takes a wise man to make—a Shakespearian fool.

No man can serve two masters.
(M 322)

[MATT. vi. 24.] *c.* **1330** WRIGHT *Pol. Songs* Camden Soc. 325 That no man may wel serve tweie lordes to queme. *a.* **1628** CARMICHAELL no. 889 (and please baith the pairties). **1642** D. ROGERS *Naaman* 166 You cannot have your will ... and Christ too; no man can serve two masters. **1853** TRENCH vi. 143 Our lord ... has said: 'No man can serve two masters' ... ; compare the Spanish proverb: *He who must serve two masters, must lie to one.* **1907** S. LEE *Gt. Eng. of 16th Cent.* 22 [Sir T. More] made ... a working reconciliation between the old religion and the new learning. ... There was inconsistency in the endeavours to serve two masters.

No man can sup and blow together.
(S 998)

1597 N. BRETON *Wits Trenchmour* Wks. Gros. II. *b* 11 Contraries cannot at one time be in one subiect: which we see otherwise doe fall out in a man, that warmes his hands and cooles his pottage, and all with one breath. **1641** FERGUSSON no. 646. **1721** KELLY 359.

No man cries stinking fish.
(M 325)

1656 L. PRICE *A Map of Merry Conceits* A4 You never heard a fish wife Cry stinking fish. **1660** JER. TAYLOR *Duct. Dubit.* (1671) 805 Does ever any man cry stinking fish to be sold? **1732** FULLER no. 3596. **1806** WOLCOT (P. Pindar) *Tristia* Wks. (1816) IV. 309 But no one, to be sure, cries 'Stinking fish'. **1912** *Spectator* 29 June, 1033 It is always foolish to cry 'stinking fish' or to lower one's prestige in the international market by appearing to confess to a weakness which does not exist.

No man dies of an ague, or without it.
(M 324)

1616 T. ADAMS *Divine Herbal* 55 But as Physicians say, no man dies of an ague, or without it: so seldome any soule dyes of pride, or without pride. **1706** STEVENS s.v. Quartana.

No man ever became thoroughly bad all at once.
(M 316)

[JUVENAL *Sat.* 2. 83 *Nemo repente fuit turpissimus.*] **1590** SIDNEY *Arcadia* I. xii. There is no man sodainely excellentlie good, or extremely evill.   **1601** JONSON *Cynth. Rev.* v. i. 12 No man is presently made bad with ill.   **1629** T. ADAMS *Serm.* (1861–2) I. 7 The violence and virulence of this venomous quality comes not at first.   *Nemo fit repente pessimus*—No man becomes worst at the first dash.   **1832** LYTTON *Eug. Aram.* v. iv. Mankind are not instantaneously corrupted.   **1850** *Id. Caxtons* III. vii. (1854) 52 'Done his duty, and reformed the unhappy wretch' ... *Nemo repentè turpissimus semper fuit* —No man is wholly bad all at once.   **1892** H. P. LIDDON *Serm. Wds. of Christ* 126 The old saying that no man becomes very bad all of a sudden— *nemo repente fuit turpissimus*—applies to the life of faith as well as of conduct.

No man fouls his hands in his own business.

1632 HERBERT *Priest to Temple* 275 The *Italian* says, *None fouls his hands in his own businesse*; and it is an honest, and just care, so it exceed not bounds, for every one to imploy himselfe to the advancement of his affairs.

No man has a lease of his life.   (M 327)

1377 LANGLAND *P. Pl.* B. x. 89 (Skeat) I. 292 For we haue no lettre of owre lyf · how longe it shal dure.   **1590–1** SHAKES. *2 Hen. VI* IV. x. 6 If I might have a lease of my life for a thousand years I could stay no longer.   *a.* **1600** *Id. Sonnet* 146 Why so large cost, having so short a lease, Dost thou vpon thy fading mansion spend? **1629** *Oxinden Letters* 1607–42 ed. D. Gardiner 46 No man has a lease of his life for tearm of yeares.   **1721** KELLY 266.   **1862** HISLOP 232 Nae man has a tack[1] o' his life. [[1] lease.]

No man has a worse friend than he brings from home.   (M 413)

1616 DRAXE no. 2162 (Where can a man haue a worse enemy).   **1623** CAMDEN 280 Where shall a man haue a worse friend, than hee brings from home.   **1678** RAY 351.   **1738** SWIFT Dial. I. E.L. 261 Well, I see there's no worse friend than one brings from home with one; and I am not the first man has carried a rod to whip himself. **1853** TRENCH vi. 146 This one ... telling of the enemy whom every one of us has the most to fear: *No man has a worse friend than he brings with him from home*; ... in striking agreement with Augustine's remarkable prayer, 'Deliver me from the evil man, from myself.'[1] [[1] *Libera me ab homine malo, a meipso*.]

No man holds you.   (M 328)

1594–8 SHAKES. *T.S.* I. i. 106 Your gifts are so good here's none will hold you.   **1595–6** R. CAREW *Exc. of Eng. Tongue* (*Eliz. Crit. Essays* ed. G. Smith ii. 292) When wee would be rid of one, wee vse to saye ... by circumlocution ... The doore is open for you, theres noe bodye holdes you.   **1631** JONSON *Staple News* III. iv. 75 Goe, as you came, here's no man holds you, There, There lies your way, you see the doore. **1738** SWIFT Dial. II. E.L. 316 Well, run on till you're weary, nobody holds you.

No man is a hero to his valet.   (M 517)

[Fr. ... *qu'il n'y avail point de héros pour les valets de chambres*. MADAME CORNUEL, 1605–94.]

1603 MONTAIGNE (Florio) III. ii. 33 Few men have beene admired of their familiars. No man hath beene a Prophet, not onely in his house, but in his owne country ... In my climate of Gascoigne they deeme it a jest to see mee in print.   **1685** COTTON *Montaigne* III. ii. Few men have been admired by their domestics.   **1759** 24 Nov. JOHNSON *Idler* no. 84 If it be true, which was said by a French prince, 'that no man was a hero to the servants of his chamber', it is equally true, that every man is yet less a hero to himself.   **1764** FOOTE *Patron* II (1774) 30 It has been said ... that no man is a hero to his valet de chambre; now I am afraid when you and I grow a little more intimate, ... you will be horribly disappointed in your high expectations.   **1818** BYRON *Beppo* xxxiii And to his very valet seemed a hero.   **1824** SIR J. PRIOR *Life of Burke* xvi. (Bohn) 490 No man, it has been said, is a hero to his valet-de-chambre; and ... few men perhaps however great in the estimation of the world, carry the same impression of greatness into the bosoms of their own families. **1841** CARLYLE *Heroes* v. (1896) 258 We ... deny altogether ... that no man is a Hero to his *valet-de-chambre*. Or if so, it is not the Hero's blame, but the Valet's.   **1910** *Times Wkly.* 21 Jan. Many men have been heroes to their valets, and most (except Pope and Poe) to their biographers.

No man is a match for a woman till he's married.

1854 SURTEES *Handley Cross* ch. 57 That no man is a match for a woman till he's married, is an axiom that most Benedicts will subscribe to.

No man is bound to criminate himself.

[A Law maxim. L. *Nemo tenetur seipsum accusare*.]   **1724** DEFOE *Behav. Servts.* 94 I hope your Worship will not be angry, ...; am I obliged to accuse myself?—Why no, you are not.   [**1868**] MONTAGUE WILLIAMS *Leaves of Life* ch. 18 (1893) 125 Mr. Baron Bramwell said ... that the witnesses might have refused to give evidence on the ground that, by so doing, they might incriminate themselves.

No man is content with his lot. *Cf.* Content with his own kevel.   (M 332)

[L. *Nemo suâ sorte contentus.*] No man is content with his lot.]   **1539** TAVERNER *Publius* A6 Noman is contented with his owne allotment and thynges.   **1576** *Susanna* 1. 721 Nemo sua sorte contentus ... not one in all this world, was with his chaunce content.   **1621** ROBINSON 19 There is no man content with his owne estate. **1639** CLARKE 73.

No man is his craft's master the first day.   (M 334)

1540 PALSGRAVE *Acolastus* 70 No man is borne a craftes man.   **1580** LYLY *Euph. & his Eng.* ii. 68 *Appelles* was no good Paynter the first day.   **1580** J. BARET *Alveary* V95 One daie is not sufficient to attaine to learning.   **1639** CLARKE 35.   **1640** HERBERT no. 654 None is borne Master.   **1678** RAY 120 ... *Nessuno nasce maestro*. Ital.

No man is wise at all times.   (M 335)

[PLINY *H. N.* 7. 40. 2 *Nemo mortalium omnibus horis sapit.* No one of mortals is wise at all times.] **1481** CAXTON *Reynard* Arb. 65 Ther is no man so wyse but he dooleth[1] other whyle. **1539** TAVERNER E5[v] Nemo mortalium omnibus horis sapit. No man in the worlde is wyse at all houres. **1586** G. WHETSTONE *Eng. Mirror* 217 The wisest of men wyll sometimes erre. **1604** J. MARSTON *Malcontent* V. ii. 177 Nemo omnibus horis sapit. No man can be honest at all howers. **1639** CLARKE 266. **1710** PALMER 55 No Man is always a Fool, but Every Man some times. **1766** GOLDSMITH *Vic. W.* ch. 10 19 I was tired of being always wise, and could not help gratifying their request, because I loved to see them happy. [[1] becomes stupid.]

No man knows when he shall die, although he knows he must die. *Cf.* **Nothing so certain as death.**   (N 311)

c. **1386** CHAUCER *Clerk's T.* l. 124 And al so certein as we knowe echoon That we shul deye, as uncerteyn we alle Been of that day whan deeth shal on us falle. *c.* **1450** *Provs. of Wisdom* (ed. Schleich) in Anglia 51. 224 We schal dye, we note, how sone. **1561** T. BECON *Sick Man's Salve* P.S. 92 Albeit nothing is more certain than death, yet is nothing more uncertain than the hour of death. **1590** GREENE *Never too Late* Wks. Gros. viii. 125 Wee haue nothing more certaine than to dye, nor nothing more vncertaine than the houre of death. **1591** ARIOSTO *Orl. Fur.* Harington XVIII. 84 Death certaine is to all the Prouerbe seath, Vncertaine is to all the houre of death. **1599** SHAKES. *J.C.* III. i. 99 That we shall die, we know; 'tis but the time And drawing days out, that men stand upon.

No man lives so poor as he was born.

[PUBL. SYR. *Nemo ita pauper vivit, quam pauper natus est.*] **1732** FULLER no. 3604.

No man makes haste to the market where there's nothing to be bought but blows.   (M 339)

1614 W. RALEIGH *Hist. of the World* Bk. 4, ch. 2, sect. 4, 148. **1670** RAY 119.

No man may poind[1] for unkindness. *Cf.* **Poind for debt.**   (M 340)

a. **1628** CARMICHAELL no. 1201. **1641** FERGUSSON no. 653. [[1] distrain.]

No man so good, but another may be as good as he.   (M 343)

1592 DELAMOTHE 17 There is no man though neuer so strong but there is a stronger. **1662** FULLER *Ches.* 173 Some will oppose to this narrow County-Proverb, an English one of greater latitude, viz. No man so good, but another may be as good as he.

No man so wise but he may be deceived.   (M 344)

c. **1200** LAYAMON *Brut* ed. Madden v. i. 32 Nis nawer man so wis mon that me ne mai beswiken.

1592 DELAMOTHE 17 (so craftie). **1616** BRETON *Crossing* A5.

No man, There is | though never so little, but sometimes he can hurt.   (M 389)

1592 DELAMOTHE 15. **1616** DRAXE no. 1257. It is a very small thing that can doe neither good nor hurt. **1651** HERBERT no 1119.

No man was ever made more healthful by a dangerous sickness, or came home better from a long voyage.

1617 MORYSON *Itin.* III. i. 5 (1908) III. 357 The wiser sort, . . . see many returne from forraine parts corrupted with vices proper to them, according to the Flemings Proverb: that no man was ever made more healthfull by a dangerous sicknesse, or came home better from a long voyage.

No man (woman) will another in the oven (kirn) seek, except that himself (herself) have been there before. (W 353)

1520 W. DE WORDE *Seven Wise Masters* 40 Yr fader soughte neuer his sone in y[e] ouen but yf he had bin therin hymselfe. **1530** PALSGRAVE 708a The good wyfe wolde neuer seke her doughter in the oven and she had nat ben there afore. **1546** HEYWOOD II. vii. I4[v] And as for yll places, thou sekest me in mo, And in woorse to, than I into any go. Wherby this prouerbe shewth the in by the weeke. . . . **1596** NASHE *Saffron W.* iii 129 Of the Good-wife . . . finding her daughter in the ouen, where she would neuer haue sought her, if she had not been there first her selfe. **1640** HERBERT no. 696 If the mother had not beene in the oven, shee had never sought her daughter there. **1641** FERGUSSON no. 664 Na man can seek his marrow[1] in the kirne,[2] sa weill as hee that hes been in it himself. [[1] partner. [2] harvest-home.]

No man's enemy but his own, He is.   (M 452)

1580 S. BIRD *A friendly communcation* H6[v] Alas (saie they) it is great pitie: he was no mans foe but his owne. **1591** ARIOSTO *Orl. Fur.* Harington VI. 33 To none an enemie but to my selfe. **1592** GREENE *A Quip for an upstart courtier* Wks. Gros. xi. 290 I think him an honest man if he would but liue within his compasse, and generally no mans foe but his own. **1616** T. ADAMS *Diseases of the Soul* 53 Prodigalitie . . . (saith the Prouerbe) is no mans foe else [but his owne]. **1639** CLARKE 21. **1749** FIELDING *Tom Jones* (1805) I. IV. v. Sophia . . . discerned that Tom . . . was nobody's enemy but his own. **1881** A. JESSOPP *Arcady* 183 Ben's life . . . has been singularly inoffensive. As the saying is, 'He has been no man's enemy but his own'.

No Man's Land.

1662 FULLER *Warwicks.* 121 There happened so grievous a Pestilence in London, that . . . the Dead might seem to Justle one another . . . Whereupon this bishop[1] . . . bought . . . Ground nigh Smithfield. It was called *No-Man's-Land*, . . . as designed and consecrated for the general sepulture of the deceased. **1719** DEFOE *Crusoe*

II. (Globe) 563 This was a kind of Border, that might be called *no Man's Land*, being a Part of . . . *Grand Tartary*. **1896** R. S. S. BADEN-POWELL *Downfall of Prempeh* 68 The Adansis . . . have been removed . . . and the district remains a No Man's Land, and practically a bush desert. **1928** *Times*, 10 Dec. 15/6 There are to-day . . . zones of what may be called, economically, No Man's Land. . . . They are too far from the market. **1929** 16 April 22/4 The narrator begins by losing him while on patrol, and then undergoes . . . dreadful experiences in 'No Man's Land'. . . . Before he can escape from his shell hole, the French launch a minor attack. [¹ Ralph de Stratford, *d.* 1354.]

No matter how but whether.   (M 759)

1639 CLARKE 216.

No mill, no meal.   (M 948)

[Gk. Ὁ φεύγων μύλον ἄλφιτα φεύγει. He who shuns the millstone shuns the meal. L. *Qui fugit molam farinam non invenit*. He who flies from the mill gets no meal.] **1639** CLARKE 163 No milne, no meale. **1732** FULLER no. 3613.

No mischief but a woman or a priest is at the bottom of it.   (M 1000–1)

[JUVENAL *Sat.* 6. 242 *Nulla fere causa est in qua non femina litem moverit*. There is scarcely any dispute but a woman has been at the bottom of it.] **1549** LATIMER *2nd Serm. bef. Edw. VI* P.S. 114 He called . . . one Abiather the hyghe prieste. For it is maruayle if any mischyefe be in hand, if a priest be not at some ende of it. **1575** LUTHER *Comm. on 'Galatians'* 26 That common prouerbe among the Germains: In Gods name beginneth all mischiefe. **1629** T. ADAMS *Medit. upon Creed* 1169 When he would peruert a whole family to superstition, hee teaches his Iesuite to begin with the woman. **1659** HOWELL *Eng. Prov.* 15a There is no mischief in the world done, But that a woman is alwayes one. **1670** RAY 50 There's not mischief in the world done, But a woman is always one. **1754** RICHARDSON *Grandison* Lett. 24 Such a plot must have a woman in it. **1830** SCOTT *Note K. in Ht. Midl.* The journal . . . proceeds thus: . . . No doubt the daughter and parson would endeavour to persuade him to decline troubling himself in the matter . . . No mischief but a woman or a priest in it—here both.

No money, no Swiss.   (M 1089)

1592 DELAMOTHE 43 No money no man. (Point d'argent, point de valet.) **1652** E. PEYTON *Secret Hist. of James I* (1811) ii. 428 As the proverb is, no money no Swiss: no money no obedience. **1670** RAY 143 No silver no servant. The *Suisses* have a Proverb among themselves, parallel to this. Point d'argent point de Suisse. No money no *Suisse*. The *Suisses* for money will serve neighbouring Princes in their wars. **1738** GAY *Fables* II. ix. 61 For these, like Swiss attend; No longer pay, no longer friend. **1840** MARRYAT *Olla Pod.* ch. 35 What a pity . . . that a nation so brave . . . should be . . . so *innately* mercenary. There never was a truer saying than 'Point d'argent, point de Suisse'.

No moon, no man.

1878 T. HARDY *Return of the Native*, Bk. 1, ch. 3 'No moon, no man'. 'Tis one of the truest sayings ever spit out. The boy never comes to anything that's born at new moon. **1878** DYER *Eng. Folk-Lore* 41 In Cornwall, when a child is born in the interval between an old moon and the first appearance of a new one, it is said that it will never live to reach the age of puberty. Hence the saying 'No moon, no man'.

No more of a cat but (than) her skin, You can have.   (M 1167)

1564 BULLEIN *Dial. agst. Fever* (1888) 9 In my fantasie it is happy to the Huntman when he haue nethyng of the Catte but the sillie skinne. [**1602**] **1637** T. HEYWOOD *Royal King* vi. 23. **1639** CLARKE 163. **1721** KELLY 371 . . . You can have no more of a Person, Or thing, than they can afford. **1738** SWIFT *Dial.* II. E.L. 315.

No more of a fox than the skin, You can have.   (M 1163)

[*c.* 1515] *c.* 1530 BARCLAY *Eclog.* ii. 1074. **1546** HEYWOOD II. ix. L2 Ye haue had of me all that I might make. And be a man neuer so greedy to wyn, He can haue no more of the foxe but the skyn. **1582** T. WATSON *Hecatompathia* lx Besides his Skinne, the Fox hath nought to pay. **1611** DAVIES *Prov.* no. 273. **1630** WESTCOTE *View of Devonsh.* 1845, xvii. I would not wish you to think to have more good of the fox than his skin.

No news is good news.   (N 152)

1616 JAMES I in *Losely MSS.* (Kempe) 403 No newis is better then evill newis. *c.* **1645** HOWELL *Lett.* II. xviii. I am of the Italians mind that said, *Nulla nuova, buona nuova*, no news' good news. **1850** SMEDLEY *Frank Fairlegh* ch. 10 Arguing . . . (on the 'no news-being good news system') that I should have heard again if anything had gone wrong, I dismissed the subject from my mind. **1864** J. PAYN *Lost Sir Massingb.* ch. 20.

No one is bound to do impossibilities.   (I 44)

1655 FULLER *Hist. Univ. Camb.* (1840) 236 Though divines, they were presumed to have so much of civil law, yea, of the law of nature, as to know, *Nemo tenetur ad impossibilia*, 'No Man is tied to impossibilities'.

No other meat, They that have | bread and butter are glad to eat.   (M 841)

1639 CLARKE 113. **1670** RAY 66.

No pains, no gains.   (P 94)

1577 J. GRANGE *Golden Aphroditis* M1 Who will the fruyte that haruest yeeldes must take the payne. **1577** BRETON *Wks. of a young wit* H4ᵛ They must take pain that look for any gayn. **1589** J. MELVILLE *Spiritual Propine* pref. sonnet None gets the gaine, bot he wha prooffe essayes. **1605–6** SHAKES. *M.* IV. i. 39 O! well done! I commend your pains, And every one shall share i' the gains. **1648** HERRICK *Hesper.* Wks. (O.U.P.) 248 *No Paines, No Gaines*. If little labour, little are our gaines: Mans fortunes . . . are according to his paines. **1721** KELLY 259 No Profit but¹ Pains. **1853** TRENCH V. 114 For the most part they courageously accept the law of labour, *No pains, no gains,* ... as the appointed law and condition of man's life. **1864** R. BROWNING *Death in Desert* 207 When pain ends, gain ends too. [¹ without.]

No paternoster, no penny.

[= no work, no pay.] **1707** HICKERINGILL *Priest-cr.* II. ii. 22 Once was—No Pater Noster, No Penny; now—No Sermons, not a Penny, not a farthing.

No penny, no pardon.   (P 198)

1531 TYNDALE *Expos. I John* P.S. 156 O Popishe forgiuenesse with whom it goeth after the comon prouerbe, no peny no pardon. *a.* **1628** CARMICHAELL no. 1187. **1641** FERGUSSON no. 663.

No penny, no paternoster.   (P 199)

[= priests insist on being paid as a condition of performing service.] **1528** TYNDALE *Obed. Chrn. Man* P.S. 245 After the common saying, 'No peny, no paternoster'. **1546** *Suppl. Commons* (1871) 87 Theyr couetouse is growne into this prouerbe, 'No peny, no pater noster'. **1621** BURTON *Anat. Mel.* I. II. iii. 15, 276. 'No penny ...', as the saying is. **1640** BASTWICK *Lord Bps.* vi. E iv b No penny, no Pater noster; they looke more to their tithes, then to their taske. **1648** HERRICK *Hesper., The Peter-penny* Wks. (O.U.P.) 251 Who at a dead lift, Can't send for a gift A Pig to the Priest for a Roster, Shall heare his Clarke say, ... *No pennie, no Pater Noster.*

No penny, no *placebo*.

c. **1548** BALE *K. Johan* 1930 Sed. No grote no pater noster, no penye no *placebo*.¹ [¹ Vespers in the Office for the Dead, from first word in first antiphon, *Placebo*, I shall be pleasing or acceptable; *Ps.* cxiv. 9 Vulg.]

No play where one greets¹ and another laughs, It is.   (P 398)

a. **1628** CARMICHAELL no. 891. **1641** FERGUSSON no. 506. **1721** KELLY 198 . . . Spoken when a Patrimony is unequally divided. [¹ weeps.]

No play without a fool (devil, woman), There is.   (P 393)

[*c.* **1587**] **1592** KYD *Span. Trag.* IV. i. 96 For whats a plaie without a woman in it? **1615** W. GODDARD *Nest of Wasps* B4ᵛ Without Divells, plaies are nothing worth. **1624** J. GEE *The Foot out of the Snare* 68 It was wont, when an Enterlude was to bee acted in a Countrey-Towne, the first question that an Hob-naile Spectator made, before hee would pay his penny to get in, was, *Whether there bee a Diuell and a foole in the play?* And if the Foole get vpon the Diuels backe, and beate him with his Cox-combe til he rore, the play is compleate. **1626** JONSON *The Staple of News* 1st Intermean 35 My husband . . . was wont to say, there was no play without a *Foole*, or a *Diuell* in it. **1639** CLARKE 149.

No priest, no mass.   (P 584)

1662 FULLER *Shropshire* 2 Plowden¹ being of the Romish perswasion some Setters² trepanned

him . . . to hear Masse. But afterwards Plowden understanding that the pretender to Officiate was no Priest, . . . 'Oh the case is altered', quoth Plowden: 'no Priest, no Mass'. **1732** FULLER no. 3618. [¹ 1518–85. ² decoys.]

No profit to honour, no honour to religion.   (P 599)

1640 HERBERT no. 759.

No purchase, no pay.

[*a.* **1700**] **1867** ADML. W. H. SMYTH *Sailor's Word-Bk.* 521 A buccaneering principle of hire, under the notion of plunder and sharing in prizes, was, *no purchase no pay.*

No receiver, no thief.   (R 53)

c. **1386** CHAUCER *Cook's T.* A l. 4415 Ther is no theef with-oute a louke¹ That helpeth him to wasten and to souke. **1546** HEYWOOD I. xii. F1 For this prouerbe preeues, Where be no receyuers, there be no theeues. **1629** T. ADAMS *Serm.* (1861–2) I. 187 The calumniator is a wretched thief, and robs man of the best thing he hath. . . . But if there were no receiver there would be no thief. **1639** CLARKE 233 The receiver makes the thief. **1641** FERGUSSON no. 800 There is na thief without a resetter. **1670** RAY 136. **1926** *Times* 22 Nov. 11/3 It had often been said in those Courts that if there were no receivers there would be no thieves. [¹ accomplice.]

No reply (plie¹) is best.   (P 407)

a. **1628** CARMICHAELL no. 1189 (play = plea). **1641** FERGUSSON no. 660 Na plie is best. **1721** KELLY 267 . . . Spoken by sedate and even temper'd Men, when abused by others. [¹ lawsuit, plea.]

No root, no fruit.

c. **1374** CHAUCER *Troilus* Bk. 4, l. 770 For which ful ofte a by-word here I seye, That 'rooteles moot grene soone deye'. **1640** J. DYKE *Worthy Commun.* 176 No roote no fruite.

No silver, no servant.   (S 456)

1616 DRAXE no. 1861. **1639** CLARKE 243. **1670** RAY 143.

No silver (gold) without his dross.

                                              (G 289. S 457)

1576 LAMBARDE *Peramb. of Kent* H3 Corne hath his chaffe, and metall his drosse. **1611** COTGRAVE s.v. Or No Gold without some drosse. **1616** DRAXE no. 680. **1631** *Celestina* tr. Mabbe T.T. 11 Glass hath it's lead; Gold it's drosse; Corne it's chaffe. **1639** CLARKE 80.

No smoke without some fire. *Cf.* No fire, no smoke.   (S 569)

c. **1375** BARBOUR *Bruce* E.E.T.S. IV. l. 123 And thair may no man fire sa covir, [Bot] low or reyk sall it discovir. *c.* **1440** LYDGATE *Wks.* E.E.T.S. I. 134 Wher no fyr maad is may no smoke aryse. **1579** LYLY *Euph.* i. 285 There can no greate smoke aryse, but there must be

some fire, no great reporte without great suspition. **1655** FULLER *Ch. Hist.* II. v. (1868) I. 232
Dunstan, by looking on his own furnace, might
learn thence, there was no smoke but some fire:
either he was dishonest or indiscreet, which gave
the ground-work to their general suspicion.
1869 TROLLOPE *He knew he was right* ch. 52 He
considered that . . . Emily . . . had behaved
badly. He . . . repeated . . . the old adage, that
there was no smoke without fire.

No song, no supper.   (S 1003*a*)

1611 BEAUM. & FL. *Kt. Burn. P.* II. i. No, Michael,
. . . let him stay at home and sing for his supper.
1894 STEVENSON & OSBORNE *Ebb-Tide* ch. 7 If
you're not there by the time named, there will
be no banquet; no song, no supper, Mr. Whish!

No sooner said than done.   (S 117)

[TER. *And.* 2.3.7 *Dictum factum*, Said [and]
done.] **1566** P. BEVERLEY *Ariodaute and Genevra*
ed. Prouty 98 So thought, so don. **1577** J.
FITJOHN *A Diamond most Precious* H2ᵛ So sayd,
and so done, is a thread well spone. **1592**
SHAKES. *T.S.* I. ii. 182 So said, so done, is well.
1608 R. ARMIN *Two Maids* I2ᵛ. **1671** J. BALTHARPE
Straights Voyage ed. Bromley 96 No sooner
said, but forthwith done. *a.* **1734** R. NORTH
Lives (Bohn ed. i. 393). **1762** 28 Dec. BOSWELL
London Journal. **1824** MOIR *Mansie W.* ch. 17
The lassie . . . cried out, 'Hide me . . . for
yonder comes my old father!' No sooner said
than done. **1888** 'ROLF BOLDREWOOD' *Robbery
under Arms* ch. 40.

No sooner up, but hand (head) in the ambry,[1] and nose in the cup.   (H 262)

1570 TUSSER H1 No soner Sunne vp But nose
in the cup. *Ibid.* Some slouens from sleping no
sooner be vp, but hand is in Aumberie, and nose
in the cup. **1639** CLARKE 136 (head). **1721**
KELLY 263 . . . *but her Head in the Ambry.*
Spoken of, or to Maidens, who have too early
a Stomach. [1 store-closet, or cupboard in a
pantry.]

No sport, no pie.   (S 777)

a. **1625** J. FLETCHER *Wom. Prize* I. iv. I'll devil
'em: by these ten bones I will: I'll bring it to
the old proverb, no sport no pie. **1678** RAY 205.

No tempest, good July, lest corn look ruely.   (T 90)

1580 TUSSER N4ᵛ Julies husbandrie. No tempest,
good Julie, Least corne lookes rulie. **1732**
FULLER no. 6208 (Lest corn come off bluely).

'No, thank you', has lost many a good butter-cake.

1873 HARLAND & WILKINSON *Lancashire Leg.*
201.

No way but one with him, There is.

                                            (W 148)

[i.e. He must die.] **1542** ERASM. tr. Udall *Apoph.*
268ᵛ Thinkyng to bee no waye but one, Caesar
opened who he was. **1545** *Precepts of Cato* 'Sage
Sayings' Thales D4ᵛ A thiefe beynge vpon the

galous and perceyuynge that there is no way
but one, and that ther is no other remedy but
that he must hange and swynge in an halter, if
he feare in this case, he doth none other but make
to him selfe a newe payne of galous . . . **1561**
T. BECON *Sick Man's Salve* P.S. 147 I perceiue
there is none other way with me but one, even
to depart from this life. [*c.* **1587**] **1590** MARLOWE
Tamb. V. ii. 138. [*c.* **1590**] **1598** *Famous Vict.
Hen. V* B4 There had bene no way but one with
vs, We should haue bene hangde. **1599** SHAKES.
Hen. V II. iii. 14 For after I saw him fumble with
the sheets, and play with flowers, and smile upon
his fingers' ends, I knew there was but one way.
1607 MIDDLETON *The Phoenix* I. vi. (Bullen i. 132).

No word but mum. *Cf.* Mum is the word.   (W 767)

1523 SKELTON *Garl. Laurel* l. 1118 Dyce i. 406
There was amonge them no worde then but
mum. **1525–9** *Godly Q. Hester* l. 481 I dare
say nothinge but mum. **1590–1** SHAKES. *2 Hen.
VI* I. ii. 89 Seal up your lips and give no words
but mum. **1597** *Id. Rich. III* III. vii. 3 The
citizens are mum, say not a word. **1611** L.
BARRY *Ram-Alley* iv. G3ᵛ No word but mum,
My warrant you shall have when time shall come.

No, No man, No more, *see also under significant
words following.*

Noah's Ark.

[A cloud-formation having some resemblance
to the outline of a ship's hull.] **1787** BEST
Angling (ed. 2) 145 Small black fragments of
clouds like smoke, flying underneath, which
some call messengers, another's, Noah's Ark.
1821 CLARE *Vill. Minstr.* II. 27 As oft from
'Noah's Ark' great floods descend. **1866**
BLACKMORE *Cradock Now.* ch. 31 Daubed with
lumps of vapour which mariners call 'Noah's
arks'.

Noah's dove.

[GEN. viii. 6–9 Noah . . . sent forth a dove . . . but
the dove found no rest for the sole of her foot,
and she returned unto him to the ark.] **1599**
SIR J. DAVIES *Nosce Teipsum* xxx. st. 26 When
the soule findes heere no true content, And like
Noah's Doue, can no sure footing take, She doth
returne from whence shee first was sent. **1853**
J. MONTGOMERY *For ever with the Lord* st. 5 Like
Noah's dove, I flit between Rough seas and
stormy skies.

Nobility, without ability, is like a pudding wanting suet.

1721 KELLY 259 . . . Both want the principal
Ingredient.

Nobility, *see also* Virtue is the only true n.

Noble housekeepers need no doors.

                                            (H 795)

1640 HERBERT no. 91.

Noble plant suits not with a stubborn ground, A.   (P 390)

1640 HERBERT no. 622. **1670** RAY 21 Noble
plants suit not a stubborn soil.

Noble, The more | the more humble.

(N 195)

1616 DRAXE no. 1504. 1639 CLARKE 212 The more humble the more honourable. 1670 RAY 19.

Noble, Jack, *see* Farewell, forty pence! J. N. is dead.

Noble (*adj.*), *see also* Serve a n. disposition . . . he will repay.

Noble(s), (*noun*), *see* Bring a n. to ninepence; Right, master, four n. a year's a crown a quarter; Yellow as the golden n.

Nobleness, *see* Virtue is the beauty (n.) of the mind.

Nobody's nails can reach the length of London.

1818 SCOTT *Ht. Midl.* ch. 4 When we had a king, and a chancellor, and parliament men o' our ain, we could aye peeble them wi' stanes when they werena gude bairns—But naebody's nails can reach the length o' Lunnon. 1896 A. CHEVIOT *Prov. Scotl.* 258 Naebody's nails can reach the length of Lunnon. . . . This saying arose after the Union of the English and Scottish Parliaments in 1707.

Nobody, *see* Caesar or n., (Either); Know not me, (If) know n.

Nod for a wise man, A | and a rod for a fool.

1678 RAY *Adag. Hebr.* 413. 1723 FULLER no. 337.

Nod from a lord, A | is a breakfast for a fool.

1732 FULLER no. 338. *a.* 1816 WOLCOT (P. Pindar) *Odes of Condol.* Wks. (1816) II. 338 As nods of lords are dinners for a *fool.*

Nod is as good as a wink to a blind horse, A.

1794 GODWIN *Caleb Williams* i. ch. 7 (1831 ed. 68). 1802 D. WORDSWORTH *Journal* (Knight) i. 129 A wink's as good as a nod with some folks. 1809 MALKIN *Gil Blas* II. ix. (Dent) I. 128 I shall say no more at present, a nod is as good as a wink. 1818 SCOTT *Ht. Midl.* ch. 16 'Ye understand my meaning?' 'Ay, . . . sir; a wink's as gude as a nod to a blind horse.' 1837–47 BARHAM *Ingol. Leg.* (1898) 488 'To a blind horse a Nod is as good as a Wink!' Which some learned Chap, . . . Perhaps would translate by the words '*Verbum Sap*!'

Nod(s), *see* Homer sometimes n.; Land of N.

Noddy, To play at.

(N 199)

1594 SHAKES. *T.G.V.* I. i. 107 Nod-ay? Why, that's noddy.—You mistook, sir. I say she did nod; and you ask me if she did nod; and I say, 'Ay'—And that set together is 'noddy'. 1600 DEKKER *Old Fort.* I. i. 59 All haile Signior tree, . . . ile sleepe vnder your leaues, . . . your backe and my browes must . . . haue a game or two at Noddie erre I wake againe. 1666 TORRIANO *Prov. Phr.* s.v. Muti 113 The English quibble in saying, To play at Noddy, which is meant either of the game at cards so call'd, or to set a sleep and nod ones head.

Noise is greater than the nuts, The.

(N 200)

1599 MINSHEU *Span. Gram.* 83, i. More afraid then hurt. 1651 HERBERT no. 1073.

Noise is so great, The | one cannot hear God thunder.

1659 HOWELL *Fr. Prov.* 16 Such a noise that one could not hear God thunder. 1853 TRENCH vi. 135.

Noise, *see also* Loves n. must buy pig.

Nolens volens.

[L. = willing or unwilling.] 1593 PEELE *Edw. I* sc. viii. 44 A little serves the friar's lust When *nolens volens* fast I must. 1665 SIR T. HERBERT *Trav.* (1677) 124 He would profer them a little money for what he liked, which if they refused, then *nolens volens* he would have it. 1815 SCOTT *Guy Man.* ch. 50 Well, *nolens volens* You must hold your tongue. 1837 HOOD *Ode to Rae Wilson* 455 Tugg'd him neck and crop Just *nolens volens* thro' the open shop.

Noli me tangere.

(N 202)

[L. *Noli me tangere*, 'touch me not', occurring in the Vulgate, *John* xx. 17.] *c.* 1380 GOWER *Mirour de l'Omme* l. 1518 EI pour cela l'en solt nommer Le mal Noli me tangere. ?*a.* 1300 LYDGATE *Pilgrimage of Life of Man* l. 1560 [Wrath *loq.*] My name callyd in ech place Ys thys, 'Noli me tangere'. *c.* 1475 *Mankind* in '*Lost Tudor Plays*' (1907) 23 He is a *noli-me-tangere.* 1634 W. WOOD *New Eng. Prosp.* (1865) 24 The Porcupine . . . stands upon his guard, and proclaims *Noli me tangere*, to man and beast. *a.* 1635 NAUNTON *Fragm. Reg.* Arb. 18 He was wont to say of them, that they were of the Tribe of Dan, and were *noli me tangeres*; implying, that they were not to be contested with. 1806 J. BERESFORD *Miseries Hum. Life* x. 'xxi. (ed. 5) I. 219 Every dish, as it is brought in, carrying a 'noli me tangere' on the face of it. [*Cf.* Fr. *Sainte nitouche.*]

Nolo episcopari.

[L. *Nolo episcopari*, 'I do not wish to be made a bishop'; now applied commonly to those who profess a reluctance for promotion which they do not feel.] 1678 DRYDEN *Limberham* III. i. Plays (1701) II. 127 But you wou'd be intreated, and say, *Nolo, nolo, nolo*, three times, like any Bishop, when your Mouth waters at the Diocese. *a.* 1816 WOLCOT (P. Pindar) *2nd Ep. to Mrs. C.* Wks. (1816) IV. 450 For, *un*like Bishops, 'tis my firm intention To cry out, 'Yes, my Liege', for Place or Pension. 1827 SCOTT *Journ.* 16 July, There may be something like affectation and *nolo episcopari* in seeming to under-rate my own

Labours. **1884** TENNYSON *Becket* Prol. Wks. (1893) 696 Take thou mine answer in bare commonplace—*Nolo episcopari*. **1941** R. R. MARETT *A Jerseyman at Oxford* ch. 15 I should have deemed it cowardly to plead a *nolo episcopari*.

Nomen, omen.

[L. *nomen*, a name.] **1662** FULLER Devon 253 John Jewell[1] ... was born ... 24th of May 1552 ... It may be said of his Sirname, *Nomen, Omen*; Jewel his Name and Pretious his Vertues. [[1] Bp. of Salisbury.]

Non est inventus. (N 204)

[L. *Non est inventus* = 'He was not found'. The answer made by the sheriff in the return of the writ when the defendant is not to be found in his bailiwick. In 16th–17th cent. often used allusively.] *c.* **1475** *Mankind* 774 in *Macro Plays* 29 ȝe must speke to þe schryne for a 'cepe coppus', Ellys ȝe must be fayn to retorn with 'non est inventus'. **1583** STUBBES *Anat. Abus.* Kj Sheriffes & officers wil returne writs with a *tarde venit* or with a *non est inuentus*. **1590** GREENE *Never too Late* (1600) H3 So long put he his hand into his purse, that at last the empty bottome returned him a writ of *Non est inuentus*. **1827** DE QUINCEY *Murder* Wks. (1854) IV. 50 He inquired after the unfortunate reporter . . .; the answer was . . . from the under-sheriff of our county—'Non est inventus'. **1850** THACKERAY *Pendennis* ch. 60 Mrs. Montague Rivers hoff to Boulogne—non est inwentus, Mr. Morgan.

Non placet. (N 205)

[L. *Non placet*, 'it does not please'; the formula used in the older universities and in ecclesiastical assemblies, in giving a negative vote upon a proposition.] **1587** J. BRIDGES *Defence* 1370 Our scrutators when they had numbred al their voyces, would returne vs a fayre Non placet. **1589** GREENE *Menaphon* Arb. 42 When I craued a finall resolution to my fatal passions, shee ... shooke me off with a *Non placet. a.* **1635** SIBBES *Christian's End* (1639) v. 110 When flesh and bloud shall put up a petition, . . . give it a *Non placet*, deny the petition. **1890** *Echoes from the Oxford Magazine* ed. 2 'L'Envoy' We have assisted the Hebdomadal Council in the establishment of the Non-Placet Society.

Non plus, He is put to a. (N 206)

1578 G. WHETSTONE 2 *Promos and Cassandra* I. vii. H1[v] Their purses will be dryuen to a nonplus. **1587** GREENE *Penelope's Web.* ed. Grosart v. 224 Set at an non plus. **1589** JANE ANGER *J.A.: Her Protection for Women* 2 Men are often drouen to non plus. **1589** T. COOPER *Admon. People Eng.* 73 He cannot be perswaded that D. Sparke will affirme, that he did put the bishop . . . (as they terme it) to a non plus. **1659** HOWELL *Fr. Prov.* 23 He was graveld or put to a nonplus.

Nonconformist conscience.

1890 *Let.* in *Times* 28 Nov. 8/6 The minimum demand of the great Nonconformist party is the ... abdication of Mr. Parnell. ... Nothing less will satisfy the Nonconformist conscience now. **1896** MAX BEERBOHM *King George the Fourth* The Nonconformist Conscience makes cowards of us all. **1929** *Times* 23 April 12/2 There is in the bones of the British people a reverence for God and the things of God. You may call it 'the Non-Conformist Conscience' or whatever you like, but it is there.

None (but, is, is so, so), *see under significant words following.*

Nonsuch, He is a. (N 207)

1670 BROOKS *Wks.* (1867) VI. 30 Job was a nonsuch in his day for holiness. **1753** RICHARDSON *Sir C. Grandison* I. xxii. (1781) 152 Then you are, as indeed I have always thought you, a nonsuch of a woman. **1895** 'SARAH TYTLER' *Macdonald Lass* 172 As for your Prince, . . . he's not a nonsuch.

Noon on one's head, To ring. (N 210)

1592–3 SHAKES. *C.E.* I. ii. 45 The clock hath strucken twelve upon the bell—My mistress made it one upon my cheek. [**1600**] **1659** J. DAY *Blind Beg.* ii. D3 I'll make your sconce and the post ring noon together. **1605** CHAPMAN *All Fools* III. i. 420 By your clock, sir, it should be almost one, for your head rung noon some half hour ago. **1605** T. HEYWOOD I. *If You Know not Me* l. 872 Go ... make their pates ring noone. **1640** JONSON *Tale Tub* II. ii. 23 This Ash-plant Had rung noone o' your pate, Mr. Broome-beard.

Nopence, *see* Nippence, n.

Norfolk dumplings. (D 641)

[**1600**] **1659** DAY & CHETTLE *Blind Beggar* D2[v] I was as naked as your *Norfolk*-Dumplin. **1608** ARMIN *Nest Nin.* Shaks. Soc. 17 Nothing was undone that might be done to make Jemy Camber a tall, little, slender man, when yet he lookt like a Norfolke dumpling, thicke and short. **1662** FULLER Norfolk 247 ... This cannot be verified of any dwarfish ... stature of people in this County .... But it relates to the fare they commonly feed on.

Norfolk, *see also* Essex stiles ... N. wiles.

Norman, *see* Row the boat, N.

North, Out of the | all ill comes forth. Cf. Three ills come from the north. (N 213)

1591 PEELE *Hunting of Cupid* (Malone Soc. Coll. i. 310) Ab aquilone omne malum. **1597** DRAYTON *England's Heroical Epistles* Wks. (Hebel) ii. 188 They say, all Mischiefe commeth from the North. **1598** SIR R. BARCKLEY *Felicitie of Man* (1631) IV. iii. 339 There hath beene an old saying, that all evils rise out of the North. *a.* **1628** CARMICHAELL no. 1524 There came never luk fra the north bot horse and fair women. **1656** FORD & DEKKER *Sun's Darling* v. 35 What such murmurings does your gall bring forth, Will you prove't true, no good coms from the North.

North country, *see* Knight of Cales.

North for greatness, The | the east for health; the south for neatness, the west for wealth. (N 211)

1656–91 J. AUBREY Royal Soc. MS. f. 24. **1662** FULLER *Dorset* 278 The Houses of the Gentry herein are built rather to be lived in, than to be looked on.... Indeed the rhime holds generally true of the English structures, 'The North for Greatness, the East for Health; The South for Neatness, the West for Wealth'.

North of England for an ox, The | the south for a sheep, and the middle part for a man. (N 212)

1662 FULLER *Wilts.* 143 I have heard a Wise man say, that an Oxe ... would, of all England, choose to live in the North, a Sheep in the South ..., and a Man in the Middle betwixt both.

North wind does blow, The | and we shall have snow.

1805 *Songs for Nursery.* **1883** ROPER 9. **1893** INWARDS 78.

North, *see also* Cold weather and knaves come out of n.; Three ills come from n.; Wind's in n. (When), fisher goes not forth.

North-east, *see* Wind is n.-e. (If the).

North-west wind, An honest man and a | generally go to sleep together.

1883 ROPER 11. **1893** INWARDS 79.

North-west, *see also* Wind is in n.-w. (Do business when).

Northampton stands on other men's legs. (N 214)

1662 FULLER *Northamp.* 279 The Town of Northampton may be said to stand chiefly on other men's Leggs; where ... the most and cheapest boots and stockens are bought in England. **1897** BP. CREIGHTON *Some Eng. Shires* 343 It was this central position that gave Northampton its trade of shoemaking, ... and hides could easily be obtained from the rich grazing meadows ... on every side. It was an old saying that 'Northampton stood on other men's legs'.

Northampton, *see also* Eat a buttered fagot; Mayor of N.

Northamptonshire for squires and spires.

1869 HAZLITT 297. **1878** *Murray's Guidebk. to Northamp.* ch. 19 Northamptonshire has been called a land of 'Squires and Spires'; and it is undoubtedly preeminent in noble examples of the latter.

Northerly wind and blubber, brings home the Greenland lubber.

1846 DENHAM 20 ... A satirical proverb made use of by sailors.

Northern cloth, shrunk in the wetting, Like. (C 432)

1594 NASHE *Terrors Night* i. 384 He shall see [the witches] shrinke faster than Northren cloath, and outstrip time in dastardly flight. [1614] **1631** JONSON *Barth. Fair* IV. iv. 14 Doe my Northerne cloth zhrinke i' the wetting? ha? **1682** N. O. *Lutrin* iii. 28 Recall your wonted worth, new frights forgetting: 'Tis York-shire Cloath, you know, that shrinks i' th' wetting'.

Northern wind (air) brings weather fair, A.

1846 DENHAM. **1883** ROPER 9. **1893** INWARDS 77.

Nose into everything (every man's pot), To put one's. (N 238)

1545 *Precepts of Cato* C4ᵛ A common rauenynge dogge that thrusteth his head in euery mans pot. **1611** COTGRAVE s.v. Nez To thrust his nose into euerie corner. **1666** TORRIANO *Prov. Phr.* s.v. Naso 114 To put his nose in every business, viz. to meddle where one is not concern'd. **1678** HEXHAM *Dict.* s.v. Besnoffelen To See, Prie, or Have his nose in every thing.

Nose of wax, A. (H 531. L 104. N 226)

[= a thing or person easily moulded.] *a.* **1529** SKELTON *Image Hypocrisy:* Dyce ii. 425 The text to turne and glose, like a welshe manes hose, or lyk a waxen nose. **1532** TYNDALE *Expos. Matt.* P.S. 103 If the Scripture be contrary, then make it a nose of wax and wrest it this way and that till it agree. **1589** T. COOPER *Admon. People Eng.* 71ᵛ The Papistes ... affirming ... that the Scriptures ... may be wrested euery way, like a nose of waxe, or like a leaden Rule. **1596** LODGE *Marg. America* Hunt. Cl. iii. 40 Iustice is made a nose of waxe warmed, and wrought according to all mens pleasures. **1621** SYLVESTER 1055 Wordes wax-nosed. **1666** TORRIANO *It. Prov.* 126 no. 12 All laws have a nose of wax. **1686** HORNECK *Crucif. Jesus* ix. 167 Oral Tradition, that nose of wax, which you may turn and set, which way you list. **1815** SCOTT *Guy Man.* ch. 5 I let ... the constable ... manage the business his ain gate, as if I had been a nose o' wax. **1821** GALT *Annals Parish* ch. 12 Her ladyship ... said that I was a nose-of-wax.

Nose out of joint, To put (thrust) one's. (N 219)

[= to displace or supplant one; to disconcert.] **1581** RICH *Farew. Milit. Profess.* K4 It could bee no other then his owne manne, that had thrust his nose so farre out of ioynt. **1585** A. MUNDAY *Fedele and Fortunio* l. 1729 My nose is ioynted. **1598** R. BERNARD tr. *Terence, Eunuch* I. ii. Fearing now lest this wench ... should put your nose out of joynt. **1662** PEPYS *Diary* 31 May The King is pleased enough with her: which, I fear, will put Madam Castlemaine's nose out of joynt. **1860** THACKERAY *Lovel* ch. 6 My dear, I guess your ladyship's nose is out of joint.

Nose swell, To make one's. (N 235)

[= to make one jealous or envious.] **1678** RAY 77 Doth your nose swell (or eek, *i.e.* itch) at

that? **1743** in HOWELL *St. Trials* (1813) XVII.
1187 He heard lord Altham say, . . . my wife
has got a son, which will make my brother's
nose swell.

Nose, To take (pull) oneself by the.
(N 237)

1535 G. JOYE *Apol. to Tyndale* Arb. 27 Take not
your selfe no more by the nose. **1540** SIR T.
ELYOT *Pasquil the Plain* B3 Nowe thou takest
thy selfe by the nose. **1586** R. CROWLEY *Father
John Francis* H1ᵛ Where you doo charge vs
with pryde, . . . I must vse an English prouerbiall
speeche, and say: Take your selfe by the nose,
and saie foole I haue caught thee. **1596** HARING-
TON *Metam. Ajax* (1927 ed.) 90 Let them take
heed that in one place or other of this pamphlet,
they doe not pull themselues by the nose, as the
prouerbe is. **1616** DRAXE no. 1618 Take thy
selfe by the nose.

Nose to make a poor man's sow, He has a good.
(N 217)

1530 PALSGRAVE 580a (to be). **1576** HOLYBAND
D8ᵛ (You are good to be). *c.* **1579** [MERBURY]
Marr. Wit and Wisdom iii. 27 I haue a good nose
to be a pore mans sowe. **1639** CLARKE 239. **1678**
RAY 262 . . . Il seroit bon truy à pauvre homme.
Gall. **1738** SWIFT Dial. III. É.L. 323.

Nose to the grindstone, To hold (keep, bring, put) one's.
(N 218)

[1525–40] **1557** *Merry Dial.* 60 I woulde haue
holden his nose to the grindstone. **1532** FRITH
Mirr. to know Thyself (1829) 273 This Text
holdeth their noses so hard to the grindstone,
that it clean disfigureth their faces. **1546** HEY-
WOOD I. v. B2 I shall to reueng former hurtis,
Hold their noses to grinstone. **1621** BURTON
Anat. Mel. III. i. III. (1651) 429 We . . . contemn,
insult, vex, torture, molest, and hold one anothers
noses to the grindstone hard. **1801** EDGEWORTH
Pop. Tales, Contrast ch. 1 I would not let my
nose be kept to the grindstone, as yours is, for
any one living. **1823** GALT *Entail* ch. 92 Leave
no stone unturned till you hae brought Mr.
Milrookit's nose to the grindstone. **1901** S.
LANE-POOLE *Sir H. Parkes in C.* i. 14 Morrison
. . . kept his nose to the grindstone, and taught
him the value of hard work.

Nose warp, You make his.
(N 245)

1678 RAY 262.

Nose will abide no jests, His.
(N 223)

1588 *Mar-Prelate Epit.* (1843) 9 I am sure their
noses can abide no iest. **1593** PEELE *Edw. I* ii.
175 We are . . . disposed to be pleasant with
thee a little; but I perceive, friar, thy nose will
bide no jest. **1659** HOWELL *Eng. Prov.* 6a His
nose will abide no jests.

Nose will not make a shoeing horn, Every man's.
(M 449)

c. **1510** STANBRIDGE *Vulgaria* 19 His nose is lyke
a shoynge horne. **1576** GASCOIGNE *Grief of Joy*
i. 518 Full well wot you, that Corinth shoeing
horns May not be made, like every noddy's nose.
1670 RAY 125. **1721** KELLY 91 . . . Spoken to

them who have found the Man with whom they
were dealing, more sagacious and cunning than
they expected.

Nose, see also Better a snotty child than n.
wiped off; Bore him through n. with cushion;
Bridge of one's n. (Make a); Clout a man will not
wipe his n. on, (It is a foul); Cut off one's n. to
spite; Dog's n. always cold; Fall on his back and
break n.; Follow one's n.; Fox has got in his n.
(When), body follow; Great n. (He that has)
thinks everybody speaking of it; Hang a n.;
Hole under his n.; Hunger drops out of his n.;
Jack would wipe his n. if had it; Know by your
n. what pottage you love; Lead one by the n.;
Little mense o' the cheeks to bite off n.; Lose the
droppings of his n. (He will not); Pay through
the n.; Pepper in the n. (Take); Plain as the n.
on man's face; See his n. cheese first; See no
further than the end of one's n.; Sees an inch
before n.; Snap (bite) one's n. off; Spite of one's
teeth (n. etc.); Tell where to turn his n. (Cannot);
Wipe one's n. on sleeve; Wipe the n. of someone;
Wipes his n. and has it not, (He that) forfeits his
face.

Nosegay to him as long as he lives, It will be a.
(N 246)

1678 RAY 262 . . . It will stink in his nostrils,
spoken of any bad matter a man hath been
engaged in.

Not God above gets all men's love.
(G 241)

[THEOGNIS 26 Οὐδὲ γὰρ ὁ Ζεὺς Οὔθ' ὕων πάντεσσ'
ἁνδάνει οὔτ' ἀνέχων. For not even Jove can
please all, whether he rains or does not rain.
ERASM. *Ad. Ne Juppiter quidem omnibus placet.*]
1616 WITHALS 568. **1639** CLARKE 147. **1721**
KELLY 267 . . . L. *Jupiter neque pluens neque
abstinens omnibus placet.*

**Not (a, a word of, able to, even, fit to, made of,
only ought, so good to, such a, till the, to, to be,
too), see** *under significant words following.*

Not worth (a, an, his), see (Brass) farthing,
Button, Cress, Curse, Dodkin, Doit, Eggshell,
Fig, Fly, Groat, Haddock, Hair, Harrington,
Haw, Ivy-leaf, Leek, Louse, Muck, Needle, Nut-
shell, Pin, Plack, Pudding, Rotten apple, Shoe-
buckles, Straw, Taking the wall of dog, Three
halfpence, Turd.

Notchel, see Cry N.

Note, see Bird is known by his n.; Musician has
forgot n. (When); Sing so merry a n.

Nothing between a poor man and a rich but a piece of an ill year.

1721 KELLY 335 . . . Because, in that space,
many things may fall out, that may make a rich
Man poor.

Nothing but is good for something.
(N 327)

a. 1500 *15c. School-Bk.* ed. W. Nelson 61 Ther is nothynge but it wyll serve for sumwhat, be it never so course. *c.* 1595 SHAKES. *R.J.* II. iii. 17 For naught so vile that on the earth doth live But to the earth some special good doth give. 1609 HARWARD 106ᵛ (somewhat). 1616 BRETON A5ᵛ. 1639 CLARKE 72. 1681 DRYDEN *Span. Friar* III. ii. Merm. 164 They say everything in the world is good for something . . . but I never knew what a friar was good for, till your pimping showed me.

Nothing but up and ride?   (N 284)

1639 CLARKE 116 What? no more but up and ride? 1670 RAY 198. 1732 FULLER no. 5497.

Nothing comes fairer (sooner) to light than that which has been long hid.
(N 286)

a. 1628 CARMICHAELL no. 1205 (sooner). 1641 FERGUSSON no. 661 (sooner). 1721 KELLY 260 . . . Spoken when People unexpectedly find what has been long hid, or discovers what has been long conceal'd.

Nothing comes of (from) nothing. *Cf.*
Nothing for nothing.   (N 285)

[L. *Ex nihilo nihil fit.*] *c.* 1380 CHAUCER *Boece* v. i. 42 For this sentence is verray and soth, that 'no thing hath his beynge of naught'. *c.* 1400 *Rom. Rose* l. 4476 Withoute yift, is not to prisc. 1551 CRANMER *Ans. to Gardiner* 369 Sicut ex nihilo nihil fit, Ita nihil in nihilum redigitur. As nothyng can be made of nought, so nothynge can be tourned into nought. [*c.* 1589] 1633 MARLOWE *Jew of Malta* I. ii. 105 Christians, what or how can I multiply? Of naught is nothing made. 1605–6 SHAKES. *K.L.* I. i. 89 Nothing will come of nothing: speak again. *Ibid.* I. iv. 132 Why, no, boy; nothing can be made out of nothing. *c.* 1606 MARSTON *What You Will* IV. i. But of nothing, nothing is bred. 1610 FIELD *Woman is a W.* II. i. Merm. 372 I remember thus much philosophy of my schoolmaster, ex nihilo nihil fit. *a.* 1704 T. BROWN to *Author of Address* in *Collect. of Poems* 97 Thou know'st the Proverb: Nothing due for naught. 1904–10 ALEX. MACLAREN *Expos., Amos* 172 The last touch in the picture is meanness, which turned everything into money. . . . Is not 'nothing for nothing' an approved maxim to-day?

Nothing costs so much as what is given us.

1732 FULLER no. 3660.

Nothing crave, nothing have. *Cf.*
Nothing have, nothing crave. (N 291)

c. 1560 *Dan Hew Monk of Leicester* (Hazlitt, *Early Pop. Poetry* iii. 137) When I haue it I wil it not craue. 1659 HOWELL *Eng. Prov.* 16b. 1732 FULLER no. 6242.

Nothing dries sooner than tears. (N 288)

[CICERO *De Part. Orat.* 17. 57 *Cito enim exarescit lacrima.*] 1560 T. WILSON *Arte of Rhet.* (1909) 134 For as Cicero doth say, nothing drieth soner then teares. 1612 WEBSTER *White Devil* V. iii. Merm. 103 These are but moonish shades of griefs or fears; There's nothing sooner dries than women's tears. 1670 RAY 147 . . . Niente più tosto se secca che lagrime. *Ital.* 1757 FRANKLIN Jan. Nothing dries sooner than a tear.

Nothing enters into a close hand.
(N 289)

1641 FERGUSSON no. 647 (in). 1721 KELLY 263 . . . Niggardly People will not procure much good will.

Nothing for nothing (and very little for a halfpenny).

1858 G. J. WHYTE-MELVILLE *Interpreter* ch. 25 Sir Harry . . . recollected the old-established principle of himself and his clique, . . . 1863 G. ELIOT *Romola* ch. 1 Nothing for nothing, young man.

Nothing freer than a gift.   (G 103)

c. 1451 *Paston Letters* (Gairdner 1904) ii. 256 And askyd here wat was freere than gyfte. *c.* 1470 HENRYSON *Mor. Fab., Fox, Wolf,* and *Husb.* 38 (1917) 107 And is thair oucht, sayis thow, frear than gift? 1639 CLARKE 222 What's freer than gift? 1721 KELLY 267. 1832 HENDERSON 28.

Nothing has no savour (flavour). (N 290)

1546 HEYWOOD I. viii. C1 But now I can smell, nothyng hath no sauer. [*c.* 1550] 1641 CAVENDISH *Wolsey* ed. Morley n.d. 128. 1614 CAMDEN 310. 1738 SWIFT *Dial.* I. E.L. 293 Has he got a good fortune with his lady? for they say something has some savour, but nothing has no flavour.

Nothing have, nothing crave. *Cf.*
Nothing crave, nothing have.   (N 291)

1659 HOWELL *Eng. Prov.* 16b.

Nothing, He has | that is not contented.
(N 257)

1616 DRAXE no. 348. 1664 CODRINGTON 195. 1674 J. SMITH *Grammatica Quadrilinguis* 67.

Nothing ill in Spain but that which speaks.   (N 293)

1642 HOWELL *For. Travel* vii. Arb. 38 *Spaine* yeeldeth to none of her neighbours in perfection of anything, but only in *Plenty*; which I beleeve was the ground of a Proverbe . . . , *No ay cosa mala en Espana, sino lo que habla,* there is nothing ill in *Spaine,* but that which speakes.

Nothing is, Where | a little does ease.
(N 336)

1546 HEYWOOD I. x. D1 (a little thyng). 1614 CAMDEN 314. 1694 D'URFEY I *Don Quix.* (1729) II. i. 24 Where nothing is, a little goes a great way.

Nothing is certain but death and quarter day (the taxes).

1789 B. FRANKLIN Letter to M. Lewis.   **1902-4** LEAN 153 There is nothing sure but death and quarter day.   **1912** *Spectator* 18 May, 785 It is not merely the . . . amount of the taxes. . . . It is their compulsory and irresistible incidence. . . . 'There are only two evils from which no man can escape—death and the king's taxes'.

Nothing is certain but the unforeseen (unexpected).

1885 C. LOWE *Bismarck* ix. (1898) 320 The fall of Bismarck was . . . one of the wonders of the century; and . . . no more unexpected event ever happened, though the French . . . will have it that nothing is so certain as the unexpected.   **1886** FROUDE *Oceana* ch. 7.   **1905** ALEX. MACLAREN *Expos., Matthew* I. 322 There is nothing certain to happen, says the proverb, but the unforeseen. Tomorrow *will have* its cares.

Nothing, He that has | need fear to lose nothing.   (N 331)

c. **1557** ROPER *Life of More* (Hitchcock) 7 He nothinge having, nothing could loose.   **1591-2** SHAKES. *3 Hen. VI* III. iii. 152 Having nothing, nothing can he lose.   **1592** NASHE *Summer's Last Will* iii. 242 *Cui nil est, nil deest*: he that hath nothing, wants nothing.   **1639** CLARKE 41.   **1732** FULLER no. 2150 (is frighted at).

Nothing is impossible to a willing heart (mind).   (N 299)

1509 HAWES *Past. Pleasure* l. 140 To wyllynge herte is nought Impossyble.   **1546** HEYWOOD I. iv. B1ᵛ.   **1641** FERGUSSON no. 658 Nothing is difficile to a well willit man.   **1670** RAY 29 (a willing mind).

Nothing is impossible to God.   (N 300)

c. **1566** CURIO W.P. *Pasquin in a Trance* 33ᵛ Christ . . . can do what he sayth, for nothing is impossible with him.   *Ibid.* 51ᵛ All things are possible with God.   **1605** T. HEYWOOD I *If You Know Not Me* l. 497 (impossible).   **1616** WITHALS 573.

Nothing, He that has | is not contented.   (N 266)

1670 RAY 19.

Nothing is old but shoes and hats.

1710 S. PALMER 231.

Nothing is stolen without hands.   (N 304)

1616 BRETON 2 *Cross. Prov.* B1 There is nothing stoln without hands.   **1639** CLARKE 149.

Nothing is, Where | the king must lose his right.   (N 338)

1546 HEYWOOD I. xii. F1 Where as nothyng is, the kynge must lose his ryght.   **1605** *Lond. Prodigal* III. iii. *Shakes. Apoc.* 208 Alas, what

good . . . To imprison him that nothing hath to pay? And where nought is, the king doth lose his due.   **1721** KELLY 358 . . . And so must the Subject but with this Difference, that the King loseth his Right in no other Case.

Nothing is to be presumed on, or despaired of.   (N 306)

1651 HERBERT no. 56a.

Nothing like, see under significant words following.

Nothing must be done hastily but killing of fleas.   (N 251)

a. **1655** N. L'ESTRANGE in *Anec. and Trad.* ed. Thoms i. 55 (Do nothing rashly).   **1666** TORRIANO *It. Prov.* 95 no. 30 There's never any thing well done in haste, but to shun the plague, to shun quarrelling, and to catch fleas.   **1678** RAY 151.   **1721** KELLY 261 Nothing to be done in haste, but gripping of Fleas. . . . Spoken when we are unreasonably urged to make haste.   **1732** FULLER no. 1309 (catching).

Nothing new under the sun.   (T 147)

[ECCL. i. 9 There is no new thing under the sun.]   *c.* **1386** CHAUCER *Knight's T.* l. 2125 Ther nys no newe gyse, that it nas old.   **1592** DELAMOTHE 7 Under the large Cope of heauen, we see not a new thing.   **1816** WOLCOT (P. Pindar) *Ode on Ancients* Wks. IV. 131 Alas! there's nothing new beneath the sun: The ancients with their hooks have reap'd the field.   **1850** KINGSLEY *Alton L.* ch. 18 There is nothing new under the sun; all that is stale and trite to a septuagenarian, who has seen where it all ends.

Nothing patent in the New Testament that is not latent in the Old.

1902-4 LEAN IV. 153 . . . In vetere novum latet, in novo vetus patet.

Nothing questions, He that | nothing learns.

1579 GOSSON *Ephemerides* 61b.   **1732** FULLER no. 2241.

Nothing seek, nothing find. *Cf.* Seeks, finds.   (N 315)

1600 NASHE *Summer's Last Will* iii. 261 Nought seeke, nought haue.   **1614** COCKS in *Cal. Col. P., E. Indies* 342 As the saying is, nothing seek nothing find.   **1616** JONSON *Ev. Man in Hum.* II. v. 116 You'ld gladly finde it, but you will not seeke it.   **1659** HOWELL *Br. Prov.* 28 Not seek, not find.

Nothing so bad (good) but it might have been worse (better).

1769 WESLEY *Journal* v. 230.   **1818** SCOTT *Rob Roy* ch. 27 There's naething sae gude on this side o' time but it might hae been better.   **1876** MRS. BANKS *Manch. Man* ch. 43 However, there is nothing so bad but it might be worse.   **1886** E. J. HARDY *How to be Happy* ch. 21 Let us resolve to look at the bright side of things. . . . 'Nothing so bad but it might have been worse'.

1908 *Times Wkly.* 9 Oct. Farmers . . . will regard the . . . meteorological changes as illustrating the ancient axiom to the effect that circumstances are never so bad that they cannot be worse.

Nothing so bad in which there is not something of good. (N 328)

1599 SHAKES. *Hen. V* IV. i. 4 There is some soul of goodness in things evil. **1623** WODROEPHE 505 No Evill without Good. **1678** RAY *Adag. Hebr.* 408.

Nothing so certain (sure) as death. *Cf.* No man knows when. (N 316)

c. **1300** *King Alisaunder* l. 918 N'is in this world so siker thyng So is deth, to olde and yyng. **1484** CAXTON *Curial* 19 Ne than the deth nothynge more certayn. **1562** SACKVILLE & NORTON *Gorboduc* IV. ii. 153 How brittle our estate, Of nothing sure, saue onely of the death. **1639** CLARKE 214 (sure).

Nothing so crouse,[1] as a new washen louse. (N 329)

1641 FERGUSSON no. 864. **1674** RAY *Collection of English Words* 12. **1721** KELLY 263 . . . Spoken of them who have been ragged, and dirty, and are proud, and fond of new, or clean Cloaths. [1 brisk.]

Nothing so necessary for travellers as languages. (N 318)

1611 COTGRAVE s.v. Rome He that can speake may trauell any way. **1616** BRETON 2 *Cross. Prov.* A5.

Nothing stake, nothing draw. *Cf.* Nought lay down.

1678 RAY 206.

Nothing succeeds like success.

1867 RICHARDSON *Beyond the Mississippi* 418. **1868** SIR A. HELPS *Realmah* ch. 5. **1872** BESANT & RICE *Ready-money M.* ch. 9 In Mr. Mortiboy's judgment, no proverb could be better than . . . 'Nothing succeeds like success'. Success dazzled him. **1903** J. MCCARTHY *Portr. of Sixties* ch. 21 Robsons's . . . dazzling success led to the waste of his physical powers and to his early death. . . . In certain cases at least, nothing fails like success. **1919** DEAN INGE *Outspoken Ess.* 88 Aristocracies do not maintain their numbers. The ruling race rules itself out; nothing fails like success.

Nothing that is violent is permanent. *Cf.* All that is sharp is short. (N 321)

1562 SACKVILLE & NORTON *Gorboduc* V. i. 76 These violent thinges may haue no lasting long. **1562** J. PILKINGTON *Aggeus and Abdias* P.S. 208 No violent thing can long endure. **1576** PETTIE ii. 62 Nothing violent is permanent. [*c.* 1590] **1633** MARLOWE *Jew of Malta* I. i. 130. **1594** SHAKES. *Lucrece* l. 894 Thy violent vanities can never last. **1595–6** *Id. Rich. II* II. i. 34 For violent fires soon burn out themselves. **1600–1**

Id. H. II. i. 103 This is the very ecstasy of love, Whose violent property fordoes itself. **1613** WITHER *Abuses* II. i. As if all euils they would quite reforme Within a moment: But things *violent* Cannot you know be long time *permanent*. **1623** J. TAYLOR (Water-P.) ¦*Mer. Wher. Fer. Voy.* Wks. (1630 ed.) 8 But nothing violent is permanent, and in short space away the Tempest went. **1861** G. J. WHYTE-MELVILLE *Inside Bar* ch. 4 There is a good old rule in mechanics which affirms '*nil violentum est perpetuum*'.

Nothing tickles that pinches not.

1603 MONTAIGNE (Florio) III. xii. 184 And good Historians avoid calme narrations, . . . to retreeve seditions and finde out warres, whereto they know we cal them.

Nothing to be got without pains. *Cf.* Pleasure without pain, No. (N 305)

1561 T. BECON *Sick Man's Salve* P.S. 150 Nothing is gotten without pain and travail. **1611** COTGRAVE s.v. Peine Nor bread, nor ought is gotten without paines. **1616** WITHALS 562 Nothing proues well except it be plyed. **1721** KELLY 262 Nothing gotten but [= without] Pains, but an ill Name. **1732** FULLER no. 3677 . . . but Poverty.

Nothing turns sourer than milk.

1830 FORBY 428 . . . *i.e.* A mild, good-humoured man is most determined, when he is thoroughly provoked.

Nothing (Nought) venture, nothing (nought) have. (N 319)

c. **1374** CHAUCER *Troilus* Bk. 2, l. 807 And seyde, 'He which that no-thing under-taketh, Nothynge ne acheveth, be hym looth or dere.' *c.* **1386** *Id. Reeve's T.* l. 4210 'Unhardy is unsely',[1] thus men sayth. **1546** HEYWOOD I. xi. E1 Noght venter noght haue. **1580** TUSSER (1878 ed. 44) Naught venter, naught haue. **1602** BRETON *Wonders* in Wks. Gros. ii. 9. **1659** TORRIANO no. 170 (hazzard . . . knaw[2]). **1777** BOSWELL *Johnson* lxi. (1848) 558 I observed, 'I am, however, generally for trying: "Nothing venture, nothing have".' **1850** LYTTON *My Novel* IV. iv. 'Learn whist—sixpenny points to begin with'. . . . Shaking my head, I called for my bill. . . . 'Poor spirit, sir! . . . Nothing venture, nothing have.' [1 unfortunate. 2 gnaw.]

Nothing venture, nothing win. (N 320)

1481 CAXTON *Reynard* Arb. 27 He that wil wynne he muste laboure and auenture. **1668** SEDLEY *Mulberry Gard.* III. ii. Who ever caught any thing with a naked hook? Nothing venture, nothing win. **1876** BLACKMORE *Cripps* ch. 43 We must all have been in France . . . if—well, never mind. Nothing venture nothing win. But happily we have won.

Nothing when you are used to it, It is.

1738 SWIFT *Dial.* III. E.L. 319 I would not keep such company for the world.—O, miss, 'tis nothing when you are used to it.

Nothing when you are used to it, It is | as the eels said when they were being skinned alive.

1829–30 M. SCOTT *T. Cring. Log* ch. 1 Who says that eels cannot be made used to skinning? The poor girls continued their little preparations with alacrity. **1902–4** LEAN IV. 19 'Tis nothing when you are used to it, as the eels said when they were being skinned alive.

Nothing worse than a familiar[1] enemy.
(P 243)

[MATT. X. 36 A man's foes shall be they of his own household.] *c.* **1386** CHAUCER *Merch. T.* l. 1784 O famulier foo, that his servyce bedeth! *c.* **1400** *Id. Test. Love* II. 343/1 Nothyng is werse . . . than . . . a famyliar enemye. *c.* **1538** *Lisle Papers* XII. art. 43 in *N. & Q.* 4th Ser. IX. 423 It hath been an old proverbe that there is no worse pestilence than a famylyar enemy. [1 of one's own household.]

Nothing, *see also* Blessed is he who expects n.; Covetousness brings n. home; Dance upon n.; Does n., does amiss; Doing n. we learn to do ill; Enough where n. was left (Never); Fools are fain of n.; Good for n., (He is); Hard gives more; Judge knows n. unless it has been explained to him three times; Know n. except that I know not, (I); Knows n., doubts n.; Little of everything, and n. in the main; Lose n. for asking; Loss (He that is not sensible of his) has lost n.; New n., (A); Name for n., (You had not your); Neck or n.; Pain to do n. than something (More); Put n. into purse (If you); Say n. than not to purpose (Better); Something is better than n.; Thank you for n.; Too much of n. but fools; Well fare n. once a year; World is n.

Notice, *see* Long foretold . . . short n. soon past.

Nottingham, *see* Smith of N.

Nought's impossible, as t'auld woman said when they told her cauf had swallowed grindlestone.[1]

1917 BRIDGE 96. [1 grindstone.]

Nought is never in danger. (N 342)

[L. *Malum vas non frangitur.* A worthless vessel does not get broken.] **1639** CLARKE 126. **1738** SWIFT *Dial.* I. E.L. 268. **1853** SURTEES *Sponge's Sport. T.* ch. 56 'He was nearly killed last time'. . . . 'Oh, nought's never in danger!' observed Bob Spangles.

Nought is that muse that finds no excuse. (M 1317)

1573 SANFORD 110. **1578** FLORIO *First F.* 33ᵛ (II). **1629** *Bk. Mer. Rid.* Prov. no. 123.

Nought is to wed with, Where | wise men flee the clog. (N 347)

1546 HEYWOOD I. xi. D2ᵛ. *a.* **1547** REDFORD *Wit and Science* l. 1046 Ye have woon a clogg

wythall . . . such as doth fall to all men that ioyne them selves in mariage in kepyng ther wyves a carefull cariage. **1614** CAMDEN 314 Where nought is to wend whit [1636 *with*], wise men flee the clog.

Nought lay down, nought take up. *Cf.* Nothing stake. (N 343)

1546 HEYWOOD I. xi. E2 He can . . . no tyme assyne, In whiche he hath laied downe one peny by myne, . . . And . . . nought ley downe, nought. take vp. **1611** DAVIES *Prov.* no. 173. **1659** HOWELL *Eng. Prov.* 5a Nothing down, nothing up.

Nought, He that has | shall have nought.

1509 BARCLAY *Ship of Fools* i. 100 He that nought hathe, shall so alway byde poor, But he that ouer moche hath, yet shall haue more. *c.* **1550** *Parl. of Byrdes* l. 221 in HAZLITT *Early Pop. Poetry* iii. 179.

Nought will be nought. (N 344)

1509 BARCLAY *Ship of Fools* i. 167 Nought wyll be nought what so euer thou do. **1570** TUSSER H2 Naught wilbe nought say and do what thou wilt.

Nought won by the one, nought won by the other. (N 345)

c. **1549** HEYWOOD I. xi. E2ᵛ.

Nought, *see also* All have but n. forego, (He would); Beauty without bounty avails n.; Best is as good as stark n.; Fault (He has but one), he is n.; Little good to stark n., (From); Make much of n.; Old n. will never be aught; Play for n. as work for n. (As good); Too good (much) is stark n.; Too much of ought good for n.; Well fare n. once a year; Work for n.; World is n. *See also* Nothing, Nowt.

Nouns, *see* God is better pleased with adverbs than with n.

Nourished, *see* Grey hairs are n. with green thoughts.

November take flail, let ship no more sail. *Cf.* Thresher take his flail. (N 348)

1570 TUSSER 24ᵛ. **1732** FULLER no. 6221.

November, *see also* First of N. . . . an end of wheat-sowing.

Now I have, *see* Ewe and a lamb; Sheep and a cow.

Now is now, and then was then (Yule's in winter). (N 350)

1530 PALSGRAVE 885a Than was than, and nowe is nowe. **1551** T. WILSON *Rule of Reason* O7 Aristotle sayth, it is mete for men to marye at .xxvj. for maidens to marie at .xviii. but then was

then, and now is now. *a.* **1558** *Jacob and Esau*
D1ᵛ Yea then was then, now is it otherwise.
1584 R. WILSON *Three Ladies of London* Hazl.-
Dods. vi. 257 Then was then, and now is now.
1615 R. BRATHWAIT *A Strappado for the Devil*
(Ebsworth) 89 The time is chang'd, now's now,
and then was then. **1721** KELLY 268. ... A Return
to them that say Now, by way of Resentment;
a Particle common in Scotland. **1846** DENHAM 6.

Now or never. (N 351)

c. **1380** CHAUCER *Troilus* Bk. 4, l. 101 But now
or nevere, if that it lyke yow, I may hire have
right sone. *c.* **1400** *Sir Gawain and the Green
Knight* ll. 2215–16 If any wyȝe oȝt wyl, wynne
hideð fast, Oþer now oþer neuer, his nedeþ to
spede. **1569** J. PHILLIP *Patient Grissill* l. 889
Nowe or els neuer. [*c.* **1587**] **1592** KYD *Span.
Trag.* III. iv. 79 Now or neuer ends Lorenzoes
doubts. [*c.* **1589**] **1594** PEELE *Battle of Alcazar*
l.1211 Now or neuer brauely execute Your resolution. **1590–1** SHAKES. *2 Hen. VI* III. i. 331 Now,
York, or never, steel thy fearful thoughts. **1608**
DAY *Humour* IV. iii. Merm. 319 You shall find
us at the south port.—Now or never, my lord.
1712 ADDISON *Spect.* no. 403 Wks. (1902) III. 381
Sharp's the word. Now or never boy. Up to
the walls of Paris directly. **1847–8** THACKERAY
Vanity F. ch. 6 Now or never was the moment,
Miss Sharp thought, to provoke the declaration
which was trembling on the timid lips of Mr.
Sedley.

Now, *see* Better keep n. than seek anon.

Nowadays, *see* World is n.

Nowt, *see* Doubt, (When in) do n.; Owt for n.

Nullum numen abest si sit prudentia, see No
divinity.

Number one.

[= oneself.] **1641** 25 Jan. SIR WILLIAM UVEDALE
Treasurer of the Chamber S.P.D. Chas. I.
cccclxxvi. 79 It is the rule that we ought to look
to our selues in the first place. **1796** EDGEWORTH
Par. Asst. (1903) 322 I'm only talking of
number one, you know. I must take care of
that first. **1816** [J. W. CUNNINGHAM] *Sancho, or
the Proverbialist* 22 Take care of Number One.
1839 DICKENS *N. Nickleby* ch. 60 The only
number in all arithmetic that I know of, as a
husband and a father, is number one. **1849**
DARWIN in *Life & Lett.* I. 369 I do not see my
way clearly, beyond humbly endeavouring to
reform Number one.

Number(s), *see* Luck in odd n.; One is no n.;
Safety in n.

Nun of Sion, with the friar of Sheen, The. (N 352)

1659 HOWELL *Eng. Prov.* 17a The Nun of *Sion*
with the Frier of *Shean*, Went under the water
to play the quean. **1787** GROSE (*Middlesex*) 209
The nun of Sion, with the friar of Shean. A
saying, meant to express birds of a feather.
Although the river Thames runs between these
two monasteries, there is a vulgar tradition that
they had a subterraneous communication.

Nun, *see also* Nice as a n.'s hen.

Nunc dimittis, see Sing *N. d.*

Nurse is valued till the child has done sucking, The.

1732 FULLER no. 4688.

Nurse's tongue is privileged to talk, The. (N 355)

1659 HOWELL *Brit. Prov.* 4. **1670** RAY 19.

Nurses put one bit in the child's mouth and two in their own. (N 356)

1639 CLARKE 39.

Nurse(s), *see also* Kiss the child for n.'s sake;
One year a n. and seven the worse.

Nurture and good manners maketh man. *Cf.* Manners maketh man.

c. **1460** *Vrbanitatis* 33 in *Babees Bk.* E.E.T.S. 14
In halle, in chambur, oρe where þou gon, Nurtur
& good maners makeþ man.

Nurture is above (passes) nature. *Cf.* Nature passes nurture. (N 357)

c. **1532** *Tales* no. 41 Lycurgus proued by experience that nourysshynge, good bryngynge vp,
and exercyse ben more apte to leade folke to
humainte and the doynge of honest thynges than
Nature her selfe. **1539** TAVERNER I *Garden* A5ᵛ
Nature (I woll well) is a thynge of great myght
and efficacye, but surely institution or bring-
ynge vp, is moche myghtier. **1572** J. PARINCHEF
Extract of Examples 84 Nature is of greate force,
but education is of greater force. **1578** *The
Joyful Receiving of the Queen's ... Majesty into
Norwich* B4 Good nurture chaungeth qualities.
1579 LYLY *Euph.* i. 264 But you see howe education altereth nature. **1586** LA PRIMAUDAYE *The
French Academy* 176 That old prouerbe was not
spoken without reason, that education goeth
beyond nature. **1592** DELAMOTHE 37–8 Nourriture passe nature. Bringing vp goeth beyond
nature. **1611** COTGRAVE s.v. Nourriture Nurture surpasseth nature. **1639** CLARKE 167.
1659 HOWELL *It. Prov.* 6 (overcomes). *Fr. Prov.*
12 (passeth).

Nuts to him (to an ape), It is. (N 363)

1578 G. WHETSTONE *Promos and Cass.* B2ᵛ As
iumpe as Apes, in vewe of Nuttes to daunce.
1600–1 SHAKES. *H.* IV. ii. 19 He keeps them,
like an ape, in the corner of his jaw; first
mouth'd, to be last swallowed. [**1619**] **1647**
FLETCHER *Mad Lover* V. 65 Such are Nuts to me.
1711–12 8 Jan. SWIFT *Jrnl. to Stella* Lord
Keeper and Treasurer teased me for a week. It
was nuts to them. **1732** FULLER no. 2970 It
is like Nuts to an Ape. **1809** MALKIN *Gil Blas*
VI. i. His disgrace or ruin will be nuts to me.
[**1812**] **1819** J. H. VAUX *Vocab. of the Flash
Language* at end of his *Memoirs* ii. 192 Nuts
upon it, to be very much pleased or gratified
with any object so a person who conceives a

strong inclination for another of the opposite sex, is said to be . . . nuts upon him or her.   **1843** DICKENS *Christmas C.* ch. I It was the very thing he liked. To edge his way along . . . warning all human sympathy to keep its distance, was . . . 'nuts' to Scrooge.   **1914** 10 May KIPLING to W. Osler C. Carrington *Life* (1955) 422 Culpepper . . . could write even if he couldn't cure for nuts.

Nut(s), *see also* Ape can crack a n., (Before an); Apple, an egg, and a n.; Crack me that n.; Cracked n. with her tail (As if she); Deaf n.; Eat the kernel must crack n.; Hard n. to crack; Hen cracks n., (As fast as a); Lost with an apple, won with a n.; Madame Parnell, crack the n.; Noise is greater than the n.; Sweet as a n.; Sweet is the n., but bitter the shell; Sweet n. if you were well cracked.

Nut-cracker, *see* Windmill dwindles into n.-c.

Nutmeg, *see* Carry a n. in pocket, married to old man.

Nutshell, Not worth a.   (N 366)

a. **1300** *Cursor M.* 23828 þair spede es noght a nute-scell.   *c.* **1390** GOWER *Conf. Amantis* II. 20 Bot al nys worth a note schale.   *a.* **1529** SKELTON *Agst. Venemous Tongues* Wks. (1843) I. 135 All is not worth a couple of nut shalis.   **1683** DRYDEN 'Vindication of the Duke of Guise' *Wks.* ed. W. Scott vii. 141 I did not disown it; but the universe to a nutshell that I did not disown it for want of success.

Nutshell, *see also* Sea with a spoon (n.), (To empty the).

Nutting on Sundays, If you go | the devil will come to help and hold the boughs for you.

1894 A. J. C. HARE *Sussex* 43 Hazel copses . . . are . . . abundant (an old Sussex proverb).

Nutting, *see also* Holyrood Day the devil goes a-n.; Speak in clusters, begot in n.

O

O Master Vier, we cannot pay you your rent, for we had no grace of God this year; no shipwreck upon our coast.   (M 740)

1659 HOWELL *Eng. Prov.* 12b . . . A saying of the *Cornish.*

Oak has been an acorn, Every.   (A 22)

1578 GOSSON *In prayse of the Booke* in Florio *First F.* 16 From slender roote . . . sometyme we see the boystrous Oke to rise.   **1579** *Id. Sch. Abuse* Arb. 38 But tal Cedars, from little graynes shoote high: great Okes, from slender rootes spread wide.   **1584** WITHALS D4 Of a nut springes an hasill, and of an Akorn an hie or tall oke.   **1732** FULLER no. 4576 The greatest Oaks have been little Acorns.   **1852** E. FITZGERALD *Polonius* v. 'Every oak must be an acorn.'   **1908** *T.L.S.* 26 June We always forget that the oak grew from an acorn.

Oak is not felled at one stroke, An. *Cf.* Strokes fell great oaks, Many.

c. **1370** [CHAUCER] *Romaunt of the Rose*, l. 3688 No man at fyrste stroke He maye nat fele down an oke.   *c.* **1430** LYDGATE *Fall Princes* I. 96 These ookis grete be nat douniþewe First at a strok.   *a.* **1530** *R. Hill's Commonpl. Bk.* E.E.T.S. 128 Hit is a febill tre that fallith at the first strok.   **1621** BURTON *Anat. Mel.* I. ii. IV. vii. (1651) 172 An old oak is not felled at a blow.   **1641** FERGUSSON no. 811 The tree fals not at the first straike.

Oak's before the ash, If the | then you'll only get a splash; if the ash precedes the oak, then you may expect a soak.

1852 *N. & Q.* 1st Ser. v. 581 When the oak comes out before the ash, there will be fine weather in harvest. I . . . find it generally correct.   **1911** *T.L.S.* 4 Aug. 285 One of the commonest weather rhymes in most parts of England deals with the budding of the oak and the ash:— When the oak's before the ash Then you'll only get a splash, When the ash is before the oak Then you may expect a soak. But in North Germany the signs are exactly inverted, and also in Cornwall.

Oaks may fall when reeds stand the storm.   (O 3)

c. **1374** CHAUCER *Troilus* Bk. 2, l. 1387 'And reed that boweth doun for every blast Ful lightly, cesse wynd, it wol aryse; But so nyl nought an ook whan it is cast'.   **1562** J. PILKINGTON *Aggeus and Abdias* P.S. 208 Yet stand fast the low bushes, when the great oaks are overthrown.   **1577** TUSSER liii. (1878) 149 Like as in tempest great, where wind doth beare the stroke, Much safer stands the bowing reede then doth the stubborn oke.   **1621** BURTON *Anat. Mel.* II. iii. III. (1651) 329 Though I live obscure, yet I live clean and honest; and when as the lofty oke is blown down, the silly reed may stand.   **1660** FULLER *Hants.* 9 Though our Lord Powlet enjoyed his place not so many years, yet did he serve more Soveraigns, in more mutable times, being (as he said of himself) 'no oake, but an osier'.   **1732** FULLER no. 3692.

Oak(s), *see also* Close (hard) as o., (As); Cut down o. and set strawberry; Grass on the top of o. tree (Look for); Heart of o.; Man in the o.; Strokes fell great o.; Willow will buy horse before o. saddle.

Oar in every man's boat (barge), To have an.   (o 4)

[= to have a hand in every one's affairs.] *c.* **1500** *Cocke Lorell's Bote* Percy Soc. 11 In Cocke's bote eche man had an ore. **1542** ERASM. tr. Udall *Apoph.* II. 180. In eche mannes bote, would be haue an ore. **1546** HEYWOOD I. X. C3 She must haue an ore in euery mans barge. **1577** STANYHURST in Holinshed *Chron. Ireland* (1587, 89a) Thomas Canon . . . was very willing to haue an ore in that bote. **1606** *Ret. from Parnassus* For his oare in every paper boate. **1631** BRATHWAITE *Whimzies* (1859) 86 He loves to fish in troubled waters, have an oar in every mans boat. **1731** COFFEY *Devil to Pay* I. ii. I will govern my own house without your putting in an oar. *c.* **1779** R. CUMBERLAND in *Lett. Lit. Men* (Camden) 412 Whilst I have such a friend to act for me, why should I put in my oar? **1809** MALKIN *Gil Blas* I. vii. par. 11 . . . put in my oar whenever I thought I could say a good thing. **1886** BESANT *Childr. Gibeon* II. xxx 'Now, don't you put your oar in, young woman. You'd best stand out of the way, you had!'

Oar(s), *see also* Boat without the o. (Ill goes).

Oath is better broken than kept, An unlawful.   (o 7)

1481 CAXTON *Reynard* Arb. 50 A bydwongen oth or oth sworn for force was none oth. **1528** TYNDALE *Obed. of a Christian Man* P.S. 206. **1542** T. BECON *Invective agst. Swearing* (n.d. H2ᵛ) The ooth, promise or vowe, that is not grounded on truth, iudgement, and ryghteousnes, ought to be broken [St. Jerome]. **1590–1** SHAKES. *2 Hen. VI* V. i. 182 It is a great sin to swear unto a sin, But greater sin to keep a sinful oath. **1594** *Id. T.G.V.* II. vi. 11 Unheedful vows may heedfully be broken. **1640** HERBERT no. 1017 An oath that is not to be made, is not to be kept. **1670** RAY 126.

Oath(s), *see also* Children deceived with comfits, men with o.; King's word more than another man's o.

Oatmeal, *see* Store of o. (Where there is), you may put enough in crock.

Oats will mow themselves.

1750 W. ELLIS *Mod. Husbandm.* v. 52 Oats are so heavy a Grain as to lie close with a little Trouble. We say, Oats will mow themselves.

Oat(s), *see also* Cut o. green; Debtors (Of ill) men take o.; Goose, (Young is) that will eat no o.; Horse that will not carry saddle; Horse will not void o.; Janiveer sows o. (Who in); Rough o.; St. David's day put o. in clay; Water trotted is as good as o.; Wild o.

Obedience is much more seen in little things than in great.

1732 FULLER no. 3693.

Obedience is the first duty of a soldier.

1846–7 J. GRANT *Rom. of War* ch. 59 'What do the wiseacres at headquarters mean in sending a detachment there?' 'I suppose they scarcely know themselves. But obedience—we all know the adage.' **1872** G. J. WHYTE-MELVILLE *Satanella* ch. 24 'The first duty of a soldier is obedience', he answered in great glee.

Obedient, *see* Money (All things o. to).

Obey(s, -ing), *see* Bound must o.; Commands enough that o. a wise man; Nature conquered by o. her.

Obligation, *see* Irishman's o.

Obliges, *see* Trusts much o. much.

Obsolete, *see* Works it's o., (If it).

Obstinate, *see* Mule, (As o. as a).

Obtains, *see* Stay (He that can) o.

Occam's razor.

[*Entia non sunt multiplicanda praeter necessitatem*, the leading principle of the nominalism of William of Occam, an Eng. scholastic philosopher of first half of 14th cent., that for purposes of explanation things not known to exist should not, unless it is absolutely necessary, be postulated as existing; usually called the Law of Parsimony.] **1836–7** SIR W. HAMILTON *Metaph.* xxxix (1859) II. 395 We are, therefore, entitled to apply Occam's razor to this theory of causality. **1929** *Let. to Times* 2 May 12/2 Is it to be a universal denomination *ante rem*, or a still more universal (!) denomination *post rem*? Has the noble lord forgotten Occam's razor?

Occasion lost cannot be redeemed, An.

1616 DRAXE no. 1522 (cannot easily). **1813** RAY 144.

Occasion, *see also* Do ill (Who would) ne'er wants o.; Takes away the o. takes away the offence, (He. that); Time (O.) by the forelock (Take).

Occupation is as good as land, An.

a. **1592** W. PERKINS *Treatise of Callings* (Wks. 1608, i. 729) (Our people haue a common saying that). **1599** MINSHEU *Span. Gram.* 83 He that hath an occupation or office, hath a benefit and a benefice.

Ocean, *see* Drink the o. dry.

O'clock, *see* Know what's o.

Odds, *see* Evil there is o. (In); Two to one is o.

Odious, *see* Comparisons are o.

Off the hooks (hinges).   (H 592)

[(*a*) = out of condition, order.] **1616** 14 Nov. J. CHAMBERLAIN *Letters* (McLure) ii. 34 The Lord Cooke [= Coke] is now quite of the hookes. **1620** SHELTON *Quix.* Pt. II. vii (ii. 232) Off the hinges. **1626** JONSON *Staple of News* III. ii. 24 To hang the States on, h' has heau'd off the hookes. **1644** J. HOWELL *Dodona's Grove* 91 (hinges). **1659** HOWELL *Fr. Prov.* 17 The world is quite off the hinges. *a.* **1659** CLEVELAND *Pet. Poem* 22 My Doublet looks Like him that wears it, quite off o' the Hooks. **1684** H. MORE *Answer* 240 But the application is, methinks, much off the Hooks. **1930** 30 Jan. D. H. LAWRENCE *Lett.* ii. 1238 Why do you think you want to razzle and drink . . .? . . . You'll always be miserable when you go off the hooks. [(*b*) = out of bounds.] **1612** *North's Plutarch* 1214 Agrippina began . . . to flye off the hookes: and coming to Nero himself, threatned to take his Empire from him. [(*c*) = out of humour or spirits, or crazy.] **1621** FLETCHER *Pilgrim* III. vi. What fit's this? The Pilgrim's off the hooks too. **1662** PEPYS *Diary* 28 Apr. One thing that hath put Sir William so long off the hooks. **1824** SCOTT *St. Ronan's* ch. 30 Everybody . . . is a little off the hooks . . . in plain words, a little crazy, or so. [(*d*) = crestfallen.] **1639** DAVENPORT *New Trick* I. ii. [(*e*) = dead or dying.] **1842** BARHAM *Ingol. Leg., Blk. Mousq.* II Our friend . . . has popp'd off the hooks! **1894** BLACKMORE *Perlycross* 293 Is it true that old Fox is dropping off the hooks?

Off with the old love before you are on with the new, It is best to be.

1801 M. EDGEWORTH *Belinda* ch. 10. **1816** MATURIN *Bertram* Motto. **1819** SCOTT *Bride Lam.* ch. 29 (the old song). **1857** TROLLOPE *Barch. Tow.* ch. 27 There is an old song which gives us some very good advice about courting: . . . **1891** A. LANG *Ess. in Little* 6 Dumas . . . met the great man at Marseilles, where . . . Alexandre chanced to be ' on with the new love' before being completely ' off with the old'.

Offence, *see* Babbling is not without o. (Much); Takes away the occasion takes away the o., (He that).

Offended (Hurt) but by himself, None is.   (O 14)

[L. *Nemo laeditur nisi a seipso.* No man is hurt but by himself.] **1640** HERBERT no. 656.

Offender never pardons, The.   (O 15)

[TAC. *Agric.* 42. 4 *Proprium humani ingenii est odisse quem laeseris.*] **1640** HERBERT no. 561. **1666** TORRIANO *It. Prov.* 176 no. 18 Who offends, ne'er forgives. **1672** DRYDEN *Conq. Gran.* Pt. 2. I. ii. Forgiveness to the injur'd does belong, But they ne'er pardon who have done the wrong. **1821** 17 Nov. BYRON *Lett.* Prothero v. 481 The moralists say that the most offending are the least forgetting. **1876** MRS. BANKS *Manch. Man* ch. 45 He was of Mrs. Ashton's mind that, ' as offenders never pardon', Augusta needed a friend.

Offenders, *see* Laws, (The more) the more o.; Pardon makes o.

Offer much, is a kind of denial, To.   (M 1292)

1611 COTGRAVE s.v. Beaucoup To offer much to him that asketh little, is flatly to denie him the little he asketh. **1631** MABBE *Celestina* T.T. 116 (a common saying).

Offer your hen for sale on a rainy day, Never.   (H 427)

1721 KELLY 373 You will not sell . . . **1846** DENHAM 3.

Offer, *see also* Fair o. no cause of feud; Refuse a good o., (Never).

Offering, *see* Long standing and small o. makes poor parsons; Priest (Such), such o.; Saint (Like), like o.

Off-fallings, *see* Gentles (Where there are), there are o.-f.

Office, He has a good | he must needs thrive.   (O 20)

1611 COTGRAVE s.v. Mestier He that hath a good trade hath a goodlie reuenue. *c.* **1640** W. S. *Countrym. Commonw.* 19 Hee that hath an Occupation or an Office, hath a Benefit and a Benefice. **1678** RAY 263.

Office, *see also* Buy an o. (They that) must sell; Cast of his o. (Give one a); Jack in o.; Jack out of o.; Out of o. out of danger. *See also* Magistracy.

Offices may well be given, but not discretion.   (O 23)

1573 SANFORD 109ᵛ. **1578** FLORIO *First F.* f. 33ᵛ. **1629** *Bk. Mer. Rid.* Prov. no. 116. **1642** TORRIANO 50 Offices are bestowed, but not the wit how to manage them.

Offspring of those that are very old, or very young, lasts not, The.   (O 24)

1640 HERBERT no. 887.

Oft ettle,[1] whiles hit.

1721 KELLY 269 . . . People who have made many Tryals to do a Thing, may hit right at last. [¹ aim.]

Often and little eating makes a man fat.   (E 55)

1657 E. LEIGH *Select & Choice Observations* 275. **1659** N. R. 84. **1670** RAY 38.

Often(er), *see also* Content lodges o. in cottages than palaces; Little and o. fills purse; Put not the bucket too o. in the well.

Oil (no oil) left in the lamp, There is.
(o 29)

1573 GASCOIGNE *Dan B. of Bath* i. 127 Who hath seene a Lampe begyn to fade, Which lacketh oyle to feede his lyngring light. **1573** *Id. Flowers* i. 43 The boxe of oyle is wasted wel, which once dyd feede my lampe. **1590** SPENSER *F.Q.* II. x. 30 True it is that when the oyle is spent, The light goes out. **1591** ARIOSTO *Orl. Fur.* Harington XXIV. 69 And as the lampe go'th out when oyle doth wast, So quietly the noble Zerbin slept. *Ibid.* XXXIII. 48 Much like a lampe when all the oile is spent. **1591–2** SHAKES. *I Hen. VI* II. v. 8 These eyes, like lamps whose wasting oil is spent, Wax dim. **1596** *Id. Rich. II* I. iii. 221 My oil-dried lamp and time-bewasted light Shall be extinct with age. **1602** *Id. A.W.* I. ii. 58 'Let me not live,' quoth he, 'After my flame lacks oil'.

Oil of angels.[1]
(o 27)

[= gold as gifts or bribes.] **1592** GREENE *Upst. Courtier* E j b The palms of their hands so hot that they cannot be coold vnlesse they be rubed with the oil of angels. **1593** NASHE *Christ's Tears* ii. 156 Lawyers . . . cannot heare except their eares be rubd with the oyle of angels. **1623** MASSINGER *Dk. Milan* III. ii I have seen . . . his stripes wash'd off With the oil of angels. [1 a gold coin worth 10s.]

Oil of baston.[1]

[= a beating.] **1602** WITHALS 308ᵛ That Remedie against that vnlustinesse, which they call the Feuer lurden, Vnguentum Baculinum, they call it vulgarly the oyle of Baston, or a sower cudgell. [1 stick.]

Oil of fool.

[= flattery used to befool a person.] **1785** WOLCOT (P. Pindar) *9th Ode to R.A.'s*, Reynolds . . . prithee, seek the Courtier's school And learn to manufacture oil of fool.

Oil of whip (strap).
(o 28)

1662 FULLER *Somerset* 21 Although oil of whip be the proper plaister for the cramp of lazinesse, yet some pity is due to impotent persons. **1693** *Poor Robin* Now for to cure such a disease as this, The oyl of whip the surest medicine is. **1847** HALLIWELL *Dict.* (1889) II. 816 Strap-oil. A severe beating. It is a common joke on April 1st to send a lad for a pennyworth of strap-oil, which is generally ministered on his own person.

Oil on the fire is not the way to quench it, Pouring.
(o 32)

c. **1580** SIDNEY I *Arc.* iv. 68 As well may thinck, with Oyle to coole the fyer. **1586** GUAZZO ii. 149 You thinke . . . to quench fire with oyle. **1592** DELAMOTHE 35 (To cast oyle into the fier). **1608** SHAKES. *C.* III. i. 196 This is the way to kindle, not to quench. **1608** *Id. P.* I. iv. 4 That were to blow at fire in hope to quench it. **1623** CAMDEN 275. **1670** RAY 126 (To cast oil in). **1875** CARLYLE *Early K. of Norway* ch. 7 Wretched Ethelred . . . offered them Danegelt . . . : a dear method of quenching fire by pouring *oil* on it.

Oil to the fire, To add.
(o 30)

c. **1386** CHAUCER *Phys. T.* l. 60 For wyn and youthe dooth Venus encresse, As men in fyr wol casten oille or greesse. **1548** HALL *Chron.* (1808 ed., 477) Thei cast oyle and pitche into a fyre. *Ibid.* 820 Malicious . . . persones who added Oyle (as the Adage sayth) to the Fornace. *c.* **1550** INGELEND *Disob. Child* Hazl.-Dods. ii. 280 And, after the proverb, we put oil to the fire. **1605–6** SHAKES. *K.L.* II. ii. 72 Bring oil to fire, snow to their colder moods. *a* **1677** SIR P. WARWICK *Memoirs* (1701) 18 To pour new oyle into this flame.

Oil upon the waters, To pour.

[= to smooth matters over.] *a.* **731** BEDE *Eccles. Hist.* Bk. 3, ch. 15 Remember to throw into the sea the oil which I give to you, when straightway the winds will abate, and a calm and smiling sea will accompany you throughout your voyage. **1847** W. B. BARING in *Croker Papers* (1884) III. xxv. 103 Lord G. [Bentinck] . . . spoke angrily. D'Israeli poured oil and calmed the waves. **1864–5** DICKENS *Mutual Friend* Bk. III, ch. 12 'His wife . . . would throw oil on the waters . . . I should fail to move him to an angry outburst, if his wife was there'.

Oil, *see also* Measures o. (He that) shall anoint fingers; Midnight o.; Old fish, old o., old friend; Palm o.; Smooth as o.; Truth and o. are ever above; Wine (Of) the middle, of o. the top.

Ointment, *see* Fly in the o.

Old acquaintance will soon be remembered.

c. **1550** R. WEVER *Lusty Juventus* Hazl.-Dods. ii. 70 I never knew, That you and I together were acquainted: But nevertheless, if you do it renew, Old acquaintance will soon be remembered.

Old age comes stealing on.
(A 70)

1530 PALSGRAVE 501a Age crepeth upon us or we be ware. **1557** TOTTELL Arb. 173 Age with stelyng steppes Hath clawed me with his crowch. **1600** DEKKER *Shoem. Hol.* III. iii. 22 Lets be merry whiles we are yong, olde age, sacke and sugar will steale vpon vs ere we be aware. *c.* **1600** SHAKES. *H.* V. i. 71 Age, with his stealing steps, Hath clawed me in his clutch. **1616** WITHALS 543 (commeth stealing vpon vs).

Old age is sickness of itself.
(A 73)

[TER *Phorm.* 575 *Senectus ipsast morbus*.] **1601** T. WRIGHT *Passions of the Mind* 73 (a perpetuall sickenesse). **1666** TORRIANO *It. Prov.* 297 no. 33 If I dye of no other disease than old age. **1672** WALKER 33 no. 93 (sickness enough of itself).

Old and cold.

1327–8 *Chester Plays, Salut. & Nativ.* Shakes. Soc. I. 98 For I am bouth oulde and coulde. *a.* **1628** CARMICHAELL no. 251 Auld and cauld, ill to ly besyde. **1721** KELLY 160 He is old and cold, and ill to lye beside. Spoken by a young Maid, when jeer'd with an old Man. **1738** SWIFT *Dial.* I. E.L. 276 Not so old, nor yet so cold—You know the rest, miss.

Old and tough, young and tender. (o 35)

1678 RAY 85. **1855** THACKERAY *Little Billee* There's little Bill as is young and tender, We're old and tough.

Old and wise, Though | yet still advise.

(A 44)

1640 HERBERT no. 134. **1732** FULLER no. 6227.

Old ape has an old eye, An. (A 272)

1633 W. ROWLEY *Match at Midn.* Hazl.-Dods. xiii. 39 Nay, an old ape has an old eye; I shall go before, an' thou woot show me a love-trick, and lock me into the garden. **1636** CAMDEN 291. **1639** CLARKE 267. **1738** SWIFT Dial. I. E.L. 276.

Old as Charing Cross, As.

1598 DELONEY 2 *Gentle Craft* Wks. (Mann) 188.

Old as Glastonbury Tor, As. (G 139)

[The Tor (550 ft.) is crowned with the tower of a chapel destroyed in 1271.] **1678** RAY 344 . . . *Somerset.* This torre, *i.e.* tower, so called from the Latine *Turris*, stands upon a round hill.

Old as Methuselah, As. (M 908)

1620 SHELTON *Quix.* II. iii ii. 208. **1687** MIÈGE s.v. Old (Mathusalem). **1706** STEVENS s.v. Sarra (Mathusalem).

Old as my tongue and a little older than my teeth.

c. **1604** DAY *Law Tricks* v. ii. I am just as old . . . as my little finger. **1738** SWIFT Dial. I. E.L. 270.

Old as Pauls (*or* Paul's steeple), As.

(P 119)

[The steeple of Old St. Paul's cathedral was destroyed by lightning in 1561 and never re-erected.] **1659** HOWELL *Prov.* Dedn. Some of them may be said to be as old as Pauls Steeple. **1662** FULLER London 199 (Paul's steeple). . . . This proverb . . . serveth . . . to be returned to such, who pretend those things to be Novell, which are known to be stale . . . and almost antiquated. **1670** RAY 206. **1738** SWIFT Dial. I. E.L. 284 She's as old as Poles.

Old as the flood, As.

1586 FERNE *Blazon of Gent.* 158 (ancient). **1828** T. H. LISTER *Herbert Lacy* ch. I.

Old as the hills.

a. **1500** *15c. School Bk.* ed. W. Nelson 37 Yf I lyff the age of malvornn hyllys. **1819** METRO-POLIS I. 58. **1820** SCOTT *Monastery* ch. 9.

Old band (ensign) is a captain's honour, An. (B 64)

1573 SANFORD 102ᵛ. **1578** FLORIO *First F.* 28 An old Ensigne is the honor of a captaine. **1629** *Bk. Mer. Rid.* Prov. no. 65.

Old be, or young die. (D 328)

1579 A. HALL *Quarrel betw. Hall and Mallorie* in *Misc. Antiq. Angl.* 47 Olde I must be or die young. **1678** RAY 182.

Old bones, She will never make.

1872 C. READE *Wandering H.* ch. 9 She is too good to last. . . . I fear she is like her father, and will ne'er make old bones.

Old brown cow laid an egg, The.

1917 BRIDGE 117 . . . Used as an answer to importunate questioners.

Old cart well used may outlast a new one abused, An. (C 108)

c. **1549** HEYWOOD I. xi. D3ᵛ Cartis well driuen . . . go longe vpright. **1732** FULLER no. 6287.

Old cat laps as much milk as a young (kitten), An. (C 160)

1623 CAMDEN 266. **1670** RAY 68 (as much as a young kitlin).

Old cat sports not with her prey, An.

(C 161)

1640 HERBERT no. 1030.

Old cat to an old rat, Put an. (C 162)

1668 DAVENANT *Man's the Master* I. i. Wks. (1874) V. 16 (As the proverb says).

Old cattle breed not. (C 195)

1614 T. ADAMS *Soul's Sickness* 30 Old breed cattell no longer, doted trees deny fruit, the tired earth becomes barren. **1670** RAY 127.

Old chains gall less than new.

1907 *Spectator* 12 Jan. 50 Prayer-book revision . . . might . . . end in a narrowing . . . of the Church. The late Master of Balliol once re-minded Liberal Churchmen that old chains gall less than new.

Old cloak makes a new jerkin, An.

c. **1592** KYD *Span. Trag.* III. vi Doost thou think to liue till his olde doublet will make thee a new trusse? **1594** BACON *Promus* 212, no. 469 Old treacle new losange. *c.* **1641** FERGUSSON MS. no. 1127 Often hath it bein sein that Eva's old kirtl hath maid old Adam a pair of new breeches. **1600-1** SHAKES. *M.W.W.* I. iii. 16 An old cloak makes a new jerkin; a withered serving-man, a fresh tapster.

Old cock crows, As the | so crows the young (the young one learns). (C 491)

c. **1350** *Douce MS.* 52 no. 43 As þe cocke croweth, so þe chekyn lernyth. **1509** BARCLAY *Ship of Fools* i. 235 The yonge Cok lerneth to crowe hye of the olde. **1546** HEYWOOD I. x. C2ᵛ Their folkis glomd on me to, by whiche it apeer-eth. The yong cocke croweth, as he the olde heereth. **1615** BRATHWAIT *Strappado for Div.*

176 Which by the proverb every man discerns, *Since as the old cock crows, the young cock learns.* **1822** SCOTT *Pirate* ch. 18 As the old cock crows the young cock learns . . . the father declares against the king's customs, and the daughter against the king's crown. **1834** MARRYAT *Jacob Faith.* ch. 25 There's an old adage which saith, 'As the old cock crows, so doth the young'.

Old debts are better than old (new) sores. (D 170)

a. **1628** CARMICHAELL no. 239 Auld debtis better nor new sairs. *Ibid.* no. 277 Better auld debts nor auld sairs. **1641** FERGUSSON no. 171 Better auld debts nor auld saires. **1659** HOWELL *Portugal Prov.* (*Span. Prov.*) 27 An old debt is better then a new sin. **1721** KELLY 275 . . . The one may be paid, and the other will ake.

Old dog barks not in vain, An. (D 498)

1573 SANFORD 102ᵛ. **1593** J. ELIOT *Ortho-Epia Gallica* ed. J. Lindsay 50 One should . . . beleeue the barking of an old dog. **1611** COTGRAVE s.v. Iapper. **1651** HERBERT no. 1099.

Old dog bites sore, An. (D 499)

1545 TAVERNER A3ᵛ The englysh prouerbe sayth thus An olde dogge byteth sore. **1546** HEYWOOD II. vi. I1 It is saide of olde, an olde dog byteth sore. **1589** *Just Censure* Marprelate Tracts Pierce 377 There is no biting to the old snake. **1721** KELLY 23 . . . Spoken to discourage one from provoking a Man of advanc'd Years; for . . . he will give a desperate Blow.

Old enough (and ugly enough) to take care of oneself.

1600 BRETON *Pasquil's Mistress* A2 Hopeing that you are olde enough to know what is good for your selfe. **1872** G. J. WHYTE-MELVILLE *Satanella* ch. 10 'Are you quite alone, on your own hook?' 'What a question!' she laughed. 'I suppose you think I'm old enough and ugly enough to take care of myself!'

Old enough to lie without doors. (D 565)

1678 RAY 77.

Old ewe dressed lamb fashion, An.

1777 *Gent. Mag.* xlvii. 187 Here antique maids of sixty three Drest out lamb-fashion you might see. **1785** GROSE s.v. Ewe . . . . an old woman, drest like a young girl. **1891** J. L. KIPLING *Beast & Man* 201 Of an old woman in gay attire they say, 'An old mare in a red rein'. Our brutal saw says, 'Old ewe, lamb fashion'.

Old fish and young flesh do feed men best. (F 369)

c. **1386** CHAUCER *Merch. T.* 1. 1418 Oold fissh and yonge flessh wolde I have fayn. . . . Bet than olde boef is the tendre veel. I wol no womman thritty yeer of age. **1546** HEYWOOD II. iv. G3 Olde fishe and yong flesh (quoth he) dooth men best feede. **1576** HOLYBAND D1ᵛ They say in our parish that yong phisitions make the churchyardes croked, and old attorneies sutes to go a wray: but to the contrary yong atturneis

and old phisitions, yong flesh, and olde fishe be the best. **1641** S. MARMION *The Antiquary* Hazl.-Dods. xiii. 432. **1670** RAY 39 Jeun chair & vieil poisson, *i.e.* Young flesh and old fish are best.

Old fish, old oil, and an old friend are the best. (F 321)

1659 HOWELL *It. Prov.* 15 Old fish, old oyl, and an old friend. **1678** RAY 41 Pesce, oglio & amico vecchio.

Old fox is not easily snared, An. (F 647)

1539 TAVERNER 28ᵛ Annosa vulpes haud capitur laqueo. An olde foxe is not taken in a snare. *Ibid.* 39 Vulpes non iterum capitur laqueo. The foxe is not eftsones taken in a snare. *c.* **1558** W. WEDLOCK *Image of Idleness* E4ᵛ The Fox . . . beinge once tangled in a trap and escapeth, wyl be so circumspecte, that he is neuer taken by any kynde of engine afterwardes. **1607** DEKKER *Whore Bab.* III. i. 55 Old Lyons hardly fall into the snare. **1621** BURTON *Anat. Mel.* II. iii. VI. (1651) 343 A little experience and practice will inure us to it; *vetula vulpes,* as the proverb saith *laqueo haud capitur*; an old fox is not so easily taken in a snare. **1659** TORRIANO no. 84 Even some old Foxes are taken in the snare. **1809** MALKIN *Gil Blas* IV. xi Justice . . . is coming . . . to lay her paw upon my person. But an old fox is too cunning to be caught in a trap.

Old foxes want no tutors. (F 648)

1639 CLARKE 267 An old fox need learne no craft. **1670** RAY 127 (as 1639). **1732** FULLER no 3712. *Ibid.* no. 644 An old Fox needs not to be taught Tricks. **1792** WOLCOT (P. Pindar) *Odes to Pitt* V Wks. (1816) II. 263 What, preach to *me* on *money*-wit! Old foxes want no tutors, Billy Pitt.

Old friends and old wine and old gold are best. (F 755)

1565 J. HALL *Court of Virtue* R7ᵛ Plato. Of all thynges the newest is best for behoue, Saue only frendshyp and frendly loue. **1575** MARCH *Cal. Span. Papers 1568–79* 492 [Queen Elizabeth told the Spanish ambassador that] 'Old wine, old bread, and old friends should be valued'. **1576** PETTIE ii. 132 You ought to like those friends best which last longest, and have lived longest with you . . . like many wines, which the older they are the better they are! *c.* **1594** BACON *Promus* 508. 1612 Vin vieux, amy vieux et or vieux sont aimez en tous lieux. **1640** HERBERT no. 136 Old wine and an old friend are good provisions. **1670** RAY 19. **1706** STEVENS s.v. Azeyte with 'oil' for 'gold'.

Old head and young hands. (H 263)

1678 RAY 347. *Somerset.*

Old head on young shoulders, An. *Cf.* Grey head . . . green shoulders. (M 500)

1591 H. SMITH *Preparative for Marriage* 14–15 It is not good grafting of an olde head vppon young shoulders. **1596** SHAKES. *M.V.* IV. i. 160 I never knew so young a body with so old a head. **1639** CLARKE 7 You set an old mans head on a yong mans shoulders. **1842** MARRYAT *Perc. Keene* ch. 19 You appear to have an old head upon very young shoulders; at one moment to be a scampish boy . . ., and at another a resolute . . . man.

Old knave (babe) is no babe (child), An. (K 132)

1528 MORE *Wks.* (1557) 242a They shal for al that fynde in some of us yt an olde knaue is no chylde. **1546** HEYWOOD II. ii. G1ᵛ (chylde). **1555** *Id. Epigr. upon Prov.* no. 148. **1626** BRETON *Soothing* A8 An old babe is no childe. **1639** CLARKE 71 (as 1626). **1641** FERGUSSON no. 84 (na bairne). **1721** KELLY 35 (*no bairn*) . . . Cunning old Companions, who are thoroughly versed in Cheating and Deceit.

Old long (well old), He that would be | must be old betimes (Old young and old long). *Cf.* Old young, young old. (O 34, 36)

[CICERO *De Senec.* 32 *Mature fieri senem, si diu velis senex esse.*] **1539** TAVERNER 10ᵛ Become an olde man betyme yf thou wylt be an olde man longe. *a.* **1628** CARMICHAELL no. 1366 Soone an old man, lang ane old man. **1639** CLARKE 190 Old young, and old long. *Ibid.* 780 They that would bee old long, must be old yong. **1640** HERBERT no. 371 (well old). **1670** RAY 34 (as 1639, 190). **1672** WALKER 39 no. 15. **1691** R. CROMWELL *Let.* in *Eng. Hist. Rev.* (1898) xiii. 109 There is an old proverb 'old yong, yong old'. **1711** STEELE *Spect.* no. 153, 25 Aug. It was prettily said, 'He that would be long an old man must begin early to be one' . . . . It is necessary that before the arrival of age we bid adieu to the pursuits of youth.

Old love will not be forgotten.

1634 T. HEYWOOD & R. BROME *Late Lancashire Witches* Heywood's Wks. (1874) iv. 201 and 216. **1675** *Letter* to Sir R. Verney *Verney Memoirs* iv (1899) 311 Ould love will not be forgotten.

Old maids lead apes in hell. (M 37)

c. **1560** *Bk. Fortune* 190 A mickle truth it is I tell Hereafter thou'st lead Apes in Hell: For she that will not when she may, When she will she shall have nay. **1573** GASCOIGNE *Posies* i. 430 I am afrayde my marryage will bee marred, and I may go lead Apes in hell. **1579** LYLY *Euph.* i. 220 But certès I will either lead a virgins life in earth (though I lead Apes in hel) or els follow thee. **1594–8** SHAKES. *T.S.* II. i. 34 I must dance bare-foot on her wedding-day, And, for your love to her, lead apes in hell. **1598–9** *Id. M.A.* II. i. 34 Therefore I will . . . lead his apes into hell . . . and there will the devil meet me . . . and say, 'Get you to heaven, Beatrice, get you to heaven; here's no place for you maids:' so deliver I up my apes. *c.* **1600** DONNE *Paradoxes and Problems* 'That Virginity is a Virtue', There is an old Proverb, That, they that dy maids, must lead Apes in Hell . . . perchance for the unprofitableness of this Beast did the proverb come up. **1605** *London Prodigal* I. ii Shakes. Apoc. 196. But tis an old prouerbe, and you know it well, That women dying maides lead apes in hell. **1738** SWIFT *Dial.* I. E.L. 292 Miss,

you may say what you please; but faith you'll never lead apes in hell.

Old man in a house is a good sign, An. (M 347)

1642 TORRIANO 14 Happy is that house that savoureth of an old man. **1659** HOWELL *It. Prov.* 4 That house is happy which smells of an old man. **1678** RAY *Adag. Hebr.* 403 . . . Old men are fit to give wise counsel.

Old man in a hurry, An.

1886 LORD RANDOLPH CHURCHILL on Gladstone. *To the Electors of South Paddington, June 1886.* [*Cf.* WELLINGTON in Greville, Aug. 1840 I have not time not to do what is right.]

Old man is a bed full of bones, An. (M 349)

1678 RAY 184. **1732** FULLER no. 648.

Old man lecher, young man liar.

c. **1250** *Ten Abuses* in *O. E. Misc.* 184 Old mon lechur, ȝunch mon lieȝer [*2nd text* lyere.]

Old man never wants a tale to tell, An.

1659 HOWELL *Span. Prov.* 10 The old man never wants stories at the fire-side or the Sunshine. **1706** STEVENS s.v. Viejo. **1732** FULLER no. 649.

Old Man of the Sea.

[In the *Arabian Nights*, the Old Man of the Sea, once seated on the shoulders of Sindbad, refused to dismount.] **1809** SCOTT *Let.* 7 Aug. in LOCKHART *Life* ch. 19 The old incumbent . . . reminds me of Sinbad's Old Man of the Sea, and will certainly throttle me if I can't somehow dismount him. **1909** *Spectator* 4 Dec. 931 If the Budget were passed, 'an Old Man of the Sea' would be sat upon the shoulders of the respectable and reputable classes in the community. **1927** *Times* 22 July 15/4 The bad habit into which we slip almost unconsciously fixes itself about our necks as firmly as any Old Man of the Sea.

Old man, when thou diest, give me thy doublet. (M 350)

1678 RAY 77.

Old man who weds a buxom young maiden, An | bids fair to become a freeman of Buckingham.

1787 GROSE 152 . . . The fabricator of this proverb, by a freeman of Buckingham, meant a cuckold.

Old man will not drink, When an | go to see him in another world. (M 410)

1659 HOWELL *It. Prov.* 15. **1664** CODRINGTON 227. **1666** TORRIANO 298 no. 17 (Look for him). **1670** RAY 20. *Ital.* **1706** STEVENS s.v. Viejo. When an old Man cannot drink They may make his Grave.

Old man's staff is the rapper of death's door, An. (M 480)

c. **1386** CHAUCER *Pardoner's T.* ll. 729–31 And on the ground, which is my moodres gate, I knokke with my staf, bothe erly and late, And seye 'leeve mooder, leet me in!' **1640** HERBERT no. 916. **1732** FULLER no. 4690.

Old mare leave flinging,[1] It is hard to make an.

1721 KELLY 193 . . . It is hard to reclaim those who have been long and habitually wicked. [[1] kicking.]

Old mare would have a new crupper, My. (M 651)

1546 HEYWOOD II. i. F3 What myne olde mare wolde haue a newe crouper. **1611** DAVIES no. 185. **1659** HOWELL *Eng. Prov.* 2a Old Mares lust after new cruppers.

Old men (soldiers) and travellers may lie by authority. *Cf.* Traveller may lie. (M 567)

1509 BARCLAY *Ship of Fools* ii. 68 Thre sortes . . . haue auctoryte to lye . . . pylgrimes . . . men aged . . . And men of hye degre Before theyr seruauntis. **1578** FLORIO *First F.* 75 Three sortes of men may lye by aucthoritie, a Phisition, an Olde man, and a Trauayler. *a.* **1607** *Lingua* D1 *Mendacio loq.* old man . . . challenge my Company by authority. **1623** CAMDEN 275 (farre trauellers). **1639** CLARKE 316. **1659** HOWELL *Eng. Prov.* 21a (Souldiers and travellers).

Old men are twice children. (M 570)

[ARISTOPH. *Nub.* 1417 Ἐγὼ δέ γ' ἀντείποιμ' ἄν, ὡς δὶς παῖδες οἱ γέροντες. I would reply that old men are twice boys. ERASM. *Ad. Bis pueri senes.*] **1527**? J. LONGLAND *Sermones* f. 704 [trans.] The proverb says of the aged, bis pueri senes. **1539** TAVERNER f. 16ᵛ Olde folke are twyse children. **1549** LATIMER *2nd Serm. bef. Edw. VI* P.S. 113 Kynge Dauid beynge . . . in hys second chyldhode, for al old men are twise chyldren, as the Prouerb is. *Senex bis puer.* **1600–1** SHAKES. *H.* II. ii. 381 They say an old man is twice a child. **1605–6** *Id. K.L.* I. iii. 19 Now by my life, Old fools are babes again. **1610** *Id. Cymb.* V. iii. 57 Two boys, an old man twice a boy. **1662** FULLER *Berks.* 93 In such Cases Native Ayr may prove Cordial to Patients, as Mothers' milk to (and old men are twice) children. **1821** GALT *Annals of Par.* ch. 16 Lady Macadam; in whom the saying was verified, that old folk are twice bairns, for . . . she was as play-rife as a very lassie at her sampler.

Old men go to death, death comes to young men. (M 572)

1625 BACON *Apoph.* Wks. (Chandos) 379 One of the fathers saith, ' That there is but this difference between the death of old men and young men; . . .'. **1732** FULLER no. 3719.

Old men, when they marry young women, make much of death. (M 348)

1539 TAVERNER *Publius* A6 An olde woman when she vseth dalyaunce, she doth nothyng els in effecte but delyteth death. **1582** WHETSTONE *Hept. Civil Disc.* T1 Greene Iuy, which catcheth an olde Tree, maketh quicke worke for the fire: and the imbracements of a faire Woman, hastneth an olde man to his Graue. [*Margin*] A yong wyfe is death to an old man. **1640** HERBERT no. 597 (scorne). **1642** TORRIANO 60 I vecchi che scherzano con le giovani, accarezzano la morte. Old men that dandle young maidens, hug death. **1659** HOWELL *It. Prov.* 14 Old men who play with with young maids, embrace death. **1659** N. R. 85 (seem young). **1748** RICHARDSON *Clarissa* iv. 121 (1785) Old men, when they marry young women, are said to make much of death.

Old man (men), *see also* Advice (If you wish good) consult o. m.; Better be an o. m.'s darling; Kindness is lost bestowed on o. m.; Wrongs not an o. m. that steals supper; Young man should not marry yet, o. m. not at all; Young man would (If) and o. m. could; Young men think o. m. fools; Young men's knocks o. m. feel.

Old muck-hills will bloom. (M 1303)

1678 RAY 77.

Old naught will never be aught, An. (N 346)

1523 SKELTON *Garl. Laurel* l. 1205: Wks. i. 410 Harde to make ought of that is nakid nought. **1574** HIGGINS *Mirr. for Mag.* ed. Campbell 112 Naught once (they saye) and euer after naught. **1678** RAY 184.

Old Nick. (N 161)

[= the Devil.] *c.* **1633** FLETCHER & SHIRLEY *The Night Walker* II. i. What's that that moves there, ith' name of—*Nicholas*? **1641** MARMION *Antiquary* Hazl.-Dods. xiii. 458 Old Nick Machiauel. *a.* **1643** in EBSWORTH *Merry Drollery* App. (1875) 394 For Roundheads Old Nick stand up now. **1668** R. L'ESTRANGE *Vis. Quev.* III. 103 They were all sent to Old Nick. **1774** GOLDSMITH *Retal.* 58 We wished him full ten times a day at Old Nick. **1788** GROSE *Class. Dict.* Old Nick The Devil; from Neken, the evil spirit of the north. **1886** BESANT *Childr. Gibeon* I. viii When you . . . made us laugh with your conceit, being always conceited as Old Nick.

Old of the moon, In the | a cloudy morning bodes a fair afternoon. (O 33)

c. **1640** *Berkeley MSS.* 31 no. 52 A misty morne in th' old o' th' moone doth alwaies bringe a faire post-noone. An hilly proverbe about Simondsall (Glouc.). **1678** RAY 48.

Old ox makes a straight furrow, An. (O 105)

1659 HOWELL *Span. Prov.* 9 (streightest). **1666** TORRIANO *It. Prov.* 30 no. 19. An old Oxe, a streight furlong. **1732** FULLER no. 650. **1823**

COLLINS 69 . . . Applicable to those persons, who, guided by their judgment and experience, conduct their affairs . . . with success.

Old ox will find a shelter for himself, An.

[L. *Bos senior caute consulit ipse sibi.*] **1706** STEVENS s.v. Buey. **1732** FULLER no. 651. **1823** COLLINS 4 'Do not seek a shelter for an old ox.' Alluding to old persons, who know from experience what they require.

Old oxen (stots) have stiff horns.

1832 HENDERSON 102 Auld stots hae stiff horns.

Old physician, An | and a young lawyer. *Cf.* Young barber and an old physician. (P 265)

1567 HOWELL *Fr. Prov.* 12 Make use of a young Chyrurgeon, but an old Physitian. **1576** HOLYBAND D1ᵛ They say in our parish that young phisitions make the churchyardes croked, and old attorneies sutes to go a wray: but to the contrary yong atturneies and old phisitions, young flesh, and olde fishe be the best. **1640** HERBERT no. 648. **1642** FULLER *H. & P. State* II. i (1841) 50 Commonly, physicians, like beer, are best when they are old; and lawyers, like bread, when they are young and new. **1670** RAY 36 . . . An old Physician because of his experience; a young Lawyer, because he . . . will have leisure enough to attend your business.

Old poacher makes the best keeper, An. (D 191)

c. **1386** CHAUCER *Physician's T.* l. 83 A theef of venisoun, that hath forlaft His likerousnesse, and al his olde craft, Kan kepe a forest best of any man. **1623** WEBSTER *Devil's Law-Case* I. ii. 214 There is no warier Keeper of a Parke, To prevent Stalkers, or your Night-walkers, Then such a man, as in his youth has been A most notorious Deare-stealer. **1655** FULLER *Ch. Hist.* IX. iii (1868) II. 596 Always set a — to catch a —; and the greatest deer-stealers make the best parkkeepers. **1864** PAYN *Lost Sir Massingb.* ch. 14 If you want to find a gentleman who in his youth . . . has been a poacher . . ., look you among the game-preservers on the bench of justice.

Old pottage (porridge) is sooner heated than new made. (P 512)

1670 RAY 47 . . . Old lovers fallen out are sooner reconciled then new loves begun. Nay the Comedian saith, *Amantium irae amoris redintegratio est.* [The quarrels of lovers are the renewal of love. TER. *Andria* 3. 3. 23.] **1732** FULLER no. 3724 (porridge . . . warmed).

Old praise dies, unless you feed it. (P 539)

1640 HERBERT no. 699.

Old sack asks much patching, An. (s 8)

1546 HEYWOOD II. ii. G1ᵛ I promyse you an olde sacke asketh much patchyng. **1586** LYLY *Endym.* v. ii. 29. **1641** FERGUSSON no. 81 An old seck craves meikle clouting.[1] [1 patching.]

Old Sarbut says (told me) so.

1894 NORTHALL *Folk-phrases* E.D.S. 20 Old Sarbut told me so. *Warw.* A local version of 'A little bird told me so'. The mythical Sarbut . . . is credited with the revealing of secrets, and as the originator of malicious statements.

Old Scratch.

[= the Devil.] **1762** SMOLLETT *L. Greaves* II. x He must have sold himself to Old Scratch. **1843** DICKENS *Christmas C.* ch. 4 'Well!' said the first. 'Old Scratch has got his own at last, hey?'

Old Serpent.

[= the Devil.] [REV. xx. 2 The old serpent, which is the Devil.] **1629** T. ADAMS *Med. upon Creed* Wks. (1861–2) III. 178 A serpent . . . is still his emblem. Every serpent is (as it were), a young devil, and the devil is called an 'old serpent'. **1817** MOORE *Lalla Rookh*; *Par. & Peri* 206, 'Some flowerlets of Eden ye still inherit, But the trail of the Serpent is over them all!'

Old serving-man, a young beggar, An. *Cf.* Young serving-man, old beggar. (s 255)

1598 I. M. *Health to Serv. Mec* C4 (I holde it an infallible rule, An olde). **1600–1** SHAKES. *M.W.W.* I. iii. 17 An old cloak makes a new jerkin; a wither'd servingman a fresh tapster. **1607** DEKKER & WEBSTER *Northw. Ho* III. ii. 130 An old Seruing-man turnes to a young beggar, whereas a young Prentise may turne to an old Alderman. [*c.* 1637] **1659** R. BROME *Eng. Moor* III. iii. 46 I am too old to seek out a new Master. I will not beg, because Ile crosse the proverb That runs upon old serving creatures. **1656** L. PRICE *Map of Merry Conceits* A6 Nothing so much out of request as an old horse.—Yes an old Servingman.

Old sin makes new shame. (s 471)

c. **1300** *Havelok* 2461 E.E.T.S. 69 Old sinne makes newe shame. *c.* **1350** *Douce MS.* 52 no. 119 Old synnys makyn new shamys. *c.* **1390** GOWER *Conf. Amantis* III. 2033 Men sein: 'Old Senne make new schame.' *a.* **1470** HARDYNG *Chron.* CXIV. xviii. Thus synnes olde make shames come full newe. **1623** WODROEPHE 522. **1629** *Bk. Mer. Rid.* Prov. no. 24 (repentance). **1659** TORRIANO no. 138 (penance). **1721** KELLY 269 (breed).

Old soldier over one, To come the.

[= to impose on one.] **1824** SCOTT *St. Ronan's* ch. 18 I should think he was coming the old soldier over me. **1861** HUGHES *Tom B. at Oxford* II. xvii. 331 But you needn't try to come the old soldier over me. I'm not quite such a fool[1] as that.

Old springs[1] give no price. (s 787)

a. **1628** CARMICHAELL no. 254. **1721** KELLY 273 . . . Spoken when old People or Things are despised. [1 tunes.]

Old Testament, *see* Testament.

Old thanks pay not for a new debt.

1642 TORRIANO I Old thanks beseem not a new gift. **1732** FULLER no. 3728.

Old, None so | that he hopes not for a year of life.   (Y 13)

[CICERO *De Senect.* 7. 24 *Nemo enim est tam senex, qui se annum non putet posse vivere.* There is no one so old but he thinks he can live a year.] *c.* **1520** *Calisto & Mel.* Hazl.-Dods. i. 78 None so old but may live a year. **1629** T. ADAMS *Serm.* (1861–2) II. 135 Though *tam senex nemo, quin putet se annum posse vivere,*—no man is so old but still he thinks he may live another year. And therefore lightly the older, the more covetous. **1678** RAY 353.

Old thief deserves (desires) a new halter, An.   (T 107)

1623 CAMDEN 265. **1670** RAY 127 (desires).

Old use and wont, legs about the fire.

1721 KELLY 273 . . . A Reflection on them who persevere in a bad Custom.

Old vessels must leak.   (V 39)

1587 *Mirr. for Mag.* (Campbell 283) So old a vessayle cannot chuse but leake. **1613** *Scoggins Jests* D7 Olde vessels must needs leake. **1666** TORRIANO *It. Prov.* 163 no. 74. **1732** FULLER no. 3729.

Old wife that wats[1] her weird,[2] She is an.

1721 KELLY 285 . . . None can know what may come of them. [[1] knows. [2] fortune.]

Old wise man's shadow is better than a young buzzard's sword, An.   (M 481)

1611 COTGRAVE s.v. Coquard The shadow of an aduised grandsire is better than the sword of an aduenturous goosecap. **1640** HERBERT no. 90. **1659** HOWELL *Fr. Prov.* 6 (is more safe then the target of the young gallant).

Old wives' tales.   (W 388)

c. **1200** *Ancrene Riwle* 88 Me seið upon ancren, þat euerich mest; haueð on olde cwene to ueden hire earen; ane maðelild þ maðeleð hire all þe talen of þe londe: [People say of anchoresses that almost every one hath an anchoresses that almost every one hath an old woman to feed her ears; a prating gossip who tells her all the tales of the land.] **1387** TREVISA tr. *Higden* (Rolls Ser.) III. 265 And useþ telynges as olde wifes doþ. **1509** BARCLAY *Ship of Fools* i. 72 A fole he is . . . to byleue the tales of an olde wife. **1542** ERASM. tr. Udall *Apoph.* (1877) Pref. xxv Old wiues foolishe tales of Robin Hoode.

Old wives were aye good maidens.

1721 KELLY 271 . . . Old People will always be boasting what fine Feats they did when they were young.

Old (Auld) wife (wives), see also ̄Need makes o. w. trot; Sorrow and an evil life makes o. w.; Tough sinew in a. w.'s heel (There is a).

Old woman in a wooden ruff, An.   (W 635)

1678 RAY 77 . . . *i.e.* in an antique dresse.

Old woman, see also Good small beer, good o. w. (No such thing as); Good things I do not love, good o. w.

Old wood is best to burn, old horse to ride, old books to read, and old wine to drink. *Cf.* Old friends.   (W 740)

1574 (1584 ed. 125) GUEVARA *Familiar Epistles* tr. Hellowes The good king Sir Alonso that tooke Naples, did vse to say that all was but trash, except drie wood to burne, an olde horse to ride, olde wine to drinke, old friendes to be conuersant, and olde bookes to read in. *c.* **1580** SIDNEY I *Arcadia* (Feuillerat) iv. 91 Old wood makes the best fire. **1589** LEO. WRIGHT *Displ. Dutie* 19 As olde wood is best to burne: old horse to ride, old bookes to reade, and old wine to drinke: so are old friends always most trusty to use. **1625** BACON *Apoph.* Wks. (Chandos) 366 Alonso of Arragon was wont to say . . ., 'That age appeared to be the best in four things: old wood best to burn; old wine to drink; old friends to trust; and old authors to read. **1773** GOLDSMITH *She Stoops to C.* I. Wks. (Globe) 645 I love everything that's old: old friends, old times, old manners, old books, old wine; and . . . I have been pretty fond of an old wife.

Old young, young old.   (O 36)

1659 HOWELL *Eng. Prov.* 4a A young man old, makes an old man young. **1670** RAY 34 They who would be young when they are old must be old when they are young. **1691** R. CROMWELL *Corr.* 109 There is an old proverb old yong, yong old.

Old, see also Devil knows many things because o.; Kindness lost on o. folks; Leaves o. way for new; Folks grow o. (When) they are not set by; Life in it (the o. horse) yet, (There is); Live to be o. (If you would not), be hanged young; Man is as o. as he feels; Never too o. to learn; Offspring of very o. lasts not; Shoe after one for luck, (To cast an o.); Shoe, (To be thrown aside like an o.); Sins grow o. (When) covetousness young; Trick to catch the o. one; Virtue never grows o.

Older and wiser.   (O 37)

1632 HAUSTED *Rival Friends* v. iv. L2ᵛ Are you auis'd of that? older and wiser. **1639** CLARKE 267 The older the wiser. **1670** RAY 126. **1697** W. POPE *Seth* [*Ward*] 125 As he was older than any of that Convention, he also thought himself wiser. **1762** WESLEY *Lett.* iv. 277 We are old enough to be wiser.

Older the worse (better), The.

1587 J. BRIDGES *Defence* 126 Antiquitie of time makes a iolie claime. Bonum quo antiquius, eo melius. A good thing the more auncient, the better. **1589** WARNER *Albion's Eng.* V. R1 The neerer to our graues, the further we from God. **1621** ROBINSON 23. **1639** CLARKE 84 . . . like my old shooes. **1823** J. GALT *Entail* ch. 4 Nae doubt, Cornie, the world's like the tod's whelp, aye the aulder the waur.

Olive, Call me not an | till thou see me gathered. (O 39)

1640 HERBERT no. 301.

Oliver, *see* Roland for O.

Omelets are not made without breaking of eggs.

[**1815** B. HAYDON *Autobiography* ch. 15 *On ne peut pas faire des omelettes sans casser les œufs.*] **1859** GEN. P. THOMPSON *Audi Alt.* II. xc. 65 We are walking upon eggs and . . . the omelet will not be made without the breaking of some. **1898** *Times* 10 Jan. 13/3 Omelettes cannot be made without breaking eggs, and war cannot be made without losses of this kind occurring.

Omittance, *see also* Forbearance.

Omne ignotum pro magnifico.

[TACITUS *Agricola* xxx. *Omne ignotum pro magnifico est.* Everything unknown is taken for magnificent.] **1819** LEIGH HUNT *Indicator* 8 Dec. It is better to verify the proverb, and take everything unknown for magnificent, rather than predetermine it to be worthless. The gain is greater. **1909** A. LLOYD *Every-day Japan* (1911) 235 *Omne ignotum pro mirifico.* . . . The Japanese . . . flock to the Hibiya Park, that they may see . . . gay-coloured flowers in the trim beds, for the park is laid out in the Western style of gardening.

Omnipotent, *see* Beauty is potent, but money is o.

Once a bishop, always a bishop. (B 409)

1655 FULLER *Ch. Hist.* VII. i. 28 (1868) II. 379 Latimer, by the courtesy of England ('once a bishop and ever a bishop'), was in civility saluted 'lord'.

Once a devil, always a devil.

1903 A. C. PLOWDEN *Grain or Chaff?* ch. 23 When a Counsel has two cases coming on at the same time in different Courts, he asks a friend to attend to one of them. Such a friend immediately becomes a 'devil'. . . . With some men it is, 'Once a devil, always a devil'; they never become anything else.

Once a knave, and ever a knave.

(K 133)

c. **1566** CURIO *Pasquin in a Trance* 107ᵛ The olde rule: he that is once a false knaue, it is maruell if euer he be honest man after. **1609** HARWARD 98ᵛ A knave will be a knave still. **1659** HOWELL *Eng. Prov.* 13a.

Once a parson (priest), always a parson (priest).

1859 G. A. SALA *Round the Clock* (1878) 290 The great case of Horne Tooke *versus* the House of Commons—'Once a priest for ever a priest.' **1865** L. STEPHEN *Lett.* 13 Jan. in *Life* (1906) ix. 158 As in this . . . country we stick to the maxim, 'once a parson, always a parson', I could not . . . go in for law. **1920** *Bookman* Sept. 192 No former celibate, with Boris's incapacity for blotting out his past, could be happy until he returned to his cell—once a priest always a priest, is a true enough motto so far as he is concerned. [On 9 Aug. 1870, an act enabling the clergy to unfrock themselves was passed. LEAN IV. 71.]

Once a thief, always a thief.

1706 STEVENS s.v. Hurtar.

Once a use and ever a custom. (U 22)

1565 COOPER *Thesaurus* s.v. Facere Use maketh a custome. **1591** STEPNEY 152 Vse bringeth a continuall custome. **1594** SHAKES. *T.G.V.* V. iv. 1 How use doth breed a habit in a man. **1621** ROBINSON 9. **1623** CAMDEN 275. **1670** RAY 153. **1732** FULLER no. 3733 Once in use, and ever after a custom.

Once a way (away) and aye a way (away).

1721 KELLY 274 . . . As a Proverb it signifies that no private Authority can stop that which has once been allowed to be a publick road. As a Phrase, it signifies that a Thing is quite gone.

Once a whore and ever a whore.

(W 321)

1613 H. PARROT *Laquei Ridiculosi* Bk. II, epi. 121. **1659** HOWELL *Eng. Prov.* 15a. **1704** SWIFT *Tale of a Tub* ed. D. Nichol Smith 101 A True Critick hath one Quality in common with a Whore and an Alderman, never to change his Title or his Nature. **1706** STEVENS s.v. Verguanças.

Once a year a man may say, on his conscience. (Y 14)

1640 HERBERT no. 971.

Once, and use it not. (U 25)

1598 DELONEY 2 *Gentle Craft* (Mann) 149. **1599** *Warning for Fair Women* B3ᵛ How ere it be, weel take it in good part For once and vse it not. **1678** RAY 263.

Once bit (bitten), twice shy.

1853 SURTEES *Sponge's Sport. T.* ch. 33 Jawleyford had been bit once, and he was not going to give Mr. Sponge a second chance. **1899** SIR A. WEST *Recoll.* ch. 13 Mr. Thomas . . . answered: 'Once bitten twice shy. I have tried one gentleman [as an apprentice] and will never try another.' **1909** *Times* 18 March The Admiralty have allowed themselves to be caught napping once, and . . . they must not be caught napping again. Once bit, twice shy.

Once born, He that is | once must die.
(B 140)

1592 DELAMOTHE 43.   **1639** CLARKE 323.   **1651**
HERBERT no. 1087.

Once deceives, He that | is ever
suspected.   (D 180)

1576 PETTIE ii. 23 Can he think to find me faithful towards him, that am faithless to mine own
father? **1578** FLORIO *First F.* 28ᵛ Who is
faultie, is suspected. *a.* **1597** LYLY *Woman in
the Moon* IV. i. 196 Once guiltie, and suspected
euermore. **1640** HERBERT no. 417.

Once hits, He that | is ever bending.
(H 476)

1640 HERBERT no. 785.   **1710** PALMER 378.

Once in a blue moon.   (M 1121)

1527 ROY & BARLOWE *Rede me, etc.* 114 Arb.
Yf they saye the mone is belewe, We must
beleve that it is true. **1607** DEKKER *Knight's
Conjuring* Percy Soc. 25 She would haue trickes
(once in a moone) to put the Diuell out of his
wits. **1707** E. WARD *Wood. World Dissect.* 17
Once in a moon, perhaps, he invites some Marine-
Lieutenant to taste of his bounty. **1823** GROSE
ed. Pierce Egan s.v. Blue Moon. In allusion to a
long time before such a circumstance happens.
1869 E. YATES *Wrecked in Port* ch. 22 (That
indefinite period). **1891** A. FORBES *Barracks Biv.
& Bat.* (1910) 107 It was only once in a blue
moon that he was seen in the saddle.

Once in ten years, one man has need
of another.   (Y 24)

1578 FLORIO *First F.* 33.   **1732** FULLER no. 3732.

Once in the year Apollo laughs. (Y 15)

[L. *Semel in anno ridet Apollo.*]   **1586** GUAZZO ii.
156 Remember that Apollo laughed once a
yeare. **1590** *The Cobbler of Canterbury* Epistle
Semel in anno ridet Apollo. **1638** R. BRATHWAIT
Barnabees Jrnl. iv. Cc (1820) II. 401 Thou err'st
(*Mirtilus*) so doe mo[1] too, If thou think'st I
never goe to *Bacchus* temple, which I follow
'Once a yeare laughs wise *Apollo.*' [¹ more.]

Once out and always out.   (O 41)

1654 E. GAYTON *Pleasant Notes upon Don Quixote*
5 (ever).   **1678** RAY 77.

Once paid (and) never craved.   (P 128)

1639 CLARKE 182.   **1641** FERGUSSON no. 61.
1721 KELLY 270 ... In the Scottish Dialect, *Anes
pay't ne'er cree't*; pay your Debts, and prevent
dunning.

Once wood[1] and aye the waur[2] (never
wise).   (W 745)

a. **1628** CARMICHAELL no. 147.   **1641** FERGUSSON
no. 60 Anes wood, never wise.   **1721** KELLY 271
... They who have once been mad will seldom
have their Senses sound and well again. [¹ mad.
² worse.]

One and all.   (O 51)

1602 *Blurt Mast. Constable* v. iii. 59 Come any
one, come all.   **1662** FULLER Devon 260 The
English Nation . . . had learnt also from the
Souldiers . . . to cry out 'One and All'; each
Shire setting forth a Remonstrance of their
grievances.   **1725** DEFOE *New Voy. round World*
Wks. (Bohn) VI. 222 Some bold rogues upon the
forecastle . . . cried out, *One and all*, which was
a cry . . . of mutiny and rebellion.   **1850**
KINGSLEY *Alton L.* ch. 10 Mind, 'One and all',
as the Cornishmen say, and no peaching.

One and none is all one.   (O 52)

1591 H. SMITH *Preparative Marriage* Wks. i. 12
We say that one is none.   *c.* **1595** SHAKES. *R.J.*
I. ii. 32 Which, on more view of many, mine,
being one, May stand in number, though in
reck'ning none.   **1611** COTGRAVE s.v. Vn As
good haue none as haue no more but one.   **1659**
HOWELL *Span. Prov.* 19.   **1664** CODRINGTON 208.
1670 RAY 20.

One (Two) and thirty, He is.   (O 64)

1592 GREENE *Groatsworth* ed. Harrison 29 Will
ye play then at cards. I said he, so it be one
and thirtie. That fooles game, said she? [The
allusion appears to be to a card game. 'Irish
one and thirty' is mentioned in *A Defence of
Conycatching*, 1592.] **1594–8** SHAKES. *T.S.* I. ii.
33 Was it fit for a servant to use his master so;
being, perhaps, for aught I see, two-and-thirty,
a pip out. [1596] **1605** *Stukeley* l. 605 Crack
his crown and that makes one and thirty.
1678 RAY 87 *Of one drunk.* . . . He is one and
thirty.

One bad general is better than two
good ones.

1861 LINCOLN *Wks.* (1953) V. 51.   **1902–3** LEAN
IV. 72 . . . To escape divided counsels.

One, but (that one) a lion.   (O 53)

[AESOP *Fables* 240 (*The Lioness and the Fox*)
'Ἕνα . . . ἀλλὰ λέοντα.] **1607** TOPSELL *Hist. Four-
footed Beasts* 465 Shee bringeth foorth indeede
but one, yet that one is a Lyon.   **1692** L'ESTRANGE
Aesop's Fab. cxxii (1738) 138 A fox cast it in
the teeth of a lioness, that she brought forth but
one whelp at a time. 'Very right,' says the other,
'but then that one is a lion.'   **1884** H. D. TRAILL
Coleridge iii. 48 The one long poem[1] which
Coleridge contributed to the collection is alone
sufficient to associate it for ever with his name.
Unum sed leonem. To any one who should have
taunted him with the infertility of his muse he
might have returned the haughty answer of the
lioness in the fable. [¹ *Ancient Mᵣ iner.*]

One day was three till liberty was
borrow.

1546 HEYWOOD I. x. C4ᵛ Eche one daie was three,
tyll lybertee was borow, For one monthis ioie
to bryng hir holle lyues sorow.

One dog, one bull.

1879 G. F. JACKSON *Shropshire Wd.-Bk.* 309 One
dog, one bull, *phr.* signifies 'fair play'. This
saying had its rise in the practice of bull-baiting
. . . which lingered in Shropshire till about . . .
1841.

One door shuts, Where | another opens.
(D 563)

1586 D. ROWLAND tr. *Lazarillo* (1924) 32 This proverbe was fulfild, when one doore is shut the other openeth. **1599** MINSHEU *Span. Dial.* 11 (a hundred doe open). **1620** SHELTON *Quix.* III. vii. i. 159 They are all sentences taken out of experience itself, . . . specially that proverb that says, 'Where one door is shut, another is opened.' **1710** PALMER 49. **1821** GALT *Annals of Par.* ch. 26. As one door shuts another opens; for scarcely were we in quietness by the decease of . . . Lady Macadam, till a full equivalent for her was given in this hot and fiery Mr. Cayenne. **1853** SURTEES *Sponge's Sport. T.* ch. 43 'When one door shuts another opens', say the saucy servants. **1853** TRENCH V. 116.

One does the scathe, and another has the scorn.
(S 129)

1611 COTGRAVE s.v. Faire. **1659** HOWELL *Eng. Prov.* 6a. **1678** RAY 186 . . . *i.e.* One doth the harm and another bears the blame.

One enemy (foe) is too many; and a hundred friends too few.
(E 141)

1640 HERBERT no. 523 One enemy is too much. **1659** TORRIANO no. 144 One enemy is too much to any great State, and a hundred friends too few. **1853** TRENCH iv. 81 (The . . . German proverb.)

One flower makes no garland.
(F 388)

1640 HERBERT no. 521.

One eye, He that has but | must be afraid to lose it.
(E 238)

1592 DELAMOTHE 45. **1609** HARWARD 117ᵛ One ey is as good as twoo but for store. **1639** CLARKE 305 (must take heed how hee). **1642** TORRIANO 31 (is evermore wiping of it). **1651** HERBERT no. 1088. **1721** KELLY 128 (must look well to that). Spoken when a Man hath but one thing of a Kind, and therefore shy to lend it.

One eye, He that has but | sees the better for it.
(E 239)

1639 CLARKE 44. **1678** RAY 134 . . . Better than he would do without it: a ridiculous saying.

One fire (heat) drives out another.
(F 277)

1580 LYLY *Euph. & his Eng.* ii. 124 The fire that burneth, taketh away the heate of the burn. **1594** SHAKES. *T.G.V.* II. iv. 188 Even as one heat another heat expels. *c.* **1595** *Id. R.J.* I. ii. 46 Tut, man, one fire burns out another's burning; One pain is less'ned by another's anguish. **1608** *Id. C.* IV. vii. 54 One fire drives out one fire; one nail, one nail. **1732** FULLER no. 4523 The Fire that burneth, taketh out the Heat of a Burn.

One foot in the grave, To have. (M 346)

1509 BARCLAY *Ship of Fools* i. 44 Thy graue is open, thy one fote in the pyt. **1566** PAINTER *Pal. of Pleasure* (Jacobs) II. 109 Takyng paines to visite him, who hath one of his feet alreadie within the graue, the other stepping after with conuenient speede. **1578** *Courtly Controv.* R3 Let vs . . . haue a longing to learne, yea euen when our owne foote shall stande vppon the graues brincke. **1586** J. CASE *Praise of Music* 24 Socrates . . . being farre stricken in yeares, and hauing in a manner one foote in the graue. **1632** MASSINGER & FIELD *Fatal Dowry* I. ii When one foot's in the grave. **1655** FULLER *Ch. Hist.* IX. vii. (1868) III. 115 A pious and godly life, which increased in his old age; so that, . . . whilst he had one foot in the grave, he had the other in heaven. **1726** SWIFT *Voy. to Laputa* x. He observed long life to be the universal desire . . . of mankind. That whoever had one foot in the grave was sure to hold back the other as strongly as he could. **1886** J. PAYN *Luck Darrells* ch. 15 He has twenty thousand a year . . . And one foot in the grave.

One foot in the straw, He that has | has another in the spittle.[1]
(F 566)

1640 HERBERT no. 438. **1642** TORRIANO 89 (one foot in the baudy house . . . hospitall). [1 hospital.]

One foot is better than two crutches.
(F 568)

1577 N. BRETON *The Works of a Young Wit* (*Poems* ed. J. Robertson 29) Better one eye, one legge, and but one hand, then be starke blinde, and cannot sturre, nor stand. **1640** HERBERT no. 769.

One [magpie] for sorrow: two for mirth: three for a wedding: four for a birth: five for silver: six for gold: seven for a secret, not to be told: eight for heaven: nine for hell: and ten for the devil's own sel.

a. **1846** B. HAYDON *Autobiography* Pt. i ch. 5 (anno 1808) The old saw, One for sorrow, two for mirth, three for a wedding, and four for death (Devonshire). **1846** DENHAM 35. **1865** *N. & Q.* 3rd Ser. VII. 304 We shall now proceed to the magpies: II. *Cornish* 'One for sorrow, two for mirth, Three for a wedding, four for a birth' *Welsh.* 'Piogen â chroesdra.'—A magpie and disappointment. . . . It is always an evil omen, and invariably 'one for sorrow' in this locality. [Cardigan.] **1913** A. C. BENSON *Along the Road* 162 I never see magpies myself without repeating the old rhyme: 'One for sorrow, Two for mirth, Three for a death, Four for a birth; Five, you will shortly be In a great company.'

One for the mouse, one for the crow, one to rot, and one to grow.

1850 *N. & Q.* 1st Ser. II. 515 *How to sow Beans.* 'One for the mouse, One for the crow, One to rot, One to grow.'

One God, no more, but friends good store. (G 242)

1616 WITHALS 583. **1639** CLARKE 26. **1670** RAY 94.

One hog, He that has | makes him fat; and he that has one son makes him a fool. (H 490)

1640 HERBERT no. 433. **1732** FULLER no. 2138.

One is no number. *Cf.* One man no man. (O 54)

[MACROB. *Comm. Somn. Scip.* 2. 8 *Monas numerus esse non dicitur.*] **1561** CASTIGLIONE *Courtier* tr. Hoby E.L. 231 One maketh no number. **1592** LYLY *Midas* III. i. 32 And haue they not perished, that there was not two left to make a number? **1598** MARLOWE *Hero & L.* i. 255 One is no number, maides are nothing then Without the sweet societie of men. **1609** SHAKES. *Sonnet* no. 136, l. 8 Among a number one is reckoned one (cf. no. 8. l. 14). *a.* **1649** DRUMMOND Muses Lib. i. 155 Poor one no number is.

One man is worth a hundred and a hundred is not worth one. (M 354)

1573 SANFORD 52. **1578** FLORIO *First F.* 32ᵛ. **1629** *Bk. Mer. Rid.* Prov. no. 42.

One man no man. (M 353)

[Gk. Εἶς ἀνήρ, οὐδεὶς ἀνήρ.] **1539** TAVERNER 17 Vnus uir nullus uir. One man no man. *a.* **1591** H. SMITH 1657 ed. 16 *Preparative to Marriage* We say that one is none, because hee cannot bee fewer than one, . . . lesse than one, . . . weaker than one. *a.* **1628** CARMICHAELL no. 131. **1642** TORRIANO 39 One mans company is no company. **1853** TRENCH vi. 135.

One man, What chances to | may happen to all men. (M 406)

1539 VIVES *Introd. to Wisdom* H8ᵛ What so euer chaunceth to one, may hap to an other. *c.* **1584** G. HARVEY *Marginalia* 101 That mai happen to many, Which doth happen to any. **1624** J. HEWES *Perfect Survey* F2. **1668** RYMER *Prince* xiv. 48 Reject not any man to whom a thing hapneth, which may sometimes befall the wisest and best men.

One man's will is another man's wit.

1597 *Politeuphuia* 37b. **1647** *Countrym. New Commonwealth* 14.

One nail (love), | drives out another. (N 17)

[AR. *Pol.* 5. 11. 3 ἥλῳ ὁ ἥλος (SC. ἐκκρούεται).] *c.* **1200** *Ancrene Riwle* (Morton) 404 Vor, al so as on neil driueð uit þen oðerne. . . . *c.* **1374** CHAUCER *Troilus* Bk. 4, l. 415. The newe love out chaceth ofte the olde. **1555** HEYWOOD *Epigr. upon Prov.* no. 111 One nayle dryueth out an other. **1579** LYLY *Euph.* i. 255 One loue expelleth an other. **1594** SHAKES. *T.G.V.* II. iv. 192 Even as one heat another heat expels, Or as one nail by strength drives out another, So the

remembrance of my former love Is by a newer object quite forgotten. **1606** CHAPMAN *Mons. d'Olive* v. i. Wks. (1874) III. 134 For one heat, all know, doth drive out another, One passion doth expel another still. **1608** SHAKES. *C.* IV. vii. 54 One fire drives out one fire; one nail, one nail. *c.* **1645** HOWELL *Lett.* 17 Sept. (1903) III. 87 Languages and words . . . may be said to stick in the memory like nails on pegs in a wainscot door, which used to thrust out one another oftentimes. **1666** TORRIANO *It. Prov.* 10, no. 36 One love expells another. **1836** MRS. CARLYLE *Lett.* April 1 One feels soaked to the very heart. . . . As one fire is understood to drive out another, I thought one water might drive out another also; and so . . . I took a shower-bath. **1900** *Althenaeum* 27 Oct. 547/2 Nail drives out nail.

One of these days is none of these days. (D 119)

1658 *Comes Facundus* 185.

One point of a good hawk, She has | she is hardy. (P 454)

1546 HEYWOOD II. iv. 64.

One poison drives out another. (P 457)

c. **1558** W. WEDLOCK *Image of Idleness* E1 The common opinion, that one poyson expelleth another. **1567** G. FENTON *Trag. Dis.* 12 T.T. ii. 218 One poyson driveth oute an other. **1573** G. HARVEY *Letter-Bk.* 50 To driue out on poison with another. **1616** DRAXE no. 1829 Euery venimous beast hath his counterpoison. **1622** MIDDLETON *Changeling* II. ii. Men of art make much of poison, Keep one to expel another. **1659** HOWELL *Brit. Prov.* 34 (expels).

One shoe will not fit all feet. *Cf.* All feet tread not in one shoe. Shoe fits not every foot, Every. (S 364)

1574 G. GRATARDUS *A Direction for the Health of Magistrates and Students* tr. T. Newton B3 Therefore sayth Galene, euen as a shoomaker cannot make one shooe to serue euery mannes foote, . . . **1602** J. H. *Work for Chimneysweepers* B3ᵛ No more then one shooe can wel serue all mens feete. **1672** WALKER 47 no. 56 To make one shoe serve for all feet.

One sows and another reaps. (S 691)

[JOHN iv. 37 One soweth, and another reapeth.] **1577** HOLINSHED *Chron.* Hen. I, 1586 ed. iii. 36 Wherein the prouerbe tooke place, that One soweth, but an other reapeth. **1579** LYLY *Euph.* i. 234 As thou hast reaped where an other hath sowen, so an other may thresh that which thou hast reaped. **1590–1** SHAKES. *2 Hen. VI* III. i. 381 From Ireland come I with my strength And reap the harvest which that rascal sow'd. **1592** DELAMOTHE 53 One soweth, that reapeth not. **1853** TRENCH i. 5 He declares, 'Herein is that saying', or that proverb, true, 'One soweth and another reapeth'.

One tale (story) is good till another is told. (T 42)

1593 GREENE *Mamillia* II Gros. 222 Tush syr quoth the Marquesse, one tale is always good

vntil another is heard. **1601** WEEVER *Mirr.
Mart.* A iij b One tale is good, untill anothers
told. **1604** w. WREDNOT *Palladis Palatium* 147.
1662 FULLER Kent 65 But one story is good till
another is heard. . . . I met since with a supplement thereunto. **1831** MACAULAY *Ess., Sadler's
Ref.* Wks. v. 482 A theory is not proved . . .
merely because the evidence in its favour looks
well at first sight. . . . 'One story is good till
another is told!'

One thing at a time.

1772 J. WESLEY *Lett.* v. 299. **1825** SYD. SMITH
in *Edinb. Rev.* Wks. (1839) II. 266 *Snail's Pace
Argument.*—'*One thing at a time! Not too fast!*'
1868 w. w. COLLINS *Moonstone* I. ch. 18 'One
thing at a time' said the Sergeant, . . . 'I must
attend to Miss Verinder first'. **1926** *Times* 27
Feb. 13/3 'One thing at a time', as Lord Grey
said.

One thing at a time, and that done well, is a very good thing, as many can tell.

1885 D. C. MURRAY *Rainbow Gold* IV. vi I'm not
going to have too many irons in the fire. You
know the old saying, Sarah: . . .

One thing (etc.) brings up another thing.

1555 J. BOEME *Fardle of Fashions* tr. W. Waterman *ij᷂ᵛ One talke bringes in another. **1572**
E. PASQUIER *Monophylo* tr. G. Fenton 19 One
matter drawes on another. *a.* **1575** HARPSFIELD
Life of More E.E.T.S. 186 One business be-
getteth another (olde proverbe). *a.* **1576**
WYTHORNE 125 On þing brings an oþer. **1591**
ARIOSTO *Orl. Fur.* Harington XLIII. 188 In speech
it often doth befall, That one thing doth another
bring to light. **1596** NASHE *Saffron W.* iii. 129
Good Lord, how one thing brings on another.
[1597] **1599** CHAPMAN *Hum. Day's Mirth* sc. iv,
l. 7 One sin will draw another quickly so. **1599**
PORTER *Angry Wom. Abing.* l. 1659 One thought
another brings. **1630** T. WESTCOTE *View oj
Devonsh.* (1845) 262 Commonly one [tale]
draws in another.

One thing said twice deserves a 'trudge'.   (T 144)

1579 LYLY *Euph.* i. 272 It is varietie that moueth
the minde of all men, and one thing sayd twice
(as wee say commonly) deserueth a trudge.[1]
[1 command to be off.]

One thing thinks the bear, and another he that leads him.

c. **1374** CHAUCER *Troilus* Bk. 4, l. 1453 And thus
men seith, that 'oon thenketh the bere. But al
another thenketh his ledere!' *c.* **1400** *MS.
Latin no. 364, J. Rylands Libr.* (ed. Pantin) in
Bull. J. R. Libr. XIV, f. 24 The berewarde and the
bere thenken not alle on.

One thing thinks the horse, and another he that saddles (rides) him.   (H 667)

1622 CÉSAR OUDIN *A Grammar Spanish and
English* tr. I. W. 251. **1631** MABBE *Celestina*
T.T. 264. **1640** HERBERT no. 387 The horse

thinkes one thing, and he that sadles him another. **1670** RAY 14 The horse thinks one thing,
and he that rides him another. **1732** FULLER
no. 3799.

One tongue is enough for a woman.
                                              (T 398)

1659 N. R. 84. **1678** RAY 59. **1738** SWIFT
Dial. II. E.L. 299 Will you please to send me a
piece of tongue?—By no means, madam:
one tongue is enough for a woman. **1837**
T. HOOK *Jack Brag* ch. 11 I am no great linguist.
I am very much of the opinion that one tongue is
sufficient for one woman.

One, two, three, four, are just half a score.   (O 58)

1678 RAY 86.

One year a nurse, and seven years the worse.   (Y 16)

a. **1628** CARMICHAELL no. 258 A yeir a nurice
seauen yeirs a daw.[1] **1641** FERGUSSON no. 31
(as *a.* 1628). **1663** P. STAMPOY 4. **1678** RAY
182 . . . Because feeding well and doing little she
becomes liquorish and gets a habit of idleness.
1721 KELLY 270. **1732** FULLER no. 6377. [1 slut.]

One year of joy, another of comfort, and all the rest of content.   (Y 17)

1678 RAY 63 . . . *A marriage wish.*

One year's seeding makes seven years' weeding.

1873 HARLAND & WILKINSON *Lancashire Leg.* 190
One year's seeding makes seven years weeding.
1917 BRIDGE 100 One year's seed Seven years'
weed. If weeds are neglected they increase very
fast and give much trouble in eradicating them.

One's too few, three too many.   (O 56)

1678 RAY 342. *Somerset.*

One, *see also* Beware of man of o. book; Kingdom
of blind o.-eyed man king; Spindles are made
(By o. and o.).

One can, cannot, drop of, good, had as good be,
has always, is not, man may, man's, may, may
be, must, never, ought to have, should, whom
the), ones, *see also under significant words
following.*

Onion, It will do with an.   (O 67)

1548 COOPER s.v. Cepa Cepas edere, to eate
oynions, was a prouerbe spoken of them, which
dydde seeme to weepe, or that do weepe often.
1583 MELBANCKE *Philot.* xiᵛ Yet can I not chuse
but weepe, with an onion in mine eye, and an
apple in my mouth. **1594–8** SHAKES. *T.S.* Ind.
i. 124 And if the boy have not a woman's gift
To rain a shower of commanded tears, An onion
will do as well for such a shift. **1602** *Id. A.W.*
V. iii. 314 Mine eyes smell onions; I shall weep
anon. **1606–7** *Id. A.C.* IV. ii. 34 Look, they

weep, And I, an ass, am onion-ey'd. 1616
WITHALS 557 To weepe with an Onyon. 1659
HOWELL *Eng. Prov.* 1b. 1678 RAY 78.

Onion, *see also* Capon (If thou hast not a), feed
on an o.; Smell of garlic takes away smell of o.

Open arms, With.

[= welcoming any chance or anybody. ERASM.
Ad. Obviis ulnis, manibus.] *a.* 1687 COTTON
Poems (1923) 186 I, for thy bounty well pre-
par'd, with open arms my blessing meet. 1735
POPE *Ep. to Arbuthnot* 142 With open arms
received one Poet more. *a.* 1761 RICHARDSON
Corr. v. 332 By whom she was received with
open arms.

Open confession is good for the soul.

(C 591)

1615 *Janua Linguarum* tr. W. Welde 17 Confession is physick to a sinner. *c.* 1641 FERGUS-
SON MS. no. 159 (Ane open confessione). 1721
KELLY 270 . . . Spoken ironically, to them that
boast of their ill deeds. 1881 J. PAYN *Grape from
Thorn* 39. Confession may be good for the
soul; but it is doubtful whether the avowal of
incapacity to the parties desirous of securing
our services is quite judicious. 1961 20 Dec.
Times 3/5 (Honest).

Open confession, open penance.

(C 592)

1559 *Mirr. for Magistrates* (Campbell) 192 Open
confession axeth open penaunce. 1608 ARMIN
Nest Ninnies (1842) 46 Take thy forfeit (Harry)
sayes the foole; open confession, open penance.

Open door may tempt a saint, An.

(D 558)

1659 HOWELL *Span. Prov.* 16 (gate). 1732 FULLER
no. 655.

Open doors dogs come in, At.   (D 564)

c. 1200 *Ancrene Riwle* 60 Hund wule in bliðeliche
hwar se he ivint hit open. *a.* 1628 CARMICHAELL
no. 226. 1641 FERGUSSON no. 47. 1721 KELLY
23 (*come benn*) And so will Thieves and impertinent Persons. 1826 SCOTT *Woodst.* ch. 37
They say in my country, when doors are open
dogs enter.

Open one's mouth wide, To.

[= to ask a high price.] 1891 C. ROBERTS
Adrift Amer. 251. To use a vulgarism, he did
not open his mouth so wide as the other, but
at once offered me a through ticket to Liverpool
for $72. 1898 *Daily News* 28 Oct. 3/1 Directly
the word England is mentioned, the mouths of
the Continental artists are opened so unconscionably wide.

Open Sesame.

[The charm used to open the door of the robbers'
den in the tale of 'Ali Baba and the Forty
Thieves'; hence a magic password.] 1785 *Arab
Nts. Entert.* 562 Ali Baba . . . perceiving the
door, . . . said 'Open Sesame'. 1806 SCOTT *Lett.*

to Ld. Dalkeith 11 Feb. in LOCKHART *Life* ch. 15
Your notoriety becomes a talisman—an 'Open
Sesame' before which everything gives way.
1876 BURNABY *Ride to Khiva* ch. 2 'From hall
porters to the mistresses of those officials who
give out the railway contracts, all have their price.
You will find gold . . . an open sesame throughout the Russian Empire.'

Open the door with an axe, To.

1623 J. LEYCESTER no. 71 To cleaue wood with
the key and open the doore with an Axe. 1813
RAY 75.

Open thy purse, and then open thy
sack.   (P 660)

1678 RAY *Adag. Hebr.* 402 Open thy purse (viz.
to receive thy money) and then open thy sack,
i.e., then deliver thy goods.

Open your mouth but you put your
foot in it, You never.

1910 P. W. JOYCE *Eng. as We Speak* 128 To
a person who habitually uses unfortunate
blundering expressions.

Open your pack, and sell no wares,
Never.

a. 1628 CARMICHAELL no. 701 He opens his pak
and sellis na wairis. 1721 KELLY 262 . . . Never
proffer your Service where it is not likely to be
accepted.

Open, *see also* Market of his ware . . . o. his shop;
Year does nothing but o. and shut.

Openshaw, *see* Constable of O.

Opinion is never wrong, Our own. (O 69)

1642 TORRIANO 62. 1732 FULLER no. 3824.

Opinion(s), *see* Complies against his will, of
same o. still; Doctor's o. (That is but one);
Lawyer's o. worth nothing unless paid for;
Plant an o. they seem to eradicate (Some);
Speers all o. comes ill speed.

Oportet comes in place (When) thou knowest
miserere has no grace, *see* Cured (What can't be)
must be endured.

Opportunity is whoredom's bawd.

(O 70)

[ERASM. *Occasione duntaxat opus improbitati.*]
1539 TAVERNER D6ᵛ Leudnes lacketh but
occasion. 1586 WARNER *Albion's Eng.* II. ix. E2ᵛ
Opportunitie can win the coyest She that is. [1600]
1631 T. HEYWOOD I *Fair Maid* ii. 267 Then put
her to't, win Oportunity, Shees the best bawd.
1604 MARSTON *Malcontent* III. ii That great
bawd opportunitie. 1616 T. ADAMS *Diseases of
the Soul* 47 Let him shunne Opportunity as his
Bawde, and Occasion as his Pandar. 1636
CAMDEN 303.

Opportunity makes the thief. (o 71)

c. **1220** *Hali Meidenhad* E.E.T.S. 17 Man seið
þat eise makeð þeof. *c.* **1440** in HIGDEN *Polychron.* (1865) VII. 379 At the laste bischop seide
to hym 'Me thenke that opportunite makethe
a thefe'. *c.* **1513** MORE *Richard III* 1821 ed. 11
[Of Richard and the murder of the princes]
Opportunitye and lykelyhoode of spede, putteth
a manne in courage of that hee neuer entended.
1576 PETTIE ii. 93 As a pleasant prey soon
enticeth a simple thief. **1623** CAMDEN 275.
1670 RAY 129 . . . *Occasio facit furem.* Therefore,
masters . . . ought to secure their moneys and
goods under lock and key; that they do not give
. . . a temptation to steal. **1791** I. D'ISRAELI *Cur.
Lit.* (1858) III. 42 At another *entrée* the proverb
was—*L'occasion fait le larron.* Opportunity
makes the thief.

Opportunity, *see also* Market of his ware . . .
watch an o. to open his shop; Necessity and o.

Oppression makes a wise man mad. (o 73)

[ECCLES. vii. 7.] **1616** BRETON 2 *Cross. Prov.* B3.
1895 DEAN PLUMPTRE *Eccles.* 162.

Oracle, *see* Speak like an o.

Orange that is too hard squeezed yields a bitter juice, The.

1732 FULLER no. 4696.

Orator, *see* Gold is an o.; Good o. who convinces
himself; Sorrow makes silence best o.

Orchard, *see* Free of fruit that wants o.; Rob an
o. when none keeps (Easy to).

Order reigns at Warsaw.

[1831] **1882** BENT *Fam. Short Say.* (ed. 8) 478
After the insurrection of Warsaw . . . was sub-
dued, . . . Sebastiani . . . announced in the
Chamber of Deputies, Sept. 16, 1831, . . . 'My
letters from Poland announce that order reigns
in Warsaw' (*Des lettres que je reçois de Pologne
m'annoncent que la tranquillité règne à Varsovie*).
1892 J. NICHOL *T. Carlyle* 202 He has no word
of censure for the more settled form of anarchy
which announced, 'Order reigns at Warsaw'.
1908 *Times Wkly.* 30 Oct. Sir Theodore Martin
. . . said . . . 'We may yet see the glitter of the
bayonet in Piccadilly. . . . Peace may only be
restored in London as in Warsaw.'

Order, *see also* Apple-pie o.

Ordinary, *see* Scotch o.

Orestes, *see* Pylades and O.

Organs, *see* Pig plays on the o.

Ornament, *see* Silence is best o. of woman.

Orphans, *see* Late children early o.

Orts[1] of good hay, Make not. (o 80)

1639 CLARKE 262. **1670** RAY 188. [[1] leavings.]

Orts, *see also* Evening o. morning fodder.

Ossa upon Pelion, To heap (cast, pile). (o 81)

[VIRGIL *Georgics* I. 281 *Imponere Pelio Ossam.*
The allusion is to the attempt of the giants, in
mythology, to scale heaven by piling Mount
Ossa upon Mount Pelion.] **1561** SENECA *Herc.
Furens* tr. Jasper Heywood K1 Let Chiron vnder
Ossa see his Pelion mowntayne grette. **1584**
R. SCOT *Discovery of Witchcraft* 559 They
imitate the old giants . . . piling vp Pelion vpon
Ossa. **1592** *Soliman and Perseda* I. iii. 158
Wouldst thou haue me a Typhon, To beare vp
Peleon or Ossa? **1609** DEKKER *Gull's Horn-
book* E3ᵛ You heape *Pelion* vpon *Ossa*, glory
vpon glory. **1633** T. HEYWOOD *Eng. Trav.* IV.
iii. Merm. 223 And, to suppress Your souls yet
lower, without hope to rise, Heap Ossa upon
Pelion. **1668** COWLEY *Essays; Of Greatness*
(1906) 433 The old Gyants are said to have made
an Heroical attempt of scaling Heaven in despight
of the gods, and they cast *Ossa* upon *Olympus*
and *Pelion* upon *Ossa*.

Ossing comes to bossing. (o 82)

c. **1350** *Douce MS.* 52 no. 117 Ossyng comys to
bossyng. **1670** RAY 52 . . . *Chesh.* Ossing, *i.e.*
offering or aiming to do. The meaning is the
same, with *Courting and woing brings dallying
and doing.*

Ostrich policy. (o 83)

1579 GOSSON *Sch. Abuse* 43 Woodcocks . . . want
not will to auoyde hurte, when they thrust theyr
heads in a Bushe, and thinke their bodyes out
of daunger. **1579** PLUTARCH tr. T. North Epil.
to Lives of Agesilaus and Pompey T.C. ed. vi.
345 Like the ostrich that hides his head in the
sand. **1623** *Someth. Written by Occas. Accid.
Blacke Friers* 14 Like the Austridge, who hiding
her little head, supposeth her great body obscured. **1837** CARLYLE *Fr. Rev.* I. i. iv Louis
XV . . . would not suffer Death to be spoken
of; avoided the sight of churchyards, funereal
monuments, and whatever could bring it to
mind. It is the resource of the Ostrich; who, hard
hunted, sticks his foolish head in the ground,
and would fain forget that his foolish unseeing
body is not unseen too. **1891** *Pall Mall G.* 12
Sept. 1/2 The facts . . . are too damning to leave
much room for an ostrich policy.

Ostrich, *see also* Stomach (Digestion) like an o.

Other man (men), *see* Beware by o. m.'s harms;
Cry Yule at o. m.'s cost; Learn at o. m.'s cost;
Northampton stands on o. m.'s legs.

Other people, *see* Toils like a dog, who roasts for
o. p.'s eating.

Other times, other manners.

[Fr. *Autres temps, autres mœurs.*] **1892** A. DOB-
SON *S. Richardson* 101 Notwithstanding the
favourite explanation of 'other times, other

manners', contemporary critics of Clarissa found very much the same fault with her history as people do to-day.

Other(s), *see also* All came from . . . o; Breaks his word, (A man that) bids o. be false to him; Finds fault with o. and does worse himself, (He); Flesh and blood as o. are, (To be); Give o. good counsel (He can) . . .; Grief is lessened when imparted to o.; Hose (In my o.).

Otherwise, *see* Some are wise and some o.

Ounce of discretion (mother wit), An | is worth a pound of wit (learning, clergy). (o 87)

1548 HALL 585 Doctor Stokesley a man that had more learning, than discrecion to be iudge. **1568** WM. CECIL cited C. Read *Mr. Sec. Cecil* 424 Marry, an ounce of advice is more worth to be executed aforehand than in the sight of perils. **1592** DELAMOTHE 55 (a pound of hardinesse). **1616** T. ADAMS *Sacr. of Thankfulness* 19 The Prouerbe is true; an Ounce of Discretion is worth a pound of Learning. **1641** FERGUSSON no. 149 An ounce of mothers wit is worth a pound of clergie. **1670** RAY 79. **1882** SYD. SMITH *Persecuting Bishops* in *Edinb. Rev.* Wks. (1850) 359 We are convinced of the justice of the old saying, that an ounce of mother wit is worth a pound of clergy.

Ounce of (good) fortune is worth a pound of forecast (discretion), An. (o 85)

c. **1576** WHYTHORNE 142 I ment not to be on of thoz who waith A chip of chauns mor then A pownds wurth of witt. **1611** COTGRAVE s.v. *Sagesse* An ounce of lucke excells a pound of wit. **1672** WALKER 42 no. 57 (discretion). **1732** FULLER no. 657 (forecast).

Ounce of mirth is worth a pound of sorrow, An. (o 86)

1567 *Trial of Treasure* A3 A little mirth is worth much sorow some say. **1576** PETTIE i. 141. Every dram of delight hath a pound of spite. **1579** LYLY *Euph.* i. 247 For euerye dramme of pleasure, an ounce of payne. *a.* **1594** *Locrine* IV. i. 102 One dramme of ioy, must haue a pound of care. **1619** B. RICH *Irish Hubbub* 4 A little mirth (they say) is worth a great deale of sorrow. **1639** CLARKE 185 ('Dramme' for 'ounce').

Ounce of practice is worth a pound of precept, An.

1845 COOPER *Chainbearer* 402 They say that 'an ounce of experience is worth a pound of theory'. **1866** BLACKMORE *Cradock N.* ch. 37 Remember that rigid probity, and the strictest punctuality . . ., are the very soul of business, and that an ounce of practice is worth a pound of precept.

Ounce of state requires a pound of gold, An. (o 88)

1573 SANFORD 51ᵛ (and a pound). **1629** *Bk. Mer. Rid.* Prov. no. 26.

Ounce of wit that's bought is worth a pound that's taught, An.

1732 FULLER no. 6495.

Our Lady, *see* Lady.

Our Lord, *see* Lord.

Ourselves, *see* Born for o. (We are not).

Out at elbow(s), To be. (E 102)

[= to be ragged.] **1586** J. FERNE *Blazon of Gentry* II. 10 2A5ᵛ [He] hath obteined the wearing of a coate by the hands of the Heralds: but I thinke before he hath done, he will weare it out at the elbowes. **1590** NASHE *Almond for a Parrot* iii. 356 Your witte wilbe welny worn thredbare, and your banquerout inuention cleane out at the elbowes. **1604** SHAKES. *M.M.* II. i. 59 He cannot [speak] Sir; he's out at elbow. **1771** SMOLLETT *Humph. Clink.* (1815) 55 Sir Ulic Mackilligut . . . is said to be much out at elbows. **1841** DICKENS *B. Rudge* ch. 27 Partaking of the character of truisms worn a little out at elbow.

Out at heels. (H 389)

1588 'Marprelate' *Epistle* ed. Pierce 74 Usurer Harvey . . . being out at the heels with all other usurers. **1588** FRAUNCE *Lawyer's Log.* I. iv. 27 To affectate such woordes as were quite worne out at heeles and elbowes long before the nativitie of Geffrey Chaucer. **1600–1** SHAKES. *M.W.W.* I. iii. 29 Well, sirs, I am almost out at heels. **1605–6** *Id. K.L.* II. ii. 152 A good man's fortune may grow out at heels. **1676** WYCHERLEY *Plain Dealer* ed. Summers III. 153 Go look out the Fellow . . . that walks with his Stockings and his Sword out at heels.

Out of all whooping (cry, ho).

c. **1374** CHAUCER *Troilus* Bk. 2, l. 1083. And after that, than gan he telle his woo; But that was endeles, withouten hoo. **1546** HEYWOOD I. xi. E1ᵛ She is one of theim to whom god bad who. **1577** *Misogonus* II. iii. 55 Thoughe you thinke him past whoo, He may yet reduce him. **1581** GUAZZO i. 246 Out of al crie. *a.* **1593** GREENE *Friar Bacon* l. 1768 Out of all hoe. **1599** SHAKES. *A.Y.* III. ii. 177 O wonderful . . .! out of all whooping! **1639** CLARKE 38 He hath noe whoe with him. **1711** SWIFT *Jrnl. to Stella* Lett. XX When your tongue runs, there's no ho with you, pray.

Out of debt, out of danger (deadly sin). (D 166–7)

1551 ROBINSON tr. *Utopia.* ii. Arb. 104 Whyche to those riche men, in whose debte and daunger they be not, do giue almost diuine honoures. **1613** T. ADAMS *The White Devil* 1861–2 ii. 247 Debt is not (as the vulgar speech is) deadly sin; a sore it may be, no sin. **1636** CAMDEN 304 (deadly sinne). **1639** CLARKE 82 (and deadly danger). **1641** H. PEACHAM *Worth of a Penny* (1667) in ARBER'S *Garner* VI. 256 How bold, confident, merry, lively, and ever in humour, are Moneyed Men. [For being out of debt, they are out of danger!] **1908** E. M. SNEYD-KYNNERSLEY *H.M.I.* (1910) ch. 21 Call it distributing capital expenditure over a term of years, and even a rural dean succumbs. 'Out of debt, out of danger', but 'out of debt, out of progress'.

Out of doors, *see* Step (The greatest) is that o. of d.

Out of God's blessing into the warm sun. (G 272)

[i.e. from better to worse.] 1540 PALSGRAVE *Acolastus* 153 From the halle in to the kitchin, or out of cristes blessing in to a warme sonne. 1546 HEYWOOD II. v. H1ᵛ In your rennyng from hym to me, ye roon Out of gods blissing into the warme soon. 1576 PETTIE ii. 146 You would . . . bring me . . . out of God's blessing into a warm sun. 1579 LYLY *Euph.* i. 322. Out of a warme Sunne into Gods blessing. 1605–6 SHAKES. *K.L.* II. ii. 156 Thou out of heaven's benediction comest to the warm sun. 1616 DRAXE no. 52. 1655 FULLER *Ch. Hist.* III. iv (1868) I. 398 But small reason had King John to rejoice, being come out of God's blessing (of whom before he immediately held the crown), into the warm sun, or rather scorching heat of the pope's protection. 1670 RAY 177 . . . *Ab equis ad asinos.* 1738 SWIFT Dial. I. E.L. 284.

Out of gunshot. (G 482)

1551 ROBINSON tr. *Utop.* Arb. 26 Being themselves . . . as sayeth the prouerbe, oute of all daunger of gonneshotte. 1613 J. STEPHENS *Cinthia's Revenge* G2 Be (out of gun-shot) most irregular. 1678 RAY 249.

Out of office, out of danger.

1633 MASSINGER *New Way* II. i. Merm. 126 In being out of office I am out of danger; Where, if I were a justice, . . . I might. . . . Run myself finely into a *premunire.*

Out of season, out of price.

1595 SOUTHWELL *Losse in Delaye* Wks. (1872) 76 Tyme and place give best advice, Out of season, out of price.

Out of sight, out of languor.[1] (S 437)

a. 1628 CARMICHAELL no. 1232. 1641 FERGUSSON no. 670. 1721 KELLY 269, Eng. Long absent, soon forgotten. [1 desire.]

Out of sight, out of mind. (S 438)

a. 1275 *Provs. of Alfred* B. 554 For he þat is ute bi-loken he is inne sone for-ʒeten. *c.* 1450 tr. *De Imitatione* I. xxiii. 30 Whan man is oute of siʒt, son he passið oute of mynde. 1545 TAVERNER D6ᵛ (Oure Englysshe prouerbe). 1608 DAY *Hum. out of B.* III. i. Merm. 299 Clean out of sight?—And out of mind too or else you have not the mind of a true woman. 1704 M. HENRY *Friendly Visits* 16 Though they are out of sight they are not out of mind. 1807–8 SYD. SMITH *Peter Plym.* iii. Wks. (1839) III. 298 Out of sight, out of mind, seems to be a proverb which applies to enemies as well as friends.

Out of the world and into Bodmin (Kippen).

1862 HISLOP 159 (Kippen). 1893 *Murray's Handbk. Cornwall* 66 Bodmin . . . seems always to have been regarded as somewhat remote and difficult of approach; and an old saw runs, 'Out of the world and into Bodmin'.

Out of the world as out of the fashion, As good be. (W 866)

1639 CLARKE 171. 1738 SWIFT Dial. II. E.L. 295 (better to be). 1837 HOOK *Jack Brag* ch. 16.

Out of the, *see also under significant words following.*

Out, *see also* Aim, (To be o. of one's); Date is o.; Element, (O. of one's); Once o. always o.

Outbid, *see* Hasty to o. another (Be not).

Outface with a card of ten, To. (C 75)

[To brag, put on a bold front. 'Face' was a term at the game of Primero, see HALLIWELL *Dict.*] 1520 WHITTINGTON *Vulg.* E.E.T.S. 93 I set very lytle or nought by hym yᵗ can not face oute his ware with a carde of .x. *c.* 1549 J. PROCTOUR *Fall of the late Arian* E6. 1594–8 SHAKES. *T.S.* II. i. 397 Yet I have fac'd it with a card of ten. *c.* 1604 DAY *Law Tricks* V. ii.

Out-run (Over-run) the constable, To. (C 615)

[At first in literal sense, later = to run into debt.] [c. 1589?] 1633 MARLOWE *Jew of Malta* V. i. 20 I cannot out-run you, constable. 1600 KEMP *Nine Daies Wonder* 15 I far'd like one that had . . . tride the use of his legs to out-run the constable. 1663 BUTLER *Hudibras* I. iii. 1367–8 Quoth Hudibras, Friend Ralph, thou hast Out-run the constable at last. 1670 RAY 169 . . . To spend more then ones allowance or income. 1689 SELDEN *Table-Talk* Arb. 76 There was another trick found out to get money, and . . . another Parliament was call'd . . ., &c. But now they have so out-run the Constable——. 1748 SMOLLETT *Rod. Rand.* ch. 23 'Harkee, my girl, how far have you overrun the constable?' I told him that the debt amounted to eleven pounds. 1906 *T.L.S.* 27 April The Englishman . . . has it . . . in his mind that the natural Irishman . . . drinks hard, outrunning the constable, living from hand to mouth.

Out-shoot a man in his own bow, To. (B 563)

a. 1585 MONTGOMERIE *Cherrie & Slae* lxxix. (1821) 42 In your awin bow ʒe are owreschot, Be mair than half ane inch. 1639 FULLER *Holy War* IV. vi (1840) 185 Because Rome maketh her universality such a masterpiece to boast of, let us see if the Greek church may not outshoot her in her own bow.

Oven, *see* Axle-tree for an o.; Butter is good for anything but stop o.; Gaping against an o. (Ill); Great doings at Gregory's; Kiln calls o. burnt-house; Little wood heat little o.; News, (You must go to the o. or the mill if you will learn); No man will another in o. seek; Set not your loaf till o. hot; Time to set in when o. comes to dough.

Over, Mayor of, *see* Mayor of Altrincham.

Over fast (sicker) over loose.   (F 77)

a. 1628 CARMICHAELL no. 1228. 1641 FERGUSSON no. 665. 1721 KELLY 271 *O'er sicker, o'er lose.* The Method taken to secure a Thing often makes it miscarry.

Over head and ears.   (H 268)

[*c.* 1515] 1530 BARCLAY *Eclog.* iv. 76 Fals in the mud both ouer head and eares. 1530 PALSGRAVE 725/2 He souced him in the water over head and eares. 1533 J. HEYWOOD *Play of Love* B4ᵛ Quyte ouer the eares in loue. *c.* 1553 UDALL *Ralph Roister D.* I. i. 40 Up is he to the harde eares in debt. *c.* 1610 SHAKES. *W.T.* I. ii. 186 Inch-thick, knee-deep, o'er head and ears a fork'd one. 1665 MANLEY *Grotius' Low C. Warres* 875 The Commonwealth . . . would run over head and ears in debt. 1749 FIELDING *Tom Jones* IV. iii The poor lad plumped over head and ears into the water. 1812 E. NARES *I'll Consider of It* i. 142 Over head and ears in debt.

Over holy¹ was hanged, but rough and sonsy² wan³ away.

1721 KELLY 271 Spoken against too precise People; as if those of less Pretensions were more to be trusted. [¹ softly. ² lucky. ³ got.]

Over hot over cold.   (H 731)

c. 1573 HARVEY *Lett. Bk.* 121 As good symtyme aver cowlde as over warme. *c.* 1641 FERGUSSON MS. no. 1113. 1668 R. B. 41.

Over jolly dow not.¹   (D 576)

a. 1628 CARMICHAELL no. 1229. 1641 FERGUSSON no. 673. [¹ doesn't last.]

Over shoes, over boots.   (S 379)

[1603] 1607 T. HEYWOOD *Woman Killed with Kindness* sc. xi, l. 114 Once o'er shoes, we are straight o'er head in sin. 1607 E. SHARPHAM *Cupid's Whirligig* E2. 1615 M. R. *A President for Young Pen-Men* D1ᵛ Not ouer bootes though ouer shooes, not gone so farre but I can come home againe. 1616 BRETON 2 *Cross Prov.* B4. 1648 SANDERSON *Serm.* (1681) II. 248 Over shoes, over boots; I know God will never forgive me, and therefore I will never trouble to seek His favour . . . this is properly the sin of despair. 1818 SCOTT *Rob Roy* ch. 26 I hae taen sae muckle concern wi' your affairs already, that it maun een be ower shoon ower boots wi' me now. 1854 R. S. SURTEES *Hand. Cross* ch. 14 Considering how far he had gone, and how he would be laughed at if he backed out, he determined to let it be 'over shoes over boots'.

Over the left shoulder.   (S 405)

[= the words used express the reverse of what is really meant.] 1596 NASHE *Saffron W.* iii. 90 Wolfe could not choose but bee a huge gainer, a hundred marke at least ouer the shoulder. 1611 BRETNOR *Almanac* April Ouer the left shoulder. 1611 COTGRAVE s.v. Espaule, Ouer the shoulder, or the wrong way. 1654 E. GAYTON *Festivous Notes on Don Quixote* 186 You shall . . . fetch your enemies over the left shoulder. 1659 HOWELL *Eng. Prov.* 17b I have gott it ore the left shoulder. 1692 L'ESTRANGE *Aesop's Fab.* cccxxxviii (1738) 351 This good office over the left shoulder, is the civility that he values himself upon. He gives her his good word (as we call it) to the very end that she may be eaten. 1837 DICKENS *Pickwick* ch. 42 Each gentleman pointed with his right thumb over his left shoulder . . . 'over the left' . . . its expression is one of light and playful sarcasm. 1838 J. C. APPERLEY *Nimrod's North. T.* 12 'Well, Mr. Guard, you made a pretty business of your last Leger'. — 'All over the left shoulder; they drawed me of forty pound'.

Over the stile ere you come at it, You would be. *Cf.* Leap over the hedge before you come at the stile.   (S 856)

1546 HEYWOOD II. ix. L2ᵛ Like one halfe lost, tyll gredy graspyng gat it, Ye wolde be ouer the style, or ye come at it. 1616 WITHALS 555. 1710 PALMER 188 Don't go over the Stile before you come at It.

Overburden, *see* Burden, (It is not the) but the o.

Overcame, Overcome(s), *see* Came, saw, and o., (I); Endures is not o. (He that); Labour o. all things.

Over-ruler, *see* Fellow-ruler.

Over-run, *see* Out-run (O.-r.) the constable.

Overseen, *see* Wisest man may fall (be o.).

Overtakes, *see* Judgement as he runs, (He that passes) o. repentance.

Overturn(s, ed), *see* Hand of man; Stone in the way o. a great wain, (A little).

Owe God a death, To.   (G 237)

c. 1581 *Dial. betw. Cath. and Cons.* l. 59 in *Bal. from MSS*, ii, pt. ii, 176 Fiat voluntas Dei, then say I, We owe a death, and once we needes must dye. 1588 G. D. *A Briefe Discovery* 125 We do all owe God a death: how shall we better pay it, then in his quarrell? 1592 *The Repentance of Robert Greene* (Harrison) 11. *a.* 1593 *Jack Straw* Hazl.-Dods. v. 381. 1597 SHAKES. *I Hen. IV.* V. i. 127 Why, thou owest God a death. 1681 ROBERTSON *Phraseol. General.* 969a I ow God a death; Debemur morti nos nostráque.

Owes, He who | is in all the wrong.

1642 TORRIANO 32 [*Chi deve, hà tutti i torti*] . . . 1732 FULLER no. 2398.

Owe(s), *see also* Devil o. me good turn; Hundred, (He that o. a); Pay what you o. and you'll know what you're worth.

Owing, *see* Sleep without supping, wake without o.

Owl flies, The.   (o 93)

1549 ERASM tr. Chaloner. *Praise of Folly* P 4
This other prouerbe, *The howlate flieth* (whereby
was ment, that lyke as *Pallas*, to whome the howlate is consecrate, was wont to geue good . . .
successe to . . . *Atheniens* purposes vnaduisedly
enterprised: So that armie which had *Timotheus*
ones for captaine, was euer victorious though
tenne to one it should haue chaunced otherwise).
[? **1562**] **1571** W. ALLEY *Poor Man's Library* 6
Noctua volauit. The owle hath floen.

Owl in an ivy-bush, An.   (o 96)

1553 UDALL *Ralph Roister D.* II. i. 23 With
toodleloodle poope As the howlet out of an
yvie bushe shoulde hoope. **1579–80** LODGE *Def.
Poet.* Shakes. Soc. 8 Your day Owl . . . hath
brought such a lot of wondering birds about
your ears, as . . . will chatter you out of your ivy
bush. *a.* **1611** BEAUM. & FL. *Four Plays in One*
Induct. Could not you be content to be an owl
in such an ivy-bush? **1738** SWIFT Dial. I. E.L.
289.

Owl is the king of the night, An.

                                                      (o 94)

1616 DRAXE no. 724. **1639** CLARKE I.

Owl sings, When the | the nightingale will hold her peace.

1603 BRETON *Packet Mad Let.* Wks. (1879) II. 12.

Owl thinks her own young fairest, The.

1576 U. FULWELL *Ars Adulandi* E I Thou knowest
the fable in Æsope, that the Oule thought her
owne birdes faierest. **1732** FULLER no. 4698
(young ones Beauties).

Owls to Athens.   (o 97)

[Ar. *Αν.* 301 *Γλαῦκ' εἰς Ἀθήνας.*] **1545** *Bibliotheca Eliotae Noctuae Athenis* Oules to Athenes.
c. **1580** J. CONYBEARE 46. **1590** SWINBURNE
Testaments Pref. I may be thought . . . to carrie
owles to Athens, and to trouble the reader with
a matter altogether needlesse and superfluous.
1591 ARIOSTO *Orl. Fur.* Harington XL. i. **1853**
TRENCH iii. 68.

Owl(s), *see also* Blind as an o.; Fly with the o.;
Give a groat for an o. (He is in great want that
will); Lived too near wood to be frightened by o.

Own hearth is gowd's worth, One's, *or* Own fire is pleasant, One's.

c. **1300** *Provs. of Hending* 14 Este bueth oune
brondes. *c.* **1350** *Douce MS.* 52 no. 54 Hit is
merry a man to syt by his owne fyre. **1862**
HISLOP 19 Ane's ain hearth is gowd's worth.

Own is own.   (o 100)

c. **1300** *Provs. of Hending* 26 Owen ys owen, and
other mennes edueth. *c.* **1450** *Provs. of Wysdom*
103 Own is own and oþere men is edwyte. **1546**
HEYWOOD II. iv. G4ᵛ For alwaie owne is owne, at
the recknyngis eend. **1583** G. BABINGTON *Exposⁿ
of the Commandments* 384 A mans owne is his

owne. **1591** *Troublesome Reign K. John* Pt. I
C3ᵛ Mine owne is mine. **1659** HOWELL *Eng.
Prov.* 7a Own is own, and home is home.

Own, *see also* Beat one at one's o. weapon, (To);
Bold with what is your o., (Be); Every man gets
his o., (When); Every man should take his o.;
Gallows will have its o.; Rod for his o. back;
Soul is my o., (I dare not say); Wise that has
wit for o. affairs.

Owner, *see* House shows o.

Owt for nowt, If tha does | do it for thysen.

1913 I Feb. D. H. LAWRENCE *Lett.* i. 183 (The
Yorkshire proverb).

Ox before, Take heed of an | of a horse behind, of a monk on all sides.   (H 376)

1640 HERBERT no. 900. **1670** RAY 20 (Asse
behind).

Ox go where he shall not labour? Whither shall the.   (o 111)

1631 MABBE *Celestina* T.T. 78 Which way shall
the oxe goe, but he must needs plough? **1640**
HERBERT no. 98. **1699** A. BOYER *Compleat French
Master* 147 (where he may be free from the
Yoke?). **1853** TRENCH V. 114 Where wilt thou
go, ox, that thou wilt not have to plough? is
the Catalan remonstrance addressed to one, who
imagines by any outward change of condition
to evade the inevitable task and toil of existence.

Ox is never woe, till he to the harrow go, The.   (o 106)

1523 FITZHERB. *Husb.* § 15 It is an olde sayinge,
The oxe is neuer wo, tyll he to the harowe goo.
1742 *An Agreeable Companion* 13 The Plough
cuts smoothly along, but the Harrow Tugs by
Jerks, whence The Ox does never know such
Woe, As when to the Harrow he does go.

Ox is taken by the horns, and a man by the tongue, An.   (M 385. O 107)

1593 J. ELIOT *Ortho-Epia Gallica* ed. J. Lindsay
68 Take men by their words and birds by a call.
1611 COTGRAVE s.v. Homme An oxe (is bound)
by the horne, a man by his word. *a.* **1628**
CARMICHAELL no. 1417 Tak a man be his word
and a kw be hir horne. **1640** HERBERT no. 967.
1641 FERGUSSON no. 853 (as *a.* 1628). **1706**
STEVENS s.v. Buey The Ox is held by the Horn,
and a Man by his Word. **1721** KELLY 320 . . . A
Reflection upon one who has broken his Word
to us.

Ox on his tongue, He has an.

[Of one who keeps silence for some weighty
reason. AESCH. *Ag.* 36 τὰ δ' ἄλλα σιγῶ, βοῦς ἐπὶ
γλώσσῃ μέγας βέβηκεν. L. *Bos in linguâ.*] **1548**
SIR T. ELYOT *Bibliotheca* Bos in lingua . . . A
prouerbe touchynge theym, which dare not
speake the truthe or wyll not, because they
haue receyued money to holde their peace. For
the Athenienses vsed a certaine coigne of money,

with an oxe figure thereon. **1911** *Times Wkly.*
24 Nov. 473 [Borrow] got to know the importance of maintaining an ox upon his tongue.

Ox, An | when he is loose, licks himself at pleasure.

1706 STEVENS s.v. Buey . . . Much us'd by Batchelors against Matrimony, which is called a Yoke.
1732 FULLER no. 659.

Ox when weariest treads surest, The.

(O 108)

[*a.* **420** JEROME *Bos lassus fortius figit pedem.*]
1539 TAVERNER 3 An olde beaten oxe fastenethe
hys fote the stronger. Hierome vsed thys
prouerbe wrytyng to S. Austyne to feare hym
that he a yonge man shulde not prouoke S.
Hierom at that tyme olde. **1611** COTGRAVE
s.v. Soëf The Ox when he is tir'd sets down his
foot fast. That is, when a Man is in Years he
does things with solidity. **1678** RAY 186. **1706**
STEVENS s.v. Buey The wearie Oxe treads gently
or gingerly; goes faire and softly.

Ox(en), *see also* Beauty draws more than o.;
Black o. has trod on his foot; Cages for o. to
bring up birds; Fling at the brod ne'er a good
o.; Lazy o. little better for goad; Muzzle not
the o.'s mouth; North of England for o.; Old
o. have stiff horns; Old o. straight furrow; Old
o. will find shelter; Plough with o. and ass;
Plough with such o. as he has; St. Luke's day
the o. have leave to play; Steal an egg will
steal an o.; Swallow an o. and be choked with
tail.

Oxford draws knife, When | England's soon at strife.

(C 375)

1662 FULLER Oxford 329 *Chronica si penses, cum
pugnent* Oxonienses *Post aliquot menses volat
ira per* Angliginenses. 'Mark the Chronicles
aright, When Oxford Scholars fall to fight,
Before many months expir'd England will with
war be fir'd.' **1874** J. R. GREEN *Short Hist.* (1892)
I. iii. 255 Every phase of ecclesiastical controversy or political strife was preluded by some
fierce outbreak in this turbulent, surging mob.
. . . A murderous town and gown row preceded
the opening of the Barons' War. 'When Oxford
draws knife', ran the old rime, 'England's soon at
strife.'

Oxford for learning, London for wit, Hull for women, and York for a tit.[1]

a. **1871** HIGSON *MSS. Coll.*, 209 in HAZLITT 326.
[[1] horse.]

Oxford is the home of lost causes.

1865 M. ARNOLD *Ess. in Criticism* Pref. xix
Oxford . . . Adorable dreamer . . .! home of lost
causes, and forsaken beliefs, and unpopular
names, and impossible loyalties. **1914** *T.L.S.*

7 Aug. 378 Oxford has often been called 'the
home of lost causes', or, as Mr. Cram puts it,
'of causes not lost but gone before'.

Oxford knives, and London wives.

(K 159)

1659 HOWELL *Eng. Prov.* 14a.

Oyster is a gentle thing, and will not come unless you sing, The.

1776 HERD *Scot. Songs*, 'The Dreg Song' II. 165
The oysters are a gentle kin, They winna tak
unless you sing. **1816** SCOTT *Antiq.* ch. 40
Elspeth chanting . . . 'But the oyster loves the
dredging sang, For they come of a gentle kind'.
1869 HAZLITT 381.

Oysters? How do you after your.

1678 RAY 78.

Oysters are only in season in the R months.

(O 117)

1577 W. HARRISON *Descr. of England* New
Sh. S. ii. 22 Our oisters are generallie forborne
in the foure hot monethes of the yeare, that is,
Maie, Iune, Iulie, and August ['which are void
of the letter R' added 1587]. **1599** H. BUTTES
Dyets Dry Dinner N I The Oyster . . . is vnseason-
able and vnholesome in all monethes, that haue
not the letter R in their name. **1602** WITHALS
38 Spoken of the Monethes wherein Oysters bee
in season, Mensibus in quibus r, as October,
Nouember, December, and the like of that letter,
Ostrea suat bona semper. **1678** RAY 349
Oysters are not good in a moneth that hath not
an R in it. **1764** CHESTERFIELD *Lett.* cccxlvi
Here is no domestic news of changes and chances
in the political world, which like oysters, are
only in season in the R months, when the Parliament sits. **1906** A. T. QUILLER-COUCH *Mayor of
T.* ch. 12 We were talking of oyster shells. . . .
You can't procure 'em all the year round. . . .
You can work at your beds whenever there's
an 'r' in the month, and then, during the
summer, take a spell.

Oysters are ungodly, because they are eaten without grace; uncharitable be-cause we leave nought but shells; and unprofitable because they must swim in wine.

(O 118)

1611 *Tarlton's Jests* Shakes. Soc. 6. **1738** SWIFT
Dial. II. E.L. 296 They say oysters are a cruel
meat, because we eat them alive: then they are
an uncharitable meat, for we leave nothing to
the poor; and they are an ungodly meat,
because we never say grace.

Oyster(s), *see also* Apple to an o. (As like as an);
Bold man that first ate o.; Gape like an o.;
Gravest fish is o.; Mayor of Northampton opens
o. with dagger.

P

P's and Q's, To mind (be on), one's.

(P 1)

[= to be very particular as to one's words or behaviour.] **1594** LYLY *Mother B.* II. iv. 21 Euerie one remember his que.—I, and his k. **1602** DEKKER *Satiro-mastix* in Wks. (1873) I. 211 Now thou art in thy Pee and Kue. **1779** MRS. H. COWLEY *Who's the Dupe?* I. i You must mind your *P*'s and *Q*'s with him, I can tell you. ?**1800** W. B. RHODES *Bomb. Fur.* iv. 30 My sword I can well use So mind your P's and Q's. *a.* **1814** *Apollo's Choice* in *Mod. Brit. Drama* IV. 208 I must be on my P's and Q's here, or I shall get my neck into a halter. **1888** C. BLATHERWICK *Uncle Pierce* ch. 1 He was rather on his p's and q's.

Pace that kills, It is the.

1850 THACKERAY *Pendennis* ch. 19 You're going too fast, and can't keep up the pace, . . . it will kill you. You're livin' as if there was no end to the money . . . at home. **1901** S. LANE-POOLE *Sir H. Parkes* 365 There is an old proverb about the pace that kills, and . . . Sir Harry was killing himself by work at high pressure.

Pace, *see also* Soft p. goes far; Stumbles and falls not mends p.

Paced like an alderman, He is. (A 98)

c. **1553** UDALL *Ralph Roister D.* IV. v. 15 No Alderman Can goe I dare say, a sadder pace than ye can. **1583** MELBANCKE 14 Vsing an aldermans pace before he can wel gange. **1612** SHELTON *Quix.* IV. xx. ii. 132 In a grave posture, and with an alderman-like pace. **1639** CLARKE 32. **1691** SEWELS 13 To walk an Aldermans pace.

Pack of cards without a knave, There is no.

1600 BRETON *Pasquils Fooles-Cappe* 26/1 Wks. Gros. I. 26 And yet is it in vaine such *world* to wish: There is no packe of Cardes without a *Knaue.* **1613** [N. BRETON] *Uncasing of Machiavel's Instructions* (*Poems* ed. Robertson 157).

Pack the cards, Many can | yet cannot play well. (C 78)

1659 HOWELL *Eng. Prov.* 19a . . . *viz.* Witty men seldom wise.

Pack to the pins, You have brought the. (P 5)

1568 FULWELL *Like Will to Like* D4 Rafe roister . . . Hath brought a pack of wul to a faire paire of hosen. *a.* **1585** MONTGOMERIE *Cherrie & Slae* xciii (1821) 49 'Suppose the pack cum to the pins, Quha can his chance eschew?' **1721** KELLY 368 . . . That is, you have dwindled away your Stock.

Pack, *see also* Every one thinks his p. heaviest; Lack what they would have in their p. (Many

men); Open your p. and sell no wares (Never); Silly p. that may not pay the custom; Small p. becomes small pedlar; Take part of pelf when p. a-dealing.

Pad in the straw, A. (P 9)

[= a lurking or hidden danger.] **1530** PALSGRAVE 595/a Though they make no never so fayre a face, yet there is a padde in the strawe. **1611** DAVIES no. 17. **1650** FULLER *Pisgah* III. II. viii. § 3 *Latet anguis in herbâ*, there is a pad in the straw, and invisible mischief lurking therein.

Paddle one's own canoe, To.

[= to make one's way by one's own exertions.] **1828** J. HALL *Lett. from West* 261 The Lady of the Lake . . . 'paddled her own canoe' very dexterously. **1844** MARRYAT *Settlers in Canada* ch. 8 I think it much better as we all go along together that every man paddle his own canoe. **1854** SARAH T. BOLTON *Song* 'Paddle Your Own Canoe'.

Paddocks, *see* Weather meet to set p. abroad in.

Padlock, *see* Wedlock is p.

Page of your own age, Make a. (P 11)

c. **1526** J. RASTELL *Nature of Four Elements* Hazl.-Dods. i. 23 Then I beshrew the page of thine age, Come hither, knave, for thine advantage. **1608** ARMIN *Nest Nin.* Shakes. Soc. 53 The next bootes Ile make a page of my own age, and carry home myselfe. **1616** DRAXE no. 333 Let him make a page of his age. **1670** RAY 189. **1738** SWIFT *Dial.* I. E.L. 293 Make a page of your own age, and do it yourself. **1818** SCOTT *Rob Roy* ch. 32 Folk may just mak a page o' their ain age, and . . . gang their ain errands.

Page, *see also* Wage will get a p.

Pagoda tree, *see* Shake the p. t.

Paigle [= cowslip], *see* Yellow as a p.

Pail, *see* God gives the milk not the p.

Pain both to pay and pray, It is a. (P 125)

c. **1516** SKELTON *Magnificence* l. 363 Had I not payde and prayd . . . I had not bene here with you this nyght. **1639** CLARKE 220 Both pay and pray? that's hard. **1641** FERGUSSON no. 520.

Pain is forgotten where gain follows. (P 19)

1530 TYNDALE *Practice of Prelates* P.S. 29 Gain joined with pain maketh pain nothing. **1548** HALL *Chron.* (1809, 56) Paine is forgotten euer where gaine foloweth [Cato]. **1636** CAMDEN 304. **1732** FULLER no. 3836.

Pain is gain.

c. 1430 LYDGATE *Minor Poems* E.E.T.S. Mercers' Mumming ll. 90–1 Grande Peyne: Grande Gayne. 1881 DEAN PLUMPTRE *Eccles.* vii. 3 *Sorrow is better than laughter.* . . . We are reminded of the Greek axiom, παθεῖν, μαθεῖν ('Pain is gain'). . . . There is a moral improvement rising out of sorrow which is not gained from enjoyment however blameless.

Pain like the gout (and toothache), There is no. (P 18)

1616 BRETON *Cross. Prov.* B1 There is no paine like the Gowt.—Yes, the Tooth-ach. 1639 CLARKE 203 (and tooth-ach).

Pain to do nothing than something, It is more. (P 17)

1640 HERBERT no. 884. 1659 HOWELL *Span. Prov.* 18.

Pains is the price that God puts upon all things. (P 22)

[HESIOD *Wks. and Days* 289 τῆς δ' ἀρετῆς ἱδρῶτα θεοὶ προπάροιθεν ἔθηκαν.] 1648 HERRICK *Hesp.* (Muses Lib.) 471 Jove will not let his gifts go from him if not bought with sweat. 1659 HOWELL *Eng. Prov.* 19b.

Pains to get, care to keep, fear to lose. (P 23)

1616 DRAXE no. 1880 There is paine in getting, care in keeping, and griefe in losing riches. 1640 HERBERT no. 975.

Pain(s), *see also* Cruelty more cruel if we defer the p.; Gains will quit the p. (The); Great p. and little gain soon weary; Great p. quickly find ease; Hoards up money; Labour for one's p. (To have one's); Like punishment and equal p. key and keyhole sustain; No p. no gains; Nothing to be got without p.; Pleasure (No) no p.; Take a p. for a pleasure.

Painted pictures are dead speakers. (P 279)

1616 BRETON 2 *Cross. Prov.* B1ᵛ Painted creatures are dead speakers. 1678 RAY 20.

Paint(s, ed), *see also* Devil is not so black as p.; Fresh as p.; Lion is not so fierce as p.; Makes much of his p. sheath; Post soon p., (A rotten); Woman and a cherry are p. for harm; Woman that p. puts up a bill.

Painter, *see* God or a p. (He is either a); Good p. can draw a devil.

Painter (of a boat), *see* Cut the p.

Painters (travellers) and poets have leave to lie. (P 28)

[HOR. *A.P.* 9 *Pictoribus atque poetis quidlibet audendi semper fuit aequa potestas.*] *c.* 1566 CURIO *Pasquin in a Trance* tr. W.P. 50 Painters and Poets haue alwayes had authoritie to deuise what they liste themselues. 1573 GASCOIGNE i. 143. 1578 *Courtly Controv.* S4ᵛ Poets . . . haue a bull of dispensation to lye, the better to sauce their fictions. 1580 *Second and Third Blasts* (*Eng. Drama and Stage*, ed. Hazlitt) 145 The notablest lier is become the best Poet. 1584 WITHALS F5 To lie belongeth vnto Astrologers, or Stargasers, and to Poets. 1586 J. CASE *Praise of Music* 87 Painters and Poets are commonly allowed to ly. 1591 HARINGTON *Apol. of Poetrie* par. 3 According to that old verse . . . Astronomers, Painters, and Poets may lye by authoritie. 1616 DRAXE no. 1334 Poets and trauellours may lie by authority. 1621 ROBINSON 38 (Poets and Painters). 1639 CLARKE 131 (Poets and painters). 1641 FERGUSSON no. 691.

Painting and fighting look aloof, On. (P 29)

1640 HERBERT no. 247. 1721 KELLY 273 (*look abigh*).[1] It is dangerous to be near the one, and if we look near the other it loseth much of its Advantage. [1 at a distance.]

Painting, *see also* Blind man's wife needs no p.; Woman's p. breed stomach's fainting (Let no).

Pair of ears draws dry a hundred tongues, One. (P 33)

1640 HERBERT no. 526. 1659 HOWELL *It. Prov.* 5 (dry up). 1659 TORRIANO no. 178 (is enough to drie up).

Pair of heels, One | is often worth two pair of hands. (P 34)

1575 *Gamm. Gurton* IV. ii. 77 If one pair of legs had not bene worth two pairc of hands He had had his bearde shaven if my nayles wold have served. [1604] 1607 DEKKER & WEBSTER *Sir T. Wyatt* IV. iii. 3 They may thank their heeles more then their hands For sauing of their liues. 1659 HOWELL *Eng. Prov.* 2a. 1678 RAY 153 . . . Always for cowards. The *French* say, Qui n'a cœur ait jambes; and the *Italian* . . . , Chi non ha cuore habbi gambe. He that hath no heart let him have heels. 1820 SCOTT *Monast.* ch. 13 I . . . made two pair of legs (and these were not mine, but my mare's) worth one pair of hands. . . . I e'en pricked off with myself.

Pair of heels, *see also* Show a fair p. of h.

Pair of shears between them, There went but a. (P 36)

[They match each other as if cut from the same piece of cloth.] 1579 LYLY *Euph.* i. 195 The *Sympathia* of affections and as it were but a payre of sheeres to goe betweene theire natures. 1604 SHAKES. *M.M.* I. ii. 26 Thou thyself art a wicked villain, despite of all grace.—Well, there went but a pair of shears between us. 1604 MARSTON *Malcontent* IV. v. 1632 *Star Chamber Cases* (Camden) 98 There went but a paire of sheeres between a Papist and a Protestant, and not a pinne to choose of what religion a man is.

Pair, *see* Couple is not a p. (Every); Stars than a p. (More).

Paisley, *see* Glasgow people . . . P. bodies.

Palace(s), *see* Content lodges oftener in cottages than p.

Palate, *see* Purse and his p. ill met.

Pale as a clout, As. (C 446)

c. **1489** CAXTON *Sons Aymon* E.E.T.S. XIX. 419 He . . . becam pale as a white cloth for the grete wrathe that he had at his herte. **1563** SACKVILLE 'Buckingham' *Mirror for Mag.* ed. Campbell 339. *c.* **1595** SHAKES. *R.J.* II. iv. 200. **1606** W. ELDERTON *A new merry News* A2ᵛ. **1841** MARRYAT *Mast. Ready* ch. 58 (a sheet).

Pale as ashes, As. (A 339)

c. **1385** CHAUCER *Leg. Gd. Women* Bk. 9, l. 2649 Deed wex her hewe and lyk as ash to sene. *c.* **1386** *Id. Knight's Tale* l. 1364 His hewe falow, and pale as asshen colde. *c.* **1592** MARLOWE *Mass. at Paris* l. 1226. **1594–5** SHAKES. *R.J.* III. ii. 54 A piteous corse, a bloody piteous corse; Pale, pale as ashes, all bedaub'd in blood. **1772** H. WALPOLE *Lett. to C'tess Ossory* (1848) i. 37 *Pale as ashes* must be one of our most ancient proverbs and in use before coals. **1813** BARRETT *Heroine* ed. Raleigh 81.

Pale as death, As. (D 134)

1557 EDGEWORTH *Sermons* P1 He was afrayde and pale as death. **1567** PAINTER *Pal. of Pleasure* Jacobs iii. 9 The colour whereof is more pale than death. **1751** FIELDING *Amelia* VI. ix She turned as pale as death. **1818** SCOTT *Ivanhoe* ch. 9 'Over God's forebode!' said Prince John, involuntarily turning . . . as pale as death.

Pale as lead, As. (L 135)

[**1503**] *c.* **1545** SKELTON *Phyllyp Sparrowe* l. 60: Wks. i. 53 My vysage pale and dead, Wanne, and blewe as lead. **1509** HAWES *Past. Pleas.* E.E.T.S. 76 And dyane derlynynge pale as ony lede. **1520** R. WHITTINGTON *Vulgaria* E.E.T.S. 20 His lyppes be as wan as lede. **1563** SACKVILLE 'Buckingham' *Mirror for Mag.* ed. Campbell 343. **1576** LEMNIUS *Touchstone of Complexions* tr. T. Newton 90 As wanne as Lead. *c.* **1595** SHAKES. *R.J.* II. v. 17.

Pale man, *see* Red man (To a) read thy rede.

Pale moon does rain, red moon does blow: white moon does neither rain nor snow. (M 1122, 1126)

1588 FRAUNCE *Lawyer's Log.* I. viii. 43ᵛ When the Moone is red, shee betokeneth wind, these common adiunctes. **1616** WITHALS (1634, 2). **1639** CLARKE 263.

Pale, (adv.), *see also* Cold (p.) as clay.

Pale, (noun), *see* Severn (Fix thy p. in).

Paleness of the pilot is a sign of a storm, The.

1594 GREENE *Looking-Glass* IV. i. Merm. 130 Our bark is batter'd by encountering storms, . . .

The steersman, pale and careful, holds his helm. **1666** TORRIANO *It. Prov.* 169 no. 31.

Palm oil.

[= bribery.] **1907** H. DE WINDT *Through Savage Europe* ch. 18 My mission . . . was eventually accomplished, chiefly by the aid of 'palm oil'. **1929** *Times* 12 Jan. 14/3 With a little 'palm oil' you have been able to . . . get back the stolen property.

Palm, *see* Straighter grows the p.

Paltock's Inn.

[= a poor place.] **1579** GOSSON *Sch. Abuse* Arb. 52 Comming to *Chenas* a blind village, in comparison of *Athens* a Paltockes Inne.

Pan, *see* Black as a pot-side (p.); Turn the cat in p.

Pancake(s), *see* Flat as a p.; Thatch Groby Pool with p.

Pandora's box. (P 40)

[Jupiter gave Pandora a box containing all human ills, which flew forth when the box was opened: but at the bottom was Hope.] **1565** J. CALFHILL *Answer* P.S. 5 You have receiued from your Jove of the Capitol a Pandora's box. **1579** GOSSON *Sch. Abuse* Arb. 44 I cannot lyken our affection better than to . . . *Pandoraes* boxe, lift vppe the lidde, out flyes the Deuill. **1621** BURTON *Anat. Mel.* I. i. I. i (1651) 2 The sin of our first parent Adam . . . shadowed unto us in the tale of Pandoras box, which, being opened through her curiosity, filled the world full of all manner of diseases. **1679** J. GOODMAN *Penit. Pardoned* II. i (1713) 264 There may be some hope left in the bottom of this Pandora's box of calamities. **1888** J. E. T. ROGERS *Econ. Interp. Hist.* (1894) ch. 17 The favours of Government are like the box of Pandora, with this important difference, that they rarely leave hope at the bottom.

Panem et circenses, see Bread and circuses.

Pannier, *see* Mock no p. men; Pig of worse p.

Pantofles,¹ To stand (be, etc.) upon (one's). (P 43)

[= to be on one's dignity.] **1569** J. PHILLIP *Patient Grissell* l. 546 For wearing my masters pantofles I wold beat them about thy pate. **1573** G. HARVEY *Letter-bk.* Camden 14 He was now altogither set on his merri pinnes and walked on his stateli pantocles. **1579** LYLY *Euph.* i. 196 For the most part they stande so on their pantuffles. [*c.* **1590**] **1594** *Taming a Shrew* B4 Then am I so Stout and takes it vpon me, and stands vpon my pantofles To them out of al crie. **1616** DRAXE no. 2219 He standeth too much on his pantofles. **1685** BUNYAN *Pharisee & Publ.* Wks. (1845) 140 Thou standest upon thy points and pantables, thou wilt not bate God on all of what thy righteousness is worth. [¹ slippers, pattens.]

Pap with a hatchet. (P 45)

c. 1557 *Jacob and Esau* G3 I would with this fauchon I might geue him pap. 1587 J. BRIDGES *Defence* 151 Did God meane, they shoulde haue suche Pappe with an Hatchet, and that Princes should be nowises on that fashion? 1589 LYLY [*Title*] Pappe with an Hatchet. 1592 G. HARVEY *Foure Lett.* ii. Wks. Gros. I. 164 I neither name Martin-mar-prelate: nor shame Papp wyth a hatchet. 1594 LYLY *Mother B.* I. iii. 104 They giue vs pap with a spoon before we can speak, and when wee speake for that wee loue, pap with a hatchet. 1615 A. NICCHOLES *Disc. Marr.* ix. 30 He that so olde seekes for a nurse so yong, shall have pappe with a Hatchet for his comfort. 1909 M. LOANE *Englishman's Castle* ch. 8 The poor are extremely sensitive to small amenities. . . . 'Pap with an hatchet' may be all very well among social equals, but more ceremony is needed when there is a gap . . . between the persons concerned.

Paper, *see* Fairer the p. fouler blot; Youth and white p. take any impression.

Papist, *see* Christian (A complete) must have works of a P.

Paradise, *see* England p. of women; Enter into P. must have good key; Fool's p.; Powys is p. of Wales.

Paramour(s), *see* Hunting, hawking, and p.; Puddings and p. should be hotly handled.

Parched pea on a griddle, Like a.

1836 HALIBURTON *Clockmaker* I. 243 As brisk as a parched pea. 1896 J. C. HUTCHESON *Crown & Anchor* ch. 4 The wiry little . . . waiter . . . was hopping about the room 'like a parched pea on a griddle'.

Pardon makes offenders. (P 50)

a. 1589 *Love and Fortune* G2ᵛ Sometime pardon breedes a second ill. 1604 SHAKES. *M.M.* II. i. 270 Pardon is still the nurse of second woe. 1639 CLARKE 182.

Pardon of Maynooth.

[1535] FROUDE *Hist. Eng.* (1856–70) II. viii The prisoners . . . under the ruins of their own den,[1] were hung up for a sign to the whole nation. . . . In the presence of this 'Pardon of Maynooth', as it was called, the phantom of rebellion vanished on the spot. [[1] the castle of Maynooth.]

Pardoning the bad is injuring the good.
1732 FULLER no. 3842.

Pardons and pleasantness are great revenges of slanders. *Cf.* Vengeance, The noblest | is to forgive. (P 51)

1640 HERBERT no. 365. 1710 PALMER 81 Forgiveness and a Smile is the best Revenge.

Pardon(s) (*noun*), *see also* Fault is (Where no) needs no p.; No penny no p.

Pardon(s) (*verb*), *see also* Offender never p.

Parent(s), *see* Children when little make p. fools, and when great mad; God, and p. . . . can never be requited.

Paring of his nails, He will not part with the. (P 52)

1546 HEYWOOD I. xi. E1ᵛ She will not part with the paryng of hir nayles. 1639 CLARKE 37. 1670 RAY 184 (lose).

Parings of a pippin are better than a whole crab, The.

1706 STEVENS s.v. Cascara The Paring of a Pippin is better than the Kernel of an Acorn. 1732 FULLER no. 4701.

Paris, *see* Americans when they die.

Parish churches, *see* Parsons (More) than p. c.

Parish clerk, *see* Too hasty to be p. c.

Parish priest forgets that ever he has been holy water (parish) clerk, The. (P 56)

c. 1513 SIR T. MORE *Rich. III* (1821) 154 The olde prouerbe, . . . the parish priest remembreth not that euer he was parishe Clarke. 1533 J. HEYWOOD *John, Tyb, &c.* Farmer 86 But now I see well the old proverb is true; That parish priest forgetteth that ever he was clerk. 1546 HEYWOOD I. xi. D4ᵛ And now nought he setteth By poore folke, For the paryshe prieste forgetteth That euer he hath bene holy water clerke. 1548 HALL *Chron.* (1809) 387 But when he was once crouned King . . . he cast aside his old cōdicions . . . verefieng ye old prouerbe, honoures chaunge maners, as the parishe prest remembreth that he was neuer parishe clerck. 1599 PORTER *Angry Wom. Abingd.* l. 707 Harke, Mother hark The Priest forgets that ere he was a Clark When you were at my yeares, . . . Your minde was to change maidenhead for wife. 1639 CLARKE 31. The Priest forgets that ever he was clarke. 1706 STEVENS s.v. Suegra The Parson forgets he was Clark.

Parish top,[1] Like a. (P 57)

[*Cf.* VIRGIL *Aen.* vii. 380 ff.] [*c.* 1580] 1590 SIDNEY *Arcadia* ed. Feuillerat i. 227 Even like a toppe . . . which nought but whipping moves. [1600] 1662 *Grim the Collier of Croydon* Hazl.-Dods. viii. 408 Every night I dream I am a town top, and that I am whipped up and down with the scourge-stick of love and the metal of affection. 1601 w. I. *The Whipping of the Satire* D6ᵛ As boyes scourge tops for sport on Lenten day; So scourges he the great towne-top of sin. 1601 SHAKES. *T.N.* I. iii. 37 He's a coward . . . that will not drink . . . till his brains turn o' the toe like a parish-top. *c.* 1616 FLETCHER & MASS. *Thierry & Theod.* II. iii A boy of twelve Should scourge him hither like a parish-top. [[1] a large top provided for the use of peasants in frosty weather.]

Parish(es), *see also* Estate in two p.; Mad p. must have a mad priest; World is a wide p.

Parleys, *see* City (Castle, Woman) that p.

Parliament can do everything but turn a boy into a girl.

1665 J. GLANVILL *Scepsis Scientifica* 95 As King James would say of Parliament, It can do any thing but make a Man a Woman.   **1902–4** LEAN IV. 79.

Parliament, *see also* Coach and four.

Parnassus has no gold mines in it.

1732 FULLER no. 3844.

Parnell, *see* Madame P. crack the nut; Tender as P. that broke her finger.

Parrot, *see* Almond for a p.; Speak like a p.

Parsley bed.　　　　　　　　　　　　　(B 6)

1622 MABBE tr. *Aleman's Guzman d'Alf.* I. 25 *margin* That phrase which we vse to little children, when we tell them they were borne in their mothers Parsly-bed.   **1796** PEGGE *Anonym.* I, § 91 (1809) 52 The child, when new-born, comes out of the persley bed, they will say in the North.

Parsley before it is born is seen by the devil nine times.　　　　　　　　　(P 62)

1658 MENNIS & SMITH *Wit Restored: Facetiae* i. 152 Or else the weed [parsley], which still before it's borne Nine times the devill sees.   **1883** BURNE *Shropsh. Folk-Lore* 248 Parsley must be sown nine times, for the devil takes all but the last.   **1908** 4 May D. H. LAWRENCE *Lett.* i. 7 People say parsley seed goes seven times (some are moderate, discarding the holy number as unfit, and say five) to the Old Lad, it is so long a-germinating.

Parsley fried will bring a man to his saddle, and a woman to her grave.
　　　　　　　　　　　　　　　　　　(P 63)
1678 RAY 345.

Parsley, *see also* Mistress is the master (Where the) the p. grows the faster; Welsh p.

Parson (Priest) always christens his own child first, The.　　　　(C 318)

1659 HOWELL *Eng. Prov.* 3b 'Tis good Christning of a mans own child first.   **1697** W. POPE *Life of Seth [Ward] Bp. of Salisbury* 93.   **1721** KELLY 310 The Priest christens his own Bairn first. An Apology for serving our selves before our Neighbours.   **1738** SWIFT *Dial.* I. E.L. 266 Miss, will you be so kind as to fill me a dish of tea? —... I'm just going to fill one for myself; and, you know, the parson always christens his own child first.   **1927** E. V. LUCAS in *Times* 15 Mar. 18/1 Jamaican proverbs ... I quote a few ... 'Parson christen him own piccaninny first.'

Parson of Saddleworth,[1] Like the | who could read in no book but his own.
　　　　　　　　　　　　　　　　　　(P 71)
1670 RAY 209 ... *Chesh.* [1 in Yorkshire, but belonging, ecclesiastically, to the parish of Rochdale, Lancs.]

Parson Smith, *see* Smith.

Parson's cow, To come home like the | with a calf at her foot.　　　(P 69)

1670 RAY 209 ... *Chesh.*   **1917** BRIDGE 333 ... Said of a girl returning home with an addition to the family. Sometimes said of one who has succeeded well in business and greatly increased his store.

Parson's pig, *see* Poor and peart like p.'s p.

Parsons are souls' waggoners.　　(P 70)

1640 HERBERT no. 938.

Parsons than parish churches, There are more.

1894 NORTHALL *Folk-phrases* E.D.S. 25.

Parson(s), *see also* Fool of the family: make a p. of him; Good enough for the p. unless parish better; House-going p., church-going people; Long standing ... makes poor p.; Michaelmas chickens and p.'s daughters; Once a p. always a p.; Pinch on the p.'s side; Tender as a p.'s leman.

Part with the crock as the porridge, She will as soon.　　　　　　　(C 830)

1678 RAY 352 *Somerset.*

Part (*noun*), *see* Art (He who has an) has everywhere a p.; Charity construes all doubtful things in good p.; Eye will have his p.; Pudding in the fire and my p. lies therein; Repairs not p. builds all; World is a stage and every man plays his p.

Part (*verb*), *see also* Baker to the pillory (Fear we p. not yet, quoth); Friends must p.; Merry meet, merry p.

Part with, *see also* Paring of his nails.

Parthian war.　　　　　　　　　　(P 80)

1600 NASHE *Summer's Last Will* iii. 235 As the Parthians fight, flying away.   c. **1609** SHAKES. *Cymb.* I. vi. 20 Like the Parthians, I shall flying fight.   **1629** T. ADAMS *Serm.* (1861–2) I. 222 The best way to conquer sin is by Parthian war, to run away. So the poet—'Sed fuge; tutus adhuc Parthus ab hoste fuga est.'   **1902** GREENOUGH & KITTREDGE *Words* 380 A 'Parthian shot' was very literal to Crassus[1] ...: to us it is only an elegant and pointed synonym for our method of 'having the last word'. [1 53 B.C.]

Parties, *see* Hear all p.; Please all p.

Parting of the ways, To be (stand) at the.

[EZEK. xxi. 21 For the King of Babylon stood at the parting of the way, at the head of the two ways, to use divination.] **1849** J. R. LOWELL *The Parting of the Ways* [Title]. **1928** *Times* 29 May 8/4 India is at the parting of the ways, and needs the services of her best sons.

Parting, *see also* Careless p. between mare and cart; Little intermeddling fair p.; Praise at p.; Sorrow is at p. if at meeting laughter.

Partington, Mrs., *see* Mrs. P. mopping up Atlantic.

Partridge (plover), As plump as a. (P 84)

1594 NASHE *Unfort. Trav.* ii. 261 As fat and plump euerie part of her as a plouer. **1678** RAY 281. **1695** RAVENSCROFT 18. **1748** SMOLLETT *Rod. Random* ch. 47.

Partridge had the woodcock's thigh, If the | it would be the best bird that ever did fly. (P 85)

1670 RAY 44. **1732** FULLER no. 6400.

Pasch, *see* Figs after peace (P.); Green Yule and white P. . . . fat churchyard; Yule feast may be done at P.

Pass of Alton, Through the | poverty might pass without peril of robbing.

['The wooded pass of Alton, on the borders of Surrey and Hampshire, . . . was a favourite ambush for outlaws.' Quoted in SKEAT P. Pl. II. 213.] **1393** LANGLAND *P. Pl.* C. xvii. 139 Thorw the pas of Altoun Pouerte myghte passe · withoute peril of robbynge.

Pass (through) the pikes, To. (P 321)

[= to pass through difficulties or dangers.] **1560** T. PALFREYMAN *A Mirror or clear glass* D5 Thou hast escaped a scowringe, or passed thorough the pykes. **1567** G. FENTON *Bandello* T.T. I. 239 At the leaste, hee wolde graunte him dispence and saffe conduit To passe thorow the pikes of his infortunat dangers. **1611** CHAPMAN *May-Day* III. ii (1874) 291 Y'ave past the pikes i' faith, and all the jails of the love-god swarm in yonder house, to salute your recovery. **1616** JONSON *Masque of Christmas* vii. 440 I bring you a Masque . . . Which say the King likes, I ha' passed the Pikes. **1785** COWPER *Let. to Lady Hesketh* 30 Nov. Wks. (1836) v. 187 So far, therefore, I have passed the pikes. The Monthly Critics have not yet noticed me.

Passage, *see* Worse the p., more welcome port.

Passes a winter's day, He that | escapes an enemy. (W 513)

[14. . Fr. *Prov. communs.* Qui passe un jour d'yver si passe un de ses ennemis mortelz.]

1611 COTGRAVE s.v. Passer A mortall foe he scapes who scapes a Winters day. **1640** HERBERT no. 864.

Passing bell, *see* Hear a toll or knell.

Passion, *see* End of p. beginning of repentance.

Past cannot be recalled, Things. (T 203)

c. **1486–1500** MEDWALL *Nature* ii. 1028 ed. Brandt in *Quellen des weltlichen Dramas* (1898) A thyng don cannot be called agayn. *c.* **1513** SIR T. MORE *Rich. III* (1821) 16 Thynges passed cannot be gaine called. **1546** HEYWOOD I. x. C4 But thingis past my handis, I can not call agein. **1548** HALL (1809 ed., 344) Thynges passed cannot be called agayne. **1580** LYLY *Euph.* i. 188 Thinges past, are paste callinge agayne. **1616** DRAXE no. 1587 That that is past, cannot be recalled or helped. **1802** EDGEWORTH *Pop. Tales, Rosanna* ch. 3 Since a thing past can't be recalled, . . . we may be content.

Past cure, past care. (C 921)

1567 J. PICKERING *Horestes* E1ᵛ Sease of syr kyng leaue morning lo, nought can it you auaylle. **1576** PETTIE i. 108 In vain it is to complain, when my care is without cure, and none can redress my wrong. **1593** GREENE *Wks.* Gros. ii. 154 Remember the olde prouerbe, past cure, past care. **1594–5** SHAKES. *L.L.L.* V. ii. 28 Great reason; for 'past cure is still past care'. **1595–6** *Id. Rich. II.* II. iii. 171 Things past redress are now with me past care. **1598** DRAYTON *Her. Epist., Rich. II to Q. Isabel* (1603) 40 Comfort is now vnpleasing to mine eare, Past cure, past care, my bed become my Beere. **1609** SHAKES. *Sonn.* 147, l. 9 Past cure I am, now Reason is past care. **1611** *Id. W.T.* III. ii. 219 What's past help Should be past grief.

Past dying of her first child, She is. (C 314)

1639 CLARKE 282 A maid after marriage, or she'l never die of her first child. **1678** RAY 240 . . . *i.e.* she hath had a bastard.

Past shame, past amendment (grace). (S 271)

a. **1547** REDFORD *Wit & Sci.* l. 920 As the sayeng is, and daylye scene—Past Shame once, and past all amendment. **1692** J. RAY *Dissoln. & Changes of World* 214 Doth not the Scripture condemn a Whore's forehead? Is it not a true Proverb, Past Shame, past Grace?

Pastime, *see* Hang yourself for p.; Hunger makes dinners, p. suppers.

Paston poor, There never was a | a Heyden a coward, nor a Cornwallis a fool. (P 93)

1678 RAY 327. Norfolk.

Pasture, *see* Break a p. makes a man (To); Change of p. makes fat calves.

Patch and long sit, build and soon flit
(*or* Botch and sit, build and flit).
(B 547)

1618 W. LAWSON *New Orchard & Garden* (1676)
9 Tenants who have taken up this proverb
Botch and, &c. **1664** CODRINGTON 209. **1670**
RAY 21.

Patch by patch is good housewifery,
but patch upon patch is plain beggary.
(P 94)

1639 *Berkeley MSS.* 1885, iii. 33 no. 91 Patch
by patch is yeomanly; but patch vpon patch is
beggerly. **1670** RAY 129 (husbandry). **1732**
FULLER no. 6181.

Pate, *see* Cup in p.

Patent, *see* Nothing p. in New Testament.

Paternoster while, A.   (P 99)

1530 PALSGRAVE 807b But a pater noster while
a go. **1594** NASHE *Terrors Night* i. 378 Euery
Pater noster while, he lookt whether in the nets
he [the devil] should be entangled. **1605** 14
June SIR T. BODLEY (*Letters* ed. Wheeler 143)
[The speech to the king] must be short and
sweete, and full of stuffe: . . . it may not exceed
the length of six Pater nosters.

Pater noster built churches, and *Our
Father* pulls them down.   (P 97)

1616 T. ADAMS *Gallant's Burden* 35 Common
Prophane persons . . . that make the profession
of the Gospell haue an euill name: hence that
Prouerbe, *Pater noster*, set vp Churches, *Our
Father*, pulles them downe. **1644** FULLER *Jacob's
Vow* in *Sel. Serm.* (1891) I. 426 Will yourselves
. . . suffer the houses of God to lie waste? Shall
Pater noster build churches, and *Our Father* pull
them down (as the proverb is)? or suffer them
to fall? **1670** RAY 70 . . . I do not look upon
the building of Churches as an argument of the
goodness of the Roman Religion, for . . . its
easier to part with ones goods then ones sins.

Paternoster, He may be in my | but he
shall never come in my creed.   (P 96)

1546 HEYWOOD II. ix. L2 He maie be in my
Pater noster in deede. But be sure, he shall
neuer come in my Creede. **1591** ARIOSTO *Orl.
Fur.* Harington XLIII. *Allegory* As the saying is,
It may be in my Paternoster indeed, But sure it
neuer shall come in my Creed. **1629** T. ADAMS
Serm. (1861–2) II. 247 [Flatterers] are . . . the
commonwealth's wolves. Put them in your
Paternoster, let them never come in your creed:
pray for them, but trust them no more than
thieves.

Paternoster, *see also* Ape's p., (To say an); No p.
no penny; No penny no p.; Patter the devil's p.

Path has a puddle, Every.   (P 100)

1640 HERBERT no. 215. **1706** STEVENS s.v.
Sendero. In every Path there is a sticking, or a
dirty place. **1818** SCOTT *Rob Roy* ch. 38 Ye hae
had your ain time o't, Mr. Syddall; but . . .
ilka path has its puddle.

Pathway, *see* Man must not leave the king's
highway for a p.

Patience, and shuffle the cards. (P 105)

1620 SHELTON *Quix.* II. xxiii. ii. 345 If it
be otherwise, O cousin, I say, patience and
shuffle. [*Note.* Card-players . . . when they
lose, cry to the dealer, 'Patience and shuffle the
cards.'] **1810** SCOTT *Let. Joanna Baillie* 23 Nov.
in LOCKHART *Life* ch. 21 But, as Durandarte
says. . . . —'Patience, cousin, and shuffle the
cards.' **1839** R. H. BARHAM *Life of R. H. Barham*
ii. 78 But 'patience and shuffle the cards' says
the Spanish proverb.

Patience[1] grow in your garden alway,
Let.   (P 116)

c. **1549** HEYWOOD I. xi. E3ᵛ. **1611** DAVIES no. 375
'Let Patience still in your Garden appeare.'
[[1] a species of Dock; *Rumex Patientia*, Linn.]

Patience, He that has | has fat thrushes
for a farthing.   (P 104)

1640 HERBERT no. 430.

Patience in adversity brings a man to
the Three Cranes in the Vintry.
(P 106)

1599 PORTER *Angry Wom. Abingd.* l. 2349 I am
patient I must needes say, for patience in
adversitie, brings a man to the three Cranes in
the Ventree. **1616** DRAXE no. 1595.

Patience is a flower that grows not in
every one's garden.   (P 117)

1616 DRAXE no. 1601 Patience is an excellent
hearbe, but it groweth not in a womans head.
1644 HOWELL *Lett.* 1 Dec. (1903) I. 96 No more,
but that I wish you patience, which is a flower
that grows not in every garden. **1670** RAY 21
. . . Herein is an allusion to the name of a Plant
so called, i.e. Rhabarbarum Monachorum.

Patience is a plaster for all sores.
(P 107)

c. **1390** GOWER *Conf. Amantis* III. 614 Pacience
. . . is the leche of alle offence, As tellen ous
these olde men. a. **1591** H. SMITH *Serm.* (1657)
Trial of the Righteous 234 Among the strange
cures of patience, David may report of his
experience what this Plaister hath done for him.
1639 CLARKE 15. **1664** W. CONYERS *Hemerologicum Astronomicum* 12 Nov. Patience is but
a dry Plaster. **1732** FULLER no. 3856 Patience is
good for abundance of Things besides the Gout.
1738 SWIFT *Dial.* III. E.L. 319 He's laid up with
the gout . . . I hear he's weary of doctoring it,
and now makes use of nothing but patience and
flannel. **1885** E. P. HOOD *World of Prov.* 72.

Patience is a remedy for every grief
(sorrow).   (P 108)

c. **1526** *Dicta Sap.* B3 Some yuels are remedy
to other some: But pacyence is a commune

leuyacion of all yuels. **1539** TAVERNER *Publius*
B4 To all maner sorowe pacience is a remedy.
[1553] **1560** T. WILSON *Art of Rhetoric* ed. Mair
206 Pacience is a remedie for euery disease.
1578 FLORIO *First F.* 44ᵛ Pacience is the best
medicine that is, for a sicke man, the most
precious plaister that is, for any wounde. **1586**
LA PRIMAUDAYE *French Academy* 308 Patience
(saith Plautus) is a remedie for all griefes.
[*Margin*] Patience is a salue for all sores. **1629**
Bk. Mer. Rid. Prov. no. 32 (the remedy of sorrow). *a.* **1763** SHENSTONE *Detached Thoughts on
Men and Manners* Patience is the Panacea; but
where does it grow and who can swallow it?

Patience is a virtue.   (P 109)

1377 LANGLAND *P. Pl.* B. xi. 370 Suffraunce is a
souereygne vertue. *c.* **1386** CHAUCER *Franklin's
T.* l. 773 Pacience is an heigh vertu, certeyn.
1594 LYLY *Mother B.* v. iii. 122. **1618** BEAUM.
& FL. *Loy. Sub.* III. ii. 105 Study your Vertue,
Patience, It may get Mustard to your Meat.
1753 RICHARDSON *Grandison* (1812) II. xvii. 137
Aunt Prue in Yorkshire . . . will be able to
instruct you, that patience is a virtue; and that
you ought not to be in haste to take a first offer,
for fear you should not have a second.

Patience perforce.   (P 111)

1504 CORNISH *Treat. Infor. and Music* (1908) l.
90, 424 Enformacione hathe taught hym to
solff thys songe: pacyence, perforce content yew
with wronge. [*a.* 1563] **1661** *Tom Tyler* l. 900.
c. **1570** *Marriage of Wit and Wisdom* (Halliwell)
2. **1575** GASCOIGNE *Patience Perforce* [title of
poem]. **1584** R. WILSON *Three Ladies of London*
Hazl.-Dods. vi. 303 He must have patience perforce, seeing there is no remedy. **1592** SHAKES.
T.G.V. II. ii. 1 Have patience, gentle Julia.—I
must, where is no remedy. **1595–6** *Id. Rich. III*
I. i. 116 Meantime, have patience.—I must perforce. **1594–5** *Id. R.J.* I. v. 87 Patience perforce
with wilful choler meeting Makes my flesh
tremble in their different greeting. **1596** SPENSER
F.Q. II. iii. 3 Patience perforce: helplesse what
may it boot To frett for anger, or for griefe to
mone? **1837** SOUTHEY *Lett. Mrs. Hughes* 7 Dec.
'Patience perforce' was what I heard of every
day in Portugal,— . . . it *must* be practised at
last, whether you like it or not.

Patience perforce is medicine for a mad
dog.   (P 112)

1606–7 SHAKES. *A.C.* IV. xv. 79 Patience is
sottish and impatience does become a dog that's
mad. **1659** HOWELL *Eng. Prov.* 9b.

Patience provoked turns to fury.
                                              (P 113)

1539 TAVERNER *Publius* C2ᵛ Pacience often
hurte becommeth a fury. Pacient bodyes if they
be often styrred, at laste they rage muche the
sorer, bycause it is longe, ere they be moued.
1591 ARIOSTO *Orl. Fur.* Harington XXXVI. *Moral.*
1659 HOWELL *Br. Prov.* 19 Long patience breaks
into passion. **1732** FULLER no. 3859.

Patience, time, and money accom-
modate all things.   (P 114)

1640 HERBERT no. 498. **1642** TORRIANO 84 (and
Moneyes, set all things right). **1659** HOWELL
It. Prov. 13.

Patience under old injuries invites new
ones.   (1 68)

1616 T. ADAMS *A Divine Herbal* 128 It hath beene
sayd, Beare one iniurie and prouoke more.
1617 MORYSON *Itin.* III. i. 25 (1907–8) III. 400
Some dissuade men from being patient in their
conversation, saying that he invites a new injury,
who bears the old patiently. **1624** J. HEWES
Perfect Survey G2 By bearing an olde iniury,
thou doest inuite a new.

Patience with poverty is all a poor
man's remedy.   (P 115)

1605 14 Sept. J. CHAMBERLAIN *Letters* (McLure)
i. 207 Patience is the poore mans vertue. **1639**
CLARKE 15. **1670** RAY 130.

Patience, *see also* God take the sun (Though),
we must have p.; Nature, time and p. . . .
physicians; Peace and p., and death with
repentance; Remedy but p. (No); Travel
through world necessary to have . . . money and
p.; Trouble brings experience (p.).

Patient as Job, As.   (J 59)

1509 BARCLAY *Ship of Fools* i. 113. **1584**
WITHALS G3. **1598** SHAKES. *2 Hen. IV* I. ii. 119
I am as poor as Job, my lord, but not so patient.
1643 MILTON *Divorce* I. viii. Wks. (1851) 39
Job the patientest of men. **1908** *Confessio
Medici* 83 Talk of the patience of Job, said a
Hospital-nurse, Job was never on night-duty.

Patient Grisel.   (G 456)

c. **1386** CHAUCER *Clerk's T.* l. 1177 Grisilde is
deed, and eek hire pacience. **1594–8** SHAKES.
T.S. II. i. 287 For patience she will prove a
second Grissel. **1818** SUSAN FERRIER *Marriage*
ch. 47 Your patient Grizzles make nothing of
it, except in little books: in real life they become
perfect packhorses, saddled with the whole
offences of the family. **1892** SIR H. MAXWELL
Meridiana 155 The part she had to play in life
is known to have been the patient Grizel'
business.

Patient men win the day.   (P 102)

c. **1382** GOWER *Vox Clam.* iii. 409 *Vincit qui
patitur; si vis vincere, disce pati. c.* **1386**
CHAUCER *Franklin's T.* l. 773 Patience . . .
venquysseth, as thise clerkes seyn, Thynges that
rigour sholde nevere atteyne. **1393** LANGLAND
P. Pl. C. xvi. 138 Quath Peers the Plouhman.
'*pacientes uincunt*'. **1639** CLARKE 242 . . .
Vincit qui patitur. **1853** TRENCH v. 116 As the
Italians say: *The World is for him who has
patience.*[1] [[1] *Il mondo è di chi ha pazienza.*]

Patient (*adj.*), *see also* Served must be p. (He
that will be).

Patient (*noun*), *see* Physician owes all to p.

Pattens, *see* Tongue runs on p.

Patter the devil's paternoster, To. *Cf.*
Ape's paternoster.   (D 315)

c. **1386** CHAUCER *Pars. T.* l. 506 Yet wol they
seyn harm and grucche and murmure priuely

for verray despit, whiche wordes men clepen the deueles Pater noster. **1530** PALSGRAVE 642a I murmure, I make a noyse, I bydde the dyuels Paster noster. **1546** HEYWOOD I. xi. E1 Pattryng the diuels Pater noster to hir selfe. **1665** J. WILSON *Projectors* II. i (1874) 231 How he mumbles the devil's *paternoster*! **1678** RAY 264 He is pattring the Devils *Pater noster*. When one is grumbling to himself and it may be cursing those that have angred or displeased him.

Paul Pry.

[*Paul Pry*; a very inquisitive character in comedy of same name by John Poole; 1825.] **1829** MACAULAY *Ess.*, *Southey* v. 348 He conceives that . . . the magistrate . . . ought to be . . . a Paul Pry in every house, spying, eaves-dropping. **1902** A. E. W. MASON *Four Feathers* ch. 13 Blindness means to all men . . . continual and irritable curiosity—there is no Paul Pry like your blind man.

Paul's pigeons.   (P 120)

[= scholars of St. Paul's School, London.] **1598** STOW *Survey* ed. Kingsford i. 75 The schollers of Paules, meeting with them of S. Anthonies, would call them Anthonie pigs, and they againe would call the other pigeons of Paules, because many pigions were bred in Paules Church, and Saint Anthonie was alwayes figured with a pigge following him. **1662** FULLER *London* 205 Nicholas Heath was . . . one of St. Anthonies Pigs therein (so were the Scholars of that School commonly called, as those of St. Paul's, Paul's pigeons).

Paul's will not always stand.   (P 121)

1593 G. HARVEY *Wks.* Gros. i. 297 Powles steeple, and a hugyer thing is doune. **1659** HOWELL *Eng. Prov.* Dedn. *We live in those destructive fatall Times, that are like to verifie a very ancient* Proverb *of that stately* Temple[1] . . . viz. Pauls cannot alwayes stand, *alluding to the lubricity of all sublunary things. Ibid.* 6a *Pauls* cannot alwayes stand. [[1] St. Paul's Cathedral.]

Paul's, *see also* Old as P.; Westminster for a wife, P. for a man (Who goes to).

Paunches, *see* Fat p. have lean pates.

Paut, *see* Ill p. with her hind foot (She has).

Paw, *see* Cat's p.

Pawn, *see* Fair p. never shamed his master.

Paws off, Pompey.

1834 MARRYAT *Jacob Faith.* ch. 12 Although she liked to be noticed so far by other chaps, yet Ben was the only one she ever wished to be handled by—it was 'Paws off, Pompey', with all the rest.

Pax Britannica.

1896 R. S. S. BADEN-POWELL *Downf. of Prempeh* 17 Mr. Chamberlain . . . put it thus: . . . 'I think the duty of this country . . . is to establish . . . *Pax Britannica*, and force these people to keep the peace amongst themselves.' **1911** *Spectator* 10 June 882 Nearly half the revenue of [South Nigeria] is derived from the duty imposed on spirits. . . . Is this to be the result of the boasted *Pax Britannica*?

Pay beforehand was never well served.
                               (W 845)

1591 FLORIO *Second F.* 39 He that paieth afore hand, hath neuer his worke well done. **1721** KELLY 278 . . . It is common to see Tradesmen, and Labourers, to go about a piece of Work with great Uneasiness, which is to pay a just Debt. **1732** FULLER no. 2245 He that payeth beforehand, shall have his Work ill done. **1819** SCOTT *Bride Lam.* ch. 3 'Your honour is the bad paymaster', he said, 'who pays before it is done.'

Pay, He that cannot | let him pray.
                               (P 125)

1577 TUSSER (1878 ed., 188) Inholders posy, For nothing paie and nothing praie, in Inne it is the gise. **1611** COTGRAVE s.v. Argent. **1670** RAY 130. **1732** FULLER no. 6362.

Pay(s, paid) for, *see* Drunk (What you do) you must p. f. sober; Purse opened not when it was p. f. (Your); Third time p. f. all.

Pay more for your schooling than your learning is worth, You.   (M 1168)

1639 CLARKE 59. **1732** FULLER no. 5955 (You may pay).

Pay not a servant his wages, If you | he will pay himself.

1732 FULLER no. 2778.

Pay one in his own coin, To.   (C 507)

1578 *Courtly Controv.* O2 Since he hadde betaken his credite unto a deceiuer, it was no meruayle though he [the devil] hadde payde hym with hys coyne, whyche is, Illusion and false semblaunte. *c.* **1583** SIDNEY *Arcadia* ed. Feuillerat i. 98 He courted this Ladie Artesia, who was as fit to paie him in his owne monie as might be. **1589** GREENE *Tullies Loue* in Wks. Gros. vii. 133 Lentulus . . . paide hir his owne coine. **1639** FULLER *Holy War* II. xxiv (1840) 80 [Baldwin] played on them freely to their faces; yea, and never refused the coin he paid them in, but would be contented . . . to be the subject of a good jest. **1655–62** GURNALL *Chrn. in Armour* (1865) I. 391 Now when he [Joseph] might have paid them in their own coin, . . . this holy man is lift above all thoughts of revenge. **1852** FROUDE *Reynard* in *Short Stud.* (1890) I. 607 If the other animals venture to take liberties with him, he will repay them in their own coin.

Pay one's debt to nature, To.   (D 168)

[*c.* 1500] **1516** FABYAN *New Chron. Eng. and Fr.* ed. H. Ellis ii. 28 Fynally he payde the dette of nature. **1578** *Courtly Controv.* Y3 The carcasse whiche nowe hadde paied the tribute of Nature. [1604] **1607** DEKKER & WEBSTER *Sir T. Wyatt* ed. Bowers v. ii. 31 Make hast to tender natures debt.

Pay (a person off) scot and lot, To.

(s 159)

[= to pay out thoroughly, to settle with.] **1494** in *Eng. Gilds* (1870) 189 I shalbe redy at scotte and lotte, and all my duties truly pay and doo. **1597** SHAKES. *1 Hen. IV* V. iv. 115 'Twas time to counterfeit, or that hot termagant Scot had paid me scot and lot too. **1844** DICKENS *M. Chuz.* ch. 24 I'll pay you off scot and lot by and bye.

Pay the piper (music, fiddler), To.

(P 349)

[= to bear the cost.] **1638** J. TAYLOR (Water-P.) *Taylor's Feast* 98 in Wks. 3rd Coll. Spens. S. Alwayes those that dance must pay the musicke. **1681** T. FLATMAN *Heraclitus Ridens* no. 29 (1713) I. 190 After all this Dance he has led the Nation, he must at last come to pay the piper himself. **1753** CHESTERFIELD *Lett.* (1792) II. 39 The other Powers cannot well dance, when neither France nor the maritime Powers can . . . pay the piper. **1833** M. SCOTT *T. Cring. Log* ch. 16 I don't defend slavery . . . but am I to be the only one to pay the piper in compassing its extinction?

Pay through the nose, To.   (N 234)

[= to be overcharged.] **1666** TORRIANO *Prov. Phr.* s.v. Gatta 71a and s.v. Salata. 176a. **1672** MARVELL *Reh. Transp.* I. 270 Made them pay for it most unconscionably and through the nose. **1782** MISS BURNEY *Cecilia* x. vi She knows nothing of business, and is made to pay for everything through the nose. **1878** J. PAYN *By Proxy* ch. 17 'You have been paying through the nose.' 'No doubt. They are all cheats.'

Pay too dear for one's whistle, To.

[= to pay much more for something than it is worth.] **1779** FRANKLIN *The Whistle* Wks. (1840) ii. 182 Poor man [a miser], said I, you pay too much for your whistle. **1851** TICKNOR *Life, Lett. & Jrnls.* (1876) II. xiii. 271 Too much, he thought, for the price of such a whistle. **1854** R. S. SURTEES *Hand. Cross* ch. 7 I should not like to pay too dear for my whistle. **1876** GEO. ELIOT *Dan. Der.* ch. 35 If a man likes to do it he must pay for his whistle.

Pay well, command well, hang well.

[**1643**] RALPH, LORD HOPTON[1] in DAV. LLOYD *Memoires* (1668) 343 His three words were, *Pay well, Command well,* and *Hang well.* [[1] a General in Charles I's army.]

Pay what you owe and you'll know what you're worth.

1706 STEVENS s.v. Pagar. **1732** FULLER no. 6352. **1875** SMILES *Thrift* 89 Who pays what he owes enriches himself.

Pay with the same dish you borrow.

(D 372)

1639 CLARKE 14.

Pay your money and you take your choice, You.

c. **1845** C. LEVER to Mr. M'Glashan in L. Stevenson *Dr. Quicksilver* (1939) 149 You have

paid your money, and you may take your choice. **1846** *Punch* x. 16. **1894** R. L. STEVENSON & LLOYD OSBORNE *The Ebb-Tide* 206 You p'ys your money and you tykes your choice. **1904** LEAN iv. 205 You pays your money and you takes your choice. You pays your moneys and what you sees is A cow or a donkey, just as you pleases.

Pay (noun), *see* No purchase no p.

Payer(s), *see* Cravers are aye ill p.; Good p. is master of another's purse.

Paymaster, *see* God is sure p.; Good p. needs no surety; Ill p. never wants excuse.

Payment, *see* Best p. is on peck bottom; County Clare p.; Misreckoning no p.; Trust is dead, ill p. killed it.

Pays last, He that | never pays twice.

(P 127)

1659 HOWELL *Eng. Prov.* 1b Who payeth last payeth but once. **1670** RAY 130. **1721** KELLY 150 . . . Spoken in Jest to one who is loth to pay his Reckoning, as if it was out of a Principle of Prudence. **1732** FULLER no. 2246.

Pays the lawing[1] choose the lodging, Let him that.

1827 SCOTT *Chron. Canon.* ch. 5 I'm nane of thae heartsome land leddies that can . . . make themsells agreeable; . . . but if it is your will to stay here, he that pays the lawing[1] maun choose the lodging. [[1] reckoning.]

Pays the physician does the cure, Who.

(P 272)

1616 DRAXE no. 1417 They that pay the Physition, shall bee cured. **1640** HERBERT no. 879.

Pays the piper may call the tune, He who. *Cf.* Pay the piper.

1895 *Daily News* 18 Dec. 9/1 Londoners had paid the piper, and should choose the tune. **1910** *Spectator* 22 Oct. 643 How the Irish Nationalist leader can combine 'loyalty' with the acceptance of Patrick Ford's dollars is a question. . . . 'He who pays the piper calls the tune.'

Pay(s), paid (verb), *see also* Beggar p. benefit with louse; Better to p. and have little; Borrows (He that) must p. again with shame or loss; Charre-folks are never p.; Day (One) will p. for all; Devil to p.; Gentleman that p. rent; Gift much expected is p. not given; Home (with heave and ho), (To p. one); Long day that never p. (They take); Once p. never craved; Pain both to p. and pray; Pitch and p.; Promises like merchant, p. like man of war; Receive before you write, write before you p.; Short Lent that must p. at Easter; Silly pack that may not p. custom; Small sum will p. short reckoning; Solomon was a wise man and Sampson . . . yet neither could p.; Sweet appears sour when we p.; Take all and p. all; Take all and p. baker.

Pea for a bean, To give a.

c. **1390** GOWER *Conf. Amantis* v. 4408 He wol
ayeinward take a bene, Ther he hath lent the
smale pese. **1896** *Folk-Lore* vii. 377.

Peace and catch a mouse.   (M 1240)

a. **1630** *The Partial Law* (ed. B. Dobell, 1908, 41)
Mumme and catch a mouse. **1639** CLARKE 302
(Whist and). **1659** HOWELL *Eng. Prov.* 11a.
1721 KELLY 289. Silence catches a Mouse.
Saying nothing, 'till you be ready to put in
Execution, is the Way to shun Prevention, and
effect your Business.

Peace and patience, and death with repentance.   (P 142)

1640 HERBERT no. 319.

Peace, He that will not have | God gives him war.   (P 141)

1640 HERBERT no. 729.

Peace, Where there is | God is.   (P 143)

1640 HERBERT no. 733.

Peace makes plenty.   (P 139)

c. **1425** *MS. Digby* 230 l. 223 b (*Reliq. Ant.*
(1841) i. 315) Pees makith Plente Plente makith
Pride Pride maketh Plee[1] Plee makith Pouert
Pouert makith Pees. *a.* **1589** PUTTENHAM *Art
Eng. Poesy* Arb. 217 Peace makes plentie,
plentie makes pride. **1599** SHAKES. *Hen. V* V. ii.
34 Peace, Dear nurse of arts, plenties, and joyful
births. **1610** *Histriomastix*, the six acts: Peace,
Plenty, Pride, Envy, War, Poverty—then Peace
again. **1626** BRETON *Soothing* A4 Peace
breeds plentie. . . . Plentie breeds pride. . . .
Pride breeds ambition. . . . Ambition breeds
warres. . . . Warre breeds pouertie. . . . Pouertie
breeds peace. **1659** HOWELL *Eng. Prov.* 19a
Through Peace cometh Plenty. [[1] plea.]

Peace, In time of | prepare for war.

                                    (T 300)

[VEGETIUS *Mil. Qui desiderat pacem, praeparet
bellum.* Generally quoted as *Si vis pacem, para
bellum.*] **1548** HALL *Chron. Edward IV*, an. 9,
209 He forgat the olde adage, Saynge in tyme of
peace prouyde for warre. **1552** LYNDSAY *Three
Estates* 2560 Into peace, ye should provyde for
weirs. **1581** W. STAFFORD *Examn. ordinary
complaints* New Sh. S. 65 In peace, looke for
warre. **1593** M. SUTCLIFFE *Practice of Arms* A2ᵛ
[*Veget.* lib.3 cap.1] He that desireth peace, he
must prepare for warres. **1617** J. SWETNAM
School of Defence 61 Wee find the wise to
prouide . . . in time of peace for wars. **1624**
BURTON *Anat. Mel.* II. iii. VI. 264. **1885** C. LOWE
Bismarck (1898) ch. 7 Lord Beaconsfield had
acted on the maxim that 'if you want peace,
you must prepare for war'.

Peace with sword in hand, 'Tis safest making.   (P 153)

1590–1 SHAKES. *2 Hen. VI* II. i. 33 I prithee,
peace . . . For blessed are the peacemakers on
earth.—Let me be blessed for the peace I make

Against this proud Protector with my sword!
1594 LIPSIUS *6 Books of Politics* tr. Jones 2A3
The olde prouerbe . . . It is best treating of peace,
with weapons in ones hand. **1609** HARWARD
110ᵛ Intreat for peace but do it with the hand
armed. **1639** CLARKE 251. To make peace with
a sword in his hand. **1699** FARQUHAR *Love & a
Bottle* v. iii.

Peace, *see also* Ask your neighbour if you shall
live in p.; Better a lean p. than fat victory;
Clothe thee in war, arm thee in p.; Disarmed p. is
weak; Figs after p.; Just war better than unjust
p.; Live in p. and rest (He that would); Pipe of
p.; Soldiers in p. like chimneys in summer; War
(Of all) p. is end; Weapons bode p.; Wisdom p.
(By).

Peaceably, *see* Live p. with all breeds good
blood.

Peacemaker, *see* Stick is surest p.

Peach will have wine and the fig water, The.   (P 156)

1573 SANFORD 104ᵛ. **1629** *Bk. Mer. Rid. Prov.*
no. 103.

Peach, *see also* Bloom is off the p.; Peel a . . . p.
for enemy.

Peacock has fair feathers, but foul feet, The.   (P 158)

1532 TYNDALE *Exposⁿ of Matthew V, VI, VII*
P.S. 74 If a peacock did look well on his feet,
. . . he would not be so proud of the beauty of
his tail. **1582** *Batman upon Bartholomew* 187
The Pecocke hath . . . a taile ful of bewty . . . and
. . . foulest feet and riueled. **1593** NASHE *Christ's
Tears* ii. 112 Dooth the Peacocke glory in his
foule feete? Dooth he not hang downe the tayle
when he lookes on them? **1599** DAVIES *Nosce
Teipsum* fin. Compare thy peacock's feet with
thy gay peacock's traine. **1616** DRAXE no. 100.

Peacock loudly bawls, When the | soon we'll have both rain and squalls.

1883 ROPER 28. **1893** INWARDS 135.

Peacock, *see also* March comes in . . . goes out
with p. tails; Proud as a p.

Pear year, a dear year, A. *Cf.* Cherry year, etc.

1742 *An Agreeable Companion* 65 A Pear Year,
a dear Year, A cherry Year, a merry year, A
plumb year, a dumb year. **1893** INWARDS 5.

Pear(s), *see also* Ask p. of an elm; Plant p. for
your heirs; Share not p. with your master;
Worst hog gets best p.

Pearl on your nail, Make a.   (P 164)

1592 NASHE *Pierce Pen.* i. 205 Drinking super
nagulum, a devise . . . which is, after a man hath
turnde up the bottom of the cup, to drop it on

hys nayle, and made a pearle with that is left; which, if it slide, . . . he must drinke againe for his penance. **1862** July *Edinburgh Review* cxvi. 247 It is not merely 'a bumper with a last drop on the nail' but the ring of the nail of each guest on the inside of his glass, to show that it is empty, and ready to do duty again. **1868** *N. & Q.* 4th Ser. I. 460 At the tables of . . . friends in Scotland and in London . . . the custom was to turn the glass with the mouth downwards, and to tap it with the thumbnail—repeating . . . *Supernaculum.*

Pearls are (Gold is) restorative. (P 166)

1580 LYLY *Euph. & his Eng.* ii. 87 I but ther is no Pearle so hard but Vinegar breaketh it. **1600** DEKKER *Old Fort.* I. i. 292 Gold is heauens phisicke, lifes restoratiue. **1600** JONSON *Ev. Man out Hum.* II. vi. 107 If thou wilt eate the spirit of gold, and drinke dissolu'd pearle in wine, 'tis for thee. **1600–1** SHAKES. *H.* V. ii. 263 The king shall drink to Hamlet's better breath; And in the cup an union shall he throw, Richer than that which four successive kings In Denmark's crown have worn. . . . Hamlet, this pearl is thine; Here's to thy health. Give him the cup. **1605** JONSON *Volpone* III. vii. 191 See, here, a rope of pearle; and each more orient Then the braue Egyptian queene carrous'd: Dissolve and drink them. **1616** BRETON *Cross. Prov.* B3 Pearles are restoratiue.

Pearls before swine, To cast. (P 165)

[MATT. vii. 6.] **1340** *Ayenbite* E.E.T.S.152 Þet we ne þrauwe naȝt oure preciouse stones touore þe zuyn. **1362** LANGLAND *P. Pl.* A. xi. 9 *Noli mittere Margeri*—perles Among hogges. *c.*1430 LYDGATE *Minor Poems* Percy Soc. 188 Men should not put . . . perles whight, To-fore rude swyne. **1526** TYNDALE *Matt.* vii. P.S. 114 Nether caste ye youre pearles before swyne. **1645** MILTON *2nd Sonn. Tetrach.* This is got by casting Pearl to Hoggs. **1655** FULLER *Ch. Hist.* II. i (1868) I. 93 The people of Rome, accounting him a precious jewel, . . . would 'not cast this pearl before swine', by hazarding him to the insolency of the Pagans. **1848** DICKENS *Dombey* ch. 23 Oh, I do a thankless thing, and cast pearls before swine!

Pearl, *see also* Black man p. in fair woman's eye.; Liberty is more worth than gold, (is a p., a jewel).

Peas, The smaller the | the more to the pot; the fairer the woman, the more the giglot.[1] (P 137)

c. **1350** *Douce MS. 52* no. 99 The smaller pesun, the more to pott; the fayrer woman, the more gylott. *c.* **1470** *Harl. MS. 3362*, f. 7b The smellere pesyn, þe mo to þe pot. *c.* **1470** *Slo. MS. 1210*, f. 134a in *Rel. Antiq.* II. 40 The smaller pese, the mo to the pott; the fayrere woman, the more gylott. **1541** *Schoolho. of Women* CI[v] The smaller pease, the mo to the pot, The fayrer woman, the more gyllot. [[1] a wanton.]

Peas, Who has many | may put the more in the pot. (P 138)

1546 HEYWOOD I. v. B2. **1616** DRAXE no. 1657. **1670** RAY 21.

Peas with the king, and cherries with the beggar, Eat. *Cf.* Share not pears. (C 279)

c. **1530** *Dialogues of Creatures* xx I counsell not seruantis to ete churyes with ther bettyrs. For they wyl haue the rype and leue them the harde. **1642** TORRIANO 78 It is not good eating of cherries with great ones Nota. For Lords and Ladies and the like, lie simpering and picking, having eaten sufficiently of solider meats before. **1642** FULLER *H. & P. State* III. v. *He that eats cherries with noblemen shall have his eyes spirted out with the stones.*—This outlandish proverb hath in it an English truth, that they who constantly converse with men far above their estates, shall reap shame and loss thereby. **1721** KELLY 100 . . . Peas are best when young, and Cherries when ripe. **1732** FULLER no. 1356.

Pea(s), pease, *see also* Children pick up words as pigeons p.; Crooked man should sow beans, wud man p.; David and Chad, sow p.; Little sap in dry p. hulls; Parched p. on a griddle; St. Benedick sow thy p.; Sow peas . . . in wane of moon; Two p. (As like as).

Pease has its veaze, Every | and a bean fifteen. (P 134)

1599 BUTTES *Diet's Dry Dinner* E7 Our common prouerb accordeth, speaking somewhat homely: Euery pease wil haue a fease; but euerie beane, fifteene. **1670** RAY 214. **1678** *Id.* 78 (Every pease). A veaze vescia in Italian is crepitus ventris. So it signifies Pease are flatulent, but Beans ten times more.

Pease, *see also* Pea(s).

Pease-cod(s), *see* Everything is good in its season (*quotation* 1591); Winter-time . . . , p. time for wooing; Woman were as little as good (If a), a p. would make her hood.

Pease-field, He is going into the.

1678 RAY 264 . . . i.e. falling asleep.

Pease-pottage, *see* Love and p.

Peat-pot[1] into the mire, Out of the.

a. **1628** CARMICHAELL no. 1233. **1721** KELLY 268. [[1] the hole out of which peat is dug.]

Pebbles, *see* Hang together like p. in halter.

Peccavi, see Cry p.

Peck (part), 'of malt, For my | set the kiln on fire. (P 74, 171)

1616 WITHALS 566. **1621** ROBINSON 20 For my part burne the kill boldly. *a.* **1628** CARMICHAELL no. 529 For my bow[1] aits, burne the kill bauldlie. **1638** J. TAYLOR *Bull, Bear, and Horse* A6. **1639** CLARKE 77 For my part, burne the kilne boldly. *Ibid.* 254. **1917** BRIDGE 58 . . . Our proverb seems to mean 'I mustn't be hasty—I am not such a fool as to burn the kiln down to get my paltry peck'. [[1] boll = measure of capacity.]

Peck of troubles, To be in a.   (P 172)

1533 UDALL *Flowers of Latin Speaking* (1560)
M5ᵛ As we saie in inglish prouerbially, in a
whole pecke of troubles. *c.* **1535** in *Archæologia*
xxv. 97 The said George . . . told hym that Mr.
More was in a pecke of troubles.   **1857** HUGHES
Tom Brown I. viii A pretty peck of troubles
you'll get into.

Peck, *see also* Best payment is on the p. bottom;
Blind man's p.; Eat a p. of dirt (Every man
must).

Pecked to death by a hen, One had as good be.   (D 156)

1678 RAY 240.

Pecks, (*verb*), *see* Ill bird that p. out dam's eyes.

Pecker, *see* Keep your p. up.

Pedigree(s), *see* Great p. (In) there are . . .
chandlers; Long as Welsh p.

Pedlar carry his own burden (pack), Let every.   (P 174)

1611 COTGRAVE s.v. Mercier Let each man his
owne burthen beare.   **1659** HOWELL *Eng. Prov.*
17b.   **1670** RAY 21.   **1732** FULLER no. 3176.

Pedlar's drouth.

1822 SCOTT *Pirate* ch. 6 My certie, . . . there is the
chapman's drouth and his hunger baith, as folks
say. (*Footnote.* The chapman's drouth, that is
the pedlar's thirst, is proverbial in Scotland because those pedestrian traders were in the use of
modestly asking only for a drink of water, when,
in fact, they were desirous of food.)

Pedlar's French.   (P 175)

1530 PALSGRAVE 727a They speke a pedlars
frenche amongest them selfe. *c.* **1536** R. COP-
LAND *Highway to the Spittle house* And thus
they babble . . . with theyr pedlyng frenche.
1567 HARMAN *Caveat* 23 Their languag—which
they terme peddelars Frenche or Canting.   **1613**
WITHER *Abuses* II. i. L3 Besides as I suppose their
lawes they pen'd, In their old *Pedlars French*
vnto this end.   **1620** SHELTON *Quix.* II. xix. ii.
312 All this to the husbandmen was heathen
Greek or pedlar's French.

Pedlar, *see also* Small pack becomes small p.

Pedley, *see* God help the fool, quoth P.; I was
by, quoth P.; Rope enough . . . said P.; Slow
and sure like P.'s mare.

Peebles for pleasure.

1890 F. ANSTEY *Pariah* I. ii 'I think Littlehampton
must be ever so much more amusing than
France is'. 'Peebles for pleasure!' remarked
Margot at hearing Lettice's opinion on the
comparative merits of France and Littlehampton.   **1919** DEAN INGE *Outspoken Ess.* 36
The local patriot thinks that Peebles, and not
Paris, is the place for pleasure, or asks whether
any good thing can come out of Nazareth.

Peel a fig for your friend and a peach for your enemy.   (F 212)

1573 SANFORD 101ᵛ (Prouide).   **1629** *Bk. Mer.
Rid.* Prov. no. 53 (as 1573).   **1678** RAY 53 Al
amico cura [g]li il fico, Al inimico il Persico.

Peel (pick) straws, Go.   (S 923)

c. **1510**? *Wealth and Health* l. 212 Mary then
I may Goe pyke strawes and take me rest.
[*c.* **1522**] *c.* **1545** SKELTON *Why Come Not to
Court* ii. 35 They make vs to pyll [peel]
strawes.   **1553** *Respublica* I. iii. 160.   **1580** S.
BIRD *Friendly Communication* G6 As much
delight . . . as they haue now in peeling of
strawes.   **1672** WALKER 21, no. 10 To sit still
and pill straws.

Peeled egg, You have come to a.

1721 KELLY 369 . . . Spoken to those who have
got an Estate, Place or Preferment ready
prepar'd for their hand; or as the English say,
Cut and dry.

Peeps through a hole, He who | may see what will vex him.

1706 STEVENS s.v. Agujero (sees his sorrow).
1707 MAPLETOFT 75.   **1710** PALMER *Moral Essays
on Proverbs* 135.

Peerage is the Englishman's Bible, The.

1850 CARLYLE *Lat.-Day Pam.* No. 7 (1885) 241
Collins's old Peerage-Book . . . is properly all
we English have for a Biographical Dictionary;
—nay, . . . for a National Bible.   **1883** W. BATES
Maclise Port.-Gallery 68 That bulky volume
which has been called the Englishman's Bible—
Burke's Peerage.

Peers, *see* Play with your p.

Peg, *see* Round p. in square hole; Take one down
a p.

Pelf, *see* Take part of the p. when pack a-dealing.

Pelion, *see* Ossa.

Pen and ink is wit's plough.   (P 182)

1626 BRETON *Soothing* B2ᵛ.   **1639** CLARKE 35.

Pen is mightier than the sword, The.

[CIC. *Off.* I. 22. 77 Cedant arma togae.]   **1571**
TIGURINUS *Instit. of a Christ. Prince* 4 There is
no sworde more to bee feared than the Learned
pen.   **1582** WHETSTONE *Heptameron* I1 The
dashe of a Pen, is more greeuous then the counter
use of a Launce.   **1586** *Id. Eng. Mirror* 210
Alexander surnamed Seuerus, would oftentimes say, that he stoode in more feare of one
writer, then of a hundred souldiers, for that the
wound of a pen remaineth after death.

Pence, *see* Take care of p.

Pendle, *see* Ingleborough.

Pendulum, *see* Swing of the p.

Penelope's web.   (P 186)

[Penelope undid at night what she had woven during the day, to defer her choice of a husband in the absence of Ulysses.] **1580** BARET *Alveary* P253 *Penelopes telam texere* . . . Homer. A Prouerbe aptly applied to those which labour, and yet can see no fruite of their trauell, or paines taking. **1559** COOPER s.v. Penelope *Penelopes telam retexere*, signifieth to doo and vndoo, to take much labour in vayn. **1591** FLORIO *Second F.* 195 If this be all you say, a fayre threed she hath sponne, For what she wrought all day, at night was all vndone. **1608** SHAKES. *C.* I. iii. 82 You would be another Penelope; yet they say all the yarn she spun in Ulysses' absence did but fill Ithaca with moths. **1614** SIR T. OVERBURY *Characters* (1890) 73 *A Melancholy Man.* He winds up his thoughts often, and as often unwinds them; Penelope's web thrives faster. **1614** T. ADAMS *Heaven & Earth Reconciled* D4ᵛ. Examples teach soonest. . . . The force of a hundred good sermons is lost by one enormity; so easy is it to weave Penelope's web. **1707** SWIFT *Facult. of Mind* Wks. (1856) II. 285 Else we shall be forced to weave Penelope's web, unravel in the night what we spun in the day. **1910** *T.L.S.* 14 Oct. 'A Penelope, who unravels by night the web she has woven all day long; . . . such', says Anthero de Quental, 'is History'.

Penetrates, *see* Prayer p. heaven, (A short).

Penniless Bench.   (P 187)

[A covered open-air seat for destitute way-farers. To sit on Penniless Bench = to be in extreme poverty.] **1560–1** in W. H. TURNER *Select. Rec. Oxf.* (1880) 284 Item, to . . . for mending the peneles benche. **1580** LYLY *Euph. & his Eng.* ii. 29 Euery stoole he sate on was penniles bench. **1604** MIDDLETON *Works* (Bullen) VIII. 27 The time was at hand, like a pickpurse, that Pierce should be called no more Pennyless, like the Mayor's bench at Oxford. [Ed. note: At the east end of old Carfax church at Oxford there was a seat for loungers which was known as *Penniless Bench.* Hence came the proverb 'To sit on Penniless Bench'.] **1632** MASSINGER *City Madam* IV. i. Bid him bear up; he shall not Sit long on Penniless-Bench. **1860** WARTER *Seaboard* II. 43 Though he have some-times to sit on the Penniless Bench.

Penniless souls maun¹ pine in pur-gatory.

1823 HENDERSON 46. [¹ must.]

Penny and penny laid up will be many.
                                                             (P 201)

1591 W. STEPNEY *The Span. Schoolmaster* One penie here, and in another place another, makes two pence. **1639** CLARKE 35. **1670** RAY 130.

Penny at a pinch is worth a pound, A.
                                                             (P 202)

1616 WITHALS 553 (better then a Pound at any other time). **1639** CLARKE 45.

Penny for your thoughts, A.   (P 203)

c. **1522** T. MORE *Four Last Things* Wks., ed. W. E. Campbell, i. 76 It often happeth, that the very face sheweth the mind walking a pilgrimage, in such wise that . . . other folk sodainly say to them: a peny for your thought. **1546** HEYWOOD II. iv. G3 Wherwith in a great musyng he was brought. Freend (quoth the good man) a peny for your thought. **1738** SWIFT *Dial.* I. E.L. 261 Here's poor miss has not a word to throw at a dog. Come, a penny for your thought. **1870** READE *Put Yourself* ch. 24 Always in the clouds, . . . A penny for your thoughts, sir!

Penny in purse will bid me drink, when all the friends I have will not.   (P 205)

1670 RAY 130. **1732** FULLER no. 3865 (Penny in Purse will make me).

Penny in the forehead, A.

[Allusion to a nursery joke in which a coin is pressed to the forehead so as to be felt as if still there after removal.] **1602** N. BRETON *Old Mad-cappes new Gallymawfrey* B2ᵛ I loue no leese, nor winke, nor wily looke, But *straight fore-right*, a penny in my face. **1607** SHARPHAM *Cupid's Whirligig* K3 Holde vp your head Tobias, and looke and you can see a penny in my browe. **1658–9** T. BURTON *Diary* 9 March Sir A. Haslerigge . . . said 'I am not bound always to look you in the face like children, to see if you have a penny in your forehead'.

Penny is well spent that saves a groat, That.   (P 210)

1591 JOHN DAVIES *O Utinam* D9ᵛ Let it not grieue thee to loose a pennie to spare a pound. **1611** COTGRAVE s.v. Bon Well is that halfepenie spent that saues a penie. **1614** CAMDEN 312. **1670** RAY 130. **1732** FULLER no. 4369. **1749** FRANKLIN March 'Tis a well spent penny that saves a groat.

Penny more buys the whistle, A.

1721 KELLY 8 . . . Spoken when one gets a Bargain for a little more than was offer'd for it; or at Cards, when a Card is taken by a Card just bigger by one. **1732** FULLER no. 341.

Penny saved is a penny gained (got), A. Cf. Penny that's saved is not gotten.
                                                             (P 206)

1640 HERBERT no. 506 A penny spared is twice got. **1662** FULLER *Hunts.* 51 By the same pro-portion that a penny saved is a penny gained, the preserver of books is a Mate for the Com-piler of them. **1695** RAVENSCROFT *Canterbury Guests* II. iv This I did to prevent expenses, for . . . A penny sav'd, is a penny got. **1712** *Spec-tator* 14 Oct. I think a speculation upon Many a Little makes a Mickle; a Penny saved is a penny got . . . would be very useful to the World. **1748** THOMSON *Castle Ind.* i st. 50 A penny saved is a penny got . . . this scoundrel maxim. **1811** BYRON *Hints fr. Horace* 516 (got). **1838** *Chamb. Edin. Jrnl.* 45.

Penny soul never came to twopence, A.

1844 *Chamb. Jrnl.* II. 225 A penny soul never came to twopence. **1859** SMILES *Self-Help* ix (1860) 235 Narrow-mindedness in living and in dealing . . . leads to failure. The penny soul never came to twopence.

Penny that's saved is not gotten, Every. *Cf.* Penny saved is a penny gained.

(P 191)

1670 RAY 139.

Penny to buy his dog a loaf (to bless him), He has not a. *Cf.* Cross (Penny) to bless himself with. (P 193)

a. 1628 CARMICHAELL no. 792 (leaf *sic* for loaf). 1641 FERGUSSON no. 437. *Of weasters and divers.*[1] . . . [[1] bankrupts.]

Penny to spend at a new ale-house, Every one has a. (P 192)

1678 RAY 181. 1732 FULLER no. 1445.

Penny wise and pound foolish. (P 218)

1607 TOPSELL *Four-f. Beasts* 609 If by covetousnesse or negligence, one withdraw from their ordinary foode, he shall be penny wise, and pound foolish. 1612–15 BP. HALL *Contempl.* IV. xxvii (1825) II. 495 Worldly hearts are penny-wise, and pound-foolish: they . . . set high prices upon . . . trash of this world; but . . . heavenly things, . . . they shamefully undervalue. 1712 ADDISON *Spect.* no. 295, par. 6 I think a Woman who will give up herself to a Man in marriage, where there is the least Room for such an Apprehension, . . . may very properly be accused . . . of being Penny Wise and Pound foolish. 1827 HARE *Gues. at Truth* (1873) i. 239 Many . . . are said to be penny-wise and pound-foolish: but they who are penny-foolish will hardly be pound-wise.

Penny (-ies), pence, *see also* Bad p. always comes back; Clean as a p.; Companion like the p. (No); Cow of his own . . . quart of milk for a p.; Cross (P.) to bless himself with; Farewell forty p.; Four p. to a groat; Friend in court better than p. in purse; In for a p.; Keep a p. (Who will not); Know by a p. how shilling spends; Look twice at a p.; Miserable (Covetous) man makes p. of farthing; No paternoster no p.; No p. no pardon; No p. no paternoster; No p. no *placebo*; Piper a p. to play (Give); Put the poor man's p. and the rich man's p. in ae purse; Put two halfpennies (p.) in a purse; Smith and his p. both are black; Take care of the p., and the pounds . . .; Thinks his p. good silver; Three p.; Touch pot touch p.; Turn the (an honest) p.

Penny-weight of love is worth a pound of law, A.

1721 KELLY 17 . . . A dissuasive from Law Suits among Neighbours; used also when we value a Man more for his good Humour than his Skill in the Laws. 1732 FULLER no. 343.

Pennyworth of ease is worth a penny, A.

(P 219)

c. 1549 ERASM. *Two Dial.* tr. E. Becke f. 11ᵛ (is euer worth). 1636 CAMDEN 291. 1732 FULLER no. 344.

Pennyworth(s), *see also* Good bargain (p.) (At a) make pause; Honesty may be dear bought; Robin Hood's p.; Ruined by buying good p.

Pens may blot, but they cannot blush.

(P 183)

c. 1574 G. HARVEY *Lett. Bk.* 172 I could not sai so mutch to your face without blussing, but literae non erubescunt. 1577 J. GRANGE *Gold Aphrod.* K2 If needes you would haue opend (quoth she) your budget of villany unto me, yet better mighte you haue done it with penne and inke, who (as the Prouerbe goeth) neuer blusheth, then with that shamefull tongue of yours. 1615 *Janua Linguarum* tr. W. Welde 15 Letters blush not. 1616 DRAXE no. 114 Pennes may blot, but they cannot blush.

Pension never enriched a young man.

(P 221)

1640 HERBERT no. 515.

Pent, *see* Grief p. up will break the heart.

Penyghent, *see* Ingleborough.

Penzance, Not a word of. (W 768)

1678 RAY 350 (Pensants). 1750 R. HEATH *Acct. of Islands of Scilly* 405 July 20, 1595, . . . *four Gallies* of the *Spaniards* appeared . . . against Mousehole. . . . *Id.* 407 note The *Cornish Inhabitants*, at this Time, behaving so ill in making Defence against the Enemy, added a Proverb more to this County.[1] *Not a Word of Pensance.* [[1] Cornwall.]

People, *see* Builds on the p.; Fame is but breath of the p.; King (prince), (Like) like p.; Priest (Like) like p.; Serves the p. (Who) serves nothing; Voice of the p. voice of God; Worst p. have most laws; Wrath of . . . and tumult of p. (Take heed of).

Pepper Gate, *see* Daughter is stolen (When), shut P. G.

Pepper in the nose, To take. (P 231)

[= to take offence, be vexed.] 1377 LANGLAND *P. Pl.* B. xv. 197 And to þere peple han peper in the nose. *c.* 1450 *Provs. of Wysdom* in *Anglia* 51. 222, l. 53 Have not pepir in þi nose. 1520 WHITTINGTON *Vulg.* (1527) 24 If ony man offende hym, he may not forthwith take peper in the nose, and show by rough words . . . that he is angred. 1579 LYLY *Euph.* ii. 141 Least you gentlewomen shoulde take pepper in the nose. 1682 BUNYAN *Holy War* 267 The peevish old gentleman took pepper in the nose.

Pepper is black and has a good smack.

(S 593)

1508 J. STANBRIDGE *Vulgaria* E.E.T.S. 23 Though peper be blacke, it hathe a good smacke. *a.* 1530 R. *Hill's Commonplace Bk.* 140 no. 17 Though peper be blake hit hath a good smakke. 1546 HEYWOOD II. iv. G3ᵛ Snow is white And lieth in the dike and euery man lets it lye. Pepper is blacke And hath a good smacke And

euery man doth it bye. **1584** WITHALS E4
Pepper is blacke, and hath a good smacke, and
euery man doth it buy: Snow is white, and meltes
in the dike, and euery man lets it lie. **1721**
KELLY 296 Snow is white . . . Spice is black . . .
An Apology for black People.

Pepper is hot in the mouth but cold in the snow. (P 234)

1579 LYLY *Euph.* i. 218 (mawe). **1588** W. BAILEY
Disc. Peppers B5 (For it is a common saying,
that pepper).

Pepper to Hindustan.

1791 I. DISRAELI *Cur. Lit.* (1858) III. 46 In the
'Bustan' of Sadi we have *Infers piper in Hindo-
stan*; 'To carry pepper to Hindostan'. **1853**
TRENCH iii. 68 The Greeks said: *Owls to Athens*,
Attica abounding with these birds; . . . the
Orientals: *Pepper to Hindostan*.

Perch, *see* Turn over the p.

Perfect, *see* Friendship cannot be without
equality, (P.); Use (Practice) makes p.

Perfidious Albion.

a. **1821** NAPOLEON I in *N. & Q.* (1921) 12th Ser.
VIII. 216 Bossuet's reference to 'La perfide
Angleterre' occurs in his 'Premier Sermon pour
la Circoncision'. The alteration from 'Angleterre' to 'Albion' has been usually attributed to
Napoleon I, who used it as the Romans used
Punica fides. **1908** *Sphere* 28 March 270 Most
of the continental states seem to recognize the
disinterested nature of the British proposal.
'Perfidious Albion' it is coming to be seen has
no selfish interest in reducing Macedonia to
peace and order.

Perfidious, *see also* Tie can oblige the p. (No).

Performance, One acre of | is worth twenty of the Land of Promise. (A 24)

1593 G. HARVEY *Pierce's Supererogation* Grosart
ii. 286. **1596** NASHE *Saffron W.* iii. 126 He
saith in one leafe that one acre of performance
is worth twentie of the Land of Promise. **1659**
N. R. 82. One acre of possession is worth a whole
land of promise. **1749** J. WESLEY *Letters* ii. 348.

Performance(s), *see also* Promises and small p.,
(Great).

Performing, *see* Promising and p. (Between).

Peril(s), *see* Forecasts all p. (He that) will never
sail sea; —— will win no worship; Four good
mothers have four bad daughters:;. . . security,
p.; Neighbour's scathe is my p.; Profit (What
is none of my) shall be none of my p.; Yellow
p.; Youth never casts for p.

Perjuries, *see* Jove laughs at lovers' p.

Perseverance kills the game.

1706 STEVENS s.v. Porfia. **1813** RAY 149.

Pershore {where do you think? / God help us!

1894 NORTHALL *Folk-phrases* E.D.S. 21 . . .
Pershore, *Worc.*, is noted for its fruit. When
there is a particularly fine crop, any native
vendor, if asked where his fruit was grown, says
boastingly, 'Parshur, where do you think but
Parshur?' If asked the same question in a bad
season, he replies, 'Parshur, God help us!'

Persians, *see* Law of Medes and P.

Person marked, Take heed of a | and a widow thrice married. (H 372)

1599 MINSHEU *Span. Gram.* 84. **1651** HERBERT
no. 1152. **1721** KELLY 311 *Take a Care of that
Man whom God has set a Mark on.* . . . The
Scots generally have an Aversion to any that
have any natural Defect or re-Dundancy. **1914**
Lady's Pict. 21 Nov. 713 The . . . crippled
sword-arm was very noticeable. A Frenchman
said: 'Distrust those that are marked by the
Creator.'

Person(s), *see* All things fit not all p.

Persuasion of the fortunate sways the doubtful, The. (P 241)

1640 HERBERT no. 630.

Pert as a sparrow, As.

1610 *Histriomastix* II. i. 311. **1837** J. F. & M.
PALMER *Devonshire Dialect* 30.

Perverseness makes one squint-eyed. (P 242)

1640 HERBERT no. 634.

Pervert, *see* Zeal like that of p. (No).

Pet, *see* Take p.

Petard, *see* Hoist with his own p.

Peter is so godly, that God don't make him thrive. (P 246)

1659 HOWELL *Span. Prov.* 15 Peter is so much
Gods, that God gets him not. **1706** STEVENS
s.v. Pedro . . . Every body imposes on him.
1732 FULLER no. 3870.

Peter of Wood, church and mills are all his. (P 247)

1670 RAY 217. *Chesh.* **1917** BRIDGE 103 . . .
I have failed to find any solution of this saying.

Peter, *see also* Difference between P. and P.;
Rob P. to pay Paul.

Peterborough, *see* Ramsey.

Petticoats woo, When | breeks may come speed.

1721 KELLY 346 . . . Spoken when Maids court
young Men.

Petticoat(s), *see also* Lass in the red p. shall pay; Near is my coat (p.) but nearer is. . . .

Philip and Cheiny. (P 251)

[i. Two or more of common people taken at random.] **1542** ERASM. tr. Udall *Apoph.* (1877) It was not his entent to bryng vnto Sylla philip and cheinie, mo then a good meiny, but to bryng hable souldiours of manhood approved and well tried to his handes. **1573** TUSSER 2 E.D.S. 8 Loiterers I kept so meanie, both Philip, Hob, and Cheanie. [ii. A woollen stuff of common quality.] **1614** FLETCHER *Wit at S. W.* II. i. Thirteene pound . . . 'Twill put a Lady scarce in Philip and Cheyney.

Philip, *see also* Appeal from P. drunk.

Philosopher, *see* Beard that makes p. (It is not).

Philosopher's stone, *see* Content is the p. s.; Thrift is the p. s.

Philosophy of the distaff, It is the.
(P 254)

1651 HERBERT no. 1039.

Phlegmatic, *see* Choleric drinks, p. sleeps.

Phoenix, *see* Rare as the p.

Physic before he is sick, He takes.
(P 257)

1585 A. DENT *Sermon of Repentance* C1ᵛ Would you haue Plaisters before you haue woundes? Would you haue Phisicke before you bee sicke? **1616** WITHALS 575. **1639** CLARKE 283. **1670** RAY 189.

Physic do not work, If | prepare for the kirk. (P 259)

c. **1386** CHAUCER *Knight's T.* l. 2759 And certeinly, ther Nature wol nat wirche, Fare wel, phisik! go ber the man to chirche! **1678** RAY 189.

Physic, *see also* Ague in the spring is p. for king; Kitchen p. is best p.; Temperance is best p.; War and p. governed by eye.

Physician, heal thyself. (P 267)

[LUKE iv. 23.] *c.* **1412** HOCCLEVE *De Regim. Princ.* (1860) 7 Cure, godeman? ye, thow art a faire leche; Cure thy self, that tremblest as thou goste. **1579** LYLY *Euph.* i. 256 If thou saye to mee, Phisition heale thy selfe. I aunswere, that I am meetly well purged of that disease. **1590–1** SHAKES. *2 Hen. VI* II. i. 53 *Medice, teipsum*; Protector, see to't well, protect yourself. **1602** [T. HEYWOOD?] *How a Man may Choose* Hazl.-Dods. ix. 9 Medice, cura teipsum. **1616** DRAXE no. 1630. **1882** BLACKMORE *Christowell* ch. 24 'Physician, heal thyself', is the hardest, and most unanswerable of all taunts.

Physician, A | is an angel when employed, but a devil when one must pay him.

1820 SCOTT *Abbot* ch. 26 I cured him . . . and now he talks of the chargeableness of medicine. . . . Old saying and true, Præmia cum poscit medicus, Sathan est. We are angels when we come to cure—devils when we ask payment.

Physician, Every man is a | save him that is sick.

c. **1534** GILES DUWES 1070 Men be wont to say every man to be a phisycion, but he that is sycke.

Physician like a true friend, No.

c. **1386** CHAUCER *Mel.* l. 2495 Catoun seith, 'If thou hast nede of help, axe it of thy freendes, for ther nys noon so good a phisicien as thy trewe freend'. [SKEAT footnote: *Cato, De Moribus*, iv. 13: 'Auxilium a noble petito, si forte laboras. Nec quisquam melior medicus quam fidus amicus.'] **1584** WITHALS N4 Not one Physician better is, Then a sure friende that trustie is.

Physician, The | owes all to the patient, but the patient owes nothing to him but a little money. (P 268)

1616 DRAXE no. 1626 The physitian oweth all to the disease, and the disease nothing to the physition. **1640** HERBERT no. 921.

Physicians, The best | are Dr. Diet, Dr. Quiet, and Dr. Merryman. (D 427)

1558 BULLEYN *Govt. of Health* 50 Cousaill was geuen me, that I should not staye myselfe vpon the pinion of any one phisicion, but rather vpon three. . . . The first was called doctor diet, the seconde doctor quiet, the thirde doctor mery mā. **1621** BURTON *Anat. Mel.* II. ii. vi. iv (1651) 301 This is one of the three Salernitan doctors, D. Merryman, D. Diet, and D. Quiet, which cure all diseases—*Mens hilaris, requies, moderata diæta.* **1738** SWIFT *Dial.* II. E.L. 307. **1909** *Spectator* 30 Jan. A proverb prescribes for sickness Dr. Diet, Dr. Quiet, and Dr. Merryman. The merry heart goes all the way in all but the worst sicknesses.

Physicians kill more than they cure.

1624 BURTON *Anat. Mel.* II. iv. I. i. 2P4ᵛ Physitians kill as many as they saue. **1703** E. WARD *Writings* ii. 328 ('an old maxim').

Physicians, Where there are three | there are two atheists.

1586 LA PRIMAUDAYE *Fr. Acad.* tr. T. Beard 161 This prouerbe, which is too true, . . . Of three Physitians one Atheist. **1643** SIR K. DIGBY *Observations upon Religio Medici* It is a common speech (but only amongst the unlearned sort) *ubi tres medici duo athei.* **1656** T. KECK *Crit. Notes app. to Sir T. Browne's 'Religio Medici'* § 1 Physicians . . . are commonly ill spoke of in this behalf. It is a common saying, *Ubi tres medici, duo athei.* **1665** J. GLANVILL *Scepsis Scientifica* 182 I daresay the Proverb, *Ubi tres Medici, duo*

Athei is a Scandal. **1837** SOUTHEY *Doctor* iv.
181 (citing the passage from Digby). **1853**
TRENCH iv. 79 A Latin medieval proverb boldly
proclaims: . . .

Physician(s), *see also* City is in bad case whose p.
has gout; Deadly disease neither p. can ease;
Feed by measure and defy p.; Few lawyers . . .
few p. live well; Fool or p.; Fool who makes p.
heir; Go not for every grief to p.; God heals and
p. has thanks; Gout, (To the) all p. are blind;
Hide nothing from thy p.; Honour a p. before
need of him; Nature, time, and patience p.; Old
p., young lawyer; Pays the p. (Who) does the
cure; Piss clear and defy p.; Pitiful surgeon (p.)
spoils sore; St. Luke was a p. yet is dead;
Words ending in *ic* mock p.; Young barber, old
p.; Young p. fattens the churchyard. *See also*
Doctor.

Pick a hole (holes) in something, To.

(H 522)

c. **1533** J. FRITH *Another ans. agst. Rastell* B6
Therwith he [Rastell] hath made a foule hole in
his kinsmans [More's] cote. **1580** MUNDAY
Zelauto N2 If they can possyble catche a hole
in a mans coate: the same wyll they lay euerie
day in his dishe. **1586** J. CASE *Praise of Music* 30
They that cannot espie an hoale in the musicians
coate for their loosenesse and effeminatie of
manners. **1588** *Mar-Prelate's Epitome* (1843) 3
There is a deuice to fynde a hole in the coat of
some of you puritanes. **1592** GREENE *Quip* ed.
Hindley 46. **1599** SHAKES. *Hen. V* III. vi. 82
If I find a hole in his coat I will tell him my
mind. **1600–1** *Id. M.W.W.* III. v. 125 There's
a hole made in your best coat, Master Ford.
1616 T. ADAMS *Three Divine Sisters* 5 *Satan* is a
subtill Lawyer, . . . and will soone picke holes
in it [the evidence]. **1632** *Pinder of Wakefield*
D2. **1639** CLARKE 80 It's easie to pick a hole
in another man's coat, if he be disposed. **1648**
NEEDHAM *Plea for King* 21 Every ambitious
popular person would be ready to pick holes in
their Coates, to bring them into disfavour of the
People. **1655–62** GURNALL *Chrn. in Armour*
(1865) I. 85 Nor is it hard for Satan to pick
some hole in the saint's coat, when he walks
most circumspectly. **1691** A. WOOD *Life &
Times* W.C. 329 Some heads of houses . . . and
fellowes are generally against it [his book]; study
to pick holes in it or at least popery. **1894**
Aspects Mod. Oxford 93 Any one can pick
holes in the University system of teaching and
examination.

Pick (suck) a person's brains, To.

[= to elicit and appropriate the results of his
thought.] **1850** WILLIS *Life* 349 I . . . sat down
to pick his brains of the little information I
wanted. *a.* **1893** JOWETT *Life* i. 435 Do you
possess the art of picking other people's brains?
1907 A. C. BENSON *From Coll. Window* (4 ed.) 48
He had an astonishing memory. . . . If one
wanted to know what books to read in any line,
one had only to pick his brains.

Pick (pluck) a rose, To.

(R 184)

1593 B. R. *Greene's News* E2 Fie for shame, will
you speakes bugges wordes? Could you not
pretily haue saide: I pray you Mother haue me

vppe to picke a Rose? **1606** DAY *Isle of Gulls*
H3 I left my little dog pearl plucking dazies.
1607 *Dobson's Dry Bobs* O2ᵛ One of the maides
. . . went into the calfehouse to pul a rose. **1678**
RAY 88 To gather a rose. To make water.

Pick up (Gather) one's crumbs, To.

(C 868)

[= to pick up or recover strength or health.]
1474 *Paston Letters* (Gairdner 1904) V. 211 But,
God thanke yow, I toke so my crommys whyls
I was wyth yow, that I felyd my sylfe . . . stronger
than I wenyd that I had ben. **1580** LYLY *Euph.
& his Eng.* ii. 78 (gather vp). **1588** A. INGRAM in
HAKLUYT *Voy.* II. II. 130 Our men beganne to
gather vp their crums and to recouer some better
strength. c. **1645** HOWELL *Lett.* 2 Feb. an. 1621
Thank God, I . . . am recovering and picking up
my crums apace. **1840** R. H. DANA *Before Mast*
ch. 27 [He] had 'picked up his crumbs' . . . and
[was] getting strength and confidence daily.
1888 W. *Somerset Word-bk.* s.v. A person or
animal improving in appearance is said to be
picking up his crumbs.

Pick(s, ed), *see also* Bear p. muscles, (As
handsomely as a); Bird to p. out his own eyes
(He has brought up a); Bone to p.; Hawks will
not p. out hawks' eyes; Peel (p.) straws, (Go);
Plays you as fair as if he p. your pocket; Wit to
p. a lock.

Pickle, To be in a sad (sweet). (P 276)

1573 TUSSER *100 Points* (1580 ed. D2) Reape
barlie with sickle, that lies in ill pickle. [1577]
1578 T. WHITE *Serm.* 9. **1587** BRIDGES *Defence*
638 (in a proper pickle). **1591** ARIOSTO *Orl.
Fur.* Harington XXI. 60 Now in what pickle
thinke you was the leach? **1603** DEKKER *et al.
Patient Grissil* IV. iii. 124 (in a pitifull pickle).
[1603] **1607** T. HEYWOOD *Woman K. with Kindness* SC. xvi, l. 114 (in a sweet pickle). **1611**
SHAKES. *Temp.* V. i. 281 How cam'st thou in
this pickle?—I have been in such a pickle, since
I saw you last, that I fear me will never out of
my bones. **1660** PEPYS *Diary* 26 Sept, i. 251
At home with the workmen all the afternoon,
our house being in a most sad pickle. **1673**
MARVELL *Reh. Transp.* GROS. 457.

Pickerel, *see* Heresy . . . beer (p.) came into
England.

Pickle, *see* Rods in p.

Pickpockets, *see* Agree like p.

Pickpurse, *see* At hand, quoth P.; Bargain is a p.
(A good); Purgatory p.

Picture of ill luck, To look like the.

(P 278)

1624 T. HEYWOOD *The Captives* l. 558 The mapp
of misfortune and very picture of ill luck. **1624**
T. BREWER *A Knot of Fools* C2ᵛ. **1639** CLARKE
119. **1678** RAY 286.

Pictures are the books of the unlearned.

(P 280)

1660 FULLER *Canterb.* 97 According to the
Maxime, 'Pictures are the Books', painted

windows were in the time of Popery the Library of Laymen; and after the Conquest grew in general use in England.

Picture(s), *see also* Painted p. are dead speakers; Speech is p. of mind.

Pie(s), *see* Finger in the p.; Humble p.; Love like pig and p.; No sport no p.; Prayers (They shall have no more of our) than we of their p.

Pie (bird), *see* High for the p. (Not too); Merry as a p.; Preach like a p.

Piece of a kid is worth two of a cat, A. (P 291)

c. 1549 HEYWOOD II. vii. K1ᵛ A peece of a Kyd is woorth two of a cat. Who the diuell will chaunge a rabet for a rat? 1547 BORDE *Introd. of Knowledge* Furnivall 274 Yonge kyddes flesshe is praysed aboue all other flesshe. 1614 CAMDEN 303. 1639 CLARKE 96. *Ibid.* 104 A bit of a kid's worth the body of a kite.

Piece(s), *see also* Churchyard (A p. of) fits every body; Worst p. in the midst.

Pie-crust, *see* Promises are like p.

Pie-lid makes people wise. (P 295)

1592 LYLY *Midas* IV. iii. 39 He hath laid the plot to be prudent: why 'tis pastie crust, eat enough and it will make you wise, an old prouerb. 1678 RAY 79 . . . Because no man can tell what is in a pye till the lid be taken up.

Pig of my own sow, A. (P 305)

c. 1535 *Gentleness and Nobility* A1ᵛ That is euyn a pyg of our own sow. 1546 HEYWOOD II. vii. I2ᵛ A pyg of myne owne sowe. 1579 GOSSON *Sch. Abuse* Arb. 40 The last, because it is knowen too be a Pig of myne owne Sowe, I will speake the lesse of it. 1731 FIELDING *Grub St. Op.* III. xiv If you come to my house I will treat you With a pig of your own sow.

Pig of the worse pannier, A. (P 301)

1533 J. HEYWOOD *John, Tyb, &c.* Farmer 89 And, peradventure, there, he and she Will make me cuckold, even to anger me; and then had I a pig in the worse panyer. 1546 HEYWOOD II. xi. M1 Who that hath either of these pygs in vre, He hathe a pyg of the woorse panier sure.

Pig plays on the organs, A. (P 306)

1616 WITHALS 580. 1639 CLARKE 7. 1670 RAY 189. 1672 WALKER 53, no. 59. 1685 WESLEY *Maggots* Grunting of Hog 22 Why should not other Piggs on Organs play, As well as They?

Pig's tail, Like a | going all day and nothing done at night.

1865 *Lancs. Proverbs* in *N. & Q.* 3rd Ser. VIII. 494. 1869 HAZLITT (1882) 271. *Lancashire.*

Pig's tail, Of a | you can never make a good shaft. (S 265)

1599 MINSHEU *Span. Gram.* 83. 1651 HERBERT no. 1104. 1659 HOWELL *Eng. Prov.* 17b (good whistle). 1742 FRANKLIN April Tom, vain's your Pains; They all will fail: Ne'er was good Arrow made of a Sow's Tail.

Pig's tail, *see also* Horn of a p. t. (Cannot make a).

Pigeon never knows woe, but when she does a-benting go, The. (P 316)

1609 T. RAVENSCROFT *Deuteromelia* F3 The pigion is neuer woe, till abenting she goe. 1611 *Melismata* in LEAN I. 432 The pigeon is never woe Till a-benting she doth go. 1670 RAY 44. 1750 W. ELLIS *Mod. Husbandman* III. 134 At this time of the year . . . the pigeons have had hardly any other field-meat besides, except the seed of bent-grass; which occasioned the old verse: The pigeon never knows pore woe, Than when he does a-benting go.

Pigeons and priests (Doves and dominies) make foul houses. (P 588)

[1386 CHAUCER *Cant. T., Shipman–Prioress Link* B² 1632 Draweth no monkes moore unto youre in. 1530 BAIF *Mimes II* in LEAN IV. 85 Chi vuol tener la casa monda Non tenga mai ne prete ne colomba.] 1610 B. RICH *New Descript. Ireland* xiii. 47 I could wish them to bee well aware of this holy brood of the *Popes* Cockrels, the prouerbe is old, and not so old as true: . . . 1641 FERGUSSON no. 1129 (Priests and doves). 1659 HOWELL *Span. Prov.* 20 Without Priest and pigeon-house thou mayst keep thy house clean. 1721 KELLY 86 Doves and Domine's leave ay a foul House. Pigeons will dirty everything where they are: and these little Fellows, whom Gentlemen bring in to educate their Children, will be intreaguing with the Maids.

Pigeons go a benting,[1] When the | then the farmers lie lamenting.

1830 FORBY 417. [1 feeding on the seeds of grasses.]

Pigeon(s), *see also* Cat among the p., (To put the); Catch two p. with one bean; Paul's p.; Shoot at a p. and kill crow.

Pigmarket, *see* Silence in the p.

Pigs fly in the air with their tails forward. (P 312)

1595 PEELE *Old Wives' Tale* l. 884 E2ᵛ Are not you the man . . . that came from a strange place in the land of Catita, where Jacke a napes flies with his taile in his mouth? 1616 WITHALS 583. 1639 CLARKE 147.

Pigs love that lie together. (P 313)

1678 RAY 189 . . . A familiar conversation breeds friendship among them who are of the most base and sordid natures.

Pigs may fly; but they are very unlikely birds.

1862 HISLOP 116 It may be that swine may flee, but it's no an ilka day's bird. An emphatic expression of incredulity at an extraordinary, or . . . improbable statement. **1885** E. P. HOOD *World Prov. & P.* 352 Here is the passage . . . with its succession of hypotheses and suppositions. . . . And so, . . . '*Pigs might fly, but they are very unlikely birds.*' **1906** W. DE MORGAN *Jos. Vance* ch. 22 Pigs may fly—you know the rest.

Pigs may whistle, but they hae an ill mouth for 't.

1832 HENDERSON 135. **1846** J. GRANT *Rom. of War* ch. 12 'I dare say the Spanish sounds very singular to your ear'. 'Ay, sir, it puts me in mind o' an auld saying o' my faither the piper. "A soo may whussle, but its mouth is no made for't."'

Pigs see the wind.   (P 311)

1678 BUTLER *Hudibras* III. ii. 1107 Had lights where better eyes were blind, As pigs are said to see the wind. **1823** BYRON *Juan* VII. lxxxiv Ask the pig who sees the wind! **1902–4** LEAN I. 437 Pigs see the wind, *i.e.* the coming tempest, which makes them the most restless of animals.

Pig(s), *see also* Buy a p. in a poke; Child's p. father's bacon; Come again as Goodyer's p. did; Cunning as a dead p.; First p. . . . is the best; God loves (Whom), his bitch brings forth p.; Goodyer's p. . . . doing mischief (Like); Hogs Norton; Hogs (P.) to a fair market; Kill a p. every day (We don't); Knows not a p. from dog; Love like p. and pie; Lubberland where the p. run about; More sauce than p.; Parson's p.; Please the p.; Poor and peart like parson's p.; Pretty p. makes ugly sow; Proud as a p.; St. Anthony's (Tantony) p.; Snug as a p.; Stare like a stuck p.; Swine (P.) (He is like a), he'll never do good while he lives; Wilful as a p.; Young p. grunts like old sow.

Pike(s), *see* Ancum p.; Pass the p.; Witham p.

Pikestaff, *see* Plain as a p.

Pilate's voice.   (P 323)

[The loud voice belonging to the part of Pilate in the mystery plays.] **1530** PALSGRAVE 837 In a pylates voyce, *a haulte voyx.* **1542** ERASM. tr. Udall *Apoph.* (1877) 382 He heard a certain oratour speaking out of measure loude and high, and altogether in Pilates voice. **1546** HEYWOOD I. x. C3ᵛ Streight after diner myne aunte had no choyce, But other burst, or burst out in pylat's voyce.

Pile up the agony, To.

1835–40 HALIBURTON *Clockm.* (1862) 444 I was actilly in a piled-up-agony. **1839** MARRYAT *Diary Amer.* Ser. l. II. 235 I do think he piled the agony up a little too high in that last scene. **1852** C. BRONTË in Mrs. Gaskell *Life* (1857) II.

xi. 267 I doubt whether the regular novel-reader will consider the 'agony piled sufficiently high' (as the Americans say).

Pile (*noun*), *see* Cross and p.

Pilgrim(s), *see* God knows well which are best p.

Pilgrimage, *see* Life is a p.

Pillar to post (Post to pillar), From.
                                                (P 328)

[i.e. from whipping-post to pillory.] *c.* **1420** LYDGATE *Ass. of Gods* 1147 Thus fro poost to pylour he was made to daunce. [*c.* **1515**] *c.* **1530** BARCLAY *Eclog.* III. l. 273 From poste vnto piller tossed shalt thou be. **1549** LATIMER *7th Serm. bef. Edw. VI* P.S. 230 A wonderful thing, how he was tost from post to pillar. *a.* **1550** *Vox Populi* 185 in HAZL. *E.P.P.* iii. 274 From piller vnto post the powr man he was tost. **1605** CHAPMAN *All Fools* III. i This light sex is tumbled and tossed from post to pillar. **1670** RAY 190 To be tost from post to pillory. **1882** BLACK-MORE *Christowell* ch. 52 Mr. Greatorex . . . had been sent from pillar to post, for a fortnight, to find out such a hole as this.

Pilling Moss, *see* God's grace.

Pillory, *see* Baker to the p. (Part not yet, quoth).

Pillows under the elbows, To sew.
                                                (P 329)

[EZEK. xiii. 18 Woe to the women that sew pillows to all armholes.] **1562** J. PILKINGTON *Aggeus and Abdias* P.S. 270 Woe then be to them that flatter, lay pillows under their elbows. **1579** LYLY *Euph.* i. 195 One flattereth an other in hys owne folly, and layeth cushions vnder the elbowe. **1640** JONSON *Magn. Lady* V. vii. 14 Softly with art, as we were sowing pillowes Vnder the Patient elbowes.

Pillow, *see* Debtor's p.; Take counsel of p.

Pills were pleasant, If the | they would not want gilding.
                                          (A 282. P 325)

1580 LYLY *Euph. & his Eng.* ii. 99 The admonition of a true friend should be like the practise of a wise Phisition, who wrappeth his sharpe pils in fine sugar. **1591** ARIOSTO *Orl. Fur.* Harington *Brief Allegory* (1607 ed., 2M2ᵛ) According (as I said in my Apologie, vsing Tassoes comparison) like to the pill that is lapped in sugar, and giuen a child for a medicine, who otherwise would not be drawne to take the simple drugge though it were to saue his life. **1616** DRAXE no. 627 If the Apothecaries pilles had a good taste, they would neuer gilde them ouer. **1639** CLARKE 108 Apothecaries would not give pilles in sugar vnlesse they were bitter. **1776** FLETCHER OF MADELEY *Wks.* vii. 111.

Pill(s), *see also* Bitter p. blessed effects; Sugar the p.

Pillvall, *see* Remedy (If there be no), welcome P.

Pilot, *see* Calm sea every man a p.; Paleness of
p. is sign of storm.

Pilson Pen, *see* Akin as Lewson Hill to P. P.

Pin, Not worth a (Flanders).   (P 334)

c. **1492** *Thrie Priests of Peblis* in *Early Pop. Poet.
Scot.* 1189 (1895) I. 163 To the thow thocht I
was not wort ane prene. *c.* **1530** H. RHODES
Bk. Nurture 420 in *Babees Bk.* 93 Yet he is not
worth a pin. *c.* **1550** WEVER *Lusty Juventus*
Hazl.-Dods. ii. 64 If I had not been, Thou
haddest not been worth a Flanders pin At this
present day. **1590** LODGE *Rosalynde* Wks. (1883)
I. 37 Aliena . . . said, the wedding was not
worth a pinne, vnles there were some cheere.
1594 SHAKES. *T.G.V.* II. vii. 55 A round hose,
madam, now's not worth a pin. **1600-1** *Id.
H.* I. iv. 65 I do not set my life at a pin's fee.
1616 WITHALS 570 (pin's end).

Pin a day is a groat a year, A.

1712 ADDISON *Spect.* no. 295, par. 4 A Pin a
Day, says our frugal proverb, is a Groat a Year.
1738 SWIFT *Dial.* I. E.L. 275. **1827** HARE *Gues.
at Truth* (1873) i. 238 Thrift is the best means of
thriving. . . . A pin a-day is a groat a-year.

Pin, See a | and let it stay (lie), you'll want a pin another day (before you die); see a pin and pick it up, all the day you'll have good luck.

1659 HOWELL *Span. Prov.* 14 Who takes not up
a pin hath no care of his wife. **1843** HALLIWELL
Nursery Rhymes 120 See a pin and let it lay,
Bad luck you'll have all the day! **1872** *N. & Q.*
4th Ser. x. 477 I have frequently heard the following in Cornwall 'To see a pin and let it lie, You'll
want a pin before you die'. **1883** BURNE &
JACKSON *Shropshire Folk-Lore* 279.

Pinch on the parson's (priest's) side.
                                           (P 67)

[= reduce your almsgiving, or tithes.] **1530**
Proper Dyaloge in *Rede me, &c.* Arb. 169 Let
him ones begynne to pynche Or withdrawe their
tithinge an ynche, For an heretike they will him
ascite. **1576** U. FULWELL *Ars Adulandi* M3ᵛ
Pinch on the parsons side my Lorde, the whor-
sons haue too much. **1614** T. ADAMS *Heaven &
Earth Reconciled* F3. This is a common slander
when the hell-hound (the covetous wretch)
pincheth on the priest's side: 'No matter, let
him talk for his living'.

Pinch(es), *see also* Jack at a p.; Nothing tickles
that p. not; Penny at a p. worth a pound;
Shoe wrings (p.).

Pine wishes herself a shrub when the axe is at her root, The.   (P 339)

1692 L'ESTRANGE *Aesop's Fab.* ccxxxvii (1738)
253 'Tell me, however, when the carpenter
comes next with the axe into the wood, to fell
timber, whether you had not rather be a bramble
than a fir tree'. **1732** FULLER no. 4705.

Pins and needles, To be on.

1811 J. POOLE *Hamlet Travestie* 8 Would it were
supper-time . . . Till then I'm sitting upon pins
and needles. **1897** STEVENSON *St. Ives* ch. 29
He was plainly on pins and needles. **1910** P. W.
JOYCE *Eng. as We Speak* 141 I was *on pins and
needles* till you came home: *i.e.* I was very uneasy.

Pins his faith upon another man's sleeve, He.   (F 32)

1548 HALL 599 He would none of his seruauntes
should hang on another mannes sleue. **1579**
LYLY *Euph.* i. 249 Art thou so pinned to their
sleeues. **1584** *Id. Sappho & Phao* II. iv. 97
Be not pinned alwais on her sleeues. **1590**
GREENE *Wks.* Gros. ix. 173 What is it for mee
to pinne a fayre meacocke and a witty milksop
on my sleeue, who dare not answere with their
swords in the face of the enemy? **1594-5**
SHAKES. *L.L.L.* V. ii. 321 This gallant pins the
wenches on his sleeve. **1660** SECKER *Nonsuch
Prof.* iii (1891) 274 That was a good saying of
Sir Thomas More: 'I will not pin my faith upon
any man's sleeve, because I know not whither
he will carry it.' **1678** RAY 342 I'll not pin my
faith on your sleeve. **1824** FERRIER *Inheritance*
II. xi There are those who pin their faith upon
the sleeve of some favourite preacher. **1867-77**
FROUDE *Short Stud.* (1890) III. 140 The Protestant
. . . refused to pin his faith upon the Church's
sleeve thenceforward.

Pin(s), *see also* Care a p. (Not to); Cleave the p.;
Heard a p. drop (Might have); Merry p., (To be
in a); Neat as a new p.; Needles and p.; Pack to
the p. (Brought the); Silvered p. fair without
foul within; Steal a p.; Stoop for a p. (He that
will not); Takes not up a p. slights wife (He
that).

Pint stoups hae lang lugs.

1818 SCOTT *Rob Roy* ch. 26 Not that I wad speak
ony ill of this MacCallum More—'Curse not
the rich in your bedchamber, . . . For a bird of
the air shall carry the clatter, and pint stoups hae
lang lugs.' **1862** HISLOP 247 . . . For a great
deal is said over them, which, but for their
influence, would not be heard.

Pint-pot, *see* Quart into a p., (To put a).

Pint stoup(s), *see also* Comes to the hand like p. s.

Pint, *see also* Bald moon . . . another p.

Pip, *see* Hen live, (Let) though it be with her p.

Pipe in (with) an ivy leaf, To.
                                           (I 110)

[= to console oneself (for failure, etc.) with
some frivolous employment.] *c.* **1370** WYCLIF
Eng. Wks. E.E.T.S. 372 The Seculer party may
go pipe with an yuy lefe for any lordeschipis that
the clerkis will geue hem agen. *c.* **1374** CHAUCER
Troilus Bk. 4, l. 1433 But, Troylus, thou mayst
now, este or weste, Pipe in an ivy leefe, if that
the leste. **1387-8** T. USK *Test. Love* III. vii (Skeat)
l. 50 Far wel the gardiner, he may pipe with an
yue leafe, his fruite is failed. *c.* **1430** LYDGATE

Churl & Bird 276 *Minor Poems* Percy Soc. 189 Thou mayst go pype in an yve-leffe. **1572** CRADOCKE *Ship of Assured Safety* 117 Touching the lybertie of oure firste creation, wee may as soone pype in an yuie leafe, as any more haue authoritie to make clayme to that. **1609** HARWARD 111.

Pipe of peace, To smoke the.

1762 FOOTE *Lyar.* I. (1786) 17 I had the first honour of smoaking the pipe of peace with the little Carpenter. **1789** WOLCOT (P. Pindar) *Subj. for Paint.* Wks. (1816) II. 3 I come to bid the hatchet's labour cease, And smoke with friends the calumet of peace. **1870** MISS BRIDGMAN *Rob. Lynne* II. xii. 261 They had better smoke the pipe of peace.

Pipe one's eye (eyes), To.

[Orig. Naut. slang = to weep.] **1789** C. DIBDIN *Song, Poor Jack* iii What argufies sniv'ling and piping your eye? *a.* **1814** *Sailor's Ret.* II. i in *New Brit. Theatre* II. 337 Lucy and he must have piped their eyes enough by this time. **1826** HOOD *Faithless Sally Brown* xv in *Whims & Odd.* (1861) 44 He heav'd a bitter sigh, And then began to eye his pipe, And then to pipe his eye.

Pipe that lacks his upper lip, He can ill
                                          (L 324)

1546 HEYWOOD II. ix. L1ᵛ (ouer lyp). **1621** JONSON *Gip. Metam.* vii. 596 Mary, a newe Collection, there's no Musique els, he can ill pipe that wants his vpper lip. **1670** RAY 131 . . . Things cannot be done without necessary helps and instruments.

Pipe(s) (*noun*), *see also* Dance to p.; Fowler's p. sweet till bird caught; Long a-tuning your p. (You are as); Put that in your p.; Put up your p.

Pipe (*verb*), *see also* No longer p. no longer dance.

Piper a penny to play, Give the | and two pence to leave off.

1732 FULLER no. 1660.

Piper of Bujalance, Like the | who got one maravedi to strike up and ten to leave off.

1846 LONGFELLOW *Span. Stud.* I. ii. Art thou related to the bagpiper of Bujalance, who asked a maravedi for playing, and ten for leaving off? **1885** J. ORMSBY *D. Quixote* II. 345 Note B.

Piper wants mickle that wants the nether chaft(s),[1] The.   (P 348)

a. **1628** CARMICHAELL no. 1449. **1641** FERGUSSON no. 796. **1721** KELLY 310 . . . Spoken when a Thing is wanting that is absolutely necessary. [¹ lower jaw.]

Piper(s), *see also* Pay the p.; Pays the p. call the tune; Speak good of p.; Tinker and p. make bad music together.

Pippin(s), *see* Crab-tree where you will (Plant), never bear p.; Parings of a p. better than whole crab.

Pirate gets nothing of another but his cask, One.   (P 353)

1659 HOWELL *Fr. Prov.* 5 'Twixt Pirat and Pirat there's nothing found but crack'd casks. **1666** TORRIANO *It. Prov.* 54 no. 24 'Twixt Pirate and Pirate, there's nothing to be had but empty barrels. **1732** FULLER no. 3790.

Pisgah sight, A.

[DEUT. xxxiv. 1–3.] **1650** FULLER *A Pisgah-sight of Palestine* [title]. **1829** SCOTT *Journal* 7 Mar. This extrication of my affairs, though only a Pisgah prospect, occupies my mind more than is fitting.

Pismire, *see* Angry as a p.

Piss clear, and defy the physician.
                                          (P 269)

1591 FLORIO *Second F.* 61 I knowe no better phisick then to pisse cleare, that so a man may bid a figg for the phisition. **1678** RAY 42 Piscia chiaro & incaca al medico, i.e. Pisse clear and defie the physician. **1706** STEVENS s.v. Color (turn away).

Piss down one's back, To.

1788 GROSE s.v. Pissing (Flattering him). **1813** RAY 66 . . . *i.e.* to flatter.

Piss in the same quill, To.   (Q 177)

c. **1640** SMYTH 32, no. 82 Things ne'ere goe ill where Jacke and Gill pisse in one quill. **1666** TORRIANO *Prov. Phr.* 217 One . . . of the same kidney, to piss thorough a quill. **1678** RAY 265. *a.* **1734** NORTH *Exam.* I. ii, § 78 (1740) 70 So strangely did Papist and Fanatic, or . . . the Anticourt Party, piss in a Quill; agreeing in all Things that tended to create Troubles and disturbances.

Piss not against the wind.   (W 427)

1642 TORRIANO 19 He who pisseth against the wind, wetteth his shirt. **1670** RAY 131 . . . Chi piscia contra il vento si bagna la commiscia, *Ital.* He that pisseth against the wind, wets his shirt. It is to a man's own prejudice, to strive against the stream.

Pissed on a nettle, He has.   (N 132)

1546 HEYWOOD II. x. L3ᵛ It seemed to hym she had pyst on a nettyl. **1592** GREENE *Upst. Courtier* B3 All these women that you heare brawling . . . and skolding thus, have seuerally pist on this bush of nettles. **1641** FERGUSSON no. 426 *Of angry persons.* He hes pisht on a nettle. *a.* **1700** B. E. *Dict. Canting-Crew* . . . he is very uneasy or much out of Humor. **1828** *Craven Gloss.* s.v. 'Thou's p—d of a nettle this morning', said of a waspish, ill-tempered person.

Pissed his tallow, He has.   (T 66)

[*c.* **1450** *M. E. Med. Book* (Heinrich) Take talow of an hert, suche as he pysseþ by twene two

seynt mary dayes.] **1600–1** SHAKES. *M.W.W.*
V. v. 12 For me, I am here a Windsor stag, . . .
send me a cool rut-time, Jove, or who can blame
me to piss my tallow. **1678** RAY 78 . . . This is
spoken of bucks who grow lean after rutting
time, and may be applied to men. **1694** MOTTEUX
Rabelais v. xxviii (1737) 132 He's nothing but
Skin and Bones; he has piss'd his Tallow.

Pisses more than he drinks, He.

1614 OVERBURY *The Wife* (1632) T3 The vaine-
glorious man pisseth more then he drinkes.
1699 B.E. *Dict. Canting-Crew* s.v. Vain-glorious.
1785 GROSE s.v. Vain-glorious.

Pistol, *see* Antwerp is p. pointed at heart of
England.

Pit, *see* Dig a p. . . ., (To); Edge of his grave
(p.'s brink), (He is upon the); Law is bottomless
p.

Pitch and pay. (P 360)

**14— ** *Piers of Fulham* 206 in HAZL. *E.P.P.* ii. 9
Yt ys full hard bothe to pyche and paye. **1559**
Mirr. Mag., Warwick (Campbell 209) I vsed
playnnes, ever pitch and pay. **1599** SHAKES.
Hen. V II. iii. 51 The word is, Pitch and pay:
trust none. **1602** WITHALS 352 Mercari Græca
fide. To buy as they doe in Greece, viz. with that
estimation, with that credit, which is, to pitch
and pay, as we tearme it. **1608** H. CLAPHAM
Errour on Left Hand 102 But you your promise
once did breake. Give me your hand, that you
will pitch and pay.

Pitch, *see also* Black as soot (p.); Devil to pay
and no p. hot; Mouse in p.; Touches p. (He that)
shall be defiled.

Pitcher (Pot) goes so often to the well (water), The | that it is broken at last. (P 501)

1340 *Ayenb.* 206 Zuo longe geþ pot to þe
wetere, þet hit comþ to-broke hom. *c.* **1350**
Douce MS. 52 no. 88 The pot goth so longe to
the water þat he comyth broke home. *a.* **1450**
Knt. de la Tour 82 It is a trew prouerbe, that
'the potte may goo so longe to water, that atte
the laste it is broken'. **1546** HEYWOOD II. vii. I4ᵛ
The pot so long to the water gothe. Tyll at the
laste it comthe home broken. **1591** GREENE *Art
Conny Catch.* II (1592) 15 Yet at last so long the
pitcher goeth to the brooke, that it commeth
broken home. *c.* **1645** HOWELL *Lett.* I. i. vi That
the Pot which goes often to the water, comes
home crack'd at last. **1670** RAY 131 The pitcher
doth not go so often to the water, but it comes
home broken at last. **1826** SCOTT *Woodst.* ch. 22
The pitcher goes oft to the well——. **1883** *Pall
Mall G.* 3 Oct. 3/2 The pitcher, however, has
gone once too often to the well, and yesterday
. . . the panorama caught fire in earnest, and
was reduced to ashes.

Pitcher strikes the stone, Whether the | or the stone the pitcher, it is bad for the pitcher. (P 362)

1620 SHELTON *Quix.* III. vi. i. 158 After what way
soever I grow angry with thee, it will be bad for

the pitcher. *Ibid.* II. xliii. iii. 116 And 'If the pot
fall upon the stone, or the stone on the pot, ill
for the pot, ill for the stone'. **1911** A. COHEN
Anct. Jew. Prov. 103 If the stone falls on the pot,
woe to the pot; if the pot falls on the stone, woe
to the pot; in either case woe to the pot. . . .
The weak always suffers. A proverb . . . current
in Spain, borrowed in all probability from the
Jews.

Pitcher(s), *see also* Little p. have great ears;
Tom p.'s broken (When), I shall have shards.

Pities another remembers himself, He that. (P 372)

1539 TAVERNER *Publius* C6ᵛ The man that is
pytiful vpon a miserable person, remembreth
hym selfe. For he vnderstandeth that he him
selfe may haue nede of helpe. **1640** HERBERT
no. 782. **1659** HOWELL *Span. Prov.* 18. **1748**
RICHARDSON *Clarissa* iv. Let. 24 Another proverb
that I picked up at Madrid . . .

Pitiful look asks enough, A. (L 427)

1640 HERBERT no. 790.

Pitiful mother makes a scald[1] head (scabby daughter), A. (M 1201)

c. **1594** BACON no. 1471 Mere pitieuse fille
rigeureuse. **1611** COTGRAVE s.v. Rongneux A
tender-hearted mother breeds a short-heeld
daughter. s.v. Mère (tender . . . scabbie). **1640**
HERBERT no. 647. **1659** HOWELL *Fr. Prov.* II.
Too pitiful a mother makes a scabby child.
1659 TORRIANO no. 74 (scabby daughter). **1706**
STEVENS s.v. Madre. A tender Mother breeds
a nasty Daughter. [¹ scabby.]

Pitiful surgeon (physician) spoils a sore, A. (P 270)

1562 BULLEIN *Bulwark Def.* Dial. 2ᵛ Soft
chyrurgiens maketh foule sores. **1573** SANFORD
107ᵛ A pitiful physition maketh a deadly
wound. **1578** FLORIO *First F.* 32 (maketh a
scald wound). **1580** S. BIRD *Friendly Communication* 71 Soft hands maketh a foule sore. **1604**
MARSTON *Malcontent* IV. ii. 95 A pitiful surgeon
makes a dangerous sore.

Pity is akin to love. (P 370)

1601 SHAKES. *T.N.* III. i. 119 I pity you.—
That's a degree to love. **1696** SOUTHERNE
Oroonoko II. i Do pity me; Pity's akin to love.
1896 F. LOCKER-LAMPSON *My Confid.* 95 They
say that Pity is akin to Love, though only a
Poor Relation; but Amy did not even pity me.

Pity (noun), *see also* Foolish p. mars a city;
Laird of p. (Looks like).

Pity (-ied) (verb), *see also* Sick man is not to be
p. who has cure.

Pivot(s), *see* Great engines.

Place for everything, and everything in its place, A. (T 169)

1640 HERBERT no. 379 All things have their place,
knew wee how to place them. **1841** MARRYAT

Mast. Ready ch. 30 In a well-conducted man-of-war . . . everything is in its place, and there is a place for everything. **1875** SMILES *Thrift* 78 Order is most useful in the management of everything. . . . Its maxim is, A place for everything and everything in its place. **1902–4** LEAN III. 401.

Place in the sun, One's.

1727 B. KENNET *Pascal's Thoughts* (ed. 2) 291 This Dog's *mine*, says the poor Child: this is *my* Place, in the Sun. From so petty a Beginning, may we trace the Tyranny and Usurpation of the whole Earth. **1911** *Times* 28 Aug. 6/3 (Wilhelm II's Speech at Hamburg, 27 Aug.) No one can dispute with us the place in the sun that is our due.

Place like home, There is no.

1573 TUSSER (1580) S1 Though home be but homely, yet huswife is taught, that home hath no fellow to such as haue aught. **1659** HOWELL *Brit. Prov.* 1 While through all places thou dost rome, yet have thy eyes still towards home. **1822** J. H. PAYNE *Song 'Home, Sweet Home'* Be it ever so humble, there's no place like home. **1859** LD. DUFFERIN *Lett. High Lat.* (1895) 241 My . . . infant walrus . . . would . . . come . . . among us again with a contented grunt, as much as to say, 'Well, after all, there's no place like *home*!' **1876** J. PAYN *Halves* ch. 21 When one was sick there was no place like home.

Place(s), *see also* Change p. but not . . . grief, (One may); Quits his p. well that leaves friend; Sit in your p., none can make you rise; Two p. at once (A man cannot be in); Wise man esteems every p. his own country; Women think p. a sweet fish; World is but a little p.

Placebo, see No penny no *p.*; Sing *p.*

Plack,[1] Not worth a.   (P 379)

a. **1550** in DUNBAR *Poems* S.T.S. 307 He wald nocht mend thame worth ane plack. *a.* **1585** A. MONTGOMERIE *Cherrie & Slae* lxxxiii (1821) 44 3e are nae prophet worth a plak. [[1] a small copper coin current in Scotland in 15th and 16th centuries.]

Placks and bawbees grow pounds.

1832 HENDERSON 16.

Plague, *see* Plenty is no p.

Plain as a pikestaff, As.   (P 8, 322)

[An alteration of *as plain as a packstaff*, in reference to its plain surface.] **1532** MORE *Wks.* (1557) 814. **1542** BECON *David's Harp* Early Wks. P.S. 276 He is as plain as a pack-staff. **1553** T. WILSON *Rhetoric* (1585 ed. Mair 141) Plaine as a packsaddle. **1591** GREENE *Disc. Coosnage* (1592) 4 A new game . . . that hath no policie nor knauerie, but plaine as a pike-staffe. **1719** D'URFEY *Pills* III. 22 When a Reason's as plain as a Pikestaff. **1818** SCOTT *Rob Roy* ch. 26 I'll make it as plain as Peter Pasley's pike-staff. **1867** TROLLOPE *Last Chron. Bars.* I. xlii. 367 The evidence against him was as plain as a pikestaff.

Plain as the nose on a man's face, As.
                                              (N 215)

a. **1576** WHYTHORNE 26 It shalnot be somuch seen az A noz in A mans fas. **1581** GUAZZO i. 173 The simple soules not perceiving that their transformation, or rather deformation, is no more seene then a nose in a man's face. **1594** SHAKES. *T.G.V.* II. i. 124 O jest unseen, inscrutable, invisible, As a nose on a man's face. **1639** CLARKE 188. **1655** H. MORE *Second Lash* 200. **1868** W. COLLINS *Moonstone* ch. 15 On evidence which is as plain as the nose on your face!

Plain dealing is a jewel.   (P 381)

a. **1573** *New Custom* A4ᵛ Then playne dealing beare [*i.e.* bore] away the price. **1587** J. BRIDGES *Def. of Gvt. of C. of E.* 124 Plaine dealing (sayeth the Prouerbe) is a Iewell. **1605–8** SHAKES. *T.Ath.* I. i. 212 How dost thou like this jewel, Apemantus?—Not so well as plain-dealing. **1685** DRYDEN *Albion & Alban.* Epil. *Plain Dealing* for a Jewel has been known; But ne'er till now the Jewel of a Crown. **1826** T. H. LISTER *Granby* iii. 92 (. . . as your father says).

Plain dealing is a jewel, but they that use it die beggars.   (P 382)

1583 MELBANCKE *Philotimus* Epist. Ded. Plaine dealing is a iewel (though they that vse it commonly die beggers). **1599** PORTER *Angry Wom. Abingd.* l. 2325 I speake plainely, for plaine dealing is a Iewell, and he that vseth it shal dye a beggar. **1608** DAY *Law Tricks* II. i Thereof grew the prouerbe, plaine dealing is a Iewell.—But he that vseth it shall die a begger. **1660** W. SECKER *Nonsuch Prof.* II (1891) 284 That is but an hall-made proverb: plain dealing is a jewel, but he who adheres to it shall die a beggar.

Plain dealing is best.   (P 383)

1575 R. B. *Appius and Virg.* E2ᵛ. **1609** HARWARD 120 (Square dealing). **1616** DRAXE no. 1639.

Plain dealing is dead, and died without issue.   (P 384)

1613 T. ADAMS *The White Devil* (1861–2, ii. 241) Plain-dealing is dead, and, what we most lament, it died without issue. **1616** B. RICH *Ladies Looking Glasse* 60 Plaine dealing: honesty is dead. **1732** FULLER no. 3879. **1750** FRANKLIN Sept. Poor Plain dealing! dead without Issue.

Plain dealing is praised more than practised.   (P 385)

1639 CLARKE 138.

Plain fashion is best, The.   (F 75)

1555 HEYWOOD *Epigr. upon Prov.* no. 201 D2.

Plain of poverty and die a beggar.
                                              (P 523)

1678 RAY 191.

Plain (*noun*), *see* Graze on the p.

Plaints (Tarrows) early that plaints (tarrows) on his kail, He. (K 3)

a. **1628** CARMICHAELL no. 760. **1641** FERGUSSON no. 366. **1721** KELLY 135 (*Tarrows*). The Scots, for their first Dish have Broth (which they call Kail) and their Flesh-meat . . . after. Spoken when Men complain before they see the utmost that they will get.

Planet(s), *see* Born under a three-halfpenny p.; Born under an unlucky p. (star); Rains by p.

Plant an opinion they seem to eradicate, Some men. (M 584)

1651 HERBERT no. 1164. **1659** N. R. 93.

Plant pears for your heirs.

1869 HAZLITT 330 . . . A proverb which no longer holds true, since pears are now made to yield well after a few years.

Plant (*noun*), *see* Confidence p. of slow growth; Noble p. suits not stubborn ground.

Plant(ed), (*verb*), *see also* Crab-tree where you will (P.); Pluck not where never p.

Plants a tree plants for posterity, He that.

a. **1640** L. CHADERTON in Dillingham's *Life* tr. E. S. Shuckburgh 1884 18 We plant for another generation. **1707** MAPLETOFT 113 Planting of Trees is England's old thrift. **1732** FULLER no. 2248 He that plants Trees, loves others besides himself.

Plants a walnut-tree, He who | expects not to eat of the fruit.

1706 STEVENS s.v. Noguera. **1732** FULLER no. 2401.

Plaster for so small a sore, That is a prodigious. (S 646)

1546 J. BALE *Examn. of Anne Askewe* P.S. 166 To lay a plaister unto the whole skin, it might appear much folly. **1593** J. RAINOLDS (Boas *Univ. Stage* 242) My plaister would be lesse a great deale then the wound. **1616** DRAXE no. 1616 The plaster must not bee greater then the wound. **1671** T. WATSON *Mischief of Sin* 21 [Sin] makes the wound broader than the plaister. **1732** FULLER no. 4347.

Plaster, *see also* Break one's head and bring p; Death is a p. for all ills; Patience is a p. for all sores.

Platter, *see* Much matter of wooden p.

Play at bowls, He that will | must expect to meet with rubbers. (B 569)

1594–5 SHAKES. *L.L.L.* IV. i. 131 Challenge her to bowl.—I fear too much rubbing. **1595–6** *Id. Rich. II* III. iv. 4 Madam, we'll play at bowls.—

'Twill make me think the world is full of rubs. **1762** SMOLLETT *Sir Launcelot Greaves* ch. 10 [heading] Which showeth that he that plays at Bowls will sometimes meet with Rubbers. **1824** SCOTT *Redg.* ch. 20 'And how if it fails?' said Darsie. 'Thereafter as it may be', said Nixon; 'they who play at bowls must meet with rubbers.'

Play at chess when the house is on fire, To. (M 497)

1592 DELAMOTHE 29. **1651** HERBERT no. 1136. **1659** HOWELL *It. Prov.* 6. **1732** FULLER no. 5539 When a Man's House is on Fire, it's Time to break off Chess.

Play booty, To. (B 539)

[= to act as decoy for confederates, practise collusion.] **1540** PALSGRAVE *Acolastus* 139 Shal not I be boty or party felow with the? **1561** AWDELAY *Frat. of Vacabondes* 9 And consent as though they will play booty against him. **1592** GREENE *Art Conny Catch.* II. 8 The bowlers cast euer booty and doth win or loose as the bet of the gripe leadeth them. **1622** MABBE tr. *Aleman's Guzman d'Alf.* I. 222 Wee are three of vs, let vs all play booty, and joyne together to coozen the Cardinall. **1771** P. PARSONS *Newmarket* I. 108 Bribing the rider to play booty, to lose the race. **1813** *Examiner* 17 May 319/1 I gave a jockey a handsome premium to play booty.

Play (at) fast and loose, To. (P 401)

[= to be unreliable or inconsistent. Fast-and-loose was an old cheating game played by gipsies and vagrants. See 1847 HALLIWELL *Dict.*] **1557** *Tottel's Misc.* Arb. 157. [Title of Epigram] Of a new married student that plaid fast or loose. **1578** WHETSTONE 1 *Promos and Cass.* II. v. C3 At fast or loose, with my Giptian, I meane to haue a cast. **1594–5** SHAKES. *L.L.L.* I. ii. 148 Let me not be pent up, sir: I will fast, being loose. —No, sir; that were fast and loose. *Ibid.* III. i. 97 To sell a bargain well is as cunning as fast and loose. **1596** *Id. K.J.* III. i. 242 Play fast and loose with faith? **1599** S. HARSNET *Discovery of fraudulent practises* 227 Here is fast and loose, as the Egyptian listeth. **1606–7** SHAKES. *A.C.* IV. xii. 25 This grave charm, . . . Like a right gipsy, hath, at fast and loose, Beguil'd me. **1630** *R. Johnson's Kingd. & Commw.* 369 The French playing fast and loose with their Salick Law. **1712** STEELE *Spect.* no. 320, par. 1 A little . . . playing fast and loose, between Love and Indifference. **1829** *Westm. Rev.* x. 185 Doctrines . . . which play at fast and loose with truth and falsehood. **1860** THACKERAY *Lovel the Wid.* vi (1869) 252 She had played fast and loose with me.

Play first (second) fiddle, To.

[= to take a leading (or subordinate) place.] **1778** *Learning at Loss* II. 79 Our Friends . . . returned, with Jack Solecism the first Fiddle as usual. **1809** MALKIN *Gil Blas* x. xi I am quite at your service to play second fiddle in all your laudable enterprises. **1822** O'MEARA *Napoleon in Exile* I. 227 He was of opinion that Prussia should never play the first fiddle in the affairs of the Continent. **1850** THACKERAY *Pendennis* (1878) II. xvii. 19 'I've played a second fiddle all through life', he said with a bitter laugh. **1909**

Times 17 May Austria–Hungary . . . last autumn took the initiative on her own account. For the first time during . . . her alliance with Germany . . . she has played the first fiddle.

Play for nought as work for nought, As good. (N 340)

1533 UDALL *Flowers for Latin Speaking* Better contented (according to the accustomed prouerbe) to plaie for naught then to werke for naught. **1546** HEYWOOD I. xi. E3ᵛ Men say, as good plai for nought as work for nought. **1548** ERASM. tr. Udall Preface. *a.* **1628** CARMICHAELL no. 298 (sit idle). **1721** KELLY 60 Better play for nought, than work for nought. **1808** SCOTT *Let. to Sharpe* 30 Dec. in LOCKHART *Life* The fee is ten guineas . . . —as good play for nothing, you know, as work for nothing.

Play off your dust. (D 649)

1604 DEKKER I *Hon. Whore* I. v. 155 Come: play't off: to me, I am your last man. **1639** CLARKE 46. **1670** RAY 216 *Drinking Phrases* . . .

Play one's cards well, To.

[= to make good use of one's resources or opportunities.] **1702** T. BROWN, etc. *Letters from the Dead to the Living* 160 How'er, all Flattery apart You've play'd your Cards with wondrous Art. **1753** FOOTE *Eng. in Paris* I. i If Lucinda plays her cards well, we have not much to fear from that Quarter. **1894** MRS. STEEL *Potter's Thumb* ch. 25 'He is a fool, and yet he is playing his cards well'.

Play rex, To. (R 96)

[= to act as lord or master. L. *Rex*, a King.] **1563** FOXE *Acts and Monum.* II. i. 355 This Theodore, being made archbishop and metropolitan of Canterbury, began to play the Rex, placing and displacing the bishops at his pleasure. **1596** WARNER *Albion's Eng.* IX. 50 Q3 Then plaid he [Lucifer] Rex ore all the Earth. **1597** BEARD *Theatre God's Judgem.* (1612) 529 The Scots that were so curbed in his fathers dayes, now played rex through his negligence. **1651** N. BACON *Disc. Govt. Eng.* II. xxxvii (1739) 168 The Prelacy . . . played Rex all the while with the people.

Play small game before he will sit out, He (The devil) will. (G 21)

1565 J. CALFHILL *Treatise of the Cross* P.S. 231 I perceiue you will play small play, rather than sit out. **1576** J. BRIDGES *Sermon at Paul's Cross* 177 So fain the Papist wold haue some thing to boast vppon, he will play small play rather than he will sitte out. **1578** G. WHETSTONE *Promus & Cassandra* D4ᵛ He will playe at Small game, or he sitte out. *a.* **1591** HY. SMITH *Serm.* (1866) II. 108 The devil, or the world, or the flesh, will play small game, as we use to say, before they will sit out. If they cannot get full possession of our hearts, then they are content to have some part of our love. **1623** CAMDEN 270. **1631** R. BRAITHWAIT *Whimzies* (1859) 148 Now for the divel he ha's so much to do With roaring boys, he'll slight such babes as thou. Yet be not too secure, but put him to't, For he'll play at small

game, e'er he sit out. **1655–62** GURNALL *Chrn. in Armour* (1865) I. 294 They would make us think, that here men played but at small game, and their souls were not at stake, as in other sins. **1721** KELLY 391 You will play small Game before you stand out. **1827** SCOTT *Canongate* ch. I Some stuck to cards, and though no longer deep gamblers, rather played small game than sat out.

Play, The less | the better. (P 396)

1641 FERGUSSON no. 834.

Play the devil in the bullimong, To. (D 301)

1670 RAY 171. **1678** RAY 239 To play the *Devil i' th' bulmong*, *i.e.* corn mingled of pease, tares, and oats [sown together for feeding cattle].

Play the devil in the horologe, To. (D 302)

[= to play pranks with the works of a clock; a type of the confusion caused by a mischievous agent in any orderly system.] **1519** HORMAN *Vulg.* 232 b Some for a tryfull pley the deuyll in the orlege. [*c.* **1553**] **1566–7** UDALL *Ralph Roister D.* III. ii. Arb. 43 What will he?—Play the deuill in the horologe. **1611** DAVIES nos. 361, 362.

Play the fool, see No man can p. the f. as wise man; Wise man who cannot (He is not); Wise men p. the f. (If).

Play the game.

c. **1386** CHAUCER *Clerk's T.* Prol. ll. 10–11 For what man that is entred in a pley, he nedes moot unto the pley assente. **1898** KIPLING *Day's Work* 248 (*Maltese Cat*) 'Play the game, don't talk'. **1904** *Daily Chron.* 2 May 4/5 Men do not talk about their honour nowadays —the call it 'playing the game'.

Play the jack, To. (J 8)

[= to play the knave, to do a mean thing.] **1567** GOLDING *Ovid* xiii. 289 Yit durst Thersites bee So bold as rayle vppon the kings, and he was payd by mee For playing so the sawcye Jacke. **1598–9** SHAKES. *M.A.* I. i. 157 Speak you this with a sad brow? or do you play the flouting Jack? **1611** BEAUM. & FL. *Kt. Burn. P.* Induct. If you were not resolved to play the Jacks, what need you study for new subjects, purposely to abuse your betters? **1611** SHAKES. *Temp.* IV. i. 198 Your fairy . . . has done little better than played the Jack with us. **1668** PEPYS *Diary* 23 Feb. Sir R. Brookes overtook us coming to town; who played the jacke with us all, and is a fellow that I must trust no more.

Play underboard, To. (P 402)

1558 CRANMER Pref. to *Confut. Unwritten Verities* tr. E.P. A4 (Alas) so long till all was playde vnder the boorde. **1564** Jan. WM. CECIL cited C. Read *Mr. Sec. Cecil* 287 Though playing under the board prove sometime the jugglers. **1591** FLORIO *Second F.* 134 Thou haste long hands, and vsest them vnderboord.

Play well if you lose, It signifies nothing to.

1732 FULLER no. 3045.

Play with a bull till you get his horn in your eye, You may.

1917 BRIDGE 158 . . . Another form of 'Do not play with edged tools'.

Play with a fool at home, and he will play with you in the market. (F 502)

1640 HERBERT no. 146. 1670 RAY 10. 1732 FULLER no. 2763 If you let a Fool play with you at Home, he'll do so with you in the Market.

Play with fire, To. (F 286)

1582 WHETSTONE *Heptameron* E3 In doing of these three thinges is great daunger, . . . to play with fire: to striue with water: and to giue a woman knowledge of our power. [1589] 1594 LODGE *Wounds* l. 453 Both blunt and bold but too much Mother wit, To play with fier where furie streames about. 1596 B. GRIFFIN *Fidessa* Sonnet xiii, *Eng. Garner* ii. 271 Compare me to the child that plays with fire. 1655 H. VAUGHAN *Garland* in *Silex Scint.* II. (1847) 132 I played with fire, did counsell spurn, . . . But never thought that fire would burn, Or that a soul could ake.

Play with the ears than the tongue, It is better to. (E 17)

1539 TAVERNER I *Garden* F6 Zeno Cittieus to a certayn yong man which was alwayes pratlyng, sayd, I trowe (good felow) thy eares be fallen into thy tonge. Declaryng herby, that it shulde be a yong mans propertie to heare moche & speake lytell. 1592 DELAMOTHE 21. 1611 DAVIES no. 217.

Play with you for shoe-buckles, I will not. (S 383)

1616 WITHALS 558 Wee play not for shoe-buckles. 1639 CLARKE 195 (as 1616). 1678 RAY 347.

Play with your peers. (P 180)

a. 1400 Sermon against Miracle Plays (*Reliq. Antiquae* ed. Wright and Halliwell, 1845, ii. 43) A lord . . . sodaynly sleeth his seruaunt for he playide to homely with him: and . . . seith to his seruaunt, 'play not with me, but play with thi pere'. [c. 1582] 1621 MONTGOMERIE *Flyting* (1629 ed.) l. 95: *Poems* 62 Play with they peir, or I'll pull thee like a paipe. a. 1628 CARMICHAELL no. 1243 Pleid [?Plaie] with your peirs quo Parkie. 1641 FERGUSSON no. 688. 1721 KELLY 281 Play with your Playfeers.[1] Spoken to young People when they offer to be roguish upon, or play too saucily with, old People. [[1] fellows.]

Play, women, and wine undo men laughing. (P 397)

1579 LYLY *Euph.* i. 256 It is play, wine and wantonnesse, that feedeth a louer as fat as a foole. 1642 TORRIANO 54 (consumes a man laughing): That is, before one is aware of either of them. 1655–62 GURNALL *Chrn. in Armour* (1865) II. 239 The Italians say that 'play, wine, and women consume a man laughing'. It is true of all pleasurable sins. 1670 RAY 21.

Play(s) (*noun*), *see also* Boys' p. (To leave); Cast be bad (If), mend by good p.; Cheat at p.; Fair p. a jewel; Good as a p.; Hand p. churls' p.; Kings are out of p.; Leave off while p. good; No p. where one greets and another laughs; No p. without fool.

Play(s) (*verb*), *see also* Blind man's buff (To p. at); Bo-peep (To p.); Cat's away mice will p.; Children and fools must not p. with edged tools; Cole-prophet (To p.); Done no ill the six days (If you have) p. the seventh; Game that two can p. at; Jacks are common to all that will p.; Least in sight (To p.); Merchant with us (To p. the); Mumbudget (To p.); Noddy (To p. at); Pigs p. on organs; Wily beguiled (P.); Woodcock (To p. the); World is a stage and every man p. his part.

Play with cats, *see* Bourd with cats.

Players, *see* Lookers-on see more than p.

Playful as a kitten, As.

1732 FULLER no. 3680 Nothing's more playful than a young Cat. 1825 SCOTT *Journ.* 21 Dec. I never saw Byron so full of fun, frolic, wit, and whim; he was as playful as a kitten.

Playing with a straw before an old cat, No. (P 406)

c. 1450 HENRYSON *Mor. Fab.* 65 It is ane olde Dog . . . that thou begyles, Thou weines to draw the stra before the Cat. 1546 HEYWOOD II. viii. K2ᵛ No plaiyng with a strawe before an olde cat, Euery tryflyng toie age can not laugh at. 1641 FERGUSSON no. 519 It is ill to draw a strea before an auld cat. 1721 KELLY 180 I am o'er old a Cat, to draw a Straw before my Nose . . . I am too old to be imposed upon. A young Cat will jump at a Straw drawn before her, but not an old one. 1818 SCOTT *Rob Roy* ch. 26 He tried if Mac Vittie and Co. wad gie him siller on them . . . but they were ower auld cats to draw that strae afore them.

Playing with short daggers, It is ill. (P 405)

1546 HEYWOOD I. xii. E4ᵛ It be yll playing with short daggers, Whiche meaneth, that euery wise man staggers, . . . to be busie or bolde With his biggers or betters. c. 1594 BACON *Promus* no. 483.

Plays best (well) that wins, He. (P 404)

1555 HEYWOOD *Epigr. upon Prov.* no. 230 D5ᵛ. 1639 CLARKE 122 (well).

Plays his money, He that | ought not to value it. (M 1045)

1640 HERBERT no. 201.

Plays more than he sees, He that | forfeits his eyes to the king.　　(E 260)

1614 CAMDEN 307.　**1670** RAY 132.　**1721** KELLY 172. . . . An Excuse for overlooking an Advantage at Game.

Plays the whore for apples, She | and then bestows them upon the sick.

(W 322)

1678 RAY *Adag. Hebr.* 407 . . . This Proverb is used against those who give Almes of what they get unjustly.

Plays you as fair as if he picked your pocket, He.　　(P 445–6)

1678 RAY 79.

Plea, *see* Ill p. should be well pleaded.

Pleaing[1] at the law is like fighting through a whin[2] bush,—The harder the blows, the sairer[3] the scarts.[4]

1832 HENDERSON 39. [[1] pleading.　[2] furze. [3] sorer.　[4] scratches.]

Pleasant, *see* Pleasure is not p. unless it cost dear.

Please all parties, It is hard to.　　(P 88)

a. **1500** *15c. School Bk.* ed. W. Nelson 89 It is full harde to please all menn.　*c.* **1565** W. WAGER *Enough* D1ᵛ.　**1566** SENECA *Octavia* tr. T. Nuce A4 There is nothing harder than to please all men.　**1616** DRAXE no. 504 One can hardly please all men.　**1721** KELLY 220 . . . *Durum est omnibus placere.*　**1844** RUSKIN *Diaries* 1835–47 274 Can't please everybody.

Please the pigs.

[= please the fates; if circumstances permit.] **1702** T. BROWN *Lett. fr. Dead* Wks. (1760) II. 198 I'll have one of the wigs to carry into the country with me, and [i.e. an't] please the pigs. **1837** J. B. KER I will do it, please the pigs.　**1891** *Blackw. Mag.* June 819/1 There I'll be, please the pigs, on Thursday night.

Please, I will | what so betide.

c. **1450** *Provs. of Wysdom* 19 'I wyll please, what so betyde'. If thou wylt please, lay truthe, a syde.

Please your eye and plague your heart.

(E 244)

1655 A. BREWER *Love-sick King* III in BANG, *Materialien* B. 18, 38 She may please your eye a little . . . but vex your heart.　**1748** SMOLLETT *Rod. Rand.* xl Many a substantial farmer . . . would be glad to marry her; but she was resolved to please her eye, if she should plague her heart.　**1829** COBBETT *Adv. to Y. Men* iii. (1906) 122 'Please your eye and plague your heart' is an adage that want of beauty invented, I dare say, more than a thousand years ago. **1876** MRS. BANKS *Manch. Man* ch. 38 But I WILL marry him, mamma—I'll please my eye, if I plague my heart.

Please(s), *see also* All men will p. (He that) shall never find ease; Benefits p. when fresh; Hard to p. a knave as a knight; Meat p. not all mouths, (All); Rise betimes that would p. everybody; Take it as you will (p.).

Pleased, If you be not | put your hand in your pocket and please yourself.

(H 81)

1678 RAY 79 . . . A jeering expression to such as will not be pleased with the reasonable offers of others.　**1732** FULLER no. 2739 (content).

Pleased, *see also* Angry without a cause, . . . p. without amends; Devil is good when p.; God is better p. with adverbs than with nouns; Never well (p.), full nor fasting; Proud (p.) as Punch.

Pleases not God, When it | the saint can do little.　　(G 258)

1659 HOWELL *Span. Prov.* 1.　**1664** CODRINGTON 223.　**1670** RAY 23 . . . *Hisp.*　**1706** STEVENS s.v. Dios. When God will not the Saint cannot.

Pleasing ware is half sold.　　(W 66)

1611 COTGRAVE s.v. Chose.　**1623** PAINTER C6 Wares will bought are euermore halfe sold. **1640** HERBERT no. 14.　*c.* **1641** FERGUSSON MS. no. 942 Lyked gear is half coft [bought].　**1721** KELLY 235 Lik'd Geer is half bought. For in that Case a Man will give a little more for his Fancy.

Pleasure is not pleasant unless it cost dear.　　(P 415)

[*c.* **1590**] **1594** LODGE & GREENE *Looking-Glass* II. I. 442 Pleasures hardly got Are sweete, if once attainde.　**1592** DELAMOTHE 33.　*a.* **1597** *Pilgr. to Parn.* II (ed. Macray) 9 Ofte pleasure got with paine wee dearlie deeme.

Pleasure long expected is dear enough sold, A.　　(P 416)

1592 DELAMOTHE 27 A pleasure is bought to deare, When it is looked for to long.　**1640** HERBERT no. 868.

Pleasure refrain, Who will in time present | shall in time to come the more pleasure obtain.　　(T 342)

c. **1549** HEYWOOD I. xi. D2ᵛ.

Pleasure without pain (repentance), No. *Cf.* Nothing to be got without pain. Take a pain for a pleasure.

(P 413, 420)

c. **1526** *Dicta Sapientum* D3ᵛ Lyghtly there is no pleasure, but that vnto it some peyne is annexed.　**1539** TAVERNER I *Garden* F2ᵛ Pleasures . . . leue behynde them repentaunce and sorowe.　**1573** SANFORD 108 No good thing is without payne.　**1576** GASCOIGNE *Grief of Joy* ii. 522 Eche pleasure hathe his payne.　**1576** PETTIE I. 142 Pleasure must be purchased with the price of pain. *c.* **1590** MARLOWE *Faustus* v. ii. 16 His store of pleasure must be sauced with pain. **1591** GREENE *Wks.* Gros. ix. 256–7 Euerie bliss hath his bane, . . . euerie pleasure hath his paine. **1598** CHAPMAN *Blind Beggar of Alex.* sc. v. **1597** *Politeuphuia* 172 Pleasure bought with sorrowe, causeth repentance. **1601** SHAKES. *T.N.* II. iv. 66 There's for thy pains . . . I'll pay thy pleasure then.—Truly, sir, and pleasure will be paid, one time or another. **1611** GRUTER 181 . 2Miij Never pleasure without repentance. **1639** CLARKE 326 Never pleasure without repentance. **1670** RAY 21 (as 1611).

Pleasures of the mighty are the tears of the poor, The. *Cf.* Dainties of the great. (P 422)

1616 DRAXE no. 1509. **1670** RAY 21. **1732** FULLER NO. 4707 The Pleasures of the Rich are bought with the Tears of the Poor.

Pleasure(s), *see also* Business before p.; Diseases are the interests of ill p.; Eat at p.; Fly that p. which pains after; Follow love (p.) and it will flee; Gentleman but his p. (What's a); Look not on p. as they come; Peebles for p.; Say to p., *Gentle Eve*; Secrets (If you would know) look for them in p.; Short p. long lament; Stolen waters (p.) are sweet; Toil of a p.; Vine brings forth three grapes: the first of p.

Pledge your own health, You must not. (H 293)

1599 JONSON *Ev. Man' out of Hum.* Induction 359 There's an old rule; No pledging your own health. **1678** RAY 152.

Plentiful as blackberries, As. (B 442)

1597 SHAKES. *1 Hen. IV* II. iv. 232 If reasons were as plentiful as blackberries, I would give no man a reason upon compulsion. **1841** CARLYLE *Heroes* v (1896) 426 Though you had constitutions plentiful as blackberries. **1855** MRS. GASKELL *North and South* ch. 29 (common).

Plenty breeds pride.

1573 GASCOIGNE *Dul. Bellum Inex.* i.ᵃ 142 Plentie brings pride. **1586** G. WHETSTONE *Eng. Mirror* M5 Plentie causeth pride. **1589** PUTTENHAM *Art of Poetry* Bk. III, ch. 19. **1615** *Janua Linguarum* tr. W. Welde 19 (disdaine). **1639** CLARKE 33.

Plenty is no dainty. (P 425)

c. **1449** PECOCK *Repr.* 184 Experience wole weel schewe that plente is no deinte, and ouermyche homelines with a thing gendrith dispising toward the same thing. **1542** RECORDE *Gr. Artes* B ij Plentie is no deintie, as the common saieying is. **1546** HEYWOOD II. iv. G3ᵛ Plentie is no deintie, ye see not your own ease. **1639** CLARKE 75.

Plenty is no plague.

1616 DRAXE no. 1658 (sore). **1832** HENDERSON 85.

Plenty makes (is) dainty. (P 426)

c. **1641** FERGUSSON MS. no. 1144 (is). **1678** RAY 190. **1721** KELLY 281 . . . When People have Variety of many Meats, or Abundance of one Sort, they are nice and delicate. **1732** FULLER no. 6375.

Plenty makes poor. (P 427)

[ov. *Met.* 3. 466 *Inopem me copia fecit.*] *c.* **1594** BACON *Promus* no. 354 Inopem me copia fecit. **1596** WARNER *Albion's Eng.* IX. 52 Q6ᵛ Vs Plentie maketh poore. **1596** SPENSER *F.Q.* I. iv. 29 Whose wealth was want, whose plenty made him poor. **1621** BRATHWAIT *Omphale* in *Nat. Embas.* (1877) 269 Forced now to surfet on her store, She prou'd this true: Much plentie made her poore. **1623** FLETCHER *Lover's Progress* I. ii. Abundance makes me poor.

Plenty of good(s), He that has | shall have more. (P 424)

1546 HEYWOOD I. xi. E4. **1614** CAMDEN 307. **1639** CLARKE 125.

Plenty will take no heed, He who of | shall find default in time of need.

c. **1450** *Prov. of Wysdom* 159, 160.

Plenty, *see also* Peace makes p.

Pliable as wax, As. (W 135)

c. **1549** ERASM. *Two Dial.* tr. E. Becke 14ᵛ Take hede . . . that thou, . . . when Christ shall laye his mighty hande vpon the be as tender as waxe, that accordynge to his eternall wyll he maye frame and fashion the with his hande. **1576** LEMNIUS *Touchstone of Complexions* tr. P. Newton 98ᵛ To vyse ye pliant is as waxe. [*Ars. Poet.* 163.] **1591** SHAKES. *3 Hen. VI* II. i. 169 Clifford and . . . Northumberland . . . Have wrought the easy-melting King like wax. **1906** W. DE MORGAN *Jos. Vance* ch. 5 Dr. Thorpe . . . but as wax in my Father's hands.

Plie, *see* No reply (p.) is best.

Plough be jogging, If your | you may have meat for your horses. (P 432)

1659 HOWELL *Eng. Prov.* 11a.

Plough deep, while sluggards sleep; and you shall have corn to sell and to keep. (B 625)

1659 HOWELL *Span. Prov.* 8 Plow deep, thou shalt have bread enough. **1706** STEVENS S.V. Pan Plow deep, and you will reap abundance of Corn. **1758** FRANKLIN in Arber *E. Garner* v. 580 . . ., says *Poor* DICK.

Plough goes not well if the ploughman hold it not, The. (P 435)

1616 WITHALS 573. **1639** CLARKE 92. **1732** FULLER no. 4710.

Plough going than two cradles, Better have one. (P 430)

1580 LYLY *Euph. & his Eng.* ii. 16 Be not hastie to marry, it is better to haue one plough going, then two cradells: and more profit to haue a barne filled then a bedde. **1600** HEYWOOD *et al. 1 Edw. IV* i. 71 Thou hast two ploughs going, and nere a cradle rocking. **1609** HARWARD 116 It is better to haue a barne full then a bedd and twoo plows going then one cradle. **1732** FULLER no. 905.

Plough stand to catch a mouse, Let (Never let) the. (P 433)

a. **1628** CARMICHAELL no. 1067 Let the pleuch stand and slay a mouse. **1678** RAY 265. **1710** PALMER 5 (Never let the Plough). **1721** KELLY 234 . . . and slay a Mouse. Lay aside, for a little, that Business that you are so earnest upon; and take a little Divertisement: Master *Palmer*[1] has one. . . . Never let the Plough stand to slay a Mouse . . . to wit, that we be not taken off from our proper Business, by every obvious Divertisement. [[1] S. Palmer, author of *Moral Essays*, 1710.]

Plough the sands, To. *Cf.* Sowing on the sand. (S 89)

[OVID *ex Ponto* 4. 2. 16 *Siccum sterili vomere litus aro.* ERASM. *Ad. Arare litus.*] **1548** COOPER s.v. Aro Arare littus, a prouerbe signifyng to labour in vayne. **1576** PETTIE ii. 95 So that I plough the barren rocks, and set my share into the shore of the sea. **1585** J. PRIME *Sermon at St. Mary's Oxon* A7 What speak I to deaf ears, which is, but to powder the flint, to plow the rocke and sow the sand, and so to loose both salt, seed, and labour? **1590** GREENE *Never too Late* Wks. Gros. viii. 166 With sweating browes I long haue plowde the sands . . . Repent hath sent me home with emptie hands. **1605** SYLVESTER (1621) 19 On thanklesse furrows of a fruitlesse sand Their seed and labour lose, with heedless hand. **1647** JER. TAYLOR *Lib. Proph.* Ep. Ded. 5 That I had as good plow the Sands, or till the Aire, as perswade such Doctrines, which destroy mens interests. **1775** WESLEY *Jrnl.* 15 Nov. I preached at Dorking. But still I fear we are ploughing upon the sand: we see no fruit of our labours.

Plough would thrive, He that by the | himself must either hold or drive. (P 431)

[*Cf.* **1557** T. TUSSER B2 If thou wilt thriue, loke thy selfe to thy barne.] **1678** RAY 191. **1758** FRANKLIN *Way to Wealth* (Crowell) 18 We must . . . not trust too much to others; for, . . .

Plough with an ox and an ass together, To. (O 109)

[DEUT. xxii. 10.] *c.* **1540** POLYDORE VERGIL *Eng. Hist.* ed. Ellis Camden Soc. nos. 29 and 46, 72 The same could be accompted nothing els but (as the old prouerbe is) to till the grounde with an oxe and an asse. **1813** RAY 212 . . . *i.e.* To sort things ill.

Plough with any one's heifer (ox, calf), To. (H 395)

[JUDGES xiv. 18.] **1584** G.B. *Beware the Cat* Ded. I doubt whether M. Stremer will be contented that other men ploughe with his oxen. **1632** MASSINGER *City Madam* II. iii I will undertake To find the north passage to the Indies sooner Than plough with your proud heifer. **1697** W. POPE *Seth* [*Ward*] 40 Mr. Busby . . . plow'd with the same Heifers.

Plough with such oxen as he has, A man must. (O 112)

1678 RAY 191. **1732** FULLER no. 5968.

Plough (*noun*), *see also* Counts all costs (He that) will ne'er put p.; Counts all the pins in the p. will never yoke (He that); Father to bough, son to p.; Lippens to lent p. his land will lie ley; Pen and ink is wit's p.; Scythe cuts and p. rives (Where), no more fairies; Speed the p.; Well worth aw, it makes p. draw.

Plough (*verb*), *see also* Whistling at going to p. (Belongs more than).

Plover, *see* Partridge (p.) (As plump as a).

Plowden, *see* Case is altered.

Pluck not where you never planted. (P 438)

1639 CLARKE 270.

Pluck the grass to know where the wind sits, To. (G 422)

[= to interpret the signs of the times.] **1596–7** SHAKES. *M.V.* I. i. 18 I should be still Plucking the grass to know where sits the wind. *a.* **1670** HACKET *Abp. Williams* II (1692) 16 No Man could pluck the Grass better, to know where the Wind sat; no Man could spie sooner from whence a Mischief did rise.

Pluck(s), *see also* Crow to p. with one; Pick (p.) a rose; Sin p. on sin.

Plum year a dumb year, A. *Cf.* Pear year, etc., Cherry year, etc. (Y 7)

1664 *Poor Robin Almanac*, quoted in LEAN, i. 419 A cherry year's a merry year, a sloe year's a woe year, a haw year's a braw year, an apple year's a drappin' year, a plum year's a glum year. **1678** RAY 52. **1732** FULLER no. 6139.

Plum, *see also* Black p. sweet as white; Bloom is off the peach (p.).

Plum-tree, *see* Higher the p. riper the plum; Knave is in a p. (When).

Plump, *see* Partridge (As p. as a).

Pluto, *see* Helmet of P.

Plutus, *see* Fearful as P.

Plymouth cloak, A. (P 443–4)

[= a cudgel or staff carried by one who walked without cloak, and thus facetiously assumed to take the place of the latter.] **1608** DEKKER *2 Hon. Whore* III. ii. 32 Shall I walke in a Plimouth Cloake, (that's to say) like a rogue, in my hose and doublet, and a crabtree cudgell in my hand? **1662** FULLER Devon 248 . . . That is, a Cane or a Staffe . . . Many a man . . . comming home from far Voiages, may chance to land here, and . . . [be] unable . . . to recruit himself with Cloaths.

Plymouth was a vuzzy[1] down, When | Plympton was a borough town.

1850 *N. & Q.* 1st Ser. II. 511. **1911** W. CROSSING *Folk Rhymes of Devon* 12 . . . Plympton is more ancient than Plymouth, although it had not become a 'borough town', until long after the latter had sprung into existence. [[1] furzy.]

Plympton, *see* Plymouth.

Poacher, *see* Old p. best keeper.

Pocket (up) an injury, To. (I 70)

[= to take an affront without showing resentment.] **1589** GREENE *Span. Masquerado* Wks. Gros. v. 273 Thus the great Generall of Spaine was content to pockette vppe this Dishonour to saue his life. [*c.* 1591] **1592** *Arden of Fev.* I. i. 309 But rather then I pocket vp this wrong—. **1596** SHAKES. *K.J.* III. i. 200 Well ruffian, I must pocket up these wrongs. **1597** *Id. I Hen. IV* III. iii. 163 And yet you will stand to it, you will not pocket up wrong. **1599** *Id. Hen. V* III. ii. 47 They would have me as familiar with men's pockets as their gloves or their handkerchers . . ., it is plain pocketing up of wrongs. **1622** MABBE tr. *Aleman's Guzman d'Alf.* I. 214 If he . . . pocket a wrong, and hold his hands, he is a coward. **1769** *Polit. Register* v. 229 Your grace would have pockctcd the affront. **1826** SCOTT *Woodstock* ch. 23 The bravest man sacrifices nothing by pocketing a little wrong.

Pocket(s), *see also* Devil dances in empty p.; Horns in p. (Better put); Last garment is made without p.; Line one's p.; Money burns in your p.; Pleased (If not) put hand in p.; Pun (He that would make) would pick p.

Poet in adversity can hardly make verses, A. (P 450)

1579 SPENSER *Sh. Cal.* Oct. l. 100 The vaunted verse a vacant head demaundes, Ne wont with crabbed care the Muses dwell. **1616** DRAXE no. 53.

Poet is born not made, A. (P 451)

[L. *Poeta nascitur, non fit.*] **1581** GUAZZO i. 182 A right Gentleman is not borne as the Poet, but made as the Oratour. *c.* **1581** SIDNEY *Apologie* Arb. 62 Therefore is it an old prouerbe, *Orator fit; Poeta nascitur.* **1620** SHELTON *Quix.* II. xvi. ii. 292 It is a true opinion that a poet is born so; . . . a poet is naturally born a poet from his mother's womb. **1624** J. HEWES *Perfect Survey* G3 No man is born an Artist. **1662** FULLER *Warw.* 126 Shakespeare . . . was an eminent instance of the truth of that Rule, 'Poeta non fit sed nascitur' (one is not made but born a Poet). **1780** J. WESLEY *Wks.* xiv. 341. **1827** HARE *Gues. at Truth* (1873) 194 It is impossible to devise any scheme of education . . . for promoting the development of poetical genius. . . . *Poeta nascitur, non fit.*

Poets, *see* Painters and p. have leave to lie.

Poetic licence.

1563 FOXE *A. and M.* (1631 ed., ii. 273a) You will excuse your selfe, per licentiam Poeticam, after the priuiledge of Poets and painters. **1591** ARIOSTO *Orl. Fur.* Harington III. 11 [*margin*] This is poeticall licence to faine it [Merlin's tomb] to be in France, for it is in Wales. **1592** NASHE *Strange News* i. 307 Poetica Licentia. **1606** *Sir Giles Goosecap* K2 Thats Poetica licentia, the verse wood haue binne too long, and I had put in the third. **1609** DANIEL *Civil Wars* Ded. [I have used] that poeticall licence, of framing speaches to the persons of men according to their occasions; as C. Salustius and T. Livius . . . haue . . . done before me.

Poetical justice.

1678 T. RYMER *Tragedies of the last Age* 23 If they had refused to succeed their Father, . . . then no Poetical Justice could have touch'd them. **1679** DRYDEN *Troilus and Cres.* Pref. We are glad when we behold his Crimes punish'd, and that Poetical Justice is done upon him. **1711** *Spectator* Apr. 16, no. 40 *King Lear* is an admirable tragedy of the same kind [in which calamities are not relieved], as Shakespeare wrote it; but as it is reformed according to the Chymerical Notion of Poetical Justice, in my humble opinion it has lost half its beauty. **1712** *Ibid.* 28 Nov. no. 548 That late invented term called *Poetical Justice.* **1765** JOHNSON *Observ. on Plays of Shakesp.* Hamlet. The poet is accused of having shown little regard to poetical justice. **1938** E. I. FRIPP *Shakesp. Man and Artist* ii. 1606 Notwithstanding painful features, it [*K. Lear*] is comedy in the sense that 'poetic justice' is done.

Poind[1] for debt but not for kindness, We can.

1721 KELLY 349 . . . If our Friends will not be kind to us, we have no Remedy at Law. [[1] distrain.]

Poind, *see also* No man may p. for unkindness.

Point(s), *see* Knows one p. more than devil; Needles' p., (To stand on); Potatoes and p.; Thorn comes forth with p. forward.

Poison, One drop of | infects the whole tun of wine.

c. **1175** *Old Eng. Homilies* (Morris) Ser. 1. 23 A lutel ater[1] bitteret muchel swete. **1579** LYLY *Euph.* i. 189 One droppe of poyson infecteth the whole tunne of Wine. [[1] venom.]

Poison is poison though it comes in a golden cup. (P 458)

[1562] 1565 SACKVILLE & NORTON *Gorboduc* II. ii *Chorus* Loe, thus it is, poyson in golde to take, And holsome drinke in homely cuppe forsake. 1566–8 R. WILMOT, etc. *Gismond of Salern* III *Chorus* 41 He geues poison so to drink in gold. 1576 PETTIE ii. 80 As in fair painted pots poison oft is put. 1579 LYLY *Euph.* i. 202 Doe we not commonly see that in paynted pottes is hidden the deadlyest poyson? 1584 RICH *Don Simonides* Part ii. O3 The painted pot [shrowdeth] the deuowrying poyson. 1584 W. WARNER *Pan his Syrinx* E3 Out of golden cuppes you will drinke poisoned draughts. 1587 GREENE *Wks.* Gros. iii. 206 Fond were that person that would think wel of him that profereth poyson though in a golden pot. 1600 N. BRETON *Melancholique Humours* (Harrison) 36 Poys'ned broth, in silver dishes. 1616 DRAXE no. 659 In golden pottes are hidden the most deadly poyson.

Poison, *see also* Bee sucks honey (Where), spider sucks p.; Bites on every weed (He that) must light on p.; Hate like p.; Horn spoon holds no p.; Meat (One man's), is another's p.; One p. drives out another; Unsound minds ... if you feed, you p.

Poke a man's fire, You may | after you've known him seven years, but not before.

1902–4 LEAN IV. 204 ... You must be a seven years' friend of the house before you dare stir the fire. [*N. & Q.*]

Poke savour of the herring, It is kindly[1] that the. (P 460)

1611 COTGRAVE s.v. Harenc The poke still of the Herring smells. *a.* 1628 CARMICHAELL no. 872 It is kyndlie the poke saure[2] of the hearin. 1641 FERGUSSON no. 494. 1721 KELLY 197 ... It is no uncommon Thing to see Children take after their Parents. Always meant in ill Things. [[1] natural. [2] savour, smell.]

Poke(s), *see also* Nichils in nine p.; Toom p. will strive; Which way to London? A p. full of plums.

Poker, *see* Stiff as a p.

Polecat, *see* Stink like a p.

Policy prevents chance (goes beyond strength). (P 462)

a. 1547 REDFORD *Wit and Science* l. 1001 Where strength lacketh policye supplieth. 1548 HALL (1809, 23) Policie preuenteth chance. *c.* 1590 G. HARVEY *Marginalia* (1913) 100 A lytle pollicy præuaileth when a great deale of strength fayleth. [1598] 1616 HAUGHTON *Englishmen for my Money* l. 2212 It is not Force, but Pollicie must serue. 1706 STEVENS s.v. Acial Policy goes beyond Strength [English].

Policy, *see also* Honesty is best p.; Ostrich p.

Polish, *see* Elbow grease gives best p.

Politeness, *see* Loses anything by p. (One never).

Pollutes, *see* Thrush when he p. bough.

Pomfret, *see* Sure as a louse in P.

Pomp the earth covers, All our. (P 464)

1563 GOOGE *Eclog. Epit. and Sonn.*, Arb. 98 All the pompe and Pryde, the Bodie tournes to dust. 1640 HERBERT no. 716. 1666 TORRIANO *It. Prov.* 285 no. 11 All our pomps, at the last the earth doth cover.

Pompey, *see* Paws off, P.

Pompous provision comes not alway of gluttony, but of pride some time. (P 617)

c. 1549 HEYWOOD II. vii. 14.

Pond(s), *see* Breams in his p. ... friend welcome; Courts (It is at) as in p.

Pons asinorum.

[= bridge of asses. A humorous name for the 5th prop. of the 1st bk. of Euclid, found difficult by beginners, hence used allusively.] 1751 SMOLLETT *Per. Pic.* I. xviii. 130 Peregrine ... began to read Euclid ... but he had scarcely advanced beyond the *Pons Asinorum* when his ardor abated. 1845 FORD *Handbk. Spain* I. 217/2 This bridge was the *pons asinorum* of the French, which English never suffered them to cross. 1870 *Eng. Mech.* 4 Feb. 502/1 He knows the operation ... to be the *pons asinorum* of incompetent workmen.

Pontifical fellow, He is a.

1528 TYNDALE *Obed. Chrn. Man* P.S. 304 We say, ... 'He is a pontifical fellow'; that is, proud and stately.

Pony, *see* Shank's mare (p.).

Pool(s), *see* Fish is cast away; Standing p. gather filth.

Poole was a fish-pool, and the men of Poole fish, If | there'd be a pool for the devil and fish for his dish.

1787 GROSE (*Dorset*) 169 ... This satyrical distich was written a long time ago. Pool is, at present, a respectable place, and has in it several rich merchants trading to Newfoundland.

Poor and liberal, rich and covetous. (P 473)

1631 MABBE *Celestina* T.T. 212 When I was poore, then was I liberall; when I was rich, then was I covetous. 1640 HERBERT no. 339.

Poor and peart like the parson's pig.

1887 T. DARLINGTON *S. Cheshire Folk Speech* E.D.S. 289. 1903 *Eng. Dialect Dict.* IV. 446 *Cheshire* ... probably refers to the times when the parson collected his tithe in kind. The pig reserved for him, being a small one and not overfed, was consequently brisk and active.

Poor and proud, fie, fie. (P 474)

[Apocrypha ECCLES. xxv. 2 Three sorts of men my soul hateth . . . a poor man that is proud.] **1558** J. FISHER *Three Dialogues* D4 Thre thynges saith Syrach my soule dooth hate . . . A poore man proude, a ryche man a lyer, An olde man a foole. **1581** GUAZZO i. 172 This saying, that three sortes of men are odious . . . a poore man proude, a riche man a lyar, and an old man a foole. **1586** WILLIAM MARQUESS OF WINCHESTER *The Lord Marquess' Idleness* 52 It is a miserie to be poore and proud. **1584** R. WILSON *Three Ladies of London* Hazl.-Dods. vi. 458 I need not tell thee they are poor and proud. **1594** LYLY *Mother B.* I. iii. 17 Your minxe had no better grandfather than a Tailer, who (as I have heard) was poore and proud. **1601** SHAKES. *T.N.* III. i. 124 O world! how apt the poor are to be proud. **1611** GRUTER 182. **1614** CAMDEN 311. *c.* **1620** *Roxburghe Ballads* ii. 580 B.S. The saying old hath oft beene told, It plain doth verifie, 'Poore and proud, still tayler-like.' **1639** CLARKE 32.

Poor (Hungry) as a church mouse (rat), As. (C 382)

1659 HOWELL *Eng. Prov.* 13b (hungry). **1670** RAY 205 (hungry). **1672** COREY *Gen. Enemies* I. 10 All that live with him Are as poor as Church-Rats. **1703** WARD *Writings* ii. 120 As poor as rats. **1731** *Pol. Ballads* (1860) II. 222 The owner, 'tis said, was once poor as church-mouse. **1833** MARRYAT *P. Simple* ch. 31 He's as poor as a rat. **1848** THACKERAY *Vanity F.* ch. 23 The young couple are as poor as church mice. **1857** DICKENS *Little Dorr.* ch. 33 'As poor as Thingummy'. 'A church mouse', Mrs. Merdle suggested with a smile. **1913** 29 Jan. D. H. LAWRENCE *Lett.* i. 181.

Poor as Job, As. (J 60)

c. **1300** BRUNNE *Chron.* 323 As Job þe pouere man. *c.* **1390** GOWER *Conf. Amantis* v. l. 2505 To ben for evere til I deie As pooere as Job, and loveles. **1530** PALSGRAVE 620a As bare as euer was Job. *Ibid.* 628a. **1553** T. WILSON *Arte of Rhet.* (1580) 210 Tushe, thou art as poore as Iob. **1598** SHAKES. *2 Hen. IV* I. ii. 119 I am as poor as Job, my lord. **1600–1** *Id. M.W.W.* V. v. 148 One that is as slanderous as Satan?—And as poor as Job? **1661** *Oxinden & Peyton Letters 1642–1670* ed. D. Gardiner 252 Job and Lazarus (Names poore to a proverb). **1822** BYRON *Werner* I. i. 401 He's poor as Job, and not so patient.

Poor beauty finds more lovers than husbands, A. (B 178)

1612 WEBSTER *White Devil* V. i. 211 Alas! poore maides get more lovers then husbands. **1640** HERBERT no. 481.

Poor but honest.

[**1553**] **1566–7** UDALL *Ralph Roister D.* III. iv. 2 May not folks be honest, pray you, though they be poore? *a.* **1557** *Wealth and Health* l. 488 Ye shal finde vs pore but true we cannot be. *a.* **1577** *Misogonus* III. i. 253 Though wear poore yet wear true and trusty. *c.* **1595** BACON *Promus* no. 120 Poore and trew. **1640** *Verney Memoirs* (1892) i. 179 Beleeve the proverbe of me, though poore yet honest. **1654** E. GAYTON *Festivous Notes on Don Quixote* 92.

Poor dog that does not know 'Come out', It is a.

1830 FORBY 428 . . . *i.e.* He is foolish, who does not know when to desist.

Poor dog that is not worth the whistling, It is a. (D 488)

1546 HEYWOOD I. xi. E3 It is, as I haue lerned in lystnyng, A poore dogge, that is not worth the whistlyng. **1603** BRETON *Packet Mad Lett.* Wks. (1879) II. 19 There are more maids than Maulkin, and I count myself worth the whistling after. **1605** SHAKES. *K.L.* IV. ii. 29 I have been worth the whistle. **1614** CAMDEN 303. **1738** SWIFT Dial. I. E.L. 272 Because, miss, you never asked me: and 'tis an ill dog that's not worth whistling for.

Poor folk (men) are fain of little. (M 356)

a. **1628** CARMICHAELL no. 1256 Pure men ar fain of richt nocht. **1641** FERGUSSON no. 687 (little thing). **1721** KELLY 279 . . . Because they have no hopes to get much.

Poor folk fare the best. (F 416)

1639 CLARKE 205.

Poor folks are glad of porridge (pottage). (F 423)

1576 U. FULWELL *Ars Adulandi* K3 Poore men are pleasde with potage ay til better vittailes fall. **1639** CLARKE 225. **1659** HOWELL *Eng. Prov.* 4a (must be glad of pottage).

Poor folks' friends soon misken them.

c. **1386** CHAUCER *Man of Law's* Prol. l. 121 If thou be povre, thy brother hateth thee, And alle thy freendes fleen fro thee, allas! **1721** KELLY 279.

Poor heart that never rejoices, It is a.

1833 MARRYAT *Peter Simple* ch. 5 'Well', continued he, 'it's a poor heart that never rejoiceth'. He then poured out half a tumbler of rum. **1843–4** DICKENS *M. Chuz.* ch. 5 'Let us be merry.' Here he took a captain's biscuit. 'It is a poor heart that never rejoices.'

Poor hen that can't scrat[1] for one chick, It is a.

1721 KELLY 181 It is a sary Hen that cannot scrape to one Burd. Spoken of them that have but one Child to provide for. **1882** E. L. CHAMBERLAIN *West Worc. Wds.* E.D.S. 39. [1 scratch.]

Poor indeed that can promise nothing, He is. (N 261)

1616 DRAXE no. 2498. **1639** CLARKE 142. **1670** RAY 132. **1732** FULLER no. 1941.

Poor kin (family) that has neither whore nor thief in it, It is a. (F 49)

1566 L. WAGER *Mary Magd.* D1 It is a stock (they say) right honorable and good, That hath neither thefe nor whore in their blood. ₁ **1639** CLARKE 160 'Tis a good kin, that none doe amiss in. **1659** HOWELL *Span. Prov.* 1 There's no family but there's a Whore or a Knave of it. **1721** KELLY 186 . . . Spoken when some of our Relations, who have done an ill Thing, is cast in our Teeth.

Poor man gets a poor marriage, A.

1609 HARWARD 112 Poore man poorely wived. *c.* **1641** FERGUSSON MS. no. 172. **1732** FULLER no. 353.

Poor man is aye put to the worst, The.

[OVID *Fast.* I. 218 *Pauper ubique iacet.* Everywhere the poor man is despised.] **1721** KELLY 314.

Poor man pays for all, The. (M 357)

c. **1561** *Poor Man Pays* in *Roxb. Bal.* ii. 334, l. 4 And, waking from my sleepe, I ⋮My dreame to mind did call: Me thought I saw before mine eyes, How poore men payes for all. *a.* **1630** Title of old ballad, entered at Stationers' Hall 12 Mar. 1630. **1639** CLARKE 99 The poore must pay for all. **1721** KELLY 323.

Poor man turns his cake, The | and another comes and takes it away.
  (M 358)

1678 RAY *Adag. Hebr.* 402.

Poor man wants some things, a covetous man all things, A. *Cf.* Poverty wants many things. (M 359)

[HORACE *Odes* Bk. III, xvi, l. 42 *Multa petentibus desunt multa.*] *c.* **1560** T. LUPTON *Money* l. 829 *Inopiae pauca desunt, auaritiae omnia,* saith Horacius: Fewe things to the needie but all wanting to the couetous. **1678** R. L.'ESTRANGE *Mor.* III. ii. 467 The Poor Man wants many things, but the Covetous Man wants All.

Poor man's cow dies, a rich man's child, A. (M 484)

1640 HERBERT no. 869.

Poor man's shilling is but a penny, The.

1721 KELLY 337 . . . Because he must buy everything at the dearest Rate.

Poor man's table is soon spread, A.
  (M 485)

1616 DRAXE no. 1465. **1670** RAY 132.

Poor man's tale cannot be heard, A.
  (M 486)

[1547–53] *c.* **1565** WEVER *Lusty Juventus* C3 A poore mans tale cannot now be heard As in

tymes past. **1616** DRAXE no. 1691. *c.* **1640** *Berkeley MSS.* 31, no. 57 A poare mans tale may now bee heard; vizt when none speakes the meanest may (Gloucest.).

Poor men go to heaven as soon as rich.
  (M 576)

1594 *Knack to Know an Honest Man* l. 1022 Poore mens soules were made for heauen, and the rich for hell. **1639** CLARKE 98.

Poor men have no souls. (M 577)

1555 HEYWOOD *Epigr. upon Prov.* no. 167 Poore men haue no soules, no but poore men had soules: Tyl the dronken soules, drownd theyr soules in ale boules. **1641** FERGUSSON no. 696 Poore men they say hes na souls. **1721** KELLY 281 . . . This is an old Proverb in the Time of Pop'ry when the Poor had no Masses, or *Dirige's* said for them.

Poor men seek meat for their stomach; rich men stomach for their meat.
  (M 366)

1586 W. WARNER *Albion's Eng.* ed. Chalmers v. 27: *Poems* 571 The rich for meate seeke stomackes, and the poore for stomackes meate. **1595** A. COPLEY *Wits, Fits and Fancies* (1614) 105 (want meat). **1659** HOWELL *Eng. Prov.* 10b The difference twixt the poor man and the rich, is that the one walketh to gett meat for his stomack, the other to get a stomack to his meat. **1678** RAY 79 (as 1659). **1732** FULLER no. 3895. **1862** HISLOP 161.

Poor man (men), *see also* Get the p. m.'s answer; Hope is p. m.'s bread; Make a p. m. a knight (Little of God's might to); Nothing between p. m. and rich but . . . ill year; Put the p. m.'s penny and the rich man's in ae purse.

Poor suffer all the wrong, The. (P 469)

c. **1532** *Tales* no. 22 The ryche hath his wyll, the pore taketh wronge. **1616** DRAXE no. 2367. **1639** CLARKE 99 Rich men use the poore as they list.

Poor that God hates, He is. (G 231)

1611 COTGRAVE s.v. Haï Poore is the man whom God abhorres. **1615** M. R. *A President for Young Pen-Men* C4 He is poore whom God hateth. **1616** DRAXE no. 1688. **1641** FERGUSSON no. 323. **1721** KELLY 138 . . . A surlish Return to them who, tauntingly, call us Poor.

Poor that has little, He is not | but he that desires much. (L 346)

1547 W. BALDWIN *Treatise Moral Philosophy* (1550) K7 Not he that hath lyttle, but he that desyreth muche is poore. **1579** *Proverbs of Sir Janus Lopez de Mendoza* tr. B. Googe 94^v Seneca saith, in an Epistle to Lucilius, that he is not poore that hath but a little, but he that desireth muche. **1595** DANIEL *Civil Wars* Bk. iii. Wks. Gros. ii. 125. **1640** QUARLES *Enchiridion* II. xvii. **1640** HERBERT no. 309. **1732** FULLER no. 1937 (craves).

Poor, *see also* Alms never make p.; Charity and pride feed the p.; Every one is weary, the p. in seeking; Fools live p. to die rich; Giving much to the p. does enrich; God help the p.; God's p. and devil's p.; Hard task to be p. and leal; Loves the p. but cannot abide beggars; Much money makes country p.; No man lives so p. as he was born; Pleasures of mighty, tears of p.; Plenty makes p.; Reasons of p. weigh not; Rich man may dine when he will, the p. man when he may; Rich men are stewards of p.; Serves the p. with thump on the back; Vine p. (Make the).

Pope by voice, a king by birth (nature), an emperor by force (power), A. (P 477)

1642 TORRIANO 83.   **1659** HOWELL *New Sayings* 9a.

Pope, If you would be | you must think of nothing else.

[*Cf.* **1659** N. R. 68 If thou mindest to be Pope, thou must have him to write in thy forehead.] **1707** MAPLETOFT 53.

Pope, *see also* King and p., lion and wolf; Know no more than P.; Sit in Rome and strive against P. (Hard to); Turk and the P. (Here is a talk of).

Popham, *see* Horner.

Porpoise plays before a storm, The. (P 483)

1577 GRANGE *Gold. Aphroditis* A4ᵛ I seeme to prognosticate thereby (as doth the Dolphin) that some storme or tempest approcheth at hande.   **1593** NASHE *Christ's Tears* ii. 9 Give mee leaue, with the sportiue Sea Porposes, pre-ludiatelie a little to play before the storme of my Teares.   **1605** CHAPMAN, JONSON, MARSTON *Eastw. Ho* III. ii (1874) 469 There was a porpoise even now seen at London-bridge, which is always the messenger of tempests, he says.   **1608** SHAKES. *P.* II. i. 21 Alas, poor souls! It grieved my heart to hear what pitiful cries they made to us to help them . . .—Nay, master, said not I as much when I saw the porpas, how he bounc'd and tumbled?   *a.* **1613** OVERBURY *Newes* Wks. (1890) 198 That the wantonnesse of a peaceable common-wealth, is like the play-ing of the porpesse before a storme.   **1623** WEBSTER *Duch. Malfi* III. iii. Merm. 188 That cardinal . . . lifts up's nose, like a foul porpoise before a storm.

Porridge, *see* Eats most p. (He that); Keep your breath to cool p.; Old pottage (p.) is sooner heated; Part with the crock as the p. (As soon); Poor folks are glad of p. *See also under* Pottage.

Port, *see* Any p. in a storm; Sailors have a p. in every storm; Worse the passage, more welcome p.

Portion, *see* Best bred have best p.; Better a p. in a wife; Fair face half a p.

Portuguese, *see* Bad Spaniard makes good P.; Three Moors to a P.

Positive, One | weighs more than twenty negatives. (P 486)

1689 PRIOR *Epist. to F. Shepherd* 131 Wks. (1858) 21 One single positive weighs more, You know, than negatives a score.

Possesses, *see* Rich that p. much, (He is not).

Possession is nine (*formerly* eleven) points of the law. (P 487)

a. **1596** *Edw. III* III. i. 109 Tis you are in posses-sion of the Crowne, And thats the surest poynt of all the Law.   **1602** R. CAREW *Survey of Corn-wall* (1769 ed. 38ᵛ) 11 poynts of the Lawe.   **1616** DRAXE no. 1692 (in).   **1623** CAMDEN 275 (eleven). **1639** FULLER *Holy War* V. xxix (1840) 297 At this day the Turk hath eleven points of the law in Jerusalem, I mean possession.   **1659** *John Ireton's Oration* 5 (nine points).   **1678** RAY 191 . . . eleven . . . and they say there are but twelve. **1712** ARBUTHNOT *John Bull* IV. iii Possession . . . would make it much surer. They say 'it is eleven points of the Law!'   **1796** EDGEWORTH *Par. Asst., Simple S.* (1903) 89 'Pardon me', said the attorney, . . . 'possession . . . is nine points of the law'.   **1880** BLACKMORE *Mary Aner.* ch. 1 There is a coarse axiom . . . that possession is nine points of the law. We have possession.

Possession is worth an ill charter. (P 488)

a. **1628** CARMICHAELL no. 1245.   **1641** FERGUSSON no. 692.   **1721** KELLY 278 . . . The Law supposes the Person in Possession to be the right Owner, till the contrary appear.

Possession, *see also* Change a cottage in p.; Fast and loose is no p.; Prospect is often better than p.

Posset-drink, *see* Twittle twattle, drink up your p.

Post soon painted, A rotten.

1599 MARSTON *Scourge of Villainy* X. 62.   **1624** T. BREWER *A Knot of Fools* B1ᵛ.   **1654** T. HALL *Loathsomeness of Long Haire* (cited *P. Stubbes* ed. New Sh. Soc. i. 255).

Post, As good speak (tell it) to the. *Cf.* Deaf as a post. (P 491)

1530 TYNDALE *Answer to More* P.S. 11 It is nothing else but to say Pater noster unto a post. **1534** *Id. Parable of Wicked Mammon* Joy's *Apol.* ed. Arber X. Some of them . . . so doted in that folye that it were as good perswade a post as to plucke that madnes oute of their braynes. *a.* **1535** T. MORE *Dial.* (*Library* 1933–4, 441 n) Bk. IV, ch. 18.   **1540** PALSGRAVE *Acolastus* 47 He were as good to tell his tale to a poste.   **1564** *Pleasant Dial. of Cap and Head* (1565 ed., (3)) I were as good tell it to the post.   **1581** J. CARTIGNY *Voyage of the Wandering Knight* tr. W. Goodyear F2 She [Virtue] preached to a post, and Folly . . . did mocke and deride her.   **1639** CLARKE 301.

Post, As good trust to a rotten. (P 492)

1609 J. WYBARNE *New Age of Old Names* 36 In the end it prooueth a rotten poste. **1616** DRAXE no. 2257. **1639** CLARKE 248.

Post of honour is the post of danger, The. (The more danger, the more honour.) (D 35)

c. **1534** BERNERS *Huon* E.E.T.S. 20, 56 Where as lyeth grete parelles there lieth grete honour. **1591** SHAKES. *3 Hen. VI* V. i. 70 The harder match'd, the greater victory! **1592** DELAMOTHE 41 Through perils, credit ought to be sought. [1592] **1596** *Edw. III* III. i. 31 But all the mightier that their number is, The greater glory reapes the victory. **1599** SHAKES. *Hen. V* IV. iii. 20 If we are mark'd to die, we are enow To do our country loss; and if we live, The fewer men, the greater share of honour. **1613** T. HEYWOOD *Brazen Age* (1874 ed. iii, 211) The greater dangers threaten The greater is his honour that breaks through. **1624** J. FLETCHER *Rule a Wife* IV. iv. Wks. (1905) III. 209 For I remembered your old Roman axiom, The more the danger, still the more the honour. **1732** FULLER no. 4658 The more Danger, the more Honour. **1832** HENDERSON 33. **1905** *Brit. Wkly.* 14 Dec. The Chancellorship of the Exchequer . . . is pre-eminently the post of danger, and therefore the post of honour in the new Government.

Post, *see also* Deaf (mute, silent) as a p.; Kiss the p.; Knight of p.; Lame p. brings truest news; Letter stay for the p. (Let your); Pillar to p.; Ride p. for puddings.

Posterity, *see* Plants a tree plants for p., (He that).

Postern door makes thief and whore, The. *Cf.* Back door. (D 560)

1573 SANFORD 107 The posterne dore destroyeth the house. **1611** DAVIES no. 71. **1616** DRAXE no. 2117 The backe doore maketh theeues. **1623** CAMDEN 279. **1732** FULLER no. 6176.

Postscript, *see* Gist of lady's letter in p.

Pot broken, Your | seems better than my whole one. (P 507)

1640 HERBERT no. 270.

Pot's full, When the | it will boil over.

1721 KELLY 357.

Pot that belongs to many is ill stirred and worse boiled, A.

1706 STEVENS s.v. Olla. **1732** FULLER no. 360.

Pot-side, *see* Black as a p. (pan).

Pot, *see also* Boil the p. (Make the p. boil); Boiling p., (To a) flies come not; Boils his p. with chips; Comes last to the p. (He that) soonest wroth; Earthen p. must keep clear brass kettle; Fair words will not make p. play;

Go not for every thirst to p.; Go to p.; God's blessing make my p. boil (Will); Good broth in old p.; Honey in his p. (He that has no); Ill weed mars a whole p.; Janiveer freeze p.; Keep the p. boiling; Kettle calls p. black-brows; Lends his p.; Little p. soon hot; Money makes the p. boil; Nose into everything, (every man's p.), (To put one's); Peas, (Who has many) may put more in the p.; Pitcher (P.) goes so often to the well; Touch p. touch penny; Watched p. never boils; Weak goes to p.; Wife that never cries for ladle till p. runs over; Year is (As the), your p. must seethe.

Potatoes and point.

1825 J. NEAL *Bro. Jonathan* I. 75 The potatoes and point of an Irish peasant. **1890** W. F. BUTLER *Napier* 81 The boasted 'wealth of England', he scornfully remarks, 'is to her vast poor and pauper classes as the potato and the "pint" of the Irish labourer'. **1910** P. W. JOYCE *Eng. as We Speak* 247 You will sometimes read . . . that each person, before taking a bite, *pointed* the potato at a salt herring or a bit of bacon hanging in front of the chimney: but this . . . never occurred in real life.

Potent, *see* Beauty is p.

Potsherd, *see* Dived deep . . . and brought up p.

Pottage of a stool-foot, With cost one may make. (C 672)

1678 RAY 70.

Pottage pot, *see* Chip in a p. p. (Like a).

Pottage, *see also* Dish while I shed my p., (Hold the); Drink in your p., cough in your grave; Free of another man's cost (p.), (To be); Herb-John (Without) no good p.; Know by your nose what p. you love; Know him not should I meet him in my p. dish; Old p. is sooner heated; Prettiness makes no p.; Rain p. (If it should), he would want dish; Scald not your lips in another's p. See also under Porridge.

Potter envies another, One. (P 514)

[HESIOD *Works & Days* 25 Καὶ κεραμεὺς κεραμεῖ κοτέει. L. *Figulus figulo invidet, faber fabro.* The potter envies the potter, the smith the smith.] **1539** TAVERNER 8ᵛ The potter enuyeth the potter, the smythe the smythe. **1581** C. THIMELTHORPE *Short Inventory* B2ᵛ Ther is an old prouerb Figulus Figulo inuidit, one Potter hateth an other. **1633** D. DYKE *Wks. Philemon* 23 In the most men the proverb is verified, *Figulus figulo invidet*; One potter envies another. But far be this envy from all Christians of what calling soever, especially of the ministry. **1891** A. LANG *Ess. in Little* 105 Artists are a jealous race. 'Potter hates potter, and poet hates poet', as Hesiod said so long ago.

Pouch, *see* Hand twice to bonnet for once to p.

Poultry, *see* Women, priests, and p. have never enough.

Pound of butter among a kennel of hounds? What is a. (P 519)

1666 TORRIANO *Prov. Phr.* s.v. Torso. **1670** RAY 66. **1732** FULLER no. 5498.

Pound(s), *see also* Care (A p. of) will not pay debt; Dab, quoth Dawkins, when he hit his wife on the arse with a p. of butter; Fetch the five p.; Hundred p. of sorrow; Lob's p.; Mischief comes by the p.; Penny wise p. foolish; Take care of pence; Thousand p. . . . all one thing at doomsday.

Pour gold on him, and he'll never thrive. (G 290)

1639 CLARKE 220.

Pour not water on a drowned mouse. (W 102)

a. **1628** CARMICHAELL no. 1851 Ye bread of them casts water on a drownd man. **1639** CLARKE 9. **1670** RAY 133 . . . *i.e.* Add not affliction to misery. **1721** KELLY 267 . . . Never insult over those who are down already. **1738** SWIFT Dial. I. E.L. 265 Take pity on poor miss; don't throw water on a drowned rat. **1832** HENDERSON 83 (It's needless to).

Pours, *see* Rains but it p., (Never).

Poverty breeds strife. *Cf.* **Want makes strife.** (P 524)

c. **1538** T. STARKEY *Dial.* I. ii. 827: *Eng. in Reign Hen. VIII* II. 50 Sche [poverty] ys the mother of envy and malice, dyssensyon and debate. **1678** RAY 354. *Somerset.* **1732** FULLER no. 6109 Want makes Strife, Between the good Man and his Wife.

Poverty comes in at (the) doors, When | love leaps out at (the) windows. (P 531)

c. **1476** CAXTON *Game Chess* III. iii. F4 Herof men say a comyn prouerbe in englond, that loue lasteth as longe as the money endurith. **1631** BRATHWAIT *Eng. Gentlewoman* (1641) 346 It hath been an old maxime; that as poverty goes in at one doore, love goes out at the other. **1639** CLARKE 25. **1721** KELLY 346 (Friendship flees out). **1732** FULLER no. 5565 (creeps out). **1823** GALT *Entail* ch. 14 'Tak thy tocherless bargain to thee. . . . But mind my words—when Poverty comes in at the door, Love jumps out at the window.' **1869** READE *Foul Play* ch. I When Mr. Wylie urged her to marry him . . . she spoke out . . . 'I've seen poverty enough in my mother's house, it shan't come in at my door to drive love out of window'.

Poverty is hateful good.

1377 LANGLAND *P. Pl.* B. xiv. 275 'Paupertas', quod Pacience 'est odibile bonum'. *c.* **1386** CHAUCER *Wife's T.* l. 1195 Poverte is hateful good, and, as I gesse, A ful greet bryngere out of bisynesse.

Poverty is (a pain, inconvenience, but) no disgrace (crime, sin). (P 526)

1591 FLORIO *Second F.* 105 Neuer be ashamed of thy calling, for Pouertie is no vice, though it be an inconuenience. **1599** MINSHEU *Span. Gram.* 84 Pouertie is no vile or vicious matter, but yet an inconuenience. **1640** HERBERT no. 844 Poverty is no sinne. **1641** PEACHAM *Worth of a Penny* in Arber *Garner* vi. 260 Women of the meanest condition may make good wives; since Paupertas non est vitium; Poverty is no vice. **1659** HOWELL *Span. Prov.* 10 Poverty is no baseness, but an inconvenience. **1721** KELLY 278 Poortha[1] is a Pain, but no Disgrace. Unless it be the Effects of Laziness, and Luxury. **1813** BARRETT *Heroine* ed. Raleigh 215 Poverty is no great disgrace, provided one comes honestly by it; for one may get poor as well as rich by knavery. **1827-48** HARE *Gues. at Truth* (1859) i. 148 *La pobreza no es vileza,* Poverty is no disgrace, says the Biscayan proverb, *Paupertas ridiculos homines facit,* says the Roman satirist. . . . Which is the wiser and better saying. . . ? **1832-8** S. WARREN *Diary of Phys.* (1854) ch. 27 You know, sir, poverty's no sin. **1838-9** DICKENS *N. Nickleby* ch. 55 (not a crime). [1 poverty.]

Poverty is not a shame; but the being ashamed of it is.

1732 FULLER no. 3908. **1749** FRANKLIN July Having been poor is no shame, but being ashamed of it, is.

Poverty, He that is in | is still in suspicion. (P 521)

1553 *Precepts of Cato* (1556) S4ᵛ They that be in pouertie and myserye Be alwayes suspected of iniquitie. **1573** SANFORD 102ᵛ. **1629** *Bk. Mer. Rid.* Prov. no. 73.

Poverty is the mother of all arts. *Cf.* **Necessity mother of invention.** (P 527)

c. **1526** *Dicta Sapientum* C3ᵛ Pouerte is ingenious, and a fynder of craftis. And after the sayeng of Ouide, Iueles that is to saye affliction and nedinesse ofte quickeneth the wytte. **1611** COTGRAVE s.v. Pain Necessitie inuented all good Artes. **1666** TORRIANO *It. Prov.* 214, no. 28 . . . and trades.

Poverty is the mother of health. (P 528)

1377 LANGLAND *P. Pl.* ᵀB. xiv. 298 Þe fyfte [pouerte] is moder of helthe. **1572** CRADOCKE *Ship of Assured Safety* 200 Pouertie maketh men healthfull and to be quickly cured when they be sicke. **1598** SIR R. BARCKLEY *Felicitie of Man* (1631) IV. iii. 335 A poore table is the mother of health. **1640** HERBERT no. 472.

Poverty parts fellowship (friends, good company). (P 529)

c. **1350** *Douce MS.* 52 no. 107 Poverte brekys company. *c.* **1386** CHAUCER *Mel.* B² l. 2749 And if thy fortune change that thou wexe povre, farewel freendshipe and felawshipe. **1406** HOCCLEVE *Male Regle* E.E.T.S. l. 133 Fy! Lak of coyn departith conpaignie. **1546** HEYWOOD I. xii. F1 Yet pouertie parteth felowshyp we see. **1594** NASHE *Unf. Trav.* ii. 210 But pouertie in the end partes friends. **1599** SHAKES. *A.Y.* II. i. 51 ''Tis right!' quoth he, 'thus misery doth part The flux of company.' **1616** BRETON 2 *Cross Prov.* B2ᵛ (good company). **1641** FERGUSSON no. 694 Povertie parts good company, and is an enemie to vertue. **1721** KELLY 278 *Poortha¹ parts friends*. At least makes them very coldrife. **1842** LOVER *Handy Andy* ch. 2 As the old song says, 'Poverty parts good company'; . . . he can't afford to know you any longer, now that you have lent him all the money you had. [¹ poverty.]

Poverty wants many things, and covetousness (avarice) all. *Cf.* Poor man wants some things.   (P 530)

[PUB. SYRUS 121 *Desunt inopiae multa, avaritiae omnia.*] **1539** TAVERNER *Publius* D2 Poertie lacketh smale thynges but couetise lacketh al thynges. **1614** SENECA *Wks.* tr. Lodge *Epistles* 443. **1668** COWLEY *Ess.* vii (1904) 82 One line of Ovid: *Desunt luxuriæ multa, avaritiæ omnia*. Much is wanting to luxury, all to avarice. To which saying, I have a mind to add . . . ; Poverty wants some, luxury many, avarice all things. **1669** PENN *No Cross, No Crown* xiii Poverty wants many things, but covetousness all.

Poverty, *see also* Bashfulness enemy to p.; Bear wealth, p. bear itself; Content in his p.; Easier to commend p. than to endure it; Pass of Alton (Through) p. might pass; Patience with p. poor man's remedy; Plain of p. and die beggar; Pride and p. ill met; Virtue that p. destroys not (No).

Pow, *see* Hale p.

Powder, *see* Trust in God but keep p. dry.

Power behind the throne, The.

[**1770** PITT *Speech* 2 Mar. There is something behind the throne greater than the King himself.] **1874** MARK TWAIN *Life on the Mississippi* ch. 15 A power behind the throne that was greater than the throne itself. **1905** VACHELL *The Hill* 198 It was his habit to consult his wife in emergencies. The chief cutter . . . said that Amelia was the power behind the throne. **1909** *T.L.S.* 23 July 269 The Duc de Morny . . . far more than the . . . Empress, was the power behind the Throne.

Power seldom grows old at court.
                                                    (P 534)
1651 HERBERT no. 1053.

Power, *see also* Knowledge is p.; Mickle p. makes many enemies; Pope by voice, . . . emperour by force (p.)

Powys is the paradise of Wales. (P 536)

1662 FULLER Montgomeryshire 45 'Pywys Paradwys Cymry'. That is, 'Powis is the Paradise of Wales'. This Proverb referreth to Teliessen¹ the Author thereof, at what time

Powis had far larger bounds than at this day, as containing all the land interjacent betwixt Wye and Severn. [¹ Taliesin, a British bard, perhaps mythic, of 6th cent.]

Practice, *see* Knowledge without p. makes but half artist; Ounce of p. worth pound of precept; Use (p.) makes perfect.

Practise what you preach.   (P 537a)

1377 LANGLAND *P. Pl.* B. v. 45 'If ȝe lyuen as ȝe leren vs . we shal leue¹ ȝow the bettere.' *Ibid.* B xiii 79 This goddes gloton . . . Hath no pyte on vs pore. He performeth yuel. That he precheth he preueth nouzt. **1596** SHAKES. *M.V.* I. ii. 15 It is a good divine that follows his own instructions. **1639** FULLER *Holy War* I. xxiii (1840) 42 The Levites . . . had forty-eight cities, . . . being better provided for than for many English ministers, who may preach of hospitality to their people, but cannot go to the cost to practise their own doctrine. **1678** R. L'ESTRANGE *Seneca's Morals* II. ii. 130 We must practise what we preach. **1812** COMBE (*Dr. Syntax*) *Consolation* xxvii 'Tis not for me, my friend, to teach You; you should practise what you preach. **1853** THACKERAY *Newcomes* ch. 14 Take counsel by an old soldier, who fully practises what he preaches, and beseeches you to beware of the bottle. [¹ believe.]

Praise a fair day at night. *Cf.* Evening crowns (praises) the day.   (D 100)

c. **1350** *Douce MS. 52* no. 10 At euene prayse þe fayre day. **1481** CAXTON *Reynard* xxix Arb. 75 Me ought not preyse to[o] moche the daye . tyl euen be come. **1616** ADAMS *Gallant's Burden* 38 Your Life is in the Noone of pride, but (we say) Prayse a faire day at Night. **1640** HERBERT no. 97 Praise day at night, and life at the end. **1721** KELLY 282 *Ruse¹ the fair Day at Night*. Commend not a Thing, or Project, till it has had its full Effect. **1853** TRENCH iv. 89 This is Spanish: Call me not 'olive', till you see me gathered; being nearly parallel to our own: Praise a fair day at night. [¹ praise.]

Praise a hill, but keep below. (H 466)

1591 FLORIO *Second F.* 99 Wonder at hills, keepe on the plaine. **1640** HERBERT no. 488.

Praise at parting.   (P 83)

c. **1410** *Towneley Plays* E.E.T.S. 108 Now prays at the partyng. *c.* **1440** *Gesta Romanorum* E.E.T.S. 39 'Preyse at þe parting', seide þe knyȝt. **1530** PALSGRAVE 677b Prove at the partynge, quod Rockley. **1580** LYLY *Euph. & his Eng.* ii. 130 I but *Philautus* prayse at the parting, if she had not liked thee, she would neuer haue aunswered thee. **1599** PORTER *Angry Wom. Abing.* l. 2721. **1611** SHAKES. *Temp.* III. iii. 38 A kind of excellent dumb discourse.— Praise in departing.

Praise by evil men is dispraise. (P 540)

c. **1526** *Dicta Sap.* A2ᵛ It forceth nat howe many, but what they be that preyse the: for to be preysed of yuell parsons is dispreyse. *c.* **1590** HARINGTON *Epig.* III. 210 The latten Prouerbe sayes, Laudari a laudatis is most praise. **1605–8** SHAKES. *T.Ath.* IV. iii. 172 I never did thee

Praise | Praising

644

harm.—Yes, thou spok'st well of me.—Call'st thou that harm?—Men daily find it. 1612 CHAPMAN *Widow's Tears* II. iii. 3 Never was man so praised with a dispraise. 1732 FULLER no. 3925 Praises from wicked Men are Reproaches.

Praise is not pudding.

1728 POPE *Dunc.* I. 54 Where, in nice balance, truth with gold she weighs, And solid pudding against empty praise. 1750 FRANKLIN Pref. Since 't is not improbable, that a Man may receive more solid Satisfaction from *Pudding*, while he is *living*, than from *Praise*, after he is *dead*. 1837–48 BARHAM *Ingol. Leg., House-Warming* (1898) 581 An old proverb says, 'Pudding still before praise!' 1885 D. C. MURRAY *Rainbow Gold* II. i Even the empty praise is problematical just yet, and the solid pudding is denied me altogether. They consent to publish . . . but they pay nothing.

Praise (Honour) is the reflection (shadow) of virtue. (P 541)

1551 WILSON *Rule of Reason* K6ᵛ Prayse foloweth vertue, as the shadow doth the bodie. 1612 BACON *Essays* (1864) xii. 258. 1617 J. DAVIES *Wit's Bedlam* B4 Honor, is Vertues Shadow.

Praise makes good men better, and bad men worse. (P 542)

1659 T. PECKE *Parnassi Puerp.* 95 Good men are made better; bad, worse by praise. 1710 PALMER 121 Praise does a Wise Man Good, but a Fool worse. 1732 FULLER no. 3918.

Praise no man till he is dead.

1540 TAVERNER A6ᵛ Vitae finem spectato Praise no man for blessed and happy till thou se the ende of his life. 1547 BALDWIN *Treatise Moral Philosophy* K1ᵛ Prayse no man before death, for death is the discouerer of all his woorkes.

Praise none too much, for all are fickle. (A 200)

1640 HERBERT no. 774.

Praise nor dispraise thyself; Neither | thy actions serve the turn. (A 26)

1581 GUAZZO i. 154 That saying, that a man ought not to speake of himselfe, eyther in prayse or in disprayse. 1640 HERBERT no. 771.

Praise (Speak well of) the bridge he goes over (that carries him over), Let every man. (M 210)

1678 RAY 106 . . . *i.e.* Speak not ill of him who hath done you a courtesie, or whom you have made use of to your benefit; or do commonly make use of. 1732 FULLER no. 3175 (that carries him over). 1850 KINGSLEY *Alton Locke* ch. 10 Every one speaks well of the bridge which carries him over. Every one fancies the laws which fill his pockets to be God's laws. 1886 G. DAWSON *Biog. Lect.* 22 Our love of compromise . . . is our little weakness, and it has also been our great strength; . . . and of course we speak well of the bridge that carries us over.

Praise the child, and you make love to the mother.

1829 COBBETT *Adv. to Y. Men* iv (1906) 154 It is an old saying, 'Praise the child, and you make love to the mother'; and it is surprising how far this will go. 1886 E. J. HARDY *How to be Happy* ch. 19 . . . and it is a thing no husband ought to overlook.

Praise (Commend) the sea, but keep on land. (S 177)

1591 FLORIO *Second F.* 99 Praise the sea, on shore remaine. 1640 HERBERT no. 489. 1659 TORRIANO no. 131 (Commend). 1706 STEVENS s.v. Mar Talk of the Sea, and be upon Land.

Praise the wine before ye taste of the grape, Ye. (W 493)

c. 1549 HEYWOOD I. x. C4ᵛ.

Praise without profit puts little in the pot.

1666 TORRIANO *It. Prov.* 131 no. 1 Praises fill not the belly. 1721 KELLY 280. 1732 FULLER no. 3922.

Praise(s) (*noun*), *see also* Lacking breeds laziness, p. breeds pith; Man's p. in his own mouth stinks; Old p. dies unless you feed it; True p. roots and spreads; Wheat will not have two p.

Praise(s, d) (*verb*), *see also* Admonish your friends in private, p. them in public; Counsel must be followed not p.; Evening p. the day; Fool (One) p. another; Neighbours (He dwells far from) that p. himself.

Praises himself, He that | spatters himself. (P 547)

1523 A. BARCLAY *Mirr. Good Manners* Sp. S. 76 For this is a prouerbe sounding to veritie Of thy proper mouth thy laud is not laudable. 1581 GUAZZO i. 95 Hee which washeth his mouth with his owne praise, soyleth himselfe with the suddes that come of it. 1640 HERBERT no. 990.

Praises Saint Peter, Who | does not blame Saint Paul. (S 57)

1640 HERBERT no. 859.

Praises who wishes to sell, He. (P 546)

1594–5 SHAKES. *L.L.L.* IV. iii. 237 To things of sale a seller's praise belongs. 1608 J. DAY *Law Tricks* l. 723 You will not buy me sure you praise me so. 1658 *Comes Facundus* 20 He that praiseth would sell, and he that blames would buy.

Praising a ford till a man be over, It is not good. (P 549)

1575 GASCOIGNE *Posies* i. 6 Yet is it true that I must take the Foord as I finde it. 1616 DRAXE no. 578. 1641 FERGUSSON no. 731 Ruse¹ the food as ye find it. 1670 RAY 92. 1818 SCOTT

Rob Roy ch. 27 But it's an ill wind blaws naebody gude—Let ilka ane ruse the ford as they
find it. [¹ praise.]

Prate is prate; but it's the duck lays
the eggs.   (P 550)

1659 HOWELL *Eng. Prov.* 13b.   **1670** RAY 215.

Prate, *see also* Hen does not p. (If the).

Pray for yourself, I am not sick.   (P 551)

c. **1549** HEYWOOD II. vii. I4ᵛ.

Pray(s), *see also* Devil p., (When); Labour as
long lived, p. as dying; Learn to p., go to sea;
Pain both to pay and p.; Pay (He that cannot)
let him p.

Prayer but little devotion, He has
much.   (P 552)

1546 HEYWOOD II. ix. L2 Aue Maria (quoth he)
howe muche mocion Here is to praiers, with
howe littell deuocion.   **1641** FERGUSSON no. 466.
1721 KELLY 170 . . . Spoken of those Men who
make great pretences to Religion, but shew
little of it in their Practice.

Prayer penetrates heaven, A short.
                                                             (P 555)

a. **1387** *Piers Plowman* C. xii. 297 Brevis oratio
penetrat celum.   *c.* **1450–1500** *The Gd. Wife wd.
a Pilgrimage* l. 84 A schort prayer wynneth
heyvyn, the Patter Noster and an Ave.   *c.* **1470**
Mankind l. 551 A schorte preyer thyrlyth hewyn.
1493 H. PARKER *Dives and Pauper* 74ᵛ It is a
common prouerbe, that a short prayer thirleth
[reaches] heuen.   **1587** J. BRIDGES *Defence* 494
Breuis oratio penetrat coelum.   **1666** TORRIANO
It. Prov. 178 no. 10 A short prayer penetrates.
1732 FULLER no. 397 A short Prayer may reach
up to the Heaven of Heavens.

Prayer should be the key of the day
and the lock of the night.   (P 554)

1620–8 O. FELTHAM *Resolves* lxvii Dent 353
Though prayer should be the key of the day,
and the lock of the night, yet I hold it more
needful in the morning, than when our bodies
do take their repose.

Prayers and provender hinder no man's
journey.   (P 556)

1599 MINSHEU *Span. Dial.* 6 Neither in going to
the Church, nor in giuing prouender to thy
horse, was there euer iourney hindred or lost.
1632 HERBERT *Country Parson* 251 At going to
bed . . . he will have prayers in the hall . . . The
like he doth in the morning, using pleasantly
the outlandish proverb, that Prayers and Provender never hinder iourney.   **1670** RAY 133.

Prayers are done, When | my lady is
ready.   (P 560)

1611 COTGRAVE s.v. Messe When prayers were
ended, Madame ends her pranking.   **1640**
HERBERT no. 71.

Prayers of the wicked won't prevail,
The.

1706 STEVENS s.v. Oración A Dog's Prayer does
not go up to Heaven. The Prayers of the
Wicked don't prevail.   **1738** SWIFT Dial. II.
E.L. 314 I wish you may be wet to the skin.—
Ay; but they say the prayers of the wicked won't
prevail.

Prayers, They shall have no more of
our | than we of their pies, quoth the
vicar of Layton.   (M 1159)

1678 RAY 191.

Prayer(s), *see also* Go home and say p.; Last p.
(She is at her); Said my p. in other corner; Says
anything but his p.

Preach at Tyburn Cross,¹ To.   (T 646)

[= to be hanged.]   **1576** GASCOIGNE *Steele Glas*
ii. 148 That Souldiours sterue, or prech at
Tiborne crosse. [¹ the place of execution.]

Preach like a pie, To.

a. **1607** *Chester Whitsun Plays; Proc. Prophet.*
273 BALAACK. Popelard! thou preachest as a
pie.¹ [¹ magpie.]

Preach(ed, es), *see* Fox p., (When); Friar p.
against stealing; Practise what you p.

Preacher(s), *see* Saturday is working day . . . of
p.; Saved (He that will not be) needs no p.;
Scholars are not the best p., (The greatest).

Preaches, He that | gives alms.   (A 224)

1640 HERBERT no. 788.

Preaches war, Who | is the devil's
chaplain.   (W 52)

1659 HOWELL *New Sayings* 8b.   **1664** CODRING-
TON 229.   **1670** RAY 27.   **1732** FULLER no. 2251
(He that preacheth up War when it might well
be avoided).

Preaches well that lives well, He.
                                                             (P 561)

1620 SHELTON *Quix.* II. xxi. ii. 326.   **1732** FULLER
no. 2006.

Precept, *see* Example better than p.; Ounce of
practice worth pound of p.

Precipices, *see* High places have p.

Presage, *see* Rainbows . . . p. rain.

Presence, *see* Absence sharpens love, p.
strengthens it; Saving your p.

Present (*adj., adv.*), *see* Absent without fault nor
p. without excuse (Neither); Fears you p. (He
that) will hate you absent; Lion when he is

absent, (Who takes a) fears a mouse p.; Pleasure refrain (Who will in time p.), shall more pleasure obtain; Things p. are judged by things past; Time like p. (No).

Presents of love fear not to be ill taken of strangers. (P 566)

1651 HERBERT no. 1162.

Press, *see* Yellow P.

Pressed men, *see* Volunteer (One) worth two p. m.

Preston, *see* Proud P.

Presumed good, All are | till they are found in a fault. *Cf.* Innocent until proved guilty. (A 120)

1640 HERBERT no. 944.

Presumed, *see also* Nothing is to be p. on.

Presumers, *see* Deservers grow p.

Pretence, *see* Want a p. to whip dog.

Pretended, *see* Holiness is double iniquity, (P.).

Prettiness dies first (quickly). (P 567)

1610 BRETNOR *Almanac* May Good days Prettie, if it would last. **1640** HERBERT no. 484. **1664** CODRINGTON 209 (quickly). **1670** RAY 21 (as 1664).

Prettiness makes no pottage. (P 568)

1678 RAY 192. **1732** FULLER no. 3931.

Pretty fellow, *see* Axle-tree for oven.

Pretty pig makes an ugly old sow, A.

[**1577** N. BRETON *The Works of a Young Wit* (*Poems*, ed. J. Robertson 77) I haue seene ere now, a prety pigge of an ill favoured Sowe.] **1721** KELLY 42 (bonny Grice). **1732** FULLER no. 363.

Pretty, *see also* Long and lazy . . . p. and proud.

Prevail, *see* Truth is mighty and will p.

Prevent(s, ing), *see* Policy p. chance; Providing is p.

Prevention is better than cure. (P 569)

c. **1240** BRACTON *De Legibus* (Rolls Ser. vi. 104) bk. v, c. 10, § 14 Cum melius et utilius sit in tempore occurrere quam post causam vulneratam quaerere remedium. **1618** T. ADAMS *Happiness Church* Wks. 598 Preuention is so much better then healing, because it saues the labour of being sicke. **1732** FULLER no. 3932 (much preferable). **1751** N. COTTON *Vis. Verse, Health*

31 Prevention is the better Cure, So says the Proverb, and 'tis sure. *a.* **1863** SIR G. C. LEWIS in BAGEHOT *Biog. Stud.* (1881) 212 'In *my* opinion, in nine cases out of ten, cure is better than prevention. . . . By looking forward to all possible evils, we waste the strength that had best be concentrated in curing the one evil which happens.'

Price is too low for a 'bear'[1] or too high for a 'bull',[2] No.

[Stock Exchange.] **1884** *Times* 28 June No price is too low for a 'bear' or too high for a 'bull' (LEAN IV. 62). [[1] one who sells stock for future delivery hoping to buy it cheap meanwhile, and therefore tries to bring prices down. [2] person trying to raise prices.]

Price, *see also* Ask but enough . . . lower the p.; Every man has his p.; Good thing cheap (He will never have) that is afraid to ask p.; Love is true p. of love; Much money makes country poor, for it sets dearer p.; Pain is p. God puts.

Prick(s) (*noun*), *see* Hit the p.; Kick against p.; Shoot nigh the p.

Prick(ed, s) (*verb*), *see* Ass p. must needs trot; Early p. that will be thorn.

Prickles, *see* Sows thistles shall reap p., (He that).

Pride and grace dwelt never in one place.

1721 KELLY 276. **1732** FULLER no. 6273.

Pride and laziness would have mickle upholding. (P 573)

1641 FERGUSSON no. 685 Pride and Sweirnesse[1] wald have meikle uphald. **1721** KELLY 277 . . . Pride requires Ornament, and Laziness Service. [[1] laziness.]

Pride and poverty are ill met, yet often seen together.

1660 *The Rump Despairing, or the Rump's Proverbs* 2 You know Pride and Poverty make a double affliction. **1732** FULLER no. 3933.

Pride breakfasted with plenty, dined with poverty, and supped with infamy.

1758 FRANKLIN in Arber *Garner* v. 584 Pride that dines on Vanity, sups on Contempt, as *Poor* RICHARD says. And in another place, . . .

Pride, but[1] profit, wear shoon[2] and go bare foot. (P 574)

1626 BRETON *Soothing* B3 Pride is without profit . . . for it spends much to gaine scorne. *a.* **1628** CARMICHAELL no. 877 (gloves). **1639** CLARKE 31 Pride without profit. **1721** KELLY 277 . . . Spoken when People have something fine about them, but the rest shabby. [[1] without. [2] shoes.]

Pride feels (finds, knows) no cold (pain).
(P 575)

1614 T. ADAMS *Fatal Banquet* II. Wks. 196 Pride is neuer without her own paine, though shee will not feele it: be her garments what they will, yet she will neuer be too hot, nor too colde. **1631** JONSON *New Inn* II. ii. 5 Thou must make shift with it. Pride feeles no pain. Girt thee hard, Prue. **1650** SIR J. BIRKENHEAD *Two Centuries of Pauls Church-yard* 59 Pride feels no cold. **1670** RAY 133. **1721** KELLY 277 Pride finds no cold. Spoken heretofore to young Women, when, in compliance with the Fashion, they went with their Breasts and Shoulders bare. **1732** FULLER no. 3935 (frost). **1837** T. HOOK *Jack Brag* ch. 18 Truly, indeed, does the proverb say that 'pride knows no pain'.

Pride goes before destruction (and shame comes after). *Cf.* Pride rides.
(P 576)

[PROV. xvi. 18: Pride goeth before destruction, and an haughty spirit before a fall.] *c.* **1350** *Douce MS.* 52 no. 135. *c.* **1440** *Jacob's Well* 70 Pride goth beforn, & schame folwyth after. *a.* **1529** SKELTON *Agst. Garnesche* 165 Wks. (Dyce) I. 131. **1546** HEYWOOD I. x. C4ᵛ Pryde wyll haue a fall. For pryde goeth before, and shame cometh after. **1605** CHAPMAN, JONSON. MARSTON *Eastw. Ho* IV. ii. 163 (Shame wil follow after). **1732** FULLER no. 3936.

Pride is as loud a beggar as want, and a great deal more saucy.

1732 FULLER no. 3941.

Pride may lurk under a threadbare cloak.
(P 579)

1542 ERASM. tr. Udall *Apoph.* (1877) 24 Pride maie as well be in sack cloth as in rich araie. **1659** HOWELL *New Sayings* 3b Pride is oftner seen through a threadbare coat then through a silk cloak. **1732** FULLER no. 3947.

Pride must be pinched.

1894 NORTHALL *Folk-phrases* E.D.S. 21 Pride must be pinched. A reproof to one who complains of tight boots, garments, &c.

Pride of the morning, The.

1827 KEBLE *Christ. Yr.*, *25th S. aft. Trin.* Pride of the dewy morning, The swain's experienced eye From thee takes timely warning Nor trusts the gorgeous sky. **1801** A. FORBES *Bar. Biv. & Bat.* (1910) 9 There had been a shower as the sun rose—the 'pride of the morning' the soldiers call the sprinkle—just sufficient to lay the dust.

Pride of the rich makes the labour(s) of the poor, The.
(P 580)

1616 BRETON *Cross. Prov.* Wks. A7. **1639** CLARKE 18.

Pride rides, When | shame lacqueys. *Cf.* Pride goes before.
(P 582)

1573 SANFORD D4ᵛ Lewis the eleuenth King of Fraunce . . . was woonte to saye, when pryde

rydeth, damage and shame goe behynde. **1592** DELAMOTHE 47 When Pryde doth ryde, shame and damage [honte et dommage] doth folow after. **1597** *Politeuphuia* 234b When pride dooth ride, shame & danger doe follow on foote. **1673** DARE *Counsellor Manners* 18 King Lewis the Eleventh was wont to say, When pride rides in the Saddle, shame and confusion rides in the crupper. **1732** FULLER no. 5567.

Pride that apes humility.

1799 COLERIDGE *Devil's Thoughts* vi And the Devil did grin, for his darling sin Is pride that apes humility. **1858** SURTEES *Ask Mamma* ch. 17 [He] divested himself of his paletot in which he had been doing 'the pride that apes humility'. **1910** *Spectator* 10 Dec. 1028 Browning's . . . simplicity was very real . . . and he was wholly free from the pride that apes humility.

Pride will have (never left his master without) a fall.
(P 581)

c. **1390** GOWER *Conf. Amantis* I. 3066 Pride . . . schal down falle and ouer the owe. **1509** BARCLAY *Ship of Fools* ii. 159 For it hath be sene is sene, and euer shall That first or last foule pryde wyll haue a fall. **1546** HEYWOOD I. x. C4ᵛ Well well (quoth myne aunte) pryde will haue a fall. **1595** SHAKES. *Rich. II* V. v. 88 Would he not stumble? Would he not fall down.—Since pride must have a fall. **1646** J. WHITAKER *Uzziah* 26 That pride will have a fall, is from common experience grown proverbiall. **1721** KELLY 276 (never left his master without). Proud People often meet with very humbling Circumstances. **1784** JOHNSON *Let.* 2 Aug. in *Boswell* I am now reduced to think . . . of the weather. Pride must have a fall.

Pride, *see also* Charity and p. feed the poor; Declaim against p. (Not sign of humility to); Despises p. with greater p.; Devil wipes tail with poor man's p.; Four good mothers have four bad daughters: . . . prosperity, p.; Plenty breeds p.; Pompous provision comes of p.

Pries into every cloud, He that | may be stricken with a thunderbolt.

1597 *Politeuphuia* 167 Hee that loues to be sifting of euery cloude, may be smitten with a thunder-stroke. **1639** CLARKE 31. **1670** RAY 134.

Priest, Like | like people.
(P 583)

[HOSEA iv. 9] **1561** PILKINGTON *Burning of Paul's Church* P.S. 486 Sicut populus ita et sacerdos . . . as the people be, so God sends them priests. **1589** *Return of Pasquil* Nashe i. 91 Like people, like Priest begins now to be verified. **1606** G. CLOSSE *The Parricide Papist* B4 The prouerbe was well shared amongst them, *such a priest, such people.* **1664** JOS. MEDE Wks. *Disc.* xxxvi. 276 Ita populus, sicut sacerdos, Such as the priest is, such will the people be; the priest cannot err, but he causeth others to err also. **1670** RAY 114. **1893** R. HEATH *Eng. Peasant* 329 He had so deep a reverence for the clergy, that it never entered into his mind that perhaps, after all, it was 'like people, like priest'.

Priest praises his own relics, Each.

c. 1400 *MS. Latin no. 394, J. Rylands Libr.* (ed. Pantin) in *Bull. J. R. Libr.* XIV i. 18 Eche preste preyseth his awgh relikes.

Priest, Such as the | such is the clerk. (p 585)

[*Cf.* ISAIAH xxiv. 2.] **1622** C. OUDIN *A Grammar Spanish & English* 269 Such as the Priest, such is the Clarke. **1624** BURTON *Anat. Mel.* I. ii. III. xv. 123 Such a Patrone, such a Clearke. **1732** FULLER no. 4279.

Priest, Such | such offering. (p 586)

a. 1628 CARMICHAELL no. 1364. **1641** FERGUSSON no. 761 Sike[1] priest, sike offering. [[1] such.]

Priest(s), *see also* Good to fetch the devil a p.; Know by a half-penny if p. take offering; Live well (If you would) . . . turn p.; Mad parish must have a mad p.; No mischief but p. at bottom; No p. no mass; Once a parson (p.) always a p.; Parish p. forgets he has been clerk; Parson (P.) always christens own child first; Pigeons and p. make foul houses; Pinch on the p.'s side; Three things are insatiable; Women, p., and poultry have never enough.

Prince hates, He whom a | is as good as dead. (p 589)

1589 SIR JOB THROCKMORTON (J. E. Neale *Eliz. and her Parl[ts]. 1584–1601* 174) I have read indeed long ago . . . that the indignation of the Prince was death. **1594** *The Wars of Cyrus* IV. iii. 1240 Wrath of princes, what is it but death? **1599** MINSHEU *Span. Gram.* To Rdr. I3[v] As the saying is, the anger of a Prince the messenger of death. **1600** T. HEYWOOD *et al. I Edw. IV* i. 73 And who knows not a princes hate is death? **1611** COTGRAVE s.v. *Mort.*

Princes are venison in heaven. (p 593)

c. 1577 J. NORTHBROOKE *Treat. agst. Dicing* (1843) 22 I pray God the olde prouerbe be not found true, that gentleman and riche men are venison in Heauen (that is), very rare and daintie to haue them come thither. **1616** T. ADAMS *Gallant's Burden* 52 A wealthy and great man, serued vp to Gods table in his kingdome, is as rare as Venison at our Boardes on earth. **1651** HERBERT no. 1156.

Princes have no way. (p 594)

1640 HERBERT no. 956.

Prince(s), *see also* Hamlet without P. of Denmark; Learning in breast of bad man (p.) as sword in hand of madman; New p. new bondage; Punctuality is politeness of p.

Print, A man (thing) in. (M 239)

c. 1576 WHYTHORNE 3 A man cannott alway speak in prynt. **1576** FLEMING *Panoplie of Epistles* 357 What soeuer is uttered in such mennes hearing, must bee done in printe; as wee say in oure common Prouerbe. **1587** J.

BRIDGES *Defence* 1316 Speake in print vpon aduised deliberation. **1594** SHAKES. *T.G.V.* II. i. 157 All this I speak in print, for in print I found it. **1594–5** *Id. L.L.L.* III. i. 163 Most sweet gardon! I will do it, sir, in print. **1599** *Id. A.Y.* V. iv. 85 O sir, we quarrel in print. **1616** DRAXE no. 611 In print, rarely, admirably, finically.

Priscian, *see* Break P.'s head.

Prison, *see* Bean in liberty better than comfit in p.; God keep me from . . . a p.; Love is foul (No.), nor p. fair.

Prisoner(s), *see* All's out is good for p.; Secret is thy p. (Thy).

Prizing of green barley, It is ill.

1721 KELLY 218 . . . It is ill prizing these Things who have not yet had an Occasion of shewing themselves; spoken of Boys, Colts, &c.

Probabilities do not make one truth, A thousand.

1707 MAPLETOFT 32.

Procession, *see* Ill battle (p.) where devil carries colours.

Procrastination is the thief of time.

1742 YOUNG *Night Thoughts* I. 393 Procrastination is the thief of time; Year after year it steals, till all are fled. **1850** DICKENS *Dav. Cop.* ch. 12 Never do to-morrow what you can do to-day. Procrastination is the thief of time.

Procrustes' bed. (p 597)

[Procrustes, a fabulous robber of Attica.] **1563** FULKE *Defence* i. P.S. 97 You play manifestly with us the lewd part of Procrustes, the thievish host, which would make his guest's stature equal with his bed's, either by stretching them out if they were too short, or by cutting off their legs if they were too long. **1618** JONSON *Conv. with Drummond* (ed. Patterson, 1924) 6 He cursed Petrarch for redacting verses to Sonnets, which he said were like that Tirrants bed, wher some who were too short were racked, others too long cut short. **1769** BURKE *Observ. on 'The Present State of Nat.'* Wks. (Bohn) I. 258 Procrustes shall never be my hero of legislation; with his iron bed, the allegory of his government. . . . Such was the state-bed of uniformity. **1796** LAMB to Coleridge, June Who shall go about to bring opinion to the bed of Procrustes? **1827** HARE *Gues. at Truth* (1878) i. 258 The man of the world is the Procrustes, who lays down his bed across the high-road, and binds all passers-by to it.

Proffered service (ware) stinks. (s 252)

[ST. JEROME *Merx ultronea putet*; and so ERASM. *Ad.*] *c.* 1350 *Douce MS.* 52 no. 33 Bodun seruycys stynkys—Omnibus oblatus sordere solet famulatus. *c.* 1386 CHAUCER *Canon's Yeom. T.* l. 1066 Ful sooth it is that swiche profred servyse Stynketh, as witnessen thise olde wyse. **1546** HEYWOOD II. iv. G2[v] I wene (quoth she) proferd seruyce stynkth. **1584** LODGE *Alarum agst. Usurers* Shakes. Soc. 45 For that I see so good a nature in you (if proferred service stinke not) I will verye willynglye . . . further you in what I may. **1612** CHAPMAN *Widow's Tears* I. ii. 53 But offered ware is not so sweet, you know. **1641** FERGUSSON no. 156 Bodin geir stinkes. **1670** RAY 134 Proffer'd service (and so ware) stinks. **1710** SWIFT *Jrnl. to Stella* 22 Oct. I stopped short in my overture, and we parted very drily. . . . Is there so much in the proverb of proffered service? When shall I grow wise? **1710** PALMER 118 Profer'd Service Stinks: Or, Profer'd Ware is sold at half Price. **1771** SMOLLETT *Humph. Clink.* 26 Apr. (1871) 481 When I go to market to sell, my commodity stinks; but when I want to buy . . . it can't be had for love or money.

Profit, What is none of my | shall be none of my peril.

1509 BARCLAY *Ship of Fools* i. 160 They haue the profyte, another hath the paynes. **1706** STEVENS s.v. Maduro Let him that hath the Profit take the Pains. **1721** KELLY 343 . . . I will not engage my self deep in a Business in which I have no Concern. L. Mihi istic nec seritur nec metitur. [PLAUTUS *Epidicus* 2. 2. 80.]

Profit(s), *see also* Go to hell for the house p.; Honour and p. not in one sack; Honour without p.; No p. to honour; Praise without p. puts little in pot; Pride but p. wear shoon but go barefoot; Small p. quick returns; Thrift goes by the p. of a yeld hen (Your).

Profitable, *see* Shrew p. may serve.

Prolong thy life: Two things do | a quiet heart and a loving wife. (T 214)

1607 T. DELONEY *Strange Histories; Wise Sentences* Percy Soc. 70.

Promise, To | and give nothing, is comfort to a fool. (N 333)

1611 COTGRAVE s.v. Promettre To promise and giue nought contents the foole. **1616** DRAXE no. 1736 To promise, and to give nought, is to comfort a foole. **1670** RAY 22.

Promise is debt. (P 603)

c. **1386** CHAUCER *Man of Law Head-link* l. 41 Biheste is dette. **14..** *Everyman* 821 Yet promyse is dette, this ye well wot. *c.* **1500** *Young Children's Bk.* 49 in *Babees Bk.* E.E.T.S. 19 Fore euery promys, it is dette, That with no falsed muste be lette. **1639** CLARKE 194 (a due debt). **1813** RAY 19 He who promises runs in debt. *Hisp.*

Promise more in a day than they will fulfill in a year, Men may.

[*c.* **1515**] **1530** BARCLAY *Ecl.* v. l. 629 Some in one houre more promes to the wyll, Than all his dayes he thynketh to fulfyll. **1545** *Precepts of Cato* E6.

Promises and small performances, Great. (P 602)

1548 HALL 774 He [Wolsey] would promise muche and performe lytle. **1560** HEYWOOD *Fourth Hundred of Epig.* no. 10 Great promyse, small performance. **1604** SHAKES. *O.* IV. ii. 184 Your words and performance are no kin together. *c.* **1607** MIDDLETON *Trick* II. i. 269 To promise much and perform little. **1639** CLARKE 194.

Promises are either broken or kept. (P 604)

1590 DEE *Diary* 37 There was never promisse made, but it was broken or kept. **1609** HARWARD 110 Every promise is either broaken or kept. **1659** HOWELL *Eng. Prov.* 13a Ther's never a promise made, but its either broken or kept. **1692** L'ESTRANGE *Aesop's Fab.* ccclxvi (1738) 383 . . . Here's a reproof to all religious cheats and impostures, that promise more than they are able to perform. **1738** SWIFT Dial. I. E.L. 273.

Promises are like pie-crust, made to be broken. (P 605)

1599 SHAKES. *Hen. V* II. iii. 51 For oaths are straws, men's faiths are wafercakes. **1706** WARD *Hud. Rediv.* v. vii. 9 Fair promises avail but little, Like too rich pye-crust they're so brittle. **1738** SWIFT Dial. I. E.L. 273. Promises and pie-crust are made to be broken. **1739** 'R. BULL' tr. *Dedekindus' Grobianus* 162 Then all the Vengeance of the Gods invoke, In case this Pye-crust Promise should be broke. **1871** TROLLOPE *Ralph the H.* ch. 23 'Promises like that are mere pie-crusts', said Ralph.

Promises like a merchant, and pays like a man of war, He. (M 885)

1639 CLARKE 194. **1670** RAY 22.

Promises mountains and performs molehills, He. (M 1217, S 187)

1573 SANFORD 104ᵛ He promiseth seas and mountaynes. **1574** *Mirr. for Mag.* Campbell ii. 208 To promise hilles of gold and in performance waxe as key full colde. **1576** PETTIE i. 75 Will he not promise golden hills and perform dirty dales? **1578** FLORIO *First F.* 29ᵛ. *c.* **1607** MIDDLETON *Trick* IV. i. 106 He would do mountains now. **1629** *Bk. Mer. Rid.* Prov. no. 105.

Promises too much, He that | means nothing. (N 272)

a. **1593** GREENE *Friar Bacon* l. 2008 She speaks least to hold her promise sure. **1611** COTGRAVE s.v. Langue Those that promise most performe least. **1616** DRAXE no. 1737 He that promiseth all, deceiueth all. **1732** FULLER no. 2253.

Promises (*noun*), *see also* Many fair p. in marriage making.

Promise(s, d) (*verb*), *see also* Loses his thanks who p. and delays; Performance (One acre of) is worth twenty of p.; Poor indeed that can p. nothing.

Promising and performing, Between | a man may marry his daughter. (P 606)

1611 COTGRAVE s.v. Promettre Betweene giuing somewhat and promising much, a man may be honestly rid of a daughter. **1659** HOWELL *Fr. Prov.* 10. **1670** RAY 22.

Promising is the eve of giving. (P 607)

1573 SANFORD 104ᵛ (vigile). **1578** FLORIO *First F.* 29ᵛ The eue to geue, is to promise. **1640** HERBERT no. 847.

Proo¹, Naunt², your mare puts. (N 52)

1678 RAY 79 ... *i.e.* pushes. [¹ a call to a cow or horse, inviting it to stand still or come near. ² aunt.]

Proof of the pudding is in the eating, The. (P 608)

c. **1300** *King Alisaunder* l. 4042 Hit is y-writein, every thyng Himseolf shewith in tastyng. **1623** CAMDEN 266 (All the proofe). **1682** N. O. tr. BOILEAU *Le Lutrin* 23 To spight his foes, yet for all's feating, The proof of th' pudding's seen i' th' eating. **1738** SWIFT *Dial.* II. E.L. 300. **1830** G. COLMAN (Jr.) *Rand. Records* I. 37 (a precept to trust only to absolute experience).

Proper (noble) that has proper (noble) conditions,¹ He is. *Cf.* **Gentleman that has proper conditions.** (C 586)

1599 PORTER *Angry Wom. Abingd.* l. 2322 But he is propper that hath propper conditions. **1600** DEKKER *Shoem. Hol.* I. ii. 49 By my troth he is a propper man, but he is proper that proper doth. **1614** CAMDEN 307. **1616** DRAXE no. 154 They are pretie, that haue pretie conditions. *Ibid.* no. 841 Hee is a gentleman that hath gentle conditions. *Ibid.* no. 1505 Hee is noble, that hath noble conditions. **1639** CLARKE 91. [¹ disposition.]

Properer man, The | the worse luck. (M 360)

1606 J. DAY *Isle of Gulls* ii. 2 (Bullen) 34 You may see the properer women the worse luck. **1613** J. CHAMBERLAIN *Letters* 18 Feb. (McLure) i. 426 The old proverb the properer men the worse luck. **1633** JONSON *T. Tub* III. vii. 20. **1670** RAY 134 The properer man (and so the honester) the worse luck.

Prophesy, *see* Dying men speak true (p.).

Prophet is not without honour save in his own country, A.

[MATT. xiii. 57.] **1603** MONTAIGNE (Florio) III. ii. 33 No man hath beene a Prophet, not only in his house, but in his owne country, saith the experience of histories. **1771** SMOLLETT *Humph. Clink.* 15 Sept. The captain, like the prophets of old, is but little honoured in his own country. **1823** GALT *Entail* ch. 98 That's just as I might hae expectit—a prophet ne'er got honour in his own country. **1879** M. PATTISON *Milton* 153 The homage which was wanting to the prophet [i.e. Milton] in his own country was more liberally tendered by foreigners.

Prophet(s), *see also* Saul among p.

Prophetess, *see* Young wench, (Take heed of a), a p.

Proposes, *see* Man p.

Prospect is often better than possession.

1732 FULLER no. 3958.

Prosperity, In time of | friends will be plenty; in time of adversity, not one amongst twenty. *Cf.* **Prosperity makes friends.** (T 301)

a. **1500** *15c. School-Bk.* ed. W. Nelson 44 A man shall knowe his frende best in adversite, ffor then all flaterers lyghtly departith. *c.* **1500** *Everyman* Hazl.-Dods. i. 113 It is said, in prosperity men friends may find, Which in adversity be full unkind. *c.* **1526** ERASM. *Dicta Sap.* A3 In tyme of prosperyte thou shalte haue many frendes. But in aduersyte fewe frendes remayne, but they be true. **1584** WITHALS 11ᵛ In prosperous times many friendes may be tolde, But when fortune fadeth, not one to behold. **1659** HOWELL *Eng. Prov.* 20a. **1732** FULLER no. 6394.

Prosperity is the blessing of the Old Testament, adversity the blessing of the New.

1625 BACON *Essays* ed. Arber 505 Prosperity is the blessing of the Old Testament, adversity is the blessing of the New, which carrieth the greater benediction and the clearer revelation of God's favour. **1908** A. C. BENSON *At Large* ch. 12 222 The Bishop seemed to have forgotten the ancient maxim that prosperity is the blessing of the Old Testament, and affliction the blessing of the New.

Prosperity lets go the bridle. (P 612)

1640 HERBERT no. 736. **1754** FRANKLIN May Nay When Prosperity was well mounted, she let go the Bridle, and soon came tumbling out of the Saddle.

Prosperity makes friends, adversity tries them. *Cf.* **Prosperity, In time of.** (P 611)

a. **1500** *15c. School-Bk.* ed. W. Nelson 44 A man shall knowe his frende best in adversite, ffor than all flaterers lyghtly departith. *c.* **1526** *Dicta Sap.* A3 In tyme of prosperyte thou shalte haue many frendes. But in aduersyte fewe frendes remayne but they be true. *Ibid.* B1ᵛ Luckye fortune maketh frendes. Aduersite maketh a profe wheder they be fayned or true. **1597** *Politeuphuia* 161ᵛ Prosperitie getteth friends, but aduersitie tryeth them. **1598** SIR R. BARCKLEY *Felicity of Man* 538 Prosperitie winneth friends, but aduersitie proueth them.

1611 SHAKES. *W.T.* IV. iv. 565 Besides, you know Prosperity's the very bond of love. **1732** FULLER no. 3962 Prosperity get Followers; but Adversity distinguishes them. **1853** TRENCH iii. 59.

Prosperity no altars smoke, In.

1853 TRENCH iv. 88 On the danger of being overset by prosperity: . . . another Italian which says: . . .

Prosperity, *see also* Four good mothers have four bad daughters: . . . p., pride.

Protection, *see* Innocence is no p.

Protestant Rome, The.

[= Geneva.] **1912** *Spectator* 27 Jan. 128 During the period of religious persecution the 'Protestant Rome' became a city of refuge into which flowed a constant stream of emigration from France. In the eighteenth century Geneva became something of a cosmopolitan centre.

Protestant(s), *see also* Bible is religion of P.; Christian must have . . . faith of a P.

Proteus, *see* Shapes as P. (As many).

Proud as a peacock, As.   (P 157)

c. **1290** *Polit. Songs* (Wright) 159 A pruest[1] proud ase a po[2]. *c.* **1386** CHAUCER *Reeve's T.* l. 3926 As eny pecok he was proud and gay. **1560** DAUS tr. *Sleidane's Comm.* 119 They are as bragge and as proude as pecockes. **1592–3** SHAKES. *C.E.* IV. iii. 75 'Fly pride', says the peacock: mistress, that you know. **1753** RICHARDSON *Grandison* Lr. 137 Lord L., proud as a peacock, is . . . come for me. [[1] priest. [2] peacock.]

Proud as a dog (pig) with two tails, As.

1834 J. B. KER 7 He is as proud as a dog with two tails. **1837** T. HOOK *Jack Brag* ch. 16 'No', interrupted Mrs. Salmon, '. . . you are as proud as a pig with two tails.'

Proud as Lucifer (the devil), As. (L 572)

c. **1394** *Polit. Poems* (Wright) I. 318 As proud as Lucifarre. **1450** *Partonope* E.E.T.S. l. 9740 As prowde as Lucifere. **1589** T. BLAND *A Bait for Momus* 19 As proude as Lucifer. *c.* **1590** PEELE *O.W.T.* l. 769 As prowd as the diuell. **1643** *Oxinden & Payton Lett.* 36 As proud as the Devill. **1675** C. COTTON *Burlesque upon Burlesque* 79. **1782** MISS BURNEY *Cecilia* IX. vi. **1820** 16 Oct. BYRON *Letters* Prothero v. 99. My Mother . . . was as haughty as Lucifer with her descent from the Stuarts. **1858** TRELAWNEY *Recollections* ch. 6.

Proud (pleased) as Punch, As.

1848 MRS. GASKELL *Mary Barton* ch. 5 (proud). *a.* **1852** THOMAS MOORE *Lett. to Lady Donegal* I was (as the poet says) as pleased as Punch. **1854** DICKENS *Hard Times* Bk. I, ch. 6 When Sissy got into the school here . . . her father was as pleased as Punch. **1860** *Id. Great Expectations* ch. 25

(proud). **1942** EVELYN WAUGH *Put out More Flags* Spring 3 Believe it or not, she's as pleased as Punch.

Proud beggar that makes his own alms, He is a.

c. **1430** LYDGATE *Minor Poems* Percy Soc. 56 A prowde hert in a beggers brest . . . it accordith nought. **1721** KELLY 152 . . . Eng. Beggars should not be Chusers.

Proud (Stout) comes behind as goes before, As.   (c 536)

1575 *Gammer Gurton's N.* v. ii. 331 As proude coms behinde, they say, as any goes before! **1655** FULLER *Ch. Hist.* III. iii (1868) I. 374 York was rather quiet than contented, pleasing itself that 'as stout came behind as went before'.

Proud eye, A | an open purse, and a light wife, bring mischief to the first, misery to the second, and horns to the third.   (E 245)

1597 *Politeuphuia* 236b. **1647** *Countrym. New Commonwealth* 35.

Proud horse that will not bear his own provender, It is a.   (H 683)

1546 HEYWOOD II. ix. L3 With good will wyfe, for it is (sayde he to her) A proude hors that wil not beare his own prouander. **1599** PORTER *Angry Wom. Abingd.* l. 2357 Hee's a proud horse will not carry his owne prouender. **1670** RAY 105 It's an ill horse will not carry his own provender. **1721** KELLY 131 (*prowan*)[1] An Excuse for doing our own Business ourselves. [[1] provender.]

Proud mind and a beggar's purse agree not well together, A.   (H 324)

c. **1430** LYDGATE *Minor Poems* Percy Soc. 56 A prowde hert in a beggers brest . . . it accordith nought. **1603** T. HEYWOOD *Woman Killed with Kindness* Wks. ii. 114. **1670** RAY 133. **1732** FULLER no. 369 A proud Mind and a poor Purse are ill met. *Ibid.* no. 6386 There's nothing agrees worse Than a Prince's Heart and a Beggar's Purse.

Proud Preston (poor people, high church, and low steeple).

1727 DEFOE *Tour* iii. 221 The Town . . . is full of Gentlemen, Attorneys, Proctors, and Notaries. . . . The People are gay here, though not perhaps the richer for that; but it has on this Account obtained the name of Proud Preston. **1818** SCOTT *Rob Roy* ch. 37 Wilfred . . . was slain at Proud Preston, in Lancashire, on the day that General Carpenter attacked the barricades. **1852** *N. & Q.* 1st Ser. VI. 496 The old lines . . . are, 'Proud Preston, Poor people, High church, And low steeple'. The name in the first line yet adheres to us; . . . the second is no longer applicable; . . . [and] in 1815 the tower of the church . . . was pulled down, and . . . one of proportionate size erected.

Proud tod[1] that will not scrape his own hole, He is a. (T 367)

a. **1628** CARMICHAELL no. 671. **1641** FERGUSSON no. 321. **1721** KELLY 146 . . . A Reproof to them who refuse to do their own proper Business, or an Excuse in them that do it. [1 fox.]

Proud, *see also* Bastard brood always p.; Beating p. folks (It is good); Fine (p.) as a lord; I p. and thou p.; Long and lazy . . . pretty and p.; Poor and p.

Prove your friend ere you have need. *Cf.* **Try your friend before you trust.** (F 718)

c. **1400** *Cato's Morals* in *Cursor M.* E.E.T.S. III. 1672 Be scarske of þi louing til hit come to prouing of þi gode frende. *c.* **1526** *Dicta Sap.* A4 Proue they frende or you haue nede. **1545** TAVERNER 14ᵛ. **1546** HEYWOOD I. xi. E4. **1611** DAVIES *Prov.* no. 115.

Prove(s), *see also* Black is white (P. that); Exception p. rule.

Provender pricks him, His. (P 615)

1546 HEYWOOD I. xi. D3 For when prouender pryckt him a little tyne, He dyd as thou didst. **1550** R. CROWLEY *Way to Wealth* E.E.T.S. 142. **1650** BROME *Jov. Crew* I. (1708) 7 I left the merry grigs (as their provender has prickt 'em) in such a *Hoigh* yonder! such a frolic! **1670** RAY 190.

Provender, *see also* Prayers and p. hinder no journey.

Proverbs, *see* Wise men make p.

Proves too much, That which | proves nothing.

1732 FULLER no. 4384.

Provide(d), *see* Fear (P. for) the worst; Money and capers, (He that has) is p. for Lent.

Providence is always on the side of the strongest battalions.

[**1770** VOLTAIRE *Let.* 6 Feb. *On dit que Dieu est toujours pour les gros bataillons.*] **1842** ALISON *Hist. Europe* X. lxxviii. 1013 Moreau expressed a fact of general application, explained according to the irreligious ideas of the French Revolution, when he said, that 'Providence was always on the side of dense battalions'. **1867–77** FROUDE *Short Stud.* (1890) II. 397 If Providence, as Napoleon scornfully said, is on the side of the strongest battalions, it provides also, as Napoleon himself found at Leipsic, that in the times of these tremendous visitations the strong battalions shall be found in defence of the cause which it intends shall conquer. **1906** ALEX. MACLAREN *Expos., Deut.* 1 *Sam.* 238 The old sneer, that 'Providence is always on the side of the strongest battalions', is . . . the very opposite of the truth.

Providence is better than rent. (P 616)

1640 HERBERT no. 254.

Providence, *see also* Fly in the face of P.; Leap into a well (If you), P. not fetch you out; Play p.

Provider, *see* Lion's p.

Providing is preventing.

1883 GEORGINA JACKSON *Shropshire Folk-Lore* 588 A collier's wife at Kelley heard that her father-in-law . . . was dangerously ill, so having an opportunity of buying cheaply, she got mourning for all her family . . .; but the old man recovered. '*Pervidin's perventin.*' The proverb may also be taken in the sense of 'forewarned is forearmed'.

Provision in season makes a rich house. (P 618)

a. **1628** CARMICHAELL no. 1249 (mak a rich maison[1]). **1641** FERGUSSON no. 698 (meason[1]). **1721** KELLY 281 . . . Because every Thing is gotten at the easiest rate. [1 house.]

Provision, *see also* Pompous p. comes not alway of gluttony.

Provoked, *see* Patience p. turns to fury.

Prudence, *see* Fear is one part of p.; No divinity is absent if P. present.

Pry, *see* Paul P.

Psalms, *see* Whistle p. to taffrail.

Public gown, *see* Puts on a p. g. (He that).

Pucksy, *see* Muxy (He got out of the).

Pudding for a friar's mouth, As fit as a. (P 620)

1568 FULWELL *Like Will to L.* (1906) 13 I will find one as fit for you as a pudding for a friar's mouth. *c.* **1570** *Juli & Julian* I. 1307 (as mett as). *c.* **1590** LYLY *Mother B.* II. i. 106 (for a dog's). **1600** DEKKER *Shoem. Hol.* IV. iv. 54 As fit as a pudding. **1602** SHAKES. *A.W.* II. ii. 25 As fit as . . . the nun's lips to the friar's mouth; nay, as the pudding to his skin. **1659** J. DAY *Blind Beg. Bethnal Green* IV Thou com'st as fit for the purpose as a Pudding for a Fryers mouth.

Pudding, If it won't | it will froize.

1830 FORBY 427 . . . *i.e.* If it won't do for one thing, it will for another.

Pudding in the fire, There is a | and my part lies therein.

1609 T. RAVENSCROFT *Pammelia* C2. **1659** HOWELL *Eng. Prov.* 13b.

Pudding (Pudding prick), Not worth a.
(P 626)

1530 TYNDALE *Answ. to More* P.S. 141 Not the value of a poding prick. [*c.* 1530] *c.* **1545** H. RHODES *Bk. Nurture* (1577 ed.) l. 489 in *Babies Bk. etc.* 95 But in the ende his peevishe pryde makes all not worth a pudding. **1600** BRETON *Pasquil's Foolscap* B4ᵛ Not worth two puddings endes.

Pudding time, He (It) comes in.
(P 634)

1546 HEYWOOD II. ix. L2ᵛ This geare comth euen in puddyng time ryghtly. **1568** FULWELL *Like Will to L.* (1906) 14 Even in pudding time Yonder cometh Ralph Roister, an old friend of mine! **1611** DAVIES no. 41 Oft things fall out in pudding time. **1738** SWIFT *Dial.* II. E.L. 298 Will you do as we do? You are come in pudding time.

Puddings and paramours should be hotly handled.
(P 633)

a. **1628** CARMICHAELL no. 1258. **1641** FERGUSSON no. 702. **1721** KELLY 277 . . . Puddings, when cold, are uneatable, and Love, when coldrife, is near the breaking off.

Pudding(s), *see also* Better some of a p.; Cake and p. to me, (It is); Claws it as Clayton clawed p.; Cold p. will settle love; Come of a blood and so is a p.; Dirty p.; Eat a p. at home, dog have skin; Eat another yard of p. first; Everything has an end, and a p. has two; Gentleman without estate; Good blood makes bad p.; Love like p.; Lucky p. (If ever you make), I'll eat the prick; Make the crow a p.; Never ate flesh (He that) thinks p. dainty; Praise is not p.; Proof of the p. in the eating; Ride post for p.; Salt to Dysart and p. to Tranent (Carry); Too much p. will choke dog; Vex a dog to see p. creep.

Pudding-prick, *see* Pudding (P.), (Not worth a); Thwitten a mill-post to p. *See also* Lucky pudding.

Puddle, *see* Path has a p. (Every).

Puddock(s), *see* Gentle p. have long toes; Mim as a May p.

Puff and blow, *see* Grampus.

Puff not against the wind.
(W 428)

1509 BARCLAY *Ship of Fools* i. 228 He bloweth in the wynde, and shall nat haue his thought. **1614** CAMDEN 311. **1639** CLARKE 154. **1747** J. WESLEY *Journal* iii. 306 One may as well blow against the wind.

Pull caps, To.

[= to quarrel, wrangle.] **1754** RICHARDSON 12 Sept. (*Corresp.* v. 27) She scrupled not . . . to pull caps in good-humoured roguery. **1778** FRANCES BURNEY *Evelina* Lett. 79 If either of you have any inclination to pull caps for the title of Miss Belmont, you must do it with all speed.

1826 SCOTT *Journ.* 3 Aug. So the two Duties may go pull caps about it. **1853** SURTEES *Sponge's Sport. T.* ch. 7 'There's nothin' talked of . . . but the rich stranger that's a comin', and the gals are all pulling caps, who's to have the first chance.'

Pull devil, pull baker.

1759 COLMAN *Rolliad* can. ii. Pull Tom, pull Nick, pull baker, and pull devil. **1819** SCOTT *Let.* to Ld. Montagu 4 Mar. in LOCKHART *Life* ch. 44 A most disagreeable see-saw—a kind of pull-devil, pull-baker contention. **1853** SURTEES *Sponge's Sport. T.* ch. 50. Mr. Sponge was now engaged with a game of 'pull devil, pull baker', with the hounds for the fox. **1909** *Spectator* 28 Aug. 293 In China . . . in financial matters there has been a game of 'Pull devil, pull baker' between the central Government and the provincial Governments, the central Government exacting as much as possible and the provincial Governments withholding as much as possible.

Pull down than to build, It is easier to.
(P 635)

1577 R. STANIHURST in Holinshed *Chron. Ireland* (1587, 88a) It is easie to raze, and hard to build. [Earl of Kildare to his son, 1533]. **1587** J. BRIDGES *Def. of Govt. in C. of E.* 518 It is a true say of olde, *Facilius est destruere quam construere*, We may quicklier pull downe with one hande, than wee can easilie builde againe with both. **1644** J. HOWELL *Dodona's Grove* 96. **1909** *Times* 28 Apr. Turkey and her new rulers . . . have astonished those who thought they knew the Turks best by . . . the vigour . . . with which the great change has been conducted. . . . But it is easier always and everywhere to pull down than to build up.

Pull down your hat on the wind('s) side.
(H 206)

1640 HERBERT no. 334. **1721** KELLY 19 As the Wind blows seek you Beel. . . . Advising us to make our Interest as the Times change. . . .

Pull not out your teeth but with a leaden instrument.
(T 427)

1678 RAY 351.

Pull out one tooth and pull out more.

1552 A. BORDE *Brev. of Health* 97 xxxviii. And beware of pullyng out any toth for pul out one, and pul out mo.

Pull the devil by the tail, To.

[= to be in difficulties or straits. Fr. *tirer le diable par la queue.*] *a.* **1832** BENTHAM *Wks.* (1838–43) X. 25 So fond of spending his money on antiquities, that he was always pulling the devil by the tail. **1864** TROLLOPE *Sm. H. at Allington* ch. 47 I've always been pulling the devil by the tail, and never yet got as much as a good hold on to that.

Pull the thorn out of your foot and put it into my own, I will not.
(T 231)

1633 D. DYKE *Wks. Philemon* 279 When thou . . . becomest surety for another, let it be for no more

than thou art willing and well able to part withall.
A man is not bound to pluck a thorn out of
another man's foot, to put it into his own. **1678**
RAY 273.

Pulleyn, *see* Raw p. . . . make churchyards fat.

Pulls an old house on his head, He.
(H 756)

[= To get oneself into trouble.] *c.* **1566** *The
Bugbears* I. ii. **1576** GASCOIGNE ii. 548 My Boye
quod he who badd the be so bolde As for to
plucke an olde house on they hedd? **1608** TOP-
SELL *Serpents* (1658) 658 You shall pull an old
house over your own head by a further provocation. **1670** RAY 188. **1739** J. HILDROP *Regul.
Freethinking* 7 He . . . will have good Luck if he
does not pull an old House upon his head. **1861**
G. ELIOT *Silas Marner* ch. 3, E.L. (1952) 36
You'll have less pleasure in pulling the house
over my head, when your own skull's to be
broken too.

Pulls with a long rope that waits for another's death, He.
(R 170)
1640 HERBERT no. 25. **1659** HOWELL *Span.
Prov.* 17.

Pull(s), *see also* Long p., and p. all together;
Nose, (To take (p.) oneself by the); Sin plucks
(p.) on sin.

Pulse beats matrimony, Her.   (P 636)
1678 RAY 265. **1732** FULLER no. 2492.

Pulse, *see also* Long time to know world's p.

Pun, He that would make a | would pick a pocket.
1722 B. VICTOR *Ep. to Sir Richard Steele* A great
Critick [Dennis] formerly . . . declared He that
would pun would pick a Pocket. **1907** HAM-
MERTON *Eng. Humourists* III If there were any
truth in that ancient saw, . . . 'He who would
make a pun, would pick a pocket', what a
capacity for pocket-picking had Francis
Burnand!

Punch coal, cut candle, set brand on end, neither good housewife, nor good housewife's friend.
(C 461)
1666 TORRIANO *It. Prov.* 242 no. 36 The English
say, Burn candle, break cole, set stick on end,
is neither good housewivery, nor yet good hous-
wives friend. **1678** RAY 295.

Punch (*noun*), *see* Many estates are spent . . .
since men for P. forsook . . .; Proud as P.

Punctuality is the politeness of princes.
[LOUIS XVIII *L'exactitude est la politesse des rois.*]
1834 EDGEWORTH *Helen* ch. 25 She dreaded,
when the General quoted 'Punctuality is the
virtue of princes', that Mr. Harley . . . would
have ridiculed so antiquated a notion. **1854**
SURTEES *Hand. Cross* ch. 35 Punctuality is the
politeness of princes, and I don't like keeping
people waiting. **1879** DOWDEN *Southey* 104
Verbeyst, the prince of booksellers, had not a
prince's politeness of punctuality.

Punctuality is the soul of business.
1843 T. C. HALIBURTON *Wise Saws* ch. 3. **1911**
W. CROSSING *Folk Rhy. of Devon* 16 Punctuality
is the soul of business, and in these days of cheap
watches there can be no excuse for anybody
failing to cultivate the habit.

Punic faith.
[= faithlessness. L. *Fides Punica*, The faith of
Carthaginians, who were supposed to be syste-
matically false; cf. LIVY 21. 4 (of Hannibal)
Perfidia plus quam Punica.] **1603** MONTAIGNE
(Florio) I. v. 30 These were true Romane pro-
ceedings, and not Grecian policies, nor Punike
wiles, with whom to vanquish by force is lesse
glorious than to conquer by treacherie. **1631**
MASSINGER *Believe as you List* II. ii The Punicque
faith is branded by Our enemies. **1645** (11 Aug.)
Mercurius Anti-Britannicus Carthage; A City
where the Publique Faith, grew to be a prouerbe
for perfidiousnesse. **1768–74** TUCKER *Lt. Nat.*
(1852) II. 318 French faith became the same
among us, as Punic faith had been among the
Romans. **1824** SCOTT *Redg.* ch. 17 A devout
belief in whatever had been said of the punic
faith of Jesuits.

Punish(es), *see* Anger p. itself; God will p.,
(When); Man p. the action, God the intention.

Punishment, Many without | but none without fault (sin).
(P 638)
1616 DRAXE no. 678. **1670** RAY 17 (sin).

Punishment is lame, but it comes.
(P 639)
[HOR. *Od.* 3. 2. 31 *Raro antecedentem scelestum
Deseruit pede poena claudo.*] **1640** HERBERT no.
249. **1853** TRENCH vi. 147 . . . rests on an image
derived from antiquity.

Punishment, *see also* Fault, (Like) like p.; Fire
of London p. for gluttony; Like p. . . . key and
keyhole sustain; Reward and p. are the walls of
a city; Sin brings its p.

Puppy, *see* First pig but last p. best.

Purchase, *see* No p. no pay.

Purgatory pickpurse.   (P 277)
[= the use made of the doctrine of purgatory to
obtain payment of masses for departed souls.]
1537 LATIMER tr. *Serm. bef. Convoc.* P.S. 50
They that begot and brought forth that our
old ancient purgatory pick-purse. *a.* **1591**
H. SMITH *Arrow agst. Ath.* (1622) 60 It may be
well and justly called Purgatorie Pickpurse; . . .
wealth and great riches of the clergy, was the
only mark they aimed at. **1721** M. HENRY
Popery Wks. (1853) II. 346/2 'Purgatory pickpurse', so it has been called. **1922** DEAN INGE
Outspoken Ess. 33 The reformers in the sixteenth century complained of 'Purgatory Pickpurse'; our revolutionists think that heaven and

hell are made to discharge the same function of bolstering up social injustice.

Purgatory, *see also* England paradise of women, p. of servants; Penniless souls maun pine in p.

Puritan, *see* Christian must have . . . words of a P.

Purple, *see* Win p. and wear p.

Purpose(s), *see* Intents and p.; Wise man needs not blush for changing p.

Purse and his palate are ill met, His.

1721 KELLY 154 . . . Spoken when a poor Man loves to eat good Meat. **1732** FULLER no. 2513.

Purse be your master, Let your.   (P 658)

1616 WITHALS 564. **1639** CLARKE 129. **1670** RAY 135. **1672** WALKER 47 no. 48.

Purse is his best friend, His.   (P 656)

c. **1425** *Castle of Perseverance* l. 2522 Thi purs schal be thi beste frende. **1623** WODROEPHE 501 Our Friends are in our Purse. So said of all vncharitable Worldlings through all Where. **1639** CLARKE 220.

Purse is made of a toad's skin, His.   (P 657)

1678 RAY 90 *A covetous person . . .*

Purse opened not (was steekit[1]) when it (that) was paid for, Your.

1721 KELLY 385 . . . A Reproof to those who abuse what is not their own. **1832** HENDERSON 151 Your purse was steikit when that was paid for. [[1] shut.]

Purse to your wife, If you sell your | give your breeks into the bargain.

1721 KELLY 195 . . . For if your Wife command your Purse, she will certainly have the Mastery in every Thing else.

Purse, *see also* Be it for better . . . do after him that bears p.; Dog is hanged . . . and man killed for p. (Many a); Drunkard's p. a bottle; Empty p. causes full heart; Empty p. fills face with wrinkles; Empty p. that is full of other men's money; Fair words make me look to my p.; Fortunatus' p.; Four and spends five (He that has but) has no need of p.; Friends tie p. with cobweb; Full p. (He that has) never wanted friend; Gain that is put in p. (All is not); Heavy p. light heart; Left his p. in his other hose; Less of your counsel, more of your p.; Light p. heavy heart; Little and often fills p.; Looks in a man's face (He that) knows not what money is in his p.; Money in thy p. (Put);

Money (He that has no) needs no p.; Open thy p. then thy sack; Penny in p.; Proud eye, open p. bring; Proud mind and beggar's p.; Put nothing into p. (If you); Put two pennies in a p.; Rusty sword and empty p. plead performance; Shows his p. longs to be rid of it; Sickness soaks the p.; Silk p. of a sow's ear; Toom p. makes blate merchant; Two friends have a common p. (When); Two hands in a dish, one in a p.

Purse-net, *see* Caught a knave in a p.

Purser's shirt on a handspike, Like a.

1810 J. MOORE *Post-Captain* v. 23 There is nothing of him left but ribs and trucks. His coat fits him like a purser's shirt upon a handspike.

Pursuits become (grow into) habits. *Cf.* Studies pass into character.

[L. *Abeunt studia in mores.*] **1605** BACON *Adv. Learn.* I. iii (Oxf.) 21 *Abeunt studia in mores*, studies have an influence and operation upon the manners of those that are conversant in them. **1926** *Times* 1 Feb. Rushbrooke . . . acquired . . . a particular bent to New Testament studies, not on their exegetical side only but also as a foundation for life. *Abierunt studia in mores.*

Put a blithe face on a black heart, It is ill to. *Cf.* Fair face and foul heart.

1721 KELLY 216 . . . It is hard to pretend Mirth, when the Heart is sorrowful.

Put a churl (carl) upon a gentleman, I will never (not).   (C 387)

1586 L. EVANS *Withals Dict. Revised* D7 Lay not a Churle vpon a Gentleman, drinke not beere after wine. **1721** KELLY 186 (Carle above) . . . Spoken when we offer Ale to them that have been drinking Claret. **1738** SWIFT *Dial.* II. E.L. 310 Will you taste a glass of October[1]?—No, faith, my lord; I like your wine, and won't put a churl upon a gentleman; your honour's claret is good enough for me. [[1] ale.]

Put a miller, a waver, and a tailor in a bag, and shake them; the first that comes out will be a thief.   (M 957)

1592 GREENE *Quip* Hindley *Old Bk. Collector's Misc.* i. 73 You weaver, the proverb puts you down for a crafty knave; you can filch and steal almost as ill as the tailor; . . . What, miller, shake hands with your brother the weaver for knavery. **1636** W. SAMPSON *Vow Breaker* I. ii Put me a Tailor, a Weaver, and a Miller into a bag.—And what then, sir?—Why, he that first comes out will be a knave. **1637** (1676 cd., B3) *Hist. of Will Sommers* The Proverb being then on foot, That there were three several Trades, that could never be free from Felony, namely, Weavers, Millers and Taylors. **1659** HOWELL *Eng. Prov.* 3b. **1706** STEVENS s.v. Sastre (will be a Knave). **1823** GROSE ed. Pierce Egan s.v. Tailor.

Put another man's child in your bosom, and he'll creep out at your elbow. (M 487)

1609 HARWARD 80 (in thy sleeve . . . at the elbow). **1670** RAY 52 . . . *Chesh.* That is, cherish or love him, he 'll never be naturally affected towards you.

Put[1] at the cart that is aye ganging, They. (C 104)

1641 FERGUSSON no. 826. **1721** KELLY 371 . . . Spoken to them whom we have been very ready to serve, when our readiness that way encourages them to put the sorer upon us. [[1] push.]

Put back the clock, To.

1867 LOWELL *Biglow Papers* Wks. (1893) VIII. 261 'T would put the clock back all o' fifty years Ef they should fall together by the ears. **1907** A. C. BENSON *Upton Lett.* (ed. 2) 61 The attempt to put back the clock, and to try and restore things as they were. **1928** *Times* 23 Oct. 12/2 This means . . . the abandonment of the idea of an All-Indian Parliament. Can the clock be put back?

Put him up in a bag, He is able to. (B 31)

1662 FULLER *Cardigan* 26 They had a kind of Play, wherein the stronger . . . put the weaker into a Sack; and hence we have borrowed our English By-word . . . 'He is able to put him up in a bagge.'

Put it on thick, and a little will stick.

1841 F. CHAMIER *Tom Bowl.* ch. 3 Captain Cornish . . . had also imbibed the vulgar but correct notion of 'put it on thick, and a little will stick', so that in plaster and in compliments the proverb is verified.

Put it together with a hot needle and burnt thread, You. (N 98)

1678 RAY 350.

Put no faith in tale-bearers.

c. **1450** *Provs. of Wysdom* 123 Be ware of hym, þat tel-þe talis. **1560** DAUS tr. *Sleidane's Comm.* 21b He admonisheth him to gyue no credit to talebearers.

Put not the bucket too often in the well.

1590 GREENE *Mourning Garment* ed. Gros. ix. 209 By drawing too oft, the Well waxed drie. **1594** LIPSIUS *Six Books of Politics* tr. Jones 39 You may so long draw water at this well, that in the end it will become drie. **1616** DEKKER *Villainies Discovered* L2 Put not the Bucket too often into the Well.

Put nothing into your house (purse), If you | you can take nothing out. (N 280)

1642 TORRIANO 17 In a new house, he that bringeth nothing in, nothing shall find. **1659** HOWELL *Span. Prov.* 10 Where they take out and

put nothing in, they quickly go to the bottom. **1732** FULLER no. 2781. **1771** J. WESLEY *Letters* v. 269 We cannot put out what we never put in.

Put off his clothes (doublet) before he goes to bed, He will not. (D 570)

1603 MONTAIGNE (Florio) II. viii. 102. That answer . . . which fathers have commonly in their mouthes: I will not put off my clothes before I be ready to goe to bed. **1662** FULLER *Cumb.* 219 Archbishop Grindall . . . was willing to put off his clothes before he went to bed, and in his life time to resigne his place to Doctor Whitgiff. **1678** RAY 239 He 'll not put' off his doublet before he goes to bed, *i.e.* part with his estate before he die. **1888** FREEMAN *Wm. the Conq.* ch. 10 Robert . . . demand[ed] . . . Normandy and Maine. William refused with many pithy sayings. It was not his manner to take off his clothes till he went to bed.

Put off the evil hour as long as you can.

1738 SWIFT *Dial.* II. E.L. 314. Come, sit down; let us put off the evil hour as long as we can.

Put off the person of a judge, He has | that puts on the person of a friend. (P 239)

1563 RAINOLDE *Found. Rhet.* 61[v] No godlie Lawe, maketh the accuser his owne Judge. **1618** T. ADAMS *Serm.* (1861–2) ii. 550 Tully tells us of a proverb:¦ *Exuit personam judicis, quisquis amici induit.*—He hath put off the person of a judge, that puts on the person of a friend.

Put off till tomorrow what may be done to-day, Never. (T 378)

c. **1386** CHAUCER *Mel.* B[2] l. 2984 'An old proverbe,' quod she, 'seith: that "the goodnesse that thou mayst do this day, do it; and abyde nat ne delaye it nat till to-morwe".' **1530** PALSGRAVE 515b It is folye to differ the thing tyll to morowe that had nede to be doone by and by. **1576** PETTIE i. 6 Qui non est hodie, cras minus aptus erit. **1616** DRAXE no. 471 Deferre not vntill to morrow, if thou canst do it to day. **1633** J. HOWELL *Lett.* 5 Sep. (Dent) II. 140 Secretary Cecil . . . would ofttimes speak of himself, 'It shall never be said of me that I will defer till to-morrow what I can do to-day'. **1712** ADDISON *Spect.* no. 487 Wks. (Bohn) III. 469 The maxim . . . should be inviolable with a man in office, never to think of doing that to-morrow which may be done to-day. **1846** DENHAM 3 Never put off till to-morrow, what you can do to-day. **1906** W. MAXWELL *From Yalu to Port A.* 7 It was added that the Chinese Government 'would not reply in haste', but would take advantage of its reputation for never doing to-day what could be put off till the morrow.

Put on one's considering (thinking) cap, To. (C 613)

[= to take time for thinking over something.] **1573** J. BRIDGES *Supremacy of Christ. Princes* D2 Ye had on some great considering cappe. **1582** T. BLENNERHASSET *Revel. of the true Minerva* C3[v] Peter put on his considering cappe. *c.* **1604**

DAY *Law Tricks* V. ii. How now, Father, haue you put on your Considering Cap and bethought you? **1607** H. ESTIENNE *World of Wonders* tr. R. C. 25 A man had need to put on his considering cap. **1657** R. LIGON *Barbadoes* (1673) 42 They fall back, and put ion their considering caps. **1738** SWIFT Dial. I. E.L. 288 Guess who it was that told me; come, put on your considering cap.

Put one to (upon) his trump (trumps), To. (T 545)

[= to oblige a card player to play out his trumps; *fig.* to put to the last expedient.] **1559** *Mir. Mag., Jack Cade* ed. Campbell, 176. Ere he took me, I put him to his trumps. **1560** *Cont. betwixt Churchyard and Camell* G3 You will put me to my trompe, with a false carde often. **1584** LYLY *Camp.* III. iv. 59 Doeth not your beauty put the painter to his trump? **1697** DAMPIER *Voy.* (1729) I. 526 The Wind . . . oft put us to our trumps to manage the Ship. **1907** W. JAMES *Pragmatism* iv. 142 A bit of danger or hardship puts us agreeably to our trumps.

Put one's finger in the fire, To. (F 230)

1546 HEYWOOD II. ii. GI[v] It were a foly for me . . . To put my fynger to far in the fyre. **1600–1** SHAKES. *M.W.W.* I. iv. 77 I'll ne'er put my finger in the fire. **1602** [T. HEYWOOD?] *How a Man may Choose* Hazl.-Dods. ix. 87 I will not thrust my finger in the fire. **1670** RAY 175 . . . *Prudens in flammam ne manum injicito*, Hieron. . . . Put not your finger needlessly in the fire. Meddle not with a quarrel voluntarily. **1828** SCOTT *F. M. Perth* ch. 7 You will needs put your finger in the fire.

Put one's money upon the wrong horse, To.

1897 MARQ. SALISBURY in *Ho. Lords* 19 Jan. Many members of this House will keenly feel the nature of the mistake that was made when I say that we all put our money upon the wrong horse.

Put out the miller's eye, To. (M 962)

1678 RAY 343 . . . Spoken by good housewives when they have wet their meal for bread or paste too much. **1834** ESTHER COPLEY *Housekpr's Guide* x. 233 If after . . . 'putting out the millers eye' by too much water, you add flour to make it stiff enough for rolling out [&c.].

Put out your tubs when it is raining.

1721 KELLY 176 It is good to have our Coag[1] out, when it rains Kail. It is good to be in the way when Things are a going. **1909** ALEX. MACLAREN *Expos. Hebrews* 353 There is a vulgar old proverb that says, 'Put out your tubs when it is raining'. Be sure that when the gift is falling you fling your hearts wide for its acceptance. [[1] dish.]

Put over the borrowing days, He will.

[i.e. the last three days of March (Old Style), said in Scottish folk-lore to have been borrowed by March from April, and supposed to be especially stormy.] **1721** KELLY 174 . . . Spoken

upon some Hopes of our sick Friend's Recovery; taken from weak Cattel, who if they out live the first nine Days of April, we hope, they will not die.

Put that in your pipe and smoke it.

[= digest or put up with that if you can.] **1836** DICKENS *Pickwick* ch. 16 Fill your pipe with that 'ere reflection. **1840** BARHAM *Ingol. Leg.* Ser. I *St. Odille* Put that in your pipe, my lord Otto, and smoke it! **1884** W. E. NORRIS *Thirlby Hall* ch. 25 It don't do to let them get the whip-hand of you, according to my experience. Put that in your pipe and smoke it, Master Charley.

Put the man to the mear[1] that can manage the mear.

1862 HISLOP 250. [[1] mare.]

Put the poor man's penny and the rich man's penny in ae purse, and they'll come out alike.

1832 HENDERSON 86.

Put to bed with a shovel, He is.

1785 GROSE s.v. Bed Put to bed with a mattock, and tucked up with a spade. **1813** RAY 213 . . . He is going to be buried.

Put tricks upon travellers, Don't. (T 521)

1611 SHAKES. *Temp.* II. ii. 55 Have we devils here? Do you put tricks upon us with savages and men of Ind? **1709** DYKES 53 But, generally speaking there's no putting of tricks upon old Travellers. **1738** SWIFT Dial. I. E.L. 287 I know better Things; Miss and I are good Friends; don't put Tricks upon Travellers. **1870** READE *Put Yourself* ch. 29 That's a lie! . . . none of your tricks upon travellers.

Put two pennies in a purse, and they will draw together. (P 215)

1601 SHAKES. *T.N.* III. i. 47 Would not a pair of these [coins] have bred, sir?—Yes, being kept together and put to use. *a.* **1628** CARMICHAELL no. 152. **1641** FERGUSSON no. 690. **1721** KELLY 281 . . . When People have purchased any little sum of Money it will easily encrease. Apply'd sometimes when rich Men marry rich Women.

Put up your pipes. (P 345)

[= desist; 'shut up'.] [*c.* **1515**] **1521** BARCLAY *Ecl.* IV. l. 491 If thou fayle promes my confort clene is lost Than may I hang my pype vpon the post. **1556** OLDE *Antichrist* 148 Then maye the B[ishop] of Rome put up his pypes. **1559** T. BECON *Display. Popish Mass Prayers* P.S. 276 Then put up your pipes, and lay you down to sleep. **1563** PILKINGTON *Confutation* P.S. 601. **1594–5** SHAKES. *R.J.* IV. v. 96 Faith, we may put up our pipes, and be gone. **1604** *Id. O.* III. i. 20 Then put up your pipes in your bag, for I'll away. **1639** CLARKE 155.

Put up your pipes, and go to Lockington wake.[1] (P 345)

1678 RAY 317 Leicestershire. . . . **1787** GROSE (*Leics.*) 189 Put up your pipes, and go to Lockington-wake. Lockington stands . . . upon the confines of Derby and Nottingham shires. [1 festival, fair.]

Put your finger in the fire, and say it was your fortune.

1721 KELLY 280 . . . Spoken to them who lay the blame of their Crimes, and Mismanagements, on their hard Fortune.

Put your hand in the creel,[1] **and take out either an adder or an eel.** (H 89)

a. **1575** T. HOWELL *New Sonnets* E3ᵛ Who hastes to wiue in hope of that, Maye grope for Eles and catch a Snake. **1589** T. BLAND *A Bait for Momus* A1 Because I go a fishing for mine accusers, do you but imagine I Bait for Eeles, & I may haplie catch the Snake. *a.* **1610** A. MONTGOMERIE *Misc. Poems; The poet reasons* (1821) 203 Bot put ȝour hand, by hazard in the creill; Zit men hes mater vharvpon to muse. For they must drau ane adder or ane eill. **1721** KELLY 278 . . . Spoken of taking a Wife, where no Cunning, Art, or Sense can secure a good Choice. **1823** GALT *Entail* ch. 25 Watty, my lad, . . . 'Marriage is a creel, where ye maun catch', as the auld byword runs, 'an adder or an eel'. [1 wicker basket for fish, etc.]

Put (*noun*), see Forced p.

Put (*verb*), *see also* Cat among the pigeons, (To p. the); Countenance, (To be p. out of); Nose into everything, (To p. one's); Shifts, (He is p. to his); Silks and satins p. out the fire.

Put, Put a (an), Put not, Put your, *see also under significant words following.*

Puts on a public gown, He that | must put off a private person. (G 388)

1641 F. QUARLES *Enchiridion* Cent. 4 no. 6 He that puts on a publique gowne, must put off a private person. **1642** FULLER *H. & P. State* IV. vii. (1841) 255 The Good Judge . . . gives sentence with uprightness. For when he put on his robes, he put off his relations to any; and, like Melchisedec, becomes without pedigree. **1732** FULLER no. 2257.

Puttock, see Eat white bread (When shall we)? When the p. is dead.

Pylades and Orestes died long ago, and left no successors.

[Two inseparable friends. Orestes was the son of Agamemnon and of Clytemnestra, whom, by the help of Pylades, he killed.] **1732** FULLER no. 3987.

Pyrrhic victory.

[A victory gained at too great a cost; in allusion to the exclamation attributed to Pyrrhus, King of Epirus, after the battle of Asculum in Apulia, in 279 B.C. . . . 'One more such victory and we are lost.'] **1602** R. CAREW *Survey of Cornwall* 1769 ed. 62 Say with Pirrhus, that many such conquests would beget his utter overthrow. **1885** *Daily Tel.* 17 Dec. Although its acceptance might secure for the moment the triumph of a party division, it would be indeed a Pyrrhic victory.

Q

Quail, see Couch like a q.

Quake, see Aspen leaf.

Quality, without quantity, is little thought of.

1604 E. GRYMESTON *Miscellanea* A3ᵛ The grauest wits . . . The qualitie, not quantitie, respect. **1721** KELLY 282.

Qualities, see Defects of q.

Quandary, To be in a. (Q 1)

c. **1576** *Common Cond.* l. 1778 G2ᵛ I stand in such a quandary that I would giue my life for two pence. *a.* **1577** *Misogonus* III. i. 90 Thou makst me in a greater quandary. **1577** J. GRANGE *Golden Aphroditis* D3ᵛ. **1579** LYLY *Euph.* i. 182 To the Gentlemen Readers, I was driuen into a quandarie. **1600–1** SHAKES. *M.W.W.* II. ii. 55 You have brought her into such a canaries as 'tis wonderful: the best courtier of them all . . . could never have brought her to such a canary. **1616** DRAXE no. 1610. **1875** JOWETT *Plato* (ed. 2) I. 229 Now I was in a great quandary at having to answer this question.

Quarrel with one's bread and butter, To.

1738 SWIFT Dial. I. E.L. 264 I won't quarrel with my bread and butter for all that; I know when I'm well. **1780** CRAIG *Mirror* no. 69 par. 1 How did she show superior sense by thus quarrelling with her bread and butter? **1883** J. PAYN *Thicker than W.* ch. 38 He thought that Edgar had shown his wisdom in not 'quarrelling with his bread and butter'.

Quarrel, *see also* Come and welcome, go by, no q.; Lambs, (He that has) has q.; Make a fire (He that can) can end q.; Two to make q.

Quarrelling dogs come halting home.

1591 I *Troublesome Reign K. John* CIᵛ Hastie curres . . . Come halting home, and meete their ouermatch. **1721** KELLY 309 Tulying¹ Dogs come halting home. **1732** FULLER no. 3988. [¹ fighting.]

Quarrelsome dogs get dirty coats.

(C 916)

1659 HOWELL *Br. Prov.* 2 A snarling dog hath a ragged coat. **1842** S. LOVER *Handy Andy* ch. 46 'You're a stout fellow, Ratty', said he, 'but remember this old saying, . . .

Quart into a pint-pot, To put a.

1896 SIR M. HICKS-BEACH *Daily News* 23 July 4/3 What he might describe in homely phrase as putting a quart into a pint pot.

Quart, *see* Cow of his own . . . q. of milk for a penny; Neighbour-q. is good q.

Quartan agues kill old men, and cure young.

(A 82)

1659 HOWELL *It. Prov.* 15. **1678** RAY 41. **1732** FULLER no. 3991.

Quarter, *see* Wind keeps not always in one q.

Quarter day, *see* Nothing is certain but . . . q. d.

Quarter-master wherever he comes, He'll be.

(Q 4)

1541 *Schoolhouse of Women* BIᵛ The yonge [wives] waxe bolde So that within a moneth they be Quarter mayster, or more then he. **1572** T. WILSON *Discourse upon Usury* (1925) 210 He . . . wilbee quarter master wyth mee I tell you, do what I can [of a forward young fellow]. **1678** RAY 266. **1732** FULLER no. 2414 He would be Quarter-Master at home, if his Wife would let him.

Quatre trey, *see* Size cinque.

Queen Anne is dead.

1722 Ballad in LADY PENNYMAN *Miscellanies* 1740 He's as dead as Queen Anne the day after she dy'd. **1840** BARHAM *Ingol. Leg.* Ser. 1. *Acc. New Play* Lord Brougham, it appears isn't dead, though Queen Anne is. **1859** THACKERAY *Virgin.* ch. 73 On which my lady cried petulantly, 'Oh, Lord, Queen Anne's dead, I suppose.' **1885** D. C. MURRAY *Rainbow G.* III. v. May happen thee hasn't heard th' other piece o' news. Queen Anne's dead.

Queen, *see also* Dead as Q. Anne; King of good fellows appointed for q. of beggars; Light as the Q.'s groat.

Queen Elizabeth is dead.

1738 SWIFT *Dial.* I. E.L. 260 What news, Mr. Neverout.—Why, madam, Queen Elizabeth's dead.

Queen's weather.

1902 GUGGISBERG *The Shop* 177 On the 22nd June, 1897, the cadets . . . proceeded to London to take part in Her Majesty's Diamond Jubilee celebration. . . . Never did the expression 'Queen's weather' more thoroughly deserve its meaning. **1910** *Times Wkly.* 9 Dec. The Coronation of King Edward took place in weather as bright as that which had come to be known as 'Queen's weather'.

Queer Street.

1811 *Lexicon balatronicum* (Grose) . . . a cant phrase, to signify that it is wrong or different to our wish. **1823** GROSE ed. Pierce Egan . . . Wrong. Improper. Contrary to one's wish. **1823** JON BEE *Slang* 'to live in . . .' to be badly off as to income. **1836** DICKENS *Pickwick* ch. 55 You would have found yourself in Queer Street before this. **1837** LYTTON *E. Maltrav.* IV. vii You are in the wrong box—planted in Queer Street, as we say in London. **1865** DICKENS *Mut. Fr.* Bk. 3, ch. 1 Queer Street is full of lodgers just at present.

Queer, *see also* Dick's hatband (Q. as).

Quench, *see* Wine in bottle does not q. thirst.

Question for question is all fair.

1773 GOLDSMITH *She Stoops to C.* I. ii (Globe) 648 No offence; but question for question is all fair, you know.

Question like answer, Like.

1584 LYLY *Camp.* I. iii. 89 Straunge questions must haue straung answeres. **1616** DRAXE no. 1786. **1659** TORRIANO no. 57. As the question, so the answer.

Question(s) (*noun*), *see also* Ask no q., told no lies; Beg the q.; Fool may ask more q.; Irishman before answering q. asks another; Never answer q. until it is asked; Spur a jade a q., she'll kick an answer; Two sides to every q.

Question(s) (*verb*), *see* Comes from above let no man q.; Nothing q., nothing learns.

Quey¹ calves are dear veal.

1737 RAMSAY III. 192 Quey caufs are dear veal. [¹ Heifer. Female calves should be kept for breeding.]

Qui facit per alium facit per se, *see* Causes to be done.

Quick and nimble, more like a bear than a squirrel.

1732 FULLER no. 3992. **1813** RAY 66 In some places they say, in drollery, . . .

Quick and nimble, 'twill be your own another day.

1678 RAY 345.

Quick as a bee, As. (B 203)

1546 HEYWOOD I .ix. C2 Home agayne hitherward quicke as a bee. **1579** J. DYOS *Sermon* B3ᵛ To the worlde as quicke as bees: to the word, as slow as snayles. *c.* **1580** *Wife in Morel's Skin* E.P.P. iv. 196. **1732** FULLER no. 666 As brisk as a Bee in a Tar-Pot.

Quick at meat, quick at work. (M 835)

1611 COTGRAVE s.v. Bon A good beast eats apace; or, as we say, good at meat good at worke. **1616** DRAXE no. 494. **1639** CLARKE 92. **1650** T. FULLER *Pisgah-Sight* 174. **1695** RAVENS-CROFT 45 (Good at). **1738** SWIFT Dial. II. E.L. 312 I have dined this half Hour.—What! quick at Meat, quick at Work, they ·say.

Quick believers need broad shoulders.
(B 270)

1640 HERBERT no. 39.

Quick returns make rich merchants.

1721 KELLY 282 . . . Often ironically apply'd to them, who having been drunk, and having slept themselves sober, go to it again.

Quick, *see also* Judge, (From a foolish) a q. sentence; Live by the q. (We must); Nimble (q.) as eel; Swift (q.) as thought; Touched him to the q.

Quickly come, quickly go. *Cf.* Light(ly) come, light(ly) go. Easy come. (C 533)

1578 G. WHETSTONE *Promus & Cassandra* Iiᵛ Who gets a pace as meryly may spend. **1583** MELBANCKE *Philotimus* V2ᵛ Quickly spent, thats easely gotten. **1631** MABBE *Celestina* T.T. 29 Quickly be wonne, and quickly be lost. **1869** HAZLITT 322.

Quickly too'd[1] and quickly go, quickly will thy mother have moe.

1659 HOWELL *Eng. Prov.* 4a Soon todd,[1] soon with God. A Northern Proverb when a child hath teeth too soon. **1670** RAY 52 . . . *Yorksh.* Some have it quickly to'd, quickly with God, as if early breeding of teeth, were a sign of a short life, whereas we read of some born with teeth in their heads, who have yet lived long enough to become famous men. [[1] toothed.]

Quickly, *see also* Gives twice who gives q.; Good and q. seldom meet.

Quiet as a wasp in one's nose, She is as.
(W 77)

1588 'MARPRELATE' *Oh read over Dr. John Bridges* (ed. Pierce 49) At the hearing of this speech, the wasp got my Brother by the nose, which made him in his rage to affirm . . . **1616** WITHALS 566 A woman is as quiet, as a waspe in a mans nose. **1659** HOWELL *Eng. Prov.* 16a. **1670** RAY 215. **1732** FULLER no. 4130 (ear).

Quiet conscience sleeps in thunder, A.
(C 609)

1584 WITHALS O4 The man whose conscience pricks him not, A quiet minde hath for his lot.

c. **1605** SHAKES. *M.* IV. i. 85 I may tell pale-hearted fear it lies, And sleep in spite of thunder. **1672** R. CODRINGTON no. 233 Clear thy conscience before thou close thine Eyes, so thou may'st have golden Dreams. **1721** KELLY 14 A safe Conscience makes a sound Sleep. And doubtless a bad Conscience will have the contrary Effect. **1732** FULLER no. 374 . . . causes a quiet Sleep. **1747** FRANKLIN July A quiet conscience sleeps in thunder, but rest and guilt live far asunder.

Quiet sow, quiet mow.

1850 *N. & Q.* 1st Ser. II. 512 . . . A saying with reference to land or lease held on lives. If the seed is sown without notice of the death of the life, the corn may be reaped, although the death took place before the sowing.

Quiet, *see also* Anything for q. life; Children stand q.; Little with q.; Physicians (Best) are Dr. Diet, Dr. Q.

Quietness is best (a great treasure).
(Q 15)

[*a.* **1521**] *c.* **1545** J. HEYWOOD *Four PP.* C1 And sure I thynke that quietnesse In any man is great rychesse. [**1587**] **1594** GREENE *Alphonsus* I. i. 146 A quiet life doth passe an Emperie. [**1587–93**] **1599** [GREENE?] *George a Green* I. 1152. **1664** CODRINGTON 209 Quietness is a great treasure. **1832** HENDERSON 137.

Quietness is best, as the fox said when he bit the cock's head off.

1886 R. HOLLAND *Cheshire Gloss.* E.D.S. 453. **1917** BRIDGE 104.

Quietness, *see also* Husband must be deaf and the wife blind to have q.; Love (Next to), q.

Quietus, To give a. (Q 16)

[Med. L. *Quietus est* = he is quit. A discharge, acquittance; death.] **1530** LATIMER *Let.* 3: *Serm. and Rem.* P.S. 309 To have . . . your quietus est sealed with the blood of our Saviour Christ. **1587** J. BRIDGES *Defence* 1387 If we receaue the like, our brethren haue here giuen vs a flat discharge, and our quietus est for this. **1594** R. CAREW *Exam. Men's Wits* (1616) XIII. 217 That steward . . . salued vp all his reckonings, and got his quietus est. **1600–1** SHAKES *H.* III. i. 75 For who would bear the whips and scorns of time, . . . When he himself might his quietus make With a bare bodkin? **1609** *Id. Sonn.* 126, l. 12 Her [Nature's] audit, though delay'd, answer'd must be, And her quietus is to render thee. **1618** BEAUM. & FL. *Loy. Subj.* II. vi. 105 You have . . . eas'd mine age, Sir; And to this care a fair *Quietus* given. **1775** SHERIDAN *Rivals* V. iii If an unlucky bullet should carry a quietus with it. **1872** BAKER *Nile Tribut.* v. 65 The shot, far from producing a quietus, gave rise to a series of convulsive struggles.

Quill, *see* Piss in same q.

Quinine is made of the sweat of ship carpenters.

1894 F. COWAN *Sea Prov.* 67 . . . Hence it is very dear.

Quis custodiet, see Keep the keepers.

Quits his place well that leaves his friend there, He.   (P 373)
1611 COTGRAVE s.v. Place He leaues a place well that leaues a friend in it.   **1640** HERBERT no. 875.

Quits, *see* Cry q.

Quit(s) (*verb*), *see also* Begins to die that q. his desires; Gains will q. the pains.

Quittance, *see* Cry quits (q.).

Quot homines tot sententiae, see Men (So many), so many minds.

R

'R' is the dog's letter.   (R I)
[= has the sound of a snarl. PERSIUS *Sat.* i. 109 *Sonat hic de nare canina Littera.* Here from the nostril sounds the canine letter.]   **1509** BARCLAY *Ship of Fools* i. 182 This man malycious . . . Nought els soundeth but the hoorse letter R . . . , he none answere hath saue the dogges letter. **1594-5** SHAKES. *R.J.* II. iv. 202 Both with an R. — Ah! mocker; that's the dog's name.   **1616** T. ADAMS *Diseases of the Soul* 29 Because R is a dogged letter.   **1636** JONSON *Eng. Gram.* (1640) 47 R is the Dogs Letter and hurreth[1] in the sound.   **1645** FULLER *Good Thoughts* (1841) 186 This scholar . . . made a Latin oration . . . without an R therein . . . to show that men might speak without being beholden to the dog's letter. [[1] snarls.]

Rabbit, He is like a | fat and lean in twenty-four hours.   (R 2)
1678 RAY 288.   **1738** SWIFT Dial. I. E.L. 282.

Rabbit for a rat? Who will change a.
                                           (R 3)
c. **1549** HEYWOOD II. vii. K I[v] A peece of a kyd is woorth two of a cat. Who the diuell will chaunge a rabet for a rat?

Rabbit hunting with a dead ferret, To go.
1732 FULLER no. 5170 To go a Coney-catching with a dead Ferrit.   **1813** RAY 213 . . . Andar a caça con huron muerto. *Hisp.*   **1897** 'H. S. MERRIMAN' *In Kedar's T.* ch. 7 The innkeeper next door displays a branch of pine, which, I notice, is more attractive. . . . One does not catch rabbits with a dead ferret.

Rabbits, *see* Godalming.

Race is got by running, The.
1732 FULLER no. 4728.

Race is not to the swift, The | nor the battle to the strong.
[ECCLES. ix. II.]   **1581** G. ELLIOTT *Report of taking E. Campion* Arber, *Eng. Garner* VIII. 212

The field is not always won by strength.   **1621** BURTON *Anat. Mel.* II. iii. VII. (1651), 351.

Race-horses, *see* Gamesters and r. never last.

Rack and manger, To lie (live) at.
                                           (R 4)
[= to live in reckless abundance.]   *c.* **1378** WYCLIF *Works* (Matthew) 435 It is yuel to kepe a wast hors in stable, . . . but it is worse to have a womman at racke and at manger.   **1541** *Schoolhouse of Women* A3 Kepe them [women] bothe at racke, and maunger.   *a.* **1625** J. FLETCHER *Lit. Fr. Law* v. i (1905) III. 451 God help the Courtiers, That lye at rack and manger. **1679** MRS. BEHN *Feign'd Curtizan* III. i Danger, . . . once o'recome, I lie at rack and manger.   **1825** SCOTT *Journ.* 9 Dec. Harriet Wilson . . . who lived with half the gay world at rack and manger. **1843** CARLYLE *Past & Pr.* II. i John Lackland . . . tearing out the bowels of St. Edmundsbury Convent . . . by living at rack and manger there.

Rack, *see also* Canterbury is higher r.

Raddleman, *see* Rutland R.

Rag of money (with varying words).
1592 NASHE *Strange News* i. 301 Valete humanae artes, heart and good will, but neuer a ragge of money.   **1592-3** SHAKES. *C.E.* IV. iv. 84 Money by me! heart and goodwill you might. But surely, master, not a rag of money.   [1602] **1637** HEYWOOD *Royal King* VI. 44 And for the Campe, there's honour cut out of the whole peece, but not a ragge of money.

Rag(s), *see also* Red r. to bull; Sluggard must be clad in r.; Tag, r., and bobtail.

Ragged as a colt, As.   (C 521)
1537 *Thersites* C2[v] As ragged as a colt.   **1863** WISE *New Forest* ch. 16 The proverb 'as ragged as a colt Pixey' is everywhere to be heard, and at which Drayton seems to hint in his *Court of Faerie*: 'This Puck seems but a dreaming dolt, Still walking like a ragged colt.'

Ragged colt may make a good horse, A.
(c 522)

1520 WHITTINGTON *Vulgaria* 108 Many a ragged colt proued to [be] a good horse. *a.* **1530** *R. Hill's Commonpl. Bk.* E.E.T.S. 128 Of a rwgged colte cwmeth a good hors. **1546** HEYWOOD I. xi. D3 Colts (quoth his man) may proue wel with tatchis yl. For of a ragged colt there comthe a good horse. **1605** CHAPMAN, JONSON, MARSTON *Eastw. Ho* v. v. 73 (may prove). **1670** RAY 72 . . . An unhappy boy may make a good man. . . . Children which seem less handsome when young, do afterwards grow into shape and comeliness. **1721** KELLY 48 . . . And so may an untoward slovenly Boy prove a decent and useful Man.

Ragged, *see also* Coat, (Under a **r.** (threadbare)) lies wisdom.

Rain always comes out of Mobberley hole, The.

1917 BRIDGE 117 The rain always comes out of Mobberley hole. [Wilmslow.] . . . The direction from which an unpleasant wind or rain comes is almost invariably termed a 'hole'.

Rain before seven: fine before eleven.

1853 *N. & Q.* 1st Ser. VIII. 218. **1909** *Spectator* 20 Mar. 452 'Rain before seven, shine before eleven', is one of the most trustworthy of all country saws.

Rain cats and dogs, To.   (c 182)

1653 R. BROME *City Wit* IV. i It shall raine . . . dogs and polecats, and so forth. **1738** SWIFT *Dial.* II. E.L. 314 Sir John will go, though he was sure it would rain cats and dogs. **1819** SHELLEY *Let. to Peacock* 25 Feb. It began raining cats and dogs. **1882** BLACKMORE *Christow.* ch. 20.

Rain comes before the wind, If the | lower your topsails, and take them in; if the wind comes before the rain, lower your topsails, and hoist them again.

1853 *N. & Q.* 1st Ser. VIII. 218.

Rain comes scouth when the wind's in the south, The.

1862 HISLOP 186 . . . 'To rain scouth', is to rain abundantly or heavily.

Rain from the east: wet two days (twenty-four hours) at least.   (R 11)

1656–91 AUBREY *Nat. Hist. Wilts.* 16 If the raine comes out of east 'Twill raine twice twenty-four howres at the least. **1830** FORBY 417 When it rains with the wind in the east, it rains for twenty-four hours at least. **1869** HAZLITT 337.

Rain lays great dust, Small.   (R 15)

1670 RAY 135. **1732** FULLER no. 4193.

Rain lays (allays) great winds, Small.
(R 16)

c. **1230** *Ancrene Wisse* E.E.T.S. 249. 66b. 15 A muche wind aliŏ wiŏ alute rein. *c.* **1500** *Melusine* XXXVI. 247 A lytel rayne leyeth doun grete wynd. **1563** SACKVILLE Induction *Mirr. for Mag.* ed. Campbell 303 Rage of rayne doth swage the stormy wynde. **1586** GUAZZO ii. 183 That Proverbe . . . That a little rain alaieth a great wind. **1591** SHAKES. *3 Hen. VI* I. iv. 145 For raging wind blows up incessant showers, And when the rage allays the rain begins. **1592** DELAMOTHE 41 Small rayne alayes great wind. **1602** SHAKES. *T.C.* IV. iv. 52 Where are my tears? Rain, to lay this wind, or my heart will be blown up by the root. **1639** CLARKE 204. **1670** RAY 135 Petite pluye abat grand vent. Small rain, or a little rain lays a great wind. *Gall.*

Rain pottage, If it should | he would want[1] his dish.   (P 510)

1583 MELBANCKE *Philot.* 2C3 All the world is otemeale, and my poke left at home. **1670** RAY 191. **1732** FULLER no. 2687. [[1] lack.]

Rain, rain, go to Spain: fair weather come again.   (R 14)

1659 HOWELL *Eng. Prov.* 20a. **1686–7** J. AUBREY *Remains of Gent. and Jud.* ed. J. Britten 180 Little children have a custome, when it raines to sing or charme away the Raine; thus they all joine in a Chorus, and sing thus, viz: 'Raine, raine, goe away, Come againe a Saterday.'

Rain rains and the goose winks, When the | little wots the gosling what the goose thinks.   (R 19)

1523 SKELTON *Garl. Laurel* 1431 Whan the rayne rayneth and the gose wynkith, Lytill wotith the goslyng what the gose thynketh.

Rain, Some | some rest. *Cf.* **More rain, more rest.**   (R 17)

1678 RAY 80 . . . *A harvest proverb.*

Rain, There is no | —the Christians are the cause.

[*a.* **413**] **1869** LECKY *Hist. Europ. Mor.* (1905) I. iii 'There is no rain—the Christians are the cause', had become a popular proverb in Rome. (ST. AUG. *De Civ. Dei* ii. 3.)

Rainbow at morn, A | put your hook in the corn: a rainbow at eve, put your head in the sheave.

1883 ROPER 11. **1893** INWARDS 112.

Rainbow in the morning, A | is the shepherd's (sailor's) warning; a rainbow at night is the shepherd's (sailor's) delight.   (R 21)

1555 L. DIGGES *Prognostication* B2 If in the mornyng the raynebow appere, it signifieth moysture . . . If in the euening it spend it self, fayr weather ensueth. **1670** RAY 43.   **1828** SIR H. DAVY *Salmonia* (1851) vi. 164 I have often observed that the old proverb is correct—A rainbow in the morning is the shepherd's warning: A rainbow at night is the shepherd's delight. **1898** R. INWARDS *Weather Lore* (ed. 3) 135 Rainbow at night, Sailor's delight; Rainbow in morning, sailors take warning.

Rainbows appear at one time, If two | they presage rain to come.

1612 A. HOPTON *Concordancy of Years* 91.   **1669** *New Help to Discourse* 293.

Rainbow, *see also* Colours of r.; End of the r. (Go to the).

Rains but it pours, It never.

1726 J. ARBUTHNOT *It cannot Rain but it Pours* [Title].   **1809** MALKIN *Gil Blas* I. ix As it never rains but it pours, I was in the front of the battle, hemmed in between the captain and the lieutenant.   **1851** KINGSLEY *Yeast* ch. 6 'It never rains but it pours', and one cannot fall in with a new fact or a new acquaintance but next day twenty fresh things shall spring up as if by magic.   **1913** *Spectator* 26 Apr. 687 'It never rains but it pours' might be said . . . of the number of books on Japan which have appeared in the last few years.

Rains by planets, It.   (P 388)

1662 FULLER Westmr. 241 Rain (which Countrypeople say goeth by Planets) goeth by Providence.   **1670** RAY 45 . . . This the Countrey people use when it rains in one place and not in another; meaning that the showers are governed by the Planets, which . . . cause such uncertain wandring of clouds and falls of rain. Or . . . the falls of showers are as uncertain as the motions of the Planets are imagined to be.   **1882** in LUCAS *Stud. Nidderdale* 206 That no two floods in Nidderdale are alike in effect, which is locally accounted for by saying, 'that the rain falls in planets'.

Rains when the sun is shining, If it | the devil is beating his wife.   (S 973)

1666 TORRIANO *It. Prov.* 79 no. 47 When it rains, and the Sun shines both at one and the same time; the French say . . . le Diable bat sa femme, the Devil is beating of his wife.   **1738** SWIFT *Dial.* I. E.L. 263 It rained and the sun shone at the same time. — Why, then the devil was beating his wife behind the door with a shoulder of mutton.   **1828** LYTTON *Pelham* ch. 61 Sharp shower coming on. 'The devil will soon be beating his wife with a leg of mutton', as the proverb says.

Rain(s) (*noun*), *see also* Bright r. makes fools fain; Cloak for the r. (Good to have); Clouds bring not r. (All); Crow croaks before the r., (The hoarse); Dirt-bird sings, we shall have r.; Easterly winds and r. bring cockles; Every day of the week a shower of r.; Farther the sight, nearer the r.; God will (When) no wind but brings r.; Gull comes against r.; Hampshire ground requires r.; Many r. many rowans;

More r. more rest; Near burr far r.; Peacock loudly bawls (When); Rainbows . . . presage r.; Right as r.; Snails on the road you see (When); Sun goes pale to bed, r. tomorrow; Swain that lets journey for r.; Three things drive man out of house; Thunder comes r., (After); Wind's in the south, it's in r.'s mouth; Wit enough to come in out of the r.

Rain(s, ing) (*verb*), *see also* Although it r. throw not away watering-pot; Butter and cheese, (It r.); Cloak to make when r. (Have not thy); Easter day, (If it r. on) . . .; Put out your tubs when r.; St. Swithin's day.

Rainy day, Lay up (Lay by *or* Keep something) against (for) a.   (D 89)

c. **1566** *The Bugbears* III. ii. 23 Wold he haue me kepe nothyng agaynst a raynye day?   **1582** C. FETHERSTON *A Dialogue against light dancing* ¶ 4 It is good sauing a penny against a wet day.   **1639** CLARKE 93 Lay up for a rainie day.   **1677** YARRANTON *Eng. Impr.* 115 In the Time of Plenty, then lay up for a Rainy-day.   **1710** PALMER 280 'Tis good to take Care for a Wet-Day.   **1841** F. CHAMIER *Tom Bowl.* ch. 39 I have got some money that I put by for a rainy day.

Rainy, *see also* First of July (If the) it be r.; Offer your hen for sale on r. day (Never).

Raise Cain, To.

1852 MRS. STOWE *Uncle Tom's C.* ch. 20 Topsy would hold a perfect carnival of confusion . . . in short as Miss Ophelia phrased it, 'raising Cain' generally.   **1882** STEVENSON *Treasure Is.* ch. 3 If I get the horrors, I'm a man that has lived rough, and I'll raise Cain.

Raise no more devils (spirits) than you can lay (conjure down).   (D 319)

1631 JONSON *New Inn* III. ii. 251 Beware you doe not coniure vp a spirit You cannot lay.   **1639** CLARKE 247 (spirits . . . conjure down).   **1655** FULLER *Ch. Hist.* x. iv (1868) III. 300 The boy, having gotten a habit of counterfeiting, . . . would not be un-deviled by all their exorcisms; so that the priests raised up a spirit which they could not allay.   **1670** RAY 135 (as 1639).   **1721** KELLY 282 . . . Do not stir up a Strife, that you will not afterward be able to appease.   **1845** MACAULAY *Speech on Maynooth* Wks. viii. 314 All those fierce spirits, whom you hallooed on . . . now . . . worry you. . . . Did you think, when . . . you called the Devil up, that it was as easy to lay him as to raise him?

Raise the devil, To.

1705 VANBRUGH *Confed.* v. ii. Sir, give me an account of my Necklace, or I'll make such a Noise in your House I'll raise the Devil in't.   **1841** LEVER *C. O'Malley* ch. 63 He was going to raise the devil.

Raise the devil than to lay him, It is easier to.

1655 FULLER *Ch. Hist.* x. iv (1868) III. 300 The boy, having gotten a habit of counterfeiting, . . .

would not be un-deviled by all their exorcisms; so that the priests raised up a spirit which they could not allay. **1777** GARRICK Prol. to *Sch. for Scandal* Alas! the devil's sooner raised than laid. **1845** MACAULAY *Speech on Maynooth* Wks. viii. 314 Did you think, when, to serve your turn, you called the Devil up, that it was as easy to lay him as to raise him? **1890** 'ROLF BOLDREWOOD' *Miner's Right* ch. 21 But exorcists of all kinds . . . have ever found the fiend more easy to invoke than to lay.

Raise the wind, To.

1785 GROSE s.v. Wind, . . . to procure money. **1789** *Loiterer* no. 42 10 He . . . never offered to pay earnest. I suppose, poor fellow, he could not raise the wind. **1857** TROLLOPE *Three Clerks* ch. 34 He came to me this morning to raise the wind.

Raisin, *see* Black plum (r.) sweet as white.

Rake hell for a bodle,[1] He would.

1832 HENDERSON 2. [[1] one-sixth of a penny.]

Rake, *see also* Better with a r. than a fork; Fork is commonly r.'s heir; Lean as a r.; Little for the r. after besom.

Ram to kill a butcher, It is possible for a.   (R 26)

1664 CODRINGTON 201. **1670** RAY 22. **1828** LYTTON *Pelham* ch. 13 Don't think of fighting the man; he is a tradesman. . . . Remember that 'a ram may kill a butcher'.

Ram, *see also* Right as a r.'s horn.

Ramehead, *see* Dudman.

Rammish, *see* Wives make r. husbands, (Rutting).

Ramsey the rich.   (R 29)

[A Benedictine Abbey, near Huntingdon, built 969. *See* LEAN I. 103.] **1607** *Pleas. Conc. Hobson* 2 in *Shakes. Jest-Bks.*, iii. 2: 1. Ramsay the rich. 2. Bond the stout. 3. Beecher the gentleman. 4. and Cooper the loute. This pleasant rime, so sodaynely spoken by Master Hobson, is to this day accounted for his proverbe in London. **1662** FULLER Huntingd. 49 . . . This was the . . . Crœsus of all our English Abbies; For having but sixty Monks to maintaine therein, the Revenues thereof, . . . amounted unto Seven Thousand pounds a year.

Ramsey, the rich of gold and of fee; Thorney, the flower of the fen country. Crowland, so courteous of meat and of drink; Peterborough the proud, as all men do think. And Sawtrey, by the way, that old abbaye Gave more alms in one day than all they.

1852 *N. & Q.* 1st Ser. VI. 350.

Ramsins, *see* Leeks in Lide and r. in May.

Rancour sticks long by the ribs.   (R 30)

1616 WITHALS 561. **1639** CLARKE 178. **1659** HOWELL *Eng. Prov.* 16a.

Rank courtesy when a man is forced to give thanks for his own, It is a.   (C 733)

1664 CODRINGTON 203. **1670** RAY 20.

Rap, Not a.

[*Rap*, a counterfeit coin passing current for a halfpenny in Ireland in the 18th cent. **1724** SWIFT *Drapier's Lett.* Wks. (1755) v. ii. 14 Copper halfpence or farthings . . . have been for some time very scarce, and many counterfeits passed about under the name of raps.] **1823** BYRON *Don Juan* Can. 11, st. 84 I have seen the Landholders without a rap. **1830** MARRYAT *King's Own* ch. 35 'You must fork out.' 'Not a rap.' **1834** AINSWORTH *Rookwood* Bk. III. ch. 5 For the mare-with-three-legs [the gallows], boys, I care not a rap. **1881** MISS BRADDON *Asphodel* ch. 14 A man who dies and leaves not a rap behind him.

Rap, *see* Cat (The likerish) gets many a r.

Rape[1] rueth, Oft.

c. **1300** *Prov. of Hending* xxxi in *Salomon & Sat.* (1848) 278 Ofte rap reweþ, quoþ Hendyng. *c.* **1390** GOWER *Conf. Amantis* III. 1525 Men sen alday þat rape reweþ. **1473** MARG. PASTON in *P. Lett.* (Gairdner 1904) v. 174 Bydde hym that he be not to hasty of takyng of orderes . . . for oftyn rape rewith. *c.* **1580** SPELMAN *Dialogue* Roxb. Cl. 2 I mynde to go safelye, least in goyinge to hastelye, we Repente more speedely. And thinges dunne in haste Bringeth spedye Repentance. [[1] haste.]

Rape (= rope), *see* Whaup in the r. (There is a).

Rare as the phoenix.   (P 256)

1568 B. GARTER *Two Eng. Lovers* 18 A thing as rare as Phenix is to see. **1578** *Courtly Controv.* O4 It is a thing rarer than the only Phenix. **1578** FLORIO *First F.* 78 One only Fenix in the cage. **1580** LYLY *Euph. & his Eng.* ii. 86 There is but one Phoenix in the world. **1581** GUAZZO i. 58 As rare on earth as the Phoenix. **1599** SHAKES. *A.Y.* IV. iii. 16 She calls me proud, and that she could not love me, Were man as rare as phoenix. **1610** *Id. Cym.* I. vi. 16 If she be furnish'd with a mind so rare, She is alone th' Arabian bird, and I Have lost the wager.

Rare, *see also* Thing which is r. is dear.

Rath[1] sower never borrows of the late, The.   (S 693)

1659 HOWELL *Eng. Prov.* 17a. [[1] early.]

Rather sell than be poor.   (S 220)

1678 RAY *Adag. Hebr.* 400.

Rats desert (forsake, leave) a falling house (sinking ship).   (M 1243)

1579 T. LUPTON *A Thousand Notable Things* ii. 87 Rats and dormice will forsake old and ruinous houses, three months before they fall [cited in note to WEBSTER *Duchess of Malfi* (Lucas) v. ii. 219–20]. **1586** G. WHETSTONE *Eng. Mirr.* 176. *a.* **1588** DR. RECORD (quoted J. HARVEY *Concerning Prophesies* (1588) 81) When a house will fall, the Mice right quicke Flee thence before. **1601** PLINY tr. Holland viii. 28 When an house is readie to tumble downe, the mice goes out of it before. **1607** TOURNEUR *Rev. Trag.* v. ii Like the mice That forsake falling houses, I would shift to other dependance. **1611** SHAKES. *Temp.* I. ii. 147 A rotten carcass of a boat, . . . the very rats Instinctively have quit it. **1625** BACON *Ess., Wisd. for Man's Self* Arb. 187 It is the *Wisedome of Rats,* that will be sure to leaue a House, somewhat before it fall. **1738** GAY *Fables* Ser. II. ix As rats, before the mansion falls, Desert late hospitable walls, In shoals the servile creatures run, To bow before the rising sun. **1824** SCOTT *St. Ronans* ch. 25 They say a falling house is best known by the rats leaving it —a falling state, by the desertion of confederates and allies—and a falling man, by the desertion of his friends. **1895** J. PAYN *In Mark. Ov.* ch. 26 This is bad news indeed about Barton's pupils. . . . It is a case of the rats leaving a sinking-ship, I fear.

Rat(s), *see also* Drowned mouse (r.); Poor as a church mouse (r.); Rabbit for r.; Rhyme r. to death; Scot, a r., travel world over; Smell a r.; Welcome death, quoth the r.

Rat-trap, Like a | easier to get into than out of.

1897 L. J. TROTTER *Life of J. Nicholson* ch. 11 November passed away before John Nicholson found himself free to quit. . . . India, he wrote, was 'like a rat-trap—easier to get into than out of'.

Raven bodes misfortune (death), The croaking.   (R 33)

1578 T. WHITE *Sermon at Paul's Cross* 3 Nov. 1577 77 It was a greate faulte in this people [the Jews] . . . to obserue dreames, singyng of byrdes, and the like paltrie as many doe nowe, . . . the crying of Rauens, the flying of Owles, a sorte of . . . olde wyues fables, whereby the Diuell deludeth manye, and weakeneth their faythe. **1584** LYLY *Sappho & Phao* III. iii. 60 I mistruste her not: for that the owle hath not shrikte at the window, or the night Rauen croked, both being fatall. [1587] **1599** PEELE *David & Beths.* iv. D1 Like as the fatall Rauen, that in his voice Carries the dreadful summons of our deaths. [*c.* 1589] **1633** MARLOWE *Jew of Malta* II. i. 1 Like the sad presaging raven, that tolls The sick man's passport in her hollow beak. **1590–1** SHAKES. *2 Hen. VI* III. ii. 40 A raven's note Whose dismal tune bereft my vital pow'rs. **1592** *Id. T.And.* II. iii. 96 Here nothing breeds, Unless the nightly owl or fatal raven. **1594** NASHE *Terrors Night* i. 346 That ill angel the Rauen . . . a Continuall messenger . . . of dole and misfortune. **1598** GUILPIN *Skialethia* A4 Like to the fatall ominous Rauen which tolls, The sicke mans dirge within his hollow beake. **1600–1** SHAKES. *H.* III. ii. 248 The croaking raven doth bellow for revenge. **1605** ROWLEY *When you See me* K4ᵛ Hell stop that fatall boding Emperors throte, That sings against vs this dismall Rauens note. **1605–6**

SHAKES. *M. I.* v. 35 The raven himself is hoarse That croaks the fatal entrance of Duncan Under my battlements. **1607** DEKKER *Whore of Babylon* III. i. 113 And on the house-tops of Nobilitie (If there they can but sit) like fatall Rauens, Or Skrich-Owles croake their fals and hoarsely bode, Nothing but scaffolds and vnhallowed graues.

Raven(s), *see also* Bitter bird (Thou art) said r. to starling; Carcase is (Where the), r. will gather; Takes the r. for guide (He that); White crow (r.).

Ravine (= rapine), *see* Ruin of one r.

Raw, *see* Johnny R.

Raw head and bloody bone.   (R 35)

[= a bugbear.] *c.* **1589** PEELE *Battle of Alcazar* I. 265 And shall we be afraide of Bassas and of bugs, Rawe head and bloudie bone? **1596** NASHE *Saffron W.* iii. 98. **1598** FLORIO *Worlde of Wordes* s.v. Mani . . . imagined spirits that nurces fraie their babes withall to make them leaue crying, as we say bug-beare, or else rawe head and bloodie bone. **1622** FLETCHER *Prophetess* IV. v But now I look Like Bloody-Bone and Raw-head, to frighten children. **1824** SCOTT *St. Ronans* ch. 19 I had . . . to walk to the Spa, bleeding like a calf, and tell a raw-head-and-bloody-bone story about a footpad. **1837** J. B. KER 36 . . . the nurse's opiate to quiet a troublesome brat.

Raw Hempstead.[1]

1902–4 LEAN I. 152 The rawness of Hempstead may possibly be attributed to its position on one of the bleakest portions of our eastern coast, and not from any want of polish on the part of its inhabitants. [¹ Norfolk.]

Raw leather will stretch.   (L 167)

1583 MELBANCKE *Philot.* G2ᵛ Yong kids lether will stretch. **1611** DAVIES no. 213. **1639** CLARKE 66.

Raw pulleyn,[1] veal, and fish, make the churchyards fat.   (V 20)

1588 W. AVERELL *Combat of Contrarieties* B4 A gluttonous Bellye makes rich Phisitions and fat Churchyardes. **1611** COTGRAVE s.v. Cimitière (Raw Veale, and Chickens). **1623** WODROEPHE 522 Ill sodden Veale, and rawe Hennes, make swollen Churchards Lust, and Death. **1659** HOWELL *Fr. Prov.* 12 Raw Veal and Pullets make the Churchyard full of graves. **1678** RAY 41. [¹ poultry.]

Razor, *see* Cut blocks with r.; Honey in the mouth, (He has) and a r. at the girdle; Occam's r.; Sharp as a r.

Read one like a book, To.

1602 SHAKES. *T.C.* IV. v. 238 O! like a book of sport thou'lt read me o'er; But there's more in me than thou understand'st. **1874** WHYTE-MELVILLE *Uncle John* ch. 5 That lady, who read him like a book, preserved an appearance of complete unconsciousness.

Read, try, judge, and speak as you find, says old Suffolk.

1813 RAY 71.

Read, *see also* New book appears (When) r. old one; Parson of Saddleworth (Like the) who could r. no book but his own; Runs may r., (He that).

Ready at an inch.   (I 58)

c. **1560** T. LUPTON *Money* l. 702 Thou wilt helpe him at an ynche.   **1569** *Marriage of Wit and Science* D2 My wyll be always prest, and ready at an ynche.   **1575** GASCOIGNE *Glass of Gov[t]*. ii. 62 Dicke wilbe at an inche with a cleane plate to proffer him.   **1575** LANEHAM *Letter* ed. Furnivall 59.   **1581** B. RICH *Fare. Mil. Prof.* 201 Attendaunt upon her,‡ and readie at an ynche to provide her of anythyng.   **1590–1** SHAKES. *2 Hen. VI* I. iv. 42 Beldam, I think we watch'd you at an inch.

Ready money is a ready medicine.
                                              (M 1091)

1559 COOPER s.v. Medicamen Pecunia praesens medicamen est praesentaneum, redie monie, redie medicine.   *c.* **1580** J. CONYBEARE *Adagia* in *John Conybeare* (1905) 46 Pecunia praesens, medicamen est praesentaneum: Redie money, redie medicine.   **1651** HERBERT no. 1038.   **1659** HOWELL *Fr. Prov.* 6 Ready money brings physick.

Ready money will away.   (M 1092)

? **1622** J. TAYLOR (Water-P.) *Trav. Twelvepence* (1630) 72 The Prouerbe true doth say That ready money euer will away.   **1659** HOWELL *Eng. Prov.* 12a.

Ready money, *see also* Cutpurse is sure trade.

Ready mouth for a ripe cherry, A.
                                              (M 1267)

a. **1628** CARMICHAELL no. 167.   **1641** FERGUSSON no. 910.   **1721** KELLY 366 . . . Spoken to those who are ready to catch at what we have.   **1732** FULLER no. 5913.

Ready, *see also* Booted are not always r.; Burst with laughing, (To be r. to); Rides ere he be r. (He that); Rough and r.

Reap, *see* Sow (As they), so let them r.; Sows thistles shall r. prickles, (He that).

Reason binds the man.   (R 44)

a. **1628** CARMICHAELL no. 1319 Reason band the man, but the devill could never bind the wyfe.   **1641** FERGUSSON no. 730.

Reason governs the wise man and cudgels the fool.

1707 MAPLETOFT 24.

Reason in all things, There's.

1602 MARSTON *Antonio and Mellida* C3[v].   **1606** CHAPMAN *Monsieur D'Olive* IV. ii. 249.

Reason in roasting of eggs, There is.
                                              (R 49)

1659 HOWELL *Eng. Prov.* 12b.   **1773** BURKE in BOSWELL *Johnson* ch. 30 *note* 'Your definition is good', said Mr. Burke, 'and I now see the full force of the common proverb, "There is *reason* in roasting of eggs".'   **1867** TROLLOPE *Last Chron. Bar.* ch. 75 But there's reason in the roasting of eggs, and . . . money is not so plentiful . . . that your uncle can afford to throw it into the Barchester gutters.

Reason, One | is as good as fifty.

1718 PRIOR *Alma* i. 513 Wks. (1858) 233 Examples I could cite you more; But be contented with these four: For, when one's proofs are aptly chosen, Four are as valid as four dozen.

Reason labours will.

1546 HEYWOOD I. v. B2 Reason laboureth wyll, to wyn wyls consent, To take lacke of beautie but as an eye sore.

Reason lies between the spur and the bridle.   (R 45)

1640 HERBERT no. 711.

Reason pist my goose, Such a.   (R 47)

1616 WITHALS 560 You speake like a Pottecary, such a reason pist my goose.   **1639** CLARKE 70.

Reason rules all things.   (R 43)

1362 LANGLAND *P. Pl.* A. I. 52 For rihtfoli he resoun schulde rulen on alle.   **1595** SHAKES. *M.N.D.* II. ii. 115 The will of man is by his reason sway'd; And reason says you are the worthier maid.   **1602** *Liberality and Prod.* v. iii E4[v] Where reason rules, there is the golden meane.   **1616** DRAXE no. 1818 Let reason rule all your actions.   **1659** HOWELL *Eng. Prov.* 9b.

Reasons of the poor weigh not, The.
                                              (R 50)

1616 DRAXE no. 1691 A poore mans tale cannot be heard.   **1640** HERBERT no. 633.

Reason(s), *see also* Affection blinds r.; Because is a woman's r.; Custom without r. ancient error; Good r. and part cause; Hearken to r.; Love is without r.; Man without r. a beast; Rhyme nor r. (Neither).

Rebound, *see* Heart is caught in r. (Many).

Recalled, *see* Past cannot be recalled (Things); Time lost cannot be r.; Words have wings, and cannot be r.

Receive before you write, write before you pay. (W 940)

c. 1576 WHYTHORNE 143. 1659 HOWELL *Span. Prov.* 19. 1678 RAY 348 Recipe scribe, scribe solve. A good rule for stewards.

Receiver is as bad as the thief, The. (R 52)

1623 WODROEPHE 509 The Concealer, is no lesse guiltie in Treason then the Theefe. 1650 SIR J. BIRKENHEAD *Two Centuries of Pauls Church-yard* 5 A Receiver is worse then a thief. 1662 FULLER Notts. 315 But, seeing The receiver is as bad as the thief, . . . the cheap Pennyworths of plundered goods may in fine prove dear enough to their Consciences. 1721 KELLY 15 A Receipter is worse than a Thief. If there were none to receive stol'n Goods, Thieves would be discouraged. 1830 MARRYAT *King's Own* ch. 11 The receiver is as bad as the thief. . . . If there were no demand there would be no supply.

Receiver, *see also* No r. no thief.

Reckless youth makes rueful age. (Y 42)

c. 1520 DUNBAR *Wks.* S.T.S. II. 309 Misgovernit yowth makis gowsty[1] age. 1641 FERGUSSON no. 733 Rackless youth, makes a goustie[1] age. 1721 KELLY 284 . . . People who live too fast when they are young, will neither have a vigorous, nor a comfortable old Age. [1 dreary, wasted.]

Reckons without his host, He that | must reckon again (twice). (H 726)

c. 1489 CAXTON *Blanchardyn* lii. 202 It ys sayd in comyn that 'who soeuer rekeneth wythoute his hoste, he rekeneth twys for ones'. 1533 MORE *Debell. Salem* Wks. 991/2 He fareth lo lyke a geste, that makyth hys rekening himselfe without hys hoste. 1579 LYLY *Euph.* i. 228 In that *Philautus* . . . shoulde accompt mee his wyfe before hee wo[o]e mee, certeinely he yis lyke for mee to make hys rec[k]oninge twice, bicause hee reconeth without hys hostesse. 1670 RAY 136 . . . Chi fa conto senza l'hoste fa conto due volte. *Ital.* Qui compte sans son hoste, il lui convient compter deux fois, *Gall.* 1824 SCOTT *St. Ronans* ch. 15 But hostess as she was herself, . . . she reckoned without her host in the present instance. 1909 *Spectator* 3 July 9 Any man who counts upon such a desire as a political asset reckons without his host.

Reckon(s), *see also* Tell (R.) money after your father.

Reckoning(s), *see* Cast up accounts (r.); Even r. long friends; Fairer the hostess, fouler r.; Keep one head for r.; Merry is feast-making till r.; Misreckoning is no payment; Short r.; Small sum will pay short r.

Recks not who is rich, Wisest is he who.

[L. (in Ellesmere MS., margin) *Inter omnes altior existit, qui non curat in cuius manu sit mundus.*] c. 1386 CHAUCER *W. of Bath's Prol.* l. 324 The wyse astrologien Dan Ptholome, that seith this proverbe in his Almageste, 'Of alle men his wisdom is the hyeste, That rekketh never who hath the world in honde'.[1] [1 i.e. who has abundant wealth.]

Recks, *see also* Sow r. not' of balm.

Recoil a little, We must | to the end we may leap the better. (L 369)

c. 1500 *Melusine* XX. E.E.T.S. 113 Wyse men goo abacke for to lepe the ferther. 1547 J. HARRISON *Exhor. to Scots* 213 As one that intendeth to make a greate lepe, I muste bee forced to ronne back to fetche my course. 1579 S. GOSSON *Ephemerides of Phialo* H6 Rams retire to strike harder. 1592 DELAMOTHE 17 We must recule a litle, to the end we leape the better. 1603 MONTAIGNE (Florio) I. xxxviii. 104 They have gone backe that they might leap the better. 1611 COTGRAVE s.v. Saulter *Il recule pour mieux saulter.* He goes backe to take burre, or to leape the better. 1616 DRAXE no. 2521. 1651 HERBERT no. 1121. 1657 S. JACOMBE *Moses his Death* 7 They who go backwards, leap the further for it. 1827 HARE *Gues. at Truth* (1859) i. 328 We must not overlook the numerous examples which history furnishes in proof that, according to the French proverb, *il faut reculer pour mieux sauter.*

Reconciled enemies (and of meat twice boiled), Take heed of. (H 373, 378)

c. 1386 CHAUCER *Mel.* B[2] l. 2371 And eek thou shalt eschewe the conseilling of thyne olde enemys that been reconsiled. c. 1526 *Dicta Sap.* B3 A reconcyled enemy is nat to be trusted by and by. 1585 ROBSON *Choice Change* K1 Three things which our auncestors haue abhorred. Meate twice sodden. A reconciled friend. A woman with a beard. 1613 R. DALLINGTON *Aphorisms* 181 There is no Sinceritie in reconciled enemies. 1621 BURTON *Anat. Mel.* II. iii. VII (1651) 360 Take heed of a reconciled enemy. c. 1622 [CHAPMAN?] *Alphonsus of Germany* 1654 ed. (Schwarz, 1913) 4 Trust not a reconciled friend. 1642 TORRIANO 42–4 From a reconciled friend . . . good Lord deliver us. 1670 RAY 22 Take heed of enemies reconcil'd, and of meat twice boil'd. 1733 FRANKLIN Sept. Beware of meat twice boiled and an old foe reconcil'd. 1777 JOHNSON 3 May in Boswell *Life* (1848) lvii. 530 Tell Mrs. Boswell I shall taste her marmalade cautiously at first. . . . Beware, says the Italian proverb, of a reconciled enemy.

Recumbentibus, To give one a. (R 58)

[= a knock-down blow.] c. 1400 *Laud Troy Bk.* 7490 He 3aff the Kyng Episcropus Suche a recumbentibus, He smot In-two both helme & mayle. c. 1549 HEYWOOD II. vii. E7[v] Had you some husbande, and snapte at hym thus, Iwys he would geue you a recumbentibus. 1599 NASHE *Lenten Stuff* iii. 167 Which leesing (had I bene let alone) I would haue put to bed with a recumbentibus. a. 1687 COTTON *Poet. Wks.* (1765) 294 Which Recumbentibus he [Hercules] got By being of an Argonaut.

Red as a cherry, As. (C 277)

c. 1425 *Disput. Mary & Cross* in *Leg. Rood* (1871) 217 Dropes rede as ripe cherrees.

c. **1440** *Bone Flor.* 1763 Wyne redd as Cherye. *c.* **1520** SKELTON *Magnificence* l. 1558. *c.* **1550** *Robin Conscience* iii. 243.

Red (rank) as a fox, As. (F 628)

c. **1386** CHAUCER *Prol.* l. 552 His berd, as any sowe or fox, was reed. **1599** NASHE *Lenten Stuff* iii. 191. **1601** SHAKES. *T.N.* II. v. 114 Though it be as rank as a fox. **1693** D'URFEY *Rich. Heiress* (1718) I. 14 Red and rank as a fox. **1837** LEVER *Harry Lorr.* ch. 6 Father Malachi's dark; but . . . the coadjutor's as red as a fox.

Red as a rose, As. (R 177)

c. **1260** *King Horn* (Camb.) l. 16 (Hall) Rose red was his colour. *c.* **1374** CHAUCER *Troilus* Bk. 2, l. 1256. 'Nay, nay!' quod she, and wex as red as rose. *c.* **1425** *Castle of Perseverance* l. 2027. **1598** SHAKES. *2 Hen. IV* II. iv. 27 Your colour, . . . is as red as any rose. **1863** KINGSLEY *Water Bab.* ch. 2 A fine old English gentleman, with a face as red as a rose. **1798** COLERIDGE *Anc. Mariner* i. 34 Red as a rose is she.

Red as a turkey-cock, As. (T 611)

1484 CAXTON *Bk. La Tour-Landry* E.E.T.S. 120, 168 He . . . was reed as a cok and had a good lyuynge colour. **1596** T. LODGE *Wit's Misery* Hunt. Cl. L1 He looks red in the gils like a Turkie cocke. *c.* **1630** BEAUM. & FL. *Faithful Friends* III. ii Blush as red as a turkey-cock. **1666** TORRIANO *Prov. Phr.* s.v. Gambero, 70. **1857** G. ELIOT *Scenes of Clerical Life* 'Amos Barton' ch. 1.

Red as blood, As. (B 455)

c. **1205** LAYAMON *Brut* l. 15940 þe oder [drake] is milc-whit . . . þe oðer is ræd alse blod. *c.* **1386** CHAUCER *Prol.* l. 635 To drynken strong wyn, reed as blood. **1574** J. BALE *Pageant of Popes* tr. J. Studley 45 The moone . . . appearing as redde as bloud all the night long. **1886** STEVENSON *Kidnapped* ch. 6 The cardinal bird that is as red as blood.

Red beard and a black head, A | catch him with a good trick and take him dead. (B 143)

1584 WITHALS L7 Thou shalte know a lewde fellow, By his bearde, eyther redde or yealow. **1599** SHAKES. *A.Y.* III. iv. 7 His very hair is of the dissembling colour.—Something browner than Judas's. **1659** HOWELL *Eng. Prov.* 12b. **1670** RAY 212. **1732** FULLER no. 1915 He is false by Nature that has a black Head and a red Beard.

Red cap, You shall have the. (C 66)

1678 RAY 352 . . . *Somerset.* (Said to a marriage-maker.)

Red clouds in the east, rain the next day.

1659 HOWELL *Span. Prov.* 22. **1883** ROPER 14. **1893** INWARDS 88.

Red cock, The.

[= incendiarism. Probably taken from the German *roter Hahn* used already by H. SACHS in this sense.] **1815** SCOTT *Guy Man.* ch. 3 'We'll see if the red cock craw not in his bonnie barnyard ae morning before daydawing.' . . . 'What does she mean?' . . . 'Fire-raising', answered the laconic Dominie.

Red cow gives good milk, A.

1917 BRIDGE 5 . . . In old medical books, when milk was ordered to be given, it was frequently specified that it should be taken from a red cow. . . . 'A draught of red cow's milk'. Walton's *Compleat Angler.*

Red herring across the track, To draw a.

[= to attempt to divert attention from the real question.] **1890** W. F. BUTLER *Sir C. Napier* 60 Englishmen, so long diverted from their own affairs by the red herring of foreign politics so adroitly drawn across the trail, would [&c.]. **1928** *Times* 7 Apr. 8/1 These ladies . . . then calmly proceed to draw various red herrings of their own across the track.

Red herring ne'er spake word but een, broil my back, but not my weamb.[1] (H 449)

1678 RAY 52. [1 belly.]

Red (narrow) lane[1], The.

1542 ERASM. tr. Udall *Apoph.* 119 Quiet and clene to swallowe down the narrow lane. **1733** *Universal Spectator* 26 May He'd never again Run, like a Fox, down the Red Lane. [1 throat.]

Red man, To a | read thy rede[1]; with a brown man break thy bread; at a pale man draw thy knife; from a black man keep thy wife. (M 155, 395)

c. **1470** *Harl. MS.* 3362, f. 17a To þe blak draw þy knyf; with þe brown led þy lyf. **1573** SANFORD 105[v] Greete a redde man and a bearded woman three myles off. *c.* **1641** FERGUSSON MS. no. 1422. **1615** R. TOFTE tr. of B. VARCHI *Blazon of Jealousie* 21 The sallow complectioned fellow with a blacke beard, . . . [is] to be suspected about Womens matters, according to the old saying: . . . Which wee expound after this manner: The Red is wise, the Browne trusty, The Pale enuious, and the Blacke lusty. **1659** HOWELL *Eng. Prov.* 16b. [1 declare thy counsel, plan.]

Red rag to a bull, Like a. (R 59)

[OVID *Met.* 12. 103 *Sua irritamina . . . poeniceas vestes.*] **1580** LYLY *Euph. & his Eng.* ii. 226 He that commeth before an Elephant will not weare bright colours, nor he that commeth to a Bul red. **1899** SIR A. WEST *Recollect.* II. xiv. 87 His appointment . . . was looked on as a job, and Mr. Gladstone, to whom a job was like a red rag to a bull, thought so. **1928** *Times* 27 June 15/1 Cyrillic type is like a red rag to a bull to the Croats in their present frame of mind.

Red sky, *see* Sky red in the morning.

Red the sun begins his race, If | expect that rain will flow apace. *Cf.* Sky red in the morning.

1659 HOWELL *Span. Prov.* 22 A red Sun hath water in his eye.   **1706** STEVENS s.v. Sol When the Sun shines red, there is Rain near at hand. **1781** J. CLARIDGE *The Shepherd of Banbury's Rules* (3rd ed.) I The old English Rule published in our first Almanacks . . . If red the Sun . . . be sure the rain will fall apace.   **1846** DENHAM II.

Red wood maks gude spindles.

1862 HISLOP 164 . . . 'Red wood', the name given to the reddish . . . and more incorruptible wood found in the heart of trees.—*Jamieson.*

Red, *see also* Evening r. and morning grey; Eyes as r. as a ferret's; Fern grows r., (When); God make me great and big, for white and r. I can make myself; Lass in the r. petticoat; Rowan tree and r. thread; Sun in r. should set (If).

Redd[1] for windlestraws, He that is | should not sleep in lees[2].   (W 452)

a. **1628** CARMICHAELL no. 730.   **1641** FERGUSSON no. 328.   **1721** KELLY 134 He that's redd for windle Straws, should not pish in Lays. Spoken to those who are afraid of small and far distant Dangers. [[1] afraid. [2] unploughed land.]

Redder's (Redding)[1] stroke, The.

1721 KELLY 159 He who meddles with Quarrels, gets the ridding Stroke.   **1737** A. RAMSAY (1750) 45 He that meddles with toolies[2] comes in for the redding streak.   **1816** SCOTT *Old Mort.* ch. 4 'If they come to lounder ilk ither, . . . suldna I call on you?' 'At no hand, Jenny; the redder gets aye the warst lick in the fray.'   **1888** MRS. OLIPHANT *Second Son* ch. 5 After receiving this redding stroke, which is inevitably the recompense of the third party, Edmund drew back a little.   **1900** LANG *Hist. Scot.* I. 325 The Earl of Crawford was mortally wounded—'got the redder's stroke'—in an attempt to stop the fighting. [[1] The redder is one who attempts to settle a dispute. [2] quarrels.]

Rede, *see* Short r. good r.

Redemption from hell, There is no.
(R 60)

1377 LANGLAND *P. Pl.* B. xviii. 152 That thyng that ones was in helle · out cometh hit neuere. For Iob[1] the parfit patriarke · repreoueth thy sawes, *Quia in inferno nulla est redempcio.* **1596** HARINGTON *Metam. Ajax* (1927 ed. 66) As for that scripture ex inferno nulla redemptio, I haue heard it oft alledged by great Clarkes, but I thinke it is in the Epistle of S. Paul to the Laodiceans, or in Nicodemus Gospel: for I neuer yet coulde finde it in the Bible.   **1622** J. TAYLOR (Water-P.) *Mer. Wher. Fer.* (1630) 12 From Hell each man sayes, Lord deliuer me, Because from Hell can no Redemption be. **1662** FULLER *Westmr.* 236 . . . There is a place . . . partly by the Exchequer Court, commonly called Hell. . . . Formerly this place was . . .

for the King's debtors, who never were freed thence, untill they had paid their uttermost due. . . . This Proverb is applyed to moneys paid into the Exchequer, which thence are irrecoverable. [[1] VULGATE *Job* vii. 9 Sicut consumitur nubes, et pertransit; sic qui descenderit ad inferos, non ascendet.]

Reeds, Where there are | there is water.

c. **1700** *Dict. Cant. Crew* s.v. Smoke No Reeds but there is some Water.   **1732** FULLER no. 5674.

Reed(s), *see also* Broken r. (Lean upon); Oaks may fall when r. stand storm.

Reek comes aye doun again however high it flees.

1837 A. LEIGHTON in *Tales of Borders* III. 335 'Set a beggar on horseback an' he'll ride to the deevil'. . . . Anither o' the same kind—'Reek comes aye doun again, however high it flees'—is just as pithy and pertinent to your case.

Reek, *see also* Kail through the r. (Give one his).

Reel, *see* Spin and r. at same time, (A man cannot).

Refer my coat and lose a sleeve.

1721 KELLY 283 . . . Arbitrators, for the better Accommodation of Business, make both Parties abate of their Pretensions.

References, *see* Always verify r.

Reflexion, *see* Praise is the r. of virtue.

Reformation, *see* Erasmus laid egg of R.

Refrain, *see* Pleasure r. (Who will in time present).

Refuse (It is good to take) a good offer, Never.   (O 17)

1591 STEPNEY 150 Refuse not a benefit when it is proffered.   **1592** DELAMOTHE 53 Some refuseth a thing, that he wisheth for after.   **1616** DRAXE no. 864 It is good to take a good offer.   **1670** RAY 136.   **1824** SCOTT *Redg.* ch. 21 'You shall have a bellyful for love. . . .' 'I shall never refuse a fair offer', said the poverty-stricken guest.

Refuse a wife with one fault, and take one with two.   (W 371)

1659 HOWELL *Brit. Prov.* 13.

Refuse with the right hand (side) and take with the left, To.   (H 100)

1572 CRADOCKE *Ship of Assured Safety* CI[v] Christian brother, . . . catche not vnto thee with the lefte hande, that whiche is raughte oute with the righte.   **1616** G. CHAPMAN *Musæus: of Hero and Leander* Ded. Howsoever the mistaking world takes ill (whose left hand euer received what I gave with my right).   **1639** CLARKE s.v. Imposturae 149.

Refuse(d), *see also* Money¯r.; Money you r .

Reins, *see* Bridle (r.), (To give one the); Lay the r. on the neck.

Reivers[1] should not be ruers.

1641 FERGUSSON no. 734. **1721** KELLY 284 ... They who are so fond of a Thing as to snap greedily at it, should not repent that they have got it. [[1] robbers.]

Relation, *see* Friend is my nearest r.

Relics, *see* Priest praises own r.

Religion a stalking-horse to shoot other fowl. (R 63)

1579 W. WILLIAMSON *Confut. Fam. Love* 70b Abusing the pretence of the Gospell as a stalking horse to leuell at others by. **1604** MARSTON *Malcontent* IV. i. 226 A fellow that makes religion his stalking-horse. **1651** HERBERT no. 1069. **1672** MARVELL *Rehearsal Transprosed* Gros. ii. 33. **1678** BUNYAN *Pilgr.* I. (1877) 115 If it be unlawful to follow Christ for loaves, . . . how much more abominable is it to make of him and Religion a Stalking-horse, to get and enjoy the world.

Religion an ill man is of, It matters not what.

1732 FULLER no. 3038.

Religion but can boast of its martyrs, No.

1732 FULLER no. 3621.

Religion, credit, and the eye are not to be touched. (R 64)

1616 DRAXE no. 658 Faith and the eye are tender. **1640** HERBERT no. 837.

Religion is the rule of life. (R 65)

1616 BRETON *Cross. Prov.* B3.

Religions is of no religion, He that is of all.

1579 CALVIN *Four Sermons* tr. J. Field Ep. Ded. There be many Newters which haue made a couenant with their owne heartes rather to be of all religions . . . then to endure the least danger. **1584** R. WILSON *Three Ladies of London* C4ᵛ Of what religion are you can ye tell? Mary sir of all religions, I know not my selfe very well. **1589** *Temporis filia veritas* B3 Let no man . . . charge me to be of no Religion, neither yet to be of all Religions. **1614** OVERBURY *Characters* (Webster, ed. Lucas iv. 34) 'A Distaster of the Time', Religion is commonly his pretence of discontent, though hee can bee of all religions: therefore truely of none. **1619** DRUMMOND *Conv. with Jonson* (Herford and Simpson i. 151) For any religion as being versed in both.

Religion, *see also* Bible is r. of Protestants; Cities seldom change r. only; Jest not with · · · r.; Man without r. like a horse.

Remedy, The best | against an ill man, is much ground between. (R 66)

1640 HERBERT no. 152.

Remedy but patience, No. (R 71)

[HOR. *Od.* I. 24. 19 *Durum: sed levius fit patientia Quidquid corrigere est nefas.*] **1530** PALSGRAVE 425b And he be ameved ones, there is no remedy but pacyence and fayre wordes. **1530** TYNDALE *Practice of Prelates* P.S. 252 We have no remedy but patiently to abide what God will do. **1548** HALL *Chron.* (1809, 129) There was no remedy but pacience. **1552** LINDSAY *Three Estates* l. 2052. **1557** *Letter of Muscovy Company* (Hakluyt, E.L. i. 381). **1566** GASCOIGNE *Supposes* i. 194. **1584** R. WILSON *Three Ladies of London* C3. **1592** SHAKES. *T.G.V.* II. ii. 2. **1616** DRAXE no. 1590. **1624** BURTON *Anat. Mel.* III. iii. IV. i. (1638) 617. **1631** T. BREWER *Merry Devil of Edmonton* F2 He saw there was no remedy but patience. **1670** RAY 190. **1680** L'ESTRANGE *Citt & Bumpkin* 6 Well, there's no remedy but patience. **1692** *Id. Aesop's Fab.* cxciii (1738) 209 The silly ass stood preaching to himself upon the text of. . . .

Remedy for all things (everything) but death, There is a. (R 69)

[MED. L. *Contra malum mortis, non est medicamen in hortis.* Against the evil of death there is no remedy in the gardens.] *c.* **1430** LYDGATE *Daunce Mac.* l. 432 Aȝens deeth is worth no medicine. **1573** SANFORD 52. **1620** SHELTON *Quix.* II. lxiv. iii. 275 'There is a remedy for everything but death', said Don Quixote. **1641** FERGUSSON no. 818 There is a remeid for all things but stark deid. **1787** COWPER *Yearly Bill of Mortality* No medicine, though it oft can cure, Can always balk the tomb. **1896** F. LOCKER-LAMPSON *My Confid.* 95 There is a remedy for everything except Death . . . , so the bitterness of this disappointment has long passed away. **1901** DEAN HOLE *Then & Now* (ed. 7) ch. 8 But . . . we hold our own at bowls, not forgetting that Contra vim mortis non est medicamen in hortis.

Remedy for everything, could men find it, There is a. (R 70. G 189)

1573 GASCOIGNE *Adventures* i. 439 There are remedies for all mischifes. **1576** *Paradise of Dainty Devices* (Lean) iv. 60 The ancient prouerb saith that none so fester'd grief Doth grow, for which the gods themselves have not ordain'd relief. **1579** LYLY *Euph.* i. 208 O ye gods haue ye ordayned for euerye maladye a medicine, for euery sore a salue, for euery payne a plaister. **1624** BURTON *Anat. Mel.* II. iv. I. ii. 298. **1642** TORRIANO 4. **1651** HERBERT no. 1142.

Remedy for injuries, is not to remember them, The. *Cf.* Neglect will kill. (N 102)

c. **1526** *Dicta Sap.* D1 To reuenge the iniuries to the done remedieth lytel but the forgettynge is most best. **1597** *Politeuphuia* 45 To forget an iniury is better then to remember it. *Ibid.* 62 It is more safetie to forget an iniurie then to

reuenge it. **1639** CLARKE 324 To forget a
wrong is the best revenge. **1642** TORRIANO 44
(is oblivion). **1647** *Countrym. New Commonw.*
16 It is more safety to forget an injury, then to
revenge it. Aurelius. **1659** HOWELL *It. Prov.* 11.

Remedy is worse than the disease, The.
(R 68)

1582 MULCASTER *Elementary* (Campagnac) 107.
1597 7 Nov. *Calendar Hatfield MSS.* vii. 541–3.
1601 DANIEL 'To Sir Thomas Egerton' l. 20.
1607–12 BACON *Ess., Seditions* Arb. 414 Lett
Princes . . . not be without some great person of
Militarye valew . . . for the repressing of seditions
. . . But lett such one, be an assured one, . . .
orels[1] the remedy is worse then the disease.
1632 S. MARMION *Holland's Leaguer* B2 That's a
cure Worse then any disease. **1896** FROUDE
Council of Trent i. 5 Rebellion against an unjust
and corrupt governmnent may be a remedy
worse than the disease. [[1] or else.]

Remedy, If there be no | then welcome Pillvall.
(R 67)

1670 RAY 189.

Remedy, *see also* Danger best r. for danger;
Death is a plaster (r.) for all ills.; Every evil
under sun (For) there is r.; Medicine (R.) for
fear (No); Patience is a r. for grief; Wrong
without r. (No).

Remember the living, We ought to.

1539 TAVERNER 11 *Viuorum oportet meminisse.*
We ought to remember the lyuyng. There be
many that loue to talke of deade men, yea and
wyth dead men as much as in them lyeth.

Remember to distrust.
(R 72)

[EPICHARMUS Νᾶφε καὶ μέμνασ' ἀπιστεῖν (in CIC.
ad Att. l. 19. 8). ERASM. *Ad. Sobrius sis ac
memineris nemini confidere.*] **1664** J. WILSON
Andron. Com. III. iii. Wks. (1874) 165 You forget
our proverb—Remember to distrust! This easy
faith Has done more mischief than it e'er did
good.

Remember you are but a man.

1673 DAV. LLOYD *Dying & Dead Men's Words* 83
Philip of Macedon had one every morning to call
upon him to remember that he was a man.
1732 FULLER no. 4014.

Remember(s), *see also* Faithful friend hard to
find (R. man); Pities another r. himself; St.
Vincent's Day (R. on); Slept well that r. not he
has slept ill; Youth is used to.(What) age r.

Remembrance of past sorrow is joyful, The.
(R 73)

[SENECA *Herc. Fur.* 656 Quae fuit durum pati,
meminisse dulce est.] *c.* **1375** BARBOUR *Bruce*
III. 560 For, quhen men oucht at liking ar, To
tell of paynys passyt by Plesys to heryng
wonderly. *c.* **1403** LYDGATE *Temple of Glas*
st. 104 Swete is swettir eftir bitternes. **1539**
TAVERNER 34ᵛ Labours ones done, be swete . . .
after paynful labours and peryls the remem-

braunce of them is to him ryght pleasaunt.
1548 T. ELYOT *Bibliotheca* s.v. Acti iucundi
labores. **1555** J. PROCTOR *Hist. of Wyatt's
Rebellion* (Antiq. Repert. iii. 1808, 68) The safe
and sure recordation of paynes and peryls past,
hath present delectation (sayeth Tullye). **1576**
PETTIE i. 79 The remembrance of the peril
past delighteth. **1584** R. WILSON *Three Ladies
of London* Hazl.-Dods. vi. 416 Comfort it is
to think on sorrow past. **1593** *Tell-Troth's
New-year's Gift* New Sh.S. 6 Durum pati
meminisse dulce. **1594–5** SHAKES. *R.J.* III. v. 52
All these woes shall serve For sweet discourses
in our time to come. **1605** MARSTON *Dutch
Courtezan* v. ii It is much joy to thinke on
sorrowes past. **1639** CLARKE 206. **1732** FULLER
no. 4385 That, which was bitter to endure, may
be sweet to remember. **1827** POLLOK *Course of
Time* i. 464 Sorrows remembered sweeten joy.

Remove an old tree and it will wither to death.
(T 491)

1523 BARCLAY *Mirr. of Good Manners* Spenser
Soc. 67 An olde tree transposed shall finde small
auantage. **1670** RAY 22. **1721** KELLY 284 . . .
Spoken by a Man who is loth to leave a Place in
his advanc'd Years, in which he had long lived.
1831 W. M. PRAED *The Old Tory* I'm near threescore; you ought to know You can't transplant
so old a tree.

Remove Mort-stone, He may. (M 1184)

1662 FULLER Devon 248 . . . There is a Bay in
this County called Mort-Bay;[1] but the Harbour
in the entrance thereof is stopped with a huge
Rock, called Mort-Stone; and the People
merrily say that none can remove it, save such
who are Masters of their Wives. [[1] SW. of
Ilfracombe.]

Remove stones, bruise their fingers, Who.
(S 897)

1611 COTGRAVE s.v. Doigt He that remoueth
stones crusheth his fingers; harsh things are
seldome stirred without harme. **1640** HERBERT
no. 40.

Remove Tottenham Wood, You shall as easily.

1631 W. BEDWELL *Brief Descript. Tottenham* iii
. . . This is, of some spoken of things impossible,
or not likely to be effected. For the Hill is not
only very high, but also it's very great.

Remove(s), *see also* Three r. as bad as fire.

Render unto Caesar the things which are Caesar's.
(C 9)

[**1611** MATT. xxii. 21 Render therefore unto
Caesar the things which are Caesar's; and unto
God the things that are God's.] **1601** BP.
BARLOW *Serm. Paul's Cross* 27 The things due
from subjects to their Caesar. **1630** T. ADAMS
Good Politic. Direct.: Wks. 836 They forsake
Christ; and will not giue Caesar his due.

Render, *see also* Evil for good, (To r.)

Rent of Dee mills, If you had the | you would spend it. (R 76)

1670 RAY 171 . . . *Chesh. Dee* is the name of the river on which the city *Chester* stands: the mills[1] thereon yield a very great annual rent. [[1] Pulled down in 1910.]

Rent, *see also* Gentleman that pays r.; Hold the greatest farms pay least r. (They that); O Master Vier, we cannot pay your r.; Providence is better than r.; Spend a whole year's r. at one meal.

Repairs not a part, He that | builds all. (P 76)

1640 HERBERT no. 344.

Repairs not his gutter, Who | repairs his whole house.

1849 RUSKIN *Seven Lamps.* VI. xix (1880) 196 A few dead leaves and sticks swept in time out of a water-course, will save both roof and walls from ruin. **1855** BOHN 567 . . . *Span.*

Repay, *see* Serve a noble disposition . . . he will r.

Repeats, *see* History r. itself; Knows little (He that) often r. it.

Repent, *see* Marry in haste, r. at leisure; Never too late to r.

Repentance comes too late. *Cf.* **Never too late to repent.**

c. **1440** LYDGATE *Fall of Princes* III. l. 915 Harm doon, to late folweth repentaunce. **1575** GASCOIGNE *Posies* i. 66 Bought witte is deare, and drest with sower salte, Repentaunce commes to late. **1590** H. ROBERTS *Defiance to Fortune* O3ᵛ Repentance commeth too late. **1605** SHAKES. *K.L.* I. iv. 257 Woe, that too late repents. **1670** RAY 22 When all is consumed, . . . **1753** WESLEY *Lett.* iii. 97 They repented when it was too late.

Repentance too dear, To buy. (R 81–2)

1508 J. FISHER *Sayings David in Psalms* 63 He answered that his lernynge was not to bye penaunce so dere. **1539** TAVERNER I *Garden* D6 Demosthenes [when Lais demanded a great sum for one night's lodgings answered] I bye not repentaunce so dere. **1590** GREENE *Mourn. Garm.* 178 You will (at last) buy repentance with too deare a price. **1611** T. HEYWOOD *Gold. Age* IV. 68 Repentance I'd not buy At that high rate, ten thousand times to dye.

Repentance, *see also* End of passion beginning of r.; Hearing (From) comes wisdom, from speaking r.; Judgement as he runs, (He that passes) overtakes r.; Late r. seldom true; Marriage rides upon the saddle and r. upon the crupper; Peace and patience and death with r.; Stool of r.

Repented speech than silence, More have. (M 1148)

1579 *The Proverbs of Sir James Lopez de Mendoza* tr. B. Googe 79 As Isocrates sayth, I haue manie time repented for woordes that I haue spoken, but for keeping silence, neuer. **1640** HERBERT no. 682. **1872** BLACKMORE *Maid of Sker* ch. 34 Seldom need any man repent for not having said more than he did; and never so needeth a Welshman.

Reply, *see* No r. is best.

Report, *see* Blister; Turns lie dead and one ill deed r. abroad does spread, (Ten good).

Repps, *see* Gimmingham.

Reproach, *see* Sting of a r. is the truth.

Reputation is commonly measured by the acre.

1614 SIR T. OVERBURY *A Wife etc.* (1622 ed., R6) Reputation is measured by the Acre. **1616** T. ADAMS *The Soldier's Honour* B2 Reputation [should] be valued by valour, not measured by the acre. **1732** FULLER no. 4023.

Reserve the master-blow. *Cf.* **Fencer has one trick in budget.** (F 187)

1642 TORRIANO 90 . . . That is, teach not all thy skil, some secret is to be reserved; lest the scholar overreach his master, or rather insult over him: this is taken from fencing. **1659** HOWELL *It. Prov.* 13 (thy master-piece). **1813** RAY 20.

Resolute, *see* Things that must be (In) . . . be r.

Resolved mind has no cares, The. (M 973)

1616 DRAXE no. 1592 All troubles welcome to a resolued minde. **1640** HERBERT no. 464 (eares).

Respect a man, he will do the more. (M 362)

1659 HOWELL *Brit. Prov.* 16.

Respect the burden.

[*a.* **1821** NAPOLEON I.] **1902–4** LEAN IV. 89 . . . (A saying of Napoleon at St. Helena when, going up a narrow ascent, he met a heavily-burthened peasant, who was told to give place.— Emerson, *Representative Men.*) **1910** *Spectator* 26 Nov. 902 No one . . . can look at the portraits hanging there without feeling how profound is Van Gogh's . . . respect for the human burden.

Respects not is not respected, He that. (R 86)

a. **1663** HERBERT *Priest to the Temple* 268. **1640** *Id.* no. 427.

Respice finem, see Look to the end.

Rest, *see* A-bed (All are not) that shall have ill r.; Desire has no r.; Lawsuits consume r.; Little business stands great r., (In); Rain (Some), some r.; Sufferance (Of) comes r.

Restorative, *see* Pearls are r.

Restoring, *see* Giving is dead, r. sick.

Retinue, *see* Captain (Such) such r.

Retreat, In a | the lame are foremost.
(R 88)
1640 HERBERT no. 883.

Return(s), *see* Home as wise as one went (To r.); Quick r. make rich merchants; Runs far that never r.; Small profits quick r.

Revenge is a dish that should be eaten cold.
1620 SHELTON *Quix.* II. lxiii. iii. 274 Revenge is not good in cold blood. **1885** C. LOWE *Bismarck* (1898) iii. 36 [Bismarck] had defended Olmütz, it is true, but . . . with a secret resolution to 'eat the dish of his revenge cold instead of hot'. **1895** J. PAYN *In Mark. Ov.* ch. 17 Invective can be used at any time; like vengeance, it is a dish that can be eaten cold.

Revenge is a morsel for God.
(V 24)
[PS. xciv. 1: O Lord God, to whom vengeance belongeth. *Id.* xi. 7 Upon the ungodly he shall rain snares, fire and brimstone.] **1596** SHAKES. *Rich. II* I. ii. 6 Put we our quarrel to the will of heaven, Who, when they see the hours ripe on earth, Will rain hot vengeance on offenders' heads. **1622** T. ADAMS *City of Peace* Wks. 1008 When the Italians heare how God hath reserued vengeance to himselfe, they say blasphemously, He knew it was too sweet a bit for man, therefore kept it for his owne tooth. **1853** TRENCH iii. 55 Italian history . . . shows them no empty words, but truest utterances of the nation's heart. . . . One of them . . . declares, *Revenge is a morsel for God.* [Vendetta, boccon di Dio.]

Revenge is sweet.
(R 90)
1566 PAINTER *Pal. of Pleasure* (Jacobs) ii. 35 Vengeance is sweet. **1609** JONSON *Sil. Wom.* IV. v 182 O reuenge, how sweet art thou! **1667** MILTON *Par. Lost* ix. 171 Revenge, at first, though sweet, Bitter ere long, back on itself recoils. **1775** SHERIDAN *St. Pat. Day* II. iv Revenge is sweet. . . . And though disappointed of my designs upon your daughter, . . . I am revenged on her unnatural father. **1861** H. KINGSLEY *Ravenshoe* ch. 36 Revenge is sweet— to some. Not to him.

Revenge of a hundred years has still its sucking teeth.
[*It.* Vendetta di cent'anni ha ancor i lattaiuoli.] **1666** TORRIANO *It. Prov.* 299 no. 27. **1853** TRENCH iii. 56 Another [Italian proverb] proclaims an immortality of hatred, . . .

Revenge(s), *see also* Dead avails not and r. vents hatred, (To lament the); Living well best r.; Neglect will kill an injury sooner than r.; Pardons and pleasantness are great r. *See also* Vengeance.

Revenged all (every) wrong, Had I | I had not worn my skirts so long.
(W 945)
a. **1530** *R. Hill's Commonpl. Bk.* E.E.T.S. 140 He that will venge euery wreth, tho longer he levith the lesse he hath. **1575** GASCOIGNE *Posies, Dulce Bel. Inex.* i. 147 But sit at home and learne this old sayde sawe Had I revenged bene of every harme, My coate had never kept me halfe so warme. **1591** J. DAVIES *O Utinam* D7ᵛ He that will be auenged on euerie wrath, the longer he liues the lesse he hath. [*c.* **1640**] **1651** Cartwright *Ordinary* V. iv. **1670** RAY 136.

Revenue, *see* Sparing is great r.; Thrift is a great r.

Reverend are ever before, The.   (R 94)
1640 HERBERT no. 891.

Reverse, *see* Medal has its r.

Revolutions are not made with rose-water.
[MARMONTEL *Mémoires d'un Père (Œuvres* 1818 ii. 294) retort of Sebastien Chamfort: Voulez-vous qu'on vous fasse des révolutions à l'eau rose.] **1819** BYRON *Letters* (Prothero) iv. 358. **1830** *Morn. Chron.* 4 Aug. But for the 1500 killed and wounded . . . this would almost have been what Mirabeau [in 1789] said was impossible: a revolution of rose-water. **1873** LYTTON *Parisians* V. vii Did I not impiy . . . that we commence our journal with politics the mildest? Though revolutions are not made with rose-water, it is rose-water that nourishes their roots. **1894** LD. AVEBURY *Use of Life* ch. 11 It is sometimes said that Revolutions are not made with rose-water. Greater changes, however, have been made in the constitution of the world by argument than by arms.

Reward and punishment are the walls of a city.
(R 95)
1629 E. BOLTON *The City's Advocate* 17 But two maine pillars of the Commonwealth, Praemium et Poena, Reward and Punishment. **1639** CLARKE 181.

Reward, *see also* Desert and r. ever far odd; Honour is the r. of virtue; Love is true r. of love; Service without r. is punishment; Virtue is own r.; Wise who first gave r.

Rex, *see* Play r.

Rhetoric, *see* Truth has no need of r.

Rheum, *see* Wealth is like r.

Rhyme, It may | but it accords not.
(R 99)
c. **1387** T. USK *Test. of Love* in SKEAT *Chaucer* vii. 51 These thinges . . . mowe wel, if men liste, ryme; trewly, they acorde nothing. *a.* **1451** LYDGATE *Minor Poems* E.E.T.S. ii. 540 It may

wele ryme, but it accordith nought. **1546**
HEYWOOD I. xi. E3ᵛ To disdeygne me, who
mucke of the worlde hoordth not, As he dooth,
it may ryme but it accordth not. **1592** SHAKES.
T.G.V. II. i. 131 Nay, I was rhyming; 'tis you
that have the reason. **1594–5** *Id. L.L.L.* I. i. 99
In reason nothing.—Something then in rhyme.
Ibid. I. ii. 103 A dangerous rhyme, master,
against the reason of white and red.

Rhyme nor reason, Neither.   (R 98)

c. **1500** *Cf.* Proverbs at Leconfield (*Antiq.
Repert.* iv, 1809, 416) Regarde not the ryme but
the reason marke well. *a.* **1529** SKELTON in
Wks. (Dyce) i. 123 For reson can I non fynde
Nor good ryme in yower mater. **1592–3**
SHAKES. *C.E.* II. ii. 49 Neither rhyme nor
reason. **1599** *Id. A.Y.* III. ii. 367 Neither rime
nor reason can express how much. **1600–1** *Id.
M.W.W.* V. v. 123 In despite of the truth of all
rhyme and reason. **1625** BACON *Apoph.* Wks.
(Chandos) 381 ' Now it is somewhat, for now it is
rhyme: whereas before it was neither rhyme nor
reason'. **1664** H. MORE *Myst. Iniq.* 415 Against
all the Laws of Prophetick Interpretation, nay
indeed against all rhyme and reason. **1678**
RAY 349 Heer's nor rhythm, nor reason. **1731**
BAILEY s.v. Rhyme Tho Rhyme be but a jingle, it
affords Delight by the Musicalness of its Cad-
ence, when for want of both Rhyme and
Reason it neither delights the Sense nor improves the Intellectuals. **1888** ' R. BOLDREWOOD'
Robbery under Arms II. xi. 181 This won't do.
There's neither rhyme nor reason about it.

Rhyme rats to death, To.   (D 158)

[With reference to the alleged killing or expulsion of Irish rats by riming.] **1581** SIDNEY
Apol. Arb. 72 I will not wish vnto you . . . to be
rimed to death, as is sayd to be doone in
Ireland. **1599** SHAKES. *A.Y.* III. ii. 165 I was
never so be-rimed since Pythagoras' time, that I
was an Irish rat. **1660** [title] Rats Rhimed to
Death, or, The Rump-Parliament Hang'd up in
the Shambles. **1735** POPE *Donne Sat.* II. 22
Songs no longer move; No rat is rhym'd to
death, nor maid to love.

Rhymed, *see* Well r., tutor, brains, and stairs.

Rib(s), *see* Rancour sticks long by the r.; Stick
by the r.

Riband, *see* St. Johnston's r.

Ribchester was as rich as any town in Christendom, It is written upon a wall in Rome.   (W 13)

1586 CAMDEN *Britannia* Lancashire 431 ·It is
written vpon a wall in Rome, Ribchester was as
rich as any Towne in Christendome.

Rice for good luck, and bauchles¹ for bonny bairns.

1896 CHEVIOT 285 . . . Refers to the custom of
throwing rice and old shoes after a newly
married couple. [¹ old shoes.]

Rich as a new-shorn sheep, As.   (S 295)

c. **1520** *Cock Lorell's Boat* l. 16 The nexte that
came was a coryar, And a cobeler, his brother,
As ryche as a newe shorne shepe. **1546** HEY-
WOOD I. xi. E2ᵛ Till time ye be as ryche as a newe
shorne sheepe. [*c.* **1591**] **1595** PEELE *O.W.T.*
l. 271 (poore). **1631** BRATHWAITE *Whimzies*
(1859) 62 His speculation in time will make
him as rich as a new-shorn sheep.

Rich as Croesus (a king, etc.), As.

(C 832)

1577 KENDALL *Flow. of Epigrams* Spens. Soc. 57
As riche as Cresus Affric is. **1578** T. LUPTON
All for Money CI (a king). **1598–9** SHAKES.
M.A. III. v. 20 If I were as tedious [*Dogberry's
mistake for* rich] as a king, I could find in my
heart to bestow it all of your worship. **1631**
DEKKER *Penny Wise* B4 (a Queene). **1683**
T. FARNABY *Troposchematologia* B7 (an Em-
perour). **1724** DEFOE *Roxana* 73 (Croesus).
1837 DISRAELI *Venetia* I. v Your la'ship knows
'tis quite a saying, As rich as a lord. **1849**
THACKERAY *Pendennis* I. ch. 12 If he had a good
coat, you fancied he was as rich as Crazes.—As
Croesus, said Mr. Bowles. **1927** 13 June
D. H. LAWRENCE *Lett.* ii. 984 (Croesus).

Rich before night, He that will be | may be hanged before noon.   (N 172)

1607 H. ESTIENNE *World of Wonders* tr. R.C. 39
This . . . prouerbiall saying, He that would
quickly be rich, must turne his backe on God.
a. **1679** J. DUPORT in interleaved copy of RAY
(1670) at Trin. Coll., Cambridge. **1692**
L'ESTRANGE *Aesop's Fab.* ccclxix (1738) 388.
'Tis a roguey kind of a saying, that . . .

Rich enough that wants nothing, He is.

(N 262)

c. **1387** T. USK *Test. of Love* in SKEAT *Chaucer*
vii. 88 Is he nat riche that hath suffisaunce.
1577 N. BRETON *Works of a Young Wit* (*Poems*
ed. J. Robertson 31) Hee onely blest, that
needeth nought at all. **1640** HERBERT no. 403.

Rich enough who lacks not bread, He is.

[s. HIERON. *Epist.* cxxv *Satis diues, qui pane non
indiget.*] **1377** LANGLAND *P. Pl.* B. vii. 86 He
hath ynough that hath bred ynough · though he
haue nou3t elles: *Satis diues est, qui non indiget
pane.*

Rich folk have many (routh¹ of) friends.

(M 580a. R 103)

c. **1386** CHAUCER *Mel.* B² l. 2748 Pamphilles
seith also ' . . . if thou be right riche, thou shalt
find a great nombre of felawes and freendes'.
1616 T. ADAMS *Diseases of the Soul* 67 Riches
make many friends. **1659** HOWELL *It. Prov.* 9.
Rich men can want no kindred. **1706** STEVENS
s.v. Pobreza He that is rich . . . is a kin to all
Men. **1721** KELLY 283 . . . Many of whom are
but flatterers. **1832** HENDERSON 54 (routh).
[¹ plenty.]

Rich knows not who is his friend, The.

(R 104)

1640 HERBERT no. 865.

Rich man may dine when he will, the poor man when he may, The.   (M 365)

1542 ERASM. tr. Udall *Apoph.* (1877, 110). 1547 WM. BALDWIN (1550) G8. 1594 BACON *Promus* no. 1477 (in French). 1623 WODROEPHE 269. 1706 STEVENS s.v. Rico.

Rich man steal? Why should a.
                                                                              (M 416)

1678 RAY 196. 1732 FULLER no. 5736.

Rich man's money hangs him often-times, A.   (M 489)

1616 WITHALS 562. 1639 CLARKE 98.

Rich men are stewards for the poor.
                                                                              (M 578)

1552 LATIMER *Serm. Lord's Prayer* v. P.S. 399 You rich men, when there cometh a poor man unto you, . . . remember that thy riches be not thy own, but thou art but a steward over them. 1616 BRETON *Cross. Prov.* B1. 1735 POPE *Moral Essays* iii. 173 Who sees pale Memnon pine amidst his store, Sees but a backward steward for the poor.

Rich men may have what they will (may do anything).   (M 579–80)

1578 G. WHETSTONE 2 *Promos and Cassandra* III. ii. 14 Men may do what them woll, that haue money. 1617 J. SWETNAM *School of Defence* 66 As the olde Prouerbe goeth, The rich men haue the Lawe in their owne hands. 1639 CLARKE 99 (doe any thing). 1869 HAZLITT 325.

Rich man (men), *see also* Akin to the r. m. (Every one); Beggars breed and r. m. feed; God send us of our own when r. m. go to dinner; Poor man's cow dies and r. m.'s child; Put the poor man's penny and the r. m.'s . . .; Scrambling at a r. m.'s dole.

Rich rogue, A | two shirts and a rag.
                                                                              (R 160)

1678 RAY 80. 1738 SWIFT *Dial.* I. E.L. 278.

Rich that possesses much, He is not but he that is content with what he has.

c. 1526 ERASM. *Dicta Sap.* A2ᵛ. c. 1577 J. NORTHBROOKE *Treatise agst. Dicing* 48. 1624 J. HEWES *Perfect Survey* M3 (but who wanteth not much).

Rich, *see also* Beg from beggars never r.; Brother had rather see sister r.; Every one is weary, the r. in keeping; Fools live poor to die r.; God help the r.; Handsome at twenty nor r. at forty will never be; Law for the r. (One); Make me a diviner, I will make thee r.; Poor and liberal, r. and covetous; Pride of r. makes labour of poor; Quick returns make r. merchants; Ramsey the r.; Recks not who is r. (Wisest who); Ribchester; Tithe and be r.; Wise that is r.

Richer the cobbler, The | the blacker his thumb, *see* Higher the plum-tree.

Riches are but the baggage of virtue (fortune).   (R 107)

1580 LYLY *Euph. & his Eng.* ii. 15 To bee rich is the gift of Fortune. 1607–12 BACON *Ess., Riches* Arb. 230 I cannot call *Riches* better than the baggage of *Vertue* (the Romaine word is better, *Impedimenta*) For as the *Baggage* is to an Army, so is Riches to vertue. 1670 RAY 22 (fortune). 1732 FULLER no. 4042 (as 1670).

Riches are like muck, which stink in a heap, but spread abroad make the earth fruitful.   (M 1071)

1564 BULLEIN *Dial. agst. Fever* (1888) 9 *Mend.* Couetous vsurers . . . like vnto greate stinkyng mucle medin hilles, whiche neuer doe pleasure vnto the Lande . . . vntill their heapes are caste abroade to the profite of many. 1599 JONSON *Ev. Man out of Hum.* III. viii. 48 I haue liued, Like an vnsauourie muck-hill to my selfe, Yet now my gathered heapes being spread abroad, Shall turne to better and more fruitfull vses. 1625 BACON *Apoph.* Wks. (Chandos) 369 Mr. Bettenham . . . used to say, that riches were like muck; when it lay in a heap it gave but a stench . . . ; but when it was spread upon the ground, then it was cause of much fruit. 1670 RAY 22.

Riches bring care and fears.   (R 109)

c. 1526 ERASM. *Dicta Sap.* A2 The richer one is, the more thoughtfull he lyueth. 1545 *Precepts of Cato* Sage Sayings Periander B3 The richer a man is in substaunce, Of cares the more is his abundaunce. 1546 HEYWOOD I. xii. E4ᵛ Riches bryngth ofte harme, and euer feare. 1552 R. HUTCHINSON *Wks.* P.S. 296 Cura divitiarum amovest somnum. Riches do drive away sleep. 1611 DAVIES no. 317 If riches brings feare, Gold's bought to deere. 1616 DRAXE no. 1876.

Riches have wings.   (R 111)

[PROVERBS xxiii. 5 Riches certainly make themselves wings; they fly away as an eagle toward heaven.] 1607–12 BACON *Ess., Riches* Arb. 238 Riches have winges, and sometymes they fly away of themselves. 1623 PAINTER B7ᵛ Wealth hath wings, and it may flye away. 1785 FLETCHER OF MADELEY *Wks.* vii. 473 Riches . . . make themselves wings.

Riches increase, When | the body decreases.   (R 114)

1611 COTGRAVE s.v. Bien When goods encrease the body decreases. 1670 RAY 22 . . . For most men grow old before they grow rich.

Riches of Egypt are for the foreigners therein, The.

1875 BURCKHARDT *Arab. Provs.* 83 . . . Since the time of the Pharaohs Egypt has never been governed by national rulers, but constantly by foreigners.

Riches serve a wise man but command a fool. (R 113)

a. **1606** CHARRON *Wisdom* tr. Lennard (1640) 84 Riches serves wise men, but command a foole. For a covetous man serves his riches, not they him. **1669** PENN *No Cross, No Crown* xiii Peter Charron,[1] a famous Frenchman, wrote . . . 'Riches serve wise men, but command a fool; for a covetous man serveth his riches, and not they him.' **1732** FULLER no. 4047. [[1] *d.* 1603.]

Riches (*noun*), *see also* Children poor men's r.; Covetousness is (R. are) the root of all evil; Good name better than r.; Health is great r. . . .; Honour is but ancient r.; Small r. have most rest.

Riches (*verb*), *see* Carl r. he wretches (As the).

Riddance, *see* Good r. to bad rubbish.

Riddle, *see* Sib as sieve and r.

Ride a hobby to death, To.

[= to overdo some pet subject.] **1881** A. JESSOPP *Arcady* 197 They got astride of this favourite hobby-horse of the doctrinaires, and . . . a hobby may be ridden to death.

Ride a horse and mare on the shoulders, an ass and mule on the buttocks. (H 685)

1659 HOWELL *It. Prov.* 2. **1678** RAY 53.

Ride a young colt, When you | see your saddle be well girt. (C 524)

1659 HOWELL *Eng. Prov.* 13b.

Ride an inch behind the tail, You shall. (I 60)

1678 RAY 266.

Ride as if you went to fetch the midwife, You. (M 920)

1678 RAY 266.

Ride (backwards) up Holborn Hill, He will. (H 507)

[1592] **1594** *Knack to know Knave* sc. xiv You must . . . be towde up Holburne hill. [1592] **1594** *Selimus* l. 2082 That had bene the way to preferment, downe Holburne vp Tiburne. **1600** C. SNUFFE [R. Armin] *Quips upon Questions* F1[v] Goe braue still, And it will bring thee soone vp Holborne hill. **1675** C. COTTON *Burlesque upon Burlesque* 16 For so small a Peccadill To send a man up Holborn-hill. **1785** GROSE *Classical Dict.* s.v. London. **1787** *Id. Prov. Glos.* (*London*) 197 He will ride backwards up Holborn-hill. He will come to be hanged. Criminals . . . were, till about the year 1784, executed at Tyburn, the way to which from Newgate, was up Holborn-hill. They were generally conveyed in carts . . . with their backs towards the horses.

Ride fair, and jaup[1] none.

1721 KELLY 283 . . . Taken from riding through a Puddle: But apply'd to too home jesting. [[1] to bespatter with mud.]

Ride post for puddings, To.

1602 WITHALS 74 With foot and wing, as they say, post haste, *Equis, et velis.* It is also spoken where haste is, and neede is, but then in the worser part, as they say, post haste for puddings. **1616** BRETNOR *Almanac* January (Evil days) Post for a pudding. **1619** MIDDLETON *Inner Temple Masque* ed. Bullen vii. 211.

Ride so near the rump, You | you'll let none get on behind you.

1721 KELLY 365 . . . You go sharply to Work, that you will let none get any Advantage by you.

Ride softly, that we may come sooner home. (R 115)

1678 RAY 204. **1732** FULLER no. 4050.

Ride the fore-horse, To. (R 120)

1664 ETHEREGE *Comical Revenge* III. v. I see you ride the fore-horse, gentlemen. [*a.* 1657] **1693** J. HACKET *Mem. Williams* I. 28 None of his Fellows had cause to repent, that he rode upon the Fore-Horse. **1738** SWIFT *Dial.* I. E.L. 283 Well, miss, you ride the fore-horse to-day. **1818** SCOTT *Rob Roy* ch. 27.

Ride (Mount) the high horse, To.

[= to put on airs.] **1721** KELLY 173 He is upon his high Horse Spoken when People fall into a Passion. **1773** VIEYRA s.v. Ai To be transported with anger, or as we say, to mount upon his great horse. **1805** F. AMES *Wks.* I. 339 I expect reverses and disasters, and that Great Britain, now on the high horse, will dismount again. **1824** MISS FERRIER *Inheritance* III. xii Fred seems to be on his high horse to-day, . . . I told you he would give himself airs. **1855** TROLLOPE *Warden* ch. 7 Though Eleanor Harding rode off from John Bold on a high horse, it must not be supposed that her heart was so elate as her demeanour.

Ride the water with, He is not a man to.

1857 DEAN RAMSAY *Remin.* V. (1911) 202 . . . A common Scottish saying to express you cannot trust such an one in trying times. May have arisen . . . where fords abounded, and the crossing them was dangerous.

Ride to Romford[1] on it, You might.

1738 SWIFT *Dial.* II. E.L. 311 One may ride to Rumford upon this knife, it is so blunt. **1901** *N. & Q.*, 9th Ser. VIII. 306 'You might ride to Romford on it'. When a youngster I often heard my old grandmother make this remark *à Propos* any blunt carving or other knife which failed to come up to expectations. [[1] Romford, in Essex, famous for breeches-making.]

Ride who will, the mare is shod. (M 652)

1541 *Sch. House of Women* C1[v] Our fyly is fetlyd vnto the sadle; Ryde who wyll, shod is our mare, And thus they eschaunge ware for ware.

Ride with the beard on the shoulder, To.

1706 STEVENS s.v. Barba To carry one's Beard on his Shoulder. That is, to be upon one's Guard. **1823** SCOTT *Peveril* ch. 7 They rode, as the Spanish proverb expresses it, 'with the beard on the shoulder', looking around, . . . and using every precaution to have the speediest knowledge of any pursuit.

Rides a tiger, He who | is afraid to dismount.

1902 A. R. COLQUHOUN *Mastery of Pacific* 410 These colonies are . . . for her [France] the tiger which she has mounted (to use the Chinese phrase), and which she can neither manage nor get rid of.

Rides behind another, He who | does not saddle when he pleases.

1706 STEVENS s.v. Cavalgar.

Rides ere he be ready, He that | wants some of his gear.   (G 56)

a. **1628** CARMICHAELL no. 826.   **1641** FERGUSSON no. 421.   **1721** KELLY 154 . . . Apply'd to him who goes about a Business without proper Tools to accomplish it.

Rides not ay when he saddles his horse, He.

1706 STEVENS s.v. Recuero . . . Put on the Pack-saddles to day and go away to morrow.   **1721** KELLY 175 . . . Spoken of them who make great Pretences to Haste, but yet linger long enough.

Rides sure that never fell, He.   (R 116)

a. **1485** MALORY *Morte d'Arthur* IX. 28 He rydeth wel that neuer fylle.   *a.* **1628** CAR-MICHAELL no. 700 He ryds sikker fell never. **1641** FERGUSSON no. 303.   **1721** KELLY 133 . . . A Man has gone through the World with a strange even Hand, that never committed a Blunder.   **1732** FULLER no. 2011 He rode sure indeed, that never caught a Fall in his Life.

Ride(s), rode, *see also* Better r. on an ass that carries me; Bodkin, (To r.); Marriage r. upon the saddle and repentance upon the crupper; Mickle to do when cadgers r.; Never r. never fell; Nothing but up and r.; Pride r., (When) shame is on the crupper; St. George . . . never r.; Two r. on a horse (If).

Rider, *see* Ill for the r. good for abider; Time is the r. that breaks youth.

Ridge, *see* Love his house (*or* the Kirk), yet not ride on r.

Ridiculous, *see* Sublime to the r.

Riding, *see* Good r. at two anchors; Half an hour's hanging hinders r.; Safe r. in good haven.

Rig, *see* Run a r.

Right as a ram's horn, As.   (R 28)

c. **1320** *Reliq. Antiquae* (1843) ii. 19 As ryt as rams orn.   *a.* **1529** SKELTON *Col. Cloute* 1200 They say many matters be borne By the right of a ram's horn.   **1562** J. PILKINGTON *Aggeus and Abdias* P.S. 256.   **1659** HOWELL *Eng. Prov.* 11b.

Right as a trivet, As.

1835 HOOD *Dead Robbery* x 'I'm right' thought Bunce, 'as any trivet'.   **1837** DICKENS *Pickwick* ch. 50 'I hope you are well, Sir.' 'Right as a trivet, Sir,' replied Bob Sawyer.

Right as my leg, As.   (L 180)

c. **1630** *Roxb. Ballads* B.S. iii. 338 That are as right's my leg.   **1638** 12 Feb. *Stationer's Register* Arb. iv. 455 *The New Married Couple or as right as my leg.*   **1639** CHAPMAN & SHIRLEY *The Ball* iv. Wks. (1889) 506 Good! right as my leg again.   **1663** J. WILSON *Cheats* II. iv All's well, and as right as my leg.—And that's crooked to my knowledge.

Right as rain, As.

[PLAUTUS *Capt.* 2. 2. 86 *Tam hoc tibi in proclivi quam imber est quando pluit.*]   **1894** W. RAYMOND *Love & Quiet Life* 108 ''Tes so right as rain, Zir,' sez I.

Right at Rome, No.   (R 124)

1639 CLARKE 172.

Right hand, He is his.   (H 73)

c. **1528–37** LD. J. BUTLER in Ellis *Orig. Lett.* ser. II ii. 48 O Connor . . . who hath maried the erle of Kildare's doghter, is his right hand.   **1581** G. ELLIOT [title] *A very true Report of the apprehension . . . of that arch-Papist Edmund Campion, the Pope his right hand.*   **1592** SHAKES. *T.G.V.* V. iv. 67 Who should be trusted [now] when one's own right hand Is perjured to the bosom?   **1598–9** *Id. M.A.* I. iii. 42 Marry, it is your brother's right hand.   **1608** J. DAY *Hum. out Breath* II. i. 22 I am his right hand.   **1640** JONSON *Tale Tub* I. vi. 45 O that same surly knave, Is his right hand: and leads my sonne amisse.

Right, He that has | fears; he that has wrong, hopes.   (R 123)

1640 HERBERT no. 429.

Right hand from his left, He knows (not) his.   (H 74)

c. **1535** BYGOD *Treat. conc. Improp. Ben.* D1 As well as I knowe my right hande from my lyfte. **1587** HOLINSHED *Chron.* III. 1354b This auoweth he that knew the man as well as the right hand from the left.   **1612** *Don Quix.* (1900) i. 127 We shall not be able to know which is our right foot.   **1619** J. FAVOUR *Antiquity triumphing* *over Novelty* 376 A child of Nineueh, that scarce knew his right hand from his left. **1620** *Don Quix.* (1900) iii. 37 Whom I know as well as I know one hand from another. **1681** ROBERTSON *Phraseol. Generalis* 1079. **1857** G. ELIOT *Scenes of Clerical Life* 'Mr. Gilfil's Love-Story' ch. 4.

Right, master, right; four nobles a year's a crown a quarter. (M 730)

1670 RAY 217 . . . *Chesh.* **1917** BRIDGE 105 . . . It seems to be a sarcastic answer to one who is very positive in asserting an inaccuracy.

Right mixture makes good mortar.

1721 KELLY 284. **1732** FULLER no. 4052.

Right side. (S 427)

1639 CLARKE 182 I will not take from my left side to give to my right. **1664** CODRINGTON 201 (as 1639). **1670** RAY 195 To take from ones right side, to give to ones left.

Right wrongs no man.

1832 HENDERSON 89.

Right, *see also* Bribe nor lose thy r. (Neither); Come r. in the wash, (It will all); Country, r. or wrong; Do r. nor suffer wrong (He will neither); Extreme law (r.) is wrong; Might is r.; Refuse with the r. hand; Rise on r. side; Wrong never comes r.

Rigorous, *see* Virtuous that is not r. (He cannot be).

Riners, *see* Shed r. with a whaver (To).

Ring of a rush. (R 128)

[i.e. of no value.] *c.* **1449** PECOCK *Repr.* II. v. 166 It is weel allowid . . . that he make a ring of a rische and putte it on his fynger. **1546** HEYWOOD I. iii. A4 I hoppyng without for a ryng of a rushe. **1602** SHAKES. *A.W.* II. ii. 20 As fit . . . as Tib's rush for Tom's forefinger. **1641** FERGUSSON no. 188 Better na ring nor the ring of a rashe. **1732** FULLER no. 918 Better no Ring, than a Ring of a Rush. **1813** ELLIS *Brand's Pop. Antiq.* II. 38 A custom . . . appears antiently to have prevailed, . . . of marrying with a Rush Ring; chiefly practised, however, by designing men.

Ring of Gyges. (R 132)

[An ancestor of Gyges, a Lydian, found a gold ring, which, worn on the finger, rendered him invisible (PLATO *Rep.* 2. 359). ERASM. *Ad. Gygis anulus.*] **1586**? LYLY *Triumphs of Trophes* iii. 430, l. 86 To walke vnseene with *Giges* ring faine they would. **1606** CHAPMAN *M. d'Olive* II. ii. 86 Thought myself as private as if I had had King Giris [sic] ring and could have gone invisible. **1662** FULLER *Heref.* 35 Civil War . . . will trace all corners, except they be surrounded with Gyges his ring. **1710** STEELE *Tatler* No. 138 (1896) 71 Gyges . . . had an enchanted ring, . . . making him who wore it visible or invisible, as he turned it to or from his body. . . . Tully . . . says

. . . , 'that a man of honour who had such a ring would act just in the same manner as he would without it'.

Ring(s) (*noun*), *see also* Honour without profit like r.; St. Martin's r.

Ring (*verb*), *see* Noon on one's head, (To r.)

Rip not up old sores. (S 649)

1553 N. UDALL *Ralph Roister Doister* 1. 698 No good turnes entwite[1] Nor olde sores recite. **1559** COOPER s.v. Cicatrix Refricare cicatricem, to rubbe or make sore that, which was almoste whole, spoken prouerbyally, of renewynge and styrrnge vp agayne, a daungerous matter. **1573** G. HARVEY *Letterbk.* Camd. Soc. 18 Besides sutch ripping up of ould matters . . . as I suppose there have sildum been seen the like. **157 6** LEMNIUS 112[v] They cannot abyde to haue olde soares rypped vp. **1589** *A Comparison of Eng. and Spanish Nation* A2 He chooseth rather to rip vp old sores. *c.* **1592** NASHE *Summer's Last Will* iii. 246, l. 410. **1639** CLARKE 303. **1679** J. GOODMAN *Penit. Pard.* III. vi (1713) 393 He will not rake in men's wounds, nor rip up old sores. **1830** GALT *Lawrie T.* IV. ix It's little my part to rip up old sores. [[1] censure.]

Ripe(ns), *see* Fruit r. not well in shade; Soon r., soon rotten.

Ripon, *see* True steel as R. rowels.

Rise betimes that will cozen the devil, He must. (D 279)

1581–90 *Timon* IV. Sh. S. ii. 62 Hee that will cheate mee must arise betimes. **1630** T. ADAMS *Faith's Encouragem.* Wks. 722 He that would deceiue the deuill, had need to rise betimes. **1659** HOWELL *Eng. Prov.* 19a.

Rise betimes that would please everybody, He had need. (N 86)

1639 CLARKE 34 They must rise betimes that please all. **1670** RAY 132. **1732** FULLER no. 1854.

Rise early that used to rise late, In vain they. (V 4)

1592 DELAMOTHE 19 In vaine he rises early, that was wont to rise late. **1611** DAVIES no. 216. **1616** DRAXE no. 413. **1639** CLARKE 67 (They can't).

Rise early, Though you | yet the day comes at his time, and not till then. (D 104)

1591 STEPNEY 148 A mans early rising bringeth day neuer the sooner. **1640** HERBERT no. 333. **1659** HOWELL *Span. Prov.* 16 For rising early the day breaks never the sooner. **1659** N.R. 98.

Rise on the right (wrong) side, To. (S 426)

[A happy, or unhappy, augury.] **1540** PALSGRAVE *Acolastus* 90. **1546** HEYWOOD II. iv. G3[v]

You rose on your right syde here right. **1633**
JONSON *T. Tub.* IV. ii. 10 We are like men that
wander in strange woods, And lose ourselves in
search of them wee seeke.—This was because
wee rose on the wrong side. **1824** SCOTT *Redg.*
ch. 20 Why, brother Nixon, thou art angry this
morning . . . hast risen from thy wrong side, I
think. **1894** BLACKMORE *Perlycross* ch. 32 I
have heard of people getting out of bed the
wrong side; and you can't make it right all day.

Rises not early, He that | never does a good day's work. *Cf.* Rises late.

1577 BRETON *Wks. of a Young Wit* (Wks. ed.
J. Robertson 62) Who lies in bedde till Dinner
tyme, gaines litle after noone. **1616** DRAXE no.
1527 (in the morning loseth his journey). **1620**
SHELTON *Quix.* Pt. II, ch. 43, T.T. iv. 41 He that
riseth not with the sun loseth the day. **1846**
DENHAM 5.

Rises over early, He | that is hanged ere noon.   (N 208)

a. **1628** CARMICHAELL no. 699. **1641** FERGUSSON
no. 329.

Rises betimes, He that | has something in his head.   (S 617)

1640 HERBERT no. 235.

Rises first, He that | is first dressed.
(R 134)

1640 HERBERT no. 202.

Rises late, He that | must trot all day. *Cf.* Rises not early, etc.

1659 HOWELL *Span. Prov.* 17. **1758** FRANKLIN
Pref.

Rise(s), *see also* Bed with the lamb (Go to) r.
with lark; Falls today, (He that) may r. to-
morrow; Thrive (He that will) must r. at five.

Rising, *see* God's help is better than early r.;
Worship the r. sun.

Rising was a seaport town, and Lynn it was a wash, but now Lynn is a seaport town, and Rising fares the worst.[1]

1851 *N. & Q.* 1st Ser. III. 206. [1 Norfolk.
See **1902–4** LEAN I. 150 Castle Rising is described in . . . 1672, as utterly decayed and its
havens filled with sand.]

Rising was, Lynn is, and Downham shall be, the greatest seaport of the three.

1851 *N. & Q.* 1st Ser. III. 206.

Riven breeks, *see* Sits full still that has r. b.

Riven dish, *see* Lost that is put into r. d.;
Simpers like a r. d.

River of Dart! O river of Dart! every year thou claimest a heart.[1]

1850 *N. & Q.* 1st Ser. II. 511 . . . It is said that a
year never passes without the drowning of one
person, at least, in the Dart. The river . . . is
liable to sudden risings, when the water comes
down with great strength and violence. **1912**
Spectator 3 Aug. 163 Perhaps it is . . . the huge
stones . . . which sets a certain cruelty about the
Dartmoor landscape; perhaps . . . it is the name
of the river, and the legend of its toll, 'every year
a heart', to rhyme with its name. [1 Devon.]

Rivers need a spring.   (R 141)

1640 HERBERT no. 600.

Rivers run into the sea, All. *Cf.* Follow the river and you'll get to the sea.   (R 140)

[ECCLES. i. 5.] [*c.* 1515] *c.* **1530** BARCLAY *Eclog.*
I. l. 1217 Likewise as streames vnto the sea do
glide. **1573** SANFORD 106ᵛ The water goeth to
the sea. **1576** PRUDENTIUS tr. Robinson *Moral
Method* A1 From Homer all Poets haue
recource, euen as all Riuers from the Ocean are.
[1592] **1596** *Edw. III* v. i. 92 All riuers haue
recourse vnto the Sea. **1593** NASHE *Christ's
Tears* ii. 63 All Riuers must runne into the Sea.
1596 SHAKES. *M.V.* V. i. 95 And then his state
Empties itself, as doth an inland brook Into the
main of waters. **1608** J. HALL *Epistles* I. v. 37
Euen little streames empty themselues into great
riuers; and they againe into the Sea. **1616**
DRAXE no. 1872. **1650** T. FULLER *Pisgah-sight* 3,
A4 Solomons rule, All rivers run into the Sea.
1732 FULLER no. 541 All Rivers do what they
can for the Sea.

River, *see also* Danger (R.) past, God forgotten;
Follow the r. get to the sea; Great man and
great r. ill neighbours; Great r. great fish (In a);
Mountain and r. good neighbours; Sea refuses
no r.

Rives the kirk to theek[1] the quire, He.
(K 101)

c. **1523** BARCLAY *Mirr. Good Manners* 30
Uncover not the church therwith to mend the
quer: Spoye not a multitude of people miserable,
To one or two persons for to be profitable.
1641 FERGUSSON no. 419. **1721** KELLY 276 Peel
the kirk, and thick the quire Eng. Rob Peter and
pay Paul. **1857** DEAN RAMSAY *Remin.* V (1911)
202 . . . Spoken of unprofitable persons who, in
the English proverb, 'rob Peter to pay Paul'.
[1 thatch.]

Rivington Pike do wear a hood, If | be sure that day will ne'er be good.
(R 142)

1670 RAY (*Lancs.*) 236 . . . A mist on the top of
that hill is a sign of foul weather.

Roads lead to Rome, All.

c. **1391** CHAUCER *Astrolabe* Prol. l. 40 Right as
diverse pathes leden diverse folk the righte way
to Rome. **1872** BLACK *Strange Adv. Ph.* ch. 6
You know all roads lead to Rome, and they say

that Oxford is halfway to Rome. **1893** BP.
MOULE *Comment. Rom.* 3 As 'all roads led to
Rome', so all roads led from Rome.

Road(s), *see also* Keeps his r. who gets rid of bad
company; Royal r. to learning (No); Snails on r.

Roar like a bull, To.   (B 715)

1545 ASCHAM *Toxoph.* Arb. 42 Roring lyke a
bull, as some lawyers do. **1597** SHAKES. *1 Hen.
IV* II. iv. 248 And, Falstaff, you ... roar'd for
mercy, and still run and roar'd, as ever I heard
bullcalf. **1598** *Id. 2 Hen. IV* III. ii. 172 Come,
prick me Bullcalf till he roar again ... What,
dost thou roar before thou art prick'd? **1600**
T. HEYWOOD *et al. 2 Edw. IV* i. 119 And roarde
and bellowd like a parish-bull. **1759** J. WESLEY
Journal iv. 319. **1840** MARRYAT *Poor Jack* ch. 13
There was one of our men hanging on the main-
stay, and roaring like a bull.

Roast a stone, To.   (S 892)

1522 SKELTON *Why not to Court?* 109 Pescoddes
they may shyll, Or elles go rost a stone. **1546**
HEYWOOD II. ii. F4ᵛ Hir carreyne carkas (saide he)
is so colde, ... I do but rost a stone. In warmyng
hir. **1611** DAVIES no. 354 Fuscus his old wife
now lies alone, When he lyes with her, he roasts
but a Stone.

Roast meat, To give one (a dog) | and beat him with the spit.   (M 147)

[To follow hospitality with harshness.] **1553**
T. WILSON *Arte of Rhet.* (1909) 72 Such are not
to be lyked that geue a man a shoulder of
mutton, and breake his head with the spitte
when they haue doen. **1636** CAMDEN 296 Give a
dog roast and beat him with the spit. **1674**
WOOD *Life* O.U.P. 210 He gave me roast meat
and beat me with the spit. *a.* **1700** B. E. *Dict.
Cant. Crew* ... to do one a Curtesy, and Twit or
Upbraid him with it. **1876** ROBINSON *Whitby
Gloss.* 182/1 'Never invite a friend to a roast
and then beat him with the spit', do not confer a
favor and then make the obligation felt.

Roast meat does[1] cattle.

1877 E. LEIGH *Chesh. Gloss.* 63 ... which means
that in dry seasons cattle, if they can only get
plenty of water often milk better than in cold
wet seasons, when there is more grass. **1917**
BRIDGE 105 ... In a very dry season, grass
which is half burnt is more fattening than grass
in a rainy season. [1 fattens.]

Roast meat, You are in your | when others are in their sod.   (M 848)

1616 WITHALS 575 (Sodden). **1639** CLARKE 115
(as 1616). **1670** RAY 190. **1732** FULLER no. 5849.

Roast, *see also* Cry r. meat; Invited you to the r.?
(Who); Loves r. meat; Rule the r.

Rob an orchard when none keeps it, It is easy to.   (O 76)

1639 CLARKE 55. **1670** RAY 23.

Rob, He that does not | makes not a robe or garment.   (R 145)

1573 SANFORD 103ᵛ. **1629** *Bk. Mer. Rid.* Prov.
no. 83.

Rob Peter to (give to, clothe) pay Paul, To.   (P 244)

c. **1380** WYCLIF *Sel. Wks.* III. 174 Lord, hou
schulde God approve þat þou robbe Petur, and
gif þis robbere to Poule in þe name of Crist?
c. **1440** *Jacob's Well* 305 þei robbyn seynt petyr
& ȝeuyn it seynt Poule. [*c.* 1515] *c.* **1530** BARCLAY
Eclog. i. E.E.T.S. 47 Fewe Princes geue that
which to them selfe attayne ... They robbe
sant Peter therewith to cloth S. Powle. **1546**
HEYWOOD I. xi. D2 Lyke a pickpurs pilgrym,
ye prie and ye proule At rouers, to robbe Peter
and paie Poule. **1581** GUAZZO ii. 99 That in my
judgment is a shamefull thyng ... to uncloath
Peter to cloath Paule. **1640** HERBERT no. 763
Give not St. Peter so much, to leave St. Paul
nothing. **1655** FULLER *Ch. Hist.* XI. vi (1868) III.
550 Much he[1] expended on the repair of Westminster Abbey church; and his answer is generally known, when pressed by Bishop Laud to a
larger contribution to St. Paul's, that he would
not rob Peter to pay Paul. **1737** *Gent. Mag.* VII.
172/1 This Scheme is ... calculated ... to Rob
Peter to pay Paul, or, to remove ye Burthen
from one Part of the Community, and lay it upon
another. **1926** *Times* 7 Jan. 9/6 Martin and
Martin had been in low water for a long time
and had recourse to the method of robbing
Peter to pay Paul. [1 Dean Williams.]

Rob(s), *see also* Table r. more than a thief;
Thief r. another (One).

Robbery, *see* Exchange no r.

Robbing the barn.

1869 HAZLITT 325 ... The good wife sometimes
does this to pay for extra finery.

Robe, *see* Bode a r. and wear it; Rob (He that
does not) makes not r.

Rob'em, *see* Starv'em.

Robert, Sir, *see* Robin that herds ... can be as
blithe as S. R.

Robin (Sparrow), The | and the wren are God's cock and hen: the martin and the swallow are God's mate and marrow.

a. **1508** SKELTON *Phil. Sparrow* ll. 598–601 Wks.
(1843) i. 69 That Phyllyp may ... treade the
prety wren, That is our Ladyes hen. **1790**
GROSE *Prov. Glossary* Pop. Superstitions 47 It is
held extremely unlucky to kill a cricket, a lady-
bug, a swallow, martin, robin red-breast, or
wren; perhaps from the idea of its being a
breach of hospitality; all those birds and insects
taking refuge in houses. There is a particular
district in favour of the robin and wren: A robin
and a wren Are God Almighty's cock and hen.
Persons killing any of the above-mentioned
birds or insects, or destroying their nests, will
infallibly, within the course of the year, break a

bone, or meet with some other dreadful misfortune. On the contrary, it is deemed lucky to
have martins or swallows build their nests under
the eaves of a house, or on the chimnies. **1826**
R. WILBRAHAM *Chesh. Glos.* 105 The following
. . . is common in Cheshire: The Robin and the
Wren Are God's cock and hen, The Martin and
the Swallow are God's mate and marrow.
1908 *Times Wkly.* 7 Feb. iii. The rhyme . . .
which asserts that the robin and the wren 'are
God's cock and hen' expresses a belief . . . that
the robin and the wren are actually the male and
female of one species.

Robin Goodfellow.   (R 147)

[= a sportive elf or goblin.] **1531** TYNDALE
Expos. 1 Ep. St. John P.S. 139 The Scripture . . .
is become a maze unto them, in which they
wander as in a mist, or (as we say) led by Robin
Goodfellow, that they cannot come to the right
way. **1567** HARMAN *Caueat for Common*
Cursetors ch. 3, ed. Viles and Furnivall 36 I
verely suppose that when they wer wel waked
with cold, they suerly thought that Robin
goodfellow (according to the old saying) had
bene with them that night. **1581** GUAZZO ii. 81
They will make it a sport to put their children
in feare with tales of Robin good fellow. **1595**
SHAKES. *M.N.D.* II. i. 34 That shrewd and
knavish sprite Call'd Robin Goodfellow. **1626**
BRETON *Soothing* B2ᵛ Robin Goodfellow was a
strange man. True, among wenches that kept
not their houses cleane. **1639** CLARKE 69 Robin
Goodfellow was a strange man.

Robin Hood could bear (stand) any wind (anything) but a thaw wind.

c. **1855** *Life & Ballads of Robin Hood* ii Every
Yorkshireman is familiar with the observation
that Robin Hood could brave all weathers but
a thaw wind. **1917** BRIDGE 105 Robin Hood
could stand anything but a thaw wind. *A thaw*
or *tho'* wind is a cold piercing wind from the S. or
SE. which often accompanies the breaking up of
a long frost.

Robin Hood's mile.

[= one of several times the recognized length.]
1559 W. CUNNINGHAM *Cosmogr. Glasse* 57 These
are Robin Hode's miles, as the prouerbe is.

Robin Hood's pennyworth (bargains).
                                           (R 149)

[= a thing or quantity sold at a robber's price,
i.e. far below the real value.] **1565** *Col. S. P.*
Dom. Eliz. i. 262 at St. John's Cambridge
'Making Robin Hoodes pennyworthes of their
copes and vestments'. **1582** G. WHETSTONE
Heptameron of Civil Discourses T2 The cunning
Lawier, that buyeth Robin hoodes pennewortes
& yet with some nice for faitures, threatneth
the seller, with continuall bondage. **1600** W.
HAUGHTON *Robin Hood's Pen'orths* (play title,
Henslowe's *Diary*, ed. Greg. ii. 215). **1614** T.
ADAMS *Serm.* (1861–2) I. 201 The devil . . . makes
the world believe that he sells Robin Hood's
pennyworths; that he hath . . . a prodigal hand,
and gives all *gratis*. **1677** W. HUGHES *Man of*
Sin II. viii. 122 In Germany, there is a Robin-
Hood's pennyworth to be had, . . . 8000 years
of Pardon both from punishment and fault.
1709 *Brit. Apollo* No. 58 3/1 When . . . a

Purchase you reap, that is wondrous Cheap,
They Robin-Hood Bargains are call'd.

Robin Hood, *see also* Good even, good R. H.;
Speak of R. H. (Many) that never shot; Tales of
R. H. are good among fools.

Robin sings in the bush, If the | then the weather will be coarse; but if the robin sings on the barn, then the weather will be warm.

1830 FORBY 416.

Robin that herds on the height can be as blithe as Sir Robert the knight.

1862 HISLOP 165.

Robin, *see also* Naked as r.

Robs a scholar, He that | robs twenty men.   (S 134)

1616 WITHALS 553. **1639** CLARKE 243. **1670**
RAY 23 . . . For commonly he borrows a cloak
of one, a sword of another, a pair of boots of a
third, a hat of a fourth, &c.

Robs, *see also* Rob(s).

Rock,¹ Thus rid the.   (R 150)

[= so was the distaff managed.] **1546** HEY-
WOOD II. ix. K4ᵛ What ye wan in thundred yer
lost in the sheere. In all your good husbandry,
thus ryd the rocke. **1555** HEYWOOD *Epig. on*
Proverbs CII Thus rydeth the rocke, yf the
rocke be rydyng. The spynsters thryft, is set a
foote slydyng. [¹ distaff.]

Rock, *see also* Firm as a r.; Tow on one's r.
(To have).

Rock lizards.

1842 BORROW *Bible in Spain* (1843) III. xiv. 269
He was . . . what is called a rock lizard, that is, a
person born at Gibraltar of English parents.

Rock scorpions.

1867 ADM. SMYTH *Sailor's Word-bk.* Rock
Scorpion, a name applied to persons born at
Gibraltar. **1891** A. FORBES *Barracks, Biv. &*
Bat. (1910) 105 The Smytches, Rock Scorpions,
Cypriotes, . . . and other miscellaneous scum of
the Levant who were serving as mule-drivers.

Rocket, *see* Go up like r.

Rocking, *see* Sleep without r.

Rod breaks no bones, The.   (R 154)

1616 DRAXE no. 1891. **1639** CLARKE 75.

Rod (staff) for his own back (breech, tail, head), He makes a.   (R 153)

c. **1374** CHAUCER *Troilus* Bk. I, l. 740 For it is
seyd, man maketh ofte a yerde With which the

maker is hymself y-beten. *c.* **1510** STANBRIDGE *Vulg.* E.E.T.S. 23 He hath ordeyned a staffe for his owne heed. **1533** FRITH *Disp. Purg.* (1829) 110 Then hath he made a rod for his own breech. **1545** TAVERNER G1ᵛ Many there be whiche make a rod for theyr owne arse. **1546** HEYWOOD I. ii. A3 Whan haste proueth a rod made for his owne tayle. **1552** HULOET T3ᵛ Make a rod for his owne ars . . . a prouerbe . . . risen of one Perellus, whyche made a brazen Bulle, ordeyened for tormente, and gaue it to Phalaris, wherein he him selfe was fyrste tormented. **1641** FERGUSSON no. 455 He brings a staff to his own head. **1650** BAXTER *Saints' Everl. Rest* III. ix And so make a rod for their own backs. **1772** FLETCHER OF MADELEY *Wks.* ii. 42 (scourge).

Rods in pickle (piss), To have.   (R 157)

[= to have punishment in store.] **1553** *Respublica* III. v. 820 Some would in no wyse to owre desyres applye. But we have Roddes in pysse for them. *c.* **1630** *The Soddered Citizen* l. 769 (Bryne). **1648** J. DILLINGHAM in *Ld. Mcntagu of Beaulieu's P.* (Hist. MSS. Comm.) 163 No doubt there are many rods in pickle against many great ones. **1714** MANDEVILLE *Fab. Bees* (1733) I. 331 I see a thousand rods in piss, and the whole posse of diminutive pedants against me. **1911** W. F. BUTLER *Autobiog.* ch. 21 The visit of Sir Alfred Milner . . . was . . . for . . . the preparation and pickling of rods for the Republic.

Rod(s), see also Give a slave a r.; Kiss the r.; Rule with r. of iron; Spare the r. spoil child; Whip for fool and r. for school.

Roe, see John Doe and Richard R.; Trip like a doe (r.).

Roger, see Sow is good mutton (Your); True R.

Rogue like to the godly rogue, No.

1732 FULLER no. 3624.

Rogue's wardrobe is harbour for a louse, A.   (R 161)

1626 BRETON *Soothing* A5. **1670** RAY 137.

Rogue(s), see also Rich r., two shirts and a rag; Thieves and r. have best luck.

Roint, see Rynt.

Roland for an Oliver, To give a.

(R 195)

[= tit for tat. Roland and Oliver were two of the paladins of Charlemagne, both famous for their exploits.] **1548** HALL *Chronicle* (1809) 266 To haue a Rowland for an Olyuer. **1549** ERASM. tr. Chaloner *Praise of Folly* M3 Set one enchaunter against an other, or an Oliver for a Rolande. **1565** J. CALFHILL *Treatise of the Cross* P.S. 374 Is not that (as the proverb hath) to have a quarrel to Rowland, and fight with Oliver? **1577** HOLINSHED *Chron.* (1808) III. 205 Bicause he knew the French King would not take the matter well, to haue a Roland for an

Oliuer; he sente solemne ambassadours to the King of England, offering him his daughter in mariage. **1670** RAY 191 . . . That is, *quid pro quo*, to be even with one. **1692** L'ESTRANGE *Aesop's Fab.* xxxi (1738) 38 'Tis allowable in all the liberties of conversation to give a man a Rowland for his Oliver, and to pay him in his own coin. **1816** SCOTT *Antiq.* ch. 35 He gave my termagant kinsman a *quid pro quo*—a Rowland for his Oliver, as the vulgar say.

Rolling eye, a roving heart, A.

1629 T. ADAMS *Serm.* (1861–2) II. 219 The eye is the pulse of the soul: as physicians judge of the heart by the pulse, so we by the eye; a rolling eye, a roving heart.

Rolling stone gathers no moss, A.

(S 885)

[ERASM. *Ad.* Λίθος κυλινδόμενος τὸ φῦκος οὐ ποιεῖ. Musco lapis volutus haud obducitur.] **1362** LANGLAND *P. Pl.* A. x. 101 Selden Moseþ þe Marbelston þat men ofte treden. *c.* **1450–1500** *Gd. Wife wd. a Pilgr.* l. 12 Syldon mossyth the ston þat oftyn ys tornnyd and wende. **1546** HEYWOOD I. xi. D2. **1618** BRETON *Courtier & Countryman* Wks. Gros. II. 8/2 I haue heard that roling stones gather no mosse. **1709** A. PHILIPS *Pastoral* 2 A rolling stone is ever bare of moss. **1720** T. BOSTON *Fourfold State* (1797) 305 A rolling stone gathers no fog. **1886** E. J. HARDY *How to be Happy* ch. 14 Servants are now rolling stones that gather no moss. **1917** BRIDGE 5 A rolling stone gathers no moss, but a tethered sheep winna get fat. Cheshiremen are rather fond of putting a tag to an ordinary proverb. In Surrey and Sussex we have the addition:—'And a sitting hen never grows fat'.

Rome brick, I found | I leave it marble.

[L. *Urbem lateritiam invenit, marmoream reliquit*[1]] **1559** J. FERRARIUS *Good Ordering of a Commonwealth* tr. W. Bavande 18ᵛ He himself [Octavian], whereas he receiued the citee of Roome built of Bricke, would leaue it all of Marble. **1581** GUAZZO i. 185 Augustus . . . sayd, I found Rome of stones and brickes, but I have left it of marble. **1783** JOHNSON *Life of Dryden* What was said of Rome, adorned by Augustus, may be applied by an easy metaphor to English poetry embellished by Dryden, *lateritiam invenit, marmoream reliquit.* He found it brick and left it marble. **1828** (Feb.) BROUGHAM *Speech in Ho. of Commons on Law Reform* It was the boast of Augustus . . . that he found Rome of brick, and left it of marble . . . Much nobler will be the sovereign's boast . . . that he found law dear, and left it cheap. [[1] Adapted from SUETONIUS *Aug.* 28.]

Rome sees a bad man, He that goes first to | he that goes the second time meets with him, he that goes the third time brings him home.   (R 162)

1619 BASSE *Help Discourse* 334. **1637** *Life & Death of Will Summers* 1676 ed. C1 The old Proverb . . . The first time after that a man hath been at Rome, and returned from thence, he is thought to be a Knave; the second time he is proved to be a Knave; but the third time he is known to be both a Knave and an Imposter.

1673 DARE *Counsellor Manners* 58 He that goes to Rome once, seeth a wicked man; he that goes twice learneth to know him; but he that goes thrice thither, brings him home with him.

Rome, When you are at | do as Rome does. (R 165)

[s. AMBROSE *Quando hic sum, non ieiuno Sabbato*; *quando Romae sum, ieiuno Sabbato* (s. AUGUSTINE, *Ep.* 36, ch. 14). JER. TAYLOR, *Si fueris Romae, Romano vivito more; Si fueris alibi, vivito sicut ibi.* If you are at Rome, live after the Roman fashion; if you are elsewhere, live as they do there.] *a.* 1530 R. *Hill's Commonpl. Bk.* E.E.T.S. 130 When thou art at Rome, do after the dome; And whan þou art els wher, do as they do ther. **1581** GUAZZO i. 65 Hee had so readie a wit to frame himselfe to the diversitie of the life and manners of other Countries, and according to the saying, When one is at Rome, to live as they doe at Rome. **1669** PENN *No Cross, No Crown* ix Her fashions, as those of France now, were as laws to the world, at least at Rome: whence it is proverbial, *Cum fueris Romæ, Romano vivito more*. 'When thou art at Rome, thou must do as Rome does.' **1849** C. BRONTË ch. 5 Don't put on the sabots again. I told you ... they were not quite the thing for this country ... do at Rome as the Romans do.

Rome was not built in a (one) day. (R 163)

[c. 1190 *Li Proverbe au Vilain* (Tobler) 43 Rome ne fut pas faite toute en un jour, ce dit li vilains.] **1545** TAVERNER D1ᵛ. **1546** HEYWOOD I. xi. D4 Rome was not bylt on a daie (quoth he) and yet stood Tyll it was fynysht. **1622** BEAUM. & FL. *Prophetess* I. iii You must have patience, Rome was not built in one day. **1641** FERGUSSON no. 737 Rome was not biggit on the first day. **1660** TATHAM *Rump* I. i (1879) 214 Why, gentlemen, Rome was not built in a day. **1748** SMOLLETT *Rod. Rand.* ch. 51 Mounting by gradual steps to the summit of your fortune. Rome was not built in a day. **1901** S. LANE-POOLE *Sir H. Parkes* ch. 17 The Japanese . . . went too fast and fell into grave commercial, monetary, and administrative troubles. Neither Rome nor New Japan could be built in a day.

Rome, *see also* All things are to be bought at R.; Better be first in a village than second at R.; Drive a snail to R.; Fiddle while R. burning; Home rule R. rule; Protestant R.; Ribchester; Right at R. (No); Roads lead to R. (All); Sit in R. and strive against Pope (Hard to).

Romford, *see* Ride to R. on it.

Room is better than his company, His. (R 168)

1577 R. STANYHURST in Holinshed *Descr. Ireland* (1587) 17a His roome had beene better than his companie. **1579** *Marr. of Wit & Wisdom* Sh. S. iii. 27 I had rather haue your roome as your componie. **1591** GREENE *Farewell to Folly* in Wks. Gros. ix. 329 I had a liefe haue their roome as their companie. **1633** D. DYKE *School of Afflict.* 216 Many, . . . are rather like the Gadarenes, loving the ministers' room better than their company. **1662** FULLER Lancs. 119 Worthington perceiving his Room more wellcome then his Company, embraced the next opportunity of Departure. **1822** SCOTT *Nigel* ch. 26 The waterman declared he would rather have her room than her company.

Room to swing a cat, Not. (c 603a)

1665 *Medela Pestilentiae* 11 They had not space enough (according to the vulgar saying) to swing a Cat in. **1666** TORRIANO *Prov. Phr.* s.v. Conscientia 44 The English say, to have a wide conscience, as one may swing a cat in't. *a.* 1679 J. DUPORT MS. note in Trin. Coll. Camb. copy of RAY 1670 A good large conscience—you may swing a cat in it. **1771** SMOLLETT *Humph. Clink.* II. 8 June At London, I am pent up in frouzy lodgings, where there is not room to swing a cat. **1927** *Times* 11 Feb. 10/3 The working rooms ... are crowded with store cases, and not a man ... has room to swing a cat.

Roost, *see* Curses come home to r.

Root (*noun*), *see* Covetousness is (Riches are) the r. of all evil; Idleness is r. of all evil; No r. no fruit.

Root(s) (*verb*), *see* Tree r. more fast which has stood blast.

Rope and butter; if one slip t'other will hold, A. (R 172)

1652 *A New Model* (single sheet) A rope and butter. **1678** RAY 267. **1732** FULLER no. 384.

Rope enough and he'll hang himself, Give a thief (him). (T 104)

1639 FULLER *Holy War* v. vii They were suffered to have rope enough, till they had haltered themselves in a *præmunire*. **1670** RAY 148. **1732** FULLER no. 1657 (him).

Rope enough, I thought I had given her | said Pedley, when he hanged his mare. (R 171)

1670 RAY 191. **1732** FULLER no. 2627.

Rope for a thief, As fit (meet) as a. *Cf.* Worth it as a thief worth a rope. (R 169)

1540 PALSGRAVE *Acolastus* 88 As mete for him as a rope is for a thefe. **1546** HEYWOOD I. x. C3 (mete). **1591** ARIOSTO *Orl. Fur.* Harington XIII. *Moral* As fit (to vse the old Prouerbe) as a rope is for a theefe.

Rope in after the bucket, Throw the. (R 173)

1599 MINSHEU *Span. Gram.* 80 To cast the rope after the caldron. **1620** SHELTON *Quix.* II. ix. ii. 243. **1631** MABBE *Celestina* T.T. 24 The rope will go after the Bucket: and one losse follow another. **1732** FULLER no. 5042.

Rope (Halter), Name not a | in his house that hanged himself (was hanged). (H 59)

1599 MINSHEU *Span. Dial.* 2 A man ought not to make mention of a halter in the house of a man that was hanged. **1612** SHELTON *Quix.* III. xi. i. 220 Why do I name an ass with my mouth, seeing one should not mention a rope in one's house that was hanged? **1640** HERBERT no. 671 Mention not a halter in the house of him that was hanged. **1670** RAY 138. **1890** J. PAYN *Burnt Mil.* ch. 32 Miss Grace, whom he pictured . . . as sensitive upon the matter, as though if her parent had been hung- she would have been to an allusion to a rope.

Ropes of sand, To make (twist). (R 174)

[ERASM. *Ad. Ex arena funiculum nectis.* You are for making a rope of sand.] **1576** E. PATRIZI *Civil Policy* tr. R. Robinson 60ᵛ The prouerbe: Of Sand an infinite quantitie take, And yet vnpossible it is a coarde to make. **1594** LIPSIUS *6 Books of Politics* tr. Jones X2 There are manye other things, which I can not easilie tye together with this corde of sand. *c.* **1594** BACON *Promus* (Pott) 275 To knytt a rope of sand. **1608** CHAPMAN *Byron's Trag.* V. iv. 55 These are but ropes of sand. **1621** BURTON *Anat. Mel.* I. ii. IV. vii (1651) 167 Make a rope of sand; to what end? **1631** JONSON *Devil is an Ass* I. i. 118 Get you e'en backe, Sir, To making of your rope of sand againe. **1662** BUTLER *Hud.* (1726) I. i. 156. 24 For he a Rope of Sand co'ld twist As tough as Learned Sorbonist. **1800** J. ADAMS *Wks.* (1854) IX. 87 Sweden and Denmark, Russia and Prussia, might form a rope of sand, but no dependence can be placed on such a maritime coalition. **1909** ALEX. MACLAREN *Ephesians* 305 Men . . . are doing what . . evil spirits were condemned to do— spinning ropes out of seasand.

Rope(s), *see also* Bitten by a serpent afraid of a r.; High r. (To be on the); Know the r.; Pulls with long r. that waits for another's death. *See also* Rape.

Rose, The fairest | at last is withered. (R 180)

a. **1487** *Thewis Gd. Women* l. 10 Farest ross takis sonest faidinge. **1591** FLORIO *Second F.* 105 The fairest and the sweetest Rose, In time must fade and beauty lose. **1592** DELAMOTHE 25. **1623** CAMDEN 279 (in three dayes). **1670** RAY 138.

Rose without a thorn, No. (R 182)

1430–40 LYDGATE *Bochas* Prol. ix There is no rose . . . in garden, but there be sum thorne. **1579** LYLY *Euph.* i. 184 The sweetest Rose hath his prickel. **1592–4** SHAKES. *I Hen. VI* II. iv. 69 Hath not thy rose a thorn, Plantagenet? **1603** MONTAIGNE (Florio) III. iii. 68 But no good without paines; no Roses without prickles. **1609** SHAKES. *Sonn.* 35. l. 2 Roses have thorns and silver fountains mud. **1647** HERRICK *Noble Numb.*; *The Rose* O.U.P. 386 But ne're the Rose without the Thorn. **1670** RAY 138. **1866** C. READE *Griffith G.* ch. 4 There was a thorn in

the rose of their wedded life: he was of the Church of England; she . . . a Roman Catholic.

Rose(s), *see also* Fresh as a r.; Lie upon r. when young; Pick a r.; Red as a r.; Stung by a nettle than a r. (Better be); Took her for a r.; Truths and r. have thorns; Under the r.

Rose-water, *see* Revolutions.

Roseberry Topping wears a cap, When | let Cleveland then beware a clap. (R 187)

1610 P. HOLLAND tr. Camden *Brit.* 721 Yorkshire North Riding Ounsbery or Rosebery Topping mounteth up a mighty height, and maketh a goodly shew a farre off, serving unto sailers for a marke of direction, and to the neighbour inhabitants for a prognostication: For, so often as the head thereof hath his cloudy cap on, lightly there followeth raine: whereupon they haue a Prouerbiall Rhime, when Rosebery Topping weares a cap. Let Cleveland then beware a clap. **1659** E. LEIGH *Eng. Descr.* 232.

Ross was, Dublin is, Drogheda shall be.

1577 R. STANYHURST in Holinshed *Descr. Ireland* (1587) 25a.

Rosse (Russe) of Potterne, *see* Live as long as old R. of P.

Rot, *see* Michaelmas r.

Rotheras, *see* Dwell at R. (Every one cannot).

Rotten apple, Not worth a.

c. **1370** CHAUCER *Romaunt of the Rose* l. 4531 Ne worth an appel. *c.* **1489** CAXTON *Sons of Aymon* E.E.T.S. 544 The sones of a traytour whiche ben not worthe a roten apple. **1538** BALE *King Johan* l. 989 (warden). **1641** *Seven Arguments Proving that Papists are Traiterous Subjects* 4 Not worth the paring of a rotten apple.

Rotten apple injures its neighbours, The. (A 294)

[L. *Pomum compunctum cito corrumpit sibi iunctum.*] **1340** *Ayenbite* 205 A roted eppel amang þe holen, makeþ rotie þe y-ȝounde. *c.* **1386** CHAUCER *Cook's T.* l. 4406 Wel bet is roten appel out of hord Than that it rotie al the remenaunt. **1576** WITHALS D4ᵛ A perished apple doth quicklye rotte the next vnto it. **1577** J. NORTHBROOKE *Treatise agst. Dicing* ed. Collier 125 A penny naughtily gotten, sayth Chrysostoms, is like a rotten apple laid among sounde apples, which will rot all the rest. **1736** FRANKLIN July The rotten apple spoils his companion.

Rotten, *see also* Boughs (Who trusts to r.) may fall; Choice in r. apples (Small); Medlars are never good till they be r.; Post (As good trust to a r.); Post soon painted (A r.); Soon ripe, soon r.

Rough and ready.

1810 F. J. JACKSON in Sir G. Jackson *Diaries & Lett.* (1873) i. 120 A more rough and ready state of things . . . than we had before been accustomed to. **1849** DICKENS *Dav. Cop.* ch. 3 You'll find us rough, sir, but you'll find us ready. **1855** BROWNING *Bp. Bloug. Apol.* You, . . . The rough and ready man, who write apace, Read somewhat seldomer, think perhaps even less. **1880** S. BARING-GOULD *Mehalah* I. ch. 5 Glory was the girl for him, rough and ready, who could row a boat, and wade in the mud.

Rough as it runs, as the boy said when his ass kicked him.

1687 T. BROWN in *Dk. Buckingham's Wks.* (1705) II. 129 If you don't like me rough, as I run, fare you well, Madam. **1763** J. BOSWELL *Let. Ld. Hailes* 16 Jul. Take me just as I am, good, or bad, or indifferent; or (as Sir Francis Dashwood said of the Cyder Bill) rough as I run. **1813** RAY 231.

Rough diamond, A.   (D 322)

1624 FLETCHER *Wife for Month* IV. ii She is very honest, And will be hard to cut as a rough diamond. **1700** DRYDEN *Pref. Fables* (Globe) 503 Chaucer . . . is a rough diamond. **1853** C.BRONTË *Villette* ch. 14 A good and gallant but unpolished man, a sort of diamond in the rough.

Rough net is not the best catcher of birds, The.   (N 129)

c. **1549** HEYWOOD I. ix. C2 It hurteth not the tounge to geue fayre wurdis. The rough net is not the best catcher of burdis. **1577** R. STANYHURST in Holinshed *Chron. Ireland* (1587) 96b Master Brereton . . . perceiuing that rough nets were not the fittest to take such peart birds. **1614** CAMDEN 313.

Rough oats, To take.

c. **1580** J. CONYBEARE 14 Rather I hadde to take rough otes (as they saye) of a bad debter then nothynge at all.

Rough with the smooth, Take the.

c. **1400** *Beryn* E.E.T.S. 37 Take yeur part as it comyth, of roughe and eke of smooth. **1882** BLACKMORE *Christowell* ch. 16 To take the rough and smooth together, is a test of magnanimity; but Howell took the rough without the smooth.

Rough, *see also* Lick with the r. side of one's tongue, (To give a).

Rouk-town's seldom a good housewife at home, A.   (R 191)

1670 RAY 52 . . . A Yorkshire Proverb. A Rouk-town is a gossiping housewife.

Round as a ball (hoop, top), As.
                                        (B 61. H 593)

1555 HEYWOOD *Epig. on Prov.* no. LXVIII Turnd round as a bal. c. **1555** *Songs and Bal. Philip and Mary* Roxb. Cl. 29, 98 Untyll she ryll as

rownd as a hoope. [**1587–93**] **1599** [GREENE?] *George a Greene* l. 467 (top).

Round of beef, *see* Tomtit on r. of b. (Like a).

Round peg in a square hole (*or vice versa*), A.

1804–6 SYDNEY SMITH *Lecture* ix We shall generally find that the triangular person has got into the square hole, the oblong into the triangular, and a square person has squeezed himself into a round hole. **1836** FONBLANQUE *Eng. under Seven Administr.* (1837) III. 342 Sir Robert Peel was a smooth round peg in a sharp-cornered square hole, and Lord Lyndhurst is a rectangular square-cut peg, in a smooth round hole. **1901** *Westm. Gaz.* 24 Dec. 2/2 Was there ever a more glaring case of square peg in round hole and round peg in square?

Round table, At a | there's no dispute of place.   (T 1)

1611 COTGRAVE s.v. Table Round tables take away contention. **1623** WODROEPHE 483 A round table yealds no debate. **1642** TORRIANO 4 (no contending for priority). **1670** RAY 138.

Round the moon there is a brugh,[1] When | the weather will be cold and rough. *Cf.* Near burr, far rain.

1631 BRATHWAIT *Whimzies* (1859) 104 A burre[1] about the moone is not halfe so certain a presage of tempest as . . . c. **1667** *Journal of James Yonge* 113 By reason of a ring about the moon this day we apprehended a storm, but it proved not so. **1843** RUSKIN *Diaries 1835–47* 239 Liverpool captains say storm is coming when the halo is *far* from the moon. **1846** DENHAM 17. [[1] halo.]

Round, *see also* Money is r.; World is r.

Roundabouts, *see* Swings (To lose on).

Roundheads, *see* Wellington R.

Rout, *see* Better to rule than be ruled by the r.

Routing[1] like a hog.   (H 497)

c. **1386** CHAUCER *Reeve's T.* l. 4162 This millere hath so wisely bibbed ale That as an hors he snorteth in his sleep, . . . Men myghte hir rowtyng heere two furlong. **1546** HEYWOOD I. x. D1ᵛ But where was your vncle . . . ? A sleepe by (quoth she) routyng lyke a hog. [[1] snoring.]

Rover, *see* Tongue run at r.

Row the boat, Norman, row.

[**1453**] **1598** STOW *Survey of Lond.* (1633) 567 Sir Iohn Norman . . . was the first Maior that was rowed by water to *Westminster*, to take his Oath. . . . The Watermen made a Song in his prayse beginning, *Row thy Boate, Norman*, &c. a. **1529** SKELTON *Bowge* 252 Wks. (1843) I. 40 Heue and how rombelow,[1] row the bote, Norman, rowe! [[1] a cry of rowers.]

Row to hoe, To have a hard (long).

1835 D. CROCKETT *Tour Down East* 69 I never
opposed Andrew Jackson for the sake of
popularity. I knew it was a hard row to hoe.
1848 LOWELL *Biglow P.* Ser. I. Wks. (1884) 213
You've a darned long row to hoe.

Row(s) (*verb*), *see also* All men r. galley way;
Carried down the stream need not r.; Looks one
way r. another.

Rowan tree and red thread make the
witches tine[1] their speed.

1846–59 *Denham Tracts* F.L.S. ii. 329 (haud the
witches a' in dread). **1896** CHEVIOT 287 . . . It
was at one time common in Scotland to attach a
cross of this wood to the byre-door with a red
thread, as a security to the cattle against witches.
[[1] lose.]

Rowan(s), *see also* Many rains many r.

Royal road to learning, There is no.

[PROCLUS *Comm. in Eucl.* 68 (Teubner) μὴ
εἶναι βασιλικὴν ἀτραπὸν ἐπὶ γεωμετρίαν, quoting
Euclid to Ptolemy I.] **1824** EMERSON *Journals*
I. 393. **1857** TROLLOPE *Barch. Tow.* ch. 20
There is no royal road to learning; no short cut
to the acquirement of any valuable art. **1894**
LD. AVEBURY *Use of Life* ch. 7 In the earlier
stages of Education . . . neither rank nor wealth
gives any substantial advantage. . . . It was long
ago remarked that there was no royal road to
learning.

Royalist, *see* More r. than the king.

Royet[1] lads (may) make sober men.

1832 HENDERSON 66. [[1] wild.]

Royston horse and a Cambridge master
of arts will give way to nobody, A.
(H 686)

1575 WM. SOONE in George Braun (or Bruin)
Civitates Orbis Terrarum vol. II, lib. ii, fol. I.
In platæis ambulantes, decedi sibi de via, non à
ciuibus solum, sed etiam à peregrino quouis,
nisi dignitate excellat, postulant: vt iam in
prouerbij locum venerit, equum Roystonium
(est autem pagus Roystonum, vnde Londinum
hordeum coctum, equis impositum peruehitur)
& Magistrum Cantabrigensem, duo esse anim-
alium genera, quæ nemini de via cædant. **1662**
FULLER *Cambs.* 150 A Boisten[1] horse and a
Cambridge Master of Art, are a couple of
Creatures that will give way to no body. This
Proverb we find in the Letter of William Zoon
written to George Bruin, in his 'Theatre of
Cities'. [[1] misprint for Royston, Cambs.]

Rub, There is (Here lies) the.   (R 196)

[= inconvenience, difficulty; comes from the
game of bowls.] **1577–8** R. STANYHURST in
Holinshed *Hist. of Ireland* (1586) 97a How
dangerous it is to be a rub, when a king is disposed to sweepe an alleie. **1600–1** SHAKES. *H.*
III. i. 65 To sleep! perchance to dream! ay,
there's the rub; For in that sleep of death what

dreams may come. **1616** T. ADAMS *Soul's
Sickness* 36 Dangers like to . . . rubbes in a
smooth way. **1641** *Oxinden Letters 1607–1642*
ed. D. Gardiner 280 This . . . is but a rub cast in
the way, to turne away the bias of my affection
from my desired Mistress. **1712** STEELE *Spect.*
no. 533, par. I But her Relations are not
Intimates with mine. Ah! there's the rub.
1822 SCOTT *Pirate* ch. 34 Here lies the rub . . .
When she hears of you she will be at you. **1830**
LYTTON *Paul Clif.* ch. 20 Expense! . . . Ay!
there's the rub!

Rub a cat on the rump, The more you |
the higher she sets up her tail.   (C 156)

1678 RAY 109. **1853** TRENCH iv. 78 No need
. . . of adulation or flattery to quicken [fools] to a
ranker growth; for The more you stroke the
cat's tail, the more he raises his back.

Rub a galled (scabbed) horse on the
back (gall) and he will wince.   (H 700)

a. **1384** WYCLIF *Wks.* Arnold III. 231 As a horse
unrubbed, that haues a sore back, wynses when
he is oght touched or rubbed on his rugge.
c. **1386** CHAUCER *W. of Bath's T.* l. 939 For
trewely, there is noon of us alle, If any wight wol
clawe us on the galle, That we nil kike. **1523**
SKELTON *Gar. Laur.* 97 Yet wrote he none ill
Sauynge he rubbid sum vpon the gall. **1541**
Schoolh. of Wom. D4 Rub a scalde horse vpon
the gall, And he wyll byte, wynse, and vente,
So wyll all people that are malyuolent. **1570**
EDWARDS *Damon & Pythias* Hazl.-Dods. iv. 28
I know the galled horse will soonest wince.
1596 *Estate of English Fugitives* 132 Let them
onely wince that feele their galled backe rubbed.
1600–1 SHAKES. *H.* III. ii. 237 Let the gall'd jade
wince, our withers are unwrung. **1611** DAVIES
no. 414 A Scab'd Horse no combe abides.
1651 HERBERT no. 1113 A scabbed horse cannot
abide the comb. **1659** HOWELL *Eng. Prov.*
6b. **1670** RAY 95. **1738** SWIFT *Dial.* I. E.L. 269
Touch a gall'd horse, and he'll wince. **1869**
HAZLITT 372.

Rub and a good (great) cast.   (C 119)

[Comes from the game of bowls.] **1608**
DEKKER *Bellman of London* F3[v] Rub & a Great
one. **1614** T. FREEMAN *Rubbe, and a great Cast*
(Title). **1667** 'RODOLPHUS' *Fortune's Uncertainty* 1959 ed. 32 Rub, rub, and a good cast, the
Proverb goes. **1678** RAY 81 . . . Be not too
hasty, and you'll speed the better.

Rub (scratch) the elbow, To. *Cf.* Claw
the elbow.   (E 100)

[= to show oneself excited, whether with
pleasure or anger.] **1594** NASHE *Unfort. Trav.*
ii. 219 Had you seene him how he . . . scratcht
his scabd elbowes at this speach. **1594–5**
SHAKES. *L.L.L.* V. ii. 109 One rubb'd his elbow
thus, and fleer'd, and swore A better speech was
never spoke before. **1597** *Id. I Hen. IV* V. i. 77
Fickle changelings and poor discontents, Which
gape and rub the elbow at the news Of hurly-
burly innovation. **1598** E. GUILPIN *Skial.* (1878)
25 He'le . . . scratch the elbow too To see two
butchers curres fight. [1600] **1639** DELONEY 2
Gentle Craft 171 Is he but a Shooemaker . . . ?
O how that word makes me scratch my elbo:
. . . See how it makes my blood rise.

Rubbing, *see* Gip with ill r.

Rubbish, *see* Good riddance to bad r.

Rubicon, To cross (pass) the.   (R 197)

[= to take a decisive step, especially at the
outset; Caesar's crossing of this stream, in N.
Italy, marked the beginning of war with Pompey.] **1626** J. MEAD in BIRCH *Crt. & Times Chas.
I* (1848) I. 180 Queen Dido did never more
importune Æneas's stay at Carthage, than his
mother and sister do his continuance here at
London. . . . But now he is past the Rubicon.
1643 J. OWEN *Death of Death* Wks. (1852) X. 150
The die being cast and Rubicon crossed. **1827**
SCOTT *Napoleon* iv. 21 [Bonaparte] would, . . .
like Caesar, have crossed the Rubicon at the
head of the popular party.

Ruck, *see* Devil always tips at biggest r.

Rudder, *see* Ruled by the r. (Who will not be);
Tongue is the r. of our ship.

Rue and thyme grow both in one garden.   (R 198)

c. **1641** FERGUSSON MS. no. 1162. **1721** KELLY
283 . . . A Persuasion to repent and give over an
Attempt before it be too late, alluding to the
Sound of the two Herbs here nam'd. **1824** S.
FERRIER *Inheritance* III. ch. 6 I wish it may last;
but 'rue and thyme grow baith in ae garden'.

Rue in thyme should be a maiden's posie.

1721 KELLY 284. [A play upon the word *thyme*
(time).]

Rue(rs), (*noun*), *see also* Reivers should not be r.;
Take the r.

Rue(s) (*verb*), *see* Better r. sit than r. flit; Rape
r. (Oft).

Ruff, *see* Old woman in wooden r.

Ruffian's-hall, He is only fit for.   (R 200)

1590 *An Almond for a Parrot* (Nashe iii. 356)
You thinke . . . Masse Martin, hath neuer broke
sword in ruffians hall. **1592** NASHE *Piers
Penniless* i. 187 Make Ruffians hall of Hell.
1631 STOW *Annals* 1023 West Smithfield for
many years called Ruffians Hall. **1662** FULLER
Lond. 199 . . . A Ruffian is the same with a
Swaggerer. . . . West Smithfield . . . was formerly
called Ruffian's hall, where such men met
casually and otherwise. . . . The Proverb [is]
only appliable to quarrelsome people . . . who
delight in brawls and blows.

Rugged stone grows smooth from hand to hand, A.   (S 886)

1640 HERBERT no. 316.

Ruin of one ravine.[1]   (R 201)

1546 HEYWOOD II. ix. L1 And sure sens we were
borne, Ruine of one rauyn, was there none
gretter. [[1] act of rapine.]

Ruin(s), *see also* Abundance like want r.;
France's r. is eve of r. of England.

Ruined by buying good pennyworths, Many have been.

1732 FULLER no. 3349. **1758** FRANKLIN *Way to
Wealth* (Crowell) 20 The bargain, by straitening
thee in thy business, may do thee more harm
than good. . . .

Rule a shrew save he that has her, Every man can.   (M 106)

1546 HEYWOOD II. vi. I1. **1621** BURTON *Anat.
Mel.* II. ii. VI. i. (1651) 291 Every man, as the
saying is, can tame a shrew, but he that hath her.
1721 KELLY 92 Every Man can guide an ill Wife,
but he that has her. Often . . . apply'd in a literal
Sense; but in a general when one apprehends
that he could order such a Station, Post, or
Business, better than he that has it.

Rule of thumb.   (R 203)

[= a roughly practical method without scientific
basis.] **1692** SIR W. HOPE *Fencing-Master* 157
What he doth, he doth by rule of Thumb, and
not by art. **1721** KELLY 257 No Rule so good
as Rule of Thumb, if it hit. But it seldom hits!
Spoken when a Thing falls out to be right,
which we did at a Venture. **1865** M. ARNOLD
Ess. Crit. v. 159 The English . . . have in all
their changes proceeded, . . . by the rule of
thumb. **1909** *Times Wkly.* I June 363 His
scientific method he shares with his countrymen,
who have long discarded the rule of thumb
which we are just discovering to be inadequate
in modern conditions.

Rule the roast, To.   (R 144)

[= to have full sway; to be master.] **14..**
Carpenter's Tools 176 in HAZLITT *E.P.P.* i. 85
What so euer 3e brage ore boste, My mayster
3et shall reule the roste. **1526** SKELTON
Magnyf. 805 In fayth, I rule moche of the rost
—Rule the roste! thou woldest, ye. **1577-8**
STANYHURST in Holinshed *Desc. of Ireland*
(1587 ed.) ii. 34a They rule the rost. **1590-1**
SHAKES. *2 Hen. VI* I. i. 104 Suffolk, the new-made
duke that rules the roast. **1778** FOOTE *Trip
Calais* II The ladies always rule the roast in this
part of the world.

Rule with a rod of iron, To.

[REV. ii. 27.] **1577** HOLINSHED (1587 ed.) iii.
173b. **1672** CLARENDON *Life* (1759, ii. 92).
1860 W. COLLINS *Woman in White* Second Epoch
W.C. 219 The rod of iron with which he rules
her never appears in company. **1871** C. KINGS-
LEY *At Last* ch. 3 Trinidad became English; and
Picton ruled it, for a while with a rod of iron.

Rule without some exception, There is no general.   (R 205)

1579 T. F. *News from the North* D1ᵛ. **1579**
NORTH *Plutarch's Alexander & Caesar* T.C. vii.
220 All rules have their exceptions. **1608** T.
HEYWOOD *Lucrece* I. ii. Merm. 335 A general
concourse of wise men! . . . Tarquin, if the
general rule have no exceptions, thou wilt have
an empty consistory. **1621** BURTON *Anat. Mel.*

I. ii. II. iii (1651) 76 No rule is so general, which admits not some exception. **1738** SWIFT *Dial. I. E.L.* 291 But I hope you won't blame the whole sex because some are bad ... —O madam; there's no general rule without an exception. **1836** MARRYAT *Mr. Midshipman Easy* ch. 12 There must be exceptions in every rule.

Rule youth well, and (for) age will rule itself. (Y 41)

1641 FERGUSSON no. 736 Rule youth weill, and eild[1] will rule the sell. **1659** HOWELL *Fr. Prov.* 6 He that corrects not youth, controlls not age. **1721** KELLY 283 . . . Youth is rash and headstrong, but Age sober and stedfast. [[1] age.]

Rule (*noun*), *see also* Exception proves r.; Religion is r. of life.

Rule(s, d) (*verb*), *see also* Better to r. than be r. by the rout; Divide and r.; Reason r. all things; Tent thee (I will) . . . if I can't r. my daughter, I'll r. my good.

Ruled by his own dame, He that will not be | shall be ruled by his stepdame. (D 19)

1509 BARCLAY *Ship of Fools* i. 203 But who that of his moders doctryne hath disdayne: Shall by his stepdame endure wo care and payne. *a.* **1530** *R. Hill's Commonpl. Bk.* E.E.T.S. 128 He that will not be warned bi his owne fader, he shall be warned bi his stepfader. **1546** HEYWOOD II. ix. K4[v]. **1641** FERGUSSON no. 304 He that wil not hear motherhead, shall hear stepmotherhead. **1721** KELLY 158 He that will not hear Mother Hood, shall hear Step-Mother Hood. That is, they who will not be prevailed upon by fair Means, shall meet with harsher Treatment.

Ruled by the rudder, Who will not be | must be ruled by the rock.

1666 TORRIANO *It. Prov.* 286 no. 20 That ship which will have no rudder, must have a rock. **1823** DISRAELI *Cur. of Lit.* (1824) 2nd Ser. i. 454 [Cited as 'a Cornish proverb']. **1853** TRENCH iii. 64 Obstinate wrongheads, who will take no warning except from calamities. **1911** B. WILBERFORCE *Secret of Quiet Mind* 79 The spiritual blindness of the people made the . . . destruction of Jerusalem, and its attendant horrors inevitable.

Ruler, *see* Fellow-ruler; Good r. (No man can be) unless.

Rump, *see* Eaten the hen's r.; Ride so near the r. (You) let none get on behind; Rub a cat on r.

Run a (the) rig, To.

[= to play pranks.] **1782** COWPER *Gilpin* xxv He little dreamt, when he set out, Of running such a rig! **1797** B. HAMILTON in BEDDOES *Contrib. Phys. & Med. Knowl.* (1799) 315 To run the rig with the boys in the street in place of going on my errand. **1837** J. B. KER 30. **1912** 28 Mar. D. H. LAWRENCE *Lett.* i. 104 Jack runs the rig . . . occasionally.

Run after two hares, If you | you will catch neither. (H 163)

[ERASM. *Ad. Duos insequens lepores neutrum capit.*] **1509** BARCLAY *Ship of Fools* i. 153 A fole is he whiche with one hande tendyth to take two hares in one instant. **1573** SANFORD 102[v] He that hunteth two Hares, looseth one, and leaueth the other. **1580** LYLY *Euph. & his Eng.* ii. 157 Yet one thing maketh [mee] to feare, that in running after two Hares, I catch neither. **1658–9** BURTON *Diary* 9 Mar. (1828) IV. 108 Keep to your debate. You have two hares afoot. You will lose both. **1659** TORRIANO no. 27 (loseth the one, and deserts the other). **1732** FULLER no. 2782.

Run amuck, To. (R 209)

[= a headlong course of attack.] **1672** MARVELL *Reh. Transp.* I. 59 Like a raging Indian . . . he runs a mucke (as they cal it there) stabbing every man he meets. **1735** POPE *Hor. Sat.* II. i. 70 I'm too discreet To run a muck, and tilt at all I meet. **1880** W. R. SMITH in *Manch. Guard.* 29 Oct. In their alarm they were determined to run amuck of everything.

Run as you drink, If you could | you might catch a hare. (H 155)

1640 HERBERT no. 373.

Run (Go) before one's horse to market, To. (M 649)

[= to count one's chickens before they are hatched.] **[1592]** **1597** SHAKES. *Rich. III* I. i. 160 But yet I run before my horse to market: Clarence still breathes, Edward still lives and reigns, When they are gone, then must I count my gains. **1709** R. KINGSTON *Apop. Curiosa* 79 Resolution without Deliberation . . . is like running before ones Mare to the Market.

Run like a deer, To.

1594–5 SHAKES. *L.L.L.* V. ii. 310 Whip to your tents, as roes run over land. **1620** SHELTON *Quix.* II. xix. ii. 313 He is the activest youth we have, . . . he runs like a deer. **1859** H. KINGSLEY *Geof. Hamlyn* ch. 40 The black lad . . . running like a deer, sped . . . across the plain.

Run one's head against a stone wall, To. (H 273)

1553 T. WILSON *Rhet.* ed. Mair 189 It is euill running against a stone wall. **1589** [? LYLY] *Pap w. Hatchet* iii. 110 But if like a restie Iade thou wilt take the bitt in thy mouth, . . . thou shalt . . . haue thy head runne against a stone wall. **1621** J. CHAMBERLAIN *Lett.* (McLure) ii. 309. **1641** *Oxinden Letters 1607–1642* ed. D. Gardiner 264 (post). **1772** R. GRAVES *Spiritual Quixote* VIII. I.

Run over, *see* Coaches won't r. o. him.

Run tap, run tapster. (T 68)

1678 RAY 86 . . . This is said of a tapster that drinks so much himself, and is so free of his drink to others that he is fain to run away.

Run that cannot go, He may ill. (R 208)

[*a.* 1415] 1468 *Mary's Betrothment* in *Coventry Myst.* Sh. S. 97 He may evyl go that is ner lame; In sothe I com as fast as I may. 1546 HEYWOOD II. ix. L1 Men saie he maie yll renne, that can not go. *c.* 1610 BEAUM. & FL. *Kt. Burn. P.* II. v. 41 Though I can scarcely go, I needs must run. 1611 DAVIES no. 280. 1636 CAMDEN 308 They hardly can run, that cannot go. 1721 KELLY 130 . . . In vain he attempts an uneasy Task, who is not equal to an easy one.

Run the gantlope (gauntlet), To.

[Orig. a military punishment in which the culprit ran, stripped to the waist, between two rows of men, who struck at him with sticks or knotted cords.] 1649 T. FORD *Lus. Fort.* *2 Being now exposed to run the Gantelope of the Worlds censure. 1709 POPE *Let. to Wycherley* 17 May Hitherto your miscellanies have safely run the gauntlet, through all the coffee-houses. 1836 *Edin. Rev.* lxiv. 71 No doubt he ran the usual gantelope of jokes. 1839 LD. BROUGHAM *Statesm. Geo. III, Eldon* (ed. 2) 254 The case had run the gauntlet of the courts.

Run to work in haste, You | as [if] nine men held you. (M 608)

1546 HEYWOOD I. xi. E2ᵛ. 1672 WALKER 20 no. 17 To go a snails gallop; . . . as if nine men pull'd you, and ten men held you. 1678 RAY 348.

Run (Hold) with the hare and hunt (run) with the hounds, To. (H 158)

c. 1440 *Jacob's Well* E.E.T.S. 263 Þou hast a crokyd tunge heldyng wyth hownd and wyth hare. 1546 HEYWOOD I. x. C3 There is no mo such titifyls¹ in Englands grounde, To holde with the hare, and run with the hounde. 1579 LYLY *Euph.* i. 247 I meane not to runne with the Hare and holde with the Hounde. 1690 *Turn-Coat of Times* in *Roxb. Ball.* (1883) IV. 515 I can hold with the Hare, and run with the Hound: Which no body can deny. 1896 M. A. S. HUME *Courtships of Q. Eliz.* 261 Leicester, as usual, tried to run with the hare and hunt with the hounds, to retain French bribes and yet to stand in the way of French objects. [¹ Titivillus, a devil. = Villain > the Vice.]

Run (noun), see Long lane (r.) no turning; Long r. (In the).

Run(s) (verb), see also Bias, (To r. against the); Fights and r. away; Glass is r., (His); Hae lad and r. lad; Judgement as he r., (He that passes) overtakes repentance; Lapwing that r. away; Long r. fox as he has feet; Mouth r. over, (His); Need makes naked man r.; Rough as it r.

Runaway monk never praises his convent, A.

1666 TORRIANO *It. Prov.* 156 no. 15 A vagrant Monk ne'r spoke well of his Convent.

Runner, You look like a | quoth the devil to the crab (lobster).

1721 KELLY 389 (*lobster*). Spoken to those who are very unlikely to do what they pretend to.

1802 WOLCOT (P. Pindar) *Middl. Elect.* i. Wks. (1816) IV. 174 *He* conquer *us*, the scab! *He,* that ne'er renn'd a race before; 'Yes, you're a *racer,* to be sure,' Cried the Devil to the crab.

Running horse is an open grave, A. (H 687)

1573 SANFORD 102ᵛ (burying). 1578 FLORIO *First F.* 28ᵛ. 1611 COTGRAVE s.v. Cheval Cheval courant est vn sepulchre ouvert: Prov. (So much danger is his necke in that rides him.) *Ibid.* s.v. Sepulchre (an open sepulcher). 1629 *Bk. Mer. Rid.* Prov. no. 68. 1666 TORRIANO *It. Prov.* 43 no. 4 (sepulchre). 1732 FULLER no. 376 A Race-Horse is an open Sepulcher.

Running leather, see Shoes are made of r. l.

Runs (goes) far that never returns (turns not again), He. *Cf.* Long lane.

1545 TAVERNER D4ᵛ The English prouerbe . . . He runneth farre, that neuer commeth agayn. 1546 HEYWOOD II. ix. K3ᵛ He runneth far that never turneth again. 1579 LYLY *Euph.* i. 322. 1606 2 *If you know not Me* l. 2440 Hee goes farre that never turnes. 1629 T. ADAMS *Serm.* (1861–2) II. 95 They go far that never return. We heard this son at the highest stair of rebellion, now . . . 'he repented and went'. 1662 FULLER *Surrey* 81 'But they go far who turn not again'; and in him the Proverb was verified, 'Naughty Boyes sometimes make good Men'.

Runs fastest gets most ground, He that. (G 465)

1616 BRETON *Cross. Prov.* A 4. 1639 CLARKE 319. 1670 RAY 138.

Runs fastest, He that | gets the ring. (R 130)

1540 PALSGRAVE *Acolastus* 19 Thynking . . . to them selfes, that bycause they haue hopped beste, that they be moste worthy to haue the rynge. 1546 HEYWOOD I. iii. A4 Where wooers hoppe in and out, long tyme may bryng Hym that hoppeth best, at last to haue the ryng. 1594–8 SHAKES. *T.S.* I. i. 136 He that runs fastest gets the ring. How say you, Signior Gremio?

Runs in the blood like wooden legs, It.

1917 BRIDGE 81 . . . Said of any family peculiarity.

Runs in the night, He that | stumbles. (N 171)

1504 CORNISH *Treat. Infor. and Music* l. 13, 422 Who gothe in the darke must stomble among. 1616 DRAXE no. 1073. 1664 CODRINGTON 196. 1670 RAY 19.

Runs may read, He that. (R 211)

[HAB. ii. 2.] 1583 G. BABINGTON *Exposⁿ of the Commandments* 348 O what a God serue we, that being able to set euerie thought wee thinke visible in our foreheads in great letters, that euerie one which runneth by, might reade them, yet most mercifully spareth vs. 1630 T. ADAMS

Politic Hunting Wks. 105 It is that gre at Booke, of so large a Character, that a man may run and read it. **1670** RAY 191.

Runs, *see also* Run(s).

Rush bush keeps the cow, The. (R 214)

a. **1542** SIR D. LINDSAY *Complaynt to K.* 407–8 Wks. (1879) I. 57 Jhone Upeland bene full blyith, I trow, Because the rysche bus kepis his kow. [*Note,* p. 256, James V[i] had made such an example of the thieves, . . . that it was a common saying, 'That he made the rush bush keep the cow'.—CHALMERS.] **1827–30** SCOTT *Tales Grandf.* ch. 27 James was said to have made 'the rush bush keep the cow'; that is to say, . . . cattle might remain on their pastures unwatched. [[1] 1513–42.]

Rush(es), *see also* Knot in a r., (To seek); Ring of a r.; Stop gaps with r.; Strew green r. for stranger.

Russian, *see* Scratch a R.

Rust(s), *see* Iron not used soon r.

Rusty sword and empty purse plead performance of covenants, The. (S 1051)

1664 CODRINGTON 216. **1670** RAY 23.

Rutland Raddleman. (R 6)

1613–22 DRAYTON *Polyolb.* xxiii. 268 (1876) III. 95 And little *Rutlandshire* is termed *Raddleman.* **1662** FULLER Rutland 347 . . . *Radleman* is a *Reddleman,* a Trade . . . onely in this County, whence men bring . . . a pack of red stones, or Oker, which they sell . . . for the marking of sheep.

Rutting, *see* Wives make rammish husbands, (R.).

Rye, *see* Sow wheat . . . and r. in dust.

Rye-dough, *see* Image of r. d., (To look like an).

Rynt you witch, quoth Besse Lockit to her mother. (W 584)

c. **1605** SHAKES. *K.L.* III. iv. 122 Aroint thee, witch. **1605–6** *Id. M.* I. iii. 6 Aroint thee, witch! the rump-fed ronyon cries. **1674** RAY *Collectn. Eng. Works* 52 *Rynt* ye: By your leave, stand handsomely. As, Rynt you Witch, quoth *Besse Locket* to her Mother, Proverb, *Chesh.* **1917** BRIDGE 106 Roint ye! witch, as Bessie Lockit said to her mother. Roint, Rynt, Runt . . . = away with you. . . . 'Runt thee' is an expression used by milkmaids to a cow when she has been milked, to get out of the way. *Wilbraham.*

S

Sack is known by the sample, The.

1584 WITHALS G1[v] When the sack is opened, it is knowne what is therein conteined. **1732** FULLER no. 5949 You may know by a Handful the whole Sack. **1869** HAZLITT 397.

Sacks to the mill, More. (S 12)

[*To bring more sacks to the mill* = to supplement argument with argument or weight with weight.] **1590** NASHE *Pasquil's Apol.* i. 123 To the next, to the next, more sacks to the Myll. **1594–5** SHAKES. *L.L.L.* IV. iii. 77 More sacks to the mill! O heavens! I have my wish. **1623** MIDDLETON *Span. Gipsy* IV. i. Merm. I. 419 Welcome welcome, welcome!—More sacks to the mill. **1738** SWIFT *Dial.* I. E.L. 277 [NEVEROUT, *as* MISS *is standing, pulls her suddenly on his lap.*] Now, colonel, come sit down on my lap; more sacks upon the mill.

Sack(s), *see also* Bad s. that abide no clouting; Bag (S.) (To give the); Bind the s. before full; Broken s. hold no corn; Collier's s., . . . (Like a); Comes nought out of s. but was there; Empty s. cannot stand; Every one thinks his s. heaviest; Grain (One) fills not s.; Old s. asks much patching; Wishes never fill s.

Sad because I cannot be glad, I am. (S 14)

[*c.* **1553**] **1566** UDALL *Ralph Roister D.* III. liii. 11 But why speake ye so faintly, or why are ye so sad?—Thou knowest the prouerbe, bycause I can not be had [glad]. **1592** SHAKES. *T.G.V.* IV. ii. 26 Now, my young guest—methinks you're allycholly. I pray you, why is it?—Marry, mine host, because I cannot be merry. **1596** *Id. M.V.* I. i. 47 Then let us say you are sad Because you are not merry.

Sad burden to carry a dead man's child, It is a. (B 726)

1655 FULLER *Ch. Hist.* II. v. § 29 (1868) I. 237 Our women have a proverb, 'It is a sad burden to carry a dead man's child'; and, surely, a historian hath no heart . . . to exemplify dead canons.

Sad, *see also* Long lives a merry man as a s.; Pickle, (To be in a s.).

Saddle on the right horse, Set the. (S 16)

1607 DEKKER & WEBSTER *Westw. Ho* v. i. 173–4 How say you wenches, haue I set the Sadle on the right horse? **1616** DRAXE no. 1141 The right saddle must bee set on the right horse. **1619** 19 June J. CHAMBERLAIN *Lett.* (McLure) ii. 246 Yt wilbe . . . difficult . . . to set the right saddle upon the right horse. *a.* **1653** GOUGE *Comm. Hebr.* xi. 37 To remove this scandal, the apostle setteth the saddle on the right horse, and sheweth, that [&c.]. **1660** W. SECKER *Nonsuch Prof.* III (1891) 276 God . . . will bring every sinner to the bar. . . . Then He will set the

saddle on the back of the right horse. **1670**
RAY 138 . . . This Proverb may be variously
applied; either thus, Let them bear the blame
that deserve it: or thus, Let them bear the
burden that are best able. **1678** DRYDEN *All for
Love* Pref. Mcrm. II. ii. I suppose he would think
it a wiser part to set the saddle on the right horse,
and choose rather to live with the reputation of
a plain-spoken, honest man, than to die with
the infamy of an incestuous villain.

Saddle, To set one beside the.   (s 18)

1542 T. BECON *Invective agst. Swearing* (n.d., F 3)
Yet by this meanes haue they obteyned their
purpose, and set the other beggarly fellowe
besydes the sadle. **1589** *Temporis Filia Veritas*
B 3ᵛ. [**1590**] **1598** *Famous Vict. Henry V* F3
It skils not though he sit beside the saddle.

Saddles lack, Where | better ride on a pad than on the horse bareback.   (s 19)

c. **1549** HEYWOOD I. x. D1.   **1611** DAVIES no. 312
(than on the Horse back).   **1732** FULLER no.
6464.

Saddle(s) (*noun*), see also Cadgers are aye
cracking of s.; Fair in cradle foul in s.; Horse
that will not carry s.; Marriage rides upon the
s. and repentance upon the crupper; Parsley
fried; Ride a young colt (When you) . . . s. well
girt; Sow to bear s. (Meet as).

Saddle(s) (*verb*), see Eats his cock alone (Who)
must s. alone; Rides behind another does not s.
when he pleases; Rides not ay when he s. horse.

Saddleworth, see Parson of S. (Like the).

Sadness and gladness succeed each other.   (s 21)

1592 DELAMOTHE 35 (doth rule one after another).
1639 CLARKE 326.   **1670** RAY 139.

Safe and sound.

[**1529**] **1533** LUPSET *Exhort.*ᴮ *Young Men* ed. Gee
261. *c.* **1530** LUCIAN *Necromantia* A8ᵛ Dely-
ueryd saue and sound.   **1577** HOLINSHED (1587)
iii. 97b.   **1591** ARIOSTO *Orl. Fur.* Harington VI.
23.   **1592–3** SHAKES. *C.E.* IV. iv. 148.

Safe as a crow (sow) in a gutter.   (c 845)

1579 FULKE *Confut. Sanders* 675 He triumpheth
like a crow in a gutter.   **1639** CLARKE 97 (a
sowe i' th gutter).   **1670** RAY 207.

Safe (snug) as a mouse in a cheese, As.   (M 1221)

c. **1610–40** *The Telltale* l. 1065 . . . or louse in
bosome.   **1666** TORRIANO *Prov. Phr.* s.v. Zucca
241 To lye close and snug, making no noise;
the English Phrases are, A Mouse in a Cheese,
or a Lord in a Hutch.   **1678** RAY 288.

Safe as a thief in a mill, As. *Cf.* Mouse in mill.   (T 102)

1606 J. DAY &c. *The Isle of Gulls* II. ii (Bullen)
37.   **1663** J. WILSON *Cheats* I. ii As safe in the
Constable's house, As a Thief in a Mill.   **1738**
SWIFT Dial. I. E.L. 274.

Safe as houses (churches).

1859 CORNWALLIS *New World* i. 79 The owner
of the weapon assured him that he was as safe
as houses.   **1891** HARDY *Tess* ch. 14 The plain
ones be as safe as churches.

Safe as the bank, As.

1857–8 DICKENS *Little Dorrit* ix As trustworthy
as the Bank of England.   **1862** *Id. Letters* (1880)
ii. 183.

Safe from the East Indies, He came | and was drowned in the Thames.

1732 FULLER no. 1817.

Safe is the word.

1721 KELLY 291 . . . Taken from the Watchword given among Soldiers, spoken when we
have gotten over some great Difficulty.   **1733**
SWIFT *On Poetry* Wks. (1856) I. 652 If still you
be disposed to rhyme, Go try your hand a second
time. Again you fail: yet Safe's the word; Take
courage, and attempt a third.

Safe riding in a good haven, It is.   (R 121)

1572 L. LAVATER *Of Ghosts* tr. R.H. E 2 When
these messengers were returned, (and as the
Prouerbe is) thoughte them selues in a safe
hauen, the noble Senate hadde commaunded
the foure Monkes to be fast kept in prison.   **1659**
HOWELL *Eng. Prov.* 16b.   **1732** FULLER no. 5083
'Tis good riding in a safe Harbour.

Safe side, It is best to be on the.

1776 FLETCHER OF MADELEY *Wks.* ii. 80 (safer).
1902–4 LEAN IV. 152.

Safe, see also Sure (s.) as louse in bosom; Way
to be s.

Safely, see Goes softly goes s.; Lives s. that lives
closely, (He).

Safety first.

1915 'Safety First' motto of the Industrial
Council for Industrial Safety.   **1929** DEAN INGE
Assess. & Anticip. 87 'Safety first' is all very
well when we are preparing to cross a street or
board an omnibus.

Safety in numbers, There is.

15.. JOHN KNOX (? cf. J. B. Black *Reign of
Elizabeth* 35).   **1680** BUNYAN *Mr. Badman* ed.
J. Brown 78 In the multitude of Counsellors
there is safety.

Saffron Walden, God help me!

1851 *N. & Q.* 1st Ser. III. 167 Many of the
mendicants who ramble the county of Suffolk
in search of relief, when asked where they come
from, reply in a pitiful tone, 'Saffron Walden,
God help me'.

Sage in May, Set | and it will grow alway.

1661 M. STEVENSON *Twelve Moneths* 23 I shall conclude with the old Proverbe, . . .

Sage, *see* Live for aye eat s. in May.

Said in the kitchen, All that is | should not be heard in the hall.

1721 KELLY 9 . . . Every thing that a Man may say of his Neighbour, . . . should not be whisper'd to him.

Said my prayers in the other corner, I have.

1869 HAZLITT 221 . . . *Devon*. This phrase is in common use in cases where a person only partially fills any utensil, as a jug or a milk-bowl.

Sail near the wind, To.

[= to come near transgressing a law or moral principle.] **1586** J. FERNE *Blazon of Gentry* 190 Herealdes in these daies, may go neare inough the winde, so shall they be the lighter Courtiers, to goe and returne, their soueraignes message. **1822** 21 Nov. BYRON *Letters* vi. 142 If Mr. Beere had been civil, and Frost honest, I should not have been obliged to go near the wind with them. **1840** H. COLERIDGE *Int. to Massinger & Ford* ch. 37 [Shakespeare's] nurse is not a very discreet guardianess for a beauty . . . her language sails a little too near the wind. **1902** A. R. COLQUHOUN *Mastery of Pac.* 192 In Australia . . . steps are to be taken against natives of India by means of an education test. As the Hindoos are British subjects, this is sailing rather near the wind.

Sail over the sea in an egg-shell, It is hard to. (s 175)

1639 CLARKE 5.

Sail, quoth the king: hold, quoth the wind.

1721 KELLY 285 . . . That unaccountable Creature, which God brings out of his Treasures, cannot be commanded by mortal Power. **1732** FULLER no. 4064. **1820** SCOTT *Monast. Ans. to Introd. Epist.* Mr. Watt . . . affording the means . . . of sailing without that wind which defied the commands . . . of Xerxes himself. *Note.*— Probably the author alludes to the national adage: The king said sail, But the wind said no.

Sail too big for the ballast, Make not your. (s 24)

1565 J. CALFHILL *Treatise of the Cross* P.S. 23 Perilous it is, to carry too high a sail upon a rotten mast. **1577–87** W. HARRISON *Description of England* (New Sh. S.) i. 129 No man hath hurt by it but himselfe, who . . . will . . . as our prouerbe saith, now and then beare a bigger saile than his boat is able to sustaine. **1592** WARNER *Albion's Eng.* VII. 36 V4ᵛ Perken . . . proudly striues to beare too high a sayle. *a.* **1609** JONSON *Ev. Man in Hum.* I. i. 83 I'ld ha' you . . . contain your selfe; Not, that your

sayle be bigger then your boat. **1748** SMOLLETT *Rod. Random* ch. 5 More sail than ballast. **1771** J. WESLEY *Lett.* v. 277 [She] was in danger of having more sail than ballast.

Sail under false colours, To.

1756 J. WESLEY *Lett.* iii. 370 Hanging out false colours. **1897** STEVENSON *St. Ives* ch. 28 If it could be managed without . . . the mention of my real name. I had so much wisdom as to sail under false colours in this foolish jaunt of mine.

Sail with every wind, To. (s 25)

[*c.* 1515] *c.* 1530 BARCLAY *Eclog.* II. l. 1145 In court must a man sayle after euery winde, Himselfe conforming to euery mans minde. **1562** RANDOLPH to Lord Rob. Dudley (T. Wright *Eliz. & her Times* i. 107) He is a man that sayleth with all wyndes. **1585** O.C. *Elizabeth Queen* How wary in Queene Maryes daies, he did himselfe behaue, And sailes which hung aloft at mast, to windes relenting gaue. **1591** ARIOSTO *Orl. Fur.* Harington xxv. 74 That foolish people might not make a iest To his reproch . . . Rogero loues to take the surer side, And turnes his sailes as fortune turnes her tide. **1605–6** SHAKES. *K.L.* I. iv. 99 An thou canst not smile as the wind sits, thou'lt catch cold shortly. **1639** CLARKE 267 A wise mariner can fit his sayles to every wind.

Sail without danger, He that would | must never come on the main sea. (D 34)

1592 DELAMOTHE 47. **1639** CLARKE 250. **1670** RAY 139.

Sail(s) (*noun*), *see also* Heal s. is good s.; Hoist your s. when wind fair; Keep a low s.; Ship under s.; Wind blows (As) set s.

Sail, (*verb*), *see also* Sea, (Being on) s.; Wind and tide, (To s. with).

Sailing in a sow's ear, To come. (s 686)

c. 1579 [MERBURY] *Marr. Wit and Wisdom* Sh. S. ii. 13 So we ware both put into a mussellbote, and came saling in a sowes yeare over sea into Kent. [1615] 1631 P. FLETCHER *Sicelides* Gros. II. vi. 42 We had neere taken a iourney in such a fly-boate, such a sow's-eare, such an egge-shell. **1670** RAY 192. **1732** FULLER no. 5146.

Sailor's warning, *see* Rainbow in the morning; Sky red in the morning.

Sailors get money like horses, and spend it like asses.

1751 SMOLLETT *Per. Pick.* ch. 2 I make good the old saying, 'We sailors get money like horses, and spend it like asses'. *a.* **1814** C. DIBDIN *Songs*, 'At Sea' (1886) 16 'Tis said that, with grog and our lasses Because jolly sailors are free, Our money we squander like asses Which like horses we earn'd when at sea.

Sailors go round the world without going into it.

1829 MARRYAT *Frank M.* ch. 27 You know her character, and you should know something about our sex; but sailors, they say, go round the world without going into it.

Sailors have a port in every storm.

1817 J. T. SMITH *Vagabondiana* 25 (according to the old adage).

Sailors' fingers must be all fish-hooks.

1840 DANA *Two Years before the Mast* (1911 ed.) 274 He was a true sailor, every finger a fishhook. **1902** A. B. LUBBOCK *Round the Horn* ch. 6 Frenzied men tore at the sail with both hands, hanging on by their eyelids . . . Truly a sailor must have each finger a fishhook, as they say.

Sailors, *see also* Heaven takes care of s.; Souters shouldna be s.

Saint (angel) abroad and a devil at home, A.   (s 31. w 702)

1541 *Schoolh. Wom.* C3 As holy as sayntes in churche they be And in strete as aungels they were At home, for all theyr ypocrysye A deuylysshe lyfe, they led all the yere. **1591** FLORIO *Second F.* 175 Women are in churches, Saints: abroad, Angels: at home, deuills. **1604** SHAKES. *O.* II. i. 110 You are pictures out of doors, Bells in your parlours, wildcats in your kitchens, Saints in your injuries, devils being offended, Players in your housewifery, and housewives in your beds. **1606** CHARRON *Wisdom* (1640 ed., 302) That proverb, An angel in the Church, a divel in the house. **1633** P. FLETCHER *Purp. Is.* VII. xxxvi. (1908) II. 94 A saint abroad, at home a fiend; and worst a saint. **1659** HOWELL *Brit. Prov.* 6 An angel in the field, a devil by the fire. **1678** BUNYAN *Pilgr.* I. (1877) 84 Thus say the common people that know him, . . .

St. Andrew the King, three weeks and three days before Christmas comes in.

1830 FORBY 418.

St. Anthony's (Tantony) pig, To follow one like a.   (s 35)

[Pigs under the protection of St. Anthony, the patron of swineherds, were allowed to roam the streets, and followed any one who fed them.] *c.* **1460** *Good Wife Would a Pilg.* l. 9 And rene thou not fro hous to house lyke an Antyny gryce.[1] **1533** J. HEYWOOD *Johan Johan* l. 5 She wyll go a gaddynge very myche Lyke an Antony pyg. **1598** STOW *Surv. Lond.* (1603) 185 Whereupon was raised a prouerbe, such a one will follow such a one, and whine as it were an Anthonie pig. **1606** CHAPMAN *Gent. Usher* IV. i Plays (1874) 100 I have followed you up and down like a Tantalus pig. **1709** *Brit. Apollo* II. no. 62 3/2 Whom all the Town follow, Like so many St. Anthony's pigs. **1738** SWIFT *Dial.* I, E.L. 283 She made me follow her last week through all the shops like a Tantiny pig. **1765** BICKERSTAFFE *Love in Village* I. ix To see you dangling after me every where, like a tantony pig. [1 pig.]

St. Barnabas, *see* B. bright.

St. Bartholomew[1] brings the cold dew.   (s 37)

1678 RAY 52. **1706** STEVENS s.v. Agósto (English). **1846** DENHAM 55 At St. Barthol'mew, Then comes cold dew. **1859** *N. & Q.* 2nd Ser. VIII. 242 St. Barthōlomew, Bring'st the cold dew. [1 24 Aug.]

St. Benedick,[1] sow thy pease, or keep them in thy rick.   (s 38)

1678 RAY 52. [1 21 March.]

St. Bernard, *see* Bernard did not see every thing.

Saint but the devil he is, He looks like a.   (s 30)

c. **1425** *Wakefield Plays* 'Judgement' l. 267 She lookys like a saynt, And wars then the deyll. **1602** WITHALS 1. **1639** CLARKE 140. **1706** STEVENS s.v. Guez All Saint without, all Devil within.

St. Chad, *see* Before St. C. every goose lays; St. Valentine's Day cast beans . . . but on St. C. sow. See also Chad.

St. David's day,[1] put oats and barley in the clay.   (s 40)

1678 RAY 346 . . . With us it is accounted a little too early to sow barley (which is a tender grain) in the beginning of March. [1 1 March.]

St. David, *see also* David.

St. Distaff's Day neither work nor play, On.   (s 41)

1648 HERRICK *Hesper.* Wks. O.U.P. 308 *Saint Distaffs day, or the morrow after Twelfth day.* Partly worke and partly play He must on S. *Distaff's* day. **1846** DENHAM 23 On St. Distaff's Day—neither work nor play. Jan. 7th: called St. Distaff's Day, or Rock Day, because (the Christmas holidays having ended) good housewives resumed . . . the distaff.

St. George to borrow.

[(i) St. G. being security for one's good faith; (ii) an asseveration, By St. G.!] **1529** SKELTON *Albany* 506 Saint George to borrowe, Ye shall have schame and sorrowe. **1548** HALL *Chron.* (1809) 416 Now sent George to borowe, let us set forward. [*c.* **1553**] **1566–7** UDALL *Ralph Roister D.* IV. viii. 77 What then? Sainct George to borrow, our Ladies Knight.

St. George, Like | who is always on horseback and never rides.   (s 42)

1575 19 April BURGHLEY to Walsingham cited C. Read *Ld. Burghley & Q. Elizabeth* 147 [B. being lame and writing four days before St. George's day] I am in doubt . . . whether to come to the Court on Friday, being not able, I fear, then to make the passage on foot. But if St. George's four nights should ride as he doth, I could better do my service. **1579** LYLY *Euph.* i. 260 Lyke St. George, who is euer on

horse backe yet neuer rideth.   *a.* 1591 HY. SMITH
Serm. (1866) II. 32 [*Satan*] is not called a tempter,
. . . a murderer, and a compasser, in vain; like
St. George, which is always on horseback, and
never rides.   1592 NASHE *Pierce Pen.* i. 174
These whelpes of the first Litter of Gentilitie, . . .
I knowe not howe, like Saint *George*, they are
alwaies mounted, but neuer moue.   1596 SHAKES.
K.J. II. i. 288 Saint George, that swing'd the
dragon, and e'er since Sits on his horse back at
mine hostess' door.   1612 T. ADAMS *The Gallant's
Burden* (1616 ed., 56) The Sword in their hands
. . . like the Picture of S. George, with his hand
vp, but neuer striking.   1738 FRANKLIN *Aug.*
Defer not thy well doing; be not like St. George,
who is always a-horseback, and never rides on.

St. Giles's[1] breed; fat, ragged and saucy.

1787 GROSE (*Lond.*) 197 . . . The people of that
parish, particularly those resident in Newton
and Dyot streets, still retain their rags and
impudence.   [[1] A district in west-central London,
long notorious for poverty and vice.]

St. Giles's cup.

[Criminals on their way to the gallows at Tyburn
were presented with a cup of water at or near
the church of St. Giles in the Fields.]   *a.* 1580
Death's Dance in COLLIER *Roxb. Bal.* (1847) 3
If Death would . . . briefly say, '. . . I bring to
you Saint Giles his bowle', 'twould put them
all in feare.   1594 CHURCHYARD *Mirror of Man*
'Trusting in friendship makes some be trust up,
Or ride in a cart to kis Saint Giles his cup'.

St. Giles, *see also* Dine with St. G.; Lame as
St. G.

St. Hugh's bones.   (s 44)

[= shoemakers' tools.]   1597 DELONEY I *Gentle
Craft* Wks. (Mann) 87.   1600 DEKKER *Shoem.
Hol.* I. iv. 70 Skomaker, haue you al your tooles
. . . your hand and thumb-leathers and good
saint Hughs bones to smooth vp your worke.
1688 R. HOLME *Acad. Armory* III. viii. 349 Let
not any of . . . the Gentle Craft, take it in ill part,
that all their Tools were not set together, seeing
St. Hughs Bones ought not to be separated.

St. James's Day[1] be come and gone, Till | you may have hops or you may have none.   (s 45)

1670 RAY 44.   [[1] July 25.]

St. John to borrow.

[St. John being security for good faith.]   *c.* 1386
CHAUCER *Squire's T.* l. 596 I hydde fro hym my
sorwe And took hym by the hond, Seint John
to borwe, And seyde thus: 'Lo, I am youres al.'

St. John to borrow!

[A Scottish formula at parting = *au revoir*.]
1423 JAS. I *Kings Q.* xxiii With mony 'fare wele'
and 'sanct Iohne to borowe'.   *c.* 1470 HENRY
Wallace III. 336 Thar leyff thai tuk, with con-
forde. . . . Sanct Iohne to borch, thai suld meyt
haille agayne.

St. John, *see also* Laid in his fuel before St. J.

St. Johnston's riband (tippet).

[Sc. A halter or hangman's rope.   *St. Johnston*
= Perth.]   1638 H. ADAMSON *Muse's Threnodie*
(1774) 119 Hence of St. Johnston's ribband
came the word.   1816 SCOTT *Old Mort.* ch. 7
To be sent to Heaven wi' a Saint Johnstone's
tippit about my hause.

St. Laurence, *see* More like the devil than St. L.

Saint (Shrine), Like | like offering.   (s 32)

1550 BALE *Eng. Votaries* II. 105 b These adages
myght then haue bene founde true, suche saynt,
suche shryne, suche bere, suche bottell.   1592
DELAMOTHE 3 Such a Saint, such an offring.
1639 CLARKE 46.

St. Lucy, *see* Lucy light.

St. Luke was a saint and a physician, and yet he died (is dead).   (s 47)

1610 SHAKES. *Cym.* V. v. 28 But I consider By
med'cine life may be prolong'd, yet death Will
seize the doctor too.   1616 DRAXE no. 1425.
1640 HERBERT no. 1008.

St. Luke's Day[1] the oxen have leave to play, On.

[The ox was the medieval symbol of St. Luke.]
1732 FULLER no. 6220.   [[1] 18 Oct.]

St. Luke's (little) summer.

[Occurring about St. Luke's Day, 18 Oct.]   1828
T. FORSTER *Circle Seasons* 293 Fair, warm, and
dry weather, often occurs about this time, and
is called St. Luke's Little Summer.   1855 *N. &
Q.* 1st Ser. XII. 366/1 A few fine days, . . . called
St. Luke's little summer; which the good folks
of Hants and Dorset always expect about the
18th of this month.

St. Martin's stuff (rings, ware).   (s 48)

[= counterfeit goods.]   *c.* 1550 BECON *Jewel of
Joy* P.S. 438 A Martin chaine the price of eight-
pence.   1566 PAINTER ed. Jacobs ii. 142 Two
yonge men . . . bearing about them counterfait
Iewels and lingots, guilt of S. Martine's touche.
1590 R. HARVEY *Pl. Perc.* 4 I doubt whether all
be gold that glistereth, sith Saint Martins rings
be but Copper inside.   1598 GUILPIN *Skial.* (1878)
41 I had thought the last mask. . . . Had . . .
Taught thee S. Martins stuffe from true gold
lace.   1648 C. WALKER *Hist. Independ.* I. 122
These letters may be St. Martins ware, counterfeit stuffe.

St. Martin's summer.

[Fine, mild weather occurring about Martinmas.]
1592–4 SHAKES. *I Hen. VI* I. ii. 131 Expect Saint
Martin's summer, halcyon days.   1864 TENNY-
SON *Aylmer's F.* 560 Then ensued A Martin's
summer of his faded love.   1880 MAHAFFY *Hist.
Gr. Lit.* i. 97 The martinmas summer of Greek
literature in Plutarch.   1888 A. T. QUILLER-
COUCH *Troy Town* ch. 7 She was . . . not young,

but rather in that St. Martin's Summer when a woman learns for the first time the value of her charms. **1896** 'H. S. MERRIMAN' *Flotsam* ch. 2 The carriage was . . . in the shadow of the trees in Trinity Square, for it was St. Martin's summer and a hot October.

St. Matthee[1] shut up the bee. (s 49)

1678 RAY 52. [[1] St. Matthias, 24 Feb.]

St. Matthew[1] get candlesticks new.

1830 FORBY 418. [[1] 21 Sept.]

St. Matthi[1] lay candlesticks by.

1830 FORBY 418. [[1] St. Matthias, 24 Feb.]

St. Matthias[1] both leaf and grass. (s 51)

1659 HOWELL *Eng. Prov.* 21b. [[1] 24 Feb.]

St. Matthie[1] all the year goes by. (s 50)

1678 RAY 52 . . . Because in Leap-year the supernumerary day is then intercalated. [[1] St. Matthias, 24 Feb.]

St. Matthie[1] sends saps into the tree. (s 52)

1678 RAY 50. [[1] St. Matthias.]

St. Mattho,[1] take thy hopper,[2] and sow. (s 53)

1678 RAY 52. [[1] St. Matthias. [2] seed-basket.]

St. Michael, *see* Burned one candle to St. M.

St. Monday.

[Used with reference to workmen being idle on Monday, as a consequence of drunkenness on the Sunday.] **1753** *Scots. Mag.* Apr. 208/1 (*title*) St. Monday; or, the tippling tradesmen. **1771** B. FRANKLIN *Autobiog.* E.L. 56 My constant attendance (I never making a St. Monday) recommended me to the master. **1804** EDGEWORTH *Pop. Tales, To-morrow* ch. 7 (1856) 408 *note* It is a custom in Ireland among shoemakers, if they intoxicate themselves on Sunday, to do no work on Monday; and this they call making a Saint Monday. **1857** GEN. P. THOMPSON *Audi Alt.* I. vii. 22 An assemblage of artisans keeping Saint Monday.

St. Nicholas' clerks. (s 54)

[i. = poor scholars.] **1553** T. WILSON *Arte of Rhet.* (1580) 155 Thei are no Churchmen, thei are maisterlesse men, or rather S. Nicolas clerkes that lacke liuyng. [ii. = highwaymen.] **1570** FOXE *A. & M.* (ed. 2) 2287 I haue heard of men robbed by S. Nicolas clerkes. **1597** SHAKES. *1 Hen. IV* II. i. 60 Sirrah, if they meet not with Saint Nicholas' clerks, I'll give thee this neck. **1662** J. WILSON *The Cheats* I. i Who should I meet with but our old Gang, some of St. Nicholas's Clerks.

St. Paul[1] be fair and clear, If | then betides a happy year. (s 55)

14th cent. ROBERT OF AVESBURY *Hist.* (Hearne) 266 *Clara dies Pauli bona tempora denotat anni.* **a. 1530** *R. Hill's Commonpl. Bk.* E.E.T.S. 134 Clara dies Pauli bona tempora denotat anni. **1584** R. SCOT *Witchcraft* XI. xv If Paul th' apostles day be clear, it doth foreshew a lucky year. **1686–7** J. AUBREY *Rem. Gent. & Jud.* (1881) 94 The old verse so much observed by Countrey people: 'If Paul's day be faire and cleare It will betyde a happy yeare.' **1732** FULLER no. 6142 If *St. Paul* be fair and clear, Then betides a happy Year; If the Wind do blow aloft, Then of Wars we shall hear full oft; If the Clouds make dark the Sky, Great store of People then will die; If there be either Snow or Rain, Then will be dear all sorts of Grain. **1846** DENHAM 24 If St. Paul's day be fine and clear, It doth betide a happy year; But if by chance it then should rain, It will make dear all kinds of grain; And if the clouds make dark the sky, Then neat[2] and fowls this year shall die; If blustering winds do blow aloft, Then wars, shall trouble the ealm full oft. **1866** *N. & Q.* 3rd Ser. IX. 118 A Huntingdonshire cottager said to me: 'We shall have a fine spring, Sir. There is an old proverb that says: "If Paul's day is fine, it will be a fine spring".' [[1] 25 Jan. [2] cattle.]

St. Paul's mariners, He is one of.

1662 FULLER *Kent* 61 Navigation is much improved . . . since Saint Paul's time; insomuch that, when a man goes bunglingly about any work in a ship, I have heard our Englishmen say, 'Such a man is one of St. Paul's Mariners'.

St. Paul, *see also* Praises St. Peter (Who) does not blame St. P. *See also* Paul's.

St. Peter's in the Poor, where no tavern, alehouse, or sign at the door. (s 58)

1662 FULLER *Lond.* 198 . . . Under Correction, I conceive it called 'in the Poor', because the Augustinian Friers, professing wilful poverty, for some hundreds of years, possessed more than a Moiety thereof. . . . This Parish[1] . . . was (not to say is) one of the richest in London. [[1] Old Broad Street. LEAN I. 142.]

St. Peter's needle, To go through.

1917 BRIDGE 134 . . . To have serious misfortune. Applied to a man who has become a bankrupt and is sold up.

St. Peter, *see also* Praises St. P. (Who) does not blame St. Paul.

St. Robert gave his cow, As freely as. (s 59)

1670 RAY 208 . . . This Robert was a Knareburgh[1] Saint. [[1] Knaresborough, Yorks.]

St. Stephen, Blessed be | there is no fast upon his even. (s 61)

1659 HOWELL *Eng. Prov.* 21a . . . Because 'tis Christmas night.

St. Stephen, *see also* Bleed your nag on S.'s day; Yule is young . . . and as old in S.

Saint swear (to anger, vex a saint), Enough to make a.   (s 28)

c. **1560** *Tom Tyler* 809. **1567** J. PICKERING *Horestes* l. 97 Would it not anger a saynt at the hart. **1577** *Misogonus* II. v We . . . could anger him an he were a verye Saynt. **1593–4** SHAKES. *T.S.* III. ii. 28 Such an injury would vex a very saint. *c.* **1599** JONSON *Case is Altered* I. vii. 17. **1608** BEAUM. & FL. *Philas.* IV. ii This would make a saint swear like a soldier. **1842** MARRYAT *Perc. Keene* ch. 26 The remonstrances . . . the badgering I have received . . . have been enough to make a saint swear. **1903** CONRAD *Typhoon* ch. 2 The weather's awful. It would make a saint swear.

St. Swithin[1] is christening the apples.

1813 BRAND *Pop. Antiq.* (Ellis, 1895) i. 342 There is an old saying that when it rains on St. Swithin's Day, it is the Saint christening the apples. **1846** DENHAM 50 . . . A common observation on this (St. Swithin's) day, should it chance to be a rainy one. **1880** HARDY *Trumpet Major* ch. 17 You country-folk call St. Swithin's their [apples] christening day, if it rains? [1 15 July.]

St. Swithin's day, if thou dost rain, for forty days it will remain; St. Swithin's day, if thou be fair, for forty days 'twill rain na mair.   (s 62)

[St. Swithun (or Swithin), bishop of Winchester, *d.* 862.] **1599** JONSON *Ev. Man out of Hum.* I. iii. 33 O, here, *Saint Swithin's*, the xv day, variable weather, for the most part raine: Why, it should raine fortie daies after, now, more or lesse, it was a rule held afore I was able to hold a plough. **1697** *Poor Robin's Alm.* in DENHAM 53 In this month is St. Swithin's day; On which, if that it rain, they say, Full xl days after it will, Or more or less some rain distill. **1716** GAY *Trivia* I. 183–6 How if on Swithin's feast the welkin lowers, And ev'ry pent-house streams with hasty showers, Twice twenty days shall clouds their fleeces drain, And wash the pavements with incessant rain. **1846** DENHAM 52.

St. Thomas à Waterings.   (s 63)

[A place used for executions in Surrey, on the Kent road, where horses were watered; dedicated to Thomas à Becket. *c.* **1386** CHAUCER *Prol.* l. 826 And forth we riden. . . . Unto the wateryng of Seint Thomas.] *c.* **1510** *Hickscorner* C3ᵛ For at saynt thomas of watrynge and they stryke a sayle. **1631** JONSON *New Inn* I. iii. 85 He may, perhaps, take a degree at Tyburn, . . . come, to read a lecture . . . at St. Thomas à Waterings.

St. Thomas[1] divine, brewing, baking, and killing of fat swine.

1742 *An Agreeable Companion* 59 Thomas Divine, Brewing and Baking, and Killing of Swine. **1797–1811** *Agricult. Com. to Bd. of Agric.* in LEAN I. 383. [1 21 Dec.]

St. Thomas[1] gray! St. Thomas gray! the longest night and the shortest day.

1859 *N. & Q.* 2nd Ser. VIII. 242. [1 21 Dec.]

St. Valentine,[1] On | all the birds of the air in couples do join.   (s 66)

c. **1380** CHAUCER *Parl. of Foules* l. 309 For this was on seynt Valentynes day, When every foul cometh ther to chese his make.[2] **1477** *Paston Letters* (Gairdner 1904) v. 266 And, cosyn, uppon Fryday is Sent Volentynes Day, and every brydde chesyth hym a make. **1595** SHAKES. *M.N.D.* IV. i. 136 Saint Valentine is past: Begin these woodbirds but to couple now? **1714** GAY *Shep. Wk.*, *Thurs.* 37 Last *Valentine*, the Day when Birds of Kind Their Paramours with mutual Chirpings find, I rearly[3] rose. **1830** FORBY 418. [1 14 Feb. 2 mate. 3 early.]

St. Valentine,[1] set thy hopper[2] by mine.   (s 64)

1678 RAY 52. [1 14 Feb. 2 seed-basket.]

St. Valentine's Day[1] cast beans in clay, On | but on St. Chad[2] sow good or bad.   (s 67)

c. **1640** SMYTH *Berkeley MSS.* 33, no. 89. [1 14 Feb. 2 2 March.]

St. Valentine, *see also* Valentine.

St. Vincent's Day,[1] Remember on | if the sun his beams display, be sure to mark the transient beam, which through the casement sheds a gleam; for 'tis a token bright and clear of prosperous weather all the year.

1584 R. SCOT *Witchcraft* XI. xv. **1846** DENHAM 24. [1 22 Jan.]

St. Vitus's day[1] be rainy weather, If | it will rain for thirty days together.

1846 DENHAM 49. [1 15 June.]

Saints in Cornwall than in heaven, There are more.

1864 *N. & Q.* 3rd Ser. v. 275 *Cornish Proverbs.*— There are more Saints in Cornwall than in Heaven. The process of creation is continued. . . . I lately, in a Cornish paper, met with *Saint Newlyn.*

Saint(s), *see also* All are not s. that go to church; Greater the sinner the greater the s.; Isle of S.; Pleases not God (When it), s. can do little; St. Luke was a s.; Young s., old devil.

Sair dung[1] bairn that dare not greet,[2] It is a.   (B 41)

a. **1628** CARMICHAELL no. 907. **1641** FERGUSSON no. 550. **1721** KELLY 117 . . . They are under great Awe, that may not complain. [1 beaten. 2 cry.]

Sairs[1] should not be fair handled.

1862 HISLOP 166 . . . That is, delicate or painful subjects should be cautiously alluded to. [¹sores.]

Sairy brewing that is not good in the newing,[1] It is a. (B 657)

a. **1628** CARMICHAELL no. 849. **1641** FERGUSSON no. 474. **1721** KELLY 181 . . . Spoken when People are much taken with new Projects. [¹ when it is new.]

Sairy collop that is taken off a capon, It is a. (C 518)

a. **1628** CARMICHAELL no. 896 (schamed collop). **1641** FERGUSSON no. 512. **1721** KELLY 189 . . . One cannot take much where there is but little.

Sairy wood that has never a withered bough in it, It is a.

1721 KELLY 186 . . . Spoken when some of our Relations, who have done an ill Thing, is cast in our Teeth.

Salad may be the prologue to a bad supper, A good. (S 69)

1642 TORRIANO 100 (is the beginning of an evil). **1659** N.R. 19 A good Sallet the beginning of a bad Supper. **1664** CODRINGTON 184 (is the beginning of an ill). **1732** FULLER no. 174.

Salad, *see also* Drinks not wine after s. (He that); Thistle is fat s. for ass.

Sale, *see* Devil on s.

Salisbury Cathedral was built upon wool-packs.

1656–91 J. AUBREY *Nat. Hist. Wilts.* (1847) 98 The old tradition is, that this church was *built upon wooll-packs.* . . . It might be that . . . when Salisbury Cathedral was building, . . . an imposition might be putt on the Wiltshire wool-packs towards the carrying on of this magnificent structure.

Salisbury Plain is seldom (never) without a thief or twain. (S 73)

1656–91 J. AUBREY *Nat. Hist. Wilts.* (1847) xiv. 69 A PROVERB: 'Salisbury Plain Never without a thief or twain.' **1659** HOWELL *Eng. Prov.* 17a.

Sallows, *see* Builds his house all of s.

Salmon and sermon have their season in Lent. (S 74)

1659 HOWELL *Fr. Prov.* 21. **1670** RAY 23 . . . *Gall.* **1917** BRIDGE 106 . . . Not exclusively a Cheshire saying but often used in the County, the Dee being a salmon river.

Salmon, *see also* Hook's well lost to catch s.

Salt beef draws down drink apace.
(M 836)

a. **1628** CARMICHAELL no. 1405 Spair never your maisters salt beif for a drink. **1633** HART *Diet Diseased* I. xviii. 71 Salted meat . . . is farre worse than fresh meat . . . howbeit a good shooing horne for a cup of good liquor. **1666** TORRIANO *It. Prov.* 25 no. 25.

Salt, Below (Above) the.

[A large salt-cellar in the middle of a dining-table formerly marked off the less honoured guests from those more honoured.] **1597** BP. HALL *Sat.* II. vi That he do, on no default, Euer presume to sit aboue the salt. **1599** JONSON *Cynthia's Rev.* (1616) II. ii. 88. Hee'neuer drinkes below the salt. **1658** *Wit Restor'd* 43 Hee . . . humbly sate Below the Salt, and munch'd his sprat.

Salt cooks bear blame, but fresh bear shame. (C 641)

1670 RAY 73. **1732** FULLER no. 6300.

Salt fish, *see* Affairs, like s. f., ought to be . . . soaking.

Salt on a bird's tail, To cast (lay, throw). (B 401)

[In allusion to the jocular advice given to children to catch birds by putting salt on their tails.] **1580** LYLY *Euph. & his Eng.* ii. 99 It is . . . a foolish bird that staieth the laying salt on hir taile. **1595** R. TURNER *Garland of a Green Wit* E3 [Foolish man,] that hauing caught a Fowle feathered to thy owne affection, and couldest not lay salt on her tayle as the saying is. **1639** CLARKE 155 You catch birds by laying salt on their tayles. **1664** BUTLER *Hudibras* II. i. 78 Such great achievements cannot fail, To cast salt on a woman's tail. **1704** SWIFT *T. Tub* vii. Men catch knowledge by throwing their wit on the posteriors of a book, as boys do sparrows by flinging salt upon their tails. **1721** KELLY 380 *You will ne'er cast salt on his tail.* That is, he has clean escap'd. **1813** SOUTHEY *Nelson* viii. If they go on playing this game, some day we shall lay salt upon their tails. **1926** Jan. D. H. LAWRENCE *Lett.* ii. 883 Will I write a fore-word? Will I put salt on its tail!

Salt or brains, Do not offer. (M 626)

1666 TORRIANO *It. Prov.* 245 no. 21. At table, one ought not to present any one, either salt, or the head of any creature. **1738** SWIFT *Dial.* II. E.L. 303 Then, madam, shall I send you the brains? I beg your ladyship's pardon; for they say, 'tis not good manners to offer brains. **1872** J. GLYDE, jr. *Norfolk Garland* 44. **1903** W. A. DUTT *Norfolk Broads* 338 That 'to help one to salt is to help one to sorrow' is as firmly credited as the belief that good luck attaches to the picking up of pins or cast horseshoes.

Salt seasons all things. (S 80)

c. **1567–8** Posy in *Loseley Manuscripts* ed. Kemp 207 As salt by kind gives things their savour So hap doth hit where fate doth favour. **1590** R. HARVEY *Plain Percival* B1ᵛ You say true, Sal

sapit omne. **1591** FLORIO *Second F.* 53 Salt
sauoureth, and seasoneth all things. **1624** J.
HEWES *Perfect Survey* V4 Salt . . . is said to
sauour each thing. **1659** HOWELL *Eng. Prov.* 9b.

Salt to Dysart and puddings to Tranent, Carry. (s 77)

[= to send things to a place where they are
already plentiful.] *a.* **1628** CARMICHAELL no.
370 Bring salt to Disert. *c.* **1641** FERGUSSON
MS. no. 583. He cals[1] salt to Dysart. **1822**
SCOTT *Let.* 10 Feb. in LOCKHART *Life* ch. 60
(1860) 472 It would be sending coals to Newcastle . . ., not to mention salt to Dysart, and
all other superfluous importations (&c.). **1862**
HISLOP 42 Carrying saut to Dysart and puddings
to Tranent. [[1] drives.]

Salt water and absence wash away love.

a. **1805** NELSON in SOUTHEY *Life* (1813) ch. 2
'Have you not often heard', says he in another
letter, 'that salt water and absence always wash
away love? Now I am such a heretic as not to
believe that faith.' **1840** MARRYAT *Poor Jack*
ch. 38 I'm very glad that we're off to-morrow—
salt water cures love, they say, sooner than anything else.

Salt water never gives cold.

1837 T. HOOK *Jack Brag* ch. 12 'Wet clothes!'
said Jack. 'Nothing—a mere flea-bite—salt
water never gives cold.'

Salt, *see also* Before you make friend eat . . . s.
with him; Black (Above) there is no colour;
Business is s. of life; Come after with s. and
spoons; Eat a peck of dirt (s.); Eat me without s.;
Egg without s., (As an); Give neither counsel nor
s.; Grain of s., (To take things with a); Sugar or
s.; Take away the s., throw flesh to the dogs;
Worth one's s.

Salute, *see* Know one another (They that) s. afar.

Salve for every sore, He has but one. (s 82)

1509 BARCLAY *Ship of Fools* i. 263 Say, blysshe
Surgyan by what experyance . . . Takest thou
on the . . . With one Salue or plaster, to heale
euery sore. **1559** T. BECON *Displ. Popish Mass
Prayers* P.S. 264 [The mass is] a salve for all
sores, a remedy for all diseases. **1566** T. DRANT
A Medicinal Moral A3 Not one kynde of musike
deliteth all passions: nor one salue for all greu-
ances. **1579** LYLY *Euph.* i. 193 Woulde you
haue one potion ministred to the burning Feuer,
and to the colde Palseye? one playster to an olde
issue and a fresh wounde? one salue for all sores?
one sauce for all meates? **1621** ROBINSON 32
He healeth all sores with one salue. **1639**
CLARKE 14 (as 1621).

Salve for every sore, There is a. (s 84)

1541 *Sch. House of Women* B3 A saulue there
is, for euery sore. **1579** LYLY *Euph.* i. 208 O
ye Gods, have ye ordeyned for every malady
a medicine, for every sore a salve, for every
paine a plaster, leaving only love remedilesse?
1591 SHAKES. *3 Hen. VI* IV. vi. 88 But let us

hence, my sovereign, to provide A salve for any
sore that may betide. **1639** CLARKE 44. **1908**
C. M. DOUGHTY *Wander. Arabia* I. vi. 102 Some
specific must he have for every disease, because
'there is a salve in nature for every sore'.

Salve, *see also* Hand that gave the wound must
give the cure (s.); Seek your s. where you got
your sore;—where you got your ail; Sore upon
sore not s.

Same boat, To be all in the. (B 491)

[CIC. *ad Fam.* 12. 25 *Una navis est iam bonorum
omnium.*] **1584** HUDSON *Judith* (J. Craigie) 51
Haue ye pain? So likewise pain haue we; For
in one boat we both imbarked be. **1857** HUGHES
Tom Brown 131 'But my face is all muddy',
argued Tom. 'Oh, we're all in one boat for that
matter.' **1858** TROLLOPE *Dr. Thorne* ch. 24 Dr.
Fillgrave and Mr. Rerechild were accustomed to
row in the same boat.

Same knife cuts bread and fingers, The. (K 157)

1579 GOSSON *Sch. Abuse* Arb. 46 The goodness
of a Knife cuts the owner's fingers. **1580** LYLY
Euph. & his Eng. ii. 28 That were as fond as
not to cut ones meate with that knife that an
other hath cut his finger. **1616** DRAXE no. 2319.
1659 HOWELL *Span. Prov.* 19.

Same, *see also* Another yet the s.; Like is the s.,
(No).

Sample, *see* Sack is known by s.

Sampson than of Solomon in him, There is more of.

1830 FORBY 430 . . . *i.e.* Great bodily strength,
but little sense.

Samson, *see* Solomon was a wise man.

Sand feeds the clay, When the | England cries Well-a-day: but when the clay feeds the sand, it is merry with England. (s 90)

1577 W. HARRISON *Description of Eng.* New
Sh. S. iii. 139–40 According to the old rude
verse set downe of England . . . When the sand
dooth serue the claie Then may we sing well
awaie; But when the claie doth serue the sand,
Then is it merie with England. **1662** FULLER
Berks. 84 . . . As Nottinghamshire is divided
into . . . the sand and the clay, all England falls
under the same *Dicotomy*; yet . . . the sand
hardly amounteth to the Fifth part thereof.
Now a wet year, which drowneth and chilleth
the clay, makes the sandy ground most fruitful
with corn, and the general Granarie of the Land.

Sand, To build on. (s 88)

[MATT. vii. 26 A foolish man, which built his
house upon the sand.] **1548–9** N. UDALL *Paraphrase of Erasmus* 2nd ded. to Queen Katherine
A1[v] Thinges not builded vpon the sand of
ambicious sekyng nor (like bubles in the rayne

water) puffed vp with an vncertain blast of worldly vanitee. **1585** MUNDAY *Fidele and Fort.* II. iv. D2 He fondly reares his fortresse on the sande. That buildes his trust vpon a womans troth.

Sand(s), *see also* Marls s.; Plough the s.; Rope s.; Sowing on the s.

Sandal tree perfumes the axe that fells it, The.

1853 TRENCH iv. 75 This Indian [proverb], suggesting that good should be returned for evil. **1865** *Id. Poems* 302 The sandal tree, most sacred tree of all, Perfumes the very axe which bids it fall.

Sands will sink a ship, Many.   (s 92)

1615 T. ADAMS *Bad Leaven* Wks. 708 Many little sands gather'd to an heape, faile not to swallow a greet vessell.   **1621** BURTON *Anat. Mel.* I. ii. IV. vii. (1651) 172 As Austin said,[1] *many grains and small sands sink a ship,* . . . Often reiterated, many dispositions produce an habit. **1639** CLARKE 11.   **1670** RAY 118 . . . We must have a care of little things. [[1] Numquid minutissima sunt grana arenae? sed si arena amplius in navem mittatur, mergit illam.]

Sandy bowrocks, *see* Build s. b. together (We will never).

Sap and heart are the best of wood.

1917 BRIDGE 106 . . . Outside and inside are equally useful.

Sap, *see also* Little s. in dry pease hulls; St. Matthie sends s. into trees.

Sarbut, *see* Old S. says so.

Sarsnick, *see* Dim S. with him.

Sarum, *see* Secundum usum S.

Satan (Vice) reproves (rebukes) sin.
                                                              (D 262)

1623 PAINTER B6 Tis more then time for iustice to come in, When vice thus openly rebuketh sinne.   **1666** TORRIANO *It. Prov.* 60 no. 99 The Devil corrects sin.   **1721** KELLY 287 . . . Spoken when we are reproved by wicked Men.   **1822** SCOTT *Nigel* ch. 32 I am afraid . . . I might have thought of the old proverb of 'Satan reproving sin'.   **1897** C. C. KING *Story of Brit. Army* 176 Napoleon . . . induced his ally, the Czar, to address King George a letter, asking him to make peace 'in the name of humanity!' It was like 'Satan reproving sin'.

Satiety, *see* Variety takes away s.

Saturday is the working day and Monday the holiday of preachers.
                                                              (s 94)

1661 FULLER *Cambs.* 159 Andrew Marvail[1] . . . preached what he had pre-studied some competent time before. Insomuch that he was wont

to say, that he would crosse the common proverb, which called 'Saturday the working day, and Munday the holy day of preachers'. [[1] Marvell.]

Saturday servants never stay, Sunday servants run away.

1851 STERNBERG *Dialect of Northants* 169.   **1917** BRIDGE 107 Servant maids do not like to go to a new place on Saturday . . . Northamptonshire.

Saturday without some sunshine, There is never a.

1835 SOUTHEY *Doctor* iii. 165.   **1866** *New Suffolk Garland* 166 There is also a saying that 'the sun is always seen on a Saturday'.

Saturday's flittings light sittings.

1854 BAKER *Northants Gloss.* s.v. Flit 'Saturday's flit will never sit' is a proverb of prediction with superstitious servants, who reluctantly enter upon a new service on that day.   **1917** BRIDGE 107 . . . Servant maids do not like to go to a new place on a Saturday as it forebodes a short stay.

Saturday's moon, A | if it comes once in seven years, it comes too soon.

1732 FULLER no. 6491.   **1864** *N. & Q.* 3rd Ser. v. 209 A Saturday or a Sunday moon Comes once in seven years too soon.

Saturday's new, and Sunday's full, was never fine and never wool.[1]

1823 E. MOOR *Suffolk Words* 494 We have a local antipathy to a Saturday *new* and Sunday *full* moon, . . . **1830** FORBY 417. [[1] will.]

Sauce for the goose is sauce for the gander, What's.   (s 102)

1670 RAY 98 That that's good sawce for a goose, is good for a gander. This is a woman's Proverb.   **1692** L'ESTRANGE *Aesop's Fab.* ccii. 264 Sauce for a Goose is Sauce for a Gander.   **1738** SWIFT *Dial.* II. E.L. 316 *Miss gives Neverout a smart pinch. . . . Never.* [*Giving Miss a pinch.*] Take that, miss; what's sauce for a gander.   **1823** BYRON *Juan* XIV. lxxxiii Teach them that 'sauce for goose is sauce for gander'.   **1894** BLACKMORE *Perlycross* ch. 35 A proverb of large equity. . . .

Sauce, To be served with the same.
                                                              (s 99)

1523–5 BERNERS *Chron. Froissart* T.T. iii. 374 If the flemynges had achyued the prise over them, they had bene served of the same sauce.   **1530** PALSGRAVE 710a I serve one of the same sauce, whiche we use in maner of a prouerbe.   **1545** *Precepts of Cato* F3ᵛ With the same sauce, serue him so agayne.   **1593** *Tell-Trothes Gift* in *Tell-Trothes New Year's Gift, etc.* 7 I will not liue alone in sorrow, but will make thee taste of the same sauce.   **1681** E. RAWLINS *Heraclitus Ridens* Feb. 22 And if poor Bob and Smug be not serv'd with the same sauce, they'l cross the Proverb.

Sauce, *see also* Crab of wood is s. good; Hunger is best s.; More s. than pig; Seek your salve (s.) where you get ail; Simonds s., (To eat of); Sweet meat . . . sour s.; Sweet s. wax sour.

Saul also among the prophets? Is.

(s 104)

[1 SAM. X. 11.] **1815** SCOTT *Guy Man.* ch. 21 Is Saul, you will say, among the prophets? Colonel Mannering write poetry! **1853** TRENCH ii. 35 . . . finds its application as often as any one reveals suddenly a nobleness which had been latent in him until now. **1882** 'F. ANSTEY' *Vice Versa* ch. 4 This is indeed finding Saul among the prophets; your sentiments, if sincere, Bultitude . . . are very creditable.

Save a stranger from the sea, and he'll turn your enemy.

1601 SHAKES. *T.N.* II. i. 20 Before you took me from the breach of the sea was my sister drowned. . . .—If you will not murder me for my love, let me be your servant. **1822** SCOTT *Pirate* ch. 7 'Are you mad . . . to risk the saving of a drowning man? Wot ye not . . . he will be sure to do you some capital injury?'

Save a thief from the gallows and he will hate (never love) you.

(T 109)

13— *Sir Beues* 1217 Deliure a þef fro þe galwe, He þe hateþ after be alle halwe! *c.* **1440** LYDGATE *Fall of Princes* VI. l. 3253 Who saueth a theef whan the rop is knet/Aboute his nekke, as olde clerkis write, With sum fals tourn the bribour wil hym quite. **1484** CAXTON *Fables of Aesop* I. x Yf ye kepe a man fro the galhows he shalle neuer loue yow after. **1583** MELBANCKE *Philot.* 163 True is the Prouerbe, saue a Thiefe from the gallowes and he will be the firste shall doe thee a mischiefe. **1583** GOLDING *Calvin on Deut.* li. 307 Saue a theefe from the gallowes and hee will helpe to hang thee. **1592** DELA-MOTHE 39 Saue a theefe from the gallowes, and he will put you in his place. **1594** NASHE *Christ's Tears* Pref. Ep. ii. 180 Saue a theef from the gallows, and hee'le be the first shall shew thee the way to Saint Gilesesse. [The church of St. Giles in the Fields was on the way to the gallows.] **1614** CAMDEN 311 Saue a theife from the gallows, and heele cut your throat. **1622** MASSINGER *Virg. Mar.* II. iii. She saved us from the gallows, and, only to keep one proverb from breaking his neck, we'll hang her. **1659** HOWELL *It. Prov.* 9 Take down a thief from the gallowes, and he will hang thee after. **1692** L'ESTRANGE *Aesop's Fab.* cccxi (1738) 334 The mouse gnawed a hole in 't, and set her at liberty; and the kite eat up the mouse for her pains. . . . *Save a thief from the gallows,* and he'll cut your throat. **1721** KELLY 61 Buy a Thief from the Gallows, and he'll help to hang your self . . . A very worthy Clergyman in Scotland, . . . saved a Villain from the Gallows: And twelve Years after, he was the first that rabbled him, and the sorest upon him. **1723** DEFOE *Col. Jack* ch. 9 Whence else came the English proverb, That if you save a thief from the gallows, he shall be the first to cut your throat.

Save one's bacon, To.

(B 24)

[= to escape injury to one's body.] **1675** DICK HALS to Sir R. Verney *Verney Memoirs* (1899) iv.

312 My last reprive . . . came durante bene placito Regis. Iff soe, itt will still save my bacon. **1691** *Weesils* i. 5 No, they'l conclude I do't to save my Bacon. **1812** COMBE (Dr. Syntax) *Pictur.* vi. 22 But as he ran to save his bacon, By hat and wig he was forsaken.

Save something for the man that rides on the white horse.[1]

(s 619)

1639 CLARKE 129. **1670** RAY 139 . . . For old age, wherein the head grows white. **1721** KELLY 226. [1 age, distress, and necessity.]

Save while you may: For age and want | no morning sun lasts a whole day.

1758 FRANKLIN in Arber *Eng. Garner* v. 585 You may think yourself in thriving circumstances; . . .

Saved, He that will not be | needs no preacher.

(P 562)

1611 COTGRAVE s.v. Cure He that will not be saued needs no preaching: aduice preuailes not with such as are carelesse of their owne good. **1670** RAY 21.

Save(s, d), *see also* Groat is ill s. that shames; Penny is well spent that s. groat; Penny s. is penny gained; Penny that's s. is not gotten (Every); Spend not where you can s.

Savers in a house do well, Some.

(s 106)

1678 RAY 198.

Saver(s), *see also* Good s. is good server.

Saves his dinner will have the more for his supper, He that.

(D 342)

1611 COTGRAVE s.v. Souper (keepes his dinner). **1616** DRAXE no. 2041. **1639** CLARKE 241. **1670** RAY 79 . . . This is a French Proverb, Qui garde son disne il a mieux à souper. He that spares when he is young, may the better spend when he is old. **1732** FULLER no. 2288.

Saving, Of | comes having. *Cf.* Sparing is the first gaining.

(s 107)

1573 TUSSER (1580) 11ᵛ Who nothing saue, shall nothing haue. **1609** HARWARD 97ᵛ Save and have. **1616** DRAXE no. 2130. *a.* **1640** SMYTH *Lives of the Berkeleys* i. 307 The Gloucestershire proverb within the hundred of Berkeley is, That sauinge must equall havinge, else want will at the yeares end bee Auditor and Accomptant. **1670** RAY 139. **1732** FULLER no. 6102.

Saving your presence.

c. **1607** BEAUM. & FL. *Kt. Burn. P.* II. ii You lookt so grim, and, as I may say it, saving your presence, more like a Giant than a mortal man. **1907** ELIZ. ROBINS *Convert.* ii. 24 There's nothing I should quite so much hate talking about as politics—saving your presence.

Saving your (one's) reverence.   (R 93)

c. **1400** MANDEVILLE E.E.T.S. 123. 22 But after
my lytyle wytt, it semeth me, sauynge here
reuerence, þat it is more. **1455** *Rolls of Parlt.*
v. 285/1 Defaime untruly (sauyng youre
reverence) leyed upon us. **1528** ROY & BARLOW
Rede me and be not wroth ed. Arber 41. **1530**
PALSGRAVE 698b. **1533** J. HEYWOOD *Johan
Johan* l. 366. **1552** HULOET Q1ᵛ Honor saued,
or sauynge your honour Dignitate tuta. a terme
spoken absolute in a poynt of reuerence, as the
vulgar saying is, sauynge your reuerence. &c.
Reuerentia salua honestate salua, etc. *Id.* 2D1
Sauing your honour, reuerence, or worship, a
terme spoken to our betters wher we talke of
a vile thing. *a.* **1593** MARLOWE *Edw. II* I. i.
Saving your reverence, you must pardon me.
c. **1596** HARINGTON *New Disc. of Stale Subject*
A4 As olde Tarlton was wont to saie, this same
excellent worde saue reuerence, makes it all
manerlie. **1596** SHAKES. *M.V.* II. ii. 25 To run
away from the Jew, I should be ruled by the
fiend, who, saving your reverence, is the devil
himself. *Ibid.* II. ii. 119 His master and he,
saving your worship's reverence, are scarce
cater-cousins. **1597** *Id. 1 Hen. IV* II. iv. 451
But that he is, saving your reverence, a whore
master, that I utterly deny. **1598–9** *Id. M.A.*
III. iv. 32 I think you would have me say,
'saving your reverence, a husband'. **1604** *Id.
M.M.* II. i. 86 Sir, she came in, great with child,
and longing,—saving your honour's reverence—
for stewed prunes.

Saving, *see also* Alchemy to s. (No); Hang s.

Savour (*noun*), *see* Best smell is bread, the best s.
salt; Nothing has no s.; Something has some s.;
Wine by the s.

Savours (*verb*), *see* Cask s. of first fill; Gain s.
sweetly from anything.

Saws, *see* Sooth s. be to lords lothe.

Sawtrey, *see* Ramsey.

Say as men say, but think to yourself.
                                          (M 581)

1616 DRAXE no. 728 Speake faire wordes, and
thinke what you will. **1639** CLARKE 327.

Say B to a battledore, He cannot. *Cf.* Knows not a B.

1599 NASHE *Lent. Stuffe* iii. 151 Euery man can
say Bee to a Battledore, and write in prayse of
Vertue. **1621** BP. MONTAGU *Diatribae* 118 Some
. . . will . . . conclude, that the Clergy of this
time were blind Bayards, and not able to say
bo to a battledore. **1896** SKEAT *Stud. Past* 62
A hornbook . . . was shaped something like a
battledore. . . . To be able to say B when B was
pointed to in the hornbook, was called 'to say
B to a battledore'.

Say *bo* to a goose, He cannot.   (B 481)

1572 *2nd Admonition to Parl.* (Frere and Douglas
128) Can scarce say (as they say) shue to a
goose. **1588** *Marprel. Ep.* Arb. 43 He is not
able to say bo to a goose. **1603** T. HEYWOOD

Wom. K. Kindness III. ii. Unless it be Nick and I,
there's not one amongst them all can say bo to
a goose. **1639** CLARKE 145 (shooh). **1748**
SMOLLETT *Rod. Rand.* ch. 54 I could not say Bo
to a goose. **1866** BLACKMORE *Cradock N.* ch. 30
Bob could never say 'bo' to a gosling of the
feminine gender.

Say little (nothing), I | but I think the more.   (L 367)

c. **1430** LYDGATE *Minor Poems* 155 (Percy Soc.)
Take no quarelle, thynk mekyl, and sey nought.
c. **1450** *Prov. of Wysdom* (Ed. Schleich) in *Anglia*
51, l. 94 Whateuer þou þenkest sey but lyte.
c. **1490** *Partonope* E.E.T.S. 84 He seyyth butte
lytell, butte more thynckyth he. **1546** HEYWOOD
II. ii. G1 I saie little (saied she) but I thynke more.
[*c.* **1587**] **1592** KYD *Span. Trag.* II. ii. 25 The
lesse I speak, the more I meditate. **1591** SHAKES.
3 Hen. VI IV. i. 83 I hear; yet say not much,
but think the more. **1599** PORTER *Angry Wom.
Abingd.* IV. iii. l. 2328. **1721** KELLY 182 I will say
nothing, but I will yerk[1] at the thinking . . . I
will at present conceal my Resentments; but I
will watch an Opportunity for Retaliation.
1666 TORRIANO *It. Prov.* 200 no. 18 (and write
less). **1738** SWIFT *Dial.* I. E.L. 269 Miss says
nothing; but I warrant she pays it off with
Thinking. **1748** SMOLLETT *Rod. Rand.* ch. 54
Speak less and think more. **1836** MARRYAT *Mr.
Midsh. Easy* ch. 14 As for Jack, he said nothing,
but he thought the more. ?**1837** Aug. DICKENS
Lett. to Forster *Lett.* ed. House i. 297 I am like
the Parrot who was doubly valuable for not
speaking, because he thought a great deal more.
[*Cf. N. & Q.* ccviii (1963), 313.] **1861** G. J.
WHYTE-MELVILLE *Market Harb.* ch. 18 Cissy . . .
said nothing; perhaps she thought the more.
[[1] be busy.]

Say 'Nay', *see* Learned timely to steal that
could not say 'Nay'; Maids s. 'Nay'.

Say 'No', *see* Always say 'No' (If you), you'll
never be married.

Say no ill of the year till it be past.
                                          (I 33)

1640 HERBERT no. 297. **1732** FULLER no. 4071.

Say no more till the days be longer, I will.   (M 1142)

1555 HEYWOOD *Epigr. on Prov.* no. clxviii.
1616 DRAXE no. 1562 (day).

Say 'No' till you are asked, Don't.

1738 SWIFT *Dial.* I. E.L. 275 Pray, don't say
no, till you are asked.

Say nothing, Better | than not to the purpose.   (N 250)

1605 30 April J. CHAMBERLAIN *Lett.* (McLure)
i. 205 As goode say nothing as to no purpose.
1732 FULLER no. 921.

Say nothing when you are dead.   (N 323)

1678 RAY 82 . . . i.e. be silent. **1813** RAY 67.

Say nothing, *see also* Hear and see and s. n.;
Say little (n.) but think more.

Say to pleasure, *Gentle Eve*, I will none
of your apple.   (P 418)
1651 HERBERT no. 1140.

Say true, You | will you swallow my
knife?   (K 158)
1678 RAY 255.

Say well, and do well, end with one
letter; say well is good, but do well is
better.   (S 122)
1536 *Remedy for Sedition* (cited Elyot's *Governor*,
ed. Croft, ii. 41) Men say wel that do wel. *c.*
1549 J. HALL *Proverbs of Salomon* A6ᵛ Saywell
from do well dyffereth a letter Saywell is good,
but do well is better.   1639 CLARKE 194.   1732
FULLER no. 6447.

Say well or be still.   (S 112)
c. 1480 *Early Miscell.* (Warton Cl., 1855) 63
Ewyre say wylle, or hold the[e] styll.   *a.* 1529
SKELTON *Agst. Comely Coyst.* 64 Wks. (1843) I.
17 A prouerbe of old, say well or be styll.

Saying and doing are two things.
(*Cf.* Saying is one thing.)   (S 119)
c. 1549 HEYWOOD II. v. H4ᵛ But it is as folke
dooe, and not as folke saie. For they saie,
saiyng and dooyng are two thyngis.   *c.* 1549
J. HALL *Proverbs of Salomon* A6ᵛ Say well, and
do well, ·are thynges twayne.   1578 FLORIO
First F. 18ᵛ From the said vnto the deed there
is a great throw.   1622 J. DE LUNA *Gram. Span.
& Eng.* tr. I.W. 233 Saying and doing are two
different things.   1706 STEVENS s.v. Dicho.

Saying goes good cheap.   (S 120)
a. 1628 CARMICHAELL no. 1329.   1641 FERGUSSON
no. 745.

Saying, Honey, Honey, It is not with |
that sweetness will¦come into the mouth.
1853 TRENCH v. 114 They courageously accept
the law of labour . . . This is Turkish.

Saying is one thing, and doing another.
Cf. Saying and doing.   (S 121)
1600–1 SHAKES. *H.* I. iii. 24 If he says he loves
you, It fits your wisdom so far to believe it As
he . . . May give his saying deed.   1603 MON-
TAIGNE (Florio) II. xxxi. 264 . . . A man must
consider the Sermon apart and the preacher
severall.   1620 SHELTON *Quix.* II. lxiv. iii. 275
'You do prettily facilitate the matter,' said
Sancho; 'but 'tis one thing to say and another
to do.'   *Ibid.* ii. 230 Great sayers are small doers.
1812 H. & J. SMITH *Rej. Addr., Drury L. Hust.*
'Tis just like the hustings, We kick up a bother,
But saying is one thing and doing's another.

Says anything but his prayers, He | and
those he whistles.
1732 FULLER no. 2014.   1738 SWIFT Dial. I. E.L.
268 Miss will say anything but her prayers, and
those she whistles.   1802 WOLCOT (P. Pindar)
Middl. Elect. ch. 3 Zay ev'ry thing bezides their
pray'rs, And those, agosh! they whistle.

Says his garner is full, None.   (G 41)
1640 HERBERT no. 657.

Say(s), said, *see also* Ape's paternoster, To s. an;
Buff nor baff, (He can neither s.); Crow is white
(To s.); Do as I s., not as I do; Do well than to s.
well, (It is better to); Easier s. than done; Goodman s. so s. we (As the); Ill s. that was not ill
taken (Never); Learn to s. before you sing; Lesson without book, (To con, s.); Little (Least,
Nothing) s. soon amended; Love best (Whom
we), to them can s. least; Many a one s. well
that thinks ill; No sooner s. than done; Sell the
cow (Who will) must s. the word; Soul is my
own, (I dare not s.); Sport is to do deed and s.
nothing; 'They s. so' is half a lie; They s.—
What s. they; Though I s. it that should not;
True that all men s.; Women will s. anything.

Scab, *see* Blab is a s.; Sloth breeds a s.

Scabbard, *see* Blade wears out s.; Draws
sword against prince (Who), must throw away s.

Scabbed horse cannot abide the comb, *see* Rub
a galled horse, etc. (1640 quotn.).

Scabbed sheep, One | will mar a whole
flock.   (S 308)
[JUVENAL *Sat.* 2. 79 *Grex totus in agris Unius
scabie cadit.* The entire flock dies in the field of
the disease introduced by one.]   *c.* 1350 *Douce
MS.* 52 no. 87 Oon scabbyd shepe makyth a
fowle flock.   1520 WHITTINGTON *Vulg.* E.E.T.S.
116 One scabbed shepe (as they say) marreth a
hole flocke.   *a.* 1530 *R. Hill's Commonpl. Bk.*
E.E.T.S. 129 One skabbid shepe infectith all the
folde.   1611 DAVIES no. 68.   1616 BRETON *Cross.
Prov.* B4 One rotten sheepe will marre a whole
flocke.   1629 T. ADAMS *Serm.* (1861–2) I. 76
They report, that once one scabbed sheep from
Spain rotted all the sheep of England. In this
manner is this poison of adultery spread from
a harlot.   1715 ISAAC WATTS *Divine Songs* (1728)
xxi. 30 From one rude Boy that's us'd to mock,
Ten learn the wicked Jest; One sickly Sheep
infects the Flock, And poysons all the rest.

Scabby heads love not the comb.
                                                  (H 689)
1592 DELAMOTHE 5 A scabed horse cannot abide
the combe.   1611 COTGRAVE s.v. Teigneux No
scauld-pate will the combe indure.   1623
WODROEPHE 516 A scabbed Head doth never
loue the Combe.   1732 FULLER no. 4072.   1796
WOLCOT (P. Pindar) *Orson & Ellen* Wks. (1816)
IV. 83 But George disliketh much to hear About
his Scottish home; Thus *scabby heads*, the proverb says, For ever hate a *comb*.

Scald[1] head is soon broken, A. (H 265)

c. **1350** *Douce MS. 52* no. 47 A scald mannys hede is lefe to breke. *c.* **1470** *Harl. MS. 3362,* f. 1a Frangitur exfacile caput infantis glabriosi— A scallyd mannys hed ys good to be broke. **1546** HEYWOOD II. iii. G2[v] But a scalde head is soone broken, and so they, As ye shall streight here, fell at a newe fraie. **1721** KELLY 11 A scal'd head is eith[2] to bleed. A thing that was but tender before, will easily be put out of Order. [[1] scabby. [2] easy.]

Scald[1] horse is good enough for a scabbed squire, A. (H 690)

1540 *Acolastus* 88 For suche a scalde squier as he is, a scabbed horse. **1546** HEYWOOD I. xi. E1[v] But hakney men saie, at mangy hackneis hyer, A scald hors is good ynough for a scabde squier. **1555** HEYWOOD *Epig. on Prov.* no. CLXI (A scalde horse . . . scalde squyre). **1611** DAVIES no. 169 (as 1546). [[1] scabby.]

Scald not your lips in another man's pottage. (L 328)

a. **1552** DOUGLAS *Aeneid* I Prol. 258 For dreid thai suld hys· lypis scald. **1598** *Servingmans Comfort in Inedited Tracts* (Hazlitt) 99 It is not good to scalde ones lyppes in other mens pottage. **1616** T. ADAMS *Diseases of the Soul* 65. *a.* **1628** CARMICHAELL no. 1340 (caill). **1670** RAY 56. **1766** *Goody Two-Shoes* [3 ed.] v. i Don't burn your lips with another man's broth. **1823** GALT *Entail* ch. 94 (kail).

Scalded cat (dog) fears cold water, A. (C 163)

1561 T. HOBY *Courtier* T.T. II. 191 As dogges, after they have bine once scaulded with hott water, are aferd of the colde. **1592** DELAMOTHE 7 A scalded Cat doth feare the coldest water. **1611** COTGRAVE s.v. Chien The scaulded dog feares euen colde water. *Id.* s.v. Chat. **1670** RAY 140. **1796** EDGEWORTH *Par. Asst.* (1903) 381 As my father said to you once—the scalded dog fears cold water. [Fr. *Chat éclaudé craint l'eau froide.*]

Scandal, *see* Everything in turn except s.

Scanderbeg's[1] sword must have Scanderbeg's arm. (S 127)

1655–62 GURNALL *Chrn. in Armour* (1865) II. 239 Not another arm could use this sword to have done thus much with it, besides the Spirit of God. . . . None could do such feats with Scanderbeg's sword as himself. **1732** FULLER no. 4077. **1779–81** JOHNSON *Lives of Poets* (Bohn) II. 212 [Congreve] . . . has the sword without the arm of Scanderbeg; he has his antagonist's coarseness, but not his strength. [[1] George Castriota, the Albanian hero, 1403–68.]

Scant of bairns that brought you up, They were.

1721 KELLY 321 . . . Spoken to ill thriven, or ill mannered Children.

Scant (Scarce) of news that told his father was hanged, He was. (N 142)

1668 R.B. *Adagia Scotica* 24. **1707** MAPLETOFT 119. **1721** KELLY 136 . . . Spoken to them that say something that may tend to the Disparagement of themselves, or Family. **1732** FULLER no. 2378. **1852** E. FITZGERALD *Polonius* 35 Cobbett used to say that people never should sit talking till they didn't know what to talk about. . . .

Scar(s), *see* Slander leaves s.; Wars bring s.; Wound be healed, s. remains.

Scarborough warning. (S 128)

[= very short notice, or no notice at all; a surprise.] **1546** HEYWOOD I. xi. E3 A daie' er I was wedde, I badde you (quoth I) Skarbrough warnyng I had (quoth he) whereby, I kept me thens. **1573** TUSSER (1580) C4 Or Skarborow warning, as ill I beleeue, when (sir I arest yee) gets hold of thy sleeue. **1582** STANYHURST *Aen.* 3 Arb. 81 Hym by his syers altars killing with skarboro warning [*incautum*]. **1603** BP. T. MATTHEW *Let.* 19 Jan. in CARDWELL *Confer.* (1840) 166 I received a message . . . that it was his Majesty's pleasure that I should preach before him upon Sunday next; which Scarborough warning did not only perplex me, but [&c.]. **1659** HOWELL *Eng. Prov.* 20a . . . viz. Not till danger knock at the door, as it once happened there from the French. **1824** SCOTT *Redg.* ch. 19 The true man for giving Scarborough warning— first knock you down, then bid you stand.

Scarce of horseflesh, They are | where two and two ride on a dog. (H 716)

1678 RAY 157.

Scarce, *see also* Good men are s.; Make much of one, good men are s.; Scant (S.) of news.

Scare, *see* Bugbears (Bugs) to s. babes.

Scarlet fever.

[= the attraction of a soldier's red coat.] **1864** J. GRANT *Rom. of War.* ch. 34 Louis . . . appeared . . . in the uniform of the Gordon Highlanders; and . . . all the young ladies were quite in love him, fairly touched with the scarlet fever. **1876** MRS. BANKS· *Manch. Man* ch. 4 Glory's scarlet fever was as rife an epidemic in Manchester as elsewhere. The town bristled with bayonets.

Scathe, *see* Neighbour's s. is my peril; One does the s., another has scorn; Scorn comes with s.

Scatter her mice, To.

1869 HAZLITT 446 . . . Said of a woman who has had a baby, and goes about to see her friends. There is a supposed liability to catch the same complaint.

Scatter with one hand, gather with two.

1659 HOWELL *Brit. Prov.* 2.

Sceptre is one thing, A | and a ladle another. (S 131)

1573 SANFORD 93ᵛ The common prouerbe: *Aliud est sceptrum, aliud plectrum*: that is, the scepter is one thing, and the harp is an other. 1586 J. CASE *Praise of Music* *4ᵛ Stratonicus answered King Ptolomy, . . . A scepter o King is one thing, and an instrument another. *c.* 1594 BACON *Promus* no. 520 Alia res sceptrum, alias plectrum.—ERASM. *Adagia* 872. 1640 HERBERT no. 545. 1670 RAY 23.

Scholar as my horse Ball, As good a. (S 132)

1639 CLARKE 145.

Scholar may waur¹ the master, The. (S 136)

1632 *Celestina* tr. T. Mabbe T.T. 144 Many times (as it is in the Proverbe) a good Scholler goes beyond his Master. 1721 KELLY 310 . . . (by a time). L. *Meliorem præsto magistro discipulum.*² [¹ be better than. ² Juvenal.]

Scholars are not the best preachers, The greatest.

1656 E. LEIGH *Treat. of Religion and Learning* A3ᵛ.

Scholar, *see also* Diligent s., the master's paid; Good master a good s.; Master that never was s., (Ill); Mere s. mere ass; Robs a s. robs twenty; Today is the s. of yesterday.

School, *see* Experience keeps dear s.; Good will (With as) as e'er boy came from s.; Tales out of s.

Schoolboys are the reasonablest people in the world; they care not how little they have for their money. (S 139)

1666 TORRIANO *Prov. Phr.* s.v. Scuola 187 As Children, who play the Truant most willingly and who are said in England to be Conscientious Persons, they care not how little they have for their Money, so they may be idle, they care not what Charges their Parents be at. 1678 RAY 81.

Schoolbutter, *see* Taste of s.

Schooling, *see* Pay more for s. than learning is worth.

Schoolmaster is abroad, The.

1828 LD. BROUGHAM *Speech* 29 Jan. The school-master is abroad! and I trust more to the school-master . . . than to the soldier. 1841 MARRYAT *Poacher* ch. 33 That is very polite for a mender of old kettles; but the school-master is abroad, which, I presume, accounts for such strange anomalies.

Schoolmaster, *see also* Father (One) more than hundred s.

Schools make subtle clerks, Sundry.

c. 1386 CHAUCER *Merch. T.* l. 1427 For sondry scoles maken sotile clerkis.

Science has no enemy but the ignorant. (S 142)

1555 L. DIGGES *Prognostication* *4 It is an olde sayd sawe, and trew: Scientia non habet inimi-cum nisi ignorantem . . . ignorancie, the grete enemie of all pure learning. 1574 G. HARVEY *Letter Bk.* 163. 1586 J. CASE *Praise of Music* 64 That common saying of the learned: Scientia neminem habet inimicum nisi ignorantem. None are so great enimies to knowledge as they that know nothing at all. 1623 WODROEPHE 514 . . . Most so, because the Vertuous Maintaine and cherish it.

Science, *see* Much s. much sorrow.

Scoff, *see* Demand is a jest, (Where the) the fittest answer is a s.

Scoggin¹ is a doctor, Among the common people. (P 222)

1616 WITHALS 559. 1639 CLARKE 143. [¹ a jester, *temp.* Edw. IV.]

Scold, Who has a | has sorrow to his sops. (S 145)

1659 HOWELL *Eng. Prov.* 15a. 1732 FULLER no. 5705.

Scold like a wych-waller, To. (W 950)

1670 RAY 208 . . . *Chesh.* That is, a boiler of salt; wych houses are salt houses, and walling is boiling. 1917 BRIDGE 142 . . . Women were formerly exclusively employed in this operation, hence the 'scolding'.

Scold like butter wives, To. (B 781)

1611 COTGRAVE s.v. Tripiere (Butter-whore). 1621 BURTON *Anat. of Mel.* (1738, 659, 4P3). 1639 CLARKE 275.

Scold, *see also* Call her whore (s., thief) first; Husbands are in heaven whose wives s. not.

Scolding wife, *see* Three things drive out of house, . . . s. w.

Scolds and infants never lin¹ bawling. (S 146)

1616 BRETON *Cross. Prov.* B3ᵛ. [¹ cease.]

Scone of a baking is enough, One.

a. 1628 CARMICHAELL no. 191. 1721 KELLY 273 . . . It is unreasonable to expect two Gratuities out of one Thing.

Score twice before you cut once. (S 149)

1688 R. HOLME *Acad. of Armory* III. vi. 292 The point on the back of the Shoemakers pareing knife is to Score, or Trace out the Leather before he venture to cut it, according to the saying, *Score twice before you Cut once.* 1917 BRIDGE 107 . . . Don't cut your leather until you feel sure that you have selected the right place. Used by the shoemakers of Chester.

Scorn a thing as a dog scorns tripe, To.
(T 157)
1670 RAY 207.

Scorn at first makes after-love the more.
(S 150)

1580 LYLY *Euph. & his Eng.* ii. 131 The more they seeme at the first to loth, the more they loue at the last. [*c.* **1589**] **1601** *Id. Love's Metam.* III. i. 78 Disdaine increaseth desire. **1594** SHAKES. *T.G.V.* III. i. 95 For scorn at first makes after-love the more.

Scorn comes commonly with scathe.
(S 151)

a. **1585** MONTGOMERIE *Cherrie & Slae* xvi (1821) 11 As skorne cummis commonlie with skaith, Sa I behufit to bide them baith. *a.* **1628** CAR-MICHAELL no. 1649 We may not have the skaith bot the scorne to. **1721** KELLY 288 . . . Spoken when one gets a Hurt, and another laughs at it.

Scorn with (at) the heels, To.

c. **1596** SHAKES. *M.V.* II. ii. 8 Scorn running with thy heels. *c.* **1599** *Id. M.A.* III. iv. 43 I scorn that with my heels. **1611** T. HEYWOOD *Golden Age* (1874) iii. 11 To skorne Akehornes with their heeles. **1612** FIELD *Woman a Weathercock* IV. ii He contemns you, he scorns you at his heels. **1827** SCOTT *Journ.* 10 Apr. Some incivility from Leith Bank, which I despise with my heels.

Scorn, *see also* One does the scathe another has s.

Scorning, *see* Mocking (S.) is catching.

Scorpion under every stone, There is (sleeps) a.
(S 894)

[SOPH. *Frag.* 35 Ἐν παντὶ γάρ τοι σκορπίος φρουρεῖ λίθῳ. Under every stone a scorpion lies hid. ERASM. *Ad. Sub omni lapide scorpius dormit.* Under every stone a scorpion sleeps.] *c.* **1522** ERASM. *Let.* Pope Adrian VI in FROUDE *Council Trent* (1896) iii. 66 Then there was only approval and encouragement, where now there is a scor-pion under every stone. People seem as if they wished to drive me into rebellion. **1545** TAVER-NER G7 Under euery stone slepeth a scorpion. **1732** FULLER no. 5444 We know not which Stone the Scorpion lurks under.

Scorpion(s), *see also* Chastise with s.; Rock S.

Scot (*proper name*), *see* Killed her for goodwill, said S.

Scot, A | a rat, and a Newcastle grind-stone travel all the world over. (M 367)

1662 FULLER *Northumb.* 303 . . . The Scots (Gentry especially), . . . travail into foreign parts, most for maintenance, many for accomplish-ment. . . . No Grindstone so good as those of Newcastle. **1821** A. CUNNINGHAM in LOCKHART *Scott* ch. 52 (1860) 457 [Mr. Bolton] said, 'That's like the old saying,—in every quarter of the world you will find a Scot, a rat, and a Newcastle grindstone'.

Scot and lot, *see* Pay s. and l.

Scot, To shoot like a.

a. **1575** J. PILKINGTON *Nehemiah* P.S. 428 If any shoot illfavouredly, we say 'he shooteth like a Scot'.

Scot will not fight till he sees his own blood, The.

1822 SCOTT *Nigel* ch. 1 'The Scot will not fight till he sees his own blood', said Tunstall, whom his north of England extraction had made familiar with all manner of proverbs against those who lay yet farther north than himself.

Scotch ordinary, The.
(S 161)

1678 RAY 81 The *Scotch* ordinary. *i.e.* The house of office.

Scot-free, To go.

[= free from payment of 'scot', tavern score, fine, etc. *fig.* exempt from injury, punishment; etc.] **1531** TYNDALE *Expos.* 1 *John* (1537) 22 The poore synner shulde go Skot fre without oughte at all. **1546** *St. Papers Hen. VIII* xi. 129 What damages their cuntrey and people had suffred by this warre, and that Your Majestie went not all scott free. *a.* **1548** HALL *Chron. Edw. IV* 233 They payed no money, but were set scot free. **1740** RICHARDSON *Pamela* (1824) I. 117 She should not, for all the trouble she has cost you, go away scot-free. **1877** BLACK *Green Past.* ch. 13 When some notorious offender has got off scot free.

Scotland, *see* France win (He that will) must with S. begin.

Scotsmen take their mark from a mischief.
(S 162)

1667 R.B. 46. *Adag. scotica.* **1721** KELLY 292 . . . Spoken when we say such a Thing fell out, when such an ill Accident came to pass. A Scottish man solicited the Prince of Orange to be made an Ensign, for he had been a Sergeant ever since his Highness run away from Groll. **1832** HENDERSON 87. Scotsmen aye reckon frae an ill hour.

Scot(s), Scotchman, Scottishman, *see also* Biting and scratching is S. wooing; Englishman is never happy . . . S. never at home; Englishman weeps . . . S. gangs while he gets it; False as a S.; Hardhearted as a S.; Lose a S. (We will not).

Scottish mist will wet an Englishman to the skin, A. (M 1016)

1589 LYLY *Pap w. Hatchet* iii. 394 We care not for a Scottish mist, though it wet vs to the skin. **1662** FULLER *Northumb.* 303 . . . Mists . . . have their fountain North, but fall South of Tweed. **1721** KELLY 18 . . . I never knew the Meaning of this . . . unless it be, that a Scottish Man will bear more foul Weather than an English.

Scouring, *see* Escape a s.

Scrambling at a rich man's dole, It is brave. (s 164)

1639 CLARKE 39. **1732** FULLER no. 5069.

Scrape(d), *see* Comes of a hen (He that) must s.; Fine as a carrot new s.

Scratch (*proper name*), *see* Old S.

Scratch, To come (bring) up to the.

[= the line drawn across the ring, to which boxers are brought for an encounter; often used fig.] **1821** *John Bull* 7 Jan. 29/3 He started a few seconds before the time and came up . . . to the scratch at the moment appointed. **1824** SCOTT *St. Ronan's* ch. 12 A dogged look of obstinacy, expressive, to use his own phrase, of a determined resolution to come up to the scratch. **1905** SIR G. O. TREVELYAN *Interludes* 155 When once natives have given way, it is almost impossible to bring them again to the scratch.

Scratch a beggar one day before you die, You will. (B 241)

1639 CLARKE 209 You'l scratch a beggar one day. **1910** P. W. JOYCE *Eng. as We Speak* 194 Tom Hogan is managing his farm in a way likely to bring him to poverty. . . . 'Tom, you'll scratch a beggarman's back yet': meaning that Tom will himself be the beggarman.

Scratch a Moore and your own blood will flow.

1913 *T.L.S.* 15 Aug. 336 George Moore . . . was . . . of impetuous temper, which vented itself in fierce and unguarded words, if not deeds. 'Scratch a Moore and your own blood will flow' is a proverb in Mayo.

Scratch a Russian and you'll find a Tartar.

1855 THACKERAY *Newcomes* ch. 63 What the Emperor Napoleon the First said respecting his Russian enemies might be applied to this lady, Grattez-la, and she appeared a Tartar. *c.* **1863** J. R. GREEN Lett. *N. & Q.* ccx (1965) 348 They say, if you scratch a Russian you always find the Tartar beneath. **1876** BURNABY *Ride to Khiva* ch. 9 Grattez le Russe et vous trouverez le Tartare. . . . It requires but little rubbing to disclose the Tartar blood so freely circulated through the Muscovite veins. **1888** MRS. OLIPHANT *Second Son* ch. 14 I don't put any faith in Russians. . . . 'Scratch a Russian and you'll come to the Tartar.' **1911** *Spectator* 2 Dec. 964 Until a short time ago the aphorism, 'Scratch a Russian and you find a Tartar', was the sum of British comprehension of the Russian character.

Scratch me (my back) and I'll scratch you (yours). *Cf.* Claw me, claw thee. Ka me, ka thee.

[DIOGENIANUS τὸν ξύοντα δ' ἀντιξύειν.] **1706** E. WARD *Wks.* iii. 145 Scratch me, says one, and I'll scratch thee. **1868** W. COLLINS *Moonstone* ch. 8 We are all getting liberal now; and (provided you can scratch me if I scratch you) what do I care . . . whether you are a Dustman or a Duke? **1929** *Times* 8 Aug. 9/1 Its members bargain among themselves to support the pet schemes of each on the principle of 'you scratch my back and I'll scratch yours'.

Scratch my breech and I'll claw your elbow.

1611 COTGRAVE s.v. Contrelouër To scratch the backe of one who hath alreadie clawed his elbow. **1616** WITHALS 564. **1670** RAY 140 . . . *Mutuum muli scabunt.* Ka me and I'll ka thee. When underserving persons commend one another.

Scratch (Claw) where it itches not, I. (M 49)

[*c.* **1515**] *c.* **1530** BARCLAY *Eclog.* IV. E.E.T.S. 143 But Codrus I clawe oft where it doth not itche. *c.* **1540** J. BALE *King Johan* l. 96 She shall rather kysse, wher as it doth no ytche. **1546** HEYWOOD II. vii. K1 Thou makest me claw where it itcheth not. **1589** PUTTENHAM *Eng.Poesie* III. xxiii. Arb. 279 The French King . . . said somewhat sharply, I pray thee good fellow clawe me not where I itch not with thy sacred maiestie. **1636** CAMDEN 299. **1678** RAY 296 It would make a man scratch where it doth not itch, To see a man live poor to die rich, *Est furor haud dubius simul et manifesta phrenesis, ut locuples moriaris egenti vivere fato.*—Juvenal [14. 136].

Scratches his head with one finger, He.

1542 ERASM. tr. Udall *Apoph.* (1877) 360 *Uno digito caput scalpere.*

Scratch(ed), *see also* Rub (S.) the elbow; Truth has a s. face.

Scratching and biting, By | cats and dogs come together. (s 165)

1546 HEYWOOD II. i. F4. **1623** CAMDEN 267.

Scratching, *see also* Biting and s. Scots' folk wooing; Eating and s. wants but beginning.

Screw loose somewhere, There is a.

[= something wrong in the condition of things; a weakness in some arrangement or (colloq.) in the head.] **1810** *Sporting Mag.* XXXVI. 166 The others . . . had got a screw loose. **1833** E. FITZGERALD Lett. (1889) I. 21 In fact, a genius with a screw loose, as we used to say. **1837** DICKENS *Pickwick* ch. 49 Something dark and mysterious was going forward, or, as he always said himself, 'there was a screw loose somewhere'. **1903** HENRY JAMES *The Beast in the Jungle* ch. 2.

Scrip, *see* Beggar's s. never filled.

Scripture, *see* Devil can cite S.

Scrub, *see* Mule (One) s. another.

Scruffel, *see* Skiddaw.

Scylla and Charybdis, Between. (s 169)

[A monster on a rock, and a whirlpool, on opposite sides of the Straits of Messina; HOMER *Od.* xii. *c.* 1180 *Walter of Lille* v. 301 Incidis in Scyllam cupiens vitare Charybdin.] *a.* 1547 SURREY ed. Padelford (1928) 20 From Cillas seas to Carribes clives. 1562 J. WIGAND *De Neutralibus* K7[v] Incidit in Scillam, cupiens vitare Charibdis. When he thought to shunne Charibdis, he dropped in to Scilla, a worse place. 1573 L. LLOYD *Pilg. of Princes* 215 To auoide Charibdis gulfe, I fall in Scillas bande. 1576 PETTIE ii. 89 But running from Charybdis he rushed upon Scilla. 1579 GOSSON *Sch. Abuse* Arb. 61 Lest that laboring to shun Sylla you light on Charibdis. 1579 LYLY *Euph.* i. 189 Thou arte heere amiddest the pykes betweene Scilla and Caribdis. 1596 SHAKES. *M.V.* III. v. 15 When I shun Scylla, your father, I fall into Charybdis, your mother. 1662 FULLER *Carnavon* 30 That Pilot is to be pitied, who, to shun Scylla, doth run on Charibdis. 1824 SCOTT *St. Ronan's* ch. 28 The Nabob made a considerable circuit to avoid ... this filthy puddle ... and by that means fell upon Scylla as he sought to avoid Charybdis ... and fell into the channel of the streamlet. 1896 M. A. S. HUME *Courtships of Q. Eliz.* 226 [Elizabeth] said, My lord, here I am between Scylla and Charybdis.

Scythe cuts and the plough rives, Where the | no more fairies and bee-bikes.[1]

1846 DENHAM 17. [[1] bees' nests.]

Scythe, *see also* Devil run through you with s.; Marries between the sickle and the s. (Who); Sickle and the s., that love I not to see.

Sea and the gallows refuse none, The. (s 178)

1614 T. GENTLEMAN *England's Way to Win Wealth* (*Social England* ed. Lang 271) The sailor's proverb, The sea and the gallows refuse none. 1703 NED WARD *Trip to New Eng.* Wks. II. 141 A man on Board cannot but be thoughtful on two Destinies, *viz.* Hanging and Drowning. ... It often put me in mind of the old Proverb, *The Sea and the Gallows* refuses none. 1866 BROGDEN *Lincolnsh. Words* 79 There is an old adage, that 'The Kirk-garth, like the gallows and the sea, receives all without asking questions'.

Sea complains it wants water, The. (s 179)

1541 *Schoolh. of Women* C1[v] Loke when the see, doth water want ... Then women cease wyll of theyr talke. 1639 CLARKE 6. 1732 FULLER no. 4740 (for want of water).

Sea has fish for every man, The. (s 180)

1575 GASCOIGNE *Ferd. and Leonora* i. 452. 1576 PETTIE i. 33. 1636 CAMDEN 308.

Sea refuses no river, The. (s 181)

[*c.* 1589] 1601 LYLY *Love's Met.* III. ii. 6 The Sea ... receiueth all things, and cannot bee

filled. 1601 SHAKES. *T.N.* I. i. 9 O spirit of love ... thy capacity Receiveth as the sea. *Ibid.* II. iv. 99 But mine [love] is all as hungry as the sea And can digest as much. 1605 *London Prodigal* I. i. *Shakes. Apoc.* 193 Brother, he is one that will borrow of any man.—Why, you see, so doth the sea: it borrowes of all the smal currents in the world, to encrease himselfe. 1609 SHAKES. *Son.* 135, l. 9 The sea, all water, yet receives rain still, And in abundance addeth to his store. 1732 FULLER no. 4741.

Sea, Being on | sail; being on land, settle. (s 171)

1640 HERBERT no. 418.

Sea, *see* Anchor of a ship, (Like the) always at s.; Calm s. (In) every man a pilot; Complains wrongfully on the s.; Devil and deep s., (Between); Drop of water in the s., (As lost as a); Fish in the s. (As good); Fishing (No) to fishing in s.; Forecasts all perils (He that) will never sail s.; Great way to the bottom of the s.; Learn to pray, go to s.; Mist comes from the ... s. (When); Old Man of the S.; Praise the s. but keep on land; Rivers run into s. (All); Save a stranger from the s. and he'll ...; Send him to the s., he will not get water; Three things are insatiable; Three ways, the Church, s., court; Travels not by s. knows not fear of God; Water in the s., (To seek); Water into the s., (To cast).

Sea with a spoon (nutshell), To empty the. (s 183)

c. 1534 GILES DUWES 1021 To lade the water out of the se. 1550 *A Notable and Marueilous Epistle* C2 As possyble as too take the whoole waater of the Sea, in one spoone, and to drynke it vp at a draught. [1616] 1631 JONSON *Devil Is Ass* v. ii. 1 Put me To ... lauing The sea dry with a nut-shell. 1662 FULLER *Northumb.* 303 Scotish Proverbs Lang or ye cut Falkland-wood with a penknife. It is spoken of such who embrace unproportionable, and improbable means, to effect the ends propounded to themselves, to as much purpose as to lave the sea with a cockle-shell.

Sea-mark, *see* Shipwreck (Let another's) be your s.

Seal(ed), *see* Sure as if s. with butter.

Seaman, A | if he carries a millstone, will have a quart out of it. (s 189)

1670 RAY 218 (quait)[1] Spoken of the common mariners, if they can come at things that may be eat or drunk. [[1] misprint in Ray 1670 and 1678 for quart.]

Season(s), *see* Constancy of the benefit in s. argues Deity; Everything is good in s.; Fools (If) do no fool it, they lose s.; Money never comes out of s. out of price; Oysters only in s. in R. months; Provision in s. makes rich house; Silly s.; Sluggard's convenient s. never comes.

Seasonably, *see* Little given s. excuses great gift.

Second side of the bread takes less time to toast, The.

1887 BLACKMORE *Springhaven* ch. 18 . . . We must not let the first side of ours be toasted; we will shun all the fire of suspicion.

Second thoughts (afterwits) are best.

(T 247)

[EUR. *Hipp.* 436 Αἱ δεύτεραί πως φροντίδες σοφώτεραι. ERASM. *Ad. Posterioribus melioribus.*] **1577** HOLINSHED (1587) iii. 94a Oftentimes it chanceth, that latter thoughts are better aduised than the first. **1579** GOSSON *Sch. Abuse* 18 After-wittes are euer best. **1581** GUAZZO i. 58 Whereby I finde verified the Proverbe, That the second thoughtes are ever the best. **1590** GREENE *Never Too Late* Gros. viii. 125 Had I wist is a great fault, and after wits are bitten with many sorrowes. **1738** SWIFT Dial. II. E.L. 305 What do you say to my wine?— I'll take another glass first; second thoughts are best. **1813** 11 Dec. BYRON *Corr.* Prothero ii. 305 In composition I do not think second *thoughts* are best, though second *impressions* may improve the first ideas. **1822** SCOTT *Pirate* ch. 4 Second thoughts are best; . . . take any port in a storm. **1852** E. FITZGERALD *Polonius* 13 'Second thoughts are best'. 'No', says the Guesser at Truth, 'First thoughts are . . . those of generous impulse'.

Second word makes the bargain, The. Cf. Two (words) to make bargain.

(W 827)

1597 BACON *Col. of G. & E.* 10 Arb. 154 In such cases the second degree seemes the worthyest, as . . .

Second, *see also* First blow makes wrong, s. makes fray; Shoot a s. arrow to find first.

Secret foe gives a sudden blow, A.

1721 KELLY 50. **1736** BAILEY *Dict.* s.v. Foe.

Secret is too little for one, enough for two, too much for three, A. (S 193)

1606 MARSTON *Fawn* III. i. When two know it how can it be a secret? **1611** COTGRAVE s.v. Trois As good let all, as three, men know a thing.

Secret is thy prisoner; Thy | if thou let it go, thou art a prisoner to it. Cf. Tells a secret. (S 195)

1678 RAY *Adag. Hebr.* 408 . . . We ought to be as careful in keeping a secret as an officer in keeping his prisoner, who makes himself a prisoner by letting his prisoner go.

Secret, Wherever there is a | there must be something wrong.

1696 ROGER NORTH *Lives* (Bohn) iii. 233 Secrecy is never without guile. **1837** LOCKHART *Life of Scott* ch. 2 (an old saying).

Secrets, If you would know | look for them in grief or pleasure. (S 197)

1640 HERBERT no. 367. **1670** RAY 23.

Secret (*adv.*), *see* Night, (As s. as the).

Secret (*noun*), *see also* Tells a s. (He that) is another's servant; Wild horses will not drag the s. from me.

Secundum usum Sarum, It is done.

(S 198)

a. **1529** SKELTON *Ware the Hauke* l. 103 Sed non secundum Sarum. **1588** 'Marprelate' *Epitome* ed. Pierce 162 He hath brought such a reason against this . . . as is just secundum usum Sarum. **1589** [LYLY] *Pap w. Hatchet* iii. 400 For the winter nights the tales shall be told *secundum usum Sarum.* **1662** FULLER Wilts. 146 . . . Many Offices or forms of service were used . . . in England . . . untill Osmond Bishop of Sarum,[1] about the year . . . 1090, made that . . . Office, which was generally received all over England. . . . It is now applyed to . . . Paterns of unquestionable Authority. [[1] 1½ m. from Salisbury, the present seat of the bishopric.]

Secure, *see* Crimes are made s. by greater crimes; Way to be safe is never to be s.

Securely, *see* Ears, . . ., (To sleep s. on both).

Security, *see* Actions are our s. (Our own); Danger next neighbour to s.; Four good mothers have four bad daughters: . . . s., peril.

Sedan, *see* Going to heaven in a s. (No).

See a churchman ill, Though you | yet continue in the church still. (C 381)

1640 HERBERT no. 698.

See a woman weep (greet), It is no more pity to | than to see a goose go bare foot. (P 365)

[c. **1275** *Prov. of Alfred* (Skeat) 31 Wummen wepeð for mod Ofter þanne for eni good.] *c.* **1548** BALE *K. Johan* ll. 173–5 Yt is as great pyte to se, a woman wepe As yt is to se a sely dodman[1] crepe, Or, as ye wold say, a sely goose go barefote. **1621** BURTON *Anat. Mel.* III. ii. III. iv. (1651) 498 And as much pitty is to be taken of a woman weeping, as of a goose going barefooted. **1641** FERGUSSON no. 533 It is na mair pittie to see a woman greit, nor to see a goose go bair fit. **1857** DEAN RAMSAY *Remin.* ch. 5 . . . A . . . reference to the facility with which the softer sex can avail themselves of tears to carry a point. [[1] snail.]

See, and approve, the better course; I | (but) I follow the worse. (B 325)

[OVID *Metamorph.* 7. 20 *Video meliora proboque; Deteriora sequor.*] **1523** A. FITZHERBERT *Husbandry* 94 He is an vnhappy man or woman, that god hath giuen bothe wyt and reason, and putteth hym in chose, and woll chose the worst parte. **1592** DANIEL *Complaint of Rosamond* ll. 433–4 We see what's good, and therto we consent, But yet we choose the worst, and soone repent. **1616** T. ADAMS *Gallant's Burden* 33. **1751** FIELDING *Amelia* VIII. X. **1827** HARE *Gues. at Truth* (1859) i. 139 The mind, when allowed its full and free play, prefers moral good, however faintly, to moral evil. Hence the old confession, *Video meliora, proboque*: and hence are we so much better judges in another's case than our own.

See, To | and to be seen.

[OVID *A.A.* l. 99 *Spectatum veniunt, veniunt spectentur ut ipsae.*] *c.* **1387** CHAUCER *W. of Bath* Prol. l. 552 And for to see and eek for to be seye. **1609** JONSON *Epithal.* (1633) 20 And they came all to see and to be seen. **1828** SCOTT *Journ.* 3 May After the dinner I went to Mrs. Scott of Harden, to see and be seen by her nieces. *a.* **1911** GILBERT *Lost Bab Ballads* 31 To see and be seen is for what we pay At Islington on the half-crown day.

See day at a little hole, One may. (D 99)

1546 HEYWOOD I. X. C4 I see daie at this little hole. **1590** LODGE *Rosalynde* Wks. (1883) I. 68 Aliena (that spied where the hare was by the hounds, and could see day at a little hole), thought to be pleasant with her Ganimede. **1594–5** SHAKES. *L.L.L.* V. ii. 712 I have seen the day of wrong through the little hole of discretion. **1609** J. WYBARNE *New Age of Old Names* 52 The heathens saw light through a narrow grate. **1623** CAMDEN 275.

See for your love (and) buy for your money. (L 540)

1563 NEWBERY *Dives Pragmaticus* A4 Come see for your loue, or come bye of me. *a.* **1568** U. FULWELL *Like will to Like* iii. 344. *c.* **1570** *The Pedlar's Prophesy* l. 160. **1572** CRADOCKE *Ship of Assured Safety* 182 Let vs see at leastwise for our loue, if it may not be bought for money. **1580** S. BIRD *Friendly Communication* F4. **1639** CLARKE 79. **1721** KELLY 299 See for love, and buy for money. A Cant among Pedlars and Hucksters.

See him need, I may | but I'll not see him bleed. (S 201)

1639 CLARKE 42. **1670** RAY 187 . . . Parents will usually say this of prodigal or undutiful children; meaning, I will be content to see them suffer a little hardship, but not any great calamity.

See his (your) nose cheese first, I will.

1721 KELLY 224 I would sooner see your nose cheese, and my self the first bite. A disdainful rejecting of an unworthy Proposal. **1728** SWIFT *Dial.* II. E.L. 296 I'll see your nose cheese first and the dogs eating it. **1816** SCOTT *Let.* 29 Apr. in LOCKHART *Life* ch. 37 He proposes they shall have the copyright *for ever.* I will see their noses cheese first.

See me, and see me not. *Cf.* Bopeep. (S 203)

1546 HEYWOOD II. V. H2ᵛ If he plaie falsehed in felowshyp, plaie yee, See me, and see me not.

. the woorst part to flee. **1548** HALL 51 The crafty hasarders which vse a plaie called seest thou me or seest thou me not. **1571** J. BRIDGES *Sermon at Paul's Cross* 29 He wil and he will not, this is boe peepe in dede, seest me and seest me not. **1613** [N. BRETON] *Uncasing of Machiavel's Instructions* ed. Robertson, 164 Play at bo-peepe, see me and see me not.

See Naples and then die.

1858 HOLMES *Aristocrat* (1892) 126. **1861** G. A. SALA *Dutch Pictures* ch. 16 (the vain-glorious saying of the Neapolitans). **1890** MRS. OLIPHANT *Kirsteen* ch. 8 This was the Highland girl's devout belief; *Vedi Napoli e poi morire;*[1] earth could not have anything to show more fair. [[1] *Vedi Napoli e poi muori.*]

See no further than the end of one's nose, To. (N 220)

c. **1594** BACON no. 1563 Il ne regard plus loin que le bout de son nez. **1659** HOWELL *Fr. Prov.* 9.

See no good near home, Some people can.

1902–4 LEAN IV. 97.

See not what is in the wallet behind, We. (W 20)

[CAT. XXII. 20, 21 Suus cuique attributus est error; sed non videmus manticae quod in tergo est.] **1545** TAVERNER H4ᵛ We loke not what is in the wallet behynde. Esope the writer of fables feyned that euery man and woman hath a wallet whereof the one parte hangeth before vs on oure brest, and the other behinde vs on oure shoulders. But into the syde which hangeth before our eyen we put other mens faultes, and oure owne faultes we put in the part behinde. By this he signifieth that we wol easely espy faultes in other men, but at our own we be wont to wynke. **1547** ERASM. tr. Chalenor *Praise of Folly* D1 (casting as sharpe an eie vpon their friendes faultes . . . not ones lokyng backe as the sachell hangynge behinde them). **1581** C. MERBURY *Brief Discourse* 22 We . . . carie alwayes two sachelles about vs, one before, to put other mens faultes in, and an other behinde, wherin to hide our owne. **1598** SIR R. BARCKLEY *Felicity of Man* 526. **1602** *The Jesuit's Catechism* ¶¶ 1ᵛ You see not that part of the wallet that hangs at your owne backes. **1648** HERRICK *Hesper.* 'Our own sinnes unseen' Wks. (1956) 253 Other mens sins wee ever beare in mind; None sees the fardell of his faults behind. **1654** E. GAYTON 93. **1732** FULLER no. 5453.

See the city for the houses, You cannot.

1597–8 BP. HALL *Satires* IV. i That *Lyncius*[1] may be match't with *Gaulard's* sight. That sees not *Paris* for the houses' height. **1877** ABP. TRENCH *Med. Ch. Hist.* ch. 1 The countryman . . . having gone for the first time to see some famous city, complained on his return home that he could not see the city for the houses. [[1] Lynceus, one of the Argonauts, famed for his sight.]

See the gowk[1] in your sleep, You will.

1846 JAMIESON *Scot. Dict.* 298 . . . A proverbial phrase denoting a change of mind. [[1] cuckoo.]

See the wood for trees, You cannot.

(W 733)

1546 HEYWOOD II. iv. G3ᵛ. **1581.** N WOODES *Conflict of Conscience* C2ᵛ. **1612–15** BP. HALL *Contempl.* IV. xii (1825) I!. 389 Let me not seem . . . an abettor of those Alcoran-like fables of our Popish doctors, who, not seeing the wood for trees, do *hærere in cortice*; 'stick in the bark'. **1738** SWIFT *Dial.* I. E.L. 259. **1912** *Spectator* 27 Jul. 121 We never get from it the sweep of narrative and the view as from a high place which we get from the greater historians. Once again, it is a case of the trees obscuring the wood.

See thy neck as long as my arm, I will first.

(N 64)

1678 RAY 261.

See what we must all come to, if we live, You.

1678 RAY 65.

See what we shall see, We shall.

1852 A. CARY *Clovernook* 264. **1895** J. PAYN *In Market Overt* ch. 14 'Well, we shall see what we shall see, when Miss Bryce comes in for her own', said Avis doggedly.

See which leg you are lame of, I now.

(L 185)

1586 D. ROULAND *Lazarillo* (1924) 40 As for me, when I perceiued upon which foot hee halted, I made hast to eat. **1732** FULLER no. 2623.

See with one's own eyes, To.

1707 J. STEVENS tr. *Quevedo's Com.* Wks. (1709) 350 I have seen it with my own Eyes. **1776** *Trial of Nuncomar* 24/2 I have seen him . . . with my own eyes take off his seal.

See you in daylight, They that | winna break the house for you at night. *Cf.* Sees thee by day, etc.

1832 HENDERSON 95 . . . (Spoken to ugly women.)

See your friend, Whensoever you | trust to yourself. *Cf.* Love your friend but look to yourself.

(F 724)

1566 PAINTER ed. Jacobs i. 87 This prouerbe olde and true . . . The thing do not expect by frends for to atchieue, which thou thyselfe canst doe, thy selfe for to relieue. [**1587**] **1592** KYD *Span. Trag.* III. ii. 118 Ile trust my selfe, my selfe shall be my freend. **1616** BRETON 2 *Crossing* A4ᵛ. **1639** CLARKE 26.

See your house in flames, When you | approach and warm yourself by it.

1853 TRENCH iii. 52 How proud a looking of calamity in the face, speaks out in . . . : When thou seest thine house in flames, approach and warm thyself by it.[1] [1 *Quando verás tu casa quemar, llegate á escalentar.*]

See(s), saw, *see also* Believe it though I s. it myself (I cannot); Believe not all that you s.; Bit what the bread is (You may s. by a); Blind as those who won't s. (None so); Blind enough who s. not through holes of sieve; Bound to s. (One is not); Came, s., and overcame; Child to hear (s.) something (To be with); Fain s. (That would I), said blind George; God will have s. (That) shall not wink; Hear and s. and say nothing; Land (To s.); Let me s., as blind man said; Lions (To s.); Live longest will s. most; Lives well (He that) s. afar; Rome s. a bad man; Speak that I may s. thee; Summer's day (As good as one may s. in a); Sun s. all things; Trust you no further than I can s. you; Wait and s.; Wolf (S. a); World to s.

See, *see also under significant words following.*

Seed, *see* Everything has its s.; Evil grain (Of) no good s.; Sows good s. shall reap good corn.

Seeding, *see* One year's s. makes seven years' weeding.

Seed-time, *see* Harvest follows s. t.

Seeing is believing.

(S 212)

1594–8 SHAKES. *T.S.* Ind. ii. 70 Am I a lord? . . . I see, I hear, I speak; I smell sweet savours and I feel soft things. Upon my life, I am a lord indeed. **1597** *Id.* *1 Hen. IV* V. iv. 135 I prithee speak. We will not trust our eyes Without our ears. **1609** HARWARD 85 Seeing is leeving. **1619** J. FAVOUR *Antiquity* 419 *Seeing is no leeving* with these men, they will take no witnesse of their owne eyes. **1639** CLARKE 90. **1678** RAY 200 . . . Chi con l'occhio vede, col cuor crede. *Ital.* **1685** DRYDEN Theoc. Idyl. XXVII (*Sylvae*). **1712** ARBUTHNOT *John Bull* II. xviii There's nothing like matter of fact; seeing is believing. **1721** KELLY 298 . . . all the World over. **1827–48** HARE *Gues. at Truth* (1859) ii. 497 *Seeing is believing*, says the proverb. . . . Though, of all our senses, the eyes are the most easily deceived, we believe them in preference to any other evidence. **1909** *T.L.S.* 28 May 198 Seeing is believing; . . . only art can make history really credible, or a great name more than a label to an abstraction.

Seek a brack[1] where the hedge is whole, You.

(B 584)

1580 LYLY *Euph. & his Eng.* ii. 150 Wild horses breake high hedges though they cannot leap over them. **1616** WITHALS 568 You break a gap where the hedge is whole. **1639** CLARKE 80 (as 1616). **1670** RAY 165. [1 breach, gap.]

Seek a hare in a hen's nest, To.

1599 PORTER *Angry Wom. Abingd.* l. 2285 Hee is gone to seeke a Hayre in a Hennes nest, . . . which is as sildome seene as a blacke Swan.

Seek grace at (of) a graceless face, You.

(G 396)

16th c. *Johnie Armstrong* in *Eng. and Scot. Pop. Bal.* 417 I haif asked grace at a graceless face,

But there is nane for my men and me. **1621**
ROBINSON 25. **1641** FERGUSSON no. 899.

Seek hot water under cold ice, You.
(W 128)

16th c. *Johnie Armstrong* in *Eng. and Scot. Pop.
Bal.* 417 To seik het water beneth cauld yce,
Surely it is a great folie. *a.* **1628** CARMICHAELL
no. 1415 (het fire). **1641** FERGUSSON no. 896.
1721 KELLY 364 . . . You court for Friendship
from them that will not befriend you.

Seek in a sheep five feet where there are but four, To.
(S 318)

1592 DELAMOTHE 5. **1651** HERBERT no. 1112.
1659 HOWELL *Fr. Prov.* 4. To seek five feet in a
Mutton.

Seek mickle, and get something; seek little, and get nothing.

1721 KELLY 291.

Seek that which may be found.

1579 *Proverbs* of Sir James Lopez de Mendoza
tr. B. Googe 93 Seeke that which thou maist
easily haue, and care not for no more. **1621**
BURTON *Anat. Mel.* II. iii. VII (1651) 360 Out of
humane authors take these few cautions, . . .
Seek that which may be found.

Seek till you find, and you'll not lose your labour.
(L 8)

1678 RAY 200. **1738** SWIFT Dial. I. E.L. 288 I
have lost the finest needle—Why, seek till you
find it, and then you won't lose your labour.

Seek your salve (sauce) where you get your sore (ail).
(S 83)

c. **1400** *Rom. Rose* l. 1965 The helthe of love
mot be founde Where as they token first her
wounde. **1580** LYLY *Euph. & his Eng.* ii. 73
There is none that can better heale your wound
than he that made it. **1641** FERGUSSON no. 764
Seik your sauce where you get your ail. **1721**
KELLY 292 . . . Spoken to them who are sick
after Drink, *alias*, Take a Hair of the Dog that
bit you. **1732** FULLER no. 4090.

Seek your salve where you got your ail, and beg your barm where you buy your ale.

1862 HISLOP 167 . . . The surly reply of a person
who has been shunned for some trivial or mistaken reason by one who is compelled by circumstances to apply to him for information or
assistance.

Seekers, *see* Losers a.

Seeks finds, He that. *Cf.* Nothing seek, nothing find.
(S 213)

[MATT. vii. 7.] **1530** PALSGRAVE xii. He that wyll
seke may fynde. *Id.* 537a. **1533** J. HEYWOOD
Play of Love C2. *c.* **1540** J. BALE *K. Johan* l. 192
Serche and ye shall fynd. **1546** HEYWOOD I. X.

C3[v]. **1581** RICH *Farewell to Militarie Prof.*
(1846) 128 As the proverbe is (he that sekes
shall finde).

Seeks trouble, He that | never misses.
(D 33. T 532)

c. **1460** *Pol., Rel., and Love Poems* E.E.T.S. 69
Who sechith sorwe, is by [his be] the receyte.
1580 S. BIRD *Friendly Communication* F3 He that
loueth daunger must needs fall into it. **1598–9**
SHAKES. *M.A.* I. i. 81 Are you come to meet your
trouble? The fashion of the world is to avoid
cost, and you encounter it. **1612** SHELTON
Quix. I. iii. vi. i. 171 He which seekes the
danger, perisheth therein. **1617** BRAITHWAIT
Solemn Disputation 49 It is written, He that
loveth danger, shall perish in it. **1640** HERBERT
no. 416. **1721** KELLY 131 He that seeks trouble,
it were a Pity he should miss it. Spoken to,
and of, Quarrelers, who commonly come by the
worst.

Seek(s), sought, *see also* Better keep now than s.
anon; Find not that you do not s. (Take heed
you); Man that s. his mare, and he riding on her;
No man will another in the oven s.; Nothing
s. nothing find; Truth s. no corners; Water in
the sea., (To s.); Woman's answer is never to s.

Seem, *see* Be what thou wouldst s. to be.

Seen, *see* Gives to be s. (He that); Heard where
he in not s.; Maid oft s.; Parsley before it is
born is s. by the devil nine times; Seldom s. soon
forgotten.

Sees an inch before his nose, He. (I 51)

a. **1628** CARMICHAELL no. 812. **1641** FERGUSSON
no. 394 Of well skilled persons. . . .

Sees thee by day will not seek thee by night, Who. *Cf.* See you in daylight.
(D 81)

1573 SANFORD 103[v]. **1659** HOWELL *Ital. Prov.* 2.

Sees, *see also* See(s).

Segging is good cope. (S 215)

[Used in echoes of the Dutch proverb *zeggen is
goedkoop*, 'talk is cheap'.] **1546** HEYWOOD II.
IX. L1 The douche man saieth, that seggyng
is good cope. **1613** F. ROBARTS *Revenue Gosp.*
104 Alasse, alasse, segging is no good coping.

Seill[1] comes not while (till) sorrow be gone (over).
(S 216)

a. **1628** CARMICHAELL no. 1341. **1641** FERGUS-
SON no. 757. **1721** KELLY 294 . . . Eng. When
Bale is highest Boot is next. [¹ happiness.]

Sel, sel, has half-filled hell.

1862 HISLOP 168 . . . 'Sel, sel', that is, the sin
of selfishness.

Seldom comes a (the) better. (B 332)

a. **1272** MS. *Temp. Hen. III* in DOUCE *Illust. of
Shaks.* (1807) II. 34 [The story is related of the

monks who, discontented with the gifts of their abbot, prayed that he might die. He did die and the gifts of the next abbot were less satisfactory than those of his predecessor. This abbot likewise died, whether in answer to the prayers of the monks or not, and a third abbot brought disappointment again. One of the monks then suggested that they should pray for this abbot to live, for who could say what a fourth one would do?] Unde solet dici 'Seilde comed se betere'. **1546** HEYWOOD I. iv. BI. [**1593**] **1597** SHAKES. *Rich. III* II. iii. 4 Ill news by'r lady; seldom comes the better. I fear, I fear, 't will prove a giddy world. **1599** PORTER *Angry Wom. Abingd.* I. 922 I pray God saue my Maisters life, for sildome comes the better. **1820** SCOTT *Abbot* ch. 6 Though he may be a good riddance in the main, yet what says the very sooth proverb, 'Seldom comes a better'.

Seldom does the hated man end (*sic* for erendeth) well.

a. **1250** *Owl & Night* 942–4 C.U.P. 80 For hit seide þe king Alfred: 'Sel[d]e erendeð wel þe loþe, an selde plaideð wel þe wroþe.' [The hated man seldom intercedes well, and the angry man seldom pleads well.] *a.* **1327** Brit. Mus. MS. Add. 35, 116 f. 24d Lex vidit iratum, iratus non vidit illam. Selde grendeth well the lothe and selde pleadeth well the wrothe.

Seldom is a long man wise, or a low man lowly. (M 370)

1556 T. HILL *Brief and Pleas. Epit. Physiog.* FI[v] The olde prouerbe . . . I haue seldom seen a long or tal man, wittye, or a little man, meeke and pacyent. **1583** MELBANCKE *Philot.* 153 I haue red that in an old smokie authour, . . . and here I meane to insert . . . I haue seldome sene a long man wise, or a lowe man lowlie. **1625** BACON *Apothegms* Wks. XIII. 410 My Lord St. Alban said, that wise nature did never put her precious jewels into a garret four stories high: and therefore that exceeding tall men had ever very empty heads.

Seldom lies the devil dead by the gate (in a ditch). (D 293)

c. **1460** *Towneley Myst., 2nd Shep. Play* 229 III. Seldom lyys the dewyll dede by the gate. *c.* **1470** HENRYSON *Mor. Fab., Fox, Wolf & C.* 113 'Heir lyis', quod he, 'the devill deid in a dyke. Sic ane selcouth[1] saw I not this sevin yeir.' **1641** FERGUSSON no. 744 (by the dyke side). **1670** RAY 79 (in a ditch). We are not to trust the Devil or his children, though they seem . . . without all power or will to hurt. . . . Perchance this Proverb may allude to the fable of the fox, which escaped by feigning himself dead. **1721** KELLY 230 Long e'er the Dee 'l lye dead by the Dike side. Spoken when we are told that some wicked Person is like to die. [[1] strange thing.]

Seldom seen, soon forgotten. *Cf.* Long absent, soon forgotten. (S 208)

c. **1350** *Douce MS.* 52 no. 89 Seldun sey, sone forȝete. *c.* **1375** *Vernon MS.* (Furnivall) 715 That selden i-seiȝe is sone forȝete. **1377** *Pol. Poems* (Rolls) I. 215 He that was ur most spede

Is selden seye and sone forȝete. *c.* **1450** *Prouerbis of Wysdom* 25 Seld i-say ys sone foreyete. *c.* **1470** *Harl. MS. 3362* (ed. Förster) in *Anglia* 42. 201 ȝelde y-seyȝe, sone forȝete. *Res raro visa procul est a corde rescisa. a.* **1530** *R. Hill's Commonpl. Bk.* E.E.T.S. 129 Selde sene, sone forgotin. **1546** HEYWOOD I. xi. D2 I haue seene this gentylman, yf I wyst where. Howe be it lo, seldome seene, soone forgotten. **1614** CAMDEN 311. **1721** KELLY 297 Sindle[1] seen, soon forgotten. [[1] Seldom.]

Self do, self have. (D 405. S 217)

a. **1500** *Prov. Wisdom* l. 37 Who so self do, self haue. **1546** HEYWOOD I. vii. CI For I did it my selfe: and selfe do, selfe haue. **1579** GOSSON *Sch. Abuse* Arb. 46 Selfe doe, selfe haue, they whette their Swoords against themselues. **1605** CHAPMAN, JONSON, MARSTON *Eastw. Ho* V. i. 123. **1641** FERGUSSON no. 754 Self deed, self fa.[1] **1721** KELLY 300 Self deed, self fa.[1] That is, as you do to others, so it will befall you. [[1] come to your share.]

Self, *see* Friend is another s.

Self-accuser, *see* Guilty conscience is a s. a.

Self-defence, *see* Self-preservation.

Self-edge makes show of the cloth, The. (S 222)

1611 COTGRAVE s.v. Maistre We say, the seluidge makes shew of the cloth. **1670** RAY 141. **1732** FULLER no. 4744.

Self-love is a mote in every man's eye. (S 218)

1597 *Politeuphuia* 4[v] Selfe-loue, the ruine of the Angels, is the confusion of men. **1616** WITHALS 564. **1639** CLARKE 254.

Self-preservation is the first law of nature. (S 219)

1613 R. DALLINGTON *Aphorisms* 160 Custom hath taught nations, and Reason men, and Nature beasts, that self-defence is alwaies lawfull. *a.* **1614** DONNE Βιαθάνατος (1644) sig. AA It is onely upon this reason, that selfe-preservation is of Naturall Law. *a.* **1678** ?MARVELL *Hodge's Vision* Self-preservation, Nature's first great law. **1681** DRYDEN *Span. Friar* IV. ii If one of you must fall, Self-preservation is the first of laws. **1822** SCOTT *Pirate* ch. 5 Triptolemus . . . had a reasonable share of that wisdom which looks towards self-preservation as the first law of nature. **1858** MRS. CRAIK *A Woman's Thoughts* 71 That 'first law of nature', self-preservation, is—doubtless, for wise purposes—imprinted pretty strongly on the mind of the male sex.

Sell for a song, To. (S 636)

1602 SHAKES. *A.W.* III. ii. 8 I know a man that had this trick of melancholy sold a goodly manor for a song. **1609** HARWARD 124[v] Unthrifts, spendthrifts, scapethrifts first sell their patrimony for a peece of an ould song. **1666** TORRIANO *Prov. Phr.* s.v. Roccrio 170 To part with his Commodities for bit of bread, for a song.

Sell his hen on a rainy day, He will not.
(H 427)

1639 CLARKE 232 I will not sell my hen i'th raine. *c.* **1641** FERGUSSON MS. no. 1575. **1721** KELLY 373 . . . You will part with nothing to your Disadvantage, for a Hen looks ill on a rainy Day. **1766** GOLDSMITH *Vicar W.* ch. 12 He knows what he is about. I'll warrant we'll never see him sell his hen of a rainy day. **1831** SCOTT *Journ.* 13 Mar. I will not sell on a rainy day, as our proverb says. **1846** DENHAM 3 Never offer your hen for sale on a rainy day.

Sell his ware after the rates of the market, A man must.
(M 284)

1584 GREENE *Wks.* Gros. iii. 224 If thou bee wise . . . make thy market while the chaffer is set to sale. **1670** RAY 23. **1732** FULLER no. 5969 You must sell as Markets go.

Sell, If it will not | it will not sour.

1721 KELLY 214 . . . Spoken when People will not give a Price for those Wares that will keep without Loss.

Sell (Buy) lawn before he can fold it, He that will | he will repent him before he have sold it.
(L 121)

[Ital. *Chi fa mercantia e no la cognosce, se trova le mane piene di mosche.*] **1546** HEYWOOD I. viii. CI. **1580** LYLY *Euph. & his Eng.* ii. 68 He that will sell lawne must learne to folde it. **1670** RAY 112 (buys).

Sell one's bacon, To.

[i.e. one's flesh or body.] **1825** CARLYLE *Schiller* III (1845) 163 To the Kaiser, therefore, I sold my bacon, And by him good charge of the whole is taken.

Sell one's birthright, To.
(B 403)

1537 Matthew's Bible, chapter-heading of GENESIS XXV Esau selleth his byrthright for a messe of potage. *a.* **1557** *Jacob and Esau* l. 623 Woulde I sell my birthright? . . . to lette it goe for a mease of pottage. **1592** NASHE *Strange News* i. 314 He will sell his birthright in learning, with Esau, for a messe of porrige. **1611** HEBREWS xii. 16 Lest there be any . . . prophane person, as Esau, who for one morsell of meat sold his birthright. **1629** T. ADAMS *Serm.* (1861–2) II. 537 There be some that *sell* their birthright: it is said of the lawyer that he hath *linguam venalem,* a saleable tongue; the covetous, *venalem animam,* a saleable soul; the harlot, *venalem carnem,* a saleable flesh.

Sell smoke, To.
(S 576)

1569 C. AGRIPPA *Vanity* (1575, 114ᵛ) The prouerbe Fumos vendere, that is, to sell smoke. **1583** MELBANCKE *Philot.* F1ᵛ He that soulde smoake, is smouldered with smoacke. **1591** ARIOSTO *Orl. Fur.* Harington XXXIII. *Allusion* Hauing taken their reward, his promise vanished into the aire like a vapour, and left the poore suters nothing but his vaine breathed words: the iust Emperour [Severus] caused him to be smothered to death with smoke, saying, Fumo

pereat, qui fumum vendidit, Let fume him choake, that selleth smoke. **1619** JOHN FAVOUR *Antiquity* 319 The Caluinist . . . sels his smoke and clouds to his Companions.

Sell the bear's (lion's) skin before one has caught the bear (lion), To. (B 132)

1578 *Courtly Controv.* N4ᵛ His eyes, greedily fixed vpon his faire Mistresse, solde vnto him (as men say) the skin before the beast is taken. **1580** LYLY *Euph. & his Eng.* ii. 53 I trusted so much, that I solde the skinne before the Beaste was taken. **1599** SHAKES. *Hen. V* IV. iii. 93 The man that once did sell the lion's skin While the beast liv'd, was kill'd with hunting him. **1662** FULLER Cornw. 196 Medina Sidonia . . . resolved [Mount-Edgecombe] for his own possession in the partage of this Kingdome[1] . . . But he had catch'd a great Cold, had he had no other Clothes to wear then those which were to be made of a skin of a Bear not yet killed. **1721** KELLY 376 You sell the Bear Skin on his Back. [[1] 1588.]

Sell the cow and sup the milk, You cannot. (C 755)

a. **1628** CARMICHAELL no. 1833. You sel the Kw and sups the milk. **1721** KELLY 379. **1732** FULLER no. 2786 If you sell the Cow, you sell her Milk too.

Sell the cow must say the word, Who will. (C 766)

1640 HERBERT no. 791.

Sell(s, ing), see also Buy and s. and live by loss; Buy at a fair, s. at home; Dust is on your feet (While), s. what have bought; Gift, (Who receives a) s. his liberty; Live by s. ware for words (One cannot); Market goes (As) wives must s.; Open your pack and s. no wares (Never); Praises who wishes to s. (He); Rather s. than be poor; Sin to s. dear (It is no), but to give ill measure; Takes gifts (She that) herself she s.; Washing his hands (For) none s. lands; Weigh justly, s. dearly.

Selthe, *see* Lith and s. are fellows.

Send and fetch. (S 223)

a. **1628** CARMICHAELL no. 1353. **1641** FERGUSSON no. 753. **1721** KELLY 288 . . . Lat. *Da, si vis accipere.*

Send him (you) to the sea and he (you) will not get (salt) water. (S 182)

1641 FERGUSSON no. 769. **1683** MERITON *Yorks. Ale* (1697) 83–7. **1721** KELLY 287 . . . Spoken when People foolishly come short of their Errand.

Send you away with a sore heart, He will never.

1721 KELLY 165 . . . Spoken of those who are ready at their Promises, but slow in their Performance.

Send, *see also* Never sigh, but s.

Send, Send a, Send not a, *see also under significant words following.*

Sends a fool, He that | expects one.
(F 488)

c. **1594** BACON no. 1547 Qui fol envoye fol attend. **1611** COTGRAVE s.v. Attendre He that imployes a foole, expects a foole. **1640** HERBERT no. 851. **1659** HOWELL *Fr. Prov.* 8.

Sends a fool, He that | means to follow him.
(F 489)

1594 LYLY *Mother B.* II. ii. 14 I sent him on my arrande, but I must goe for an answere my selfe. **1611** COTGRAVE s.v. Fol He that imployes a foole may follow him for companie. **1640** HERBERT no. 51. **1659** HOWELL *Eng. Prov.* 3b Who sendeth a fool upon an errand, must goe himself after.

Senhouse, Dick, *see* Spite of the devil and D. S.

Senseless, *see* Block, Dull (S.) as a.

Sentence, *see* Judge, (From a foolish) a quick s.

September blow soft till fruit be in loft.
(S 224)

1573 TUSSER ch. 15 Ei Septembre blowe soft, Till fruite be in loft. **1732** FULLER no. 6214. **1928** *Daily Mail* 3 Sept. 10/2 'September blow soft till the apple's in the loft' is what we desire of this traditionally beautiful month.

Sepulchre, *see* Flatterer's throat is open s.

Sermon, *see also* Salmon and s. have season in Lent.

Serpent has bitten, Whom a | a lizard alarms.
(A 33)

1666 TORRIANO *It. Prov.* 257 no. 1 *Whom an adder bites, dreads a lyzard.* **1853** TRENCH iii. 70.

Serpent, A | unless it has devoured a serpent, does not become a dragon.
(S 228)

[ERASM. *Ad.* Ὄφις εἰ μὴ φάγοι ὄφιν, δράκων οὐ γενήσεται. Serpens, ni edat serpentem, draco non fiet.] **1598** BARCKLEY *Fel. Man* V. 396 There hath beene a common saying: Serpens, ni serpentem edat, draco non fiet. Vnhappy are they that make the miseries of others riches to themselues. **1611** JONSON *Catiline* III. l. 523 A serpent, ere he comes to be a dragon, Do's eate a bat. **1613** BEAUM. & FL. *Honest Man's Fort.* III. i. The snake that would be a dragon and have wings, must eat. **1625** BACON *Ess., Fortune* Arb. 375 No Man prospers so suddenly, as by Others Errours. *Serpens nisi Serpentem comederit non fit Draco.* **1679** DRYDEN *Oedipus* III. i. A serpent ne'er becomes a flying dragon, Till he has eat a serpent.

Serpent than the dove, To have more of the.
[MATT. X. 16 Be ye therefore wise as serpents, and harmless as doves.] *c.* **1592** MARLOWE *Jew of Malta* II. iii. 36 Now will I show myself To have more of the serpent than the dove; That is—more knave than fool. **1642** D. ROGERS *Naaman* 210 Many professors defile the ointment of sweete Christianity, with their overmuch pollicy.... They put more of the Serpent, then the Dove into the confection. **1910** A. M. FAIRBAIRN *Stud. Relig. & Theol.* 167 If Lightfoot had had more of the serpent and less of the dove in him, he would have kept clear himself of the Clementine literature.

Serpent, *see also* Bitten by a s. afraid of rope; Old S.; Strike s.'s head with enemy's hand; Tongue stings (is more venomous than s.'s sting); Trail of the s.

Servant and a cock must be kept but a year, A.
1706 STEVENS s.v. Gallo. **1732** FULLER no. 389.

Servant before one can be a master, One must be a. *Cf.* Good ruler. (S 237)
1592 DELAMOTHE 41 In seruing well, and being faithfull, one may become of a good seruaunt, a good master. **1616** DRAXE no. 1941. **1629** *Bk. Mer. Rid. Prov.* no. 81 He that hath not serued knoweth not how to command.

Servant has two, He that has one | he that has two has but half a one, and he that has three has none at all. (S 234)
1543 G. COUSIN *Office of Seruants* B8ᵛ. **1666** TORRIANO *It. Prov.* 258 no. 9.

Servant is known by his master's absence, A.
(S 238)
1595 PLAUTUS *Menaechmi* tr. w.w. v. The proofe of a good servant, is to regard his maisters businesse as well in his absence, as in his presence. **1642** TORRIANO 78. **1659** HOWELL *It. Prov.* 12. **1732** FULLER no. 390.

Servant must come when you call him, A good | go when you bid him, and shut the door after him. (S 232)
1609 HARWARD 115 Servants dutyes. Do what I say, comme when I call and shutt the dores after thee, especially rule thy tongue well. **1628** HOWELL *Let.* I. v. 13, I. 264 (will come). **1738** SWIFT *Dial.* I. E.L. 290 (Remember, that a good servant must always come when he's called, do what he's bid, and).

Servant, He that has no | must serve himself.
c. **1386** CHAUCER *Reeve's* [T. l. 4027 Hym boes[1] serve hym-self that has na swayn, Or elles he is a fool, as clerkes sayn. **1659** HOWELL *Brit. Prov.* 2 Who so cannot endure a servant, must be his owne servant. [[1] behoves.]

Servant, A good | should have the back of an ass, the tongue of a sheep, and the snout of a swine. *Cf.* Travel through the world.   (s 233)

1589 L. WRIGHT *Display of Dutie* 37 It is required in a good seruant, to haue the backe of an Asse, to beare all things patiently: the tongue of a sheepe, to keepe silence gently: and the snout of a swyne, to feede on all things heartily.   **1593** G. HARVEY Pierce's *Supererogation* 166 The wisest Oeconomy maketh especiall account of three singular members, a marchants eare; a pigges mouth; and an Asses backe.   **1595** LYLY *Woman in Moon* I. i. 169 I see that seruants must haue Marchants eares.

Servant, A good | should never be in the way and never out of the way.

[Said by Chas. II of Sidney Godolphin: *see* LEAN III. 289.]   **1896** F. LOCKER-LAMPSON *My Confid.* 403 Margaret, . . . was . . . a good servant (never in and never out of the way).

Servant, If you would have a good | take neither a kinsman nor a friend.   (s 236)

a. **1598** BURGHLEY *Ten Precepts* Be not served with kinsmen, or friends, . . . for they expect much and do little.   **1640** HERBERT no. 794 A kinsman, a friend, or whom you entreate, take not to serve you, if you will be served neately.   **1642** TORRIANO 92 Never intreat a servant to dwell with thee, intertain not a kinsman or a friend into thy service, if thou meanest to be well served.

Servants make the worst masters.

1902–4 LEAN IV. 93.

Servants (Slaves), So many | so many enemies.   (s 242)

[CATO *Quot servi, tot hostes.*]   **1539** TAVERNER 34 *Quot seruos habemus, totidem habemus hostes.* Loke how many bondmen we haue and so many enemyes we haue.   **1543** G. COUSIN *Office of Servants* B2 That prouerbe . . ., As many slaues so many ennemies.   **1581** GUAZZO ii. 101 We have so many enemies as we have servantes.   **1603** MONTAIGNE (Florio) II. viii. 110 Old Cato was wont to say, So many servants, so many enemies.   **1869** LECKY *Hist. Eur. Mor.* (1905) I. ii. 302 The servile wars . . . had shaken Italy to the centre, and the shock was felt in every household. 'As many enemies as slaves', had become a Roman proverb.   **1892** BP. LIGHTFOOT *Philemon* 320 The universal distrust had already found expression in a common proverb, 'As many enemies as slaves'. [*Note.*—Senec. *Ep. Mor.* 47 '. . . totidem hostes esse quot servos'.]

Servant(s), *see also* Beg of . . . a beggar (Neither) nor serve s.; Choose none for thy s. who have served betters; Common s. no man's s.; Give little to his s. (He can) that licks his knife; Grandfather's s. never good; Ill s. never good master; Master and s., (Every one is); Master of straw eat s. of steel; Money is good s.; No silver no s.; Pay not a s. his wages (If you), will pay himself; Saturday s. never stay, Sunday s. run away; Sleepy master, s. a lout; Smiling boy seldom good s.; Spaniard is bad s.

Serve a great man, and you will know what sorrow is.

1706 STEVENS s.v. Señor.

Serve a noble disposition, though poor, the time comes that he will repay thee.   (D 382)

1611 COTGRAVE s.v. Bon He that serues a good master looks for a good reward.   **1640** HERBERT no. 368.

Serve the devil for God's sake, To.

1820 SCOTT *Abbot* ch. 24 Do you suppose I would betray my mistress, because I see cause to doubt of her religion?—that would be a serving, as they say, the devil for God's sake.

Serve the tod[1], As long as you | you must bear up his tail.   (T 366)

1641 FERGUSSON no. 112 As long as ye serve the tod, ye man bear up his tail.   **1721** KELLY 26 . . . When you have engaged in any Man's Service, you must not think yourself too good for anything he employs you in. [[1] fox.]

Served, He that will be | must be patient.   (s 247)

1640 HERBERT no. 354.

Served, He that would be well | must know when to change his servants.

1707 MAPLETOFT 27.

Served, If you would be well | serve yourself. *Cf.* Thou canst do it. Want a thing well done.   (s 248)

1659 TORRIANO no. 145 Who hath a mind to any thing let him go himself, if not let him send.   **1706** STEVENS s.v. Querer.   **1869** J. E. AUSTEN-LEIGH *Mem. of Jane Austen* 35 (quoted as a homely proverb).

Serves God for money, He that | will serve the devil for better wages. (G 234)

1692 L'ESTRANGE *Aesop's Fab.* cv (1738) 121 (the old saying).

Serves God, serves a good master, He who.   (G 235)

1611 COTGRAVE s.v. Maistre The seruant of God hath a good maister.   *c.* **1641** FERGUSSON MS. no. 575.   **1853** TRENCH vi. 146.

Serves, He that | must serve.   (s 245)

1640 HERBERT no. 786.   **1659** HOWELL *Fr. Prov.* 11 He serveth ill, Who serve's not thoroughly.

Serves the poor with a thump on the
back with a stone, He.   (P 467)

1678 RAY 90 *A covetous person.* . . .

Serves the people, He who | serves
nothing.   (P 226. S 244)

1573 SANFORD 103ᵛ (the Common wealthe,
serueth none). **1578** FLORIO *First F.* 29 (the
commons serueth no body). **1606–7** SHAKES.
A.C. I. ii. 179 Our slippery people, Whose love
is never link'd to the deserver Till his deserts are
past. **1611** COTGRAVE *s.v.* Servir The seruant
of a Comminaltie finds enow to correct his
errors, but none to reward his deserts. **1611**
DAVIES no. 237 Who serues the People nothing
serues. **1642** TORRIANO 20 He who serveth all
men, hath wages of no man. **1706** STEVENS *s.v.*
Comun He that does any thing for the Publick,
does it for no body.

Serves well, He that | needs not (be
afraid to) ask his wages.   (W 2)

1640 HERBERT no. 798. **1732** FULLER no. 2296
(be afraid to).

Serve(s, d), *see also* After a sort, as Costlet s. the
King; Altar, (He that s. at the) ought to live by
the altar; Beg of . . . a beggar (Neither) nor s.
servant; Every man will have his own turn s.;
First come, first s.; Good master shall have good
wages, (He that s. a); Many a man s. thankless
master; Master must s.; No man can s. two
masters; Pay beforehand never well s.; Youth
will be s.

Service a child does his father is to make
him foolish, The first.   (S 249)

1640 HERBERT no. 463.

Service is no inheritance.   (S 253)

1412 HOCCLEVE *Reg. of Princes* E.E.T.S. 31 l. 841
Seruyse, I wot well, is non heritage. *a.* **1500**
15c. School-Bk. ed. W. Nelson 61. **1509** BAR-
CLAY *Ship of Fools* i. 106 Thus worldly seruyce
is no sure herytage. **1602** SHAKES. *A.W.* I. iii.
25 In Isbel's case and mine own. Service is no
heritage. **1631** BRATHWAIT *Whimzies* (1859) 98
But service is no inheritance, lest therefore . . .
he should grow weary of his place, or his place
of him; . . . he begins to store up against winter.
1721 KELLY 298 . . . An Argument for Servants
to seek out for some Settlement. **1824** SCOTT
S . Ronan's ch. 10 '[You] call yourself the friend
and servant of our family'. . . . 'Ay, . . . —but
service is nae inheritance; and as for friendship,
it begins at hame.' **1830** MARRYAT *King's Own*
ch. 10 There was a club established for servants
out of place. . . . Our seal was a bunch of green
poplar rods, with 'Service is no inheritance' as
a motto.

Service to the king's, No.   (S 251)

1484 CAXTON *Chartier's Curial* E.E.T.S. 19 Ne
seruyse lyke to the kyng souerayn. *c.* **1580** G.
HARVEY *Marginalia* (1913) 142 No fisshing to
yᵉ Sea . nor seruice to A King. **1618** N. BRETON
Courtier & Countryman Wks. Gros. ii. 10
Though there is no service to the King, nor no

fishing to the Sea, yet there are [&c.]. **1639**
CLARKE 98. [*See also quotations under* Fishing
to fishing *in the sea.*]

Service without reward is punishment.
                                          (S 254)

1616 DRAXE no. 1942. **1640** HERBERT no. 1015.

Service, *see also* Child's s. is little, yet fool that
despises; Good s. great enchantment; Proffered
s. stinks; Trade is better than s.; Yeoman's s.

Serving-man, *see* Old s., young beggar; Young s.,
old beggar.

Sesame, *see* Open S.

Set a person on his legs, To.

1624 SANDERSON *Serm.* i. 251 Set him upon his
legs and make him a man for ever. **1679–1715**
SOUTH *Serm.* 2 fin. The excellency of Christian
religion . . . to set fallen man upon his legs again.

Set (Fall together) by the ears, To.
                                          (E 23)

[= to put or be at variance.] **1530** TYNDALE
Practise of Prelates P.S. 266 This Lewis left
three sons, . . . which . . . fell together (as we say)
by the ears. **1539** TAVERNER 2 *Garden* C5ᵛ He
[Cambyses] set a yonge lyon and a very eger
dogge togither by the eares. **1542** ERASM. tr. Udall
Apoph. (1877, 27). **1546** HEYWOOD II. i. F4
Togyther by the eares they come (quoth I)
cherely. **1553** T. WILSON *Arte of Rhet.* (1909) 37
When is the law profitable? Assuredly, . . .
especially in this age, when all men goe together
by the eares, for this matter, and that matter.
1602 SHAKES. *A.W.* I. ii. 1 The Florentines and
Senoys are by the ears. **1603** KNOLLES *Hist.
Turkes* 1184 They fell together by the eares
about the matter. **1608** SHAKES. *C.* I. i. 231 Were
half to half the world by the ears . . . I'd revolt.
1636 S. WARD *Serm.* (1862) 77 The devil . . .
threw in these bones to set us together by the
ears. **1725** DEFOE *Voy. round W.* (1840) 67 They
would fall together by the ears about who should
go with you. **1868** G. DUFF *Pol. Surv.* (1868) 40
Does it [Turkey] fancy that it will obtain security
for itself by setting Greek and Bulgarian by the
ears?

Set in, *see* Time to s. i. when oven comes to
dough.

Set not your loaf in till the oven's hot.

1732 FULLER no. 4110.

Set one's cap at, To.

[Said of a woman who sets herself to gain the
affections of a man.] **1772** R. GRAVES *Spiritual
Quix.* III. x. I know several young ladies who
would be very happy in such an opportunity of
setting their caps at him. **1788** GROSE *s.v.* Cap
Acquaintance A woman who endeavours to
attract the notice of any particular man, is said
to set her cap at him. **1822** BYRON *Juan* xi.
lxxx Some, who once set their caps at cautious
dukes. **1848** THACKERAY *Vanity F.* ch. 3 That
girl is setting her cap at you.

Set one's face like a flint, To.   (F 18)

[= firmly, steadfastly.] [ISAIAH I. 7. There-fore have I set my face like a flint, and I know that I shall not be ashamed.] **1586** J. OVERTON *Jacob's Journey* 60 The wicked . . . haue set their hartes as hard as an adamant stone, and made their faces like flint to do al kinde of mischiefe. **1688** BUNYAN *Wk. of Jesus Christ* Wks. (1855) I. 180 He . . . sets his face like a flint to plead for me with God. **1859** KINGSLEY *Misc.* (1860) I. 321 Set his face like a flint.

Set one's house on fire only to roast one's eggs (to run away by the light of it), To.   (H 757. 783)

1530 PALSGRAVE 710b I can do some thyng, for I can set a house a fyre and ronne awaye by the lyght, whan I have done. **1584** A. MUNDAY *Watchword to England* 37a What were it else, but to set a house on fire, and run away by the light. **1612** BACON *Ess., Of Wisdom* Arb. 186 And certainely it is the nature of extreme selfe louers, as they will set an house on fire, and it were but to rost their egges. **1629** T. ADAMS *Serm.* (1861–2) II. 259 They . . . would set their neighbour's house on fire and it were but to roast their own eggs. **1692** L'ESTRANGE *Aesop's Fab.* clxviii (1738) 181 Those that . . . set their country afire for the roasting their own eggs. **1751** FRANKLIN Jan. Pray don't burn my House to roast your Eggs. **1858** TRELAWNEY *Recollections* ch. 7.

Set the Thames on fire, To.

[= to do something remarkable.] **1778** FOOTE *Trip Calais* III. iii Matt Minnikin . . . an honest burgoise, . . . won't set fire to the Thames. **1785** GROSE *Dict. Vulg. T.* s.v. Thames He will not find out a way to set the Thames on fire; he will not make any wonderful discoveries. **1863** KINGSLEY *Water Bab.* ch. 8 The Pantheon of the Great Unsuccessful, . . . in which . . . projectors [lecture] on the discoveries which ought to have set the Thames on fire. **1909** *T.L.S.* 27 Aug. The vast majority . . . are decidedly unimaginative . . . The Thames will never be set on fire . . . by the . . . [Masonic] Grand Lodge of England.

Set their horses together, They cannot.   (H 717)

1608 DAY *Law Tricks* I. ii Souldiers and Scollers could neuer set their horses together, especially in this kicking age. **1639** CLARKE 94 (i' th' same stable). **1670** RAY 181. **1697** W. POPE *Life of Seth* [Ward] 40 Impossible for those two, as the saying is, to set their Horses together.

Set trees at Allhallontide[1] and command them to prosper: set them after Candlemas[2] and entreat them to grow.   (A 299)

1656–91 J. AUBREY *Nat. Hist. Wilts* (1847) 105. **1678** RAY 52 . . . This Dr. J. Beal alledgeth as an old English and Welch Proverb, concerning Apple and Pear-trees, Oak and Hawthorn quicks. **1822** SCOTT *Letter* 15 May in LOCKHART *Life* ch. 56 Except evergreens, I would never transplant a tree betwixt March and Martinmas. . . . Plant a tree before Candlemas, and *command* it to grow—plant it after Candlemas, and you must *entreat* it. [[1] All Hallows'-tide, the season of All Saints, the first week in November. [2] Feast of Purif. of Virg. Mary, 2 Feb.]

Set trees poor and they will grow rich, set them rich and they will grow poor.   (T 510)

1678 RAY 350 . . . Remove them always out of a more barren into a fatter soil.

Set up (in) one's staff (of rest), To.   (S 804)

[To settle down in a place, take up one's abode. Another meaning of 'To set up one's rest', not illustrated here, is 'to stake one's all', a metaphor from the card-game of primero. Occasionally both meanings are intended.] **1573** HARVEY *Letter-Book* Camden Soc. 4 He hath set down his staf, and made his reckning. **1592–3** SHAKES. *C.E.* III. i. 51 Have at you with a proverb: Shall I set in my staff? *c.* **1595** *Id. R.J.* V. iii. 110 O! here Will I set up my everlasting rest. **1594** NASHE *Unf. Trav.* ii. 232 Heere I was in good hope to set vpp my staffe for some reasonable time. **1609** BODLEY *Life* (1647) 15 I concluded at the last to set up my Staffe at the Library doore in Oxford. **1815** SCOTT *Guy Man.* ch. 19 Here, then, Mannering resolved, for some time at least, to set up the staff of his rest. **1860** TROLLOPE *Framley P.* ch. 48 They appeared in London and there set up their staff.

Set your heart at rest.   (H 327)

1595 SHAKES. *M.N.D.* II. i. 121. **1670** RAY 190.

Set your wit against a child, Don't.   (W 547)

1738 SWIFT *Dial.* I. E.L. 265 Why so hard upon poor miss? Don't set your wit against a child.

Set, *see also* Beans in the wane of the moon, (S.); Saddle, (To s. one beside the); Sow dry and s. wet.

Set (a, the), *see also under significant words following.*

Settling an island, In | the first building erected by a Spaniard will be a church; by a Frenchman, a fort; by a Dutchman, a warehouse; and by an Englishman, an alehouse.

1787 GROSE (*Glos., Eng.*) 149.

Seven deadly sins.

1340 *Ayenbite* 9 Lecheire . . . is one of þe ʒeuen dyadliche ʒennes. *c.* **1386** CHAUCER *Parson's T.* l. 387 Now is it bihovely thyng to telle whiche been the sevene deedly synnes, this is to seyn, chieftaynes of synnes. **1604** SHAKES. *M.M.* III. i. 111 Sure it is no sin; Or of the deadly seven it is the least. *a.* **1711** KEN *Hymnotheo* Poet. Wks. (1721) III. 269 The seven curs'd deadly Sins. . . . Pride, Envy, Sloth, Intemp'rance, Av'rice, Ire, And Lust.

Seven hours' sleep will make a clown (the husbandman) forget his design.

1732 FULLER no. 4112. 1846 DENHAM 5 (the husbandman).

Seven Sleepers.

a. 1633 DONNE *The Good-Morrow* Or snorted we in the Seven Sleepers' den? 1837 CARLYLE *Fr. Rev.* II. III. i. The whole French people . . . bounce up . . . like amazed Seven-sleepers awakening. 1861 H. KINGSLEY *Ravenshoe* ch. 38 He made noise enough to waken the seven sleepers. 1869 S. BARING-GOULD *Cur. Myths* 101 The Seven Sleepers of Ephesus, who had been slumbering two hundred years in a cavern of Mount Celion, . . . had . . . turned themselves over on their left sides.

Seven years, This.   (Y 25)

[For a long period.] [1475–1500] 1572 *Rauf Coilyear* l. 725, 25 Thair suld n' man be sa wyse, To gar me cum to Parise, To luke quhair the King lyis, In faith, this seuin yeir! 1533 SIR T. MORE *Debellation* 1557 ed. 936b And he seeke thys seuen yere, he shall . . . fynde you no suche wordes of mine. 1546 HEYWOOD II. v. H3ᵛ This seven yeres, daie and night to watche a bowle. 1599 SHAKES. *A.Y.* III. ii. 298 Time's pace is so hard that it seems the length of seven year. 1674 J. HOWARD *Eng. M.* II. 25 I have not seen you this seven years. 1778 MISS BURNEY *Evelina* Lett. 23 I don't think I shall speak to you again these seven years.

Seven(s), *see also* All in the s. (It is); Keep a thing s. years; Man may lose more in an hour than he can get in s.; Sixes and s.

Seventh heaven, The.

[= a state of bliss.] [By the Jews seven heavens were recognized, the highest being the abode of God and the highest angels.] 1824 SCOTT *St. Ronan's* ch. 26 He looked upon himself as approaching to the seventh heaven. 1844 KINGLAKE *Eothen* ch. 17 The Sheik . . . rolled his eyes . . . between every draught, as though the drink . . . had come from the seventh heaven. 1833 RITA *After Long Grief* ch. 22 Lady Ramsey was in the seventh heaven of delight.

Severity is better than gentleness, Sometimes.   (S 258)

1609 HARWARD 90ᵛ Gentlenesse will do more then rigour. 1616 DRAXE no. 1947. 1664 CODRINGTON 210.

Severn, Fix thy pale in | Severn will be as before.   (P 36a)

1662 FULLER Montgom. 46 'Fixt thy pale (with intent to force out his water) in Severn, Severn will be as before'. Appliable to such who undertake projects above their power to perform, or grapple in vain against Nature.

Severn, *see also* Blessed is the eye betwixt S. and Wye; Sip up the S. as soon.

Seville, He who has not seen | has not seen a wonder.

1706 STEVENS s.v. Sevilla. 1748 SMOLLETT tr. *Gil. Blas* X. x. (1907) II. 269 Thou wilt not be sorry to see that capital of Andalusia. He that hath not Seville seen (saith the proverb[1]) Is no traveller, I ween. [¹ Quien no ha visto a Sevilla, No ha visto maravilla.]

Sew(ed), *see* Little to s. when tailors true; Pillows under the elbows, (To s.); Tailor that s. for nothing.

Sexton has shaked his shoo[1] at him, The.

1917 BRIDGE 120 . . . Said of any one who is ill and not likely to get better. [¹ shovel or spade.]

Sexton is a fatal musician, The. (S 260)

1626 BRETON *Soothing* A3ᵛ. 1639 CLARKE 215.

Shade, *see* Fruit ripens not well in s.

Shadow(s), *see* Afraid of his own s.; Catch not at the s.; Coming events cast their s.; Every light has its s.; Fight with s.; Follow one like one's s.; Hair so small but has s. (No); Life is a s.; Old wise man's s. better than buzzard's sword; Praise is the reflexion (s.) of virtue; Staff be crooked (If) s. cannot be straight; Sun is highest (When the) he casts the least s.; Sun without s. (No); Ware, knave, quoth Tomkins to his s.

Shaft[1] or a bolt[2] of it, I will make a.   (S 264)

[= I will take the risk, whatever may come of it.] 1594 NASHE *Terror of Night* i. 368 To make a shaft or a bolt of this drumbling subject of dreames. 1600–1 SHAKES. *M.W.W.* III. iv. 24 I'll make a shaft or a bolt on 't. 'Slid, 'tis but venturing. 1608 MIDDLETON *Trick to Catch* II. i. I'll quickly make a bolt or a shaft on 't. 1687 R. L'ESTRANGE *Answ. Dissenter* 46 One might have made a Bolt or a Shaft on 't. 1819 SCOTT *Ivanhoe* ch. 27 footnote Hence the English proverb 'I will either make . . .'. [¹ arrow for a longbow. ² arrow for a cross-bow.]

Shaft, *see also* Pig's tail (Of) never make good s.

Shake a bridle over a Yorkshire tike's grave, and he'll rise again.   (B 669)

1677 *Smithfield Jockey* 4 (Hence grew the Proverb; Shake a). 1787 GROSE (*Yorks.*) 235 . . . An allusion to the fondness for horses, shown by almost every native of this county. 1822 SCOTT *Pirate* ch. 4 His father observed that Trip could be always silenced by jingling a bridle at his ear. From which he used to swear . . . that the boy would prove true Yorkshire.

Shake a Leicestershire man by the collar, and you shall hear the beans rattle in his belly.   (M 372)

15th cent. *Rel. Antiq.* (1841) i. 269 Leicesterschir, full of benys. 1613–22 DRAYTON *Polyolb.* xxiii.

265 (1876) III. 95 *Bean belly, Lestershire* her attribute doth bear. **1662** FULLER Leic. 126 But those Yeomen smile at what is said to rattle in their bellies, whilst . . . good silver ringeth in their Pockets. **1818** SCOTT *Ht. Midl.* ch. 29 An ye touch her, I'll gie ye a shake by the collar shall make the Leicester beans rattle. **1881** A. B. EVANS *Leicest. Wds.* 299 'Shake a Leicestershire man by the collar, and you shall hear the beans rattle in his belly' . . . is still current, as is also the answer . . .; 'Yoi, lad, but 'ew doo'st?'

Shake a loose (free) leg, To.

[= to lead an irregular life, live freely.] **1834** AINSWORTH *Rookwood* III. ix. (1878) 233 While luck lasts, the highwayman shakes a loose leg! **1856** MAYHEW *Gt. World Lond.* 87 Those who love to 'shake a free leg', and lead a roving life, as they term it. **1876** MRS. BANKS *Manch. Man* ch. 28 It was doubly satisfactory to find the comforts of their home appreciated . . . and to be able to refute Mr. Ashton's theory that 'all young men like to shake a loose leg'.

Shake in one's shoes, To.

1818 COBBETT *Polit. Reg.* XXXIII. 497 This is quite enough to make Corruption and all her tribe shake in their shoes. **1889** R. L. STEVENSON *Mast. of Ball.* ch. 9 Any face of death will set me shaking in my shoes.

Shake the dust off one's feet, To.

[MATT. x. 14.] **1553** T. BECON *Jewel of Joy* P.S. 419.

Shake the elbow, To.   (E 101)

[= to play at dice.] **1623** WEBSTER *Devil's Law-Case* II. i. 178 This comes of your . . . Shaking your elbow at the Taule-board. **1699** *Dict. of Canting Crew.* s.v. Elbow He lives by shaking of the Elbow; a Gamester. **1705** HEARNE *Collect.* 26 Nov. (1885–6) I. 100 Money which . . . he squander'd away in shaking his elbow. **1826** J. WILSON *Noct. Ambr.* Wks. (1855) I. 127 Many good and great men have shook the elbow.

Shake the pagoda[1] tree, To.

[= to make a fortune rapidly in India.] **1836** T. HOOK *G. Gurney* I. 45 The amusing pursuit of 'shaking the pagoda-tree' once so popular in our oriental possessions. **1912** *Spectator* 17 Feb. 273 Rennell['s] . . . contemporaries had won handsome fortunes by 'shaking the Pagoda Tree', by the private trade that then was permitted to John Company's servants. [[1] Indian gold coin.]

Shake your ears (heels), You may go and.   (E 16)

[= to show contempt or displeasure.] **1537** *Comparison between the Old Learning and the New* A2ᵛ Let the heretikes go and shake theyr cares, with theyr new learnynge. **1573** G. HARVEY *Letter-bk.* Camden Soc. 42 As for gentle M. Gawber, his Mastership may go shake his eares elsewhere. **1581** N. WOODES *Conflict of Conscience* C2ᵛ Goe shake your eares both, like slaues as your be. bee. **1601** SHAKES. *T.N.* II. iii. 116 She [my lady] shall know of it, by this hand. —Go shake your ears. **1620** SHELTON *Quix.* II. i.

ii. 196. *c.* **1645** HOWELL *Lett.* (1655) I, § i. xxi. 32 They shut their Gates against him, and made him go shake his ears, and to shift for his lodging. **1690** D'URFEY *Collin's W.* iv. 177 If this be true as it appears, Why dost not rouse and shake thy Ears? **1813** RAY 215 . . . Spoken to one who has lost his money.

Shake(s), *see also* All that s. falls not.

Shaking of the sheets, To dance the.

a. **1577** *Misogonus* II. iv. 272. **1579** GOSSON 33. **1602** [T. HEYWOOD?] *How a Man may Choose* Hazl.-Dods. ix. 41 Now, come, let's dance the shaking of the sheets. [**1603**] **1607** T. HEYWOOD *Woman Killed with Kindness* I. i. 2. **1604** *Meeting of Gallants* (DEKKER *Plague Pamphlets* 125). *c.* **1608** D. BARRY *Ram Alley* Hazl.-Dods. x. 365.

Shallow streams (waters) make most din.   (W 130)

1576 SIDNEY *Lady of May* Feuillerat iii. 233 Shallow brookes do yeeld the greatest sound. *c.* **1580** *Id.* I *Arcadia* iv. 54 Shallow brookes murmur moste, Depe sylent slyde away. **1594** SHAKES. *Lucrece* l. 1329 Deep sounds make lesser noise than shallow fords. **1657** W. LONDON *Catalogue of the most vendable books* D1 They are the shallowest Rivers which make the greatest noise. **1721** KELLY 289 Shaal[1] Waters make the greatest Sound. And empty Fellows make the greatest Noise. **1832** HENDERSON 90. [[1] shallow.]

Shallow, *see also* Water is s. (Where), no vessel will ride.

Sham Abra(ha)m, To.

[Orig. *Naut. slang* = to feign sickness.] **1752** *Gentl. Mag.* Mar. 140/2 As he [Capt. Lowry] went along some sailors cry'd out . . . that He must not sham Abram (a cant sea phrase when a sailor is unwilling to work on pretence of sickness . . .). **1760** GOLDSMITH *Cit. World* cxix The boatswain . . . swore . . . that I shammed Abraham merely to be idle. **1827** SCOTT *Surg. Dau.* ch. 6 It's good enough . . . for a set of lubbers, that lie shamming Abraham. **1863** C. READE *Hard Cash* ch. 31 He's shamming Abraham.

Shame fall on him that speers[1] and kens sae weel.

1691 J. WILSON *Belphegor* v. ii. (1874) 372 What are ye?—Shame fa' him that speers and kens sae weel. [[1] inquires.]

Shame fall the gear and the blad'ry[1] o't.

1721 KELLY 296 . . . The Turn of an old Scottish Song, spoken when a young, handsome Girl marries an old Man, upon the account of his Wealth. [[1] trumpery.]

Shame in a kindred cannot be avoided.   (S 273)

1636 CAMDEN 305.

Shame is past the shedd[1] of your hair.
(s 275)

1578 ROLLAND *Seven Sages* S.T.S. l. 1188, 44 Schame is past the sched of thair hair, as weill we knaw. *a.* 1628 CARMICHAELL no. 1402. 1641 FERGUSSON no. 768. 1721 KELLY 287 . . . Spoken to People impudent, and past blushing. [1 parting.]

Shameful (Shameless) craving must have shameful nay.
(c 808)

c. 1549 HEYWOOD I. xi. D3[v] (Shameful). 1611 DAVIES no. 377. 1670 RAY 141 (Shameless).

Shameful leaving is worse than shameful eating.

1721 KELLY 63. 1894 NORTHALL *Folk Phrases* E.D.S. 22.

Shames, He that | shall be shent. (s 282)

a. 1628 CARMICHAELL no. 749. 1641 FERGUSSON no. 348. 1721 KELLY 159 (let him be shent) . . . A Wish that he who exposes his Neighbour, may come to shame himself.

Shame take him, *see* Ill be to him . . . [*Honi soi qui mal y pense*].

Shame to steal, It is a | but a worse to carry home. (s 269)

c. 1570 *Marr. Wit and Science* IV. i. C3[v] You must aduenture both, spare to speake, spare to speede, What tell you me of shame, it is shame to steale a horse. 1639 CLARKE 190 (but a greater shame to bring again). 1670 RAY 141. 1732 FULLER no. 2875.

Shame, *see also* Better die with honour than live with s.; Loss embraces s.; Past s. past amendment; Poverty is not a s.; Pride goes before, s. comes after; Pride rides, s. lacqueys; Single long, s. at length.

Shank's (Shanks's) mare (nag, pony).

[= one's own legs as a means of conveyance.] *a.* 1628 CARMICHAELL no. 1711 Ye are fairdie,[1] ye bread[2] of Henrie Schanks meirs.[3] *a.* 1774 FERGUSSON *Poems* (1808) 333 And auld shanks-naig wad tire, I dread, To pace to Berwick. 1785 GROSE To ride shanks naggy, to travel on foot. (Scotch). *a.* 1795 S. BISHOP *Poet. Wks.* (1796) I. 204 I'd rather . . . ride on Shanks's mare. 1359 G. A. SALA *Twice Round Clock* (1878) 87 The humbler conveyances known as 'Shanks's mare', and the 'Marrowbone Stage'—in more refined language, walking. 1898 WATTS-DUNTON *Aylwin* XII. iii. I'll start for Carnarvon on Shanks's pony. |[1 active. 2 breed. 3 mares.]

Shape a coat for the moon, You may as soon. (c 475)

1647 N. WARD *Simple Cobbler* 27 He that makes Coates for the Moone, had need take measure every noone. 1656 *Trepan* 34 I conclude with her Religion, which to tell you what it is, were to shape a Coat for the Moon. 1678 RAY 260.

Shape coat and sark[1] for them, We can | but we cannot shape their weird.

1721 KELLY 356 . . . Spoken when People of good Education fall into Misfortunes, or come to untimely Ends. 1832 HENDERSON 3 We can shape our bairns' wyliecoat,[2] but canna shape their weird. (We can shape our children's clothes, but not their fate.) [1 shirt. 2 a flannel vest.]

Shape (*noun*), *see* Good s. is in shears' mouth; Lick into s.

Shapes (*verb*), *see also* God makes and man s.; God s. back for burden.

Shapes as Proteus, As many. (s 285)

[A sea-deity of many shapes.] *c.* 1370 CHAUCER *Romaunt of the Rose* l. 6319 For Protheus, that cowde hym chaunge, In every shap homely and straunge. *c.* 1550 T. BECON *Diversity Prayers* P.S. 488 Proteus neuer turned himself into as many fashions as that antichrist of Rome did. 1591 SHAKES. *3 Hen. VI* III. ii. 192 I can . . . change shapes with Proteus. 1600 *Sir J. Old-castle* I. ii. I have as many shapes as Proteus had. 1761 CHURCHILL *Rosciad* Wks. (1868) 14 The Proteus shifts, bawd, parson, auctioneer.

Share and share alike (some all, some never a whit). (s 286)

1571 R. EDWARDS *Damon & Pythias* l. 1727 Ley vs into the Courte to parte the spoyle, share and share like. 1611 COTGRAVE s.v. Escot Whereat euerie guest payes his part, or share and share like. 1616 WITHALS 562 Share and share like, some all, some neuer a whit. 1817 EDGEWORTH *Ormond* ch. 25 The woman . . . was dividing the prize among the *lawful owners*, 'share and share alike'.

Share not pears with your master, either in jest or in earnest. *Cf.* Peas with the king.
(c 280)

1611 COTGRAVE s.v. Seigneur He that eats Peares with his Lord, picks none of the best. 1659 HOWELL *Span. Prov.* 5. 1706 STEVENS s.v. Burlas. 1732 FULLER no. 4117.

Share (*noun*), *see* God oft has s. in house; Lion's s.

Shares honey with the bear, He who | has the least part of it. (H 551)

1601 FULBECKE *Parallel Civ. Law* I. v. 28[v] According to the common prouerbe, a man should deuide honie with a Beare. 1642 TORRIANO 19. 1659 HOWELL *It. Prov.* 10. 1732 FULLER no. 2403.

Shark, *see* Dover s.

Sharp as a needle, As. (N 95)

a. 1000 *Souls Address* 120 O.E.D. 3ifⱦr hatte se wyrm, þe þa eaȝlas beoð nædle scearpran. 1552 HULOET *Abced.* 2E1 Sharpe lyke a nedle. 1843 SURTEES *Handley Cross* ch. 7. 1902 DOBSON *Richardson* 31 She [Pamela] is only fifteen, but she is as sharp as a needle.

Sharp as a razor, As.   (R 36)

c. **1370** CHAUCER *Romaunt of the Rose* l. 1885
Kene grounde as ony rasour. **1519** HORMAN
Vulg. f. 277 My wodknyfe is as sharp as a rasur.
1530 TYNDALE *Supper of the Lord* P.S. 249.
1611 DAVIES *Prov.* no. 381 (keene).   **1771** WESLEY
Letters v. 249 Not so sharp as razors.

Sharp (keen) as vinegar, As.   (V 63)

1601 SHAKES. *T.N.* III. iv. 137 Here's the chal-
lenge; read it. I warrant there's vinegar and
pepper in't.   *a.* **1607** *Lingua* D3 There's a
Mustard-maker lookes as keene as Viniger.
1615 H. CROOKE *Microcosmographia* (1631) 632
Sowre and sharpe as Vineger. **1636** QUARLES
Elegie Wks. Gros. III. 11/1 We . . . sadly rise
With the sharp vinegre of suffused eyes.

Sharp stomach makes short devotion, A.   (S 873)

1639 CLARKE 112. **1721** KELLY 293 Sharp
stomachs make short graces.

Sharp's the word and quick's the motion (action).

1709 CIBBER *Rival Fools* I Sharp's the word!
We'll have half ours too.   **1712** ADDISON *Spect.*
no. 403 Wks. (Bohn) III. 381 'Sharp's the word.
Now or never boy. Up to the walls of Paris
directly.'   **1837** T. HOOK *Jack Brag* ch. 2 'Be
alive, my fine fellow! . . . no nonsense—sharp's
the word and quick's the motion, eh?'

Sharper the storm, The | the sooner it's over.

1872 9 June *Kilvert's Diary* ii. 207 The harder
the storm the sooner 'tis over.   **1913** *Folk-Lore*
xxiv. 76.

Sharp(er), *see also* All that is s. is short; Hunger
is s. than thorn.

Shave an egg, It is very hard to.   (E 76)

1592 DELAMOTHE 23.   **1639** CLARKE 243.   **1648**
HERRICK *Hesper.* 558 (1893) I. 262 Eggs Ile
not shave.   **1670** RAY 84 . . . Where nothing
is, nothing can be had.   **1861** C. READE *Cloist. &*
Hearth ch. 58 We Dutchmen are hard bargainers.
We are the lads . . . 'to shave an egg'.

Shaving against the wool, It is ill.
(F 14. S 287)

1546 HEYWOOD I. xi. D4 What shuld your face
thus agayn the woll be shorne?   **1555** *Id. Epigr.*
on Prov. no. clii Thy face is shorne ageynst
the wooll.   *c.* **1580** G. HARVEY *Marginalia* 113
As it were shorne against the wooll.   *c.* **1584**
D. FENNER *Counter Poison* 73 In the other poynt
he is forced to goe against the wool.   **1636**
CAMDEN 300.   **1670** RAY 141.

Shave(s, -ing, -en), *see also* Bald head soon s.;
Barber learns to s. by s. fools; Barber s. another
gratis; Barber s. so close but another finds work;
Beard will pay for s.; Handsaw good thing.

Sheaf of a stook[1] is enough, One.

1721 KELLY 34 . . . An Answer to those who
propose to Match twice into the same Family:
and hits the Patter if the first Match was not
very fortunate. [[1] group of sheaves.]

Shear sheep that have them.   (S 310)

1678 RAY 210.

Shear your sheep in May, and shear them all away.   (S 311)

1670 RAY 41.   **1732** FULLER no. 6195 (clear them
all away).

Shear, *see also* Sheep to s., (You have no more).

Shearer, *see* Bad s. never had good sickle.

Shears, *see* Pair of s. between them (Went but a).

Sheath, *see* Blade wears out s.; Leaden sword in
ivory s.; Makes much of painted s.; Swear
dagger out of s.; Sword (One) keeps another in s.

Shed riners with a whaver, To.

1826 WILBRAHAM *Chesh. Glos.* 68 'To shed riners
with a whaver' . . . means, to surpass anything
skilful or adroit by something still more so.
1917 BRIDGE 143 To shed riners with a whaver.
Shed = to divide or surpass. *Riner* = *toucher.*
Used at Quoits. A *Riner* is when the quoit
touches the peg or mark. *Whaver* is when it
rests upon the peg and hangs over and consequently wins the cast.

Shed, *see also* Dish while I s. my pottage, (Hold
the).

Sheen, *see* Nun of Sion with friar of S.

Sheep and a cow, Now I have a | every-body bids me 'Good morrow'. *Cf.* Ewe and a lamb.   (S 307)

1659 HOWELL *Span. Prov.* 10 (Now that I have
a Sheep and an Ass).   **1757** FRANKLIN *Poor Rich.*
Improved; Alm. for 1758 in ARBER *Garner* v. 581
Industry gives comfort, and plenty, and respect.
. . . *Now I have a sheep and a cow Everybody bids*
me 'Good morrow'.

Sheep follows another, One.   (S 309)

1599 T. HEYWOOD *I Edw. IV* (1874) i. 20 Muddy
clownes, Whose courage but consists in multitude, Like sheepe and neat that follow one
another.   **1606** J. DAY *Isle Gulls* A3 Why doost
thinke thy audience like a flock of sheepe, that
one cannot leape ouer a hedge, but all the rest
will follow.   **1678** RAY *Adag. Hebr.* 405 . . . So
one thief, and any other evil doer, follows the ill
example of his companion.   **1706** STEVENS s.v.
Cabra Where one Goat goes they all will go.
Like Sheep, which if one leaps into the Water,
will all follow.

Sheep hang by his (its) own shank, Let every.

1706 STEVENS s.v. Carnero Every Sheep hangs by its own Foot. **1721** KELLY 240 ... Every Man must stand by his own Endeavour, Industry, and Interest. **1818** SCOTT *Rob Roy* ch. 26 Na, na! let every herring hing by its ain head, and every sheep by its ain shank.

Sheep in the flock, He that has one | will like all the rest the better for it.

1721 KELLY 137 ... Spoken when we have a Son at such a School, University, Army, or Society, we will wish the Prosperity of these respective Bodies, upon his account.

Sheep leap o'er the dyke[1], If one | all the rest will follow.

1721 KELLY 179 ... Shewing the Influence of evil Example. **1816** SCOTT *Old Mort.* ch. 36 Call in the other fellow, who has some common sense. One sheep will leap the ditch when another goes first. [[1] ditch.]

Sheep of Berry; it is marked on the nose, It is a. (S 304)

1611 COTGRAVE s.v. Mouton C'est vn mouton de Berry, il est marqué sur le nez. He hath gotten a rap ouer the nose. Whereon the Shepheardes of Berry marke their Sheepe. **1651** HERBERT no. 1040 (applyed to those that have a blow). **1867** *N. & Q.* 3rd Ser. XII. 488 ... A sheep is often marked on the nose to show to what barn it belongs.

Sheep, swine, and bees, He that has | sleep he, wake he, he may thrive. (S 321)

1523 FITZHERBERT 121 (an olde saying).

Sheep to shear, You have no more. (S 322)

1678 RAY 344 ... *Somerset.*

Sheep's clothing, *see* Wolf in s. c.

Sheep's eye at (upon), To cast (throw) a. (S 323)

[= to look amorously or longingly at.] **1529** SKELTON *Agst. Garnesche* iii. 54 When ye kyst a shepys ie, ... [At] mastres Andelby. *a.* **1586** SIDNEY *Arcadia* II (Sommer) 107 Mopsa throwing a great number of sheeps eyes vpon me. **1738** SWIFT *Dial. I. E.L.* 269 How do you like Mr. Spruce? I swear I have often seen him cast a sheep's eye out of a calf's head at you. **1809** MALKIN *Gil Blas* I. iv. (Rtldg.) 9 I could not help casting a sheep's eye at the gold and silver plate peeping out of the different cupboards. **1848** THACKERAY *Vanity F.* ch. 27 The horrud old Colonel, ... was making sheep's eyes at a half-caste girl there.

Sheep's flesh, *see* Loves well s. f. (mutton) that wets bread in wool.

Sheep, *see also* Better give the wool than the s.; Black s. is a biting beast; Black s. in every flock; Black s. keep the white (Let); Black s., (To know one from a); Butcher does not fear many s.; Carrion crows bewail dead s.; Death of wolves is safety of flock; Dust raised by s. does not choke wolf; Every hand fleeces (Where), s. goes naked; Every time s. bleats loses mouthful; Foolish s. makes wolf confessor; Hanged for a s. as a lamb; Keep s. by moonlight; Lazy s. thinks wool heavy; Lion among s. and a s. among lions; Lone s. in danger of wolf; Makes himself a s. (He that), eaten by wolf; North of England for ox, south for s.; Rich as a new-shorn s.; Scabbed s. will mar flock; Seek in a s. five feet; Shear s.; Shear your s.; Shrew than a s. (Better to be *or* to marry); Some good some bad as s. come to fold; Soon goes the young s. to the pot; Steals a s. and gives back trotters; Troubles a wolf how many s. (Never); Wolf eats the s. (By little); Wolf eats often s. that have been told; Wolf to keep the s. (Set the).

Sheet(s), *see* Better wear out shoes than s.; Difference is wide that s. will not decide; Makes much of his painted s.; Shaking of the s., (To dance the); Stand in a white s.; Three s. in the wind.

Sheffield Park is ploughed and sown, When | then little England hold thine own. (S 325)

1678 RAY 340 Yorkshire. ... It hath been plow'd and sown these six or seven years.

Shell, To be in (out of) the. *Cf.* Like the lapwing.

1542 ERASM. tr. Udall *Apoph.* (1877, 371) This feloe ... that came but yesterdaie in maner out of the shel. **1551** T. WILSON *Rule of Reason* O7ᵛ In this wolde a child shal scant be out of his shel, but he shalbe suer to one or other. *a.* **1576** WYTHORNE 190 Sum yoong heir that iz newly start owt of the shell. **1583** MELBANCKE E1ᵛ To commit wealth to him which yesterday came out of the shell. **1587** J. BRIDGES *Defence* 1178 The moste of them that are moste busy nowe, were then but in the shell (as they say) or but yong hatched. **1587** D. FENNER *Def. of Godly Ministers* 42–5 Thou boye beardlesse boye, yesterday birde, newe out of the shell. **1857** T. HUGHES *Tom Brown's Schooldays* pt. II, ch. 2 'There you go off as usual, with a shell on your head,' struck in East.

Shell, *see also* Contempt pierces through s. of tortoise; Half an egg is better than an empty s.; Kernel and leap at the s., (To lose); Lapwing that runs away with the s. on its head, (Like a); Soon enough to cry 'Chuck' when out of s.; Sweet is the nut, but bitter the s.

Shelter, *see* Good tree is good s.

Sheltering under an old hedge, It is good. (H 358. S 327)

1639 CLARKE 25 ⌐Better to keep under an old

hedge, than creepe under a new furr-bush. **1674** *Learne to lye Warm; or An Apology for that Proverb, 'Tis good sheltering under an Old Hedge* [title of tract]. **1678** RAY 351.

Shepherd's warning, *see* Rainbow in the morning; Sky red in the morning.

Shepherd(s), *see* Good s. must fleece . . . not flay; Sike as the s. sike his sheep; Wolves rend sheep when s. fail.

Sherramuir (Sheriff-muir), *see* Mair lost at S.

Shield, *see* Cover yourself with your s.

Shift may serve long, A good | but it will not serve for ever.   (S 333)

1678 RAY 201.

Shift to want, It is no.

1721 KELLY 210 . . . Spoken when in Necessity we take what we have use for.

Shifts, He is put (driven) to his.

1542 A. BORDE *Dietary of Health* E.E.T.S. 240. **1551** CRANMER *Ans. to Gardiner* 103 He . . . now beyng at a pynche driuen to his shiftes, crieth for helpe vpon you. **1567** PAINTER ii. 178 The standers by that marked the game, perceiued that hee was dryuen to his shiftes. **1577** BEZA *Abraham's Sacrifice* C4 Foyle him in feeld, or put him to his shift. **1581** A. MANUTIUS *Phrases Linguae* 29 Euery man is driuen to his shiftes. **1592** SHAKES. *T.And.* IV. ii. 177 It is you that puts us to our shifts.

Shift(s), *see also* Bad excuse (s.) better than none; Hang him that has no s.; Make a s., as Macwhid with preaching; Spinner has a large s. (Diligent).

Shilling, *see* Bad penny (s.) comes back; Better give a s.; Cut off with a s.; Know by a penny how s. spends; Ninepence to s.; Poor man's s. is but a penny; Take the (King's) s. *See also* Five shillings.

Shin(s), *see* Against the s.; Fast for fear of breaking your s. (Not too); Lies not in your gate breaks not your s. (It that).

Shine(s), *see* Bright that s. by himself; Burns most (He that) s. most; Sun s. on all alike.

Ship, a woman (and a lute) are ever repairing, A.   (S 350)

1578 FLORIO *First F.* 30 Who wil trouble hym selfe all dayes of his life, Let hym mary a woman, or buy hym a shyp. **1589** NASHE *Anat. Absurd.* i. 13 Marcus Aurelius compared women to shyps, because to keepe them wel and in order, there is alwayes somewhat wanting. **1594** *Mirr. Policy* (1599) X2 Is it not an old Prouerbe. That Women and Shippes are neuer so perfect but still there is somewhat to hee amended. **1602–3** MANNINGHAM *Diary* Camden Soc. 12 To furnish a shipp requireth much trouble, But to furnishe

a woman the charges are double. **1609** HARWARD 115[v] A shipp, a wiff, and a lute do stand always in some want. They still need somme rigging. **1640** HERBERT no. 780. **1840** DANA *Two Years bef. Mast* ch. 3 As has often been said, a ship is like a lady's watch, always out of repair.

Ship comes home, When my.

[= when one comes into one's fortune.] **1851** MAYHEW *Lond. Labour* I. 175 One [customer] always says he'll give me a ton of taties when his ship comes home. **1857** MISS MULOCK *Jno. Halifax* ch. 22 'Perhaps we may manage it some time.' 'When our ship comes in.' **1920** 4 Jan. D. H. LAWRENCE *Lett.* i. 604 (Keep it till your).

Ship, As broken a | has come to land.   (S 344)

a. **1628** CARMICHAELL no. 30 Als brokin a ship hes commed to land. **1641** FERGUSSON no. 139. **1725** A. RAMSAY *Gentle Shep.* III. ii. **1732** FULLER no. 668. **1824** SCOTT *St. Ronans* ch. 9 'My sister will never marry.' . . . 'That's easily said, . . . but as broken a ship's come to land.'

Ship (*orig. and prop.* Sheep, Ewe, Hog), To lose (spoil) the | for a halfpennyworth of tar.   (H 495)

[= to lose an object, spoil an enterprise, or court failure, by trying to save in a small matter of detail, referring to the use of tar to protect sores or wounds on sheep from flies: *sheep* is dialectically pronounced *ship* over a great part of England.] [1600] **1659** DAY & CHETTLE *Blind Beggar* v. K1 To him Father, never lose a hog for a halfp'worth of tar. **1623** CAMDEN 265 A man will not lose a hog, for a halfeperth of tarre. **1631** J. SMITH *Advert. Planters* XIII. 52 Rather . . . to lose ten sheepe, than be at the charge of a halfe penny worth of Tarre. **1636** J. CRAWSHEY *Countryman's Instructor* Ep. ded. Hee that will loose a Sheepe (or a Hogge) for a pennyworth of Tarre, cannot deserve the name of a good husband. **1670** RAY 103 Ne're lose a *hog* for a half-penny-worth of tarre. [ed. **1678** 154 *adds* Some have it, lose not a sheep, &c. Indeed tarr is more used about sheep then swine.] **1672** J. PHILLIPS *Moronides* VI. 22 And judge you now what fooles those are, Will lose a Hog for a ha'porth of tar. **1841** MARRYAT *Mast. Ready* ch. 14. **1861** READE *Cloist. & Hearth* ch. 1 Gerard fell a thinking how he could spare her purse. . . . 'Never tyne[1] the ship for want of a bit of tar, Gerard', said this changeable mother. **1886** E. J. HARDY *How to be Happy* ch. 13 People are often saving at the wrong place, and spoil the ship for a halfpenny worth of tar. **1910** *Spectator* 19 Feb. 289 The ratepayers . . . are accused of . . . cheeseparing, of spoiling the ship for a ha'p'orth of tar, of being penny wise and pound foolish. [[1] lose.]

Ship of the desert, The.

[= the camel.] **1823** BYRON *Island* II. viii. note The 'ship of the desert' is the oriental figure for the camel. **1844** KINGLAKE *Eothen* ch. 17 Gaza . . . bears towards [the desert] the same kind of relation as a seaport bears to the sea. It is there that you *charter* your camels ('the ships of the Desert') . . . for the voyage.

Ship under sail, a man in complete armour, a woman with a great belly are three of the handsomest sights, A.

(s 351)

1609 HARWARD 119 A shipp vnder sayle, a woman great bellyed and a feeld loaden with corne are in their prime of pride. **1659** HOWELL *Eng. Prov.* 2b . . . Whereunto the Spaniard addeth two more; viz. A Bishop in a Pulpit, and a theif on the gallowes.

Ship(s), *see also* Anchor of a s., (Like the); Dear s. long in haven; Every wind is ill to broken s.; Great s. asks deep waters; Leak will sink great s.; November . . . let s. no more sail; Rats desert sinking s.; Sands will sink s.; Simon and Jude all s. home crowd; Thresher take his flail, and s. no more sail; Venture (Take your) as many a good s.

Shipman, *see* Conscience as large as a s.'s hose.

Shipmate, *see* Messmate before s.

Shipped the devil, He that has | must make the best of him. (D 280)

1678 RAY 125. **1720** DEFOE *Capt. Singleton* (1906) 8 He that is shipped with the devil must sail with the devil. **1732** FULLER no. 2152 (purchas'd . . . most).

Ships fear fire more than water.

1640 HERBERT no. 909.

Shipshape and Bristol fashion.

1823 COOPER *Pioneers* ch. 6 It was ship-shape, and Brister-fashion. **1826** SCOTT *Chron. of Canongate* Introd. Stretching our fair canvas to the breeze, all ship-shape and Bristol fashion. **1840** DANA *Two Years bef. Mast* ch. 22 Her decks were wide and roomy. . . . There was no foolish gilding and gingerbread work, . . . but everything was 'ship-shape and Bristol fashion'.

Shipwreck be your sea-mark, Let another's. (s 355)

1640 F. QUARLES *Enchiridion* II. xxxi. Let another's passion be a lecture to thy reason, and let the shipwracke of his understanding be a seamarke to thy passion. **1662** FULLER *Derbysh.* 234 Seeing *Nocumenta, Documenta*; and that the shipwrecks of some are Sea-marks to others: even this Knight's[1] miscarriage proved a direction to others. **1670** DRYDEN *Cong. Gran.* I. III. i. Merm. 63 I am your sea-mark; and, though wrecked and lost, My ruin stands to warn you from the coast. **1910** *T.L.S.* 9 Dec. 491 If he[2] makes other's shipwrecks his seamarks, . . . all will be well with the great Dependency. [[1] Sir Hugh Willoughby. [2] Lord Hardinge.]

Shipwreck, *see also* Complains wrongfully on sea that twice suffers s.; O Master Vier . . . no s. upon our coast; Slander is a s.

Shire, *see* Lost in the hundred found in s.

Shires, To come out of the.

1736 PEGGE *Kenticisms, Prov.* 71 E.D.S. 78 . . . A proverbial saying relative to any person who comes from a distance. . . . The word *shire* is not annexed to any one of the counties bordering upon Kent.

Shirt full of sore bones, I will give you a.

c. **1680** ROGER NORTH *Lives of the Norths* (Bohn) i. 179 Give him 'a serk full of sere benes', that is a shirt full of sore bones. **1732** FULLER no. 2637.

Shirt knew my design, If my | I'd burn it. (s 357)

1578 *Courtly Controv.* 2O3[v] If he had thought his shirt had knowen his meaning, he had burnt it. **1583** MELBANCKE *Philot.* H2 One askinge Hannibal, what his purpose was to do the next daye, when he remoued camp, had this answere, that if the cote on his owne backe knewe his intent, he woulde disrobe himselfe and burne it. **1592** DELAMOTHE 49 If our shirt know our secrets, it were to be burned. **1616** DRAXE no. 1919 If our shirt knew our secrecie, it were to be burnt. **1633** JONSON *T. Tub* I. i. 66 My Cassock sha' not know it; If I thought it did, Ile burne it. **1710** SWIFT *Jrnl. to Stella* 30 Nov. He know my secrets? No; as my Lord Mayor said, 'No; if I thought my shirt knew', &c. **1732** FULLER no. 2695.

Shirt of Nessus.

[The garment dipped in the blood of the centaur Nessus, sent by Deianeira to Hercules, whose flesh it consumed.] **1606** SHAKES. *A.C.* IV. xii. 43 The shirt of Nessus is upon me. **1905** WEYMAN *Starvecrow F.* ch. 32 Remorse is the very shirt of Nessus. It is of all mental pains the worst. It seizes upon the whole mind.

Shirt(s), *see also* Near is my coat but nearer my s.; Near is my coat (s.) but nearer my skin; Purser's s. on a handspike (Like a); Smocks than s. in a bucking (He that has more).

Shitten luck is good luck. (L 581)

1639–61 *Rump Songs* (1662, repr. 1874) Pt. I. 137. **1670** RAY 141. **1894** NORTHALL *Folkphrases* E.D.S. 22 Sh . . . n luck is good luck. Said by one who treads accidentally into excrement, or is befouled by mischance. This . . . probably owes its existence to an ancient term for ordure—*gold* or *gold dust* . . . 'The name *gold finder* or *gold farmer*, [was] given as late as the seventeenth century to the cleaners of privies.'

Shive[1] of a cut loaf, It is safe taking a. *Cf.* Cut large shives of another's loaf.

(s 359)

1592 SHAKES. *T.And.* II. i. 87 Easy it is Of a cut loaf to steal a shive. **1639** CLARKE 118. **1670** RAY 52. [[1] slice.]

Shive[1] of my own loaf, A.

1670 RAY 188. [[1] slice.]

Shive(s), *see also* Cut large s. of another's loaf; Fiddle for s.

Shock, *see* Corn is in s.

Shod in the cradle, barefoot in the stubble. (C 793)

a. **1628** CARMICHAELL no. 1350. **1641** FERGUSSON no. 140. **1721** KELLY 289 . . . Spoken of those who are tenderly used in their Infancy, and after meet with harsher Treatment.

Shod, *see also* Hosed and s. (He came in); More bare (Worse s.) than shoemaker's wife and smith's mare (None).

Shoe after one for luck, To cast an old. (S 372)

1546 HEYWOOD I. ix. C2. **1577** *Art of Angling* B2ᵛ I am gladde now that I did throw an olde shooe after you in the morning. **1699** R. E. s.v. Shoe-makers-stocks: To throw an old Shoe after one, or wish them good Luck in their Business.

Shoe fits not every foot, Every. *Cf.* All feet tread not in one shoe. One shoe will not fit all feet. (S 364)

1587 J. BRIDGES *Def. of Gvt. of C. of E.* 86 Diuerse feete haue diuerse lastes. The shooe that will serue one, may wring another. **1616** B. RICH *Looking Glasse* 21 Euery shooe is not fit for euery foote. **1721** KELLY 96 . . . Every Condition of Life, every Behaviour, every Speech and Gesture becomes not every Body; that will be decent in one, which will be ridiculous in another.

Shoe the goose (gander, gosling), To. *Cf.* Meddles in all things. (G 354)

[= to spend one's time in trifling or unnecessary labour: *Bodl. misc.* 264, *c.* 1340, shows a miniature: shoeing the swan (GREEN *Short Hist.* ill. ed. II. 481).] *c.* **1410** HOCCLEVE *Poems* (1796) 13 Ye medle of al thyng, ye moot shoo the goos. **14—** *Why I cant be Nun* 254 in *E.P.P.* (1862) 144 He schalle be put owte of company, and scho the gose. **1546** HEYWOOD II. iii. G2 Who medleth in all thyng, maie shooe the goslyng. **1583** STUBBES *Anat. Abus.* II. (1882) 31 Then may he go sue ye goose, for house gets he none. **1594** NASHE *Unf. Trav.* ii. 230 Galen might goe shooe the Gander for any good he could doo. **1641** FERGUSSON no. 296 Go shoe the goose. **1804** EDGEWORTH *Pop. Tales, Lame Jervas* ch. 3 A blacksmith once said to me, when . . . asked why he was not both blacksmith and whitesmith, 'The smith that will meddle with all things may go shoe the goslings.'

Shoe (Ride) the wild (mockish) mare, To. (M 655)

[A childish Christmas game.] *a.* **1529** SKELTON *Colin Clout* 180 For let see who that dare Shoe the mockish mare. **1598** SHAKES. *2 Hen. IV* II. iv. 235 [He] drinks off candles' ends for flapdragons, and rides the wild mare with the boys. **1609** ARMIN *Maids of More-Cl.* (1880) 92 Christ-

mas gambuls, father, shooing the wilde mare. **1611** COTGRAVE s.v. Asne Desferer l'asne. To unshoe the Asse; wee say, to ride the wild mare.

Shoe (a cast-off glove), To be thrown aside like an old.

1600 DEKKER *Shoem. Hol.* I. i. 142 She shal be laid at one side like a paire of old shooes. **1826** T. H. LISTER *Granby* ii. 222 I would be your friend . . . but not in mere appearance, . . . thrown aside like a cast off glove.

Shoe will hold with the sole, The. (S 371)

1546 HEYWOOD II. v. H1ᵛ Folke say of olde, the shoe will holde with the sole. **1580** LYLY *Euph. & his Eng.* ii. 83 I wil sticke as close to thee, as the soale doth to the shoe. *a.* **1612** DEKKER & MIDDLETON *The Roaring Girl* C2ᵛ As fast as your sole to your boote or shooe sir. **1639** CLARKE 286. **1642** TORRIANO 70 The sole holdeth with the upper leather.

Shoe wrings me (pinches), I know best where. (M 129)

[PLUTARCH *Vita Aemilii* c. 5; S. JEROME *Aev. Iov.* i. 48 *Nemo scit praeter me ubi me (soccus) premat.*] *c.* **1386** CHAUCER *Merch. T.* l. 1553 But I woot best where wryngeth me my sho. *c.* **1510** DUNBAR *Wks.* (Schipper) 356 Thow knawis best quhair bindis the thi scho. **1546** HEYWOOD II. v. H2ᵛ My selfe can tell best, where my shooe doth wryng mee. **1620** SHELTON *Quix.* IV. v. i. 309 As though I knew not . . . where the shoe wrests me now. **1641** FERGUSSON no. 551 I wat where my awn shoe bindes me. **1749** SMOLLETT *Gil Blas* VIII. vi. I did not feel where the shoe pinched. **1895** J. PAYN *In Market O.* ch. 26 Dives . . . does not see where the shoe of poverty pinches; and this ignorance . . . is often the cause of deplorable sins of omission.

Shoe(s), shoon, *see also* All feet tread not in one s.; Better cut the s.; Better wear out s. than sheets; Craft lies in clouted s.; Dead men's s.; Die in one's s., (To); Easy as an old s.; Find fault with my s. and give no leather; Great s. fits not little foot; Hertfordshire s.; Horse cast a s.; Iron s., (He should wear . . .); Mare's s. and horse's s. alike; Meal cheap and s. dear; Meddle with your old s.; Nothing is old but s. and hats; One s. not fit all feet; Over s. over boots; Pride, but profit, wear s. and go barefoot; Shake in one's s.; Too big for one's boots (s.); Tread one's s. awry; Want of a nail s. is lost; Wife down in her wedding s., (To take a); Worthy to wipe (buckle) his s. (Not). *See also* Wooden shoes.

Shoe-buckles, Not worth. (S 382)

1670 RAY 192.

Shoe-buckles, *see also* Play with you for s.-b.

Shoe-leather, As honest a man as ever trod on. (M 66)

[**1545** TAVERNER H7 The starkest knaue that goeth on two legges.] **1560–77** *Misogonus* IV.

i. 158 As vp right a fellowe as ere trod on netes lether.   *c.* **1590** PEELE *O.W.T.* l. 582 As good a fellow as euer troade vppon Neats leather.   **1594** LYLY *Mother B.* I. iii. 45 As neate a stripling as euer went on neats leather.   *Ibid.* II. iii. 19 I haue as fayre a face as euer trode on shoo sole.   **1599** SHAKES. *J.C.* I. i. 27 As proper men as ever trod upon neat's leather have gone upon my handi-work.   **1599** *Id. Hen. V* IV. vii. 136 His reputa-tion is as arrant a villain and a Jacksauce as ever his black shoe trod upon God's ground and his earth, in my conscience, la!   **1608** MIDDLE-TON *Mad World* III. ii. 195 As comfortable a man to woman as ever trod shoe-leather.   *c.* **1610** SHAKES. *Temp.* II. ii. 68 A present for any emperour that ever trod on neat's leather.   **1622** MABBE tr. *Aleman's Guzman d'Alf* ii. 163 As arrant a villaine as ever trode upon a shooe of leather.   **1670** RAY 181 (shoe leather).

Shoeing, see Winter-time for s.

Shoeing-horn to help on his gloves, He calls for a.

c. **1700** B. E. *Dict. Cant. Crew* s.v. *Hobbist* Sir *Posthumus Hobby*, one that Draws on his Breeches with a Shoeing-horn.   **1732** FULLER no. 1816.

Shoeing horn, see also Nose will not make s. h.

Shoemaker's stocks, In the.   (s 385)

[*c.* 1602] **1637** T. HEYWOOD *Royal King* III. 44 Come bare-foot to a Shooemaker, tho' he be a Constable, he will not put us into his Stocks.   **1678** RAY 347.   **1699** B. E. Shoemakers-stocks, pincht with strait Shoes.

Shoemaker, see also More bare (Worse shod) than s.'s wife (Who goes); Six awls make a s.

Shoes are made of running leather, His.   (s 376)

1575 CHURCHYARD *Chippes* (Collier) 130 My Minde could never rest at hoem, My shoes wear maed of running leather suer.   **1639** CLARKE 159.   **1691** W. SEWEL 288.

Shoes, see also Shoe(s).

Shoot a second arrow to find the first, To.   (A 325)

c. **1596** SHAKES. *M.V.* I. i. 140 When I had lost one shaft, I shot his fellow of the self-same flight The self-same way, with more advised watch To find the other forth, and by adventuring both, I oft found both.   **1600** 'C. SNUFFE' [= R. ARMIN] *Quips upon Questions* D1.   **1601** J. CHAMBERLAIN *Letters* (McLure) i. 115.   **1616** DEKKER *Villainies Discovered* K1 He shot a second Arrow to finde the first.   **1659** HOWELL *Eng. Prov.* 19b Shoot the second shaft, and perhaps thou maist find again the first.   **1706** STEVENS s.v. *Virote* To send one Shaft after another.   When one Servant is sent to fetch another, and both stay: Or when a Man throws away good Money after bad.

Shoot at a pigeon and kill a crow, To.   (P 317)

1639 CLARKE 2.   **1670** RAY 189.   **1830** LD. LYTTON *Brachylogia* in *Paul Clifford* (1848) 445 A law is a gun, which if it misses a pigeon al-ways kills a crow;—if it does not strike the guilty it hits some one else.   **1866** BLACKMORE *Cradock N.* ch. 27 You . . . must be prepared to meet some horrible accusations. . . . Very likely he is innocent.   Perhaps they are shooting at the pigeon in order to hit the crow.

Shoot higher who shoots at the moon (sun) than he who aims at a tree, He will.   (M 1115)

1590 SIDNEY *Arcadia* II. vi. 2 (1912) 184 Who shootes at the mid-day Sunne, though he be sure he shall never hit the marke; yet as sure he is he shall shoote higher, than who ayms but at a bush.   **1632** HERBERT *Priest to Temple*, Auth. to Rdr. 224 I have resolved to set down the Form and Character of a true Pastour, that I may have a Mark to aim at: which also I will set as high as I can, since hee shoots higher that threatens the Moon, than hee that aims at a Tree.   **1655–62** GURNALL *Chrn. in Armour* (1865) I. 365 He that aims at the sky, shoots higher than he that means only to hit a tree.   **1721** KELLY 136 He will shoot higher that shoots at the Moon, than he that shoots at the Midding, though he never hit the Mark.   Spoken as an Encouragement to noble Designs and Endea-vours.

Shoot Niagara, To.

[= attempt desperate adventure.]   **1867** CARLYLE *Shooting Niagara* (title) in *Macmil. Mag.*   **1868** LES. STEPHEN in *Life & Lett.* (1906) xi. 203 The Reform Bill will change all this, it may be, and we shall shoot Niagara.

Shoot nigh the prick, To.   (P 571)

1546 HEYWOOD I. vi. B3 Now ye shoote ny the pricke.   **1551** CRANMER *Ans. to Gardiner* 304 You . . . haue taken great payne to shoote away all your boltes in vaine, missynge quite and cleane bothe the pricke and the whole butte. . . . like vnto a man that had shotte all his shaftes cleane wide from the butte, and yet wold beare al men in hand that he had hitte the pricke.   **1562** J. WIGAND *De Neutralibus* E2 If thou haue hit this prick so straight, that thou maiest truly make thy boast of these matters.   **1594–5** SHAKES. *L.L.L.* IV. i. 124 'A mark,' says my lady! Let the mark have a prick in't, to mete at, if it may be . . .—Indeed 'a must shoot nearer.

Shoot the cat, To.

[= to vomit, especially from too much drink.]   **1785** GROSE s.v. *Shoot.*   **1830** MARRYAT *King's Own* ch. 32 I'm cursedly inclined to shoot the cat.

Shoot the moon, To.

[= to make a moonlight flitting.]   **1837** COL. HAWKER *Diary* (1893) II. 123 He having just 'shot the moon', I had to follow him to a cock-loft in St. Giles's.   **1882** W. BESANT *All Sorts* ch. 4 I told him who were responsible tenants;

I warned him when shooting of moons seemed likely.

Shoot wide of the mark, To.   (M 668)

c. **1550–60** J. THORNE Poems in J. O. Halliwell's ed. of *Wit and Science* 103 Sum shotte wyde and sum shotte shorte, yet all in fyne do mys the marke. **1555** HEYWOOD *Epig. on Prov.* lxxxviii He shooteth wyde . . . he seeth not the marke. **1578** [? **1563**] T. GARTER *Susanna* l. 636 How wyde I shot, when I shot at this marke.

Shoot with a silver gun, To.

1823 COBBETT *Rural Rides* 1 Aug. Shooting with *a silver gun* is a saying amongst game-eaters. That is to say, *purchasing* the game. A . . . fellow that does not know how to prime and load will, in this way, beat the best shot in the county.

Shoot zaftly,[1] doey now.

1787 GROSE (*Dorset*) 109 Shoot zaftly, doey now. A privateer of [Poole] having . . . loaded their guns, on their return to port, wished to draw out the shot, but . . . could [not] think of any other method, than that of firing them off, and receiving the shot in a kettle: the person employed to hold the kettle . . . prayed for his companion, who was to discharge the gun, to shoot zaftly. [1 softly.]

Shoot, shot, *see also* Arrow s. upright falls on the shooter's head; Dead s. at yellow-hammer; Feathers, (To be s. with one's own); Scot, (To s. like a).

Shooting, *see* Far s. never killed; Kittle s. at corbies and clergy; Short s. loses game.

Shoots oft at last shall hit the mark, He that.   (S 388)

[CICERO *Div.* 2. 59. 121 *Quis est enim, qui totum diem iaculans, non aliquando collineat*?] **1551** ROBINSON tr. *More's Utop.* Arb. 52 He made the prouerbe true, which saieth: he that shoteth oft, at the last shal hit the mark. **1624** J. HEWES *Perfect Survey* K1 no. 28 Who is it that shooting all the day, doth not sometimes hit the marke? **1732** FULLER no. 2276 He that's always shooting, must sometimes hit.

Shoots well that hits the mark, He.   (M 667)

1656 L. PRICE *A Map of Merry Conceits* A5ᵛ He shoots well that hits the mark. **1659** HOWELL *Eng. Prov.* 20b.

Shop, *see* Fair s. and little gain; Goodwin Sands, (To set up s. on); Keep your s. and your s. will keep you; Market of his ware . . . open his s.; Singing man keeps s. in throat; Stomach an apothecary's s., (Make not thy). See *also* Shut up s.

Shop windows, *see* Shut up s.

Shopkeepers, *see* English are nation of.

Shore, *see* Lean to the wrong s. (To).

Shorn, *see* God tempers the wind; Wool (Go out for) and come home s.

Short acquaintance brings repentance.   (A 23)

1670 RAY 142.

Short and sharp, *see* All that is sharp is short.

Short and sweet.   (S 396)

1533 SIR T. MORE *Debellation* 955 a It is a good swete sermon and a short. **1545** TAVERNER I4 The englyshe prouerbe . . . Short and swete. **1579–80** LODGE *Def. of Plays* 28 I should preferr Wilsons Shorte and sweete if I were judge, a peece surely worthy prayse. **1623** MIDDLETON *Span. Gip.* IV. iii. Both short and sweet some say is best. **1721** KELLY 59 Better short and sweet, than long and lax. **1882** BLACKMORE *Christowell* ch. 19 'Short, but not sweet', said Mr. Gaston lifting his eyebrows, as he read indignantly—'I beg to return your rigmarole.' **1902** F. VILLIERS *Pict. of Many Wars* 3 A short interview. But a very sweet one to me. I left . . . with a bag of sovereigns in my pocket.

Short and sweet, like a donkey's gallop.

1894 NORTHALL *Folk-phrases* E.D.S. 22 Short and sweet, like a donkey's gallop. Some say, like a roast maggot. **1914** K. F. PURDON *Folk of Furry F.* ch. 8 Dan . . . started the old donkey off as well as he could. Short and sweet like an ass's gallop, as the saying is, and she soon failed at it.

Short boughs, long vintage.   (B 556)

1573 SANFORD 109 A short bow [*Ramo curto*], a long grape time, or store of grapes. **1640** HERBERT no. 508.

Short folk are soon angry.

1721 KELLY 285 . . . It is alledged that People of a low Stature are pettish, passionate, and fiery.

Short folk's heart is soon at their mouth.

1721 KELLY 285 . . . It is alledged that People of a low Stature are pettish, passionate, and fiery.

Short follies are best.   (F 439)

1589 *Admonition given by one of the Duke of Savoy's Council* C1 The shortest follies are best. *c.* **1594** BACON no. 148 The shortest folly is the best. **1611** COTGRAVE s.v. Court.

Short harvests make short adlings.[1]

1846 DENHAM 54. [1 earnings.]

Short horse is soon curried, A. *Cf.* Bonny bride is soon buskit, etc.   (H 691)

c. **1350** *Douce MS.* 52 no. 17 Short hors is son j-curryed. *c.* **1500** *Sloane MS. 747* (ed. Förster) in *Anglia* **42**. 204 Short horse ys sone coryed. **1546** HEYWOOD I. x. C2ᵛ. **1659** HOWELL *Eng. Prov.* 4a (little). **1820** SCOTT *Abbot* ch. 11 A short tale is soon told—and a short horse soon curried.

Short Lent, He has but a | that must pay money at Easter. (L 204)

1642 TORRIANO 34. **1658** *Comes Facundus* 23 He that would have a short Lent, let him take money to be paid at Easter. **1659** HOWELL *It. Prov.* 11. **1732** FULLER no. 1865. **1758** FRANKLIN in ARBER *E. Garner* v. 585 TIME will seem to to have added wings to his heels, as well as shoulders. Those have a short Lent, saith Poor RICHARD, who owe money to be paid at Easter.

Short life and a merry one, A. (L 261)

1654 GAYTON *Pleasant Notes Don Q.* 101 The indicted cry a merry life and a short. **1660** J. TATHAM *The Rump* I. i. (1879) 204 A short life and a merry life. **1745** SWIFT *Dir. Servts.* IV. Wks. (1856) II. 363 Go upon the road . . . ; there you will . . . live a short life and a merry one. **1870** READE *Put Yourself* ch. 24 'We prefer a short life and a merry one, Mr. Little', said the father of all file-cutters.

Short pleasure, long lament (repentance, pain). (P 419)

1468 *Coventry Plays* Shakes. S. 32 Schort lykyng xal be longe bought. **1539** TAVERNER I *Garden* F2ᵛ The same Aristotle aduertysed men to consydre and marke pleasours not commynge but departynge, that is to saye, not before, but behynde. For when pleasures be commynge, with theyr peynted faces they flatter vs, but when they departe, they leue behynde them repentaunce and sorowe. **1556** G. COLVILE tr. *Boethius* (1897) 66 Or, as a man woulde saye: for a lytle pleasure, long payne. **1597** *Politeuphuia* 169ᵛ For a short pleasure, long repentance is the hier. **1670** RAY 142 . . . De court plaisir long repentir, *Gall.* **1732** FULLER no. 4155 Short Pleasures, long Pains.

Short reckonings are soon cleared.

1732 FULLER no. 4156.

Short reckonings (accounts) make long friends. (R 56)

1537 R. WHITFORD *Werke for Householders* sig. A6 The commune prouerbe is that ofte rekeninge holdeth longe felawshyppe. **1641** FERGUSSON no. 668 Oft compting makes good friends. **1721** KELLY 271 Oft counting keeps Friends long together. **1804** EDGEWORTH *Pop. Tales; Out of Debt* ch. 2 Short accounts, they say, make long friends; and . . . it would be very convenient if he could be got to settle with Mr. Ludgate. **1842** LOVER *Handy A.* ch. 8 There must be no nonsense about the wedding. . . . Just marry her off, and take her home. Short reckonings make long friends. **1892** HENLEY & STEVENSON *Adml. Guinea* II. i. Short reckonings make long friends, hey? Where's my change?

Short rede, good rede.[1]

a. **1235** ROGER OF WENDOVER *Chron.* E.H.S. II. 18 Unus ex illis cujus arbitrium omnes ex-

spectabant, præcipitanter patria lingua dixit, 'Schort red, god red; slea ye the bischop'. **1828** SCOTT *F. M. Perth* ch. 7 'What shall we do?' 'Short rede, good rede', said the Smith. 'Let us to our Provost, and demand his . . . assistance.' **1888** FREEMAN *William the Conq.* ch. 10 On May 14, 1080, a full Gemot . . . was held at Gateshead. . . . There was no vote, no debate; the shout was 'Short rede good rede, slay ye the Bishop.' And . . . Walcher himself and his companions . . . were slaughtered. [¹ counsel.]

Short shooting loses the game. (S 390)

1546 HEYWOOD II. ix. L2ᵛ No hast but good (quoth she) Short shootyng leeseth your game, ye maie see. *c.* **1580** G. HARVEY *Marginalia* (1913) 147 Lett not short shooting loose yoᵘ game . aime straight, draw home . risoluto per tutto. **1601** *Letters of Philip Gawdy* 114. **1611** DAVIES no. 42 (the set). **1639** CLARKE 40.

Shortest answer is doing, The. (A 252)

1640 HERBERT no. 552.

Short(est), *see also* All that is sharp is s.; Art is long life is s.; Day s., work much; Discourse makes s. days and nights; Long and s. of it; Prayer penetrates heaven, (A s.); St. Thomas gray, . . . s. day; Take a man up s.

Shortly as a horse will lick his ear, As. (H 630)

1546 HEYWOOD II. ix. L1 Ye will get it agayn (quoth she) I feare, As shortely as a hors will lycke his eare. *a.* **1558** *Jacob and Esau* IV. v. l. 1149 Here again I trow, ere an horse licke his eare.

Shot my bolt, I have. *Cf.* Fool's bolt soon shot. (B 512)

[= made my endeavour.] *c.* **1475** *Mankind* l. 775 My bolte ys schott. **1577** STANYHURST in Holinshed *Descr. Irel.* (1586) 11 But if I may craue your patience till time you see me shoot my bolt. **1853** G. J. WHYTE-MELVILLE *Digby Grand* ch. 2 The grey horse had evidently shot his bolt. **1901** *Daily Express* 28 Feb. 4/5 The home players had shot their bolt, and in thirty minutes the Birmingham team added two goals. **1944** *Times* 29 Dec. 4/1 All the indications now are that Rundstedt has shot his bolt in the Ardennes.

Shoulder of mutton and English beer, make the Flemings tarry here. (S 404)

1617 MORYSON *Itin.* III. ii. 99 (1907-8) IV. 62 They [the Dutch] greatly esteeme English Beere. . . . So in the Sea townes of England they sing this English rime; . . .

Shoulder of mutton draws (drives) down another, One. (S 402)

1611 COTGRAVE s.v. Appetit. **1657** TORRIANO *It. Dial.* 213 One glass draws on another. **1670** RAY 128. **1738** SWIFT *Dial.* II. E.L. 303 I think the more I eat the hungrier I am.—Why, colonel, they say, one shoulder of mutton drives down another. **1811** JANE AUSTEN *Sense &*

Sensib. ch. 30 (Mrs. Jennings) 'One shoulder of mutton, you know, drives another down'.   **1828** LYTTON *Pelham* ch. 25 I am sure if you were to go there, you would cut and come again—one shoulder of mutton drives down another. **1833** TENNYSON to Spedding, 9 Feb. Are we not quits then, or in the language of Mrs. Jennings, 'Does not one shoulder of mutton drive down another?'

Shoulder of mutton for a sick horse, As fit as a.   (s 399)

1541 *Schoolh. of Wom.* A2ᵛ As holesome for a man, is a womans corse As a sholder of motton, for a sycke horse. [*c.* **1609**] **1616** JONSON *Ev. Man in Hum.* II. i. 73 But counsel to him is as good as a shoulder of mutton to a sick horse. **1670** RAY 204.   **1732** FULLER no. 1179 Counsel is as welcome to him as . . .

Shoulder of mutton is going, When the | 'tis good to take a slice.   (s 406)

1678 RAY 350.

Shoulder of veal, In a | there are twenty and two good bits.   (s 401)

1676 W. WYCHERLEY *The Plain Dealer* III. i. The two and thirty good Bits in a shoulder of Veal. **1678** RAY 83 . . . This is a piece of country wit. They mean by it, There are twenty (others say forty) bits in a shoulder of veal, and but two good ones.   **1738** SWIFT Dial. II. E.L. 297 They say there are thirty and two good bits in a shoulder of veal.—Ay, colonel, thirty bad bits and two good ones.

Shoulder to the wheel, Put your.

(s 403)

1621 BURTON *Anat. Mel.* II. i. II. (1651) 222 Like him in Æsop, that, when his cart was stalled, lay flat on his back, and cryed, aloud, 'Help, Hercules!' but that was to little purpose, except, as his friend advised him, . . . he whipt his horses withal, and put his shoulder to the wheel.   **1864** TROLLOPE *Sm. H. at Allington* ch. 46 Putting your shoulder to the wheel when the coach gets into the mud. That's what I've been doing all my life.   *a.* **1889** C. MACKAY *Cheer! Boys, cheer!* (Song). If you'll only put your shoulder to the wheel.   **1907** *Spectator* 2 Mar. 333 National progress is impossible unless the individuals who compose the nation themselves put their own shoulders to the wheel.

Shoulder(s), *see also* Cold s.; Dogs run away with whole s.; Dwarf on giant's s.; Head and s., (To thrust out by); Over the left s.; Ride with beard on s.

Shouting, *see* All is over but the s.

Shovel, Shoo, *see* Put to bed with a s.; Sexton has shaked his s.

Show a fair (clean) pair of heels, To.

(P 31)

[= to run away.] **1546** HEYWOOD II. vii. I2ᵛ Except hir mayde shewe a fayre payre of heeles,

She haleth her by the booy rope.   [**1594–1600**] **1615** T. HEYWOOD *Four Prentices* ii. 173 I would show him as fine a paire of heeles . . . as any the neatest cork shoe in all the Towne turnes vp. **1597** SHAKES. *1 Hen. IV* II. iv. 44 Darest thou . . . play the coward with thy indenture and show it a fair pair of heels and run from it?   **1613** T. ADAMS *White Devil* (1861–2) ii. 247 But for these shackles, debt would often shew credit a light pair of heels.   **1768** RAY 89 He hath shewen them a fair pair of heels.   **1819** SCOTT *Ivanhoe* ch. 40 Or Folly will show a clean pair of heels, and leave Valour to find out his way.

Show a good man his error, and he turns it to a virtue; but an ill, it doubles his fault.   (M 374)

1640 HERBERT no. 655.

Show me a liar, and I will show thee (you) a thief. *Cf.* Lie will steal, He that will.   (L 220)

1615 T. ADAMS *Mystical Bedlam* Wks. 505 The Prouerbe giues the Lier, the inseparable society of another sinne. *Da mihi mendacem, et ego ostendam tibi furem*: Shew me a Lier, and I will shew thee a thiefe.   **1639** CLARKE 148.   **1670** RAY 113.

Show me not (Look not on) the meat, but show me (look on) the man. (M 838)

1534 HEYWOOD *Play of Love* l. 1230 (Brandl *Quellen* 198).   **1546** *Id.* II. iv. G3 And though your pasture look bareynly and dull, Yet loke not on the meate, but loke on the man.   **1581** W. AVERELL *Charles and Julia* A3 Let the meate be seene in the man, the Tree in his fruite. **1639** CLARKE 84.   **1650** FULLER *Pisgah-Sight* II. (1869) 201 Our English proverb saith, 'Show me not the meat, but show me the man.' The well battling of the giants bred in Philistia . . . Sufficiently attests the fertility of their soil.   **1721** KELLY 259 . . . If a Man be fat, plump, and in good liking, I shall not ask what keeping he has had.

Show me the man, and I'll show you the law.   (M 375)

a. **1628** CARMICHAELL no. 1411.   **1641** FERGUSSON no. 773.   **1721** KELLY 289 . . . The Sentences of Judges may vary, according to the Measure of their Fear, Favour, or Affection.   **1819** SCOTT *Bride Lam.* ch. 2 A case of importance scarcely occurred, in which there was not some ground for bias or partiality on the part of the judges, who were so little able to withstand the temptation, that the adage 'Show me the man, and I will show you the law', became as prevalent as it was scandalous.

Show than substance, More.   (s 408)

1594 NASHE *Terrors of the Night* i. 353 The spirits of the aire . . . are in truth all show and no substance.   *c.* **1595** SHAKES. *R.J.* III. ii. 77 Despised substance of divinest show!   **1609** *Id. Son.* 5, l. 13 But flowers distill'd . . . Leese but their show—their substance still lives sweet. **1721** KELLY 255.

Show the bull-horn, To.

[= to make a show of resistance.] **1838** GALT in *Fraser's Mag.* VIII. 655 He shewed, when he durst, the bull-horn.

Show (*noun*), *see* Flaming figure (Fair s.) in country church (It will make).

Show (*verb*), *see also* Cards to s. for it, (He has good); Cloven hoof (To s.); Dare not s. his head; Good manners to s. learning before ladies (Not); White feather (To s.).

Shower in July, A | when the corn begins to fill, is worth a plow of oxen, and all belongs there till.

1721 KELLY 43. **1732** FULLER no. 6468. **1893** INWARDS 30.

Shower(s), *see also* April s. . . . May flowers; Cornwall will bear a s. every day; Every day of the week a s. of rain; Hat is not made for one s.; Many drops make s.

Shows all his wit at once, He. (W 554)

1616 DRAXE no. 767. **1670** RAY 199.

Shows his purse, He that | longs to be rid of it (bribes the thief). (P 654)

1611 JONSON *Catiline* II. 217 And keepe your beautie, within locks, and barres, here, Like a fooles treasure?—True, shee was a foole, When, first, shee shew'd it to a thiefe. **1621** ROBINSON 18 He that sheweth his goods longeth to be rift. **1639** CLARKE 176. **1721** KELLY 129 (bribes the Thief). **1732** FULLER no. 2299 He that sheweth his Wealth to a Thief is the Cause of his own Pillage.

Shreds, *see* Tailor's s. are worth the cutting.

Shrew profitable may serve a man reasonable, A. (S 414)

1577 N. BRETON *The workes of a young wyt* IIv I hearde my father once say, . . . (might serue). **1616** *Id. Cross. Prov.* BIv A shrew profitable, is good for a man reasonable. **1623** CAMDEN 265. **1662** FULLER Shrops. 2 A Profitable Shrew may well content a reasonable-man, the Poets feigning Juno chaste and thrifty, qualities which commonly attend a shrewd nature.

Shrew than a sheep, It is better to be (marry) a. (S 412)

[*Cf. c.* **1560** *Tom Tyler* l. 710 Though some be sheep, yet some be shrowes.] **1562** G. LEGH *Accidence of Armoury* 229 Trye when you will, and you shall find a shrew or a shepe. **1573** TUSSER 157 Now be she lambe or be she eaw, Giue me the sheepe, take thou the shreaw. **1575** GASCOIGNE *Glass Govt.* ii. 44 It is an olde saying, one shrew is worth two sheep. **1614** CAMDEN 308. *c.* **1645** HOWELL *Lett.* (1650) I. 110 It is better to marry a Shrew than a Sheep; for though silence be the dumb Orator of beauty, . . . yet a Phlegmatic dull Wife is fulsom and fastidious.

Shrew(s), *see also* Eye is a s.; Fair weather when the s. have dined; Leap an inch from a s. (She cannot); Rule a s. (Every man can); Stretton in the Street, where s. meet.

Shrift, He has been at. (S 415)

1528 TYNDALE *Obed. Chrn. Man* P.S. 304 Of him that is betrayed, and wotteth not how, we say, 'He hath been at shrift'.

Shrine, *see* Saint (S.) (Like) like offering.

Shrink in the wetting, To. *Cf.* Northern cloth. Three ills. (W 278)

1540 PALSGRAVE *Acolastus* 147 Where is my golden chain . . . it is shrunk in the wetynge. **1592** NASHE *Strange News* i. 274 The fourth [son] is shrunke in the wetting, or else the Print shoulde haue heard of him. **1609** J. WYBARNE A4. **1664** W. CONYERS *Hemerologium Astronicum* 2 July It's better to shrink in the wetting, then waste in the warming. **1680** R. L'ESTRANGE *Citt and Bumpkin* 8 Provided you stand to your Tackle, y'are a Made man already; but if you shrink in the wetting, y'are lost.

Shrub(s), *see* Cedars fall when low s. remain, (High); Pine wishes herself s.

Shrug, *see* Neapolitan s.

Shrunk, *see* Northern cloth, s. in the wetting.

Shuffle, *see* Patience and s. the cards.

Shunning, *see* Smoke (S. the) they fall into the fire.

Shuns the man that knows him well, He.

a. **1250** *Owl. & Night.* 235 For Alured King hit seide 2 wrot: 'He schunet þat hine [vu]l wot.'

Shut the stable-door when the steed is stolen, It is too late to. (S 838)

[L. *Maxima pars pecore amisso praesepia claudit* (MARCELL. PALINGEN. *Zodiacus Vitae* ix. 287). *c.* **1190** *Li Proverbe au Vilain* A tart ferme on l'estable, quant li chevauz est perduz, ci dit li vilains.] *c.* **1350** *Douce MS.* no. 22 When þe hors is stole steke þe stabull-dore. *c.* **1390** GOWER *Conf. Amantis* IV. 903 For whan the grete stiede Is stole, thanne he taketh hiede, And makth the stable dore fast. *c.* **1490** *Provs. in Sloane MS.* 747 (ed. Förster) in *Anglia* 42. 204 Whan the stede ys stole than shytte the stable-dore. *a.* **1530** R. *Hill's Commonpl. Bk.* E.E.T.S. 128 Whan the stede is stolen, shit the stabill dore. **1546** HEYWOOD I. x. C4 To late (quoth myne aunt) this repentance shewd is, Whan the steede is stolne shut the stable durre. **1579** LYLY *Euph.* i. 188 But thinges past, are paste callinge agayne: it is to late to shutte the stable doore when the steede is stolen. **1602** *Narcissus* (1893) 264 It is too late, When steede is stolne to shutt the stable gate. **1719** DEFOE *Crusoe* II (Globe) 387 It was only shutting the

Stable Door after the Stead was stoln. **1817**
LAMB to the Kenneys, Oct. 'Tis too late when
the steed is stole, to shut the stable door.

Shut up shop (windows), To.   (s 394)

c. **1530** BARCLAY *Eclog.* IV. l. 493 Then may
I . . . shet the shopwindowes for lacke of
marchaundice. *a.* **1547** R. EDWARDES *Damon
and Pithias* l. 959 I wyll knock down this your
Lantern, and shut vp your shop window too.
[i.e. execute him.] **1599** DEKKER *Shoem. Hol.*
(1610) v. ii. We may shut up our shop and make
holiday. **1650** VAUGHAN *Silex Scint., Faith* 19
Stars shut up shop, mists pack away, And the
Moon mourns. **1659** N. R. 58 He that hath
not his Craft let him shut up shop. **1678** RAY
89 *A Bankrupt.* He has shut up shop-windows.

Shut, *see also* Servant must . . . **s.** the door after
him (A good).

Shut up shop, *see also* Craft (He that has not
the); Wares be gone (When), **s. u. s.** windows.

Shuttle, *see* Life is a **s.**

Siamese twins.

[Two male natives of Siam, Chang and Eng
(1814–74), who were united by a tubular band
in the region of the waist.] **1867** H. SIDGWICK
Misc. Ess. & Add. (1904) 273 There seems no
adequate reason why Latin and Greek should
be regarded as a sort of linguistic Siamese twins,
which nature has joined together, and which
would wither if separated. **1899** *Daily News*
15 Mar. 4/4 The death of M. Erckmann . . .
removes the last of the Siamese twins of French
fiction.

Sib[1] as sieve and riddle[2], As much | that grew in the same wood together.   (s 434)

1508 DUNBAR *Test. of A. Kennedy* l. 55 We were
als sib as seue and riddill, In vna silua que
creuerunt. *a.* **1628** CARMICHAELL no. 199. **1670**
RAY 207 As much sib'd as sieve and ridder, that
grew both in a wood together. **1721** KELLY 31
As sib as Sive and Riddle that grew both in one
Wood. Spoken to them who groundlessly
pretend Kindred to great Persons. **1824** SCOTT
Redg. Lett. 13 Whilk . . . sounds as like being
akin to a peatship & sherriffdom, as a sieve is
sib to a riddle. [[1] related. [2] a course wire sieve.]

Sick, He who never was | dies the first fit.

1732 FULLER no. 2409.

Sick of the sullens.   (s 964)

1580 LYLY *Euph. & his Eng.* ii. 63 She was
solitaryly walking, with hir frowning cloth, as
sick lately of the solens. **1584** *Id. Sappho and
Phao* III. i. 26. **1606–7** SHAKES. *A.C.* I. iii. 13
I am sick and sullen. **1671** CLARKE *Phras. Puer.*
s.v. Sad 288 Sick of the sullens.

Sick Man.

[*i.e.* Turkey.] [**1853** NICHOLAS I.] **1855** HAMLEY
War in Crimea (ed. 3) 11 The true design of the
Czar . . . had been made clear . . . in various
conversations in . . . 1853. 'We have on our
hands a sick man. . . . I repeat to you that the
sick man is dying.' **1909** *Spectator* 2 Oct. The
ambitions of Greeks, when Turkey was only the
'Sick Man', may have had a reasonable hope
of being realized, . . . but . . . Turkey has
rejuvenated herself.

Sick man is not to be pitied who has his cure in his sleeve, That.

1732 FULLER no. 4371.

Sick nor sorry, Neither.

1818 SCOTT *Rob Roy* ch. 12 Among the best good
fellows of the time . . . could carry off their six
bottles under their belt . . . and be neither sick
nor sorry the next morning. **1894** NORTHALL
Folk-phrases 20 . . . Said of one who has caused
annoyance or trouble and takes the matter
lightly. Some understand 'sorry' in the old
sense of *sore.* **1907** SIR W. BUTLER *From Naboth's
V.* 182 The devil is sick and sorry to-day in
South Africa, but his sorrow is for himself. It
does not extend to others.

Sick of a fever lurden,[1] He that is | must be cured by the hazel gelding.   (F 197)

c. **1500** in HAZLITT *Early Pop. Poetry* i. 93 I trow
he was infecte with the faitour, or the
fever lordeyn. **1633** D. DYKE *Com. upon Philemon* 134 Yet sometimes, the fever-lurden having
caught her, she begins to be lazy, and to have no
list to work. **1678** RAY 172. [[1] laziness.]

Sick of the idle crick, and the belly-wark in the heel.   (c 824)

1666 TORRIANO *Prov. Phras.* 218 s.v. Torcicollo
To be sick of a crick in the neck, viz. to play the
Hypocrite, who turns his neck a side in a posture
of Devotion. **1678** RAY 254 . . . Bellywark,
i.e. belly-ake. It is used when People complain
of sickness for a pretence to be idle upon no
apparent cause.

Sick of the idles.   (I 4)

1616 WITHALS 558. **1638** J. CLARKE *Phraseol.
Puerilis* C7 Sicke of the idle. **1639** CLARKE 144.

Sick of the Lombard fever.   (L 413)

[= a fit of idleness.] [*c.* **1553**] **1566–7** UDALL
Ralph Roister D. II. ii. 23 If he haue not one
Lumbardes touche, my lucke is bad. **1659**
HOWELL *Eng. Prov.* 11b. **1670** RAY 215 (feaver,
or of the idles).

Sick of the mulligrubs with eating chopped hay.   (M 1307)

[= ill-tempered and grumbling.] *c.* **1620**
BEAUM. & FL. *Mons. Thomas* II. iii. Whose dog
lies sick o' the mulligrubs? **1670** RAY 218.
1738 SWIFT *Dial.* I. E.L. 280.

Sick of the silver dropsy.   (D 620)

[= inordinate desire for silver.] [*a.* **1511**] **1570**
HENRYSON *Fox, Wolf, and Cadger: Fab.,* ed.
G. G. Smith 150 Ye ar siluer seik, I wait richt

weill.   c. 1548 *Praise of such as sought common-wealths* A3ᵛ Ouide in libro fastorum sayth: that couetousnes is lyke vnto the dropsye.   **1616** DRAXE no. 372 He hath the siluer dropsie.   **1639** CLARKE 40.

Sick, *see also* Healthful man can give counsel to the s.; Physic before he is s. (Takes); Physician, (Every man is a) save him that is s.; Pray for yourself, I am not s.; Yellows, (To be s. of the).

Sicker, *see* Over fast (s.) over loose.

Sickle and the scythe, The | that love I not to see, but the good ale tankard, happy might it be.   (s 421)

1602 WITHALS 7.   **1639** CLARKE 47.

Sickle into another man's corn (harvest), To put one's.   (s 420)

1387 TREVISA tr. Higden viii. 183 (Rolls Ser.) And seide to hym, þou hast no leve to sette þyn hook in oþer men ripe.   **1576** LAMBARDE *Kent* 3A1 (Haruest).   **1578** *Courtly Controv.* X3 To put his sythe into an other mans haruest.   c. **1592** KYD *Span. Trag.* additions l. 1693.   **1659** HOWELL *It. Prov.* 9.

Sickle, *see* Marries between s. and scythe.

Sickness of the body may prove the health of the soul, The.   (s 423)

1624 J. HEWES *Perfect Survey* G2 Sicknesse doth wound or afflict the flesh, but it cures the soule. **1666** TORRIANO *It. Prov.* 119 no. 3.

Sickness shows (tells) us what we are.

1732 FULLER no. 4161.   **1908** S. PAGET *Confessio Medici* 19 Sickness, as Lucretius says of impending death, shows us things as they are: the mask is torn off, the facts remain.

Sickness soaks the purse.   (s 424)

1616 BRETON *Cross. Prov.* B2ᵛ.   **1639** CLARKE 205.

Sickness, *see also* Chamber of· s. is chapel of devotion; Foul dirty ways and long s. (Take heed of); Health and s. men's double enemies; Health is not valued till s.; No man was ever more healthful from s.; Old age is s. of itself.

Side of the hedge, To be on the right (better, safe) *or* wrong.   (s 428)

1600 HOLLAND *Pliny* lxix. Epil. 1246 One who ever loved to be on the better side of the hedge. **1653** BAXTER *Worc. Petit. Def.* 24 If you say, We have too much in any of these particulars; then we are on the safer side of the hedge.   **1697** W. POPE *Seth* [Ward] 40.   **1816** AINSWORTH *Lat. Dict.* s.v. To be on the wrong side of the hedge, or mistaken, *hallucinor, erro.*

Side(s), *see also* Angels (On the s. of the); Better s. the worse; Faults on both s.; Hear all parties (both s.); Jack of both s.; Kindness lies not in

one s.; Laugh on wrong s.; Lick with the rough s. of tongue; Mother's s. is surest; Refuse with the right hand (s.); Right s.; Rise on right (wrong) s.; Safe s.; Two s. to every question; Weak s.

Sieve, To be (leak) like a.   (s 435)

1576 LEMNIUS *Touchstone of Complexions* tr. T. Newton 130ᵛ Pratlers and praters . . . as close as a sieue.   **1592** *Arden of Fev.* v. i. 134 Then stab him till his flesh be as a siue.   [*c.* 1605] **1630** DEKKER 2 *Hon. Whore* I. ii. 132 Is she poore? . . . Then she's a right Strumpet . . . Siues can hold no water, no Harlots hoord vp money.   **1666** TORRIANO *Prov. Phr.* s.v. Vaglio 224 To be like a Sive, viz. which doth not retain, but all goes through.   **1861** C. READE *Cloister and H.* ch. 57 The captain left the helm and came amidships pale as death . . . 'She leaks like a sieve.'

Sieve(s), *see* Blind enough who sees not through s.; Deals in the world (He that) needs four s.; Sib as s. and riddle; Water in a s. (Carry).

Sift him grain by grain and he proves but chaff.   (G 401)

1616 DRAXE no. 525.   **1639** CLARKE 289.

Sigh (*verb*), *see* Never s. but send.

Sight for sore eyes, A.

1738 SWIFT *Dial.* I. E.L. 261 The sight of you is good for sore eyes.   **1826** HAZLITT *Of Persons one Would Wish to have Seen* Wks. (Howe) XVII. 129 What a *sight for sore eyes* that would be [*viz.* to see Garrick act].   **1955** W. P. MILNE *Eppie Eldrick* 264 Ye're a sicht for sair een.

Sight of a man has the force of a lion, The.   (s 439)

1640 HERBERT no. 617.

Sight, *see also* Farther the s. nearer the rain; Least in s., (To play); Love not at first look (s.); Out of s. out of languor; Out of s. out of mind; Pisgah s.; Ship under sail, . . . handsomest s.; Woos a maid.

Sign invites you in, The | but your money must redeem you out.

1642 TORRIANO 7 As you come in the signe inviteth you, but as you go out, you must have money or moneyes worth.   **1732** FULLER no. 4746.

Sike¹ a man as thou wald²· be, draw thee to sike¹ company.   (M 382)

a. **1628** CARMICHAELL no. 1362.   **1641** FERGUSSON no. 742. [¹ such. ² would.]

Sike¹ as the shepherd, sike be his sheep.   (s 328)

1579 SPENSER *Shep. Cal.* Sept. Wks. (Globe) 474 Sike as the shepheards, sike bene her sheepe.

1581 T. LUPTON *Siuquila* 101 Such Shepheard such Sheepe. [¹ such.]

Silence does seldom harm.   (S 445)

c. **1549** J. HALL *Proverbs of Salomon* A5ᵛ For wordes oftimes men haue ben shente, For sylence kept, fewe them repent. **1630** BRATHWAITE *Eng. Gent.* &c. (1641) 51 Silence . . . may doe good, but can doe little harme. **1639** CLARKE 284 Silence never did man harme. **1670** RAY 24. **1732** FULLER no. 4170 Silence seldom hurts.

Silence gives consent.   (S 446)

c. **1380** WYCLIF *Sel. Wks.* III. 349 Oo maner of consent is, whanne a man is stille & telliþ not. *c.* **1490** *Partonope* E.E.T.S. 467 This proverbe was seide full longe a-go: 'Who so holdeth hym still dothe assent.' **1551** CRANMER *Ans. to Gardiner* 114 The lawe saithe, Qui tacet, consentire videtur. **1591** LYLY *Endym.* v. iii. 211 Silence, Madame, consents. **1611** COTGRAVE s.v. Consentir He consents enough that sayes nothing; (Many, who know not much more Latine, can say, *Qui tacet consentire videtur.*¹) **1651** HOBBES *Leviath.* II. xxxvi. 138 Silence is sometimes an argument of Consent. **1721** KELLY 299. **1847–9** HELPS *Friends in C.* Ser. ix I have known a man . . . bear patiently . . . a serious charge which a few lines would have entirely answered. . . . Silence does not give consent in these cases. **1883** FROUDE *Short Stud.* IV. I. vii. 77 The archbishop [Becket] answered that there was a proverb in England that silence gave consent. [*c.* 1200 in *Materials Hist. Becket* (Rolls) I. 68.] [¹ BONIFACE VIII. *Sexti Decret. Lib.* V. xii.]

Silence in the pigmarket, and let the old sow have a grunt.

1894 NORTHALL *Folk-phrases* E.D.S. 22.

Silence (is) the best ornament of a woman.   (S 447)

[SOPH. *Ajax* 293.] **1539** TAVERNER 50 *Mulierem ornat silentium.* Silence garnysheth a woman. **1547** BALDWIN (1550) K7ᵛ Silence in a woman, is a great and a goodly vertue. *a.* **1619** DANIEL *To Lady Anne Clifford* 85 Through silence women never ill became. **1659** HOWELL *Eng. Prov.* 11a.

Silence, *see also* Repented speech than s. (More); Sorrow makes s. best orator; Speech is silvern, s. golden; Wisdom to s. (No).

Silent as death (the grave).   (D 135)

1377 LANGLAND *P. Pl.* B. x. 137 As doumbe as deth. **1604** SHAKES. *O.* V. ii. 96 Ha! no more moving? Still as the grave. **1826** T. H. LISTER *Granby* ii. 290 Still as death. **1829** SCOTT *Jrnl.* 1 July The house . . . became silent as the grave. **1889** R. L. STEVENSON *Master of Ball.* ch. 3 As silent as the grave.

Silent, He that is | gathers stones.

1599 MINSHEU *Span. Dial.* 20 Although I hold my peace, I gather vp stones. **1706** STEVENS s.v. Piedra. **1813** RAY 159.

Silent Highway, The.

[= the Thames.] **1859** G. A. SALA *Twice Round Clock* (1878) 87 The Silent Highway has been their travelling route. On the broad . . . bosom of Father Thames, they have been borne in swift, grimy little steamboats.

Silent Sister.

1834 FATHER PROUT in *Fraser* I Aug. The silent and unproductive Trinity College Dublin [at that time producing few books]. **1896** W. O'C. MORRIS *Ireland 1494–1868*, 245 The University of Dublin . . . was not supported by great public schools, . . . and it was long known by the name of the 'Silent Sister'.

Silent, *see also* Beware of a s. dog (man); Fools are wise as long as s.; Night, (As secret (s.) as the); Speak fitly or be s. wisely; Wise men s. fools talk.

Silk and scarlet walks many a harlot, In.

1869 HAZLITT 234. **1892** NORTHALL *Eng. Folk Rhymes* 547 A certain lady . . . observing a mason carefully working said, 'By *line* and rule, works many a fool, . . .' To which the man readily responded, 'In silk and scarlet walks many a harlot, . . .'

Silk, The fairest | is soonest stained.
                                               (S 450)

1575 GASCOIGNE *Glass of Gov.* ii. 59 The finest Silkes, do seeld continue freshe. **1579** LYLY *Euph.* i. 189 (soyled). **1639** CLARKE 83 (as 1579). **1670** RAY 88 . . . The handsomest women are soonest corrupted, because they are most tempted. It may also be applied to good natures, which are more easily drawn away by evil company.

Silk purse (Velvet) out of a sow's ear, You cannot make a.   (P 666)

c. **1514** BARCLAY *Eclog.* v. 360 None can . . . make goodly silke of a gotes flece. **1579** GOSSON *Ephemerides* 62b Seekinge . . . too make a silke purse of a Sowes eare, that when it shoulde close, will not come togeather. **1659** HOWELL *Eng. Prov.* 13a You will never make a Sattin purse of a Sowes ear. **1670** RAY 152 (make velvet). **1738** SWIFT *Dial.* II. E.L. 315. **1762** STERNE *T. Shandy* ch. 4 Slawkenburgius's Tale, As certainly as you can make a velvet-cap out of sow's ear. **1834** MARRYAT *P. Simple* ch. 12 The master, . . . having been brought up in a collier, he could not be expected to be very refined; . . . 'it was impossible to make a silk purse out of a sow's ear'. **1875** BROWNING *Inn Album* i. Still silk purse Roughs finger with some bristle sow-ear-armed.

Silks and satins put out the fire in the chimney (kitchen fire).   (S 452)

1640 HERBERT no. 912. **1721** KELLY 293 (kitchen fire). Commonly spoken by Servants, when they think that their Masters' and Mistresses' extravagant Cloaths make their Meat and Drink something scarcer. **1758** FRANKLIN in ARBER E.

Garner v. 583 Many a one, for the sake of finery on the back, has gone with a hungry belly, and half starved their families. Silks and satins, scarlet and velvets, as Poor RICHARD says, put out the kitchen fire!

Silk, *see also* Adam's children (we are all), but s. makes the difference; Eats leaves and voids s.; Silver in his purse (He that has not), should have s. on tongue.

Sillier than a crab, that has all his brains in his belly, He is.

1642 TORRIANO 97 (paunch). 1659 HOWELL *It. Prov.* 16. Thou art a greater fool then the Crab, who carrieth his brains in his pocket. 1732 FULLER no. 1944.

Silly Billy.

[1836] 1881 GOLDW. SMITH *Lect. & Ess.* 193 Old William, Duke of Gloucester, the King's uncle, being rather weak in intellect, was called 'Silly Billy'.

Silly[1] child is soon ylered.[2]   (B 44)

c. 1300 *Prov. of Hending* 9 Sely child is sone ylered. *c.* 1386 CHAUCER *Prior. T.* l. 1701 And he forgate it naught, For sely child wol alday soone leere. *c.* 1400 *Latin MS. 394, John Rylands Libr.* (ed. Pantin) in *Bull. J. R. Libr.* XIV, f. 17*a* Sely chylde sone lerned. 1641 FERGUSSON no. 750 Sillie bairns are eith to lear. [[1] good, forward. [2] taught.]

Silly fish that is caught twice with the same bait, It is a.   (F 316)

1581 N. WOODES *Conflict of Conscience* B4ᵛ The Fish once taken, and scaped from baight, Will euer heareafter, beware of the hooke. 1732 FULLER no. 2879.

Silly (Sairy, Sorry) flock where the ewe bears the bell, It is a.   (F 377)

a. 1628 CARMICHAELL no. 858 (sarie flock quhair the yow). 1641 FERGUSSON no. 482 (zowe)[1]. 1721 KELLY 181 (sairy). It is a bad House where the Wife commands. 1732 FULLER no. 2885. [[1] ewe.]

Silly Jockey, There never was a | but there was as silly a Jenny.

ã. 1628 CARMICHAELL no. 1527 There was never sa sarie a Jokkie bot he gat as sarie a Jeanie. 1821 J. GALT *Annals of Par.* ch. 27 Take a lady of your own. . . . There never was a silly Jock, but there was as silly a Jenny. 1832 HENDERSON 142.

Silly man that can neither do good nor ill, He is a.

1721 KELLY 137 Used as a Dissuasive from disobliging any, even the meanest, for some time or other it may be in his Power to do you Service, or Disservice.

Silly pack that may not pay the custom, It is a.   (P 6)

a. 1628 CARMICHAELL no. 954. 1641 FERGUSSON no. 546. 1721 KELLY 178 It's an ill pack that's no worth the Custom. It is a bad Thing that is not worth any small Pains, or Cost, that it may require.

Silly season.

[August & Sept., when newspapers, for lack of real news, discussed trivial topics.] 1871 *Punch* 9 Sept. 102/2 The present time of the year has been named 'the silly season'. 1884 *Illustr. Lond. News* 23 Aug. 171/1 The 'silly season' having begun . . . , the newspapers are, as a necessary consequence, full of instructive and amusing matter.

Silly Suffolk.

1867 J. G. NALL *Gt. Yarm. & Glos. E. Angl.* 720 'Silly Suffolk' and 'Essex Calves' are local amenities liberally bestowed on each other by the natives.

Silly Sutton.

1892 *Eastern Ev. News*, Norwich 15/11 in LEAN I. 152 In this district we had . . . 'Silly Sutton' . . . Sutton is awarded its . . . title from the tradition that its aged natives . . . put their hands out of their bedroom windows to feel if it was daylight.

Silver in his purse, He that has not | should have silk on his tongue.   (S 455)

1611 COTGRAVE s.v. Avoir Qui n'a argent en bourse ait du moins du miel en bouche. Let him that cannot spend freely speake faire. 1659 HOWELL *It. Prov.* 5 Who hath not money in his purse, let him have honey in his mouth. 1721 KELLY 143 . . . He that cannot pay his Debts should at least give good Words. 1732 FULLER no. 2149 (Silver on his Tongue).

Silver key can open an iron lock, A.   (K 24)

1607 DEKKER & WEBSTER *Westw. Ho* II. ii. 39 Here is golden keyes T'vnlock thy lips. 1618 *The Owl's Almanack* 39 Siluer keyes open any doores. 1732 FULLER no. 400.

Silver streak.

[*i.e.* the English Channel.] 1879 *Even. Standard* 11 Nov. The answer of the citizens of London to the 'silver-streak' politicians. 1903 H. B. GEORGE *Relat. of Geog. & Hist.* 136 The value of the 'silver streak', as a defence for England against her enemies, scarcely needs demonstration in words. 1909 *Sphere* 27 Mar. 'The silver streak' can be crossed in little over an hour from Folkestone or Dover.

Silver will have a silver sound.   (S 458)

1594–5 SHAKES. *R.J.* IV. v. 129 Silver hath a sweet sound. 1616 DRAXE no. 2488. 1639 CLARKE 112.

Silver, *see also* Angle with s. hook; Born with a s. spoon; Cloud has s. lining; No s. no servant;

No s. without dross; Shoot with s. gun; Sick of the s. dropsy; Tip the cow's horn with s.; White s. draws black lines.

Silvered pin, fair without but foul within, He is like a.

1813 RAY 237.

Simile runs on all fours, No.   (S 460)

[L. *Nullum simile quatuor pedibus currit.*] **1551** CRANMER *Ans. to Gardiner* 338 Similitudes maye not be pressed in all pointes, but in the purpose wherfore they be broght. **1598** CHAPMAN *Iliad* ii (comm.) That a simile must *semper uno pede claudicare* [from Spondanus] . . . only sheweth how vain vulgar tradition is. **1607** R. WILKINSON *The Merchant Royal. A Sermon* 12 As the saying is in the schooles, Similitudo non currit quatuor pedibus: Many things may be like, yet nothing like in all things. **1629** T. ADAMS *Serm.* (1861–2) I. 376 No metaphor should of necessity run like a coach on four wheels. **1692** BENTLEY *Phalaris* (Bohn) 13 quotes 'the English proverb'. **1825** MACAULAY *Ess. on Milton* It is not easy to make a simile go on all fours. **1905** ALEX. MACLAREN *Expos., Matthew* III. 39 No metaphor of that sort goes on all fours, and there has been a great deal of harm done . . . by carrying out too completely the analogy between money debts and our sins against God.

Simon, *see* Simple S.; Sup, S.

Simon and Jude[1] all the ships on the sea home they do crowd.

1902–4 LEAN I. 381. [1 SS. Simon & Jude, Oct. 28.]

Simonds (Symonds, Simondsall) sauce, To eat of.   (S 96)

1582 W. W. *True and just Record* A4ᵛ (and C5ᵛ) If you will not be ruled, you shall haue Simonds sauce. *c.* **1640** SMYTH *Berkeley MSS.* no. 34, 30 Vsuall To note a guest bringinge an hungry appetite to our table. Or when a man eates little, to say hee wants some of Simondsall sauce. The farme of Simondsall stands on the highest place and purest aire of all that country [Gloucestershire].

Simper-de-cocket.   (S 462)

[An affected, coquettish air; a woman characterized by this; a flirt.] *a.* **1529** SKELTON *E. Rummyng* 55 She wyll iet. . . . In her furred flocket, And gray russet rocket, With symper the cocket. *a.* **1530** HEYWOOD *Weather* 877 (Brandl), I saw you dally with your symper de cokket. **1546** *Id.* II. i. F2ᵛ Vpright as a candell standth in a socket, Stoode she that daie, so sympre de coket. **1621** JONSON *Gypsies Metam.* vii. 571 Diuing the pockettes And sounding the socketts Of Simper-the Cocketts. **1707** tr. *Wks. C'tess D'Anois* (1715) 384 I have here in my Custody, said she, a little Simper de cockit that will not let me be at quiet.

Simpers like a bride on her wedding-day, She.   (B 664)

1678 RAY 288. **1699** A. BOYER *Compleat French Master* 131 As troublesom to set out as a Bride on her Wedding Night.

Simpers like a furmity kettle, She.
(F 789)

1530 PALSGRAVE 718a I symper, as lycour dothe on the fyre byfore it begynneth to boyle. **1565** J. PHILLIP *Patient Grissil* C3 l. 429 Symper like a fyrmentie pot. **1566** PAINTER ed. Jacobs ii. 144 To whom she said (smiling like a frumenty pot) . . . **1594** NASHE *Unf. Trav.* ii. 225 I sympered with my countenance like a porredge pot on the fire when it first begins to seethe. **1678** RAY 289. **1738** SWIFT *Dial.* I. E.L. 273 Her tongue runs like the clapper of a mill. . . .—And yet she simpers like a firmity kettle.

Simpers like a mare when she eats thistles, She.   (M 653)

1575 R. LANEHAM *Lett.* ed. Furnivall 23. **1639** CLARKE 120.

Simpers like a riven dish, She.   (D 373)

1678 RAY 288.

Simple man is the beggar's brother, The.

1832 HENDERSON 92.

Simple Simon.

1665 PLAYFORD *Dancing Master* 'Simple Simon' a tune. *c.* **1685** *Simple Simon's Misfortunes* [a ballad]. **1785** GROSE *Dict. Vulgar T.* s.v. Simple Simon a natural, a silly fellow. **1899** *Westm. Gaz.* 12 June 5/1 A tall, ungainly Simple Simon of a peasant.

Simple, *see also* Innocent (s.) as a dove.

Simples, *see* Battersea; Cut for the s.

Sin brings its punishment with it, Every.   (S 467)

1616 DRAXE no. 1782 As a man sinneth, so is his punishment. **1640** HERBERT no. 760. **1756** J. WESLEY *Letters* iii. 164 One sin will punish another till the day of grace is at an end. **1834** MARRYAT *Jacob Faith.* ch. 14 That is the punishment of making free with the bottle, . . . but if it is an offence, then it carries its own punishment.

Sin plucks (pulls) on sin. *Cf.* Crimes are made secure by greater crimes.
(C 826)

[SENECA *Ag.* l. 115: Per scelera semper sceleribus tutum est iter.] *c.* **1425** *Castle of Perseverance* l. 1035 Euery synne tyllyth in other. [*c.* **1587**] **1592** KYD *Span. Trag.* III. xiii. 6 Per scelus semper tutum est sceleribus iter . . . . Euils vnto ils conductors be. [1592] **1597** SHAKES. *Rich. III* IV. ii. 66 Sin will pluck on sin. **1596** F. SABIE *David and Beersheba* Thus euermore sinne leadeth vnto sinne. *c.* **1607** HEYWOOD & ROWLEY *Fortune by Land and Sea* I. ii. Hazl.-Dods. vi. 378 Sin pulls on sin. **1620** SHELTON *Quix.* II. lx. iii. 248 One horror brings on another, and one sin.

Sin that is hidden is half-forgiven.
(s 472)

1567 G. FENTON *Bandello* T.T. ii. 149 Me thinkes a falte don in secrett is halfe perdoned. **1629** *Bk. Mer. Rid.* Prov. no. 25.

Sin to sell dear, It is no | but a sin to give ill measure.

1721 KELLY 189 . . . When you sell the Buyers are on their Guard, but Measures and Weights are left to your Conscience. **1732** FULLER no. 2993 It is not a sin to sell dear, but it is to make ill measure.

Sin(s), *see also* Charity covers s.; Fall into s. is human; Fear nothing but s.; Gluttony s. of England; Hospitality (S. against); Idleness is root of s.; Law grows of s.; Lie against the devil (S. to); Old s. new shame; Punishment (Many without), none without s.; Satan reproves s.; Seven deadly s.; Sorrow is good for nothing but s.; Swims in s. shall sink in sorrow; Ugly as s. *See also* Sins.

Sinew, *see* Tough s. in auld wife's heel.

Sinews of war, *see* Money is the s.

Sing before breakfast, If you | you'll cry before night. *Cf.* Laugh before breakfast.
(M 1176)

1530 PALSGRAVE 776 You waxe mery this morning, God gyve grace you wepe nat or nyght.

Sing *lachrymae*, To.
(L 15)

[= to lament. Refers to John Dowland's 'Lachrimae or Seaven Teares', London, 1605.] **1614** SIR T. OVERBURY *Characters* Wks. (1890) 155 *A Prison.* Every man here sings *Lachrymae* at first sight.

Sing like a lark, To.
(L 70)

1590 SPENSER *F.Q.* II. vi. 3 Sometimes she sung, as loud as larke in aire. *c.* **1592** SHAKES. *T.And.* III. i. 158 Did ever raven sing so like a lark. **1596** *Id. M.V.* V. i. 102 The crow doth sing as sweetly as the lark When neither is attended. **1620** SHELTON *Quix.* II. xix. ii. 313 He . . . sings like a lark, plays a gittern as if he made it speak. **1621** JONSON *Gypsies Metam.* vii. 600. **1847–8** THACKERAY *Vanity F.* ch. 5 Amelia came . . . singing like a lark.

Sing (one's) *nunc dimittis*, To.

[= to declare glad acceptance of release from life or some employment. The first words of the Song of Simeon in *Luke* ii. 29.] **1642** NETHERSOLE *Consid. upon Affairs* 8 I should . . . cheerfully sing my *Nunc dimittis.* **1776** J. ADAMS Wks. (1854) IX. 391 When these things are once completed, I shall . . . sing my *nunc dimittis*, return to my farm [&c.]. **1825** HAN. MORE in W. ROBERTS *Mem.* (1834) IV. 257 If I could see the abolition of the slavery . . . in the West Indies . . . I could sing my *nunc dimittis* with joy. **1859** DARWIN *Life & Lett.* (1887) II. 232 I am now contented, and can sing my 'nunc dimittis'.

Sing *placebo*, To.
(P 378)

[= to play the sycophant, be time-serving. L. *Placebo.* I shall be pleasing or acceptable. *Placebo Domino in regione vivorum, Ps.* cxiv. 9 Vulg.] **1340** *Ayenb.* 60 þe uerþe zenne is þet huanne hi alle zingeþ 'Placebo', þet is to zigge: 'mi lhord zayþ zoþ, mi lhord deþ wel'. *c.* **1386** CHAUCER *Pars. T.* I. l. 616 Flatereres been the deueles Chapelleyns that syngen euere Placebo. *c.* **1534** GILES Duwes l. 1676. **1607–8** BACON *Gen. Naturaliz.* Wks. (1879) I. 467 If any man shall think that I have sung a placebo, for mine own particular, I would have him know that I am not so unseen in the world. **1818** SCOTT *Let.* 12 Nov. in LOCKHART *Life* ch. 43 He is too much addicted to the *placebo* . . . too apt to fear to give offence by contradiction.

Sing so merry a note, Who can | as he that cannot change a groat?
(N 249)

1546 HEYWOOD I. xii. E4ᵛ. And who can syng so mery a note, As maie he, that can not chaunge a grote. Ye (quoth he) beggers maie syng before theeues. **1611** DAVIES no. 318. **1659** HOWELL *Eng. Prov.* 3b.

Sing the same (another) song, To.
(s 637–8)

[TERENCE *Phormio* 3. 2. 10 *Cantilenam eandem canis.* You sing the same song.] **1390** GOWER *Conf. Amantis* I. 260 O thou, which hast desesed The Court of France be thi wrong, Now schalt thou singe an other song. **1483** TERENCE *Vulgaria* Q3ᵛ Thou syngeste alwey oon songe. **1548** HALL 796 The Lady Katerine . . . euer continued in her old song. **1588** J. UDALL *Diotrephes* Arb. 18 If they had euen my experience, they would sing another song. **1670** RAY 192 . . . Nothing more troublesom and ungrateful then the same thing over and over. **1711** W. KING tr. *Naude's Ref. Politics* iii. 91 The Jesuits began to play their part, and sing another song.

Sing(s), *see also* Beggar may s. before thief; Bird loves to hear herself s.; Dirt-bird s., we shall have rain; Learn to say before you s.; Little birds that can s.; Many a man s. that wife home brings; Nightingale with a thorn against one's breast, (To sit (s.) like a); Robin s. in bush (If); Swan s. when death comes.

Singed cat, He is like the | better than he's likely.[1]

a. **1628** CARMICHAELL no. 1760 Ye bred of a singet cat ye are better nor ye are like. **1737** RAMSAY 40. **1914** K. F. PURDON *Folk of Furry F.* ch. 2 Maybe I'm like the singed cat, better than I look! [1 of good appearance.]

Singest like a bird called a swine, Thou.
(B 383)

1678 RAY 269.

Singing man keeps his shop in his throat, The.
(M 376)

1640 HERBERT no. 918.

Single long, shame at length. (s 278)

1659 HOWELL *Brit. Prov.* 21.

Sings on Friday, He that | will weep on Sunday. (F 680)

1640 HERBERT no. 411. **1642** FULLER *Fast Serm. on Innoc. Day* (1891) I. 241 Let not old men . . . be transported with their follies. . . . The French proverb saith, They that laugh on Friday, shall cry on Sunday. [Fr. Tel qui rit vendredi, dimanche pleurera.]

Sings to the deaf (at a deaf man's door), He. *Cf.* **Knock at a deaf man's door. Tale to a deaf man.** (M 499)

1542 T. BECON *Invective against Swearing* (n.d., B4ᵛ) Some . . . shal laugh at this my laboure as a songe sunge to them that are deafe cared. **1550** R. CROWLEY *One and Thirty Epigrams* E.E.T.S. 11 This my tale is to deafe men tolde. **1562** A. BROOKE *Romeus and Juliet* l. 2409 In vain vnto the deaf she calls. **1567** PAINTER ed. Jacobs ii. 247 What follies doe I vaunt by singing to the deafe. *Ibid.* iii. 113 The poore olde Woman . . . sange a song vnto the deafe. **1616** DRAXE no. 433. **1631** DEKKER *Penny-Wise, Pound-Foolish* B2] The musicke of their enchanting tongues but songs to the deafe. **1638** J. CLARKE *Phraseol. Puerilis* E2ᵛ. **1693** W. ROBERTSON *Phraseol. Generalis* 429a.

Sings, *see also* Sing(s).

Sink or swim. (s 485)

c. **1368** CHAUCER *Compl. Pity* l. 110 Ye rekke not whethyr I flete or sinke. **1386** *Id. Knight's T.* l. 2397 She . . . reccheth neuere wher I synke or fleete. *c.* **1475** 'Play of Robin Hood' Malone Soc. *Coll.* i. 130. **1538** STARKEY *England* I. iii. 85 They care not (as hyt ys com mynly sayd) 'whether they synke or swyme'. **1597** SHAKES. *I Hen. IV* I. iii. 194 If he fall in, good night, or sink or swim! **1668** R. STEELE *Husbandman's Calling* iii. (1672) 29 I will be just and honest, sink or swim. **1818** SCOTT *Ht. Midl.* ch. 26 Sink or swim, I am determined to gang to Lunnon. **1889** 'R. BOLDREWOOD' *Robbery under Arms* ch. 23 It's sink or swim with all of us.

Sinner, *see* Greater the s. the greater the saint.

Sins and our debts are often more than we think, Our. (s 476)

1642 TORRIANO 59. **1658** *Comes Facundus* 23. **1659** HOWELL *It. Prov.* 1 Our sinnes and our debts are alwayes more then we take them to be. **1721** KELLY 273 . . . We are too apt to have too good an Opinion of our Condition both in reference to this World, and another.

Sins are not known till they be acted. (s 477)

1593–4 SHAKES. *Luc.* l. 527 The fault unknown is as a thought unacted. **1640** HERBERT no. 942.

Sins grow old, When all | covetousness is young. (s 479)

1557 EDGEWORTH 2Y1ᵛ It is a very true saiynge: *Omnibus viciis senescentibus sola auaritia iuuenescit.* When all vices waxe olde, couetise onely waxeth yonge againe. **1560** BECON *Catechism* P.S. 373 Covetousness is a vice appropriated . . . to old men, according to this old saying: *Cum omnia vitia senescunt, sola avaritia juvenescit:* 'When all vices wax old, covetousness alone waxeth young.' **1640** HERBERT no. 18.

Sins, *see also* Sin(s).

Sion, *see* Nun of S.

Sip up the Severn and swallow Malvern, You may as soon. (s 259)

1659 HOWELL *Eng. Prov.* 20a . . . meant of impossibilities. **1787** GROSE (*Worcs.*) 231 . . . That is, sip up a great river, and swallow a range of hills.

Sip, *see also* Blow first, s. afterwards.

Sir, *see* Call one s. and something else.

Sir Robert, *see* Robert.

Sire, *see* Litter is like to s. and dam.

Sirrah[1] your dogs, sirrah not me; for I was born before you could see. (D 502)

1670 RAY 192 Sirrah your dogs. **1732** FULLER no. 6496. [[1] a contemptuous form of address.]

Sister of the Charterhouse,[1] She is a. (s 489)

1528 TYNDALE *Obed. Chrn. Man* P.S. 305 Of her that answereth her husband six words for one, we say, 'She is a sister of the Charter house': as who should say, 'She thinketh that she is not bound to keep silence; their silence shall be a satisfaction for her.' [[1] a Carthusian monastery with severe discipline.]

Sister(s), *see also* Brother had rather see s. rich; Silent S.; Three s.

Sisyphus, *see* Stone of S.

Sit awhile and go a mile. (w 300)

1530 PALSGRAVE 436b Rest a whyle and ronne a myle. **1639** CLARKE 235.

Sit in Rome and strive against the Pope, It is hard to. (R 166)

a. **1628** CARMICHAELL no. 1847. Ye may not sit in Rome and strive with the Pape. **1641** FERGUSSON no. 901 (as *a.* 1628). **1721** KELLY 194 . . . It is foolish to strive with our Governours, Landlords, or those under whose Distress we are. **1904–10** A. MACLAREN *Expos., Daniel* 58 'It is ill sitting at Rome and striving with the Pope'. Nebuchadnezzar's palace was not precisely the place to dispute with Nebuchadnezzar.

Sit in the chair that have malt to sell,
They may. (C 215)

1639 CLARKE 99.

Sit in your place, and none can make
you rise. (P 375)

1611 COTGRAVE s.v. Seoir He needs not feare
to be chidden that sits where he is bidden. **1640**
HERBERT no. 372. **1721** KELLY 299 Sit in your
seat, and none will raise you. Spoken to those
who have gotten an Affront for presuming
beyond their Station. **1853** TRENCH V. 115
Genuine modesty and manly self-assertion are
united in this: Sit in your own place, and no
man can make you rise.

Sit near the fire when the chimney
smokes, It is best to.

1729 FENTON'S *Waller: Observations* etc. 141.
1779–81 JOHNSON *Lives of Poets* (Napier) I. 236
Roscommon, foreseeing that some violent con-
cussion of the State was at hand, purposed to
retire to Rome, alleging, that it was best to sit
near the chimney when the chamber smoaked.
1826 SCOTT *Woodst.* ch. 21 It is best sitting near
the fire when the chimney smokes; . . . Woodstock, . . . in the vicinity of the soldiers, will be
less suspected . . . than more distant corners.

Sit on (upon *or* in) one's skirts, To.
(S 513)

[= to press hard upon one; punish severely.]
1546 HEYWOOD I. v. B2 Hold their noses to
grinstone, and syt on theyr skurtis, That erst
sate on myne. **1583** G. BABINGTON *Expos*[n]. *of
Commdmts.* P.S. 511 As our . . . might and
power is, we sitte vpon his skirtes. **1654** H.
L'ESTRANGE *Chas. I* (1655) 184 Many began . . .
to sit upon the Bishops skirts, that is,to controvert
the motes and bounds of their authority. **1755**
SMOLLETT *Quix.* II. iii. xv. (1803) IV. 75 If my
government holds, . . . I will sit upon the skirts
of more than one of these men of business.

Sit on your thumb till more room do
come.

1894 NORTHALL *Folk-phrases* E.D.S. 22 . . .
A reply to a child that continually says, 'Where
shall I sit?'

Sits above that deals acres (land), He.
(A 25)

c. **1300** *Provs. of Hend.* in *Anglia* 51. 267 Heye
he sit þat akeres deleþ. *a.* **1628** CARMICHAELL
no. 654 (akers). **1641** FERGUSSON no. 351.
1721 KELLY 162 . . . An Appeal to the Divine
Providence, Justice, and Omniscience.

Sits full still that has riven breeks, He.
(B 649)

a. **1628** CARMICHAELL no. 779. **1641** FERGUSSON
no. 383. **1721** KELLY 149 . . . A Man who is
not very clamorous in his Complaints, may lye
under as great Inconveniencies as they that do.
It took its rise from the Earl of Angus, who
being in an Engagement,[1] . . . stayed till all his
Men were drest, and then told them that he was

wounded himself, by repeating this Proverb.
1822 SCOTT *Nigel* ch. 35 Poortith takes away
pith, and the man sits full still that has a rent in
his breeks. **1852** E. FITZGERALD *Polonius* 63 The
Guilty Man. May escape, but he cannot rest
sure of doing so.—*Epicurus.* Riven breeks sit
still. [[1] Shrewsbury, 1403.]

Sits not sure that sits too high, He.
(S 493)

1611 COTGRAVE s.v. Asseuré. He is not safe
that's got too high.

Sits well, He that | thinks ill. (S 494)

1573 SANFORD 50[v]. **1578** FLORIO *First F.* 28.
1629 *Bk. Mer. Rid.* Prov. no. 10.

Sit(s), *see also* Better rue s. than rue flit; Better
s. still than rise and fall; Discontented man
knows not where to s. easy; Do as thy master
commands thee and s. down at table; Frog on
chopping-block (S. like); Lowly s. richly warm;
Nightingale with a thorn against one's breast,
(To s. like a); Patch and long s.; Wire-drawer
(S. like).

Sitting, *see* Cheap s. as standing.

Six awls make a shoemaker. (A 407)

1668 SKIPPON *Diary* Sept. 15, 163 (Six alls).
1670 RAY 216.

Six days shalt thou labour and do all
that thou art able, and on the seventh
—holystone the decks and scrape the
cable.

1840 DANA *Two Years bef. Mast* ch. 3 Some
officers . . . have set them to . . . scraping the
chain cables. The 'Philadelphia Catechism' is,...

Six feet of earth make all men equal.
(F 582)

1563 *Mirr. for Mag.* ed. Campbell 375 Myne
heritage but seven foote of earth. **1579** LYLY
Euph. i. 314 Philip falling in the dust, and seeing
the figure of his shape perfect in shewe: Good
God sayd he, we desire the whole earth and see
how little serueth. **1584** *Id. Camp.* v. iv. 50
How much ground would content thee? . . . the
length of my body. [**1589**] **1592** *Id. Midas* III.
i. 12 What should I doo with a world of ground,
whose bodie must be content with seauen foote
of earth? *c.* **1595–6** SHAKES. *K.J.* IV. ii. 99 That
blood which owed the breadth of all this isle,
Three foot of it doth hold. **1597** *Id. I Hen. IV*
V. iv. 91 Two paces of the vilest earth is room
enough. **1659** HOWELL *It. Prov.* 8. **1785** WESLEY
Journal vii. 182 And what has he [Marquis of
Rockingham] now? Six feet of earth.

Six hours' sleep for a man, seven for a
woman, and eight for a fool.
(*Cf.* H 746)

1623 WODROEPHE 310 The Student sleepes six
Howres, the Traueller seuen; the Workeman
eight, and all Laizie Bodies sleepe nine houres

and more. **1642** TORRIANO 38 The traveller sleepeth five houres, the scholar seaven, the merchant eight, and every knave eleven. **1864** FRISWELL *Gentle Life* 259 John Wesley . . . considered that five hours' sleep was enough for him or any man. . . . The old English proverb, so often in the mouth of George III, was 'six hours for a man, seven for a woman, and eight for a fool'. **1908** *Spectator* 19 Dec. Is there not a proverb that a man requires six hours' sleep, a woman seven, a child eight and only a fool more? If this be true, thousands of great men were, and are, fools.

Six of one and half a dozen of the other.

[= little or no difference between two (sets of) persons or things.] **1836** MARRYAT *Pirate* ch. 4 I never knows the children. It's just six of one and half-a-dozen of the other. **1864** J. PAYN *Lost Sir M.* ch. 16 'There were faults on both sides; it was six of one, and—'. **1889** 'R. BOLDREWOOD' *Robbery under Arms* ch. 11 It's six of one and half-a-dozen of the other, so far as being on the square goes.

Six strings, *see* Whip with s. s.

Sixes and sevens, To be (set all) at.
(A 208)

[= To be careless of consequences, or let things go to disorder: the original form, *on six and seven*, is based on dicing.] *c.* **1340** *Avowyne of Arthur* Camden Soc. st. 65 Alle in Sundur hit brast in six or in seuyn. *c.* **1374** CHAUCER *Troilus* Bk. 4, l. 622 Let nat this wrechched wo thyn herte gnawe, But manly set the world on sexe and seuene. *c.* **1410** *Towneley Plays* xvi, l. 128 I shall, and that in hy set all on sex and seuen. *a.* **1500** *15c. School-Bk.* ed. W. Nelson 18 He . . . settes all at sixe and sevyn. **1535** JOYE *Apol. Tindale* Arb. 43 Yet had he leuer marre and destroy al, and (as they saye) set all at six and seuen, then [&c.]. **1595–6** SHAKES. *Rich. II* I. ii. 121 All is uneven, And everything is left at six and seven. [1600] **1631** T. HEYWOOD I *Fair Maid* ii. 280 I will bring them in a reckning at six and at sevens. **1629** T. ADAMS *Serm.* (1861–2) III. 61 He that sits on the throne is not idle; to let all things in the world run at sixes and sevens. **1655–62** GURNALL *Chrn. in Armour* (1865) I. 154 Calling left at six and sevens; yea, wife and children crying, may be starving; while the wretch is . . . wasting their livelihood. **1712** ARBUTHNOT *John Bull* II. i. His Affairs went on at sixes and sevens. **1843** MRS. CARLYLE in *New Lett.* (1903) I. 219 With her departure everything went to sixes and sevens. **1848** THACKERAY *Vanity F.* ch. 54 There's a regular shinty in the house; and everything at sixes and sevens.

Sixpence, *see* Loses his wife and s. (He that).

Size cinque will not, and deuce ace cannot, then quatre trey must, If.
(S 496)

[Taken from dicing.] **1602–3** *Diary of Jno. Manningham* Camden Soc. 81 'Size ace will not, deux ace cannot, quater tree must', quothe Blackborne, when he sent for wine; a common phrase of subsidies and such taxes, the greate ones will not, the little ones cannot, the meane men must pay for all. **1678** RAY 348 . . . The

middle sort bear publick burthens, Taxes, &c. most. Deux ace non possunt & size cinque solvere nolunt: Est igitur notum quatre trey solvere totum.

Skaiths, *see* Better two s. than one sorrow.

Skatt, *see* Haldon has a hat, (When), let Kenton beware of a s.

Skeer your own fire.

1917 BRIDGE 109 . . . Skeer = to rake out. Mind your own business.

Skein, *see* Tangled s. to wind off.

Skeleton at the feast, The.

[HDT. 2. 78. PETRON. 35.] **1651** JER. TAYLOR *Holy Dying* ii. § 1 (1850) 330 All the wise and good men of the world, . . . chose to throw some ashes into their chalices . . . Such was . . . the Egyptian skeleton served up at feasts. **1839** MRS. CARLYLE *Let.* 20 May Poor Mrs. Edward Irving . . . in her weeds, . . . seemed to me . . . like the skeleton which the old Egyptians placed at table, in their feasts, to be a memorial of their latter end. **1909** E. PHILLPOTTS *The Haven* I. iii. Dick . . . was a skeleton at the feast of life in Brixham.

Skeleton in the closet (cupboard), The.

[A secret source of shame or pain to a family or person.] **1845** THACKERAY *Punch in the East* Wks. O.U.P. viii. 27 There is a skeleton in every house. **1855** *Id. Newcomes* ch. 55 Some particulars regarding the Newcome family, which will show us that they have a skeleton in their closets, as well as their neighbours. **1859** W. COLLINS *Q. of Hearts* (1875) 62 Our family had a skeleton in the cupboard. **1884** 'F. ANSTEY' *Giant's Robe* ch. 25 His skeleton came out of the cupboard and gibbered at him. What right had he, with this fraud on his soul, to be admitted . . . to the . . . friendship of a high-minded girl? **1928** *Times* 20 Jan. 13/6 The skeleton of religious division . . . came out of its cupboard yesterday and rattled its bones in the Senate Chamber.

Skiddaw has a cap, If | Scruffel [Criffel] wots full well of that.
(S 497)

1586 CAMDEN *Britannia, Cumb.* (1722) I. 1006. **1662** FULLER *Cumb.* 217 . . . These are two neighbour hills, the one in this County, the other in Anandale in Scotland. If the former be capp'd with clouds and foggy mists, it will not be long before rain falls on the other. **1791** I. D'ISRAELI *Curios. Lit.* (1858) III. 55 When Scotland, in the last century, felt its allegiance to England doubtful, and when the French sent an expedition to the Land of Cakes, a local proverb was revived to show the identity of interests which affected both nations; if Skiddaw hath a cap, Scruffel wots full well of that. **1818** SCOTT *Ht. Midl.* ch. 40 When a Sarkfoot wife gets on her broomstick, the dames of Allonby are ready to mount, just as sure as the byword gangs o' the hills—If Skiddaw hath a cap, Criffel wots full weel of that.

Skiddaw,[1] Lauvellin, and Casticand, are the highest hills in all England. (s 498)

1586 CAMDEN *Britannia, Cumb.* (1722) II. 1006 The Inhabitants . . . have this rhyme . . . concerning the height of this and two other mountains in those parts. [[1] 3,054 ft.]

Skilfullest wanting money is scorned, The. (s 503)

1670 RAY 18.

Skill and confidence are an unconquered army. (s 500)

1640 HERBERT no. 626.

Skill in horseflesh, He has good | to buy a goose to ride on. (s 499)

1670 RAY 181. **1738** SWIFT *Dial.* I. E.L. 284 Is it possible she could take that booby, Tom Blunder for love?—She had good skill in horseflesh that could choose a goose to ride on.

Skill of man and beast, You have | you were born between the Beltanes[1].

1721 KELLY 376 . . . A Ridicule on them that pretend to Skill. [[1] the 1st and 8th of May.]

Skill, *see also* All things require s. but appetite; Try your s. in galt first; Will is no s.

Skimmington,[1] To ride. (s 504)

1609 C. BUTLER *Fem. Mon.* iv (1623) Ij Yet when they have it [*sc.* their desire] let them use poore Skimmington as best they may, especially in publike, to hide his shame. **1633-4** HEYWOOD & BROME *Late Lancashire Witches* iv. 230 A Skimmington, A Skimmington. **1886** HARDY *Mayor of Casterbridge* ch. 36 'Tis a' old foolish thing they do in these parts when a man's wife is . . . not too particularly his own. [[1] An exhibition designed to ridicule a man with an unfaithful wife.]

Skin a louse, and send the hide to market, He would. (L 473)

1591 FLORIO *Second F.* 117 He was such a couetous miser, that he would haue fleade a louse to saue the skin of it. **1623** WODROEPHE 285 He would haue flayed a Louse for her skin, he was so couetous. **1659** HOWELL *It. Prov.* 7 He is such a miser, that he would flay a louse to sell the skin. **1813** RAY 323 (and fat).

Skin and bone, He is nothing but. (N 260)

c. **1430** *Hymns Virgin* (1867) 73 Ful of fleissche Y was to fele, Now . . . Me is lefte But skyn & boon. **1555** HEYWOOD *Three Hund. Epigr.* no. 42, A7[v] And yet art thou skyn and bone. **1576** LEMNIUS *Touchstone of Complexions* tr. T. Newton 75 Nothing almost on their bodyes, but skinne and boane. **1617** MORYSON *Itin.* I.

251 My self being nothing but skin and bone, as one that languished in a Consumption. **1691** SEWELS 57 He is all skin and Bones. *a.* **1770** H. BROOKE *Fool of Quality* (1770) i. 64.

Skin of one's teeth, With (By) the. (s 510)

[= narrowly, barely.] [JOB xix. 20 I am escaped with the skin of my teeth.] **1647** CLARENDON *Contempl. Ps.* Tracts (1727) 510 He reckoned himself only escaped with the skin of his teeth, that he had nothing left. **1794** SALA *Lond. Up to Date* 66 I got in by the skin of my teeth.

Skin (*noun*), *see also* Dog is hanged for his s., (Many a); Flay a louse for its s.; Honest as the s. between his brows; Lion's s.; Near is my coat but nearer my s.; No more of a cat but s. (You can have); No more of a fox than s. (You can have); Sell the bear's s. before caught; Sleeping in a whole s. (Good); Soon goes young lamb's s. to market (As); Tail follow s. (Let); Wish your s. full of holes (Long ere you); Wolf must die in own s.

Skin (*verb*), *see also* Flay (S.) a flint.

Skin-deep, *see* Beauty is but s. d.

Skirts of straw, Who has | needs fear the fire. (s 514)

1659 HOWELL *Span. Prov.* 17. **1664** CODRINGTON 226. **1666** TORRIANO *It. Prov.* 184 no. 33 Who hath his tail of straw is afraid of fire. **1670** RAY 25.

Skirt(s), *see also* Sit on one's s.

Skulls, *see* Golgotha are s. of all sizes (In).

Sky fall? What if the. (s 516)

1533-4 N. UDALL *Flowers* 174[v] [TERENCE *Heaut.* IV. iii] Quid si coelum ruat? What & if the skie fal? **1581-90** *Timon* II. v. Take heede leaste thou fall. What, if the skie fall? **1602** WITHALS 1 If thou touchest Heauen, or if the skie fall.

Sky falls we shall catch (have) larks, If the. (s 517)

[**1534** RABELAIS I. xi. Si les nues tomboient esperoyt prandre les alouettes.] *a.* **1530** *R. Hill's Commonpl. Bk.* E.E.T.S. 140 And hevyn fell we shall have meny larkys. **1546** HEYWOOD I. iv. B1[v]. **1567** *Appius & Virginia* Mal. Soc. l. 407 If hap the skie fall, we hap may haue Larkes. **1597** LYLY *Wom. in Moon* IV. i. 290. **1611** DAVIES no. 294. *a.* **1619** FLETCHER *Mad Lover* I. ii. 104. **1670** RAY 143. **1721** KELLY 343 What if the lift[1] fall, you may gather Laverocks.[2] Spoken when People make silly, frivolous Excuses and Objections. **1837** CARLYLE *Fr. Rev.* I. VII. i. If the King gets this Veto, what is the use of National Assembly? . . . Friends, if the sky fall, there will be catching of larks! [[1] sky. [2] larks.]

Sky red in the morning is a sailor's (shepherd's) warning; sky red at night is the sailor's (shepherd's) delight.

(M 1175. S 515)

[MATT. xvi. 2 When it is evening, ye say, It will be fair weather: for the sky is red.] **1551** T. WILSON *Rule of Reason* M4ᵛ The skie was very red this mornyng. Ergo we are like to haue rayne or nyght. **1555** L. DIGGES *Prognostication* B1 The element redde in the euenyng, the next daye fayr, but in the morning redde, wynde and rayne. **1583** J. PRINCE *Fruitful and Brief Disc.* 201 Naturall men can iudge the face of the euening, if it be red, they saie we shall haue a faire day, if the morning red, we shall haue raine. **1584** R. SCOT *Witchcraft* XI xv The skie being red at evening Foreshews a faire and clear morning; But if the morning riseth red, Of wind or raine we shall be sped. **1593** SHAKES. *V.A.* ll. 453–5 Like a red morn, that ever yet betoken'd Wrack to the seaman, tempest to the field, Sorrow to shepherds. **1893** INWARDS 53.

Sky, *see also* Mackerel s.; Winter never rots in s.

Slain that had warning, He was | not he that took it.   (W 72)

1592 DELAMOTHE 49 Wise is the man that beleeues him, that giues him a good warning. **1659** HOWELL *Brit. Prov.* 3.

Slander, It may be a | but it is no lie. *Cf.* Slander with a matter of truth. Tongue is no slander.   (S 520)

1546 HEYWOOD II. vii. K1 For sclaunder perchaunce (quoth she) I do not denie. It maie be a sclander, but it is no lie. **1583** MELBANCKE 96 But I had better slaunder them trulye, which is no Slaunder indeede, then flatter them falsely as thou doest. **1594–5** SHAKES. *R.J.* IV. i. 33 That is no slander, sir, which is a truth. **1613** *Id. Hen. VIII* II. i. 153 But that slander, sir, Is found a truth now.

Slander is a shipwreck by a dry tempest.   (S 521)

1651 HERBERT no. 135a.

Slander leaves a score[1] (scar) behind it.
(S 522)

c. **1350** *How the Gd. Wife* l. 22 A sclaundre þat is reised is euil to stille. **1616** DRAXE no. 1990 (skarre). **1670** RAY 24 *Calumniare fortiter, aliquid adhærebit.* **1721** KELLY 286 Slander always leaves a Slur. Eng. Throw much Dirt some will stick. Lat. *Calumniare audacter, aliquid adhærebit.* [¹ mark.]

Slander one with a matter of truth, To. *Cf.* Slander (It may be) but no lie. Tongue is no slander.

1578 T. WHITE *Sermon at Paul's Cross* 3 Nov. (1577) 63 We . . . deale liberally, and therefore this is a slaunder (in a mater of truth say I for the greatest number). **1596** NASHE *Saffron W.* iii. 88 It is a worlde to heare how malicious

tongues will slaunder a man with truth. **1603** *Bachelor's Banquet* (F. P. Wilson) 107 [margin] Slaundred with a matter of truth. **1619** J. FAVOUR *Antiquity Triumphing over Novelty* 318. **1678** RAY 269.

Slander(s), *see also* Pardons . . . are revenges of s.; Tongue is no s.

Slanning, *see* Charles's Wain.

Slave(s), *see* Give a s. a rod; Servants (S.) (So many), so many enemies.

Slavery, *see* Think no labour s. that brings penny.

Slay(s), slain, *see* Knife (man may s. himself with his own); Lie where he was s. (He will not); Sword of lead, (To s. with a).

Sleep is the brother (cousin) of death.
(S 526)

[HOMER *Iliad* xiv. 231 ῎Ενθ' ῞Υπνῳ ξύμβλητο, κασιγνήτῳ Θανάτοιο. There she fell in with Sleep, brother of Death.] **1535** T. LUPSET *Exhortⁿ to Young Men* ed. Gee 246 Slepe is deth for the tyme. **1558** PHAER *Aeneid* vi. 294 Q1ᵛ Than Death himself; whose neigbor next Was Slepe that kinsman is to Death. **1563** *Mirr. Mag.* ed. Campbell 308 By him lay heavy slepe, the cosin of death. **1573** BARET *Alveary* s.v. Death Sleepe is deathes coosen. **1632** *Holland's Leaguer* B2 Sleepe is too neere a kinseman to death. **1718** POPE *Iliad* xiv. 265 The cave of Death's half-brother, Sleep. **1813** SHELLEY *Queen Mab* i How wonderful is Death, Death and his brother Sleep!

Sleep is the image of death.   (S 527)

1534 LUPSET *Treat. Dying Well* ed. Gee 275 Nowe than what shall we saye of dethe? the whiche by hym selfe is not vnlyke to an endles slepe of the bodye. **1539** VIVES *Introd. to Wisdom* G8 Slepe, a very expresse token of deathe. **1577** J. BISHOP *Beautiful Blossoms* 2A 2ᵛ Sleepe is an Image of death. *a.* **1593** MARLOWE *Ovid's Amores* II. ix. 41 Fool, what is sleep but image of cold death? **1606** SHAKES. *M.* II. iii. 74 Sleep, death's counterfeit. **1609** *Id. Cym.* II. ii. 31 O sleep, thou ape of death. **1612** A. STAFFORD *Meditations* 73 They say there is a kind of resemblance betweene Sleepe and Death. **1616** T. ADAMS *The Soul's Sickness* 21 Sleepe is the image of death, sayth the Poet. **1639** CLARKE 322.

Sleep like a top, To.   (T 440)

1613 SHAKES. *T.N.K.* III. iv. 26 I shall sleep like a top else. **1666** TORRIANO *Prov. Phr.* s.v. Zocco 240 To sleep like a logg, viz. soundly, so as not to be sensible of any thing, to sleep like a Dormouse, or a Town-Top. **1693** CONGREVE *Old Bachelor* I. ed. Summers i. 176 Should he seem to rouse, 'tis but well lashing him, and he will sleep like a Top. **1820** BYRON *Letters* v. 115. **1841** DICKENS *B. Rudge* ch. 33 Johnny's dropped off.—Fast as a top. **1860** PEACOCK *Gryll Grange* ch. 5 He slept like a top.

Sleep to all, I don't.

c. **1580** J. CONYBEARE 56 *Non omnibus dormio,*
I sleepe not to all mennc, I am not readye at
euery mans challenge.   **1725** BAILEY tr. *Erasmus'
Colloq.* 487 You know the old proverb, I don't
sleep to all.

Sleep with one eye (one's eyes) open, To.   (E 250)

1581 GUAZZO ii. 41 Which sleepeth (as they say)
her eies being open.   **1607–8** FLETCHER *Faithful
Shep.* II. i.   **1732** FULLER no. 1947 He is so
wary, that he sleeps like a Hare, with his Eyes
open.   **1836** MARRYAT *Midsh. Easy* ch. 18 It
may be as well to sleep with one eye open. . . .
Suppose we keep watch and watch, and have our
pistols out ready?

Sleep without rocking, I shall.   (R 152)

1631 R. BRATHWAIT *Whimzies* (1859) 106 Hee
sleepes soundly without rocking.   **1738** SWIFT
Dial. III. E.L. 325.   **1844** DICKENS *M. Chuz.*
ch. 17 You'll sleep without rocking to-night,
sir.

Sleep without supping, and wake without owing.   (S 1006)

1640 HERBERT no. 93.

Sleep (*noun*), *see also* Hour's s. before midnight; Man is known mortal by s. and lust;
Seven hours' s. make clown forget design; Six
hours' s. for a man; Take it out in s.

Sleeper(s), *see* Net of the s. catches fish; Seven S.

Sleeping dogs, *see* Let s. d. lie; Waken s. d.
(Ill to).

Sleeping enough in the grave, There will be.

1758 FRANKLIN in ARBER *Garner* v. 579 How
much more than is necessary do we spend in
sleep? forgetting that . . . there will be sleeping
enough in the grave, as Poor RICHARD says.

Sleeping in a whole skin, It is good.
                                                                                         (S 530)

1542 T. BECON *Invective agst. Swearing* (n.d.,
A4ᵛ) It is good sleapyng in an whole skynne.
1546 HEYWOOD II. v. H2ᵛ Sens by stryfe, ye
maie lose, and can not wyn, Suffer. It is good
slepyng in a whole skyn.   **1620** SHELTON *Quix.*
II. xli. iii. 97 'Tis good sleeping in a whole
skin; I mean, I am very well at home in this
house.   **1684** BUNYAN *Pilgr.* II. (1877) 210
Mrs. *Bat's-eyes* . . . If he was here again, he
would rest him content in a whole skin, and
never run so many hazards for nothing.   **1745**
A. SKIRVING *Johnnie Cope* Fy now, Johnnie, get
up and rin; . . . It's best to sleep in a hale skin.
1837 CARLYLE *Fr. Rev.* III. I. iii Patriotism is
good; but so is . . . sleeping in whole skin.

Sleeps all the morning, He who | may go a begging all the day after.   (M 1172)

1642 TORRIANO 37.   **1659** HOWELL *It. Prov.* 11.
1732 FULLER no. 2404.

Sleeps as dogs do when wives sift meal, He.   (D 536)

a. **1628** CARMICHAELL no. 1831.   **1641** FERGUS-
SON no. 472 *Of hypocrites.* . . .   **1721** KELLY 127
(when Wives bakes; or when Wives sift Meal).
Apply'd to those who pretend to be asleep, or
unconcern'd, who are all the while making their
Remarks.

Sleeps too sound, (wishes to sleep well), Let him that | borrow (buy) the debtor's pillow (bed).   (B 510)

1659 J. HOWELL *Span. Prov.* Letter to Sir
Lewis Dives Quien quiere bien dormir que
compre la cama de un deudor.   **1753** JOHNSON
Adventurer no. 41 I never retired to rest without
feeling the justness of the Spanish proverb, 'Let
him who sleeps too much, borrow the pillow of a
debtor'.   **1813** RAY 21 He who desireth to
sleep soundly, let him buy the bed of a bankrupt.
Hisp.   **1910** *T.L.S.* 28 Oct. 398 The dun, the
lawyer's letter, the writ, . . . are an old story in
the annals of authors by trade. There is a
Spanish proverb, 'Let him that sleeps too sound
borrow the debtor's pillow'.

Sleep(s, ing), (*verb*), *see also* Child s. upon
bones (Let not); Ears, . . ., (To s. securely on
both); Fern is as high (When the) . . . you may s.;
Log, (To s. like a); Lubberland where they have
half a crown for s.; Man s. (When), his head is in
stomach; Scorpion under every stone, (There is
(s.) a); Sheep, swine, and bees, (He that has)
s. he, wake he, he may thrive; Walk groundly
. . . s. soundly.

Sleepy fox has seldom feathered breakfasts, The.   (F 649)

1611 COTGRAVE s.v. Emplumé.   **1659** HOWELL *Fr.
Prov.* 7 The Fox who sleeps in the morning
hath not his tongue feathered.   **1758** FRANKLIN
in ARBER *Garner* v. 579 How much more
than is necessary do we spend in sleep? forgetting
that the sleeping fox catches no poultry.

Sleepy master makes his servant a lout, A.   (M 731)

1640 HERBERT no. 766.

Sleeve, To have in one's.   (S 534)

1545 *Precepts of Cato* A4ᵛ Least any such band-
dogge chaunce to open his mouth at vs nowe, we
wyll be sure to haue in our sleue eyther some
lytle corde to tye hym vp in a kennel, or els we
wyl cast him in a gobbet of meat to stop his
throte, that he may leaue his barking.   **1581**
GUAZZO ii. 77 The father hath not alwayes his
sonne in lawe in his sleeve, mariages (as they
say) are made in heaven, and are guided by
destiny.   **1585** A. DENT *Sermon of Repentance*
C4ᵛ.   **1589** PUTTENHAM *Art Eng. Poesy* III. xxv.
300 Whereby the better to winne his purposes
and good aduantages, as now and then to haue a
iourney or sicknesse in his sleeue, thereby to
shake of other importunities of greater consequence.

Sleeve(s), *see also* Broken s. holds arm back;
Conscience as large as a friar's s., (He has a);

Fool in his s.; Laugh in one's s.; Pins faith on another man's s.; Spits on own s.; Stretch your arm no further than s.; Tailor must cut three s.

Sleeveless[1] errand, A.   (E 180)

1546 HEYWOOD I. vii. B4ᵛ He tooke in hande, To make to my house, a sleeuelesse errande. **1600** *Look about You* l. 956 To tell a sleueles tale. **1602** SHAKES. *T.C.* V. iv. 9 Might send that Greekish whoremasterly villain with the sleeve back to the . . . drab of a sleeveless errand. **1655** FULLER *Ch. Hist.* IV. iii. (1868) I. 603 Warwick . . . had taken so much pains about nothing, . . . employed about a sleeveless errand. [[1] useless; Apperson quotes from Lady Charlotte Guest's tr. of the *Mabinogion* ('Dream of Mayen Wledig') an explanation of this word, relating to the sleeve worn by messengers on their caps as a sort of passport and protection.]

Sleight, *see* Might or s.

Slender in the middle as a cow in the waist, As.   (M 919)

1582 R. STANYHURST *First Four Bookes of Virgil* O3 She limps in the going, this slut with a cammoysed haucks nose, And as a Cow wasted plods on, with an head lyke a lutecase. **1583** MELBANCKE C3ᵛ Made in the wast like a cowe with calue. **1621** BURTON *Anat. Mel.* III. ii. 608 Euery louer admires his mistris, though she be . . . lame, splea-footed, as slender in the middle as a cowe in the waste. **1670** RAY 207. **1732** FULLER no. 727.

Slept well, He has | that remembers not he has slept ill.

1679 *Baconiana* 61 (from the *Mimi* of Publius Syrus). **1732** FULLER no. 1897.

Slice, *see* Shoulder of mutton is going (When), good to take s.

Sliddery[1] stone before the hall[2] door, There is a.

1721 KELLY 305 . . . Signifying the Uncertainty of Court Favour, and the Promises of Great Men. [[1] slippery. [2] great man's house.]

Slight, *see* Laird s. the lady (If the) so will kitchen boys.

Sling, *see* Killing a crow with empty s.

Slip(s), *see* Better the foot s. than the tongue; Cup and the lip (Many a s. between); Cut (s.) the painter; Neck out of collar (S.); Stands not surely that never s.

Slippery as an eel, As.   (E 60)

[ERASM. *Chil. Adag.* Ἀπ᾽ οὐρᾶς τὴν ἔγχελυν ἔχεις. You have got the eel by the tail.] *c.* **1384** CHAUCER *Ho. Fame* Bk. 3, l. 2154 And stampen, as men doon after eles. *c.* **1412** HOCCLEVE *Reg. Princes* l. 1985 Mi wit is also slippir as an eel. **1589** · *Pasquil and Marforius* [Nashe] i. 98. [*c.* **1591**] **1598** GREENE *James IV* IV. iv. 1627

(scittish). **1641** FERGUSSON no. 536 I have a sliddrie eill by the tail. **1670** RAY 173 There is as much hold of his word, as of a wet eel by the tail. **1728** POPE *Dunciad* i. 279 How index-learning turns no student pale, Yet holds the eel of science by the tail. **1855** MRS. GASKELL *North & South* ch. 17.

Sloe tree is as white as a sheet, When the | sow your barley whether it be dry or wet.   (S 540)

1678 RAY 49. **1732** FULLER no. 6482.

Slop, *see* Sow in the s.

Sloth breeds a scab.   (S 541)

1546 HEYWOOD I. iii. A4ᵛ. **1597** *Politeuphuia* 22ᵛ It is a scabbe of the worlde to bee enuious of vertue. **1611** DAVIES no. 303. **1639** CLARKE 109 It will prove a scab i' th' end.

Sloth, like rust, consumes faster than labour wears.

1758 FRANKLIN in ARBER *E. Garner* v. 579 Sloth, by bringing on diseases, absolutely shortens life. *Sloth, like Rust, consumes faster than Labour wears.*

Slothful is the servant of the counters,[1] The.   (S 543)

1640 HERBERT no. 610. [[1] prisons.]

Slothful man is the beggar's brother, The.   (M 378)

a. **1628** CARMICHAELL no. 171. **1641** FERGUSSON no. 3. **1663** P. STAMPOY 2. **1707** MAPLETOFT 121. **1721** KELLY 315.

Slovens, *see* Sluts are good enough to make s.' pottage.

Slow and (but) sure.   (S 544)

1562 G. LEGH *Accidence of Armoury* 97 Although the Asse be slowe, yet is he sure. **1587** *Letters of Philip Gawdy* 26 Though he be suer, yet he is very slow. **1592** DELAMOTHE 31 Hastinesse is hurtfull, but slownesse is sure. **1594-5** SHAKES. *R.J.* II. iii. 94 Wisely and slow. They stumble that run fast. **1604** MARSTON *Malcontent* IV. v. Vengeance, tho't comes slow, yet it comes sure. **1606** *Id. The Fawn* III. i. 95 This snail['s] slow, but sure. *c.* **1608-9** MIDDLETON *Widow* II. ii. Martino, we ride slow.—But we ride sure, sir; Your hasty riders often come short home. **1639** CLARKE 325. **1692** L'ESTRANGE *Aesop's Fab.* ccclxix (1738) 388 Slow and sure in these cases, is good counsel. . . . He that will be rich before night may be hanged before noon. **1727** GAY *Fables* iv. 28 The hound is slow, but always sure. **1838-9** DICKENS *N. Nickleby* ch. 42 (and steady). **1882** BLACKMORE *Christowell* ch. 14 You go on so fast, when you want to slur a point. Slow and sure is my style of business.

Slow and sure, like Pedley's mare.

1732 FULLER no. 4188.

Slow and (but) sure (steady) wins the race.

1859 SMILES *Self-Help* 358 Provided the dunce has persistency and application he will inevitably head the cleverer fellow without those qualities. Slow but sure wins the race. **1894** NORTHALL *Folk-phrases* E.D.S. 22 Slow and steady wins the race.

Slow to bed, *see* Sluggard's guise.

Sluggard must be clad in rags, The.
(s 546)

1636 CAMDEN 307. **1683** G. MERITON *Yorkshire Dialogue* 16 Ill Husbands and Sluggards mun gang in Raggs.

Sluggard takes an hundred steps because he would not take one in due time, A.

1666 TORRIANO *It. Prov.* 208 no. 23 A lazy sluggard A lazy body, because he will not go one step, is fain to go a hundred. **1707** MAPLE-TOFT 22.

Sluggard's convenient season never comes, The.

1732 FULLER no. 4750.

Sluggards' guise, slow to bed, and slow to rise.
(s 547)

1639 CLARKE 292 Ever sick of th' slouthfull guise. *c.* **1640** J. SMYTH *Berkeley MSS.* 32, no. 65 Hee is tainted with an evill guise, Loth to bed and lother to rise.

Sluggards, *see also* Every day is holiday with s.; Plough deep, while s. sleep.

Slumber finds (invites) another, One.
(s 549)

1605 ERONDELLE *Fr. Garden* 60 The more I sleep, the more I would sleep. **1611** COTGRAVE s.v. Attraire One sleepe draws on another. **1640** HERBERT no. 528. **1670** RAY 20 (invites).

Sluts are good enough to make slovens' pottage.
(s 553)

c. **1623** *Y. Man's Careless Wooing* in *Roxb. Bal.* viii. 869 A Slut's good enough to make Sloven's porridge. **1639** CLARKE 287. **1670** RAY 143. **1732** FULLER no. 4190.

Slut(s), *see also* Leap an inch from a s. (She cannot); Tame beasts (Of all) I hate s.

Smack, *see* Pepper is black, and has a good s.

Small as a wand, As.
(w 23)

1530 PALSGRAVE 469a. **1550** CROWLEY *Epig.* l. 1313 Wks. 45 Hyr mydle braced in, as smal as a wande. **1592** SHAKES. *T.G.V.* II. iii. 21 She is as white as a lily and as small as a wand.

Small beer, *see* Chronicle s. b.; Good s. b. (There is no such thing as); Good things I do not love, good s. b.; Think no s. b. of oneself.

Small birds must have meat.
(B 397)

[JOB xxxviii. 41 Who provideth for the raven his food? PS. cxlvii. 9 He giveth to the beast his food, and to the young ravens which cry.] **1600–1** SHAKES. *M.W.W.* I. iii. 32 Young ravens must have food. **1602** JONSON *Poetaster* III. iv. 258 For sparrowes must haue foode. **1639** CLARKE 246. **1670** RAY 63 . . . Children must be fed, they cannot be maintained with nothing.

Small invitation will serve a beggar.

1659 N. R. 92.

Small pack becomes a small pedlar, A.
(P 7)

1592 DELAMOTHE 3. **1611** COTGRAVE s.v. Mercier The little Pedler a little packe doth serue. **1623** WODROEPHE 475 A litle pedler, a litle Packe. **1670** RAY 143 . . . Petit mercier, petit panier, *Gall.* **1802** WOLCOT (P. Pindar) *Middl. Elect.* i Little packs Become a little pedlar.

Small profits and quick returns.

1721 KELLY 282 Quick Returns make rich Merchants. Eng. Many Ventures make a full Fraught. **1899** SIR ALG. WEST xxxi His mission had been conducted on strictly commercial lines of small profits and quick returns.

Small riches hath most rest.

[*c.* **1515**] *c.* **1530** BARCLAY *Eclog.* III. l. 765 Small riches hath most rest, In greatest seas moste sorest is tempest.

Small sorrows speak; great ones are silent. *Cf.* Grief is lessened. Grief pent up.
(s 664)

[SENECA *Hippol.* 607 Curae leves loquuntur, ingentes stupent.] **1565** T. COOPER *Thesaurus* (1573) s.v. Cura Small sorow complayneth, great care is astonied. **1581** SENECA *Hippol.* tr. J. Studley T.T. i. 158 Light cares have words at will, but great doe make us sore agast. **1587** T. HUGHES *Misf. Arthur* Clar. Press IV. ii. 14 Small griefes can speake: the great astonisht stand. **1590** SPENSER *F.Q.* I. vii. 41 Great griefe will not be tould. **1592** KYD *Span. Trag.* I. iii. 7 Deepest cares break neuer into teares. **1592** NASHE *Strange News* i. 314 Curae leues loquuntur . . . Maiores stupent. *c.* **1605** CHAPMAN *The Widow's Tears* IV. i. 114–15 These griefs that sound so loud, prove always light, True sorrow evermore keeps out of sight. **1605** MARSTON *Dutch Courtezan* IV. iv. Deare woes cannot speake. **1605** SHAKES. *M.* IV. iii. 209 The grief that does not speak Whispers the o'erfraught heart and bids it break. *a.* **1618** SYLVESTER (1621) 1209 Small griefes speake, but great are dumb. *a.* **1642** KYNASTON in Saintsbury *Carol. Poets* ii. 142 Small sorrows speak, the greatest still are dumb. **1864** FRISWELL *Gentle Life* 164 Not one of us is there but would exchange all his little troubles for some heavy one . . . 'Light cares cry out: the heavier are dumb'.

Small sum will serve to pay a short reckoning, A.   (s 965)

1607-40 *Politeuphuia* s.v. Proverbs. **1639** CLARKE 128. **1732** FULLER no. 413.

Small, *see also* Beginnings come great things, (From s.); Choice in rotten apples (There is s.); Many s. make a great; Play a s. game before he will sit out; Promises (Great) and s. performances; Spark a great fire (Of a s.).

Small, *see also under significant words following.*

Smell a rat, To.   (R 31)

[= to have suspicions.] **1533** *Ballads from MSS.* B.S. i. 182 For yf they smell a ratt . . . *a.* **1550** SKELTON *Image Hypocr.* I. 51 (1843) II. 414/2 Yf they smell a ratt, They grisely chide and chatt. **1595** *Locrine* II. v. 93 But, oh, I smel a foxe. [1603] **1607** T. HEYWOOD *Wom. K. Kindness* sc. xii. l. 7 Now you talk of a cat, Sisley, I smell a rat. **1663** BUTLER *Hudibras* I. i. 821 Quoth Hudibras, I smell a rat; Ralpho, thou dost prevaricate. **1712** ARBUTHNOT *John Bull* II. xi. The good old gentlewoman was not so simple as to go into his projects—she began to smell a rat. **1874** G. J. WHYTE-MELVILLE *Uncle John* ch. 20 A young . . . smelt a rat, and followed him out of the house.

Smell fire, Well may he | whose gown burns.   (F 289)

1640 HERBERT no. 138.

Smell of garlic (leeks) takes away the smell of onions etc., The.   (s 556)

[Sir T. More's medicament.] **1599** BUTTES *Diet's Dry Dinner* H7 To take away the smell of Onions, eate Leekes: and to conuince your Leekes eat a clowe or two of Garlicke: and if then Garlicke breath be strong, choke him with a piece of a T. with a u. with an r. with a d. **1609** J. MELTON *Six-Fold Pol.* 35 According to the prouerbe the smell of Garlick takes away the stink of dunghills.

Smell of the inkhorn, To.   (I 77)

[= to be pedantic.] **1542** ERASM. tr. Udall *Apoph.* (1877) 243 These wordes . . . smellen all of the inkhorne. **1587** GOLDING *De Mornay* xxvi. 396 Proclamations set forth in such a stile, . . . smelling too much of the Inkehorne.

Smell, *see also* Best s. is bread; Faint at s. of wallflower.

Smells best that smells of nothing, He (She).   (W 664)

[PLAUT. *Most.* I. iii. 116 *Mulier tum bene olet ubi nihil olet.*] **1529** HYRDE *Instr. Chr. Wom.* IX. 77 Plautus saieth, A woman euer smelleth best whan she smelleth of nothing. **1598** MERES *Palladis* f. 32 As women do Smell well which

smel of nothing. **1599** DAVIES *Nosce Teipsum* Sith they smell best that do of nothing smell. **1607** [Tomkis] *Lingua* IV. iii None can weare Ciuet, but they are suspected of a proper badde sent, where the prouerbe springs, hee smelleth best, that doth of nothing smell. **1621** BURTON *Anat. Mel.* III. ii. III. iii (1651) 477 *Mulier recte olet, ubi nihil olet*; then a woman smells best, when she hath no perfume at all.

Smells of the lamp (oil), It.   (c 43)

[PYTHEAS (PLUTARCH, *Demosth.* 8. 2) Ἐλλυχνίων ὄζειν αὐτοῦ τὰ ἐνθυμήματα. His impromptus smell of the lamp. L. *Olet lucernam.*] **1542** ERASM. tr. Udall *Apoph.* (1877) 370 One Pythias obiected to Demosthenes, that his argumentes . . . smelled all of the candle: signifiyng, that he pronounced none oracion but out of writyng, and made with greate studie, by Candle in the night time. **1603** MONTAIGNE (Florio) I. x. 53 Some compositions . . . smell of the oile, and of the lampe, by reason of a certaine harshnesse, . . . which long plodding labour imprints in them that be much elaborated. **1605** BACON *Adv. Learn.* I. ii. (Oxf. 1900) 16 Æschines[1] . . . told him[2] *That his orations did smell of the lamp.* **1625** JONSON *Staple News* Prol. A work not smelling of the lamp tonight, But fitted for your Majesty's disport. **1907** *Times Wkly.* 8 Feb. Nothing but the rapt fervour which he brought to his researches could have saved 'John Inglesant' from the smell of the lamp. [[1] Pytheas, not Æschines.   [2] Demosthenes.]

Smell(s), *(verb), see also* Elbow-grease, (It smells of).

Smelt where all stink, One is not.

1629 T. ADAMS *Serm.* (1861-2) I. 76 They that will quarter themselves with the wicked must drink of their poison. If you ask how haps it that their infection is not smelt, Bernard answers: *Ubi omnes sordent, unus minime sentitur,*—One is not smelt, where all stink.

Smelts, *see* Westward for s.

Smile(s) *(noun), see* Better the last s. than first laughter.

Smile(s) *(verb), see* Fortune s. (When); Laugh (S.) on the wrong side.

Smiling boy seldom proves a good servant, A.   (B 578)

1659 HOWELL *Eng. Prov.* 16b. **1670** RAY 24. **1721** KELLY 53 A laughing fac'd Lad makes a lither Servant. It is supposed such are too full of Roguery to be diligent. **1852** FITZGERALD *Polonius* ch. 53 Softness of smile indicates softness of character. . . . 'A smiling boy is a bad servant.'

Smith *(prop. name), see* There or thereabouts, as Parson S. says.

Smith and his penny both are black, The.   (s 561)

1640 HERBERT no. 195. **1655-62** GURNALL *Chrn. in Armour* (1865) I. 504 'The smith', we say, 'and his penny, both are black.' So wert thou with all thy duties and performances, while unreconciled in his eye. **1875** SMILES *Thrift* 178 'The smith and his penny are both black'. But the penny earned by the smith is an honest one.

Smith forges a very weak knife, Often a full dexterous.

c. **1200** *Ancrene Riwle* Camden Soc. 52 Ofte a ful hawur smið smeoðið a ful woc knif.

Smith has always a spark in his throat, The. (s 562)

1678 RAY 90. **1721** KELLY 334 The Smith has ay a Spark in his Haise.[1] And they often take pains to quench it, but to no purpose. **1865** G. MACDONALD *Alec Forbes* ch. 62 'Jist rax down the bottle, gudewife' . . . 'Ye're a true smith, man: ye hae aye a spark i' yer throat.' [1 throat.]

Smith of Nottingham, The little | who does the work that no man can. (s 565)

1609 C. BUTLER *Fem. Monarchie* B3 The little smith of Nottingham (whose art is thought to excel al art of man). **1662** FULLER *Notts.* 216 II. 570 . . . I . . . have cause to suspect that this . . . is a periphrasis of *Nemo, Oὖτις*, or a person who never was. And the Proverb . . . is applied to such who, being conceited of their own skill, pretend the achieving of impossibilities.

Smith's dog, Like the | that sleeps at the noise of the hammer, and wakes at the crashing (crunching) of teeth. (s 563)

1595 COPLEY *Wits, Fits* I. 15 Sir, you are welcome, though resembling the Smithes dog, euermore awake at meale, and asleepe at the Anuill. **1666** TORRIANO *It. Prov.* 36 no. 16 The Smiths dog falls asleep at the strokes of the hammer. **1692** L'ESTRANGE *Aesop's Fab.* cxvii (1738) 133 A blacksmith took notice of a cur he had, that would be perpetually sleeping, so long as his master was at his hammer; but whenever he went to dinner, the dog would be sure to make one. **1732** FULLER no. 3236. **1862** HISLOP 139 (sleep at the sound o' the hammer, and wauk at the crunching o' teeth.)

Smith, *see also* More bare (Worse shod) than s.'s mare (Who goes); Water in a s.'s forge.

Smithfield bargain, A. (s 564)

[= a roguish bargain; also, a marriage of interest, not love.] **1604** B. RICH *The Fruits of long Experience* H2ᵛ Will you then fetch him [your soldier] from Bridewell? That were to buy a horse out of Smithfield. **1624** BURTON *Anat. Mel.* III. iii. IV. ii. 3S3ᵛ He that marries a wife out of a suspected Inne or Alehouse, buyes a horse in Smithfield . . . shall likely have a Jade to his horse. **1662** J. WILSON *Cheats* V. v. Your daughter has married a gentleman:—is not this better than a Smithfield bargain? **1697** W. POPE *Seth* [Ward] 89 He never was without proffers of Wives, much beyond his deserts; as the Markets go in Smithfield. **1710–11** SWIFT *Jrnl. to Stella* 10 Mar. He was such a fool as to offer him money . . . and a

hundred pounds is too much in a Smithfield bargain. **1775** SHERIDAN *Rivals* v. i. To find myself made a mere Smithfield bargain of at last! **1826** T. H. LISTER *Granby* i. 228.

Smithfield, *see also* Westminster for a wife (Who goes to) . . . S. for a horse.

Smithwick, You been like | either clemmed or borsten. (s 566)

1678 RAY 291 . . . *Chesh.* **1917** BRIDGE 157 You bin like Smithwick, either clemmed or bossten. . . . Either starved or bursting.

Smock, *see* Lapped in his mother's s.; Near is my coat (petticoat) but nearer my s.

Smocks than shirts in a bucking, He that has more | had need be a man of good forelooking. (s 567)

1678 RAY 353.

Smoke follows the fairest, The. (s 571)

[ARISTOPHAN. Fr. 4 Κονδύλους πλάττειν δὲ Τελαμών, τοὺς καλοὺς πειρᾶν καπνός.] *c.* **1640** SMYTH *Berkeley MSS. 31*, no. 11 If many gossips will sit against a smokey chimney the smoke will bend to the fairest. **1646** SIR T. BROWNE *Eng. into Vulg. & Common Err.* in Wks. (1835) III. 166 That smoke doth follow the fairest, is an usual saying with us . . . yet is it the continuation of a very ancient opinion, as . . . observed from a passage in Athenæus; wherein a parasite thus describeth himself: . . . Like smoke unto the fair I fly. **1721** KELLY 314 (Reek) . . . This is in Aristophanes, and signifies that Envy is a Concomitant of Excellency. **1738** SWIFT *Dial.* I. E.L. 266 *A puff of smoke comes down the chimney.* . . . Does your ladyship's chimney smoke?—No, madam; but they say smoke always pursues the fair, and your ladyship sat nearest. **1832** HENDERSON 86 Reek follows the fairest, bear witness to the crook.[1] [1 The chain and hooks by which vessels are hung over the fire.]

Smoke of a man's own country (house) is better than the fire of another's, The. (s 572)

[ERASM. *Patriae fumus igni alieno luculentior.* The smoke of our own country is brighter than the fire of another.] **1539** TAVERNER 6ᵛ The smoke of a mans owne countrey, is much clearer than the fyer in a straunge countrey. **1632** MASSINGER *City Madam* V. i Merm. 483 We desire A competence.—And prefer our country's smoke Before outlandish fire. **1670** RAY 20 (house). *Hispan.* **1721** KELLY 307 (The Reek of my own House). **1818** SCOTT *Rob Roy* ch. 38 Our ain reek's better than other folk's fire.

Smoke of Charren. (s 573)

1659 HOWELL *Eng. Prov.* 21a The smoak of Charren; A Proverb relating to a wife who had beat her husband, and he going out weeping, said it was for the smoake that his eyes watered.

Smoke, Shunning the | they fall into the fire. *Cf.* Frying pan.   (s 570)

[ERASM. *Adag.* 184c: Fumum fugiens, in ignem incidi.] *c.* 1530 LUCIAN *Necromantia* A3ᵛ As the comen prouerb is of euery man Out of the smoke into the fyre I ran. 1535 T. LUPSET *Exhort. Young Men* ed. Gee 256 What faute so euer you may do, let it not be defended with a false tale: for that were to fle out of the smoke in to the fire. 1549 H. BULLINGER *Treatise or Sermon* B4 Magistrates had nede of much . . . feare of god, in takyng vp or in laying downe their warres, lest perchaunse in flying the smoke thei fall into the fyre. 1576 PETTIE ii. 89 Thinking to quench the coals of his desire, he fell into hot flames of burning fire. 1599 SHAKES. *A.Y.* I. ii. 266 Thus must I from the smoke into the smother. 1666 TORRIANO *Prov.* 96 no. 22 Many an one flies the smoke, who afterward falls into fire.

Smoke, To feed oneself with.   (s 575)

1549 ERASM. tr. Chalenor *Praise of Folly* Q1 Fedde with smoke. 1604 SIR J. BEAUMONT *Met. of Tobacco* E4ᵛ The Gods . . . doe feed on smoke (as Lucian sayes). 1666 TORRIANO *Prov. Phr.* s.v. Speranza 199 . . . To be deceiv'd.

Smoke you, I will.   (s 577)

c. 1552 *Manifest Detection Dice Play* ed. Halliwell 26 Always to beware that we cause him not smoke. *Ibid.* 39 When the money is lost, the cousin begins to smoke. [1598] 1601 JONSON *Every Man In Hum.* IV. i. 35 I fayth (I am glad) I haue smokt you yet at last. 1602 SHAKES. *A.W.* IV. i. 26 They begin to smoke me. 1693 CONGREVE *Old Bachelor* III. 190 Oh! I begin to smoak ye. 1699 B.E. *Dict. Canting Crew* Smoke, to Smoke or smell a Design.

Smoke(s), *see also* Chimneys (Many), little s.; Consume your own s.; Fire (Make no), raise no s.; Life is a shadow (s.); Much s., little fire; No s. without fire; Pipe of peace (S.); Sell s.; Sit near the fire when chimney s.; Three things drive out of house, s. . . .

Smooth as a die.   (D 325)

1530 PALSGRAVE 629b Make this borde as smothe as a dyce. 1550 HEYWOOD *100 Epigrams* no. 27 Thy waie, both faire and smooth as a die is. 1575 LANEHAM *Lett.* ed. Furnivall 40 (clean). 1583 MELBANCKE *Philot.* F1 (fit). [1591] 1593 PEELE *Edw. I* Bullen i. 140 (fit). 1666 TORRIANO *Prov. Phr.* s.v. Dado 51 As plain as a die, viz. even, level, without ascent, or descent; the English say, as smooth as a die.

Smooth as a millpond.

1697 DAMPIER *Voy.* i. 217 It was quite calm and the Sea as smooth as a Mill-pond. 1766 SMOLLETT *Trav.* I. xix. 301. 1836 MARRYAT *Midsh. Easy* ch. 14.

Smooth as oil.   (O 25)

1579 LYLY *Euph.* i. 224. *Ibid.* i. 295 As softe as Oyle. 1597 SHAKES. *I Hen. IV* I. iii. 7. *a.* 1637 JONSON *Underwoods* viii. 280.

Smooth, *see also* Rough with s.; Still (s.) waters run deep.

Snacks, *see* Go s.

Snail slides up the tower at last, The | though the swallow mounteth it sooner.   (s 581)

1575 GASCOIGNE *Glass of Govt.* Epilogue. ii. 89 Much like the snaile, which clymes the Castle wall. 1580 LYLY *Euph. & his Eng.* ii. 178 The slow Snaile clymeth the tower at last, though the swift Swallowe mount it. 1595 *Locrine* II. i. 1 *Shaks. Apoc.* 44 At length the snaile doth clime the highest tops, Ascending vp the stately castle walls. 1732 FULLER no. 4757.

Snail's gallop (pace), To go (at) a.   (s 583)

a. 1400–50 *Alexander* l. 4095 þan sny3es¹ þar, out of þat snyth² hill as with a snayles pas, A burly best. 1533 HEYWOOD *Johan Johan* l. 419 As fast as a snayle. 1546 *Id.* I. ix. C2 I will . . . thitherward hie me in haste like a snaile. 1691 SEWEL 211 (a snails pace). 1793 D'ARBLAY *Lett.* 12 Sept. That snail's pace with which business is done by letters. 1901 *Scotsman* 5 Nov. 6/8 For a time they were able to get along at a snail's gallop, men leading the horses with torches and lanterns. [¹ creeps. ² ?smooth.]

Snails on the road you see, When black | then on the morrow rain will be.

1883 ROPER 31.   1893 INWARDS 144.

Snail(s), *see also* Drive a s. to Rome; Tramp on a s., she'll shoot out horns.

Snake (Viper) in one's bosom, To nourish a.   (V 68)

[Refers to the ingratitude and treachery of the snake in Aesop's Fable (I. x).] *c.* 1386 CHAUCER *Summoner's T.* l. 1993 Be war from hire that in thy bosom crepeth. *Id. Merch. T.* l. 1786 Lyk to the naddre in bosom sly untrewe. 1580 BARET C784 Colubrum in sinu fouere. A Prouerbe applied to those which foster and cherishe an vngratefull and thankelesse person: who will breake out in the ende as a snake in a mans bosome. 1590 *Mar-Martin* A1ᵛ The frozen snake for cold that cannot creepe, Restorde to strength a stinging stur will keepe. 1590–1 SHAKES. *2 Hen. VI* III. i. 343 I fear me you but warm, the starved snake, Who, cherish'd in your breasts, will sting your hearts. 1595–6 *Id. Rich. II* III. ii. 131 Snakes, in my heart-blood warm'd, that sting my heart. 1671 MILTON *Samson* 763 Drawn to wear out miserable days. Entangl'd with a poysnous bosom snake. 1721 KELLY 61 *Eng.* Put a Snake in your Bosom, and it will sting when it is warm. 1732 FULLER no. 5210. 1763 JOHNSON 8 Dec. in BOSWELL (1848) xviii. 162 Every desire is a viper in the bosom, who, while he was chill, was harmless; but when warmth give him strength, exerted it in poison. 1865 KINGSLEY *Hereward* ch. 9 The wild Viking would have crushed the growing snake in his bosom.

Snake in the grass. (s 585)

[After VIRGIL *Ecl.* iii. 93 *Latet anguis in herba.*] *c.* **1290** WRIGHT *Pol. Songs John to Edw. II* Camden Soc. 172 Cum totum fecisse putas, latet anguis in herba. *c.* **1386** CHAUCER *Summoner's T.* l. 1994 War fro the serpent that so slily crepeth Under the gras, and styngeth subtilly. *c.* **1420** LYDGATE *Troy Bk.* I. 185 Lyche an addre vnder flouris fayre. **1579–80** LODGE *Def. Poet.* (1853) 22 *Latet anguis in herba,* under your fair show of conscience take heed you cloak not your abuse. **1590–1** SHAKES. *2 Hen. VI* III. i. 228 Or as the snake rolled in a flowering bank . . . doth sting a child. **1594–5** *Id. R.J.* III. ii. 73 O serpent heart, hid with a flow'ring face. **1595–6** *Id. Rich. II* III. ii. 19 And when they from thy bosom pluck a flower, Guard it, I pray thee, with a lurking adder. **1605–6** *Id. M.* I. v. 62 Look like the innocent flower, But be the serpent under it. **1677** YARRANTON *Eng. Impr.* 101 Hold, hold, you drive too fast; there is a snake in the Bush. **1696** [C. LESLIE] *(title)*, The Snake in the Grass. **1709** HEARNE *Collect.* O.H.S. II. 173 There is a Snake in the Grasse, and the designe is mischievous. **1868** W. COLLINS *Moonstone* ch. 14 Those enquiries took him (in the capacity of snake in the grass) among my fellow-servants.

Snake, *see also* Eaten a s.; Head like s.

Snakes in Iceland.

1778 JOHNSON in *Boswell* (1848) lxiv. 589 A complete chapter of 'The Natural History of Iceland', from the Danish of *Horrebow,* . . . chap. lxii.—*Concerning Snakes.* 'There are no snakes to be met with throughout the whole island.' **1906** *Spectator* 5 May 'The Value of a Public School Education' reminds one of the chapter on the snakes in Iceland. . . . 'So far as the school at large is concerned every Greek and Latin book should be destroyed'.

Snap (bite) one's nose off, To. (N 241)

1598–9 SHAKES. *M.A.* V. i. 115 We had like to have had our two noses snapped off with two old men without teeth. **1599** NASHE *Lenten Stuff* iii. 200 Shee was a shrewish snappish bawd, that wold bite off a mans nose with an answere. **1604** SHAKES. *M.M.* III. i. 109 That thus can make him bite the law by th' nose. **1678** RAY 348 Will you snap (or bite) off my nose? **1709** MRS. CENTLIVRE *Busie Bodie* I. i I . . . asked him if he was at leisure for his Chocolate, . . . but he snap'd my Nose off; no, I shall be busy here these two Hours.

Snapping so short makes you look so lean. (s 586)

c. **1649** *There I Mumpt You* 41 in *Cav. and Pur.* 299 Alas, good Sir, your snapping short do's make you look so lean. **1678** RAY 345. **1738** SWIFT Dial. I. E.L. 294 (Snap short).

Snare(d), *see* Birds once s. (limed) fear all bushes; Dig a pit (Make a s.).

Snatch and away, A. (s 587)

1547 BALE *Three Laws* IV. EI Yea, poore marryed men, haue very moch a do, I counte hym wysest, that can take a snatche and to go.

1570 TUSSER HI[v] Brekfast. A snatch and to worke fellowes, tarry not here. **1581** C. THIMELTHORPE *Short Inventory* G5[v] The warninge of a wyse manne to leaue the Racke, and Maunger, and to take a snatch and away. **1582** MUNDAY *Eng. Rom. Life* HI[v] (Content with). **1592** SHAKES. *T.And.* II. i. 95 Why, then, it seems some certain snatch or so Would serve your turns. **1594** *Id. L.L.L.* III. i. 19 Keep not too long in one tune, but a snip and away. [1602] **1637** T. HEYWOOD *Royal King* vi. 51. **1609** DEKKER *Gulls Hornbook* Grosart ii. 258 A licke at all sorts of learning and away. **1621** BURTON *Anat. Mel.* III. ii. v. v. (1638) 584.

Sneck before one's snout, To put a.

1583 MELBANCKE FI Neither hatch before dore, nor snecke before his snout. **1607** *Dobson's Dry Bobs* L4 He found a snecke before his snowt. *c.* **1770** PEGGE *Derbicisms* E.D.S. 65 The sneck is the latch itself and not the string, Hence the proverb: 'to put a sneck before one's snout'.

Sneeze, *see* Friend at a s. . . . God bless you.

Sneezed at, Not to be.

[= not to be under-valued.] **1813** SCOTT 24 Aug. in LOCKHART *Life* As I am situated, £300 or £400 a-year is not to be sneezed at. **1860** SURTEES *Plain or Ringlets*? ch. 35 Their Jasper was not a young man to be sneezed at. **1891** N. GOULD *Double Event* 82 A thousand pounds . . . was not to be sneezed at.

Snipe, *see* Winter enough for the s.

Snite[1] need not the woodcock betwite[2], The. (s 588)

1581 J. BELL *Haddon's Answ. Osorius* 374 Ill may the Snight the Woodcock twight, for his long bill. **1678** RAY 344 . . . *Som.* [¹ snipe. ² upbraid.]

Snotty, *see* Better a s. child.

Snout, *see* Sneck before one's s.

Snow for a se'nnight is a mother to the earth, for ever after a stepmother. (s 592)

1642 TORRIANO 69. **1659** HOWELL *It. Prov.* 14 (for eight dayes). **1659** TORRIANO no. 180 (as Howell).

Snow in harvest, As welcome as. (s 590)

[PROV. xxv. 13, xxvi. 1.] **1565** J. HALL *Court of Virtue* R8 As vnmete is honor fooles to assayle, As snowe in sommer, or in haruest hayle. *c.* **1568** WAGER *Longer thou livest* F3 As snow in haruest is untimelie. **1641** FERGUSSON no. 451 *Of untymous persons.* . . . **1670** RAY 202 As seasonable as snow in summer.

Snow year, a rich year, A. (Y 18)

1580 J. FRAMPTON tr. Monardes T.T. ii. 162 For this it is said, The yeare of snow, the yeare of fertilitie. **1640** HERBERT no. 125. **1659** HOWELL *Fr. Prov.* 21 A snowie year, a fruitful year. **1706** STEVENS s.v. Año.

Snow(s), snaw(s), (*noun*), *see also* Boil s. or pound it, can have but water; Candlemas-day is come (When) s. lies; Corn hides itself in s. as old man in furs; Filth under s. sun discovers; Fire from ice (s.), (To strike); Many haws many s.; Pepper is hot in mouth but cold in s.; Under water famine, under s. bread.

Snows (*verb*), *see* Tell me it s.

Snowdon will yield sufficient pasture for all the cattle of Wales put together.
                                                             (S 597)

1586 CAMDEN *Britannia, Caernarvon* (1722) II. 795 It is a common saying among the Welsh, That the mountains of Eryreu would, in case of necessity, afford Pasture enough for all the Cattel in Wales. **1662** FULLER Carnarvon 30 Craig Eriry, or Snow-don . . . importing, by help of an Hyperbole, the extraordinary fruitfulness of this place.

Snuff, To be up to.

[= knowing, sharp.] **1811** POOLE *Hamlet Trav.* II. i He knows well enough The game we're after: Zooks he's up to snuff. **1837** DICKENS *Pickwick* ch. 12 Up to snuff and a pinch or two over—eh? **1894** BLACKMORE *Perlycross* ch. 24 The Parson was up to snuff—if the matter may be put upon so low a footing.

Snuff, To take (take in).   (S 598)

[= to take offence at a thing.] **1560** DAUS *Sleidane's Comm.* 463 A brute went that the Pope toke it in snuffe [L. *indigne tulisse*] that this truce was made. **1565** ALLEN *Def. Purg.* xiv. 262 Aërius, . . . taking snoffe that he could not get a bishoprike, fell in to the hæresy of Arius. **1594-5** SHAKES. *L.L.L.* V. ii. 22 You'll mar the light by taking it in snuff. **1597** *Id. 1 Hen. IV* I. iii. 41 Who [the nose] therewith angry . . . took it in snuff. **1617** MORYSON *Itin.* III. 28 Englishmen, especially being young and unexperienced, are apt to take all things in snuffe. **1692** L'ESTRANGE *Aesop's Fab.* I. clxxxv. 156 Jupiter took Snuff at the Contempt, and Punish'd him for't. **1716** T. WARD *Eng. Reform.* 129 Pray take it not, you old Cur-mudgeon, So much in snuff and evil dudgeon.

Snug as a bug in a rug, As.

1769 *Stratford Jubilee* II. i If she has the mopus's, I'll have her, as snug as a bug in a rug. **1833** T. HOOK *Love and Pride* ch. 6 You might sit as snug as a bug in a rug.

Snug as a pig in pease-straw, As. (P 296)

[1603] **1607** T. HEYWOOD *Wom. K. Kindness* sc. xii. l. 29 To bed, . . . and let us sleep as snug as pigs in pease-straw. c. **1662** *Jovial Crew* l. 89 in *Bagford Bal.*, B.S. i. 198 Like Piggs in the pease-straw, intangld they lie.

Snug's the word.

1714 STEELE *Lover* no. 7. 11 Mar. *Select. Clar.* Press 279 I here lay *Incog.* for at least three seconds; snug was the word. **1738** POPE *Imit. Hor.* Ep. I. 146, 7 'Away, away! take all your scaffolds down For *Snug's the word*: My dear! we'll live in Town.'

Snug, *see also* Safe (s.) as a mouse in a cheese.

So far, so good.

1721 KELLY 300 . . . So much is done to good purpose. **1753** RICHARDSON *Grandison* v. x (1812) 389. **1921** M. HEWLETT *Wiltshire Ess.* 108 Not the most gallant way of putting it, perhaps; but so far, so good.

So got, so gone.   (G 89)

1677 E. RICHARDSON *Cert. Mor. Savings: Anglo-Belgica* II. 31 So gotten, so spent. **1678** RAY 349.

So many, *see under significant words following.*

So much is mine as I enjoy.   (M 1290)

1573 SANFORD 50.ᵛ **1629** *Bk. Mer. Rid.* Prov. no. 17 So much is mine as I possesse, and give, or lose, for God's sake. **1642** TORRIANO 94 (injoy, and give away for Gods sake). **1732** FULLER no. 4198 (and give away for God's sake).

Sober (Grave) as a judge, As.   (J 93)

1682 D'URFEY *Injured Princess* 5 Sober as a judge. **1685** S. WESLEY *Maggots* 2 As grave as judge that's giving charge. c. **1798-1803** R. B. SHERIDAN Letter (Sotheby Sale Cat. 19 July 1955, 82) I truly have been and truly will be sober as a Judge. **1850** DICKENS *Household Words* 'The Detective Police' Fikey walks . . . round it [a horse and cart] as grave as a judge. **1855** MRS. GASKELL *North and South* ch. 20 (calm).

Sober, *see also* Honest (S.) by Act of Parliament (Cannot make people).

Sober men, *see* Royet lads make s. m.

Soberness conceals, What | drunkenness reveals.   (H 333. S 600)

[L. *Quod in corde sobrii, id in linguâ ebrii.*] c. **1386** CHAUCER *Man of Law's T.* l. 776 Ther dronkenesse regneth in any route, Ther is no conseil hyd withouten doute. **1539** TAVERNER 30 The thynge that lyeth in a sobre mans hart, is in the tongue of the dronkarde. **1579** LYLY *Euph.* i. 279 It is an olde Prouerbe, Whatsoeuer is in the heart of the sober man, is in the mouth of the drunckarde. **1616** WITHALS 578 (that drunkennesse reveales). **1639** CLARKE 47. **1687** MIÈGE s.v. Drunkenness.

Socket, *see* Body is s. of soul; Candle burns within the s.

Sod, *see* Roast meat (You are in) when others in s.

Sodden, *see* Cabbage twice cooked (s.) is death.

Sodom apples outwardly fair, ashes at the core.   (A 300)

[= fruit, dissolving into ashes; any disappointing, specious thing.] **1400** MANDEVILLE ch. 12 There beside [the Dead Sea] grow trees that bear full fair apples, and fair of colour to beholde; but whoso breaketh them or cutteth them in two, he shall find within them coals and cinders. **1533** ELYOT *Of Know.* ed. Schroeder, v. 100 Or be lyke unto apples of the deed se', whiche be delicate in colour without, but within ther is nothing but coles and powder unsavery. **1583** J. PRIME *Fruitful and Brief Disc.* 8 These faire apples of Gomorrha . . . will fal straight all to dust. **1596** SHAKES. *M.V.* I. iii. 96 A goodly apple rotten at the heart. **1615** BRATHWAIT *Strappado for Div.* (1878) 48 See painted Sodom-apples faire to th'eye, But being tucht they perish instantly. **1616** T. ADAMS *The Divine Herbal* 66. **1634** RAINBOW *Labour* (1635) Those apples of Sodom which dye betwixt the hand and the mouth. **1679–1715** SOUTH *Sermons* (1842) i. 255 An apple of Sodom which, though it may entertain his eye with a florid, jolly white and red, yet, upon the touch, it shall fill his hand only with stench and foulness. **1905** W. J. ROLFE *Shaks. Sonn.* 19 The ashes to which the Sodom-apples of illicit love are turned in the end.

Soft answer turneth away wrath, A.

[PROV. XV. 1] **1382** WYCLIF *Prov.* xv. 1 A soft answere brekith ire. *c.* **1382** GOWER *Vox Clam.* l. 1509 *Iram multociens frangit responsio mollis. c.* **1420** *Peter Idle's Instructions to his Son* (Miessner) l. 190 A softe worde swagith Ire. **1586** *Maxwell Younger MS.* in HENDERSON *Scot. Prov.* (1832) Pref. xli Ane meik answer slokinnis melancholie. **1826** SOUTHEY 19 July *Lett.* (1912) 414.

Soft fire makes sweet malt.   (F 280)

a. **1530** R. *Hill's Commonpl. Bk.* E.E.T.S. 128 A softe ffyre makyth swete malte. **1545** TAVERNER D5ᵛ. [*c.* 1553] **1566–7** UDALL *Ralph Roister D.* I. ii Arb. 20 Soft fire maketh sweete malte, good Madge. **1599** PORTER *Angry Wom. Abingd.* l. 874 Haste makes waste, softe fire makes sweete malt. **1648** HERRICK *Hesper., Con. Flores* 50 (1921) 218 Extremes have still their fault; *The softest Fire makes the sweetest Mault.* **1663** BUTLER *Hudibras* I. iii. 1251 Hold, hold (quoth Hudibras), soft fire, They say, does make sweet malt.

Soft pace goes far.   (P 3)

1576 HOLYBAND D8ᵛ Soft passe goeth farre. **1598** MERES *Palladis* f. 259. **1669** *Politeuphuia* 182.

Soft place in one's head, To have a. *Cf.* **Sound head, etc.**   (P 376–7)

1666 TORRIANO *Prov. Phr.* s.v. Matto 102 To be born a fool, to have had a knock in the cradle, else to have a soft place in ones head. **1670** RAY 193.

Soft wax will take any impression. *Cf.* **Melt like wax. Pliable as wax.**   (W 136)

a. **1500** *15c. School-Bk.* ed. W. Nelson 20 Then [in childhood] the myn of a yong mann is as waxe, apte to take all thynge. *c.* **1550** *Nice Wanton* C2 Chyldren in theyr tender age, ye may worke them like waxe, to your own entent. **1551** WILSON *Rule of Reason* C7ᵛ Euen as wax chaufed with the hande, is made softer, euen so some partes of man are made by vs more apte to compasse any thing. **1578** LEMNIUS *Touchstone of Complexions* 17ᵛ Like to very moyst and softe waxe, that wil not easely take [i.e. for long] anye printe or forme. **1579** LYLY *Euph.* i. 187 The tender youth of a childe is lyke the temperinge of newe waxe apte to receiue any forme. **1590** H. ROBERTS *Defiance to Fortune* D3 Knowe you not that the new wrought dough wil receaue any impression. [1592] **1594** *Knack to Know a Knave* Hazl.-Dods. vi. 569 Pliny writes, women are made like wax, Apt to receive any impression. **1595** SHAKES. *M.N.D.* I. i. 49 You are but as a form in wax, By him imprinted, and within his power To leave the figure, or disfigure it.

Soft words and hard arguments.   (W 821)

1670 RAY 158. **1766** *Goody Two-Shoes* (ed. 3) ii. Use soft words and hard arguments.

Softly, see Fair and s., as lawyers to heaven; Fair and s. goes far.; Goes s. goes safely.

Sold, see Bought and s.; Pleasing ware is half s.

Soldier's wind—there and back again, A.

1855 KINGSLEY *Westward Ho!* ch. 19 The breeze . . . was 'a soldier's wind, there and back again', for either ship. **1899** J. K. LAUGHTON *From Howard to Nelson* 114 The 'favourable gale' which took the English ships in and out of the harbour seems to have been . . . a 'soldier's wind', there and back again.

Soldiers in peace are like chimneys in summer.   (S 605)

1595 A. COPLEY *Wits, Fits, etc.* (1614) 34. *a.* **1598** LD. BURLEIGH *Advice to Son* in KNIGHT *Half-Hours* IV. 75 Neither . . . shalt thou train them up in wars. . . . It is a science no longer in request than in use. For soldiers in peace are like chimneys in summer. *a.* **1600** *Tarlton's Jests* Pt. I, Sh. Soc. ed. 11. **1732** FULLER no. 4207.

Soldier(s), see also French s.; Obedience is duty of s.; Old men (s.) may lie by authority; Old s. over one (To come); Water, fire, and s. make room.

Sole(s), see Cleveland in clay; Shoe will hold with s.

Solitary man is either a beast (brute, devil) or an angel (saint, god), A.

(M 216, 380)

1547 BALDWIN *Moral Philosophy* O6ᵛ (a god or a beast). **1570** *Id. Beware the Cat* (1584) C5 margin. **1597** *Politeuphia* 127 (either a God or a beast). **1621** BURTON *Anat. Mel.* I. ii. II. vi. (1638) 90 As the saying is, *homo solus aut Deus,* *aut Dæmon*: a man alone is either a Saint or a Diuell. **1732** FULLER no. 418 (either a Brute or an Angel).

Solitude, *see* Great city great s.

Solomon was a wise man, and Sampson was a strong man, yet neither of them could pay money before they had it. (s 86)

1623 PAINTER B2 Though Salomon were wise, and Sampson strong, They neither could their yeares one day prolong. **1659** HOWELL *Eng. Prov.* 21a. **1666** TORRIANO *It. Prov.* 164 no. 125 (As the English say ... Sampson). **1732** FULLER no. 4066 Samson was a strong Man, yet could not pay Money before he had it.

Solomon's wise, loath to go to bed, but ten times loather to rise.

1882 E. L. CHAMBERLAIN *West Worc. Wds.* 39.

Solomon, *see also* Good wife's a prize (saith S.); Sampson than S. in him (More of).

Solvitur ambulando.

[*i.e.* It is solved by walking.] **1863** CONINGTON *Horace Odes* xxviii How easily the *Solvitur ambulando* of an artist like Mr Tennyson may disturb a whole chain of ingenious reasoning on the possibilities of things. **1906** F. W. MAITLAND *Lesl. Stephen* ch. 17 He would have to proceed empirically. *Solvitur ambulando*—the motto of the philosophic tramp—had also to be the motto of the editor. **1931** *Times* 16 Feb. 13/5 There has been nothing so perfect since Zeno's proof that motion is an impossibility and the answer in both cases is the same: *Solvitur ambulando*, or 'get a move on'.

Some are wise, and some are otherwise, (wiser than some).

1601 JONSON *Poetaster* III. iv. 23 Some wiser then some. **1658** *Comes Facundus* 308. **1659** HOWELL *Eng. Prov.* Ia. **1738** SWIFT Dial. I. E.L. 267.

Some good, some bad, as sheep come to the fold. (s 313)

1577 J. FITJOHN *A Diamond most precious* G3ᵛ They ... are as the prouerb sayth, some good, some bad. **1678** RAY 247.

Somerton ending. (s 615)

1678 RAY 347 ... *Somerset. i.e.* When the difference between two is divided.

Something (Somewhat) has some savour. *Cf.* Nothing has no savour. (s 620)

[JUVENAL *Sat.* 14. 204 *Lucri bonus est odor, ex re Qualibet.* Good is the smell of gain, come from what it may.] **1576** U. FULWELL *Ars Adulandi* sig. C2 As somewhat hath some sauor, so nothing doth no harme. **1577** N. BRETON *Wks.*

of a Young Wit (*Poems* ed. J. Robertson 29). *c.* **1607** MIDDLETON *Trick to Catch* III. i. 91 This has some savour yet. **1616** WITHALS 563 Somewhat hath some sauour, so we get the chincke,¹ we wil beare with the stinke. **1738** SWIFT Dial. I. E.L. 293 Has he got a good fortune with his lady? for they say something has some savour, but nothing has no flavour. [¹ coin.]

Something (somewhat) in the wind, There is. (s 621)

1571 R. EDWARDS *Damon & Pythias* B3ᵛ (sumwhat). **1592-3** SHAKES. *C.E.* III. i. 69 There is something in the wind, that we cannot get in. **1681** DRYDEN *Span. Friar* III. i. ed. Saintsbury vi. 456 There's something in the wind, I'm sure. *a.* **1687** C. COTTON *Poems* ed. Beresford 345.

Something, *see also* All things in their being good for s.; Always a s.; Child to hear (see) s., (To be with); Somewhat (S.) is better than nothing.

Somewhat (Something) is better than nothing. (s 623)

1546 HEYWOOD I. ix. D1 And by this prouerbe apeerth this o thyng, That alwaie somwhat is better then nothyng. **1612** SHELTON *Quix.* III. 7 i. 162 I will wear it as I may, for something is better than nothing.

Somewhat like, That is.

c. **1553** UDALL *Ralph Roister D.* l. 1003. *c.* **1565** W. WAGER *Enough* C3 This is some what like the matter. **1590** *Almond for a Parrot* Nashe iii. 350. **1601** CHETTLE & MUNDAY *Downfall E. of Huntington* Hazl.-Dods. viii. 195. **1748** RICHARDSON *Clarissa* (1811) vi. 241 Why this is talking somewhat like. **1859** G. ELIOT *A. Bede* ch. 8 It's summat-like to see ...

Son full and tattered, The | the daughter empty and fine. (s 629)

1640 HERBERT no. 214. **1659** HOWELL *Fr. Prov.* 6. Thy son well fed, and ill cloth'd, but thy daughter well cloth'd, and ill fed; a rule in breeding children. **1706** STEVENS s.v. Hijo.

Son is my son, My | till he has got him a wife; but my daughter's my daughter all the days of her life. (s 628)

1670 RAY 53. **1732** FULLER no. 6076. **1857** D. M. MULOCK *John Halifax* ch. 32 There is often a pitiful truth ... in the foolish rhyme, ...—'My son's my son till he gets him a wife, My daughter's my daughter all her life.' **1863** C. READE *Hard Cash* ch. 5 'Oh, mamma,' said Julia warmly, 'and do you think all the marriage in the world ... can make me lukewarm to my ... mother? ... Your son is your son till he gets him a wife: but your daughter's your daughter, all the days of her life.'

Son of a bachelor, He is the. (s 630)

1678 RAY 66 ... i.e. a bastard.

Son(s) of a (the) white hen. (s 632)

[= very fortunate.] [JUVENAL *Sat.* 13. 141 *Gallinae filius albae.*] **1540** PALSGRAVE *Acolastus* 80 May not I by ryghte be estemed the sonne of a whyte henne . i . maye not men . . . thinke, that I was borne in a good howre? **1602** WITHALS 143 The Chicken of a white hen, spoken of him that is fortunate, as they say, the sonne of Fortune, Albae gallinae filius. **1631** JONSON *New Inn* I. iii. 100 Yet all, Sir, are not sonnes o' the white Hen: Nor can we . . . all . . . be wrapt . . . in fortune's smock. **1706** STEVENS s.v. Blanco.

Son of his own works, Every man is the. (s 624)

1612 SHELTON *Quix.* I. iv. i. 23 There may be knights of the Haldudos; and what is more, every one is son of his works. **1659** HOWELL *It. Prov.* 6 (work).

Son(s), *see also* Brings up his s. to nothing (He that); Clergymen's s. turn out badly; Father, (That is for the), but not s.; Father (One) enough to govern hundred s.; Father (Like) like s.; Great men's s.; Marry your s. when you will; Mother's s., (Every); One hog (He that has) . . . one s. makes him fool; Will is good s.

Song, *see* Begins the s. (Let him that) make an end; Cuckoo has but one s.; End of an old s.; Made a s. of (She is not to be); No s. no supper; Sell for a s.; Sing the same s.

Soon as man is born he begins to die, As. (M 73)

[MANIL. 4. 16 *Nascentes morimur, finisque ab origine pendet. Cf.* AUG. *Civ. Dei* 13. 10.] **1576** PETTIE i. 62 We are born to die, and even in our swathe-clouts death may ask his due. **1579** LYLY *Euph.* i. 252 Our lyfe is . . . of suche vncerteintie, that we are no sooner borne, but wee are subiecte to death, the one foote no sooner on the grounde, but the other ready to slippe into the graue. **1594–5** SHAKES. *R.J.* III. iv. 4 Well, we were born to die. **1596** *K. Edw. III* IV. iv. For, from the instant we begin to live, We do pursue and hunt the time to die. **1629** T. ADAMS *Serm.* (1861–2) I. 292 As soon as we are born, we begin to draw to our end. **1742** YOUNG *Night Thoughts* V. 717 While man is growing, life is in decrease, And cradles rock us nearer to our tomb. Our birth is nothing but our death begun.

Soon as syne, As good.

a. **1610** *Birth of Hercules* IV. ii. 46. **1818** SCOTT *Rob Roy* ch. 18 Better soon as syne.

Soon deemeth, He that | soon repenteth (shall soon repent).

c. **1386** CHAUCER *Mel.* l. 2220 For the commune proverbe seith thus: 'He that soone deemeth, soone shal repente'.

Soon enough, if well enough. (s 640)

[L. *Sat cito, ṭs sat bene.*] **1545** ASCHAM *Toxoph.* Arb. 114 Men whiche labour more spedily to make manye bowes . . . then they woorke diligently to make good bowes, . . . not layinge before theyr eyes, thys wyse prouerbe. *Sone ynough, if wel ynough.* **1592** DELAMOTHE 5. *a.* **1628** CARMICHAELL no. 1453. **1651** HERBERT no. 1109 We do it soon enough, if that we do be well. **1659** HOWELL *It. Prov.* 10 What's well done is done soon enough.

Soon enough to cry 'Chuck'[1] when it is out of the shell.

1721 KELLY 288 . . . It is time enough to reckon on a Thing when you are sure of it. [[1] the hen's call to a chicken.]

Soon goes the young sheep to the pot as the old, As.

1599 PORTER *Angry Wom. Abingd.* l. 921 Take heed, as soone goes the yong sheep to the pot as the olde.

Soon goes the young lamb's skin to the market as the old ewe's, As. (L 39)

c. **1520** *Calisto & Melibea* B3 As sone goth to market the lambys fell As the shyppes. **1546** HEYWOOD II. iv. G2ᵛ As soone goth the yonge lamskyn to the market As tholde yewes. **1561** BECON *Sick Man's Salve* P.S. 118 As the common proverb is As soon to the market for to be sold Cometh the young sheep as the old. **1620** SHELTON *Quix.* II. vii. ii. 231 (to the roast). **1641** FERGUSSON no. 65. **1819** SCOTT *Bride Lam.* ch. 5 I thought Sir William would have verified the auld Scottish saying, 'as soon comes the lamb's skin to market as the auld tup's'.

Soon gotten, soon spent. (G 91)

1546 HEYWOOD II. vi. I1ᵛ. *a.* **1628** CARMICHAELL no. 1376. **1639** CLARKE 115.

Soon hot, soon cold. (H 732)

c. **1450** BURGH (& LYDGATE) *Secretes* E.E.T.S. 60. *a.* **1502** *Not-Browne Mayd* in PERCY *Reliques* It is sayd of olde, Sone hote, sone colde; And so is a woman. **1530** PALSGRAVE 885a. **1639** CLARKE 116. **1732** FULLER no. 4228.

Soon learnt, soon forgotten.

c. **1374** CHAUCER *Troilus* Bk. 2, l. 1238 Forwhy men seyth 'impressiounes lighte Ful lightly been ay redy to the flighte'.

Soon ripe, soon rotten. (R 133)

[L. *Cito maturum cito putridum.*] **1393** LANGLAND *P. Pl.* C. xiii. 223 And that that rathest[1] rypeth . roteth most saunest.[2] **1546** HEYWOOD I. x. C4ᵛ In youth she was towarde and without euill. But soone rype soone rotten. **1594** GREENE *Fr. Bacon* D1ᵛ Timely ripe is rotten too-too soon. **1642** D. ROGERS *Naaman* x. 288 Some indeed . . . are moved to . . . disdain by their inferiors' forwardness, calling them hastings, soon ripe, soon rotten. **1832** HENDERSON 137 Ripe fruit is soonest rotten. **1887** SMILES *Life & Labour* ch. 6 Very few prize boys and girls stand the test of wear. Prodigies are almost always uncertain; they illustrate the proverb of 'soon ripe, soon rotten'. [[1] earliest. [2] soonest.]

Soon up, soon down.

1642 D. ROGERS *Naaman* 229 Carnall reason is no torrent, soone up soone downe; but a gulfe. **1659** HOWELL *Brit. Prov.* 4 Soon get up, soon goe down.

Sooner begun, sooner done.

1578 *Comedy of Susanna* l. 948 The sooner that we do begin, the sooner is it done. **1872** TROLLOPE *Golden Lion* ch. 20.

Sooner break than bow, It will.   (B 636)

c. **1523** BARCLAY *Mirr. Good Manners* Sp. S. 24 For sooner breake then bowe great trees of long age. **1541** H. BULLINGER *Christ. State Matrimony* tr. Coverdale (1543) M1 Yong braunches wyl be bowed as thou lysteth, but olde trees wyl sooner breake than bow. **1555** *Institut. of Gentleman* A7ᵛ. **1623** WODROEPHE 509 (then bend). *a.* **1640** J. SMYTH *Lives of the Berkeleys* i. 151 Hee was a Lord that would make way for his will ... breake he might, bend hee would not.

Sooner fall than rise, One may. *Cf.* Descend (Fall) than to ascend (rise), It is easier to.   (F 37)

1616 DRAXE no. 602. **1639** CLARKE 164. **1670** RAY 9.

Sooner named, sooner come.   (N 33)

1581 *Conflict of Conscience* Hazl.-Dods. vi. 66 But I marvel what doth him from hence so long stay, Sooner named, sooner come, as common proverbs say.

Sooner the better, The.   (S 641)

c. **1475** *Mankind* l. 254 The sonner the leuer. **1528** JOHN WEST (cited Arber Roy and Barlow's *Rede me* 14). **1590–1** SHAKES. *2 Hen. VI* I. iv. 14 To this gear, the sooner the better. **1605** *Fair Maid Bristow* C1 I sweet hart, name you the time, The sooner the better. **1841** DICKENS *B. Rudge* ch. 37.

Soon(er, est), *see also* Easier (S.) said than done; Flowers s. fade, (The fairest); Kingdoms divided s. fall; Post s. painted (Rotten); Well done, s. done.

Soot, *see* Black as s.

Sooth as God is king.

c. **1386** CHAUCER *Merch. T.* l. 1267 As soth as God is king.

Sooth bourd is no bourd.   (B 559)

1386 CHAUCER *Cook's Prol.* l. 4356 'Thou seist ful sooth', quod Roger, 'by my fey! But "sooth pley¹ quaad² pley", as the Flemyng seith.' **1546** HEYWOOD II. viii. K2 It is yll iestyng on the soothe. Sooth bourd is no bourd, in ought that mirth doothe. **1591** HARINGTON *Apol. Poet.* in *Orl. Fur* ¶vj As the old saying is sooth boord is no boord. **1721** KELLY 3 ... Spoken when People reflect too

satyrically upon the real Vices, Follies, and Miscarriages of their Neighbours. **1824** SCOTT *Redg.* ch. 12 This sally did not take quite as well as former efforts of the Laird's wit. The lady drew up, and the Provost said, half aside, 'The sooth bourd is nae bourd'. ['play, jest. ²evil, bad: Dutch *kwaad*.]

Sooth saws be to lords lothe.

c. **1412** HOCCLEVE *De Regim. Princ.* Roxb. Cl. 106 And, for sothe sawes ben to lordes lothe, Nought wole he sothe seyne, he hathe made his othe.

Sooth, *see* True (S.) as gospel.

Soothsayer, *see* Make me a diviner.

Sop to Cerberus, To give a.   (S 643)

[= to give something to stop for the moment the mouths of Cerberus, the three-headed dog, in mythology, which guards the entrance to Hades.] **1513** DOUGLAS *Aeneid* VI. vi. 69 Cerberus, the hidduus hund. ... Quham till the prophetes. ... A sop stepit intill hunny ... gan cast. **1695** CONGREVE *Love for L.* I. iv. 17 If I can give that Cerberus a sop, I shall be at rest for one Day. **1825** HOR. SMITH *Gaieties & Grav.* I will throw down a napoleon, as a sop to Cerberus.

Sops, *see* Gangs up i' s. (When it), it'll fau down in drops; Scold (Who has a); Sorrow to his s.

Sore fight wrens as cranes, As.   (W 938)

1641 FERGUSSON no. 77. **1721** KELLY 36 ... Little People (if rightly match'd) will fight as bitterly ... as those who are stronger or bigger.

Sore upon sore is not a salve.   (S 647)

1572 E. PASQUIER *Monophylo* tr. G. Fenton 3ᵛ A pinching sore cannot abide a smarting playster. **1592** DELAMOTHE 37. **1639** CLARKE 197.

Sore(s), *see also* Empty leech sucks s.; Healing of an old s. (Ill); Keep something for s. foot; Old debts better than old s.; Plaster for small s., (Prodigious); Rip not up old s.; Salve for every s., (He has but one); Send you away with a s. heart (He will never); Shirt full of s. bones; Store is no s.; Touch me not on s. heel. *See also* Sairs.

Sorrow and an evil (ill) life makes soon an old wife.   (S 652)

1602 [COOKE] *How Man May Choose* B2. **1621** ROBINSON 33. **1639** CLARKE 279. **1670** RAY 144. **1721** KELLY 286.

Sorrow be in the house that you're beguiled in.   (S 653)

c. **1641** FERGUSSON MS. no. 1215. **1721** KELLY 298 ... Spoken to sharp expert People who have their Interest in their Eye.

Sorrow, Of thy | be not too sad, of thy joy be not too glad.

c. 1450 *Provs. of Wysdom* 51.

Sorrow (and ill weather) comes (come) unsent for. (s 654)

[L. *Mala ultro adsunt.* Misfortunes come unsought.] 1579 SPENSER *Shep. Cal.* May l. 152 Sorrowe ne neede be hastened on, For he will come, without calling, anone. 1602 H. CHETTLE *Hoffman* l. 268 You are bred of ill weather, come before you are sent for. 1639 CLARKE 101. *Ibid.* 165 Like ill weather, . . . 1721 KELLY 290 Spoken when a Person is coming to your House, whose Company you do not care for.

Sorrow is always dry. (s 656)

[Fr. 14— *Provs. communs.* Assez boit qui a deuil.] *c.* 1548 BALE *K. Johan* l. 2458 I woulde I were now at Rome at the sygne of the Cuppe, For heavynesse is drye. 1594–5 SHAKES. *R.J.* III. v. 57 Either my eyesight fails, or thou look'st pale.—And trust me, love, in my eye so do you. Dry sorrow drinks our blood. *c.* 1612 BEAUM. & FL. *Scornf. Lady* II. ii. 90 Off with thy drink, thou hast a spice of sorrow makes thee dry. 1644 W. BROWNE *Lidford Journey* Wks. Roxb. Lib. II. 352 To see it thus much grieved was I, The proverb says, Sorrow is dry; So was I at this matter. 1714 GAY *Shep. Wk., Frid.* 151, 2 For Gaffer Treadwell told us, by the bye, Excessive sorrow is exceeding dry. 1885 D. C. MURRAY *Rainbow G.* v. vi That's a public-house. Sorrow's dry, and so am I.

Sorrow is asleep, When | wake it not. (s 662)

1595 SHAKES. *M.N.D.* III. ii. 84 So sorrow's heaviness doth heavier grow For debt that bankrupt sleep doth sorrow owe; Which now in some slight measure it will pay, If for his tender here I make some stay [*Lies down and sleeps*]. *Ibid.* III. ii. 435 And sleep, that sometimes shuts up sorrow's eye, Steal me awhile from mine own company. 1659 HOWELL *Eng. Prov.* 16a. 1732 FULLER no. 5569. 1852 MISS M. A. STODDART *Song, When sorrow sleepeth wake it not.*

Sorrow is at parting if at meeting there be laughter.

c. 1460 *Towneley Myst., Proces. Talent* (Surtees) 243 Thus sorow is at partyng, at metyng if ther be laghter.

Sorrow is good for nothing but sin. (s 657)

1605 CAMDEN (1637) 287 Sorrow is good for nothing save sin onely. 1658 *Comes Facundus* 194. 1659 HOWELL *Eng. Prov.* 2a.

Sorrow is soon enough when it comes. (s 659)

1576 PETTIE ii. 70 Every evil bringeth grief enough with it when it cometh. 1721 KELLY 291 . . . Spoken to them who vex themselves with future dismal Expectations.

Sorrow makes silence her best orator.

1595 S. DANIEL *Civil Wars* ii. 93. 1597 *Politeuphuia* 131b Sorrow makes silence her best ayde, & her best Orator.

Sorrow rode in my cart.

1830 FORBY 429 . . . I did ill, but I had reason to repent it afterwards.

Sorrow to his (my) sops. *Cf.* Scold, Who has a. (s 661)

1546 HEYWOOD II. viii. K2 But two daies after this came in vre,[1] I had sorow to my sops ynough be sure. 1788 GROSE *Dict. Vulg. T.* (ed. 2) Sorrow shall be his sops. He shall repent this. [[1] use.]

Sorrow will pay no debt. (s 660)

1578 G. WHETSTONE *Promos and Cassandra* B2ᵛ Sorrowe wyll not serue . . . thou must needes prouide thee else where. 1621 ROBINSON 27 Sorrow neuer helped man. 1659 HOWELL *Letter before Span. Prov.* 1 Sorrow quits no score. 1669 *New Help to Discourse* 310 Sorrow quits no scores. 1670 RAY 144.

Sorrow wit you wat[1] where a blessing may light.

1721 KELLY 291 . . . You know not but I may have a better Fortune than you think, or expect. [[1] you can by no means know, equivalent to 'Deil Kens'.]

Sorrows gars[1] websters spin. (s 655)

1641 FERGUSSON no. 748. [[1] makes.]

Sorrow(s) (*noun*), *see also* Better a little loss than long s.; Better two skaiths than one s.; Fat s. better than lean; God send you joy, for s. come fast enough; Good to be sent for s. (You are); Grief (s.) drives out the less, (The greater); Hang care (s.); Hundred pounds of s. pays not debt; Lay s. to your heart (Never); Much science much s.; Need makes . . . and s. makes websters spin; Remembrance of past s. is joyful; Scold (Who has a) has s.; Seill comes not while s. be gone; Serve a great man and you will know s.; Small s. speak; Swims in sin shall sink in s.; Thunders in March, (When it) it brings s.; Two s. of one (Make not); Vine brings forth three grapes: . . . third of s.; Weal pricks (Whom) s. . . . licks; Worth s. (He is) that buys it. *See also* Grief.

Sorrows (*verb*), *see* Lives not well one year (He that) s. seven.

Sorry for you, I am | but I cannot weep. (c 872)

1584 R. WILSON *Three Ladies of Lond.* Hazl.-Dods. vi. 319 Alas! Lucre, I am sorry for thee, but I cannot weep. [*c.* 1587] 1592 KYD *Span. Trag.* Hazl.-Dods. v. 84. 1611 BEAUM. & FL. *Kt. Burn. P.* I. i. I'm sorry for your losses, But as the proverb says, I cannot cry. 1827 SCOTT *Journ.* 4 June Sorry for it, but I can't cry.

Sorry, *see also* Better be sure than s.; Sick nor s. (Neither); Thief is s. that he is hanged, but not that he is thief.

Sorts, *see* All s. to make world.

Sough, *see* Keep a calm s.

Soul above buttons, To have a.

1795 G. COLMAN *Sylv. Daggerwood* i (1808) 10 My father was an eminent Button-Maker . . . but I had a soul above buttons . . . I panted for a liberal profession. 1833 MARRYAT *P. Simple* ch. 1 My father, who was a clergyman . . . had . . . a 'soul above buttons', if his son had not.

Soul is my own, I dare not say my.

(S 667)

a. 1628 CARMICHAELL no. 998. 1640 BRAITH-WAIT *Art Asleep Husb.* 215 One who is . . . so sheepish, as shee dare not say her soule is her owne. 1857 G. ELIOT *Scenes* 'Amos Barton' ch. 4 Though his soul was a very little one . . . he would not have ventured to call it his own.

Soul is not where it lives, but where it loves, The.

1580 LYLY *Euph. & his Eng.* ii. 48 I feare my friends sore, will breed to a *Fistula*: for you may percciue that he is not where he liues, but wher he loues. 1662 FULLER *Westmoreland* 140 The Proverb is, Homo non est ubi animat, sed amat, One is not to be reputed there where he lives, but where he loves. 1732 FULLER no. 4761. 1908 ALEX. MACLAREN *Expos., Acts* I. 139 In the inmost depth of reality, the soul that loves is where it loves, and has whom it loves ever with it.

Soul needs few things, The | the body many.

(S 668)

1640 HERBERT no. 640. 1659 HOWELL *It. Prov.* I.

Soul(s), *see also* Body is more dressed than s.; Body is socket of s.; Brevity is s. of wit; Charge of s. (He that has); Corn is cleansed . . . and the s. by chastenings; Corporations have neither s. to be saved . . .; Counsellors (Though thou hast) do not forsake counsel of s.; Garby whose s. neither God nor devil would have; Holy habit cleanses not foul s.; Life and s. together, ('To keep); Iron entered into s.; Little body harbours great s.; Little troubles the eye, less the s.; Penniless s. maun pine in purgatory; Penny s. never came to twopence; Sickness of body . . . health of s.; Women have no s.

Sound as a bell, As.

(B 272)

1557 EDGEWORTH 2R8 If it [a mason's stone] rynge and sounde close like a Bell. 1576 LEMNIUS *Touchstone of Complexions* tr. T. Newton 109ᵛ They be people commonly healthy, and as sounde as a Bell. 1598-9 SHAKES. *M.A.* III. ii. 12 He hath a heart as sound as a bell. 1616 DRAXE no. 952. 1659 HOWELL *It. Prov.* 15 As sound as a fish, or a bell.

Sound head that has not a soft piece in it, It is a. *Cf.* Soft place in one's head.

1721 KELLY 133.

Sound love is not soon forgotten.

(L 542)

1591 STEPNEY L4ᵛ Who so heartely loueth, hardly forgetteth. 1611 COTGRAVE s.v. Aimer. 1659 HOWELL *Fr. Prov.* 6 Who loves well is long a forgetting. 1659 N. R. 91. 1664 CODRINGTON 210 (and true). 1894 NORTHALL *Folk Phrases* E.D.S. 23.

Sound mind in a sound body, A.

(M 974)

[JUV. *Sat.* 10. 356 *Orandum est, ut sit mens sana in corpore sano.*] 1578 L. LEMNIUS *Touchstone of Complexions* tr. T. Newton A2 That worthy saying of the Poet Iuuenal. Most chiefly ought our prayers to be made, For healthy minde within a body sound. 1586 *Maxwell Younger MS.* no. 32 in HENDERSON *Scot. Prov.* (1832) Pref. The dispositioun of the mynd followeth the constitutioun of the body. 1692 L'ESTRANGE *Aesop's Fab.* (1738) cccxxv. 337 A sound mind in a sound body is the perfection of human bliss. 1749 FIELDING *T. Jones* XII. iv. 1912 *Times Wkly.* 16 Feb. 127 Conditions which will give to the native a sound mind in a sound body.

Sound travelling far and wide, a stormy day will betide.

1883 ROPER 25 A good hearing day is a sign of wet *and* Much sound in the air is a sign of rain. 1893 INWARDS 106.

Sound, *see also* Empty vessels . . . greatest s.; Safe and s.; Silver will have silver s.

Soup and love, Of | the first is the best.

1706 STEVENS s.v. Sopa. 1732 FULLER no. 3699.

Sour as a crab (as wer[1]).

(C 783)

1530 PALSGRAVE 325a Sower as a crabbe is. 1616 DRAXE no. 2019. 1674 RAY *Collection of Eng. Words* 52 As sowre as wharre, *Chesh.* 1809 BYRON *Lett.* (Prothero) i. 230. 1917 BRIDGE As sour as wer (or wharre). [[1] = crab-apples.]

Sour apple-tree, *see* Tied to the s. a.-t.

Sour as whig.[1]

1589 LYLY *Pap with a Hatchet* iii. 406 More sower than wig. 1854 BAKER *Northants Gloss.* s.v. Whig . . . a common proverbial simile. [[1] sour whey.]

Sour(er), *see also* Grapes are s.; Love is sweet in beginning, s. in ending; Nothing turns s. than milk; Sell (If it will not), it will not s.; Sweet appears s. when we pay; Sweet in on-taking, s. in off putting; Sweet meat s. sauce; Sweet sauce begins to wax s.; Sweet with the s. (Take the).

Source, *see* Stream cannot rise above s.

Souter gave the sow a kiss; The | Humph, quoth she, it's for a birse.[1]

1721 KELLY 338 . . . Spoken of those whose Service we suppose to be mercenary. **1815** SCOTT *Let.* to Dk. of Buc. in LOCKHART *Life* ch. 36 The following lines are . . . from an ancient Scottish canzonetta . . . 'The sutor ga'e the sow a kiss: Grumph! quo' the sow, it's a' for my birss'. [[1] bristle.]

Souters shouldna be sailors, wha can neither steer nor row.

1832 HENDERSON 90.

South, *see* North for greatness, s. for neatness; North of England for ox, s. for sheep; Wind is s. (When), it blows bait into fish's mouth; Wind's in the s. (When), it's in rain's mouth.

South Darne, *see* Sutton.

Southerly wind and a cloudy sky, A | proclaim a hunting morning.

1846 DENHAM 8. **1869** G. A. SALA *Rome & Venice* ch. 32 . . . to which I may venture to add that 'You all know Tom Moody, the whipper-in, well'.

Southerly wind with showers of rain will bring the wind from west again, A.

1883 ROPER 691. **1893** INWARDS 82.

Southwark ale.

c. **1386** CHAUCER *Miller's Prol.* l. 3140 If that I mysspeke or seye, Wyte it the ale of Southwerk, I you preye. **1665** R. BRATHWAIT *Comments upon Chaucer's Tales* (1901) 6 Where the best Ale is . . . was made good long ago, as may appear by that overworn Proverb, The nappy strong Ale of Southwirke Keeps many a Gossip fra the Kirke.

Sow beans in the mud, and they'll grow like (a) wood.   (B 122)

1639 CLARKE 307. **1647** FULLER *Gd. Thoughts in Worse T.* viii (1863) 124 I saw in seedtime a husbandman at plough, in a very rainy day; asking . . . why he would not rather leave off than labour in such foul weather, his answer was . . . : Sow beans in the mud, And they'll come up like a wood. **1846** DENHAM 40.

Sow beans in the wind, To.   (B 125)

[= labour in vain.] **1568** *Marr. Wit & Wisdom* 45 It is not for idlenis that men sow beanes in the wind.

Sow by the ear, To have (take) the right (wrong).   (S 685)

1546 HEYWOOD II. ix. K4. Ye tooke The wrong waie to wood, and the wrong sow by theare. **1598** JONSON *Every Man in Hum.* II. i. 78 When he is got into one o' your city pounds, the counters, he has the wrong sow by the ear. **1630** J. TAYLOR (Water-P.) *Wit & Mirth* Wks. II. 180b I knew when he first medled with your Ladyship, that hee had a wrong Sow by the eare. **1690** D'URFEY *Collin's Walk* iv. 168 Thought Strumpet, since the Wind sits there, I'le take the right Sow by the Ear. **1857** E. FITZGERALD in BENSON *Ed. FitzGerald* (1905) 98 I am not always quite certain of always getting the right sow by the ear.

Sow by the right ear, To have the.   (S 684)

1570 FOXE *A. & M.* (ed. 2) 2034/1 I perceiue . . . that that man hath the sow by the right eare. **1605** CHAPMAN, JONSON, MARSTON *Eastw. Ho* II. ii. 278 You have the sow by the right ear, sir.

Sow dry and to set wet, This rule in gardening never forget to.   (S 689)

1573 TUSSER (1580 ed., ch. 35) By sowing in wet is little to get. **1660** S. RIDERS *Riders: 1600 British Merlin* [Observ. on April] In gardning never this rule forget To sowe dry, and set wet. **1678** RAY 49.

Sow four beans in a row, one for cowscot[1] and one for crow, one to rot and one to grow.

1932 *Times* 23 May 20/6 Pigeons do attack beans. . . . A saying here[2] indicates how experience forestalls the mischief by a liberal sowing . . . [[1] Cushat. [2] Guisborough, Yorks.]

Sow in beans, As still as a.

1706 STEVENS s.v. Negra (our English proverb).

Sow in the slop, 'twill be heavy at top.

1823 MOOR *Suffolk Words* 376. **1830** FORBY 417 . . . *i.e.* Wheat sown when the ground is wet, is most productive.

Sow is good mutton, Right, Roger, your.   (R 159)

1639 CLARKE 147 It's hard to make mutton of a sow. **1658** E. PHILLIPS *Mysteries of Love and Eloquence* 159. **1670** RAY 191. **1732** FULLER no. 4054.

Sow or set beans in Candlemas waddle.   (B 123)

1523 FITZHERBERT *Husbandry* (Skeat 21–2) Bothe pees and beanes . . . to begyn sone after Candelmasse is good season, . . . And specially let them be sowen in the olde of the mone. **1678** RAY 343 . . . *i.e.* Wane of the Moon. *Somerset.*

Sow peas and beans in the wane of the moon; who soweth them sooner, he soweth too soon.

1573 TUSSER Nov. ch. 12 Set garlicke and beanes at S. Edmond the King, the Moone in the, wane, thereon hangeth a thing. *Ibid.* Feb.

ch. 34 Sowe peason and beanes in the wane of the Moone, who soweth them sooner, he soweth too soone. **1846** DENHAM 42.

Sow playing on a trump, Like a.

1721 KELLY 232 . . . Spoken when People do a Thing ungracefully. **1818** SCOTT *Rob Roy* ch. 25 Never look like a sow playing upon a trump for the luve o' that, man . . . ye'll cool and come to yoursell. **1823** GALT *Entail* ch. 78.

Sow recks not of balm, The.

1577 HOLINSHED *Descr. Scotland* (1587, 19a) Herein also the prouerbe was proued true, that the sow recks not of balme.

Sow, As they | so let them reap.
(s 687)

[GALAT. vi. 7.] *a.* **900** CYNEWULF *Christ. Anglo-Saxon Poetic Records* ed. Knapp and Dobbie i, l. 85–6 Swa eal manna bearn sorgum sawað, swa eft ripað. *c.* **1275** *Provs. of Alfred* (1907) A82 Hwych so þe mon soweþ, al swuch he schal mowe. *c.* **1475** *Mankind* 175 But such as thei haue sowyn, such xall thei repe. **1664** BUTLER *Hudibras* II. ii. 503 And look before you ere you leap; For as you sow, you're like to reap. **1871** FROUDE *Short Stud., Calvinism* (1900) II. 12 As men have sown they must still reap. The profligate . . . may recover . . . peace of mind . . . ; but no miracle takes away his paralysis.

Sow (Swine) teaching Minerva, A.
(s 680)

[ERASM. *Ad. Sus Minervam.*] **1542** ERASM. tr. Udall *Apoph.* 342b A swyne to teache Minerua, was a prouerbe. **1569** *Epitaph on Dr. Bonner* (Harl. Misc. 1744, i. 597) *Sus* taught Mineruam there to long, Whiche held usurped place. **1586** LA PRIMAUDAYE A1.

Sow the wind and reap the whirlwind, To.
(w 437)

[HOSEA ix. 7 For they have sown the wind, and they shall reap the whirlwind.] **1583** J. PRINCE *Fruitful & Brief Disc.* 203 They who sowed a winde, shall reap a whirl-winde. **1837** CARLYLE *Fr. Rev.* III. v. i They . . . are at work, *sowing the wind.* And yet, as God lives, they shall *reap the whirlwind.* **1929** DEAN INGE *Assessmts. & Anticip.* 144 Class-hatred and class-warfare are preached . . . by middle-class *enragés,* . . . These rascals sow the wind; the next generation reaps the whirlwind.

Sow thin and mow (shear) thin. (s 690)

1557 EDGEWORTH *Sermons* 3G4 He that soweth spareli and thin, shal reape thin. **1593** P. STUBBES *Motive to Good Works* 192 He that soweth little shall reape little. **1641** FERGUSSON no. 751 Saw thin, and maw thin. **1721** KELLY 299. **1846** DENHAM 33 Sow thin shear thin.

Sow to a fiddle, A. *Cf.* Ass play on a harp.
(s 679)

[ERASM. *Ad. Asinus ad lyram*: An ass listening to a lyre.] *c.* **1380** CHAUCER *Troilus* Bk. I, l. 731 Or artowe lyk an asse to the harpe? **1616** WITHALS 552. **1639** CLARKE 5. **1670** RAY 193.

Sow to bear a saddle, As meet as a. *Cf.* Becomes it as well.
(s 672)

1492 *Dial. of Salomon & Marcolphus* ed. Duff 12 It becomyth not a dogge to bere a sadyll. **1546** HEYWOOD II. i. F3 She is nowe, To become a bryde, as meete as a sowe To beare a saddle. **1565** J. HALL *Court of Virtue* T8 As yf a sowe should spin and twist Of from a lynnen rocke. **1599** MINSHEU *Span. Dial.* 8 I haue as good knowledge therein as a sowe in a bridle. **1681** S. COLVIL *Whiggs Supp.* 39 Which them becomes, as all avow, As well as a saddle doth a sow. **1738** SWIFT Dial. II. E.L. 304 It became him, as a saddle becomes a sow.

Sow to her own trough, Every. (s 675)

1678 RAY 204.

Sow wheat in dirt, and rye in dust.
(w 283)

1557 TUSSER A4 Sowe wheate as thou mayst, but sowe rye in the dust. **1573** *Id.* (1878 ed., 39) Sowe timely thy whitewheat, sowe rie in the dust. **1721** KELLY 298 . . . A wet Season agrees with the one, and a dry with the other.

Sow with the hand, and not with the whole sack.
(H 91)

[PLUTARCH τῇ χειρὶ δεῖ σπείρειν, ἀλλὰ μὴ ὅλῳ τῷ θυλάκῳ. One must sow with the hand, not from the sack's mouth. Corinna's advice to Pindar.] **1591** HARINGTON *Apol. Poet.* in *Orl. Fur.* 8ᵛ For as men vse to sow with the hand and not with the whole sacke, so I would haue the eare fed, but not cloyed with these pleasing and sweet falling meeters. **1629** T. ADAMS *Serm.* (1861–2) II. 464 That stock lasts that is neither hoarded miserably nor dealt out indiscreetly. We sow the furrow, not by the sack, but by the handful. **1853** TRENCH v. 112 The Greeks, who never lost sight of measure and proportion, . . . said, . . .

Sowed cockle reaped no corn. *Cf.* Sows thistles.

c. **1386** CHAUCER *Man of Law* End-link l. 1183 He wolde sowen som difficulte, Or springen cokkel in our clene corn. **1594–5** SHAKES. *L.L.L.* IV. iii. 379 Sow'd cockle reap'd no corn; and justice always whirls in equal measure. **1608** *Id. C.* III. i. 69 The cockle of rebellion, insolence, sedition, Which we ourselves have plough'd for, sow'd and scatter'd.

Sower, *see* Rath s. never borrows.

Sowing on the sand, He is. *Cf.* Plough the sands.
(s 87)

a. **1529** SKELTON *Speke, Parrot* Dyce ii. 17 To sowe corne in the see sande, ther wyll no crope growe. *c.* **1580** SIDNEY I *Arcadia* Wks. (Feuillerat) iv. 69 Hee water plowes and soweth in the sande. *a.* **1594** SELINUS l. 1366 I sow not seeds vpon the barren sand. **1604** MARSTON *Malcontent* IV. i. 123 Go sow the ingratefull sand, and love a woman. **1616** DRAXE no. 2305 He soweth on the sand. **1813** RAY 75.

Sowlegrove sil lew.

1686-7 J. AUBREY *Rem. Gent. & Jud.* (1881) 9
The Shepheards, and vulgar people in South
Wilts call Februarie Sowlegrove: and have this
proverbe of it: viz. Sowlegrove sil lew. February
is seldome warme.

Sows good seed, He that | shall reap
good corn.   (s 209)

[GALAT. vi. 7 Whatsoever a man soweth, that
shall he also reap.]   **1492** *Dial. of Salomon &
Marcolphus* ed.   Duff 7 He that sowyth chaf
shal porely mowe.   *c.* **1569** W. WAGER *Longer
Thou Livest* A2 But commonly of good See
procedeth good Corne.   **1557** TUSSER *100
Good Points* 'September' Be carefull for sede,
for such sede as thou sowe: as true as thou
liuest, loke iustly to mowe.   **1616** DRAXE no. 117.
1700 TRYON *Lett.* I. 3 If the Seed he Sowes be
good . . . his Crop is according . . . if he Sows
Tares . . . will he expect Wheat?

Sows in the highway, He that | tires his
oxen and loses his corn.   (H 458)

1616 DRAXE no. 2312 He that soweth in the high
way, wearieth his oxen, and looseth his labour.
1706 STEVENS s.v. Camino. **1732** FULLER no.
2305.

Sows, He that | trusts in God.   (c 662)

1640 HERBERT no. 342.   **1670** RAY 24 Who sows
his corn in the field trusts in God.   **1706**
STEVENS s.v. Dios.

Sows thistles shall reap prickles, He
that. *Cf.* Sowed cockle.   (T 228)

1583 J. PRIME *Fruitful & Brief Disc.* 33 Of a
thistle a prick, of a bramble commeth a bryer.
1611 COTGRAVE s.v. Chardon (reapes thornes).
1659 HOWELL *Span. Prov.* 19 (reaps).

Sows virtue, He that | reaps fame. (v 70)

1573 SANFORD 52ᵛ.   **1629** *Bk. Mer. Rid.* Prov.
no. 48.   **1642** TORRIANO 23.

Sow(s) (*noun*), *see also* Barren s. was never good
to pigs; Cow (s.) has calved (pigged); Grease the
fat s.; Lay the head of the s. to tail of grice;
Little knows fat s. what lean doth mean; Love a
woman (He that does not) sucked a s.; Mutton
of a s., (It is hard to make); Nose to make
poor man's s. (He has); Pig of my own s.;
Pretty pig makes ugly s.; Safe as a crow (s.) in a
gutter; Sailing in a s.'s ear; Silence in the pigmarket and let s. grunt; Silk purse of a s.'s ear;
Souter gave the s. a kiss; Still s. eats up draff.

Sow(s), sowing, sown (*verb*), *see also* David and
Chad s. peas; Dragon's teeth; Early s. early
mow; Forbear not s. because of birds; Many
things grow in garden never s.; One s., another
reaps; Quiet s. quiet mow; St. Mattho take
hopper and s.; Speaks (He that) s., holds his
peace gathers; Thick s. thin come up; Thrush
when he pollutes . . . s. seeds of woe; Weeds want
no s.; Wild oats.

Space comes grace, In.   (s 697-8)

a. **1530** WOLSEY in *Letters & Papers Hen. VIII.*
iv. 6182 (cited A. F. POLLARD *Wolsey* 323).   **1541**
BULLINGER *Christian State Matrimony* tr.
Coverdale (1543) I6ᵛ.   **1546** HEYWOOD I. iv.
B1.   **1591** HY. SMITH *Serm.* (1866) I. 22 He must
not look to find a wife without a fault, . . . and if
he find the proverb true, That in space cometh
grace, he must rejoice . . . when she amendeth.
1641 FERGUSSON no. 479.   **1670** RAY 144.   **1732**
FULLER no. 6167.

Spade, *see* Call a s. a s.

Spain, *see* Castles in S.; Death come to me from
S.; Live in Italy, die in S.; Nothing ill in S. but
that which speaks; Rain go to S.; Succours of S.

Span new, *see* Spick and span.

Span, *see* Life is a s.; Spick and s.

Spaniard is a bad servant, but a worse
master, The.   (s 702)

1616 T. ADAMS *Sacrifice of Thankfulness* 6 Hee
that serues the Flesh serues his fellow . . . Wee
may say of him, as of the Spaniard, Hee is a
bad Seruant, but a worse Maister.

Spaniard, *see also* Bad S. makes good Portuguese.

Spaniel, A | a woman, and a walnut-
tree, the more they're beaten the better
they be.   (w 644)

[L. *Nux, asinus, mulier verbere opus habent.*]
1581 GUAZZO ii. 39 I have redde, I know not
where, these verses, A woman, an asse, and a
walnut-tree, Bring the more fruit, the more
beaten they bee.   **1650** Letter to Sir Ralph
Verney *Verney Memoirs* (1894) iii. 147 He
[Tom Verney] is of the Spaniell kind, the more
he is beaten the more he fawnes and per contra.
1670 RAY 50 (the better still).   **1692** L'ESTRANGE
Aesop's Fab. (1738) cccxvi. 329 A company of
young fellows were cudgelling a walnut tree. . . .
Says one of the lads, ''Tis natural for asses,
women, and walnut-trees to mend upon beating'.
1902-4 LEAN I. 455 A woman, a whelp, and a
walnut-tree, the more you bash 'em the better
they be.   **1913** *Spectator* 15 Mar. 440 If it were
only a case of a spaniel, a wife or a walnut tree
we might be capable of the ultimate brutality of
the proverb.

Spaniels that fawn when beaten, will
never forsake their masters.   (s 705)

1579 LYLY *Euph.* i. 249 Wilt thou resemble the
kinde Spaniell, which the more he is beaten the
fonder he is.   **1580** *Id. Euph. & his Eng.* ii. 155
The Spaniel that fawneth when he is beaten will
neuer forsake his maister, the man that do[a]teth
when he is disdained, will neuer foregoe his
mistres.   **1592** SHAKES. *T.G.V.* IV. ii. 14 Spaniel-
like, the more she spurns my love, The more
it grows, and fawneth on her still.   **1595** *Id.
M.N.D.* II. i. 202 I am your spaniel; and,
Demetrius, The more you beat me, I will fawn
on you.   **1732** FULLER no. 4236.   **1764** CHUR-
CHILL *Independence* 327 He, like a thorough

true-bred spaniel, licks The hand which cuffs him, and the foot which kicks.

Spaniel(s), *see also* Fawn like a s.; Flattering as a s.

Spare at the spigot, and let it out at the bung-hole. (S 750)

1642 TORRIANO 50 He holdeth in at the spicket, but letteth out at the bunghole. **1670** RAY 193. **1721** KELLY 299 . . . Spoken to them who are careful and penurious in some trifling Things, but neglective in the main Chance. **1886** E. J. HARDY *How to be Happy* ch. 13 People are often saving at the wrong place. . . . They spare at the spigot, and let all run away at the bunghole.

Spare the rod and spoil the child. (R 155)

[PROV. xiii. 24.] *c.* **1000** ÆLFRIC *Hom.* II. 324 Se ðe sparað his ȝyrde, he hatað his cild. **1377** LANGLAND *P. Pl.* B. v. 38 41 'Salamon seide . . . *Qui parcit virge, odit filium.* The English of this latyn is . . . Who-so spareth the sprynge[1]. spilleth his children.' **1382** WYCLIF *Prov.* xiii. 24 He that sparith the ȝerde, hatith his sone. **1577** *Misogonus* in BRANDL *Quellen* II. iii. 442 He that spareth the rode, hates the childe, as Solomon writes. **1605** ROWLEY *When you see me* l. 1845 A good rodde make a good boy. **1639** CLARKE 161. **1664** BUTLER *Hudibras* II. i. 843 Love is a boy, by poets styled; Then spare the rod and spoil the child. **1876** MRS. BANKS *Manch. Man* ch. 24 'Spare the rod and spoil the child' had not been abolished from the educational code fifty-five years back. [[1] rod.]

Spare to speak (and) spare to speed. (S 709)

c. **1350** *Douce MS.* 52 no. 27 Who-so sparyth to speke, sparyth to spede. *c.* **1390** GOWER *Conf. Amantis* i. 1293 For specheles may no man spede. *a.* **1500** *15c. School-Bk.* ed. W. Nelson 59. **1545** *Precepts of Cato* Publius M4ᵛ The comon saiynge is, spare speche and spare spede. **1546** HEYWOOD I. xi. E1. **1721** KELLY 5 . . . Unless a Man make Interest, and importune, he will not readily come to Profit, Honour, or Advancement. **1788** BURNS *The Blue-eyed Lass*. *a.* **1863** ARCHBP. WHATLEY *Commonpl. Bk.* (1865) 201 Another goes on the maxim . . . of 'spare to speak and spare to speed'.

Spare well and have (spend) well. (S 707)

1541 BULLINGER *Christ. State Matrimony* tr. Coverdale (1543) I3 To spare that thou mayest haue to spend. **1832** HENDERSON 16.

Spare when the bottom is bare (all is spent), It is too late to. (B 551)

[HESIOD *Op.* 367 δειλὴ δ᾽ ἐνὶ πυθμένι φειδώ. SENECA *Epist.* I *Sera in fundo parsimonia.*] **1539** TAVERNER f. 32 It is to late sparinge at the bottome. **1541** BULLINGER *Christ. State Matrimony* tr. Coverdale (1543) L4ᵛ Sparing is but vayne, when thou arte come to the bottome. *a.* **1594** *Selimus* l. 492 Alasse I spare when all my store is gone. **1639** CLARKE 283. **1662** FULLER

Sussex 105 By his magnificent prodigality, he spent the greatest part, till he seasonably began to spare, growing neer to the bottom of his Estate. **1736** AINSWORTH *Thesaurus* I. s.v. It is too late to spare when all is spent. **1853** TRENCH v. 120 There is another ancient proverb,[1] which in English runs thus: *It is* too late to spare when all is spent. [[1] Sera in imo parsimonia.]

Spare when you're young, and spend when you're old. (S 710)

1541 BULLINGER *Christ. State Matrimony* tr. Coverdale (1543) I3ᵛ Spare for thyne age. **1611** COTGRAVE s.v. Souper. **1670** RAY 79 He that spares when he is young, may the better spend when he is old. **1721** KELLY 297.

Sparing is a great revenue.

1539 TAVERNER I *Garden* B6 Magnum uectigal parsimonia, Sparyng is great rentes or reuenues. **1541** BULLINGER *Christ. State Matrimony* tr. Coverdale (1543) ed. I.4ᵛ Sparynge is a rytche purse. **1572** T. WILSON *Discourse upon Usury* (1925) 338 In sparing is great gettynge. **1732** FULLER no. 1631 Frugality is an Estate alone.

Sparing is the first gaining. *Cf.* Saving (Of) comes having. (S 712)

1573 SANFORD 105. **1578** FLORIO *First F.* 29ᵛ The first gaine or profite is to spare. **1580** LYLY *Euph. & his Eng.* ii. 16 Sparing, is good getting. **1659** HOWELL *It. Prov.* I.

Spare(s, d, -ing), *see also* Better s. at brim; Better s. than ill spent; Better s. to have of thine own; Daft that has to do and s. for every speech; Enough and none to s.; Friars observant s. their own; Know when to spend and when to s.; Lion s. the suppliant; Lost the large coat for the hood (Oft for s.); Spend and God will send, s. ever bare; Spend not where may save, s. not where must spend; Up hill s. me.

Spark a great fire, Of a small. (S 714)

1412–20 LYDGATE *Troy Book*, Bk. i. l. 785 And of sparkys that ben of syghte smale, Is fire engendered that devoureth al. **1509** BARCLAY *Ship of Fools* i. 194 A small sparcle often tyme doth augment It selfe: and groweth to flames peryllous. *a.* **1530** *R. Hill's Commonpl. Bk.* E.E.T.S. 131 Of a lytill sparkyll, commeth a gret fyre. **1591** SHAKES. *3 Hen. VI* IV. viii. 7 A little fire is quickly trodden out, Which, being suffer'd, rivers cannot quench. **1607** DEKKER *Whore Bab.* II. ii. 83 Cities with sparkes as small haue oft beene burn'd. **1666** TORRIANO *It. Prov.* 97 no. 11 Of a small spark oft cometh a great fire.

Spark(s), *see also* Heart is a fire (When) some s. fly; Smith has always s. in throat.

Sparrow(s), *see* Lustful as a s.; Pert as a s.; Two s. on one ear of corn make ill agreement.

Spatters, *see* Praises himself (He who) s. himself.

Speak and speed, ask and have. *Cf.*
Ask and have. (s 719)

c. 1547 J. BALE *Three Laws* E8 Who first speake
first spede. 1615 L. ANDREWES *Sermons* 5 Aug.
1615 (1635 ed. 835) Petite & dabitur Speake and
speed . . . Ave et habe, wish and haue. 1639
CLARKE 40. 1664 W. CONYERS *Hemerologicum
Astronomicum* 10 Sept. Speak and spead.

Speak as if you would creep into my
mouth, You. (M 1250)

1546 HEYWOOD II. ix. LIᵛ Ye speake now, as ye
wolde creepe into my mowth, In pure peinted
processe, as false as fayre. 1616 WITHALS 574
(bosome).

Speak as one finds, To. (s 724)

1594-8 SHAKES. *T.S.* II. i. 66 Mistake me not; I
speak but as I find. [1602] 1637 T. HEYWOOD
Royal King vi. 29 Give me free leave to speake
but as I finde. 1666 TORRIANO *It. Prov.* 294
no. 115 The English say, Let every one speak as
he finds. 1838 DICKENS *N. Nickleby* ch. 5.

Speak (Not to speak) as one thinks, To.
(s 725)

[TERENCE *Heaut.* Dico quod videt mihi.] *c.* 1500
Proverbs at Leconfield (*Antiq. Report* iv, 1809,
415) Many thynke not as they speke. *c.* 1520
RASTELL *Four Elements* Hazl.-Dods. i. 20 I speke
as I thynke. 1533-4 N. UDALL *Flowers* 163
I say as I thinke: . . . or, I speke as my mynde is.
1552 HULOET 2F5 Speake one thing, and thinke
another. Profari. *c.* 1565 W. WAGER *Enough* B2
Doo you speak as you think? 1590-1 SHAKES.
2 Hen. VI III. i. 247 Say as you think and
speak it from your souls. 1592-4 *Id. I Hen. VI*
V. iii. 141 Speaks Suffolk as he thinks? 1595
Id. M.N.D. III. ii. 191 You speak not as you
think. 1604 MARSTON *Malcontent* 'To the
Reader' It is my custome to speake as I thinke,
and write as I speake. 1738 SWIFT Dial. I. E.L.
290 Faith, miss, if you speak as you think, I'll
give you my mother for a maid.

Speak that I may see thee.

[ERASM. *Apoph.* (*Opera* 1540, iv. 148) Tum
Socrates ad puerum, Loquere igitur, inquit,
adolescens, ut te videam.] *a.* 1637 JONSON
Disc. viii. 625 Language most shewes a man:
speake that I may see thee. 1819 SCOTT *Bride o,
Lamm.* ch. 1 'The ancient philosopher was wont
to say, "Speak, that I may know thee;" and how
is it possible for an author to introduce his
personae dramatis to his readers in a more
interesting and effectual manner than by the
dialogue.'

Speak, You never | but your mouth
opens. (M 1249)

1639 CLARKE 133. 1670 RAY 193.

Speak by the card, To.

[= to express oneself with care and nicety.]
1600-1 SHAKES. *H.* V. i. 132 We must speak by
the card, or equivocation will undo us. 1875
JOWETT *Plato* (ed. 2) IV. 315 I speak by the card
in order to avoid entanglement of words.

Speak fair and think what you will.
(s 720)

1598 SIR R. BARCKLEY *Discourse of Felicity of
Man* A8 Farewell, and speake well, and
thinke as ye list. 1611 GRUTER 183. 1614
CAMDEN 312.

Speak false Latin, To. (L 88)

[*Fig.* to commit a breach of manners.] 1607
Puritan Widow I. i Shaks. *Apoc.* 222 I lou'd my
father well, too; but to say, Nay, vow, I would
not marry for his death—Sure, I should speake
false Lattin, should I not? 1665 G. HAVERS
P. della Valle's Trav. E. India 186 He (the King)
bid us several times put on our Hats; but our
Captain . . . answer'd that he would not, that
they should not cause him to commit that false
Latine.

Speak fitly, or be silent wisely. (s 721)

1611 COTGRAVE s.v. Taire Better no words then
words unfitly placed. 1640 HERBERT no. 625.

Speak for yourself.

1902-4 LEAN IV. 99 . . . *i.e.* don't compromise
others by unauthorized admissions.

Speak good of archers, for your father
shot in a bow.

a. 1628 CARMICHAELL no. 1412 (archers, your
father was ane). 1721 KELLY 292 . . . Spoken
to them who despise the Trade, Profession, or
way of Living, that their Father had.

Speak good of pipers, your father was a
fiddler.

1832 HENDERSON 138.

Speak ill of others is the fifth element,
To. (I 36)

1573 SANFORD 104. 1578 FLORIO *First F.* f. 29.
1611 DAVIES no. 59 . . . Nature needs but fowre;
then, the fift'sᵢ an Excrement.

Speak in clusters; You | you were begot
in nutting. (C 456)

1678 RAY 346. 1732 FULLER no. 6009.

Speak (prate) like a parrot, To. (P 60)

1521 SKELTON *Speak, Parrot.* [title]. 1575
GASCOIGNE *Glass of Govt.* ii. 5 Yong men of
quicke capacitie, do (Parrotte like) very quickly
learne the rules without booke. 1587 *Mirr. for
Mag.* 'Cardinal Wolsey' (ed. Campbell 502)
Shee had not such credite as I gate, Although a
King would heare the parret prate. 1591
LYLY *Endym.* v. iii. 219 Speakes the Parrat?
shee shall nod heere-after with signes. 1604
SHAKES. *O.* II. iii. 271 Drunk! And speak
parrot! And squabble, swagger, swear! 1630
JONSON *New Inn* I. iii. 4 He prates Latine, And
'twere a parrat, or a play-boy. 1639 CLARKE
133 He prates like a parrot. 1706 STEVENS s.v.
Papagayo To talk like a Parrot, That is, Either
to talk very much, or to talk nothing to the
purpose.

Speak like an oracle, To. (o 74)

1563 FOXE *A. & M.* (1632) 274a Let vs imagine all to be Oracles that he saith. [**1599**] **1600** DEKKER *Old Fort.* I. i. 228 And thou (like Phebus) shalt speake Oracle. **1600** JONSON *Cynthia's Revels* III. iv. 16 One that will speake More darke and doubtful then six oracles. **1676** SOUTH *Serm.* (1715) 341 He only now-a-days speaks like an oracle, who speaks tricks and ambiguities. **1770** WESLEY *Journal* v. 352.

Speak much who cannot speak well, Many. (s 718)

1597 *Politeuphuia* A3 Wee ought to haue an especiall regard, not howe much we speake, but howe well. **1616** DRAXE no. 106.

Speak not of a dead man at the table. (M 381)

1640 HERBERT no. 672. **1642** TORRIANO 81.

Speak not of my debts, unless you mean to pay them. (D 171)

1640 HERBERT no. 998. **1902–4** LEAN IV. 57.

Speak of my drink, that never consider my drouth,[1] They. *Cf. the following proverb.*

1721 KELLY 312 . . . They censure my doing such a Thing, who neither consider my Occasions of doing it, or what Provocations I had to do it. [[1] drought, thirst.]

Speak of my great drinking, Many but few of my sore thirst. (D 611)

a. **1628** CARMICHAELL no. 1112 (meikle drink). **1641** FERGUSSON no. 1054.

Speak (Talk) of Robin Hood, Many | that never shot in his bow. (R 148)

c. **1374** CHAUCER *Troilus* Bk. 2, l. 861 Swich maner folk, I gesse, Defamen love, as no-thing of him knowe; Thei speken, but thei benten nevere his bowe. **1401** *Reply of Friar Daw Topias in* T. WRIGHT *Pol. Poems* (1859–61) II. 59 Many men speken of Robyn Hood, and shot nevere in his bowe. **1546** HEYWOOD II. vi. I1. **1631** R. BRATHWAIT *Whimzies* (1859) 19 He cites . . . as if they were his familiars Euclid, Ptolemie . . . But many have spoke of Robin Hood, that never shot in his bow. **1670** RAY 137 . . . And many talk of Little John that never did him know.

Speak of the fair as things went with them there, Men. (M 557)

1631 MABBE *Celestina* IV. 84 And as you find your penniworths, so you speake of the Faire. **1640** HERBERT no. 151.

Speak of what you understand. (s 722)

1639 CLARKE 11. **1659** HOWELL *Span. Prov.* 9.

Speak, spend, and speed, quoth Jon of Bathon.

[*c.* **1381**] **1652** TWYSDEN *Hist. Angl. Script.* X. 2638 Speke, spende and spede, quoth Jon of Bathon.

Speak to a fasting man, Never. (M 314)

1621 ROBINSON 16. **1639** CLARKE 178.

Speak to the man at the wheel, Don't.

1897 BADEN-POWELL *Matabele Camp.* 235 The maxim, 'Do not speak to the man at the wheel', should ever be . . . acted up to, by those with a column who think they know better than the guide.

Speak well of the dead. (D 124)

[CHILON *Diog. Laert.* I. 3. 2. 70 Τὸν τεθνηκότα μὴ κακολογεῖν. Speak no evil of the dead. L. *De mortuis nil nisi bonum.* Say nothing of the dead but what is good.] **1540** ERASM. tr. Taverner *Flores sententiarum* A6 Rayle not upon him that is deade. **1579** A. HALL *Letter Misc. Ant. Ang.* 1815–16 3 As De absentibus nil nisi bonum, so, De mortuis nil nisi optimum. **1597** *Politeuphuia* 91ᵛ Slaunder not them that be dead. **1609** S. HARWARD 81ᵛ Speake not evill of the dead. *c.* **1628** J. SMYTH *Lives of the Berkeleys* ii. 294 I hate the tooth that bites the dead. **1642** TORRIANO 6 One ought not to wrong the absent, or the dead. **1648** HERRICK *Hesper., No despight to the dead.* Reproach we may the living; not the dead. **1669** PENN *No Cross, No Crown* xix Chilon . . . would say, . . . 'Speak well of the dead'. **1779–81** JOHNSON *Lives Poets* (Bohn) III. 321 He that has too much feeling to speak ill of the dead, . . . will not hesitate . . . to destroy . . . the reputation . . . of the living. **1902** *Spectator* 1 Nov. The dislike to speak ill of those lately dead has been proverbial for ages.

Speak well of your friend, of your enemy say nothing.

1707 MAPLETOFT 2.

Speak well, He cannot | that cannot hold his tongue. (P 146)

1545 *Precepts of Cato* B7ᵛ Pittacus. He to speake wel shalbe nothynge connynge, That wyl not knowe howe to leaue his bablynge. **1547** BALDWIN *Treatise Moral Philosophy* K8 He knoweth not howe to speake, that knoweth not howe to holde his peace. **1581** GUAZZO i. 121 Hee who knoweth not how to holde his peace, knoweth not howe to speake. **1597** *Politeuphuia* 145ᵛ He that knowes not when to hold his peace knowes not when to speake. **1666** TORRIANO *It. Prov.* 279 no. 14. **1732** FULLER nos. 1820 and 2210.

Speak when you are spoken to. (s 723)

1586 LA PRIMAUDAYE *French Academy* tr. T. Bowes Ep. Ded. Vᵛ It is unseemly for a maid-servant . . . to speake before she be spoken vnto. **1599** PORTER *Angry Wom. Abingd.* l. 917 Who speakes to you? you may speake when ye are spoken to. **1670** RAY 145 Speak when you

are spoke to, come when you are call'd. **1721**
KELLY 293 Speak when you're spoken to, do
what you're bidden. Come when you're call'd,
and you'll not be chidden. A Cant of Mistresses
to their Maid Servants. **1876** MRS. BANKS
Manch. Man. ch. 13 Girls of fifteen were then
. . . taught only to 'speak when spoken to'.

Speak with your gold, You may | and make other tongues dumb. (G 295)

[HOR. *Auro loquente, nihil pollet quaevis oratio.*]
1581 GUAZZO i. 187 It is said, . . . that the tongue
hath no force when gold speaketh. **1623** J.
LEICESTER no. 23. **1659** TORRIANO no. 135
Where gold speaks every tongue is silent. **1670**
RAY 12 . . . *Ital.*

Speak without (within) book, To. (B 532)

1551 CRANMER *Ans. to Gardiner* 279 Where you
speake of the humiliation of Christ in the sacrament, you speake without the boke. *c.* **1566**
CURIO *Pasquin in a Trance* tr. W.P. 57ᵛ Such as
speake clarkely and within booke. **1575** R.
LANEHAM *Letter* ed. Furnivall 31 (Captain Cox)
can talk az much without book, az any Inholder
betwixt Brainford and Bagshot. **1599** PORTER
Angry Wom. Abingd. l. 1517 Me thinkes you
speake without the booke, To place a fower-
wheele waggon in my looke. **1601** SHAKES.
T.N. II. iii. 137 He . . . cons state without book,
and utters it by great swarths. **1855** MRS.
GASKELL *North and South* ch. 10 I am not speaking without book.

Speaks as if every word would lift a dish, He.

1721 KELLY 154. **1732** FULLER no. 2024.

Speaks ill, Of him that | consider the life more than the word.

1640 HERBERT no. 761.

Speaks ill of the mare would buy her, He that. (M 648)

1599 MINSHEU *Span. Dial.* 60 It is as they say,
he that dispraiseth the mare carrieth her away.
1659 HOWELL *Span. Prov.* 17 Who speaks ill
of the Mare buyes her. **1721** KELLY 130 (lacks
my mare) . . . Buyers commonly discommend
what they have a Mind to; apply'd when a Man
discommends a Maid, whom he would gladly
marry, if he could get her.

Speaks in his drink what he thought in his drouth,[1] He.

1721 KELLY 134 . . . Eng. What Sobriety conceals, Drunkennes reveals. Lat. Quod in corde
Sobrii, more Ebrii. [¹ thirst.]

Speaks lavishly, He that | shall hear as knavishly. *Cf.* Says what he likes. (S 726)

c. **1595** PERKINS *Gvt. Tongue* (1608) Wks. i. 449a
He that will speake what he will, shall heare
what he would not. [citing Offic. Lib.I]. **1616**
WITHALS 577. **1670** RAY 144. **1732** FULLER no.
6367. **1773** VIEYRA s.v. Açongue.

Speaks me fair and loves me not, He that | I'll speak him fair and trust him not. (S 727)

1580 MUNDAY *Zelauto* L3 They which speak vs
fayre and looue vs not: We will speake them
as fayre, and trust them not. **1616** DRAXE no.
733. **1670** RAY 24.

Speaks sows, He that | and he that holds his peace gathers. (P 147)

1640 HERBERT no. 435. **1642** TORRIANO 32
(reapeth). **1853** TRENCH iv. 86 Speech is silvern,
silence is golden; with which we may comnare
the Italian: Who speaks sows; who keeps silence,
reaps.

Speaks the thing he should not, He that | hears the thing he would not. (S 115)

[TERENCE *Qui pergit ea quae vult dicere, ea quae
non vult audiet.*] **1530** PALSGRAVE 583b. He
that dothe otherwyse than he ought to do hereth
that we wolde be lothe of. **1539** TAVERNER 2
He that speaketh what he woll, shall heare what
he woll not. Let men beware how they rail.
1581 GUAZZO i. 72 He which saieth what
pleaseth him, heareth that which displeaseth
him. **1588** GREENE *Pandosto* Wks. (1881–3) IV.
293 Peace husband . . .: speake no more than
you should, least you heare what you would not.
1600 T. HEYWOOD *et al. 2 Edw. IV* i. 100 He that
will do . . . what he should not, Must and shall
heare of me what he would not. *a.* **1628** CAR-
MICHAELL no. 717. **1641** FERGUSSON no. 311.
1853 TRENCH iv. 86 Who says what he likes,
shall hear what he does not like, gives a further
motive for self-government in speech.

Speaks well, He that | fights well.

c. **1250** *Owl & Night.* l. 1074 'Wel fiȝt þat wel
specþ' seide Alured.

Speak(s), spoke(n), *see also* Actions s. louder
than words; Ale will make cat s.; All men s.
(When), no man hears; Bad cause that none s.
in; Bear-garden, (He s.); Clouds, (To s. in the);
Dying men s. true; Effect s., tongue need not;
First think then s.; Fool may sometimes s.
to purpose; Friends, (All are not) that s. us fair;
Good friend that s. well of us; Hear much, s.
little; Hears much and s. not at all (He that)
shall be welcome; Knows most (Who) s. least;
Leave to s. (Must have) who cannot hold tongue;
Losers leave to s. (Give); Mickle s. part maun
spill; Mouse in cheese (S. like); Post, (As good s.
to the); Read, try, s. as you find; Spare to s.;
Think that dares not s.; Time to s. (There is a);
Usurer at table (To s. of); Well-bred youth
neither s. of himself; Well s. that is well taken.

Speaking, *see* Full man and fasting (Ill s.
between).

Spear of Achilles could both wound and heal, The. (S 731)

[Telephus, king of Mysia, wounded by the
spear of Achilles, was told by an oracle that he
could only be cured by the weapon that gave

the wound.] **1579** LYLY *Euph.* i. 247 Achilles speare could as well heale as hurte. **1590–1** SHAKES. *2 Hen. VI* V. i. 100 Whose smile and frown, like to Achilles' spear Is able . . . To kill and cure. **1621** BURTON *Anat. Mel.* III. ii. v. iv. (1638) 568 Many fly to . . . Philters, Amulets, . . . which as a wound with the speare of Achilles, if so made and caused, must so be cured. **1900** C. BIGG in *The Church, Past & Pres.* 40 Evolution may be compared to the speare of Achilles; it heals at any rate some of the wounds which it causes . . . by telling . . . how . . . the lower must always prepare the way for the higher.

Spear, *see also* Good s. (He that has), let him try it; Ithuriel's s.

Spectacles are death's harquebuze.

(S 733)

1640 HERBERT no. 950.

Spectators, *see* Sport is sweetest when no s.

Speech is silvern, silence is golden.

1831 CARLYLE *Sart. Res.* III. iii. As the Swiss Inscription says: *Sprechen ist silbern, Schweigen ist golden* (Speech is silvern, Silence is golden). **1868** *Silent Hours* i. 4 Speech is, after all, not the silvern but the golden thing, when rightly used.

Speech is the picture (index) of the mind.

(S 735)

[DION. *Hal.* I. i. Εἰκόνας εἶναι τῆς ἑκάστου ψυχῆς τοὺς λόγους. ERASM. *Adag.* Hominis figura oratione agnoscitur.] **1545** *Precepts of Cato* L2ᵛ Nothynge doth more shewe and declare the lyfe and disposycion of man, then his communicacion. **1573** SANFORD 56 A Mans wordes are the image of his mynde. **1576** PRUDENTIUS tr. R. Robinson *Moral Method* A1 Nothing better sheweth what a man is then his speech. **1589** T. COOPER *Adman. People Eng.* F2ᵛ Sermo est index animi. that is, Such as the speeche is, such is the minde. **1591** H. SMITH *Preparative to Marriage* (1659, 21) The eye and the speech are the minds glasses. **1616** DRAXE no. 2042. *a.* **1637** JONSON *Disc.* viii. 625 Language most shewes a man: speake that I may see thee. **1637** *Hist. of Will Sommers* (1676) A2ᵛ Men are found by their speech and behaviour, whether they be wise or foolish. **1639** CLARKE 238 Speech showes what a man is. **1670** RAY 24. *a.* **1791** J. WESLEY Sermon C (*Wks.* 1829, vii. 146) Let your words be the very picture of your heart.

Speech, *see also* Repented s. than silence (More).

Speed is in the spurs, All the.

(S 736)

a. **1628** CARMICHAELL no. 213. **1641** FERGUSSON no. 57. **1721** KELLY 24 . . . Spoken when a Man rides a lazy Horse, . . . or must ride hard or lose his Business. **1732** FULLER no. 556.

Speed the plough, God.

(G 223)

c. **1450** 'God Speed the Plough' Poem in MS. Arch. Selden B. 26 *Historical Poems* ed. R. H. Robbins 97 God spede þe plowe al day! **1472** *Paston Letters* (Gairdner 1904) v. 147 God sped

plowghe. *c.* **1500** *Spede the Plough* 8 I pray to God, spede wele the plough. **1602** DEKKER I *Hon. Whore* v. ii. 180 God speed the Plow, thou shalt not speed me. **1891** J. E. T. ROGERS *Ind. & Commer. Hist.* II. iv The English farmer . . . wherever he may be . . . chronicles his opportunity of proposing the British toast of 'Speed the Plough'. **1896** SKEAT *Stud. Pastime* 79 'God speed the plough' does not mean 'God hasten the plough', but 'God prosper the plough'.

Speed (*noun*), *see also* Haste. (The more), less s.; —worse s.; More haste than s.; Speers all opinions comes ill s.

Speed, sped (*verb*), *see also* Spare to speak and spare to s.; Speak and s., ask and have; Speak, spend, s., quoth Jon of Bathon; Tod never s. better than own errand.

Speers all opinions, He that | comes ill speed.

1721 KELLY 167 . . . Because their different Advices will confuse, and distract him.

Speers the gate he knows full well, Many a man.

(M 311)

a. **1628** CARMICHAELL no. 1133. **1641** FERGUSSON no. 635.

Speer(s), *see also* Shame fall him that s. and kens.

Spell Yarmouth steeple right, You cannot.

1787 GROSE (*Norfolk*) 210 . . . This is a play on the word *right*. Yarmouth spire is awry or crooked, and cannot be set right or straight by spelling.

Spend a whole year's rent at one meal's meat, He will.

(Y 20)

1640 HERBERT no. 305.

Spend and be free, but make no waste.

(W 80)

1616 WITHALS 564. **1639** CLARKE 129. **1670** RAY 24. **1732** FULLER no. 4247.

Spend, and God will send; spare, and ever bare.

(G 247)

c. **1350** *Douce MS.* 52 no. 16 Spende and God wyl sende; spare and euer bare—Expendas late, mittet tibi Deus omnia grate. **1546** HEYWOOD II. v. H1 Euer spare and euer bare (saieth he) by and by. Spend, and god shall send (saieth he) saith tholde ballet. **1575** GASCOIGNE *Flowers* i. 64 The common speech is, spend and God will send, But what sends he? a bottell and a bagge. **1623** CAMDEN 268 Euer spare, and euer bare. **1721** KELLY 290 . . . Solomon says, There is that scattereth, and yet aboundeth: And there is some that withholdeth more than is meet and it tendeth to Poverty.

Spend as you get. (s 738)

1530 R. WHITFORD *Werk for Housholders* H3ᵛ
Fyrst get and brynge in and than spende. **1595**
H. CHETTLE *Piers Plainness* D4ᵛ How euer any
market went, as it came he spent it. **1639**
CLARKE 212.

Spend me and defend me. (D 192)

1590 PAYNE *Brief Descr. Ireland* (1841) 4 They
have a common saying which I am persuaded
they speak vnfeinedly, which is, Defend me
and Spend me. **1596** SPENSER *State Irel.* Wks.
(Globe) 624/1 They . . . are very loth to yeld
any certayne rent, but onely such spendinges,
saying commonly, 'Spend me and defend me'.
1619 HOWELL *Lett.* I May (1903) I. 17 [In
Amsterdam] monstrous exercises . . . are imposed upon all sorts of commodities . . .; it
goes . . . to preserve them from the Spaniards,
so that the saying is truly verified here, 'Defend
me and spend me'. **1678** RAY 351 Defend me
and spend me (*saith the* Irish *churle*). **1853**
TRENCH iii. 61 . . . expresses their idea of what
they owed to their native chiefs, and what these
owed in return to them.

Spend much, If you can | put the more to the fire. (M 1279)

1641 FERGUSSON no. 491. **1721** KELLY 181 . . .
That is, if you have a great Income spend
accordingly. Some have it Put the more to the
Fore, that is, lay up the more, and do accordingly.

Spend not where you may save; spare not where you must spend. (s 739)

1678 RAY 348.

Spender, To a good | God is the treasurer. (s 743)

1640 HERBERT no. 530.

Spenders are bad lenders, Great. (s 744)

1626 BRETON *Soothing* B1ᵛ (are but). **1639**
CLARKE 262.

Spending lies the advantage, In. (s 745)

1640 HERBERT no. 85.

Spends before he thrives, Who | will beg before he thinks. (s 740)

1597 *Politeuphuia* 236ᵛ. **1732** FULLER no. 5720.

Spends his Michaelmas rent in Midsummer moon, He. (R 75)

1617 SWETNAM *School of Defence* 79 Spend
not Michaelmasse rent in Midsummer quarter
abroade. **1623** CAMDEN 270. **1670** RAY 186.

Spends more than he should, shall not have to spend when he would, Who.

1664 CODRINGTON 226. **1670** RAY 25. **1732**
FULLER no. 6074.

Spends the traveller more than the abider, Much. (T 475)

1640 HERBERT no. 276.

Spent we had; What we | what we gave, we have; what we left, we lost. (s 742)

[Supposedly inscribed on the tomb at Tiverton
which existed till the late sixteenth century of
Edward de Courtenay third Earl of Devonshire
who died in 1419. It is based on 'Quod expendi,
habui' etc. quoted by John Weever: see C.
Bühler *Renaissance News* viii (1955) 10.] **1579**
Gloss to SPENSER *Shep. Cal.* May, Much like the
epitaph of a good old Erle of Devonshire . . .
the rymes be these; Ho, ho! Who lies here?
I the good Earle of Devonshere And Maulde my
wife that was ful deare . . . That we spent, we
had; That we gave, we have: That we lefte we
lost. **1669** *New Help to Discourse* 250 (What
we lent is lost). **1773** 12 Aug. JOHNSON *Lett.*
(Chapman) i. 338 [Monument of Robert of
Doncaster]. **1862** 15 Dec. *The Times* 'Field and
Factory' The most common maxim of the rank
and file of British industry is that what you
spend you have, for it alone cannot be taken
away from you.

Spend(s, -t), *see also* Better spared than ill s.;
Covetous s. more than liberal; Do not all you
can, s. not all you have; Four and s. five, (He
that has but) has no need of a purse; Gain
teaches to s.; Gains well and s. well (He that);
House and land are s. (When), learning is
excellent; Know when to s.; Life is half s.;
Little good is soon s.; More than he is worth
does s. (Who); Narrow gathered widely s.;
Penny is well s. that saves; Soon gotten, soon s.;
Spare well and s. well; Spare when young, s.
when old; Speak, s., speed, quoth Jon of
Bathon.

Spice is black, but it has a sweet smack.

1721 KELLY 296 . . . An Apology for black
People.

Spice, He that has the | may season as he list. (s 747)

1640 HERBERT no. 424. **1670** RAY 25 Who hath
spice enough may season his meat as he pleaseth.

Spice, *see also* Beat s., it will smell sweeter.

Spick and span, *or* Spick and span new (*formerly* Span new). (s 748)

c. 1300 *Havelok* 968 The cok bigan of him to
rewe, And bouthe him cloþes, al spannewe.
c. 1374 CHAUCER *Troilus* Bk. 3, l. 1665 This tale
was ay span-newe to bygynne. *a.* 1579–80
NORTH *Plutarch* (1895) II. 217 They were all
in goodly gilt armours, and brave purple
cassocks upon them, spicke, and spanne newe.
c. 1590 Forewords to STUBBES' *Anat.* (1877) 38
A spicke and spanne new Geneua Bible. **1665**
PEPYS *Diary* 15 Nov. My Lady Batten walking
through the dirty lane with new spicke and
span white shoes. **1691** RAY *S. & E. Co. Words*
114 *Span New*, very new: that was never worn
or used. **1846** THACKERAY *Crit. Rev. Wks.*

(1886) XXIII. 159 Benvenuto, spick and span in his very best clothes. **1886** 'MAXWELL GRAY' *Silence Dean Maitland* I. i. 9 A dog-cart, . . . driven by a spick-and-span groom.

Spider lost her distaff, and is ever since forced to draw her thread through her tail, The.
1732 FULLER no. 4766.

Spider(s), *see also* Bee sucks honey (Where), s. sucks poison; Killed the blue s. in Blanch powder land; Swallowed a s.; Thrive (He who would wish to) must let s. run alive.

Spies are the ears and eyes of princes.
(S 795)
1651 HERBERT no. 1067.

Spies, The life of | is to know, not to be known. (L 257)
1651 HERBERT no. 1068.

Spigot, *see* Spare at the s.

Spill, *see* Mickle spoken part maun s.

Spilt (Puddled) wine is worse than water. (W 469)
1616 DRAXE no. 1105 (Puddled). **1721** KELLY 295 . . . Spoken when a Thing is spoil'd and not put to its proper Use.

Spin a fair (fine) thread, To. (T 252)
c. **1412** HOCCLEVE *Reg. Princes* E.E.T.S. 64, l. 1763 Alasse! this likerous dampnable errour, In this londe hath so large a threde I-sponne, That wers peple is non vndir the sonne. **1546** HEYWOOD II. v. H2 In beyng your owne foe, you spin a fayre threede. *c.* **1550** *Jacob & Esau* C3. **1606** MARSTON *Fawn* IV. i. **1660** TATHAM *The Rump* IV. i. Wks. (1879) 246 Cain has kill'd his brother, Coll. Cordmayner. He has spun a fine thread to-day.

Spin and reel at the same time, A man cannot. (M 227)
1678 RAY 205. **1732** FULLER no. 2591 (spin and weave).

Spin(s), span, spun, *see also* Adam delved and Eve s.; Kiss than s. (She had rather); Labours and thrives s. gold; Spoil before you s. (Must); Thread is s.

Spindle and thy distaff ready, Get thy | and God will send thee flax. (S 753)
1659 HOWELL *New Sayings* 8. **1670** RAY 11. **1721** KELLY 119 Get your Spindle and Roke ready, and God will send you Tow. Use proper Means, and depend upon God for the Blessing.

Spindles are made, By one and one the.
(O 43)
1573 SANFORD 102. **1578** FLORIO *First F.* 27ᵛ. **1629** *Bk. Mer. Rid.* no. 62.

Spinner has a large shift, The diligent.
(S 757)
1659 HOWELL *Span. Prov.* 11 Who spins well hath a large smock. **1758** FRANKLIN in Arber *E. Garner* v. 581 Industry gives comfort, and plenty, and respect. . . .

Spinola's pleasure, *see* Kirkbie's castle.

Spins well that breeds her children, She. (C 343)
1640 HERBERT no. 144. **1706** STEVENS s.v. Tela. She spins a good Web who breeds up her Son.

Spirit is willing, The | but the flesh is weak. (S 760)
[MATT. xxvi. 41 The spirit indeed is willing. . . .] **1608** ARMIN *Nest Ninnies* Wks. 54 I am willing, but flesh is weake. **1666** TORRIANO *It. Prov.* 268 no. 19 The spirit is ready, but the body is lame. **1827** SCOTT *Journ.* 23 July The spirit is willing but the flesh is weak, so I must retreat into the invalided corps.

Spirit of building is come upon him, The. (S 761)
1678 RAY 67.

Spirits, *see also* Raise no more devils (s.) than you can lay.

Spit and a stride, A. (S 763)
[1621] **1647** FLETCHER *Pilg.* ed. Glover and Waller II. ii. 176 Wilt thou take a spit and a stride, and see if thou canst outrun us? **1656** 17 Jan. SIR T. PEYTON to H. Oxinden *Oxinden & Peyton Letters 1642–1670* ed. D. Gardiner 213 'Tis not I that am Author of this saying but a man about a spit and a stride wiser, learned Causabon. **1666** TORRIANO *Prov. Phr.* s.v. Trotto 223a A small distance the English say, A Spit and a Stride, not far.

Spit in (on) his hand and do full ill, A man may. (M 269)
1641 FERGUSSON no. 100. **1721** KELLY 26 . . . A Man . . . will spit in his Hand, that he may hold the Cudgel the faster: Meaning, that a Man may make good Offers to act stoutly whose Heart may yet misgive him after all.

Spit in his mouth, and make him a mastiff. (M 1259)
1576 FULWELL *Ars Adulandi* VIII. 13ᵛ I thinke those men of honour and worship, vse you as men vse their waterspaniels: that is, they make you their instrument to fetch and bringe vnto them such commodities, as you by the corrupting of your conscience may compasse, and . . . for your labour they spitte in your mouth. **1606**

DANIEL *Arcadia* Gros. I. ii. 221 And if she meet but with my dog, she takes And strokes him on the head, playes with his eares, Spits in his mouth, and claps him on the backe. *a.* 1633 JONSON *T. Tub* II. iv. 10 A Spaniel, And scarce be spit i' th'mouth for 't. 1670 RAY 216.

Spit in your hand and take better hold (hold fast). (H 120–1)

1546 HEYWOOD II. iv. G4ᵛ. Naie, I will spyt in my handes, and take better holde. 1577 GRANGE *Gold. Aphrod.* H j b If I haue anoynted your palmes with hope, spitte on your handes and take good holde. 1591 I *T. Reign K. John* B1ᵛ Spit in your hand and to your other proofes. 1670 RAY 194. 1686–7 J. AUBREY *Remains of Gent. & Jud.* ed. Britten 197 I remember in Kent, when a person in a declining condition recovers and is likely to live longer, it is a proverb to say of him that he has spit in his hand, and will hold out the nother year. 1721 KELLY 291 . . . hold fast. Spoken to Wives, when they speak of their Husband's second Marriage. 1738 SWIFT *Dial.* I. E.L. 268 Nought's never in danger. I warrant miss will spit in her hand, and hold fast. 1866 BLACK-MORE *Cradock N.* ch. 33 Spit on your grapples, my lads of wax, and better luck the cast after.

Spit in your mouth, Let me. (M 1255)

1581 C. THIMELTHORPE *Short Inventory* H8 He [a fool] will not greatly sticke in anye companye what soeuer, to spyt in your mouth when you passe the Streetes talkinge with your friend, . . . to come and colle you about the necke. *Ibid.* 15ᵛ Since upon thys small familiaritie vouchsafed vpon you . . . you begin to creep vpon my backe, no doubt you wil shortly . . . spit into my mouth. 1602 MARSTON *Antonio & Mel.* II. i. 93 I'll spit in thy mouth, and thou wilt, to grace thee. 1609 HARWARD 120ᵛ Stroke his head and spitt in his mouth. He is like a windmill. He will go no longer then flattering doth blow him forward. 1639 CLARKE 186.

Spit of, The very. *Cf.* Like one as if he had been spit out of his mouth.

[The exact image, likeness, or counterpart of (a person, &c.)] 1825 KNAPP & BALDWIN *Newgate Cal.* III. 497/2 A daughter, . . . the very spit of the old captain. 1836 T. HOOK *G. Gurney* I. 202 You are a queer fellow—the very spit of your father. [*Cf.* Fr. *tout craché* (LA FONTAINE, *Contes, Deux Amis*).] 1912 8 Mar. D. H. LAWRENCE *Lett.* i. 103 It's the spit and image of him.

Spit on a (the) stone, (and) it will be wet at the last. (S 887)

a. 1628 CARMICHAELL no. 1377. 1641 FERGUSSON no. 746. 1721 KELLY 300 . . . Constant and perpetual doing, though slow, yet may at last effect great Things.

Spit one's venom, To. (V 28)

c. 1200 *Ancrene Riwle* 86 The uorme cumeð al openliche, & seið vuel bi anoðer, & speoweð ut his atter¹. *c.* 1386 CHAUCER *Pard. T.* Prol. l. 421 Thus spitte I out my venym vnder hewe Of hoolynesse, to semen hooly. *c.* 1450 *Myrr. our Ladye* 205 God gaue mankynde fowde of lyfe wherein the enemy spued venym by a worde of

lesyng. 1639 CLARKE 54. 1701 FARQUHAR *Sir H. Wildair* I. i. Let 'em spit their venom among themselves, and it hurts nobody. [¹ venom.]

Spit upon the same stone, To.

1777 BRAND *Pop. Antiq.* 101 *note* We have too a kind of popular Saying, when Persons are of the same Party, or agree in Sentiment, 'they spit upon the same stone'.

Spit (*noun*), *see also* Eggs on the s.; God's blessing make . . . my s. go (Will); Irishman on s.; Loves roast meat that licks s.; Roast meat (Give one) and beat him with s.

Spit(s) (*verb*), *see also* Bitter in his mouth (Who has) s. not all sweet; Like one as if s. out of his mouth; Long as I live I'll s. in my parlour.

Spital, Spittle (i.e. hospital), *see* God keep me from . . . s.; One foot in the straw (He that has) has another in s.

Spite of one's teeth (beard, head, heart, nose), In. (S 764)

c. 1489 CAXTON *Sons Aymon* III. 109 Reynawde toke Alarde oute of his enemyes handes, mawgre theyr teeth. [1525–40] 1557 *Mer. Dial.* 68 (beards). 1533 T. LUPSET *Exhortatⁿ. Young Men* ed. Gee 259 These small gyftes of fortune, mawgre our heed, be taken from vs. 1565 J. HALL *Court of Virtue* R6 Spyght of her [Anger's] beard they put her to flight. 1568 TILNEY *Duties in Marriage* B6 He shall enioy hir in dispite of hir husbands beard. 1570–1 L.H. *Dict. Fr. and Eng.* Maulgré que i'en aye, in spite of my teeth, against my will. 1600–1 SHAKES. *M.W.W.* V. v. 123 In despite of the teeth of all rhyme and reason. 1611 COTGRAVE s.v. Barbe Mauger his beard, in despight of him. 1650 BURROUGHES *Gospel Worship* VI. 98 In spight of thy heart thou canst not cover any thing from the Lords eyes. 1655 C. COTTON *Scarron.* IV. 114 He would go 'spite of all their Noses.

Spite of the devil and Dick Senhouse,¹ It will do, in.

1794 W. HUTCHINSON *Hist. Cumberland* II. 269 They were a constant family of gamesters . . . The doctor playing with a stranger, he tipped the die so pat, that the other exclaimed, 'Surely it is either the devil or Dick Senhouse!' A common saying, . . . [¹ Richard Senhouse, Bishop of Carlisle, 1624–6.]

Spits against heaven (the wind), Who | it falls in his face. (H 356)

1557 NORTH *Dial. of Princes* 106 As he whiche spitteth into the element and the spittel falleth againe into his eies. 1578 J. YVER *Courtly Controv.* tr. H. Wotton P3 Thou shalte be like him that spitteth againste the winde, whose slauer fleeth in his owne face. 1612 WEBSTER *White Devil* III. i. Merm. 48 For your names Of whore and murderess, they proceed from you, As if a man should spit against the wind; The filth returns in 's face. 1629 T. ADAMS *Serm.* (1861–2) I. 391 God shall . . . at last despise you, that have despised him in us. *In expuentis recidit faciem, quod in cælum expuit*—That which a man spits against heaven shall fall back on his own face.   **1640** HERBERT no. 346.

Spits on his own blanket (sleeve), He.
(B 447. S 536)

1611 COTGRAVE s.v. Manche C'estoit du temps qu'on se mouchoit encor à la manche. It was in the dayes of simplicitie, or ignorance; it was at a time when people either knew not, or cared not for good manners. **1621** ROBINSON 24 (sleeue). **1639** CLARKE 54 You spit on your owne sleeve. **1641** FERGUSSON no. 416. Of misnurtured persons. . . . **1721** KELLY 367 What you say reflects upon yourself, or Family. Eng. You spit on your own Blanket (lap). **1828** LYTTON *Pelham* ch. 77 Mr. Pelham, who is a long-headed gentleman, and does not spit on his own blanket, knows well enough that one can't do all this for five thousand pounds.

Spits, *see also* Spit(s).

Spitting in the church, Some make a conscience of | yet rob the altar. (C 610)

1591 FLORIO *Second F.* 13 Who sometimes make it a matter of conscience to spit in the Church, and at another time will beray the altar.   **1640** HERBERT no. 650.

Spleen, *see* Fly has her s.; Good for the liver bad for s.

Splice the main-brace, To.

[= to serve out grog.]   **1805** *Naval Chron.* XIII. 480 Now splice the main brace.   **1833** MARRYAT *P. Simple* ch. 15 Mr. Falcon, splice the main-brace, and call the watch.   **1841** CHAMIER *Tom Bowl.* ch. 27 I'm not going to splice the main-brace, my lads; we must have no Dutch courage.

Split, *see* Cut (S.) the hair.

Spoil before you spin, You must.
(S 767)

1621 ROBINSON 15.   **1639** CLARKE 110.   **1732** FULLER no. 5970 (spin well).

Spoil the Egyptians, To.

[EXODUS xii. 35, 36 They borrowed of the Egyptians jewels of silver, and jewels of gold, and raiment. . . . And they spoiled the Egyptians.]   **1818** SCOTT *Rob Roy* ch. 18 'How does a man of your strict principles reconcile yourself to cheat the revenue?' 'It's a mere spoiling o' the Egyptians', replied Andrew. **1872** C. READE *Wand. Heir* ch. 4 But I doubt me whether that would be fair trade. . . . Is it lawful to spoil the Egyptians?

Spoils, *see* Too much s.

Spoke an angel, There.   (A 242)

[An angel was a gold coin worth 10s.; often used, as here, in quibbles.]   c. **1590–5** Sir Thos. More I. i. *Shaks. Apoc.* 387 Lets freendly goe and drinke together . . .—There spake an angell.   c. **1594** SHAKES. *K.J.* V. ii. 65 And even there

methinks, an angel spake.   **1599** PORTER *Angry Wom. Abing.* l. 1389.   **1605** CHAPMAN, JONSON, MARSTON *East. Ho.* II. ii. 272 The bloud-hound Securitie will smell out ready money for you instantly.—There spake an Angell.

Spoke in his wheel, It is the best.

1721 KELLY 223.

Spoke in one's wheel, To put a. (S 769)

1580 LYLY *Euph. & his Eng.* ii. 173 Camilla not thinking to be silent, put in hir spoke as she thought into the best wheele.   **1601** JONSON *Poetaster* II. i. 47 You would haue your spoke in my cart!   **1853** G. J. WHYTE-MELVILLE *Digby Grand* ch. 8 I will put a spoke in your wheel, take my word for it.

Spoke, *see also* Worst s. breaks first.

Sponge, *see* Throw up s.

Spoon in every man's dish, To have a. *Cf.* Oar in every man's boat.

1577 HOLINSHED (1587) iii. 100b His spoon in euerie mans dish.   **1609** HARWARD 75ᵛ Have not a).

Spoon(s), *see* Born with a silver s.; Come after with salt and s.; Fern is as high as a s., (When); Fill the mouth with empty s.; Gives fair words feeds with empty s.; Horn s. holds no poison; Long s. that sups with devil; Make a s. or spoil a horn; Sea with a s., (To empty the); Sup with a cutty than want a s. (Better to).

Sport is sweetest when there be no spectators.   (S 779)

1616 WITHALS 555 (lookers on).   **1639** CLARKE 326.

Sport, The best of the | is to do the deed, and say nothing.   (B 323)

1640 HERBERT no. 812.

Sport, *see also* Age is jocund (When) it makes s. for death; Good s. that fills belly; Make s. (He that cannot) should mar none; Mischief (More) the better s.; No s. no pie; War is s. of kings.

Sports and journeys men are known, In.
(S 780)

1640 HERBERT no. 399.

Spots (even) in (on) the sun, There are.
(S 782)

1665 R. BOYLE *Occasional Reflections* IV. xi. Wks. ii. 196 Our late astronomers, being assisted with good glasses, are allowed to tell us, that they discern spots even in the sun it self. **1732** FULLER no. 4434 The brightest of all Things, the Sun, hath its Spots. **1843–4** DICKENS *M. Chuz.* ch. 4 You are . . . a strange instance of the little frailties that beset a mighty mind . . . I should have been quite certain from my observation of you, Chiv. that there were spots on the sun.   **1907** s. LEE *Gt. of 16th Cent.* 7 But in the case of Bacon and Shakespeare, such errors are spots on the sun.

Spot(s), *see also* Enemy (In an) s. soon seen; Ermine (In an) s. soon discovered; Leopard cannot change his s.; Leopard (In a) the s. not observed.

Sprat, Jack, *see* Jack S. he loved no fat; J. S. would teach grandame.

Sprat now-a-days calls itself a herring, Every.

1732 FULLER no. 1464.

Sprat to catch a mackerel (herring, whale), Throw out a.

1810 J. POOLE *Hamlet Travestie* (1811, 30).   **1827** HONE *Ev. Day Book* ii. 1410 It is but 'giving a sprat to catch a herring', as a body may say. **1832** MARRYAT *N. Forster* ch. 44 'Depend upon it, that's his plan. A sprat to catch a mackerel.' **1843–4** DICKENS *M. Chuz.* ch. 8 It was their custom . . . never to throw away sprats, but as bait for whales.   **1926** *Times* 31 Mar. 5/7 The firm is doing that for a purpose. . . . That is in the nature of a sprat to catch a mackerel.

Sprat, *see also* Fish for herring and catch s.

Spread the table, and contention will cease. (T 2)

1678 RAY *Adag. Hebr.* 413.

Spring at his elbow, He has a. (s 786)

1678 RAY 351 He hath a spring in his elbow. Spoken of a Gamester.

Spring from the year, To take away the.

1623 J. LEYCESTER no. 214.   **1813** RAY 75.

Spring (Be sprung) of a (the) stone, To.

[= to indicate the absence of any known ancestry of kinsfolk.]   **1297** R. GLOUC. (Rolls) 6720 Seint Edward in normandie was þo bileued al one As bar, as wo seiþ, of þe kunde as he sprong of þe stone.   a. **1300** *K. Horn* (Camb.) 1026 Horn him ȝede alone, Also he sprunge of stone. a. **1400** *Sir Perc.* 1043 Als he ware sprongene of a stane, Thare na mane hym kende.

Spring, *see also* Ague in s.; Blossom in the s. (That which does); Rivers need a s.; Tread on nine daisies, s. has come.

Spring(s) (= tune), *see* Old s. give no price; Take a s. of his own fiddle (Let him).

Springe to catch a woodcock, A. (s 788)

1579 GOSSON *School of Abuse* Arber 72 Cupide sett vpp a Springe for Woodcockes.   c. **1600–1** SHAKES. *H.* I. iii. 115.   **1607** E. SHARPHAM *The*

Fleir G4 The Springle of her beautie hath all readie caught the woodcocke of his affections. c. **1610** SHAKES. *W.T.* IV. iii. 34 If the springe hold, the cock's mine.   **1617** J. SWETNAM *School of Defence* B1ᵛ They fall into the springle with the woodcocke.

Spun, If it will not be | bring it not to the distaff. (s 755)

1640 HERBERT no. 665 That which will not be spun, let it not come betweene the spindle and the distaffe.   **1732** FULLER no. 2726.

Spur a free horse, Do not. (A running (forward) horse needs no spur). *Cf.* Untimeous spurring. (H 638, 688)

OVID *Ars. Am.* 2. 732 Nolle admisso subdere calcar equo.   **1477** *Paston Lett.* (Gairdner 1904) v. 294 It shall never neede to prykk nor threte a free horse.   **1595–6** SHAKES. *Rich. II* IV. i. 72 How fondly dost thou spur a forward horse. **1599** JAMES VI *Basil. Dor.* Arb. 156 Pastimes, wherewith men by driving time, spur a free and fast enough running horse (as the proverb is). **1616** DRAXE no. 2409 A running horse needeth no spurre.   **1623** J. BALMFORD *Reply to Gataker* 41 A running horse (say they) needeth no spurring.   a. **1628** CARMICHAELL no. 119 A gentil horse sould not be over sair spurred. **1633** JONSON *T. Tub* III. iv. Spur a free horse, he'll run himself to death.   **1659** HOWELL *Span. Prov.* 9 A forward Horse needs no Spur. *Ibid. Eng. Prov.* 17a ('Tis ill spurring).   **1670** RAY 145. **1732** FULLER no. 156 A good Horse should be seldom spurr'd.   **1750** W. ELLIS *Mod. Husbandm.* VII. 95 The roots will after this often cutting . . . wear out and die before their natural Time, according to the Proverb, One may ride a free Horse to Death.

Spur a hamshackled[1] horse, It is idle to.

1828 SCOTT *F. M. Perth* ch. 33 'It is but idle to spur a horse when his legs are ham-shackled', said the Highlander haughtily. 'Her own self cannot fight even now, and there is little gallantry in taunting her thus.' [1 shackled, by having its head tied to one of its forelegs.]

Spur a jade a question, and (s)he'll kick you an answer.

1692 L'ESTRANGE *Aesop's Fab.* cccxvi (1738) 329 . . . People should not be too inquisitive, without considering how far they themselves may be concerned in the answer to the question.

Spur and a whip for a dull horse, A. (s 790)

1580 T. CHURCHYARD *Churchyards Charge* (ed. Collier 35) A dulled horse that will not sturre Must be remembered with a spurre.   **1582** *Batman upon Bartholomew* 74ᵛ A slowe horse must haue a quicke spur.   **1616** DRAXE no. 1005 To a lazie horse a good spurre.   **1639** CLARKE 76.

Spur in the head is worth two in the heel, A. (s 791)

1668 SKIPPON *Diary* 162 A sparre in the head is as good as two in the heele.   **1670** RAY 218.

1721 KELLY 49 . . . A Man when drunk rides hard. **1738** SWIFT *Dial.* II. E.L. 312 Stay till this bottle's out . . . a cup in the pate is a mile in the gate, and a spur in the head is worth two in the heel. **1812** EDGEWORTH *Absentee* ch. 10 That's four good miles; but 'a spur in the head is worth two in the heel'. **1853** G. J. WHYTE-MELVILLE *Digby Grand* ch. 19 (the old Scotch proverb).

Spur of the moment, On the.

1806 A. DUNCAN *Nelson's Funeral* 43 The contrivance of Mr. Wyatt, on the spur of the moment. **1831** BLAKEY *Free Will* 152 A speaker who gives us a ready reply upon the spur of the moment.

Spur, Upon the.   (s 789)

a. **1576** WHYTHORNE 206 Shee being whot in the sear and of the spur. **1613** T. ADAMS *The White Devil* (1862) ii. 224 Either he must be unmerciful or over-merciful; either wholly for the reins, or all upon the spur. **1639** CLARKE 116 (He's all on).

Spur(s), *see also* Bridle and s. makes good horse; Love in his breast (He that has) has s.; Reason lies between s. and bridle; Speed is in the s.; Win s.

Spurring, *see* Untimeous s. spills the steed.

Spy faults if your eyes were out, You would.   (F 124)

1678 RAY 271.

Spy-faults, *see* Mend-fault.

Square, *see* Inch breaks no s.; Just as a s.

Squeak, *see* Young one s. (Make the).

Squeeze a cork, you will get but little juice, If you.

1732 FULLER no. 2791.

Squib, *see* Angry as an ass with s. in breech.

Squint-eyed, *see* Perverseness makes one s.

Squire, *see* Scald horse for scabbed s.

Squires and spires, *see* Northamptonshire.

Stabbed with a Bridport dagger.   (D 5)

1662 FULLER *Dorset* 278 . . . That is, hanged . . . at the Gallowes; The best . . . Hemp . . . growing about Brydport, a Market Town in this County. **1910** *T.L.S.* 21 Oct. 384 Leland . . . jots down, 'At Bridporth be made good daggers'. Nowadays, at any rate, a Bridport dagger is a grimly humorous euphemism for a hangman's rope.

Stable-door, *see* Shut the s.-d. when steed stolen (Too late to).

Staff and wallet, To come to the.
                                              (s 799)

[To be beggared.] **1541** BULLINGER *Christian State Matrimony* tr. Coverdale (1543) H4 A rytche man . . . commeth immediately to the staffe and wallet. **1546** HEYWOOD II. v. H1. **1639** CLARKE 243 (staffe and the wallet).

Staff be crooked, If the | the shadow cannot be straight.   (s 801)

1640 HERBERT no. 583.

Staff (Stick) (stone to throw at a dog), to beat a dog, It is an easy thing to find a.   (T 138)

1563 BECON *Early Wks.* P.S. Pref. 28 How easy a thing it is to find a staff if a man be minded to beat a dog. **1581** GUAZZO ii. 100 It is an easie matter to finde a staffe to beate a dog. **1590–1** SHAKES. *2 Hen. VI* III. i. 171 A staff is quickly found to beat a dog. **1616** BRETON *Cross. Prov.* B3. **1626** *Id. Soothing* B3 It is easie to finde a stone to throw at a dogge. **1639** CLARKE 80 (as 1626). **1692** L'ESTRANGE *Aesop's Fab.* (1738) iii. 3 . . . Innocence is no protection against . . . a tyrannical power. **1875** SMILES *Thrift* 328 Excuses were abundant. . . . It is easy to find a stick to beat a sick dog. **1908** *T.L.S.* 6 Nov. 391 The reviewer seems . . . predisposed to the view that any stick is good enough to beat a dog with.

Staff's (stave's) end, To hold (keep) at. *Cf.* World still he keeps at staff's end.
                                              (s 807)

1596 LODGE *Wit's Misery* 83 The most chollericke and troublesome woman liuing vpon the earth, shee was alwaies at the staffes end with my father. **1601** SHAKES. *T.N.* V. i. 276 He holds Belzebub at the stave's end. **1680** BUNYAN *Mr. Badman* Wks. iii. 616 I would have held him a little at stave's-end, till I had far better proof of his manners to be good.

Staff, *see also* Blind man casts his s.; Bread is s. of life; Broken reed (s.) (Lean upon); End of the s. (To have the better *or* worse); Horse, (Who has no) may ride on s.; Keep the s. in own hand; Literature is good s.; Married man turns s. into stake; Old man's s. rapper of death's door; Set up one's s.; World still he keeps at his s.'s end.

Stafford blue.

[= some kind of blue cloth.] *c.* **1410** 'Pluck of her bells and let her fly' (Poem in *Rel. Ant.* i. 27) Clothe here well yn stafford blewe. *c.* **1460** *Towneley Myst.* iii. 200 Thou were worthi be cled In stafford blew. [=you deserve a beating].

Stafford law.   (s 808)

[= 'club law'.] **1557** *A Merry Dialogue* B1ᵛ Yf that she woulde not be rewled by wordes (a goddess name take Stafforde lawe). [*c.* 1570] **1595** *The Pedlar's Prophecy* l. 125 Mars eased them with stafford laws. **1589** *Hay any Work* A3 I threatned him with blowes, and to deale by stafford law. **1611** COTGRAVE s.v. Festin.

He hath had a triall in Stafford Court. **1615**
BEDWELL *Moham. Impost.* I, § 26 The Alkoran
of Mohammed established by Stafford law.
1623 T. HEYWOOD *Captives* III. ii.

Stag (= gander), *see* Full flock.

Stag(s), *see* Army of s. led by lion.

Stage, *see* World is a s.

Stagger like a drunken man, To.
                                        (M 399)

[PS. cvii. 27]. **1530** PALSGRAVE 732a I staggar,
as a dronkyn man dothe. **1606** T. HEYWOOD 2
If you Know not Me l. 2619 His Ordinance . . .
made their war-like Shippes Like drunkards
reele, and tumble side to side. **1837** CHAMIER
Saucy Areth. ch. 11 The ship rolled over the
waves, but . . . as she recovered herself she
seemed to stagger like a drunken man.

Staggerer, *see* Lame goes as far as s.

Stain(ed), *see* Silk is soonest s. (Fairest); True
blue will never s.

Stake, The loath (ill, loose) | stands long (longest).
                                        (S 812)

1546 HEYWOOD II. iv. G2ᵛ. *c.* **1594** BACON
Promus no. 485. **1611** DAVIES no. 371 (most
long). **1639** CLARKE 44 (loose). **1670** RAY 14
(ill . . . longest).

Stake that cannot stand one year in a hedge (the ground), It is an ill (poor).
                                        (S 811)

1546 HEYWOOD II. iv. G2ᵛ So is it an yll stake
(I haue herde amonge) That cannot stande one
yere in a hedge. **1640** HERBERT no. 553 It's a
poore stake that cannot stand one yeare in the
ground. **1659** HOWELL *Brit. Prov.* 3.

Stake, To be bound to a.
a. **1500** *15c. School-Bk.* ed. W. Nelson 46 As
men say, he is bounde at a stake that may not
do but as he is bidde. **1606** SHAKES. *M.* V. vii.
1 They have tied me to a stake: I cannot fly.

Stake (*noun*), *see also* Bear goes to the s. (As
willingly as the); Eaten (Swallowed) a s.;
Married man turns staff into s.; Stiff as a s.;
Stopford law, no s. no draw; Water a s.

Stake (*verb*), *see* Nothing s. nothing draw.

Stalk (Streak) of carl hemp¹ in you, You have a.

1721 KELLY 373 . . . Spoken to sturdy and
stubborn Boys. **1862** HISLOP 215 (streak).
Figuratively this means that a person possesses
firmness, or strength of mind. [¹ male hemp.]

Stalking-horse, *see* Religion a s. to shoot other
fowl.

Stamford, *see* Mad as the baiting bull of S.

Stamps like a ewe upon yeaning,¹ She.
                                        (E 210)

1678 RAY 344 . . . *Somerset.* [¹ bringing forth
young.]

Stand in a white sheet, To.
[= to do penance.] **1587** HARRISON *England* II.
xi. 185/1 in Holinshed Harlots and their mates
by . . . doing of open penance in streets, in
churches and market steeds are . . . put to
rebuke. **1597** *Pilgr. Parnass.* V. 546 An honest
man that nere did stande in sheete. **1607**
MIDDLETON *Fam. Love* IV. iv. I can describe how
often a man may lie with another man's wife
before 'a come to the white sheet.

Stand in one's own light, To.   (L 276)

[= to prejudice one's chances.] *a.* **1522**
DOUGLAS *Aeneid* 9 Prol. 84 Syne pardon me,
sat sa far in my lycht. **1538** J. BALE *Temptation
of our Lord* E2ᵛ If all come to passe, I maye syt
as moch in your light. **1546** HEYWOOD II. iv.
G3ᵛ Howe blyndly ye stande in your owne lyght.
1551 CRANMER *Ans. to Gardiner* 351 This standyng in your owne conceyte, is nothyng els
but to stande in your owne lyght. **1579** LYLY
Euph. i. 195 Heere ye may beholde gentlemen,
how lewdly wit standeth in his owne lyght.
1616 DRAXE no. 2414 Hee standeth in his owne
light. **1664** COTTON *Scarron.* iv. 65 Y'have . . .
stood too much in your own light. **1738** SWIFT
Dial. I. E.L. 263 Mr. Neverout, methinks you
stand in your own light.—Ah! madam, I have
done so all my life.

Stand Moses (*slang*), To.
1796 GROSE *Dict. Vulg. T.* s.v. A man is said
to stand *Moses* when he has another man's
bastard child fathered upon him, and he is
obliged by the parish to maintain it.

Stand on one's own legs, To.   (L 194)

1582 L. FIORAVANTI *Comp. of National secrets* tr.
J. Hester *2ᵛ To stand vppon our owne feete,
to feele with our owne handes, and to see with
our own eyes. **1619** G. HERBERT Letter in *Wks.*
370. **1626** JONSON *Staple of News* I. i. 20. **1808**
E. HAMILTON *Cottagers of Glenburnie* ch. 5.

Stand to one's guns, To.
[= to maintain one's position.] **1769** BOSWELL
in Johnson *Life* ch. 22 (1848) 201 Mrs. Thrale
stood to her gun with great courage, in defence
of amorous ditties. **1909** *Spectator* 24 Apr. 661
The Quakers . . . stood to their guns (their
principles) and, without any resort to brute
force, finally won all along the line. **1912** D. H.
LAWRENCE *Lett.* i. 123 I like the way you [Frieda]
stick to your guns.

Stand to one's tackling, To.   (T 7)

1534 MORE *Dial. of Comfort* E1. **1550** HEYWOOD
100 Epig. no. LIV (stick). **1613** BEAUM. & FL.
Kt. Burn. Pestle V. i. Stand to your tacklings
lads, and shew to the world, you can as well
brandish a sword, as shake an Apron. **1613**
FLETCHER & (?) SHAKES. *T.N.K.* II. iii. 55 We'll see

the sports; then every man to's tackle! **1633**
J. FORD *'Tis Pity* (1966) I. ii. Come sir, stand to
your tackling, if you prove Crauen, I'le make
you run quickly. .

Standers-by, *see* Lookers-on.

Standing pools (dubs¹) gather filth.
(P 465)
1579 GOSSON *Sch. Abuse* Arb. 52 Standing
streames geather filth; flowing riuers, are euer
sweet. **1596** SHAKES. *M.V.* I. i. 88 There are a
sort of men whose visages Do cream and mantle
like a standing pond. **1597** *Politeuphuia* 167
(streames). **1605–6** SHAKES. *K.L.* III. iv. 131
Drinks the green mantle of the standing pool.
1639 CLARKE 144. **1721** KELLY 299 (Mud).
1832 HENDERSON 13 Standing dubs gather dirt.
[¹ pools.]

Standing, *see also* Higher s., lower fall; Leave
neither stick nor stone s., (To); Long s. . . .
makes poor parsons.

Stands not surely that never slips, He.
(S 820)
1611 COTGRAVE s.v. Mescheoir (did neuer slip).
1640 HERBERT no. 68.

Stand(s), *see also* Friendship cannot s. on one
side; Little business s. great rest, (In); Mammering, (I s. in a); Needles' points (To s. on);
Pantofles (To stand upon); Paul's will not
always s.; Stake that cannot s. one year; Tub
must s. on own bottom.

Stare like a stuck pig, To.   (P 307)
[*c.* 1625] **1637** FL. & MASSINGER *Elder Brother*
ed. Glover and Waller, II. ii. 16 Ask 'em any
thing out of the Element of their understanding,
and they stand gaping like a roasted Pig. **1694**
MOTTEUX *Rabelais* V. ix. 41 Panurge stared at
him like a dead pig. **1720** GAY *New S. New
Sim.* Like a stuck pig I gaping stare. **1837**
DISRAELI *Corr. w. Sister* 21 Nov. Gibson Craig
. . . rose, stared like a stuck pig, and said nothing.

Staring, *see* Difference between s. and stark
blind.

Stark dead, Nothing like. *Cf.* Stone-dead has no fellow.
1721 KELLY 262 . . . First used by Captain James
Stewart, against the Noble Earl of Morton;¹ and
afterwards apply'd to . . . Strafford, and . . .
Laud. Lat. Mortui non mordent. [¹ *d.* 1581.]

Stark dead be thy comfort.   (C 543)
1659 HOWELL *Eng. Prov.* 11b.

Stars than a pair, There are more.
c. **1382** CHAUCER *Parl. Foules* l. 595 'There ben
mo sterres, god wot, than a payre!'

Star(s), *see also* Born under an unlucky planet
(s.); Gaze at the moon (s.); Stones against the

wind (s.), (To throw); Sun, moon, and seven s.
against us.

Starve in a cook's shop, To.   (C 639)
1611 COTGRAVE s.v. Aimer He that loues another
better than himselfe starues in a Cookes shop.
1629 T. ADAMS *Serm.* (1861–2) II. 535 We see
others *esuriente in popina*, as the byword is,
starving in a cook's shop—wretched in their
highest fortunes. **1659** HOWELL *Eng. Prov.* 5b
What, shall we starve in a Cooks-shop, and a
shoulder of mutton by? **1738** SWIFT *Dial.* II.
E.L. 304 I am very glad you like it; and pray
don't spare it.—No, my lord; I'll never starve
in a cook's shop.

Starv 'em, Rob 'em, and Cheat 'em.
1787 GROSE (*Kent*) 186 Starv 'em, Rob 'em,
and Cheat 'em. Stroud, Rochester, and Chatham. A saying in the mouths of the soldiers and
sailors, in allusion to the impositions practised
upon them.

State, *see* Ounce of s. requires pound of gold.

States have their conversions and periods as well as natural bodies.
(S 832)
1651 HERBERT no. 1166.

Stave, *see* Staff's (s.'s) end.

Stay a little, and news will find you.
(L 364)
1640 HERBERT no. 330. **1659** HOWELL *Span.
Prov.* 16. For newes never trouble thy selfe, thou
shalt know it time enough.

Stay a while, that we may make an end the sooner.
(W 301)
1580 SIDNEY *Arcadia* (1893) i. 63 His horse . . .
taught him that 'discreet stays make speedy
journeys'. **1625** BACON *Apoph.* Wks. (Chandos)
365 Sir Amyas Pawlet, when he saw too much
haste made in any matter, was wont to say,
'Stay a while, that we may make an end the
sooner'. **1732** FULLER no. 4263 (Stop a little,
to make).

Stay, and drink of your browst.¹
1721 KELLY 289 . . . Take a Share of the Mischief
that you have occasioned. [¹ brewing.]

Stay, If any thing | let work stay.
(W 846)
1678 RAY 278.

Stay, He that can | obtains.
(B 749. S 835)
1611 COTGRAVE s.v. Attendre He that can stay
his time shall compasse any thing. **1640** HER-
BERT no. 852. *Ibid.* no. 188 He that staies does
the businesse. **1721** KELLY 138 He that well
bides well betides. He that waits patiently, may
come to be well served at last.

Stays in the valley, He that | shall never get over the hill. (V 11)

1616 DRAXE no. 477. **1670** RAY 152.

Stay(s), *see also* God s. long, but strikes at last; Horse (One) s. for another; Nay, s., quoth Stringer; Tide s. for no man.

Steady, *see* Slow and s. wins race.

Steal a goose and give the giblets in alms, To. (G 364)

1659 HOWELL *Eng. Prov.* 1a. **1670** RAY 25. **1859** G. ELIOT *Scenes* 'Mr. Gilfil's Love-Story' ch. 1.

Steal a goose and stick down a feather, To. (G 365)

1545 W. TURNER *The Rescuing of the Romish Fox* G4 Ye do accordyng to the prouerbe stele a gous and for hyt stik down a fether. **1546** HEY-WOOD I. xi. E2ᵛ As dyd the pure penitent that stale a goose And stak downe a fether. **1616** G. HAKEWILL *Answer to a Treatise by Dr. Carier* 177. **1658** J. SPENCER *Things New & Old* (1868) 574 Like those that steal a goose and stick down a feather, or those that have undone many, then build a hospital for some few. **1659** TORRIANO no. 32 Whosoever steals a goose at Court, ere the year comes about payes for the feathers. **1706** STEVENS s.v. Puerco. **1714** JNO. WALKER *Sufferings of Clergy* ii. 331 For the Managers of those times thought fit, when they *Stole the Goose, To stick down the Feather,* and allow the *Sequestred's Wife* and *Children* the *Fifths* To live on. **1773** VIEYRA s.v. Amor.

Steal a hog and give the feet in alms, To. *Cf.* Steals a sheep, etc. (H 498)

1609 HARWARD 117 (a pigg . . . for gods sake). **1640** HERBERT no. 237. **1659** HOWELL *Span. Prov.* 14 (give the Pettitoes in almes). **1670** RAY 25 (*Hispan.*). **1732** FULLER no. 2028.

Steal a horse, One man may | while another may not look over a hedge. (H 692)

1546 HEYWOOD II. ix. K4 This prouerbe, . . . Which saith, that some man maie steal a hors better, Than some other maie stande and looke vpone. **1591** LYLY *Endym.* III. iii. 65 Some man may better steale a horse, then another looke ouer the hedge. **1670** RAY 128 . . . If we once conceive a good opinion of a man, we will not be perswaded he doth any thing amiss; but him whom we have a prejudice against, we are ready to suspect on the sleightest occasion. **1748** CHESTERFIELD *Lett.* 26 July, In that respect the vulgar saying is true. . . . **1891** A. LANG *Ess. in Little* 30 Nobody has bellowed 'Plagiarist!' Some people may not look over a fence: Mr. Stevenson, if he liked, might steal a horse. **1894** LD. AVEBURY *Use of Life* ch. 2 The Graces help a man almost as much as the Muses . . . 'One man may steal a horse, while another may not look over a hedge'; . . . because the one does things pleasantly, the other disagreeably.

Steal a march, To.

[= to get a secret advantage over a rival or opponent.] **1740** CIBBER *Apol.* (1756) I. 143 After we had stolen some few days march upon them. **1771** SMOLLETT *Humph. Clink.* 6 May (1815) 73 She yesterday wanted to steal a march of poor Liddy. **1856** READE *Never too Late* ch. 22 Happening to awake earlier than usual, he stole a march on his nurses, and . . . walked out.

Steal a pin, He that will | will steal a better thing. (P 332)

1537 R. WHITFORD *Werke for Householders* D7 The chylde yt begineth to pike at a pynne or a poynte wyl pyke a penny or a pounde. **1670** RAY 145. **1732** FULLER no. 6087.

Steal an egg, He that will | will steal an ox. (E 73)

1592 DELAMOTHE 45. **1639** CLARKE 148. **1659** HOWELL *Brit. Prov.* 1 (steal a hen).

Steal for others, If you | you shall be hanged yourself.

1642 TORRIANO 20. **1732** FULLER no. 2790.

Steal not my kail, If thou | break not my dyke. (K 4)

a. **1628** CARMICHAELL no. 262 An ye do na evill do na evil like and ye steill not my kaill brek not my dyke. **1641** FERGUSSON no. 490.

Steal the horse, and carry home the bridle. (H 693)

1618 T. ADAMS *Happiness Church* Wks. 596 To steale the bridle, as to steale the horse, is Tam, though not Tantum: such a sinne, though not so great a sinne. **1678** RAY 342.

Steals a sheep and gives back the trotters for God's sake, He. *Cf.* Steal a hog. (S 319)

1601 R. JOHNSON *Kingdoms and Commonw.* ii. 104 He steales the Sheepe and giues the Tratters for Gods sake. **1602** R. CAREW *Survey of Cornwall* (1769) 24 It resteth, that hereafter, not the dammes Foale, but the dammes Trotters, be trusted vnto. **1604** R. DALLINGTON *The View of France* R2 Hee steales the sheepe, and giues the Tratters for Gods sake. **1655** FULLER *Ch. Hist.* VI. iv. (1868) II. 287 The expression of a late Bishop of Norwich is complained of, . . . that 'King Henry took away the sheep from that cathedral, and did not restore so much as the trotters unto it'. **1891** J. E. T. ROGERS *Indust. & Com. Hist.* II. viii. Mary Tudor . . . felt herself constrained to allow the alienation of the abbey lands. The nobles of the day, as the Spanish proverb goes, stole the sheep and kept it, but gave God the trotters.

Steals can hide, He that.

1642 TORRIANO 80 It is not enough to know how to steal, one must know how to hide too. **1721**

KELLY 140 . . . Yes, and forswear too, a Discouragement to search stoln Goods. **1732** FULLER no. 2315.

Steals honey, He that | should beware of the sting.

1721 KELLY 163.

Steal(s, ing, stolen), *see also* Beg than s., (Better); Cat shuts eyes while s. cream; Daugher is s. (When) shut Pepper Gate; Friar preached against s.; Knows what may be gained (He that) never s.; Learned timely to s. that could not say nay; Lie will s. (He that will); Nothing is s. without hands; Old age comes s. on; Rich man s. (Why should); Shame to s., but worse to carry home; Wit to . . . s. horse, wisdom to let alone; Wrongs not an old man that s. supper.

Steed, *see* Untimeous spurring spills the s.

Steel in my needle eye, There is | though there be little of it.   (S 844)

c. **1641** FERGUSSON MS. no. 1404 Ther is good steel in my needl ey. **1721** KELLY 321 . . . Spoken when a Thing, commendable for its Kind, is fou.id Fault with for its Quantity.

Steel to the back.   (S 842)

1579 LYLY *Euph.* i. 247 I knowe Curio to be steele to the backe. *c.* **1590** SHAKES. *T.And.* IV. iii. 47 We are . . . steel to the very back. **1615** *Work for Cutlers* ed. Sieveking 38 You shall finde Sworde mettle to the very backe. *c.* **1630** *The Soddered Citizen* l. 2154 Steele to the hard backe.

Steel, *see also* Tongue is not s. yet cuts; True as s.; True s. as Ripon rowels.

Steeple, *see* Grantham s.; Tenterden s.

Steersman, *see* Gunner to his linstock.

Step after step the ladder is ascended.   (S 847–8)

1611 COTGRAVE s.v. Pas Step after step goes farre. **1640** HERBERT no. 393. **1732** FULLER no. 4260.

Step, The greatest (first) | is that out of doors (is the hardest).   (S 846)

1590–5 MUNDAY *et al. Sir T. More* II. iv. 73 Would I were so far on my journey. The first stretch is the worst methinks. **1616** WITHALS 576 The first step is as good as halfe ouer. **1639** CLARKE 171 (as 1616). **1640** HERBERT no. 461. **1655–62** GURNALL *Chrn. in Armour* (1865) l. 206 The greatest step to heaven, is out of our own doors, over our own threshold. **1659** HOWELL *It. Prov.* 7 The hardest step is that over the threshold, viz, the beginning. **1668** COWLEY *Ess.* X (1904) 105 Begin; the getting out of doors is the greatest part of the journey. Varro[1] teaches us that Latin proverb, *portam itineri longissimam esse.* **1783** J. WESLEY *Letters* vii.

166. The first steps you take will be of the utmost importance. **1788** B. FRANKLIN *Autobiog.* E.L. 130 After getting the first hundred pound, it is more easy to get the second. **1928** 3 Feb. D. H. LAWRENCE *Lett.* ii. 1037 C'est le premier pas qui coûte. [[1] *De Re Rust.* Lib. i.]

Stepdame, *see* Ruled by own dame.

Stepped, *see also* Wheamow . . . when she s. into milk bowl.

Stepmother: Take heed of a | the very name of her suffices.   (H 374)

1599 MINSHEU *Span. Gram.* 84. **1651** HERBERT no. 1155. **1659** HOWELL *Span. Prov.* 15.

Stepmother, *see also* Fortune is mother to one, to another s.

Steps, *see* Sluggard takes a hundred s.

Stern chase is a long chase, A.

1824 COOPER *Pilot* 416. **1836** MARRYAT *Midsh. Easy* ch. 29 The Aurora . . . had neared the chase about two miles. 'This will be a long chase, a stern chase always is.'

Stew, *see* Fry (S.) in one's own grease (juice).

Steward abroad when there is a windfrost, There is a good.

1830 FORBY 431 . . . *i.e.* You have no occasion to look to your labourers, they must work to keep themselves warm.

Stick by the ribs, To.   (R 101)

1603 *The Bachelor's Banquet* (Wilson) 84 Some one . . . hath offred her such Kindnes, as sticks by her ribs a good while after. **1616** WITHALS 561. **1670** RAY 194.

Stick is the surest peacemaker, The.

1902–4 LEAN IV. 139. [**1610** GRUTER *Floril.* 189 A Yiddish proverb says 'A stick in the hand is better than a tongue in the mouth.']

Sticking[1] goes not by strength, but by guiding of the gully.[2]   (S 854)

c. **1641** FERGUSSON MS. no. 1230 Stiking goes not be strenth. **1721** KELLY 292 . . . Matters are carried on rather by Art than Strength. [[1] stabbing. [2] knife.]

Sticks and stones will break my bones, but names will never hurt me.

1894 NORTHALL *Folk-phrases* E.D.S. 23 . . . Said by one youngster to another calling names.

Stick(s) (*noun*), *see also* Cross as two s.; Dog for your friend, and in your other hand a s., (Keep a); Dress up a s. and it does not appear as s.; End of the staff (s.) (To have the wrong); Fiddle but not the s.; Leave neither s. nor stone standing,

(To); Little s. kindle fire; Staff (S.) is quickly found to beat dog; Straight s. crooked in water; Trust to a dry s. (No); Two dry s. kindle green one.

Stick(s) (*verb*), *see also* Ball does not s. to the wall (If); Bird caught in lime strives, (The more the)/the faster he s.; Dirt enough (Fling) and some will s.; Hap (Some have the), some s. in gap; Put it on thick a little will s.

Sticklers, *see* Story without s. (No).

Stiff as a board.   (B 485)

[*c.* 1515] *c.* 1530 BARCLAY *Eclogues* I. B1ᵛ My handes are . . . styfe as a borde by warke contynuall.   1840 RUSKIN *Dairies 1835–47* 126.

Stiff as a poker.

1706 STEVENS s.v. Virote As stiff as if he had swallow'd a Stake.   1792 *Letters of S. T. Coleridge* (ed. E. H. Coleridge) i. 30.   1797 COLMAN JR. *Heir at Law* III. ii. Stuck up as stiff as a poker.   1886 J. E. C. WELLDON *The Rhetoric of Aristotle Translated* 272 'The porter who carried the beam' was a typical Greek instance of stiffness like 'the man who has swallowed a poker' in English.

Stiff as a stake, As.   (s 809)

1563 SENECA *Oedipus* tr. A. Neville B1 Blud and flesh congeled stands, in face as stiffe as stake.   1565 R. SHACKLOCK *Beginning of Heresies* D2ᵛ (Southern 115).   1566 *Albion Kn.* Malone Soc. Collections i. 236.   1706 STEVENS s.v. Garrote.

Stiff upper lip, To keep (carry) a.

1825 J. NEAL *Brother Jonathan* I. 157 Keepin' a good stiff upper lip.   1833 *Id. Down Easters* I. ii. 15 'What's the use o' boo-hooin'? . . . keep a stiff upper lip.   1837 HALIBURTON *Clockm.* Ser. I. xxv She used to carry a stiff upper lip and make him and the broomstick acquainted together.

Stile(s), *see* Best dog leap s. first; Essex (Suffolk) s.; Go over the s. (He that will not); Leap over hedge before you come at s.; Over the s. ere you are at it (You would be).

Still sow eats up all the draff, The.

(s 681)

c. 1225 *Trin. MS. O. II. 45* (ed. Förster) in *Eng. Stud.* 31. 6 The stille sohghe het, þare gruniende, mete. *Sus taciturna vorat, dum garrula voce laborat.*   *c.* 1250 *Digby MS. 53,* f. 8, in *Eng. Stud.* 31. 15 The stille sue æt gruniende hire mete.   *c.* 1400 *MS. Latin no. 394,* J. Rylands Libr. (ed. Pantin) in *Bull. J. R. Libr.* XIV. 29 The stylle sowȝe etus alle þe draffe.   1546 HEYWOOD I. x. C4ᵛ Well the styll sowe eats vp all the draff.   1600 1 SHAKES. *M.W.W.* IV. ii. 93 'Tis old but true, Still swine eats all the draff.   1633 JONSON *T. Tub* III. v. I'll ne'er trust smooth-faced tileman for his sake.—Mother, the still sow eats up all the draff.   1721 KELLY 313 . . . Spoken to Persons who look demurely, but are roguish.   1828 LYTTON *Pelham* ch. 61 'You won't bet, Mr. Pelham? close and shy . . . ; well, the silent sow sups up all the broth.'

Still tongue makes a wise head, A.

(T 401)

1562 HEYWOOD *Sixth Hund. Epigr.* no. 86, 214 Hauyng a styll toung he had a besy head.   1892 QUILLER-COUCH *Three Ships* ch. 7 A still tongue makes a wise head, and 'twill be time enough to talk . . . when, &c.

Still (Smooth) waters run deep.   (w 123)

c. 1400 *Cato's Morals* in *Cursor M.* E.E.T.S. l. 1672 There the flode is deppist the water standis stillist.   *c.* 1430 LYDGATE *Churl & Bird* Percy Soc. 186 Smothe waters ben ofte sithes depe.   *c.* 1435 *Burgh's Cato* v. 1050 In floodis stille is watir deep and hihe.   1545 *Precepts of Cato* L6ᵛ Where the floodes is calme there perchaunce the water lyeth deaper.   1580 LYLY *Euph. & his Eng.* ii. 65 I perceiue *Issida* that where the streame runneth smoothest, the water is deepest.   1590–1 SHAKES. *2 Hen. VI* III. i. 53 Smooth runs the water where the brook is deep.   1616 DRAXE no. 1853 Where riuers runne most stilly, they are the deepest.   1721 KELLY 287 (Smooth).   1858 MRS. CRAIK *A Woman's Thoughts* 291 In mature age, . . . the fullest, tenderest tide of which the loving heart is capable, may be described by those 'still waters' which 'run deep'.   1869 TROLLOPE *He knew he was right* ch. 35 'What do you call Dorothy Stanbury? That's what I call still water. She runs deep enough. . . . So quiet, but so—clever.'

Still waters, Take heed of | the quick pass away.

1623 WODROEPHE 276 Flee from still waters, for in running water thou mayst enter assuredly.   1640 HERBERT no. 171.

Still, *see also* Be s. and have thy will; Beware of a silent dog and s. water; Say well and be s.; Sow in beans, (As s. as a).

Stillest humours are always the worst, The.   (H 807)

1664 CODRINGTON 216 (waters, and humours).   1670 RAY 25.

Sting is in the tail, The.   (s 858)

[REV. ix. 10 They have tails like unto scorpions, and stings; and in their tails is their power to hurt men.]   1594–8 SHAKES. *T.S.* II. i. 211 If I be waspish, best beware my sting. My remedy is, then, to pluck it out.—Ay, if the fool could find out where it lies.—Who knows not where a wasp does wear his sting? In his tail.   1615 T. ADAMS *England's Sickness* 17 Hee is like a Bee or an Epigram, all his sting is in his tail.   1657 in *Verney Mem.* (1907) II. 52 His letter to you I hope will be full of douceur without a stinge at the tayle of it.   1926 *Times* 7 Sept. 17/5 But the sting of this book is in its tail.

Sting of a reproach is the truth of it, The.

1732 FULLER no. 4769.   1909 *T.L.S.* 17 Dec. 491 This merciless exposition of American military weakness will prove very unpleasant reading for American citizens. The sting . . . lies in its truth.

Sting (*noun*), *see also* After your fling watch for
s.; Bees that have honey in mouth; Tongue
stings (is more venomous than a serpent's s.).

Stings (*verb*), *see* Tongue s.

Stink like a brock,[1] To.   (B 679)

c. **1400** *Ywaine & Gaw.* l. 98 It es ful semeli, als
me think, A brok omang men forto stynk.   *a.*
1528 SKELTON *Agst. Garnesche* l. 55 She seyd
your brethe stank lyke a broke.   **1552** LINDSAY
Three Estates l. 2489. [1 badger.]

Stink like a goat, To.

c. **1386** CHAUCER *Can. Yeo. T.* l. 886 For al the
world they stynken as a goot.

Stink like a polecat, To.   (P 461)

1533 J. HEYWOOD *Johan Johan* 73 That she shall
stynke lyke a pole-kat.   **1630** DEKKER 2 *Hon.
Whore* IV. iii. 79 Sh'as a breath stinkes worse
than fifty Polecats.   **1648** *Key to the Cabinet of
the Parliament* 7 They stinke like Polecats in a
Gyn.

Stink (*noun*), *see* Chink (So we get) bear with s.;
Devil always leaves s.

Stink(s) (*verb*), *see also* Fish begins to s. at head;
Garlic makes a man s.; Man's praise in his own
mouth s.; Proffered service s.; Smelt where all s.
(One is not); Stir it (The more you), worse it s.;
What serves dirt for if it do not s.?

Stinking fish, *see* No man cries s. f.

Stir it (a turd), The more you | the worse it stinks.   (T 603)

1546 J. BALE *Exam^n Anne Askewe* P.S. 180.
1546 HEYWOOD II. vi. I2 Let hym pas, for we
thynke, The more we stur a tourde, the wours
it will stynke.   **1620** SHELTON *Quix.* II. xiii.
ii. 266 I have spoken, . . . but let it alone; the
more it is stirred, the more it will stink.   **1639**
CLARKE 200 The more you stirre it, the worse it
stinkes.   **1670** RAY 194 The more you stir, the
worse you stink.   **1710** S. PALMER 150 A Stink
is still Worse for the Stirring.

Stir one's stumps,[1] To.   (S 946)

[= to walk or dance briskly.]   **1535** LAYTON in
Lett. Suppress. Monast. (Camden) 76 His hore
. . . bestyurde hir stumpis towardes hir startyng
hirlles.   **1559** *Mirr. Mag.* ed. Campbell 'Jack
Cade' 176 But hope of money made him stur
his stumpes, And to assault me valiauntly and
bolde.   **1596** COLSE *Penelope* (1880) 164 I doubt
not but poore shepheards will stirre their stumps
after my minstrelsie.   **1832** MARRYAT *N. Forster*
ch. 10 Come this way, my hearty—stir your
stumps.   **1876** BLACKMORE *Cripps* ch. 13 Look
alive, woman! Stir your stumps! [1 legs.]

Stir, *see also* Wasp's (hornet's) nest, (To s. a).

Stirling gets a hat, When the castle of |
the carse of Corntown pays for that.

1857 DEAN RAMSAY *Remin.* V. (1911) 205 . . .
When the clouds descend so low as to envelop
Stirling Castle, a deluge of rain may be expected
in the adjacent country.

Stitch[1] against, To have (take) a.
(S 865)

a. **1591** H. SMITH *Serm.* (1594) 224 Therefore
his Maiestie hath a stitch against her, as Salomon
had to Shimei.   *a.* **1639** W. WHATELEY *Proto-
types* II. xxx. (1640) 100 We sometimes take
such a stitch and spleene against those whom
nature hath tyed to us. [1 a grudge, dislike.]

Stitch in time saves nine, A.

1732 FULLER no. 6291 (may save).   **1793**
Friendly Addr. Poor 14 A stitch in time may
save nine.   **1869** READE *Foul Play* ch. 9 Repairing the ship. Found a crack or two in her inner
skin. . . . A stitch in time saves nine.

Stitch, *see also* Stop s. while I put needle in;
Tailor that makes not knot loses s.

Stock, lock, and barrel.

[= the entirety of any thing.]   **1817** SCOTT in
LOCKHART *Life* V. 238 Like the Highlandman's
gun, she wants stock, lock, and barrel, to put
her into repair.   **1853** G. J. WHYTE-MELVILLE
Digby Grand ch. 24 When a woman is a trump
there is nothing like her; but when she does go
to the bad, she goes altogether, 'stock, lock and
barrel'.   **1912** *Spectator* 6 Jan. 24 He condemns
fiscal autonomy—lock, stock, and barrel—as
ignoring the lessons of the past.

Stock(s), *see also* Buy no s.; Constable of
Openshaw . . . s. at Manchester; Grafting on a
good s.; Lacks a s. (Who), his gain is not worth
chip; Look to him gaoler . . . frog in s.; Shoemaker's s.

Stockfish, *see* Beat one like a s.

Stocking(s), *see* Given them green s.; Yellow s.

Stolen goods never thrive.   (G 307)

1608 J. DAY *Law Tricks* I. i.   **1659** HOWELL
Brit. Prov. 5 Plundred ware, never thrive.

Stolen waters (pleasures) are sweet.
(W 131)

[PROV. ix. 17.]   *c.* **1548** *The Wyll of the
Deuyll* B4 This saiyng of the retcheles woman
in Salomon (Stollen waters ar sweete . . .).
1607-8 FLETCHER *Faithful Shep.* III. i. Some
place, where out of sight We freely may enjoy
our stoln delight.   **1629** T. ADAMS *Serm.* (1862)
I. 159 Sin shows you a fair picture—'Stolen
waters are sweet'.   **1632** MASSINGER *City Madam*
II. i And pleasure stolen, being sweetest.   **1721**
KELLY 298 . . . People take great Delight in that
which they can get privately.   **1737** A. RAMSEY
58 Stown dints' are sweetest.   **1824** SCOTT *Redg.
Letter* 10 His eyes dancing with all the glee of

a forbidden revel; and his features . . . confessing the full sweetness of stolen waters.   [¹ occasions.]

Stolen, *see also* Nothing is s. without hands.

Stomach an apothecary's shop, Make not thy.

1574 *A Form of Christian Policy* tr. G. Fenton 51 It is not good that euerye one make a Custome and common recourse to Phisicke, reducing the disposition of their Stomackes to a Pothicarye shoppe.   **1609** HARWARD 111.

Stomach, To have a | and lack meat: to have meat and lack a stomach: to lie in bed and cannot rest: are great miseries.   (s 875)

1636 CAMDEN 307.

Stomach (Digestion) like an ostrich, A.
(1 97)

1495? *Bartholomaeus anglicus* tr. Trevisa xii. 33. **1579** LYLY *Euph.* i. 260 The Estrich disgesteth harde yron to preserue his healthe.   **1584** COGAN *Haven Health* ix. (1636) 33 Rusticks, who have stomachs like ostriges, that can digest hard yron. **1590–1** SHAKES. *2 Hen. VI* IV. x. 27 I'll make thee eat iron like an ostrich . . . ere thou and I part.   **1658** WALL *Comm. Times* 63 Estridge Consciences, that can digest Iron but not straw. **1819** SCOTT *Let.* 15 Apr. in LOCKHART *Life* ch. 44 At least till my stomach recovers its tone and ostrich-like capacity of digestion.

Stomach makes all the meat bitter, An ill.   (s 871)

1587 J. BRIDGES *Defence* 343 [citing Marloratus *in Apocal.* ch. 2] So long as the stomake is sicke, health is provided to the other members to no purpose.   **1616** DRAXE no. 1344.   **1732** FULLER no. 4218 Some Stomachs nauseate even sweet Meats.

Stomachs to eat, He has two | and one to work.

1706 STEVENS s.v. Hazer.   **1813** RAY 104 . . . The Spaniards say, *Al hacer temblar y al comer sudar.* To quake at doing, and sweat at eating.

Stomach(s), *see also* Army marches on its s.; Honey cloys s., (Too much); Poor men seek meat for their s.; Sharp s. makes short devotion.

Stone in a well is not lost, A.   (s 888)

1640 HERBERT no. 845.

Stone in the way overturns a great wain (may make a tall man stumble), A little.   (s 884)

c. **1375** BARBOUR *Bruce* Bk. xi, l. 24 A litell stane, as men sayis, May ger weltir ane mekill wane. **1580** MUNDAY *Zelauto* ¶3ᵛ A little stone may make a tall man stumble.   **1622** MABBE *Rogue* II. II. ix. IV. 5 A little stone in the way overturns a great wain.

Stone of Sisyphus.

[In Greek mythology, Sisyphus was condemned to roll daily to the top of a hill a huge stone, which thereupon rolled down again.]   **1576** F. PATRICIUS tr. R. Robinson *Moral Method* Ep. Ded. Yet ceassed I not with Sysiphus to roule the stone.   **1581** SENECA *Thyestes* tr. Jasper Heywood in *Ten Tragedies* Act I, l. 5790 Shal Sisyphus his stone, That slipper restles, rolling payse vppon my backe be borne?   **1621** BURTON *Anat. Mel.* I. ii. III. xi. (1638) 112 Commonly, they that, like Sisyphus, roïe this restlesse stone of Ambition, are in a perpetuall agony.   **1670** DRYDEN *Conq. Gran.* III. ii. ii. What'er I plot, like Sisyphus, in vain I heave a stone, that tumbles down again.   **1909** *T.L.S.* 16 July 260 'The task of Sisyphus has to be begun again by all . . . rulers of empires; and the stone of civiliza-tion which has been painfully rolled up the mountain side tumbles back into the pit.'

Stone that lies not in your gate breaks not your toes, The.

1721 KELLY 308 . . . Spoken against meddling in the Business in which we have no Concern. **1732** FULLER no. 4770 The Stone, that lieth not in your Way, need not offend you.

Stones against the wind (stars), To throw.   (s 896)

1541 *Schoolh. of Wom.* C2ᵛ As good, throwe stones at the wynde.   **1565** J. CALFHILL *Treatise of the Cross* P.S. 85 (air).   **1587** WHETSTONE *Censure of Loyal Subject* E3ᵛ As vaine . . . as to throwe stones against the starres.   *c.* **1613** MIDDLETON *No Wit, No Help* III. i. 121 (wind).

Stone(s), *see also* Ask for bread and be given s.; Boil s. in butter; Buys land buys many s.; Constant dropping wears s.; Dog bites s.; Fells two dogs with one s.; Fool may throw s.; Gently over the s.; Hard as a flint (s.); Hold my peace and gather s.; Leave neither stick nor s. standing, (To); Leave no s. unturned; Mark with a white s.; Never take a s. to break egg; No man can flay a s.; Pitcher strikes s.; Remove s. bruise fingers (Who); Roast a s.; Rolling s. no moss; Rugged s. grows smooth; Scorpion under every s.; Silent gathers s.; Sliddery s. before hall door; Spit on a s.; Split upon same s.; Spring of a s. (To); Stumbles twice at one s.; Swim like a s.; Tree loaded with fruit people throw s.; Trick for trick and a s. in thy foot besides; Water (Blood) from a s.; Word and a s. cannot be called back; Word (S.) to throw at a dog.

Stone wall(s), *see* Hard with hard makes not s. w.; Hunger breaks s. w.; Love will go through s. w.; Run one's head against s. w.

Stone-dead has no fellow. *Cf.* Stark dead, Nothing like.   (s 898)

c. **1633** *Soddered Citizen* v. iv Is your ffather dead?—Laid with both Leggs Sir, in one lynnen bootehose That has noe fellowe, stone dead. [**1641**] **1828** MACAULAY *Ess., Hallam* Wks. V. 185 Essex said, . . . with more truth than elegance, 'Stone-dead hath no fellow'.   **1926** *Times* 27

Aug. 11/3 The execution of the death sentence had been postponed for a week, an unusual period in a country where the adage 'stone-dead hath no fellow' wins general support.

Stook, *see* Sheaf of a s.

Stool in the sun; Put a | when one knave rises, another comes.   (s 899)

1659 HOWELL *Eng. Prov.* 2a . . . *viz.* To places of preferment.   **1732** FULLER no. 4105.

Stool of repentance.

[A stool formerly placed in Scottish churches for offenders (especially against chastity); also called *Cutty-stool*.] *a.* **1674** CLARENDON *Hist. Reb.* xiii. § 48 To stand publickly in the Stool of Repentance, acknowledging their former transgressions. *a.* **1704** T. BROWN *Walk round London* Wks. (1709) III. 34 When the Fumes of Melancholy or Wine set them on the Stool of Repentance.   **1884** *Christian World* 2 Oct. 737/1 *The Times* . . . seats itself as it were in shame on the stool of repentance.

Stool(s), *see also* Between two s.; Comb head with three-legged s.; Fools set s. for wise folk to stumble; Lay the s.'s foot in water.

Stool-foot, *see* Pottage of a s.-f. (With cost one may make).

Stoop for a pin, He that will not | shall never be worth a point (pound). (P 331)

1609 HARWARD 101 (Take vppe a pinne).   **1618** BRETNOR *Almanac* July Evil days.   **1668** PEPYS *Diary* 2 Jan. (Globe) 600 Sir W. Coventry answered: 'I see your Majesty do not remember the old English proverb, "He that will not stoop for a pin, will never be worth a pound".'   **1670** RAY 131.

Stoop that has a low door, He must.
                                          (D 555)

1678 RAY 206.   **1732** FULLER no. 1995.

Stoop when the head is off, It is no time to.   (T 305)

1470 HENRYSON *Moral Fab.* in Wks. S.T.S. II. 130 The nek to stoup, quhen it the straik sall get Is sone aneuch.   **1641** FERGUSSON no. 486. **1721** KELLY 197 . . . That is, Care, Wariness, and Saving, is to no purpose when all is gone. **1737** RAMSAY III. 183 It is past jouking[1] when the head's aff. [[1] bowing the head.]

Stooping, *see* Come, but come s.

Stop every man's mouth, He who will | must have a great deal of meal. (M 453)

1509 BARCLAY *Ship of Fools* i. 208 One must have moche mele, to stoppe eche mannys mouthe.   **1584** WITHALS 201.   **1707** MAPLETOFT 6.

Stop gaps with rushes, To.   (G 29)

[= a futile effort.] *c.* **1549** HEYWOOD II. ix. L1[v] Ye will (quoth she) as soone stop gaps with russhes.

Stop one's mouth, To.   (M 1264)

1527 J. SKELTON *Replication* l. 114 Wolde God . . . That wyse Harpocrates Had your mouthes stopped.   **1534** S. GARDINER to Paget *Letters* ed. Muller 180.   **1545** *Ibid.* to Duke of Richmond 59. **1546** HEYWOOD II. iv. G4[v] That shall not stop my mouth, ye maie well gesse.   **1598–9** SHAKES. *M.A.* II. i. 279 Stop his mouth with a kiss. **1680** FLAVEL *Method Grace* xxix. 448 Your inoffensive carriage is the only means to stop the mouths of Detractors.

Stop stitch while I put a needle in.

1847 HALLIWELL *Dict.* (1889) II. 808 . . . a proverbial phrase applied to any one when one wishes him to do anything more slowly.

Stop two gaps with one bush, To.
                                          (G 30)

1548 HALL *Chron.* (1809 ed., 503) The kyng entendinge to stope two gappes with one bushe. *c.* **1549** HEYWOOD II. ix. L1[v].   **1600** HOLLAND *Livy* XXIII. iii. 474 Therefore with one bush (as they say) ye are to stop two gaps, and to do both at once.   **1639** FULLER *Holy War* v. xxii (1840) 280 These Italians stopped two gaps with one bush; they were merchant pilgrims, and together applied themselves to profit and piety.

Stop two mouths with one morsel, To.
                                          (M 1269)

1616 WITHALS 556.   **1639** CLARKE 45.

Stopford[1] law; no stake, no draw.
                                          (s 901)

1678 RAY 301 *Cheshire.*   **1787** GROSE (*Chesh.*) 157 . . . Commonly used to signify that only such as contribute to the liquor, are entitled to drink of it.   **1917** BRIDGE 110 Stopport[1] law, no stake no draw.... Only those who contribute to an undertaking may reap any benefit from it. . . . Stockport is half in Lancashire and half in Cheshire. [[1] Stockport.]

Stopped, *see* Stream s. swells the higher.

Store is no sore.   (s 903)

1471 RIPLEY *Comp. Alch.* XII. viii in *Ashm.* (1652) 186 For wyse men done sey store ys no sore. **1546** HEYWOOD I. v. B2 Gredynesse, to drawe desyre to this lore, Saieth, . . . store is no sore. **1633** MASSINGER *New Way* III. ii. Merm. 149 Let my dressers crack with the weight Of curious viands.—'Store indeed's no sore', sir. **1639** CLARKE 74.

Store of butter, They that have got good | may lay it thick on their bread.
                                          (s 904)

1639 CLARKE 49.

Store of oatmeal, Where there is | you may put enough in the crock. (s 906)

1678 RAY 352 . . . *Somerset.*

Store, *see also* Fair and the foul, by dark are like s.; Honey and gall in love there is s., (Of); Worst s., maid unbestowed.

Stork, *see* Log nor a s. (Neither a).

Storm, As welcome as a. (s 909)

1583 MELBANCKE X2ᵛ As welcome . . . as a storme of winde to the moneth of March. 1597 DELONEY 1 *Gentle Craft* 73 As welcome to me, as a storme to a distressed Mariner. 1732 FULLER no. 746.

Storm in a teacup, A.

[CICERO *Leg.* 3. 16. 36 *Excitare fluctus in simpulo.*] 1678 DK. ORMONDE *Let. Earl Arlington* in *Hist. MSS. Comm., Ormonde MSS.* IV. 292 Our skirmish . . . compared with the great things now on foot, is but a storm in a cream bowl. 1854 W. B. BERNARD Title of farce. 1872 BLACK *Strange Adv. Ph.* ch. 19 She has raised a storm in a tea-cup by her . . . unwarranted assault. 1900 G. C. BRODRICK *Mem. & Impr.* 360 Here the storm in the Oxford tea-cup raged as furiously as in the open sea.

Storm(s), *see* After a s. a calm (*or vice versa*); Fair day in winter mother of s.; Porpoise plays before s.; Sailors have a port in every s.; Sharper the s. sooner over; Stuffing holds out s.; Vows made in s. forgotten in calms.

Stormy, *see* Sound travelling far and wide.

Story without sticklers,[1] No. (s 911)

1659 HOWELL *Brit. Prov.* 35. [1 strong supporters.]

Story, *see also* Cock-and-bull s.; One tale (s.) is good till another told.

Stot(s), *see* Old oxen (s.) have stiff horns.

Stoup(s), *see* Pint s. hae lang lugs; Water s. hold no ale.

Stout (Strong), As you are | be merciful.

1721 KELLY 39 . . . Spoken in a taunting manner to them that threaten us. 1738 SWIFT Dial. I. E.L. 260. 1884 D. C. MURRAY *Way of World* ch. 29 But, Clare, as you are strong be merciful.

Stout, *see* Hard (S.) heart against hard hap (to stey brae); I proud (s.) and thou proud (s.); Proud (S.) comes behind as goes before.

Stow on the Wold,[1] where the wind blows cold.

1844 J. O. HALLIWELL *Nursery Rh. of Eng.* 1852 *N. & Q.* 1st Ser. v. 375. 1853 HALLIWELL *Nursery Rh. of Eng.* in LEAN I. 39. [1 a small market town in the Cotswold Hills.]

Straight as a line. (L 303)

c. 1380 CHAUCER *Troilus* Bk. 2, l. 1461. 1412–20 LYDGATE *Troy Book* Bk. 2, l. 6739 The wey hem ladde To the paleis, streight as any lyne. 1546 HEYWOOD I. xi. D3 As ryght as a lyne. c. 1549 *Ibid.* I. xi. D3 As tight as a lyne. 1591 ARIOSTO *Orl. Fur.* Harington VI. 19 Straight as a line bending to neither side.

Straight stick is crooked in the water, A. (s 850)

1589 NASHE *Anat. of Absurd.* i. 24 The straightest things beeing put into water, seeme crooked. 1603 MONTAIGNE (Florio) I. xl. 148 To judge of high and great matters, a high and great minde is required. . . . A straight oare being under the water seemeth to be crooked. 1647 FULLER *Serm.* (1891) I. 546 Take a straight stick and put it into the water; then it will seem crooked. Why? Because we look upon it through two mediums, air and water. 1732 FULLER no. 425.

Straight trees have crooked roots. (T 511)

1580 LYLY *Euph. & his Eng.* ii. 99 For experience teacheth me, that straight trees haue crooked rootes. 1732 FULLER no. 4264.

Straight, *see also* Cedar, (As s. as a).

Straighter grows the palm, etc., The. (P 37)

1540 PALSGRAVE *Acolastus* 17 The palme tree . . . the more weight is layd vpon it, the more it ryseth hygher or resisteth. 1547 S. GARDINER to Somerset (*Letters* ed. Muller 427) That is in dede lyke as the palme tree that beareth towards the borden upwarde and from it downward, as other woodes do. 1548–9 N. UDALL *Paraphrases of Erasmus* Ded. before *Acts* 3A2 The Paulme tree the more weight and burden is layed vpon it, the more it ariseth and shootheth vpright. 1551 T. WILSON *Rule of Reason* M8 Some good felowes . . . tell strange tales . . . when there is not one woorde true. As the palme tree beyng ouerlaide with weightes, riseth higher, and buddeth vpward more freshelye: so a noble stomake vexed with muche aduersite is euermore the stouter. 1579 LYLY *Euph.* i. 191 It is proper for the Palme tree to mounte; the heauyer you loade it the higher it sprowteth. 1591 ARIOSTO *Orl. Fur.* Harington XXXIV. 41 (The thicker do the vnder branches grow). 1625 F. MARKHAM *Bk. of Honour* 12 Fame like a Palme tree, growes by suppressing.

Strain at (out) a gnat and swallow a camel, To. (G 150)

[MATT. xxiii. 24 Ye blind guides, which strain out the gnat, and swallow the camel.] c. 1200 *Ancrene Riwle* 8 ȝe beon ase sum deð . . . þe isihð þene gnet & swoluweð þe uliȝe. [fly.] 1526 TYNDALE *Matt.* xxiii. 24 Ye blinde gydes, which strayne out a gnat, and swalowe a cammyll. 1594 J. KING *On Jonas* (1599) 284 They have verified the old proverbe in strayning at gnats and swallowing downe camells. 1612–15 BP.

HALL *Contempl.* IV. xxxi (1825) II. 517 Do ye fear to be defiled with the touch of Pilate's pavement? doth so small a gnat stick in your throats, while ye swallow such a camel of flagitious wickedness? **1928** *Times* 31 Jan. 5/3 Factor said in effect: 'I will swallow all the camels you have said about me, but I strain at this gnat.'

Strand on the Green, thirteen houses, fourteen cuckolds, and never a house between. (s 913)

1602 R. CAREW *Survey of Cornwall* (1769) 108ᵛ Crasthole ... through an inueterate byword ... is peopled with 12 dwellings, and 13 cuckolds. **1659** HOWELL *Eng. Prov.* 21b ... For the father and son lay in one house.

Strange beast that has neither head nor tail, It is a. (B 155)

1616 DRAXE no. 2103.   **1639** CLARKE 8.

Strange than true, It is no more. (s 914)

a. **1534** J. HEYWOOD *Love* A3 The case as ye put it I thynke more straunge Then true. **1575** R. LANEHAM *Letter* ed. Furnivall 46. **1590–5** MUNDAY *et al. Sir T. More* V. iii. 50 It's very strange.—It will be found as true. **1595** SHAKES. *M.N.D.* V. i. 2 More strange than true. **1604** *Id. M.M.* V. i. 44 This is all as true as it is strange. **1687** MIÈGE s.v. Strange.

Stranger is for the wolf, The.

1908 C. M. DOUGHTY *Wander. in Arabia* (1908) I. vii. 117 There is not ... a man ... had not slain thee.... The stranger is for the wolf! you heard not this proverb in your own country?

Stranger(s), *see also* Presents of love; Save a s. from sea; Strew green rushes for s.

Strap, *see* Oil of whip (s.).

Strathbogie, *see* Miscall a Gordon.

Straw, Not worth a. (s 918)

c. **1300** *Havelok* E.E.T.S. 10, I. 315 He let his oth al ouer-ga, þerof ne yaf he nouth a stra. *c.* **1390** GOWER *Conf. Amantis* Bk. 3 l. 666 And seith, that such an Housebonde Was to a wif noght worth a Stre. *c.* **1412** HOCCLEVE *De Reg. Princ.* l. 1670 Swiche vsage is Not worþ a strawe. **1522** *Mundus et Infans* 355 (1903) 365 All thy techynge is not worthe a straye. **1730** SWIFT *On Stephen Duck* Wks. (1856) I. 637 Though 'tis confess'd that those who ever saw His poems think them all not worth a straw!

Straw, To be in (out of) the. (s 920)

[= in childbed: recovered after child bearing.] **1602** 23 Oct. J. CHAMBERLAIN *Letters* ed. McLure. **1609** HARWARD 120ᵛ She is downe in the straw. **1614** J. HOSKYNS *Wks.* ed. L. B. Osborn 70. **1662** FULLER Lincs. 145 Our English plain Proverb, 'De Puerperis' they are in the Straw. **1705** [E. WARD] *Hudibras Rediv.* IV 18 We sipp'd our Fuddle, As Women in the Straw do Caudle. **1772** *Grimston Papers* (MS.) I hope your neighbour, Mrs. G., is safe out of the straw, and the child well. **1832** MARRYAT *N. Forster* ch. 15 They found the lady *in the straw.*

Straw to his dog and bones to his ass, He gives.

1813 RAY 75.

Straws show which way the wind blows. (s 924)

[*a.* **1654**] **1689** SELDEN *Table-Talk, Libels* Arb. 67 Take a straw and throw it up into the Air, you shall see by that which way the Wind is ... More solid things do not show the Complexion of the times so well, as Ballads and Libels. **1823** BYRON *D. Juan* XIV. viii You know, or don't know that great Bacon saith 'Fling up a straw, 'twill show the way the wind blows'. **1835** LYTTON *Rienzi* II. iii The Provençal, who well knew how to construe the wind by the direction of straws. **1861** READE *Cloist. & Hearth* ch. 56 And such straws of speech show how blows the wind. **1907** S. LEE *Gt. Eng. of 16th Cent.* 224 Bacon set forth these views as mere *ballons d'essai,* as straws to show him which way the wind blew.

Straw(s), *see also* Barley s. good fodder when cow gives water; Bricks without s.; Care a s. (Not to); Corn lies under the s. (Much); Cradle s. are scarce out of his breech; Drowning man catch at s.; Eyes draw s.; Fire cannot be hidden in flax (s.); Fire of s.; Foot further than the whittle ... into the s.; Ill man lie in thy s. (Let an); Last s.; Law for wagging of s. (Will go to); Long journey (In a) s. weighs; Man of s.; Master of s.; One foot in the s.; Pad in the s.; Peel s., (Go); Playing with s. before old cat (No); Skirts of s. (Who has) fear the fire; Strike with a s.; Stumble at a s. and leap block; Time and s. make medlars ripe; Wagging of a s.

Strawberry, *see* Cut down an oak.

Streak, *see* Silver s.

Stream cannot rise above its source, The. (s 931)

1578 T. PROCTOR *et al. Gorg. Gallery* ed. Rollins 12 Beleeue this to bee true, that streames shall soner turne, Or frosen Ice to fier coales, on blasing flame to burne. **1591** ARIOSTO *Orl. Fur.* Harington XLIV. 59 First shall the streames runne back vnto their bed, Ere I will iustly such a blame desarue. [**1634**] **1655** MASSINGER *Very Woman* Epil. ed. H. Coleridge 390 All that I can say Will never turn the stream the other way. **1700** DRYDEN *Wife of Bath* 388–9 Then what can Birth, or mortal Men bestow, Since Floods no higher than their Fountains flow? **1732** FULLER no. 4771 The Stream can never rise above the Springhead. **1905** VACHELL *The Hill* 84 Clever chap, ... but one is reminded that a stream can't rise higher than its source. **1921** T. R. GLOVER *The Pilgrim* 125 It is held that a stream cannot rise above its source; but ... [a] river may have many tributaries, and one of them may change the character of what we call the main stream.

Stream (current, tide) stopped swells the higher, The.   (S 929)

1563 *Mirr. for Mag.* ed. Campbell 389 The more ye stop streames the hygher they flowe. **1576** PETTIE i. 98 As the swift running stream if it be not stopped runneth smoothly away without noise, but if there be any dam . . . to stay the course thereof, it rageth and roareth and swelleth above the banks. **1579** LYLY *Euph.* i. 209 Hast thou not redde Euphues, that . . . hee that stoppeth the streame forceth it to swell higher? **1590** GREENE *Never Too Late* Gros. 103 I have read sweete Love, in the Aphorismes of the Philosophers, that heate suppressed is more violent, the streame stopt makes the greater Deluge, and passions concealed, procure the deeper sorrowes. **1592-3** SHAKES. *V.A.* l. 331 An oven that is stopp'd, or river stay'd, Burneth more hotly, swelleth with more rage. **1594** *Id. T.G.V.* II. vii. 25 The current that with gentle murmur glides . . . being stopp'd, impatiently doth rage. **1608** *Id. C.* III. i. 249 Like interrupted waters, and o'erbear What they are us'd to bear.   [1636] **1655** STRODE *Float. Island* I. ii. 151 Water it selfe if bounded in too streight, Will foame and swell and breake thick bonds of Rock.

Stream(s), see also Carried down s. need not row; Cross the s. where it is ebbest; Little s. drives light mill; Shallow s. make most din; Striving against s. (Ill).

Street, see Man in s.

Strength enough to bear the misfortunes of one's friends, One has always.

1773 GOLDSMITH *She Stoops to C.* III. Wks. (Globe) 661 You must learn resignation. . . . See me, how calm I am.—Ay, people are generally calm at the misfortunes of others. **1853** TRENCH v. 104 This Russian, . . . The burden is light on the shoulders of another; with which the French may be compared: . . .

Strength, see also Policy . . . (goes beyond s.); Sticking goes not by s.; Tower of s.; Union (concord) is s.; Wisdom is better than s.

Strengthens, see Absence sharpens love, presence s. it.

Stretch without a halter, You.

1738 SWIFT *Dial.* I. E.L. 278 Why, colonel, you break the King's laws; you stretch without a halter.

Stretch your arm (Put your hand) no further than your sleeve will reach.
                                                                        (A 316)

1541 COVERDALE *Chr. State Matr.* XIX. I3ᵛ Strech out thine arme no farther then thy sleve wyll retche. **1549** LATIMER *2nd Serm. bef. Edw. VI* P.S. 108 Mayntayn no greater port, then thou art able to bear out and support of thyne owne provision. Put they hand no further then thy sleue will reache. **1590** GREENE *Mourning Garment* Wks. (Huth) IX. 216 My sutes were silke, my talke was all of State, I stretcht beyond the compasse of my sleeye. **1639** CLARKE 21.

1721 KELLY 277 Put your Hand no farther than your Sleeve will reach. That is, spend no more than your Estate will bear. **1822** J. GALT *Provost* ch. 2 I replied, 'Dinna try to stretch your arm, gude-wife, further than your sleeve will let you.' **1881** W. WESTALL *Old Factory* ch. 21 It would leave me short of working capital, and . . . I mustn't stretch my arm further than th' coat-sleeve will reach.

Stretch your legs according to your coverlet.   (L 189)

a. **1253** GROSTESTE *Bk. of Husbandry* in RILEY *Mem. of London* 8, note 4 Whoso streket his fot forthere than the whitel¹ wil reche, he schal streken in the straw. *c.* **1300** *Walter of Henley's Husbandry* (1890) 4 Wo þat strechet forþerre þan his wytel¹ wyle reche in þe straue his fet he mot streche. [He that stretches farther than his whittle will reach, in the straw his feet he must stretch.] **1393** LANGLAND *P. Pl.* C. xvii. 76 When he streyneth hym to strecche . the straw is hus whitel. **1550** W. HARRYS *Market or Fair of Usurers* D5ᵛ. **1640** HERBERT no. 147 Every one stretcheth his legges according to his coverlet. **1670** RAY 25. **1897** 'H. S. MERRIMAN' *Kedar's Tents* ch. 4 'Every one stretches his legs acccrding to the length of his coverlet', he said. [¹ blanket.]

Stretching and yawning lead to bed.
                                                                        (S 932)

1659 HOWELL *Eng. Prov.* 17b. **1678** RAY 81.

Stretch(ed, ing), see also Foot further than the whittle, (He that s.) will s. into the straw; Hanging's s.; Strings high s. . . . soon crack.

Stretton in the Street, where shrews meet.   (S 933)

1678 RAY 333 Rutlandshire.

Strew green rushes for the stranger.
                                                                        (R 213)

[Before the introduction of carpets the rushes on the floor were renewed for a visitor.] **1546** HEYWOOD II. iii. G2 She bad vs welcome and merily toward me, Greene rushes for this straunger, strawe here (quoth she). **1589** GREENE *Menaphon* Arb. 85 When you come you shall have greene rushes, you are such a straunger. **1594-8** SHAKES. *T.S.* IV. i. 40 Is supper ready, the house trimmed, rushes strewed, cobwebs swept? **1738** SWIFT *Dial.* I. E.L. 261 If we had known of your coming, we should have strewn rushes for you.

Stricken deer withdraws himself to die, The.   (D 189)

a. **1547** *Surrey* ed. Padelford (1928) 28. 21 As the striken deere withdrawes him selfe alone. **1563** SACKVILLE 'Buckingham' *Mirr. for Mag.* ed. Campbell 326. **1578** J. YVER *Courtly Controv.* tr. H. Wotton 2E1ᵛ As the striken Hart not finding any Dittany to heale his wounde, languishing seeketh the next Fountayne to yeelde his deadly gaspe. **1583** MELBANCKE *Philot.* 167. **1592** SHAKES. *T.And.* III. i. 89 Seeking to hide.

herself, as doth the deer, That hath receiv'd some unrecuring wound. [*c.* **1592**] **1594** MARLOWE *Edw.* II ll. 2120–1. **1599** SHAKES. *A.Y.* II. i. 33 To the which place [brook] a poor sequest'red stag, That from the hunter's aim had ta'en a hurt, Did come to languish . . . and the big round tears Cours'd one another down his innocent nose In piteous chase. **1600–1** *Id. H.* III. ii. 265 Why, let the strucken deer go weep, The hart ungalled play. **1785** W. COWPER *The Task* III. 108 I was a stricken deer that left the herd Long since.

Stricken the ball under the line, Thou hast. (B 62)

[*i.e.* not played according to the rules.] *c.* **1533** J. FRITH *Another Ans. agst. Rastell* A4ᵛ It is not Inoughe for a man playinge at tennes to tosse the ball agayn . . . he muste take hede that he neyther smyte to shorte of the lynne nor yet vnder for then it is a losse and he had ben better to let it goe. *Ibid.* C3 Here Rastell hath smyte the ball quyte vnder the corde. *c.* **1549** HEYWOOD I. xi. E2ᵛ Thou hast striken the ball, vnder the line. **1611** SHAKES. *Temp.* IV. i. 237 Mistress line, is not this my jerkin? Now is the jerkin under the line. **1616** DRAXE no. 1724 Hee hath strooke the ball vnder the line.

Stricken, *see also* Pries into every cloud may be s. (He that); Threatened than s. (More).

Stride, *see* Spit and a s.

Strife, *see* Devil has cast bone to set s.; God stint all s.; Poverty breeds s.; Weight and measure take away s.; Wife, (He that has) has s.

Strike all of (on *obs.*) a heap, To.

[= to paralyse, to cause to collapse.] **1711** *Brit. Apollo* III. no. 133. 2/1 A Young Woman . . . struck me all on a heap. **1741** RICHARDSON *Pamela* I. 205 This alarm'd us both; and he seem'd quite struck of a Heap. **1818** SCOTT *Rob Roy* ch. 24 The interrogatory seemed to strike the honest magistrate, to use the vulgar phrase, 'all of a heap'. **1875** JOWETT *Plato* (ed. 2) III. 120 Some one who . . . will not be struck all of a heap like a child by the vain pomp of tyranny.

Strike as ye feed, and that's but soberly.

1721 KELLY 286 . . . A Reproof to them that correct those over whom they have no Power.

Strike, but hear.

[PLUTARCH *Themistocles* xi Πάταξον μὲν, ἄκουσον δέ. L. *Verbera sed audi.*] [480 B.C.] **1579** NORTH *Plutarch, Themistocles* Dent II. 18 Eurybiades[1] having a staff in his hand lift it up, as though he would have stricken him. Strike and thou wilt, said he,[2] so thou wilt hear me. [[1] Spartan commander of the Grecian fleet at Artemisium. [2] Themistocles.]

Strike, Dawkin; the devil is in the hemp. (D 53)

1678 RAY 70.

Strike the serpent's head with your enemy's hand, It is good to.

1732 FULLER no. 2945.

Strike while the iron is hot. (I 94)

c. **1374** CHAUCER *Troilus* Bk. 2, l. 1275 Pandare, which that stood hir faste by, Felte iren hoot, and he began to smyte. *c.* **1386** *Id. Mel.* l. 1036 Whil that iren is hoot, men sholden smyte. **1546** HEYWOOD I. iii. A4 And one good lesson to this purpose I pyke From the smithis forge, whan thyron is hote stryke. **1580** LYLY *Euph. & his Eng.* ii. 133 Omitting no time, least the yron should coole before he could strike, he presently went to *Camilla.* **1591** SHAKES. *3 Hen. VI* V. i. 49 Strike now, or else the iron cools. **1611** CHAPMAN *Il.* 16. 352 Patroclus then did strike while steel was hot. **1614** CAMDEN 309 (It is good to). **1682** BUNYAN *Holy War* ii. Wks. (Offor) III. 260 Finding . . . the affections of the people warmly inclining to him, he, as thinking it was best striking while the iron is hot, made this . . . speech unto them.

Strike with a straw, To.

1579 GOSSON *Apology* ed. Arber 74. **1813** RAY 75.

Strikes my dog, He that | would strike me if he durst.

1588 *Discourse upon the present state of France* 27 Whilest hee dare not strike the maister, hee striketh the Dogge. **1721** KELLY 143 . . . Spoken with Resentment to them who injure any Thing that belongs to us. **1732** FULLER no. 2318.

Strikes with his tongue, He that | must ward with his head. (T 385)

1640 HERBERT no. 313. **1732** FULLER no. 2319.

Strikes with the sword, He that | shall be stricken (beaten) with the scabbard. (S 1047)

[*c.* **1515**] *c.* **1530** BARCLAY *Eclog.* v. 41 All suche as with the sworde do strike Feare to be serued with the scaberd like. **1546** HEYWOOD II. vii. 12ᵛ The prouerbe saith he that striketh with the swoorde, Shalbe strikyn with the scaberde. **1591** ARIOSTO *Orl. Fur.* Harington XXVIII. 80. **1599** PORTER *Angry Wom. Abingd.* l. 1836 Blessed are the peace-makers; they that strike with the sword, shall be beaten with the scabberd. **1611** DAVIES no. 208.

Strike(s, th), *see also* Fire from ice, (To s.); God stays long, but s. at last; God s. not with both hands; God s. with finger; Many s. on anvil (When) they must s. by measure; Mint ere you s.

Strings high stretched either soon crack or quickly grow out of tune. (L 201)

c. **1594** BACON no. 612 Spanish En fin la soga quiebra por el mas delgado. **1595** R. TURNER *Garland of a Green Wit* D1 Strings high stretched, eyther soone cracke, or quickly grow out of tune. **1616** DRAXE no. 1771 Where strings are high set, they breake or grow out of tune. **1659**

HOWELL *Br. Prov.* 2 The more a string is stretcht, the sooner it breaks. *Ibid.* 8 When the string is streightest it breaks with stretching.

String(s), *see* Go to heaven in a s.; Harp on one s.; Harp on s. that gives no melody; Knot is loose (Where) s. slips; Two s. to one's bow; World in a s. (To have the).

Stringer, *see* Nay, stay, quoth S.

Strip it, Thou'lt | as Slack stript the cat, when he pull'd her out of the churn.
(s 519)
1678 RAY 289.

Strive(s), *see* Bird caught in lime s., (The more the)/the faster he sticks.

Striving against the stream, It is ill (evil).
(s 927)
[*Iesus Sirach* 4. 31. *Vulg. Ecclus.* 4. 22. ERASM. *Ad.* 3. 2. 9.] c. **1275** *Prov. of Alfred* (Skeat) A 145 Strong hit is to rowe ayeyn the see that floweth So hit is to swynke ayeyn un-ylimpe[1]. c. **1300** *Cato's Dist.* (Furnivall) iv. 585 Aȝeyn þe strem ne strive þou nouȝt. c. **1390** GOWER *Conf. Amantis* Bk. IV, l. 1780 Betre is to wayte upon the tyde than rowe ayein the stremes stronge. c. **1460** *Wisdom* l. 1091 I woll no more row ageyn þe floode. **1539** TAVERNER 14 It is euyll stryuyng against the streme, that is to saye, It is greate folye to struggle agaynste such thynges as thou canst not ouercome. **1593** SHAKES. *V.A.* l. 772 All in vain you strive against the stream. **1599** GREENE *Alphonsus* III. iii. Merm. 45 In vain it is to strive against the stream; Fates must be follow'd and the gods' decree Must needs take place. **1614** CAMDEN 308 (hard). **1641** FERGUSSON no. 894 Ye strive against the stream. a. **1721** PRIOR *Dialog. of Dead* (1907) 250 *Vic. of Bray.* Never strive against the stream, always drive the nail that will go. [[1] misfortune.]

Strokes be good to give, If | they are good to get.
1721 KELLY 186 . . . Spoken to those whom we beat for beating others. **1732** FULLER no. 2700.

Strokes fell great (tall) oaks, Many (Little). *Cf.* Oak is not felled at one stroke.
(s 941)
[ERASM. *Ad. Multis rigida quercus domatur ictibus.*] c. **1370** CHAUCER *Rom. of Rose* l. 3688 No man at fyrste stroke He maye nat fele down an oke. **1539** TAVERNER 26ᵛ Wyth many strokes is an oke ouerthrowne. **1579** LYLY *Euph.* i. 225 Many strokes ouerthrow the tallest Oke. **1587** T. HUGHES *Misfortunes of Arthur* II. iii. 103 The smallest axe may fell the hugest oake. **1591** SHAKES. *3 Hen. VI* II. i. 54 And many strokes, though with a little axe, Hews down, and fells the hardest-timber'd oak. By many hands your father was subdu'd. **1670** RAY 115 *Multis ictibus dejicitur quercus.* Many strokes fell, &c. Assiduity overcomes all difficulty. **758** FRANKLIN *Way to Wealth* (Crowell) 17 St ick to it steadily and you will see great effects; for . . . Little strokes fell great oaks.

Stroke(s), *see also* Fools . . . among his kindred, (Who has neither) was born of a s. of thunder; Great s. make not music; Oak is not felled at one s.; Redder's s.; Words go with the wind, but s. out of play.

Strong as a horse, As.
1703 WARD *Writings* ii. 81.

Strong town (castle) is not won in an hour, A.
(T 455)
[**1587**] **1599** GREENE *Alph. of Aragon* v. iii. l. 1810 Castles are not wonne At first assault. **1599** MINSHEU *Span. Gram.* 84 Rome was not built in a day. c. **1640** W.S. *Countrym. Commonw.* 45 No sudden storme or affliction dants a valiant minde: for a strong Towne is not wonne in an houre, nor was Rome built vpon one day.

Strong, *see also* Handsome at twenty, nor s. at thirty (He that is not); Stout (S.) be merciful (As you are).

Struck at Tib, but down fell Tom, He.
(T 280)
1639 CLARKE 1. **1672** WALKER 59, no. 66.

Strumpet, *see* Never was s. fair.

Strut, *see* Turkey-cock.

Stuarts, *see* All S. not sib to the king.

Stuck a knife to my heart, If you had | it would not have bled.
1721 KELLY 192 . . . Intimating that the Thing was a great Surprize. **1858** READE *Jack of All Trades* ch. 12 A chill came over me. If you had stuck a knife in me I shouldn't have bled.

Students, *see* Thrive as New College s.

Studied, *see* Whittington's College (He has s. at).

Studies his content, He that | wants it.
(c 627)
1611 COTGRAVE s.v. Aise Hee that studies his contentment ouermuch, euer wants it. **1640** HERBERT no. 4.

Studies pass into his character, A man's.
[OVID *Heroides* 15. 83 *Abeunt studia in mores.*] **1586** G. WHETSTONE *The Eng. Mirr.* 237 14 . . . Sic studium mores . . . From studie so, doth perfect manners spring. **1612** BACON *Ess., Studies* Arb. 11 *Histories* make one wise, *Poets* wittie, . . . *Abeunt studia in mores.* **1889** J. W. HALES Introd. to Johnson *Lives of Poets* xxvi Perhaps we may invert. . . . 'Studia abeunt in mores', that is, 'A man's studies pass into his character', and read, 'Mores abeunt in studia', . . . 'A man's character passes into his studies', expresses itself inevitably in his writings.

Study, *see* Addendum p. 930, (S., To be in a brown).

Stuff a cold and starve a fever. (F 195)

1574 WITHALS I2 Fasting is a great remedie in feuers. **1586** GUAZZO ii. 135 It is better to feede a fever, then weaknesse. **1642** TORRIANO 51 (as 1586). **1659** HOWELL *It. Prov.* 15 'Tis better feed a fever then feebleness. **1852** E. FITZGERALD *Polonius* 9 In the case of . . . a Cold— 'Stuff a cold and starve a fever', has been grievously misconstrued, so as to bring on the fever it was meant to prevent. **1881** *N. & Q.* 6th Ser. IV. 54 'Stuff a cold', &c. The expression is elliptical, for '[if you] stuff a cold, [you will have to] starve a fever'.

Stuff, *see* St. Martin's s.

Stuffing holds out storm.

1721 KELLY 293 . . . Advising Men to take some good Thing, before they travel in a bad Day.

Stumble at a straw and leap over a block, To.   (S 922)

1526 *Hund. Mer. Tales* v. B. iii. As ye *commen* prouerbe is they *stumble* at a straw & lepe ouer a blok. **1530** PALSGRAVE 736b Thou lepest over a bloke and stomblest at a strawe. **1547** *Homilies, Works* D4 They were of so blynd iudgemente, that they stombled at a strawe, & leped ouer a blocke. **1653** W. RAMESEY *Astrol. Restored,* To Rdr. 17 To skip over blocks, and stumble at straws. **1721** KELLY 288 Start at a Straw, and loup o'er a Bink.[1] Scruple at small Things, and be guilty of greater. [[1] bench.]

Stumble may prevent a fall, A.

1732 FULLER no. 424.

Stumbles and falls not, He that | mends his pace.   (P 2)

1611 COTGRAVE s.v. Choper He that stumbles without falling gets the more forward. **1636** HOWELL *Lett.* 15 Aug. (1903) II. 105 We find that a stumble makes one take firmer footing. . . . Kit hath now overcome himself, therefore I think he will be too hard for the devil hereafter. **1640** HERBERT no. 7. **1655** FULLER *Ch. Hist.* VIII. i. (1868) II. 456 Archbishop Cranmer . . . recanted his subscription, and valiantly burned at the stake. Thus, he that stumbleth, and doth not fall down, gaineth ground thereby; as this good man's slip mended his pace to his martyrdom. **1676** MARVELL *Mr. Smirke* Grosart 59 (gains a step).

Stumbles twice over one stone, He that | deserves to break his shins.   (S 882)

[ZENOBIUS 3. 29 δὶς πρὸς τὸν αὐτὸν αἰσχρὸν προσκρούειν λίθον.] **1539** TAVERNER 39 He that wyse is, woll not the seconde tyme stomble at the same stone. **1580** LYLY *Euph. & his Eng.* ii. 92 A burnt childe dreadeth the fire, he that stumbleth twice at one stone is worthy to breake his shins. **1659** HOWELL *Span. Prov.* 12 (deserves to have a broken face). **1706** STEVENS s.v. Piedra (it is no wonder if he breaks his Head, for his Heedlesness).

Stumble, *see also* Horse may s.; Stone in the way . . . may make a tall man s., (A little); Threshold, (To s. at the).

Stumps, *see* Stir one's s.

Stung by a nettle than pricked by a rose, It is better to be.

1580 LYLY *Euph. & his Eng.* ii. 95 I can better take a blister of a Nettle, then a prick of a Rose. **1659** HOWELL *Eng. Prov.* 18b 'Tis better to be stung by a Nettle, then prickt by a Rose; *viz.* To *be wronged by a foe, then a friend.* **1732** FULLER no. 878.

Sturt[1] pays no debt.   (S 948)

a. **1628** CARMICHAELL no. 1380. **1641** FERGUSSON no. 749. **1721** KELLY 292 . . . Spoken with Resentment, to them who storm when we crave of them our just Debts. [[1] haughtiness, indignation.]

Stye, The worse their | the longer they lie.

1724 SWIFT 'Blunders of Quilca' ed. Davis v. 221 A Proverb on the Laziness and Lodgings of the Servants . . . .

Style is the man, The.

[L. *Stylus virum arguit.* The style shows the man. ERASM. *Ad. Qualis vir, talis oratio.* **1753** BUFFON *Discours sur le style,* Le style est l'homme même.] **1621** BURTON *Anat. Mel.* To the Reader BI *Stylus virum arguit,* our stile bewrayes us. **1827–48** HARE *Gues. at Truth* (1859) ii. 343 Shakespeare was always alive . . . to the truth of the maxim, *le style est l'homme même.* **1901** ALEX. WHYTE *Bib. Char. Stephen,* &c. civ. 72 If the style is the man in Holy Scripture also, . . . we feel a very great liking for Luke.

Subject's love is the king's lifeguard, The.

[SENECA *De Clementia* I. 19. 6.] *c.* **1386** CHAUCER *Mel.* B² l. 2529 For thus seith Tullius, that 'there is a maner garnison that no man ne venquisse ne disconfite, and that is, a lord to be biloved of hise citezeins and of his peple'. **1578** B. GARTER *Receiving of the Queen into Norwich* (Nichols 1823, ii. 141) We come . . . for that whiche in right is our owne, the heartes and true allegeaunces of our subjects, whiche are the greatest riches of a kingdome. **1592** DELAMOTHE 29 The loue of the subiect, is the strongest pillar of the prince. **1597** *Politeuphia* 72ᵛ The strength of a Prince, is the friendship and loue of his people. **1616** DRAXE no. 1297 (as 1592). **1640** QUARLES *Enchiridion* I. xlv The strongest castles a Prince can build . . . is in the hearts of his subjects. **1721** KELLY 338.

Subject(s), *see* Hated of his s.; Heretic and good s.

Sublime to the ridiculous, There is but one step from the.

[*c.* **1799** MARMONTEL Le ridicule touche au sublime. **1812** NAPOLEON in DE PRADT, *Hist. de l'Ambassade dans le Grand-duché de Varsovie en 1812* Du sublime au ridicule il n'y a qu'un pas.] **1794** T. PAINE *Age of Reason* ii Note The sublime and the ridiculous are often so nearly related, that it is difficult to class them separately. One step above the sublime makes the ridiculous, and one step above the ridiculous makes the sublime again. **1879** M. PATTISON *Milton* 116 The Hague tittle-tattle . . . is set forth in the pomp of Milton's loftiest Latin. . . . The sublime and the ridiculous are here blended without the step between. **1909** *T.L.S.* 17 Dec. 492 In the case of Louis XVIII, indeed, the ridiculous was, as it is commonly said to be, only a step removed from the sublime.

Submitting to one wrong brings on another, The.

[L. *Veterem injuriam ferendo, invitas novam.* By submitting to an old injury, you invite a new one.] **1692** L'ESTRANGE *Aesop's Fab.* cclxxxv (1738) 299 A snake . . . appealed to Jupiter . . . who told him . . . 'If you had but bit the first man that affronted ye, the second would have taken warning by't'. . . . The putting up of one affront draws on another. **1706** STEVENS s.v. Agravio The taking of one Wrong brings on another. Because those that will do wrong grow upon our Patience.

Substance, *see* Catch not at the shadow; Show than s., (More).

Subtle, *see* Devil is s.

Subtlety is better than force.   (s 952)

1616 T. ADAMS *Souldier's Honour* A4 This must not be done *Marte sed Arte*; not by force but by fraud. **1616** DRAXE no. 2435. **1664** CODRINGTON 210. **1736** BAILEY *Dict.* s.v.

Success makes a fool seem wise.

1707 MAPLETOFT III.

Success, *see* Failure teaches s.; Nothing succeeds like s.

Succours of Spain, either late or never.

1853 TRENCH iii. 53 *Succours of Spain, either late or never.*[1] Any one who reads the despatches of England's Great Captain during the Peninsular War will find in almost every page of them justifications of this proverb. [[1] *Socorros de España, ó tarde, ó nunca.*]

Such, *see also* Sike.

Such . . ., such . . ., *see under significant words following.*

Sucked evil from the dug, He.   (E 198)

1531 ELYOT *Governor* I. iv. 29 Often times the childe soukethe the vice of his nouryse with the milk of her pappe. **1579** LYLY *Euph.* i. 266 The common bye worde of the common people . . . which is: This fellow hath sucked mischiefe euen from the teate of his nursse. *a.* **1591** H. SMITH *Serm.* (1866) I. 32 . . . that is, as the nurse is affected in her body or in her mind, commonly the child draweth the like infirmity from her. [**1592**] **1597** SHAKES. *Rich. III* II. ii. 30 He is my son. . . . Yet from my dugs he drew not this deceit. **1678** RAY 354.

Sucked not this out of my fingers' ends, I.   (F 244)

1546 HEYWOOD I. xi. E3. **1550** CRANMER *Def. of Doct. of Sacrament* 57 Least the Papistes shuld say, that we sucke this out of our own fyngers, the same shalle be proued by testimonye of all the olde authors. **1588** E. BULKELEY *An Answer* 23 You rather sucke that out of your owne fingers, then find it *in Luthers* works. **1616** DRAXE no. 1328. **1670** RAY 25.

Suck(s, ed), *see also* Bee s. honey out of the bitterest flowers; Empty leech s. sore; Children s. mother when young, and father when old; Lambs, (Like) you do nothing but s.; Looks as if s. his dam through hurdle; Love a woman (He that does not) s. a sow; Pick (S.) a person's brains.

Sudden friendship, sure repentance.

1721 KELLY 285. **1732** FULLER no. 4281.

Sudden joy kills sooner than excessive grief.   (J 86)

1548 N. UDALL *Paraphrase* A5ᵛ Muche sooner and sorer doeth immoderate ioye drounde mannes reason, then immoderate dolour. **1620** SHELTON *Don Quix.* II. lii. IV. 118 'Tis usually said, That sodaine joy as soon kils as excessive griefe. **1732** FULLER no. 4283.

Sudden, *see also* Nature hates s. changes.

Suds, To be (leave, lie) in the.   (s 953)

[= in difficulties.] *c.* **1560** BOCCACCIO *Hist. of Galeano, Cymon & Iphigenia* tr. T.C. A3ᵛ From top of whirlyng wheele she [Fortune] throwes him in the suddes. **1573** GASCOIGNE *Posies* i. 161 He . . . sought with victuall to supplie Poore Myddleburgh which then in suddes did lie. **1653** H. MORE *Conject. Cabbal.* (1713) 230 After the hurry of his inordinate pleasures and passion, when he was for a time left in the suds, as they call it. **1730** SWIFT *Death & Daphne* Misc. (1735) V. 109 Away the frighted Spectre scuds And leaves my Lady in the Suds. **1775** S. J. PRATT *Liberal Opin.* cxxxiv (1783) IV. 216 This proves, *logicè*, that you are in the suds; which is *Anglicè*, that you will be hanged.

Sue a beggar, and get a louse.   (B 240)

1583 MELBANCKE 2D4 He that helpes a begger out of the ditch shalbe stung with his lyce. **1639** CLARKE 72. **1659** HOWELL *Eng. Prov.* 2a Goe to Law with a beggar, thou shalt gett a lowse. **1819** SCOTT *Bride Lam.* ch. 3 I guess it is some law phrase—but sue a beggar, and—your honour knows what follows'.

Suet, *see* Gentleman without estate.

Suffer a calf to be laid on thee, If thou | within a little they'll clap on the cow.

1659 TORRIANO no. 3 (to be clapt on thy shoulders, suddenly they'l . . . also). **1853** TRENCH iii. 68 The Italian, . . . Undue liberties are best resisted at the outset.

Suffer and expect.   (s 954)

1640 HERBERT no. 702.

Suffer the ill and look for the good. *Cf.* Every commodity.

c. **1526** *Dicta Sapientum* C2ᵛ Thou must other-whyle suffre an incommodite, to thende thou mayst enioye a commodite. **1573** SANFORD 109ᵛ. **1578** FLORIO *First F.* 33ᵛ (tary for).

Suffer(s), *see also* Bear (Take, S.) this, bear (take, s.) all; Better s. ill than do ill; Do right nor s. wrong (He will neither); Lives long (He that) s.; Poor s. all the wrong.

Sufferance, Of | comes ease (rest).
(s 955)

c. **1386** CHAUCER *Merchant's T.* l. 2115 Passe over is an ese, I sey na-more. *c.* **1390** GOWER *Conf. Amantis* Bk. 3, l. 1639 Suffrance haþ euere be þe beste To wissen him þat secheþ reste. **1546** HEYWOOD I. ix. C2 Sens ye can nought wyn, if ye can not plcase, Best is to Suffer: For of suffrance comth ease. [**1589**] **1633** MARLOWE *Jew of Malta* I. ii. 239 Sufferance breeds ease. *a.* **1591** HY. SMITH *Serm.* (1866) I. 229 Even those which cannot suffer that they might have rest, yet sing the patient proverb, In sufferance is rest. **1598** SHAKES. *2 Hen. IV* V. iv. 24 O, that right should thus overcome might! Well, of sufferance comes ease. **1607** MARSTON *What you will* Prol. Ile give a proverbe—'Sufferance giveth ease'.

Sufferance, *see also* Forbearance.

Suffered to do more than is fitting, He that is | will do more than is lawful.
(M 1140–1)

1664 CODRINGTON 195.   **1670** RAY 9.

Suffering, It is not the | but the cause which makes a martyr.   (s 956)

1576 LAMBARDE *Kent* 2G4ᵛ The cause only, and not the death, maketh a Martyr. **1596** WARNER *Albion's Eng.* ix. 51 Q5ᵛ Not the pain, but cause, doth make the Marter. **1597** *Politeuphuia* 81ᵛ (as 1596). **1644** S. TORSHELL *Hypocrite Discovered* I. xii. 44 That saying which hath gone current through all Antiquity, That it is not the suffering but the cause which makes a Martyr, will hold good still. **1655** FULLER *Ch. Hist.* X. iv (1868) III. 284 To Smithfield he was brought to be burned . . . : it is neither the pain, nor the place, but only the cause, makes a martyr.

Suffices, That which | is not little.
(s 957)

1640 HERBERT no. 876.

Sufficient unto the day is the evil thereof.

[MATT. vi. 34.] **1784** J. WESLEY *Jour.* vi. 497. Sufficient for this day was the labour thereof. **1824** SCOTT *St. Ronan's* ch. 11 You must not . . . plague me with any of the ceremonial for your fête—'sufficient for the day is the evil thereof'.

1836 MRS. CARLYLE *Let.* to Miss Welsh, 1 Apr. In the meanwhile there were no sense in worrying over schemes for a future, which we may not live to see. 'Sufficient for the day is the evil thereof.' **1857** TROLLOPE *Barch. Tow.* ch. 15 'We shall be poor enough, but you will have absolutely nothing.' 'Sufficient for the day is the evil thereof', said Bertie.

Suffolk, Old, *see* Read, try, speak as you find, quoth o. S.

Suffolk cheese.   (c 273)

[*c.* **1625**] **1633** MASSINGER *New Way to Pay Old Debts* IV. ii. 73 A peece of *Suffolke* cheese, or Gammon of Bacon. **1661** PEPYS *Diary* 4 Oct. I found my wife vexed at her people for grumbling to eat Suffolk cheese. **1699** E. WARD *World Bewitched* 183 in LEAN I. 194 Many London prentices will be forced to eat Suffolk cheese that their master's daughters may be kept at a boarding school. **1787** GROSE (*Suffolk*) 224 Hunger will break through stone walls, or any thing except a Suffolk cheese. Suffolk cheese is . . . by some represented as only fit for making wheels for wheelbarrows. **1830** FORBY 424 *Suffolk Cheese.* . . . The cheese speaks: Those that made me were uncivil, for they made me harder than the d—l. Knives won't cut me; fire won't sweat me; Dogs bark at me, but can't eat me.

Suffolk fair maids.   (M 38)

1594 GREENE *Friar Bacon* A3ᵛ A bonier wench all Suffolke cannot yeeld. **1622** DRAYTON *Polyol.* XXIII Fayre Suffolke Mayds and Milke. **1662** FULLER Suffolk 55 . . . It seems the God of Nature hath been bountiful in giving them beautiful complexions.

Suffolk is the land of churches.

1867 NALL *Gt. Yarmouth, &c.* 224 Suffolk has been called the land of churches. . . . In Domesday Book whilst only one church is recorded as existing in Cambridgeshire, and none in Lancashire, Cornwall, or Middlesex, 364 are enumerated in Suffolk.

Suffolk milk.   (M 937)

1622 *See quot. under* 'Suffolk fair maids' *supra.* **1662** FULLER Suffolk 55 . . . No County in England affords better and sweeter of this kind. **1818** R. BLOOMFIELD in *Suffolk Garland* 374 Hence Suffolk dairy-wives run mad for cream, And leave their milk with nothing but its name; Its name derision and reproach pursue, And strangers tell of 'three times skimm'd sky-blue'.

Suffolk whine.

1787 GROSE (*Suff.*) 223 The Suffolk whine. The inhabitants of this county have a kind of whining tone in their speech, much resembling that of a person in great mental distress.

Suffolk, *see also* Read . . . as you find, says old S.; Silly S.

Sugar or salt, Not made of.

[= not to be disconcerted by wet weather.] **1738** SWIFT *Dial.* I, E.L. 263 Did you walk through the Park in the rain?—Yes, madam, we were neither sugar nor salt; we were not afraid the rain would melt us. **1786** *Har'st Rig* (1794) 27 But Highlanders ne'er mind a douk, For they're na'e sawt. **1855** CARLYLE in *E. FitzGerald's Lett.* (1889) I. 235 I persist in believing the weather will clear, . . . at any rate I am not made of sugar or of salt.

Sugar (gild) the pill (word), To. (P 325)

1539 TAVERNER I *Garden* D4ᵛ His wordes were more sugered then salted, more delectable then profitable. **1557** T. NORTH *Dial Princes* II. xvi. 1582 ed. T4ᵛ For the faire woemen are lyke vnto the golden pilles: the which in sight are very pleasaunt, and in eatinge very noysome. **1583** MELBANCKE *Philot.* I4ᵛ Pills ywrapt in sugar yeeld no bitter relishe. *a.* **1608** W. PERKINS *Gvt. of Tongue* Wks. 1608, i. 445 When a man shal sweare in his talke I shall not need alwaies to say, Ye do very ill to sweare . . . but I wil lap it vp in the forme of an exhortation, as pills are lapt in sugar. **1666** TORRIANO *It. Prov.* 324 no. 21 Bitter Medicines are cover'd over with Sugar.

Sugar, *see also* Time has turned white s. to white salt (When).

Suit at law and a urinal bring a man to hospital, A. (s 961)

1616 DRAXE 112 Suites in Law, and oft taking of physicke undoeth many. **1642** TORRIANO 4 I wish a woman, a sute, and an urinall befall him, who wisheth me any evil. **1664** CODRINGTON 184. **1670** RAY 15 (*Hispan.*). **1732** FULLER no. 6238.

Suit is best that best fits me, That. (s 960)

1639 CLARKE 16. **1670** RAY 146.

Suit of law, One | breeds twenty. (w 919)

1640 HERBERT no. 253 The worst of law is, that one suit breedes twenty. **1732** FULLER no. 3796.

Suitor, *see* Last s. wins maid.

Suits hang half a year in Westminster Hall; at Tyburn, half an hour's hanging endeth all. (s 962)

1560 HEYWOOD *Fourth Hund. Epig.* no. 12 Sutes hange halfe a yere in Westminster hall, At Tyburne, halfe an howres hangyng endeth all.

Sullen man, *see* Keep out of . . . a s. m.'s way.

Sullens, *see* Sick of the s.

Sum, *see* Small s. will pay short reckoning.

Summer, No | but has its winter.

1641 F. QUARLES *Enchiridion* Cent. 3, no. 97. **1846** DENHAM 48.

Summer in winter, and a summer's flood, never boded England good.

1846 DENHAM 68.

Summer is a seemly time.

1721 KELLY 289.

Summer's day, As good as one shall see in a. (s 967)

1594 LYLY *Mother B.* I. iii. 44 He is as goodly a youth as one shall see in a Summers daie. **1595** SHAKES. *M.N.D.* I. ii. 76 A proper man as one shall see in a summer's day. **1599** *Id. Hen. V* III. vi. 62 I'll assure you 'a utt'red as prave words at the pridge as you shall see in a summer's day. **1599** PORTER *Angry Wom. Abingd.* l. 2320. **1742** FIELDING *Andrews* IV. 15 (As fine a fat thriving child as).

Summer, *see also* Dream of a dry s.; English s. three hot days; Good winter good s.; Grass (S.) on the top of oak (Look for); Indian s.; St. Luke's s.; St. Martin's s.; Swallow (One) does not make s.; Winter (After rainy) plentiful s.; Winter eats what s. lays up; Winter is s.'s heir; Winter's thunder and s.'s flood never boded good.

Summoned before the Mayor of Halgaver,[1] He is to be. (m 775)

1602 CAREW *Survey of Cornwall* (1769) 126ᵛ Hence is sprung the prouerb, when we see one slouenly apparelled, to say, He shall be presented in Halgaver Court. **1662** FULLER *Cornwall* 198 . . . This is a joculary and imaginary Court, wherewith men make merriment . . ., presenting such Persons as go Slovenly in their Attire, . . . Where judgement in formal terms is . . . executed more to the scorn than hurt of the persons. **1821** SCOTT *Kenilw.* ch. 4 We'll have you summoned before the Mayor of Halgaver. [[1] Halgaver Moor, Bodmin.]

Sun can be seen by nothing but its own light, The.

1732 FULLER no. 4774.

Sun does not shine on both sides of the hedge at once, The.

1879 R. JEFFERIES *Wild Life in South. County* ch. 17 The hedge . . . forms the basis of many proverbs . . . such as, 'The sun does not shine on both sides of the hedge at once'.

Sun enters, Where the | the doctor does not.

1928 *Times* 6 June 12/4 There is an Italian proverb which says, 'Dove va il sole non va il medico' ('Where the sun enters the doctor does not'). . . . I saw gangs of Italian roadmen acting on that proverb by lying halfclad on the roadside after their midday meal.

Sun goes pale to bed, If the | 'twill rain tomorrow, it is said.

1883 ROPER 7. **1893** INWARDS 52.

Sun has set; The | no night has followed.

[*a.* **1220** GIRALDUS CAMBRENSIS. *Sol occubuit; nox nulla secuta est.*] *a.* **1626** SIR J. DAVIES Wks.

Gros. 467 By that Eclipse which darken'd our Apollo, Our sunne did sett, and yett noe night did follow [James I's death]. **1860** RILEY *Dict. Lat. Quot.* 435 'The sun has set; no night has ensued'. A piece of flattery addressed to a son, and equally complimentary to his father. . . . Ascribed to Giraldus, and refers to the succession of Richard on the death of Henry II.

Sun in red should set, If the | the next day surely will be wet; if the sun should set in grey, the next will be a rainy day. *Cf.* Sky red, etc.

1846 DENHAM 10.

Sun is highest, When the | he casts the least shadow.   (s 989)

1577 GRANGE *Gold. Aphroditis* E4ᵛ The higher the Sun, the lesser our shadowes are. **1580** LYLY *Euph. & his Eng.* ii. 179 When the Sunne is at the highest . . . then is my shadowe at the shortest. **1608** CHAPMAN *Byron's Tragedy* v. i. 140 As the sun At height and passive o'er the crowns of men . . . Casts but a little or no shade at all. **1608** SHAKES. *C.* I. i. 258 Such a nature, Tickled with good success, disdains the shadow Which he treads on at noon. **1645** J. MARSH *Marsh his Mickle Monument* A2ᵛ Shadows . . . cease when the Sun is at the highest. **1732** FULLER no. 5607.

Sun is never the worse for shining on a dunghill, The.   (s 982)

[TERTULL. *de Spect.* 20 *Sane sol et in cloacam radios suos defert, nec inquinatur.*] **1303** BRUNNE *Handl. Synne* l. 2299 The sunne, hys feyrnes neuer he tynes, þogh hyt on þe muk hepe shynes. *c.* **1386** CHAUCER *Parson's T.* l. 911 Though that holy writ speke of horrible sinne, certes, holy writ may nat been defouled, na-more than the sonne that shyneth on the mixen. **1579** LYLY *Euph.* i. 193 The Sun shineth vppon the dunge-hill and is not corrupted. **1600–1** SHAKES. *M.W.W.* I. iii. 59 Sometimes the beam of her view gilded my foot, sometimes my portly belly.— Then did the sun on dunghill shine. **1633** PRYNNE *Histrio-Mastix* II. 961 If any here reply . . . : That the sun shines on a dung-hill, and yet its beams are not defiled by it: . . . for unto the pure all things are pure.

Sun may do its duty, The | though your grapes are not ripe.

1732 FULLER no. 4778.

Sun, moon, and seven stars are against us, The.

[*Cf.* GENESIS xxxvii. 9.] ?**1543** T. BECON Pref. to *Dial. betw. the Christian Knight & Satan* P.S. 623 Truly the wicked have against them whatsoever and whosoever is of God . . . but also the moon and seven stars as they use to say. **1567** PAINTER *Pal. of Pleasure* Jacobs iii. 294 There were against him the Moone and the vii starres. **1570** *July and Julian* l. 1170 My master thinkes the mone and vii stares work in his mind [= thinks he has the world at will]. **1592–1602** *Thomas Lord Cornwall* I. i. 8 He keepes such a quile [= coil] in his studie, with the Sunne, and the Moone, and the seauen starres, that I do

verily thinke heele read out his wits. **1601** A. DENT *Plain Man's Pathway* 285 Wee haue (as they say) the Sunne, Moone, and seuen Starres against vs. **1616** DRAXE no. 27.

Sun of one, To get the.   (s 987)

1548 HALL (1809) 418 Betwene both armies ther was a great marryse which therle of Richemond left on his right hand, for this entent that it should be on that syde a defence for his part, and in so doyng he had the sonne at his backe and in the faces of his enemies. **1581** W. AVERELL *Charles and Julia* H4ᵛ By tracing ground, they got of them, bothe winde and shining Sun. Sir Phoebus blerde the Rebels eyes, his glistering beames so shinde. **1594–5** SHAKES. *L.L.L.* IV. iii. 365 Be first advis'd, In conflict that you get the sun of them. **1596** *Edw. III* II. ii. 69 D3 Ah but alas she winnes the sunne of me. **1666** TORRIANO *It. Prov.* 263 no. 6 The sun in ones eyes, a sad battel. *Ibid.* 276 no. 156 Armies are mightily disadvantag'd by the Sun, if it strike in their eyes.

Sun rises in the morning, In every country the.   (c 710)

1640 HERBERT no. 621.

Sun rises, When the | the disease will abate.   (s 990)

1678 RAY *Adag. Hebr.* 400 . . . It is said . . . there was a pretious stone which did hang on the neck of *Abraham*, which when the sick man looked on he was presently healed; And that when *Abraham* died God placed this stone in the Sun.

Sun sees all things and discovers all things, The.   (s 984)

1542 ERASM. tr. Udall *Apoph.* (1877) 344 *Cicero* thought in his merie conceipte, that forasmuch as according to the prouerbe, *Sol omnia videt ac revelat*, the sunne seeth all thinges and discouereth all things, &c.

Sun sets bright and clear, When the | an easterly wind you need not fear.

1846 DENHAM 20.

Sun sets in a bank,[1] When the | a westerly wind we shall not want.

1846 DENHAM 12. [[1] a heavy, dark cloud.]

Sun shines upon all alike (everywhere), The.   (s 985)

[MATT. v. 45 He maketh his sun to rise on the evil and on the good, and sendeth rain on the just and on the unjust.] **1552** LATIMER *Serm.* 19 P.S. 363 He letteth his sun shine as well over the wicked as over the good. **1553** T. WILSON *Arte of Rhet.* (1909) 32 The Sunne shineth indifferently ouer all. **1580** LYLY *Euph. & his Eng.* ii. 199 The Sunne when he is at his hight shineth as wel vpon course carsie [kersey] as cloth of tissue. **1601** SHAKES. *T.N.* III. i. 36 Foolery, sir, does walk about the orb like the sun; it shines everywhere. *c.* **1611** *Id. W.T.* IV. iv. 436 The selfsame sun that shines upon his court Hides not his visage from our cottage, but Looks on alike. **1659** HOWELL *Span. Prov.* 3 The Sergeant and the Sun are everywhere. **1882** BESANT *All Sorts* ch. 7 The sun shines everywhere, even, as Mr. Bunker remarked, in an Almshouse.

Sun with a candle, To set forth the.
(s 988)

[ERASM. *Ad. Lumen soli mutuas.*] **1540** PALSGRAVE *Acolastus* 11 What meane I . . . which . . . seme here to be thus farre abused, as to be aboute to shewe lyght vnto the bryght shynynge sonne? *a.* **1547** SURREY ed. Padelford (1928) 18.30 To matche the candle with the sonne. **1551** MORE *Utopia* tr. Robinson (Lupton) 23 Unles I wolde seme to shew and set furth the brightenes of the sonne wyth a candell, as the Prouerbe sayth. *c.* **1570** J. SAPARTON *Saparton's Alarum* (ballad) Match not the candle with the sun. **1578** J. YVER *Courtly Controv.* tr. H. Wotton F1ᵛ So probable reasons, as shall not bee repugnable, excepte you will demaunde torche-light at highe noone. **1585** A. DENT *Serm. of Repentance* A3 It may seem as a Candle lighted at noone day. **1596** SHAKES. *K.J.* IV. ii. 14 With taper-light To seek the beauteous eye of heaven to garnish Is wasteful and ridiculous excess. **1602** [? KYD] *Span. Trag.* III. xiiA 28 Light me your torches at the mid of noone. **1616** DEKKER *Artillery Garden* C4 Bringes but a candle to the mid-day light. **1639** *Publ. Ovid. De Tristibus* tr. Z. Catlin A3 To commend the Authour, were to hold up a Taper to the Sunne. **1667** *Life of Duke of Newcastle* 149. *a.* **1728** YOUNG *Satire* vii. 97 How commentators each dark passage shun, And hold their farthing candle to the sun.

Sun without a shadow, No.   (s 996)

1597 *Politeuphuia* 224ᵛ Euery light hath his Shadowe. **1639** CLARKE 326.

Sun(s), *see also* Although the s. shine leave not thy cloak; Bride the s. shines on (Happy is); Butter before the s., (To melt like); Clear as the s.; Day still while s. shines; Doctor cures (If) s. sees it; Eagle can gaze at the s., (Only the); Every light is not the s.; Filth under snow s. discovers; Gazes upon the s., (He that) shall at last be blind; God take the s. . . . (Though), we must have patience; March s.; Moon's not seen where s. shines; Morning s. never lasts a day; Morning s. . . . seldom end well; Motes in the s., (As many as there are); Out of God's blessing into warm s.; Place in the s.; Red the s. begin his race (If); Spots in the s.; Stool in the s., when one knave rises other comes; Two s. cannot shine in one sphere; Walk much in the s. will be tanned at last; Wind follows s.'s course; Worship the rising s.

Sunday comes it will be holy day, When.   (s 994)

1616 BRETON 2 *Crossing of Prov.* A4ᵛ. **1639** CLARKE 19.

Sunday's wooing draws to ruin.

1597 T. DELONEY *Gentle Craft* Wks. ed. Mann 104 I maruell how the Deuill thou camest to be

so bold with her? Surely thou hast drawn on her shooes on Sunday, I may say, thou hast left so good a token [a child] behind. **1832** HENDERSON 9.

Sunday(s), *see also* Alike every day, clout on S.; Begin a journey on S.; Come day . . . God send S.; Every day braw makes S. a daw; Hanged himself on S.; Month of S.; Mothering S.; Nutting on S. the devil will help; Saturday servants . . . S. servants run away; Saturday's new and S.'s full [sc. moon]; Two S. come together (When).

Sun-dial in the grave (shade)? What's the good of a.

a. **1633** DONNE 'The Will' Grierson i. 58 And all your graces no more use shall have, Then a Sun dyall in a grave. **1732** FULLER no. 5507 What's a Sun-dial in the shade good for? **1750** FRANKLIN Oct. Hide not your Talents, they for Use were made. What's a Sun-Dial in the Shade? **1761** S. JOHNSON *Thoughts on the Coronation* Wks. (1825) v. 451 Magnificence in obscurity is equally vain with a sundial in the grave.

Sung well before he broke his left shoulder with whistling, He could have.
(s 400)

1678 RAY 82.

Sunshine, *see* Heat (S.) that melts wax harden clay; Saturday without s. (Never a).

Sup kail with him, He would not | unless he broke the dish on his head.

1721 KELLY 134 . . . A disdainful Answer to them who compare our Friend to some unworthy inferior Fellow.

Sup, Simon, the best is at the bottom (here's good broth).   (s 461)

1598 DELONEY *Thomas of Reading* Wks. (Mann) 232 Sup Simon, theres good broth. **1607** *The Puritan* III. v Sup, Simon, now! eat porridge for a month. **1639** CLARKE 46. **1678** RAY 88 Prov. Phrases . . . belonging to . . . drinking.

Sup with a cutty than want a spoon, It is better to.

1721 KELLY 210 . . . It is better to have a Thing, not quite so good in its Kind, than to want altogether.

Sup, *see also* Hot s. hasty swallow; No man can s. and blow.

Supernaculum, *see* Pearl on your nail.

Superstition, *see* Devil divides . . . between atheism and s.

Supperless, *see* Better go to bed s.; Goes to bed s. all night tosses.

Suppers, By | more have been killed than Galen ever cured. *Cf.* Gluttony kills.   (S 1004)

1640 HERBERT no. 272. **1659** HOWELL *Span. Prov.* 22 (Avicen).

Supper(s), *see also* After dinner sit; Fared worse than when I wished for s., (I never); Hole in the groat and s. to seek; Hope is good breakfast but bad s.; Hunger makes dinners, pastime s.; No song no s.; Salad may be prologue to bad s.; Wrongs not an old man that steals s.

Supping, *see* Sleep without s.

Suppliant, *see* Lion spares the s.

Sups ill who eats all at dinner, He.
                                                    (A 183)

1586 GUAZZO ii. 136 If thou hadst dyned so poorelie . . . thou wouldest not haue supped so slenderlie. **1611** COTGRAVE s.v. Disner *Mal soupe qui tout disne*: Hee suppes ill that dines all; after a gluttonous and disordinat youth, followes a needie and hungrie age. **1678** RAY 125.

Sure as check.   (C 261)

1591 R. GREENE *Greene's Farewell to Folly* ed. Grosart ix. 231. **1611** BRETNOR *Almanac* April (a check). **1612** *Ibid.* Nov. (check). **1670** RAY 207 As sure as Check, or Exchequer pay. This was a Proverb in Queen Elisabeths time, the credit of the Exchequer beginning in, and determining with her reign.

Sure as death.   (D 136)

1592 SHAKES. *T.And.* I. i. 486 And sure as death I swore I would not part a bachelor from the priest. **1602** JONSON *Ev. Man in Hum.* I. iv. 97 That I were iealous: nay, as sure as death, Thus they would say. **1670** RAY 207 As sure as a gun, [or as death].

Sure as a gun, As.   (G 480)

1622 BEAUM. & FL. *Prophetess* I. iii You are right master, Right as a gun. **1654** E. GAYTON *Festivous Notes on Don Quixote* 55. **1656** S. HOLLAND *Wit & Fancy in a Maze* 161 He is dead as sure as a Gun. **1730** FIELDING *T. Thumb* III. ii Sure as a gun I'll have thee laid. **1849–50** THACKERAY *Pendennis* ch. 58 In every party of the nobility his name's down as sure as a gun.

Sure (safe) as louse in bosom, As. (L 467)

c. **1610–40** *The Telltale* l. 1065 As safe as . . . louse in bosome. **1666** TORRIANO *Prov. Phr.* 175. **1670** RAY 208 *Chesh.*

Sure as a louse in Pomfret, As.   (L 466)

1638 BRATHWAIT *Barnabees Jrnl.* A *Louse* in *Pomfrait* is not surer, Then the Poor through Sloth securer.

Sure as eggs is eggs, As.   (E 84)

1680 OTWAY *Caius Marius* IV. 43 'Twas to seek Lord Marius, as sure as Eggs be Eggs. **1699** B.E. *Dict. Cant. Crew* As sure as eggs be eggs. **1768** GOLDSMITH *Goodn. Man* iv And, as sure as eggs is eggs, the bridegroom and she had a miff. **1837** DICKENS *Pickwick* ch. 43 (Romance) And the Bishop says 'Sure as eggs is eggs, This here's the bold Turpin?' **1857** HUGHES *T. Brown* II. vi I shall come out bottom of the form as sure as eggs is eggs!

Sure (firm) as fate, As.   (F 81)

1600 JONSON *Cynthia's Revels* IV. iii. 223 As sure as fate, 't is so. **1604** MARSTON *Malcontent* II. v. (firm as fate). **1701** FARQUHAR *Sir H. Wildair* V. v 'Her Ghost! Ha, ha, ha. . . .'—'As sure as fate, it walks in my House.' **1826** T. H. LISTER *Granby* i. 35.

Sure as God's in Gloucestershire, As.
                                                    (G 174)

1655 FULLER *Ch. Hist.* VI. ii. (1868) II. 212 Of all counties . . . Gloucestershire was most pestered with monks. . . . Hence the . . . proverb . . . **1902–4** LEAN I. 86 *i.e.* the relic of Christ's blood preserved at Hailes Abbey.

Sure as if it had been sealed with butter, As.   (B 769)

1546 HEYWOOD II. vii. K1ᵛ Euery promyse that thou therin doest vtter, Is as sure as it were sealed with butter. **1577** *Art of Angling* A4 Your warrant is as good, as an obligation sealed with butter. **1587** J. BRIDGES *Def. of Gvt. of C. of E.* 1288. **1616** WITHALS 583 A warrant sealed with butter.

Sure as you live, As.   (L 374)

1590–1 SHAKES. *2 Hen. VI* III. ii. 153 As surely as my soul intends to live With that dread King. **1594** *Id. T.G.V.* IV. iv. 18 Sure as I live, he had suffer'd for't. [**1596**] **1605** *Stukeley* l. 2042 Sure as I live. **1710–11** 24 Feb. SWIFT *Jour. to Stella* Letter 16 This letter certainly goes this evening, sure as you're alive, young women.

Sure card, A.   (C 74)

c. **1537** *Thersites* E1 Nowe thys is a sure carde, nowe I may well saye. **1579** LYLY *Euph.* i. 324 A cleere conscience is a sure carde, truth hath the prerogatiue to speak with plainnes. *c.* **1592** SHAKES. *T.And.* V. i. 100 As sure a card as ever won the set. **1616** DRAXE no. 2083 He hath a sure c d. **1838–9** DICKENS *N. Nickleby* ch. 24.

Sure of your watch on deck, You are always | but never sure of your watch below.

1903 W. C. RUSSELL *Overdue* ch. 2 It's a true saying that you're always sure of your watch on deck, but never sure of your watch below.

Sure: It is good to be | toll it again, quoth the miller.   (M 958)

c. **1386** CHAUCER *Cant. T.* Prol. l. 562 Wel koude he [the Miller] stelen corn and tollen thries. *c.* **1500** MEDWALL *Nature* F2ᵛ It ys good to be sure euer more. **1678** RAY 91. **1721** KELLY 189 It is good to be sure, quoth the Miller, when he moultered[1] twice. [¹ took the toll.]

Sure, *see* Better be s. than sorry; Coat is on one's back, (As s. as the); Death is s. to all; Make all s.; Rides s. that never fell; Sits not s.; Slow and s.

Surety for another, He that will be a | shall pay.   (S 1009)

[PROV. xi. 15: He that hateth suretiship is sure.] **1539** TAVERNER 20ᵛ Be suretie for an other and harme is at hande. **1592** DELAMOTHE 45. **1651** HERBERT no. 1091. **1721** KELLY 272 *Oft times the Cautioner[1] pays the Debt.* Not only a Caution against Suretiship, but often a Return to them who say they'll be Caution (that is, Bail) that we will come to some ill Accident. [¹ surety, bail.]

Surety wants a surety, Your. (S 1010)

1678 RAY *Adag. Hebr.* 404 . . . This Proverb is used of an infirm argument that is not sufficient to prove what it is alleged for. **1911** A. COHEN *Anct. Jew. Prov.* 114 Thy guarantee needs a guarantee. Applied to an unreliable authority.

Surety, *see also* Certainty (s.) and leans to chance.

Surfeits of too much honesty, A man never.   (M 288)

1616 WITHALS 570. **1639** CLARKE 213 Too much honesty did never man harm. **1670** RAY 13. **1732** FULLER no. 3597. No Man ever surfeited on too much Honesty.

Surgeon must have an eagle's eye, a lion's heart, and a lady's hand, A good.
(S 1013)

1585 ROBSON *Choice Change* M2ᵛ Three things very requisite in a Chirurgion. A haukes eye. A lions heart. A ladies hand. **1589** L. WRIGHT *Display of Duty* 37 In a good chirurgian, a Hawkes eye: a lyons heart: and a ladies hand. **1592** GREENE 2 *Cony-Catching* (Harrison 34) (an Eagles eie, a Lady hand, and a Lions heart). **1616** T. ADAMS *The Soldier's Honour* 21 Wee say of the Chirurgian, that he should haue a Ladies hand, and a Lyons heart: but the Christian Souldier should haue a Ladies heart, and a Lyons hand. **1670** RAY 36. **1837** T. HOOK *Jack Brag* ch. 9 A surgeon ought to have an eagle's eye, a lion's heart, and a lady's hand.

Surgeon, *see also* Pitiful s. spoils sore.

Surnames, *see* 'Ford' (In), in 'ham' . . . most English s. run.

Surprised with the first frost, He that is | feels it all the winter after.   (F 771)

1640 HERBERT no. 992.

Surprised, *see also* Man assaulted is half taken.

Suspects, *see* Fault (guilty) s. everybody, (Who is in).

Suspicion has double eyes.   (S 1017)

1597 SHAKES. *1 Hen. IV* V. ii. 8 Suspicion all our lives shall be stuck full of eyes. **1605** DANIEL *Philotas* Gros. iii. 145 Suspition full of eyes, and full of eares. *c.* **1680** in *Roxb. Ballads* B.S. VI. 317 It is a proverb of old 'Suspicion hath double eyes'.

Suspicion, *see also* Caesar's wife must be above s.; Poverty (He that is in) is in s.; Virtue of a coward is s.; Weed amongst corn nor s. in friendship, (Neither).

Sussex moon.

1928 *Times* 7 Dec. 19/6 Even the old horn lantern, the 'Sussex moon' of the country jape, blurred the eyes to its mild splendours.

Sussex weeds.

1869 HAZLITT 348 Sussex weeds. *i.e.* Oaks, which are particularly common in that county.

Sutton for good mutton, Cheam for juicy beef, Croydon for a pretty girl, and Mitcham for a thief.

1852 *N. & Q.* 1st Ser. v. 374.

Sutton for mutton, Carshalton for beeves; Epsom for whores, and Ewell for thieves.

1787 GROSE (*Surrey*) 91 . . . The downs near Sutton . . . produce delicate small sheep, and the rich meadows about Cashalton are remarkable for fattening oxen. Epsom . . . mineral waters . . . were . . . resorted to . . . particularly by ladies of easy virtue. Ewel is a poor village, about a mile from Epsom.

Sutton[1] for mutton, Kirby[2] for beef, South Darne[3] for gingerbread, Dartford for a thief.

1902–4 LEAN I. 114. [¹ Sutton at Hone. ² Horton Kirby. ³ S. Darenth (all on the river Darenth, in Kent).]

Sutton for mutton, Tamworth for beef, Walsall for bandy legs, and Brummagem[1] for a thief.

a. **1871** Higson's *MSS. Coll.* No. 175 in HAZLITT 361. [¹ Birmingham.]

Sutton Wall and Kentchester Hill, are able to buy London were it to sell.
(S 1021)

1659 HOWELL *Eng. Prov.* 20b . . . Two fruitful places in Herefordshire. **1678** RAY 311.

Sutton, *see also* Silly S.; York excels foul S.

Swain, He is no good | that lets[1] his journey for the rain. (For a morning. rain, leave not your journey.)

(R 10. S 1022)

a. **1530** *R. Hill's Commonpl. Bk.* E.E.T.S. 131 He is no good swayn, þat lettith his jorney for þe rayn. *a.* **1628** CARMICHAELL no. 810 (a feible swaine). **1640** HERBERT no. 976 For a morning raine leave not your journey. [[1] gives up.]

Swallow a tavern token, To.   (T 79)

[**1598**] **1601** JONSON *Ev. Man in Humour* i. iii. 48 Drunk sir? . . . perhaps he swallow'd a tauerne token. **1604** *Meeting of Gallants* (Dekker's *Plague Pamphlets* ed. Wilson 122) This strange Wine-sucker . . . had swallowed downe many Tauerne-tokens. **1655** J. COTGRAVE *Wit's Interpreter* 2E3ᵛ.

Swallow an ox, and be choked with the tail, To.   (O 110)

1659 HOWELL *Eng. Prov.* 13a. **1670** RAY 194. **1732** FULLER no. 5238.

Swallow (gape for) gudgeons, To.

(G 473)

1577 HOLINSHED *Chron. Ireland* (1587) 916 Doo you thinke Iames was so mad, as to gape for gogions? **1579** LYLY *Euph.* i. 238 You haue made both mee and Philautus to swallow a Gudgen. **1583** MELBANCKE E3 Gapers for gudgeons are soone choked. **1602** WITHALS 36 To gape Gogeon-like, which is as wide as his chappes will let him. **1605** CHAPMAN *All Fools* III. i. 95 And do you think he'll swallow down the gudgeon? **1607** T.W. *Optic Glass of Humours* ¶7ᵛ Thou vsest not to gape after gougins. **1613** T. ADAMS *The White Devil* (1862 ed. ii. 224) He could swallow a gudgeon, though he kecks at a fly. **1659** HOWELL *Fr. Prov.* 19 He is cousened, or he hath swallowed a gudgeon. **1664** BUTLER *Hudibras* II. iii. 923 (1854) i. 197 To swallow gudgeons ere they're catch'd, And count their chickens ere they're hatch'd. **1666** TORRIANO *Prov. Phr.* 93 To make one believe any thing, to make one to swallow gudgeons. **1773** VIEYRA s.v. Affronta To bear an affront; commonly to swallow a gudgeon.

Swallow, One | does not make a summer.

(S 1025)

[Gk. Μία χελιδὼν ἔαρ οὐ ποιεῖ. ERASM. *Ad. Una hirundo non facit ver.* One swallow does not make spring.] **1539** TAVERNER 25 It is not one swalowe that bryngeth in somer. It is not one good qualitie that meketh a man good. **1546** HEYWOOD II. v. H3. **1593** J. ELIOT *Ortho-Epia Gallica* ed. J. Lindsay 60 (spring). **1636** CAMDEN 303. **1642** D. ROGERS *Matr. Hon.* 28 One swallow makes no summer, neither ought it to prescribe a precedent unto others. **1690** D'URFEY *Collin's W.* iii One Swallow makes ('tis true) no Summer, Yet one Tongue may create a Rumour.

Swallow (noun), *see also* Robin and the wren; Snail slides up tower though s. mounts it sooner; Swift as a s.

Swallowed a fly, He has.

1721 KELLY 175 . . . Spoken of Sots who are always drunk, as if there was a Fly in their Throat which they endeavoured to wash down.

Swallowed a spider, He has.   (S 749)

1659 HOWELL *Eng. Prov.* 6a. viz. He hath plaid the bankrupt. **1678** RAY *Prov.* 89 *A Bankrupt.*

Swallowed the devil, If you have | you may swallow his horns.

1853 TRENCH vi. 151.

Swallow(s, ed) (verb), *see also* Eaten (S.) a stake; Say true (You), will you s. my knife.

Swan sings when death comes, The.

(S 1028)

[CICERO *Tusc. Disp.* l. 30. 73 (*Commemorat ut*) *cygni . . . providentes quid in morte boni sit, cum cantu et voluptate moriantur.* The swan, foreseeing how much good there is in death, dies with song and rejoicing.] *c.* **1382** CHAUCER *Parl. Foules* l. 342 The jalous swan, ayens his deth that syngeth. *c.* **1430** LYDGATE *Against Self-love* in *Minor Poems* Percy Soc. 157 The yelwe swan famous and aggreable, Ageyn his dethe melodyously syngyng. **1594** SHAKES. *Lucrece* l. 1611 And now this pale swan in her watery nest Begins the sad dirge of her certain ending. **1596** *Id.* *K.J.* V. vii. 21 I am the cygnet to this pale faint swan, Who chants a doleful hymn to his own death. **1604** *Id. O.* V. ii. 250 I will play the swan, And die in music. **1650** SIR T. BROWNE *Pseud. Ep.* III. xxvii (1894) 357 From great antiquity . . . the musical note of swans hath been commended, and that they sing most sweetly before their death. **1732** FULLER no. 4779.

Swan(s), *see also* Black s.; Geese are s. (All).

Swap horses when crossing a stream, Don't.

1864 ABRAHAM LINCOLN in E. R. JONES *Lincoln.* &c. (1876) 59 I am reminded . . . of a story of an old Dutch farmer, who remarked . . . 'that it was not best to swap horses when crossing a stream'. **1889** W. F. BUTLER *Gordon* 17 Clothing and equipment were then undergoing a vigorous process of 'swopping' at the moment the animals were in the mid-stream of the siege of Sebastopol.

Swarm of bees all in a churm (Humble bee in a churn), Like a.

1863 J. R. WISE *New Forest* ch. 16 'Charm', or rather 'churm', signifying . . . noise or disturbance. . . . We meet it . . . in the common Forest proverb, 'Like a swarm of bees all in a churm'. **1894** NORTHALL *Folk-phrases* 19 Like a humble bee in a churn. Spoken of one whose voice is indistinct.

Swarm of bees in May, A | is worth a load of hay, but a swarm in July is not worth a fly.   (S 1029)

1617 G. MARKHAM *Country Housew. Gard.* x. 100 A Mayes swarme is worth a Mares Foale. **1655**

HARTLIB *Reformed Commonwealth of Bees* 26 It being a Proverb, that a Swarm of Bees in May is worth a Cow and a Bottle of Hay, whereas a Swarm in July is not worth a Fly. **1670** RAY 41. **1879** R. JEFFERIES *Wild Life South. Co.* ch. 7 'A swarm in May is worth a load of hay; a swarm in June is worth a silver spoon; but a swarm in July is not worth a fly'—for it is then too late ... to store up honey before the flowers begin to fade.

Swarston Bridge, *see* Driving his hogs over S. B.

Swear by no beggars (bugs), To. (B 248)

1573 GASCOIGNE *Dan B. of Bath* i. 127 The messenger sware by no bugges I trowe. **1579** GOSSON *Sch. Abuse* 33 Caligula ... swore by no bugs, that he would make him a consul. **1579** A. HALL *Quarrel betw. Hall & Mallorie* in *Misc. Antiq. Ang.* 43 (swearing by no beggers). **1581** GUAZZO ii. 13. **1617** MORYSON *Itinerary* I. II. iii. i. 343 Be content with this answere, otherwise (I sweare by no beggars) I will praise you to your face.

Swear dagger out of sheath, He will.
(D 3)
1678 RAY 271.

Swear like a carter (abbot, cutpurse, falconer, gentleman, tinker), To. (A 4)

1599 TASSO *Marriage & Wiving* E4 She will ... sweare like a Cutpursse. **1607** H. ESTIENNE *World of Wonders* tr. R. C. 70 He sweareth like a carter (gentleman). **1611** COTGRAVE s.v. Chartier He sweares like a Carter; (we say, like a Tinker). **1612** WEBSTER *White Devil* V. I. Merm. 88 A new up-start; one that swears like a falconer. **1623** T.G. *Friar's Chron.* F1ᵛ It was a Prouerbe, a common Prouerbe in those times, Hee sweareth like an Abbott. **1706** STEVENS s.v. Carretero (carter). *c.* **1645** MS. Proverbs in *N. & Q.* 154. 27.

Swear like a lord, To.

1531 ELYOT *Gov.* Croft i. 275 They wyll say he that swereth depe, swereth like a lorde. **1738** SWIFT *Polite Conv.* Introd. E.L. 247 A Footman can swear; but he cannot swear like a Lord. He can swear as often: But, can he swear with equal Delicacy, Propriety, and Judgment? No, certainly.

Swear like a trooper, To.

1821 J. GALT *Annals of Parish* ch. 8 He swore like a trooper, that he would get an act of parliament to put down the nuisance. **1824** MOIR *Mansie W.* ch. 14 He swore like a trooper that ... he would run in spite of their teeth. **1896** M. A. S. HUME *Courtships of Q. Eliz.* 323 Calling Cecil as a witness to her words, she renewed her vows, swearing like a trooper.

Swear the devil out of hell, He will.
(D 283)
1678 RAY 271.

Swear (Look) through an inch board, He will.
(I 61)
c. **1623** *Welsh Ambass.* l. 349 Theres my Cozen a scrivener (that can looke through an inch bourd his eyes are so sharpe). **1666** TORRIANO *Prov. Phr.* 195 As the English say of a Pillory, To make one to look thorough an inch Board. **1678** RAY 271. **1728** EARL OF AILESBURY *Mem.* (1890) 372 Then he went through thick and thin, according to an old English phrase, swore through a two-inch board.

Swear till one is black in the face, To.

1778 F. BURNEY *Evelina* Lett. 47 However, if you swear till you're black in the face, I shan't believe you. **1750** THACKERAY *Pendennis* ch. 55 I'd swear, till I was black in the face, he was innocent, rather than give that good soul pain.

Swear Walsingham, To. (W 21)

[= to swear by our Lady of Walsingham, in Norfolk, there being a noted shrine of the Virgin at that place.] **1599** PORTER *Angry Wom. Abingd.* ll. 2304–5 I warrant, when he was in, he swore Walsingham, and chafte terrible for the time.

Swear, He that will | will lie. (S 1030)

1530 R. WHITFORD *A werke for housholders* D1ᵛ Euery lyer is commonly a swerer, for else the lye shulde not be coloured dubbed & painted sufficiently to seme treue. **1601** A. DENT *Plain Man's Pathway* 168 Swearing and lying, be of very neare kindred. **1606** *Murder committed by Annis Dell* B3 Who knowes not lying and swearing are partners. **1616** DRAXE no. 2094 He that sweareth oft, foresweareth. **1630** J. TAYLOR (Water-P.) *Wks.* 189.

Swear, If you | you'll catch no fish. (F 315)

1607 HEYWOOD *Fair Maid of Exchange* in *Wks.* (1874) II. 69 What are you cursing too? then we catch no fish. *a.* **1625** J. FLETCHER *Mons. Thomas* I. iii. No swearing; He'll catch no fish else. **1630** J. TAYLOR (Water-P.) *Wks.* I. 117/2 The Prouerbe sayes, If you sweare you shall catch no fish. **1790** WOLCOT (P. Pindar) *Benev. Ep. to Sylv. Urb.* Besides, a proverb, suited to my wish, Declares that swearing never catcheth fish.

Swear, *see also* Saint s.

Swearing came in at the head, and is going out at the heels (tail).

1812 J. BRADY *Clavis Calend.* I. 339 ... in allusion to its having once been the vice of the great, though ... it had descended to the most low and vulgar of the people.

Sweat like a bull, To. (B 713)

1551 R. CROWLEY *Philargyrie* C1 He gan swete As it had bene a bull. **1566** ERASM. *Diversoria* tr. E. H[ake], ed. H. de Vocht 11. **1666** TORRIANO *Prov. Phr.* s.v. Toro 218 To be as strong as a Bull, viz. main strong; the English useth the Phrase, To Sweat like a Bull.

Sweat of other men's brows, To live by the. (S 1032)

1559 T. BECON *Displ. of Popish Mass* P.S. *Prayers* 261 Be nourished of the sweat of other men's brows. **1576** PETTIE ii. 138 You . . . liue . . . by the sweet of other men's sweat. *c.* **1577** J. NORTHBROOKE *Treatise agst. Dicing* 57 Liuing vpon the sweat of other mens trauels. **1616** DRAXE no. 1050 (liueth on).

Sweat, *see also* Eat till you s.; Ground s. cures all disorders; Quinine made of s. of ship carpenters; Sweet without s. (No).

Sweep before his own door, If each would | we should have a clean city (street). (D 561)

1629 T. ADAMS *Serm.* (1861–2) II. 307 When we would have the street cleansed, let every man sweep his own door, and it is quickly done. **1650** FULLER *Pisgah Sight* III. v. 327 How soon are those streets made clean, where every one sweeps against his own door? **1666** TORRIANO *It. Prov.* 41 no. 19 If every one will sweep his own house, the City will be clean. **1732** FULLER no. 4296 Sweep before your own Door. **1856** ABP. WHATELY *Annot. Bacon's Ess.* (1876) 287. **1930** *Times* 25 Mar. 10/5 It appears to be hard to draw a clear distinction between deciding a question of right and wrong for one's self and deciding it for others. . . .—'If every man would sweep his own doorstep the city would soon be clean.'

Sweeps, swept, *see* Tall maid is stooping (While) little one has s.

Sweet appears sour when we pay. (S 1037)

1659 HOWELL *Brit. Prov.* 21.

Sweet as a nut. (N 358)

c. **1599** *Club Law* I. iv. 13. **1685** N. THOMPSON *A Collection of 86 Loyal Poems* 23. **1855** MRS. GASKELL *North and South* ch. 16.

Sweet as honey. (H 544)

[PS. cxix. 103 Thy words . . . sweeter than honey to my mouth.] *c.* **1475** *Mankind* l. 218 Swetere then hony. **1506** PYNSON *Kal. of Shepherds* (1892) 75 Swete as hony in oure mouth. **1541** *Schoolh. of Women* D1 Dulce as honye. [*c.* 1553] **1566–7** UDALL *Ralph Roister D.* 'Song' at end of play. **1639** CLARKE 285.

Sweet beauty with sour beggary. (B 176)

1546 HEYWOOD I. xiii. F1ᵛ Sweete beautee with soure beggery, naye I am gon, To the welthy wythred wydow.

Sweet in the bed, and sweir up in the morning, was never a good housewife.

1721 KELLY 290 . . . A jocose Reproof to young Maids, when they lye long A-bed.

Sweet in the mouth is oft sour (bitter) in the maw (stomach), What is. (M 1265)

[REV. x. 9–10.] **1592** DELAMOTHE 5 What is sweet in the mouth, is oft bitter at the hart.

1594 SHAKES. *Lucrece* l. 699 His taste delicious, in digestion souring. *c.* **1595** *Id. Rich. II* I. iii. 236 Things sweet to taste proue in digestion sour. **1597** *Politeuphuia* 158 What is sweet in the mouth, is better in the stomack. *a.* **1628** CARMICHAELL no. 1404 Sueit in the mouth, sowre in the bellie.

Sweet in the on taking, but sour in the off putting.

1721 KELLY 297 . . . Spoken of Debt for the most part, but apply'd to Sin, sensual Pleasure, and the like.

Sweet is the nut, but bitter (hard) is the shell. (N 360)

1566 P. BEVERLEY *Ariodanto and Genevra* A2ᵛ The harde shell shrowdeth the sweet curnell. **1579** LYLY *Euph.* i. 202 The sweete kernell lyeth in the hard shell. **1599** SHAKES. *A.Y.* III. ii. 99 Sweetest nut hath sourest rind, Such a nut is Rosalinde. **1648** J. ACONTIUS *Satan's Stratagems* a2 Let the goodness of the Kernel, excuse the hardness of the Shell.

Sweet meat will have sour sauce. (M 839)

c. **1400** *Beryn* E.E.T.S. 29 ffor 'aftir swete, the soure comith, ful offt, in many a plase'. **1546** HEYWOOD I. viii. C1 And allthough it were sweete for a weeke or twayne, Sweete meate will haue sowre sawce, I see now playne. **1594–5** SHAKES. *R.J.* II. iv. 77 Thy wit is a very bitter sweeting; it is a most sharp sauce.—And is it not well served to a sweet goose? **1607** HIERON *Wks.* (1614) I. 20 The sweet meats of wickedness will have the sowre sauce of wretchedness and misery.

Sweet nut if you were well cracked, You are a. (N 362)

1583 MELBANCKE *Philotimus* 160 You are a swete nut, the Deuill cracke you. **1595** *Locrine* III. iii. 60. **1721** KELLY 389 . . . Ironically spoken to bad Boys.

Sweet sauce begins to wax sour. (S 97)

1546 HEYWOOD II. i. F3ᵛ When she sawe sweete sauce begyn to waxe sowre, She waxt as sowre as he.

Sweet things are bad for the teeth.

1607 DEKKER *Whore Bab.* 12 Sweet meates that rotte the eater. **1612** WEBSTER *White Devil* III. ii. 84 Sweete meates which rot the eater. **1738** SWIFT *Dial.* II. E.L. 306 Miss, I would have a bigger glass [of jelly]. . . .—But you know, sweet things are bad for the teeth.

Sweet tooth, To have a. (T 420)

1580 LYLY *Euph. & his Eng.* ii. 83 I am glad that my *Adonis* hath a sweete tooth in his head. **1590** LODGE *Rosalynde* Hunt. Cl. 136 I haue a longing tooth . . . that makes me crie. **1594** SHAKES. *T.G.V.* III. i. 319 'Item, She hath a sweet mouth.' **1629** T. ADAMS *Serm.* (1861–2) II. 354 Thou hast . . . a sweet tooth in thy head, a liquorish appetite to delicate meats and intoxicating wines. **1876**

MRS. BANKS *Manch. Man* ch. 17 'I know you've a sweet tooth, . . . but . . . nothing half so good as Mrs. Clowes's toffy takes you there'.

Sweet with the sour, Take the. (s 1038)

1509 BARCLAY *Ship of Fools* i. 39 Take ye in good worth the swetnes with the Sour. **1546** HEYWOOD II. iv. G3ᵛ Content ye (quoth she) take the sweete with the sowre. **1582** *Love & Fortune* l. 132. **1706** STEVENS s.v. Maduro.

Sweet without (some) sweat, No.
                                        (s 1036)

1576 PETTIE ii. 138 You . . . live . . . by the sweet of other men's sweat. **1639** CLARKE 87. **1667** FLAVEL *Saint Indeed* (1754) 129 He that will not have the sweat, must not expect the sweet of religion. **1670** RAY 146 No sweet without some sweat. *Nul pain sans peine, Gall.*

Sweet(er), *see also* Beetle flies over many a s. flower; Deeper the s.; Deserves not the s. that will not taste the sour; Good in the maw that is s. in mouth; Lay the s. side of your tongue to it; Life is s.; Lost his taste (To him that has) s. is sour; Love is s. in beginning; Mutton is s.; Pickle, (To be in a sad (s.)); Revenge is s.; Short and s.; White has its black and s. its sour.

Sweet-heart and bag-pudding. (s 1039)

1585 A. MUNDAY *Two It. Gent.* l. 81 Sweet hart and bag pudding goe you so swiftly? [c. **1597**] **1609** JONSON *Case Is Altered* IV. vii. 43 Sweet hart, sweet hart?—And bag pudding, ha, ha, ha? **1659** HOWELL *Eng. Prov.* 6a. **1670** RAY 214.

'Sweet-heart' and 'Honey-bird' keeps no house. (s 1040)

1678 RAY 57.

Sweetness, *see* Saying Honey, Honey (It is not with) s. will come.

Sweir, *see* Work for nought makes folk s.

Swell like a toad, To. (T 362)

1541 *Schoolh. of Wom.* A2 They . . . swell as a tode, for feruent yre. **1546** HEYWOOD I. xi. E1 And streight as she sawe me, she swelde lyke a tode. **1579** J. CALVIN *Thirteen Sermons* D7ᵛ The Iewes . . . were swolne as Todes with a diuelish kinde of pride. **1599** TASSO *Marriage & Wiving* E4 She will swell like a toad. **1639** CLARKE 235.

Swell(s), *see also* Nose s., (To make); Stream stopped s. the higher.

Swift as a swallow, As. (s 1023)

1551 T. WILSON *Rule of Reason* R8ᵛ We vse to saye, he is as swifte as a swallowe. **1592** SHAKES. *T.And.* IV. ii. 173 Now to the Goths, as swift as swallow flies. **1672** WALKER 16, no. 44.

Swift as an arrow, As. (A 322)

1551 T. WILSON *Rule of Reason* R8ᵛ We vse to saye he is as swifte as a swallowe, he flieth like an arrowe out of a bowe. **1563** FULKE *Meteors* 111, 68 The matter . . . beateth the cloud before it and so it carried as an arrow out of a bow. **1577** *Art of Angling* D4ᵛ. **1581** SENECA *Thebais* tr. T. Newton T.T. i. 122 She runnes apace . . . No Arrow swifter out of Bow. **1591** ARIOSTO *Orl. Fur.* Harington IX. 72 Orlando with such speed doth him pursue, As doth an arrow from a bow of Yue. **1595** SHAKES. *M.N.D.* III. ii. 101 Swifter than arrow. **1672** WALKER 16, no. 44 As swift as a swallow; as the wind; as an arrow out of a bow.

Swift (quick) as thought, As. (T 240)

a. **1225** *Ancrene R.* l. 94 Ase swifte ase is nu monnes þouht. **1468** *Coventry Mys.* 298 (Sh. S.) I am as whyt [quick] as thought. *c.* **1590** [GREENE?] *John of Bordeaux* l. 1153 As swift as thought can fli. **1594** NASHE *Terrors of Night* i. 349 As quicke as thought. **1594–5** SHAKES. *Luc.* l. 1216 For swift-wing'd duty with thought's feathers flies. **1599** *Id. A.Y.* IV. i. 125 A woman's thought runs before her actions.—So do all thoughts; they are wing'd. **1600–1** *Id. H. I.* v. 29 I, with wings as swift As meditation or the thoughts of love, May sweep to my revenge. **1612** DEKKER *If It Be Not Good* II. i. 210 Swift as mans thought.

Swift, *see also* Race is not to s.

Swim like a cork, To.

1869 C. READE *Foul Play* ch. 10 Throw that madman into the sea; then we can pick him up. He swims like a cork.

Swim like a fish (duck), To. (F 328)

1552 HULOET 2H1ᵛ Swymme lyke a ducke. Tetrinno. **1591** ARIOSTO *Orl. Fur.* Harington XXIX. 47 Orlando nakt and light, swam like a fish. **1611–12** SHAKES. *Temp.* II. ii. 120 I can swim like a duck. **1620** SHELTON *Quix.* II. XXX. iii. 20 (goose). **1622** J. FLETCHER *Sea-Voyage* I. i I can swim like a fish. **1624** HEYWOOD *Captives* l. 623 (ducks). **1852** SMEDLEY *Lewis Arundel* ch. 56 He follows the calling of a gondolier, . . . and swim like a fish. **1866** BLACKMORE *Cradock N.* ch. 54 What a lovely deep pool! I can swim like a duck.

Swim like a stone, To. (s 893)

1666 TORRIANO *Prov. Phr.* 237 To swim like a Coulter, viz. not to swim in the least; spoken Ironically; the English say, To swim no more than a stone. **1866** BLACKMORE *Cradock N.* ch. 54 I can swim like a duck; and you like a stone, I suppose.

Swim, He must needs | that is held up by the chin. (C 349)

a. **1530** R. *Hill's Commonpl. Bk.* E.E.T.S. 129 He mai lightli swim, that is hold up by þe chin. **1530** PALSGRAVE 451a (that is borne up by the chynne). **1563** NEWBERY *Dives Pragmaticus* B3ᵛ I wyll hould you vp, euen by the chinne. **1580** LYLY *Euph. & his Eng.* ii. 6 If your Lordship with your lyttle finger doe but holde me vp by

the chinne, I shall swimme.   **1614** BEAUM. & FL.
Wit at S.W. I. i Well he may make a padler i'
th' world, . . . but never a brave swimmer, Borne
up by th' chin.   **1655** FULLER *Ch. Hist.* IV. i.
(1868) I. 531 Whose safety, . . . is not so much
to be ascribed to his own strength in swimming,
as to such as held him up by the chin.   **1721**
KELLY 129 He may well swim that's held up
by the Chin. Spoken of the thriving Condition
of those, who have some to support, assist, and
raise them.

Swim without bladders (a cork), He can.   (B 443)

[HOR. *Sat.* I. iv. 120 Nabis sine cortice.]   **1535**
G. JOYE *Apol. to Tyndale* Arber 23 I wolde the
scripture were so . . . translated that it neded
nether note . . . nor scholia, so that the reder
might once swimme without a corke.   **1609**
HARWARD To the Reader Yf any be not so good
a linguist that he cann swimme without a cork
then he may yf he please vse the helpe of the
later volume.   **1639** *Publ. Ovid De Tristibus* tr.
Z. Catlin A3ᵛ To them that can swim without
bladders, this translation will . . . bring them in
delight and profit both.   **1649** HOWELL *Pre-em.
Parl.* 17 My whole life (since I was left to my
self to swim, as they say without bladders).
1706 STEVENS S.V. Corcho To swim without
Corks.   **1732** FULLER no. 1821.

Swim, *see also* Anchor of a ship . . . never learns
to s.; Apples s.! (See how we); Duck s.; Fish
must s. thrice; Knows not to s. goes to bottom;
Sink or s.; Taught you to s. (I) and now you'd
drown me. *See also* Swims.

Swimmers, *see also* Good s. at length drowned.

Swims in sin shall sink in sorrow, Who.

1563 GOOGE *Eclogs* viii. Arb. 67 The wretched.
man . . . Whom Deth hymself flyngs ouer bord,
amyd the Seas of syn, The place wher late, he
swetly swam, now lyes he drowned in.   **1579** LYLY
Euph. i. 312 They that couet to swimme in vice,
shall sinke in vanitie.   **1766** *Goody Two-Shoes*
(ed. 3) v. i. A Moral Lesson. He that swims in
sin will sink in sorrow.

Swine (Pig), He is like a | he'll never do good while he lives.   (M 1005)

1564 BULLEIN *Dial. agst Fever* (1888) 9 Covetous
usurers, which be like fat unclean swine, which
do never good until they come to the dish.   **1599**
MINSHEU *Span. Gram.* 82 A dead hog tasteth
best when he is eaten.   *a.* **1600** *Gernutus* in Percy
Reliques I. ii. (1857) 106 His life was like a
barrow hogge, that liveth many a day, Yet never
once doth any good, until men will him slay.
1621 W. MASON *Handf. Essaies* 47 Of Couetousnes . . . Vntil this earthworme come vnto the
earth, hee minds nothing but earthly things, like
a Swine he neuer doth good till his death.   **1629**
T. ADAMS *Serm.* (1861–2) I. 482 The covetous
man is like a two-legged hog: while he lives he is
ever rooting in the earth, and never doth good
till he is dead.   **1678** RAY 90 (untill he come to the
knife).   **1733** FRANKLIN April A rich rogue is
like a fat hog, who never does good till as dead
as a log.

Swine over fat, is the cause of his own bane, A.   (S 1043)

c. **1549** HEYWOOD II. vii. I4.   **1614** CAMDEN 303.
a. **1628** CARMICHAELL no. 77 (procures his awin
death).   **1639** CLARKE 200 (too fat).

Swine, women, and bees cannot be turned.   (S 1044)

1678 RAY 212.   **1732** FULLER no. 4299.

Swine's gone through it, The.

1721 KELLY 330 . . . Spoken when an intended
Marriage is gone back, out of a superstitious
Conceit, that if a Swine come between a Man
and his Mistress, they will never be married.
1809 SCOTT *Let.* 23 Mar. in LOCKHART *Life*
ch. 18 He suffered the pigs to run through
the business, when he might in some measure
have prevented them.   **1823** GALT *Entail* ch. 66
'If it's within the compass o' a possibility, get
the swine driven through't, or it may work . . .
as his father's moonlight marriage did.'

Swine, *see also* Dogs will redd s.; Draff is good
enough for s.; Pearl before s., (Cast); Sheep, s.,
and bees, (He that has) . . . may thrive; Singest
like a bird called a s.

Swing of the pendulum.

a. **1694** TILLOTSON in DOWDEN *Puritan & Anglican*
335 Nothing is more natural than for extremes
in religion to beget one another, like the vibra-
tions of the pendulum, which the more violently
you swing it one way, the farther it will return
the other.   **1851** HELPS *Compan. of Solit.* iii. 26
The pendulous folly of mankind oscillates as far
in this direction as it has come from that.   **1906**
Brit. Wkly. 15 Nov. Mr. Watts-Dunton says:
'George Eliot's fame has suffered from the
"swing of the pendulum" against that excessive
laudation of which during life she was made
the subject. . . . A reaction against her was
inevitable.'

Swing (*noun*), *see also* Youth will have its course
(s.).

Swing (*verb*), *see* Room to s. a cat.

Swinge, To bear (have) a great.   (S 1045)

1530 TYNDALE *Ans. to More* P.S. 12 Holy
church hath borne a great swinge.   **1551** CRAN-
MER *Ans. to Gardiner* 179 The papisticall
churche . . . now many yeres hath borne the
whole swynge.   **1562** J. WIGAND *De Neutralibus*
A8ᵛ Those most noysome myschiefes . . . grow,
and beare the swynge more and more.   *Ibid.*
B2ᵛ Those that beare the swinge of the church
and all the hole world.   **1579** J. CALVIN *Thirteen
Sermons* 64ᵛ We in the meane time will haue
our swinge in this worlde, wee will haue all our
desires.   **1580** *Second and Third Blasts* (*Eng.
Drama & Stage* ed. Hazlitt 135) On the holie-
daies . . . wee permit our youth to haue their
swinge.   **1697** DRYDEN *Georgics* Ded. ed. Saintsbury xiv. 2 He had, (according to our homely
Saying) his full swing at this Poem.

Swings, To lose on the | and make up on the roundabouts.

1910 P. R. CHALMERS *Green Days & Blue Days* 19 What's lost upon the roundabouts we pulls up on the swings! **1927** *Times* 24 Mar. 15/5 By screwing more money out of tax-payers he diminishes their savings, and the market for trustee securities loses on the swings what it gains on the roundabouts. **1929** *Times* 9 Aug. 11/6 The recent decision . . . to abolish all entrance fees into State galleries and museums will be appreciated. . . . What the Government may lose on the swings it will more than make up on the roundabouts. **1944** G. B. SHAW *Everybody's Polit. What's What* ch. 15 I lost on the swings what I gained on the roundabouts.

Swiss, see No money no S.

Switzers, see Law, logic, and the S. fight for anybody.

Swoop, At one fell.

1605 SHAKES. *M.* IV. iii. 216 Oh Hell-Kite! All? What, all my pretty chickens and their dam At one fell swoop? **1612** WEBSTER *White Devil* I. i. 6 If she [Fortune] give ought, she deales it in smal percels, That she may take away all at one swope. **1819** BYRON *D. Juan* I. 45 For there we have them all at one fell swoop.

Sword (knife) in a madman's (child's) hand, It is ill putting a.

(P 669. S 1050)

1539 TAVERNER 38 Commytte not a swearde to a chylde. Who so euer putteth a chylde, or a foolyshe and ignoraunt person . . . in authoritie and office, commytteth a swerde to a chylde. *Ibid.* 39 Truely, quoth the kynge [Henry VII], me thought that a naked swerde was commytted to the handes of a madde man. **1541** BULLINGER *Christian State of Matrimony* tr. Coverdale (1543) D5 As muche as to gyue a mad man a swerd, and a knyfe to a yong chyld. **1546** HEYWOOD II. viii. K2 It is (as olde men right well under-stande) Ill puttyng a nakt swoord in a mad mans hande. **1565** SACKVILLE & NORTON *Gorboduc* III. i. 63–64 Was this not wrong, yea yll aduised wrong, To giue so mad a man so sharpe a swoorde. **1583** MELBANCKE *Philot.* E1ᵛ A sword must not be giuen into a childes hand, least he hurte himselfe. **1590–1** SHAKES. *2 Hen. VI* III. i. 347 You put sharp weapons in a madman's hands. **1681** S. COLVIL *Whiggs Sup.* I. 69 A sword put in a wood[1] man's hand, Bred meikle

trouble to the land. **1721** KELLY 264 Never put a Sword in a Wood[1] Man's Hand. Lat. Ne puero gladium. [[1] mad.]

Sword of lead, To slay (cut one's throat) with a. (S 1054)

1533–4 N. UDALL *Flowers* 184 Plumbeo iugulare gladio, to cutte ones throte with a sworde of lead. **1559** COOPER s.v. Plumbeus To cut ones throte with a leaden swoorde: by translation to conuince with a weake argument. **1580** BARET P-527 Plumbeo iugulare gladio . . . A Prouerbe aptlie to be vsed to those which are ouercome with an easie argument.

Sword, One | keeps another in the sheath (scabbard). (S 1049)

1625 PURCHAS *Pilgrims* (1905–7) XIX. 254 Prudence . . . armeth herself against fears of war, forewarning and forearming men by the sword drawn to prevent the drawing of swords. **1640** HERBERT no. 723. **1836** F. CHAMIER *Ben Brace* ch. 1 The proverb 'One sword drawn keeps the other in the scabbard' was verified, the hostile preparations led to negociations, and the question was settled without fighting. **1853** TRENCH iii. 70 (scabbard).

Sword(s), see also Choosing a wife and . . . s. not trust to another; Draws his s. against his prince (Who); Gluttony kills more than s.; Horse, a wife, and s. may be shewed, not lent; Hunger is sharper than thorn (the s.); Leaden s. in ivory sheath; Learning in breast of bad man as s. in hand of madman; Love rules kingdom without s.; Old wise man's shadow better than buzzard's s.; Peace with s. in hand; Pen is mightier than s.; Rusty s. and empty purse plead performance; Scanderbeg's s.; Strikes with the s. (He that); Words cut more than s.

Sworn at Highgate, He has been.

c. **1720** J. SMEDLEY in *Somers Tracts* (1811) xiii. 825 Dined, and was sworn at Highgate. **1787** GROSE (*Middx.*) 209 He had been sworn at Highgate. A saying used to express that a person preferred strong beer to small; an allusion to an ancient custom . . . in this village, where the landlord of the Horns . . . used to swear . . . passengers, upon a pair of horns, stuck on a stick . . . They should not kiss the maid, when they could kiss the mistress; nor drink small beer when they could get strong.

Syne, see Soon as s., (As good).

T

Table robs more than a thief, The.

(T 3)

1640 HERBERT no. 636. **1732** FULLER no. 4782 The Table is a great Robber.

Table(s), *see also* Armour is light at˙ t.; Do as thy master commands thee and sit down at t.;

Feet under another's t.; Good man from home (When) . . . t. soon spread; Knock under t.; Poor man's t. soon spread; Round t. no dispute of place; Turn the t.; Wine makes all sorts at t.

Table-cloth, *see* Dish-clout my t.-c. (Not make).

Tabor, *see* Hunt for hare with t.

Tace is Latin for a candle. (T 6)

[*Tace* is the Latin for 'Be silent'. The saying is a hint to keep silent about something.] **1605** Camden *Rem.* 162 (*Impreses*) Edmund of Langley . . . asked . . . his sonnes . . . what was Latine for a fetter-locke: Whereat when the yong gentleman studied, the father said, well then you cannot tell me, I will tell you, Hic haec hoc taceatis, as advising them to be silent and quiet. **1676** SHADWELL *Virtuoso* I I took him up with my old repartee: Peace, said I, *Tace* is *Latin* for candle. **1697** *Dampier's Voy.* 356 Trust none of them for they are all Thieves, but Tace is Latin for a Candle. **1752** FIELDING *Amelia* I. x. '*Tace*, Madam', answered Murphy, 'is Latin for a candle; I commend your prudence'. **1827** SCOTT *Journ.* 23 Mar. So *Tace* is Latin for a candle. **1897** STEVENSON *St. Ives* ch. 10 'Ye must tell me nothing of that. I am in the law, you know, and *tace* is the Latin for a candle.'

Tackling, *see* Stand to one's t.

Tacks, *see* Brass t. (To come down to).

Taffeta, *see* Fret like gummed t.

Taffrail, *see* Whistle psalms to t.

Tag, rag, and bobtail (cut and long tail). (T 9, 10)

[A contemptuous term for people of all sorts.] **1553** *Vocacyon of John Bale* in *Harl. Miscell.* VI. 459 Than was all the rable of the shippe, hag tag, and rag, called to the reckeninge. **1575** LANEHAM *Letter* (1871) 25 Tag and rag, cut and long tail. **1577** R. STANYHURST in Holinshed *Descr. Ireland* (1587) 25b Tag and rag, cut and long taile. **1579** GOSSON *Sch. Abuse* Arb. 45 Euerye one which comes to buye their Iestes, shall haue an honest neighbour, tagge and ragge, cutte and longe tayle. **1599** SHAKES. *J.C.* I. ii. 257 If the tag-rag people did not clap him and hiss him. **1608** *Id. C.* III. i. 247 Will you hence, Before the tag return? **1639** CLARKE 236 Tag and rag, cut and long tayle every one that can eat an egge. **1645** *Just Defence John Bastwick* 15 That rabble rout tag ragge and bobtaile. **1670** *Mod. Account of Scotland* in *Harl. Miscell.* VI. 138 The young couple, being attended with tag rag and bobtail, gang to kirk. **1850** THACKERAY *Pendennis* ch. 7 'Fancy marrying a woman of a low rank of life, and having your house filled with her confounded tag-rag-and-bobtail relations!' **1883** LD. R. GOWER *My Remin.* I. xiii. 251 The mounted police charged the crowd . . . and our party had to fly before them along with tag, rag, and bob-tail.

Tail broader than thy wings, Make not thy. (T 14)

1597 BACON *Ess., Followers* Arb. 32 Costly followers are not to be liked, least while a man maketh his traine longer, hee make his wings shorter. **1659** HOWELL *Eng. Prov.* 18b . . . *viz.* Keep not too many attendants. **1710** S. PALMER 358.

Tail does often catch the fox, The. (T 15)

1573 SANFORD 106ᵛ The tayle condemneth many times the Foxe to die, for beeing ouerlong. **1611** DAVIES no. 70. **1616** DRAXE no. 790.

Tail follow the skin, Let the.

1721 KELLY 236 . . . Let the Appurtenance follow the main Bulk.

Tail will catch the chin-cough,[1] His. (T 12)

1678 RAY 82 His tail will catch the kincough. Spoken of one that sits on the ground. [¹ or kinkcough, whooping-cough.]

Tail(s), *see also* Ape is of his t. (As free as an); Bear wants t. and cannot be lion; Bees that have honey in mouth have sting in t.; Better be the head of a dog (lizard, pike, ass, yeomanry) than t. of a lion (sturgeon, horse, gentry); Come cut and long t.; Cow knows not what her t. is worth; Cow with iron t.; Cracked nuts with her t. (Goes as if she); Crow flies (When) her t. follows; Cut off a dog's t.; Devil wipes t.; Dog that has lost t. (Look like); Dogs wag t. in love to bread; Fox that having lost its t.; Head nor t. (It has neither); Heads I win; Holds a wet eel by the t.; Lambs (Like) you do nothing but . . . wag t.; Pig's t.; Pigs fly with t. forward; Ride an inch behind the t.; Salt on bird's t.; Sting in t.; Tag, rag, and bob-t.; Tod gets in wood; Wite your teeth if your t. be small; Woman has an eel by t. (Who has a); Words have long t. *See also* Cow's t., Foxtail, Pig's t.

Tailor-like.

c. **1560** *Tom Tyler* l. 310 Tom Tayler, how dost thou?—After the old sort, in mirth and jolly sport, Tayler-like I tell you. **1601** CORNWALLIS *Essayes* II (1610) Dd 6 What is his gaine but the marke of an ideot? What his knowledge, but tailor-like and light?

Tailor makes the man, The. (T 17)

[ERASM. *Ad.* (quoting Gk. Εἵματα ἀνήρ) *Vestis virum facit.* The garment makes the man.] **1602** SHAKES. *A.W.* II. v. 17 Pray you, sir, who's his tailor?—Sir!—O, I know him well. Ay sir; he, sir, 's a good workman, a very good tailor. **1605–6** *Id. K.L.* II. ii. 51 A tailor made thee.— Thou art a strange fellow; a tailor make a man? **1607** DEKKER *North. Hoe* II. i. 9 They say three Taylors go to the making vp of a man, but Ime sure I had foure Taylors and a halfe went to the making of me thus. **1609–10** SHAKES. *Cymb.* IV. ii. 81 Know'st me not by my clothes?—No, nor thy tailor, rascal, Who is thy grandfather: he made those clothes, Which, as it seems, made thee. **1625** JONSON *Staple of N.* I. ii. 108 Belieue it, Sir, That clothes doe much vpon the wit, . . . and thence comes 'your prouerbe; The Taylor makes the man. **1861** G. J. WHYTE-MELVILLE *Market Harbor.* ch. 24 Dress works wonders, and the tailor, . . . doubtless helps to make the man.

Tailor must cut three sleeves to every woman's gown, The. (T 18)

1552 LYNDSAY *Satyre of the Thrie Estatis* l. 4118 I leirit Tailgeours in euerie town, To schaip fyue quarters in ane gown. **1583** R. D. *The Mirror of Mirth* M3ᵛ Tailor . . . would cut out . . . three sleeues in a cloke, and sowe on but

twooe. **1662** *Common Cries of London* in
COLLIER *Roxb. Ballads* (1847) 209 The weaver
and the taylor, cozens they be sure, They cannot
work but they must steal, to keep their hands in
ure; For it is a common proverb thorowout the
town, The taylor he must cut three sleeves to
every womans gown.

Tailor that makes not a knot, The | loses a stitch.

1642 TORRIANO 90.   **1732** FULLER no. 4786.

Tailor, Like the | that sewed for nothing, and found thread himself.

1706 STEVENS s.v. Sastre.   **1732** FULLER no. 3237.
1885 J. ORMSBY *D.Quix.* IV. 391 The tailor of El
Campillo who stitched for nothing and found
thread.

Tailor's shreds are worth the cutting, A.

(T 20)

1626 BRETON *Soothing* A4ᵛ.   **1639** CLARKE 72.

Tailors and writers must mind the fashion.

(T 24)

1579 LYLY *Euph.* i. 182 In my mynde Printers
and Taylors are bound chiefely to pray for
Gentlemen, the one hath so many fantasies to
print, the other such diuers fashions to make,
that the pressing yron of the one is neuer out of
the fyre, nor the printing presse of the other any
tyme lyeth still.   **1732** FULLER no. 4301.

Tailors of Tooley Street, Three.

[*a.* **1827** CANNING.]   **1872** BREWER *Dict. Phr. &
F.* 875 *The three tailors of Tooley Street.*
Canning says that three tailors of Tooley Street,
Southwark, addressed a petition of grievances
to the House of Common, beginning—'We, the
people of England'.   **1885** C. LOWE *Bismarck*
ii. (1898) 25 The second German parliament[1] ...
only contained delegates from Prussia and some
of the other minor states ... The Teutonic
tailors of Tooley Street, so to speak, had again
assembled.   **1909** *Times Wkly.* 20 Aug. Our
Correspondent 'has been misled into taking the
clamours of the Toronto variety of the "three
tailors of Tooley-Street" for the voice of
Canada'.   [[1] 1850.]

Tailor(s), *see also* Devil among t.; Knavery in all
trades, most in t.; Little to sew when t. true;
Nine t. make a man; Put a miller ... and a t. in
bag, first that comes out will be thief; Trust a t.
that doesn't sing, (Never).

Take a leaf out of (a person's) book, To.

[= to imitate one.]   **1809** MALKIN *Gil Blas* VII.
ii (Rtldg.) 12 I took a leaf out of their book.
1861 HUGHES *Tom Br. at Oxford* I. ii. 32 It is a
great pity that some of our instructors ... will
not take a leaf out of the same book.   **1926**
Times 19 July 11/1 France ... might well take
a leaf out of Germany's discarded book.

Take a man up short, To.

(M 400)

1582 WHETSTONE *Heptameron* S2 The Doctor
more rougher then the rest, tooke him vp ...

short.   **1639** CLARKE s.v. Rigor 274 To take
a man up as short as a dog in a halter.

Take a pain for a pleasure all wise men can. *Cf.* Pleasure without pain (No).

(P 412)

1509 HAWES *Past Pleas.* 16, Percy S. 70. Who
wyll have pleasure he must fyrst apply To take
the payne wyth hys cure besely.   **1546** HEYWOOD
I. v. B2ᵛ.

Take a spring[1] of his own fiddle, and dance to it when he has done, Let him.

1721 KELLY 240 ... Let him go in his own way,
and bear the Effects of it.   **1818** SCOTT *Rob Roy*
ch. 29 'Aweel, aweel, sir,' said the Bailie, 'you're
welcome to a tune on your ain fiddle; but see if
I dinna gar ye dance till't afore a's dune.'
[[1] tune.]

Take all and pay all.

(A 203)

1600–1 SHAKES. *M.W.W.* II. ii. 104 Never a wife
in Windsor leads a better life than she does: do
what she will, ... take all, pay all, ... all is as
she will.   [**1600**] **1601** MARSTON *Jack Drum* i B3
Rule all, pay all, take all without checke or suit.
1620 WEBSTER *Devil's Law-Case* III. i. 14.   **1642**
D. ROGERS *Matrim. Hon.* 92 Your heirs must
be fain to take all, and pay all, and so flecce
the rest.

Take all, and pay the baker.

(A 204)

1678 RAY 348.   **1721** KELLY 331 *Take it all pay
the Maltman* (*Baker*). Spoken jocosely when we
give all of such a thing.   **1732** FULLER no. 4303.

Take away the salt, If you | you may throw the flesh to the dogs.

(S 79)

1678 RAY *Adag. Hebr.* 402.   **1911** A. COHEN *Anc.
Jew. Prov.* 33 Shake the salt off and throw the
meat to the dog. ... When the soul leaves the
body what remains is worthless. The soul is
the preservative of the body in the same way as
all salt is a preservative for meat.

Take by the hand, *see* Dance (When you), take
heed whom you t. by the h.

Take care of Dowb.

c. **1854** MINCHIN *Our Pub. Sch.* (1901) 42 'Take
care of Dowb' ... has become a synonym for
unblushing nepotism. ... Dowbiggin joined the
army and went out to the Crimea. His uncle, as
Secretary for War, despatched a cablegram ...
'Take care of Dowbiggin etc. etc.' The cable ...
broke off at the first syllable, and 'Take care of
Dowb' got into the papers.   **1858** SURTEES *Ask
Mamma* ch. 40 The next was larger, ... urging
him as before to take care of Dowb (meaning
himself).   **1890** W. F. BUTLER *Sir C. Napier* 187
'The world' thought he could do it a good turn
in the matter of its brothers and sons and
nephews ... 'Dowb' had to be 'taken care of'.

Take care of the pence, and the pounds will take care of themselves.

[*a.* **1724**] **1750** LD. CHESTERFIELD *Lett.* 5 Feb.
(1774) I. 551 Old Mr. Lowndes, the famous

Secretary of the Treasury, . . . used to say, . . . **1760** STERNE *Tristram Shandy* II. ch. 19 And wherefore, he would add, are we needy?—From the neglect, he would answer, of our pence and halfpence:—our banknotes, sir, are guineas,— nay, our shillings take care of themselves. **1827** HARE *Gues. at Truth* (1859) i. 229 Thrift is the best means of thriving. . . . **1846** JOWETT to R. R. W. Lingen 18 Aug. A tradesman's [emphatic] motto ought to be 'Take care . . .'

Take counsel of (consult with) one's pillow, To. (C 696)

[= to take a night to reflect.] **1530** PALSGRAVE 508a I wyll debate this mater with myselfe, and take counsayle of my pylowe, or I gyve you an answere. **1540** *Id. Acolastus* 25 Tourne me on the other syde to rounde with my pyllowe. **1573** G. HARVEY *Letter-bk.* Camden Soc. 21 You counsel me to take counsel of mi pillow. **1642** FULLER *H. & P. State* v. xvi (1841) 394 Others . . . feared, there being so many privy to the plot, that, if they suffered them to consult with their pillows, their pillows would advise them to make much of their heads. **1709** STEELE *Tatler* no. 60. par. 1 [He] frequently consulted his Pillow to know how to behave himself, on such important Occasions.

Take half in hand and the rest by and by, It is best to. (H 48)

1678 RAY 354 . . . (The tradesman that is for ready money).

Take hares with foxes, To.

1577 STANYHURST in Holinshed *Descr. Irel.* (1586) VI. 36b But in deed it is hard to take hares with foxes.

Take heed does surely speed, Good. (T 32)

1639 CLARKE 266.   **1670** RAY 147.

Take heed is a fair thing (good rede[1]). (T 33)

c. **1374** CHAUCER *Troilus* Bk. 2, l. 343 Avysement is good before the nede.   **1546** HEYWOOD II. viii. K2ᵛ Take heede is a fayre thyng. Beware this blyndnesse.   **1587** J. BRIDGES *Defence* 641 This *take heed* is a faire thing (as they say).   **1599** PORTER *Angry Wom. Abingd.* l. 1839 I could haue said to you, syr, Take heede is a good reede.   **1614** CAMDEN 312 (good reede). [1 counsel.]

Take heed (of), *see also under significant words following.*

Take it as you will (list, please). (T 27)

a. **1530** J. HEYWOOD *Witty & Witless* ed. Fairholt 6 Tak yt howe ye lyst.   **1580** LYLY *Euph. & his Eng.* ii. 94 And this my flat and friendly deling if thou wilt not take as I meane, take as thou wilt.   *c.* **1595** SHAKES. *R.J.* I. i. 40 I will frown as I pass by, and let them take it as they list.   **1601** *Id. T.N.* II. iii. 177 If I do not, never trust me, take it how you will.   **1738** SWIFT *Dial.* I. E.L. 282 Take it as you please; but, I swear, you are a saucy Jack, to use such expressions.

Take it or leave it. (T 28)

1576 LAMBARDE *Kent* 2D3ᵛ I . . . do leaue the Reader to his free choice, to take or leaue the one, or the other.   **1605–6** SHAKES. *K.L.* I. i. 202 Will you . . . Take her, or leave her? . . . Then leave her, Sir.   **1664** KILLIGREW *Thomaso* I. IV. ii That is the price, and less I know, in curtesie you cannot offer me; take it or leave it.   **1762** J. WESLEY *Letters* iv. 182.   **1930** *Times* 25 Mar. 17/2 The Commons . . . are informed of the result of each event after it is over, and have no option, as the saying is, to take it or leave it.

Take it out in sleep.

1902–4 LEAN IV. 106 . . . The consolation of the supperless. Qui dort dîne.

Take it (money) with you (when you die), You can't.

1841 MARRYAT *Mast. Ready* ch. 31.

Take me not up before I fall. (T 30)

1583 MELBANCKE *Philotimus* L1 Thou louest me well that takest me up before I fall.   **1617** J. SWETNAM *School of Defence* 183.   **1655** FULLER *Ch. Hist.* III. viii. (1868) I. 481 The pope . . . predisposed such places to such successors as he pleased . . . He took up churches before they fell, yea before they ever stumbled.   **1658** MARGARET ELMES to Sir R. Verney *Verney Memoirs* iii (1894) 431 I may justly make yous of the owlde fraise and say you tooke me up be foare I was downe.   **1721** KELLY 336 . . . Do not . . . give an Answer to my Discourse, before you hear me out.   **1738** SWIFT *Dial.* I. E.L. 261 What! Mr. Neverout, you take me up before I'm down.   **1818** SCOTT *Ht. Midl.* ch. 18 'Sir, . . . ye take me up before I fall down. I canna see why I suld be termed a Cameronian.'

Take no more on you than you're able to bear.

1721 KELLY 305.

Take one as you find him, To. *Cf.* Take things as you find them. (T 29)

1548 HALL *Chron.* (1809 ed. 330) Myne advice is, let all men trust them as thei fynde them. [*c.* **1553**] **1566–7** UDALL *Ralph Roister D.* l. 1253 I can be content To take you as you are.   **1580** MUNDAY *Zelauto* H2ᵛ In the meane whyle, take as you finde.   **1596** HARINGTON *Metam. Ajax* 19 And becaus as the saying is, loquendum cum vulgo, wee must nowe take him as we finde him, with all his faults.   **1624** T. BREWER *A Knot of Fools* A2 For their Characters, take them as you find them.

Take one down a peg or two (a peg, *or* a button-hole, etc., lower), To. (P 181)

[= to humble him.]   *c.* **1550** BECON *Catechism, &c.* P.S. 561 This doctrine plucketh them down one staff lower than they were before.   **1589** LYLY *Pap w. Hatchet* iii. 394 Now haue at you all my gaffers of the rayling religion, tis I that must take you a peg lower.   **1592** NASHE *Pierce Penniless* i. 204 (button hole).   *a.* **1593** PEELE *Ed. I* (Bullen i. 148) I'll take you down a button-hole.   **1594–5** SHAKES. *L.L.L.* V. ii. 688 Master,

let me take you a button-hole lower. **1604** *Id.
O.* II. i. 197 O, you are well tun'd now! But
I'll set down the pegs that make this music, As
honest as I am. **1664** BUTLER *Hudibras* II. ii. 522
We still have worsted all your holy Tricks, . . .
And took your Grandees down a peg. **1781**
C. JOHNSTON *Hist. J. Juniper* II. 247 An oppor-
tunity for letting him down a peg or two. **1886**
G. A. SALA *America Revis.* 373 The Grand Pacific
clerk . . . thought he would take him down a
peg or two.

Take one's ease in one's inn, To. (E 42)

[= to enjoy oneself as if one were at home.]
1546 HEYWOOD I. v. B2 To let the worlde wag,
and take myne ease in mine yn. **1577** *Art of
Angling* D2ᵛ I loue to take mine ease in mine
inn. **1588** W. AVERELL *Combat of Contrarieties*
A4 Neither will I step ouer the threshold . . .
but meane to take my rest in mine Inne. **1591**
ARIOSTO *Orl. Fur.* Harington XXVII. 103. **1597–8**
SHAKES. *1 Hen. IV* III. iii. 80 Shall I not take
mine ease in mine inn but I shall have my pocket
picked? **1639** CLARKE 292.

Take part of the pelf, when the pack is a-dealing. (P 78)

a. **1628** CARMICHAELL no. 1421 (pak is gane *or*
poke is open). **1641** FERGUSSON no. 783.

Take pet, To.

1590 LODGE *Rosalynde* Wks. (Gros.) IV. 90
Some while they thought he had taken some
word vnkindly, and had taken the pet. **1606**
CHAPMAN *Mons. d'Olive* II. i Fled backe as it
came and went away in Pett. **1660** PEPYS
Diary 6 Dec. Which did vex me . . . and so I
took occasion to go up and to bed in a pet. **1699**
New Help to Discourse 252 He thereupon took
pet, and so did die. **1773** VIEYRA S.V. Affrontar
To take pet, to take huff, or exception.

Take tea in the kitchen, To.

1894 NORTHALL *Folk-phrases* E.D.S. 30 To take
tea in the kitchen = To pour tea from the cup
into the saucer, and drink it from this.

Take the bear by the tooth, To. (B 131)

1601 DENT *Path. Heauen* 62 To put his finger
into the Lion's mouth, and . . . take the Beare
by the Tooth. **1670** RAY 163 (You dare as well).
1736 BAILEY S.V. You dare as well take a Bear
by the Tooth, That is, You dare not attempt it.

Take the bit (bridle) in the teeth, To. (B 424)

[= to be beyond restraint.] **1546** HEYWOOD II.
viii. K2 I gaue hir the bridell at begynnyng. And
nowe she taketh the brydle in the teeth, And
runth awaie with it. **1586** J. OVERTON *Jacob's
Journey* J2 To take the bitte between their teeth,
and so to run forwards and neuer to be pluckt
back. **1589** LYLY *Pap w. Hatchet* iii. 410 But
if like a resty iade thou wilt take the bit in thy
mouth, and then run over hedge and ditch,
thou shalt be broken as Prosper broke his horses.
1600 ABP. ABBOT *Exp. Jonah* 521 Neither yet
taking the bit perversely in his teeth. **1666**
TORRIANO *Prov. Phr.* S.V. Denti 52 To take the

bit with ones teeth, viz. to fret, and be devilish
angry. **1927** *Times* 30 Jul. 10/2 If . . . Congress should take the bit in its teeth and authorize
an imposing addition to the United States Naval
strength, would he . . . intervene with his veto?

Take the bread out of one's mouth, To. (B 629)

[= take away his living by competition.] **1601**
J. WHEELER *Treat. Commerce* 37 Eating as it
were the bread out of his mouth. **1666** TOR-
RIANO *Prov. Phr.* S.V. Pane 130b To take bread
out of ones mouth or hand, viz. to take from
him his livelyhood and subsistence for himself
and his family. **1708** MOTTEUX *Rabelais* IV. xvi.
You little Prigs, will you offer to take the Bread
out of my mouth? **1845** J. W. CROKER in *Papers*
(1884) III. xxiv. 47 Lord Johnny dashed forward
to take the bread out of his [Peel's] mouth.

Take the bull by the horns, To.

[= to meet a difficulty rather than to evade it.]
1659 HOWELL *Span. Prov.* 5 Take a Bull by the
horn, and a man by his word. **1711** SWIFT
Conduct of the Allies Davis vi. 40 (As the old
Duke of Schomberg expressed it) to engage with
France, was to take a Bull by the Horns. **1816**
SCOTT *Old Mort.* ch. 25. **1822** GALT *Provost*
ch. 28 It would never do to take the bull by the
horns in that manner. **1850** LYTTON *Caxtons*
II. i. Dr. Herman, in his theory of education, began
at the beginning! he took the bull fairly by the
horns. **1869** TROLLOPE *He knew he was right*
ch. 91 Nora would have faced the difficulty, and
taken the bull by the horns, and asked her father
to sanction her engagement in the presence of her
lover.

Take the fat with the lean, You must.

1813 RAY 218.

Take the gilt off the gingerbread, To.

[= to deprive something of its attractive qualities.] **1830** FORBY 432 It will take the gilding
off the gingerbread. **1874** G. J. WHYTE-MELVILLE
Uncle John ch. 12 He marvelled how this angel
could have come down from heaven to be his
own! For him the gilt was yet on the gingerbread, the paint on the toy, the dew on the
flower. **1884** J. PAYN *Canon's W.* ch. 11 He . . .
embarrassed his grandmother by his plain
speaking. . . . He was always rubbing the gilt
off some gingerbread theory which other children
swallow without enquiry. **1927** 31 Oct. D. H.
LAWRENCE *Lett.* ii. 1015 When one comes to
dead cities with exhausted people, the gilt goes
off the gingerbread.

Take the law into one's own hands, To. (L 111)

1599 PORTER *Angry Wom. Abingd.* l. 2290 But
they may do as they list, the law is in their owne
hands. **1604** SHAKES. *O.* I. iii. 67 The bloody
book of law You shall yourself read in the bitter
letter After your own sense; yea, though our
proper son Stood in your action. **1606** DEKKER
Sev. Sinnes 35 They . . . take the lawe into their
owne handes, and doe what they list. **1840**
MARRYAT *Poor Jack* ch. 28 He has taken the law
into his own hands already by mast-heading me
for eight hours, and now he makes a complaint

to you. **1881** E. B. TYLER *Anthropology* (1889) 418 The avenger of blood . . . would now be himself punished as a criminal for taking the law into his own hands.

Take the rue, To.

[= to repent.] **1789** *Shepherd's Wedding* 10 E.D.D. I own, indeed, I've ta'en the rue, My mind is fairly alter'd. **1816** SCOTT *Old Mort.* ch. 28 Tam Halliday took the rue, and tauld me a' about it. **1848** MRS. GASKELL *Mary Barton* ch. 12 It would be to give him a hint you'd taken the rue, and would be very glad to have him now.

Take the (King's) (Queen's) shilling, To.

[= to enlist as a soldier by accepting a shilling from a recruiting officer. **1707** HEARNE *Collect.* 27 Mar. (O.H.S.) II. 2 He did take a shilling, but not with any intent of listing.] **1852** THACKE-RAY *Esmond* Bk. III. ch. 5 One fellow was jilted by his mistress, and took the shilling in despair. **1886** FARJEON *Three Times Tried* I I took the Queen's shilling, and became a soldier. **1901** *Scotsman* 4 Mar. 8/1 A contingent of Volunteer Engineers was sworn in for service in South Africa. Each was presented . . . with the King's shilling.

Take the wind out of the sails of, To.

[= to put at a disadvantage.] **1822** SCOTT *Nigel* ch. 9 He would take the wind out of the sail of every gallant. **1883** *Harper's Mag.* Feb. 339/2 A young upstart of a rival, Llanelly . . . which has taken a great deal of the wind out of the sails of its older neighbour. **1911** *Spectator* 30 Dec. 1141 Dr. . . . aims at taking the wind out of his critics' sails by giving the nation a lead in regard to relations with England.

Take things as they are (be) meant.

1571 R. EDWARDS *Damon & Pithias* Prol. Hazl.-Dods. iv. 13 But, worthy audience, we you pray, take things as they be meant.

Take things as they come.   (T 196)

1509 A. BARCLAY *Ship of Fools* ii. 319 That man folowes hye wysdome whych takys all thynges as they come. **1530** PALSGRAVE 614b I take the worlde as it cometh and love God of all. **1592** DELAMOTHE 15 We must needes take the tyme as it doth come. **1611** DAVIES Prov. no. 296 Take all things as they come, and bee content.

Take things as you find them. *Cf.* Take one as you find him.

1828 T. H. LISTER *H. Lacy* i. ch. 6 As for their manners, we must take them as we find them. **1836** MARRYAT *Mr. Midshipman Easy* ch. 1 We must take things as we find them in this world. **1902–4** LEAN IV. 105.

Take to a thing like a duck to water, To.

1894 SIR J. ASTLEY *Fifty Years of My Life* i. 22 I always took to shooting like a duck to water. **1901** G. W. STEEVENS *In India* 94 In Bengal . . . the native took to European education as a duck to water.

Take to one's heels, To.   (H 394)

1530 PALSGRAVE 749a I take my legges, I ronne away. **1548** HALL 1809 ed., 853 They ranne a waie, and trusted some to their Horsses, and some to their legges like tall felowes. **1566** SENECA *Medea* tr. J. Studley E1ᵛ Take thou thy heles to scape them both. **1573** GASCOIGNE *Flowers* i. 69 Clim of the Clough then takes his heeles. **1585** A. MUNDAY *Fedele and Fortunio* D1ᵛ II. iii. Shee tooke to her heeles. **1588** J. ASKE *Elizabetha Triumphans* (Nichols, *Eliz.* 1823 ii. 579) The other ships . . . thinke it best to trust unto their heeles. **1591** ARIOSTO *Orl. Fur.* Harington VII. 69 They tooke their heeles when as their hearts them failed. **1721** KELLY 145 He has taken his Heels.

Take up the cudgels (bucklers), To.   (C 898)

[= to attack or defend vigorously.] **1603** CHETTLE, DEKKER, HAUGHTON *Patient Grissil* II. i. 234 If we quarrel sheele take vp the bucklers. **1639** *Publ. Ovid. de Tristibus* tr. Z. Catlin A3ᵛ Old Entellus takes up the Bats and Bucklers, against young Dares. **1649** SELDEN *Laws Eng.* I. lix (1739) 109 The Clergy took up the bucklers, and beat both King and Commons to a retreat. **1662** FULLER *Westmorld.* 140 Mr. Chillingworth, a great Master of defence in School divinity, took up the Cudgell against him. **1691** WOOD *Ath. Oxon.* II. 61 John dying before he could make a reply . . . Dr. Franc. White took up the bucklers. **1788** WOLCOT (P. Pindar) *Sir J. Banks* Wks. (1816) I. 473 I must take up the cudgels for my client. **1826** SCOTT *Journ.* 4 Feb. Here I am taking up the cudgels and may expect a drubbing in return. **1876** SIR G. O. TREVELYAN *Life & Let. Macaulay* ch. 3 George Babington . . . was always ready to take up the Tory cudgels.

Take what you find or what you bring.   (T 26)

c. **1386** CHAUCER *Reeves T.* l. 4129 I have herd seyd, man sal taa of twa thinges, Slyk as he fyndes, or taa slyk as he bringes. [A man must take (one) of two things, either such as he finds, or such as he brings. These lines imitate the dialect of the North of England.—Skeat.] **1599** GREENE *George a Greene* IV. iv. 1002 If this like you not, Take that you finde, or that you bring, for me. **1862** HISLOP 107 If ye dinna like what I gie ye, tak what ye brought wi' ye.

Taken by a morsel, I was | says the fish.   (M 1179)

1640 HERBERT no. 627.

Taken my horse and left me the tether, He has.   (H 652)

1672 WALKER 17, no. 61.

Takes away the occasion takes away the offence, He that.   (O 8)

c. **1554** LINDSAY *Three Estates* l. 2346 Quhen ye ken the occasioun, That maks them sic persuasioun, Ye may expel the cause. **1599** MINSHEU *Span. Gram.* 84.

Takes gifts, She that | herself she sells, and she that gives, does not else. (M 24)

1611 COTGRAVE s.v. Fille A maid that gives is easily gotten. A maid that takes (much) is as good as taken. *a.* **1628** CARMICHAELL no. 1345 Sche that takes gifts for hir self sche sellis and sche that gives dois not els. **1641** F. QUARLES *Euchiridion* III. lvi He that presents a gift buyes the receiver; he that takes a gift sells his liberty. **1641** FERGUSSON no. 771. **1721** KELLY 294.

Takes his wife, As a man | — for better, for worse. (M 65)

1552 *Book of Common Prayer, Solemnization of Matrimony.* **1666** TORRIANO *Prov. Phr.*, s.v. Moglie 106 To have taken a wife that one might not be miserable alone, . . . the English say, for better, or for worse. **1668** COWLEY *Essays* i (1904) 7 We enter into the bonds of it, like those of matrimony; . . . and take it for better or worse. **1738** SWIFT *Dial.* I. E.L. 280 Colonel, you must take it for better for worse, as a man takes his wife.

Takes not up a pin, He that | slights his wife. (P 330)

1640 HERBERT no. 361. **1706** STEVENS s.v. Alfiler. **1732** FULLER no. 2324.

Takes the devil into his boat, He that | must carry him over the sound. (D 282)

1678 RAY 125. **1732** FULLER no. 2326.

Takes the raven for his guide, He that | will light on carrion.

1865 ABP. TRENCH *Poems* 302 Who doth the raven for a guide invite, Must marvel not on carcases to light.

Taking (Getting) the breeks off a bare arse (a Hielandman), It is ill. (B 644, 650)

1546 HEYWOOD I. ix. CI[v] There is nothyng more vayne . . . than to beg a breeche of a bare arst man. **1641** FERGUSSON no. 500 It is ill to take a breik off a bair arse. **1818** SCOTT *Rob Roy* ch. 27 It will be nonsense fining me, . . . that hasna a grey groat to pay a fine wi'—it's ill taking the breeks aff a Hielandman. **1857** DEAN RAMSAY *Remin.* V. (1911) 194 It's ill getting the breeks aff the Highlandman . . . savours . . . of a Lowland Scotch origin. Having suffered loss at the hands of their neighbours from the hills, . . . there was little hope of redress from those who had not the means of supplying it. **1863** C. READE *Hard Cash* ch. 41 What . . . was . . . poor Dr. Wolf to do? Could he sub-embezzle a Highlander's breeks? **1917** BRIDGE 84 (a bare leg). Spoken of a bankrupt.

Taking the wall of a dog, Not worth.

1639 CLARKE 228.

Take(n, s, taking), *see also* Always t. out of the meal-tub . . . soon comes to bottom; Bear (T., Suffer) this, bear (t., suffer) all; Counsel to give (t.) than to t. (give), (We have better); Everything is as it is t.; Give a thing and t. a thing; Give and t.; Give others good counsel but will t. none himself (He can); Giving and t.; Lion when he is absent (Who t.); Little t. a little (Of a); Longer (longest) liver t. all; Net (trap) (To be t. in one's own); New lease of life (To t. out a); Refuse with the right hand and t. with the left; Smell of garlic (leeks) t. away smell of onions; Soft wax will t. any impression; Spring from the year (To t. away); Tale (word) out of one's mouth (To t.); Things are as they be t.; Touch and t.; Trip (To t. one in a); Variety t. away satiety; Well spoken that is well t.

Take, To, *see also under significant words following.*

Tale if it were told in Greek, A good. (T 37)

1616 WITHALS 571. **1639** CLARKE 231.

Tale ill told is marred in the telling, A good. (T 38)

[L. *Male narrando fabula depravatur.*] *c.* **1532** SIR ADRIAN FORTESCUE no. 59 A good tale yll toldd is spyllt in the telling. *c.* **1549** HEYWOOD II. vii. 14[v]. **1605–6** SHAKES. *K.L.* I. iv. 32 I can . . . mar a curious tale in telling it. **1614** CAMDEN 302. **1721** KELLY 244 Many a good Tale is spoil'd in the telling. Apply'd often when a good Sermon is ill delivered.

Tale is none the worse for being twice told, A good. (T 39)

1577 R. STANYHURST in Holinshed *Descr. Ireland* (1587) 88b A good tale maie be twice told. **1681** S. COLVIL *Whiggs Suppl.* 42 It's not superfluous and vain To tell a good tale ov'r again. **1721** KELLY 33 . . . An Apology for them that say Grace twice, unawares. **1816** SCOTT *Old Mort.* ch. 7 It's very true the curates read aye the same words . . . ; and . . . what for no? A gude tale's no the waur o' being twice tauld.

Tale never loses in the telling, A. (T 43)

c. **1535** SIR T. MORE *Dialogue Comf.*, ed. P. S. Allen 238 A tale that fleeth through many mouths catcheth many feathers. **1541** *Schoolh. of Women* A4[v] What soeuer commeth to memorye shall not be loste, for the tellinge. **1581** *Stationers' Register* (Arb.) ii. 388 A good tale cannot too often be told. **1609** HARWARD 121 Tales lose nothing by the cariadge. **1616** DRAXE no. 1836 A tale in the carying is made more. **1710** PALMER 177 A Story never loses by Carrying. **1721** KELLY 55 . . . Fame or Report . . . commonly receives an Addition as it goes from Hand to Hand. **1907** *Spectator* 16 Nov. 773 A story never loses in the telling in the mouth of an Egyptian.

Tale of a roasted horse, A. (T 44)

1569–70 *Marriage of Wit & Science* C2[v] You tell vs a tale of a rosted horse. **1575** GASCOIGNE *Cert. Notes Instruct.* in *Steele Glas, &c.* i. 470 The verse that is to easie is like a tale of a rosted horse. **1611** COTGRAVE s.v. Cicogne *Contes de la cicogne*, idle histories; . . . tales . . . of a rosted horse.

Tale of a tub, A.   (T 45)

[**1525–4**] **1557** *A Merry Dialogue* 82. **1532** MORE *Confut. Tindale* Wks. 576/1 Thys is a fayre tale of a tubbe tolde vs of hys electes. **1546** HEYWOOD II. ix. LI[v]. **1567** PAINTER iii. 339. **1633** JONSON *T. Tub* I. iv. 25 A meere tale of a Tub. Lend it no eare I pray you. **1724** DEFOE *Mem. Cavalier* (1840) 97 Having entertained the fellow with a tale of a tub.

Tale of two drinks, It is a.

1721 KELLY 177 . . . It is a Thing that requires Deliberation; at least as long as the Glass may go twice about.

Tale (word) out of one's mouth, To take the.   (T 50)

1530 PALSGRAVE 751a It is no good maner to take the worde out of my mouthe, or I have made an ende of my tale. **1581** J. CARTIGNY *Voyage of Wandering Knight* tr. W. Goodyear E4 This painted Pecocke . . . puts foorth hir selfe to speake before me alwaies, and to take the tale out of my mouth. *c.* **1589** LYLY *Love's Met.* I. ii. 89. **1599** SHAKES. *Hen. V* IV. vii. 40 It is not well done, mark you now, to take the tales out of my mouth. **1666** TORRIANO *Prov. Phr.* 17a To interrupt one in his discourse, and take the word out of his mouth.

Tale runs as it pleases the teller, The.

1732 FULLER no. 4783.

Tale to a deaf man, You tell a.   (T 51)

1533–4 N. UDALL *Flowers* 128. *c.* **1538** T. STARKEY *Dial.* II. iii. 575 *Eng. in Reign Hen. VIII* ii. 212 Hyt ys as you wold tel a tale to a deffe man. **1583** MELBANCKE K4[v] Meaning no more . . . to . . . wast my wordes to a deafe man. **1605** T. HEYWOOD I *If You Know Not Me* l. 714 You preach well to deaf men. **1672** WALKER 52, no. 36.

Tale(s), *see also* Believe no t. from enemy; Canterbury t.; Dead men tell no t.; Half a t. enough; Keep my mind . . . tell my t. to wind (I will); Old man never wants a t.; Old wives' t.; One t. is good till another told; Poor man's t. cannot be heard; Tell another t.; Tell you a t. and find you ears; Thereby hangs a t.

Tale-bearer is worse than a thief, A.
                                                           (T 55)

a. **1628** CARMICHAELL no. 206 (tailtellar). **1721** KELLY 37. **1736** BAILEY *Dict.* s.v.

Tale-bearers, *see* Put no faith in t.-b.

Tale-tellers, *see* Ale sellers should not be t.-t.

Tales of Robin Hood are good among fools.   (T 53)

[*c.* **1405–10**] **1492** *Dives et Pauper* MS Douce 295, f. 45a quoted H. G. Pfander *Library* Dec. 1933

308 Han leuir to gon to the tauerne . . . to heryn a tale or a songe of robyn hode or of sum rubaudry than to heryn messe or matynes. **1509** BARCLAY *Ship of Fools* ii. 155 All of fables and lestis of Robyn hode. **1546** HEYWOOD II. ix. LI[v]. **1527** TYNDALE *Parable of Wicked Mammon* P.S. 80. **1528** *Id. Obed. Christ. Man* P.S. 306 Of no greater value than a tale of Robin Hood. **1581** GUAZZO ii. 81 They will make it a sport to put their children in feare with tales of Robin good fellow. **1670** RAY 137 Tales of Robin Hood are good enough for fools. . . . [Robin] Hood was a famous robber in the time of King Richard the first.

Tales out of school, Tell no.   (T 54)

1530 TYNDALE *Pract. of Prelates* P.S. 249 So that what cometh once in may never out, for fear of telling tales out of school. *c.* **1549** HEYWOOD I. x. C31 To tell tales out of schoole, that is hir great lust. **1616** WITHALS 573 (out of the Tauerne). **1639** CLARKE 132. *Ibid.* 133 (out of the taverne). **1679** SHADWELL *True Widow* IV. i. Fie, miss! fie! tell tales out of school. **1721** KELLY 303 Tell no School Tales. Do not blab abroad what is said in drink, or among Companions. **1876** MRS. BANKS *Manch. Man* ch. 15 All attempts to make known school troubles and grievances were met with 'never tell tales out of school'.

Tales, *see also* Tale(s).

Talk as Dutch[1] as Daimport's[2] (Darnford's) dog, To.

1879 G. F. JACKSON *Shropshire Wordbk.* 129 "'E talks as *Dutch* as Darnford's dog': proverbial saying heard in the neighbourhood of Whitchurch. **1917** BRIDGE 144. [[1] fine, affected. [2] Davenport.]

Talk (Prate) is but talk (prate); but 'tis money buys land. *Cf.* Words are but sands. Words are but words.   (T 59)

1639 SHIRLEY *Ball* V. i. 78 You may hear talk; but give me the man that has measured 'em: talk's but talk. **1678** RAY 177 (Prate is but prate, it's). *Ibid.* 346 (lands). **1681** ROBERTSON 1203.

Talk like a book, To.

1821 SCOTT *Lives of Novelists* (1887) 412 His talk too stiffly complimentary, too like a printed book, to usage a Scottish phrase. **1900** G. C. BRODRICK *Mem. & Impress.* 205 I do not mean that 'talking like a book' has ceased to be fashionable— . . . but that slang is the order of the day.

Talk like an apothecary, To.   (A 280)

1540 SIR T. ELYOT *Pasquil the Plain* B3[v] You speake lyke a potticury. **1616** WITHALS 560 You speake like a Pottecary, such a reason pist my goose. **1639** CLARKE 133 He prates like a poticary. *Ibid.* 178 (He chafes like). **1659** HOWELL *Eng. Prov.* 15b You speak like a Pothecary, viz. Ignorantly. **1670** RAY 195.

Talk much, and err much, says the Spaniard.   (S 703)

1599 MINSHEU *Span. Dial.* 31 Prating and lying

are nere of kinne. **1640** HERBERT no. 649. **1706** STEVENS s.v. Hablar. Great Talkers speak much Nonsense.

Talk of an angel and you'll hear his wings.

1902–4 LEAN IV. 106.

Talk of Christmas so long, that it comes, They. (C 373)

1611 COTGRAVE s.v. Noel So long is Christmas cried that at length it comes. **1640** HERBERT no. 840.

Talk of the devil, and he is sure to appear. (D 294)

1591 LYLY *Endym.* I. iii. 4 *Et ecce autem*—Wyl you see the deuill? **1666** TORRIANO *It. Prov.* 134 no. 78 The English say, Talk of the Devil, and he's presently at your elbow. **1678** RAY 125 (he'll either come or send). **1721** PRIOR *Hans Carvel* 71 Forthwith the devil did appear (For name him, and he's always near). **1721** KELLY 299 Speak of the Dee'l, and he'll appear. Spoken when they, of whom we are speaking, come in by Chance. **1772** R. GRAVES *Spiritual Quix.* VIII. ch. 5 (and he will appear). **1830** MARRYAT *King's Own* ch. 25 The unexpected appearance of Mrs. Rainscourt made him involuntarily exclaim, 'Talk of the devil—' 'And she appears, sir', replied the lady. **1853** TRENCH vi. 149.

Talk than trouble, There is more. (T 60)

1611 BRETNOR *Almanac* June Good days More prattle then practise. **1640** HERBERT no. 265.

Talk the hind leg off a donkey (horse), To.

1844 H. COCKTON *Sylvester S.* ch. 31 He'd talk a horse's hind leg off, sir; and then wouldn't be quiet. **1877** BESANT *This Son of V.* I. xiii I believe you'd talk a donkey's hind leg off, give you time. **1878–9** A. TROLLOPE *John Caldigate* ch. 51 She'd talk the hind-legs off a dog, as we used to say out there [Australia]. **1909** *Times Wkly.* 15 Jan. 41 Socialists . . . would argue the hind leg off a donkey, to drop into their own vernacular vein.

Talk to the wind, To. (W 438)

c. **1565** *Bugbears* IV. iv. 15 Trifle owt the tyme and tel a tale to the winde. **1604** *Wit Woman* C2 Nowe let mee talke a little to the winde: for I hope there is no body heares mee. **1713** SWIFT *Jour. to Stella* no. 63 10 Apr., Davis ii. 658 This I tell her, but talk to the winds. **1819** 25 May BYRON *Letters* Prothero iv. 305 You may as well talk to the Wind.

Talk(s), *see also* Hold your tongue and let me t.; Think with wise, t. with vulgar; Tongue t. at head's cost; Walk groundly, t. profoundly.

Talkers (crakers), The greatest | are (always) the least doers. (T 64)

1509 BARCLAY *Ship of Fools* i. 198 (crakers). **1526** *Hundred Merry Tales* no. 42. **1537** *Ther-*

sites [title-page] The greatest boesters are not the greatest doers. [**1592**] **1597** SHAKES. *Rich. III* I. iii. 350 Talkers are no good doers: be assur'd We go to use our hands and not our tongues. **1614** CAMDEN 312. **1670** RAY 147 (always).

Talkers, *see also* Women are great t.

Talking pays no toll. (T 65)

1640 HERBERT no. 485. **1732** FULLER no. 4317.

Talks much of his happiness, He that | summons grief. (H 139)

1640 HERBERT no. 856.

Talks to himself, He that | speaks to a fool.

1721 KELLY 139 . . . Because none but Fools will do so. **1732** FULLER no. 2328.

Talks, *see also* Talk(s).

Tall maid is stooping, While the | the little one hath swept the house. (M 29)

1666 TORRIANO *It. Prov.* 108 no. 18 Whilst a tall Meg of Westminster is stooping, a short wench sweeps the house.

Tallow, *see* Pissed his t.

Tame beasts, Of all | I hate sluts. (B 159)

1678 RAY 81.

Tame, *see also* Beasts, The most deadly of wild, is a backbiter (tyrant), of t. ones a flatterer; Tod's bairns ill to t.

Tammie Norie o' the Bass canna kiss a bonny lass.

1842 R. CHAMBERS *Pop. Rhymes Scot.* (1870) 190 The Puffin.—Tammie Norie o' the Bass Canna kiss a bonny lass. . . . Said jocularly, when a young man refuses to salute a rustic coquette. The puffin, which builds . . . on the Bass Rock, is a very shy bird. . . . It is also customary to call a stupid-looking man a *Tammie Norie*.

Tamworth, *see* Sutton.

Tangled skein of it to wind off, You have a.

1732 FULLER no. 2603.

Tankard, *see* Sickle . . . love I not to see, but the good ale t., happy might it be; Tears of the t.

Tantallon, *see* Ding doun T.

Tantony, *see* St. Anthony.

Tap, *see* Run t. run tapster.

Tar, *see* Ship (To lose) for halfpennyworth of t.

Tar-box, *see* Capers like a fly in a t.-b.

Tarred with the same brush (stick), All.
(P 359)

1581 GUAZZO i. 59 Of one selfe pitch, we all have a touch. **1623** WODROEPHE 287 Ye are all stained with one Pitch. **1818** SCOTT *Ht. Midl.* ch. 42 The worshipful gentleman was . . . tarred wi' the same stick . . . as mony of them, . . . a hasty . . . temper. **1880** BLACKMORE *Mary Aner.* ch. 29 They are . . . all tarred with one brush—all stuffed with a heap of lies.

Tarrows, *see* Plaints (T.) early that plaints on his kail.

Tarry breeks pays no fraught.

1721 KELLY 318 . . . People of a Trade assist one another mutually.

Tarrying, *see* Long t. takes thanks away.

Tarry-long brings little home.

1721 KELLY 389 You have tarried long and brought little home. **1732** FULLER no. 4320.

Tartar, *see* Catch a T.; Scratch a Russian.

Task, *see* Hard t. to be poor.

Taste of schoolbutter, To.   (S 140)

[= A thrashing.] *c.* **1570** *Juli and Julian* l. 314 mr Dicke had some scholbutter to Day. **1585** A. MUNDAY *Fedele & Fortunio* l. 1545 O that I had some of Pediculus Schoole-butter to make me a lip salue. **1604** *Pasq. Jests* Warning for Tale Tellers in *Shakes. Jest-Bks.* iii. 24 An unhappy boy, willing to have one of his fellowes taste of such schoole-butter as hee had often broke his fast with.

Tastes differ.

1868 W. COLLINS *Moonstone* ch. 15 Tastes differ . . . I never saw a marine landscape that I admired less.

Taste(s) (*noun*), *see also* Accounting for t. (No); Every man to his t.; Lost his t. (To him that has) sweet is sour.

Taste (*verb*), *see also* Husbandman ought first to t. of the new grown fruit.

Tatter(ed), *see* Linen often to water, soon to t.; Son full and t.

Taught you to swim, I | and now you'd drown me.

1732 FULLER no. 2626.

Taught, *see also* Better fed than t.

Taunt one tit over thumb, To.

1546 HEYWOOD II. iv. G4 And ye taunt me tyt ouer thumb (quoth shee).

Taunton, *see* Nertown was a market town.

Taunton Dean, *see* 'Ch was bore at T. D.

Tavern, *see* God keep me from . . . t.; St. Peter's in the Poor, where no t.

Tavern token, *see* Swallow a t. t.

Tawse, *see* Never take the t. when a word will do.

Tax(es), *see* Nothing is certain but . . . t.

Te Deum, see Correct *Magnificat* before one has learnt *T.D.*

Tea, *see* Many estates are spent . . . for t.; Take t. in the kitchen.

Teach an old dog tricks (Make an old dog stoop), It is hard to.   (D 489, 500)

1523 FITZHERBERT *Husbandry* E.D.S. 45 The dogge must lerne it when he is a whelpe, or els it wyl not be; for it is harde to make an olde dogge to stoupe. *c.* **1549** HEYWOOD II. vii. E8 But it is harde to make an olde dog stoupe. **1557** EDGEWORTH *Sermons* 4G1v (old dog stoop). **1636** CAMDEN 300. **1670** RAY 127 An old dog will learn no tricks. It's all one to physick the dead, as to instruct old men. **1761** STERNE *T. Shandy* III. xxxiv The same renitency against conviction which is observed in old dogs, 'of not learning new tricks'. **1819** SCOTT *Bride Lam.* ch. 26 I am ower auld a dog to learn new tricks, or to follow a new master. **1857** TROLLOPE *Barch. Tow.* ch. 13 There can be nothing wrong in your wishing to make yourself useful . . . As for myself . . . 'It's bad teaching an old dog tricks.'

Teach the cat the way to the kirn,[1] To.

1721 KELLY 93 Eith[2] to learn the Cat to the Kirn. An ill Custom is soon learn'd, but not so soon forgotten. **1820** SCOTT *Monast.* ch. 35 I gave her . . . a yard of that very black say,[3] to make her a couvre-chef; but I see it is ill done to teach the cat the way to the kirn. [1 churn. 2 easy. 3 silk.]

Teach your father to get children. (F 94)

1641 FERGUSSON no. 900 Ye learn your father to get bairns. **1670** RAY 9.

Teach your grandame to grope[1] (her) ducks.   (G 407)

1611 COTGRAVE s.v. Apprendre (An idle, vaine, or needless labour) we say, to teach his grandame to grope ducks. **1616** WITHALS 575 Pisces natare doces. You teach your good Maister: teach your grandam to grope her duck. **1670** RAY 178 . . . Teach me to do that I know how to do much better then your self. [1 To handle (poultry) in order to find whether they have eggs.]

Teach your grandame to sup sour milk.
(G 409)

1670 RAY 178.

Teach your grandmother to suck eggs.

1707 J. STEVENS tr. *Quevedo's Com.* Wks. (1709) 348 You would have me teach my Grandame to suck eggs. **1738** SWIFT *Dial.* I. É.L. 277 I'll mend it, miss.—You mend it! go, teach your grannam to suck eggs. **1797** WOLCOT (P. Pindar) *Ode to Liv. London* ii. (1816) III. 140 Those fellows talk to *me*— . . . They teach, forsooth, their grannum to *suck eggs!* **1882** BLACKMORE *Christow.* ch. 21 A . . . twinkle, which might have been interpreted—'instruct your grandfather in the suction of gallinaceous products'.

Teaches himself, He that | has a fool for his master. (F 490)

a. **1637** JONSON *Timber* viii. 563 But very few men are wise by their owne counsell; or learned by their owne teaching. For hee that was onely taught by himselfe, had a foole to his Master. **1655–62** GURNALL *Chrn. in Armour* (1865) II. 225 'He that is his own teacher', saith Bernard, 'is sure to have a fool for his master.' **1741** FRANKLIN *Jan.* Learn of the skilful: He that teaches himself, hath a fool for his master.

Teaches ill, He | who teaches all. (A 184)

1605 CAMDEN He doth not teach well which teacheths all; leaving nothing to subtill wits to sift out. **1611** SANFORD *Span. Tongue* v. 64 He teacheth ill that teacheth all; which made me carefull to cutte off Impertinencies. **1659** HOWELL *Eng. Prov.* 2b. **1670** RAY 147. **1732** FULLER no. 2035.

Teach(es, ing), *see also* Dead or t. school (He is either); Gain t. to spend; Love needs no t.

Teacup, *see* Storm in t.

Teague's cocks, Like | that fought one another, though all were of the same side.

1732 FULLER no. 3234.

Teams, *see* Nature draws more than ten t.

Tears of the tankard, The. (T 85)

1666 TORRIANO *Prov. Phr.* 216b To drink till the tears trickle down ones eyes; which tears the English call. The drops of the Tankard; spoken by way of disparagement. **1678** RAY 82.

Tear(s) (noun), *see also* Crocodile t.; Dainties of great, t. of poor; Lass with the t. in her eye; Nothing dries sooner than t.; Pleasures of mighty, t. of poor.

Teeth are longer than your beard, Your.

1591 *A Wonderful Prognostication* in Nashe's *Wks.* iii. 394 Diuerse men shall haue their teeth longer than their beards.

Teeth forward (outward), From the. (F 691. T 423)

1532 T. MORE *Conf. Tyndale's Ans.* II. ii. 148 He lawgheth but from the lyppes forwarde. *c.* **1549** FRASM. *Two Dial.* tr. E. Becke It is . . . a poynte of a pharesey . . . when a man prayeth . . . with the lyppes only and from the tethe outward. *a.* **1575** J. PILKINGTON *Nehemiah* P.S. 314 (from the teeth outward). **1576** LAMBARDE *Peramb. Kent* (1826) 420 They met . . . and from the teeth forwarde departed good friends againe. **1584** R. WILSON *Three Ladies of London* E2ᵛ Thou canst not loue but from the teeth forward. **1595** LIPSIUS *Constancy* tr. Stradling D1ᵛ Speak you that from your heart, or onlie from the teeth outward? *c.* **1607** SHAKES. *A.C.* III. iv. 9 When the best hint was given him, he not took't, Or did it from his teeth. **1616** WITHALS 562 A friend from the teeth outward. **1721** KELLY 105 . . . That is, not inwardly, and from my Heart. **1898** CUNNINGHAME GRAHAM *Mogreb-El-Acksa* 25 Christ and Mohammed never will be friends. . . . Even the truce they keep is from the teeth outwards.

Teeth guard the tongue, Good that the. (T 424)

1572 CRADOCKE *Ship of Assured Safety* 31 The tongue . . . to the intente it might be the better fashioned, and not poured out to much at random, it is compased (as it were) about with a double wal, both of the teeth and the lips. **?1574** SIR H. SIDNEY to Philip Sidney *Harl. Misc.* vii. 566 Remember how Nature hath, as it were, rampired up the Tongue with Teeth, Lips, yea, and Hair without the Lips, and all betoken Reins and Bridles to the Restraining the Use of that Member. **1579** LYLY *Euph.* i. 279 We maye see the cunning and curious worke of Nature, which hath barred and hedged nothing in so stronglye as the tongue, with two rowes of teeth, therewith two lyppes. *c.* **1580** P. SIDNEY I *Arcadia* iv. 223 Lippes . . . Whichen ever parte but that they showe, Of precyous partes the Duble Rowe, The second sweetely fenced warde, Her heuenly dewed Tounge to garde. **1586** LA PRIMAUDAYE tr. T. Bowes 130 It seemeth that nature would teach vs [the dangers of the tongue] by fortifing the toong better than any other part of the body, and by setting before it the bulworke of the teeth, that . . . we might . . . chastice the impudencie thereof with blouddy biting. **1596** SHAKES. *Rich. II* I. iii. 166 Within my mouth you have enjail'd my tongue, Doubly portcullis'd with my teeth and lips. **1659** HOWELL *Br. Prov.* 10.

Teeth, *see also* Bite. (If you cannot) never show your t.; Cast in the t.; Dragon's t.; Spite of one's t.

Tell a lie and find a (the) truth. (L 237)

c. **1594** BACON *Promus* no. 610 Di mentira y saqueras verdad. (Tell a lye to know a truth.) **1596** SHAKES. *K.J.* III. i. 275 Though indirect, Yet indirection thereby grows direct, And falsehood falsehood cures, as fire cools fire. **1600–1** *Id. H.* II. i. 64 And thus we do . . . By indirections find directions out. **1605** BACON *Adv. Learn.* II. ii. 18 There are few men so true to themselves and so settled, but that, . . . they open themselves; specially if they be put to it with a counter-dissimulation, according to the proverb of Spain, Di mentira, y sacaras verdad: Tell a lie and find a truth. **1678** RAY 75 (the troth). **1732** FULLER no. 4324 (find out).

Tell another tale, To make one. (T 49)

1481 CAXTON *Reynard* ch. 32, Arb. 94 I shal telle hym a nother tale. **1530** PALSGRAVE 596a

And I catche you, I wyll make you tell me another tale. *c.* **1577** J. NORTHBROOKE *Treat. agst. Dicing* 159 Marke the effects thereof, and then you shall tell me another tale. **1600–1** SHAKES. *M.W.W.* I. i. 67 And here [is] young Master Slender, that peradventures shall tell you another tale, if matters grow to your liking. **1602** *Id. T.C.* I. ii. 80 You shall tell me another tale when th'other's come to 't. **1604** *Id. O.* V. i. 125 Come, mistress, you must tell 's another tale. **1678** RAY 348 You will tell another tale when you are tryed.

Tell how many holes be in a scummer, You. (H 524)

1616 WITHALS 553. **1639** CLARKE 146.

Tell me it snows. (T 86)

1585 A. MUNDAY *Fedele & Fortunio* l. 1194 Tush, ... I had as liue you tolde me that it snew. **1639** CLARKE 8 Fiddle, faddle, tell me it snowes. **1670** RAY 193.

Tell me news. (N 154)

1547 SENECA *De Remediis Fortuitorum* Eng. trans. A3 I thought thou woldest haue shewd me some newes. **1586** ELIZABETH to Lords & Commons (Neale *Eliz. & her Parl. 1584–1601*) I believe therein their meaning was to tell me news: and news it is to me indeed. **1603** RALEIGH in *Criminal Trials* (1832) i. 408 All this while you tell me news, Mr. Attorney. **1622** J. DE LUNA *Grammar Span. & Eng.* 261 You tell me no newes. **1670** RAY 187.

Tell me with whom thou goest, and I'll tell thee what thou doest. (T 87)

1581 GUAZZO i. 57 Tel me with whom thou doest goe, and I shall know what thou doest. **1678** RAY 147. **1706** STEVENS s.v. Dezir Tell me your Company and I'll tell you who you are. **1710** PALMER 36.

Tell (Reckon) money after your own father (kin). (M 1093)

1604 S. HIERON *The Preacher's Plea* (1605) 236 We have a Prouerbe, that a man must tell mony euen after his owne father. **1616** DRAXE no. 2175 A man must tell golde after his owne father. **1639** CLARKE 90. **1692** L'ESTRANGE *Aesop's Fab.* cccxl (1738) 353 One gave him a fee of forty broad pieces: he took 'em, and counted 'em (as *a man may count money after his father,* they say). **1721** KELLY 284 Reckon Money after all your Kin.

Tell not all you know, all you have, or all you can do.

1642 TORRIANO 77 Never tell what thou knowst, what thou hast, or what thou canst do. **1659** HOWELL *It. Prov.* 12 Never tell all thou knowest, thou canst, or hast. **1739** FRANKLIN Oct. Proclaim not all thou knowest, all thou owest, all thou hast, nor all thou canst.

Tell that to the marines!

1805 J. DAVIS *Post Captain* ch. 5. **1823** BYRON *Island* II. xxi Right, quoth Ben, that will do for the marines. **1824** SCOTT *Redg.* ch. 14 Tell that to the marines—the sailors won't believe it. **1850** THACKERAY *Pendennis* ch. 67 'Tell that to the marines, Major', replied the valet, 'that cock won't fight with me'. **1928** *Times* 21 Jul. 17/5 He said that I should ... most likely be shot. I ventured to suggest that he should tell that to the Marines.

Tell thy foe that thy foot aches (sleeps), Never. (F 412)

c. **1300** *Prov. of Hending* 12 Tel thou neuer thy fo that they fot aketh. **1641** FERGUSSON no. 858 Thou should not tell thy foe when thy fit slides. **1721** KELLY 317 Tell not thy Foe when thy Foot's sleeping, nor thy Stepminny when thou'rt sore hungry. **1862** HISLOP 156 Ne'er tell your fae when your fit sleeps.

Tell truth and shame the devil. (T 566)

1548 PATTEN *Exped. Scotl. (Eng. Gar.* iii. 61) An epigram ..., the which I had, or rather (to say truth and shame the devil, for out it will) I stale ... from a friend of mine. **1576** GASCOIGNE *Grief of Joy* ii. 555 I will tell trewth, the devyll hymselfe to shame, Although therby I seeme to purchase blame. **1597** SHAKES. *I Hen. IV* III. i. 58 And I can teach thee, coz, to shame the devil By telling truth: tell truth and shame the devil. **1611** GRUTER 186 Truth shameth the divell. **1614** CAMDEN 313 (as 1611). **1738** SWIFT Dial. I. E.L. 288 Well, but who was your author? Come, tell truth and shame the devil. **1853** TRENCH vi. 129.

Tell where to turn his nose, He cannot. (N 216)

c. **1570** *A Balade of a Preist* in *Anct. Ballads & Broadsides* (1867) 211 The prouerbe is true in you, I suppose,—He cannot tell where to turne his nose.

Tell you a tale and find you ears too? Must I. (T 41)

1546 HEYWOOD II. ix. K3ᵛ Who euer with you any time therein weares, He must both tell you a tale, and fynde you eares. **1670** RAY 195 Tell you a tale, and find you ears. **1738** SWIFT Dial. I. E.L. 275.

Tell you, you are an ass, If one, two, or three | put on a bridle (tail).

1678 RAY *Adag. Hebr.* 396 If any say that one of thine ears is the ear of an ass, regard it not: If he say so of them both, procure thyself 'a bridle: That is, it is time to arm ourselves with patience when we are greatly reproached. **1732** FULLER no. 2697 (Tail). **1903** *Brit. Wkly* 9 Apr. 673 The outsider's judgment is usually safe. It is written in the Talmud, 'If thy friends agree in calling thee an ass, go and get the halter round thee'. **1911** A. COHEN *Anct. Jew. Prov.* 89 If one person tell thee thou hast ass's ears, take no notice; should two tell thee so, procure a saddle for thyself.

Tell¹ your cards, and then tell me what you have won. (C 80)

1548 W. PATTEN *Exped. into Scotland* (Tudor Tracts 65) Now, where they will have it no Field, let them tell their cards, and count their winning. *c.* **1549** HEYWOOD I. xi. D4.   **1678** RAY 68. When you have counted your cards you'll find you have gained but little.   **1732** FULLER no. 5628 When you have counted your cards, you'll find you have little left. [¹ count.]

Teller, *see* Tale runs as it pleases t.

Tells a secret, He that | is another's servant. *Cf.* Secret is thy prisoner.
(S 192)

1581 GUAZZO i. 71 He bringeth him selfe in subjection to another, which telleth his secret to him who knewe it not.   **1585** A. MUNDAY *Fedele & Fortunio* I. 1 He that discloseth to a freend the secrets of his minde: Dooth rob him selfe of libertie.   **1623** WODROEPHE 277 To him thou tellest thy Secret, thou giuest also thy Liberty. **1640** HERBERT no. 512.   **1647** HOWELL *Lett.* 14 Feb. (1903) II. 257 I find it now true, that he who discovers his secrets to another sells him his liberty and becomes his slave.   **1659** TOR-RIANO no. 218 Who tels his secrets makes himself a slave.   **1706** STEVENS S.V. Puridad To him you tell your Secret, to him you resign your Liberty.   **1773** VIEYRA S.V. Amigo Tell thy friend the secret, and h'll lay his foot on thy throat.

Tells his wife news, He that | is but newly married.
(W 347a, 362)

c. **1275** *Provs. of Alfred* (Skeat) A 269 Ne wurth thu neuer so wod, ne so wyn-drunke, That euer segge thine wife alle thine wille. [Never be so mad or so drunken as to tell all thy counsel to thy wife.]   **1541** *Schoolh. of Women* D2ᵛ Be wyse and ware, wake ye or wynke And tell not your wyfe all that ye thynke.   **1640** HERBERT no. 987.   **1642** FULLER *H. & P. State* I. iii. He keeps her in the wholesome ignorance of un-necessary secrets. . . . He knows little, who will tell his wife all he knows.   **1732** FULLER no. 2330 (omitting 'news').

Tell(s), told, *see also* Ass kicks you (When) never t. it; Bird t. me; Do not all you can, t. not all you know; Glass t. you (What your) will not be t. by counsel; Kiss and t.; Know all (Since you) t. me what I dreamed; Post, (As good speak (t. it) to the); Tale ill t. marred in telling; Tale to a deaf man, (You t. a); When? Can you t.?

Tell-truth, *see* Tom T.-t.

Temperance is the best physic.
1520 WHITTINGTON *Vulg.* E.E.T.S. 45 He that foloweth temperaunce . . . nedeth no physicyons.

Tempers (*verb*), *see* God t. the wind.

Tempest, *see* No t. good July.

Temple brough, *see* Winkabank.

Tempt(ed), *see* Busy (He that is) is t. by one devil; Devil t. all but idle man t. devil; Open door may t. a saint.

Ten, *see* Bayard of t. toes.; Commandments; Turns lie dead . . . (T. good).

Tenants, *see* Aching teeth, (Who has) has ill t.

Tender as a parson's leman, As. (P 68)
1546 HEYWOOD I. x. C4.   **1571** J. BRIDGES *Sermon at Paul's Cross* 125.   **1659** HOWELL *Eng. Prov.* 15a.

Tender as Parnell, that broke her finger in a posset-curd, As. (P 58)
1678 RAY 289.   **1785** GROSE S.V. Tender.

Tender Gordons, You are one of the | that dow¹ not be hanged for galling their neck.
1721 KELLY 380 . . . Spoken to those who readily complain of Hurts and Hardships. [¹ could.]

Tenham, *see* Live a little while.

Tent¹ thee, I will | quoth Wood: if I can't rule my daughter, I'll rule my good. (W 744)
1670 RAY 52 . . . *Chesh.* [¹ attend to, take heed.]

Tenterden steeple is the cause of Goodwin Sands. (T 91)
[The land now represented by these quicksands, opposite Sandwich, was submerged, about 1100, because, it is said, the stones for its sea-wall were used by the abbot of St. Augustine's, Canterbury, for the tower of Tenterden church.] **1528** MORE *Dialogue* in Wks. (1557) 278 col. 1. **1550** LATIMER *Last Serm. bef. Edw. VI* P.S. 251 'Forsooth, sir', quoth he, 'I am an old man; I think that Tenterton steeple is the cause of Goodwin sands'.   **1662** FULLER *Kent* 65 (of the Breach in). It is used Commonly in derision of such who, being demanded to render a reason of some important Accident, assign . . . a Ridiculous and improbable cause thereof. . . . But . . . the old man had told a rational tale, had he found but the due favour to finish it.

Tenterhooks, To be on.
[= in a state of painful suspense.] **1748** SMOLLETT *Rod. Rand.* ch. 45 I left him upon the tenter-hooks of impatient uncertainty.   **1761** A. MURPHY *Old Maid* Wks. (1786) II. 160 The heart . . . flutters upon the tenterhooks of expectation.   **1887** *Sat. Rev.* 25 Dec. 754/1 The author keeps . . . the reader . . . on tenter-hooks.

Term time in the court of conscience, It is always.
1732 FULLER no. 2914.

Testament(s), *see* Nothing patent in New T.; Tochers (The greatest) make not greatest t.; Weime (That which is in my) is not in my t.

Tester, *see* Handsome head of hair.

Testoons are gone to Oxford to study in Brasenose.[1]   (T 92)

[Henry VIII debased the coins to ⅓ silver and ⅔ alloy. The testoons (shillings) having the king's full face soon began to show the inferior metal at the end of the nose.] **1562** HEYWOOD *Fourth Hund. Epig.* no. 63, Testons be gone to Oxforde, god be their speede: To studie in Brazennose there to proceede. **1662** FULLER Oxf. 328 . . . This Proverb began about the end of the raign of King Henry the eighth . . . . *Testons* especially . . . [were] *allayed* . . . with Copper (which common people confound with Brass). [1 Brasenose College was founded in 1509.]

Tether, *see* End of one's t., (To reach the); Hair to make a t.

Tewkesbury mustard.   (M 1333)

[**1500** ERASM. *Sinapi victitare.*] *c.* **1594** BACON no. 813 To feed upon mustard . . . of the crabbed and gloomy. **1594** NASHE *Terrors of the Night* i. 350. **1596** *Id. Saffron W.* iii. 25. **1598** SHAKES. *2 Hen. IV* II. iv. 230 His wit is as thick as Tewkesbury mustard. **1662** FULLER *Glos.* 353 He looks as if he had liv'd on Tewkesbury Mustard. It is spoken partly of such who always have a sad, severe, and tetrick countenance.

Thames, *see* Ducks fare well in T.; Safe from the E. Indies, drowned in T.; Set the T. on fire.

Thanet, *see* England wrings (When), T. sings.

Thank you for nothing.   (N 277)

1594 LYLY *Mother B.* II. iii. 95 I thank you for nothing, because I vnderstand nothing. *a.* **1595** PLAUTUS *Menaechmi* tr. W. W. IV. God a mercy for nothing. *Ibid.* v. I thanke ye for nothing **1668** SHADWELL *Sullen Lov.* v. iii. Merm. 110 Thank you for nothing. Is this the honour you have for me . . . ? **1712** ADDISON *Spect.* no. 391 Wks. (Bohn) III. 366 One . . . promised Jupiter . . . a silver cup. Jupiter thanked him for nothing. **1847–8** THACKERAY *Vanity F.* ch. 24 It's you who want to introduce beggars into my family. Thank you for nothing, Captain.

Thank you for the next, I will | for this I am sure of.   (N 157)

[*c.* **1591**] **1595** PEELE *O.W.T.* 1. 281 Holily praised neighbour, as much for the next. *a.* **1637** JONSON *Tale Tub* I. i. 88 I thanke you Squires-worship, Most humbly (for the next, for this I am sure of). **1678** RAY 273. **1738** SWIFT Dial. II. E.L. 313 Your wine is excellent good, so I thank you for the next, for I am sure of this.

Thank (*verb*), *see also* God and my cunning, (I t.).

Thankless, *see* Many a man serves t. master.

Thanks, *see* Gets little t. for losing his own; Keep your t. to feed your cat; Loses his t. who delays; Old t. pay not new debt; Rank courtesy when man forced give t. for own.

That is for that, and butter's for fish.

1721 KELLY 336 . . . Spoken when a thing fits nicely what it was design'd for. **1738** SWIFT Dial. I. E.L. 283 Well, so much for that, and butter for fish.

Thatch Groby Pool[1] **with pancakes, Then I'll.**   (G 460)

1678 RAY 317 (*Leics.*). **1787** GROSE (*Leics.*) 192 . . . Spoken when something improbable is promised or foretold. **1818** SCOTT *Ht. Midl.* ch. 29 'I hope there is nae bad company on the road, sir?' . . . 'Why, when it's clean without them I'll thatch Groby pool wi' pancakes.' [1 a large sheet of water near Leicester.]

Thatched his house, When I have | he would throw me down.   (H 787)

1639 CLARKE 170. **1732** FULLER no. 5559 (he would have hurl'd me from the Roof).

Thatches his house with turds, He that | shall have more teachers than reachers.   (H 761)

1678 RAY 209. **1721** KELLY 147 . . . He that is engaged in a difficult and troublesome Business, will have more to give him their Advice than their Assistance. **1762** SMOLLETT *Sir Launcelot Greaves* ch. 15.

Thatch(ed, es), *see also* Head is down (When my), house is t.; Long as he is lither (If he were), he might t. a house.

There or thereabouts, as Parson Smith says.   (P 72)

1643 CHAS. I (to Rupert): *Pythouse Papers* I. I So desyring you to have care of the Armes and Clothes there and thereabouts. **1678** RAY 343 . . . Proverbial about Dunmow in Essex.

Thereby hangs (lies) a tale.   (T 48)

1523 SKELTON *Garl. Laurel* l. 1200 Yet, thoughe I say it, therby lyeth a tale. **1594–8** SHAKES. *T.S.* IV. i. 50 Out of their saddles into the dirt, and thereby hangs a tale. **1599** *Id. A.Y.* II. vii. 28 And then from hour to hour we rot and rot, And thereby hangs a tale. **1600–1** *Id. M.W.W.* I. iv. 132 Have not your worship a wart above your eye? . . . And thereby hangs a tale. **1604** *Id. O.* III. i. 8 Are these, I pray you, wind-instruments?—Ay, marry, are they, sir.—O! thereby hangs a tail.—Whereby hangs a tale, sir?—Marry, sir, by many a wind-instrument that I know. *a.* **1642** SUCKLING *Ballad on Wed.* The maid (and thereby hangs a tale).

Therm, *see* Wide t. had never long arm.

'They say so', is half a lie (liar). (T 99)

1666 TORRIANO *It. Prov.* 30 no. 32 To have heard say, is half a lye. **1710** PALMER 261 I heard One SaySo is half a Lye or They Say is half a Lye. **1732** FULLER no. 4970. **1853** TRENCH i. 13 (half a liar).

They say!—What say they?—Let them say.

[From a late engraved Roman gem: Λέγουσιν
ἃ θέλουσιν· λεγέτωσαν· οὐ μέλ[ε]ι μοι.] *c.* 1593
KEITH, EARL MARISCHAL in W. WATT *Aberdeen
& Banff* (1900) 179 The defiant motto which
the fifth earl inscribed on . . . his college[1] in
Aberdeen—'They haif said: Quhat say thay?
Lat thame say.' [¹ Marischall Coll. in the
University of Aberdeen.]

Thick and thin, Through.   (T 101)

[= through everything that is in the way.] *c.*
1000 *Exeter Bk. Riddles* in *Anglo-Saxon Poetic
Records* ed. Krapp & Dobbie no. 59 ll. 35–6 . . .
þaet ic mid ryhte reccan moste þicce and þynne.
c. **1386** CHAUCER *Reeve's T.* l. 4064 Whan the
hors was loos, he ginneth gon Toward the fen,
. . . thurgh thikke and thurgh thenne. **1530**
PALSGRAVE 827b. **1543** GRAFTON *Contn. Harding* 544 Kyng Richard . . . purposed to goo
thorow thicke and thinne in this mater. **1782**
COWPER *Gilpin* 45 Six precious souls, and all
agog To dash through thick and thin.

Thick and threefold.   (T 100)

1533 SIR T. MORE *Debellation* 1557 ed. 930a But
than herde I shortely that thicke and thre folde
the pennes went to worke. **1548** HALL *Hen.
VIII: Chron.* 186 Afterward, when mo new
Testamentes were imprinted, they came thicke
and threfold into England. **1549** ERASM. tr.
Chaloner *Praise of Folly* L4ᵛ. **1650** FULLER
Pisgah Sight II. ix. Disaster . . . which afterwards
fell thick and threefold upon it. **1759** STERNE
Tristram Shandy II. xxxviii. 170.

Thick as thieves, As.

1833 T. HOOK *Parson's Dau.* II. ii. She and my
wife are as thick as thieves, as the proverb goes.

Thick sown thin come up.   (S 692)

1564 *A Pleasant Dial. betw. the Cap & the Head*
(1565 ed.) A3 Such Heades are thick sowne but
come thin vp. **1580** LYLY *Euph. & his Eng.* ii.
134 Faire women are set thicke, but they come
vp thinne. *a.* **1637** JONSON *Tale of a Tub* III. vi.
43 Husbands, they say, grow thick; but thin
are sowne. **1671** CLARKE *Phras. Puer.* s.v.
Seldome 304 Such men come up thin.

Thick, *see also* Fast (T.) as hops; Put it on t., a
little will stick.

Thief does fear each bush an officer,
The. *Cf.* Thinks every bush a boggard.
                                    (T 112)
1563 SACKVILLE 'Buckingham' *Mirr. for Mag.*
(Campbell 325) Much like the felon that pursued
by night, Startes at eche bushe as his foe were
in sight. **1583** MELBANCKE *Philot.* 166 Tush,
thou art like a Thiefe, that thinkes euerye Tree
a true man. **1591** SHAKES. *3 Hen. VI* V. vi. 12
Suspicion always haunts the guilty mind; The
thief doth fear each bush an officer. **1594** NASHE
Unf. Trav. ii. 319 A theefe, they saie, mistakes
euerie bush for a true man.

Thief for the widdy[1], It is as meet as a.
                                    (T 106)
1641 FERGUSSON no. 538. [¹ gallows.]

Thief is sorry he is to be hanged, but
not that he is a thief, The.

1732 FULLER no. 4788.

Thief knows a thief as a wolf knows a
wolf, A.   (T 115)

1539 TAVERNER 35 The thefe knoweth the thefe,
and the wolfe the wolfe. **1616** DRAXE no. 1160
One thiefe knoweth another. **1732** FULLER
no. 430.

Thief passes for a gentleman when
stealing has made him rich, A.

1732 FULLER no. 431. **1802** WOLCOT (P. Pindar)
Middl. Elect. ch. 3 A thief may be a gentleman
That git'th estates by stealing.

Thief robs (will not rob) another, One.
                                    (T 108)
1539 TAVERNER 9 One false merchaunte de-
ceyueth an other. *a.* **1575** J. PILKINGTON
Nehemiah P.S. 460 One thief will not rob
another. **1600** *Sir J. Oldcastle* III. iv (*Shaks.
Apoc.*) 146 Wel, if thou wilt needs haue it, there
tis: iust the prouerb, one thiefe robs another.
1672 WALKER 45 no. 8 One thief accuseth
another.

Thief to catch (take) a thief, Set a.
                                    (T 110)
1654 GAYTON *Pleas. Notes Don Quix.* IV. ii. 178
As they say, set a fool to catch a fool; a Proverb
not of that gravity (as the Spaniards are), but
very usefull and proper. **1655** FULLER *Ch. Hist.*
IX. iii. (1868) II. 596 Many were his lime-twigs
to this purpose. . . . Always set a —— to catch
a ——; and the greatest deer-stealers make the
best park-keepers. **1670** RAY 148. **1778** LANG-
TON in BOSWELL *Johnson* lxvi (1848) 611 'A fine
surmise. Set a thief to catch a thief.' **1812**
EDGEWORTH *Absentee* ch. 17 'You have been
all your life evading the laws . . .; do you think
this has qualified you peculiarly for being a
guardian of the laws?' Sir Terence replied, 'Yes,
sure; set a thief to catch a thief is no bad maxim.'

Thieves and rogues have the best luck,
if they do but scape hanging.   (T 120)
1670 RAY 118.

Thieves and whores meet at the gallows.

1626 BRETON *Soothing* B3ᵛ. **1639** CLARKE 207.

Thieves fall out, When | true (honest)
men come to their own.   (T 122)

1546 HEYWOOD II. ix. L1 Whan theeues fall out,
true men come to their goode. **1616** BRETON
Cross. Prov. A3ᵛ When theeues fall out, true
men come by their goods. **1629** T. ADAMS *Serm.*
(1861–2) II. 395 This is eventually one good
effect of many controverted points: the way is

cleansed for others, though not for themselves. Thieves falling out, true men come by their goods. **1681** S. COLVIL *Whiggs Sup.* II. 53 When thieves reckon, it's oft-times known That honest people get their own. **1710** PALMER 327 (knaves). **1721** KELLY 345 When Thieves reckon leal[1] Folks come to their Geer.[2] **1866** KINGSLEY *Hereward* ch. 15 The rogues have fallen out, and honest men may come by their own. [[1] honest. [2] goods.]

Thieves, All are not | that dogs bark at.
(A 117)

1577 PEACHAM *Garden of Eloquence* (1593) 30 All are not theeves that dogges barke at. **1616** DRAXE no. 542. **1639** CLARKE 54. **1670** RAY 56.

Thieves' handsel ever unlucky. *Cf.* Ill-gotten goods.

1686-7 J. AUBREY *Remains of Gent. & Jud.* ed. J. Britten 120 (a proverb).

Thief (-ves), *see also* Ask my fellow if I be t.; Beggar may sing before t.; Bolder than miller's neckcloth (What is); Brings up his son to nothing (He that); Building is a t.; Call her whore (scold, t.) first; Careless hussy makes many t.; Ease makes t.; Every man gets his own (When), t. will get widdie; Friends are t. of time; Great t. hang little ones; Hole calls the t.; Honour among t.; Hop whore pipe t.; Ill layers up make t.; Liar worse than t.; Looks as the wood were full of t.; Marries a widow and two children, marries three t. . . .; Men of all trades (Of the) they hang t.; Miller (Many a) many a t.; No receiver no t.; Old t. new halter; Once a t., always a t.; Opportunity makes the t.; Poor kin that has neither whore nor t.; Postern door makes t.; Procrastination t. of time; Put a miller . . . in a bag, the first will be t.; Receiver is as bad as t.; Rope enough (Give a t.); Rope for a thief (Meet as); Safe as a t. in a mill; Save a t. from the gallows and . . .; Salisbury plain seldom without t.; Show me a liar and I will show t.; Tale-bearer is worse than t.; Thick as t.; Thunders (When it) t. becomes honest; True man and a t. think not the same; War makes t., peace hangs them; Whores and t. go by clock; Worth it as a t. worth a rope.

Thimble, *see* Four farthings and a t.; Tine t. tine thrift.

Thin as Banbury cheese, As. *Cf.* Banbury zeal.
(C 268)

1562 HEYWOOD *Sixth Hund. Epig.* no. 24, 204 I neuer saw Banbery cheese thicke enough. **1600-1** SHAKES. *M.W.W.* I. i. 115 (to Slender) You Banbery Cheese. **1601** *Pasquil & Kath.* III. 178 Put off your clothes, and you are like a Banbery cheese, Nothing but paring.

Thin end of the wedge is to be feared, The.

1858 TROLLOPE *Dr. Thorne* ch. 31 [ch. heading] The Small End of the Wedge. **1884** BLACKMORE

Tom. Upmore ch. 17 My father kept calling him . . . the thin end of the wedge, and telling dear mother . . . not . . . to let him in. **1908** *Spectator* 15 Feb. 263 The Mission inserted the thin end of its wedge when it set up constant communications with a Legate from the Emperor.

Thin meadow is soon mowed, A.
(M 781)

a. **1659** FULLER *Serm.* (1891) II. 570 By his vastation to leave . . . footing for foreign enemies to fasten on this country. . . . And no wonder if a thin meadow were quickly mown. **1670** RAY 26.

Thin, *see also* Thick and t.; Thick sown t. come up.

Thing in it, There is a | (quoth the fellow when he drank the dish-clout).
(T 146)

1639 CLARKE 8. **1732** FULLER no. 4884 (drunk Dish-clout and all).

Thing that's done has an end (is not to do), The.
(T 149)

1605-6 SHAKES. *M.* I. vii. 1 If it were done when 'tis done, then 'twere well It were done quickly. *a.* **1637** JONSON *Tale of a Tub* II. i. 1 Cheare up, the better leg avore: This is a veat is once done, and no more. *c.* **1641** FERGUSSON MS. no. 1362 The thing that is don is not to do. **1666** TORRIANO *It. Prov.* 55 no. 14 The thing done hath an end.

Thing that's, *see also under significant words following.*

Things are at the worst they will mend, When.
(T 216)

1582 WHETSTONE *Hept. Civil Disc.* U3 Let this comfort you: that thinges when they are at the worst, begin again to amend. The Feauer giueth place to health, when he hath brought the pacyent to deathes doore. *c.* **1594** BACON no. 1456 When things are at the periode of yll they turne agayne. **1596** SHAKES. *K.J.* III. iv. 114 Evils that take leave, On their departure most of all show evil. **1600** *Sir J. Oldcastle* IV. iii. (*Shaks. Apoc.*) 153 Patience, good madame, things at worst will mend. **1605-6** SHAKES. *M.* IV. ii. 24 Things at the worst will cease, or else climb upward To what they were before. **1615** J. CHAMBERLAIN *Letters* i. 596. **1623** WEBSTER *Duch. of M.* IV. i. Merm. 200 Things being at the worst begin to mend. **1858** SURTEES *Ask Mamma* ch. 25 Certainly, things got to their worst in the farming way, before they began to mend. **1885** R. G. MOULTON *Shaks. as Dram. Art.* 46 Proverbs like . . . 'When things come to the worst they are sure to mend', exactly express moral equilibrium.

Things present are judged by things past.
(T 205)

1573 SANFORD 52. **1578** FLORIO *First F.* 30. **1629** *Bk. Mer. Rid.* Prov. no. 36.

Things that are above us, The | are nothing to us. (T 206)

[ERASM. *Quae supra nos nihil ad nos.*] **1539**
TAVERNER 19ᵛ The thynges that be aboue vs,
belonge nothynge vnto vs. This was the saying
of Socrates. **1545** *Precepts of Cato* G4 That
whiche is aboue vs, belongeth not vnto vs. **1547**
BALDWIN P3ᵛ Socrates, Suche thinges as are
aboue vs, pertayne not vnto vs. **1571** R.
EDWARDES *Damon & Pythias* l. 35. **1580** LYLY
Euph. & his Eng. ii. 41. **1583** STUBBES *Anat.* N.
Sh. S. II. i. 56 It is an olde saieng, . . . *Quae
supra nos, nihil ad nos,* Those things that are
aboue our reach, conserne vs not, and therefore
we ought not to enter into the bowels and
secrets of the Lord. *c.* **1592** GREENE *Friar Bacon*
l. 195. **1616** GREENE *Mourn. Garm.* Gros. ix.
185 His Aphorisms are too farre fetcht for me,
and therefore, *Quae supra nos, nihil ad nos.*
1621 BURTON *Anat. Mel.* I. ii. I. ii. (1638) 45 But
be they [sublunary devils] more or lesse, *Quod
supra nos nihil ad nos* (what is beyond our comprehension does not concern us).

Things that are below us, The | are nothing to us.

1860 RILEY *Dict. Lat. Quot.* 353 *Quae infra
nos nihil ad nos. Prov.* 'The things that are below
us are nothing to us.' We must look upwards.

Things that are, Things of, *see also under
significant words following.*

Things that must be, In | it is good to be resolute.

1732 FULLER no. 2830.

Thing which is rare is dear, That. (T 145)

1597 *Politeuphuia* 152 The things that are most
skant to be gotten are most deere of price, and
the things seldom spoken of, most desired. **1606**
J. FORD *Honor Triumphant* 24 Rara praeclara;
according to the proverbe, that the fairest are
the rarest, that is, the best and best to be estemed.
1666 TORRIANO *It. Prov.* 55 no. 13.

Thing(s), *see also* All t. are good unseyit; All t.
are to be bought at Rome; All t. fit not all
persons; All t. in their being are good for something; All t. require skill but appetite; All t.
thrive at thrice; All t. to all men; Beginnings
(From small) come great t.; Borrowed t. will
home again; Cap after a t., (To throw); Every
man likes his own t. best; Give a t. and take a t.;
Good t. are hard; Good t. soon caught up;
Little t.; Many t. happen unlooked for; Modest
words to express immodest t.; Money has what
he wants (most t.) (He that has); Neighbour
(An ill) is an ill t.; One t. at a time; One t.
brings up another t.; Poor man wants some t.,
covetous man all t.; Reason in all t.; Time cures
all t.; Time devours all t.; Time discloses all t.;
Time for all t.

Think a calf a muckle beast that never saw a cow, They.

1832 HENDERSON 95.

Think no labour (travail) slavery that brings in penny saverly.[1] (W 841)

1573 TUSSER 17 To count no trauell slauerie,
that brings in peny sauerlie. **1813** RAY 42.
[1 by saving.]

Think no small beer of oneself, To.

1837 SOUTHEY *Doctor* IV. 381 It is clear . . . that
the Author does not in vulgar parlance, think
Small Beer of himself. **1840** DE QUINCEY *Style*
Wks. XI. 174 Should express her self-esteem by
the popular phrase, that she did not 'think
small beer of herself'.

Think none ill, They that | are soonest beguiled. (T 221)

1546 HEYWOOD II. v. H4ᵛ. **1590** SPENSER *F.Q.*
III. ii. 54 Who meanes no guile, beguiled soonest
shall. **1600–1** SHAKES. *H.* IV. vii. 135 He, being
remiss, Most generous, and free from all con-
triving, Will not peruse the foils; so that . . . you
may choose A sword unbated, and, in a pass of
practice, Requite him for your father. **1604** *Id.
O.* I. iii. 393 The Moor is of a free and open
nature That thinks men honest that but seem
to be so. **1605–6** *Id. K.L.* I. ii. 170 A brother
noble, Whose nature is so far from doing harms
That he suspects none. **1613** CHAPMAN *Rev.
Bussy D'Amb.* IV. iii. 81 Your noblest natures
are most credulous. **1659** HOWELL *Fr. Prov.* 6
He is easily deceived who thinks no hurt.

Think of ease, but work on. (E 40)

1640 HERBERT no. 178.

Think, One may | that dares not speak. *Cf.* First think. Say little. (T 220)

1605–6 SHAKES. *M.* V. i. 77 I think, but dare not
speak. **1616** DRAXE no. 239. **1639** CLARKE 64.
1659 N.R. 81 One may think what he dares not
speak.

Think there is bacon, Where you | there is no chimney. (B 25)

1640 HERBERT no. 99. **1706** STEVENS S.V.
Tocino. Where I thought to find Flitches of
Bacon, I found not so much as the Pins to hang
. . . them on.

Think well of all men. (M 588)

1659 HOWELL *Eng. Prov.* 10a.

Think with the wise, but talk with the vulgar. (W 530)

1545 ASCHAM *Toxoph.* Arb. 18 He that wyll
wryte well in any tongue, muste folowe thys
counsel of Aristotle, to speake as the common
people do, to thinke as wise men do. **1605**
BACON *Adv. Learn.* II. xiv. 11 (Oxf. 1900) 163
Although we . . . prescribe it well *loquendum
ut vulgus sentiendum ut sapientes.* **1662** FULLER
Lond. 200 Common people (we must speak with
the *volge,* and think with the wise) call it Guttur
Lane. *a.* **1682** Motto of SIR HENRY BLOUNT
(1602–82, Aubrey's *Lives*). **1871** J. HAY *Pike
County Ballads* Speak with the speech of the
world, think with the thoughts of the few.

Thinking is very far from knowing.

1706 STEVENS s.v. Pensar.   1707 MAPLETOFT 50.
1719 DE ALVARADO 96.

**Thinks amiss, He that | concludes
worse.**   (T 222)

1651 HERBERT no. 1046.

Thinks every bush a boggard, He.
Cf. **Thief does fear each bush an officer.**
                                                  (B 738)

1534 MORE *Dial. of Comfort* E.L. 205 In the
night eueri bushe to hym that waxeth once aferd,
semeth a theefe.   1579 GOSSON *Apology* Arb. 65
I am not so childishe to take euery bushe for a
monster.   1594 SHAKES. *Lucr.* l. 972 Let . . . the
dire thought of his committed evil Shape every
bush a hideous shapeless devil.   1595 *Id. M.N.D.*
V. i. 22 Or in the night, imagining some fear,
How easy is a bush suppos'd a bear!   *c.* 1660
R. WATKYNS *The Righteous is Confident as a Lyon*
The guilty conscience fears, when there's no
fear, and thinks that every bush contains a bear.
1678 RAY 232 He thinks every bush a boggard,
i.e. a bugbear or phantasm.

**Thinks his business below him, He that
| will always be above his business.**

1732 FULLER no. 2333.

**Thinks his feet be, He | where his head
shall never come.**   (F 577)

c. 1549 HEYWOOD I. xi. D3ᵛ.   1557 EDGEWORTH
Sermons 4G4 Not to haue any hy opinion of
our selues, thinkynge our feete there, as our
head wil neuer come.   1611 DAVIES no. 343.

**Thinks his penny (farthing, half-
penny) good silver, He.**   (P 194)

[= has a good opinion of himself.]   1546 HEY-
WOOD I. x. C4ᵛ She thinkth her farthyng good
syluer I tell you.   1575 GASCOIGNE *Glass Govt.* ii.
24 I think my halfpenny as good silver as
another doth.   1579 LYLY *Euph.* i. 195 He
deemeth no pennye good siluer but his owne,
preferring . . . his owne witte before all mens
wisedomes.   1590 SIDNEY *Arcadia* II. xiv. I,
simple though I sit here, thought once my penny
as good silver, as some of you do.   1603 BRETON
Packet Mad Let. liv (1879) 20/1 There are more
Batchelors than Roger, and my peny is as|good
siluer as yours.   1721 KELLY 172 He counts
his Halfpenny good Silver. That is, he thinks
much of himself with little Reason.

**Thinks not well, He | that thinks not
again.**   (T 224)

1611 COTGRAVE s.v. Penser He thinks not
well that. . . thinks not more then once.   1640
HERBERT no. 836.

Think(s, ing), thought (*verb*), *see also* End before
you begin, (T. on the); First t. then speak; Fool
says, Who would have t. it; Fool that t. not
that another t.; God by the toe, (When they t.

they have); Ill be to him that t. ill; Lancashire t. today, (What); Mackissock's cow did
(Will do as), I'll t. more than I say; One thing t.
the bear; One thing t. the horse; Put on considering (t.) cap; Say as men say but t.; Say
little but t. the more; Says nothing (Though he),
he pays with t.; Sits well t. ill; Speak (Not to
speak) as one t.; Speak fair and t. what you will;
Speaks in his drink what he t. in his drouth;
Spends before he thrives (Who) will beg before he
t.; Warm (He that is) t. all so; Weal or woe as he
t. himself so.

Third is a charm, The.

1721 KELLY 331 . . . Spoken to encourage those
who have attempted a thing once and again to
try a third time.

**Third of April, On the | comes in the
cuckoo and nightingale.**

1659 HOWELL *Span. Prov.* 21 The third of April
the Cuckow is to come, if he comes not the
eighth day, he is taken or dead.   1732 FULLER
no. 6136.   1846 DENHAM 41.

Third time's lucky, The. *Cf.* **All things
thrive at thrice.** **Luck in odd numbers.**

1840 R. BROWNING to J. Macready (*Lett.* of R.B.
ed. T. L. Hood 1933) 'The luck of the third
adventure' is proverbial.   1862 HISLOP 194.

Third time pays for all, The.   (T 319)

1350 *Seven Sages* l. 2062 Men sais the thrid
time throwes best.   *c.* 1370 *Sir Gawain and the
Green Knight* l. 1680 Thrid tyme throwe best.
1574 HIGGINS *Mirr. for Magist.* I 'Q. Elstride'
st. 23 in *Brit. Bibliographer* 68 The third payes
home, this prouerbe is to true.   1601 SHAKES.
T.N. V. i. 32 Primo, secundo, tertio, is a good
play; and the old saying is, 'the third pays for
all'.   1917 BRIDGE 120 The third time pays· for
all. Never despair.

Thirst, *see* First glass for t.; Speak of my
drinking (Many), but few of my t.

Thirsty, *see* Goes to bed t. (He that).

**Thirteen of you may go to the dozen
well enough.**   (T 227)

1588 'MARPRELATE' *Epistle: Marpr. Tracts* 79 And
pay it you with aduantage, at least thirteen to
the dozen.   1656 *Trepan* 31 Here is·a Stanza of
thirteen to the dozen.   [*a.* 1660] 1693 URQUHART
Gargantua III. xxiv. T.T. iii. 126 That is a pretty
jolly Vow of Thirteen to the Dozen.   1721
KELLY 323 . . . Spoken to worthless Fellows.

**Thistle is a fat salad for an ass's mouth,
A.**

[1642] 1647 CLEVELAND *To P. Regent* l. 50 A
Gelding-Earle Gives no more relish to thy
Female Palat, Then to that Asse did once the
Thistle-Sallat.   1721 KELLY 241 [*Eng.*].   1732
FULLER no. 435.   1802 WOLCOT (P. Pindar)
Middl. Elect. iii. A disell, by an ass's jaws, Is
thoft a pretty sallet.

Thistle(s), *see also* Ass loaded with gold still eats t.; Brain sows not corn (If), plants t.; Good harvest (He that has) content with some t.; Grapes of thorns or figs of t., (One cannot gather); Need of a blessing that kneel to a t.; Simpers like a mare when she eats t.; Sows t. shall reap prickles, (He that).

Thither as I would go, I can go late; thither as I would not go, I know not the gate. (G 45)

1678 RAY 296.

Thole[1] well is good for burning.

a. **1628** CARMICHAELL no. 1517. **1721** KELLY 312 . . . Eng. *Patience and Posset-Drink cures all Maladies.* [[1] bear.]

Thomson, *see* John T.'s man.

Thong(s), *see* Buckle and t.; Buckle and bare t.; Cut large t. of other men's leather (Men); Cut one's t. according to one's leather; Tine the whinger for t.

Thorn comes forth with the point forwards, The. (T 234)

1640 HERBERT no. 238.

Thorn springs not a fig (grape), Of a. (G 411)

[MATT. vii. 16 Do men gather grapes of thorns, or figs of thistles?] **1537** W. TURNER *Old Learn. & New* B3ᵛ How can a thorne tre brynge forth a grape. **1545** BRINKLOW *Lament* (1874) 90 Do briers bring forth figges, and thorns grapes? **1573** *Brief Discourse of murther of George Saunders* (R. Simpson, *School of Sh.* ii. 234) The twiggs of a thorne or bramble can beare no grapes.

Thorn-bush, *see* Dwell (Wherever a man) t.-b. near his door.

Thorney, *see* Ramsey.

Thorns, To be (sit, stand) upon. (T 239)

1528 MORE *Dial. conc. Heresy* Wks. (1557) 234a I long by my trouth, quod he, and euen syt on thornes tyll I see that constitucion. **1561** T. HOBY tr. *Castiglione's Courtyer* ii. (1900) 114 The poore gentilwoman stood upon thornes, and thought an houre a thousande yeare, till she were got from him. *c.* **1580** JEFFERIE *Bugbears* III. ii. in *Archiv. Stud. Neu. Spr.* (1897) I sytt all on thornes till that matter take effect. *a.* **1599** SHAKES. *Son.* no. 99 The roses fearfully on thorns did stand. *c.* **1611** *Id. W.T.* IV. iv. 577. **1768** EARL CARLISLE in *JESSE Selwyn & Contemp.* (1843) II. 316 I should have been upon thorns till you had wrote.

Thorns make the greatest crackling.

[ECCLES. vii. 6 As the crackling of thorns under a pot, so is the laughter of the fool.] **1732** FULLER no. 5031.

Thorns whiten, yet do nothing. (T 237)

1640 HERBERT no. 943.

Thorn(s), *see also* Barefoot must not plant t.; Cuckoo comes to bare t., (When); Early pricks that will be t.; Grapes of t. . . . , (One cannot gather); Handles t. (He that); Honey that is licked from t.; Hunger is sharper than t.; Lie upon roses . . . upon t. when old; Nightingale with a t. against one's breast, (To sit like a); Pull the t. out of your foot (I will not); Rose without t. (No); Truths and roses have t.

Thou thyself canst do it, If | attend no other's help or hand. *Cf.* Served, If you would be well. Want a thing (well) done. (D 401)

1541 COVERDALE *Christ. State Matrimony* 64ᵛ That whych thou cannest do conueniently thy selfe commytte it not to another. **1566** PAINTER *Pal. of Pleasure* i. 87 (Jacobs) This prouerbe olde and true . . . The thing do not expect by frends for to atchieue: which thou thyselfe canst doe, they selfe for to relieue. **1640** HERBERT no. 813. **1705** *Pleas. Art* 150 Rely not an Another, for what thou can'st do thy self. **1710** PALMER 152 For what you can do your Self don't depend on Another.

Though I say it that should not say it. (S 114)

a. **1400** LANGLAND *Piers Plowman* B.V. 556 For thouze I saye it my-self I serue hym [Truth] to paye. *a.* **1500** DIGBY 'Slaughter of the Innocents' 139 Though I sey it my self I am a man of myght. *a.* **1500** *The Nine Worthies* (Tanner MS. 407 f. 32ᵛ Herford & Simpson's *Jonson* ix. 432) And in romaunce often am I [Alexander] leyt As conquerour gret thow I seyt. [c. **1553**] **1566–7** UDALL *Ralph Roister D.* l. 1149 For though I say it, a goodly person ye bee. *a.* **1577** *Misogonus* III. i. Though I sait and should not sait. **1587** *Mirr. for Mag.* ed. Campbell 464 and 263 Hee lou'de me for my fight and person, (though I say). **1594** LYLY *Mother B.* v. iii. 15 Though I say it that should no, haue bene a minstrell these thirties yeeres. **1596** SHAKES. *M.V.* II. ii. 46. *c.* **1610** *Id. W.T.* IV. iv. 176. Though I report it, That should be silent. **1721** KELLY 316 Though you say it, that should not say it, and must say it, if it be said. A Ridicule upon them that commend themselves. **1809** HANNAH MORE *Cœlebs* ch. 5 Though I say it, who should not say it, they are as highly accomplished as any ladies at St. James's. **1818** SCOTT *Ht. Midl.* ch. 27 'I am not able to dispute with you'. 'Few folk are—. . . though I say it that shouldna say it,' returned Bartoline, with great delight.

Thought has good legs, The | and the quill a good tongue. (T 243)

1640 HERBERT no. 612. **1732** FULLER no. 4790 (wings).

Thought is free. (T 244)

c. **1390** GOWER *Conf. Amantis* v. 4485 I have herd seid that thoght is fre. *c.* **1490** *Partonope* E.E.T.S. 440, l. 10884 Therfore þis proverbe

is seide full truly: þought to·a man is euer ffre.
1546 HEYWOOD II. ii. G1 I say little (said she)
but I thinke more. Thought is free. **1580** LYLY
Euph. & his Eng. ii. 60 Why then quoth he,
doest thou thinke me a foole, thought is free
my Lord quoth she. **1601** SHAKES. *T.N.* I. iii.
64 Now, sir, 'thought is free'. **1604** *Id. M.M.*
V. i. 451 Thoughts are no subjects. **1604** *Id. O.*
III. iii. 139 I am not bound to that all slaves are
free to. Utter my thoughts? **1611** *Id. Temp.* III.
ii. 118 Thought is free. **1636** CAMDEN 307
Thoughts be free from toll. **1738** SWIFT *Pol.
Conv.* Introd. E.L. 244 It hath been universally
allowed, that Thought is free. **1874** G. MAC-
DONALD *Malcolm* ch. 39 'How do you come
to think of such things?' 'Thocht's free, my
lord.'

Thought to have asked you, I had.
                                            (T 225)
[A mocking retort.] **1592** SHAKES. *C.E.* III. i. 55
I thought to have ask'd you. **1594** LYLY *Mother
B.* II. iii. 64 (to aske you). *Ibid.* IV. ii. 36.

Thoughts close and your countenance loose, Your.   (T 248)
1612 CHARRON *Of Wisdom* tr. Lennard (1640)
335 *Frons aperta, lingua parca, mens clausa,
nulli fidere*: His face open, his tongue silent,
his mind secret, and to trust none. [**1638**
Letter from SIR HENRY WOTTON to John Milton
printed before *Comus*, *I pensieri stretti e il viso
sciolto* will go safely over the whole World.]
1651 HERBERT no. 1183. **1707** MAPLETOFT 21.
1748 CHESTERFIELD *Lett.* 19 Oct. The height of
abilities is to have *volto sciolto* and *pensieri
stretti*. **1825** SCOTT *Journ.* 28 Nov. He [Lock-
hart] sometimes reverses the proverb and gives
the *volte strette e pensiere sciolti* [sic].

Thought(s) *(noun)*, *see also* Grey hairs are
nourished with green t.; Knave and a fool never
take t.; Penny for your t.; Second t. are best;
Swift (quick) as t. *For* Thought *(verb) see* Think.

Thousand pounds, A | and a bottle of hay, is all one thing at doomsday.
                                            (P 520)
1659 HOWELL *Eng. Prov.* 1b. **1670** RAY 26.
1732 FULLER no. 6398.

Thousand pounds (worth) of law, In a | there's not an ounce of love (a shilling's worth of pleasure).   (P 517)
1611 COTGRAVE S.V. Amour In a hundred pound
of law there's not a halfepenny weight of loue.
1670 RAY 15. **1732** FULLER no. 2811 (a
Shilling's worth of Pleasure).

Thraw[1] the wand[2] while it is green.
                                            (W 27)
1457 HARDING *Chron.* 746 Men . . . writhe the
wande while it is yonge and grene. **1580** LYLY
Euph. & his Eng. ii. 224 Wandes are to be
wrought while they are greene, least they rather
break then bende when they be drye. *a.* **1628**
CARMICHAELL no. 1539. **1641** FERGUSSON no.
789. [[1] twist. [2] rod.]

Thrawn[1] faced bairn that is gotten against the father's will, It is a. (B 42)
a. **1628** CARMICHAELL no. 1571. **1721** KELLY
188 . . . Kindness extorted come[s] always with
an ill Grace. [[1] distorted.]

Thread breaks where it is weakest, The.
                                            (T 251)
1640 HERBERT no. 596. **1706** STEVENS S.V. Hilo
(in the thinnest place). **1732** FULLER no. 5647.

Thread is spun, His.   (T 249)
1565 J. HALL *Court of Venus* M3[v] My hartes
intent, Is to prayse God omnipotent, Whoe of
our helth the thred hath spunne. **1584** HERO-
DOTUS 'Euterpe' tr. B.R. ed. Lang 129 His
thread was almost spoon. **1590** LODGE *Rosalynde* ed. Greg 6 My thriedd is spun, and my
foot is in the grave. **1605** JONSON *Volpone* V. iii.
11 Mosca? Is his thred spunne? **1681** *Roxb.
Ballads* v. 45 Give them what they deserve,
their thread is spun.

Thread will tie an honest man better than a rape[1] will do a rogue, A.
1832 HENDERSON 33. [[1] rope.]

Thread, *see also* Friends tie purse with cobweb t.;
Hair (t.) (To hang by); Put it together with . . .
burnt t.; Rowan tree·and red t.; Spin a fair t.;
Tailor that found t.

Threadbare, *see* Coat, (Under a ragged (t.)) lies
wisdom.

Threadneedle St., The old lady of.
[= the Bank of England.] **1797** 22 May *Punch*
[Title of caricature] The Old Lady in Threadneedle Street in Danger. **1864** J. PAYN *Lost Sir
Massingb.* ch. 27 I trust you are not come about
any fresh wrongs against the Old Lady of
Threadneedle Street.

Threatened folk(s) (men) live long. Cf. Warned folks may live.   (F 425)
c. **1555** COLLMAN *Ballads, &c.* Roxb. Cl. 69 It
is a true prouerbe: the threatned man lyues long.
1560 T. CHURCHYARD *Contention between Churchyard & Camell* B4[v] It is a true prouerbe: the
threatned man lyues·long. **1599** PORTER *Angry
Wom. Abingd.* l. 2337 I, brags a good dog;
threatned folkes liue long. **1614** CAMDEN 313.
1655 FULLER *Ch: Hist.* VIII. iii (1868) II. 476
Gardiner . . . vowed . . . to stop the sending of
all supplies·unto them. . . . But threatened folk
live long. **1865** THORNBURY *Haunted London*
ii Temple Bar was doomed to destruction by
the City as early as 1790. . . . 'Threatened men
live long.' . . . Temple Bar[1] still stands. [[1] taken
down in 1878.]

Threatened men eat bread, says the Spaniard.   (M 589)
1599 MINSHEU *Span. Gram.* 83 Threatned men
eat bread, ∴ The threatned men liue long. **1651**
HERBERT no. 1081.

Threatened than stricken, There are more men. (M 586)

1640 HERBERT no. 256.

Threatens many that hurts any, He. (T 255)

1539 TAVERNER *Publius* D6 He threteneth many that dothe wronge to one. **1572** SIR HUGH PLATT *Flowers of Philosophy* (cited G. Harvey, *Marginalia* 101) He threatenith many That hurtith any. **1604** JONSON *Sejanus* II. i. 476 He threatens many, that hath iniur'd one. **1642** TORRIANO 19 He who punisheth one threatneth a hundred. **1732** FULLER no. 2372.

Three acres and a cow.

[**1885**] **1894** SIR H. MAXWELL *Life of W. H. Smith* 274 The anxiety to secure support from the newly enfranchised labourers gave prominence to Mr. Jesse Collings's formula of 'three acres and a cow', which became the battle-cry of the Liberal party. **1902** DEAN HOLE *Then & Now* ch. 11 An honest man who had worked long and well should have 'three acres and a cow'.

Three blue beans in a blue bladder. (B 124)

[*c.* **1590**] **1594** GREENE *Orl. Fur.* player's part of Orl. l. 136 Thre blew beans a blewe bladder, rattle bladder rattle. *c.* **1591** PEELE *O.W.T.* l. 819 (as *c.* 1590). **1640** *Wit's Recreations* no. 684 As there are three blue . . . There are three Universities. **1686–7** J. AUBREY *Remains of Gent. & Jud.* ed. J. Britten 12. **1715** PRIOR *Alma* c. i, l. 29 They say . . . That, putting all his words together, 'Tis·three blue beans in one blue bladder. **1804** ANNA SEWARD *Mem. of Darwin* 310 It is to the ear no whit more agreeable than 'Three blue . . .' **1827** MOORE *Diary* 12 Sept. Porson's Greek version τρεῖς κύανοι κύαμοι.

Three classes of clergy: Nimrods, ramrods, and fishing-rods.

1902–4 LEAN IV. 159. [i.e. men fond of hunting, shooting, and fishing.]

Three cranes in the Vintry, *see* Patience in adversity.

Three dear years will raise a baker's daughter to a portion. (Y 26)

1678 RAY 86 . . . 'Tis not the smalness of the bread, but the knavery of the baker.

Three failures and a fire make a Scotsman's fortune.

1896 CHEVIOT 369.

Three flails and cuckoo.

1917 BRIDGE 123 . . . A farmer who at the return of the cuckoo can keep three flails at work cannot want for capital or be otherwise than prosperous.

Three halfpence, Not worth.

1540 SIR T. ELYOT *Pasquil the Plain* C4ᵛ Not worth thre halfpens. **1576** AELIAN tr. A. Fleming E1 Skarse woorth three halfpence. **1617** J. SWETNAM *School of Defence* 173 Not . . . worth twopence. **1672** WALKER 26, no. 99.

Three helping one another, bear the burthen of six. (T 256)

1640 HERBERT no. 135.

Three ills come from the north, a cold wind, a shrinking cloth, and a dissembling man. *Cf.* Northern cloth. Shrink in the wetting. (I 38)

1659 HOWELL *Eng. Prov.* 1a. **1670** RAY 19. **1697** MERITON 166 Three great ills come out of the North, A cawd wind, a cunning knave, and a shrinking cloth.

Three L's.

1867 ADM. W. H. SMYTH *Sailor's Word-bk.* 427 The three L's were formerly vaunted by seamen who despised the use of nautical astronomy; viz. lead, latitude, and look-out.

Three letters, A man of. (M 295)

[PLAUTUS *Aulularia* II. iv. 46 *Homo trium literarum.* A man of three letters (i.e. 'fur', a thief).] **1559** COOPER s.v. Homo Homo trium literarum, signifieth sometyme in mockage a man of noble linage, because noble men wrote theyr fornames, their names and surnames with three letters, as. P.Cor. Scipio . . . It is somtyme taken for a thefe, because Fur, hath in it but thre letters. **1888** J. E. T. ROGERS *Econ. Interp. Hist.* II. xxii The various settlers, . . . the aggregate of whom is implied by Juvenal in his word of three letters.

Three Moors to a Portuguese; three Portuguese to an Englishman. (M 1132)

1625 PURCHAS *Pilgrims* (1905–7) I. 35 Even the Indians (which yield commonly in martial, always in Neptunian affairs to the Moors) have a proverb, three Moors to a Portugal, three Portugals to an Englishman.

Three pence, If you make not much of | you'll ne'er be worth a groat. (M 1278)

1609 HARWARD 101 He that will not make much of a litle shall never be maister of much. **1678** RAY 210.

Three R's.

[Toast said to have been first given by Alderman Curtis, hero of Peter Pindar's *Fat Knight and Petition*.] **1828** *Mirror* v. 75/1 The three R's. Reading, Writing, and Rithmetic. **1908** E. M. SNEYD-KYNNERSLEY *H.M.I.* (1910) vi. It was seldom that the examination . . . went beyond the three elementary subjects commonly known as the Three R's. (What philosopher . . . first found out that reading, writing, and arithmetic all began with R?)

Three removes are as bad as a fire.

1736 FRANKLIN *Way to Wealth Wks.* ed. Bigelow i. 445. **1758** *Id.* in ARBER *E. Garner* v. 581 As POOR RICHARD says, I never saw an oft removed tree, Nor yet an oft removed family, That throve so well, as those that settled be. And again, Three Removes are as bad as a Fire. **1839** 14 Nov. DICKENS Letter to Samuel Rogers There is an old proverb that . . . **1852** MRS. CARLYLE *Let.* 25 Sept. Three flittings, they say, is equal to a fire; but a 'thorough repair' is equal to three fires. **1929** *Times* 16 Feb. 10/1 There used to be a saying that three removals were equal to a fire. This applies to householders . . . the handling of their furniture apparently having always involved a serious amount of destruction.

Three sheets in the wind.

[= very drunk.] **1821** EGAN *Real Life* I. xviii. 385 Old Wax and Bristles is about three sheets in the wind. **1840** R. H. DANA *Two Years Bef. Mast* ch. 20 He talked a great deal about . . . steadiness, . . . but seldom went up to the town without coming down 'three sheets in the wind'.

Three skips of a louse (pie[1]), Not worth.
                                                        (S 512)

[*a.* 1529] **1542–8** SKELTON *Agst. Scots* l. 100, Wks. i. 185 (pye). **1545** *Precepts of Cato* Publius M7 Scarse worth thre skyppes of an olde doggue. *c.* **1624** *Marvelous Medicine* in *Roxb. Bal.* viii. 426 And temper it with three leaps of a lowse. [1633] **1640** JONSON *Tale Tub* II. ii. 64 I care not I, Sir, not three skips of a Lowse for you. **1700** SWIFT *Mrs. Harris's Petition: Misc. Poems* 53 'Tis not that I value the money three skips of a louse. **1706** STEVENS s.v. Bayle. [[1] magpie.]

Three sisters.   (S 490)

[The Fates or Parcae.] *c.* **1374** CHAUCER *Troilus* Bk. 3, l. 733 O fatale sustrin! which, er eny clothe Me shapyn was, my destyne me sponne. **1402** LYDGATE *Compl. Bl. Knight* l. 489 Or I was born, my desteny was sponne By Parcas sustren, to slee me, if they come. *c.* **1449** PECOCK *Repr.* II. iv. 155 This opinioun, that iiij. sistris (whiche ben spiritis) comen to the cradilis of infants, forto sette to the babe what schal bifalle to him. **1559** *Mirr. Mag.* (1563) B ij Whose fatall threde false fortune needes would reele, Ere it were twisted by the susters thre. **1595** SHAKES. *M.N.D.* V. i. 327 O, sisters Three, Come, come to me. **1596** *Id.* *M. V.* II. ii. 55 The young gentleman,—according to . . . the Sisters Three and such branches of learning,— is, indeed, deceased. **1598** *Id.* *2 Hen. IV* II. iv. 189 Why then, let grievous, ghastly, gaping wounds Untwine the Sisters Three!

Three things are insatiable, priests, monks, and the sea.

c. **1560** WRIGHT, *Songs, &c.* Philip and Mary (Roxb. Cl.) 208. **1607** H. ESTIENNE *World of Wonders* tr. R.C. 48 . . . Howbeit I haue heard old folkes name these three, Priests, women, and the sea. **1649** TORRIANO 74 The sea, women, and fire, are three evils.

Three things are thrown away in a bowling-green—time, money, and oaths.

1628 EARLE *Microcosmographie* no. xxx A bowl-alley is the place where there are three things thrown away beside bowls, to wit, time, money, and curses, and the last ten to one. **1822** SCOTT *Nigel* ch. 12 The field . . . soon resounded with . . . 'Run, run—rub, rub—hold bias, you infernal trundling timber!' thus making good the saying, that three things are thrown away in a bowling-green, namely, time, money, and oaths.

Three things cost dear: the caresses of a dog, the love of a whore, and the invitation of a host.   (T 208)

1659 TORRIANO no. 148 Three things always brings cost, the fawning of a dog, the love of a whore, and the invitation of a host. **1659** N. R. 105 (a whore). **1707** MAPLETOFT *Ital. Prov.* 3 (a miss).

Three things drive a man out of his house—smoke, rain, and a scolding wife.   (H 781)

[Perhaps the original form of this commonly quoted proverb is this:—'Tria sunt enim quae non sinunt hominem in domo permanere: fumus, stillicidium, et mala uxor'; Innocens Papa, *De Contemptu Mundi*, i. 18. [Compiled] from Prov. x. 26, xix. 13, and xxvii. 15. Note by SKEAT *P. Pl.* (1886) II. 246.] *c.* **1386** CHAUCER *Mel.* l. 1086 Thre thinges dryven a man out of his hous; that is to seyn, smoke, dropping of reyn, and wikked wyves. **1393** LANGLAND *P. Pl.* C. xx. 297–304 Ac thre thynges ther beeth · that doth a man to sterte Out of his owene hous · . . . a wikkede wif · . . . and reyne on hus bedde, . . . Ac when smoke and smorthre · smerteth hus syghte. **1492** *Dial. of Salomon & Marcolphus* ed. Duff 9 An angry housewyf, the smoke, the ratte and a broken plater, are often tymes unprofitable in an howse. **1576** GASCOIGNE *Drum Dooms.* ii. 227 There are three things that suffer not a man to abyde in his owne house. Smooke, Rayne, and an evil wyfe. **1597** SHAKES. *1 Hen. IV* III. i. 158 O! he's as tedious As a tired horse, a railing wife; Worse than a smoky house. **1659** HOWELL *Span. Prov.* 15 Smoak, a dropping gutter, and a scold, cast the good man out of his hold. **1706** STEVENS s.v. Humo.

Three things there be full hard to be known.   (S 349)

[PROV. xxx. 18 There be three things which are too wonderful for me, yea, four which I know not: The way of an eagle in the air; the way of a serpent upon a rock; the way of a ship in the midst of the sea; and the way of a man with a maid.] **1417** *Reliq. Antiquae* (1841) l. 233 There ben thre thinges full hard to be knowen which waye they woll drawe. The first is of a birde sitting upon a bough. The second is of a vessell in the see. And the thirde is the waye of a yonge man. **1509** BARCLAY *Ship of Fools* ii. 7–8 There be thynges thre Right harde to knowe, . . . whan a byrde doth fle Alonge in the ayre . . . The way of a Shyp in the se . . . the way of a serpent ouer a stone. **1541** *Schoolh. of Women* D3[v] Whiche waye, a byrde wyll flee Or of a serpent, sprent from a stone What hauen a shyppe shal be dryue vpon, The crafte of a hore. **1578** FLORIO *First F.* 22ᵛ There be three things that can not be knowen, and the fourth no man is able to vnderstand, The steps of an Eagle . . . the waye of a Serpent ouer a Rocke, the path of a ship in the sea, and the life of a young man led in his youth. **1581** GUAZZO i. 170. **1616** ADAMS *Sacrifice of Thankfulness* 26 The Course of a Dolphin in the Water, of a Buzzard in the Ayre, of a Whore in the Citie.

Three ways: There are | the church (universities), the sea, the court.
(w 178)

1612 SHELTON *Quix.* IV. xii. ii. 39 There is an old proverb in this our Spain, . . . 'The Church, the Sea, or the Court'. **1640** HERBERT no. 383 (the Vniversities). **1706** STEVENS s.v. Cosa. Three things make a Man thrive; Learning, the Sea, and the Court.

Three women (and a goose) make a market.
(w 690)

1581 GUAZZO i. 240 Doe not you knowe the Prouerbe that three women make a mercat? **1665** J. WILSON *Projectors* III. i. Wks. (1874) 249 If two women and a goose make a market, I see no reason why three may not make a council. **1666** TORRIANO *It. Prov.* 76 no. 15 Three geese, and three women, make up a market. **1678** RAY 59 Three women and a goose make a market. This is an Italian one, Tre donne & un occa fan un mercato. **1738** SWIFT *Dial. III.* E.L. 323 Miss, did you never hear that three women and a goose are enough to make a market?

Three words, he is at the top of the house, At.
(w 783)

1546 HEYWOOD II. v. H1 He is at thre words vp in the house roufe. **1616** DRAXE no. 89. **1659** HOWELL *Eng. Prov.* 15a In three words she is at the roof of the house.

Three, *see also* Judge knows nothing unless it has been explained to him t. times; One's too few, t. too many; Secret is . . . too much for t.; Servant . . . (He that has t.) has none at all.

Threefold, *see* Thick and t.

Thresh(ed), *see* Barn's full (When), you may t. before door; I do what I can . . . when he t. in his cloak.

Thresher take his flail, Let the | and the ship no more sail. *Cf.* November take flail.

1626 BRETON *Fantasticks* Gros. 10 It is now November, and according to the old prouerbe, Let the thresher &c. **1661** M. STEVENSON *The Twelve Moneths*, Nov. 51 Now wheels the Proverb about, *Let the* Thresher take his Flayl, and the Ship no more Sayl; for the high winds, and the rough seas will try the Ribs of the Ship, and the hearts of the Saylors.

Thresher, To eat like a.

1773 VIEYRA s.v. Alarve (We say, he eats).

Threshold, To stumble at the.
(T 259)

1377 LANGLAND *P. Pl.* B.v. 357 He stumbled on the thresshewolde. **1579** SPENSER *Sheph. Cal.* 2 May, l. 229 Tho went the pensife Damme out of dore, And chaunst to stomble at the threshold flore: Her stombling steppe some what her amazed, (For such, as signes of ill luck bene dispraised). **1591** SHAKES. *3 Hen. VI* IV. vii. 10 I like not this! For many men that stumble at the threshold Are well foretold that danger lurks within. [1592–3] **1597** *Id. Rich. III* III. iv. 86 Three times to-day my footcloth horse did stumble . . . O Margaret, Margaret, now thy heavy curse Is lighted on poor Hastings' wretched head! **1672** MARVELL *Rehearsal Transprosed* Grosart ii. 14 He himself stumbles so notoriously upon the very same fault at his own threshold.

Thrice, *see* All things thrive at t.; Measure t. what thou buyest.

Thrift and he are at fray.
(T 261)

1546 HEYWOOD I. xi. E3 How be it whan thrift and you fell fyrst at a fray, You played the man for ye made thrift ren away. **1639** CLARKE 261.

Thrift goes by the profit of a yeld¹ hen, Your.

1721 KELLY 378 . . . A Taunt upon them who boast of what they have wrought. **1862** HISLOP 228 Your thrift's as gude as the profit o' a yeld hen. [¹ barren.]

Thrift is a great revenue.
(P 61)

[CICERO *Paradoxa* 6. 3. 49 *Non intelligunt homines quam magnum vectigal sit parsimonia.* Men do not realize how great a revenue thrift is.] **1659** HOWELL *Fr. Prov.* 15 Parsimony is the best revenue. **1930** *Times* 10 Oct. 13/5 Thrift which is not only a great virtue but also 'a great revenue', as Tacitus told us long ago when he wrote *magnum vectigal est parsimonia.*

Thrift is in the town, When | you are in the field.
(T 262)

1546 HEYWOOD II. ix. K4 Whan thrift is in the towne, ye be in the feelde. But contrary, you made that sence to sowne, Whan thryfte was in the feelde, ye were in the towne. **1611** DAVIES no. 37. **1670** RAY 196 When thrift's in the field, he's in town.

Thrift is the philosopher's stone.

1732 FULLER no. 5040.

Thrift of you, and the wool of a dog, would make a good web, The. *Cf.* Wit of you.

1721 KELLY 331 . . . Spoken in jest to them that pretend to be thrifty.

Thrift, *see also* Inch of his will for span of his t. (He will not give).

Thrive as New College students, who are golden Scholars, silver Bachelors, and leaden Masters, They.　　(S 944)

1659 HOWELL *Eng. Prov.* 20b.

Thrive in all haste, You would.

1546 HEYWOOD II. ix. L1ᵛ Now thrifte is gone, now would ye thryue in all haste.

Thrive, He that will | must ask leave of his wife.　　(L 169)

c. 1470 *Songs & Carols* (Percy Soc. no. 73) 87 Fore he that cast hym for to thryve, he must ask off his wiffe leve. *c.* 1549 HEYWOOD I. xi. D3ᵛ. 1641 FERGUSSON no. 110 A man cannot thrive except his wife let him. 1670 RAY 49 A man must ask his wife leave to thrive. 1784 FRANK-LIN *Autobiog.* E.L. 95 . . . It was lucky for me that I had one as much dispos'd to industry and frugality as myself. 1858 R. S. SURTEES *Ask Mamma* ch. 10 His wife, by whose permission men thrive, was a capital manager.

Thrive, He who would wish to | must let spiders run alive.

1867 *N. & Q.* 3rd Ser. XI. 32 The proverb so often used in Kent: 'He who would wish to thrive Must let spiders run alive.'

Thrive, He that will | must rise at five; he that has thriven, may lie till seven; but he that will never thrive may lie till eleven.　　(T 265)

c. 1584 G. HARVEY *Marginalia* (1913) 102. *a.* 1628 CARMICHAELL no. 711. 1639 CLARKE 93. *c.* 1640 w.s. *Countrym. Commonw.* 17 He that hopes to thriue must rise at fiue: he that hath thriuen, may lie till sequen: But he that will neuer thriue, may lie till eleuen. 1766 *Goody Two-Shoes* i. 1807 SCOTT *Let. to Southey* Nov. in LOCKHART *Life* ch. 16 The only difference . . . is on the principle contained in the old pro-verb: . . .

Thrives he whom God loves, Well.

c. 1350 *How the Gd. Wife* l. 5 Wele thryuet þat God louet.

Thrive(s), *see also* All things t. at thrice; First t. then wive; Good man t. (If a), all t. with him; Labours and t. (He that); Leave to t. for throng (You cannot get); Office (He has a good), he must t.; Plough would t. (He that by the); Sheep, swine, and bees, (He that has) . . . may t.; Spends before he t., (Who) will beg before he thinks; Stolen goods never t.; Wise with whom all things t. (Seems); Wive and t. in a year (Hard to).

Throat(s), *see* Belly thinks t. is cut; Cut one's own t.; Flatterer's t.; Lie in one's t.; Singing man keeps shop in t.; Small house has wide t.; Sword of lead, (To cut one's t. with a); Tickle my

t. with feather; Wash their t. before they washed their eyes; Whet a knife for own t.

Throne, *see* Power behind the t.

Throng, *see* Leave to thrive for t. (You cannot get).

Throw (Send) good money after bad, To.

1706 STEVENS s.v. Virote When a Man throws away good Money after bad. 1854 SURTEES *Handley Cross* ch. 37 (It's no use throwin'). 1884 J. PAYN *Canon's Ward* ch. 25 If they would confess it, and forget it, and start free, instead of sending their good money after bad—how much happier would be this world of ours! 1931 *Times* 15 Jul. 14/3 It would be throwing good money after bad if France came to the rescue without very definite guarantees for the preservation of peace.

Throw him into the Nile and he will come up with a fish in his mouth.

1853 TRENCH i. 20 Of a man whose good luck seems never to forsake him, . . . the Arabs say: . . .

Throw no gift again at the giver's head.　　(G 101)

1546 HEYWOOD I. xi. D4ᵛ Throw no gyft agayne at the geuers head, For better is halfe a lofe than no bread. 1555 *Id. Epig. on Proverbs* lviii. 1611 DAVIES no. 103.

Throw of the dice, The best | is to throw them away.

a. 1591 HY. SMITH *Serm.* (1866) II. 242 If thou dost not only venture thy money, but hazard thy soul; then the best cast at dice is, to cast them quite away.

Throw that bone to another dog.

1620 SHELTON *Quix.* IV. v. i. 309 'There were never such knights in the world, nor such adventures and ravings happened in it.' 'Cast that bone to another dog', quoth the innkeeper, 'as though I knew not how many numbers are five.' 1706 STEVENS s.v. Perro.

Throw up one's (the) cards, To.　　(C 79)

[= to abandon a course.] 1639 FULLER *Holy War* II. xviii (1840) 73 Others, being crossed by the world by some misfortune, sought to cross the world again in renouncing of it. These, like furious gamesters, threw up their cards, not out of dislike of gaming but of their game. *a.* 1721 PRIOR *Dial. of Dead* (1907) 256 What think you of . . . Regulus, Cato, and Brutus? . . . Whenever the game did not go well they always threw up the cards.

Throw up the sponge, To.

[= to confess oneself beaten.] *a.* 1861 CHAMBER-LAIN *My Confession* (1956) 261 I . . . threw down the sponge, surrendered at discretion. 1888 'R. BOLDREWOOD' *Robbery under Arms* ch. 31 We must stand up to our fight now, or throw up the sponge. **1909** ALEX. MACLAREN *Philippians* 366 If ever you are tempted to say . . . 'I am beaten and I throw up the sponge', remember Paul's wise exhortation.

Throw(n), *see also* Cap after (at) a thing (at the moon) (To t. one's); Cap in the wind (To t. one's); Dust in man's eyes (To t.); Even hand to t. a louse in the fire (He has an); Gauntlet (To t.); Hatchet (To t.); House out of windows (To t.); Shoe (To be t. aside like an old); Stones against the wind (To t.); Thatched his house (When I have), he would t. me down.

Throw, To, *see also under significant words following.*

Thrown would ever wrestle, He that is.
(T 269)

1640 HERBERT no. 797.   **1710** PALMER 378.

Thrum caps (buttons), To.

1594 NASHE *Unfort. Trav.* ii. 217 The King stood not long a thrumming of buttons there. **1598** R. JOYNER *Itis* [title] Shall I stand thrumming of caps all the daye? Shall I not as other take leaue to playe. **1606** *Wily Beguiled* G2 I am none of these sneaking fellowes that wil stand thrumming of Caps, and studying vppon a matter, . . . but if I begin with wooing, Ile ende with wedding. **1607** DEKKER & WEBSTER *North. Ho* v. i. 443.

Thrush when he pollutes the bough sows for himself the seeds of woe, The.
(T 270)

[L. *Turdus ipse sibi malum cacat.* The thrush voids evil for itself.] **1612–15** BP. HALL *Contempl.* IX. viii. (1825) I. 248 The Schechemites . . . raised [Abimelech] unjustly to the throne, they are the first that feel the weight of his sceptre. The foolish bird limes herself with that which grew from her own excretion. **1635** SWAN *Spec. Mundi* (1665) 246 The berries . . . voided out again in her excrements, grow into a bush, the bush bringeth forth berries, and of the berries the fowler maketh birdlime, wherewith after he taketh the thrush: and thus, Turdus sibi cacat malum.

Thrushes, *see* Patience (He who has) has fat t. for farthing; Wishes were t. (If).

Thumb, To be under (a person's).

[= At the disposal of, subservient to.] **1754** RICHARDSON *Grandison* IV. xxix. 181 She . . . is obliged to be silent. I have her under my thumb. **1809** MALKIN *Gil Blas* VII. xiii, par. 6 Authors . . . are under the thumb of booksellers and players. **1889** JESSOPP *Coming of Friars* ii. 65 The lord was a petty king, having his subjects very much under his thumb.

Thumb is under my belt, Thy. (T 271)

a. **1628** CARMICHAELL no. 1154 My thumb is not under your belt, nor yet my dock[1] under your danger. **1641** FERGUSSON no. 848. [[1] breech.]

Thumb(s), *see also* Bite one's t.; Bites the mare by the t.; Cow's t.; Fash one's t.; Finger and t. (They are); Fingers are all t. (His); Hit one over t.; Miller has golden t.; Miller's t. (No bigger than a); Rule of t.; Sit on your t.; Taunt one tit over t.

Thunder (wind) comes rain, After.
(T 275)

1539 TAVERNER I *Garden* B6 [Socrates's wife] Xantippe . . . beynge more out of pacyence by his quyetnes and gentle sufferaunce, streyghte out of the wyndowe powred downe a pysse-bowle vppon his hedde. . . . Socrates . . . smyled, sayenge. I easyly gessed that after so great thunderynges, we shulde haue rayne. **1541** *Schoolh. of Women* B3[v] Socrates . . . his wyues twayne . . . A pyspot they brake, vpon his pate . . . sayde he . . . true it is, that all men fayne That after thonder, commeth rayne. **1548** E. HALL *Hen. IV: Chron.* 16 As the old prouerbe saith, after wynde commeth rayn. **1557** EDGEWORTH *Sermons* 3E4[v] After thunder clappes woulde come a showre. **1591** SHAKES. *3 Hen. VI* I. iv. 146 And when the rage allays the rain begins. **1592–4** *Id. 1 Hen. VI* II. v. 85 See, see what show'rs arise, Blown with the windy tempest of my heart. **1672** WALKER 55 no. 2.

Thunder lasted, While the | two bad men were friends.

1908 A. C. BENSON *At Large* iii. 42 'While the thunder lasted', says the old Indian proverb, 'two bad men were friends.' That means that a common danger will sometimes draw even malevolent people together.

Thunders in March, When it | it brings sorrow.

1659 HOWELL *Fr. Prov.* 21 (we may cry alas). **1893** INWARDS *Weather Lore* 7.

Thunder, Dunder (noun), *see also* Black as t.; D. do gally the beans; Dying duck in t.; Escaped the t. and fell into lightning; Fools . . . among his kindred (Who has neither), was born of a stroke of t.; Lightning lightly before t.; Winter t. summer hunger; Winter's t. . . . ; never boded good; Winter's t. makes summer's wonder.

Thunder (verb), *see also* Noise is so great.

Thunderbolt has but his clap, The.
(T 278)

1579 LYLY *Euph.* i. 209. **1605** JONSON *Sejanus* II. 205 Thunder speakes not till it hit. **1616** DRAXE no. 2251. **1639** CLARKE 166. **1670** RAY 148. **1732** FULLER no. 4793.

Thunderbolt, *see also* Pries into every cloud (He that).

Thunders, When it | the thief becomes honest.
(T 118)

1640 HERBERT no. 690.

Thursday come, and the week is gone.
(T 279)
1640 HERBERT no. 587.

Thwitten[1] a mill-post to a pudding-prick, He has. (M 964)

1528 MORE *Dialog. concernynge Heresyes* in Wks. (1557) Now forsoth . . . , here was a gret post wel thwyted to a pudding pricke. **1573** G. HARVEY *Letter-bk.* Camden Soc. 26 Meaning belike to . . . make a great monsterus milpost of his litle pudding prick. **1602** MARBECK *Def. of Tabacco* G4ᵛ This terrible accusation, is much like to a Sampsons post, thwited to a pudding pricke, as the Prouerbe is. **1611** COTGRAVE s.v. Arbre (We say of one that hath squandered away great wealth) . . . **1659** HOWELL *Eng. Prov.* Ia (brought). [[1] whittled.]

Thyme, *see* Rue and t. grow in one garden; Rue in t. a maiden's posie.

Thynne, *see* Horner; Portman.

Thyrsus-bearers, Many are the | but the bacchants are few.

[Gk. Πολλοί τοι ναρθηκοφόροι, παῦροι δέ τε βάκχοι.] **1853** TRENCH vi. 144 . . . .; many assume the outward tokens of inspiration, whirling the thyrsus[1] aloft; but those whom the god indeed fills with his spirit are few. . . . And there is the classical Roman proverb: Non omnes qui habent citharam, sunt citharoedi. **1892** SIR H. MAXWELL *Meridiana* 244 'Many are the thyrsus-bearers, but few are the mystics.' There are plenty who take books in their hands, but few who care to commune with the writer. [[1] a staff which was the attribute of Bacchus.]

Tib, *see* Struck at T. down fell Tom.

Tib's (Tibb's) eve.

[= never. See suggestions as to origin in *N. & Q.* 2nd Ser. XI. 269 and possibly cf. **1586** CAMDEN *Britannia* (1616) *Rutlandshire* 419 Tibbia, minorum gentium Diua, quasi Diana ab aucupibus, . . . colebatur.] **1785** GROSE *Dict. Vulg. T.* s.v. Saint Tibb's evening, the evening of the last day, or day of judgement; he will pay you on St. Tibb's eve (*Irish*). **1837** W. H. MAXWELL *Bivouac* III. iii He would return and claim her hand on 'Tib's eve'—an irish festival which is stated to occur 'neither before nor after Christmas'. **1882** W. P. IAGO *Dialect of Cornwall* 323 St. Tibb's Eve, neither before nor after Christmas, i.e. at no time. 'I'll do et St. Tibb's Eve.'

Tick, *see* Empty leech (t.) sucks sore.

Tickle it with a hoe and it will laugh into a harvest.

1907 SIR W. F. BUTLER *From Naboth's V.* 210 It used to be said of the Egyptian Delta that if you tickled it with a hoe it would laugh into a harvest.

Tickle my throat with a feather, and make a fool of my stomach. (T 267)
1678 RAY 210.

Tickle(s), *see also* Nothing t. that pinches not.

Tide keeps its course, The. (T 282)
1659 HOWELL *Eng. Prov.* 10a.

Tide must be taken when it comes, The. (T 283)

1559 COOPER s.v. Occasio Occasio praemenda, a prouerbe, when the sunne shinneth make hay: the tide muste be taken when it commeth. **1599** SHAKES. *J.C.* IV. iii. 218 There is a tide in the affairs of men Which, taken at the flood, leads on to fortune. **1830** MARRYAT *King's Own* ch. 23 'There is a tide in the affairs of men', and it was on this decision . . . that depended the future misery or welfare of M'Elvina. **1868** H. SMART *Breezie Lang.* ch. 4 It is no use meditating on when 'the tide in your affairs' took place. . . . You did not take it at the turn.

Tide never goes out so far but it always comes in again, The.

1864 *N. & Q.* 3rd Ser. VI. 494 Cornish Proverbs.

Tide stays (tarries) for no man, The. *Cf.* Time and tide tarry, etc. (T 323)

c. **1440** LYDGATE *Fall of Princes* III, l. 2801 The tid abit nat for no maner man, Nor stynt his cours for no creature. **1546** HEYWOOD I. iii. A4 The tide tarieth no man. [*c.* **1553**] **1566–7** UDALL *Ralph Roister D.* I. ii. Arb. 13 Farewell . . . the tyme away dothe waste And the tide they say, tarieth for no man. **1580** LYLY *Euph. & his Eng.* ii. 185 *Euphues* knowing the tyde would tarrye for no man, . . . determined sodeinly to departe. **1589** *Pasquil of Eng.* Nashe i. 84 The Winde and the Tide will staie for no Man. **1592–3** SHAKES. *C.E.* IV. i. 46 Both wind and tide stays for this gentleman. **1594** *Id. T.G.V.* II. iii. 33 Away, ass! you'll lose the tide if you tarry any longer. **1614** CAMDEN 313.

Tide(s), *see also* Ebb will fetch off what t. brings; Stream (t.) stopped swells the higher; Time and t. tarry no man; Turn with the wind (t.); Wind and t. (To sail with the); Work double t.

Tie can oblige the perfidious, No. (T 286)
1651 HERBERT no. 1066.

Tie it well, and let it go. (T 287)
1640 HERBERT no. 642.

Tied a knot with his tongue that he cannot untie with his teeth, He has. (K 167)

1580 LYLY *Euph. & his Eng.* ii. 220 That before this good company, we might knit that knot with our tongues, that we shall neuer vndoe

with our teeth. **1594** *Id. Mother B.* III. iii. 22
Accius tongue shall tie all Memphio's land to
Silena's dowrie, let his father's teeth vndoo them
if hee can. **1625** HOWELL *Lett.* 5 Feb. (1903) I.
249 Marriage . . . may make you or mar you.
. . . The tongue useth to tie so hard a knot that
the teeth can never untie. **1670** RAY 183. **1738**
SWIFT *Dial.* I. E.L. 293 Is . . . Ned Rattle
married?—Yes, . . .; he has tied a knot with
his tongue that he can never untie with his
teeth. **1831** SCOTT *Diary* 6, 7, 8 May in *Life* X.
58 I cannot conceive that I should have tied a
knot with my tongue which my teeth cannot
untie. We shall see.

Tied by the tooth.

1621 BURTON *Anat. Mel.* III. i. II. i. (1638) 414
They were tied to thee [the rich man] by the
teeth. **1917** BRIDGE 124 . . . Sheep and cattle
will not break through fences or try to wander if
the pasture in which they are grazing is very good.
They are '*tied by the tooth*'.

Tied to the sour apple-tree, To be.

(A 304)

1670 RAY 193 . . . *i.e.* To be married to an ill
husband.

Tied up, *see* Mastiff grows the fiercer for being
t. u.

Tiger, *see* Rides a t. afraid to dismount.

Tike, *see* Yorkshire t.

Tile, To wash a. (T 289)

1548 COOPER s.v. Later Thou wasshest a tyle.
A prouerbe, signifiyng, thou labourest in vayne.
1556 W. WOLFGANG *Of lawful and unlawful usury*
translator's preface A2ᵛ As it is sayde by a
prouerbe, to wassh tyle stones. *c.* **1613** SHAKES.
T.N.K. III. v. 40 We have, as learned authors
utter, wash'd a tile; We have been fatuous, and
laboured vainly.

Timber, *see* Knotty t.

Time and art, With | the leaf of the mulberry-tree becomes satin.

1659 HOWELL *New Sayings* 3b With Time, and
Art, the Mulberry leafs grow to be sattin. **1865**
ABP. TRENCH *Poems; Provs., Turk. & Pers.* xxi.
303 What will not time and toil?—by these a
worm Will into silk a mulberry leaf transform.

Time and I against any two.

1712 ARBUTHNOT *John Bull* [1727] *Postscript*
Wks. (1892) 290 ch. 16 Commentary upon
the Spanish proverb, 'time and I against any
two'.

Time, He that has | and looks for time, loses time. (T 292)

1562 A. BROOKE *Romeus & Juliet* l. 891 Who
takes not time . . . when time well offered is,
Another time shall seek for time, and yet of
time shall miss. **1573** SANFORD 103 He that
hath tyme, looketh not for tyme. **1578** FLORIO
First F. 28ᵛ (Who hath tyme, and tarieth for).

1599 MINSHEU *Span. Gram.* 84 He that hath
time, and lookes for better time, Time comes
that he repent himselfe of time. **1636** CAMDEN
297. **1659** HOWELL *Span. Prov.* 12 Who hath
time and waits for time, the time will come he
will repent. **1732** FULLER no. 2162 (for a better
Time, loseth Time).

Time and straw make medlars ripe.

(T 321)

1578 FLORIO *First F.* 14 With time and with
straw, Medlers are made ripe. **1578** J. IVER
Courtly Controv. 2L2 The Italian prouerbe *Col
tempo & la paglia, si matura la mela*: videlicet,
with time and strawe men make melowe apples.
1659 TORRIANO no. 110. **1670** RAY 149. **1710**
PALMER 12.

Time and tide tarry (stay, wait for) no man. *Cf.* Tide stays, etc. (T 323)

c. **1386** CHAUCER *Clerk's T.* l. 118 For thogh
we slepe or wake, or rome or ryde, Ay fleeth the
tyme, it nil no man abyde. [*c.* 1500] *a.* **1520**
Everyman A4 For wete you well the tyde
abydeth no man. [*c.* **1553**] **1566–7** UDALL
Ralph Roister D. I. ii. 10 Farewell . . . the tyme
away dothe waste And the tide they say, tarieth
for no man. **1592** GREENE *Disput.* 22 Tyde nor
time tarrieth no man. **1639** CLARKE 233. **1655**
FULLER *Ch. Hist.* IV. iii. (1868) I. 590 The press
(like time and tide) staying for no man, I have
not been so happy seasonably to receive it. **1816**
SCOTT *Antiq.* ch. I 'Time and tide tarry for no
man; and so, . . . we'll have a snack here at
the Hawes.' **1852** E. FITZGERALD *Polonius* 89
'Time and tide wait for no man', still to be
seen on the Temple sundial.

Time (Occasion) by the forelock, Take | (for she is bald behind). (T 311)

[The Greek God Καιρός, *Occasio*, used to be
represented with a full forelock. ERASM. *Ad.
Fronte capillata, post haec occasio calva.*] **1539**
TAVERNER C4ᵛ They made her [Time] a goddesse
. . . beynge on the former parte of her hed all
heavy and on the hynder parte balde, so that
by the fore parte she maye easely be caughte,
but by the hynder parte, not so. **1548** HALL
Chron. (1809, 124) It is wisdome to take occasion
when the hery side and not the balde side is proferd. **1567** PAINTER (Jacobs) iii. 10 It is wel
known that she [Occasion] being balde behinde,
hath no place to sease vpon when desire moueth
vs to lay hold vpon hir. **1576** PETTIE ii. 185 Let
not sluppe occasion, for it is bauld behynde, it
cannot be pulled back agayne by the hayre.
1587 MARLOWE *2 Tamburlaine* V. iii. 238 The
nature of these proud rebelling jades Will take
occasion by the slenderest hair. **1591** GREENE
Farewell to Folly Wks. Gros. ix. 311 Take time
now by the forehead, she is bald behinde.
1592–3 SHAKES. *C.E.* II. ii. 70 The plain bald
pate of Father Time himself. *Ibid.* II. ii. 105
Time himself is bald. **1594** SPENSER *Amoretti*
lxx The ioyous time will not be staid, Unlesse
she doe him by the forelock take. **1595** SHAKES.
K.J. III. i. 324 Old Time the clock-setter, that
bald sexton. **1602** *Id. A.W.* V. iii. 39 Let's
take the instant by the foremost top. **1604** *Id.
O.* III. i. 48 To take the saf'st occasion by the
front To bring you in again. **1606** BRYSKETT
Civ. Life 9 If he may once lay hold upon that
locke, which, men say, Occasion hath growing

on her forehead, being bald behind.   **1611** CHAP-
MAN *May Day* Occasion is bald, take her by the
forelock.   **1625** BACON *Ess., Delays* Arb. 525
Occasion . . . turneth a Bald Noddle, after she
hath presented her locks in Front, and no hold
taken.   **1633** SHIRLEY *Witty Fair One* IV. iii.
(*Song*) Enforce time itself to stay, And by the
forelock hold him fast, Lest occasion slip away.
1824 SCOTT *St. Ronan's* ch. 26 Time was—time
is—and, if I catch it not by the forelock as it
passes, time will be no more.   **1882** BLACKMORE
Christowell ch. 47 He had taken time by the
forelock now, so far as to seize and hide the
cash-box, before the intrusion of lawyers.   **1909**
ALEX. MACLAREN *Expos., Ephesians* v. 336
Occasion is bald behind, and is to be grasped
by the forelock.

Time cures all things (is a healer). (T 325)

c. **1380** CHAUCER *Troilus* Bk. 5, l. 350 As tyme
hem hurt, a tyme doth hem cure.   **1483** *Vulgaria*
(1529) B5 It is a comyn sayeinge. Longe
tyme slaketh or taketh awaye mennes sorowe.
1539 TAVERNER 38 Tyme taketh away greuaunce.
1591 SHAKES. *3 Hen. VI* III. iii. 76 For though
usurpers sway the rule awhile, Yet heav'ns
are just and time suppresseth wrongs.   **1591**
ARIOSTO *Orl. Fur.* Harington VI. ii. He hurt the
wound which time perhaps had healed.   **1616**
DRAXE no. 2150 (euery disease).   **1634** PEACHAM
Compleat Gentleman 34 Time, the Physician of
all things.   **1930** 14 Feb. D. H. LAWRENCE *Lett.*
ii. 1244 Time is the best healer, when it isn't a
killer.

Time devours (consumes) all things.
(T 326)

[OVID *Metam.* XV. 234 *Tempus edax rerum.*
Time, the devourer of all things.]   **1549** W.
THOMAS *Hist. Italy* 28 Some other ascribe the
fault to tyme, mother and consumer of all
thyngs.   **1559** J. FERRARIUS tr. W. Bavande
Good Ordering of a Common weale 101 Time
that all deuoures.   **1578** J. IVER *Courtly Controv.*
tr. H. Wotton 2M2 Tyme, which consumeth
all things.   **1594–5** SHAKES. *L.L.L.* I. i. 4 Spite
of cormorant devouring Time.   *c.* **1607** FLETCHER
Scornful Lady II. iii. 40 Time, that wears all
things out, wore out this husband.   **1613**
FLETCHER *et al. Honest Man's Fortune* II. ii. 281
Tyme the devourer of all things.   **1616** DRAXE
no. 2146 (consumeth).   **1813** BARRETT *Heroine*
ed. Raleigh Lett. 21, 114 Time changeth all
things, as the proverb saith.

Time discloses (reveals) all things.
(T 333)

[ERASM. *Ad. Tempus omnia revelat.*]   **1530** PALS-
GRAVE 470a Tyme bringeth the truthe to lyght.
1539 TAVERNER 37 *Tempus omnia reuelat.* Tyme
discloseth all thynges. Nothynge is couered,
but shalbe reueld, nothynge is hyd, that shal
not be known, sayeth Christ.   **1548** HALL
(1809 ed. 210) In conclusion tyme reueled truth.
1601 SHAKES. *T.N.* II. ii. 38 O Time, thou must
untangle this, not I; It is too hard a knot for
me t'untie!   **1616** DRAXE no. 2138 (reueleath).

'Time enough' lost the ducks.

1910 P. W. JOYCE *Eng. as we Speak* 114 . . . The
ducks should have been secured at once, as it
was known that a fox was prowling about.

Time flies (flees away without delay, has wings). (T 327)

[L. *Tempus fugit.*]   *c.* **1386** CHAUCER *Clerk's T.*
l. 118 For though we slepe or wake, or rome,
or ryde, Ay fleeth the tyme, it nil no man abyde.
c. **1581** *Tim. of Athens* v. i Howers haue wings.
1603 CHETTLE, DEKKER, HAUGHTON *Patient
Grissil* I. ii. 74 Time apace weares.   **1639** CLARKE
308 Time flyeth away without delay.   **1732**
FULLER no. 6090 Time fleeth away, Without
Delay.   **1776** FLETCHER OF MADELEY *Wks.* i. 197
Time flies!   **1807** CRABBE *Sir Eust. Grey* 44
Some twenty years, I think, are gone (Time
flies, I know not how, away).   **1842** MARRYAT
Perc. K. ch. 20 How time flies away . . . You
have been afloat nearly three years.

Time for all things (everything), There is a. (T 314)

[VULGATE *Eccles.* iii. 1 *Omnia tempus habent.*
1382 WYCLIF *Eccles.* iii. 1 Alle thingis han
tyme.]   *c.* **1386** CHAUCER *Clerk's T.* Prol. l. 6
But Salomon seith 'every thyng hath tyme' . . .
It is no time for to studien heere.   *a.* **1450** *Ratis
Raving* III. 3497 E.E.T.S. 100 Al thing has tyme
wald men tak heid.   *c.* **1460** *Wisdom* 401 All
thynge has dew tymes.   **1539** CRANMER Preface
to 'Great Bible' There is tyme for euerye thyng.
1592–3 SHAKES. *C.E.* II. ii. 63 Well, sir, learn
to jest in good time: there's a time for all things.
1594 LYLY *Mother B.* v. iii. 15 Boy, no more
words! theres a time for al things.   **1671** MILTON
P.R. iii. 183 And time there is for all things,
Truth hath said.   **1732** FULLER no. 1466 Every
thing hath its Time, and that Time must be
watch'd.   **1832** MACAULAY *Ess., Mirabeau* Wks.
v. 620 The highest glory of the statesman is to
construct. But there is a time for everything,—
a time to set up, and a time to pull down.

Time, He that has | has life (Gain time, gain life). (T 293)

1573 SANFORD 50ᵛ.   **1578** FLORIO *First F.* 28.
1596 NASHE *Saffron W.* iii. 48.   **1628** SIR EDWARD
CECIL, Viscount Wimbledon (*Times* 19 Apr.
1943, 6/5) As the proverb saith, Gain time
gain life.   **1629** *Bk. Mer. Rid.* Prov. no. 14.
1710 PALMER 380 He that gains time gains all
things.

Time has turned white sugar to white salt, When. (T 341)

1546 HEYWOOD I. ii. A3 Whan tyme hath
tourned white suger to white salte.   **1580** LYLY
Euph. & his Eng. ii. 228 Vntil time might turne
white salt into fine sugar.   *a.* **1600** R. WITE
Against the wilfull Inconstancy of E.T. [STC
25873] B3 Ease by Disease hath made me to
halt, Time hath so turned my Sugar to Salt.

Time is a file that wears and makes no noise. (T 328)

1666 TORRIANO *It. Prov.* 282 no. 41 Time is a
still file.

Time is money. (T 329)

[THEOPHR. in D. *Laert.* 5. 2. 10. 40: πολυτελὲς
ἀνάλωμα εἶναι τὸν χρόνον.]   **1572** T. WILSON *A
Discourse upon Usury* (1925) 228 They saye

tyme is precious. **1607–12** BACON *Essays*
'Despatch' Time is the measure of business, as
money is of wares. [**1625**] **1647** FLETCHER
Chances I. ix. 75 Time is precious. **1748** BENJ.
FRANKLIN *Adv. to Young Tradesman* in Wks.
(1793) 2. 55. **1840** LYTTON *Money* III. vi. You
don't come often to the club, Stout? — No; time
is money. **1859** SMILES *Self-Help* ch. 9 Men of
business are accustomed to quote the maxim
that Time is money. **1887** LD. AVEBURY *Pleas.
of Life* I. vi Time is often said to be money, but
it is more—it is life.

Time is the father of truth.   (T 329*a*)

1561 CASTIGLIONE *Courtier* tr. Hoby Epistle
E.L. 14 Time . . . is father to truth. **1567**
PAINTER (Jacobs) iii. 109 Tyme, the mother of
Truth. **1573** SANFORD 52ᵛ. **1578** FLORIO *First
F.* 32ᵛ. **1629** *Bk. Mer. Rid.* Prov. no. 47.

Time is the rider that breaks youth.
(T 330)

1640 HERBERT no. 615. **1666** TORRIANO *It. Prov.*
282 no. 39 Time is the coult-breaker, which
tames youth.

Time is tickle.¹   (T 331)

1546 HEYWOOD I. iii. A4. **1616** DRAXE no. 2143
Time is ticklish. [¹ uncertain.]

Time is, time was, and time is past.

1589 GREENE *Friar Bacon* xi. 55–76 (Ward) 94–5
The Brazen Head. Time is . . . Time was . . .
Time is past. *a.* **1603** BACON *Apologie* in
Spedding (1868) III. 152 I must speak to you as
Friar Bacon's head spake, . . . *Time is,* and then
Time was, and *Time would never be*: for certainly
(said I) it is now far too late. **1614** SIR T. OVER-
BURY *Characters* Wks. (1890) 99 *A Bawde.* The
burden of her song is like that of *Frier Bacons*
head; . . . **1930** *Times* 7 Nov. 15/5 Cannot
British statesmanship rise to the height of this
great occasion? 'Time is.' I need not finish
the quotation.

Time like the present, No.   (T 310)

1562 G. LEGH *Accidence of Armoury* 228ᵛ Mary
sir no time better then euen now. **1696** MANLEY
Lost Lover IV. i. 23. **1771** SMOLLETT *Humph.
Clink.* 28 Sept. Wks. (1871) 564 'There is no
time like the present time', cried Mr. Bramble.
1790 TRUSLER *Prov. Exempl.* 152 . . ., a thousand
unforeseen circumstances may interrupt you at
a future time. **1888** MRS. OLIPHANT *Second Son*
ch. 4.

Time lost (past) cannot be recalled
(won again).   (T 332)

c. **1374** CHAUCER *Troilus* Bk. 4, l. 1283 For time
y-lost may nought recovered be. **1546** HEY-
WOOD II. i. F2ᵛ And that tyme loste, agayne we
can not wyn. **1579** GASCOIGNE *Hemates* ii. 476
Tyme past can not be called agayne. **1580** LYLY
Euph. & his Eng. ii. 74 And time lost [past] may
well be repented, but neuer recalled. **1621**
BURTON *Anat. Mel.* III. ii. VI. v. (1638) 577 *Volat
irrevocabile tempus,* time past cannot be recal'd.
1748 FRANKLIN *Jan.* Lost time is never found
again.

Time out of mind.

1414 *Rolls of Parl.* iv. 60 By old tyme, . . . tyme
oute of mynde. **1560** CHURCHYARD *Cont.
between Churchyard and Camel* CIᵛ. **1578**
Courtly Controv. 2C3. **1594–5** SHAKES. *R.J.*
I. iv. 69 Time out o' mind the fairies' coach-
makers.

Time stays not the fool's leisure.
(T 335)

1611 COTGRAVE s.v. *Jour* Time stayeth not on
fools; or, though the foole stay, time staies not.
1659 N.R. 112.

Time (and thinking) tames the strong-
est grief.   (T 322)

[TERENCE *Heaut.* 3. 1. 13. ERASM. *Ad. Dies adimit
ægritudinem.*] *c.* **1374** CHAUCER *Troilus* Bk. 5,
l. 350 As tyme hem hurt, a tyme doth hem cure.
1539 TAVERNER 38 *Dies adimit ægritudinem.*
Tyme taketh awaye greuaunce. There is no
dyspleasure so great, . . . no sorowe so im-
moderat, but tyme asswageth it. **1594** SHAKES.
T.G.V. III. ii. 14 A little time, my lord, will
kill that grief. **1721** KELLY 333 (and thought).
1832 HENDERSON 57. **1887** BLACKMORE *Springhaven* ch. 32 Sad tidings, which would make the
rest of her life flow on in shadow. So . . . she
thought, forgetful . . . that time and the tide of
years submerge the loftiest youthful sorrow.

Time to cock your hay and corn, It is |
when the old donkey blows his horn.

1836 *Farmer's Mag.* IV. 447 in *N. & Q.* (1861)
2nd Ser. XII. 304. **1849** HALLIWELL *Pop. Rhymes*
157 . . . The braying of the ass is said to be an
indication of rain or hail.

Time to set in, It is | when the oven
comes to the dough.   (T 306)

1678 RAY 186 . . . *i.e.* Time to marry when the
maid wooes the man.

Time to speak and a time to be silent,
There is a.   (T 316)

[ECCLES. iii. 7 A time to keep silence, and a
time to speak.] **1485** CAXTON *Charles the Grete*
E.E.T.S. 56 The comyn prouerbe—sayth that
there is a tyme of spekyng and tyme of beyng
stylle. **1616** DRAXE no. 15 (to holde ones
peace). **1670** RAY 103 *Amyclas silentium perdidit.* . . . The Amycleans . . . disquieted with
vain reports of the enemies coming, made a
law that no man should bring . . . such news.
. . . When the enemies did come indeed, they
were surprised and taken. There is a time to
speak as well as to be silent.

Time to wink as well as to see, There
is a.   (T 317)

a. **1628** CARMICHAELL no. 1635 There is time to
glie¹ and time to looke even. *a.* **1699** L'ESTRANGE
Aesop's Fab. cxvii There's a Time to Sleep
(says the Dog) and a Time to Wake. **1721**
KELLY 339 (as *a.* 1628). **1732** FULLER no. 4885.
[¹ look a-squint.]

Time to yoke, It is | when the cart comes to the caples. (T 308)

1670 RAY 48 . . . *i.e.* horses. *Chesh.* That is, it's time to marry when the woman wooes the man.

Time tries all (things). (T 336)

1553 *Republica* Prol. Yet tyme trieth all. **1599** PORTER *Angry Wom. Abingd.* l. 2313 Time and trueth tryes all. **1599** SHAKES. *A.Y.* IV. i. 178 Time is the old justice that examines all such offenders, and let time try. **1611** *Id. W.T.* IV. i. [Time] l, that please some, try all. *a.* **1625** J. FLETCHER *Mons. Thomas* IV. ii. Time tries all then. **1639** CLARKE 308 Time trieth all things.

Time tries truth. (T 338)

1546 HEYWOOD II. v. H4 Let tyme trie. tyme tryeth trouth in euery dout. **1563** *Mirr. for Magistrates* (Campbell) 370 Time trieth out both truth and also treason. **1589** PUTTENHAM *Arb.* 185 Time tried his truth, his travails and and his trust. **1641** FERGUSSON no. 793.

Time undermines us. (T 339)

1640 HERBERT no. 923.

Time when time comes (while time serves), Take. (T 312)

[*c.* **1535**] **1602** LINDSAY *Three Estates* l. 711, E.E.T.S. 401 Till tak our tyme, quhill wee may get it. **1546** HEYWOOD I. iii. A4. **1548** HALL (1809, 253) Mynding to take time when time serued. **1555** HEYWOOD *Two Hundred Epig.* no. 285, E1. **1585** MUNDAY *Fedele and Fort.* II. v. D4 And therefore while time serues me to take the same I were best. *a.* **1585** MONTGOMERIE *Cherrie & Slae* xxxvi (1821) 21 Tak time in time, time be tint,[1] For tyme will not remaine. **1599** SHAKES. *A.Y.* V. iii. 28 Take the present time. **1666** TORRIANO *Prov. Phr.* s.v. Festa 61 To make a prudent use of ones time, to take time when time is. [1 lost.]

Time when time comes, Take | lest time steal away. (T 313)

[*a.* **1529**] **1545** SKELTON *On Time*, l. 7 Dyce i. 137 Take tyme when tyme is, for tyme is ay mutable, **1546** HEYWOOD I. iii. A4. **1611** SHAKES. *Temp.* I. ii. 180 And by my prescience I find my zenith doth depend upon A most auspicious star, whose influence If now I court not, but omit, my fortunes Will ever after droop. **1639** CLARKE 233 Take time while time is, for time will away. **1670** RAY 149 ('when time is' and as 1639).

Time works wonders.

1588 A. MARTEN *Exhortation* Harl. Misc. 1744, i. 271b If you shall think that Time will work Wonders, though you yourselves follow your own Pleasures. **1815** BYRON 7 Jan. *Corr.* ed. J. Murray 1922, i. 293 Time does wonders. **1845** D. W. JERROLD *Time Works Wonders* (Title of play). **1872** G. J. WHYTE-MELVILLE *Satanella* ch. 24 'I want you to like me'. . . . 'They say time works wonders, . . . and I feel I shall.'

Timely blossom, timely ripe. (B 468)

1639 CLARKE 171 (beare). **1670** RAY 149. **1732** FULLER no. 5057 (fruit).

Times change and we with them. (T 343)

1579 LYLY *Euph.* i. 276 The tymes are chaunged as Ouid sayeth, and wee are chaunged in the times. **1583** G. BABINGTON *Expos. of the Commandments* P.S. 222 Times are changed to and fro, and chaunging times haue chaunged vs too. **1598** I. M. *Health to Serv. Men* E3ᵛ Tempora mutantur, et nos mutamur in illis. [**1602**] **1637** T. HEYWOOD *Royal King* vi. 32 You see the times change.

Time(s), *see also* Best use of their t. (Those that make) have none to spare; Busiest men have most t.; Crutch of t. . . . club of Hercules; Done at any t. will be done no t.; Friends are thieves of t.; God will send t.; Good t. coming; Health (Chief box of) is t.; Judge knows nothing unless it has been explained to him three t.; Last my t.; Lawsuits consume t.; Lose your t. cannot get gain Nature, t. . . . great physicians; Other t. other manners; Parsley before it is born is seen by the devil nine t.; Patience, t. and money; Rainbows appear at one t. (If two) they presage rain; Stitch in t.; Truth is t.'s daughter.

Tine[1] cat, tine game.

1721 KELLY 325 . . . An Allusion to a Play called *Cat i' the Hole.* . . . Spoken when Men at Law have lost their principal Evidence. [1 lose.]

Tine[1] half-mark whinger[2] for the halfpenny thong (whang[3]), Many. (W 302)

a. **1628** CARMICHAELL no. 1145 Manie for ane halfpennie quhang tynes the four Ss dager. **1641** FERGUSSON no. 638 Monie tynes the halfe marke whinger, for the halfe pennie whange. **1721** KELLY 360 You tine the Tuppeny Belt for the Twapeny Whang. . . . People lose often things of a great Value, for not being at a small Expence. [1 lose. 2 short dagger. 3 thong.]

Tine heart, tine all.

1721 KELLY 142 Have you geer, have you none, tine heart and all is gone. Spoken to dissuade People from desponding in any Case. **1778** A. ROSS *Helenore* (ed. 2) 83 We manna[1] weary at thir rugged braes; Tyne heart, tyne a'. **1818** SCOTT *Ht. Midl.* ch. 50 'When ye deal wi' thae folk, it's tyne heart tyne a'.' [1 must not.]

Tine needle, tine darg[1] (dark[1]).

1721 KELLY 325 (dark). Spoken to young Girls when they lose their Needle. [1 day's work.]

Tine thimble, tine thrift.

1862 HISLOP 200.

Tinker and a piper make bad music together, A. (T 346)

1626 BRETON *Soothing* B1 A Piper and Tinker make a bad peece of musicke. **1639** CLARKE 5 (make bad music together).

Tinker's budget[1] is full of necessary tools, A. (T 349)

1626 BRETON *Soothing* A4ᵛ. 1639 CLARKE 72. [¹ sack.]

Tinkers, Banbury | who in mending (stopping) one hole make three (two), Like. (T 347, 351)

c. 1430 LYDGATE *Minor Poems* E.E.T.S. ii. 675 Thome Tynker with alle hees pannes olde, And alle the wyres of Banebury that he solde. 1564 T. DORMAN *Proof of Certain Articles* V. 1–2 He . . . is like the false tincker that mendeth one hole and maketh two newe. 1576 *Common Conditions* l. 221 Hay tisty tosty Tinkers good fellowes they bee. In stopping of one hole they vse to make three. *Ibid.* 267 You howresun Banbery slaue. 1621 BURTON *Anat. of Mel.* II. ii. iii. (1638) 256 As a Tinker stops one hole and makes two. 1644–7 CLEVELAND *Char. Lond. Diurn.* 8 What did this Parliament ever go about to reforme, but Tinkerwise, in mending one hole they made three? 1647 MILES CORBET *Speech* in *Harl. Misc.* i. 266 The Malignants do compare this Commonwealth to an old Kettle with here and there a Fault or a Hole . . . in it, and that we (in Imitation of our worthy Brethren of Banbury) were intrusted to mend the said Kettle; but, like deceitful and cheating Knaves, we have, instead of stopping one Hole, made three or four Score. 1659 HOWELL *Eng. Prov.* 14b. 1663 *A Merry-Conceited Fortune-Teller* A4ᵛ Tinkers shall have the fortune to stop one hole and make three, and yet they shall be accounted Lads of mettal, and if they escape Banbury they may have a better fortune. 1678 RAY 329. 1738 SWIFT *Dial.* I. E.L. 287 You have mended as a tinker mends a kettle; stop one hole and make two.

Tinker(s), *see also* Cobblers and t. best ale-drinkers.

Tinsel (= craw), *see* Winning (Your) is not in my t.

Tint[1] never a cow, He | that grat[2] for a needle. (C 754)

c. 1350 RYLANDS Latin MS. 394 *Bulletin* xiv. 92 Seldon dyeth his oxe þat wepeth for a kok. *a.* 1628 CARMICHAELL no. 1480. 1641 FERGUSSON no. 380. 1721 KELLY 149 . . . It is a Token that a Man had never a great Loss, who is immoderately griev'd for a small one. [¹ lost. ² wept.]

Tint (Lost) thing, For a | care not. *Cf.* Crying over spilt milk. (T 127)

1484 CAXTON *Aesop* (Jacobs) ii. 270 The thyrd [doctrine] is that thow take no sorowe of the thynge lost whiche may not be recouered. 1641 FERGUSSON no. 265. 1678 RAY 366 (lost).

Tip the cow's horn with silver, To.

1917 BRIDGE 144 When a butcher pays for the cow he has bought, he expects a 'luck-penny' to be returned to him which . . . is usually a shilling and is technically called 'tipping the cow's horn with silver'.

Tippet, *see* St. Johnston's t.; Tyburn t.

Tit for tat. (T 356)

[App. a variation of *tip for tap* = one stroke in return for another; retaliation.] 1546 HEYWOOD II. iv. G4. 1552 HULOET 2B6ᵛ Requite as tick for tacke. 1556 HEYWOOD *Spider & F.* xxxvii. 26 That is tit for tat in this altricacion. 1573 GASCOIGNE *Hundreth Sundry Flowers* i. 431 (tip for tap). 1710 ADDISON *Tatler* no. 229, par. 3 I was threatened to be answered Weekly Tit for Tat. 1881 SAINTSBURY *Dryden* iv. 80 A fair literary tit-for-tat in return for the *Rehearsal*.

Tit, *see also* Little t. all tail; Taunt one t. over thumb.

Tithe and be rich. (T 357)

[ECCLES. XXV. 9–11.] *c.* 1626 J. SMYTH *Lives of Berkeleys* (1883) i. 67 The Hebrewe proverbe mentioned in the Jewes writings at this daye, pay tythes justly that thou mayest bee ritch. 1651 HERBERT no. 1147.

Tither, *see* Good t. good thriver.

Tittle-tattle, give the goose more hay. (T 359)

1659 HOWELL *Eng. Prov.* 11a. 1678 RAY 82 (*Joculatory*). 1732 FULLER no. 5058.

Tividale men have libers, lemans and lier-bys. (M 877)

[= Teviotdale. *Mid. Eng.* Teuidale.] 1583 MELBANCKE 2A2ᵛ It is a Prouerbe in Englande that the men of Tiuidal borderers on yᵉ English midle marches, haue likers, lemmons, and lyerbies.

Toad (frog, paddock) said to the harrow, The | cursed be so many lords. (F 764. M 735)

c. 1150–1200 B.M. MS. Cotton Faustina A. x f. 100ᵛ Ad traeam dixit pereant tot buffo magistri. þa tadda cw̄ to þa eiþa a Forwurþa swa fola maistres. *c.* 1380 WYCLIF *Serm.* Sel. Wks. II. 280 Cristene men may seye, as þe poete seiþ in prouerbe—þe frogge seide to þe harwe, cursid be so many lordis. *a.* 1628 CARMICHAELL no. 1123 Manie maister quo the padok to the harrow quhen ilka yrtynd gat her a knok. 1641 FERGUSSON no. 609. 1659 HOWELL *Brit. Prov.* 21 As the Frog frets under the harrow. 1721 KELLY 243 (*gave her a tig*)[1] Spoken by those whom Persons, inferior to their Masters, presume to reprove, command, or correct. 1808–12 BENTHAM *Rationale of Evidence* (1827) i. 385 Note, Kept like toads under a harrow. 1818 SCOTT *Rob Roy* ch. 27 Andrew was compelled to submit, only muttering between his teeth, 'Ower mony maisters,—ower mony maisters, as the paddock said to the harrow, when every tooth gae her a tig.' 1859 SMILES *Self-Help* iv. While in this employment he endured much hardship—living, as he used to say, 'like a toad under a harrow'. 1897 M. A. S. HUME *Sir W. Ralegh* 10 The country gentry had lived like toads under a harrow for the last three reigns. [¹ twitch.]

Toad, To hate one like a.   (T 361)

1548 HALL 413 Diuerse other noble personages . . . inwardely hated kynge Richard worsse then a toade or a serpent. **1550** LATIMER *Serm.* 15, P.S. 289 Indeed neither loved other, but hated each other as a toad. **1584** WITHALS M3 Drunkennesse . . . blabs abroade, That which the hart loues, or hates as a tode. *c.* **1591** *Arden of Feversham* III. vi. 19 I hate them as I hate a toade. **1592** SHAKES. *T.And.* IV. ii. 67 As loathsome as a toad. *c.* **1595** *Id. R.J.* III. v. 31 Some say the lark and loathed toad change eyes. **1645** MILTON *Colasterion* Wks. iv. 252 Although there bee not easily found such an antipathy, as To hate one another like a toad or poison, yet . . . there is oft such a dislike . . . to conjugal love.

Toad, *see also* Purse is made of a t.'s skin; Swell like a t.

Toast, As hot (warm) as a.   (T 363)

c. **1430** *Two Cookery-Bks.* 12 Seene forth alle hote as tostes. *a.* **1529** SKELTON *Image Hypocrisy,* Wks. ii. 415 Chafyng lyke myne hoste, As hott as any toste. **1565** *Bugbears* II. iv. 27. **1639** CLARKE 286. **1841** DICKENS *B. Rudge* ch. 12 The room's as warm as any toast in a tankard. **1860** READE *Cloist. & Hearth* ch. 25 They were soon as warm as toast, and fast asleep.

Toast, *see also* Second side bread less time to t.

Toasted cheese has no master.   (C 274)

1678 RAY 82.

Tobacco-hic, if a man be well, it will make him sick; tobacco-hic, will make a man well if he be sick.   (T 365)

1678 RAY 296.

Tocherless[1] dame sits long at hame, A.

1721 KELLY 32 . . . A Maid without a Portion will be long unmarried. [[1] portionless.]

Tochers,[1] The greatest | make not the greatest testaments.[2]

1721 KELLY 333. [[1] portion, dowry. [2] will.]

Tochers, *see also* Maidens' t. are aye less than called.

Tod[1] gets to the wood, When the | he cares not who keek[2] in his tail.

1721 KELLY 345 . . . Spoken when a Villain has so cleanly escap'd that he cares not who look after him. [[1] fox. [2] peep.]

Tod never sped better than when he went his own errand, The.

1721 KELLY 311 . . . Every Man is most zealous for his own Interest; spoken to advise a Man to go about such a Business himself.

Tod's bairns (whelps) are ill to tame, The.

1721 KELLY 329 . . . Apply'd to them who are descended of an ill Parentage, or curs'd with a bad Education: Such are hard to be made good or virtuous.

Tod(s), *see also* Breed of t.'s bairns; Hare (T.) or bracken bush; Proud t. that will not scrape own hole; Serve the t. (As long as you) bear up his tail.

Today a man, tomorrow a mouse.

(M 403)

1609 HARWARD 88. **1666** TORRIANO *It. Prov.* 59 no. 79. **1670** RAY 77. **1732** FULLER no. 5152.

Today a man, tomorrow none.   (M 404)

a. **1500** *R. Hill's Commonpl. Bk.* E.E.T.S. 129 This dai a man, to-morow non. *c.* **1500** *Proverbs in Lodgings at Leconfield* (*Antiq. Rep.* iv, 1809, 398) Today a man in golde, tomorow closyde in clay. **1539** TAVERNER 35 Nothynge is more frayle . . . than y[e] lyfe of man. [*c.* **1553**] **1566–7** UDALL *Ralph Roister D.* 2 To day a man, to morow John. **1659** TORRIANO no. 223 Today in a posture, or shape, tomorrow in ones grave.

Today is the scholar of yesterday. (T 372)

[PUB. SYRUS 124 *Discipulus est prioris posterior dies.*] **1601** J. WHEELER *A Treatise of Commerce* 24 One day still being a Schoole-master vnto the other. **1613** SHAKES. *Hen. VIII* I. i. 16 Each following day Became the next day's master. **1732** FULLER no. 5153 To-Day is Yesterday's Pupil. **1853** TRENCH v. 122 The Latin proverb, . . . Let our 'to-day' learn of our 'yesterday'. **1909** *Times* 7 Jan. The present has always to be read in the light of the past. To-day is what yesterday made it.

Today, One | is worth two tomorrows.

(T 370)

1641 F. QUARLES *Enchiridion* cent. 4 no. XCV. **1660** W. SECKER *Nonsuch Prof.* II (1891) 292 Many think not of living any holier, till they can live no longer: but one to-day is worth two to-morrows.

Today will not, If | tomorrow may.

(T 369)

1591 STEPNEY L3[v] That which is not done to day may be done to morow. **1732** FULLER no. 2725.

Today, *see also* Here t., gone tomorrow; Hour t. worth two tomorrow; I t., you tomorrow.

Toe(s), *see* Bayard of ten t.; God by the t. (When they think they have); Stone that lies not in your gate breaks not your t.

Toil of a pleasure, I will not make a | (quoth the good man when he buried his wife).   (T 374)

1603 N. BRETON *Dial. full of Pith,* Wks. ii. 7 I

doo not loue so to make a toyle of a pleasure. **1721** KELLY 192 . . . A Man going under his Wife's Head to the Grave, was bid go faster, because the Way was long, and the Day short; [he] answered, I will not make a Toil of a Pleasure.

Toil so for trash, If you | what would you do for treasure?   (T 470)

1639 CLARKE 194.

Toiling dog comes halting home, A.

1721 KELLY 27.   **1732** FULLER no. 441.

Toils like a dog in a wheel, He | who roasts meat for other people's eating.

(M 87)

1614 SIR T. OVERBURY *Newes* Wks. (1890) 200 A covetous man is like a dog in a wheele, that toiles to roast meat for other mens eating.   **1748** RICHARDSON *Clarissa H.* (1785) IV. 120 What is a covetous man to be likened to so fitly, as to a dog in a wheel, which roasts meat for others? **1813** RAY 72.

Told me, So you.   (T 89)

[**1497**] *c.* **1512–16** MEDWALL *Fulgens & Lucres* l. 1088 Ye, so I harde you say.   **1594–5** SHAKES. *L.L.L.* I. ii. 134 I love thee. — So I heard you say. **1594–8** *Id. T.S.* IV. ii. 53 Ay, and he'll tame her. — He says so, Tranio.   **1606** J. DAY *Isle Gulls* E1ᵛ Ide loue you, sweet. — Sowre, so I heard you say.   [**1614**] **1631** JONSON *Barth. Fair* III. v. 53 Yet these will serue to picke the pictures out o' your pockets . . . — So, I heard 'hem say.¶ **1659** HOWELL *Eng. Prov.* 14a Spoken ironically. **1738** SWIFT Dial. I. E.L. 265 Miss, give me a Blow, and I'll beat him. — So she prayed me to tell you.   *Ibid.* I. E.L. 275 Madam, I find you live by ill neighbours, when you are forced to praise yourself.—So they pray'd me to tell you.

Told you so, I.   (S 111)

1604 SHAKES. *M.M.* II. i. 231 If you live to see this come to pass, say, Pompey told you so. **1827–48** HARE *Gues. at Truth* If a misfortune which a man has prognosticated, befalls his friend, the monitor . . . will often exclaim . . . *Didn't I tell you so?* **1872** W. BLACK *Adv. Phaeton* ch. 15 The man who would triumph over the wife of his bosom merely to have the pleasure of saying 'I told you so', does not deserve . . . such tender companionship.

Told, *see also* Tell(s).

Toll (noun), *see* Forsake not· market for the t.; Hear a t. or knell (When you do) think on passing bell; Talking pays no t.

Toll (verb), *see* Sure (Good to be), t. it again.

Tom, Dick, and Harry.   (T 376)

1554 LINDSAY *Dial. betw. Experience & Courtier* I. 19 Quharefore to Colzearis, Cairtaris, and to Cukis,—To Iok and Thome,—my Ryme sall be diractit.   **1596** SHAKES. *1 Hen. IV* II. iv. 9 I am sworn brother to a leash of drawers, and can

call them by their names, as Tom, Dick, and Francis.   **1604** JAMES I at Hampton Court Conference reported in Fuller *Church Hist.* x. i. 18 Then Jack, and Tom, and Will, and Dick shall meet and censure me and my Council. **1622** J. TAYLOR *Sir Greg. Nonsense,* Wks. F. 164 I neither care what Tom, or Iacke, or Dicke sed. **1641** *Oxinden Lett. 1607–1642* 257 Of no more account then Jack or Tom.   **1661** A. BROME *Royalist's Answer: Poems* 657 Though Dick, Tom and Jack, Will serve you and your pack. **1734** *The Vocal Miscellany* i. 332 cited *N. & Q.* Dec. **1962,** 455 Farewell, Tom, Dick, and Harry, Farewell, Moll, Nell, and Sue.   **1762** J. OTIS *Vindication of House of Representatives Massachusetts-Bay* Boston 21 That I should die very soon after my head should be cut off, whether by a sabre or a broad sword, whether chopped off to gratify a tyrant by the christian name of Tom, Dick or Harry is evident.   **1815** *Farmer's Almanack* (Boston, Mass.) in Kittredge *Old Farmer* (1904) 88 So he hired Tom, Dick and Harry, and at it they all went.   **1857** T. HUGHES *Tom Brown's Schooldays* pt. ii, ch. 5 Every one . . . has his enemies, . . . be they . . . Russians, or Border-ruffians, or Bill, Tom, or Harry.   **1883** M. TWAIN *Life on the Mississippi* A target for Tom, Dick and Harry.

Tom Fool, *see* More know T. F.

Tom of Lincoln, *see* Loud as T. of L.

Tom Pitcher's broken, When | I shall have the shards.   (T 381)

1678 RAY 351 . . . (*i.e.* Kindness after others have done with it; or refuse).

Tom Tell-truth.   (T 382)

1377 LANGLAND *P. Pl.* B. III. 320 Thanne worth Trewe-tonge a tidy man.   *Ibid.* B. IV. 17 Tomme Trewe-tonge-tille-me-no-tales.   **1550** LATIMER *Serm. Stamford* P.S. 289 Master, we know that thou art Tom Truth, and thou tellest the very truth.   **1580** H. GIFFORD *Gilloflowers* (1875) 147 Is not Tom teltroath euerywhere, A busie cockcombe deem[d]e?   **1639** CLARKE 308 Time is Tom tell-troth.   **1646** *Ex-ale-tation of Ale* 7 Tom tell troth lies hid in a [pot of good Ale]. **1721** KELLY 303 Tom tell Truth lies without. **1738** SWIFT Dial. III. E.L. 320 You know, I'm old Telltruth; I love to call a spade a spade. **1862** HISLOP 271 Tam-tell-truth's nae courtier.

Tom Tiddler's ground.

[= any place where money, etc., is 'picked up' readily.]   **1823** E. MOOR *Suffolk Wds. & Phr.* 437. **1838–9** DICKENS *N. Nickleby* ch. 34 I am here, my soul's delight, upon Tom Tiddler's ground, picking up the demnition gold and silver.   **1848** *Id. Dombey* ch. 36 The spacious dining-room with . . . the glittering table, . . . might have been taken for a grown-up exposition of Tom Tiddler's ground, where children pick up gold and silver. **1861** MISS YONGE *Stokesley Secret* ii. 34 She heard the joyous cry behind her—'I'm on Tommy Tittler's ground Picking up gold and silver'.   **1890** 'R. BOLDREWOOD' *Col. Reformer* (1891) 290 He . . . had come on to . . . Tom Tidler's ground, . . . gold . . . was sticking out of the soil everywhere.   **1907** A. C. BENSON *From Coll. Window* (ed. 4) 182 I would rather regard literature as a kind of Tom Tiddler's ground, where there is gold as well as silver to be picked up.

Tomb, *see* Womb to the t.

Tomkins (*prop. name*), *see* Ware, knave, quoth T. to his shadow.

Tomorrow come never.   (T 379)

1539 TAVERNER 9 To morowe to morowe they saye we wol begyn, but thys to morowe is euer commynge but neuer present. **1602** J. CHAMBERLAIN *Letters* 8 May (McLure) i. 142 Tomorrow comes not yet. **1639** *Stationers' Register* 28 June Arb. iv. 470 A book, Too late to call back yesterday and tomorrow comes not yet. **1678** RAY 343. **1738** SWIFT Dial. I. E.L. 272 I'll send it you to-morrow —. . . I suppose, you mean to-morrow come never. **1830** MARRYAT *King's Own* ch. 26 'To-morrow you shall see that with your own eyes.' 'To-morrow come never!' muttered the coxswain.

Tomorrow is a new day.   (T 380)

c. **1520** *Calisto & Mel.* Hazl.-Dods. i. 86 Well, mother, to-morrow is a new day. **1594** LYLY *Mother B.* v. iii. 19 Let vs not brabble but play: to morrow is a new daie. **1603** MONTAIGNE (Florio) II. iv. 57 A letter . . . being delivered him . . . at supper, he[1] deferred the opening of it, pronouncing this by-word: *To-morrow is a new day.* **1738** SWIFT Dial. I. E.L. 272 I'll send it you to-morrow. — Well, well; to-morrow's a new day. **1824** SCOTT *St. Ronan's* ch. 33 We will say no more of it at present . . . , to-morrow is a new day. [[1] Archias, at Thebes, 379 B.C.]

Tomorrow morning I found a horse-shoe.   (M 1177)

1620 SHELTON *Quix.* II. xliii. iii. 113 I bid thee leave thy proverbs, . . . that are as much to the purpose as To-morrow I found a horseshoe. **1732** FULLER no. 5208.

To-morrow(s), *see also* Business t.; Catch birds t. (Shall); Friend asks (When), there is no t.; Here today, gone t.; Hour today worth two t.; Put off till t. (Never); Today a man, t. none; Today (One) worth two t.; Today will not (If), t. may; Trust (This day no), but come t.

Tomson, Tommy, *see* Contentibus.

Tomtit on a round of beef, Like a.

1849 NORTHALL *Folk-phrases* 19 . . . A little person is said to look so when situated on some coign of vantage.

Tong, *see* Live a little while . . . go to T.

Tongs, *see* Find it where Highlandman found t.; Hammer and t.; Touch him with a pair of t.

Tongue breaks bone, and herself has none.   (T 403)

[PROV. XXV. 15 A soft tongue breaketh the bone.] *c.* **1225** *Trin. MS. O. 11. 45* in *Eng. Stud.* 31. 6 Tunge bregþ bon, þegh heo nabbe hire silf non. *a.* **1250** *Provs. of Alfred* A. 425 (Skeat) 38 For ofte tunge brekeþ bon, þeyh heo seolf nabbe non. *c.* **1300** *Prov. of Hending* XIX Tonge breketh bon, and nath hire-selue non. *c.* **1350** *Douce MS. 52* no. 42 The tonge brekyth bon, And hath hym sylfe non. *c.* **1390** GOWER *Conf. Amantis* III. 465 For men sein that the harde bon, Althogh himselven have non, A tunge brekth it al to pieces. *c.* **1425** *Eng. Conq. Irel.* 46 Tong breketh bon, thegh hym-self ne hawe none. *c.* **1470** *Harl. MS. 3362,* f. 1b Tunge brekyth bon, þat hyr self haue non. **1546** HEYWOOD II. v. H2 Tong breaketh bone, it selfe hauyng none. **1659** TORRIANO no. 31 A tongue hath no bone in it, yet it breaks ones back. **1659** HOWELL *Eng. Prov.* 2a.

Tongue does lie that speaks in haste, That.   (T 400)

1573 SANFORD 107. **1611** DAVIES no. 74.

Tongue ever turns to the aching tooth, The.   (T 404)

1586 GUAZZO ii. 201 The more they are in loue, the more they tell things that are not apparantlie credible, and yet are most true, because according to the Proverbe. The tongue rolles there where the teeth aketh. **1659** HOWELL *It. Prov.* 8. **1732** FULLER no. 4796.

Tongue in one's head, To keep a good.   (T 402)

1542 ERASM. tr. Udall *Apoph.* (1877 ed., of 1564 ed.) 288. *a.* **1606** *Nobody & Somebody* l. 488. **1611** SHAKES. *Temp.* III. ii. 33 Trinculo, keep a good tongue in your head. *Ibid.* III. ii. 108 But while thou liv'st, keep a good tongue in thy head.

Tongue is ill (well) hung, His.

1639 CLARKE 52 (ill). **1738** SWIFT Dial. I. E.L. 260 (well).

Tongue is made of very loose leather, Your.

1721 KELLY 382 You have o'er mickle lose Leather about your Lips. **1732** FULLER no. 6062.

Tongue is no slander, His (Your). (T 389)

c. **1600** *Club Law* ed. Moore Smith III. ix. 61 Ffie on thee, fie on thee, but thy tongue is no slander. **1601** SHAKES. *T.N.* I. v. 88 There is no slander in an allowed fool, though he do nothing but rail. *a.* **1602** W. PERKINS *Treatise of Christian Equitie* (Wks. iii. (1609) 513) Many mens tonges are no slander. **1616** DRAXE no. 1993. **1670** RAY 196. **1692** L'ESTRANGE *Aesop's Fab.* cccc (1738) 547 The best on't is, sirrah, *Your tongue's no slander.* **1721** KELLY 390 . . . Because you are known to be a Lyar. **1738** SWIFT Dial. I. E.L. 267 Well, my comfort is, your tongue is no slander.

Tongue is not steel yet it cuts, The.   (T 405)

c. **1386** CHAUCER *Manciple's T.* l. 340 Right as a swerd forkutteth and forkerveth. . . . A tonge

kutteth freendshipe al a-two. **1546** HEYWOOD
I. x. C3 Her tong is no edge toole, but yet it will
cut. **1640** HERBERT no. 838. **1853** TRENCH vi.
146.

Tongue is the rudder of our ship, The.
(T 406)

[EPISTLE OF ST. JAMES iii. 4.] **1539** VIVES *Introd.
to Wisdom* 16ᵛ James the Apostle dothe resemble it [the tongue] very well to the sterne of
a shyp. **1560** BIBLE Gloss in Geneva version
He sheweth by two similitudes, the one taken
from the bridles of horses, the other from the
rudder of shippes, how great matters may be
brought to passe by the good moderation of
the tongue. **1642** TORRIANO 68 (is like). **1666**
Id. It. Prov. 129, no 6 (of the body). **1732**
FULLER no. 4798.

Tongue run at rover, Let not your.

[= at random, unrestrained.] **1546** HEYWOOD
II. v. H2ᵛ Be silent. Leat not your tong ron
at rouer.

Tongue runs before his (your) wit, His (Your).
(T 412)

c. **1350** *Pearl* (1921) l. 294 Thy worde by-fore
þy wytte con fle. **1539** VIVES *Introd. to Wisdom*
18ᵛ Let not thy tounge goo before thy wit. **1546**
HEYWOOD II. iv. G4. **1659** HOWELL *Eng. Prov.* 7a.
1710 STEELE *Tatler* no. 235 If Mrs. Rebecca is
not so talkative . . . she knows better what she
says when she does speak. If her wit be slow,
her tongue never runs before it.

Tongue runs like the clapper of a mill, Her.
(T 388)

1616 ADAMS *Three Divine Sisters* 23 The Tongue
is mans clapper. **1738** SWIFT *Dial.* I. E.L. 273.

Tongue runs nineteen to the dozen, Your.

1785 GROSE *Dict. Vulg. T.* s.v. Chatterbox one
whose tongue runs twelve score to the dozen.
1854 BAKER *Northants Gloss.* s.v. Nineteen A
Common expression when any one talks too fast.

Tongue runs on pattens (wheels), Her.
(T 387)

c. **1450** *Partonope* E.E.T.S. l. 10123 Suche
mennes tonges gone euer on wheles. **1546**
HEYWOOD II. vii. I2ᵛ. [*c.* **1553**] **1566–7** UDALL
Ralph Roister D. I. iii. Arb. 20 Yet your tongue
can renne on patins as well as mine. **1575** *Gam.
Gurton's N.* II. iv. 34 How she began to scolde!
The tonge it went on patins. **1639** CLARKE 133.
1670 RAY 196 His tongue runs on wheels (or
at random).

Tongue stings (is more venomous than a serpent's sting), The.
(T 407)

1591 LYLY *Endym.* v. iii. 203 The very waspe of
all women, whose tongue stingeth as much as
an Adders tooth. [*c.* **1605**] **1630** DEKKER 2 *Hon.
Whore* II. i. 199 Thy blacke tongue doth swell
With venome, to hurt him that gaue thee bread.
1616 DRAXE no. 2157.

Tongue talks at the head's cost, The.
(T 408)

1616 DRAXE no. 2163 Let not thy tongue speake,
that thy head shall smart for. **1640** HERBERT
no. 312. **1659** HOWELL *Brit. Prov.* 4. The toung
will cause beheading. **1706** STEVENS s.v. Lengua.
1732 FULLER no. 4801.

Tongue walks where the teeth speed not, The.
(T 409)

1609 DEKKER *Gull's Hornbook* D4ᵛ Let your
tongue walke faster then your teeth. **1640**
HERBERT no. 102.

Tongue's end, To have at one's. (T 413)

1539 VIVES *Introd. to Wisdom* 18ᵛ This sayeing,
what so euer fyrst cometh to the tongues ende,
which Cicero spake vnto Titus of Athenes, ought
selde or neuer to be admitted. **1596** NASHE
Saffron W. iii. 73 I haue a tale at my tungs end.
1598 [LYLY?] *Entertainment at Mitcham* ed. L.
Hotson 17 Soe shall you haue her hartes bottome
at her tonges ende. **1607** WALKINGTON *Optic
Glass* I. 2 Pythagoras . . . had this golden poesie
ever on his tongues end.

Tongue(s), *see also* Arthur could not tame
woman's t.; Blister upon t. that tells lie; Child
has red t. like father; Devil makes Christmas
pies of lawyers' t.; Eat above t. like calf; Effect
speaks, t. need not; False t. hardly speak truth;
Fool's t. long enough; Foolish t. talk by dozen;
Good t. is good weapon; Good t. (Who has not)
ought to have good hands; Good t. that says no
ill; Heart thinks (What the), t. speaks; Hold
one's t. in ill time; Honey t., heart of gall; Ill
t. may do much; Keep one's t. within teeth;
Lame t. gets nothing; Lay the sweet side of t.
to it; Lick with the rough side of one's t. (To
give a); Lickerish of t.; Little can a long t. lein;
Long t. short hand; Lost the t. of the trump;
Nature has given . . . one t.; Nurse's t. privileged;
Old as my t.; One t. is enough for woman; Ox is
taken by horns, man by t.; Ox on his t.; Play
with the ears than t. (Better); Speak with your
gold and make other t. dumb; Still t. wise head;
Strikes with his t. (He that); Teeth guard the t.
(Good that the); Thought has good legs and
quill good t.; Tied a knot with his t.; Venom to
that of t. (No); Wae's the wife that wants the t.;
Wide ears short t.; Woman's t. in his head (He
has a); Woman's t. is last thing . . . that dies;
Woman's t. wags like a lamb's tail. *See also*
Hold his tongue.

Too big for one's boots, To be.

1887 *S. Chesh. Gloss.* s.v. Shoe Too big for one's
shoon. **1894** SIR H. MAXWELL *Life W. H. Smith*
34 Sometimes a young man, 'too big for his
boots', would . . . sniff at being put in charge
of a railway bookstall. **1897** CONRAD *Nigger of
the Narcissus* ch. 4.

Too clever by half.

1889 W. WESTALL *Birch Dene* (1891) 144 'He's
a good scholar, and nobody can deny as he's
clever.' 'Ay, too clever by half.'

Too far east is west.   (E 44)

1664 BUTLER *Hudibras* II. i. 271 Th' extremes
of glory and of shame, Like east and west
become the same. **1853** TRENCH (1905) 93
Extremes meet, or its parallel, Too far East is
West, reaches very far into the heart and centre
of things.

Too free to be fat.   (F 667)

1639 CLARKE 260.   **1670** RAY 176.

Too (much) good is stark naught. *Cf.*
Little good to stark nought.

1592 DELAMOTHE 55 To much is starke naught.
1738 SWIFT Dial. II. E.L. 309 The only Fault I
find is, that they are too good. — O madam;
I have heard 'em say, that too good is stark
naught.

Too good to be true, This news is.
                                             (N 156)

1578 WHETSTONE *Promos & Cassandra* B3 I
thought thy talke was too sweete to be true.
1580 T. LUPTON *Siuquila. Too good to be true*
[title]. **1594** LYLY *Mother B.* IV. ii. 4 It was
too good to be true. **1606** DANIEL *Queen's
Arcadia* 2383 Besides 'tis too good to be true.
1638 T. HEYWOOD *Wise W. of Hogs* IV. iv. Merm.
310 The name of that news is called 'too good
to be true'. **1908** W. S. CHURCHILL *My Afr.
Jrny.* ch. 5 It *is* too good to be true. One can
hardly believe that such an attractive spot can
be cursed with malignant attributes.

Too hasty to be a parish clerk.   (P 55)

1616 DRAXE no. 93 (Parish Priest).   **1639** CLARKE
116.   **1670** RAY 180.

Too hot to hold.   (H 514)

1607 GRESHAM *Almanac* Jan. Too hote, to last
long.   **1639** CLARKE 178.   **1678** RAY 346 . . .
Moderata durant.

Too late aware.

c. **1386** CHAUCER *Troilus* Bk. 2, ll. 397–8 Lat
this prouerbe a lore unto you be: 'Too late
ywar', quod Beautee, whan it paste.

**Too late to, *see* Grieve when chance past; Shut
the stable-door; Spare when bottom bare.**

Too many cooks spoil the broth. (C 642)

1575 GASCOIGNE *Life Sir P. Carew* 33 There
is the proverb, the more cooks the worse potage.
1662 GERBIER *Princ.* (1665) 24 Too many cooks
spoil the broth.   **1706** STEVENS s.v. Olla Too
many Cooks spoil the Meat. **1851** KINGSLEY
Yeast ch. 3 'Get out of the way, my men!'
quoth the colonel. 'Too many cooks spoil the
broth.'

**Too much for one, and not enough for
two, like the Walsall man's goose.**

1880 POOLE *Arch. & Prov. Words of Staff.* 25
in NORTHALL *Folk-phrases* (1894) 31 A Walsall
man, when asked if he and his wife were going

to have a goose for their Christmas dinner,
replied 'No; . . . the goose was a silly bird—
too much for one to eat, and not enough for two '.

Too much liberty spoils all.   (L 225)

1533 UDALL *Flowers for Latin Speaking* (1560)
T4ᵛ We be all the worse by hauying to much
libertee.   **1547** BALDWIN *Moral Philos.* Bk. III.
D5 To muche libertie turneth into bondage.
1587 HOLINSHED iii. 1354b Companie and libertie
bring manie to miserie.   **1597** *Politeuphuia* 137ᵛ
Through too much libertie, all things run to
ruine.   **1592** SHAKES. *C.E.* II. i. 15 Headstrong
liberty is lash'd with woe.   **1611** COTGRAVE s.v.
Bandon   Much libertie brings men to the
gallowes.   **1681** ROBERTSON 822.

**Too much of nothing but of fools and
asses.**   (N 334)

1616 DRAXE no. 746.   **1639** CLARKE 73.

**Too much of one (a good) thing is not
good (good for nothing).**   (T 158)

c. **1386** CHAUCER *Canon's Yeom. Prol.* l. 645
That that is overdoon, it wol nat preeve Aright,
as clerkes seyn; it is a vice.   *c.* **1500** Proverbs
at Leconfield (*Antiq. Repert.* iv (1809) 414) Too
much is naught.   *c.* **1526** ERASM. *Dicta Sap.*
A4ᵛ. To moche is nought.   **1546** HEYWOOD II.
iv. G4ᵛ Well (quoth I) to muche of one thyng
is not good, Leaue of this.   **1599–1600** SHAKES.
A.Y. IV. i. 108 Why then, can one desire too
much of a good thing?   **1616** BRETON 2 *Cross.*
A3 Too much of any thing is good for nothing.
1659 HOWELL *It. Prov.* 3 Too much of good is
distasteful.   **1706** STEVENS s.v. Olla (good for
nothing).   **1738** SWIFT Dial. I. E.L. 283 Fie,
miss; you said that once before; and, you know,
too much of one thing is good for nothing.
1885 R. G. MOULTON *Shakes. as Dram. Art.* 46
'Too much of a good thing' suggests that the
Nemesis on departures from the golden mean
applies to good things as well as bad.   **1961**
W. H. DUNN *J. A. Froude* citing L. James 38
Freedom is good, but you can have too much
even of a good thing.

Too much of ought is good for nought.

1871 *N. & Q.* 4th Ser. VIII. 506 Common
Lancashire Proverbs.— . . .

Too much pudding will choke a dog.

1830 G. COLMAN (jun.) *Random Records* in
Broad Grins 421 (a caution against excess).
1841 S. WARREN *Ten Thous. a Year* ch. 16 All
this might be very well in its way, began to think
Miss Tagrag—but it was possible to choke a
dog with pudding.   **1917** BRIDGE 141 Too much
pudding would sade¹ a dog. [¹ sate or surfeit.]

**Too much spoils, too little does not
satisfy.**   (M 1294)

1573 GASCOIGNE *Posies* i. 64 To much and to
little bothe bee shente.   **1642** TORRIANO 64 (not
sufficient).   **1659** HOWELL *It. Prov.* 12.   **1732**
FULLER no. 5268 (is nothing).

Too much taking heed is loss.   (T 36)

1640 HERBERT no. 889.

Too much water drowns the miller.

1823 SCOTT *Peveril* ch. 21 A jug of home-brewed ale . . . was warranted . . . as excellent; 'for', said she, 'we know by practice that too much water drowns the miller, and we spare it on our malt as we would in our mill-dam'.

Too much, *see also* Money makes one mad (T. m.)

Too-too will in two. (T 435)

1670 RAY 149. **1678** *Id.* 210 . . . *Chesh. i.e.* Strain a thing too much and it will not hold.

Too wise to live long. (L 384)

1576 PETTIE ii. 160 Those children which are destined to death in the prime time of their life, are far more witty, discreet, and perfect every way, than those who have long time granted them to live on earth. **1586** TIM. BRIGHT *Treat. Melancholy* xi. 52 Wherupon I take it, the prouerbe ariseth: that they bee of short life, who are of wit so pregnant: because their bodies doe receaue by nature so speedye a ripenes, as thereby age is hastened. [**1592**] **1597** SHAKES. *Rich. III* III. i. 79 So wise so young, they say, do never live long. **1607** MIDDLETON *Phœnix* I. i A little too wise, a little too wise to live long.

Too'd (= Toothed), *see* Quickly too'd and quickly go.

Took her for a rose, I | but she proved a burr (nettle). (R 181)

1546 HEYWOOD I. x. C4 I toke hir for a rose, but she breedth a burre. She comth to sticke to me nowe in hir lacke. **1570** G. TURBERVILE *Epitaphs, Epigrams Songs & Sonnets* 117ᵛ Thou pluckst a Nettle for a Rose. **1659** HOWELL *Eng. Prov.* 4a.

Tool(s), *see* Bad workman quarrels with t.; Edged t.; Tinker's budget is full of necessary t.; Whetstone . . . makes t. cut; Workman, like t. (Like); Workman without his t. (What is).

Tooley Street, *see* Tailors of T. S.

Toom¹ bags rattle. (B 33)

a. **1628** CARMICHAELL no. 1544 (rattles ay). **1641** FERGUSSON no. 781. [¹ empty.]

Toom pokes will strive.

1721 KELLY 313 . . . When a married Couple are pinch'd with Poverty they will be apt to jarr.

Toom¹ purse makes a blate² merchant, A. (P 665)

a. **1628** CARMICHAELL no. 204. **1674** RAY *Coll. of Eng. Words* 6 . . . *Scot. Prov.* That is, an empty purse makes a shamefac't Merchant. **1678** RAY 356. [¹ empty. ² bashful.]

Tooth and nail. (T 422)

1533 ʹERASM. *Enchiridion* R8ᵛ Take and holde this with toth and nayle, that to be honour onely which springeth of true vertue. *c.* **1548** *The Will of the Devil* B2 Fightyng with toothe and nayle. **1548** HALL *Chron.* (1809 ed. 269). **1561** T. BECON *Sick Man's Salve* P.S. 165 Cleave both tooth and nail (as they use to say) to . . . God. **1579** W. WILKINSON *Confut. Familye of Love* 51 M. Harding fighteth for it tooth and nail. **1591** ARIOSTO *Orl. Fur.* Harington XXVII. 63 I will defend my right with tooth and naile. *Margin* A latin prouerb Dentibus et vnguibus. **1909** *Times Wkly.* 14 May Herr von Holstein . . . fought tooth and nail for the acquisition of Samoa.

Tooth, teeth, *see also* Aching t. at one (To have an); Aching t. (Who has) has ill tenants; Any t., good barber; Bear's (hound's) t. (As white as a); Cast in the t.; Colt's t.; Dragon's t.; Never bite unless . . . t. meet; Old as my tongue, older than t.; Pull not out your t. but with leaden; Pull out one t. and pull out more; Revenge . . . has its sucking t.; Skin of one's t.; Spite of one's t.; Sweet things bad for t.; Sweet t.; Take the bear by the t.; Take the bit in the t.; Tied by the t.; Tongue ever turns to aching t.; Tongue walks where t. speeds not; Trust not a horse's heel nor dog's t.; Wite your t. if your tail be small; Wolf may lose his t. but never memory.

Toothache is more ease than to deal with ill people, The. (T 433)

1640 HERBERT no. 558.

Toothache, *see also* Music helps not t.; Pain like . . . t. (No).

Tooth-drawer, He looks like a. (T 434)

1608 BEAUM. & FL. *Philas.* I. i Here is a fellow has some fire in's veins; The outlandish prince looks like a tooth-drawer. **1678** RAY 83 . . . *i.e.* very thin and meager.

Top and topgallant, With. (T 437)

c. **1589** PEELE *Battle of Alcazar* (Bullen i. 268) He cometh . . . Top and top-gallant, all in brave array. **1593** NASHE *Christ's Tears* ii. 137. *c.* **1600** DEKKER *et al. Patient Grissil* H4. *c.* **1600** *Merry Devil of E.* I. i. **1614** JONSON *Barth. Fair* IV. v. 48.

Top (head) to toe (heel), From. (T 436)

c. **1425** *Wakefield Plays* Second Shepherds l. 265. *c.* **1425** *Castle of Perseverance* l. 615. **1489** CAXTON *Blanchardyn* XXXVII E.E.T.S. 139 And all armed fro top to too. **1562** BROOKE *Romeus & Jul.* l. 2146, 210 With manly courage arme thy selfe, from heele unto the head. **1597** SHAKES. *Rich. III* III. i. 156 He is all the mother's, from the top to toe. **1618** JONSON *Hon. of Wales* l. 21.

Top, *see* Drive a t. over tiled house; Parish t. (Like a); Round as a ball (t.); Sleep like a t.

Topgallant, *see* Top and t. (With).

Torch, *see* Light a t. gives (The more).

Torment(s), *see* Fortune t. me (If) hope contents me; Love is a sweet t.

Tortoise to catch the hare, To set the.

1798 MALTHUS *Popul.* (1817) III. 117 It would appear to be setting the tortoise to catch the hare.

Tortoise wins the race while the hare is sleeping, The.

[From *Aesop's Fables*.] **1850** THACKERAY *Pendennis* ch. 21 He had slept and the tortoise had won the race. He had marred at its outset what might have been a brilliant career.

Tortoise, *see also* Contempt pierces shell of t.

Tottenham is turned French.   (T 444)

1536 NORFOLK to Cromwell, in *Cal. Lett. etc. Henry VIII* i, no. 233 It is further written to me that a bruit doth run that I should be in the Tower of London. When I shall deserve to be there Totynham shall turn French. **1546** HEYWOOD I. vii. B4 Their faces told toies, that Totnam was tournd frenche. **1662** FULLER *Middlesex* 178 ... French Mechanicks swarmed in England, ... which caused the insurrection in London, ... Anno Dom. 1517. Nor was the City onely, but Country Villages for four miles about, filled with French fashions and infections.

Tottenham wood is all on fire, When | then Tottenham street is nought but mire.   (T 445)

1631 W. BEDWELL *Brief Descrip. of Tottenham* iii ... It is obserued, That whensoeuer a foggy thicke mist doth arise out of this wood, and hang ouer it ... in maner of a smoake, That it's generally a signe of raine and foule weather.

Tottenham Wood, *see also* Remove T. W. (As easily).

Touch and go.

[= a risky or ticklish case or state of things.] **1815** R. WARDLAW *Let.* in ALEXANDER *Life* vi. (1856) 166 'Twas touch and go—but I got my seat. **1831** MISS FERRIER *Destiny* ch. 4 So it was with Glenroy and his lady. It had been touch-and-go with them for many a day; and now ... ended in a threatened separation. **1842–3** W. H. MAXWELL *Hector O'Halloran* ch. 25 You had a close escape. Well, 'touch and go' is good pilotage they say.

Touch and take.   (T 447)

1591 FLORIO *Second F.* 197 Euery finger a limetwig, touch and take, take and holde. **[1600] 1657** *Lust's Dominion* Hazl.-Dods. xiv. 141 For my powder, 'tis but touch and take. **1609** HARWARD 120 Spy sport non spy touch and take a trick of such as be limefingred. **1619** FLETCHER & MASSINGER *Barnevelt* I. 2741. **1670** NARBOROUGH *Jrnl.* in *Acc. Sev. Late Voy.* I. (1694) 14 One blinded with a Cloth serv'd euery Man as they were called to touch and take. **1805** NELSON *Let. to J. D. Thomson* 5 Sept. The Enemy have a shoal of frigates with their fleet. ... My Motto shall be Touch and Take.

Touch him with a pair of tongs (barge-pole, etc.), I would not.   (P 32)

1639 CLARKE 34 Not to be handled with a paire of tongues. **1658** J. SMITH *Wit Restor'd* (Hotten) 281 Without a payre of tongs no man will touch her. **1670** RAY 196. **1683** T. FARNABY *Troposchematologia* B8 (with a pair of hedging-mittins). **1688** BUNYAN *Jer. Sinner Saved* Wks. (1855) I. 98 We are scarce for touching of the poor ones that are left behind; no, not with a pair of tongs. **1801** EDGEWORTH *Out of Debt* ch. 1 She, who had formerly been heard to say 'she would not touch him with a pair of tongs', now unreluctantly gave him her envied hand at a ball. **1854** DICKENS *Hard Times* ch. 4 I was so ragged and dirty, that you wouldn't have touched me with a pair of tongs. **1931** 8 Mar. S. BALDWIN on the editor of the *Daily Mail* (T. Driberg *Beaverbrook* (1956) 214) An action for libel would lie ... I should get an apology and heavy damages. The first is of no value, and the second I would not touch with a barge-pole.

Touch me not on the sore heel (toe).   (H 387)

1621 ROBINSON 36 (sore toe). **1639** CLARKE 11 (sore toe). **1641** FERGUSSON no. 851 (sair heel). **1721** KELLY 320 ... Do not jest too near with my Honour and Interest. **1771** J. WESLEY *Letters* v. 246 I doubt they touch a sore point; I am afraid the shoe pinches.

Touch pot, If you | you must touch penny.   (P 506)

1654 GAYTON *Pleasant Notes Don Q.* 83 Touch pot touch penny. **1678** RAY 351 ... Somers. (Pay for what you have.) **1822** SCOTT *Nigel* ch. 16 Every man ... with his purse in his hand is as free to make new laws as he, ... since touch pot touch penny makes every man equal.

Touch wood; it's sure to come good.

[To touch wood is supposed to be a charm to avert misfortune, especially after untimely boasting.] **1906** *N. & Q.* 10th Ser. VI. 231. **1908** *Westmr. Gaz.* 30 Dec. 2/3 On the next occasion when we read of Christmas with spring weather or of the changing seasons we shall 'touch wood'. **1909** *Times Wkly.* 11 June 377 I witnessed on June 2 a diligence accident ... 'Have you ever had an accident?' ... 'No signor, ... and I have driven this coach for 15 years.' But he did not touch wood.

Touch your eye but with your elbow, You should never.   (D 360)

1640 HERBERT no. 203 Diseases of the eye are to bee cured with the elbow. **1670** RAY 39. **1856** ABP. WHATELY *Annot. Bacon's Ess.* (1876) xxii. 252 The granting of some permission, coupled with some condition which ... cannot or will not be fulfilled, is practically a prohibition. ... According to the proverbial caution 'You should never rub your eye except with your elbow'.

Touch-box, *see* Glimmer in the t.

Touched him to the quick, He has. (Q 13)

[c. 1517] **1533** SKELTON *Magn.* E3 As yf a man fortune to touche you on the quyke, Then feyne yourselfe dyseased and make yourselfe seke.

1548 T. ELYOT *Bibliotheca* Ad vivum resecare, to touche it to the quicke. A prouerbe taken of paryng of nayles, untill the bloud dooth appere. Which signifieth to touche a thyng neerer than need requyreth. **1551** ROBINSON *Utopia* (1556 Arb.) 53 For he . . . beynge thus touched on the quicke, and hit on the gaule, . . . fumed and chafed. **1592-3** SHAKES. *C.E.* II. ii. 129 How dearly would it touch thee to the quick, Shouldst thou but hear I were licentious. **1592** *Id. T. And.* IV. ii. 28 Lines, that wound, beyond their feeling, to the quick. *Ibid.* IV. iv. 36 But, Titus, I have touch'd thee to the quick. **1600-1** *Id. H.* II. ii. 593 I'll tent him to the quick: if he but blench I know my course. **1611** *Id. Temp.* V. i. 25 With their high wrongs I am struck to the quick.

Touches pitch shall be defiled, He that.

(P 358)

[APOCRYPHA *Ecclus.* xiii. 1 He that toucheth pitch shall be defiled therewith.] *c.* **1300** BRUNNE *Handl. Synne* l. 6578 Who-so handlyth pycche wellyng hote, He shal haue fylthe therof sumdeyl. *c.* **1386** CHAUCER *Parson's T.* l. 854 As who-so toucheth warm pych, it shent his fyngres. **1579** LYLY *Euph.* i. 250 Hee that toucheth pitche shall be defiled. **1597** SHAKES. *1 Hen. IV.* II. iv. 402 This pitch, as ancient writers report, doth defile. **1598-9** *Id. M.A.* III. iii. 52 I think they that touch pitch will be defiled. **1655** FULLER *Ch. Hist.* x. iv. (1868) III. 278 Vorstius had . . . received several letters from certain Samosatenian heretics . . . and . . . had handled pitch so long that at last it stuck to his fingers. **1852** ED. FITZGERALD *Polonius* 157 'Touch pitch and be daubed.' Never wholly separate in your mind the merits of any political question in from the Men who are concerned in it. *Burke.*

Touchstone tries gold, As the | so gold tries men.

(T 448)

1540 TAVERNER tr. *Erasm. Flores Sententiarum* A7 The touche stone tryeth golde, gold tryeth man. **1567** *Amorous Tales* tr. Sanford E4ᵛ The stone proueth golde, golde proueth a man. **1579** LYLY *Euph.* i. 219 But as the true golde is tryed by the touch . . . so the loyall heart of the faithfull louer is knowen by the tryal of his Lady. **1593** GREENE *Wks.* Gros. ii. 215 As the touchestone trieth the golde, so adversitie prooueth friends. **1625** BACON *Apoph.* Wks. (Chandos) 377 Chilon would say, 'That gold was tried with the touch-stone, and men with gold'. **1642** FULLER *Holy State* IV. vii. (1841) 256 Integrity is the proper portion of a judge. Men have a touchstone whereby to try gold, but gold is the touchstone whereby to try men. **1732** FULLER no. 736.

Touchstone, see also Calamity (Extremity) is the t. of a brave mind (unto wit).

Tough as leather, As. (L 166)

1533 ERASM. *Enchiridion* (1905) 161 As tough as white leather. **1611** COTGRAVE s.v. Corias. **1678** RAY 290 (whitleather).

Tough sinew in an auld wife's heel, There is a.

1737 RAMSAY III. 196.

Tough, see also Old and t.

Toulouse, see Gold of T.

Tout, see New t. in old horn.

Tow on one's distaff (rock), To have.

(T 450-1)

[= to have business to attend to.] *c.* **1386** CHAUCER *Miller's T.* l. 3774 This Absolon . . . hadde moore tow on his distaf Than Gerueys knew. **1412** HOCCLEVE *Reg. of Princes* E.E.T.S. 45, l. 1226 Tow on my distaf haue I for to spynne, Morë, my fadir, than ye wot of yit. *c.* **1460** *Townely Myst.* xiii. 389 I have tow on my rok more than euer I had. **1546** HEYWOOD II. v. H4ᵛ Some of them shall wyn More towe on their distaues, then they can well spyn. **1721** KELLY 182 I have other Tow on my Roke. **1756** MRS. CALDERWOOD in *Coltness Collect.* (Maitl. Club) 155 'In good faith', says John, . . . 'the Dutch has some other tow in their rock.' **1817** SCOTT *Rob Roy* ch. 39 They had other tow on their rock. **1818** *Id. Fam. Letters* (1894) II. 4 Above all, I had too much flax on my distaff.

Tow, see also Fire and t.

Tower of strength, A.

[PROV. xviii. 10 The name of the Lord is a strong tower.] [1592] **1597** SHAKES. *Rich. III* V. iii. 12 The King's name is a tower of strength. **1852** TENNYSON *Ode on Death of Duke of Wellington* canto 4 O fall'n at length that tower of strength. **1861** TROLLOPE *Framley Parsonage* ch. 20 The Prime Minister . . . has again added to himself another tower of strength.

Tower, see Snail climbs t.

Town bull is as much a bachelor as he, The.

(B 716)

1591 ARIOSTO *Orl. Fur.* Harington XXXVIII *Moral* Imagine some man so chast (as Caesar. was called), Omnium mulierum vir, or to vse our homely English phrase (as the towne Bull of the Parish). **1598** SHAKES. *2 Hen. IV* II. ii. 149 A proper gentlewoman, sir, and a kinswoman of my master's. — Even such kin as the parish heifers are to the town bull. **1666** TORRIANO *Prov. Phr.* s.v. Gallo 70 To be the cock of the parish, viz. to be a great whore-master, to be the town bull. **1678** RAY 66 Then the town-bull is a Batchelour. i.e. as soon as such an one.

Town but had a mire at one end of it, There was never a good.

1721 KELLY 312 . . . The Deficiency and Unsatisfactoriness of every created Being, has given occasion to this, and many other Proverbs.

Town in May, He that is in a | loses his Spring.

(T 453)

1640 HERBERT no. 988.

Town, see also Strong t. not won in an hour; Thrift is in the t. (When), you are in field.

Toy to mock an ape, A.   (T 456)

1571 THACKHAM *Defence* in *Narr. Reform.* V. 120
In deede S. Paul (whose examples for a shewe
to mocke an ape withall you bryng in) was never
a tyrant. **1579** FULKE *Heskins et al. Overthr.*
292 He nameth the accidents of things for the
thinges them selues, which is a toy to mocke an
ape. **1591** ARIOSTO *Orl. Fur.* Harington XXV.
60. **1599** *Look About You* l. 960. **1616** JONSON
Ev. Man in Hum. IV. ii. 10 Mary, an Elegie, an
Elegie, an odde toy — To mock an ape withall.

Traces, *see* Kick over the t.

**Tracys have always the wind in their
faces, The.**   (T 457)

1630 T. WESTCOTE *View of Devonsh.* (1845) 259–
60 This knight [Sir William Tracey] came into
this place [Morthoe Tracey] . . . the Pope
banning, cursing . . . then so formidable and
powerful, that it made the wind to blow always
in his face; whereby grew a common proverb
in this tract to those who had adverse fortune
or ill chance,—thou art like Sir William Tracey,
wind and weather is always against thee. **1662**
FULLER Glouc. 353 . . . Tradition . . . reporteth
that ever since Sir William Tracey was most
Active amongst the four Knights, which killed
Thomas Becket,[1] it is imposed on Tracies for
miraculous Penance, that . . . the Wind is ever
in their faces. [[1] 1170.]

Trade follows the flag.

1888 J. E. T. ROGERS *Econ. Interp. of Hist.* (1894)
II. xiii. 291 The English . . . began to build up
a new colonial empire, . . . under a new . . .
maxim, that trade follows the flag. **1902** H. J.
MACKINDER *Britain & Brit. Seas* 345 Britain . . .
derives profit from her daughter states. In
Canada and Australia trade has undoubtedly
tended to follow the flag.

Trade is better than service, A. (T 462)

1640 HERBERT no. 1005.

Trade is the mother of money. (T 463)

1616 DRAXE no. 2165. **1670** RAY 27. **1732**
FULLER no. 5271.

Trades live, Let all.

1721 KELLY 241 . . . Spoken when we have
broken an Utensil, which must employ a Tradesman to mend it, or make a new one. **1772** R.
GRAVES *Spiritual Quix.* IV. 1 Sure all trades
must live. **1832** HENDERSON 131 'Let a' trades
live', quo' the wife, when she burnt her besom.

**Trade, Who has a | has a share every-
where.**   (T 461)

1539 TAVERNER 22ᵛ Art or kunnynge euery
countrey nourysheth, that is to say, kunnynge
men and such as haue any facultie or science,
whether so euer they goo: shall lacke no liuyng.
1560 T. BECON *Catechism* P.S. 355 This common
proverb. Artem quaevis terra alit; that is to
say, A man having an occupation shall be
able to live wheresoever he become. *a.* **1580**
Wife in Morel's Skin Hazl. E.P.P. iv. 189 A good
Crafte I haue, pardee, To get our liuing in any

land. **1659** HOWELL *Fr. Prov.* 23 He that hath
a good trade will have his share. **1732** FULLER
no. 2386.

Trade(s), *see also* Cutpurse sure t.; Drives a
subtle t.; Every man must walk in own t.;
Good t. (He that has no), it is to his loss;
Handful of t. handful of gold; Jack of all t.;
Knavery in all t., most in tailors; Learns a t.
has a purchase; Many t. (Man of) begs; Men of
all t.; Two of a t. seldom agree; Virtue and a t.
best for children.

Tradesmen live upon lack.   (T 465)

1626 BRETON *Soothing* B3ᵛ. **1639** CLARKE 125.

Tradesmen, *see also* Break or wear out (If things
did not) how would t. live.

Traduttori, traditori (Translators,
traitors).

1607 H. ESTIENNE *World of Wonders* tr. R.C. 13
He performed not the office of a *traduttore*, but
of a *traditore*, that is, . . . he played not the part
of a *translator*, but of a traitor. **1853** TRENCH
i. 20 [An] Italian proverb . . . *Traduttori, traditori*
. . . *Translators, traitors*: so untrue very often
are they to the genius of their original. **1929**
Times 7 Aug. 6/3 The visitor . . . ought to be
able to speak fluently the language of the country
visited. Working through an interpreter is
roundabout and in many cases hopeless. As the
Italian proverb says: *Traduttore traditore.*

Trail of the serpent, The.

[In reference to GENESIS iii.] **1817** MOORE *Lalla
R., Par. & Peri* 206 Some flow'rets of Eden ye
still inherit, But the trail of the Serpent is over
them all! **1909** *Spectator* 2 Oct. 488 These
essays are avowedly an *olla podrida*, and . . . we
are painfully conscious of the trail of the
journalistic serpent.

**Traitors at the table, Are there | that
the loaf is turned the wrong side
upwards?**   (T 466)

1678 RAY 82. **1827–30** SCOTT *Tales Grandf.* ch. 7
The signal . . . was when one of his pretended
friends, who betrayed him,[1] should turn a loaf
. . . with its bottom or flat side uppermost.
[[1] Wallace, in 1305.]

Traitors' Bridge, *see* Loyal heart.

Traitor(s), *see also* King loves treason but hates
t.; *Traduttori.*

**Tramp on a snail, and she'll shoot out
her horns.**

1721 KELLY 302 . . . The meanest, when injured,
will show their Resentment.

**Tramp on a turd, The more you | the
broader it grows.**   (T 604)

1641 FERGUSSON no. 812. **1721** KELLY 316 . . .
Spoken when People make a great Stir about

scandalous Words which they are supposed to have deserv'd.

Tranent, *see* Salt to Dysart and puddings to T. (Carry).

Translators, *see Traduttori.*

Transplanted, *see* Tree often t. bears not much fruit.

Trap, To understand (be up to). (T 469)

[i.e. knows his own interest.] **1679** [LEANERD] *Counterfeits* III. i. 24 You're deceiv'd in old Gomez, he understands Trap. **1681** T. FLATMAN *Heraclitus Ridens* no. 5 (1713) I. 30 Well, Brother, I understand Trap. **1785** COWPER *Lett. to Lady Hesketh* 15 Dec. He understands booksellers' trap as well as any man. **1842** S. LOVER *Handy Andy* ch. 2 A clever, ready-witted fellow up to all sorts of trap.

Trap, *see also* Easy to fall into t.; Net (t.), (To be taken in one's own).

Trash, *see* Toil so for t. (If you).

Travel makes a wise man better, but a fool worse. (T 473)

1620–8 FELTHAM *Resolves* (1904) 240 Yet I think it not fit, that every man should travel. It makes a wise man better, and a fool worse. **1732** FULLER no. 5272.

Travel through the world, To | it is necessary to have the mouth of a hog, the legs of a stag, the eyes of a falcon, the ears of an ass, the shoulders of a camel, and the face of an ape, and overplus, a satchel full of money and patience. *Cf.* Servant (A good). (w 888)

1580 LYLY *Euph. & his Eng.* ii. 25 Recorde with thy selfe the inconueniences that come by trauailing . . . when at all times thou must haue the back of an Asse to beare all, and the snowt of a swine to say nothing. **1591** FLORIO *Second F.* 93 If you will be a traueller . . . haue alwayes the eies of a Faulcon . . . the eares of an Asse . . . the face of an Ape . . . the mouth of a Hog . . . the shoulder of a Camell . . . the legges of a Stagg . . . and see that you neuer want two bagges very full, that is one of pacience . . . and another of money. **1594** NASHE *Unfort. Trav.* ii. 297 A traueller must haue the backe of an asse to beare all, a tung like the taile of a dog to flatter all, the mouth of a hogge to eate what is set before him, the eare of a merchant to heare all and say nothing. **1617** FYNES MORYSON *Itinerary* III. 1. iii. iii. 453 We in England vulgarly say, that a Traveller to Rome must have the backe of an Asse, the belly of a Hogge, and a conscience as broad as the Kings high way. **1659** HOWELL *It. Prov.* 6 A Traveller must have the snout of a Hog, the legs of a Deer, and the back of an Asse. **1666** TORRIANO *It. Prov.* 157, no. 15.

Travel (*noun*), *see also* Little wit meikle t.

Traveller may lie with authority, A. *Cf.* Old men and travellers. (T 476)

c. **1362** LANGLAND *P. Pl.* A. Prol. 46 Pilgrymes and palmers . . . hedden leue to lyʒen heere lyf aftir. [*a.* 1521] *c.* **1545** HEYWOOD *Four PP* A3 [The Pardoner tells the Palmer that] Ye May lye by aucthoryte And all that hath wandred so farre That no man can be theyr controller. **1594** MARLOWE *Edw. II* I. i. 33 What art thou?—A traveller.—. . . Thou would'st do well to . . . tell me lies at dinner-time. **1602** SHAKES. *A.W.* II. v. 27 A good traveller is something at the latter end of a dinner; but one that lies three thirds . . . should be once heard and thrice beaten. **1608** DAY *Law Tricks* II. i (of scholars). **1611** SHAKES. *Temp.* III. iii. 26 Travellers ne'er did lie, Though fools at home condemn 'em. **1614** CAMDEN 303. **1616** DRAXE no. 1334 (Poets and trauellours). **1706** FARQUHAR *Recruit. Off.* III. i. Add but the traveller's privilege of lying; and even that he abuses. **1721** KELLY 23 A traveled Man has leave to lie.

Travellers change climates, not conditions. (T 477)

[HORACE *Epist.* I. II. 27 *Coelum non animum mutant, qui trans mare currunt.* Those who cross the sea, change their clime but not their character.] **1591** ARIOSTO *Orl. Fur.* Harington XXVII. 102 To his owne natiue soyle his course he bent, But changing place, could not his sorrow moue, Nor trauels paine, his paine of mind relent. **1624** J. HEWES *Perfect Survey* G4 They change the Climate not their minde, who flye beyond the Sea. **1655** FULLER *Ch. Hist.* III. ii. (1868) I. 366 *cælum non animum.* 'Travellers change climates, not conditions.' Witness our Becket; stubborn he went over, stubborn he staid, stubborn he returned.

Traveller(s), *see also* Lame t. should get out betimes; Nothing so necessary for t. as languages; Old men and t. lie by authority; Painters (t.) have leave to lie; Put tricks upon t. (Don't); Spends the t. more than abider (Much).

Travels far, He that | knows much. (M 1276)

1620 SHELTON *Quix.* II. XXV. ii. 362 He that reads much and travels much sees much and knows much. **1639** CLARKE 276. **1670** RAY 149.

Travels not by sea, He who | knows not what the fear of God is. *Cf.* Learn to pray, go to sea. (S 185)

1573 SANFORD 103 (He that hath not ben on the sea). **1623** WODROEPHE *Spared Houres* 230. **1666** TORRIANO *It. Prov.* 143, no. 8 (Who goes not by sea).

Travel(s) (*verb*), *see also* Rides behind another does not t. when he pleases; Way to t. is towards heaven (The best).

Tre, Pol, and Pen, you shall know the Cornish men, By. (T 479)

1548 BORDE *Introduction* E.E.T.S. 122 To sew Tre poll pen, for wagging of a straw. **1602**

CAREW *Survey of Cornwall* (1769) 55. **1662**
FULLER Cornw. 197 ... *Tre* signifieth a *Town* ...
Pol an *Head* ... *Pen* a *Top*. **1821** SCOTT *Kenilw*.
ch. I A worthy name ... of Cornish lineage;
for ... 'By Pol, Tre, and Pen, You may know
the Cornish men'. **1864** *N. & Q*. 3rd Ser. v. 208
Cornish Provs. .... By Tre, Pol, and Pen, Ros,
Caer and Lan, You shall know all Cornish men.
The second line of the old saw is frequently
omitted.

Tread on a worm and it will turn.

(W 909)

[Even the humblest will resent extreme ill-
treatment.] **1546** HEYWOOD II. iv. G4[v] Tread a
woorme on the tayle, and it must turne agayne.
1548 HALL *Chron*. (1809 ed. 270). **1591** SHAKES.
3 Hen. VI II. ii. 17 The smallest worm will turn,
being trodden on. **1611** DAVIES no. 115 Presse
a worme on the taile, and t'will turne againe.
a. **1628** CARMICHAELL no. 1397 Stramp on a
snail, sche will steir with her taill. **1748**
RICHARDSON *Clar. H*. (1785) I. vii. 41 How can
one be such a reptile as not to turn when trampled
upon. **1864** BROWNING *Mr. Sludge* 72 Tread
on a worm, it turns, sir! If I turn, Your fault!

Tread on nine daisies at once, When you can | spring has come.

1862 CHAMBERS *Bk. of Days* (1869) I. 312 Still
we can now plant our 'foot upon nine daisies'
and not until that can be done do the old-
fashioned country people believe that spring is
really come. **1910** *Spectator* 26 Mar. Spring
is here when you can tread on nine daisies at
once on the village green; so goes one of the
country proverbs.

Tread one's shoe awry, To. (S 367, 373)

[To fall from virtue.] **1530** PALSGRAVE 571b
I go a wrie, as one dothe that treadeth nat their
shoe a ryght. *c*. **1542** WYATT *Complaint of
Falseness* Wks. 96 Farewell all my welfare!
My shoe is trod awry. **1572** CRADOCKE *Ship of
Assured Safety* C2[v] If my shoe tread not always
streighte, I forbidde not a brotherly admonition.
1599 T. HEYWOOD *2 Edw. IV* 139 Pity that ere
awry she trod her shoe! **1678** RAY 81 He
knows not whether his shooe goes awry.

Tread, *see also* Eggs (To t. upon).

Treason, *see* King loves the t. but hates the
traitor; Trust is t. (In).

Treasure consisted of coals, The. (T 484)

1540 PALSGRAVE *Acolastus* 69 He is dysapoynted,
that loketh for treasoure, and findeth coles.
1616 JONSON *Mercury Vindicated* vii. 411 A
child o' the Scullery steales all their coales for
'hem too, and he is bid sleepe secure, hee shall
finde a corner o' the Philosophers stone for't,
vnder his bolster, one day, and haue the Prouerbe inuerted.

Treasure, *see also* Health is great riches (a jewel,
a t.); Measure is t.

Tree, Up a.

[= in a difficulty or 'fix'.] **1825** J. NEAL *Bro.
Jonathan* II. 103 If I didn't—I'm up a tree—

that's a fact. **1839** THACKERAY *Maj. Gahagan*
ch. 5 I had her in my power—up a tree, as the
Americans say.

Tree but bears (some) fruit, There is no.

(T 495)

c. **1521** BARCLAY *Eclogues* iv. 321 Euery tree
hath fruit after his Kinde. **1616** BRETON *2 Cross*.
A2[v] There is no tree but beareth fruit. **1639**
CLARKE 198.

Tree is fallen, When the | every one runs to it with his axe (hatchet). (T 502)

[MENANDER *Monosticha* 123 Δρυὸς πεσούσης πᾶς
ἀνὴρ ξυλεύεται. When an oak has fallen every
man becomes a woodcutter. L. *Dejectâ arbore,
quivis ligna colligit*. When the tree is fallen,
every one runs to it with his axe.] **1586** GUAZZO
ii. 172 This is a most true saying, That the tree is
no sooner fallen downe to the grounde, but
everie one is readie to runne vppon it with his
Hatchette. **1642** TORRIANO 5 When a tree is
once a falling, everyone crieth, Down with it,
Down with it. **1732** FULLER no. 4804 The Tree
is no sooner down but every one runs for his
Hatchet. **1791** I. D'ISRAELI *Curios. Lit*. (1858)
III. 444 The dissolution of the foundations of
deans and chapters would open an ample
source to pay the king's debts, and scatter the
streams of patronage. .... He[1] quoted a Greek
proverb, 'that when a great oak falls, every
neighbour may scuffle for a faggot'. [[1] Preston,
Master of Emmanuel Coll.]

Tree is known by its fruit, A. (T 497)

[MATT. xii. 33 The tree is known by his fruit.]
1528 TYNDALE *Obed. of a Christian Man* P.S.
252 Judge the tree by his fruit, and not by his
leaves. *c*. **1548** (? *c*. **1545**) J. BALE *Chron. of
L. Cobham* P.S. 10 (margin) Judge the ill tree
by his fruit. **1573** TUSSER 160 How euer tree
groweth, the fruit the tree showeth. **1598**
SHAKES. *I Hen. IV* II. iv. 414 If then the tree
may be known by the fruit, as the fruit by the
tree. **1670** RAY 11 ... and not by the leaues.
1896 FROUDE *Council of Trent* iv. 77 Lutherans
said the tree is known by its fruit. Teach a pure
faith, and abuses will disappear, and a righteous
life grow out of it as the fruit grows.

Tree, Like | like fruit. (T 494)

[MATT. vii. 17 Every good tree bringeth forth
good fruit; but a corrupt tree bringeth forth
evil fruit.] *c*. **1300** *Cursor M*. l. 38 O gode
pertre coms god peres, Wers tre, wers fruit it
beres. *c*. **1386** CHAUCER *Mel.–Monk Link* B[2]
l. 3146 Of fieble trees ther comen wrecched
ympes [grafts]. *Id Leg. Goo Women* l. 239
That wiked fruit cometh of a wiked tre, That
may ye fynde, if that it like yow. **1402** HOCCLEVE
Minor Poems E.E.T.S. 79 For swiche the frute
ys as that is the tre. *a*. **1529** SKELTON *Replyc*.
155 For it is an auncyent brute, Suche apple
tre, suche frute. **1573** *Brief Discourse of Murther
of George Saunders* (R. Simpson, *School of
Shakes*. ii. 234) Suche as the roote is, such are
the braunches. **1639** CLARKE 224. **1670** RAY
149 Such as the tree is, such is the fruit.

Tree loaded with fruit, It is only at the | that people throw stones.

1858 TRELAWNEY *Recollections* ch. I The proverb

'No person throws a stone at a tree that does not bear fruit'. **1865** ABP. TRENCH *Poems; 'Proverbs'* xvi Be bold to bring forth fruit, though stick and stone At the fruit-bearing trees are flung alone.

Tree often transplanted, A | bears not much fruit.   (T 499)

1609 HARWARD 123 A Tree too oft remooved groweth no where.   **1611** COTGRAVE s.v. Plante The ouer-oft remoued plant's not plentifull. **1666** TORRIANO *It. Prov.* 12 no. 28 (is never loaden with fruit).

Tree roots more fast, The | which has stood a rough blast.

1657 S. JACOMBE *Moses his Death . . . a Sermon . . . at the Funeral of Mr. Edward Bright* 7 A tree shaken by the wind roots it self the faster. **1856** ABP. WHATELY *Annot. Bacon's Ess.* (1876) v. 76 'The tree roots more fast, which has stood a rough blast'. . . . The agitation of a tree . . . by winds . . . causes it to put out more and stronger roots. Even so, every temptation that has been withstood . . . strengthens the roots of good principle.

Tree that God plants, The | no wind hurts it.   (T 500)

1640 HERBERT no. 691.

Tree that grows slowly, The | keeps itself for another.   (T 501)

1640 HERBERT no. 198.

Trees eat but once.   (T 512)

1640 HERBERT no. 933.

Tree(s), *see also* Bark and t. (Put not hand between); Bark up wrong t.; Crooks the t. (Timely) that will good cammock be; Do these things in a green t. (If they); Good fruit of a good t.; Good t. is good shelter; Good t. that has neither knap nor gaw; Great t. are good for shade; Great t. keep down little ones; Highest t. has greatest fall; Loves the t. loves branch; Man lives (As a) . . . as a t. falls so shall it lie; Plants a t. plants for posterity (He that); Remove an old t. and it will wither; See the wood for the t. (Cannot); Set. t. at Alll·llontide; Set t. poor; Straight t. have crooked roots; Withy t. (Old) would have new gate.

Trelawny, *see* Never a Granville wanted.

Tremble, *see* Aspen leaf.

Trencher friends are seldom good neighbours.   (F 762)

1576 LEMNIUS *Touchstone of Complexions* tr. T. Newton 101 Trencher frends and Coseners. **1590** GREENE *Never too late* Grosart viii. 130 Flattering Gnatos, that only are time pleasers and trencher friends. **1605–8** SHAKES. *T.Ath.* II. ii. 170 Ah, when the means are gone that

buy this praise, The breath is gone whereof this praise is made. Feast-won, fast-lost. **1611** COTGRAVE s.v. Voisin.   **1623** WODROEPHE 521 Hold him not for a good Nighbour, That's at Table and wine at eu'ry Houre.   **1732** FULLER no. 3573 No Friendship lives long, that owes its Rise to the Pot.

Trencher, *see* Little and good fills the t.; Muckhill on my t.; Trim as a t.

Trencherman, A good.   (T 515)

1590 GREENE *Francesco's Fortunes* Grosart viii. 199 Mullidor tried himselfe so tall a trencher man, that his mother perceiued by his drift he would not die for loue.   **[1598] 1616** HAUGHTON *Englishmen for my Money* l. 896 Lets too't . . . and try who's the best Trencher-man.   **1598–9** SHAKES. *M.A.* I. i. 41 You had musty victual, and he hath holp to eat it. He is a very valiant trencher-man; he hath an excellent stomach. **1616** DRAXE no. 879.   **1626** BRETON *Soothing* A5ᵛ A tall trencher-man had not need be a poore man.

Trevannion, *see* Charles's Wain.

Treve, The, *see* Every man's man had a man . . . made the T. fall.

Trial, *see* Truth loves t.

Tribe of Levi must have no mind to the tribe of Gad, The.   (T 516)

[A play upon the word *gad*.]   **1629** T. ADAMS *Serm.* (1861–2) I. 455 Ministers must be like stars fixed in their orbs; ours is a stable profession, not a gadding ministry. . . . He spake merrily that said, the tribe of Levi must have no mind to the tribe of *Gad*.   **1738** SWIFT *Dial.* I. E.L. 286 I think your ladyship is one of the tribe of Gad.

Trick for trick, and a stone in thy foot besides, quoth one pulling a stone out of his mare's foot, when she bit him upon the back, and he her upon the buttock.   (T 519)

1659 HOWELL *Eng. Prov.* 4a.

Trick the colt gets at his first backing, The | will, while he continueth, never be lacking.   (T 520)

1611 COTGRAVE s.v. Poulain.   **1721** KELLY 63. [*English.*]

Trick (The way) to catch the old one,'A.   (W 149)

[1598] 1616 HAUGHTON *Englishmen for my Money* l. 2000 Now for a tricke to ouerreach the Diuell.   **1606** J. DAY *Isle Gulls* E3 We are in the way to catch the old one, and then our ayme deceiues not.   **1608** MIDDLETON *A Trick to Catch the Old One* [Title].   **1639** CLARKE 127

This is the way to catch the old one. **1678** RAY 87 (the way . . . on the nest).

Trick worth two of that, A. (T 518)

1597 SHAKES. *1 Hen. IV* II. i. 36 I know a trick worth two of that. **1608** DAY *Hum. out of Br.* IV. ii. Tut, I can tell you a trick worth two of that. **1619** *Sir J. Barnavelt* IV. i. *fin.* I know a trick worth ten of that. **1772** R. GRAVES *The Spiritual Quix.* III. xv. She said, whe knew a trick worth two of that. **1837** DICKENS *Pickwick* ch. 27 He knows a trick worth a good half dozen of that.

Tricks as (than) a dancing bear, He has as many (more). (T 522)

1666 TORRIANO *Prov. Phr.* s.v. Scimia 185 To be full of ridiculous gestures, and making of faces, more tricks than a dancing bear. **1667** 'RODUL-PHUS' *Fortune's Uncertainty* (1959) 13 He had as many tricks as a dancing bear. **1670** RAY 163. **1738** SWIFT *Dial.* I. E.L. 277 I wish you would be quiet, you have more tricks than a Dancing Bear. **1837** J. B. KER 45 He is as whimsical as a dancing bear.

Trick(s), *see also* Dog's t.; Fencer has one t. in his budget; Put t. upon travellers (Don't); Teach an old dog t.

Trim as a trencher. (T 513)

1542 ERASM. tr. Udall *Apoph.* 246b Fillyng vp as trymme as a trencher ye space that stood voide. **1548** BALE *K. Johan* l. 2514, 128 Trymme as a trencher, hauynge hys shoes of golde. [*a.* **1558**] **1568** *Jacob and Esau* IV. iii. E2.

Trim tram, like master like man. (T 525)

1571 J. BRIDGES *Sermon at Paul's Cross* 109 It is now the old prouerbe vp and downe, trim tram, such maister, suche man. **1583** MEL-BANCKE D3ᵛ Trim tram, neither good for God nor man. **1617** MIDDLETON & ROWLEY *Fair Quarrel* II. ii. Merm. 231 My name is Trimtram, forsooth; look what my master does, I use to do the like. **1659** HOWELL *Eng. Prov.* 13b. **1790** TRUSLER *Provs. Exempl.* 28 Even the slave who follows him, is infected with his master's pride; and . . . illustrates the proverb, *Trim tram, like Master like Man.*

Tring,[1] Wing,[2] and Ivinghoe,[2] for striking of a blow Hampden did forego, and glad he could escape so.

1830 SCOTT *Ivanhoe* Introd. A rhyme recording three names of the manors forfeited by the ancester of the celebrated Hampden, for strik-ing the Black Prince a blow with his racket, when they quarrelled at tennis:—Tring, Wing, and Ivanhoe, For striking of a blow, Hampden did forego, And glad he could escape so. **1864** *N. & Q.* 3rd Ser. v. 176 As the Messrs. Lysons remark, 'this tradition . . . will not bear the test of examination; for it appears, by record, that neither the manors of Tring, Wing, or Ivan-hoe, ever were in the Hampden family'. (*Bucks,* vol. i, pt. iii, p. 571.) [[1] Herts. [2] Bucks.]

Tring,[1] Wing[2] and Ivinghoe,[2] three dirty villages all in a row, and never without a rogue or two. Would you know the reason why? Leighton Buz-zard[3] is hard by.

1852 *N. & Q.* 1st Ser. v. 619. [[1] Herts. [2] Bucks. [3] Beds.]

Trip like a doe (roe), To. (D 431)

1530 PALSGRAVE 762b She hath a light herte, she tryppeth and it were a doe. *c.* **1563** *Jack Juggler* B1 She tryppeth like a do. [*c.* **1590**] **1599** PEELE *David & Bethsabe* l. 121 Now comes my louer, tripping like the Roe. **1678** RAY 83 To trot like a Doe.

Trip, To take one in a. (T 526)

1539 TAVERNER *Publius* B2 He loseth well money, which when he is taken in a tryppe gyueth to the iudge or ruler some reward for his indemnitie. **1541** *Schoolh. of Women* D3 Saba, the gorgyous quene . . . enuyed kynge Salomon To proue his wysdome, and take with a tryppe Passed the sees. **1546** HEYWOOD II. iii. G2 Also hardly, if ye can Take me in any tryp. **1551** T. WILSON *Rule of Reason* X2 Thei thought to take hym in a trip. **1611** DAVIES no 352 Phryne is often tane in a trip.

Tripe's good meat if it be well wiped. (T 527)

1678 RAY 50.

Tripe, *see also* Scorn a thing as a dog scorns t.

Tripoli, To come from.

['To vault and tumble with activity. It was, I believe, first applied to the tricks of an ape, or monkey, which might be supposed to come from that part of the world.' Nares. There may also be a pun on 'trip' = to caper or dance.] **1609** JONSON *Sil. Woman* V. i. 44 I protest, sir John, you came as high from Tripoly as I doe. *a.* **1625** FLETCHER *M. Thomas* IV. ii. 69 Get up to that window there, and presently . . . come from Tripoli. **1827** SCOTT *Journ.* 3 Apr. I drank a glass or two of wine more than usual, got into good spirits, and *came from Tripoli* for the amusement of the good company.

Triumph before the victory, Do not. (V 50)

1545 TAVERNER H7 Ye triumphe before the vyctorye. Such there be not fewe whiche glory of thinges to sone, before they haue fully brought them to effecte. **1551** CRANMER *Ans. to Gardiner* 294 You triumph before the victorie. **1579** LYLY *Euph.* i. 323 But I will not vaunt before the victorie. **1599** SHAKES. *A.Y.* I. ii. 187 You mean to mock me after. You should not have mock'd me before. **1599** *Id. Hen. V* III. vii. [In this scene Shakespeare portrays the folly of the French who boast before the battle.] *a.* **1628** CARMICHAELL no. 1580. **1649** TORRIANO 98.

Trivet, *see* Right as a t.

Trojans became wise too late, The.
(T 528)

[ERASM. *Ad. Sero sapiunt Phryges.*] **1539**
TAVERNER A2ᵛ Sero sapiunt phryges. The
Troyans are wyse to late. . . . Euen so it is of
many at thys daye. They be wyse, but to late.
1579 LYLY *Euph.* i. 188 The Troyans repented to
late when their towne was spoiled. **1860** RILEY
Dict. Lat. Quot. 418 . . . When their city was on
the point of being taken, they began to think
of restoring Helen. **1895** SIR H. MAXWELL *Post
Meridiana* 49 *Sero sapiunt Phryges*—knowledge
comes, but wisdom tarries, [lingers][1] as was
said long ago. [[1] *Locksley Hall.*]

Trojans were, We.
(T 529)

[VIRGIL *Aen.* ii. 324.] **1545** S. GARDINER to Paget
(*Letters* ed. Muller 160) As he that hath made
an ende of his oration, may saye, *dixi*, soo, for
myn owne pleasour in the worlde, I may saye,
vixi, *fuimus Troes*. *c.* **1594** BACON no. 776 We
Trojans were—i.e. have now ceased to be.

Trooper, *see* Swear like a t.; Young t. should have
old horse.

Trot (*proper name*), *see* John T.

Trot (*verb*), *see* Ass pricked must needs t.; Dog
that t. about finds bone; Mother t., (If the) how
can the daughter amble?; Need makes old wife t.

Trotters, *see* Steals a sheep, gives t.

Trouble brings experience (patience) and experience brings wisdom.
(T 535)

1550 COVERDALE *Spiritual Pearl* P.S. 120. **1557**
EDGEWORTH *Sermons* 3E4ᵛ True it is that trouble
worketh patience. **1581** WOODES *Confl. Consc.*
I. ii. B2 For trouble bring forth pacience, from
pacience dooth insue Experience, from experience
Hope, of health the ankor true.

Troubles a wolf how many the sheep be, It never.
(W 604)

1625 BACON *Ess., Great. of Kingd.* Arb. 473 Nay
Number (it selfe) in Armies, importeth not
much, where the People is of weake Courage:
for (as *Virgil* saith) *It neuer troubles a Wolfe,
how many the sheepe be.*[1] **1786** MRS. PIOZZI
Anec. of S. Johnson (1892) 18 I said to him,
'Why there happens to be no less than five
Cambridge men in the room now'. 'I did not'
(said he) 'think of that till you told me; but the
wolf don't count the sheep.' [[1] VIRGIL *Ecl.* vii.
52.]

Trouble(s), *see also* Company in t. (Good to
have); Meet t. half-way (Don't); Peck of t.;
Seeks t. never misses; Seeks t. pity he should
miss it; Talk than t. (More); War, hunting . . .
full of t.; Young bear with his t. before him
(Like a).

Troublesome, *see* Better be unmannerly than t.

Trough, *see* Sow to own t.

Trout, *see* Chevin to the t. (Said the); Lose a fly
to catch a t.; Whole (Sound) as a t.

Trowel, *see* Lay it on with t.

Troy was.
(T 540)

[VIRGIL *Aen.* iii. 11 *Troja fuit.*] **1620** SHELTON
Quix. II. lxvi. iii. 284 As they went out of
Barcelona, Don Quixote beheld the place
where he had his fall, and said, '"Hic Troja
fuit"; here . . . my fortune fell, never to rise
again'. **1754** WESLEY *Journ.* Jul. [at ruins of
Old Sarum] Troy was. **1828** LAMB to Cowden
Clarke, 25 Feb. They all live in my mind's
eye . . . Troja fuit.

Trucks (*verb*), *see* Fair chieve all where love t.

Trudge, *see* One thing said twice deserves a t.

True as a turtle to her mate, As.
(T 624)

c. **1380** CHAUCER *Parl. of Fowls* l. 355 The
wedded turtel with her herte trewe. **1590**
SPENSER *F.Q.* III. xi. 2 As trew in loue, as Turtle
to her make. **1602** SHAKES. *T.C.* III. ii. 174 As
true as . . . turtle to her mate. *c.* **1608–9** MIDDLE-
TON *Widow* I. i. Mine own wit this, and 'tis as
true as turtle. **1639** CLARKE 268.

True as God is in heaven, As.
(G 175)

1475 *Mankind* l. 654 As sekyr as Gode ys in
hewyn. **1569** J. PHILLIP *Patient Grissill* l. 1002
As sure as God doth lyue, and sitt in heauen
aboue. **1573** BARET *Alveary* s.v. True. **1600**
DEKKER *Shoem. Hol.* IV. iv. 40. **1670** RAY 208.

True (Sooth) as gospel.
(G 378)

13.'. *Minor Poems fr. Vernon MS.* xxiii. 796
Soþ as gospelle. *c.* **1380** *Romaunt of the Rose*
l. 5453 And trowe been as the Evangile. *c.*
1440 *Partonope* 153 And that hit were as sothe
as gospell. **1509** BARCLAY *Ship of Fools* i. 100.
[c. **1515**] *c.* **1530** *Id. Eclog.* I. 637. *c.* **1520** SKELTON
Magnificence l. 218 As trewe as the crede.
c. **1520** J. RASTELL *Four Elements* E2 As trewe as
the gospell. **1538** J. BALE *Three Laws* E4. **1567**
PAINTER (Jacobs) iii. 208. **1591** ARISOTO *Orl.
Fur.* Harington xxxiv. *Allegorie.*

True as I am his uncle, That is as.
(U 4)

1678 RAY 83.

True as steel, As.
(S 840)

a. **1300** *Siriz* 95 in *Anec. Lit.* (1844) 5 Oure love
is also trewe as stel, Withouten wou. *c.* **1300**
BRUNNE *Handl. Synne* l. 2338 And to the ded
was as trew as steyl. *c.* **1350** *How the Gd. Wife.*
l. 80. *c.* **1385** CHAUCER *Leg. G.W.* l. 334 That
ben as trewe as euer was any steel. *c.* **1425**
Wakefield Plays Second [Shepherds l. 226. **1575**
GASCOIGNE *Posies* i. 143 Though it have been
thought as true as steel. **1594–5** SHAKES. *R.J.*
II. iv. 192 I warrant thee my man's as true as
steel. **1595** *Id. M.N.D.* II. i. 197 My heart Is
true as steel. **1602** *Id. T.C.* III. ii. 173. **1705**
DUNTON *Life & Err.* 244 He's as true as steel
to his word. **1839** DICKENS *N. Nickleby* ch. 61.

Page 841

**True as that the cat crew, That is as |
and the cock rocked the cradle.**

1732 FULLER no. 4351.

True blue. *Cf.* Coventry blue. **True
blue will never stain.** (T 542)

1600 JONSON *Cynth. Rev.* v. i Steal into his hat
the colour whose blueness doth express trueness.
1650 COWLEY *Guardian* v. v Bess, poor wench,
is married to a chandler; but she's true blue
still. 1663 BUTLER *Hudibras* I. i. 191 'Twas
Presbyterian true blue. 1890 W. F. BUTLER *Sir
C. Napier* 95 A conspiracy among the . . . True
Blues of their party to shut out the Princess
Victoria from the throne.

True blue will never stain. *Cf.* Coventry
blue. **True blue.** (T 543)

1579 LYLY *Euph.* i. 226 I find it nowe for a
setled truth, which earst I accompted for a
vaine talke, that the Purple dye will neuer
staine. 1659 HOWELL *Eng. Prov.* 11a. 1670
RAY 166 . . . Coventry had formerly the reputation for dying of blues; insomuch that true
blue became a Proverb to signifie one that was
always the same and like himself. 1721 KELLY
303 . . . A Man of fix'd Principles, and firm
Resolutions, will not be easily induc'd to do
an ill, or mean thing.

True love kythes[1] in time of need.
(L 548)

a. 1628 CARMICHAELL no. 1550. 1641 FERGUSSON
no. 837. 1721 KELLY 326 . . . L. *Amicus certus
in re incerta cernitur.* [[1] shows itself.]

**True man, A | and a thief think not the
same.**

1386 CHAUCER *Squire's T.* F[1] l. 537 A trewe wight
and a theef thenken nat oon. 1598–9 SHAKES.
M.A. III. iii. 46 If you meet a thief, you may
suspect him . . . to be no true man.

True praise roots and spreads. (P 545)
1640 HERBERT no. 538.

True Roger.

1611 COTGRAVE s.v. Iaquet, Tu dis vray Iaquet.
True Roger, say we, and vse it (as the French
that) in scorne, and to the disgrace, of a lyer.

True steel as Ripon rowels, As. (S 841)
1625 JONSON *Staple of News* I. iii. 52 Why,
there's an angel. If my Spurres Be not right
Rippon—. 1662 FULLER *Yorks.* 190 . . . It is
said of trusty Persons, men of metall, faithful
in their imployments. . . . The best Spurs . . .
are made at Rippon.

True that all men say, It is. (M 204)
1520 WHITTINGTON *Vulg.* E.E.T.S. 72 It is lyke
to be true that euery man sayth. 1545 TAVERNER
H1[v] The englyshe prouerbe . . . It is like to be
true that euery man sayeth. 1546 HEYWOOD I.
xi. D4[v] It must needes be true, that euery man

sayth. 1611 DAVIES no. 29. 1623 CAMDEN 272
1670 RAY 150 . . . *Vox populi vox Dei.* 1721
KELLY 187 It may be true that some Men say;
but it must be true that all Men say. 1840
MARRYAT *Poor Jack* ch. 33 Every one declared
that she was the handsomest creature that ever
they had seen; and what every one says must
be true. 1905 ALEX. MACLAREN *Matthew* II. 246
'What everybody says must be true' is a cowardly
proverb . . . What most people say is usually
false.

True word is spoken in jest, Many a.
(W 772)

c. 1386 CHAUCER *Monk-Nun's Priest Link* B[2]
l. 1353 Be nat wrooth, my lord, for that I pleye.
Ful ofte in game a soothe I have herd seye!
1605–6 SHAKES. *K.L.* V. iii. 71 Jesters do oft
prove prophets. *a.* 1628 CARMICHAELL no. 1099
Manie suith word said in bourding.[1] 1738
SWIFT Dial. I. E.L. 294. 1877 ABP. TRENCH *Med.
Ch. Hist.* (1879) ix. 130 Damiani . . . fondly calls
him[2] his *Sanctus Satanas*, . . . and . . . as the
proverb tells us, many a true word has been
uttered in jest. 1928 9 Mar. D. H. LAWRENCE
Lett. ii. 1043 Juliette . . . suggested rather
savagely I should call it: John Thomas and
Lady Jane. Many a true word spoken in spite.
[[1] jesting. [2] Hildebrand.]

**Truest jests sound worst in guilty ears,
The.** (J 44)

1599 MINSHEU *Span. Gram.* 84 True iests are
ill, i. It is ill to iest at that which was done in
deed. 1659 HOWELL *Span. Prov.* 7 The worst
jest is the true jest. *Ibid.* Fr. *Prov.* 10 True jests
are the worst. 1664 CODRINGTON 215. 1670
RAY 14. 1706 STEVENS s.v. Burlas No jest like
a true jest.

True (r, st), *see also* Belly is the t. clock; Dying
men speak t.; False (T.) as God is t., (AS);
Love's-knot, (A t.); New is not t.; Newer is
t.; Strange than t., (It is no more); Velvet t.
heart. *See also* Sooth.

Trump, *see* Lost the tongue of the t.; Sow
playing on t. (Like a).

Trump(s) (at cards), *see* Clubs are t.; Money is
. . . t.; Put one to his t.; Turn up t.

Trumpet, *see* Blow one's own t.

Trumpeter is dead, Your. *Cf.* Blow your
own trumpet.

1721 KELLY 375 . . . Spoken when people commend themselves. 1729 FRANKLIN *Busy-Body*
no. 1 in Wks. (Bigelow) i. 29 I am cautious of
praising myself, lest I should be told my
trumpeter's dead. 1788 GROSE *Dict. Vulg. T.*
s.v. Trumpeter . . . he is therefore forced to sound
his own trumpet.

Trumpeter, *see also* Die (When you), your t. will
be buried; Dry cough t. of death.

Trunch, *see* Gimmingham.

Truss up all his wit in an eggshell, You
may.   (W 573)

1678 RAY 84 [*Joculatory*]. **1732** FULLER no.
5957.

Trust a tailor that does not sing at his
work, Never.

[**1607**] **1613** BEAUM. & FL. *Kt. Burn. P.* II. viii.
(Dent) 64 Never trust a tailor that does not sing
at his work; his mind is of nothing but filching.

Trust before you try, If you | you may
repent before you die.   (T 558)

c. **1560** HUTH *Ancient Ballads* (1867) 221 Who
trusts before he tries may soon his trust repent.
1670 RAY 149. **1732** FULLER no. 6084.

Trust, This day there is no | but come
tomorrow.   (D 103)

1594 LYLY *Mother B.* IV. ii. 24 I cannot help
you at this time, I praie you come againe to
morrow. **1642** TORRIANO 58 This day there is
no trusting, but tomorrow. **1658** *Comes
Facundus in Via* 15–16. **1732** FULLER no. 4999.

Trust him no further than I can fling
him (throw a mill-stone), I will.   (T 556)

1618 HARINGTON *Epigrams* Bk. ii no. 74 That
he might scant trust him so farre as to throw
him. **1670** RAY 197. **1678** *Id.* 274 . . . or
then I can throw a millstone. **1732** FULLER no.
5286 (than you can throw him).

Trust him with untold gold (money),
You may.   (G 296)

[*a.* **1558**] **1568** *Jacob & Esau* E3 Ye may trust
her with gold Though it were a bushell, and not
a peny tolde. **1616** DRAXE no. 2185. **1639**
CLARKE 116 (money). **1670** RAY 197.

Trust in God, Put your | but keep your
powder dry.

a. **1658** CROMWELL in HAYES *Ballads of Ireld.*
(1855) I. 191 Cromwell . . . when his troops
were about crossing a river . . . concluded an
address . . . with these words—'put your trust
in God; but mind to keep your powder dry'.
1908 *T.L.S.* 6 Nov. 383 In thus keeping his
powder dry the bishop acted most wisely, though
he himself ascribes the happy result entirely to
observance of the other half of Cromwell's
maxim.

Trust is dead, ill payment killed it.
                                                     (T 554)

1666 TORRIANO *It. Prov.* 184 no. 19.

Trust is the mother of deceit.   (T 555)

c. **1400** *Rom. Rose* l. 3932 For he may best, in
every cost, Disceyve, that men tristen most.
a. **1530** R. *Hill's Commonpl. Bk.* E.E.T.S. 130
In whom I trust most, soonest me deseyvith.
1611 SHAKES. *Temp.* I. ii. 93 My trust, Like a

good parent, did beget of him A falsehood in
its contrary as great As my trust was. **1636**
CAMDEN 307.

Trust is treason, In.   (T 549)

c. **1450** *Mankind* l. 743 In trust ys treson, *t*his
promes ys not credyble. *c.* **1450–1500** *Gd.
Wife wd. a Pilgrimage* l. 38. **1531** SIR T. ELYOT
Governour ii. 139 Ye, your truste is the cause
that I haue conspired agayne you this treason.
1546 HEYWOOD II. v. H1ᵛ Shall I trust hym then?
nay in trust is treason. **1559** *Mirror for Mag.*
(Campbell) 92 For often we see in trust is
treason. **1614** CAMDEN 308. **1639** CLARKE 90.

Trust is truth, In.   (T 550)

1639 CLARKE 116.

Trust me, but look to thyself.

1721 KELLY 239 (Lippen to me). **1732** FULLER
no. 5288.

Trust not a horse's heel, nor a dog's
tooth.   (H 711)

[L. *Ab equinis pedibus procul recede*. Keep at a
distance from a horse's heels.] *c.* **1383** FORDUN
Scotichronicon (1759) Bk. 14 ch. 32 Till
horsis fote thou never traist, Till hondis tooth,
no womans faith. **1577** PEACHAM *Garden of
Eloquence* (1593) 87. **1605** SHAKES. *K.L.* III. vi.
17 He's mad that trusts in the tameness of a
wolf, a horse's health [?heels], a boy's love, or a
whore's oath. **1678** RAY 158. **1910** P. W.
JOYCE *Eng. as we Speak* 110 Three things are
not to be trusted—a cow's horn, a dog's tooth,
and a horse's hoof.

Trust not a new friend nor an old
enemy.

a. **1450** *Ballad* 288 in *Ratis Raving, etc.* E.E.T.S.
9 Thi enemys auld trow neuer in. *c.* **1450**
Provs. of Wysdom 21 Never trust neuer in thyn enmy.
c. **1513** MORE *Rich. III* (1821 ed.) 21 None of vs
I beleue is so vnwyse, ouersone to truste a newe
frende made of an olde foe. **1721** KELLY 262
Never trust much to a new Friend, or an old
Enemy.

Trust not a woman when she weeps.
                                                     (W 638)

1597 *Politeuphuia* 27 (for it is her nature to
weepe when shee wanteth her will). **1604**
DEKKER I *Hon. Whore* V. i. 34 Trust not a
woman when she cryes, For sheele pump water
from her eyes. **1605–8** SHAKES. *T.Ath.* I. ii. 63
Immortal gods . . . Grant I may never prove so
fond To trust . . . a harlot for her weeping. **1659**
HOWELL *Span. Prov.* 7 (woman that weeps, nor
a dog that pisseth).

Trust to a dry stick, No.   (T 552)

1616 BRETON 2 *Cross.* A3ᵛ.

Trust to the dog, While you | the wolf
slips into the sheepfold.

1732 FULLER no. 5690.

Trust you no further than I can see you,
I will.   (T 557)

1565 QUEEN ELIZABETH to Sir Henry Sidney
(Nichols *Progresses* 1823, ii. 304) He [Desmond]
hathe so well performed his Englesche vowes,
that I warne you trust him no longer than you
see one of them.   *c.* **1593** *Fair Em.* l. 396 Why,
darest thou not trust me?—Yes faith, euen as
long as I see thee.   **1594** *True Trag. Rich. III*
iv. Cɪᵛ Ile trust neuer . . . a Duke in the world,
further then I see him.   **1606** J. DAY *Isle Gulls*
C2 Wil you trust him?—Yes as farre as I see
him.   **1639** CLARKE 90.

Trusted (Get credit) with a house full of
unbored millstones, He may be. (H 792)

1641 FERGUSSON no. 408 Of false persons. He
will get credit of a house full of unbored mil-
stones.   **1721** KELLY 151 . . . That is, only with
what he cannot carry away.

Trusts in a lie, He that | shall perish in
truth.   (L 231)

1640 HERBERT no. 569.   **1642** TORRIANO 26.

Trusts much, He that | obliges much,
says the Spaniard.   (S 701)

1651 HERBERT no. 1045.

Trusts not, He who | is not deceived.
                                                   (T 559)

1597 *Politeuphuia* 243 He that neuer trusteth,
is neuer deceiued.   **1616** DRAXE no. 2182.   **1642**
TORRIANO 24.   **1707** MAPLETOFT 66.   **1732** no.
2406.

Trust(s, ed), *see also* Better known than t.;
Boughs, (Who t. to rotten)/may fall; First try
then t.; God provides for him that t.; Post, (As
good t. to a rotten); See your friend (Whensoever you), t. to yourself; Sows (He that) t. in
God; Speaks me fair and loves me not . . . t. him
not; Try before you t.

Trust (noun), *see* Breaks his t., (To him that)/
let t. be broken.

Truth and oil are ever above.   (T 568)

1620 SHELTON *Quix.* II. i. iii. 174 I have told
you the truth, which shall always prevail above
lies, as the oil above the water.   **1640** HERBERT
no. 234.

Truth fears no colours. *Cf.* Truth needs
no colours.   (C 520)

[= fears no enemy.]   **1592** NASHE *Strange News*
i. 280 Helter skelter, feare no colours, course
him, trounce him.   **1594–5** SHAKES. *L.L.L.* IV.
ii. 140 Sir, tell me not of the father; I do fear
considerable colours.   **1598** *Id. 2 Hen. IV* V.
v. 86 Sir, I will be as good as my word . . . Fear
no colours.   **1601** *Id. T.N.* I. v. 8 I can tell thee
where that saying was born of, 'I fear no colours'.
1613 MARSTON *Insat. Count.* II. I Then came in
after him one that, it seem'd, feared no colours.

1664 COTTON *Scarron.* (1715 ed. 3) Must they
go on fearing no Colours?   **1678** RAY 347.

Truth finds foes, where it makes none.
                                                   (T 570)

[AUSONIUS *Ludus Septem Sapientum, Bias,
Veritas odium parit.* Truth produces hatred.]
c. **1530** TERENCE *Andria* A4   Trewth getteth
hatred.   *c.* **1560** BALE *K. Johan* l. 2208 Treuthe
ingendereth hate.   **1572** T. WILSON *Discourse
upon Usury* (1925) 188 It is a common saying,
Veritas odium parit, Truth purchaseth hatred.
1576 PETTIE ii. 113 Truth getteth hatred.   **1581**
N. WOODES *Confl. of Consc.* l. 338 That olde
said saw, . . . Obsequium amicos, by flateries
friends are prepared: But veritas odium parit,
. . . For speaking the trueth, many hated haue
beene.   **1588** TERENCE *Andria* tr. Kyffin Flatry
gaynes Freinds, and Truthe gets Foes.   **1670**
RAY 150.

Truth has a good face, but bad (ill)
clothes.   (T 571)

1597 *Politeuphuia* 9 Truth delighteth when it is
apparrailed worst.   **1591** FLORIO *Second F.* 99
Vertue often times is hid, vnderneath a base
weede.   **1639** FULLER *Holy War* III. xix Strange
that any should fall in love with that profession,
whose professors were so miserable! But truth
hath always a good face, though often but bad
clothes.   **1659** HOWELL *Eng. Prov.* 3b (ill).

Truth has a scratched face.   (T 572)

1584 LYLY *Camp.* IV. iii. 26 Truth is neuer
without a scratcht face.   **1609** HARWARD 121ᵛ
Truth is seldom without a skared face.   **1875**
CHEALES *Proverb. Folk-Lore* 118.

Truth has always a fast bottom.   (T 573)

1678 RAY 211.   **1732** FULLER no. 5300 (sure).

Truth has no answer.   (T 574)

1642 TORRIANO 65 . . . That is, it is but a folly
to object against it.   **1732** FULLER no. 5294
Truth and Matter of Fact have no Answers.

Truth has no need of rhetoric (figures).
                                                   (T 575)

1535 G. JOYE *Apol. to Tyndale* Arber 20 The
trowth knoweth no fucated polesshed and
paynted oracion.   **1562** J. WIGAND *De Neutralibus* 13 It is an old said saw: Truth speaketh
playnly.   **1566** GASCOIGNE & F. KINWELMERSH
Jocasta II. i. 300 [*margin*] Truth pleadeth simply
when falsehood vseth eloquence.   **1589** WARNER
Albion's Eng. Chalmers iv. 578b Good causes
need not curious termes.   **1591** *2 Troublesome
Reign K. John* B4ᵛ Shining truth Plainely to
paint as truth requires no art.   *a.* **1597** *Pilg. to
Parn.* ed. W. D. Macray 2 Plaine dealing needs
not Retoricks tinklinge bell.   **1597** *Politeuphuia*
10 Truth is a good cause, and needes no help of
oratorie.   **1600–1** SHAKES. *H.* II. ii. 95 More
matter, with less art.   **1608** MIDDLETON *Family
Love* V. iii. 340 Truth needs not the foil of
rhetoric.   **1622** G. MARKHAM & SAMPSON *Herod
and Antipater* 1 B4ᵛ Truth hath no need of
figures.

Truth is always green, The.   (T 577)

1659 HOWELL *Span. Prov.* 5 Truth is green. **1835** TRENCH iv. 76 There may be poetry in a play upon words . . . as . . . in that exquisite Spanish proverb: *La verdad es siempre verde* . . . **1894** BLACKMORE *Perlycross* ch. 13 Ivory—. . . which . . . whitens with the lapse of years, though green at first, as truth is.

Truth is God's daughter.

1706 STEVENS s.v. Verdad. **1732** FULLER no. 5301.

Truth is lost, In too much dispute.
     (D 384)

c. **1526** *Dicta Sap.* D3ᵛ By moderate arguyng the trouth is bulted out; but by immoderate it goth by. **1611** COTGRAVE s.v. Debatre (By too much arguing). *Ibid.* ǀs.v. Verité Too much debating makes truth to be lost. **1653** A. WILSON *Hist. of Gt. Britain* 291 But *nimium altercando Veritas amittitur*, Truth may be lost in a croud. **1659** HOWELL *Fr. Prov.* 1.

Truth is mighty and will prevail. (T 579)

[I ESD. iv. 41 Great is Truth, and mighty above all things.] *c.* **1390** GOWER *Conf. Amantis* Prol. l. 369 Trowthe mot stonde ate laste. *c.* **1400** *Beryn* l. 2037 For, aftir comyn seying-evir atte ende The trowith woll previd, how-so men evir trend. **1576** FULWELL *Ars Adulandi* IV E4 Trueth in the ende shall preuayle. **1582** S. GOSSON *Plays Confuted* F3ᵛ Greate is the trueth, and it doth preuaile. *c.* **1591** MARLOWE *Edw. II* III. iii. 5 Right will preuaile. **1616** DRAXE no. 2189. *c.* **1640** W.S. *Countrym. Commonw.* 15 Truth . . . is strong, and will preuaile.

Truth (fact) is stranger than fiction.

1823 BYRON *Juan* XIV. ci Truth is always strange; Stranger than fiction. **1843** R. H. BARHAM in R. H. D. Barham's *Life* ii. 158. **1910** A. M. FAIRBAIRN *Stud. in Relig. & Theol.* 395 Forgetting the fact which is stranger than fiction, that the sagest man in the theory of the State may be the unwisest man in statecraft.

Truth is time's daughter.   (T 580)

[A. GELLIUS I. 2. 9 *Veritatem Temporis filiam esse.*] **1532** S. GARDINER to Cromwell (*Let.* ed. Muller 50) Truth is called tymes daughter. **1553** *Respublica* I. 33 Veritie, the daughter of sage old Father Tyme. **1567** BALDWIN *Moral Philos.* 2B 8ᵛ Truth is the daughter of time. **1592** GREENE *Wks.* Gros. xi. 189 Now doo I proove that true by experience, which earst I held onelye for a bare prouerbe, that trueth is the daughter of time. **1597** *Politeuphuia* 9 Truth is the daughter of Time and the guide of all goodnesse. **1647** HOWELL *Fam. Lett.* (1903) III. 22 As Time begets her [Truth], so he doth the obstetritious office of a Midwife to bring her forth. **1663** BUTLER *Hudibras* II. iii. 663 'Tis not Antiquity, nor Author, that makes truth truth, although time's daughter.

Truth is truth.   (T 581)

c. **1566** CURIO tr. W. P. *Pasquin in a Trance* 3ᵛ The truth can not be but truth. [*margin*] Truth will be truth how so euer it be called. **1576**

GASCOIGNE *Philomene* ii. 192 But truth is truth, and muste be tolde Though daunger keepe the dore. *c.* **1594–5** SHAKES. *L.L.L.* IV. i. 48. [**1597**] **1599** CHAPMAN *Hum. Day's Mirth* sc. 4 l. 179 That which is truth is truth. **1604** SHAKES. *M.M.* V. i. 45 Truth is truth To th' end of reck'ning. **1732** FULLER no. 5303 Truth is Truth, in spite of Custom's Heart.

Truth lies at the bottom of a well (pit).
     (T 582)

[DIOGENES LAERTIUS Ἐτεὸν δὲ οὐδὲν ἴδμεν· ἐν βυθῷ γὰρ ἡ ἀλήθεια. We know nothing certain; for truth is hidden in the bottom of an abyss. LACTANTIUS *Inst.* 3. 28. 13 *In puteo . . . veritatem iacere submersam.*] **1547** BALDWIN *Moral Philos.* N1ᵛ Wysedome is lyke a thyng fallen into the water, whiche no man can fynde, except he searche it at the bottom. **1562** J. WIGAND *De Neutralibus* G6ᵛ The truth lyeth yet still drowned in the depe, as Democritus⸱ was wont to say. **1572** E. PASQUIER tr. G. Fenton *Mono-phylo* 42ᵛ The truth lyeth drowned in the bottome of the pitte. **1578** J. IVER *Courtly Controv.* tr. H. Wotton N1ᵛ I shall conduct you . . . vnto the Mansion where the truth so long hidden dothe inhabite, the which sage Democritus searched in the bottome of a well. **1601** T. WRIGHT *The Passions of the Mind* 232 *Veritas in profundo latet*, veritie lieth in the bottome. **1625** BACON *Apoph.* no. 263 Truth lies in profound pits, and when it is got, it needs much refining. **1635** HOWELL *Fam. Lett.* (1903) II. 112 As if truth were got into some dungeon; or, as the old Wizard said, into some deep Pit. *a.* **1721** PRIOR *Dial. of Dead* (1907) 225 You know the ancient philosophers said Truth lay at the bottom of a well. **1822** SHELLEY in SYMONDS *Life* (1878) ch. 6 Trelawny fished him out, and when he had taken breath he said: 'I always find the bottom of the well, and they say Truth lies there'.

Truth loves (fears no) trial.   (T 583)

1581 T. HOWELL *Devises* ed. Raleigh 92 Truth feareth no tryall. **1595** SHAKES. *Rich. II* I. iii. 95 As gentle and as jocund as to jest Go I to fight. Truth hath a quiet breast. **1639** CLARKE 316 (loveth).

Truth may be blamed, but cannot be shamed.   (T 584)

c. **1450** *Coventry Myst.* Shaks. Soc. 367 Trewthe dyd nevyr his maystyr shame. **1541** *Schoolh. of Women* A1ᵛ The truth is often blamed Yet in no wyse trueth may be shamed. **1565** J. HALL *Court of Virtue* P5 Blamd, but not shamd, the prouerbe is. **1571** J. BRIDGES *Sermon at Paul's Cross* 33 Truth neuer shames his master. **1583** G. BABINGTON *Expos. of Commts* 478 Truth may be blamed, but it can neuer be shamed. **1623** PAINTER B5ᵛ. **1655** FULLER *Ch. Hist.* IV. i (1868) I. 548 Here, if ever, did the proverb take effect, 'Truth may be blamed, but cannot be shamed'; for, although . . . condemned . . . he was beheld as loyalty's confessor, speaking . . . in discharge of his conscience. **1670** RAY 150 (but't shall never). **1706** STEVENS s.v. Verdad.

Truth needs no colours. *Cf.* Truth fears no colours.   (T 585)

1519 HARMAN *Vulg.* (James) 91 Treuthe nedeth no peynted or colored termes. **1580** J. BARET

Alveary P 925 Truth and honestie need no cloke.
c. 1600 *Edmund Ironside* l. 1198 Truth needes noe cullors.

Truth seeks no corners.   (T 587)

1564 BULLEIN *Dial.* E.E.T.S. 81 Well, man, well; truth seketh no corners. *Ibid.* 89 Veritas non querit angulos. **1621** ROBINSON 38 (seeketh not by wayes). *c.* **1622** *Two Noble Ladies* l. 451. **1663** F. HAWKINS *New Youths Behaviour* G3.

Truth shows best being naked, The.
                                                              (T 589)

c. **1390** GOWER *Conf. Amantis* I. 284 For trowthe hise wordes wol noght peinte. **1579** LYLY *Euph.* i. 181 A naked tale doth most truely set foorth the naked truth. **1605–8** SHAKES. *T.Ath.* V. i. 62 I, am rapt, and cannot cover The monstrous bulk of this ingratitude With any size of words. — Let it go naked; men may see't the better. *c.* **1613** J. TAYLOR (Water-P.) *Watermens Suit* (1630 ed.) 176 Thus (because the truthe shewes best being naked) I haue plainely set downe how farre I proceeded in my suite. **1732** FULLER no. 5314 Truth's best Ornament is Nakedness.

Truth, The | the whole truth, and nothing but the truth.   (T 590)

1580 LYLY *Euph. & his Eng.* ii. 101 Speake no more then the trueth, vtter no lesse. **1600** *Livy* tr. Holland To Reader That which most of all commendeth an historie, which . . . ought especially to deliuer with synceritie the whole truth and nothing but the truth. **1659** HEYLIN *Animadversions* in FULLER *Appeal Inj. Innoc.* (1840) 651 Let us see therefore what he saith of this prelate, and how far he saith truth, the whole truth, and nothing but the truth.

Truth will come to light (break out).
                                                              (T 591)

1539 TAVERNER *Publius* B1 The thyng that good is (as trouth and iustice) thoughe it be suppressed and kepte and vnder for a tyme, yet is it not quenched vtterly, but at length wyll breake out agayne. **1558** *Wealth & Health* l. 934 Truth wyll appeare. **1582** WHETSTONE *Heptameron* Li* I sowrrow to tell the rest, but trueth will haue passage. **1596** SHAKES. *M.V.* II. ii. 73 Truth will come to light; murder cannot be hid long—a man's son may, but in the end truth will out. [*a.* 1600] **1662** I.T. *Grim Collier Croydon* II. i. G10 It were a shame to speak this, but Truth will come to light.

Truths and roses have thorns about them.

1707 MAPLETOFT 61.

Truths too fine spun are subtle fooleries.

1707 MAPLETOFT 52.

Truth(s), *see also* All t. are not to be told; Better speak t. rudely; Craft must have clothes; Devil sometimes speaks t.; Face to face, the t. comes out; Fair fall t.; Follow not t. too near the heels; Fool may sometimes speak, (tell t.); Four good mothers have four bad daughters; t., hatred

E e

. . .; Greater the t. greater the libel; Half the t. a great lie; Lies like t.; Many words (In) the t. goes by; Probabilities (Thousand) do not make t.; Slander one with matter of t.; Sting of a reproach is the t.; Tell t. and shame devil; Time is the father of t.; Time tries t.; Trust is t. (In); Wine in, t. out; Wine there is t. (In).

Try all ways to the wood, You.   (W 180)

1546 HEYWOOD II. ix. L1 What wyfe . . . I will assaie all the waies to the wood. **1616** WITHALS 573. **1639** CLARKE 163.

Try (Try your friend) before you trust. *Cf.* Friend is never known till a man have need. Prove your friend ere you have need.   (T 595)

c. **1450–1500** *Gd. Wife wd. a Pilgrimage* l. 59 Asay or euer þow trust. *c.* **1500** *Wisdom* l. 30 (assay thy frend). **1578** *Parad. D. Deuises* (repr.) 38 *Trye before you trust* (Title). **1580** LYLY *Euph. & his Eng.* ii. 143 Friendes are tryed before they are to be trusted. *a.* **1600** TURBERVILLE *To Browne* Beware my Browne of light beliefe, trust not before you trie. **1616** BRETON *2 Cross.* A4v Try and then trust. **1633** SHIRLEY *Witty Fair One* IV. ii. Merm. 55 Try me, and trust me after. **1639** CLARKE 24 Try your friend before you trust him.

Try your skill in galt[1] first, and then in gold.   (S 501)

1639 CLARKE 60. **1670** RAY 95 . . . Practise new and doubtful experiments in cheap commodities, or upon things of small value. [[1] clay.]

Try, tried, tries, *see also* First t. then trust; Gold is t. in the fire; Know what you can do till you t. (You never); Time t. all; Trust before you t. (If).

Trysts, *see* Fools set far t.

Tu quoque, see You are another.

Tub (Vat) must stand on its own bottom, Every.   (T 596)

1564 BULLEIN *Dial. agst. Fever* E.E.T.S. 65 Let euerie Fatte stande vpon his owne bottome. **1583** G. BABINGTON *Expos. of the Commandments* 156 Let euerie vessell stande vppon his owne botome. *Ibid.* 278 (vat). **1639** CLARKE 66. **1670** RAY 102 . . . Every man must give an account for himself. **1678** BUNYAN *Pilgr.* I. (1877) 37 Presumption said, *Every Fat must stand upon his own bottom.* **1866** READE *Grif. Gaunt* ch. 6 There is an old saying, 'Let every tub stand on its own bottom'.

Tub to the whale, To throw out a.
                                                              (T 597)

[= to create a diversion.] **1572** *Brief Coll. . . . gathered out of Sebastian Munster* 24v. **1591** I *Troublesome Reign K. John* D1 The marriner, Spying the hugie Whale, . . . That throwes out emptie vessells, so to stay His furie,

while the ship doth saile away.   **1651** JER. TAYLOR
Holy Dying I. iii (Bohn) 313 He is at first entertained with trifles . . . and little images of things
are laid before him, like a cock-boat to a whale,
only to play withal.   **1704** SWIFT *T. Tub* Author's
Pref. 14 Sea-men have a Custom when they
meet a Whale, to fling him out an empty Tub,
. . . to divert him from laying violent Hands
upon the Ship.   **1810** W. B. RHODES *Bombastes
Fur.* i (1873) 16 A tub thrown to a whale, To
make the fish a fool.   **1912** *Nation* 29 June 465/2
He throws a tub to the High Church whale.

Tubs, *see* Put out your t. when raining; Tale of t.

Tug of war, *see* Greek meets Greek.

Tumult, *see* Wrath of . . . and t. of people (Take
heed of).

Tune the old cow died of, The.

[**1732** FULLER no. 4360 That is the old Tune
upon the Bag-Pipe.]   **1836** MARRYAT *Japhet* ch.
68 This tune, which the old cow died of, as the
saying is, used to be their horror.   **1859** C.
READE *Love me Little* ch. 3 'David, . . . that is
enough of the tune the old cow died of; take
and play something to keep our hearts up.'

Tune (-ing), *see also* Good t. on old fiddle
(Many); Long a-tuning your pipes (You are as);
Strings high stretched quickly grow out of t.

Turd, Not worth a.   (T 605)

c. **1390** CHAUCER Prol. to *Melibeus* l. 2120 Nat
worth a tord.   c. **1425** *Castle of Perseverance* l.
2227.   **1541** *Schoolh. of Women* A2ᵛ.   **1578**
WHETSTONE *Promos & Cassandra* FI Care not
a Tinkers torde.

Turd(s), *see* Ill weed mars pottage; Stir it (The
more you), the worse it stinks; Thatches his
house with t. (He that); Tramp on a t. (The
more you), the broader it grows. *See also* Horse-
turd.

Turf, On the | all men are equal—and under it.

[i.e. on the race-course and in the grave.]   **1854**
SURTEES *Hand. Cross* ch. 59 'On the turf and
under the turf all men are obliged to be equal',
mused our master.   **1896** 'H. S. MERRIMAN'
Sowers ch. 3 It appears that beneath the turf
or on it all men are equal; so no one could object
to the presence of Billy Bale, the man . . . who
could give you the straight tip on any race.

Turf, *see also* Need of a besom that sweep with t.
(They have).

Turk and the Pope, Here is a talk of the | but my next neighbour does me more harm than either of them both.   (T 57)

1651 HERBERT no. 1173.   **1659** HOWELL *Eng.
Prov.* 2a (doth me the hurt).

Turk's horse once treads, Where the | the grass never grows.   (T 610)

1639 FULLER *Holy War* v. xxx. (1840) 297 The
Turkish empire is the greatest . . . the sun ever
saw. . . . Populous it is not, for . . . it lieth waste,
according to the old proverb, Grass springeth
not where the grand signior's horse setteth his
foot.   **1659** HOWELL *Eng. Prov.* 6b.   **1902** F.
VILLIERS *Pict. of Many Wars* 11 Each day's
bloody work added to the night's lurid glow, for
the Turks . . . destroyed everything . . . as they
advanced, illustrating the aphorism: 'Where
the hoof of the Turkish horse treads no blade
of grass ever grows.'

Turk, *see also* Turn T.; Unspeakable T.

Turkey-cock, To strut (swell) like a.   (T 612)

1599 SHAKES. *Hen. V* V. i. 15 Why, here he
comes, swelling like a turkey-cock.   **1601** A.
DENT *Plain Man's Pathway* 333 They swell like
Turkey-cockes.   **1689** SHADWELL *Bury Fair* III.
i. Merm. 407 What, like one of those odious
creatures, will you dress at me? . . . and strut
like a turkey-cock, and prune yourself?   **1857**
TROLLOPE *Barch. Tow.* ch. 39 They all swelled
into madam's drawing-room, like so many
turkey cocks.

Turkey-cock, *see also* Red as t.-c.

Turkeys, *see also* Driving t. to market.

Turn (over) a (new) leaf, To.   (L 146)

[= to adopt a different line of conduct, now
in a good sense.]   **1540** SIR T. ELYOT *Pasquil the
Plain* A8ᵛ Now tourne the lefe.   **1546** HEYWOOD
II. iv. G4 Nay, she will tourne the leafe.   **1562**
A. BROOKE *Romeus & Juliet* l. 947 And joyful
Juliet another leaf must turn.   **1592** *Arden of
Fevers.* III. i. 7 Shaks. *Apoc.* 15 No question
then but she would turn the leafe And sorrow
for her desolation.   **1597** BEARD *Theatre God's
Judgem.* (1631) 92 But as soone as he was
exalted to honor, he turned over a new leafe,
and began . . . furiously to afflict . . . the . . .
faithful servants of Christ.   **1861** HUGHES *Tom
B. of Oxford* ch. 42.   **1909** ALEX. MACLAREN
Ephesians iv. 22 How many times have you said
. . . 'I have played the fool . . . but I now turn
over a new leaf'.

Turn a narrow adlant, To.

1879 JACKSON *Shrops. Word-Book* 3 To 'turn
on a mighty narrow adlant' is a proverbial
saying expressive of a very narrow escape.   **1917**
BRIDGE 145 . . . To have a narrow escape from
death or some calamity. . . . Adlant is the head-
land of a field.

Turn about is fair play.

1755 *Life of Capt. Dudley Bradstreet* ed. Taylor
216.   **1834** C. A. DAVIS *Lett. of J. Downing* 275
Turn and turn about was fair play.   **1854** SUR-
TEES *Handley Cross* ch. 18.   **1892** STEVENSON
Wrecker ch. 24 You had your chance then;
seems to me it's mine now. Turn about's fair
play.

Turn in his grave, To make a person.

1864 J. PAYN *Lost Sir Massingb.* ch. 34 This
holiday-making and mixture of high and low
here, are themselves enough to make Sir
Massingberd turn in his grave. **1888** BRYCE
Amer. Commonw. I. xii. 159 Jefferson might
turn in his grave if he knew of such an attempt
to introduce European distinctions of rank into
his democracy. **1927** *Times* 28 Nov. 15/5 If
the tune is changed at that service I shall turn
in my grave.

Turn one's coat (tippet), To.   (T 353)

[= to change sides, desert.] **1546** HEYWOOD II.
i. F4 So turned they theyr tippets by waie of
exchaunge, From laughyng to louryng. **1551**
CRANMER *Ans. to Gardiner* 452 He anone after
tourned his typpet, and sange an other songe.
1565 SHACKLOCK *Hatchet of Heresies* 74 How
many times Melancthon hath turned his coat
in this one opinion. **1650** TRAPP *Comm. Exod.*
xii. 38 Strangers, that took hold of the skirts
of these Jews . . . but afterwards turned their coat.
1655 FULLER *Ch. Hist.* IX. vii. § 24 That all the
Protestants would either turn their coats, copies,
arms, or fly away. **1819** SCOTT *Leg. Mont.* ch. 17
Sir John Urrie, a soldier of fortune . . ., had
already changed sides twice during the Civil
War, and was destined to turn his coat a third
time before it was ended.

Turn or burn.   (T 620)

1616 WITHALS 576 Rather turne then burne.
1639 CLARKE 222 (as 1616). **1675** BUNYAN *Saved
by Grace* Wks. (Offor) I. 351 They now began
to see that they must either turn or burn. [*Footnote*. These terms are taken from Foxe's *Mar-
tyrology*. It was frequently the brutal remark of
the Judges, You must turn or burn. Bunyan
here applies it to turning from sin or burning in
hell.—ED.] **1855** KINGSLEY *Westw. Ho!* ch. 7
The Inquisition . . . claims the bodies and souls
of all heretics . . . and none that it catches . . . but
must turn or burn.

Turn over the perch, To.

[To 'do' for one.] **1594** NASHE *Unfort. Trav.*
ii. 228. **1601** A. DENT *Plain Man's Pathway* 171
Hoist a man and turn him over the perke. **1609**
DEKKER *Gulls Hornbk.* Gros. ii. 216. **1637**
HEYWOOD & ROWLEY *Fortune by Land & Sea* vi.
398 If he should peak over the pearch now.

Turn (Twist) (a person) round one's (little) finger, To.   (F 232)

1680 R. L.'ESTRANGE *Citt and Bumpkin* 25 You
cann't imagine Citt, how he windes him about's
Finger. **1698** COLLIER *Immor. Stage* 279 To
play People out of their Senses . . . and wind their
Passions about their Fingers as they list. **1706**
STEVENS s.v. Embolver To wind a Man about
ones Finger, to have an entire Ascendant over
him. **1818** SCOTT *Bride Lamm.* ch. 21 I am
told the mother can wind them both round her
little finger. **1841** DICKENS *B. Rudge* ch. 6
Women may twist me round their fingers at
their pleasure. **1855** MOTLEY *Dutch Rep.* v. iii.
(1866) 698 Margaret . . . had already turned
that functionary round her finger.

Turn the cat in the pan, To.   (C 172)

[= (*a*) to reverse the order of things so dexterously as to make them appear the very opposite
of what they really are; to turn a thing right
about; (*b*) to change one's position, change
sides, from motives of interest, &c.] *a.* **1384**
WYCLIF *Works* (Arnold) III. 332 Many men of
lawe . . . bi here suteltes turnen the cat in the
panne. *c.* **1552** *Manifest Detection Dice Play*
(1850) 18 These vile cheaters turned the cat in
the pan, giving to diverse vile, patching thefts,
an honest and goodly title, calling it by the name
of a law. **1543** BECON *Invect. agst. Swearing*
Wks. (1843) 353 God saith, 'Cry, cease not',
but they turn cat in the pan, and say 'Cease,
cry not'. **1622** T. STOUGHTON *Chr. Sacrif.* vii.
91 How do they shrinke? yea, how foully do
they . . . turne cat in pan, and become themselves
persecuters of others. **1625** BACON *Essays* 'Of
Cunning', There is a Cunning, which we in
England call, The Turning of the Cat in the Pan;
which is, when that which a Man sayes to
another, he laies it, as if Another had said it
to him. **1675** CROWNE *City Polit.* II. 1 Come,
Sirrah, you are a villain, have turn'd cat-in-
pan, and are a Tory. *a.* **1720** *Song, Vicar of Bray*
I turned the cat in pan once more, And so
became a Whig, sir. **1721** KELLY 151 He has
turn'd his Cloak on the other Shoulder. He
has chang'd his Side, Party, or Interest. The
English say he has turn'd Cat i' the Pan: The
reason of which Expression I do not know.
1816 SCOTT *Old Mort.* ch. 35 O, this precious
Basil will turn cat in pan with any man.

Turn the money in your pocket when you hear the cuckoo.

1850 *N. & Q.* 1st Ser. II. 164 When the cry of the
cuckoo is heard for the first time in the season,
it is customary to turn the money in the pocket,
and wish. **1869** HAZLITT 441 Turn your money
when you hear the cuckoo, and you'll have
money in your purse till the cuckoo come again.

Turn the (an honest) penny, To.   (P 211)

[= to employ one's money profitably; or, to
gain money.] **1525** *Maid Emlyn* l. 77 in *Early
Pop. Poetry* iv. 85 His wyfe made hym so wyse,
That he wolde tourne a peny twyse, And then
he called it a ferthynge. **1546** HEYWOOD II. ix.
K4ᵛ Towne ware was your ware, to tourne
the peny. **1548** HALL 575 It is merye to turne
the penye. *c.* **1645** HOWELL *Lett.* (1754) 76
There is no State that winds the Penny more
nimbly, and makes quicker returns. **1676**
WYCHERLEY *Pl. Dealer* III. Wks. (Rtldg.) 125/2
You must call usury and extortion God's
blessing, or the honest turning of the penny.
1838 DICKENS *Oliver T.* ch. 37 I suppose, a
married man . . . is not more averse to turning
an honest penny when he can, than a single one.
1887 JESSOPP *Arcady* vii. 216 He turns an honest
penny by horse hire.

Turn the tables, To.   (T 4)

[= to reverse the relation between two persons
or parties, from the notion of players reversing
the position of the board.] **1612** CHAPMAN
Widow's Tears I. iii. 27 I may turn the tables
with you ere long. **1634** SANDERSON *Serm.* II.
290 Whosoever thou art that dost another

wrong, do but turn the tables; imagine thy
neighbour were now playing thy game, and
thou his. **1647** DIGGES *Unlawf. Taking Arms* iii.
70 The tables are quite turned, and your friends
have undertaken the same bad game, and play
it much worse. **1713** ADDISON *Guard.* no. 134,
par. 4 In short, Sir, the tables are now quite
turned upon me. **1893** SELOUS *Trav. S.E. Africa*
33 They had won the first match, though I
hoped I might yet turn the tables on them in
the return.

Turn Turk, To.   (T 609)

[= to change completely as from a Christian to
an infidel.] [c. **1590**] **1592** *Soliman and Perseda*
III. v. 7 What say these prisoners? will they turne
Turke, or no? **1592** NASHE *Strange News* i. 291
Is it not a sinfull thing for a Scholler and a
Christian to turne Tully? a Turke would neuer
do it. **1598–9** SHAKES. *M.A.* III. iv. 49 Well,
an you be not turned Turk, there's no more
sailing by the star. **1600–1** *Id. H.* III. ii. 270 If
the rest of my fortunes turn Turk with me. **1629**
J. M. tr. *Fonseca's Dev. Contempl.* 403 The
Souldier, he will turne Turke vpon point either
of profit, or of honor.

Turn up one's nose, To.   (N 232)

[= to show disdain.] **1545** W. TURNER *Rescuing
of the Romish Fox* A5ᵛ Your castyng of your
nose in the winde lyke a storke doth in hyr nest.
1562 J. WIGAND *De Neutralibus* D5ᵛ The Papistes
caste vp the nose into the wynde and crake, that
the churche is tyed to the Byshoppe of Rome
and hys College. **1579** TOMSON *Calvin's Serm.
Tim.* 228/1 Let women holde vppe their noses
no more: for all their presumption is sufficiently
beaten downe here. **1779** MME. D'ARBLAY *Diary*
20 Oct. Mr. Thrale . . . turned up his nose with
an expression of contempt. **1836** MARRYAT
Midsh. Easy ch. 24 Miss Julia, who turned up
her nose at a midshipman.

Turn up trump(s), To.   (T 544)

1621ᵛBURTON *Anat. Mel.* III. iii. I. ii. (1638) 602
They turned up trumpe, before the Cards were
shufled. **1642** FULLER *H. & P. State* IV. viii The
cards were so shuffled that two kings were turned
up trump at once, which amazed men how to
play their game. **1862** WILKIE COLLINS *No Name*
IV. viii Instances . . . of short courtships and
speedy marriages, which have turned up trumps
—I beg your pardon—which have turned out
well, after all.

Turn with the wind (tide), To.   (W 439)

c. **1550** R. SMITH *Confutation* cited 1551 Cranmer
Ans. to Gardiner 453 They turne and will turne
as the wynde turneth. **1565** *Albion Knight* l.
108 It wyll turne with euery wynde. **1569** T.
PRESTON *Cambises* B4. *c.* **1576** *Common Cond.*
l. 622 C2ᵛ Roome for a turne coate, that will
turne as the wynde. **1670** RAY 197 (wind, or
tide).

Turns lie dead and one ill deed report abroad does spread, Ten good.   (T 619)

1539 TAVERNER I *Garden* F1ᵛ Demaunded, what
thynge waxeth sone olde, he [Aristotle] answered,
thanke. Meanyng that the remembraunce of
iniurye sticketh very fast, but the memorie of a

good turne is gone anone. **1578** WHETSTONE
I *Promos and Cass.* III. iv. D2ᵛ The Prouerbe
saies, that tenne good turnes lye dead, And one
yll deede, tenne tymes beyonde pretence, By
enuious tongues, report abrode doth spread.
1599 SHAKES. *J.C.* III. ii. 75 The evil that men
do lives after them; The good is oft interred with
their bones.

Turn (*noun*), *see* Devil owes me good t.; Every
man will have his own t. served; Everything in
t.; Good t. for it, (I will watch you a); Good t.;
Ill t.; Loses by doing good t. (One never).

Turn(s, ed), (*verb*), *see also* Bias again (He t. to
his old); Deaf ear (To t. a); Great businesses
t. on little pin; Great engines t. on small
pivots; Patience provoked t. to fury; Runs far
that t. not again; Tell where to t. his nose
(He cannot); Way to t. him (He knows not
which); World is round (t. as a ball).

Turnagain lane.   (H 755)

1531 TYNDALE *Expos. St. John* P.S. 140 It is
become turn-again lane with them. **1560** HEY-
WOOD *Fourth Hund. Epig.* no. 69 Fynde meanes
to take a house in turne agayne lane. **1662**
FULLER Lond. 200 'He must take him a House
in Turn-again Lane'. This, in old Records, is
called Wind-again Lane, and lyeth in the Parish
of St. Sepulchre's, going down to Fleet-Dike;
which men must turn again the same way they
came, for there it is stopped. The Proverb is
applied to those who . . . must seasonably alter
their manners.

Turncoat, *see* Wine is t.

Turnips like a dry bed but a wet head.

1917 BRIDGE 147 Turnips like a dry bed but
a wet head. They do not grow well on undrained
land.

Turnips, *see also* Given him t. (She has).

Turtle, *see* True as a t. to her mate.

Tweedledum and Tweedledee, The difference between.

[Used originally of two rival musicians, and now
in reference to differences held to be insignificant.]
1725 BYROM *Handel & Bononcini* Poems (1773)
I. 344 Strange all this Difference should be,
'Twixt Tweedle-dum and Tweedle-dee! **1851**
THACKERAY *Eng. Hum.* v. (1876) 304 Swift could
not see the difference between tweedle-dee and
tweedle-dum. **1911** *Chr. Endeavour Times* 10
Aug. 724/1 A . . . war of words over tweedledees
of subtle doctrinal differences and tweedle-dums
of Church polity.

Twelfth Day the days are lengthened a cock-stride, At.   (T 628)

1659 HOWELL *It. Prov.* 14 At Saint Thomas the
day is lengthened a cock-stride. **1678** RAY 52
The Italians say at Christmas.

Twenty-four hours in the day, There are only.

1902–4 LEAN IV. 145 . . . Against those who attempt too much.

Twenty-fourth of August be fair and clear, If the | then hope for a prosperous autumn that year.

1732 FULLER no. 6470.

Twice clogs, once boots.

1871 *N. & Q.* 4th Ser. VII. 472 Clogs to clogs is only three generations. A Lancashire proverb implying that, however rich a poor man may eventually become, his great-grandson will certainly fall back to poverty and clogs. **1875** SMILES *Thrift* 306 Hence the Lancashire proverb, 'Twice clogs, once boots'. The first man wore clogs, and accumulated a 'power o' money'; his rich son spent it; and the third generation took up the clogs again.

Twice, *see also* Done t. (If things were to be); Gives t. who gives quickly; Look t. at a penny; One thing said t. deserves trudge; Tale none the worse for being t. told; War (In) it is not permitted t. to err; Well done is t. done.

Twig(s), *see* Bend while it is a t.; Birchen t. break no ribs; Hop the t.

'Twill not be why for thy.   (W 330)

1678 RAY 345 *Somerset.* Of a bad bargain or great loss for little profit.

Twinkling of a bedpost (bed-staff), In the.   (T 634)

1660 *Charac. Italy* 78 In the twinkling of a Bedstaff he disrobed himself. **1833** MARRYAT *P. Simple* ch. 36 Won't I get you out of purgatory in the twinkling of a bedpost? **1871** M. COLLINS *Mrg. & Merch.* III. iii. 78 In the twinkling of a bedpost Is each savoury platter clear.

Twinkling of an eye, In the.   (T 635)

c. **1300** *Vernon MS.* E.E.T.S. 286 In a twynclyng of an eiȝe ffrom erþe to heuene þon maiȝt styȝe. **1380** WYCLIF *I Cor.* XV. 52 In a moment in the twynkelynge of an yȝe. **1528** TYNDALE *Obed. of a Christian Man* P.S. 142. **1549** LATIMER *4th Serm. bef. Edw. VI* P.S. 161 I will not deny, but that he may in the twinkling of an eye, save a man. **1593–4** SHAKES. *T.S.* II. i. 303 In a twink she won me to her love. **1596** *Id. M.V.* II. ii. 153 I'll take my leave of the Jew in the twinkling. **1670** RAY 197.

Twins, *see* Siamese t.

Twist, *see* Turn (T.) round one's finger.

Twittle twattle,[1] drink up your posset-drink. *Cf.* Tittle tattle.   (T 637)

1670 RAY 253 . . . This Proverb had its original in *Cambridge*, and is scarce known elsewhere. [1 idle talk.]

Two and thirty, *see* One and thirty.

Two and two make four.   (T 641)

1562 J. WIGAND *De Neutralibus* B8ᵛ That twyce twoo are foure, a man may not lawfully make a doubt of it, bicause that manner of knowledge is grauen into mannes nature. **1696** J. TOLAND *Christianity Myst.* ii. 11 First, When the Mind, without the Assistance of any other Idea, immediately perceives the Agreement or Disagreement of two or more Ideas, as that Two and Two is Four, that Red is not Blew; it cannot be call'd Reason, though it be the highest Degree of Evidence. **1697** COLLIER *Ess. Mor. Subj.* II (1703) 85 The . . . Notion . . . is as clear as that Two and Two makes Four. **1779** JOHNSON in Boswell *Life* (1848) lxviii. 624 You may have a reason why two and two should make five; but they will still make but four. **1927** *Times* 1 Mar. 19/6 The rules of arithmetic—the law that two and two make four . . . are the laws that sentimental economists are always unconsciously trying to evade.

Two anons and a by-and-bye, is an hour and a half.   (A 249)

1636 CAMDEN 308.

Two attorneys can live in a town, when one cannot.

1902–4 LEAN IV. 169 . . . *i.e.* they make work for each other. Quoted by Pollock, barrister on circuit, Sept. 1880.

Two bachelors drinking to you at once; you'll soon be married.

1738 SWIFT *Dial.* II. E.L. 308 Well, miss, you'll certainly be soon married; here's two bachelors drinking to you at once.

Two bigs will not go in one bag.   (B 344)

1659 HOWELL *Brit. Prov.* 22.

Two bits (bites) of a cherry, To make.   (B 423)

1666 TORRIANO *Prov. Phr.* 184b To play the Hypocrite, and be demure, are that will make two bits of one Chery, but in private can devour a pound and more. *Ibid.* 81b . . . swallow you a liver at a mouth-full. **1694** MOTTEUX *Rabelais* v. xxviii By Jingo, I believe he wou'd make three bits of a cherry. **1827** SCOTT *Two Drovers* ch. 2 Take it all, man—take it all—never make two bites of a cherry.

Two blacks do not make a white.

1721 KELLY 321 Two Blacks make no White. An Answer to them who, being blam'd, say others have done as ill or worse. **1822** SCOTT to Lord Montague (*Lett.* ed. Grierson vii. 96) To try whether I cannot contradict the old proverb of 'Two blackies [sic: Lockhart printed 'blacks'] not making a white'. **1881** AINGER *C. Lamb* 136 As two blacks do not make a white, it was beside the mark to make laborious fun over Southey's youthful ballads.

Two cats and a mouse, two wives in one house, two dogs and a bone, never agree in one. (C 186)

c. 1417 *Lansdowne MS. 762* in *Reliq. Antiq.* (1841) I. 233 Two wymen in one howse, Two cattes and one mowce, Two dogges and one bone, Maye never accorde in one. *a.* 1628 CARMICHAELL no. 1559 (never ane of others was faine). 1670 RAY 151. 1732 FULLER no. 6095.

Two daughters and a back door are three arrant (stark) thieves. *Cf.* Marries a widow. (D 48)

a. 1628 CARMICHAELL no. 1547 (stark). 1641 FERGUSSON no. 778 (stark). 1670 RAY 51. 1721 KELLY 304 (stark) Daughters are expensive, and Back-doors give Servants Opportunity to purloyn their Master's Goods.

Two dismal days, the day of death and the day of doom. (D 122)

1626 BRETON *Soothing* B3 Two dayes are most dreadfull to the wicked . . . the day of death, and the day of doome. 1639 CLARKE 215.

Two dogs strive for a bone, and a third runs away with it. (D 545)

c. 1386 CHAUCER *Knight's T.* l. 1177 We stryve as dide the houndes for the boon, . . . Ther cam a kyte, whyl that they were so wrothe, And bar away the boon. 1534 MORE *Dial. of Comfort* E.L. 129. 1575 GASCOIGNE *Posies* i. 475 It hath bin an old saying, that whiles two doggs do strive for a bone, the thirde may come and carrie it away. 1592 *Arden of Fevers.* III. vi. 30 *Shaks. Apoc.* 20 I pray you, sirs, list to Esops talk: Whilest two stout dogs were striuing for a bone, There comes a cur and stole it from them both. 1721 KELLY 308 . . . Spoken when two, by their mutual Contentions, hinder each other of a Place, and Preferment, and it has falen to a third by that Means.

Two dry sticks will kindle a green one. (S 852)

1678 RAY 213.

Two (four) eyes can see more than one (two). (E 268)

1577 BRETON *Wks. of a Young Wit* (*Poems* ed. J. Robertson) 30 The man that sees with both his eyes, dooth thinke a man with one eye sees but ill. 1587 J. BRIDGES *Defence* 678 Plus vident oculi, quam oculus; one man sees not all. 1591 A. COLYNET *True Hist. of Civil Wars of France* 37 Two eyes doo see more then one. 1592 DELAMOTHE 45 (Foure . . . two). *c.* 1594 BACON *Promus* no. 946 (are better). 1599 MINSHEU *Span. Gram.* 83 Foure eies see better then two. 1600 HAKLUYT *Navig. & Disc. of Eng. Nat.* (2 ed.) III Ep. Ded (1903) I. lxxvi Commonly a souldier observeth one thing, and a mariner another, and as your honour knoweth, Plus vident oculi, quam oculus. 1614 CAMDEN 313. 1642 FULLER *H. & P. State* IV. v. (1841) 246 Matters of inferior consequence he will communicate to a fast friend, and crave his advice;

for, two eyes see more than one. 1691 SEWEL 177 (Two eyes . . . better than one). 1898 F. MAX MÜLLER *Auld Lang Syne* 80 But who has ever examined any translation from any language, without finding signs of . . . carelessness or ignorance? Four eyes see more than two.

Two faces (heads) in one hood, To bear (carry, have). (F 20)

a. 1425 *Rom. Rose* 738 With so gret devotion They made her confession, that they had ofte, for the nones, Two hedes in one hood at ones. *a.* 1449 LYDGATE *Minor Poems* I. 69 God lovyd neuer two facys in oon hood. *c.* 1460 *Wisdom* l. 721 Jorowur [juror] in on hoode berith to facis. 1544 H. STALBRIDGE [= J. Bale] *Epistle Exhortatory* Apdx. D6ᵛ An wholsome counsellor with. ii. faces in an whoode. 1550 LEVER *Serm.* Arb. 99 These flatterers be wonders perilous felowes, hauynge two faces under one hoode. 1639 CLARKE 140 He carrieth two faces under one hood. 1668 SHADWELL *Sul. Lov.* IV. i. Merm. 83 Hypocrisy is an abominable vice. —'Tis indeed, to be a Pharisee, and carry two faces in a hood, as the saying is. 1888 'R. BOLDREWOOD' *Robbery under Arms* ch. 2 We . . . scorned to look pious and keep two faces under one hood.

Two false knaves need no broker. *Cf.* Crafty knave. (K 147)

1546 HEYWOOD I. xi. D3ᵛ. 1592 SHAKES. *T.G.V.* III. i. 262 My master is a kind of a knave: but that's all one, if he be but one knave. 1611 A. NOWELL *Sword against Swearers* B3 As two false knaves need no Broker, for they can easily enough agree in wickednesse *Sine mediante.* 1732 FULLER no. 5322 (Two cunning knaves).

Two fools in one house are too many. (F 555)

1580 LYLY *Euph. & his Eng.* ii. 62 Me thinketh it were no good match, for two fooles in one bed are too many. 1641 FERGUSSON no. 809 Twa fooles in ane house is over many. 1732 FULLER no. 5328 . . . by a Couple.

Two fools met, There. (F 554)

1672 W. WALKER 14, no. 10 Two fools well met. 1721 KELLY 338 . . . Spoken to them that say they refused such a considerable Price for such a Penyworth. That is, he was a Fool that offered it, and you a Fool that refus'd it. 1732 FULLER no. 5679 Where two Fools meet, the Bargain goes off.

Two forenoons in the same day, You cannot have.

1854 *N. & Q.* 1st Ser. IX. 527 In answer to some remarks . . . on the necessary infirmities of old age, one of them replied, 'You cannot have two forenoons in the same day'.

Two friends have a common purse, When | one sings and the other weeps.

1707 MAPLETOFT 59.

Two friends with one gift, To make.
(F 757)

1616 WITHALS 556 (one fauour). **1642** TORRIANO 45. **1732** FULLER no. 5205.

Two hands in a dish, and one in a purse.
(H 123)

1616 BRETON *Cross. Prov.* A4 One hand is enough in a purse. **1623** CAMDEN 279. **1626** BRETON *Soothing* A5ᵛ (as 1616). **1738** SWIFT *Dial.* II. E.L. 297 Then pray, Tom, carve for yourself: They say, Two Hands in a Dish, and One in a Purse. **1809** MALKIN *Gil Blas* X. x There was my bag! Two hands in a dish and one in a purse, was not one of her proverbs; so that finding the contents in crowns and pistoles, she thought . . . the money . . . hers.

Two (Many) hands (wits) are better than one.
(H 281)

c. **1390** GOWER *Conf. Amantis* Prol. 157 Althogh a man be wys himselue, Yit is the wisdom more of tweluc. *Id.* i. 1020 Two han more wit then on. **1530** PALSGRAVE 495a Two wyttes be farre better than one. **1546** HEYWOOD I. ix. C2ᵛ But of these two thynges he wolde determyne none Without ayde. For two heddis are better than one. **1563** *Mirr. for Mag.* Campbell 243 Moe wits are better then one. **1591** SPENSER *M. Hubberd* 82 Two is better than one head. **1641** FERGUSSON no. 825 Twa wits is better nor ane. **1721** KELLY 247 (Many). *Ibid.* 335 (Wits). *Plus vident oculi, quam oculus.* **1772** FOOTE *Nabob* i. Wks. (1799) II. 289 Here comes brother Thomas; two heads are better than one; let us take his opinion. **1818** SCOTT *Rob Roy* ch. 8 Oh, certainly; but two heads are better than one; you know. **1893** S. BUTLER (Festing Jones *Life* 1920 ed. ii. 8) 'Two are better than one'. I head someone say this and replied: 'Yes, but the man who said that did not know my sisters.'

Two heads are better than one, even if the one's a sheep's.

1864 'Cornish Proverbs' in *N. & Q.* 3rd Ser. VI. 494 Two heads are better than one if only sheeps' heads. **1894** NORTHALL *Folk-phrases* E.D.S. 32 . . . 'A sheep's' head in folk figure, means a daft or unreasoning head.

Two heads are better than one, quoth the woman, when she had her dog with her to the market.
(H 281)

1732 FULLER no. 5331.

Two is company, but three is none.

1706 STEVENS s.v. Compañía A Company consisting of three is worth nothing. It is the Spanish Opinion, who say that to keep a Secret three are too many, and to be Merry they are too few. **1866** MRS. GASKELL *Wives & Daughters* ch. 11 Two is company, Three is trumpery. **1871** *N. & Q.* 4th Ser. VIII. 506 Common Lancashire Proverbs. . . . When a lover meets his intended with her companion, the latter will say, 'Two are company, but three are none', and pass on another road. **1876** J. PAYN *Halves* ch. 21 The proverb that 'Two is company, but three is none', had great weight with me just

then. **1880** MRS. PARR *Adam & Eve* ix. 124 'Two's company and three's trumpery, my dear.'

Two men, *see also* Amongst good men t. m. suffice.

Two negatives make an affirmative.
(N 101)

c. **1580** SIDNEY *Astrophel & Stella* Wks. (Feuillerat) II. 377 For Grammer sayes (to Grammer who sayes nay) That in one speech, two negatives affirme. **1593** G. HARVEY in Wks. Gros. i. 293 But euen those two Negatiues . . . would be conformable enough, to conclude an Affirmatiue. **1596** HARINGTON *Metam. of Ajax* (1814) 126 For in one speech two negatives affirm. **[1600] 1657** *Lust's Dominion* Hazl.-Dods. xiv. 98 No, no says ay; and twice away says stay. **1601** SHAKES. *T.N.* V. i. 18 If your four negatives make your two affirmatives, why then, the worse for my friends and the better for my foes. **1647** FULLER *Gd. Thoughts in Worse T.* xvii (1863) 190.

Two of a trade seldom agree.
(T 643)

[*c.* 1605] **1630** DEKKER 2 *Hon. Whore* IV. i. 363 It is a common rule, and 'tis most true, Two of one trade neuer loue: no more doe you. **1678** RAY 212. **1727** GAY *Fables* I. xxi. 43 (1859) 197 In every age and clime we see, Two of a trade can ne'er agree. **1891** ANDREW LANG *Essays in Little* 105 Artists are a jealous race. 'Potter hates potter and poet hates poet', as Hesiod said so long ago.

Two peas, As like as.
(P 136)

1580 LYLY *Euph. & his Eng.* ii. 5 The Twinnes of Harpocrates (who wer as lyke as one pease is to an other). **1778** FRANCES BURNEY *Evelina* Lett. 21 Why it's as like the twelve-penny gallery at Drury-Lane . . . as two peas are to one another. **1813** BARRETT *Heroine* ed. Raleigh Lett. 37, 215 As like . . . as one pea is like another.

Two places at once, A man cannot be in. *Cf.* No man can do two things at once.
(M 221)

1509 BARCLAY *Ship of Fools* i. 160 No man can be always in euery place. *c.* **1566** CURIO *Pasquin in a Trance* tr. W.P. 57 Maruell . . . how it is possible that they may be in two places at once. **1611** COTGRAVE s.v. Moulin One cannot be in two places, or follow two businesses, at once. **1655–62** GURNALL *Chrn. in Armour* (1865) I. 206 You cannot be found in two places at once. Choose whether you will be found in your own righteousness or in Christ's. **1659** HOWELL *Fr. Prov.* 7 He cannot be at once at the Mill and the Bakers. **1842** W. H. MAXWELL *Hector O'H.* ch. 12 As . . . nothing can be in two places at once . . . it was quite clear that neither of the Prymes could be at one and the same time in bed and in the street.

Two ride on a horse, If | one must ride behind.
(T 638)

1598–9 SHAKES. *M.A.* III. v. 34 An two men ride of a horse, one must ride behind. *c.* **1640** SMYTH *Berkeley MSS.* (1885) 32 no. 67. That in each contention one must take the foile. **1874**

WHYTE-MELVILLE *Uncle John* ch. 10 (An old adage). **1927** *Times* 16 Feb. 10/4 'When two men ride a horse, one must ride behind'. . . . It is . . . the wife who must yield when conflict arises.

Two sides to every question, There are.

1742 J. RALPH *The Other Side of the Question* [title]. **1853** G. J. WHYTE-MELVILLE *Digby Grand* ch. 4. **1863** C. KINGSLEY *Water Bab.* ch. 6 Let them recollect this, that there are two sides to every question.

Two sorrows of one, Make not. (s 663)

c. **1430** LYDGATE *Chorle & Bird* in *Minor Poems* Percy Soc. 187 For who takethe sorowe for losse in that degree, Reknethe first his loose & aftir rekyn his peyne, And of oon sorowe, makethe he sorowes tweyne. *c.* **1540–50** J. HEYWOOD Poem in J. O. Halliwell's ed. of *Wit & Science.* **1546** HEYWOOD II. v. H4 And reason saieth, make not two sorows of one. **1609** JONSON *Case Altered* I. ix. 11 Passion's duld eye can make two grieues of one.

Two sparrows on one ear of corn make an ill agreement. (s 717)

1599 MINSHEU *Span. Gram.* 83. **1609** HARWARD 78 (in one tare do agree but badly). **1651** HERBERT no. 1074. **1706** STEVENS s.v. Pardal (cannot agree).

Two (Many, etc.) strings to one's bow, To have. (s 937)

c. **1477** CAXTON *Jason* E.E.T.S. 57 I wil wel that euery man be amerous & loue . but that he haue .ij. strenges on his bowe. **1546** HEYWOOD I. xi. D4 Ye haue many stryngis to the bowe. **1568** QUEEN ELIZABETH to Mary Queen of Scots cited C. Read *Mr. Sec. Cecil* 397 Those who have two strings to one bow may shoot strongly but they rarely shoot straight. **1579** LYLY *Euph.* i. 255 My counsaile is that thou haue more strings to thy bow, then one. **1585** QUEEN ELIZABETH *Let.* to James VI, June I . . . hope that you wyl remember, that who seaketh two stringes to one bowe, he may shute strong, but never strait. **1678** BUTLER *Hudibras* III. i. 3 As he that has two strings t' his bow, And burns for love and money too. **1771** SMOLLETT *Humph. Clink.* 8 June, Wks. (1871) 507 A right Scotchman has always two strings to his bow, and is *in utrumque paratus* [prepared for either alternative]. **1857** TROLLOPE *Barch. Tow.* ch. 27 It was hard to say which was the old love and which the new. . . . But two strings to Cupid's bow are always dangerous to him on whose behalf they are to be used.

Two Sundays come together (meet), When. (s 995)

[**1598**] **1616** HAUGHTON *Englishmen for my Money* D2 Art thou so mad as to turne French? —Yes marry when two Sundayes come together. **1639** CLARKE 229 (fall together). **1678** RAY 271 When two Sundays meet, i.e. never.

Two suns (kings in one kingdom) cannot shine in one sphere (reign at once). (s 992)

1542 ERASM. tr. Udall *Apoph.* (1877) 209 Vnto Darius he [Alexander] made aunswere in this maner, that neither the yearth might endure or abyde two sonnes, nor the countree of Asia, two kinges. **1586** GUAZZO ii. 171 Two kinges in one kingdome doe not agree well together. *c.* **1591** MARLOWE *Edw. II* v. i. 58 Two kings in England cannot raigne at once. **1592** SHAKES. *T.And.* V. iii. 17 What, hath the firmament moe suns than one? **1593** NASHE *Christ's Tears* ii. 40 The Sunne . . . can endure no more Sunnes but it selfe. **1597** *Politeuphuia* 53ᵛ Two sunnes are not adored in one skye, nor many Kings admired in one throne. **1597** SHAKES. *1 Hen. IV* V. iv. 65–6 Two stars keep not their motion in one sphere; Nor can one England brook a double reign. **1609** DEKKER *Work for Armourers* Gros. iv. 105 *Non capit Regnum duos*, A Kingdome is heauen, and loues not two suns shining in it. **1609** HARWARD 98 Kingdomes in their governments do endure no parlement. One Sunn, one king.

Two (words) to make a bargain, It takes. *Cf.* More words than one. Second word makes, etc. (w 827)

1579 LYLY *Euph.* i. 228 As ther can bee no bargaine where both be not agreede, neither any Indentures sealed where the one will not consent. **1608–9** MIDDLETON *Widow* v. i. Merm. II. 479 There's two words to a bargain ever, . . . and, if loue be one, I'm sure money's the other. *a.* **1633** JONSON *T. Tub* II. iv. 76. **1732** FULLER no. 3465 More Words than one to a Bargain. **1766** GOLDSMITH *Vicar W.* ch. 31 'Hold, hold, Sir,' cried Jenkinson, 'there are two words to that bargain.' **1858** R. S. SURTEES *Ask Mamma* ch. 75 Unfortunately, it requires two parties to these bargains, and Mrs. Yammerton wouldn't agree to it.

Two to make a quarrel, It takes.

1706 STEVENS s.v. Barajar When one will not, two do not Quarrel. **1765** J. WESLEY *Letters* iv. 293 Two must go to a quarrel, and I declare I will not be one. **1859** H. KINGSLEY *Geof. Hamlyn* ch. 30. **1912** A. MACLAREN *Expos., Romans,* 298 . . . it takes two to make peace also. **1919** DEAN INGE *Outspoken Ess.* (1920) 42 In spite of the proverb, it takes in reality only one to make a quarrel. It is useless for the sheep to pass resolutions in favour of vegetarianism, while the wolf remains of a different opinion.

Two to one in all things against the angry man.

1732 FULLER no. 5336.

Two to one is odds. (T 644)

1576 GASCOIGNE *Grief of Joy* ii. 540. Ytt hathe bin sayd, long synce . . . Come one to one, and that makes prety playe, But two to one, can be no equall lott. **1592** NASHE *Strange News* i. 298 Three to one . . . is oddes. **1599** PORTER *Angry Wom. Abingd.* l. 2887 It is hard when there is two to one, Especially of Women. **1616** N. BRETON *Wks.* Gros. I *t* 24. **1659** HOWELL *Eng. Prov.* 4a (odds at foot-ball). **1670** RAY 151. **1706** STEVENS s.v. Paja (as 1659).

Two will, That which | takes effect. (T 639)

c. **1386** CHAUCER *Pard. T.* l. 825 And two of us shal strenger be than oon. *c.* **1596** MARLOWE

Ovid's Elegies in Wks. (Dyce) II. cl. 3 327 What two determine never wants effect. **1640** HERBERT no. 705.

Two wives in one house, *see under* Two cats.

Two wolves may worry one sheep.

(w 619)

a. **1628** CARMICHAELL no. 1542. **1611** COTGRAVE s.v. Brebis Two wolues deuour one sheepe with ease. **1641** FERGUSSON no. 808.

Two wrongs don't make a right.

1840 HALIBURTON *Clockmaker* III. 22 Can two wrongs make a right? **1875** CHEALES *Proverb Folk-Lore* 120. **1905** S. WEYMAN *Starvecrow Fm.* ch. 24 After all, two wrongs don't make a right. **1906** *Spectator* 23 June Two wrongs can never make a right, and therefore we cannot accept the ill-doing of the Nonconformist extremists as an excuse for Churchmen who have forgotten their duty.

Two, *see also* Beast with t. backs, (To make the); Never be angry at (T. things); No man can do t. things at once; Rainbows appear at one time (If t.); Secret is . . . enough for t. . . .; Servant has t. (He that has one), he that has t. has but half . . .; Too-too will in t.

Twyford; My name is | I know nothing of the matter.

(N 29)

1694 MOTTEUX *Rabelais* (1897) v. xiii Has not the fellow told you he does not know a word of the business? His name is Twyford. **1706** STEVENS s.v. Viña . . . When a Man will not know, or be concern'd in what has happen'd, he pleads

he has been absent, out a Town at his Vineyard. **1732** FULLER no. 3502.

Tyburn tippet, A.

(T 647)

[= hangman's rope: Tyburn was the place of public execution for Middlesex until 1783.] **1549** LATIMER *2nd Serm. bef. Edw. VI* P.S. 119 He should have had a Tyburn tippet, a half-penny halter, and all such proud prelates. **1550** R. COWLEY *One & Thirty Epigrams* E.E.T.S. 30 They deserued a Tiburne typpet. **1577** HARRISON *Descr. of England* Furnivall i. 284 Trussed vp in a Tiburne tippet. **1680** C. NESSE *Church Hist.* 143 The cart at Tyburn drives away when the tippet is fast about the necks of the condemned.

Tyburn, *see also* Dance the T. jig; Low ebb at Newgate, afloat at T.; Preach at T. Cross; Suits hang . . . in Westminster Hall, at T. . . .

Tympany[1] with two heels, She has (is cured of) a.

(T 648)

c. **1566** *The Bugbears* III. iii. 38 Her greatest disease is a spice of the timpanye. **1579** *Marr. of Wit & Wisdom* Shak. Soc. 15 Nay, by S. Anne, I am afraid it is a timpany with two legges! **1678** RAY 275 (is cured of). **1732** FULLER no. 4127. [[1] swelling: a euphemism for pregnancy.]

Tyrant is most tyrant to himself, A.

(T 649)

1640 HERBERT no. 888.

Tyrant, *see also* Beasts, (The most deadly of wild) is a backbiter (t.); Cruelty is a t. attended with fear.

U

Ugly as sin (the devil, hell), As.

(s 465)

[1600] **1657** *Lust's Dominion* Hazl.-Dods. xiv. 99 Ugly as hell. **1666** TORRIANO *Prov. Phr.* 137b To be uglier than sin, viz. most ugly. **1725** ERASM. *Fam. Colloquies* tr. N. Bailey (1733), 416 A Face as ugly as the Devil. **1804** EDGEWORTH *Pop. Tales, Out of Debt* (1805) I. 315 Why, she is as ugly as sin!

Ugly, *see also* Old enough and u. enough.

Ulysses, *see* Bow of U.

Unbidden guest knows not where to sit (must bring his stool with him), An.

(G 476)

c. **1350** *Douce MS. 52* no. 53 Unboden gest not, where he shall sytte. **1546** HEYWOOD I. ix. C1[v]. **1579** LYLY *Euph.* i. 200 I will either bring a stoole on mine arme for an vnbidden guest, or a visard on my face. *c.* **1590** SHAKES. *1 Hen. VI* II. ii. 55 I have heard it said, unbidden guests

Are often welcomest when they are gone. **1612** WEBSTER *White Devil* ed. Lucas. III. ii. 6 An unbidden guest Should travaile as dutchwomen go to Church, Beare their stooles with them. **1659** HOWELL *Eng. Prov.* 15b An unbidden guest must bring his stool with him.

Unblessed, *see* Ungirt, u.

Unborn, *see* Better u. than unbred.

Uncalled, *see* Come not to counsel u.; Comes u. sits unserved.

Uncertainty of the law, The glorious.

1759-93 MACKLIN *Love à la mode* II. i. 27 The law is a sort of hocus-pocus science . . . and the glorious uncertainty of it is of mair use to the professors than the justice of it.

Uncle, *see* Aunt had been a man (If my) she'd have been my u.; Call the bear 'u.'; Dog worry my u.; Dutch u. (Talk like a); True as I am his u.; She is one of mine aunts that made mine u. go a-begging.

Uncouth, *see* Unknown (U.) unkissed.

Under the rose.   (R 185)

[= in secret: there is reason to believe that the phrase originated in Germany. L. *sub rosa*] **1546** *State Papers Hen. VIII* XI. 200 The sayde questyons were asked with lysence, and that yt shulde remayn under the rosse, that is to say, to remayn under the bourde, and no more to be rehersyd. **1622** FLETCHER *Beggar's Bush* II. iii If this make us speak Bold words, anon, 'tis all under the Rose forgotten. **1654** GAYTON *Pleas. Notes* III. v. 93 What ever thou and the foul pusse did doe (*sub Rosa* as they say). **1708** *Brit. Apollo* no. 112. 3/1 But when we with caution a secret Disclose, We cry Be it spoken (Sir) under the Rose. **1899** A. W. WARD *Eng. Dram. Lit.* III. 298 *Hudibras* . . . merely repeated . . . the comments which during the rule of Puritanism men had been making 'under the rose'.

Under water, famine; under snow, bread.   (W 115)

1640 HERBERT no. 516. **1721** KELLY 358 (dearth) . . . Great Rains in Winter wash and impoverish the Ground; but Snow is supposed to cherish it.

Underboard, *see* Play u.

Underling, *see* Friday will be king or u.

Undermines, *see* Time u. us.

Understanding, *see* God will punish, (When); Heart (U.), (Who has not).

Understands ill, Who | answers ill. *Cf.* Ill hearing. Wrong hears.   (U 6)

1611 COTGRAVE s.v. Mal He that vnderstands ill answers vnfitly. **1642** TORRIANO 30 He who understandeth amisse, answereth worse. **1736** BAILEY s.v. Understand.

Understand(s), *see also* Good language which all u. not (Not); Speak of what you u.; Trap (He u.).

Undone, *see* Done cannot be u. (Things).

Unexpected, *see* Nothing is so certain as the u.; Unforeseen (U.) that happens (It is).

Unforeseen (Unexpected) that always happens, It is the.

[PLAUTUS *Most.* I. 3. 40 *Insperata accidunt magis quam speres.*] **1886** E. J. HARDY *How to be Happy* ch. 25 It is the unexpected that constantly happens. **1909** *Times Wkly.* 12 Nov. No place in the world is more familiar than the House of Commons with 'the unforeseen that always happens'.

Unforeseen, *see also* Nothing is certain but the u.

Unfurnished, *see* Cockloft is u.]

Ungirt, unblessed.   (U 10)

c. **1477** CAXTON *Book of Curtesye* E.E.T.S. 45 Vngyrte . vnblyssed . seruyng atte table Me semeth hym a seruant nothing able. **1596** SPENSER *F.Q.* IV. v. 18 Fie on the man, that did it first inuent, To shame vs all with this, 'Vngirt vnblest'. **1612–15** BP. HALL *Contempl.* IV. xii. (1825) II. 385 'Ungirt, unblest', was the old word; as not ready till they were girded, so not till they had prayed. **1690** C. NESSE *O. & N. Test.* I. 451 Here, if ever, doth that proverb Ungirt, Unblest, hold true.

Unhappy man's cart is eith[1] to tumble[2], An.   (M 495)

a. **1628** CARMICHAELL no. 241. **1641** FERGUSSON no. 32. **1721** KELLY 22 . . . Spoken of an infortunate Man, when Misfortunes follow him. [[1] easy. [2] overturn.]

Union (concord) is strength, In.   (U 11)

[HOMER *Iliad.* Bk. 12, l. 237 συμφερτὴ δ' ἀρετὴ πέλει ἀνδρῶν καὶ μάλα λυγρῶν.] *c.* **1526** *Dicta Sap.* A4ᵛ Concorde maketh those thynges that are weake, mighty and stronge. **1548** HALL (1809), 52 I haue red, and heard great clarckes say, that strengthe knitte and combined together is of more force and efficacie then when it is seuered and dispersed. **1562** G. LEGH *Accidence of Armoury* 216ᵛ Thinges deuyded, cary theyr onely strength, which being together, double theyr enduring. **1596** SHAKES. *K.J.* II. i. 446 This union shall do more than battery can To our fast-closed gates. **1621** *Grievous Groans for the Poor* A3 It is an old, and yet a true Prouerbe, Vis vnita fortior, Vnited force is most vigorous. **1877** WALFORD *Tales of Gt. Fam.* (1890) 156 The prosperity of the House of Rothschild [is due to] the unity which has attended the co-partnership of its members, . . . a fresh example of the saying that 'union is strength'.

Union, *see also* Henry was the u. of the roses (In).

Universities, *see* Three ways, the church (u.), sea, court.

Unkind, *see* Unkissed, u.

Unkindness, *see* Cut to u. (No); No man may poind for u.

Unkissed, unkind.   (U 13)

1584 PEELE *Arraign. of Paris* I. v. B2ᵛ And I will haue a louers fee they saie, vnkist, vnkinde. **1611** DAVIES no. 314 Farewell vnkist. That farwel's vnkinde.

Unkissed, *see also* Unknown u.

Unknown (Uncouth) unkissed.   (U 14)

1374 CHAUCER *Troilus* Bk. I, l. 809 Vnknowe vnkyst and lost that is vn-sought. **1401** *Pol. Poems* (Rolls) II. 59 On old Englis it is said, unkissid is unknowun. **1546** HEYWOOD I. xi. E1

Vnknowne vnkyst . it is loste that is vnsought. *c.* **1582** NASHE *Mar-Martine* xxii Thou caytif kerne, vncouth thou art, vnkist thou eke sal bee. *a.* **1697** AUBREY *Lives* (1898) II. 254 He . . . ransackt the MSS. of the church of Hereford (there were a great many that lay uncouth and unkiss).

Unknown, *see also Ignotum.*

Unlooked for, *see* Many things happen u.

Unlucky, *see* Born under an u. planet (star); Lucky at cards, u. in love; Lucky in life, u. in love; Thieves' handsel ever u.

Unmannerly, *see* Better be u. than troublesome.

Unminded, unmoaned.   (U 16)
1546 HEYWOOD I. ix. C2 Vnmynded, vnmoned, go make you mone.   **1659** HOWELL *Eng. Prov.* 4b.

Unmoaned, *see* Unminded u.

Unsafely, *see* Lives u. that looks too near.

Unseyit, *see* All things are good u.

Unsonsy[1] fish aye gets the unlucky bait, The.
1832 HENDERSON 141. [¹ unlucky.]

Unsought, *see* Lost that is u.

Unsound minds, like unsound bodies, if you feed, you poison.   (M 977)
1651 HERBERT no. 1076.

Unspeakable Turk, The.
1876 GLADSTONE in MAXWELL *Life of W. H. Smith* (1894) 151 Mr. Gladstone . . . published an article in the 'Contemporary Review' advocating the expulsion of the 'unspeakable Turk, bag and baggage', from Europe.   **1907** H. DE WINDT *Through Savage Europe* viii Nearly thirty years had now elapsed since Servia last fought to free herself from the yoke of the unspeakable Turk.

Unstable (false) as water.   (W 86)
[GEN. xlix. 4 Unstable as water, thou shalt not excel.]   *c.* **1380** WYCLIF *Sel. Wks.* II. 90 þis Emperour . . . was vnstable as watir.   **1526** BONDE *Pilgr. Perf.* 104 More flowynge and vnstable than the waters of the see.   **1591** ARIOSTO *Orl. Fur.* Harington XVI. 15 Vnchast and false, as euer water wet.   **1602** SHAKES. *T.C.* III. ii. 187 As false As air, as water, wind, or sandy earth.   **1604** *Id. O.* V. ii. 137 She was false as water.   **1824** SCOTT *St. Ronan's* ch. 15 Ye have got an idea that every thing must be changed— Unstable as water, ye shall not excel.

Unstable, *see also* World is u.

Untaught, *see* Better u. than ill taught.

Unthankful, *see* Call a man no worse than u. (You can).

Unthrift, *see* Blames their wife for own u.; Drift as bad as u.

Untimeous[1] spurring spills[2] the steed. *Cf.* Spur a free horse, Do not.   (S 794)
1581 GUAZZO i. 134 By too much spurring, the horse is made dull.   *a.* **1585** MONTGOMERIE *Cherrie & Slae* 397 (1645) 29 15 (Quoth DANGER) Huilie,[3] Freind, take heed, Untymous spurring spills the Steed.   **1596** SHAKES. *Rich. II* II. i. 36 He tires betimes that spurs too fast betimes.   **1721** KELLY 343 . . . That is, too much haste spoils Business. [¹ untimely. ² spoils. ³ softly.]

Unwashed, The great.
1596 SHAKES. *K.J.* IV. ii. 201 Another lean unwash'd artificer.   **1864** J. PAYN *Lost Sir Massingb.* ch. 1 There were no such things as 'skilled workmen', or 'respectable artisans', in those days. The 'people' were 'the Great Unwashed'.

Unwashed, *see also* Hands, (With u.)

Unworthy of life that causes not life in another, He is.
1633 D. DYKE *Six Evangel. Hist.* 98 Life, when grown to strength, is generative. . . . *Nascitur indigne per quem non nascitur alter*; . . .

Unworthy to live who lives only for himself, He is.
1732 FULLER no. 1952.

Up and down, *see* Wants in u. and d. (What she).

Up hill, spare me; down hill bear (forbear) me; plain way, spare me not; let me not drink when I am hot.
1721 KELLY 358 . . . A Rule in Jockeyship how to use a Horse in a Journey.

Up the hill favour me, down the hill beware thee.   (H 470)
1639 CLARKE 22.   **1721** KELLY 359 Up Hill spare me, down Hill take tent[1] to thee. For if you ride fast down a Hill the Horse will be fair to stumble. [¹ heed.]

Up to one's gossip, To be.
1785 GROSE *Dict. Vulg. T. Up to their Gossip*, to be a match for one who attempts to cheat, or deceive, to be on a footing, or in the Secret. **1828** CARR *Craven Dialect.* i. 193.

Up to the ears.
[*c.* **1553**] **1566-7** UDALL *Ralph Roister D.* Ii A3 If any woman smyle . . . Vp is he to the harde eares in loue. [**1588**] **1591** LYLY *Endym.* I. iii. 1 In loue vp to the eares.   **1594** BARNFIELD *Affect.*

Sheph. Percy Soc. 8 But leave we him in love up to the eares. **1611** COTGRAVE S.V. Oreille He is vp to the eares in, or hath his whole fill of.

Up, *see also* Early u. never nearer; First u., last down; Soon u., soon down; Take me not u. before I fall.

Upper hand, To get (have) the.   (H 95)

c. **1430** LYDGATE 'Mumming at Hertford' *Minor Poems* E.E.T.S. ii. 679 Cleyming of right to haue the hyegher hande. [*a.* 1470] **1481** TIPTOFT *Tulle Old Age* 79 [He] had the vppir-hande and victorye of the men of Cartage. **1530** PALSGRAVE 582a We have the upper hande of our enemyes. **1541** *Schoolh. of Women* C3ᵛ. **1557** EDGEWORTH *Sermons* (haue the ouerhand ouer). [**1592**] **1597** SHAKES. *Rich. III* IV. iv. 37 Let my griefs frown on the upper hand. **1604** DEKKER I *Hon. Whore* IV. iii. 46 Ile shoulder with him for the vpper hand. **1681** W. ROBERTSON 1269 Where men agree well together, they are more like to have the upper hand.

Upper ten thousand, The.

1844 N. P. WILLIS *Necessity for a Promenade Drive* in New York *Evening Mirror*, 11 Nov. 2a At present there is no distinction among the upper ten thousand of the city. **1860** JOWETT in *Life* ch. 3 The world, that is to say the upper 10,000. **1870** F. S. COZZENS *Sayings* 53 Willis did originate some phrases, . . . such as 'the upper ten thousand'. You see how it has been trimmed down to 'the upper ten'. **1878** J. PAYN *By Proxy* ch. 36 Warren . . . is a *novus homo*, and only a Conservative on that account; it being the quickest method to gain admission among the Upper Ten. **1905** SIR G. O. TREVELYAN ·*Interludes* 286 A rout which . . . embraces a tithe of the Upper Ten Thousand, is conventionally described . . . by the epithets 'small' and 'early'.

Upright, *see also* Arrow shot u. falls on the shooter's head.

Ups and downs, To have many. (U 19)

1637 RUTHERFORD *Let.* 106, 177 But oh, the windings, the turnings, the ups and the downs that he hath led me through. **1659** BUNYAN *Doctrine Law and Grace* Wks. i. 553 The very saints of God have . . . many ups and downs·in this their travel towards heaven. **1782** 4 June JOHNSON *Lett.* (Chapman) ii. 487 Wisely was it said by him who said it first, that this·world is all ups and downs. **1891** HARDY *Tess* ch. 40 Take the ups wi' the downs. **1913** D. H. LAW-RENCE *Lett.* i. 190 I've had my ups and downs . . . with Frieda.

Upset, *see* Apple-cart (To u. the).

Urinal, *see* Suit at law and u.

Use is all.   (U 23)

[*c.* 1592] **1600** NASHE *Summer's Last Will* iii. 249 T'is vse is all in all. **1609** HARWARD 124 Vse and practise is all. **1631** JONSON *Staple of News* v. vi. 26. **1638** CLARKE *Phraseologia Puerilis* F2ᵛ.

Use legs and have legs.   (L 195)

a. **1576** WHYTHORNE 8 Yvz limz, and hav limz. *c.* **1582** G. HARVEY *Marginalia* (1913) 188 Vse Legges, & haue Legges: Vse Law and haue Law. Vse nether & haue nether. **1636** S. WARD *Sermons* (1862) 25 Graces, gifts, virtues . . . the principal beauty and benefit of them consists in use. . . . Use limbs, and have limbs; the more thou dost, the more thou mayest. **1670** RAY 153. **1721** KELLY 342 Work Legs, and win Legs; hain¹ Legs, and tine² Legs. [¹ save, spare. ² lose.]

Use makes mastery.   (U 24)

1340 *Ayenbite* E.E.T.S. 178 Uor wone makeþ maister. **1477** NORTON *Ord. Alch.* vii in ASHM. *Theat. Chem. Brit.* (1652) 105 Use maketh Masterie. **1545** TAVERNER D8 The common prouerbe which we haue in englishe: Use maketh maystryes. **1546** HEYWOOD II. ii. F4ᵛ. **1706** STEVENS S.V. Usar (masters).

Use (*later* Practice) makes perfect (perfectness).   (U 24)

[L. *Usus promptum facit.* Practice makes perfect.] **1560** T. WILSON *Arte of Rhet.* (1909) 5 Eloquence was vsed, and through practise made perfect. **1562** A. BROOKE *Romeus & Juliet* l. 1494. **1564** BULLEIN *Dial. agst Fever* (1888) 66 Use maketh perfectnes; we will teach you to swim by art as well as we do by Nature. **1599** PORTER *Angry Wom. Abingd.* l. 913 Forsooth as vse makes·perfectnes, so seldome seene is soone forgotten. **1810** CRABBE *The Borough* xix (1908) 186 *Practice makes perfect*; when the month came round, He dropp'd the cash, nor listen'd for a sound. **1829** SCOTT *Jrnl.* 27 Jan. Use makes perfectness. **1863** C. READE *Hard Cash* ch. 44 He lighted seven fires, skilfully on the whole, for practice makes perfect. **1902** *Spectator* 10 May Practice never makes perfect. It improves up to a point.

Use one like a dog, To.   (D 514)

1530 PALSGRAVE 680b He rebuked me and I had ben a dogge. **1589** R. HAKLUYT E.L. vi. 110 Using them more like dogs then men. **1595** SHAKES. *M.N.D.* II. i. 210 What worser place can I beg in your love . . . Than to be used as you use your dog. **1612** BRINSLEY *Ludus Litera-rius* (1627, ed. Campagnac) 291 To use them worse, then we would use a dogge, as they say. **1614** JONSON *Barthol. Fair* IV. ii. 77 I would not ha' vsed a dog o' the name, so. **1619** W. HORNBY *Scourge of Drunkennes* A4 Ile vse thee like a dogge, a Iew a slave. **1688** SHADWELL *Squire Alsatia* I. i. Merm. 242 I'll endure 't no longer! . . . I'll teach him to use his son like a dog. **1714** STEELE *Lover* no. 7, 11 Mar. I was terribly afraid that . . . if she caught me at such an advantage, she would use me like a dog.

Use one like a Jew, To.   (J 52)

1619 W. HORNBY *Scourge of Drunkennes* A4 Ile vse thee like a dogge, a Iew, a slave. **1662** FULLER *Lond.* 198 'I will use you as bad as·a Jew'. . . . That poor Nation (especially on Shrove Tuesday) being intollerably abused by the English. **1700** BP. PATRICK *Comm. Deut.* xxviii. 37 Better we cannot express the most cut-throat dealing, than thus, You use me like a Jew.

Use (*noun*), *see also* Best u. of time; Everything is of u. to housekeeper; Iron with u. grows bright; Keep a thing seven years, find u. for it; Lay things by, they may come to u.; Old u. and wont, legs about the fire; Once a u. ever a custom; Worst u. can put man to is to hang him.

Use (*verb*), *see* Choose for yourself and u. for yourself; Means (U. the) and God give blessing; Once and u. it not.

Used key is always bright, The. (K 26)

1561–2 *Kitt Hath Lost Key* in *Extr. Stationers' Co.* ed. Collier i. 55 My key is bright, not rusty, It is soe oft applied. **1602** *Poet. Rhap.* 11, ed. Rollins i. 52 For vse . . . euer shineth brighter. **1758** FRANKLIN in Arber *E. Garner* v. 579 Sloth, like Rust, consumes faster than Labour wears; while the used key is always bright.

Used to, *see* Nothing when you are u. to it; Youth is u. to (What), age remembers.

Uses me better than he is wont, He that | will betray me. (U 26)

1573 SANFORD 50ᵛ. **1611** DAVIES no. 231 Who vseth mee better then hee was vs'd, By him I am, or shall be abus'd. **1732** FULLER no. 2180 He that is kinder than he was wont, hath a Design upon thee.

Usurer at the table, To speak of a | mars the wine. (U 27)

1640 HERBERT no. 974.

Usurers are always good husbands. (U 30)

1616 BRETON *Cross.* B2.

Usurers live by the fall of heirs, as swine by the dropping of acorns.

1607 G. WILKINS *Mis. of Enf. Marriage* III. Hazl.-

Dods. ix. 509 To see that we and usurers live by the fall of young heirs, as swine by the dropping of acorns. **1639** R. CHAMBERLAIN *Nocturnal Lucubrations* III. 18.

Usurer(s), *see also* God keep me from . . . u.'s [house].

Uther-Pendragon[1] do what he can, Let | The river Eden will run as it ran. (U 33)

1659 HOWELL *Eng. Prov.* 20a. **1662** FULLER Westm. 135 . . . Uter-Pendragon had a design to fortifie the Castle of Pen-dragon in this County . . . whereunto, with much art and industry, he invited . . . the River of Eden to forsake his old chanel, and all to no purpose . . . *Naturam expellas Furcâ licet, usque recurret.* [1 a mythical Welsh prince.]

Utopia.

[The title of the book published by Sir T. More, in 1516, describing an imaginary island with a perfect system of government, hence an ideally perfect place or state of things. (= nowhere, from Gk. οὐ not+τόπ-ος a place).] **1570** FOXE *A. & M.* (ed. 2) 1156/2 I do not . . . thinke, that . . . there is any such fourth place of Purgatory at all (vnles it be in M. More's Vtopia). **1613** PURCHAS *Pilgrimage* (1614) 708 The reports of this his voyage savour more of an Vtopia, and Plato's Commonwealth, then of true Historie. **1621** BURTON *Anat. Mel.* To the Reader (1638) 60 I will yet to satisfie and please my selfe, make an Vtopia of mine owne, a new Atlantis, a poeticall Commonwealth of mine owne. *a.* **1734** NORTH *Lives* II. 364 Young men, for want of experience, . . . create Utopias in their own imagination. **1837** MACAULAY *Ess., Lord Bacon* (1903) 402 An acre in Middlesex is better than a principality in Utopia. The smallest actual good is better than the most magnificent promise of impossibilities.

V

Vacuum, *see* Nature abhors v.

Vain, *see* Labour in v.

Vainglory blossoms but never bears. (V 6)

1611 COTGRAVE s.v. Gloire Vaineglorie hauing blossomd, perisheth. **1616** DRAXE no. 2209 Vaine glory is a floure that beareth no corne. **1732** FULLER no. 5342.

Vale best discovers the hill, The. (V 7)

1594 BACON *Promus* no. 145. **1597–8** *Id. Ess., Followers* Arb. 38 To take aduise of friends is euer honorable: . . .

Valentine's Day,[1] On | will a good goose lay; if she be a good goose, her dame well to pay, she will lay two eggs before Valentine's Day. (V 9)

1678 RAY 51. [1 14 Feb.]

Valet, *see* No man is a hero to v.

Valiant man's look is more than a coward's sword, A. (M 496)

1640 HERBERT no. 708.

Valiant, *see also* Dog is v. at own door; Wise (v.) man esteems every place his own country.

Valley, *see* Stays in the v. (He that).

Valour can do little without discretion. (V 12)

1664 CODRINGTON 223. **1670** RAY 27.

Valour would fight, but discretion would run away. (V 15)

1678 RAY 214. **1732** FULLER no. 5344.

Valour, *see also* City (V.) that parleys; Discretion; Virtue (V.) is the beauty of the mind.

Value(d), *see* Know the v. of ‑a ducat (If you would); Nurse is v. till.

Variant, *see* Fortune is v.

Variety is charming.

1539 TAVERNER 12ᵛ It is moost pleasaunt rowynge nere the lande, and walkynge nere the see. Man is much delyted wyth varietie. **1632** *Holland's Leaguer* C4ᵛ Variety is pleasant. **1822** COBBETT *Rural Rides* 24 Nov. They say that 'variety is charming', and this day I have had of scenes and of soils a variety indeed! **1861** G. J. WHYTE-MELVILLE *Tilbury N.* ch. 25 'Variety is charming', and that charm no one can deny to the different kinds of weather which successively constitute an English summer's day.

Variety takes away satiety. (V 18)

1579 LYLY *Euph.* i. 272 It is varietie that moueth the minde of all men. **1592** DELAMOTHE 37 Nature hath pleasure in diuersitie. **1599** MINSHEU *Span. Dial.* 10 Others say varietie breedes delight. **1606–7** SHAKES. *A.C.* II. ii. 240 Age cannot wither her nor custom stale Her infinite variety. **1609** HARWARD 124 Variety taketh away tediousnes. **1624** J. HEWES *Perfect Survey* P1 Variety doth alwayes refresh wearisomnesse. **1639** CLARKE 315 (sacietie). **1784** COWPER *Task* II. 606 Variety's the very spice of life, That gives it all its flavour.

Varlet, *see* Ape's an ape, a v.'s a v.

Vat, *see* Tub (V.) must stand on own bottom.

Vaunter and a liar are near akin, A. (V 19)

c. **1374** CHAUCER *Troilus* Bk. 3, l. 309 A vauntor and a lier, al is on. *a.* **1628** CARMICHAELL no. 230 (baith ane thing). **1641** FERGUSSON no. 4 (both one thing). **1721** KELLY 36 . . . when a Man once takes a humour of boasting . . . , he will not stop at the most palpable Lies.

Veal will be cheap: calves fall. (V 21)

1678 RAY 83 . . . A jeer for those who lose the calves of their legs by &c. **1823** GROSE ed. Pierce Egan s.v. Calves.

Veal, *see also* Calf (Greatest) is not sweetest v.; Raw pulleyn, v., make churchyards fat; Shoulder of v. (In a) . . . good bits.

Vease thee, I will. (V 22)

c. **890** *Laws Edward & Guthrum* xi Donne fysie hi man of earde. *c.* **1400** *Beryn* Prol. 351 Shall I com þen, Cristian, & fise a-wey þe Cat? *c.* **1594** SHAKES. *T.S.* Ind. i. I'll pheeze you, in faith. **1678** RAY 345 I'll vease the (i.e. *hunt, drive thee*). Somerset.

Veaze, *see* Pease has its v., (Every).

Velvet, On.

1769 BURKE *Obs. Pres. St. Nat.* Wks. ii. 142 Not like our author, who is always on velvet, he is aware of some difficulties. **1785** GROSE *Dict. Vulg. T.* . . . to have the best of a bet or match. **1826** SCOTT *Journ.* 4 March Though I have something to pay out of it, I shall be on velvet for expense. **1897** *Daily News* 1 June 3/5 Is that what you call being 'On velvet' when you are sure to win something?—Yes.

Velvet true heart, He is a. (H 308)

[*c.* 1602] **1608** *Merry Dev. of Ed.* IV. i. 33 Thou speak'st as true as velvet. **1678** RAY 83 . . . *Chesh.*

Velvet, *see also* Fret like gummed v.; Iron hand in v. glove; Silk purse (V.) out of sow's ear.

Venomous, *see* Tongue stings (is more v. than serpent's sting).

Vengeance, The noblest | is to forgive. *Cf.* Pardons and pleasantness. (R 92)

1547 BALDWIN O4 Forgeuenes is a valyaunt kynde of reuengeaunce. **1573** SANFORD 10 The diuine Petrach sayde . . . *Nobilissimum vindictae genus est parcere.* The noblest kind of reuengement is to forgiue. **1580** LYLY *Euph. & his Eng.* ii. 207 Thinking no reuenge more princely, then to spare when she might spill. **1666** TORRIANO *It. Prov.* 202 no. 7 To pardon, is a divine revenge. **1710** PALMER 81 Forgiveness and a Smile is the best Revenge. **1853** TRENCH i. 13.

Vengeance of the law, The.

1881 E. B. TYLOR *Anthrop.* (1889) 417 Reading . . . of a Corsican 'vendetta', we hardly . . . think of it as a relic of ancient law . . . , as is still plain . . . [from] such phrases as 'the vengeance of the law'.

Vengeance, *see also* Vice is (Where), v. follows. See also Revenge.

Venice-glass broken, *see* Credit lost.

Venison, *see* Flesh (All) is not v.; Princes are v. in heaven.

Venom to that of the tongue, There is no. (V 29)

1659 HOWELL *Eng. Prov.* 11b.

Venom, *see also* Spit one's v.; Viper so little (No), but has its v.

Vent(s), *see* Dead avails not and revenge v. hatred, (To lament the).

Venture a small fish to catch a great one. (F 329)

1592 DELAMOTHE 19 We must aduenture a small fish, to take a great one. **1611** COTGRAVE s.v. Hasarder Il faut hasarder vn petit poisson pour prendre vn grand. A little, for a great gaine must be hazarded. **1639** CLARKE 41. **1659** HOWELL *Fr. Prov.* 9 You may well lose a Menow to take a Salmon. **1670** RAY 152. **1796** EDGEWORTH *Par. Asst., Lit. Merch.* ch. 1 Venture a small fish, as the proverb says, to catch a great one.

Venture, Take your | as many a good ship has done.

1721 KELLY 304 . . . Spoken when Advice is asked in a Case where the Success may be dubious.

Venture it, I will | as Johnson did his wife, and she did well. (J 72)

1678 RAY 83. **1732** FULLER no. 1367 E'en venture on, as Johnson did on his Wife.

Venture not all in one bottom.[1] *Cf.* Eggs in one basket. (A 209)

[ERASM. *Ad. Ne uni navi facultates.*] **1513** SIR T. MORE *Rich. III* 1821 ed., 61 What wise merchaunt aduentureth al his good in one ship? **1592–4** SHAKES. *1 Hen. VI* IV. vi. 32 O, too much folly is it, well I wot, To hazard all our lives in one small boat! **1596** *Id. M.V.* I. i. 42 My ventures are not in one bottom trusted. **1617** J. SWETNAM *Sch. of Defence* 56 He is a foole which will adventure all his goods in one ship. **1623** WEBSTER *Duch. Malfi* III. v. Merm. 193 Let us not venture all this poor remainder In one unlucky bottom. **1639** CLARKE 95. **1732** FULLER no. 5349. [1 vessel.]

Venture(s), *see also* Many v. make full freight; Nothing v. nothing have; Nothing v. nothing win.

Venus, *see* Ceres and Bacchus (Without), V. grows cold.

Verdingales[1] to Broad-gates[2] in Oxford, Send. (F 73)

1560 HEYWOOD *Fourth Hund. Epig.* no. 55 Alas poore verdingales must lye in the streete: To house them, no doore in the citee made meete. Syns at our narow doores they in cannot wyn, Send them to Oxford, at Brodegates to get in. **1662** FULLER *Oxf.* 329 . . . With these *Verdingales* the Gowns of Women beneath their waists were pent-housed out far beyond their bodies; . . . the first inventress . . . a light House-wife, who, . . . sought to cover her shame and the fruits of her wantonness. . . . Their wearers could not enter (except going sidelong) at any ordinary door; which gave the occasion to this Proverb. [1 hooped petticoats (farthingales). 2 Broadgates Hall, Oxford, was superseded in 1624 by Pembroke College.]

Verify, *see* Always v. your references.

Verses, *see* Poet in adversity can hardly make v.

Vessel, The greatest | has but its measure.

1732 FULLER no. 4580.

Vessel(s), *see also* Empty v. make greatest sound; Ill v. seldom miscarry; Old v. must leak; Water is shallow (Where) no v. can ride; Weaker v. *See also* Cask.

Vex a dog to see a pudding creep, It would. (D 491)

c. **1629** F. D. *Excell. Medley* l. 51 in *Roxb. Bal.* i. 58 Would not a dog for anger swell, to see a pudding creepe. **1659** HOWELL *Eng. Prov.* 21a. **1738** SWIFT Dial. II. E.L. 312 I have a Mind to eat a Piece of that Sturgeon; but fear it will make me sick. . . . Let it alone, and I warrant it won't hurt you.—Well, but it would vex a Dog to see a Pudden creep.

Vicar of Bowdon, Every man cannot be. (M 108)

1678 RAY 301 *Chesh.* . . . Bowden . . . is one of the greatest livings near Chester.

Vicar of Bray will be vicar of Bray still, The. (V 40)

1662 FULLER Berks. 82 The Vivacious Vicar hereof living under King Henry the 8. King Edward the 6. Queen Mary, and Queen Elizabeth, was first a Papist, then a Protestant, then a Papist, then a Protestant again. . . . Being taxed . . . for being a Turn-coat . . .—'Not so', said he; 'for I alwaies kept my Principle, which is this, to live and die the Vicar of Bray.' *c.* **1720** *Song, Vicar of Bray* That whatsoever King shall reign, I'll still be Vicar of Bray, Sir. **1735** BROME in *Lett. by Eminent Persons* (1813) II. 100 It is Simon Aleyn or Allen, who was Vicar of Bray about 1540 and died 1588.

Vicar of fools is his ghostly father, The. (V 41)

1560 HEYWOOD *Fourth Hund. Epig.* no. 19 Whens come all these? From the vicar of saint fooles. **1564** BULLEIN *Dial. agst. Fever* (1888) 27 The vicar of S. Fooles be your ghostly father. Are you so wise? **1660** TATHAM *Rump.* v. i. Wks. (1879) 268 Sure the vicar of fools was his ghostly father. Be beat without a blow, there's a mystery indeed!

Vicar, *see also* Devil be a v. (If), you will be clerk; Devil gets up belfry by v.'s skirts.

Vice is often clothed in virtue's (liberty's) habit. (V 44)

1557 EDGEWORTH *Sermons* 2Z2ᵛ Not as the seruauntes of the flesh or the worlde, coueringe vices vnder the cloke of libertie. **1569** C. AGRIPPA *Vanity of Arts & Sciences* *2 Vices often times put on the colour of vertue. *c.* **1590** HARVEY

Marginalia 99 Eueri Vice hath a cloak: and preasith, or creepith in, under yᵉ maske of A vertu. **1616** DRAXE no. 523 Vice in vertues habite. **1664** CODRINGTON 223.

Vice is, Where | vengeance follows.
(v 48)

[HORACE *Odes* 3. 2. 31 *Raro antecedentem scelestum Deseruit pede pœna claudo*. Rarely has punishment, with halting foot, failed to overtake the evil-doer in his flight.] **1611** COTGRAVE s.v. Supplice No vice without its punishment; or, each vice is to it selfe a punishment. **1623** WODROEPHE 505 No Vice with [without?] Punishment. **1639** CLARKE 325.

Vice(s), *see also* Covetousness starves other v.; Hates not the person but the v.; Idleness is root of all v.; Maintains one v. (What) would bring up two children.

Victory, He gets a double | who conquers himself.
(v 51)

1539 TAVERNER *Publius* B1ᵛ He that can ouercome himselfe in victory, that is to say, vse moderatly the victory, ouercommeth twyse, fyrst his enemy, seconde his owne mynd. **1545** *Precepts of Cato* F8 He hath a double victorye, Who ouercometh him selfe and his enimye. **1591** ARIOSTO *Orl. Fur.* Harington XIII *Historie* That excellent wise saying, it is a greater vertue to conquer ones owne affections then to win cities. **1639** CLARKE 319 Selfe conquest is the greatest.

Victory that comes without blood, It is a great.
(v 52)

1591 ARIOSTO *Orl. Fur.* Harington xv. *Moral* It cannot be denied but bloudy conquests are no praise to the conquerour. *a.* **1593** MARLOWE tr. Ovid's *Amores* II. xii. 5 That victory doth chiefly triumph merit, Which without bloodshed doth the prey inherit. **1598–9** SHAKES. *M.A.* I. i. 8 A victory is twice itself when the achiever brings home full numbers. **1640** HERBERT no. 227. **1666** TORRIANO *It. Prov.* 313 no. 11 Great is the victory without bloudshed, and hath greatest glory.

Victory, *see also* Better a lean peace; Moors (The more), better v.; Pyrrhic v.; Triumph before the v. (Do not).

Victualled my camp, I have.

1678 RAY 345 I have victualled my camp (*filled my belly*).

Victuals, Of all | drink digests the quickest.

1721 KELLY 274 *Of all Meat in the World. Drink goes the best down.* A facetious Bull when we drink heartily after Meat. **1738** SWIFT Dial. II. E.L. 304 Of all vittles drink digests the quickest: give me a glass of wine.

Victuals in England, There is more good | than in seven other kingdoms.
(v 53)

1621 ROBINSON 15. **1639** CLARKE 74.

Video meliora proboque, deteriora sequor, see See and approve the better course.

Vier, *see* O Master V.

Village, *see* Better be first in a v.

Vine brings forth three grapes: the first of pleasure, the second of drunkenness, the third of sorrow, The.
(v 60)

1539 TAVERNER I *Garden* F5 (thre cloisters . . . the thyrde of displeasure). **1568** TILNEY *Duties in Marriage* C1ᵛ Anacharsis the Philosopher sayde, that the Vine bare three kindes of grapes, the first of pleasure, the seconde of dronkennesse, and the thirde of sorrowe. **1586** GUAZZO ii. 152 The Vine carrieth likewise . . . three sorts of greapes. **1601** SHAKES. *T.N.* I. v. 132 What's a drunken man like, fool?—Like a drown'd man, a fool, and a madman. One draught above heat makes him a fool, the second mads him, and a third drowns him. **1666** TORRIANO *It. Prov.* 318 no. 23 A grape hath three grape-seeds, one of Health, another of Mirth, and the third of Drunkenness.

Vine embraces the elm, The.
(v 61)

1565 J. HALL *Court of Virtue* R6ᵛ Lyke as the vyne that flourysheth, with lyuely grapes and leaues most green, The small tree neuer despyseth: That beares hym vp. **1569** E. FENTON *Certain Secret Won. Nat.* 68ᵛ As we may see of the Vine, who imbraceth the Elme, ioying and reioycing much at hes presence. [c. **1587**] **1592** KYD *Span. Trag.* II. iv. 45 Thus Elmes by vines are compast till they fall. **1592–3** SHAKES. *C.E.* II. ii. 173 Thou art an elm, my husband; I am a vine. **1595** *Id. M.N.D.* IV. i. 40 The female ivy so Enrings the barky fingers of the elm.

Vine of a good soil, Take a | and the daughter of a good mother.
(v 59)

1642 TORRIANO 45. **1659** HOWELL *It. Prov.* 15 Plant thy Vine in a good soyl, and take a wife of a good race. **1813** RAY 45.

Vine poor, Make the | and it will make you rich.
(v 58)

1678 RAY 350 . . . Prune off its branches.

Vinegar of sweet wine, Take heed of the.
(H 382)

1573 SANFORD 105ᵛ Take you heede of vineger, and sweet wyne, that is, of the anger of a quiet man. **1578** FLORIO *First F.* 30ᵛ Beware of vineger and sweete wine, and of the anger of a peaceable man. **1579** LYLY *Euph.* i. 197 For as the best wine doth make the sharpest vinaigre, so the deepest loue tourneth to the deadliest hate. **1589** L. WRIGHT *Display of Duty* 20 The best wine, maketh the sharpest viniger. **1612** WEBSTER *White Devil* IV. i. Merm. 74 Best natures do commit the grossest faults, When they're given o'er to jealousy, as best wine, Dying, makes strongest vinegar. **1640** HERBERT no. 451. **1754** FRANKLIN Jan. Take heed of the Vinegar of sweet Wine, and the Anger of Good-nature. **1852** E. FITZGERALD *Polonius* 9 'It is . . . the sweet wine that makes the sharpest vinegar', says an old proverb.

Vinegar, *see also* Cries wine sells v.; Sharp as v.

Vineyard, *see* Fear looks to the v.; Naboth's v.

Vintage, *see* Short boughs long v.

Vintry, Three cranes in the, *see* Patience in adversity.

Violent, *see* Nothing that is v. is permanent.

Violet(s), *see* A-mothering (Who goes) finds v.

Viper so little, but has its venom, No.
(v 67)

1666 TORRIANO *It. Prov.* 257 no. 5 Every serpent hath its venom. **1732** FULLER no. 3639.

Viper, *see also* Snake (V.) in the bosom.

Virgin, *see* Maid and a v. is not all one.

Virtue and a trade are the best portion for children.
(v 76)

1640 HERBERT no. 107.

Virtue flies from the heart of a mercenary man.
(v 77)

1592 DELAMOTHE 23. **1651** HERBERT no. 1133.

Virtue has all things in itself.
(v 78)

[PLAUTUS *Amph.* l. 652 Virtus omnia in sese habet.] *a.* **1500** *15c. Sch-Bk.* ed. W. Nelson 56 Vertue . . . which whosoever hath, for to use plautes proposicion, he hath all thynge. **1594** LIPSIUS *6 Books of Politics* tr. Jones B1ᵛ Vertue . . . in her selfe containeth all things. **1736** BAILEY *Dict.* s.v. Virtue.

Virtue is a jewel of great price.
(v 79)

c. **1594** BACON no. 63 Vertue like a rych gemme, best plaine sett. **1616** BRETON *Cross.* A7ᵛ.

Virtue is found in the middle (mean).
(v 80)

1557 EDGEWORTH *Sermons* G2ᵛ All vertues consisteth in the meane and middle betwixt two vices. **1591** FLORIO *Second F.* 49 Vertue consists in the midst, quoth the diuell, when hee found himselfe between two Nonnes. **1596** SHAKES. *M.V.* I. ii. 7 It is no mean happiness, therefore, to be seated in the mean. **1605-6** *Id. T.Ath.* IV. iii. 300 The middle of humanity thou never knewest, but the extremity of both ends. **1620** J.C. *Two Mer. Milk-Maids* V. iii. P2 The Prouerbe, In Medio consistet virtus. **1666** TORRIANO *It. Prov.* 310 no. 31 Virtue is fix'd in the very middle.

Virtue is her own reward.
(v 81)

1509 BARCLAY *Ship of Fools* i. 12 Vertue hath no rewarde. **1596** SPENSER *F.Q.* III. xii. 39 Your vertue selfe her owne reward shall breed, Euen immortall praise, and glory wyde. **1619** JONSON *Pleasure Reconciled to Virtue* vii. 491 Vertue . . . she being his owne reward. **1642** SIR T. BROWNE *Relig. Med.* I. xlvii. (1881) 74 *Ipsa sui pretium virtus sibi,*[1] that Vertue is her own reward, is but a cold principle. **1643** Letter of COL. HUTCHINSON (*Memoirs* ed. Firth 412). **1692** PRIOR *Ode in Imit. of Horace* 146 And virtue is her own reward. **1813** BYRON *Journal Corr.* Prothero ii. 313 . . . It certainly should be paid well for its trouble. [[1] CLAUDIAN *De Mallii Theod. Consul.* v. 1.]

Virtue is more important than blood.
(v 82)

1581 GUAZZO i. 224 It is a common saying, that the bondes of vertue binde more straightly, then the bondes of blood. [*c.* **1597**] **1607** JONSON *Case Is Altered* I. x. 37 Didst thou neare read in difference of good, Tis more to shine in vertue then in bloud?

Virtue (Valour) is the beauty (nobleness) of the mind.
(v 83)

1601 SHAKES. *T.N.* III. iv. 351 In nature there's no blemish but the mind; . . . Virtue is beauty, but the beauteous evil Are empty trunks o'erflourished by the devil. **1616** BRETON *Crossing* A7 Valour is the noblenes of the minde. **1732** FULLER no. 5381 (of the Soul).

Virtue is the only true nobility.
(v 85)

1591 ARIOSTO *Orl. Fur.* Harington II. 58 [*margin* Virtus vera nobilitas*] For onely vertue noblenesse doth dignifie. **1592** DELAMOTHE 5 T'is vertue onely that giues nobilitie. **1697** W. POPE *Seth* [Ward] 4 Vertuous Actions, not great Names, are the best ensigns of nobility. **1706** STEVENS s.v. Cuerpo Virtue is the true Beauty. **1732** FULLER no. 5383. **1812** E. NARES *I'll Consider of It* ii. 179. **1813** BARRETT *Heroine* Lett. 4, ed. Raleigh 20 Virtue alone is true nobility.

Virtue never grows old.
(v 87)

1611 COTGRAVE s.v. Menton Vertue neuer grew old; the vigor thereof did neuer decay. **1639** CLARKE 321 Only vertue never dies. **1640** HERBERT no. 64.

Virtue of a coward is suspicion, The.
(v 89)

1651 HERBERT no. 1179.

Virtue of necessity, Make a.
(v 73)

[QUINTIL. I. 5 *Laudem virtutis necessitati damus.* ST. JEROME *In Libros Rufini,* III. 2. *Facis de necessitate virtutem.* (You make a virtue of necessity.)] *c.* **1374** CHAUCER *Troilus* Bk. 4, l. 1586 Thus maketh vertu of necessite! *c.* **1412** HOCCLEVE *Reg. Princes* E.E.T.S. 46, l. 1252 Make of necessite, reed I, vertu. **1532** HENRYSON *Test. Cress.* 478 I counsale thee mak vertew of ane neid. *c.* **1586** *Maxwell Younger MS.* in HENDERSON (1832) xli. no. 172 Neide oft makis wertew. **1594** SHAKES. *T.G.V.* IV. i. 62 Are you content . . . To make a virtue of necessity And live, as we do, in this wilderness? **1595-6** *Id. Rich. II* I. iii. 278 There is no virtue like necessity. **1641** FERGUSSON no. 648 Need makes vertue. **1642** J. HOWELL *Inst. For. Trav.* xiii. Arb. 62 Industrious people . . . making a rare vertue of necessity, for the same thing which makes a Parrot speake, makes them to labour.

Virtue that poverty destroys not, There is no. (v 75)

1573 SANFORD 108. **1578** FLORIO *First F.* 32 . . . but pouertie wyl marre it. **1629** *Bk. Mer. Rid.* Prov. no. 8.

Virtue, *see also* Blushing is v.'s colour; Honour is the reward of v.; Modesty be a v. (Though); Money, wit, and v. (Of) believe one fourth; Patience is a v.; Praise is the reflexion of v.; Riches are but baggage of v.; Show a good man his error, he turns it to v.; Sows v. shall reap fame; Vice is often clothed in v.'s habit; Youth (Who that in) no v. uses; Zeal when v. dangerous.

Virtuous, He cannot be | that is not rigorous. (v 91)

1640 HERBERT no. 664.

Visage, *see* Blithe heart makes a blooming v.

Visible church, The.

[*i.e.* Harrow on the Hill.] *a.* **1685** CHARLES II in DEFOE *Tour through Gt. Brit.* (1748) II. iv. 214 *Harrow*; the Church of which standing on the Summit of an Hill, and having a very high Spire, they tell us, King Charles II, ridiculing the warm Disputes . . . concerning the *Visible* Church of *Christ* upon Earth, used to say, This was it. **1790** G. ROSE s.v. Middx. The visible church; i.e. Harrow on the Hill. King Charles II, speaking on a topic then much agitated among divines of different persuasions, namely, which was the visible church, gave it in favour of Harrow on the Hill, which, he said, he saw, go where he would.

Visit(s), *see* Angel v.

Visor to hide an ill-favoured face, A well-favoured. (v 92)

1545 W. TURNER *Rescuing of the Romish Fox* I3ᵛ An old prouerbe, the Pope home agayn into our own dores, and that without a viser whereas yit he is partly covered. **1546** HEYWOOD II. i. F2ᵛ Many soon wishte, for beautifying that bryde, . . . Some well fauourd visor, on hir yll fauourd face. *c.* **1595** SHAKES. *R.J.* I. iv. 29 Give me a case to put my visage in. A visor for a visor! *Ibid.* II. iv. 102 My fan, Peter.—Good Peter, to hide her face; for her fan's the fairer face.

Vixere fortes ante Agamemnona see Brave men before A.

Voice is the best music, The. (v 94)

1616 BRETON *2 Cross.* A8 What Musique is sweet?—The voyce. **1639** CLARKE 57.

Voice of the people, the voice of God, The. (v 95)

a. **804** ALCUIN *Opp.* (Froben, 1777) cxxvii. t. I, p. 191 *Nec audiendi sunt ii qui volent dicere, vox populi vox Dei, cum tumultuositas vulgi semper insaniae proxima est. c.* **1378** GOWER *Mir. de l'Omme,* l. 12725 Au vois commune est acordant La vois de dieu. *c.* **1412** HOCCLEVE *Reg. Princes* E.E.T.S. 104, l. 2886 For peples vois is goddes voys, men seyne. **1575** GASCOIGNE *Posies* i. 143 Yet could I never any reason feele, To think *Vox populi vox Dei est.* **1738** POPE *Imit. Hor.* II. i. 89, 90 All this may be; the people's voice is odd, It is, and it is not, the voice of God. **1827–48** HARE *Gues. at Truth* (1859) i. 164 That *vox populi,* which, when it bursts from the heaving depths of a nation's heart, is in truth *vox Dei.* **1853** TRENCH vi. 130 The Latin proverb, *The voice of the people, the voice of God* . . . rests on the assumption that the foundations of man's being are laid in the truth. . . 'The general and perpetual voice of men is as the sentence of God himself.' [HOOKER *Eccles. Pol.* i, § 8.]

Voice, *see also* Pilate's v.; Pope by v.

Volunteer, One | is worth two pressed[1] men.

1705 LD. SEYMOUR in HEARNE *Collect.* 31 Oct. O.H.S. I. 62, 100 Voluntiers are better than 200 press'd men. **1834** MARRYAT *Jacob Faith.* ch. 13 'Shall I give you a song?' 'That's right, Tom; a volunteer's worth two pressed men.' **1837** CHAMIER *Saucy Areth.* ch. 3. Don't fancy you will be detained against your will; one volunteer is worth two pressed men. [[1] impressed for the King's or Government service.]

Vomit, *see* Dog returns to his v.

Vote, *see* Voyage never has luck where each one has v.

Vows made in storms are forgotten in calms. (v 97)

1530 PALSGRAVE 473b So long as the storme lasted he called upon God and all his saintes. **1639** FULLER *Holy War* II. xlvi. (1840) 114 The cardinals lamented out of measure. . . . But this their passion spent itself . . . , and these mariners' vows ended with the tempest. **1642** TORRIANO 52 The vow no sooner made, but the Saint deluded: Nota, As soon as the storm is over, God is no longer invoked, but neglected. **1732** FULLER no. 5408.

Vox populi, vox Dei, see Voice of the people.

Voyage never has luck where each one has a vote, That. (v 99)

a. **1585** MONTGOMERIE *Cherrie & Slae* li (1821) 28 'They say, that voyage never luckis, Quhar ilke ane hes ane vote.'

Voyage, *see also* Goes and comes makes good v. (He that); No man was ever . . . better from v.

Vulgar will keep no account of your hits, but of your misses, The.

1732 FULLER no. 4816.

W

Wabster, Jock, *see* Devil goes ower J. W.

Wade's Mill, *see* Ware and W. M.

Wading in an unknown water, No safe.
(w 1)

c. 1552 *Manifest Detection* Percy Soc. 6 Ye seem to be a man that wadeth not so unadvisedly in the deep, but that always ye be sure of an anchor hold. 1588 GREENE *Wks.* Gros. ix. 67 Wade not too far where the foorde is vnknowne. 1589 *Ibid.* vii. 160 Wade not there where the ford hath no footing. 1612 T. ADAMS *Wks.* (1616) 50. 1639 CLARKE 250. 1670 RAY 153. 1721 KELLY 261 (uncouth[1]). It is no Wisdom to engage with Dangers that we are not acquainted with. 1732 FULLER no. 3627. [[1] strange.]

Wae's[1] the wife that wants the tongue, but weel's the man that gets her.

1832 HENDERSON 64. [[1] woe's.]

Wag as the bush wags, He will.

1721 KELLY 140 (wags with him). That is, he will comply with all Changes of Times, and Parties.

Wage will get a page.

1721 KELLY 358 . . . If I be able to hire Servants I will get them to hire.

Wages, *see also* Good master shall have good w. (He that serves); Serves well, (He that) needs not ask w.

Wagging of a straw, To be angry at (laugh at, be afraid of the). *Cf.* Law for wagging of a straw.
(w 5)

[= ·a mere trifle.] *c.* 1374 CHAUCER *Troilus* Bk. 2, l. 1745 In titeryng, and pursuyte, and delayes, The folk devyne at waggyng of a stree. *c.* 1517 [1533] SKELTON *Magnif.* l. 1026 Wks. (1843) I. 258 Sometyme I laughe at waggynge of a strawe. 1520 WHITTINGTON *Vulgaria* 98 Of all the world I hate suche cowardes that . . . be aferde of euery waggynge of a strawe. 1530 PALSGRAVE 604a I can make hym laughe at the waggynge of a strawe. [*c.* 1553] 1566–7 UDALL *Ralph Roister D.* IV. vii. 47 G4 That tender heart of yours wyll marre altogether, Thus will ye be turned with waggyng of a fether. [1592] 1597 SHAKES. *Rich. III* III. v. 7 I can . . . Tremble and start at wagging of a straw. 1639 CLARKE 34 Angry at the wagging of a straw.

Wag(s), wagging, *see also* Afraid of w. of feathers; Law, (He will go to) for w. of straw; World w.

Waggoners, *see*·Parsons are souls' w.

Wagon, *see* Hitch your w. to a star.

Wags a wand in the water, He. (w 25)

1641 FERGUSSON no. 420 Of unprofitable foolish persons. . . .

Wagtail, *see* Makes his mistress a goldfinch.

Wain, *see* Charles's W.; Stone in the way overturns a great w., (A little).

Wait and see.

1839 DICKENS *N. Nickleby* ch. 55 'Very good, my dear', replied Mrs. Nickleby, with great confidence, 'Wait and see'. *Ibid.* ch. 63 [Mrs. N. again] 'Never mind; wait and see'. 1915–16 A phrase generally associated with Asquith as Premier at that date, a catchword from the legal chambers of Sir Henry James, where he worked. G. Robey in his song 'In Other Words' (Asquith supposed speaking): Remain inert and dormant just like me, and cultivate spontaneous quiescence, In other words, Wait and See! 1945 A. J. CUMMINGS in *News Chron.* 24 Aug. They [the Labour party in Parliament] are prepared to 'wait and see'.

Wait till you're asked.

1888 MRS. OLIPHANT *Second Son* ch. 14 'I have never been at a dance. . . . Oh, papa, let me go'. 'You had better wait till you're asked,' said the Squire.

Wait(s), *see also* Everything comes to him who w.; Pulls with a long rope that w. another's death; Wash my hands and w. upon you.

Wake not a sleeping lion. (L 317)

1581–90 *T. of Ath.* III. iii. To wake a sleeping lyon, what it is, I'le make thee knowe. 1593 SIDNEY *Arcadia* Feuillerat ii. 90 Not thinking it good to awake the sleeping Lyon. 1672 WALKER 13 no. 1 You will rave in a wasps nest; wake a sleeping Lion; bring an old house over your head.

Wake, *see also* Hope is but dream of those that w.; Sheep, swine, and bees, (He that has) sleep he w. he, he may thrive; Sorrow is asleep (When) w. it not.

Wakefield, *see* Merry W.

Waking men, *see* War must be waged by w. m.

Waldrons, *see* Clent (People of).

Wales, *see* Anglesea is the mother of W.; Knight of Cales; Powys is paradise of W.; Snowden sufficient pasture for all cattle of W.

Walk (*noun*), *see* Cock of w.; Fisherman's w.

Walk, drab, walk! *Cf.* Walk, knave, walk!

[= begone.] 1525 *Widow Edyth* 11th Jest (HAZLITT iii. 91) No man can tel, Where she is

become, with Walk queane walk. **1546** HEY-
WOOD II. iv. G4 Walke drab[1] walke. [[1] slut,
harlot.]

Walk groundly; talk profoundly; drink roundly; sleep soundly.

1562 HEYWOOD *Sixth Hundred of Epigrams*,
no. 29. **1869** HAZLITT 446.

Walk, knave, walk! *Cf.* Walk, drab, walk! (K 140)

[= begone] **1529** MORE *Dyaloge* I. xiv. 18b He
bad hym walk faytoure. **1530** TYNDALE *Pract.
Prelates* G vb The Cardinall bad him walcke
a vilayne. *c.* **1532** *Tales* no. 102 His enuyer
greatlye disdayninge sayde: walke knaue with a
myschiefe, where hast thou ben nourtered.
c. **1533** J. FRITH *Disp[n] of Purgatory* C2 If you se
a poore man shyuerynge for colde in the streete,
you may bydde hym walke a knaue and bere
hym in hande that he feeleth no harme. **1540**
Acolastus 116 This is wyne walke a knaue.
1546 HEYWOOD II. iv. G4 Nay (quoth she) walke
knaue walke Saieth that terme. *a.* **1558** *Jack
Juggler* l. 455 Pike and walke a knaue here a
waye is no passage. *c.* **1655** *Roxburghe Ballads*
Ballad Soc. vi. 211 'Walk, knave!' is a parrot's
note.

Walk much in the sun, They that | will be tanned at last. (S 972)

1553 T. WILSON *Arte of Rhet.* (1909) 5 They that
walke much in the Sunne, and thinke not of it,
are yet for the most part Sunne burnt. **1579**
GOSSON *Sch. Abuse* Arb. 59 We walke in the
Sun many times for pleasure, but our faces are
tanned before we returne: though you go to
theaters to se sport, Cupid may catche you ere
you departe. **1579–80** E. KIRKE Ded. of *Shep.
Cal.* in Spenser Wks. (Globe) 441 How could it
be, . . . but that walking in the sonne, . . . he
mought be sunburnt; and, having the sound of
those auncient Poetes still ringing in his eares,
he mought . . . hit out some of theyr tunes. **1670**
RAY 146.

Walk(s) *(verb)*, *see also* Goes (w.) softly w.
safely; Needles' points, (to stand (w.) on).

Walking over my grave, Some one is.

1738 SWIFT Dial. I. E.L. 286 Lord! there's somebody walking over my grave.

Walking with a horse in one's hand, It is good. (W 10)

[1588] **1591** LYLY *Endym.* IV. ii. 50 Why, is it not
saide: It is good walking when one hath his
horse in his hand? **1721** KELLY 196 . . . It is
good when a Man of any Art, Trade, or Profession, has an Estate to support him, if these
should fail. **1738** SWIFT Dial. II. E.L. 300 I
hear you are a great walker. . . .—No, . . . ;
I always love to walk with a horse in my hand.

Wallet, *see* Count not four unless in w.; Kingdom of a cheater (In the); See not what is in w.
behind; Staff and w., (To come to the).

Wallflower, *see* Faint at the smell of a w.

Walls have ears. *Cf.* Fields have eyes. (W 19)

1573 GASCOIGNE *Supposes* i. 189 The tables . . .
beds . portals, yea and the cupbords themselves
have eares . . . the windowes and the doores.
1591 ARIOSTO *Orl. Fur.* Harington XXII. 32 For
posts have eares, and walls haue eyes to see.
1594 *True Trag. Rich. III* l. 1103, E2[v] Hedges
haue eyes, and high-wayes haue eares. **1595**
SHAKES. *M.N.D.* V. i. 207 No remedy, my lord,
when walls are so wilful to hear without warning.
1600 *Look about You* G2[v] They say bushes haue
eares and eyes. **1620** SHELTON *Quix.* IV. vii. 53
They say Walls have ears. **1706** STEVENS s.v.
Pared.

Wall(s), *see also* Ball does not stick to the w.,
(If the); Bare w. make giddy housewives;
England's wooden w.; Flea stick in w., (Let
that); Further than the w. he cannot go; Hard
with hard makes not w.; Line to the w. (Bring
your); Look on the w. and it will not bite; Men
not w. make a city safe; Reward and punishment are the w. of a city; Run one's head
against w.; Taking the w. of dog (Not worth);
Weakest goes to w.; White w. fool's paper;
Writing on w.

Walnut-tree, *see* Plants a w.-t. expects not to
eat fruit (Who); Spaniel, a woman, and a w.-t.

Walsall, *see* Sutton.

Walsall man's goose, *see* Too much for one.

Walsingham, *see* Swear W.

Waltham, *see* Wise as W.'s calf.

Wame, *see* Lay your w. to your winning. *See also*
Weime.

Wand[1] ding[2] him, Let his own. (W 26)

1641 FERGUSSON no. 388 He is sairest dung when
his awn wand dings him. **1721** KELLY 233 . . .
Let him reap the Fruits of his own Folly. [[1] rod.
[2] beat.]

Wand, *see also* Small as a w.; Thraw the w. while
green; Wags a w. in the water.

Wane, *see* Beans in the w. of the moon, (Set).

Wanswell, *see* Maids in W. may dance in an
eggshell, (All the).

Want a pretence to whip a dog, If you | it is enough to say he eat up the frying-pan.

1706 STEVENS s.v. Perro If you want an excuse to
whip a Dog, it is enough to say he eats Iron . . .
Or in English, You need never want a Stick to
beat a Dog. **1732** FULLER no. 2794.

Want a thing (well) done, If you | do it yourself. *Cf.* Served (If you would be well) serve yourself. Thou thyself can do it.   (M 195)

1541 BULLINGER *Christ. State Matrimony* tr. Coverdale (1543) L4ᵛ If thou wylte prospere, then looke to euery thyng thyne owne selfe. **1611** COTGRAVE s.v. Attendre Nothing is well done where one altogether trusts vnto, or relyes vpon, another. **1616** DRAXE no. 1695 If a man will haue his businesse well done, he must doe it himselfe. **1858** LONGFELLOW *Miles Standish* ii That's what I always say; if you want a thing to be well done, You must do it yourself. **1902–4** LEAN IV. 3. **1927** *Times* 14 Nov. 15/3 Lastly there is the illustration of the great principle: if you want a thing done, do it yourself.

Want (wish) a thing done, If you | go; if not, send.   (B 750)

1666 TORRIANO *It. Prov.* 319 no. 2 Who will have a thing, let him go, who will not have it, let him send. **1743** FRANKLIN Nov. If you'd have it done, Go: If not, send. **1858** MRS. CRAIK *A Woman's Thoughts* ch. 2 'If you want a thing done, go yourself; if not send'. This pithy axiom, of which most men know the full value, is by no means so well appreciated by women.

Want in meat, What they | let them take out in drink.   (M 845)

1590 LODGE *Rosalynde* Hunt. Cl. 26 What they wanted in meat, was supplyed with drinke. **1597–8** SHAKES. *2 Hen. IV* V. iii. 28 What you want in meat we'll have in drink. [**1600**] **1631** T. HEYWOOD I *Fair Maid* ii. 280 The old proverbe, What they want in meate, let them take out in drinke.

Want is the worst of it.

1721 KELLY 347 . . . Spoken when one must take a mean Thing or want all.

Want of a nail the shoe is lost; For | for want of a shoe the horse is lost; for want of a horse the rider is lost. (W 29)

Cf. c. **1390** GOWER *Conf. Amantis* V. 4785 For sparinge of a litel cost Ful ofte time a man hath lost The large cote for the hod. **1629** T. ADAMS *Serm.* (1861–2) II. 359 The Frenchmen have a military proverb: 'The loss of a nail, the loss of an army.' The want of a nail loseth the shoe, the loss of a shoe troubles the horse, the horse endangereth the rider, the rider breaking his rank molests the company so far as to hazard the whole army. **1640** HERBERT no. 499. **1880** SMILES *Duty* 270 'Don't care' was the man who was to blame for the well-known catastrophe:— 'For want of a nail the shoe was lost, for want of a shoe the horse was lost, and for want of a horse the man was lost.'

Want of a wise man (wise men), For | a fool is set in the chair (fools sit on benches).   (W 30)

c. **1400** *Wisdom of Solomon* E.E.T.S. 23, l. 765 I saw ful set one segis of honore, and wysmen set one lawar segis. c. **1450** HENRYSON *Want of Wise Men* 16 Poems & Fab. (1845) 36 Sen want of wyse men makis fulis sitt on bynkis. *a.* **1628** CARMICHAELL no. 519 For falt of wise men fooles sits on binks. **1639** CLARKE 137. **1721** KELLY 105 For fault of wise Men Fools sit on Benks. Spoken when we see unworthy Persons in Authority.

Want of company, For | welcome trumpery.   (W 31)

1678 RAY 69. **1721** KELLY 54 After Company welcome Thrump'ry. Spoken by them who are not well pleas'd that you took not notice of them as soon as other Company. Or when People come to visit us that we care not for.

Want of money, want of comfort.
                                        (W 35)

1616 DRAXE no. 273. **1664** CODRINGTON 226. **1736** BAILEY *Dict.* s.v. Want.

Want of wit is worse than want of gear.

1721 KELLY 357.

Want the thing you have, You. (T 160)

1573 SANFORD 110ᵛ. **1629** *Bk. Mer. Rid.* Prov. no. 130.

Want when I have, and when I haven't too, I will not.   (W 36)

1666 TORRIANO *Prov. Phr.* s.v. Oro 124 To want when one hath, as well as when one hath not, to die for love, and starve in a Cooks shop. **1678** RAY 344 . . . *Somerset.* **1732** FULLER no. 2650 I will not want, when I have it; and have it not too.

Want will be my (your) master.

1738 SWIFT *Dial.* I. E.L. 278 Miss, I want that diamond ring of yours.—Why then, want's like to be your master. **1869** READE *Foul Play* ch. 50 Wylie . . . replied stoutly that it was pretty well known . . . what he wanted in that quarter. 'Well, then,' said Nancy, 'want will be your master. . . . Get out o' my sight, do.'

Want (*noun*), **see also** Abundance, like w., ruins many; Pride is as loud a beggar as w.; Save while you may (For age and w.); Waste makes w.; Wealth is best known by w.; Woe to w. (No); Worth of a thing known by w. of it.

Wanted me and your meat, If you | you would want one good friend. (M 821)

1641 FERGUSSON no. 552. **1721** KELLY 198 . . . Facetiously meaning, by the one good Friend, his Meat.

Want(s, ed) (*verb*), **see also** Leal folks never w. gear; Meat than guests or company, (Better to w.); Money has what he w., (He that has); Poor man w. some things, a covetous man all things; Rich enough that w. nothing; Shift to w. (It is no); Waste not, w. not; York, you're w.

Wanton as a calf (with two dams), As.

1576 LEMNIUS *Touchstone of Complexions* tr. T. Newton 97 As wanton as Calues. *Ibid.* 98 As wanton and toying as a yonge Calfe. **1678** RAY 290. **1880** BLACKMORE *Mary Aner.* ch. 13 Like the celebrated calf that sucked two cows, Carroway had drawn royal pay... upon either element.

Wanton kittens (may) make sober cats.

1732 FULLER no. 5415 Wanton Kitlins may make sober old Cats. **1832** HENDERSON 97 Wanton kittens mak douce[1] cats. [[1] sedate.]

Wants a mule without fault, He who | must walk on foot.

1599 MINSHEU *Span. Gram.* A3ᵛ (Let him be without her). **1706** STEVENS s.v. Mula. **1707** MAPLETOFT 50. **1854** R. SURTEES *Hand. Cross* ch. 17 'There is an old saying in Spain, that a man wot would buy a mule without a fault must not buy one at all, and faultless 'osses are equally rare.'

Wants in up and down, What she | she has in round about (to and fro). (w 38)

[L. *Quod alibi diminutum, exsequatur alibi.* What is wanting in one way may be made up in another.] **1666** TORRIANO *Prov. Phr.* s.v. Scarpe 183 The English say ... drollingly, What one loses in the Up and Down, to get it again in the Too and Fro. **1678** RAY 346. **1721** KELLY 346 What you want up and down, you have to and fro. Spoken to them who are low of Stature, but broad and squat.

Wants, *see also* **Want(s).**

War, All may begin a | few can end it.

1548 HALL 747–8. **1589** J. FREGEUILLE *Reformed Politic* 65 It is an easie matter to marke the time when warre beginneth, but it is not easie to know when it will end. [1592] **1596** *Ed. III* I. i. 119 Warre is soone begun, But not so quickely brought vnto an end.

War and physic are governed by the eye. (w 45)

1640 HERBERT no. 906.

War begins, When | then hell opens. (w 51)

1642 TORRIANO 87. **1651** HERBERT no. 1141. **1659** HOWELL *It. Prov.* 13.

War, hunting, and law (love), are as full of trouble as pleasure. (w 46)

1640 HERBERT no. 228 In war, hunting, and love, men for one pleasure a thousand griefes prove. **1670** RAY 28. **1732** FULLER no. 5416 War, Hunting, and Love have a thousand Troubles for their Pleasure.

War is death's feast. (w 47)

1611 COTGRAVE s.v. Feste Warre is the dead mans holyday. **1640** HERBERT no. 822.

War is not done so long as my enemy lives, The. (w 48)

1651 HERBERT no. 1051.

War is sweet to them that know it not. (w 58)

1539 TAVERNER 49ᵛ *Dulce bellum inexpertis.* Batell is a swete thynge to them that neuer assayed it. **1575** GASCOIGNE *Posies* i. 170 Yet proves it still ... That *war seems sweet to such as know it not.* **1587** HUGHES *et al. Misfort. Arthur* II. iii. 118 Warre seemeth sweete to such as haue not tried. **1621** BURTON *Anat. Mel.* III. ii. v. iii. (1638) 562 *Dulce bellum inexpertis,* as the proverb [Erasm.] is, 'tis fine talking of warre ... till it be tried. **1816** SCOTT *Antiq.* ch. 28 'A soldier! then you have slain and burnt, and sacked and spoiled?' ... 'It's a rough trade—war's sweet to them that never tried it.'

War is the sport (trade) of kings.

1691 DRYDEN *King Arthur* II. ii. (trade). **1907** A. T. QUILLER-COUCH *Mayor of Troy* ch. 5 'War is a terrible business'. 'It has been called the sport of kings', answered the Major.

War, In | it is not permitted twice to err. (w 43)

[ERASM. *Ad. Bis peccare in bello non licet;* said of Lamachus, PLUT. *Apoph. Reg.*] **1550** TAVERNER *Flowers* A8 It is nat lawfull in battell to make a faulte twyse. **1594** LIPSIUS *Six Bks. of Politics* tr. Jones Y2ᵛ [Cato apud Veget. I. 13.] **1606** CHARRON (1640 ed., 420) Faults may not twice bee committed in warre. **1777** JOHNSON in Boswell *Life* (1848) lxi. 564 Quoting the saying, '*In bello non licet bis errare*': and adding, 'this equally true in planting'.

War makes thieves, and peace hangs them. (w 49)

c. **1594** BACON no. 1535 La guerre fait les larrons et la paix les moines au gibbet. **1598** SIR R. BARCKLEY *Of the Felicity of Man* 370 The Italian hath a prouerbe; warres make theeues, and peece hangeth them vp. **1640** HERBERT no. 471. **1721** KELLY 358 ... This has relation to the Border Wars betwixt the two Nations, which was the great Nursery of Thieves. **1732** FULLER no. 5418.

War must be waged by waking men. (w 50)

1639 CLARKE 318. **1732** FULLER no. 5419 (Men asleep).

War(s), Of all | peace is the end. (w 55)

1399 GOWER *In Praise of Peace* 66 Wks. O.U.P. iii. 483 For of bataile the final ende is pees. **1609** HARWARD 127ᵛ The trew end of warrs is to enioy peace. **1612** SHELTON *Quix.* I. xi. ii. 32. **1641** FERGUSSON no. 675 Of all war peace is the finall end. **1721** KELLY 275 Spoken by them who would compose a Law Suit, or reconcile those who have had an Outfall.

War to the knife.

[= relentless war, after Sp. *guerra al cuchillo*.]
1812 BYRON *Ch. Har.* I. lxxxvi War, war is still
the cry, 'War even to the Knife!' **1842** MARRYAT
Perc. Keene ch. 18 He was . . . very strict about
the lights being put out. This was the occasion
of war to the knife between the midshipmen
and Mr. Culpepper. **1876** GLADSTONE *Relig.
Thought* in *Contemp. Rev.* June 7 'Catholicism'
has . . . declared war to the knife against modern
culture.

War with all the world, and peace with England.

1659 HOWELL *Span. Prov.* I With all the World
have War, But with England do not jar. Con
todo el Mundo guerra, Y paz con Ingalatierra.
1913 *Spectator* 20 Sept. 413 The sixteenth-
century Spaniards embodied a . . . maxim of
State policy . . . in the following distisch, . . .
'Con todo el mundo guerra Y paz con Inglaterra'.

War without a woman, No.   (w 44)

1639 CLARKE 117.

War(s), *see also* Advise none to . . . go to w.;
Clothe thee in w.; Just w. better than unjust
peace; Keeps his own makes w.; Love's w.;
Makes a good w., makes a good peace; Parthian
w.; Peace (He that will not have) God gives him
w.; Peace (In time of) prepare for w.; Preaches
w. is devil's chaplain.

Wardour-street English.

[**1861** TROLLOPE *Framley Pars.* ch. 8 The vast
hall [of Gatherum Castle] adorned with trophies
—with marble busts from Italy and armour from
Wardour Street. **1918** F. MUIRHEAD *London* 161
Wardour Street, once noted for . . . its spurious
antiques, extends from Coventry St. to Oxford
St.] **1888** A. BALLANTYNE in *Longm. Mag.* Oct.
585 (title) *Wardour-Street English. Ibid.* 589 This
is Wardour-Street Early English—a perfectly
modern article with a sham appearance of the
real antique about it. **1910** *Times Lit. Sup.* 18
Nov. Both this chapter and an excursion into
Wardour-street English in describing the book
trade in 1530, are blemishes in a book which is
otherwise written with taste and care.

Wardrobe, *see* Carries all his w.; Rogue's w. is
harbour for a louse.

Ware and Wade's Mill are worth all London.   (w 69)

[A play on the name *Ware*, a town in Herts., as
if it meant *goods*; 2 m. to the N. is the village of
Wade's Mill.] *a.* **1561** *Queen Hester* l. 566 By
Wade's Mill. **1588** A. FRAUNCE *Lawier's Logike*
f. 27 Ware and Wadesmill bee worth all London.
1662 FULLER Herts. 18 . . . This . . . is a Master-
piece of the Vulgar wits in this County. . . . The
Fallacy lieth in the Homonymy of Ware, here . . .
taken . . . appellatively for all vendible Commodities.

Ware (the) hawk.   (H 227)

[A phrase applied to an officer of the law, who
pounces upon criminals.] *a.* **1529** SKELTON

(title) *Ware the Hauke.* **1620** SHELTON *Quix.*
II. x. ii. 248. **1631** JONSON *Staple News* V. v.
56 See! the whole Couy is scatter'd, 'Ware,
'ware the Hawke. I loue to see him flye. **1673**
S' too him Bayes 31 But now ware hawk!

Ware, knave, quoth Tomkins to his shadow.

1583 MELBANCKE Rˣ . . . to whom hee gaue
many a good bang.

Wares be gone, When the | shut up the shop windows.   (s 394. W 68)

c. **1521** BARCLAY *Eclog.* IV. 493 Shet the
shopwindowes for lack of marchaundice. **1560**
T. BECON *Catechism* P.S. 396 There is no more
buying when the mart is done, and when the
shop-windows are shut up. **1605** CAMDEN 255-6
Sir Thomas More *loq.*: When the wares are
gone, and the tooles taken away, we must shut
vp shop. **1612** WEBSTER *White Devil* V. iv. 105
Now the wares are gone, we may shut up shop.
1639 CLARKE 119. **1670** RAY 153.

Ware(s), *see also* Good w. quick markets; Ill
w. never cheap; Market of his w., (He that
desires to make) must watch an opportunity
to open his shop; Pleasing w. half sold; St.
Martin's w.; Sell his w. after rates of market.

Warm as wool, As.   (W 751)

[1591] **1593** PEELE *Edw. I* II. ii. 99. **1639** CLARKE
286. **1692** R. L'ESTRANGE *Fables* 438, I. 411
A Vengeance on ye, says he, Y'are as warm as
Wooll.

Warm one in his armour, It is absurd to.   (A 320)

1640 HERBERT no. 775.

Warm, He that is | thinks all so.   (A 189)

1640 HERBERT no. 80.

Warm *(adj.)*, *see also* Clothe thee w.; Head and
feet keep w.; Lowly sit richly w.; Toast, (As hot
(w.) as a); Wise enough that can keep w.

Warms too near that burns, He.   (W 70)

1611 COTGRAVE s.v. Brusler Hee warmes· himselfe too neere that burnes himselfe. **1640**
HERBERT no. 815.

Warm(s) *(verb)*, *see also* Leg w. (While), boot
harms; See your house in flames (When), w.
yourself by it.

Warned folks may live. *Cf.* Threatened folks.   (F 429)

1578 Parts added to *Mirror for Mag.* ed. Campbell 441. **1639** CLARKE 202.

Warning(s), *see* Cassandra w.; Scarborough w.;
Rainbow in the morning; Sky red in the morning; Slain that had w.

Warp, *see* Make ab or w. of the business; Nose w., (To make).

War-path, To be (go) on the.

1775 ADAIR *Hist. Amer. Ind.* 396 I often have rode that war path alone. **1841** J. F. COOPER *Deerslayer* ch. 15 The great serpent of the Mohicans must be worthy to go on the warpath with Hawkeye.

Warrant you for an egg at Easter, I will. (E 75)

1577 [W. SAMUEL] *Art of Angling* A4. **1659** HOWELL *Eng. Prov.* 2b. **1670** RAY 214.

Warrant, *see also* Innocent actions carry w.; Wrong has no w.

Wars bring scars. (W 59)

1639 CLARKE 44. **1732** FULLER no. 6096. **1826** SCOTT *Woodst.* ch. 27 Myself am in some sort rheumatic—as war will leave its scars behind, sir.

Wars, He that is not in the | is not out of danger. (W 54)

1640 HERBERT no. 999.

Warsaw, *see* Order reigns at W.

Wash an Ethiop (blackamoor, Moor), white, To. (E 186)

[LUCIAN *Adversus Indoctum* 28 Αἰθίοπα σμήχειν ἐπιχειρῶ. I am endeavouring to wash an Ethiopian white. ERASM. *Ad. Æthiopem lavas* (or *dealbas*).] **1543** BECON *Early Wks.* P.S. 49 Here, therefore, do ye nothing else than, as the common proverb is, go about to make an Ethiop white. **1548** T. ELYOT *Bibliotheca* Aethiopem lauas, Thou wasshest a Mooren or Moore. **1621** ROBINSON 9 (Blackamoore). **1621** BRATH-WAITE *Omphale* (1877) 275 'To wash the Moore, is labouring in vaine, For th' colour that he h'as, is d'id in graine'. **1684** BUNYAN *Pilgr. P.* II. (1877) 336 They saw one *Fool* and one *Want-wit* washing of an Ethiopian with intention to make him white, but the more they washed him the blacker he was. **1799** WOLCOT (P. Pindar) *Postscript to Nil Admirari* (1816) III. 430 I have exhibited my imbecility in trying to wash the blackamoor white.

Wash dirty linen in public, To.

[= to give publicity to family disputes or scandals.] **1815** NAPOLEON *Speech* [on return from Elba] C'est en famille, ce n'est pas en publique, qu'on lave son linge sale. **1867** TROLLOPE *Last Chron. Barset.* ch. 44 Nothing ... so bad as washing one's dirty linen in public. **1886** E. J. HARDY *How to be Happy* ch. I Married people ... should remember the proverb about the home-washing of soiled linen. **1895** *Globe* 23 May People who ought to wash their dirty linen at home will not be satisfied with a less public laundry than Piccadilly. **1931** *Times* 3 Aug. 9/1 If the Government had made tactful ... representations ... to the Holy See, ... the whole matter could have been quietly settled without any washing of dirty linen in public.

Wash my hands and wait upon you, I will. (H 118)

[1600] **1659** J. DAY *Blind Beg.* ii. D2ᵛ I'll wash mine hands and wait on you [said in scorn]. **1678** RAY 353. **1738** SWIFT *Dial.* I. E.L. 279.

Wash one's face in an ale-clout, To. (F 19)

[= to get drunk.] *c.* **1549** HEYWOOD I. x. C4 As sober as she seemth, fewe daies come about But she will onece wasshe hir face in an ale clout.

Wash one's hands of a thing, To. (H 122)

[MATT. xxvii. 24 Pilate . . . took water, and washed his hands ... saying, I am innocent of the blood of this just person.] **1554** LADY JANE GREY *Words on Scaffold Harl. Misc.* III. 115 I wil wash my hands giltles thereof. **1572** G. FENTON tr. E. Pasquier *Monophyle* 8ᵛ I wype my handes of such iudgement. **1693** CONGREVE *Old Bachelor* ii. 179 Mony is but Dirt, Sir Joseph.—Mere Dirt.—But I profess, 'tis a Dirt I have washed my Hands of at present. **1838-9** DICKENS *N. Nickleby* ch. 49.

Wash out ink with ink, You. (I 76)

1616 WITHALS 563. **1639** CLARKE 197.

Wash their throats before they washed their eyes, Our fathers which were wondrous wise, did. (F 99)

1613 WITHER *Abuses* II. i Prethee let me intreat thee for to drinke. Before thou wash; Our fathers that were wise, Were wont to say, 'tis wholesome for the eyes. **1659** HOWELL *Eng. Prov.* 6a.

Wash your hands often, your feet seldom, and your head never. (H 124)

1574 G. GRATAROLUS *Direction for the Health of Magistrates and Students* tr. T. Newton E1ᵛ An olde sayinge, ... neuerthelesse for the moste parte vntrue, ... **1609** HARWARD 93 Hands, the physicians praecept, Ut tu sis sanus saepe lavato manus. **1670** RAY 38.

Washes an ass's head, He that | loses both his lye[1] (soap) and his labour. (A 370)

1578 FLORIO *First F.* 34 Who washeth an Asses head, loseth both labour and sope. **1592** LODGE *Euphues Shadow* (1882) 53 Who washeth the Asses eares, looseth both his Sope and his labour. **1639** CLARKE 155. **1659** TORRIANO no. 15 (looses his sope, and who preacheth in a wilderness, loseth his speech). **1672** MARVELL *Rehearsal Transprosed* Grosart ii. 6 Chi lava la testa al asino perde il sapone. **1789** WOLCOT (P. Pindar) *Expost. Odes* xiv To try to wash an ass's face, Is really labour to misplace; And really loss of time as well as sope. **1861** HUGHES *Tom B. at Oxford* ch. 23 Simon ... summed up ... by the remark that ''Twas waste of soap to lather an ass'. [¹ cleansing agent.]

Washing his hands, For | none sells his lands.   (w 75)

1611 COTGRAVE s.v. Laver Pour laver ses mains on n'en vend pas sa terre: Prov. Neuer did cleanlinesse any man vndoe. **1640** HERBERT no. 54.

Wash (*noun*), *see* Come right in the w., (It will all).

Wash(ing), (*verb*), *see also* Crow never whiter for w. often; Hand (One) w. another; Hand (One) will not w. another; Tile (To w. a).

Wasp's (hornet's) nest, To stir a.   (w 79)

1601 JONSON *Poetaster* 'To Reader' l. 71 What was therein it could . . . stirre so many hornets? **1648** H. C. DAVILA *Civil Wars of France* 675 The Queen . . . spoke this conceit in the Italian tongue: Bisogna coprirsi bene il viso inanzi che stuzzicare il bespaio. [margin] He that will stir up a Wasp's nest, had first need to cover his face well. **1659** HOWELL *Br. Prov.* 18 Down now with the wasps nest.

Wasp(s), *see* Angry as a w.; Quiet as a w. in nose; Women are like w. in anger.

Waste (Wilful waste) makes (woeful) want.   (w 81)

1576 R. EDWARDES *Par. Dainty Dev.* in *Brit. Bibliogr.* (1812) III. 88 For want is next to waste and shame doeth synne ensue. **1592** GREENE *Groatsworth* ed. Harrison 32 Till wast bring woe. **1721** KELLY 353 Wilful waste makes woe-ful want. **1732** FULLER no. 5423. **1835** J. M. WILSON *Tales of Borders* I. 202 She never suffered herself to forget . . . that . . . 'wilful waste makes woful want'.

Waste not, want not.

1772 J. WESLEY *Lett.* v. 334. He will waste noth-ing; but he must want nothing. **1796** EDGE-WORTH *Par. Asst.* (1903) 232 The following words . . . were written . . . over the chimney-piece in his uncle's spacious kitchen.—'Waste not, want not.' **1855** KINGSLEY *Westward Ho!* ch. 8 Waste not want not is my doctrine; so you and I may have a somewhat to stay our stomachs.

Waste (*noun*), *see also* Haste makes w.; Spend and be free, but no w.

Watch one as a cat watches a mouse, To.   (c 128)

c. **1534** *Bk. Merchants* E1 They haue a C. eyes euer open to watch as the cat for a mouse. **1563** *Mirror for Mag.* ed. Campbell 363 Which watched and wayted as duely for theyr pray, As euer dyd the Cat for the Mouse taking. **1570** TUSSER G3ᵛ The huswife . . . must tende on her profite as Cat on the Mouse. **1579–80** LODGE *Def. Poetry* Shaks. Soc. 44 As the catte watcheth the praye of the mouse, so dilygentlye intendes hee to the compassing of some young novice. **1602** WITHALS 65. **1623** HOWELL *Lett.* 10 July (1903) I. 186 It was no handsome comparison of Olivarez, that he watched her as a cat doth a

mouse. **1738** SWIFT *Dial.* III. E.L. 318 I am told, she watches him, as a Cat would watch a Mouse. **1853** G. J. WHYTE-MELVILLE *Digby Grand* ch. 2.

Watch (*noun*), *see* Constable in midsummer w.; Good w. prevents misfortune; Sure of your w. on deck (You are always); Wise man though you can't make a w.

Watch (*verb*), *see also* Good turn for it, (I will w. you a); Harm w. harm catch; Market of his ware, (He that desires to make) must w. an opportunity to open his shop.

Watched pot (pan) never boils, A.

1848 GASKELL *M. Barton* ch. 31. **1908** *Spectator* 12 Dec. 988 He remarks to himself that a watched pot never boils.

Water a stake (post), To.   (s 814)

[= useless labour.] **1636** S. WARD *Serm.* (1862) 107 Who waters a dry stake with any heart? What comfort hath Peter to pray for Simon Magus in the gall of bitterness? **1639** CLARKE 153 You bestow water on a gate-post. **1732** FULLER no. 5897 You do but water a dead Stake.

Water afar off quenches not fire.
                                          (w 116)

1586 GUAZZO ii. 145 Water a farre of doth not quench fier that is nigh. **1605** DANIEL *Philotas* I. i. Gros. 112 Water farre off quenches not fire neere hand. **1640** HERBERT no. 398.

Water bewitched.   (w 118)

[= excessively diluted liquor; now chiefly, very weak tea.] **1678** RAY 84 Water bewitch't. *i.e.* very thin beer. **1694** S. JOHNSON *Notes Past. Let. Bp. Burnet* I, Pref. 2 There was not one drop of Wine in it, it was all Water Bewitch't. **1699** T. BROWN *L'Estrange's Colloq. of Erasm.* Add. v. 53 The Broth was nothing in the world but Water bewitched [L. *mera aqua*], if it deserved so good a name. **1738** SWIFT *Dial.* I. E.L. 267 Your Ladyship is very sparing of your Tea; I protest, the last I took, was no more than Water bewitch'd. **1840** R. H. DANA *Two Years before the Mast* ch. 5 Hot tea (or, as the sailors significantly call it, 'water bewitched'). **1858** TRELAWNEY *Recollections* ch. 6 He [Byron] drank . . . a single glass of grog; which when I mixed it for him I lowered to what sailors call 'water bewitched'.

Water, fire, and soldiers, quickly make room.   (w 119)

1640 HERBERT no. 514. **1659** HOWELL *Eng. Prov.* 6b (and war).

Water (Blood, Milk) from a flint (stone), To get (wring).   (w 107)

a. **1542** WYATT *Defence* Wks. ed. Gilfillan, xxxii Thou shalt as soon find out oil out of a flint stone as find any such thing in me. **1559** COOPER s.v. Pumex A pumice aquam querere, To seeke a thynge of a man that he hath not. **1580** LYLY *Euph. & his Eng.* ii. 139 But if thou attempt

againe to wring water out of the Pommice, thou
shalt but bewraye thy falshoode, and augment
thy shame, and my seueritie. [*c.* **1591**] **1599**
[GREENE?] *George a Green* E4ᵛ Faith, I see it is as
hard to get water out of a flint, As to get him to
haue a bout with me. **1609** J. WYBARNE *New Age
of Old Names* 39 Skilfull to suche Milke out of
a Flint. **1666** TORRIANO 161 There's no getting of
bloud out of that wall. **1850** DICKENS *Dav. Cop.*
ch. 11 Blood cannot be obtained from a stone,
neither can anything on account be obtained . . .
from Mr. Micawber. **1855** MRS. GASKELL *North
& South* ch. 37 (milk out of a flint). **1881** A. JESSOP
Arcady 157 If these . . . Norfolk landlords have
no more than their land, you may as well try
to get blood out of a stone as try and make
them build houses for other people's labourers.

Water goes by the mill that the miller knows not of, Much.   (w 99)

1546 HEYWOOD II. v. H4ᵛ. **1592** SHAKES. *T.And.*
II. i. 85 What, man! more water glideth by the
mill Than wots the miller of. **1641** FERGUSSON
no. 618 Meikle water runs where the millar
sleeps. **1670** RAY 121. **1721** KELLY 256 . . .
That is, People who have much among their
Hands, will have Things broken, lost, and pur-
loyned, of which they will not be sensible. **1814**
HOGG to Byron 11 Oct. Muckle water rins while
the miller sleeps.

Water has run under the bridge since then, Much.

1927 *Times* 27 July 15/3 A good deal of water
has flowed under the Thames bridges since the
report of . . . last December.

Water his horse at Highgate, I will make him.   (H 669)

1678 RAY 86 . . . *i.e.* I'll sue him, and make him
take a journey up to London.

Water in a sieve, To carry (draw, fetch).   (w 111)

[ERASM. *Ad. Cribro aquam haurire.*] **1477** NOR-
TON *Ord. Alch.* i. in Ashm. (1652) 17 As he that
fetcheth Water in a Sive. **1509** BARCLAY *Ship
of Fools* i. 245 Wymen ar no kepars of councell
It goeth through them as water through a syue.
1589 GREENE *Menaph.* Arb. 48 Suppose she were
a Vestall, . . . shee might carie water with Amulia
in a siue. **1598–9** SHAKES. *M.A.* V. i. 5 Thy
counsel . . . falls into mine ears as profitless As
water in a sieve. **1602** *Id. A.W.* I. iii. 193 Yet,
in this captious and intenible sieve I still pour
in the waters of my love. **1686** HORNECK *Crucif.
Jesus* xxii. 741 That's no better, than taking up
water in a sieve. **1732** FULLER no. 5979 You
pour Water into a Sieve. **1764** A. MURPHY *No
One's Enemy* I. Wks. (1786) ii. 335 To trust him,
is taking up water with a sieve.

Water in a smith's forge, As | that serves rather to kindle than quench.   (w 87)

1535 J. FISHER *Serm. Good Friday: Eng. Wks.* 424
The colde water when it is cast into the Fyer,
causeth the Fyer to be much more fearse and
violent. **1576** PETTIE i. 154 But as the smith his

forge, by casting on cold water, burneth more
fiercely, so their love by those delays increased
more vehemently. **1579** LYLY *Euph.* i. 209 He
that casteth water on the fire in the smith's forge,
maketh it to flame fiercer. *c.* **1595** *Edmond
Ironside* l. 665 Cold water Cast on burninge
Coles doth make the fier more fervently to
flame. **1639** CLARKE 158.

Water in the sea, To seek.   (w 113)

1530 MORE *Dialogue* Bk. III, ch. 8 He that should
. . . study for that, should study where to find
water in the sea. **1666** TORRIANO *Prov. Phr.*
s.v. Acqua 1 . . . To do an easie business.

Water into a ship, As welcome as.
                                               (w 89)

1520 R. WHITTINGTON *Vulg.* E.E.T.S. 88. [*c.*
1553] **1566–7** UDALL *Ralph Roister D.* III. ii. Arb.
40 For it liked hir as well to tell you no lies, As
water in hir shyppe. **1580** LYLY *Euph. & his Eng.*
ii. 146 My counsell is no more welcome vnto
thee then water into a ship. **1641** FERGUSSON no.
450 Of untymous persons . . . He is as welcome
as water in a rivin ship.

Water into one's shoes, As welcome as.
                                               (w 126)

1621 R. BURTON *Anat. Mel.* II. II. i. ii. (1638) 236
401 To some men nothing can be more offen-
sive; they had better . . . pour so much water
in their shoes. **1659** HOWELL *Eng. Prov.* 11a.
1678 RAY 281.

Water into the sea (Thames), To cast.
                                               (w 106)

1377 LANGLAND *P. Pl.* B. xv. 332 And went
forth with that water . to woke with Themese
[= to moisten the Thames with]. **1509** BARCLAY
Ship of Fools i. 166 Or in the se cast water,
thynkynge it to augment. **1546** HEYWOOD I. xi.
E1 It is, to geue him, as much almes or neede
As caste water in Thems. **1590** SWINBURNE
Testaments Pref. I may be thought to powre
water into the Sea, to carry owles to Athens, and
to trouble the reader with a matter altogether
needlesse and superfluous. **1625** PURCHAS
Pilgrims (1905–7) II. 55 Foolishly do I further
pour water into this sea, into which Pope
Alexander's bull hath brought me. **1706**
STEVENS s.v. Villano.

Water is as dangerous as commodious.

1579 GOSSON *Sch. Abuse* Arb. 23. **1669** *Politeuphuia* 184.

Water is shallow, Where the | no vessel will ride.   (w 125)

1597 *Politeuphuia* 166. **1639** CLARKE 245.

Water is the eye of a landscape.

1902–4 LEAN IV. 175.

Water makes all clean, Fair.   (w 91)

1605–6 SHAKES. *M.* II. ii. 67 A little water clears
us of this deed. How easy is it then! **1616**

BRETON *Cross.* A5 Faire water makes all cleane. No, not a foule minde. **1639** CLARKE 66.

Water off (on) a duck's back, Like.

1533 MORE *Debellation* Wks. (1557) 762b Yet goeth euer thys water ouer this gooses backe, and for any thing that anye man can dooe, no man can make it synke vnto the skynne that she may once feele it, but euer she shaketh suche playn proues of with her fethers of Some say and they say the contrary. **1824** MAGINN *Maxims of Sir M. O'Doherty* (1849) 128 He only laughed . . . and the thing passed off like water from a duck's back. **1866** BLACKMORE *Cradock N.* ch. 39 Irony . . . antithesis . . . metaphor . . . all these are like water on a duck's back when the heart won't let the brain work. **1912** *Spectator* 20 July 82 No one would listen to our arguments. They fell like water off a duck's back.

Water stoups hold no ale.

1721 KELLY 339 . . . An Apology for not drinking strong Liquor, because we have not been accustomed to it.

Water trotted is as good as oats.

(w 124)

1640 HERBERT no. 131. **1867** *N. & Q.* 3rd Ser. XII. 488 . . . Giving a horse on a journey a drink of water, provided you trot afterwards, is as good as a feed of oats.

Water where the stirk[1] drowned, There was aye some.

1721 KELLY 309 . . . There was certainly some Occasion for so much Talk, Rumour, and Suspicion. [[1] a young bullock.]

Water will never reave the widdy, The, *see* Born to be hanged, He that is | will never be drowned.

Waterings, *see* St. Thomas à W.

Water(s), (*noun*), *see also* Beat w. in mortar; Beware of . . . still w.; Blood thicker than w.; Carries fire in one hand and w. in other; Cast not out the foul w. till; Christened with pump w.; Cost hot w. (It will); Deepest w. best fishing; Devil loves no holy w.; Draw w. to mill; Drink w. (Let none say I will not); Drop of· w. in sea (As lost as); Fire and w. (Go through); Fire and w. good servants; Fire and w. have no mercy; Fish do the w. (To love it as well as); Fish mars w.; Fish out of w.; Fishing in troubled w. (Good); Fools lade w.; Foul w. as soon as fair will quench; Go to the well against his will . . . w. will spill; Hole in the w.; House is burned down (When) you bring w.; King over the w.; Know the worth of w. till well dry (We never); Lay the stool's foot in w.; Linen often to w., soon to tatter; Look to (a person's) w.; Mill cannot grind with w. past; Mills will not grind if you give them not w.; Mix w. with fire; Moonshine in w.; Muckle w. rins while miller sleeps; Oil upon w.; Pour not w. on drowned mouse; Reeds (Where there are) there is w.; Ride the w. with (He is not man to); Salt w.

and absence wash away love; Sea complains it wants w.; Send him to the sea, he will not get w.; Still w. (Take heed of); Still w. run deep; Stolen w. are sweet; Too much w. drowns miller; Under w. famine; Unstable (false) as w.; Wading in unknown w. (No safe); Wind and w. (Shoot between).

Water(ing), (*verb*), *see also* Fools grow without w.; Green cheese (You see no) but teeth w.; Make one's mouth w.

Watering-pot, *see* Although it rain throw not away.

Watkin, Be good to.

[Ironical answer to an outrageous remark.] **1586** R. CROWLEY *Friar John Francis* A2ᵛ Bona verba queso. Good sir, be good to Watkin. What not any one freende amongst vs all?

Waveney, *see* Castle of Bungay.

Wavering as the wind, As.   (w 412)

c. **1500** Proverbs at Leconfield (*Antiq. Rep.* iv. 420) Vayne wordis unstedfast as the wynde. **1546** HEYWOOD II. i. F4 For in one state they twayne could not yet settyll. But waueryng as the wynde, in docke out nettyll. **1550** HEYWOOD *100 Epig.* no. LXX Whos wit like the winde hath been waueryng euer. [**1582**] **1589** *Love & Fortune* I. 168. [*c.* **1591**] **1595** *Selimus* I. 1682 (vnconstant). **1594–5** SHAKES. *R.J.* I. iv. 99 Which [fantasy] is as thin of substance as the air, And more inconstant than the wind. **1769** J. WESLEY *Letters* V. 152 Variable as the wind.

Wax, *see* Dog (man) of w.; Head of w. (He that has); Melt like w.; Nose of w.; Pliable as w.; Soft w. will take any impression.

Way is an ill neighbour, The.   (w 169)

1640 HERBERT no. 915.

Way of all flesh, The.   (w 166)

[JOSH. xxiii. 14 I am going the way of all the earth.] **1337–8** EDWARD III Doc. cited by J. Smyth *Lives of the Berkeleys* i 336 And so also for his own soule the day that hee shall goe the way of all flesh. *a.* **1557** *Jacob & Esau* l. 953 I must go the way of all mortall fleshe. **1605** MARSTON *The Dutch Courtesan* I. i. 88. **1606** CHAPMAN *Mons. D'Olive* I. i. 344 Send her the way of all flesh. **1607** DEKKER *Westward Hoe* D1. **1607–8** D. BARRY *Ram Alley* Hazl.-Dods. X. 282. **1609** DEKKER *Raven's Almanack* C3ᵛ. **1611** T. HEYWOOD *Golden Age* III If I go by land, and miscarry, then I go the way of all flesh. **1631** *Id. Fair Maid of West* II. IV. She . . . by this is gone the way of all flesh. **1776** FLETCHER OF MADELEY *Wks.* vii. 418.

Way to an Englishman's heart is through his stomach, The.

1845 R. FORD *Handbk. Spain* ch. 1 The way to many an honest heart lies through the belly. **1857** MRS. CRAIK *John Halifax* ch. 30 'Christmas dinners will be much in request'. 'There's a saying that the way to an Englishman's heart is through his stomach.'

Way to Babylon will never bring you to Jerusalem, The.

1732 FULLER no. 4819.

Way to be gone is not to stay here, The. (W 151)

1678 RAY 72.

Way to be safe is never to be secure, The. (He that is secure is not safe). (W 152)

1585 J. PRIME *Sermon in St. Mary's Oxon.* A7 Securitie makes fools. [**1603**] **1607** T. HEYWOOD *Woman Killed with Kindness* sc. viii, l. 218 And when they think they may securely play, They are nearest to danger. **1596** SHAKES. *Rich. II* II. i. 266 And yet we strike not, but securely perish. **1602** *Id. T.C.* II. ii. 14 The wound of peace is surety, Surety secure. **1605–6** *Id. K.L.* IV. i. 19 Full oft 'tis seen Our means secure us, and our mere defects Prove our commodities. **1605–6** *Id. M.* III. v. 32 And you all know security Is mortals' chiefest enemy. [*c.* **1613**] **1632** T. HEYWOOD 2 *Iron Age* IV. 410 Obserue it, they are still securest whom the Diuell driues to ruine. **1640** F. QUARLES *Enchyridion* IV. lxiii, Wks. i. 45. **1732** FULLER no. 2195 He that is too secure, is not safe. *Ibid.* no. 4820. **1748** FRANKLIN 25 He that's secure is not safe. **1780** 30 May JOHNSON *Lett.* (Chapman) ii. 364 Security will produce danger.

Way to heaven is alike in every place, The. (W 171)

[CIC *Tusc.* l. 43. 104 *Undique ad inferos tantundem viae est.*] **1516** MORE *Utopia* Arb. 30 *Undique ad superos tantundem est viae.* **1551** RALPH ROBINSON *Utopia* Arb. I. 30 The way to heauen out of all places is of like length and distaunce. **1583** J. PRIME *Fruitful & Brief Disc.* 122 The way to heauen is but single, and one and the same to all. **1669** PENN *No Cross, No Crown* xix To one bewailing himself that he should not die in his own country: 'Be of comfort', saith he,[1] 'for the way to heaven is alike in every place.' [1 Diogenes.]

Way to heaven is as ready by water as by land, The. (W 171)

[**1532**] ELSTOWE in Froude *Hist. Eng.* (1856) I. 373 Essex told them they deserved to be . . . thrown into the Thames. 'Threaten . . . rich and dainty folk . . .', answered Elstowe . . . 'we know the way to heaven to be as ready by water as by land.' **1570** G. TURBERVILLE *Epitaphs, Epigrams Songs & Sonnets* 129 As nie a way To Heauen as by Land they say. **1583** SIR HUM. GILBERT in Fuller Devon 261 A terrible Tempest did arise; and Sir Humphrey said cheerfully . . ., 'We are as neer Heauen here at Sea as at Land'.

Way to travel is towards heaven, The best.

1616 BRETON 2 *Cross. of Prov.* (1632) A6ᵛ. **1639** CLARKE 272.

Way to turn (him), He knows not which. (W 141)

1577 HOLINSHED (1587) iii. 190a The barons . . . knew not which way to turne them, nor how to seeke for releefe. **1616** DRAXE no. 547. **1639** CLARKE 248.

Ways of dressing a calf's head, There are many.

1902–4 LEAN IV. 145 There are many ways of dressing a calf's head (*i.e.* of showing your folly). At the Calf's Head Club it was served in every imaginable guise.

Ways to fame, There are many. (W 177)

1640 HERBERT no. 539.

Ways to kill a dog (cat) than hanging (choking her with cream), There are more. (W 156)

1678 RAY 127. **1721** KELLY 253 Many ways to kill a Dog, and not to hang him. There be many ways to bring about one and the same Thing, or Business. **1855** KINGSLEY *Westw. Ho!* ch. 20 (cat . . . cream).

Ways to the wood than one, There are more. (W 179)

1533–4 UDALL *Flowers* 163 (As we say prouerbially in englysshe) bene there no mo wayes to the wood but one? **1546** HEYWOOD II. ix. L1 What wife there be mo waies to the wood than one. [**1596**] **1605** *Stukeley* l. 302 There is a nearer way to the wood than all this. **1611** DAVIES *Prov.* no. 282. **1659** HEYLIN *Animadv.* in FULLER *Appeal Inj. Innoc.* (1840) 524 But there are more ways to the wood than one; and they had wit enough to cast about for some other way, since the first had failed them.

Way(s), *see also* Beggar never out of his w.; Block in another's w. (To lay a); Companion in a long w. (Man knows); Every man in his w.; Fair w. (To be in a); Farthest w. about, nearest w. home; Foul dirty w. (Take heed of); Good land, evil w.; Great w. to bottom of sea; Half the w. to know the w.; Leaves old w. for new; Lion in w.; Long w. long lies; Looks one w. and rows another; Love will find w.; Nearest w. commonly foulest; No w. but one with him; Once a w. and aye a w.; Parting of w.; Princes have no w.; Servant (A good) should never be in w. or out of w.; Stone in the w. overturns great wain (A little); Trick (W.) to catch the old one; Try all w. to the wood; Will (Where) there's a w.; Wrong w. to the wood (Go); Wrong w. to work (Go).

Waykenning, *see* Ill of his harbory good of w.

Wayside, *see* House built by w. too high or too low.

We hounds slew the hare, quoth the messan.[1] (H 737)

a. **1628** CARMICHAELL no. 1652. **1641** FERGUSSON

no. 880. **1721** KELLY 349 . . . Spoken to insignificant Persons, when they attribute to themselves any part of a great Atchievement. **1732** FULLER no. 5443 We Hounds killed the Hare, quoth the Lap-Dog. [¹ lap-dog.]

Weabley, *see* Lemster bread and W. ale.

Weak men had need be witty. (M 594)

1639 CLARKE 42.

Weak side, Every man has his. (M 118)

1692 L'ESTRANGE *Aesop's Fab.* cccxcii (1738) 415 Every man, in fine, has a weak side, if a body could but hit upon't. **1850** KINGSLEY *Alton Locke* ch. 24 But every man has his weak side; and . . . his was a sort of High-Church Radicalism.

Weak, *see also* Wiles help w. folk.

Weaker goes to the pot, The. (w 183)

1546 HEYWOOD II. v. H2 Where the smalle with the great, can not agree, The weaker goth to the potte, we all daie see.

Weaker has the worse, The. (w 184)

1481 CAXTON *Reynard* xiv. Arb. 31 Hit went with hem as it ofte doth the feblest hath the worst. **1546** HEYWOOD I. x. C2ᵛ But the weaker hath the wurs we all daie see. **1611** DAVIES no. 407 (The weake).

Weaker vessel, *see* Woman is.

Weakest goes to the wall, The. (w 185)

a. **1500** *Coventry Plays* E.E.T.S. 47 The weykist gothe eyuer to the walle. **1579** LYLY *Euph.* i. 201 He that worst may is alwaye enforced to holde the candell, the weakest must still to the wall. **1594–5** SHAKES. *R.J.* I. i. 17 That shows thee a weak slave; for the weakest goes to the wall. **1623** CAMDEN 279 The weakest goe to the walles. **1833** MARRYAT *P. Simple* ch. 5 You will be thrashed all day long . . .; the weakest always goes to the wall there. **1867–77** FROUDE *Short Stud., Cat's Pilg.* (1890) I. 645 My good Cat, there is but one law in the world. The weakest goes to the wall.

Weal and women cannot pan, but woe and women can. (w 189)

1639 CLARKE 118 Weale and women never sam, but sorrow and they can. **1678** RAY 355 *Northern Proverbs.* Weal and women cannot pan, i.e. *close together.* But woe and women can.

Weal (Well) or woe as he thinks himself so, A man is. (M 254)

1533 SIR T. ELYOT *Knowledge which maketh a Wise Man* M3ᵛ Nothing unto a man is miserable, but if he so think it. **1549** ERASM. tr. Chaloner *Pr. Folly* F3 For what hurteth the, the peoples hissing, as long as thou clappest thy selfe on the backe? **1573** J. CARDAN *Cardanus Comfort* tr. T. Bedingfield A8 A man is nothinge but his mynde: if the mynde be discontented, the man is

al disquiet though al the reste be well, and if the minde be contented though all the rest misdoe it forseeth little. **1591** NASHE *Pref.* Sidney's *Astr. & Stella.* iii. 332 So that our opinion (as Sextus Empiricus affirmeth) giues the name of good or ill to euery thing. **1596** SPENSER *F.Q.* VI. ix. 30 It is the mynd, that maketh good or ill, That maketh wretch or happie, rich or poore. **1597** *Politeuphuia* 60ᵛ There is nothing greeuous if the thought make it not. **1600–1** SHAKES. *H.* II. ii. 248 There is nothing either good or bad but thinking makes it so. **1604** *Id. O.* II. iii. 261 You have lost no reputation at all unless you repute yourself such a loser. **1639** CLARKE 125 A man may be happy if he will himself. **1721** KELLY 25 (well) . . . A contented Mind will sweeten every Condition, and a repining Heart will produce the contrary effects. **1732** FULLER no. 6312.

Weal pricks, Whom | sorrow comes after and licks. (w 190)

1636 CAMDEN 305. **1659** N.R. 125.

Weal without woe, No. (w 188)

a. **1400** *Le Morte Arthur* 1. 1891 Aftyr the welc to take the woe. *c.* **1470** MALORY ed. Vinaver iii. 1171 Ye shall take the woo wyth the weall. [*c.* **1470**] **1485** MALORY *Morte d'Arthur* xx. v. 804 We wil take the woo with the wele. **1578** FLORIO *First F.* 33. **1572** CRADOCKE *Ship of Assured Safety* 84 Our weale is neuer so welthy and well liking, but that stound mele it is enterlaced and wrapte with woe.

Weal, *see also* Worth no w. that can bide no woe.

Wealth is best known by want.

1631 DEKKER *Penny-wise, Pound-foolish* A3 Wealth is not regarded till we come to Beggerie. **1732** FULLER no. 5463.

Wealth, The greatest | is contentment with a little. (c 629. w 194)

1550 HEYWOOD *100 Epig.* LXXIV Is not the poore man riche, that is contented. **1565** W. WAGER *Enough* B1ᵛ A minde wel content, Is great riches as wise king Salomon dooth say. **1565** J. HALL *Court of Virtue* B1 He (sayth Seneca) is ryche and welthy, which is contented with his pouertie. **1567** *Trial of Treasure* D1ᵛ. **1616** DRAXE no. 349 Contentment is great riches. **1659** HOWELL *Eng. Prov.* 6b. **1670** RAY 28.

Wealth is like rheum, it falls on the weakest parts. (w 199)

a. **1633** HERBERT 'Confession' *Wks.* 126 God's Afflictions . . . are too subtill for the subt'llest hearts; And fall, like rheumes, upon the tendrest parts. **1640** *Id.* no. 475.

Wealth makes wit waver. (w 201)

a. **1628** CARMICHAELL no. 1646 (Welth gars¹). **1641** FERGUSSON no. 873 (as *a.* 1628). **1721** KELLY 340 . . . Spoken when People have many advantageous Offers, and are at a loss which to take. **1824** SCOTT *St. Ronan's* ch. 15. [¹ makes.]

Wealth makes worship. (w 202)

1616 BRETON *Cross.* A7ᵛ Wealth makes the worship of the world. **1639** CLARKE 99. **1732** FULLER no. 5464 (wants not for).

Wealth, *see also* Bear w., poverty will bear itself; Bring home w. of the Indies; Health better than w.; Knowledge makes one laugh, but w. dance; Little w. little care; Marries for w. sells liberty; Men get w. and women keep it; Wine and w. change wise men's manners; North for greatness, west for w.; Wisdom (Without) w. is worthless; Wit than w. (Better); World's w. (If we have not), we have ease.

Weapons bode (breed) peace. (w 206)

a. **1530** R. *Hill's Commonpl. Bk.* 13. 128 Wepin makith pese diwers times. *a.* **1575** J. PILKINGTON *Nehemiah* P.S. 436 (as the common saying is). **1609** HARWARD 125ᵛ (breed). *a.* **1628** CARMICHAELL no. 1640.

Weapons of war (Arms of England) will not arm fear, All the. (w 205)

1573 SANFORD 50ᵛ All the wepons of *Brescia* can not arme feare. **1578** FLORIO *First F.* 32 (of London). **1611** DAVIES no. 78. **1640** HERBERT no. 722 (Armes of England).

Weapon(s), *see also* Beat one at one's own w.; Conquering w.; Necessity is hard w.; Wight man never wanted w.; Wise man never wants w.

Wear a horn and blow it not. (H 618)

15th c. GREENE *Early Eng. Carols* 234 I hold hym wyse and wel itaught Can bar an horn and blow it naught. **1571** R. EDWARDES *Damon & Pithias* F3ᵛ I can weare a horne and blow it not. **1639** CLARKE 142. **1691** W. SEWEL 233 He cannot Hold a horn in his mouth but must blow it.

Wear clothes, Ever since we | we know not one another. (C 435)

1640 HERBERT no. 168. **1667** MILTON *P.L.* iv. 740 These troublesome disguises which we wear.

Wear like a horseshoe, the longer the brighter, She will.

1721 KELLY 300 . . . Spoken of ill-coloured Girls who they hope will clear up when they are married.

Wear the willow, To. (w 403)

[= to mourn loss or absence of one's beloved, formerly indicated by a garland of willow leaves.] *c.* **1550** HEYWOOD in J. O. Halliwell's edn. of *Wit & Science* 87 All a grene wyllow is my garland. **1563** B. GOOGE *Eglogs* vi. Arb. 52 Let Wyllows wynde aboute my hed (a Wrethe for Wretches mete). **1591** SHAKES. *3 Hen. VI* III. iii. 228 Tell him . . . I'll wear the willow garland for his sake. *Ibid.* IV. i. 100. **1598–9** *Id. M.A.* II. i. 193 I offered him my company to a willow tree, . . . to make him a garland, as being forsaken. **1604** *Id. O.* IV. iii. 49 Sing all a green willow must be my garland. **1884** BLACKMORE *Tommy Up.* ch. 33 You are quite wrong . . . in supposing that I have any call . . . to wear the willow. . . . Miss Windsor . . . never has been to me more than a bubble.

Wears a whole lordship on his back, He. (L 452)

1576 GASCOIGNE *Steel Glass* ii. 173 On their backs, they beare . . . Castles and Towres, revenewes and receits, Lordships, and manours, fines, yea fermes and al. **1580** LYLY *Euph. & his Eng.* ii. 121 An other layeth all his lyuing vppon his. backe. **1588** W. AVERELL *Combat of Contrarieties* B4 I will not say the Backe is a Monster, that can carrie vppon his shoulders, Landes, Castles, and Towns. *c.* **1590** SHAKES. *2 Hen. VI* I. iii. 78 She bears a duke's revenues on her back. [*c.* **1590**] **1605** *King Leir* II. iii. 27 Sheele lay her husbands Benefice on her back, Euen in one gowne, if she may haue her will. [**1592**] **1594** MARLOWE *Edw. II* l. 737 He weares a lords reuenewe on his back. **1596** SHAKES. *K.J.* II. i. 69 Have sold their fortunes at their native homes, Bearing their birthrights proudly on their backs, To make a hazard of new fortunes here. **1599** *Id. A.Y.* II. vii. 74 What woman in the city do I name, When that I say the city woman bears The cost of princes on unworthy shoulders? **1613** *Id. Hen. VIII* I. i. 83 O, many Have broke their backs with laying manor on 'em For this great journey. **1639** CLARKE 262.

Wears black must hang a brush at his back, He that. (B 437)

1639 CLARKE 201. **1670** RAY 63. **1732** FULLER no. 6298.

Wears the breeches, She. *Cf.* Master (Most) wears no breech. (B 645)

[= where the wife rules the husband.] **1567–8** T. HOWELL *New Sonnets: Poems* 151 He is a cokes: and worthy ·strokes, whose wife the Breeches beare. **1591** SHAKES. *3 Hen. VI* V. v. 26 That you might still have worn the petticoat, and ne'er have stol'n the breech from Lancaster. **1592** GREENE *Quip for Upstart Courtier* Gros. xi 219 I saw a great many of women vsing high wordes to their husbandes; some striuing for the breeches. **1606** *Choice, Chance & C.* (1881) 22 She that is master of her husband must weare the breeches. **1666** TORRIANO *Prov. Phr.* s.v. Marito 100 To make him [her husband] subject unto her, to wear the breeches. **1807** W. IRVING *Salmag.* (1824) 102 The violent inclination she felt to wear the breeches.

Wears the bull's feather, He. (B 717)

1533 *Ballads from MSS.* B.S. i. 199 Lyke cokold foles to-gether. . . we wer an oxes fether. **1662** J. WILSON *The Cheats* II. iv Let no man disorder his rest, By believing bull's feathers in's crest. **1678** RAY 67 . . . This· is a French Proverb, for·a cuckold.

Wear(s, ing), *see also* Better to w. out than rust out; Better w. out shoes than sheets; Blade w. out scabbard; Break or w. out (If things did not); Cap fits (If· the) w. it; Everything is worse for w.; Gown is his that w. it; Iron shoes,

(He should w.) . . .; Wedding ring w., (As), cares will w. away; Wide will w., narrow will tear; Win and w.

Wearies, *see* Does well (He that) w. not.

Weary (-iest),·*see* Burden makes w. bones, (Too long); Every one is w.; Giff gaff was a good fellow; Go a long way w. (One can); Never be w. of well doing; Ox when w. treads surest.

Weasel and the cat make a marriage, When the | it is a very ill presage.
(W 212)

1678 RAY *Adag. Hebr.* 406 . . . When evil men, who were formerly at variance, and are of great power, make agreement, it portends danger to the innocent. . . . Thus upon the agreement of *Herod* and *Pilot* the most innocent bloud is shed.

Weasel, *see also* Catch a w. asleep.

Weather is ill, No | if the wind be still.
(W 220)

c. **1593** SHAKES. *L.L.L.* IV. ii. 31 Many can brook the weather that love not the wind. **1623** CAMDEN 279. **1639** CLARKE 263. **1670** RAY 42.

Weather meet to set paddocks[1] abroad in.
(W 222)

1546 HEYWOOD I. xiii. F2 We haue had . . . Weather, meete to sette paddockes[1] abroode in. Rain, more than enough. [1 toads, frogs.]

Weather, Take the | as it comes.

1349 *The Papelard Priest* ed. A. H. Smith in *London Med. Studies* ii. l. 86 Take þe wedur as hit cometz, cloudi and clere.

Weather, *see also* After black clouds clear w.; April w. rain and sunshine; Calm w. in June; Change of w. discourse of fools; Child (To a) all w. is cold; Clerk of the w.; Cock moult before hen; Cold w. . . . come out of north; Come wind, come w.; Fair w.; Farewell frost, fair w. next; Field requires three things; fair w., etc.; Leeward for fine w. (Look not to); March many w.; Queen's w.; Sorrow and ill w. come unsent for; Wind and w. do thy worst.

Weathercock in the wind, Like a.
(W 223)

c. **1340** *Ayenbite of Inwyt* E.E.T.S. 180 Hi byeth ase the wedercoc that is ope the steple, thet him went mid eche wynde. *c.* **1386** CHAUCER *Clerk's T.* l. 996 O stormy peple! unsad and evere untrewe! Ay undiscreet and chaungynge as a vane. *c.* **1475** *Mankind* l. 742. **1558** E. P. Pref. to T. Cranmer *Refut*[n] *Unwritten Verities* C5 [margin] These are wauering redes, and perfecte wether ·ockes, that turne with euery winde. **1580** LYLY *Euph. & his Eng.* ii. 98. **1621** ROBINSON 35 He is as fickle as the Weather-cocke. *c.* **1641** FERGUSSON MS. no. 713 He is lyk ane widder cok in the wind. **1655** FULLER *Ch. Hist* V. ii. 48 As wavering as the Weather-cock.

Weathercock, *see also* Woman is a w.

Weather-eye, *see* Keep your w. open.

Weavers' beef of Colchester, The.
(W 224)

1662 FULLER Essex 320 . . . These are Sprats, caught hereabouts, . . . in incredible abundance, whereon the poor Weavers (numerous in this City) make much of their repast, . . . as lasting in season well nigh a quarter of a year.

Weaver(s), *see also* Devil would have been w. but for Temples; Put a miller, a w. . . . in a bag, first that comes out will be thief.

Web of a bottle[1] of hay, It is hard to make a good.
(W 225)

c. **1640** W.S. *Countrym. Commonw.* I A strong web [is never made] of a bottell of hay. **1670** RAY 154. [1 bundle.]

Web (Weft), *see also* Devil is subtle, yet weaves coarse w.; Ill-spun w. will out; Penelope's w.

Webster(s), *see* Need makes . . . and sorrow makes w. spin; Sorrows gars w. spin.

Wed(s), *see* Better w. over the mixen; Early w. early dead; More folks are w. than keep good houses; Nought is to w. with (Where) . . . flee the clog; Old man who w.; Wiser now you're w.; Woo where he will, w. where his hap is.

Wedded to one's will, To be.
(W 392)

1546 HEYWOOD II. XI. M1 I was wedded vnto my wyll. How be it, I will be deuorst, and be wed to my wyt. **1548** HALL 756 The king . . . knewe well, that the queene was wedded to her owne opinion. **1594–5** SHAKES. *L.L.L.* II. i. 209 Is she wedded or no?—To her will, sir, or so.

Wedding begets another, One.
(W 231)

c. **1634** M. PARKER *Wooing Maid* Roxb. Bal. iii. 54 'Tis said that one wedding produceth another. **1713** GAY *Wife of Bath* I. i One Wedding, the Proverb says, begets another. **1848** DICKENS *Dombey & Son* ch. 31 One wedding makes many. **1929** *Daily Mail* 19 Sept. 10/2 It is apparent that weddings do breed weddings, and that bridesmaids are particularly apt to find themselves early involved in matrimony.

Wedding ring wears, As your | your cares will wear away.
(W 233)

1678 RAY 344. *Somerset.* **1732** FULLER no. 6146 You'll wear off your Cares.

Wedding (*adj.*), *see also* Wife down in her w. shoes, (To take a).

Wedding, (*noun*), *see also* After a dream of a w.; Hanging and w. go by destiny; Never but once at a w.; Wooing was day after w.

Wedge, There goes the | where the
beetle drives it.   (w 235)

a. **1637** JONSON *Tale Tub* I. v. 25 The Beetle and
Wedges will, where you will heve 'hem. **1678**
RAY 216. **1732** FULLER no. 4869.

Wedge(s), *see also* Fool that makes a w. of fist;
Knotty timber must have sharp w.; Thin end of
w.

Wedlock is a padlock.   (w 236)
1678 RAY 56. **1732** FULLER no. 6261.

Wedlock, *see also* Age and w. tames.

Weed amongst corn nor suspicion in
friendship, Neither.   (w 239)

a. **1530** *Calisto & Melibea* l. 462 Wedes among
corn Nor suspecions with fryndes dyd neuer
well. **1616** DRAXE no. 1066. **1659** HOWELL
Span. Prov. 1 Nor weeds in thy corn, nor
scruples in thy friend.

Weeding, *see* One year's seeding.

Weeds overgrow the corn, The. (w 242)

c. **1450** *MS. Harl. 5396* in *Reliq. Antiq.* (1843)
II. 240 Therfor eny man may care, Lest the wede
growe over the whete. *a.* **1534** *Hyckscorner*
545 Lo, lordes, they may curs the tyme they
were borne For the wedes that over-groweth the
corne. **1641** FERGUSSON no. 794 (overgaes).
1721 KELLY 319 . . . The bad are the most
numerous.

Weeds want no sowing.   (w 243)
1659 N. R. 127 You need not sow weeds. **1732**
FULLER no. 5466.

Weed(s), *see also* Bites on every w.; Fat land
grow w. (On); Garden without w.; Ill w. grow
apace; Ill w. mars a whole pot; Sussex w.

Week, *see* Friday and the w.; In by the w., (He
is); Thursday come and w. is gone.

Weel bides, weel betides.   (B 343)
a. **1628** CARMICHAELL no. 1616. *c.* **1641** FERGUS-
SON MS. no. 1475.

Weel kens the mouse (when) the cat's
out of the house.   (M 1239)

a. **1628** CARMICHAELL no. 1645 (Weill wat the
mouse). **1641** FERGUSSON no. 878 (as *a.* 1628).
1721 KELLY 342. **1821** J. GALT *Annals of Parish*
ch. 37 I saw that it would be necessary . . . for
me to take another wife . . . on account of the
servant lasses, who grew out of all bounds,
verifying the proverb, 'Well kens the mouse,
when the cat's out of the house'.

Weel's him and wae's him that has a
bishop in his kin.   (B 410)

1530 PALSGRAVE 458a He never felte wo or
never shall blynne, that hath a bysshoppe to his

kynne. **1574** J. BALE *Pageant of Popes* tr. J.
Studley 143ᵛ The old saying: Cum moritur
praesul, cognatio tota fit exul. When as a prelate goes awaye, then all the kindred do decaye.
a. **1628** CARMICHAELL no. 1670. **1641** FERGUSSON
no. 889. **1721** KELLY 347 . . . Because such may
be advanc'd, and perhaps disappointed.

Weening is not measure.   (w 246)
1640 HERBERT no. 811.

Weep for joy is a kind of manna, To.
(J 87)

1596 SHAKES. *M.A.* I. i. 26 How much better is
it to weep at joy than to joy at weeping. **1605–6**
Id. M. I. iv. 33 My plenteous joys, Wanton in
fulness, seek to hide themselves In drops of
sorrow. **1640** HERBERT no. 462.

Weep Irish, To.   (w 247)

[= to feign sorrow.] **1577** STANYHURST in Holinshed *Descr. Irel.* (1587), 44b They follow the
dead corpse to the graue with howling and
barbarous outcries . . .; whereof grew, as I
suppose, the prouerbe: To weepe Irish [orig.
Hibernice lacrimari]. **1612** WEBSTER *White
Devil* IV. ii. What! dost weep? Procure but ten
of thy dissembling trade, Ye'd furnish all the
Irish funerals With howling past wild Irish.
1681 ROBERTSON *Phraseol. Gen.* 1305 To weep
Irish, or to feign sorrow.

Weep (Drop) millstones, To.   (M 967)

[= said of a hard-hearted person.] *c.* **1400**
Beryn Prol. l. 35 Teris . . . As grete as eny
mylstone. **1587** J. BRIDGES *Defence of the Govt.*
3 All their chiefest mourning and lamentation
is for this, if indeed they weepe and mourne at
all, and that euery teare be not (as they say) as
big as a milstone. [**1592**] **1597** SHAKES. *Rich. III*
I. iii. 353 Your eyes drop millstones, when fools'
eyes fall tears. *Ibid.* I. iv. 236 He will weep.—
Ay, millstones. **1602** *Id. T.C.* I. ii. 137 Queen
Hecuba laughed that her eyes ran o'er.—With
millstones. **1632** MASSINGER *City Madam* IV. iii.
Merm. 469 He, good gentleman, Will weep
when he hears how we are used.—Yes, millstones. **1820** SHELLEY *Oed. Tyr.* 334 And
every tear turned to a millstone.

Weeping come into the world, We | and
weeping hence we go.   (w 889)

1576 H. KERTON ded. to Innocent III *Mirror of
Man's Life* ¶3 Wee lamente in firste minute, and
rewe to the laste moment. **1590** SIDNEY I
Arcadia III. xii. i. 227 The man that feeling
knowes, with cries first borne, the presage of
his life. **1605–6** SHAKES. *K.L.* IV. vi. 179 We
came crying hither; Thou know'st, the first time
that we smell the air We wawl and cry. **1666**
TORRIANO *It. Prov.* 115 no. 30 Man comes into
the World weeping, lives laughing, and dyes
sighing.

Weeping Cross, To go home by. (w 248)

1564 BULLEIN *Dial. agst. Fever* E.E.T.S. 78 In
the ende thei go home . . . by weepyng cross.
1579 GOSSON *Sch. Abuse* Arb. 46 They . . .
returne home by weeping Crosse, and fewe of
them come to an honest ende. **1603** MONTAIGNE

(Florio) III. v. 108 Few men have wedded their . . . paramours or mistresses, but have come home by weeping Crosse. **1659** HOWELL *Eng. Prov.* 3b. **1670** RAY 199 . . . This weeping cross which gave occasion to this phrase, is about two miles distant from the town of Stafford.

Weep(s, ing), *see also* Better children w. than old men; Englishman w.; Learn w. shall gain laughing; See a woman w. (No more pity than goose go barefoot); Sorry for you, but cannot w.; Trust not a woman when she w.; Women laugh when they can, and w. when they will.

Weevil in a biscuit, Like a.

1899 A. T. QUILLER-COUCH *Ship of Stars* ch. 13 Suppose you put me to work in the vestry? There's only one window . . . : you can block that up with a curtain, and there I'll be like a weevil in a biscuit.

Weigh justly and sell dearly.   (w 250)

1573 SANFORD 109 Make iust waight and sell deere. **1578** FLORIO *First F.* 33 Weigh iust, and sel deere. **1640** HERBERT no. 500.

Weigh(s), *see also* Carries well to whom it w. not.

Weight and measure take away strife.
                                                  (w 254)

1640 HERBERT no. 213. **1721** KELLY 247. **1732** FULLER no. 5468 Weight, Measure, and Tale take away Strife.

Weight(s), *see also* Great w. on small wires; Knows the w. of another's burden (None); Worth one's w. in gold.

Weime,[1] That which is in my | is not in my testament.

1721 KELLY 324 . . . An Excuse for eating rather than keeping what is before us. [[1] belly.]

Weird (*noun*), *see* Old wife that wats her w.; Shape coat and sark (We can) but not w.

Welcome death, quoth the rat, when the trap fell down.   (D 159)

1659 HOWELL *Eng. Prov.* 10a. **1732** FULLER no. 5469.

Welcome evil (mischief), if thou comest alone.   (E 205. I 32)

1595 COPLEY *Wits, Fits* v. 144 One vsed to compare follies to mischances, for that they seldome come alone: And therefore whensoeuer hee sawe any man doe or say a follie, he would stil say: Wel fare it if it come alone. **1620** SHELTON *Quix.* II. lv. iii. 206 I . . . think that every moment I shall fall into a deeper profoundity than this former, that will swallow me downright. 'Tis a good ill that comes alone. **1640** HERBERT no. 140. **1706** STEVENS s.v. Mal (mischief). **1732** FULLER no. 5471 (mischief).

Welcome fares well, He that is.

a. **1628** CARMICHAELL no. 715. **1641** FERGUSSON no. 309. **1721** KELLY 158 . . . An Apology for giving to, or receiving from, a hearty Friend, an ordinary Entertainment. **1736** BAILEY *Dict.* s.v. Welcome.

Welcome is the best cheer.   (w 258)

[Gk. Ξενίων δέ τε θυμός ἄριστος. In hospitality it is the spirit that is the chief thing.] *c.* **1430** LYDGATE *Isopes* E.E.T.S. l. 434 As men seyen & reporte, at þe leste, Nat many deyntees, but good chere makeþ a feste. *c.* **1550** HEYWOOD'S poem in J. O. Halliwell's ed. *Wit & Science* 112 Welcum is the best dysh. **1578** G. WHETSTONE I *Promos and Cassandra* III. vi. D4ᵛ Your good welcome Sir, your best cheere will be. **1584** R. WILSON *Three Ladies of London* Hazl.-Dods. vi. 290 Welcome, thy best fare. **1590** H. R. *Defiance to Fortune* D1 Your cates shall not be dainty, homelie, cleanly, and welcome your principal dish. **1592–3** SHAKES. *C.E.* III. i. 21 I hold your dainties cheap, sir, and your welcome dear. *Ibid.* III. i. 26 Small cheer and great welcome makes a merry feast. **1611** COTGRAVE s.v. Chere A heartie welcome is worth halfe a feast. **1670** RAY 154. **1721** KELLY 349 Welcome is the best Dish in the Kitchen.

Welcome, Such | such farewell.   (w 256)

1546 HEYWOOD II. vii. I4. **1639** CLARKE 288.

Welcome that bring, They are.

a. **1628** CARMICHAELL no. 1481. **1641** FERGUSSON no. 797. **1642** TORRIANO 10 He who bringeth ought, findeth the door open. **1659** HOWELL *It. Prov.* 8 He is welcome who brings something. **1841** MARRYAT *Mast. Ready* ch. 46 We do not go back empty-handed, and therefore, as the saying is, we shall be more welcome.

Welcome when you go.   (w 259)

1546 HEYWOOD II. vii. I3ᵛ Welcome when thou goest . thus is thine errand sped.

Welcome, *see also* Bold than w. (More); Breams in his pond . . . friend w.; Come and w.; Eat and w.; Ewe and a lamb (Now I have) everyone cries w. Peter.

Welcome as, *see* Flowers in May; Snow in harvest; Storm; Water into a ship; Water into one's shoes.

Well and them cannot, then ill and them can, If.   (w 267)

1670 RAY 155. *Yorks.*

Well begun is half done (ended). *Cf.* Good beginning.   (B 254)

[HORACE *Ep.* I. 2. 40 *Dimidium facti, qui coepit, habet.* He who has made a beginning, has half done.] *a.* **1500** *15c. School.-Bk.* ed. Nelson 21 It was a noble saying of Aristotle: Begynnynge is more than halfe the worke. **1539** TAVERNER 9 *Principium dimidium totius.* The begynnynge is halfe the hole. **1548** W. PATTEN *Exped[n] into*

Scotland (Tudor Tracts 143) They say, 'a match well made, is half won'. **1597** BACON *Col. of G. & E.* 10 (Arb.) 153 Hence grew the common place of extolling the beginning of euery thing, Dimidium qui bene coepit habet. **1642** D. ROGERS *Naaman* ix. 256 A work well entered is truly said to be half done. **1908** ALEX. MACLAREN *Acts* I. 176 Satan spoils many a well-begun work. . . . Well begun is half—but only half—ended.

Well doing, *see* Never be weary of w. d.

Well done is twice (ever) done, That which is. (T 153)

1530 PALSGRAVE 648b The thyng that is well doone is twyse done, and the thyng that is yeull done muste be begon agayne. **1548** W. PATTEN *Exped^n into Scotland* (Tudor Tracts 127) We well remembered that ·a thing once well done, is twice done. **1606** DAY *Ile of Gulls* V For, saies my mother, a thinge once wel done is twice done. **1630** J. TAYLOR *Wks.* L5ᵛ When a thing is well done (tis an old saying) it is twice done. **1658** E. WILLIAMSON *J. Cleaveland Revived* (1668) A3 There is a saying, Once well done, and ever done. **1659** HOWELL *Eng. Prov.* 9a. **1670** RAY 154. **1732** FULLER no. 4381.

Well fare nothing (nought) once a (by the) year. (N 335)

1597 DOWLAND *First Bk. Songs or Airs* in *Eng. Garn.* iv. 48 If doubt do darken things held dear, Then Well fare nothing! once a year. **1600** *Weakest to Wall* B3. **1639** J. SMITH of Nibley Berkeley MSS. 30, no. 38 (ffaire fall nothinge). **1639** CLARKE 244 Well fare nought once by the yeere. **1659** HOWELL *Eng. Prov.* 18b . . . For then he is not subject to plundering. **1678** RAY 182 Fair fall nothing once by the year. It may sometimes be better to have nothing then something. So said the poor man, who in a bitter snowy morning could lie still in his warm bed, when as his neighbours who had sheep·and other cattel, were fain to get up betimes and abroad, to look after and secure them.

Well-favoured, *see* Visor to hide an ill-favoured face, (A w.f.).

Well fitted abide, Things. (T 207)

1640 HERBERT no. 483.

Well for him who feeds a good man.

c. **1300** *Havelok* l. 1693 Wel is him þat god man fedes!

Well for him who has a good child.

c. **1300** *Havelok* l. 2983 Him stondes wel þat god child strenes.[1] [1 begets.]

Well-furnished, *see* House w. f. makes a woman wise.

Well is full, When the | it will run over. (W 261)

1641 FERGUSSON no. 729. **1721** KELLY 357 . . . That is, when People are much wrong'd they

will shew their Resentments. **1738** BAILEY *Dict.* s.v. Well.

Well is, that well does. (D 415)

a. **1628** CARMICHAELL no. 1681 Weill is them that weill dois, few folks monis[1] them. **1707** MAPLETOFT 120 (Scotch proverb). **1721** KELLY 353. [1 admonish].

Well married, She is | who has neither mother-in-law nor sister-in-law by her husband. *Cf.* Happy is she who marries.

1706 STEVENS s.v. Suegra.

Well, He that would be | needs not go from his own house. (H 762)

1611 COTGRAVE s.v. Bouger *Qui bien est ne bouge*: Prov. Let not him budge that finds himselfe well seated. **1640** HERBERT no. 442.

Well off, *see* Know when one is well (w. o.); Wise man who, when w. o., can keep so.

Well rhymed, tutor, brains and stairs. (T 625)

1639 CLARKE 70. **1678** RAY 67 . . . Now used in derision of such as make paltry ridiculous rhythmes.

Well since he is in heaven, He is. (H 347)

c. **1595** SHAKES. *R.J.* IV. v. 75 O, in this love, you love your child so ill That you run mad, seeing that she is. well . . . Dry up your tears and stick your rosemary On this fair corse. *Ibid.* V. i. 15 How fares my Juliet? That I ask again, For nothing can be ill if she be well.—Then·she is well . . . Her body sleeps in Capels' monument. **1598** *Id.* 2 *Hen. IV* V. ii. 3 How doth the King?—Exceeding well; his· cares are now all ended.—I hope, not dead.—He's walk'd the way of nature, And, to our purposes, he lives no more. [c. 1600] **1631** T. HEYWOOD I *Fair Maid* ii. 299 You told me he was well, And shall I not rejoyce?—Hee's well in heaven, For Mistrisse, he is dead. **1602** SHAKES. *A.W.* II. iv. 2 She is not well, but yet· she has her health. She's very merry, but yet she is not well. But thanks be given, she's very well and wants nothing i' th' world. But yet she is not well . . . she's very well indeed, but for two things . . . One, that she's not in heaven, whither God send her quickly! the other, that she's in earth, from whence God send her quickly! **1605–6** *Id. M.* IV. iii. 176 How does my wife?—Why, well.—And all my children?—Well too . . . your wife and babes savagely slaughter'd. **1725** N. BAILEY *Canonization Reuclin: Familiar Colloq.* 109 Our Reuclin is well . . . he is so well recovered that he will never be sick again.

Well spoken that is well taken, That is. (S 730)

1599 PORTER *Angry Wom. Abingd.* l. 57 Things are well-spoken, if they be well taken. **1600** JONSON *Cynth. Rev.* IV. iii. 151 Whatsoeuer they speake is well-taken; and whatsoeuer is well-taken is well-spoken. **1639** CLARKE 111. **1662**

FULLER *Som.* 26 'Had I', said he, 'failed of my design, I would have killed the Kings and all in the place'; words well spoken because well taken, all persons present being then highly in good humour.

Well that ends well, All is.   (A 154)

c. 1300 *Prov. of Hending* no. 1 Wel is him, þa wel ende mai. *a.* 1530 *R. Hill's Commonpl. Bk.* E.E.T.S. 110 'All ys well þat endyth well' said þe gud wyff. 1546 HEYWOOD I. x. C3ᵛ Well·aunt (quoth Ales) all is well that endes well. 1602 SHAKES. *A.W.* IV. iv. 35 All's well that ends well: still the fine's the crown. *Ibid.* V. i. 25 All's well that ends well yet. 1655 FULLER *Ch. Hist.* III. i. (1868) I. 319 But all is well that ends well; and so did this contest. 1836 MARRYAT *Midsh. Easy.* ch. 6 I had got rid of the farmer, . . . dog, . . . bull, and the bees—all's well that ends well.

Well to work and make a fire, it does care and skill (discretion) require.
(F 290. W 854)

1640 HERBERT no. 225 Working and making a fire doth discretion require. 1664 CODRINGTON 227. 1670 RAY 28.

Well used, Where men are | they'll frequent there.   (M 597)

1659 HOWELL *Eng. Prov.* 10a. 1670 RAY 27. 1732 FULLER no. 5649 Where Men are kindly used they will resort.

Well well, is a word of malice.   (W 269)

1595 SHAKES. *Rich. II* II. iii. 152 Well, well, I see the issue of these arms. I cannot mend it, I must needs confess. *Ibid.* III. iii. 170 Well, well, I see I talk but idly, and you laugh at me. 1670 RAY 154 . . . *Chesh.* In other places, if you say well well, they will ask, whom you threaten.

Well with him who is beloved of his neighbours, All is.   (A 157)

1611 COTGRAVE s.v. Voisin He that hath neighbors loue liues well at home. 1640 HERBERT no. 10.

Well with me, Where it is | there is my country. *Cf.* Wise man esteems every place.   (M 468)

[L. *Ubi bene, ibi patria.*] 1547 SENECA *De Remediis Fortuitorum* Eng. trans. B2 Patria est vbicunque bene est, My countre is in euery place where it is well. 1576 PETTIE i. 40 I count any place my country where I may live well and wealthily. 1579 LYLY *Euph.* i. 316 The wiseman lyueth as well in a farre country as in his owne home. [1590] 1592 *Soliman & Perseda* IV. ii. 7 Where a man liues well, there is his countrie. 1597 *Politeuphuia* 125ᵛ (as 1590). 1639 CLARKE 121 A good heart may doe well any where. 1909 A. LLOYD *Every-day Japan* (1911) Pref. *Ubi bene est ibi patria.* The wonderful kindness I have always received in Japan has made me understand how true the phrase is.

Well worth aw (awe, all), it (that) makes (gars)[1] the plough draw.
(A 404–5)

1621 ROBINSON 11 Well with [sic] awe, maketh the carle draw. *a.* 1628 CARMICHAELL no. 1650 Weill is aw garris the pleuch draw. 1639 CLARKE 93 Aw makes Dun draw. 1721 KELLY 354 . . . Spoken when People are over-aw'd to do a thing, which otherways they would not do. 1862 HISLOP 205 Weel worth a' that gars the plough draw. *Anglice,* Good luck to everything by which we earn money. 1881 EVANS *Leics. Words, &c.* E.D.S. 95 Au Au! an exclamation to horses to bid them turn to the left or near side. 'Aw makes Dun draw' is a punning proverb quoted by Ray [1670 58]. [1 makes.]

Well (*adj.*, *adv.*), see also Do w. and doubt no man; Do w. and have w.; Do w. than to say w. (It is better to); Does w. (He that) wearies not; Know when one is w.; Leave w. alone; Live w. for week, month, all life; Lives not w. one year; Lives w. is learned enough; Lives w. that w. lurked; Living w. best revenge; Long (It is not how) but how w. we live; Loves w. sees afar off; Man has his mare again (All is w.); Never w., full or fasting; One thing at a time . . . done w.; Say w. and do w. end with one letter; Say w. or be still; Spare w. and have w.; Tongue is ill (w.) hung; Want a thing w. done (If you); Weal (W.) or woe as he thinks (Man is); Wisdom counsels (W. goes case when); Wise that knows when he's w. enough.

Well(s) (*noun*), see also Buckets in a w.; Deep as a w.; Dirt into the w. (Cast no); Dog in the w.; Drawn w. seldom dry; —— have sweetest water; Fool may throw stone in w.; Go the w. against his will . . . water will spill; Know the worth of water till w. dry (We never); Leap into w., (If you); Many w. many buckets; Pitcher goes to w.; Put not the bucket too often in the w.; Stone in w. not lost; Truth lies at bottom of w.

Well-bred youth neither speaks of himself, nor, being spoken to, is silent, A.
(Y 50)

1640 HERBERT no. 278.

Wellington Roundheads.[1]   (R 192)

1678 RAY 353 . . . Proverbial in *Taunton* for a violent fanatick. [1 members of the Parliamentary party in the Civil War of the 17th century, who wore their hair cut short, Puritan fashion.]

Welly[1] brosten,[2] I am.

1738 SWIFT *Dial.* II. E.L. 311 A *footman brings a great whole cheese* . . . Well: I'm welly brosten, as they say in Lancashire. [1 almost. 2 burst.]

Welsh ambassador.   (A 233)

[A name for (*a*) the cuckoo; (*b*) the owl.] 1608 MIDDLETON *Trick to catch Old One* iv. H1 Thy Sound is like the cuckowe, the welch Embassador. *c.* 1620 *Welsh Embass.* iv. 1501 Malone Soc.

Pray m^r Reese . . . what is the reason that wee english men when the Cuckoe is vppon entrance saie the welsh embassador is Cominge. **1683–4** in MACRAY *Reg. Magd. Coll.* N.S. IV (1904) 135 Mr. Clerke, commoner, complain'd of Sir Charnock, demy, for abusing him . . . , calling him foole, Welsh ambassadour (an expression for an owle). **1917** BRIDGE 121 . . . This is the general Cheshire name for the cuckoo which is heard first from the Welsh quarter.

Welsh bait. (H 644)

[= a rest, without other refreshment, given to a horse on reaching the top of a hill; also *fig.*] **1603** T. POWELL (*title*) Welch Bayte to spare Prouender. Or, A looking backe vpon the Times past. **1658** HARRINGTON *Prerog. Pop. Govt.* I. vi. 32 In this place he takes a Welsh bait, and looking back makes a Muster of his Victories.

Welsh (English) blood is up, His. (B 462)

1590–5 MUNDAY *et al. Sir Thomas More* I. iii. 58 If the English blood be once but up. **1631** SHIRLEY *Love Tricks* V. iii. i. 90 Her Welsh plood is up, look you. **1662** FULLER Wales 7.

Welsh mile. (M 925)

[= a long and tedious mile, chiefly proverbial.] *c.* **1450** *Merlin* XV. 247 All the contrey was of hem covered the length of a walshe myle. **1652** J. TAYLOR (Water-P.) *Journ. Wales* (1859) 21 I hired a guide who brought me to Swansey (sixteen well stretch'd Welch mountainous miles). **1785** GROSE *Dict. Vulg. T.* (1796) 'Welch Mile' Like a Welch mile, long and narrow.

Welsh parsley. (W 273)

a. **1625** FLETCHER *Elder Brother* I. ii In tough Welsh Parsly, which in our vulgar Tongue, is strong Hempen Halters. **1638** RANDOLPH *Hey for Honesty* IV. i. (1651) 30 This is a Rascal deserves . . . To dance in Hemp *Derricks Caranto*: Lets choke him with Welch Parsley.

Welsh, *see also* Long as W. pedigree.

Welshman had rather see his dam on the bier, than to see a fair Februeer, The. (W 271)

1678 RAY 44.

Welshman keeps nothing until he has lost it, The. (W 272)

1662 FULLER Cardig. 26 . . . When the British recovered the lost Castles from the English, they doubled their diligence and valour, keeping them more tenaciously than before.

Welshman, The older the | the more madman. (W 270)

1659 HOWELL *Brit. Prov.* 31.

Welshman's cow, little and good, Like the.

1850 KINGSLEY *Alton Locke* ch. 27 We're just of a size, you know; little and good, like a Welshman's cow.

Welshman's hose of, To make.

[= to wrest the meaning of a word or sentence.] *a.* **1529** *Colin Cloute* 780 A thousand thousande other, That . . . make a Walshmans hose Of the texte and of the glose. **1559** *Mirr. Mag.*, ed. Campbell 77 And wurds that wer most plaine . . . we turned by construction lyke a welchmans hose.

Welshman, *see* also Heart of an Englishman towards W.; Irishman for a hand.

Welt or guard, Without. (W 274)

[= without ornamentation or trimming; also used *fig.*] [**1589**] **1594** GREENE *Fr. Bacon* H4^v Marke you maisters, heers a plaine honest man, without welt or garde. **1592** *Id. Upst. Courtier* B3b I sawe they were a plaine payre of Cloth breeches, without eyther welt or garde. **1594** NASHE *Unf. Trav.* ii. 210 He kept a plaine ale-house without welt or gard of anie iuybush. **1602** WITHALS 144 Without welt or gard, Playne, of it owne color. **1620** SHELTON *Quix.* II. v. ii. 220 I was christened Teresa, without welt or gard, nor additions of Don or Dona. **1639** CLARKE 30.

Wench(es), *see* Wine and w. empty men's purses; Wine makes old wives w.; Young w. make old wrenches; Young w., (Take heed of a).

Wept when I was born, I | and every day shows why. (D 82)

1605–6 SHAKES. *K.L.* IV. vi. 183 When we are born, we cry that we are come To this great stage of fools. **1640** HERBERT no. 199. **1768** GOLDSMITH *Good-nat. Man* I (Globe) 613 Nothing can exceed the vanity of our existence, but the folly of our pursuits. We wept when we came into the world, and every day tells us why.

Wer, *see* Sour as a crab (as w.).

West, *see* East or w., home best; Longer east, shorter w.; North for greatness, w. for wealth; Wind is w. (When), fish bite best; Wind's in the w., weather at best.

Westminster for a wife, Who goes to | to Paul's for a man, and to Smithfield for a horse, may meet with a whore, a knave, and a jade. (W 276)

1585 ROBSON *Choice Change* L3^v A man must not make choice of 3. things in 3. places. Of a wife in Westminster. Of a seruant in Paules. Of a horse in Smithfield. Least he chuse a queane, a knaue, or a iade. **1593** *Passionate Morrice* N.Sh.S. 83 It is more vncertaine . . . whether a Smithfeelde horse will proue good or iadish. **1598** SHAKES. *2 Hen. IV* I. ii. 45 Where's Bardolph? . . . I bought him in Paul's, and he'll buy me a horse in Smithfield: an I could get me but a wife in the stews, I were manned, horsed, and wived. **1617** MORYSON *Itin.* III. i. 53 (1908) III. 463 The Londoners pronounce woe to him, that buys a horse in Smithfield, that takes a servant in Paul's church, that marries a wife out of Westminster. **1659** HOWELL *Eng.*

Prov. 14a. **1699** *Dict. Canting Crew* Westminster-Wedding, a Whore and a Rogue Married together. **1706** STEVENS s.v. Ruyn A Westminster Wedding, a Whore and a Rogue.

Westminster Hall, *see* Suits hang half a year in W. H., at Tyburn . . .

Westward for smelts.   (S 559)

1607 DEKKER &c. *Westw. Hoe* II. iii. 79 But wenches, with what pullies shall wee slide . . . out of our husbandes suspition, being gone Westward for smelts all night. **1608** *Great Frost* in ARBER *E. Garner* i. 85 (1877) Say, have none gone 'westward for smelts' as our proverbial phrase is? **1620** *Westward for Smelts, or the Waterman's Fare of Mad, Merry, Western Wenches, &c.* [title].

Wet finger, With a.   (F 234)

[= with the utmost ease.] **1519** HORMAN *Vulg.* f. 195 I wyll helpe all this besines with a wete fynger. **1542** ERASM. tr. Udall *Apoph.* To Rdr. Readie waie and recourse maie with a weate finger easily be found out. **1602** DEKKER I *Hon. Whore* V. i. 34 Trust not a woman when she cryes, For sheele pump water from her eyes With a wet finger. **1611** CHAPMAN *May Day* I. i. 315 I am able to pay it with a wet finger. **1748** RICHARDSON *Clarissa* (1750) V. 152 If thou likest her, I'll get her for thee with a wet finger, as the saying is. **1754** FOOTE *Knights* I. Wks. (1799) I. 69 If Dame Winifred were here she'd make them all out with a wet finger.

Wet one's whistle, To.   (W 312)

[= to take a drink.] *c.* **1386** CHAUCER *Reeve's T.* 4155 So was hir ioly whistle wel ywet. *c.* **1425** *Wakefield Plays* Second Shepherds l. 103 Had she oones wett hyr whystyll, she couth syng full clere Hyr Pater Noster. **1530** PALSGRAVE 780b I wete my whystell, as good drinkers do, *je crocque la pie.* **1653** WALTON *Angler* iii. 75 Lets . . . drink the other cup to wet our whistles, and so sing away all sad thought. **1787** WOLCOT (P. Pindar) *Ode upon Ode* Wks. (1812) I. 447 Nor damn thy precious soul to wet thy whistle.

Wether, *see* Belled w. break the snow (Let the).

Wetting, *see* Northern cloth, shrunk in the w.; Shrink in the w. (To).

Whale, *see* Sprat to catch w.; Tub to the w. (Throw); White as a w. bone.

Wharlers, *see* Carleton w.

What d'ye lack?   (L 20)

[A salesman's cry.] **1563** NEWBERY *Dives Pragmaticus* A3ᵛ What lacke ye sir, what seke you, what wyll you bye? **1581** MUNDAY *Zelauto* D4 Euery body sayd, a mad term that they [Londoners] had, What lack ye, what lack ye . . . they asked me what I would buye. **1614** JONSON *Barth. Fair* II. ii. 29 What doe you lacke? what is't you buy? . . . Rattles, Drums, Halberts [&c.]. **1668** DRYDEN *Evening's Love* V. i. Wks.

(1883) III. 363 To draw us in, with a what-do-you-lack, as we passed by.

What has been, may be.

1603 MONTAIGNE (Florio) Notes V. 357 To . . . Reader What is that that hath beene? That that shall be. **1732** FULLER no. 5491. **1760** J. WESLEY *Letters* iv. 108.

What is he (she), It is not | but what has he (she).   (H 218)

1621 R. BRAITHWAIT *Sheph. Tales* II. i (1877) 233 Alas poor Swaine; 'tis true what th' prouerbe saith, We aske not what he is, but what he hath. **1721** KELLY 224 . . . Spoken of the Choice of Wives, where the Portion is often more look'd after than either the Person or the Virtues. **1738** SWIFT *Dial.* I. E.L. 82 They say her Father was a Baker.—Ay; but it is not, What is she? but what has she? now-a-days.

What rake[1] the feud where the friendship dow[2] not.

1641 FERGUSSON no. 892. **1721** KELLY 349 . . . Signifying our Contempt of mean Persons, whose Hatred we defy, and whose Friendship we despise. [[1] signifies. [2] avails, profits.]

What serves dirt for if it do not stink?   (D 350)

a. **1628** CARMICHAELL no. 1270 Quhat dow dirt, bot gif it stink. *a.* **1641** FERGUSSON MS. no. 1439. **1721** KELLY 354 . . . Spoken . . . when mean, base born People, speak proudly, or behave themselves saucily.

What the king wills, that the law wills (Laws go as kings like).   (K 72)

1539 TAVERNER I *Garden* C7ᵛ Quod principi placuit legis, habet uigorem: that is to saye: That lyketh the prynce hath the strengthe of lawe. **1581** GUAZZO i. 198 Princes . . . are Lordes over Lawes, and injoyne them to others. **1591–2** SHAKES. *3 Hen. VI* IV. i. 50 [Edward IV] For this once my will shall stand for law. **1591** I *Troublesome Reign K. J.* G3ᵛ [K. John] Nay murmur not, my will is law enough. **1611** COTGRAVE s.v. Roy. The King and Law haue but one will and pleasure; the Law is wholly gouerned by the King. **1659** HOWELL *Fr. Prov.* 17 That which the King wills the Law wills. **1706** STEVENS s.v. Ley. The Laws go which way Kings please. **1885** J. ORMSBY tr. *Quixote* xlv. (II. 301) 'May I never share heaven', said the poor barber, 'if your worships are not all mistaken; but, "laws go"—I say no more.' [Alfonso VI at Toledo settled the question as to which of the rival rituals, the French or the Musarabic, was to be adopted, by flinging the latter into the fire. Hence the proverb.]

Whaup in the rape, There is a.

1721 KELLY 305 . . . There is something amiss. **1862** A. HISLOP 189 . . . There is a knot in the rope—there is something wrong.

Whaver, *see* Shed riners with a w.

Wheamow, I am very | quoth the old woman, when she stepped into the milk bowl. (W 629)

1670 RAY 217 . . . Yorksh. wheamow, i.e. nimble. 1917 BRIDGE 79 I'm very wheamow (active) as the old woman said when she stept into the middle of the bittlin (milk-bowl). . . . As *wheamow* is not a common Cheshire word the proverb has doubtless come to us from a neighbouring county.

Wheat will not have two praises. (W 284)

1678 RAY 348 . . . (*Summer and Winter*.)

Wheat, *see also* May makes or mars w.; Sow w. in dirt.

Wheat-sowing, *see* First of November . . . an end of w.-s.

Wheatears, *see* May never goes without w.

Wheelbarrow, *see* Drunk as a w.; Go to heaven in w.; Music on a w. (Make as good).

Wheels within wheels, There are. (W 289)

[EZEK. i. 16 Their work was as it were a wheel in the middle of a wheel.] 1642 D. ROGERS *Matrim. Honour*, To Reader This wheele of our conversation . . . including many lesser wheeles in, and under it. 1670 I. WALTON *George Herbert* Let us consider that the Prophet Ezekiel says, There is a wheel within a wheel. 1709 SHAFTSB. *Charac.* (1711) I. 114 Thus we have Wheels within Wheels. And in some National Constitutions . . . we have one Empire within another. 1824 L. MURRAY *Engl. Gram.* (ed. 5) I. 457 They are wheels within wheels; sentences in the midst of sentences. 1900 'H. S. MERRIMAN' *Isle of Unrest* ch. 6 There are wheels within wheels . . . in the social world of Paris.

Wheel(s), *see also* Charles' Wain, (The four w. of); Fifth w. to coach; Fly sat upon the axletree; Fortune to be pictured on w. (Not only ought); Greases his w. helps oxen; Shoulder to w.; Speak to man at w., (Don't); Spoke in w.; World goes on w.; Worst w. creaks most.

Whelp of the same litter (hair), A. (W 293)

1530 TYNDALE *Practise of Prelates* P.S. 335 A whelp that goeth not out of kind from his sire. 1575 J. HIGGINS in Udall *Flowers for Latin Speaking* Y8ᵛ This is a whelpe of the same heere, or one of that crewe. 1577 HOLINSHED (1587) iii. 170b All the whelps of that litter [papal legates]. 1590 LODGE *Rosalynde* ed. Greg 64 Whelps of one litter are ever most loving. 1599 RAINOLDS *Overthrow Stage Plays* 8 Were it not a whelpe too of the same litter. 1624 T. BREWER *Knot of Fools* C4 (colour). 1639 CLARKE 288.

Whelp, *see also* Expect a good w. from ill dog (We may not); First pig, last w. is the best.

When? Can you tell? (T 88)

[1590] 1592 *Soliman and Perseda* II. ii. 3 I must betraie my maister? I, but when, can you tell? *c.* 1590 A. MUNDAY *John a Kent* l. 62. 1592–3 SHAKES. *C.E.* III. i. 52 Have at you with another; that's—When? can you tell? 1592 *Id. T.And.* I. i. 202 Titus, thou shalt obtain and ask the empery.—Proud and ambitious Tribune, canst thou tell? 1597 *Id. I Hen. IV* II. i. 37 I pray thee lend me thine.—Ay, when? canst tell? *c.* 1622 FLETCHER *Beggar's Bush* II. i. 184.

Where one is bred, Not | but where he is fed. (B 647)

1557 T. NORTH *Dial Princes* II. xviii. 242 The proverb Not from whence thou commest, but whereof thou feedest. 1620 SHELTON *Quix.* II. x. ii. 248 Thou art known by him that doth thee feed, not by him that doth thee breed. 1662 FULLER I. 60 The Latines have a Proverb, 'non ubi nascor, sed ubi pascor'; making that place their Mother, not which bred but which fed them.

Whet a knife for one's own throat, To.

1639 FULLER *Holy War* II. xl. (1840) 1c. Thus princes who make their subjects overgreat, whet a knife for their own throats.

Whet brings no let. (W 296)

1616 DRAXE no. 1826 Whetting (viz. of kniues and sithes) is no letting. 1639 CLARKE 271 Whetting is no letting. 1654 FULLER *Serm.* (1891) l. 75 A whet is no let, saith the proverb: mowers lose not any time which they spend in whetting . . . their scythes. 1659 HOWELL *Eng. Prov.* 2a Whett brings no lett, *viz.* When a mower whets his sithe.

Whet his knife on the threshold of the Fleet, He may. (K 154)

1662 FULLER Lond. 200 . . . The Fleet is . . . a Prison . . . so called . . . from a Brook running by. . . . The Proverb is appliable to those who never owed ought; or else, having run into debt, have crept out of it; so . . . may defie danger and arrests.

Whet(s), *see also* Iron w. iron; Knife w. another, (One).

Whether I would not I cannot the way. (W 173)

1611 DAVIES no. 31. 1616 DRAXE no. 2317.

Whetstone, To deserve (have, lie for) the. (W 298)

[= to be a great liar: in allusion to the former custom of hanging a whetstone round the neck of a liar.] 1364 *Liber Albus* (Rolls) iv. 601 Juggement de Pillorie par iii heures, ove un ague pier entour soun col, pur mensonges controeves. *c.* 1410 *Towneley Plays* xxi. 80 A, good sir, lett hym oone; he lyes for the quetstone. 1418 *Cal. Let.-Bks. Lond., Let.-Bk. I* (1909) 197 He, as a fals lyere . . . shal stond . . . upon þe pillorye . . . wiþ a Westone about his necke. 1577 FULKE

Confut. Purg. 437 You haue sayd enough, M. Allen, to winne the whetstone.   **1616** DRAXE no. 1330 He will lie for the whetstone.   **1658** [H. EDMUNDSON] *Fellow-trav.* 285 A great Person . . . had in a frolick set on some wanton wits to lye for the Whetstone.   **1678** RAY 89 He deserves the whetstone. He 'll not let any body lye by him.   **1778** *Exmoor Courtship* E.D.S. 79 What a gurt Lee es thate! . . . thek Man shou 'd a had the Whitstone.

Whetstone, though it can't itself cut, makes tools cut, A.   (w 299)

[HOR. *A.P.* 304 *Fungar vice cotis acutum Reddere quae ferrum valet exsors ipse secandi*, I will perform the function of a whetstone, which, itself incapable of cutting, can make iron sharp.] *c.* **1374** CHAUCER *Troilus* Bk. I, l. 631 A wheston is no kerving instrument. But yit it maketh sharpe kerving toles.   **1533–4** UDALL *Flowers* 176ᵛ [transl. Horace *A.P.*].   **1539** TAVERNER I *Garden* F7ᵛ Whetstones, quoth he [Isocrates], them selfes can not cutte, yet they make knyfes and weapons sharpe & able to cut other thynges.   **1545** R. ASCHAM *Toxophilus* ed. Wright XV A whettestone whiche is blunte, can make the edge of a knife sharpe.   **1579** LYLY *Euph.* i. 196 These nouises that thincke to haue learning without labour . . . not remembring, that the finest edge is made with the blunt whetstone.   **1588** *Disc. upon present state of France* 66 He serueth for nothing else but to edge tools.   **1599** SHAKES. *A.Y.* I. ii. 50 For always the dulness of the fool is the whetstone of the wits.   **1621** BURTON *Anat. Mel.* III. iv. 1. ii. (1638) 648 Yet as so many whetstones to make other tooles cut, but cut not themselves, though they be of no religion at all, they will make others most devout and super-stitious.   **1732** FULLER no. 455.

Which way (How many miles) to London ? A poke¹ full of plums. (w 174)

1542 RECORDE *Ground Arts* 35 (How many miles).   **1580** J. BARET *Alveary* F63 *Falces postulabas*. . . . A Prouerbe vsed, when a man asking a question, answere is made quite contrarie to his demand : as thus : which is the way to London ? answere is made, A poke full of plumbes.   **1583** MEL-BANCKE L3 God geue you good euen, which is the way to Poclinton, a pokeful of plummes. *a.* **1628** CARMICHAELL no. 789 (How manie myle to St. Jhonston).   **1639** CLARKE 19.   **1666** TOR-RIANO *Prov. Phr.* s.v. Albanese 3 To answer absurdly, and from the purpose, as, how many miles to London, a poke full of plums.   [¹ bag, sack.]

Whiff and away.

1593 P. FOULFACE *Bacchus' Bounty* C3ᵛ Whip snatch and away.   **1624** T. BREWER *A Knot of Fools* C4ᵛ. [Of a smoker].

Whig, *see* Sour as w.

While (*noun*), *see* Paternoster w.

Whiles¹ thou, whiles I, so goes the bailery.²   (B 36)

a. **1628** CARMICHAELL no. 1301.   **1641** FERGUSSON no. 716.   **1721** KELLY 352 . . . Spoken when

Persons, and Parties, get Authority by turns. [¹ sometimes.   ² magistracy.]

Whin, *see* March wind . . . blooms the w.

Whine, *see* Bite and w.; Suffolk w.

Whinger, *see* Tine the w. for thong.

Whip and bell.   (w 303)

[= something that detracts from one's comfort or pleasure : the Romans attached a whip and a bell to the triumphal chariot of a general, to drive away evil.]   **1644** CLEVELAND *Char. Lond. Diurn.* 4 In all this Triumph there is a whip and a Bell.   **1684** OTWAY *Atheist* I. i To get rid of that Whip and a Bell, call'd thy Wife.

Whip and whirr never made good fur.¹   (w 304)

[*c.* **1553**] **1566–7** UDALL *Ralph Roister D.* I. iii. Arb. 20 No haste but good, . . . for whip and whurre The olde prouerbe doth say, neuer made good furre.   [¹ furrow.]

Whip for a fool, A | and a rod for a school, is always in good season.   (w 305)

1605 S. ROWLEY *When you see me* E4ᵛ A rod in schoole, a whip for a foole, is alwaies in season.   **1609** BRETNOR *Almanac* Oct. (Evil Days) A Whip for a Foole.   **1670** RAY 212.

Whip the cat, To.   (C 173)

[= to be drunk.]   **1550–1700** *Master Malt Is Gentleman* l. 123 in *Roxb. Bal.* ii. 382 But Mault made hym the cat to whip.   **1599** MINSHEU *Span. Dial.* 19 Whosoeuer loues good wine, *hunts the Fox once a yeere *i.e. Whips the cat, or is drunke once a yeere.   **1600** *Weakest to Wall* E3ᵛ Adieu mine host lick-spigot, . . . When you meet with the Cat, for my sake whip her.   **1611** COTGRAVE s.v. Bertrand To be drunke . . . to whip the cat.

Whip with six strings.   (w 306)

[= the severe religious Act of the Six Articles, 1539.]   *a.* **1548** HALL *Chron., Hen. VIII* 234 This act established chiefly sixe articles, whereof . . . of some it was named the whip with sixe strynges.   **1655** FULLER *Ch. Hist.* V. v. (1868) II. 112 The Six Articles . . . that whip with six knots, each one, as heavily laid on, fetching blood from the backs of poor protestants.

Whip(s), *see also* Chastise with scorpions; Oil of w.; Spur and a w. for dull horse; Want a pre-tence to w. a dog (If you).

Whipping cheer, You shall have.   (w 308)

1573 *New Custom* I. i. A4 To have whipping cheere.   **1575** J. HIGGINS in Udall *Flowers* 2C7ᵛ.   **1586** R. CROWLEY *Friar John Francis* *4 I wyll doo what I shall be able to doo, in helping him to some whipping cheere in our Bridewell.   **1598**

SHAKES. *2 Hen. IV* V. iv. 6 She shall have whipping cheer enough, I warrant her. [1602] **1637** T. HEYWOOD *Royal King* vi. 32 Whipping cheere is best for him. **1616** WITHALS 574 (must haue).

Whip-hand of, To have the. (w 307)

[= to have the advantage, upper hand of.] **1680** ALSOP *Mischief Impos.* ii. 8 When once they are got into the Saddle, and have the whip-hand of the poor Laity. **1690** CHILD *Disc. Trade* Pref. C. 8 Before the Dutch get too much the whip-hand of us. **1849** DE QUINCEY *Engl. Mail-Coach* Wks. (1890) XIII. 307 In the art of conversation, . . . he admitted that I had the whip-hand of him.

Whirl the eyes too much, shows a kite's brain, To. (E 267)

1626 BRETON *Soothing* A4 Trowling eyes make rowling wits. **1640** HERBERT no. 717.

Whisker, *see* Dam of that was a w.; March w. never good fisher.

Whispering there is lying, Where there is. (w 310)

1584 WITHALS M2ᵛ They whiche oft times do whisper together, Do tumble and heape vp lies altogether. **1659** *Baron Tomlinson's Learned Speech* (*Phoenix Britannicus*, 1732, 271) (The Proverb says, That . . .). **1678** RAY 348. **1738** SWIFT *Dial. I. E.L.* 281 There's no Whispering, but there's Lying.

Whistle for a wind (breeze), To. (w 440)

c. 1510 *Cock Lorel's Boat* l. 344 Some whysteled after the wynde. **1686–7** J. AUBREY *Remains of Gent. & Jud.* ed. J. Britten 21 The seamen will not endure to have one whistle on shipboard: believing that it rayses winds. **1834** MARRYAT *Jacob Faith.* ch. 39 We must whistle for a breeze. In the mean time, Mr. Knight, we will have the boats all ready.

Whistle (go whistle) for it, You may. (w 313)

1513 SIR T. MORE *Rich. III* (1821) 45 There thei spende and bidde their creditours gooe whistle them. **1607** TOMKIS *Lingua* II. i. C3ᵛ The senses might haue whistled for the victory. **1611** SHAKES. *W.T.* IV. iv. 687 This being done, let the law go whistle. **1613** *Id. T.N.K.* III. v. 39 We may go whistle; all the fat's i' th' fire.

Whistle like a blackbird, To.

1663 BUTLER *Hudibras* I. i. 53, 4 That Latin was no more difficile, Than to a blackbird 'tis to whistle. **1887** BLACKMORE *Springhaven* ch. 6 You can whistle like a blackbird when you choose.

Whistle (sing) psalms to the taffrail (a dead horse), To.

1836 CROCKETT *Exploits* 81 He mought just as well have sung psalms to a dead horse, for my mind was made up. **1898** ANSTED *Dict. Sea Terms* 310 . . . An expression signifying the throwing away of good advice upon some person who may be about as susceptible to its influence as is the taffrail of his yacht.

Whistle (*noun*), *see* Clean as a w.; Make an end of your w. though cart overthrow; Pay too dear for one's w.; Penny more buys w.; Wet one's w.

Whistle(s, d) (*verb*), *see also* Everybody's dog that w. (I am not); Gled w. (Never for nothing that the); Halloo (W.) until one is out of wood (Not to); Pigs may w.; Says anything but prayers and those he w.

Whistling maid, *see* Crooning cow.

Whistling to going to plough, There belongs more than. (M 1156)

1678 RAY 191.

Whistling, *see also* Poor dog that is not worth the w.; Sung well before he broke shoulder with w.

Whit, *see* Never a w.

White as a kerchief, As.

1571 J. BRIDGES *Serm. at Paul's Cross* 125. **1578** LEMNIUS tr. T. Newton 13. **1579** NORTH'S Plutarch 'Demetrius' T.C. viii. 314.

White as a whale's bone, As. (w 279)

1515 A. BARCLAY *Life of St. George* l. 1150. As white as bone of whale. **1594–5** SHAKES. *L.L.L.* V. ii. 332. This is the flow'r that smiles on every one To show his teeth as white as whales-bone.

White as ivory, As. (I 109)

[*c.* 1565] *c.* 1620 T. ROBINSON *Mary Magd.* l. 199, E.E.T.S. 16 Her louely tresses of embellish'd haire, Kist her soft necke, and shoulders iu'ry white. **1591** ARIOSTO *Orl. Fur.* Harington XI. 54 (smooth). **1592** WARNER *Albion's Eng.* VII. 36 Vi. **1592–3** SHAKES. *V.A.* l. 363 Ivory in an alablaster band—So white a friend engirts so white a foe. **1596** *Id. M.V.* III. i. 33 There is more difference between thy flesh and hers than between jet and ivory.

White black, To make. (B 440)

[JUV. 3. 30: *Qui nigrum in candida vertunt.*] **1580** LYLY *Euph. & his Eng.* ii. 178 You would faine with your witte cast a white vpon blacke. **1584** R. WILSON *Three Ladies London* B4 I can make blacke white, and white blacke againe. [1591] **1594** MARLOWE *Edw. II* I. iv. 247 Such reasons make white black, and dark night day. **1605–8** SHAKES. *T.Ath.* IV. iii. 28 Thus much of this will make black white, foul fair. **1612–13** *Id. Hen. VIII* I. i. 209 That dye is on me Which makes my whit'st part black. **1706** STEVENS s.v. Blanco To make white black and black white. **1732** FULLER no. 5206 (as 1706).

White (White-headed) boy. (B 579)

[= a favourite.] **1539** TAVERNER 48 He that can flatter and save as I say, shalbe myne owne whyte sonne. **1541** COVERDALE *Confut. Standish*

(1547) lii b Maruaill not . . . though . . . I call you . . . her owne whyte sonne. [*c.* 1553] 1566-7 UDALL *Ralph Roister D.* I. i. Be his nowne white sonne. 1599 PORTER *Angry Wom. Abingd.* l. 1531 Whose white boy is that same? 1581-90 *Timon* I. iii. 10 . . . What speake the virgines of me? . . . —They terme you delight of men, white boye. 1639 FULLER *Holy War* I. xiii (1840) 22 The pope was loath to adventure his darlings into danger; those white boys were to stay at home with his holiness. 1690 C. NESSE *O. & N. Test.* I. 377 Joseph . . . was not only his earthly fathers white-boy, but his heavenly's also. 1823 LAMB *All Fools' Day* fin. So many darlings of absurdity, minions of the goddess, and her white boys. 1894 HALL CAINE *Manxman* II. xi He was always my white-headed boy, and I stuck to him with life.

White crow (raven), A.   (c 859)

[1525-40] 1557 *A Merry Dial.* 75 We haue as greate plentie of suche housbandes as of white crowes. 1579 GOSSON *Sch. Abuse* ed. Arber 30 For any chaste liuer to haunt them was a black swan, and a white crowe. 1639 CLARKE 271 (raven). 1666 TORRIANO *It. Prov.* 47 no. 2 A black Swan, a white crow.

White feather, To show the.

1785 GROSE s.v. White feather, He has a white f. he is a coward, an allusion to a game cock, where hauing a white feather, is a proof he is not of the true game breed. 1824 SCOTT *St. Ronan's* ch. 8 'To him, man . . . he shows the white feather.' 1850 THACKERAY *Pendennis* ch. 40 It was reported . . . he . . . had certainly shown the white feather in his regiment.

White foot, One | —buy him: two white feet—try him: three white feet— look well about him: four white feet— go without him.

1659 HOWELL *Fr. Prov.* 14 He is the horse of four white feet, viz. he promiseth fair, but performs nothing. 1882 *N. & Q.* 6th Ser. v. 427. Horsedealing Proverb.

White has its black, and every sweet its sour, Every.

c. 1400 *Beryn* E.E.T.S. 29 For 'aftir swete, the soure comyth, ful offt, in many a plase'. *a.* 1765 *Sir Cauline* II. i. in PERCY *Reliques* I. 39 Everye white will have its blacke, And everye sweete its sowre. 1818 MISS FERRIER *Marriage* ch. 55 'Every white white has its black, And every sweet its sour', as Lady Juliana experienced. Her daughter was Duchess of Altamont, but Grizzy Douglas had arrived in Bath!

White hen, *see* Son of a w. h.

White horse and a fair wife, He that has a | never wants trouble.   (H 657)

1581 GUAZZO ii. 10 It is yet an ordinary saying, That he that hath a white Horse, and a fayro woman, is never without trouble.

White horse, *see also* Save something for man that rides w. h.

White legs would aye be rused.[1]

1721 KELLY 340 . . . Spoken when People fish for Commendations, by disparaging a little their Persons, or Performances. [[1] praised.]

White man's grave, The.

[1873] SIR W. BUTLER *Autobiog.* ch. 9. What did it matter if the Gold Coast had been the White Man's Grave ever since Columbus had been there? One never dreamt of asking whether a climate was good or bad. 1910 *Times Lit. Sup.* 25 Feb. 65 The colony of Sierra Leone is happily no longer known as 'The White Man's Grave'. . . . Europeans can now live on the coast and in the hinterland under reasonably healthy conditions.

White silver draws black lines.   (s 459)

1576 PETTIE i. 142 White silver is wrought in black pitch. 1579 GOSSON *Sch. Abuse* Arb. 23 Whyte siluer, drawes a blacke lyne. 1580 LYLY *Euph. & his Eng.* ii. 167 Beautie, though it bee amiable, worketh many things contrarye to hir fayre shewe, not vnlyke vnto Syluer, which being white, draweth blacke lynes. 1670 RAY 142.

White wall is a fool's paper, A.   (w 17)

1573 SANFORD 108. 1611 DAVIES *Prov.* no. 77 A Fooles Paper is a white Wall: But, it was not so in Baltazar's hall. 1636 CAMDEN 292. 1662 FULLER *Lancs.* 107 'A wall is the fool's paper', whereon they scribble their Fancies. 1706 STEVENS s.v. Pared He that writes Sentences on the Wall . . . is a Fool.

White, *see also* Bear's (hound's) tooth, (As w. as a); Black and w.; Black best sets forth w.; Black is to w., (As like as); Calf with the w. face, (You would have the); Crow is w., (To say); God made w. man; God make me great and big, for w. and red I can make myself; Grey (W.) hairs death's blossoms; Son of a w. hen; Wool so w. but dyer can make black (No).

Whiten, *see* Thorns w.

Whither go you, *see* How does your.

Whither goest, grief? Where I am wont.
                                             (G 451)

1640 HERBERT no. 96.

Whiting, *see* Fine as if you had a w. hanging at your side; Leaped a haddock (w.).

Whittington's College, He has studied at.

1592 *The Defence of Conny catching . . . By Cuthbert Cunny-catcher, Licenciate in Whittington College* [title]. 1602 S. ROWLANDS *'Tis Merry when Gossips Meet* A2ᵛ Commence Bachelor in Whittington College. 1787 GROSE (*Lond.*) 204 . . . That is, he has been confined in Newgate, which was rebuilt A.D. 1423, according to the will of Sir Richard Whittington; by . . . his executors.

Whittle, (blanket), *see* Foot further than the w. (He that stretches).

Whitworth (Madge), *see* Go here away.

Who's the fool now?

1588 *Stationers' Register* 9 Nov. Arb. ii. 506 Martyn said to his man, whoe *is* the foole now. **1600** 'C. SNUFFE' *Quips upon Questions* B3ᵛ Who's the Foole now? **1600** DEKKER *Old Fort.* I. ii. 115 Wisemen . . . crie who's the foole now? **1609** T. RAVENSCROFT *Deuteromelia* D1ᵛ Martin: Fie man, fie, who's the foole now? Thou hast well drunken man, who's the foole now. **1695** E. RAVENSCROFT 56.

Who wats who may keep sheep another day.

1721 KELLY 345 . . . Who knows but it may be in my Power to do you good or harm hereafter, and as you use me, so will I you.

Whoave, *see* Kill but w., (We will not).

Whole (Sound) as a trout (fish), As.
(F 301. T 536)

a. **1300** *Cursor M.* 11884 (Cott.) Bi þat þou þar-of cum vte þou sal be hale sum ani trute [*v. r.* troute]. *c.* **1450** *Mirk's Festial* l. 265 Anon þe lepur fel from hym and he was hole as a fysche. *c.* **1517** SKELTON *Magnyf.* 1624, I am forthwith as hole as a troute. **1594** SHAKES. *T.G.V.* II. v. 17 Both as whole as a fish. **1635** SWAN *Spec. M.* (1670) 347 When we speak of one who is sound indeed, we say that he *is* sound as a Trout. **1678** RAY 289 (sound).

Whole from the broken, Keep the.

1563 T. NEWBERY *Dives Pragmaticus* B3ᵛ (The oulde Prouerbe is).

Whole, *see also* Cut out of w. cloth, (To); Go the w. hog; Half is more than w.; Half shows what w. means; Lick w.

Wholesomest meat is at another man's cost, The.

1659 HOWELL *Eng. Prov.* 19a. **1670** RAY 1.

Whooping, *see* Out of all w.

Whore in a fine dress is like a clean entry to a dirty house, A.

1721 KELLY 51. **1736** BAILEY *Dict.* s.v.

Whoredom and grace dwelt ne'er in one place.
(W 328)

a. **1628** CARMICHAELL no. 645 (cannot byde in). **1721** KELLY 355.

Whoredom, *see also* Opportunity is w.'s bawd.

Whores affect not you but your money.
(W 326)

1541 BULLINGER tr. Coverdale *Christian State of Matrimony* (1543) F5 Among whores is way-styng and expenses moost regarded, nether art thou welcome but thy money. No more money, no more loue. **1611** COTGRAVE s.v. Aimer Whoores affect your purse, not you. **1659** N. R. 120 (as 1611). **1664** CODRINGTON 225 (as 1611). **1670** RAY 28. **1732** FULLER no. 5726.

Whores and thieves go by the clock.

1607 DEKKER & WEBSTER *Northw. Ho* C2 They say Whores and bawdes go by clocks. **1678** RAY 68.

Whores in Hose than honest women in Long Clawson, There are more.

1787 GROSE (*Leic.*) 191 . . . Hose and Long Clawton are neighbouring villages . . . : Howes, or Hose, is but a small place, Long Claxton, Clayston, or Clawston, is . . . near a mile long. . . . The entendre lies in the word Hose, which here is meant to signify stockings.

Whore(s), *see also* Call her w. (scold, thief) first; Drives an ass and leads a w., (Who), has toil; Fools nor . . . w. among his kindred, (Who has neither) was born of a stroke of thunder; Hop w. pipe thief; Once a w. ever a w.; Plays the w. for apples, then bestows; Poor kin that has neither w. nor thief; Postern door makes w.; Thieves and w. meet at the gallows.

Whoring and bawdry do often end in beggary.
(W 329)

1614 T. ADAMS *Fatal Banquet* iv. Wks. 226 The old Prouerbe conioynes venery and beggery. **1664** CODRINGTON 230 (doe alwayes end). **1670** RAY 28.

Whose mare is dead?
(M 657)

1595 *Maroccus Extaticus* Percy Soc. 5 Holla, Marocco, whose mare is dead, that you are thus melancholy? **1598** SHAKES. *2 Hen. IV* II. i. 40 How now? Whose mare's dead? What's the matter. **1738** SWIFT *Dial.* I. E.L. 280 What's the matter? whose mare's dead now?

Why has a wherefore, Every.
(W 331)

1573 GASCOIGNE *Supp.* i. 189 I have given you a wherefore for this why many times. **1592–3** SHAKES. *C.E.* II. ii. 45 Ay, sir, and wherefore; for they say every why hath a wherefore. *Ibid.* III. i. 39 I'll tell you when, an you'll tell me wherefore. **1678** RAY 348 There is never a why but there's a wherefore. **1822** SCOTT *Nigel* ch. 3.

Why, *see also* 'Twill not be w. for thy.

Wicked book is the wickeder because it cannot repent, A.

1732 FULLER no. 457.

Wicked (wretched), It is an ill thing to be | but worse to be known ·so (to boast of it).   (T 140)

1592–3 SHAKES. *C.E.* III. ii. 9 Let not my sister read it in your eye; Be not thy tongue thy own shame's orator. **1606** T. HEYWOOD 2 *If You Know Not Me* l. 738 Tis bad to do euill, but worste to boast of it. **1609** SHAKES. *Son.* no. 121, l. 1 'Tis better to be vile than vile esteemed. **1611** COTGRAVE s.v. Recognoistre To doe euill, and then brag of it, is a double wickednesse. **1637** SHIRLEY *Gamester* II. i. 205 You know 'tis ill to do a thing that's wicked; But 'twere ·a double· sin to talk on't too. **1640** HERBERT no. 577 (Tis hard to be wretched). **1642** TORRIANO 49 It is an evil thing to be wicked, but a worse to be known ·so.

Wicked man is his own hell, A. (M 417)

[c. 1592] **1604** MARLOWE *Faustus* II. i. 122 Hell hath no limits, nor is circumscribed In one self place; but where we are is Hell. **1642** BROWNE *Rel. Med.* I (1881) 81 I feel sometimes a hell within my self. **1667** MILTON *Par. Lost* IV. 75 Which way I fly is hell; my self am hell. **1732** FULLER no. 460 . . . and his Passions and Lusts the Fiends that torment him. **1773** FLETCHER OF MADELEY *Wks.* vii. 294 His own mind would be his hell.

Wicked man's gift has a touch of his master, A. (M 498)

1640 HERBERT no. 162. **1706** STEVENS s.v. Dadiva A base Man's Gift is like its owner. That is, the gift shows the generosity, or the poor Spirit of the giver.

Wicked, The more | the more fortunate (lucky).

1552 LATIMER *Serm. Lincolnsh.* i. P.S. 466 And therefore there is a common sayinge The more wicked, the more lucky.

Wicked thing to make a dearth one's garner, It is a. (T 137)

1640 HERBERT no. 898. **1732** FULLER no. 2890.

Wicked woman and an evil is three halfpence worse than the devil, A.
                                                    (W 641)

1576 T. T. *The Schoolmaster* (1583) P2 A wicked woman fraught with all euill is by three farthings worse then the Deuill. **1621** ROBINSON 30. **1639** CLARKE 118. **1670** RAY 50. **1732** FULLER no. 6406.

Wicked world, It is a | and we make part of it.

1732 FULLER no. 5063.

Wicked, *see also* Prayers of w. won't prevail.

Wickedly, *see* Lives w. can hardly die honestly.

Widdie[1] hold thine own.

1721 KELLY 353 . . . Spoken when we see a bad Man in danger, as if he owd his Life to the Gallows. [[1] gallows.]

Widdie or Widdy, *see* Every man gets his own (When); thief will get w.; Highest in court nearest the w.; Laughing to girn in a w. (It is nae); Thief for w. (Meet as); Water will never reave the w.

Wide at the bow hand. (B 567)

1590–5 *Sir T. More* III. iii. 246 O Wit, thou art now on the bow hand, And blindly in thine own opinion dost stand. **1594–5** SHAKES. *L.L.L.* IV. i. 126 Wide o' the bow-hand. I'faith, your hand is out. **1604** DEKKER 1 *Hon. Whore* I. ii. 86 Y' are wide ath bow hand still brother: my longings are not wanton, but wayward. [c. 1620] **1654** WEBSTER [and T. HEYWOOD] *Appius and Virg.* III. iv. 9 I take thee to be an honest good fellow.—Wide of the bow-hand ·still: Corbulo is no such man. [1625] **1647** FLETCHER *Chances* I. viii. 18 You are as far o' th' bow-hand now.

Wide ears and a short tongue. (E 26)

1597 *Politeuphuia* 88[v] Vse thyne eares more then thy tongue. **1616** DRAXE no. 1979. **1639** CLARKE 302.

Wide therm[1] had never a long arm, He that has a.

a. **1628** CARMICHAELL no. 231. **1721** KELLY 137 . . . Gluttonous People will not be liberal of their Meat. [[1] belly.]

Wide will wear, but narrow will tear.
                                                    (W 334)

1609 HARWARD 128[v]. **1678** RAY 217. **1732** FULLER no. 6097. **1856** ABP. WHATELY *Annot. Bacon's Ess.* (1876) 510 The rule should be . . . not a severe one; lest, like over-severe laws, . . . it should be violated; according to the Proverb, that 'Wide will wear, but tight will tear'.

Widecombe folks are picking their geese, faster, faster, faster.

1850 *N. & Q.* 1st Ser. II. 512 . . . A saying among the parishes of the south coast during a snow-storm. **1911** W. CROSSING *Folk Rhymes of Devon* 29 . . . Widecombe-in-the-Moor is an extensive Dartmoor parish. . . . The village of the same name lies in a deep valley. . . . A writer . . . has suggested that the name of the moorland village . . . is merely a corruption of . . . 'widdi-cote', an old Devonshire term for the sky.

Widows are always rich (Wooers and widows are never poor). (W 342)

[*a.* 1553] **1566–7** UDALL *Ralph Roister D.* I. ii. A4[v] Wowers and Widowes are neuer poore. *a.* **1628** CARMICHAELL no. 1541 There was never a pure wower nor a rich deid man. **1678** RAY 57. **1732** FULLER no. 5740.

Widow(s), *see also* Keep yourself from . . . w. thrice married; Long a w. weds with shame; Maid, wife, nor w., (She is neither); Marries a w. and two children (He that); Marries a. w. and two daughters (He that); Marries a w. (He that), dead man's head in dish; Marry a w. before she leaves mourning; Marry a w. (Never), unless first husband hanged; Person marked (Take heed of) and w. thrice married.

Wife, Next to no | a good wife is best.
(w 369)

c. **1497** H. MEDWALL *Fulgens & Lucres* l. 785 He is well at ease that hath a wyf, yet he is better that hath none by my lyf. **1642** FULLER *H. & P. State* III. xxii. (1841) 205 A bachelor was saying, 'Next to no wife, a good wife is best'. 'Nay,' said a gentle-woman, 'next to a good wife, no wife is the best.'

Wife an ass, If you make your | she will make you an ox.
1732 FULLER no. 2772.

Wife and children are bills of charges.
(w 379)

1607–12 BACON *Ess., Marriage* Arb. 266 There are some other that esteeme wife, and children but as Bills of Charges. **1659** HOWELL *Eng. Prov.* 18a.

Wife and children, He that has a | has given hostages to fortune.
(w 380)

[LUCAN 7. 660 *Coniunx est mihi, sunt nati; dedimus tot pignora fatis.*] **1612** BACON *Ess., Mar. & Sing. Life* Arb. 264 He that hath wife, and children, hath given hostages to fortune, for they are impedimentes to great enterprizes. **1678** BUTLER *Hudibras* III. i. 809 For what secures the civil life But pawns of children, and a wife? That lie, like hostages, at stake, To pay for all men undertake. **1732** FULLER no. 5742 Wife and Children are Hostages given to Fortune.

Wife and children, He that has a | wants not business.
(w 355)

1640 HERBERT no. 778. **1732** FULLER no. 2157.

Wife, He that has no | beats her oft.
(w 357)

1573 SANFORD 103. **1629** *Bk. Mer. Rid.* Prov. no. 79.

Wife cries five loaves a penny, My.
(w 368)

1678 RAY 71 . . . *i.e.* She is in travel.[1] [[1] travail.]

Wife (shrew) down (up) in her (one's) wedding shoes, To take a.

[= rebuke.] **1545** *Precepts of Cato* Publius H2 Happy and also wyse is he that can take her [a shrewish wife] vp in her weddyng shoes. [**1603**] **1607** T. HEYWOOD *Woman Killed with Kindness* I. i. 47 In a good time that man both wins and woos That takes his wife down in her wedding shoes. **1605** DEKKER 2 *Hon. Whore* I. iii. 100 This wench (your new wife) will take you downe in your wedding shooes, vnlesse you hang her vp in your wedding garters.

Wife, He that has a | has a master.
1721 KELLY 138.

Wife, He that has a | has strife.
(w 356)

c. **1486–1500** MEDWALL *Nature* ii. 825 Now he that wold haue warre or stryfe I pray god sende hym a shrewde wyfe and then shall he haue I now. **1559** BERCHER *Nobility Women* I. 21, 127 Thear is another common proverbe. who hathe no controversye hathe no wyffe. **1611** COTGRAVE s.v. Noise He that a wife hath strife hath. **1721** KELLY 138 He that has a Wife, has a Master. . . . Eng. He that has a Fellow-Ruler, has an Over-Ruler.

Wife is the key of the house, The.
(w 383)

1616 DRAXE no. 1014 A woman is the key of the house and a man the soule of it. *Ibid.* no. 2387. **1640** HERBERT no. 904. **1732** FULLER no. 4828.

Wife that kept her supper for her breakfast, There was a | and she died ere day.
1721 KELLY 317 . . . Spoken when you are bid keep such a Thing for another Meal.

Wife that never cries for the ladle till the pot runs over, Like the.
1862 HISLOP 139 . . . That is, never asks for an article until it is too late.

Wife (Wives), *see also* Bachelors' w. well taught; Best or worst . . . is choosing good or ill w.; Better a portion in a w.; Blames w. for own unthrift; Blind man's w. needs no painting; Caesar's w. must be above suspicion; Child's bird and knave's w.; Choose a w. on a Saturday; Choose not a w. by the eye only; Choosing a w. not trust to another; Commend not your w.; Cunning w. makes husband apron; Dab, quoth Dawkins, when he hit his w. . . . ; Dawted daughters daidling w.; Devil is dead (When) there's a w. for Humphrey; Ding the Deil into a w. (You may); Fair w. . . . breed quarrels; Fair w. (Who has) needs more than two eyes; Fault of a w. (He has) that marries mam's pet; First w. is matrimony; Go down ladder when marry a w.; Good husband makes good w.; Good lasses, but whence bad w.; Good w. and health; Good w. in the country (There is one) and every man thinks; Good w. makes good husband; Good w.'s a goodly prize; Groaning horse and groaning w.; Hope better, quoth Benson, when w. bade him come in cuckold; Horse, a w., and a sword shewed not lent; Horse made and w. to make; House, a w., and fire to put her in; Husband drinks to w.; Husband (In) wisdom, in w. gentleness; Husband must be deaf and the w. blind to have quietness; Husbands are in

heaven whose w. scold not; Lets his horse . . .
and w. to every wake; Little house . . . little w.
well willed; Long-tongued w. go long with
bairn; Loses his w. and sixpence; Maid, w., nor
widow, (She is neither); Many a man sings that
w. home brings; Market goes (As), w. must sell;
Mills and w. ever wanting; Nice w. . . . make
rich man poor; Prolong thy life, quiet heart
loving w.; Proud eye . . . light w. bring; Purse to
your w. (If you sell your), give your breeks;
Refuse a w. with one fault; Scold like butter w.;
Sorrow and ill life makes old w.; Takes his w.
(As a man), for better, for worse; Tells his w.
news is newly married; Thrive (He that will)
must ask his w.; Two cats . . . two w. in a house
never agree; Venture it, as Johnson did his w.;
Wae's the w. that wants the tongue; White
horse and a fair w. (He that has); Wite yourself
if w. with bairn; Women (W. and wind) are
necessary evils; World and his w. *See also* Old
(Auld) wife (wives), Scolding wife.

Wight[1] man never wanted a weapon, A. *Cf.* Wise man never wants a weapon. (M 418)

c. 1470–80 HENRYSON *Moral Fables* ed. H. Wood
l. 2108 Ane wicht man wantit neuer, and he
wer wyis.   1616 T. ADAMS *The Soldier's Honour*
10 *Furor arma ministrat*, wrath will quickly
affoord weapons.   *a.* 1628 CARMICHAELL no. 232.
1641 FERGUSSON no. 10.   1721 KELLY 6 . . .
A Man of Sense . . . will make a Tool of the
first thing that comes to his Hands. [[1] strong,
bold.]

Wigs on the green, There will be.

[A colloq. expression (orig. Irish) for coming
to blows or sharp altercation.]   1856 *Chamb.
Jrnl.* 1 Mar. 139/1 If a quarrel is foreseen as a
probable contingency, it is predicted that 'there'll
be wigs on the green'.   1893 STEVENSON *Catriona*
ch. 17 Mr. David Balfour has a very good
ground of complaint, and . . . if his story were
properly redd[1] out . . . there would be a number
of wigs on the green. [[1] put in order.]

Wigs, *see also* Judges' w.

Wild as a buck, As. (B 692)

1530 PALSGRAVE 439b.   1592–3 SHAKES. *C.E.*
III. i. 72 It would make a man mad as a buck
to be so bought and sold.   1618 BELCHIER *Hans
Beer-Pot* D1 Thou wilt be like To Pasquill,
wilde as a Bucke, or Liueret Bred in March.

Wild boar, The rage of a | is able to spoil more than one wood. (R 7)

1592 DELAMOTHE 23.   1639 CLARKE 257.

Wild cat out of a bush, He looks like a.

1721 KELLY 173.   1732 FULLER no. 1973.

Wild goose chase, To run the. (W 390)

[= a foolish, fruitless, or hopeless quest.]
1594–5 SHAKES. *R.J.* II. iv. 69 Nay, if our wits run

the wild-goose chase, I am done.   1599 PORTER
Angry Wom. Abingd. l. 333 Shee's cunning
in the wilde goose race.   1606 CHAPMAN *Mons.
D'Olive* I. i. Plays (1889) 117 We may . . . talk
satire, and let our wits run the wild-goose chase
over Court and country.   1754 H. WALPOLE to
Bentley 20 Nov. Don't let me think, that if you
return, you will set out upon every wild-goose
chase, sticking to nothing.   1876 F. E. TROLLOPE
Charming Fellow ch. 12 His journey to London
on such slender encouragement is a wild-goose
chase!   1894 BLACKMORE *Perlycross* ch. 24 The
English public . . . always exult in a wild-goose
chase.

Wild horses will not drag (pluck) the secret from me.

1591 ARIOSTO *Orl. Fur.* Harington xx. 93 But
first I will with horses wild be torne, And suffer
all the paines of earth and hell, Before that I
will condescend to show it, Or then by me you
euer come to know it.   1592 SHAKES. *T.G.V.* III.
i. 265 He lives not now that knows me to be
in love; yet I am in love; but a team of horse
shall not pluck that from me.   1601 *Id. T.N.* II.
v. 60 Though our silence be drawn from us with
cars, yet peace.   1922 15 May D. H. LAWRENCE
Lett. ii. 703 How I hated a great deal of my
time in Ceylon . . . Not wild horses would drag
me back.

Wild oats, To sow one's. (O 6)

[= to indulge in youthful vices.]   1542 BECON
Nosegay: Early Wks., P.S. 204 That they may
satisfy the foolish desire of certain light brains
and wild oats, which are altogether given to new
fangleness.   1560–77 *Misogonus* II. iii. 37 He
hath yet sowne all his wilde otes he is but yonge
trulie he must needes runne his race.   1576
LEMNIUS *Touchstone* tr. T. Newton II. ii. 99 That
wilfull and vnruly age, which lacketh rypenes
and discretion, and (as wee saye) hath not sowed
all theyr wyeld Oates.   1577 TUSSER (1878 ed.
17) To bridle wild otes fantasie.   1577 BRETON
Wks. of a Young Wit ed. Robertson 63.   1638
T. HEYWOOD *Wise W. Hogsd.* II. i. Merm. 268
And will these wild oats never be sown?   1829
COBBETT *Adv. to Y. Men* Lett. I, par. 36 These
vices of youth are varnished over by the saying,
that there must be time for 'sowing the wild
oats'.   1861 T. HUGHES *Tom B. at Oxford* ch. 6
'A young fellow must sow his wild oats'. . . .
You can make nothing but a devil's maxim of it.

Wild, *see also* Beasts, The most deadly of w. is a
backbiter (tyrant), of tame ones a flatterer;
Shoe the w. mare.

Wiles help weak folk. (W 391)

a. 1628 CARMICHAELL no. 1667.   1641 FERGUSSON
no. 869.

Wiles, *see also* Fox's w.; Wise men are caught
in w.

Wilful as a pig; As | he'll neither lead nor drive. (P 298)

1678 RAY 291.   1864–5 DICKENS *Mut. Friend*
Bk. III, ch. 9 I [Bella] am naturally as obstinate
as a Pig.

Wilful man had need be very wise, A.
(M 419)

1616 DRAXE no. 2411 He is more wilful then wise. *c.* **1641** FERGUSSON MS. no. 141. **1721** KELLY 2. **1732** FULLER no. 465.

Wilful man will have his way, A.

1818 SCOTT *Rob Roy* ch. 28 The Hecate . . . ejaculated, 'A wilfu' man will hae his way'. **1906** W. DE MORGAN *Jos. Vance* ch. 25 A wilful chiel maun hae his wull.

Wilfulness, *see* Lawyers' gowns lined with w. of clients.

Will and wit strive with you (for the victory).

1590 R. WILSON *Three Ladies of London* Hazl.-Dods. vi. 380 Wit and Will are at strife. **1721** KELLY 347 . . . You are at a stand whether to do the pleasantest or the most profitable. Lat. *Aliud appetitus, aliud sapientia suadet.* **1736** BAILEY *Dict.* s.v. Wit Wit and will strive for the victory.

Will, As I | so I command (Will is his law).

[JUVENAL *Sat.* vi. 223: Hoc volo, sic jubeo, sit pro ratione voluntas.] **1586** G. WHETSTONE *Eng. Mirr.* 52 Sic volo, sic iubeo, stet pro ratione voluntas. So I will, so I commaund For lawe, let my pleasure stand. [**1587**] **1590** MARLOWE I *Tamburlaine* III. iii. 41 Will and Shall best fitteth Tamburlaine; *Ibid.* IV. ii. 91 This Is my mind and I will have it so. **1592** GREENE *Groatsworth* ed. Harrison 43 Is it pestilent Machiuilian pollicy that thou [Marlowe] hast studied? . . If Sic volo, sic iubeo, hold in those that are able to commaund . . . onely Tyrants should possesse the earth. **1592** SHAKES. *T.G.V.* V. iv. 13 [Of outlaws] These are my mates, that make their wills their law. **1624** CAPT. JOHN SMITH *Virginia* i. 76 When he listeth his will is a law and must be obeyed.

Will buys and money pays.
(w 395)

1573 SANFORD 110ᵛ. **1578** FLORIO *First F.* 34 Wyl maketh the market but money maketh payment. **1629** *Bk. Mer. Rid.* Prov. no. 133.

Will for the deed, Take the.
(w 393)

[OV. *Ex Ponto* 4. 8. 5 *Meritum velle iuvare voco.*] *a.* **1438** *Bk. of Margery Kempe* 212 I receyue euery good wyl as for dede. *a.* **1450** *Ratis Raving* 294 E.E.T.S. 98 The wyll Is reput for the deid. **1542** T. BECON *Invective agst. Swearing* (n.d.) H1ᵛ *Voluntas reputatur pro facto.* There wyll was taken for the very acte. **1567** *Id. Catechism* P.S. 224 St. Bernard likewise saith: 'The will is taken for the deed, when necessity excludeth the deed'. **1567** E. HAKE tr. *Imitation of Christ* A4ᵛ (1568) Either he will make thee able, or else accept thy desire, for the dede that thou desirest to do. **1606–7** SHAKES. *A.C.* II. v. 8 And when good will is show'd, though 't come too short, The actor may plead pardon. **1612–15** BP. HALL *Contempl.* I. iv. (1825) I. 17 That God, which (in good) accepts the will for the deed, condemns the will for the deed in evil. **1738**

SWIFT *Dial.* II. E.L. 298 If we had known we should have such good Company, we should have been better provided; but you must take the Will for the Deed. **1883** J. PAYN *Thicker than W.* ch. 31 The necessity for the self-sacrifice had not arisen, but by Beryl Paton the will was taken for the deed.

Will is a good boy when Will is at home.
(w 399)

1584 R. WILSON *Three Ladies of London* Hazl.-Dods. vi. 379 Will is a good boy, where better is none. **1639** CLARKE 253.

Will is a good son, and will is a shrewd boy.

1546 HEYWOOD I. xi. D3ᵛ Will is a good sonne, and will is a shrewde boy. And wilfull shrewde will hath wrought the this toy. *a.* **1576** WHY-THORNE 38.

Will is no skill.

c. **1517** SKELTON *Magnf.* l. 148 But haue ye not herde say that Wyll is no Skyll? *c.* **1528** HEYWOOD *Four PP* B2ᵛ What helpeth wyll where is no skyll.

Will is ready, Where your | your feet are light.
(w 394)

1640 HERBERT no. 448.

Will is the cause of woe.
(w 396)

1616 BRETON I *Cross.* A7. **1639** CLARKE 253. **1732** FULLER no. 5757.

Will may win my heart.

1546 HEYWOOD I. iv. B1ᵛ Will maie wyn my herte, herein to consent, To take all thinges as it comth, and be content.

Will not, If one | another will; (so are all maidens married).
(O 62)

1546 HEYWOOD I. iii. A4 Sens that that one wyll not, an other wyll. **1584** R. WILSON *Three Ladies of London* Hazl.-Dods. vi. 263. **1609** HARWARD 84 That which one will not an other may. That maketh all meates eaten and all maydes maryid. *a.* **1628** CARMICHAELL no. 600 Gif ye will not, ane other will, the morne is the nixt day. **1639** CLARKE 17 What one will not, another will. **1670** RAY 158 The world was never so dull but . . . **1721** KELLY 182 . . . so are all Maidens married.

Will not, If one | another will; the morn's the market day.

1721 KELLY 182.

Will not when he may, He that | when he would he shall have nay.
(N 54)

10th cent. *A.-S. Homily* quoted in SKEAT *Early Eng. Prov.* vi þe læs, gif he nu nelle þa hwile þe he mæge, eft þonne he late wille, þæt he ne mæge. *c.* **1175** *Poema Morale* MS. Lambeth 35 þe wel ne deð þe hwile he mai ne scal weane

he walde. *a.* **1180** ST. BASIL in JOHN OF SALISBURY
Polycrat. viii. 17 *Qui non vult cum potest, non
utique poterit cum volet. c.* **1200** *Ancrene Riwle*
(1853) 296 Hwo ne deth hwon he mei, he ne
schal nout hwon he wolde. **1303** R. BRUNNE
Handl. Synne 4795 Hyt ys seyd al day, for thys
skyl, 'He that wyl nat whan he may He shal
nat, when he wyl'. *c.* **1350** *Douce MS. 52* no. 57
Who-so wylle not, when he may, He shall not,
when he wylle. *a.* **1506** HENRYSON *Rob. & Mak.*
The man that will nocht quhen he may, Sall
haif nocht quhen he Wald. **1546** HEYWOOD I.
iii. A3ᵛ. **1621** BURTON *Anat. Mel.* III. ii. VI. v.
(1638) 573 But commonly they omit opportunities, . . . He that will not when he may,
When he will he shall have nay. **1893** STEVEN-
SON *Catriona* ch. 19 That young lady, with whom
I so much desired to be alone again, sang . . .
'He that will not when he may, Whcn he will
he shall have nay'.

Will, Where there's a | there's a way.

1640 HERBERT no. 730 To him that will, ways
are not wanting. **1822** HAZLITT 'The Fight'
New Monthly Mag. Feb. Where there's a will,
there's a way. I said so to myself, as I walked
down Chancery-lane . . . to inquire . . . where the
fight the next day was to be. **1927** *Times* 9
Aug. 11/5.

Will will have will, though will woe win.   (w 397)

1546 HEYWOOD I. xi. D3ᵛ But lo, wyll wyll haue
wyll, though will wo wyn. **1732** FULLER no.
5758.

Will (*noun*), *see also* Be still and have thy w.;
Complies against his w. is of same opinion still;
Go to the well against his w. (If the lad) . . .
water will spill; Good w., (With as); Ill w.
never said well; Inch of his w. (He will not
give) for span of thrift; Killed for her good w.;
Kindness comes of w.; One man's w. another
man's wit; Reason labours w.; Wedded to one's
w.; Welcome (Good w.) is the best cheer; Wit
and w. strive for victory; Wit at w.; World at
w., (To have the).

Willing horse, All lay load on the.

(A 158)

1546 HEYWOOD I. xi. E2ᵛ Whan ought was to
doo, I was common hackney, Folke call on the
hors that will cary alwey. **1609** HARWARD 95
Call not vpon the horse that always draweth.
1670 RAY 116. **1732** FULLER no. 532. **1926**
Times 24 Apr. 16/6 He was . . . the 'willing
horse' upon whom every one of the many duties
. . . were laid.

Willing, *see also* Fate leads the w.

Willow will buy a horse before the oak will pay for a saddle, The.   (w 405)

1662 FULLER *Cambs.* 144 [The willow] groweth
incredibly fast; it being a by-word in this County,
'that the profit by Willows will buy the Owner
a Horse, before that by other Trees will pay for
his Saddle'.

Willows are weak, yet they bind other wood.   (w 404)

1640 HERBERT no. 594. **1754** FRANKLIN Aug.
Willows are weak, but they bind the faggot.
1912 *Spectator* 2 Mar. 343 Ella Fuller Maitland
. . . has written . . .—'Withy is weak' the proverb
tells, 'But many woods he binds': And in the
truth that therein dwells My heart some comfort
finds.

Willow(s), *see also* Hang one's harp on w.;
Wear the w.

Wills the end, He who | wills the means.

1679–1715 SOUTH *Sermons* (1842) i. 206 That
most true aphorism, 'That he who wills the end,
wills also the means'. **1910** *Spectator* 29 Oct.
677 We won at Trafalgar . . . because we not
only meant to win, but knew how to win—
because we understood . . . the maxim, 'He who
wills the end wills the means'.

Will(s) (*verb*), *see also* All must be as God w.;
Do what one's own self w. (Easy to); Rich man
may dine when he w.; Two w. (That which
takes effect).

Wiltshire moonrakers.

1787 GROSE (*Wilts.*) 230 . . . Some Wiltshire
rustics, as the story goes, seeing the figure of the
moon in the pond, attempted to rake it out.
1819 J. C. HOBHOUSE *Let.* in SMILES *J. Murray*
(1891) I. xvi. 409 I have been . . . immersed in
the miserable provincial politics of my brother
moon-rakers of this county. **1863** J. R. WISE
New Forest ch. 15 'Hampshire and Wiltshire
moon-rakers' had its origin in the Wiltshire
peasants fishing up the contraband goods at
night, brought through the Forest, and hid in
the various ponds.

Wily beguiled with himself, He has played.   (w 406)

1555 LATIMER in STRYPE *Eccl. Mem.* (1721) III.
App. xxxvi. 103. **1566** J. BARTHLET *Pedegrew of
Popish Heretiques* P1ᵛ So playing wily beguily,
he beguileth himselfe. *c.* **1566** CURIO *Pasquin
in a Trance* tr. W. P. 95ᵛ Wilie begyle themselues
that think they goe to Purgatorie and go streight
to Hell. **1616** DRAXE no. 454. **1678** RAY 84.
1732 FULLER no. 1895 He hath play'd a wiley
Trick, and beguil'd himself.

Wimble,¹ The little | will let in the great auger.   (w 407)

1636 FEATLEY *Clavis Myst.* xxix. 377 As the
Wimble bores a hole for the auger. **1732** FULLER
no. 4632. [¹ gimlet.]

Wimble, *see also* Gifts enter everywhere without
w.

Wimple¹ in a lawyer's clew,² There is aye a.

1818 SCOTT *Ht. Midl.* ch. 24 The Judge didna
tell us a' . . . about the application for pardon

. . . ; there is aye a wimple in a lawyer's clew.
[¹ twist. ² ball of thread.]

Win and wear.   (w 408)

c. 1552 *Manifest Detection of Dice-Play* A1ᵛ There
is my xx. li. win it and weare it.   1573 G. HARVEY
Letter Bk. (Camden Soc.) 114 Thou hast woone
her—weare her.   [1589] 1633 MARLOWE *Jew
of M.* II. iii. 293 This is thy diamond; tell me
shall I have it?—Win it and wear it, it is yet un-
soiled.   1598 SHAKES. *2 Hen. IV* IV. v. 220 You
won it, wore it, kept it, gave it me.   1598–9 *Id.
M.A.* V. i. 82 Win me and wear me.   1622 J.
FLETCHER *Span. Cur.* II. i. Wks. (1905) II. 75 I'l
win this Diamond from the rock and wear her.
1847 MARRYAT *Childr. N. Forest* ch. 27 As for
his daughter . . . you have yet to 'win her and
wear her', as the saying is.

Win at first and lose at last.   (F 297)

1659 HOWELL *Span. Prov.* 29 To win at the
beginning is a bait to lose: Because it allures
one to give himself to gaming.   1678 RAY 349.

Win gold and wear gold.   (G 294)

1562 G. LEGH *Accidence of Armoury* 132ᵛ Nowe
we haue a comon saying winne golde and weare
it.   1581 THIMELTHORPE *Short Inventory* 17ᵛ It
is a prouerbe olde, the winners may best weare
the gold.   1583 MELBANCKE *Philot.* C4 Thou
hast woon goulde, now weare gould.   1587
Letters of Philip Gawdy 23 (and eat gold).   1614
CAMDEN 315 Win gold and wear gold.   1660
TATHAM *The Rump* III. i. Wks. (1879) 244 He
that wins gold, let him wear gold, I cry.   1748
RICHARDSON *Clarissa* III. 350 I, who have won
the gold, am only fit to wear it.

Win purple and wear purple.   (P 640)

1650 FULLER *Pisgah Sight* IV. vi. § 1 Earned
with her industry (and good reason—win purple
and wear purple).   1853 TRENCH V. 114.

Win (one's *or* the) spurs, To.   (S 792)

[= to gain knighthood; *fig.* gain distinction.]
c. 1425 LYDGATE *Assembly of Gods* l. 980 These
xiiii Knyghtes made Vyce that day; To wynne
theyr spores they seyde they wold asay.   1530
TYNDALE *Answer to More* P.S. 17 He weeneth
that he hath won his gilden spurs.   1551 T.
WILSON *Logic* (1580) 74b Sennacherib that
wicked kyng, thought . . . to winne his spurres
against Jerusalem.   1600 HOLLAND *Livy* xxx.
xxxii. 762 Resolute that day either to winne the
spurres or loose the saddle.   1639 CLARKE 31.

Win the horse or lose the saddle, Either.   (H 639)

c. 1549 HEYWOOD II. ix. L1ᵛ Recouer the hors or
lese the saddle too.   1554 J. CHRISTOPHERSON
Exhortation C1 Eyther . . . will they wynne the
horse (as the prouerbe is) or els loose bothe the
horse and the sadle to.   1575 GASCOIGNE *Posies*
i. 169 It was my full entent, To loose the sadle
or the horse to winne.   1592 GREENE 2 *Cony-
catching* Grosart x. 100 What they get in the
bridle they lost in the saddle.   1599 NASHE *Lenten
Stuff* iii. 187 Win the horse or lose the saddle
(as it runs in the Prouerb).   1609 HARWARD 126
He will either winne the horse or lose the bridle.

desperate play.   1670 RAY 199.   1721 KELLY 96
(tine the Saddle). Spoken as an Encouragement
to a noble Attempt.

Win(s, won), *see also* Daughter w. (He that
would the); Gear that is gifted . . . that is w.;
Heads I w.; Laughs who w.; Looks as if neither
w. nor lost; Lost (W.) in the hundred found
(lost) in the shire; Nought w. by the one;
Patient men w. day; Plays best that w.;
Women (All) may be w.

Winchester goose.   (G 366)

[= a certain venereal disease; also, a prostitute.]
1543 W. TURNER *Hunting of the Romish Fox* A8
Ye holde styll that the masse . . . is profytable
for . . . the frenche pox, for the goute in the to,
and also for a winchester goose.   1554 H. HILARIE
[John Bale] *Resurrection of the Mass* A3 A
wynchester goose to heale is my gyse.   1559
BECON in *Prayers, &c.* P.S. 284 Making whole
of a Winchester goose.   1592–4 SHAKES. *1 Hen.
VI* I. iii. 53 Gloster, thou wilt answer this before
the Pope.—Winchester Goose, I cry, a Rope, a
Rope.   1602 *Id.* *T.C.* V. x. 52 My fear is this,
Some galled goose of Winchester would hiss.
1611 COTGRAVE s.v. Clapoir, a botch in the
Groyne, or yard; a Winchester Goose.   1630
J. TAYLOR (Water-P.) *Taylors Goose* 105b Then
ther's a goose that breeds at Winchester, And
of all Geese, my mind is least to her.   1778 *Eng.
Gazetteer* (ed. 2) s.v. *Southwark* In the times of
popery here were no less than 18 houses on the
Bankside, licensed by the Bishops of Winchester
. . . to keep whores, who were, therefore, commonly called Winchester Geese.

Winchester, *see also* Canterbury is the higher
rack.

Wind, To have one in the.   (w 434)

1540 PALSGRAVE *Acolastus* 78 I haue in the
wynde, some good sauour of gayne.   1546 HEY-
WOOD I. xi. E1ᵛ I smelde hir out, and had hir
streight in the wynde.   1602 SHAKES. *A.W.* III.
vi. 104 By this same coxcomb that we have i'
the wind.

Wind and tide, To sail with the. (w 429)

1546 HEYWOOD I. xi. D4 A tyme I will spy, To
take wynde and tyde with me.   1590–1 SHAKES.
3 Hen. VI V. i. 53 Sail how thou canst, haue
wind and tide thy friend.   1591 FLORIO *Second
F.* 97 For wisdome sailes with winde and tide.
[1592] 1594 *Selimus* l. 270 Wisedome commands
to follow tide and winde.   1709 HARWARD 120
Thou rowest agaynst wind and tyde.   1623
PAINTER B5ᵛ Tis best to sayle with current and
with the wind.

Wind and water, To shoot between.
                                            (w 436)

1588 *Cert. Advert. Losses Sp. Navie Irel.* B2 One
of the shot was betweene the winde and the
water, whereof they thought she would haue
sonke.   *c.* 1607 T. HEYWOOD & W. ROWLEY
Fortune by Land and Sea IV. iii. You gave not
one shot betwixt wind and water in all this
skirmish.   1608 BEAUM. & FL. *Philas.* IV. i The
wench has shot him between wind and water.

1639 FULLER *Holy War* IV. xxiv. (1840) 222 Sea-
fights are more bloody . . . since guns came up,
whose shot betwixt wind and water . . . is commonly observed mortal. **1774** BURKE *Sp. on
Amer. Tax.* 19 Apr. Charles Townshend . . . hit
the house just between wind and water.

Wind and weather, do thy worst.

(w 446)

1678 RAY 277. **1732** FULLER no. 5743 (your
utmost).

Wind blew you hither? What. (w 441)

c. **1374** CHAUCER *Troilus* Bk. 2, l. 1104 What
manere wyndes gydeth yow now here? *c.* **1489**
CAXTON *Sonnes of Aymon* E.E.T.S. 106 Lordes,
what ye be, and what wynde dryveth you hyther.
1546 HEYWOOD I. x. C3ᵛ Ye huswife, what wind
blowth ye hyther thus right? **1598** SHAKES. *2
Hen. IV* V. iii. 84 What wind blew you hither,
Pistol? **1602** WITHALS 335 (draue). **1664**
COTTON *Scarron.* iv. 1715 ed. 98 He askt what
Wind had blown her thither. **1824** SCOTT *Redg.*
ch. 21 Pengwinion, you Cornish chough, has
this good wind blown you north?

Wind blows not down the corn, Every.

(w 415)

1546 HEYWOOD II. ix. L1. **1611** DAVIES no. 283.

Wind blows, As the | you must set your
sail.

1846 DENHAM 3.

Wind follows sun's course, If | expect
fair weather.

1883 ROPER 10. **1893** INWARDS 71.

Wind in one's face makes one wise, The.

(w 447)

1640 HERBERT no. 717. **1659** HOWELL *It. Prov.*
5 Wind in the visage makes one sage: viz.
adversity. **1710** PALMER 190.

Wind in that door (corner)? Is the.

(w 419)

1470–85 MALORY *Arthur* VII. xxxv 'What!
neuewe, is the wynde in that dore?' **1546** HEY-
WOOD II. v. H2 If the winde stande in that doore,
it standth awry. **1589** *Marprel. Epit.* B iv. Is
the winde at that dore with you brother deane?
1598 SHAKES. *1 Hen. IV* III. iii. 87 Is the wind in
that door, i' faith? **1598–9** *Id. M.A.* II. iii. 91
Sits the wind in that corner? *a.* **1625** BEAUM. &
FL. *Coronation* II. i. Is the wind in that corner?
1668 DRYDEN *Evening's Love* IV. i. Is the Wind
in that Door? Here's like to be fine doings.

Wind is in the east, When the | it is
neither good for man nor beast.

(w 442)

1600 R. CAWDREY *Treas. of Similes* 750 The east
wind is accounted neither good for man or
beast. **1609** HARWARD 86 The Wind East is
neither good for man nor beast. **1659** HOWELL

Eng. Prov. 19b. **1670** RAY 41 . . . The East-wind
with us is commonly very sharp, because it comes
off the Continent. **1927** *Times* 21 Nov. 15/4
Science is beginning a new incursion into . . .
such wisdom as is contained in the lines When
the wind is in the East 'Tis neither good for man
nor beast.

Wind is in the east on Candlemas Day,[1]
When the | there it will stick till the
second of May.

1852 *N. & Q.* 1st Ser. v. 462. [¹ 2 Feb.]

Wind is in the north, When the | the
skilful fisher goes not forth.

1846 DENHAM 17. **1869** INWARDS 48.

Wind is in the north-west, Do business
with men when the.

1883 ROPER 10. **1893** INWARDS 78.

Wind is in the south, When the | it's
in the rain's mouth.   (w 444)

1639 CLARKE 263. **1670** RAY 42. **1721** KELLY
353 (rain will be forth¹). [¹ in abundance.]

Wind is in the west, When the | the
weather is at the best.   (w 445)

1606 CHAPMAN *Gent. Usher* II. i. 36 The wind
must blow at west still or she'll be angry. *c.*
1685 AUBREY *Nat. Hist. of Wilts* 16 A Wiltshire
proverb When the wind is north-west The
weather is at the best. **1721** KELLY 353. **1732**
FULLER no. 6223.

Wind is north-east, If the | three days
without rain, eight days will pass
before south wind again.

1883 ROPER 9. **1893** INWARDS 78.

Wind is on Martinmas Eve, Where the
| there it will be the rest of winter.

1883 ROPER 23 If the wind is south-west at
Martinmas, It keeps there till after Christmas.
1893 INWARDS 37.

Wind is south, When the | it blows your
bait into a fish's mouth.   (w 443)

1653 WALTON *Angler* v. (Clar. Press) 115 For
the wind . . . the south wind is said to be the
best. One observes, that—When the wind is
south, It blows your bait into a fish's mouth.
1732 FULLER no. 6226.

Wind is west, When the | the fish bite
best.

1883 ROPER 11. **1893** INWARDS 77.

Wind keeps not always in one quarter,
The.   (w 448)

1579 GOSSON *Ephemerides* 15 The wind is not
euer in one quarter. **1590** T. LODGE *Rosalynde*

ed. Greg 103 The wind cannot be tied within his quarter. **1616** WITHALS 568 (in one corner). **1639** CLARKE 124. **1670** RAY 156. **1732** FULLER no. 4831.

Wind shakes no corn, All this. (W 410)

1546 HEYWOOD I. xi. D4 What man all this wynd shakes no corne. Let this wynde ouerblow . a tyme I will spy, to take wynde and tyde with me. **1557** EDGEWORTH *Sermons* 3M2ᵛ. **1612–15** BP. HALL *Contempl.* VII. iii. (1825) I. 168 What if he had been suffered to go and curse? What corn had this wind shaken, when God meant to bless them? **1620** SHELTON *Quix.* II. lxviii. iii. 298 This wind winnows no corn.

Wind that comes in at a hole, and a reconciled enemy, Take heed of. *Cf.* Reconciled enemies, Take heed of.
(H 384)

1599 MINSHEU *Span. Gram.* 84. **1651** HERBERT no. 1154. **1659** HOWELL *Span. Prov.* 15 God guard me from the wind through a hole, and from a reconciled friend.

Wind up your bottom,[1] To. (B 553)

[= to sum up, conclude, drink up.] **1590–5** MUNDAY *et al. Sir Thomas More* III. i. 19 To be great Is, when the thread of hazard is once spun, A bottom great wound up, greatly undone. **1603** DEKKER *Wonderful Year* (Plague Pamphlets ed. Wilson 48) She . . . vnraueld the bottome of her frailtie at length. **1633** *Banquet of Jests* Pt. 2 148–9 Wind up your bottom. **1639** CLARKE 46 [Drinking term]. **1678** RAY 88 She's not a good house-wife that will not wind up her bottom, i.e. take off her drink. **1698** S. CLARK *Script. Just.* 112 It's high Time now to wind up my Bottoms. **1826** SCOTT *Diary* 15 Mar. in LOCKHART *Life* ch. 70 Must work hard for a day or two. I wish I could wind up my bottom handsomely. [¹ ball of thread.]

Wind veers against the sun, When the | trust it not, for back 'twill run.

1883 ROPER 10. **1893** INWARDS 71.

Wind(s), *see also* Blow the w. never so fast; Cap in the w., (To throw one's); Catch the w. in a net; Cold w. reach you through a hole; Come w., come weather; Come with the w., go with the water; Corn cleansed with w.; Devil busy in high w.; Devil never sent w. but he would sail with it; Down the w.; Easterly w. and rain bring cockles; Every w. is ill to broken ship; Fancy flees before w.; Fight against the w.; Free as the w.; God tempers the w.; God will (When), no w. but brings rain; Good w. that blows to the wine; Great w. upon high hills; Hoist your sail when w. is fair; Ill w. that blows nobody good; Keep yourself from . . . w. at a hole; Kick the w.; Know which way the w. blows; Little kens the wife . . . the w. blows cold on Hurleburle-swyre; Little w. kindles fire; March sun causes dust and w. blows it; March w. kindles adders; Mill will go with all w.; North w. does blow; Northerly w.; Northern w. brings weather fair; North-west w. (Honest man and a); Pigs

see the w.; Piss not against w.; Pluck the grass to know where w. sits; Puff not against w.; Pull down your hat on w. side; Rain comes before the w.; Rain comes scouth when w.'s in south; Rain lays great w.; Raise the w.; Robin Hood could stand any w. but thaw w.; Sail near w.; Sail, quoth the king, hold, quoth the w.; Sail with every w.; Soldier's wind, there and back; Something in the w., (There is); Southerly w. with showers of rain; Southerly w. hunting morning; Sow beans in the w.; Sow the w. and reap the whirlwind; Spits against the w.; Stones against the w., (To throw); Straws show which way w. blows; Sun sets bright (When), easterly w. you need not fear; Sun sets in a bank (When), westerly w.; Take the w. out of the sails; Talk to the w.; Thunder (w.) comes rain, (After); Tracys have always w. in their faces; Tree that God plants no w. hurts; Turn with the w.; Wavering as the w.; Weather is ill (No) if w. still; Weathercock in the w.; Whistle for w.; Woman's mind and winter w. change oft; Women are as changeable as w.; Women (Wives and w.) are necessary evils; Words and feathers w. carries away; Words are but w.; Wroth as the w.

Wind-frost, *see* Steward abroad when there is w. (There is good).

Windlestraws, *see* Redd for w. (He that is) should not sleep in lees.

Windmill dwindles into a nutcracker, Your. (W 454)

c. **1380** CHAUCER *House of Fame* l. 1280 I saugh him carien a Wind-melle Under a walsh-note shale. **1678** RAY 277 (nut-crack). **1732** FULLER no. 6064.

Windmill go with a pair of bellows, You cannot make a. (W 453)

1640 HERBERT no. 676.

Windmill, *see also* Bradshaw's w.

Windmills[1] in one's head, To have.
(W 455)

[Referring to Don Quixote's fight with the windmills (I. viii). Span. *acometer molinos de viento*.] **1612** SHELTON *Quix.* I. viii. i. 48 Windmills in his brains. **1622** MASSINGER & DEKKER *Virg. Mart.* II. iii Thy head is full of Windemils. **1639** CHAPMAN & SHIRLEY *The Ball* v. Chapman *Plays* (1874) 494 I do love One that has windmills in his head — How, madam? — Projects and proclamations. **1665** J. WILSON *Project.* I. i. Wks. (1874) 220 If they will set up windmills in their heads, contribute my assistance to cut out the sails. **1754** RICHARDSON 21 Aug. (*Corresp.* III. 212) But she had a windmill in her head, and away the air of it carried her upwards of one hundred miles from her Doctor. [¹ impossible or impracticable schemes.]

Window(s), *see* Air of a w. is as . . . crossbow; Come in at the w.; Eye is the w. of the heart;

Fair day (To a) open the w.; Goods in the w., (To keep all one's); House out of w. (Throw the); John Roper's w., (To look in at); Love comes in at w.; Shop w.; Woman that loves to be at w.

Windy March and a rainy April make a beautiful May, A. (M 644)

1657 E. LEIGH *Select & Choice Observations* 270. 1659 HOWELL *Span. Prov.* 21. 1706 STEVENS s.v. Marco. 1732 FULLER no. 468.

Wine and wealth change wise men's manners. (W 472)

1584 WITHALS B7. 1639 CLARKE 33.

Wine and wenches empty men's purses. (W 473)

1626 BRETON *Soothing* B1. 1639 CLARKE 28.

Wine and women. (W 474)

[ECCLUS. xix. 2 *Vinum et mulieres apostatare faciunt sapientes.*] *c.* 1387 CHAUCER *Monk's T.* l. 2644 Sav wyn and wommen, no thyng myghte aswage. 1604 W. WAEDNOT *Palladis Palatium* 134 Wine and women make men runnagates. 1607 DEKKER & WEBSTER *Westw. Ho* v. i. G3 To see what wine and women can do, the one makes a man not to haue a word to throw at a Dogge, the other makes a man to eat his owne words. 1609 HARWARD 126 Wine and weomen make wise men madd. 1616 DRAXE no. 2428 Wine and women make wisemen runagates. 1621 BURTON *Anat. Mel.* I. ii. III. xiii. (1638) 120 Those two maine plagues, and common dotages of human kind, Wine and Women, which have infatuated and besotted Myriades of people. They goe commonly together. 1727 GAY *Begg. Op.* II. i. Women and wine should Life employ. 1819 BYRON *Juan* II. clxxviii Let us have wine and women, mirth and laughter. 1862 THACKERAY *Philip* ch. 7 As Doctor Luther sang, Who loves not wine, women, and song He is a fool his whole life long.

Wine and youth increase love.

c. 1386 CHAUCER *Phys. T.* l. 59 For wyn and youthe dooth Venus encresse, As men in fyr wol casten oille or greesse.

Wine by the barrel, You cannot know. (W 492)

1611 COTGRAVE s.v. Cercle The goodnes of wine is not known by the fashion, or strength of the hoops that begird it. 1640 HERBERT no. 20. 1732 FULLER 5884 (cask).

Wine by the savour, bread by the colour (heat). (W 475)

1573 SANFORD 105. 1578 FLORIO *First F.* 29ᵛ (bread by the heate). 1666 TORRIANO *It. Prov.* 186 no. 17 Bread by the colour, and wine by the taste.

Wine ever pays for his lodging. (W 476)

1640 HERBERT no. 930.

Wine in the bottle does not quench thirst. (W 479)

1640 HERBERT no. 616. 1642 TORRIANO 61. 1732 FULLER no. 5745 (hogshead).

Wine (ale) in, truth (wit) out. *Cf.* **Wine there is truth, In.** (W 471)

c. 1386 CHAUCER *Pard. T.* l. 560 In whom that drynke hath dominacioun He kan no conseil kepe. *c.* 1390 GOWER *Conf. Amantis* VI. 535 For wher that wyn doth wit aweie, Wisdom hath loste the rihte weie. 1528 MORE *Dial. agst. Tyndale* ed. W. E. Campbell 246 When the wine were in and the wit out. 1555 HEYWOOD *Epig. upon Prov.* no. CLXIII When ale is in, wyt is out. 1560 BECON *Cat.* P.S. 375 When the wine is in, the wit is out. 1598–9 SHAKES. *M.A.* III. v. 33 When the age is in, the wit is out. 1710 PALMER 18 (the Wit's out). 1839 DICKENS *N. Nickleby* ch. 27 'Oh, ho!' thought our knowing Lady [Mrs. Nickleby]; 'Wine in, truth out.' 1858 SURTEES *Ask Mamma* ch. 58 It was just the wine being in and the wit being out . . . that led him away.

Wine is a turncoat (first a friend, then an enemy). (W 480)

1640 HERBERT no. 929.

Wine is a whetstone to wit. (W 491)

1581–90 *Timon* II v. 39 Wine's valours whetstone. 1597 *Politeuphuia* 38. 1647 *Countryman's New Commonwealth* 14. 1736 BAILEY *Dict.* s.v. Whetstone.

Wine is drawn; The | it must be drunk.

1853 TRENCH ii. 43 At the siege of Douay, in 1667, Louis XIV . . . under a heavy cannonade . . . was about . . . to retire; when M. de Charost . . . whispered . . . in his ear: *The wine is drawn; it must be drunk.* [Le vin est tiré; il faut le boire.] 1891 J. L. KIPLING *Beast & Man* 123 A Bengal saying recalling the French 'When the cork is drawn, the wine must be drunk' is, 'Milk once drawn from the dug never goes back'.

Wine is not common, Where | commons must be sent. *Cf.* **Coin is not common.** (C 508)

1611 GRUTER 187. 1614 CAMDEN 314. 1659 HOWELL *Eng. Prov.* 10a.

Wine is old men's milk. (W 483)

1584 COGAN *Haven of Health* (1636) 244 To old men, wine is as sucke to young children, and is therefore called of some *Lac senum.* 1586 GUAZZO ii. 154. 1659 HOWELL *Fr. Prov.* 13. 1809 MALKIN *Gil Blas* x. i You reprobate the ignorance of those writers who dignify wine with the appellation of old men's milk.

Wine is the best liquor to wash glasses in.

1738 SWIFT *Dial.* II. E.L. 317 John, bring clean glasses. — I 'll keep mine; for I think wine is the best liquor to wash glasses in.

Wine is the master's, The | the good-
ness is the butler's (drawer's). (w 482)

1639 CLARKE 204 (drawers). **1678** RAY *Adag.
Hebr.* 401.

Wine is the glass of the mind. (w 481)

[ERASM. *Ad.* quoting Aesch. fr. 288 Κάτοπτρον
εἴδους χαλκός ἐστ', οἶνος δὲ νοῦ.] **1580** LYLY
Euph. & his Eng. ii. 83. **1584** *Id. Sappho & Phao*
II. iv. 80 Grapes are minde glasses.

Wine makes all sorts of creatures at
table. (w 484)

1640 HERBERT no. 931.

Wine makes old wives wenches.
(w 485)

1639 CLARKE 192.

Wine savours (will taste) of the cask,
The.

1579 LYLY *Euph.* i. 191 Season the woode neuer
so well the wine will taste of the caske. **1621**
BURTON *Anat. Mel.* I. ii. v. i (1638) 173 As wine
savours of the caske wherein it is kept; the soul
receives a tincture from the body, through which
it workes. **1662** FULLER Wilts. 155 If any fusti-
ness be found in his Writings, it comes not from
the Grape, but from the Cask. The smack of
Superstition in his books is . . . to be imputed . . .
to the Age wherein he[1] lived. [[1] William of
Malmesbury.]

Wine sinks, When | words swim.

1721 KELLY 354. **1732** FULLER no. 5622.

Wine that cost nothing is digested
before it be drunk. (w 489)

1640 HERBERT no. 932. **1732** FULLER no. 5750.

Wine, Of | the middle, of oil the top,
and of honey the bottom, is the best.
(w 467)

[MACROB. *Saturn.* VII. 12. *Quaero igitur, Cur
oleum quod in summo est, vinum quod in medio,
mel quod in fundo optimum esse credantur.*] **1580**
LYLY *Euph. & his Eng.* ii. 219 The oyle that
swimmeth in the top is the wholsomest . . . the
honny that lieth in the bottome is the sweetest
. . . the wine which is in the middest . . . the finest.
1603 PLUTARCH *Moralia* tr. Holland 'Of Sym-
posiaques' vii. 3 What is the cause, that the mids
of wine, the top of oile, and the bottome of
honie, is best. **1659** HOWELL *It. Prov.* 15. **1662**
FULLER Hants. 2 It is an old and true rule, 'the
best Oyle is in the top; the best Wine in the
middle; and the best Hony in the bottome.'
1678 RAY 41 Vino di mezzo, oglio di sopra &
miele di sotto.

Wine there is truth, In. (w 465)

[Gk. Ἐν οἴνῳ ἀλήθεια.—L. *In vino veritas.*] **1545**
TAVERNER H5[v] *In uino ueritas.* In wyne is
trouthe. *c.* **1590** LYLY *Mother B.* III. iii. 31 I
perceiue sober men tel most lies, for *in vino*

veritas. If they had drunke wine, they would
haue tolde the truth. **1597** DELONEY I *Gentle
Craft* Wks. (Mann) 129 Wine is the bewrayer
of secrets. **1598–9** SHAKES. *M.A.* III. iii. 98
Borachio. [Span. a drunkard] I will, like a true
drunkard, utter all to thee. **1611** COTGRAVE
s.v. Mentir Wine telleth truth and should not be
belyed. **1772** BOSWELL in *Johnson* xxvii (1848)
242 I . . . had recourse to the maxim, *in vino
veritas,* a man who is well warmed with wine
will speak truth. **1869** TROLLOPE *He knew he
was right* ch. 51 There is no saying truer than
that . . . there is truth in wine. Wine . . . has the
merit of forcing a man to show his true colours.

Wine washes off the daub.

1732 FULLER no. 5752.

Wine wears no breeches. (w 490)

1611 COTGRAVE s.v. Vin Wine wanteth, or goeth
without, breeches; *viz.* bewrayeth a mans
infirmities. **1659** HOWELL *Eng. Prov.* 7a.

Wine, *see also* Ale (W.) is in (When), wit is out;
Ask mine host whether he have good w.; Best
w. comes out of old vessel; Best w. is . . . at
another's cost; Commend not your w.; Counsels
in w. seldom prosper; Cries w., sells vinegar;
Drink w. and have gout; Drinks not w. after
salad (He that); Gaming, women, and w.; Good
wind that blows to w.; Good w. engendres good
blood; Good w. needs no bush; Milk says to w.
welcome; Old friends and old w. are best; Old
wood is best . . . old w. to drink; Peach will have
w.; Play, women, and w. undo; Poison (One
drop) infects tun of w.; Praise the w. before
. . .; Spilt w. worse than water; Women and w.
. . . make the wealth small; Vinegar of sweet w.
(Take heed of).

Wing (*proper name*), *see* Tring.

Wing(s), *see* Ant had w. to her hurt; Bill under
w.; Bird must flighter that flies with one w.;
Clip the w. of; Covers me with his w.; Fear
gives w.; Flying without w. (No); Gives thee a
capon; Lies have no w.; Ignorant has eagle's w.;
Mischief has swift w.; Riches have w.; Tail
broader than thy w. (Make not); Words have w.

Wink and choose. (w 501)

a. **1576** WHYTHORNE 203 Hee that will marry
must wink and drink, and tak the good or ill
fortiun that God will send him. *c.* **1614** WEBSTER
Duch. of Malfi I. i. 390 Let old wives report I
winckèd and chose a husband. **1621** BURTON
Anat. Mel. Democr. to Rdr. (1638) 46 Goe backward or forward, choose out of the whole pack,
wink and choose: you shall find them all alike.
1678 RAY 347 One may wink and choose.

Wink at small faults. (F 123)

1543 G. COUSIN *Office of Servants* B1[v] On thone
part, auaileth the masters ieutilnes, and (as who
saith) winking at smal faultes. **1558** CRANMER
Confutn tr. E.P. G6[v] They wynke one at anothers
faultes, and helpe to cloke the same. **1599**
SHAKES. *Hen. V* II. ii. 55 If little faults, . . . Shall

not be wink'd at, how shall we stretch our eye
When capital crimes, . . . Appear before us?
1639 CLARKE 225.   **1721** KELLY 341 . . . for you
have great ones yourself.

Wink (*noun*), *see* Nod is as good as w.

Winkabank and Temple brough will buy all England through and through.
(w 502)

1678 RAY 340 *Yorkshire.* . . . *Winkabank* is a
wood upon a hill near Sheffield where there are
some remainders of an old Camp. *Temple
brough* stands between the *Rother* and the *Don.*
. . . It is a square plat of ground encompassed
by two trenches.

Winks with one eye, He that | and looks with the other, I will not trust him though he were my brother. (E 241)

c. **1390** GOWER *Conf. Amantis* I. 1. 384 Betre is
to winke than to loke.   **1530** PALSGRAVE 782.
c. **1549** HEYWOOD I. xi. EI[v].   **1614** CAMDEN 307.
a. **1628** CARMICHAELL no. 1000 (Quho lookes up
with the ane eye and doun with the other).   **1721**
KELLY 169 He that looks with one Eye, and
winks with another, I will not believe him,
though he was my Brother. If the Man naturally
squint, my Countrymen have an Aversion to
him, and all who have any Thing disagreeable, if
he wink, or nod, they look upon him to be a
false Man.

Wink(s), *see also* Cat w. (When), little wots
mouse; Garlic makes a man w.; Rain rains and
the goose w. (When), little wots gosling; Time
to w. as well as to see.

Winner, *see* Games it is good leave off a w.

Winneral (Winnold), *see* First comes David.

Winning is not in my tinsel,[1] Your.
(w 505)

1668 R.B. 57.   **1721** KELLY 378. [1 craw.]

Winning, *see also* Lay your wame to your w.

Winter, After a rainy | a plentiful summer.

1706 STEVENS s.v. Invierno.   **1893** INWARDS
Weather Lore 9.

Winter eats (finds out) what summer lays up.
(w 510)

c. **1450–1500** *The Gd. Wife wd. a Pilgrimage* l. 78
Wynttor ettyþe þat somor gettyþ.   **1678** RAY
219 (finds out).

Winter enough for the snipe and wood-cock too, There is.

1732 FULLER no. 4939.

Winter is summer's heir.
(w 511)

1678 RAY 218.

Winter never died in a ditch.

1883 ROPER 33.   **1893** INWARDS 8.

Winter never rots in the sky.
(w 512)

1612–15 BP. HALL *Contempl.* XIII. i. (1825) I. 368
God . . . chooses out a fit season for the execution. As we use to say of winter, the judgments
of God do never rot in the sky, but shall fall, if
late, yet surely, yet seasonably.   **1642** D. ROGERS
Naaman ix. 264 Beware therefore of extremities,
and till the Lord hath truly brought down thy
winter out of the sky, know it will never rot
there.

Winter thunder (bodes) summer hunger.

1721 KELLY 353.   **1846** DENHAM 3 Winter
thunder bodes summer hunger.

Winter's thunder and summer's flood never boded Englishman good.
(w 514)

1659 HOWELL *Eng. Prov.* 17a.   **1670** RAY 44.
1732 FULLER no. 6479.

Winter's thunder makes summer's (old man's) wonder.
(T 277. W 515)

1605 R. VERSTEGAN *Restitution Decayed Intelligence* (1673) ch. 7.   **1611** COTGRAVE s.v. Tonner.
1636 CAMDEN 310.   **1639** CLARKE 263 Winter
thunder, is old mens wonder.   **1658** T. WILLS-
FORD *Natures Secrets* 113 Thunder and lightning
in Winter . . . is held ominous . . . and a thing
seldome seen, according to the old Adigy,
Winters thunder, is the Sommers wonder.

Winter, *see also* Age (W.) and wedlock tames;
Good w. good summer; Green w. fat churchyard; Hard w. when wolf eats another; Life of
man is a w.'s way and w.'s day; Mile is two in
w.; Passes a w.'s day escapes an enemy;
Summer but it has a w. (No); Woodcock does
not make w. (One).

Winter-time for shoeing, peascod-time for wooing.

1841 BRAND *Pop. Antiq.* (Bohn) ii. 100 [quoted
as 'an old proverb in a MS.' Devon Glossary].
1846 DENHAM 64.

Wipe one's nose on one's sleeve, To.
(N 243)

c. **1436** *Libelle of Englyshe Polycye* in Wright
Polit. Poems II. 176 And thus they wold, if we
will beleve, Wypen our nose with our owne sleve.
1546 HEYWOOD II. ix. L2[v] And I maie set you
besyde the cushyn yit, And make ye wype your
nose vpon your sleeue.   **1575** J. HIGGINS in
Udall *Flowers for Latin Speaking* Y2[v] Possibly
he shall go without, or shall wype his nose on
his sleeve.   **1577** R. STANYHURST in Holinshed
Desc. Ireland (1587) 18b For anie recompense
he is like to haue at mine hands, he may wipe
his nose on his sleeue.   **1659** HOWELL *Fr. Prov.*
22 He wiped his nose with his own sleeve, viz.
he cousened him neatly.

Wipe the nose of someone, To. (N 244)

[= deprived, defrauded of something.] **1563** J.
PILKINGTON *Questions* P.S. 643 Daila has wiped
his [Goliath's] nose. **1577** HOLINSHED *Chron.* ii.
323b Hee deuised a shifte howe to wype the
bysshoppes nose of some of his golde. **1598** R.
BERNARD *Terence, Eunuch* I. i The very destruction of our substance: who wipes our noses of
all that we should have. **1611** CHAPMAN *May
Day* v. i. 267 Wilt thou suffer thy nose to be
wiped of this great heir? **1667** PEPYS *Diary* 17
July That the King [might] own a marriage . . .
with the Queen, and so wipe their noses of the
Crown. **1678** RAY 343 I wip't his nose on it.
1721 CIBBER *Rival Fools* Wks. II. 1754 I. 29 I
durst lay my life thou wipest this foolish knight's
nose of his mistress at last.

**Wipes his nose and has it not, He that |
forfeits his face to the king.** (N 221)

1591 *Wonderful Prognost.* Nashe iii. 387 (as
1592). **1592** NASHE *Pierce Penn.* i. 181 He that
wipes his nose, and hath it not, shall forfeit
hys whole face. **1609** HARWARD 106ᵛ. **1672**
WALKER 9 no. 28. **1678** RAY 86 (He that snites
[wipes] his nose). A man can do no more then
he can.

**Wipes the child's nose, He that | kisses
the mother's cheek.** (C 323)

1640 HERBERT no. 1032. **1659** HOWELL *Span.
Prov.* 18. **1706** STEVENS s.v. Hijo He who wipes
my Son's Nose kisses my Face; that is, the small
Kindness shown to my Child, I take as a double
one to my self.

Wipe(s), *see also* Clout a man will not w. his
nose on, (It is a foul); Never kiss a man's wife
nor w. his knife.

**Wire-drawer under his work, To sit
like a.** (W 517)
1670 RAY 217. *Yorksh.*

Wires, *see* Death upon w.

**Wisdom counsels, Well goes the case
when.**

1707 MAPLETOFT 126 (Welsh). **1736** BAILEY *Dict.*
s.v. Wisdom.

**Wisdom (Constancy) has one foot on
land, and another on sea.**
(C 618. W 525)

1598–9 SHAKES. *M.A.* II. iii. 58 Men were
deceivers ever, One foot in sea, and one on
shore; To one thing constant never. **1640**
HERBERT no. 611. **1659** N.R. 119. **1664** COD-
RINGTON 190 (Constancy). *Ibid.* 229 (Wisdome...
at Sea).

Wisdom is better than strength.
(W 527)

c. **1200** LAYAMON *Brut* l. 17210 Hit was isaid wile/
þat betere his sleahþe/ þane vuele strengþe.

c. **1250** *Owl & Nightingale* ed. E. G. Stanley l.
762 Vor soþ, hit is þat seide Alured: 'Ne mai
no strengþe aȝen red.' *c.* **1250** *Ancrene Riwle*
120. **1591** ARIOSTO *Orl. Fur.* Harington XV.
Moral So much they preferred wisedome that
is peculiar to man, before strength that is common to beasts. **1611** COTGRAVE s.v. Engin
Better be wise then strong. **1616** DRAXE no.
2436. **1664** CODRINGTON 224. **1736** BAILEY
Dict. s.v. Wisdom (goes beyond).

Wisdom, What is not | is danger.
(W 521)

1659 HOWELL *Brit. Prov.* 2 (wisdom (or discretion)). **1707** MAPLETOFT 125 (Welsh). **1878**
J. PLATT *Morality* 34.

Wisdom peace, By | by peace plenty.
(W 518)

1611 GRUTER 175. **1614** CAMDEN 304. **1621**
ROBINSON 31 (. . . by plenty warre).

**Wisdom to find out one's own folly, It
is a great point of.**

1732 FULLER no. 2860.

Wisdom to silence, No. (W 519)

[PLUTARCH *De Liberis educ.* 14. 10E Σοφὸν γὰρ
εὔκαιρος σιγὴ καὶ παντὸς λόγου κρεῖττον. There
is wisdom in timely silence which is better than
all speech.] **1620** J.C. *Two Mer. Milk-Maids* II.
ii. F3 Silence Lady is the best part of Wisdome.
1659 HOWELL *Br. Prov.* 27. **1732** FULLER no.
4169 Silence is Wisdom, when speaking is Folly.

Wisdom, Without | wealth is worthless.

[PROV. xvi. 16 How much better is it to get
wisdom than gold!] *c.* **1275** *Provs. of Alfred*
(Skeat) A 119 Wyþ-vte wysdome is weole wel
vnwurþ. [Without wisdom wealth is of little
value.]

Wisdom, *see also* Coat, (Under a ragged) lies w.;
Experience mother of w.; Haste and w. far odd;
Hearing (From) comes w.; Husband (In) w.;
Money, w., and good faith (Of) less than count
upon; Trouble brings . . . w.; Wit and w.; Wit to
pick lock and steal horse, w. to let alone.

Wise after the event, It is easy to be.
(E 192)

c. **1584** G. HARVEY *Marginalia* ed. Moore Smith
99 Had I wist, cummith too late: It is good,
to be wise before the Mischiff. **1609** JONSON *Silent
Wom.* II. iv. 81 Away, thou strange iustifier of
thyselfe, to bee wiser then thou wert, by the euent!
1666 TORRIANO *It. Prov.* 249 no. 23 After the business is over, every one is wise. **1900** A. LANG
Hist. Scot. I. i To the wisdom which comes after
the event the map of Scotland seems, in part, a
prophecy of her history. **1900** A. C. DOYLE *Boer
War* (1902) ch. 19 It is easy to be wise after the
event, but it does certainly appear that . . . the
action at Paardeberg was as unnecessary as it
was expensive.

Wise and great, He that is truly | lives both too early and too late.

1856 ABP. WHATELY *Annot. Bacon's Ess.* (1876) 240 A man . . . will often be mortified at perceiving that he has come too late for some things, and too soon for others. . . . Hence the proverb—. . .

Wise as a daw, As.   (D 50)

c. **1525** [J. RASTELL?] *Gentleness & Nobility* C2ᵛ Then fare ye well as wyse as two dawys. *c.* **1592** SHAKES. *1 Hen. VI* II. iv. 18 Good faith, I am no wiser than a daw. **1609** HARWARD 80ᵛ Construe Logick and spell law And then proove as wise as a daw.

Wise as a goose, As.   (G 348)

1509 BARCLAY *Ship of Fools* i. 179 As wyse as a gander. **1528** MORE *Wks.* (1557) 179b And all as wise as wilde geese. **1530** PALSGRAVE 873b.

Wise as a man of Gotham, As.   (M 636)

[Ironical.] *c.* **1410** *Towneley Plays* 106 Sagh I neuer none so fare bot the foles of gotham. **1526** *Hundr. Merry Tales* (Oesterley) no. xxiv. 45 (title) Of the III wyse men of gotam. **1659** HOWELL *Eng. Prov.* 6a You are as wise as the men of Gotham, who went to build a wall about the wood to keep out the Cuckow. **1662** FULLER Notts. 315 . . . It passeth publickly for the Periphrasis of a Fool; and a hundred Fopperies are . . . fathered on the Town-folk of Gotham, . . . in this County. **1720** SWIFT *Prop. for Univ. Use of Irish Manuf. Wks.* ed. Davis ix. 15 A Volume as large as the History of the wise Men of Goatham. **1824** MOIR *Mansie W.* ch. 12 It was an agreed . . . thing among . . . these wise men of Gotham, to abolish all kings, clergy, and religion.

Wise as a wisp, As.   (W 540)

1530 PALSGRAVE 873b. **1548–50** BALE *Eng. Votaries* II. 84 As wyse as ii wyspes, and as godly as ii goselynges.   —

Wise as a woodcock, As.   (W 746)

c. **1512** *Hickscorner* C3 I was as wyse as a woodcock. **1520** R. WHITTINGTON *Vulg.* E.E.T.S. 60 He hath . . . as many braynes as a woodcok. **1670** RAY 203 (a wisp, or woodcock).

Wise as Waltham's calf, As.   (W 22)

[Ironical.] *c.* **1525** SKELTON *Col. Cloute* l. 811 As wyse as Waltom's calfe. **1543** BARNES *In the Defence of the Berde* ll. 115–16 Who goth a myle to sucke a bull, Comes home a fole, and yet not full. **1546** HEYWOOD II. iii. G2. **1562** J. WIGAND *De Neutralibus* K8ᵛ These . . . Iackes of both sydes . . . would not be compted for blocke heades, nor to speake as wise as a Calfe. **1586** R. CROWLEY *Friar John Francis* A4 As wyse as Waltams Calfe that ranne nine miles to sucke a Bull. **1639** CLARKE 285 (wattom's calfe). **1659** HEYLIN *Animadv. on Ch. Hist.* in FULLER's *Appeal Inj. Innoc.* (1840) 596 But certainly our author showed himself 'no wiser than Waltham's calf, who ran nine miles to suck a bull, and came home athirst', as the proverb saith.

Wise behind the hand, To be.

1567–83 *Satirical Poems* S.T.S. no. XLIII, l. 212 As Scottismans wisdome dois behinde the hand. **1621** ROBINSON 35. *a.* **1628** CARMICHAELL no. 97 (A foole is). **1820** SCOTT in Lockhart's *Life* v. 42 The next night, being, like true Scotsmen, wise behind the hand, the bailies had a sufficient force . . . and put down every attempt to riot.

Wise, None is so | but the fool overtakes him.   (F 500)

1640 HERBERT no. 734. **1659** HOWELL *Fr. Prov.* 7 There's none so wise, but women may besot him.

Wise child that knows its own father, It is a.   (C 309)

[HOM. *Od.* I. 216 Οὐ γάρ πώ τις ἐὸν γόνον αὐτὸς ἀνέγνω.] **1584** WITHALS L4 Wise sonnes they be in very deede, That knowe their Parentes who did them breede. **1589** GREENE *Wks.* Gros. vi. 92 For wise are the children in these dayes that know their owne fathers. **1596** SHAKES. *M.V.* II. ii. 69 It is a wise father that knows his own child. **1607** TOURNEUR *Rev. Trag.* II. i The world's so changed into another, It is a wise child now that knows his mother. **1613** WITHER *Abuses; Of Desire* v. 27 Is't not hence this common proverb grows, 'Tis a wise child that his own father knows? **1762** GOLDSMITH *The Mystery Revealed* Wks. (1912) II. 472 She called her father John instead of Thomas, . . . but perhaps she was willing to verify the old proverb, that 'It is a wise child that knows its own father'. **1827** SCOTT *Surg. D.* ch. 9 It is not every child that knows its own father, nor how can every man be so sure of his own name?

Wise enough that can keep himself warm, He is.   (K 10)

1537 *Thersites* C4 Sonne, ye be wise, kepe ye warme. **1546** HEYWOOD II. ii. F4ᵛ Ye are wise enough (quoth he) yf ye kepe ye warme. **1594–8** SHAKES. *T.S.* II. i. 258 Am I not wise?—Yes; keep you warm. **1598–9** *Id. M.A.* I. i. 56 If he have wit enough to keep himself warm. **1614** JONSON *Barth. Fair* v. iv. 364 In a Scriuener's furred gowne, which shewes he is no foole. For therein he hath wit enough to keepe himselfe warme. **1670** RAY 28.

Wise erred not, If the | it would go hard with fools.   (W 529)

1640 HERBERT no. 510. **1642** TORRIANO 92 If the wise man should never miscarry, the fool would burst. **1707** MAPLETOFT 110.

Wise fear begets care.

c. **1626** J. SMYTH *Lives of the Berkeleys* i. 275 The proverbe That to abstaine and distrust are two mayne sinewes of wisdome. **1707** MAPLETOFT 8 Wise Distrust is the Parent of Security. **1732** FULLER no. 6355.

Wise hand does not all that the foolish mouth speaks, The.   (H 105)

1640 HERBERT no. 246.

Wise head makes a close mouth, A.
(H 276)

c. **1386** CHAUCER *Miller's T.* l. 3598 Men seyn thus 'sende the wise, and sey no thyng'. *c.* **1590** *John of Bordeaux* l. 1086 Him count I wise that well his tung can kepe. **1678** RAY 219. **1732** FULLER no. 469 (hath a close mouth to it).

Wise man by day is no fool by night, He that is a.
(M 173)

1642 TORRIANO 26 He who is accounted a wise man in the day time, is no fool in the night. **1659** HOWELL *It. Prov.* 6 Who is wise in the day can be no fool in the night.

Wise man cares not for what he cannot have, A.
(M 600)

1640 HERBERT no. 662. **1670** RAY 29.

Wise man changes his mind, a fool never, A.
(M 420)

c. **1390** CHAUCER *T. Melibee* l. 1064 No folie to chaunge conseil whan the thyng is chaunged. **1570** BALDWIN *Beware the Cat* (1584) A7 A wise man may in some things chaunge his opinion. **1631** MABBE *Celestina* T.T. 104 A wise man altreth his purpose, but a foole persevereth in his folly. **1659** HOWELL *Span. Prov.* 9 The wise man changeth counsel, the fool perseveres. **1817** 9 May BYRON *Letters* Prothero iv. 118 Opinions are made to be changed, or how is truth to be got at?

Wise man commonly has foolish children, A.
(M 421)

1545 TAVERNER H2ᵛ Our common Englyshe prouerbe sayeth, that the wisest men haue moost foles to theyr chyldren. **1594** LYLY *Mother B.* v. iii. 111 A wise man . . . commonly hath a foole to his heyre. **1608** *Ram Alley* IV. i. Hazl.-Dods. x. 352 Why may not I, a fool, get a wise child, as well as wise men get fools?

Wise (valiant) man esteems every place to be his own country, A.
(M 426)

1539 TAVERNER I *Garden* E8ᵛ Demaunded, what countryman he [Diogenes] was, he aunswered, a worldly man. Signyfienge that a wyse man, where so euer in the worlde he be, liueth in his owne countrey. **1562** A. BROOKE *Romeus & Juliet* l. 1443 Unto a valiant heart there is no banishment. All countries are his native soil beneath the firmament. **1579** LYLY *Euph.* i. 314 Socrates would . . . call him selfe . . . a Citizen of the world. Plato . . . noted that euery place was a countrey to a wise man, and all partes a pallaice to a quiet minde. *c.* **1594** SHAKES. *Rich. II* I. iii. 275 All places that the eye of Heaven visits Are to a wise man ports and happy havens. **1602** MARSTON *Antonio's Revenge* l. 696 A wise mans home is wheresoere he is wise. **1605** JONSON *Volpone* II. i. 1 To a wise man all the world's his soil. **1706** STEVENS s.v. Varon Any Country is a Native Soil to a good Man. A wise and good man is easie in all Countries.

Wise man is a great wonder, A. (M 423)

1624 BURTON *Anat. Mel.* Democr. to Reader 36. **1639** CLARKE 314 (a wonder). **1732** FULLER no. 472.

Wise man is never less alone than when he is alone, A.
(A 228)

[CIC. *De Offic.* 3. 1, quoted by **1642** BROWNE *Rel. Med.* Pt. II (1881) 114.] *c.* **1555** *Songs and Bal. Philip and Mary* 6, Roxb. Cl. 22 Never was I lesse alone then beyng alone. **1567** PAINTER ed. Jacobs ii. 150 The saying which Tullie aduoucheth of Publius Scipio . . . that he was . . . neuer lesse alone, than when he was alone. **1581** GUAZZO i. 49 Scipio sayd that he was neuer lesse alone then when he was alone. **1595** LIPSIUS 2 *Bks. of Constancy* K1 I am neuer less solitarie (said he) then when I am alone: nor neuer less idle then when I am at leisure. **1601** SHAKES. *T.N.* I. iv. 36 Some four or five attend him—All, if you will; for I myself am best When least in company. **1621** BURTON *Anat. of Mel.* I. ii. ii. vi. (1638) 89. **1669** PENN *No Cross, No Crown* xix Scipio Africanus . . . used to say, That he was never less alone, than when he was alone. **1707** SWIFT *Facult. of Mind* Wks. (1904) 416 Contemplation . . . exceeds action. And therefore a wise man is never less alone than when he is alone: *Nunquam minus solus, quam cum solus.* **1819** 10 Dec. BYRON *Corres.* ed. J. Murray 1922 ii. 130 I am . . . never more alone than when alone.

Wise man may sometimes (He is not wise who cannot) play the fool, A. *Cf.* No man can play the fool so well.
(M 428)

c. **1500** *Proverbs at Wressell* (*Antiq. Rep.* iv. (1809), 415) It is no wysdome allway to seme sage, but sumtyme as be pretens to shew foly . . . Sumtyme to be unwyse in apparens, Amonge the wyse is called grete prudens. **1545** *Precepts of Cato* H2ᵛ Some tyme to playe the foole is a poynt of wyt. **1549** ERASM. tr. Chaloner *Praise of Folly* Q1ᵛ This verse of Cato . . . It is most wysedome for a man in place to counterfaicte Folie. **1557** EDGEWORTH *Sermons* 203ᵛ Thys comon prouerbe: Stultitiam simulare loco prudentia summa est, To fayne foolishnesse in some case, is very highe wisedome. **1597** *Politeuphuia* 29ᵛ To play the foole well, is a signe of wisedom. **1601** SHAKES. *T.N.* III. i. 64 Folly that he wisely shows, is fit. **1601** JONSON *Poetaster* IV. v. 46 I haue reade in a booke, that to play the foole wisely, is high wisdome. **1640** F. QUARLES *Enchiridion* Cent. 4 no. 96 It is a great part of wisdome, sometimes to seem a fool. **1732** FULLER no. 1929 He is no wise Man, that cannot play the Fool upon Occasion.

Wise man must carry the fool upon his shoulders, The.
(M 430)

1573 SANFORD 104. **1623** WODROEPHE 489.

Wise man needs not blush for changing his purpose, A.
(M 431)

1545 *Precepts of Cato* E3ᵛ In a wyse man it is no maner of cryme, His maners to chaunge, accordynge to the tyme. **1573** SANFORD 52ᵛ

(ought not to be ashamed to change). **1629**
Bk. Mer. Rid. Prov. no. 43 (ought not to be
ashamed to alter). **1640** HERBERT no. 613.

Wise man never wants a weapon, A.
Cf. Wight man, *etc.*

1736 BAILEY *Dict.* s.v. Weapon.

**Wise man on an errand, Send a | and
say nothing to him.** (M 371)

c. **1386** CHAUCER *Miller's T.* l. 3598 Men seyn
thus 'send the wyse, and sey no thyng'. **1461**
July DENYS to M. Paston (Gairdner 1904)
Paston Let. iii. 285 Men sey, send a wiseman on
thy erand, and sey litell to hym, wherfor I write
brefly and litell. **1616** DRAXE no. 2084 (on your
errand). **1640** HERBERT no. 217.

**Wise man though you can't make a
watch, You may be a.** (M 439)

1664 CODRINGTON 231. **1670** RAY 29.

**Wise man, He is a | who, when he is
well can keep so.** (H 512)

1587 J. BRIDGES *Def. of Gvt. of C. of E.* 149 It
is good keeping themselues well when they are
well. **1616** DRAXE no. 353 A man must keepe
himselfe well when he is well. *a.* **1628** CAR-
MICHAELL no. 674 He is wyse that quhen he is
weill can hald him sua. **1641** FERGUSSON no.
322 He is wise when he is well, can had[1] him
sa. **1721** KELLY 357 When you are well hold
you so. A Discouragement from hazarding the
Alteration of our Condition by new Projects.
[1 hold.]

Wise men are caught in (with) wiles.
(M 599)

1205 LAYAMON *Brut* (Madden) I. 32 Nis nawer
nan so wis mon That me ne mai biswiken.
[There is nowhere so wise a man that one may
not deceive.] *c.* **1600** *Mer. Devil of Ed.* v. i. 71
The wisest man that is may be o'erreached.
1639 CLARKE 266. **1721** KELLY 360 (caught with).
I have writ down this proverb as the English have
it, because in Scotch it is smutty.

**Wise men have their mouth in their
heart, fools their heart in their mouth.**
(M 602)

1477 RIVERS *Dictes & Sayings* (1877) 140 And
another said the tonge of a discrete man is in
his herte & the herte of a foole is in his tonge.
1579 LYLY *Euph.* i. 279 It is an olde Prouerbe:
Whatsoeuer is in the heart of the sober man, is in
the mouth of the drunckarde. **1630** BRATHWAIT
Eng. Gent. (1641) 47 These are those fooles,
which carry their Hearts in their Mouthes; and
farre from those wise men, which carry their
Mouthes in their Hearts.

**Wise men learn by other men's harms
(mistakes); fools, by their own.** (M 615)

[PLAUTUS *Mercator* iv. 7. 40 (interpolated)
Feliciter is sapit qui periculo alieno sapit. He

is happy in his wisdom, who is wise at the
expense of another. ERASM. *Ad. Felix quem
faciunt aliena pericula cautum.*] *c.* **1374** CHAUCER
Troilus Bk. 3, l. 329 For wyse ben by foles harm
chastysed. **1583** G. BABINGTON *Ten Commandments* (1588, 384). **1732** FULLER no. 5779.

**Wise men make proverbs and fools
repeat them.** (M 604)

1710 PALMER Pref. viii Wise men make Proverbs,
but Fools Repeat 'em. **1857** DEAN RAMSAY
Remin. v. (1911) 198 *Fules mak' feasts, and wise
men eat em* ... was said to a Scottish nobleman
... who readily answered, 'Ay, and *Wise men
make proverbs and fools repeat 'em*'.

**Wise men play the fool, If | they do it
with a vengeance.**

1707 MAPLETOFT 20.

Wise men propose, and fools determine.
(M 605)

1625 BACON *Apophthegms* no. 231 (dispose).
1692 L'ESTRANGE *Aesop's Fab.* cxxii (1738) 139
Right reason deliberates. ... The old saying is
a shrewd one; that ...

Wise men silent, fools talk. (M 606)

a. **1561** *Queen Hester* D2 Fooles will tell all and
that trobleth sore, And wyse men will say nought
at al till al be gone and more. **1590–5** MUNDAY
et al. Sir T. More III. i. 38 Who prates not much
seems wise, his wit few scan; While the tongue
blabs tales of the imperfect man. **1624** BURTON
Anat. Mel. Democr. to Reader 30. **1639**
CLARKE 5.

Wise (wisest) man (men), *see also* Bridges were
made for w. m.; Clerks (The greatest) be not the
w. m.; Fool does in the end (What), w. m.
in beginning; Fool wanders, w. m. travels;
Fools bite one another, but w. m. agree; Fools
build houses, but w. m. live in them; Fools cut
fingers, but w. m. thumbs; Fools lade water,
but w. m. catch fish; Fools make feasts, and
w. m. eat them; Fools tie knots and w. m. loose
them; No man can play fool as w. m.; No man
so w. but he may be deceived; Nod for a w. m.;
Old w. m.'s shadow better than buzzard's
sword; Oppression makes w. m. mad; Reason
governs w. m.; Riches serve a w. m.; Travel
makes a w. m. better; Want of a w. m. (For)
fool set in chair; Word to w. m. enough;
Words are w. m.'s counters.

**Wise that has wit enough for his own
affairs, He is.**

c. **1386** CHAUCER *Monk's T.* l. 3329 Ful wys is he
that kan hymselven knowe! **1732** FULLER no.
1954.

Wise that is honest, He is. (W 533)

1616 BRETON I *Cross.* A7ᵛ. **1639** CLARKE 127.
1670 RAY 13.

Wise that is rich, He is. (w 534)

c. 1525 J. RASTELL *Nat. Four Elem.* A3 That man
is holdyn Moste wyse, whiche to be ryche
studyeth only. 1609 DEKKER *Work for Armour-*
ers E2ᵛ Hee is wise enough that hath wealth
enough. 1616 BRETON 2 *Cross.* A5. 1629 T.
ADAMS *Serm.* (1861–2) II. 128 It is even a maxim
in common acceptation, . . .

Wise that is ware in time, He is. (T 291)

1303 R. BRUNNE *Handl. Synne* 8085 He wys is,
that ware ys. *c.* 1374 CHAUCER *Troilus* Bk. 2,
l. 343 Avysement is good before the nede.
a. 1530 R. *Hill's Commonpl. Bk.* 109, E.E.T.S.
139 He ys wyse that ys ware or he harm fele.
1600–1 SHAKES. *M.W.W.* II. iii. 10 He is dead
already, if he be come.—He is wise, Sir; he knew
your worship would kill him if he came. 1741
FERGUSSON no. 324. 1721 KELLY 156 (wary)
. . . That is, who foresees Harm before it come,
and provides against it.

Wise that ·knows when he's well enough, He is. (E 163)

1493 *Dives et Pauper* A1 It is an olde prouerbe.
He is well atte ease that hath ynough & can saye
ho. 1519 HORMAN *Vulgaria* 104 He is a foole that
cannat holde hym selfe content when he is well
at ease. *c.* 1549 HEYWOOD II. vii. E6 He that
knoweth when he hath enough, is no foole.
1721 KELLY 163 . . . That is a pitch of Wisdome
to which few attain. 1732 FULLER no. 2475.

Wise who first gave a reward, He was very.

12 . . SIR TRISTREM 626 (1886) 18 He was· ful
wise, y say, þat first ʒaue ʒift in land. *c.* 1300
Havelok 1635 He was ful wis þat first yaf mede,[1]
And so was hauelok ful wis here. [1 reward.]

Wise, He is not | who is not wise for himself. (w 532)

[Gk. Μισῶ σοφιστὴν ὅστις οὐχ αὑτῷ σοφός. I
hate the wise man who is not wise for himself.
CIC. *ad Fam.* 7. 6 *Qui ipsi sibi sapiens prodesse*
non quit, nequiquam sapit.] *c.* 1532 *Tales* no. 26
Cicero saythe: That wyse men, that can nat
profytte him selfe, hath but lytell wysdome.
1539 TAVERNER 18 *Nequicquam sapit qui sibi non*
sapit. He is in vayne wyse that is not wyse for
hym selfe. 1576 G. WAPULL *Tide* B1 Ne quisque
sapit, qui sibi non sapit . . . One not wise . . .
1590 LODGE *Rosalynde* Wks. (1883) I. 39 *Non*
sapit, qui non sibi sapit is fondly spoken in such
bitter extreames. [*c.* 1590] 1594 GREENE
Looking-Glass II. ii. 614 You know the old
Proverb, He is not wise that is not wise for himselfe. 1639 CLARKE 22 He is wise that's wyse
for himself.

Wise with whom all things thrive, He seems. (T 184)

1642 TORRIANO 2. 1658 *Comes Facundus* 309.
1732 FULLER no. 2016.

Wise(r, st), *see also* Adversity makes man w.;
Better be happy than w.; Few words to the w.
suffice; Fools are w. as long as silent; Handsome

at twenty nor w. at fifty (He that is not);
Home as w. as one went, (To return); House
well-furnished makes a woman w.; Italians w.
before deed; Love and be w. (Cannot); Marries
ere he be w.; Merry and w.; Mete and measure
make all w.; Money is w.; More nice than w.; No
man is w. all times; Old and w., (Though); Older
and w.; Pie-lid makes w.; Recks not who is rich
(W. is he who); Seldom is long man w.; Some
are w., some otherwise; Think with the w., talk
with the vulgar; Too w. to live long; Trojans
became w. too late; Wind in one's face makes
w.; World is w.

Wiser now you're wed, You will be. (w 228)

1639 CLARKE 266.

Wisest man may fall (be overseen), The. (M 432)

1599 PORTER *Angry Wom. Abingd.* l. 995 The
wisest of us all may fall. [*c.* 1602] 1608 *Merry*
Devil of Edmonton v. i. 71 The wisest man that
is may be o'erreached. 1616 DRAXE no. 2439
No man·so discreet, but that he may be ouer-
scene. 1818 SCOTT *Rob Roy* ch. 23 The best
·and wisest may err.

Wish and wish on.

1852 E. FITZGERALD *Polonius* 13 'Wish and wish
on'. . . . Who has many wishes has generally
but little will. Who has energy of will has few
diverging wishes.

Wish is father to the thought, The, *see* Believe
what we desire (We soon).

Wish one at Jericho, To.

[= to wish one elsewhere.] 1635 T. HEYWOOD
Hier. Bless. Angels iv. 208 Bid such young boys
to stay in Jericho Vntill their beards were grown.
1778 D'ARBLEY *Diary* i. 31 (Mrs. Thrale) They
wish the poor children at Jericho. 1811 E. NARES
Thinks-I-To-Myself i. 23 'I wish they were
further,' says. my dear mother;—'I wish they
were at Jericho' says my dear father. 1850
LYTTON *Caxtons* v. ii I wish Uncle Jack had been
at Jericho before he had brought me up to
London. 1878 J. PAYN *By Proxy* ch. 34 She
wishes you were . . . at Jericho—anywhere else,
in short, than at Sandybeach.

Wish the burn dry because it weets·our feet, We maunna.

1832 HENDERSON 19.

Wish your skin full of holes, It will be long enough ere you. (s 508)

1599 PORTER *Angry Wom. Abingd.* l. 2971 Twill
be a good while, ere you wish your skin full of
llet holes. 1678 RAY 219.

Wish(ed, es), *see also* Better to have than w.;
Fared worse than when I w. for supper (I
never); Praises who w. to sell (He); Want
(W.) a thing done (If you).

Wishers and woulders be no good householders.   (w 539)

c. **1510** STANBRIDGE *Vulg.* E.E.T.S. 30 Wysshers and wolders be small housholders. **1546** HEY-WOOD I. xi. D2ᵛ Sonne (quoth he) as I haue herd of myne olders, Wishers and wolders be no good householders. **1614–16** *Times Whistle* vii. 3276–8 But the olde proverbe is exceeding true, 'That these great wishers, & these common woulders, Are never (for the moste part) good house-holders'. **1641** FERGUSSON no. 870 Wishers and walders are poore housealders. **1870** SCHAFF *Comm. Prov.* xxi. 25–6 Wishers and woulders are neither good householders nor long livers.

Wishes never can fill a sack.

1666 TORRIANO *It. Prov.* 29 no. 20 By longing thou shalt never fill up thy sack.

Wishes were butter-cakes, If | beggars might bite.   (w 536)

1678 RAY 219.

Wishes were horses, If | beggars would ride.   (w 538)

a. **1628** CARMICHAELL no. 140 (pure¹ men wald ryde). **1721** KELLY 178. **1844** HALLIWELL *Nursery Rhymes of Eng.* 217 If wishes were horses, Beggars would ride; If turnips were watches, I would wear one by my side. **1912** *Brit. Wkly.* 18 Jan. If wishes were horses Unionists would ride rapidly into office. [¹ poor].

Wishes were thrushes (truths), If | then beggars would eat birds.   (w 537)

1610 T. MILLES *Catalogue of Honor* Ep. Ded. If wishes were Thrushes, that Beggers might eat Black-birds. **1623** CAMDEN 272 (truths). **1636** *Ibid.* 300.

Wishes would bide, If | beggars would ride.   (w 538)

1611 COTGRAVE s.v. Pastoureau If wishes might succeed poore men would Princes be. **1659** HOWELL *Fr. Prov.* 11 If wishes were true, Coblers had been Kings. **1670** RAY 157 ... Si souhaits furent vrais pastoureaux seroyent rois, *Gall.* If wishes might prevail, shepherds would be kings.

Wisp, *see* Wise as a w.

Wist, *see* Blab is w.; Had I w.

Wit and wisdom is good warison.¹

c. **1300** *Provs. of Hending* 3 (*Rel. Antiq.* (1841) i. 109) Wyt and wysdom is god warysoun. [¹ provision or store.]

Wit at will, He has.   (w 552)

c. **1470** *Songs and Carols* 37 Percy S. no. 73 If thou haue wysdom at thi wyll. [*c.* **1589**] **1594** LODGE *Wounds* l. 1639 Both of you haue words and scoffs at will. **1593** *The Passionate Morrice* New Sh. S. 75 Though shee had wit at will, and was very proper. **1738** SWIFT *Dial.* I. E.L. 260 She's very handsome, and has wit at will. **1822** SCOTT *Pirate* ch. 14 'He is an Orkney goose, if it

please you, Mr. Dryden', said Tim, who had wit at will.

Wit (wisdom) at will, He has | that with an angry heart can hold him still. (w 553)

c. **1450** *Prov. Counsel* in *Bks. on Courtesy* 69 He hathe wysdom at hys will that can with Angry harte be stylle. **1481** CAXTON *Reynard* Arber 110 Therfore he is wyse that can in his angre mesure hym self and not be ouer hasty. *c.* **1549** HEYWOOD I. xi. C5 He maie shew wisdome at wyll, That with an angry hert can holde his tongue styll. *a.* **1628** CARMICHAELL no. 664 (wisdom). **1732** FULLER no. 6434.

Wit bought is better than two for nought.   (w 543)

1621 ROBINSON 19. *a.* **1628** CARMICHAELL no. 279 Better a wit coft¹ nor tua for nocht. **1732** FULLER no. 6272 (is worth). [¹ bought.]

Wit enough to come in out of the rain, To have.   (F 537)

1580 LYLY *Euph. & his Eng.* ii. 70 In deede so much wit is sufficient for a woman, as when she is in the raine can warne hir to come out of it. **1599** BUTTES *Diet's Dry Dinner* B4 Fooles ... haue the wit to keepe themselues out of the raine. **1601** SHAKES. *T.N.* I. iii. 68 It's dry, sir. —Why, I think so. I am not such an ass but I can keep my hand dry. **1640** BRATHWAITE *Art Asleep Husb.* 293 To have no more wit than to goe out o' th' raine.

Wit in his head, He has no more | than you in both your shoulders.   (w 548)

c. **1592** SHAKES. *C.E.* II. ii. 38 I shall seek my wit in my shoulders. **1602** *Id. T.C.* II. i. 42 Thou sodden-witted lord! thou hast no more brain than I have in mine elbows. **1670** RAY 217 (*Yorks*).

Wit in his little finger, He has more | than you have in your whole hand (body). (w 549)

1563? (**1631** ed., ii. 653a) FOXE *A. & M.* He [Edward VI] hath more diuinity in his little finger, than all wee haue in all our bodies. **1591** H. SMITH *Restitution Nebuchadnezzar* Wks. i. 197 (than the rest in their whole body). **1721** KELLY 173. **1738** SWIFT *Dial.* II. E.L. 304 (goodness in ... whole body).

Wit, He has some | but a fool has the keeping of it.   (w 551)

1577 STANYHURST in Holinshed *Chron. Ireland* (1587) 97b A yoong man not deuoid of wit, were it not ... that a foole had the keeping thereof. **1707** MAPLETOFT 114. **1766** *Goody Two-Shoes* (1881) 40. **1813** RAY 174. Wit is folly, unless a wise man hath the keeping of it.

Wit of a woman is a great matter, The.   (w 568)

1533 T. LUPSET *Treatise of Charity* ed. Gee 224 The common prouerbe ... womens wyttes in dede be shorte. **1589** *Jane Anger her Protection for Women* C2. **1599** BRETON *Wks.* II, ch. 59 (the common proverbe).

Wit of you, The | and the wool of a blue dog, will make a good medley. *Cf.* Thrift of you. (w 569)

1659 HOWELL *Eng. Prov.* 11b (will make a piece of lincy-woolsie). **1732** FULLER no. 4836.

Wit once bought is worth twice taught. *Cf.* Bought wit.

1639 R. CHAMBERLAIN *Conceits, Clinches* no. 118. **1670** RAY 157.

Wit than a coot (stone, stool, etc.), No more. (w 550, 561)

c. **1548** BALE *K. Johan* l. 178 Thow semyste by thy wordes, to haue no more wytt than a coote. **1581** N. WOODES *Confl. of Consc.* l. 1395 Thou hast no more wit, I see then this stoole. **1591–2** WILMOT *Tancred and Gism.* IV. ii. E2 As a senceles stone I lay, For neither wit nor tongue could ... expresse the passions of my pained heart. **1601** SHAKES. *T.N.* I. v. 79 I saw him put down ... with an ordinary fool that has no more brain than a stone. **1672** WALKER 11, no. 61 He hath no more wit than a stone; no more brains than a burbourt. He is a very Cods-head.

Wit than wealth, Better. (w 544)

1567 BALDWIN P5 It is better to want ryches then witte. **1610** BRETNOR *Almanac* Dec. Good days Wit rather then wealth. **1736** BAILEY *Dict.* s.v. Better. **1818** SCOTT *Rob Roy* ch. 23 Wit is better than wealth.

Wit to pick a lock and steal a horse, but wisdom to let them alone, It is. (w 557)

1659 HOWELL *Fr. Prov.* 3. **1670** RAY 30.

Wit, whither wilt thou? (w 570)

[Phrase addressed to one who is talking too much or foolishly.] **1539** VIVES *Introd. to Wisdom* 18ᵛ How fowle, howe peryllous, a thynge is, Lingua quo vadis? Tunge whether goest thou? **1575** J. HIGGINS in UDALL *Flowers for Latin speaking* [Gloss on Terence *Adelph.* v. i. 7 Verba fundis, sapientia] Wisdome, you speake in vaine, Wyt whither wilt thou. **1599** SHAKES. *A.Y.* I. ii. 51 How now, wit! whither wander you? *Ibid.* IV. i. 148 A man that hath a wife with such a wit, he might say, 'Wit, whither wilt?' **1600** KEMP *Kemp's Nine Day's Wonder* (G. B. Harrison) 26. **1613** T. ADAMS *The White Devil* (1861–2, ii. 241) Many a Pope sings that common ballad of hell, Ingenio perii, qui miser ipse meo [Ovid, Tristia II. 1–2.] 'Wit, whither wilt thou? Woe is me; My wit hath wrought my misery.' **1617** *Greene's Groat's W. Wit* Pref. A2 This olde Ballad made in Hell: *Ingenio perij, qui miser ipse meo*: Wit, whither wilt thou? woe is me. **1624** T. BREWER *A Knot of Fools.* C3. **1659** HOWELL *Eng. Prov.* 3a.

Wit will never worry you, Your.

1721 KELLY 383.

Wit without learning is like a tree without fruit.

1567 BALDWIN P4. **1647** *Countryman's New Commonwealth*, 15.

Wit(s), *see also* Ale is in (When) w. is out; All the w. in the world (If you had), fools would fell you; Born when w. was scant; Bought w. is dear; Bought w. is the best; Brevity is soul of w.; Bush natural, more hair than w.; Calamity (Extremity) is the touchstone of a brave mind (unto w.); Constable for your w. (You might be a); German's w. in fingers; God send you more w.; Good w., if a wise man had keeping; Good w. jump; Great w. short memories; Idleness turns edge of w.; Little w. and it does you good; Little w. in head, work for heel; Little w., meikle travel; Little w. serve fortunate; Love makes w. of fool; Man may learn w. every day; Men (So many), so many w.; Mickle head, little w.; Money, w. (Of), believe one fourth; Moon's in the full (When) w.'s in the wane; One man's will another man's w.; Ounce of discretion worth a pound of w.; Ounce of w. that's bought; Oxford for learning, London for w.; Set your w. against child (Don't); Shows all his w. at once; Tongue runs before his w.; Truss up his w. in eggshell (You may); Two heads (w.) better than one; Want of w. worse than want of gear; Wealth makes w. waver; Will and w. strive with you; Wine is a whetstone to w.; Wise that has w. enough for own affairs; Wood in wilderness ... w. in poor man are little thought of. *See also* After wit.

Witch, I believe you are a. (w 585)

1616 DRAXE no. 859 He is a witch. **1631** HEYWOOD 2 *Fair Maid of West* I. i. I thinke you are a witch ... A foolish proverbe we use in our country. **1738** SWIFT *Dial.* III. E.L. 320. [Often an ironical comment on some obvious answer.] A Boy, I suppose.—No, ... guess again.—A Girl then.—You have hit it; I believe you are a Witch.

Witches' Sabbath.

[A midnight meeting of witches, presided over by the Devil, held as an orgy or festival.] *a.* **1660** F. BROOKE tr. *Le Blanc's Trav.* 312 Divers Sorcerers ... have confessed that in their Sabbaths, ... they feed on such fare. **1735** POPE *Ep. Lady* 239 As Hags hold Sabbaths, less for joy than spite, So these their merry, miserable Night. **1883** *Harper's Mag.* 831/2 It might have been ... a veritable Witches' Sabbath.

Witch(es), *see also* Burn you for w. (They that) will lose coals; Go in God's name, so ride no w.; Lancashire w.; Rowan tree and red thread; Rynt you w., quoth Bessie Lockit.

Wite[1] God, You need not | if the Deil ding you over.[2]

1721 KELLY 384 ... Spoken to them that have great big Legs. [[1] blame. [2] throw you down.]

Wite[1] your teeth if your tail be small.

1721 KELLY 355 . . . Spoken to them that have
good Meat at their Will. [¹ blame.]

**Wite[1] yourself if your wife be with
bairn.**

1721 KELLY 357 . . . Spoken when People's
Misfortunes come by their own Blame. [¹ blame.]

**Witham eel, and Ancum (Ancolme)
pike, in all the world there is none syke.**

1587 HARRISON in Holinshed *Descr. of Britain*
(cited *Wks.* Drayton v. (1941) 243) Ancolme
ele, and Witham pike Search all England and
find not the like. **1613–22** DRAYTON *Polyolb.*
XXV. 307–10 (1876) III. 151 *As Kestiven* doth
boast, her *Wytham* so have I, My *Ancum* (only
mine) whose fame as far doth fly, For fat and
dainty *Eels*, as hers doth for her *Pyke*, Which
makes the proverb up, the world hath not the
like. (Selden's note:—*Wytham Eele*, and
Ancum Pyke, In all the world there is none syke.)

Witham pike: England has none like.
(P 320)

1662 FULLER Lincs. 144 English pikes, wherein
this County is eminent, especially in that River
which runneth by Lincolne, whence . . . Witham
Pike England hath nene like. **1896** BEALBY
Dau. of Fen viii The fish fully justified the local
saying, 'Witham pike, none like'. It was big and
fat and beautifully marked.

Witham, *see also* Little W., (He was born at).

Withdraw, *see* Choleric man w. a little (From a).

Withered, *see* Rose (Fairest) at last w.

Within, *see* Better were w. (If), better would
come out; Collier's sack, . . . worse w., (Like a).

**Withy[1] tree would have a new gate
hung at it, The old.**   (W 589)

1678 RAY 184. [¹ willow.]

Witness everywhere, There is a.
(W 590)

[L. *Nullum locum putes sine teste: semper adesse
Deum cogita.*] **1621** BURTON *Anat. Mel.* II. iii.
VII (1638) 356 Think no place without a witnesse.
1732 FULLER no. 4886.

Witness, With a.   (W 591)

[With a vengeance.] **1578** THOMAS WHITE *Serm.
at Paul's Cross* 3 Nov. 1577 34 To him it is to
sinne with a witnesse. **1588** 'Marprelate' *Epist.*
Pierce 30 My book shall come with a witness,
before the High Commision. [1591] **1593** PEELE
Edw. I Bullen i. 181 Thou defiest me with a witness. **1602** WITHALS 18. **1665** GLANVILL *Scepsis
Scient.* xvi. 99 Every Religion hath its bare
Nominals: and that Pope was one with a witness,
whose saying it was.

Witness(es), *see* Conscience is a thousand w.;
Lie with a w.

Wits are a wool-gathering, Your.
(W 582)

[= absent-mindedness.] **1553** T. WILSON *Rhet.*
II. 59 Hackyng & hemmyng as though our wittes
and our senses were a woll gatheryng. **1591**
PEELE *Hunting of Cupid* Malone Soc. *Coll.* i. 312.
1621 BURTON *Anat. Mel.* I. ii. III. xv. (1638) 129
Th. Aquinas, supping with King Lewis of France,
upon a sudden . . . cryed, *conclusum est contra
Manichæos*; his wits were a wool-gathering (as
they say), and his head busied about other
matters. **1677** YARRANTON *Eng. Improvement*
100 My Brains shall go with yours a Wool-
gathering this one bout. **1815** SCOTT *Guy Man.*
ch. 47 'I crave pardon, honourable sir! but my
wits'—'Are gone a wool-gathering, I think.'

Wits' end, He is at his.   (W 575)

c. **1374** CHAUCER *Troilus* Bk. 3, l. 931 At dulcarnon, right at my wittes ende. *c.* **1420** LYD-
GATE *Ass. of Gods* E.E.T.S. 49 They were
dreuyn to her wyttes ende. *c.* **1510** STANBRIDGE
Vulg. E.E.T.S. 22 I am at my wyttes ende. **1576**
PETTIE i. 172 The learned physicians . . . were
at their wits' end. **1641** FERGUSSON no. 395 Of
wilful persons. . . .

Witty, *see* Every one is w. for own purpose;
Weak men had need be w.

**Wive and thrive both in a year, It is
hard to.**   (Y 12)

1349 *The Papelard Priest* ed. A. H. Smith in
London Med. Stud. ii. l. 90 I may noust wyue
and þriue al in a ȝere. *c.* **1410** *Towneley Plays*
xii l. 97 It is sayde full ryfe 'a man may not wyfe'
and also 'thryfe and all in a year'. **1573** TUSSER
lvi. 153 It is too much we dailie heare, To wiue
and thriue both in a yeare. **1580** LYLY *Euph. &
his Eng.* ii. 222 Although in one yeare to mar[r]ie
and to thr[i]ue it be hard. **1614** CAMDEN 308.
1721 KELLY 49 . . . For Courting, Marriage, and
their Appurtenance, occasions an Expence that
one Year cannot retrieve. **1738** SWIFT Dial. I.
E.L. 286 You can't expect to wive and thrive
in the same year.

Wive, *see also* First thrive then w.

**Wives make rammish husbands, Rut-
ting.**

1577 R. STANYHURST in Holinshed *Descr. Ireland*
(1587) 26a Rutting wiues make often rammish
husbands, as our prouerb dooth inferre.

**Wives must be had, be they good or
bad.**   (W 386)

1639 CLARKE 328.

**Wiving and thriving a man should take
counsel of all the world, In.**   (W 592)

a. **1591** HY. SMITH *Serm.* (1866) I. 9 They say,
that in wiving and thriving a man should take
counsel of all the world, lest he light upon a
curse while he seeks for a blessing.

Wiving, *see also* Hanging and w. go by destiny.

Woe to him that is alone. (w 598)

[ECCLES. iv. 10 Woe to him that is alone when
he falleth. **1382** WYCLIF *Ibid.* Wo to hym that is
aloone, for whanne he fallith, he hath noon
reisynge him.] *c.* **1200** *Ancrene Riwle* Camden
Soc. 252 Wo is him thet is euer one, uor hwon
he ualleth he naueth hwo him areare.[1] *c.* **1374**
CHAUCER *Troilus* Bk. 1, ll. 694–5 The wyse seyth,
wo him that is allone, For, and he falle, he hath
noon help to ryse. **1581** GUAZZO i. 48 Wo be to
the lone man, who when he shalbe fallen downe,
shall have none to helpe him up. [[1] to raise.]

Woe to the house where there is no chiding. (w 599)

1640 HERBERT no. 450. **1642** TORRIANO 56
(where the family agreeth). **1710** S. PALMER 203.
1732 FULLER no. 5801.

Woe to want, No. (w 594)

1581 C. THIMELTHORPE *Short Inventory* K1ᵛ The
rich man . . . Sayth . . . no woe to want when
I am old. **1590** R. GREENE *Wks.* Gros. ix. 312
He felt . . . that there was no greater woe than
want. **1597** *Politeuphuia* 122ᵛ Pouerty is the
sister to distresse, and there is no greater woe
then want. **1623** CAMDEN 278. **1639** CLARKE
244.

Woe worth ill company, quoth the kae[1] of Camnethen.

1721 KELLY 345 . . . Spoken when we have been
drawn by ill Company into an ill thing. A Jack-
Daw in *Camnethen* learned this Word from a
Guest in the House when he was upon his
Penitentials after hard drinking. [[1] Jack-daw.]

Woe's to them that have the cat's dish, and she aye mewing.

1721 KELLY 343 . . . Spoken when People owe
a Thing to, or detain a Thing from needy People,
who are always calling for it.

Woeful is the household that wants a woman.

c. **1460** *Towneley Myst., 2nd Shep. Play* 420
Ffull wofull is the householde That wantys a
woman.

Woes unite foes.

1832 HENDERSON 20.

Woe(s), *see also* Hasty man never wants w.;
Weal and women cannot pan, but w. and
women can; Weal or w. as he thinks; Weal
without w., (No); Will is the cause of w.

Wogan, *see* King comes to W. (Shall be done
when).

Wolf, To see (have seen) a. (w 621)

[THEOCR. 14. 22, etc. λύκον ἰδεῖν = to be tongue-
tied, from the belief that a man on seeing a wolf
lost his voice. *Cf.* VIRG. *Ecl.* 9. 53 *Lupi Moerin
videre priores.*] *c.* **1554** W. TURNER *Hunting of
the Romish Wolf* E5 If the Wolfe se the man,
before the man se the wolfe, then is the man by
the syght of the wolfe made dum, or at the least
so horse, that he can hardly speake. **1562** G.
LEGH *Accidence of Armoury* 98 It is sayde, if a
man be seene of hym [a wolf] first, the man
looseth his voyce. **1650** COTGRAVE Howell's
Epistle Ded., When one is growne hoarse they
use to say Il a vu le loup, hee hath seen the
wolf, wheras that effect is wrought in one whom
the wolf hath seen first, according to Plinie, and
the Poet,—Lupi illum videre priores. **1697** DRY-
DEN *Virg. Past.* ix. 75 My Voice grows hoarse;
I feel the Notes decay; As if the Wolves had seen
me first to Day. **1823** SCOTT *Quentin D.* ch. 18
Our young companion has seen a wolf, . . . and
he has lost his tongue in consequence.

Wolf and fox are both of one counsel, The. (w 611)

1591 STEPNEY 152 (the craftie fox are both of
one counsell). *c.* **1594** BACON no. 606 El lobo
et la vulpeja son todos d'una conseja. **1706**
STEVENS s.v. Lobo The Wolf and the Fox are both
of a Gang. **1732** FULLER no. 4837 (both privateers).

Wolf by the ears, To have (hold) a. (w 603)

[APOLLOD. CARYST. *Epid.* 5 Τῶν ὤτων ἔχω τὸν
λύκον . . . I have got a wolf by the ears, I can
neither hold him nor let go. TERENCE *Phormio* 3.
2. 21 *Auribus teneo lupum.*] *c.* **1386** CHAUCER
Mel. B² l. 2732 And Salomon seith that 'he
that entre metteth him of the noyse or stryf of
another man is lyk to him that taketh an hound
by the eres'. . . . For . . . he that taketh a straunge
hound by the eres is outherwhyle biten with the
hound. **1528** SIR T. WYATT Plutarch's *Quiet of
Mind* C8 As tho he held the wolfe by the eres,
as the prouerbe saith. *c.* **1560** DAUS tr. *Sleidane's
Comm.* 425 The Bishop of Rome, . . . as the
prouerbe is, helde the woulfe by both eares, . . .
he coueted to gratifie the Kyng, and also feared
themperours displeasure. **1563** *Mirr. for Mag.*
ed. Campbell 409 He hath a raging Wolfe fast
by the eares. *c.* **1566** CURIO tr. W.P. *Pasquin in
a Trance* 33ᵛ Thou holdest the Woulfe by the
eares, whom thou darest neyther holde still nor
yet let goe. **1616** DRAXE no. 216 A medlar is
as he that taketh a wolfe by the eares. **1621**
BURTON *Anat. Mel.* Democr. to Rdr. (1638) 50
He that goes to law (as the proverb is) holds a
wolfe by the eares; . . . if he prosecute his cause,
he is consumed: if he surcease his suit he loseth
all. **1631** QUARLES *Samson* xi. 63 I have a
Wolfe by th' eares; I dare be bold, Neither with
safety, to let goe, nor hold. **1884** *Times* 29 Oct.
9/3 These expressions come from a man who
has a wolf by the ears, whose task is well-nigh
desperate.

Wolf does something every week that hinders him from going to church on Sundays, The.

1706 STEVENS s.v. Lobo. **1732** FULLER no. 4838.

Wolf eats often of the sheep that have been told[1] (warned), The. (w 612)

1592 DELAMOTHE 25. **1639** CLARKE 271. **1651**
HERBERT no. 1134 (warned). **1659** TORRIANO no.

18 (feeds even of). **1666** *Id. It. Prov.* 132 no. 21 The wolf worries sheep, for all that they are told. **1706** STEVENS s.v. Lobo (eats of what is counted). [¹ i.e. counted.]

Wolf eats the sheep (goose), By little and little the. (L 339)

1611 COTGRAVE s.v. Manger (Goose). **1616** DRAXE no. 134. **1659** HOWELL *Fr. Prov.* 11 By degrees the Wolf eats up the Goose.

Wolf for his mate, Who has a | needs a dog for his man. (w 610)

1611 COTGRAVE s.v. Loup. **1623** WODROEPHE 276 If thou makest the Wolfe thy Fellow, cary a Dog vnder thy Cloake. **1640** HERBERT no. 57.

Wolf in sheep's clothing (a lamb's skin), A. (w 614)

[MATT. vii. 15 Beware of false prophets, which come to you in sheep's clothing, but inwardly they are ravening wolves.] *c.***1460** *Wisdom* l. 490 51 Ther ys a wolffe in a lombys skyn. **1509** BARCLAY *Ship of Fools* ii. 7 She is perchaunce A wolfe or gote within a Lammys skyn. **1533** C. SAINT-GERMAN cited Sir T. More *Debellation* (1533) 1034a A wolfe may looke simply lapt in a sheepes skynne. **1546** HEYWOOD I. x. C4ᵛ Of trouth she is a wolfe in a lambes skyn. **1566** J. BARTHLET *Pedegrew of Popish Heretiques* 21ᵛ Seeming holy in outwarde appearance, Wolues in sheepes skinnes. **1590–1** SHAKES. *2 Hen. VI* III. i. 77 Is he a lamb? His skin is surely lent him, For he's inclined as is the ravenous wolf. **1590–1** *Id. 1 Hen. VI* I. iii. 55 Thee I'll chase hence, thou wolf in sheep's array. **1641** FERGUSSON no. 469 Of hypocrites . . . He is a wolfe in a lamb's skin. **1706** STEVENS s.v. Dios.

Wolf knows what the ill beast thinks, The. (w 615)

1611 COTGRAVE s.v. Loup Le loup scait bien que male beste pense: Prov. One lewd fellow is well acquainted with the purposes, or sleights of another. **1640** HERBERT no. 16.

Wolf may lose his teeth, but never his nature (memory), The. (w 620)

1616 DRAXE no. 2449 (memory). **1666** TORRIANO *It. Prov.* 132 no. 29 The woolf loseth his tooth, but not his instinct. **1670** RAY 30 Wolves lose their teeth, but not their memory. **1732** FULLER no. 5802. **1832** HENDERSON 93.

Wolf must die in his own skin, The. (w 617)

c. **1400** *Rom. Rose* C. l. 7313 Men ne may in no manere Teren the wolf out of his hide Till he be flayn, bak and side. **1611** COTGRAVE s.v. Loup A knaue will die in a knaues skinne, if hee formerly loose it not. **1640** HERBERT no. 849.

Wolf to keep the sheep, To set the. (w 602)

[TER. *Eun.* v. i. 16 Ovem lupo commisisti.] *c.* **1513** MORE *Rich. III* 1821 35 The Duke of Gloucester . . . was made . . . protectoure of the king and hys realme, so that (were it destenye or were it foly) the lamb was betaken to the wolfe to keepe. **1533–4** UDALL *Flowers* 94 You have entrusted the sheep to the wolf. *c.* **1566** C. A. CURIO *Pasquin in a Trance* The Wolues should not be made Shepheardes, nor such dogs as can not barke. **1576** F. PATRIZI *Civil Policy* tr. R. Robinson I2ᵛ It is most dangerous as it is spoken in the Prouerbe: To betake a sheepe into the custodye of a wolfe. **1576** PETTIE i. 60 He committed the silly sheep to the rauening wolf. **1577** HOLINSHED *Chron. Ireland* (1587) 94a To betake their mastiues into the custodie of the woolues. **1579** GOSSON *Sch. Abuse* Arb. 47. **1594** SHAKES. *T.G.V.* IV. iv. 87 Alas, poor Proteus! thou hast entertain'd A fox to be the shepherd of thy lambs. **1639** CLARKE 95 You have given the wolf the weather to keep. **1641** FERGUSSON no. 291 Give never the wolfe the wedder to keep. **1863** READE *Hard Cash* ch. 41 A lunatic . . . protected by that functionary, is literally a lamb protected by a wolf.

Wolves rend sheep when the shepherds fail.

[Cf. JOHN X. 12. ALANUS DE INSULIS *Liber Parabolarum* i. 31 *Sub molli pastore capit lanam lupus, et grex Incustoditus dilaceratur eo.*] *c.* **1386** CHAUCER *Phys. T.* l. 101 Under a shepherde softe and necligent The wolf hath many a sheep and lamb to-rent. **1592** DELAMOTHE 37 An ill shepheard, doth often feede the wolfe.

Wolf (-ves), *see also* Bear, (w.), (If it were a) it would bite you; Cry w.; Cut down the woods, catch w.; Dark as a w.'s mouth; Death of a young w. never too soon; Death of w. safety of sheep; Dog (w.) barks in vain at the moon; Dust raised by sheep not choke w.; Foolish sheep makes w. confessor; Growing youth has w. in belly; Hard winter when w. eats another; Howl with the w.; Hunger drives w. out of woods; Keep w. from door; Keeps company with w. (Who) will learn to howl; Kid that keeps above is in no danger of w.; Life of the w. is death of lamb; Lone sheep in danger of w.; Man is to man a w.; Stranger is for the w.; Thief knows a thief as w. knows w.; Troubles a w. how many sheep (Never); Trust to dog (While you), w. slips into sheepfold; Two w. may worry one sheep.

Woman and a cherry are painted for their own harm, A. (w 645)

1659 HOWELL *Span. Prov.* 18 (paint themselves for their own hurt). **1666** TORRIANO *It. Prov.* 75 no. 21 A woman and a cherry is coloured to its prejudice.

Woman and a glass are ever in danger, A. (w 646)

1535 BERNERS *Gold. Bk.* 241 There be some women so bryttell, that as a glasse, with a fylloppe wyll breke. **1576** PETTIE ii. 106 Women having lost their chastity are like broken glasses which are good for nothing. **1599** SHAKES. *Pass. Pilg.* no. 13 As broken glass no cement can redress: So beauty blemish'd once, for ever lost. **1604** *Id. M.M.* II. iv. 124 Nay, women are frail too.—Ay, as the glasses where they view themselves, Which are as easy broke as they make forms. **1612** SHELTON *Quix.* I. IV. vi. ii. 72 Truely woman is of glasse, Therefore no man ought to trie If she broke or not might bee. **1621** HOWELL *Lett.* I June (1903) i. 68 A saying . . ., 'That the first handsome woman . . . was made of Venice glass', . . . implies beauty, but brittleness with all (and Venice is not unfurnished with some of that mould, for no place abounds more with lasses and glasses). **1640** HERBERT no. 244. **1706** STEVENS s.v. *Muger.* **1721** KELLY 113 Glasses and Lasses are bruckle [brittle] Wares. Both apt to fall, and both ruined by falling.

Woman conceals what she knows not, A. (w 649)

c. **1386** CHAUCER *Mel.* B²l. 2274 Ye seyn that the ianglerie of wommen kan hyde thynges that they woot not as who seith, that a woman can nat hyde that they noght wot. **1589** NASHE *Anat. Absurdity* i. 14 Who will commit any thing to a womans tatling trust, who conceales nothing but that shee knowes not? **1597** SHAKES. *I Hen. IV* II. iii. 105 Constant you are, But yet a woman . . . for I well believe Thou wilt not utter what thou dost not know. **1640** HERBERT no. 1031. **1721** KELLY 347 Women and bairns lain[1] what they know not. But what they know. they'll blab out. [[1] conceal.]

Woman either loves or hates in extremes, A. (w 651)

c. **1526** *Dicta Sap.* B1 Aut amat aut odit mulier, nihil est tertium. A woman to eyther part is inclined ouer vehemently. **1539** TAVERNER *Publius* A2 A woman eyther loueth or hateth, there is no thyrde. Woman kynde for most parte is in extremes and to vehement vpon eyther parte. She hath no meane. [**1582**] **1589** *Love & Fortune* ll. 1267–8 A right woman, either loue like an Angell, Or hate like a Deuill, in extreames so to dwell. **1592–3** SHAKES. *V.A.* l. 987 Thy weal and woe are both of them extremes. **1600–1** *Id. H.* III. ii. 162 For women's fear and love holds quantity, In neither aught, or in extremity. **1639** CLARKE 118. *c.* **1640** *Countryman's Comm.* 6 Woemen . . . are either too curst or too kinde, according to that verse in Mantuan: Aut te ardenter amat, aut te capitaliter odit; that is, a woman loues feruently, or hates deadly.

Woman has an eel by the tail, Who has a. *Cf.* Hold of his word. (w 640)

a. **1576** WHYTHORNE 23 [Of a woman] Hee had but A slippery eell . . . by the tayll. **1613** ?SHAKES. *T.N.K.* III. v. 48 An eel and woman, A learned poet says, unless by th' tail And with thy teeth thou hold, will either fail. **1616** BEAUM. & FL. *Scornful Lady* II. i. 111 (He that holds a woman). **1616** DRAXE no. 2461 Women like to wet Eeles. **1640** SHIRLEY *Arcadia* V i. 238 But I see a woman and a wet eel have both slippery tails.

Woman has an eye more than a man, A.

1622 MIDDLETON *Changeling* III. iii (A woman, they say, . . .).

Woman is a weathercock, A. (w 653)

1518 *Frederyke of Jennen* ed. J. Raith (1936) 109 A womans nature is to be vnstedfast, and

tourneth as the wynde dooth. **1548** HALL (1809 ed., 208) The Quene his [Henry VI's] wife . . . had one poynt of a very woman: for often tyme, when she was vehement and fully bente in a matter, she was sodainly like a wethercocke, mutable, and turnyng. [**1598**] **1616** HAUGHTON *Englishmen for my Money* E2ᵛ. **1607** MIDDLETON *Family of Love* I. ii. 59 Women . . . are but windy turning vanes. **1612** N. FIELD *A Woman is a Weather-cock* [title]. **1616** DRAXE no. 2460.

Woman is flax, A | man is fire, the devil comes and blows the bellows.

1666 TORRIANO *It. Prov.* 75 no. 24. **1874** WHYTE-MELVILLE *Uncle John* ch. 6. The tow and tinder of which men and women are proverbially composed, only wait a*chance spark, a rising breeze, to become a bonfire.

Woman is the confusion (woe) of man. (w 656)

[VINCENT DE BEAUVAIS[1] *Spec. Hist.* x. 71 *Mulier est hominis confusio.*] *c.* **1386** CHAUCER *Mel.* B² l. 2294 If that wommen were nat goode, . . . our Lord God . . . wolde nevere hav wroght hem, ne called hem help of man, but rather confusioun of man. *Id. Nun's Priest's T.* B²l. 4354 *Mulier est hominis confusio.* *c.* **1549** HEYWOOD II. vii. E7 A woman. As who saieth, wo to the man. **1576** PETTIE ii. 126 I think them [women] made of God only for a plague and woe unto men, as their name importeth. *c.* **1637** WHITING in *Caroline Poets* iii. 479 She is woe to man, a woman to me. **1667** MILTON *P.L.* xi. 633 But still I see the tenor of man's woe Holds on the same, from Woman to begin. [[1] Died *c.* 1264.]

Woman is the weaker vessel, A. (w 655)

[I PETER iii. 7 Giving honour unto the wife, as unto the weaker vessel.] *c.* **1548** *Praise of suche as sought commonwealths* A6ᵛ O weaker vessell [Esther]. Where may one in these dayes finde a man that hateth his preeminencie. **1594–5** SHAKES. *L.L.L.* I. i. 255 Jaquenetta—so is the weaker vessel called. **1594–5** *Id. R.J.* I. i. 15 Women, being the weaker vessels, are ever thrust to the wall. **1598** *Id. 2 Hen. IV* II. iv. 58 You are the weaker vessel, as they say, the emptier vessel. **1599** *Id. A.Y.* II. iv. 5 I must comfort the weaker vessel, as doublet and hose ought to show itself courageous to petticoat. **1639** CLARKE 118.

Woman kissed is half won, A. (w 657)

1607 SHARPHAM *Cupid's Whirl.* I 13 (is halfe inioyed). **1642** TORRIANO 46 A woman saluted, is half conquered. Nota, As saluting is accounted of in Italy, not in England. **1659** HOWELL *It. Prov.* 11.

Woman need but look on her apron-string to find an excuse, A. (w 659)

1577 GRANGE *Gold. Aphroditis* C2 Who first fixed hir eyes vpon hyr apernestrings . . . straight foorth had a ready answere. **1607** SHARPHAM *Cupid's Whirl.* I. 15 Wit of a Woman now assist me, O aperne stringes be now auspitious. **1738** SWIFT *Dial.* III. E.L. 321 They say, a woman need but look on her apron-string to find an excuse.

Woman she is fair, Tell a | and she will soon turn fool. (w 153)

1659 HOWELL *Span. Prov.* 18 The way to make a woman a fool, is to commend her beauty. **1664** CODRINGTON 219 (as 1659). **1707** MAPLETOFT 5 (wondrous fair).

Woman that deliberates (hesitates) is lost, The.

1713 ADDISON *Cato* IV. i When love once pleads admission to our hearts (In spite of all the virtue we can boast) The woman that deliberates is lost. **1887** BLACKMORE *Springhaven* ch. 42 'May I tell you my ideas about that matter?' . . . Dolly hesitated, and with the proverbial result.

Woman that loves to be at the window, A | is like a bunch of grapes on the highway. (w 647)

1666 TORRIANO *It. Prov.* 74 no. 33 A woman at a window, as grapes on the highway. **1869** HAZLITT 39.

Woman that paints, A | puts up a bill that she is to be let. (w 663)

1658 [EDMONDSON] *Comes Fac. in Via* 217 The reason why they [women] paint or patch is notorious to a Proverb, They who whiten their house mean to let it. **1659** HOWELL *It. Prov.* 3 Who paints her face thinks on her tail. *Ibid.* 15 A woman who paints will do more then piss. **1700** WARD *London Spy* (1924) 420 For she that paints will doubtless be a whore. **1732** FULLER no. 481.

Woman were as little as she is good, If a | a pease-cod would make her a gown and a hood. (w 630)

1591 FLORIO *Second F.* 175. **1659** HOWELL *It. Prov.* 7 (a cap and a hood). **1678** RAY 64.

Woman's advice is best at a dead lift, A. (w 669)

c. **1425** *Wakefield Plays* Second Shepherds' l. 342 A woman auyce helpys at the last. **1659** HOWELL *Eng. Prov.* 6b.

Woman's advice is no great thing, A | but he who won't take it is a fool. (w 671)

1620 SHELTON *Quix.* II. vii. ii. 230 I say a woman's advice is but slender, yet he that refuseth it is a madman.

Woman's answer is never to seek, A. (w 670)

1526 *Hundr. Merry Tales* (Oesterley) no. xxxiii. 29. *c.* **1555** *Jacob & Esau* B4ᵛ Yea, womens answeres are but fewe times to seeke. **1599** SHAKES. *A.Y.* IV. i. 154 You shall never take her without her answer unless you take her without her tongue.

Woman's eye, *see* Black man is a pearl in fair w.'s e.

Woman's mind and winter wind (Winter weather and women's thoughts) change oft, A. (w 673)

15th c. *Sloane MS. 381* in *Early Eng. Carols* 255 Wynteris wether and wommanys thowt And lordis loue schaungit oft. **1590** GREENE *Royal Exch.* Gros. vii. 292 Wherevnto alludeth our old English prouerbe. Wynters wether, and womens thoght. And gentlemens purposes chaungeth oft. **1616** DRAXE no. 2459 Womens thoughts oft change. *a.* **1628** CARMICHAELL no. 1701 Winters nicht and womans thocht and lords purpose changes oft. **1639** CLARKE 118 Winter weather and womens thoughts change oft. **1721** KELLY 17 A Winter's Night, a Woman's Mind, and a Laird's Purposes, change oft. *Ibid.* A Woman's Mind is like the Wind in a Winter's Night. *a.* **1796** BURNS *Women's Minds* Tho' women's minds like winter winds May shift and turn, and a' that.

Woman's painting breed thy stomach's fainting, Let no. (w 666)

1611 COTGRAVE s.v. Femme. **1664** CODRINGTON 204. **1670** RAY 20. **1732** FULLER no. 6243 (thy Heart's fainting).

Woman's tongue in his head, He has a.

1616 T. ADAMS *Three Divine Sisters* 36 The Prouerbe came not from nothing, when we say of a brawling man . . .

Woman's tongue is the last thing about her that dies, A. (w 676)

1612 CHAPMAN *Widow's Tears* IV. ii When a man dies the last thing that moves is his heart; in a woman her tongue. **1738** SWIFT *Dial.* III. E.L. 323 Well, miss, they say a woman's tongue is the last thing about her that dies.

Woman's tongue wags like a lamb's tail, A. (w 678)

c. **1597** DELONEY *Jack of Newbery* ed. Mann 50 Considering that womens tongues are like Lambs tayles, which seldome stand still. **1670** RAY 49. **1721** KELLY 387 Your Tongue goes like a lamb's tail. Spoken to People that talk much, and to little purpose.

Woman's work is never at an end (never done), A. (w 679)

1570 BALDWIN *Beware the Cat* (1584) C2 The good Huswiues Candle neuer goeth out. **1570** TUSSER G2 Some respite to husbands the weather doth send, but huswiues affaires haue neuer none ende. **1629** Title of ballad entered *Stationers' Register* 1 June Arb iv. 213. **1670** RAY 50. **1678** *Id.* 60 A womans work is never at an end. Some add, And washing of dishes. **1920** *Times Wkly.* 12 Mar. 209. 'Women's work is never done'. . . We shall never hear the whole of woman's work during the war.

Womb to the tomb, From the. (w 726)

1576 GASCOIGNE *The Drum of Doomsday* ii. 217 Transferred from the Wombe to the Tombe.

1639 CLARKE 3. 1662 FULLER Yorks. 209 Infants
. . . from the Wombe to the Winding sheet.

Women and dogs set men together by the ears (cause much strife). (w 694)

1541 *Schoolh. of Women* C3ᵛ The prouerbe olde,
accordeth ryght: Women and dogges, causeth
moche stryfe. 1639 CLARKE 117. *c.* 1640 W.S.
Countrym. Commonw. 35 In woemen, wine, and
dogs, these vertues are. They seldome do breed
peace, but often warre. 1666 TORRIANO 52 no.
26 Many women and dogs cause contention.

Women and geese, Where there are | there wants no noise. (w 691)

1492 *Dial. of Soloman and Marcolphus* ed. Duff 6
Where women be there are wordys. 1616 DRAXE
no. 2456 Where there are women, there is much
tatling. 1659 HOWELL *It. Prov.* 16. 1678 RAY
64. 1732 FULLER no. 5684 Where Women are
and Geese, there wants no gagling.

Women and hens are lost by gadding. (w 695)

1591 STEPNEY 156 A stragling henne and a
wandring wife, deserue small commendation of
their life. 1611 COTGRAVE s.v. Poule Women
and hennes, that gad oremuch, are quickly lost.
1620 SHELTON *Quix.* II. xlix. iii. 165 The honest
maid [is] better at home with a bone broken
than a-gadding; the woman and the hen are
lost with straggling. 1666 TORRIANO *It. Prov.*
10 no. 42 Women and hens, by too much
gadding are lost. 1706 STEVENS s.v. Muger
(The Woman and the Hen).

Women and music should never be dated.

1773 GOLDSMITH *She Stoops to C.* III (Globe) 663
I must not tell my age. They say . . .

Women and wine, game and deceit, make the wealth small, and the wants great.

1591 FLORIO *Second F.* 73 Women, Wine, and
Dice will bring a man to Lice. 1721 KELLY 353
. . . This is the Translation of an old Munkish
Rhyme. Pisces, perdices, vinum, nec non
meritrices Corrumpunt cistam, & quicquid ponis
in istam. 1732 FULLER no. 6416.

Women are as wavering (changeable) as the wind. *Cf.* Woman is a weathercock. (w 698)

1546 HEYWOOD II. i. F4 For in one state they
twayne could not yet settyll, But waueryng as
the wynde. *c.* 1560 L. WAGER *Mary Magdalen*
G3 Womens heartes turne oft as doth the wynde.
c. 1566 *The Bugbears* V. ii You know women's
Clackes will walke with euery winde. 1579
LYLY *Euph.* i. 203 Women are to be wonne with
euery wynde. 1706 STEVENS s.v. Muger Woman,
Wind, and Fortune soon change; . . . Women in
all Countries have the ill Fate to be compar'd
to the Wind.

Women are born in Wiltshire, brought up in Cumberland, lead their lives in Bedfordshire, bring their husbands to Buckingham, and die in Shrewsbury.[1] (w 699)

1658 *Wit Restor'd* 99. 1662 FULLER Shrops. 2
'He that fetcheth a wife from Shrewsbury must
carry her into Staffordshire, or else shall live in
Cumberland.' The Staple-wit of this vulgar
Proverb, consisting solely in similitude of sound,
is scarce worth the inserting. 1738 FRANKLIN
Mar. Jack's wife was born in *Wiltshire*, brought
up in *Cumberland*, led much of her life in
Bedfordshire, sent her husband into *Huntingdonshire* in order to send him into *Buckinghamshire*.
But he took courage in *Hartfordshire*, and carried
her into *Staffordshire*, or else he might have lived
and died in *Shrewsbury*. [1 Puns on wilt (self-
willed); cumber (care); bed; buck (cuckold);
shrew.]

Women are great talkers. (w 701)

c. 1400 *Pride of Life* l. 207 ʒe, dam, þou hast
wordis fale [many], hit cometh þe of kinde.
1509 BARCLAY *Ship of Fools* i. 109 They [women]
. . . ar as coy and styll As the horle wynde or
clapper or a mylle. 1611 JONSON *Cat.* III. 679
You say, Women are greatest talkers. 1666
TORRIANO *It. Prov.* 87 no. 34 Women and magpies are alwaies prating.

Women are like wasps in their anger. *Cf.* Angry as a wasp. (w 705)

1594–8 SHAKES. *T.S.* III. i. 208 Come, come, you
wasp; i'faith, you are too angry. 1616 BRETON
2 *Cross.* B2. 1639 CLARKE 217 Women be
waspes, if angered.

Women (Wives and wind) are necessary evils. (w 703)

[MENANDER *Minor Fragments* 651 K (Loeb) Τὸ
γαμεῖν, ἐάν τις τὴν ἀλήθειαν σκοπῇ, κακὸν μέν
ἐστιν, ἀλλ' ἀναγκαῖον κακόν. Marriage if one will
face the truth, is an evil but a necessary evil.]
1547 BALDWIN O5. 1576 PETTIE ii. 166 You,
Gentlemen, may learn hereby . . . to use them
[women] as necessary evils. 1581 C. THIMEL-
THORPE *Short Inventory* E5ᵛ Wee haue an other
old saying with vs, . . . that fire, water, and a
woman be three of the most necessary euils in
the world. 1599 TASSO *Marr. & Wiving* G2
Chrisostome writeth, that she [woman] is . . . a
bad necessarie euill. 1639 CLARKE 118. 1721
KELLY 355 Wives and Wind are necessary Evils.

Women are the devil's nets. (w 707)

1520 *Calisto & Melibea* A iijb Yt is an old
sayeing That women be the deuells netts, and
hed of syn.

Women have no souls. (w 709)

1566 L. WAGER *Mary Magd.* E4ᵛ Women haue
no soules, this saying is not newe. 1590 *Almond
for a Parrot* B3ᵛ (Nashe iii. 348). [*a.* 1680]
1759 S. BUTLER *Gen. Rem.* i 246 The Souls of
Women are so small, That some believe th'
have none at all.

Women in mischief are wiser than men.
(W 711)

c. **1526** *Dicta Sap.* D2ᵛ (In thynges yll women are). **1547** BALDWIN O5ᵛ. **1597** *Politeuphuia* 25. **1647** *Countryman's New Commonwealth* II.

Women in state affairs are like monkeys in glass-shops. (W 712)

1659 HOWELL *Eng. Prov.* 12b.

Women laugh when they can, and weep when they will. (W 713)

[**1570**] **1584** BALDWIN *Beware the Cat* E1 Women can weep when they will. **1611** COTGRAVE s.v. Femme. **1640** HERBERT no. 821.

Women look in their glass, The more | the less they look to their house.
(W 688)

1623 'DAWE' *Vox Grac.* 43 So that I may iustly take vp this Spanish Prouerbe . . . That these painted Puppets, the more curious they are about their faces, the more carelesse they are about their houses. **1640** HERBERT no. 250. **1641** JONSON *Timber* viii. 569 A woman, the more curious she is about her face is commonly the more carelesse about her house. **1659** HOWELL *Span. Prov.* 17. **1732** FULLER no. 4669 (into their Glass, the less they look into their Hearts).

Women may be won, All. (W 681)

1579 LYLY *Euph.* i. 211 There is no woeman, Euphues, but shee will yeelde in time. **1583** MELBANCKE *Philot.* R4 Wherefore neuer geuing ouer, which Ouid commaundes vs in his Art of louing. **1584** LYLY *Sappho and Phao* II. iv. 62 Imagine with thy selfe all [women] are to bee won. **1588** GREENE *Wks.* Gros. vii. 68 Melissa was a woman and therefore to be woone. **1589** *Id.* xii. 31 and 78 Argentina is a woman, and therefore to be wooed, and so to be won. **1591–2** SHAKES. *1 Hen. VI* V. iii. 78 She's beautiful, and therefore to be woo'd; She is a woman, therefore to be won. **1592–3** *Id. Rich. III* I. ii. 228 Was ever woman in this humour won? **1593** *Id. T.And.* II. i. 82 She is a woman, therefore may be woo'd; She is a woman, therefore may be won. **1611** CHAPMAN *May Day* I. i. 151 She's a woman, is she not? . . . then let me alone with her. **1620** J. FORD *Line Life* 59 Women were in their creation ordained to bee wooed, and to be won.

Women (men) may blush to hear what they were not ashamed to act (do). (M 553)

c. **1558** W. WEDLOCKE *Image of Idleness* E6ᵛ The common prouerbe saith, that women loue better to haue it, then to heare spek of it. [c. 1602] **1637** T. HEYWOOD *Royal King* II. (1874 ed.) 23 And even the modest wives, this know we too, Oft blush to speake what is no shame to doe. **1605** R.F. *Sch. Slov.* I. 196 21 What kinde of men are these? true reason soone will prove them mad Which will not speake the words, but do the deedes, which is as bad. **1605–6** SHAKES.

K.L. IV. vi. 120 Yond simp'ring dame . . . That minces virtue, and does shake the head To hear of pleasure's name. The fitchew nor the soiled horse goes to 't With a more riotous appetite. **1666** TORRIANO *It. Prov.* 85 no. 4 That which is dishonest to do, believe not that it is honest to speak.

Women must have their wills while they live, because they make none when they die. *Cf.* **Women will have.**
(W 715)

1602–3 MANNINGHAM *Diary* Camden Soc. 92 Women, because they cannot have their wills when they dye, they will have their wills while they live. **1678** RAY 63.

Women naturally deceive, weep and spin. (W 716)

[Med. L. *Fallere, flere, nere, dedit Deus in muliere.*] *c.* **1386** CHAUCER *W. of Bath's Prol.* l. 401 Deceite, wepyng, spynnyng god hath yive To wommen kyndely, whyl they may lyve. *c.* **1430** LYDGATE *Of Deceitful Women* 29–33 in SKEAT *E.E.P.* 113 Women, of kinde, have condicions three; The first is, that that they be fulle of deceit; To spinne also is hir propertee; And women have a wonderful conceit, They wepen oft, and al is but a sleight. **1589** PUTTENHAM *Eng. Poesie* I. vii. Arb. i. 29 This . . . was written (no doubt by some forlorne louer, or els some old malicious Monke). . . *Fallere flere nere mentiri nilque tacere Hæc quinque vere statuit Deus in muliere.*

Women, priests, and poultry, have never enough. (W 717)

1659 HOWELL *It. Prov.* 7. **1670** RAY 30.

Women think *place* a sweet fish. (W 719)

1658 E. PHILLIPS *Myst. Love & Eloq.* 204 What is the name of that fish, which of all others, please women best?—Plase. **1678** RAY 59.

Women will have the last word. (W 722)

1541 *Schoolh. of Wom.* A2ᵛ Yet wyll the woman, haue the laste worde. **1563** B. GOOGE *Eglogs* no. vii. **1591** LYLY *Endym.* II. ii. 40 You meane to haue the last worde. **1738** SWIFT. *Dial.* I. E.L. 276 Miss, you have shot your Bolt: I find, you must have the last Word.

Women will have their wills. *Cf.* **Women must have, etc.** (W 723)

1541 *Schoolh. of Wom.* C3 They [women] wyl folowe theyr owne wyll, now and then. **1547** A. BORDE *Brev. of Helthe* (1557) f. lxxxii Let euery man please his wyfe in all matters, and . . . let her haue her owne wyll, for that she wyll haue who so euer say nay. [**1598**] **1616** HAUGHTON *Englishmen for my Money* l. 372 The prouerbe . . . Women and Maydes, must alwayes haue their will. **1639** CLARKE 329.

Women will say anything.

1611 SHAKES. *W.T.* I. ii. 131 Women say so, That will say anything.

Women's counsel is cold.

[Icelandic prov. Köld eru opt kvenna-ráð (cold, *i.e.* fatal, are often women's counsels).]   *c.* 1275 *Provs. of Alfred* (Skeat) A 336 Cold red is quene red (cold advice is women's advice).   *c.* 1386 CHAUCER *Nun's Priest's T.* l. 4446 Wommennes counseils been ful ofte colde; Wommannes counseil broghte us first to wo, And made Adam fro paradys to go.

Woman (Women), *see also* All w. are good; Ass climbs a ladder (When), may find wisdom in w.; Bad w. is worse than bad man; Because is w.'s reason; Choose neither a w. by candle-light; City (W.) that parleys; Dally not with w.; Dead w. will have four to carry her; Discreet w. have neither eyes; Fair w. and a slashed gown; Fair w. without virtue; Find a w. without an excuse; First advice of a w. (Take); Gaming w. and wine; Honest w.; House well-furnished makes a w. wise; Lancashire fair w.; Love a w.; Man is as old as he feels, w. as she looks; Man of straw worth w. of gold; Man, w., and devil are three degrees; Many w. many words; Married w. has nothing of her own but; Meat and good drink (If it wasn't for) w. might gnaw sheets; Men get wealth and w. keep it; Morning sun . . . and Latin-bred w.; Mother's (W.'s) side is surest; Name of an honest w. is mickle worth; No man is a match for a w.; No mischief but a w. is at bottom; Old w.; Old w. in wooden ruff; One tongue is enough for w.; Peas (The smaller the) . . . the fairer the w. the more the giglot; Play, w., and wine undo; See a w. weep (No more pity to) than goose go barefoot; Ship and a w. ever repairing; Ship under sail, . . . w. with a great belly, . . .; Silence is best ornament of w.; Spaniel, a w., and a walnut-tree; Swine, w., and bees cannot be turned; Trust not a w. when she weeps; War without a w. (No); Weal and w. cannot pan; Wicked w. worse than devil; Wine and w.; Wit of a w. a great matter; Woeful is a household that wants a w.; Wonders of England (Three).

Won with the egg and lost with the shell.

1575 GASCOIGNE *Posies* i. 450 Nor woman true but even as stories tell, Wonne with an egge, and lost againe with shell. 1582 C. FETHERSTON *Dial. against Dancing* C6. 1639 CLARKE 159.

Won, *see also* Strong town not w. in an hour; Woman kissed is half w.

Wonder at nothing, *see* Nil admirari.

Wonder is the daughter of ignorance.
(W 727)

1573 SANFORD 52ᵛ (Maruell). 1629 *Bk. Mer. Rid.* Prov. no. 44 (Maruell). 1615 T. ADAMS *England's Sickness* 95. Wonder you at this? Wonder is the daughter of ignorance, ignorance of nature.

Wonder lasts but nine days, A. (W 728)

c. 1374 CHAUCER *Troilus* Bk. 4, l. 588 For wonder last but nine night nevere in toune! 1525 ARCHBP. WARHAM (to Card. Wolsey) in *Original Let.* III, ed. Ellis 128, i. 375 It is a prouerbe not a wondre dureth but ix dayes. 1546 HEYWOOD II. i. F3ᵛ This wonder (as wonders last) lasted nine daies. 1590–1 SHAKES. *2 Hen. VI* II. iv. 69 These few days' wonder will be quickly worn. 1591 *Id. 3 Hen. VI* III. ii. 114 That would be ten days' wonder at the least.—That's a day longer than a wonder lasts. 1599 *Id. A.Y.* III. ii. 162 I was seven of the nine days out of the wonder before you came. 1602 [T. HEYWOOD?] *How a Man may Choose* Hazl.-Dods. ix. 74 (but a nine-days' talk). 1633 MASSINGER *New Way* IV. ii That were but nine day wonder. 1764 CHURCHILL *Ghost* III. 547 He would be found . . . A nine day's wonder at the most. 1879 W. MINTO *Defoe* 135 Selkirk, whose solitary residence on . . . Juan Fernandez was a nine days' wonder.

Wonders of England, Three | the churches, the women, the wool. (W 729)

1612–15 BP. HALL *Contempl.* IV. xi. (1825) II. 378 There were wont to be reckoned three wonders of England, ecclesia, fœmina, lana; 'the churches, the women, the wool'.

Wonders will never cease.

1776 *Garrick Corresp.* (1823) ii. 174. 1836 HALIBURTON *Clockmaker* I. 100. 1842 LEVER *Jack Hinton* ch. 20. The bystanders . . . looked from one to the other, with expressions of mingled surprise and dread . . . 'Blessed hour, . . . wonders will never cease'. 1885 C. LOWE *Bismarck* (1898) x. 339 Bismarck had . . . been kissed and hugged by his Majesty. . . . The world had been again reminded . . . that wonders, truly, would never cease.

Wonder(s), *see also* Seville (He who has not seen) has not seen a w.; Time works w.; Wise man great w.

Wont, *see* Uses me better than he is w. (He that) will betray me.

Woo but[1] cost? Who may. (C 671)

a. 1628 CARMICHAELL no. 1262 Quha may wow but coste. 1641 FERGUSSON no. 715. 1721 KELLY 352 . . . That is, no great matter can be easily attain'd or atchiev'd. [1 without.]

Woo, To | is a pleasure in a young man, a fault in an old. (P 421)

1664 CODRINGTON 217. 1670 RAY 30. 1732 FULLER no. 5254 (a Phrenzy in an old).

Woo where he will, A man may | but he will wed where his hap is. (M 271)

1641 FERGUSSON no. 114. 1721 KELLY 27 A Man may woo where his will, but wed where his Wife is. Spoken of a Man who having courted many Mistresses, has at last married to his Disadvantage.

Woo, *see also* Petticoats w. (When), breeks may come speed.

Wood (*proper name*), *see* Hunt's (W.'s) dog
(Like); Peter of W., church and mills are his;
Tent thee, quoth W.

Wood, To be in a.   (w 732)

[= to be bewildered.] **1595** SHAKES. *M.N.D.*
III. i. 136 If I had wit enough to get out of this
wood, I have enough to serve mine own turn.
1608 DAY *Law Tricks* v. i 1me in a wood. **1608**
MIDDLETON *Mad World* v. ii. 143. *c.* **1616**
BEAUM. & FL. *Mad Lover* IV. i. 95 Help the boy;
He's in a wood, poor child.

Wood half-burnt is easily kindled.

(w 742)

1557 G. CAVENDISH *Life of Card. Wolsey* (1893)
142 Nowe ye may perceyve the old malice
begynnyth to breake owt, & newely to kyndell
the brand that after proved to a great fier. **1640**
HERBERT no. 606.

Wood in a wilderness, moss in a mountain, and wit in a poor man's breast, are little thought of. (w 742)

a. **1628** CARMICHAELL no. 1633 (dois na gude).
1641 FERGUSSON nos. 887 and 888 Wood in
wildernesse, and strength in a fool. Wit in a
poore mans head, mosse in a mountain availes
nothing. **1721** KELLY 347.

Wood, Like | like arrows.   (w 739)

1616 DRAXE no. 1236.

Wood(s), *see also* Arrows (Not to know of what
w. to make); Crab of the w. . . . w. of the crab;
Cut down the w., catch wolf; Cut Falkland w.
with penknife; Fields have eyes; Game cheaper
in market; Green w. makes hot fire; Halloo
until out of the w. (Not to); Lay on more w.,
ashes give money; Little w. heat little oven;
Lived too near a w. to be frightened by owls;
Lives longest must fetch w. farthest; Looks as
the w. were full of thieves; Mares in w.; New
beer . . . green w. makes hair grow through
hood; Old w. is best to burn; Red w. makes
gude spindles; Sairy w. that has never withered
bough; Sap and heart are best of w.; See the w.
for trees (Cannot); Touch w.; Ways to the w.
than one (More).

Wood (= mad), *see* Horn mad (w.); Once w.
and aye the waur.

Woodcock does not make a winter, One.   (w 747)

1617 J. SWETNAM *School of Defence* 171 One
Swallow maketh not a Summer, nor two Woodcocks a Winter. **1636** CAMDEN 303 One swallow
maketh not summer Nor one Woodcocke a
winter. **1659** N. R. 84 (as 1636). **1662** J.
WILSON *Cheats* I. ii. One woodcock makes
no winter. **1670** RAY 128 One swallow makes
not a spring, nor one woodcock a winter.

Woodcock, To play the.   (w 748)

1582 WHETSTONE *Heptameron* Q3 The rule of
his Wife, is warrant sufficient, for the wise to
ouer rule him for a Woodcocke. **1594-8** SHAKES.
T.S. I. ii. 157 O this woodcock, what an ass it
is! **1666** TORRIANO *Prov. Phr.* 115a To play
the fool, or to play the woodcock; to do worse
and worse.

Woodcock, *see also* Partridge had w.'s thigh (If);
Snite need not w. betwite; Springe to catch a w.;
Winter enough for the snipe and w.; Wise as a
w.

Wooden dagger, I will not wear the.

(D 4)

1670 RAY 198. *i.e.* lose my winnings.

Wooden, *see* Counsel of fools (To), a w. bell; No
Jews, no w. shoes; Runs in the blood like w.
legs.

Wood-pile, *see* Nigger in the w.-p.

Wooers, *see* Maiden with many w.

Wooing for woeing; banna for banning.

c. **1549** HEYWOOD II. vii. 14ᵛ Had I not been
witcht, . . . The termes that long to weddyng had
warnde me First wooyng for woyng, banna for
bannyng.

Wooing that is not long a-doing, Happy is the.   (w 749)

1576 *Parad. of D. Devices* in *Brit. Bibliog.* (1812)
iii. 71 Thrise happie is that woying That is not
long a doyng. **1599** H. PORTER *Angry Wom.
Abingd.* l. 2569 Short woeing is the best. **1621**
BURTON *Anat. Mel.* III. ii. v. v. (1638) 578 Blessed
is the wooing, That is not long a-doing. As the
saying is, when the parties are sufficiently knowne
to each other, . . . let her meanes be what they
will, take her without any more adoe. **1670** RAY
48. **1721** KELLY 153 . . . I have seldom seen . . .
a suddain Match, prove comfortable or prosperous. **1753** RICHARDSON *Grandison* I. ix. (1812)
13 What signifies shilly-shally? What says the
old proverb?—'Happy is the wooing, That is
not long a-doing.'

Wooing was a day after the wedding, The.   (w 750)

1579 LYLY *Euph.* i. 228 I cannot but smile to
hear that . . . the woeing should bee a day after
the weddinge. **1732** FULLER no. 4840.

Wooing, *see also* Courting and w. bring dallying;
Sunday's w. draws to ruin.

Wool, Many go out for | and come home shorn.   (w 754)

1599 MINSHEU *Span. Dial.* 61 You will goe for
wooll, and returne home shorne. **1612** SHELTON
Quix. I. vii. i. 43 To wander through the
world, . . . without once considering how many
there go to seek for wool that return again shorn
themselves? **1678** RAY 220. **1824** SCOTT *St.
Ronan's* ch. 36 You are one of the happy sheep
that go out for wool, and come home shorn.
1910 G. W. E. RUSSELL *Sketches & Snap.* 315
Some go [to Ascot] intent on repairing the
ravages of Epsom or Newmarket; and in this

speculative section not a few . . . who go for wool come away shorn.

Wool over (a person's) eyes, To draw (pull).

1838 HALIBURTON *Clockmaker* II. II (draw). **1855** FRANCES M. WHITCHER *Widow Bedott* ch. 15 He ain't so big a fool as to have the wool drawd over his eyes in that way. **1884** HOWELLS *Silas Lapham* ch. 7 I don't propose he shall pull the wool over my eyes.

Wool so white but a dyer can make it black, There is no.   (w 755)

1567 J. JEWELL *Def. of the Apology of the C. of E.* B6 It is very course woole, that wil take no coloure. **1576** PETTIE ii. 69 I see there is no wool so coarse but it will take some colour. **1580** LYLY *Euph. & his Eng.* ii. 101 There is no wooll so white but the Diar can make blacke. **1642** TORRIANO 17 That is evil wool, that will not hold dying. **1732** FULLER no. 4927. **1802** WOLCOT (P. Pindar) *Middl. Elect.* iii. Wks. (1816) IV. 194 E'en let mun all their poison spit, My lord, there is no wooll zo whit, That a dyer caan't make *black*.

Wool, *see also* Better give the w. than the sheep; Cap be made of w. (If his); Feet of deities shod with w.; Go to a goat for w.; Great cry little w.; Lemster w.; Loves well sheep's flesh who . . . bread in w.; Shaving against the w.; Thrift of you and w. of dog good web; Warm as w.; Wit of you and w. of blue dog good medley; Wonders of England (Three).

Wool-gathering, *see* Wits are w.-g.

Woolpack(s), *see* London Bridge.

Wool-seller knows a wool-buyer, A.
                                        (w 757)

a. **1628** CARMICHAELL no. 245. **1641** FERGUSSON no. 52. **1670** RAY 159 (Yorksh.). **1721** KELLY 341 Wool Sellers ken ay Wool Buyers. Roguish People know their own Consorts.

Woolward, To go.

[= without linen.]` *c.* **1315** SHOREHAM *Poems* i. 1024 Baruot go, Wolle-ward and wakynge. **1377** LANGLAND *P. Pl.* B. xviii. 1 Wolleward and wete-shoed went I forth after. *c.* **1489** *Id. Sonnes of Aymon* xxvii. 574 He is goon his wayes wulwarde and barefote. **1530** PALSGRAVE 846b Wolwarde, without any lynnen nexte ones body. *c.* **1552** T. BECON *Treatise of Fasting* P.S. 536 Some in their fast go woolward, bare-footed and bare-legged. *c.* **1594** SHAKES. *L.L.L.* V. ii. 697 The naked truth of it is: I have no shirt; I go woolward for penance.

Woos a maid, He that | must seldom come in her sight; but he that woos a widow must woo her day and night.
                                        (w 338)

c. **1576** WHYTHORNE 191 Hee who doth wo A maid shalnot bee the wurs welkum thoh hee

kum but now and then to her, az in iij or iiij daiz, but hee that woeth A widow, must ply her daily. [*c.* 1597] **1619** DELONEY *Jack Newberry* ch. 11, 65 He that will wooe a widow, must take time by the forelocke. **1639** CLARKE 27 He that will win a maid must seldome come in her sight. **1670** RAY 49. **1732** FULLER no. 6403.

Word and a blow, A.   (w 763)

1563 R. RAINOLDE *Foundation of Rhetoric* D1 Richard duke of Gloucester . . . quicke and liuely, a worde and a blowe. *c.* **1568** WAGER *Longer thou Livest* D1 This is manhoode to make thee bolde, Let there be but a worde and a blow. **1594-5** SHAKES. *R.J.* III. i. 40 Make it a word and a blow. **1678** BUNYAN *Pilgr.* I. (1877) 74 He was but a word and a blow, for down he knocked me, and laid me for dead. **1821** BYRON *Letters* Prothero v. 451.

Word and a stone let go (word spoken) cannot be called back, A.   (w 777)

[HOR *A.P.* 390 *Nescit vox missa reverti.*] *c.* **1386** CHAUCER *Manc. T.* l. 355 Thing that is seyd, is seyd; and forth it gooth Though hym repente, or be hym nevere so looth. **1509** BARCLAY *Ship of Fools* i. 108 A worde ones spokyn reuoked can nat be. **1548** W. PATTEN *Exped. into Scotland* (Tudor Tracts 154) The word thus uttered cannot be called again. **1579** LYLY *Euph.* i. 279 What so is kept in silence is husht, but whatsoeuer is babbled out cannot agayne be recalled. **1584** WITHALS 14ᵛ If a word flit, no calling back serueth, no reuoking of it. **1616** DRAXE no. 2482. **1639** CLARKE 51 A word spoken is past recalling. **1732** FULLER no. 485.

Word before (in time) is worth two behind (afterwards), A.   (w 778)

a. **1628** CARMICHAELL no. 255. **1641** FERGUSSON no. 48. **1659** HOWELL *Br. Prov.* 17 Better one word in time, then afterwards two.

Word is in your mouth, While the | it is your own; when 'tis once spoken 'tis another's.   (w 776)

1509 BARCLAY *Ship of Fools* i. 110 Whan a worde is nat sayd, the byrde is in the cage . . . whan thy worde is spoken . . . Thou arte nat mayster but he that hath it harde. **1547** BALDWIN K6ᵛ A man hath power ouer hys wordes till they be spoken, but after they be vttered they haue power ouer hym. **1600-1** SHAKES. *H.* III. ii. 94 I have nothing with this answer, Hamlet. These words are not mine.—No, nor mine now. **1646** A. BROME *Roxb. Ballads* B.S. viii. 109 Our words are our own if we keep them within.

Word to a wise man is enough, A. (Few words to the wise suffice).   (w 781)

[L. *Verbum sat sapienti.*] *c.* **1275** *Provs. of Alfred* (Skeat) A38 Mid fewe worde wis mon fele biluken wel con. *c.* **1475** *Mankind* l. 102 Few wordis: few and well sett! *c.* **1530** HEYWOOD *Witty & Witless* ed. Fairholt 22 Few words wher reason ys. *c.* **1532** *Tales* no. 34 The noble wyse men loue fewe wordes. **1546** HEYWOOD II. vii. I4ᵛ Fewe woord is to the wise suffice to be spoken. *c.* **1568** V. FULWELL *Like will to like* B2ᵛ Few words are best among

freend̃s. **1576** HOLYBAND Eɪᵛ Few wordes
among wise men suffiseth. **1577** RHODES *Boke
of Nature* in *Babees Book* E.E.T.S. 88 For few
wordes to wise man is best. **1578** SIDNEY *Wks.*
(Feuillerat) iii. 124 Few wordes are beste. **1584**
WITHALS H8ᵛ Mylde and few wordes beseeme a
woman. **1594** *King Leir* III. v. 109. [1597?]
1609 JONSON *Case is Altered* I. i. 21 Go to, a
word to the wise. *c.* **1600** *Roxb. Ballads* (Hindley) i. 157 It is an old saying that few words are
best. **1614** CAMDEN 306 Few words to the wise
suffice. **1662** FULLER *Westmor.* Kendal 135
I hope the Towns-men thereof (a word is enough
to the wise) will make their commodities . . .
substantiall. **1678** RAY 220. Few words are
best . . . A fool's voice is known by multitude of
words. **1837–47** BARHAM *Ingol. Leg.* (1898) 488
Which some learned Chap . . . perhaps would
translate by the words 'Verbum Sap!'

Word to deed is a great space, From. (w 802)

1573 SANFORD 104. **1599** MINSHEU *Span. Dial.*
11 (a great distance). **1642** TORRIANO 44 (a
great distance).

Word (Stone) to throw at a dog, He hasn't a. (w 762)

[*c.* 1590] **1598** *Famous Vict. Henry V* G1 We
haue not a French word to cast at a Dog by
the way. **1593** G. HARVEY *Wks.* Gros. ii. 53
Shall not bee allowed a woord to cast at a dogg.
1599 SHAKES. *A.Y.* I. iii. 3 Not a word?— Not
one to throw at a dog.—No, thy words are too
precious to be cast away upon curs. **1600–1** *Id.
M.W.W.* I. iv. 103 He shall not have a stone
to throw at his dog. **1639** CLARKE 302 He hath
not a word to cast at a dog. **1738** SWIFT *Dial.* I.
E.L. 261 Here's Miss, has not a Word to throw
at a Dog. **1837** LOVER *Rory O'More* ch. 22
This last monosyllable 'annihilated' the Frenchman, . . . 'he hadn't a word to throw to a dog'.
1890 HENLEY & STEVENSON *Beau Austin* I. i She
falls away, has not a word to throw at a dog,
and is ridiculously pale.

Words and feathers the wind carries away. (w 831)

c. 1570 *The Pedlar's Prophecy* l. 782 Words wey
not, but are light, and fly in the winde. **1591**
STEPNEY *Span. Schoolmaster* E3ᵛ Words are
more light then feathers, that are caried with
euery swift winde. **1599** MINSHEU *Span. Gram.*
84. **1651** HERBERT no. 1103. **1706** STEVENS s.v.
Palabra (. . . that is, Words are but wind).

Words and not of deeds, A man of | is like a garden full of weeds. (M 296)

1659 HOWELL *Eng. Prov.* 20a. **1670** RAY 211.

Words are but wind. (w 833)

c. 1200 *Ancrene Riwle* 122 Hwat is word bute
wind? *c.* 1390 GOWER *Conf. Amantis* III. 2768
For word is wynd, bot the maistrie Is that a man
himself defende Of thing which is noght to
commende. **1509** BARCLAY *Ship of Fools* i. 207
Wordes ar but wynde. **1591** ARIOSTO *Orl. Fur.*
Harington X. 6 Their othes but words, their
words are all but wind. **1592–3** SHAKES. *C.E.*
III. i. 75 A man may break a word with you,

sir, and words are but wind. **1594–5** *Id. L.L.L.*
IV. iii. 64 Vows are but breath, and breath a
vapour is. **1598–9** *Id. M.A.* V. ii. 45 Foul
words is but foul wind. **1616** DRAXE no. 2126.
1650 COWLEY *Guardian* I. iii I'm . . . given to
jeering: but what, man? words are but wind.
1652 FULLER *Com. on Christ's Tempt.* in *Sel.
Serm.* (1891) II. 44 Some will say, *Wordes are
but wind*; but God's are real words, such as fill
and fat those that depend upon them.

Words are but wind, but blows unkind (dunts¹ are the devil). (w 834)

1616 DRAXE no. 1108. **1641** FERGUSSON no. 871
(dunts are the devil). **1659** HOWELL *Eng. Prov.*
14b. **1721** KELLY 340 Words go with the
Wind, but dunts are the Devil. [¹ hard blows.]

Words are but words (sands), but money buys land. *Cf.* Talk is but talk. (w 832)

1590–5 MUNDAY *et al. Sir T. More* IV. iv. 1
Woords are but wordes and payes not what men
owe. **1619** FLETCHER & MASS. *Little Fr. Lawyer*
I. i Words are but words. **1659** HOWELL *Eng.
Prov.* 11b (sands). **1666** TORRIANO *Prov. Phr.*
116 Words are words, but money buys Land,
saith the English.

Words are wise men's counters, the money of fools. (w 835)

1651 HOBBES *Leviathan* I. iv. (1904) 18 Words are
wise mens counters, they do but reckon by them:
but they are the mony of fooles, that value them
by the authority of an *Aristotle*, a *Cicero*, or a
Thomas. **1903** JAS. BRYCE *Biograph. Stud.*, Ld
Beaconsfield 40 In his fondness for particular
words and phrases there was a touch . . . of the
cynical view that words are the counters with
which the wise play their game.

Words bind men.

[L. *Verba ligant homines, taurorum cornua funes.*]
1621 BURTON *Anat. Mel.* III. ii. III. iv. (1638) 480
It was Cleopatras sweet voice, and pleasant
speech which inveigled Anthony. . . . *Verba
ligant hominem, ut Taurorum cornua funes*, as
Bulls hornes are bound with ropes, so are mens
hearts with pleasant words.

Words cut (hurt) more than swords. (w 839)

[PHOCYLIDES *Sententiae* 124 Ὅπλον τοι λόγος
ἀνδρὶ τομώτερόν ἐστι σιδήρου. The tongue is
a sharper weapon than the sword.] *c.* 1200
Ancrene Riwle 74 Mo sleað word þene sweord.
1584 LYLY *Camp.* l. 549. **1584** WITHALS N3ᵛ.
c. 1594 SHAKES. *T.And.* I. i. 314 These words are
razors to my wounded heart. **1621** BURTON
Anat. Mel. I. ii. IV. iv. (1638) 148 It is an old
saying, *A blow with a word strikes deeper then a
blow with a sword.* **1659** HOWELL *Eng. Prov.* 13a.
1670 RAY 158 Many words hurt more then
swords. **1878** J. A. SYMONDS *Sidney* 13, 15 A
letter written by Sir Henry Sidney to his son . . .
may here be cited . . . 'A wound given by a word
is oftentimes harder to be cured than that which
is given with the sword.'

Words ending in *ic*, The | do mock the
physician; as hectic, paralytic, apoplec-
tic, lethargic.   (w 836)

1651 HERBERT no. 1044. **1659** HOWELL *Fr. Prov.*
12 Diseases ending in ik shame the Physitian,
as Paralytik, Hydropik, etc.

Words go with the wind, but strokes
are out of play.

1721 KELLY 340.

Words have long tails, and have no
tails.   (w 837)

1678 RAY 221.

Words have wings, and cannot be
recalled. *Cf.* Word spoken.   (w 838)

1590 GREENE *Royal Exch.* Gros. vii. 232 Words
had wings, which once let slyp could never be
recalled. **1593** J. RAINOLDS (Boas, *Univ. Drama*
242) Woordes haue winges, and flie away, mans
writings doe remaine. **1687** MIÈGE s.v. Word.

Words may pass, but blows fall heavy.
                                        (w 840)

1678 RAY 354. *Somerset.*

Words will not fill a bushel (fill not the
firlot[1]), Many.   (w 817)

1641 FERGUSSON no. 627 Mony words fils not
the furlot. **1659** HOWELL *Eng. Prov.* 9a. **1692**
BUNYAN *Christ a Complete Sav.* Wks. (1855) I.
213 For the more compliment, the less sincerity.
Many words will not fill a bushel. **1695** RAVENS-
CROFT 17 (Fair words). **1721** KELLY 251 Many
words fill not the farlet. [[1] a dry measure.]

Words would have much drink, Many.
                                        (w 818)

[*c.* 1515] *c.* 1530 BARCLAY *Eclog.* III. l. 3 Many
wordes requireth much drinke. *a.* 1628
CARMICHAELL no. 1134 (wald have meikle drink).
1641 FERGUSSON no. 624 (as *a.* 1628). **1824**
SCOTT *St. Ronan's* ch. 32 Ye hae garr'd the poor
wretch speak till she swarfs.[1] . . . Let me till her
wi' the dram—mony words mickle drought, ye
ken. [[1] swoons.]

Word(s), *see also* Actions speak louder; Bare w.
no bargain; Bird is known by his note, man by
his w.; Breaks his w., (A man that) bids others
be false to him; Changing of w.; Children pick
up w. as pigeon peas; Deeds are fruits, w. are
leaves; Deeds are males, w. females; Deeds, not
w.; Difference between w. and deed, (There is
great); Eat one's w.; Evening w. not like
morning; Fair w. and foul deeds cheat; —— and
foul play cheat; —— butter no parsnips; ——
in flyting (Never a). Few w., many deeds;
Fine w. dress ill deeds; First w. of flyting (You
have got); First w. stand (Let the); Gives
fair w.; Good as one's w., (To be as); Good w.
costs no more; Good w. and ill deeds deceive;

Good w. anoint us; —— cool more; —— cost
nought; —— fill not a sack; —— good cheap;
—— without deeds; Half a w. enough; Hard w.
break no bones; Honest man's w.; Ill w. asks
another; Ill w. meets another; Keep off and
give fair w.; King of your w. (Ye should be);
King's w. is more than another man's oath;
Last w.; Lie or two may escape (In many w.);
Live by selling ware for w. (One cannot); Mad
w. deaf ears; Many w.; Modest w. to express
immodest things, (It is hard to find); More w.
than one to bargain; Never take the tawse
when w. will do; Nine w. at once; No w. but
mum; Penzance (Not a w. of); Safe is the w.;
Second w. makes bargain; Sharp's the w.; Snug's
the w.; Soft w. hard arguments; Speaks as if
every w. would lift dish; Tale (w.) out of one's
mouth, (To take the); Three w. (At); True w.
spoken in jest; Two (w.) to a bargain; Wine
sinks (When) w. swim; Women will have last
w.; Wranglers never want w.

Work and no play makes Jack a dull
boy, All.   (w 842)

1659 HOWELL *Eng. Prov.* 12b. **1670** RAY 158.
1859 SMILES *Self-Help* ch. 11 'All work and no
play makes Jack a dull boy'; but all play and
no work makes him something greatly worse.

Work cut out, To have one's.

1574 *Form of Christ. Policy* tr. G. Fenton 152
The Ritch man . . . hath (as it were) his worke
cut out, if (as he ought) hee discharge the dutye
of his estate towardes God. **1672** MARVELL
Rehearsal Transprosed ed. Grosart 165.

Work double tides, To.

1788 MME D'ARBLAY *Diary* 1 July I was most
content to work double tides for the pleasure
of his company. **1832** *Examiner* 745/2 The
artisans work double tides, that is, they perform
two days' labour in one. **1852** MISS YONGE
Cameos (1877) II. vii. 95 There is not a spinster
in Brittany who will not spin double tides until
my purchase-money be raised.

Work (etc.) for a dead horse, To.
                                        (H 699)

1638 BROME *Antipodes* I. Wks. (1873) III. 234
His land . . . 'twas sold to pay his debts; All went
that way, for a dead horse, as one would say.
1609 HARWARD 108 He woorketh (as he sayth)
for a dead horse [Of one that gets paid beforehand.] **1670** RAY 171 . . . To work out an old
debt, or without hope of future reward. **1706**
STEVENS s.v. Dinero. People will not work for
Money paid before hand: we say, it is bad
working for a dead Horse. **1857** *N. & Q.* 2nd
Ser. IV. 192/1 . . . He has so much unprofitable
work to get through in the ensuing week, which
is called 'dead horse'.

Work for nought makes folk dead
sweir.[1]

a. **1628** CARMICHAELL no. 1661. **1721** KELLY
341. [[1] lazy.]

Work hard, To | live hard, die hard, and go to hell after all, would be hard indeed!

1840 R. H. DANA *Two Years bef. Mast* ch. 6 Sailors . . . seldom get beyond the common phrase which seems to imply that their sufferings and hard treatment here will excuse them here-after—. . .

Work in the morning may trimly be done, Some | that all the day after may hardly be won.

1573 TUSSER 75 E.D.S. 167.

Work like a galley-slave, To.

1841 F. CHAMIER *Tom Bowl.* ch. 2 I made up my mind to be contented in my situation, and . . . worked away like a galley-slave.

Work like a horse, To.

1710 SWIFT *Jrnl. to Stella* 9 Sept. Lord Wharton . . . is working like a horse for elections.   **1857** HUGHES *Tom Brown* II. viii The Marylebone men played carelessly in their second innings, but they are working like horses now to save the match.

Work, He that will not | shall not eat.
(L 10)

[2 THESS. iii. 10.] **1530** *Dial. betw. Gentlemen & Husbandmen* Arber 143 Saynt Paules doctryne Qui non laborat, non manducet. **1548** R. CROWLEY *Information agst. the Oppressors of the Poor Commons* A4 I woulde wysh that no man were suffered to eate, but such as woulde laboure in theyr occasion and callyng. **1552** LINDSAY *Three Estates* 2600 Qui non laborat non manducet, . . . Quha labouris nocht he sall not eit. **1616** DRAXE no. 1176. **1639** CLARKE 163 (will want).

Work that kills, It is not | but worry.

1879 D. M. CRAIK *Young Mrs. Jardine* Bk. 3 ch. 9. **1908** E. M. SNEYD-KYNNERSLEY *H.M.I.* ch. 18 The work is often very heavy, but it is not work that kills: it is worry.   **1909** *Brit. Wkly.* 8 July 333 It is worry that kills, they say, and not work . . . The canker of care seems to eat the life away.

Work wisely lest a man be prevented, It is good to.
(M 199)

1616 DRAXE no. 2432. **1664** CODRINGTON 224. **1846** DENHAM 3.

Work with the Government (dockyard) stroke, To.

1873 W. ALLINGHAM *Rambles* II. 60 'Working with a dockyard stroke' . . . means . . . taking the longest time to do as little as possible. **1909** *Spectator* 22 May 807 Working with 'the Government stroke' . . . mean[s] that when a man is working for the Government he works less strenuously than when working for a private employer.

Work(s) *(noun)*, *see also* All in the day's w.; Changing of w. lighting of hearts; Church w. goes on slowly; Cobble and clout (They that) shall have w.; Day is short, w. is much; Doctor (One) makes w. for another; Fools and bairns . . . half-done w.; Great gain makes w. easy; Little wit in head makes w.; Love makes one fit for any w.; Rises not early never does good day's w.; Run to w. in haste; Son of his own w.; Stay (If anything) let w. stay; Stomachs to eat, (He has two), one to w.; Woman's w. never done; Workman is known by his w.

Worker(s), *see* Ill w. are aye good to-putters.

Work-hard, *see* Forecast is better.

Working, *see also* Kills himself with w.

Workman is known by his work, The.
(W 860)

1490 VINCENTIUS tr. Caxton (1529 ed., C1^v) By the work is the workeman knowen.   **1592** DELAMOTHE 1 At the end of his worke, we iudge of a workeman.   **1666** TORRIANO *It. Prov.* 177 no. 27 The work commends the Master.

Workman, like tool, Like.

1577 *Art of Angling* A4^v.   **1609** HARWARD 122^v. **1617** SWETNAM *Sch. of Defence* 9 A Prouerbe, A workeman is knowne by his tooles. [i.e. he should keep them in good order.]

Workman, The better | the worse husband.
(W 856)

1616 DRAXE no. 685 (the worser husband).   **1670** RAY 158 . . . It is an observation generally true (the more the pity) and therefore . . . I put it down.

Workman without his tools? What is a.
(W 859)

1546 HEYWOOD II. ix. L1^v.   **1559** BECON *Prayers &c.* P.S. 260 Ye cannot consecrate aright. Ye have not all your tools. . . . For what is a workman without his tools?   **1614** CAMDEN 314.

Workman, *see also* Bad w. quarrels with tools; Good w. seldom rich; Little let lets an ill w.

Works after his own manner, He that | his head aches not at the matter.

1640 HERBERT no. 421.   (M 634)

Works it's obsolete, If it.

1961 22 Sept. *Times* . . . Lord Mountbatten . . . used this modern American proverb to-day to bring home to a study conference on defence administration the rapacious march of science.

Work(s, ed) *(verb)*, *see* Corn him well, he'll w. the better; Eat till you sweat, w. till you freeze; Night comes (When) no man can w.; St. Distaff's Day neither w. nor play; Think of ease but w. on; Well to w. and make a fire does care require.

World and his wife, All the.

1738 SWIFT *Dial.* III. E.L. 318 Who were the company?—Why there was all the world and his wife. **1816** BYRON to Moore 29 Feb. I am at war with all the world and his wife.

World, This is the | and the other is country. (w 881)

1678 RAY 84. (*Joculatory.*)

World at will, To have the. (w 869)

15c. *Early Eng. Carols* ed. R. L. Greene 340 Yyf a man . . . haue not the world at will. **1534** T. LUPSET *Treat. Dying Well* ed. Gee 284 It must be a bytter thyng to make an ende of all his pleasures, and in this case be . . . they that haue this worlde at their wyll. **1540** PALSGRAVE *Acolastus* 98. **1545** TAVERNER I2 Thou haste the worlde at will. **1573** GASCOIGNE *Supposes* i. 197. **1621** BURTON *Anat. Mel.* II. iii. iii. iii. (1638) 318. **1629** *Bk. Mer. Rid.* Prov. no. 52 He that hath the world at will seemes wise.

World goes (runs) on wheels, The. (w 893)

a. **1500** *15c. School-Bk.* ed. Nelson 2 Nowe the worlde rennyth upon another whele. **1528** ROY & BARLOW *Rede me & be not wroth* ed. Arber 61 Fortune with prestes runneth on wheles. **1542** A. BORDE *Dyetary* E.E.T.S. 250 The malt worme playeth the deuyll so fast in the heade, that all the worlde rouneth rownde about on wheles. **1546** HEYWOOD II. vii. I2ᵛ. **1594** SHAKES. *T.G.V.* III. i. 307 Then may I set the world on wheels. **1603** MONTAIGNE (Florio) III. ii. 26 The world runnes all on wheels. All things therein moove without intermission. **1606-7** SHAKES. *A.C.* II. vii. 97 The third part of the world . . . is drunk. Would it were all, That it might go on wheels! **1629** T. ADAMS *Serm.* (1861-2) I. 87 The proud gallant . . . and his adorned lady . . . are riders too. . . . The world with them runs upon wheels; and they . . . outrun it.

World (fortune, love) in a string, To have the. (w 886)

[= to have it under control.] **1580** LYLY *Euph. & his Eng.* ii. 92 Al fire is not quenched by water, thou hast not loue in a string. **1580** J. BARET *Alveary* F926 When any man hath fortune as it were in a string. **1583** MELBANCKE *Philot.* I Those that walke as they will, . . . perswading themselues that they haue the worlde in a string. **1584** R. WILSON *Three Ladies of London* Hazl.-Dods. vi. 335 I think you lead the world in a string. **1681** H. MORE *Exp. Dan.* 162 He [Alex. the Great] had the world in a string, as our English Proverbial Phrase is. **1894** F. BARRETT *Justif. Lebrun* viii. 66 When they believed they had the world on a string.

World is a ladder for some to go up and some down, The. (w 897)

1481 CAXTON *Reynard* ch. 33, Arb. 97 I wente dounward and ye cam vpward . . . thou saidest thus fareth the world that one goth vp and another goth doun. **1642** TORRIANO 63 (is made latherwise). **1659** HOWELL *It. Prov.* I The world is like a ladder, one goeth up, the other down. **1732** FULLER no. 4841.

World is a long journey, The. (w 894)

1616 BRETON *Cross.* A6.

World is a stage and every man plays his part, This. (w 882)

c. **1530** LUCIAN *Necromantia* BIᵛ Mannes lyfe wel be lykenid might To a stage play where it fortunyth alway That they that be the players shalbe that day Apparelyd in dyuers straunge clothyng As rych aray for hym that playeth the kyng . . . Another is dressyd in seruauntis aray One lokyth bewtiouse fresh and gay . . . a play ought to be Of all maner of kyndis and of euery degre. **1571** R. EDWARDES *Damon & Pythias* C2 Pythagoras said that this world was like a stage, whereon many play their parts. **1584** WITHALS I5 This life is a certaine enterlude or playe, the world is a stage ful of change euery way, Euerye man is a player, and therein a dealer. **1596** SHAKES. *M.V.* I. i. 77 I hold the world but as the world, Gratiano — A stage, where every man must play a part, And mine a sad one. **1599** *Id. A.Y.* II. vii. 139 All the world's a stage, And all the men and women merely players. **1605** J. HALL *Medit.* II. 30 (1621 ed. 102) The world is a stage; Every man an actor; and playes his part heere either in Comedie or Trajedy. **1605-6** SHAKES. *M.V.* v. 24 Life's but a walking shadow, a poor player, That struts and frets his hour upon the stage And then is heard no more. **1639** CLARKE 322 We all must act our part.

World is a wide parish (place), The. (w 895)

1581 W. FULKE *Brief Confutation* 17ᵛ The worlde is wide. **1659** HOWELL *Brit. Prov.* 12. **1738** SWIFT *Dial.* II. E.L. 307 I believe there is not such another in the varsal¹ world.—O, miss, the world's a wide place. [¹ universal.]

World is but a little place, after all, The.

1886 G. A. SALA *America Revisited* (ed. 6) 431 Thirty-one years afterwards I find him in San Francisco . . . ; and yet it is not such a large world after all. **1902-4** LEAN IV. 143 The world is but a little place, after all (or, The world is round). Spoken when two casually meet, and find that they have many mutual friends.

World is full of fools (knaves), The. (w 896)

[CICERO *Epist. ad Fam.* lx. 22 Stultorum plena sunt omnia.] **1591** R.W. *Martin Mar-Sixtus* C2 Stultorum plena sunt omnia; not a wise word in a whole Oration. **1596** HARINGTON *Metam. Ajax* 55 And for the foole, the olde prouerbe may serue vs, Stultorum plena sunt omnia, the world is full of fooles. **1609** DEKKER *Gulls' Hornbk.* [title-page] Stultorum plena sunt omnia. **1616** WITHALS 582 (knaues). **1743** FRANKLIN ed. T. H. Russell 21 (of fools and faint hearts).

World is his that enjoys it, The, *see* Gown is his that wears it.

World is nought, The. (w 899)

1591 W. PERKINS *Treat. of Callings* Wks. (1608) i. 748b. **1639** CLARKE 219.

World is nothing, This | except it tend to another.   (w 883)

1640 HERBERT no. 382. **1909** ALEX. MACLAREN *Ephesians* i. 18 This world means nothing worthy, except as an introduction to another.

World is nowadays, God save the conqueror, The.   (w 900)

1591 STEPNEY 150. **1651** HERBERT no. 1075.

World is round (turns as a ball), The.
                                                (w 901)

a. **1500** *Prov. Wisdom* l. 33 The world turnythe, as a ball. **1575** BURGHLEY to Walsingham cited C. Read *Ld. Burghley & Q. Elizabeth* 146 The world is made of a round substance, that it cannot stand still. **1613** T. ADAMS *White Devil* Wks. 57 For (as it is well obserued) the world is round. **1732** FULLER no. 5001 This World is ever running its round.

World is unstable, This | so saith sage: therefore gather in time, ere thou fall into age.

[Prov. attached to Caxton's ed. of Lydgate's *Stans Puer ad Mensam.* HAZLITT (1907) 455.] *c.* **1450** *Salomon's Proverbs* in *Cambridge M.E. Lyrics* ed. Person 1962 l. 27 Thys worlde is mutabyll, so seyth sage, Therfor gedyr yn tyme, or thow fall yn age.

World is well amended with him, The.
                                                (w 902)

a. **1558** *Jacob & Esau* C4ᵛ The worlde is now metely well amended in deede. **1562–3** *Stationers' Register* Arb. i. 205 'The world is well amended quoth little Jack a Lent' [ballad]. **1566** ERASM. *Diversoria* ·r. E.H. ed. de Vocht i. 374 They haue some stiffer meate til suche time as the world beinge well amended with them, they set roste on the table. **1594** NASHE *Unfort. Trav.* ii. 214. **1599** J. CHAMBERLAIN *Letters* (McLure) Aug. 23, i. 82. **1616** DRAXE no. 37 The world is somewhat amended for him. **1670** RAY 200.

World is wiser than it was, The.

a. **1788** WESLEY *Sermons* ii. 276 (than ever it was). **1794** WOLCOT (P. Pindar) *Ode* (in *Pindariana*) Wks. (1816) III. 274 As everybody says, 'the world grows wiser'.

World on your chessboard, Had you the | you could not fill all to your mind.

1640 HERBERT no. 701.   (w 867)

World still he keeps at his staff's end that needs not to borrow and never will lend, The.   (w 904)

1546 HEYWOOD I. xi. F2ᵛ I lyue here at staues ende, Where I nede not borrow, nor I will not lende. *a.* **1576** WHYTHORNE 34 Poverty . . . I kan keep at stavz end. **1611** DAVIES no. 177 (neede). **1616** DRAXE no. 2037 (nor nothing

will lend). **1641** FERGUSSON no. 386 He is weill staikit[1] thereben, that will neither borrow nor len. [[1] stocked, provided.]

World, the flesh, and the devil, The.

[BOOK OF COMMON PRAYER, *Athanasian Creed. Collect for 18th Sunday after Trinity.*] **1530** R. WHITFORD *Werk for Householders* E4ᵛ Our thre ghostly enemies, the deuyll, the worlde, and the flesshe. **1562** G. LEGH *Accidence of Armoury* 211ᵛ Vanquishing the deuill, the worlde, and the Fleshe. **1596** A. COPLEY *Fig for Fortune* 54 The flesh, the world, and fierce insulting deuill. **1596** NASHE *Saffron W.* iii. 61 The world, the flesh, and the diuell. **1606** MARSTON *What You Will* v. i. **1621** BURTON *Anat. Mel.* I. ii. III. xv. (1638) 43 [Where the learned clerk has acquired a small benefice] our misery begins afresh, we are suddenly encountered with the flesh, world, and Divell, with a new onset.

World to see, It is a.   (w 878)

c. **1475** *Assembly of Ladies* in SKEAT'S *Chaucer* VII. 397 For yonge and olde, and every maner age, It was a world to loke on her visage. *a.* **1500** *15c. School-Bk.* ed. Nelson 3. **1515** BARCLAY *Life of St. George* E.E.T.S. l. 289. **1519** RASTELL *Four Elements* Hazl.-Dods. i. 35 It is a world to see her whirl, Dancing in a round. **1579** LYLY *Euph.* i. 254 . . . how commonly we are blynded with the collusions of woemen. **1594–8** SHAKES. *T.S.* II. i. 303 'Tis a world to see, How tame. . . . A meacock wretch can make the curstest shrew. **1598–9** *Id. M.A.* III. v. 33 God help us! it is a world to see.

World wag (slide, shog[1]), Let the.

                                                (w 879)

c. **1425** *Wakefield Plays* Second Shepherds l. 120 Whoso couthe take hede and lett the warld pas. *c.* **1525** RASTELL *Four Elements* Hazl.-Dods. i. 20 Let the wide world wind! *a.* **1529** *Gentleness & Nobility* l. 1028 Syth it so is I wyll let the world wagg and home wyll I goo. *a.* **1529** SKELTON *Sp. Parrot* 90 In flattryng fables men fynde but lyttyl fayth: But *moveatur terra,* let the world wag. **1550** CROWLEY *Epigr.* 361 Let the worlde wagge, we must neades haue drynke. **1576** LEMNIUS *Touchstone of Complexions* tr. T. Newton 141ᵛ (slyde). **1594–8** SHAKES. *T.S.* Ind. I. vi Therefore . . . Let the world slide. *Ibid.* Ind. II. 139 Come, madam wife, sit by my side, And let the world slip. **1602** WITHALS 4 To passe ouer time: to let the world slide. **1611** COTGRAVE s.v. Chargé To take no thought, passe the time merrily, let the world slide. **1616** DRAXE no. 1920 He letteth the world wag, or slide. **1637** SANDERSON *Serm.* (1681) II. 73 Solomons sluggard, . . . who foldeth his hands together, and letteth the world wag as it will. **1719** RAMSAY *Ep. Hamilton* Answ. iii. 20 Be blythe, and let the Warld e'en shog, as it thinks fit. **1721** KELLY 240 Let the world shogg.[1] Spoken by them who have a Mind to do as they have resolv'd, be the Issue what will. **1877** W. BLACK *Green Past.* ch. 42 Let the world wag on as it may. [[1] shake, roll from side to side.]

World wags, I wot well how the | he is best loved that has most bags. (w 874)

1621 ROBINSON 13 (I know not . . . maniest bags). **1639** CLARKE 97. **1887** BLACKMORE *Springhaven* ch. 31 We must wag as the world does; and you know the proverb, 'What makes the world wag, but the weight of the bag?'

World will be gulled, If the | let it be gulled. (w 876)

[J. A. DE THOU *Historia* 17. 7 *Quandoquidem populus iste vult decipi, decipiatur.* Remark by Cardinal Caraffa on his entry into Paris (1556) greeted with reverence. (King's *Classical Quot.*).] **1621** BURTON *Anat. Mel.* III. iv. I. ii. (1638) 649 *Si mundus vult decipi, decipiatur.*

World will not last alway, The. (w 884)

c. **1384** CHAUCER *Ho. Fame* Bk. 3, l. 1147 But men seyn 'what may ever laste?' **1615** T. ADAMS *Wolf Worrying Lambs* Wks. (1630) 385 (last euer). **1639** CLARKE 233. **1641** FERGUSSON no. 561 This warld will not last ay.

World's end, see Great journey to.

World's wealth, If we have not the | we have the world's ease.

1721 KELLY 213 . . . Spoken by those who live happily, in a mean Condition.

World(s), see also All sorts to make w.; Athanasius against the w.; Beforehand with the w., (To be); Best of both w.; Deals in w. needs four sieves; Devil divides w. between atheism and superstition; Die (When I), w. dies with me; Every man is master (Where), w. goes to wrack; Giddy, (He that is) thinks w. turns round; Good w., but they are ill that are on it; Good w. if it hold; Gown is his . . . and w. is his that enjoys it; Half the w. knows not; Long time to know w.'s pulse; Love makes w. go round; Mad w., my masters; Mirth of w. dureth but a while; Muck of the w.; Out of the w. out of fashion; Sailors go round w.; Travel through the w. (To) . . . money and patience; War with all the w., peace with England; Weeping come into the w.; Wicked w. and we make part of it; Worst w. that ever was, some man won; ——, malt-man got his sack again.

Worm in his brain, He has a. (w 907)

a. **1534** HEYWOOD *Love* CI[v] Our louer in whose hed By a frantyk worme his opinion is bred. **1548** HALL *Chron.* (1809 ed., 302) The Essex men hauynge wylde whaye wormes in their heddes. *a.* **1558** *Jacob & Esau* A2. **1585** MUNDAY *Two It. Gent.* l. 67. **1666** TORRIANO *Prov. Phr.* s.v. Grilli 79 To be whimsycal, to have worms in his pate. **1678** RAY 278.

Worm, see also Naked as w.; Tread on a w. and it will turn.

Worry, see Kings and bears oft w. keepers; Wit will never w. you; Work that kills (Not) but w.

Worse appear the better cause (reason), To make the.

[PLATO *Apol.* 18B τὸν ἥττω λόγον κρείττω ποιεῖν, charge against Socrates.] **1605** BACON *Adv.*

Learning I. ii. I To make the worse matter seem the better, and to suppress truth by force of eloquence and speech. **1749** LD. CHESTERFIELD *Lett.* clxxv. (1774) I. 517 Like Belial, in Milton[1], 'he made the worse appear the better cause'. [[1] *P.L.* ii. 113.]

Worse luck now, The | the better another time.

1721 KELLY 323 . . . Spoken to hearten losing Gamesters. **1732** FULLER no. 4847.

Worse the passage, The | the more welcome the port.

1732 FULLER no. 4848.

Worse, see also Better the w; Collier's sack, bad without and w. within, (Like a); Everything is w. for wearing; Finds fault with others and does w. himself; Gamester (Better) w. man; Longer the w.; More bare (W. shod) than the shoemaker's wife; Nothing so bad; Older the w.; Stye, (The w. their), the longer they lie; Weaker has w.

Worship the rising sun, Men use to. (s 979)

[L. *Plures adorant solem orientem quam occidentem.* More worship the rising than the setting sun.] **1553** T. WILSON *Arte of Rhet.* (1909) 67 All men commonly more reioyce in the Sunne rising, then they doe in the Sunne setting. **1561** QU. ELIZ. cited C. Read *Mr. Sec. Cecil* 229 I know the inconstancy of the people of England . . . *Plures adorant solem orientem quam occidentalem.* **1639** CLARKE 12. **1655** FULLER *Ch. Hist.* VIII. i. (1868) II. 428 Some are so desirous to worship the rising sun, that . . . they will adore the dawning day. **1670** RAY 137 . . . *Plures adorant solem orientem quam occidentem.* They that are young and rising have more followers, then they that are old and decaying. This consideration . . . withheld Queen *Elizabeth* . . . from declaring her successour. **1738** GAY *Fables* II. ix. 109 (1859) 282 In shoals the servile creatures run, To bow before the rising sun. **1754** GARRICK on Pelham's death, Let others hail the rising sun.

Worship, see also Forecasts all perils will win no w. (He that); Good bearing begins w. (In); Love (W.) the ground he treads on; Wealth makes w.

Worst carver in the world: I am the | I should never make a good chaplain.

1738 SWIFT Dial. II. E.L. 302 I can just carve pudding and that's all; I am the worst carver in the world; I should never make a good chaplain.

Worst dog that is wags his tail, The. (D 519)

1578 FLORIO *First F.* 33. **1611** DAVIES no. 190.

Worst goes foremost, The. (w 917)

a. **1640** MASSINGER *Old Law* III. ii You shall be first; I'll observe court rules: Always the worst goes foremost. **1902–4** LEAN IV. 144 . . . *i.e.* is produced and put forward first, as the lowest in rank is in a procession.

Worst hog often gets the best pear, The.

1659 TORRIANO no. 20 Very oft the best pears drop into the mouth of swine. **1666** *Id. It. Prov.* 212 no. 27 The worst hog lights on best pear. **1706** STEVENS s.v. Puerco Sometimes a bad Hog eats the best Acorns.

Worst is behind, The.   (W 918)

1546 HEYWOOD II. ii. G1 The woorst is behynd, we come not where it grew. **1600–1** SHAKES. *H.* III. iv. 179 Thus bad begins and worse remains behind. **1659** HOWELL *Eng. Prov.* 6b.

Worst may, He that | shall (must) hold the candle.   (C 40)

c. **1534** *Coventry Plays* (Craig) 47 He thatt ma wast of all The candyll ys lyke to holde. **1546** HEYWOOD II. ii. G1. **1551** T. WILSON *Rule of Reason* Q8ᵛ When one hath lost al the money in his purse, and for lacke of coyne is fayne to holde the candel. **1594–5** SHAKES. *R.J.* I. iv. 38 For I am proverb'd with a grandsire phrase; I'll be a candle-holder, and look on. **1614** CAMDEN 307 (must). **1670** RAY 159 (still holds) . . . *Au plus debile la chandelle a la main. Gall.*

Worst misfortunes are those which never befall us, Our.

1817 JEFFERSON *Lett. to Charles Clay* How much pain have cost us the things which have never happened. **1885** E. P. HOOD *World of Prov.* 131 It is Emerson who says—'. . . What torments of pain you endured From the griefs that never arrived'. **1907** A. C. BENSON *From Coll. Wind.* 35 Lord Beaconsfield once said that the worst evil one has to endure is the anticipation of the calamities that do not happen.

Worst people have most (worst) laws, The.

c. **1425** *Wakefield Plays* 'Judgement' l. 194 It is said in olde sawes—'Wars pepill wars lawes'.

Worst piece is in the midst, The.   (P 292)

1609 HARWARD 129 Woorst peece in the midst. **1616** WITHALS 577 Brauely attired, but the worst peece is in the middest. **1671** CLARKE *Phras. Puer.* 22.

Worst spoke in a cart breaks first, The.   (S 770)

1678 RAY 205. **1732** FULLER no. 4851.

Worst store, The | a maid unbestowed.   (S 907)

1659 HOWELL *Brit. Prov.* 15.

Worst use you can put a man to is to hang him, The.

a. **1639** SIR H. WOTTON in *Reliq. Wotton.* (1651) 69 And he believed doubtlesse, that Hanging

was the worse use man could be put to. **1830** LYTTON *Paul Clif.* ch. 36.

Worst wheel of a cart creaks most (makes most noise), The.   (W 287)

c. **1400** *MS. Latin no. 394,* J. Rylands Libr. (ed. Pantin) in *Bull. J. R. Libr.* XIV. 106 Euer þe worst spoke of þe cart krakes. **1581** GUAZZO i. 222 Those whiche knowe least, speake, contend, and crie the lowdest. Whereof belike ariseth this Prouerbe, That the brokenest wheele of the charriot maketh alwaies the greatest noyse. **1642** TORRIANO 69 The worst wheel about the cart, is that which creeketh most. **1659** FULLER *Appeal Inj. Innoc.* in *Hist. Camb. Univ.* (1840) 305 That spoke in the wheel which creaketh most doth not bear the greatest burden in the cart. The greatest complainers are not always the greatest sufferers. **1692** L'ESTRANGE *Aesop's Fab.* cccxxxvi (1738) 349 A waggoner took notice upon the creaking of a wheel, that it was the worst wheel of the four that made most noise. . . . 'They that are sickly are ever the most piping and troublesome.' **1737** FRANKLIN July The worst wheel of the cart makes the most noise.

Worst world that ever was, The | some man won.   (W 905)

a. **1628** CARMICHAELL no. 1470. **1641** FERGUSSON no. 701. **1721** KELLY 318.

Worst world that ever was, The | the maltman got his sack again.   (W 906)

a. **1628** CARMICHAELL no. 1589. **1721** KELLY 308.

Worst, *see also* Best things w. to come by; Corruption of best becomes w.; Fear (Provide for) the w.; Know the w. (To) is good; Things at w. mend; Want is w. of it.

Worth a Jew's eye, To be.   (J 53)

[= to be of much value: *orig.* worth while for a Jewess's eye to look at.] **1593** G. HARVEY *Wks.* Gros. II. 146 As dear as a Iewes eye. **1596** SHAKES. *M.V.* II. v. 41 There will come a Christian by, Will be worth a Jewess's eye. **1833** MARRYAT *P. Simple* ch. 2. Although the journey . . . would cost twice the value of a gold seal, . . . in the end it might be worth a Jew's eye.

Worth doing at all, What is | is worth doing well.

1746 9 Oct., LD. CHESTERFIELD *Lett.* **1875** CHEALES *Prov. Folk-Lore* 138. **1893** *Lett. of C. Dickens* Pref. [Dickens] would take as much pains about the hanging of a picture . . . as . . . about the more serious business of his life; thus carrying out . . . his favourite motto of. . . .

Worth it as a thief is worth a rope (halter), As well.   (T 103)

1596 LODGE *Wit's Misery* 37 A rope is well bestowed to hang a theef. **1599** PORTER *Angry Wom. Abingd.* l. 879 As well worth a shilling, as a theefe woorth a halter. **1639** CLARKE 70. **1678** RAY 290.

Worth no weal that can bide no woe, He is. *Cf.* Deserves not the sweet.
(w 187)

a. 1628 CARMICHAELL no. 1617. 1641 FERGUSSON no. 353. 1721 KELLY 133.

Worth of a thing is best known by the want of it, The. (w 924)

1586 G. WHETSTONE *The Eng. Myrror* 110 The goodnesse of a thing is knowne by the depriuement thereof. 1598–9 SHAKES. *M.A.* IV. i. 220 What we have we prize not to the worth Whiles we enjoy it, but being lack'd and lost . . . we find The virtue that possession would not show us Whiles it was ours. 1611 COTGRAVE s.v. Cogneu The worth of things is knowne when they be lost. 1616 DRAXE no. 7 A man knoweth not the worth of a thing before that he wanteth it. 1670 RAY 159 . . . The cow knows not what her tail is worth, till she hath lost it. 1850 LYTTON *Caxtons* XVII. i Ay, one don't know the worth of a thing till one has lost it.

Worth of a thing is what it will bring, The. (w 925)

1569 C. AGRIPPA *Vanity of Arts & Sciences* (1575) 160 The thinge is so muche worthy as it maye be solde for. 1664 BUTLER *Hudibras* II. i. 465 (1854) I. 126 For what is worth in any thing, But so much money as 'twill bring? 1813 SOUTHEY *Nelson* ch. 2 Vouchers, he found in that country were no check whatever; the principle was, that 'a thing was always worth what it would bring'. 1818 *Letters of Keats* (M. B. Forman 1935) 111 Tradesmen say every thing is worth what it will fetch. 1908 *Spectator* 4 Apr. 'The real worth of anything, is just as much as it will bring'. You cannot get beyond that piece of ancient wisdom as to the determination of value.

Worth one's salt, To be.

[= efficient, capable.] 1830 MARRYAT *King's Own* ch. 3 The captain . . . is not worth his salt. 1857 HUGHES *Tom Brown* bk. 2 ch. 5 Every one who is worth his salt has his enemies. 1868 w. COLLINS *Moonst.* ch. 16 We shouldn't be worth salt to our porridge.

Worth one's weight in gold, To be.
(w 253)

15th c. *Sir Eger, Sir Graham, Sir Graysteel* l. 431, ed. D. Laing 15 A bed then I would had rather, Than my weight of gold and silver. *c.* 1500 MEDWALL *Nature* l. 936 Nay ye ar worth thy weyght of gold. 1608 DAY *Law Tricks* IV. ii. G2ᵛ That boy is worth his weight in pearle. 1636 S. WARD *Serm.* (1862) 146 A thankful man is worth his weight in the gold of Ophir. 1923 A. RAWLINSON *Advent. in Near East* 158 A railway officer and twenty men, who now were worth their weight in gold.

Worth sorrow, He is well | that buys it with his silver. (s 651)

a. 1628 CARMICHAELL no. 876 It is weill waired [deserved] they have sorrow that byes it with their silver. 1641 FERGUSSON no. 498 (as 1628). 1721 KELLY 130 He's well worth Sorrow that buys it with his Silver. Spoken to them that have been at some Pains, to inconvene themselves.

Worth the hearing, It is. (H 300)

1587 J. BRIDGES *Defence* 1302 The Decrees . . . are published to the open viewe of euery man, if our Bretheren as yet can burthen them with any grosse or palpable errour, or with any errour at all, . . . it were worth the hearing. 1590–5 MUNDAY *et al. Sir Thomas More* I. ii. 24 That's worth the hearing. 1597 SHAKES. *I Hen. IV* II. iv. 204 It is worth the list'ning to. 1616 WITHALS 538. *a.* 1770 H. BROOKE *Fool of Quality* i. xxxii.

Worth, *see also* Girl w. gold; Liberty is more w. than gold; Ounce of fortune w. pound of forecast; Pay what you owe and you'll know what you're w.; Tailor's shreds are w. the cutting; Threepence (If you make not much of), ne'er w. a groat; Trick w. two; Word before w. two behind. *See also* Not w.

Worthy to be named the same day, Not. (D 95)

1609 JONSON *Epig.* no. 131 l. 12. 1616 WITHALS 561 (on the same day with him). 1642 D. ROGER'S *Naaman* 139 Not worthy to be named the same day . . . with God.

Worthy to bear (carry) his books after him, Not. (B 533)

1616 WITHALS 561 (carrie his books after him). 1639 CLARKE 72.

Worthy to wipe (buckle, unbuckle) his shoes, Not. (S 378)

[JOHN i. 27 He it is, who coming after me is preferred before me, whose shoe's latchet I am not worthy to unloose.] *c.* 1386 CHAUCER *Squire's T.* l. 555 Ne were we worthy vnbokelen his galoche. *c.* 1410 *Towneley Plays* E.E.T.S. 196 I am not worthy for to lawse the leste thwong that longys to his shoyne. 1569 HUTH *Anc. Ballads* (1867) 21 For I . . ., Vnworthie most maie seeme to bee, To undoo the lachet of her shooe. 1670 RAY 200. 1826 SCOTT *Journ.* 11 Dec. The blockheads talk of my being like Shakespeare—not fit to tie his brogues. 1829 LAMB to Gilman 26 Oct. He [Thomas Aquinas] comes to greet Coleridge's acceptance, for his shoe-latchets I am unworthy to unloose. 1857 G. ELIOT *Scenes* ch. 8 A stuck-up piece of goods, . . . as isn't fit to black the missis's shoes.

Wots not whether he bears the earth, or the earth him, He.

1721 KELLY 174 . . . Spoken of excessive proud People.

Wotton under Weaver, where God came never. (w 926)

1610 CAMDEN *Britannia* tr. Holland 587 This Moreland . . . keepeth snow lying upon it a long while: in so much as that of a little country village named *Wotton* lying here uner *Woverhil* the neighbour inhabitants haue this rime rife in their mouth . . . *Wotton* under *Wever*, Where God came never.

Would *No, I thank you* had never been made. (N 201)
1678 RAY 77.

Would, *see also* Young man w. (If the) and old man could.

Would have, *see* All have and nought forego, He w.; Lack what they w. h. in their pack (Many men).

Wound be healed, Though the | yet a scar remains. (W 929)
a. **1542** SIR T. WYATT 'Wyatt being in prison, to Bryan', Sure am I, Brian, this wound shall heale again: But yet, alas, the skarre shall still remaign. **1575** GASCOIGNE *Posies* i. 159 Striketh with a sting, And leaves a skarre although the wound be heald. **1594** SHAKES. *Lucr.* l. 731 Bearing away the wound that nothing healeth, The scar that will despite of cure remain. **1612–15** BP. HALL *Contempl.* III. v. (1825) I. 65 As wounds once healed leave a scar behind them, so remitted injuries leave commonly in the actors a guilty remembrance. **1660** W. SECKER *Nonsuch Prof.* II. (1891) 358 It is best that dissension should never be born among brethren. . . . Members rent and torn cannot be healed without a scar.

Wound that bleeds inwardly is most dangerous, The. (W 930)
1579 LYLY *Euph.* i. 210 'Seeing the wound that bleedeth inwarde is most daungerous, . . . it is high time to vnfolde my secret loue to my secrete friende. **1592** SHAKES. *T.G.V.* V. iv. 71 The private wound is deepest. **1631** *Celestina* tr. Mabbe 24. **1732** FULLER no. 4852.

Wound(s), *see also* Afraid of w. (He that is); Green w. is soon healed; Hand that gave the w. must give the cure; Ill w. is cured, not ill name.

Wrack, *see* Wrong comes to w.

Wranglers never want words. (W 933)
1616 DRAXE no. 2510 A wrangler neuer wanteth words. **1670** RAY 31. **1732** FULLER no. 5833.

Wrap (a thing) up in clean linen, To. (L 306)
1678 RAY 84 . . . To deliver sordid or uncleanly matter in decent language.

Wrapped, *see* Lapped (W.) in mother's smock (He was).

Wrath of a mighty man, Take heed of the | and the tumult of the people. (H 383)
1599 MINSHEU *Span. Gram.* 84. **1651** HERBERT no. 1148.

Wrath, *see also* God gives his w. by weight; Soft answer turneth away w.

Wrekin, *see* Friends round the W.

Wren(s), *see* Everything helps; Robin and w. God's cock and hen; Sore fight w. as cranes.

Wrenches, *see* Young wenches make old w.

Wrestle, *see* Thrown would ever w.

Wrinkle(s), *see* Nicks (W.) in her horn (She has).

Write down the advice of him who loves you, though you like it not at present.
1666 TORRIANO *It. Prov.* 51 no. 20 The counsel of one who wisheth thee well, write it down, though it seem cross.

Write like an angel, To.
1774 GARRICK in *Mem. of Goldsmith* (Globe) lv Here lies Poet Goldsmith, . . . Who wrote like an angel, but talked like poor Poll. **1908** *Times* 30 Nov. Ruskin . . . wrote like an angel when he was not provoked to scream like a child.

Write, *see also* Receive before you w., w. before you pay.

Writers, *see* Tailors and w. must mind fashion.

Writes a hand like a foot, He.
1738 SWIFT *Dial.* I. E.L. 268 That's a billet-doux from your mistress.—. . . . I don't know whence it comes; but who'er writ it, writes a hand like a foot.

Writing destroys the memory.
1642 TORRIANO 28 He who writeth, hath no memory. **1674** J. SMITH *Grammatica Quadrilinguis* 125 He that writes hath no memory. **1697** W. POPE *Life of Seth* [Ward] 192 The Italian Saying . . . Chi Scrive, non ha Memoria. That is, Writing destroys the Memory.

Writing (Handwriting) on the wall, The.
[DANIEL v. 5.] **1720** SWIFT *Run Upon Bankers* l. 52. 'Tis like the Writing on the Wall. **1837** LOCKHART *Scott* ch. 27 This hand which, like the writing on Belshazzar's wall, disturbed his hour of hilarity. **1866** KINGSLEY *Hereward* ch. 18 William went back to France. . . . But . . . the handwriting was on the wall, unseen by man; and he, and his policy, and his race, were weighed in the balance, and found wanting. **1878** J. PAYN *By Proxy* ch. 38 He stared at those pregnant words till . . . they seemed to be written, like Belshazzar's warning on the wall, in letters of fire.

Writing you learn to write, By.
[L. *Scribendo disces scribere.*] **1583** MELBANCKE EI^v With writinge I maye learne to write. **1763** JOHNSON *Lett.* 16 April Chapman i. 150 If at the end of seven years you write good Latin, you will excel most of your contemporaries. Scribendo disces scribere, it is only by writing ill that you can attain to write well.

Written letter remains, *see Littera scripta manet.*

Wrong box, To be in the.

[⇒ awkwardly placed.] **1546** HEYWOOD II. ix. K4 And therby in the wronge boxe to thriue ye weare. *a.* **1555** RIDLEY *Wks.* 163 If you will hear how St. Augustine expoundeth that place, you shall perceive that you are in a wrong box. *a.* **1659** CLEVELAND *Coachman* 12 Sir, faith you were in the wrong Box. **1734** CAREY *Chronon.* iii Egad, we're in the wrong box. **1836** MARRYAT *Midsh. Easy* ch. 10 Take care your rights of man don't get you in the wrong box. **1837–8** DICKENS *O. Twist* ch. 43 Don't yer take liberties with yer superiors, . . . or yer'll find yerself in the wrong shop.

Wrong comes to wrack (will end), All.
(W 942)

c. **1300** *Walter of Henley's Husbandry* 1890 ed. 4 On ȝeer oþer to wrongge wylle on honde go. Ant euere aten hende wrong wile wende. [One year or two, wrong will on hand go, and ever at an end, wrong will wend.] **1659** HOWELL *Br. Prov.* 31. **1730** BAILEY s.v. Wrong.

Wrong has no warrant.
(W 947)

a. **1628** CARMICHAELL no. 1657. **1641** FERGUSSON no. 865. **1721** KELLY 349 . . . No Man can pretend Authority to do an ill thing.

Wrong hears, wrong answer gives. *Cf.* Ill hearing. Understands ill.
(W 948)

1611 COTGRAVE s.v. Respondre He that conceiues amisse answers amisse. *a.* **1628** CARMICHAELL no. 486 Evil heiring maks wrang ansering. **1641** FERGUSSON no. 876. **1659** HOWELL *Span. Prov.* 17 Who hearkens well, answers well.

Wrong laws make short governance.

c. **1470** HARDING *Chron.* lxxxvi. v.

Wrong never comes right.

1853 TRENCH i. 8. **1882** BLACKMORE *Christowel* ch. 22 Bad work cannot be turned into good; any more than wrong can be turned into right, in this world. **1888** MRS. OLIPHANT *Second Son* ch. 2 'Then it all comes right again.' 'What's wrong can never be right,' said Pax.

Wrong side of the blanket, Born on the.

[⇒ of illegitimate birth.] **1771** SMOLLETT *Humph. Clink.* II. 185 I didn't come on the wrong side of the blanket, girl. **1815** SCOTT *Guy Man.* ch. 9 Frank Kennedy, he said, was a gentleman, though on the wrang side of the blanket.

Wrong way to the wood, You go (take) the.
(W 167)

1546 HEYWOOD II. ix. K4 In mistakyng me, ye may see, ye tooke The wrong way to wood. **1580** LYLY *Euph. & his Eng.* ii. 66 *Fidus* you goe the wrong way to the Woode. in making a gappe, when the gate is open. **1587** J. BRIDGES *Defence* 520 Our Brethren haue another way to the woode.

Wrong way to work, You go the.
(W 168)

1475 JOHN PASTON to Margaret Paston (Gairdner 1904) v. 241 Me thynk he takyth a wronge wey, if he go so to werk. **1611** COTGRAVE s.v. Biais He went not the right way to worke. **1639** CLARKE 8. **1773** VIEYRA s.v. Ahi.

Wrong without a remedy, No.

[L. *Ubi jus, ibi remedium.* Law Max.—Where there is a right, there is a remedy.] **1910** *Spectator* 10 Dec. 1016 Again and again . . . English judges have invented artifices in order to give effect to the excellent legal maxim that there shall be no wrong without a remedy.

Wrongs not an old man that steals his supper from him, He.
(M 181)

1640 HERBERT no. 311. **1659** HOWELL *Span. Prov.* 22. **1737** FRANKLIN Jan. He that steals the old man's supper do's him no wrong.

Wrongs of a husband or master are not reproached, The.
(W 949)

1640 HERBERT no. 139.

Wrong(s), *see also* Absent are always in w.; Bark up a w. tree; Beg at the w. door; Claps his dish at w. man's door; Country, right or w.; Disputants (Of two) warmer in w.; Do w. once and never hear the end; Extreme law is w.; Laugh on w. side of face; King can do no w.; Opinion is never w. (Our own); Owes (Who) is in all the w.; Poor suffer all the w.; Put one's money on w. horse; Revenged all w. (Had I); Right (He that has) fears, w. hopes; Rise on the w. side; Secret (Wherever) something w.; Submitting to one w. brings another; Two w. don't make a right.

Wrongs, *(verb), see also* Right w. no man.

Wroth as the wind.

13 . . *E. E. Allit. P. C.* 410 He wex[1] as wroth as þe wynde towarde oure lorde. **1393** LANGLAND *P. Pl.* C. iv. 486 As wroth as the wynd. wex[1] Mede ther-after. [[1] became.]

Wroth, *see also* Comes last . . . soonest w.

Wry mouth, To make a.

1605 DEKKER *2 Hon. Whore* II. i. 6 I should ha made a wry mouth at the World like a Playce. **1611** COTGRAVE s.v. Moue We say of one that's hanged, he makes a wry mouth. **1785** GROSE s.v. Wry.

Wych-waller, *see* Scold like a w.-w.

Wye, *see* Blessed is the eye betwixt Severn and W.; Naughty Ashford, surly W.

Wyndham, *see* Horner.

Y

Yard, *see* Measure everyone by own y.

Yarmouth, *see* Spell Y. steeple right (Cannot).

Yate for another, good fellow, One.
(Y 3)

1678 RAY 263 The Earl [of Rutland] riding by himself one day . . . a Countreyman . . . open'd him the first gate they came to, not knowing who the Earl was. When they came to the next gate the Earl expecting . . . the same again, Nay soft, saith the Countreyman, *One yate for another, Good fellow.*

Yawning, *see* Stretching and y. leads to bed.

Year is, As the | your pot must seethe.
(Y 6)
1640 HERBERT no. 335.

Year sooner to the begging, It is but a.

1721 KELLY 217 . . . Facetiously spoken, when we design to be at a little more Expence than we thought.

Year does nothing else but open and shut, The.
(Y 19)
1640 HERBERT no. 901.

Year, A good | will not make him, and an ill year will not break him.
1658 *Comes Facundus* 24.   **1721** KELLY 36.

Yeared, It is.
(Y 28)
1678 RAY 344 . . . *Spoken of a desperate debt.*

Years know more than books.
(Y 27)
1640 HERBERT no. 928.

Year(s), *see also* All one a hundred y. hence; Birds of this y. in last y.'s nests; Cherry y. merry y.; Child for the first seven y.; Christmas all the y. (They keep); Christmas comes but once a y.; Cuckoo sings all y.; Day better than y. (Oft times one); Died half a y. ago dead as Adam; Dies this y. is excused for the next (Who); Fair lasts all y.; Fewer his y. fewer his tears; Four things (Of) man has more than he knows; Good y. corn is hay; Ill y.; Leap y. never sheep y.; Let your house to enemy (First y.); Men's y. and faults are more than they own; More thy y. nearer thy grave; Old (None so) that he hopes not for a y.; One y. a nurse; One y. of joy; One y.'s seeding; Pear y.; Plum y. dumb y.; Promise more in a day than fulfil in a y.; St Matthie all the y. goes by; Say no ill of the y. till; Servant and a cock must be kept but a y.; Seven y. (This); Snow y. rich y.; Spend a whole y.'s rent at one meal; Spring from the y. (Take away).

Yellow as a kite's foot, As.
(K 115)
1509 BARCLAY *Ship of Fools* I. 287 Though he be yelowe as kyte Is of his fete.   **1576** LEMNIUS *Touchstone of Complexions* tr. T. Newton 69 and 128ᵛ.   **1630** DAVENANT *Just Italian* I Yellow as foot of kite.

Yellow as a paigle,[1] As.
(P 13)
1678 RAY 355 As blake² as a paigle.   *a.* **1697** G. MERITON *Yorks. Ale* 83 As Blake² as a paigle.   **1735** PEGGE *Kenticisms* in E.D.S. no. 12, 40.   **1791** *Id. Derbicisms* E.D.A. 114. [¹ cowslip. ² yellow.]

Yellow as the golden noble, As.
(N 193)
1587 HARRISON *Descr. of England* New Sh. Soc. i. 160 The beere . . . yellow as the gold noble, as our potknights call it.   **1678** RAY 350.

Yellow bellies.

1787 GROSE (*Linc.*) 193 . . . This is an appellation given to persons born in the Fens, who, it is jocularly said, have yellow bellies, like their eels.   **1895** ADDY *Household Tales* Introd. xxix.   Dr. Morton . . . who was born in a Lincolnshire village, . . . never thought that the Yellow Bellies 'were . . . yellow, but something of a bronze shade'.   **1896** BEALBY *Daughter of Fen* ch. 13 'That's allus the waay wi' you yaller-bellies, I noätice', chimed in Brewster Bletherwell.

Yellow Jack.

[= yellow fever.] **1833** MARRYAT *P. Simple* ch. 29 With regard to Yellow Jack, as we calls the Yellow fever, it's a devil incarnate.

Yellow peril.

[= a supposed danger of invasion of Europe by Asiatic peoples.] **1900** *Daily News* 21 July 3/5 The 'yellow peril' in its most serious form.   **1911** *Spectator* 2 Dec. 936 In . . . *The Air Scout* . . . [the] 'Yellow Peril' has come upon the 'White World'. It is not Japan that is threatening the West. . . . It is China that has awoke.

Yellow Press, The.

[Applied to newspapers of a sensational character. Derived from the figure of a child in a yellow dress in a cartoon issued in 1895 by the *New York World*.] **1898** *Daily News* 2 Mar. 7/2 The yellow Press is for a war with Spain at all costs.   **1906** A. T. QUILLER-COUCH *Cornish W.* 52 Whatever nation your Yellow Press happens to be insulting at this moment.

Yellow stockings, To wear.
(S 868)
[= to be jealous.] **1584** PEELE *Arr. Paris* I. iii. A3ᵛ A rare deuice; and Flora well perdie, Did painte her yellow for her iellozie.   *c.* **1590** *Tarlton's News out of Purgatory* D2 He resolues with the crue of the Yellow hosde companions . . . that *Mulier* . . . is a woorde of vnconstancie.   *c.* **1598** DELONEY *Thomas of Reading* Wks. (Mann)

217 Fie, vpon these yellow hose. **1600** *Look about You* H4ᵛ Ha sirra, you'l be master, you'l weare the yellow. **1601** SHAKES. *T.N.* II. v. 145 My lady loves me. She did commend my yellow stockings of late, she did praise my leg being cross-garter'd. **1606** DEKKER *News from Hell* C1ᵛ If he put on yellow stockings. **1608** DAY *Law Tricks* III. i If you have me, you must not put on yellowes. **1736** BAILEY *Dict.* s.v. Yellow.

Yellow's forsaken, and green's forsworn, but blue and red ought to be worn.

1862 HISLOP 334 . . . In allusion to the superstitious notions formerly held regarding these colours.

Yellows. To be sick of the.

[1596] **1605** *Stukeley* l. 587. **1600–1** SHAKES. *M.W.W.* I. iii. 97 I will possess him with yellowness. [Ile poses him with Iallowes. *Q*]

Yellow, *see also* Jaundiced eye (To) all things y.

Yellow-hammer, *see* Dead shot at.

Yelping curs will raise mastiffs. (C 919)

1623 PAINTER A2ᵛ I haue hope as the old prouerbe spake, That barking curs oft times great mastifs wake. **1721** KELLY 360 . . . Spoken when mean and unworthy People, by their private Contentions, cause Difference among greater Persons.

Yeoman's service.

1600–1 SHAKES. *H.* V. ii. 36 It did me yeoman's service. **1824** SCOTT *St. Ronan's* ch. 19. I have wanted it [your help] already, and that when it might have done me yeoman's service. **1826** *Id. Journ.* 16 Nov. It [note by Wellington] is furiously scrawled . . . but it *shall* do me yeoman's service.

Yesterday, It is too late to call back. (Y 31)

a. **1529** SKELTON *Magnf.* l. 2057 Ye, syr, yesterday wyll not be callyd agayne. **1546** HEYWOOD II. ix. K3ᵛ Well well (quoth she) what euer ye now saie, It is too late to call agayne yesterdaie. **1601** *Letters of Philip Gawdy* 114 It was too late too call backe yesterdaye. [1603] **1607** T. HEYWOOD *Woman K. with Kindness* sc. xiii, l. 52 O God, O God, that it were possible To undo things done, to call back yesterday. **1616** N. BRETON I *Cross*. A5ᵛ No man can call againe yesterday. **1692** L'ESTRANGE *Aesop's Fab.* ccv. (1738) 221 'Tis to no purpose to think of recalling yesterday.

Yesterday, *see also* Born y., (I was not); Every day is not y.

Yew bow in Chester, There is more than one. (Y 33)

1662 FULLER *Flint.* 37 'Mwy nag un bwa yro Ynghaer'. That is, more then one Yugh-Bow in Chester. Modern use applieth this Proverb to such who seize on other folk's goods . . . mistaken with the similitude thereof to their own goods. **1917** BRIDGE 118 . . . Mwy nag un bwa yew ynghaer. Many a Welshman on the border has found out the truth of this saying, and . . . the Welsh . . . were not allowed to carry bows themselves when they visited the City. . . . Now if a man boasts of some unique possession, he is sometimes told that 'there is more than one yew bow in Chester', *i.e.* it is not so rare as he thinks.

Yoke, *see* Time to y. when cart comes to caples.

York excels foul Sutton, As much as.

1545 P. ASCHAM *Toxophilus* ed. Wright 19 As lyke . . . as Yorke is foule Sutton. **1607** R. CAREW in Epistle to Reader in H. ESTIENNE *A World of Wonders* A1ᵛ If the life of our Ministers be compared with that of their triers, it will be found to exceed theirs as farre as *Yorke* doth foule *Sutton*, to vse a Northerne phrase. **1732** FULLER no. 715.

York, you're wanted.

1816 T. MORTON *The Slave* I. i What, you won't go? Holloa, York you're wanted.— . . . Who is that?—His name is Sharpest: he's his Yorkshire mentor. **1866** *N. & Q.* 3rd Ser. x. 355 'York, you're wanted.'—This phrase is commonly used on board a man-of-war when something goes wrong by reason of the absence of 'the right man' from the 'right place'.

York, *see also* Lincoln was; Oxford for learning . . . Y. for a tit.

Yorkshire (= a sharp fellow), He is.

1734 *Joe Miller's Jests* 156 I'se Yorkshire, said the Fellow, an ha' lived Sixteen Years here. I wonder, reply'd the Gentleman, that . . . so clever a Fellow as you seem to be, have not come to be Master of the Inn yourself. Ay, said the Hostler, But Maister's Yorkshire too. **1790** GROSE s.v. Yorkshire Master's Yorkshire too. *a.* **1806** WOLCOT (P. Pindar) *Pitt's Flight* Wks. (1816) III. 64 But, hang the fellow, 'he was Yorkshire too'. **1813** RAY 223 . . . The Italians say, *E Spoletino*. He's of Spoleto: intimating, he's a cunning blade. **1844** KINGLAKE *Eothen* ch. 24 'The father of lies' . . . an appellation not implying blame, but merit; the 'lies' . . . are feints and cunning stratagems . . . The expression . . . has nearly the same meaning as the English word 'Yorkshireman'.

Yorkshire on one, To come (put).

[= to cheat, dupe, overreach him.] **1700** *Step to the Bath* 10 I ask'd what Countrey-Man my Landlord was? Answer was made full North; and Faith 'twas very Evident; for he had put the Yorkshire most Damnably upon us. **1785** GROSE To come Yorkshire over anyone, to cheat him. **1838–9** DICKENS *N. Nickleby* ch. 42 Wa'at I say, I stick by.—And that's a fine thing to do, . . . though it's not exactly what we understand by 'coming Yorkshire over us' in London.

Yorkshire tike. (Y 34)

[A native of Yorkshire.] [*a.* 1600] **1612** DELONEY *T. Reading* 230 Do you thinke that any can

beare the flirts and frumps, which that Northerne tike gaue me the last time he was in towne.
1699 B.E. Yorkshire-Tike, a Yorkshire manner of
Man.   **1817** SCOTT *Rob Roy* ch. 4 Thou kens
I'm an outspokea Yorkshire tyke.

Yorkshireman, *see* Give a Y. a halter; Shake a
bridle over Y.'s grave.

Young are not always with their bow bent, The.   (Y 35)

1678 RAY 353 . . . *i.e.* Under rule.

You are such another.   (A 250)

[L. *Tu quoque*, 'thou also' = Eng. slang 'you're
another!', a retort upon one's accuser.]   [*c.*
1517] **1533** SKELTON *Magnf.* D1 Cockys bonys
herde ye euer syke another.   [*c.* **1553**] **1566–7**
UDALL *Ralph Roister D.* III. v. If it were an other
but thou, it were a knaue.—Ye are an other your
selfe, sir.   **1598–9** SHAKES. *M.A.* III. iv. 75 Yet
Benedick was such another.   **1598–1601** *Id.*
M.W.W. I. iv. 134 Thereby hangs a tale:—good
faith, it is such another Nan.   **1602** *Id. T.C.* I.
ii. 293 You are such another!   **1602** [T. HEY-
WOOD?] *How a Man may Choose* Hazl.-Dods.
ix. 30.   **1614** J. COOKE (*title*) *Greenes Tu Quoque.*
1749 FIELDING *Tom Jones* IX. vi 'I only said
your conclusion was a non sequitur.' 'You are
another,' cries the sergeant.   **1838** LYTTON *Alice*
III. iv No man knew better the rhetorical effect
of the *tu quoque* form of argument.

Young barber and an old physician, A. *Cf.* Old physician, young lawyer. (B 72)

1573 SANFORD 50.   **1578** FLORIO *First F.* 32.
1666 TORRIANO *It. Prov.* 21 no. 29.

Young bear, Like a | with all his troubles before him.

1833 MARRYAT *P. Simple* ch. 2 I replied that I
had never been at sea . . . but that I was going.
'Well, then, you're like a young bear, all your
sorrows to come'.

Young cocks love no coops.   (C 492)

1636 CAMDEN 310.

Young colts will canter.

1824 SCOTT *St. Ronan's* ch. 1 'They were daft
callants,'[1] she said, . . .; 'a young cowt will
canter, be it up hill or down'. [[1] youths.]

Young courtier, A | an old beggar. *Cf.* Young serving-man.   (C 737)

[*c.* **1515**] *c.* **1530** BARCLAY *Eclog.* II. l. 1056.   **1553**
T. BECON *Jewel of Joy* P.S. 442.   **1577** J. FITZJOHN
Diamond most Precious B2 (The old Prouerbe
is true).   **1598** *Health to the Gentlemanly Prof.*
C4 For, I holde it an infallible rule, an olde
Seruing man, a young Beggar.   **1600** [T. HEY-
WOOD *et al.*?] *1 Edw. IV* i. 50.   **1607** TOURNEUR
Rev. Trag. IV. iv O, when women are young
courtiers, They are sure to be old beggars.   **1616**
BRETON *2 Cross* B3.   **1642** FULLER *Holy State* I.
vii. 6 Hadst thou an occupation (for service is
no heritage; a young courtier, an old beggar),

I could find it in my heart to cast her away upon
thee.   **1659** HOWELL *Eng. Prov.* 12a An old
Serving-man, a young beggar.

Young enough to mend, Ye be | but I am too old to see it.   (A 236)

1546 HEYWOOD II. ix. K3ᵛ.

Young man idle, A | an old man needy, *see* Idle youth, &c., 1642 quotn.

Young man should not marry yet, A | an old man not at all.   (M 696)

1542 ERASM. tr. Udall *Apoph.* (1877) 139 To one
demanding when best season were to wedde
a wife: For a young man, (quoth he[1]) it is to
soone, and for an olde manne ouerlate.   **1607–
12** BACON 'Of Marriage and Single Life' He was
reputed one of the Wise Men, that made
aunsweare to the question When a Man should
marrie, A younger Man not yet, an elder Man
not at all.   *c.* **1640** W.S. *Countrym. Commonw.*
35.   [[1] Diogenes.]

Young man would, If the | and the old man could, there would be nothing undone.   (M 197)

1642 TORRIANO 91 If the young man did but
know, and the old man were but able, there is
nothing but might be effected.   **1736** BAILEY
Dict. s.v. Would.

Young man, *see also* Woo is a pleasure in a y. m. (To).

Young men die many, Of | of old men scape not any. *Cf.* Young men may die.   (M 566)

1659 TORRIANO no. 172.   **1659** N. R. 83.   **1670**
RAY 127.   **1732** FULLER no. 6379.

Young men may die, but old must die. *Cf.* Young men die many.   (M 609)

1534 MORE *Dial. of Comforte* in Wks. (1557)
1139/2 For as we well wot, that a young man
may dye soone: so be we very sure than an olde
man cannot liue long.   **1586** LA PRIMAUDAYE
French Academy 205ᵛ That sentence of Plato, . . .
That yong men die very soone, but that olde
men cannot liue long.   **1594–8** SHAKES. *T.S.* II.
i. 385 May not young men die as well as old?
1623 CAMDEN 276.   **1732** FULLER no. 6039.

Young men think old men fools, and old men know young men to be so.   (M 610)

c. **1576** WHYTHORNE 4 When I was A yoong man,
weening then, that yong men were as wyse as the
olde experienced men be . . . but now I wott
though I am not verye olde that there remayns
many follies in yoong men.   **1577** J. GRANGE
Golden Aphroditis O2ᵛ.   **1580** LYLY *Euph. & his
Eng.* ii. 26 Such a quarrel hath ther alwaies bin
betwene the graue and the cradle, that he that
is young thinketh the olde man fond, and the
olde knoweth the young man to be a foole.

1605 CAMDEN (1637) 281 quoted as the saying of Dr. (Nicholas) Metcalfe (d. 1539). 1605 CHAPMAN *All Fools* v. i. (1874) 75 What, I say! Young men think old men are fools; but old men know young men are fools. 1639 CLARKE 181. 1710 STEELE *Tatler* no. 132 11 Feb. He is constantly told by his uncle, . . . 'Ay, ay, Jack, you young men think us fools; but we old men know you are.'

Young men's knocks old men feel.
(M 620)

[L. *Quae peccamus juvenes ea luimus senes.* We pay when we are old for the misdeeds of our youth.] 1670 RAY 38.

Young one squeak, Make the | and you'll catch the old one.

1732 FULLER no. 3326.

Young physician fattens the churchyard, A.
(P 273)

1576 HOLYBAND C8ᵛ They say in our parish that yong phisitions make the churchyardes croked and old attorneies sutes to go a wray. 1609 HARWARD 129 Yong physicions do make vneauen churchyeards, and ould lawyers crooked actions. 1666 TORRIANO *It. Prov.* 147 no. 38 Ignorant Physicians make a bumping Churchyard. *Ibid.* 148 no. 22.

Young pig grunts like the old sow, The. *Cf.* Old cock crows.
(P 309)

1583 MELBANCKE Ded. to Inns of Court 1 The yong cat cries mew as well as the old one. 1678 RAY 184.

Young saint, old devil.
(S 33)

c. 1400 *Middle Eng. Sermons* from MS Royal 18 B xxiii E.E.T.S. (1940) 159 Itt is a comond prouerbe bothe of clerkes and of laye men, 'younge seynt, old dewell'. c. 1470 *Hart. MS. 3362* (ed. Förster) in *Anglia* 42 ʒoung seynt, old deuyl. a. 1530 DUNBAR *Merle & Nycht.* 35 Of yung sanctis growis auid feyndis but faill. 1546 HEYWOOD I. x. C4ᵛ. But soon rype, soone rotten, yong saynt olde deuill. 1552 LATIMER *7th Serm. Lord's Prayer* P.S. 431 The old proverb, 'Young saints, old devils' . . . is . . . the devil's own invention; which would have parents negligent in bringing up their children in goodness. 1567 O. FENTON *Certain Trag. Discourses* ed. Douglas ii. 97 The French adage . . . of a young saint proceeds an old Sathan. 1636 S. WARD *Serm.* (1862) 81 Young saints will prove but old devils. . . . But . . . such were never right bred. Such as prove falling stars never were aught but meteors.

Young serving-man, A | an old beggar. *Cf.* Old serving-man. Young courtier.
(S 256)

1564 *Pleasant Dial. of Cap & Head* (1565 ed., C1ᵛ) A yong seruing man an olde beggar. 1587 HARRISON *Descr. of England* New Sh. S. i. 134 There runneth a prouerbe; Yoong seruing men, old beggars. [1488] 1590 R. WILSON *Three Ladies of London* Hazl.-Dods. vi. 398 Hadst not thou

better . . . learn a trade to live another day, than to be a serving-boy in thy youth, and to have no occupation in thine age. 1670 RAY 160.

Young trooper should have an old horse, A.

1611 COTGRAVE s.v. Soldat A young souldier would be fitted with an old horse. 1642 TORRIANO 3 (souldier). 1732 FULLER 493.

Young wench, Take heed of a | a prophetess, and a Latin woman.
(H 375)

1599 MINSHEU *Span. Gram.* 84. 1659 HOWELL *It. Prov.* 20 God deliver me from a winching Mule, from the bleak North-wind, and from a Latine woman. From a woman that pretendeth to be too wise. 1659 *Ibid. Span. Prov.* 15 From a prognosticating Maid, and a Latine Wife, the Lord preserve me.

Young wenches make old wrenches.
(W 275)

1626 BRETON ̄*Soothing* A3ᵛ (wrinches). 1639 CLARKE 174.

Younger brother has the more wit, The.
(B 687)

1607 SHARPHAM *Cupid's Whirligig* (1926) III. 42 The younger brothers (according to the old wiues tailes) alwaies prooued the wisest men. 1678 RAY 85.

Younger brother is the better gentleman (soldier), The.
(B 688)

1615 *Work for Cutlers* ed. Sieveking 43 Oftentimes the younger brother prooues the better Souldier. 1642 FULLER *Holy State* xv. (1840) 37 The Younger Brother. Some account him the better gentleman of the two, because son to the more ancient gentleman. 1678 RAY 85 The younger brother is the ancienter Gentleman. 1738 SWIFT *Dial.* I. E.L. 286 You are a younger brother.—Well, madam, the younger brother is the better gentleman.

Younger brother of him, He has made a.
(B 686)

1597 *Discouerie of Knights of the Poste* C2 Thou must not thinke to make a younger brother of me. 1599 SHAKES. *A.Y.* III. ii. 345 What were his marks?— . . . A beard neglected, which you have not: but I pardon you that, for, simply, your having in beard is a younger brother's revenue. 1678 RAY 85.

Younger, You will never be (labour).
(Y 36)

c. 1549 HEYWOOD I. ix. B2 Set forward, ye shall neuer labour yonger. 1566 L. WAGER *Mary Magd.* B2 One thyng is this, you shal neuer be yonger in dede. 1579 LYLY *Euph.* i. 212 Take hart at grasse, younger thou shalt neuer be. 1594-8 SHAKES. *T.S.* Ind. II. 139 Let the world slip: we shall ne'er be younger. 1611 DAVIES no. 400 Faire Candida can neuer labour yonger: For, shee's in labour being Thirteene vnder.

1738 SWIFT *Dial.* I. E.L. 274 Let'm laugh, they'll ne'er laugh younger.

Young(er), *see also* Learn y., learn fair; Learns y. (Whoso) forgets not; Offspring of . . . very y. lasts not; Old y., y. old; Old and tough, y. and tender; Old be, or y. die; Soon goes the y. lamb's skin to market (As); Spare when y.

Youth and age will never agree. (Y 43)

c. **1390** CHAUCER *Miller's T.* l. 3230 Youthe and elde is often at debaat. *c.* **1450** *Towneley Plays* x. 170 It is ill cowpled of youth and elde. **1550** HEYWOOD *100 Epigrams* no. 33 Age and youth to gether can seeld agree. *c.* **1599** [SHAKES.] *Pass. Pilgr.* xii. 1 Crabbed age and youth cannot live together. **1641** FERGUSSON no. 902.

Youth and white paper take any impression. (Y 44)

1579 LYLY *Euph.* i. 187 The tender youth of a childe is . . . apte to receiue any forme. **1594** SHAKES. *T.G.V.* III. i. 34 Tender youth is soon suggested. **1670** RAY 31. **1796** EDGEWORTH *Par. Asst., Lit. Merch.* ch. 1 Youth and white paper, as the proverb says, take all impressions. The boy profited much by his father's precepts, and more by his example.

Youth in a basket. (Y 51)

1600–1 SHAKES. *M.W.W.* IV. ii. 101 Set down the basket, villains! Somebody call my wife. Youth in a basket! **1606** BRETON *Choice* Gros. 29 I . . . was fallen vpon, by a young gallant in shewe . . . this youth in a basket with a face of Brasse . . . comes to me, with this salutation. [*c.* 1607–25] **1632** W. ROWLEY *New Wonder* Hazl.-Dods. xii. 163 Speak, sweet Mistress, am I the youth in a basket?

Youth is used to, What | age remembers.

1303 BRUNNE *Handl. Synne* 7674 (Yn a proverbe of olde Englys)—That yougthe wones, Yn age mones; That thou dedyst ones, Thou dedyst eftsones. (That which youth is used to, in age (one) remembers; that which thou didst once, thou didst again.) [Skeat.]

Youth knew what age would crave, If | it would both get and save. (Y 39)

1611 COTGRAVE s.v. *Jeunesse* If youth knew what to doe, and age could doe what it knowes, no man would euer be poore. **1670** RAY 160.

Youth never casts for peril (is reckless).

c. **1400** *Beryn* l. 1052 3owith is recheles. **1641** FERGUSSON no. 894. **1721** KELLY 374 . . . Signifying that Youth is rash and headstrong.

Youth, Who that in | no virtue uses, in age all honour him refuses. (Y 37)

c. **1450** *Provs. of Wysdom* 9, 10 Who that in youth no vertew vsyþe, In age all honowre hym refusythe. **1526** W. MORE *Journ.* 34 (no Vertu will youse in age all honour will hym Refuse). **1558** J. FISHER *Three Dialogues* B4ᵛ He that in youthe no vertue wyll vse As the commun pro-

uerbe dooth say In age all goodnesse wyll him refuse.

Youth will be served.

1851 BORROW *Lavengro* iii. 291 Youth will be served, every dog has his day, and mine has been a fine one. **1900** A. C. DOYLE *Green Flag &c.* 125 There were . . . points in his favour. . . . There was age—twenty-three against forty. There was an old ring proverb that 'Youth will be served'. **1928** *Times* 30 Aug. 15/6 This visit was to initiate a novice in the mysteries of the dry fly. And, as youth must be served, it would never have done to begin his education . . . where . . . there is no rise till the evening.

Youth will have its course (swing). (Y 48)

1562 G. LEGH *Accidence of Armoury* Pref. 14 Of these that runne so farre as will not turne, old weomen wil say, such youth wil haue their swinge, and it bee but in a halter. **1579** LYLY *Euph.* i. 261 We haue an olde (Prouerb) youth wil haue his course. **1587** HARRISON in Holinshed *Desc. of England* i. 284. [*c.* 1589] **1594** LODGE *Wounds* l. 850 Youth will beare the sway. **1639** CLARKE 183 (swing).

Youth, *see also* Abundance of money ruins y.; Flax from fire and y. from gaming, (Keep); Growing y. has wolf in belly; Idle y. needy age; *Maxima debetur*; Reckless y. makes rueful age; Rule y. well; Time is the rider that breaks y.; Wine and y. increase love.

Yowe, *see* Ewe.

Yule feast may be done (or quit) at Pasch,[1] A.

a. **1628** CARMICHAELL no. 260 (quit). **1641** FERGUSSON no. 126 (quat). **1662** FULLER *Northumb.* 304. . . . That is, Christmas cheer may be digested, and the party hungry again, at Easter. **1721** KELLY 27 . . . A good Office, done at one time, may be requit at another. **1857** DEAN RAMSAY *Remin.* V (1911) 198 (done). Festivities . . . need not . . . be confined to any season. [[1] Easter.]

Yule is come, and Yule is gone, and we have feasted well; so Jack must to his flail again, and Jenny to her wheel.

1846 DENHAM 67.

Yule is good on Yule even. (Y 54)

1639 CLARKE 307.

Yule is young in Yule even, and as old in Saint Stephen.[1]

1721 KELLY 378 . . . Spoken when People are much taken with Novelties, and as soon weary of them. [26 Dec.]

Yule, *see also* Cry Y. at other men's cost; Fool that marries wife at Y.; Green Y. . . . fat churchyard; Now is now and Y.'s in winter.

Yule-day, *see* Every day's no Y.-d.

Z

Zeal like that of a pervert, No.

1872 *N. & Q.* 4th Ser. x. 108 Those who are likest in disposition disagree most hotly when a difference arises. . . . 'There is no hate like that of a brother'; no zeal like that of a pervert.

Zeal, when it is a virtue, is a dangerous one.

1732 FULLER no. 6071.

Zeal without knowledge.   (z 3)

[ROMANS x. 2 They have a zeal for God, but not according to knowledge.] **1527** TYNDALE *Parable of Wicked Mammon* P.S. 105 No zeal without knowledge is good. **1611** DAVIES no. 57 'Zeale without knowledge is sister of Folly': But though it be witlesse, men hold it most holly. **1732** FULLER no. 6069 Zeal without Knowledge is Fire without Light.

Zeal, *see also* Banbury z.

ADDENDUM

Study, To be in a brown

[= a state of mental abstraction.] **1532** *Dice-Play* 6 Lack of company will soon lead a man into a brown study. **1579** LYLY *Euphues* (Arb.) 80 You are in some brown study, what coulours you might best weare for your Lady. **1712** STEELE *Spectator* No. 286, par. 3 He often puts me into a brown Study how to answer him. **1871** BLACKIE *Four Phases* i. 13 He had been standing there in a brown study.

NOTES

NOTES

NOTES

NOTES

NOTES

NOTES